The
DA CAPO CATALOG
of
CLASSICAL MUSIC
COMPOSITIONS

The
DA CAPO CATALOG
of
CLASSICAL MUSIC
COMPOSITIONS

Jerzy Chwiałkowski

DA CAPO PRESS • NEW YORK

Library of Congress Cataloging in Publication Data

Chwialkowski, Jerzy.
  The Da Capo catalog of classical music compositions / Jerzy ᛫
Chwialkowski.
      p.   cm.
  Includes bibliographical references.
  ISBN 0-306-79666-X (hard: alk. paper).—ISBN 0-306-80701-7 (pa-
per: alk. paper)
  1. Music—bibliography. I. Title.
ML113.C59   1996
016.78—dc20   95-53230
                                                                CIP

ISBN 0-306-80701-7 (paperback)
ISBN 0-306-79666-X (hardcover)

Published by Da Capo Press, Inc.
A Subsidiary of Plenum Publishing Corporation
233 Spring Street, New York, N.Y. 10013

Manufactured in the United States of America

To
MARGARET,
for 25 wonderful years,
and to
LUIZA and SANDRA,
with all my love.

CONTENTS

INTRODUCTION

This catalog is the only source available to classical music lovers that exhaustively lists the works of 132 major composers, from Monteverdi, Vivaldi, and Bach to Webern, Cage, and Stockhausen. Whether you simply collect favorite recordings and enjoy books about composers and their music, or whether you are a true connoisseur, this catalog will be as indispensable an investment as a philatelic catalog is to the postage stamp collector.

While individual composers and their work have been thoroughly treated in other books, there has never been a volume that collects and organizes all essential information about classical compositions. Similarly, while other books provide plots and lists of characters of operas—useful for operagoers but not quite sufficient for those who listen at home—only this volume dissects numerous stage works into building blocks so that the reader can easily place a particular aria in the context of the whole opera, or quickly grasp the structure of an oratorio. And *The Da Capo Catalog* also includes lost works, fragments, projects, doubtful and spurious compositions, and arrangements of other composers' works.

For the novice, the catalog will serve as a notebook and guide:

—You can highlight in it all the compositions you already own to see which works would complete your collection of, say, Mozart's serenades or Dvořák's string quartets.

—You can label your collection using the numbering system on the left of each entry.

—When you hear a radio announcer speak of Beethoven's Piano Sonata No. 14, you can instantly check whether it is the "Moonlight" or the "Waldstein" sonata.

—When you can find in your record store Perahia's recordings of all of Mozart's piano concertos from No. 1 through No. 9 and No. 11 through No. 27, you can instantly discover herein why he did not record Mozart's Piano Concerto No. 10.

—If you collect symphonies or string quartets only, you can trace lesser-known ones. You will discover, for example, three symphonies by Borodin and twenty string quartets by the operatic composer Donizetti.

As your expertise grows, so will the power of this book. The connoisseur will appreciate having at his or her fingertips quick answers to questions such as these:

—How many years after Beethoven's "Eroica" did Tchaikovsky compose his "Pathétique"?

—At what age did Brahms compose his first symphony?

—What was Schumann working on when Berlioz published his "Symphonie fantastique"?

—What other works by Beethoven share the musical themes of "Eroica"?

—What American folk tunes, popular melodies, and fragments of other composers' works did Ives build into his compositions?

—What other composers besides Schubert set to music Goethe's "Gretchen am Spinnrade," and who besides Mendelssohn wrote music to Shakespeare's "A Midsummer Night's Dream"?

Each catalog entry consists of the title of the work of the composer, along with the date of composition (or first performance/publication), the source of the lyrics to vocal works, the instruments for which the piece was composed, additional information regarding the provenance of the work, arrangements, orchestration, etc., and its opus and/or catalog numbers. Instrumental compositions which can be considered as collections of individual pieces (e.g., instrumental suites) have been broken down into their constituent sections, and other compositions, like symphonies or string quartets, list the titles of the movements if they contain programmatic information. When the text of a vocal or stage composition was also used by other composers listed in the catalog, this has also been noted.

The compositions have been grouped first by composer (arranged alphabetically), then in genres: stage music, symphonies, other orchestral, concertos, string quartets, other chamber music, piano, organ, church music, choral, other vocal, songs, arrangements of works of other composers. Within each genre, the compositions are arranged either chronologically or according to the numbering system of the most definitive catalog of the composer's works (e.g. BWV numbers for J.S. Bach). Additional headings and subheadings are introduced when necessary: for example, stage works are subdivided into operas, ballets, incidental music, radio, and film; chamber music is subdivided according to the number of instruments, with separate subheadings for more popular ensembles. And each composition is given its full description, so that regardless of how others may abbreviate the title, you will be able to identify it quickly in the catalog.

While using this catalog, please keep in mind that you are travelling through several centuries of classical music history, through generations of musicians and composers, through many countries and languages. In time, the meanings of words used to describe compositions changed (compare Vivaldi's cantatas for one voice and continuo with the elaborate cantatas of the nineteenth and twentieth centuries for solo voices, chorus, orchestra, and often organ), new genres of music were created (the symphony, the string quartet), new instruments were invented (piano) and old ones improved (valves were added to the horn).

Titles of compositions were evolving as well. Originally a composition may have had a short title and perhaps a long descriptive subtitle, but a substitute title may then have been added. In time a substitute title may have become the main title. A composition may have been given a nickname, which in time may have pushed the original name aside (as is the case with the "Eroica Variations"). Some compositions were composed in one country and published elsewhere with titles in another language (some Russian composers were first published in France). Later, they might have been translated from the original into a third language.

This evolution—reflected in spelling, capitalization, numbering, and use of foreign words (e.g. praeludium, präludium, prélude, prelude; symphony, simphonie, sinfonia)—is part of our cultural heritage, and the catalog tries to preserve it, occasionally at the expense of uniformity or consistency. For the knowledgeable reader, these variations carry valuable information regarding the place and time of composition, the character of the piece, its structure, and more. Therefore only for works well established under their English names has preference been given to the English language. In many cases the work's title in the original language is followed in brackets by its English title (given to the work at the time it entered the repertoire of the English-speaking world, and not necessarily a straight translation).

This catalog was prepared with the classical music lover in mind: the listener, the reader, the collector of recordings. It omits information important mainly to scholars, such as the location of manuscripts or their state of preservation. The bibliography lists catalogs of individual composers should you require more information. The catalog does not address the numerous scholarly controversies surrounding titles of composition, dating, instruments, authorship of arrangements, etc.—it follows the most authoritative sources, all listed in the bibliography.

The format is as user-friendly as I could make it. (For example, the catalog lists all the BWV numbers of J. S. Bach compositions—even the unused ones—so that the user does not have to wonder what composition a missing number denotes.) The abbreviations listed at the front of the volume are commonly used in books about classical music and are probably already familiar to the reader.

The main focus of the catalog is the well-defined period in music history from Bach and Handel to Schoenberg and Webern. However, the Baroque is also quite well represented, especially with composers who have strong "connections" with the Classic and Romantic eras. There are a few forays into contemporary music, which deserves a separate volume, updated every few years. Some composers were omitted because research into their work is not yet at the stage where each composition could be individually identified, which is the aim of this catalog. Others clearly fell beyond its scope. I regret that for lack of space I could not include such important and prolific composers as Telemann and Palestrina from the Baroque era; Cui, one of "The Mighty Five" of nineteenth-century Russia (the other four are included); Humperdinck, who wrote the ever-popular opera "Hänsel und Gretel"; or Schaeffer, who brought us *musique concrète*. I am solely responsible for the choice of composers; this choice was, inevitably, personal, and I hope that exclusions will be forgiven.

When I started this catalog many years ago for my own private use, I was astonished and disappointed by the inadequacy and inconsistency of the existing reference sources. They span many decades, originated in different countries, represent different standards, and—or so it seems—were often not subjected to the sharp eye of an editor. Even in the multi-volume *New Grove Encyclopedia* the lists are remarkably incomplete, the format changes from composer to composer, and the text is cluttered with information important primarily to archivists, making it difficult to use by ordinary classical music lovers such as myself.

I began to write complete lists of compositions based on available scholarly work and to come up with a format that would make using the catalog as easy as changing CDs in a CD player. After researching all the available books about each composer, I would base my list on the most authoritative one, and then check each composition with the other sources. For many composers I had to tap contacts in other countries and often use information available only in the language of the composer. As the work grew, I changed and improved the format of the catalog continuously until I was satisfied that it had become flexible yet coherent enough to accomodate bodies of work as different as those of Chopin and Stockhausen, transparent enough for the average reader yet with sufficient depth for experts, and informative enough to relay the character and significance of each composition. I then tried to reconcile my catalog with catalogs of available recordings such as *The Schwann Catalogue, The Gramophone Classical Catalogue*, and *The New Penguin Guide to Compact Discs and Cassettes*, which involved cross-listing entries by every conceivable numbering and labeling system used there, so that Mozart symphonies do not end at No. 41, "Jupiter"—chronologically his last—but at No. 55; and one Beethoven sonata can be found listed as Op. 27 No. 2, Piano Sonata No. 14, Piano Sonata in C sharp minor, and simply "Moonlight" Sonata.

So here it is, the first of its kind, a catalog for classical music lovers. In its various stages of completion, it has served me and continues to serve me well. Now I share it with you in the hope that it will become a well-appreciated companion in your journeys through musical history, and that it will enrich your experience of the highest achievements of human talent and spirit.

EXPLANATORY NOTES

The typical entry in the catalog contains three parts and is explained here on the basis of examples from Mendelssohn.

1.7   "Die Heimkehr aus der Fremde" (Son and Stranger), 1 act operetta (c1829, Klingemann) Op.89

The first part of the entry pertains to the title of the composition. After *The Da Capo Catalog* number—1.7—is the proper title of the work—"Die Heimkehr aus der Fremde." It is followed in parentheses by the English title—"Son and Stranger." If the text in brackets is in the same language as the proper title of the composition, it indicates another name under which the composition is known. For example:

8.13   "Recitativo" (Largo) in D minor (c1820) ....

"Recitativo" in D minor is also known as "Largo" in D minor; in various sources you may find it listed either way, but it is the same work composed in 1820. Some instrumental compositions were given nicknames: these are placed in double quotation marks after the *key* of the composition. For example:

8.43   No. 2 "Andante espressivo," in A minor, "Regrets" ....

The nickname is "Regrets."

Many of the entries for songs and other vocal works list the first words of the composition. These are shown in double quotation marks following the title (or titles) of the composition, and are preceded by a colon. For example:

17.3   "Die Nachtigall": "Da ging ich hin" (c ?1821–2) ....

The name of the song is "Die Nachtigall." The first words are "Da ging ich hin."

To go back to our main example, Mendelssohn 1.7, the next words—1 act operetta—describe the genre of the composition in greater detail. This first part of the entry always ends at the parenthesis before the date of composition.

If a title is generic (Symphony, String Quartet, Piano Sonata) it is not listed in quotation marks, and is often followed by a number. In many instances this number has been assigned by the recording industry, often based on numbers in published collections. For example, Chopin's mazurkas received numbers from 1 to 62. The first numbers, 1 to 49, follow a more or less chronological order, while numbers 50 to 62 represent mazurkas previously unknown or unnoticed (generally earlier versions of those previously known), in no particular order except that of their inclusion in the body of performed works. Another instance is Mozart's violin sonatas, numbered from 1 to 36, where a group of six so-called "Aurnhammer-Sonaten" (Nos. 17 and 24–28) were not given consecutive numbers. Scholars usually spurn these numbers as "not valid" because obviously they were never sanctioned by the composer, but the listener is constantly confronted with them on recordings and in the catalogs of recordings. Since the industry quite notoriously shortens composition titles (for lack of space), often omitting catalog numbers, and since books by scholars omit the numbering systems of the recording industry, the classical music lover trying to correlate both worlds is left in a vacuum. *The Da Capo Catalog* fills this void by including all applicable numbers.

The second part of the entry gives the basic information about the composition. In our main example, this consists of its date of composition—1829—and the name of the librettist—Klingemann. Sometimes after the date of composition is the date of revision. For example:

13.4   "Die erste Walpurgisnacht," cantata (c1832, r1843, Goethe; ch & orch)...Op.60

For ballets and incidental music, instead of the name of the librettist that of the playwright is given; for songs, that of the poet; for film scores, that of the principal screenwriter or director. Following this source information is often detail about the instrumental or vocal ensemble (always preceded by a semi-colon). The above cantata, Mendelssohn 13.4, was composed for chorus and orchestra. This information may in turn be followed by additional information about the work. For example:

3.8   "Trauermarsch," in A minor (c1836; milit band, in memory of N. Burgmüller)...Op.13

And this information may, after a semi-colon, be followed by information regarding other compositions or arrangements the composition influenced or in which its material was used.

Please keep in mind that double quotation marks (") indicate titles of works or the first words of a vocal composition; single quotation marks (') indicate a quotation related to a work which is not its title.

The third part of the entry consists of the opus number and (if there is one) the catalog number of the work. In the case of our main example, Mendelssohn 1.7, this is simply the opus number: Op. 89. Some opus numbers are shown in parentheses, which signifies that the number is used by association with another form of the same work and that the other form was originally published with that opus number. Other opus numbers are shown as "op." rather than "Op."; this usually indicates an abandoned numbering of a composer's juvenile works.

Opus numbers were assigned by composers or publishers to published compositions; because this practice was often haphazard at best, missing (unused) numbers do not indicate missing compositions. Many compositions without opus numbers were never officially published but were circulated and performed from copies prepared by copyists (now an extinct profession) or were discovered after the composer's death and were published without an opus number (although in some cases works were published as opus posthumous, with a consecutive number, shortly after the composer's death).

This catalog includes the numbering systems (wherever available) of scholars who have devoted their professional lives to cataloging works of individual composers. W. Schmieder cataloged the works of J. S. Bach; his catalog is known as *Bach Werke Verzeichnis*, and his catalog numbers are thus preceded by the letters BWV. Dr. L. R. von Köchel cataloged works by Mozart; his catalog is known as *Köchel Werke Verzeichnis*, and his catalog numbers are preceded by the letters KWV, or K for short. O. E. Deutsch cataloged works of Schubert, and his catalog numbers are preceded by the letter D. (For example, Schubert's song cycle "Die schöne Müllerin" was published as Opus 25 and is listed in Deutsch's catalog under number 795; we therefore refer to the cycle as Op. 25, D795.) The *Da Capo Catalog* lists all numbers of all the individual catalogs presently in use and identifies these catalogs at the end of the list of each composer's work. Appendix (App) or, in German catalogs, Anhang (Anh) numbers refer to the appendices found in those catalogs.

Sections of works are listed in different manners according to the nature of the work.

The numbering of sections of or selections from **stage works** follows precisely the numbering (often seemingly incomplete or inconsistent) found in the definitive catalogs of the individual composers. In some instances, where no such numbering is given, the *Da Capo Catalog* uses the numbers assigned by the recording industry in *The Gramophone Classical Catalogue*, and these are clearly marked as such. For the convenience of the reader, the breakdown of stage works into their component sections is usually listed under a separate heading (e.g. 1a).

In composite works such as **suites, sets, cycles of songs, or works consisting of short pieces**, each component part has been given its own *Da Capo Catalog* number (at the far left of the entry). The first component part of the suite or set is inserted between the second and third part of the main catalog entry. For example:

8.27   "7 Characteristic Pieces" (p1827): No.1 "Sanft und mit Empfindung," in E minor Op.7

Here "Sanft und mit Empfindung" in E minor is the first piece of "7 Characteristic Pieces." The third part of the main entry—the opus number, Op. 7—is assigned to all seven pieces, and thus "Sanft und mit Empfindung" is commonly referred to as Op. 7 No. 1. In **instrumental** suites, sets, etc., the number of the component part is preceded by "No.," while in **vocal** works the "No." is left out; in this manner, a quick glance at a page which contains such works will indicate to the reader whether or not he/she is looking at vocal or instrumental works.

Component parts of **integrated compositions** (e.g. symphonies), which you would not expect to be performed separately from the other parts, are listed in the catalog only if they contain programmatic information, and are not given *Da Capo Catalog* numbers on the left (for example, see Mendelssohn 2.15 or 12.29). These parts are numbered without the letters "No."

(Where sections were left unnumbered in the composer's catalog, they are preceded simply by a dot instead of a number.)

Lastly, **works listed in *italics*** are either: a) compositions you can read about but cannot listen to, such as lost works, fragments, and projects; b) works which were thought to be composed by the composer in question and were once included in catalogs but have since been proven spurious or of doubtful authenticity; or c) arrangements by other composers (some of which are better known than the original works).

ACKNOWLEDGMENTS

I wish to express my gratitude to Luiza Ch. for her research in the Eda Kuhn Loeb music library at Harvard University in Cambridge, Massachusetts and for overall help with the catalog; to Margaret Ch., Sandra Ch., and Anna Kowalska-Chałupka for their research on Polish composers; to Karl H. Seyffer for his help with translating German sources; to Jenny Singer for her help with Spanish sources; to Grant Neufeld, computer wizard, for technical assistance.

I am indebted to my editor, Yuval Taylor, for his thoughtful comments which allowed me to improve the catalog even where I would never have considered it possible.

I am grateful to the following for proofreading parts of the catalog written in their mother tongues: Karl H. Seyffer in German, Charles Borsenberger in French, Domenico Perri in Italian, Jenny Singer in Spanish, Attila Bódis in Hungarian, Natalia Greslikova in Czech and Slovak, Margaret Ch. in Polish, and Yuval Taylor in English. Of course, any errors or misspellings remain my sole responsibility.

Finally I wish to express my very special thanks to the staff of the National Library of Canada in Ottawa for their unequalled courtesy and professional help.

—J. Ch.
Ottawa, November 1995

COMPOSERS

/	or	mS	mezzo-soprano (voice)
=	same	no.	number
		nos.	numbers
A	alto (voice)		
a	alto (instr)	ob	oboe
acc	accompaniment	obbl	obbligato
add	additional / added	Op.	opus
ad lib	ad libitum	orch	orchestra
Anh	Anhang (appendix)	orchd	orchestrated
anniv	anniversary	org	organ
anon	anonymous	orig	originally
App	appendix	Ov	overture
arr	arranged by		
arrs	arrangements	p (stage works)	produced
assembl	assembled by	p (non-stage works)	published
attr	attributed	part	partial
		p ca	produced (published) circa
B	bass (voice)	perc	percussion
b	bass (instr)	perf	performed
Bar	baritone (voice)	pf	piano
bn	bassoon	pic	piccolo
Boh	Bohemian	Pol	Polish
b rec	bass recorder	posth	posthumous
		pseud	pseudonym
c	composed	pubd	published
c?	date unknown		
ca	(composed) circa	qnt	quintet
ch	chorus	qt	quartet
child ch	children's chorus		
cl	clarinet	r	revised
collab	in collaboration with	rec	recorder
	/ collaborative	recit	recitative
compl	completed by	reconstr	reconstructed
Conc	concerto	red	reduction / reduced
cont	basso continuo	Rom	Romanian
cT	counter-tenor (voice)	Russ	Russian
d	double	S	soprano (voice)
ded	dedicated	sax	saxophone
destr	destroyed	sec	seconds
		Son	sonata
ed	edited by	spur	spurious
Eng	English	str	string
ens	ensemble	strings	string orchestra
		suppl	supplement
fem ch	female chorus	Swed	Swedish
fl	flute	Sym	symphony
Fr	French	sym	symphonic
frag	fragment		
		T	tenor (voice)
Ger	German	t	tenor (instr)
gui	guitar	timp	timpani
		tpt	trumpet
harm	harmonium	trad	traditional
hn	horn	transcr	transcribed
hpd	harpsichord	transl (tr)	translated by
Hung	Hungarian	trbn	trombone
		tr instr	treble instrument
inc	incomplete	tr v	treble voice
incid	incidental		
incl	included / including	unacc	unaccompanied
incorp	incorporated	unfin	unfinished
instr	instrument	unperf	unperformed
insts	instruments	unpubd	unpublished
It	Italian		
		v	voice
kbd	keyboard	va	viola
		var	variations
Lat	Latin	vc	violoncello
Lith	Lithuanian	vers	version
		vle	violone
maj	major	vn	violin
mand	mandolin	Vol.	volume
m ch	male chorus	vv	voices
mech	mechanical		
milit	military	w/	with
min (tonal works)	minor	WoO	work w/ out opus no.
min (atonal works)	minutes		
misc	miscellaneous		
movt	movement		

1. STAGE WORKS

Operas:

1.1	*"Cuánto más viejo," 1 act zarzuela (c early, lost)* ....
1.2	*"Catalanes de gracia," 1 act zarzuela (c early, lost)* ....
1.3	*"El canto de salvacion," 2 act zarzuela (c early, lost)* ....
1.4	*"El Cristo," oratorio (c early, lost)* ....
1.5	"The Magic Opal," 2 act comic opera (p1893, Law) ....
1.6	Additional Nos. for Millöcker: Poor Jonathan (c1893) ....
1.7	"San Antonio de la Flórida" (L'ermitage fleuri), 1 act zarzuela (p1894, Sierra) ....
1.8	"Henry Clifford," 3 act opera (p1895, Money-Coutts) ....

"King Arthur," opera trilogy:

1.9	I. "Merlin," 3 act opera (c1903, Money-Coutts) ....
1.10	*II. "Lanzarote" (inc)* ....
1.11	*III. "Ginebra" (not composed)* ....
1.12	"Pepita Jiménez," 2 act lyric comedy (p1896, Money-Coutts after Valera's novel) ....

2. ORCHESTRAL WORKS

2.1	"Escenas sinfónicas catalanas," 3 pieces (perf1889) ....
2.2	"Catalonia, suite populaire" (1st part perf1899, 2nd & 3rd inc) ....
2.3	*"Iberia," suite (orchd Arbos from: Iberia for pf): No.1 "Evocación"* ....
2.4	*No.2 "El corpus en Sevilla"*
2.5	*No.3 "Triana"*

3. PIANO CONCERTOS, PIANO & ORCH

3.1	*"Rapsodia española" (orchd Enescu 1911 from orig for pf)* .... *(Op.70)*
3.2	*Piano Concerto in A minor, "Concierto fantástico" (orchd Trayter 1887; arr for 2pf)* *Op.78*

4. CHAMBER MUSIC

4.1	"Sextet" (Suite de concert): No.1 "Scherzo" (c before 1889) ....
4.2	No.2 "Serenata morisca"
4.3	No.3 "Capricho Cubano"
4.4	Trio No.1 in F major (c before 1889) ....

5. PIANO SONATAS

5.1	Piano Sonata No.1 in A-flat major (c before 1884, Scherzo p1883, other movts lost) Op.28, B4
5.2	*Piano Sonata No.2 (lost)* *A9*
5.3	Piano Sonata No.3 in A-flat major (c before 1886) Op.68, B14
5.4	Piano Sonata No.4 in A major (c before 1887) Op.72, B20
5.5	Piano Sonata No.5 in G-flat major (c before 1887): Op.82, B27

    1. "Allegro non troppo," in G-flat major
    2. "Minuetto del gallo: Allegro assai," in C-sharp minor (pubd separately)
    3. "Revene et allegro: Andante," in D major
    4. "Allegro," in G-flat major

5.6	*Piano Sonata No.6 (lost)* *A10*
5.7	Piano Sonata No.7 in E-flat major (c before ?1890, Minuetto only) Op.111, B34

6. OTHER PIANO WORKS

Early works allegedly c by Albéniz (cited Laplane):

6.1	*"Marcha militar" (para piano por el niño de ocho años Isaac Albéniz)* *A1*
6.2	*"Burgos" (mentioned Collet)* *A2*
6.3	*"2 Caprichos"* *A3*
6.4	*"2 Caprichos Andaluces"* *A4*
6.5	*"2 Grandes estudios de concierto"* *A5*
6.6	*"3 Mazurkas"* *A6*
6.7	*"Marcha nupcial"* *A7*
6.8	*"Pavana española" (mentioned Iglesias, = ?Op.12 or Op.83)* *A8*
6.9	*"Suite morisca" (mentioned Marliave, quoted Collet): No.1 "Marcha de la caravana"* *A11*
6.10	*No.2 "La noche"*
6.11	*No.3 "Danza de las esclavas"*
6.12	*No.4 "Zambra"*

Mature works:

6.13	"Pavana capricho," in E minor (c1883 or earlier)	Op.12, B1
6.14	"Barcarole Catalane," in D-flat major (c before 1885)	Op.23, B2
6.15	"6 pequeños valses" (c before 1884): No.1 in A-flat major	Op.25, B3
6.16	No.2 in E-flat major	
6.17	No.3 in A major	
6.18	No.4 in E-flat major	
6.19	No.5 in F major	
6.20	No.6 in A-flat major	
6.21	"Serenata árabe," in A minor (c before 1886)	B5
6.22	"El Deseo: Estudio de concierto," in E minor (c1883–6)	Op.40, B6
6.23	"Suite española" (No.1): No.1 "Granada," serenata in F major (c1886)	Op.47, B7
6.24	No.2 "Cataluña," corranda in G minor (c1886)	
6.25	No.3 "Sevilla," sevillanas in G major (c before 1886)	
6.26	No.4 "Cádiz," canción in D-flat major (ca1890, = Op.181, added ca1918)	
6.27	No.5 "Asturias," leyenda in G minor (ca1896, = Op.232/1, added ca1918)	
6.28	No.6 "Aragón," fantasía in F major (c before 1889, = Op.164/1, added ca1918)	
6.29	No.7 "Castillas," seguidillas in F-sharp major (ca1896, = Op.232/5, added ca1918)	
6.30	No.8 "Cuba," capricho in E-flat major (c1886)	
6.31	"Suite antigua" (No.1) (c before 1886): No.1 "Gavota," in G minor	Op.54, B8
6.32	No.2 "Minuetto," in A-flat major	
6.33	"Estudio impromptu," in B minor (c before 1886)	Op.56, B9
6.34	"Suite antigua No.2" (ca1886): No.1 "Sarabanda," in G minor	Op.64, B10
6.35	No.2 "Chacone," in C minor	
6.36	"7 estudios en los tonos naturales mayores" (ca1886): No.1 in C major	Op.65, B11
6.37	No.2 in G major	
6.38	No.3 in D major	
6.39	No.4 in A major	
6.40	No.5 in E major	
6.41	No.6 in B major	
6.42	No.7 in F major	
6.43	"6 Mazurkas de salón" (c before 1886): No.1 "Isabel," in A-flat major	Op.66, B12
6.44	No.2 "Casilda," in F minor (= First Mazurka, Op.140/1)	
6.45	No.3 "Aurora," in A major	
6.46	No.4 "Sofía," in A-flat major	
6.47	No.5 "Christa," in E major (= Second Mazurka, Op.140/2)	
6.48	No.6 "María," in G major	
6.49	"Rapsodia cubana," in G major (c before 1886; orchd1887)	Op.66, B13
6.50	"Angustia: Romanza sin palabras," in E minor (ca ?1886)	B15
6.51	"Minuetto No.3," in A-flat major (ca ?1886)	B16
6.52	"Rapsodia española," in D minor (ca1887; see orchd Enescu 1911)	Op.70, B17
6.53	"Recuerdos de viaje" (ca1886): No.1 "En el mar," barcarola in A-flat major	Op.71, B18
6.54	No.2 "Leyenda," barcarola in E-flat major	
6.55	No.3 "Alborada," in A major	
6.56	No.4 "En la Alhambra," in A minor	
6.57	No.5 "Puerta de Tierra," bolero in D major (pubd as: Andalucia)	
6.58	No.6 "Rumores de la Caleta," malagueña in D min / A Phrygian	
6.59	No.7 "En la playa," in A-flat major	
6.60	"Cadiz-gaditana," in D min / A Phrygian (c between ?1886–1890)	B19
6.61	"Suite antigua" No.3 (c1886): No.1 "Minuetto," in G minor	B21
6.62	No.2 "Gavotte," in D minor	
6.63	"Minuetto," in G minor (c before 1887)	B22
6.64	"6 Danzas españolas" (c before 1887): No.1 in D major (pubd as: Habanera)	B23
6.65	No.2 in B-flat major	
6.66	No.3 in E-flat major (pubd as: Serenata andaluza)	
6.67	No.4 in G major (pubd as: Danza)	
6.68	No.5 in A-flat major (pubd as: Recuerdo)	
6.69	No.6 in D major	
6.70	"Champagne" (Carte blanche), waltz in E-flat major (c before 1887; No.1 of Album: Cotillon)	B24
6.71	"Recuerdos," mazurka in G-flat major (c before 1887)	Op.80, B25
6.72	"Mazurka de salón," in E-flat major (c before 1887)	Op.81, B26
6.73	"Pavana fácil para manos pequeñas," in C minor (c before 1887)	Op.83, B28
6.74	"12 Piezas Caractéristicas" (ca1888): No.1 "Gavota," in G major	Op.92, B29
6.75	No.2 "Minuetto a Silvia," in A major	
6.76	No.3 "Ciel sans nuages," barcarola in E-flat major	
6.77	No.4 "Plegaria" (Prière), in E-flat major	
6.78	No.5 "Conchita," polka in F major	
6.79	No.6 "Pilar," waltz in A major	
6.80	No.7 "Zambra," granadina in G minor	
6.81	No.8 "Pavana," in F minor	
6.82	No.9 "Polonesa," in E-flat major	
6.83	No.10 "Mazurka," in G minor	
6.84	No.11 "Staccato," capricho in A major	
6.85	No.12 "Torre Bermeja," serenata in E major	

* * * * *

B =   Pola Baytelman: "Isaac Albéniz. Chronological List and Thematic Catalog of His Piano Works."
        Harmonie Park Press. Michigan, 1993.
        A = Appendix A in Baytelman's Catalog.

1. STAGE WORKS (operas)

1.1	*"Zenobia, regina de' Palmireni" (p1694, Marchi; used in pasticcio: Il vinto trionfante 1717)* ....
1.2	*"Il prodigio dell'innocenza" (p1695, Gualazzi, lost)* ....
1.3	*"Zenone, imperator d'oriente" (p1696, Marchi, lost)* ....
1.4	*"Il Tigrane, re d'Armenia" (p1697, Corradi, lost)* ....
1.5	*"Primislao primo, re di Boemia" (p1697, Corradi, lost)* ....
1.6	*"L'ingratitudine gastigata" (p1698, Silvani, r1712 as: Alarico, lost)* ....
1.7	*"Radamisto" (p1698, Marchi, lost)* ....
1.8	*"Diomede punito da Alcide" (p1700, Aureli, lost)* ....
1.9	*"L'inganno innocente" (p1701, Silvani, r1702 as: Rodrigo in Algeri, several arias extant)* ....
1.10	*"L'arte in gara con l'arte" (p1702, Silvani, lost)* ....
1.11	*"Griselda" (p1703, Zeno, 3 arias extant)* ....
1.12	*"Aminta" (p1703, Zeno, lost)* ....
1.13	"Il più fedel tra i vassalli" (p1705, Sorietti) ....
1.14	*"Le prosperità d'Elio Sejano" (p1707, Minato, lost)* ....
1.15	*"La fede tra gl'inganni" (p1707, Silvani, lost)* ....
1.16	*"Astarto" (p1708, Zeno & Pariati, several arias extant)* ....
1.17	(Vespetta e) "Pimpinone," intermezzi for opera: Astarto (p1708, Pariati; r1717 as: La serva astuta) ....
1.18	"Engelberta" (p1709, Zeno & Pariati) ....
1.19	*"Il tradimento tradito" (p1709, Silvani, lost)* ....
1.20	*"Ciro" (p1710, Pariati, lost)* ....
1.21	*"Il tiranno eroe" (p1711, Cassani, several arias extant)* ....
1.22	*"Il Giustino" (p1711, Beregani, r by Pariati, lost)* ....
1.23	*"Le gare generose" (p1712, Zaniboni, 5 arias extant)* ....
1.24	*"Lucio Vero" (p1713, Zeno, lost)* ....
1.25	*"L'amor di figlio non conosciuto" (p1716, Lalli, lost)* ....
1.26	*"Eumene" (p1717, Salvi, 1 aria extant)* ....
1.27	*"Meleagro" (p1718, Bernadoni, lost)* ....
1.28	"Cleomene" (p1718, Cassani) ....
1.29	*"Gli eccessi della gelosia" (p1722, Lalli; r1724 as: La Mariane, several arias extant)* ....
1.30	*"I veri amici" (p1722, Silvani & Lalli, several arias extant)* ....
1.31	*"Il trionfo d'amore," componimento poetico (p1722, Pariati, lost)* ....
1.32	*"Eumene" (p1723, Zeno, 2 arias extant)* ....
1.33	*"Ermengarda" (p1723, Lucchini, lost)* ....
1.34	*"Antigono, tutore di Filippo, re dei Macedoni" (p1724, Piazzon, collab Porta, lost)* ....
1.35	*"Scipione nelle Spagne" (p1724, Zeno, lost)* ....
1.36	*"Laodice" (p1724, Schietti, 2 arias extant)* ....
1.37	*"I rivali generosi" (p1725, Zeno, lost)* ....
1.38	*"Didone abbandonata" (p1725, Metastasio, lost)* ....
1.39	"L'impresario delle Canarie," intermezzi for opera: Didone abbandonata (p1725, Metastasio) ....
1.40	*"Alcina delusa da Ruggero" (p1725, Marchi, r1732 as: Gli evenimenti di Ruggero, lost)* ....
1.41	"La Statira" (p1726, Zeno & Pariatti) ....
1.42	*"Malsazio e Fiammetta," intermezzi for: La Statira (p1726, lost)* ....
1.43	*"Il trionfo di Armida" (p1726, Colatelli, lost)* ....
1.44	"L'incostanza schernita" (p1727, Cassani; r1729 as: L'infedelta delusa, words Filandro) ....
1.45	*"Le due rivali in amore" (p1728, Aureli, lost)* ....
1.46	*"Il Strapone," comic intermezzi (p1729, Salvi, lost)* ....
1.47	*"La fortezza al cimento" (p1729, Silvani, lost)* ....
1.48	*"Gli stratagemmi amorosi" (p1730, Passerini, lost)* ....
1.49	*"Elenia" (p1730, Bergalli, lost)* ....
1.50	*"Merope" (p1731, Zeno, lost)* ....
1.51	*"Il più fedel tra gli amanti" (p1731, Sorietti, lost)* ....
1.52	*"Ardelinda" (p1732, Vitturi, 5 arias extant)* ....
1.53	*"Candalide" (p1734, Vitturi, lost)* ....
1.54	*"Artamene" (p1741, Vitturi, lost)* ....

2. SINFONIAS (2vn, va & bass)

2.1	Sinfonia in D major	Si1
2.2	Sinfonia (p1694; tpt, 2vn, 2va, vc & vle/hpd, to Act I of opera: Zenobia)	
2.3	"Sonata con violini e tromba a 6"	
2.4	"Sinfonia a 6"	
2.5	"Sonata di concerto a 7 vocibus"	
2.6	Sinfonia in F major (p1709, to Act I of opera: Engelberta)	Si2
2.7	Sinfonia in A major	Si3
2.8	"Sonata," in A major (2vn, va & vle/org, anon pubd ca1709–12 as No.3 in: 6 Sonates a 4, 5 & 6 parties; identical in part to: Sinfonia in A major, Si3)	Si3a
2.9	Sinfonia in D major (c1714)	Si4
2.10	Sinfonia in A major	Si5
2.11	Sinfonia in B-flat major	Si6
2.12	Sinfonia in G minor	Si7
2.13	Sinfonia in G major	Si8
2.14	Sinfonia in F major	Si9

3. INSTRUMENTAL WORKS (w/ opus numbers)

3.1	12 "Suonate a tre" (p1694; 2vn, vc & org): No.1 in D minor	Op.1
3.2	No.2 in F major	
3.3	No.3 in A major	
3.4	No.4 in G minor	
3.5	No.5 in C major	
3.6	No.6 in A minor	
3.7	No.7 in G major	
3.8	No.8 in B minor	
3.9	No.9 in D major	
3.10	No.10 in F minor	
3.11	No.11 in C minor	
3.12	No.12 in B-flat major	
3.13	6 "Sinfonie e (6) concerti a cinque" (p1700; 1/2vn, 2va, vc & cont): No.1 Sonata No.1 in G major	Op.2
3.14	No.2 Concerto No.1 in F major	
3.15	No.3 Sonata No.2 in C major	
3.16	No.4 Concerto No.2 in E minor	
3.17	No.5 Sonata No.3 in A major	
3.18	No.6 Concerto No.3 in B-flat major	
3.19	No.7 Sonata No.4 in C minor	
3.20	No.8 Concerto No.4 in G major	
3.21	No.9 Sonata No.5 in B-flat major	
3.22	No.10 Concerto No.5 in C major	
3.23	No.11 Sonata No.6 in G minor	
3.24	No.12 Concerto No.6 in D major	
3.25	12 "Balletti a tre" (p1701; 2vn, vc & hpd): No.1 "Preludio," in C major	Op.3
3.26	No.2 "Allemanda," in E minor	
3.27	No.3 "Preludio," in G major	
3.28	No.4 "Preludio," in A major	
3.29	No.5 "Allemanda," in D minor	
3.30	No.6 "Preludio," in F major	
3.31	No.7 "Preludio," in D major	
3.32	No.8 "Allemanda," in C minor	
3.33	No.9 "Preludio," in G minor	
3.34	No.10 "Preludio," in E major	
3.35	No.11 "Allemanda," in A minor	
3.36	No.12 "Preludio," in B-flat major	
3.37	12 "Concerti a cinque" (p1707; 3vn, 2va, vc & hpd): No.1 in B-flat major	Op.5
3.38	No.2 in F major	
3.39	No.3 in D major	
3.40	No.4 in G major	
3.41	No.5 in A minor	
3.42	No.6 in C major	
3.43	No.7 in D minor	
3.44	No.8 in F major	
3.45	No.9 in E minor	
3.46	No.10 in A major	
3.47	No.11 in G minor	
3.48	No.12 in C major	
3.49	12 "Trattenimenti (Sonatas) armonici per camera" (p ca1711; vn, vc & hpd): No.1 in C major	Op.6
3.50	No.2 in G minor	
3.51	No.3 in B-flat major	
3.52	No.4 in D minor	
3.53	No.5 in F major	
3.54	No.6 in A minor	
3.55	No.7 in D major	
3.56	No.8 in E minor	
3.57	No.9 in G major	
3.58	No.10 in C minor	
3.59	No.11 in A major	
3.60	No.12 in B-flat major	
3.61	12 "Concerti a cinque" (p1715; 2vn, va, vc & cont): No.1 in D major	Op.7
3.62	No.2 in C major (+ 2ob)	
3.63	No.3 in B-flat major (+ ob)	
3.64	No.4 in G major	
3.65	No.4a "Sinfonia," in G major	
3.66	No.5 in C major (+ 2ob)	
3.67	No.6 in D major (+ ob)	
3.68	No.7 in A major	
3.69	No.8 in D major (+ 2ob)	
3.70	No.9 in F major (+ ob)	
3.71	No.10 in B-flat major	
3.72	No.10a in B-flat major	
3.73	No.10b in B-flat major	

3.74	No.11 in C major (+ 2ob; music = Concerto in C major, Co2)
3.75	No.12 in C major (+ ob)
3.76	6 "Balletti e (6) sonate a tre" (p1722; 2vn, vc & org): No.1 Sonata No.1 in B-flat major Op.8
3.77	No.2 Allemanda No.1 in D minor
3.78	No.3 Sonata No.2 in A major
3.79	No.4 Allemanda No.2 in F major
3.80	No.5 Sonata No.3 in C major
3.81	No.6 Allemanda No.3 in D major
3.82	No.7 Sonata No.4 in G minor
3.83	No.8 Allemanda No.4 in B-flat major
3.84	No.9 Sonata No.5 in F major
3.85	No.10 Allemanda No.5 in C major
3.86	No.11 Sonata No.6 in C minor
3.87	No.12 Allemanda No.6 in G minor
3.88	12 "Concerti a cinque" (p1722): No.1 in B-flat major (3vn, va, vc & cont) Op.9
3.89	No.2 in D minor (ob, 2vn, va, vc & cont)
3.90	No.3 in F major (2ob, 2vn, va, vc & cont)
3.91	No.4 in A major (3vn, va, vc & cont)
3.92	No.5 in C major (ob, 2vn, va, vc & cont)
3.93	No.6 in G major (2ob, 2vn, va, vc & cont)
3.94	No.7 in D major (3vn, va, vc & cont)
3.95	No.8 in G minor (ob, 2vn, va, vc & cont)
3.96	No.9 in C major (2ob, 2vn, va, vc & cont)
3.97	No.10 in F major (ob, 2vn, va, vc & cont)
3.98	No.11 in B-flat major (ob, 2vn, va, vc & cont)
3.99	No.12 in D major (2ob, 2vn, va, vc & cont)
3.100	12 "Concerti a cinque" (p ?1735–6; 3vn, va, vc & org): No.1 in B-flat major Op.10
3.101	No.2 in G minor
3.102	No.3 in C major
3.103	No.4 in G major
3.104	No.5 in A major
3.105	No.6 in D major
3.106	No.7 in F major
3.107	No.8 in G minor
3.108	No.9 in F major
3.109	No.10 in C major
3.110	No.11 in C minor
3.111	No.12 in B-flat major

4. CONCERTOS (3vn, va & bass)

4.1	Concerto in D major (+ vle)	Co1
4.2	Concerto in C major (ca1717; music = No.11 in: Concerti à cinque, Op.7)	Co2
4.3	Concerto in C major	Co2a
4.4	Concerto in C major	Co2b
4.5	*Concerto in D major (lost)*	*Co3*
4.6	Concerto in G major	Co4
4.7	Concerto in A major	Co5

5. SONATAS

5.1	"Sonata à sei con tromba," in C major (tpt, 2vn, va, vle & org)	So1
5.2	"Balletti a cinque" (2vn, 2va, vc & org): No.1 "Introduzione," in B-flat major	So2
5.3	No.2 "Introduzione," in G minor	So3
5.4	No.3 "Introduzione," in E minor	So4
5.5	No.4 "Introduzione," in F minor	So5
5.6	No.5 "Introduzione," in A major	So6
5.7	No.6 "Introduzione," in F major	So7
5.8	"Balletti a quattro" (2vn, va & cont): No.1 in G major	So8
5.9	No.2 in B minor	So9
5.10	No.3 in D major	So10
5.11	No.4 in A major	So11
5.12	No.5 in C major	So12
5.13	No.6 in E minor	So13
5.14	No.7 in F major	So14
5.15	No.8 in A minor	So15
5.16	No.9 in B-flat major	So16
5.17	No.10 in D minor	So17
5.18	No.11 in E major	So18
5.19	No.12 in G minor	So19
5.20	"Sonate a tre" (2vn, vc & org): No.1 in C major	So20
5.21	No.2 in B-flat major	So21
5.22	No.3 in F major	So22

6. MISC INSTRUMENTAL (attributed to Albinoni but not certain)

7. SACRED VOCAL

8. ORATORIOS

9. SERENATAS

10. CANTATAS (1v & cont)

* * * * *

Si, Co, So, Mi = Michael Talbot: "Albinoni. Leben und Werk." Edition Kunzelmann. Switzerland, 1980.

1. STAGE WORKS

Operas:

1.1 "Przygoda króla Artura" (The Adventure of King Arthur), radio comic opera (c1959, Fischer; TV vers 1960)

Ballets:

1.2 "Z chlopa król" (The Peasant King), ballet (c1953–4, Swinarski after Baryka)..

1.3 "Esik w Ostendzie" (Esik in Ostend), comic ballet (c1964, Terpiłowski after Boy-Żeleński) ....

1.4 "Pożądanie" (Desire), ballet (c1968–9, Bibrowski after Picasso: Désir attrapé par la queue) ....

Incid music:

1.5 "Farfarello," radio play (c1945, based on Zeromski: Róża) ....

1.6 "O Janku co psom szył buty" (c1945, Słowacki)..

1.7 "Konrad Wallenrod" (c1950, Mickiewicz) ....

1.8 "Nieboska Komedia" (c1959, Krasiński) ....

1.9 "Macbeth" (c1960, Shakespeare transl Korzeniewski) (also see operas c by Bloch & Verdi, incid music c by Khachaturian, Milhaud Op.175, Spohr WoO 55 & Sullivan) ....

1.10 "Troilus and Cressida" (c1960, Shakespeare transl Korzeniewski) ....

1.11 "Sprawa" (c1961, Suchowo-Kobylin) ....

1.12 "Mazepa" (c1965, Słowacki)..

1.13 "Balladyna" (c1965, Słowacki) ....

Radio (orch):

1.14 "Mazur" (Mazurka) (c1944)..

1.15 "Pod strzechą" (Under the Thatch) (c1945)..

1.16 "Suite" (c1946; strings) ....

1.17 "Ze starej muzyki" (From Old Music) (c1946) ....

1.18 "Polish Dance No.2" (c1948) ....

1.19 "Szkice ludowe" (Folk Sketches) (c1948) ....

1.20 "Groteska" (c1949) ....

1.21 "Oberek" (c1949, transcription) ....

1.22 "Waltz" (c1949) ....

1.23 "Easy Pieces for Clarinet & Orchestra" (c1949) ....

1.24 "Polish Caprice" (c1949, transcription) ....

1.25 "Krakowiak" (c1950) ....

1.26 "Serenada" (c1950) ....

1.27 "Suita tańców polskich" (Polish Dance Suite) (c1950) ....

1.28 "Wiwat" (Quintet for clarinet & strings) (c1950) ....

1.29 "Mazovian dance" (c1951, transcription) ....

1.30 "Nocturne" (c1951, from: Violin Sonata No.5) ....

1.31 "Oberek noworoczny" (Oberek for the New Year) (c1952) ....

1.32 "Songs for Children" (c1959–60, various) ....

Film:

1.33 Music for children's films (c1957, 1959, 1960) ....

2. SYMPHONIES

2.1 *Symphony (c1933, lost)* ....

2.2 *Symphony (c1938, lost)* ....

2.3 Symphony No.1 (c1945) ....

2.4 Symphony (c1946; strings)..

2.5 Symphony No.2 (c1951)..

2.6 Symphony No.3 (c1952)..

2.7 Symphony No.4 (c1953)..

3. OTHER ORCHESTRAL WORKS

3.1 "Sinfonietta" (c1929; chamber orch) ....

3.2 "Suite" (c1931; strings) ....

3.3 "Sinfonietta" (c1932) ....

3.4 "3 Karykatury" (3 Caricatures) (c1932) ....

3.5 "Pochód radości" (Procession of Joy), sym poem (c1933) ....

3.6 "Sinfonietta" (c1935; strings) ....

3.7 "Overture" (c1943) ....

3.8 "Introduction & Caprice" (c1947) ....

3.9 "Concerto" (c1948; strings) ....

3.10 "Polish Overture" (c1954) ....

4. CONCERTOS, SOLO INSTR & ORCH

Pf & orch:

Vn & orch:

Va & orch:

Vc & orch:

Other:

5. STRING QUARTETS

6. OTHER CHAMBER MUSIC

4 or more insts:

3 insts:

6.9   "Trio" (c1965; ob, harp & perc) ....

Vn & pf:

6.10   "Song for Violin & Piano" (c1927) ....
6.11   Violin Sonata (No.1) (c1929) ....
6.12   "Partita" (c1930) ....
6.13   "Une pièce pour violin et piano" (c1931) ....
6.14   "Caprice" No.1 (c1932) ....
6.15   "Witraż" (Stained Glass) (c1932) ....
6.16   "Andante & allegro" (c1934) ....
6.17   "Caprice" No.2 (c1934) ....
6.18   "Pieśń litewska" (Lithuanian Song) (c1934) ....
6.19   "Theme and Variations" (c1934) ....
6.20   "Partita" (c1935) ....
6.21   "Allegro" (c1936) ....
6.22   "Concertino" (c1945) ....
6.23   "Legenda" (c1945) ....
6.24   "Sonata da Camera" (Vn Son No.1) (c1945; 4th movt Andante sostenuto arr for va/vc & org)............
6.25   "Łatwe utwory" (Easy Pieces) (Exercise Book I) (c1946) ....
6.26   "Caprice" (c1946) ....
6.27   Violin Sonata No.2 (c1946) ....
6.28   Violin Sonata No.3 (c1947) ....
6.29   "Taniec polski" (Polish Dance) (c1948, encore piece; pubd as No.1 of: 3 Dances) ....
6.30   "Melody" (c1949, encore piece) ....
6.31   "Oberek" No.1 (c1949, encore piece) ....
6.32   Violin Sonata No.4 (c1949) ....
6.33   "Taniec antyczny" (Antique Dance) (c1950) ....
6.34   Violin Sonata No.5 (c1951) ....
6.35   "Taniec mazowiecki" (Mazovian Dance) (c1951, encore piece; pubd as No.2 of: 3 Dances; arr for vc & pf)
6.36   "Kołysanka" (Lullaby) (c1952, encore piece) ....
6.37   "Oberek" No.2 (c1952, encore piece) ....
6.38   "Taniec słowiański" (Slavic Dance) (c1952, encore piece; pubd as No.3 of: 3 Dances) ....
6.39   "Humoresque" (c1953, encore piece) ....
6.40   "Partita" (No.2) (c1955; also see orch work) ....

Other 2 insts:

6.41   "Easy Pieces" (c1932; various insts) ....
6.42   Oboe Sonata (c1936; ob & pf) ....
6.43   "Suite" (c1943; 2vn) ....
6.44   "Easy Duets on Folk Themes" (c1945; 2vn) ....
6.45   "Easy Pieces" (c1948; cl & pf) ....
6.46   "Oberek" No.1 (c1949; cl & pf) ....
6.47   "Polish Caprice" (c1952; cl & pf) ....
6.48   Sonatina (c1955; ob & pf) ....

Vn solo:

6.49   "Sonata" (c1929) ....
6.50   "Sonata" (c1932) ....
6.51   "Sonata" No.1 (c1941) ....
6.52   "Scherzo" (c1945) ....
6.53   "Polish Caprice" (c1949, encore piece) ....
6.54   "Caprice" No.2 (c1952) ....
6.55   "Sonata" No.2 (c1958; transcr for va) ....
6.56   "4 Caprices" (c1968; transcr for va) ....

7. PIANO SONATAS

7.1   Piano Sonata (c1930)..
7.2   Piano Sonata (c1935)..
7.3   Piano Sonata (c1938)..
7.4   Piano Sonata (c1942)..
7.5   Piano Sonata No.1 (c1949) ....
7.6   Piano Sonata No.2 (c1955) ....

8. OTHER PIANO WORKS

8.1   "March" (c1920) ....
8.2   "4 Preludes" (c1921)..
8.3   "Theme & Variations" (c1924) ....
8.4   "Preludium & fugue" (c1927) ....

8.5	"Preludium" (c1928) ....
8.6	"Allegro" (c1929) ....
8.7	"Adagio & fugue" (c1931) ....
8.8	"2 Miniatures" (c1931) ....
8.9	"Andante & allegro" (c1932) ....
8.10	"Trois pièces caractéristiques" (c1932) ....
8.11	"Toccata" (c1932) ....
8.12	"Sonatina" (c1933) ....
8.13	"Suita dziecięca" (Children's Suite) (c1933) ....
8.14	"Scherzo" (c1934) ....
8.15	"3 Burlesques" (c1935) ....
8.16	"3 Preludes" (c1941) ....
8.17	"Krakowiak koncertowy" (c1949) ....
8.18	"3 Etudes" (ca1949, 1952 & 1955) ....
8.19	"Etiuda tercjowa" (Study in Thirds) (c1952) ....
8.20	"10 Etudes" (c1956) ....
8.21	"Maly tryptyk" (Little Triptych) (c1965) ....

9. ORGAN

| 9.1 | "Esquisse" (c1966) .... |

10. CHORAL WORKS

10.1	"Fugue for double choir" (c1928; ch) ....
10.2	"Fugue for 4 voices" (c1931; ch) ....
10.3	"De profundis," cantata (c1932; vv, ch & orch) ....
10.4	"Kantata olimpijska" (Olympic Cantata) (c1948, Pindar; ch & orch) ....
10.5	"Acropolis," cantata (c1964, Wyspiański: Akropolis; ch & orch, for 600th anniv of Jagieloński University) ....
10.6	"Flirtations" (Song for choir) (c1968; ch) ....

11. VOICE & ORCHESTRA

11.1	"3 Songs" (c1938, 10th cent Arabic transl Staff; T & orch/pf): 1. "Illusion" ....
11.2	2. "Another one"
11.3	3. "Loneliness"

12. SONGS (w/ pf)

12.1	"Pink, trailing wild flowers" (c1929) ....
12.2	"Oh, Mother" (c1930) ....
12.3	"Trzy róże" (Three Roses) (c1934, Arabic transl Staff) ....
12.4	"Mów do mnie, miły" (Speak to me, Beloved) (c1936, Tagore transl Kasprowicz) ....
12.5	"Oto jest noc" (Here is the Night) (c1947, Gałczyński) ....
12.6	"Smuga cienia" (Trail of Shadow) (c1949, Broniewski) ....
12.7	"Rozstanie" (Parting) (c1949, Tagore transl Kasprowicz) ....
12.8	"Usta i pelnia" (Lips and Fullness) (c1949, Gałczyński) ....
12.9	"Boli mnie glowa" (My Head Aches) (c1955, Bacewicz) ....
12.10	"Dzwon i dzwonki" (Bell and Little Bells) (c1955, Mickiewicz) ....
12.11	"Nad wodą wielką i czystą" (Over the Wide, Clear Water) (c1955, Mickiewicz) ....
12.12	"Sroczka" (Little Magpie) (c1956, trad) ....

13. ARRANGEMENTS OF WORKS OF OTHERS

13.1	Szymanowski: "Harnasie," ballet Op.55, M68 (red1935; 2pf) ....
13.2	Paganini: Caprice No.4, Op.1/4 (transcr1946; vn & pf) ....
13.3	Szymanowski: Prelude No.1 in B minor, Op.1/1, M1/1 (transcr1948; vn & pf) ....
13.4	Grieg: "Nocturne," in C major, Op.54/4 (transcr1950; vn & pf) ....
13.5	Campagnoli: Capriccio No.17 (Theme with variations) (transcr1952; va & pf) ....

* * * * *

1. SINFONIAS

2. CONCERTOS & SONATINAS

3. CHAMBER MUSIC (w/ kbd obbl)

4. SOLO SONATAS

5. TRIO SONATAS

6. OTHER CHAMBER MUSIC

7. KEYBOARD

7.10	No.4 in E minor	Wq64/4, H10
7.11	No.5 in D major	Wq64/5, H11
7.12	No.6 in E-flat major	Wq64/6, H12

c1735:

7.13	Keyboard Sonata in E minor (r1743)	Wq65/5, H13
7.14	"Minuet (c by Locatelli) with Variations," in G major	Wq118/7, H14

c1736–8:

7.15	"5 Keyboard Sonatas" (r1743–4): No.1 in G major	Wq65/6, H15
7.16	No.2 in E-flat major	Wq65/7, H16
7.17	No.3 in C major	Wq65/8, H17
7.18	No.4 in B-flat major	Wq65/9, H18
7.19	No.5 in A major	Wq65/10, H19

c1739:

7.20	Keyboard Sonata in B-flat major	Wq62/2, H20
7.21	Keyboard Sonata in G minor	Wq65/11, H21

c1740:

7.22	Keyboard Sonata in D major	Wq62/3, H22
7.23	Keyboard Sonata in G major	Wq65/12, H23
7.24	6 "Prussian Sonatas" (c1740–2): No.1 in F major	Wq48/1, H24
7.25	No.2 in B-flat major	Wq48/2, H25
7.26	No.3 in E major	Wq48/3, H26
7.27	No.4 in C minor	Wq48/4, H27
7.28	No.5 in C major	Wq48/5, H28
7.29	No.6 in A major	Wq48/6, H29

c1742–3:

7.30	6 "Württemberg Sonatas" (No.6 = Wq49/6, H36): No.1 in A minor	Wq49/1, H30
7.31	No.2 in A-flat major	Wq49/2, H31
7.32	No.3 in B-flat major	Wq49/4, H32
7.33	No.4 in E minor	Wq49/3, H33
7.34	No.5 in E-flat major	Wq49/5, H34
7.35	Keyboard Sonata in B minor (c1743)	Wq65/13, H35

c1744:

7.36	Keyboard Sonata in B minor (= No.6 of: 6 Württemberg Sonatas, Wq49)	Wq49/6, H36
7.37	Keyboard Sonata in F-sharp minor	Wq52/4, H37
7.38	"4 Keyboard Sonatas": No.1 in D minor	Wq62/4, H38
7.39	No.2 in E major	Wq62/5, H39
7.40	No.3 in F minor	Wq62/6, H40
7.41	No.4 in C major	Wq62/7, H41
7.42	Keyboard Sonata in D major	Wq65/14, H42

c1745

7.43	Keyboard Sonata in G major	Wq65/15, H43
7.44	"Minuetto con variationi," in C major	Wq118/3, H44
7.45	"Sinfonia," in G major (= kbd red of: Sinfonie in G major, Wq173, H648)	Wq122/1, H45

c1746:

7.46	"4 Keyboard Sonatas" (c1746–8): No.1 in C major	Wq65/16, H46
7.47	No.2 in G minor	Wq65/17, H47
7.48	No.3 in F major	Wq65/18, H48
7.49	No.4 in F major	Wq65/19, H49

c1747:

7.50	Keyboard Sonata in E-flat major	Wq52/1, H50
7.51	"2 Keyboard Sonatas": No.1 "Grande Sonate," in B-flat major	Wq65/20, H51
7.52	No.2 in F major	Wq65/21, H52
7.53	Keyboard Sonata "a due tastature," in D minor	Wq69, H53
7.54	"Arioso con 7 variazioni," in F major	Wq118/4, H54

c1748:

7.55	"3 Keyboard Sonatas": No.1 in F major	Wq62/8, H55
7.56	No.2 in G major	Wq65/22, H56
7.57	No.3 in D minor	Wq65/23, H57

c1749:

7.58	"4 Keyboard Sonatas": No.1 in F major	Wq62/9, H58

7.59	No.2 in C major	Wq62/10, H59
7.60	No.3 in D minor	Wq65/24, H60
7.61	No.4 in C major	Wq65/25, H61

c1750:

7.62	Keyboard Sonata in G major	Wq51/6, H62
7.63	Keyboard Sonata in G major	Wq62/11, H63
7.64	Keyboard Sonata in G major	Wq65/26, H64
7.65	"Allegretto con 6 variazioni," in C major	Wq118/5, H65

c1751:

7.66	Keyboard Sonata in E minor	Wq62/12, H66

c1752:

7.67	"2 Keyboard Sonatas": No.1 in D major	Wq62/13, H67
7.68	No.2 in G minor	Wq65/27, H68
7.69	"24 Veränderungen über das Lied: Ich schlief," in F major	Wq118/1, H69

c1753:

7.70	"18 Probestücke in 6 Sonaten": No.1 in C major	Wq63/1, H70
7.71	No.2 in D minor	Wq63/2, H71
7.72	No.3 in A major	Wq63/3, H72
7.73	No.4 in B min / D maj / F-sharp minor	Wq63/4, H73
7.74	No.5 in E-flat major	Wq63/5, H74
7.75	No.6 in F minor (3rd movt: 'Hamlet' Fantasia in C minor)	Wq63/6, H75

c1754:

7.76	"Duo in contrap. ad 8, 11 & 12 mit Anmerkungen," in A minor	Wq119/1, H76
7.77	"2 Keyboard Sonatas": No.1 in G major	Wq62/14, H77
7.78	No.2 in E-flat major	Wq65/28, H78
7.79	"La Borchward," polonaise in G major	Wq117/17, H79
7.80	"La Pott," minuet in C major	Wq117/18, H80
7.81	"La Boehmer," in D major	Wq117/26, H81
7.82	"La Gause," in F major	Wq117/37, H82

c1755:

7.83	Keyboard Sonata in E major	Wq65/29, H83
7.84	"4 Organ Sonatas" (org solo): No.1 in F major	Wq70/3, H84
7.85	No.2 in A minor	Wq70/4, H85
7.86	No.3 in D major	Wq70/5, H86
7.87	No.4 in G minor	Wq70/6, H87
7.88	"Fuga a 3," in G minor	Wq112/19, H88
7.89	"La Gleim," rondeau in A minor	Wq117/19, H89
7.90	"La Bergius," in B-flat major	Wq117/20, H90
7.91	"La Prinzette," in F major	Wq117/21, H91
7.92	"L'Herrmann," in G minor	Wq117/23, H92
7.93	"La Buchholz," in D minor	Wq117/24, H93
7.94	"La Stahl," in D minor	Wq117/25, H94
7.95	"L'Aly Rupalich," in C major	Wq117/27, H95
7.96	"La Philippine," in A major	Wq117/34, H96
7.97	"La Gabriel," in C major	Wq117/35, H97
7.98	"La Caroline," in A minor	Wq117/39, H98
7.99	"Fuga a 2," in D minor	Wq119/2, H99
7.100	"Fuga a 3," in F major	Wq119/3, H100
7.101	"Fuga a 3 mit Anmerkungen," in A major	Wq119/4, H101
7.102	"Fuga a 4, org. mit Anmerkungen," in E-flat major	Wq119/6, H102
7.103	"Fantasia e fuga a 4," in C minor	Wq119/7, H103
7.104	"Sinfonia," in F major (= kbd red of: Sinfonia in F major, Wq175, H650)	Wq122/2, H104

c1756:

7.105	"2 Keyboard Sonatas": No.1 in D minor	Wq62/15, H105
7.106	No.2 in E minor	Wq65/30, H106
7.107	"Preludio," in D major (org)	Wq70/7, H107
7.108	"Andantino," in F major	Wq116/18, H108
7.109	"La Complaisante," in B-flat major	Wq117/28, H109
7.110	"Les Langueurs tendres" (La memoire raisonée), in C minor	Wq117/30, H110
7.111	"L'Irrésoluë," in G major	Wq117/31, H111
7.112	"La Journalière," in C minor	Wq117/32, H112
7.113	"La Capricieuse," in E minor	Wq117/33, H113
7.114	"La Louise," in D major	Wq117/36, H114
7.115	*"Sinfonia," in E minor (= lost kbd red of: Sinfonia in E minor, Wq177, H652)*	*Wq122/3, H115*

c1757:

7.116	"5 Keyboard Sonatas": No.1 in B-flat major	Wq62/16, H116
7.117	No.2 in E major	Wq62/17, H117
7.118	No.3 in G minor	Wq62/18, H118
7.119	No.4 in G major	Wq62/19, H119
7.120	No.5 in C major	Wq62/20, H120
7.121	Keyboard Sonata in C minor	Wq65/31, H121
7.122	"L'Auguste," polonaise in F major	Wq117/22, H122
7.123	"La Xénophon et La Sybille," in C-sharp major	Wq117/29, H123
7.124	"L'Ernestine," in D major	Wq117/38, H124
7.125	"La Sophie," aria in B-flat major	Wq117/40, H125

c1758:

7.126	Keyboard Sonata in B-flat major	Wq50/5, H126
7.127	"3 Keyboard Sonatas": No.1 in C minor	Wq51/3, H127
7.128	No.2 in D minor	Wq51/4, H128
7.129	No.3 in E minor	Wq52/6, H129
7.130	Keyboard Sonata in F major	Wq55/2, H130
7.131	"2 Keyboard Sonatas": No.1 in A minor	Wq62/21, H131
7.132	No.2 in B minor	Wq62/22, H132
7.133	"2 Keyboard Sonatas" (org): No.1 in A major	Wq70/1, H133
7.134	No.2 in B-flat major	Wq70/2, H134
7.135	Keyboard Sonata in A major	Wq65/32, H135

c1759:

7.136	"5 Keyboard Sonatas": No.1 in F major	Wq50/1, H136
7.137	No.2 in G major	Wq50/2, H137
7.138	No.3 in A minor	Wq50/3, H138
7.139	No.4 in D minor	Wq50/4, H139
7.140	No.5 in B-flat major	Wq50/6, H140
7.141	"2 Keyboard Sonatas": No.1 in F major	Wq51/5, H141
7.142	No.2 in D minor	Wq52/2, H142
7.143	Keyboard Sonata in A minor	Wq65/33, H143
7.144	"Fantasia," in D major	Wq112/2, H144
7.145	"Solfeggio," in G major	Wq112/4, H145
7.146	"Fantasia," in B-flat major	Wq112/8, H146
7.147	"Solfeggio," in C major	Wq112/10, H147
7.148	"Fantasia," in F major	Wq112/15, H148
7.149	"Solfeggio," in G major	Wq112/18, H149

c1760:

7.150	"3 Keyboard Sonatas": No.1 in C major (r as No.2 in: 2 Kbd Sonatas, Wq65/36, H157)	Wq51/1, H150
7.151	No.2 in B-flat major	Wq51/2, H151
7.152	No.3 in B-flat major	Wq65/34, H152
7.153	"Allegro," in C major	Wq116/21, H153
7.154	"Polonoise," in G minor	Wq116/22, H154
7.155	"Clavierstück mit (22) Veränderungen," in A major	Wq118/2, H155
7.156	"2 Keyboard Sonatas": No.1 in C major	Wq65/35, H156
7.157	No.2 in C major (r of H150)	Wq65/36, H157

c1761:

7.158	Keyboard Sonata in G minor	Wq52/3, H158

c1762:

7.159	"Minuet," in E-flat major	Wq116/1, H159
7.160	"Polonaise," in E-flat major	Wq116/2, H160
7.161	"Minuet," in C major	Wq116/15, H161
7.162	"Fantasia," in D major (pubd in: Versuch)	Wq117/14, H162
7.163	"3 Keyboard Sonatas": No.1 in E major	Wq52/5, H163
7.164	No.2 in C major	Wq53/1, H164
7.165	No.3 in C minor	Wq53/5, H165
7.166	"Veränderungen und Auszierungen über einige meiner Sonaten"	Wq68, H166
7.167	"Minuet," in D major	Wq112/3, H167
7.168	"Alla polacca," in A minor	Wq112/5, H168
7.169	"Minuet," in D major	Wq112/9, H169
7.170	"Alla polacca," in G minor	Wq112/11, H170
7.171	"Minuet," in A major	Wq112/16, H171
7.172	"Alla polacca," in D major	Wq112/17, H172

c1763:

7.173	Keyboard Sonata in F minor	Wq57/6, H173
7.174	"5 Keyboard Sonatas": No.1 in A major	Wq65/37, H174

7.175	No.2 in B-flat major	Wq65/38, H175
7.176	No.3 in E minor	Wq65/39, H176
7.177	No.4 in D major	Wq65/40, H177
7.178	No.5 in C major	Wq65/41, H178
7.179	Keyboard Sonata in D minor	Wq112/7, H179

c1764:

7.180	"4 Keyboard Sonatas": No.1 in B-flat major	Wq53/2, H180
7.181	No.2 in A minor	Wq53/3, H181
7.182	No.3 in B minor	Wq53/4, H182
7.183	No.4 in F major	Wq53/6, H183

c1765:

7.184	"2 Keyboard Sonatas": No.1 in D minor	Wq54/3, H184
7.185	No.2 in D major	Wq54/5, H185
7.186	"2 Keyboard Sonatas": No.1 in A major	Wq55/4, H186
7.187	No.2 in G major	Wq55/6, H187
7.188	"2 Keyboard Sonatas": No.1 in E minor	Wq58/4, H188
7.189	No.2 in E-flat major	Wq65/42, H189
7.190	"Concerto," in C major (hpd solo)	Wq112/1, H190
7.191	"Sinfonia," in G major (hpd solo, red of: Sinfonia in G major, Wq180, H655)	Wq112/13, H191
7.192	Keyboard Sonata in A major	Wq65/43, H192
7.193	"Kurze und leichte Klavierstücke": No.1 "Allegro," in G major	Wq113/1, H193
7.194	No.2 "Arioso," in A minor	Wq113/2, H194
7.195	No.3 "Fantasia," in D minor	Wq113/3, H195
7.196	No.4 "Minuet," in F major	Wq113/4, H196
7.197	No.5 "Alla polacca," in C major	Wq113/5, H197
7.198	No.6 "Allegretto," in D minor	Wq113/6, H198
7.199	No.7 "Alla polacca," in D major	Wq113/7, H199
7.200	No.8 "Allegretto," in A major	Wq113/8, H200
7.201	No.9 "Andante e sostenuto," in G minor	Wq113/9, H201
7.202	No.10 "Presto," in B-flat major	Wq113/10, H202
7.203	No.11 "Allegro," in D minor	Wq113/11, H203

c1766:

7.204	"4 Keyboard Sonatas": No.1 in F major	Wq54/1, H204
7.205	No.2 in C major	Wq54/2, H205
7.206	No.3 in B-flat major	Wq54/4, H206
7.207	No.4 in A major	Wq54/6, H207
7.208	Keyboard Sonata in D minor	Wq57/4, H208
7.209	Keyboard Sonata in C minor	Wq60, H209
7.210	"4 Keyboard Sonatas": No.1 in F major	Wq62/23, H210
7.211	No.2 in C major	Wq65/44, H211
7.212	No.3 in B-flat major	Wq65/45, H212
7.213	No.4 in A major	Wq65/46, H213
7.214	"Minuet," in D major	Wq116/3, H214
7.215	"Alla polacca," in C major	Wq116/4, H215
7.216	"Minuet," in C major	Wq116/5, H216
7.217	"Alla polacca," in D major	Wq116/6, H217
7.218	"Minuet," in F major	Wq116/7, H218
7.219	"Alla polacca," in G major	Wq116/8, H219
7.220	"3 Solfeggios": No.1 in C minor	Wq117/2, H220
7.221	No.2 in E-flat major	Wq117/3, H221
7.222	No.3 in A major	Wq117/4, H222
7.223	"3 Fantasias": No.1 in G major	Wq117/11, H223
7.224	No.2 in D minor	Wq117/12, H224
7.225	No.3 in G minor	Wq117/13, H225
7.226	"Romance 'avec 12 variations,' " in G major	Wq118/6, H226
7.227	"Sinfonia," in F major (hpd solo)	Wq122/5, H227

c1767:

7.228	"Allegro molto," in D minor	Wq114/1, H228
7.229	"Andantino e grazioso," in B-flat major	Wq114/2, H229
7.230	"Presto," in C minor	Wq114/3, H230
7.231	"Minuet," in G major	Wq114/4, H231
7.232	"Alla polacca," in D major	Wq114/5, H232
7.233	"Alla polacca," in E-flat major	Wq114/6, H233
7.234	"Fantasia," in D minor	Wq114/7, H234
7.235	"Allegro," in E major	Wq114/8, H235
7.236	"Allegretto," in A major	Wq114/9, H236
7.237	"Andante," in C major	Wq114/10, H237
7.238	"Poco allegro," in E minor	Wq114/11, H238

c1768:

7.239   "Polonaise," in G major H239

c1769:

7.240   "Clavier-Sonate mit veränderten Reprisen," in F major Wq62/24, H240

c1770:

7.241   "Clavierstück für die rechte oder linke Hand allein," in A major Wq117/1, H241
7.242   "Concerto" (hpd solo) H242

c1772:

7.243   "5 Keyboard Sonatas": No.1 in F major Wq55/5, H243
7.244   No.2 in C major Wq55/1, H244
7.245   No.3 in B minor Wq55/3, H245
7.246   No.4 in G major Wq56/2, H246
7.247   No.5 in A minor Wq57/2, H247

c1775:

7.248   "Sechs leichte Clavier-Stückgen": No.1 in C major Wq65/47, H248
7.249   No.2 in F major H249
7.250   No.3 in D major H250
7.251   No.4 in G major H251
7.252   No.5 in B-flat major H252
7.253   No.6 in D major H253
7.254   "Minuet," in F major H254
7.255   "Allegro," in D major H255
7.256   "Allegro," in F major H256
7.257   "Allegretto," in D major H257
7.258   "Minuet," in F major H258

c1777:

7.259   "Variationen mit veränderten Reprisen," in C major Wq118/10, H259

c1778:

7.260   "3 Rondos": No.1 in C major Wq56/1, H260
7.261   No.2 in D major Wq56/3, H261
7.262   No.3 in A minor Wq56/5, H262
7.263   12 "Variationes über die Folie d'Espagne," in D minor Wq118/9, H263
7.264   80 "Cadenzen" (for his own concertos & sonatas) Wq120, H264

c1779:

7.265   "4 Rondos": No.1 in E major Wq57/1, H265
7.266   No.2 in F major Wq57/5, H266
7.267   No.3 in B-flat major Wq58/5, H267
7.268   No.4 in G major Wq59/2, H268

c1780:

7.269   "2 Keyboard Sonatas": No.1 in F major Wq56/4, H269
7.270   No.2 in A major Wq56/6, H270
7.271   "Rondo," in G major Wq57/3, H271

c1781:

7.272   "Abschied von meinem ... Claviere, in einem Rondo," in E minor Wq66, H272
7.273   Keyboard Sonata in G maj / E major Wq58/2, H273
7.274   "Rondo," in E major Wq58/3, H274
7.275   "Canzonetta der Herzogin von Gotha," in F major Wq118/8, H275

c1782:

7.276   "Rondo," in A major Wq58/1, H276
7.277   "3 Fantasias": No.1 in E-flat major Wq58/6, H277
7.278   No.2 in A major Wq58/7, H278
7.279   No.3 in F major Wq59/5, H279

c1783:

7.280   "Sonata fürs Bogen-Clavier," in G major Wq65/48, H280

c1784:

7.281   "2 Keyboard Sonatas": No.1 in E minor Wq59/1, H281
7.282   No.2 in B-flat major Wq59/3, H282
7.283   "Rondo," in C minor Wq59/4, H283

7.284	"Fantasia," in C major	Wq59/6, H284
7.285	"Fughetta on the name 'C. P. E. Bach,' " in F major	H285

c1785:

7.286	"2 Keyboard Sonatas": No.1 in D major	Wq61/2, H286
7.287	No.2 in G major	Wq61/5, H287
7.288	"Rondo," in E-flat major	Wq61/1, H288
7.289	"Fantasia," in B-flat major	Wq61/3, H289
7.290	"Rondo," in D minor	Wq61/4, H290
7.291	"Fantasia," in C major	Wq61/6, H291

c1786:

7.292	"6 sonatine nuove": No.1 in G major	Wq63/7, H292
7.293	No.2 in E major	Wq63/8, H293
7.294	No.3 in D major	Wq63/9, H294
7.295	No.4 in B-flat major	Wq63/10, H295
7.296	No.5 in F major	Wq63/11, H296
7.297	No.6 in D minor	Wq63/12, H297
7.298	"2 Keyboard Sonatas": No.1 in E-flat major	Wq65/49, H298
7.299	No.2 in G major	Wq65/50, H299

c1787:

7.300	"Freie Fantasie fürs Clavier," in F-sharp minor (also see: Clavier-Fantasie, Wq80, H536)	Wq67, H300

c varies:

7.301	"Allegretto," in F major	Wq116/19, H301
7.302	"Allegro," in D major	Wq116/20, H302
7.303	"Minuet," in G major	Wq116/29, H303
7.304	"Minuet," in G major	Wq116/30, H304
7.305	"Minuet," in G major	Wq116/31, H305
7.306	"Minuet," in F major	Wq116/32, H306
7.307	"Minuet," in D major	Wq116/33, H307
7.308	"Polonaise," in A major	Wq116/34, H308
7.309	"Minuet," in D major	Wq116/35, H309
7.310	"Allegro di molto," in A major	Wq116/36, H310
7.311	"Allegro," in E major	Wq116/37, H311
7.312	"Allegro," in B-flat major	Wq116/38, H312
7.313	"Presto," in A minor	Wq116/39, H313
7.314	"Minuet," in D major	Wq116/40, H314
7.315	"4 Polonaises": No.1 in F major	Wq116/41, H315
7.316	No.2 in A major	Wq116/42, H316
7.317	No.3 in B-flat major	Wq116/43, H317
7.318	No.4 in E-flat major	Wq116/44, H318
7.319	"2 Marches": No.1 in F major	Wq116/45, H319
7.320	No.2 in D major	Wq116/46, H320
7.321	"2 Minuets": No.1 in C major	Wq116/47, H321
7.322	No.2 in G major	Wq116/48, H322
7.323	"Polonaise," in D major	Wq116/49, H323
7.324	"Langsam und traurig," in A minor	Wq116/50, H324
7.325	"Allegro," in C major	Wq116/51, H325
7.326	"Allegro ma non troppo," in E-flat major	Wq116/52, H326
7.327	"Allegro," in C major	Wq116/53, H327
7.328	"Allegro," in G major	Wq116/54, H328
7.329	"Allegro," in E-flat major	Wq116/55, H329
7.330	"Allegro," in D major	Wq116/56, H330
7.331	"Allegretto grazioso," in C major	Wq116/57, H331
7.332	Keyboard Sonata in D major	H332
7.333	"La Juliane," in F major	H333
7.334	"Variations," in C major (late work)	H334
7.335	"Adagio per il organo a 2 claviere e pedal," in D minor	H335
7.336	"5 Choräle mit ... Mittelstimmen" (kbd, no text): No.1 "O Gott"	H336
7.337	No.2 "Ich bin ja Herr in deiner Macht"	
7.338	No.3 "Jesus meine Zuversicht"	
7.339	No.4 "Wer nur den Lieben Gott"	
7.340	No.5 "Komm heiliger Geist"	
7.341	"Chorale: Wo Gott zum Haus nicht gibt, a 4"	H337

Doubtful:

7.342	*2 unattributed movts (?spur): No.1 "Allegro," in A major*	*H338*
7.343	*No.2 "Allegro," in G major*	
7.344	*"Fantasia," in E-flat major (ca1755)*	*H339*
7.345	*"Garten-Sonata," in D major (c by 1762, ?spur)*	*H340*
7.346	*Keyboard Sonata in E minor (c by 1762, ?spur)*	*H341*

8. CHORAL WORKS

9. SOLO VOICE (w/ kbd)

9.1	"3 Arias" (c by ?1738): 1. "Edle Freiheit, Götterglück" Wq211, H669
9.2	2. "Himmels Tochter, Ruh der Seelen"
9.3	3. "Reiche bis zum Wolkensitze" (T, strings & cont)
9.4	"3 Songs": 1. "Schäferlied": "Eilt, ihr Schäfer" (c1741, Ziegler) Wq199/2, H670
9.5	2. "Der Zufriedne": "Entfernt von Gram und Sorgen" (c1743, Stahl) Wq199/10, H671
9.6	3. "Ihr misvergnügten Stunden" (c1743, Steinhauer) Wq199/12, H672
9.7	"3 Songs" (c1750-3): 1. "Die Küsse": "Dass ich bey meiner Lust" (Giseke) Wq199/4, H673
9.8	2. "Trinklied": "Den flüchtigen Tagen" (Gleim) Wq199/5, H674
9.9	3. "Amint": "Sie fliehet fort" (Kleist) Wq199/11, H675
9.10	"Die märkische Helene": "Ehret, Brüder, meine Schöne" (c1754, Lessing) Wq199/14, H676
9.11	"2 Songs" (c1754 or 5): 1. "Die sächsische Helene": "Herr Bruder meine Schöne" Wq199/1, H677
9.12	2. "Dorinde": "Amor sagte zu Cythere" (Gleim) Wq199/7, H678
9.13	"2 Songs" (c1756): 1. "Lied eines jungen Mädchens": "Noch bin ich jung" (?Lessing) Wq199/3, H679
9.14	2. "Der Morgen": "Uns lockt die Morgenröthe" (Hagedorn) Wq199/6, H680
9.15	"4 Songs" (c1756-7): 1. "Die Biene": "Als Amor in den güldnen Zeiten" (Lessing) Wq199/9, H681
9.16	2. "Die Küsse": "Ein Küsschen das ein Kind mir schenket" (Lessing) Wq199/13, H682
9.17	3. "Der Stoiker": "Ein fauler Freund der Fröhlichkeit" Wq199/8, H683
9.18	4. "Serin": "Serin, der hochberühmte Mann" Wq199/15, H684
9.19	"La Sophie," aria (c1757) H685
	54 "Geistliche Oden und Lieder mit Melodien" (c1757-8, Gellert): Wq194, H686
9.20	1. "Abendlied": "Für alle Güte sey gepreist" ....
9.21	2. "Zufriedenheit mit seinem Zustande": "Du klagst und fühlest die Beschwerde" ....
9.22	3. "Das Glück eines guten Gewissens": "Besitz ich nur ein ruhiges Gewissen" ....
9.23	4. "Vom Worte Gottes": "Gott ist mein Hort" ....
9.24	5. "Weihnachtslied": "Auf, schicke dich" ....
9.25	6. "Geduld": "Ein Herz, o Gott" ....
9.26	7. "Prüfung am Abend": "Der Tag ist wieder hin" ....
9.27	8. "Danklied": "Du bists, dem Ruhm und Ehre gebühret" ....
9.28	9. "Bitten": "Gott, deine Güte reicht so weit" (also see Beethoven Op.48/1) ....
9.29	10. "Osterlied": "Jesus lebt, mit ihm auch ich" ....
9.30	11. "Der thätige Glaube": "Wer Gottes Wort nicht hält" ....
9.31	12. "Der Schutz der Kirche": "Wenn Christus seine Kirche schützt" ....
9.32	13. "Um Ergebung in den göttlichen Willen": "O Herr, mein Gott" ....
9.33	14. "Passionslied": "Erforsche mich, erfahr mein Herz" ....
9.34	15. "Morgengesang": "Mein erst Gefühl sey Preis und Dank" ....
9.35	16. "Gottes Macht und Vorsehung": "Gott ist mein Lied" ....
9.36	17. "Trost des ewigen Lebens": "Nach einer Prüfung kurzer Tage" ....
9.37	18. "Die Ehre Gottes aus der Natur": "Die Himmel rühmen des Ewigen Ehre" (also see Beethoven Op.48/4)
9.38	19. "Die Liebe des Nächsten": "So jemand spricht: Ich liebe Gott!" ....
9.39	20. "Auf die Himmelfahrt des Erlösers": "Jauchzt, ihr Erlösten" ....
9.40	21. "Das Gebet": "Dein Heil, o Christ" ....
9.41	22. "Osterlied": "Freywillig hab ichs dargebracht" ....
9.42	23. "Passionslied": "Herr, stärke mich" ....
9.43	24. "Trost eines schwermüthigen Christen": "Du klagst, o Christ" ....
9.44	25. "Betrachtung des Todes": "Wie sicher lebt der Mensch" ....
9.45	26. "Preis des Schöpfers": "Wenn ich, o Schöpfer, deine Macht" ....
9.46	27. "Von der Quelle der guten Werke": "Wenn zur Vollführung deiner Pflicht" ....
9.47	28. "Ermunterung die Schrift zu lesen": "Soll dein verderbtes Herz" ....
9.48	29. "Trost der Erlösung": "Gedanke, der uns Leben giebt" ....
9.49	30. "Warnung vor der Wollust": "Der Wollust Reiz" ....
9.50	31. "Abendlied": "Herr, der du mir das Leben" ....
9.51	32. "Das natürliche Verderben des Menschen": "Wer bin ich von Natur" ....
9.52	33. "Die Güte Gottes": "Wie gross ist des Allmächt'gen Güte" ....
9.53	34. "Der Weg des Frommen": "Wer Gottes Wege geht" ....
9.54	35. "In Krankheit": "Ich hab in guten Stunden" ....
9.55	36. "Vom Tode": "Meine Lebenszeit verstreicht" ....
9.56	37. "Lied am Geburtstage": "Dir dank ich heute für mein Leben" ....
9.57	38. "Versicherung der Gnade Gottes": "So hoff ich denn mit festem Muth" ....
9.58	39. "Gelassenheit": "Was ists, dass ich mich quäle" ....
9.59	40. "Allgemeines Gebet": "Ich komme vor dein Angesicht" ....
9.60	41. "Osterlied": "Erinnre dich, mein Geist, erfreut" ....
9.61	42. "Weinachtslied": "Diess ist der Tag, den Gott gemacht" ....
9.62	43. "Am Communiontage": "Ich komme Herr, und suche dich" ....
9.63	44. "Am neuen Jahre": "Er ruft der Sohn" ....
9.64	45. "Busslied": "An dir allein, an dir hab ich gesündigt" (also see Beethoven Op.48/6) ....
9.65	46. "Die Liebe der Feinde": "Nie will ich dem zu schaden suchen" ....
9.66	47. "Demuth": "Herr, lehre mich" ....
9.67	48. "Wider den Übermuth" ....
9.68	49. "Wider den Aufschub der Bekehrung": "Willst du die Busse noch" ....
9.69	50. "Vertrauen auf Gottes Vorsehung": "Auf Gott, und nicht auf meinen Rath" ....
9.70	51. "Beständig Erinnerung des Todes": "Was sorgst du ängstlich" ....
9.71	52. "Der Kampf der Tugend": "Oft klagt dein Herz" ....

9.138   8. "Der 23. Psalm": "Gott ist mein Hirt, im Schatten seiner Güte" ....
9.139   9. "Der 25. Psalm": "Herr, mein einziges Verlangen" ....
9.140   10. "Der 30. Psalm": "Dich preis ich, Gott; denn du hast mich erhoben" ....
9.141   11. "Der 32. Psalm": "Heil dem, den nicht die Furcht, gestraft zu werden" ....
9.142   12. "Der 33. Psalm": "Jauchzt, ihr Gerechten, dem Herrn, und lasset" ....
9.143   13. "Der 38. Psalm": "Lass mich nicht deinen Zorn empfinden" ....
9.144   14. "Der 42. Psalm": "Wie der Hirsch in schwüler Zeit" ....
9.145   15. "Der 46. Psalm": "Der Herr ist unsre Macht" ....
9.146   16. "Der 47. Psalm": "Frohlocket, ihr Völker, frohlocket mit Händen" ....
9.147   17. "Der 65. Psalm": "Dich, Gott zu Zion" ....
9.148   18. "Der 67. Psalm": "Herr, unser Gott, dem wir vertrauen" ....
9.149   19. "Der 86. Psalm": "Herr, erhöre meine Klagen!" ....
9.150   20. "Der 88. Psalm": "Tag und Nacht, du Heil der Frommen" ....
9.151   21. "Der 90. Psalm": "Herr, unser Gott, du warst" ....
9.152   22. "Der 91. Psalm": "Wie selig ist, der Gott vertraut" ....
9.153   23. "Der 93. Psalm": "Jehova herrscht, ein König über alle" ....
9.154   24. "Der 96. Psalm": "Erhebet Gott durch neue Lieder" ....
9.155   25. "Der 97. Psalm": "Jehova regieret: Es jauchze die Erde" ....
9.156   26. "Der 99. Psalm": "Der Herr regiert; die Völker zittern" ....
9.157   27. "Der 100. Psalm": "Es jauchze Gott und preise Gott alle" ....
9.158   28. "Der 103. Psalm": "Lobsinge Gott! Erwecke deine Kräfte" ....
9.159   29. "Der 104. Psalm": "Erheb, erheb, o meine Seele" ....
9.160   30. "Der 110. Psalm": "Jehova sprach zu Gott, dem Sohne" ....
9.161   31. "Der 111. Psalm": "Gelobt sey Gott! Ihm will ich fröhlich" ....
9.162   32. "Der 116. Psalm": "Dess freu ich mich, dass Gott zu meinen" ....
9.163   33. "Der 119. Psalm": "Heil denen, welche sich unsträflich" ....
9.164   34. "Der 121. Psalm": "Sieh, mein Auge, nach den Bergen" ....
9.165   35. "Der 128. Psalm": "Die Gnade Gottes sey mit allen" ....
9.166   36. "Der 130. Psalm": "Aus der Tiefe ruf ich dir, Höre" ....
9.167   37. "Der 139. Psalm": "Herr, du erforschest mich! Du kennst mich!" ....
9.168   38. "Der 142. Psalm": "Gott, es seufzet meine Stimme" ....
9.169   39. "Der 145. Psalm": "Ich will, mein Gott, du König dir lobsingen" ....
9.170   40. "Der 146. Psalm": "Es werde Gott von uns erhoben!" ....
9.171   41. "Der 148. Psalm": "Preis sey dem Gotte Zebaoth!" ....
9.172   42. "Der 150. Psalm": "Erhebt, erhebet den Herrn" ....

9.173   "Der Frühling, an Röschen": "O seht, die liebe Sonne lacht" (c ?1773–82, Miller) Wq200/9, H734
9.174   "Die Grazien," cantata (c1774, Gerstenberg) Wq200/22, H735
9.175   "Die Schlummernde": "Eingewiegt von Nachtigallentönen" (c1774, Voss) Wq200/G/1, H736
9.176   "Lyda": "Dein süsses Bild, o Lyda" (c1774, Klopstock) Wq200/G/2, H737
9.177   "Trinklied für Freye": "Mit Eichenlaub den Hut bekränzt" (c1775, Voss) Wq202/I/1, H738
9.178   "Selma": "Sie liebt, mich liebt die Auserwählte" (c1775–6, Voss) Wq202/I/2, H739
9.179   "4 Songs": 1. "Trinklied": "Ein Leben wie im Paradies" (c1775–82, Hölty) Wq200/13, H740
9.180   2. "An Doris": "Des Tages Licht hat sich verdunkelt" (c1775–6, Haller) Wq200/2, H741
9.181   3. "Auf den Flügeln des Morgenroths" (c ?1775–6, Cramer) Wq202/O/1, H742
9.182   4. "Da schlägt des Abschieds Stunde" (c ?1775–6, Metastasio) Wq202/O/4, H743
9.183   "An den Schlaf": "Geliebter Schlaf, du Freund von meinem Herzen" (c1776) Wq202/H, H744
9.184   "Todtengräberlied": "Grabe, Spaten, grabe" (c1776–82, Hölty) Wq200/1, H745
9.185   "Selma": "Eil, o May, mit deinem Brautgesange" (c1777, Voss) Wq202/J, H746
9.186   "Aus einer Ode zum neuen Jahr": "Der Weise blickt" (c ?1777–82) Wq200/14, H747
9.187   "An die Grazien und Musen": "Ihr Musen, seht den Amor" (c ?1778–82, Gleim) Wq200/5, H748

        30 "Geistliche Gesänge" (c1780, Sturm): Wq197, H749

9.188   1. "Demüthigung vor Gott": "Betet an vor Gott" ....
9.189   2. "Passionslied": "Einst, als dich im Gerichte" ....
9.190   3. "Loblied für das Seelenleiden Jesu": "Sieh, Gotteslamm, wir fallen" ....
9.191   4. "Osterlied": "Amen! Lob und Preis und Stärke" ....
9.192   5. "Pfingstlied": "Sey, Weltversöhner, sey gepreist" ....
9.193   6. "Passionslied": "Da stehest du, Sohn Gottes" ....
9.194   7. "Gottes Grösse in der Natur": "Gross ist der Herr" ....
9.195   8. "Die Würde des Christen": "Ich bin ein Christ" ....
9.196   9. "Todesfreudigkeit": "Gott, dem ich lebe" ....
9.197   10. "Der gestirnte Himmel": "Mit heilgem Grauen" ....
9.198   11. "Weihnachtslied": "Vom Grab, an dem wir wallen" ....
9.199   12. "Beschleunigung der Busse": "Christ, sey achtsam" ....
9.200   13. "Der Tag des Weltgerichts": "Wann der Erde Gründe beben" ....
9.201   14. "Der Frühling": "Erwacht zum neuen Leben" ....
9.202   15. "Erndtelied": "So weit der Fluren Gränzen blühen" ....
9.203   16. "Frohe Erinnerung der Lehre Jesu": "Auch mich, o Herr" ....
9.204   17. "Sonntagslied": "Dir, Jesu, dir sey dieser Tag geweihet" ....
9.205   18. "Der Weg zum Himmel": "Schmal ist der Pfad" ....
9.206   19. "Neujahrslied": "Schon wieder ist von meiner Zeit" ....
9.207   20. "Sommerlied": "Allgütiger, dich will ich fühlen" ....
9.208   21. "Die Fortdauer der Lehre Jesu": "Umsonst empört die Hölle sich" ....
9.209   22. "Dieses und jenes Leben": "Ein Pilger bin ich" ....

* * * * *

Wq = A. Wotquenne: "Thematisches Verzeichnis der Werke von C. P. E. Bach." Leipzig, 1905/ r1972.
H = E. Helm: "A New Thematic Catalog of the Works of Carl Philip Emanuel Bach."

1. STAGE WORKS

Operas (3 acts):

Material inserted in operas & pasticcios:

7. "Obliar l'amato sposo," aria
8. "La sventura del figlio," scena

1.32	*"Amelia," pasticcio (p1771, Cumberland: The Summer's Tale, music lost)* ....
1.33	"The Flitch of Bacon," pasticcio (p1778, Shield): T245/2
	. "No, 'twas neither," aria

Spurious:

1.34	*"Arrestatevi olà barbare furie," scena for: Ifigenia (?spur)* ....
1.35	*"Tu parti, mio ben," duet for pasticcio: Cleonice (p1763, ?spur)* *T253/4*
1.36	*"Non dura," aria for opera: Demofoonte (p1765, Metastasio, ?spur)* ....
1.37	*"Quel labbro adorato," for opera: L'Olimpiade (not the T231/3, ?spur)* *T253/2*

2. SYMPHONIES & OVERTURES

2.1	Overture in D major (p1763; 2ob, 2hn & strings) T277/4
2.2	"6 Favourite overtures" (p1763, from operas): No.1 "Orione," in D major (from opera T237) T272/2
2.3	No.2 "La calamità," in D major (from opera T272/5)
2.4	No.3 "Artaserse," in D major (from opera T217)
2.5	No.4 "Il tutore e la pupilla," in C major (from pasticcio T273/2)
2.6	No.5 "La cascina," in G major (from pasticcio T273/5)
2.7	No.6 "Astarto," in G major (from pasticcio T273/81, = Ov in opera: Alessandro nell'Indie, T212)
2.8	Symphony in C major (p ?1763; 2ob, 2hn & strings) Op.12, T276/3
2.9	"6 Sinfonias" (p1765; 2ob, 2hn & strings; arr for hpd): No.1 in C major Op.3, T262/1
2.10	No.2 in D major
2.11	No.3 in E-flat major
2.12	No.4 in B-flat major
2.13	No.5 in F major
2.14	No.6 in G major
2.15	"An overture in 8 parts," in D major (p1766; 2ob, 2hn & strings) T275/3
2.16	"6 Sinfonias" (p1770; 2ob, 2hn & strings): No.1 in G major Op.6, T264/1
2.17	No.2 in D major
2.18	No.3 in E-flat major (= Op.8/1)
2.19	No.4 in B-flat major (= Op.8/5)
2.20	No.5 in E-flat major (= Op.8/6)
2.21	No.6 in G minor
2.22	Symphony in E-flat major (p by 1769; 2ob, 2hn & strings) T266/1
2.23	"6 Sinfonias 'périodiques' " (p1770; 2ob, 2hn & strings): No.1 in E-flat major (= Op.6/3) Op.8, T266/4
2.24	No.2 in G major
2.25	No.3 in D major
2.26	No.4 in F major
2.27	No.5 in B-flat major (= Op.6/4)
2.28	No.6 in E-flat major (= Op.6/5)
2.29	"3 Sinfonias" (p1773; 2fl/ob, 2hn ad lib & strings): No.1 in B-flat major Op.9, T268/3
2.30	No.2 in E-flat major (= Overture to opera: Zanaida, T241; Andante arr for pf known as: La Céleste)
2.31	No.3 in B-flat major
2.32	"Symphonie périodique," in E-flat major (p ?1773; 2fl/ob, 2hn & strings) T274/4
2.33	Symphony in D major (p ?1781; 2fl, 2ob, 2hn & strings) T283/6
2.34	"6 Grand Overtures" (Sinfonias) (p1781; d orch): No.1 in E-flat major Op.18, T269/4
2.35	No.2 in B-flat major, "Lucio Silla" (= Overture to opera: Lucio Silla, T232)
2.36	No.3 in D major (= Overture to serenata: Endimione, T248/3)
2.37	No.4 in D major (= No.2 of: Deux sinfonies, T271/5)
2.38	No.5 in E major
2.39	No.6 in D major
2.40	"Deux sinfonies" (p ca1785; d winds & strings): No.1 in D major (= Ov to: La clemenza, T229) T271/5
2.41	No.2 in D major (= No.4 of: 6 Grand Overtures, Op.18/4, T269/4)
2.42	Symphony in F major (2ob, 2hn & strings) T279/4
2.43	Symphony in F major (2ob, 2tpt & strings) T279/7
2.44	Symphony in E-flat major (2ob, 2hn & strings) T282/5
2.45	Symphony in E-flat major (hns, trombe di querra & strings) T282/7
2.46	Symphony in E-flat major (2ob, 2hn & strings) T282/10
2.47	Symphony in E-flat major ....
2.48	"2 Minuets" (orch w/ hns) T361/7

Spurious:

2.49	*Symphony in C major (2ob, 2cl & strings, ?spur)* *T276/6*
2.50	*Symphony in D major (strings, ?spur)* *T277/7*
2.51	*Symphony in D major (2ob, 2hn & strings, ?spur)* *T278/9*
2.52	*Symphony in D major (2ob, 2hn & strings, ?spur)* *T279/1*
2.53	*Symphony in D major (2ob, 2hn & strings, ?spur)* ....
2.54	*Symphony in D major (2ob, 2hn & strings, ?spur)* ....
2.55	*Symphony in D major (2hn & strings, ?spur)* ....
2.56	*Symphony in D major (?spur)* ....

3. CONCERTED SYMPHONIES ('&' separates concertino from ripieno insts)

Spurious:

4. CONCERTOS, SOLO INSTR & ORCH

Hpd/pf & orch:

Other:

Spurious:

4.30	*Oboe Concerto in F major (ob, 2hn & strings; ?spur)*	*T287/4*
4.31	*"2 Harpsichord Concertos" (p ca1776; hpd & strings, ?spur): No.1 in E-flat major*	*T297/1*
4.32	*No.2 in A major (?spur)*	
4.33	*Keyboard Concerto in A major (hpd & strings, ?spur)*	*T300/1*
4.34	*Keyboard Concerto in E major (?spur)*	*T300/4*
4.35	*Keyboard Concerto in F minor (hpd & strings, ?spur)*	*T301/4*
4.36	*Keyboard Concerto in D major (?spur)*	

5. MARCHES (winds)

5.1	"Sei sinfonie" (p1782; 2cl, 2hn & bn/2bn): No.1 in E-flat major	T285/3
5.2	No.2 in B-flat major	
5.3	No.3 in E-flat major	
5.4	No.4 in B-flat major	
5.5	No.5 in E-flat major	
5.6	No.6 in B-flat major	
5.7	"Quintettos," military pieces (p ca1794; 2cl, 2hn & bn): No.1 in E-flat major	
5.8	No.2 in E-flat major	
5.9	No.3 in B-flat major	
5.10	No.4 in E-flat major	
5.11	"3 Military marches," in E-flat major (2ob/fl, 2hn & bn): No.1 "March ... de Prince Ernst"	T359/3
5.12	No.2 "Marche du Régiment de Braun"	
5.13	No.3 "Marche du Régiment de Wurmb"	
5.14	"2 Marches" (2ob, 2cl, 2hn & 2bn): No.1 in E-flat major	T360/1
5.15	No.2 in E-flat major	
5.16	"Due Marce ... Prince Wallis" (2cl, 2hn & 2bn): No.1 in F major	T360/3
5.17	No.2 in F major	
5.18	"Due Marce ... della Maestà Regina" (2hn, 2ob, 2cl & bn): No.1 in F major	T360/5
5.19	No.2 in F major	
5.20	"6 Marches": No.1 in F major	T361/1
5.21	No.2 in E-flat major	
5.22	No.3 in E-flat major	
5.23	No.4 in F major	
5.24	No.5 in E-flat major	
5.25	No.6 in B-flat major	
5.26	"2 Entradas" (hns): No.1 in F major (c1767)	T361/7
5.27	No.2 in C major (c1769)	

6. CHAMBER MUSIC

6 insts:

6.1	"Sestetto," in C major (p1783; ob, 2hn, vn, vc & hpd/pf)	Op.3, T302/1

5 insts:

6.2	Quintet in B-flat major (p1770; 2vn/ob, va, vc/bn & cont)	T305/1
6.3	"6 Quintettos" (p1774; fl, ob, vn, va & cont): No.1 in C major	Op.11, T303/1
6.4	No.2 in G major	
6.5	No.3 in F major	
6.6	No.4 in E-flat major	
6.7	No.5 in A major	
6.8	No.6 in D major	
6.9	"2 Quintettes" (p1785): No.1 in D major (fl, ob, vn, vc & hpd/pf)	Op.22, T304/6
6.10	No.2 in F major (ob, vn, va da gamba, vc & hpd/pf)	

4 insts:

6.11	"6 Quartettos" (p1772; fl, vn, va & vc): No.1 in C major	Op.8, T306/1
6.12	No.2 in D major	
6.13	No.3 in E-flat major	
6.14	No.4 in F major	
6.15	No.5 in G major	
6.16	No.6 in B-flat major	
6.17	"6 Quartettos" (p1776; fl/vn, vn, va & cont, 3 quartets only c by J. C. Bach): No.1 in D major	T309
6.18	No.2 in C major	
6.19	No.3 in A major	
6.20	"6 Quartetti" (p by 1779; 2vn, va & cont, arr of: Vn Son in G major, Op.10/3, T322/1)	
6.21	"Quartetto," in G major (p1783; vn, 2vc & kbd)	T310/9
6.22	"4 Quartettos" (p1784): No.1 in C major (2fl, va & vc)	Op.19 posth, T307/4
6.23	No.2 in D major (2fl, va & vc)	

6.24	No.3 in G major (2fl, vn & vc)
6.25	No.4 in C major (fl, ob/fl, va & vc)
6.26	"4 Sonatas" (p1783; vn, fl, ob, vc & hpd; adapt Luther for hpd/pf & vn): No.1 in D major T310/1
6.27	No.2 in C major
6.28	No.3 in F major
6.29	No.4 in G major
6.30	"3 Quartets & 1 Quintet" (vn, fl, ob, vc & hpd; adapt Luther for hpd/pf & vn): No.1 in D major T311/2
6.31	No.2 in C major
6.32	No.3 in F major
6.33	No.4 in G major

3 insts:

6.34	Sonata in B-flat major (p1777; 2vn & vc, = No.1 of 6 Sonatas; Nos.2–6 c by others) T311/6
6.35	Sonata in B-flat major (p ?1796; harp, vn & vc/hpd) T330/5
6.36	Flute Trio in C major (fl, fl/vn & vc, = No.1 of: 2 Flute Trios selected by Monzani p ca1800) T317/2
6.37	"6 Sonatas" (c1763; hpd, vn/fl & vc): No.1 in F major T313
6.38	No.2 in G major
6.39	No.3 in D major
6.40	No.4 in C major
6.41	No.5 in D major
6.42	No.6 in E-flat major
6.43	"6 Trios" (hpd/pf & vn): No.1 in C major T316
6.44	No.2 in G major
6.45	No.3 in B-flat major
6.46	No.4 in E major
6.47	No.5 in F major
6.48	No.6 in D major
6.49	"6 Trios" (p1764; 2vn & va/cont): No.1 in B-flat major .... Op.2 (also as Op.4), T314/5
6.50	No.2 in A major
6.51	No.3 in E-flat major
6.52	No.4 in G major
6.53	No.5 in D major
6.54	No.6 in C major
6.55	"6 Trio Sonatas" (p1766; 2vn & cont): No.1 in G major T317/5
6.56	No.2 in D major
6.57	No.3 in E major
6.58	No.4 in F major
6.59	No.5 in B-flat major
6.60	No.6 in E-flat major
6.61	Trio sonata in G major (2fl/2vn & bass) T317/7
6.62	*Trio sonata in F major (2va & cont, lost) T318/8*
6.63	"6 Trio Sonatas" (p1764; hpd, vn/fl &vc): No.1 in F major Op.2, T313/1
6.64	No.2 in G major
6.65	No.3 in D major
6.66	No.4 in C major
6.67	No.5 in A major
6.68	No.6 in E-flat major

2 insts:

6.69	"6 Sonatas" (p1773; hpd/pf & vn): No.1 in B-flat major Op.10, T322/1
6.70	No.2 in C major
6.71	No.3 in G major
6.72	No.4 in E major
6.73	No.5 in F major
6.74	No.6 in D major
6.75	"6 Duetts" (p by 1775; 2vn): No.1 in D major T335/1
6.76	No.2 in G major
6.77	No.3 in E-flat major
6.78	No.4 in B-flat major
6.79	No.5 in A major
6.80	No.6 in C major
6.81	"4 Sonatas" (p1778; hpd/pf, vn &vc): No.1 in C major Op.15/1–4, T323/5
6.82	No.2 in A major
6.83	No.3 in D major
6.84	No.4 in B-flat major
6.85	"6 Sonatas" (p1779; hpd/pf & vn/fl): No.1 in D major.. Op.16, T325/1
6.86	No.2 in G major
6.87	No.3 in C major
6.88	No.4 in A major
6.89	No.5 in D major
6.90	No.6 in F major
6.91	"4 Sonatas" (p1781; hpd/pf & vn/fl): No.1 in C major... Op.18, T326/3
6.92	No.2 in D major

6.93	No.3 in E-flat major	
6.94	No.4 in G major	
6.95	"4 Canzonettes" (2vn, arr of Nos.1, 4, 3 & 2 of: 6 Canzonette a 2, T260/2): No.1 in F major	T336/6
6.96	No.2 in E-flat major	
6.97	No.3 in G major	
6.98	No.4 in B-flat major	
6.99	Sonata in D major (p1771; hpd &vn)	T331/2
6.100	"7 Sonatas" (hpd & vn; ed1969): No.1 in F major	T332/4
6.101	No.2 in D major	
6.102	No.3 in G major	
6.103	No.4 in A major	
6.104	No.5 in G major	
6.105	No.6 in D major	
6.106	No.7 in F major	

Misc:

6.107	"Quartetto" (= Concerto for hpd & 2vn, Op.1/2)	
6.108	Sonata in A major (hpd & vn)	
6.109	"Sonata con cembalo o spinetta," in F major (?vn & cont)	

Spurious:

6.110	*Sonata in F major (ob, vn, va & vc, ?spur)*	
6.111	*Sonata in D major (2vn, va & vc, ?spur)*	
6.112	*Sonata in E-flat major (Eng hn, vn, va & vc, ?spur)*	
6.113	*"4 Trio sonatas" (2vn & vc, ?spur): No.1 in C major*	
6.114	*No.2 in F major*	
6.115	*No.3 in A major*	
6.116	*No.4 in E-flat major*	
6.117	*"3 Sonatas" (hpd, vn & vc, ?spur): No.1 in D major*	
6.118	*No.2 in F major*	
6.119	*No.3 in C minor*	
6.120	*"2 Sonatas" (hpd & vn, ?spur): No.1 in B-flat major*	
6.121	*No.2 in G major*	
6.122	*"6 Sonatas" (hpd &vn, ?spur): No.1 in C major*	
6.123	*No.2 in G major*	
6.124	*No.3 in F major*	
6.125	*No.4 in B-flat major*	
6.126	*No.5 in E-flat major*	
6.127	*No.6 in D major*	
6.128	*Trio sonata in F major (2vn & cont, ?spur)*	*T279/10*
6.129	*Trio sonata in B-flat major (2vn & cont, ?spur)*	*T319/4*
6.130	*Trio sonata in B-flat major (2vn & cont, ?spur)*	*T319/7*
6.131	*"Divertimento," in B-flat major (2vn & cont, ?spur)*	*T319/9*
6.132	*Trio sonata in B-flat major (2vn & cont, ?spur)*	*T320/1*
6.133	*Trio sonata in E-flat major (2vn & cont, ?spur)*	*T320/4*
6.134	*Trio sonata in E-flat major (2vn & cont, ?spur)*	*T320/6*
6.135	*Trio sonata in B-flat major (fl, vn & bass, ?spur)*	*T320/9*
6.136	*Trio sonata in E-flat major (hpd & 2vn, ?spur)*	*T321/1*
6.137	*Sonata (p ca1770; gui & vn, ?spur)*	
6.138	*"6 Sonatas" (p1783; hpd/pf & vn/fl, ?spur): No.1 in C major*	*Op.19, T327/5*
6.139	*No.2 in G major*	
6.140	*No.3 in D major*	
6.141	*No.4 in A major*	
6.142	*No.5 in E-flat major*	
6.143	*No.6 in B-flat major*	
6.144	*"3 Sonatas" (p ca1785; hpd/pf & vn, ?spur): No.1 in C major*	*Op.20 posth, T329/1*
6.145	*No.2 in D major*	
6.146	*No.3 in F major*	
6.147	*"3 Sonatas" (p ca1785; hpd/pf & vn, ?spur): No.1 in G major*	*Op.21 posth, T329/1*
6.148	*No.2 in A major*	
6.149	*No.3 in B-flat major*	
6.150	*Sonata in F major (hpd & fl, ?spur)*	*T332/1*
6.151	*Sonata in D major (vn & cont, ?spur)*	*T331/6*
6.152	*"3 Sonatas" (fl & vn, ?spur): No.1 in D major*	*T337/1*
6.153	*No.2 in G major*	
6.154	*No.3 in C major*	
6.155	*"3 Sonatas" (p after 1785; hpd/pf & vn, ?spur): No.1 in E-flat major*	*Op.21, T344/4*
6.156	*No.2 in B-flat major*	
6.157	*No.3 in D major*	

7. KEYBOARD

7.71	*"Variazioni," in F major (kbd duet, spur)*	
7.72	*"6 Sonates" (p ca1764; kbd duet, ?spur, lost): No.1 in E-flat major* *T353/2*	
7.73	*No.2 in G major*	
7.74	*No.3 in B-flat major*	
7.75	*No.4 in D major*	
7.76	*No.5 in C major*	
7.77	*No.6 in F major*	

8. ARRANGEMENTS FOR KEYBOARD

From operatic music & overtures:

8.1	"Air de ballet," in D major (from opera: Amadis des Gaules, T215) ....
8.2	"Air de Chasse," in D major (from opera: Amadis des Gaules, T215) ....
8.3	Overture & ballet music (hpd/pf & harp, from opera: Amadis des Gaules, T215) ....
8.4	"5 Opera overtures" (hpd/org): No.1 in D major ....
8.5	No.2 in B-flat major
8.6	No.3 in D major
8.7	No.4 in G major
8.8	No.5 in G major

From symphonies:

8.9	"Overture," in D major ....
8.10	"6 Symphonies," Op.3, T262/1: No.1 in D major ....
8.11	No.2 in C major
8.12	No.3 in E-flat major
8.13	No.4 in B-flat major
8.14	No.5 in F major
8.15	No.6 in G major

From orch dances:

8.16	"Minuet" (of 1767), in F major ....
8.17	"Minuet" (of 1769), in C major ....

Arrs of works for large chamber orch:

8.18	"Quartet," in A major (hpd, 2vn & vc, transcr of: Hpd Conc in A major, Op.1/2, T292/1) ....
8.19	"Quartet," in A major (hpd, 2vn & vc, transcr of: Sonata in E major, Op.10/4, T322/1) ....

From kbd concertos:

8.20	"6 Sonatas" (hpd, from: Sei concerti, Op.7, T293/4): No.1 in C major..
8.21	No.2 in F major
8.22	No.3 in D major
8.23	No.4 in B-flat major
8.24	No.5 in E-flat major
8.25	No.6 in G major
8.26	"Variations," in D major (on God save the King, from: Hpd Conc in G major, Op.1/6, T292/1) ....
8.27	"Variations," in G major (on Saw you my Father, from: Pf Conc in D major, Op.13/2, T295/1) ....
8.28	"Variations," in B-flat major (on The Yellow Hair'd Laddie, from: Pf Conc in B-flat major, Op.13/4, T295/1) .

From operatic music for kbd w/ acc:

8.29	"2 Marches" (hpd, fl & 2fl, from opera: La clemenza di Scipione, Op.14, T229): No.1 in G major ....
8.30	No.2 in D major

From chamber works for kbd w/ acc:

8.31	Sonata in D major (hpd & vn, from: String Trio in D major, Op.2/5, T314/5) ....
8.32	"4 Sonatas" (Sextet, 2 Quartets & Quintet arr for hpd/pf & vn): No.1 in C major ....
8.33	No.2 in D major
8.34	No.3 in F major
8.35	No.4 in G major
8.36	"4 Sonatas" (hpd/pf & vn/fl, from: 4 Quartettos, Op.19 posth, T307/4): No.1 in C major ....
8.37	No.2 in D major
8.38	No.3 in G major
8.39	No.4 in C major

Arrs for pf duet:

8.40	"Overture," in D major (hpd/pf duet, from opera: Orione, T237) ....
8.41	"Grand Overture," in E-flat major (pf/hpd duet, from Op.18/1, T269/4) ....

9. SACRED VOCAL

10. CANTATAS

10.1 "Ode on the ... Arrival ... of ... Charlotte": "Thanks be to God" (c ?1761, Lockman) T244/6
10.2 "Cantata a 3 voci per ... natalizio ... Maestà cattolica" (p1762, ?Passeri) ....
10.3 "Gli orti esperidi" (p1765, ?Passeri, lost) ....
10.4 "Endimione," serenata a quattro (p1772, after Metastasio) T248/3
10.5 "Amor vincitore" (p1774, ?Verazi) T247/2
10.6 "Scene & Rondo" (on the Duke de Nivernois air: Infelice, invan mi lagno) T246/1
10.7 "La tempesta" (p ca1776, Metastasio) ....
10.8 "Rinaldo ed Armida," scena con aria (p1778, part lost) T250/2
10.9 "Happy Morn, auspicious rise" T243/1
10.10 "Aurora," cantata T247/3
10.11 "L'Olimpe" (?spur) *T249/7*

11. OTHER VOCAL

Chamber duets:

11.1 "9 Duetti" (ca ?1760; 2S & cont): 1. "Chi mai di questo core" ....
11.2   2. "Che ciascun per te sospiri"
11.3   3. "Trova un sol"
11.4   4. "Io lo sò"
11.5   5. "Ascoltami, oh Clori" (r as 6. of: 6 Canzonette a 2, Op.4, T259/1)
11.6   6. "Eccomi alfin"
11.7   7. "Parlami pur"
11.8   8. "Lascia chi'io posso" (r as 1. of: 6 Canzonette a 2, Op.4, T259/1)
11.9   9. "Ah che nel dirti addio"
11.10 "6 Canzonette a 2" (p1765; 2S & cont): 1. "Già la notte s'avvicine" Op.4, T259/1
11.11   2. "Ah rammenta oh bella Irene"
11.12   3. "Pur nel sonno almen talora"
11.13   4. "T'intendo si mio cor"
11.14   5. "Che ciascun per te sospiri"
11.15   6. "Ascoltami, oh Clori"
11.16 "6 Canzonette a 2" (p1770; 2S & cont): 1. "Torna in quel l'onda" Op.6, T260/2
11.17   2. "Io lo sò"
11.18   3. "E pur fra le tempeste"
11.19   4. "Trova un sol"
11.20   5. "Chi mai di questo core"
11.21   6. "S'infida tu mi chiami"

Misc arias:

11.22 "Infelice ... Là nei regni" (p ca1783; mS & kbd duet) T247/1
11.23 "Abbiamo penato e ver" T250/5
11.24 "Ascender mi sento" T250/6
11.25 "Ah che gli stessi numi ... Cara ti lascio" (p ca1785; A & orch) ....
11.26 "A quei sensi di gloria" ....
11.27 "Al mio bène a lei ch'adoro" T251/1
11.28 "Caro, caro mio bene" T251/2
11.29 "O Venere vezzosa" (p ca1775, Horace transl Bottarelli) T252/3
11.30 "When an angry woman's breast with revenge" (p ca1775) T256/3
11.31 "No more with unavailing woe," air (from opera: Gioas, T226) T256/4
11.32 "No, 'twas neither shape nor feature" T257/1
11.33 "While Cecilia we admire" (from opera: Carattaco, T221) T258/1
11.34 "Scena aus Egisto": 1. "La sventura del figlio," recit T251/5
11.35   2. "Dal suo bene," coro T251/6
11.36 "Scena con Rondo": 1. "Miscordo i torti miei," recit T251/7
11.37   2. "Dolci aurette," aria T251/8
11.38 "Arie aus Demofonte": 1. Misera, misera" T252/1
11.39   2. "Misero pargoletto" T252/2

Spurious:

11.40 "Amiche solitudine ... Verdi prati" (?spur) ....
11.41 "A! si barbaro colpo ... Morte vieni" (?spur) ....
11.42 "Fosca Nube, che in alto s'aggira" (?spur) ....
11.43 "Hvad fasligt qval mitt hjerta plagar" (?spur) *T251/3*
11.44 "La sorte spietata" (in Mengozzi: Méthode, ?spur) *T251/4*
11.45 "Nel cammin di nostra vita" (S & orch, ?spur) ....
11.46 "Non temer, bell'idol mio" (S, ob & orch, ?spur) ....
11.47 "Parto, ma se tu m'ami" (?spur) *T252/6*
11.48 "Principe non temer," recit & "Con si bel nome," aria (?spur) *T252/7*
11.49 "Se quel folle ... Figlia, oh dio!" (S & orch, ?spur) ....
11.50 "9 Solfeggi, del Sig. Giovanni Bach in Genova" (p1781; S & cont, ?spur) ....

11.51	*"Questa date l'ho impregata" (?spur)*	
11.52	*"Sospiri del mio cor"*	*T253/3*
11.53	*"Una semplice agnelletta" (?spur)*	*T253/5*
11.54	*"Sventurata in van mi lagno" (c after 1773; S, 2hn obbl & orch, ?spur)*	
11.55	*"Vieni, dell'amorosa Glicera ... Di gioventù desia" (?spur)*	
11.56	*"Vo solcando" (S & orch, ?spur)*	
11.57	*"Vo cercando" (?spur)*	

Vauxhall songs:

11.58	"4 Favourite Songs" (perf1766): 1. "By my sighs"	T254/1
11.59	2. "Cruel Strephon"	
11.60	3. "Come, Colin"	
11.61	4. "Ah, why shou'd love"	
11.62	"4 Favourite Songs," II (perf1767): 1. "In this shady blest retreat"	T254/5
11.63	2. "Smiling Venus"	
11.64	3. "Tender virgins shun deceivers"	
11.65	4. "Lovely yet ungrateful swain"	
11.66	"4 Favourite Songs," III (perf1771): 1. "Midst silent shades"	T255/2
11.67	2. "Ah seek to know"	
11.68	3. "Would you a female heart inspire"	
11.69	4. "Cease awhile, ye winds, to blow"	
11.70	"Blest with thee, my soul's dear treasure" (c ?1780)	T255/6
11.71	"Farewell, ye soft scenes" (p ?1790, Eng r of pasticio: L'Olimpiade, T231/3)	T256/2
11.72	"See the kind indulgent gales" (p ca1780, Eng r of opera: Zanaida, T241/3)	T257/2

Folksong settings:

11.73	The Braes of Ballenden: "Beneath a green shade" (p1779, Blacklock; A, ob, vn, va, vc & pf)	
11.74	The Broom of Cowdenknows: "How blyth" (p ca1784; A, 2fl, 2vn & cont)	T257
11.75	"I'll never leave thee" (p ca1784, Crawford; A, 2fl, 2vn & cont)	
11.76	"Lochaber" (p ca1785, Ramsay; A, 2fl, 2vn & cont)	T256
11.77	*"The Yellow-hair'd Laddie" (p1786, lost)*	

Transcriptions:

11.78	"Ebben si vada," acc recit & rondo (transcr1778; mS, ob, pf & orch, from T245/2)	T250/2
11.79	"Al mio bène," rondo (p1779, after Roccaforte; mS, pf & orch)	T251/1
11.80	"Wenn nach der Stürme Toben," aria (p1785; S & kbd, from T229/4)	T253/6

* * * * *

T = C. S. Terry: "John Christian Bach." London, rev. 2/1967 by H. C. R. Landon. (T numbers—page no./no. of incipit on page; only first incipit of group given.)

BACH, Johann Sebastian
1685–1750

1. ORCHESTRAL WORKS

4 Orchestral Suites:

1.1 Orchestral Suite No.1 in C major (ca1718–23; 2ob, bn & strings, cont): BWV1066
    1. "Ouverture"
    2. "Courante"
    3. "Gavotte," I & II
    4. "Forlane"
    5. "Menuet," I & II
    6. "Bouree," I & II
    7. "Passepied," I & II
1.2 Orchestral Suite No.2 in B minor (ca1718–23 or 35; fl & strings, cont): BWV1067
    1. "Ouverture"
    2. "Rondeau" (Gavotte)
    3. "Sarabande"
    4. "Bouree," I & II
    5. "Polonaise"
    6. "Double"
    7. "Menuet"
    8. "Badinerie"
1.3 Orchestral Suite No.3 in D major (ca1729–31; 3tpt, timp, 2ob, strings & cont): BWV1068
    1. "Ouverture"
    2. "Air" (famous as: Air on the G String) (rewritten by A. Wilhelmj for vn & pf 1871)
    3. "Gavotte," I & II
    4. "Bourée"
    5. "Gigue"
1.4 Orchestral Suite No.4 in D major (ca1718–23; 3tpt, timp, 3ob, bn, strings & cont): BWV1069
    1. "Ouverture"
    2. "Bouree," I & II
    3. "Gavotte"
    4. "Menuet," I & II
    5. "Réjouissance"

Other:

1.5   *Overture in G minor (spur: c by ?C. P. E. Bach)* *BWV1070*
    (Sinfonia in F major—version of Brandenburg Concerto No.1 in F major, BWV1046, assigned
    a new number BWV1046a, see: 'Brandenburg Concertos') BWV1071

2. CANONS & LATE CONTRAPUNTAL WORKS

2.1 "Canon trias harmonica" (c?) BWV1072
2.2 "Canon à 4 perpetuus" (c1713) BWV1073
2.3 "Canon à 4" (c1727) BWV1074
2.4 "Canon à 4 perpetuus" (c1734) BWV1075
2.5 "Canon triplex" (c1746) BWV1076
2.6 "Canone doppio sopr'il Soggetto" (c1747) BWV1077
2.7 "Canon super Fa Mi a 7 post Tempus Musicum" (c1749) BWV1078
2.8 "The Musical Offering" (c1747): BWV1079
    1. "Ricercar a 3"
    2. "Ricercar a 6"
    2a. "Ricercar a 6" (older vers)
    2b. "Ricercar a 6" (younger vers)
    3. "Sonata a traversa" (vn & cont)
    4a. "Canon 1 a 2 cancrizans"
    4b. "Canon 2 a 2 Violini in unisono"
    4c. "Canon 3 a 2 per Motum contrarium"
    4d. "Canon 4 a 2 per Augmentationem, contrario Motu"
    4e. "Canon 5 a 2 per Tonos"
    4f. "Fuga Canonica in Epidiapente"
    4g. "Canon perpetuus super Thema Regium"
    4h. "Canon perpetuus"
    4i. "Canon a 2"
    4k. "Canon a 4"
2.9 "The Art of Fugue" (ca1745–50, inc): BWV1080
    1. "Contrapunctus 1"
    2. "Contrapunctus 2"
    3. "Contrapunctus 3"
    4. "Contrapunctus 4"
    5. "Contrapunctus 5"
    6. "Contrapunctus 6, a 4, im Stile francese"
    7. "Contrapunctus 7, a 4, per Augmentationem et Diminutionem"
    8. "Contrapunctus 8, a 3"

       9. "Contrapunctus 9, a 4, alla Duodecima"
      10. "Contrapunctus 10, a 4, alla Decima"
      11. "Contrapunctus 11, a 4"
      12a. "Contrapunctus 12, a 4" (rectus)
      12b. "Contrapunctus 12, a 4" (inversus)
      13a. "Contrapunctus 13, a 3" (rectus)
      13b. "Contrapunctus 13, a 3" (inversus)
      14. "Canon per Augmentationem in contrario motu"
      15. "Canon alla Ottava"
      16. "Canon alla Decima"
      17. "Canon alla Duodecima in Contrapuncto alla Quinta"
      18a. "Fuga a 2 Clav."
      18b. "Alio modo. Fuga a 2 Clav."
      19. "Fuga a 3 Soggetti" (inc)
      10a. "Contrapunctus 14, a 4"

      1. "Canon simplex"
      2. "all' roverscio"
      3. "Beede vorigen Cannones zugleich, motu recto e contrario"
      4. "motu contrario e recto"
      5. "Canon duplex à 4"
      6. "Canon simplex über besagtes Fundament"
      7. "Idem à 3"
      8. "Canon simplex à 3, il soggetto in Alto"
      9. "Canon in unisono post semifusam à 3"
      10. "Alio modo, per syncopationes et per ligaturas à 2"
      11. "Canon duplex übers Fundament à 5"
      12. "Canon duplex über besagte Fundamental—Noten à 5"
      13. "Canon triplex à 6"
      14. "Canon à 4 per Augmentationen et Diminutionem"

3. CONCERTOS, SOLO INSTR / INSTS & STRINGS

Violin Concertos:

6 "Brandenburg Concertos":

Clavier Concertos:

4. CHAMBER MUSIC

Lute solo:

4.1	Lute Suite No.1 in E minor (ca1708–17): No.1 "Praeludio"	BWV996
4.2	No.2 "Allemande"	
4.3	No.3 "Courante"	
4.4	No.4 "Sarabande"	
4.5	No.5 "Bourrée"	
4.6	No.6 "Gigue"	
4.7	Lute Suite No.2 in C minor (ca1737–41): No.1 "Preludio"	BWV997
4.8	No.2 "Fuga"	
4.9	No.3 "Sarabande"	
4.10	No.4 "Gigue"	
4.11	No.5 "Double"	
4.12	Lute Suite No.3 in G minor (ca1727–31): No.1 "Prelude"	BWV995
4.13	No.2 "Allemande"	
4.14	No.3 "Courante"	
4.15	No.4 "Sarabande"	
4.16	No.5 "Gavotte," I	
4.17	No.6 "Gavotte," II (en Rondeau)	
4.18	No.7 "Gigue"	
4.19	Lute Suite No.4 in E major (ca1740, transcr of BWV1006): No.1 "Prélude"	BWV1006a
4.20	No.2 "Loure"	
4.21	No.3 "Gavotte en Rondeau"	
4.22	No.4 "Menuett," I	
4.23	No.5 "Menuet," II	
4.24	No.6 "Bourée"	
4.25	No.7 "Gigue"	
4.26	"Prelude, fugue & allegro," in E-flat major (ca1740–5; lute/clavier)	BWV998
4.27	"Prelude," in C minor (ca1720)	BWV999
4.28	"Fugue," in G minor (ca1725)	BWV1000

6 (Unaccompanied) Violin Sonatas & Partitas (ca1718–23):

4.29	Sonata No.1 in G minor: No.1 "Adagio"	BWV1001
4.30	No.2 "Fuga"	
4.31	No.3 "Siciliana"	
4.32	No.4 "Presto"	
4.33	Partita No.1 in B minor: No.1 "Allemanda"	BWV1002
4.34	No.2 "Double"	
4.35	No.3 "Courante"	
4.36	No.4 "Double"	
4.37	No.5 "Sarabande"	
4.38	No.6 "Double"	
4.39	No.7 "Tempo di Borea"	
4.40	No.8 "Double"	
4.41	Sonata No.2 in A minor: No.1 "Grave"	BWV1003
4.42	No.2 "Fuga"	
4.43	No.3 "Allegro"	
4.44	No.4 "Allegro"	
4.45	Partita No.2 in D minor: No.1 "Allemande"	BWV1004
4.46	No.2 "Courante"	
4.47	No.3 "Sarabande"	
4.48	No.4 "Gigue"	
4.49	No.5 "Chaconne"	
4.50	Sonata No.3 in C major: No.1 "Adagio"	BWV1005
4.51	No.2 "Fuga"	
4.52	No.3 "Largo"	
4.53	No.4 "Allegro assai"	
4.54	Partita No.3 in E major: No.1 "Preludio"	BWV1006
4.55	No.2 "Loure"	
4.56	No.3 "Gavotte en Rondeau"	
4.57	No.4 "Menuet," I	
4.58	No.5 "Menuet," II	
4.59	No.6 "Bourrée"	
4.60	No.7 "Gigue"	

6 (Unaccompanied) Cello Suites (ca1718–23):

4.61	Cello Suite No.1 in G major: No.1 "Prélude"	BWV1007
4.62	No.2 "Allemande"	
4.63	No.3 "Courante"	
4.64	No.4 "Sarabande"	
4.65	No.5 "Menuet," I	

4.66	No.6 "Menuet," II	
4.67	No.7 "Gigue"	
4.68	Cello Suite No.2 in D minor: No.1 "Prélude"	BWV1008
4.69	No.2 "Allemande"	
4.70	No.3 "Courante"	
4.71	No.4 "Sarabande"	
4.72	No.5 "Menuett," I	
4.73	No.6 "Menuet," II	
4.74	No.7 "Gigue"	
4.75	Cello Suite No.3 in C major: No.1 "Prélude"	BWV1009
4.76	No.2 "Allemande"	
4.77	No.3 "Courante"	
4.78	No.4 "Sarabande"	
4.79	No.5 "Bourrée," I	
4.80	No.6 "Bourrée," II	
4.81	No.7 "Gigue"	
4.82	Cello Suite No.4 in E-flat major: No1. "Prélude"	BWV1010
4.83	No.2 "Allemande"	
4.84	No.3 "Courante"	
4.85	No.4 "Sarabande"	
4.86	No.5 "Bourrée," I	
4.87	No.6 "Bourrée," II	
4.88	No.7 "Gigue"	
4.89	Cello Suite No.5 in C minor: No.1 "Prélude"	BWV1011
4.90	No.2 "Allemande"	
4.91	No.3 "Courante"	
4.92	No.4 "Sarabande"	
4.93	No.5 "Gavotte," I	
4.94	No.6 "Gavotte," II	
4.95	No.7 "Gigue"	
4.96	Cello Suite No.6 in D major: No.1 "Prélude"	BWV1012
4.97	No.2 "Allemande"	
4.98	No.3 "Courante"	
4.99	No.4 "Sarabande"	
4.100	No.5 "Gavotte," I	
4.101	No.6 "Gavotte," II	
4.102	No.7 "Gigue"	

Other:

4.103	"Partita," in A minor (c1722–3; fl): No.1 "Allemande"	BWV1013
4.104	No.2 "Corrente"	
4.105	No.3 "Sarabande"	
4.106	No.4 "Bourée anglaise"	
4.107	"6 Violin Sonatas" (ca1718–23; vn & clavichord): No.1 in B minor	BWV1014
4.108	No.2 in A major	BWV1015
4.109	No.3 in E major	BWV1016
4.110	No.4 in C minor	BWV1017
4.111	No.5 in F minor	BWV1018
4.112	. Variant of BWV1018 (3 movt)	BWV1018a
4.113	No.6 in G major	BWV1019
4.114	. Variant of BWV1019 (3–5 movts)	BWV1019a
4.115	*Violin Sonata in G minor (vn/fl & clavichord, spur: c by C. P. E. Bach)*	*BWV1020*
4.116	Violin Sonata in G major (ca1718–23; vn & cont)	BWV1021
4.117	*Violin Sonata in F major (vn & clavichord, ?spur)*	*BWV1022*
4.118	Violin Sonata in E minor (ca1718–23; vn & cont)	BWV1023
4.119	*Violin Sonata in C minor (vn & cont, ?spur)*	*BWV1024*
4.120	*"Suite," in A major (vn & clavichord, ?spur: c by ?C. P. E. Bach)*	*BWV1025*
4.121	*"Fugue," in G minor (c1717–23; vn & clavichord, spur)*	*BWV1026*
4.122	"3 Viola da Gamba Sonatas" (c1717–23; va da gamba & clavichord): No.1 in G major	BWV1027
4.123	*. "Trio," in G major (?spur transcr of 3rd movt of BWV1027)*	*BWV1027a*
4.124	No.2 in D major	BWV1028
4.125	No.3 in G minor	BWV1029
4.126	"6 Flute Sonatas": No.1 in B minor (ca1718–23; fl & clavichord)	BWV1030
4.127	*No.2 in E-flat major (fl & clavichord, ?spur: c by ?C. P. E. Bach)*	*BWV1031*
4.128	No.3 in A major (c1718–23; fl & clavichord)	BWV1032
4.129	*No.4 in C major (fl & cont, ?spur: c by ?C. P. E. Bach)*	*BWV1033*
4.130	No.5 in E minor (ca1718–20; fl & cont)	BWV1034
4.131	No.6 in E major (ca1718–20; fl & cont)	BWV1035
4.132	*"4 Trio Sonatas": No.1 in D minor (2vn & cont, ?spur: c by ?C. P. E. Bach)*	*BWV1036*
4.133	*No.2 in C major (fl, vn & cont, spur: c by ?Goldberg)*	*BWV1037*
4.134	*No.3 in G major (fl, vn & cont; spur: c by ?C. P. E. Bach)*	*BWV1038*
4.135	No.4 in G major (ca1720; 2fl & cont)	BWV1039
4.136	Movement (Trio) in F major (ca ?1713; vn, ob & cont)	BWV1040

5. ORGAN

5.74	"Canzona," in D minor (ca1715)	BWV588
5.75	"Alla breve pro organo pleno," in D major (ca1709)	BWV589
5.76	"Pastorale," in F major (c before 1710)	BWV590
5.77	*"Kleines harmonisches Labyrinth" (spur: c by ?Heinichen)*	*BWV591*
5.78	"6 Organ Concertos" (c ?1713–4; solo org): No.1 in G major (after Ernst)	BWV592
	. Version of BWV592 for kbd	BWV592a
5.79	No.2 in A minor (after Vivaldi's Op.3/8, RV522)	BWV593
5.80	No.3 in C major (after Vivaldi's Op.7/11, RV208)	BWV594
5.81	No.4 in C major (after Ernst)	BWV595
5.82	No.5 in D minor (after Vivaldi's Op.3/11, RV565, incl: Sicilienne)	BWV596
5.83	*No.6 in E-flat major (?spur)*	*BWV597*
5.84	"Pedal Exercise," in G minor (c?, improvisation by Bach, notated by Thieme)	BWV598

The Neumeister Collection of Chorale Preludes (c early, Yale University Manuscript LM 4708):

5.85	"Wir Christenleut"	BWV1090
5.86	"Das alte Jahr vergangen ist"	BWV1091
5.87	"Herr Gott, nun schleuss den Himmel auf"	BWV1092
5.88	"Herzliebster Jesu, was hast du verbrochen"	BWV1093
5.89	"O Jesu, wie ist dein Gestalt"	BWV1094
5.90	"O Lamm Gottes unschuldig"	BWV1095
5.91	"Christe, der du bist Tag und Licht" (Wir danken dir, Herr Jesu Christ)	BWV1096
5.92	"Ehre sei dir, Christe, der du leidest Not"	BWV1097
5.93	"Wir glauben all einen Gott"	BWV1098
5.94	"Aus tiefer Not schrei ich zu dir"	BWV1099
5.95	"Allein zu dir, Herr Jesu Christ"	BWV1100
5.96	"Durch Adams Fall, ist ganz verderbt"	BWV1101
5.97	"Du Friedefürst, Herr Jesu Christ"	BWV1102
5.98	"Erhalt uns, Herr, bei deinem Wort"	BWV1103
5.99	"Wenn dich Unglück tut greifen an"	BWV1104
5.100	"Jesu, meine Freude"	BWV1105
5.101	"Gott ist mein Heil, mein Hilf und Trost"	BWV1106
5.102	"Jesu, meines Lebens Leben"	BWV1107
5.103	"Als Jesus Christus in der Nacht"	BWV1108
5.104	"Ach Gott, tu dich erbarmen"	BWV1109
5.105	"O Herre Gott, dein göttlich Wort"	BWV1110
5.106	"Nun lasst uns den Leib begraben"	BWV1111
5.107	"Christus, der ist mein Leben"	BWV1112
5.108	"Ich hab mein Sach Gott heimgestellt"	BWV1113
5.109	"Herr Jesu Christ, du höchstes Gut"	BWV1114
5.110	"Herzlich lieb hab ich dich, o Herr"	BWV1115
5.111	"Was Gott tut, das ist wohlgetan"	BWV1116
5.112	"Alle Menschen müssen sterben"	BWV1117
5.113	"Werde munter, mein Gemüte"	BWV1118
5.114	"Wie nach einer Wasserquelle"	BWV1119
5.115	"Christ, der du bist der helle Tag"	BWV1120
	previously known: . "Ach Gott und Herr" (= BWV714)	
	. "Der Tag, der ist so freudenreich" (= BWV719)	
	. "Ein Kindelein so löbelich" (= BWV719)	
	. "Ach Herr, mich armen Sünder" (= BWV742)	
	. "Herzlich tut mich verlangen" (= BWV742)	
	. "Machs mit mir, Gott, nach deiner Güt" (= BWV957)	

"Orgelbüchlein"—Chorale preludes (c1713–7):

5.116	No.1 "Nun komm der Heiden Heiland" (Advent)	BWV599
5.117	No.2 "Gott, durch deine Güte" (Advent)	BWV600
5.118	No.3 "Herr Christ, der ein'ge Gottes-Sohn" (Advent)	BWV601
5.119	No.4 "Lob sei dem allmächtigen Gott" (Advent)	BWV602
5.120	No.5 "Puer natus in Bethlehem" (Christmas)	BWV603
5.121	No.6 "Gelobet seist du, Jesu Christ" (Christmas)	BWV604
5.122	No.7 "Der Tag, der ist so freudenreich" (Christmas)	BWV605
5.123	No.8 "Vom Himmel hoch da komm' ich her" (Christmas)	BWV606
5.124	No.9 "Vom Himmel kam der Engel Schar" (Christmas)	BWV607
5.125	No.10 "In dulci jubilo" (Christmas)	BWV608
5.126	No.11 "Lobt Gott, ihr Christen, allzugleich" (Christmas)	BWV609
5.127	No.12 "Jesu, meine Freude" (Christmas)	BWV610
5.128	No.13 "Christum wir sollen loben schon" (Christmas)	BWV611
5.129	No.14 "Wir Christenleut' " (Christmas)	BWV612
5.130	No.15 "Helft mir Gottes Güte preisen" (New Year)	BWV613
5.131	No.16 "Das alte Jahr vergangen ist" (New Year) (c after ?1740)	BWV614
5.132	No.17 "In dir ist Freude" (New Year)	BWV615
5.133	No.18 "Mit Fried und Freund ich fahr dahin" (Purification)	BWV616
5.134	No.19 "Herr Gott, nun schleuss den Himmel auf" (Purification)	BWV617
5.135	No.20 "O Lamm Gottes, unschuldig" (Passiontide)	BWV618

5.136	No.21 "Christe, du Lamm Gottes" (Passiontide)	BWV619
5.137	No.22 "Christus, der uns selig macht" (Passiontide) (also earlier vers BWV620a)	BWV620
5.138	No.23 "Da Jesus an dem Kreuze stund" (Passiontide)	BWV621
5.139	No.24 "O Mensch, bewein dein Sünde gross" (Passiontide)	BWV622
5.140	No.25 "Wir danken dir, Herr Jesu Christ" (Passiontide)	BWV623
5.141	No.26 "Hilf Gott, dass mir's gelinge" (Passiontide)	BWV624
5.142	No.27 "Christ lag in Todesbanden" (Easter)	BWV625
5.143	No.28 "Jesus Christus, unser Heiland" (Easter)	BWV626
5.144	No.29 "Christ ist erstanden" (Easter; 3 vers)	BWV627
5.145	No.30 "Erstanden ist der heilge Christ" (Easter)	BWV628
5.146	No.31 "Erschienen ist der herrliche Tag" (Easter)	BWV629
5.147	No.32 "Heut triumphieret Gottes Sohn" (Easter)	BWV630
5.148	No.33 "Komm, Gott Schöpfer, heiliger Geist" (Whit Sunday)	BWV631
5.149	No.34 "Herr Jesu Christ, dich zu uns wend" (Trinity Sunday)	BWV632
5.150	No.35 "Liebster Jesu, wir sind hier" (Trinity Sunday)	BWV633
5.151	No.36 "Liebster Jesu, wir sind hier" (Trinity Sunday, variant of BWV633)	BWV634
5.152	No.37 "Dies sind die heilgen zehn Gebot" (The Catechism)	BWV635
5.153	No.38 "Vater unser im Himmelreich" (The Catechism)	BWV636
5.154	No.39 "Durch Adams Fall ist ganz verderbt" (Penitence & Amendment)	BWV637
5.155	No.40 "Es ist das Heil uns kommen her" (Penitence & Amendment)	BWV638
5.156	No.41 "Ich ruf zu dir, Herr Jesu Christ" (Conduct & Experience)	BWV639
5.157	No.42 "In dich hab ich gehoffet, Herr" (In Time of Trouble)	BWV640
5.158	No.43 "Wenn wir in höchsten Nöten sein" (In Time of Trouble)	BWV641
5.159	No.44 "Wer nur den lieben Gott lässt walten" (In Time of Trouble)	BWV642
5.160	No.45 "Alle Menschen müssen sterben" (Death & the Grave)	BWV643
5.161	No.46 "Ach wie nichtig, ach wie flüchtig" (The Life Eternal)	BWV644

Schübler's Book—Chorale preludes (ca1747):

5.162	No.1 "Wachet auf, ruft uns die Stimme"	BWV645
5.163	No.2 "Wo soll ich fliehen hin" (or: Auf meinen lieben Gott)	BWV646
5.164	No.3 "Wer nur den lieben Gott lässt walten"	BWV647
5.165	No.4 "Meine Seele erhebet den Herren"	BWV648
5.166	No.5 "Ach bleib bei uns, Herr Jesu Christ"	BWV649
5.167	No.6 "Kommst du nun, Jesu, vom Himmel herunter"	BWV650

18 Leipzig Chorale preludes (c1708–17, r1747–9):

5.168	No.1 "Komm, heiliger Geist," fantasia	BWV651
5.169	Variant of BWV651	BWV651a
5.170	No.2 "Komm, heiliger Geist" (alio modo)	BWV652
5.171	Variant of BWV652	BWV652a
5.172	No.3 "An Wasserflüssen Babylon"	BWV653
5.173	Variant of BWV653 (simplified vers)	BWV653a
5.174	Variant of BWV653 (orig vers)	BWV653b
5.175	No.4 "Schmücke dich, o liebe Seele"	BWV654
5.176	Variant of BWV654	BWV654a
5.177	No.5 "Herr Jesu Christ, dich zu uns wend," trio	BWV655
5.178	Variant of BWV655	BWV655a
5.179	*Variant of BWV655 (?spur: 19th cent adaptation)*	*BWV655b*
5.180	*Variant of BWV655 (?spur)*	*BWV655c*
5.181	No.6 "O Lamm Gottes unschuldig"	BWV656
5.182	Variant of BWV656	BWV656a
5.183	No.7 "Nun danket alle Gott"	BWV657
5.184	No.8 "Von Gott will ich nicht lassen"	BWV658
5.185	Variant of BWV658	BWV658a
5.186	No.9 "Nun komm, der Heiden Heiland"	BWV659
5.187	Variant of BWV659	BWV659a
5.188	No.10 "Nun komm, der Heiden Heiland," trio	BWV660
5.189	Variant of BWV660	BWV660a
5.190	*Variant of BWV660 (?spur)*	*BWV660b*
5.191	No.11 "Nun komm, der Heiden Heiland"	BWV661
5.192	Variant of BWV661	BWV661a
5.193	No.12 "Allein Gott in der Höh sei Ehr"	BWV662
5.194	Variant of BWV662	BWV662a
5.195	No.13 "Allein Gott in der Höh sei Ehr"	BWV663
5.196	Variant of BWV663	BWV663a
5.197	No.14 "Allein Gott in der Höh sei Ehr," trio	BWV664
5.198	Variant of BWV664	BWV664a
5.199	Variant of BWV664 (orig vers)	BWV664b
5.200	No.15 "Jesus Christus, unser Heiland"	BWV665
5.201	Variant of BWV665	BWV665a
5.202	No.16 "Jesus Christus, unser Heiland" (alio modo)	BWV666
5.203	Variant of BWV666	BWV666a
5.204	No.17 "Komm, Gott Schöpfer, heiliger Geist"	BWV667

5.205	Variant of BWV667	BWV667a
5.206	Variant of BWV667 (orig vers)	BWV667b
5.207	No.18 "Vor deinen Thron tret ich hiermit" (inc)	BWV668
5.208	Variant of BWV668: "Wenn wir in höchsten Nöten sein"	BWV668a

Catechism preludes, Clavierübung III (also incl BWV552) (p1739):

5.209	No.1 "Kyrie, Gott Vater in Ewigkeit"	BWV669
5.210	No.2 "Christe, aller Welt Trost"	BWV670
5.211	No.3 "Kyrie, Gott heiliger Geist"	BWV671
5.212	No.4 "Kyrie, Gott Vater in Ewigkeit"	BWV672
5.213	No.5 "Christe, aller Welt Trost"	BWV673
5.214	No.6 "Kyrie, Gott heiliger Geist"	BWV674
5.215	No.7 "Allein Gott in der Höh sei Ehr"	BWV675
5.216	No.8 "Allein Gott in der Höh sei Ehr"	BWV676
5.217	*Variant of BWV676 (?spur)*	*BWV676a*
5.218	No.9 "Allein Gott in der Höh sei Ehr," fughetta	BWV677
5.219	No.10 "Dies sind die heil'gen zehn Gebot"	BWV678
5.220	No.11 "Dies sind die heil'gen zehn Gebot," fughetta	BWV679
5.221	No.12 "Wir glauben all an einen Gott" (Giant Fugue)	BWV680
5.222	No.13 "Wir glauben all an einen Gott," fughetta	BWV681
5.223	No.14 "Vater unser im Himmelreich"	BWV682
5.224	No.15 "Vater unser im Himmelreich" (alio modo)	BWV683
5.225	*Variant of BWV683 (?spur)*	*BWV683a*
5.226	No.16 "Christ, unser Herr, zum Jordan kam"	BWV684
5.227	No.17 "Christ, unser Herr, zum Jordan kam" (alio modo)	BWV685
5.228	No.18 "Aus tiefer Not schrei ich zu dir"	BWV686
5.229	No.19 "Aus tiefer Not schrei ich zu dir" (alio modo)	BWV687
5.230	No.20 "Jesus Christus unser Heiland"	BWV688
5.231	No.21 "Jesus Christus unser Heiland," fugue	BWV689

Kirnberger's Collection—Chorale preludes:

5.232	"Wer nur den lieben Gott lässt walten" (ca ?1708–17)	BWV690
5.233	"Wer nur den lieben Gott lässt walten" (ca ?1720)	BWV691
5.234	*Variant of BWV691 (?spur)*	*BWV691a*
5.235	*"Ach Gott und Herr" (spur: c by Walther)*	*BWV692*
5.236	*Variant of BWV692 (spur: c by Walther)*	*BWV692a*
5.237	*"Ach Gott und Herr" (spur: c by Walther)*	*BWV693*
5.238	"Wo soll ich fliehen hin" (c before 1708)	BWV694
5.239	"Christ lag in Todesbanden," fantasia (ca1708–17)	BWV695
5.240	*Variant of BWV695 (?spur)*	*BWV695a*
5.241	"Christum wir sollen loben schon," fughetta (c before 1708)	BWV696
5.242	"Gelobet seist du, Jesu Christ," fughetta (c before 1708)	BWV697
5.243	"Herr Christ, der ein'ge Gottes-Sohn," fughetta (c before 1708)	BWV698
5.244	"Nun komm der Heiden Heiland," fughetta (c before 1708)	BWV699
5.245	"Vom Himmel hoch da komm' ich her" (c before 1708)	BWV700
5.246	"Vom Himmel hoch da komm' ich her," fughetta (c before 1708)	BWV701
5.247	*"Das Jesulein soll doch mein Trost" (spur)*	*BWV702*
5.248	"Gottes Sohn ist kommen," fughetta (c before 1708)	BWV703
5.249	"Lob sei dem allmächt'gen Gott," fughetta (c before 1708)	BWV704
5.250	*"Durch Adam' Fall ist ganz verderbt" (spur)*	*BWV705*
5.251	"Liebster Jesu, wir sind hier" (ca1708–17)	BWV706
5.252	*"Ich hab mein Sach Gott heimgestellt" (spur)*	*BWV707*
5.253	*"Ich hab mein Sach Gott heimgestellt" (spur)*	*BWV708*
5.254	*Variant of BWV708 (?spur)*	*BWV708a*
5.255	"Herr Jesu Christ, dich zu uns wend" (ca1708–17)	BWV709
5.256	"Wir Christenleut" (ca1708–17)	BWV710
5.257	"Allein Gott in der Höh sei Ehr" (ca1708–17)	BWV711
5.258	"In dich hab ich gehoffet, Herr" (c1708–17)	BWV712
5.259	"Jesu, meine Freude," fantasia (c1708–17)	BWV713
5.260	*Variant of BWV713 (?spur)*	*BWV713a*

Misc Chorale preludes:

5.261	"Ach Gott und Herr," canon (ca1708–17)	BWV714
5.262	"Allein Gott in der Höh sei Ehr" (c before 1708)	BWV715
5.263	*"Allein Gott in der Höh sei Ehr," fugue (spur)*	*BWV716*
5.264	"Allein Gott in der Höh sei Ehr" (ca1708–17)	BWV717
5.265	"Christ lag in Todes Banden" (c before 1708)	BWV718
5.266	"Der Tag, der ist so freudenreich" (Ein Kindelein so löbelich)	BWV719
5.267	"Ein feste Burg ist unser Gott" (c ?1709)	BWV720
5.268	"Erbarm dich mein, o Herre Gott" (c before 1708)	BWV721
5.269	"Gelobet seist du, Jesu Christ" (c before 1708)	BWV722
5.270	Variant of BWV722 (ca1703–7)	BWV722a

6. CLAVIER

Inventions & duets:

6.14	No.13 in A minor	BWV784
6.15	No.14 in B-flat major	BWV785
6.16	No.15 in B minor	BWV786
6.17	"3-Part Inventions" (Sinfonien) (ca1720): No.1 in C major	BWV787
6.18	No.2 in C minor	BWV788
6.19	No.3 in D major	BWV789
6.20	No.4 in D minor	BWV790
6.21	No.5 in E-flat major	BWV791
6.22	No.6 in E major	BWV792
6.23	No.7 in E minor	BWV793
6.24	No.8 in F major	BWV794
6.25	No.9 in F minor	BWV795
6.26	No.10 in G major	BWV796
6.27	No.11 in G minor	BWV797
6.28	No.12 in A major	BWV798
6.29	No.13 in A minor	BWV800
6.30	No.14 in B-flat major	BWV801
6.31	No.15 in B minor	BWV802
6.32	"4 Duets" (c before 1739, from: Clavierübung III): No.1 in E minor	BWV803
6.33	No.2 in F major	BWV804
6.34	No.3 in G major	BWV805
6.35	No.4 in A minor	

"English Suites" (ca ?1715–21):

6.36	English Suite No.1 in A major: No.1 "Prélude"	BWV806
6.37	No.2 "Allemande"	
6.38	No.3 "Courante," I	
6.39	No.4 "Courante," II	
6.40	No.4a "Double," I	
6.41	No.4b "Double," II	
6.42	No.5 "Sarabande"	
6.43	No.6 "Bourrée," I	
6.44	No.7 "Bourrée," II	
6.45	No.8 "Gigue"	
6.46	Version of English Suite No.1 in A major (avec Prélude): No.1 "Prélude"	BWV806a
6.47	No.2 "Allemande"	
6.48	No.3 "Courante," I	
6.49	No.4 "Courante," II	
6.50	No.4a "Courante precedent avec la Basse Simple"	
6.51	No.5 "Sarabande"	
6.52	No.6 "Bourrée"	
6.53	No.7 "Gigue"	
6.54	English Suite No.2 in A minor: No.1 "Prélude"	BWV807
6.55	No.2 "Allemande"	
6.56	No.3 "Courante"	
6.57	No.4 "Sarabande"	
6.58	No.4a "Les agréments de la même Sarabande"	
6.59	No.5 "Bourrée," I	
6.60	No.6 "Bourrée," II	
6.61	No.7 "Gigue"	
6.62	English Suite No.3 in G minor: No.1 "Prélude"	BWV808
6.63	No.2 "Allemande"	
6.64	No.3 "Courante"	
6.65	No.4 "Sarabande"	
6.66	No.4a "Les agréments de la même Sarabande"	
6.67	No.5 "Gavotte alternativement"	
6.68	No.6 "Gavotte," II (ou la Musette)	
6.69	No.7 "Gigue"	
6.70	English Suite No.4 in F major: No.1 "Prélude"	BWV809
6.71	No.2 "Allemande"	
6.72	No.3 "Courante"	
6.73	No.4 "Sarabande"	
6.74	No.5 "Menuet," I	
6.75	No.6 "Menuet," II	
6.76	No.7 "Gigue"	
6.77	English Suite No.5 in E minor: No.1 "Prélude"	BWV810
6.78	No.2 "Allemande"	
6.79	No.3 "Courante"	
6.80	No.4 "Sarabande"	
6.81	No.5 "Passepied," I (en Rondeau)	
6.82	No.6 "Passepied," II	
6.83	No.7 "Gigue"	
6.84	English Suite No.6 in D minor : No.1 "Prélude"	BWV811
6.85	No.2 "Allemande"	

6.86	No.3 "Courante"	
6.87	No.4 "Sarabande"	
6.88	No.4a "Double"	
6.89	No.5 "Gavotte," I	
6.90	No.6 "Gavotte," II	
6.91	No.7 "Gigue"	

"French Suites" (ca1720–2):

6.92	French Suite No.1 in D minor (2 vers): No.1 "Allemande"	BWV812
6.93	No.2 "Courante"	
6.94	No.3 "Sarabande"	
6.95	No.4 "Menuet," I	
6.96	No.5 "Menuet," II	
6.97	No.6 "Gigue"	
6.98	French Suite No.2 in C minor (also vers w/ 2nd Menuet): No.1 "Allemande"	BWV813
6.99	No.2 "Courante"	
6.100	No.3 "Sarabande"	
6.101	No.4 "Air"	
6.102	No.5 "Menuet"	
6.103	No.6 "Gigue"	
6.104	French Suite No.3 in B minor (also vers w/ different Trio, BWV814a): No.1 "Allemande"	BWV814
6.105	No.2 "Courante"	
6.106	No.3 "Sarabande"	
6.107	No.4 "Gavotte"	
6.108	No.5 "Menuet" (alternativement)	
6.109	No.6 "Trio"	
6.110	No.7 "Gigue"	
6.111	French Suite No.4 in E-flat major (2 vers): No.1 "Allemande"	BWV815
6.112	No.2 "Courante"	
6.113	No.3 "Sarabande"	
6.114	No.4 "Gavotte"	
6.115	No.5 "Air"	
6.116	No.6 "Menuet" (only in 2nd vers)	
6.117	No.7 "Gigue"	
6.118	Variant of BWV815: No.1 "Praeludium"	BWV815a
6.119	No.2 "Courante"	
6.120	No.3 "Sarabande"	
6.121	No.4 "Gavotte"	
6.122	No.5 "Air"	
6.123	No.6 "Gavotte," II	
6.124	No.7 "Aria"	
6.125	French Suite No.5 in G major (2 vers): No.1 "Allemande"	BWV816
6.126	No.2 "Courante"	
6.127	No.3 "Sarabande"	
6.128	No.4 "Gavotte"	
6.129	No.5 "Bourrée"	
6.130	No.6 "Loure"	
6.131	No.7 "Gigue"	
6.132	French Suite No.6 in E major (2 vers): . "Prélude" (in 2nd vers only)	BWV817
6.133	No.1 "Allemande"	
6.134	No.2 "Courante"	
6.135	No.3 "Sarabande"	
6.136	No.4 "Gavotte"	
6.137	No.5 "Polonaise"	
6.138	No.6 "Bourrée"	
6.139	No.7 "Gigue"	
6.140	No.8 "Menuet"	

Other suites:

6.141	"Suite," in A minor (ca1722): No.1 "Allemande"	BWV818
6.142	No.2 "Courante"	
6.143	No.3 "Sarabande simple"	
6.144	No.3a "Sarabande double"	
6.145	No.4 "Gigue"	
6.146	Variant of BWV818 (newer vers): No.1 "Fort gai"	BWV818a
6.147	No.2 "Allemande"	
6.148	No.3 "Courante"	
6.149	No.4 "Sarabande"	
6.150	No.5 "Menuett"	
6.151	No.6 "Gigue"	
6.152	"Suite," in E-flat major (ca1722): No.1 "Allemande"	BWV819
6.153	No.2 "Courante"	
6.154	No.3 "Sarabande"	

6.155	No.4 "Bourrée"
6.156	No.5 "Menuett," I (altern)
6.157	No.6 "Menuett," II (Trio)
6.158	Variant of BWV819 (newer vers: No.1 = different Allemande) BWV819a
6.159	"Ouverture" (Suite), in F major (ca ?1709): No.1 "Ouverture" BWV820
6.160	No.2 "Entrée"
6.161	No.3 "Menuett"
6.162	No.4 "Trio"
6.163	No.5 "Bourrée"
6.164	No.6 "Gigue"
6.165	*"Suite," in B-flat major (?spur)* *BWV821*
6.166	*"Suite," in G minor (?spur)* *BWV822*
6.167	"Suite," in F minor (ca ?1708–14, inc): No.1 "Prélude" BWV823
6.168	No.2 "Sarabande en Rondeau"
6.169	No.3 "Gigue"
6.170	*"Suite," in A major (spur: c by Telemann)* *BWV824*

7 Partitas (Clavierübung I) (ca1725–30):

6.171	Partita No.1 in B-flat major, "German Suite": No.1 "Praeludium" BWV825
6.172	No.2 "Allemande"
6.173	No.3 "Corrente"
6.174	No.4 "Sarabande"
6.175	No.5 "Menuet," I
6.176	No.6 "Menuet," II
6.177	No.7 "Giga"
6.178	Partita No.2 in C minor, "German Suite": No.1 "Sinfonia" BWV826
6.179	No.2 "Allemande"
6.180	No.3 "Courante"
6.181	No.4 "Sarabande"
6.182	No.5 "Rondeaux"
6.183	No.6 "Capriccio"
6.184	Partita No.3 in A minor, "German Suite": No.1 "Fantasia" BWV827
6.185	No.2 "Allemande"
6.186	No.3 "Courante"
6.187	No.4 "Sarabande"
6.188	No.5 "Burlesca"
6.189	No.6 "Scherzo"
6.190	No.7 "Gigue"
6.191	Partita No.4 in D major, "German Suite": No.1 "Ouverture" BWV828
6.192	No.2 "Allemande"
6.193	No.3 "Courante"
6.194	No.4 "Aria"
6.195	No.5 "Sarabande"
6.196	No.6 "Menuet"
6.197	No.7 "Gigue
6.198	Partita No.5 in G major, "German Suite": No.1 "Praeambulum" BWV829
6.199	No.2 "Allemande"
6.200	No.3 "Courante"
6.201	No.4 "Sarabande"
6.202	No.5 "Tempo di Minuetta"
6.203	No.6 "Passepied"
6.204	No.7 "Gigue"
6.205	Partita No.6 in E minor, "German Suite": No.1 "Toccata" BWV830
6.206	No.2 "Allemanda"
6.207	No.3 "Courante"
6.208	No.4 "Air"
6.209	No.5 "Sarabande"
6.210	No.6 "Tempo di Gavotta"
6.211	No.7 "Gigue"
6.212	Partita No.7 in B minor, "French style" (ca1734, from: Clavierübung II): No.1 "Ouverture" BWV831
6.213	No.2 "Courante"
6.214	No.3 "Gavotte," I
6.215	No.4 "Gavotte," II
6.216	No.5 "Passepied," I
6.217	No.6 "Passepied," II
6.218	No.7 "Sarabande"
6.219	No.8 "Bourrée," I
6.220	No.9 "Bourrée," II
6.221	No.10 "Gigue"
6.222	No.11 "Echo"
6.223	Version of BWV831 (ca1730, earlier vers) BWV831a

Other:

6.224	"Suite," in A major (ca ?1708–14): No.1 "Allemande"	BWV832
6.225	No.2 "Air" (pour les Trompettes)	
6.226	No.3 "Sarabande"	
6.227	No.4 "Bourrée"	
6.228	No.5 "Gigue"	
6.229	*"Praeludium et Partita del terzo tuono," in F major (spur: c by Pasquini)*	*BWV833*
6.230	*"Allemande," in C minor (spur)*	*BWV834*
6.231	*"Allemande," in A minor (spur: c by Kirnberger)*	*BWV835*
6.232	*"Allemande," in G minor (spur: c by W. F. Bach)*	*BWV836*
6.233	*"Allemande," in G minor (spur: c by W. F. Bach)*	*BWV837*
6.234	*"Allemande & Courante," in A major (spur: c by Graupner)*	*BWV838*
6.235	*"Sarabande," in G minor (spur)*	*BWV839*
6.236	*"Courante," in G major (spur: c by Telemann)*	*BWV840*

3 Menuets (ca1720, from Klavierbüchlein for W. F. Bach):

6.237	"Menuet," in G major (ca1720)	BWV841
6.238	"Menuet," in G minor (ca1720)	BWV842
6.239	"Menuet," in G major (ca1720)	BWV843

Other:

6.240	*"Scherzo," in D minor (2nd vers, spur: c by W. F. Bach)*	*BWV844*
6.241	*Variant of BWV844, in E minor (1st vers, spur: c by W. F. Bach)*	*BWV844a*
6.242	*"Gigue," in F minor (spur)*	*BWV845*
6.243	"The Well-tempered Clavier," I (24 Preludes & fugues) (ca1718–22): No.1 in C major	BWV846
6.244	. Version of BWV846 (Prelude)	BWV846a
6.245	No.2 in C minor	BWV847
6.246	No.3 in C-sharp major	BWV848
6.247	No.4 in C-sharp minor	BWV849
6.248	No.5 in D major	BWV850
6.249	No.6 in D minor	BWV851
6.250	No.7 in E-flat major	BWV852
6.251	No.8 in E-flat minor (D-sharp minor)	BWV853
6.252	No.9 in E major	BWV854
6.253	No.10 in E minor	BWV855
6.254	. Variant of BWV855 (Prelude)	BWV855a
6.255	No.11 in F major	BWV856
6.256	No.12 in F minor	BWV857
6.257	No.13 in F-sharp major	BWV858
6.258	No.14 in F-sharp minor	BWV859
6.259	No.15 in G major	BWV860
6.260	No.16 in G minor	BWV861
6.261	No.17 in A-flat major	BWV862
6.262	No.18 in G-sharp minor	BWV863
6.263	No.19 in A major	BWV864
6.264	No.20 in A minor	BWV865
6.265	No.21 in B-flat major	BWV866
6.266	No.22 in B-flat minor	BWV867
6.267	No.23 in B major	BWV868
6.268	No.24 in B minor	BWV869
6.269	"The Well-tempered Clavier," II (24 Preludes & fugues) (ca1738–42): No.1 in C major	BWV870
6.270	. Variant of BWV870 (Prelude & fughetta)	BWV870a
6.271	. Variant of BWV870 (Prelude)	BWV870b
6.272	No.2 in C minor	BWV871
6.273	No.3 in C-sharp major	BWV872
6.274	. Variant of BWV872 (Prelude & fughetta)	BWV872a
6.275	No.4 in C-sharp minor	BWV873
6.276	No.5 in D major	BWV874
6.277	No.6 in D minor	BWV875
6.278	. Variant of BWV875 (Prelude)	BWV875a
6.279	No.7 in E-flat major	BWV876
6.280	No.8 in E-flat minor (D-sharp minor)	BWV877
6.281	No.9 in E major	BWV878
6.282	No.10 in E minor	BWV879
6.283	No.11 in F major	BWV880
6.284	No.12 in F minor	BWV881
6.285	No.13 in F-sharp major	BWV882
6.286	No.14 in F-sharp minor	BWV883
6.287	No.15 in G major	BWV884
6.288	No.16 in in G minor	BWV885
6.289	No.17 in A-flat major	BWV886
6.290	No.18 in G-sharp minor	BWV887

6.366	*"Fugue," in G major (?spur)*	*BWV957*
6.367	"Fugue," in A minor (ca1710)	BWV959
6.368	*"Fugue," in E minor (spur, inc)*	*BWV960*
6.369	*"Fughetta," in C minor (?spur)*	*BWV961*
6.370	*"Fugato," in E minor (spur: c by Albrechtsberger)*	*BWV962*
6.371	"Sonata," in D major (ca1704)	BWV963
6.372	*"Sonata," in D minor (spur: arr ?W. F. Bach of Vn Sonata, BWV1003)*	*BWV964*
6.373	"Sonata," in A minor (ca1718–23, after Reincken)	BWV965
6.374	"Sonata," in C major (ca1718–23, after Reincken)	BWV966
6.375	"Sonata," in A minor (ca1704, 1 movt)	BWV967
6.376	*"Adagio," in G major (spur: arr W. F. Bach of 1st movt of: Vn Sonata, BWV1005)*	*BWV968*
6.377	*"Andante," in G minor (spur)*	*BWV969*
6.378	*"Presto," in D minor (spur: c by W. F. Bach)*	*BWV970*
6.379	"Italian Concerto," in F major (c before 1735, from: Clavierübung II)	BWV971

"16 Concertos after other Masters" (arrs) (arr for hpd 1713–6):

6.380	Concerto No.1 in D major (from Vivaldi's Op.3/9, RV230)	BWV972
6.381	Concerto No.2 in G major (from Vivaldi's Op.8/8, RV332)	BWV973
6.382	Concerto No.3 in D minor (from Marcello: Ob Conc)	BWV974
6.383	Concerto No.4 in G minor (form Vivaldi's Op.4/6, RV316)	BWV975
6.384	Concerto No.5 in C major (from Vivaldi's Op.3/12, RV265)	BWV976
6.385	Concerto No.6 in C major (?)	BWV977
6.386	Concerto No.7 in F major (from Vivaldi's Op.3/3, RV310)	BWV978
6.387	Concerto No.8 in B minor (from ?Torelli)	BWV979
6.388	Concerto No.9 in G major (from Vivaldi's Op.4/1, RV381)	BWV980
6.389	Concerto No.10 in C minor (from Marcello's Op.1/2)	BWV981
6.390	Concerto No.11 in B-flat major (from Ernst's Op.1/1)	BWV982
6.391	Concerto No.12 in G minor (from anon)	BWV983
6.392	Concerto No.13 in C major (from Ernst)	BWV984
6.393	Concerto No.14 in G minor (from Telemann)	BWV985
6.394	Concerto No.15 in G major (from anon)	BWV986
6.395	Concerto No.16 in D minor (from Ernst's Op.1/4)	BWV987

Other:

6.396	"Goldberg Variations" (ca1741, Clavierübung IV):	BWV988

   . "Aria"
    1. "a 1 Clav."
    2. "a 1 Clav."
    3. "Canone all'Unisono. a 1 Clav."
    4. "a 1 Clav."
    5. "a 1 Clav."
    6. "Canone alla Seconda. a 1 Clav."
    7. "a 1 ovvero 2 Clav. Al tempo di Giga"
    8. "a 2 Clav."
    9. "Canone alla Terza. a 1 Clav."
    10. "Fughetta. a 1 Clav."
    11. "a 2 Clav."
    12. "Canone alla Quarta. (a 1 Clav.)"
    13. "a 2 Clav."
    14. "a 2 Clav."
    15. "Canone alla Quinta. a 1 Clav. Andante"
    16. "Ouverture. a 1 Clav."
    17. "a 2 Clav."
    18. "Canone alla Sesta. a 1 Clav."
    19. "a 1 Clav."
    20. "a 2 Clav."
    21. "Canone alla Settima. (a 1 Clav.)"
    22. "a 1 Clav. Alla breve"
    23. "a 2 Clav."
    24. "Canone all'Ottava. a 1 Clav."
    25. "a 2 Clav. Adagio"
    26. "a 2 Clav."
    27. "Canone alla Nona"
    28. "a 2 Clav."
    29. "a 1 ovvero 2 Clav."
    30. "Quodlibet. a 1 Clav."
   . "Aria da Capo"

6.397	"Aria variata" (alla maniera italiana), in A minor (ca1709)	BWV989
6.398	*"Sarabande con Partite," in C major (spur)*	*BWV990*
6.399	*"Aria with variations," in C minor (ca1722, frag)*	*BWV991*
6.400	"Capriccio on the Departure of His Most Beloved Brother," in B-flat major (ca1704)	BWV992
6.401	"Capriccio in honorem Johann Christoph Bachii," in B-flat major (ca1704)	BWV993
6.402	"Applicatio," in C major (ca1720, from: Klavierbüchlein for W. F. Bach)	BWV994

7. CHURCH CANTATAS (vv, ch & orch)

7.1   Cantata No.1: "Wie schön leuchtet der Morgenstern" (c1725, Annunciation): BWV1
     1. "Wie schön leuchtet der Morgenstern," chorus
     2. "Du wahrer Gottes und Marien Sohn," recit (T)
     3. "Erfüllet, ihr himmlischen göttlichen Flammen," aria (S)
     4. "Ein ird'scher Glanz, ein leiblich Licht, recit (B)
     5. "Unser Mund und Ton der Saiten," aria (T)
     6. "Wie bin ich doch so herzlich froh," choral

7.2   Cantata No.2: "Ach Gott, vom Himmel sieh darein" (c1724, Trinity 2): BWV2
     1. "Ach Gott, vom Himmel sieh' darein," chorus
     2. "Sie lehren eitel falsche List," recit (T)
     3. "Tilg', o Gott, die Lehren," aria (A)
     4. "Die Armen sind verstört," recit (B)
     5. "Durchs Feuer wird das Silber rein," aria (T)
     6. "Das woll'st du, Gott, bewahren rein," choral

7.3   Cantata No.3: "Ach Gott, wie manches Herzeleid" I (c1725, Epiphany 2): BWV3
     1. "Ach Gott, wie manches Herzeleid" (ch)
     2. "Wie schwerlich lässt sich Fleisch und Blut," recit (w/ ch)
     3. "Empfind' ich Höllenangst und Pein," aria (B)
     4. "Es mag mir Leib und Geist verschmachten," recit (T)
     5. "Wenn Sorgen auf mich dringen," duet (S, A)
     6. "Erhalt mein Herz im Glauben rein," choral

7.4   Cantata No.4: "Christ lag in Todesbanden" (ca1707–8, Easter Day): BWV4
     1. "Sinfonia"
     2. "Christ lag in Todesbanden," chorus
     3. "Den Tod niemand zwingen kann," duet (S, A)
     4. "Jesus Christus, Gottes Sohn" (T)
     5. "Es war ein wunderlicher Krieg" (ch)
     6. "Hier ist das rechte Osterlamm" (B)
     7. "So feiern wir das hohe Fest," duet (S, T)
     8. "Wir essen und leben wohl," choral

7.5   Cantata No.5: "Wo soll ich fliehen hin?" (c1724, Trinity 19): BWV5
     1. "Wo soll ich fliehen hin," chorus
     2. "Der Sünden Wust hat mich nicht nur befleckt," recit (B)
     3. "Ergiesse dich reichlich," aria (T)
     4. "Mein treuer Heiland tröstet mich," recit (A)
     5. "Verstumme, Höllenheer," aria (B)
     6. "Ich bin ja nur der kleinste Theil der Welt," recit (S)
     7. "Führ auch mein Herz und Sinn," choral

7.6   Cantata No.6: "Bleib' bei uns, denn es will Abend werden" (c1725, Easter Monday): BWV6
     1. "Bleib' bei uns, denn es will Abend werden," chorus
     2. "Hoch gelobter Gottessohn," aria (A)
     3. "Ach bleib' bei uns, Herr Jesu Christ," choral (S)
     4. "Es hat die Dunkelheit an vielen Orten," recit (B)
     5. "Jesu, lass uns auf dich sehen," aria (T)
     6. "Beweis' dein Macht, Herr Jesu Christ," choral

7.7   Cantata No.7: "Christ unser Herr zum Jordan kam" (c1724, St. John Baptist): BWV7
     1. "Christ unser Herr zum Jordan kam" (ch)
     2. "Merkt und hört, ihr Menschenkinder," aria (B)
     3. "Dies hat Gott klar mit Worten," recit (T)
     4. "Des Vaters Stimme liess sich hören," aria (T)
     5. "Als Jesus dort nach seinem Leiden," recit (B)
     6. "Menschen, glaubt doch dieser Gnade," aria (A)
     7. "Das Aug' allein das Wasser sieht," choral

7.8   Cantata No.8: "Liebster Gott, wenn werd' ich sterben?" (c1724, Trinity 16): BWV8
     1. "Liebster Gott, wenn werd' ich sterben" (ch)
     2. "Was willst du dich, mein Geist, entsetzen," aria (T)
     3. "Zwar fühlt mein schwaches Herz," recit (A)
     4. "Doch weichet ihr tollen vergeblichen Sorgen," aria (B)
     5. "Behalte nur, o Welt das Meine," recit (S)
     6. "Herrscher über Tod und Leben," choral

7.9   Cantata No.9: "Es ist das Heil uns kommen her" (ca1732–5, Trinity 6): BWV9
     1. "Es ist das Heil uns kommen her" (ch)
     2. "Gott gab uns ein Gesetz," recit (B)
     3. "Wir waren schon zu tief gesunken," aria (T)
     4. "Doch musste das Gesetz erfüllet werden," recit (B)
     5. "Herr, du siehst statt guter Werke," duet (S, A)
     6. "Wenn wir die Sünd aus dem Gesetz erkennen," recit (B)
     7. "Ob sich's anliess', als wollt' er nicht," choral

7.10   Cantata No.10: "Meine Seel' erhebt den Herrn" (c1724, Visitation): BWV10
     1. "Meine Seel' erhebt den Herrn" (ch)
     2. "Herr, der du stark und mächtig bist," aria (S)
     3. "Des Höchsten Güt und Treu," recit (T)
     4. "Gewaltige stösst Gott vom Stuhl," aria (B)

5. "Er denket der Barmherzigkeit," duet (S, A)
6. "Was Gott den Vätern alter Zeiten," recit (T)
7. "Lob und Preis sei Gott dem Vater und dem Sohn," choral

7.11 Cantata No.11: "Lobet Gott in seinen Reichen" (Ascension Oratorio) (c1735, Ascension Day): BWV11
1. "Lobet Gott in seinen Reichen," chorus
2. "Der Herr Jesus hub seine Hände auf," recit (T)
3. "Ach, Jesu, ist dein Abschied schon so nah?," recit (B)
4. "Ach, bleibe doch, mein liebstes Leben," aria (A)
5. "Und ward aufgehoben zusehens," recit (T)
6. "Nun lieget Alles unter dir," choral
7a. "Und da sie ihm nach sahen," recit (T, B)
7b. "Ach, ja! So komme bald zurück," recit (A)
7c. "Sie aber beteten ihn an," recit (T)
8. "Jesu, deine Gnadenblikke," aria (S)
9. "Wann soll es doch geschehen," choral

7.12 Cantata No.12: "Weinen, Klagen, Sorgen, Zagen" (c1714, Easter 3): BWV12
1. "Sinfonia"
2. "Weinen, Klagen, Sorgen, Zagen," chorus
3. "Wir müssen durch viel Trübsal," recit (A)
4. "Kreuz und Krone sind verbunden," aria (A)
5. "Ich folge Christo nach," aria (B)
6. "Sei getreu, alle Pein," aria (T)
7. "Was Gott tut, das ist wohlgetan," choral

7.13 Cantata No.13: "Meine Seufzer, meine Tränen" (c1726, Epiphany 2): BWV13
1. "Meine Seufzer, meine Tränen," aria (T)
2. "Mein liebster Gott lässt mich," recit (A)
3. "Der Gott, der mir hat versprochen," choral (A)
4. "Mein Kummer nimmet zu," recit (S)
5. "Ächzen und erbärmlich Weinen," aria (B)
6. "So sei nun, Seele, deine," choral

7.14 Cantata No.14: "Wär Gott nicht mit uns diese Zeit" (c1735, Epiphany 4): BWV14
1. "Wär Gott nicht mit uns diese Zeit," chorus
2. "Unsre Stärke heisst zu schwach," aria (S)
3. "Ja, hätt es Gott nur zugegeben," recit (T)
4. "Gott, bei deinem starken Schützen," aria (B)
5. "Gott Lob und Dank, der nicht zugab," choral

7.15   Cantata No.15: "Denn du wirst meine Seele," (spur: c by J. L. Bach) BWV15
7.16 Cantata No.16: "Herr Gott, dich loben wir" (c1726, New Year): BWV16
1. "Herr Gott, dich loben wir," chorus
2. "So stimmen wir bei dieser frohen Zeit," recit (B)
3. "Lasst uns jauchzen, lasst uns freuen," aria & chorus (B)
4. "Ach treuer Hort," recit (A)
5. "Geliebter Jesu, du, du allein," aria (T)
6. "All solch dein Güt wir preisen," choral

7.17 Cantata No.17: "Wer Dank opfert, der preiset mich" (c1726, Trinity 14): BWV17
I: 1. "Wer Dank opfert, der preiset mich," chorus
2. "Es muss die ganze Welt," recit (A)
3. "Herr, deine Güte reicht so weit der Himmel ist," aria (S)
II: 4. "Einer aber unter ihnen," recit (T)
5. "Welch Übermass der Güte," aria (T)
6. "Sieh meinen Willen an," recit (B)
7. "Wie sich ein Vat'r erbarmet," choral

7.18 Cantata No.18: "Gleich wie der Regen und Schnee" (ca1714 & 1724, Sexagesima): BWV18
1. "Sinfonia"
2. "Gleich wie der Regen und Schnee vom Himmel fällt," recit (B)
3. "Mein Gott, hier wird mein Herze sein," recit & chorus (S, T, B)
4. "Mein Seelenschatz ist Gottes Wort," aria (S)
5. "Ich bitt', o Herr, aus Herzens Grund," choral

7.19 Cantata No.19: "Es erhub sich ein Streit" (c1726, St. Michael): BWV19
1. "Es erhub sich ein Streit," chorus
2. "Gottlob! der Drache liegt," recit (B)
3. "Gott schickt uns Mahanaim zu," aria (S)
4. "Was ist der schnöde Mensch," recit (T)
5. "Bleibet, ihr Engel, bleibt bei mir," aria (T)
6. "Lasst uns das Angesicht," recit (S)
7. "Lass dein' Engel mit mir fahren," choral

7.20 Cantata No.20: "O Ewigkeit, du Donnerwort" (c1724, Trinity 1): BWV20
I: 1. "O Ewigkeit, du Donnerwort," chorus
2. "Kein Unglück ist in aller Welt zu finden," recit (T)
3. "Ewigkeit, du machst mir bange," aria (T)
4. "Gesetzt, es dau'rte der Verdammten Qual," recit (B)
5. "Gott ist gerecht," aria (B)
6. "O Mensch, errette deine Seele," aria (A)
7. "Solang ein Gott im Himmel lebt," choral
II: 8. "Wacht auf, verlornen Schafe," aria (B)

        5. "Kommt, ihr angefochtnen Sünder," aria (A)
        6. "Eine Stimme lässt sich hören," choral
    II: 7. "So bist du denn, mein Heil, bedacht," recit (B)
        8. "Ich will nun hassen, und Alles lassen," aria (B)
        9. "Und ob wohl sonst der Unbestand," recit (S)
     10. "Eilt, ihr Stunden, kommt herbei," aria (S)
     11. "Geduld! Der angenehme Tag," recit (T)
     12. "Freue dich, geheilgte Schar," chorus

7.31   Cantata No.31: "Der Himmel lacht! Die Erde jubilieret" (c1715, Easter Day): BWV31
        1. "Sonata"
        2. "Der Himmel lacht! Die Erde jubilieret," chorus
        3. "Erwünschter Tag! sei, Seele, wieder froh," recit (B)
        4. "Fürst des Lebens, starker Streiter," aria (B)
        5. "So stehe denn, du Gottergebne Seele," recit (T)
        6. "Adam muss in uns verwesen," aria (T)
        7. "Weill denn das Haupt sein Glied," recit (S)
        8. "Letze Stunde, brich herein," aria (S)
        9. "So fahr ich hin zu Jesu Christ," choral

7.32   Cantata No.32: "Liebster Jesu, mein Verlangen" (c1726, Epiphany 1): BWV32
        1. "Liebster Jesu, mein Verlangen," aria (S)
        2. "Was ist's, was ist's, dass du mich gesuchet?," recit (B)
        3. "Hier, in meines Vaters Stätte," aria (B)
        4. "Ach, heiliger und grosser Gott," recit (S, B)
        5. "Nun verschwinden alle Plagen," duet (S, B)
        6. "Mein Gott, öffne mir die Pforten," choral

7.33   Cantata No.33: "Allein zu dir, Herr Jesu Christ" (c1724, Trinity 13): BWV33
        1. "Allein zu dir, Herr Jesu Christ," chorus
        2. "Mein Gott und Richter," recit (B)
        3. "Wie furchtsam wankten meine Schritte," aria (A)
        4. "Mein Gott, verwirf mich nicht," recit (T)
        5. "Gott, der du die Liebe heisst," duet (T, B)
        6. "Ehr sei Gott in dem höchsten Thron," choral

7.34   Cantata No.34: "O ewiges Feuer, O Ursprung der Liebe" (c ?1740, Whit Sunday): BWV34
        1. "O ewiges Feuer, o Ursprung der Liebe," chorus
        2. "Herr! unsre Herzen halten dir," recit (T)
        3. "Wohl euch, ihr auserwählten Seelen," aria (A)
        4. "Erwählt sich Gott die heil'gen Hütten," recit (B)
        5. "Friede über Israel! Dankt den höchsten Wunderhänden"

7.35   Cantata No.34a: "O ewiges Feuer, o Ursprung der Liebe" (c1726, a wedding, inc): BWV34a
        1. "O ewiges Feuer," chorus
        2. "Wie dass der Liebe hohe Kraft," recit (B)
        3. "Siehe, also wird gesegnet der Mann," duet (A, T)
        4. "Friede über Israel," chorus
        5. "Wohl euch, ihr auserwählten Schafe," aria (A)
        6. "Das ist vor dich, o ehrenwürd'ger Mann," recit (S)
        7. "Gib, höchster Gott," chorus

7.36   Cantata No.35: "Geist und Seele wird verwirret" (c1726, Trinity 12): BWV35
    I: 1. "Sinfonia"
        2. "Geist und Seele wird verwirret," aria (A)
        3. "Ich wundre mich, denn Alles, was man sieht," recit (A)
        4. "Gott hat Alles wohl gemacht," aria (A)
    II: 5. "Sinfonia"
        6. "Ach, starker Gott, lass mich doch dieses stets bedenken," recit (A)
        7. "Ich wünsche mir, bei Gott zu leben," aria (A)

7.37   Cantata No.36/1: "Schwingt freudig euch empor" (ca1726–30 & 1731, Advent 1): BWV36/1
        1. "Schwingt freudig euch empor," chorus
        2. "Die Liebe zieht mit sanften Schritten," aria (T)
        3. "Sei mir willkommen, werter Schatz," aria (B)
        4. "Auch mit gedämpften, schwachen Stimmen," aria (S)
        5. "Wie bin ich doch so herzlich froh," choral

7.38   Cantata No.36/2: "Schwingt freudig euch empor" (ca1726–30 & 1731, Advent 1): BWV36/2
    I: 1. "Schwingt freudig euch empor," chorus
        2. "Nun komm, der Heiden Heiland," choral
        3. "Die Liebe zieht mit sanften Schritten," aria (T)
        4. "Zwingt die Saiten in Cythara," chorus
    II: 5. "Willkommen, werter Schatz," aria (B)
        6. "Der du bist dem Vater gleich," choral (T)
        7. "Auch mit gedämpften, schwachen Stimmen," aria (S)
        8. "Lob sei Gott dem Vater ton," choral

7.39   Cantata No.37: "Wer da gläubet und getauft wird" (c1724, Ascension Day): BWV37
        1. "Wer da gläubet und getauft wird," chorus
        2. "Der Glaube ist das Pfand der Liebe," aria (T)
        3. "Herr Gott Vater, mein starker Held," choral (S, A)
        4. "Ihr Sterblichen, verlanget ihr mit mir," recit (B)
        5. "Der Glaube schafft der Seele Flügel," aria (B)

      6. "Den Glauben mir verleihe an dein' Sohn, Jesum Christ," choral

7.40   Cantata No.38: "Aus tiefer Not schrei ich zu dir" (c1724, Trinity 21): BWV38
      1. "Aus tiefer Not schrei' ich zu dir," chorus
      2. "In Jesu Gnade wird allein der Trost," recit (A)
      3. "Ich höre mitten in dem Leiden," aria (T)
      4. "Ach! dass mein Glaube noch so schwach," recit a battuta (S)
      5. "Wenn meine Trübsal als mit Ketten," trio (S, A, B)
      6. "Ob bei uns ist der Sünden viel," choral

7.41   Cantata No.39: "Brich dem Hungrigen dein Brot" (c1726, Trinity 1): BWV39
    I: 1. "Brich dem Hungrigen dein Brot," chorus
       2. "Der reiche Gott," recit (B)
       3. "Seinem Schöpfer noch auf Erden," aria (A)
    II: 4. "Wohlzutun und mitzuteilen," aria (B)
       5. "Höchster, was ich habe," aria (S)
       6. "Wie soll ich dir, o Herr," recit (A)
       7. "Selig sind, die aus Erbarmen," choral

7.42   Cantata No.40: "Darzu ist erschienen der Sohn Gottes" (c1723, 2nd day of Christmas): BWV40
      1."Darzu ist erschienen der Sohn Gottes," chorus
      2. "Das Wort ward Fleisch und wohnet in der Welt," recit (T)
      3. "Die Sünd'macht Leid," choral
      4. "Höllische Schlange, wird dir nicht bange," aria (A)
      5. "Die Schlange, so im Paradise," recit (A)
      6. "Schüttle deinen Kopf und sprich," choral
      7. "Christenkinder, freuet euch," aria (T)
      8. "Jesu, nimm dich deiner Glieder," choral

7.43   Cantata No.41: "Jesu, nun sei gepreiset" (c1725, New Year): BWV41
      1. "Jesu, nun sei gepreiset," chorus
      2. "Lass uns, o höchster Gott," aria (S)
      3. "Herr! Deine Hand, dein Segen muss allein," recit (A)
      4. "Woferne du den edlen Frieden," aria (T)
      5. "Doch weil der Feind bei Tag und Nacht," recit (S, A, T, B)
      6. "Dein ist allein die Ehre," choral

7.44   Cantata No.42: "Am Abend aber desselbigen Sabbats" (c1725, Easter 1): BWV42
      1. "Sinfonia"
      2. "Am Abend aber desselbigen Sabbats"
      3. "Wo Zwei und Drei versammlet," aria (A)
      4. "Verzage nicht," choral (S, T)
      5. "Man kann hiervon ein schön Exempel sehen," recit (B)
      6. "Jesus ist ein Schild der Seinen," aria (B)
      7. "Verleih' uns Frieden gnädiglich," choral

7.45   Cantata No.43: "Gott fähret auf mit Jauchzen" (c1726, Ascension Day): BWV43
    I: 1. "Gott fähret auf mit Jauchzen," chorus
       2. "Es will der Höchste," recit (T)
       3. "Ja, tausendmal Tausend," aria (T)
       4. "Und der Herr," recit (S)
       5. "Mein Jesus hat nunmehr," aria (S)
    II: 6. "Es kommt der Helden Held," recit (B)
       7. "Er ist's, der ganz allein," aria (B)
       8. "Der Vater hat ihm ja," recit (A)
       9. "Ich sehe schon im Geist," aria (A)
      10. "Er will mir neben sich," recit (S)
      11. "Du Lebensfürst, Herr Jesu Christ," choral

7.46   Cantata No.44: "Sie werden euch in die Bann tun" I (c1724, Ascension 1): BWV44
      1. "Sie werden euch in die Bann," duet (T, B)
      2. "Es kömmt aber die Zeit," chorus
      3. "Christen müssen auf der Erden," aria (A)
      4. "Ach Gott, wie manches Herzeleid," choral (T)
      5. "Es sucht der Antichrist," recit (B)
      6. "Es ist und bleibt der Christen Trost," aria (S)
      7. "So sei nun, Seele," choral

7.47   Cantata No.45: "Es ist dir gesagt, Mensch, was gut ist" (c1726, Trinity 8): BWV45
    I: 1. "Es ist dir gesagt, Mensch, was gut ist," chorus
       2. "Der Höchste lässt mich," recit (T)
       3. "Weiss ich Gottes Rechte," aria (T)
    II: 4. "Es werden Viele zu mir sagen," arioso (B)
       5. "Wer Gott bekennt aus wahrem Herzensgrund," aria (A)
       6. "So wird denn Herz und Mund," recit (A)
       7. "Gib, dass ich tu' mit Fleiss," choral

7.48   Cantata No.46: "Schauet doch und sehet, ob irgend" (c1723, Trinity 10): BWV46
      1. "Schauet doch und sehet, ob irgend ein Schmerz sei," chorus
      2. "So klage du, zerstörte Gottesstadt," recit (T)
      3. "Dein Wetter zog sich auf von weiten," aria (B)
      4. "Doch bildet euch, o Sünder," recit (A)
      5. "Doch Jesus will auch bei der Strafe," aria (A)
      6. "O grosser Gott der Treu," choral

7.49   Cantata No.47: "Wer sich selbst erhöhet, der soll erniedriget werden" (c1726, Trinity 17): BWV47
           1. "Wer sich selbst erhöhet, der soll erniedriget werden," chorus
           2. "Wer ein wahrer Christ will heissen," aria (S)
           3. "Der Mensch ist Kot, Staub, Asch und Erde," recit (B)
           4. "Jesu beuge doch mein Herze," aria (B)
           5. "Der zeitlichen Ehr will ich gern entbehr'n," choral
7.50   Cantata No.48: "Ich elender Mensch, wer wird mich erlösen" (c1723, Trinity 19):............................ BWV48
           1. "Ich elender Mensch, wer wird mich erlösen," chorus
           2. "O Schmerz, o Elend! so mich trifft," recit (A)
           3. "Soll's ja so sein," choral
           4. "Ach, lege das Sodom der sündlichen Glieder," aria (A)
           5. "Hier aber tut des Heilands Hand," recit (T)
           6. "Vergiebt mir Jesus meine Sünden," aria (T)
           7. "Herr Jesu Christ, einiger Trost," choral
7.51   Cantata No.49: "Ich geh' und suche mit Verlangen" (c1726, Trinity 20):..BWV49
           1. "Sinfonia"
           2. "Ich geh' und suche mit Verlangen," aria (B)
           3. "Mein Mahl ist zubereit'," recit (B, S)
           4. "Ich bin herrlich, ich bin schön," aria (S)
           5. "Mein Glaube hat mich selbst so angezogen!," recit (S, B)
           6. "Dich hab ich je und je geliebet," duet (S, B)
7.52   Cantata No.50: "Nun ist das Heil und die Kraft" (c ?1723, ?St. Michael, inc)..................... BWV50
7.53   Cantata No.51: "Jauchzet Gott in allen Landen" (c ?1730, Trinity 15): BWV51
           1. "Jauchzet Gott in allen Landen!," aria (S)
           2. "Wir beten zu dem Tempel an," recit (S)
           3. "Höchster, mache deine Güte ferner," aria (S)
           4. "Sei Lob und Preis mit Ehren," choral (S)
           5. "Alleluja," aria (S)
7.54   Cantata No.52: "Falsche Welt, dir trau' ich nicht" (c1726, Trinity 23): BWV52
           1. "Sinfonia"
           2. "Falsche Welt, dir trau' ich nicht," recit (S)
           3. "Immerhin, immerhin," aria (S)
           4. "Gott ist getreu!," recit (S)
           5. "Ich halt' es mit dem lieben Gott," aria (S)
           6. "In dich hab' ich gehoffet," choral
7.55   *Cantata No.53: "Schlage doch, gewünschte Stunde," aria (A, spur: c by Hoffmann)* *BWV53*
7.56   Cantata No.54: "Widerstehe doch der Sünde" (c ?1714, Trinity 7): BWV54
           1. "Widerstehe doch der Sünde," aria (A)
           2. "Die Art verruchter Sünden ist zwar," recit (A)
           3. "Wer Sünde tut, der ist vom Teufel," aria (A)
7.57   Cantata No.55: "Ich armer Mensch, ich Sündenknecht" (c1726, Trinity 22):......................BWV55
           1. "Ich armer Mensch, ich Sündenknecht," aria (T)
           2. "Ich habe wider Gott gehandelt," recit (T)
           3. "Erbarme dich," aria (T)
           4. "Erbarme dich! Jedoch nun tröst' ich mich," recit (T)
           5. "Bin ich gleich von dir gewichen," choral
7.58   Cantata No.56: "Ich will den Kreuzstab gerne tragen" (c1726, Trinity 19): BWV56
           1. "Ich will den Kreuzstab gerne tragen," aria (B)
           2. "Mein Wandel auf der Welt," recit (B)
           3. "Endlich, endlich wird mein Joch," aria (B)
           4. "Ich stehe fertig und bereit," recit (B)
           5. "Komm, o Tod, du Schlafes Bruder," choral
7.59   Cantata No.57: "Selig ist der Mann" (c1725, 2nd day of Christmas): BWV57
           1. "Selig ist der Mann," aria (B)
           2. "Ach, dieser süsse Trost," recit (S)
           3. "Ich wünschte mir den Tod," aria (S)
           4. "Ich reiche dir die Hand," recit (S, B)
           5. "Ja, ja, ich kann die Feinde schlagen," aria (B)
           6. "In meinem Schoss liegt Ruh' und Leben," recit (S, B)
           7. "Ich ende behende mein irdisches Leben," aria (S)
           8. "Richte dich, Liebste," choral
7.60   Cantata No.58: "Ach Gott, wie manches Herzeleid" II (c1727, 1733–4, Sunday after New Year): BWV58
           1. "Ach Gott, wie manches Herzeleid," duet (S, B)
           2. "Verfolgt dich gleich die arge Welt," recit (B)
           3. "Ich bin vergnügt in meinem Leiden," aria (S)
           4. "Kann es die Welt nicht lassen," recit (S)
           5. "Ich hab' für mir ein' schwere Reis'," duet (S, B)
7.61   Cantata No.59: "Wer mich liebet, der wird mein Wort halten" I (c1724, Whit Sunday):......................BWV59
           1. "Wer mich liebet, der wird mein Wort halten," duet (S, B)
           2. "O! was sind das für Ehren," recit (S)
           3. "Komm, heiliger Geist," choral
           4. "Die Welt mit allen König reichen," aria (B)
7.62   Cantata No.60: "O Ewigkeit, du Donnerwort" (c1723, Trinity 24): BWV60
           1. "O Ewigkeit, du Donnerwort," duet (A, T)
           2. "O schwerer Gang zum letzten Kampf und Streite," recit (A, T)

3. "Mein letztes Lager will mich schrecken," duet (A, T)
4. "Der Tod bleibt doch der menschlichen Natur verhasst," recit (A, B)
5. "Es ist genug," choral

7.63   Cantata No.61: "Nun komm, der Heiden Heiland" I (c1714, Advent 1): BWV61
1. "Overture: Nun komm, der Heiden Heiland," chorus
2. "Der Heiland ist gekommen," recit (T)
3. "Komm, Jesu, komm zu deiner Kirche," aria (T)
4. "Siehe, siehe! Ich stehe," recit (B)
5. "Öffne dich, mein ganzes Herze," aria (S)
6. "Amen! Komm du schöne Freuden," choral

7.64   Cantata No.62: "Nun komm, der Heiden Heiland" II (c1724, Advent 1): BWV62
1. "Nun komm, der Heiden Heiland," chorus
2. "Bewundert, o Menschen," aria (T)
3. "So geht aus Gottes Herrlichkeit," recit (B)
4. "Streite," aria (B)
5. "Wir ehren diese Herrlichkeit," recit (S, A)
6. "Lob sei Gott, dem Vater," choral

7.65   Cantata No.63: "Christen, ätzet diesen Tag" (c1713 & 1723, Christmas Day): BWV63
1. "Christen, ätzet diesen Tag," chorus
2. "O sel'ger Tag!," recit (A)
3. "Du hast es wohl geflüget," duet (S, B)
4. "So kehret sich nun heut' das bange Leid," recit (T)
5. "Ruft und fleht den Himmel an," duet (A, T)
6. "Verdoppelt euch dem nach," recit (B)
7. "Höchster, schau' in Gnaden an," chorus

7.66   Cantata No.64: "Sehet, welch eine Liebe" (c1723, 3rd day of Christmas): BWV64
1. "Sehet, welch eine Liebe hat uns der Vater erzeiget," chorus
2. "Das hat er Alles uns getan," choral
3. "Geh', Welt! behalte nur das Deine, recit (A)
4. "Was frag ich nach der Welt," choral
5. "Was die Welt in sich hält," aria (S)
6. "Der Himmel bleibet mir gewiss," recit (B)
7. "Von der Welt verlang ich nichts," aria (A)
8. "Gute Nacht, o Wesen, das die Welt erlesen," choral

7.67   Cantata No.65: "Sie werden aus Saba alle kommen" (c1724, Epiphany): BWV65
1. "Sie werden aus Saba alle kommen," chorus
2. "Die Kön'ge aus Saba kamen dar," choral
3. "Was dort Jesaias vorhergesehn," recit (B)
4. "Gold und Ophir ist zu schlecht," aria (B)
5. "Verschmähe nicht," recit (T)
6. "Nimm mich dir zu eigen hin," aria (T)
7. "Ei nun, mein Gott," choral

7.68   Cantata No.66: "Erfreut euch, ihr Herzen" (c1724, Easter Monday): BWV66
1. "Erfreut euch, ihr Herzen!," chorus
2. "Es bricht das Grab und damit unsre Not," recit (B)
3. "Lasset dem Höchsten ein Danklied erschallen," aria (B)
4. "Bei Jesu Leben freudig sein," recit (A, T)
5. "Ich fürchte zwar des Grabes Finsternissen," duet (A, T)
6. "Alleluja!," choral

7.69   Cantata No.67: "Halt im Gedächtnis Jesum Christ" (c1724, Easter 1): BWV67
1. "Halt im Gedächtnis Jesum Christ," chorus
2. "Mein Jesus ist erstanden," aria (T)
3. "Mein Jesu, heissest du des Todes Gift," recit (A)
4. "Erschienen ist der herrlich' Tag," choral
5. "Doch scheinet fast," recit (A)
6. "Friede sei mit euch" (ch)
7. "Du Friedefürst, Herr Jesu Christ," choral

7.70   Cantata No.68: "Also hat Gott die Welt geliebt" (c1725, Whit Monday): BWV68
1. "Also hat Gott die Welt geliebt," chorus
2. "Mein gläubiges Herze," aria (S)
3. "Ich bin mit Petro nicht vermessen," recit (B)
4. "Du bist geboren mir zugute," aria (B)
5. "Wer an ihn glaubet, der wird nicht gerichtet" (ch)

7.71   Cantata No.69: "Lobe den Herrn, meine Seele" (ca1743–8, Council Election, from BWV69a): BWV69
1. "Lobe und vergiss nicht," chorus
2. "Wie gross ist Gottes Güte doch," recit (S)
3. "Meine Seele, auf, erzähle," aria (A)
4. "Der Herr hat grosse Ding an uns getan," recit (T)
5. "Mein Erlöser und Erhalter," aria (B)
6. "Es danke, Gott, und lobe dich," choral

7.72   Cantata No.69a: "Lobe den Herrn, meine Seele" (c1723, Trinity 12, orig vers): BWV69a
1. "Lobe und vergiss nicht," chorus
2. "Ach, dass ich tausend Zungen hätte," recit (S)
3. "Meine Seele, auf, erzähle," aria (T)
4. "Gedenk ich nur zurück," recit (A)

5. "Mein Erlöser und Erhalter," aria (B)
6. "Was Gott tut, das ist wohlgetan," choral
7.73   Cantata No.70: "Wachet! betet! betet! wachet!" (c1723, Trinity 26): BWV70
    I: 1. "Wachet, wachet, wachet, wachet," chorus
        2. "Erschrecket, ihr verstockten Sünder!," recit (B)
        3. "Wann kommt der Tag," aria (A)
        4. "Auch bei dem himmlischen Verlangen," recit (T)
        5. "Lass der Spötter Zungen schmähen," aria (S)
        6. "Jedoch! bei dem unartigen Geschlechte," recit (T)
        7. "Freu' dich sehr, o meine Seele," choral
    II: 8. "Hebt euer Haupt empor," aria (T)
        9. "Ach, soll nicht dieser grosse Tag," recit (B)
     10. "Seligster Erquikkungstag," aria (B)
     11. "Nicht nach Welt, nach Himmel," choral
7.74   *Cantata No.70a: "Wachet! betet! betet! wachet!" (c1716, Advent 2, lost)* *BWV70a*
7.75   Cantata No.71: "Gott ist mein König" (c1708, Council Election): BWV71
        1. "Gott ist mein König," chorus
        2. "Ich bin nun achtzig Jahr," aria (S, T)
        3. "Dein Alter sei wie deine Jugend," chorus
        4. "Tag und Nacht," arioso (B)
        5. "Durch mächtige Kraft," aria (A)
        6. "Du wollest dem Feinde," chorus
        7. "Das neue Regiment" (ch)
7.76   Cantata No.72: "Alles nur nach Gottes Willen" (c1715 & 1726, Epiphany 3): BWV72
        1. "Alles nur nach Gottes Willen," chorus
        2. "O sel'ger Christ," recit, arioso & aria (A)
        3. "So glaube nun!," recit (B)
        4. "Mein Jesus will es tun," aria (S)
        5. "Was mein Gott will," choral
7.77   Cantata No.73: "Herr, wie du willt, so schicks mit mir" (c1724, Epiphany 3): BWV73
        1. "Herr, wie du willt, so schicks mit mir," chorus
        2. "Ach, senke doch den Geist der Freuden," aria (T)
        3. "Ach, unser Wille bleibt verkehrt," recit (B)
        4. "Herr, so du willt," aria (B)
        5. "Das ist des Vaters Wille," choral
7.78   Cantata No.74: "Wer mich liebet, der wird mein Wort halten" II (c1725, Whit Sunday): BWV74
        1. "Wer mich liebet, der wird mein Wort halten," chorus
        2. "Komm, komm, mein Herze steht dir offen," aria (S)
        3. "Die Wohnung ist bereit," recit (A)
        4. "Ich gehe hin," aria (B)
        5. "Kommt! kommt! eilet," aria (T)
        6. "Es ist nichts Verdammliches," recit (B)
        7. "Nichts kann mich erretten," aria (A)
        8. "Kein Menschenkind hier," choral
7.79   Cantata No.75: "Die Elenden sollen essen" (c1723, Trinity 1): BWV75
    I: 1. "Die Elenden sollen essen," chorus
        2. "Was hilft des Purpurs Majestät," recit (B)
        3. "Mein Jesus soll mein Alles sein," aria (T)
        4. "Gott stürzet und erhöhet," recit (T)
        5. "Ich nehme mein Leiden mit Freuden," aria (S)
        6. "Indess schenkt Gott ein gut Gewissen," recit (S)
        7. "Was Gott tut, das ist wohlgetan," choral
    II: 8. "Sinfonia"
        9. "Nur eines kränkt ein christliches Gemüte," recit (A)
     10. "Jesus macht mich geistlich reich," aria (A)
     11. "Wer nur in Jesu bleibt," recit (B)
     12. "Mein Herze glaubt," aria (B)
     13. "O Armut, der kein Reichtum gleicht!," recit (T)
     14. "Was Gott tut, das ist wohlgetan," choral
7.80   Cantata No.76: "Die Himmel erzählen die Ehre Gottes" (c1723, Trinity 2): BWV76
    I: 1. "Die Himmel erzählen die Ehre Gottes," chorus
        2. "So lässt sich Gott nicht unbezeuget!," recit (T)
        3. "Hört, ihr Völker," aria (S)
        4. "Wer aber hört," recit (B)
        5. "Fahr' hin, abgöttische Zunft," aria (B)
        6. "Du hast uns, Herr," recit (A)
        7. "Es woll' uns Gott genädig sein," choral
    II: 8. "Sinfonia"
        9. "Gott segne noch die treue Schar," recit (B)
     10. "Hasse nur, hasse mich recht," aria (B)
     11. "Ich fühle schon im Geist," recit (A)
     12. "Liebt, ihr Christen, in der Tat," aria (A)
     13. "So soll die Christenheit," recit (T)
     14. "Es danke, Gott, und lobe dich," choral

7.81   Cantata No.77: "Du sollst Gott, deinen Herren, lieben" (c1723, Trinity 13): BWV77
         1. "Du sollst Gott, deinen Herren, lieben," chorus
         2. "So muss es sein!," recit (B)
         3. "Mein Gott, ich liebe dich," aria (S)
         4. "Gib mir dabei, mein Gott! ein Samariter Herz," recit (T)
         5. "Ach, es bleibt in meiner Liebe," aria (A)
         6. "Du stellst, mein Jesu," choral
7.82   Cantata No.78: "Jesu, der du meine Seele" (c1724, Trinity 14): BWV78
         1. "Jesu, der du meine Seele," chorus
         2. "Wir eilen mit schwachen," duet (S, A)
         3. "Ach! ich bin ein Kind der Sünden," recit (T)
         4. "Dein Blut, so meine Schuld durch streicht," aria (T)
         5. "Die Wunden, Nägel, Kron' und Grab," recit (B)
         6. "Nun, du wirst mein Gewissen stillen," aria (B)
         7. "Herr! ich glaube, hilf mir Schwachen," choral
7.83   Cantata No.79: "Gott, der Herr, ist Sonn' und Schild" (c ?1725, Reformation Festival): BWV79
         1. "Gott, der Herr, ist Sonn' und Schild," chorus
         2. "Gott ist unser Sonn' und Schild!," aria (A)
         3. "Nun danket Alle Gott," choral
         4. "Gott Lob! Wir wissen den rechten Weg zur Seligkeit," recit (B)
         5. "Gott, ach Gott, verlass," aria a due (S, B)
         6. "Erhalt uns in der Wahrheit," choral
7.84   Cantata No.80: "Ein' feste Burg ist unser Gott" (c ?1724, Reformation Festival): BWV80
         1. "Ein' feste Burg ist unser Gott," chorus
         2. "Mit unsrer Macht," aria (S, B)
         3. "Erwäge doch, Kind Gottes," recit (B)
         4. "Komm in mein Herzenshaus," aria (B)
         5. "Und wenn die Welt voll Teufel wär'," choral
         6. "So stehe denn bei Christi blutgefärbter Fahne," recit (T)
         7. "Wie selig sind doch sie," duet (A, T)
         8. "Das Wort sie sollen lassen stahn," choral
7.85   *Cantata No.80a: "Alles, was von Gott geboren" (c1715, lost)* *BWV80a*
7.86   *Cantata No.80b: "Ein' feste Burg ist unser Gott" (c1723, lost except for 2 frags)* *BWV80b*
7.87   Cantata No.81: "Jesus schläft, was soll ich hoffen?" (c1724, Epiphany 4): BWV81
         1. "Jesus schläft, was soll ich hoffen?," aria (A)
         2. "Herr! warum bleibest du so ferne?," recit (T)
         3. "Die schäumenden Wellen von Belials Bächen," aria (T)
         4. "Ihr Kleingläubigen," arioso (B)
         5. "Schweig', aufgetürmtes Meer!," aria (B)
         6. "Wohl mir! mein Jesus spricht ein Wort," recit (A)
         7. "Unter deinen Schirmen," choral
7.88   Cantata No.82: "Ich habe genug" (c1727, 31, 35 & after 1745, Purification; 3–4 vers): BWV82
         1. "Ich habe genug," aria (B)
         2. "Ich habe genug!," recit (B)
         3. "Schlummert ein, ihr matten Augen," aria (B)
         4. "Mein Gott! wann kommt das schöne Nun!," recit (B)
         5. "Ich freue mich auf meinen Tod," aria (B)
7.89   Cantata No.83: "Erfreute Zeit im neuen Bunde" (c1724, Purification): BWV83
         1. "Erfreute Zeit im neuen Bunde," aria (A)
         2. "Herr, nun lässest du deinen," intonation & recit (B)
         3. "Eile, eile," aria (T)
         4. "Ja, merkt dein Glaube noch," recit (A)
         5. "Er ist das Heil und selig' Licht," choral
7.90   Cantata No.84: "Ich bin vergnügt mit meinem Glücke" (c1727, Septuagesima): BWV84
         1. "Ich bin vergnügt mit meinem Glükke," aria (S)
         2. "Gott ist mir ja nichts schuldig," recit (S)
         3. "Ich esse mit Freuden mein weniges Brot," aria (S)
         4. "Im Schweisse meines Angesichts," recit (S)
         5. "Ich leb' indess in dir vergnüget," choral
7.91   Cantata No.85: "Ich bin ein guter Hirt" (c1725, Easter 2): BWV85
         1. "Ich bin ein guter Hirt," aria (B)
         2. "Jesus ist ein guter Hirt," aria (A)
         3. "Der Herr ist mein getreuer Hirt," choral (S)
         4. "Wenn die Miethlinge schlafen," recit (T)
         5. "Seht, was die Liebe tut!," aria (T)
         6. "Ist Gott mein Schutz und treuer Hirt," choral
7.92   Cantata No.86: "Wahrlich, wahrlich, ich sage euch" (c1724, Easter 5): BWV86
         1. "Wahrlich, wahrlich, ich sage euch," aria (B)
         2. "Ich will doch wohl Rosen brechen," aria (A)
         3. "Und was der ewig güt'ge Gott," choral (S)
         4. "Gott macht es nicht," recit (T)
         5. "Gott hilft gewiss," aria (T)
         6. "Die Hoffnung wart' der rechten Zeit," choral
7.93   Cantata No.87: "Bisher habt ihr nichts gebeten in meinem Namen" (c1725, Easter 5): BWV87
         1. "Bisher habt ihr nichts gebeten," aria (B)

      2. "O Wort, das Geist und Seel' erschreckt!," recit (A)
      3. "Vergib, o Vater, vergib unsre Schuld," aria (A)
      4. "Wenn unsre Schuld bis an den Himmel steigt," recit (T)
      5. "In der Welt habt ihr Angst," aria (B)
      6. "Ich will leiden, ich will schweigen," aria (T)
      7. "Muss ich sein betrübet," choral

7.94   Cantata No.88: "Siehe, ich will viel Fischer aussenden" (c1726, Trinity 5): BWV88
     I: 1. "Siehe, ich will viel Fischer aussenden," aria (B)
         2. "Wie leichtig könnte doch," recit (T)
         3. "Nein! Gott ist allezeit geflissen," aria (T)
     II: 4. "Jesus sprach zu Simon," aria (T, B)
         5. "Beruft Gott selbst," duet (S, A)
         6. "Was kann dich denn," recit (S)
         7. "Sing', bet' und geh' auf Gottes Wegen," choral

7.95   Cantata No.89: "Was soll ich aus dir machen, Ephraim?" (c1723, Trinity 22): BWV89
      1. "Was soll ich aus dir machen, Ephraim?," aria (B)
      2. "Ja, freilich sollte Gott," recit (A)
      3. "Ein unbarmherziges Gerichte," aria (A)
      4. "Wohlan! mein Herze legt," recit (S)
      5. "Gerechter Gott, ach, rechnest du," aria (S)
      6. "Mir mangelt zwar sehr viel," choral

7.96   Cantata No.90: "Es reisset euch ein schrecklich Ende" (c1723, Trinity 25): BWV90
      1. "Es reisset euch ein schrecklich Ende," aria (T)
      2. "Des Höchsten Güte wird von Tag," recit (A)
      3. "So löschet im Eifer," aria (B)
      4. "Doch Gottes Auge sieht," recit (T)
      5. "Leit' uns mit deiner rechten Hand," choral

7.97   Cantata No.91: "Gelobet seist du, Jesu Christ" (c1724, Christmas Day): BWV91
      1. "Gelobet seist du, Jesu Christ," chorus
      2. "Der Glanz der höchsten Herrlichkeit," recit & choral (S)
      3. "Gott, dem der Erdenkreis zu klein," aria (T)
      4. "O Christenheit!," recit (B)
      5. "Die Armut, so Gott auf sich nimmt," duet (S, A)
      6. "Das hat er Alles uns getan," choral

7.98   Cantata No.92: "Ich hab' in Gottes Herz und Sinn" (c1725, Septuagesima): BWV92
      1. "Ich hab' in Gottes Herz und Sinn," chorus
      2. "Es kann mir fehlen nimmermehr," recit & choral (B)
      3. "Seht, seht! wie bricht, wie reisst, wie fällt," aria (T)
      4. "Zudem ist Weisheit und Verstand," choral (A)
      5. "Wir wollen nun nicht länger zagen," recit (T)
      6. "Das Brausen," aria (B)
      7. "Ei nun, mein Gott, so fall' ich dir," choral & recit
      8. "Meinem Hirten bleib' ich treu," aria (S)
      9. "Soll ich denn auch des Todes Weg," choral

7.99   Cantata No.93: "Wer nur den lieben Gott lässt walten" (c ?1724, Trinity 5): BWV93
      1. "Wer nur den lieben Gott lässt walten," chorus
      2. "Was helfen uns die schweren Sorgen?," recit & choral (B)
      3. "Man halte nur ein wenig stille," aria (T)
      4. "Er kennt die rechten Freudenstunden," duet & choral (S, A)
      5. "Denk' nicht in deiner Drangsalshitze," recit & choral (T)
      6. "Ich will auf den Herren," aria (S)
      7. "Sing', bet' und geh' auf Gottes Wegen," choral

7.100   Cantata No.94: "Was frag' ich nach der Welt" (c1724, Trinity 9): BWV94
      1. "Was frag' ich nach der Welt," chorus
      2. "Die Welt ist wie ein Rauch," aria (B)
      3. "Die Welt sucht Ehr' und Ruhm," recit & choral (T)
      4. "Betörte Welt," aria (A)
      5. "Die Welt bekümmert sich," recit & choral (B)
      6. "Die Welt kann ihre Lust und Freud'," aria (T)
      7. "Es halt' es mit der blinden Welt," aria (S)
      8. "Was frag' ich nach der Welt!," choral

7.101   Cantata No.95: "Christus, der ist mein Leben" (c ?1723, Trinity 16): BWV95
      1. "Christus, der ist mein Leben," chorus
      2. "Nun, falsche Welt," recit (S)
      3. "Valet will ich dir geben," choral
      4. "Ach, könnte mir doch bald," recit (T)
      5. "Ach, schlage doch bald," aria (T)
      6. "Denn ich weiss dies," recit (B)
      7. "Weil du vom Tod erstanden bist," choral

7.102   Cantata No.96: "Herr Christ, der ein'ge Gottessohn" (c1724, Trinity 18): BWV96
      1. "Herr Christ, der ein'ge Gottessohn," chorus
      2. "O Wunderkraft der Liebe," recit (A)
      3. "Ach, ziehe die Seele," aria (T)
      4. "Ach, führe mich, o Gott," recit (S)
      5. "Bald zur Rechten, bald zur Linken," aria (B)

6. "Ertöt' uns durch dein' Güte," choral

7.103   Cantata No.97: "In allen meinen Taten" (c1734): BWV97
1. "In allen meinen Taten," chorus
2. "Nichts ist es spat und frühe," aria (B)
3. "Es kann mir nichts geschehen," recit (T)
4. "Ich traue seiner Gnaden," aria (T)
5. "Er wolle meiner Sünden," recit (A)
6. "Leg' ich mich späte nieder," aria (A)
7. "Hat er es denn beschlossen," duet (S, B)
8. "Ihm hab' ich mich ergeben," aria (S)
9. "So sei nun, Seele," choral

7.104   Cantata No.98: "Was Gott tut, das ist wohlgetan" I (c1726, Trinity 21): BWV98
1. "Was Gott tut, das ist wohlgetan," chorus
2. "Ach Gott! wann wirst du mich," recit (T)
3. "Hört, ihr Augen, auf zu weinen," aria (S)
4. "Gott hat ein Herz," recit (A)
5. "Meinen Jesum lass' ich nicht," aria (B)

7.105   Cantata No.99: "Was Gott tut, das ist wohlgetan" II (c1724, Trinity 15): BWV99
1. "Was Gott tut, das ist wohlgetan," chorus
2. "Sein Wort der Wahrheit stehet," recit (B)
3. "Erschütt're dich nur nicht verzagte Seele," aria (T)
4. "Nun, der von Ewigkeit geschloss'ne Bund," recit (A)
5. "Wenn des Kreuzes Bitter," duet (S, A)
6. "Was Gott tut, das ist wohlgetan," choral

7.106   Cantata No.100: "Was Gott tut, das ist wohlgetan" III (ca1732–4): BWV100
1. "Was Gott tut, das ist wohlgetan," chorus
2. "Was Gott tut, das ist wohlgetan," duet (A, T)
3. "Was Gott tut, das ist wohlgetan," aria (S)
4. "Was Gott tut, das ist wohlgetan," aria (B)
5. "Was Gott tut, das ist wohlgetan," aria (A)
6. "Was Gott tut, das ist wohlgetan," choral

7.107   Cantata No.101: "Nimm von uns, Herr, du treuer Gott" (c1724, Trinity 10): BWV101
1. "Nimm von uns, Herr, du treuer Gott," chorus
2. "Handle nicht nach deinen Rechten," aria (T)
3. "Ach! Herr Gott, durch die Treue," recit & choral (S)
4. "Warum willst du so zornig sein," aria (B)
5. "Die Sünd' hat uns verderbet," recit & choral (T)
6. "Gedenk' an Jesu bittern Tod," duet (S, A)
7. "Leit' uns mit deiner rechten Hand," choral

7.108   Cantata No.102: "Herr, deine Augen sehen nach dem Glauben" (c1726, Trinity 10): BWV102
I: 1. "Herr, deine Augen sehen nach dem Glauben," chorus
2. "Wo ist das Ebenbild," recit (B)
3. "Weh! der Seele," aria (A)
4. "Verachtest du den Reichtum," arioso (B)
II: 5. "Erschrekke doch," aria (T)
6. "Beim Warten ist Gefahr," recit (A)
7. "Heut' lebst du, heut' bekehre dich," choral

7.109   Cantata No.103: "Ihr werdet weinen und heulen" (c1725 & 1731, Easter 3): BWV103
1. "Ihr werdet weinen und heulen," chorus
2. "Wer sollte nicht in Klagen untergehn," recit (T)
3. "Kein Arzt ist ausser dir zu finden," aria (A)
4. "Du wirst mich nach der Angst," recit (A)
5. "Erholet euch," aria (T)
6. "Ich hab' dich einen Augenblick," choral

7.110   Cantata No.104: "Du Hirte Israel, höre" (c1724, Easter 2): BWV104
1. "Du Hirte Israel, höre" (ch)
2. "Der höchste Hüter sorgt für mich," recit (T)
3. "Verbirgt mein Hirte sich zu lange," aria (T)
4. "Ja, dieses Wort ist meiner Seelen Speise," recit (B)
5. "Beglückte Herde, Jesu Schafe," aria (B)
6. "Der Herr ist mein getreuer Hirt," choral

7.111   Cantata No.105: "Herr, gehe nicht ins Gericht mit deinem Knecht" (c1723, Trinity 9): BWV105
1. "Herr, gehe nicht ins Gericht," chorus
2. "Mein Gott, verwirf mich nicht," recit (A)
3. "Wie zittern und wanken der Sünder Gedanken," aria (S)
4. "Wohl aber dem, der seinen Bürgen weiss," recit (B)
5. "Kann ich nur Jesum," aria (T)
6. "Nun, ich weiss, du wirst mir stillen," choral

7.112   Cantata No.106: "Gottes Zeit ist die allerbeste Zeit" (Actus tragicus) (c ?1708, funeral cantata): ... BWV106
1. "Sonatina"
2. "Gottes Zeit ist die allerbeste Zeit," chorus
3. "In deine Hände," duet (A, B)
4. "Glorie, Lob, Ehr' und Herrlichkeit," chorus

7.113   Cantata No.107: "Was willst du dich betrüben" (c1724, Trinity 7): BWV107
1. "Was willst du dich betrüben," chorus

2. "Denn Gott verlässet Keinen," recit (B)
3. "Auf ihn magst du es wagen," aria (B)
4. "Wenn auch gleich aus der Höllen," aria (T)
5. "Er richt's zu seinen Ehren," aria (S)
6. "Drum ich mich ihm ergebe," aria (T)
7. "Herr, gib, dass ich dein' Ehre ja," choral

1. "Es ist euch gut, dass ich hingehe," aria (B)
2. "Mich kann kein Zweifel stören," aria (T)
3. "Dein Geist wird mich also regieren," recit (T)
4. "Wenn aber jener, der Geist der Wahrheit," chorus
5. "Was mein Herz von dir begehrt," aria (A)
6. "Dein Geist, den Gott vom Himmel gibt," choral

1. "Ich glaube, lieber Herr," chorus
2. "Des Herren Hand ist ja noch nicht verkürzt," recit (T)
3. "Wie zweifelhaftig ist mein Hoffen," aria (T)
4. "O fasse dich," recit (A)
5. "Der Heiland kennet ja," aria (A)
6. "Wer hofft in Gott und dem vertraut," choral

1. "Unser Mund sei voll Lachens," chorus
2. "Ihr Gedanken und ihr Sinnen," aria (T)
3. "Dir, Herr, ist Niemand gleich," recit (B)
4. "Ach Herr! was ist ein Menschenkind," aria (A)
5. "Ehre sei Gott," duet (S, T)
6. "Wacht auf!," aria (B)
7. "Alleluja! gelobt sei Gott," choral

1. "Was mein Gott will, das g'scheh' allzeit," chorus
2. "Entsetze dich, mein Herze," aria (B)
3. "O Törichter!," recit (A)
4. "So geh' ich mit beherzten Schritten," duet (A, T)
5. "Drum wenn der Tod," recit (S)
6. "Noch eins, Herr, will ich bitten dich," choral

1. "Der Herr ist mein getreuer Hirt," choral
2. "Zum reinen Wasser er mich weist," aria (A)
3. "Und ob ich wandert," recit (B)
4. "Du bereitest für mir einen Tisch," duet (S, T)
5. "Gutes und die Barmherzigkeit," choral

1. "Herr Jesu Christ, du höchstes Gut," chorus
2. "Erbarm dich mein in solcher Last," choral
3. "Für wahr, wenn mir das kömmet ein," aria (B)
4. "Jedoch dein heilsam Wort," recit w/ choral (B)
5. "Jesus nimmt die Sünder an," aria (T)
6. "Der Heiland nimmt die Sünder an," recit (T)
7. "Ach Herr, mein Gott, vergib mir's doch," duet (S, A)
8. "Stärk mich mit deinem Freudengeist," choral

1. "Ach lieben Christen, seid getrost" (ch)
2. "Wo wird in diesem Jammertale," aria (T)
3. "O Sünder trage mit Geduld," recit (B)
4. "Kein Frucht das Weizenkörnlein bringt," choral
5. "Du machst, o Tod," aria (A)
6. "Indess bedenke deine Seele," recit (T)
7. "Wir wachen oder schlafen ein," choral

1. "Mache dich, mein Geist, bereit," chorus
2. "Ach schläfrige Seele, wie?," aria (A)
3. "Gott, so vor deine Seele wacht," recit (B)
4. "Bete aber auch dabei," aria (S)
5. "Er sehnet sich nach unserm Schreien," recit (T)
6. "Drum so lasst uns immerdar," choral

1. "Du Friedefürst, Herr Jesu Christ," chorus
2. "Ach, unaussprechlich," aria (A)
3. "Gedenke doch, o Jesu," recit (T)
4. "Ach, wir bekennen unsre Schuld," trio (S, T, B)
5. "Ach, lass uns durch die scharfen Ruten," recit (A)
6. "Erleucht auch unser Sinn und Herz," choral

1. "Sei Lob und Ehr' dem höchsten Gut," chorus
2. "Es danken dir die Himmelsheer," recit (B)

    3. "Was unser Gott geschaffen hat," aria (T)
    4. "Ich rief dem Herrn in meiner Not," choral
    5. "Der Herr ist noch und nimmer," recit (A)
    6. "Wenn Trost und Hülf ermangeln muss," aria (B)
    7. "Ich will dich allmein Leben lang," aria (A)
    8. "Ihr, die ihr Christi Namen nennt," recit (T)
    9. "So kommet vor sein Angesicht," chorus

7.124   Cantata No.118: "O Jesu Christ, mein's Lebens Licht" (c1736–7, funeral motet; 2 vers) BWV118

7.125   Cantata No.119: "Preise, Jerusalem, den Herrn" (c1723, Council Election): BWV119
    1. "Preise, Jerusalem, den Herrn," chorus
    2. "Gesegnet Land!," recit (T)
    3. "Wohl dir," aria (T)
    4. "So herrlich stehst du," recit (B)
    5. "Die Obrigkeit ist Gottes Gabe," aria (A)
    6. "Nun! nun, wir erkennen es," recit (S)
    7. "Der Herr hat Gut's an uns getan," chorus
    8. "Zuletzt! Da du uns, Herr, zu deinem Volk gesetzt," recit (A)
    9. "Hilf deinem Volk," choral

7.126   Cantata No.120: "Gott, man lobet dich in der Stille" (ca1728–9, Council Election): BWV120
    1. "Gott, man lobet dich in der Stille," aria (A)
    2. "Jauchzet, ihr erfreuten Stimmen," chorus
    3. "Auf, du geliebte Lindenstadt!," recit (B)
    4. "Heil und Segen soll und muss zu aller Zeit," aria (S)
    5. "Nun, Herr, so weihe selbst dein Regiment," recit (T)
    6. "Nun hilf uns, Herr," choral

7.127   Cantata No.120a: "Herr Gott, Beherrscher aller Dinge" (c ?1729, wedding cantata): BWV120a
    I: 1. "Herr Gott, Beherrscher aller Dinge," chorus
        2. "Wie wunderbar, o Gott," recit (B)
        2a. "Nun danket alle," chorus
        3. "Leit, o Gott, durch deine Liebe," aria (S)
    II: 4. "Sinfonia"
        5. "Herr Zebaoth, Herr, unser Vater Gott," recit (T)
        6. "Herr, fange an und sprich den Segen," duet (A, T)
        7. "Der Herr, Herr unser Gott sei so mit euch," recit (B)
        8. "Lobe den Herren," choral

7.128   *Cantata No.120b: "Gott, man lobet dich in der Stille" (c1730, music lost)* *BWV120b*

7.129   Cantata No.121: "Christum wir sollen loben schon" (c1724, 2nd day of Christmas): BWV121
    1. "Christum wir sollen loben schon," chorus
    2. "O du von Gott erhöhte Creatur," aria (T)
    3. "Der Gnade unermesslichs Wesen," recit (A)
    4. "Johannis freudenvolles Springen," aria (B)
    5. "Doch wie erblickt es dich in deiner Krippe," recit (S)
    6. "Lob, Ehr und Dank sei dir gesagt," choral

7.130   Cantata No.122: "Das neugebor'ne Kindelein" (c1724, Sunday after Christmas): BWV122
    1. "Das neugebor'ne Kindelein," chorus
    2. "O Menschen, die ihr täglich sündigt," aria (B)
    3. "Die Engel, welche sich zuvor vor euch," recit (S)
    4. "Ist Gott versöhnt," trio (S, A, T)
    5. "Dies ist ein Tag," recit (B)
    6. "Es bringt das rechte Jubeljahr," choral

7.131   Cantata No.123: "Liebster Immanuel, Herzog der Frommen" (c1725, Epiphany): BWV123
    1. "Liebster Immanuel," chorus
    2. "Die Himmels Süssigkeit, der Auserwählten Lust," recit (A)
    3. "Auch die harte Kreuzesreise," aria (T)
    4. "Kein Höllenfeind kann mich schlingen," recit (B)
    5. "Lass, o Welt, mich aus Verachtung," aria (B)
    6. "Drum fahrt nur immer hin ihr Eitelkeiten!," choral

7.132   Cantata No.124: "Meinen Jesum lass' ich nicht" (c1725, Epiphany 1): BWV124
    1. "Meinen Jesum lass' ich nicht," chorus
    2. "So lange sich ein Tropfen Blut," recit (T)
    3. "Und wenn der harte Todesschlag," aria (T)
    4. "Doch, ach! welch schweres Ungemach empfindet," recit (B)
    5. "Entziehe dich eilends," duet (S, A)
    6. "Jesum lass ich nicht von mir," choral

7.133   Cantata No.125: "Mit Fried' und Freud' ich fahr' dahin" (c1725, Purification): BWV125
    1. "Mit Fried' und Freud' ich fahr' dahin," chorus
    2. "Ich will auch mit gebrochnen Augen nach dir," aria (A)
    3. "O Wunder, dass ein Herz vor der dem Fleisch verhassten Gruft," recit (B)
    4. "Ein unbegreiflich Licht," duet (T, B)
    5. "O unerschöpfter Schatz der Güte," recit (A)
    6. "Er ist das Heil und selge Licht," choral

7.134   Cantata No.126: "Erhalt' uns, Herr, bei deinem Wort" (c1725, Sexagesima): BWV126
    1. "Erhalt' uns, Herr, bei deinem Wort," chorus
    2. "Sende deine Macht von oben," aria (T)
    3. "Der Menschen Gunst und Macht," recit (A, T)

4. "Stürze zu Boden," aria (B)
5. "So wird dein Wort," recit (T)
6. "Verleih uns Frieden gnädiglich," choral

7.135   Cantata No.127: "Herr Jesu Christ, wahr' Mensch und Gott" (c1725, Quinquagesima): BWV127
1. "Herr Jesu Christ, wahr' Mensch und Gott," chorus
2. "Wenn Alles sich zur letzten Zeit," recit (T)
3. "Die Seele ruht in Jesu Händen" schallen, aria (S)
4a. "Wenn einstens die Posaunen," recit (B)
4b. "Führwahr, euch sage ich," aria (B)
5. "Ach Herr, vergib all' unsre Schuld," choral

7.136   Cantata No.128: "Auf Christi Himmelfahrt allein" (c1725, Ascension Day): BWV128
1. "Auf Christi Himmelfahrt allein," chorus
2. "Ich bin bereit," recit (T)
3. "Auf, auf, mit hellem Schall," aria (B)
4. "Sein Allmacht zu ergründen," duet (A, T)
5. "Als dann so wirst du mich zu deiner Rechten stellen," choral

7.137   Cantata No.129: "Gelobet sei der Herr, mein Gott" (c1726, Trinity Sunday): BWV129
1. "Gelobet sei der Herr, mein Gott, mein Heil," chorus
2. "Gelobet sei der Herr, mein Gott, mein Heil," aria (B)
3. "Gelobet sei der Herr, mein Gott, mein Heil," aria (S)
4. "Gelobet sei der Herr, mein Gott, mein Heil," aria (A)
5. "Dem wir das Heilig itzt mit Freuden lassen klingen," choral

7.138   Cantata No.130: "Herr Gott, dich loben alle wir" (c1724, St Michael): BWV130
1. "Herr Gott, dich loben alle wir," chorus
2. "Ihr heller Glanz," recit (A)
3. "Der alte Drache brennt vor Neid," aria (B)
4. "Wohl aber uns," recit (S, T)
5. "Lass, o Fürst der Cherubinen," aria (T)
6. "Darum wir billig loben dich," choral

7.139   Cantata No.131: "Aus der Tiefen rufe ich, Herr, zu dir" (c ?1707, ?funeral cantata): BWV131
1. "Aus der Tiefen ruf' ich, Herr, zu dir," chorus
2. "So du willst," duet (B, S)
3. "Ich harre des Herrn," chorus
4. "Meine Seele wartet," duet (T, A)
5. "Israel, hoffe auf den Herrn," chorus

7.140   Cantata No.132: "Bereitet die Wege, bereitet die Bahn" (c1715, Advent 4): BWV132
1. "Bereitet die Wege, bereitet die Bahn," Aria (S)
2. "Willst du dich Gottes Kind," recit (T)
3. "Wer bist du?," aria (B)
4. "Ich will, mein Gott, dir frei heraus bekennen," recit (A)
5. "Christi Glieder, ach, bedenket," aria (A)
6. "Ertöt uns durch dein Güte," choral

7.141   Cantata No.133: "Ich freue mich in dir" (c1724, 3rd day of Christmas): BWV133
1. "Ich freue mich in dir," chorus
2. "Getrost! es fasst ein heil'ger Leib," aria (A)
3. "Ein Adam mag sich voller Schrecken," recit (T)
4. "Wie lieblich klingt es in den Ohren," aria (S)
5. "Wohlan! Des Todes Furcht und Schmerz," recit (B)
6. "Wohlan! so will ich mich an dich, o Jesu, halten," choral

7.142   Cantata No.134: "Ein Herz, das seinen Jesum lebend weiss" (c1724, 31 & 35, Easter Tuesday): ...BWV134
1. "Ein Herz, das seinen Jesum lebend weiss," recit (T, A)
2. "Auf, Gläubige," aria (T)
3. "Wohl dir, Gott hat an dich gedacht," recit (T, A)
4. "Wir danken, wir preisen dein brünstiges Lieben," duet (A, T)
5. "Doch wirke selbst den Dank," recit (T, A)
6. "Erschallet, ihr Himmel," chorus

7.143   Cantata No.135: "Ach Herr, mich armen Sünder" (c1724, Trinity 3): BWV135
1. "Ach Herr, mich armen Sünder," chorus
2. "Ach heile mich, du Arzt der Seelen," recit (T)
3. "Tröste mir, Jesu," aria (T)
4. "Ich bin von Seufzen müde," recit (A)
5. "Weicht all, ihr Übeltäter, weicht," aria (B)
6. "Ehr sei in's Himmels Throne," choral

7.144   Cantata No.136: "Erforsche mich, Gott, und erfahre mein Herz" (c1725, Trinity 8): BWV136
1. "Erforsche mich, Gott, und erfahre mein Herz," chorus
2. "Ach, dass der Fluch," recit (T)
3. "Es kommt ein Tag," aria (A)
4. "Die Himmel selber sind nicht rein," recit (B)
5. "Uns treffen zwar der Sünden Flecken," duet (T, B)
6. "Dein Blut, der edle Saft," choral

7.145   Cantata No.137: "Lobe den Herren, den mächtigen König der Ehren" (c1732, Trinity 12): BWV137
1. "Lobe den Herren, den mächtigen König der Ehren," chorus
2. "Lobe den Herren, der Alles so herrlich regieret," aria (A)
3. "Lobe den Herren, der künstlich und fein dich bereitet," duet (S, B)
4. "Lobe den Herren," aria (T)

                5. "Bleib' auch, mein Gott, in mir," recit (T)
                6. Choral (w/ out text, perf w/ 'Führ' auch mein Herz und Sinn')
7.158   Cantata No.149: "Man singet mit Freuden vom Sieg" (c1728, St. Michael): BWV149
                1. "Man singet mit Freuden," chorus
                2. "Kraft und Stärke sei gesungen," aria (B)
                3. "Ich fürchte mich vor tausend Feinden nicht," recit (A)
                4. "Gottes Engel weichen nie," aria (S)
                5. "Ich danke dir, mein lieber Gott," recit (T)
                6. "Seid wachsam, ihr heiligen Wächter," duet (A, T)
                7. "Ach Herr, lass dein lieb Engelein," choral
7.159   Cantata No.150: "Nach dir, Herr, verlanget mich" (ca1708–10, ?funeral cantata): BWV150
                1. "Sinfonia"
                2. "Nach dir, Herr, verlanget mich," chorus
                3. "Doch bin und bleibe ich vergnügt," aria (S)
                4. "Leite mich und lehre mich," chorus
                5. "Cedern müssen von den Winden," trio (A, T, B)
                6. "Meine Augen sehen stets," chorus
                7. "Meine Tage in den Leiden" (Ciacona), chorus
7.160   Cantata No.151: "Süsser Trost, mein Jesus kömmt" (c1725, 3rd day of Christmas): BWV151
                1. "Süsser Trost, mein Jesus kömmt," aria (S)
                2. "Erfreue dich, mein Herz," recit (B)
                3. "In Jesu Demut kann ich Trost," aria (A)
                4. "Du teurer Gottessohn," recit (T)
                5. "Heut schleusst er wieder auf die Tür," choral
7.161   Cantata No.152: "Tritt auf die Glaubensbahn" (c1714, Christmas 1): BWV152
                1. "Concerto"
                2. "Tritt auf die Glaubensbahn," aria (B)
                3. "Der Heiland ist gesetzt in Israel," recit (B)
                4. "Stein, der über alle Schätze," aria (S)
                5. "Es ärgre sich die kluge Welt," recit (B)
                6. "Wie soll ich dich, Liebster der Seelen," duet (S, B)
7.162   Cantata No.153: "Schau, lieber Gott, wie meine Feind" (c1724, Sunday after New Year):.............BWV153
                1. "Schau, lieber Gott, wie meine Feind," choral
                2. "Mein liebster Gott," recit (A)
                3. "Fürchte dich, ich bin mit dir," aria (B)
                4. "Du sprichst zwar, lieber Gott," recit (T)
                5. "Und obgleich alle Teufel," choral
                6. "Stürmt nur, stürmt, ihr Trübsalswetter," aria (T)
                7. "Getrost, mein Herz," recit (B)
                8. "Soll ich meinen Lebenslauf," aria (A)
                9. "Drum will ich, weil ich lebe noch," choral
7.163   Cantata No.154: "Mein liebster Jesus ist verloren" (c1724, Epiphany 1): BWV154
                1. "Mein liebster Jesus ist verloren," aria (T)
                2. "Wo treff ich meinen Jesum an," recit (T)
                3. "Jesu, mein Hort und Erretter," choral
                4. "Jesu, lass dich finden," aria (A)
                5. "Wisset ihr nicht, dass ich sein muss in dem," arioso (B)
                6. "Dies ist die Stimme meines Freundes," recit (T)
                7. "Wohl mir, Jesus ist gefunden," duet (A, T)
                8. "Meinen Jesum lass ich nicht," choral
7.164   Cantata No.155: "Mein Gott, wie lang', ach lange" (c1716, Epiphany 2): BWV155
                1. "Mein Gott, wie lang', ach lange?," recit (S)
                2. "Du musst glauben, du musst hoffen," duet (A, T)
                3. "So sei, o Seele," recit (B)
                4. "Wirf, mein Herze," aria (S)
                5. "Ob sichs anliess," choral
7.165   Cantata No.156: "Ich steh' mit einem Fuss im Grabe" (c1729, Epiphany 3): BWV156
                1. "Sinfonia"
                2. "Ich steh' mit einem Fuss im Grabe," aria w/ choral (S)
                3. "Mein Angst und Not," recit (B)
                4. "Herr, was du willt soll mir gefallen," aria (A)
                5. "Und willst du, dass ich nicht soll kranken," recit (B)
                6. "Herr, wie du willt," choral
7.166   Cantata No.157: "Ich lasse dich nicht, du segnest mich denn" (c1727, Purification): BWV157
                1. "Ich lasse dich nicht, du segnest mich denn," duet (T, B)
                2. "Ich halte meinen Jesum feste," aria (T)
                3. "Mein lieber Jesu du," recit (T)
                4a. "Ja, ja, ich halte Jesum feste," aria (B)
                4b. "Ei, wie vergnügt ist mir mein Sterbekasten," recit (B)
                5. "Meinen Jesum lass ich nicht," choral
7.167   Cantata No.158: "Der Friede sei mit dir" (ca1730–5, Easter Tuesday & Purification): BWV158
                1. "Der Friede sei mit dir," recit (B)
                2. "Welt, ade! ich bin dein müde," aria w/ choral (S)
                3a. "Nun Herr, regiere meinen Sinn," recit (B)
                3b. "Da bleib ich, da hab ich Vergnügen zu wohnen," arioso (B)

4. "Hier ist das rechte Osterlamm," choral

7.168   Cantata No.159: "Sehet, wir geh'n hinauf gen Jerusalem" (1729, Quinquagesima): BWV159
1a. "Sehet, sehet," arioso (B)
1b. "Komm, schaue doch mein Sinn," recit (A)
2. "Ich folge dir nach," aria w/ choral (A, S)
3. "Nun will ich mich," recit (T)
4. "Es ist vollbracht," aria (B)
5. "Jesu, deine Passion ist mir lauter Freude," choral

7.169   *Cantata No.160: "Ich weiss, dass mein Erlöser lebt" (spur: c by Telemann)* *BWV160*

7.170   Cantata No.161: "Komm, du süsse Todesstunde" (c1715 & 1735, Trinity 16): BWV161
1. "Komm, du süsse Todesstunde," aria (A)
2. "Welt, deine Lust ist Last," recit (T)
3. "Mein Verlangen ist, den Heiland zu umfangen," aria (T)
4. "Der Schluss ist schon gemacht," recit (A)
5. "Wenn es meines Gottes Wille," chorus
6. "Der Leib zwar in der Erden," choral

7.171   Cantata No.162: "Ach, ich sehe, itzt, da ich zur Hochzeit gehe" (c1715, Trinity 20): BWV162
1. "Ach, ich sehe, itzt, da ich zur Hochzeit gehe," aria (B)
2. "O grosses Hochzeitfest," recit (T)
3. "Jesu, Brunnquell aller Gnaden," aria (S)
4. "Mein Jesu, lass mich nicht zur Hochzeit unbekleidet kommen," recit (A)
5. "In meinem Gott bin ich erfreut," duet (A, T)
6. "Ach, ich habe schon erblikket," choral

7.172   Cantata No.163: "Nur jedem das Seine" (c ?1725, Trinity 23): BWV163
1. "Nur jedem das Seine," aria (T)
2. "Du bist mein Gott," recit (B)
3. "Lass mein Herz die Münze sein," aria (B)
4. "Ich wollte dir, o Gott," recit.duet (S, A)
5. "Nimm mich mir und gib mich dir," duet (S, A)
6. "Führ auch mein Herz und Sinn," choral

7.173   Cantata No.164: "Ihr, die ihr euch von Christo nennet" (c ?1725, Trinity 13): BWV164
1. "Ihr, die ihr euch von Christo nennet," aria (T)
2. "Wir hören zwar," recit (B)
3. "Aria" (A)
4. "Ach, schmelze doch durch deinen Liebesstrahl," recit (T)
5. "Händen, die sich nicht verschliessen," duet (S, B)
6. "Ertöt uns durch dein Güte," choral

7.174   Cantata No.165: "O heil'ges Geist- und Wasserbad" (c1715, Trinity Sunday): BWV165
1. "O heil'ges Geist- und Wasserbad," concerto (aria) (S)
2. "Die sündige Geburt verdammter Adams Erben," recit (B)
3. "Jesu, der aus grosser Liebe," aria (A)
4. "Ich habe ja, mein Seelenbräutigam," recit (B)
5. "Jesu, meines Todes Tod," aria (T)
6. "Sein Wort, sein Taufe," choral

7.175   Cantata No.166: "Wo gehest du hin?" (c1724, Easter 4): BWV166
1. "Wo gehest du hin," aria (B)
2. "Ich will an den Himmel denken," aria (T)
3. "Ich bitte dich, Herr Jesu Christ," choral
4. "Gleich wie die Regenwasser bald verfliessen," recit (B)
5. "Man nehme sich in Acht," aria (A)
6. "Wer weiss, wie nahe mir mein Ende," choral

7.176   Cantata No.167: "Ihr Menschen, rühmet Gottes Liebe" (c1723, St. John Baptist): BWV167
1. "Ihr Menschen, rühmet Gottes Liebe," aria (T)
2. "Gelobet sei der Herr Gott Israel," recit (A)
3. "Gottes Wort," duet (S, A)
4. "Des Weibes Samen kam," recit (B)
5. "Sei Lob und Preis mir Ehren," choral

7.177   Cantata No.168: "Tue Rechnung! Donnerwort" (c1725, Trinity 9): BWV168
1. "Tue Rechnung! tue Rechnung," aria (B)
2. "Es ist nur fremdes Gut," recit (T)
3. "Capital und Interessen," aria (T)
4. "Jedoch, erschrocknes Herz," recit (B)
5. "Herz, zerreiss des Mammons Kette," duet (S, A)
6. "Stärk mich mit deinem Freudengeist," choral

7.178   Cantata No.169: "Gott soll allein mein Herze haben" (c1726, Trinity 18): BWV169
1. "Sinfonia"
2a. "Gott soll allein mein Herze haben," arioso (A)
2b. "Zwar merk ich an der Welt," recit (A)
3. "Gott soll allein mein Herze haben," aria (A)
4. "Was ist die Liebe Gottes?," recit (A)
5. "Stirb in mir," aria (A)
6. "Doch meint es auch dabei," recit (A)
7. "Du süsse Liebe," choral

7.179   Cantata No.170: "Vergnügte Ruh', beliebte Seelenlust" (c1726, Trinity 6): BWV170
1. "Vergnügte Ruh', beliebte Seelenlust," aria (A)

2. "Die Welt, das Sündenhaus," recit (A)
3. "Wie jammern mich doch die verkehrten Herzen," aria (A)
4. "Wer sollte sich," recit (A)
5. "Mir ekelt mehr zu leben," aria (A)

7.180   Cantata No.171: "Gott, wie dein Name, so ist auch dein Ruhm" (c1729, New Year): BWV171
1. "Gott, wie dein Name, so ist auch dein Ruhm" (ch)
2. "Herr, so weit die Wolken gehen," aria (T)
3. "Du süsser Jesusname du," recit (A)
4. "Jesus soll mein erstes Wort," aria (S)
5. "Und da du, Herr, gesagt," recit (B)
6. "Lass uns das Jahr vollbringen," choral

7.181   Cantata No.172: "Erschallet, ihr Lieder" (c1714 & 1731, Whit Sunday): BWV172
1. "Erschallet, ihr Lieder, erklinget ihr Saiten," chorus
2. "Wer mich liebet," recit (B)
3. "Heiligste Dreieinigkeit," aria (B)
4. "O Seelen Paradies," aria (T)
5. "Komm, lass mich nicht länger warten," duet (S, A)
6. "Von Gott kommt mir ein Freudenschein," choral

7.182   Cantata No.173: "Erhöhtes Fleisch und Blut" (c1724, Whit Monday): BWV173
1. "Erhöhtes Fleisch und Blut," recit (T)
2. "Ein'ge heiligtes Gemüte," aria (T)
3. "Gott will, o ihr Menschenkinder," aria (A)
4. "So hat Gott die Welt geliebt," duet (S, B)
5. "Unendlichster, den man doch Vater nennt," recit duet (S, T)
6. "Rühre, Höchster, unsern Geist," chorus

7.183   Cantata No.174: "Ich liebe den Höchsten von ganzem Gemüte" (c1729, Whit Monday): BWV174
1. "Sinfonia" (Concerto)
2. "Ich liebe den Höchsten von ganzem Gemüte," aria (A)
3. "O Liebe, welcher keine gleich!," recit (T)
4. "Greifet zu, fasst das Heil," aria (B)
5. "Herzlich lieb' hab' ich dich, o Herr," choral

7.184   Cantata No.175: "Er rufet seinen Schafen mit Namen" (c1725, Whit Tuesday): BWV175
1. "Er rufet seinen Schafen mit Namen," recit (T)
2. "Komm, leite mich," aria (A)
3. "Wo find ich dich?," recit (T)
4. "Es dünket mich," aria (T)
5. "Sie vernahmen aber nicht," recit (A, B)
6. "Öffnet euch, ihr bei den Ohren," aria (B)
7. "Nun, werter Geist, ich folg' dir," choral

7.185   Cantata No.176: "Es ist ein trotzig und verzagt Ding" (c1725, Trinity Sunday): BWV176
1. "Es ist ein trotzig und verzagt Ding," chorus
2. "Ich meine, recht verzagt," recit (A)
3. "Dein sonst hell beliebter Schein," aria (S)
4. "So wundre dich, o Meister, nicht," recit (B)
5. "Ermuntert euch," aria (A)
6. "Auf dass wir also allzugleich," choral

7.186   Cantata No.177: "Ich ruf' zu dir, Herr Jesu Christ" (c ?1732, Trinity 4): BWV177
1. "Ich ruf' zu dir, Herr Jesu Christ," chorus
2. "Ich bitt noch mehr," aria (A)
3. "Verleih, dass ich aus Herzens Grund," aria (S)
4. "Lass mich kein Lust noch Furcht," aria (T)
5. "Ich lieg im Streit und wiederstreb," choral

7.187   Cantata No.178: "Wo Gott der Herr nicht bei uns hält" (c1724, Trinity 8): BWV178
1. "Wo Gott der Herr nicht bei uns hält," chorus
2. "Was Menschen Kraft und Witz," recit (A)
3. "Gleich wie die wilden Meeres-Wellen," aria (B)
4. "Sie stellen uns wie Ketzern nach," choral
5. "Auf sperren sie den Rachen weit," choral & recit
6. "Schweig, schweig, schweig nur, schweig," aria (T)
7. "Die Feind sind all in deiner Hand," choral

7.188   Cantata No.179: "Siehe zu, dass deine Gottesfurcht nicht Heuchelei sei" (c1723,Trinity 11): BWV179
1. "Siehe zu, dass deine Gottesfurcht nicht Heuchelei sei," chorus
2. "Das heut'ge Christentum ist leider schlecht bestellt," recit (T)
3. "Falscher Heuchler Ebenbild," aria (T)
4. "Wer so von innen wie von aussen ist," recit (B)
5. "Liebster Gott, erbarme dich," aria (S)
6. "Ich armer Mensch, ich armer Sünder," choral

7.189   Cantata No.180: "Schmücke dich, o liebe Seele" (c1724, Trinity 20): BWV180
1. "Schmücke dich, o liebe Seele," chorus
2. "Ermuntre dich," aria (T)
3a. "Wie teuer sind des heil'gen Mahles Gaben," recit (S)
3b. "Ach wie hungert mein Gemüte," arioso (S)
4. "Mein Herz fühlt in sich Furcht und Freude," recit (A)
5. "Lebens Sonne, Licht der Sinnen," aria (S)
6. "Herr, lass an mir dein treues Lieben," recit (B)

7. "Jesu, wahres Brot des Lebens," choral
7.190   Cantata No.181: "Leichtgesinnte Flattergeister" (c1724, Sexagesima):.. BWV181
    1. "Leichtgesinnte Flattergeister," aria (B)
    2. "O unglückselger Stand verkehrter Seelen," recit (A)
    3. "Der schädlichen Dornen unendliche Zahl," aria (T)
    4. "Von diesen wird die Kraft erstickt," recit (S)
    5. "Lass, Höchster, uns zu allen Zeiten des Herzens Trost," chorus
7.191   Cantata No.182: "Himmelskönig, sei willkommen" (c1714 & 1724, Palm Sunday; 2 vers): BWV182
    1. "Sonata" (Concerto)
    2. "Himmelskönig, sei willkommen," chorus
    3. "Siehe, siehe, ich komme," recit (B)
    4. "Starkes Lieben," aria (B)
    5. "Leget euch dem Heiland unter," aria (A)
    6. "Jesu, lass durch Wohl und Weh," aria (T)
    7. "Jesu, deine Passion ist mir lauter Freude," choral
    8. "So lasset uns gehen in Salem der Freuden," ending chorus
7.192   Cantata No.183: "Sie werden euch in den Bann tun" II (c1725, Ascension 1): BWV183
    1. "Sie werden euch in den Bann tun," recit (B)
    2. "Ich fürchte nicht des Todes Schrecken," aria (T)
    3. "Ich bin bereit mein Blut und armes Leben," recit (A)
    4. "Höchster Tröster, heil'ger Geist," aria (S)
    5. "Du bist ein Geist, der lehret," choral
7.193   Cantata No.184: "Erwünschtes Freudenlicht" (c1724, Whit Tuesday): BWV184
    1. "Erwünschtes Freudenlicht," recit (T)
    2. "Gesegnete Christen," duet (S, A)
    3. "So freuet euch," recit (T)
    4. "Glück und Segen sind bereit," aria (T)
    5. "Herr, ich hoff je," choral
    6. "Guter Hirte, Trost der Deinen" (ch)
7.194   Cantata No.185: "Barmherziges Herze der ewigen Liebe" (c1715, Trinity 4): BWV185
    1. "Barmherziges Herze der ewigen Liebe," duet (S, T)
    2. "Ihr Herzen, die ihr euch in Stein und Fels verkehret," recit (A)
    3. "Sei bemüht in dieser Zeit," aria (A)
    4. "Die Eigenliebe schmeichelt sich," recit (B)
    5. "Das ist der Christen Kunst," aria (B)
    6. "Ich ruf' zu dir, Herr Jesu Christ," choral
7.195   Cantata No.186: "Ärgre dich, o Seele, nicht" (c1723, Trinity 7):.. BWV186
  I: 1. "Ärgre dich, o Seele, nicht," chorus
    2. "Die Knechtsgestalt, die Not, der Mangel," recit (B)
    3. "Bist du, der mir helfen soll," aria (B)
    4a. "Ach, dass ein Christ so sehr," recit (T)
    4b. "Drum, wenn der Kummer gleich," arioso (T)
    5. "Mein Heiland lässt sich merken," aria (T)
    6. "Ob sichs anliess, als wollt er nicht," choral
  II: 7. "Es ist die Welt die grosse Wüstenei," recit (B)
    8. "Die Armen will der Herr umarmen," aria (S)
    9. "Nun mag die Welt mit ihrer Lust vergehen," recit (A)
    10. "Duet" (S, A)
    11. "Die Hoffnung wart' der rechten Zeit," choral
7.196   *Cantata No.186a: "Ärgre dich, o Seele, nicht" (c1716, Advent 3, music lost)* *BWV186a*
7.197   Cantata No.187: "Es wartet alles auf dich" (c1726, Trinity 7):.. BWV187
  I: 1. "Es wartet alles auf dich," chorus
    2. "Was Creaturen hält das grosse Rund der Welt," recit (B)
    3. "Du Herr, krönst allein das Jahr mit deinem Gut," aria (A)
  II: 4. "Darum sollt ihr nicht sorgen noch sagen," aria (B)
    5. "Gott versorget alles Leben," aria (S)
    6. "Halt ich nur fest an ihm," recit (S)
    7. "Gott hat die Erd schön zugericht," choral
7.198   Cantata No.188: "Ich habe meine Zuversicht" (c1728, Trinity 21):.. BWV188
    1. "Sinfonia"
    2. "Ich habe meine Zuversicht," aria (T)
    3a. "Gott meint es gut mit jedermann," recit (B)
    3b. "Drum lass ich ihn nicht," arioso (B)
    4. "Unerforschlich ist die Weise," aria (A)
    5. "Die Macht der Welt verlieret sich," recit (S)
    6. "Auf meinen lieben Gott trau ich in Angst und Not," choral
7.199   *Cantata No.189: "Meine Seele rühmt und preist" (spur: c by ?Hoffmann)* *BWV189*
7.200   Cantata No.190: "Singet dem Herrn ein neues Lied" (c1724, New Year): BWV190
    1. "Singet dem Herrn ein neues Lied," chorus
    2. "Herr Gott, dich loben wir," choral & recit
    3. "Lobe, Zion, deinen Gott," aria (A)
    4. "Es wünsche sich die Welt," recit (B)
    5. "Jesus soll mein alles sein," duet (T, B)
    6. "Nun, Jesus gebe, dass mit dem neuen Jahr," recit (T)
    7. "Lass uns das Jahr vollbringen," choral

7.201   *Cantata No.190a: "Singet dem Herrn ein neues Lied!" (c1730, music lost)* *BWV190a*
7.202   Cantata No.191: "Gloria in excelsis Deo" (ca1740–2, Christmas Day, from BWV232): BWV191
        1. "Gloria in excelsis Deo," chorus
        "Post Orationem": 2. "Gloria Patri, gloria," duet (S, T)
        3. "Sicut erat in principio," chorus
7.203   Cantata No.192: "Nun danket alle Gott" (c ?1730, ?Reformation Festival, inc): BWV192
        1. "Nun danket alle Gott," chorus
        2. "Der ewig reichte Gott," duet (S, B)
        3. "Lob, Ehr und Preis sei Gott," chorus
7.204   Cantata No.193: "Ihr Tore zu Zion" (c ?1727, inauguration of town council, inc): BWV193
        1. "Ihr Tore zu Zion," chorus
        2. "Der Hüter Israel entschläft noch schlummert nicht," recit (S)
        3. "Gott, wir danken deiner Güte," aria (S)
        4. "O Leipziger Jerusalem," recit (A)
        5. "Sende, Herr, den Segen ein," aria (A)
7.205   Cantata No.194: "Höchsterwünschtes Freudenfest" (c1723, Trinity Sunday): BWV194
        I: 1. "Höchsterwünschtes Freudenfest," chorus
            2. "Unendlich grosser Gott," recit (B)
            3. "Was des Höchsten Glanz erfüllt," aria (B)
            4. "Wie könnte dir," recit (S)
            5. "Hilf, Gott, dass es uns gelingt," aria (S)
            6. "Heil'ger Geist ins Himmels Throne," choral
        II: 7. "Ihr Heiligen, erfreuet euch," recit (T)
            8. "Des Höchsten Gegenwart allein," aria (T)
            9. "Kann wohl ein Mensch," recit duet (S, B)
          10. "O wie wohl ist uns geschehn," duet (S, B)
          11. "Wohl an dem nach, du heilige Gemeine," recit (B)
          12. "Sprich Ja zu meinen Taten," choral
7.206   Cantata No.195: "Dem Gerechten muss das Licht" (c1741 & 1747–8, wedding cantata): BWV195
        "Vor der Trauung": 1. "Dem Gerechten muss das Licht," chorus
        2. "Dem Freuden Licht gerechter," recit (B)
         3. "Rühmet Gottes Güt und Treu," aria (B)
         4. "Wohl an, so knüpfet denn ein Band," recit (S)
         5. "Wir kommen, deine Heiligkeit," chorus
         "Nach der Trauung": 6. "Nun danket all und bringet Ehr," choral
7.207   Cantata No.196: "Der Herr denket an uns" (c ?1708, wedding cantata): BWV196
        1. "Sinfonia"
        2. "Der Herr denket an uns," chorus
        3. "Er segnet," aria (S)
        4. "Der Herr segne euch," duet (T, B)
        5. "Ihr seid die Gesegneten," chorus
7.208   Cantata No.197: "Gott ist unsre Zuversicht" (ca1742, wedding cantata): BWV197
        "Vor der Trauung": 1. "Gott ist unsre Zuversicht," chorus
        2. "Gott ist und bleibt der best Sorger," recit (B)
         3. "Schläfert allen Sorgen," aria (A)
         4. "Drum folget Gott und seinem Triebe," recit (B)
         5. "Du süsse Lieb, schenk uns deine Gunst," choral
         "Nach der Trauung": 6. "O du angenehmes Paar," aria (B)
        7. "So wie es Gott," recit (S)
         8. "Vergnügen und Lust," aria (S)
         9. "Und dieser frohe Lebenslauf," recit (B)
        10. "So wandelt froh auf Gottes Wegen," choral
7.209   Cantata No.197a: "Ehre sei Gott in der Höhe" (c1728, Christmas Day, part lost): BWV197a
        1. "Ehre sei Gott in der Höhe" (ch) (music lost)
        2. "Erzählet, ihr Himmel, die Ehre Gottes," aria (music lost)
        3. "O Liebe, der kein Lieben gleicht," recit (music lost)
        4. "O du angenehmer Schatz," aria (A)
        5. "Das Kind ist mein und ich bin sein," recit (B)
        6. "Ich lasse dich nicht," aria (B)
        7. "Wohl an! so will ich mich an dich," choral
        Cantata No.198 (see: Secular Cantatas) BWV198
7.210   Cantata No.199: "Mein Herze schwimmt im Blut" (c1714, Trinity 11): BWV199
        1. "Mein Herze schwimmt im Blut," recit (S)
        2. "Stumme Seufzer, stille Klagen," aria (S)
        3. "Doch Gott muss mir genädig sein," recit (S)
        4. "Tiefgebückt und voller Reue," aria (S)
        5. "Auf die Schmerzens," recit (S)
        6. "Ich Dein betrübtes Kind," choral
        7. "Ich lege mich in diese Wunden," recit (S)
        8. "Wie freudig ist mein Herz," aria (S)
7.211   Cantata No.200: "Bekennen will ich seinen Namen" (ca1742, Purification, inc): BWV200
        . "Bekennen will ich seinen Namen," aria (A)
7.212   *Cantata No.217: "Gedanke, Herr, wie es uns gehet" (spur)* *BWV217*
7.213   *Cantata No.218: "Gott der Hoffnung erfülle euch" (spur: c by Telemann)* *BWV218*
7.214   *Cantata No.219: "Siehe, es hat überwunden der Löwe" (spur: c by Telemann)* *BWV219*

8. LITURGICAL WORKS

Motets:

Masses, mass sections & magnificats:

    I. "Kyrie": 1. "Kyrie eleison" (ch)
            2. "Christe eleison," duet (S, T)
            3. "Kyrie eleison" (ch)
    II. "Gloria": 4. "Gloria in excelsis" (ch)
            5. "Et in terra pax" (ch)
            6. "Laudamus te," aria (S)
            7. "Gratias agimus tibi" (ch)
            8. "Domine Deus," duet (S, T)
            9. "Qui tollis peccata mundi" (ch)
           10. "Qui sedes ad dextram," aria (A)
           11. "Quoniam tu solus sanctus," aria (B)
           12. "Cum sancto spiritu" (ch)
    III. "Symbolum Nicenum": 13. "Credo in unum Deum" (ch)
           14. "Patrem omnipotentem" (ch)
           15. "Et in unum Dominum Jesum Christum," duet (S, A)
           16. "Et incarnatus est" (ch)
            17. "Crucifixus" (ch)
           18. "Et resurrexit" (ch)
           19. "Et in spiritum sanctum," aria (B)
           20. "Confiteor" (ch)
           21. "Et expecto" (ch)
    IV. "Sanctus": 22. "Sanctus" (ch)
           23. "Pleni sunt coeli" (T)
    V. "Osanna, Benedictus. Agnus Dei et Dona nobis pacem": 24. "Osanna in excelsis" (d ch)
           25. "Benedictus qui venit," aria (T)
           26. "Agnus Dei qui tollis," aria (A)
           27. "Dona nobis pacem" (ch)

           1. "Magnificat," chorus
           2. "Et exultavit spiritus meus," aria (S)
           3. "Quia respexit humilitatem," aria (S)
           4. "Omnes generationes," chorus
           5. "Quia fecit mihi magna," aria (B)
           6. "Et misericordiam," duet (A, T)
           7. "Fecit potentiam," chorus
           8. "Deposuit," aria (T)
           9. "Esurientes implevit bonis," aria (A)
           10. "Suscepit Israel puerum suum," trio (2S, A)
           11. "Sicut locutus est," chorus
           12. "Gloria Patri," chorus

Passions:

8.22   "St. Matthew Passion" (c1729 & 1736): BWV244
   I: 1. "Kommt, ihr Töchter," chorus
     2. "Da Jesus diese Rede vollendet" (T, B)
     3. "Herzliebster Jesu," chorus
     4a. "Da versammelten sich die Hohenpriester" (T)
     4b. "Ja nicht auf das Fest," chorus
     4c. Da nun Jesus war zu Bethanien" (T)
     4d. "Wozu dienet dieser Unrat?," chorus
     4e. "Da das Jesus merkete" (T, B)
     5. "Du lieber Heiland du," recit (A)
     6. "Buss' und Reu'," aria (A)
     7. "Da ging hin der Zwölfen einer" (T, B)
     8. "Blute nur," aria (S)
     9a. "Aber am ersten Tage" (T)
     9b. "Wo willst du?," chorus
     9c. "Er sprach" (T, B)
     9d. "Und sie wurden sehr betrübt" (T)
     9e. "Herr, bin ich's," chorus
     10. "Ich bin's ich sollte büssen," choral
     11. "Er antwortete und sprach" (T, B)
     12. "Wiewohl mein Herz," recit (S)
     13. "Ich will dir mein Herze schenken," aria
     14. "Und da sie den Lobgesang gesprochen hatten" (T, B)
     15. "Erkenne mich," choral
     16. "Petrus aber antwortete" (T, B)
     17. "Ich will hier bei dir stehen," choral
     18. "Da kam Jesus mit ihnen" (T, B)
     19. "O Schmerz!," recit & choral (T)
     20. "Ich will bei meinem Jesu wachen," aria (2ch)
     21. "Und ging hin ein wenig" (T, B)
     22. "Der Heiland fällt vor seinem Vater nieder," recit (B)
     23. "Gerne will ich," aria (B)
     24. "Und er kam zu seinen Jüngern" (T, B)
     25. "Was mein Gott will," choral
     26. "Und er kam und fand" (T, 2B)
     27a. "So ist mein Jesus," aria (2ch)
     27b. "Sind Blitze, sind Donner in Wolken verschwunden"
     28. "Und siehe, Einer aus denen" (T, B)
     29. "O Mensch, bewein' dein' Sünde gross," choral (d ch)
   II: 30. "Ach, nun ist mein Jesus hin!," aria
     31. "Die aber Jesum gegriffen hatten" (T)
     32. "Mir hat die Welt," choral
     33. "Und wiewohl viel falsche Zeugen" (T, B)
     34. "Mein Jesus schweigt," recit (T)
     35. "Geduld, Geduld," aria (T)
     36a. "Und der Hohepriester antwortete" (T, 2B)
     36b. "Er ist," chorus
     36c. "Da speieten sie aus in sein Angesicht" (T)
     36d. "Weisage" (d ch)
     37. "Wer hat dich so geschlagen," choral
     38a. "Petrus aber sass draussen" (S, T, B)
     38b. "Wahrlich, du bist auch einer von denen," chorus
     38c. "Da hub er an" (T, B)
     39. "Erbarme dich," aria (A)
     40. "Bin ich gleich von dir gewichen," choral
     41a. "Des Morgens aber hielten alle Hohenpriester" (T, B)
     41b. "Was gehet uns das an?" (d ch)
     41c. "Und er warf die Silberlinge in den Tempel" (T, 2B)
     42. "Gebt mir meinen Jesum wieder," aria (B)
     43. "Sie hielten aber einen Rat" (T, 2B)
     44. "Befiehl du deine Wege," choral
     45a. "Auf das Fest aber hatte der Landpfleger" (S, T, B)
     45b. "Lass ihn kreuzigen" (d ch)
     46. "Wie wunderbarlich," choral
     47. "Der Landpfleger sagte" (T, B)
     48. "Er hat uns allen wohlgetan," recit (S)
     49. "Aus Liebe will mein Heiland sterben," aria (S)
     50a. "Sie schrieen aber noch" (T)
     50b. "Lass ihn kreuzigen" (d ch)
     50c. "Da aber Pilatus sahe," recit (T, B)
     50d. "Sein Blut komme über uns" (d ch)
     50e. "Da gab er ihnen Barabbam los" (T)
     51. "Erbarm' es Gott!," recit (A)

52. "Können Tränen meiner Wangen," aria (A)
53a. "Da nahmen die Kriegsknechte" (T)
53b. "Gegrüsset"
53c. "Und speieten ihn an" (T)
54. "O Haupt voll Blut und Wunden," choral
55. "Und da sie an die Stätte" (T)
56. "Ja! freilich will," recit (B)
57. "Komm, süsses Kreuz," aria (B)
58a. "Und da sie an die Stätte kamen" (T)
58b. "Der du den Tempel" (d ch)
58c. "Desgleichen auch die Hohenpriester spotteten sein" (T)
58d. "Andern hat er geholfen" (d ch)
58e. "Desgleichen schmäheten" (T)
59. "Ach, Golgatha," recit (A)
60. "Sehet, Jesus hat die Hand," aria (d ch)
61a. "Und von der sechsten Stunde" (T, B)
61b. "Der rufet dem Elias," chorus
61c. "Und bald lief einer unter ihnen" (T)
61d. "Halt, halt, lass sehen," chorus
62. "Wenn ich einmal soll scheiden," choral
63a. "Und siehe da" (T)
63b. "Wahrlich, dieser ist Gottes Sohn gewesen" (unison d ch)
63c. "Und es waren viel Weiber da" (T)
64. "Am Abend, da es kühle war," recit (B)
65. "Mache dich, mein Herze," aria (B)
66a. "Und Joseph nahm den Leib" (T)
66b. "Herr, wir haben gedacht" (d ch)
66c. "Pilatus sprach zu ihnen" (T, B)
67. "Nun ist der Herr," recit (S, A, T, B)
68. "Wir setzen uns mit Tränen nieder" (d ch)

    I: 1. "Herr, unser Herrscher," chorus
        2a. "Jesus ging," recit (T, B)
        2b. "Jesum von Nazareth!," chorus
        2c. "Jesus spricht," recit (T)
        2d. "Jesum von Nazareth," chorus
        2e. "Jesus antwortete," recit (T)
        3. "O grosse Lieb," choral
        4. "Auf dass das Wort," recit (T)
        5. "Dein Will gescheh," choral
        6. "Die Schar aber," recit (T)
        7. "Von den Stricken," aria (A)
        8. "Simon Petrus aber," recit (T)
        9. "Ich folge dir," aria (S)
       10. "Der selbige Jünger," recit (S, T, B)
       11. "Wer hat dich so geschlagen," choral
       12a. "Und Hannas sandte ihn," recit (T)
       12b. "Bist du nicht seiner Jünger einer," chorus
       12c. "Er leugnete aber," recit (T, B)
       13. "Ach, mein Sinn," aria (T)
       14. "Petrus, der nicht denkt zurück," choral
    II: 15. "Christus, der uns selig macht," choral
       16a. "Da führeten sie Jesum," recit (T, B)
       16b. "Wäre dieser nicht ein Übeltäter," chorus
       16c. "Da sprach Pilatus," recit (T, B)
       16d. "Wir dürfen niemand töten," chorus
       16e. "Auf dass erfüllet," recit (T, B)
       17. "Ach grosser König," choral
       18a. "Das sprach Pilatus," recit (T, B)
       18b. "Nicht diesen," chorus
       18c. "Barrabas aber war ein Mörder," recit (T)
       19. "Betrachte, meine Seel," arioso (B)
       20. "Erwäge," aria (T)
       21a. "Und die Kriegsknechte," recit (T)
       21b. "Sei gegrüsset," chorus
       21c. "Und gaben ihm Backenstreiche," recit (T, B)
       21d. "Kreuzige!," chorus
       21e. "Pilatus sprach zu ihnen," recit (T, B)
       21f. "Wir haben ein Gesetz," chorus
       21g. "Da Pilatus," recit (T, B)
       22. "Durch dein Gefängnis," choral
       23a. "Die Juden aber schrien und sprachen," recit (T)
       23b. "Lässest du diesen los," chorus
       23c. "Da Pilatus das Wort hörete," recit (T, B)

23d. "Weg, weg mit dem," chorus
23e. "Spricht Pilatus zu ihnen," recit (T, B)
23f. "Wir haben keinen König," chorus
23g. "Da überantwortete ihn," recit (T)
24. "Eilt, ihr angefocht'nen Seelen," aria (B)
25a. "Allda kreuzigten sie ihn," recit (T)
25b. "Schreibe nicht," chorus
25c. "Pilatus antwortet," recit (T, B)
26. "In meines Herzens Grunde," choral
27a. "Die Kriegsknechte aber," recit (T)
27b. "Lasset uns," chorus
27c. "Auf dass erfüllet," recit (T, B)
28. "Er nahm Alles wohl in acht," choral
29. "Und von Stund' an nahm sie der Jünger zu sich," recit (T, B)
30. "Es ist vollbracht," aria (A)
31. "Und neigte," recit (T)
32. "Mein teurer Heiland," aria (B)
33. "Und siehe da," recit (T)
34. "Mein Herz! in dem die ganze Welt," arioso (T)
35. "Zerfliesse, mein Herze," aria (S)
36. "Die Juden aber," recit (T)
37. "O hilfe, Christe," choral
38. "Darnach bat Pilatum," recit (T)
39. "Ruht wohl," chorus
40. "Ach Herr, lass dein lieb Engelein," choral

Oratorios:

I. "For the 1st Day of Christmas": 1. "Jauchzet, frohlocket!," chorus
2. "Es begab sich aber zu der Zeit," recit (T)
3."Nun wird mein liebster Bräutigam," recit (T)
4. "Bereite dich, Zion," aria (A)
5. "Wie soll ich dich empfangen," choral
6. "Und sie gebar ihren ersten Sohn," recit (T)
7. "Er ist auf Erden kommen arm," choral
8. "Grosser Herr und starker König," aria (B)
9. "Ach mein herzliebes Jesulein!," choral
II. "For the 2nd Day of Christmas": 10. "Sinfonia"
11. "Und es waren Hirten," recit (T)
12. "Brich an, o schönes Morgenlicht," choral
13. "Und der Engel sprach," recit (T, S)
14. "Was Gott dem Abraham verheissen," recit (B)
15. "Frohe Hirten, eilt," aria (T)
16. "Und das habt zum Zeichen," recit (T)
17. "Schaut hin!," choral
18. "So geht denn hin!," recit (B)
19. "Schlafe, mein Liebster," aria (A)
20. "Und alsobald war da bei dem Engel," recit (T)
21. "Ehre sei Gott in der Höhe," chorus
22. "So recht, ihr Engel," recit (B)
23. "Wir singen dir in deinem Heer," choral
III. "For the 3rd Day of Christmas": 24. "Herrscher des Himmels," chorus
25. "Und da die Engel von ihnen gen Himmel fuhren," recit (T)
26. "Lasset uns nun gehen gen Bethlehem," chorus
27. "Er hat sein Volk getröst'," recit (B)
28. "Dies hat er alles uns getan," choral
29. "Herr, dein Mitleid, dein Erbarmen," duet (S, B)
30. "Und sie kamen eilend," recit (T)
31. "Schliesse, mein Herze," aria (A)
32. "Ja, ja! mein Herz soll es bewahren," recit (A)
33. "Ich will dich mit Fleiss bewahren," choral
34. "Und die Hirten," recit (T)
35. "Seid froh, dieweil," choral
IV. "For the Feast of the Circumcision": 36. "Fallt mit Danken," chorus
37. "Und da acht Tage um waren," recit (T)
38. "Immanuel, o süsses Wort!," recit (S, B)
39. "Flösst, mein Heiland," aria (2S—echo)
40. "Wohlan! Dein Name soll allein," recit arioso (S, B)
41. "Ich will nur dir zu Ehren leben," aria (T)
42. "Jesus richte mein Beginnen," choral
V. "For the 1st Sunday in the New Year": 43. "Ehre sei dir, Gott, gesungen," chorus
44. "Da Jesus geboren," recit (T)

45. "Wo ist der neugeborne König der Juden?," chorus
46. "Dein Glanz all'Finsternis verzehrt," choral
47. "Erleucht' auch meine finstre Sinnen," aria (B)
48. "Da das der König Herodes hörte," recit (T)
49. "Warum wollt ihr erschrecken?," recit (A)
50. "Und liess versammeln alle Hohenpriester," recit (T)
51. "Ach, wenn wird die Zeit erscheinen?," trio (S, A, T)
52. "Mein Liebster herrschet schon," recit (A)
53. "Zwar ist solche Herzensstube," choral
VI. "For the Feast of Epiphany": 54. "Herr, wenn die stolzen Feinde schnauben," chorus
55. "Da berief Herodes," recit (T)
56. "Du Falscher, suche nur den Herrn zu fällen," recit (S)
57. "Nur ein Wink," aria (S)
58. "Als sie nun den König," recit (T)
59. "Ich steh an deiner Krippen hier," choral
60. "Und Gott befahl ihnen im Traum," recit (T)
61. "So geht! genug, mein Schatz," recit (T)
62. "Nun mögt ihr stolzen Feinde schrekken," aria (T)
63. "Was will der Hölle Schrecken nun," recit (S, A, T, B)
64. "Nun seid ihr wohl gerochen," choral

8.28   "Easter Oratorio": "Kommt, eilet und laufet" (c1725: 1st vers, text r1726 & 1795): BWV249
1. "Sinfonia"
2. Adagio"
3. "Kommt, eilet und laufet," duet/chorus (T, B)
4. "O kalter Männer Sinn!," recit (S, A, T, B)
5. "Seele, deine Specereien," aria (S)
6. "Hier ist die Gruft," recit (A, T, B)
7. "Sanfte soll mein Todeskummer," aria (T)
8. "In dessen seufzen," recit (S, A)
9. "Saget mir geschwinde," aria (A)
10. "Wir sind erfreut," recit (B)
11. "Preis und Dank," chorus

Chorals (ch, insts & cont):

186 harmonized chorals from C. P. E. Bach's collection (p1784–7; ch, insts & cont):

8.66	"Dank sei Gott in der Höhe" (Mühlmann 1618)	BWV287
8.67	"Das alte Jahr vergangen ist" (?Steuerlein 1588)	BWV288
8.68	"Das alte Jahr vergangen ist" (?Steuerlein 1588)	BWV289
8.69	"Das walt Gott Vater ind Gott Sohn" (Böhme 1608)	BWV290
8.70	"Das walt mein Gott" (?Frötsch 1613)	BWV291
8.71	"Den Vater dort oben" (Weisse 1531)	BWV292
8.72	"Der du bist drei in Einigkeit" (Luther 1543)	BWV293
8.73	"Der Tag, der ist so freudenreich" (German vers of: Dies est laetitiae)	BWV294
8.74	"Des heil'gen Geistes reiche Gnad' " (German vers of: Spiritus sancti)	BWV295
8.75	"Die Nacht ist kommen" (Herbert 1566)	BWV296
8.76	"Die Sonn hat sich mit ihrem Glanz" (Stegmann ?1630)	BWV297
8.77	"Dies sind die heilgen zehn Gebot" (Luther 1524)	BWV298
8.78	"Dir, dir, Jehova, will ich singen" (Crasselius 1697)	BWV299
8.79	"Du grosser Schmerzensmann" (Thebesius before 1652)	BWV300
8.80	"Du, o schönes Weltgebäude" (Franck 1653)	BWV301
8.81	"Ein feste Burg ist unser Gott" (Luther 1529)	BWV302
8.82	"Ein feste Burg ist unser Gott" (Luther 1529)	BWV303
8.83	"Eins ist Noth, ach Herr, dies Eine" (Schröder 1697)	BWV304
8.84	"Erbarm dich mein, o Herre Gott" (Hegenwalt 1524)	BWV305
8.85	"Erstanden ist der heil'ge Christ" (from: Surrexit Christus)	BWV306
8.86	"Es ist gewisslich an der Zeit" (Nun freut euch ...) (Ringwald 1582)	BWV307
8.87	"Es spricht der Unweisen Mund wohl" (Luther 1524)	BWV308
8.88	"Es stehn vor Gottes Throne" (Helmbold 1585)	BWV309
8.89	"Es wird schier der letzte Tag herkommen" (Weisse 1531)	BWV310
8.90	"Es woll' uns Gott genädig sein" (Luther 1524)	BWV311
8.91	"Es woll' uns Gott genädig sein" (Luther 1524)	BWV312
8.92	"Für Freuden lasst uns springen" (unknown)	BWV313
8.93	"Gelobet seist du, Jesu Christ" (Luther 1524)	BWV314
8.94	"Gib dich zufrieden und sei stille" (Gerhardt 1666)	BWV315
8.95	"Gott, der du selber bist das Licht" (Rist 1641)	BWV316
8.96	"Gott der Vater wohn uns bei" (Luther 1524)	BWV317
8.97	"Gottes Sohn ist kommen" (Horn 1544)	BWV318
8.98	"Gott hat das Evangelium" (Alberus 1548)	BWV319
8.99	"Gott lebet noch" (Zihn 1692)	BWV320
8.100	"Gottlob, es geht nunmehr zu Ende" (Weisse 1531)	BWV321
8.101	"Gott sei gelobet und gebenedeiet" (Luther 1524)	BWV322
8.102	"Gott sei uns gnädig und barmherzig" (from: Genese)	BWV323
8.103	"Meine Seele erhebet den Herrn" (Luke I, 46–55)	BWV324
8.104	"Heilig, heilig, heilig" (Sanctus, sanctus, sanctus)	BWV325
8.105	"Herr Gott, dich loben alle wir" (Eber ?1554)	BWV326
8.106	"Für deinen Thron tret ich hiermit" (Hodenberg 1648)	BWV327
8.107	"Herr Gott, dich loben wir" (unknown)	BWV328
8.108	"Herr, ich denk an jene Zeit" (Mylius 1650)	BWV329
8.109	"Herr, ich habe missgehandelt" (Franck ca1649)	BWV330
8.110	"Herr, ich habe missgehandelt" (Franck ca1649)	BWV331
8.111	"Herr Jesu Christ, dich zu uns wend' " (Wilhelm II 1651)	BWV332
8.112	"Herr Jesu Christ, du hast bereit't" (Kinner 1644)	BWV333
8.113	"Herr Jesu Christ, du Höchstes Gut" (Ringwaldt 1588)	BWV334
8.114	"Herr Jesu Christ, meins Lebens Licht" (Behm 1610)	BWV335
8.115	"Herr Jesu Christ, wahr Mensch und Gott" (Eber 1562)	BWV336
8.116	"Herr, nun lass in Friede" (Behme before 1657)	BWV337
8.117	"Herr straf mich nicht in deinem Zorn" (unknown 1640)	BWV338
8.118	"Herr, wie du will't, so schick's mit mir" (Bienemann 1582)	BWV339
8.119	"Herzlich lieb hab ich dich, o Herr" (Schalling 1571)	BWV340
8.120	"Heut ist, o Mensch, ein grosser Trauertag" (Löwenstern 1644)	BWV341
8.121	"Heut triumphiert Gottes Sohn" (Förtsch 1601)	BWV342
8.122	"Hilf, Gott, dass mir's gelinge" (Züphen before 1531)	BWV343
8.123	"Hilf, Herr Jesu, lass gelingen" (Rist 1642)	BWV344
8.124	"Ich bin ja, Herr, in deiner Macht" (Dach ca1648)	BWV345
8.125	"Ich dank dir, Gott, für all Wohltat" (Freder 1552)	BWV346
8.126	"Ich dank dir, lieber Herre" (Kolrose 1535)	BWV347
8.127	"Ich dank dir, lieber Herre" (Kolrose 1535)	BWV348
8.128	"Ich dank dir schon durch deinem Sohn" (Berwaldt 1582)	BWV349
8.129	"Ich danke dir, o Gott, in deinem Throne" (Crüger 1640)	BWV350
8.130	"Ich hab mein Sach Gott heimgestellt" (Leon ca1589)	BWV351
8.131	"Jesu, der du meine Seele" (Rist 1641)	BWV352
8.132	"Jesu, der du meine Seele" (Rist 1641)	BWV353
8.133	"Jesu, der du meine Seele" (Rist 1641)	BWV354
8.134	"Jesu, der du selbsten wohl" (Bapzien ca1656)	BWV355
8.135	"Jesu, du mein habstes Leben" (Rist 1642)	BWV356
8.136	"Jesu, Jesu, du bist mein" (Meininger Gesangbuch 1697)	BWV357
8.137	"Jesu, meine Freunde" (Franck 1650)	BWV358
8.138	"Jesu, meiner Seelen Wonne" (Jahn 1671)	BWV359
8.139	"Jesu, meiner Seelen Wonne" (Jesu, meiner Freuden ...) (Jahn 1671)	BWV360
8.140	"Jesu, meines Herzens Freud' " (Flitner 1661)	BWV361

8.216   "Wir glauben all an einen Gott" (Luther 1524) BWV437
8.217   "Wo Gott zum Haus nicht gibt sein' Gunst" (?Kolross 1525) BWV438

Other:

8.218   "Credo in unum Deum" (ca1735–40, inserted in Bassani: Mass No.5, Acroama Missale) BWV1081
8.219   "Suscepit Israel puerum suum" (arr for ch, 2vn & cont, from 3rd movt of Caldara: Magnificat
          in C major) BWV1082
8.220   "Tilge, Höchster, mein Sünden" (arr1741–6; S, A, strings & cont, from Pergolesi: Stabat mater)..BWV1083

9. SECULAR CANTATAS

9.1   "Angenehmes Wiederau, freue dich in deinen Auen" (c1737, Picander): BWV30a
          1. "Angenehmes Wiederau," chorus
          2. "So ziehen wir in diesem Hause hier," recit (S, A, T, B)
          3. "Willkommen im Heil, willkommen in Freuden," aria (B)
          4. "Da heute dir, gepriesner Hennikke dein," recit (A)
          5. "Was die Seele kann ergötzen," aria (A)
          6. "Und wie ich jederzeit bedacht mit aller Sorg und Macht," recit (B)
          7. "Ich will dich halten und mit dir walten," aria (B)
          8. "Und obwohl sonst der Unbestand mit mir verschwistert und verwandt," recit (S)
          9. "Eilt, eilt, eilt ihr Stunden," aria (S)
          10. "So recht! ihr seid mir werte Gäste," recit (T)
          11. "So wie die Tropfen zolle, dass mein Wiedrau grünen solle," aria (T)
          12. "Drum, angenehmes Wiederau, soll dich kein Blitz," recit (S, A, T, B)
          13. "Angenehmes Wiederau, prange nun in," chorus
9.2   "Steigt freudig in die Luft" (c ?1726): BWV36a
          1. "Steigt freudig in die Luft," aria (chorus) (= BWV36c/1)
          2. "Durchlauchtigste," recit
          3. "Die Sonne zieht mit sanftem Triebe," aria (= BWV36c/3)
          4. "Die Dankbarkeit," recit
          5. "Sei uns willkommen, schönster Tag," aria (= BWV36c/5)
          6. "Wiewohl das ist noch nicht genung," recit
          7. "Auch mit gedämpften, schwachen Stimmen," aria (= BWV36c/7)
          8. "Doch ehe wir noch deinen Thron," recit
          9. "Grüne, blühe, lebe lange," aria & recit (= BWV36c/9 w/ revisions)
9.3   "Die Freude reget sich" (c ?1735): BWV36b
          1. "Die Freude reget sich," chorus
          2. "Ihr seht, wie sich das Glücke, des teuersten Rivins," recit (T)
          3. "Aus Gottes milden Vater händen," aria (T)
          4. "Die Freunde sind vergnügt," recit (A)
          5. "Das Gute, das dein Gott beschert," aria (A)
          6. "Wenn sich die Welt mit deinem Ruhme trägt," recit (S)
          7. "Mit zarten und vergnügten Trieben," aria (S)
          8. "Was wir dir vor Glükke gönnen, wünscht man," chorus
9.4   "Schwingt freudig euch empor" (c ?1725): BWV36c
          1. "Schwingt freudig euch empor," chorus
          2. "Ein Herz, in zärtlichem Empfinden," recit (T)
          3. "Die Liebe führt mit sanften Schritten," aria (T)
          4. "Du bist es ja, o hochverdienter Mann," recit (B)
          5. "Der Tag, der dich vordem gebar," aria (B)
          6. "Nur dieses Einz'ge sorgen wir," recit (S)
          7. "Auch mit gedämpften schwachen Stimmen," aria (S)
          8. "Bei solchen freudenvollen Stunden," recit (T)
          9. "Wie die Jahre sich verneuen, so verneue sich dein Ruhm," chorus
9.5   *"Der Himmel dacht auf Anhalts Ruhm und Glück" (c1718, lost)* *BWV66a*
9.6   "Die Zeit, die Tag und Jahre macht" (c1719): BWV134a
          1. "Die Zeit, die Tag und Jahre macht," recit (T, A)
          2. "Auf, Sterbliche," aria (T)
          3. "So bald, als dir die Sterne hold," recit (A, T)
          4. "Es streiten, es siegen," duet (A, T)
          5. "Bedenke nur, beglücktes Land," recit (A, T)
          6. "Der Zeiten Herr hat viel vergnügte Stunden," aria (A)
          7. "Hilf, Höchster, hilf," recit (A, T)
          8. "Ergötzet auf Erden," chorus
9.7   "Durchlauchster Leopold" (c ?1722): BWV173a
          1. "Durchlauchtster Leopold, es singet Anhalts Welt," recit (S)
          2. "Güldner Sonnen frohe Stunden," aria (S)
          3. "Leopolds Vortrefflichkeiten," aria (B)
          4. "Unter seinem Purpursaum ist die Freude," duet (S, B)
          5. "Durchlauchtigster, den Anhalt Vater nennt," recit (S, B)
          6. "So schau dies holden Tages Licht," aria (S)
          7. "Dein Name gleich der Sonnen geh'," aria (B)
          8. "Nimm auch, grosser Fürst, uns auf," chorus

12. "Was Lust! Was Freude! Welch Vergnügen!," recit (Pallas, Pomona, Zephyrus)
13. "Zweig und Äste," duet (Pomona, Zephyrus)
14. "Ja, ja! ich lad euch selbst zu dieser Feier ein," recit (Pallas)
15. "Vivat! Vivat," chorus

9.17   *"Blast Lärmen, ihr Feinde! verstärket die Macht," dramma per musica (c1734, lost)* *BWV205a*

9.18   "Schleicht, spielende Wellen, und murmelt gelinde," dramma per musica (c1736): BWV206
1. "Schleicht, spielende Wellen, und murmelt gelinde," chorus
2. "O glückliche Veränderung," recit (Weichsel)
3. "Schleuss des Janustempels Türen," aria (Weichsel)
4. "So recht! beglückter Weichselstrom," recit (Elbe)
5. "Jede Woge meiner Wellen ruft," aria (Elbe)
6. "Ich nehm zugleich an deiner Freude Teil," recit (Donau)
7. "Reis, von Habsburgs hohem Stamme," aria (Donau)
8. "Verzeiht, bemooste Häupter starker Ströme," recit (Pleisse)
9. "Hört doch! der sanften Flöten Chor," aria (Pleisse)
10. "Ich muss, ich will gehorsam sein," recit (Weichsel, Elbe, Donau)
11. "Die himmlische Vorsicht der ewigen Güte," chorus

9.19   "Vereinigte Zwietracht der wechselnden Saiten," dramma per musica (c1726): BWV207
1. "Vereinigte Zwietracht der wechselnden Saiten," chorus
2. "Wen treibt ein edler Trieb zu dem," recit (Fleiss)
3. "Zieht euren Fuss nur zurükke," aria (Fleiss)
4. "Dem nur allein soll meine Wohnung offen sein," recit (Ehre, Glück)
5. "Den soll mein Lorbeer schützend dekken," duet (Glück, Ehre)
5a. "Ritornello"
6. "Es ist kein leeres Wort," recit (Dankbarkeit)
7. "Ätzet dieses Angedenken," aria (Dankbarkeit)
8. "Ihr Schläfrigen, herbei!," recit (Fleiss, Ehre, Glück, Dankbarkeit)
9. "Kortte lebe, Kortte blühe," chorus

9.20   "Auf, schmetternde Töne der muntern Trompeten," dramma per musica (c ?1735): BWV207a
1. "Auf, schmetternde Töne der muntern Trompeten," chorus
2. "Die stille Pleisse spielt," recit (T)
3. "Augustus 'Namenstages Schimmer," aria (T)
4. "Augustus 'Wohl ist der treuen Sachsen Wohlergehn," recit (S, B)
5. "Mich kann die süsse Ruhe laben," duet (S, B)
5a. "Ritornella"
6. "Augustus schützt die frohen Felder," recit (A)
7. "Preiset, späte Folge gezeiten," aria (A)
8. "Ihr Fröhlichen, herbei," recit (T, B, S)
9. "August lebe, lebe, König," chorus
. "Marcia" (Zusatz)

9.21   "Hunt Cantata": "Was mir behagt, ist nur die muntre Jagd" (c1713): BWV208
1. "Was mir behagt, ist nur die muntre Jagd!," recit (Diana)
2. "Jagen ist die Lust der Götter," aria (Diana)
3. "Wie, schönste Göttin, wie?," recit (Endymion)
4. "Willst du dich nur mehr ergetzen," aria (Endymion)
5. "Ich liebe dich zwar noch!," recit (Diana, Endymion)
6. "Ich, der ich sonst ein Gott in diesen Feldern bin," aria (Pan)
7. "Ein Fürst ist seines Landes Pan!," aria (Pan)
8. "Soll den der Pales Opfer hier das letzte sein," recit (Pales)
9. "Schafe können sicher weiden," aria (Pales)
10. "So stimmt mit ein," recit (Diana)
11. "Lebe, Sonne dieser Erden," chorale
12. "Entzükket uns beide," duet (Diana, Endymion)
13. "Weil die wollenreichen Herden," aria (Pales)
14. "Ihr Felder und Auen" (Pan)
15. "Ihr lieblichste Blikke!," chorus

9.22   *Cantata No.208a: "Was mir behagt, ist nur die muntre Jagd" (c ?1740–2, lost)* *BWV208a*

9.23   *Cantata No.209: "Non sa che sia dolore" (spur: c by Telemann)* *BWV209*

9.24   "O holder Tag, erwünschte Zeit," wedding cantata (ca1741): BWV210
1. "O holder Tag, erwünschte Zeit, recit (S)
2. "Spielet, ihr beseelten Lieder," aria (S)
3. "Doch haltet ein," recit (S)
4. "Ruhet hie, matte Töne," aria (S)
5. "So glaubt man denn," recit (S)
6. "Schweigt, ihr Flöten schweigt," aria (S)
7. "Was Luft? was grab?," recit (S)
8. "Grosser Gönner, dein Vergnügen," aria (S)
9. "Hochteuer Mann," recit (S)
10. "Seid beglückt," aria (S)

9.25   *Cantata No.210a: "O angenehme Melodei!" (ca1738–40, frag)* *BWV210a*

9.26   "Coffee Cantata": "Schweiget stille, plaudert nicht" (ca1734–5): BWV211
1. "Schweiget stille, plaudert nicht," recit (Erzähler)
2. "Hat man nicht mit seinen Kindern," aria (Schlendrian)
3. "Du böses Kind, du loses Mädchen," recit (Lieschen)
4. "Ei! wie schmeckt der Coffee süsse," aria (Lieschen)

    5. "Wenn du mir nicht den Caffee läss't," recit (Lieschen)
    6. "Mädchen, die von harten Sinnen," aria (Schlendrian)
    7. "Nun folge, was dein Vater spricht," recit (Lieschen, Schlendrian)
    8. "Heute noch, lieber Vater, tut es doch," aria (Lieschen)
    9. "Nun geht und sucht der alte Schlendrian," recit (Erzähler)
    10. "Die Katze lässt das Mausen nicht," chorus (Lieschen, Erzähler, Schlendrian)

9.27 "Peasant Cantata": "Mer hahn en neue Oberkeet" (c1742): BWV212
    1. Instrumental piece
    2. "Mer hahn en neue Oberkeet," duet (S, B)
    3. "Nu, Miecke, gib dein Guschel immer her," recit (S, B)
    4. "Ach es schmeckt doch gar zu gut," aria (S)
    5. "Der Herr ist gut," recit (B)
    6. "Ach Herr Schösser, geht nicht gar zu schlimm," aria (B)
    7. "Es bleibt dabei," recit (S)
    8. "Unser trefflicher lieber Kammerherr," aria (S)
    9. "Er hilft uns allen alt und jung," recit (S, B)
    10. "Das ist galant," aria (S)
    11. "Und unsre gnäd'ge Frau ist nicht ein prinkel stolz," recit (B)
    12. "Fünfzig Taler bares Geld," aria (B)
    13. "Im Ernst ein Wort!," recit (S)
    14. "Kleinzschocher müsse so zart und süsse," aria (S)
    15. "Das ist zu klug vor dich," recit (B)
    16. "Es nehme zehn tausend Ducaten," aria (B)
    17. "Das klingt zu liederlich," recit (S)
    18. "Gib, Schöne, viel Söhne von art'ger Gestalt," aria (S)
    19. "Du hast wohl recht," recit (B)
    20. "Dein Wachstum sei feste und lache vor Lust," aria (B)
    21. "Und damit sei es auch genung," recit (S, B)
    22. "Und dass ihrs alle wisst," aria (S)
    23. "Mein Schatz, erraten," recit (S, B)
    24. "Wir gehn nun wo der Tudelsack," chorus

9.28 "Herkules auf dem Scheidewege": "Lasst uns sorgen," dramma per musica (c1733): BWV213
    1. "Lasst uns sorgen," chorus
    2. "Und wo? Wo ist die rechte Bahn," recit (Hercules)
    3. "Schlafe, mein Liebster," aria (Wollust)
    4. "Auf! folge meiner Bahn," recit (Wollust)
    5. "Treues Echo," aria (Hercules)
    6. "Mein hoffnungsvoller Held!," recit (Tugend)
    7. "Auf meinen Flügeln sollst du schweben," aria (Tugend)
    8. "Die weiche Wollust lokket zwar," recit (Tugend)
    9. "Ich will dich nicht hören," aria (Hercules)
    10. "Geliebte Tugend, du allein sollst meine Leiterin beständig sein," recit (Hercules)
    11. "Ich bin deine," duet (Hercules, Tugend)
    12. "Schaut, Götter, dieses ist ein Bild," recit (Mercur)
    13. "Lust der Völker, Lust der Deinen, blühe," chorus

9.29 "Tönet, ihr Pauken! Erschallet, Trompeten!," dramma per musica (c1733): BWV214
    1. "Tönet, ihr Pauken! Erschallet, Trompeten!," chorus
    2. "Heut ist der Tag," recit (T)
    3. "Blast die wohlgegriffnen Flöten," aria (S)
    4. "Mein knallen des Metall," recit (S)
    5. "Fromme Musen! Meine Glieder," aria (A)
    6. "Unsre Königin im Lande," recit (A)
    7. "Kron und Preis gekrönter Damen," aria (B)
    8. "So dringe in das weite Erdenrund," recit (B)
    9. "Blühet, ihr Linden in Sachsen," chorus

9.30 "Preise dein Glücke, gesegnetes Sachsen," dramma per musica (c1734): BWV215
    1. "Preise dein Glükke, gesegnetes Sachsen," chorus
    2. "Wie können wir, Grossmächtigster August," recit (T)
    3. "Freilich trotzt Augustus' Name," aria (T)
    4. "Was hat dich sonst, Sarmatien, bewogen," recit (B)
    5. "Rase nur, verwegner Schwarm," aria (B)
    6. "Ja, ja! Gott ist uns noch mit seiner Hülfe nah," recit (S)
    7. "Durch die von Eifer entflammeten Waffen," aria (S)
    8. "Sifter der Reiche," chorus

9.31 "Vergnügte Pleissen-Stadt," wedding cantata (c1728, inc): BWV216
    1. "Vergnügte Pleissen-Stadt," duet (S, A)
    2. "So angenehm auch mein Revier," recit (S)
    3. "Angenehme Hempelin," aria (S)
    4. "Erspare den Verdruss," recit (A)
    5. "Mit Lachen und Schmerzen," aria (A)
    6. "Wie lieblich wird sie nun," recit (A)
    7. "Heil und Segen," duet (S, A)

9.32 *"Apollo et Mercurius": "Erwählte Pleissenstadt" (c after 1728, lost) BWV216a*
9.33 *"Entfliehet, verschwindet, entweichet, ihr Sorgen" (c1725, lost) BWV249a*
9.34 *"Verjaget, zerstreuet, zerrüttet, ihr Sterne" (Die Feier ...) (c1726, lost)...................BWV249b*

10. SOLO VOICE (Lieder, arias & quodlibet)

69 hymns from Schemelli's Gesangbuch (p1736; 1v & cont):

10.1	"Ach, dass nicht die letzte Stunde"	BWV439
10.2	"Auf, auf! die rechte Zeit"	BWV440
10.3	"Auf, auf! mein Herz"	BWV441
10.4	"Beglückter Stand"	BWV442
10.5	"Beschränkt, ihr Weisen"	BWV443
10.6	"Brich entzwei, mein armes Herze"	BWV444
10.7	"Brunnquell aller Güter"	BWV445
10.8	"Der lieben Sonne Licht und Pracht"	BWV446
10.9	"Der Tag ist hin"	BWV447
10.10	"Der Tag mit seinem Lichte"	BWV448
10.11	"Dich bet' ich an, mein höchster Gott"	BWV449
10.12	"Die bittre Leidenszeit"	BWV450
10.13	"Die goldne Sonne"	BWV451
10.14	"Dir, dir, Jehova"	BWV452
10.15	"Einst ist Not! ach Herr, dies Eine"	BWV453
10.16	"Ermuntre dich"	BWV454
10.17	"Erwürgtes Lamm"	BWV455
10.18	"Es glänzet der Christen"	BWV456
10.19	"Es ist nun aus"	BWV457
10.20	"Es ist vollbracht"	BWV458
10.21	"Es kostet viel"	BWV459
10.22	"Gib dich zufrieden"	BWV460
10.23	"Gott lebet noch"	BWV461
10.24	"Gott, wie gross ist deine Güte"	BWV462
10.25	"Herr, nicht schicke deine Rache"	BWV463
10.26	"Ich bin ja, Herr, in deiner Macht"	BWV464
10.27	"Ich freue mich in dir"	BWV465
10.28	"Ich halte treulich still"	BWV466
10.29	"Ich lass dich nicht"	BWV467
10.30	"Ich liebe Jesum alle Stund' "	BWV468
10.31	"Ich steh an deiner Krippen hier"	BWV469
10.32	"Jesu, Jesu du bist mein"	BWV470
10.33	"Jesu, deine Liebeswunden"	BWV471
10.34	"Jesu, meines Glaubens Zier"	BWV472
10.35	"Jesu, meines Herzens Freud"	BWV473
10.36	"Jesus ist das schönste Licht"	BWV474
10.37	"Jesus, unser Trost und Leben"	BWV475
10.38	"Ihr Gestirn, ihr hohen Lüfte"	BWV476
10.39	"Kein Stündlein geht dahin"	BWV477
10.40	"Komm, süsser Tod"	BWV478
10.41	"Kommt, Seelen, dieser Tag"	BWV479
10.42	"Kommt wieder aus"	BWV480
10.43	"Lasset uns mit Jesu ziehen"	BWV481
10.44	"Liebes Hertz, bedenke doch"	BWV482
10.45	"Liebster Gott, wann werd ich sterben"	BWV483
10.46	"Liebster Herr Jesu"	BWV484
10.47	"Liebster Immanuel"	BWV485
10.48	"Mein Jesu, dem die Seraphinen"	BWV486
10.49	"Mein Jesu, was für Seelenweh"	BWV487
10.50	"Meines Lebens letzte Zeit"	BWV488
10.51	"Nicht so traurig"	BWV489
10.52	"Nur mein Jesus"	BWV490
10.53	"O du Liebe meiner Liebe"	BWV491
10.54	"O finstre Nacht"	BWV492
10.55	"O Jesulein süss, o Jesulein mild"	BWV493
10.56	"O liebe Seele"	BWV494
10.57	"O wie selig seid ihr doch	BWV495
10.58	"Seelenbräutigam, Jesu"	BWV496
10.59	"Seelenweide, meine Freude"	BWV497
10.60	"Selig, wer an Jesum denkt"	BWV498
10.61	"Sei gegrüsset, Jesu gütig"	BWV499
10.62	"So gehst du nun"	BWV500
10.63	"So gehst du nun" (vers of BWV500)	BWV500a
10.64	"So gibst du nun"	BWV501
10.65	"So wünsch' ich mir"	BWV502
10.66	"Steh' ich bei meinem Gott"	BWV503
10.67	"Vergiss mein nicht, dass ich dein nicht vergesse"	BWV504
10.68	"Vergiss mein nicht, vergiss mein nicht," aria	BWV505
10.69	"Was bist du doch"	BWV506
10.70	"Wo ist mein Schäflein"	BWV507

Arias & Lieder from Anna Magdalena Bach's Clavierbüchlein II (p1725):

10.71	*"Bist du bei mir," aria (spur: c by ?Stölzel)*	*BWV508*
10.72	*"Gedenke doch, mein Geist," aria (spur)*	*BWV509*
10.73	*"Gib dich zufrieden," choral in F major (spur)*	*BWV510*
10.74	"Gib dich zufrieden," choral in G minor	BWV511
10.75	"Gib dich zufrieden," choral in E minor	BWV512
10.76	"O Ewigkeit, du Donnerwort!," choral	BWV513
10.77	*"Schaffs mit mir, Gott," choral (spur)*	*BWV514*
10.78	*"So oft ich meine Tabakspfeife," aria (spur: c by G. H. Bach)*	*BWV515*
10.79	*"So oft ich meine Tabakspfeife," aria (vers in G minor)*	*BWV515a*
10.80	*"Warum betrübst du dich," aria (spur)*	*BWV516*
10.81	*"Wie wohl ist mir," aria (spur)*	*BWV517*
10.82	*"Willst du dein Herz mir schenken" (spur: c by ?Giovannini)*	*BWV518*

5 Sacred Songs (c?, ?spur):

10.83	*1. "Hier lieg ich nun"*	*BWV519*
10.84	*2. "Das walt mein Gott"*	*BWV520*
10.85	*3. "Gott, mein Herz dir Dank zusendet"*	*BWV521*
10.86	*4. "Meine Seele, lass es gehen"*	*BWV522*
10.87	*5. "Ich gnüge mich"*	*BWV523*

10.88	"Quodlibet" (ca1707, Treiber; S, A, T, B & cont, for wedding, inc)	BWV524

* * * * *

BWV = W. Schmieder: "Thematisch-systematisches Verzeichnis der musikalischen Werke von Johann Sebastian Bach." 2., überarbeitete und erweiterte Ausgabe. Breitkopf & Härtel. Wiesbaden, 1990.

BACH, Wilhelm Friedemann
1710–1784

1. ORCHESTRAL WORKS

1.1	Sinfonia in C major (c1733–46; strings)	F63
1.2	Sinfonia in D major (c1746–64; strings & winds; used as: Introduction to church cantata F85)	F64
1.3	Sinfonia in D minor (p1910; 2fl & strings)	F65
1.4	*Sinfonia in D minor, "Ricercata" (ca1800; strings & cont, anon arr of fugues F31/8,5 & F37)*	*F66*
1.5	"5 Sinfonias" (c1733–46): No.1 in F major (strings)	F67
1.6	No.2 in G major (ob, bn & strings)	F68
1.7	No.3 in G major (strings)	F69
1.8	No.4 in A major (ob, bn & strings)	F70
1.9	No.5 in B-flat major (strings)	F71
1.10	*Sinfonia in A minor (c1758, cited Blume)*	

2. CONCERTOS, SOLO INSTR & ORCH

2.1	Harpsichord Concerto in D major (c1733–46; hpd, strings & cont)	F41
2.2	Harpsichord Concerto in E-flat major (ca1750; hpd, strings & cont, inc; r as: Introd to cantata F88)	F42
2.3	Harpsichord Concerto in E minor (c before ?1767; hpd, strings & cont)	F43
2.4	Harpsichord Concerto in F minor (c1733–46; hpd, strings & cont)	F44
2.5	Harpsichord Concerto in A minor (c?; hpd, strings & cont)	F45
2.6	Double Harpsichord Concerto in E-flat major (p1894; 2hpd, strings, hns, timp & tpts)	F46
2.7	*Concerto in F minor (cited Kast)*	
2.8	*Concerto in G minor (?spur)*	
2.9	*Concerto in C minor (spur)*	
2.10	*Organ Concerto in D minor (spur: = J. S. Bach, BWV596: arr of Vivaldi, Op.3/11, RV565)*	

3. CHAMBER MUSIC

3 insts:

3.1	4 "Trio Sonatas" (c before ?1762; 2fl & cont): No.1 in D major	F47
3.2	No.2 in D major	F48
3.3	*No.3 in A minor (frag)*	
3.4	No.4 in B-flat major	F49
3.5	Trio Sonata in B-flat major (2vn & cont)	F50
3.6	*"Sonata," in G major (2fl & va, spur)*	
3.7	*"Sonata," in C major (2fl & cont, spur)*	
3.8	*"Sonata," in F major (vn/fl & hpd or vn, fl & cont, spur)*	

2 insts:

3.9	*"3 Sonatas" (p1761; fl & cont, lost): No.1 in F major*	*F51*
3.10	*No.2 in A minor*	*F52*
3.11	*No.3 in D major*	*F53*
3.12	"6 Duets" (2fl): No.1 in E minor (c1733–46)	F54
3.13	No.2 in E-flat major (c1733–46)	F55
3.14	No.3 in E-flat major (c after 1770)	F56
3.15	No.4 in F major (c1733–46)	F57
3.16	No.5 in F minor (c after 1770)	F58
3.17	No.6 in G major (c1733–46)	F59
3.18	"3 Duets" (c after 1770; 2va): No.1 in C major	F60
3.19	No.2 in G major	F61
3.20	No.3 in G minor	F62
3.21	*"Trio," in B major (vn & hpd, ?spur)*	
3.22	*"Trio," in C minor (va & hpd, ?spur)*	

4. KEYBOARD (hpd)

4.1	Keyboard Sonata in C major (ca1745; 2 vers)	F1
4.2	Keyboard Sonata in C major (ca1778; 2nd & 3rd movts r in No.2 of: 10 Fantasias, F15)	F2
4.3	Keyboard Sonata in D major (p1745, No.1 of intended: Sei sonate)	F3
4.4	Keyboard Sonata in D major (ca1778)	F4
4.5	"Sonate pour le clavecin," in E-flat major (p1748)	F5
4.6	"4 Keyboard Sonatas" (c by 1745): No.1 in F major (3 vers)	F6
4.7	No.2 in G major	F7
4.8	No.3 in A major	F8
4.9	No.4 in B-flat major	F9
4.10	*Keyboard Sonata in D major (2kbd; lost)*	*F11*
4.11	*"6 Keyboard Sonatas" (cited Kast)*	
4.12	"12 Polonaises" (ca1765): No.1 in C major	F12
4.13	No.2 in C minor	
4.14	No.3 in D major	

5.8   "7 Chorale preludes": No.1 "Nun kommt der Heiden Heiland" F38/1
5.9   No.2 "Christe, der du bist Tag und Licht"
5.10   No.3 "Jesu, meine Freude"
5.11   No.4 "Durch Adams Fall ist ganz verderbt"
5.12   No.5 "Was mein Gott will"
5.13   No.6 "Wir Christenleut"
5.14   No.7 "Wir danken dir, Herr Jesu Christ"
5.15   Trio, on: "Allein Gott in der Höh sei Ehr" F38/2
5.16   "Canons & studies" F39

6. CHURCH MUSIC

Masses & mass sections:

6.1   "Deutsche Messe" (Kyrie & Agnus Dei) F98
6.2   "Amen—Halleluja" F99
6.3   *"Kyrie" (?spur)* *F100*

Church cantatas (c1746–64; 4vv & insts):

6.4   "Wer mich liebet" (c1746) F72
6.5   "Der Herr zu deiner Rechten" (c1747) F73
6.6   "Wir sind Gottes Werke" (c1748) F74
6.7   "Gott fähret auf" (c1748) F75
6.8   "Wohl dem, wohl dem, der den Herren fürchtet" F76
6.9   "Vergnügte Ruh" (part parody of J. S. Bach, BWV170 & BWV147) F77
6.10   "Heilig und Alle Lande" F78
6.11   "Lasset uns ablegen" (c1749) F80
6.12   "Der Herr wird mit Gerechtigkeit richten" (c before 1756) F81
6.13   "Ihr Lichter jener schönen Höhn" (Wie schön leucht uns) (part parody) F82
6.14   "Erzittert und fallet" F83
6.15   "Dienet dem Herrn mit Freuden" (c1755, Psalm 100) F84
6.16   "Diess ist der Tag, da Jesu Leidenskraft" F85
6.17   "Der Höchste erhöret" (c1756, part parody) F86
6.18   "Verhängnis, Dein Wüten" (c after 1756, part parody) F87
6.19   "Ertönet, ihr seligen Völker" (part parody) F88
6.20   "Es ist eine Stimme eines Predigers" F89
6.21   "Wo geht die Lebensreise hin" F91
6.22   "O Wunder, wer kann dieses fassen," Christmas cantata F92
6.23   "Ach, dass du den Himmel zerreissest," Christmas cantata F93
6.24   "Heraus, verblendeter Hochmut" (part parody) F96
6.25   *"Blast Lärmen, ihr Feinde" I (music lost, ?borrowed from J. S. Bach's cantata BWV205a)* *F101*
6.26   *"Blast Lärmen, ihr Feinde" II (music lost)* *F102*
6.27   *"Ja, Ja! Es hat mein Gott" (music lost)* *F103*
6.28   *"Halleluja, wohl diesem Volk" (music lost)* *F104*
6.29   *"Viele sind berufen" (music lost)* *F105*
6.30   *"Wertes Zion, sei getrost" (music lost, ?spur: c by ?J. S. Bach)* ....
6.31   *"Lobe den Herrn in seinem Heiligtum" (music lost, ?spur: from J. S. Bach)* ....
6.32   *"Gott is unsre Zuversicht und Stärke" (music lost, ?spur: from J. S. Bach)* ....
6.33   *"Man singet mit Freuden" (c1756, music lost, parody of J. S. Bach's cantata BWV149, cited Blume)* ...
6.34   *"Es ist das Heil uns kommen her" (music lost, parody of J. S. Bach's cantata BWV9, cited Blume)* ....
6.35   *"Gaudete omnes populi" (music lost, part parody of J. S. Bach's cantata BWV80, cited Blume)* ...
6.36   *"Nimm von uns, Herr" (music lost, parody of J. S. Bach's cantata BWV101, cited Blume)* ...
6.37   "Cantata for Easter" (c1747) F96
6.38   *"Jesu, deine Passion" (spur)* ....

7. SECULAR VOCAL

7.1   *"... Gnade finden," aria (frag)* *F79*
7.2   "O Himmel, schöne," cantata (c1758, for birthday of Frederick the Great, part parody) F90
7.3   "Zerbrecht, zerreisst," aria (S, hn & org) F94
7.4   "Auf, Christen, posaunt," cantata (c1763, celebration of the end of 7 Year War, part parody) F95
7.5   "Herz, mein Herz, sei ruhig," Cantilena nuptiarum consolatoria (c1774–84) F97
7.6   *"Lausus und Lydie," opera (c1778–9, Plümicke after Marmontel, lost)* *F106*
7.7   *"Behutsam sei und schweige" (spur)* ....
7.8   *"Kein Hälmlein wächst auf Erden," Lied (Brachvogel, spur)* ....

* * * * *

F=   Falck, M.: "Wilhelm Friedemann Bach. Sein Leben und seine Werke mit thematischem Verzeichnis
     seiner Kompositionen und zwei Bildern." II. Auflage. C. F. Kahnt. Leipzig, 1919.

1. STAGE WORKS

Operas:

1.1   *"The Firebird" (c1864, frag)* ....

Incid music:

1.2   "King Lear" (c1858–61, r1902–5, Shakespeare) (also see incid music c by Debussy L109, Dupré,
Khachaturian & Shostakovich Op.58a, film score c by Shostakovich Op.137): ....
I: . "The Procession"
II: . "Prelude. Lear's evil daughters"
1. "Gloucester"
2. "Kent"
III: . "Prelude"
. "Lear and the clown in the desert"
. "The storm"
IV: . "Prelude"
. "Lear wakes in Cordelia's tent"
6.– 7. "Gloucester and Edgar"
V: . "Prelude"
. "The battle"
. "Lear's death and apotheosis"
1. "The camp near Dover"
2. (scene)
3. "The British camp near Dover"

2. SYMPHONIES

2.1   Symphony No.1 in C major (c1864–6 & 1893–7; arr for 2 pf) ....
2.2   Symphony No.2 in D minor (c1900–8) ....

3. OTHER ORCHESTRAL WORKS

3.1   "Overture on a Spanish March Theme" (c1857, r1886) ....
3.2   "Polonaise-Fantaisie" (c1857, unfin) ....
3.3   "Overture on the Themes of 3 Russian Songs" (c1858, r1881; arr for pf duet) ....
3.4   "Russia" (2nd Overture on Russian Themes), sym poem (c1863–4, r1884) Op.10
3.5   "Overture on Czech Themes" (In Bohemia), sym poem (c1867, r1905) ....
3.6   "Tamara," sym poem (c1867–82) ....
3.7   "Suite," in B minor (c1901–8; compl Lyapunov): No.1 "Préambule" ....
3.8   No.2 "Quasi valse"
3.9   No.3 "Tarantella"
3.10   "Suite" (c1909, on pieces c by Chopin): No.1 "Préambule" (Étude) ....
3.11   No.2 "Mazurka"
3.12   No.3 "Intermezzo" (Nocturne)
3.13   No.4 "Finale" (Scherzo)

4. PIANO CONCERTOS, PIANO & ORCH

4.1   "Grande Fantasie" (c1852, on Russian folksongs) Op.4
4.2   Piano Concerto No.1 (Concerto-movement) in F-sharp minor (c1855–6) Op.1
4.3   Piano Concerto No.2 in E-flat major (c1861–2, r1906–9; compl Lyapunov) ....

5. STRING QUARTETS

5.1   String Quartet, "Quatuor original russe" (c1854–6, unfin) Op.2

6. OTHER CHAMBER MUSIC

6.1   *Septet (c1852; fl, cl, 2vn, va, vc & pf, lost)* ....
6.2   *Octet (c1855–6; fl, ob, hn, 2vn, va, vc & pf, frag)* *Op.3*
6.3   "Romance" (c1856; vc & pf) ....

7. PIANO SONATAS

7.1   Piano Sonata No.1 in B-flat minor (c1855–6, adapted from an early work: Bolshaya Sonata) Op.5
7.2   Piano Sonata in B-flat minor (c1900–5; 2nd movt = 2nd movt of Op.5 also pubd as: Mazurka No.5) ....

8. OTHER PIANO WORKS

Impromptus:

8.1	"Impromptu," in F minor (ca1850–60) ....
8.2	"Impromptu" (c1907, on the themes of 2 Preludes c by Chopin, Op.28/14 & 11) ....

Mazurkas:

8.3	Mazurka No.1 in A-flat major (c1861, r ca1884) ....
8.4	Mazurka No.2 in C-sharp minor (c1861, r ca1884) ....
8.5	Mazurka No.3 in B minor (c1886) ....
8.6	Mazurka No.4 in G-flat major (c1886) ....
8.7	Mazurka No.5 in D major (c1900; orig part of: Piano Sonata in B-flat minor of 1900–5) ....
8.8	Mazurka No.6 in A-flat major (c1902) ....
8.9	Mazurka No.7 in E-flat minor (c1906) ....

Nocturnes:

8.10	Nocturne No.1 in B-flat minor (c1856, r1898) ....
8.11	Nocturne No.2 in B minor (c1901) ....
8.12	Nocturne No.3 in D minor (c1902) ....

Scherzos:

8.13	Scherzo No.1 in B minor (c1856) ....
8.14	Scherzo No.2 in B-flat minor (c1900, uses parts of: Octet, Op.3 & Pf Son No.1 in B-flat minor, Op.5) ....
8.15	Scherzo No.3 in F-sharp major (c1901) ....

Waltzes:

8.16	Waltz No.1 in G major, "Valse di bravura" (c1900) ....
8.17	Waltz No.2 in F minor, "Valse mélancolique" (c1900) ....
8.18	Waltz No.3 in D major, "Valse Impromptu" (c1901) ....
8.19	Waltz No.4 in B-flat major, "Valse de Concert" (c1902) ....
8.20	Waltz No.5 in D-flat major (c1903) ....
8.21	Waltz No.6 in F-sharp minor (c1903–4) ....
8.22	Waltz No.7 in G-sharp minor (c1906) ....

Other:

8.23	"Fantasy" (c1854–5, r1899, on themes from Glinka's opera: Life for the Tsar) ....
8.24	"Fandango-Étude" (c1856) ....
8.25	"Polka," in F-sharp minor (c1859) ....
8.26	"The Lark" (ca1864, r1900, based on Glinka's song) ....
8.27	"Islamey—Oriental Fantasy" (c1869, r1902; orchd) ....
8.28	"Au jardin," in D-flat major (c1884) ....
8.29	"The Wilderness" (c1898, arr of 2. of: 10 Songs of 1895–6) ....
8.30	"Dumka," in E-flat minor (c1900) ....
8.31	"Berceuse," in D-flat major (c1901) ....
8.32	"Gondellied," in A minor (c1901) ....
8.33	"Tarantella," in B major (c1901) ....
8.34	"Spanish Melody," in D-flat major (c1902) ....
8.35	"Spanish Serenade" (c1902, r vers of: Fandango-Étude of 1856) ....
8.36	"Toccata," in C-sharp minor (c1902) ....
8.37	"Tyrolienne," in F-sharp major (c1902) ....
8.38	"Capriccio," in D major (c1902) ....
8.39	"Novellette," in A major (c1906) ....
8.40	"Chant du pêcheur," in B minor (c1903) ....
8.41	"Humoresque," in D major (c1903) ....
8.42	"Phantasiestück," in D-flat major (c1903) ....
8.43	"Rêverie," in F major (c1903) ....
8.44	"La fileuse," in B-flat minor (c1906) ....
8.45	"Esquisses," in G major (c1909) ....

Pf duet:

8.46	"On the Volga" (ca1863) ....
8.47	"Russian Folksongs" (c1898, arr of 6., 8. & 27. of: 30 Songs of the Russian People; transcr for ch) ....
8.48	"Suite" (c1909): No.1 "Polonaise" ....
8.49	No.2 "Little Song without Words"
8.50	No.3 "Scherzo"

9. CHORAL WORKS

9.1   "Song: The yellow leaf trembles" (c begun ca1861, Lermontov; ch; also see 8. of: 10 Songs of 1903–4) ....
9.2   "6 Anthems" (ca1880–90, Bibl; ch): 1. "Rest with the Holy Ones" (Requiem) ....
9.3   2. "From Heaven the prophets"
9.4   3. "Thy soul is regenerated"
9.5   4. "Song of the Cherubim"
9.6   5. "All flesh is silent"
9.7   6. "It is worthy"
9.8   . "Christ is risen" (ca1887, Bibl; fem/child vv) ....
9.9   "Hymn in honour of the Grand Duke of Vladimir G. Vsevolodovich" (c1889, Likhachov; ch & pf) ....
9.10 "Leaving song of the pupils of the Polotsky Girls' College" (c1891, Yasherova; fem ch) ....
9.11 "Hymn in honour of the Empress Maria Fyodorovna" (c1898, Yasherova; fem ch & pf) ....
9.12 "Beneath the shadow of Thy overflowing mercy" (c1899, Likhachov; fem ch) ....
9.13 "The Prayer of the Russians" (c1899, Pushkin; 4 fem vv or fem ch) ....
9.14 "Praise to Almighty God," hymn (c1902, Samochernova; fem ch) ....
9.15 "We sing you a hymn, O dear school," school hymn (c1902, Lebedinsky, fem/child ch) ....
9.16 "Cantata for the unveiling of the Glinka Memorial in St Petersburg" (c1902–4, Glebov; S, ch & orch) ....
9.17 "2nd leaving song of the pupils of the Polotsky Girls' College" (c1908, Bekarevich; fem ch) ....

10. SONGS (w/ pf)

10.1   "3 Forgotten Songs" (c1855): 1. "Thou art so captivating" (Golovinsky) ....
10.2   2. "The link" (Tumansky)
10.3   3. "Spanish song" (Mikhailov)
10.4   "20 Songs" (c1858–65): 1. "Brigand's song" (c1858, Koltsov) ....
10.5   2. "Embrace, kiss" (c1858, Koltsov)
10.6   3. "Barcarolle" (c1858, Arsenev after Heine)
10.7   4. "Cradle song" (c1858, Arsenev; arr for fem/child ch & small orch/pf)
10.8   5. "The bright moon" (c1858, Yatsevich)
10.9   6. "When thou playest, carefree child" (c1858, Vilde)
10.10 7. "The knight" (c1858, Vilde)
10.11 8. "I'm a fine fellow" (c1858, Koltsov)
10.12 9. "My heart is torn" (c1858, Koltsov)
10.13 10. "Come to me" (c1858, Koltsov)
10.14 11. "Selim's song" (c1858, Lermontov)
10.15 12. "Lead me, O night!" (c1859, Maykov)
10.16 13. "Hebrew melody": "My soul is dark" (c1859, Lermontov after Byron) (also see
        Schumann Op.25/15)
10.17 14. "Rapture" (c1859, Koltsov)
10.18 15. "Why?" (c1860, Lermontov)
10.19 16. "Song of the golden fish" (c1860, Lermontov)
10.20 17. "Old man's song" (c1865, Koltsov)
10.21 18. "When I hear thy voice" (c1863, Lermontov)
10.22 19. "Song of Georgia" (c1863, Pushkin; orchd1860s)
10.23 20. "The dream" (c1864, Mikhailov after Heine)
10.24 "10 Songs" (c1895–6): 1. "Over the lake" (Golenishchev-Kutuzov) ....
10.25 2. "The wilderness" (Zhemchuzhnikov; arr for pf 1898)
10.26 3. "The sea does not foam" (Tolstoy)
10.27 4. "When the yellow cornfield waves" (Lermontov)
10.28 5. "I loved him" (Koltsov)
10.29 6. "The pine-tree" (Lermontov after Heine)
10.30 7. "Nachtstück" (Khomiakov)
10.31 8. "The putting-right" (Mey; orchd Lyapunov)
10.32 9. "Mid autumn flowers" (Aksakov)
10.33 10. "The rosy sunset fades" (Kulchinsky)
10.34 "10 Songs" (c1903–4): 1. "Prologue" (Mey; orchd) ....
10.35 2. "The dream" (Lermontov; orchd)
10.36 3. "Starless midnight coldly breathed" (Khomiakov)
10.37 4. "7th November" (Khomiakov)
10.38 5. "I came to thee with greeting" (Fet)
10.39 6. "Look, my friend" (Krasov)
10.40 7. "A whisper, a timid breath" (Fet)
10.41 8. "Song: The yellow leaf trembles" (c begun ca1861, Lermontov, also see Choral works)
10.42 9. "Under the mysterious mask" (Lermontov)
10.43 10. "Sleep!" (Khomiakov)
10.44 "Dawn" (c1909, Khomiakov) ....
10.45 "The rock" (c1909, Lermontov) ....

11. FOLKSONG COLLECTIONS

11.1   "Collection of (40) Russian Folksongs" (c1865–6) ....
11.2   "30 Songs of the Russian People" (c1898; songs 6., 8. & 27. arr for pf duet; arr for ch) ....

12. ARRANGEMENTS OF WORKS OF OTHERS

For orch:

12.1	Chopin: Mazurka No.5 in B-flat major, Op.7/1, B61/1 (arr1885; strings) ....
12.2	Chopin: Piano Concerto No.1 in E minor, Op.11, B53 (reorchd & partly rewritten 1910) ....
12.3	Glinka: "Eastern Dances," from opera: Russlan and Ludmila (arr ca1868) ....
12.4	Lvov: Overture to Undine (orchd1900) ....
12.5	Cui, Dargomizhsky, Glinka, Gussakovsky & Liszt: short works (orchd) ....

For pf:

12.6	Beethoven: "Cavatina," from: Str Qt No.13 in B-flat major, Op.130 (arr1859) ....
12.7	Beethoven: "Allegretto," from 2nd movt of: Str Qt No.11 in F minor, Op.95 (arr1862) ....
12.8	Beethoven: Str Qt No.11 in F minor, Op.95 (arr1862; 2pf) ....
12.9	Berlioz: "Introduction," to: La fuite en Égypte, H128 (arr1864) ....
12.10	Berlioz: "Harold en Italie," Op.16, H68 (arr1876; pf duet) ....
12.11	Chopin: "Romance," from: Pf Conc, Op.11, B53 (arr1905) ....
12.12	Dargomizhsky: 2 excerpts from opera: Rogdana (arr1908; pf duet) ....
12.13	Glinka: "Kamarinskaya," fantasia on 2 Russian folksongs (arr1863; pf duet; arr1902; pf) ....
12.14	Glinka: "Jota aragonesa" (arr1864; pf/pf duet) ....
12.15	Glinka: "Prince Kholmsky," incid music (arr1864; pf duet) ....
12.16	Glinka: "Night in Madrid" (arr1864; pf/pf duet) ....
12.17	Glinka: Quartet in F major (arr1877; pf duet) ....
12.18	Glinka: "Chernomor's (Oriental) March," from opera: Ruslan & Ludmila (arr1890, collab Liszt) ....
12.19	Glinka: "Do not speak," song (arr1903) ....
12.20	Lvov: Overture to Undine (arr1900; pf duet) ....
12.21	Paganini: Violin Caprice, Op.1/3 (arr ca1872) ....
12.22	Taneyev: 2 Valses-Caprices: in A-flat major & D-flat major (arr1900) ....
12.23	Zapolsky: "Rêverie" (arr ca1900) ....

Choral transcriptions:

12.24	Glinka: "Cradle Song" (arr ca1887, Kukolnik) ....
12.25	Chopin: 2 Mazurkas (arr ca1887, Khomyakov): 1. Mazurka No.4 in E-flat minor, Op.6/4, B60/4 ....
12.26	2. Mazurka No.29 in A-flat major, Op.41/4, B126/3
12.27	Glinka: "Venetian Night," song (arr ca1887, Kozlov) ....
12.28	"2 Legends" (arr1902): 1. "Nikita Romanovich" (= 6. of: 30 Songs of the Russian People) ....
12.29	2. "The King's Son from Krakow" (= 8. of: 30 Songs of the Russian People)
12.30	"Oh! my heart" (arr1902, = 27. of: 30 Songs of the Russian People) ....

For 1v & orch/pf:

12.31	Dargomizhsky: "Paladin" (arr ca1860–70) ....
12.32	Glinka: "Bolero" (O my beautiful maid) (arr ca1860–70) ....
12.33	Glinka: "Midnight Review" (arr1860) ....
12.34	Glinka: "Oriental Dances," from opera: Ruslan & Lyudmila (arr1868) ....

For 1v & pf:

12.35	Dargomizhsky: 2 excerpts from opera: Rogdana (arr ca1870–2) ....

* * * * *

1. STAGE WORKS

Operas:

1.1	"The Rose Tree" (c1920, Noble)	
1.2	"Vanessa," 4 acts (c1957, Menotti) Op.32	
1.3	"A Hand of Bridge," chamber opera (9 min) (c1959, Menotti; S, A, T, B & chamber orch) Op.35	
1.4	"Antony and Cleopatra," 3 acts (c1965–6; Zefirelli after Shakespeare) (also see Castelnuovo-Tedesco's overture Op.134) Op.40	

Ballets:

1.5	"Medea" (c1946, Graham; 2 vers): Op.23
	. Version 1: "Serpent heart," 9 sections (c1946, perf1947 as: Cave of the Heart)
	. Version 2: "Medea," 7 sections (r1947; expanded orch, pubd1949, see Orch works)
1.6	"A Blue Rose" (perf1955 as a ballet; orig: Souvenirs, suite for pf duet, Op.28 orchd1953) ....

Incid music:

1.7	"One Day of Spring" (c1935, Kennedy) ....

1a. SELECTIONS FROM STAGE WORKS (Nos. of sections in The Gramophone)

1a.4	"Antony and Cleopatra," opera: Op.40

I: 1. "Prologue: From Alexandria"
 2. "These strong Egyptian fetters"
 3. "I am sick and sullen"
 4. "Orchestral Interlude"
 5. "Ah! Hail, Marcus Antonius!"
 6. "Give me some music"
 7. "The most infectious pestilence upon you!"
 8. "A sister I bequeath you"
 9. "When first she met Mark Antony"
 10. "Where's my serpent of old Nile?"
II: 11. "Contemning Rome, he has done all this"
 12. "Lord Alexas, sweet Alexas"
 13. "Hush, here come the Queen and Antony"
 14. "The night is shiny"
 15a. "Inside the tent"
 15b. "Oh take, oh take those lips away"
 16. "On to our ships"
 17. "Hark! the land bids me tread no more upon it"
 18. "Most kind ambassador"
 19. "Oh, bear me witness"
 20. "O sov'reign mistress of true melancholy"
 21. "Orchestral Interlude"
 22. "The last she spoke"
 23. "Where's Antony?"
III: 24. "O Charmian, I will never go from hence"
 25. "My lord, my lord!" (On the death of Antony)
 26. "The breaking of so great a thing"
 27. "Prelude"
 28. "He words me, girls"
 29. "Here is a rural fellow"
 30. "Give me my robe"
 31. "Death of Cleopatra: She looks like sleep"

2. SYMPHONIES

2.1	Symphony No.1 (in One Movement) (c1935–6) Op.9
2.2	Symphony No.2 (c1944, r1947): Op.19
2.3	. "Night Flight" (2nd movt of Sym No.2, Op.19) Op.19a

3. OTHER ORCHESTRAL WORKS

3.1	"Overture" (c1931–3, to Sheridan: The School for Scandal) Op.5
3.2	"Music for a Scene from Shelley" (c1933) Op.7
3.3	"Adagio for Strings" (c1936, arr from 2nd movt of: Str Qt No.1, Op.11; also see: Agnus Dei): .... (Op.11)
	. Arr Strickland for org 1949
	. Arr Caillet for clarinets 1964
	. Arr O'Reilly for woodwinds 1967
3.4	"Essay for Orchestra" No.1 (c1937) Op.12

3.5	"Essay for Orchestra" No.2 (c1942)	Op.17
3.6	"Commando March" (c1943; milit band)	
3.7	"Funeral march" (c1943, on the Army Air Corps Song)	
3.8	"Medea" (The Cave of the Heart), suite (c1947; 15 insts, vers of ballet): No.1 "Parados"	Op.23
3.9	No.2 "Choros"	
3.10	No.3 "Young Princess dance and Dance of Jason"	
3.11	No.4 "Choros"	
3.12	No.5 "Medea's dance"	
3.13	No.6 "Kanticos Agomas"	
3.14	No.7 "Exodus" (w/ fanfare of tpts)	
3.15	"Medea's Meditation & Dance of Vengeance" (c1955, = Op.23 rescored into 1 continuous movt)	Op.23a
3.16	"Horizon" (c1954)..	
3.17	"Adventure" (c1954)	
3.18	"Prelude & Intermezzo" (c1958, from opera: Vanessa, Op.32)	
3.19	"Die Natali" (Chorale preludes for Christmas) (c1960)	Op.37
3.20	"Fadograph of a Yestern Scene" (c1971, on Joyce's Finnegans Wake)	Op.44
3.21	"Essay for Orchestra" No.3 (c1978)	Op.47

4. CONCERTOS, SOLO INSTR & ORCH

Pf & orch:

4.1	*Piano Concerto (c1930, lost)*	
4.2	Piano Concerto (c1962)	Op.38

Vn & orch:

4.3	Violin Concerto (c1939–40)	Op.14

Other:

4.4	"Capricorn Concerto" (c1944; fl, ob, tpt & strings)	Op.21
4.5	Cello Concerto, in A minor (c1945)	Op.22
4.6	*"Canzonetta" (c1977–8; ob & strings, 1 movt in sketches; orchd Turner 1981)*	*Op.48*

5. STRING QUARTETS

5.1	"Serenade" (c1929; arr for strings 1944)	Op.1
5.2	String Quartet No.1 (c1936; 2nd movt arr as famous: Adagio for Strings, Op.11)	Op.11
5.3	String Quartet No.2 (c1948)	Op.27
5.4	String Quartet (c1949, 2nd movt only)...	

6. OTHER CHAMBER MUSIC

3 or more insts:

6.1	"Commemorative (Wedding) March" (c1941; vn, vc & pf)	
6.2	"Summer Music" (c1955; woodwind qnt)	Op.31
6.3	"Mutations from Bach" (Meditations) (c1967; brass & timp, on plainsong: Christ, Thou Lamb of God)	
6.4	"Variations on Happy Birthday" (c1970; brass & timp, for E. Ormandy's 70th birthday)	

Vn & pf:

6.5	*Violin Sonata (c1928, lost)*	
6.6	Violin Sonata (c1931)	Op.4
6.7	"Canzone" (= 2nd movt of: Pf Conc, Op.38 arr for vn/fl & pf 1961)	Op.38a

Other:

6.8	Cello Sonata (c1932)	Op.6

7. PIANO SONATAS

7.1	Piano Sonata in E-flat minor (c1949)..	Op.26

8. OTHER PIANO WORKS

8.1	"Melody," in F major (c1917)	
8.2	"Sadness" (c1917)	
8.3	"Largo" (c1918)..	

8.4	"War Song" (c1918) ....
8.5	"At Twilight" (c1919) ....
8.6	"Lullaby" (c1919) ....
8.7	"Themes" (ca1923) ....
8.8	"3 Sketches" (c1923–4): No.1 "Love Song" ....
8.9	No.2 "To my Steinway"
8.10	No.3 "Minuet"
8.11	Untitled work (Laughingly and briskly) (ca1924) ....
8.12	"Petite Berceuse" (ca1924) ....
8.13	"Prelude to a Tragic Drama" (c1925) ....
8.14	"Fresh from West Chester" (Some Jazzing): No.1 "Poison Ivy," a Country Dance (c1925) ....
8.15	No.2 "Let's sit it out, I'd rather watch" (c1926)
8.16	"3 Essays" (c1926) ....
8.17	"To Aunt Mamie on her birthday" (c1926) ....
8.18	"Main Street" (ca1926)...
8.19	2- and 3-part fugues (c1927) ....
8.20	"2 Interludes" (Intermezzi) (c1931–2): No.1 "Intermezzo" ....
8.21	No.2 "Interlude II"
8.22	"Excursions" (c1942–4): No.1 "Un poco Allegro" (boogie-woogie style) Op.20
8.23	No.2 "In slow blues tempo"
8.24	No.3 "Allegretto" (Western Song with variations over ostinato harmonies)
8.25	No.4 "Allegro molto" (square dance)
8.26	"Nocturne" (Homage to John Field) (c1959) Op.33
8.27	"After the Concert" (ca1973)...
8.28	"Ballade" (c1977) Op.46

Pf duet:

8.29	"Souvenirs," suite (c1951; arr for pf; orchd1953, used in ballet: A Blue Rose): No.1 "Waltz" Op.28
8.30	No.2 "Schottische"
8.31	No.3 "Pas de deux"
8.32	No.4 "Two-step"
8.33	No.5 "Hesitation Tango"
8.34	No.6 "Galop"

2 Pf:

8.35	"Fantasie" (c1924; 2pf) ....

Carillon:

8.36	"Suite for Carillon" (c1930–1, at the Bok Tower Gardens): No.1 "Legend" ....
8.37	No.2 "Round"
8.38	No.3 "Dirge"
8.39	No.4 "Allegro"
8.40	"5 Pieces for a Singing Tower" (c1931–3) ....

9. ORGAN

9.1	"To Longwood Gardens" (c1925) ....
9.2	"Chorale for a New Organ" (c1926) ....
9.3	"3 Chorale Preludes & Partitas" (c1927) ....
9.4	"Prelude & Fugue," in B minor (c1927)...
9.5	"Wondrous Love," variations on a shape-tone hymn (c1958) Op.34
9.6	"Toccata Festiva" (c1960; org & orch) Op.36

10. CHORAL WORKS

10.1	"Christmas Eve" (c1924; w/ solos)..
10.2	"Motetto on words from the Book of Job" (c1930; 4- & 8-part ch) ....
10.3	"The Virgin Martyrs" (c1935, Gembloux transl Waddell; fem ch) Op.8/1
10.4	"Let down the bars, O Death" (c1936, Dickinson; ch) Op.8/2
10.5	"Mary Ruane" (c1936, Stephens) ....
10.6	"Peggy Mitchell" (c1936, Stephens) ....
10.7	"God's Grandeur" (c1938, Hopkins) ....
10.8	"Agnus Dei" (c1967; ch & org/pf, from: Adagio for Strings, Op.11) .... (Op.11)
10.9	"O the mind, the mind has mountains" (ca1939, Hopkins, unfin) ....
10.10	"Ave Maria" (c1940, after J. Desprez) ....
10.11	"A Stopwatch and an Ordnance Map" (c1940, Spender; m ch, brass & timp)...................... Op.15
10.12	"Reincarnation" (Stephens; ch): 1. "Mary Hynes": "She is the sky of the sun!" (c1937)..... Op.16
10.13	2. "Anthony O'Daly": "Since your limbs were laid out" (c1940)
10.14	3. "The Coolin' ": "Come with me, under my coat" (c1940)
10.15	"Sure on this shining night" (arr for ch & pf 1941 from song Op.13/3) ....

10.16	"Ad bibinum cum me rogaret ad cenam" (c1943, Fortunatus, for C. Engel) ....
10.17	"Long Live Louise and Sidney Homer" (c1944) ....
10.18	"Prayers of Kierkegaard" (c1954; S, A ad lib, T ad lib, ch & orch) Op.30
10.19	"Heaven, Heaven" (arr for ch 1961 from song Op.13/1) ....
10.20	"Chorale for Ascension Day" (c1964) ....
10.21	"Twelfth Night": "No night could be darker than this night" (c1968, Lee) Op.42/1
10.22	"To be sung on the water" (c1968, Bogan)... Op.42/2
10.23	"The Lovers" (c1971, from Neruda's 20 Love Poems; Bar, ch & orch): . "Prelude" (pf) Op.43
10.24	1. "Body of a woman"
10.25	2. "Lithe girl, brown girl"
10.26	3. "In the hot depth of this summer"
10.27	4. "Close your eyes"
10.28	5. "The Fortunate Isles"
10.29	6. "Sometimes"
10.30	7. "We have lost even this twilight"
10.31	8. "Tonight I can write"
10.32	9. "Cemetery of kisses" (from Neruda's A Song of Despair)

11. VOICE & ORCHESTRA

11.1	"Dover Beach": "The sea is calm to-night" (c1931, Arnold; mS/Bar & str qt) (also see Vaughan Williams' 1. of: Fragments in a sketch-book of 1897–1902) Op.3
11.2	"Song for a New House" (c1941, Shakespeare; 1v, fl & pf)..
11.3	"Knoxville: Summer of 1915" (c1947, Agee; S & orch; arr for S & chamber orch 1950) Op.24
11.4	"Andromache's Farewell" (c1962, from Euripides: The Trojan Women; S & orch) Op.39

12. SONGS (w/ pf)

12.1	"Sometime" (c1917) ....
12.2	"Why Not?" (c1917, Parsons) ....
12.3	"In the firelight" (c1918, Field) ....
12.4	"Isabel" (c1919, Whittier) ....
12.5	"Prayer" (c1921, for his mother) ....
12.6	"An old song" (c1921, Kinsley) ....
12.7	"Hunting song" (ca1921, Bennett; w/ cornet) ....
12.8	"Thy Will be done," a sacred solo (ca1922, 3 verses from: The Wanderer; 1v & org)................
12.9	"Mother Goose Rhymes set to music," nursery songs (c1920–3) ....
12.10	"October—Weather" (ca1923, Barber) ....
12.11	"Dere Two Fella Joe" (c1924) ....
12.12	"Minuet" (ca1924; 2vv) ....
12.13	"My Fairyland" (ca1924, Kerlin) ....
12.14	"Summer is Coming" (ca1924, after Tennyson; 3vv) ....
12.15	"2 Poems of the Wind" (c1924, Macleod): 1. "Little children of the wind" ....
12.16	2. "Longing"
12.17	"A Slumber song of the Madonna" (c1925, Noyes; 1v & org)...
12.18	"Fantasy in purple" (c1925, Hughes) ....
12.19	"Lady, when I behold the roses" (c1925, anon) ....
12.20	"La nuit" (c1925, Meurath) ....
12.21	"2 Songs of youth" (c1925): 1. "Never thought that youth would go" (Rittenhouse) ....
12.22	2. "Invocation to youth" (Binyon)
12.23	"An earnest suit to his unkind mistress not to forsake him" (c1926, Wyatt)............................
12.24	"Ask me to rest" (c1926, Teury) ....
12.25	"Au clair de la lune" (c1926) ....
12.26	"Hey Nonny No" (Christ Church MS) (c1926) ....
12.27	"Man" (c1926, Wolfe) ....
12.28	"Music, when soft voices die" (ca1926, Shelley) ....
12.29	"Thy love" (c1926, Browning) ....
12.30	"Watchers" (c1926, Cornwell) ....
12.31	*"Dance" (c1927, Stephens, lost)* ....
12.32	"Mother I cannot mind my wheel" (c1927, Landor)...
12.33	"Only of Thee and me" (ca1927, Untermeyer) ....
12.34	"Rounds for 3 voices" (c1927): 1. "A lament" (Shelley) ....
12.35	2. "To Electra" (Herrick)
12.36	3. "Dirge": "Weep for the World's Wrong" (anon 1350)
12.37	. "Farewell"
12.38	. "Not I" (Stevenson)
12.39	. "Of a rose is Myn song" (anon 1350)
12.40	. "Sunset" (Stevenson)
12.41	. "The Moon" (Shelley)
12.42	. "Sun of the sleepless" (Byron)
12.43	. "The Throstle" (Tennyson)
12.44	. "When day is gone" (Burns)
12.45	. "Late, late, so late" (Tennyson)

12.46   "There's nae lark" (c1927, Swinburne) ....
12.47   "3 Songs": 1. "The Daisies": "In the scented bud of the morning O" (c1927, Stephens) Op.2
12.48   2. "With rue my heart is laden" (c1928, from Housman's A Shropshire Lad) (also see Vaughan
                Williams' 9. of the song cycle: Along the Field)
12.49   3. "Bessie Bobtail": "As down the road she wambled slow" (c1934, Stephens)
12.50   "The shepherd to his love" (c1928, Marlowe) ....
12.51   "The nymph's reply to the shepherd" (c1928, Raleigh) ....
12.52   "The song of Enitharmon over los" (ca1934, W. Blake; inc) ....
12.53   "Love at the door" (c1934, from Meleager, transl Symonds) ....
12.54   "Serenader" (c1934, Dillon) ....
12.55   "Love's caution" (c1935, Davies) ....
12.56   "Night Wanderers" (c1935, Davies) ....
12.57   "Peace" (c1935, from: Bhartorihari, transl More) ....
12.58   "Stopping by woods on a snowy evening" (c1935, Frost) ....
12.59   "Of that so sweet imprisonment" (c1935, Joyce) ....
12.60   "Strings in the earth and air" (c1935, Joyce) ....
12.61   "Who carries corn and crown" (ca1935) ....
12.62   "3 Songs" (from Joyce's Chamber Music): 1. "Rain Has Fallen": "Rain has fallen all the day" (c1935) Op.10
12.63   2. "Sleep Now": "Sleep now, o sleep now, o you unquiet heart!" (c1935)
12.64   3. "I Hear an Army": "I hear an army charging upon the land" (c1936; orchd)
12.65   "Beggar's song" (c1936, Davies) ....
12.66   "In the dark pinewood" (c1937, Joyce) ....
12.67   "4 Songs": 1. "A Nun takes the Veil": "I have desired to go" (c1937, Hopkins) Op.13
12.68   2. "The Secrets of the Old": "I have old women's secrets now" (c1938, Yeats)
12.69   3. "Sure on This Shining Night" (c1938, from Agee's Permit Me Voyage; orchd)
12.70   4. "Nocturne": "Close my darling both your eyes" (c1940, from Prokosch's The Carnival; orchd)
12.71   *"Between Dark and dark" (c1942, Chapin, lost)* ....
12.72   "2 Songs": 1. "The Queen's Face on the Summery Coin" (c1942, Horan) Op.18
12.73   2. "Monks and Raisins" (c1943, Villa; orchd)
12.74   "Nuvoletta" (c1947, from Joyce's Finnegan's Wake) Op.25
12.75   "Mélodies passagères" (c1950–1, Rilke): 1. "Puisque tout passe" Op.27
12.76   2. "Un cygne"
12.77   3. "Tombeau dans un parc"
12.78   4. "Le clocher chante"
12.79   5. "Départ"
12.80   "Hermit Songs" (c1952–3, trad Irish): 1. "At Saint Patrick's Purgatory" Op.29
12.81   2. "Church Bell at Night"
12.82   3. "St Ita's Vsion"
12.83   4. "The Heavenly Banquet"
12.84   5. "The Crucifixion" (from The Speckled Book)
12.85   6. "Sea-snatch"
12.86   7. "Promiscuity"
12.87   8. "The Monk and His Cat": "Pangur, white Pangur"
12.88   9. "The Praises of God": "How foolish the man"
12.89   10. "The Desire for Hermitage"
12.90   "Despite and Still," cycle (c1968): 1. "A Last Song": "A last song, and a very last" (Graves) Op.41
12.91   2. "My Lizard": "My lizard, my lively writher" (Roethke)
12.92   3. "In the Wilderness": "Christ of his gentleness" (Graves)
12.93   4. "Solitary Hotel": "Solitary hotel in mountain pass" (from Joyce's Ulysses)
12.94   5. "Despite and Still": "Have you not read the words in my head" (Graves)
12.95   "3 Songs" (c1972): 1. "Now have I fed and eaten up the rose" (Keller transl Joyce) Op.45
12.96   2. "A Green Lowland of Pianos": "In the evening as far as the eye can see" (Harasymowicz
                transl Miłosz)
12.97   3. "O boundless, boundless evening" (Heym transl Middleton)

* * * * *

1. STAGE WORKS

Operas:

1.1 "A kékszakállú Herceg Vára" (Duke Bluebeard's Castle), 1 act (c1911, r1912 & 1918, Balázs; transcr for 1v & pf) Op.11, Sz48

Ballets:

1.2 "A fából faragott királyfi" (The Wooden Prince), 1 act (c1914–6, Balázs; orchd1917; transl in Eng & Ger; transcr for pf) Op.13, Sz60
1.3 "A csodálatos mandarin" (The Miraculous Mandarin), 1 act pantomime (c1918–9, Lengyel; orchd1923, r1924 & 1926–31) Op.19, Sz73

2. SYMPHONIES

2.1 *Symphony in E-flat major (c1902, in pf extract only; Scherzo in C major orchd)* *DD68*

3. OTHER ORCHESTRAL WORKS

3.1 "Valcer" (c ?1900, = orig 1st & 2nd dance of: 6 Dances for pf, DD60a) DD60b
3.2 "Scherzo," in B-flat major (ca1901) DD65
3.3 "Kossuth," sym poem (c1903; Funeral March arr for pf, DD75b) DD75a
3.4 Suite No.1 (c1905, r ca1920; full orch, 5 movts) Op.3, Sz31
3.5 Suite No.2 (c1905–7, r1920 & 1943; small orch; arr for 2 pf): No.1 "Comodo" Op.4, Sz34
3.6   No.2 "Allegro scherzando"
3.7   No.3 "Andante"
3.8   No.4 "Comodo"
3.9 "Images" (c1910; transcr for pf): No.1 "In full flower" Op.10, Sz46
3.10   No.2 "Village dance"
3.11 "Romanian dance" (c1911, arr of Sz43/1) Sz47a
3.12 "4 Pieces" (c1912; orchd1921): No.1 "Preludio" Op.12, Sz51
3.13   No.2 "Scherzo"
3.14   No.3 "Intermezzo"
3.15   No.4 "Marcia funebre"
3.16 "The Wooden Prince," suite (c1921: 3 dances; r1931–2 as a longer suite) .... (Op.13, Sz60)
3.17 "7 Rumanian Folk Dances" (c1917, arr from Sz56): No.1 "Jocul cu bâta" Sz68
3.18   No.2 "Brâul"
3.19   No.3 "Pe Loc"
3.20   No.4 "Buciumeana"
3.21   No.5 "Poarga Româneasca"
3.22   No.6 "Maruntel" (from Belebyes)
3.23   No.7 "Maruntel" (from Nyagra)
3.24 "The Miraculous Mandarin," concert suite (c1927, from pantomime Op.19, SZ73) .... (Op.19, Sz73)
3.25 "Dance Suite" (c1923, for 50th anniv of merging Pest, Buda & Obuda into the city of Budapest; also for pf): No.1 "Moderato" Sz77
3.26   No.2 "Allegro molto"
3.27   No.3 "Allegro vivace"
3.28   No.4 "Molto tranquillo"
3.29   No.5 "Comodo"
3.30   No.6 "Finale"
3.31 "Rhapsody No.1" (c1928; orig for vn & pf, Sz86) Sz87
3.32 "Rhapsody No.2" (c1928; orig for vn & pf, Sz89) Sz90
3.33 "Transylvanian Dances" (c1931, arr of Sz55): No.1 "Bagpipers" Sz96
3.34   No.2 "Bear dance"
3.35   No.3 "Finale"
3.36 "Hungarian Sketches" (c1931, arr from pf): No.1 "An Evening at the Village" (= Sz39/5) Sz97
3.37   No.2 "Bear dance" (= Sz39/10)
3.38   No.3 "Air" (= Sz45/2)
3.39   No.4 "A bit tipsy" (= Sz47/2)
3.40   No.5 "Dance of the Ürög swineherds" (= Sz42/vol.II/42)
3.41 "Hungarian Peasant Songs" (c1933, arrs): No.1 "Ballade: Tema con variazioni" (= Sz71/6) Sz100
3.42   No.2 "Allegro" (= Sz71/7)
3.43   No.3 "Allegretto" (= Sz71/8)
3.44   No.4 "Allegretto" (= Sz71/9)
3.45   No.5 "L'istesso tempo" (= Sz71/10)
3.46   No.6 "Assai moderato" (= Sz71/11)
3.47   No.7 "Allegretto" (= Sz71/12)
3.48   No.8 "Allegro" (= Sz71/14)
3.49   No.9 "Allegro" (= Sz71/15)
3.50 "Music for Strings, Percussion and Celesta" (c1936) Sz106
3.51 "Divertimento" (c1939; strings) Sz113
3.52 "Concerto for Orchestra" (c1943, r1945; transcr for pf; for pf duet; for 2pf) Sz116

4. CONCERTOS, SOLO INSTR & ORCH

Pf & orch:

4.1	"Rhapsody" (c1904, transcr of Sz26 for pf; 2 vers; transcr for 2 pf)	Op.1, Sz27
4.2	"Scherzo" (Burlesque) (c1904)	Op.2, Sz28
4.3	Piano Concerto No.1 in A major (c1926, r until 1929; transcr for 2pf)	Sz83
4.4	Piano Concerto No.2 in G major (c1930–1; transcr for 2 pf)	Sz95
4.5	Piano Concerto No.3 in E major (c1945, unfin: final 17 bars scored Serly)	Sz119

Vn & orch:

4.6	Violin Concerto No.1 (c1907–8; 1st movt r as Sz37/1; 2nd movt arr for vn & pf)	Sz36
4.7	"2 Portraits": No.1 "One ideal" (c1907–8, = r of 1st movt of: Vn Conc No.1, Sz36)	Op.5, Sz37
4.8	No.2 "One grotesque" (c1911, = Sz38/14)	
4.9	Rhapsody No.1 (c1928, arr of Sz86)	Sz87
4.10	Rhapsody No.2 (c1928, r1944, arr of Sz89)	Sz90
4.11	Violin Concerto No.2 in B minor (c1937–8; transcr for vn & pf)	Sz112

Other:

4.12	Double Piano Concerto (c1940, transcr from: Sonata for 2pf & perc, Sz110)	Sz115
4.13	Viola Concerto (c1945; compl Serly 1949)	Sz120

5. STRING QUARTETS

5.1	*String Quartet in B major (c1896, lost)*	*DD42*
5.2	*String Quartet in C minor (c1896, lost)*	*DD43*
5.3	String Quartet in F major (c1898)	DD52
5.4	"Scherzo" (in sonata form), in B-flat minor (ca1900)	DD58
5.5	String Quartet No.1 (c1908)	Op.7, Sz40
5.6	String Quartet No.2 (c1915–7)	Op.17, Sz67
5.7	String Quartet No.3 (c1927)	Sz85
5.8	String Quartet No.4 (c1928)	Sz91
5.9	String Quartet No.5 (c1934)	Sz102
5.10	String Quartet No.6 (c1939)	Sz114
5.11	*String Quartet No.7 (sketch)*	

6. OTHER CHAMBER MUSIC

3 or more insts:

6.1	*Piano Quintet in C major (c1897, lost)*	*DD46*
6.2	Piano Quartet (in C) (c1898)	DD52
6.3	Quartet in F major (c1898)	DD56
6.4	Piano Quintet (c1903–4, r ?1920)	DD77
6.5	"Sonata" (c1937; 2pf & perc; transcr for 2pf & orch, Sz115)	Sz110
6.6	"Contrasts," 3 pieces (c1938; vn, cl & pf): No.1 "Recruiting dance"	Sz111
6.7	No.2 "Relaxation"	
6.8	No.3 "Fast dance"	

Vn & pf:

6.9	"A Duna folyása" (The Flow of the Danube) (c1894, vn part = arr of Op.20 for pf)	DD20a
6.10	Violin Sonata (c1895)	DD37
6.11	*Violin Sonata (c1897, pf part of 2nd movt in sketch only)*	*DD49*
6.12	"Albumblatt," (Andante) in A major (c1902)	DD70
6.13	Violin Sonata in E minor (c1903)	DD72
6.14	Violin Sonata No.1 (c1921)	Op.21, Sz75
6.15	Violin Sonata No.2 (c1922)	Sz76
6.16	"Rhapsody No.1" (c1928; transcr for vn & orch, Sz87; also for vc & pf, Sz88)	Sz86
6.17	"Rhapsody No.2" (c1928; transcr for vn & orch, Sz90)	Sz89

Other instr & pf:

6.18	"From Gyergyó," 3 Hungarian folksongs (c1907; rec & pf; transcr for pf, Sz35a): No.1 "Rubato"	Sz35
6.19	No.2 "L'istesso tempo"	
6.20	No.3 "Poco vivo"	
6.21	"Rhapsody" (c1928; vc & pf, arr of: Rhapsody No.1, Sz86)	Sz88

2 Vn:

6.22	Duo (Canon) (c1902)	DD69

6.23	"44 Duos" (c1931): I: No.1 "Teasing song"	Sz98
6.24	No.2 "Dance"	
6.25	No.3 "Menuetto"	
6.26	No.4 "Midsummer night song"	
6.27	No.5 "Slovak song," I	
6.28	No.6 "Hungarian song," I	
6.29	No.7 "Romanian song"	
6.30	No.8 "Slovak (Tót) song," II	
6.31	No.9 "Play"	
6.32	No.10 "Ruthenian song"	
6.33	No.11 "Lullaby"	
6.34	No.12 "Hay-harvesting song"	
6.35	No.13 "Wedding song"	
6.36	No.14 "Cushion dance"	
6.37	II: No.15 "Soldier's song"	
6.38	No.16 "Burlesque" (transcr for pf, Sz105)	
6.39	No.17 "Marching song," I	
6.40	No.18 "Marching song," II	
6.41	No.19 "Fairy tale"	
6.42	No.20 "Song"	
6.43	No.21 "New Year's greeting" I	
6.44	No.22 "Mosquito dance"	
6.45	No.23 "Wedding song"	
6.46	No.24 "Gay song"	
6.47	No.25 "Hungarian song"	
6.48	III: No.26 "Teasing song"	
6.49	No.27 "Limping dance"	
6.50	No.28 "Sorrow" (transcr for pf, Sz105)	
6.51	No.29 "New Year's Greeting" II	
6.52	No.30 "New Year's Greeting" III	
6.53	No.31 "New Year's Greeting" IV	
6.54	No.32 "Dance from Maramaros"	
6.55	No.33 "Harvest song"	
6.56	No.34 "Counting song"	
6.57	No.35 "Ruthenian 'kolomejka' "	
6.58	No.36 "Bagpipes" (transcr for pf, Sz105)	
6.59	IV: No.37 "Prelude & canon"	
6.60	No.38 "Romanian whirling dance" (Forgatós) (transcr for pf, Sz105)	
6.61	No.39 "Serbian dance" (Zaplet)	
6.62	No.40 "Wallachian dance"	
6.63	No.41 "Scherzo"	
6.64	No.42 "Arabian song"	
6.65	No.43 "Pizzicato" (transcr for pf, Sz105)	
6.66	No.44 "Transylvanian dance" (Ardeleana)	

Vn solo:

6.67	*Pieces for violin (c1895, lost)*	*DD39*
6.68	*"Fantasia" (c1896, lost)*	*DD40*
6.69	*"Fantasia" (c1896, lost)*	*DD41*
6.70	"Sonata" (c1944)	Sz117

7. PIANO SONATAS

7.1	Piano Sonata (No.1) in G minor (c1894)	DD32
7.2	*Piano Sonata No.2 in F major (c1895, frag, Dille's reconstruction)*	*DD35*
7.3	*Piano Sonata No.3 in C major (c1895, lost)*	*DD38*
7.4	*Piano Sonata (c1898, lost)*	*DD51*
7.5	Piano Sonata (c1926)	Sz80

8. OTHER PIANO WORKS

Early works:

8.1	"Walczer" (c1890)	DD1
8.2	"Variable piece" (c1890)	DD2
8.3	"Mazurka" (c1890)	DD3
8.4	"Budapest Athletic Competition" (c1890)	DD4
8.5	"Sonatina No.1" (c1890)	DD5
8.6	"Romanian piece" (c1890)	DD6
8.7	"Fast polka" (c1891)	DD7
8.8	"Béla," polka (c1891)	DD8
8.9	"Katinka," polka (c1891)	DD9

8.82	No.6 "Hungarian folksong"
8.83	No.7 "Dawn"
8.84	No.8 "Slovakian folksong"
8.85	No.9 "Five-finger exercise"
8.86	No.10 "Bear dance" (orchd, Sz97/2)
8.87	"2 Elegies": No.1 "Grave" (c1908) Op.8b, Sz41
8.88	No.2 "Molto adagio, sempre rubato" (c1909)
8.89	"For Children" (c1908–9, r1945): I (Hungarian): No.1 "Play": "Let's bake something" Sz42
8.90	No.2 "Children's song": "Dawn, o day"
8.91	No.3 "I lost my young couple"
8.92	No.4 "Pillow dance": "I lost my handkerchief"
8.93	No.5 "Play": "Kitty, kitty"
8.94	No.6 "Study for the left hand": "Hey, tulip, tulip"
8.95	No.7 "Play song": "Look for the needle"
8.96	No.8 "Children's game": "Hey, görbénye, görbénye"
8.97	No.9 "Song": "White lily"
8.98	No.10 "Children's dance": "The Wallachians wear wooden shoes"
8.99	No.11 "I lost my young couple"
8.100	No.12 "Chain, chain, floral chain"
8.101	No.13 "Ballad": "A lad was killed"
8.102	No.14 "The poor lads of Csanád"
8.103	No.15 "Teeny-weeny is the street of Istvánd"
8.104	No.16 "Old Hungarian tune": "I never stole in my whole life" (transcr for 1v & pf, Sz109)
8.105	No.17 "Round dance": "My little graceful girl"
8.106	No.18 "Soldier's song": "In the harbor of Nagyvárad"
8.107	No.19 "When I go into the inn at Doboz"
8.108	No.20 "Drinking song"
8.109	No.21 "Allegro robusto"
8.110	II (Hungarian): No.22 "One ought to go to Debrecen"
8.111	No.23 "Dance song": "You must walk this way, that way"
8.112	No.24 "Water, water, water"
8.113	No.25 "Three apples and a half"
8.114	No.26 "Go round, sweetheart, go round"
8.115	No.27 "Allegramente" (Fast)
8.116	No.28 "Fehér László stole a horse"
8.117	No.29 "Oh! Hey! What do you say"
8.118	No.30 "Choral": They brought up the rooster"
8.119	No.31 "Pentatonic tune": "Mother, dear mother"
8.120	No.32 "Jerring song": "The sun shines into the church"
8.121	No.33 "Stars, stars, brightly shine"
8.122	No.34 "White lady's eardrop"
8.123	No.35 "I picked flowers in the garden"
8.124	No.36 "Margitta is not far away"
8.125	No.37 "When I go up Buda's big mountain"
8.126	No.38 "Drunkard song": "Ten litres are inside"
8.127	No.39 "Swine-heard's song": "The cricket marries"
8.128	No.40 "Winter Solstice song": "May the Lord"
8.129	No.41 "Do you go, darling? I should think so"
8.130	No.42 "Swine-herd's dance": "The cricket marries" (orchd, Sz97/5)
8.131	III (Slovakian): No.1 "If there were cherries"
8.132	No.2 "Kite settled on the branch"
8.133	No.3 "Under the tree"
8.134	No.4 "Wedding song": "Hey, Lado, Lado"
8.135	No.5 "Variations": "Flew the peacock, flew"
8.136	No.6 "Rondo," I (Round dance): "There is an old witch"
8.137	No.7 "Sorrow"
8.138	No.8 "Dance song": "Hey, two pigeons sit on the tower of Presov"
8.139	No.9 "Round dance," II: "Unfold yourself, blossom, blossom"
8.140	No.10 "Funeral song": "In the barracks of Mikulás"
8.141	No.11 "On the field of Bystrov"
8.142	No.12 "Mother of my lover"
8.143	No.13 "Anicka Mlynárova"
8.144	No.14 "Plowing, plowing are six oxen"
8.145	No.15 "Bagpipe tune," I: "Dance, maiden, dance"
8.146	No.16 "Lament"
8.147	No.17 "The girl was the priest's maidservant"
8.148	No.18 "Teasing song": "Once I was your lover"
8.149	No.19 "Romance": "Bird on the branch"
8.150	No.20 "Game of tag": "Don't go at dawn, Hanulienka, to the thorny bush"
8.151	No.21 "Pleasantry": "She flew down and was in tears"
8.152	No.22 "Revelry": "The lads caught a goat"
8.153	IV (Slovakian): No.23 "I am already an old shepherd"
8.154	No.24 "I passed through the forest"
8.155	No.25 "Bird on the branch"
8.156	No.26 "Scherzando Allegretto"

8.157	No.27 "Teasing song"
8.158	No.28 "Peasant's flute"
8.159	No.29 "Pleasantry," II
8.160	No.30 "I have wandered a lot"
8.161	No.31 "Canon"
8.162	No.32 "Bagpipe," II: "Little garden, little garden"
8.163	No.33 "The orphan": "Hey forest, forest, green forest"
8.164	No.34 "Romance": "I know a little forest"
8.165	No.35 "The highway robber": "Jánosik is a big bully"
8.166	No.36 "If I knew where my darling mows"
8.167	No.37 "The Danube's bank is green at Bratislava"
8.168	No.38 "Farewell": "I look back upon you once more"
8.169	No.39 "Ballad": "Janko drives out two oxen"
8.170	Nos.40–41 "Rhapsody": "Blow, you summer wind; Hey! What a beautiful house"
8.171	No.42 "Dirge"
8.172	No.43 "Mourning song": "There in the deep valley"
8.173	"2 Rumanian Dances" (c1909–10, r1945): No.1 "Allegro vivace" (orchd, Sz47a) Op.8a, Sz43
8.174	No.2 "Poco allegro"
8.175	"7 Sketches" (c1908–10): No.1 "Portrait of a young girl" Op.9b, Sz44
8.176	No.2 "See-saw, dickory-daw"
8.177	No.3 "Lento"
8.178	No.4 "Non troppo lento"
8.179	No.5 "Romanian folksong"
8.180	No.6 "In Wallachian style"
8.181	No.7 "Poco lento"
8.182	"4 Dirges" (c1909–10): No.1 "Adagio" Op.9a, Sz45
8.183	No.2 "Andante" (orchd, Sz97/3)
8.184	No.3 "Poco lento"
8.185	No.4 "Assai andante"
8.186	"3 Burlesques": No.1 "Quarrel" (c1908) Op.8c, Sz47
8.187	No.2 "A bit tipsy" (c1911; orchd, Sz97/4)
8.188	No.3 "Molto vivo capriccioso" (c1910)
8.189	"Allegro barbaro" (c1911) Sz49
8.190	"Piano Method" (c1913, collab Reschofsky) Sz52
8.191	"The First Term at the Piano" (c1913): No.1 "Moderato" (= Sz52/21) Sz53
8.192	No.2 "Moderato" (= Sz52/22)
8.193	No.3 "Dialogue" (= Sz52/24)
8.194	No.4 "Dialogue" (= Sz52/26)
8.195	No.5 "Moderato" (= Sz52/36)
8.196	No.6 "Moderato" (= Sz52/40)
8.197	No.7 "Folksong" (= Sz52/44)
8.198	No.8 "Andante" (= Sz52/51)
8.199	No.9 "Andante" (= Sz52/59)
8.200	No.10 "Folksong" (= Sz52/68)
8.201	No.11 "Minuet" (= Sz52/89)
8.202	No.12 "Swineherd's dance" (= Sz52/77)
8.203	No.13 "Folksong" (Where have you been little lamb?) (= Sz52/95)
8.204	No.14 "Andante" (= Sz52/105)
8.205	No.15 "Wedding dance" (= Sz52/116)
8.206	No.16 "Peasant dance" (= Sz52/115)
8.207	No.17 "Allegro deciso" (= Sz52/118)
8.208	No.18 "Waltz" (Keringő) (= Sz52/119)
8.209	"Danse orientale" (c ?1913) ....
8.210	"Sonatina" (c1915, on Rumanian folk tunes; orchd, Sz96).. Sz55
8.211	"Romanian Folkdances" (c1915; orchd, Sz68): No.1 "Stick dance" Sz56
8.212	No.2 "Sash dance"
8.213	No.3 "In one spot"
8.214	No.4 "Horn dance"
8.215	No.5 "Romanian polka"
8.216	No.6 "Fast dance"
8.217	"Romanian Christmas Carols" (c1915): Series I: No.1 "Allegro" (Pa cel plai de munte) Sz57
8.218	No.2 "Allegro" (Intreaba si'intreaba)
8.219	No.3 "Allegro" (D-oi roaga sa roaga)
8.220	No.4 "Andante" (Ciucur verde de matasa)
8.221	No.5 "Allegro moderato" (Coborât-o coborât-o)
8.222	No.6 "Andante" (In patru cornuti de lume)
8.223	No.7 "Andante" (La lina fântâna)
8.224	No.8 "Allegretto" (Noi umblam d-a corindare)
8.225	No.9 "Allegro" (Noi acum artacilor)
8.226	No.10 "Piu allegro" (Tri crai dela r asaritu)
8.227	II: No.1 "Molto moderato" (Colo'n jos la munte'n josu)
8.228	No.2 "Moderato" (Deasupra pa r asaritu)
8.229	No.3 "Andante" (Creste-mi Doamne crestiu)
8.230	No.4 "Andante" (Sculati, sculati boieri mari)
8.231	No.5 "Moderato" (Ai, Colo'n josu mai din josu)

8.232	No.6 "Andante" (Si-o luat, luata)
8.233	No.7 "Variante della precedente" (Colo sus, mai susu)
8.234	No.8 "Allegro" (Colo sus pa dupa luna)
8.235	No.9 "Allegretto" (De ce-i domnul bunu)
8.236	No.10 "Allegro" (Hai cu totii sa suimu)
8.237	"Suite" (c1916): No.1 "Allegretto" Op.14, Sz62
8.238	. *"Andante" (withdrawn)*
8.239	No.2 "Scherzo"
8.240	No.3 "Allegro molto"
8.241	No.4 "Sostenuto"
8.242	"Hungarian Folksong" (c ?1914–7 or ?1923; orig: one of the pieces from Sz71)................................. Sz65
8.243	"3 Hungarian Peasant Songs" (ca1914–7, orig: part of Sz71): No.1 "The peacock" Sz66
8.244	No.2 "At the Jánoshida fairground"
8.245	No.3 "White lily"
8.246	"15 Hungarian Peasant Songs" (c1914–8), Old laments: No.1 "Rubato" (Megkötöm lovamat) Sz71
8.247	No.2 "Andante" (Kit virágot rózsám adott)
8.248	No.3 "Poco rubato" (Aj, meg kell a búzának érni)
8.249	No.4 "Andante" (Kék nefelejts ráhajlik a vállamra)
8.250	No.5 "Scherzo" (Feleségem olyan tiszta)
8.251	No.6 "Ballade: Tema con variazioni" (Angoli Borbála) (orchd, Sz100)
8.252	Old dance tunes: No.7 "Allegro" (Arra gyere, amőrre én) (orchd, Sz100)
8.253	No.8 "Allegretto" (Fölmentem a szilvafára) (orchd, Sz100)
8.254	No.9 "Allegretto" (Erre kakas, arra tyúk) (orchd, Sz100)
8.255	No.10 "L'istesso tempo" (Zöld erdöben a prücsök) (orchd, Sz100)
8.256	No.11 "Assai moderato" (Nem vagy legény, nem vagy) (orchd, Sz100)
8.257	No.12 "Allegretto" (Beteg asszony, fáradt legény) (orchd, Sz100)
8.258	No.13 "Poco piu vivo—allegretto" (Sári lovam, a fakó)
8.259	No.14 "Allegro" (Ēsszegyűltek, ēsszegyűltek az izsapi lányok) (orchd, Sz100)
8.260	No.15 "Allegro" (Bagpipe air without words) (orchd, Sz100)
8.261	"3 Studies" (c1918): No.1 "Allegro molto" Op.18, Sz72
8.262	No.2 "Andante sostenuto"
8.263	No.3 "Rubato; Tempo giusto, capriccioso"
8.264	"8 Improvisations on Hungarian Peasant Songs" (c1920): No.1 "Molto moderato"................... Op.20, Sz74
8.265	No.2 "Molto capriccioso"
8.266	No.3 "Lento rubato" (Imhol kerekedik)
8.267	No.4 "Allegretto scherzando" (Kályha vállán az ice)
8.268	No.5 "Allegro molto"
8.269	No.6 "Allegro moderato, molto capriccioso" (Jaj istenem, ezt a vént)
8.270	No.7 "Sostenuto, rubato" (Beli fiam, beli) (ded to the memory of Claude Debussy)
8.271	No.8 "Allegro" (Télen nem jó szántani)
8.272	"Dance Suite" (c1925, red of orch suite, Sz77): No.1 "Moderato" ....(Sz77)
8.273	No.2 "Allegro molto"
8.274	No.3 "Allegro vivace"
8.275	No.4 "Molto tranquillo"
8.276	No.5 "Comodo"
8.277	No.6 "Finale"
8.278	"Out of Doors" (c1926): No.1 "With drums and pipes" Sz81
8.279	No.2 "Barcarolla"
8.280	No.3 "Musettes"
8.281	No.4 "The night music"
8.282	No.5 "The chase"
8.283	"9 Little Pieces" (c1926): I. "Four dialogues": No.1 "Moderato" Sz82
8.284	No.2 "Andante"
8.285	No.3 "Lento"
8.286	No.4 "Allegro vivace"
8.287	II: No.5 "Menuetto"
8.288	No.6 "Air"
8.289	No.7 "Marcia delle bestie"
8.290	No.8 "Tambourine"
8.291	III: No.9 "Preludio—All'ungherese"
8.292	"3 Rondos on Slovak Folktunes": No.1 "Andante" (c1916) Sz84
8.293	No.2 "Vivacissimo" (c1927)
8.294	No.3 "Allegro molto" (c1927)
8.295	"Petite Suite" (c1936, arr of Sz98/28, 38, 43, 16, 36 & 32): No.1 "Slow tune"....................Sz105
8.296	No.2 "Whirling dance"
8.297	No.3 "Quasi pizzicato"
8.298	No.4 "Ruthenian dance"
8.299	No.5 "Bagpipes"
8.300	"Mikrokosmos," progressive pieces (c1926, 1932–39), I: Nos.1–6 "6 unison melodies" Sz107
8.301	No.7 "Dotted notes"
8.302	No.8 "Repetition"
8.303	No.9 "Syncopation"
8.304	No.10 "With alternate hands"
8.305	No.11 "Parallel motion"
8.306	No.12 "Reflection"

8.307		No.13 "Change of position"
8.308		No.14 "Question and answer"
8.309		No.15 "Village song"
8.310		No.16 "Parallel motion and change of position"
8.311		No.17 "Contrary motion"
8.312		Nos.18–21 "4 unison melodies"
8.313		No.22 "Imitation and counterpoint"
8.314		No.23 "Imitation and inversion"
8.315		No.24 "Pastorale"
8.316		No.25 "Imitation and inversion"
8.317		No.26 "Repetition"
8.318		No.27 "Syncopation"
8.319		No.28 "Canon at the octave"
8.320		No.29 "Imitation reflected"
8.321		No.30 "Canon at the lower fifth"
8.322		No.31 "Little dance in canon form"
8.323		No.32 "In Dorian mode"
8.324		No.33 "Slow dance"
8.325		No.34 "In Phrygian mode"
8.326		No.35 "Chorale"
8.327		No.36 "Free canon"
8.328		App. Exercises 1–4
8.329	II:	No.37 "In Lydian mode"
8.330		No.38 "Staccato and legato"
8.331		No.39 "Staccato and legato"
8.332		No.40 "In Yugoslav mode"
8.333		No.41 "Melody with accompaniment"
8.334		No.42 "Accompaniment in broken triads"
8.335		No.43 "In Hungarian style" (2 vers, 2nd for 2 pf)
8.336		No.44 "Contrary motion" (2 pf)
8.337		No.45 "Meditation"
8.338		No.46 "Increasing—diminishing"
8.339		No.47 "Big fair"
8.340		No.48 "In Mixolydian mode"
8.341		No.49 "Crescendo—diminuendo"
8.342		No.50 "Minuetto"
8.343		No.51 "Waves"
8.344		No.52 "Unison divided"
8.345		No.53 "In Transylvanian style"
8.346		No.54 "Chromatic"
8.347		No.55 "Triplets in Lydian mode" (2 pf)
8.348		No.56 "Melody in tenths"
8.349		No.57 "Accents"
8.350		No.58 "In Oriental style"
8.351		No.59 "Major and minor"
8.352		No.60 "Canon with sustained notes"
8.353		No.61 "Pentatonic melody"
8.354		No.62 "Minor sixths in parallel motion"
8.355		No.63 "Buzzing"
8.356		No.64 "Line and point" (2 vers)
8.357		No.65 "Dialogue" (w/ 1v)
8.358		No.66 "Melody divided"
8.359		App. Exercises 5–18
8.360	III:	No.67 "Thirds against a single voice"
8.361		No.68 "Hungarian dance" (2 pf)
8.362		No.69 "Chord study"
8.363		No.70 "Melody against double notes"
8.364		No.71 "Thirds"
8.365		No.72 "Dragons' dance"
8.366		No.73 "Sixths and triads"
8.367		No.74 "Hungarian song" (2 vers, 2nd w/ 1v)
8.368		No.75 "Triplets"
8.369		No.76 "In three parts"
8.370		No.77 "Little study"
8.371		No.78 "Five-tone scale"
8.372		No.79 "Hommage à J. S. B."
8.373		No.80 "Hommage à R. Sch."
8.374		No.81 "Wandering"
8.375		No.82 "Scherzo"
8.376		No.83 "Melody with interruptions"
8.377		No.84 "Merriment"
8.378		No.85 "Broken chords"
8.379		No.86 "Two major pentachords"
8.380		No.87 "Variations"
8.381		No.88 "Duet for pipes"

8.382	No.89 "In four parts"
8.383	No.90 "In Russian style"
8.384	No.91 "Chromatic invention" I
8.385	No.92 "Chromatic invention" II
8.386	No.93 "In four parts"
8.387	No.94 "Tale"
8.388	No.95 "Song of the fox" (2 vers, 2nd w/ 1v)
8.389	No.96 "Stumblings"
8.390	App. Exercises 19–31
8.391	IV: No.97 "Notturno"
8.392	No.98 "Thumb under"
8.393	No.99 "Crossed hands"
8.394	No.100 "In the style of a folksong"
8.395	No.101 "Diminished fifth"
8.396	No.102 "Harmonics"
8.397	No.103 "Minor and major"
8.398	No.104 "Through the keys" (2 vers)
8.399	No.105 "Playsong"
8.400	No.106 "Children's song"
8.401	No.107 "Melody in the mist"
8.402	No.108 "Wrestling"
8.403	No.109 "From the Island of Bali"
8.404	No.110 "Clashing sounds"
8.405	No.111 "Intermezzo"
8.406	No.112 "Variations on a folk tune"
8.407	No.113 "Bulgarian rhythm" I
8.408	No.114 "Theme and inversion"
8.409	No.115 "Bulgarian rhythm" II
8.410	No.116 "Melody"
8.411	No.117 "Bourree"
8.412	No.118 "Triplets in 9-8 time"
8.413	No.119 "Dance in 3-4 time"
8.414	No.120 "Fifth chords"
8.415	No.121 "Two-part study"
8.416	App. Exercises 32–33
8.417	V: No.122 "Chords together and opposed"
8.418	No.123 "Staccato and legato" (2 vers)
8.419	No.124 "Staccato"
8.420	No.125 "Boating"
8.421	No.126 "Change of time"
8.422	No.127 "New Hungarian folk-song" (w/ 1v)
8.423	No.128 "Peasant dance"
8.424	No.129 "Alternating thirds"
8.425	No.130 "Village joke"
8.426	No.131 "Fourths"
8.427	No.132 "Major seconds broken and together"
8.428	No.133 "Syncopation"
8.429	No.134 "Studies in double notes" (1–3)
8.430	No.135 "Perpetuum mobile"
8.431	No.136 "Whole-tone scale"
8.432	No.137 "Unison"
8.433	No.138 "Bagpipe"
8.434	No.139 "Merry Andrew"
8.435	VI: No.140 "Free variations"
8.436	No.141 "Subject and reflection"
8.437	No.142 "From the diary of a fly"
8.438	No.143 "Divided arpeggios"
8.439	No.144 "Minor seconds, major sevenths"
8.440	No.145 "Chromatic invention" (2 vers, playable on 2 pf)
8.441	No.146 "Ostinato"
8.442	No.147 "March"
8.443	Nos.148–153 "6 dances in Bulgarian rhythm"

2 Pf:

8.444	"7 pieces from Mikrokosmos" (arr1940): No.1 "Bulgarian rhythm" (= Sz107/113) Sz108
8.445	No.2 "Chord study" (= Sz107/69)
8.446	No.3 "Perpetuum mobile" (= Sz107/135)
8.447	No.4 "Canon and inversion" (= Sz107/123)
8.448	No.5 "New Hungarian folk-song" (= Sz107/127)
8.449	No.6 "Chromatic invention" (= Sz107/145)
8.450	No.7 "Ostinato" (= Sz107/146)
8.451	"Suite for 2 Pianos" (c1941, free transcr of orch work: Suite No.2, Op.4, Sz34) Op.4b, Sz115a
8.452	Cadenzas for Mozart: Double Piano Concerto in E-flat major, K365 (c ?1940) Sz121

9. CHORAL WORKS

10. VOICE & ORCHESTRA

| 10.5 | 4. "Complaint" |
| 10.6 | 5. "Humorous song" |

11. SONGS (w/ pf)

11.1	"3 Songs" (c1898): 1. "Im wunderschönen Monat Mai" (Heine) DD54
11.2	2. "Nacht am Rheine" (Siebel)
11.3	3. "Die Gletscher leuchten im Mondenlicht"
11.4	6 "Love Songs" (c1900): 1. "Du meine Liebe, du mein Herz" (Goethe).. DD62
11.5	2. "Diese Rose pflück ich hier" (Lenau)
11.6	3. "Du geleitest mich zum Grabe"
11.7	4. "Ich fühle deinen Odem" (Lenau)
11.8	5. "Wie herrlich leuchtet" (Goethe)
11.9	6. "Herr! der du alles wohl gemacht"
11.10	"4 Songs" (c1902, Pósa): 1. "Autumn Breeze" (arr for pf ?1905–7) DD67
11.11	2. "They are accusing me of"
11.12	3. "There is no greater sorrow"
11.13	4. "Oh dear, oh dear"
11.14	"Evening" (c ?1903, Harsányi) DD73
11.15	*"4 Songs" (c1903, lost)* *DD76*
11.16	"Hungarian Folksongs" (c1904–5): 1. "They have mowed the pasture already" Sz29
11.17	2. "Kiss me, for I have to leave" (arr for pf 1905–7)
11.18	3. "Fehér László stole a horse"
11.19	4. "The horses of Eger are all grey"
11.20	"Székely Folksong": "The red apple has fallen in the mud" (c1905) Sz30
11.21	"To the little 'tót,' " 5 Hungarian children's songs (c1905): 1. "I am sleepy my dear mother".................. Sz32
11.22	2. "Oh, oh, look here"
11.23	3. "The little bird has soft and warm feathers"
11.24	4. "Bim, bam, bim bam, rings the bell"
11.25	5. "The rain is falling on the dry trees"
11.26	"Hungarian Folksongs," I (c1906, r1938; 11.–20. c by Kodály): 1. "I left my fair homeland" Sz33
11.27	2. "I would cross the Tisza in a boat"
11.28	3a. "Fehér László stole a horse"
11.29	3b. "Fehér László stole a horse"
11.30	4a. "Behind the garden of Gyula"
11.31	4b. "Behind the garden of Kertmeg"
11.32	5. "The street is on fire"
11.33	6. "In my window shone the moonlight"
11.34	7. "From the withered branch no rose blooms"
11.35	8. "I walked to the end of the great street in Tarkany"
11.36	9. "Not far from here is Kis Margitta"
11.37	10. "My sweetheart is plowing"
11.38	"Hungarian Folksongs," II (c1906): 1. "On this side of the Tisza, on that side of the Danube" Sz33a
11.39	2. "Woods, valleys, narrow parks"
11.40	3. "The snow is melting"
11.41	4. "Down at the tavern"
11.42	5. "Fehér László stole a horse" (arr for pf, Sz42/II/28)
11.43	6. "My glass is empty"
11.44	7. "This maiden threading beads of glass"
11.45	8. "The young soldier"
11.46	9. "And they still say, Oh, Ah"
11.47	10. "My dear daughter" (arr for pf, Sz42/I/17)
11.48	"2 Hungarian Folksongs" (c ?1906): 1. "My mother's rosebush" Sz33b
11.49	2. "My sweetheart, you are beyond the Málnás woods"
11.50	"4 Slovakian Folksongs" (ca1907): 1. "Roses in the fields" Sz35b
11.51	*2. "Pod lipko, nad lipko" (lost)*
11.52	3. "Dirge"
11.53	4. "The message"
11.54	"9 Rumanian Songs" (c1915; compl Suchoff): 1. "I went off" Sz59
11.55	2. "Ev'ry lad wants me to perish"
11.56	3. "Woe is me"
11.57	4. "See the verdant silken tassel"
11.58	5. "In the village hall"
11.59	6. "While I still lived with my mother"
11.60	7. "You are far away from me"
11.61	8. "Many thoughts have come into mind"
11.62	9. "Those who have bad luck"
11.63	"5 Songs" (c1915–6; orchd Kodály 1962): 1. "Spring: My love" (Gombossy)............................ Op.15, Sz61
11.64	2. "Summer" (Gombossy)
11.65	3. "Night of desire" (Gleiman)
11.66	4. "Winter: In vivid dreams" (?Gombossy)
11.67	5. "Autumn: Here, in the valley" (Gombossy)
11.68	"5 Songs" (c1916, Ady): 1. "Three autumn tears" Op.16, Sz63
11.69	2. "Sounds of autumn"

11.70	3. "My bed calls me"
11.71	4. "Alone with the sea"
11.72	5. "I cannot come to you"
11.73	"Slovakian Folksong": "Tony whirls the spindle" (c ?1916) Sz63a
11.74	"8 Hungarian Folksongs" (c1907–17): 1. "Black is the earth" Sz64
11.75	2. "My God, my God, make the river swell"
11.76	3. "Wives, let me be one of your company"
11.77	4. "So much sorrow lies on my heart"
11.78	5. "If I climb yonder hill"
11.79	6. "They are mending the great forest highway"
11.80	7. "Up to now my work was plowing in the springtime"
11.81	8. "The snow is melting"
11.82	"5 Village Scenes" (Falun) (c1924, Slovakian; 1 fem v & pf): 1. "Hay-making" Sz78
11.83	2. "At the bride's"
11.84	3. "Wedding" (arr for fem ch & small orch, Sz79)
11.85	4. "Lullaby" (arr for fem ch & small orch, Sz79)
11.86	5. "Lads' dance" (arr for fem ch & small orch, Sz79)
11.87	"20 Hungarian Folksongs" (c1929), I. "Sad songs": 1. "In prison" (orchd, Sz101) Sz92
11.88	2. "Old lament" (orchd, Sz101)
11.89	3. "The fugitive"
11.90	4. "Herdsman's song"
11.91	II. "Dancing-songs": 5. "Slow dance"
11.92	6. "Fast dance"
11.93	7. "Swineherd's dance"
11.94	8. "Six-florin dance"
11.95	III. "Diverse songs": 9. "The shepherd"
11.96	10. "Joking song"
11.97	11. "Nuptial serenade" (orchd, Sz101)
11.98	12. "Humorous song" (orchd, Sz101)
11.99	13. "Dialogue song"
11.100	14. "Complaint" (orchd, Sz101)
11.101	15. "Drinking song"
11.102	IV. "New style songs": 16. "Allegro" (Oh, my dear mother)
11.103	17. "Piu allegro" (Ripening cherries)
11.104	18. "Moderato" (Long ago at Doboz fell the snow)
11.105	19. "Allegretto" (Yellow cornstalk)
11.106	20. "Allegro non troppo" (Wheat, wheat)
11.107	Hungarian Folksong (c ?1936, arr of pf work, Sz42/I/16) Sz109
11.108	Ukrainian Folksong: "The husband's grief" (c1945)............................Sz118
11.109	"Ukrainian Folksongs," cycle (c1945, inc): 1. "I was not alone" ....
11.110	2. "I shall not drink the water"
11.111	3. "Not in a ditch, lads"

12. ARRANGEMENTS OF WORKS OF OTHERS

Transcr of Italian kbd music (arr ca1926–8; pf):

12.1	Marcello: Sonata in B-flat major ....
12.2	Rossi: Toccata No.1 in C major ....
12.3	Rossi: Toccata No.2 in A minor ....
12.4	Rossi: "Tre correnti" ....
12.5	Della Ciaia: Sonata in G major: ....
	1. "Toccata"
	2. "Canzone"
	3. "Primo tempo"
	4. "Secondo tempo"
12.6	Frescobaldi: Toccata in G major ....
12.7	Frescobaldi: Fuga in G minor ....
12.8	Zipoli: Pastorale in C major ....

Other:

12.9	Bach, J. S.: Sonata No.6, BWV530 (arr ca1930; pf) ....

Misc:

12.10	Cadenza for Beethoven: Pf Conc No.3 in C minor, Op.37, 1st movt............................
12.11	"Rakoczi March" (arr1896; 2pf) ....
12.12	*Strauss, R.: "Don Quichote," Op.35 (arr1902; vn, 2 frags)* ....
12.13	Beethoven: "Erlkönig," WoO 131 (orchd ca1905) ....
12.14	Zipoli: "Suite" (arr for 2 pf) ....

13. MISC WORKS

* * * * *

Sz =   András Szöllösy: "Bibliographie des oeuvres musicales et écrits musicologiques de Béla Bartók."
(In Szabolcsi, ed.: "Bartók—Sa vie et son oeuvre." 2nd edition. Budapest, 1968.)

DD =   Denis Dille: "Thematisches Verzeichnis der Jugendwerke Béla Bartóks 1890–1904." Budapest:
Akadémiai Kiadó, 1974.

BEACH (née Cheney), Amy Marcy (Mrs. H. H. A. / Mrs. Henry Harris Aubrey)
1867–1944

1. STAGE WORKS

1.1   "Cabildo," 1 act opera (c1932, Stephens; vv, ch, speaker, vn, vc & pf)... Op.149

2. SYMPHONIES

2.1   Symphony in E minor, "Gaelic" (c1894–6) Op.32, B170

3. PIANO CONCERTOS, PIANO & ORCH

3.1   Piano Concerto in C-sharp minor (c1899; arr for 2pf p1900) .... Op.45, B66 & B171

4. STRING QUARTETS

4.1   String Quartet (c1929, in 1 movt, orig issued as Op.79) Op.89, B162

5. OTHER CHAMBER MUSIC

3 or more insts:

5.1   Piano Quintet in F-sharp minor (c1907) Op.67, B160
5.2   "Theme and Variations" (c1916, p1920; fl & str qt) Op.80, B163
5.3   "2 Compositions" (c1921): No.1 "Pastorale" (vc & org) Op.90, B164
5.4   No.2 "The Water Sprites" (fl, vc & pf)
5.5   Piano Trio in A minor (c1938, p1939).. Op.150, B167
5.6   "Pastorale" (p1942; woodwind qnt) Op.151, B168

Vn & pf:

5.7   "Romance" (c1893) Op.23, B156
5.8   Violin Sonata in A minor (c1896, p1899) Op.34, B157
5.9   "3 Compositions" (c1898; arr for vc p1903): No.1 "La captive" Op.40, B158
5.10   No.2 "Berceuse"
5.11   No.3 "Mazurka"
5.12   "Invocation" (p1904; vn, pf/org & vc obbl) Op.55, B159
5.13   "Lento espressivo" (c1920) Op.125, B165
5.14   "Barcarolle" B166

Vc & pf:

5.15   "Dreaming" (arr from No.3 of: 4 Sketches for pf, Op.15, B61) B169

6. PIANO

6.1   Cadenza to Beethoven's Piano Concerto No.3 in C minor, Op.37 (1st movt) (c1888).................. Op.3, B57
6.2   "Valse-caprice" (p1889) Op.4, B58
6.3   "Ballad," in D-flat major (p1894) Op.6, B60
6.4   "4 Sketches" (c1892): No.1 "In Autumn" Op.15, B61
6.5   No.2 "Phantoms"
6.6   No.3 "Dreaming" (arr for vc & pf, B169)
6.7   No.4 "Fireflies"
6.8   "Bal Masque" (p1894; also for orch perf1893) Op.22, B62
6.9   "Children's Carnival" (p1894): No.1 "Promenade" Op.25, B63
6.10   No.2 "Columbine"
6.11   No.3 "Pantalon"
6.12   No.4 "Pierrot and Pierrette"
6.13   No.5 "Secrets"
6.14   No.6 "Harlequin"
6.15   "3 morceaux caractéristiques" (c1894, r1922): No.1 "Barcarolle" Op.28, B64
6.16   No.2 "Menuet italien"
6.17   No.3 "Danse des fleurs"
6.18   "Children's Album" (p1897): No.1 "Minuet" Op.36, B65
6.19   No.2 "Gavotte"
6.20   No.3 "Waltz"
6.21   No.4 "March"
6.22   No.5 "Polka"
6.23   "Transcription for Pianoforte: The Serenade of Richard Strauss" (c1902) B67
6.24   "2 Compositions" (p1903): No.1 "Scottish Legend" Op.54, B68
6.25   No.2 "Gavotte fantastique"
6.26   "Variations on a Balkan Themes" (c1904, p1906, r1936, 1943; arr for orch 1906; 2pf p1937) Op.60, B69

6.27   "4 Characteristic Pieces" (4 Eskimo Pieces) (c1907, reissued 1935, 1943): No.1 "Arctic Night" . Op.64, B70
6.28   No.2 "The Returning Hunter"
6.29   No.3 "Exiles"
6.30   No.4 "With Dog Teams"
6.31   "Les rêves de Columbine" (Suite Française) (c1907): No.1 "La fée de la fontaine" Op.65, B71
6.32   No.2 "Le prince gravieux"
6.33   No.3 "Valse amoureuse"
6.34   No.4 "Sous les étoiles"
6.35   No.5 "Danse d'arlequin"
6.36   "Prelude and Fugue" (p1918) Op.81, B72
6.37   "From Blackbird Hills" (An Omaha Tribal Dance) (p1922) Op.83, B73
6.38   "Fantasia fugata" (p1923) Op.87, B74
6.39   "The Fair Hills of Éiré" (Old Irish Melody) (p1922; also as prelude for org, B59) Op.91, B75
6.40   "2 Pieces" (p1922): No.1 "The Hermit Thrush at Eve" Op.92, B76
6.41   No.2 "The Hermit Thrush at Morn"
6.42   "From Grandmother's Garden" (p1922): No.1 "Morning Glories" Op.97, B77
6.43   No.2 "Heartsease"
6.44   No.3 "Mignonette"
6.45   No.4 "Rosemary and Rue"
6.46   No.5 "Honeysuckle"
6.47   "2 Pieces" (p1924): No.1 "Farewell Summer" Op.102, B78
6.48   No.2 "Dancing Leaves"
6.49   "The Chapel by Moonlight" (p1924) Op.106, B79
6.50   "Nocturne" (p1924) Op.107, B80
6.51   "A Cradle Song of the Lonely Mother" (p1924) Op.108, B81
6.52   "From Olden Times" Op.111
6.53   "By the Still Waters" (p1925) Op.114, B82
6.54   "Tyrolean Valse-fantasie" (p1926) Op.116, B83
6.55   "A Bit of Cairo" (p1928) B84
6.56   "3 Pieces" (p1932): No.1 "Young Birches" Op.128, B85
6.57   No.2 "Scherzino—A Peterborough Chipmunk"
6.58   No.3 "A Humming Bird"
6.59   "Out of the Depths" (p1932) Op.130, B86
6.60   "5 Improvisations" (p1938): No.1 "Lento molto tranquillo" Op.148, B87
6.61   No.2 "Allegretto grazioso delicatezza"
6.62   No.3 "Allegro con delicatezza"
6.63   No.4 "Molto lento e tranquillo"
6.64   No.5 "Largo maestoso"

Pf duet:

6.65   "Summer Dreams" (p1901): No.1 "The Brownies" Op.47, B89
6.66   No.2 "Robin Redbreast"
6.67   No.3 "Twilight"
6.68   No.4 "Katy-dids"
6.69   No.5 "Elfin Tarantelle"
6.70   No.6 "Goodnight"
6.71   "Variations on Balkan Themes" (c1904, transcr from pf work Op.60, B69) B90
6.72   "From Six to Twelve," 6 pieces for children (p1927): No.1 "Sliding on the Ice" Op.119, B92
6.73   No.2 "The First Mayflowers"
6.74   No.3 "Canoeing"
6.75   No.4 "Secrets of the Attic"
6.76   No.5 "A Camp-Fire Ceremonial"
6.77   No.6 "Boy Scouts' March"

2 Pf:

6.78   "Suite for 2 Pianos Founded upon Old Irish Melodies" (p1924, orig lost: Iverniana, Op.70
          perf1910): No.1 "Prelude" Op.104, B91
6.79   No.2 "Old-Time Peasant Dance"
6.80   No.3 "The Ancient Cabin"
6.81   No.4 "Finale"

7. ORGAN

7.1   "Prelude on an Old Folk Tune, The Fair Hills of Éiré" (p1922; also for pf, Op.91, B75; also see B88) B59
7.2   "Prelude on an Old Irish Tune" (r1943 from B59) B88

8. CHORAL WORKS

8.1   Mass in E-flat major (c1890; vv, ch & orch) Op.5, B93
8.2   "O praise the Lord, all ye nations" (p1891, Psalm 117; ch & org) Op.7, B94
8.3   "Choral Responses" (p1891; ch & org): 1. "Nunc dimittis" (Luke ii.29) Op.8, B95

8.4	2. "With prayer and supplication" (Philippians iv.6–7)
8.5	3. "Peace I leave with you" (John iv.27)
8.6	"The Little Brown Bee" (c1891, Eytinge; fem ch) Op.9, B96
8.7	"The Minstrel and the King: Rudolph von Hapsburg" (p1890, Schiller; T, B, m ch & orch) Op.16, B97
8.8	"Festival Jubilate," oratorio (c1891, Psalm 100; ch & orch/pf) Op.17, B98
8.9	"Bethlehem" (p1893, Hugg; ch & org) Op.24, B100
8.10	"Alleluia, Christ is risen" (p1895, after Weisse, Gellert, Scott, Gibbons; ch; w/ vn obbl p1904) . Op.27, B101
8.11	"The Rose of Avon-Town," oratorio (p1896, Mischka; S, A, fem ch & orch) Op.30, B102
8.12	"3 Flower Songs" (p1896, Deland; fem ch & pf): 1. "The Clover" Op.31, B103
8.13	2. "The Yellow Daisy"
8.14	3. "The Bluebell"
8.15	"Teach me thy way" (c1895, Psalm 86.11–12; ch) Op.33, B104
8.16	"Peace on earth" (p1897, Sears; ch & org) Op.38, B105
8.17	"3 Shakespeare Choruses" (p1897; fem ch & pf): 1. "Over hill, over dale" Op.39, B106
8.18	2. "Come unto these yellow sands"
8.19	3. "Through the house give glimmering light"
8.20	"Song of Welcome" (p1898, Blossom; ch & pf) Op.42, B107
8.21	"Far Awa' " (= 4. of: 5 Burns Songs, Op.43, B16 arr for fem ch/ch & pf p1928) B108
8.22	"The year's at the spring" (= 1. of: 3 Browning Songs, Op.44, B17 arr for fem ch & pf p1909) B109
8.23	"Ah, love, but a day" (= 2. of: 3 Browning Songs, Op.44, B17 arr for fem ch/ch & pf p1927) B110
8.24	"Sylvania: a Wedding Cantata" (p1901, Bancroft after Bloem; 2S, A, T, B, ch & pf/orch) Op.46, B111
8.25	"A Song of Liberty" (c1902, Stanton; ch & orch; arr for m ch & pf p1917) Op.49, B112
8.26	"Help us, O God" (p1903, Psalms 79.9, 45.6 & 44.26; 5-part ch, a capella) Op.50, B113
8.27	"Juni" (= 3. of: 4 Songs, Op.51, B19 arr for fem ch/ch & pf p1931) B114
8.28	"A Hymn of Freedom: America" (c1913; r w/ text: O Lord, our God, arise 1931; new ed 1944) Op.52, B115
8.29	"Shena Van" (= 4. of: 4 Songs, Op.56, B20 arr for fem ch/m ch & pf p1917) B116
8.30	"2 Compositions" (p1904, Hughes; fem ch): 1. "Only a Song" Op.57, B117
8.31	2. "One Summer Day"
8.32	"The Sea Fairies," cantata (c1904, Tennyson; S, A, fem ch & pf/orch) Op.59, B118
8.33	"Service in A" (S, A, T, B, ch & org): A. "Te Deum" (p1905) Op.63, B119
8.34	B. "Benedictus" (p1905)
8.35	C. "Jubilate Deo" (p1906)
8.36	D. "Magnificat" (p1906)
8.37	E. "Nunc dimittis" (p1906)
8.38	"The Chambered Nautilius" (c1907, Holmes; S, A, fem ch, orch & org ad lib) Op.66, B120
8.39	"Panama Hymn" (All hail the power of Jesus' name) (p1915, Stafford; ch & orch; arr w/ org/pf) . Op.74, B121
8.40	"4 Canticles" (p1916; ch & org; also listed as Op.78): 1. "Bonum est, confiteri" (Psalm 92.1–4) Op.76, B122
8.41	2. "Deus misereatur" (Psalm 67)
8.42	3. "Cantate Domino" (Psalm 98)
8.43	4. "Benedic, anima mea" (Psalm 103)
8.44	"Thou knowest, Lord" (p1915, Borthwick; T, B, ch & org) Op.77, B123
8.45	"Dusk in June" (p1917, Teasdale; fem ch & pf) Op.82, B124
8.46	"Te Deum in F" (p1922; T, m ch & org) Op.84, B125
8.47	"May Eve" (p1933; ch & pf) Op.86, B126
8.48	"3 School Songs" (p1933; ch) Op.94, B127
8.49	"The Lord is my shepherd" (p1923, Psalm 23; fem ch & org) Op.96, B128
8.50	"Indian Lullaby" (p1895; fem ch, also listed as Op.57/3) B129
8.51	"I will lift up mine eyes," a capella motet (c1932, Psalm 121; SATB groupings of 3, 4 & 5 vv) .. Op.98, B130
8.52	"Peter Pan," cycle (p1923, Andrews; fem ch & pf) Op.101, B131
8.53	"Benedictus es Domine / Benedictus" (c1924, Luke i.67–81; ch) Op.103, B132
8.54	"Let this mind be in you" (p1924, Philippians ii.5–11; S, B, ch & org) Op.105, B133
8.55	"Lord of the worlds above" (p1925, Watts; S, T, B, ch & org) Op.109, B134
8.56	"The Greenwood": "Oh! when 'tis Summer weather ..." (p1925, Bowles; ch) Op.110, B135
8.57	"Around the manger" (p1925, Davis; ch & org/pf, r w/ fem ch p1925, r vers p1929, from
	song Op.115, B38) .... (Op.115), B136
8.58	"The Moonboat" (p1929; ch & pf) Op.118/1, B137
8.59	"Who has seen the wind" (p1930, Rossetti; school ch) Op.118/2
8.60	"Benedicite, omnia opera Domini" (p1928, Daniel iii.56–8; ch & pf) Op.121, B138
8.61	"Communion Responses" (p1928; S, A, T, B, ch & pf) Op.122, B139
8.62	"The Canticle of the Sun" (p1928, St. Francis of Assisi transl Arnold; S, mS, T, B, ch & orch) Op.123, B140
8.63	"2 Compositions" (c1930; ch & pf): 1. "Spirit of Mercy" (anon) Op.125, B141
8.64	2. "Evening Hymn": "The shadows of the evening hours" (arr as song B41; reissued for ch 1939)
8.65	"Sea Fever" (c1931, Masefield; m ch & pf) Op.126/1, B142
8.66	"The Last Prayer" (p1931; m ch & pf) Op.126/2
8.67	"When the last sea is sailed" (p1931, Masegield; m ch) Op.127, B143
8.68	"Drowsy Dream Town" (A Song of Mothers) (p1932, Norwood; S, fem ch & pf) Op.129, B144
8.69	"Christ in the universe," sacred cantata (p1931, Meynell; A, T, ch & org) Op.133, B145
8.70	"Hearken unto me" (p1934, Isaiah 51.1, 3, 43.1–3, 40.28, 31; S, A, T, B, ch & org) Op.139, B146
8.71	"We who sing have walked in glory" (p1934, Bridgman; ch & pf) Op.140, B147
8.72	"O Lord, God of Israel" (c1936, 1 Kings viii.23, 27–30, 34; S, A, B, ch & org)....................... Op.141, B148
8.73	"This morning very early" (p1937, Hills; fem ch & pf) Op.144, B149
8.74	"Agnus Dei" (O Lamb of God) (c1936; fem ch & pf) Op.145, B150
8.75	"Lord of all being" (p1938, Holmes; ch & org) Op.146, B151
8.76	"I will give thanks" (p1939, Psalm 111; S, ch & org).. Op.147, B152
8.77	"Pax nobiscum" (p1944; ch, fem ch, m ch & pf) B153

9. VOICE & ORCHESTRA

9.1	"Jephthah's Daughter," aria (c1902, Mollevaut after Judges XI.38, transl Beach; S & pf/orch; Italian transl Martinez) Op.53, B154
9.2	"Eilende Wolken, Segler der Lüfte" (Wand'ring Clouds) recit & aria (c1891, Schiller; A & orch) ..Op.18, B99

10. DUETS

10.1	"Songs of the Sea" (p1890): 1. "A Canadian Boat Song" (Moore; S, B & pf) Op.10, B52
10.2	2. "The Night Sea" (Spofford; 2S & pf)
10.3	3. "Sea Song" (Channing; 2S & pf)
10.4	"Far awa' " (= 4. of: 5 Burns Songs, Op.43, B16 arr for 2vv & pf p1918) B53
10.5	"Ah, love but a day" (= 2. of: 3 Browning Songs, Op.44, B17 arr for S, T & pf p1917) B54
10.6	"Give me not love" (p1905, Coates; S, T & pf) Op.61, B55
10.7	"Spirit Divine" (p1922, Read; S, T & org) Op.88, B56

11. SONGS (w/ pf)

11.1	"The Rainy Day" (c1880, Longfellow) B1
11.2	"4 Songs" (p1885–7): 1. "With violets" (p1885, Vannah) Op.1, B2
11.3	2. "The four brothers" (p1887, Schiller)
11.4	3. "Jeune fille et jeune fleur" (p1887, Chateaubriand)
11.5	4. "Ariette" (p1886, Shelley)
11.6	"3 Songs" (c1887–1891, Beach): 1. "Twilight" (p1887) Op.2, B3
11.7	2. "When far from her" (p1889)
11.8	3. "Empress of night" (p1891)
11.9	"3 Songs" (p1889–90, Henley): 1. "Dark is the Night": "Out of the night that covers me" (p1890) . Op.11, B4
11.10	2. "The Western Wind": "Bring her again, O western wind" (p1889)
11.11	3. "The Blackbird": "The nightingale has a lyre of gold" (p1889) (also see Delius RTv/25)
11.12	"3 Songs" (p1887, Burns): 1. "Wilt thou be my Dearie?" Op.12, B5
11.13	2. "Ye banks and braes o' bonnie doon"
11.14	3. "My luve is like a red, red rose" (also see Berg's 33. of: 70 Jugendlieder, Schumann Op.27/2 & Weber J302)
11.15	"Hymn of Trust" (p1891, Holmes; r1901 w/ vn obbl) Op.13, B6
11.16	"4 Songs" (c1890): 1. "The Summer Wind" (W. Learned) Op.14, B7
11.17	2. "Le secret" (Resseguier; r vers p1901)
11.18	3. "Sweetheart, sigh no more" (Aldrich; r vers p1901)
11.19	4. "The Trush" (Sill)
11.20	"3 Songs" (c1893): 1. "For me the jasmine buds unfold" (Coates) Op.19, B8
11.21	2. "Ecstasy" (Beach; w/ vn obbl)
11.22	3. "Golden Gates"
11.23	"Across the World: Villanelle" (p1894, E. M. Thomas) Op.20, B9
11.24	"3 Songs" (c1893): 1. "Chanson d'amour" (Hugo) Op.21, B10
11.25	2. "Ecstasy" (Extase / Exaltation) (Hugo)
11.26	3. "Elle et moi" (My Sweetheart and I / Mia Bella) (Bovet)
11.27	"4 Songs" (c1894): 1. "My Star" (Fabbri) Op.26, B11
11.28	2. "Just for this" (Fabbri)
11.29	3. "Spring" (Fabbri)
11.30	4. "Wouldn't that be queer" (Cooley; arr for fem ch & pf p1919)
11.31	"4 Songs" (c1895): 1. "Within thy heart" (Beach) Op.29, B12
11.32	2. "The Wandering Knight's Song": "My ornaments are arms" (anon Spanish transl Lockhart)
11.33	3. "Sleep, little darling" (Spofford)
11.34	4. "Haste, O beloved" (Sparrow)
11.35	"4 Songs" (c1897): 1. "Nachts" (Scherenberg) Op.35, B13
11.36	2. "Allein!" (Heine)
11.37	3. "Nähe des Geliebten" (Goethe)
11.38	4. "Forget-Me-Not" (Beach)
11.39	"3 Shakespeare Songs" (p1897): 1. "O mistress mine" Op.37, B14
11.40	2. "Take, O take those lips away" (also see Castelnuovo-Tedesco Op.24/IV/2 & Vaughan Williams' song of 1925)
11.41	3. "Fairy Lullaby" (arr for fem ch p1907)
11.42	"3 Songs" (p1898): 1. "Anita" (Fabbri) Op.41, B15
11.43	2. "Thy beauty" (Spofford)
11.44	3. "Forgotten" (Fabbri)
11.45	"5 Burns Songs" (p1899): 1. "Dearie" (reissued 1907) Op.43, B16
11.46	2. "Scottish Cradle Song"
11.47	3. "Oh were my love yon lilac fair!"
11.48	4. "Far awa' " (arr for 2S & pf, B53; arr for fem ch & pf, B108)
11.49	5. "My lassie"
11.50	"3 Robert Browning Songs" (p1900): 1. "The year's at the spring" (arr for fem ch & pf, B109) (also see Ives Ky2 & Vaughan Williams' 440. of: The Songs of Praise p1925) Op.44, B17
11.51	2. "Ah, love but a day" (arr for S, T & pf, B54; arr w/ vn obbl p1920)
11.52	3. "I send my heart up to thee, all my heart"

11.53	"4 Songs" (p1902): 1. "Come, ah come!" (Beach) Op.48, B18
11.54	2. "Good Morning" (Lockhart)
11.55	3. "Good Night" (Lockhart)
11.56	4. "Canzonetta" (Sylvestre)
11.57	"4 Songs" (p1903): 1. "Ich sagete nicht" (Wissman) Op.51, B19
11.58	2. "Wir drei" (Eschelbach)
11.59	3. "Juni" (Jansen) (arr for fem ch/ch, B114)
11.60	4. "Je demande à l'oiseau" (Sylvestre)
11.61	"4 Songs" (c1904): 1. "Autumn Song" (Beach) Op.56, B20
11.62	2. "Go not too far" (Coates)
11.63	3. "I know not how to find the spring" (Coates)
11.64	4. "Shena Van" (Black; arr w/ vn obbl p1919; arr for fem ch/m ch & pf, B116)
11.65	"When soul is joined to soul" (p1905, E. Browning) Op.62, B21
11.66	"After" (p1909, Coates) Op.68, B22
11.67	"2 Mother Songs" (p1908): 1. "Baby" (MacDonald) Op.69, B23
11.68	2. "Hush, baby dear" (Hughes)
11.69	"3 Songs" (p1910): 1. "A Prelude" (Beach) Op.71, B24
11.70	2. "O sweet content" (Dekker)
11.71	3. "An Old Love-Story" (Stathem)
11.72	"2 Songs" (p1914): 1. "Ein altes Gebet" (An Old Prayer) Op.72, B25
11.73	2. "Deine Blumen" (Flowers and Fate) (Zacharias)
11.74	"2 Songs" (p1914, Zacharias): 1. "Grossmütterchen" (With Granny) Op.73, B26
11.75	2. "Der Totenkranz" (The Children's Thanks)
11.76	"3 Songs" (p1914): 1. "The Candy Lion" (Brown; p1915 for fem ch) Op.75, B27
11.77	2. "A Thanksgiving Fable"
11.78	3. "Dolladine" (Rands; p1915 for fem ch)
11.79	4. "Prayer of a Tired Child"
11.80	"2 Songs" (p1914): 1. "Separation" (Stoddard) Op.76, B28
11.81	2. "The Lotos Isles" (Tennyson)
11.82	"2 Songs" (p1916): 1. "I" (Fanning) Op.77, B29
11.83	2. "Wind o' the Westland" (Burnett)
11.84	"3 Songs" (p1917): 1. "Meadow-Larks" (Coolbrith) Op.78, B30
11.85	2. "Night Song at Amalfi" (Teasdale)
11.86	3. "In Blossom Time" (Coolbrith)
11.87	"A Song for Little May" (c1922, Miller) ....
11.88	"The Arrow and the Song" (c1922, Longfellow) ....
11.89	"Clouds" (c1922, Sherman) ....
11.90	"In the Twilight" (c1922, Longfellow) Op.85, B31
11.91	"Message" (p1922, Teasdale) Op.93, B32
11.92	"Constant Christmas" (p1922, Brooks; 1v & org; also listed for S, A, ch & org) Op.95, B33
11.93	"4 Songs" (p1923): 1. "When Mama Sings" (Beach) Op.99, B34
11.94	2. "Little Brown-Eyed Laddie" (Greenwood)
11.95	3. "The Moonpath" (Adams)
11.96	4. "The Artless Maid" (Barili)
11.97	"2 Songs" (p1924; w/ vn obbl): 1. "A Mirage" (Ochsner) Op.100, B35
11.98	2. "Stella viatoris" (Nettleton; S, vn, vc & pf)
11.99	"Jesus, my Saviour" (p1925, Elliot) Op.112, B36
11.100	"Mine be the lips!" (p1921, Speyer) Op.113, B37
11.101	"Around the Manger" (p1925, Davis; 1v & pf/org; also choral work B136) Op.115, B38
11.102	"3 Songs" (p1925, Lee): 1. "The Singer" Op.117, B39
11.103	2. "The Host"
11.104	3. "Song in the Hills"
11.105	"Rendevous" (p1928, Speyer; w/ vn obbl) Op.120, B40
11.106	"Springtime" (p1929, Heywood) Op.124, B41
11.107	"On a Hill" (Negro Spiritual) B42
11.108	"Evening Hymn" (arr1934 from choral work Op.125/1, B141) B43
11.109	"Dark Garden" (p1932, Speyer) Op.131, B44
11.110	"I shall be brave" I (c1932, Adams) Op.132, B45
11.111	"To one I love" (p1932) Op.135, B46
11.112	"Fire and Flame" (c1932, Moody) Op.136, B47
11.113	"Baby" (c1932, Quick) Op.137/1
11.114	"May Flowers" (A Song for Mother's Day) (c1932, Moody) Op.137/2, B48
11.115	"I sought the Lord" (p1937, anon; 1v & org) Op.142, B49
11.116	"I shall be brave" II (p1932, Adams, reissue of Op.132) Op.143, B50
11.117	"Though I Take the Wings of Morning" (p1941, Spencer; 1v & org/pf) Op.152, B51
11.118	"The heart that melts" ....
11.119	"The Icicle Lesson" ....
11.120	"If women will not be inclined" ....
11.121	"Time has wings and swiftly flies" ....
11.122	"Whither" (Müller, after Chopin: Etude No.27 in D-flat major, B130/3) ....

* * * * *

B = "Catalog of Music" in Jeanell Wise Brown: "Amy Beach and Her Chamber Music. Biography, Documents, Style." The Scarecrow Press, Inc. Metuchen, N.J., & London, 1994.

1. STAGE WORKS

Operas:

1.1 "Fidelio oder Die eheliche Liebe" (Leonore), 2 acts (p1805, Sonnleithner & Treitschke after
 Bouilly: Léonore ou L'amour conjugal; 2nd vers 1806; 3rd vers 1814) Op.72
1.2 "Germania," Finale of Treitschke's Singspiel: Die gute Nachricht (p1814) .... WoO 94
1.3 "Es ist vollbracht," Finale of Treitschke's Singspiel: Die Ehrenpforten (p1815) .... WoO 97

Ballets:

1.4 "Ritterballet" (c1790–1, Waldstein) .... WoO 1
1.5 "Die Geschöpfe des Prometheus" (The Creatures of Prometheus) (c1800–1, Viganò) Op.43

Incid music:

1.6 "Vestas Feuer" (c1803, Schikaneder, frag: 1st scene only) .... Hess 115
1.7 "Egmont" (c1809–10, Goethe) Op.84
1.8 "Die Ruinen von Athen" (The Ruins of Athens) (c1811, Kotzebue) Op.113
1.9 "König Stephan" (King Stephen) (c1811, Kotzebue) Op.117
1.10 "Tarpeja" (c1813, Kuffner) .... WoO 2
1.11 "Leonore Prohaska" (c1815, Duncker) ....:.. WoO 96
1.12 "Die Weihe des Hauses" (Consecration of the House) (c1822, Meisl, adapt of: Die Ruinen, Op.113) Op.114

1a. SELECTIONS FROM STAGE WORKS

1a.1 "Fidelio oder Die eheliche Liebe" (Leonore), opera (3rd vers): Op.72
 . "Overture" (= Op.72c)
 I: 1. "Jetzt, Schätzchen, jetzt sind wir allein," duet (Marzelline, Jaquino)
 2. "O wär ich schon mit dir vereint," aria (Marzelline)
 3. "Mir ist so wunderbar," quartet (Marzelline, Leonore, Jaquino, Rocco)
 4. "Hat man nicht auch Gold beineben," aria (Rocco)
 5. "Gut Söhnchen gut," trio (Marzelline, Leonore, Rocco)
 6. "Marsch"
 7. "Ha! Ha! Ha! welch ein Augenblick," aria w/ chorus (Pizarro)
 8. "Alter, jetzt hat es Eile!," duet (Pizarro, Rocco)
 9a. "Abscheulicher! Wo eilst du hin?," recit (Leonore)
 9b. "Komm, Hoffnung, lass den letzten Stern," aria (Leonore)
 10. "O welche Lust," finale
 II: 11a. "Gott! welch Dunkel hier!," introduction (Florestan)
 11b. "In des Lebens Frühlingstagen," aria (Florestan)
 12a. "Wie kalt ist es," melodrama (Leonore)
 12b. "Nur hurtig fort, nur frisch gegraben!," duet (Leonore, Rocco)
 13. "Euch werde Lohn," trio (Leonore, Florestan, Rocco)
 14. "Er sterbe!," quartet (Leonore, Florestan, Pizarro, Rocco)
 15. "O namen-, namenlose Freude!," duet (Leonore, Florestan)
 16. "Heil! Heil! Heil sei dem Tag," finale

1a.4 "Ritterballet," ballet: .... WoO 1
 1. "March"
 2. "German Song"
 3. "Hunting Song"
 4. "Love Song," romance
 5. "War Song"
 6. "Drinking song" (Mihi est propositum)
 7. "German Dance"
 8. "Coda"

1a.5 "Die Geschöpfe des Prometheus," ballet: Op.43
 . "Overture"
 . "Introduction" (La tempesta)
 1. "Poco adagio"
 2. "Adagio—Allegro con brio"
 3. "Allegro vivace"
 4. "Maestoso—andante"
 5. "Adagio—andante quasi Allegretto"
 6. "Un poco Adagio—Allegro"
 7. "Grave"
 8. "Allegro con brio"
 9. "Adagio"
 10. "Pastorale. Allegro"
 11. "Andante"
 12. "Solo di Gioja. Maestoso"
 13. "Allegro"

14. "Solo della Cassentini. Andante"
15. "Solo di Vigano. Andantino"
16. "Finale. Allegretto"

1a.7   "Egmont," incid music: Op.84
. "Overture"
1. "Lied": "Die Trommel gerühret!" (Klärchens Lied 1)
2. "Entr'acte I"
3. "Entr'acte II"
4. "Lied": "Freudvoll und leidvoll" (Klärchens Lied 2) (also see Liszt S280 & Schubert D210)
5. "Entr'acte III"
6. "Entr'acte IV"
7. "Clärchen's Tod bezeichnend"
8. "Melodrama": "Süsser Schlaf"
9. "Siegessymphonie"

1a.8   "Die Ruinen von Athen" (The Ruins of Athens), incid music: Op.113
. "Overture"
1. "Tochter des mächtigen Zeus!," chorus
2. "Ohne Verschulden," duet (Ein Grieche, eine Griechin)
3. "Du hasst in deines Ärmels Falten," chorus of dervishes
4. "Turkish March" (theme used in: 6 Variations in D major, Op.76)
5. "Harmonie auf dem Theater," off stage music
6. "Schmückt die Altäre," march & chorus
6a. "Mit reger Freude," recit (Oberpriester)
7. "Wir tragen empfängliche Herzen," chorus & aria w/ chorus
8. "Heil unserm König, Heil!," chorus

1a.9   "König Stephan" (King Stephen), incid music: Op.117
. "Overture"
1. "Ruhend von seinen Taten" (m ch)
2. "Auf dunklem Irrweg" (m ch)
3. "Siegesmarsch"
4. "Wo die Unschuld Blumen streute" (fem ch)
5. "Melodrama I": "Du hast dein Vaterland, dein Fürstenhaus verlassen"
6. "Eine neue strahlende Sonne," chorus
7. "Melodrama II": "Ihr edlen Ungarn"
8. "Geistliche Marsch, Chorus & Melodrama": "Heil unserm Könige!"
9. "Final Chorus": "Heil unserm Enkeln!"

1a.10   "Tarpeja," incid music: .... WoO 2
. "Triumphmarsch"
. "Introduction to Act II"

1a.11   "Leonore Prohaska," incid music: .... WoO 96
1. "Krieger-Chor": "Wir bauen und sterben"
2. "Es blüht eine Blume im Garten," romance
3. "Melodrama"
4. "Funeral March"

1a.12   "Die Weihe des Hauses," incid music: Op.114
. "Overture" (= Op.124)
. "March," in E-flat major (arr from: Die Ruinen von Athen, Op.113)
. "Wo sich die Pulse," chorus .... WoO 98

2. SYMPHONIES

2.1   Symphony No.1 in C major (c1799–1800, sketches 1795) Op.21
2.2   Symphony No.2 in D major (c1801–2) Op.36
2.3   Symphony No.3 in E-flat major, "Eroica" (c1803; also see No.7 of: 12 Contredances, WoO 14) Op.55
2.4   Symphony No.4 in B-flat major (c1806–7) Op.60
2.5   Symphony No.5 in C minor, "Fate" (c1806–8, sketches 1804) Op.67
2.6   Symphony No.6 in F major, "Pastoral" (c1808): Op.68
1. "Awakening of cheerful feelings on arriving in the country"
2. "Scene by the brook"
3. "Jolly gathering of country folk"
4. "Thunderstorm"
5. "Shepherd's song and thankful feelings after the storm"
2.7   "Wellingtons Sieg" (Wellington's Victory) / "Die Schlacht bei Vittoria" (The Battle of Vittoria) (c1813) Op.91
2.8   Symphony No.7 in A major (c1811–2) Op.92
2.9   Symphony No.8 in F major (c1811–2) Op.93
2.10   Symphony No.9 in D minor, "Choral" (c1822–4, 4th movt's chorus from Schiller's An die Freude (Ode
        to Joy): 'O Freunde, nicht diese Töne!'; S, A, T, B, ch & orch, adopted as EC Anthem) (also see
        Schubert Op.posth 111/1, D189 & Tchaikovsky's cantata: Ode to Joy) Op.125
2.11   Symphony "No.10," in E-flat major (1st movt sketches 1812–25; realized/compl Cooper 1988) ....

3. OVERTURES

3.1	"The Creatures of Prometheus" (c1800–1, for ballet Op.43)	(Op.43)
3.2	"Coriolan," in C minor (c1807, for Collin's play: Coriolan)	Op.62
3.3	"Leonore No.2" (p1804–5, intended for opera: Fidelio, Op.72)	Op.72a
3.4	"Leonore No.3," in C major (p1805–6, p1827, intended for opera: Fidelio, Op.72)	Op.72b
3.5	"Fidelio" (p1814, for opera: Fidelio, Op.72)	Op.72c
3.6	"Egmont" (c1809–10, for incid music Op.84)	(Op.84)
3.7	"The Ruins of Athens" (c1811, for incid music Op.113)	(Op.113)
3.8	"Namensfeier" (Name-Day of Kaiser Franz), in C major (c1814–5)	Op.115
3.9	"King Stephen" (c1811, for incid music Op.117)	(Op.117)
3.10	"Consecration of the House" (c1822, for incid music Op.114)	Op.124
3.11	"Leonore No.1," in C major (c1807, intended for Prague production of opera: Fidelio, Op.72)	Op.138

4. OTHER ORCHESTRAL WORKS

4.1	"Gratulations-Menuet," in E-flat major (c1822)	WoO 3
4.2	"12 Minuets" (c1795): No.1 in D major	WoO 7
4.3	No.2 in B-flat major	
4.4	No.3 in G major	
4.5	No.4 in E-flat major	
4.6	No.5 in C major	
4.7	No.6 in A major	
4.8	No.7 in D major	
4.9	No.8 in B-flat major	
4.10	No.9 in G major	
4.11	No.10 in E-flat major	
4.12	No.11 in C major	
4.13	No.12 in F major	
4.14	"12 German Dances" (c1795): No.1 in C major	WoO 8
4.15	No.2 in A major	
4.16	No.3 in F major	
4.17	No.4 in B-flat major	
4.18	No.5 in E-flat major	
4.19	No.6 in G major (w/ Trio)	
4.20	No.7 in C major	
4.21	No.8 in A major (w/ Trio)	
4.22	No.9 in F major (w/ Trio)	
4.23	No.10 in D major (w/ Trio)	
4.24	No.11 in G major	
4.25	No.12 in C major	
4.26	*"12 Minuets" (c1799, ?spur)*	*WoO 12*
4.27	*"12 German Dances" (lost; see pf vers WoO 13)*	*WoO 13*
4.28	"12 Contredances" (c1800–2): No.1 in C major	WoO 14
4.29	No.2 in A major	
4.30	No.3 in D major	
4.31	No.4 in B-flat major	
4.32	No.5 in E-flat major	
4.33	No.6 in C major	
4.34	No.7 in E-flat major (used in Finale of: Creatures, Op.43 & Sym No.3 in E-flat maj, 'Eroica,' Op.55)	
4.35	No.8 in C major	
4.36	No.9 in A major	
4.37	No.10 in C major	
4.38	No.11 in G major	
4.39	No.12 in E-flat major	
4.40	*"12 Ecossaises" (c1807, spur)*	*WoO 16*
4.41	*11 "Mödlinger Tänze" (c1819; 2cl, 2hn, 2vn & d bass, spur)*	*WoO 17*

Wind band:

4.42	"March," in F major, "Für die böhmische Landwehr" (c1809, Trio added 1823)	WoO 18
4.43	"March," in F major (c1810, Trio added 1823)	WoO 19
4.44	"March," in C major (c before 1823, w/ Trio)	WoO 20
4.45	"Polonaise," in D major (c1810)	WoO 21
4.46	"Ecossaise," in D major (c1810)	WoO 22
4.47	"Ecossaise," in G major (c ?1810)	WoO 23
4.48	"March," in D major (c1816)	WoO 24
	"March," in B-flat major (listed in chamber w/ out pf WoO 29)	WoO 29

5. CONCERTOS, SOLO INSTR & ORCH

Pf & orch:

5.1	Piano Concerto in E-flat major (c1784, pf part only)	WoO 4
5.2	Piano Concerto No.1 in C major (c ?1798, r ?1800)	Op.15
5.3	Piano Concerto No.2 in B-flat major (c1793, r1794–5 & 1798)	Op.19
5.4	"Rondo," in B-flat minor (c before 1794; orig Finale of Op.19; solo part compl Czerny)	WoO 6
5.5	Piano Concerto No.3 in C minor (c1800, r until 1803)	Op.37
5.6	Piano Concerto No.4 in G major (c1805–6)	Op.58
5.7	Transcription of Vn Concerto in D major, Op.61 as Piano Concerto (c1807, cadenzas ?1809)	Op.61a
5.8	Piano Concerto No.5 in E-flat major, "Emperor" (c1809)	Op.73

Vn & orch:

5.9	"Allegro con brio," in C major (ca1790–2, frag of Vn Conc)	WoO 5
5.10	Romance No.1 in G major (c ?1801–2)	Op.40
5.11	Romance No.2 in F major (c ?1798)	Op.50
5.12	Violin Concerto in D major (c1806)	Op.61

Other:

5.13	*Oboe Concerto in F major (c ?1792–3, lost)*	*Hess 12*
5.14	*"Romance," in E minor (c1786; pf, fl, bn & orch, frag)*	*Hess 13*
5.15	"Triple Concerto," in C major (c1803–4; pf, vn, vc & orch)	Op.56

6. STRING QUARTETS

6.1	"Minuet," in A-flat major (ca1790; also for pf)	Hess 33
6.2	String Quartet in F major (c1801–2, arr of: Pf Sonata No.9 in E major, Op.14/1)	Hess 34

The "early" string quartets (c1798–1800):

6.3	String Quartet No.1 in F major	Op.18/1
6.4	String Quartet No.2 in G major, "Compliments"	Op.18/2
6.5	String Quartet No.3 in D major	Op.18/3
6.6	String Quartet No.4 in C minor	Op.18/4
6.7	String Quartet No.5 in A major	Op.18/5
6.8	String Quartet No.6 in B-flat major	Op.18/6

The "middle period" string quartets:

6.9	String Quartet No.7 in F major, "Rasumovsky 1" (c1805–6)	Op.59/1
6.10	String Quartet No.8 in E minor, "Rasumovsky 2" (c1805–6):	Op.59/2
	quoted: Russian peasant song 'Near the dish'—used in folk divination ceremonies) (also quoted Rimsky-Korsakov in: Be Praised, Op.21 & Musorgsky in the Prologue to opera: Boris Godunov)	
6.11	String Quartet No.9 in C major, "Hero" / "Rasumovsky 3" (c1805–6)	Op.59/3
6.12	String Quartet No.10 in E-flat major, "Harp" (c1809)	Op.74
6.13	String Quartet No.11 in F minor, "Serioso" (c1810)	Op.95

The "late" string quartets:

6.14	String Quartet No.12 in E-flat major (c1823–4)	Op.127
6.15	String Quartet No.13 in B-flat major, "Leib" (c1825, new Finale c1826)	Op.130
6.16	"Grosse Fuge," in B-flat major (c1825; orig Finale of: Str Qt in B-flat major, Op.130)	Op.133
6.17	String Quartet No.14 in C-sharp minor (c1826)	Op.131
6.18	String Quartet No.15 in A minor, "Heiliger Dankgesang" (c1825)	Op.132
6.19	String Quartet No.16 in F major (c1826)	Op.135

7. CHAMBER MUSIC WITHOUT PIANO

8 insts:

7.1	Octet in E-flat major (c ?1792–3; 2ob, 2cl, 2hn & 2bn)	Op.103
7.2	"Rondino," in E-flat major (c1793; 2ob, 2cl, 2hn & 2bn)	WoO 25

7 insts:

7.3	Septet in E-flat major (c1799–1800; cl, hn, bn & vn, va, vc & d bass)	Op.20

6 insts:

7.4	Sextet in E-flat major (c1796; 2cl, 2hn & 2bn)	Op.71

7.5	Sextet in E-flat major (c ?1795; 2hn & str qt)	Op.81b
7.6	"March," in B-flat major (c1798; 2cl, 2hn & 2bn; also pf vers)	WoO 29

String Quintets:

7.7	String Quintet in E-flat major (c1795, after: Wind Octet in E-flat major, Op.103)	Op.4
7.8	String Quintet in C major, "Storm" (c1801; 2vn, 2va & vc)	Op.29
7.9	String Quintet in C minor (c1817, arr of: Pf Trio in C minor, Op.1/3)	Op.104
7.10	"Fugue," in D major (c1817)	Op.137
7.11	"Prelude," in D minor (c ?1817)	Hess 40
7.12	*String Quintet in C major (c1826, frag: only in pf transcr as: The Last Musical Thought, WoO 62)*	*Hess 41*

Other 5 insts:

7.13	*Quintet in E-flat major (c ?1793; ob, 3hn & bn, frag)*	*Hess 19*
7.14	Flute Quintet (c1810, arr from: Vn Sonata No.8 in G major, Op.30/3)	
7.15	"3 Equali" (c1812; 4 trbn): No.1 in D minor	WoO 30
7.16	No.2 in D major	
7.17	No.3 in B-flat major	

String Trios:

7.18	String Trio No.1 in E-flat major (c before 1794)	Op.3
7.19	"6 Minuets" (c ?1795; 2vn & bass): No.1 in E-flat major	WoO 9
7.20	No.2 in G major	
7.21	No.3 in C major	
7.22	No.4 in F major	
7.23	No.5 in D major	
7.24	No.6 in G major	
7.25	"Serenade," in D major (c1796–7)	Op.8
7.26	String Trio No.2 in G major (c1797–8):	Op.9/1
7.27	*. Another Trio for Minuet of Str Trio No.2 in G major, Op.9/1 (c1797–8)*	*Hess 28*
7.28	String Trio No.3 in D major (c1797–8)	Op.9/2
7.29	String Trio No.4 in C minor (c1797–8)	Op.9/3

Other 3 insts:

7.30	"Variations on: La ci darem," in C major (c ?1795; 2ob & Eng hn, from Mozart's opera: Don Giovanni, K527)	WoO 28
7.31	"Serenade," in D major (c1801; fl, vn & va)	Op.25
7.32	Trio in C major (c1795; 2ob & Eng hn; arr for str trio)	Op.87

2 insts:

7.33	"Allegro & Minuet," in G major (c1792; 2fl)	WoO 26
7.34	*"3 Duos" (c ?1810–5; cl & bn): No.1 in C major (?spur)*	*WoO 27*
7.35	*No.2 in F major (?spur)*	
7.36	*No.3 in B-flat major (?spur)*	
7.37	"Duo" (Sonatensatz), in E-flat major, "With Two Eyeglasses Obbligato" (c1796–7; va & vc)	WoO 32
7.38	"Duet," in A major (c1822; 2vn)	WoO 34
7.39	"Canon," in A major (c1825; ?2vn)	WoO 35

8. CHAMBER MUSIC WITH PIANO

5 insts:

8.1	Quintet in E-flat major (c1796; pf, ob, cl, bn & Fr hn)	Op.16

Piano Quartets:

8.2	Piano Quartet in E-flat major (c1796, arr of: Quintet in E-flat major, Op.16)	(Op.16)
8.3	"3 Piano Quartets" (c1785; pf, vn, va & d bass): No.1 in E-flat major	WoO 36
8.4	No.2 in D major	
8.5	No.3 in C major	

Piano Trios:

8.6	Arr of Sextet in E-flat major, Op.81b	
8.7	Piano Trio No.1 in E-flat major (c1794–5)	Op.1/1
8.8	Piano Trio No.2 in G major (c1794–5)	Op.1/2
8.9	Piano Trio No.3 in C minor (c1794–5)	Op.1/3
8.10	Piano Trio No.4 in B-flat major, "Street Song" (c1797; pf, cl/vn & vc)	Op.11
8.11	Arr of Septet in E-flat major, Op.20 (c ?1803; pf, cl/vn & vc)	Op.38
8.12	Arr of String Quintet in E-flat major, Op.4	Op.63

8.68	No.5 "Air tirolien"
8.69	No.6 "Air écossais"
8.70	No.7 "Air russe"
8.71	No.8 "Air écossais"
8.72	No.9 "Air écossais"
8.73	No.10 "Air écossais"

Vn solo:

8.74   Cadenza for Violin Concerto, Op.61 (c1822, lost until 1954, for Léon de Saint-Lubin) ....

9. PIANO SONATAS

9.1	3 "Kurfürsten Sonaten" (Electoral) (c ?1783): No.1 in E-flat major .... WoO 47
9.2	No.2 in F minor
9.3	No.3 in D major
9.4	Piano Sonata in F major (c before 1793, 2 movts only) .... WoO 50
9.5	Piano Sonata No.1 in F minor (c1793–5) Op.2/1
9.6	Piano Sonata No.2 in A major (c1794–5) Op.2/2
9.7	Piano Sonata No.3 in C major (c1794–5) Op.2/3
9.8	Piano Sonata No.4 in E-flat major, "Grand Sonata" (c1796–7) Op.7
9.9	Piano Sonata No.5 in C minor (c ?1795–7) Op.10/1
9.10	Piano Sonata No.6 in F major (c1796–7) Op.10/2
9.11	Piano Sonata No.7 in D major (c1797–8) Op.10/3
9.12	Piano Sonata in C major, "Eleonorem Sonate" (c1797–8, inc: 2 movts only, 2nd compl Ries) .... WoO 51
9.13	Piano Sonata No.8 in C minor, "Pathétique" (c ?1797–8) Op.13
9.14	Piano Sonata No.9 in E major (c1798) Op.14/1
9.15	Piano Sonata No.10 in G major (c ?1799) Op.14/2
9.16	Piano Sonata No.11 in B-flat major (c1800) Op.22
9.17	Piano Sonata No.12 in A-flat major, "Funeral March Sonata" (c1800–1, 3rd movt: Funeral March) Op.26
9.18	Piano Sonata No.13 in E-flat major, "Quasi una fantasia" (c1800–1) Op.27/1
9.19	Piano Sonata No.14 in C-sharp minor, "Moonlight" (c1801) Op.27/2
9.20	Piano Sonata No.15 in D major, "Pastoral" (c1801) Op.28
9.21	Piano Sonata No.16 in G major (c1802) Op.31/1
9.22	Piano Sonata No.17 in D minor, "Tempest" (c1802) Op.31/2
9.23	Piano Sonata No.18 in E-flat major, "The Hunt" (c1802) Op.31/3
9.24	Piano Sonata No.19 in G minor (c ?1797) Op.49/1
9.25	Piano Sonata No.20 in G major (c1795–6) Op.49/2
9.26	Piano Sonata No.21 in C major, "Waldstein" (c1803–4) Op.53
9.27	Piano Sonata No.22 in F major (c1804) Op.54
9.28	Piano Sonata No.23 in F minor, "Appassionata" (c1804–5) Op.57
9.29	Piano Sonata No.24 in F-sharp major (c1809) Op.78
9.30	Piano Sonata No.25 in G major, "Cuckoo" (c1809) Op.79
9.31	Piano Sonata No.26 in E-flat major, "Les adieux" (c1809–10) Op.81a
9.32	Piano Sonata No.27 in E minor (c1814) Op.90
9.33	Piano Sonata No.28 in A major (c1816) Op.101
9.34	Piano Sonata No.29 in B-flat major, "Hammerklavier" (c1817–8) Op.106
9.35	Piano Sonata No.30 in E major (c1820) Op.109
9.36	Piano Sonata No.31 in A-flat major (c1821–2) Op.110
9.37	Piano Sonata No.32 in C minor (c1821–2) Op.111

10. PIANO VARIATIONS

10.1	"9 Variations on a March by Dressler," in C minor (c1782) .... WoO 63
10.2	"6 Easy Variations on a Swiss song," in F major (c before 1793; pf/harp) .... WoO 64
10.3	"24 Variations on Righini's arietta 'Venni amore,' " in D major (c1790–1) .... WoO 65
10.4	"13 Variations on arietta 'Es war einmal,' " in A maj (c1792, from Dittersdorf: Das rote Käppchen) . WoO 66
10.5	"12 Variations on 'Menuett à la Viganò,' " in C major (c1795, from Haibel: Le nozze disturbate) ..... WoO 68
10.6	"9 Variations on aria 'Quant'è più bello,' " in A major (c1795, from Paisiello: La molinara) .... WoO 69
10.7	"6 Variations on duet 'Nel cor più,' " in G major (c1795, from Paisiello: La molinara) .... WoO 70
10.8	"12 Variations on Russian Dance," in A major (c1796–7, from Wranitzky: Das Waldmädchen) .... WoO 71
10.9	"8 Variations on 'Une fièvre brulante,' " in C major (c ?1795, from Grétry: Richard Coeur de Lion) . WoO 72
10.10	"10 Variations on 'La stessa, la stessissima,' " in B-flat major (c1799, from Salieri: Falstaff) .... WoO 73
10.11	"7 Variations on 'Kind, willst du,' " in F major (c1799, from Winter: Das unterbrochene Opferfest) .. WoO 75
10.12	"8 Variations on Trio 'Tändeln und scherzen,' " in F major (c1799, from Sussmayer: Soliman II)..... WoO 76
10.13	"6 Variations on an original theme," in G major (c1800) .... WoO 77
10.14	"6 Variations on an original theme," in F major (c1802) Op.34
10.15	"Eroica Variations" (15 Variations & fugue on a theme from 'Prometheus'), in E-flat major (c1802) Op.35
10.16	"7 Variations on 'God save the King,' " in C major (c1802–3) .... WoO 78
10.17	"5 Variations on 'Rule Britannia,' " in D major (c1803) .... WoO 79
10.18	"32 Variations on an original theme," in C minor (c1806) .... WoO 80
10.19	"6 Variations on an original theme," in D major (c1809, same theme in: Turkish March, Op.113/4) Op.76
10.20	"Diabelli Variations" (33 Variations on a waltz by Diabelli), in C major (c1819) Op.120

11. OTHER PIANO WORKS

W/ opus number:

11.1	"7 Bagatelles" (c1801–2): No.1 in E-flat major	Op.33
11.2	No.2 in C major	
11.3	No.3 in F major	
11.4	No.4 in A major	
11.5	No.5 in C major	
11.6	No.6 in D major	
11.7	No.7 in A-flat major	
11.8	"2 Preludes through all 12 major keys" (c1789; pf/org)	Op.39
11.9	"2 Rondos": No.1 in C major (c ?1796–7)	Op.51
11.10	No.2 in G major (c ?1798)	
11.11	"Fantasia," in G minor (c1809)	Op.77
11.12	"Polonaise," in C major (c1814)	Op.89
11.13	"11 Bagatelles" (c by 1820–2): No.1 in G minor	Op.119
11.14	No.2 in C major	
11.15	No.3 in D major	
11.16	No.4 in A major	
11.17	No.5 in C minor	
11.18	No.6 in G major	
11.19	No.7 in C major	
11.20	No.8 in C major	
11.21	No.9 in A minor	
11.22	No.10 in A major	
11.23	No.11 in B-flat major	
11.24	"6 Bagatelles" (c1823–4): No.1 in G major	Op.126
11.25	No.2 in G minor	
11.26	No.3 in E-flat major	
11.27	No.4 in B minor	
11.28	No.5 in G major	
11.29	No.6 in E-flat major	
11.30	"Rondo a capriccio," in G major, "Rage over a Lost Penny" (c1795)	Op.129

W/ out opus number:

11.31	"6 Minuets" (c ?1795): No.1 in C major	WoO 10
11.32	No.2 in G major	
11.33	No.3 in E-flat major	
11.34	No.4 in B-flat major	
11.35	No.5 in D major	
11.36	No.6 in C major	
11.37	"7 Ländler," all in D major (c ?1798)	WoO 11
11.38	"12 German Dances" (orig for orch lost): No.1 in D major	WoO 13
11.39	No.2 in B-flat major	
11.40	No.3 in G major	
11.41	No.4 in D major	
11.42	No.5 in F major	
11.43	No.6 in B-flat major	
11.44	No.7 in D major	
11.45	No.8 in G major	
11.46	No.9 in E-flat major (Country Dance)	
11.47	No.10 in C major	
11.48	No.11 in A major	
11.49	No.12 in D major	
11.50	"Rondo," in C major (c1783)	WoO 48
11.51	"Rondo," in A major (c ?1783)	WoO 49
11.52	"Presto," in C minor (c ?1795)	WoO 52
11.53	"Fugue," in C major (c1795)	Hess 64
11.54	"Allegretto," in C minor (c1796–7)	WoO 53
11.55	"Lustig—Traurig," 2 pieces (c ?1802): No.1 "Lustig," in C major	WoO 5
11.56	No.2 "Traurig," in C minor	
11.57	"Prelude," in F minor (c before 1785; pf/org)	WoO 55
11.58	"Allegretto," in C minor (c1796–7)	Hess 69
11.59	"Allegretto," in C major (c1803)	WoO 56
11.60	"Andante favori," in F major (c1803, intended as 2nd movt of: Pf Son No.21, 'Waldstein,' Op.53)	WoO 57
11.61	2 Cadenzas to Mozart: Piano Concerto No.20 in D minor, K466 (c1802–5 or 1808–9)	WoO 58
11.62	"Bagatelle," in A minor, "Für Elise" (c1808, 1810)	WoO 59
11.63	"Bagatelle," in B-flat major (c1818)	WoO 60
11.64	"Allegretto," in B minor (c1821)	WoO 61
11.65	"Allegretto quasi andante," in G minor (c1825)	WoO 61a
11.66	"Allemande," in A major (c1793)	WoO 81
11.67	"Minuet," in E-flat major (c before 1805)	WoO 82
11.68	*"6 Ecossaises," all in E-flat major (c ?1806, ?spur)*	*WoO 83*

11.69   "Concert Finale," in C major (c1820–1, arr of Coda to Finale of: Pf Conc No.3 in C minor, Op.37) .. Hess 65
11.70   "Waltz," in E-flat major (c1824) .... WoO 84
11.71   "Waltz," in D major (c1825) .... WoO 85
11.72   "Ecossaise," in E-flat major (c1825) .... WoO 86
11.73   Theme "O Hoffnung" (c1821, for: 40 Variations c by Archduke Rudolpf) .... WoO 200

     Cadenzas to Piano Concertos:

11.74   3 Cadenzas to 1st movt of: Piano Concerto No.1 in C major, Op.15 (c1807–9, for ?Archduke Rudolph) .....
11.75   1 Cadenza to 1st movt of: Piano Concerto No.2 in B-flat major, Op.19 (ca1809) ....
11.76   1 Cadenza to 1st movt of: Piano Concerto No.3 in C minor, Op.37 (ca1809) ....
11.77   3 Cadenzas to: Piano Concerto No.4 in G major, Op.58 (ca1809): No.1 Cadenza to 1st movt...................
11.78   No.2 Cadenza to 1st movt
11.79   No.3 Cadenza to 3rd movt
11.80   2 Cadenzas to: Pf Transcr of Vn Concerto in D major, Op.61a (ca1809): No.1 Cadenza to 1st movt..........
11.81   No.2 Cadenza to 3rd movt
11.82   "Other 3 cadenzas," to: Piano Concerto No.4 in G major, Op.58 (ca1809): No.1 Cadenza to 1st movt ....
11.83   No.2 Short transition in the rondo
11.84   No.3 Short cadenza to 3rd movt
11.85   "Other 2 cadenzas," to: Pf Transcr of Vn Conc, Op.61a (ca1809): No.1 Short transition in the rondo ....
11.86   No.2 Cadenza to rondo

     Pf duet:

11.87   "8 Variations on a theme by Count Waldstein," in C major (c ?1792) .... WoO 67
11.88   "Sonata," in D major (c1796–7) Op.6
11.89   "6 Variations on song 'Ich denke dein,' " in D major (c1799, 1803; see song WoO 74) .... (WoO 74)
11.90   "3 Marches" (c ?1803): No.1 in C major Op.45
11.91   No.2 in E-flat major
11.92   No.3 in D major

     2 Pf:

11.93   Arr of "Grosse Fugue," in B-flat major, Op.133 (c1826; orig for str qt) Op.134

12. ORGAN

12.1   "Fugue," in D major (c1783) .... WoO 31

13. CHORAL WORKS

     W/ orch:

13.1   "Cantata on the Death of the Emperor Joseph II" (c1790, Averdonk; S, A, T, B, ch & orch): .... WoO 87
           1. "Todt! Todt!" (vv, ch)
           2a. "Ein Ungeheuer, sein Name Fanatismus," recit (B)
           2b. "Da kam Joseph," aria (B)
           3. "Da stiegen die Menschen," aria (S, ch)
           4a. "Er schläft," recit (S)
           4b. "Hier schlummert seinen stillen Frieden," aria (S)
           5. "Todt! Todt!" (vv & ch)
13.2   "Cantata on the Accession of the Emperor Leopold II" (c1790, Averdonk; S, A, T, B, ch & orch): ... WoO 88
           1a. "Er schlummert," recit (S, ch)
           1b. "Fliesse, Wonnezähre fliesse," aria (S)
           2. "Ihr staunt, Völker der Erde!," recit (B)
           3a. "Wie bebt mein Herz vor Wonne!," recit (T)
           3b. "Ihr, die Joseph ihren Vater nannten," trio (S, T, B)
           4. "Stürzet nieder, Millionen," chorus
13.3   "Fantasia" (Choral Fantasy), in C minor (c1808, Kuffner; pf, ch & orch) Op.80
13.4   "Christus am Ölberge" (The Mount of Olives), oratorio (c1803, r1804, Huber; S, T, B, ch & orch): Op.85
           1. "Introduction"
           . "Jehovah, du, mein Vater!, recit (Jesus)
           . "Meine Seele ist erschüttert," aria (Jesus)
           2. "Erzittre Erde Jehovas Sohn liegt hier," recit (Seraph)
           . "Preist, preist des Erlösers Güte," aria (Seraph)
           . "O Heil euch! Heil euch ihr Erlösten," chorus (Seraph und Engel)
           3. "Verkündet, Seraph mir Dein Mund," recit (Jesus)
           . So ruhe denn mit ganzer Schwere," duet (Jesus, Seraph)
           4. "Willkommen Tod!," recit (Jesus)
           . "Wir haben ihn gesehen," chorus (Krieger)
           5. "Die mich zu fangen ausgezogen sind," recit (Jesus)
           . "Hier ist er," chorus (Krieger und Jünger)
           6. "Nicht ungestraft soll der Verwegnen Schar," recit (Jesus, Petrus)

. "In meinen Adern wühlen," trio & chorus (Jesus, Seraph, Petrus, Krieger, Jünger)
. "Welten singen," final chorus (Engel)

13.5 Mass in C major (c1807; S, A, T, B, ch & orch):.. Op.86
    1. "Kyrie"
    2. "Gloria"
    3. "Credo"
    4. "Sanctus"
    5. "Benedictus"
    6. "Agnus Dei"

13.6 "Meeresstille und glückliche Fahrt" (Calm Sea & Prosperous Voyage), cantata (c1814–5, Goethe): Op.112
    1. "Meeresstille": "Tiefe Stille herrscht im Wasser"
    2. "Glückliche Fahrt": "Die Nebel zerreisset"

13.7 "Opferlied": "Die Flamme lodert" II (c1823–4, Matthisson; S, ch & orch; 1st vers c1822) Op.121b

13.8 "Bundeslied": "In allen guten Stunden" (c1823–4, Goethe; S, A, ch & winds)................................... Op.122

13.9 "Missa solemnis," in D major (c1819–23; S, A, T, B, ch, orch & org): Op.123
    1. "Kyrie"
    2. "Gloria"
    3. "Credo"
    4. "Sanctus"
    5. "Benedictus"
    6. "Agnus Dei"

13.10 "Der glorreiche Augenblick," cantata (c1814, Weissenbach; 2S, T, B, ch & orch): Op.136
    1. "Europa steht!" (ch)
    2a. "O seht sie nah und näher treten!," recit (Führer des Volkes, Genius)
    2b. "Vienna, Vienna" (ch)
    3a. "O Himmel, welch Entzükken!," recit (Vienna)
    3b. "Alle die Herrscher darf ich grüssen," aria (Vienna, ch)
    4a. "Das Auge schaut," recit (Seherin)
    4b. "Dem die erste Zähre," cavatina (Seherin, ch)
    5a. "Der den Bund im Sturme festgehalten," recit (Seherin)
    5b. "In meinen Mauern bauen," quartet (Vienna, Seherin, Genius, Führer des Volkes)
    6. "Es treten hervor die Scharen der Frauen," chorus

13.11 "Chor auf die verbündeten Fürsten": "Ihr weisen Gründer" (c1814, Bernard) .... WoO 95

W/ pf:

13.12 "Cantata campestre": "Un lieto Brindisi" (c1814, Bondi; S, 2T, B & pf) .... WoO 103
13.13 "Hochzeitslied": "Auf, Freunde, singt dem Gott" (c1819, Stein; 1v, ch & pf; 2 vers)...................... WoO 105
13.14 "Lobkowitz Birthday Cantata": "Es lebe unser teurer Fürst" (c1816; S, ch & pf) .... WoO 106

Unacc ch:

13.15 "Abschiedsgesang": "Die Stunde schlägt" (c1814, Seyfried; m ch) .... WoO 102
13.16 "Gesang der Mönche" (Song of the Monks): "Rasch tritt der Tod" (c1817; m ch, from Schiller's
    Wilhelm Tell) .... WoO 104

14. VOICE & ORCHESTRA, UNACC VOCAL

1–4vv & orch:

14.1 "Prüfung des Küssens": "Meine weise Mutter spricht," aria (ca1790–2; B & orch) .... WoO 89
14.2 "Mit Mädeln sich vertragen," aria (ca1790–2, Goethe; B & orch) .... WoO 90
14.3 2 Arias for Umlauf's Singspiel: Die schöne Schusterin (c ?1796):.. WoO 91
    1. "O welch ein Leben! ein ganzes Meer," aria (T)
    2. "Soll ein Schuh nicht drükken," aria (S)
14.4 "Primo amore piacer del ciel," scene & "Tal amor, piacer del ciel," aria (ca1790–2; S & orch) .... WoO 92
14.5 "Ah perfido!," scene & "Per pieta, non dirmi addio," aria (c1795–6, Metastasio; S & orch) Op.65
14.6 "Tremate, empi, tremate," trio (c1801–2, Bettoni; S, T, B & orch) Op.116
14.7 "No, non turbati!," scene & "Ma tu tremi, o mio tesoro!," aria (c1801–2, Metastasio; S & strings) .. WoO 92a
14.8 "Nei giorni tuoi felici," duet (c1802–3, Metastasio; S, T & orch) .... WoO 93
14.9 "Sanft wie du lebtest," elegiac song (c1814; S, A, T, B & str qt/pf) Op.118

26 unacc Italian duets, trios and quartets: .... WoO 99

14.10 1. "Bei labbri che amore" (ca1792–4, Metastasio: La gelosia; S, T; r by Salieri) ....
14.11 2. "Sei il mio ben" (c by 1800, Metastasio: Cantata 24; S, T) ....
14.12 3. "Scrivo in te" (ca1795–6, Metastasio: Il nome; S, T) ....
14.13 4. "Fra tutte le pene" (c1796–7, Metastasio: Zenobia; T, B) ....
14.14   *5. "Fra tutte le pene" (2nd vers of 4. r by Salieri)* ....
14.15 6. "Salvo tu vuoi lo sposo?" (c1796–7, Metastasio: Zenobia; S, T) ....
14.16   *7. "Languisco e moro per te" (c1802–3; S, T, sketch)* ....
14.17 8. "Ma tu tremi" (c1792–4, Metastasio: La tempesta; S, A, T) ....
14.18 9. "Giura il nocchier" (c1792–4, Metastasio: La gelosia; S, A, B) ....
14.19 10. "Per te d'amico aprile" (c1792–6, Metastasio: Il nome; S, A, B) ....

14.20	11. "Fra tutte le pene" (c1796–7, Metastasio: Zenobia; S, A, T)..
14.21	*12. "Fra tutte le pene" (2nd vers of 11. r by Salieri)* ....
14.22	13. "Quella cetra ah pur tu sei" (c1796–7, Metastasio: Cantata a Maria Teresa; S, T, B) ....
14.23	14. "Chi mai di questo core" (c before 1799, Metastasio: Il ritorno; S, T, B) ....
14.24	15. "Già la notte s'avvicina" (c1802, Metastasio: La pesca; A, T, B) ....
14.25	16. "Nei campi e nelle selve" I (c1792–6, Metastasio: Cantata 27; S, A, T, B) ....
14.26	17. "Nei campi e nelle selve" II (c1792–6, Metastasio: Cantata 27; S, A, T, B) ....
14.27	18. "Fra tutte le pene" (c1796–7, Metastasio: Zenobia; S, A, T, B) ....
14.28	*19. "Fra tutte le pene" (2nd vers of above r by Salieri)* ....
14.29	20. "Quella cetra ah pur tu sei," in G major (c1796–7, Metastasio: Cantata a M. Teresa; S, A, T, B) ....
14.30	21. "Quella cetra ah pur tu sei," in F major (c1796–7, Metastasio: Cantata a M. Teresa; S, A, T, B) ....
14.31	22. "Giura il nocchier," in C major (c1795–1800, Metastasio: La gelosia; S, A, T, B) ....
14.32	23. "Giura il nocchier," in B-flat major (c1800–2, Metastasio: La gelosia; S, A, T, B) ....
14.33	24. "Già la notte s'avvicina" (c1802, Metastasio: La pesca; S, A, T, B) ....
14.34	*25. "Silvio, amante disperato" (c1792–1802, Metastasio: Cantata 27, sketch, lost)* ....
14.35	26. "E pur fra le tempeste" (c before 1800, Metastasio: La tempesta; T solo) ....

15. SONGS (w/ pf)

c early:

| 15.1 | "Schilderung eines Mädchens": "Schildern, willst du Freund" (c ?1783, Bürger) .... WoO 107 |
| 15.2 | "An einem Säugling": "Noch weisst du nicht wess Kind du bist" (c1784, Döhring) .... WoO 108 |

c1790:

15.3	"Klage": "Dein Silber schien durch Eichengrün" (Hölty)... WoO 113
15.4	"Trinklied (beim Abschied zu singen)": "Erhebt das Glas mit froher Hand" (w/ unison ch) .... WoO 109
15.5	"Punschlied": "Wer nicht, wenn warm von Hand zu Hand der Punsch" (w/ unison ch) .... WoO 111
15.6	"Traute Henriette" (Metastasio) .... Hess 151
15.7	"An Laura": "Freud' umblühe dich auf allen Wegen" (Matthisson).. WoO 112

c1792:

15.8	"Selbstgespräch": "Ich, der mit flatterndem Sinn" (Gleim) .... WoO 114
15.9	"An Minna": "Nur bei dir, an deinem Herzen" .... WoO 115
15.10	"Elegie auf den Tod eines Pudels": "Stirb immerhin, es welken ja so viele" .... WoO 110

c1793:

| 15.11 | "Que le temps me dure" (Rousseau; 2 vers: Hess 129 & 130) .... WoO 116 |
| 15.12 | "Der freie Mann": "Wer ist ein freier Mann?" (Pfeffel, w/ unison ch) .... WoO 117 |

c1794:

15.13	"O care selve," canzonetta (Metastasio, w/ unison ch)... WoO 119
15.14	"Opferlied": "Die Flamme lodert" (c1794, r1801–2, Matthisson; see choral Op.121b) .... WoO 126
15.15	"2 Songs" (Bürger): 1. "Seufzer eines Ungeliebten": "Hast du nicht Liebe zugemessen" .... WoO 118
15.16	2. "Gegenliebe": "Wüsst ich, dass du mich"
15.17	"Adelaide": "Einsam wandelt dein Freund im Frühlingsgarten" (Matthison) Op.46

c1795:

| 15.18 | "Zärtliche Liebe": "Ich liebe dich, so wie du mich" (Herrosee) .... WoO 123 |
| 15.19 | "La partenza": "Ecco quel fiero istante!" (Metastasio) .... WoO 124 |

c1796:

| 15.20 | "Abschiedsgesang an Wiens Bürger": "Keine Klage soll erschallen" (Friedelberg)...................... WoO 121 |

c1797:

| 15.21 | "Kriegslied der Österreicher": "Ein grosses deutsches Volk" (Friedelberg) .... WoO 122 |

c1798:

15.22	"Neue Liebe, neues Leben": "Herz, mein Herz, was soll das geben" (Goethe).............................. WoO 127
15.23	"La Tiranna": "Ah grief to think! ah woe to name" (transl Wennington) .... WoO 125
15.24	"Plaisir d'aimer": "Plaisir d'aimer besoin d'une âme tendre" .... WoO 128
15.25	"Ich denke dein" (Goethe, song with 6 Variations in D major; see WoO 74 for pf duet)................... WoO 74

c1800:

15.26	"Man strebt die Flamme zu verhehlen" .... WoO 120
15.27	"6 Songs" (Gellert): 1. "Bitten": "Gott, deine Güte reicht so weit" (also see C. P. E. Bach Wq194/9) .. Op.48
15.28	2. "Die Liebe des Nächsten": "So jemand spricht: Ich liebe Gott!"
15.29	3. "Vom Tode": "Meine Lebenszeit verstreicht"
15.30	4. "Die Ehre Gottes aus der Natur": "Die Himmel rühmen des Ewigen Ehre" (also see C. P. E. Bach Wq194/18)
15.31	5. "Gottes Macht und Vorsehung": "Gott ist mein Lied"

15.32   6. "Busslied": "An dir allein, an dir hab' ich gesündigt" (also see C. P. E. Bach Wq194/45)

c1803:

15.33   "Der Wachtelschlag": "Ach mir schallt's dorten so lieblich hervor!" (Sauter) .... WoO 129
15.34   "8 Songs": 1. "Urians Reise um die Welt": "Wenn jemand" (c before 1793, Claudius) Op.52
15.35   2. "Feuerfarb' ": "Ich weiss eine Farbe" (c1792, r1793–4, Mereau)
15.36   3. "Das Liedchen von der Ruhe": "Im Arm der Liebe ruht sich's wohl" (c1793, Ueltzen)
15.37   4. "Maigesang": "Wie herrlich leuchtet mir die Natur" (c before ?1796, Goethe)
15.38   5. "Mollys Abschied": "Lebe wohl, du Mann der Lust und Schmerzen" (Bürger)
15.39   6. "Die Liebe": "Ohne Liebe lebe wer da kann" (c before 1793, Lessing)
15.40   7. "Marmotte": "Ich komme schon durch manches Land" (ca ?1790–2, Goethe)
15.41   8. "Das Blümchen Wunderhold": "Es blüht ein Blümchen irgendwo" (Bürger)
15.42   "Das Glück der Freundschaft": "Der lebt ein Leben wonniglich" Op.88

c1805:

15.43   "An die Hoffnung" I: "Die du so gern in heilgen Nächten feierst" (from Tiedge's Urania) Op.32

c1806:

15.44   "Als die Geliebte sich trennen wollte": "Der Hoffnung letzter Schimmer" (?Hoffmann) .... WoO 132

c1807:

15.45   "In questa tomba oscura lasciami riposar," arietta (Carpani) .... WoO 133

c1808:

15.46   "Sehnsucht": "Nur wer die Sehnsucht kennt" (Goethe; 4 vers) (also see Schubert Op.62/4, D877,
     Schumann Op.98a/3, Tchaikovsky Op.6/6 & Wolf's 6. of: Goethe Lieder) .... WoO 134
     . Version 1 (Andante poco agitato)
     . Version 2 (Poco Andante)
     . Version 3 (Poco Adagio)
     . Version 4 (Assai Adagio)

c1809:

15.47   "Andenken": "Ich denke dein" (Matthisson) (also see Wolf's song of 1877) .... WoO 136
15.48   "Lied aus der Ferne": "Als mir noch die Träne" (Reissig) .... WoO 137
15.49   "Der Jüngling in der Fremde": "Der Frühling entblühet dem Schoss der Natur" (Reissig) .... WoO 138
15.50   "Der Liebende": "Welch ein wunderbares Leben" (Reissig) .... WoO 139
15.51   "6 Songs": 1. "Mignon": "Kennst du das Land wo die Zitronen blüh'n" (from Goethe's Wilhelm
     Meister) (also see Liszt S275, Schubert D321, Schumann Op.79/28 & Wolf's 9. of:
     Goethe Lieder) Op.75
15.52   2. "Neue Liebe, neues Leben": "Herz, mein Herz, was soll das geben?" (Goethe)
15.53   3. "Aus Goethe's Faust": "Es war einmal ein König" (Goethe's Faust, Part I) (also see Busoni
     K278 & Musorgsky: The Song of the Flea)
15.54   4. "Gretels Warnung": "Mit Liebesblick und Spiel und Sang" (Halem)
15.55   5. "An den fernen Geliebten": "Einst wohnten süsse Ruh" (Reissig)
15.56   6. "Der Zufriedene": "Zwar schuf das Glück hienieden" (Reissig)
15.57   "4 Ariettas & 1 Duet": 1. "Hoffnung": "Dimmi, ben mio che m'ami" Op.82
15.58   2. "Liebes-Klage": "T'intendo, si, mio cor" (Metastasio)
15.59   3. "L'amante impaziente": "Che fa il mio bene?," arietta buffa (Metastasio)
15.60   4. "L'amante impaziente": "Che fa il mio bene?," arietta assai seriosa (Metastasio)
15.61   5. "Lebens-Genuss": "Odi l'aura che dolce sospira," duet (Metastasio; S, T)

c1810:

15.62   "3 Songs" (Goethe): 1. "Wonne der Wehmut": "Trocknet nicht, trocknet nicht" (also see Schubert
     Op.posth 115/2, D260) Op.83
15.63   2. "Sehnsucht": "Was zieht mir das Herz so?" (also see Schubert D123)
15.64   3. "Mit einem gemalten Band": "Kleine Blumen, kleine Blätter"

c1811:

15.65   "An die Geliebte": "O dass ich dir vom stillen Auge" (Stoll; 2 vers) (also see Schubert D303) .... WoO 140

c1813:

15.66   "Der Gesang der Nachtigall": "Höre, die Nachtigall singt" (Herder) .... WoO 141
15.67   "Der Bardengeist": "Dort auf dem hohen Felsen sang" (Hermann) .... WoO 142

c1814:

15.68   "Des Kriegers Abschied": "Ich zieh' ins Feld von Lieb' entbrannt" (Reissig) .... WoO 143
15.69   "Merkenstein": "Merkenstein! Wo ich wandle" (Rupprecht) .... WoO 144

c1815:

15.70   "Merkenstein": "Merkenstein! Wo ich wandle," duet (Rupprecht) Op.100
15.71   "An die Hoffnung" II: "Ob ein Gott sei?" (from Tiedge's Urania) Op.94

15.72   "Die laute Klage": "Turteltaube, du klagest so laut" (Herder) .... WoO 135
15.73   "Das Geheimnis": "Wo blüht das Blümchen, das nie verblüht?" (Wessenberg) .... WoO 145

c1816:

15.74   "Sehnsucht": "Die stille Nacht umdunkelt erquikkend Tal und Höh" (Reissig) .... WoO 146
15.75   "An die ferne Geliebte," cycle (Jeitteles): 1. "Auf dem Hügel sitz ich spähend" Op.98
15.76   2. "Wo die Berge so blau"
15.77   3. "Leichte Segler in den Höhen"
15.78   4. "Diese Wolken in den Höhen"
15.79   5. "Es kehret der Maien, es blühet die Au"
15.80   6. "Nimm sie hin denn, diese Lieder"
15.81   "Der Mann von Wort": "Du sagtest, Freund, an diesen Ort" (Kleinschmid) Op.99
15.82   "Ruf vom Berge": "Wenn ich ein Vöglein wär" (Treitschke) .... WoO 147

c1817:

15.83   "So oder so": "Nord oder Süd!" (Lappe) .... WoO 148
15.84   "Resignation": "Lisch aus, lisch aus, mein Licht! Was dir gebricht" (Haugwitz) .... WoO 149

c1820:

15.85   "Gedenke mein": "Gedenke mein! Ich denke Dein!" (c ?1804–5, r1819–20) .... WoO 130
15.86   "Abendlied unterm gestirnten Himmel": "Wenn die Sonne nieder sinket" (Goebel) .... WoO 150

c1822:

15.87   "Der Kuss": "Ich war bei Chloen ganz allein," arietta (Weisse) Op.128

c1823:

15.88   "Der edle Mensch sei hülfreich und gut" (Goethe) .... WoO 151

16. FOLKSONG ARRANGEMENTS (w/ pf trio)

16.1   "25 Irish Songs" (p1813): 1. "The return to Ulster": "Once again—but how chang'd" .... WoO 152
16.2   2. "Sweet power of song," duet
16.3   3. "Once more I hail thee"
16.4   4. "The morning air plays on my face"
16.5   5. "On the Massacre of Glencoe": "O! tell me, Harper, wherefore flow"
16.6   6. "What shall I do," duet
16.7   7. "His boat comes on the sunny tide"
16.8   8. "Come draw we round a cheerful ring"
16.9   9. "The Soldier's dream": "Our bugles sung truce—for the night-cloud had lowered"
16.10   10. "The Deserter": "If sadly thinking and spirits sinking"
16.11   11. "Thou emblem of faith"
16.12   12. "English bulls" (The Irishman in London): "Oh! have you not heard"
16.13   13. "Musing on the roaring ocean"
16.14   14. "Dermot and Shelah": "O who sits so sadly"
16.15   15. "Let brain-spinning swains"
16.16   16. "Hide not thy anguish"
16.17   17. "In vain to this desert," duet
16.18   18. "They bid me slight my Dermot dear," duet
16.19   19. "Wife, children and friends": "When the blackletter'd list to the gods," duet
16.20   20. "Farewell bliss and farewell Nancy," duet
16.21   21. "Morning a cruel turmoiler is"
16.22   22. "From Garyone, my happy home"
16.23   23. "A wand'ring gypsy, Sirs, am I"
16.24   24. "The Traugh Welcome": "Shall a son of O'Donnel be cheerless and cold"
16.25   25. "Oh harp of Erin": "Oh harp of Erin thou art now laid low"
16.26   "20 Irish Songs" (p1814, 1816): 1. "When eve's last rays in twilight die," duet .... WoO 153
16.27   2. "No riches from his scanty store"
16.28   3. "The British light dragoons": " 'twas a Maréchal of France, and he fain would honour gain"
16.29   4. "Since greybeards inform us that youth will decay"
16.30   5. "I dream'd I lay where flow'rs were springing," duet
16.31   6. "Sad and luckless was the season"
16.32   7. "O soothe me, my lyre"
16.33   8. "Norah of Balmagairy": "Farewell mirth and hilarity" (w/ ch)
16.34   9. "The kiss, dear maid, thy lip has left"
16.35   10. "Oh! thou hapless soldier," duet
16.36   11. "When far from the home of our youth we have rang'd"
16.37   12. "I'll praise the Saints with early song"
16.38   13. "Sunshine": " 'tis sunshine at last, come, my Ellen, sit near me"
16.39   14. "Paddy O'Rafferty, merry and vigorous"
16.40   15. " 't is but in vain, for nothing thrives"
16.41   16. "O might I but my Patrick love"
16.42   16. "Come, Darby dear, easy, be easy"

16.43	18. "No more, my Mary, I sigh for splendour"
16.44	19. "Judy, lovely matchless creature"
16.45	20. "Thy ship must sail, my Henry dear"
16.46	"12 Irish Songs" (p1816): 1. "The elfin fairies": "We fairyelves in secret dells" .... WoO 154
16.47	2. "O harp of Erin": "O harp of Erin, thou art now laid low"
16.48	3. "The farewell song": "Oh Erin, to thy harp divine"
16.49	4. "The pulse of an Irishman ever beats quicker"
16.50	5. "O! who, my dear Dermot"
16.51	6. "Put round the bright wine"
16.52	7. "From Garyone, my happy home"
16.53	8. "Save me from the grave and wise" (w/ ch)
16.54	9. "Oh! would I were but that sweet linnet," duet
16.55	10. "The hero may perish his country to save," duet
16.56	11. "The soldier in a foreign land": "The piper who sat on his low mossy seat," duet
16.57	12. "He promis'd me at parting," duet
16.58	"26 Welsh Songs" (p1817) 1. "Sion, the son of Evan": "Hear the shouts," duet .... WoO 155
16.59	2. "The monks of Bangor's march": "When the heathen trumpet's clang," duet
16.60	3. "The cottage maid": "I envy not the splendour fine"
16.61	4. "Love without hope": "Her features speak the warment heart"
16.62	5. "A golden robe my love shall wear"
16.63	6. "The fair maid of Mona": "How, my love, coulds hapless doubts o'er take thee"
16.64	7. "O let the night my blushes hide"
16.65	8. "Farewell, farewell thou noisy town"
16.66	9. "To the Aeolian harp": "Harp of the Winds! in airy measure"
16.67	10. "Ned Pugh's farewell": "To leave my dear girl"
16.68	11. "Merch Megan": "In the white cot where Peggy dwells"
16.69	12. "Waken, lords and ladies gay" (also see Mendelssohn Op.120/1)
16.70	13. "Helpless Woman": "How cruel are the parents who riches only prize"
16.71	14. "The dream": "Last night worn with anguish that tortur'd my breast," duet
16.72	15. "When mortals all to rest retire"
16.73	16. "The damsels of Cardigan": "Fair Tivy, how sweet are thy waves gently flowing"
16.74	16. "The dairy-house": "A spreading hawthorn shades the seat"
16.75	18. "Sweet Richard": "Yes, thou art chang'd since first we met"
16.76	19. "The vale of Clwyd": "Think not I'll leave fair Clwyd's vale"
16.77	20. "To the Blackbird": "Sweet warbler of a strain divine"
16.78	21. "Cupid's kindness": "Dear brother, yes, the nymph you wed"
16.79	22. "Constancy": "Tho' cruel fate should bid us part," duet
16.80	23. "The old strain": "My pleasant home beside the Dee!"
16.81	24. "Three hundred pounds": "In yonder sung cottage, beneath the cliff's side"
16.82	25. "The parting kiss": "Laura, thy sighs must now no more"
16.83	26. "Good night": "Ere yet we slumbers seek"
16.84	"25 Scotch Songs" (p1818) 1. "Music, Love, Wine": "O let me Music hear, Night and Day!" Op.108
16.85	2. "Sunset": "The sun upon the Weirdlaw hill"
16.86	3. "Oh! sweet were the hours"
16.87	4. "The Maid of Isla": "O Maid of Isla from yon cliff"
16.88	5. "The sweetest lad was Jamie"
16.89	6. "Dim, dim is my eye"
16.90	7. "Bonnie laddie, highland laddie": "Where got ye that silver moon"
16.91	8. "The lovely lass of Inverness"
16.92	9. "Behold, my love, how green the groves" (also see Haydn HobXXXIa/152)
16.93	10. "Sympathy": "Why, Julia, say, that pensive mien?"
16.94	11. "Oh! thou art the lad of my heart"
16.95	12. "O, had my fate been join'd with thine"
16.96	13. "Come fill, fill, my good fellow"
16.97	14. "O, how can I be blithe and glad" (also see Schumann Op.25/20)
16.98	15. "O cruel was my father"
16.99	16. "Could this ill world have been contriv'd"
16.100	17. "O Mary, at thy window be" (also see Sullivan's song: Mary Morison of 1874)
16.101	18. "Enchantress, fare well, who so oft has decoy'd me"
16.102	19. "O swiftly glides the bonny boat"
16.103	20. "Faithfu' Johnie": "When will you come again, my faithfu' Johnie"
16.104	21. "Jeannie's distress": "By William late offended"
16.105	22. "The highland watch": "Old Scotia, wake thy mountain strain"
16.106	23. "The Shepherd's song": "The gowan glitters on the sward"
16.107	24. "Again, my Lyre"
16.108	25. "Sally in our alley": "Of all the girls that are so smart"
16.109	"12 Scottish Songs": 1. "The Banner of Buccleuch": "From the brown crest of Newark its summons extending," trio (p1822) .... WoO 156
16.110	2. "Duncan Grey": Duncan Grey came here to woo," trio (p1824–5)
16.111	3. "Up! quit thy bower, late wears the hour," trio (p1824–5, from Joanna Baille's play: The Beacon)
16.112	4. "Ye shepherds of this pleasant vale," trio (p1824–5)
16.113	5. "Cease your funning, force or cunning" (p1839)
16.114	6. "Highland Harry": "My Harry was a galant gay" (p1839; also see WoO 157/9, music not related)
16.115	7. "Polly Stewart": "O lovely Polly Stewart" (p1841)
16.116	8. "Womankind": "The hero may perish his country to save," trio (p1824–5)

16.117	9. "Lochnagar": "Away, ye gay landscapes, ye gardens of roses," trio (p1824–5)
16.118	10. "Glencoe": "Oh! tell us, Harper wherefore flow," trio (p1841)
16.119	11. "Auld lang syne": "Should auld acquaintance be forgot," trio (p1841) (also see Schumann Op.55/4)
16.120	12. "The quaker's wife": "Dark was the morn and black the sea," trio (p1824–5)
16.121	"12 Songs of Various Nationality": 1. "God save the King" (p1839, English; w/ ch) .... WoO 157
16.122	2. "The soldier" (The Minstrel Boy): "Then, soldier! come, fill high the wine" (p1816, Irish)
16.123	3. "O Charlie is my darling," trio (p1822, Scottish)
16.124	4. "O sanctissima, o piissima," trio (Sicilian)
16.125	5. "The Miller of the Dee": "There was a joly miller once," trio (p1824–5, English)
16.126	6. "A health to the brave," duet (p1816, Irish)
16.127	7. "Robin Adair": "Since all thy vows, false maid, are blown to air," trio (Irish) (also see Haydn HobXXXIa/202)
16.128	8. "By the side of the Shannon" (p1816, Irish)
16.129	9. "Highlander's lament": "My Harry was a gallant gay" (Scottish; w/ ch; also see WoO 156/6, music not related)
16.130	10. "Sir Johnie Cope": "Sir Johnie Cope trod the north right far" (?Scottish)
16.131	11. "The wandering minstrel": "I am bow'd down, with years" (p1816, Irish; w/ ch)
16.132	12. "La gondoletta": "La biondina in gondoletta" (Venetian)
16.133	"23 Songs of Various Nationality" (p by 1943): 1. "Ridder Stig" (Danish) .... WoO 158a
16.134	2. "Horch auf, mein Liebchen" (German)
16.135	3. "Wegen meiner bleib d'Fräula" (German)
16.136	4. "Wann i in der Früh aufsteh" (Tirolean)
16.137	5. "I bin a Tyroler Bua" (Teppichkrämerlied) (Tirolean)
16.138	6. "A Madel, ja a Madel" (Tirolean)
16.139	7. "Wer solche Buema afipackt" (Tirolean)
16.140	8. "Ih mag di nit" (Aria) (Tirolean)
16.141	9. "Oj upiłem się w karczmie" (Polish)
16.142	10. "Poszła baba po popiół i diabeł ją utopił" (Polish)
16.143	11. "Já no quiero embarcarme" (Portuese)
16.144	12. "Seus lindos olhos," duet (Portuese)
16.145	13. "Vo losochke komarochkov mnogo rodilos" (Russian)
16.146	14. "Ah, ruchenky, ruchenky" (Russian)
16.147	15. "Kak poshli nashi po druzhki" (Russian)
16.148	16. "Schöne Minka, ich muss scheiden!" (Ukrainian)
16.149	16. "Lilla Carl, sov sött i frid!" (Swedish)
16.150	18. "An ä Bergli bin i gesässe" (Swiss)
16.151	19. "Una paloma blanca" (Bolero a solo) (Spanish)
16.152	20. "Como la mariposa" (Bolero a due), duet (Spanish)
16.153	21. "La tiranna se embarca" (Tiranilla española) (Spanish)
16.154	22. "Édes kinos emlékezet" (Hungarian)
16.155	23. "Da brava, Catina" (Venetian)
16.156	"7 British Songs": 1. "Adieu my lov'd harp" (Irish) .... WoO 158b
16.157	2. (text unknown), quartet (Irish)
16.158	3. "Oh was not I a weary wight" (Scottish)
16.159	4. "Red gleams the sun" (Scottish)
16.160	5. "Erin! oh, Erin!" (Irish or Scottish)
16.161	6. "O Mary ye's be clad in silk" (Scottish)
16.162	7. "Lament for Owen Roe O'Neill" (Irish)
16.163	"6 Songs of Various Nationality": 1. "When my hero in court appears" .... WoO 158c
16.164	2. "Non, non, Collette n'est point trompeuse"
16.165	3. "Mark yonder pomp of costly fashion" (Scottish) (also see Haydn HobXXXIa/229)
16.166	4. "Bonnie wee thing, canie wee thing," trio (Scottish) (also see Haydn HobXXXIa/102, bis, ter)
16.167	5. "From thee, Eliza, I must go," trio (Scottish)
16.168	6. (text unknown)
16.169	"Air francais" (text unknown) .... Hess 168
16.170	2 Austrian folksongs (p1865; w/ pf) ....
16.171	"Das liebe Kätzchen" .... Hess 133
16.172	"Der Knabe auf dem Berge" .... Hess 134

17. CANONS & MUSICAL JOKES

17.1	"Im Arm der Liebe ruht sich's wohl" (c ?1795; 3vv) .... WoO 159
17.2	"2 Canons" (c ?1795): 1. "O care selve" (3vv) .... WoO 160
17.3	2. (w/ out text) (4vv)
17.4	Canon (c1796–7; 3vv) ....
17.5	"Herr Graf, ich komme zu fragen" (c ?1797; 3vv) .... Hess 276
17.6	"Schuppanzigh ist ein Lump" (c1801, not canonic; T, 2B & 4vv) .... WoO 100
17.7	"Graf, Graf, Graf, Graf" (c1802, not canonic; 3vv) .... WoO 101
17.8	Canon (c1803; 2vv) .... Hess 274
17.9	"Languisco e moro" (c1803; 2vv) .... Hess 229
17.10	Canon (c1803; 2vv) .... Hess 275
17.11	"Ewig dein" (c?; 3vv) .... WoO 161
17.12	*"Ta, ta, ta ... lieber Mälzel" (c ?1812; spur)* .... *WoO 162*

18. MUSICAL CLOCK

* * * * *

WoO = Werk ohne Opuszahl (work without opus number) in G. Kinsky and H. Halm: "Das Werk Beethovens." Munich and Duisburg, 1955.

Hess = W. Hess: "Verzeichnis der nicht in der Gesamtausgabe veröffentlichten Werke Ludwig van Beethovens." Breitkopf & Härtel. Wiesbaden, 1957.

1. STAGE WORKS (operas)

1.1 "Adelson e Salvini," 3 act semiseria (p1825, Tottola; 2 act vers 1826) ....

1.2 "Bianca e Gernando," 2 act seria (p1826, Gilardoni) ....

1.3 "Bianca e Fernando," 2 acts (p1828, Romani after Gilardoni, vers of above) ....

1.4 "Il pirata" (The Pirate), 2 act seria (p1827, Romani) ....

1.5 "La straniera" (The Stranger), 2 act seria (p1829, Romani) ....

1.6 "Zaira," 2 act seria (p1829, Romani) ....

1.7 "I Capuleti ed i Montecchi" (The Capulets and the Montagues), 2 act seria (p1830, Romani)......................

1.8 "Ernani" (c1830, Romani, inc) ....

1.9 "La sonnambula" (The Sleepwalker), 2 act seria/semiseria (p1831, Romani)...

1.10 "Norma," 2 act seria (p1831, Romani) ....

1.11 "Beatrice di Tenda," 2 act seria (p1833, Romani) ....

1.12 "I puritani" (The Puritans), 3 act seria (p1835, Pepoli on Ancelot & Joseph-Xavier-Boniface: Têtes Rondes et Cavaliers, who based on Scott's novel) ....

1.13   "Il fu ed il sara" (p1832, Ferretti, lost) ....

1a. SELECTIONS FROM STAGE WORKS (Nos. of sections in The Gramophone)

1a.4 "Il pirata," opera: ....

excerpts: 1. "Overture"
    I: 2. "Ciel! Qual procelle orribile"
            3. "Io vivi ancor!"
            4. "Nel furor delle tempeste"
            5. "Sorgete, è in me dover"
            6. "Lo sognai ferito"
            7. "Viva! Allegri!"
            8. "Ebben?"
            9. "Se in giorno"
            10. "Pietosa al padre!"
            11. "Bagnato dalle lagrime"
            12. "Più temuto, più splendido nome"
            13. "Sì vincemmo, e il pregio io sento"
            14. "Mi abbraccia, o donna"
            15. "Parlati ancora per poco"
            16. "Ebbenn: cominci, o barbara"
            17. "Ah! partiamo, i miei tormenti"
    II: 18. "Che rechi tu?"
            19. "Tu m'apristi in cor ferita"
            21. "Lasciami, forma umana"
            22. "Vieni: cerchiam pe' mari"
            23. "Cedo al destino orribile"
            24. "Lasso! Perir così"
            25. "Giusto ciel!"
            26. "Tu vedrai la sventura"
            27a. "Oh! s'io potessi"
            27b. "Col sorriso d'innocenza"

1a.7 "I Capuleti ed i Montecchi," opera:...

excerpts: 1a. "Overture"
    I: 1b. "Aggiorna appena"
            2a. "E' serbata a questa acciaro"
            2b. "L'amo, ah, l'amo, e mi è più cara"
            3. "Se Romeo t'uccise un figlio"
            4. "La tremenda ultrice spada"
            5a. "Eccomi in lieta vesta"
            5b. "Oh! quante volte"
            6. "Si fuggire: a noi non resta"
            7. "Vieni, ah!, vieni, e in me riposa"
            8. "Lieta notte avventurosa"
            9. "Sorcorso, sostegno"
            10. "Se ogni speme è a nio rapita"
            11. "Morte io non tremo"
            12. "Ah! non poss'io partire"
            13. "Solto! ad un sol mio grido"
            14. "Svena, ah! svena un disperato"
            16. "Sorgi, mio ben"
            17a. "Tu sola, o mia Giulietta"
            17b. "Deh! tu, deh!, tu, bell'anima"

1a.9 "La sonnambula," opera: ....

excerpts: I: 1. "Viva Amina!"
          2. "Tutto è gioia"
          3. "In Elvezia non v'ha rosa"

    4a. "Care compagne"
    4b. "A te, diletta tenera madre"
    4c. "Come per me sereno"
    4d. "Sopra il sen"
    5. "Io più di tutti, o Amina"
    6a. "Perdono, o mia diletta"
    6b. "Elvin, che rechi?"
    6c. "Prendi: l'anel ti dono"
    6d. "Ah! vorrei trovar parole"
    7a. "Qual rumore"
    7b. "Il mulino!"
    7c. "Vi ravviso, o luoghi ameni"
    7d. "Tu non sai con quei begli occhi"
    8a. "Contezza del paese avete voi, Signor"
    8b. "A fosco cielo, a notte bruna"
    8c. "Basta così"
    9a. "Elvino! E me tu lasci"
    9b. "Son geloso del zefiro errante"
    10. "Davver, non mi dispiace"
    11. "Che veggio?"
    12. "Osservate! L'uscio è aperto"
    13. "È menzogna"
    14a. "D'un pensiero e d'un accento"
    14b. "Non più nozze"
II: 15. "Qui la selva è più folta"
    16a. "Reggimi, o buono madre"
    16b. "Tutto è sciolto"
    16c. "Pasci il guardo e appaga l'alma"
    17a. "Viva il Conte!"
    17b. "Ah! perchè non posso odiarti"
    18a. "Lasciami: aver compreso"
    18b. "De'lieti auguri a voi son grata"
    19a. "Signor Conte, agli occhi miei"
    19b. "V'han certuni che dormendo"
    19c. "Piano, amici, non gridate"
    20. "Lisa mendace anch'essa!"
    21a. "Signor, che creder deggio?"
    21b. "Chi? Mira ... ella stessa"
    22a. "Oh! se una volta sola"
    22b. "Ah! non credea mirarti"
    22c. "Ah! non giunge"

1a.10   "Norma," opera: ....
    excerpts: 1. "Sinfonia"
  I: 2. "Ite sul colle, o Druidi," introduction (Oroveso)
    3a. "Svanir le voci!," recit (Polio, Flavius)
    3b. "Meco all'altar di Venere," cavatina (Pollio)
    3c. "Me protegge me difende" (Pollio)
    4a. "Norma viene" (Chorus)
    4b. "Sediziose voci," scene (Norma, Oroveso)
    4c. "Casta diva," cavatina (Chorus)
    4d. "Fine al rito" (Norma)
    4e. "Ah! bello a me ritorna" (Norma)
    5. "Sgombra è la sacra selva," scene (Adalgisa)
    6a. "Eccola! Va, mi lascia," recit (Pollio)
    6b. "Va, crudele," duet (Adalgisa, Pollio)
    7a. "Vanne, e li cela entrambi," recit (Norma)
    7b. "Oh, Rimembranza!" (Norma)
    7c. "Sola, furtiva al tempio"
    8a. "Tremi tu? E per chi? ... Oh, non tremare"
    8b. "Oh! di qual sei tu vittima," trio (Norma, Adalgisa, Pollio)
    8c. "Perfido! ... Or basti"
  II: 9. "Dormono entrambi," introduction & scene
    10a. "Me chiami, o Norma?," recit
    10b. "Mira, o Norma"
    10c. "Cedi! Deh, cedi!"
    10d. "Sì, fino all'ore estreme"
    11a. "Non parti!" (Chorus)
    11b. "Guerrieri," recit
    11c. "Ah! del Tebro," aria w/ chorus
    12. "Ei tornerà sì," recit
    13. "Guerra, guerra!" (Chorus)
    14a. "In mia man," duet
    14b. "Ah! Crudele"
    15a. "All'ira vostra"

15b. "Qual cor tradisti," duet
15c. "Deh! Non volerli vittime"

1a.11   "Beatrice di Tenda," opera: ....
       excerpts: 1a. "Prelude"
       I: 1b. "Tu, signor, lasciar sì presto" (Courtiers)
            1c. "Ah! non pensar che pieno" (Agnese)
            2a. "Silenzio e notte intorno" (Agnese)
            2b. "Sì: rivale ... rival regnante" (Agnese)
            3a. "Respiro io qui" (Beatrice)
            3b. "Oh! mie fedeli!" (Beatrice)
            4a. "Ma la sola, ohimè! son io" (Beatrice)
            4b. "Ah! la pena in lor piombò" (Beatrice)
            5a. "Tu qui, Filippo?" (Beatrice)
            5b. "E quali? quali? spergiura! ingrata!" (Filippo)
            5c. "Qui di ribelli sudditi" (Filippo)
            6. "Lo vedeste?" (Men-at-arms)
            7a. "Il mio dolore" (Beatrice)
            7b. "Deh! se mi amasti un giorno" (Beatrice)
            8a. "Ciascun! ciascun! non io" (Orombello)
            8b. "A ciuscun fidar vorrei" (Beatrice)
            9a. "Parti" (Beatrice)
            9b. "Vedi? Traditori!" (Agnese, Filippo)
       II: 10. "Lassa! e può il ciel permettere" (Maids of Honour)
            11. "Omai del suo destino" (Filippo)
            12. "Venga la rea ... Di grave accusa il peso" (Judges & Nobles, Beatrice)
            13. "Orombello! Oh sciagurato!" (Beatrice)
            14. "Filippo! ... Tu! ti appressa ..." (Agnese, Filippo)
            15a. "Qui m'accolse oppresso, errante" (Filippo)
            15b. "Non son io che la condanno" (Filippo)
            16a. "Ah! no, non sia la misera" (Maids of Honour, Friends)
            16b. "Nulla io dissi" (Beatrice)
            16c. "Angiol di pace all'anima" (Orombello)
            17. "Chi giunge?" (Beatrice)
            18a. "Ah! se un'urna è a me concessa" (Beatrice)
            18b. "Ah! la morte a cui m'appresso" (Beatrice)

1a.12   "I puritani," opera: ....
       excerpts: 1a. "Sinfonia"
       I: 1b. "All'erta!"
            2. "O di Cromvel guerrieri"
            3. "A festa!"
            4a. "Or dove fuggo"
            4b. "Ah! per sempre"
            4c. "Bel sogno beato"
            5a. "O amato zio"
            5b. "O Ciel! E fia vero"
            6. "Ad Arturo onore"
            7. "A te, o cara"
            8. "Il rito augusto"
            9. "Son vergin vezzosa"
            10a. "Sulla verginea"
            10b. "Ferma invan"
            11. "Arturo! Tu ritorni"
            12. "Ma tu già mi fuggi"
       II: 13. "Ah! dolor!"
            14. "Cinta di fiori"
            15. "E di morte"
            16a. "O rendetemi la speme"
            16b. "Qui la voce sua soave"
            16c. "Vien, diletto"
            17a. "Il rival salvar"
            17b. "Suoni la tromba"
       III: 18a. "Son salvo"
            18b. "A una fonte"
            19a. "Son già lontani"
            19b. "Fini! Me lassa!"
            19c. "Nel mirarti un solo istante"
            20. "Vieni, fra queste braccia"
            21a. "Ascolta ancora"
            21b. "Credeasi, misera"

2. ORCHESTRAL WORKS (c before 1825; small orch)

2.1   Sinfonia in D major (c1818) ....
2.2   Sinfonia in D minor (ca1822) ....
2.3   "Capriccio, ossia Sinfonia per studio," in C minor (ca1822) ....
2.4   Sinfonia in E-flat major (ca1823) ....
2.5   Sinfonia in D major (ca1823) ....
2.6   Sinfonia in B-flat major (ca1823) ....
2.7   Sinfonia in E-flat major (ca1823) ....

3. CONCERTOS, SOLO INSTR & ORCH

3.1   Oboe Concerto in E-flat major ....

4. PIANO

4.1   "Allegretto," in G minor (11 measure albumleaf) ....
4.2   "Pensiero musicale" ....
4.3   "Theme with introduction and coda," in F minor (ca1834) ....

Pf duet:

4.4   Piano Sonata in F major ....
4.5   "Capriccio," in G major ....
4.6   "Polacca" ....

5. ORGAN

5.1   Organ Sonata in G major...

6. CHURCH MUSIC (c before 1825)

6.1   9 "Versetti da cantarsi il Venerdi Santo" (c1815) ....
6.2   "Ombre pacifiche" (c ?1818)..
6.3   "Gratias agimus" (c1817–8; 4vv & orch) ....
6.4   "Gratias agimus" (c1817–8; S & orch) ....
6.5   "Tantum ergo" (2vv) and "Genitori," in F major (c1817; 4vv & orch) ....
6.6   "Tantum ergo" and "Genitori," in G major (c1818; 4vv & orch)....................................
6.7   "Litanic pastorale" (in honour of B.V.M.) (c1817–8; 2S & org).....................................
6.8   "Pange lingua" (c1817–8; 2vv & org) ....
6.9   Mass (Kyrie—Gloria) in G major (c1818; ch & orch) ....
6.10   Mass (Kyrie—Gloria) in D major (c1818; ch & orch) ....
6.11   "Salve regina," in F min / major (c1818; B, org & orch) ....
6.12   "Salve regina," in F minor (c1810–19; S & org) ....
6.13   "Tantum ergo" (S) and "Genitori," in B-flat major (c1818; ch & orch) ....
6.14   "Tantum ergo," in F major (c1810–19; S) ....
6.15   "Tantum ergo" and "Genitori," in E-flat major (c1810–19; S) ....
6.16   "Magnificat" (c1818–20; ch & orch) ....
6.17   "Tecum principium," in G major (c after 1819; S & orch) ....
6.18   Mass in A minor (ca1821; ch & orch) ....
6.19   "Tantum ergo," in G major (c1823; S & orch)..
6.20   "Tantum ergo," in E major (c1823; ch & orch) ....
6.21   "Tantum ergo," in F major (c1823; 2vv & orch) ....
6.22   "Tantum ergo," in D major (c1823; B & orch) ....
6.23   "Credo," in C major (c ?1824; ch & orch)..
6.24   "Dixit Dominus," psalm (c1824; vv, ch & orch) ....
6.25   "Te Deum," in C major (c1824; ch & orch)...
6.26   Mass in G minor (c1824) ....
6.27   "Te Deum" in E-flat major (c1819–26; ch & orch)..
6.28   "Salve regina," in A major (c1820–5; ch & orch) ....

7. MISC VOCAL

7.1   Canon for Cherubini's album (c1835; 2vv & pf) ....
7.2   Canon for Zimmerman's album (c1835; 4vv)..
7.3   "Coro," in E-flat major (wordless, 4vv & orch) ....

8. SECULAR VOCAL (1v & acc)

8.1 "Farfalletta," canzonetta (c1813) ....

8.2 "Si per te, gran nume eterno," cavatina (c1818; S & orch) ....

8.3 "Scena ed aria di Cecere" (c1818; S & orch)..

8.4 "E nello stringerti," cabaletta (c1818; S & orch) ....

8.5 "Questa e la valle," arietta (ca1821) ....

8.6 "Quando incise su questo marmo," aria (ca1821; S & orch) ....

8.7 "No, traditor," aria (c1820–6; S & pf) ....

8.8 "Dolente immagine di figlia mia," aria (c1821, Genoino; S & pf) ....

8.9 "Sogno d'infanzia," romanza (c1824; mS & pf) ....

8.10 "6 ariette da camera" (c1829): 1. "Malinconia, ninfa gentile" ....

8.11   2. "Vanne, o rosa fortunata"

8.12   3. "Bella Nice, che d'amore"

8.13   4. "Almen se non poss'io" (Metastasio)

8.14   5. "Per pietà, bel'idol mio" (Metastasio)

8.15   6. "Ma rendi pur contendo" (Metastasio)

8.16   *"Se il mio nome," arietta (spur: c by Rossini in: Il barbiere di Siviglia)* ....

8.17   *"Tu che al pianger," romanza (spur: c by Florimo in: Le dernier soir)* ....

8.18 "So che un sogno," aria (c1820–6; S) ....

8.19 "Torna, vezzosa Fillide," romanza (c1826; S & pf) ....

8.20 "L'abbandono" (L'ultima veglia), romanza (c1827–35; mS & pf) ....

8.21 "Il fervido desiderio," arietta (c1827–33; mS & pf) ....

8.22 "Vaga luna, che inargenti," arietta (c1827–35; mS & pf) ....

8.23 "A palpitar d'affanno," romanza (c1827–35; S & pf) ....

8.24 "Era felice un di," arietta (c1827–35; mS & pf) ....

8.25 "L'allegro marinaro," ballata in G major (c1827–35; mS & pf) ....

8.26 "La ricordanza," sonetto (c1834, Pepoli) ....

9. WORKS LOST

9.1   *"Gallus cantavit" (c1807)* ....

9.2   *"La mammoletta," arietta (ca1830)* ....

9.3   *"Ah! Non pensai," arietta (ca1830)* ....

9.4   *"3 Sonetti" (c1834, Pepoli): 1. "Amore"* ....

9.5   *2. "Malinconia"*

9.6   *3. "La speranza"*

9.7   *"Alla luna," Sapphic ode (c1834, Pepoli)* ....

*   *   *   *   *

1. STAGE WORKS (operas)

1.1 "Wozzeck," 3 acts (c1917–22, after Büchner's play: Woyzeck) Op.7
1.2 "Lulu," 3 acts (c1929–35, after Wedekind's play: Lulu; Act III compl Cerha 1978) ....

1a. SELECTIONS FROM OPERAS

1a.1 "Wozzeck," opera: Op.7
    I. "5 Character-Pieces": 1. "Suite"
        2. "Rhapsody"
        3. "Military March and Lullaby"
        4. "Passacaglia"
        5. "Andante affettuoso" (quasi Rondo)
    II. "Symphony in 5 Movements": 1. "Sonata Movement"
        2. "Fantasy and Fugue"
        3. "Largo"
        4. "Scherzo"
        5. "Rondo con introduzione"
    III. "6 Inventions": 1. "Invention on a theme"
        2. "Invention on one note"
        3. "Invention on a rhythm"
        4. "Invention on a chord of six notes"
    Orch Interlude: "Invention on a key"
        5. "Invention on quaver figure"

2. ORCHESTRAL WORKS

2.1 "3 Orchestral Pieces" (c1913–5, r1929): No.1 "Prelude" Op.6
2.2 No.2 "Rounds"
2.3 No.3 "March"
2.4 "Lyric Suite," 3 pieces (arr1928; strings, arr from Nos.2–4 of: Lyric Suite for str qt) ....

3. CONCERTOS, SOLO INSTR & ORCH

3.1 "Chamber Concerto" (c1923–5; pf, vn & 13 wind insts) ....
3.2 Violin Concerto, "To the Memory of an Angel" (c1935) ....

4. STRING QUARTETS

4.1 String Quartet (c1910) Op.3
4.2 "Lyric Suite" (12-tone method) (c1925–6; see arr for strings): No.1 "Allegro gioviale" ....
4.3 No.2 "Andante amoroso"
4.4 No.3 "Allegro mysterioso"
4.5 No.4 "Adagio appassionato"
4.6 No.5 "Presto delirando"
4.7 No.6 "Largo desolato"

5. OTHER CHAMBER MUSIC

5.1 "Fugue" (with 3 subjects) (str qnt & pf) Op.5
5.2 "4 Pieces" (c1913; cl & pf): No.1 "Mässig—Langsam" Op.5
5.3 No.2 "Sehr langsam"
5.4 No.3 "Sehr rasch" (w/ Ländler as Trio)
5.5 No.4 "Langsam"
5.6 "Adagio" (vn, cl & pf, arr of 2nd movt of: Chamber Concerto of 1923–5) ....

6. PIANO SONATAS

6.1 Piano Sonata (c ?1907–8) Op.1
6.2 *Piano Sonata in D minor (c1907–9, frag)* ....
6.3 *Piano Sonata in E-flat major (c1907–9, frag)* ....

7. OTHER PIANO WORKS

7.1 *"Clavierstück," in F minor (c1907–8, frag)* ....
7.2 "Impromptu," in C minor (c1907–8) ....
7.3 "Klavierstück," in B minor (c1907–9) ....
7.4 "Klavierstück," in C minor (c1907–9) ....

7.5	"Klavierstück," in F major (c1907–9) ....
7.6	"Klavierstück," in F minor (c1907–9) ....
7.7	"Minuet," in C minor (c1907–9) ....
7.8	"Minuet," in F major (c1907–9) ....
7.9	"Scherzo," in C minor (c1907–9) ....
7.10	"12 Variations," in C major (c1907–9) ....
7.11	"Variations," in F major (c1907–9) ....
7.12	"Variations," in F minor (c1907–9) ....
7.13	"Waltz," in G major (c1907–9) ....

8. VOICE & ORCHESTRA

8.1	"Altenberg Lieder" (c1912, Altenberg): 1. "Seele, wie bist du schöner" Op.4
8.2	2. "Sahst du nach dem Gewitterregen"
8.3	3. "Über die Grenzen des All"
8.4	4. "Nichts ist gekommen"
8.5	5. "Hier ist Friede!"
8.6	"3 Bruchstücke from 'Wozzeck' " (p1924; S & orch, from opera Op.7): 1. "Tchin bum! Soldaten" ....
8.7	2. "Und ist kein Betrug"
8.8	3. "Ringel, Ringel"
8.9	"Der Wein," concert aria (c1929, 3 poems by Baudelaire transl George; S & orch) ....
8.10	"Lulu," suite (c1934; S & orch, from opera): 1. "Rondo" (Andante & hymn) ....
8.11	2. "Ostinato" (Allegro)
8.12	3. "Lulu's song" (Comodo)
8.13	4. "Variations" (Moderato)
8.14	5. "Adagio" (Sostenuto, lento, grave)
8.15	"Alban Berg an das Frankfurter Opernhaus," 4-part canon (c1930, Berg) ....

9. SONGS (w/ pf)

70 "Jugendlieder" (c early):

9.1	1. "Heilige Himmel" (c1900, Evers) ....
9.2	2. "Herbstgefühl" (ca1902, Fleischer) ....
9.3	3. "Unter der Linden" (c1900, Vogelweide) ....
9.4	4. "Spielleute" (ca1902, Ibsen) ....
9.5	5. "Wo der Goldregen steht" (ca1902, Lorenz) ....
9.6	6. "Lied des Schiffermädels" (ca1902, Bierbaum) ....
9.7	7. "Abschied" (ca1902, Monsterberg) ....
9.8	8. "Liebeslied" (ca1902, Dolorosa) ....
9.9	9. "Über meinen Nächten" (ca1902, Dolorosa) ....
9.10	10. "Sehnsucht" I (ca1902, Hohenberg) ....
9.11	11. "Sternenfall" (ca1902, Wilhelm) ....
9.12	12. "Er klagt, dass der Frühling so korz blüht" (ca1902, Arno Holz) ....
9.13	13. "Ich und du" (ca1902, Busse) ....
9.14	14. "Über Nacht" (ca1902, Rognetti) ....
9.15	15. "Verlassen" (ca1902, Bohemian folksong) ....
9.16	16. "Traurigkeit" (ca1902, Altenberg) ....
9.17	17. "Hoffnung" (ca1902, Altenberg) ....
9.18	18. "Flötenspielerin" (ca1902, Altenberg) ....
9.19	19. "Spaziergang" (ca1902, Mombert) ....
9.20	20. "Soldatenbraut" (ca1902, Mörike) ....
9.21	21. "So regnet es sich langsam ein" (ca1902, Cäsar Flaischlen) ....
9.22	22. "Grenzen der Menschheit" (ca1902, Goethe) ....
9.23	23. "Ballade des äusseren Lebens" (ca1902, Hofmannsthal) ....
9.24	24. "Im Walde" (ca1902, Bjørnson) ....
9.25	25. "Viel Träume" (ca1902, Amerling) ....
9.26	26. "Tiefe Sehnsucht," duet (c1904 or 5, Liliencron) ....
9.27	27. "Über den Berg" (ca1902, Busse) ....
9.28	28. "Am Strande" (ca1902, Scherer) ....
9.29	29. "Reiselied" (ca1902, Hofmannsthal) ....
9.30	30. "Spuk" (ca1902, Hebbel) ....
9.31	31. "Aus Pfingsten" (ca1902, Evers) ....
9.32	32. "Winter" (ca1902, Johannes Schlaf) ....
9.33	33. "O wär' mein Lieb' ein Röslein rot" (ca1902, Burns) (also see Beach Op.12/3, B5/3, Schumann Op.27/2 & Weber J302)
9.34	34. "Sehnsucht" II (ca1902, Hohenberg) ....
9.35	35. "Ich liebe dich" (c1904–5, Grabbe) ....
9.36	36. "Ferne Lieder" (c1904–5, Rückert) ....
9.37	37. "Ich will die Fluren meiden" (Rückert) ....
9.38	38. "Geliebte Schöne" (c1904–5, Heine) ....
9.39	39. "Schattenleben" (c1904–5, Graf) ....
9.40	40. "Am Abend" (c1904–5, Geibel) ....

9.41   41. "Wenn Gespenster aufstehen" (c1904–5, Felix Dörmann) ....
9.42   42. "Vom Ende" (c1904–5, Marie Madeleine) ....
9.43   43. "Vorüber" (c1904–5, Wiesbacher) ....
9.44   44. "Scheidelied" (c1904–5, Baumbach) ....
9.45   45. "Eure Weisheit" (c1904–5, Fischer) ....
9.46   46. "Schlummerlose Nacht" (c1904–5, Greif) ....
9.47   47. "Nachtgesang" (c1904–5, Bierbaum) ....
9.48   48. "Es wandelt, was wir schauen" (c1904–5, Eichendorff) ....
9.49   49. "Liebe" (c1904–5, Rilke) ....
9.50   50. "Wandert, ihr Wolken" (c1904–5, Avenarius) ....
9.51   51. "Im Morgengrauen" (c1904–5, Stieler) ....
9.52   52. "Grabschrift" (c1904–5, Jakobowski) ....
9.53   53. "Traum" (c1904–5, Semmler) ....
9.54   54. "Furcht" (c1904–5, Palma) ....
9.55   55. "Augenblicke" (c1904–5, Hamerling) ....
9.56   56. "Trinklied" (c1904–5, Rückl) ....
9.57   57. "Fromm" (c1904–5, Gustav Falke) ....
9.58   58. "Leben" (c1904–5, Evers) ....
9.59   59. "Näherin" (c1904–5, Rilke) ....
9.60   60. "Erster Verlust" (c1904–5, Goethe) ....
9.61   61. "Süss sind mir die Schollen des Tales" (c1904–5, Knodt) ....
9.62   62. "Der milde Herbst Anno 45" (c1904–5, Max Mell) ....
9.63   63. "Menschenherz" (c1904–5, delle Grazie) ....
9.64   64. "Holophan" (c1904–5, Wallpach) ....
9.65   65. "Mignon" (c1904–5, Goethe) ....
9.66   66. "Läuterung" (c1904–5, Hohenberg) ....
9.67   67. "Die Sorglichen" (c1904–5, Falke) ....
9.68   68. "Das stille Königreich" (c1904–5, Busse) ....
9.69   69. "Trinklied" (c1904–5, Henckell) ....
9.70   70. "An Leukon": "Rosen pflükke, Rosen blühn" (c1908, Gleim) ....

9.71   "7 Early Songs" (c1905–8—his early years of studies with Schoenberg; r & orchd1928): 1. "Im Zimmer":
        "Herbstsonnenschein" (c1905, Schlaf) ....
9.72   2. "Die Nachtigall": "Das macht, es hat die Nachtigall die ganze Nacht gesungen" (c1905–6, Storm)
9.73   3. "Liebesode": "Im Arm der Liebe schliefen wir selig ein" (c1906, Hartleben)
9.74   4. "Traumgekrönt": "Das war der Tag der weissen Chrysanthemen" (c1907, Rilke)
9.75   5. "Sommertage": "Nun ziehen Tage über die Welt" (c1908, Hohenberg)
9.76   6. "Nacht": "Dämmern Wolken über Nacht und Tal" (c1908, Hauptmann)
9.77   7. "Schilflied": "Auf geheimem Waldespfade schleich' ich gern im Abendschein" (c1908, Lenau)
9.78   "Schliesse mir die Augen beide" I (c1909, Storm) ....
9.79   "4 Songs" (c ?1909–10) (this work marks Berg's final rejection of tonality): 1. "Schlafen, schlafen, nichts
        als schlafen!" (Hebbel) Op.2
9.80   2."Schlafend trägt man mich in mein Heimatland" (Mombert)
9.81   3. "Nun ich der Riesen Stärksten überwand" (Mombert)
9.82   4. "Warm die Lüfte, es spriesst Gras auf sonnigen Wiesen" (Mombert)
9.83   "Schliesse mir die Augen beide" II (c1925, Storm) ....

10. ARRANGEMENTS OF WORKS OF OTHERS

10.1   Schreker: "Der ferne Klang" (vocal score 1911) ....
10.2   Schoenberg: "Gurrelieder" (vocal score 1912) ....
10.3   Schoenberg: "Litanei & Entrückung," from: Str Qt, Op.10 (arr1912; 1v & pf) ....
10.4   Schoenberg: "Chamber Symphony," Op.9 (arr1913–5; pf) ....

* * * * *

1. STAGE WORKS

Operas:

1.1	*"Estelle et Némorin" (c1823, Gerono after Florian, lost)*	*H17*
1.2	"Les Francs-Juges," 3 acts (c1825–6, r1829, Ferrand, inc)	H23a
1.3	"Le cri de guerre du Brisgaw," 1 act intermezzo (c1833–4, based on H23a, inc)	H23c
1.4	"Benvenuto Cellini," 2 act semi-seria (c1836–8, Wailly & Barbier; r1852 in 3 acts)	Op.23, H76a
1.5	"Erigone," intermède antique (ca1835–9, after Ballanche; vv, ch & orch, inc)	H77
1.6	"La nonne sanglante," 3 acts (c1841–7, Scribe & Delavigne after Lewis, inc)	H91
1.7	"Les troyens" (The Troyans), 5 acts (c1856–8, r1859–60, Berlioz after Virgil)................	H133a
1.8	"Béatrice et Bénédict," 2 acts (c1860–2, Berlioz after Laroche's transl of Shakespeare's Much Ado)..	H138

Incid music:

1.9	*"Hamlet" (c1844, Shakespeare transl Wailly, project, frags)*	*(H102–103)*

1a. SELECTIONS FROM OPERAS

1a.2	"Les Francs-Juges," opera:	H23a

    . "Ouverture" (c1826)
      I: 1. "Arnold, entends nos fers," chorus
             2. "Conrad s'arma," duo (Christiern, Olmerik)
             3a. "Va! je t'abhorre," recit (Conrad) (music lost)
             3b. "Noble amitié," aria (Conrad) (music lost)
             4. "La nuit voilant pour nous," élégie (Amélie) (music lost)
             5. "Frais vallons où dorment nos pères" (Arnold, Conrad, Amélie, Elmire) (music lost)
      II: 6. "L'ombre descend dans la vallée," choeur des bergers
             7. "Vois-tu le soleil s'enfuir," trio pastoral (Nise, Méry, Arnold) (see choral works H23b)
             8. "N'espère plus, Arnold," duet (Amélie, Arnold) (music lost)
             9. "Marche des gardes" (music lost)
             10. "Finale" (music lost)
      III: *11a. "Voici l'endroit fatal," recit (Arnold) (frags)*
             11b. "Descends et viens," invocation (frags)
             12. "Hymne des Francs-Juges": "Des célestes décrets"
             13. Reprise of hymn
             14. "Fier Germain, reprends ces vallons" chorus (frags)

1a.4	"Benvenuto Cellini," opera (2 act vers of 1836–8, Nos. of sections in The Gramophone) Op.23, H76a

    excerpts: 1. "Ouverture"
      I/1: 2. "Teresa! Mais où peut-elle être?" (Balducci)
            3. "Tra la la la, De profundis!," chorus
            4a. "Les belles fleurs!," recit (Teresa)
            4b. "Entre l'amour et le devoir," romance (Teresa)
            5. "Ô Teresa, vous que j'aime plus que ma vie" (Cellini)
            6. "Ah! mourir, chère belle"
            7. "Ah! maître drôle, ah! libertin!," chorus
      I/2: 8a. "Une heure encore," recit (Cellini)
            8b. "La gloire était ma seule idole," romance (Cellini)
            9a. "À boire, à boire, à boire," chorus
            9b. "Si la terre aux beaux se couronne"
            10. "Que voulez-vous? la cave est vide" (Le Cabaretier)
            11. "Cette somme t'est due," air (Ascanio)
            12. "Ah! qui pourrait me résister?" (Fieramosca)
            13. "Vous voyez, j'espère" (Balducci)
            14. "Venez, venez, peuple de Rome"
      II/1: 15. "Ah, qu'est-il devenu?" (Teresa)
            16. "Rosa purpurea"
            17. "Teresa! ... Ma dague en main, protégé par la nuit" (Cellini)
            18. "Ah! le ciel, cher époux"
            19. "Quand des sommets de la montagne," duet (Teresa, Cellini)
            20. "Ah! je te trouve enfin"
            21. "Le Pape ici! de la prudence!"
            22. "Justice à nous"
            23. "Ah! ça, démon!"
            24. "Ah! maintenant de sa folle impudence"
      II/2: 25. "Tra la la ... Mais qu'ai-je donc?," air (Ascanio)
            26a. "Seul pour lutter," recit (Cellini)
            26b. "Sur les monts," air (Cellini)
            27. "Bienheureux les matelots," chorus
            28. "Peuple ouvrier, que l'atelier vite se ferme," chorus
            29. "Du métal! du métal!" (Fieramosca)

"Benvenuto Cellini," opera (3 act vers of 1852): Op.23, H76a
. "Ouverture"
I: 1a. "Introduction"
1b. "Teresa! Mais où peut-elle être?" (Balducci)
2. "Entre l'amour et le devoir," air (Teresa)
3. "Ô Teresa, vous que j'aime plus que ma vie," duet & trio (Teresa, Cellini, Fieramosca)
4. "Final": "À nous voisines et servantes!" (Teresa)
II: 5. "La gloire était ma seule idole," romance (Cellini)
6. "À boire, à boire, à boire," scene & chorus
7. "Ah! qui pourrait me résister?," air (Fieramosca)
8. "Final: Le Carnaval": "Vous voyez, j'espère" (Barducci)
III: 9. "A l'atelier rentrons sans plus attendre," entr'acte & chorus
10. "Bienheureux les matelots, ces enfants des flots," scene (Teresa & chorus)
11. "Tra la la," air (Ascanio)
12. "Rosa purpurea Maria sancta mater ora pro nobis," scene & chorus
13. "Quand des sommets de la montagne," duo (Teresa, Cellini)
14. "Ah! je te trouve enfin," scene & sextet (Balducci)
15. "Sur les monts les plus sauvages," air (Cellini)
16. "Final. La Fonte": "Son Éminence attend. Allons, commence!" (Un Officier)

1a.6 "La nonne sanglante," opera: H91
II: (1.) "De Dieu sur quel drapeau descendit la colère," recit (Rodolphe, Hubert)
. "Sans espérance quand la souffrance," air (Hubert)
. "C'en est donc fait plus d'espérance," recit (Rodolphe, Hubert)
(2.) "Oui, oui, ma voix doit être entendue," air (Rodolphe)
. "Rodolphe! Agnès!," recit (Agnès, Rodolphe)
(3.) "Je meurs, je meurs si vous m'êtes ravie," duo (Agnès, Rodolphe)
(4.) "Avant minuit les portes sont ouvertes," légende (Rodolphe)

1a.7 "Les troyens," opera (Nos. of sections in The Gramophone): H133a
Part I. "La prise de Troie," Act I: 1. "Ha! Ha! Après dix ans" (Choeur de la populace troyenne)
2a. "Les Grecs ont disparu!," recit (Cassandre)
2b. "Malheureux Roi! dans l'éternelle nuit," aria (Cassandre)
3a. "Chorèbe! il faut qu'il parte et quitte la Troiade" (Cassandre)
3b. "Reviens à toi, vierge adorée!" (Chorèbe)
3c. "Si tu m'aimes, va-t'en" (Cassandre)
4. "Dieux protecteurs de la ville éternelle," march & hymn (Choeur)
5. "Combat de ceste—Pas de lutteurs"
6. "Andromaque et son fils!," pantomime (Choeur)
7. "Du peuple et des soldats, ô roi!," narration (Énée)
8. "Châtiment effroyable!," octet & d chorus
9. "Que la déesse nous protège," recit & chorus (Énée)
10. "Non, je ne verrai pas la déplorable fête," aria (Cassandre)
11a. "Du roi des dieux, ô fille aimée" (Trojan March) (Choeur)
11b. "Arrêtez! arrêtez! Oui, la flamme, la hache!" (Cassandre)
II: 12a. "O lumière de Troie!" (Énée)
12b. "Ah!... fuis, fils de Vénus" (L'ombre d'Hector)
13. "La ville ensanglantée" (Panthée)
14. "Ah! Puissante Cybèle" (Prière) (Choeur des Troyennes)
15a. "Tous ne périront pas" (Cassandre)
15b. "O digne soeur d'Hector!" (Choeur)
16. "Complices de sa gloire" (Choeur, Cassandre, Un chef grec)
Part II. "Les troyens à Carthage," Act III: 17a. "Prélude"
17b. "De Carthage les cieux semblent bénir la fête!" (Choeur)
18. "Gloire à Didon, notre reine chérie!" (Chant national) (Choeur)
19a. "Nous avons vu finir sept ans à peine," recit (Didon)
19b. "Chers Tyriens," aria (Didon)
19c. "Cette belle journée" (Didon)
20. "Entrée des constructeurs"
21. "Entrée des matelots"
22. "Entrée des laboureurs"
23. "Peuple! tous les honneurs," recit (Didon)
24a. "Les chants joyeux," recit (Didon)
24b. "Sa voix fait naître dans mon sein," duet (Didon, Anna)
25a. "La porte du palais n'est jamais défendue," recit (Didon)
25b. "Errante sur les mers," aria (Didon)
26. "Trojan March"
27. "Auguste reine," recit (Ascagne)
28. "Reine, je sui Énée!" (Énée)
IV: 29. "Royal Hunt and Storm"
30a. "Dites, Narbal, qui cause vos alarmes?," recit (Anna)
30b. "Pour nous de ce côté plus rien n'est redoutable" (Narbal)
31. "De quels revers menaces-tu Carthage," aria & duet (Narbal, Anna)
32. "Marche pour l'entrée de la reine"
Ballets: 33a. "Pas des Almées"

33b. "Danse des Esclaves"
33c. "Pas d'Esclaves nubiennes"
34. "O blonde Cérès" (Iopas)
35a. "Pardonne, Iopas, ta voix même" (Didon)
35b. "Ô pudeur! Tout conspire" (Didon)
36a. "Mais bannissons ces tristes souvenirs " recit (Énée)
36b. "Tout n'est que paix et charme," septet (Didon, Énée, Ascagne, Anna, Iopas, Narbal, Panthée)
37. "Nuits d'ivresse!," duet (Didon, Énée)
V: 38. "Vallon sonore" (Chanson d'Hylas)
39. "Préparez tout, il faut partir enfin" (Panthée)
40. "Par Bacchus! ils sont fous," duet (1re Sentinelle, 2e Sentinelle)
41a. "Inutiles regrets!" (Énée)
41b. "Ah! quand viendra l'instant," air (Énée)
42. "Énée! ... Encor ces voix!" (Choeur d'ombres, Énée)
43. "Debout, Troyens, éveillez-vous, alerte!" (Énée)
44. "Errante sur tes pas," duet (Didon, Énée)
45. "Va, ma soeur, l'implorer" (Didon)
46a. "En mer, voyez!" (Choeur)
46b. "Dieux immortels!" (Didon)
47. "Je vais mourir," monolog (Didon)
48. "Adieu, fière cité," aria (Didon)
49. "Dieux de l'oubli" (Choeur de Prétres de Pluton)
50a. "D'un malheureux amour" (Didon)
50b. "Mon souvenir vivra" (Didon)
51. "Quels cris!" (Choeur)
52a. "Imprécation"
52b. "Haine éternelle" (Choeur)

1a.8 "Béatrice et Bénédict," opera: H138
. "Ouverture"
I: 1. "Le More est en fuite" I, chorus
2. "Le More est en fuite" II, chorus
2bis. "Sicilienne"
3. "Je vais le voir" (Héro)
4. "Comment le dédain pourrait-il mourir?," duet (Béatrice, Bénédict)
5. "Me marier? Dieu me pardonne!," trio (Bénédict, Claudio, Don Pedro)
6. & 6bis. "Mourez, tendres époux," épithalame grotesque
7. "Ah! je vais l'aimer," rondo (Bénédict)
8. "Vous soupirez, madame?," duet-nocturne (Héro, Ursule)
. "Entr'acte: Sicilienne"
II: 9. "Le vin de Syracuse," improvisation (Somarone & Choeur à boire)
10a. "Dieu! Que viens-je d'entendre?," air (Béatrice)
10b. "Il m'en souvient"
11. "Je vais d'un coeur aimant," trio (Héro, Béatrice, Ursule)
12. "Viens, de l'hyménée" (Choeur loinain, derrière la scène)
13. "Dieu qui guidas nos bras," marche nuptiale
14. "Ici l'on voit Bénédict," enseigne
15. "L'amour est un flambeau," scherzo duettino (Béatrice, Bénédict)

2. SYMPHONIES

2.1 "Symphonie fantastique: épisode de la vie d'un artiste" (c1830; inspired in part by T. De Quincey's
Confessions of an English opium-eater, transl Musset, pubd in London Magazine 1821; also see
choral sequel: Le retour à la vie, Op.14bis, H55a): Op.14, H48
1. "Rêveries, Passions"
2. "A Ball" (Valse)
3. "Scene in the Country"
4. "March to the Scaffold"
5. "Dream of a Witches' Sabbath"
2.2 "Harold en Italie" (Harold in Italy) (c1834, inspired by Byron's Childe Harold's Pilgrimage;
w/ va solo): Op.16, H68
1. "Harold in the Mountains: Scenes of Sadness, Happiness, and Joy"
2. "March of the Pilgrims, Singing Their Evening Prayers"
3. "Serenade of a Mountaineer of the Abruzzi to His Mistress"
4. "Orgy of the Brigands: Memories of Past Scenes"
2.3 "Roméo et Juliette," sym dramatique (c1839, r until 1847, Deschamps based on Garrick's edition of
Shakespeare's play; A, T, B, ch & orch; staged as 'opéra-ballet' in Paris 1955) (also see opera
c by Gounod, ballet c by Prokofiev Op.64, incid music c by Kabalevsky, Milhaud Op.161
& R. Strauss AV86, film score c by Khachaturian): Op.17, H79
1. "Combat. Tumult. Intervention of the Prince"
2. "Roméo Alone. Sadness. Distant Sounds of Music and Dancing Festivities at the Capulets"
3. "Night. The Capulets' Garden. The Young Capulets on Their Way Home. Love Scene"
4. "Queen Mab, the Spirit of Dreams"
5. "Juliet's Funeral": "Jetez des fleurs pour la vierge expirée"

6. "Roméo at the Tomb of the Capulets"
7. "Finale": "Quoi! Roméo de retour?," air (Friar Laurence)
2.4   "Grande symphonie funèbre et triomphale" (c1840, Deschamps; 3 vers): Op.15, H80
   . Version 1 (c1840; milit band)
   . Version 2 (c1842, Deschamps; band, w/ orch & ch ad lib)
   . Version 3 of the Apothéose (c1848; mS/T, ch & pf)

3. OTHER ORCHESTRAL WORKS

3.1   "Grande Ouverture des Francs-Juges" (c1826) Op.3, H23d
3.2   "Grande Ouverture de Waverley" (c1826–8, inspired by Scott's Waverley) Op.1, H26
3.3   "Ouverture de La Tempête" (c1830; ch & orch, incorp into: Le retour à la vie, Op.14bis, H55a) H52
3.4   "Grande Ouverture du Roi Lear" (c1831) Op.4, H53
3.5   "Intrata di Rob-Roy MacGregor" (c1831, inspired by Scott's Rob Roy, used in Harold
    en Italie, Op.16, H68) H54
3.6   *"Fête musicale fenèbre" (c1835, inc, lost)* *H72*
3.7   "Grande Ouverture de Benvenuto Cellini" (c1838) H76b
3.8   "Le carnaval romain. Ouverture caractéristique" (c1843–4, based on: Benvenuto Cellini, Op.23) H95
3.9   "Ouverture du Corsaire" (c1844, orig sketches of 1831 titled: La tour de Nice; 2 vers) (also see ballet
    Il Corsaro in Donizetti's opera: Belisario, Schumann's opera: Der Corsar, Verdi's opera: Il Corsaro
    & Wolf: Ouvertüre zu Byrons 'Der Korsar'): Op.21, H101
   . Version 1, "La tour de Nice" (c1844)
   . Version 2, "Le corsaire rouge" (c1846–51, renamed 1852 as: Le corsaire after Fenimore
      Cooper's novel: The Red Rover, the change in title influenced perhaps by the popularity
      of Byron's The Corsair)
3.10 "La fuite en Égypte," overture (c1850) H128/1
3.11 "Béatrice et Bénédict," overture (c1860–2) ....
3.12 "Marche troyenne" (arr for concert 1864 from Act I of opera: Les troyens, H133a)........................... H133b

4. VIOLIN CONCERTOS, VIOLIN & ORCH

4.1   "Rêverie et caprice" (c1841; vn & orch/pf, from withdrawn cavatina of: Benvenuto Cellini, Op.23)Op.8, H88

5. CHAMBER MUSIC

5.1   *"Potpourri concertant sur des thèmes italiens" (c1817–8; fl, hn & str qt, lost)* *H1*
5.2   *"2 Quintets" (c1818–9; fl & str qt, lost)* *H2–3*
5.3   *"Là ci darem la mano," variations (ca1828; gui, on the theme of Mozart, lost)* *H30*

6. HARMONIUM

6.1   "Sérénade agreste à la madone sur le thème des pifferari romains" (c1844) H98
6.2   "Toccata" (c1844) H99
6.3   "Hymne pour l'élévation" (c1844) H100

7. CHORAL WORKS

7.1   *"Le passage de la mer rouge," oratorio (c1823–4, Latin text from Bible, lost)* *H18*
7.2   "Messe solennelle" (c1824, Latin text; B, ch & orch, recently rediscovered in Belgium): H20a
      1. "Kyrie"
      2. "Gloria"
      3. "Credo"
      4. "Crucifixus"
      5. "Et Resurrexit" I
      6. "Domine Salvum"
      7. "Salutaris"
      8. "Sanctus"
      9. "Agnus Dei"
7.3   "Resurrexit" II (Le jugement dernier) (c1828, 2nd vers of H20a/5)... H20b
7.4   "La révolution grecque" I, scène héroïque (c1825–6; ch & orch): H21a
      1. "Introduction, récitative et air (un chef grec)": "Lèvetoi, fils de Sparte! Allons!"
      2. "Choeur des guerriers": "Mais la voix du Dieu des armées"
      3. "Choeur de femmes": "Astre terrible et saint"
      4. "Final (choeur général)": "Des sommets de l'Olympe aux rives de l'Alphée"
7.5   "La révolution grecque" II, scène héroïque (arr1833; ch & milit band): H21b
      1. "Choeur de femmes": "Astre terrible et saint"
      2. "Choeur général": "Des sommets de l'Olympe aux rives de l'Alphée"
7.6   "Nocturne": "Le ciel et les voluptées" (c1828, 2nd vers of No.7 of opera: Les Francs-Juges, H23a) ... H23b
7.7   "La mort d'Orphée," cantata (c1827, Berton; T, ch & orch, for Prix de Rome): H25
      1. "Introduction": "Prêtresses de Bacchus, votre haine inflexible" (Orphée)

        12b. "Quelle céleste image"
        13. "Choeur de soldats. Choeur d'étudants": "Villes entourées ... Jam nox stellata"
  III: 14. "La retraite" (Tambours et trompettes sonnant la retraite)
        15a. "Air de Faust dans la chambre de Marguerite": "Merci doux crépuscule"
        15b. "Je l'entends"
        16a. "Que l'air est étouffant!"
        16b. "Le Roi de Thulé. Chanson gothique": "Autrefois un roi de Thulé"
        17. "Evocation": "Esprits des flammes" (Méphistophélès)
        18. "Menuets des follets"
        19a. "Sérénade de Méphistophélès avec choeur de follets": "Devant la maison"
        19b. "Grands dieux! que vois-je?"
        20. "Trio & Chorus": "Allons! il est trop tard!"
  IV: 21a. "Romance de Marguerite": "D'amour l'ardente flamme"
        21b. "Au son des trompettes"
        22. "Nature immense" (Invocation de Faust à la nature)
        23. "Récitatif et Chasse": "À la voûte azurée"
        24. "La Course à l'abyme. Duo": "Dans mon coeur retentit"
        25a. "Pandemonium. Choeur de damnés et de démons": "Ha! Irimiru Karabrao"
        25b. "Epilogue": "Alors l'Enfer se tut"
        26a. "Le Ciel. Choeur d'esprits célestes": "Laus! Hosanna!"
        26b. "Apothéose de Marguerite": "Remonte au ciel"

7.30   "Prière du matin" (c1846, Lamartine; child ch & pf) H112
7.31   "La menace des Francs": "Ah! si le sceptre en main" (c1848; 4 m vv, ch & pf/orch)............... H117
7.32   "Te Deum" (c1849, Liturgy; T, 3ch, orch, brass bands & org): Op.22, H118
        1. "Te Deum," hymne
        2. "Tibi omnes," hymne
        . "Prélude" (tambours militaires, for milit ceremonies only)
        3. "Dignare," prière
        4. "Christe, rex gloriae," hymne
        5. "Te ergo quaesumus," prière
        6. "Judex crederis," hymne et prière
        7. "Marche pour la présentation des drapeaux"
7.33   "La fuite en Égypte," mystère en style ancien (c1850; T, ch & orch, incorp in: L'enfance, Op.25): H128
        1. "Ouverture"
        2. "L'Adieu des bergers à la Sainte Famille": "Il s'en va loin de la terre," chorus
        3. "Le Repos de la Sainte Famille": "Les pélerins étant venus" (Le Récitant)
7.34   "L'enfance du Christ" (Trilogie sacrée), oratorio (c1853–4, Berlioz; vv, ch & orch): Op.25, H130
    I. "Herod's Dream": . "Dans la crèche, en ce temps, Jésus venait de naître," recit
        1. "Marche nocturne"
        2. "Toujours ce rêve!," air (Hérode)
        3. "Lâches, tremblez!," recit (Hérode, Polydorus)
        4. "Les sages de Judée, ô roi," recit (Hérode, les Devins)
        5. "O mon cher fils," duo
        6. "Joseph! Marie!" (Les Anges invisibles. Sainte Marie, St. Joseph)
    II. "The Flight into Egypt": . "Ouverture"
        . "L'Adieu des bergers à la Sainte Famille" (Shepherds' Farewell)
        . "Le Repos de la Sainte Famille"
    III. "The Arrival at Sais": . "Depuis trois jours," recit
        1. "Dans cette ville," duo (Sainte Marie, St. Joseph)
        2a. "Entrez, entrez, pauvres Hébreux!" (Père de Famille)
        2b. "Trio" (2fl & harp)
        2c. "Vous pleurez, jeune mére," recit (Le Père)
        2d. "Allez dormir, bon père," air (Le Père)
        3. "Ce fut ainsi que par un infidèle" (Récitant, Choeur)
7.35   "L'impériale": "Du peuple entier les âmes," cantata (c1854, Lafont; 2ch & orch) Op.26, H129
7.36   "Hymne pour la consécration du nouveau tabernacle": "Bien que le ciel" (c1859; ch & pf/org) H135
7.37   "Le temple universel": "La Liberté se lève sur le monde" (Vaudin; 2 vers): H137
        . Version 1 (c1861; 2ch & org)
        . Version 2 (ca1867–8; ch)
7.38   "Veni creator," motet (ca1861–8, Liturgy; 3vv & ch) H141
7.39   "Tantum ergo," motet (ca1961–8, Liturgy; 3vv, ch & org) H142

8. VOICE & ORCHESTRA (orchd versions of songs included in Songs)

8.1   *"Le cheval arabe," cantata (c1822, Millevoye; 1v & orch, lost)* *H12*
8.2   *"Beverley, ou le joueur," dramatic scene (c1823–4, Saurin after Moore; B & orch, lost)* *H19*
8.3   "Herminie," scène lyrique (c1828, Vieillard; S & orch, for Prix de Rome): H29
        1a. "Introduction"
        1b. "Ah! si de la tendresse," air (Herminie)
        2. "Arrête!," air (Herminie)
        3. "Venez, venez," air (Herminie)
        4. "Dieu des chrétiens," prière (Herminie)
8.4   "La mort de Cléopâtre," scène lyrique (c1829, Vieillard; S & orch, for Prix de Rome): H36
        1a. "Introduction"

1b. "C'en est donc fait!," recit (Cléopâtre)
2a. "Air"
2b. "Ah! qu'ils sont loin ces jours," recit (Cléopâtre)
3. "Méditation": "Grands Pharaons nobles Lagides" (Cléopâtre)
8.5   "Aubade": "Assez dormir, ma belle" (Musset; 2 vers): H78
. Version 1 (c1839; 1v & 2hn)
. Version 2 (later vers for 1v & brass: 2 cornets & 4hn)

9. SONGS (w/ pf; also orchd)

9.1   *"Romances" (c1818–9, lost)* *H4*
9.2   *"Je vais donc quitter pour jamais" (ca1819, Florian, destr; reconstr Tiersot & Temperley)* *H6*
9.3   "Le dépit de la bergère," romance (ca1819, anon) H7
9.4   Le maure jaloux: "Je vais revoir," romance (ca1819–21, Florian; 2 vers): H9
. Version 1 entitled: "L'arabe jaloux" (p1822)
. Version 2 (pubd prior to dépôt légal in April 1822)
9.5   "Amitié reprends ton empire," romance (ca1819–21, Florian; 2S, Bar & pf; 2 vers): H10
. Version 1 entitled: "Invocation à l'amitié"
. Version 2 (pubd prior to dépôt légal in February 1823)
9.6   "Pleure pauvre Colette": "Aupès de moi Colette," romance (c before 1822, Bourgerie; 2vv & pf) H11
9.7   *"Canon à trois voix" (c1822, lost)* *H13*
9.8   "Canon libre à la quinte": "La nuit de son voile épais" (c1822, Bourgerie; A, Bar & pf) H14
9.9   "Le montagnard exilé": "Loin de la sauvage," chant élégiaque (c1822–3, Du Boys; 2S & pf/harp) H15
9.10   "Toi qui t'aimas verse des pleurs": "Sous le saule de la prairie," romance (c1822–3, Du Boys) H16
9.11   "Nocturne": "Je veux dans l'inconstance passer mes premiers ans" (ca1818–30; 2vv & gui) H31
9.12   "Le pêcheur," ballade (ca1827, Goethe transl Du Boys; T & pf, incorp in: Le retour à la vie,
           Op.14bis, H55a) .... (Op.14bis)
9.13   "Le roi de Thulé": "Autrefois un roi de Thulé" (c1828; S & pf, from 6. of: 8 scènes de Faust, H33) H33a
9.14   "Le coucher du soleil": "Que j'aime cette heure," rêverie (c1829, Moore transl Gounet) H39
9.15   "Hélène": "Qui ne se souvient" (Moore transl Gounet; 2 vers): H40
. Version 1 (c1829; 2vv & pf)
. Version 2 (c1844; ch & orch)
9.16   "La belle voyageuse": "Elle s'en va," ballade (c1829, Moore transl Gounet; 4 vers): H42
. Version 1 (c1829; 1v & pf)
. *Version 2 (c1834; 4 m vv & orch, lost)*
. Version 3 (c1842; mS & orch)
. Version 4 (c1851; ch & orch)
9.17   "L'origine de la harpe": "Cette harpe chérie," ballade (c1829, Moore transl Gounet) H45
9.18   "Adieu Bessy": "Sweetest love!," romance anglaise et française (Moore transl Gounet; 2 vers): H46
. Version 1 in A-flat major (c1829)
. Version 2 in G major (c1849)
9.19   "Elégie en prose": "Quand delui qui t'adore" (c1829, Moore transl Belloc; T & pf) H47
9.20   "La captive" (Orientale): "Si je n'étais captive" (Hugo; 6 vers): Op.12, H60
. Version 1 (c1832; 1v & pf)
. Version 2 (ca1832; 1v & pf)
. Version 3 (c1832; 1v, vc ad lib & pf)
. Version 4 (c1834; S & orch)
. Version 5 in E major (c1848; A/mS & orch)
. Version 6 in D major (c1848; A/mS & orch)
9.21   "Le jeune pâtre breton": "Dès que la grive est éveillée" (Brizeux; 4 vers): H65
. Version 1: "Le paysan breton" (c1833; 1v & pf)
. *Version 2: "Le jeune paysan breton" (c1834; S & orch, lost)*
. Version 3 (c1834; 1v, hn ad lib & pf)
. Version 4 (c1835; 1v & orch)
9.22   *"Romance de Marie Tudor" (c1833, Hugo; B & pf, lost)* *H66*
9.23   "Les champs": "Rose partons! Voici l'aurore," romance (Béranger; 2 vers): H67
. Version 1 (c1834)
. Version 2 (c1850)
9.24   "Je crois en vous": "Quand mon âme ravie," romance (c1834, Guérin, used in: Benvenuto, Op.23) H70
9.25   "Le chant des bretons": "Oui, nous sommes encor" (Brizeux; ch/T & pf; 2 vers): H71
. Version 1 (c1835)
. Version 2 (c1849)
9.26   "Chansonette": "Au levant là-bas est une île" (c1835, Wailly, used in opera: Benvenuto Cellini, Op.23) H73
9.27   "Les nuits d'été," cycle (Gautier; 2 vers): Op.7, H81
. Version 1 (c1840–41; mS/T & pf)
. Version 2 (c1843, 1855–6, German transl Cornelius; vv & orch)
9.28   1. "Villanelle": "Quand viendra la saison nouvelle" H82
9.29   2. "Le spectre de la rose": "Soulève ta paupière close" H83
9.30   3. "Sur les lagunes. Lamento": "Ma belle amie est morte" H84
9.31   4. "Absence": "Reviens, reviens, ma bien-aimée!" H85
9.32   5. "Au cimetière. Claire de lune": "Connaissez-vous la blanche tombe" H86
9.33   6. "L'île inconnue. Barcarolle": "Dites, la jeune belle, où voulez-vous aller?" H87

9.34   "La mort d'Ophélie": "Auprès d'un torrent," ballade (c1842, Legouvé; 2 vers): H92
     . Version 1 (c1842; 1v & pf)
     . Version 2 (c1848; fem ch & orch)
9.35   "La belle Isabeau": "Dans la montagne" (c1843, Dumas pére; mS, ch ad lib & pf; 2 vers): H94
     . Version 1 (c1843; mS, ch ad lib & pf)
     . Version 2 (p1844; w/ ch)
9.36   "La chasseur danois": "Entendez-vous dans la bruyère?" (Leuven; 2 vers): H104
     . Version 1 (c1844; B & pf)
     . Version 2 (c1845; B & orch)
9.37   "Zaïde": "Ma ville, ma belle ville," boléro (c1845, R. Beauvoir; 2 vers): H107
     . Version 1 (c1885; S & pf)
     . Version 2 (c1845; S & orch, castanets ad lib)
9.38   "Le trébuchet": "Lison guettait une fauvette," scherzo à 2 (c1846, Bertin & Deschamps) H113
9.39   "Nessun maggior piacere," albumleaf (c1847, Berlioz after Dante) H114
9.40   "Le matin": "Pour chanter le retour du jour," romance (c1850, Bouclon) H125
9.41   "Petit oiseau": "Pour chanter le retour du jour," chanson de paysan (c1850, Bouclon) H126

10. PUBLISHED COLLECTIONS

10.1   "Neuf mélodies" (Irlande) (p1830): Op.2, H38
      1. "Le coucher du soleil": "Que j'aime," rêverie (= H39)
      2. "Hélène": "Qui ne se souvient," ballade (= H40)
      3. "Chant guerrier": "N'oublions pas ces champs" (= H41)
      4. "La belle voyageuse": "Elle s'en va," ballade (= H42)
      5. "Chanson à boire": "Amis la coupe écume" (= H43)
      6. "Chant sacré": "Dieu tout puissant!" (= H44)
      7. "L'origine de la harpe": "Cette harpe," ballade (= H45)
      8. "Adieu Bessy": "Sweetest love!," romance anglaise & française (= H45)
      9. "Elégie en prose": "Quand celui qui t'adore" (= H47)
10.2   "Tristia" (2 vers): H119
     Version 1 (p1849, 2 works):
      1. "Méditation religieuse" (= H56 red Matteman for ch & pf trio)
      2. "La mort d'Ophélie" (= H92a)
     Version 2 (p1851, 3 works): Op.18, (H119)
      1. "Méditation religieuse" (= H56b)
      2. "La mort d'Ophélie" (= H92b)
      3. "Marche funèbre pour la dernière scène d'Hamlet" (= H103)
10.3   "Vox populi" (p1849): Op.20, H120
      1. "La menace des Francs" (= H117)
      2. "Hymne à la France" (= H97)
10.4   "Feuillets d'album" (p1850): Op.19, H121
      1. "Zaïde," boléro (= H107b)
      2. "Les champs," chansonette (= H67b)
      3. "Chant des chemins de fer" (= H110)
     (intended as part of collection, pubd separately):
      4. "Prière du matin" (= H112)
      5. "La belle Isabeau, conte pendant l'orage" (= H94b)
      6. "Le chasseur danois" (= H104a)
10.5   "Fleurs des landes" (p1850): Op.13, H124
      1. "Le matin," romance (= H125)
      2. "Petit oiseau," chanson de paysan (= H126)
      3. "Le trébuchet," scherzo (= H113)
      4. "Le jeune pâtre breton," romance (= H65c)
      5. "Le chant des bretons," choeur (= H71b)
10.6   "Collection de 32 mélodies" (p1863, all previously pubd separately): H139
      1. "Villanelle," mélodie (= H82a)
      2. "Le spectre de la rose," mélodie (red of H83b)
      3. "Sur les lagunes," lamento (= H84a)
      4. "Absence," mélodie (= H85a)
      5. "Au cimetière," clair de lune (red of H86b)
      6. "L'île inconnue," mélodie (= H87a)
      7. "Le coucher du soleil," rêverie (= H39)
      8. "Hélène," ballade à 2 voix (= H40a)
      9. "Chant guerrier," solo et choeur (= H41)
      10. "La belle voyageuse," légende irlandaise (= H42a)
      11. "Chanson à boire," solo et choeur (= H43)
      12. "Chant sacré," solo et choeur (= H44a)
      13. "L'origine de la harpe" (= H45)
      14. "Adieu Bessy," romance (= H46b)
      15. "Élégie" (en prose) (= H47)
      16. "Hymne à la France," solo et choeur (red of H97)
      17. "La menace des francs," marche et choeur (red of H117)
      18. "La captive," rêverie
      19. "Sara la baigneuse," ballade à 2 voix (red of H69c)

20. "Tristia," méditation religieuse (red of H56b)
21. "La mort d'Ophélie," ballade (red of H92b)
22. "Le matin," romance (= H125)
23. "Petit oiseau," chanson de paysan (= H126)
24. "Le Trébuchet," scherzo à 2 voix (= H113)
25. "Le jeune pâtre breton," romance (= H65c)
26. "Le chant des bretons," choeur (= H71b)
27. "Zaïde," boléro (red of H107b)
28. "Les champs," aubade (= H67b)
29. "Chant des chemins de fer," solo et choeur (red of H110)
30. "Choeur d'enfants," prière du matin (= H112)
31. "Le chasseur danois," chant pour voix de basse (= H104a)
32. "La belle Isabeau," conte pendant l'orage (= H94b)

11. MISC WORKS

12. ARRANGEMENTS OF WORKS OF OTHERS

12.20	19. "Romance de l'Opéra des Blaïse et Babet": "Lise chantait dans" (from Dezède's opera: Blaise et Babet, words Boutet de Monvel)
12.21	20. "Romance de Naderman": "Je pense à vous quand la douce aurore" (c by Naderman, words Naderman)
12.22	21. "Faut l'oublier" (c by anon, words anon)
12.23	22. "Romance favorite de Henri quatre": "Viens aurore" (c by Lélu, words anon)
12.24	23. "Le rivage de Vaucluse": "Du rivage" (c by Boieldieu, words ?)
12.25	24. "Le sentiment d'amour": "N'avoir sans y songer qu'une seule pensée" (c by Meissonnier, words Meissonnier)
12.26	25. "Minverne au tombeau de Ryno": "En vain la mort" (c by anon, words Chenier)
12.27	Lisle: "Hymne des Marseillais": "Allons enfants de la patrie" (2 vers): H51
	. Version 1 (arr1830; d ch & orch)
	. Version 2 (arr1848; T, ch & pf)
12.28	Lisle: "Chant du neuf Thermidor": "Aux prodiges de la victoire" (arr1830; T, ch & orch) H51bis
12.29	*Weber: "La chasse de Lutzow": "Quels feux lointains" (arr1833; ch, strings & pf, lost) H63*
12.30	Huber: "Le chasseur des chamois": "Sur les Alpes, quel délice!" (2 vers): H64
	. Version 1 (arr1833; ch, ?strings & pf)
	. Version 2 (arr for 1v & gui)
12.31	Weber: "Der Freischütz," opera, J277 (recitatives added 1841, transl Pacini): Op.28, H89
	1. "Que vois-je" (before 2. Trio & Chorus) (Kuono, Kilian, Gaspard, Max)
	2. "En vérité c'est un brave homme" (before 3. Valse) (Kilian, Max)
	3. "Encor là, camarade?" (before 5. Ronde) (Gaspard, Max)
	4. "Mais à ton tour fais briller ton talent" (between strophes of 5.) (Gaspard, Max)
	5. "Ton brave aïeul ainsi restera" (before 8. Ariette) (Annette, Agathe)
	6. "Ô les noeuds charmants à merveille" (before 9. Scène & Air) (Annette, Agathe)
	7. "Te voilà donc enfin" (before 10. Trio) (Agathe, Annette, Max)
	8. (Spoken lines within 11. Final)
	9. "As-tu bien reposé?" (before 14. Romance) (Annette, Agathe)
	10. "Je rends grâces" (before 15. Ronde favorite) (Agathe, Annette, ch)
	11. "Faisons trêve au banquet" (before 18. Final) (Ottokar, Kuono, Gaspard, Max)
12.32	Weber: "L'invitation à la valse," Op.65, J260 (arr1841; orch) H90
12.33	Meyer: "Marche marocaine" (arr1845; orch) H105
12.34	*Meyer: "Marche d'Isly" (arr1845; orch, lost) H108*
12.35	"Marche de Rákóczy" (arr1846; ch, from Hung, incorp in: La damnation de Faust, Op.24, H111) H109
12.36	*Mehul: "Chant du départ" (arr1848; ch & pf, lost) H115*
12.37	*Lisle: "Mourons pour la patrie" (arr1848; ch & pf, lost) H116*
12.38	Bortnyansky: "Chant des chérubins": "Adoremus" (arr1850; ch & orch) H122
12.39	Bortnyansky: "Pater noster" (arr1850; ch) H123
12.40	Martini: "Plaisir d'amour" (arr1859; 1v & orch) H134
12.41	Schubert: "Le roi des aulnes" (Der Erlkönig) (arr1860; 1v & orch, transl Bouscatel) H136
12.42	Couperin: "Invitation à louer Dieu," from: Soeur Monique, Suite No.18/3 (arr ca1861–8; ch & pf) H143

* * * * *

H = D. Kern Holoman: "Catalogue of the Works of Hector Berlioz." Bärenreiter, 1987.
A = Appendix in Holoman's catalog.

1. STAGE WORKS

Operas:

1.1	"On The Town," 2 act musical comedy (c1944, Comden & Green, idea Robbins) ....
1.2	"Trouble in Tahiti," 1 act (c1951, Bernstein, incorp in opera: A Quiet Place) ....
1.3	"Wonderful Town," 2 act musical comedy (c1953, Fields & Chodorov, lyrics Comden & Green) ....
1.4	"Candide," 2 act operetta (after Voltaire; 4 vers): ....

. *Original Version (p1956, Hellman after Voltaire, withdrawn)*
. Chelsea Version (p1973, Wheeler, lyrics Wilbur, La Touche, Sondheim, Bernstein)
. Opera House Version (p1982, Wheeler, lyrics Wilbur, Sondheim, La Touche, Bernstein)
. Scottish Opera Version (p1988, = Opera House Version r by Mauceri, Miller & Wells)

1.5	"West Side Story," musical (p1957, Laurents, lyrics Sondheim, concept Robbins) ....
1.6	*"By Bernstein," a musical cabaret (p1975, Comden & Green, withdrawn)* ....
1.7	*"1600 Pennsylvania Avenue," musical (c1976, Lerner, withdrawn)* ....
1.8	"The Madwoman of Central Park West," musical (p.1979, Newman & Laurentis, collab w/ others): ....

c by Bernstein: . "Up, Up, Up" (Comden & Green)
. "My New Friends" (Bernstein)

1.9	"A Quiet Place," 4 acts (c1983, Wadsworth; 3 vers): ....

. *Orig Version, 4 acts (withdrawn)*
. Revised Version, 3 acts (r1984, incl opera: Trouble in Tahiti)
. "Ruh und Frieden" (= Version of 1984 transl into German 1987)

1.10	"The Race to Urga," musical (c1987) ....

Ballets:

1.11	"Fancy Free" (p1944, Robbins) ....
1.12	"Facsimile" (3 vers): ....

. Version 1: "Facsimile" (p1946, Robbins)
. Version 2: "Parallel Lives" (p1986, Charles)
. Version 3: "Dancing On" (p1988, Breuer)

1.13	"Dybbuk" (Dybbuk Variations) (c1974, Robbins) ....

Ballets based on Bernstein's music:

1.14	*"Jeremiah" (p1948, King)* ....
1.15	*"The Age of Anxiety" (p1950, Robbins; 2nd vers 1979)* ....
1.16	*"Serenade" (after Plato: Symposium; 3 vers):* ....

. *Version 1 (p1959, Ross)*
. *Version 2: "Voyager" (p1984, Bolender)*
. *Version 3 (p by Aterballetto, Torino, Italy)*

1.17	*"On The Waterfront," sym suite (p1964, Grego)* ....
1.18	*"Prelude, Fugue and Riffs" (6 vers):* ....

. *Version 1 (p1969, Clifford)*
. *Version 2: "Patrasolifutricatramerifu" (p1978, Uthoff)*
. *Version 3: "Kansas City Original—Opus Hot" (p1979, Sequoio)*
. *Version 4 (p1984, Villella)*
. *Version 5: "Awesome" (p1987, Small)*
. *Version 6: in 'And Now This' (p1988, Sappington; see: And Now This)*

1.19	*"Mass" (p1974, Hanger)* ....
1.20	*"Songfest" (p1979, Neumeier)* ....
1.21	*"The Commitment" (p1979, Butler; solo dancer, music = 3 Meditations From Mass)* ....
1.22	*"Kaddish" (p ?1980, Marcus)* ....
1.23	*"Chichester Psalms" (p1980, Gladstein)* ....
1.24	*"Candide" (p1984, Tanner, songs arr for orch)* ....
1.25	*"Presto Barbaro" (p1984, Curry, from: On the Waterfront)* ....
1.26	*"Divertimento" (p1986, Berdes; 2nd vers: Dancing On 1988, Breuer)* ....
1.27	*"And Now This" (p1988, Sappington)* ....

incl: . *"Overture to Candide"*
. *"Lonely Town: Pas de Deux" (No.2 of: 3 Dance Episodes from: On The Town)*
. *"Prelude, Fugue and Riffs"*

Incid music:

1.28	"The Birds" (c1938, Aristophanes, juvenilia) ....
1.29	"The Peace" (c1940, Aristophanes, juvenilia) ....
1.30	"Peter Pan" (c1950, Barrie, add music c by Rittman) ....
1.31	"The Lark" (p1955, cT & ch or 7vv for Hellman's vers of Anouilh's play: L'Alouette) ....
1.32	*"Salomé" (c1955, Wilde; vv & chamber orch, withdrawn)* ....
1.33	*"The Firstborn" (c1958, Fry, withdrawn):* ....

1. *"Moses and Israelites" (1v & ch, in Hebrew)*
2. *"Tensret's Song" (in English)*

Film:

1.34   "On The Town" (p1949, film vers of the musical): ....
        incl: 1. "Feel Like I'm Not Out of Bed Yet"
                2. "New York, New York"
                5. "Taxi Number: Come Up to My Place"
                19. Ballet: . "Imaginary Coney Island" (orig: Gabey in the Playground of the Rich)
                . "Subway Ride: Dance of the great Lover"
                . "Pas de Deux"
1.35   "On The Waterfront" (p1954, Kazan) ....
1.36   "West Side Story" (p1961, film vers of the musical) ....

1a. SELECTIONS FROM STAGE WORKS (Nos. of sections in The Gramophone)

1a.1   "On The Town," musical comedy: ....
        excerpts: I: 1. "Feel Like I'm Not Out of Bed Yet"
                2. "New York, New York"
                3. "Chase Music"
                4. "Miss Turnstiles Variations" (She's a Home Loving Girl)
                5. "Taxi Number: Come Up to My Place"
                6. "Carried Away"
                7. "Lonely Town"
                8. "Carnegie Hall Pavane"
                9. "Do-Do-Re-Do"
                10. "Dance: Lonely Town" (orig: Sailor's On the Town)
                11. "I Can Cook Too"
                12. "Lucky To Be Me"
                13. "Dance: Times Square" (Finale)
            II: 14.–18. "Night Club Sequence": 14. "So Long Baby"
                15. "I Wish I Was Dead"
                16. "I'm Blue"
                17. "You Got Me"
                18. "I Understand" (Pitkin's Song)
                19. "Ballet": . "Imaginary Coney Island" (orig: Gabey in the Playground of the Rich)
                . "Subway Ride: Dance of the great Lover"
                . "Pas de Deux"
                20. "Some Other Time"
                21. "Dance: The Real Coney Island"
                22. "Finale"

1a.3   "Wonderful Town," musical comedy: ....
        excerpts: I: 1. "Christopher Street"
                2. "Ohio"
                3. "Conquering the City"
                4. "One Hundred Easy Ways"
                5. "What a Waste"
                6. "Story Vignettes: Rexford / Mr. Mallory / Danny / Trent"
                7. "A Little Bit in Love"
                8. "Pass That Football"
                9. "Conversation Piece"
                10. "A Quiet Girl"
                11. "Conga!"
            II: 12. "My Darlin' Eileen"
                13. "Swing"
                14. "It's Love"
                15. "Ballet at the Village Vortex"
                16. "The Wrong Note Rag"

1a.4   "Candide," operetta: ....
        Original Version (p1956, Hellman after Voltaire, not available for performance: withdrawn):
                excerpts: I: 1. "Overture"
                2. "The Best of All Possible Worlds"
                3. "Oh, Happy We"
                4. "Wedding Procession, Chorale and Battle Scene"
                5. "Candide Begins His Travels"
                6. "It Must Be So / Me"
                7. "Lisbon Sequence"
                8. "Paris Waltz"
                9. "Glitter and Be Gay"
                10. "You Were Dead, You Know"
                11. "Pilgrim's Procession"
                12. "My Love"
                13. "I Am Easily Assimilated" (Buenos Aires)
                14. "Finale" (Quartet)

II: 15. *"Quiet"*
   16. *"The Ballad of Eldorado"*
   17. *"Bon Voyage"*
   18. *"Raft Sequence"*
   19. *"Venice Gambling Scene"*
   20. *"What's The Use?"*
   21. *"The Venice Gavotte"*
   22. *"Return to Westphalia"*
   23. *"Make Our Garden Grow"*
  Unperf: . "Dear Boy" (Wilbur)
  For London production of 1959: . "We Are Women" (Bernstein)

Chelsea Version (p1973, Wheeler after Voltaire, lyrics Wilbur, La Touche, Sondheim & Bernstein):
   1. "Overture"
   2. "Life is Happiness Indeed"
   3. "The Best of All Possible Worlds"
   4. "Oh, Happy We"
   5a. "It Must Be So"
   5b. "O Miserere"
   6. "Glitter and Be Gay"
   7. "Auto da Fé" (What a Day)
   8. "This World"
   9. "You Were Dead, You Know"
   10. "I Am Easily Assimilated"
   11. "My Love"
   12. "Barcarolle"
   13. "Alleluia"
   14. "Eldorado: Sheep's Song"
   16. "Bon Voyage"
   17. "Constantinople" (partial reprises of 3. & 9.)
   18. "Make Our Garden Grow"

Opera House Version (p1982, Wheeler after Voltaire, lyrics Wilbur, Sondheim, La Touche & Bernstein):
excerpts: I: 1. "Overture"
   2. "Life is Happiness Indeed"
   3. "The Best of All Possible Worlds"
   4. "Oh Happy We"
   5. "It Must Be So"
   6. "Fanfare, Chorale and Battle"
   7. "Glitter and Be Gay"
   8. "Dear Boy"
   9. "Auto da Fé"
   10. "Candide's Lament"
   11. "You Were Dead, You Know"
   12. "I Am Easily Assimilated"
   13. "Finale" (Quartet)
II: 14. "To The New World"
   15. "My Love"
   16. "The Old Lady's Tale" (Barcarolle)
   17. "Alleluia"
   18. "Sheep Song"
   19. "Governor's Waltz"
   20. "Bon Voyage"
   21. "Quiet"
   22. "What's The Use"
   23. "Make Our Garden Grow"

Scottish Opera Version (p1988, = Opera House Version r by Mauceri, Miller & Wells): ....
Add Nos. (lyrics Wilbur, Hellman, Parker & Bernstein): . "Martin's Laughing Song"
   . "Nothing More Than This"
   . "We Are Women"
   . "Venice Gambling Scene"
   . "Venice Gavotte"
   . "The King's Barcarolle"
   . "The Ballad of Eldorado"
   . "Ring-Around-A-Rosy"

1a.5   "West Side Story," musical: ....
   excerpts: I: 1. "Prologue"
   2. "Jet Song"
   3. "Something's Coming"
   4. "The Dance at the Gym" (Blues, Promenade, Mambo, Cha-Cha, Meeting Scene, Jump)
   5. "Maria"
   6. "Tonight" (Balcony Scene)
   7. "America"
   8. "Cool"
   9. "One Hand, One Heart"

10. "Tonight" (Quintet)
11. "The Rumble"
II: 12. "I Feel Pretty"
13a. "Ballet Sequence"
13b. (transition to Scherzo)
13c. "Scherzo"
13d. "Somewhere"
13e. "Procession and Nightmare"
14. "Gee, Officer Krupke"
15. "A Boy Like That / I Have a Love"
16. "Taunting Scene"
17. "Finale"

1a.6   *"By Bernstein," musical cabaret (withdrawn):* ....
1. *"Welcome" (Comden & Green)*
2. *"Gabey's Comin' " (Comden & Green, from: On The Town)*
3. *"Lonely Me" (Comden & Green, from: On The Town)*
4. *"Say When" (Comden & Green, from: On The Town)*
5. *"I'm Afraid It's Love" (Comden & Green, from: On The Town)*
6. *"Like Everybody Else" (Sondheim, from: West Side Story)*
7. *"Another Love" (Comden, Green & Bernstein)*
8. *"I Know a Fellow" (Bernstein)*
9. *"It's Gotta Be Bad to Be Good" (Bernstein)*
10. *"Dream with Me" (Bernstein, from: Peter Pan)*
11. *"Ring-Around-A-Rosy" (La Touche, from: Candide)*
12. *"Captain Hook's Soliloquy" (Bernstein, from: Peter Pan)*
13. *"Rio Bamba" (Comden, Green & Bernstein)*
14. *"The Intermission's Great" (Comden & Green, from: On The Town)*
15. *"The Story of My Life" (Comden & Green, from: Wonderful Town)*
16. *"Ain't Got No Tears Left" (Bernstein)*
17. *"The Coolie's Dilemma" (Leiber, from: A Pray by Blecht)*
18. *"In There" (Sondheim, from: A Pray by Blecht)*
19. *"Here Comes the Sun" (Comden & Green, from: The Skin of Our Teeth)*
20. *"Spring Will Come Again" (Comden & Green, from: The Skin of Our Teeth)*

1a.7   *"1600 Pennsylvania Avenue," musical (withdrawn):* ....
excerpts: I: 1. "Rehearse!"
2. *"On Ten Square Miles By the Potomac River"*
3. *"If I Was a Dove"*
4. *"Welcome Home, Miz Adams"*
5. *"Take Care of This House" (arr Freed for ch; also see: Voice & Orch)*
6. *"The President Jefferson Sunday Luncheon Party March"*
7. *"Scena"*
8. *"Sonatina": . "Allegro con brio"*
. *"Tempo di Menuetto" (incl: To Anacreon in heaven, later: Star Spangled Banner)*
. *"Rondo"*
9. *"Lud's Wedding: I Love My Wife"*
10. *"Auctions: The Little White Lie"*
11. *"Mark Of a Man"*
12. *"We Must Have a Ball"*
13. *"The Ball"*
II: 14. "Bright and Black"
15. *"Duet for One" (The First Lady Of the Land)*
16. *"The Robber-Baron Minstrel Parade"*
17. *"Pity the Poor"*
18. *"Red White and Blues"*
19. *"Proud"*
Not used: . "The Nation That Wasn't There"
. *"The grand Old Party"*
. *"American Dreaming"*
. *"Forty Acres"*
. *"Hail Garfield"*
. *"Middle C"*
. *"Monroviad"*

1a.11   "Fancy Free," ballet: ....
. "Big Stuff," juke box song (opens the ballet, words Bernstein)
1. "Enter Three Sailors"
2. "Scene at the Bar"
3. "Enter Two Girls"
4. "Pas de Deux"
5. "Competition Scene"
6. Variation 1: "Galop"
. Variation 2: "Waltz"
. Variation 3: "Danzon" (transcr Krance for concert band)

7. "Finale"

1a.30　"Peter Pan," incid music: ....
　　　　excerpts: songs (c by Bernstein): 1. "Who Am I?"
　　　　　　　　2. "My House"
　　　　　　　　3. "Peter, Peter"
　　　　　　　　4. "Never-Land"
　　　　choruses (c by Bernstein; m ch): 1. "Pirate Song"
　　　　　　　　2. "Plank Round"

1a.32　*"Salomé," incid music (withdrawn):* ....
　　　　I. French Choruses (Medieval French; w/ hand drum): 1. "Spring Song" (used in: Missa Brevis)
　　　　　　　2. "Court Song"
　　　　　　　3. "Soldier's Song"
　　　　II. Latin Choruses (Roman Mass liturgy; w/ bells; used in: Missa Brevis): 1. "Prelude"
　　　　　　　2. "Benedictus"
　　　　　　　3. "Sanctus"
　　　　　　　4. "Requiem"
　　　　　　　5. "Gloria"

2. SYMPHONIES

2.1　Symphony No.1, "Jeremiah" (c1942, text from: Lamentations; mS & orch): ....
　　　　　　1. "Prophecy"
　　　　　　2. "Profanation" (transcr Bencriscutto for concert band)
　　　　　　3. "Lamentation" (arr for 1v & pf/org)
2.2　Symphony No.2, "The Age of Anxiety" (c1949, r1965, inspired by Auden's The Age of Anxiety: A Baroque
　　　　Eclogue; pf & orch; red for 2pf): ....
　　　　I:　　1. "The Prologue"
　　　　　　　2. "The Seven Ages" (Variations 1–7)
　　　　　　　3. "The Seven Stages" (Variations 8–14)
　　　　II:　 1. "The Dirge" (p1948)
　　　　　　　2. "The Masque"
　　　　　　　3. "The Epilogue"
2.3　Symphony No.3, "Kaddish" (c1963, r1977; S, speaker, ch, boys' ch & orch; red for vv & pf): ....
　　　　　　1. "Invocation" (Kaddish 1)
　　　　　　2. "Din-Torah" (Kaddish 2)
　　　　　　3. "Scherzo, Finale" (Kaddish 3)

3. OTHER ORCHESTRAL WORKS

3.1　"3 Dance Episodes from On The Town" (c1945): No.1 "The Great Lover Displays Himself" ....
3.2　　　　No.2 "Lonely Town: Pas de Deux"
3.3　　　　No.3 "Times Square: 1944"
3.4　*"Fancy Free," suite (p1945, same as ballet less No.3 & 5, Finale changed, withdrawn)* ....
3.5　"3 Dance Variations from Fancy Free" (p1946, from ballet): No.1 "Galop" ....
3.6　　　　No.2 "Waltz"
3.7　　　　No.3 "Danzon"
3.8　"Facsimile, Choreographic Essay" (c1946, concert vers of ballet): No.1 "Solo" ....
3.9　　　　No.2 "Pas de Deux"
3.10　　　 No.3 "Pas de Trois"
3.11　　　 No.4 "Coda"
3.12　"On The Waterfront," sym suite (c1955, from film; also see: Presto Barbaro) ....
3.13　"Candide," overture (c1956, for operetta; transcr Grundman for concert band) ....
3.14　"Symphonic Dances" (c1960, from: West Side Story; orchd w/ Ramin & Kostal): No.1 "Prologue" ....
3.15　　　 No.2 "Somewhere"
3.16　　　 No.3 "Scherzo"
3.17　　　 No.4 "Mambo"
3.18　　　 No.5 "Cha-Cha"
3.19　　　 No.6 "Meeting Scene"
3.20　　　 No.7 " 'Cool'—Fugue"
3.21　　　 No.8 "Rumble"
3.22　　　 No.9 "Finale"
3.23　"Fanfare" (c1961; brass ens, for the inauguration of J. F. Kennedy) ....
3.24　"Fanfare" (c1961; brass ens, for the 25th Anniversary of the High School of Music & Art in New York) ....
3.25　*"Presto Barbaro" (transcr Erickson for brass, perc & pf 1965 from suite: On The Waterfront)* ....
3.26　"2 Meditations" (c1971, from: Mass; also see: 3 Meditations for vc & orch) ....
3.27　*"Meditation No.3" (p1972, not in stage vers but compiled from material in: Mass, withdrawn)* ....
3.28　"Suite No.1 from Dybbuk" (c1974; w/ T & B/Bar, from ballet): No.1 "Invocation & Trance" ....
3.29　　　 No.2 "The Pledge"
3.30　　　 No.3 "Kabbalah"
3.31　　　 No.4 "Possession"
3.32　　　 No.5 "Pas de Deux"

3.33	No.6 "Exorcism"
3.34	"Suite No.2 from Dybbuk" (c1974, from ballet): No.1 "The Messenger" ....
3.35	No.2 "Leah"
3.36	No.3 "5 Kabbalah Variations"
3.37	No.4 "Dream" (Pas de Deux)
3.38	"Slava! A Political Overture" (c1977; transcr Grundman for sym band) ....
3.39	*"CBS Music" (c1977, for 50th anniversary of CBS, withdrawn): No.1 "Fanfares and Titles" ....*
3.40	*No.2 "Quiet Music"*
3.41	*No.3 "Blues"*
3.42	*No.4 "Waltz"*
3.43	*No.5 "Chorale"*
3.44	"Divertimento" (c1980): No.1 "Sennets and Tuckets"..
3.45	No.2 "Waltz"
3.46	No.3 "Mazurka"
3.47	No.4 "Samba"
3.48	No.5 "Turkey Trot"
3.49	No.6 "Sphinxes"
3.50	No.7 "Blues"
3.51	No.8 "In Memoriam; March: 'The BSO Forever' "
3.52	"A Musical Toast" (c1980; transcr Grundman for sym band)...
3.53	"Jubilee Games" (Concerto for Orchestra) (c1986, r1988; w/ Bar): No.1 "Free-Style Events" ....
3.54	No.2 "Benediction" (= Opening Prayer, incl in r vers)
3.55	No.3 "Diaspora Dances"
3.56	"Variations on an Octatonic Theme" (c1989) ....
3.56	"Concerto for Orchestra" (c1989): ....
	incl: . "Diaspora Dances" (from: Jubilee Games of 1986)
	. "Opening Prayer" (from: Jubilee Games of 1986)
	. "Variations on an Octatonic Theme" (of 1989)

4. CONCERTOS, SOLO INSTR & ORCH

4.1	"Prelude, Fugue & Riffs" (c1949, r1955; cl & jazz ensemble) ....
4.2	"Serenade" (c1954, after Plato's Symposium; vn, harp, perc & strings; red for vn & pf): ....
	1. "Phaedrus: Pausanias"
	2. "Aristophanes"
	3. "Eryximachus"
	4. "Agathon"
	5. "Socrates: Alcibiades"
4.3	"3 Meditations" (c1977; vc & orch, from: Mass; red for vc & pf; also see: 2 Meditations of 1971)................
4.4	"Halil," nocturne (c1981; solo fl, piccolo, alto fl, perc, harp & perc; red for fl, pf & perc) ....

5. CHAMBER MUSIC

4 or more insts:

5.1	"4 Studies" (ca1940; 2cl, 2bn & pf, juvenilia): No.1 "Prelude" ....
5.2	No.2 "Fughetta"
5.3	No.3 "Chorale"
5.4	No.4 "Finale"
5.5	"Shivaree" (c1969; d brass ens & perc; used in Kyrie of: Mass) ....

3 insts:

5.6	Piano Trio (c1937, juvenilia) ....

Vn & pf:

5.7	Violin Sonata (c1940, juvenilia): ....
	1. "Moderato assai" (used as part of the principal theme in: Facsimile)
	2. 6 "Variations" (one variation became Variation 3 in: The Age of Anxiety)

Other 2 insts:

5.8	Clarinet Sonata (c1941–2; cl & pf)...
5.9	"Brass Music" (c1948): No.1 "Rondo for Lifey" (tpt & pf) ....
5.10	No.2 "Elegy for Mippy I" (hn & pf)
5.11	No.3 "Elegy for Mippy II" (trbn solo)
5.12	No.4 "Waltz for Mippy III" (tuba & pf)
5.13	No.5 "Fanfare for Bima" (tpt, hn, trbn & tuba)
5.14	"2 Meditations" (c1971; vc & pf, from: Mass; also see: 3 Meditations for vc & orch) ....
5.15	*"Red, White and Blues" (transcr Wastall for tpt & pf 1984 from song in: 1600 Pennsylvania) ....*

6. PIANO SONATAS

6.1   Piano Sonata (c1938, juvenilia) ....

7. OTHER PIANO WORKS

7.1   "Music for the Dance I" (c1938, juvenilia) ....
7.2   "Music for the Dance II" (c1938, juvenilia) ....
7.3   "7 Anniversaries" (c1943): No.1 "For Aaron Copland" ....
7.4   No.2 "For My Sister, Shirley"
7.5   No.3 "In Memoriam: Alfred Eisner"
7.6   No.4 "For Paul Bowles"
7.7   No.5 "In Memoriam: Nathalie Koussevitzky"
7.8   No.6 "For Sergei Koussevitzky"
7.9   No.7 "For William Schuman"
7.10   "4 Anniversaries" (c1948): No.1 "For Felicia Montealegre" ....
7.11   No.2 "For Johnny Mehegan"
7.12   No.3 "For David Diamond"
7.13   No.4 "For Helen Coates"
7.14   "5 Anniversaries" (c1949–51): No.1 "For Elisabeth Rudolf" ....
7.15   No.2 "For Lucas Foss"
7.16   No.3 "For Elisabeth B.Ehrman"
7.17   No.4 "For Sandy Gelhorn"
7.18   No.5 "For Susanna Kyle"
7.19   "Touches" (Chorale, 8 Variations & Coda) (c1981, test piece for the 1981 Van Cliburn Piano Competition)
7.20   "Moby Diptych" (c1981, for Kuerti): No.1 "Sarabande" ....
7.21   No.2 "Spout"
7.22   "13 Anniversaries" (c1988): No.1 "For Shirley Gabis Perle" ....
7.23   No.2 "In Memoriam: William Kapell"
7.24   No.3 "For Stephen Sondheim"
7.25   No.4 "For Craig Urquhart"
7.26   No.5 "For Leo Smit"
7.27   No.6 "For Nina Bernstein"
7.28   No.7 "For Helen Coates"
7.29   No.8 "In Memoriam: Goddard Lieberson"
7.30   No.9 "For Jessica Fleischmann"
7.31   No.10 "In Memoriam: Constance Hope"
7.32   No.11 "For Claudio Arrau"
7.33   No.12 "For Aaron Stern"
7.34   No.13 "In Memoriam: Ellen Goetz"

Pf duet:

7.35   "Scenes From the City of Sin," 8 miniatures (c1939, juvenilia) ....

2 Pf:

7.36   "Largo—Andante & Allegro" (c1937, juvenilia) ....

8. CHORAL WORKS

8.1   "Hashkiveinu" (c1945, words in Hebrew from Friday Evening Service; T, ch & org) ....
8.2   "Reena," Hebrew folksong (arr1947; ch & orch)..
8.3   "Yigdal," Hebrew liturgical melody (c1950, words from Sabbath Evening Service; ch & pf) ....
8.4   *"2 Harvard Choruses" (c1957, Lerner, withdrawn): 1. "Dedication"* ....
8.5   *2. "Lonely men of Harvard" (Lament & March)*
8.6   "Chichester Psalms" (c1965; 1 high v, ch & orch): 1. "Urah, haneval, v'chinor!" (Psalm 108/2 & 100) ....
8.7   2. "Adonai ro-i, lo ehsar" (Psalm 23 & 2/1–4)
8.8   3. "Adonai, Adonai" (Psalm 131 & 133/1)
8.9   "Warm-up," a round (c1970, Bernstein; ch, bell & scat sounds, used in: Mass) ....
8.10   "Mass," theatre piece (p1971, Liturgy, Schwartz & Bernstein; chamber vers arr Ramin 1972): ....
             1. "Kyrie Eleison"
             2. "A Simple Song"
             3. "Alleluia" (= Warm-Up of 1970 for ch)
             4. "Prefatory Prayers"
             5. "Dominus Vobiscum"
             6. "In Nomine Patris"
             7. "Almighty Father"
             8. "Epiphany"
             9. "Confiteor"
            10. "I Don't Know"
            11. "Easy"
            12. "Meditation No.1"

13. "Gloria Tibi"
14. "Gloria in Excelsis"
15. "Half of the People"
16. "Thank You"
17. "Meditation No.2"
18. "The Word of the Lord"
19. "God Said"
20. "Credo in unum Deaum"
21. "Non Credo"
22. "Hurry"
23. "World Without End"
24. "I Believe in God"
25. "De Profundis"
26. "Our Father"
27. "I Go On"
28. "Sanctus"
29. "Agnus Dei"
30. "Things Get Broken"
31. "Secret Songs" (Pax / Communion)

8.11	"A Little Norton Lecture" (if you can't eat you got to) (c1973, r1977; T & m ch; incl in: Songfest) ....
8.12	"Candide," suite (c1977, Bernstein & others; vv, ch & orch, from operetta), Part I: 1. "Overture" ....
8.13	2. "Oh Happy We"
8.14	3. "Wedding Procession and Chorale"
8.15	4. "Candide Begins His travels"
8.16	5. "It Must Be So"
8.17	6. "Paris Waltz Scene"
8.18	7. "Glitter and Be Gay"
8.19	8. "You Were Dead You Know"
8.20	9. "Pilgrims' Procession"
8.21	10. "Governor's Serenade" (My Love)
8.22	Part II: 11. "I am Easily Assimilated"
8.23	12. "Candide's Return From Eldorado"
8.24	13. "Ballad of Eldorado"
8.25	14. "Bon Voyage"
8.26	15. "Into the Raft"
8.27	16. "Money, Money"
8.28	17. "What's the Use?"
8.29	18. "Candide's Lament"
8.30	19. "Make Our Garden Grow"
8.31	"Canon" (p1979; boys' ch, from Kaddish 3 of: Symphony No.3) ....
8.32	*"Olympic Hymn" (c1981, Kunert, based on: Proud, from: 1600 Pennsylvania Ave, withdrawn)* ....
8.33	"Missa Brevis" (c1988; A, ch & perc or 7 solo vv & perc, based on: The Lark of 1955): ....

1. "Kyrie Eleison" (w/ 2 timp ad lib)
2. "Gloria" (w/ bells)
3. "Sanctus"
3a. "Benedictus" (w/ bells, cymbals & tam-tam)
4. "Agnus Dei"
4a. "Dona Nobis Pacem" (w/ tabor, hand drum, tambourine et al)

9. VOICE & ORCHESTRA

9.1	"Glitter and Be Gay" (c1956, Wilbur; S & orch, from operetta: Candide; also w/ pf) ....
9.2	"Take Care Of This House" (c1976, Lerner, from: 1600 Pennsylvania Avenue; also w/ pf) ....
9.3	"Songfest," cycle (c1977; 6vv & orch; also w/ pf), I. "Sextet": 1. "To the Poem" (F. O'Hara) ....
9.4	II. "3 Solos": 2. "The Pennycandystore Beyond The El" (L. Ferlinghetti)
9.5	3. "A Julia de Burgos" (J. de Burgos)
9.6	4. "To What You Said ..." (W. Whitman)
9.7	III. "3 Ensembles": 5. "Duet": "I, Too, Sing America" (L. Hughes)
	. "Okay 'Negroes' " (J. Jordan)
9.8	6. "Trio": "To My Dear and Loving Husband" (A. Bradstreet)
9.9	7. "Duet": "Storyette H.M." (G. Stein)
9.10	IV. "Sextet": 8. "if you can't eat you got to" (e. e. cummings)
9.11	V. "3 Solos": 9. *"Music I heard with You" (c by Aiken)*
9.12	10. "Zizi's Lament" (G. Corso)
9.13	11. "Sonnet": "What lips my lips have kissed ..." (E. St. Vincent Millay)
9.14	VI. "Sextet": 12. "Israel" (E. A. Poe)
9.15	"Opening Prayer" (c1986, Bible; Bar & small orch; used in r vers of: Jubilee Games) ....

10. SONGS (w/ pf)

10.1	"Psalm 148" (ca1932, juvenilia) ....
10.2	"I Hate Music" (5 Kid Songs), cycle (c1943, Bernstein; S & pf): 1. "My Name is Barbara" ....
10.3	2. "Jupiter has Seven Moons"

10.4	3. "I Hate Music"
10.5	4. "A Big Indian and a Little Indian" (Riddle Song)
10.6	5. "I'm a Person Too"
10.7	*"Lamentation" (Finale of Jeremiah Symphony) (arr Campbell-Watson for mS & pf/org 1943)* ....
10.8	*"Afterthought" (c1945, Bernstein, withdrawn)* ....
10.9	"La Bonne Cuisine: 4 Recipes" (c1947, Bernstein after Dutoit): 1. "Plum Pudding" ....
10.10	2. "Queues de Boeuf" (Ox Tails)
10.11	3. "Tavouk Guenksis"
10.12	4. "Civet à Toute Vitesse" (Rabbit at Top Speed)
10.13	"2 Love Songs" (c1949, Rilke): 1. "Extinguish My Eyes" ....
10.14	2. "When My Soul Touches Yours"
10.15	"Silhouette" (Galilee) (c1951, Bernstein: words & music of a Lebanese folksong) ....
10.16	*"On the Waterfront," song (c1954, La Touche; arr for dance band, withdrawn)* ....
10.17	*"Get Hep!," marching song (c1955, Bernstein, withdrawn)* ....
10.18	"So Pretty" (c1968, Comden & Green, from musical: West Side Story) ....
10.19	*"Haiku Souvenirs," 5 songs (c by Gottlieb 1978, words Bernstein)* ....
10.20	"My New Friends" (c1979, Bernstein, from: The Madwoman of Central Park West) ....
10.21	"Piccola Serenata," vocalise (c1979, Bernstein, for Karl Bohm's 85th birthday) ....
10.22	"Sean Song" (c1986, Yoko Ono & Lennnon; w/ vn, va, vc, harp or w/ pf) ....
10.23	"My Twelve-Tone Melody" (c1988, Bernstein, for Irvin Berlin's 100th birthday) ....
10.24	"Arias and Barcarolles" (c1988, Bernstein except 4. & 7.; 1v/2vv & pf duet): 1. "Prelude" ....
10.25	2. "Mr. and Mrs. Webb Say Goodnight"
10.26	3. "Greeting"
10.27	4. "Little Smary" (Jennie Bernstein)
10.28	5. "Telephonic Double-Duet"
10.29	6. "The Love Of My Life"
10.30	7. "Oif Mayn Khas'neh" (At My Wedding) ((Yankev-Yitskhok Segal, in Yiddish)
10.31	8. "Love Duet"
10.32	9. "Nachspiel"

Compilations of songs:

10.33	*"An Album of Songs" (1st compilation) (p1974, withdrawn)* ....
	. "La Bonne Cuisine"
	. 4 Songs from: Peter Pan
	. "Silhouette"
	. "What a Movie!" (from: Trouble in Tahiti)
	. 4 Songs from: Candide
	. "2 Love Songs"
	. 3 Songs from: Mass
10.34	"Bernstein on Broadway," compilation (p1981): ....
	. 8 Songs from "On the Town"
	. 4 Songs from "Peter Pan"
	. 9 Songs from "Wonderful Town"
	. 10 Songs from "Candide"
	. 8 Songs from "West Side Story"
	. 1 Song from "The Madwoman of Central Part West"
10.35	"Song Album" (2nd compilation) (p1988): ....
	. "I Hate Music"
	. "La Bonne Cuisine"
	. "2 Love Songs"
	. "So Pretty"
	. "Piccola Serenata"
	. "Silhouette"
	. "A Simple Song" (from: Mass)
	. "I Go On" (from: Mass)
	. "Take Care Of This House" (from: 1600 Pennsylvania Avenue)
	. "It Must Be So" (from: Candide)
	. "Candide's Lament" (from: Candide)
	. 4 Songs from: Peter Pan

11. ARRANGEMENTS OF WORKS OF OTHERS

11.1	Copland: "El Salón México" (arr1941; pf/2pf) ....
11.2	*Weiner: "Simchu Na," Hebrew folksong (arr1947; ch & orch/pf, withdrawn)* ....

* * * * *

1. STAGE WORKS

Operas & operettas:

1.1	*"La maison du docteur," 1 act opéra-comique (c early, Boitteau, vocal score only)* ....
1.2	"Le Docteur Miracle," 1 act operetta (c1856, Battu & Halévy) ....
1.3	*"Parisina," Italian opera (c1858, Romani, project)* ....
1.4	*Unnamed 1 act opéra-comique (c1858, About, project)* ....
1.5	"Don Procopio," 2 act Italian opera buffa (c1858–9, Cambiaggio) ....
1.6	*"Esmeralda" (c1859, Hugo, from: Notre-Dame de Paris, project)* ....
1.7	*"Le tonnelier de Nuremberg," 3 acts (c1859, after Hoffmann, project)* ....
1.8	*"Don Quichotte" (c1859, after Cervantes, project)* ....
1.9	*"L'amour peintre," opéra-comique (c1860, after Molière, unfin, ?destroyed)* ....
1.10	*"La prêtresse," 1 act operetta (c ?1861, Gille, sketch)* ....
1.11	*"La guzla de l'émir," 1 act opéra-comique (c1862, Barbier & Carré, ?destroyed)* ....
1.12	"Ivan le Terrible" (Ivan IV) (c1862–3, r1864–5, Leroy & Trianon, Act V unfin) ....
1.13	"Les pêcheurs de perles" (The Pearl Fishers), 3 acts (c1863, Carré & Cormon) ....
1.14	*"Nicolas Flamel" (c ?1865, Dubreuil, sketch for pf)* ....
1.15	"La jolie fille de Perth" (The Fair Maid of Perth), 4 acts (c1866, Saint-George & Adenis after Scott) ....
1.16	"Malbrough s'en va-t-en guerre," 4 act operetta (c1867, Siraudin & Busnach, Act I only) ....
1.17	*Unnamed opera (c1868, Leroy & Sauvage, project)* ....
1.18	"La coupe du roi de Thulé," 3 acts (c1868–9, Gallet & Blau, inc) ....
1.19	*"Les templiers," 5 acts (c ?1868, Halévy & Saint-George, project)* ....
1.20	"Noé" (c1868–9, Saint-Georges, unfin opera c by Halévy compl Bizet) ....
1.21	*"Vercingétorix" (c1869, Délérot, project)* ....
1.22	*"Calendal," 4 act opéra-comique (c1870, Ferier, project)* ....
1.23	*"Rama," 4 acts (ca1870, Crépet, project)* ....
1.24	*"Clarissa Harlowe," 3 act opéra-comique (c1870–1, Gille & Jaime, sketches)* ....
1.25	*"Grisélidis," 3 act opéra-comique (c1870–1, Sardou, sketches)* ....
1.26	"Djamileh," 1 act opéra-comique (c1871, Gallet) ....
1.27	*"Sol-si-ré-pif-pan," 1 act operetta (c1872, Busnach, ?destroyed)* ....
1.28	"Don Rodrigue," 5 acts (c1873, Gallet & Blau on de Castro: La Jeunese du Cid, unfin) ....
1.29	"Carmen," 4 act opéra-comique (c1873–74, Meilhac & Halévy on Mérimée) ....

Incid music:

1.30	"L'arlésienne" (c1872, Daudet) ....

1a. SELECTIONS FROM OPERAS

1a.13   "Les pêcheurs de perles," opera (Nos. of sections in The Gramophone): ....
  excerpts: I: 1a. "Sur la grève en feu" (Les Pêcheurs)
       1b. "Mais qui vient là?" (Les Pêcheurs)
       2a. "C'est toi qu'enfin je revois," recit (Zurga)
       2b. "Au fond du temple saint," duet (Nadir, Zurga)
       3. "Que vois-je?" (Zurga)
       4. "Sois la bienvenue" (Le Choeur)
       5. "Seule au milieu de nous" (Zurga)
       6a. "A cette voix quel trouble agitait tout mon être!" (Nadir)
       6b. "Je crois entendre encore" (Nadir)
       7. "Le ciel est bleu!" (Le Choeur)
       8a. "O Dieu Brahma" (Leïla)
       8b. "Dans le ciel sans voile" (Leïla)
    II: 9. "L'ombre descend des cieux" (Le Choeur)
       10a. "Me voilà seule dans la nuit" (Leïla)
       10b. "Comme autrefois, dans la nuit sombre" (Leïla)
       11. "De mon amie, fleur endormie," chanson (Nadir)
       12a. "Par cet étroit sentier" (Leïla)
       12b. "Ton coeur n'a pas compris le mien" (Nadir)
       13. "Ah! revenez à la raison," finale (Leïla)
    III: 14a. "L'orage s'est calmé" (Zurga)
       14b. "O Nadir, tendre ami de mon jeune âge" (Zurga)
       15a. "Qu'ai-je vu? Oh! ciel, quel trouble!" (Zurga)
       15b. "Je frémis, je chancelle, de son âme cruelle" (Leïla)
       16. "Entends au loin ce bruit de fête" (Nourabad)
       17. "Dès que le soleil" (Le Choeur)
       18. "Sombres divinités" (Nourabad)
       19. "O lumière sainte" (Nadir, Leïla)

1a.15   "La jolie fille de Perth," opera: ....
      . "Prélude"
    I: 1. "Que notre enclume," choeur et scène (Les Forgerons)
       1bis. "Enfin me voilà seul!... seul avec mon amour," récit (Smith)
       2. "Catherine est coquette" (Couplets)

       2bis. "Elle viendrait ce soir," scène et récit (Smith)
       3. "Vive l'hiver et vive son cortège," air (Catherine)
       3bis. "Ces plaisirs-là ne me vont pas," récit (Glover)
       4. "Deux mots encore," duo (Smith, Catherine)
       5. "Ainsi donc, plus de jalousie?...," trio (Catherine, Smith, L'Étranger)
       6. "Ah! la rencontre est imprévue!," quatuor (Le Duc, Smith, Catherine, Mab)
       7. "Vous voudrez bien, je pense," chanson et scène finale (Catherine)
  II: 8. "Bons citoyens, dormez!," marche et choeur (La Patrouille, Glover)
       9. "Carnaval! carnaval!," choeur et récit (Le Choeur, Le Duc)
       10. "Tout boit, amis, dans ce monde," chanson à boire (Le Duc, Le Choeur)
"Divertissement": 11. "Danse bohémienne"
       11bis. "Je donne en mon palais une fête de nuit ...," scène (Le Duc, Mab)
       12. "Les seigneurs de la cour" (Couplets)
       12bis. "Tu seras mon bon ange ...," reprise du choeur (Le Duc, Mab, Le Choeur)
       13. "Partout des cris de joie et des éclats de rire!," sérénade (Smith)
       13bis. "Qui va là?... Ah! c'est vous, maître!," récit (Un Ouvrier)
       14. "Tra, la, la, la, tra, la, la, la! Quand la flamme de l'amour," air (Ralph)
       14bis. "Eh! camarade!... à pareille heure," scène finale (Le Majordome)
  III: 15. "Nuit d'amour et de folle ivresse," choeur et scène (Le Choeur)
       16. "Elle sortait de sa demeure," cavatine (Le Duc, Le Choeur)
       16bis. "Et tenez, écoutez," scène (Le Duc, Les Seigneurs, La Femme Masquée)
       17. "Nous voilà seuls," duo (Le Duc, La Femme)
       18. "C'est donc ici, sans honte et sans pudeur," air (Smith)
       19. "Nuit d'amour et folle ivresse," final (Le Choeur)
  IV: 20. "Smith, tu nous connais tous," duo et choeur (Les Artisans)
       21. "Ils verront si je mens!," duo (Smith, Catherine)
       22. "Maître, là-bas, on vous attend," scène (Un Ouvrier de Smith)
       23. "Aux premiers rayons du matin" (Choeur des Garçons, Les jeunes Filles)
       23bis. "Catherine Glover?... il faut que je la voie," scène (Mab, Glover, Le Choeur)
       24. "Echo, viens sur l'air embaumé," ballade (Catherine, Le Choeur)
       25. "Le jour de la Saint-Valentin," final (Catherine, Glover, Smith, Les Garçons, Les jeunes Filles)

1a.29   "Carmen," opera (Nos. of sections in The Gramophone): ....
     excerpts: 1. "Prélude"
   I: 2. "Sur la place, chacun passe" (Soldats)
       3. "Avec la garde montante" (Choeur des Gamins)
       4a. "La Cloche a sonné, nous, des ouvrières" (Jeunes Gens)
       4b. "La voilà! Voilà la Carmencita!" (Tous)
       5. "L'amour est un oiseau rebelle" (Habanera) (Carmen w/ chorus)
       6. "Carmen! sur tes pas" (Les Jeunes Gens)
       7. "Parle-moi de ma mère!" (Don José)
       8. "Au secours!" (Choeur)
       9. "Voyons, brigadier"
       10a. "Près des remparts de Séville" (Séguidilla) (Carmen)
       10b. "Voici l'orde" (Zuniga)
  II: 11a. "Entr'acte"
       11b. "Les tringles des sistres tintaient" (Gypsy Song) (Carmen)
       11c. "Danse bohémienne"
       11d. "Vous avez quelque chose"
       12a. "Vivat, vivat le toréro!" (Choeur)
       12b. "Votre toast ... je peux vous le rendre" (Toreador's Song) (Escamillo)
       13. "Nous avons en tête une affaire!" (Dancaïre)
       14. "Halte-là! Qui va là?" (Don José)
       15a. "Je vais danser en votre honneur" (Carmen)
       15b. "Au quartier! pour l'appel" (Carmen)
       15c. "La fleur que tu m'avais jetée" (Flower Song) (Don José)
       15d. "Non! tu ne m'aimes pas!" (Carmen)
       16. "Holà! Carmen!" (Zuniga)
  III: 17a. "Entr'acte"
       17b. "Écoute, compagnon, écoute" (Les Contrebandiers)
       17c. "Notre métier est bon" (Les Six)
       18a. "Mêlons! Coupons!" (Card Scene) (Mercédès, Frasquita)
       18b. "Voyons, que j'essaie à mon tour"
       18c. "En vain, pour éviter les réponses amères" (Carmen)
       19. "Quant au douanier c'est notre affaire" (Carmen, Mercédès, Frasquita et Femmes)
       20. "Je dis que rien ne m'épouvante" (Micaëla's Aria)
       21. "Je suis Escamillo" (Escamillo)
  IV: 22a. "Entr'acte"
       22b. "A deux cuartos!" (Choeur)
       23. "Les voici, voici la quadrille" (Choeur)
       24. "Si tu m'aimes, Carmen" (Escamillo)
       25. "C'est toi!," final duet (Carmen, Don José)

2. SYMPHONIES

2.1	Symphony in C major (c1855) ....
2.2	*Symphony (c1859, 2 vers begun, destroyed)* ....
2.3	Symphony No.1 in C major, "Roma" (c1860–8, r1871) ....

3. ORCHESTRAL SUITES

3.1	"The Fair Maid of Perth," suite (from opera): No.1 "Prélude" ....
3.2	No.2 "Serenade"
3.3	No.3 "Marche"
3.4	No.4 "Danse bohémienne"
3.5	"L'arlésienne," 2 suites (from incid music), I (orchd1872): No.1 "Prélude" ....
3.6	No.2 "Menuet"
3.7	No.3 "Adagietto"
3.8	No.4 "Carillon"
3.9	*II (orchd Guiraud ?1876): No.5 "Pastorale"*
3.10	*No.6 "Intermezzo" (also vocal arr as: Agnus Dei)*
3.11	*No.7 "Minuet" (from: La jolie fille de Perth)*
3.12	*No.8 "Farandole"*
3.13	"Jeux d'enfants: petite suite" (c1871, arr from work for pf duet Op.22): No.1 "Marche" (= Op.22/6) ....
3.14	No.2 "Berceuse" (= Op.22/3)
3.15	No.3 "Impromptu" (= Op.22/2)
3.16	No.4 "Duo" (= Op.22/11)
3.17	No.5 "Galop" (= Op.22/12)
3.18	"Carmen," suite (from opera): No.1 "Prélude" (Les toréadors), Act I ....
3.19	No.2 "Entr'actre" (Les dragons d'Alcala) (Act II)
3.20	No.3 "Entr'acte" (Intermezzo) (Act III)
3.21	No.4 "Entr'acte" (Aragonaise) (Act IV)
3.22	No.5 "Seguedille" (Act I)
3.23	No.6 "Avec la garde montante" (Act I)
3.24	No.7 "Habanera" (Act I)
3.25	No.8 "Danse bohème" (Act II)
3.26	No.9 "Marche des Contrebandiers" (Act III)
3.27	No.10 "Nocturne" (Micaëla's aria) (Act III)
3.28	No.11 "Chanson de Toréador"

4. OTHER ORCHESTRAL WORKS

4.1	"Ouverture," in A min / major (ca1855) ....
4.2	"Scherzo & Marche funèbre," in F minor (c1860–1; Scherzo used in: Sym No.1 in C major, 'Roma') ....
4.3	*"La chasse d'Ossian," overture (c1861, lost)* ....
4.4	"Marche funèbre," in B minor (c1868–9; orig Prelude to opera: La coupe du roi de Thulé) ....
4.5	"Patrie," overture (c1873) Op.19

5. PIANO

5.1	"Quatre préludes" (c1854): No.1 in C major ....
5.2	No.2 in A minor
5.3	No.2 in G major
5.4	No.4 in E minor
5.5	"Valse," in C major (c very early) ....
5.6	"Thème brillant," in C major (c very early) ....
5.7	"Caprice original No.1," in C-sharp minor (c ?1860s) ....
5.8	"Romance sans paroles," in C major (c ?1860s) ....
5.9	"Caprice original No.2," in C major (c ?1860s) ....
5.10	"Grande valse de concert," in E-flat major (c1854) ....
5.11	"Nocturne" (No.1), in F major (c1854) ....
5.12	"Trois esquisses musicales" (c ?1858; pf/harm): No.1 "Ronde turque" ....
5.13	No.2 "Sérénade"
5.14	No.3 "Caprice"
5.15	"Chasse fantastique" (c ?1865) ....
5.16	"Chants du Rhin" (c1865, Méry): No.1 "L'aurore" ....
5.17	No.2 "Le départ"
5.18	No.3 "Les rêves"
5.19	No.4 "La bohémienne"
5.20	No.5 "Les confidences"
5.21	No.6 "Le retour"
5.22	"Marine" (c ?1868, orig: La chanson du matelot, souvenir d'Ischia) ....
5.23	"Variations chromatiques de concert" (c1868) ....
5.24	"Nocturne" (No.2), in D major (c1868) ....
5.25	"Promenade au clair de lune" (c after 1868, ?after Verlaine, Nos.3 & 5 of set) ....

Pf duet:

5.26	"Jeux d'enfants" (Children's games) (c1871): 1. "L'escarpolette," rêverie Op.22
5.27	2. "La toupie," impromptu
5.28	3. "La poupée," berceuse
5.29	4. "Les chevaux de bois," scherzo
5.30	5. "Le volant," fantaisie
5.31	6. "Trompette et tambour," marche
5.32	7. "Les bulles de savon," rondino
5.33	8. "Les quatre coins," esquisse
5.34	9. "Colin-Maillard," nocturne
5.35	10. "Saute-Mouton," caprice
5.36	11. "Petit Mari, petite femme," duo
5.37	12. "Le bal," galop

2 Pf:

5.38   Arr of Finale of: Symphony No.1 in C major, "Roma" (c1871; 2pf 8hands) ....

6. CHORAL WORKS

6.1	"Choeur d'étudiants" (c early, Scribe; m ch & orch)...
6.2	"Valse," in G major (c1855; ch & orch) ....
6.3	"L'ange et Tobie," cantata (ca1855–7, Halévy, unfin) ....
6.4	"Héloïse de Montfort," cantata (ca1855–7, Deschamps, unfin) ....
6.5	"Le chevalier enchanté," cantata (ca1855–7, Pastoret, unfin) ....
6.6	"Herminie," cantata (ca1855–7, Vinaty, unfin)
6.7	"Le retour de Virginie," cantata (ca1855–7, Rollet, unfin) ....
6.8	*"David," cantata (c1856, d'Albano, 2nd Prix de Rome, ?lost)* ....
6.9	"Le golfe de Bahia" (c1856, Lamartine; S/T, ch & pf, Prix de Rome; used in opera: Ivan le Terrible)
6.10	"La chanson du rouet" (c1857, Lisle; 1v, ch & pf, Prix de Rome)
6.11	"Clovis et Clotilde," cantata (c1857, Burion, 1st Prix de Rome) ....
6.12	"Te Deum" (c1858, Liturgy; S, T, ch & orch)
6.13	*"Ulysse et Circé," ode-symphony (c1859, after Homer, project)*
6.14	"Vasco de Gama," ode-symphony (c1859–60, Delatre after Camões) ....
6.15	*"Carmen saeculare," cantata (c1860, Horace, unfin, ?destroyed)* ....
6.16	"Saint-Jean de Pathmos," part-song (c ?1866, Hugo; m vv)
6.17	"Chants des Pyrénées," choral accompaniments to 6 folksongs (c ?1867, trad; also see songs)
6.18	*"Les noces de Prométhée," cantata (c1867, Cornut, lost)*
6.19	*Hymn (c1867, lost)*
6.20	"La mort s'avance," cantique (c1869, Pellegrin; ch & orch) ....
6.21	*"Ave Maria" (c?, Grandmougin; ch & orch, ?lost)* ....
6.22	*"Geneviève de Paris," dramatic legend (c1875, Gallet, project: libretto only)* ....

7. SONGS (w/ pf)

7.1	"L'âme triste est pareille au doux ciel" (c very early, Lamartine) ....
7.2	"Petite Marguerite" (c ?1854, Rolland; repubd w/ new words by Silvestre as: En avril 1888) ....
7.3	"La rose et l'abeille" (c ?1854, Rolland; repubd w/ new words by Silvestre as: Rive d'amour 1888) ....
7.4	"La foi, l'espérance et la charité" (ca1854, Lagrave)
7.5	"Vieille chanson" (c1865, Millevoye)..
7.6	"Adieux de l'hôtesse arabe": "Puisque rien ne t'arrête en cet heureux pays" (c1866, Hugo) ....
7.7	"Après l'hiver" (c1866, Hugo)
7.8	"Douce mer" (c1866, Lamartine) ....
7.9	"Chanson d'avril": "Lève-toi! lève-toi! le printemps vient de naître" (c ?1866, Bouilhet) ....
7.10	"Feuilles d'album" (c1866): 1. "A une fleur" (Musset) ....
7.11	2. "Adieux à Suzon" (Musset)
7.12	3. "Sonnet" (Ronsard)
7.13	4. "Guitare" (Hugo)
7.14	5. "Rose d'amour" (Millevoye)
7.15	6. "Le grillon" (Lamartine)
7.16	"Chants des Pyrénées," 6 folksongs (c ?1867): 1. "Mon doux ami" ....
7.17	2. "Là-haut sur la montagne"
7.18	3. "De mes brebis la plus charmante"
7.19	4. "La haute montagne"
7.20	5. "Rossignolet"
7.21	6. "Connaissez-vous ma bergère?"
7.22	"Pastorale" (c1868, Regnard) ....
7.23	"Rêve de la bien-aimée" (c1868, Courmont) ....
7.24	"Ma vie a son secret" (c1868, Arvers) ....
7.25	"Berceuse" (c1868, Desbordes-Valmore)..
7.26	"La chanson du fou" (c1868, Hugo) ....
7.27	"La coccinelle" (c1868, Hugo) ....

7.28   "La sirène" (c1868, Mendes, dramatic frags from opera: La coupe du roi de Thulé) ....
7.29   "Le doute" (c by 1868, Ferrier) ....
7.30   "L'Esprit Saint" (p1869) ....
7.31   "Absence" (p1872, Gautier) ....
7.32   "Chant d'amour" (p1872, Lamartine) ....
7.33   "Tarantelle" (p1872, Pailleron) ....
7.34   "La fuite" (p1872, Gallet) ....
7.35   "Vous ne priez pas" (p1873, Delavigne; orig title: L'âme du Purgatoire) ....
7.36   "Le colibri" (ca1868–73, Flan) ....
7.37   "Oh quand je dors," sérénade (c by 1873, Hugo) ....
7.38   "Voeu" (c?, Hugo) ....
7.39   Excerpts from unfin stage works, w/ new words, after Bizet's death (p1886): . "Voyage" (Gille) ....
7.40   . "Aubade" (Ferrier)
7.41   . "La nuit" (Ferrier)
7.42   . "Conte" (Ferrier)
7.43   . "Aimons, rêvons!" (Ferrier)
7.44   . "La chanson de la rose" (Barbier)
7.45   . "Le gascon" (Mendès)
7.46   . "N'oublions pas!" (Barbier)
7.47   . "Si vous aimez!" (Gille)
7.48   . "Pastel" (Gille)
7.49   . "L'abandonnée" (Mendès)
7.50   . "La sirène" (Mendès)
7.51   "Le retour," duet (p1887, dramatic frags w/ new words by Barbier after composer's death) ....
7.52   "Rêvons," duet (p1887, dramatic frags w/ new words by Barbier, incl: Aimons, rêvons) ....
7.53   "Le nymphes des bois," duet (p1868, dramatic frags w/ new words by Barbier, incl: La nuit) ....

8. MISC WORKS

8.1   "Vocalise," in C major (c1850; S) ....
8.2   "Vocalise," in F major (c1850; 2S) ....
8.3   Various fugues and exercises (c1850–4, corrections by Halévy) ....
8.4   "Five 4-part fugues": No.1 in A major (subject by Halévy) ....
8.5   No.2 in A minor (c1854, subject by Auber)
8.6   No.3 in F minor (c1855, subject by Auber)
8.7   No.4 in G major (c1856)
8.8   No.5 in E minor (c1857, subject by Thomas)
8.9   Fugue in 2 parts (c1866, ?lost) ....
8.10   "Duet," in C minor (c1874, test piece for Conservatoire; bn & vc) ....

9. ARRANGEMENTS OF WORKS OF OTHERS

9.1   Gounod: "Ulisse," 6 transcriptions (p1855; pf) ....
9.2   Gounod: Symphony No.1 in D major (p1855; pf duet) ....
9.3   Gounod: "La nonne sanglante" (p1855; 1v & pf) ....
9.4   Gounod: "Philémon et Baucis" (p1859; 1v & pf) ....
9.5   Gounod: "La reine de Saba" (p1862; 1v & pf) ....
9.6   Gounod: "Ave Maria" (p1865; pf) ....
9.7   Gounod: "Six choeurs célèbres" (p1866; pf) ....
9.8   Gounod: "Roméo et Juliette" (p1867; 1v & pf duet) ....
9.9   Gounod: "Méditation sur le 1er Prélude de J. S. Bach" (p1869; 1v & pf duet) ....
9.10   Gounod: "Jeanne d'Arc" (p1873; pf; also for 1v & pf 1877) ....
9.11   Gounod: "Gallia: Lamentation" (transcr for pf duet) ....
9.12   Handel: "L'harmonieux forgeron" (transcr for pf duet) ....
9.13   Marcello: "Signore non tardi dunque," psalm (transcr for pf) ....
9.14   Masse: "Le fils du brigadier" (p1867; pf) ....
9.15   Massenet: "Scènes hongroises," suite No.2 (orchd) ....
9.16   Massenet: "Scènes de bal," Op.17 (transcr for pf) ....
9.17   Mozart: "Don Juan," complete score (p1866; pf) ....
9.18   Mozart: "Don Juan," overture & excerpts (p ?1867; pf/pf duet) ....
9.19   Mozart: "L'oie du Caïre" (p1867; pf) ....
9.20   Nicolai: "The Merry Wives of Windsor" (p1866; 1v & pf) ....
9.21   Reyer: "Erostrate" (p1862; for pf) ....
9.22   Rossini: "Trio pour violon, piano et orgue sur Guillaume Tell" (unpubd) ....
9.23   Saint-Saëns: "Le timbre d'urgent," drama (p1879; 1v & pf) ....
9.24   Saint-Saëns: Piano Concerto No.2 in G minor, Op.22 (transcr for pf) ....
9.25   Saint-Saëns: "Introduction and Rondo capricioso," in A minor, Op.28 (transcr for pf) ....
9.26   Schumann: "6 Etudes," Op.56 (transcr for pf) ....
9.27   Thalberg: "L'art du chant appliqué au piano" (p1872; simplified edition for pf/pf duet) ....
9.28   Thomas: "Mignon" (p1867; pf) ....
9.29   Thomas: "Hamlet" (p1869; 1v & pf) ....

* * * * *

1. STAGE WORKS

1.1   "Macbeth," 3 act opera (c1904–9, Fleg after Shakespeare; Interludes I & III arr for 1v & pf) (also see opera c by Verdi, incid music c by Bacewicz, Khachaturian, Milhaud Op.175, Spohr WoO 55 & Sullivan) ....

2. SYMPHONIES

2.1   Symphony in C-sharp minor (c1901–2) ....

2.2   "Israel" Symphony (c1912–6; w/ 2S, 2A, B) ....

2.3   "Sinfonia breve" (c1952) ....

2.4   Symphony (c1954; trbn/vc & orch/pf) ....

2.5   Symphony in E-flat major (c1954–5) ....

3. OTHER ORCHESTRAL WORKS

3.1   "Hiver—Printemps," 2 sym poems (c1904–5) ....

3.2   "3 Jewish Poems" (c1913): No.1 "Danse" ....

3.3   No.2 "Rite"

3.4   No.3 "Cortège funèbre"

3.5   "In the Night" (c1922; also for pf) ....

3.6   "Poems of the Sea" (c1922; also for pf): No.1 "Waves" ....

3.7   No.2 "Chantey"

3.8   No.3 "At Sea"

3.9   "4 Episodes" (c1926; chamber orch): No.1 "Humoresque macabre" ....

3.10   No.2 "Obsession"

3.11   No.3 "Calm"

3.12   No.4 "Chinese"

3.13   "Helvetia" (Symphonic Fresco) (c1900–29) ....

3.14   "Evocations," sym suite (c1937; also for 2pf): No.1 "Contemplation" ....

3.15   No.2 "Houang Ti, God of War"

3.16   No.3 "Renouveau"

3.17   "Suite symphonique" (c1944): No.1 "Ouverture" ....

3.18   No.2 "Passacaglia"

3.19   No.3 "Finale"

3.20   "In Memoriam" (c1952; also for org) ....

4. CONCERTOS, SOLO INSTR & ORCH

Pf & orch:

4.1   "Concerto Grosso No.1" (c1924–5; strings & pf obbl): No.1 "Prelude" ....

4.2   No.2 "Dirge"

4.3   No.3 "Pastorale & Rustic dances"

4.4   No.4 "Fugue"

4.5   "Concerto symphonique" (c1947–8; pf & orch; also for 2pf) ....

4.6   "Scherzo fantasque" (c1946–8; pf & orch; also for 2pf) ....

Vn & orch:

4.7   Violin Concerto (c1937–8; also w/ pf) ....

Va & orch:

4.8   "Suite" (c1918–9; va & orch/pf): No.1 "Lento" ....

4.9   No.2 "Allegro ironico"

4.10   No.3 "Lento"

4.11   No.4 "Molto vivo"

4.12   "Suite hébraïque" (c1951; va/vn & orch/pf): No.1 "Rhapsody" ....

4.13   No.2 "Processional"

4.14   No.3 "Affirmation"

Vc & orch:

4.15   "Schelomo" (Solomon—Hebrew Rhapsody) (c1915–6; vc & orch/pf) ....

4.16   "Voice in the Wilderness," sym poem (c1936; w/ cello obbl; also for vc & pf): No.1 "Moderato" ....

4.17   No.2 "Poco lento"

4.18   No.3 "Moderato"

4.19   No.4 "Adagio piacevole"

4.20   No.5 "Poco agitato—Cadenza"

4.21   No.6 "Allegro giocoso"

Other:

4.22	"Concertino" (c1948; fl, va & strings/pf) ....
4.23	"Concerto Grosso No.2" (c1952; str qt & strings) ....
4.24	"Proclamation" (c1955; tpt & orch/pf) ....
4.25	"Suite modale" (c1956; fl & strings/pf): No.1 "Moderato" ....
4.26	No.2 "L'istesso tempo"
4.27	No.3 "Allegro giocoso"
4.28	No.4 "Adagio—Allegro deciso"
4.29	"2 Last Poems" (c1958; fl & orch; arr w/ pf): No.1 "Funeral music" ....
4.30	No.2 "Life again"

5. STRING QUARTETS

5.1	String Quartet No.1 in B minor (c1916) ....
5.2	"In the Mountains" (c1925): No.1 "Dusk" ....
5.3	No.2 "Rustic dance"
5.4	"Night" (c1925) ....
5.5	"Landscapes" (Paysages) (c1925): No.1 "North" ....
5.6	No.2 "Alpestre"
5.7	No.3 "Tongataboo"
5.8	"Prelude" (Recuillement) (c1925; arr Marsh for org 1946) ....
5.9	String Quartet No.2 (c1945) ....
5.10	"2 Pieces": No.1 "Andante moderato" (c1938) ....
5.11	No.2 "Allegro molto" (c1950)
5.11	String Quartet No.3 (c1952) ....
5.12	String Quartet No.4 (c1953) ....
5.13	String Quartet No.5 (c1956) ....

6. OTHER CHAMBER MUSIC

3 or more insts:

6.1	Piano Quintet No.1 (c1921–3) ....
6.2	Piano Quintet No.2 (c1957) ....
6.3	"Music for Clarinet & String Quartet" (c1984–5) ....
6.4	"3 Nocturnes" (c1924; pf trio) ....

Vn & pf:

6.5	Violin Sonata No.1 (c1920) ....
6.6	"Baal Shem" (3 Pictures of Chassidic Life), suite (c1923; orchd1939): No.1 "Vidui" (Contrition) ....
6.7	No.2 "Nigun" (Improvisation)
6.8	No.3 "Simchas Torah" (Rejoicing)
6.9	"Exotic Night" (c1924) ....
6.10	Violin Sonata No.2, "Poème mystique" (c1924) ....
6.11	"Abodah: a Yom Kippur Melody" (c1929) ....
6.12	"Melody" (c1923) ....

Va & pf:

6.13	"Suite" (c1919; va & pf): ....
	Programmatic info suppressed by composer: No.1 "In the Jungle" (Life in the Primitive World)
	No.2 "Grotesques" (Simian Stage)
	No.3 "Nocturne"
	No.4 "Land of the Sun" (China)
6.14	"2 Pieces" (c1951): No.1 "Meditation" ....
6.15	No.2 "Processional"

Vc & pf:

6.16	"From Jewish Life," 3 sketches (c1924): No.1 "Prayer" (orchd Antonini) ....
6.17	No.2 "Supplication"
6.18	No.3 "Jewish Song"
6.19	"Méditation hébraïque" (c1924) ....
6.20	*"Nigun" (arr Schuster for vc & pf 1947, from: Baal Shem) ....*

1 instr:

6.21	Violin Suite No.1 (c1958) ....
6.22	Violin Suite No.2 (c1958) ....
6.23	Viola Suite (c1958): ....
	1. "Andante"

10. CHORAL WORKS

10.1   "America: an Epic Rhapsody" (c1926; ch & orch/pf/org): ....
       1. "... 1620. The Soil—The Indians—(England)—The Mayflower—The Landing of the Pilgrims"
       2. "1861–1865. Hours of Joy—Hours of Sorrow"
       3. "1926 ... The Present. The Future"
10.2   "Avodath Hakodesh—Sacred Service" (c1930–33; Bar, ch & orch/pf/org): ....
       I. "Meditation": 1. "Mah Tovu" (How goodly are thy tents)
         2. "Borechu" (Sing His praise)
         3. "Shema Yisroel" (O hear, Israel)
         4. "Ve' ohavto" (And thou shalt love Him)
         5. "Mi Chomocho" (Who is like Thee)
         6. "A donoy Yimloch" (And the Lord shall reign)
         7. "Tzur Yisroel" (Rock of Israel)
       II. "Kedushah" (Sanctification): 8. "Nekadesh" (Sanctified be Thy name evermore)
         9. "Kodosh" (Holy, holy, holy)
         10. "Adir Adireinu" (O God ever mighty)
         11. "Echod Hu, Eloheinu" (For One is the Lord our God)
         12. "Yimloch Adonoy Le' olom" (Shalt reign, Adonoy, evermore)
       III. "Silent Devotion" (and Response): 13. "Yihu Lerotzon" (O Lord, may the words of my mouth)
         14. "Se' u She' orim" (Lift up your heads)
         . (Taking the Scroll from the Ark)
         15. "Toroh Tziroh" (The Torah, which God gave through Moses)
         16. "Shema Yisroel" (O hear, Israel, our God)
         17. "Lecho Adonoy" (And Thine, Adonoy, is the greatness)
       IV. "Returning the Scroll to the Ark": 18. "Gadelu Ladonoy" (Praise the Lord with me)
         19. "Hodo al Eretz" (Earth sees His glory)
         20. "Toras Adonoy" (The Law of the Lord is perfect)
         21. "Etz Chayim" (A Peace Song) (The Torah is a Tree of Life)
       V. "Adoration": 22. "Va' anachnu" (We adore Thee)
         23. "Bayom Hahu" (And on that day the Lord shall be One)
         24. "Tzur Yisroel" (God of Israel! Arise to the help of Israel!)
         25. "Adon Olom" (Eternal God, who reigned supreme)
         26. "Benediction" (Now may the Lord bless you)

11. VOICE & ORCHESTRA

11.1   "Poèmes d'automne," 4 songs (c1906, Rodes; mS & orch/pf): 1. "The Vagabond" ....
11.2   2. "The Waning"
11.3   3. "The Shelter"
11.4   4. "Invocation"
11.5   "Prelude & 2 Psalms" (Nos.137 & 114) (c1912–4; S & orch/pf) ....
11.6   "Psalm 22" (c1914; A/Bar & orch) ....

12. SONGS (w/ pf)

12.1   "Historiettes au crépuscule" (c1904, Mauclair): 1. "Légende" ....
12.2   2. "Les fleurs"
12.3   3. "Ronde"
12.4   4. "Complainte"
12.5   "Adonai, Elohim" (c1912–6; 2S, 2A, B & pf, from last movt of: 'Israel' Symphony) ....

*   *   *   *   *

BOCCHERINI, (Ridolfo) **Luigi**
1743–1805

1. STAGE WORKS

Operas:

1.1	"La Clementina," 2 act zarzuela (c1786, Cruz)	G540

Ballets:

1.2	"Cefalo e Procri," ballo eroico-tragico-pantomimo (c1778)	G524
1.3	"10 Minuets per un ballo," suite (c1788; large orch)	Op.41, G525
1.4	"Ballet espagnol" (ca1773)	G526

2. SYMPHONIES

Small orch:

2.1	Symphony in D major (Overture "La buona figliola") (p ca1775, = Overture to cantata G543; used as Overture in oratorio G538; used as Interlude for Piccini's opera: La buona figliola, G527)	G490 (G527)
2.2	"Concerto" (Sinfonia concertante), in C major (c1769; 2vn & orch)	Op.7, G491
2.3	"6 Divertimenti" (= 6 Sextets, Op.16, G461–G466)	G492
2.4	"6 Symphonies" (c1775): No.1 in B-flat major	Op.21, G493
2.5	No.2 in E-flat major	G494
2.6	No.3 in C major	G495
2.7	No.4 in D major	G496
2.8	No.5 in B-flat major	G497
2.9	No.6 in A major	G498
2.10	"Symphonie concertante," in G major (= Octet, Op.38/4, G470)	G499
2.11	*"Premiere Symphonie," in D major (p1767 w/ 2 hunting hns ad lib, ?spur)*	*G500*
2.12	*Symphony in G major (unpubd, ?spur)*	*G576*

Large orch:

2.13	"6 Symphonies" (c1771): No.1 in D major	Op.12, G503
2.14	No.2 in E-flat major	G504
2.15	No.3 in C major	G505
2.16	No.4 in D minor, "Della Casa del diavolo" (Finale based on Gluck's ballet: Don Juan)	G506
2.17	No.5 in B-flat major	G507
2.18	No.6 in A major	G508
2.19	"6 Symphonies" (c1782): No.1 in D major	Op.35, G509
2.20	No.2 in E-flat major	G510
2.21	No.3 in A major	G511
2.22	No.4 in F major	G512
2.23	No.5 in E-flat major	G513
2.24	No.6 in B-flat major	G514
2.25	"4 Symphonies" (c1786): No.1 in C major	Op.37, G515
2.26	*No.2 in D major (lost)*	*G516*
2.27	No.3 in D minor, "La divina"	G517
2.28	No.4 in A major	G518
2.29	Symphony in C minor (c1788)	Op.41, G519
2.30	Symphony in D major (c1789)	Op.42, G520
2.31	Symphony in D major (c1790)	Op.43, G521
2.32	Symphony in D minor (c1792)	Op.45/5, G522
2.33	Symphony in C major (arr of: Symphony in C major, Op.21/3, G495)	G523

3. OTHER ORCHESTRAL WORKS

3.1	"Serenade," in D major (p1777)	G501
3.2	*"2 Minuets" (p ca1775, spur: arr Marescalchi): No.1 in C major (from: Str Qt, Op.2/6, G164)*	*G502*
3.3	*No.2 in E-flat major (from: Str Trio, Op.4/1, G83)*	

4. CONCERTOS, SOLO INSTR & ORCH

Hpd & orch:

4.1	Harpsichord Concerto in E-flat major (unpubd)	G487

Vn & orch:

4.2	*Violin Concerto in G major (unpubd, spur)*	*G485*
4.3	*Violin Concerto in D major (unpubd, spur; ed1924)*	*G486*
4.4	*Violin Concerto in F major (unpubd, ?spur, inc)*	*G574*

Vc & orch:

4.5	Cello Concerto No.1 in E-flat major (c by ?1770–2, unpubd)	G474
4.6	Cello Concerto No.2 in A major (unpubd)	G475
4.7	Cello Concerto No.3 in D major (unpubd)	G476
4.8	Cello Concerto No.4 in C major (p1770)	G477
4.9	*Cello Concerto No.5 in D major (unpubd, part adapted from: Vc Conc No.4 in C major, G477, cantata: La confederazione dei Sabini con Roma, G543 & Symphony in D major, G490, ?spur)*	*G478*
4.10	Cello Concerto No.6 in D major (p1770)	G479
4.11	Cello Concerto No.7 in G major (p1770)	G480
4.12	Cello Concerto No.8 in C major (p1771)	G481
4.13	Cello Concerto No.9 in B-flat major (unpubd; celebrated vers arr Grützmacher ed1895)	G482
4.14	Cello Concerto No.10 in D major (p1785, w/ 2vn di concerto & 2 vn ripieni)	Op.34, G483
4.15	*"Concertino," in G major (vc & pf/orch, spur arr from: Str Trio, Op.1/5, G81 & Str Trio, Op.34/2, G102; p ca1950)*	*G484*
4.16	Cello Concerto No.11 in C major (unpubd)	G573
4.17	*Cello Concerto No.12 in E-flat major (?spur)*	

Fl & orch:

4.18	*Flute Concerto in D major (p ca ?1780, spur)*	*G489*
4.19	*Flute Concerto in D major (unpubd, common material with: Vc Conc No.6 in D major, G479, ?spur)*	*G575*
4.20	Flute Concerto in D major (c ?1767, discovered 1981)	G489

5. STRING SEXTETS

5.1	"6 String Sextets" (c1776; 2vn, 2va & 2vc): No.1 in E-flat major	Op.23, G454
5.2	No.2 in B-flat major	G455
5.3	No.3 in E major	G456
5.4	No.4 in F minor	G457
5.5	No.5 in G major	G458
5.6	No.6 in F major	G459
5.7	*String Sextet in D major (3vn, va & 2vc, unpubd, ?spur)*	*G460*

6. STRING QUINTETS

2vn, va & 2vc:

6.1	"6 String Quintets" (c1771): No.1 in A major	Op.10, G265
6.2	No.2 in E-flat major	G266
6.3	No.3 in C minor	G267
6.4	No.4 in C major	G268
6.5	No.5 in E-flat major	G269
6.6	No.6 in D major	G270
6.7	"6 String Quintets" (c1771): No.1 in B-flat major	Op.11, G271
6.8	No.2 in A major	G272
6.9	No.3 in C major	G273
6.10	No.4 in F minor	G274
6.11	No.5 in E major (3rd movt = celebrated Minuet)	G275
6.12	No.6 in D major, "L'uccelliera" (The Aviary)	G276
6.13	"6 String Quintets" (c1772): No.1 in E-flat major	Op.13, G277
6.14	No.2 in C major	G278
6.15	No.3 in F major	G279
6.16	No.4 in D minor	G280
6.17	No.5 in A major	G281
6.18	No.6 in E major	G282
6.19	"6 String Quintets" (c1774): No.1 in C minor	Op.18, G283
6.20	No.2 in D major	G284
6.21	No.3 in E-flat major	G285
6.22	No.4 in C major	G286
6.23	No.5 in D minor	G287
6.24	No.6 in E major	G288
6.25	"6 String Quintets" (c1775): No.1 in C minor	Op.20, G289
6.26	No.2 in D major	G290
6.27	No.3 in E-flat major	G291
6.28	No.4 in C major	G292
6.29	No.5 in D minor	G293
6.30	No.6 in E major	G294
6.31	"6 String Quintets" (c1778): No.1 in D minor	Op.25, G295
6.32	No.2 in E-flat major	G296
6.33	No.3 in A major	G297
6.34	No.4 in C major	G298
6.35	No.5 in D major	G299

6.106	"6 String Quintets" (c1795): No.1 in A major	Op.50, G370
6.107	No.2 in E-flat major	G371
6.108	No.3 in B-flat major	G372
6.109	No.4 in E major	G373
6.110	No.5 in C major	G374
6.111	No.6 in B-flat major	G375
6.112	"2 String Quintets" (c1795): No.1 in E-flat major	Op.51, G376
6.113	No.2 in C minor	G377
6.114	*String Quintet in C major (p ca ?1954, spur, collected from Str Qnts G349, G314, G318, G325 & G310)*	*G368*

2vn, 2va & vc ('double viola quintets'):

6.115	String Quintet in E minor (unpubd, transcr from: Pf Qnt, Op.56/1, G407; also see G451)	G379
6.116	String Quintet in F major (unpubd, transcr from: Pf Qnt, Op.56/2, G408; also see G452)	G380
6.117	String Quintet in E-flat major (unpubd, transcr from: Pf Qnt, Op.56/4, G410; also see G452)	G381
6.118	String Quintet in A minor (unpubd, transcr from: Pf Qnt, Op.56/6, G412; also see G452)	G382
6.119	String Quintet in D major (unpubd, transcr from: Pf Qnt, Op.56/5, G411; also see G452)	G383
6.120	String Quintet in C major (unpubd, transcr from: Pf Qnt, Op.56/3, G409; also see G453)	G384
6.121	String Quintet in D minor (p1816–7, transcr from: Pf Qnt, Op.57/4, G416; also see G445)	G385
6.122	String Quintet in E minor (p1816–7, transcr from: Pf Qnt, Op.57/5, G417; also see G446)	G386
6.123	String Quintet in B-flat major (unpubd, transcr from: Pf Qnt, Op.57/2, G414; also see G447)	G387
6.124	String Quintet in A major (unpubd, transcr from: Pf Qnt, Op.57/1, G413)	G388
6.125	String Quintet in E minor (unpubd, transcr from: Pf Qnt, Op.57/3, G415)	G389
6.126	String Quintet in C major (unpubd, transcr from: Pf Qnt, Op.57/6, G418)	G390
6.127	"6 String Quintets" (c1801; 2vn, 2va & vc): No.1 in C major	Op.60, G391
6.128	No.2 in B-flat major	G392
6.129	No.3 in A major	G393
6.130	*No.4 in E-flat major (lost)*	*G394*
6.131	No.5 in G major	G395
6.132	No.6 in F major	G396
6.133	"6 String Quintets" (c1802; 2vn, 2va & vc): No.1 in C major	Op.62, G397
6.134	No.2 in E-flat major	G398
6.135	No.3 in F major	G399
6.136	No.4 in B-flat major	G400
6.137	No.5 in D major	G401
6.138	No.6 in E major	G402
6.139	*"6 String Quintets" (unpubd, spur transcr from: 6 Str Qnts, Op.10, G265–270): No.1 in A maj (from G265)*	*G403*
6.140	*No.2 in E-flat major (from G266)*	
6.141	*No.3 in C minor (from G267)*	
6.142	*No.4 in C major (from G268)*	
6.143	*No.5 in E-flat major (from G269)*	
6.144	*No.6 in D major (from G270)*	
6.145	*"6 String Quintets" (unpubd, spur transcr from: 6 Str Qnts, Op.11, G271–276): No.1 in C min (from G271)*	*G404*
6.146	*No.2 in D m ajor (from G272)*	
6.147	*No.3 in E-flat major (from G273)*	
6.148	*No.4 in C major (from G274)*	
6.149	*No.5 in D minor (from G275)*	
6.150	*No.6 in E major (from G276)*	
6.151	*String Quintet in E-flat major (mentioned Picquot, not traced)*	*G406*

7. STRING QUARTETS

7.1	"6 String Quartets" (c1761): No.1 in C minor	Op.2, G159
7.2	No.2 in B-flat major	G160
7.3	No.3 in D major	G161
7.4	No.4 in E-flat major	G162
7.5	No.5 in E major	G163
7.6	No.6 in C major	G164
7.7	"6 String Quartets" (c1769): No.1 in D major	Op.8, G165
7.8	No.2 in C minor	G166
7.9	No.3 in E-flat major	G167
7.10	No.4 in G minor	G168
7.11	No.5 in F major	G169
7.12	No.6 in A major	G170
7.13	"6 String Quartets" (c1770): No.1 in C minor	Op.9, G171
7.14	No.2 in D minor	G172
7.15	No.3 in F major	G173
7.16	No.4 in E-flat major	G174
7.17	No.5 in D major	G175
7.18	No.6 in E major	G176
7.19	"6 String Quartets" (c1772): No.1 in D major	Op.15, G177
7.20	No.2 in D minor	G178
7.21	No.3 in E major	G179
7.22	No.4 in F major	G180

8. STRING TRIOS (2vn & vc)

9. OTHER CHAMBER MUSIC

Octets:

Sextets:

Piano Quintets (pf, 2vn, va & vc):

Flute & Flute/Oboe Quintets (fl/ob, 2vn, va & vc):

Guitar Quintets (gui, 2vn, va & vc, Boccherini's transcriptions, Nos.1–6 unpubd):

Harpsichord/Piano Quartets (hpd/pf, vn, va & vc):

Flute Quartets (fl, vn, va & vc):

Wind Quartets (cl, fl, hn & bn):

Harpsichord/Piano Trios (hpd/pf, vn & vc):

Piano Trios (pf, vn & va):

Flute Trios (fl, vn & vc):

Other Trios (2fl & bass):

9.101	*"Trio," in C major (unpubd, spur, arr from: Str Trio, Op.4/2, G84)*	*G157*
9.102	*"Trio," in D major (unpubd, spur, arr from: Str Trio, Op.4/5, G87)*	*G158*

Vn & cont:

9.103	*"6 Violin Sonatas" (p ?1775, Vc Sonatas pubd as Vn Sonatas): No.1 in A major (= Vc Son No.13, G13)*	*G20*
9.104	*No.2 in C major (= Vc Son No.6, G6)*	
9.105	*No.3 in G major (= Vc Son No.5, G5)*	
9.106	*No.4 in E-flat major (= Vc Son No.10, G10)*	
9.107	*No.5 in F major (= Vc Son No.1, G1)*	
9.108	*No.6 in A major (= Vc Son No.4, G4a)*	

Vn & pf/hpd:

9.109	"6 Sonatas" (c1768): No.1 in B-flat major	Op.5, G25
9.110	No.2 in C major	G26
9.111	No.3 in B-flat major	G27
9.112	No.4 in D major	G28
9.113	No.5 in G minor	G29
9.114	No.6 in E-flat major	G30
9.115	*"6 Violin Sonatas" (pubd by Artaria of Vienna in 1788, = ?Op.5/?arr/insufficient info)*	*G31*
9.116	*"3 Violin Sonatas" (Paris, Sieber, 'livre 3') (mentioned Picqut, not found)*	*G32*
9.117	*"3 Violin Sonatas" (Paris, Sieber, 'livre 4') (mentioned Picqut, not found)*	*G33*
9.118	*Violin Sonata in C major (p ca ?1780, spur: arr Billington from: Str Trio, Op.10/4, G268)*	*G34*
9.119	*Violin Sonata in E major (p ca ?1780, spur: arr Billington from: Str Trio, Op.4/3, G85)*	*G35*
9.120	*Violin Sonata in B-flat major (p ca ?1780, spur: arr Billington from: Str Trio, Op.4/2, G84)*	*G36*
9.121	*Violin Sonata in E-flat major (p ca ?1780, spur: arr Billington from: Str Trio, Op.4/1, G83)*	*G37*
9.122	*Violin Sonata in A major (p ca ?1780, spur: arr Billington from: Str Trio, Op.6/3, G91)*	*G38*
9.123	*Violin Sonata in D maj (p ca ?1780, spur: arr Billington from: Str Trio, Op.1/4, G80 & Str Qt, Op.8/1, G165)*	*G39*
9.124	*Violin Sonata in C major (p1778, spur: arr ?Naderman from: Str Qt, Op.2/6, G164 & Fl Qnt, Op.17/2, G420)*	*G40*
9.125	*Violin Sonata in B-flat major (p1778, spur: arr ?Naderman from: Str Qt, Op.17/4, G422)*	*G41*
9.126	*Violin Sonata in D minor (p1778, spur: arr ?Naderman from: Str Qt, Op.9/2, G172 & Fl Qnt, Op.17/1, G419)*	*G42*
9.127	*Violin Sonata in C minor (p1778, spur: arr ?Naderman from: Str Qt, Op.2/1, G159)*	*G43*
9.128	*Violin Sonata in B-flat major (p1778, spur: arr ?Naderman from: Str Qt, Op.2/2, G160)*	*G44*
9.129	*Violin Sonata in C min (p1778, spur: arr ?Naderman from: Str Qnt, Op.9/1, G171 & Fl Qnt, Op.17/6, G424)*	*G45*
9.130	*Violin Sonata in C min (p1782, spur: arr Mlle Le Jeune from: Str Qt, Op.2/1, G159 & Str Qt, Op.9/1, G171)*	*G46*
9.131	*Violin Sonata in D major (p1782, spur: arr Mlle Le Jeune from: Str Qt, Op.8/1, G165)*	*G47*
9.132	*Violin Sonata in B-flat major (p1782, spur: arr Mlle Le Jeune from: Str Trio, Op.6/1, G89 & Str Qt, Op.8/3, G167)*	*G48*
9.133	*Violin Sonata in A major (p1782, spur: arr Mlle Le Jeune from: Str Trio, Op.4/3, G85, Str Qt, Op.2/3, G161 & Str Qnt, Op.10/2, G266)*	*G49*
9.134	*Violin Sonata in E-flat major (p1782, spur: arr Mlle Le Jeune from: Str Qt, Op.2/4, G162 & Str Trio, Op.6/2, G90)*	*G50*
9.135	*Violin Sonata in E major (p1782, spur: arr Mlle Le Jeune from: Str Qnt, Op.13/6, G282)*	*G51*
9.136	*Violin Sonata in B-flat major (p ca1775, spur: arr Robinson from: Str Trio, Op.4/2, G84 & Str Trio, Op.1/2, G78)*	*G52*
9.137	*Violin Sonata in E-flat major (p ca1775, spur: arr Robinson from: Str Trio, Op.4/1, G83)*	*G53*
9.138	*Violin Sonata in E major (p ca1775, spur: arr Robinson from: Str Trio, Op.4/3, G85)*	*G54*
9.139	*"Rondo," in G major (p1782; hpd & vn, spur arr from: Str Trio, Op.6/5, G93)*	*G55*
9.140	*Violin Sonata (unpubd, ?spur)*	*G570*

2 Vn:

9.141	"6 Duets" (c1761): No.1 in G major	Op.3, G56
9.142	No.2 in F major	G57
9.143	No.3 in A major	G58
9.144	No.4 in B-flat major	G59
9.145	No.5 in E-flat major	G60
9.146	No.6 in D major	G61
9.147	Duet No.7 in E-flat major, "La bona notte" (unpubd)	G62
9.148	Duet No.8 in G major (p1798, arr from: Str Trio, Op.54/2, G114)	G63
9.149	Duet No.9 in E major (p1798, arr from: Str Trio, Op.34/6, G106)	G64
9.150	Duet No.10 in F minor (p1798, arr from: Str Trio, Op.34/1, G101)	G65
9.151	Duet No.11 in C major (p1798, arr from: Str Trio, Op.34/5, G105)	G66
9.152	Duet No.12 in E-flat major (arr from: Str Trio, Op.54/3, G115)	G67
9.153	Duet No.13 in D min (p1798, arr from: Str Qnt, Op.46/2, G360 & Str Qnt, Op.49/1, G365)	G68
9.154	*Duet in C major (unpubd, ?spur)*	*G69*
9.155	*Duet in C major (unpubd, ?spur)*	*G70*
9.156	*Duet in D major (p1788, ?spur, arr from: Str Trio, G122)*	*G71*
9.157	*"6 Duets" (mentioned Picquot, spur: c by Agus)*	*G72*

Vc & cont (p ca1770):

9.158	Cello Sonata No.1 in F major (arr for vn & cont, G20/5)	G1
9.159	Cello Sonata No.2 in C minor (2 vers)	G2a, b
9.160	Cello Sonata No.3 in C major	G3
9.161	Cello Sonata No.4 in A major (2nd vers unpubd; arr for vn & cont, G20/6)	G4a, b
9.162	Cello Sonata No.5 in G major (arr for vn & cont, G20/3)	G5
9.163	Cello Sonata No.6 in C major (arr for vn & cont, G20/2; arr w/ strings as: Adagio & Allegro in A major)	G6
9.164	Cello Sonata No.7 in C major	G7
9.165	Cello Sonata No.8 in B-flat major	G8
9.166	Cello Sonata No.9 in F major	G9
9.167	Cello Sonata No.10 in E-flat major (arr for vn & cont, G20/4)	G10
9.168	Cello Sonata No.11 in E-flat major	G11
9.169	Cello Sonata No.12 in B-flat major	G12
9.170	Cello Sonata No.13 in A major (arr for vn & cont, G20/1)	G13
9.171	Cello Sonata No.14 in E-flat major	G14
9.172	Cello Sonata No.15 in G major	G15
9.173	Cello Sonata No.16 in E-flat major	G16
9.174	Cello Sonata No.17 in C major	G17
9.175	Cello Sonata No.18 in C minor	G18
9.176	Cello Sonata No.19 in F major	G19

Vc & cont (unpubd):

9.177	Cello Sonata No.20 in G minor	G562
9.178	Cello Sonata No.21 in G major	G563
9.179	Cello Sonata No.22 in D major	G564
9.180	Cello Sonata No.23 in B-flat major (sketch of celebrated: Vc Conc No.9, G482; 2 vers)	G565a, b
9.181	Cello Sonata No.24 in E-flat major	G566
9.182	Cello Sonata No.25 in E-flat major	G567
9.183	Cello Sonata No.26 in E-flat major	G568
9.184	Cello Sonata No.27 in C major	G569
9.185	Cello Sonata No.28 in F major	G579
9.186	*Cello Sonata No.29 in D major (?spur)*	*G580*

2 Vc:

9.187	*"6 Fugues" (2vc/2bn, instructional exercises, unpubd, ?spur): No.1 in C major*	*G73*
9.188	*No.2 in F major*	
9.189	*No.3 in B-flat major*	
9.190	*No.4 in E-flat major*	
9.191	*No.5 in A major*	
9.192	*No.6 in E major*	
9.193	Cello Sonata in C major (unpubd; modern edition ca1945)	G74
9.194	Cello Sonata in E-flat major (p ca ?1785, = G10)	G75
9.195	*Cello Sonata in D major (?spur/?early work, unpubd, discovered Carmirelli)*	*G571*
9.196	*Cello Sonata in D major (?spur/?early work, unpubd, discovered Carmirelli)*	*G572*

10. HARPSICHORD (or pf)

10.1	*"Sinfonia," in E-flat major (pf, spur)*	*G21*
10.2	*"Sonata," in E-flat major (hpd, actually hpd part of: Sonata for hpd & vn, Op.5/6, G30)*	*G22*
10.3	*"6 Sonatas" (hpd/pf, ?hpd/pf parts of ?spur: 6 Trio Sonatas for hpd/pf, vn & vc): No.1 in C major (of G143)*	*G23*
10.4	*No.2 in E minor (of G144)*	
10.5	*No.3 in E-flat major (of G145)*	
10.6	*No.4 in D major (of G146)*	
10.7	*No.5 in B-flat major (of G147)*	
10.8	*No.6 in G minor (of G148)*	
10.9	*"6 Sonatas" (hpd & vn ad lib, spur arrs from: 6 Str Trios, Op.14, G95–100): No.1 in F major (from G95)*	*G24*
10.10	*No.2 in C minor (from G96)*	
10.11	*No.3 in A major (from G97)*	
10.12	*No.4 in D major (from G98)*	
10.13	*No.5 in E-flat major (from G99)*	
10.14	*No.6 in F major (from G100)*	

2 Hpd:

10.15	*"6 Duets" (18th cent transcr of: 6 Str Quartets, Op.26, G195–200, unpubd): No.1 in B-flat major*	*G76*
10.16	*No.2 in G minor*	
10.17	*No.3 in E-flat major*	
10.18	*No.4 in A major*	
10.19	*No.5 in F major*	
10.20	*No.6 in F minor*	

11. SACRED MUSIC

Masses & mass sections:

11.1	*"Missa solemnis" (p1800; 4vv & insts, lost)*	*Op.59, G528*
11.2	"Kyrie" (ca1764–6; 4vv & orch, unpubd)	G529
11.3	"Gloria" (ca1764–6; 4vv & orch, unpubd)	G530
11.4	"Credo" (ca1764–6; 4vv & orch, unpubd)	G531

Motets:

11.5	"Stabat mater," sequence (c1781; S & strings; 2nd vers for 3vv & strings 1780)	Op.61, G532
11.6	"Dixit Dominus" (ca1764–6, Psalm 110; 4vv & orch, unpubd)	G533
11.7	"Domine ad adjuvandum" (ca1765; 4vv & orch, unpubd)	G534
11.8	*"Christmas Cantata" (c1802, lost)*	*Op.63, G535*
11.9	*"Cantata for the feast of Saint Louis" (unpubd, ?spur)*	*G536*

Oratorios:

11.10	"Gioas, re di Giudea" (ca1765, Metastasio; vv, ch & orch)	G537
11.11	"Il Giuseppe riconosciuto" (ca1765, Metastasio; vv, ch & orch)	G538

Villancicos (half sacred & half secular carols, based on popular tunes, sung in Spain for Christmas):

11.12	"9 Villancicos" (ca1783; ch & orch, inc, unpubd): 1. "Introduccion"	G539
11.13	2. "Allegro giusto"	
11.14	3. "Allegro"	
11.15	4. "Presto"	
11.16	5. "Cantabile"	
11.17	6. "Allegro"	
11.18	7. "Lento"	
11.19	8. "Amoroso"	
11.20	9. "Allegro" (Despedida)	

12. SECULAR CHORAL

12.1	"La confederazione dei Sabini con Roma," cantata (c1765, Trenta; vv, ch & orch)	G543

13. VOICE & ORCHESTRA

Operatic:

13.1	"Scene from 'Ines de Castro' " (c1798; S & orch)	G541
13.2	*"Aria for an opera 'L'Almeria' " (?spur: mentioned Hamilton, not supported by any references)*	*G542*

"15 Arie Accademiche" (Concert arias) (c ?1792, Metastasio; S/T & orch, unpubd):

13.3	1. "Si veramente io deggio," recit (S, T) & "Ah, non lasciarmi, no, bell'idol mio," aria	G544
13.4	2. "Se non ti moro allato idolo del cor mio," aria	G545
13.5	3. "Deh, respirar lasciatemi," aria	G546
13.6	4. "Caro, son tua così che per virtù d'amor," aria	G547
13.7	5. "Misera dove son," recit & "Ah non son io che parlo," aria	G548
13.8	6. "Care luci che regnate sugl'affetti del mio cor," aria	G549
13.9	7. "Infelice in van mi lagno qual dolente tortorella," aria	G550
13.10	8. "Numi, se giusti siete, rendete," aria	G551
13.11	9. "Caro Padre,a me non dei," aria	G552
13.12	10. "Ah che nel dirti addio mi sento il cor dividere," aria	G553
13.13	11. "Di giudice severo," recit (3vv) & "Per quel paterno amplesso," aria	G554
13.14	12. "Tu di saper procura," aria	G555
13.15	13. "Mi dona, mi rende quell'alma pietosa,"	G556
13.16	14. "Se d'un amor tiranno, credei di trionfar," aria	G557
13.17	15. "Tornate sereni," aria (ca1770–5, discovered Carmirelli)	G558

2vv & orch/instr:

13.18	"La destra ti chiedo mio dolce" (un Duetto Accademico) (Metastasio; S, A & orch)	G559
13.19	*"In 'sto giorno d'allegro" (2vv & bass, ?spur, unpubd)*	*G560*
13.20	*"Ah, che nel dirti addio" (2A & bass, ?spur, unpubd)*	*G561*

* * * * *

G = Yves Gérard: "Thematic, Bibliographical and Critical Catalogue of The Works of Luigi Boccherini." Transl A. Mayor. Oxford University Press. London, 1969.

1. STAGE WORKS (operas)

1.1   "The Bogatirs" (The Valiant Knights), 5 act opera-farce (c1867, Krylov) ....
1.2   *"The Tsar's Bride" (c1867–8, after Mey's drama, unfin, transf to other works)* ....
1.3   "Prince Igor," 4 acts (c1869–70, 1874–87; unfin; compl Rimsky-Korsakov & Glazunov) ....
1.4   "Mlada," Act IV of ballet-opera (1872, Krylov after Gedeonov's scenario; Acts I–III c by Cui, Musorgsky & Rimsky-Korsakov) ....

1a. SELECTIONS FROM STAGE WORKS (Nos. of sections in The Gramophone)

1a.3   "Prince Igor," opera: ....
       excerpts: Prologue: 1. "Overture"
                          2. "To the sun in his glory"
                 I: 3. "I hate a dreary life" (Galitzky's aria)
                       4. "For long past" (Yaroslavna's aria)
                 II: 5. "The prairie flowered" (Song of the Polovtsian maidens)
                       6. "Dance of the Polovtsian maidens"
                       7. "Daylight is fading" (Vladimir's aria)
                       8. "Do you love?," duet
                       9. "No sleep, no rest" (Igor's aria)
                       10. "How goes it Prince?" (Konchak's aria)
                       11. "Polovtsian Dances"
                 III: 12. "Polovtsian March" (Prelude)
                 IV: 13. "I shed bitter tears" (Yaroslavna's lament)

2. SYMPHONIES

2.1   Symphony No.1 in E-flat major (c1862–7) ....
2.2   Symphony No.2 in B minor (c1869–75, r until 1879) ....
2.3   Symphony No.3 in A minor, "Unfinished" (c1882, 1886–7; compl Glazunov) ....

3. OTHER ORCHESTRAL WORKS

3.1   "In the Steppes of Central Asia," musical picture (c1880) ....
3.2   *"Nocturne" (arr Sargent for strings, from: Str Qt No.2)* ....

4. STRING QUARTETS

4.1   String Quartet No.1 in A major (c1874–9; transcr Rahter for pf duet 1887) ....
4.2   String Quartet No.2 in D major (c1881; transcr Blumenfeld for pf duet) ....
4.3   "Spanish Serenade," for collab work: Str Qt, "B-la-F" (c1886, for the Name-day of Belayev; arr for pf duet):
       String Quartet in B-flat major, "B-la-F" (Belayev): *1. "Sostenuto assai et Allegro" (c by Rimsky-Korsakov)*
                       2. "Scherzo" (c by Lyadov)
                       3. "Spanish Serenade" (c by Borodin)
                       4. "Finale" (c by Glazunov)
4.4   "Scherzo," in D major (c1882, incl in collab work: The Fridays & in: Sym No.3 in A minor, 'Unfinished') ......

5. OTHER CHAMBER MUSIC

       6 insts:

5.1   String Sextet in D minor (c1860–1, inc: 2 movts only, 3rd & 4th lost) ....

       5 insts:

5.2   String Quintet in F minor (c1853–4; 2vn, va & 2vc) ....
5.3   Piano Quintet in C minor (c1862) ....

       4 insts:

5.4   Quartet in D major (c1852; fl, ob, va & vc, 1st & 4th movt based on Haydn) ....
5.5   "Miniature Quartet," in D major (c1852–6; fl, ob, va & vc) ....

       3 insts:

5.6   String Trio No.1 in G major (c1847; 2vn & vc, from Meyerbeer's opera: Robert le diable) ....
5.7   String Trio No.2 in G major, "Grand Trio" (c1852–6; 2vn & vc, unfin: 2 movts only) ....
5.8   String Trio No.3 in G minor (c?1855; 2vn & vc, on folksong: How did I grieve thee?; arr for pf duet) ....
5.9   String Trio No.4 in G major (c?1850–60, single movt) ....
5.10 Piano Trio in D major (c1860–1, unfin: 3 movts only) ....

2 insts:

5.11	*Flute Concerto in D maj / minor (c1847; fl & pf, lost)* ....
5.12	Cello Sonata in B minor (c1860, based on J. S. Bach's fugue from: Sonata No.1 in G minor, BWV1001) ....

6. PIANO

6.1	"Fantasy" (c ?1849, on a theme of Hummel) ....
6.2	"Le courant," study (c ?1849) ....
6.3	"Adagio patetico," in A-flat major (c ?1849) ....
6.4	"Fugues" (c1851–2) ....
6.5	*"Scherzo," in B-flat minor (c1852, lost)* ....
6.6	"Pot-pourri," in A major (c ?1852–5, on a theme from Donizetti's opera: Lucrezia Borgia) ....
6.7	*"Fugue" (c1862, lost)* ....
	4 Pieces for collab work: Chopsticks Paraphrases (c1878): ....
	"Chopsticks Paraphrases": *No.1 "24 Variations & Finale" (c by Rimsky-Korsakov, Cui & Lyadov)*
6.8	No.2 "Polka" (c by Borodin)
6.9	No.3 "Marche funèbre" (c by Borodin)
	No.4 "Valse" (c by Lyadov)
	No.5 "Berceuse," in C major (c by Rimsky-Korsakov, on children's folksong: There goes a goat with horns)
	No.6 "Galop" (c by Lyadov)
	No.7 "Gigue" (c by Lyadov)
	No.8 "Little Fugue on B-A-C-H," in C major (c by Rimsky-Korsakov)
	No.9 "Tarantella," in C major (c by Rimsky-Korsakov)
	No.10 "Minuet," in C major (c by Rimsky-Korsakov)
	No.11 "Valse" (c by Cui)
6.10	No.12 "Requiem" (c by Borodin)
	No.13 "Carillon," in C major (c by Rimsky-Korsakov)
6.11	No.14 "Mazurka" (c by Borodin)
	No.15. "Comic Fugue," in C major (c by Rimsky-Korsakov)
	Added later: *No.16 "Cortège triomphal" (c by Lyadov, added 1893)*
	No.17 "Bigarrures. Petit supplement" (c by Shcherbachev, added 1893)
6.12	"Petit Suite" (c1885; orchd Glazunov 1889): No.1 "In the monastery," in C-sharp minor ....
6.13	No.2 "Intermezzo," in F major
6.14	No.3 "Mazurka," in C major
6.15	No.4 "Mazurka," in D-flat major
6.16	No.5 "Daydreams," in D-flat major
6.17	No.6 "Serenade," in D-flat major
6.18	No.7 "Nocturne," in G-flat major
6.19	"Scherzo," in A-flat major (c1885; orchd Glazunov as Finale of: The Miniature Suite) ....

Musical jokes & improvisations (unfin):

6.20	"Southern night," a parody on a ballad by Rimsky-Korsakov (c ?1866) ....
6.21	"60 Variationen ...," on a pseudo-Czech theme by Balakirev (c1867, 1 variation composed) ....
6.22	Waltz, on a theme of Varlaam's Song from Musorgsky: Boris Godunov (c ?1870s) ....
6.23	Quadrille, on motifs from Rimsky-Korsakov: Maid of Pskov (c ?1870s) ....
6.24	A musical joke, on a motif of a well-known ballad: Gusar, na sabliu opirayas (c ?1870s) ....
6.25	"Lancer," in church modes ....
6.26	"Kuchki," humorous waltz (c1874) ....

Pf duet:

6.27	"Hélène," polka in D minor (c1843; orig for pf) ....
6.28	"Allegretto," in D-flat major (c1861, adapt of Trio from 3rd movt of: Str Qnt in F minor) ....
6.29	"Scherzo," in E major (c1861)
6.30	"Tarantella," in D major (c ?1862) ....
6.31	*"Ey ukhnem," transcr of a folksong: The Volga boatsmen (c ?1870, sketch)* ....
6.32	Piece in E-flat major (c ?1879) ....

7. CHORAL WORKS

7.1	"God save Kirill! God save Methodius!" (c ?1862; m ch, unfin) ....

8. MISC VOCAL

8.1	"Miserere me! Barbaro sorte" (ca1850, anon; T, B & pf, unfin) ....
8.2	"Serenade in honour of a lady by four cavaliers," humorous quartet (c ?1868–71; 4 m vv & pf) ....

9. SONGS (w/ pf)

9.1   "Merciful God," aria (c ?1852–5) ....

9.2   "Why art thou so early, dawn?" (c ?1852–5, anon folksong adapt Lamm) ....

9.3   "The beautiful fisher maiden" (c1854–5, Heine transl Kropotkin; w/ vc obbl) ....

9.4   "The pretty girl no longer loves me" (c ?1853–5, Vinogradov; w/ vc obbl) ....

9.5   "Listen to my song, little friend" (c ?1853–5, Kruse; w/ vc obbl) ....

9.6   "The sleeping princess," a fairy tale (c1867, Borodin; orchd Rimsky-Korsakov) ....

9.7   "Song of the dark forest," an old song (c1867–8, Borodin; arr for m ch & pf; orchd Glazunov) ....

9.8   "The sea princess," ballad (c1868, Borodin) ....

9.9   "The false note" (c1868, Borodin) ....

9.10   "My songs are poisoned," ballad (c1868, Heine transl Mey) ....

9.11   "The sea," ballad (c1870, Borodin; orchd Rimsky-Korsakov) ....

9.12   "From my tears," ballad (c1870–1, Heine transl Mey) ....

9.13   "Arabian Melody" (c1881, Borodin, based on folk-melody) ....

9.14   "For the shores of thy fair native land" (c1881, Pushkin) ....

9.15   "Those Folk" (At home among real people) (c1881, Nekrasov; 1v & orch; arr Dütsch for 1v & pf) ....

9.16   "Pride," ballad (c ?1884, Tolstoy) ....

9.17   "Septain" (The Magic Garden), ballad (c1885, Collin transl Borodin) ....

* * * * *

BOULEZ, Pierre

born 1925

page: 1

1. STAGE WORKS

Incid music:

1.1	"L'Orestie" (c1948, Aeschylus/Obey; 1v & insts)	J21
1.2	"Ainsi parla Zarathoustra" (c1972, Nietzsche/Barrault; 1v & insts)	J37

Radio:

1.3   "Le soleil des eaux" (4 vers): J11
        . Version 1 (c1948, Char; 1v & orch, for radio)
        . *Version 2 (c1948, Char; S, T, B, ch & orch, withdrawn)*
        . Version 3 (c1958, Char; S, T, B, ch & orch)
        . Version 4 (c1965, Char; S, ch & orch)

1.4   "Le crépuscule de Yang Koueï-Feï" (c1967, Louise Fauré) J24

Film:

1.5   "La Symphonie mécanique" (c1955, Jean Mitry) J22

2. ORCHESTRAL WORKS

2.1	"Polyphonie X" (c1950–1; 18 insts, part of projected: Polyphonie for 49 insts)	J16
2.2	"Doubles" (c1957–8; large orch)	J27a
2.3	"Figures—Doubles—Prismes" (c1963; large orch)	J27b
2.4	"Figures—Doubles—Prismes" (c1968; large orch)	J27c
2.5	"Poesie pour pouvoir" (Michaux; orch & 5-track tape)	J28
2.6	"Éclat" (c from 1965; 15 insts)	J31a
2.7	"Éclat / Multiples" (c1965–70; 27insts)	J31b
2.8	"e. e. cummings ist der Dichter" (2 vers):	J34

        . Version 1 (c1970; small orch & chamber orch)
        . Version 2 (c1986)

2.9   "Rituel in memoriam Bruno Maderna" (c1974–5; 8 orch groups) J36
2.10 12 "Notations" (c1977–8; large orch) J39

3. PIANO CONCERTOS, PIANO & ORCH

3.1   *"Symphonie concertante" (c1947, lost)* *J9*

4. STRING QUARTETS

4.1   "Livre pour quatuor à cordes" (3 vers): J13
        . Version 1 (c1948–9; str qt)
        . Version 2 (orchd1968)
        . Version 3 (r1989)

5. OTHER CHAMBER MUSIC

5.1	*"Quartet" (c1945–6; 4 ondes martenot, withdrawn)*	*J5*
5.2	"Sonatine" (c1946; fl & pf)	J6
5.3	*"3 Essais" (c1950; perc, withdrawn)*	*J15*
5.4	"2 Études" (c1951–2; single track tape): No.1 "Étude sur un son"	J17
5.5	No.2 "Étude sur un accord de sept sons"	
5.6	"Strophes" (c1957; lute, inc)	J25
5.7	*"Marges" (c1962–4; perc ensemble, sketches)*	*J30*
5.8	"Domaines" (c1961–8; 2 vers):	J32

        . Version 1 (cl solo)
        . Version 2 (cl & 6 insts groups)

5.9   "For Dr. Kalmus" (c1969; fl, cl, va, vc & pf, contribution to: A Garland for Dr. K.) J33
5.10 "... explosante—fixe ..." (3 vers): J35
        . Version 1 (c1971; variable ensemble)
        . Version 2 (c from 1972; fl, cl, tpt, harp, vib, vn, va, vc & electro-acoustic equipment)
        . Version 3 (c from1989; fl & electronic equipment)

5.11	"Messagesquisse" (c1976; vc solo & 6vc)	J38
5.12	"Répons" (c from 1981; 6 instr soloists, instr ensemble & electro-acoustic equipment)	J40
5.13	"Dérive" (c1984; fl, cl, vn, vc, vibraphone & pf)	J41
5.14	"Dialogue de l'ombre double" (c1985; cl & electro-acoustic equipment)	J42

6. PIANO SONATAS

7. OTHER PIANO WORKS

2 Pf:

8. VOCAL & CHORAL

. Version 1 (c1946–7; S, A, 2 ondes martenot, pf & perc)
. Version 2 (c1951–2; S, A, fem ch & orch)
. Version 3 (c1989; S, A, fem ch & orch)
8.6   1b. "Don" (S & orch)
8.7   2a. "Improvisation I" (S & perc ens)
8.8   2b. "Improvisation I" (S & orch)
8.9   3. "Improvisation II" (S & small ens)
8.10   4a. "Improvisation III" (S & orch)
8.11   4b. "Improvisation III" (S & orch, r1983–4)
8.12   4c. "Improvisation III" (c1984–5; S & orch, definitive vers)
8.13   5. "Tombeau" (c1959–62; large orch)

* * * * *

J = D. Jameux: "Pierre Boulez." Transl Susan Bradshaw. Harvard University Press, 1991.

1. SYMPHONIES

1.1	*Symphony in D minor (c1954–5, unfin, lost; used in: Pf Conc No.1, Op.15 & German Requiem, Op.45)*	*..Anh.IIa/2*
1.2	Symphony No.1 in C minor (c1862–76, r1877) (Hans von Bülow called it 'Beethoven's Tenth')	Op.68
1.3	Symphony No.2 in D major (c1877)	Op.73
1.4	Symphony No.3 in F major (c1883; arr for 2pf)	Op.90
1.5	Symphony No.4 in E minor (c1884–5)	Op.98

2. OTHER ORCHESTRAL WORKS

2.1   Serenade No.1 in D major (c1859–60, from: Nonet of 1858) Op.11
2.2   Serenade No.2 in A major (c1860, r1875; orch w/out violins) Op.16
2.3   "Variations on a Theme of Haydn," in B-flat major, "St Anthony Variations" / "Haydn Variations"
      (c1873; orig for 2pf, Op.56b): Op.56a
      quoted: . 2nd movt of Haydn's Feldpartita, HobII/46 (based on the old Austrian pilgrim's song:
          Chorale St Anthony)
2.4   "Academic Festival Overture," in C minor (c1879): Op.80
      quoted: . "Wir hatten gebauet," student song
           . "Der Landesvater," student song
           . "Was kommt dort von der Hoh'," student song
           . "Gaudeamus igitur," student hymn
2.5   "Tragic Overture," in D minor (c1880, r1881, sketches from late 1860s) Op.81
2.6   *"Overture," in F major (c ?1880, ?inc, lost)* *Anh.IIa/3*
2.7   21 "Hungarian Dances" (p1874; orig for pf duet): No.1 in G minor (orchd Brahms 1873) .... (WoO 1)
2.8   *No.2 in D minor (orchd Hallén)*
2.9   No.3 in F major (orchd Brahms 1873)
2.10   *No.4 in F-sharp minor (orchd Juon)*
2.11   *No.5 in G minor (orchd Parlow)*
2.12   *No.6 in D major (orchd Parlow)*
2.13   *No.7 in F major (orchd Schmeling)*
2.14   *No.8 in A minor (orchd Schollum)*
2.15   *No.9 in E minor (orchd Schollum)*
2.16   No.10 in F major (orchd Brahms 1873)
2.17   *No.11 in D minor (orchd Parlow)*
2.18   *No.12 in D minor (orchd Parlow)*
2.19   *No.13 in D major (orchd Parlow)*
2.20   *No.14 in D minor (orchd Parlow)*
2.21   *No.15 in B-flat major (orchd Parlow)*
2.22   *No.16 in F minor (orchd Parlow)*
2.23   *No.17 in F-sharp minor (orchd Dvořák)*
2.24   *No.18 in D major (orchd Dvořák)*
2.25   *No.19 in B minor (orchd Dvořák)*
2.26   *No.20 in E minor (orchd Dvořák)*
2.27   *No.21 in E minor (orchd Dvořák)*

3. CONCERTOS, SOLO INSTR & ORCH

Pf & orch:

3.1   Piano Concerto No.1 in D minor (c1856–9) (associated by Brahms w/ Schumann's misfortunes,
      2nd movt—portrait of Clara) Op.15
3.2   Piano Concerto No.2 in B-flat major (c1881) Op.83

Vn & orch:

3.3   Violin Concerto in D major (c1878) Op.77
3.4   *"Adagio & Scherzo" (c1878, intended for Op.77, lost)* *Anh.IIa/1*

Other:

3.5   Double Concerto in A minor (c1887; vn, vc & orch) Op.102

4. STRING QUARTETS

4.1   *String Quartet in B-flat major (ca1852–3, lost)* *Anh.IIa/5*
4.2   String Quartet No.1 in C minor (ca1868–73) Op.51/1
4.3   String Quartet No.2 in A minor (ca1868–73) Op.51/2
4.4   String Quartet No.3 in B-flat major (c1876) Op.67

5. OTHER CHAMBER MUSIC

9 insts:

5.1   *Nonet in D major (c1858, early vers of Serenade No.1, Op.11, lost)* ....

String Sextets:

5.2   String Sextet No.1 in B-flat major (c1859–60; arr Kirchner for pf trio 1883) Op.18
5.3   String Sextet No.2 in G major (c1864–5, farewell to his love to Agathe von Siebold; arr Kirchner
    for pf trio 1883) Op.36

5 insts:

5.4   *String Quintet in F minor (c1862, lost; used in: Sonata in F minor for 2pf, Op.34b)* ....
5.5   Piano Quintet in F minor (c1864; arr from: Sonata in F minor for 2pf, Op.34b)............................... Op.34a
5.6   String Quintet No.1 in F major, "Spring" (c1882–3, from: Sarabande, WoO 5/2 & Gavotte, WoO 3/2) Op.88
5.7   String Quintet No.2 in G major (c1890) Op.111
5.8   Clarinet Quintet in B minor (c1891; cl/va & str qt) Op.115

Piano Quartets:

5.9   *"Adagio" (Andante), in C-sharp minor (c1856; pf qt, lost; reused in: Pf Qt No.3 in C minor, Op.60)*........Anh.IIa/4
5.10   Piano Quartet No.1 in G minor (c1859, r until 1861; orchd Schoenberg 1937) Op.25
5.11   Piano Quartet No.2 in A major (c1861–2) Op.26
5.12   Piano Quartet No.3 in C minor, "Werther" (c1875, radical r of: Adagio in C-sharp minor, Anh.IIa/4) ... Op.60

3 insts:

5.13   *"Phantasie," in D minor (ca1851; vn, vc & pf, lost)* Anh.IIa/6
5.14   Trio (Hymne in Veneration of the Great Joachim) (c1853; 2vn & d bass/vc) Anh.III/1
5.15   Piano Trio No.1 in B major (c1854, r1889) Op.8
5.16   Horn Trio in E-flat major (c1865; vn & hn/vc/va & pf) Op.40
5.17   *Piano Trio in E-flat major (c1880, 1 movt only, lost)* Anh.IIa/7
5.18   Piano Trio No.2 in C major (c1882) Op.87
5.19   Piano Trio No.3 in C minor (c1886) Op.101
5.20   *Piano Trio No.4 in A major (ca1856 or earlier, p1938, ?spur)*...Anh.IV/5
5.21   Clarinet Trio in A minor (c1891; cl/va, vc & pf) Op.114

Vn & pf:

5.22   *Violin Sonata in A minor (ca1852–3, lost)*..Anh.IIa/8
5.23   "Scherzo," for collab: "F-A-E" Vn Sonata (c1853): .... WoO posth 2
    "F-A-E" Violin Sonata ('F-A-E': initials of Joachim's personal motto: Frei aber einsam—Free but lonely;
    Brahms's own motto: 'F-A-F': Frei aber froh—Free but glad):
        1. (Untitled) in A minor (c by Dietrich)
        2. "Intermezzo," in F major (c by Schumann)
        3. "Scherzo," in C minor (c by Brahms)
        4. "Finale" (c by Schumann)
5.24   Violin Sonata No.1 in G major (c1878–9; arr Klengel for vc & pf p1897) Op.78
5.25   Violin Sonata No.2 in A major, "Meistersinger" (c1886) Op.100
5.26   Violin Sonata No.3 in D minor (c1886–8) Op.108

Vc & pf:

5.27   *"Duo" (ca1851, lost)* Anh.IIa/10
5.28   *"Adagio" (ca1862; orig slow movt of Op.38, lost)*...Anh.IIa/9
5.29   Cello Sonata No.1 in E minor (c1862–5) Op.38
5.30   Cello Sonata No.2 in F major (c1886) Op.99

Other:

5.31   *"12 Trumpet Etudes" (ca late 1840 or early 1850s, p1928, ?spur)* Anh.IV/1
5.32   "2 Clarinet Sonatas" (c1894; cl/va & pf; also r vers for vn & pf 1895): No.1 in F minor Op.120
5.33   No.2 in E-flat major

6. PIANO SONATAS

6.1   *Piano Sonata (? in G minor) (c1844, lost)* Anh.IIa/15
6.2   Piano Sonata No.1 in C major (c1852–3)... Op.1
6.3   Piano Sonata No.2 in F-sharp minor (c1852) Op.2
6.4   Piano Sonata No.3 in F minor (c1853) Op.5

7. OTHER PIANO WORKS

7.1	*"Phantasie über eine geliebten Waltzer" (c1849, lost)*	*Anh.IIa/13*
7.2	"Scherzo," in E-flat minor (c1851)	Op.4
7.3	14 "Variations on a Hungarian Song," in D major (c1853)	Op.21/2
7.4	*"Rákóczi-Marsch," arrangement (ca1853, frag)*	*Anh.III/10*
7.5	*"Blätter aus dem Tagebuch," I (c1854, lost): No.1 "Menuett oder?," in A-flat minor*	*Anh.IIa/11*
7.6	*No.2 "Scherzino oder?," in B minor*	
7.7	*No.3 "Piece," in D minor*	
7.8	*No.4 "Andenken an M.B.," in B minor (M.B. = Mendelssohn Bartholdy)*	
7.9	"Variations on a Theme of Schumann," in F-sharp minor (c1854; incl in lost: Blätter, Vol.II)	Op.9
7.10	"4 Ballades" (c1854): No.1 in D minor, "Edward" (after Herder's Scottish ballade: Edward)	Op.10
7.11	No.2 in D major	
7.12	No.3 in B minor (Intermezzo)	
7.13	No.4 in B major	
7.14	"2 Gavottes": No.1 in A minor (c1854)	WoO posth 3
7.15	No.2 in A major (c1855, part lost; compl Pascall)	
7.16	"2 Gigues" (c1855): No.1 in A minor	WoO posth 4
7.17	No.2 in B minor	
7.18	"2 Sarabandes" (c1854–5): No.1 in A major	WoO posth 5
7.19	No.2 in B minor	
7.20	*"Prelude & Aria," in A minor (c1855, lost; orig part of: Suite in A minor)*	*Anh.IIa/14*
7.21	"Kreis-Kanon" (c1856)	Anh.III/3
7.22	11 "Variations on an Original Theme," in D major (c1856–7)	Op.21/1
7.23	*"Hungarian Dances" (played by Clara Schumann in 1858, lost)*	*Anh.IIa/16*
7.24	Piano piece in B-flat major (c1859–62, p1979)	Anh.III/4
7.25	"Theme & Variations," in D minor (c1860, p1927, arr of slow movt of: Str Sextet No.1 in B-flat, Op.18)	
7.26	25 "Variations & Fugue on a Theme of Handel" (Handel Variations), in B-flat major (c1861)	Op.24
7.27	"Paganini Variations" (28 Variations on a Theme by Paganini), in A minor (c1862–3)	Op.35
7.28	*Canon in F minor (c1864, no insts specified; ed Pascall as a piano piece 1979)*	*Anh.III/2*
7.29	"16 Waltzes" (arr1867; see orig for pf duet, Op.39)	(Op.39)
7.30	"Variation on a Theme of Schumann" (Albumblatt for M. Wieck) (c1868, same theme in Op.9)	Anh.III/6
7.31	"8 Pieces" (c1871–8), Vol.I: No.1 "Capriccio," in F-sharp minor	Op.76
7.32	No.2 "Capriccio," in B minor	
7.33	No.3 "Intermezzo," in A-flat major	
7.34	No.4 "Intermezzo," in B-flat major	
7.35	II: No.5 "Capriccio," in C-sharp minor	
7.36	No.6 "Intermezzo," in A major	
7.37	No.7 "Intermezzo," in A minor	
7.38	No.8 "Capriccio," in C major	
7.39	"2 Rhapsodies" (c1879): No.1 in B minor	Op.79
7.40	No.2 in G minor	
7.41	"7 Fantasias" (c1891–2 or earlier), Vol.I: No.1 "Capriccio," in D minor	Op.116
7.42	No.2 "Intermezzo," in A minor	
7.43	No.3 "Capriccio," in G minor	
7.44	II: No.4 "Intermezzo," in E major	
7.45	No.5 "Intermezzo," in E minor	
7.46	No.6 "Intermezzo," in E major	
7.47	No.7 "Capriccio," in D minor	
7.48	"3 Intermezzi" (ca1892 or earlier): No.1 in E-flat major	Op.117
7.49	No.2 in B-flat minor	
7.50	No.3 in C-sharp minor	
7.51	"6 Pieces" (c1892–3 or earlier): No.1 "Intermezzo," in A minor	Op.118
7.52	No.2 "Intermezzo," in A major	
7.53	No.3 "Ballade," in G minor	
7.54	No.4 "Intermezzo," in F minor	
7.55	No.5 "Romance," in F major	
7.56	No.6 "Intermezzo," in E-flat minor	
7.57	*Piano piece in C minor (c1892, ?intended for Opp.118 & 119, lost)*	*Anh.IIa/12*
7.58	"4 Pieces" (ca1893 or earlier): No.1 "Intermezzo," in B minor	Op.119
7.59	No.2 "Intermezzo," in E minor	
7.60	No.3 "Intermezzo," in C major	
7.61	No.4 "Rhapsody," in E-flat major	

Studies & exercises:

7.62	*"Study" (c early; left hand, after Schubert: Impromptu in E-flat, D899; p1927, ?spur)*	*Anh.IV/2*
7.63	"5 Studies": No.1 "Etude," after Chopin: Etude in F minor, Op.25 (p1869)	Anh.Ia/1
7.64	No.2 "Rondo," after Weber: Finale of Sonata in C major, Op.24 (c1852, p1869)	
7.65	No.3 "Presto" I, after Bach: Violin Sonata in G major (p1879)	
7.66	No.4 "Presto" II, after Bach: Violin Sonata in G major (p1879, 2nd vers of No.3)	
7.67	No.5 "Chaconne," after Bach: Violin Partita in D minor (c1877, p1879; left hand alone)	
7.68	"Gavotte," in A major, from Glück: Iphigenie en Aulide (p1871, for: Paride ed Elena)	Anh.Ia/2
7.69	51 "Exercises" (p1893, ?accumulated over many years, many others not accounted for)	WoO 6

Cadenzas:

7.70	Cadenzas (p1927) for: . Bach: Clavier Concerto No.1 in D minor, BWV1052 .... WoO posth 11
7.71	. Beethoven: Pf Concerto No.4 in G major, Op.58 (2 cadenzas) (p1907) .... WoO posth 12
7.72	. Mozart: Pf Concerto No.17 in G major, K453 (2 cadenzas).................................... WoO posth 13
7.73	. Mozart: Pf Concerto No.20 in D minor, K466 (after Clara Schumann) .... WoO posth 14
7.74	. Mozart: Pf Concerto No.24 in C minor, K491 .... WoO posth 15
7.75	*Cadenzas for Mozart: Pf Conc No.20 in D minor, K466 (perf Badura-Skoda 1980, ?spur) Anh.IV/4*
7.76	*Cadenzas for Beethoven: Pf Concerto No.3 in C minor, Op.37 (spur: c by Moscheles)............................ Anh.IV/7*

Pf duet:

7.77	*"Souvenir de la Russie" (ca1850, ?spur): No.1 "Hymne national russe de Lvoff" Anh.IV/6*
7.78	*No.2 "Chansonette de Titoff"*
7.79	*No.3 "Romance de Warlamoff"*
7.80	*No.4 " 'Le rossignol' de A. Alabieff"*
7.81	*No.5 "Chant bohémien"*
7.82	*No.6 " 'Koca'—chant bohémien"*
7.83	10 "Variations on a Theme of Schumann," in E-flat major (c1861; arr Kirchner for pf 1878) Op.23
7.84	"16 Waltzes" (c1865; arr for pf 1867): No.1 in B major (arr for 2pf) Op.39
7.85	No.2 in E major (arr for 2pf)
7.86	No.3 in G-sharp minor
7.87	No.4 in E minor
7.88	No.5 in E major
7.89	No.6 in C-sharp major
7.90	No.7 in C-sharp minor
7.91	No.8 in B-flat major
7.92	No.9 in D minor
7.93	No.10 in G major
7.94	No.11 in B minor (arr for 2pf)
7.95	No.12 in E major
7.96	No.13 in B major
7.97	No.14 in G-sharp minor (arr for 2pf)
7.98	No.15 in A-flat major (arr for 2pf)
7.99	No.16 in C-sharp minor
7.100	18 "Liebeslieder Waltzes" (p1874, w/ out vocal): No.1 in E major Op.52a
7.101	No.2 in A minor
7.102	No.3 in B-flat major
7.103	No.4 in F major
7.104	No.5 in A minor
7.105	No.6 in A maj / F major
7.106	No.7 in C minor
7.107	No.8 in A-flat major
7.108	No.9 in E major
7.109	No.10 in G major
7.110	No.11 in C minor
7.111	No.12 in C minor
7.112	No.13 in A-flat major
7.113	No.14 in E-flat major
7.114	No.15 in A-flat major
7.115	No.16 in F minor
7.116	No.17 in D-flat major
7.117	No.18 in B-flat min / E maj / C-sharp min / C-sharp major
7.118	15 "Neue Liebeslieder Waltzes" (p1875, arr from vocal vers): No.1 in A minor Op.65a
7.119	No.2 in A min / A major
7.120	No.3 in A major
7.121	No.4 in D minor
7.122	No.5 in D minor
7.123	No.6 in F major
7.124	No.7 in C major
7.125	No.8 in E-flat major
7.126	No.9 in G minor
7.127	No.10 in G major
7.128	No.11 in G major
7.129	No.12 in G min / major
7.130	No.13 in E major
7.131	No.14 in A min / major
7.132	No.15 in F major
7.133	21 "Hungarian Dances" (p1880; see arr for orch; arr for pf), Vol.I (c1858–68): No.1 in G minor .... WoO 1
7.134	No.2 in D minor
7.135	No.3 in F major
7.136	No.4 in F-sharp minor
7.137	No.5 in G minor
7.138	II (c1858–68): No.6 in D major
7.139	No.7 in A major

7.140   No.8 in A minor
7.141   No.9 in E minor
7.142   No.10 in F major
7.143   III (c1879): No.11 in D minor
7.144   No.12 in D minor
7.145   No.13 in D major
7.146   No.14 in D minor
7.147   No.15 in D minor
7.148   IV (c1879): No.16 in F minor
7.149   No.17 in F-sharp minor
7.150   No.18 in D major
7.151   No.19 in B minor
7.152   No.20 in E minor
7.153   No.21 in E minor

2 Pf:

7.154   Sonata in D minor (c1854, unfin, lost; used in: Symphony in D minor, Anh.IIa/2) ....
7.155   Sonata in F minor (c1863–4, arr Brahms from lost: String Quintet of1862) Op.34b
7.156   "Variations on a Theme of Haydn," in B-flat major, "St. Anthony Variations" / "Haydn Variations"
               (c1873; orchd as Op.56a) Op.56b

8. ORGAN

8.1   "Choral prelude & fugue on 'O Traurigkeit, O Herzeleid,' " in A minor (c1856) .... WoO 7
8.2   "Fugue," in A-flat minor (c1856) .... WoO 8
8.3   "Prelude & fugue" (No.1), in A minor (c1856) .... WoO posth 9
8.4   "Prelude & fugue" (No.2), in G minor (c1857) .... WoO posth 10
8.5   "11 Choral preludes" (c1896 & earlier): No.1 "Mein Jesu, der du mich".................................. Op.posth 122
8.6   No.2 "Herzliebster Jesu"
8.7   No.3 "O Welt, ich muss dich lassen" I
8.8   No.4 "Herzlich tut mich erfreuen"
8.9   No.5 "Schmücke dich, o liebe Seele"
8.10   No.6 "O wie selig seid ihr doch, ihr Frommen"
8.11   No.7 "O Gott, du frommer Gott"
8.12   No.8 "Es ist ein Ros entsprungen"
8.13   No.9 "Herzlich tut mich verlangen" I
8.14   No.10 "Herzlich tut mich verlangen" II
8.15   No.11 "O Welt, ich muss dich lassen" II

9. CHORAL WORKS

W/ acc:

9.1   "Kyrie," in G major (c1856; ch & cont) .... WoO posth 17
9.2   "Ave Maria," in F major (c1858, Liturgy; fem ch & orch/org; arr for pf) Op.12
9.3   "Brautgesang": "Das Haus benedei ich" (c1858, Uhland; S, fem ch & orch, frag) *Anh.III/12*
9.4   "Begräbnisgesang" (Funeral Hymn): "Nun lasst uns den Leib" (c1859, Weisse; ch, winds & timp;
               arr for pf) Op.13
9.5   "4 Choruses" (c1859–60; fem ch, 2hn & harp): 1. "Es tönt ein voller Harfenklang" (Rupert) Op.17
9.6   2. "Lied von Shakespeare": "Komm herbei, komm herbei, Tod!" (from Twelfth Night, transl
               Schlegel) (also see Castelnuovo-Tedesco Op.24/I/1, Holst Op.9a/4, H48/4 & Vaughan
               Williams' partsong of 1899)
9.7   3. "Der Gärtner": "Wohin ich geh und schaue" (Eichendorff)
9.8   4. "Gesang aus Fingal": "Wein' an den Felsen der brausenden Winde" (from Ossian's Fingal)
9.9   "Psalm 13": "Herr, wie lange willst du mich" (c1859, Bible; fem ch, org/pf & strings ad lib) Op.27
9.10   "Geistliches Lied": "Lass dich nur nichts nicht dauren" (c1856, Flemming; ch & org/pf) Op.30
9.11   "Ein deutsches Requiem" (German Requiem) (c1863–67, Bible transl Luther; S, Bar, ch & orch): Op.45
               1. "Selig sind die da Leid tragen," chorus
               2. "Denn alles Fleisch es ist wie Gras," chorus
               3. "Herr, lehre doch mich" (Bar & ch)
               . "Der gerechten Seelen sind in Gottes Hand," fugue (T)
               4. "Wie lieblich sind deine Wohnungen," chorus
               5. "Ihr habt nun Traurigkeit" (c1869; S & ch)
               6. "Denn wir haben hier keine bleibende statt," chorus
               . "Herr, du bist würdig," fugue (A)
               7. "Selig sind die Toten," concluding chorus
9.12   "Rinaldo," cantata (c1863, Goethe; T, m ch & orch): Op.50
               1. "Zu dem Strande!" (Introduction & ch)
               2a. "Stelle her der gold'nen Tage" (T)
               2b. "Nein, nicht länger ist zu säumen," chorus
               3. "Zurück nur, zurücke!," chorus
               4a. "Zum zweitenmale" (T)

4b. "Schon sind sie erhöret," chorus
5. "Auf dem Meere": "Segel schwellen!," final chorus (c1868; see lost orig vers Anh.IIa/18)
9.13   *"Rinaldo: Final Chorus" (c1863, for cantata Op.50, orig vers lost)* *Anh.IIa/18*
9.14   "Liebeslieder," suite (arr1869–70; ch/4vv & orch, from Op.52/1–2, 4–6, 8–9, 11): 1. "Rede Mädchen," in E major ....
        2. "Am Gesteine rauscht die Fluth," in A minor
        4. "Wie des Abends schöne Röthe," duet in F major (S, A)
        5. "Die Grüne Hopfenranke," in A minor
        6. "Ein kleiner hübscher Vogel nahm," in A maj / F major
        8. "Wenn so lind dein Auge mir," in A-flat major
        9. "Am Donaustrande," in E major
        11. "Nein, es ist nicht auszukommen," in C minor
9.15   "Alto Rhapsody" (c1869, Goethe; A, m ch & orch): Op.53
        1. "Aber abseits, wer ist's?," in C minor
        2. "Ach, wer heilet die Schmerzen," in C minor
        3. "Ist auf deinem Psalter," in C major
9.16   "Hyperions Schicksalslied" (Song of Destiny) (c1868–71, Hölderlin; ch & orch): Op.54
        1. "Ihr wandelt droben im Licht"
        2. "Doch uns ist gegeben"
        3. "Postlude" (orch)
9.17   *"Psalm 22" (c1870; Bar, ch & orch, lost)* *Anh.IIa/17*
9.18   "Triumphlied" (Song of Triumph) (c1870–1, Book of Revelations; Bar, d ch, orch & org ad lib): Op.55
        1. "Hallelujah! Heil und Preis"
        2. "Lobet unsern Gott"
        3. "Und ich sahe den Himmel aufgethan"
       . "Ein König aller Könige," final chorus
9.19   "Nänie": "Auch das Schöne muss sterben" (c1880–1, Schiller; ch, orch & harp ad lib) Op.82
9.20   "Gesang der Parzen" (Song of the Fates): "Es fürchte die Götter" (c1882, Goethe; ch & orch, in Act IV of: Iphigenie) Op.89
9.21   "Tafellied. Dank der Damen": "Gleich wie Echo" (c1884, Eichendorff; d ch & pf) Op.93b

    W/ out acc:

9.22   *"3 Songs" (c1847; m ch, lost): 1. "Abschied von Winsen an der Luhe" (?Brahms)* *Anh.IIa/23*
9.23   *2. "Postillions Morgenlied" (Fallersleben)*
9.24   *3. "ABC"*
9.25   "Missa Canonica," in C major (c1856–61, inc): .... WoO posth 18
        1. "Sanctus," in A-flat major
        2. "Benedictus," in F major
        3a. "Agnus Dei," in F minor
        3b. "Dona nobis pacem," in C major
9.26   *"Credo" (c1856–61, for: Missa Canonica in C major, WoO posth 18, lost)* *Anh.IIa/20*
9.27   "Marienlieder" (c1859, trad German): 1. "Der englische Gruss": "Gegrüsset" Op.22
9.28   2. "Marias Kirchgang": "Maria wollt zur Kirche gehn"
9.29   3. "Marias Wallfahrt": "Maria ging aus wandern"
9.30   4. "Der Jäger": "Es wollt gut Jäger jagen"
9.31   5. "Ruf zur Maria": "Dich, Mutter Gottes, ruf' wir an"
9.32   6. "Magdalena": "An dem österlichen Tag"
9.33   7. "Marias Lob": "Maria, wahre Himmelsfreud"
9.34   "2 Motets" (ca1859–60): 1. "Chorale & fugue": "Es ist das Heil uns kommen her" (Speratus) Op.29
9.35   2. "Schafe in mir, Gott, ein rein Herz" (Psalm 51)
9.36   *"Motette" (c1860, lost)* *Anh.IIa/22*
9.37   "3 Sacred Choruses," motets (p1865, Liturgy; fem ch): 1. "O bone Jesu" (c1859) Op.37
9.38   2. "Adoramus te, Christe" (c1859)
9.39   3. "Regina coeli laetare" (c by 1863)
9.40   "Dein Herzlein mild" (c1860, Heyse; fem ch, no relation to Op.62/4 w/ same text) .... WoO posth 19
9.41   "5 Lieder" (c1860–2; m ch, lost): 1. "Ich schwing mein Horn ins Jammerthal" (Old German) Op.41
9.42   2. "Freiwillige her!" (Lemcke)
9.43   3. "Geleit": "Was freut einen alten Soldaten?" (Lemcke)
9.44   4. "Marschieren": "Jetzt hab ich schon zwei Jahre lang" (Lemcke)
9.45   5. "Gebt Acht! Es harrt der Feind" (Lemcke)
9.46   "3 Songs" (c1859–60): 1. "Abendständchen": "Hör, es klagt die Flöte wieder" (Brentano) Op.42
9.47   2. "Vineta": "Aus des Meeres tiefem Grunde" (Müller)
9.48   3. "Darthulas Grabesgesang": "Mädchen von Kola, du schläfst!" (Ossian transl Herder)
9.49   "12 Lieder & Romances" (c1859–66; fem ch & pf ad lib): 1. "Minnelied": "Der Holdseligen" (Voss) Op.44
9.50   2. "Der Bräutigam": "Von allen Bergen nieder" (Eichendorff)
9.51   3. "Barcarole": "O Fischer auf den Fluten" (trad Italian)
9.52   4. "Fragen": "Wozu ist mein langes Haar mir dann?" (trad Slavic)
9.53   5. "Die Müllerin": "Die Mühle, die dreht ihre Flügel" II (Chamisso; also see song Anh.III/13)
9.54   6. "Die Nonne": "Im stillen Klostergarten" (Uhland)
9.55   7. "Nun stehn die Rosen in Blüte" (from Heyse's Jungbrunnen)
9.56   8. "Die Berge sind spitz" (from Heyse's Jungbrunnen)
9.57   9. "Am Wildbach die Weiden" (from Heyse's Jungbrunnen)
9.58   10. "Und gehst du über den Kirchhof" (from Heyse's Jungbrunnen)
9.59   11. "Die Braut": "Eine blaue Schürze hast du mir" (Müller)

9.60	12. "Märznacht": "Horch! wie brauset der Sturm" (Uhland)
9.61	"Dar geit en Bek" (ca1860, Plattdeutsch text by Groth; fem ch, vers of: Am Wildbach, Op.44/9) ... (Op.44/9)
9.62	"7 Lieder" (ca1860–3): 1. "Rosmarin": "Es wollt die Jungfrau" (from Des Knaben Wunderhorn) Op.62
9.63	2. "Von alten Liebesliedern": "Spazieren wollt ich reiten" (from Des Knaben Wunderhorn)
9.64	3. "Waldesnacht": "Waldesnacht, du wunderkühle" (from Heyse's Jungbrunnen)
9.65	4. "Dein Herzlein mild": "Dein Herzlein mild, du liebes Bild" (from Heyse's Jungbrunnen)
9.66	5. "All meine Herzgedanken" (from Heyse's Jungbrunnen)
9.67	6. "Es geht ein Wehen durch den Wald" (from Heyse's Jungbrunnen)
9.68	7. "Vergangen ist mir Glück und Heil" (Old German)
9.69	*"Morgenständchen" (c1865, for birthday of Pauline Viardot-Garcia, lost) Anh.IIa/21*
9.70	"2 Motets": 1."Warum ist das Licht gegeben dem Mühseligen?" (c1877, Bible transl Luther).............. Op.74
9.71	2. "O Heiland, reiss die Himmel auf" (ca1863–70, anon)
9.72	"Dem dunkeln Schoss der heil'gen Erde" (c before 1864, Schiller) .... WoO posth 20
9.73	"6 Lieder & Romances" (c1883–4): 1. "Der bucklichte Fiedler": "Es wohnet" (trad) Op.93a
9.74	2. "Das Mädchen": "Stand das Mädchen" (Kapper from Serbian, = Op.95/1)
9.75	3. "O süsser Mai": "O süsser Mai, der Strom ist frei" (Arnim)
9.76	4. "Fahr wohl!": "Fahr wohl, o Vöglein, das nun wandern soll" (Rückert)
9.77	5. "Der Falke": "Hebt ein Falke sich empor" (Kapper from Serbian)
9.78	6. "Beherzigung": "Feiger Gedanken, bängliches Schwanken" (Goethe, Brahms's title)
9.79	"5 Songs" (c1886–8; vocal sextet): 1. "Nachtwache" I: "Leise Töne der Brust" (Rückert).................. Op.104
9.80	2. "Nachtwache" II: "Ruhn sie? rufet das Horn des Wächters" (Rückert)
9.81	3. "Letztes Glück": "Leblos gleitet Blatt um Blatt" (Kalbeck)
9.82	4. "Verlorene Jugend": "Brausten alle Berge" (Wenzig from Bohemian)
9.83	5. "Im Herbst": "Ernst ist der Herbst" (Groth)
9.84	3 "Fest- und Gedenksprüche" (c1886–8, Bible; d ch): 1. "Unsere Väter hofften auf dich" Op.109
9.85	2. "Wenn ein starker Gewappneter"
9.86	3. "Wo ist ein so herrlich Volk"
9.87	"3 Motets" (c1889): 1. "Ich aber bin elend" (Luther) Op.110
9.88	2. "Ach, arme Welt, du trügest mich" (anon)
9.89	3. "Wenn wir im höchsten Nöthen sein" (Eber)

Folksong arrs (ch & pf ad lib):

9.90	"14 Volkslieder," I: 1. "Von edler Art, auch rein und zart" (arr by 1863–4)........................ WoO 34
9.91	2. "Mit Lust tät ich ausreiten" (arr1857)
9.92	3. "Bei nächtlicher Weil" (arr1857)
9.93	4. "Vom heiligen Märtyrer Emmerano": "Komm Mainz, komm Bayrn" (arr by 1863–4)
9.94	5. "Täublein weiss": "Es flog ein Täublein" (arr by 1863–4)
9.95	6. "Ach lieber Herre Jesu Christ" (arr by 1863–4)
9.96	7. "Sankt Raphael": "Tröst die Bedrängten" (arr by 1863–4)
9.97	II: 8. "In Stiller Nacht, zur ersten Wacht" (arr1857)
9.98	9. "Abschiedslied": "Ich fahr dahin, wenn es muss sein" (arr1857)
9.99	10. "Der tote Knabe": "Es pocht ein Knabe sachte" (arr1857)
9.100	11. "Die Wollust in den Maien" (arr1857)
9.101	12. "Morgengesang": "Wach auf, mein Kind" (arr by 1863–4)
9.102	13. "Schnitter Tod": "Es ist ein Schnitter" (arr1857)
9.103	14. "Der englische Jäger": "Es wollt gut Jäger jagen" (arr by 1863–4)
9.104	"12 Volkslieder": 1. "Scheiden": "Ach Gott, wie weh tut Scheiden" (arr1857) .... WoO posth 35
9.105	2. "Wach auf!" I: "Wach auf, meins Herzens Schöne" (arr1857)
9.106	3. "Erlaube mir, feins Mädchen" (arr1857)
9.107	4. "Der Fiedler": "Es wohnet ein Fiedler zu Frankfurt" (arr1857)
9.108	5. "Da unten im Tale" (arr1857)
9.109	6. "Des Abends kann ich nicht schlafen gehn" (arr1857)
9.110	7. "Wach auf!" II: "Wach auf, meins Herzens Schöne" (arr ca1873)
9.111	8. "Dort in den Weiden": "Dort in den Weiden steht ein Haus" (arr ca1873)
9.112	9. "Altes Volkslied": "Verstohlen geht der Mond auf" (p1926)
9.113	10. "Der Ritter und die Feine": "Es stunden drei Rosen auf einem Zweig" (p1926)
9.114	11. "Der Zimmergesell": "Es war einmal ein Zimmergesell" (p1926)
9.115	12. "Altdeutsches Kampflied": "Wir stehen hier" (p1926)
9.116	"8 Volkslieder" (c1859–62; fem ch): 1. "Totenklage": "In stiller Nacht" .... WoO posth 36
9.117	2. "Minnelied": "So will ich frisch und fröhlich sein"
9.118	3. "Der tote Knabe": "Es pocht ein Knabe sachte"
9.119	4. "Ich hab die Nacht geträumet"
9.120	5. "Altdeutches Minnelied": "Mein Herzlein thut mir gar zu weh!"
9.121	6. "Es waren zwei Königskinder"
9.122	7. "Spannung": "Guten Abend"
9.123	8. "Drei Vögelein": "Mit Lust tät ich ausreiten durch einen grünen Wald"
9.124	"16 Volkslieder" (ca1859–62; fem ch): 1. "Schwesterlein, wann gehn wir" .... WoO posth 37
9.125	2. "Ich hörte ein Sichlein rauschen"
9.126	3. "Der Ritter und die Feine": "Es stunden drei Rosen"
9.127	4. "Ich stand auf hohem Berge"
9.128	5. "Gunhilde": "Gunhilde lebt gar still und fromm"
9.129	6. "Der buckligte Fiedler": "Es wohnet ein Fiedler zu Frankfurt am Main"
9.130	7. "Die Versuchung": "Feinsliebchen, du sollst mir nicht barfuss geh'n"
9.131	8. "Altes Minnelied": "Ich fahr dahin, wenn es muss sein"

9.132	9. "Die Wollust in den Maien"
9.133	10. "Trennung": "Da unten im Tale läufts Wasser"
9.134	11. "Der Jäger": "Bei nächtlicher Weil, an eins Waldes Born"
9.135	12. "Scheiden": "Ach Gott, wie weh tut Scheiden"
9.136	13. "Zu Strassburg auf der Schanz"
9.137	14. "Wach auf, mein Hort"
9.138	15. "Der Ritter": "Es ritt ein Ritter wohl durch das Ried"
9.139	16. "Ständchen": "Wach auf, meins Herzens Schöne"
9.140	"20 Volkslieder" (ca1859–62; fem ch): 1. "Die Entführung": "Auf! Schätzelein" .... WoO posth 38
9.141	2. "Gang zur Liebsten": "Des Abends kann ich nicht schlafen geh'n"
9.142	3. "Schifferlied": "Dort in den Weiden steht ein Haus"
9.143	4. "Erlaube mir, feins Mädchen"
9.144	5. "Schnitter Tod": "Es ist ein Schnitter, der heisst Tod"
9.145	6. "Die Bernauerin": "Es reiten drei Reiter"
9.146	7. "Das Lied vom eifersüchtigen Knaben": "Es stehen drei Sterne am Himmel"
9.147	8. "Der Baum im Odenwald": "Es steht ein Baum im Odenwald"
9.148	9. "Des Markgrafen Töchterlein": "Es war ein Markgraf über'n Rhein"
9.149	10. "Die stolze Jüdin": "Es war eine stolze Jüdin"
9.150	11. "Der Zimmergesell": "Es war einmal ein Zimmergesell"
9.151	12. "Liebeslied": "Gar lieblich hat sich gesellet"
9.152	15. "Ich schwing' mein Horn"
9.153	13a. "Heimliche Liebe" I: "Kein Feuer, keine Kohle"
9.154	13b. "Heimliche Liebe" II: "Kein Feuer, keine Kohle"
9.155	14. "Altes Liebeslied": "Mein Herzlein tut mir gar zu weh!"
9.156	15. "Dauernde Liebe": "Mein Schatz, ich hab es erfahren"
9.157	16. "Während der Trennung": "Mein Schatz ist auf die Wanderschaft hin"
9.158	17. "Morgen muss ich fort von hier"
9.159	18. "Scheiden": "Sind wir geschieden, und ich muss leben"
9.160	19. "Vor dem Fenster": "Soll sich der Mond nicht heller scheinen"
9.161	20. "Ständchen": "Verstohlen geht der Mond auf"
9.162	Add arrs (ca1859–60; fem ch, part lost; tunes p1968): . "Ade von hinnem" ....
9.163	. "Mein feins Lieb"
9.164	. "Die wundergefündene Tochter"
9.165	. "Gottesgericht"
9.166	. "Liebesklage"
9.167	. "Pfaffenschlich"
9.168	. "Wenn ich ein Vöglein wär" (orig composition)

10. CANONS

10.1	"13 Canons" (p1894; fem vv): 1. "Göttlicher Morpheus" (c1860–3, Goethe; 4vv) Op.113
10.2	2. "Grausam erweiset sich Amor an mir!" (c1860–3, Goethe; 3vv)
10.3	3. "Sitzt a schöns Vögerl auf'm Dannabaum" (c1858, trad; 4vv)
10.4	4. "Schlaf, Kindlein, schlaf!" (c1858, trad; 3vv)
10.5	5. "Wille wille will, Der Mann ist kommen" (c1858, trad; 4vv)
10.6	6. "So lange Schönheit wird bestehn" (Greek transl Fallersleben; 4vv)
10.7	7. "Wenn die Klänge nahn und fliehen" (Eichendorff; 3vv)
10.8	8. "Ein Gems auf dem Stein" (c1860–3, Eichendorff; 4vv)
10.9	9. "Ans Auge des Liebsten" (ca1868, Arabic transl Rückert; 4vv)
10.10	10. "Leise Töne der Brust" (c1860–3, Rückert; 4vv)
10.11	11. "Ich weiss nicht, was im Hain die Taube girret?" (c1860–3, Rückert; 4vv)
10.12	12. "Wenn Kummer hätte zu töten Macht" (c1860–3, Arabic transl Rückert; 3vv)
10.13	13. "Einförmig ist der Liebe Gram" (Rückert; 6vv)
10.14	"Grausam erweiset sich Amor" (c1881 or earlier, text = Op.113/2; 4 fem vv) .... WoO posth 24
10.15	"Mir lächelt kein Frühling," puzzle-canon (c1881 or earlier, anon; 4 fem vv) .... WoO 25
10.16	"O wie sanft!" (c1881 or earlier, text = Op.52/10; 4vv) .... WoO posth 26
10.17	"Spruch": "In dieser Welt des Trugs und Scheins" (ca1857–9, Fallersleben; 1v & va) .... WoO posth 27
10.18	"Töne, lindernder Klang" (c1859, Knebel; 4vv; 2 vers) .... WoO 28
10.19	"Wann?": "Wann hört der Himmel auf" (ca1883, Uhland; S, A) .... WoO posth 29
10.20	"Zu Rauch muss werden" (c?, Rückert; 4vv; 2 vers) .... WoO posth 30
10.21	*"Is denn mei Vater ein Leiersmann" (c?, ?spur)* *Anh.IV/3*

11. VOCAL QUARTETS (w/ pf)

11.1	"3 Quartets": 1. "Wechsellied zum Tanze": "Komm mit, o Schöne" (c1859, Goethe) Op.31
11.2	2. "Neckereien": "Fürwahr, mein Liebchen, ich will nun frein" (c1863, trad Moravian)
11.3	3. "Der Gang zum Liebchen": "Es glänzt der Mond nieder" (c1863, trad Czech)
11.4	"Liebeslieder Waltzes" (c ?1868–9, Daumer's Polidora; w/ pf duet): 1. "Rede, Mädchen," in E major Op.52
11.5	2. "Am Gesteine rauscht die Fluth," in A minor
11.6	3. "O die Frauen, O die Frauen," duet in B-flat major (T, B)
11.7	4. "Wie des Abends schöne Röthe," duet in F major (S, A)
11.8	5. "Die Grüne Hopfenranke," in A minor
11.9	6. "Ein kleiner hübscher Vogel nahm," in A maj / F major

11.10	7. "Wohl schön bewandt," duet in C minor (S, A)
11.11	8. "Wenn so lind dein Auge mir," in A-flat major
11.12	9. "Am Donaustrande," in E major
11.13	10. "O wie Sanft die Quelle sich," in G major (Russo-Polish song transl Daumer)
11.14	11. "Nein, es ist nicht auszukommen," in C minor
11.15	12. "Schlosser auf!," in C minor
11.16	13. "Vöglein durch-rauscht die Luft," duet in A-flat major (S, A)
11.17	14. "Sieh', wie ist die Welle klar," duet in E-flat major (T, B)
11.18	15. "Nachtigall, sie singt so schön," in A-flat major
11.19	16. "Ein dunkler Schacht ist Liebe," in F minor
11.20	17. "Nicht wandle, mein Licht," in D-flat major
11.21	18. "Es bebet das Gesträuche," in B-flat min / E maj / C-sharp min / C-sharp major
11.22	"3 Quartets": 1. "An die Heimat": "Heimat! Heimat!" (c1862–3, Sternau) Op.64
11.23	2. "Der Abend": "Senke, strahlender Gott, die Fluren dürsten" (c1874, Schiller)
11.24	3. "Fragen": "Mein liebes Herz, was ist dir?" (c1874, Daumer)
11.25	"Neue Liebeslieder," 15 waltzes (c1874, from Daumer's Polidora; w/ pf duet): 1. "Verzicht," in A min Op.65
11.26	2. "Finstere Schatten der Nacht," in A min / A major
11.27	3. "An jeder Hand die Finger," in A major (S)
11.28	4. "Ihr schwarzen Augen," in D minor (B)
11.29	5. "Wahre, wahre deinen Sohn," in D minor (A)
11.30	6. "Rosen steckt mir an die Mutter," in F major (S)
11.31	7. "Vom Gebirge Well' auf Well'," in C major
11.32	8. "Weiche Gräser im Revier," in E-flat major
11.33	9. "Nagen am Herzen fühl," in G minor (S)
11.34	10. "Ich kose süss, mit der und der," in G major (T)
11.35	11. "Alles, alles in den Wind," in G major (S)
11.36	12. "Schwarzer Wald, dein Schatten," in G min / major
11.37	13. "Nein, Geliebter, setze dich," duet in E major (S, A)
11.38	14. "Flammenauge, dunkles Haar," in A min / major
11.39	15. "Zum Schluss": "Nun, ihr Musen, genug!," in F major (Goethe)
11.40	"4 Quartets": 1. "O schöne Nacht": "Am Himmel märchenhaft erglänzt" (c1877, Daumer) Op.92
11.41	2. "Spätherbst": "Der graue Nebel tropft so still" (c1884, Allmers)
11.42	3. "Abendlied": "Friedlich bekämpfen" (c1884, Hebbel)
11.43	4. "Warum?": "Warum doch erschallen" (Goethe)
11.44	*"Notturno" (c1877, intended as No.5 of Op.92, rejected, lost) Anh.IIa/19*
11.45	"Zigeunerlieder" (Gypsy Songs) (c1887, Conrat from Hungarian): 1. "He, Zigeuner" Op.103
11.46	2. "Hochgetürmte Rimaflut, wie bist so trüb"
11.47	3. "Wisst ihr, wann mein Kindchen am allerschönsten ist?"
11.48	4. "Lieber Gott, du weisst, wie oft bereut ich hab"
11.49	5. "Brauner Bursche führt zum Tanze"
11.50	6. "Röslein dreie in der Reihe blühn so rot"
11.51	7. "Kommt dir manchmal in den Sinn, mein süsses Lieb"
11.52	8. "Horch, der Wind klagt in den Zweigen"
11.53	9. "Weit und breit schaut niemand mich an"
11.54	10. "Mond verhüllt sein Angesicht"
11.55	11. "Rote Abendwolken ziehn am Firmament"
11.56	"6 Quartets" (c1888–91): 1. "Sehnsucht": "Es rinnen die Wasser Tag und Nacht" (Kugler) Op.112
11.57	2. "Nachtens": "Nächtens wachen auf die irren" (Kugler)
11.58	3. "Himmel strahlt so helle und klar" (Conrat after Hungarian)
11.59	4. "Rote Rosenknospen" (Conrat after Hungarian)
11.60	5. "Brennessel steht an Weges Rand" (Conrat after Hungarian)
11.61	6. "Liebe Schwalbe, kleine Schwalbe" (Conrat after Hungarian)
11.62	"Kleine Hochzeitskantate": "Zwei Geliebte" (c1874, Keller; arr for ch & pf p1927) .... WoO posth 16

12. VOCAL DUETS

12.1	"3 Duets" (c1858–60; S, A & pf): 1. "Weg der Liebe" I: "Über die Berge" (Herder) Op.20
12.2	2. "Weg der Liebe" II: "Den gordischen Knoten, den Liebe sich band" (Herder)
12.3	3. "Die Meere": "Alle Winde schlafen auf dem Spiegel der Fluth" (trad Italian)
12.4	"4 Duets" (c1860–2; A, Bar & pf): 1. "Die Nonne und der Ritter": "Da die Welt" (Eichendorff) Op.28
12.5	2. "Vor der Thür": "Tritt auf, den Riegel von der Thür" (Old German)
12.6	3. "Es rauschet das Wasser" (Goethe)
12.7	4. "Der Jäger und sein Liebchen": "Ist nicht der Himmel so blau?" (Fallersleben)
12.8	"4 Duets" (c1874; S, A & pf): 1. "Die Schwestern": "Wir Schwestern zwei" (Mörike) Op.61
12.9	2. "Klosterfräulein": "Ach, ach, ich armes Klosterfräulein!" (Kerner)
12.10	3. "Phänomen": "Wenn zu der Regenwand Phöbus sich gattet" (Goethe)
12.11	4. "Die Boten der Liebe": "Wie viel schon der Boten" (Wenzig from Bohemian)
12.12	"5 Duets" (p1875; S, A & pf): 1. "Klänge" I: "Aus der Erde quellen Blumen" (Groth) Op.66
12.13	2. "Klänge" II: "Wenn ein müder Leib begraben" (Groth)
12.14	3. "Am Strande": "Es sprechen und blicken die Wellen" (Hölty)
12.15	4. "Jägerlied": "Jäger, was jagst du die Häselein?" (Candidus)
12.16	5. "Hüt du dich!": "Ich weiss ein Mädlein hübsch und fein" (from Des Knaben Wunderhorn)
12.17	"4 Ballades & Romances" (c1877–8): 1. "Edward": "Dein Schwert wie ists" (Herder; A, T & pf) Op.75
12.18	2. "Guter Rat": "Ach Mutter, liebe Mutter!" (from Des Knaben Wunderhorn; S, A & pf)

12.19	3. "So lass uns wandern!": "Ach Mädchen, liebes Mädchen" (from Bohemian)
12.20	4. "Walpurgisnacht": "Lieb Mutter, heut Nacht heulte Regen und Wind" (Alexis; 2S & pf)

13. SONGS (w/ pf)

c1853 or earlier (many other early songs from late 1840s lost):

13.1	"6 Songs": 1. "Liebestreu": "O versenk' versenk' dein Leid, mein Kind," in E-flat minor (Reinick) Op.3
13.2	2. "Liebe und Frühling" I: "Wie sich Rebenranken," in B major (Fallersleben, r1882)
13.3	3. "Liebe und Frühling" II: "Ich muss hinaus, ich muss zu dir," in B major (Fallersleben)
13.4	4. "Lied aus dem Gedicht 'Ivan' ": "Weit über das Feld," in E-flat minor (Bodenstedt)
13.5	5. "In der Fremde": "Aus der Heimath hinter den Blitzen roth," in F-sharp minor (Eichendorff) (also see Schumann Op.39/1)
13.6	6. "Lied": "Lindes Rauschen in den Wipfeln," in A major (Eichendorff)
13.7	"6 Songs": 1. "Spanisches Lied": "In dem Schatten meiner Lokken," in A minor (Heyse) Op.6
13.8	2. "Der Frühling": "Es lockt und säuselt um den Baum," in E major (Rousseau)
13.9	3. "Nachwirkung": "Sie ist gegangen, die Wonnen versanken," in A-flat major (Meissner)
13.10	4. "Juchhe!": "Wie ist doch die Erde so schön, so schön!," in E-flat major (Reinick)
13.11	5. "Wie die Wolke nach der Sonne," in B major (Fallersleben)
13.12	6. "Nachtigallen schwingen lustig ihr Gefieder," in A-flat major (Fallersleben)
13.13	*"Die Müllerin" I (c1853, Chamisso, frag; compl Draheim p1983; also see Op.44/5) Anh.III/13*
13.14	"6 Songs": 1. "Treue Liebe": "Ein Mägdlein sass am Meeresstrand," in F-sharp minor (Ferrand) Op.7
13.15	2. "Parole": "Sie stand wohl am Fensterbogen," in E minor (Eichendorff)
13.16	3. "Anklänge": "Hoch über stillen Höhen," in A minor (Eichendorff)
13.17	4. "Volkslied": "Die Schwälbe ziehet fort," in E minor (trad)
13.18	5. "Die Traurernde": "Mei Mueter mag mi net," in A minor (trad)
13.19	6. "Heimkehr": "O brich nicht, Steg, du zitterst sehr," in B minor (c1851, Uhland)
13.20	"Mondnacht": "Es war, als hätt der Himmel die Erde still geküsst," in A-flat major (p1854, Eichendorff) (also see Schumann Op.39/5) .... WoO 21

c1858:

13.21	"8 Lieder & Romances": 1. "Vor dem Fenster": "Soll sich der Mond," in G minor (trad) Op.14
13.22	2. "Vom verwundeten Knaben": "Es wollt ein Mädchen früh aufstehn," in A minor (trad)
13.23	3. "Murrays Ermordung": "O Hochland und o Südland!," in A minor (Herder from Percy's Reliques)
13.24	4. "Ein Sonett": "Ach könnt' ich, könnte vergessen sie," in A-flat maj (Herder from 13th cent French)
13.25	5. "Trennung": "Wach auf, wach auf, du junger Gesell," in F major (trad)
13.26	6. "Gang zur Liebsten": "Des Abends kann ich nicht schlafen gehn," in E minor (trad)
13.27	7. "Ständchen": "Gut Nacht, gut Nacht, mein liebster Schatz," in F major (trad)
13.28	8. "Sehnsucht": "Mein Schatz ist nicht da," in E minor (trad)
13.29	"5 Poems": 1. "Der Kuss": "Unter Blüten des Mai's spielt ich mit ihrer Hand," in B-flat major (Hölty) .. Op.19
13.30	2. "Scheiden und Meiden": "So soll ich dich nun meiden," in D major (Uhland)
13.31	3. "In der Ferne": "Will ruhen unter den Bäumen hier," in D min / D major (Uhland)
13.32	4. "Der Schmied": "Ich hör meinen Schatz," in B-flat major (Uhland)
13.33	5. "An eine Äolsharfe": "Angelehnt an die Epheuwand," in A-flat min / A-flat major (Mörike) (also see Wolf's 11. of: Mörike Lieder)

c1864:

13.34	"9 Lieder & Songs": 1. "Wie rafft ich mich auf in der Nacht," in F minor (Platen) Op.32
13.35	2. "Nicht mehr zu dir zu gehen," in D minor (Daumer)
13.36	3. "Ich schleich umher betrübt und stumm," in D minor (Platen)
13.37	4. "Der Strom, der neben mir verrauschte," in C-sharp minor (Platen)
13.38	5. "Wehe, so willst du mich wieder," in B minor (Platen)
13.39	6. "Du sprichst, dass ich mich täuschte," in C minor (Platen)
13.40	7. "Bitteres zu sagen denkst du," in F major (Daumer after Hafiz—14th cent Persian poet)
13.41	8. "So stehn wir, ich und meine Weide," in A-flat major (Daumer after Hafiz)
13.42	9. "Wie bist du, meine Königin," in E-flat major (Daumer after Hafiz)

c1868 and earlier:

13.43	"15 Romances" (Magelone-Lieder) (from Tieck's Die schöne Magelone), I: 1. "Keinen hat es noch gereut," in E-flat major Op.33
13.44	2. "Traun! Bogen und Pfeil sind gut für den Feind," in C minor
13.45	3. "Sind es Schmerzen, sind es Freuden," in A-flat major (also see Weber Op.30/6, J156)
13.46	II: 4. "Liebe kam aus fernen Landen," in D-flat major
13.47	5. "So willst du des Armen," in F major
13.48	6. "Wie soll ich die Freude," in A major
13.49	III: 7. "War es dir, dem diese Lippen bebten," in D major
13.50	8. "Wir müssen uns trennen," in G-flat major
13.51	9. "Ruhe, Süssliebchen, im Schatten," in A-flat major
13.52	IV: 10. "Verzweiflung": "So tönet denn, schäumende Wellen," in C minor
13.53	11. "Wie schnell verschwindet so Licht als Glanz," in F minor
13.54	12. "Muss es eine Trennung geben," in G minor
13.55	V: 13. "Sulima": "Geliebter, wo zaudert ein irrender Fuss?," in E major
13.56	14. "Wie froh und frisch mein Sinn sich hebt," in G major
13.57	15. "Treue Liebe dauert lange," in E-flat major

13.58	"4 Songs": 1. "Von ewiger Liebe": "Dunkel, wie dunkel in Wald und in Feld!," in B min (Fallersleben) Op.43
13.59	2. "Die Mainacht": "Wann der silberne Mond ," in E-flat major (Hölty)
13.60	3. "Ich schell mein Horn ins Jammerthal," in B-flat major (Old German)
13.61	4. "Das Lied vom Herrn von Falkenstein": "Es reit der Herr," in C minor (Uhland)
13.62	"Regenlied": "Regentropfen aus den Bäumen," in G minor (c1866, text = Op.59/4) .... WoO posth 23
13.63	"4 Lieder": 1. "Die Kränze": "Hier ob dem Eingang," in D-flat major (from Daumer's Polydora) Op.46
13.64	2. "Magyarisch": "Sah dem edlen Bildnis," in A major (Daumer)
13.65	3. "Die Schale der Vergessenheit": "Eine Schale des Stroms," in E major (Hölty)
13.66	4. "An die Nachtigall": "Geuss nicht so laut der liebentflammten Lieder," in E major (Hölty) (also see Schubert Op.posth 172/3, D196)
13.67	"5 Lieder": 1. "Botschaft": "Wehe, Lüftchen, lind und lieblich," in D-flat major (Daumer after Hafiz) Op.47
13.68	2. "Liebesgluth": "Die Flamme hier," in F min / F major (Daumer after Hafiz)
13.69	3. "Sonntag": "So hab ich doch die ganze Woche," in F major (Uhland)
13.70	4. "O liebliche Wangen, ihr macht mir Verlangen," in D major (Flemming 1609–40)
13.71	5. "Die Liebende schreibt": "Ein Blick von deinen Augen in die meinen," in E-flat major (Goethe) (also see Mendelssohn Op.86/3 & Schubert Op.posth 165/1, D673)
13.72	"7 Lieder": 1. "Der Gang zum Liebchen": "Es glänzt der Mond nieder," in E minor (Wenzig from Bohemian) Op.48
13.73	2. "Der Überläufer": "In den Garten wollen wir gehen," in F-sharp minor (from Des Knaben Wunderhorn
13.74	3. "Liebesklage des Mädchens": "Wer sehen will zween," in B major (from Des Knaben Wunderhorn)
13.75	4. "Gold überwiegt die Liebe": "Sternchen mit dem trüben Schein," in E minor (from Bohemian)
13.76	5. "Trost in Thränen": "Wie kommts, dass du so traurig bist," in E maj / E minor (Goethe) (also see Schubert D120)
13.77	6. "Vergangen ist mir Glück und Heil," in D minor (Old German)
13.78	7. "Herbstgefühl": "Wie wenn im frost'gen Windhauch tödlich," in F-sharp minor (Schack)
13.79	"5 Lieder": 1. "Am Sonntag Morgen zierlich angethan," in E minor (Italian transl Heyse) Op.49
13.80	2. "An ein Veilchen": "Birg, o Veilchen, in deinem blauen Kelche," in E major (Hölty)
13.81	3. "Sehnsucht": "Hinter jenen dichten Wäldern," in A-flat major (Wenzig from Bohemian)
13.82	4. "Wiegenlied": "Guten Abend, gut Nacht," in E-flat major (from Des Knaben Wunderhorn)
13.83	5. "Abenddämmerung": "Sei willkommen, Zwielichtstunde!," in E major (Schack)

c1871:

13.84	"8 Lieder & Songs" (Daumer): 1. "Von waldbekränzter Höhe," in G major Op.57
13.85	2. "Wenn du nur zuweilen lächelst," in E-flat major (after Hafiz)
13.86	3. "Es träumte mir, ich sei dir teuer," in B major (from Spanish)
13.87	4. "Ach, wende diesen Blick, wende dies Angesicht!," in F minor
13.88	5. "In meiner Nächte Sehnen," in E minor
13.89	6. "Strahlt zuweilen auch ein mildes Licht," in E major
13.90	7. "Die Schnur, die Perl an Perle," in B major (from Sanskrit)
13.91	8. "Unbewegte, laue Luft, tiefe Ruhe der Natur," in E major
13.92	"8 Lieder & Songs": 1. "Blinde Kuh": "Im Finstern geh ich suchen," in G minor (Kopisch from Italian) Op.58
13.93	2. "Während des Regens": "Voller, dichter tropft, ums Dach da," in D-flat major (Kopisch)
13.94	3. "Die Spröde": "Ich sahe eine Tigrin im dunklen Haine," in A major (Kopisch from Calabrian)
13.95	4. "O komme, holde Sommernacht verschwiegen," in F-sharp major (Grohe)
13.96	5. "Schwermut": "Mir ist so weh ums Herz," in E-flat minor (Candidus)
13.97	6. "In der Gasse": "Ich blikke hinab in die Gasse," in D minor (Hebbel)
13.98	7. "Vorüber": "Ich legte mich unter den Lindenbaum," in F major (Hebbel)
13.99	8. "Serenade": "Leise um dich nicht zu wecken," in A minor (Schack)

c1873 and earlier:

13.100	"8 Lieder & Songs": 1. "Dämmrung senkte sich von oben," in G minor (Goethe) Op.59
13.101	2. "Auf dem See": "Blauer Himmel, blaue Wogen," in E major (Simrock)
13.102	3. "Regenlied": "Walle Regen, walle nieder," in F-sharp minor (Groth)
13.103	4. "Nachklang": "Regentropfen aus den Bäumen fallen in das grüne Gras," in F-sharp min (Groth)
13.104	5. "Agnes": "Rosenzeit, wie schnell vorbei," in G minor (Mörike) (also see Wolf's 14. of: Mörike Lieder)
13.105	6. "Eine gute, gute Nacht," in A minor (Daumer from Russian)
13.106	7. "Mein wundes Herz verlangt nach milder Ruh," in E minor (Groth)
13.107	8. "Dein blaues Auge hält so still," in E-flat major (Groth)
13.108	"5 Songs of Ophelia" (from Shakespeare's Hamlet, transl Schlegel) (also see Castelnuovo-Tedesco Op.24/VII/1–2, Elgar Op.21/1, Shostakovich Op.127/1 & R. Strauss Op.67): 1. "Wie erkenn ich dein Treulieb?," in F major .... WoO posth 22
13.109	2. "Sein Leichenhemd weiss wie Schnee," in D minor
13.110	3. "Auf morgen ist sankt Valentins Tag," in B-flat major
13.111	4. "Sie trugen ihn auf der Bahre bloss," in G major
13.112	5. "Und kommt er nicht mehr zurück?," in F minor

c1873–4:

13.113	"9 Lieder & Songs": 1. "Frühlingstrost": "Es weht um mich," in A major (Schenkendorf) Op.63
13.114	2. "Erinnerung": "Ihr wunderschönen Augenblicke," in C major (Schenkendorf)
13.115	3. "An ein Bild": "Was schaust du mich so freundlich an," in A-flat major (Schenkendorf)
13.116	4. "An die Tauben": "Fliegt nur aus, geliebte Tauben!," in C major (Schenkendorf)

13.117	5. "Junge Liebe" I: "Meine Liebe ist grün wie der Fliederbusch," in F-sharp major (F. Schumann)
13.118	6. "Junge Liebe" II: "Wenn um den Holunder der Abendwind kost," in D major (F. Schumann)
13.119	7. "Heimweh" I: "Wie traulich war das Fleckchen," in G major (Groth)
13.120	8. "Heimweh" II: "O wüsst ich doch den Weg zurück," in E major (Groth)
13.121	9. "Heimweh" III: "Ich sah als Knabe Blumen blühn," in A major (Groth)

c1877 and earlier:

13.122	"9 Songs": 1. "Klage" I: "Ach! mir fehlt," in D major (Wenzig from Bohemian) Op.69
13.123	2. "Klage" II: "O Felsen, lieber Felsen," in A minor (Wenzig from Slovakian)
13.124	3. "Abschied": "Ach! mich hält der Gram gefangen," in E-flat major (Wenzig from Bohemian)
13.125	4. "Des Liebsten Schwur": "Ei, schmollte mein Vater," in F major (Wenzig from Bohemian)
13.126	5. "Tambourliedchen": "Den Wirbel schlag ich gar so stark," in A major (Candidus)
13.127	6. "Vom Strande": "Ich rufe vom Ufer," in A minor (Eichendorff from Spanish)
13.128	7. "Über die See, fern über die See ist mein Schatz gezogen," in E minor (Lemcke)
13.129	8. "Salome": "Singt mein Schatz wie ein Fink," in C major (Keller)
13.130	9. "Mädchenfluch": "Ruft die Mutter, ruft der Tochter," in A minor (Kapper from Serbian)
13.131	"4 Songs": 1. "Im Garten am Seegestade," in G minor (Lemcke) Op.70
13.132	2. "Lerchengesang": "Ätherische ferne Stimmen," in B major (Candidus)
13.133	3. "Serenade": "Liebliches Kind, kannst du mir sagen?," in B major (Goethe)
13.134	4. "Abendregen": "Langsam und schimmernd fiel ein Regen," in A min / C major (Keller)
13.135	"5 Songs": 1. "Es liebt sich so lieblich im Lenze!": "Die Wellen blinken," in D major (Heine) Op.71
13.136	2. "An den Mond": "Silbermond, mit bleichen Strahlen," in B minor (Simrock)
13.137	3. "Geheimnis": "O Frühlings-Abenddämmerung!," in G major (Candidus)
13.138	4. "Willst du, dass ich geh'?": "Auf der Heide weht der Wind," in D minor (Lemcke)
13.139	5. "Minnelied": "Holder klingt der Vogelsang," in C major (Hölty) (also see Mendelssohn Op.8/1 & Schubert D429)
13.140	"5 Songs": 1. "Alte Liebe": "Es kehrt die dunkle Schwalbe," in G minor (Candidus) Op.72
13.141	2. "Sommerfäden": "Sommerfäden hin und wieder," in C minor (Candidus)
13.142	3. "O kühler Wald": "O kühler Wald, wo rauschest du?," in A-flat major (Brentano)
13.143	4. "Verzagen": "Ich sitz am Strande der rauschenden See," in F-sharp minor (Lemcke)
13.144	5. "Unüberwindlich": "Hab ich tausendmal geschworen," in A major (Goethe)

c1878:

13.145	"5 Romances & Lieder" (1/2vv): 1. "Sommerabend": "Geh' schlafen, Tochter," in D minor (Schmidt) . Op.84
13.146	2. "Der Kranz": "Mutter, hilf mir, armen Tochter," in G minor (Schmidt)
13.147	3. "In den Beeren": "Singe, Mädchen, hell und clar," in E-flat major (Schmidt)
13.148	4. "Vergebliches Ständchen": "Guten Abend, mein Schatz," in A major (trad)
13.149	5. "Spannung": "Gut'n Abend, gut'n Abend, mein tausiger Schatz," in A minor (trad)
13.150	"6 Lieder": 1. "Sommerabend": "Dämmernd liegt der Sommerabend," in B-flat major (Heine) Op.85
13.151	2. "Mondenschein": "Nacht liegt auf den fremden Wegen," in B-flat major (Heine)
13.152	3. "Mädchenlied": "Ach, und du mein kühles Wasser!," in A minor (Kapper from Serbian)
13.153	4. "Ade!": "Wie schienen die Sternlein so hell," in B minor (Kapper from Bohemian)
13.154	5. "Frühlingslied": "Mit geheimnisvollen Düften," in G major (Geibel)
13.155	6. "In Waldeseinsamkeit": "Ich sass zu deinen Füssen," in B minor (Lemcke)
13.156	*"2 Frühlingslieder" (Geibel, lost)* *Anh.IIa/25*
13.157	"6 Lieder": 1. "Therese": "Du milchjunger Knabe," in D major (Keller) (also see Wolf's 3. of: Alte Weisen) Op.86
13.158	2. "Feldeinsamkeit": "Ich ruhe still im hohen grünen Gras," in F major (Allmers)
13.159	3. "Nachtwandler": "Störe nicht den leisen Schlummer," in C major (Kalbeck)
13.160	4. "Über die Haide": "Über die Haide hallet mein Schritt," in G minor (Storm)
13.161	5. "Versunken": "Es brausen der Liebe Wogen," in F-sharp major (Schumann)
13.162	6. "Todessehnen": "Ach, wer nimmt von meiner Seele," in F-sharp minor (Schenkendorf)

c1884:

13.163	"2 Songs" (w/ va & pf): 1. "Gestillte Sehnsucht": "In goldnen Abendschein," in D major (Rückert) Op.91
13.164	2. "Geistliches Wiegenlied": "Die ihr schwebet," in F major (Geibel after Vega)
13.165	"5 Lieder": 1. "Mit vierzig Jahren ist der Berg erstiegen," in B minor (Rückert) Op.94
13.166	2. "Steig auf, geliebter Schatten," in E-flat minor (Halm)
13.167	3. "Mein Herz ist schwer, mein Auge wacht," in G minor (Geibel)
13.168	4. "Sapphische Ode": "Rosen brach ich Nachts mir am dunklen Hage," in D major (Schmidt)
13.169	5. "Kein Haus, keine Heimat," in D minor (Halm)
13.170	"7 Lieder": 1. "Das Mädchen": "Stand das Mädchen," in B minor (Kapper from Serbian) Op.95
13.171	2. "Bei dir sind meine Gedanken," in A major (Halm)
13.172	3. "Beim Abschied": "Ich müh mich ab," in D major (Halm; 2 vers)
13.173	4. "Der Jäger": "Mein Lieb ist ein Jäger," in F major (Halm)
13.174	5. "Vorschneller Schwur": "Schwor ein junges Mädchen," in D minor (Kapper from Serbian)
13.175	6. "Mädchenlied": "Am jüngsten Tag ich aufersteh," in F major (Heyse from Italian)
13.176	7. "Schön war, das ich dir weihte," in F minor (Daumer from Turkish)
13.177	"4 Lieder": 1. "Der Tod, das ist die kühle Nacht," in C major (Heine) Op.96
13.178	2. "Wir wandelten, wir zwei zusammen," in D-flat major (Daumer from Hungarian)
13.179	3. "Es schauen die Blumen," in B minor (Heine)
13.180	4. "Meerfahrt": "Mein Liebchen, wir sassen beisammen," in A minor (Heine)

c1885:

13.181	"6 Lieder": 1. "Nachtigall": "O Nachtigall, dein süsser Schall," in F minor (Reinhold).........................Op.97
13.182	2. "Auf dem Schiffe": "Ein Vögelein fliegt über den Rhein," in A major (Reinhold)
13.183	3. "Entführung": "O Lady Judith, spröder Schatz," in D minor (Alexis)
13.184	4. "Dort in den Weiden steht ein Haus," in D major (trad Swabian)
13.185	5. "Komm bald": "Warum denn warten von Tag zu Tag?," in A major (Groth)
13.186	6. "Trennung": "Da unten im Tale läufts Wasser so trüb," in F major (trad Swabian)
13.187	*"Nachtigall": "O Nachtigall, dein süsser Schall" (Reinhold, text = Op.97/1, lost) Anh.IIa/26*
13.188	*"Wie der Mond" (Heine, lost) Anh.IIa/27*
13.189	*"Winternacht": "Um mich ist Nacht und Dunkel" (Halm, lost) Anh.IIa/28*
13.190	*"Brautlied": "Welch ein Scheiden ist seliger" (Heyse, lost) Anh.IIa/29*

c1886 and later:

13.191	"Gypsy Songs" (arr from: 11 Gypsy Songs for vocal qt, Op.103/1–7, 11): 1. "He! Zigeuner" ....(Op.103)
13.192	2. "Hochgetürmte Rimafluth, wie bist so trüb' "
13.193	3. "Wisst ihr, wann mein Liebster am besten mir gefällt?"
13.194	4. "Lieber Gott du weisst, wie oft in stiller Nacht"
13.195	5. "Brauner Bursche führt zum Tanze"
13.196	6. "Röslein dreie in der Reihe blühn so roth"
13.197	7. "Kommt dir manchmal in den Sinn, mein süsses Lieb"
13.198	11. "Rothe Abendwolken ziehn am Firmament"
13.199	"5 Lieder": 1. "Wie Melodien zieht es mir leise durch den Sinn," in A major (Groth) Op.105
13.200	2. "Immer leiser wird mein Schlummer," in C-sharp minor (Lingg)
13.201	3. "Klage": "Feins Liebchen, trau du nicht," in F major (trad Lower Rhennish)
13.202	4. "Auf dem Kirchhofe": "Der Tag ging regenschwer und sturmbewegt," in C minor (Liliencron)
13.203	5. "Verrat": "Ich stand in einer lauen Nacht," in B minor (Lemcke)
13.204	"5 Lieder": 1. "Ständchen": "Der Mond steht über dem Berge," in G major (Kugler) Op.106
13.205	2. "Auf dem See": "An dies Schifflein schmiege," in E major (Reinhold)
13.206	3. "Es hing der Reif im Lindenbaum," in A minor (Groth)
13.207	4. "Meine Lieder": "Wenn mein Herz beginnt zu klingen," in F-sharp minor (Frey)
13.208	5. "Ein Wanderer": "Hier wo sich die Strassen scheiden," in F minor (Reinhold)
13.209	"5 Lieder": 1. "An die Stolze": "Und gleichwohl kann ich anders nicht," in A major (Flemming) Op.107
13.210	2. "Salamander": "Es sass ein Salamander," in A minor (Lemcke)
13.211	3. "Das Mädchen spricht": "Schwalbe sag' mir an," in A major (Gruppe)
13.212	4. "Maienkätzchen": "Maienkätzen erster Gruss," in E-flat major (Liliencron)
13.213	5. "Mädchenlied": "Auf die Nacht in der Spinnstub'n da singen die Mädchen," in B minor (Heyse)
13.214	*"Aphorismus": "Doch was hör ich?" (c1891; 1v, frag) Anh.III/7*

c1896:

13.215	"Vier ernste Gesänge" (4 Serious Songs) (Bible; B & pf): 1. "Denn es gehet dem Menschen," in D minor...Op.121
13.216	2. "Ich wandte mich, und sahe an alle," in G minor
13.217	3. "O Tod, o Tod, wie bitter bist du," in E minor
13.218	4. "Wenn ich mit Menschen- und mit Engelszungen redete," in E-flat major

14. FOLKSONG COLLECTIONS (w/ pf)

14.1	"Volks-Kinderlieder" (c1858 or earlier): 1. "Dornröschen": "Im tiefen Wald im Dornenhag" ....WoO 31
14.2	2. "Die Nachtigall": "Sitzt a schöns Vögerl aufm Danabaum"
14.3	3. "Die Henne": "Ach, mein Hennlein, bi-bi-bi!"
14.4	4. "Sandmännchen": "Die Blümelein sie schlafen"
14.5	5. "Der Mann": "Wille wille will, der Mann ist kommen"
14.6	6. "Heidenröslein": "Sah ein Knab ein Röslein stehn, Röslein"
14.7	7. "Das Schlaraffenland": "In Polen steht ein Haus"
14.8	8a. "Beim Ritt auf dem Knie": "Ull Mann wull riden"
14.9	8b. "Beim Ritt auf dem Knie": "Alt Mann wollt reiten"
14.10	9. "Der Jäger im Walde"
14.11	10. "Das Mädchen und die Hasel": "Es wollt ein Mädchen brechen gehn"
14.12	11. "Wiegenlied": "Schlaf, Kindlein schlaf! Der Vater hüt die Schaf"
14.13	12. "Weihnachten": "Uns leuchtet heut der Freude Schein! Auf Jubelklang!"
14.14	13. "Marienwürmchen": "Marienwürmchen, setze dich"
14.15	14. "Dem Schutzengel": "O Engel, mein Schutzengel mein"
14.16	15. "Sommerlied": "Tra-ri-ro! Der Sommer der ist do!"
14.17	"28 Volkslieder" (c1858): 1. "Die Schnürbrust": "Die Maid sie wollt'nen Buhlen wert" ....WoO 32
14.18	2. "Der Jäger": "Bei nächtlicher Weil, an eins Waldes Born"
14.19	3. "Drei Vögelein": "Mit Lust tät ich ausreiten"
14.20	4. "Auf, gebet uns das Pfingstei"
14.21	5. "Des Markgrafen Töchterlein": "Es war ein Marksgraf überm Rhein"
14.22	6. "Der Reiter": "Der Reiter spreitet seinen Mantel aus"
14.23	7. "Die heilige Elisabeth an ihrem Hochzeitsfeste"
14.24	8. "Der englische Gruss": "Gegrüsset Maria"
14.25	9. "Ich stund an einem Morgen"
14.26	10. "Gunhilde": "Gunhilde lebt gar stille und fromm in"

14.27	11. "Der tote Gast": "Es pochet ein Knabe leise an Feinsliebchens Fensterlein"
14.28	12. "Tageweis von einer schönen Frauen": "Wach auf, mein Hort, vernimm mein Wort"
14.29	13. "Schifferlied": "Dort in den Weiden steht ein Haus"
14.30	14. "Nachtgesang": "Wach auf, mein Herzensschöne"
14.31	15. "Die beiden Königskinder": "Ach Elselein, liebes Elselein mein"
14.32	16. "Scheiden": "Ach Gott, wie weh tut Scheiden"
14.33	17. "Altes Minnelied": "Ich fahr dahin, wenn es muss sein"
14.34	18a. "Der getreue Eckart" I: "In der finstern Mitternacht"
14.35	18b. "Der getreue Eckart" II: "In der finstern Mitternacht"
14.36	19. "Die Versuchung": "Feinsliebchen, du sollst mir nicht barfuss gehn"
14.37	20. "Der Tochter Wunsch": "Och Mutter ich well en Ding han!"
14.38	21. "Schnitter Tod": "Es ist ein Schnitter, heisst der Tod"
14.39	22. "Marias Wallfahrt": "Maria ging aus wandern"
14.40	23. "Das Mädchen und der Tod": "Es ging ein Maidlein zarte"
14.41	24. "Es ritt ein Ritter wohl durch das Ried"
14.42	25. "Liebeslied": "Gar lieblich hat sich gesellet"
14.43	26. "Guten Abend, mein tausiger Schatz"
14.44	27. "Die Wollust in den Maien"
14.45	28. "Es reit ein Herr und auch sein Knecht"
14.46	"Neapolitanische Canzonetta": "So bello non so bello" (c1882, trad Italian) Anh.III/8
14.47	"49 Deutsche Volkslieder" (c by 1894), I: 1. "Sagt mir, o schönste Schäfrin mein" .... WoO 33
14.48	2. "Erlaube mir, feins Mädchen"
14.49	3. "Gar lieblich hat sich gesellet"
14.50	4. "Guten Abend, mein tausiger Schatz"
14.51	5. "Die Sonne scheint nicht mehr"
14.52	6. "Da unten im Tale"
14.53	7. "Gunhilde": "Gunhilde lebt gar stille und fromm"
14.54	II: 8. "Ach, englische Schäferin"
14.55	9. "Es war eine schöne Jüdin"
14.56	10. "Es ritt ein Ritter"
14.57	11. "Jungfräulein, soll ich mit euch gehn"
14.58	12. "Feinsliebchen, du sollst mir nicht barfuss gehn"
14.59	13. "Wach auf, mein Hort"
14.60	14. "Maria ging aus wandern"
14.61	III: 15. "Schwesterlein, Schwesterlein, wann gehn wir"
14.62	16. "Wach auf mein Herzensschöne"
14.63	17. "Ach Gott, wie weh tut scheiden"
14.64	18. "So wünsch ich ihr ein gute Nacht"
14.65	19. "Nur ein Gesicht auf Erden lebt"
14.66	20. "Schönster Schatz, mein Engel"
14.67	21. "Es ging ein Maidlein zarte"
14.68	IV: 22. "Wo gehst du hin, du Stolze?"
14.69	23. "Der Reiter": "Der Reiter spreitet seinen Mantel aus"
14.70	24. "Mir ist ein schöns brauns Maidelein"
14.71	25. "Mein Mädel hat einem Rosenmund"
14.72	26. "Ach, könnt ich diesen Abend"
14.73	27. "Ich stand auf hohem Berge"
14.74	28. "Es reit ein Herr und auch sein Knecht"
14.75	V: 29. "Es war ein Markgraf überm Rhein"
14.76	30. "All mein Gedanken"
14.77	31. "Dort in den Weiden steht ein Haus"
14.78	32. "So will ich frisch und fröhlich sein"
14.79	33. "Och Moder, ich well en Ding han!"
14.80	34. "Wie kumm' ich dann de Pooz erenn"
14.81	35. "Soll sich der Mond nicht heller scheinen"
14.82	VI: 36. "Es wohnet ein Fiedler zu Frankfurt am Main"
14.83	37. "Du mein einzig Licht"
14.84	38. "Des Abends kann ich nicht schlafen gehn"
14.85	39. "Schöner Augen, schöne Strahlen"
14.86	40. "Ich weiss mir'n Maidlein hübsch und fein"
14.87	41. "Es steht ein Lind"
14.88	42. "In stiller Nacht, zur ersten Wacht"
14.89	VII (w/ ch ad lib): 43. "Es stunden drei Rosen"
14.90	44. "Dem Himmel will ich klagen"
14.91	45. "Es sass ein schneeweiss Vögelein"
14.92	46. "Es war einmal ein Zimmergesell"
14.93	47. "Es ging sich unsre Fraue"
14.94	48. "Nachtigall, sag, was für Grüss"
14.95	49. "Verstohlen geht der Mond auf"

15. ARRANGEMENTS OF WORKS OF OTHERS

For pf:

15.1   Schubert: "20 Ländler," D366 & D814 (p1869; pf/pf duet) Anh.Ia/6
15.2   Schumann: "Scherzo," from Piano Quintet in E-flat major, Op.44 (arr1854) Anh.Ia/7
15.3   Schumann: "Papillons," for pf, Op.2/7 (canonic arrangement 1855) Anh.III/5
15.4   Schubert: "2 Marches," in C major, Op.121, D968b (D886) for pf duet (arr1855, lost) Anh.IIb/3
15.5   Bach, J. S.: "Toccata" (Prelude), in F major, BWV540 (arr1856, lost) Anh.IIb/1
15.6   Beethoven: Finale of String Quartet No.9 in C major, 'Rasumovsky 3,' Op.59/3 (perf1867, lost) Anh.IIb/2
15.7   Schubert: Scherzo from Octet, Op.166, D803 (arr1867, lost) Anh.IIb/4

For pf duet:

15.8   Joachim: Overture to: Hamlet, Op.4 (arr1853–4) Anh.Ia/3
15.9   Schumann: Piano Quintet in E-flat major, Op.44 (arr1854, lost) Anh.IIb/5
15.10   Schumann: Piano Quartet in E-flat major, Op.47 (arr1855) Anh.Ia/8

For 2 pf:

15.11   Litolff: Overture to: Maximilien Robespierre, Op.55 (arr early; pf & harm, frag) Anh.III/9
15.12   Joachim: Overture to: Grimm's Demetrius, Op.6 (arr1854–5) Anh.Ia/4
15.13   Joachim: Overture to: Henry IV, Op.7 (arr1854) Anh.Ia/5

For ch:

15.14   Bach, J. S.: "Ach Gott, wie manches Herzeleid," choral from Cantata No.44 (p1933; ch) Anh.Ia/9
15.15   Schubert: "Ellens zweiter Gesang," Op.52/2, D838 (2 vers): Anh.Ia/17
       . Version 1 (arr1862; ch, 4hn & 3bn)
       . Version 2 (arr1873; S, fem ch, 4hn & 2bn)
15.16   Schubert: Mass in E-flat major for ch & orch, D950 (p1865; red w/ pf) Anh.Ia/18

For 1v/vv & orch:

15.17   Schubert: "Nachtstück," D672 (arr1862; 1v, pf/harp & small orch, frag) Anh.III/11
15.18   Handel: 7 Duets and 2 Trios (cont realizations, for Handel-Gesamtausgabe Vol.32) Anh.Ia/10
15.19   Handel: 6 Duets (p1880; cont realizations, Handel-Gesamtausgabe Vol.32, 2nd edition) Anh.Ia/11
15.20   Schubert: "An Schwager Kronos," Op.19/1, D369 (arr1862; 1v & orch) Anh.Ia/12
15.21   Schubert: "Memnon," Op.6/1, D541 (arr1862; 1v & orch) Anh.Ia/13
15.22   Schubert: "Gruppe aus dem Tartarus," Op.24/1, D583 (p1937; 1v/unison ch & orch) Anh.Ia/14
15.23   Schubert: "Geheimes," Op.14/2, D719 (arr for 1v, hn & strings) Anh.Ia/15
15.24   Schubert: "Greisengesang," Op.60/1, D778 (arr1862; 1v & orch) Anh.Ia/16

*   *   *   *   *

WoO =   Werk ohne Opuszahl (Work without opus number) in M. I. McCorkle: "J. Brahms.
       Thematisch-bibliographisches Werkverzeichnis." G. Henle Verlag. München, 1984.
      Anh. = Anhang (Appendix) in McCorkle's catalog.

1. STAGE WORKS

Operas:

1.1	"Paul Bunyan," 2 act operetta (c1941, r1974, Auden)	Op.17
1.2	"Peter Grimes," 3 acts (c1944–5, Slater after Crabbe's Letter XXII: The Poor of the Borough)	Op.33
1.3	"The Rape of Lucretia," 2 act chamber opera (c1946, r1947, Duncan after Obey's play)	Op.37
1.4	"Albert Herring," 3 act comic chamber opera (c1947, Crozier after Maupassant)	Op.39
1.5	"The Beggar's Opera," ballad opera (c1948, after Gay's opera of 1728)	Op.43
1.6	"The Little Sweep," 1 act children's opera (c1949, Crozier on Blake's poem; orig part of play: Let's Make an Opera!—which illustrates the preparations & rehearsal of The Little Sweep performed in Act III)	Op.45
1.7	"Billy Budd," 4 acts (c1951, r1960, Forster & Crozier after Melville)	Op.50
1.8	"Gloriana," 3 acts (c1953, Plomer)	Op.53
1.9	"The Turn of the Screw," 2 act chamber opera (c1954, Piper after H. James)	Op.54
1.10	"Noye's Fludde," 1 act children's opera (c1957, Chester miracle play)	Op.59
1.11	"A Midsummer Night's Dream," 3 acts (c1960, Britten & Pears after Shakespeare) (also see Castelnuovo-Tedesco's overture Op.108, Mendelssohn's incid music Op.61, Orff's music drama, Purcell's semi-opera: The Fairy Queen, Z629 & Satie's incid music: 5 Grimaces)	Op.64
1.12	"The Golden Vanity," vaudeville (c1966, Graham; boys' vv & pf)	Op.78
1.13	"Owen Wingrave," 2 act television opera (c1970, Piper after H. James)	Op.85
1.14	"Death in Venice," 2 acts (c1973, Piper after Mann)	Op.88

Church parables:

1.15	"Curlew River," 1 act (c1964, Plomer)	Op.71
1.16	"The Burning Fiery Furnace," 1 act (c1966, Plomer)	Op.77
1.17	"The Prodigal Son," 1 act (c1968, Plomer)	Op.81

Ballets:

1.18	"The Prince of the Pagodas," 3 acts (c1956, Cranko)	Op.57

Incid music:

1.19	"Timon of Athens" (c1935, Shakespeare) (also see masque c by Purcell Z632 & overture c by Sullivan)
1.20	*"Easter 1916" (c1935, Slater, lost)*
1.21	"Stay Down Miner" (c1936, Slater)
1.22	"Agamemnon" (c1936, Aeschylus transl MacNeice)
1.23	"The Ascent of F6" (c1937, Auden & Isherwood; also see 2. of: 4 Cabaret Songs)
1.24	"Pageant of Empire" (c ?1937, Slater)
1.25	"Out of the Picture" (c1937, MacNeice)
1.26	*"Spain," puppet play (c1938, Slater, lost)*
1.27	"On the Frontier" (c1938, Auden & Isherwood)
1.28	"They Walk Alone" (c1938, Catto)
1.29	"Johnson over Jordan" (c1939, Priestley; suite arr Hindmarsh 1988)
1.30	"This Way to the Tomb" (c1945, Duncan)
1.31	"The Eagle Has Two Heads" (c1946, Cocteau transl Duncan)
1.32	*"The Duchess of Malfi" (c1946, Webster, adapted Auden, lost)*
1.33	*"Stratton" (c1949, Duncan, lost)*
1.34	"Am Stram Gram," canon only (c1954, Roussin)
1.35	"The Punch Revue" (c1955, Duncan):

        1. "Tell me the truth about love" (c1938, Auden)
        2. "Old friends are best" (c1955, Plomer)
        3. "Waltz" (pf, based on song: Old friends are best)

Radio:

1.36	"King Arthur" (c1937, Bridson)
1.37	"The Company of Heaven" (c1937, Ellis Roberts)
1.38	"Hadrian's Wall: An Historical Survey" (c1937, Auden)
1.39	"Lines on the Map," a series of programmes (c1938):

        1. "Communication by Land" (Potter)
        2. "Communication by Sea" (Miller)
        3. "Communication by Wireless" (Aitken & Alway)
        4. "Communication by Air" (Potter)

1.40	"The Chartists' March" (c1938, Miller)
1.41	"The World of the Spirit" (c1938, Ellis Roberts)
1.42	"The Sword in the Stone" (c1939, Helweg from White's novel)
1.43	"The Dark Valley," monologue for Dame May Whitty (c1940, Auden; 2 songs c by Britten)
1.44	"The Dynasts" (c1940, Hardy)
1.45	"The Rocking-Horse Winner" (c1941, Auden & Stern after short story by D. H. Lawrence)
1.46	"Appointment" (c1942, Corwin)
1.47	"An American in England, I: London by Clipper" (c1942, Corwin)
1.48	"An American in England, II: London to Dover" (c1942, Corwin)
1.49	"An American in England, III: Ration Island" (c1942, Corwin)

1.50   "The Man Born To Be King, X: The Princes of this World" (c1942, Sayers) ....
1.51   "Lumberjacks of America" (c1942, MacDougall) ....
1.52   "An American in England, IV: Women of Britain" (c1942, Corwin) ....
1.53   "An American in England, V: The Yanks Are Here" (c1942, Corwin) ....
1.54   "An American in England, VI: The Anglo-American Angle" (c1942, Corwin) ....
1.55   "The Man Born To Be King, XI: King of Sorrows" (c1942, Sayers) ....
1.56   "Britain to America, Series I No.9: Britain Through American Eyes" (c1942, MacNeice) ....
1.57   "Britain to America, Series II No.4: Where Do I Come In?" (c1942, MacNeice) ....
1.58   "Britain to America, Series II No.13: Where Do We Go From Here?" (c1942, MacNeice) ....
1.59   "The Four Freedoms, No.1: Pericles" (c1943, MacNeice) ....
1.60   "The Rescue" (c1943, Sackville-West on Homer's Odyssey) ....
1.61   "A Poet's Christmas" (c1944, Auden & others) ....
1.62   "The Dark Tower" (c1946, MacNeice) ....
1.63   "Men of Goodwill: The Reunion of Christmas" (c1947, Gilliam & Cottrell) ....

Film:

1.64   "The King's Stamp" (c1935, Coldstream) ....
1.65   "Coal Face" (c1935, Cavalcanti)..
1.66   "Telegrams" (c1935, Britten's music composed but not used) ....
1.67   "The Tocher" (Dowry) (c1935, Cavalcanti) ....
1.68   "C.T.O.—The Story of the Central Telegraph Office" (c1935, Legg) ....
1.69   "Gas Abstract" (?Coal Abstract) (c1935) ....
1.70   "God's Chillun" (c1935, Auden, commentary set as recit) ....
1.71   "Men Behind the Meters" (Title Music I) (c1935, Elton) ....
1.72   "Dinner Hour" (Title Music II) (c1935, Anstey) ....
1.73   "Title Music" III (c1935)...
1.74   "How the Dial Works" (c1935, Elton & Morrison) ....
1.75   "Conquering Space—The Story of Modern Communications" (c1935, Legg) ....
1.76   "Sorting Office" (c1935, Watt) ....
1.77   "The Savings Bank" (c1935, Legg)..
1.78   "The New Operator" (c1935, Legg) ....
1.79   "Night Mail" (c1935–6, Watt & Wright) ....
1.80   "GPO Title Music" I & II (c1935) ....
1.81   "Calendar of the Year" (c1936, Spice) ....
1.82   "Peace of Britain" (c1936, Rotha) ....
1.83   "Around the Village Green" (c1936, Grierson & Spice) ....
1.84   "Men of the Alps" (c1936, Cavalcanti; incl music c by Rossini arr Britten & Leigh) ....
1.85   "The Line to the Tschierva Hut" (c1936, Cavalcanti) ....
1.86   "Message from Geneva" (c1936, Cavalcanti) ....
1.87   "Four Barriers" (c1936, Watt; incl music c by Foulds) ....
1.88   "The Saving of Bill Blewitt" (c1936, Cavalcanti)..
1.89   "Love from a Stranger" (c1936, Lee) ....
1.90   "The Way to the Sea" (c1936, Holmes) ....
1.91   "Book Bargain" (c ?1937, McLaren) ....
1.92   "Mony a Pickle" (c ?1938, Cavalcanti & Massingham; incl music c by Foulds & V. Yates) ....
1.93   "Advance Democracy" (c1938, Bond) ....
1.94   "The Instruments of the Orchestra" (c1945, Mathieson) ....

1a. SELECTIONS FROM STAGE WORKS

1a.2   "Peter Grimes," opera (Nos. of sections in The Gramophone): Op.33
     excerpts: 1. "Prologue"
     I: 2. "Interlude" (Dawn) (= Op.33a/1)
        3. "Oh, hang at open doors the net"
        4. "Good morning, good morning!"
        5. "I have to go from pub to pub"
        6. "Let her among you without fault"
        7. "And do you prefer the storm"
        8. "Picture what that day was like"
        9. "They listen to money"
        10. "What harbour shelters peace"
        11. "Interlude" (Storm) (= Op.33a/4)
        12a. "Past time to close!"
        12b. "A joke's a joke"
        13. "We live and let live"
        14. "Now the great Bear and Pleiades"
        15. "Old Joe has gone fishing"
     II: 16. "Interlude" (Sunday morning) (= Op.33a/2)
        17. "Glitter of waves"
        18. "Grimes is at his exercise"
        19. "We planned that our lives should have a new start"
        20. "From the gutter"
        21. "Passacaglia"

22. "Go there!"
23. "In dreams I've built myself some kindlier home"
24. "The whole affair"
III: 25. "Interlude" (Moonlight) (= Op.33a/3)
26a. "Assign your prettiness to me"
26b. "Mr Keene! Can you spare a moment"
27. "Good night! It's time for bed"
28. "Embroidery in childhood"
29. "Mister Swallow"
30. "Who holds himself apart"
31. "Interlude"
32. "Steady! There you are!"
33. "Final Scene"

1a.18   "The Prince of the Pagodas," ballet: Op.57
1. "Prelude"
2. "March & Gavotte"
3. "The Four Kings" (North—East—West—South)
4. "Belle Epine and Belle Rose"
5. "Variations of the Prince and Belle Rose"
6. "Finale"

2. SYMPHONIES

2.1   "Simple Symphony" (c1933–4; strings): Op.4
1. "Boisterous Bourée"
2. "Playful Pizzicato" (arr Ferguson for pf duet)
3. "Sentimental Saraband" (arr Ferguson for pf duet)
4. "Frolicsome Finale"
2.2   "Sinfonia da Requiem" (c1940, in memory of his parents): Op.20
1. "Lacrimosa"
2. "Dies irae"
3. "Requiem aeternam"
2.3   "Cello Symphony" (c1963; vc & orch) Op.68

3. OTHER ORCHESTRAL WORKS

3.1   "Sinfonietta" (c1932; chamber orch) Op.1
3.2   "Russian Funeral" (c1936; brass & perc, from incid music: The Eagle has Two Heads) ....
3.3   "Soirées musicales" (Rossini Suite No.1), suite (c1936, from music c by Rossini): No.1 "March" Op.9
3.4   No.2 "Canzonetta"
3.5   No.3 "Tirolese"
3.6   No.4 "Bolero"
3.7   No.5 "Tarantella"
3.8   "Variations on a Theme by Frank Bridge" (Frank Bridge Variations) (c1937; strings): Op.10
. "Introduction and Theme"
1. "Adagio"
2. "March"
3. "Romance"
4. "Aria Italiana"
5. "Bouree Classique"
6. "Wiener Walzer"
7. "Moto Perpetuo"
8. "Funeral March"
9. "Chant"
10. "Fugue and Finale"
3.9   "Mont Juic," suite of Catalan dances (c1936–7, collab Berkeley) (titled after the name of the park in
Barcelona where they heard the tunes): No.1 "Andante maestoso" Op.12
3.10   No.2 "Allegro grazioso"
3.11   No.3 "Lament (Barcelona, July 1936). Andante moderato"
3.12   No.4 "Allegro molto"
3.13   "Canadian Carnival" (Kermesse Canadienne), overture (c1939) Op.19
3.14   "Matinées musicales" (Rossini Suite No.2), suite (c1941, from music c by Rossini): No.1 "March" Op.24
3.15   No.2 "Nocturne"
3.16   No.3 "Waltz"
3.17   No.4 "Pantomime"
3.18   No.5 "Moto Perpetuo" (Solfeggi e Gorgheggi)
3.19   "An Occasional Overture," in C major (c1941; pubd1985 as: An American Overture) Op.38
3.20   "Prelude & Fugue" (c1943; 18 strings) Op.29
3.21   "4 Sea Interludes" (c1944, from opera: Peter Grimes, Op.33): No.1 "Dawn" Op.33a
3.22   No.2 "Sunday morning"
3.23   No.3 "Moonlight"
3.24   No.4 "Storm"

3.25	"Passacaglia" (c1944, from opera: Peter Grimes, Op.33)	Op.33b
3.26	"The Young Person's Guide to the Orchestra," variations & fugue on a theme of Purcell (c1946)	Op.34
3.27	"Men of Goodwill," variations on carol: God rest ye merry gentlemen (p1982, from music c1947)	
3.28	"Variations on an Elisabethan Theme 'Quick and gay,' " Variation No.4 (c1953, collab w/ others)	
3.29	"Gloriana," sym suite (p1954; T/ob & orch, from opera Op.53): No.1 "The Tournament"	Op.53a
3.30	No.2 "The Lute Song"	
3.31	No.3 "The Courtly Dances"	
3.32	No.4 "Gloriana moritura"	
3.33	"Pas de Six" (p1957, from ballet: The Prince of the Pagodas, Op.57)	Op.57a
3.34	"A Time there was," suite on English folksongs (c1966 & 1974): No.1 "Cakes and Ale"	Op.90
3.35	No.2 "The Bitter Withy"	
3.36	No.3 "Hankin Booby" (c1966)	
3.37	No.4 "Hunt the Squirrel"	
3.38	No.5 "Lord Melbourne"	

4. CONCERTOS, SOLO INSTR & ORCH

Pf & orch:

4.1	Piano Concerto in D major (c1938, r1945, 4 movts: Toccata—Waltz—Impromptu—March):	Op.13
4.2	"Diversions on a Theme" (c1940, r1954; pf left hand & orch):	Op.21
	. "Theme"	
	Var. 1 "Recitative"	
	Var. 2 "Romance"	
	Var. 3 "March"	
	Var. 4 "Arabesque"	
	Var. 5 "Chant"	
	Var. 6 "Nocturne"	
	Var. 7 "Badinerie"	
	Var. 8 "Burlesque"	
	Var. 9a "Toccata I"	
	Var. 9b "Toccata II"	
	Var. 10 "Adagio"	
	. "Finale—Tarantella"	

Vn & orch:

4.2	Violin Concerto in D minor (c1939, r1958)	Op.15

Other:

4.3	"Young Apollo" (c1939, pf, str qt & strings)	Op.16
4.5	"Scottish Ballad" (c1941; 2 pf & orch)	Op.26
4.6	"Lachrimae, reflections on a song of Dowland" (c1976; va & strings, arr of work for va & pf, Op.48)	Op.48a

5. STRING QUARTETS

5.1	"Rhapsody" (c1929)	
5.2	"Quartettino" (c1930)	
5.3	String Quartet in D major (c1931, r1974)	
5.4	"Alla marcia" (c1933)	
5.5	"3 Divertimenti" (c1933, r1936, from unfin: Go play, boy, play): No.1 "March"	
5.6	No.2 "Waltz"	
5.7	No.3 "Burlesque"	
5.8	String Quartet No.1 in D major (c1941)	Op.25
5.9	String Quartet No.2 in C major (c1945)	Op.36
5.10	String Quartet No.3 (c1975)	Op.94

6. OTHER CHAMBER MUSIC

3 or more insts:

6.1	"Phantasy," in F minor (c1932; str qnt)	
6.2	"Phantasy Quartet" (c1932; ob & str trio)	Op.2
6.3	"Alpine Suite" (c1955; recorder trio): No.1 "Arrival of Zermatt"	
6.4	No.2 "Swiss Clock"	
6.5	No.3 "Nursery slopes"	
6.6	No.4 "Alpine scene"	
6.7	No.5 "Moto perpetuo; Down the Piste"	
6.8	No.6 "Farewell to Zermatt"	
6.9	"Scherzo" (c1955; recorder qt)	
6.10	"Fanfare for St Edmundsbury" (c1959; 3tpt)	

6.11   "Gemini Variations" (c1965; fl, vn & pf duet) Op.73

Vn & pf:

6.12   "Suite" (c1934–5): No.1 "Introduction: March" Op.6
6.13   No.2 "Moto Perpetuo"
6.14   No.3 "Lullaby"
6.15   No.4 "Waltz"
6.16   "Reveille," concert study (c1937) ....

Va & pf:

6.17   "Lachrymae, reflections on a song by Dowland" (c1950; see arr w/ strings) Op.48

Vc & pf:

6.18   Cello Sonata in C major (c1961) Op.65

Other 2 insts:

6.19   "2 Insect Pieces" (c1935; ob & pf): No.1 "The Grasshopper" ....
6.20   No.2 "The Wasp"
6.21   "Temporal Variations" (c1936; ob & pf): ....
          . "Theme" (Andante rubato)
             1. "Oration"
             2. "March"
             3. "Exercises"
             4. "Commination"
             5. "Chorale"
             6. "Waltz"
             7. "Polka"
             8. "Resolution"
6.22   "Morris Dance" (2 descant recorders, from opera: Gloriana, Op.53) ....
6.23   "Timpani Piece for Jimmy (James Blades)" (c1955; timp & pf) ....
6.24   "Hankin Booby," folk dance (c1966; wind & drums; incorp in: A time there was, Op.90) ....

Vc solo:

6.25   Cadenza for Haydn: Cello Concerto No.1 in C major, HobVIIb/1 (c1964)...
6.26   Cello Suite No.1 (c1964): No.1 "Canto primo" Op.72
6.27   No.2 "Fuga"
6.28   No.3 "Lamento"
6.29   No.4 "Canto secondo"
6.30   No.5 "Serenata"
6.31   No.6 "Marcia"
6.32   No.7 "Canto terzo"
6.33   No.8 "Bordone"
6.34   No.9 "Moto perpetuo e Canto quarto"
6.35   Cello Suite No.2 (c1967): No.1 "Declamato: Largo" Op.80
6.36   No.2 "Fuga: Andante"
6.37   No.3 "Scherzo: Allegro molto"
6.38   No.4 "Andante lento"
6.39   No.5 "Ciaccona: Allegro"
6.40   Cello Suite No.3 (c1971, on Russian themes from Tchaikovsky's folk arrs): No.1 "Introduzione" Op.87
6.41   No.2 "Marcia"
6.42   No.3 "Canto"
6.43   No.4 "Barcarola"
6.44   No.5 "Dialogo"
6.45   No.6 "Fuga"
6.46   No.7 "Recitativo"
6.47   No.8 "Moto perpetuo"
6.48   No.9 "Passacaglia"
6.49   "Tema-Sacher" (c1976) ....

Other 1 instr:

6.50   "Elegy" (c1930; va) ....
6.51   "6 Metamorphoses after Ovid" (c1951; ob): No.1 "Pan" Op.49
6.52   No.2 "Phaeton"
6.53   No.3 "Niobe"
6.54   No.4 "Bacchus"
6.55   No.5 "Narcissus"
6.56   No.6 "Arethusa"
6.57   "Nocturnal after J. Dowland" (reflections on: Come, heavy sleep) (c1963; gui; ed Bream): Op.70
             1. "Musingly"

          2. "Very agitated"
          3. "Restless"
          4. "Uneasy"
          5. "March-like"
          6. "Dreaming"
          7. "Gently rocking"
          8. "Passacaglia"
6.58   "Harp Suite," in C major (c1969; harp; ed Ellis): No.1 "Overture" Op.83
6.59   No.2 "Toccata"
6.60   No.3 "Nocturne"
6.61   No.4 "Fugue"
6.62   No.5 "Hymn" (St. Denio)

7. PIANO

7.1   "12 Variations on a theme" (c1931) ....
7.2   "Holiday Diary," suite (c1934): No.1 "Early Morning Bathe" Op.5
7.3   No.2 "Sailing"
7.4   No.3 "Fun-Fair"
7.5   No.4 "Night"
7.6   "Sonatina Romantica" (c1940) ....
7.7   "Night Piece" (Notturno) (c1963) ....
7.8   "5 Waltzes" (c1923–5, recomposed 1969): No.1 "Rather fast and nervous" (c1925) ....
7.9   No.2 "Quick, with wit" (c1924)
7.10   No.3 "Dramatic" (c1925)
7.11   No.4 "Rhythmic; not fast" (c1924)
7.12   No.5 "Variations: quiet and simple" (c1923)
7.13   Cadenza for Mozart: Piano Concerto No.22 in E-flat major, K482 (c1966) ....

        2 Pf:

7.14   "2 Pieces": No.1 "Introduction & Rondo alla burlesca" (c1940) Op.23
7.15   No.2 "Mazurka elegiaca" (c1941)

8. ORGAN

8.1   "Prelude & Fugue on a Theme of Vittoria" (c1946) ....

9. CHORAL WORKS

9.1   "A Hymn to the Virgin" (c1930, r1934, trad 14th cent) ....
9.2   "A Wealden Trio: The Song of the Women": "When ye've got a child'ats whist for want of food," carol
            (c1929, r1967, Ford; fem ch) ....
9.3   "I saw three ships," carol (c1930, r1934, anon; ch; see r1967 as: The sycamore tree) ....
9.4   "Sweet was the Song the Virgin sung," carol (c1931, r1966, trad; ch) ....
9.5   "Three 2-part Songs" (c1932, de la Mare; boys'/fem ch): 1. "The Ride-by-Nights": "Up on their brooms
            the Witches stream" ....
9.6   2. "The Rainbow": "I saw the lovely arch"
9.7   3. "The Ship of Rio": "There was a ship of Rio" (also for 1v & pf)
9.8   "A Boy was Born," choral variations (c1933; ch): Op.3
            . "A Boy was Born" (Theme) (anon 16th cent German)
            1. "Lullay, Jesu" (anon before 1536)
            2. "Herod" (anon 15th cent)
            3. "Jesu, as Thou art our Saviour" (anon 15th cent)
            4. "The Three Kings" (anon 15th cent)
            5. "In the bleak mid-winter" (Rossetti from anon 15th cent) (also see Holst H73/1)
            6. "Noël!" (Finale) (anon 15th cent, Tusser & Quarles)
9.9   "Two 2-part Songs" (c1933; ch & pf): 1. "I lov'd a lass" (Withers) ....
9.10   2. "Lift Boy": "Let me tell you the story" (Graves)
9.11   "Te Deum," in C major (c1934, Liturgy; 1v, ch & org or strings & harp/pf) ....
9.12   "Jubilate Deo," in E-flat major (c1934; ch & org) ....
9.13   "May," song (c1934, anon; unison ch & pf) ....
9.14   "Friday Afternoons" (c1935, from Tom Tiddler's Ground, ed de la Mare; child ch & pf), I: 1. "Begone,
            dull care" (anon) Op.7
9.15   2. "A tragic story": "There lived a sage in days of yore" (Thackeray)
9.16   3. "Cuckoo" (Taylor)
9.17   4. "Ea-oh!" (anon)
9.18   5. "A New Year carol" (anon; arr for fem ch & pf 1971)
9.19   6. "I must be married on Sunday" (Udall)
9.20   II: 7. "There was a man of Newington" (anon)
9.21   8. "Fishing song" (Walton)
9.22   9. "The useful plough" (anon)

9.23	10. "Jazz-man" (Farjeon)
9.24	11. "There was a monkey" (anon)
9.25	12. "Old Abram Brown" (anon)
9.26	"Company of Heaven," cantata (c1937, Roberts; 2 speakers, S, T, ch, timp, org & strings) ....
9.27	"Pacifist March" (c1937, Duncan; unison ch & pf) ....
9.28	"Advance Democracy" (c1938, Swingler; ch) ....
9.29	"Ballad of Heroes" (c1939, Auden & Swingler; 1 high v, ch & orch): Op.14

               1. "Funeral March"
               2. "Scherzo" (Dance of Death)
               3. "Recitative and Choral"
               4. "Epilogue" (Funeral March)

9.30	"A.M.D.G." (Ad Majorem Dei Gloriam), 7 settings (c1937, Hopkins; ch, withdrawn): 1. "Heaven-Haven":
	"I have desired to go" Op.17
9.31	2. "O Deus, ego amo te": "O God I love thee"
9.32	3. "Rosa Mystica"
9.33	4. "The Soldier"
9.34	5. "Prayer"
9.35	6. "God's Grandeur": "The world is charged with the grandeur of God"
9.36	7. "Prayer" I
9.37	"Hymn to St Cecilia" (c1942, Auden; ch): Op.27

               1. "In a garden shady"
               2. "I cannot grow"
               3. "O ear whose creatures cannot wish to fall"
               4. "O cry created as the bow of sin"

9.38	"Rejoice in the Lamb" (Jubilate Agno), festival cantata (c1943, Smart; vv, ch & org): Op.30

               1. "Rejoice in God, O ye Tongues"
               2. "Let Nimrod, the mighty hunter"
               3. "For I will consider my Cat Jeoffry"
               4. "For the Mouse"
               5. "For the flowers are great blessings"
               6. "For I am under the same accusation"
               7. "For He is the spirit"
               8. "For at that time malignity ceases"

9.39	"The Ballad of little Musgrave and lady Barnard" (c1943; m ch & pf) ....
9.40	"Shepherd's Carol": "O lift your little pinkie" (c1944, Auden; S, A, T, B & ch) ....
9.41	"Festival Te Deum" (c1944, Liturgy; ch & org) Op.32
9.42	"Old Joe has gone fishing," round (c1944; ch & pf, from opera: Peter Grimes, Op.33)......................
9.43	"Song of the fishermen" (c1944; ch & pf, from opera: Peter Grimes, Op.33) ....
9.44	"Deus in adjutorium meum," motet (c1945; ch, from incid music: This Way to the Tomb) ....
9.45	"Saint Nicolas," cantata (c1948, Crozier; T, choruses & strings): Op.42

               1. "Introduction: Our eyes are blinded by the holiness you bear"
               2. "The Birth of Nicolas"
               3. "Nicolas devotes himself to God"
               4. "He journeys to Palestine"
               5. "Nicolas comes to Myra and is chosen Bishop"
               6. "Nicolas from prison"
               7. "Nicolas and the pickled boys"
               8. "His Piety and Marvellous Works"
               9. "The Death of Nicolas"

9.46	"Spring Symphony" (c1949; S, A, T, boys' ch, ch & orch): Op.44

          I: . "Introduction"
               . "Shine out" (anon 16th cent)
               . "The merry cuckoo" (Spenser)
               . "Spring, the sweet spring" (Nashe)
               . "The driving boy" (Peele & Clare)
          II: . "The Morning Star" (Milton)
               . "Welcome maids of honour" (Herrick)
               . "Waters above" (Vaugham)
          III: . "Out on the lawn I lie in bed" (Auden)
               . "When will my May come" (Barnefield)
               . "Fair and fair" (Peele)
               . "Sound the flute" (from Blake's Songs of Innocence)
          IV: . "Finale"
               . "London, to thee I do present"
               . "Soomer is icoomen in" (Beaumont, Fletcher & anon)

9.47	"Wedding Anthem": "Amo ergo sum" (c1949, Duncan; S, T, ch & org) Op.46
9.48	"5 Flower Songs" (c1950; ch): 1. "To Daffodils" (Herrick) Op.47
9.49	2. "The succession of the four sweet months" (Herrick)
9.50	3. "Marsh Flowers": "Here the strong mallow strikes her slimy root" (Crabbe)
9.51	4. "The Evening Primrose": "When once the sun sinks in the west" (Clare)
9.52	5. "Ballad of Green Broom" (anon)
9.53	"6 Choral Dances" (ch, from opera: Gloriana, Op.53): 1. "Time" Op.53
9.54	2. "Concord"
9.55	3. "Time and concord"
9.56	4. "Country girls"

10.7	2. "Messalina" (anon)
10.8	3. "Dance of Death" (Hawking for the partridge) (Ravenscroft)
10.9	. "Epilogue": "Our hunting fathers" (Auden)
10.10	. "Funeral march"
10.11	"Les Illuminations," cycle (c1939, Rimbaud; S/T & strings): 1. "Fanfare" Op.18
10.12	2. "Villes"
10.13	3a. "Phrase"
10.14	3b. "Antique"
10.15	4. "Royauté"
10.16	5. "Marine"
10.17	6. "Interlude"
10.18	7. "Being beauteous"
10.19	8. "Parade"
10.20	9. "Départ"
10.21	"A Ceremony of Carols" (c1942; 1 high v & harp): 1. "Procession": "Hodie Christus natus est" Op.28
10.22	2. "Wolcum Yole!": "Wolcum be thou hevenè king" (anon)
10.23	3. "There is no rose": "There is no rose of such vertu" (anon)
10.24	4a. "That yongë child": "That yongë child when it gan weep" (anon)
10.25	4b. "Balulalow": "O my deare hert, young Jesu sweit" (J. & R. Wedderburn)
10.26	5. "As dew in Aprille": "I sing of a maiden that is makèles" (anon)
10.27	6. "This little Babe": "This little Babe so few days old" (Southwell)
10.28	7. "Interlude" (harp solo)
10.29	8. "In freezing winter night": "Behold, a silly tender babe" (Southwell)
10.30	9. "Spring Carol": "Pleasure it is to hear iwis the Birdès sing" (Cornish)
10.31	10. "Deo Gracias": "Deo gracias! Deo gracias! Adam lay ibounden" (anon)
10.32	11. "Recessional": "Hodie Christus natus est"
10.33	"Serenade" (c1943; T, hn & strings): Op.31
	. "Prologue"
	1. "Pastoral": "The day's grown old" (Cotton)
	2. "Nocturne": "The splendour falls" (from Tennyson's The Princess) (also see Holst Op.20a, H80, Delius RTiv/6, Sullivan's opera: Princess Ida & Vaughan Williams' song of 1905)
	3. "Elegy": "O Rose, thou art sick!" (Blake)
	4. "Dirge": "This ae nighte" (anon 15th cent)
	5. "Hymn": "Queen and huntress, chaste and fair" (Jonson)
	6. "Sonnet": "O soft embalmer of the still midnight" (Keats) (also see Castelnuovo-Tedesco's work for unacc ch: To sleep)
	. "Epilogue"
10.34	*"Now sleeps the crimson petal" (c1943, Tennyson, discarded from: Serenade, Op.31; ed Matthews) ....*
10.35	"3 Songs" (c1944, Duncan, from incid music: This Way to theTomb): 1. "Evening" ....
10.36	2. "Morning"
10.37	3. "Night"
10.38	"3 Arias" (from opera: Peter Grimes, Op.33): 1. "Peter's dreams" (T & pf/orch) ....
10.39	2. "Embroidery aria" (S & pf/orch)
10.40	3. "Church scene" (Ellen's Aria) (S & pf/orch)
10.41	"3 Arias" (from opera: The Rape of Lucretia, Op.37): 1. "Flower song" (A & pf/orch) ....
10.42	2. "The ride" (T & pf/orch)
10.43	3. "Slumber song" (mS & pf/orch)
10.44	"Nocturne" (c1958; T, 7 obbl insts & strings): Op.60
	1. "On a poet's lips I slept" (Shelley)
	2. "Below the thunders of the upper deep" (Tennyson)
	3. "Encinctured with a twive of leaves" (Coleridge)
	4. "Midnight's bell goes ting" (Middleton)
	5. "When that night on my bed I lay" (Wordsworth)
	6. "She sleeps on soft, last breaths" (Owen)
	7. "What is more gentle than a wind in summer?" (Keats)
	8. "When most I wink, then do mine eyes best see" (Shakespeare's Sonnet 43)
10.45	"Bottom's dream" (c1960; B/Bar & pf/orch, from opera: A Midsummer Night's Dream, Op.64) ....
10.46	"Phaedra," dramatic cantata (c1975, Racine transl Lowell; mS, strings, perc, vc & hpd) Op.93

11. SONGS (w/ pf)

11.1	"3 Early Songs" (c1922–6, r1968, p1985): 1. "Beware" (Longfellow after German).....................................
11.2	2. "O that I had ne'er been married" (Burns)
11.3	3. "Epitaph: The Clerk" (Asquith)
11.4	"The Birds": "When Jesus Christ was four years old" (c1929, r1934, Belloc) ....
11.5	"The Ship of Rio" (c1963, de la Mare; orig for boys'/fem ch 1932)...
11.6	"Tit for Tat," cycle (c1928–31, r1968, de la Mare): 1. "A Song of Enchantment": "A song of enchantment I sang me there" (c1929) ....
11.7	2. "Autumn": "There is a wind where the rose was" (c1931)
11.8	3. "Silver": "Slowly, silently, now the moon" (c1928)
11.9	4. "Vigil": "Dark is the night" (c1930)
11.10	5. "Tit for Tat": "Have you been catching of fish, Tom Noddy?" (c1928)
11.11	"4 Cabaret Songs for Hedli Anderson" (c1937, Auden): 1. "O Tell Me the Truth About Love": "Some say" ..
11.12	2. "Funeral Blues": "Stop all the clocks, cut off the telephone" (also in incid music: The Ascent of F6)

11.13	3. "Johnny": "O the valley in the summer"
11.14	4. "Calypso": "Driver, drive faster"
11.15	"On this Island," cycle (c1937, Auden; also Fr transl Pourchet): 1. "Let the florid music praise!" Op.11
11.16	2. "Now the leaves are falling fast"
11.17	3. "Seascape": "Look, stranger"
11.18	4. "Nocturne": "Now through night's caressing grip"
11.19	5. "As it is, plenty"
11.20	"Fish in the unruffled lakes" (c1937, Auden) ....
11.21	"2 Ballads" (c1937; 2vv & pf): 1. "Mother comfort" (Slater) ....
11.22	2. "Underneath the abject willow" (Auden)
11.23	"7 Sonnets of Michelangelo" (c1940): 1. "Si come nella penna" (XVI) Op.22
11.24	2. "Ah che più debb'io mai l'intensa voglia" (XXXI)
11.25	3. "Veggio co' bei vostri occhi" (XXX)
11.26	4. "Tu sa' ch'io so, signior mie" (LV)
11.27	5. "Rendete agli occhi miei" (XXXVIII)
11.28	6. "S'un casto amor, s'una pietà superna" (XXXII)
11.29	7. "Spirto ben nato, in cui si specchia e vede" (XXIV)
11.30	"Holy Sonnets of John Donne," cycle (c1945): 1. "Oh my blacke Soule" Op.35
11.31	2. "Batter my heart"
11.32	3. "O might those sighes and teares"
11.33	4. "Oh, to vex me"
11.34	5. "What if this present"
11.35	6. "Since she whom I loved"
11.36	7. "At the round earth's imagined corners"
11.37	8. "Thou hast made me"
11.38	9. "Death, be not proud"
11.39	"Canticle I: My Beloved Is Mine" (c1947, Quarles; S/T & pf, in memory of Dick Sheppard) Op.40
11.40	"A Charm of Lullabies," cycle (c1947; mS & pf): 1. "A Cradle Song": "Sleep beauty bright" (Blake).... Op.41
11.41	2. "The Highland Balou": "Hee-balou, my sweet" (Burns) (also see Schumann Op.25/14)
11.42	3. "Sephestia's Lullaby" (Greene)
11.43	4. "A Charm" (Randolph)
11.44	5. "The Nurse's Song" (Philip)
11.45	"Canticle II: Abraham and Isaac" (c1952, from: Chester miracle play; A, T & pf) Op.51
11.46	"Winter Words," cycle (c1953, Hardy; T & pf): 1. "At Day-Close in November": "The ten hours' light" Op.52
11.47	2. "Midnight on the Great Western": "In the third-class seat sat the journeying boy"
11.48	3. "Wagtail and Baby": "A baby watched a ford, whereto a wagtail came for drinking"
11.49	4. "The Little Old Table": "Creak, little wood thing, creak"
11.50	5. "The Choirmaster's Burial": "He often would ask us that, when he died"
11.51	6. "Proud Songsters": "The thrushes sing as the sun is going"
11.52	7. "At the Railway Station, Upway": "There is not much that I can do"
11.53	8. "Before Life and After": "A time there was—as one may guess"
11.54	"Canticle III: Still Falls the Rain" (c1954, Sitwell; T, hn & pf) Op.55
11.55	"Songs from the Chinese," cycle (c1957, transl Waley; S/T & gui): 1. "The Big Chariot" Op.58
11.56	2. "The Old Lute"
11.57	3. "The Autumn Wind"
11.58	4. "The Herd-boy"
11.59	5. "Depression"
11.60	6. "Dance Song"
11.61	"6 Hölderlin Fragments," cycle (c1958; T & pf): 1. "Menschenbeifall" (The Applause of Men) Op.61
11.62	2. "Die Heimat" (Home)
11.63	3. "Sokrates und Alcibiades"
11.64	4. "Die Jugend" (Youth)
11.65	5. "Hälfte des Lebens" (The Middle of Life)
11.66	6. "Die Linien des Lebens" (Lines of Life)
11.67	"Songs & Proverbs of W. Blake," cycle (c1965): 1. "London": "I wander thro' each charter'd street" (Proverb 1: The pride of the peacock is the glory of God) (also see Vaughan Williams' 4. of: 10 Blake Songs)... Op.74
11.68	2. "The Chimney-sweeper": "A little black thing among the snow" (Proverb 2: Prisons are built with stones of Law, Brothels with bricks of Religion)
11.69	3. "A Poison Tree": "I was angry with my friend" (Proverb 3: The bird a nest, the spider a web, man friendship)
11.70	4. "The Tyger": "Tyger Tyger, burning bright" (Proverb 4: Think in the morning, Act in the noon, Eat in the evening, Sleep in the night)
11.71	5. "The Fly" (Proverb 5: The tygers of wrath are wiser than the horses of instruction)
11.72	6. "Ah, Sun-flower! Weary of Time" (Proverb 6: The hours of folly are measur'd by the clock, but of wisdom: no clock can measure)
11.73	7. "Every Night and Every Morn" (Proverb 7: To see a world)
11.74	"The Poet's Echo," cycle (c1965, 6 poems of Pushkin set in Russian): 1. "Echo" Op.76
11.75	2. "My heart ..."
11.76	3. "Angel"
11.77	4. "The nightingale and the rose"
11.78	5. "Epigram"
11.79	6. "Lines written during a sleepless night"
11.80	"Who are these Children?," cycle (c1969, lyrics, rhymes & riddles W. Soutar): 1. "A Riddle (The Earth)": "There's pairt o' it young" Op.84

11.81   2. "A Laddie's Sang": "O! it's owre the braes abûne our toun"
11.82   3. "Nightmare": "The tree stood flowering in a dream"
11.83   4. "Black Day": "A skelp frae his teacher"
11.84   5. "Bed-time": "Cuddle-down, my bairnie"
11.85   6. "Slaughter": "Within the violence of the storm"
11.86   7. "A Riddle (The Child You Were)": "It was your faither and mither"
11.87   8. "The Larky Lad": "The larky lad frae the pantry"
11.88   9. "Who Are These Children": "With easy hands upon the rain"
11.89   10. "Supper": "Steepies for the bairnie"
11.90   11. "The Children"
11.91   12. "The Auld Aik": "The auld aik's doun"
11.92   "Canticle IV: The Journey of the Magi": "A cold coming we had of it" (c1971, Eliot; A, T, Bar & pf) Op.86
11.93   "Canticle V: The Death of St Narcissus" (c1974, Eliot; T & harp) Op.89
11.94   "A Birthday Hansel," cycle (c1975, Burns; T & harp): 1. "Birthday Song": "Health to the Maxwel's
         veteran Chief!" Op.92
11.95   2. "My Early Walk": "A rosebud by my early walk"
11.96   3. "Wee Eillie Gray": "Wee Willie Gray, an' his leather wallet"
11.97   4. "My Hoggie": "What will I do gin my Hoggie die"
11.98   5. "Afton Water": "Flow gently, sweet Afton, among thy green braes"
11.99   6. "The Winter": "The winter it is past, and the summer's come at last"
11.100   7. "Leezie Lindsay": "Will ye go to the Highlands Leezie Lindsay"

12. FOLKSONG ARRANGEMENTS

12.1   Vol.I "British Isles" (p1943; 1v & pf): 1. "The Sally Gardens" (orchd; also for unison ch & pf) ....
12.2   2. "Little Sir Williams"
12.3   3. "Bonny Earl o' Moray" (orchd)
12.4   4. "O can ye sew cushions?" (orchd)
12.5   5. "The trees they grow so high"
12.6   6. "The ash grove"
12.7   7. "Oliver Cromwell" (orchd; also for unison ch & pf)
12.8   Vol.II "France" (p1946; 1v & pf): 1. "La Noël passée" (orchd) ....
12.9   2. "Voici le printemps"
12.10   3. "Fileuse" (orchd)
12.11   4. "Le roi s'en va-t-en chasse" (orchd)
12.12   5. "La belle est au jardin d'amour" (orchd)
12.13   6. "Il est quelqu'un sur terre"
12.14   7. "Eho! Eho!" (orchd)
12.15   8. "Quand j'étais chez mon père" (orchd)
12.16   Vol.III "British Isles" (p1947;1v & pf): 1. "The plough boy" (melody Shield; orchd) ....
12.17   2. "There's none to soothe"
12.18   3. "Sweet Polly Oliver"
12.19   4. "The miller of Dee"
12.20   5. "The foggy, foggy dew"
12.21   6. "O Waly, Waly" (orchd)
12.22   7. "Come you not from Newcastle?" (orchd)
12.23   Vol.IV "Moore's Irish Melodies" (p1960; 1v & pf): 1. "Avenging and bright" ....
12.24   2. "Sail on, sail on"
12.25   3. "How sweet the answer"
12.26   4. "The minstrel boy"
12.27   5. "At the mid hour of night"
12.28   6. "Rich and rare"
12.29   7. "Dear harp of my country"
12.30   8. "Oft in the stilly night"
12.31   9. "The last rose of summer"
12.32   10. "O the sight entrancing"
12.33   Vol.V "British Isles" (p1961; 1v & pf): 1. "The brisk young widow" ....
12.34   2. "Sally in our alley"
12.35   3. "The Lincolnshire poacher"
12.36   4. "Early one morning"
12.37   5. "Ca' the yowes" (also see Vaughan Williams: Folksong & Carol Arrs & Haydn HobXXXIa/221)
12.38   Vol.VI "England" (S/T & gui): 1. "I will give my love an apple" ....
12.39   2. "Sailor-boy"
12.40   3. "Master Kilby"
12.41   4. "The soldier and the sailor"
12.42   5. "Bonny at morn"
12.43   6. "The shooting of his dear"
12.44   "The Holly and the Ivy" (c1957; ch) ....
12.45   "King Herod and the Cock" (c1965; unison ch & pf) ....
12.46   "8 British folksongs" (c1976; 1v & harp): 1. "Lord! I married me a wife" ....
12.47   2. "She's like the swallow"
12.48   3. "Lemady"
12.49   4. "Bonny at morn"
12.50   5. "I was lonely and forlorn"

12.51	6. "David of the White Rock"
12.52	7. "The false knight upon the road"
12.53	8. "Bird scarer's song"

13. ARRANGEMENTS OF WORKS OF OTHERS

Purcell realizations from Orpheus Britannicus (collab Pears):

13.1	"5 Songs" (1v & pf): 1. "I attempt from love's sickness to fly" ....
13.2	2. "I take no pleasure"
13.3	3. "Hark the ech'ing airl"
13.4	4. "Take not a woman's anger ill"
13.5	5. "How blest are shepherds"
13.6	"Suite of Songs" (arr1947; S/T & orch): 1. "Let sullen discord smile" (Tate) ....
13.7	2. "Why should men quarrel?" (Dryden & Howard)
13.8	3. "So when the glittering Queen of Night" (D'Urfey)
13.9	4. "Thou tun'st this world" (Brady)
13.10	5a. " 'Tis Holiday" (Betterton)
13.11	5b. "Sound, Fame thy brazen trumpet" (Betterton)
13.12	"7 Songs" (p1947; 1v & pf): 1. "Fairest isle" ....
13.13	2. "If music be the food of love" (3rd vers)
13.14	3. "Turn then thine eyes"
13.15	4. "Music for a while"
13.16	5. "Pious Celinda"
13.17	6. "I'll sail upon the Dog-Star"
13.18	7. "On the brow of Richmond Hill"
13.19	"6 Songs" (p1948; 1v & pf): 1. "Mad Bess" ....
13.20	2. "If music be the food of love" (1st vers)
13.21	3. "There's not a swain of the plain"
13.22	4. "Not all my torments"
13.23	5. "Man is for the woman made" (pubd separately)
13.24	6. "Sweeter than roses"
13.25	"6 Duets" (2vv & pf): 1. "Sound the trumpet" ....
13.26	2. "I spy Celia"
13.27	3. "Lost is my quiet"
13.28	4. "What can we poor females do?"
13.29	5. "No, no, resistance is but vain"
13.30	6. "Shepherd, leave decoying"
13.31	"3 Songs" (S/T & orch): 1. "Hark the ech'ing airl!" ....
13.32	2. "Not all my torments"
13.33	3. "Take not a woman's anger ill"

Purcell realizations from Harmonia sacra (collab Pears):

13.34	"The Blessed Virgin's Expostulation" (p1947; S/T & pf) ....
13.35	"Job's Curse" (p1950; S/T & pf) ....
13.36	"Saul and the Witch at Endor" (S, T, B & pf) ....
13.37	"3 Divine Hymns" (1v & pf): 1. "We sing to Him" ....
13.38	2. "Evening hymn"
13.39	3. "Lord, what is man?"
13.40	"2 Divine Hymns and Alleluja" (S/T & pf): 1. "A morning hymn" ....
13.41	2. "Alleluia"
13.42	3. "In the black dismal dungeon of despair"

Other Purcell realizations:

13.43	"The Queen's Epicedium," elegy on the death of Queen Mary (S/T & pf, collab Pears) ....
13.44	"Dido and Aeneas," 3 act opera (p1951, collab Holst) ....
13.45	"The Fairy Queen," concert version (p1967, collab Holst, Ledger & Pears) ....
13.46	"When night her purple veil had softly spread" (Bar, 2vn & cont) ....
13.47	"Chacony," in G minor (str qt/strings) ....
13.48	"The Golden Sonata" (2vn, vc & pf) ....

Other arrs:

13.49	"The National Anthem" (p1961; ch & orch) ....
13.50	Bach, J. S.: "5 Spiritual Songs" (p1969; 1v & pf, w/Pears): 1. "Gedenke dich, mein Geist, zurücke" ....
13.51	2. "Komm, Seelen, dieser Tag"
13.52	3. "Liebster Herr Jesu"
13.53	4. "Komm, süsser Tod"
13.54	5. "Bist du bei mir"
13.55	"God Save the Queen," national anthem (p1971; orch) ....
13.56	"What the wild flowers tell me" (orch red of 2nd movt of Mahler: Sym No.3 in D minor 1941) ....

* * * * *

1. STAGE WORKS (operas)

1.1	"Scherz, List und Rache," 1 act comic opera (p1858, Bischoff after Goethe)	Op.1
1.2	"Die Loreley," 4 act romantic opera (p1863, Geibel):	Op.16
	pubd separately: . "Lied der Lenore": "Siehst du ihn glühen"	
1.3	"Hermione," 4 acts (p1872, Hopffer after Shakespeare's The Winter's Tale)	Op.40

2. SYMPHONIES

2.1	Symphony No.1 in E-flat major (p1870)	Op.28
2.2	Symphony No.2 in F minor (p1870)	Op.36
2.3	Symphony No.3 in E major (p1887)	Op.51

3. OTHER ORCHESTRAL WORKS

3.1	"Suite on Russian Folk Melodies" (Russian Suite) (p1905)	Op.79b
3.2	"Suite No.2" (Nordland Suite) (c1906, material derived from: Lieder und Tänze, Op.79)	
3.3	"Serenade on Swedish Melodies" (c1916; strings, reworking of: Suite No.2)	Op.89

4. CONCERTOS, SOLO INSTR & ORCH

Vn & orch:

4.1	Violin Concerto No.1 in G minor (c1866, sketches from 1857)	Op.26
4.2	"Romanze," in A minor (p1874)	Op.42
4.3	Violin Concerto No.2 in D minor (p1878)	Op.44
4.4	"Scottish Fantasy" (p1880, ded to Sarasate)	Op.46
4.5	"Adagio appassionato," in C-sharp minor (p1891; vn & orch/pf)	Op.57
4.6	Violin Concerto No.3 in D minor (p1891, ded to Joachim)	Op.58
4.7	"In Memoriam" (Adagio) (p1893)	Op.65
4.8	"Serenade," in A minor (p1900)	Op.75
4.9	"Konzertstück" (Allegro appassionato & Adagio), in F-sharp minor (p1911; vn & orch/pf)	Op.84

Va & orch:

4.10	"Romanze," in F major (p1911)	Op.85

Vc & orch:

4.11	"Kol Nidrei—Adagio on Hebrew melodies" (p1881; w/ harp)	Op.47
4.12	"Canzone," in B major (p1891; vc & orch/pf)	Op.55
4.13	"Adagio on Celtic Melodies" (p1891)	Op.56
4.14	"Ave Maria" (p1892, on a theme from cantata: Das Feuerkreuz, Op.52)	Op.61

Other:

4.15	Clarinet & Viola Concerto in E minor (c1911; cl, va & orch; vers for 2pf, Op.88a)	Op.88

5. STRING QUARTETS

5.1	String Quartet No.1 in C minor (p1859)	Op.9
5.2	String Quartet No.2 in E major (p1860)	Op.10

6. OTHER CHAMBER MUSIC

3 or more insts:

6.1	Septet in E-flat major (c1849–50)	
6.2	Piano Trio in C minor (p1858)	Op.5
6.3	"8 Trio Pieces" (p1910; cl, va/vc & pf or pf trio): No.1 in A minor	Op.83
6.4	No.2 in B minor	
6.5	No.3 in C-sharp minor	
6.6	No.4 in D minor	
6.7	No.5 in F minor	
6.8	No.6 in G minor	
6.9	No.7 in B major	
6.10	No.8 in E-flat minor	
6.11	"Song of Spring" (2vn, pf & harm ad lib)	

Vn & pf:

6.12   "Swedish Dances" (p1892; orchd; arr for pf 1892): No.1 in D minor Op.63
6.13   No.2 in D major
6.14   No.3 in D minor
6.15   No.4 in B-flat major
6.16   No.5 in G minor
6.17   No.6 in E-flat major
6.18   No.7 in B-flat major
6.19   No.8 in F minor
6.20   No.9 in F major
6.21   No.10 in D major
6.22   No.11 in B minor
6.23   No.12 in G major
6.24   No.13 in A minor
6.25   No.14 in A minor
6.26   No.15 in D minor
6.27   9 "Lieder und Tänze" (p1903, on popular airs), I: No.1 "Prisoner's Song" (Russian) Op.79
6.28   No.2 "Muzhchik's Song" (Russian)
6.29   No.3 "Dance," in B-flat major (Swedish)
6.30   No.4 "Funeral March" (Russian)
6.31   No.5 "Song and Dance" (Russian)
6.32   II: No.6 "Song," in E-flat major (Swedish)
6.33   No.7 "Dance," in G minor (Swedish)
6.34   No.8 "Song," in E minor (Little Russian)
6.35   No.9 "Dance," in D minor (Russian)

Vc & pf:

6.36   "4 Stücke" (p1897): No.1 "Aria" (on melody c by his son Max Felix; orchd Harmann) Op.70
6.37   No.2 "Finnländisch. Melodie"
6.38   No.3 "Schwedisch. Tanz"
6.39   No.4 "Schottisch. Melodie"

7. PIANO

7.1   "6 Pieces" (p ?1861): No.1 in B-flat major Op.12
7.2   No.2 in G minor
7.3   No.3 "Impromptu," in G major
7.4   No.4 in D minor
7.5   No.5 "Waltz," in F-sharp major
7.6   No.6 in E major
7.7   "2 Pieces" (p ?1862): No.1 "Romanze" Op.14
7.8   No.2 "Phantasiestück"

Pf duet:

7.9   "Capriccio" (p ?1858) Op.2

2 Pf:

7.10   "Fantasia," in D minor (p1861) Op.11
7.11   Version of: Clarinet & Viola Concerto in E minor, Op.88 .... Op.88a

8. SACRED CHORAL

8.1   "Jubilate—Amen" (c1856, Moore transl Freiligrath; S, ch & orch/pf) Op.3
8.2   "Die Flucht der heiligen Familie" (p ?1864, Eichendorff; ch & orch) Op.20
8.3   "Song of the 3 Holy Kings" (p ?1864, Schenkendorf; 3vv, m ch & orch) Op.21
8.4   "Rorate coeli" (p1870, Simrock; ch, orch & org) Op.29
8.5   "Die Flucht nach Ägypten" (The Flight into Egypt) (p1870, Reinick; S, fem ch & orch) Op.31/1
8.6   "Morgenstunde" (p1870, Lingg; S, fem ch & orch) Op.31/2
8.7   "Messensätze: Kyrie, Sanctus & Agnus Dei" (p1870; 2S, ch, orch & org ad lib) Op.35
8.8   "Gruss an die heilige Nacht!" (Salute to Christmas) (p1892, Prutz; A, ch, orch & org) Op.62
8.9   "Hymne" (p1893, Bible; vv, ch, orch & org ad lib) Op.64
8.10   "Moses," oratorio (p1895, Spitta; S, T, B, ch & orch w/ harp) Op.67
8.11   "Sei getreu bis in den Tod" (p1896, Bible; ch & org) Op.69
8.12   "Easter Cantata" (p1908, after Mörike & Geibel; S, ch, orch & org) Op.81
8.13   "Das Wessobrunner Gebet" (p1910, 8th cent text; ch, orch & org, arr from secular choral Op.19) Op.82
8.14   6 "Christkindlieder" (p ?1917, M. Bruch; S, A, fem ch & pf): 1. "O holder Herr, O Jesulein" Op.92
8.15   2. "Christi Geburt"
8.16   3. "Zwei Seelen begegnen sich zur Christnacht im Walde"
8.17   4. "Auf einem goldbraunen Reh"

8.18   5. "Gebet"
8.19   6. "Christkinds Garten"

9. SECULAR CHORAL

9.1   "Die Birken und die Erlen" (c1857, from Pfarrius: Waldlieder; S, ch & orch, w/ solo vn in Finale) Op.8
9.2   4 "Männerchöre" (p ca1863, Lingg; ch): 1. "Römischer Triumphgesang" (m ch & orch) Op.19
9.3   2. "Das Wessobrunner Gebet" (m ch & brass)
9.4   3. "Lied der Städte" (m ch & brass)
9.5   4. "Scotland's Tears" (m ch & brass)
9.6   "5 Lieder" (ch, based on folksongs) Op.22
9.7   "Frithjof: Szenen aus der Frithjof-Sage" (p1864, Tegnèr; S, Bar, m ch & orch): Op.23
        1. "Frithjofs Heimfahrt"
        2. "Ingeborgs Brautzug zu König Ring"
        3. "Frithjofs Rache. Tempelbrand. Fluch"
        4. "Frithjofs Abschied von Nordland": "Sonne so schön steigt über Höh'n"
        5. "Ingeborgs Klage": "Herbst ist es nun!"
        6. "Frithjof auf der See"
9.8   "Schön Ellen": "Nun gnade dir Gott," cantata (p1867, Geibel; S, Bar, ch & orch) Op.24
9.9   "Salamis: Siegesgesang der Griechen": "Schmücket die Schiffe" (p ?1868, Lingg; vv, m ch & orch).. Op.25
9.10   "Frithjof auf seines Vaters Grabhügel" (p1870, Tegnèr; Bar, fem ch & orch) Op.27
9.11   "Normannenzug": "Da Abend kommt" (p1870, Scheffel; Bar, unison m vv & orch) Op.32
9.12   "Römische Leichenfeier": "Traurig, mit gesenkten Flügeln" (p1870, Lingg; ch & orch) Op.34
9.13   "Das Lied vom deutschen Kaiser": "Durch tiefe Nacht ein Brausen zieht" (p1871, Geibel; ch & orch) Op.37
9.14   "5 Lieder" (p ?1871; ch): 1. "Waldpsalm": "Auf, zu psalliren in frohem Choral" (Scheffel) Op.38
9.15   2. "Der Wald von Traquair": "Im schönen Walde von Traquair" (Scottish folksong)
9.16   3. "Tannhäuser": "Frau Venus, Frau Venus, o lass mich geh'n geschwinde" (Lingg)
9.17   4. "Rheinsage": "Am Rhein, am grünen Rheine" (Geibel)
9.18   5. "Feierliches Tafellied": "Wohl perlet im Glase" (Schiller)
9.19   "Dithyrambe": "Nimmer, das glaubt mir, erscheinen die Götter" (p ?1871, Schiller; T, ch & orch) Op.39
9.20   "Odysseus: Szenen aus der Odyssee" (p1872, Graff; vv, ch & orch) Op.41
9.21   "Arminius," oratorio (c1877, Küppers; vv, ch & orch) Op.43
9.22   "Das Lied von der Glocke" (c1879, Schiller; 4vv, ch, orch & org) Op.45
9.23   4 "Männerchöre" (p1881; m ch; arr for d ch): 1. "Morgenständchen": "In den Wipfeln frische Lüfte"... Op.48
9.24   2. "Trinklied": "Wir sind nicht mehr am ersten Glas"
9.25   3. "Friede den Schlummernden" (Peace to the slumberers!) (Moore transl Freiligrath)
9.26   4. "Media Vita" (The Battle Song of the Monks): "Ach, unser Leben ist nur halbes Leben":
        . "The Monks of Reichenau" (Tenor ch)
        . "The Monks of St. Gallen" (Bass ch)
        . "Conclusion," in D major (Tenor ch & Bass ch)
9.27   "Achilleus" (c1885, Bulthaupt; vv, ch & orch) Op.50
9.28   "3 Hebrew Songs" (p1888, Nathan after Byron; ch, orch & org): 1. "She walks in beauty, like the night" ......
9.29   2. "On Jordan's banks the Arabs' camels stray"
9.30   3. "O weep for those that wept by Babel's stream"
9.31   "Das Feuerkreuz" (The Cross of Fire), cantata (p1889, Bulthaupt after Scott; vv, ch & orch) Op.52
9.32   "Thermopylae," 2 choruses (m ch & orch): 1. "To the Fallen at Thermopylae" Op.53
9.33   2. "Battle Song" (Tyrtaeus of Athens transl Geibel)
9.34   "9 Songs" (p1892, various poets; ch) Op.60
9.35   "Leonidas" (p1894, Bulthaupt; Bar, m ch & orch) Op.66
9.36   "Neue Männerchöre" (p1896; m ch & orch): 1. "Song of the Pirates" (from Kruse's The Countess) Op.68
9.37   2. "Psalm 23"
9.38   3. "Kriegsgesang" (from Goethe's Des Epimenides Erwachen)
9.39   "7 Choral Songs" (p1897, trad, Scheffel; ch): 1. "Summer delights" Op.71
9.40   2. "The happy musician"
9.41   3. "To Music"
9.42   4. "A parcel of fools"
9.43   5. "The sound of Music"
9.44   6. "Spring come again"
9.45   7. "Morning song"
9.46   "In der Nacht" (p1897, Tersteegen; m ch) Op.72
9.47   "Gustav Adolf," oratorio (p1898, Hackenberg; vv, ch & orch) Op.73
9.48   "Herzog Moritz" (p1899, Storch; m ch) Op.74
9.49   "Der letzte Abschied des Volkes" (p1901, Grotthus; m ch, orch & org) Op.76
9.50   "Damajanti" (p1903, anon Indian poem; S, ch & orch) Op.78
9.51   "6 Volkslieder" (p ?1908, Welsh & Scottish; m ch) ....
9.52   "6 Songs" (p1911, M. Bruch—his daughter, Moore; ch, orch & org): 1. "Ackeley" (M. Bruch) Op.86
9.53   2. "Kleine Maria" (M. Bruch)
9.54   3. "German Spring" (M. Bruch)
9.55   4. "Go, where fame beckons you" (Irish, from Moore)
9.56   5. "In the Mosel valley" (M. Bruch)
9.57   6. "Far across the sea" (from Moore)
9.58   "Die Macht des Gesanges" (p1912, Schiller; Bar, ch, orch & org) Op.87
9.59   "Heldenfeier" (p ?1915, M. Bruch; ch, orch & org) Op.89
9.60   "5 Lieder" (ch): 1. "Im Himmelreich" (Old German) Op.90

9.61	2. "The gardener as a lancer"	
9.62	3. "Lullaby in Chiemgau" (Wartime 1914)	
9.63	4. "On the grave of a German rifleman"	
9.64	5. "Evening calls" (Vorberg)	
9.65	"Die Stimme der Mutter Erde" (p ?1916, anon Polish; ch, orch & org)	Op.91
9.66	"Trauerfeier für Mignon" (p1919, Goethe; vv, d ch, orch & org)	Op.93

10. VOICE & ORCHESTRA

10.1	"Die Priesterin der Isis in Rom" (A & orch)	Op.30
10.2	"Szene der Marfa" (p1906, from Schiller's Demetrius; mS & orch)	Op.80

11. SONGS (w/ pf)

11.1	"6 Songs" (p1859, various poets)	Op.7
11.2	"Hymnus": "Dem, der von allen Nächten der Stern" (p1862, Kolte; S & pf)	Op.13
11.3	"4 Lieder" (p ?1862): 1. "Lausche, lausche!": "War's ein Säuseln aus der Höh' " (Bone)	Op.15
11.4	2. "Gott!": "Über die Bäume möcht' ich mich schwingen" (Bone)	
11.5	3. "Im tiefen Thale" (Bone)	
11.6	4. "Goldne Brücken" (Geibel)	
11.7	"10 Lieder," 3 books (p ?1863), I. "3 geistliche Lieder aus dem Spanischen" (Geibel): 1. "An die heilige Jungfrau"	Op.17
11.8	2. "Der heilige Joseph singt"	
11.9	3. "An den Jesusknaben"	
11.10	II. "4 weltliche Lieder aus dem Spanischen und Italienischen" (Geibel & Heyse): 1. "Von den Rosen komm' ich": "An den Ufern jenes Wassers"	
11.11	2. "Carmosenella": "Ach, wie schön ist Carmosenella"	
11.12	3. "Verlassen": "Hast einsam mich verlassen"	
11.13	4. "Parte la nave": "Bald stösst vom Lande"	
11.14	III. "3 Lieder gedichtet von Hermann Lingg": 1. "Tannhäuser": "Frau Venus, Frau Venus"	
11.15	2. "Der junge Invalide": "Leb wohl du guter Reiterdienst"	
11.16	3. "Klosterlied": "Blumen an den Wegen"	
11.17	"4 Songs" (p ?1863, Mainz; Bar & pf): 1. "Volker's Nachtgesang" (Geibel)	Op.18
11.18	2. "Der Landsknecht" (Geibel)	
11.19	3. "An die heilige Jungfrau" (Spanish folksong transl Heyse)	
11.20	4. "Provençalisches Liebeslied" (Troubadour's Song)	
11.21	"12 Scottish Folksongs" (p ?1863; text in Ger & Eng): 1. "Marion": "Willst du geh'n zu den Schafen?"	
11.22	2. "Johnie und Jenny": "Johnie sprach zu Jenny: Jenny willst du mich?"	
11.23	3. "Mary's Traum": "Der Mond erglänzt' in stiller Pracht"	
11.24	4. "Der Hochzeittag": "Im Bette lag Collin des Schlafes beraubt"	
11.25	5. "Lord Gregory": "O öffne die Thür"	
11.26	6. "O, sah'st du den Vater"	
11.27	7. "Der alte Rob Morris"	
11.28	8. "Hey tutti taiti": "Auf zu Kampf und Siege"	
11.29	9. "Bei den rothen Rosen": "Bin früh hinausgegangen"	
11.30	10. "Hochlandsknabe": "Die Burschen hier im Niederland"	
11.31	11. "Ruhelos, rastlos und nirgends zufrieden"	
11.32	12. "Gieb, Liebster, ein Zeichen"	
11.33	"4 Lieder" (p1870, Scheffel; Bar & pf): 1. "Biterolf encamped before Akkon"	Op.33
11.34	2. "An old German harvest dance"	
11.35	3. "I think of you, Margaretha"	
11.36	4. "May night"	
11.37	7 "Lieder und Gesänge" (p1882): 1. "Frage. Lied des Rugentino": "Liebliches Kind, kannst du mir sagen" (Goethe)	Op.49
11.38	2. "Der Einsiedler": "Komm, Trost der Welt" (Eichendorff)	
11.39	3. "Ungarisch": "Leise zieht ein Kahn zum Strande," folksong	
11.40	4. "Serenade": "Wenn dich die Sorgen des Lebens bedrücken" (Kruse)	
11.41	5. "Weg der Liebe" (Part I): "Über die Berge" (Herder from English)	
11.42	6. "Weg der Liebe" (Part II): "Den gordischen Knoten, den Liebe sich band" (Herder from English)	
11.43	7. "Kleonike's letzter Wille": "Wirst du Kleonikens Stimme kennen" (Kruse)	
11.44	5 "Siechentrost Lieder" (p1891, Heyse; 1–4vv, vn & pf): 1. "Wie mochte je mir wohler sein" (B)	Op.54
11.45	2. "Mai! die wunderschöne Zeit" (Bar)	
11.46	3. "Gott woll' dass ich daheime wär," duet (T, B)	
11.47	4. "Wer weiss, woher das Brünnlein quillt," duet (T, B)	
11.48	5. "Schlussgesang": "Wie mochte je mir wohler sein," quartet (S, A, T, B)	
11.49	"5 Lieder" (p1892; Bar & pf; also in English by Dole): 1. "Um Mitternacht": "Gelassen stieg die Nacht an's Land" (Mörike)	Op.59
11.50	2. "Kophtisches Lied": "Lasset Gelehrte sich zanken und streiten" (Goethe)	
11.51	3. "Zweites Kophtisches Lied": "Geh, gehorche meinen Winken!" (Goethe)	
11.52	4. "Die Auswanderer. I. Flucht": "Es zieht das Schiff auf hohen Wogen" (Stieler)	
11.53	5. "Die Auswanderer. II. Heimathbild": "Im deutschen Land daheim am Heerde" (Stieler)	
11.54	"5 Songs" (p1921): 1. "My darling comes to pluck flowers" (Spanish folksong)	Op.97
11.55	2. "Through the cloudy springtime night" (Geibel)	

11.56	3. "By my window" (M. Bruch)
11.57	4. "Morgenlied" (from Goethe's Claudine von Villabella)
11.58	5. "A girl and a glass of wine" (from Goethe's Jeri and Baetelg)

Duets:

11.59	"3 Duets" (S, A & pf): 1. "You lovely larks 'Good day' " (Schlippenbach) Op.4
11.60	2. "Old German Winter Song": "Mir ist leide"
11.61	3. "In the Wood"
11.62	"7 Little Songs" (p1859; 2/3 fem vv & pf): 1. "Glückwunsch": "Seid glücklich wann die Veilchen blüh'n" Op.6
11.63	2. "Der Wald": "Heil'ger Tempel ist der Wald"
11.64	3. "Frühlingsmuth": "Alle Vögel sind schon da"
11.65	4. "Nachtlied": "Abend sinkt still auf die Flur"
11.66	5. "Im Frühling": "Blümlein, seid gegrüsset"
11.67	6. "Jesus der Morgenstern" (In der Christnacht): "Morgenstern der finstern Nacht"
11.68	7. "Beim Pfingstreigen": "Pfingsten ist kommen"

12. UNPUBLISHED WORKS

12.1	"Ach bleib mit deiner Gnade" (c1897) ....
12.2	"Altenberger Hymne" (Hymnus für die Geier im bergischen Dom zu Altenberg am 16. Juli 1913) (c1913) ...
12.3	"Am Rhein" ....
12.4	"Canzonetta" (c1862; orch) ....
12.5	"Claudine von Villabella" ....
12.6	"Dramatischen Szenen aus Scheffels Ekkehard" ....
12.7	"Durch Nacht zum Licht" (c1919) ....
12.8	"Geistlich gesinnt sein" (c1873; orchd1893) ....
12.9	"Gesänge bei der Trauung Else Tuczek und Franz von Ankert am März 1897" (c1897; ch) ....
12.10	"Hymne" (c1902) ....
12.11	"Hymne an das Vaterland" ....
12.12	"Japsenlied": "Seht doch das Völkchen im Kimono" (c?; 1v & pf) ....
12.13	"Kaiser Wilhelm-Lied zum 22 März 1897" ....
12.14	"Kleine Präludium" (c1897; org/harm, for Hildegard Zanders) ....
12.15	"Lied an die Eltern": "Für die Eltern, für die theuern" (c1847) ....
12.16	"Das Lied der Deutschen in Oesterreich" (c1882; 1v & pf) ....
12.17	"Militärmärsche" ....
12.18	"Mindener Fantasie" (c1881; pf duet) ....
12.19	Piano Quintet in G minor (c1886) ....
12.20	String Octet (c1920) ....
12.21	String Quintet in A minor (c1919) ....
12.22	Suite No.3 (c1904–15; orch w/ org) ....
12.23	"Venetian Serenade" ....
12.24	"Wächterlied in der Neujahrsnacht" (c1888) ....
12.25	"Zum 31. 8. 1900" (c1900; vv & ch) ....

Unpublished lost works:

12.26	"Begrüssungshymne" (for Maria and Richard Zanders) ....
12.27	"Concert Overture" (c1814) ....
12.28	"Die Gratulanten" ....
12.29	"Festpräludium" (c1920; 11 winds & timp) ....
12.30	"Hosanna" ....
12.31	"Jery und Baetely" (c1854, first dramatic attempt) ....
12.32	Mass (c1858) ....
12.33	"Die Jungfrau von Orleans," overture (c1856) ....
12.34	Piano Quintet (c1858) ....
12.35	Piano Trio (c1849) ....
12.36	Piano Trio (ca1852) ....
12.37	Piano Trio in E-flat major (c1855) ....
12.38	"Rinaldo," cantata (c1854) ....
12.39	"Romanze" (pf) ....
12.40	Cello Sonata (c1862) ....
12.41	String Quartet (c1862) ....
12.42	String Quintet in E-flat major (c1919) ....
12.43	Suite No.4 (orch) ....
12.44	Suite No.5 (orch) ....
12.45	"Bilder aus dem Norden," sym poem (ca1908) ....
12.46	Symphony in F major (c1852) ....

* * * * *

BRUCKNER, (Josef) **Anton**
1824–1896

1. SYMPHONIES

1.1	Symphony (No.00) in F minor, "Study Symphony" (c1863, student work)	WAB99
1.2	Symphony (No.0) in D minor, "Die Nullte" (ca1863–4, r1869; used in: Sym No.3, WAB103)	WAB100
1.3	Symphony No.1 in C minor, "The Saucy Maid" (c1865–6):	WAB101

. Linz Version (perf1868)
. Vienna Version (perf1891)

| 1.4 | *Symphony in B-flat major (c1869, inc sketch of 1 movt)* | *WAB142* |
| 1.5 | Symphony No.2 in C minor, "Symphony of Pauses" (c1871–2, small r1879 & 91): | WAB102 |

. Original Version (perf1873 in Vienna)
. Herbeck Version (perf1876)

| 1.6 | Symphony No.3 in D minor, "Wagner" (c1872–3): | WAB103 |

. First Definitive Version (perf1877):
   quoted: . "Die Walküre"
      . "Tristan und Isolde"
. Schalk Version (r1888–9 w/ Schalk)
. Final Version (pubd1890)

| 1.7 | Symphony No.4 in E-flat major, "Romantic": | WAB104 |

. Original Version (c1874, unperf, unpubd)
. Vienna Version (r & new Scherzo 1878, r of Finale 1879–80, perf1881 in Vienna)
. Karlsruhe Version (perf1881 in Karlsruhe, small revisions; pubd1936)
. New York Version (perf1886 in New York)
. Schalk & Löwe Version (r by Schalk & Löwe 1886–7, perf1888 in Vienna)

| 1.8 | Symphony No.5 in B-flat major, "Tragic" / "Church of Faith" / "Pizzicato" (c1875–6): | WAB105 |

. Original Version (r until 1878, unperf; pubd1939)
. Schalk & Zottman reduction (red for 2pf 1887)
. Schalk Version (r by Schalk for perf1894 in Graz, pubd1896)

| 1.9 | Symphony No.6 in A major, "Philosophic" (c1879–81): | WAB106 |

. Original Version (2 middle movts perf1883)
. Mahler Version (drastically cut & r by Mahler for perf1899 in Vienna)

| 1.10 | Symphony No.7 in E major, "Lyric" (c1881–3, perf1884 in Leipzig) | WAB107 |
| 1.11 | Symphony No.8 in C minor, "Apocalyptic" / "The German Michel": | WAB108 |

. First definitive Version (c1884–7, unperf)
. Schalk Version (r w/ Schalk 1889–90, perf1892 in Vienna)

| 1.12 | Symphony No.9 in D minor, "Unfinished" (c1887–96; unfin): | WAB109 |

. Löwe Version (r for perf1903)
. Carragan Version (compl Carragan 1983)

| 1.13 | *Finale of Symphony No.9 (c1895 until death, sketches)* | *WAB143* |

2. OTHER ORCHESTRAL WORKS

2.1	*"Apollo March," in E-flat major (c ?1862; milit band, ?spur)*	*WAB115*
2.2	"March," in D minor (c1862)	WAB96
2.3	"3 Pieces" (c1862): No.1 in E-flat major	WAB97
2.4	No.2 in E minor	
2.5	No.3 in F major	
2.6	"Overture," in G minor (c1862–3)	WAB98
2.7	"March," in E-flat major (c1865; band)	WAB116
2.8	"Scherzo," in G minor (c1865; intended for: Sym No.1, WAB101)	
2.9	"Adagio," in A-flat major (c1865–6, orig vers of 2nd movt of: Sym No.1 in C minor, WAB101)	
2.10	Trio in F major (c1889; intended for Scherzo of: Sym No.9 in D minor, WAB109)	

3. STRING QUARTETS

3.1	String Quartet in C minor (c1861–2)	WAB111

4. OTHER CHAMBER MUSIC

3 or more insts:

4.1	"Aequale," in C minor (c1847; A-trbn, T-trbn & B-trbn)	WAB114
4.2	"Aequale," in C minor (c1847; A-trbn, T-trbn & B-trbn)	WAB149
4.3	String Quintet in F major (c1878–9)	WAB112
4.4	"Intermezzo," in D minor (c1879; str qnt, alternative for Scherzo of: Str Qnt in F major, WAB112)	WAB113

Vn & pf:

4.5	"Abendklänge," in E minor (c1866)	WAB110

5. PIANO

5.1   "Lancier-Quadrille," in C major (ca1850) WAB120
5.2   "Steiermärker," in G major (ca1850) WAB122
5.3   "Klavierstück," in E-flat major (ca1856) WAB119
5.4   3 Sonata first movements (c1861–2, student works): No.1 in F major.......................................
5.5   No.2 in F minor
5.6   No.3 in G minor
5.7   "Adagio," in F major (c1861–2)..
5.8   "Stille Betrachtung an einem Herbstabend," in F-sharp minor (c1863) WAB123
5.9   "Erinnerung," in A-flat major (ca1868) WAB117
5.10   "Fantasie," in G major (c1868)...WAB118

       Pf duet:

5.11   "3 kleine Vortragsstücke" (c1852–4): No.1 in G major WAB124
5.12   No.2 in G major
5.13   No.3 in F major
5.14   "Quadrille," in A major (ca1854) WAB121

6. ORGAN

6.1   *"4 Preludes," in E-flat major (c1836, ?spur)* *WAB128*
6.2   "Prelude," in E-flat major (ca1837) WAB127
6.3   "Prelude," in D minor (ca1846 or ca1852) WAB130
6.4   "Prelude & fugue," in C minor (c1847) WAB131
6.5   "Postlude," in D minor (ca1852)...WAB126
6.6   "Fugue," in D minor (c1861) WAB125
6.7   "Prelude" (Preg Prelude), in C major (c1884).. WAB129

7. CHORAL WORKS—SACRED

       Larger works:

7.1   Mass (Windhaager Mass), in C major (c1842; A, 2hn & org) WAB25
7.2   "Christus factus est" (I) (Chorale Mass), in F major (c1844, for Maundy Thursday; ch) WAB9
7.3   "Messe ohne Gloria" (Kronstorfer Messe), in D minor (c1844; ch).................................... WAB146
7.4   *"Requiem" (c1845; m ch & org, lost)* *WAB133*
7.5   "Missa pro Quadragesima," in G minor (ca1843–5; ch, trbn & org, inc) WAB140
7.6   Mass in E-flat major (ca1846; ch, 2ob, 3trbn & org) WAB139
7.7   "Requiem," in D minor (c1848–9, r1892; S, A, T, B, ch, orch & org) WAB39
7.8   "Magnificat," hymn in B-flat major (c1852; S, A, T, B, ch, orch & org) WAB24
7.9   "Psalm 22": "Der Herr regieret mich," in E-flat major (ca1852; ch & pf) WAB34
7.10   "Psalm 114": "Alleluja! Liebe erfüllt mich," in A major (c1852; ch & 3trbn) WAB36
7.11   "Missa Solemnis," in B-flat major (c1854; S, A, T, B, ch & orch)....................................WAB29
7.12   "Psalm 146": "Alleluja: Lobet den Herrn," in A major (c1860; S, A, T, B, d ch & orch) WAB37
7.13   "Psalm 112": "Alleluja! Lobet den Herrn," in B-flat major (c1863; d ch & orch) WAB35
7.14   Mass No.1 in D minor (c1864; S, A, T, B, ch, orch & org) WAB26
7.15   Mass No.2 in E minor (c1866, r1876, 1882, 1885, 1896; ch & winds) WAB27
7.16   Mass No.3 in F minor, "Great" (c1867–8, r1876, 1877, 1881,1890–3; S, A, T, B, ch, orch & org).....WAB28
7.17   *"Requiem-Fragment," in D minor (c1875, sketches: beginning only)* *WAB141*
7.18   "Te Deum," hymn in C major (c1881–4; S, A, T, B, ch, orch & org) WAB45
7.19   "Psalm 150": "Halleluja! Lobet den Herrn, in C major (c1892; S, ch & orch) WAB38

       Smaller works:

7.20   *"Domine, ad adjuvandum me" (c1835; ch & strings, sketches, ?spur: c by ?Weiss)* *WAB136*
7.21   "Pange lingua," hymn in C major (ca1835–43; ch; 2nd vers 'restored' in 1891)................ WAB31
7.22   "Pange lingua" (Tantum ergo), hymn in D major (ca1843; ch) WAB32
7.23   "Libera me, Domine," in F major (ca1843; ch & org) WAB21
7.24   *"Salve Maria" (ca1844, lost)* *WAB134*
7.25   *"Litanei" (ca1844 or ca1858; ch & winds, lost)* *WAB132*
7.26   *Herz Jesulied: "Aus allen Herzen," in B-flat major (ca1845; ?Marinelli; ch & org, ?spur)* *WAB144*
7.27   *"O du liebes Jesukind," in F major (ca1845; T & org, ?spur)* *WAB145*
7.28   2 "Asperges me" (ca1843–5; ch & org): 1. in Aeolian mode WAB3
7.29   2. in F major
7.30   4 "Tantum ergo" (ca1846, r1888; ch): No.1 in E-flat major... WAB41
7.31   No.2 in C major
7.32   No.3 in B-flat major
7.33   No.4 in A-flat major
7.34   "Tantum ergo" (No.5), in D major (ca1846, r1888; ch & org)...WAB42
7.35   "In jener letzten der Nächte," choral in F minor (ca1848; ch) WAB17
7.36   "Tantum ergo," in A major (ca1848–9; ch & org) WAB43

7.37	"Entsagen," cantata in B-flat major (ca1851, from Redwitz: Amaranth; S/T, ch & org/pf)	WAB14
7.38	"Totenlied No.1": "O ihr, die ihr heut mit mir zum Grabe geht," in E-flat major (c1852; ch)	WAB47
7.39	"Totenlied No.2": "O ihr, die ihr heut mit mir zum Grabe geht," in F major (c1852; ch)	WAB48
7.40	"Tantum ergo," in B-flat major (c1854 or 5; ch, 2vn & 2tpt & org)	WAB44
7.41	"Libera me, Domine" (II), in F minor (c1854; ch, 3trbn & org)	WAB22
7.42	"Vor Arneths Grab": "Brüder, trocknet eure Zähren," in F minor (c1854, Marinelli; m ch & 3trbn)	WAB53
7.43	"Festgesang": "Sankt Jodok spross aus edlem Stamm," in C major (c1855; S, T, B, ch & pf)	WAB15
7.44	"Ave Maria" I, in F major (c1856; S, A, ch, vc & org)	WAB5
7.45	"Am Grabe": "Brüder trocknet eure Zählen," in F minor (c1861, Marinelli; m ch)	WAB2
7.46	"Ave Maria" II, in F major (c1861; ch)	WAB6
7.47	"Dir, Herr, dir will ich mich ergeben," choral in A major (ca1858–68; ch)	WAB12
7.48	"Afferentur regi," offertory in F major (c1861; ch & 3trbn; orig for ch & org)	WAB1
7.49	"Festkantate": "Preiset den Herrn," in D major (c1862, Pammesberger; Bar/B, ch & winds)	WAB16
7.50	"Trauungslied": "O schöner Tag," in F major (c1865, Proschko; 4vv, ch & org)	WAB49
7.51	"Asperges me," in F major (ca1868; ch)	WAB4
7.52	"Pange lingua et Tantum ergo," in Phrygian mode (c1868; ch)	WAB33
7.53	"In St Angelum custodem": "Jam lucis orto sidere," hymn in Phrygian mode (c1868; ch)	WAB18
7.54	"Inveni David" (I), offertory in F minor (c1868; m ch & 4trbn)	WAB19
7.55	"Locus iste," gradual in C major (c1869; ch)	WAB23
7.56	"Tota pulchra es, Maria," antiphon in Phrygian mode (c1878; T, ch & org)	WAB46
7.57	"Zur Vermählungsfeier": "Zwei Herzen haben sich gefunden," in D major (c1878, Mattig)	WAB54
7.58	"Os justi," gradual in Lydian mode (c1879; ch)	WAB30
7.59	"Christus factus est" (II), gradual in D minor (c1879; ch, 2vn & 3trbn; see for ch 1884)	WAB10
7.60	"Inveni David" (II), Gregorian choral (c1879; unison ch & org)	WAB20
7.61	"Ave Maria" III, in F major (c1882; A & org/harm)	WAB7
7.62	"Christus factus est" (III), in D minor (c1884, r1896; ch, from orig of 1879)	WAB11
7.63	"Salvum fac populum," antiphon (c1884; ch)	WAB40
7.64	"Veni creator spiritus," Gregorian choral (ca1884, org acc harmonized)	WAB50
7.65	"Ecce sacerdos," antiphon in A minor (c1885; ch, 3trbn & org)	WAB13
7.66	"Virga Jesse," gradual in E minor (c1885; ch)	WAB52
7.67	"Ave regina coelorum," Gregorian choral (ca1886; unison ch & org)	WAB8
7.68	"Vexilla regis prodeunt," hymn in Phrygian mode (c1892; ch)	WAB51
7.69	"Veni Sancte Spiritus," choral in F major (discovered in 1931)	

8. CHORAL WORKS—SECULAR

W/ acc:

8.1	"Vergissmeinnicht": "Es blühten wunderschön," cantata (c1845, Marinelli; 3 vers):	WAB93
	. Version 1: "Musikalicher Versuch nach dem Kammer-Styl ... für Sänger" (& pf)	
	. Version 2: "Musikalicher Versuch nach dem Kammer-Styl ... für Sing-Partien" (& pf)	
	. Version 3: "Vergissmeinnicht" (S, A, T, B, ch & pf)	
8.2	"Auf Brüder! auf, zur frohen Feier," cantata (c1852; S, A, 2T, 2B & brass; text: 3 vers):	WAB61
	. Version 1: "Auf, Brüder, auf zur frohen Feier" (Marinelli, for Michael Arenth)	
	. Version 2: "Heil, Vater, Dir zum frohen Feste" (Marinelli, for Friedrich Mayer)	
	. Version 3: "Heil Dir zum schönen Erstlingsfeste" (Piringer)	
8.3	"Lasst Jubeltöne laut erklingen," in E-flat major (c1854, Weiss; m ch, 2hn, 2tpt & 4trbn)	WAB76
8.4	"Auf, Brüder, auf! Und die Saiten zur Hand!," cantata (c1855, Marinelli; 4 m vv, d ch & brass)	WAB60
8.5	"Germanenzug": "Germanen durchschreiten," in D minor (c1863, Silberstein; ch & brass)	WAB70
8.6	"Um Mitternacht" I, in F minor (c1864, Prutz; A, m ch & pf)	WAB89
8.7	"Herbstlied": "Durch die Wälder streif' ich munter," in F-sharp minor (c1864, Sallet; 2S, ch & pf)	WAB73
8.8	"Mitternacht": "Die Blumen glüh'n," in A-flat major (c1870, J. Mendelssohn; T, m ch & pf)	WAB80
8.9	"Das hohe Lied": "Im Tale rauscht die Mühle," in A-flat major (c1876, Mattig; 2 vers):	WAB74
	. Version 1 (2T, Bar & 4 m ch)	
	. Version 2 (T, 4 m ch & brass)	
8.10	"Nachruf": "Vereint bist, Töneheld und Meister," in C minor (c1877; m ch & org)	WAB81
8.11	"Trösterin Musik": "Musik! Du herrliches Gebilde," in C minor (c1877, Seuffert; m ch & org)	WAB88
8.12	"Abendzauber": "Der See träumt, in G-flat major (c1878, Mattig; Bar, ch, 3 yodellers & 4hn)	WAB57
8.13	"Das deutsche Lied": "Wie durchs Bergtal," in D minor (c1892, Fels; ch & brass)	WAB63
8.14	"Helgoland": "Hoch auf der Nordsee," in G minor (c1893, Silberstein; ch & orch)	WAB71

W/ out acc:

8.15	"An dem Feste," in D-flat major (c1843, Knauer; m ch; r1893 as: Tafellied)	WAB59
8.16	"Festlied": "Freudig lasst das Lied erschallen," in D major (c1843; m ch)	WAB67
8.17	"Tafellied": "Durch des Saales bunte Scheiben," in D-flat major (c1843, r1893, Ptak)	WAB86
8.18	"Das Lied vom deutschen Vaterland": "Wohlauf ihr Genossen," in D-flat major (ca1845)	WAB78
8.19	"Ständchen": "Wie des Bächleins Silberquelle," in G major (ca1846; T & 4 m vv)	WAB84
8.20	"Der Lehrerstand": "Die Zeit weiset auf einen Stand," in E-flat major (c1847, ?Marinelli)	WAB77
8.21	"Sternschnuppen": "Wenn Natur die sanften Lider," in F major (c1848, Marinelli)	WAB85
8.22	"Das edle Herz" I: "Wer im Busen nicht die Flamme," in A major (ca1851, Marinelli)	WAB65
8.23	"Die Geburt": "Es landet ein Fremdling im Hafen der Welt," in D-flat major (c1851)	WAB69
8.24	"2 Sängersprüche" (Motti) (c1851): 1. "Ein jubelnd Hoch in Leid," in D major	WAB83
8.25	2. "Lebt wohl, ihr Sangesbrüder," in A major	

9. SONGS (w/ pf)

* * * * *

WAB = Renate Grasberger: "Werkverzeichnis Anton Bruckner." Hans Schneider. Tutzing, 1977.

1. STAGE WORKS

Operas:

1.1	"Sigune oder Das stille (vergessene) Dorf," 2 act opera (c1885–9, Soyaux after Baumbach, unfin)	K231
1.2	*"Einleitungsmusik zum Wunder des Heiligen Antonius. Der Leichenschmaus" (c1908–11, sketches)*	*K250*
1.3	"Die Brautwahl" (The Bridal Choice), 3 acts (c1906–11, Busoni after Hoffmann)	K258
1.4	*"Musiche di scena per la Franziska di F. Wedekind," operetta (c1912, Wedekind, sketches)*	*K260*
1.5	"Arlecchino" (ein theatralisches Capriccio) (The Windows), 1 act (c1914–16, Busoni)	Op.50, K270
1.6	"Turandot" (Ein chinesisches Fabel), 2 acts (p1917, Busoni after Gozzi; arr Jarnach for pf)	K273
1.7	"Doktor Faust" (c1916–24, Busoni after Marlowe; compl Jarnach 1925)	K303

Incid music:

1.8	"Turandot" (p1911, Gozzi transl Vollmoeller, from: Turandot Suite, Op.41)	

1a. SELECTIONS FROM STAGE WORKS

1a.3	"Die Brautwahl," opera:	K258

I: . "Vorspiel"
      . "Alla Marcia"
     1. "Ja, Natur, Gespräch und Tabaksblatt" (Kommissionsrat)
     2. "Darf ich nun den zweiten nehmen?" (Kommissionsrat)
      . "Ein Flüstern, Rauschen," duet (Albertine, Edmund)
     3. "Da geht er hin" (Leonhard)
      . "Verwandlungsmusik"
     4. "Könnt ich mich so verspäten?!" (Thusman)
      . "Ihr himmlischen Heerscharen!" (Thusman)
      . "Ihr seid doch ein besonderer Herr" (Leonhard)
     5. "Orchester-Zwischenspiel" ('Manasse')
      . "Seh ich Euch wieder nach langen Jahren?!" (Leonhard)
      . "Bedächtig, vorsichtig!" (Thusman)
      . "Bemerken Sie doch wieder würdige Autor" (Thusman)
      . "Da Ihr Euch gern mit den alten Historien befasset" (Grausige Historie vom Münzjuden Lippold)
      . "Man fand das Zauberbuch" (Leonhard)
      . "Ihr wollt das schöne blutjunge Mädel," finale (Leonhard)
      . "Rettig, Rettig, schwarzer Rettig" (Manasse)
II: . "Vorspiel" (Spuk- und Wirbelwalzer)
     6. "Ein gutes Bild, ein Kunstwerk!" (Kommissionsrat)
     7. "Auf dem geregelten Heimweg" (Thusman)
      . "Deine Tochter" (Thusman)
      . "und als der Morgen neblig dämmert" (Thusman)
      . "Wie du beschriebest die Zechgesellen" (Kommissionsrat)
     8. "Herr des Himmels! 's ist der Jude" (Thusman)
      . "Mein Neffe Benjamin ist in Berlin" (Manasse)
     9. "Ein Flüstern, Rauschen, Singen geht durch den Frühlingshain" (Albertine)
    10. "Aber!" (Thusman)
    11. "Nie und nimmer werd' ich die Seine" (Albertine)
      . "Also 'ne saubere Liebschaft" (Kommissionsrat)
    12. "Hä! Hä, hä, hä! Hä, bestes Mädchen, hier bin ich selber nun" (Bensch)
    13. "Das ist einer deiner Streiche" (Manasse)
      . "Siehe! ein Tänzchen" (Thusman)
      . "Nun höre, Melchior Voswinkel" (Manasse)
      . "Lasst euch nicht" (Leonhard)
III: . "Vorspiel"
    14. "Oh! du unglücklicher" (Thusman)
    15. "O, Gerechter, was erblick ich" (Thusman)
    16. "Hei ja hei, hoi didel del" (Thusman)
      . "Ich rat Euch, Thusman" (Leonhard)
      . "Vorspiel"
      . "Wär kaum zu wundern, wenn mir die Galle" (Kommissionsrat)
      . "Seht, so sind Menschen und zumal Kommissionsräte" (Leonhard)
      . "Das Lächeln ist vergrämlicht" (die erste Gefahr) (Leonhard)
      . "Eu'r Schulgenosse" (die zweite Gefahr) (Leonhard)
      . "Thusman, der Geheime"
      . "Am Alten habt Ihr, weist Ihr den Neffen ab" (die dritte Gefahr) (Leonhard)
    17. "Was musst ich hören!" (Albertine)
    18. "Lass ab von der Betrübnis, liebes Mädchen" (Leonhard)
      . "dort steht seine Zukunft" (Traumvision) (Leonhard)
      . "Nachspiel"
    19. "Ich eile auf Amors Flügel her" (Thusman)
      . "Dich, mein Geheimer" (Kommissionsrat)
      . "Sind wir einig?" (Kommissionsrat)
    20. "Ein Pfirsich kaum gereift ist sie" (Thusman, Edmund, Bensch)

. "Welch schön verschlung'ne Schrift!" (Thusman)
. "Steckt das Buch in Eure Tasche" (Leonhard, Thusman)
. "Herr Thusman hat verspielt" (Bensch)
. "Väter! her mit der Tasche!" (Manasse)
. "So ward's noch nicht entschieden" (Edmund)
. "Alles hat sich wohl gefügt" (Kommissionsrat)

1a.5   "Arlecchino," opera: Op.50, K270
Part I. "Arlecchino als Schalk": 1. "Einleitung"
. "Es bleibt doch die schönste, die ergreifendste Stelle!" (Matteo)
. "Wetterwendisch ist das Schlachtenglück," Liedchen (Arlecchino)
2. "Und noch hab' ich euch zu danken," duet (Abbate, Dottore)
3. "Von was? Die Barbaren ...," trio (Matteo, Abbate, Dottore)
Part II. "Arlecchino als Kriegsmann": 4. "Marsch"
. "Ora incomincian le dolenti note" (Matteo)
Part III. "Arlecchino als Ehemann": 5a. "Herr Kapitän" (Colombina)
. "Ach da bist du wieder," aria (Colombina)
5b. "Wie ist Ihr Schlaf, Madame?," arietta (Arlecchino, Colombina)
6a. "Mit dem Schwerte, mit der Laute," romance (Leandro)
6b. "O Colombina, nach dir hab ich," dialogue (Leandro, Colombina)
6c. "Contro l'empio traditore," duettino (Colombina, Leandro)
6d. "O Colombina, so soll heute diese Zunge," dialogue (Colombina, Leandro)
6e. "Venus sicht auf uns hernieder," cavatina (Leandro)
6f. "Wer ist es, der also die Dissonanz schleudert" (Leandro, Columbina, Arlecchino)
Part IV. "Arlecchino als Sieger": 7. "Es ist schon ganz finster" (Dottore)
. "Lasst uns beten," quartet (Abbate)
. "Glück auf zur Fahrt," melodrama (Arlecchino)
8. "Wahrlich ich weiss nicht mehr aus noch ein!," monologue (Matteo)
9. "Umzug und Schlusstanz"

1a.6   "Turandot" (Ein chinesisches Fabel), opera: K273
I/1:   1. "Introduction"
. "Peking!," scene (Kalaf, Barak)
2. "O o o o o," lamento (Königin-Mutter, Barak, Mädchen-Chor)
3. "Barak, Barak, o du tükkischer Alter," arioso (Kalaf, Barak)
4. "Pantomima e Finale" (Kalaf, Barak)
I/2:   1. "Introduction"
. "Rechts zunächst der grosse Thron," arietta (Truffaldino)
3. "Einzug des Kaisers"
4. "Kon-fut-se, dir hab ich schworen," aria (Altoum) (p as: Altoum's Prayer, Op.49/1, K277)
5. "Steh auf, unkluger Jüngling!," dialogue (Altoum, Kalaf)
6. "Entweiche, entweich' der Gefahr," quartet (Altoum, Kalaf, Pantalone, Tartaglia)
7. "Lieber möcht ich gar," march & scene (Pantalone & others)
8. "Was kriecht am Boden" (Die drei Rätsel) (Turandot)
9. "Wes Stamms und Namens," finale (Kalaf, die Doktoren, Chor)
II/3:   1. "La la la la" (Vorsängerin, Frauenchor)
2. "Tanz und Gesang" (Frauenchor)
3. "Genug! mein Kopf steht nach andren Dingen! ... Es pocht mein Herz," recit & aria (Turandot)
4. "Hören wir zunächst," intermezzo dialogato (Adelma, Turandot, Truffaldino)
5. "Ich schlich geschickt und unerblickt," aria (Truffaldino, Turandot)
6. "Heimliche Kunde kam mir zu," arioso (Altoum, Turandot, Pantalone, Tartaglia)
7. "Adelma, meine Freundin," duet (Turandot, Adelma)
8. "Intermezzo orchestrale"
II/4:   9. "Hört mir nur das klägliche Getrommel!" (Tartaglia, Pantalone, Kalaf, Altoum, Frauenchor)
10. "Vatermörderin!," finale (Altoum & others)

1a.7   "Doktor Faust," opera: K303
. "Symphonia"
Vorspiel I: . "Wagner, wahrhaftig! ich mag so nicht weiter" (Faust)
. "Dieses Buch leg ich in Eure Hand" (Erster Student)
Vorspiel II: . "Wie kommt es alsobald gelingen?" (Faust)
. "Lewis" (Zweite Stimme)
. "Ich eile" (Dritte Stimme)
. "Ich bin Fürst Belzebuth" (Vierte Stimme)
. "Schaue hier Megäros" (Fünfte Stimme)
. "Welchem Wahn gab ich mich hin!" (Faust)
. "Konnt ich soviel erhoffen?" (Faust)
. "Beschaffe mir für meines Lebens Rest" (Faust)
. "Draussen stehn die Gläubiger zu Hauf" (Mephistopheles)
. "Et resurexit ... Secundum scripturam" (ch)
Intermezzo: . "Du nicht allein der Gott der Milde" (Soldat)
. "Der Mann sinnt auf Deinen Tod" (Mephistopheles)
. "Möchtest du mir nicht beichten?" (Mephistopheles)
I: . "Cortège. In Carattere d'una Polacca"
. "Nach dieser Feste rauschend bunter Reihe" (Zeremonienmeister)

. "Wagen, und dabei gewinnen" (Mephistopheles)
. "Er naht ... Mit ihm" (ch)
. "Was wünscht die schöne Herrin zu erschauen?," parlando (Faust)
. "Ein würdiges Bild" (Herzog)
. "Samson, Dalila, in Lieb' umschlungen" (Herzog)
. "Ich führe Dich in die Unermesslichkeit der Welten" (Faust)
. "Er ruft mich wie mit tausend Stimmen" (Herzogin)
. "Symphonisches Intermezzo. Sarabande"
II: . "In modo di Minuetto rustico"
. "So lang man Jugend hat, lebt man als Nimmersatt" (ch)
. "Nichts ist bewiesen" (Faust)
. "den Spruch eines Abtrünnigen" (Erster Student)
. "Dass Wein, dass Frauen, Kunst und Liebe" (Faust)
. "Te Deum laudamus" (Chor der Katholiken)
. "Qui Tu fecisti vinum, qui feminam creavisti" (Chor der Katholiken)
. "Lasst Euch nicht stören" (Mephistopheles)
. "Dort war ein dummer Herzog der freit' " (Mephistopheles)
. "Also verbrenn ich" (Mephistopheles)
. "Junges Gelände" (Faust)
III: . (Andante sostenuto)
. "Ritornello"
. "Wenn das Wissen mit der Tugend," serenata (ch)
. "Das Haus ist mir bekannt" (Faust)
. "O, beten" (Faust)
. "Hilf, Sehnsucht" (Faust)
. "So wirk ich weiter in dir und du zeuge fort" (Faust)

2. ORCHESTRAL WORKS

3. CONCERTOS, SOLO INSTR & ORCH

Pf & orch:

4. STRING QUARTETS

5. OTHER CHAMBER MUSIC

3 or more insts:

Vc & pf:

Fl & pf:

Cl & pf:

6. PIANO SONATAS

7. OTHER PIANO WORKS

7.97	"Tre pezzi nello stile antico" (c1880): No.1 "Minuetto"	Op.10, K159
7.98	No.2 "Sonatina"	
7.99	No.3 "Gigue"	
7.100	*"Scherzo," in C major (c1880, lost)*	*K160*
7.101	*"Fantasiestück" (c1880, lost)*	*K163*
7.102	*"Preludio e Fuga," in D ?minor (c1880, lost)*	*K165*
7.103	"Preludio e Fuga," in G minor (c1880)	K166
7.104	*"Studio," in A minor (c1880, frags)*	*K175*
7.105	*"Preludio e Fuga" (c ?1881, lost)*	*K178*
7.106	"Preludio e Fuga," in A minor (c1881)	K179
7.107	"Preludio e Fuga," in C major (c1881)	Op.36, K180
7.108	"24 Preludes" (c1879–80): No.1 "Moderato"	Op.37, K181
7.109	No.2 "Andantino sostenuto"	
7.110	No.3 "Andante con moto"	
7.111	No.4 "Allegretto"	
7.112	No.5 "Vivace assai quasi presto"	
7.113	No.6 "Moderato"	
7.114	No.7 "Allegro vivace"	
7.115	No.8 "Allegro moderato"	
7.116	No.9 "Allegretto vivace e con brio"	
7.117	No.10 "Vivace ed energico"	
7.118	No.11 (w/ out tempo markings)	
7.119	No.12 "Andantino"	
7.120	No.13 "Allegretto scherzando"	
7.121	No.14 "Lento"	
7.122	No.15 "Andantino sostenuto con espressione"	
7.123	No.16 "Maestoso"	
7.124	No.17 "Allegretto vivace"	
7.125	No.18 "Allegretto con moto"	
7.126	No.19 "Allegro vivo"	
7.127	No.20 "Allegro moderato"	
7.128	No.21 "Andantino sostenuto"	
7.129	No.22 "Vivace e scherzoso"	
7.130	No.23 "Allegro vivace"	
7.131	No.24 "Presto"	
7.132	*"Fuga," in C major (c1881, lost)*	*K182*
7.133	"Una festa di villaggio," 6 pieces (c1881): No.1 "Preparazione alla festa"	Op.9, K185
7.134	No.2 "Marcia trionfale"	
7.135	No.3 "In chiesa"	
7.136	No.4 "La fiera"	
7.137	No.5 "Danza"	
7.138	No.6 "Notte"	
7.139	Fugue in F major (c1882)	K188
7.140	"Danza notturna," in D major (p1882)	K189
7.141	"Marcia di Paesani e Contadine" (ca1882, add piece for: Una festa di villaggio, Op.9, K185)...	Op.32, K193
7.142	"Macchiette Medioevali" (Medieval Figures) (c1882–3): No.1 "Dama"	K194
7.143	No.2 "Cavaliere"	
7.144	No.3 "Paggio"	
7.145	No.4 "Guerriero"	
7.146	No.5 "Astrologo"	
7.147	No.6 "Trovatore"	
7.148	*"Macchiette Medioevali No 2/B. Cavaliere Reiter" (ca1882–3, sketches, not used in K194)*	*K195*
7.149	"3 morceaux" (c ?1881–2): No.1 "Scherzo"	Op.4, K197/1
7.150	No.2 "Prélude et Fugue"	Op.5, K197/2
7.151	No.3 "Scène de ballet"	Op.6, K197/3
7.152	"Etude 15. en forme d'Adagio d'une Sonate," in D-flat major (c1882–3)	K198
7.153	"Etude 16." (Nocturne), in B-flat minor (c1882–3)	K199
7.154	"Studio 18.," in F minor (c1883)	K200
7.155	"6 Etudes" (c1883): No.1 in C major	Op.16, K203
7.156	No.2 in A minor	
7.157	No.3 in G major	
7.158	No.4 in E minor	
7.159	No.5 in D major (Fuga)	
7.160	No.6 in B minor (Scherzo)	
7.161	"Étude en forme de variations," in C-sharp minor (c1883)	Op.17, K206
7.162	"Zweite Ballettszene" (c1884):	Op.20, K209
	1. "Veloce e leggiero"	
	2. "Tempo di Valse, con grazia"	
	3. "Quasi presto"	
7.163	"Variations & Fugue on Chopin's Prelude" (No.20 in C minor, Op.28/20, B107) (c1884–5)	Op.22, K213
7.164	"10 Variations on Chopin's Prelude" (c1922, r vers of K213)	(Op.22), K213a
7.165	"Invenzione," in D minor (c1885)	K214
7.166	"Preludio," in A minor (c ?1885)	K220
7.167	"5 Variationen zu Siegfired Ochs' Variationen über das Lied 'Kommt a Vogerl g'flogen' " (c1886)	K222
7.168	*"Kanon" (c1887, lost)*	*K224*

7.239   No.4 in G major
7.240   No.5 in C minor
7.241   Version of 5 Short Pieces for the Study of Part-Playing, K296 (p1925): No.1 "Preludietto," in E major .....
7.242   No.2 in E minor (= No.1 of 1923)
7.243   No.3 in A minor (= No.2 of 1923)
7.244   No.4 in D minor (= No.3 of 1923)
7.245   No.5 in G major (= No.4 of 1923)
7.246   No.6 in C minor (= No.5 of 1923)
7.247   No.7 "Mit Anwendung des III. Pedals"
7.248   Version of: 5 Short Pieces for the Study of Part-Playing, K296 (p1954, = Nos.1–6 of 1925 version) ....
7.249   "Prélude et Etude en Arpèges" (c1923) K297

Pf duet:

7.250   *Piece (c ?1879, inc, lost)* *K109*
7.251   *"Ouverture," in E major (c ?1880, frag, lost)* *K128*
7.252   "Fuge über das Volkslied 'O, du mein lieber Augustin' " (c1888) K226
7.253   "Finnish Folk Tunes" (Finnländische Volksweisen), 2 pieces (c1888) Op.27, K227

2 Pf:

7.254   "Preludio e Fuga," in C minor (c1878) K99
7.255   "Capriccio," in G minor (c1879) K104
7.256   *"Introduzione e Capriccio" (c1879, lost)* *K125*
7.257   "Improvisation on Bach's Chorale: Wie wohl ist mir, o Freund der Seele" (BWV517) (c1916) K271
7.258   Version 4 of: Fantasia contrappuntistica, K256 (c1922; also see K255, K256 & K256a for pf) K256b

8. ORGAN

8.1   "Fuga a tre voci," in C minor (c1876; harm/org) K35
8.2   "Praeludium (Basso ostinato) und Fuge (Doppelfuge zum Choral)," in A minor (c1880) Op.7, K157

9. CHORAL WORKS (& sacred vocal)

W/ orch:

9.1   "Gott erbarme sich unser," mottetto (c1880, Psalm 67; ch & orch; r by Mayer-Remy) K174a
9.2   "Requiem" (c1881, Liturgy; vv, ch & orch, inc) K183
9.3   "Le quattro stagioni" (Four Seasons) (c1882, dall'Ongaro; vv, m ch & orch/pf): 1. "Primavera" Op.40, K191
9.4   2. "Estate"
9.5   3. "Autunno"
9.6   4. "Inverno"
9.7   "Il sabato del villaggio," cantata (c1882, Leopardi; vv, ch & orch): K192
            1. "Preludio" (pastorale)
            2. "La donzelletta vien dalla campagna" (S)
            3. "Siede con le vicine" (A)
            4. "Già tutta l'aria in bruna" (ch)
            5. "Orla squilla da segno" (B)
            6. "Orlo squillo da segno" (2 vers of the beginning)
            7. "Intermezzo sinfonica Danza"
            8. "E intanto riede alla sua parca mensa" (B)
            9. "E quando in torno" (S)
           10. "Questo di sette il più gradito" (S)
           11. "Doman tristezza e noia" (S)
           12. "Altro dirti non vò mala tua festa," coda
9.8   "So lang man jung" (c1884, Worms; T, m ch & orch) K205

Other:

9.9   "Preghiera alla Madonna" (c1873, Ferdinando Busoni—his father; 2 fem vv & pf) K8
9.10   *"Deh ci guarda benedetta" (c1877, Busoni; ch, frag)* *K56*
9.11   "Salve decus Patriarcharum," antiphon (c1877; S, mS, Bar & harm) K63
9.12   "Pater Noster" (c1877; mS, m ch & pf/harm) K69
9.13   "Pater Noster" (c1878; S, A, Bar) K82
9.14   "Tota pulchra es Maria," antiphon (c1878; S, A, T, B) K87
9.15   "Ave Maria," antiphon (c1878; 1v & str qt) K67a
9.16   "Salve Regina," antiphon (mS & str qt) K68a
9.17   "Benedicta et venerabilis es" (Graduale delle Messe ... della Madonna) (c1878; mS, 4vv obbl & org/pf) K90
9.18   "Ave Maria quatuor vocibus cantanda," antiphon (c1878; S, A, T, B) K95
9.19   "Missa I. Quatuor vocibus Cantanda" (c1879; S, A, T, B) K103
9.20   "Benedicta et venerabilis es," gradual (c1879; S, A, Bar) K105
9.21   *"Stabat Mater," sequence (c1879; 2S, A, T, 2B & str qnt, lost)* *K119*
9.22   *"Kyrie" (c1879; ch, lost)* *K127*

12. CADENZAS

13. ORCHESTRAL ARRANGEMENTS OF WORKS OF OTHERS

For orch:

For 1 instr & orch:

For chamber ens:

14. PIANO ARRANGEMENTS OF WORKS OF OTHERS

14.12   No.3 "Toccata," in D minor (from BWV565)
14.13   No.4 "Toccata," in C major (from BWV564)
14.14   No.5 "10 Chorale Preludes"
14.15   No.6 "Chaconne" (5th movt from: Partita No.2 in D minor, BWV1004)
14.16   IV. "Compositions & Free Transcriptions": No.1 "Fantasia alla memoria di mio padre" (c1909)
14.17   No.2 "Preludio, fuga e fuga figurata" (from: An die Jugend, K254)
14.18   No.3 "Capriccio sopra la lontananza del fratello dilettissimo" (BWV992)
14.19   No.4 "Fantasia, adagio e fuga" (BWV906 & BWV968)
14.20   No.5 "Fantasia contrappuntistica," II & III (c1910–2)
14.21   V. "Das Wohltemperierte Klavier," I: w/ appendix, Prelude & fugue in E minor (BWV548) (c1894)
14.22   VI. "Das Wohltemperierte Klavier," II (BWV870–BWV893)
14.23   VII. "Nachträge zu Band I–IV": No.1 "Toccata," in E minor (BWV914)
14.24   No.2 "Toccata," in G minor (BWV915)
14.25   No.3 "Toccata," in G major (BWV916)
14.26   No.4 "Fantasia and Fugue," in A minor (BWV904)
14.27   No.5 "Fantasia, Fugue, Andante and Scherzo" (BWV905, BWV969 & BWV844)
14.28   No.6 "Chromatic Fantasia and Fugue" (BWV903) (arr for vc & pf)
14.29   No.7 "Improvisation über Bachs Chorallied 'Wie wohl ist mir' " (BWV517) (arr1916; 2pf)
14.30   No.8 "Kanonische Variationen und Fuge" (BWV1079)
14.31   No.9 "Sonatina No.5"

Beethoven:

14.32   "Ecossaises"; WoO 83 (p1889) B47

Brahms:

14.33   "6 Chorale preludes," for org, Op.122 (p1902) B50

Chopin:

14.34   Polonaise No.6 in A-flat major, Op.53, B147 (reworked) B51

Cornelius:

14.35   "Fantasia," on themes from opera: Barber of Bagdad (p1886) B52

Cramer:

14.36   "8 Etudes" (ed1897) B53

Gade:

14.37   "Novelletten," Op.29 (p1889; 2 pf) B54

Goldmark:

14.38   "Konzert-Fantasie on theme from opera Merlin" (arr1887) B55
14.39   "Merlin," vocal score of opera (pf reduction p1889) B56

Liszt:

14.40   "Coeli enarrant," for m ch & orch (arr for 2pf) B57
14.41   "Fantasia & fugue," on: Ad nos, ad salutarem, from Meyerbeer: Le prophète (p1897; arr for org 1909) . B59
14.42   "Hungarian Rhapsody No.20" (ca1900, orig: Allegro vivace in G minor, S242/20) B60
14.43   "Mephisto Waltz" (p1904) B61
14.44   "Heroischer Marsch" (arr1905) B62
14.45   "Pace non trovo," pf acc of: Petrarca's Sonnet 104 (also transcr for orch) B63
14.46   Polonaise No.2 in E major (p1909, also additional final cadenza) B64
14.47   *"Franziskus-Legende" (ca1910, lost)* *B65*
14.48   "Fantasia," on 2 motives from Mozart's opera: Le nozze di Figaro, K492 (p1912) B66
14.49   "Etude No.6," in A minor (after Paganini's Tema e variazioni) (transcription-study 1913) B67
14.50   "La campanella Etüde No.3," in G-sharp minor (after Paganini's Rondo) (p1916) B68
14.51   "Valse oubliée," for piano (p1917; also arr for vc & pf) B69
14.52   "Andantino capricioso. Etüde No.2," in E-flat major (after Papanini's Caprices) (arr1916) B70
14.53   "Reminiscences de Don Juan" (arr1917) B71
14.54   "Totentanz" (also arr for pf & orch 1918) B72
14.55   "Hungarian Rhapsody No.19" (p1920) B73
14.56   "Arpeggio. Etüde No.4," in E major (after Paganini's Caprices) (p1923) B74
14.57   "Tremolo. Etüde No.1," in G minor (after Paganini's Caprices) (arr1923 or 4) B75
14.58   "La chasse. Etüde No.5," in E major (after Paganini's Caprices) (arr1923 or 4) B76
14.59   "Scherzo," in G minor for pf (ed1922) B114
14.60   "Tarantella di bravura" (Liszt's arrangement of Auber: Tarantelle de la Muette de Portici) B115

Mendelssohn:

14.61   Symphony No.1 in C minor, Op.11 (arr for 2pf—8hands) B77

Mozart:

14.62   Symphony No.30 in D major, K186b (K202) (p1888) B78

14.63	Symphony No.32 in G major, K318 (p1888)	B79
14.64	Symphony No.37 in G major, K425a (K444) (p1888)	B80
14.65	Overture to opera: The Magic Flute, K620 (transcr ?1908; pianola)	B83
14.66	"Andantino," from: Pf Conc No.9 in E-flat major, K271 (arr1913)	B84
14.67	"Duettino concertante," after Finale of Pf Conc No.19 in F major, K459 (arr1919; 2pf)	B88
14.68	*Pf Sonata in D major, K375a (K448) and Fugue in C minor, K426, for pf duet (arr1921, lost)*	*B89*
14.69	"Fantasia," in F minor for a mech organ, K608 (arr1922; 2pf)	B91
14.70	Pf Conc No.17 in G major, K453 (orch part arr Petri)	B92
14.71	Overture to opera: The Magic Flute, K620 (transcr1923; 2pf)	B93
14.72	*Fugue from Str Qt in C minor, K546 (frag)*	*B94*

Nováček:

14.73	"Scherzo," from: Str Qt No.1 (p1893)	B95
14.74	*"Walzersuite" (ca1905, lost)*	*B96*

Schönberg:

14.75	Piano piece, Op.11/2 (concert vers 1909)	B97

Schubert:

14.76	"Overture," in D major, D4 (p1888, to opera: Der Teufel als Hydraulicus)	B98
14.77	"Overture," in D major, D26 (p1888)	B99
14.78	"Overture," in B-flat major, D470 (p1888)	B100
14.79	"5 Minuets," D89 (p1888)	B101
14.80	"5 Deutsche," D90 (p1888)	B102
14.81	"Overture," in D major, D556 (p1889)	B103
14.82	"Overture," in E minor, D648 (p1889)	B104
14.83	"Overture in the Italian style," in D major, D590 (p1889)	B105
14.84	"Overture in the Italian style," in C major, D591 (p1889)	B106

Schumann:

14.85	"Concert Allegro," in D minor, Op.134 (arr1888; 2pf)	B109

Wagner:

14.86	"Siegfried's Funeral March," from opera: Götterdämmerung, WWV86D (p1883)	B111

Weill:

14.87	"Frauentanz. 7 Gedichte des Mittelalters," for S & insts (p1925; red for pf & text)	B112

Unknown:

14.88	"Fugue," in A minor for org (arr ?1888)	B113

* * * * *

K = Jürgen Kindermann: "Thematisch-chronologisches Verzeichnis der Werke von Ferruccio Busoni." Regensburg. Gustav Bosse Verlag, 1980.
B = "Verzeichnis der Kadenzen, Bearbeitungen und Ausgaben" in Kindermann's catalog.

1. CHAMBER MUSIC

1.1	7 "Suonate" (Trio Sonatas) (p ?1694; 2vn, va da gamba & hpd): No.1 in F major	Op.1, B252
1.2	No.2 in G major	B253
1.3	No.3 in A minor	B254
1.4	No.4 in B-flat major	B255
1.5	No.5 in C major	B256
1.6	No.6 in D minor	B257
1.7	No.7 in E minor	B258
1.8	7 "Suonate" (Trio Sonatas) (p ?1694; 2vn, va da gamba & hpd): No.1 in B-flat major	Op.2, B259
1.9	No.2 in D major	B260
1.10	No.3 in G minor	B261
1.11	No.4 in C minor	B262
1.12	No.5 in A major	B263
1.13	No.6 in E major	B264
1.14	No.7 in F major	B265
1.15	"Sonata," in C major (2vn, va da gamba & cont)	B266
1.16	"Sonata," in D major (va da gamba, vle & cont)	B267
1.17	"Sonata," in D major (va da gamba & cont)	B268
1.18	"Sonata," in F major (2vn, va da gamba & cont)	B269
1.19	*"Sonata," in F major (2vn & cont, frag)*	*B270*
1.20	*"Sonata," in G major, "zur Kirchen und Tafel-Musik" (2vn, va da gamba & cont, frag)*	*B271*
1.21	"Sonata," in A minor (vn, va da gamba & cont)	B272
1.22	"Sonata," in B-flat major (vn, va da gamba & cont, early vers of B255 + suite)	B273
1.23	*"Sonaten" (zur Kirchen- u. Tafel-Music bequemlich, Lübeck) (2/3vv, va da gamba & cont, lost)*	*B274*
1.24	*"Sonatina forte con molti violini doi Oboi" (c1705, lost)*	*B275*

2. KEYBOARD

Keyboard Suites:

2.1	Keyboard Suite in C major: No.1 "Allemande"	B226
2.2	No.2 "Courante"	
2.3	No.3 "Sarabande"	
2.4	No.4 "Sarabande, La Seconde"	
2.5	No.5 "Gigue"	
2.6	Keyboard Suite in C major: No.1 "Allemande"	B227
2.7	No.2 "Courante"	
2.8	No.3 "Sarabande"	
2.9	No.4 "Gigue"	
2.10	Keyboard Suite in C major: No.1 "Allemande"	B228
2.11	No.2 "Courante"	
2.12	No.3 "Sarabande"	
2.13	No.4 "Double"	
2.14	No.5 "Gigue"	
2.15	Keyboard Suite in C major: No.1 "Allemande"	B229
2.16	No.2 "Courante"	
2.17	No.3 "Sarabande"	
2.18	Keyboard Suite in C major: No.1 "Allemande"	B230
2.19	No.2 "Courante"	
2.20	No.3 "Sarabande"	
2.21	No.4 "Gigue"	
2.22	Keyboard Suite in C major: No.1 "Allemande"	B231
2.23	No.2 "Courante"	
2.24	No.3 "Sarabande"	
2.25	Keyboard Suite in D major: No.1 "Allemande"	B232
2.26	No.2 "Courante"	
2.27	Keyboard Suite in D minor, "d'Amour": No.1 "Allemande d'amour"	B233
2.28	No.2 "Courante"	
2.29	No.3 "Sarabande d'amour"	
2.30	No.4 "Sarabande"	
2.31	No.5 "Gigue"	
2.32	Keyboard Suite in D minor: No.1 "Allemande"	B234
2.33	No.2 "Double	
2.34	No.3 "Courante"	
2.35	No.4 "Double"	
2.36	No.5 "Sarabande"	
2.37	No.6 "Sarabande"	
2.38	Keyboard Suite in E minor: No.1 "Allemande"	B235
2.39	No.2 "Courante"	
2.40	No.3 "Sarabande"	
2.41	No.4 "Gigue"	
2.42	Keyboard Suite in E minor: No.1 "Allemande"	B236
2.43	No.2 "Courante"	

4. SACRED CHORAL & VOCAL

6. DOUBTFUL & FALSELY ATTRIBUTED

Doubtful:

Falsely attributed:

* * * * *

B =   "Thematisch-systematisches Verzeichnis der musikalischen Werke von Dietrich Buxtehude:
           Buxtehude-Werke-Verzeichnis (BuxWV)." G. Karstädt, ed. Breitkopf & Härtel. Wiesbaden, 1974.
           Anh = Anhang (Appendix) in the BuxWV catalog.

1. AUDIO-VISUAL WORKS

1.1 "The Seasons" (Ballet in One Act) (c1947; orch; transcr for pf, only pf vers pubd) ....

1.2 "Water Music" (6 min) (c1952; pianist using radio, whistles & other means).......................................

1.3 "Music Walk" (c1958; 1 or more pianists at 1pf using radios &/or recordings; used in dance performances)

1.4 "Sounds of Venice" (c1959; solo TV performance) ....

1.5 "Water Walk" (3 min) (c1959; solo TV performance) ....

1.6 "Theatre Piece" (c1960; up to 8 performers) ....

1.7 "Variations V" (c1965, 37 remarks on an audio-visual performance) ....

1.8 "Musicircus" (c1967; diverse performers) ....

1.9 "Reunion" (c1968; diverse performers) ....

1.10 "HPSCHD" (c1969; up to 7hpd, up to 51 tapes & other phenomena ad lib, collab Lejaren Hiller) ....

1.11 "Les Chants de Maldoror pulverisés par l'assistance même" (c1971; francophone audience) ....

1.12 "WGBH-TV" (c1971; composer & technicians).......................................

1.13 "Bird Cage" (c1972; tapes w/ solo performer) ....

1.14 "Lecture on the Weather" (c1975; 12 performers w/ independant sound-systems, recordings & film) ....

1.15 "49 Waltzes for the 5 Boroughs" (c1977; 1 or more performers/listeners/record makers) ....

1.16 "A Dip in the Lake: 10 Quicksteps, 62 Waltzes, & 56 Marches for Chicago and Vicinity" (c1978; 1 or more performers/listeners/record makers) ....

1.17 "Four Walls," 2 act dance-play (Cunningham; S & pf) ....

2. ORCHESTRAL WORKS

2.1 "Atlas Eclipticalis" (c1961–2; up to 86 insts; used in dance performances) ....

2.2 "Etcetera" (c1973; orch of any size & tape) ....

2.3 "Quartets I–VIII" (c1976; 24, 41 or 93 insts; vers for concert band & 12 amplified vv 1976: I, 1977: V, VI) ...

2.4 "Renga" (c1976; up to 78 insts &/or vv) ....

2.5 "30 Pieces for 5 Orchestras" (c1981) ....

2.6 "58" (c1992; 58 insts).......................................

2.7 "Thirteen" (c1992).......................................

3. CONCERTOS, SOLO INSTR & ORCH

3.1 "Concerto" (19$\frac{1}{2}$ min) (c1951; prepared pf & chamber orch).......................................

3.2 "Concerto" (c1957–8; pf & orch, solos for pf & 13 other insts played in any combination).......................................

4. STRING QUARTETS

4.1 "String Quartet in Four Parts" (20 min) (c1949–50):.......................................
  1. (subject: summer in France)
  2. (subject: fall in America)
  3. (subject: winter expressed as a canon)
  4. (subject: spring expressed as a quodlibet)

4.2 "30 Pieces for String Quartet" (c1983) ....

4.3 "Music for Four" (c1987, r1988) ....

5. OTHER CHAMBER MUSIC

3 or more insts:

5.1 "Music for Wind Instruments" (12-tone method, 8 min) (c1938; winds): No.1 "Trio" (fl, cl & bn) ....

5.2   No.2 "Duo" (ob & hn)

5.3   No.3 "Quintet" (fl, ob, cl, hn & bn)

5.4 "16 Dances" (53 min) (c1951; fl, tpt, vn, vc & perc qt) ....

5.5 "Music for Six" (c1984; fl, cl, trbn, 2pf & perc) ....

5.6 "Hymnkus" (c1986; fl, cl, bn, trbn & 2pf) ....

5.7 "Five" (c1988; fl, cl, d bass & 2perc) ....

5.8 "Fourteen" (c1990; 14insts) ....

5.9 "Ten" (c1991; 10insts) ....

5.10 "Seven 2" (c1992; b fl, cl, trbn, vc, d bass & 2perc).......................................

5.11 "Ryoanji" (c1983–95; fl, trbn, perc & other combinations) ....

Vn & pf:

5.12 "Nocturne for Violin and Piano" (4 min) (c1947) ....

5.13 "6 Melodies" (15 min) (c1950) ....

Other 2 insts:

5.14 "3 Pieces for Flute Duet" (6 min) (c1935; 2fl, studies in two-part chromatic writing) ....

5.15 "Etudes boréales" (c1978–9; vc &/or pf).......................................

5.16   "TWO5" (c1991; trbn & pf) ....

1 instr:

5.17   "Sonata for Clarinet" (6 min) (c1933; cl) ....
5.18   "Sliding Trombone" (c1957–8) ....
5.19   "Imitations II" (c1976; cl) ....
5.20   "Chorals" (c1978; vn) ....
5.21   "Etudes Boreales" (c1978; vc) ....
5.22   32 "Freeman Etudes" (I–XVI c1978, XVII–XXXII c from 1979; vn) ....

6. PERCUSSION & ELECTRONIC DEVICES

6.1   "Quartet" (20 min) (c1935) ....
6.2   "Trio" (12 min) (c1936; skin & wood insts): No.1 "Allegro" ....
6.3   No.2 "March"
6.4   No.3 "Waltz" (used as 3rd movt in: Amores of 1943—see prepared pf)
6.5   "Imaginary Landscape No.1" (6 min) (c1939; perc qt w/ 2 variable-speed gramophones) ....
6.6   "First Construction (in Metal)" (c1939; perc sextet w/ assistant) ....
6.7   "Second Construction" (6 min) (c1940; perc qt) ....
6.8   "Living Room Music," suite (6 min) (c1940, Stein; perc & speech qt): No.1 "To Begin With" ....
6.9   No.2 "A Story"
6.10   No.3 "To End With"
6.11   "Third Construction" (15 min) (c1941; perc qt) ....
6.12   "Double Music" (6 min) (c1941; perc qt, collab Lou Harrison) ....
6.13   "March No.1" (Imaginary Landscape No.2) (7 min) (c1942; perc qnt w/ electric devices)...........
6.14   "Imaginary Landscape No.3" (3 min) (c1942; perc sextet w/ electric devices) ....
6.15   "Credo in Us" (12 min) (c1942; perc qt incl pf; used in dance performances) ....
6.16   "Imaginary Landscape No.4" (March No.2) (4 min) (c1951; 12 radios, 24 players & conductor) ....
6.17   "Imaginary Landscape No.5" (4 min) (c1952; any 42 recordings; used in dance performances) ......
6.18   "Speech" (42 min) (c1955; 5 radios & news-reader) ....
6.19   "Radio Music" (6 min) (c1956; up to 8 performers, each at one radio) ....
6.20   "Cartridge Music" (c1960; amplified sounds, any number of players; used in dance performances) .....
6.21   "Music for Amplified Toy Pianos" (c1960; any number of readings for a given performance) ....
6.22   "Variations III" (c1962–3; 1 or any number of people performing any actions) ....
6.23   "Variations IV" (c1963; any number of players, any sound or combination of sounds by any means,
                 w/ or w/ out other activities) ....
6.24   "Variations VI" (c1966; plurality of sound systems: any sources, components, and loud-speakers) ....
6.25   "Variations VII" (c1966; various means) ....
6.26   "Variations VIII" (c1978; no music or recordings) ....

7. MAGNETIC TAPE

7.1   "Williams Mix" (4 min) (c1952) ....
7.2   "Fontana Mix" (c1958; any means; also 17 min tape vers 1958–9) ....
7.3   "WBAI" (c1960; auxiliary score for use w/ lecture or other pieces) ....
7.4   "Music for 'The Marrying Maiden' " (c1960, for Jackson MacLow's play; also 9 min tape vers)..........
7.5   "Where Are We Going? And What Are We Doing?" (c1960; set of 4 tapes) ....
7.6   "Rozart Mix" (c1965; tape loops) ....
7.7   "Newport Mix" (c1967; tape loops) ....

8. MISC SOLO OR ENSEMBLE

8.1   "6 Short Inventions" (7 min) (c1933; alto fl, B-flat cl, B-flat tpt, vn, 2va & vc) ....
8.2   "Solo with Obbl. Acc of 2 Voices in Canon, and 6 Short Inventions on the Subject of the Solo" (15 min)
                 (c1933; any 3 or more insts, chromatic composition) ....
8.3   "Sonata for 2 Voices" (c1933; any 2 or more insts, chromatic composition in 3 movts)............
8.4   "Composition for 3 Voices" (4 min) (c1934; any 3 or more insts) ....
8.5   "She Is Asleep," concert (15 min) (c1943): No.1 "Quartet" (12 tom-toms) ....
8.6   No.2 "Duet" (vocalise; 1v & prepared pf)
8.7   No.3 "A Room" (pf/prepared pf, conventional notation)
8.8   "4' 33" " (No.1) (a graph) (c1952; any instr/ensemble, no sounds intentionally produced) (at its premiere
                 D. Tudor sat silently at the piano for 4 min and 33 sec—sounds of the audience were the music).......:....
8.9   "59½" For a String Player" (a graph) (c1953) ....
8.10   "26' 1.1499" For a String Player" (c1955) ....
8.11   "27' 10.554" For a Percussionist" (a graph) (c1956) ....
8.12   "Variations I" (c1958, any number of players, any sound-producing means) ....
8.13   "Variations II" (c1961, any number of players, any sound-producing means) ....
8.14   "4' 33" " No.2 or "0' 00" " (c1952; solo in any way by anyone) ....
8.15   "Sound Anonymously Received" (c1969; unsolicited instr) ....
8.16   "33½" (c1969; records & gramophones) ....
8.17   "Score (40 Drawings by Thoreau) and 23 Parts" (c1974; any insts &/or vv) ....

8.18	"Child of Tree" (Improvisation I) (c1975; percussionist using amplified plant materials) ....
8.19	"Apartment House 1776" (c1976; any number of musicians) ....
8.20	"Branches" (c1976; perc solo or ensemble using amplified plant materials" ....
8.21	"Inlets" (Improvisation II) (c1977; 4 conch players & the sound of fire) ....
8.22	"Pools" (c1978; conch shells & tape) ....
8.23	"Some of 'The Harmony of Maine' " (c1978; org w/ assistants): ....

         1. "Alpha C. M."
         2. "Majesty C. M."
         3. "Harmony C. M."
         4. "Creation L. M."
         5. "Hallowell S. M."
         6. "Advent C. M."
         7. "Turner C. M."
         8. "Sunday C. M."
         9. "St. John's C. M."
        10. "Invitation L. M."
        11. "Transmigration"
        12. "Chester L. M."
        13. "The Lilly P. M."

8.24	"Il treno," 3 happenings (c1978; prepared trains) ....
8.25	"Someday," 10-hour radio event (c1978) ....
8.26	"- - - - -, - - - - - - - - Circus on - - - - - - - - - -," (means for translating a book into music) (c1979): ....
	. Realization: "Roaratorio, an Irish Circus on Finnegans Wake" (collab John Fulleman)
8.27	"Improvisation III" (c1980) ....
8.28	"Improvisation IV" (c1980) ....

9. PIANO

9.1	"Music for Xenia" (c1934) ....
9.2	"Quest" (c1935, only 2nd movt pubd)
9.3	"2 Pieces" (ca1935, r1974) ....
9.4	"Metamorphosis" (12-tone method, 15 min) (c1938, in 5 movts) ....
9.5	"Our Spring Will Come" (c1943) ....
9.6	"A Room" (2 min) (pf/prepared pf, = No.3 of concert: She Is Asleep of 1943—see Various solos) ....
9.7	"Ophelia" (5 min) (c1946; used in dance performances) ....
9.8	"2 Pieces" (c1946) ....
9.9	"The Seasons" (15 min) (c1947; orig orch score for ballet; only pf vers pubd) ....
9.10	"Dream" (5 min) (c1948; used in dance performances) ....
9.11	"In a Landscape" (8 min) (c1948; pf/harp; used in dance performances) ....
9.12	"Suite for Toy Piano" (8 min) (c1948; toy pf/pf; used in dance performances) ....
9.13	"Music of Changes," 4 Vols (43 min) (c1951) ....
9.14	"Waiting" (1 min) (c1952; used in dance performances) ....
9.15	"7 Haiku" (3 min) (c1952, based on 17-syllabe Japanese poem-structure; used in dance performances) ....
9.16	"For M.C. and D.T." (2 min) (c1952) ....
9.17	"Music for Piano 1" (4 min) (c1952; used in dance performances) ....
9.18	"Music for Piano 2" (4 min, tempo & dynamics free) (c1953; used in dance performances) ....
9.19	"Music for Piano 3" (tempo & dynamics free) (c1953) ....
9.20	"Music for Piano 4–19" (tempo & dynamics free) (c1953; solo/ens) ....
9.21	"Music for Piano 20" (tempo & dynamics free) (c1953) ....
9.22	"Music for Piano 21–36; 37–52," 2 groups of 16 pieces (length in time free) (c1955; solo/ens) ....
9.23	"Music for Piano 53–68," a group of 16 pieces (c1956; solo/ens) ....
9.24	"Music for Piano 69–84," a group of 16 pieces (c1956; solo/ens; used in dance performances)...................
9.25	"Winter Music" (c1957; 20 pages for one or shared by up to 20 pianists; used in dance performances) ......
9.26	"For Paul Taylor and Anita Dencks" (3 min) (c1957; used in dance performances) ....
9.27	"TV Köln" (c1958; noises produced on the interior/exterior of the piano, also auxiliary means) ....
9.28	"Electronic Music for Piano" (c1964; pf w/ electronics) ....
9.29	"Cheap Imitations" (c1969; arr for orch of 24, 59 or 95 players 1972; also for vn 1969) ....
9.30	"Etudes Australes" (c1974–5) ....
9.31	"ASLSP" (c1985) ....

     2 Pf:

9.32	"Experiences I" (6 min) (c1945–8; used in dance performances) ....

10. PREPARED PIANO

10.1	"Bacchanale" (6 min) (c1938, 1st free piece for prepared pf; used in dance performances) ....
10.2	"And the Earth Shall Bear Again" (c1942) ....
10.3	"In the Name of the Holocaust" (c1942) ....
10.4	"Amores" (9 min) (c1943): No.1 "Solo for Prepared Piano" (1 min)..
10.5	No.2 "Trio" (3 min) (9 tom-toms, pod rattle)
10.6	No.3 "Trio" (1 min) (7 woodblocks, not Chinese, = Waltz from: Trio of 1936)
10.7	No.4 "Solo for Prepared Piano" (4 min)

10.8   "Tossed as it is Untroubled" (c1943) ....
10.9   "Totem Ancestor" (2 min) (c1943, written for the dance) ....
10.10   "The Perilous Night," 6 piece suite (12 min) (c1943–4) ....
10.11   "Meditation" (3 min) (c1943; used in dance performances) ....
10.12   "Prelude for Meditation" (1 min) (c1944) ....
10.13   "Root of an Unfocus" (4 min) (c1944; used in dance performances)...
10.14   "Spontaneous Earth" (c1944) ....
10.15   "The Unavailable Memory of" (c1944) ....
10.16   "A Valentine out of Season," 3 piece suite (4 min) (c1944; used in dance performances) ....
10.17   "Daughters of the Lonesome Isle" (12 min) (c1945, conventional notation; used in dance performances) ...
10.18   "Mysterious Adventure" (8 min) (c1945, written for the dance, conventional notation) ....
10.19   "Music for Marcel Duchamp" (5 min) (c1947; used in film: Dreams that Money Can Buy of 1948)...............
10.20   "Sonatas and Interludes" (70 min) (c1946–8, expression of the 'permanent emotions' of Indian tradition)....
10.21   "2 Pastorales" (14 min) (c1951–2; used in dance performances) ....
10.22   "31' 57.9864" For a Pianist" (c1954) ....
10.23   "34' 46.776" For a Pianist" (c1954) ....

2 Prepared pf:

10.24   "A Book of Music" (30 min) (c1944, 1 piece in 2 parts) ....
10.25   "3 Dances" (20 min) (c1944–5, written for virtuosos; used in dance performances) ....

11. CARILLON

11.1   "Music for Carillon No.1" (graph score, 4 min) (c1952; also 2 vers: 2-octave & 3-octave) ....
11.2   "Music for Carillon No.2" (graph score—w/ No.3) (c1954; also 2-octave vers—1 min) ....
11.3   "Music for Carillon No.3" (graph score—w/ No.2) (c1954; also 2-octave vers—1 min) ....
11.4   "Music for Carillon No.4" (10 min) (c1961; electronic instr & electronic acc) ....
11.5   "Music for Carillon No.5" (c1967)..

12. ORGAN

12.1   "Souvenir" (c1983) ....

13. VOCAL

13.1   "3 Songs" (c1932, Stein; 1v & pf): 1. "Twenty Years After" ....
13.2   2. "It is as it was"
13.3   3. "At east and ingredients"
13.4   "5 Songs" (unorthodox 12-tone method, 12 min) (c1938, e. e. cummings; A & pf): 1. "little four paws" ....
13.5   2. "little Christmas tree"
13.6   3. "in Just-"
13.7   4. "hist whist"
13.8   5. "another comes"
13.9   "Forever and Sunsmell" (5 min) (c1942, e. e. cummings; 1v & perc duo; used in dance performances) ......
13.10   "The Wonderful Widow of Eighteen Springs" (2 min) (c1942, Joyce; 1v & closed pf) ....
13.11   "Experiences II" (3 min) (c1945–8, e. e. cummings; 1v; used in dance performances) ....
13.12   "A Flower" (4 min) (c1950, textless; 1v & closed pf; used in dance performances) ....
13.13   "Solo for Voice 1" (to be used alone or with any parts of Concert) (c1958; 1v) ....
13.14   "Aria" (to be used alone or with Fontana Mix, or any parts of Concert) (c1958; 1v)......................
13.15   "Solo for Voice 2" (to be used alone or with Concert, Fontana Mix, Cartridge Music) (c1960; 1v) ....
13.16   "Song Books" (Solos for Voice 3–92) (c1970) ....
13.17   "Mureau" (c1970; 1v) ....
13.18   "62 Mesostics re Merce Cunningham" (c1971; 1v) ....
13.19   "Letters to Erik Satie" (c1978; 1v & tape) ....
13.20   "Hymns and Variations" (c1978; 12 amplified vv) ....
13.21   "Litany for the Whale" (c1980; 2vv) ....
13.22   "Eight Whiskus" (c1984, from Chris Mann; 1v)..
13.23   "Mirakus" (c1984, from Marcel Duchamp; 1v) ....
13.24   "Music for Two (by One)" (c1984) ....
13.25   "Nowth upon Nacht" (c1984, Joyce; 1v & pf) ....
13.26   "Sonnekus" (c1985, Genesis; 1v & pf)..
13.27   "New York City" (c1994; sounds recorded outside Cage's apartment) ....
13.28   "Diary: How to improve the World (You will only make matters worse)" (unfin) ....

* * * * *

Performance times given by the composer in: "John Cage." Edited by Robert Dunn. Henmar Press Inc.
373 Park Avenue South. New York, N.Y., 1962.

1. STAGE WORKS

Operas:

1.1	"La mandragola; commedia musicale fiorentina," 3 acts (c1920–23, after Machiavelli's comedy)	Op.20
1.2	"Il mercante di Venezia" (The Merchant of Venice), 3 acts (c1956, after Shakespeare; also see overture Op.76) (also see incid music c by Moniuszko & Sullivan)	Op.181
1.3	"All's Well that Ends Well" (c1955–8, after Shakespeare)	Op.182
1.4	"Saul" (c1958–60, Alfieri)	Op.191
1.5	"The Importance of Being Earnest," chamber opera (c1961–2, Wilde)	
1.6	"Aucassin et Nicolette," marionette fable (c1919–38)	
1.7	"The Song of Songs," rustic wedding idyll (c1954–5)	

Ballets:

1.8	"Bacco in Toscana" (p1931, after Redi's poem; 2vv, ch & orch)	Op.39
1.9	"Pesce turchino" (p1937, after pf piece)	
1.10	"Bas-relief: La reine Nefertiti" (p1938)	
1.11	"The Octoroon Ball" (c1947, Dunham)	Op.136
1.12	"Naomi and Ruth" (c1947)	

Incid music:

1.13	"Savonarola" (p1935, Alessi)	Op.81
1.14	"I giganti della montagna" (p1937, Pirandello)	Op.94
1.15	"Morning in Iowa" (c1954, Nathan)	

Film:

1.16	"And Then There Were None" (c1945, dir Rene Clair)	
1.17	"The Day of the Fox" (c1947)	

2. ORCHESTRAL WORKS

Overtures to Shakespeare's plays:

2.1	"La bisbetica domata" (The Taming of the Shrew) (c1930)	Op.61
2.2	"La dodicesima notte" (Twelfth Night) (c1933) (also see opera c by Smetana: Viola, T133 & incid music c by Sibelius Op.60)	Op.73
2.3	"Il mercante di Venezia" (The Merchant of Venice) (c1933; also see opera Op.181)	Op.76
2.4	"Giulio Cesare" (c1934) (also see incid music c by Milhaud Op.158 & Ov c by Schumann Op.128) ...	Op.78
2.5	"Il racconto d'inverno" (The Winter's Tale) (c1934, used music from song: The Pedlar, Op.24/VIII/1)	Op.80
2.6	"A Midsummer Night's Dream" (c1940) (also see Britten's opera Op.64, Mendelssohn's incid music Op.61, Orff's music drama, Purcell's semi-opera: The Fairy Queen, Z629 & Satie's incid music: 5 Grimaces)	Op.108
2.7	"King John" (c1941)	Op.111
2.8	"Antony and Cleopatra" (c1947) (also see opera c by Barber Op.40)	Op.134
2.9	"The Tragedy of Coriolanus" (c1947)	Op.135
2.10	"Much Ado about Nothing" (c1953)	Op.164
2.11	"As You Like It" (c1953) (also see work for radio c by Kabalevsky)	Op.166

Other orch works:

2.12	"Le dance del re David" (c1925)	
2.13	"Cipressi" (p1940)	
2.14	"The Birthday of the Infanta," suite (c1942, after Wilde)	Op.115
2.15	"Indian Songs & Dances" (c1942)	Op.116
2.16	"5 Humoresques on themes of Foster" (c1943)	Op.121
2.17	"An American Rhapsody" (c1943)	
2.18	"Love's Labour's Lost," 4 dances (c1953): No.1 "Sarabande (for the King of Navarre)"	Op.167
2.19	No.2 "Gavotte (for the Princess of France)"	
2.20	No.3 "Spanish Dance (for Don Adriano de Armado)"	
2.21	No.4 "Russian Dance (Masque)"	

3. CONCERTOS, SOLO INSTR & ORCH

Pf & orch:

3.1	Piano Concerto No.1 (c1927)	Op.46
3.2	Piano Concerto No.2 in G major (c1936–7)	Op.92

Vn & orch:

3.3	Violin Concerto No.1 in G minor, "Concerto italiano" (c1924)	Op.31

3.4	"Symphonic Variations" (c1928)	Op.48
3.5	Violin Concerto No.2, "I profeti" (The Prophets) (c1931)	Op.66
3.6	Violin Concerto No.3 (c1939)	Op.102
3.7	"Larchmont Woods," poem (c1942)	Op.112

Vc & orch:

| 3.8 | Cello Concerto (c1932–3) | Op.72 |

Gui & orch:

3.9	Guitar Concerto No.1 in D major (c1939)	Op.99
3.10	Guitar Concerto No.2 in C major (c1953)	Op.160
3.11	"Capriccio diabolico" (c1945, after gui work Op.85)	Op.85b
3.12	"Serenade" (c1943; gui & chamber orch)	Op.118
3.13	Double Guitar Concerto (c1962; also red w/ pf)	Op.201

Other:

| 3.14 | "Concertino" (c1937; harp, str qt & 3cl, also for harp & chamber orch) | Op.93 |
| 3.15 | "Concerto da camera" (c1950; ob, 3hn, strings & timp ad lib) | Op.146 |

4. STRING QUARTETS

4.1	String Quartet No.1 (c1929)	Op.58
4.2	String Quartet No.2 in G major (c1948)	Op.139
4.3	String Quartet No.3, "Casa al dono" (c1963)	Op.203

5. OTHER CHAMBER MUSIC

5 or more insts:

5.1	Piano Quintet No.1 (c1931–2)	Op.69
5.2	Guitar Quintet (c1950; gui & str qt)	Op.143
5.3	Piano Quintet No.2 (c1934–51)	Op.155

3 insts

5.4	Piano Trio No.1 (c1928)	Op.49
5.5	Piano Trio No.2 (c1932)	Op.70
5.6	String Trio (c1950)	Op.147
5.7	"Eclogues" (fl, Eng hn & gui)	Op.206

Vn & pf:

5.8	"Capitan Fracassa" (c1921)	Op.16
5.9	"Notturno Adriatico" (c1924)	Op.34
5.10	Violin Sonata (c1928)	Op.50
5.11	Violin Sonata, "Quasi una fantasia" (c1929)	Op.56

Vc & pf:

5.12	Cello Sonata in E-flat major (c1928)	
5.13	"I nottambuli: variazioni fantastiche" (c1927; orchd1960)	Op.47
5.14	"Toccata" (Introduzione, aria e finale) (c1935)	Op.83
5.15	"Figaro" (p1963, concert transcription from Rossini's opera: The Barber of Seville)	

Other 1–2 insts & greeting cards:

5.16	"Divertimento (c1943; 2fl)	Op.119
5.17	Clarinet Sonata (c1945)	Op.128
5.18	"Sonata" (c1945; vn & va)	Op.128
5.19	Basoon Sonatina (c1946)	Op.130
5.20	"Sonata," in C minor (c1950; va & vc)	Op.144
5.21	"Fantasia" (c1950; gui & pf)	Op.145
5.22	"Sonata" (c1950; vn & vc)	Op.148
5.23	Greeting cards (c1954–67, small pieces for 1-4 insts)	Op.170
5.24	"2 Trumpet Sonatas" (c1955)	Op.179
5.25	"Sonatina" (c1965; fl & gui)	Op.205
5.26	"Sonata" (c1967; vc & harp)	Op.208
5.27	"The Harp of David," rhapsody (harp)	Op.209

6. GUITAR

7. PIANO SONATAS

8. OTHER PIANO WORKS

4. "The massacre of the Innocents"
5. "The flight into Egypt"
6. "Child Jesus and the Doctors"
II. "The Life": 7. "The Baptism on the Jordan"
8. "The dance of Salome"
9. "By the sea of Galilee"
10. "Jesus walking on the waves"
11. "The woman of Samarca at the well"
12. "The resurrection of Lazarus"
13. "Mary Magdalene"
14. "Jesus and the Money-Changers"
III. "The Words": 15. "The sermon on the mount"
16. "Pater Noster" (Our Father who art in Heaven)
17. "Sinite parvulos venire ad me" (Jesus and the little children)
18. "Invective" (Woe into you Scribes and Pharises, hypocrites!)
19. "The wise virgins and the foolish virgins" (A parable)
20. "The lost sheep" (A parable)
21. "The return of the prodigal son" (A parable)
IV. "The Passion": 22. "Hosanna" (The Entrance into Jerusalem)
23. "The Last Supper"
24. "Gethsemane" (The prayer in the garden)
25. "Crucifige" (before Pontius Pilate)
26. "Golgotha" (on the way to the Calvary)
27. "The Last Words"
28. "The Resurrection"

8.44	"6 Canons" (c1950)	Op.142
8.45	"6 Pieces in Form of Canons" (c1952): No.1 "Cradle Song" (Ninna-nanna)	Op.156
8.46	No.2 "Little March" (Marcetta)	
8.47	No.3 "Toccata"	
8.48	No.4 "Elegy" (Hommage à Fauré)	
8.49	No.5 "Valse" (Hommage à Chabrier)	
8.50	No.6 "Tarantella" (Hommage à Casella)	
8.51	"El encanto" (c1953)	Op.165
8.52	"Sonatina zoologica" (Libellule—La chiocciola—Lucertolina—Formiche) (c1960, 3rd movt c1916)	Op.187

2 Pf:

8.53	2 Pieces (c1945, 1959)	

9. ORGAN

9.1	"Prayers my grandfather wrote," 6 preludes (on theme of Bruto Senigaglia)	
9.2	"Prelude on the twelve tone row"	

10. CHORAL WORKS

Oratorios:

10.1	"Il libro di Ruth" (c1949)	Op.140
10.2	"Il libro di Giona" (c1951)	Op.151
10.3	"The Book of Esther" (c1962)	Op.200
10.4	"Tobias and the Angel," scenic oratorio (c1964–5, Tobit)	Op.204

Other choral works w/ insts:

10.5	2 "Laudi" (c1935; ch & pf)	
10.6	"Sacred Synagogue Service" (c1943, r1950; Bar, ch & org)	Op.122
10.7	"Upon Westminster Bridge": "Earth has not anything to show more fair" (c1943, Wordsworth; ch & pf)	
10.8	"Kol Nidrei" (c1944; cantor, ch, org & vc)	
10.9	"December" (c1944, Keats; fem ch & pf)	
10.10	"Proud Maisie" (c1944, Scott; ch & pf)	
10.11	"A Serenade": "Ah! County Guy, the hour is nigh" (c1944, Scott; ch & pf) (also see Sullivan's song of 1867)	
10.12	"Pibroch of Donuil Dhu" (c1946, Scott; ch & pf)	
10.13	"Naomi and Ruth," cantata (c1947; fem vv & pf/org)	Op.137
10.14	"Coronach": "He is gone on the mountain" (c1948, Scott; ch & pf)	
10.15	"Songs and processionals for a Jewish wedding" (c1951; ch & pf/org)	Op.150
10.16	"Romancero Gitano" (7 poems of F. Garcia Lorca) (c1951, Lorca; ch & gui)	Op.152
10.17	"Music, when soft voices die" (c1951, Shelley; fem ch & pf) (also see Vaughan Williams' work of 1891)	
10.18	"Naaritz'cho" (c1952; cantor, ch & org)	
10.19	"4 Christina Rossetti Settings" (c1952, Rossetti; fem ch & pf)	
10.20	"The Queen of Sheba," cantata (c1953; fem vv & pf)	Op.161
10.21	"Song of the Oceanides" (c1954, from Aeschylus: Prometheus bound; 2 fem ch, 2fl & harp)	Op.171
10.22	"Lament": "O world! O life! O time!" (c1954, Shelley; fem ch & pf)	

10.23	"The Moon": "And like a dying lady" (c1954, Shelley; fem ch & pf) (also see Hindemith's 17. of: 25 Songs)
10.24	"3 Shelley Songs" (c1955, Shelley; fem ch & pf): . "When the lamp is shattered" Op.173
10.25	. "The fountains mingle with the river" (also see Delius RTv/12:2 & Gounod's song of 1871)
10.26	. "One word is too often profaned"
10.27	"On the Grasshoper and Cricket": "The poetry of earth is never dead" (c1955, Keats; fem ch & pf) ....
10.28	"Psyche": "O Goddess! hear these tuneless numbers, wrung" (c1957, Keats; ch & pf)...............................
10.29	"The Fiery Furnace," cantata (c1958, Book of Daniel; narrator, child ch, pf/org & perc) Op.183
10.30	"Memorial Service for the Departed" (c1960; cantor, ch & org) Op.192
10.31	"The Owl": "When cats run home and light is come" (c1962, Tennyson; ch & pf) ....
10.32	"The Song of Songs" (p1963) ....

Unacc chorus:

10.33	"2 Madrigali a galatea" (c1914, Virgil) ....
10.34	"2 Canti greci" (c1916) ....
10.35	"Lecho dodi" (c1936; T & m ch; arr for T, ch & org) Op.90
10.36	"Goccius" (Laudi di S Efisio) (c1937; S & ch) Op.96
10.37	"The Mermaid Tavern": "Souls of Poets dead and gone" (c1942, Keats) ....
10.38	"Homer": "Much have I travell'd in the realms of gold" (c1944, Keats) Op.113/1
10.39	"Venice": "Once did She hold the gorgeous East in fee" (c1948, Wordsworth; m ch) ....
10.40	"The Dove": "I had a dove and the sweet dove died" (c1954, Keats) ....
10.41	"To Sleep": "O soft embalmer of the still midnight" (c1954, Keats) (also see Britten Op.31/6) ....
10.42	"Two or Three" (c1954, Keats) ....
10.43	"Happy is England! I could be content" (c1955, Keats; m ch) ....
10.44	"Old Meg": "Old Meg she was a gypsy" (c1955, Keats; m ch) ....
10.45	"To one who has been long in city pent" (c1955, Keats; m ch) ....
10.46	"Endymion" (c1960, Keats; 7-part ch) (also see Holst Op.41, H155) ....

11. VOICE & ORCHESTRA

11.1	"2 Liriche dal 'Gardiniere' " (c1917, Tagore) ....
11.2	"3 Fioretti di San Francesco" (c1919–20) ....
11.3	"6 Scottish Songs" (c1939, Scott; S, T, harp & strings) Op.100
11.4	"Lullaby" (c1943; vv & orch, on themes of Foster)...
11.5	"The Princess & the Pea," miniature opera (c1943; narrator & orch) Op.120
11.6	"Noah's Ark" (Flood), for collab cantata: Genesis (Creation) (c1944; narrator & orch) (other sections
	c by Schoenberg, Milhaud & Stravinsky) ....

12. MISC VOCAL

12.1	"La sera fiesolana" (c1923, d'Annunzio; 1v, vc & pf) ....
12.2	"3 Shakespeare Duets" (c1937; S, T & pf; orchd1938) Op.97
12.3	"Song of the Shulamite" (c1953, Bible; 1v, fl, harp & str qt) Op.163
12.4	"2 Schiller Balladen" (c1961; narrator, 2pf & perc) Op.193

13. SONGS (w/ pf or gui where indicated)

13.1	"Le roi Loys" (c1914, medieval French; orchd1930).. Op.3
13.2	"Stelle cadenti," cycle (c1915–8, trad Tuscan) Op.6
13.3	"Coplas," cycle (c1915, trad Spanish; orchd1967) Op.7
13.4	"Briciole" (c1915–6, Palazzeschi) Op.8
13.5	"L'infinito" (c1921, Leopardi) Op.22
13.6	"Shakespeare Songs" (c1921–25) Vol.I: 1. "Old Song": "Come away, death" (Twelfth Night) (also
	see Brahms Op.17/2, Holst Op.9a/4, H48/4 & Vaughan Williams' partsong of 1899) Op.24
13.7	2. "Fancy": "Tell me where is fancy bred" (Merchant of Venice) (also see song c by Poulenc,
	choral works c by Britten & Kodály)
13.8	3. "Fairies": "Ye spotted snakes" (Midsummer Night's Dream)
13.9	II (from As You Like It): 1. "Under the greenwood tree"
13.10	2. "Winter Wind": "Blow, blow, thou winter wind"
13.11	3. "Springtime": "It was a lover and his lass" (also see Delius RTv/30/1, Holst H59, Sullivan's
	partsong of 1857 & Vaughan Williams' partsong of 1922)
13.12	III: 1. "Orpheus" (Henry VIII) (also see Vaughan Williams' songs of 1903 & 1925)
13.13	2. "Silvia": "Who is Silvia?" (Two Gentlemen of Verona) (also see Schubert Op.106/4, D891)
13.14	3. "For the rain it raineth" (Twelfth Night) (also see Schumann Op.127/5)
13.15	IV: 1. "Sigh no more, ladies" (Much Ado) (also see Sullivan's 3. of: 5 Shakespeare Songs)
13.16	2. "Seals of Love": "Take, O take those lips away" (Measure for Measure) (also see Beach
	Op.37/2, B14/2 & Vaughan Williams' song of 1925)
13.17	3. "O mistress mine" (Twelfth Night) (also see Sullivan's 2. of: 5 Shakespeare Songs & Vaughan
	Williams' 3. of: 3 Elisabethan Songs)
13.18	V: 1. "Autolycus": "When daffodils begin to peer" (Winter's Tale)
13.19	2. "The Willow": "The poor soul sat sighing by a sycamore tree" (Othello) (also see Vaughan
	Williams' 2. of: 3 Elizabethan Songs)

13.20	3. "Roundel": "Fie on sinful fantasy!" (Merry Wives of Windsor)
13.21	VI: 1. "Apemantus's Grace": "Immortal gods" (Timon of Athens)
13.22	2. "Arise!": "Hark! hark! the lark" (Cymbeline) (also see Schubert D889)
13.23	3. "The Soldier Drinks": "And let me the canakin clink, clink" (Othello)
13.24	VII: 1. "The Clown in the Churchyard": "In youth when I did love" (Hamlet)
13.25	2. "Ophelia": "How should I your true love know" (Hamlet) (also see Brahms WoO posth 22, Elgar Op.21/1, Shostakovich Op.127/1 & R. Strauss Op.67)
13.26	3. "The Cuckoo and the Owl": "When daisies pied" (Love's Labour's Lost) (also see Stravinsky's 3. of: 3 Songs from Shakespeare of 1953)
13.27	VIII: 1. "The Pedlar": "Lawn as white as driven snow" (Winter's Tale)
13.28	2. "Come to Dust": "Fear no more the heat o' the sun" (Cymbeline)
13.29	3. "Two Maids Wooing a Man": "Get you hence, for I must go" (Winter's Tale)
13.30	IX: 1. "Merry Heart": "But shall I go mourn for that" (Winter's Tale)
13.31	2. "Heavily!": "Pardon, goddess of the night" (Much Ado About Nothing)
13.32	3. "The Horn": "What shall he have that kill'd the deer?" (As You Like It)
13.33	X (King Lear): "The Fool," 6 short songs linked together
13.34	XI (The Tempest): 1. "Merrily": "Where the bee sucks"
13.35	2. "The Sailor Drinks": "I shall no more to sea"
13.36	3. "Ariel": "Come unto these yellow sands" (also see Stravinsky's 2. of: 3 Shakespeare Songs & Vaughan Williams' 1. of: 3 Shakespeare Songs)
13.37	4. "Caliban": "No more dams I'll make for fish"
13.38	XII (The Tempest): "Epithalamium": "Honour, riches, marriage-blessing" (w/ Nuptial March for pf)
13.39	"8 Scherzi per musica" (c1924–5, Redi) Op.35
13.40	"Indian Serenade": "I arise from dreams" (c1925, Shelley) (also see Delius RTv/12:1 & Respighi P090/5) ..
13.41	"Heine Lieder" (c1926) Op.40
13.42	"4 Sonetti da La vita nuova" (c1926, Dante) Op.41
13.43	"Heine Lieder" (c1929) Op.60
13.44	"6 Odi di Orazio" (c1930) Op.62
13.45	"Ballade des biens immeubles" (c1931, Gide; orchd1934) Op.68
13.46	"Louisiana, Leaves of Grass, Ocean" (c1936, Whitman) Op.81
13.47	"3 Fragments de Marcel Proust" (c1936) Op.88
13.48	"28 Shakespeare Sonnets" (c1944–7; 3 add for ch; 4 add 1963) (also see Britten Op.60/8, Kabalevsky Op.52, Shostakovich Op.62/5 & Vaughan Williams' choral work of 1896) Op.125
13.49	"5 Poesie romanesche" (c1946, dell'Arco) Op.131
13.50	"Ballata dell'esiglio" (c1956, Cavalcanti; w/ gui) ....
13.51	"Vogelweide," cycle (c1958, Vogelweide; Bar & gui/pf): 1. "Schlimme Zeiten" Op.186
13.52	2. "Magdeburger Weihnacht"
13.53	3. "Die Römische Opfersteuer"
13.54	4. "Gott unergründlich"
13.55	5. "Unnatur"
13.56	6. "Reimar, der Mensch und der Künstler"
13.57	7. "Preislied"
13.58	8. "Wahre Liebe"
13.59	9. "Der Traum"
13.60	10. "Unter der Linde"
13.61	"Platero y yó" (Platero and I), melodrama (c1960, Jiménez; narrator & gui): 1. "Platero" Op.190
13.62	2. "Melancolia"
13.63	3. "Angelus"
13.64	4. "Golondrinas"
13.65	5. "La Arrulladora"
13.66	6. "Retorno"
13.67	7. "El Pozo"
13.68	8. "El Canario Vuela"
13.69	9. "La Primavera"
13.70	10. "A Platero en el Cielo de Moguer"
13.71	"Il bestiaro" (c1960, Loria) Op.188
13.72	"The Divan of Moses-ibn-Ezra," cycle (c1966; S & gui), I: 1. "When the morning of life has passed" Op.207
13.73	2. "The dove that nests in the tree-tops"
13.74	3. "Wrung with anguish"
13.75	II: 4. "Sorrow shatters my heart"
13.76	5. "Fate has blocked the way"
13.77	6. "O brook"
13.78	III: 7. "Drink deep, my friend"
13.79	8. "Dull and sad is the sky"
13.80	9. "The garden dons a coat of many"
13.81	IV: 10. "Men and children of this world"
13.82	11. "The world is like a woman of folly"
13.83	12. "Only in God I trust"
13.84	V: 14. "I have seen upon the earth"
13.85	15. "Let man remember all his days"
13.86	16. "Come now, to the Court of Death"
13.87	17. "Peace upon them"
13.88	18. "I behold ancient graves"
13.89	19. "Wouldst thou look upon me in my grave?"

* * * * *

CAVALLI, Francesco (CALETTI-BRUNI, Pier Francesco)
1602–1676

1. STAGE WORKS (operas)

1.1	"Le nozze di Teti e di Peleo," 3 act opera scenica (p1639, Persiani) ....
1.2	"Gli amori di Apollo e di Dafne," 3 acts (p1640, Busenello) ....
1.3	"La Didone," 3 acts (p1641, Busenello) ....
1.4	*"Narciso ed Ecco immortali" (p1642, Persiani, spur: c by Marazzoli & Vitali, music lost)* ....
1.5	"L'Amore innamorato," 5 act favola (p1642, Fusconi from plot by Loredano & poetry by Michiele) ....
1.6	"La virtù de' strali d'amore," 3 act opera tragicomica musicale (p1642, Faustini) ....
1.7	"L'Egisto," 3 act favola dramatica musicale (p1643, Faustini) ....
1.8	*"La Deidamia," 3 act opera musicale (p1644, Herrico, ?spur, music lost)* ....
1.9	"L'Ormindo," 3 act favola regia (p1644, Faustini) ....
1.10	*"Il Romolo e 'l Remo," 3 act drama (p1645, Strozzi, ?spur, music lost)* ....
1.11	"La Doriclea," 3 act drama musicale (p1645, Faustini) ....
1.12	*"Il Titone," 3 act drama per musica (p1645, Faustini, music lost)* ....
1.13	*"La prosperità infelice di Giulio Cesare dittatore," 5 act opera musicale (p1646, Busenello, ?spur, music lost)* .....
1.14	*"La Torilda," 3 act drama (p1648, Bissari, ?spur, music lost)* ....
1.15	"Il Giasone," 3 act drama musicale (p1649, Cicognini) ....
1.16	*"L'Euripo," 3 act drama per musica (p1649, Faustini, music lost)* ....
1.17	*"Il Bradamante," 3 act drama per musica (p1650, Bissari, ?spur, music lost)* ....
1.18	"L'Orimonte," 3 act drama per musica (p1650, Minato) ....
1.19	"L'Oristeo," 3 act drama per musica (p1651, Faustini) ....
1.20	"La Rosinda," 3 act drama per musica (p1651, Faustini) ....
1.21	*"L'Armidoro," 3 act drama per musica (p1651, Castoreo, ?spur, music lost)* ....
1.22	"La Calisto," 3 act drama per musica (p1651, Faustini) ....
1.23	"L'Eritrea," 3 act drama (p1652, Faustini) ....
1.24	"Veremonda, l'amazzone di Aragona," 3 act drama (p1652, Zorzisto—pseud of Strozzi, from Cicognini's Celio) ....
1.25	*"L'Helena rapita da Theseo," 3 act drama musicale (p1653, Badoaro, ?spur, music lost)* ....
1.26	"L'Orione," 3 act drama (p1653, Melosio) ....
1.27	"Il Ciro" (c1654, Sorrentino r by ?Aureli, music c by Provenzale, Cavalli added prologue & some arias) ......
1.28	"Xerse," 3 act drama per musica (p1655, Minato) ....
1.29	"La Statira, principessa di Persia," 3 act drama per musica (p1656, Busenello) ....
1.30	"L'Erismena," 3 act drama per musica (p1656, Aureli) ....
1.31	"Artemisia," 3 act drama per musica (p1656, Minato) ....
1.32	"L'Hipermestra," 3 act festa teatrale (p1658, Moniglia) ....
1.33	*"Antioco," 3 act drama per musica (p1659, Minato, music lost)* ....
1.34	"Elena," 3 act drama per musica (p1659, Faustini compl Minato) ....
1.35	*"La pazzica al trono" (p1660, Gisberti, ?spur, music lost)* ....
1.36	"L'Ercole amante," 5 act tragedia (p1662, Buti) ....
1.37	"Scipione Africano," 3 act drama per musica (p1664, Minato) ....
1.38	"Muzio Scevola," 3 act drama per musica (p1665, Minato) ....
1.39	"Pompeo Magno," 3 act drama per musica (p1666, Minato) ....
1.40	"Eliogabalo" (c1668, anon & Aureli, not perf) ....
1.41	*"Il Coriolano," drama (p1669, Ivanovich, music lost)* ....
1.42	*"Massenzio" (c1673, Bussani, not perf, music lost)* ....

2. CHURCH MUSIC

"Musiche Sacre concernenti messa, e salmi concertati con istromenti, imni, antifone et sonate a due, 3, 4, 5, 6, 8, 10 e 12 voci" (p1656), incl:

2.1	"Messa" (8vv, 2vn, vc & other insts ad lib) ....
2.2	"Alma Redemptoris mater" (2S, A, T, B) ....
2.3	"Ave maris stella" (A, T, B, 2vn & vc) ....
2.4	"Ave regina coelorum" (T, B) ....
2.5	"Beatus vir" (A, T, B, 2vn & vc) ....
2.6	"Confiteor tibi Domine" (8vv, 2vn & vc) ....
2.7	"Credidi" (2S, A, T, B, 2vn & vc) ....
2.8	"Deus tuorum militum" (A, T, B, 2vn & vc) ....
2.9	"Dixit Dominus" (8vv, 2vn, vc & other insts ad lib) ....
2.10	"Domine probasti" (S, A, B, 2vn & vc) ....
2.11	"Exultet orbis" (4vv, 2vn & vc) ....
2.12	"In convertendo" (2S, A, T, B) ....
2.13	"Iste confessor" (2S, 2vn & vc) ....
2.14	"Jesu corona virginum" (A, T, B, 2vn & vc) ....
2.15	"Laetatus sum" (A, T, B, 2vn & 3va) ....
2.16	"Lauda Jerusalem" (8vv, 2vn, vc & other insts ad lib) ....
2.17	"Laudate Dominum" (8vv, 2vn & vc) ....
2.18	"Laudate pueri" (2S, A, T, B, 2vn & vc) ....
2.19	"Magnificat" (8vv, 2vn, vc & other insts ad lib) ....
2.20	"Nisi Dominus" (4vv, 2vn & vc) ....
2.21	"Regina caeli" (A, T, B) ....
2.22	"Salve regina" (A, 2T, B) ....
2.23	"Canzoni (Sonate) a 3, 4, 6, 8, 10 & 12" ....

"Vesperi a 8 voci" (p1675; 8vv & cont), incl:

2.24   I. "Vespero della Beata Vergine": 1. "Dixit Dominus" ....

2.25   2. "Laudate pueri"

2.26   3. "Laetatus sum"

2.27   4. "Nisi Dominus"

2.28   5. "Lauda Jerusalem"

2.29   6. "Magnificat"

2.30   II. "Vespero delle Domeniche, et altri Salmi" (con li salmi correnti di tutto l'anno): 1. "Dixit Dominus" ....

2.31   2. "Confitebor"

2.32   3. "Beatus vir"

2.33   4. "Laudate pueri"

2.34   5. "In exitu Israel"

2.35   6. "Laudate Dominum"

2.36   7. "Credidi"

2.37   8. "In convertendo"

2.38   9. "Domine probasti"

2.39   10. "Beati omnes"

2.40   11. "De profundis"

2.41   12. "Memento"

2.42   13. "Confitebor Angelorum"

2.43   14. "Magnificat"

2.44   III. "Vespero delle Cinque Laudate" (ad uso della Capella di S. Marco): 1. "Laudate pueri" ....

2.45   2. "Laudate Dominum omnes gentes"

2.46   3. "Laudate anima mea"

2.47   4. "Laudate Dominum quoniam bonus"

2.48   5. "Lauda Jerusalem"

2.49   6. "Magnificat"

"Ghirlanda Sacra" (p1625, ed Simonetti), incl:

2.50   "Cantate Domino" (1v & cont) ....

"Motetti a voce sola di diversi Eccelentissimi Autori" (p1645), incl:

2.51   "O quam suavis," motetto (1v & cont) ....

"La Sacra Corona" (p1656, ed Marcesso), incl:

2.52   "In virtute tua" (3vv & cont) ....

2.53   "O bone Jesu" (2vv & cont; reprinted in: Sacri Concerti, ed Silvani 1668) ....

2.54   "Plaudite, cantate" (3vv & cont; reprinted in: Sacri Concerti, ed Silvani 1668) ....

Other:

2.55   "Missa pro defunctis" (Requiem) (8vv & cont) ....

2.56   "Il giuditio universale," oratorio (c1681, ?spur) ....

3. MISC VOCAL

Secular cantatas:

3.1   "Arm'il petto d'orgoglio" ....

3.2   "Chi non fa il giardinier" (c1662) ....

3.3   "Ho un cor che non sa" (Amante veridico) (c1662) ....

3.4   "Levamiti davanti" (Vanità in amore) (c1662) ....

3.5   "Se laggiù negli abissi" ....

Arias:

3.6   "Son ancor pargoletta" (c1634) ....

3.7   "E rimedio al mal d'amore" (c1656) ....

3.8   "Dolce colpo d'un sguardo amoroso" ....

3.9   "In amor non ho fortuna" ....

3.10 "O dolce servitù" ....

3.11   "Dolce amor" (?spur) ....

4. ARRANGEMENTS OF WORKS OF OTHERS

4.1   Monterverdi: "Magnificat" (6vv, 2vn & cont; pubd in Monteverdi: Messa a 4 voci, et salmi, ed Cavalli 1650)

* * * * *

1. STAGE WORKS

Operas:

Operettas:

1a. SELECTIONS FROM STAGE WORKS (Nos. of sections in The Gramophone)

2. ORCHESTRAL WORKS

3. CONCERTOS, SOLO INSTR & ORCH

4. PIANO

Pf duet:

4.27 "Souvenirs de Munich," quadrille (c1885–6, on themes from Wagner's opera: Tristan & Isolde, WWV90) ...

2 Pf:

4.28 "3 valses romantiques" (c1883; 2pf/orch): No.1 "Très vite et impétueusement" ....
4.29   No.2 "Mouvement modéré de valse"
4.30   No.3 "Animé"

5. CHORAL WORKS

5.1 "La sulamite," scène lyrique (c1884, Richepin; mS, fem ch & orch)..
5.2 "Ode à la musique" (c1890, Rostand; S, fem ch & orch/pf) ....

6. MISC VOCAL

6.1 "2 Comic Duets" (c1877–9; 2vv & orch): 1. "Cocodette et Cocorico" ....
6.2   2. "Monsieur et Madame Orchestre"
6.3 "Duo (bouffe) de l'ouvreuse de l'Opéra-Comique et de l'employé du Bon Marché" (c1888) ....

7. SONGS (w/ pf)

7.1 "9 (Early) Songs" (c1862): 1. "Couplets de Mariette" (Laprade)...
7.2   2. "L'enfant" (Laprade)
7.3   3. "Ronde gauloise"
7.4   4. "Le sentier sombre" (Renaudiére)
7.5   5. "Lied" (Banville)
7.6   6. "Chants d'oiseaux" (Laprade)
7.7   7. "Sérénade" (Châtillon)
7.8   8. "Adieux à Suzon" (Musset)
7.9   9. "Ah petit démon" (Musset)
7.10 "Sérénade de Ruy Blas" (c1863, Hugo) ....
7.11 "Les lèvres closes" (c1867) ....
7.12 "L'invitation au voyage" (c1870, Baudelaire) ....
7.13 "Sommation irrespectueuse" (c1880, Hugo) ....
7.14 "Tes yeux bleus" (c1883, Rollinat) ....
7.15 "Crédo d'amour" (c1883, Silvestre) ....
7.16 "Chanson pour Jeanne" (c1886, Mendès) ....
7.17 "6 mélodies" (c1890): 1. "Villanelle des petits canards" (Gerard)..
7.18   2. "Ballade des gros dindons" (Rostand) ....
7.19   3. "Pastorale des cochons roses" (Rostand) ....
7.20   4. "L'île heureuse" (Mikhaël) ....
7.21   5. "Les cigales" (Gérard) ....
7.22   6. "Toutes les fleurs" (Rostand) ....
7.23 "3 Songs" (from opera: L'étoile): 1. "À la musique" ....
7.24   2. "España"
7.25   3. "Romance"
7.26 "2 Songs" (from opera: Le roi malgré lui): 1. "Chanson de l'alouette" ....
7.27   2. "Chanson tzigane"
7.28 "Lied: Nez au vent" (p1897, Mendès) ....

*   *   *   *   *

1. STAGE WORKS

Pastorals, divertissements & operas:

2a. SELECTIONS FROM STAGE WORKS

    4. "Laissons là sa gloire"
    5a. "Chanson d'Alcidon": "Ah! cruelle bergère"
    5b. "Fin de la chanson d'Alcidon"
    6. "Chanson de Lysandre": "Au bord d'une fontaine"

1a.3   "Les plaisirs de Versailles," divertissement: H480
    1. "Ouverture"
    2. "Scène Première": "Que tout cède aux douceurs de mes accords charmants"
    3. "Scène seconde": "Quel objet importun à mes yeux se présente?"
    4. (Scène 3e): "Venez, dieu des festins!"
    5. "Scène 4e": "Si les cartes, les dés, l'innocent trou-madame"

1a.4   "Actéon, Pastorale en musique," pastorale: H481
    1. "Ouverture de l'opéra d'Actéon"
    2. "Bruit de chasse aprés l'ouverture"
    3. "Scène première": "Allons, marchons, courons"
    4. "Scène seconde": "Nymphes, retirons-nous dans ce charmant bocage"
    5. "Scène 3e": "Amis, les ombres racourcies"
    6a. "Scène 4e": "Mon coeur autrefois intrépide"
    6b. "Plainte" (insts)
    7. "Scène cinquième": "Jamais troupe de chasseurs"
    8. "Scène sixième": "Chasseurs, n'appelez plus"

1a.5   "Actéon changé en biche," pastorale: H481a
    1. "Ouverture pour Actéon changé en biche"
    2. (Chanson de Diane): "Ah! qu'on évite de langueurs"
    3a. "Scène 3e": "Amis, les ombres raccourcies"
    3b. "Approchons-nous"
    4. "Plainte d'Actéon au lieu de celle qui est trop longue"

1a.6   "Sur la naissance de Notre Seigneur Jésus Christ Pastorale," pastorale:.. H482
    1. "Ouverture"
    2. "Scène première": "Qu'il est charmant, qu'il a d'appas"
    3. "Scène 2de": "D'où venez-vous, bergers?"

1a.7   "Pastorale sur la naissance de Notre Seigneur Jésus Christ," pastorale H483
    1. "Ouverture"
    Part I: 2. "Scène première": "Que nos soupirs, Seigneur"
    3. "Symphonie"
    4. "Scène seconde": "Règnez, calme profond"
    5. "Scène 3e": "Celestes compagnons, trones"
    6. "Scène 4e": "Gloire dans les hauts lieux"
    Part II: 7. "Scène 5e": "Pasteurs, éveillez-vous"
    8. "Scène 6e": "Joignons nos flûtes et nos voix"

1a.8   "Seconde partie du noël français qui commence par 'Que nos soupirs' ": H483a
    1. "Scène 5e": "Heureux bergers, voici le lieu"
    2. "Scène 6e": "Qu'il a de majesté!"
    3. "Scène 7e": "Votre tendresse est équitable"

1a.9   "Seconde partie du noël français qui commence par 'Que nos soupirs, Seigneur' ": H483b
    1. "Prélude"
    2. "Scène 5e" (Choeur de vergers revenant): "Le soleil recommence à dorer nos montagnes"

1a.10   "Il faut rire et chanter: dispute de bergers," pastorale:.. H484
    1. "Ouverture"
    2. "Brouillards, glaçons, neige, frimas"
    3. "Que l'aimable printemps pour toujours recommence"
    4. "Pauvres mortels que vous êtes"
    5. "Je brave sans souci la fortune obstinée"
    6. "Gavotte en rondeau" (insts)
    7. "Je suis vaincu, je le confesse"
    8. "Gigue" (insts)

1a.11   "La fête de Rueil," pastorale: H485
    1. "Scène première": "Que je sens de plaisir"
    2. "Scène seconde": "Mais vois-je pas de leurs coteaux"
    3. "Scène 3e": "Heureux bergers qui coulez votre vie"
    4. "Scène 4e": "Les satyres" (insts)
    5. "Scène 5e": "Ils se sont retirés"
    6. "Scène 6e": "J'aime ces aimables bergères"
    7. "Scène 7e": "Mais le dieu des bergers s'avance"

1a.12   "La couronne de fleurs," pastorale: H486
    1. "Ouverture"

        3. (Premier intermède): "Nott'e dì"
        4. (Second intermède): "... oui, suivons"

1a.30   Version 3 of "La malade imaginaire," H495: H495b
        1. "Prélude pour Notte e dì" (= H495a/3)
        2. (Orchestral air 'jusqu'au second acte')
        3. "Satyres pour la fin du prologue du Malade imaginaire"
        4. "Second air pour les tapissiers du Malade imaginaire reformé pour la 3e fois"

1a.31   "Profitez du printemps," air: H495c
        1. "Profitez du printemps"
        2. "Les plaisirs les plus charmants"
        3. "Ne perdons pas"

1a.32   "Circé," overture, incid music & intermèdes: H496
        1. "Ouverture"
     Prologue: 2. "Prélude pour faire (entrer) les arts et les plaisirs"
        3. "Pour divertir Louis, unissons-nous"
     I: 4. "(Chanson du) premier satyre": "Deux beaux yeux me charment"
        5. "(Chanson du) second satyre": "Un jour la jeune Lisette"
     "Entr'acte du premier au second acte": 6. (Sarabande en rondeau)
        7. "Deux beaux yeux me charment" (insts)
        8. "Un jour la jeune Lisette" (insts)
     II: 9. "Dialogue de Tircis et de Sylvie": "Pourquoi me fuyez-vous, o beauté?"
        10. "Seconde partie du dialogue (9.) qu'on laisse si l'on veut": "La liberté m'était un bien si doux"
     "Intermède du second au 3e acte": 11. "Passecaille" (insts)
     "Entr'acte du troisième au quatrième acte": 12. "Menuet ('Les singes') (et) bourée"
     IV: 13. "(Chanson de) la dryade": "Vous étonnez-vous"
        14. "Ritornelle de Vous étonnez-vous"
        15. (Ritornel) (?substitute for 14.)
     "Intermède entre le 4e et le 5e acte": 16. "Prélude pour faire entrer les divinités des forêts"
        18. "Récit d'un des dieux des forêts": "Tout aime, tout aime"
        19. "Choeur des divinités des forêts": "Les plaisirs sont de tous les âges"
        20. "Divinités des forêts et de la mer" (insts)
        21. "Mes soupirs vous le font trop entendre"
        22. "Rondeau pour trois figures" (insts)

1a.33   Parodies of 2 airs from: Circé, H496: H496a
        1. "D'où viens-tu, cher voisin?" (setting of: Seconde Loure, Act IV)
        2. "Lorsque je suis au cabaret" (setting of: Prélude des Vents, Act IV)

1a.34   Parodies of 8 airs from: Circé, H496: H496b
        1. "Je ne connais point la tendresse" (setting of: Premier Menuet, Prologue)
        2. "Ce vin rit dans le verre," duet (parody of: Tout rit dans ce boccage, Prologue)
        3. "Le vin chasse la tristesse" (parody of: Les plaisirs suivent les peines, Prologue)
        4. "Je fais ma félicité / D'entamer quelque grand paté" (parody of: je fais ma félicité / D'une
           douce tranquillité, Act I)
        5. "Que ce jus divin / Est propre à charmer" (setting of: première Loure, Act IV)
        6. "D'où viens-tu, cher voisin?" (setting of: Seconde Loure, Act IV)
        7. "Lorsque je suis au cabaret" (setting of: Prélude des Vents, Act V)
        8. "Dans un festin avec sa maîtresse" (setting of: Menuet des Néreides, Act V)

1a.38   "Sérénade pour Le sicilien," overture & incid music: H497
        1. "Ouverture"
        2. "(Air) pour le premier musicien": "Beauté dont la rigeur s'acharne"
        3. (Duo): "Voulez-vous, beauté bizarre"
        4. "Esclaves du sicilien" (insts)

1a.39   "Ouverture du prologue de Polyeucte pour le Collège d'Harcourt," overture & ballet: H498
        1. (Ouverture)
        2. "Amours profanes: jeux et plaisirs"
        3. "Pantomimes pour les mêmes"
        4. "La grâce et les vertus"
        5. "Le désespoir"
        6. "Les crocheteurs"
        7. "Sentiments généreux et lâches"
        8. "Amours forgerons"
        9. "Marche de triomphe"
        10. "La joie seule"
        11. "Pourquoi n'avoit [?] pas le coeur tendre retourné"
        12. "Combattants"

1a.40   "Ouverture du prologue de l'Inconnu," overture & ballet: H499
        1. "Ouverture"
        2. "Les furies"

      3. "Les démons"
      4. "Fanfare pour le trompettes"
      5. "Les combattants"
      6. "Marches pour les flûtes (et les hautbois)"
      7. "Les plaisirs"
      8. "Naïades et dryades"
      9. "Pour le dieu Pan"
     10. "Plaisirs et Flore," menuet
     11. "Satyres"
     12. "Fanfare à deux trompettes"

1.43   "Les fous divertissants, comédie," overture, incid music & intermèdes: H500
      1. "Ouverture"
    "Premier intermède": 2. "Prélude pendant lequel entrent en rêvant deux fous pour chanter ce qui suit"
      3. "Hélas, nous nous plaignons tous deux"
      4. "Le villageois" (insts)
      5. "Que ces jeunes coeurs après leur disgrâce"
      6. "Bourée" (insts)
    "Second intermède": 7. "Marche pendant laquelle entrent quatre fous dansants et trois chantants"
      8. "L'amour étend ses conquêtes"
      9. "Les fous déchaînés" (insts)
     10. "Les geôliers" (insts)
     11. "Les trois musiciens"
    III: 12. "Pour les comédiens" (insts)
     13. "(Air de) Léandre": "Ce n'est qu'entre deux amants"
     14. "Pour la bohémienne" (insts)
     15. (Air d'Angélique): "Quand la flamme est dans un âme"
     16. (Air d'un musicien): "Bacchus et l'amour font débauche"
     17. "Seconde chanson pour le même": "L'amour vous récompense"
     18. "Marche des fous" (insts)
     19. "Chanson du fou musicien": "Amants, vous faîtes bien de quitter ce séjour"
     20. "Les fous à marottes" (insts)
     21. "Dialogue de deux fous amoureux": "Je ne saurais vivre sans toi"
     22. "Dernière entrée sur un autre air / les mêmes" (i.e. les fous à marottes)
     23. "Menuet (qui) se doit jouer à lieu de celui qui est écrit après la chanson de Léandre" (= 14.)

1a.44   "La pierre philosophale," divertissement: H501
      1. "Choeur des quatre éléments": "Les sages"
      2. "Menuet pour la petite gnomide"
      3. "(Chanson du) sylphe": "Je suis d'un élément"
      4. "Les éléments" (insts)
      5. "Duo pour le feu et l'eau": "Le spectacle"
      6. "Dernier choeur quand la gnomide sort de terre": "Croissez, gnomide"

1a.45   "Endimion, tragédie mêlée de musique," overture, incid music & intermèdes: H502
      1. "Ouverture devant que de lever la toile"
    (?Prologue): 2. "(Prélude) pour donner le temps aux bergers d'entrer"
      3. (Choeur des bergers): "Amour, tu ressens en ces lieux"
    "Intermède du premier au second acte": 4. "Fantaisie" (insts)
    II: 5. "L'Aurore (dans la quatrième scène)": "Séparez-vous, jeunes amants"
      6. "Scène 5te": "Heureux Endimion, voici l'astre du jour"
    "Intermède du 2d au 3e acte": 7. "Sarabande grave"
      8. "Gavotte pour allonger l'intermède du 2d au troisième acte d'Endimion"
    "Intermède entre le 3e et 4e acte": 9. "Gaillarde"
    IV: 10. "Scène 1re": "Je me rends, mon berger, à tes charmes"
     11. "Scène 7e": "Tendres amants, c'est trop longtemps"
    "Intermède du 4e au 5e acte": 12. "Gigue"

1a.47   "Andromède, tragédie," overture, incid music & intermèdes: H504
    Prologue: 1. "Ouverture"
      2. "Pendante que Melpomène vole dans le char d'Apollon, Prélude"
      3. "Récit d'Apollon": "Cieux, écoutez"
      4. "Choeur de bergers": "D'un héros qu'en tous lieux a suivi la victoire"
      5. (= 1.)
    I: 6. "Scène 3; Choeur des suivants du roi et de la reine; reine d'Erice et d'Amathonte"
      7. "Récit d'un de la suite du roi": "Peux-tu voir que de l'onde"
      8. (= 6. w/ out prelude)
      9. (Choeur): "Ainsi toujours sur tes autels"
    "Intermède du premier au second acte": 10. "Rondeau"
    II: 11. "(Air d') un de la suite de Phinée": "Qu'elle est lente, cette journée"
     12. "Air de Liriope": "Phinée est plus aimé"
     13. "Dialogue": "Heureux amant! / Heureuse amante!"
     14. "Choeur de la suite de Phinée et d'Andromède": "Joignons nos voix"
    "Intermède du second au troisième acte": 15. "Les vents" (insts)
    III: 16. "Choeur d'éthiopiens": "Le monstre est mort"

    17. "Une de la suite du roi": "Quand le danger presse"
    "Intermède du 3e au 4e acte": 18. "Caprice"
  IV: 19. "Scène 6e; Choeur du peuple": "Vivez, vivez, heureux amants"
    "Intermède du 4e au 5e acte": 20. "Premier air" (insts)
    21. "Second air," gigue anglaise
  V: 22. "Choeur": "Maître des dieux, hâte-toi"
    23. "Choeur": "Allez, amants, sans jalousie"

1a.51   "Vénus et Adonis," overture, incid music & intermèdes: H507
    1. "Ouverture"
    Prologue: 2. "Chanson de la bergère": "Il faut aimer"
    3. (= 1.)
    "Intermède du premier au second acte": 4. "Air de la bergère effrayée": "Ah! mortelles frayeurs"
    5. "Dialogue (du berger et de la bergère)": "Aimons sans alarmes"
    6. "Rondeau pour jouer jusqu'au second acte" (insts)
    "Intermède du 2d au 3e acte": 7. "Air de la bergère": "Ah! Tircis, qu'il est dangereux"
    8. "Réponse du berger": "Qu'un amant est heureux"
    9. "Chaconne pour jouer jusqu'au 3e acte" (insts)
    "Intermède du 3e au 4e acte": 10. "Menuet pour la bergère": "Gardons-nous, délivrez notre âme"
    11. "Second couplet (varié) du menuet de la bergère": "Lorsque sous l'amoureux empire"
    12. "(Menuet en) rondeau" (insts)
    13. "Passepied pour jouer jusqu'au 4e acte" (insts)
    "Intermède du 4e au 5e acte": 14. "Prélude pour la plainte de la bergère" (insts)
    15. "Prélude pour la plainte de la bergère au lieu du précédent"
    16. "Plainte de la bergère": "Nymphes, ne songez plus"
    17. "Caprice pour jouer jusqu'au 5e acte" (insts)

2. INSTRUMENTAL WORKS

Sacred:

2.1   "Symphonies pour un reposoir" (Fête-Dieu cérémonial music) (c1673; strings): No.1 "Ouverture" H508
2.2   No.2 "Tantum ergo"
2.3   No.3 "Quand les prêtres auront chanté Tantum ergo"
2.4   No.4 "Quand les prêtres auront chanté Genitori Amen"
2.5   No.5 "Allemande grave"
2.6   "Symphonie devant Regina coeli" (Prelude a 3) (c1673–4; 2vn & cont) H509
2.7   (?)"Prélude" (c1673–4; 2vn & cont) H510
2.8   "Prélude pour: O filii et filiae" (c1674; 2vn & cont) H511
2.9   (?)"Prélude" (c1674; 2vn & cont) H512
2.10   "Messe pour plusieurs insts au lieu des orgues" (c1674–6; winds, strings & cont, inc): No.1 "Kyrie" ... H513
2.11   No.2 (Gloria)
2.12   No.3 "Offerte à deux choeurs" (woodwinds, strings)
2.13   No.4 "Sanctus pour tous les instruments" (?beginning only)
2.14   No.5 (?Agnus Dei) (conclusion only)
2.15   "Offerte" (c1670–1; 2fl, 2ob, strings & org) H514
2.16   "Symphonies pour un reposoir" (c1672; strings & cont): No.1 "Ouverture dès qu'on voit la bannière" . H515
2.17   No.2 "Pange lingua à 4 parties de violons"
2.18   No.3 "In supremae pour le petit choeur"
2.19   No.4 "Tantum ergo pour les violons"
2.20   No.5 "Amen pour les violons"
2.21   "Aprés Confitebor," antienne in D minor (c1675; 2fl, strings & cont) H516
2.22   "Aprés Beati omnes," antienne in G major (c1675; strings & cont) H517
2.23   "Pour le sacre d'un évêque," overture & offertory (c1679; strings) H518
2.24   "Symphonies pour le Jugement de Salomon" (c1679; strings, for lost dramatic motet, inc): No.1
        (Ritornelle après) "Postula, Salomon, a me" (récit de Dieu) H519
2.25   No.2 "Après le récit de Salomon: quia non petisti"
2.26   No.3 "Après Non est ita, ritornelle"
2.27   "Prélude menuet et passepied devant l'ouverture" (c1679; 2fl, 2ob & bns) H520
2.28   "Prélude pour ce qu'on voudra non encore employé" (c1679; strings) H521
2.29   "Offerte non encore exécutée," offertory (c1679; 2fl, 2ob, strings & bn) H522
2.30   "Pour un reposoir: Ouverture dès que la procession paraît" (c1683; 3fl, strings & cont) H523
2.31   "Ouverture pour l'église" (c1683; strings & cont) H524
2.32   "Antienne" (c ?1690; 2fl, strings & cont) H525
2.33   "Antienne" (c ?1690; 2fl, strings & cont) H526
2.34   "Prélude pour Sub tuum praesidium" (c ?1690–1; 2vn & cont) H527
2.35   "Prélude," in G minor (c ?1690–1; fl, strings & cont) H528
2.36   "Symphonie," in G minor (c ?1690–1; 2vn/fl & cont) H529
2.37   "Prélude," in C major (c ?1690–1; fls & strings) H530
2.38   "3 Noëls" (c ?1690; fl, strings & cont): No.1 "O Créateur" H531
2.39   No.2 "Laissez paître vos bêtes"
2.40   No.3 "Vous qui désirez sans fin"
2.41   "Antienne pour les violons, flûtes et hautbois à 4 parties" (c ?1691; fl, ob, strings & cont) H532
2.42   "Prélude pour le second Magnificat" (c ?1693; 2tr insts & cont, for H80) H533

       3. (Credo): "Patrem omnipotentem"
       4. "Sanctus"
       5. "Agnus Dei"
       6. "Domine salvum"

3.2   "Messe pour les trépassés à 8" (c1671–2; vv, 2fl, strings & cont; also see H234): H2
       1. "Kyrie"
       2. "Sanctus"
       3. (Elévation): "Pie Jesu" (= H234)
       4. "Benedictus"
       5. "Agnus Dei"

3.3   "Messe à 8 voix et 8 violons et flûtes" (c1670–1; vv, ch, 2fl, strings & cont): H3
       1. "Kyrie"
       2. "Gloria"
       3. (Credo): "Patrem omnipotentem"
       4. "Sanctus"
       5. "Elévation" (= H236)
       6. "Benedictus"
       7. "Agnus Dei"
       8. "Domine salvum" (= H283)

3.4   "Messe à 4 choeurs" (c1672; vv, 4ch, strings & cont; also see H285): H4
       1. "Kyrie"
       2. "Gloria"
       3. (Credo): "Patrem omnipotentem"
       4. "Sanctus ... Benedictus"
       5. "Agnus Dei"
       8. "Domine salvum" (= H285)

3.5   "Messe, pour le Port Royal" (c1687; 3vv or ch & cont): H5
       1. "Introit pour Ste Marguerite": "Me expectaverunt peccatores"
       2. "Introit pour St François": "Os justi meditabitur sapientam"
       3. "Kyrie"
       4. (Gloria): "Et in terra pax"
       5. "Graduel pour Ste Marguerite": "Adjuvabit eam Deus"
       6. "Graduel pour St François": "Os justi meditabitur sapientiam"
       7. (Credo): "Patrem omnipotentem"
       8. "Offertoire pour Ste Marguerite": "Diffusa est gratia"
       9. "Offertoire pour St François": "Jubilate Deo fideles"
      10. "Sanctus ... Benedictus"
      11. "Agnus Dei"
      12. "Communion pour Ste Marguerite": "Feci judicium et justitiam"
      13. "Communion pour St François": "Fidelis servus et prudens"

3.6   "Messe pour Mr Mauroy" (c ?1691; vv, ch, 2fl, 2ob, strings & cont): H6
       1. "Kyrie"
       2. (Gloria): "Et in terra pax"
       3. (Credo): "Patrem omnipotentem"
       4. (Sanctus)"
       5. (Agnus Dei)
       8. "Domine salvum" (= H299)

3.7   "Messe des morts à 4 voix" (c ?1692–3; vv, ch & cont): H7
       1. "Kyrie"
       2. "Sanctus"
       3. "Elévation" (= H263)
       4. (Benedictus)
       5. "Agnus Dei"
       6. "De profundis ... Requiem" (= H213)

3.8   . Variant of Agnus Dei of H7: "... tollis peccata mundi" (c after ?1693; vv, ch & cont) H7a

3.9   "Messe pour le samedi de Pâques à 4 voix" (c ?1693; vv, ch & cont): H8
       1. "Kyrie II"; "Christe"
       2. (Gloria): "Et in terra pax"
       3. "Sanctus II"

3.10   "Messe de minuit à 4 voix, flûtes et violons, pour Noël" (c ?1694; vv, ch, 2fl, strings & cont): H9
       1. "Kyrie"
       2. (Gloria): "Et in terra pax"
       3. (Credo): "Patrem omnipotentem"
       4. "Sanctus ... Benedictus"
       5. "Agnus Dei"

3.11   "Messe des morts à 4 voix et symphonie" (c ?1695; vv, ch, 2fl, ob, strings & cont; also see H269): H10
       1. "Kyrie"
       2. "Prose des morts": "Dies irae"
       3. "Sanctus"
       4. (Elévation) (= H269)
       5. "Benedictus"
       6. "Agnus Dei"

3.12   "Assumpta est Maria. Missa 6 vocibus cum simphonia" (c1702; vv, ch, strings & cont; 2nd vers H11a): H11
       1. "Kyrie"
       2. (Gloria): "Et in terra pax"

3. (Credo): "Patrem omnipotentem"
4. (Sanctus)
5. "Agnus Dei"
6. "Domine salvum" (= H303)

4. OTHER LITURGICAL WORKS

Sequences:

4.1   "Prose des Morts": "Dies irae, dies illa" (c1671–2; vv, vn, strings & cont):... H12
        1. "Dies irae, dies illa"
        2. "Tuba mirum"
        3. "Mors stupebit"
        4. "Liber scriptus"
        5. "Juste judex"
        6. "Oro supplex"
4.2   "Prose pour le jour de Pâques": "Victimae paschali laudes" (c1671; 3vv & cont) H13
4.3   "Prose du Saint Sacrement": "Lauda Sion Salvatorem" (c1678–9; 3vv, 2tr insts & cont) H14
4.4   "Stabat Mater pour des religieuses": "Stabat mater dolorosa" (c?; 1v/ch & cont): H15
        1. "Stabat Mater dolorosa"
        2. "Cujus animam gementem"

Antiphons:

4.5   (Antienne): "Regina coeli laetare" (c1671; 2vv & cont) H16
4.6   "Autre (antienne)": "Veni sponsa Christi" (c1671; 2vv, fl & cont) H17
4.7   "Salve Regina" (c1671–3; 3vv & cont) H18
4.8   "Ave Regina coelorum" (c1671–3; 3vv & cont) H19
4.9   "Sub tuum praesidium" (c1674–6; 3vv & cont) H20
4.10 "Alma Redemptoris mater" (c1677; 2vv & cont) H21
4.11 "Ave Regina" (c1677; 2vv & cont) H22
4.12 "Salve Regina à 3 voix pareilles" (c1677; 3ch & cont; also: Prélude, H23a) H23
4.13 "Salve Regina à 3 choeurs" (c1677–8; vv, ch & cont): H24
        1. "Salve regina"
        2. "Ad te clamamus"
        3. "Eia, eia ergo"
4.14 "Antiphona in honorem Beatae Virginis": "Beata es Maria" (c1679; 2vv, 2tr insts & cont) H25
4.15 (Antienne): "Inviolata, integra et casta es Maria" (c1680; 3vv & cont) H26
4.16 "Salve Regina des Jésuites" (c1680; 1v & cont) H27
4.17 "Antiphona sine organo ad Virginem": "Sub tuum praesidium" (c1682; 3vv) H28
4.18 "Antiphona in honorem beate Genovefae": "Gloriosam Christi sponsam" (c ?1686; 1v & cont) H29
4.19 "Regina coeli laetare" (c ?1688–90; 3vv & cont) H30
4.20 "Regina coeli, voce sola cum flauti" (c ?1688–90; 1v, 2fl & cont) H31
4.21 "Antienne à la Vierge à 2 dessus": "Regina coeli laetare" (c ?1691; 2vv & cont) H32
4.22 "Antiphon cycle" (c ?1692–3): "1ère antienne": "Domine, quinque talenta" (3vv & cont) H33
4.23   . "3ème antienne": "Fidelis servus et prudens" (2vv, 2vn & cont) H34
4.24   . "5ème antienne": "Serve bone et fidelis" (2vv & cont) H35
4.25 "Salut de la veille des O et les 7 O suivant le romain" (c ?1693): "O salutaris hostia" (3vv & cont) H36
4.26   . "1er O": "O Sapienta" (3vv & cont) H37
4.27   . "2nd O": "O Adonai" (3vv & cont) H38
4.28   . "3ème O": "O radix Jesse" (3vv & cont) H39
4.29   . "4ème O": "O clavis David" (3vv, ch, strings & cont) H40
4.30   . "5ème O": "O Oriens" (3vv, ch, strings & cont) H41
4.31   . "6ème O": "O Rex gentium" (1v, 2vn & cont) H42
4.32   . "7ème O": "O Emmanuel Rex" (3vv & cont) H43
4.33 "Marian antiphon cycle" (c ?1694–5; 3vv, ch, 2vn & cont): 1. "Alma Redemptoris mater" H44
4.34   2. "Ave regina coelorum" H45
4.35   3. "Regina coeli laetare" H46
4.36   4. "Salve regina" H47
4.37 "Antienne à la Vierge": "Inviolata, integra et casta es" (c ?1696; 3vv & cont) H48
4.38 "Antienne à 3 voix pareilles pour la veille des O": "O admirable commercium" (c ?1695; 3vv & cont) ... H49
4.39 "Antiennes" (c?): 1. "Après Dixit Dominum": "Assumpta est Maria" (1v, 2vn & cont) H50
4.40   2. "Après Laetatus sum": "In odorem unguentorum" (1v, 2fl & cont) H51
4.41   3. "Après Lauda Jerusalem": "Pulchra es et decora" (3vv & cont) H52

Hymns:

4.42 "Jesu corona Virginum," hymn for the Common of Virgins (c1670; 2vv, fl & cont): H53
        1. "Jesu corona Virginum"
        2. "Qui pascis inter lilia"
        3. "Quocumque tendis" (music = 1.)
        4. "Te deprecamur supplices"
        5. "Laus honor" (music = 1.)
        6. "Amen"

5. "Sit salus illi decus atque virtus"

Magnificat (Canticle of the B.V.M.) settings:

4.61   "Magnificat" (c1670–1; vv, ch, 2tr insts & cont): H72
        1. "Magnificat anima mea Dominum"
        2. "Quia respexit humilitatem"
        3. "Et misericordia ejus"
        4. "Fecit potentiam"
        5. "Deposuit potentes"
        6. "Esurientes"
        7. "Suscepit Israel"
        8. "Sicut locutus est"
        9. "Gloria Patri"
4.62   "Magnificat" (c1670–1; 3vv, 2tr insts & cont) H73
4.63   "Magnificat à 8 voix et 8 instruments" (c1681–2; vv, ch, 2fl, ob, strings & cont) H74
        1. "Prélude"
        2. "Magnificat anima mea Dominum"
        3. "Quia fecit mihi magna"
        4. "Et misericordia ejus"
        5. "Fecit potentiam"
        6. "Suscepit Israel"
        7. "Sicut locutus est"
        8. "Gloria Patri"
4.64   "Magnificat à 3 dessus" (c1683–4; 3vv & cont) H75
        1. "Magnificat anima mea Dominum"
        2. "Suscepit Israel ... Gloria Patri ..."
4.65   "Canticum BVM" (c ?1688–90; 3vv, ch & cont; also: Prélude, H76a) H76
4.66   "Magnificat" (c ?1688–90; vv, ch, 2fl, strings & cont): H77
        1. "Prélude pour Magnificat"
        2. "Magnificat anima mea Dominum"
        3. "Quia respexit humilitatem"
        4. "Quia fecit mihi magna"
        5. "Et misericordia ejus"
        6. "Fecit potentiam"
        7. "Suscepit Israel"
        8. "Sicut locutus est"
        9. "Gloria Patri"
4.67   "Magnificat" (c ?1690; vv, ch, 2fl, strings & cont): H78
        1. "Prélude"
        2. "Magnificat anima mea Dominum"
        3. "Quia respexit humilitatem"
        4. "Quia fecit mihi magna"
        5. "Suscepit Israel"
        6. "Gloria Patri"
4.68   "3ème Magnificat à 4 voix avec instruments" (c ?1692–3; 8vv, ch, 2fl, strings & cont): H79
        1. "Prélude"
        2. "Magnificat anima mea Dominum"
        3. "Et misericordia"
        4. "Suscepit Israel ... Gloria Patri ..."
        6. "Gloria Patri"
4.69   "Magnificat" (c?; 4vv, ch & cont) H80
4.70   "Magnificat, Pour le Port Royal" (c ?1687; 3vv, ch & cont): H81
        1. "Magnificat anima mea Dominum"
        2. "Et exultavit spiritus meus"
        3. "Quia respexit humilitatem"
        4. "Quia fecit mihi magna" (music = 2.)
        5. "Et misericordia ejus"
        6. "Fecit potentiam" (music = 2.)
        7. "Deposuit potentes"
        8. "Esurientes" (music = 2.)
        9. "Suscepit Israel"
      10. "Sicut locutus est" (music = 2.)
      11. "Gloria Patri"
      12. "Sicut erat" (music = 2.)

Litany of Loreto settings:

4.71   "Litanies de la Vierge à 3 voix pareilles" (c1681–2; 3vv & cont): H82
        1. "Kyrie eleison"
        2. "Fili Redemptor"
        3. "Sancta Maria"
        4. "Virgo prudentissima"
        5. "Rosa mistica"
        6. "Salus infirmorum"

Te Deum settings:

        1. (Prélude) (= Prélude; H145a)
        2. "Te Deum laudamus"
        3. "Te gloriosus"
        4. "Tu Rex gloriae"
        5. "Dignare Domine"
        6. "In te Domine speravi"
        1. "Prélude"
        2. "Te Deum laudamus"
        3. "Te aeternum Patrem"
        4. "Te per orbem"
        5. "Tu devicto"
        6. "Aeterna fac"
        7. "Dignare Domine"
        8. "Fiat misericordia tua"
        9. "In te Domine speravi"
        1. "Te Dominum confitemur"
        2. "Te gloriosus"
        3. "Tu Rex gloriae"
        4. "Per singulos dies"
        1. "Te Dominum confitemur"
        2. "Te gloriosus"
        3. "Tu Rex gloriae"
        4. "Per singulos dies"

5. PSALMS

        1. "Laudate pueri Dominum"
        2. "Sit nomen Domini"
        3. "A solis ortu"
        4. "Excelsus super omnes gentes"
        5. "Quis sicut Dominus Deus"
        6. "Suscitans a terra"
        7. "Ut collocet eum"
        8. "Qui habitare fecit"
        9. "Gloria Patri"
        1. "Nisi Dominus"
        2. "Vanum est vobis"
        3. "Cum dederit dilectis suis"
        4. "Sicut sagittae"
        5. "Beatus vir"
        6. "Gloria Patri"
        1. "Confitebor tibi Domine"
        2. "Magna opera Domini"
        3. "Confessio et magnificentia"
        4. "Memoriam fecit mirabilitum"
        5. "Memor erit"
        6. "Ut det illis"

5.42   "Psalmus 109us": "Dixit Dominus" (c1683–4; vv, ch, 2fl, ob, strings & cont): H190
     1. "Prélude"
     2. "Dixit Dominus"
     3. "Virgam virtutis"
     4. "Tecum principium"
     5. "Dominus a dextris tuis"
     6. "De torrente"
     7. "Gloria Patri"

5.43   "Psalmus 147": "Lauda Jerusalem Dominum" (c1683–4; vv, ch, strings & cont): H191
     1. "Prélude"
     2. "Lauda Jerusalem Dominum"
     3. "Qui emittit eloquium suum"
     4. "Qui annuntiat verbum suum ... Gloria Patri ..."

5.44   "Psalm 46": "Omnes gentes plaudite manibus" (c1683–4; 3vv, 2tr insts & cont): H192
     1. "Omnes gentes plaudite manibus"
     2. "Subjecit populos nobis"
     3. "Psallite Deo nostro"
     4. "Regnabit Deus"
     5. (= 3.)

5.45   "Psalmus David 50us / Miserere mei des Jésuites": "Miserere mei Deus" (c1685; vv, ch, 2tr insts
   & cont, 2 vers; also: Prélude, H193a): H193
     1. "Prélude"
     2. "Miserere mei Deus"
     3. "Amplius lava me"
     4. "Ecce enim in iniquitatibus"
     5. "Asperges me"
     6. "Averte faciem tuam"
     7. "Ne projicias me"
     8. "Libera me de sanguinibus"
     9. "Sacrificium Deo"

5.46   "Psalmus David 99us": "Jubilate Deo omnis terra" (c1685; 3vv, 2tr insts & cont): H194
     1. "Jubilate Deo omnis terra"
     2. "Introite in conspectu ejus"
     3. "Populus ejus"
     4. "Laudate nomen ejus"

5.47   "Psalmus David 91us": "Bonum est confiteri Domino" (c1687; vv, ch, 2tr insts & cont): H195
     1. "Praeludium"
     2. "Bonum est confiteri Domino"
     3. "Quam magnificata sunt opera tua"
     4. "Justus, ut palma"
     5. "Et bene patientes erunt"

5.48   "Psalmus David 12us": "Usquequo Domine" (c1687; vv, 3fl & cont): H196
     1. "Usquequo Domine"
     2. "Usquequo exaltabitur inimicus"
     3. "Qui tribulant me"

5.49   "Psalmus David 109us": "Dixit Dominus" (c ?1688–90; 3vv, ch & cont; also: Prélude, H197a): H197
     1. "Dixit Dominus"
     2. "Tecum principium"
     3. "Dominus a dextris tuis ... Gloria Patri ..."

5.50   "Psalmus David 4us": "Cum invocarem exaudivit me" (c ?1688–90; vv, ch, fl, strings & cont): H198
     1. "Prélude pour Cum invocarem écrit au dos de cette page"
     2. "Cum invocarem exaudivit me"
     3. "Filii hominum"
     4. "A fructu frumenti"
     5. "Quoniam tu Domine"
     6. "Gloria Patri"

5.51   "Psalmus David 111us": "Beatus vir" (c ?1688–90; vv, ch & cont; also: Prélude, H199a): H199
     1. "Beatus vir"
     2. "Gloria et divitiae"
     3. "Exortum est"
     4. "Peccator videbit"
     5. "Gloria Patri"

5.52   "Psaume 110ème": "Confitebor" (c ?1688–90; vv, ch & cont; also: Prélude, H200a): H200
     1. "Confitebor tibi Domine"
     2. "Memoriam fecit"
     3. "Fidelia omnia ... Gloria Patri ..."

5.53   "Psalmus David 34us": "Judica Domine nocentes me" (c ?1688–90; 4vv, 2tr insts & cont): H201
     1. "Judica Domine nocentes me"
     2. "Fiant tamquam pulvis"

5.54   "Psalmus David 109us": "Dixit Dominus" (c ?1688–90; 4vv, ch, 2fl, ob, strings & cont): H202
     1. "Prélude"
     2. "Dixit Dominus"
     3. "Tecum principium"
     4. "Judicabit in nationibus"
     5. "Gloria Patri"

5.55   "Psalmus 112us": "Laudate pueri" (c ?1690; vv, ch & cont; also: Prélude, H203a): H203
         1. "Laudate pueri Dominum"
         2. "Excelsus super omnes gentes"
         3. "Qui habitare facit"
         4. "Gloria Patri"

5.56   "Psaume 109": "Dixit Dominus" (c ?1690; vv, ch, fl, strings & cont): H204
         1. "Prélude"
         2. "Dixit Dominus"
         3. "Tecum principium"
         4. "Dominus a dextris tuis"
         5. "Gloria Patri"

5.57   "Gloria Patri pour le De profundis" (c ?1690; vv, ch, fl, strings & cont) H205

5.58   "Psalmus David 75us": "Notus in Judea Deus" (c ?1691; vv, ch, 2fl, strings & cont, r vers of H179): ... H206
         1. (Prélude)
         2. "Notus in Judea deus"
         3. "Dormierunt somnus suum"
         4. "Tu terribilis es"
         5. "Ut salvos faceret omnes"
         6. "Quoniam cogitatio"

5.59   "Psalmus David 87us": "Domine Deus salutis meae" (c ?1691; vv, ch, 2fl, strings & cont): H207
         1. "Prélude"
         2. "Domine Deus salutis meae"
         3. "Posuerunt me in lacu"
         4. "Clamavi ad te"
         5. "Et ego ad te, Domine"
         6. "Circumdederunt me"

5.60   "Psalmus David 111us": "Beatus vir qui timet Dominum" (c ?1691; vv, ch, 2fl, ob, strings & cont): H208
         1. (Prélude)
         2. "Beatus vir"
         3. "Exortum est in tenebris"
         4. "In memoria aeterna"
         5. "Peccator videbit"
         6. "Gloria Patri"

5.61   "Psalmus David 115us": "Credidi propter" (c ?1692–3; vv, ch & cont; also: Prélude, H209a): H209
         1. "Credidi propter quod locutus sum"
         2. "Vota mea Domino ... Gloria Patri ..."

5.62   "Psalmus David 147us": "Lauda Jerusalem" (c ?1692–3; 4vv, ch, strings & cont): H210
         1. "Lauda Jerusalem Dominum"
         2. "Emittet verbum suum"
         3. "Gloria Patri"

5.63   "Psalmus David 129us / Requiem aeternam": "De profundis" (c ?1692–3; vv, ch & cont): H211
         1. "De profundis clamavi ad te"
         2. "Fiant aures"
         3. "Si iniquitates observaveris Domine"
         4. "Quia apud Dominum"
         5. "Requiem aeternam"

5.64   "Psalmus David 129us 4 vocibus": "De profundis ... Requiem aeternam ..." (c ?1692–3; vv, ch & cont): H212
         1. "De profundis clamavi ad te"
         2. "Fiant aures"
         3. "Si iniquitates abservaveris"
         4. "Sustinuit anima mea"
         5. "Et ipse redemit Israel"
         6. "Rquiem aeternam"

5.65   "Psalm 129 & Requiem aeternam": "De profundis (c ?1692–3; 5vv, ch & cont, part of H7): H213
         1. "De profundis clamavi ad te"
         2. "Fiant aures"
         3. "Quia apud te"
         4. "A custodia matutina"
         5. "Et ipse redemit Israel"
         6. "Requiem aeternam"

5.66   Variant of "De profundis," H213 (c after ?1693; 5vv, ch & cont, inc, c in conjunction w/ H7a) H213a

5.67   "Psalmus David 116us": "Laudate Dominum omnes gentes" (c ?1693–4; 3vv, ch & cont) H214

5.68   "Psalmus David 67us": "Exurgat Deus" (c ?1693–4; 3vv, ch, 2tr insts & cont): H215
         1. "Prélude"
         2. "Exurgat Deus"
         3. "Et justi epulentur"
         4. "Ecce dabit voci suae"

5.69   "Psalmus David 121us": "Laetatus sum" (c ?1693–4; 3vv, ch, 2tr insts & cont): H216
         1. "Laetatus sum"
         2. "Illuc enim ascenderunt"
         3. "Propter fratres meos"

5.70   "Psalmus David 123us": "Nisi quia Dominus" (c ?1693–4; 3vv, ch, 2tr insts & cont): H217
         1. "Nisi quia Dominus"
         2. "Benedictus Dominus"
         3. "Adjutorium nostrum"

5.71   "Psalmus David 45us": "Deus noster refugium" (c ?1693–4; 3vv, ch, 2tr insts & cont): H218
         1. "Deus noster refugium"
         2. "Fluminis ompetus"
         3. "Venite et videte"

5.72   "Psalmus 50 à 4 voix et 4 instruments": "Miserere mei" (c ?1694; vv, ch, 2fl, strings & cont): H219
         1. "Prélude"
         2. "Miserere mei Deus"
         3. "Et secundum multitudinem"
         4. "Quoniam iniquitatem meam"
         5. "Ecce enim veritatem"
         6. "Asperges me"
         7. "Averte faciem tuam"
         8. "Ne projicias me"
         9. "Domine, labia mea aperies"
         10. "Sacrificium Deo"
         11. "Benigne fac Domine"
         12. "Tunc acceptabis sacrificium"

5.73   "Psalmus David 110us à 4 voix": "Confitebor tibi Domine" (c ?1694–5; vv, ch & cont): H220
         1. "Confitebor tibi Domine"
         2. "Memoriam fecit mirabilium"
         3. "Fidelia omnia"
         4. "Gloria Patri"

5.74   "Psalmus David 111us à 4 voix": "Beatus vir" (c ?1694–5; vv, ch & cont): H221
         1. "Beatus vir"
         2. "In memoria aeterna"
         3. "Peccator videbit"
         4. "Gloria Patri"

5.75   "(Psalm 129 & Requiem aeternam) Court De profundis": "De profundis" (c ?1696; 3vv, ch & cont) H222

5.76   "Psalm 116": "Laudate Dominum omnes gentes" (c ?1695; 4vv, ch, 2fl, strings & cont): H223
         1. "Prélude"
         2. "Laudate Dominum omnes gentes"
         3. "Gloria Patri"

5.77   "Psalm 111": "Beatus vir qui timet Dominum" (c ?1695; 5vv, ch, 2fl, strings & cont): H224
         1. "Prélude"
         2. "Beatus vir"
         3. "Potens in terra"
         4. "Exortum est in tenebris"
         5. "In memoria aeterna"
         6. "Dispersit, dedit pauperibus"
         7. "Peccator videbit"
         8. "Prélude"
         9. "Gloria Patri"

5.78   "(Psalm 110) Confitebor à 4 voix ...": "Confitebor tibi" (c ?1696; 3vv, ch, 2fl, strings & cont): H225
         1. "Confitebor tibi Domine"
         2. "Memoriam fecit mirabilium"
         3. "Ut det illis"
         4. "Sanctum et terribile"
         5. "Intellectus bonus"
         6. "Gloria Patri"

5.79   "(Psalm 109) Dixit Dominus pour le Port Royal": "Dixit Dominus" (c ?1687; 3vv, ch & cont): H226
         1. "Dixit Dominus"
         2. "Donec ponam inimicos tuos" (set in falsobordone style)
         3. "Virgam virtutis tuae"
         4. "Tecum principium" (music = 2.)
         5. "Juravit Dominus"
         6. "Dominus a dextris tuis" (music = 2.)
         7. "Judicabit in nationibus"
         8. "De torrente" (music = 2.)
         9. "Gloria Patri"
         10. "Sicut erat" (music = 2.)

5.80   "Psalm 116": "Laudate Dominum omnes gentes" (c ?1687; 3vv, ch & cont): H227
         1. "Laudate Dominum omnes gentes"
         2. "Quoniam confirmata est"
         3. "Gloria Patri"

5.81   "Psalmus David 70us": "In te Domine speravi" (c1699; vv, ch, strings & cont): H228
         1. "In te Domine speravi"
         2. "Ne projicias me"
         3. "Deus docuisti me"
         4. "Exultabunt labia mea"

5.82   "Psalmus David 26us": "Dominus illuminatio mea" (c1699; vv, ch, strings & cont): H229
         1. "Dominus illuminatio mea"
         2. "Circuivi, et immolavi"
         3. "Ne tradideris me"

5.83   "Psalmus David 15us": "Conserva me Domine" (c1699; vv, ch, strings & cont): H230
         1. "Conserva me Domine"

2. "Dominus pars hereditatis meae"
3. "Propter hoc laetatum est"
4. "Notas mihi"

6. MOTETS

Elévation motets:

7. SECULAR VOCAL

Airs sérieux et à boire:

Cantatas:

8. WRITINGS

* * * * *

H = H. W. Hitchcock: "The Works of Marc-Antoine Charpentier. Catalogue Raisonné." Picard. Paris, 1982.

1. STAGE WORKS

Operas:

1.1	*"L'amore artigano," intermezzo (p1773; lost)* ....
1.2	"Il giuocatore," intermezzo (c1775) ....
1.3	Untitled intermezzo for a 'theatre de société' (p1778) ....
1.4	"Quinto Fabio," 3 acts (p1780, Zeno, lost; 2 setting p1783) ....
1.5	"Armida abbandonata," 3 acts (p1782, Duranti) ....
1.6	*"Adriano in Siria," 3 acts (p1782, Metastasio, lost)* ....
1.7	"Mesenzio re d'Etruria," 3 acts (p1782, Casori, final chorus lost) ....
1.8	"Lo sposo di tre, marito di nessuna," 2 act opera buffa (p1783, Livigni) ....
1.9	"Olimpiade," 3 acts (ca1783, Metastasio, dubious) ....
1.10	*"Idalide," 2 acts (p1784, Moretti, extant sinfonia only)* ....
1.11	*"L'Alessandro nelle Indie," 2 acts (p1784, Metastasio, frags)* ....
1.12	*"Demetrio," pasticcio (p1785, ?Metastasio, frags)* ....
1.13	*"La finta principessa," 2 act buffa (p1785, Livigni, lost)* ....
1.14	"Il Giulio Sabino," 2 acts (p1786, Metastasio) ....
1.15	"Ifigenia in Aulide," 3 acts (p1788, Moretti) ....
1.16	"Démophoon," 3 act tragédie-lyrique (p1788, Marmontel) ....
1.17	"La Molinarella," parody (c1789, 5 of 9 arias in Paisiello: La Molinara) ....
1.18	*"Marguerite d'Anjou" (c1790, inc, lost)* ....
1.19	"Lodoïska," 3 act commedia eroica (p1791, Loreaux; 2 Entr'actes added 1805) ......
1.20	*"Koukourgi," 3 acts (c1793, Duveyrier-Mélesville, lost; 4 pieces used in: Ali-Baba)*
1.21	*"Le congrès des roix," 3 act pasticcio (p1794, Desmaillots, collab w/ others, lost)*
1.22	"Elisa, ou Le voyage aux glaciers du Mont St-Bernard," 2 acts (p1794, Saint-Cyr) ..
1.23	"Médée" (Medea), 3 acts (p1797, Hoffmann) ....
1.24	"L'hôtellerie portugaise," 1 act opera comica (p1798, Aignan) ....
1.25	"La punition," 1 act (p1799, Desfaucherets) ....
1.26	"La prisonnière" (Emma), 1 act pasticcio (p1799, Jouy & others) ....
1.27	"Les deux journées ou Le porteur d'eau" (The Water Carrier), 3 acts (p1800, Bouilly) ..
1.28	"Épicure," 3 acts (p1800, Demoustier, collab Mehul) ....
1.29	"Anacréon, ou L'amour fugitif," 2 act opéra-ballet (p1803, Mendouze & St. Aignan) ..
1.30	"Achille à Scyros," ballet-pantomime (pasticcio) (p1804, Gardel) ....
1.31	"Faniska," 3 acts (p1806, Sonnleithner, new March in Act III 1831) ....
1.32	"Pimmaglione," 1 act (p1809, Vestris after Rousseau) ....
1.33	"Le crescendo," 1 act (p1810, Sewrin) ....
1.34	"Les abencérages, ou L'étendard de Grenade," 3 act opera-ballet (p1813, Jouy) ......
1.35	"Bayard à Mézières," 1 act comic pasticchio (p1814, Dupaty & Chazot) ....
1.36	"Blanche de Provence" (La Cour des Fées), 1 act pasticcio (p1821, Théaulon & Rance) ..
1.37	"La marquise de Brinvilliers," pasticcio (c1831, Scribe & Castil-Blaze) ....
1.38	"Ali Baba, ou Les quarante voleurs," 4 acts (p1833, Scribe & Mélesville) ....

Incid music:

1.39	*"La Mort de Mirabeau" (c1791, Pujoulx, lost)* ....

1a. SELECTIONS FROM STAGE WORKS (Nos. of sections in The Gramophone)

1a.23   "Médée," opera: ....

   I: 1a. "Overture"
      1b. "Che? Quando già corona"
      1c. "Io cedo alla buona preghiera"
      1d. "O Amore, vieni a me"
      1e. "No, non temer"
      2a. "O bella Glauce"
      2b. "Colco! Pensier"
      3a. "Or che più non vedrò"
      3b. "Ah, già troppo turbò"
      4a. "Pronube dive"
      4b. "Signor! Ferma una donna"
      5a. "Qui tremar devi tu"
      5b. "Taci, Giason"
      6a. "Dei tuoi figli la madre"
      6b. "Son vane qui minacce"
      7. "Nemici senza cor"
   II: 8a. "Introduction"
      8b. "Soffrir non posso"
      9a. "Data almen, per pietà"
      9b. "Medea! o Medea!"
      10a. "Solo un pianto"
      10b. "Creonte a me solo"
      11a. "Figli miei"
      11b. "Hai dato pronto ascolto"

III:
12. "Ah! Triste canto ... Dio dell'Amor!"
13a. "Introduction"
13b. "Numi, venite a me"
14a. "Del fiero duol"
14b. "D'amore il raggio ancora"
15. "E che? Io son Medea!"

2. SYMPHONIES

2.1   Symphony in D major (p1815, for London Philharmonic Society) ....

3. OTHER ORCHESTRAL WORKS

3.1   *"Chaconne" (c1785; ?orch, lost)* ....
3.2   "March for Prefect of Eure-et-Loire Chartres" (c1800; band) ....
3.3   "March for Prefect's Return" (c1800; ?band) ....
3.4   "2 Sonatas" (Studies) (c1804; 2ob, 2hn & strings) ....
3.5   "March," in F major (c1805; winds, for Baron de Braun) ....
3.6   "Trio" (c ?1807) ....
3.7   "March" (c1808; winds) ....
3.8   "6 Contredanses" (c1808) ....
3.9   "Minuet" (c1808) ....
3.10   "Aria di danza" (c1808) ....
3.11   "March" (c1809; winds) ....
3.12   "3 Contredanses" (c1809) ....
3.13   "March" (c1810; winds) ....
3.14   "Aria di danza" (c1810) ....
3.15   "2 Contredanses" (c1810) ....
3.16   "2 Trios" (c1810) ....
3.17   "March for National Guard" (c1814; band) ....
3.18   "Pas redoublé" (c1814; band, for National Guard music) ....
3.19   "6 Pas redoublés & 2 Marches for Prussian Regiment" (c1814; tpt, 3hn & trbn) ....
3.20   "Overture," in G major (c1815, for London Philharmonic Society) ....
3.21   "Funeral March" (c1820, for royal chapel) ....

4. STRING QUARTETS

4.1   String Quartet No.1 in E-flat major (c1814) ....
4.2   "Souvenir pour quatuor," in E-flat major (c1828, albumleaf for Baillot) ....
4.3   String Quartet No.2 in C major (c1829, red of: Sym in D major—new Adagio replaces Larghetto) ....
4.4   String Quartet No.3 in D minor (c1834) ....
4.5   String Quartet No.4 in E major (c1834–5) ....
4.6   String Quartet No.5 in F major (c1835) ....
4.7   String Quartet No.6 in A minor (c1835–7) ....

5. OTHER CHAMBER MUSIC

5.1   "2 Pieces" (c1818, for Conservatoire competition): No.1 Oboe piece ....
5.2   No.2 Bassoon piece
5.3   Bassoon piece (c1823, for Conservatoire competition) ....
5.4   Clarinet piece (c1824, for Conservatoire competition) ....
5.5   String Quintet No.1 in E minor (c1837) ....

6. PIANO

6.1   "6 Harpsichord Sonatas" (c1780): No.1 in F major ....
6.2   No.2 in C major
6.3   No.3 in B-flat major
6.4   No.4 in G major
6.5   No.5 in D major
6.6   No.6 in E-flat major
6.7   *"Capriccio," study (c1789, lost)* ....
6.8   "2 Romances" (c1808) ....
6.9   "La rose," romance (c1809) ....
6.10   "Romance" (c1809) ....
6.11   "Fantasia," in C major (c1810; pf/org) ....
6.12   "Stances for l'album d'Isabey" (c1811) ....
6.13   "Le mystère," romanze (c1811, for M. Guerin's album) ....

7. ORGAN

7.1	*"Sonata for 2 organs" (c1780, lost)*	....
7.2	*"Sonata" (c1805; cylinder org, frag)*	....
7.3	"Air à écho" (c1806; panharmonicon)	....

8. MASSES

8.1	*Mass No.1 in D minor (c1773; ch & orch, lost)*	....
8.2	*Mass No.2 in C major (c1774; ch & orch, lost)*	....
8.3	*Mass No.3 in C major (c1775; ch & orch, lost)*	....
8.4	*Mass (c1776; ch & orch, lost)*	....
8.5	*"Te laudamus Domine" (Mass) (c1779; ch & org, lost)*	....
8.6	Mass No.4 in F major, "di Chimay" (c1808; ch & orch)	....
8.7	Mass No.5 in D minor (c1811; ch & orch)	....
8.8	Mass No.6 in C major (c1816; ch & orch)	....
8.9	"Gloria" (Mass No.7), in E-flat major (c1816; ch & orch, not named by Cherubini)	....
8.10	Requiem No.1 in C minor (c1816; ch & orch, for anniv of death of Louis XVI)	....
8.11	*"Petite messe de la Sainte Trinité," in D minor (c1816; ch, ?spur; w/ org by Sèjan ca1835)*	....
8.12	Mass No.8 in E minor (c1818; ch & orch)	....
8.13	Mass No.9 in G major (c1819; ch & orch, for coronation of Louis XVIII)	....
8.14	Mass No.10 in B-flat major (c1821; ch)	....
8.15	Mass No.11 in A major (c1825; ch & orch, for coronation of Charles X)	....
8.16	Requiem No.2 in D minor (c1836; m ch & orch)	....

9. SMALL SACRED WORKS

9.1	*"Dixit," psalm (c1774; ch & orch, lost)*	....
9.2	*"Dixit," psalm (c1775; 1v, ch, & org, lost)*	....
9.3	*"Magnificat" (c1775; ch & orch, lost)*	....
9.4	*"Tantum ergo" (c1775; T & orch, lost)*	....
9.5	*2 "Lamentations of Jeremiah" (c1776; ch & orch, lost)*	....
9.6	*"Miserere" (c1776; ch & orch, lost)*	....
9.7	*Motet (c1777; ch & orch, from Mass No.1, lost)*	....
9.8	*Oratorio (c1777, lost)*	....
9.9	*"Te Deum" (c1777; ch & orch, lost)*	....
9.10	"9 Antiphons" (à la Palestrina) (c1778, on plain chant): 1. "Montes et Colles" (4vv & orch)	....
9.11	*2. "Angelus ad patrem" (5vv, lost)*	
9.12	*3. "Venit Dominus" (6vv, lost)*	
9.13	4. "Lauda Jerusalem" (4vv)	
9.14	5. "Lauda Jerusalem" (4vv)	
9.15	6. "Beati omnes" (4vv)	
9.16	7. "A viro iniquo libera me" (4vv)	
9.17	*8. "Expectabo Dominum" (4vv, lost)*	
9.18	9. "Petrus apostolus" (6vv)	
9.19	"8 Antiphons," on plain chant (à la Palestrina) (c1779): 1. "Vox clamantis" (4vv)	....
9.20	2. "Non confundetur" (4vv)	
9.21	3. "Salva nos, Domine" (4vv)	
9.22	4. "Lumen" (4vv)	
9.23	5. "Ipse invocabit me" (4vv)	
9.24	6. "Leva, Jerusalem" (4vv)	
9.25	*7. "Venit Dominus" (4vv, lost)*	
9.26	*8. "Expectabo Dominum" (5vv, lost)*	
9.27	*"Litanies" (c1780, ch, lost)*	....
9.28	"Per unum hominem," offertory (c1779)	....
9.29	*"Ad cultum fidei," antiphon (c1780; ch, lost)*	....
9.30	*"Regnavit, exultet" (c1780; ch, lost)*	....
9.31	*"Parasti" (c1780; 2ch, lost)*	....
9.32	*Motet (c1781; S & orch, for Luigi Marchesi, lost)*	....
9.33	"Nemo gaudeat," motet (c1781; 2ch & 2org)	....
9.34	*2 Choruses for oratorio (c1784; material from operas, lost)*	....
9.35	"Tutto d'orror m'ingombra," aria for oratorio (c1784; T)	....
9.36	"5 Sacred pieces" (c1790; ch): 1. "O Salutaris"	....
9.37	2. "Domine Salvum"	
9.38	3. "Adoremus"	
9.39	4. "Regina Coeli"	
9.40	5. "O Filii"	
9.41	"Credo" (c1806; ch & org, begun in Italy in 1778/9)	....
9.42	"Litanie de la Sainte Vierge" (c1810; ch & orch)	....
9.43	"11 Pieces" (c1816, for royal chapel): 1. "Kyrie"	....
9.44	2. "Kyrie"	
9.45	3. "Kyrie"	
9.46	4. "Laudate," recit (w/ ch)	

9.47	5. "Sanctus"
9.48	6. "Kyrie" (2vv)
9.49	7. "Kyrie" (4vv)
9.50	8. "Pater noster" (4vv)
9.51	9. "O salutaris" (mS & orch)
9.52	10. "O salutaris" (3vv & orch)
9.53	11. "Pater noster" (4vv, ch & org/pf)
9.54	"Ecce panis angelorum," offertory (c1816; T & orch) .....
9.55	"Ave Maria" (c1816; S, cl/Eng hn & orch) .....
9.56	"Lauda Sion," offertory (c ?1816; 2S & orch) .....
9.57	"2 Pieces" (c1816; ch & orch, for royal chapel): 1. "Gloria" (= Mass No.7) .....
9.58	2. "Credo"
9.59	"Ave verum" (c ?1816; 3S) .....
9.60	"O sacrum convivium" (c ?1816; ch & orch) .....
9.61	"Iste dies" (c ?1816; 4vv & orch) .....
9.62	"8 Pieces" (c1817, for royal chapel): 1. "Tantum ergo" (ch & orch) .....
9.63	2. "Tantum ergo" (T, ch & orch)
9.64	3. "Kyrie" (m ch & orch)
9.65	4. "O salutaris" (3vv & bn & vc)
9.66	5. "Agnus Dei" (4vv & orch)
9.67	6. "Sanctus" (T/S & orch)
9.68	7. "O salutaris" (T/S & orch)
9.69	8. "Gloria" (1v, ch & orch)
9.70	"4 Pieces" (c1818, for royal chapel): 1. "Regina coeli" (4vv & orch) .....
9.71	2. "O filii," hymn (4vv)
9.72	3. "O salutaris" (4vv, ch & orch)
9.73	4. "Adjutor in opportunitatibus," motet (4vv & orch)
9.74	*"3 Pieces" (c1818, for royal chapel, lost): 1. "Kyrie" (ch)* .....
9.75	*2. "Christe" (ch)*
9.76	*3. "Kyrie" (ch)*
9.77	"3 Pieces" (c1820, for royal chapel): 1. "In paradisum" (ch & orch) .....
9.78	2. "Litany of our Lady" (ch & orch) .....
9.79	3. "Domine, Dominus noster," aria (S & ob, from opera: Elisa, w/ alterations) .....
9.80	"2 Pieces" (c1821; 4vv & orch, for royal chapel): 1. "O salutaris" .....
9.81	2. "Agnus Dei"
9.82	"2 Pieces" (c1822, for royal chapel): 1. "Litany of our Lady" (ch) .....
9.83	2. "O fons amoris spiritus," hymn (T/S & ch) .....
9.84	"Sanctus" (c1822, new Sanctus for: Mass No.5 in D minor) .....
9.85	"3 Pieces" (c1823, for royal chapel): 1. "Kyrie" (ch & orch) .....
9.86	2. "Laetare Jerusalem," motet (ch, ch & orch)
9.87	3. "Inclina Domine," introit (ch & orch)
9.88	"Exaudi Domine," introit (c1824; ch / recit & ch, for royal chapel) .....
9.89	"Adjutor et susceptor meus" (c1824; ch) .....
9.90	"Adoremus," hymn (c1824; ch) .....
9.91	"Christum sempiternum," offertory (c1825; ch) .....
9.92	"O salutaris" (c1826; Bar & orch, for royal chapel) .....
9.93	"O salutaris" (c1826; ch & acc ad lib) .....
9.94	"O salutaris" (c1827; ch) .....
9.95	"O filli," hymn (c1828; ch) .....
9.96	"Credo" (c1828; ch & orch) .....
9.97	"2 Motets" (c1830, for royal chapel): 1. "Sciant gentes" (ch & orch) .....
9.98	2. "Esto mihi" (ch & orch)

10. CANTATAS & CEREMONIAL WORKS

10.1	*"La pubblica felicità," cantata in honour of Peter Leopold II (p1774; 4vv & ch, lost)* .....
10.2	*"Il trionfo dell'Arno," cantata (p1784; 3vv, lost)* .....
10.3	*"Amphion," masonic cantata for Loge Olympique (c1786, lost)* .....
10.4	*"Circé," cantata at concert of Loge Olympique (c1789, Rousseau, lost)* .....
10.5	"Hymne à la fraternité": "Nous avons chanté la victoire" (c1793, Desorgues; 1v & ch) .....
10.6	"Le salpêtre républicain": "Descendons dans nos souterrains" (c1794; ch, for opening of saltpetre mines)..
10.7	"Clytemnestre," cantata (c1794; 1v & ?orch) .....
10.8	"Hymne au Panthéon" (c1794, Chenier; ch & winds) .....
10.9	*"Hymne du combat" (c1794, Davrigny, lost)* .....
10.10	"Chant pour le Dix Août" (1792 anniv): "S'il en est qui veuillent un maître" (c1795, Lebrun; 4vv & orch) .....
10.11	"Cantata for inauguration of statue of Apollo in concert hall" (c1796, inc) .....
10.12	*"Hymne de l'agriculture" (c1796, Pipelet, lost)* .....
10.13	*"Hymne à la Victoire" (c1796, Flins, ?spur)* .....
10.14	"Ode sur le 18 Fructidor" (c1797, Andrieux; 3vv & orch, 18 Fructidor—conspiracy of poignards) .....
10.15	"Hymne et marche funèbre": "Du haut de la voûte éternelle" (c1797, Chénier, on the death of Gen. Hoche)
10.16	"Hymne pour la fête de la Jeunesse" (c1798, Parny; T & ch) .....
10.17	"Hymne pour la fête de la Reconnaissance" (c1798, Mahérault; 1v, ch & orch) .....
10.18	"Cher aux amours," funeral hymn (c1799, Chaussard, from: Hoche's Hymn, for General Joubert) .....
10.19	"Chant sur la mort d'Haydn" (c1805; S, 2T & orch) .....

10.20	"Ode à l'Hymen" (c1810, for Napoleon's marriage) ....
10.21	"Cantata for Opening New Conservatoire Concert-Hall" (c1811, Arnault, collab Méhul & Catel) ....
10.22	"Cantate pour 'La Goulette' " (c1812) ....
10.23	"Cantata in Honour of the National Guard" (c1814, Rougemont; 3vv & orch) ....
10.24	"Cantata in Honour of Louis XVIII" (c1814, Millevois; vv, ch & orch) ....
10.25	"Hymn to Spring," cantata (c1815, Vestri; 4vv & orch) ....
10.26	"Chorus and Couplets for St. Louis's Day" (c1815) ....
10.27	"Cantata for Banquet by Royal Guard in Presence of Louis XVIII" (c1816; vv, ch & orch) ....
10.28	"Le mariage de Salomon," cantata (c1816, Malle; 1v, ch & orch) ....
10.29	"Cantata for the Duke of Bordeaux's Baptism" (c1821, Baour-Lormian; vv & ch) ....
10.30	*"Stanzas" (c1823; vv & ch, for return of Duke of Angouleme, from: Il Quinto Fabio, lost)* ....

11. OTHER VOCAL WORKS

11.1	*"Rondo" (p1776, lost)* ....
11.2	*"Duet" (p1776, lost)* ....
11.3	*"Aria buffa" (p1776, lost)* ....
11.4	"3 Pieces" (c1780, in opera: Quinto Fabio): 1. "Tu quella vita in dono," aria ....
11.5	2. "Vado a morir, ben mio," rondeau
11.6	3. "Padre, deh! resta," recit & aria
11.7	*"Amato padre, addio!," recit & aria (c1781, lost)* ....
11.8	*"5 Arias" (c1781, for opera by another composer, lost): 1. "Se vi giunge il tristo avviso"* ....
11.9	*2. "Caro consorte amato"*
11.10	*3. "Distaccati al primo cenno"*
11.11	*4. "Questa è causa d'onore"*
11.12	*5. "Agitata tutta io sono"*
11.13	*"2 Pieces" (c1781, for inc opera, lost): 1. "Caro padre," aria* ....
11.14	*2. "Morte, morte fatal," recit & duet*
11.15	"Sapro scordarmi ingrata," aria (c1782, for Crescentini in opera: Adriano in Siria) ....
11.16	*"4 Nocturnes" (c1782; 2S & pf/harp, lost): 1. "Solitario bosco ombroso"* ....
11.17	*2. "Compagni, amor lasciate"*
11.18	*3. "Il pastor se torna aprile"*
11.19	*4. "Il rivedrò sovente"*
11.20	"6 Nocturnes" (c1782; 2vv & pf, ded to Signor Corsi) ....
11.21	*"2 Octaves" (c1782, Marino; 1v & pf, lost): 1. "Io che languir"* ....
11.22	*2. "E mentre dolcemente"*
11.23	*"Ella dinanzi al petto," octave (c1782, Tasso; 1v & pf, lost)* ....
11.24	*"Bella rosa porporina," canzonetta (c1782, Chiabrera; 1v & pf, lost)* ....
11.25	"3 Canons" (c1782; 3–4vv & pf): 1. "Non mi negate" ....
11.26	2. "Perfida Clori"
11.27	3. "Evviva Bacco"
11.28	"2 Duets" (c1782; 3S): 1. "Solitario bosco" ....
11.29	2. "La mia filie"
11.30	*2 Duets for George Nassau Clavering 3rd Earl Cowper (c1782; 2vv & 2 corni d'amore, lost)* ....
11.31	*"Non bramo il merito," aria (c1782, for Babbini, in pasticcio: Semiramide, lost)* ....
11.32	*"2 Arias" (c1783; T, lost): 1. "Forza è pur bell' idol mio," comic aria* ....
11.33	*2. "Pensate che la femmina," comic aria*
11.34	*Comic aria (c1783; B, lost)* ....
11.35	"Ninfa crudele," madrigal (c1783; 4vv & cont) ....
11.36	"6 Pieces" (c1785, in pasticcio: Demetrio): 1. "In questa guisa, oh Dio!," recit & duet ....
11.37	2. "Non fidi al mar che freme," aria
11.38	3. "Va cediamo al destin," recit
11.39	4. "Che mai feci!," finale
11.40	*5. "Se tutti i mali miei," aria (lost)*
11.41	*6. "Fra cento affanni e cento," aria (lost)*
11.42	*"6 Pieces" (c1786, in opera: Il Marchese Tulipano, lost): 1. "Al mio bene, al mio tesoro," aria* ....
11.43	*2. "Nobile al par che bella," duet*
11.44	*3. "Per salvarti, oh mio tesoro!," rondeau*
11.45	*4. "Madamina, siete bella," aria*
11.46	*5. "Assediato è Gibilterra," aria*
11.47	*6. "Cosa vuole il marchesino" (added to 1st Finale)*
11.48	"2 Arias" (p1787, in Cimarosa's opera: Giannina e Bernardone): 1. "A tanto amore" ....
11.49	2. "Aria"
11.50	"18 Romances" (c1787; 2vv & pf/harp, on Florian: Estella): 1. "Solitario bosco ombroso" ....
11.51	2. "Compagni, amor lasciate"
11.52	3. "Il pastor se torna aprile"
11.53	4. "Io rivedrò sovente"
11.54	5. "Io che languir"
11.55	6. "E mentre dolcemente"
11.56	7. "Ella dinanzi al petto"
11.57	8. "Bella rosa porporina"
11.58	9. "Dors, mon enfant"
11.59	10. "Le portrait de Thémire"
11.60	11. "Le veuf inconsolable"

11.61	12. "Viens voir sur l'écorce légère"
11.62	13. "Blessé par noire perfidie"
11.63	14. "Une chanson pour une fête"
11.64	15. "Voyez cette naissante rose"
11.65	16. "L'écho"
11.66	17. "Un jour échappé de Cythère"
11.67	18. "La cintura d'Armida"
11.68	"A voi torno, sponde, amate," aria (c1788, in opera: Ifigenia in Aulide) ....
11.69	"Misera Ifigenia," recit obbl (c1788, in opera: Ifigenia in Aulide) ....
11.70	"Che ascoltai qual fredda mano" (c1788, S, T, B & orch) ....
11.71	*"Sarete alfin contenti," recit & aria (c1788, for Mme Todi at Lôge Olympique, lost) ....*
11.72	"Ma che vi fece, oh stella," scena & aria (c1788, for Mlle Baletti) ....
11.73	"2 Sonnets" (c1788; 2S & insts): 1. "Conservati fedele"
11.74	2. "Vuoi ch'oi viva"
11.75	*"Ti lascio, adorato mio ben," recit & rondo (c1789, lost) ....*
11.76	*"Non so più dove io sia," recit & aria (c1789, lost) ....*
11.77	"Arias" (c1789, in Paisiello: La Molinara): 1. "D'un alma incostante" ....
11.78	2. "Mi sta nell' anima"
11.79	3. "Vedrai nel suo bel viso"
11.80	4. "Piano, piano"
11.81	5. "Scritti addio"
11.82	6. "Ah! ho male al cuore"
11.83	7. "Del caro ben che adoro"
11.84	8. "Or m'accorgo dell'errore"
11.85	9. "Viva amor," last finale
11.86	*"Aria for Mme Galli" (p1789, in Cimarosa's opera: Il fanatico Burlato, lost) ....*
11.87	"Se il duol che il cor m'affanna," aria (c1789, in Guglielmi: La pastorella nobile) ....
11.88	"8 Pieces" (c1790, in opera: Marguerite d'Anjou): 1. "Respires tu?," aria ....
11.89	2. "Tout doucement," trio
11.90	3. "O reine infortunée!," aria
11.91	4. "Couplets," aria
11.92	5. "Non ce n'est pas," aria
11.93	6. "Princes et rois," aria
11.94	7. "Ne jugez, pas," chorus
11.95	8. "Finale"
11.96	*"2 Pieces" (p1790, in Paisiello: La grotta di Trofonio, lost): 1. "D'un dolce amor la face," aria ....*
11.97	*2. "Che avenne! che fu!," duet*
11.98	"2 Arias" (p1790, in Guglielmi: Le due gemelle): 1. "Di valore armato il petto" ....
11.99	2. "Mirate! oh Dio, mirate!"
11.100	*"2 Arias" (p1790, in Paisiello: La frascatana, lost): 1. "Fa ch' io veda il dolce aspetto" ....*
11.101	*2. "Perdonate mio signore"*
11.102	"3 Pieces" (p1790, in Anfossi: I viaggiatori felici): 1. "Volgi a cara, amorosetto," aria (lost) ....
11.103	2. "Cara da voi dipende" (4vv)
11.104	*3. "Evviva amore," finale (lost)*
11.105	"6 Pieces" (p1790, in Cimarosa's opera: L'italiana in Londra): 1. "Al par dell' onda infida," aria (lost) ....
11.106	*2. "Senza il caro mio tesoro," aria (lost)*
11.107	3. "Lungi del caro bene," aria
11.108	4. "Son tre, sei, nove," trio
11.109	5. "Van girando per la testa," aria
11.110	*6. "Al generoso amico," recit obbl (lost)*
11.111	*2 Allegros of arias (p1790, for Mlle Baletti, lost): 1. In Sarti: La gelosie villane ....*
11.112	*2. In Guglielmi: La bella pescatrice*
11.113	"Romance d'Essex à Elisabeth" (c1790, Tilly; w/ gui) ....
11.114	*"6 Romances" (c1791; 1v & pf, lost) ....*
11.115	*"Dors mon enfant," romance (c1791, Berquin, lost) ....*
11.116	*"Le portrait de Thémire," romance (c1791, lost) ....*
11.117	"Le veuf inconsolable," romance (c1791, Lamaisonfort) ....
11.118	*"2 Arias" (p1791, in Paisiello: Il tamburo notturno, lost): 1. "Moro, manco" ....*
11.119	*2. "Fuggite, o donne, amore"*
11.120	"2 Pieces" (c1791, for opera: Lodoiska): 1. "A ces traits je connais ta rage," duet (altered) ....
11.121	2. "Cette indigne barbarie," air (not used)
11.122	*"Penso, riffletto," aria (p1791, in Martini: Il burbero di buoncore, lost) ....*
11.123	*"Ti rasserena oh cara" (p1791, added to sextet in Gazzaniga: Le vendemmie, lost) ....*
11.124	*"Quest' è l'ora," recit obbl (p1791, in Paisiello: La pazza d'amore, lost) ....*
11.125	Finale of sextet in Gazzaniga: Il finto cieco (c1791) ....
11.126	"Ah quelle ivresse," cavatina (p1791; S, for Paisiello: La pazza d'amore) ....
11.127	*"L'amitié," aria (c1792, for Mlle Tourette, lost) ....*
11.128	*"Non ti fidar, o misera," quartet (p1792, for Gazzaniga: Don Giovanni, lost) ....*
11.129	"Di qual rigido marmo," recit & duet (p1792, in Martini: La cosa rara) ....
11.130	*"5 Pieces" (p1792, in Salieri: La locandiera scaltra, lost): 1. "Le dolci sue maniere," aria ....*
11.131	*2. "Ma se tu fossi amore," aria)*
11.132	*3. "Io mi sento un non so che," aria*
11.133	*4. "Il core col pensiero," trio*
11.134	*5. "Compassione ad una donna," duet*
11.135	"Aria for Mme Morichelli" (c1792, in Cimarosa's opera: Giannina e Bernardone) ....

11.136 "Duets" (c1793, Metastasio; 2vv & pf): 1. "La libertà" ....
11.137   2. "La palinodia a Nice"
11.138 "2 Trios" (c1793; w/ vn, lost) ....
11.139 "Berenice che fai," recit & arias (c1793, for Mme Ethis, lost) ....
11.140 "L'exil," romance (c1793, for Mme Ethis, lost) ....
11.141 "Romance de Selico" (c1794, inc) ....
11.142 "4 Romances" (c1798): 1. "Viens voir sur l'écorce légère" ....
11.143   2. "Blessé par noire perfidie" (lost)
11.144   3. "Une chanson pour une fete" (lost)
11.145   4. "Voyez cette naissante rose" (lost)
11.146 2 "Anacreonic Odes" (c1799, set to the Greek; 1v) ....
11.147 "Le réveil," romance (c1801, Ferrary) ....
11.148 "Solitario bosco ombroso," nocturne (c1801; 2vv & pf) ....
11.149 "L'écho," romance (c1801) ....
11.150 "Un jour échappé de Cythère," romance (c1801) ....
11.151 "Tu les brisas, ces noeuds charmants," romance (c1801, Longchamps)...........................
11.152 "La cintura d'Armida" (c1801, from Tasso: Jerusalem Delivered; S & pf) ....
11.153 "Duet & chorus" (c1802, for an unnamed, unfin comic opera)..
11.154 "Aria" (c1804, Bouilly, for unfin opera: Les arrêts) ....
11.155 "10 Canons" (c1806; 3vv) ....
11.156 "Credimi si mio sole," recit & aria (c1806, for Crescentini) ....
11.157 "Chorus & melodrama" (c1807, for unfin opera) ....
11.158 "12 Canons" (c1779–1807; 2–4vv) ....
11.159 "Le mystère," romance (c1808, Bernard, for Count Metternich, lost) ....
11.160 "Romance" (c1811, Nivernois)...
11.161 "Romance sur un enfant" (c1811, Mme de Genlis) ....
11.162 "Madrigal" (c1811; 4vv) ....
11.163 "Canon" (c1811; 8vv, for Neukomm's album)..
11.164 "La ressemblance," romance (c1813, for Mme Louis) ....
11.165 "Chant guerrier," aria (p1814, Arnault; in: La rançon de Duguesclin).............................
11.166 "English aria for Mme Chinnery" (c1815) ....
11.167 "Vive le roi!," aria (c1815; w/ pf) ....
11.168 "Je ne t'aime plus," romance (c1818; 2vv & pf) ....
11.169 "Hymn to Bacchus," drinking song (c1819; 3vv)...
11.170 "Scène de table" (c1820; 2vv & pf ad lib) ....
11.171 "Canon" (c1820; 2vv, for Cherubini's album, lost) ....
11.172 "L'amant trompé," romance (c1823, for Mlle C's album, lost) ....
11.173 "Le bon Médore," romance (c1823, for M. Berat's album, lost) ....
11.174 "Trio" (c1825; unacc, for Mme M., lost) ....
11.175 "Piece" (c1828; 4vv, for Baillot's album, lost) ....
11.176 "Canon" (c1829; 3vv, lost) ....
11.177 "Arietta" (c1830) ....
11.178 "Exhortation villageoise," canzonetta (c1834, de Beauchesne) ....
11.179 "Octave" (c1834; 1v, vn & pf; in Tasso: Gerusalemme liberata) ....
11.180 "2 Italian ariettas" (c1835): 1. "Ch'io mai vi possa" (2nd setting 1837).........................
11.181   2. (lost)
11.182 "Romance" (c1835, de Veres) ....
11.183 "Vive le bric-à-brac," canon (c1835; 2vv, for Sauvageot, lost) ....
11.184 Arietta (c1839, lost) ....
11.185 "Canons" (c1779–1841) ....
11.186 "Souhaits heureux" (c1841; 1v, for New Year 1842) ....
11.187 "O Ingres amabile," canon (c1842; 3vv) ....

12. PEDAGOGICAL WORKS

12.1 "39 Figured basses" (c1798) ....
12.2 65 "Solfèges," for all keys (c1795–99; 1–4vv) ....
12.3 "Methode de chant" (c1800) ....
12.4 "Solfèges contenant des leçons" (p1838)..
12.5 "Figured basses" (c1818–40) ....
12.6 "52 Leçons d'harmonie" (p1904 ed P. Vidal) ....
12.7 Other solfèges (c1800–40, lost) ....

* * * * *

CHOPIN, Fryderyk (Franciszek)
1810–1849

page: 1

1. STAGE WORKS

Operas (c by others, w/ Chopin's music):

1.1   *"Fuego Fatuo" (Firefly), 3 acts (c by Falla 1918–9, Martínez Sierra; also as suite p1976):* ....
        quoted music of Chopin (orchd):
        I: 1a. Waltz No.8 in A-flat major, Op.64/3, B164/3
            1b. Scherzo No.2 in B-flat min / D-flat major, Op.31, B111
            2. Scherzo No.4 in E major, Op.54, B148 (central section)
            3. Mazurka No.15 in C major, Op.24/2, B89/2
            4. "Bolero," in C maj / A major, Op.19, B81
            5. Mazurka No.25 in B minor, Op.33/4, B115/4
            6. Scherzo No.2 in B-flat min / D-flat major, Op.31, B111
        II: 1. "Berceuse" (c by Falla, in the style of Chopin)
            2. Etude No.3 in E major, "Tristesse," Op.10/3, B74
            3. Mazurka No.8 in A-flat major, Op.7/4, B61/4
            4. Ballade No.1 in G minor, Op.23, B66
            5a. Waltz No.5 in A-flat major, "Grande valse," Op.42, B131
            5b. Mazurka No.51 in A minor (ded to Gaillard), Op.posth, B140
            6. Etude No.12 in C minor, "Revolutionary," Op.10/12, B67
        III: 1. "Tarantelle," in A-flat major, Op.43, B139
            2. "Mazurka" (from Liszt's transcr of No.6 of: Songs, Op.74)
            3. "Berceuse," in D-flat major (Variantes), Op.57, B154
            4. Ballade No.4 in F minor, Op.52, B146
            5. "Barcarolle," in F-sharp major, Op.60, B158

Ballets (c by others, w/ Chopin's music):

1.2   *"A Month in the Country" (Ashton after Turgenev, = Opp.13, 22 & 2 arr Lanchbery)* ....
1.3   *"Les sylphides" (Chopiniana) (p1909, conceived by Fokin, orch arr by others; arr Douglas 1936):*
        1. "Prelude" (= Prelude No.7 in A major, Op.28/7, B100)
        2. "Nocturne" (= Nocturne No.10 in A-flat major, Op.32/2, B106/2)
        3. "Waltz" (= Waltz No.11 in G-flat major, Op.70/1, B92)
        4. "Mazurka" (= Mazurka No.23 in D major, Op.33/2, B115/2)
        5. "Mazurka" (= Mazurka No.44 in C major, Op.67/3, B93/2)
        6. "Prelude" (= Prelude No.7 in A major, Op.28/7, B100)
        7. "Waltz II" (= Waltz No.7 in C-sharp minor, Op.64/2, B164/2)
        8. "Waltz" (= Waltz No.1 in E-flat major, Op.18, B62)

2. PIANO CONCERTOS, PIANO & ORCH

2.1	"Variations on 'Là ci darem,' " in B-flat major (c1827, from Mozart's opera: Don Giovanni, K527) Op.2, B22	
2.2	"Fantasia on Polish airs," in A major (c1828)	Op.13, B28
2.3	"Krakowiak—Concert Rondo," in F major (c1828)	Op.14, B29
2.4	Piano Concerto No.2 in F minor (c1829–30)	Op.21, B43
2.5	Piano Concerto No.1 in E minor (c1830)	Op.11, B53
2.6	"Grande Polonaise," in E-flat major (1830–1, usually perf w/ Andante spianato, B88)	Op.22, B58

3. CHAMBER MUSIC

3.1	"Variations on 'Non più mesta,' " in E major (c1824; fl & pf, from Rossini's opera: La Cenerentola)	B9
3.2	Piano Trio in G minor (c1828–9)	Op.8, B25
3.3	"Introduction & Polonaise brillante," in C major, "La gaieté" (c1829–30; vc & pf)	Op.3, B41 & B52
3.4	"Grand Duo Concertante," in E major (c1832; vc & pf, on Meyerbeer's opera: Robert le diable)	B70
3.5	Cello Sonata in G minor (c1845–6)	Op.65, B160

4. PIANO SONATAS

4.1	Piano Sonata No.1 in C minor (c1828)	Op.4, B23
4.2	Piano Sonata No.2 in B-flat minor, "Funeral March Sonata" (c1839, 3rd movt = Funeral March, B114)	Op.35, B128
4.3	Piano Sonata No.3 in B minor (c1844)	Op.58, B155

5. BALLADES (pf)

5.1	Ballade No.1 in G minor, "Polish Ballade" (c1831–5)	Op.23, B66
5.2	Ballade No.2 in F major, "La gracieuse" (c1836–9)	Op.38, B102
5.3	Ballade No.3 in A-flat major (c1840–1)	Op.47, B136
5.4	Ballade No.4 in F minor (c1842)	Op.52, B146

6. ETUDES (pf)

7. IMPROMPTUS (pf)

8. MAZURKAS (pf)

8.35	Mazurka No.35 in C minor (c1843)	Op.56/3, B153/3
8.36	Mazurka No.36 in A minor (c1845)	Op.59/1, B157/1
8.37	Mazurka No.37 in A-flat major (c1845)	Op.59/2, B157/2
8.38	Mazurka No.38 in F-sharp minor (c1845)	Op.59/3, B157/3
8.39	Mazurka No.39 in B major (c1846)	Op.63/1, B162/1
8.40	Mazurka No.40 in F minor (c1846)	Op.63/2, B162/2
8.41	Mazurka No.41 in C-sharp minor (c1846)	Op.63/3, B162/3
8.42	Mazurka No.42 in G major (c1835)	Op.67/1, B93/1
8.43	Mazurka No.43 in G minor (c1849)	Op.67/2, B167
8.44	Mazurka No.44 in C major (c1835)	Op.67/3, B93/2
8.45	Mazurka No.45 in A minor (c1846)	Op.67/4, B163
8.46	Mazurka No.46 in C major (c1829)	Op.68/1, B38
8.47	Mazurka No.47 in A minor (c1827)	Op.68/2, B18
8.48	Mazurka No.48 in F major (c1829)	Op.68/3, B34
8.49	Mazurka No.49 in F minor (c1849)	Op.68/4, B168
8.50	Mazurka No.50 in A minor, "Notre temps" / "The Cracow Mazurka" (c1840)	B134
8.51	Mazurka No.51 in A minor (c1840, for Gaillard)	B140
8.52	Mazurka No.52 in D major (c?1820)	B4
8.53	Mazurka No.53 in A-flat major (c1825, orig vers of: Mazurka No.8, Op.7/4, B61/4)	B7
8.54	Mazurka No.54 in A minor, "The Little Jew" (c1825, orig vers of: Mazurka No.13, Op.17/4, B77/4)	B8
8.55	Mazurka No.55 in G major (c1826)	B16/1
8.56	Mazurka No.56 in B-flat major (c1826)	B16/2
8.57	Mazurka No.57 in G major (c1829)	B39
8.58	Mazurka No.58 in A minor (c1829, 1st vers of: Mazurka No.6, Op.7/2, B61/2)	B45
8.59	Mazurka No.59 in B-flat major (c1832, for A. Wołowska)	B73
8.60	Mazurka No.60 in D major (c1832)	
8.61	Mazurka No.61 in C major (c1833)	B82
8.62	Mazurka No.62 in A-flat major (c1834, for Szymanowska)	B85

9. NOCTURNES (pf)

9.1	Nocturne No.1 in B-flat minor, "Murmures de la Seine 1" (c1830–1)	Op.9/1, B54/1
9.2	Nocturne No.2 in E-flat major, "Murmures de la Seine 2" (c1830–1)	Op.9/2, B54/2
9.3	Nocturne No.3 in B major, "Murmures de la Seine 3" (c1830–1)	Op.9/3, B54/3
9.4	Nocturne No.4 in F major, "Les zéphyrs 1" (c1830–1)	Op.15/1, B55/1
9.5	Nocturne No.5 in F-sharp major, "Les zéphyrs 2" (c1830–1)	Op.15/2, B55/2
9.6	Nocturne No.6 in G minor, "Les zéphyrs 3" (c1833)	Op.15/3, B79
9.7	Nocturne No.7 in C-sharp minor, "Les plaintives 1" (c1835)	Op.27/1, B91
9.8	Nocturne No.8 in D-flat major, "Les plaintives 2" (c1835)	Op.27/2, B96
9.9	Nocturne No.9 in B major, "Il lamento e la consolazione 1" (c1836–7)	Op.32/1, B106/1
9.10	Nocturne No.10 in A-flat major, "Il lamento e la consolazione 2" (c1836–7)	Op.32/2, B106/2
9.11	Nocturne No.11 in G minor (c1838)	Op.37/1, B119
9.12	Nocturne No.12 in G major (c1839)	Op.37/2, B127
9.13	Nocturne No.13 in C minor (c1841)	Op.48/1, B142/1
9.14	Nocturne No.14 in F-sharp minor (c1841)	Op.48/2, B142/2
9.15	Nocturne No.15 in F minor (c1843)	Op.55/1, B152/1
9.16	Nocturne No.16 in E-flat major (c1843)	Op.55/2, B152/2
9.17	Nocturne No.17 in B major (c1846)	Op.62/1, B161/1
9.18	Nocturne No.18 in E major (c1846)	Op.62/2, B161/2
9.19	Nocturne No.19 in E minor (c1827)	Op.72/1, B19
9.20	Nocturne No.20 in C-sharp minor, "Reminiscence" (c1830)	B49
9.21	Nocturne No.21 in C minor (c1837)	B108

10. POLONAISES (pf)

10.1	*"2 Polonaises" (c1818, for Empress M. Fyodorovna, lost)*	
10.2	Polonaise No.1 in C-sharp minor, "Les favorites 1" (c1834–5)	Op.26/1, B90/1
10.3	Polonaise No.2 in E-flat minor, "Les favorites 2" (c1834–5)	Op.26/2, B90/2
10.4	Polonaise No.3 in A major, "Military" / "Les favorites 3" (c1838)	Op.40/1, B120
10.5	Polonaise No.4 in C minor, "Les favorites 4" (c1839)	Op.40/2, B121
10.6	Polonaise No.5 in F-sharp minor, "Tragic" (c1840–1)	Op.44, B135
10.7	Polonaise No.6 in A-flat major, "Héroïque" (c1842)	Op.53, B147
10.8	Polonaise No.7 in A-flat major, "Polonaise-fantaisie" (c1845–6)	Op.61, B159
10.9	Polonaise No.8 in D minor (c ?1825)	Op.71/1, B11
10.10	Polonaise No.9 in B-flat major (c1828)	Op.71/2, B24
10.11	Polonaise No.10 in F minor (c1828)	Op.71/3, B30
10.12	Polonaise No.11 in B-flat minor, "Adieu à Guillaume Kolberg" (c1826, farewell to W. Kolberg)	B13
10.13	Polonaise No.12 in G-flat major (c1829)	B36
10.14	Polonaise No.13 in G minor (c1817, for Skarbek)	B1
10.15	Polonaise No.14 in B-flat major (c1817)	B3
10.16	Polonaise No.15 in A-flat major (c1821, for Zywny)	B5
10.17	Polonaise No.16 in G-sharp minor (c1822, for Dupont)	B6

11. PRELUDES (pf) (Nos.2–24 c1836–9)

11.1	Prelude No.1 in C major, "Reunion" (c1831)	Op.28/1, B124
11.2	Prelude No.2 in A minor, "Presentiment of Death"	Op.28/2, B123
11.3	Prelude No.3 in G major, "Thou Art So Like a Flower"	Op.28/3, B107
11.4	Prelude No.4 in E minor, "Suffocation"	Op.28/4, B123
11.5	Prelude No.5 in D major, "Uncertainty"	Op.28/5, B107
11.6	Prelude No.6 in B minor, "Tolling Bells"	Op.28/6, B107
11.7	Prelude No.7 in A major, "The Polish Dance"	Op.28/7, B100
11.8	Prelude No.8 in F-sharp minor, "Desperation"	Op.28/8, B107
11.9	Prelude No.9 in E major, "Vision"	Op.28/9, B107
11.10	Prelude No.10 in C-sharp minor, "The Night Moth"	Op.28/10, B123
11.11	Prelude No.11 in B major, "Dragon Fly"	Op.28/11, B107
11.12	Prelude No.12 in G-sharp minor, "Duel"	Op.28/12, B107
11.13	Prelude No.13 in F-sharp major, "Loss"	Op.28/13, B107
11.14	Prelude No.14 in E-flat minor, "Fear"	Op.28/14, B107
11.15	Prelude No.15 in D-flat major, "Raindrop" (according to G. Sand—depiction of rainstorm at Valldemosa)	Op.28/15, B107
11.16	Prelude No.16 in B-flat minor, "Hades"	Op.28/16, B107
11.17	Prelude No.17 in A-flat major, "A Scene on the Place de Notre Dame de Paris"	Op.28/17, B100
11.18	Prelude No.18 in F minor, "Suicide"	Op.28/18, B107
11.19	Prelude No.19 in E-flat major, "Heartfelt Happiness"	Op.28/19, B107
11.20	Prelude No.20 in C minor, "Funeral March"	Op.28/20, B107
11.21	Prelude No.21 in B-flat major, "Sunday"	Op.28/21, B123
11.22	Prelude No.22 in G minor, "Impatience"	Op.28/22, B107
11.23	Prelude No.23 in F major, "A Pleasure Boat"	Op.28/23, B107
11.24	Prelude No.24 in D minor, "The Storm"	Op.28/24, B107
11.25	Prelude No.25 in C-sharp minor (c1841)	Op.45, B141
11.26	Prelude No.26 in A-flat major (c1834, for Wolff)	B86

12. RONDOS (pf)

12.1	Rondo in C minor, "L'adieu à Varsovie" (c1825)	Op.1, B10
12.2	Rondo in F major, "à la Mazur" / "La posiana" (c1826)	Op.5, B15
12.3	Rondo in C major (c1828; also see: Rondo in C major for 2 pf, Op.73, B27)	B26
12.4	"Introduction (in C minor) & Rondo (in E-flat major)" (Rondo elégante) (c1832)	Op.16, B76
12.5	Rondo in C major (c1828; 2pf; see orig for pf, B26)	Op.73, B27

13. SCHERZOS (pf)

13.1	Scherzo No.1 in B minor, "Le banquet infernal" (c1831–2)	Op.20, B65
13.2	Scherzo No.2 in B-flat minor / D-flat major (c1837)	Op.31, B111
13.3	Scherzo No.3 in C-sharp minor (c1839)	Op.39, B125
13.4	Scherzo No.4 in E major (c1842)	Op.54, B148

14. WALTZES (pf)

14.1	*Waltz in C major (c1824, lost)*	
14.2	Waltz in C major (c1825)	
14.3	*Waltz in A-flat major (c1827, lost)*	
14.4	Waltz in E-flat major (c1827)	
14.5	*Waltz in D minor (c1828, lost)*	
14.6	*Waltz in A-flat major (c1829, lost)*	
14.7	*Waltz in A minor (c1829, sketch)*	B40b
14.8	Waltz No.1 in E-flat major, "Grande valse brillante" / "L'Invitation pour la danse" (c1831)	Op.18, B62
14.9	Waltz No.2 in A-flat major, "Valse brillante" (c1835)	Op.34/1, B94
14.10	Waltz No.3 in A minor (c1831)	Op.34/2, B64
14.11	Waltz No.4 in F major, "Valse brillante" / "Cat Waltz" (c1838)	Op.34/3, B118
14.12	Waltz No.5 in A-flat major, "Grande valse" (c1840)	Op.42, B131
14.13	Waltz No.6 in D-flat major, "Minute" / "Dog Waltz" (c1846–7)	Op.64/1, B164/1
14.14	Waltz No.7 in C-sharp minor (c1846–7)	Op.64/2, B164/2
14.15	Waltz No.8 in A-flat major (c1846–7)	Op.64/3, B164/3
14.16	Waltz No.9 in A-flat major, "L'adieu valse" (c1835)	Op.69/1, B95
14.17	Waltz No.10 in B minor (c1829)	Op.69/2, B35
14.18	Waltz No.11 in G-flat major (c1835)	Op.70/1, B92
14.19	Waltz No.12 in F minor (c1841)	Op.70/2, B138
14.20	Waltz No.13 in D-flat major (c1829)	Op.70/3, B40
14.21	Waltz No.14 in E minor (c1830)	B56
14.22	Waltz No.15 in E major (c1829)	B44
14.23	*Waltz No.16 in A-flat major (c1827, ed Hoesick 1902)*	B21
14.24	Waltz No.17 in E-flat major (c1829–30)	B46
14.25	Waltz No.18 in E-flat major, "Sostenuto" (c1840)	B133

14.26	*Waltz No.19 in A minor (c ?1843, ed S. & D. Chainaye 1955)*	*B150*
14.27	Waltz in B major (c1848, for Erskine, discovered 1952)	B166

15. MISC WORKS (pf)

15.1	*"Military March" (c1817, lost)*	*B2*
15.2	"Funeral March," in C minor (c1827)	Op.72/2, B10
15.3	"3 Ecossaises" (c1826): No.1 in D major	Op.72/3, B12
15.4	No.2 in G major	
15.5	No.3 in D-flat major	
15.6	"Introduction & Variations on a German air 'The Swiss Boy,' " in E major (c1826)	B14
15.7	"Contredanse," in G-flat major, "Kulawy" (Lame) (c ?1827; ed M. Idzikowski 1943)	B17
15.8	*"Ecossaise," in B-flat major (c1827, lost)*	
15.9	*"Andante dolente," in B-flat minor (c1827, lost)*	
15.10	"Souvenir de Paganini," variations in A major (c1929)	B37
15.11	"Allegro de Concert," in A major (c1831, movt of Pf Conc; r vers for pf 1841)	Op.46, B72
15.12	"Variations brillantes on rondo from Halevy's 'Ludovic,' " in B-flat major (c1833)	Op.12, B80
15.13	"Bolero," in C maj / A major, "Souvenir d'Andalousie" (c1833)	Op.19, B81
15.14	"Cantabile," in B-flat major (c1834)	B84
15.15	"Andante spianato" (c1834; perf as Introduction to: Grand Polonaise, Op.22, B58)	B88
15.16	"Largo," in E-flat major (c ?1837)	B109
15.17	"Variation No.6 on march from Bellini's 'I puritani,' " in E major (c1837, in: Hexameron)	B113
15.18	"Funeral March," in B-flat minor (c1837, = 3rd movt of: Pf Sonata No.2, Op.35, B128)	B114
15.19	"Andantino," in G minor (c1838, pf transcr of song: Spring, Op.74/2)	B117
15.20	"Canon," in F minor (c ?1839, manuscript sold in Geneva in 1957 by Rauch)	
15.21	"Tarantelle," in A-flat major (c1841)	Op.43, B139
15.22	"Fantasia," in F min / A-flat major (c1841)	Op.49, B137
15.23	"Fugue," in A minor (c1841–2)	B144
15.24	"Albumleaf 'Moderato,' " in E major (c1843)	B151
15.25	"Berceuse," in D-flat major (Variantes) (c1843–4)	Op.57, B154
15.26	"Barcarolle," in F-sharp major (c1845–6)	Op.60, B158
15.27	"2 Bourrées" (c1846): No.1 in G minor	B160b
15.28	No.2 in A major	
15.29	"Galop Marquis," in A-flat major (c1846, after G. Sand's dog named Marquis)	
15.30	*"Veni Creator" (c1846, lost)*	

Pf duet:

15.31	"Introduction, Theme & Variations," in D major (c1826)	B12a
15.32	*"Variations," in F major (c1826, for Wojciechowski, lost)*	

16. SONGS (w/ pf)

16.1	"17 Songs": 1. "The Wish": "Were I the sun in the sky," in G major (c1829, Witwicki)	Op.74, B33
16.2	2. "Spring": "The dew glistens," in G minor (c1838, Witwicki; see arr for pf, B117)	B116
16.3	3. "The Sad Stream": "A stream flowing," in F-sharp minor (c1831, Witwicki)	B63/1
16.4	4. "Merrymaking": "Serving maid, take care," in G major (c1830, Witwicki)	B50/1
16.5	5. "There Where She Loves": "A stream loves the vale," in A major (c1829, Witwicki)	B32
16.6	6. "Out of My Sight!," in F min / A-flat major (c1830, Mickiewicz)	B48
16.7	7. "The Envoy": "The early herb broke forth," in D major (c1830, Witwicki)	B50/2
16.8	8. "Handsome Lad": "Strong, tall and young," in D major (c1841, Zaleski)	B143
16.9	9. "Melody": "From the mountains they bore," in G maj / E minor (c1847, Krasiński)	B165
16.10	10. "The Warrior": "My bay horse neighs," in A-flat major (c1830, Witwicki)	B47
16.11	11. "The Double End": "They loved for a year," in D minor (c1845, Zaleski)	B156/1
16.12	12. "My Darling": "When you are happily singing," in G-flat major (c1837, Mickiewicz)	B112
16.13	13. "I Want What I Have Not": "Mist before my eyes," in A minor (c1845, Zaleski)	B156/2
16.14	14. "The Ring": "Thy nurses sing sadly for thee" (c1836, Witwicki)	B103
16.15	15. "The Bridegroom": "The wind rose ..." (c1831, Witwicki)	B63/2
16.16	16. "Lithuanian Song": "Very early in the morning," in F major (c1831, Osiński)	B63/3
16.17	17. "Hymn From the Tomb": "Leaves are falling," in E-flat minor (c1836, Pol)	B101
16.18	"Spells": "This is witchcraft, surely witchcraft," in D minor (c1830, Zaleski)	B51
16.19	"Reverie": "Mist before my eyes," in A minor (c1840, Zaleski, in Witwicki's album)	B132

Arrs by others:

16.20	*"Aspiration," song (arr unknown from: Nocturne No.2 in E-flat major, Op.9/2, B54/2)*	
16.21	*"Messagero amoroso," song (arr Buzzi-Peccia from: Waltz No.6 in D-flat major, 'Minute,' Op.64/1, B164/1)*	

*   *   *   *   *

B = M. Brown: "Chopin. An Index of his Works in Chronological Order." 2nd ed., Da Capo Press. New York, 1972.

1. STAGE WORKS

Opera:

1.1	"The Second Hurricane," 2 act school play-opera (c1936, Denby) ....
1.2	"The Tender Land," 2/3 acts (c1952–4, r1954–5, Everett after Johns) ....

Ballets:

1.3	"Grogh," 1 scene choreographic fantasy (c1922–5) ....
1.4	"Hear Ye! Hear Ye!," 2 acts (c1934, Page) ....
1.5	"Billy the Kid," 1 act (c1938, Loring) ....
1.6	"Rodeo," 1 act (c1942, Mille): ....

      1. "Buckaroo Spring"
      2. "Corral Nocturne"
      3. "Saturday Night Waltz"
      4. "Hoe-Down"

1.7	"Appalachian Spring" 1 act (c1943–4, Graham; 13 insts) ....
1.8	"Dance Panels," 7 sections (c1959–62, Rosen) ....

Incid music:

1.9	"Miracle at Verdun" (c1931, Chlumberg) ....
1.10	"The Five Kings" (c1939, O. Welles after Shakespeare's Henry IV Part 1 & 2, Henry V & Richard II; 5 insts)
1.11	"Quiet City" (c1939, Shaw; cl, sax, tpt & pf) ....
1.12	"From Sorcery to Science," puppet show (c1939; orch) ....
1.13	"The World of Nick Adams," television drama (c1957, on Hemingway's stories) ....

Film:

1.14	"The City," documentary (c1939, Lorenz, Fodakiewicz & Serling) ....
1.15	"Of Mice and Men" (c1939, Roach after Steinbeck's novel) ....
1.16	"Our Town" (c1940, Lesser after Wilder's play) ....
1.17	"Fiesta" (p1942) ....
1.18	"North Star" (c1943, Hellman) ....
1.19	"The Cummington Story," documentary (c1945) ....
1.20	"Fiesta" (p1947, based on orch work: El Salon Mexico of 1933–6) ....
1.21	"The Red Pony" (c1948, Milestone after Steinbeck's story) ....
1.22	"The Heiress" (c1948, Wyler, screenplay R. & A. Goetz after H. James's novel: Washington Square) ....
1.23	"Something Wild" (c1961, Garfine after Karmel's novel) ....

2. SYMPHONIES

2.1	"Symphony for Organ & Orchestra" (c1924) ....
2.2	Symphony No.1 (c1928, = Sym for Organ & Orch arr w/ out org; 1st movt Prelude arr for small orch) ....
2.3	"Dance Symphony" (c1930, from ballet: Grogh) ....
2.4	Symphony No.2, "Short Symphony" (c1932–3; also see: Sextet) ....
2.5	Symphony No.3 (c1944–6, also see: Fanfare for the Common Man) ....

3. OTHER ORCHESTRAL WORKS

3.1	"Cortège Macabre" (c1922–3, from ballet: Grogh) ....
3.2	"Music for the Theatre," suite (c1925; small orch): No.1 "Prologue" ....
3.3	No.2 "Dance"
3.4	No.3 "Interlude"
3.5	No.4 "Burlesque"
3.6	No.5 "Epilogue"
3.7	"Symphonic Ode" (c1927–9, r1955) ....
3.8	"2 Pieces" (arr for strings 1928; see orig for str qt): No.1 "Rondino" (on the Name of G. Fauré) ....
3.9	No.2 "Lento molto" ....
3.10	"Statements" (c1932–5): No.1 "Militant" ....
3.11	No.2 "Cryptic"
3.12	No.3 "Dogmatic"
3.13	No.4 "Subjective"
3.14	No.5 "Jingo"
3.15	No.6 "Prophetic"
3.16	"El Salón México" (c1933–6): ....

    arrs by others: . Arr Bernstein for pf
       . Arr Bernstein for 2pf
       . Arr Hindsley for winds 1972
       . Arr Mikhashoff for cl, bn, tpt, trbn, pf, perc, 1–4vn & d bass 1983

3.17	"Music for Radio" (Saga of the Prairies) (c1937, music for Radio Prairie Journal) ....

3.18   "Billy the Kid," orch suite (arr1940, from ballet): No.1 "The Open Prairie" ....
3.19   No.2 "Street in a Frontier Town"
3.20   No.3 "Card Game at Night" (Prairie Night)
3.21   No.4 "Gun Battle"
3.22   No.5 "Celebration Dance after Billy's Capture"
3.23   No.6 "Billy's Death"
3.24   No.7 "The Open Prairie Again"
3.25   "Waltz: Billy and his Sweetheart" (from ballet: Billy the Kid) ....
3.26   "An Outdoor Overture" (c1937; arr for band 1941) ....
3.27   "Our Town," suite (c1940, from film; see excerpts arr for pf 1944) ....
3.28   "John Henry, a Railroad Ballad" (c1940, r1952; chamber orch) ....
3.29   "Quiet City" (arr1941; Eng hn, tpt & strings, from incid music) ....
3.30   "Rodeo—4 Dance Episodes" (arr1942, from ballet): No.1 "Buckaroo Holiday" ....
3.31   No.2 "Corral Nocturne"
3.32   No.3 "Saturday Night Waltz"
3.33   No.4 "Hoe Down"
3.34   "Music for Movies," suite (arr1942): No.1 "New England Countryside" (from: The City) ....
3.35   No.2 "Sunday Traffic" (from: The City)
3.36   No.3 "Barley Wagons" (from: Of Mice and Men)
3.37   No.4 "Story of Grovers Corners" (from: Our Town)
3.38   No.5 "Threshing Machines" (from: Of Mice and Men)
3.39   "Lincoln Portrait" (c1942; speaker & orch) ....
3.40   "Fanfare for the Common Man" (c1942; brass & perc, from: Sym No.3) ....
3.41   "Letter from Home" (c1944, r1962) ....
3.42   "Jubilee Variations" (c1944, on theme by Goossens) ....
3.43   "Appalachian Spring," concert suite (c1945, from ballet) ....
3.44   "The Red Pony," suite (arr1948, from film): No.1 "Morning on the Ranch" ....
3.45   No.2 "The Gift"
3.46   No.3 "Dream March and Circus Music"
3.47   No.4 "Walk to the Bunkhouse"
3.48   No.5 "Grandfather's Story"
3.49   No.6 "Happy Ending"
3.50   "Preamble for a Solemn Occasion" (c1949; speaker & orch; see arr for org 1953) ....
3.51   "The Tender Land," suite (arr1957, from opera): No.1 "Introduction and Love Music" ....
3.52   No.2 "Party Scene"
3.53   No.3 "Finale: The Promise of Living"
3.54   "Orchestral Variations" (c1957, based on: Pf Variations of 1930) ....
3.55   "2 Mexican Pieces" (c1959, later = Nos.2–3 of: 3 Latin-American Sketches) ....
3.56   "Connotations" (c1961–2) ....
3.57   "Music for a Great City" (c1963–4, based on film: Something Wild): No.1 "Skyline" ....
3.58   No.2 "Night Thoughts"
3.59   No.3 "Subway Jam"
3.60   No.4 "Toward the Bridge"
3.61   "Emblems" (c1964; concert band) ....
3.62   "Down a Country Lane" (arr1965; school orch; orig pf piece of 1962) ....
3.63   "CBS 'Television Playhouse' Theme" (c1966) ....
3.64   "Inscape" (c1967) ....
3.65   "Variations on a Shaker melody" (arr1967, from ballet: Appalachian Spring) ....
3.66   "Happy Anniversary" (c1969, for the 70th birthday of E. Ormandy) ....
3.67   "Ceremonial Fanfare" (c1969; brass, for the New York City Metropolitan Museum centenary) ....
3.68   "Inaugural Fanfare" (c1969, r1975; winds & perc, commissioned by The City of Grand Rapids) ....
3.69   "3 Latin-American Sketches" (c1959–71; see: 2 Mexican Pieces of 1959): No.1 "Estribillo" ....
3.70   No.2 "Paisaje Mexicano"
3.71   No.3 "Danza de Jalisco"

4. CONCERTOS, SOLO INSTR & ORCH

4.1   Piano Concerto (c1926) ....
4.2   Clarinet Concerto (c1947–8; cl & strings w/ harp, pf) ....

5. STRING QUARTETS

5.1   Movement (Lent—Assez Vif) (c1924) ....
5.2   "2 Pieces" (see arr for strings): No.1 "Rondino" (on the Name of G. Fauré) (c1923) ....
5.3   No.2 "Lento molto" (c1928)
5.4   *"American Landscapes," I (arr Mikhashoff from pf): No.1 "Sunday Afternoon Music"* ....
5.5   *No.2 "The Young Pioneers"*
5.6   *No.3 "Down a Country Lane" (arr from orch vers)*
5.7   *"American Landscapes," II (arr Mikhashoff from pf): No.1 "Midsummer Nocturne"* ....
5.8   *No.2 "Conversation at the Soda Fountain"*
5.9   *No.3 "In Evening Air"*

6. OTHER CHAMBER MUSIC

Early works:

6.1	"Capriccio" (ca1916; vn & pf)	....
6.2	"Poème" (c1918; vc & pf)	....
6.3	"Lament" (ca1919; vc & pf, unfin)	....
6.4	Prelude No.1 (ca1919; vn & pf)	....
6.5	Prelude No.2 (c1921; vn & pf)	....
6.6	Piano Trio (ca1916–21, inc)	....

Mature works:

6.7	"2 Pieces" (c1926; vn & pf): No.1 "Nocturne"	....
6.8	No.2 "Ukelele Serenade"	....
6.9	"Vitebsk, Study on a Jewish Theme" (c1928; pf trio)	....
6.10	*"Elegies" (c1932; vn & va, withdrawn)*	....
6.11	Sextet (c1937; cl, str qt & pf, chamber red of: Symphony No.2)	....
6.12	Violin Sonata (c1942–3)	....
6.13	Piano Quartet (c1950)	....
6.14	Nonet (c1960; 3vn, 3va & 3vc)	....
6.15	Duo (c1971; fl & pf)	....
6.16	"2 Threnodies" (fl & str trio): No.1 "In memoriam Igor Stravinsky" (c1971)	....
6.17	No.2 "In memoriam Beatrice Cunningham" (c1973)	....

7. PIANO SONATAS

7.1	Piano Sonata in G major (c1920–1, early work)	....
7.2	Piano Sonata (c1939–41)	....

8. OTHER PIANO WORKS

Early works:

8.1	"Moment Musicale" (c1917)	....
8.2	"Waltz Caprice" (c1918)	....
8.3	"3 Sonnets": No.1 "Sonnet I" (c1918)	....
8.4	No.2 "Sonnet II" (c1919)	
8.5	No.3 "Sonnet III" (c1920)	
8.6	"Moods," 3 esquisses (c1920–1): No.1 "Amertume" (Embittered)	....
8.7	No.2 "Pensif" (Wistful)	
8.8	No.3 "Jazzy"	
8.9	. Supplement: "Petit portrait"	

Mature works:

8.10	"The Cat and the Mouse" (Scherzo Humoristique) (c1920)	....
8.11	"Passacaglia" (c1921–2)	....
8.12	"2 Blues" (c1926): No.1 "Sentimental Melody"	....
8.13	No.2 "Blues No.2" (= No.4 of: 4 Piano Blues)	
8.14	"Piano Variations" (c1930; basis for: Orch Variations of 1957)	....
8.15	"2 Children's Pieces" (c1935; also see: American Landscapes for str qt): No.1 "Sunday Afternoon Music"..
8.16	No.2 "The Young Pioneers"	
8.17	*"Billy the Kid," excerpts (arr Foss, from ballet): No.1 "The Open Prairie"*	....
8.18	*No.2 "Street Scene"*	
8.19	*No.3 "Billy and his Sweetheart"*	
8.20	*No.4 "Celebration"*	
8.21	"Our Town," 3 excerpts (arr from orch suite of 1944): No.1 "Story of Our Town"	....
8.22	No.2 "Conversation at the Soda Fountain"	
8.23	No.3 "The Resting—Place on the Hill"	
8.24	"4 Piano Blues": No.1 "Freely poetic" (c by 1947)	....
8.25	No.2 "Soft and languid" (c1934)	
8.26	No.3 "Muted and sensuous" (c1948)	
8.27	No.4 "With bounce" (= No.2 of: 2 Blues of 1926)	
8.28	"Midsummer Nocturne" (c1947)	....
8.29	"Midday Thoughts" (c1947; compl Peekskill 1982)	....
8.30	"Piano Fantasy" (c1955–7)	....
8.31	"Down a Country Lane" (c1962; see arr for orch)	....
8.32	"Rodeo" (arr1962, from ballet): No.1 "Buckaroo Holiday"	....
8.33	No.2 "Transition—Corral Nocturne"	
8.34	No.3 "Saturday-Night Waltz"	
8.35	"Dance Panels" (arr1965, from ballet)	....
8.36	"In Evening Air" (c1966, from film: The Cummington Story, r by Peekskill 1972)	....

| 8.37 | "Nights Thoughts—Homage to Ives" (c1972) .... |
| 8.38 | "Proclamation" (c1973; compl Peekskill 1982; orchd Ramey 1985) .... |

Pf duet:

| 8.39 | "Danse caractéristique" (c1918; pf duet/orch, early work) .... |
| 8.40 | "Danzón Cubano" (c1942; orchd1945) .... |

2 Pf:

8.41	"Billy the Kid," suite (c1938, from ballet) ....
8.42	"Danza de Jalisco" (arr1967, from No.3 of: 3 Latin-American Sketches for orch) ....
8.43	"Dance of the Adolescent" (arr from ballet: Grogh) ....

9. ORGAN

| 9.1 | "Episode" (c1940) .... |
| 9.2 | "Preamble for a Solemn Occasion" (arr1953, from orch piece of 1949) .... |

10. CHORAL WORKS

10.1	"4 Motets" (c1921, Bible; ch): 1. "Have mercy on us, O my Lord" ....
10.2	2. "Help us, O Lord"
10.3	3. "Sing ye praises to our King"
10.4	4. "Thou, o Jehovah, abideth forever"
10.5	"2 Choruses" (c1925): 1. "The House on the Hill" (from Robinson's Children of the Night; fem ch) ....
10.6	2. "An Immortality" (from Pound's Lustra; S, fem ch & pf) ....
10.7	"What do we plant?" (c1935, Abbey; junior high ch & pf) ....
10.8	"Lark" (c1938, Taggard; Bar & ch) ....
10.9	"Las Agachadas" (The Shake-down Song) (c1942, trad Spanish; SATB solo group & ch) ....
10.10	"Song of the Guerrillas" (c1943; Bar, m ch & pf/orch, from film: North Star) ....
10.11	"The Younger Generation" (c1943; ch & pf, from film: North Star) ....
10.12	"In the Beginning" (c1947, from Genesis; mS & ch) ....
10.13	*"Old American Songs" I (arr Fine for ch/m ch & pf; 2 vers)* ....
10.14	"Canticle of Freedom" (c1954, r1966, Barbour; ch & orch) ....

11. SONGS (w/ pf)

Early works:

11.1	"Melancholy" (a song à la Debussy) (c1917, Farnol) ....
11.2	"Spurned Love" (c1917, Aldrich) ....
11.3	"After Antwerp" (c1917, Cammaerts) ....
11.4	"3 Songs" (c1918, Schaffer): 1. "A Summer Vacation" ....
11.5	2. "My heart is in the East"
11.6	3. "Night Song"
11.7	"Simone" (c1919, Gourmont) ....
11.8	"Music I heard" (c1920, Aitken) ....

Mature works:

11.9	"Old Poem" (Mélodie Chinoise) (c1920, trad Chinese transl Waley) ....
11.10	"Pastorale" (c1921, Arabic transl Mathers) ....
11.11	"As it fell upon a day" (c1923, Barnefield; S, fl & cl) ....
11.12	"Alone" (c1923, Mathers) ....
11.13	"Poet's Song" (Song) (c1927, e. e. cummings) ....
11.14	"Vocalise-etude" (c1928, wordless; arr Dwyer for fl & pf 1972) ....
11.15	"Into the Streets May First" (c1934, Hayes) ....
11.16	"12 Poems of Emily Dickinson," cycle (c1949–50): 1. "Nature, the gentlest mother" (orchd1970) ....
11.17	2. "There came wind like a bugle" (orchd1970)
11.18	3. "Why do they shut me out of heaven?"
11.19	4. "The world feels dusty" (orchd1970)
11.20	5. "Heart, we will forget him" (orchd1970)
11.21	6. "Dear March, come in" (orchd1970)
11.22	7. "Sleep is supposed to be" (orchd1970)
11.23	8. "When they come back"
11.24	9. "I felt a funeral in my brain"
11.25	10. "I've heard an organ talk sometimes"
11.26	11. "Going to heaven" (orchd1970)
11.27	12. "The chariot" (orchd1958–70)
11.28	"Old American Songs" (arr1950; orchd1955), I: 1. "The Boatsmen's dance" (Emmett 1843) ....
11.29	2. "The Dodger" (collected Lomax)

* * * * *

CORELLI, Arcangelo
1653–1713

1. CONCERTI GROSSI

1.1	"Concerti grossi" (p1714; concertino: 2vn, vc & ripieno: 2vn, va, bass): No.1 in D major Op.6
1.2	No.2 in F major
1.3	No.3 in C minor
1.4	No.4 in D major
1.5	No.5 in B-flat major
1.6	No.6 in F major
1.7	No.7 in D major
1.8	No.8 in G minor, "Christmas Concerto"
1.9	No.9 in F major
1.10	No.10 in C major
1.11	No.11 in B-flat major
1.12	No.12 in F major
1.13	*"12 Concerti grossi" (concertino: 2vn, vc & ripieno: 2vn, va, bass, ?spur)... Anh1–12*

2. SONATAS A QUATRO

2.1	"Sonata a 4" (2vn, violetta & bass) .... WoO 2
2.2	*"Sonata a 4" (2vn, violetta & bass, frag) .... WoO 3*
2.3	"Sonata a 4" (tromba sola, 2vn & bass) .... WoO 4
2.4	*"Concerto a quatro" (vn & 2tpt or 2vn & bass, ?spur) Anh13*
2.5	*"Sonata a 4" (ob, 2vn & bass, ?spur) Anh14*

3. TRIO SONATAS

3.1	"Sonate da chiesa a tre" (p1681; 2vn, violone/archlute & org): No.1 in F major Op.1
3.2	No.2 in E minor
3.3	No.3 in A major
3.4	No.4 in A minor
3.5	No.5 in B-flat major
3.6	No.6 in B minor
3.7	No.7 in C major
3.8	No.8 in C minor
3.9	No.9 in G major
3.10	No.10 in G minor
3.11	No.11 in D minor
3.12	No.12 in D major
3.13	"Sonate da camera a tre" (p1685; 2vn & violone/hpd): No.1 in D major Op.2
3.14	No.2 in D minor
3.15	No.3 in C major
3.16	No.4 in E minor
3.17	No.5 in B-flat major
3.18	No.6 in G minor
3.19	No.7 in F major
3.20	No.8 in B minor
3.21	No.9 in F-sharp minor
3.22	No.10 in E major
3.23	No.11 in E-flat major
3.24	No.12 in G major
3.25	"Sonate da chiesa a tre" (p1689; 2vn, violone/archlute & org): No.1 in F major Op.3
3.26	No.2 in D major
3.27	No.3 in B-flat major
3.28	No.4 in B minor
3.29	No.5 in D major
3.30	No.6 in G major
3.31	No.7 in E minor
3.32	No.8 in C major
3.33	No.9 in F minor
3.34	No.10 in A minor
3.35	No.11 in G minor
3.36	No.12 in A minor
3.37	"Sonate da camera a tre" (p1694; 2vn & violone/hpd): No.1 in C major Op.4
3.38	No.2 in G minor
3.39	No.3 in A major
3.40	No.4 in D major
3.41	No.5 in A minor
3.42	No.6 in E major
3.43	No.7 in F major
3.44	No.8 in D minor
3.45	No.9 in B-flat major
3.46	No.10 in G major
3.47	No.11 in C minor

4. VIOLIN SONATAS

5. MISC INSTRUMENTAL

6. MISC VOCAL

* * * * *

WoO = Hans Joachim Marx: "Archangelo Corelli. Historisch-kritische Gesamtausgabe der
       musikalischen Werke. Supplementband. Die Überlieferung der Werke Arcangelo Corellis.
       Catalogue raisonné." Arno Volk Verlag—Hans Gerig KG Köln, 1980.
Anh = Anhang (Appendix) in Marx's catalog.

1. CHAMBER MUSIC

Trio Sonatas:

1.1   "La pucelle," in E minor (ca1692; 2vn, bass-viol & cont; r as La françoise in: Les nations) ....

1.2   "La Steinquerque," in B-flat major (ca1692; 2vn, bass-viol & cont) ....

1.3   "La visionnaire," in C minor (ca1693; 2vn & cont; r as L'espagnole in: Les nations) ....

1.4   "L'astrée," in G minor (ca1693; 2vn, bass-viol & cont; r as La piemontoise in: Les nations) ....

1.5   "La superbe," in A major (ca1693; 2vn, bass-viol & cont) ....

1.6   "L'impériale," in D minor (ca1710–5; 2vn, bass-viol & cont, preserved as trio sonata only in: Les nations) ..

Sonatas à quatro:

1.7   "La sultane," quartet/quintet in D minor (ca1695; 2vn, 2 bass-viols & cont) ....

Apothéoses:

1.8   "Le Parnasse, ou L'apothéose de Corelli," Grand Trio Sonata in B minor (p1724; 2vn, bass-viol & cont).....

1.9   "Concert en forme d'apothéose de Lully," in G minor (p1725; 2vn, 2fl & unspec insts, double pastiche): .....
          1. (Lully in the Elysian Fields, in Concert with the Lyric Spirits)
          2. (Air for the Same)
          3. (Descent of Apollo, Who Comes to Offer Lully His Violin and His Place on Mount Parnassus)
          4. (Underground Rumblings Caused by the Composers Who Are Lully's Contemporaries)
          5. (Ascension of Lully to Parnassus)
          6. (Lully's Thanks to Apollo)
          7. (Air léger for Two Violins, with Lully Playing the Subject, and Corelli the Accompaniment)
          8. (Second Air, with Corelli Now Playing the Subject, Which Lully Accompanies)
          9. (The peace of Parnassus, Made Under Conditions Required by the French Muses, That
             Henceforth, in Their Language, One Will Use the Terms 'Sonade' and 'Cantade,' Just As
             One Says 'Ballade,' 'Sérénade,' etc.)

"Les nations" (Sonades et suites de symphonies en trio) (p1726; 2vn, bass-viol & cont, r vers of trio
    sonatas w/ added dance suite to each):

1.10   "La françoise," trio sonata & suite in E minor (from: La pucelle) ....

1.11   "L'espagnole," trio sonata & suite in C minor (from: la visionnaire) ....

1.12   "La piémontoise," trio sonata & suite in G minor (from: L'astrée) ....

1.13   "L'impériale," trio sonata & suite in D minor..

"Concerts royaux" (p1722; strings, winds & cont):

1.14   "Premier concert," in G major: No.1 "Prélude" ....
1.15   No.2 "Allemande"
1.16   No.3 "Sarabande"
1.17   No.4 "Gavotte"
1.18   No.5 "Gigue"
1.19   "Deuxième concert," in D major: No.1 "Prélude" ....
1.20   No.2 "Allemande fuguée"
1.21   No.3 "Air tendre"
1.22   No.4 "Air contrefugué"
1.23   No.5 "Echos"
1.24   "Troisième concert," in A major: No.1 "Prélude" ....
1.25   No.2 "Allemande"
1.26   No.3 "Courante"
1.27   No.4 "Sarabande grave"
1.28   No.5 "Gavotte"
1.29   No.6 "Musette"
1.30   No.7 "Chaconne légère"
1.31   "Quatrième concert," in E minor: No.1 "Prélude" ....
1.32   No.2 "Allemande"
1.33   No.3 "Courante française"
1.34   No.4 "Courante à l'italienne"
1.35   No.5 "Sarabande"
1.36   No.6 "Rigaudon"
1.37   No.7 "Forlane. Rondeau"

"Les goûts-réûnis (The Union of Styles), ou Nouveaux concerts" (p1724):

1.38   "Cinquième concert," in F major: No.1 "Prélude" ....
1.39   No.2 "Allemande"
1.40   No.3 "Sarabande grave"
1.41   No.4 "Gavotte"
1.42   No.5 "Musette dans le goût de carillon. Rondeau"
1.43   "Sixième concert," in B-flat major: No.1 "Prélude" ....
1.44   No.2 "Allemande à quatre temps"

1.45   No.3 "Sarabande mesurée"
1.46   No.4 "Air de Diable"
1.47   No.5 "Sicilienne"
1.48   "Septième concert," in G minor: No.1 "Prélude" ....
1.49   No.2 "Allemande"
1.50   No.3 "Sarabande grave"
1.51   No.4 "Fuguéte"
1.52   No.5 "Gavotte"
1.53   No.6 "Sicilienne"
1.54   "Huitième concert," in G major, "dans le goût théâtral": No.1 "Overture" ....
1.55   No.2 "La Grande Ritournelle"
1.56   No.3 "Air"
1.57   No.4 "Air tendre"
1.58   No.5 "Air léger"
1.59   No.6 "Louré"
1.60   No.7 "Air"
1.61   No.8 "Sarabande grave et tendre"
1.62   No.9 "Air tendre"
1.63   No.10 "Air de Bacchantes"
1.64   "Neuvième concert," in E major, "Ritratto dell'amore": No.1 "Le charme" ....
1.65   No.2 "L'enjouement"
1.66   No.3 "Les grâces. Courante française"
1.67   No.4 "La je-ne-sçay-quoy"
1.68   No.5 "La vivacité"
1.69   No.6 "La noble fierté. Sarabande"
1.70   No.7 "La douceur"
1.71   No.8 "L'et coetera, ou Menuets" (2 parts)
1.72   "Dixième concert," in A minor: No.1 "Prélude" ....
1.73   No.2 "Air tendre et louré"
1.74   No.3 "Plainte pour les violes ou autres instruments à l'unisson" (2 parts)
1.75   No.4 "Tromba"
1.76   "Onzième concert," in C minor: No.1 "Prélude" ....
1.77   No.2 "Allemande"
1.78   No.3 "Courante"
1.79   No.4 "Deuxième courante"
1.80   No.5 "Sarabande"
1.81   No.6 "Gigue lourée"
1.82   No.7 "Rondeau"
1.83   "Douzième concert," in A major, "à deux violes ou autres instruments à l'unisson" ....
1.84   "Treizième concert," in G major, "à deux instruments à l'unisson": No.1 "Prélude" ....
1.85   No.2 "Air"
1.86   No.3 "Sarabande"
1.87   No.4 "Chaconne"
1.88   "Quatorzième concert" (et dernière de cet oeuvre), in D minor: No.1 "Prélude" ....
1.89   No.2 "Allemande"
1.90   No.3 "Sarabande grave"
1.91   No.4 "Fuguéte"

         "Pièces de violes" (p1728; 2va & cont):

1.92   Suite No.1 in E minor: No.1 "Prélude" ....
1.93   No.2 "Allemande"
1.94   No.3 "Courante"
1.95   No.4 "Sarabande grave"
1.96   No.5 "Gavotte"
1.97   No.6 "Gigue"
1.98   No.7 "Passacaille ou Chaconne"
1.99   Suite No.2 in A major: No.1 "Prélude" ....
1.100   No.2 "Fuguéte"
1.101   No.3 "Pompe funèbre"
1.102   No.4 "La chemise blanche"

2. HARPSICHORD

         "Pièces de clavecin ... premier livre" (p1713):

2.1   Suite No.1 in G min / major: No.1 "L'auguste," allemande ....
2.2   No.2 "Premier courante"
2.3   No.3 "Seconde courante"
2.4   No.4 "La majestueuse," sarabande
2.5   No.5 "Gavotte"
2.6   No.6 "La milordine," gigue
2.7   No.7 "Menuet" (w/ double)
2.8   No.8 "Les silvains," rondeau

2.78	. "Quatrième prélude," in F major
2.79	. "Cinquième prélude," in A major
2.80	. "Sixième prélude," in D minor
2.81	. "Septième prélude," in B-flat major
2.82	. "Huitième prélude," in E minor

"Le second livre de pièces de clavecin" (p1716–7):

2.83	Suite No.6 in B-flat major: No.1 "Les moissonneurs" ....
2.84	No.2 "Les langueurs-tendres"
2.85	No.3 "Le gazouillement"
2.86	No.4 "La Bersan"
2.87	No.5 "Les baricades mistérieuses"
2.88	No.6 "Les bergeries"
2.89	No.7 "La commére"
2.90	No.8 "Le moucheron"
2.91	Suite No.7 in G maj / minor: No.1 "La Ménetou" ....
2.92	No.2 "Les petits âges":
	1. "La muse naissante"
	2. "L'enfantine"
	3. "L'adolescente"
	4. "Les délices"
2.93	No.3 "La basque"
2.94	No.4 "La Chazé"
2.95	No.5 "Les amusemens," rondeaux
2.96	Suite No.8 in B minor: No.1 "La Raphaéle" ....
2.97	No.2 "L'Ausoniéne," allemande
2.98	No.3 "Courante"
2.99	No.4 "Seconde courante"
2.100	No.5 "L'unique," sarabande
2.101	No.6 "Gavotte"
2.102	No.7 "Rondeau"
2.103	No.8 "Gigue"
2.104	No.9 "Passacaille"
2.105	No.10 "La Morinéte"
2.106	Suite No.9 in A maj / minor: No.1 "Allemande à deux clavecins" ....
2.107	No.2 "La rafraîchissante"
2.108	No.3 "Les charmes"
2.109	No.4 "La Princesse de Sens"
2.110	No.5 "L'olimpique"
2.111	No.6 "L'insinuante"
2.112	No.7 "La séduisante"
2.113	No.8 "Le bavolet-flotant"
2.114	No.9 "Le petit-deuil, ou les trois veuves"
2.115	No.10 "Menuet"
2.116	Suite No.10 in D maj / minor: No.1 "La triomphante": ....
	1. "Bruit de guerre; Combat"
	2. "Allegresse des vainqueurs"
	3. "Fanfare"
2.117	No.2 "La Mézangére"
2.118	No.3 "La Gabriéle"
2.119	No.4 "La Nointéle"
2.120	No.5 "La fringante"
2.121	No.6 "L'amazône"
2.122	No.7 "Les bagatelles"
2.123	Suite No.11 in C min / major: No.1 "La castelane" ....
2.124	No.2 "L'etincelante ou La bontems"
2.125	No.3 "Les graces naturéles, Suite de la bontems"
2.126	No.4 "La zénobie"
2.127	No.5 "Les fastes" (5 piéces)
2.128	Suite No.12 in E maj / minor: No.1 "Les juméles" ....
2.129	No.2 "L'intîme," courante
2.130	No.3 "La galante"
2.131	No.4 "La coribante"
2.132	No.5 "La Vauvré"
2.133	No.6 "La fileuse"
2.134	No.7 "La boulonoise"
2.135	No.8 "L'atalante"

"Le troisième livre de pièces de clavecin" (p1722):

2.136	Suite No.13 in B minor: No.1 "Les lis naissans" ....
2.137	No.2 "Les rozeaux"
2.138	No.3 "L'engageante"

2.139	No.4 "Les folies françoises, ou Les dominos":
	1. "La virginité sous le domino couleur d'invisible. Premier couplet"
	2. "La pudeur sous le domino couleur de roze. 2e couplet"
	3. "L'ardeur sous le domino incarnat. 3e couplet"
	4. "L'esperance sous le domino vert. 4e couplet"
	5. "La fidélité sous le domino bleu. 5e couplet"
	6. "La pérséverance sous le domino gris de lin. 6e couplet"
	7. "La langueur sous le domino violet. 7e couplet"
	8. "La coquéterie sous diférens dominos. 8e couplet"
	9. "Les vieux galans et les trésoriers suranées sous des dominos pourpres et feuilles
	mortes. 9e couplet"
	10. "Les coucous bénévoles sous des dominos jaunes. 10e couplet"
	11. "La jalousie taciturne sous le domino gris de Maure. 11e couplet"
	12. "La frénésie ou le désespoir sous le Domino noir. 12e couplet"
2.140	No.5 "L'âme-en-peine"
2.141	Suite No.14 in D maj / minor: No.1 "Le rossignol-en-amour" (w/ Double) ....
2.142	No.2 "La Linote éfarouchée"
2.143	No.3 "Les fauvétes plaintives"
2.144	No.4 "Le rossignol-vainqueur"
2.145	No.5 "La Juillet"
2.146	No.6 "Le carillon de Cithére"
2.147	No.7 "Le petit-rien"
2.148	Suite No.15 in A maj / minor: No.1 "La régente ou la Minerve" ....
2.149	No.2 "Le dodo ou L'amour au berçeau, Pièce-croisée"
2.150	No.3 "L'evaporée"
2.151	No.4 "Muséte de Choisi"
2.152	No.5 "Muséte de Taverni"
2.153	No.6 "La douce et piquante"
2.154	No.7 "Les vergers fleuris"
2.155	No.8 "La Princesse de Chabeuil, ou La muse de Monaco"
2.156	Suite No.16 in G maj / minor: No.1 "Les graces incomparables ou La Conti" ....
2.157	No.2 "L'himen-amour"
2.158	No.3 "Les vestales"
2.159	No.4 "L'aimable Thérése"
2.160	No.5 "Le drôle de corps"
2.161	No.6 "La distraite"
2.162	No.7 "La Létiville"
2.163	Suite No.17 in E minor: No.1 "La superbe ou la Forqueray" ....
2.164	No.2 "Les petits moulins à vent"
2.165	No.3 "Les timbres"
2.166	No.4 "Courante"
2.167	No.5 "Les petites chrémiéres de Bagnolet"
2.168	Suite No.18 in F min / major: No.1 "La Verneüil," allemande ....
2.169	No.2 "La Verneuilléte"
2.170	No.3 "Soeur Monique"
2.171	No.4 "Le turbulant"
2.172	No.5 "L'atendrissante"
2.173	No.6 "Le tic-toc-choc ou Les maillotins, Pièce croisée"
2.174	No.7 "Le gaillard boiteux"
2.175	Suite No.19 in D min / major: No.1 "Les Calotins et les Calotines, ou La pièce à tretous" ....
2.176	No.2 "Les Calotines"
2.177	No.3 "L'ingénue"
2.178	No.4 "L'artiste"
2.179	No.5 "Les culbutes"
2.180	No.6 "La muse—Palantine"
2.181	No.7 "L'enjouée"
	"Le quatrième livre de pièces de clavecin" (p1730):
2.182	Suite No.20 in G maj / minor: No.1 "La Princesse Marie" (3 piéces) ....
2.183	No.2 "La boufonne"
2.184	No.3 "Les chérubins ou L'aimable Lazure"
2.185	No.4 "La Croûilli ou La Couperinéte"
2.186	No.5 "La fine Madelon"
2.187	No.6 "La douce Janneton"
2.188	No.7 "La Sezile, Pièce croisée pour le grand clavier"
2.189	No.8 "Les tambourins"
2.190	Suite No.21 in E minor: No.1 "La reine des coeurs" ....
2.191	No.2 "La bondissante"
2.192	No.3 "La Couperin"
2.193	No.4 "La harpée, Pièce dans le goût de la harpe"
2.194	No.5 "La petite pince-sans-rire"
2.195	Suite No.22 in D maj / minor: No.1 "Le trophée" ....
2.196	No.2 "Premier air pour La suite du trophée"
2.197	No.3 "2e air"

2.198   No.4 "Le point du jour," allemande
2.199   No.5 "L'anguille"
2.200   No.6 "Le croc-en-jambe"
2.201   No.7 "Menuets croisés":
      1. "1e menuet"
      2. "2e menuet"
2.202   No.8 "Les tours de passe-passe"
2.203   Suite No.23 in F major: No.1 "L'audacieuse" ....
2.204   No.2 "Les tricoteuses"
2.205   No.3 "L'arlequine"
2.206   No.4 "Les gondoles de Délos"
2.207   No.5 "Les satires chevre-pieds"
2.208   Suite No.24 in A min / major: No.1 "Les vieux seigneurs," sarabande grave ....
2.209   No.2 "Les jeunes seigneurs"
2.210   No.3 "Les dars-homicides"
2.211   No.4 "Les guirlandes"
2.212   No.5 "Les brinborions"
2.213   No.6 "La divine Babiche, ou Les amours badins"
2.214   No.7 "La belle Javotte, autre fois l'Infante"
2.215   No.8 "L'amphibie," mouvement de passacaille
2.216   Suite No.25 in E-flat maj / C maj / minor: No.1 "La visionaire" ....
2.217   No.2 "La misterieuse"
2.218   No.3 "La Montflambert"
2.219   No.4 "La muse victorieuse"
2.220   No.5 "Les ombres errantes"
2.221   Suite No.26 in F-sharp minor: No.1 "La convalescente" ....
2.222   No.2 "Gavotte"
2.223   No.3 "La Sophie"
2.224   No.4 "L'epineuse"
2.225   No.5 "La pantomime"
2.226   Suite No.27 in B minor: No.1 "L'exquise," allemande ....
2.227   No.2 "Les pavots"
2.228   No.3 "Les chinois"
2.229   No.4 "Saillie"
2.230   "Sicilienne," in G major ....

3. ORGAN

3.1   "Messe des paroisses," organ mass (c1690): ....
    "Kyrie": 1. "Plain-chant du premier Kyrie, en taille"
      2. "Fugue sur les jeux d'anches. Deuxième couplet"
      3. "Récit de chromhorne. Troisième couplet"
      4. "Dialogue sur la trompette et le chromhorne. Quatrième couplet"
      5. "Plain-chant. Cinquième et dernier couplet"
    "Gloria": 6. "Plein jeu. Et in terra pax"
      7. "Petite fugue sur le chromhorne. Deuxième couplet du Gloria"
      8. "Duo sur les tierces. Troisième couplet"
      9. "Dialogue sur les trompettes, clairons et tierces du grand clavier et le bourdon avec le larigot du
        positif. Quatrième couplet"
     10. "Trio à deux dessus de chromhorne et la basse de tierce. Cinquième couplet"
     11. "Tierce en taille. Sixième couplet"
     12. "Dialogue sur la voix humaine. Septième couplet"
     13. "Dialogue du trio du cornet et de la tierce. Huitième couplet"
     14. "Dialogue sur les grands jeux. Neuvième et dernier couplet"
    "Offertory": 15. "Offertoire sur les grands jeux"
    "Sanctus": 16. "Plain-chant du premier Sanctus en canon"
     17. "Récit de cornet. Deuxième couplet"
    "Benedictus": 18. "Benedictus. Chromhorne en taille"
    "Agnus Dei": 19. "Plain-chant de l'Agnus Dei en basse et en taille alternativement"
     20. "Dialogue sur les grands jeux. Troisième couplet de l'Agnus"
    "Deo gratias": 21. "Petit plein jeu"
3.2   "Messe des couvents," organ mass (c1690): ....
    "Kyrie": 1. "Plein jeu. Premier couplet du Kyrie"
      2. "Récit de chromhorne"
      3. "Trio à deux dessus de chromhorne et la basse de tierce. Quatrième couplet du Kyrie"
      4. "Dialogue sur la trompette du grand clavier, et sur la montre, le bourdon, et le nazard du
        positif. Cinquième et dernier couplet du Kyrie"
    "Gloria": 5. "Plein jeu. Premier couplet du Gloria"
      6. "Petite fugue sur le chromhorne. Deuxième couplet"
      7. "Duo sur les tierces. Troisième couplet"
      8. "Basse de trompette. Quatrième couplet"
      9. "Chromhorne sur la taille. Cinquième couplet"
     10. "Dialogue sur la voix humaine. Sixième couplet"
     11. "Trio. Les Dessus sur la tierce et la basse sur la trompette. Septième couplet"

12. "Récit de tierce. Huitième couplet"
13. "Dialogue sur les grands jeux. Dernier couplet"
"Offertory": 14. "Premiere partie," in G major
15. "Deuxième partie," in G minor
16. "Troisième partie"
"Sanctus": 17. "Premier couplet du Sanctus. Plein jeu. Récit de cornet. Deuxième couplet"
"Élévation": 18. "Premier couplet du Sanctus. Plein jeu. Récit de cornet. Deuxième couplet"
"Agnus Dei": 19. "Plein jeu"
20. "Dialogue sur les grands jeux. Dernier couplet d'Agnus Dei"
"Deo gratias": 21. "Petit plein jeu"

4. SACRED VOCAL

4.1	"Motet": "Laudate pueri Dominum" (c1693–7, p1697; 2S, B, 2vn & cont): 1. "Laudate pueri Dominum" ....
4.2	2. "Sit nomen Domini benedictum"
4.3	3. "A solis ortu"
4.4	4. "Excelsus super omnes gentes"
4.5	5. "Quis Sicut Dominus"
4.6	6. "Suscitans terra inopem"
4.7	7. "Ut colloquium eum"
4.8	8. "Qui habitare facit"
4.9	"Motet de Sainte-Suzanne": "Veni sponsa Christi" ....

Versailles manuscript:

4.10	"Motet de Saint-Barthélemy": "Laetentur coeli" (2 tr vv & cont) ....
4.11	"Motet de Sainte-Anne": "Festiva laetis" (1 tr v, cT, B & cont) ....
4.12	"Motet de Saint-Augustin": "Jucunda vox ecclesiae" (2 tr vv, B & cont) ....
4.13	"Élévation": "O misterium ineffabile" (S, B & cont)
4.14	"Élévation": "O amor, O gaudium" (cT, T, B & cont) ....
4.15	"Élévation": "O Jesu amantissime" (cT, T, B & cont) ....
4.16	"Élévation": "Venite exultemus Domine" (1 tr v, low tr v & cont)..............................
4.17	"Élévation": "Quid retribuam tibi Domine" (cT & cont)
4.18	"Élévation": "Audite omnes et expavescite" (cT, 2vn & cont) ....
4.19	"Motet pour le jour de Pâques": "Victoria, Christo resurgenti" (2S & cont) ....
4.20	"Magnificat" (2 tr vv & cont)
4.21	"Motet": "O Domine quia refugiam" (2Bar, B & cont) ....
4.22	"Dialogus inter Deum et hominem": "Accedo ad te" (cT, B & cont) ....

The Manuscript of the Count of Toulouse (Tenbury manuscript):

4.23	"Tantum ergo sacramentum" (2 tr vv, B & cont) ....
4.24	"Domine salvum fac regem" (1 tr v, B & cont) ....
4.25	"Élévation": "Lauda Sion Salvatorem" (2 tr vv & cont) ....
4.26	"Respice in me" (cT & cont) ....
4.27	"Salve Regina" (for solo voice) (cT & cont) ....
4.28	"Regina coeli, laetare" (2 tr vv & cont) ....
4.29	"Usquequo, Domine" (cT) ....
4.30	"Salvum me fac Deus" ....
4.31	"Ad te levavi oculos meos" (B, 2vn & cont) ....
4.32	"Ornate aras" (inc)
4.33	"Resonent organa" (inc) ....
4.34	"Exultent superi," (1 tr v, cT, B, 2vn & cont, inc) ....

Motets written at the order of the king:

4.35	"Qui dat nivem" (Verset from the Motet of the previous year sung by Mlle Couperin at her debut) (c1702) ..
4.36	"Mirabilia testimonia" (4 Versets d'un motet) (c1703, Psalm 118): 1. "Tabescere me fecit zelus" ....
4.37	2. "Ignitum eloquium tuum"
4.38	3. "Adolescentulus sum"
4.39	4. "Justitia tua"
4.40	"Benedixisti Domine" (7 Versets du motet) (c1704, Psalm 84): 1. "Converte nos" ....
4.41	2. "Numquid in aeternum irasceris nobis"
4.42	3. "Ostende nobis"
4.43	4. "Audiam quid loquatur in me"
4.44	5. "Misericordia et Veritas"
4.45	6. "Veritas de terra"
4.46	7. "Et enim Dominus"
4.47	"Qui Regis Israel" (7 Versets du motet) (c1705, Psalm 79): 1. "Qui Regis Israel" ....
4.48	2. "Excita potentiam tuam"
4.49	3. "Vineam de Aegypto"
4.50	4. "Dux itineris fuisti"
4.51	5. "Operuit montes"
4.52	6. "Extendit palmites Suos"
4.53	7. "Deus virtutum convertere"

Leçons de Ténèbres:

4.54	"Leçons de Ténèbres du mercredi" (c1714, for Maundy Thurs): 1. "Incipit lamentatio Jeremiae prophetae"
4.55	2. "Et egressus est filia" ....
4.56	3. "Manum suam misit hostis" ....
4.57	*"Leçons de Ténèbres du jeudi" (c1714, for Good Friday, lost)* ....
4.58	*"Leçons de Ténèbres du vendredi" (ca1712, for Holy Saturday, lost)* ....

5. SECULAR VOCAL

1v & cont:

5.1	"Qu'on ne me dise plus," air sérieux (c1697) ....
5.2	"Doux liens de mon coeur," air sérieux (c1701) ....
5.3	"Zéphire, modère en ces lieux," brunette, air sérieux (c1711) ....

2vv & cont:

5.4	"Epitaphe d'un paresseux": "Jean s'en alla comme il était venu," air à boire (c1706) ....
5.5	"La pastorelle": "Il faut aimer," air sérieux (c1711) ....
5.6	"Les solitaires": "Dans l'île de Cythère," air sérieux (c1711) ....
5.7	"Musette": "A l'ombre d'un ormeau," air sérieux (c1711) ....
5.8	"Les pellerines": "Au temple de l'amour," air sérieux (c1712) ....

3vv & cont:

5.9	"Vaudeville": "Faisons du temps," air sérieux (c1712) ....
5.10	"Trois vestales champêtres et trois Poliçons": "Quel bruit soudain" ....
5.11	"La femme entre deux draps," canon à 3, air à boire ....
5.12	"A moy! Tout est perdu!," canon à 3, air à boire ....

Cantatas:

5.13	*"Ariane abandonée" (c1716, lost)* ....

6. THEORETICAL WORKS

6.1	"Le traité d'accompagnement" ....
6.2	"L'art de toucher le clavecin" (p1716; Ger & Eng transl 1933) ....

* * * * *

1. STAGE WORKS

Operas:

Ballets:

Incid music:

Projects:

1a. SELECTIONS FROM STAGE WORKS

      3. "Je suis perdu aussi"
      4. "Voici ce qu'il écrit à son frère Pelléas"
      5. "Qu'en dites-vous?"
      6. "Interlude"
      7. "Il fait sombre danses jardins"
      8. "Hoé! Hisse Hoé"
II: 9. "Vous ne savez pas où je vous ai menée?"
      10. "C'est au bord d'une fontaine"
      11. "Interlude"
      12. "Ah! Ah! Tout va bien"
      13. "Voyons, donne-moi ta main"
      14. "Interlude"
      15. "Oui, c'est ici nous y sommes"
III: 16. "Mes longs cheveux"
      17. "Non, non, nous n'avons pas été coupables"
      18. "Que faites-vous ici?"
      19. "Prenez garde: par ici, par ici"
      20. "Ah! je respire enfin"
      21. "Interlude"
      22. "Viens, nous allons nous asseoir ici"
      23. "Qu'ils s'embrassent, petit père?"
IV: 25. "Maintenant que le père de Pelléas"
      26. "Pelléas part ce soir"
      27. "Ne mettez pas ainsi votre main à la gorge"
      28. "Interlude"
      29. "Oh! Cette pierre est lourde"
      30. "C'est le dernier soir"
      31. "Nous sommes venus ici il y a bien longtemps"
      32. "In dirait que ta voix"
      33. "Quel est ce bruit?"
V: 34. "Ce n'est pas de cette petite blessure"
      35. "Attention; je crois qu'elle s'éveille"
      36. "Mélisande, as-tu pitié de moi"
      37. "Non, non, nous n'avons pas été coupables"
      38. "Qu'avez-vous fait?"
      39. "Qu'y a-t-il?"
      40. "Attention ... attention"

1a.13   "Chansons de Bilitis," incid music: L96
         1. "Chant pastoral"
         2. "Les Comparaisons"
         3. "Les contes"
         4. "Chanson"
         5. "La partie d'osselets"
         6. "Bilitis"
         7. "Le tombeau sans nom"
         8. "Les courtisanes égyptiennes"
         9. "L'eau pure du bassin"
        10. "La danseuse aux crotales"
        11. "Le souvenir de Mnasidica"
        12. "La pluie du matin"

1a.17   "La martyre de Saint Sébastien," incid music (Nos. of sections in The Gramophone): L124
         excerpts: I. "La Cour des Lys": 1. "Prélude"
                   2. "Sébastien!"
                   3. "Danse extatique de Sébastien"
             II. "La chambre magique": 4. "Prélude"
                   5. "Je fauchais l'épi de froment"
                   6. "Qui pleure mon enfant si doux"
            III. "Le concile des faux dieux": 7. "Prélude"
                   8. "Païan, Lyre d'or, Arc d'argent!"
                   9. "Avez-vous vu celui que j'aime?"
                  10. "Ne pleurez plus!"
                  11. "Io! Io! Adoniastes!"
                  12. "Il est mort, le bel Adonis"
             IV. "Le Laurier blessé": 13. "Prélude"
                  14. "Il est là, la Pasteur. Regardez"
                  15. "Hélas!"
              V. "Le Paradis": 16. "Interlude"
                  17. "Gloire!"

2. SYMPHONIES

2.1   *Symphony in B minor (c1880, pf score only; orchd Faldner; Allegro arr for pf duet 1890)* *L10*
2.2   *Symphony (c1890, after Poe, project, lost)* ....

3. OTHER ORCHESTRAL WORKS

3.1   *"Le triomphe de Bacchus," suite (ca1882, lost; extant: Allegro & Andante cantabile):* *L38*
        . *"Allegro" (arr Gaillard for pf; also orchd1928)*
        . *"Andante cantabile" (orchd Gaillard 1928)*
3.2   "Orchestral Suite No.1" (ca1883; arr for pf): No.1 "Fête" L50
3.3   No.2 "Ballet"
3.4   No.3 "Rêve"
3.5   No.4 "Bacchanale"
3.6   *"Printemps," sym suite (c1887; fem ch & orch, lost; arr for pf duet 1904; orchd Büsser)* *L61*
3.7   *"Trois scènes au crépuscule" (c1892–3, after Regnier, sketches; used in: 3 Nocturnes, L91)* *L83*
3.8   "Nocturnes" (Triptyque symphonique) (c1897–9; arr Ravel for pf duet): No.1 "Nuages" L91
3.9   No.2 "Fêtes"
3.10   No.3 "Sirènes" (w/ wordless fem ch)
3.11   "La mer" (The Sea), 3 sym sketches (c1903–5; arr for pf duet): No.1 "De l'aube à midi sur la mer" L109
3.12   No.2 "Jeux de vagues" (Play of the Waves)
3.13   No.3 "Dialogue du vent et de la mer"
3.14   "Images" (c1905–12): No.1 "Gigues" (c1909–12; compl Caplet) L122
3.15   No.2 "Ibéria" (c1905–8):
            a. "Par les rues et par les chemins"
            b. "Les parfumes de la nuit"
            c. "Le matin d'un jour de fête"
3.16   No.3 "Rondes de printemps" (c1905–9)
3.17   *"La martyre de Saint Sébastien," sym frags (arr Caplet, from incid music): No.1 "La cour de lys"* ....
3.18   *No.2 "Danse extatique"*
3.19   *No.3 "La chambre magique"*
3.20   *No.4 "La passion"*
3.21   *No.5 "Le laurier blessé"*
3.22   *No.6 "Le bon pasteur"*

4. CONCERTOS, SOLO INSTR & ORCH

4.1   "Intermezzo" (c1882; vc & orch, frag of inc suite; arr for pf duet) L27
4.2   "Fantaisie" (c1889–90; pf & orch) L73
4.3   "Prélude à L'après-midi d'un faune" (Prelude to 'The Afternoon of a Faun') (c1892–4, fl & orch, after
        Mallarmé's poem; arr for 2pf) (the opening w/ fl solo 'arabesque'—free ornamental melody of 'natural
        curves') L86
4.4   *"Poéme" (Violin Concerto) (ca1894; vn & orch, project)* ....
4.5   *"Trois nocturnes" (ca1894; vn & orch, project)* ....
4.6   "Rapsodie" (c1901–8; sax & orch/pf; compl Roger-Ducasse p1919) L98
4.7   "Deux danses" (c1904; harp/pf & strings; arr for pf duet): No.1 "Danse sacrée" L103
4.8   No.2 "Danse profane"

5. STRING QUARTETS

5.1   String Quartet in G minor (c1893) Op.10, L85
5.2   *String Quartet No.2 (c1894, project)* ....

6. OTHER CHAMBER MUSIC

3 insts:

6.1   Piano Trio No.1 in G major (c1880) L3
6.2   Sonata No.2 (c1915; fl, va & harp) L137
6.3   *Sonata (No.4) (c1915; ob, hn & hpd, project)* ....
6.4   *Sonata (No.5) (c1915; cl, bn, tpt & pf, project)* ....
6.5   *Sonata (No.6) (c1915; pf & ensemble, project)* ....

Vn & pf:

6.6   *Violin Sonata (c1894, project)* ....
6.7   (Violin) Sonata No.3 in G minor (c1916–7) L140

Other 2 insts:

6.8   "Nocturne et scherzo" (c1882; vc & pf) L26

7. PIANO

7.64   No.9 "Hommage à S. Pickwick Esq. P.P.M.P.C." (inspired by Dickens: The Posthumous Papers
of the Pickwick Club)
7.65   No.10 "Canope"
7.66   No.11 "Les tièrces alternées"
7.67   No.12 "Feux d'artifice"
7.68   "Berceuse héroïque" (c1914; orchd1915) L132
7.69   "Pièce pour l'oeuvre du 'Vêtement du blessé' " (c1915, pubd as: Page d'album) L133
7.70   "Étude retrouvée" I (Pour les arpèges composés) (c1915, 1st vers of: Étude No.11, L136/11)....................
7.71   "Douze études" (c1915), I: No.1 "Pour les cinq doigts" (after Czerny) L136
7.72   No.2 "Pour les tierces"
7.73   No.3 "Pour les quartes"
7.74   No.4 "Pour les sixtes"
7.75   No.5 "Pour les octaves"
7.76   No.6 "Pour les huit doigts"
7.77   II: No.7 "Pour les degrés chromatiques"
7.78   No.8 "Pour les agréments"
7.79   No.9 "Pour les notes répétées"
7.80   No.10 "Pour les sonorités opposées"
7.81   No.11 "Pour les arpèges composés" II
7.82   No.12 "Pour les accords"
7.83   "Élégie" (c1915) L138

Pf duet:

7.84   "Andante cantabile" (ca1880) ....
7.85   "Andante cantabile" (ca1882, sold at Paris auction in 1979) ....
7.86   "Intermezzo" (ca1882, 1 single movt) ....
7.87   "Divertissement" (ca1882; pf duet/2pf) L36
7.88   "Petite Suite" (c1886–9; orchd Büsser 1907): No.1 "En bateau" L65
7.89   No.2 "Cortège"
7.90   No.3 "Menuet"
7.91   No.4 "Ballet"
7.92   "Marche écossaise sur un thème populaire" (The Earl of Ross March) (c1891; orchd1906) L77
7.93   "Six épigraphes antiques" (c1914, derived from L96; arr for pf): No.1 "Pour invoquer Pan" L131
7.94   No.2 "Pour un tombeau sans nom"
7.95   No.3 "Pour que la nuit soit propice"
7.96   No.4 "Pour la danseuse aux crotales"
7.97   No.5 "Pour l'égyptienne"
7.98   No.6 "Pour remercier la pluie au matin"

2 Pf:

7.99   "Lindaraja" (c1901) L97
7.100   "En blanc et noir" (c1915): No.1 (Poetic epigraph: Qui reste à sa place) (Barbier & Carré) L134
7.101   No.2 (Poetic epigraph: Prince, porté soit des serfs Éolus) (Villon)
7.102   No.3 (Poetic epigraph: Yver, vous n'estes qu'un vilain) (Charles d'Orleans)

8. CHORAL WORKS

8.1   "Hélène": "Franchis les mers icariennes," scène lyrique (ca1881–2, Lisle; S, ch & orch, inc) L20bis
8.2   "Le printemps": "Salut, printemps" (c1882, Ségur; fem ch & orch; arr Gaillard for pf 1928).................... L24
8.3   *"Choeur des brises": "Réveillez-vous" (ca1882; S & 3 fem vv, sketch; extract pubd1950)* *L35*
8.4   "Invocation": "Élevez-vous, voix de mon âme" (c1883, Lamartine; m ch & orch) L40
8.5   "Le printemps": "L'aimable printemps ramène dans la plaine" (c1884, Barbier; ch & orch) L56
8.6   "La damoiselle élue," poème lyrique (c1887–8, r1902, Rossetti transl Sarrazin; S, fem ch & orch;
also Eng adaptation to Rossetti's original poem by Damrosch) L62
8.7   "Trois chansons de Charles d'Orléans" (ch): 1. "Dieu! qu'il la fait bon regarder!" (c1898) L92
8.8   2. "Quand j'ai ouy le tambourin" (c1908)
8.9   3. "Yver, vous n'estes qu'un villain" (c1898)
8.10   "Ode à la France": "Les troupeaux vont" (c1916–7, Laloy; S, ch & orch; compl Gaillard 1928)............ L141

9. VOICE & ORCHESTRA

9.1   "Daniel": "Versez, que de l'ivresse," cantata (ca1881, Cécile; 3vv & orch, inc)...................................... L20
9.2   "Le gladiateur": "Mort aux Romains," cantata (c1883, Moreau; 3vv & orch) L41
9.3   "L'enfant prodigue": "L'année, en vain," scène lyrique / cantata (c1884, r1906–8, Guinand; vv & orch,
Prix de Rome 1884): L57
         1. "Cortège et air de danse" (arr for pf duet)
         2. "Récit. et air de Lia"
9.4   *"Zuleima," ode symphonique (c1885–6, Boyer after Heine; ?1v & orch, lost)* *L59*
9.5   "La saulaie" (c1896–1900, Rossetti transl Louÿs; Bar & orch) (also see Vaughan Williams' cantata:
Willow-wood) L89

10. SONGS (w/ pf)

10.74 "3 Chansons de France" (c1904): 1. "Rondel I": "Le temps a laissié son manteau" (d'Orléans) L102
10.75   2. "La grotte": "Auprés de cette grotte sombre" (l'Hermite; = L118/1)
10.76   3. "Rondel II": "Pour ce que Plaisance est morte" (d'Orléans)
10.77 "Fêtes galantes," Set II (c1904, Verlaine): 1. "Les Ingénus": "Les hauts talons luttaient" L104
10.78   2. "Le Faune": "Un vieux faune de terre cuite"
10.79   3. "Colloque sentimental": "Dans le vieux parc solitaire et glacé"
10.80 "Le promenoir des deux amants," cycle (l'Hermite): 1. "La grotte" (= L102/2) L118
10.81   2. "Crois mon conseil chère Climène" (c1910)
10.82   3. "Je tremble voyant ton visage" (c1910)
10.83 "Trois ballades de François Villon" (c1910; orchd): 1. "Balade de Villon à s'amye": "Faulse beauté" L119
10.84   2. "Ballade que Villon feit à la requeste de sa mère pour prier Nostre-Dame": "Dame du ciel"
10.85   3. "Ballade des femmes de Paris": "Quoy qu'on tient belles langagières"
10.86 "Trois poèmes de Stephane Mallarmé" (c1913): 1. "Soupir": "Mon âme vers ton front où rêve" L127
10.87   2. "Placet futile": "Princesse! à jalouser le destin d'une Hébé"
10.88   3. "Éventail": "O rêveuse, pour que je plonge"
10.89 "Noël des enfants qui n'ont plus de maisons": "Nous n'avons plus" (c1915, Debussy) L139

11. MISC WORKS

Exercises for the Paris Conservatory:

11.1   1. Melody and realized bass (c1878, for harmony exam) ....
11.2   2. "Chant donné and basse donnée" (c1879, for harmony exam) ....
11.3   3. Melody for harmonization (c1879, in class of Émile Durand) ....
11.4   4. "Chant donné; basse donnée" (c1880, for harmony exam) ....
11.5   5. "Leçon" (c1880, for harmony class of Émile Durand) ....
11.6   6. Fugue (c1881, for Concours de Fugue 1881) ....
11.7   7. "Fugue à 4 voix" (c1882, subject by Gounod, for exam leading to Prix de Rome competition) ....
11.8   8. "Fugue à 4 voix" (c1882, for final round in Prix de Rome competition) ....
11.9   9. Fugue (c ?1883, for the exam leading to Prix de Rome competition) ....
11.10   10. Fugue (c1883, for Concours de Fugue de 1883. Sujet de M) ....
11.11   11. "Fugue à 4 voix" (c1884, for exam leading to Prix de Rome competition) ....
11.12   12. "Fugue à 4 voix" (c1884, preparatory fugue, prior to: Le printemps & L'enfant prodigue) ....
11.13   13. "Pièces sans date. Partitions de Debussy donné par J. Durand" ....
11.14   14. "Fugue d'école sur un thème de Th. Dubois" ....

Musical Greetings:

11.15   1. "Je vous la souhaite bonne et heureuse" (ca1882; 1v & pf, New Year's greeting) ....
11.16   2. "Marche nuptiale pour le mariage de Pierre Louÿs" (c1899; 1v & org) ....
11.17   3. "Noël pour célébrer Pierre Louÿs pour toutes les voix" (c1903) ....
11.18   4. "Les accords de septième regrettent!" (c1905; pf, for birthday of Emma Debussy) ....
11.19   5. Piano fragment (c1905, for Emma Bardac's birthday) ....
11.20   6. "Petite cantate sur grand papier pour le jour de sa fête Emma" (c1907; S, Bar, ch, bells & pf) ....
11.21   7. "Chant des matelots du vaisseau" (c1911; 1st & 2nd basses, on a greeting card) ....
11.22   8. "Noël pour 1914 ..." (c1914; 1v & pf) ....
11.23   9. "La neige sur le village. Poème symphonique en 5 mesures" (c1916; bells, for Emma) ....

12. ARRANGEMENTS OF WORKS OF OTHERS

For orch:

12.1 Satie: "Deux gymnopedies" (arr1896, Nos.1 & 3 of: Trois gymnopedies) ....

For pf:

12.2 Raff: "Humoresque en forme de valse" (arr1893) ....
12.3 Saint-Saëns: Extracts from opera: Étienne Marcel ....
12.4 Schumann: "Am Springbrunnen" (À la fontaine), Op.85/9 (arr1903) ....

For pf duet:

12.5 Tchaikovsky: 3 Dances from ballet: The Swan Lake (arr1880): No.1 "Danse russe" ....
12.6   No.2 "Danse espagnole"
12.7   No.3 "Danse napolitaine"
12.8 Saint-Saëns: "Caprice," on the airs of ballet in Gluck's opera: Alceste, Wq44 (arr1889) ....

For 2 pf:

12.9 Saint-Saëns: "Introduction et Rondo capriccioso," Op.28 (arr1889) ....
12.10 Saint-Saëns: Symphony No.2 in A minor, Op.55 (arr1890) ....
12.11 Saint-Saëns: Airs from ballet in opera: Étienne Marcel (arr1890): ....
  1. "Introduction"

2. "Entrée des ecoliers"
3. "Musette guerrière"
4. "Pavane"
5. "Valse"
6. "Entrée des bohémiens"
7. "Finale: Allegro"

12.12   Schumann: "6 études en forme de canon," Op.56 (transcr1891) ....

12.13   Wagner: Overture to opera: The Flying Dutchman, WWV63 (arr1890) ....

Editions of works of others:

12.14   Rameau: "Les fêtes de Polymnie" (p1908, r & red for pf) ....

12.15   Chopin: "Oeuvres complètes pour piano," 12 vols (p1915–7) ....

12.16   Bach, J. S.: "6 sonates pour violon et clavecin and 3 Sonates pour piano et violoncelle" (p1923) ....

*   *   *   *   *

L = Fr. Lesure: "Catalogue de l'oeuvre de Claude Debussy." Éditions Minkoff. Genève, 1977.

DELIUS, Frederick (Fritz) (Theodore Albert)
1862–1934

1. STAGE WORKS

Operas:

1.1	*"Zanoni" (c1888, sketches)*	*RTi/1*
1.2	"Irmelin," 3 acts (c1890–2, Delius)..	RTi/2
1.3	"The Magic Fountain" (Der Wunderborn), 3 acts (c1894–5, Delius)	RTi/3
1.4	"Koanga," 3 acts (c1895–7, Keary after Cable's novel: The Grandissimes) RTi/4
1.5	"A Village Romeo and Juliet," 6 scene lyric drama (c1900–1, Delius & Keary after Keller's tale: Die Leute von Seldwyla)	RTi/6
1.6	"Margot la rouge," 1 act lyric drama (c1902, Rosenval, vocal score by M. Ravel)	RTi/7
1.7	"Fennimore and Gerda," 11 scenes (c1909–10, after Jacobsen's novel: Niels Lyhne)	RTi/8

Incid music:

1.8	"Folkeraadet" (The Council of the People), satiric drama (c1897, Heiberg; see: Norw Suite, RTi/5)	RTi/5
1.9	"Hassan or The Golden Journey to Samarkand" (c1920–3, Flecker)...	RTi/9

1a. SELECTIONS FROM STAGE WORKS (Nos. of sections in The Gramophone)

1a.5   "A Village Romeo and Juliet," opera: RTi/6
     excerpts: I. "September. A strip of land on a hill": 1. "Prelude"
             2. "A shame it is, to let such good land lie waste"
             3. "How strange the wind sounds"
             4. " 'Twixt us, methinks, will lie the bidding"
       II. "Six years later. Outside Marti's house": 5. "Prelude"
             6. "Vreli!... Sali!"
             7. "Interlude—Prelude to Scene 3"
       III. "The Wildland": 8. "I knew we'd meet again"
             9. "O Sali, I'm afraid!"
             10. "Shameless hussy!"
       IV. "Interior of Marti's house": 11. "Prelude"
             12. "Ah, the night is approaching"
             13. "Dearest, I'll you no more"
             14. "The dream of Sali and Vrenchen" (Wedding Scene)
             15. "Ah! it was a dream"
       V. "The Fair": 16. "Prelude"
             17. "O Sali, see what beautiful things!"
             18. "Well, well, gracious me, if it isn't Vreli Marti and Sali Manz"
             19. "Interlude—The Walk to the Paradise Garden"
       VI. "The Paradise Garden": 20. "Dance along"
             21. "So you want to know, how the strife began"
             22. " 'Tis almost night"
             23a. "Come and live with us and taste the cream of life!"
             23b. "What say you, Vreli?"
             24. "Halleo! Halleo!"
             25. "See, the moonbeams kiss the woods"

1a.9   "Hassan or The Golden Journey to Samarkand," incid music: RTi/9
     excerpts: 1. "Prelude"
       I: 2. "Interludes between Scenes 1 and 2"
            3. "Scene 2: Moonlight—The Street of Felicity"
            4. "Serenade" (vn solo)
            5. "Hassan falls under the shadow of the fountain"
            6. "Chorus behind the scene"
            7. "Serenade" (T solo)
       II: 8. "Prelude to Scene 1"
            9a. "Fanfare preceding the Ballet"
            9b. "Ballet—Dance of the Beggars"
            10. "Chorus of Women"
            11. "Divertissement"
            12. "General Dance"
            13. "Chorus of Beggars and Dancing Girls"
            14. "Scene 2: The Street of Felicity"
            15. "Music accompanying Ishak's poem"
       III: 16. "Prelude to Scene 1"
            17. "Scene 1: Curtain"
            18. "Interludes between Scenes 1 and 2"
            19. "Scene 2: The War Song of the Saracens"
            20. "Fanfares—Entry of the Caliph"
       IV: 21. "Prelude to Scene 1"
            22. "Interlude between Scenes 1 and 2"
       V: 23a. "Prelude"
            23b. "The Garden of the Caliph's palace"

23c. "Sunset"
23d. "The Song of the Muezzin at Sunset"
24. "Procession of Protracted Death"
25. "Prelude to the last scene"
26. "Closing scene: We take the Golden Road to Samarkand"

2. ORCHESTRAL WORKS

2.1	"Florida" (Tropical Scenes for Orchestra), suite (c1887): No.1 "Daybreak—Dance"	RTvi/1
2.2	No.2 "By the River" (r1889)	
2.3	No.3 "Sunset—Near the Plantation"	
2.4	No.4 "At Night"	
2.5	"Hiawatha," tone poem (c1888, after poem by Longfellows)	RTvi/2
2.6	"Rhapsodic Variations" (c1888, unfin)	RTvi/3
2.7	*"3 Pieces" (c1888, ?lost/not composed)*	*RTvi/4*
2.8	"Idylle de printemps" (Morceau symphonique) (c1889)	RTvi/5
2.9	"Petite suite d'orchestre" (Little Suite) (c1889–90): No.1 "Marche," in C major (c1889, r1890)	RTvi/6
2.10	No.2 "Berceuse," in G major	
2.11	No.3 "Scherzo," in G major	
2.12	No.4 "Duo," in B minor	
2.13	No.5 "Tema con variazione," in E minor	
2.14	"Suite de 3 morceaux caracteristiques" (c1889–90): No.1 "La quadroone," in F-sharp minor	RTvi/6a
2.15	No.2 "Scherzo," in E major	
2.16	No.3 "Marche caprice," in C major	
2.17	"Marche française" (c1890)	RTvi/6b
2.18	"3 Small Tone Poems" (c1890): No.1 "Summer Evening"	RTvi/7
2.19	No.2 "Winter Night" (Sleigh Ride) (see lost orig vers for pf, RTix/3)	
2.20	No.3 "Spring Morning"	
2.21	Orch fragment (c ?1890, incl section: À l'amore or À l'aurore, inc)	RTvi/8
2.22	"Petite suite d'orchestre" (c1890; small orch): No.1 "Allegro ma non troppo," in G minor	RTvi/9
2.23	No.2 "Con moto," in G minor	
2.24	No.3 "Allegretto," in E major	
2.25	"Paa Vidderne" (On the Mountains), sym poem (c1890–2, after Ibsen)	RTvi/10
2.26	"Over the Hills and Far Away," fantasy overture (c1893–7)	RTvi/11
2.27	"Appalachia" (American Rhapsody) (c1896, common material w/ RTii/2)	RTvi/12
2.28	"Norwegian Suite" (c1897, from incid music: Folkraadet, RTi/5): No.1 "Vorspiel 1ste Akt. Bewegt," in C major	(RTi/5)
2.29	No.2 "Lustig bewegt," in G major	
2.30	No.3 "Allegro energico," in C major	
2.31	No.4 "Marcia, lento solenne," in C min / major	
2.32	"La ronde se déroule" (The Dance Goes On), sym poem (c1899; see: Life's Dance, RTvi/15)	RTvi/13
2.33	"Paris: A Nocturne" (The Song of a Great City) (c1899)	RTvi/14
2.34	"Life's Dance" (Lebenstanz), sym poem (c1901, r1912; orig: The Dance goes on, RTvi/13)	RTvi/15
2.35	"Brigg Fair" (An English Rhapsody) (c1907)	RTvi/16
2.36	"In a Summer Garden," rhapsody (c1908, r1909)	RTvi/17
2.37	"A Dance Rhapsody" (No.1) (c1908)	RTvi/18
2.38	"2 Pieces" (small orch): No.1 "On Hearing the first Cuckoo in Spring" (c1912)	RTvi/19
2.39	No.2 "Summer Night on the River" (c1911)	
2.40	"North Country Sketches" (c1913–4): No.1 "Autumn" (The wind soughs in the trees)	RTvi/20
2.41	No.2 "Winter Landscape"	
2.42	No.3 "Dance"	
2.43	No.4 "The March of Spring" (Woodlands, Meadows and silent Moors)	
2.44	"Air and Dance" (c1915; strings)	RTvi/21
2.45	"A Dance Rhapsody" (No.2) (c1916)	RTvi/22
2.46	"Eventyr" (Once upon a Time), ballad (c1917, after Asbjørnsen's fairy tales)	RTvi/23
2.47	"A Song before Sunrise" (c1918; small orch)	RTvi/24
2.48	"A Poem of Life and Love" (c1918, inc)	RTvi/25
2.49	"A Song of Summer" (c1929–30, adapted from: A Poem of Life and Love, RTvi/25)	RTvi/26
2.50	"Irmelin. Prelude" (Intermezzo from 'Irmelin') (c1931, rewritten from opera: Irmelin, RTi/2)	RTvi/27
2.51	"Fantastic Dance" (c1931)	RTvi/28

Arrs by others:

2.52	*"2 Aquarelles" (arr Fenby for strings 1936, from 2 songs: 'to be sung of a summer night,' RTiv/5)*	
2.53	*"La Calinda" (Dance from Act II of: Koanga) (arr Fenby for orch, from opera RTi/4)*	
2.54	*"Late Swallows" (arr Fenby for strings p1963, from 3rd movt of: Str Qt No.2, RTviii/8)*	
2.55	*"Sonata for Strings" (arr Fenby for strings, from Str Qt No.2, RTviii/8, includes: Late Swallows)*	
2.56	*"Fenimore and Gerda Intermezzo" (arr Fenby for orch, from Interludes to Scenes 10 & 11, RTi/8)*	

3. CONCERTOS, SOLO INSTR & ORCH

Pf & orch:

3.1	"Sagen" (Legends) (c1890, unfin)	RTvii/2

3.2 Piano Concerto in C minor (3 vers): RTvii/4
. Version 1 (c1897, orig vers in 3 movts)
. Version 2 (revised in 1 movt p1907)
. Version 3 (in 1 movt, further revisions)
3.3 *"Rhapsody" (ca1900–10s, unfin draft)* *RTvii/4a*

Vn & orch:

3.4 "Suite" (c1888): No.1 "Pastorale," in E minor RTvii/1
3.5 No.2 "Intermezzo," in C major
3.6 No.3 "Elegie," in G major
3.7 No.4 "Finale," in G major
3.8 "Légende," in E-flat major (c1892–5; red for vn & pf) RTvii/3
3.9 Violin Concerto (c1916) RTvii/6

Vc & orch:

3.10 Cello Concerto (c1921) RTvii/7
3.11 "Caprice & Elegy," 2 pieces (c1930; vc & chamber orch) RTvii/8

Other:

3.12 Double Concerto (c1915–6; vn, vc & orch) RTvii/5

4. STRING QUARTETS

4.1 String Quartet (c1888, inc: 1st movt lost) RTviii/1
4.2 String Quartet No.1 (c1892–3) RTviii/4
4.3 String Quartet No.2 (c1916; see 3rd movt arr Fenby for strings as: Late Swallows) RTviii/8

5. OTHER CHAMBER MUSIC

Vn & pf:

5.1 "Romance" (c1889) RTviii/2
5.2 Violin Sonata in B major (c1892) RTviii/3
5.3 Violin Sonata No.1 (c1905–14) RTviii/6
5.4 Violin Sonata No.2 (c1923; arr Tertis for va & pf) RTviii/9
5.5 Violin Sonata No.3 (c1930) RTviii/10

Vc & pf:

5.6 "Romance" (c1896) RTviii/5
5.7 Cello Sonata (c1916, in 1 movt) RTviii/7

6. PIANO

6.1 "Zum Carnival Polka" (c1885) RTix/1
6.2 "Pensées mélodieuses" (c1885) RTix/2
6.3 *"Norwegian Sleigh Ride" (c1887, lost; see orch vers: No.2 of: 3 Small Tone Poems, RTvi/7)* *RTix/3*
6.4 "Badinage," in D-flat major (c ?1880s or 1890s) RTix/4
6.5 "2 Pieces" (c1889–90): No.1 "Valse" (early vers of No.3 of: 5 Pieces, RTix/7) RTix/5
6.6 No.2 "Reverie" (unfin)
6.7 "5 Pieces" (c1922–3): No.1 "Mazurka for a Little Girl," in F major RTix/7
6.8 No.2 "Waltz for a Little Girl," in C major
6.9 No.3 "Waltz," in G major (= r vers of No.1 of: 2 Pieces, RTix/5)
6.10 No.4 "Lullaby for a Modern Baby," in D major (arr for vn & pf 1929)
6.11 No.5 "Toccata," in A minor
6.12 "3 Preludes" (c1923): No.1 "Scherzando," in D major RTix/8
6.13 No.2 "Quick," in D major
6.14 No.3 "Con moto," in D major

Hpd:

6.15 "Dance," in A minor (c1919) RTix/6

7. CHORAL WORKS

W/ orch:

7.1 "Zarathustra's Night-song" (1898, Nietzsche; Bar, m ch & orch, later incl in: A Mass of Life, RTii/4) ... RTii/1

7.2   "Appalachia" (Variations on an old slave song) (c1902, trad; Bar, ch & orch) RTii/2
7.3   "Sea Drift" (c1903–4, from Whitman's Out of the cradle endlessly rocking; Bar, ch & orch) RTii/3
7.4   "Eine Messe des Lebens" (A Mass of Life) (c1904–5, Nietzsche; S, A, T, Bar, ch & orch): RTii/4
     words from Nietzsche's Also sprach Zarathustra: I: 1. from 'Von alten und neuen Tafeln' (d ch)
              2. from 'Von höheren Menschen' (recit—B)
              3. from 'Das Eselsfest' (Tutti)
              4. from 'Das trunkne Lied' (Bar, ch)
              5. from 'Das Nachtlied' (Bar, ch)
       II: 1. from 'Das Zeichen, Von alten und neuen Tafeln, Vom Gesindel' (vv, d ch)
              2. from 'Das trunkne Lied' (Bar)
              3. from 'Das Tanzlied' (Bar, fem vv)
              4. from 'Mittags' (Tutti)
              5. from 'Das trunkne Lied' (Bar, ch)
              6. from 'Das trunkne Lied' (Bar, tutti)
7.5   "Songs of Sunset" (c1906–7, Dowson; mS, Bar, ch & orch; also Ger transl J. Rosen): 1. "A song of the
           setting sun!" RTii/5
7.6   2. "Cease smiling, Dear! a little while be sad"
7.7   3. "Pale amber sunlight falls across the reddening October trees"
7.8   4. "Exceeding sorrow consumeth my sad heart!"
7.9   5. "By the sad waters of separation"
7.10   6. "See how the trees and the osiers lithe are green bedecked"
7.11   7. "I was not sorrowful, I could not weep"
7.12   8. "They are not long, the weeping and the laughter"
7.13   "The Song of the High Hills" (c1911, wordless; ch & orch)... RTii/6
7.14   "An Arabesque" (c1911, r1915, Jacobsen transl Heseltine; Bar, ch & orch) RTii/7
7.15   "Requiem" (c1913–6, Delius; S, Bar, d ch & orch) RTii/8
7.16   "Songs of Farewell" (c1930, Whitman; d ch & orch): 1. "How sweet the silent" RTii/9
7.17   2. "I stand as on some mighty eagle's beak"
7.18   3. "Passage to you"
7.19   4. "Joy, shipmate, joy!"
7.20   5. "Now finalè to the shore"

W/ pf:

7.21   "2 Songs for Children" (c1913): 1. "What does little birdie say?" (Tennyson; unison ch) (also see
           Sullivan's song of 1867) RTv/29
7.22   2. "The streamlet's slumber song"

Unacc ch:

7.23   "6 German Partsongs" (c by 1887): 1. "Lorelei von H. Heine," in A minor (c ?1885) RTiv/1
7.24   2. "O Sonnenschein!," in G major (c1886–7, Reinick)
7.25   3. "Durch den Wald," in D-flat major (c1886–7, Schreck)
7.26   4. "Ave Maria," in E-flat major (c1887)
7.27   5. "Sonnenscheinlied," in F major (c1887, Björnsen)
7.28   6. "Frühlingsanbruch," in C major (c1887, Andersen)
7.29   "On Craig Dhu" (An Impression of Nature): "The sky through the leaves of the bracken" (c1907,
           Symons) RTiv/2
7.30   "Wanderer's Song": "I have had enough of women" (c1908, Symons; m ch) RTiv/3
7.31   "Midsummer Song" (c1908, wordless) RTiv/4
7.32   "To be sung of a summer night on the water" (1917, wordless): 1. "Slowly, but not dragging" RTiv/5
7.33   2. "Gaily but not quick"
7.34   "The splendour falls on castle walls" (c1923, from Tennyson's The Princess) (also see Britten
           Op.31/2, Holst Op.20a, Sullivan's opera: Princess Ida & Vaughan Williams' song of 1905) RTiv/6

8. VOICE & ORCHESTRA

8.1   "Paa Vidderne" (On the Heights), declamation / melodrama (c1888, Ibsen; reciter & orch) RTiii/1
8.2   "Sakuntala" (c1889, Drachmann; T & orch) RTiii/2
8.3   "Maud," cycle (c1891, Tennyson; T & orch): 1. "Birds in the high Hall-garden" RTiii/3
8.4   2. "I was walking a mile"
8.5   3. "Go not, happy day" (also see Liszt S335)
8.6   4. "Rivulet crossing my ground"
8.7   5. "Come into the garden, Maud" (also see Massenet's song of 1876–81)
8.8   "7 Danish Songs" (c1897; also w/ pf): 1. "Silken shoes" (Jacobsen)... RTiii/4
8.9   2. "Irmelin Rose" (Jacobsen)
8.10   3. "Summer Nights": "On the sea-shore" (Drachmann)
8.11   4. "In the Seraglio Garden" (Jacobsen)
8.12   5. "Wine Roses" (Jacobsen transl Delius)
8.13   6. "Red Roses": "Through the long, long years" (That for which we longed) (Jacobsen)
8.14   7. "Let Springtime come" (Jacobsen transl Delius)
8.15   "Cynara": "Last night, ah, yesternight, betwixt her lips and mine" (c1907, Dowson; Bar & orch,
          finished w/ Fenby 1929) RTiii/5

8.16   "A Late Lark" (Die Lerche am Abend): "A late lark twitters from the quiet skies" (c1924–9, Henley;
         T & small orch) RTiii/6
8.17   "Idyll": "Once I passed thro' a populous City" (c1932, Whitman; S, Bar & orch) RTii/10

9. SONGS (w/ pf)

9.1   "When other lips shall speak" (c ?1880) RTv/1
9.2   "Over the Mountains High" (c1885, Bjørnson) RTv/2
9.3   "Two Brown Eyes" (c1885, Andersen) RTv/3
9.4   "Der Fichtenbaum" (c1886, Heine) RTv/4
9.5   "5 Songs from the Norwegian" (c1888): 1. "Slumber Song" (Bjørnson) RTv/5
9.6   2. "The Nightingale" (Wellhaven)
9.7   3. "Summer Eve" (Paulsen)
9.8   4. "Longing" (Kjerulf)
9.9   5. "Sunset" (Munck)
9.10   "Hochgebirgsleben" (c1888, Ibsen) RTv/6
9.11   "O schneller mein Ross" (Plus vite, mon cheval) (c1888, Geibel) RTv/7
9.12   "Chanson de Fortunio" (c1889, Musset) RTv/8
9.13   "7 Songs from the Norwegian" (c1889–90) 1. "Craddle Song" (Ibsen; orchd Gibson) RTv/9
9.14   2. "The Homeward Journey" (Vinje; orchd Sondheimer)
9.15   3. "Evening Voices" (Twilight Fancies) (Bjørnson transl Copeland; orchd; also orchd Beecham)
9.16   4. "Sweet Venevil" (Bjørnson; orchd Beecham)
9.17   5. "Minstrel" (Ibsen)
9.18   6. "Secret Love" (Bjørnson)
9.19   7. "The Bird's Story" (Ibsen transl Grist; orchd; also orchd Gibson)
9.20   "Skogen gir susende langsam besked" (Softly the forest) (c1891, Bjørnson) RTv/10
9.21   "4 Songs" (c1890–1, Heine): 1. "Mit deinen blauen Augen" RTv/11
9.22   2. "Ein schöner Stern geht auf in meiner Nacht"
9.23   3. "Hör' ich das Liedchen klingen"
9.24   4. "Aus deinen Augen fliessen meine Lieder"
9.25   "3 English Songs" (c1891, Shelley): 1. "Indian Love Song" (Indisches Liebeslied): "I arise from
                         dreams of thee" (Ger transl Rosen) (also see Castelnuovo-Tedesco: Indian Serenade
                         & Respighi P090/5) RTv/12
9.26   2. "Love's Philosophy" (Liebesphilosophie): "The fountains mingle with the river" (Ger transl
                         Rosen) (also see Castelnuovo-Tedesco's choral work & Gounod's song of 1871)
9.27   3. "To the Queen of my Heart" (An meines Herzens Königin) (Ger transl Tischer)
9.28   "Dreamy Nights" (Lyse Naetter): "On Shore how still" (c1891, Drachmann) RTv/13
9.29   "Jeg havde en nyskaaren Seljefløjte" (I once had a newly cut willow pipe) (c ?1891, Krag) RTv/14
9.30   "Nuages" (c1893, Richepin) RTv/15
9.31   "Deux mélodies" (c1895, Verlaine transl Dowson; orchd Heseltine): 1. "Il pleure dans mon coeur" ... RTv/16
9.32   2. "Le ciel est, par-dessus le toit"
9.33   "The Page sat in the lofty Tower" (c ?1895, Jacobsen) RTv/17
9.34   "Traum Rosen" (c1898, Marie Heinitz) RTv/18
9.35   "Nietzschelieder" (c1898, Nietzsche): 1. "Nach neuen Meeren" RTv/19
9.36   2. "Der Wanderer"
9.37   3. "Der Einsame"
9.38   4. "Der Wanderer und sein Schatten"
9.39   "In bliss we walked with laughter" (c1898, Drachmann) RTv/20
9.40   "2 Danish Songs" (c1900): 1. "The Violet" (Holstein; orchd1908) RTv/21
9.41   2. "Autumn" (Jacobsen)
9.42   "Black Roses" (c1901, Josefson; orchd Del Mar) RTv/22
9.43   "I hear in the night" (c1901, Drachmann) RTv/23
9.44   "Summer Landscape" (c1902, Drachmann; orchd1903) RTv/24
9.45   "The nightingale has a lyre of gold" (c1910, Henley; orchd Del Mar) (also see Beach Op.11/3, B4) .. RTv/25
9.46   "La lune blanche" (c1910, Verlaine transl Bottomley; orchd Heseltine) RTv/26
9.47   "Chanson d'automne" (c1911, Verlaine) RTv/27
9.48   "I-Brasîl": "There's sorrow on the wind, my grief" (c1913, Macleod; orchd Heseltine) RTv/28
9.49   "4 Old English Lyrics": 1. "It was a lover and his lass" (c1916, from Shakespeare's As You Like It;
                         orchd Warlock) (also see Castelnuovo-Tedesco Op.24/II/3, Holst H59, Sullivan's
                         partsong of 1857 & Vaughan Williams' partsong of 1922) RTv/30
9.50   2. "So white, so soft, so sweet is she" (c1915, Jonson; arr Beecham for strings)
9.51   3. "Spring, the sweet Spring" (c1915, Nashe; orchd Lambert)
9.52   4. "To Daffodils" (c1915, Herrick; orchd Beecham; orchd Del Mar; orchd Fenby)
9.53   "Avant que tu ne t'en ailles" (c1919, Verlaine) RTv/31

*   *   *   *   *

         RT =   R. Threlfall: "A Catalogue of the Compositions of Frederick Delius." Delius Trust. London, 1977.
                 Updated in: R. Threlfall: "Frederick Delius. A Supplementary Catalogue." Delius Trust. London, 1986.

1. STAGE WORKS

Operas:

1.1	"Die Bergknappen" (c1891, Körner, not perf)	
1.2	"Tante Simona," 1 act comic opera (c1910, Heindl)	Op.20
1.3	"A vajda tornya" (The Tower of the Voivod), 3 act romantic opera (c1915–22, Lanyi)	Op.30
1.4	"Der Tenor," 3 act comic opera (c1927–9, Góth after Sternheim)	Op.34
1.5	"Murányi Vénusz" (Venus of Murano) (c after 1931, Csanády, inc)	

Ballets:

1.6	"Der Schleier der Pierrette" (The Veil of Pierrette), 3 part pantomime (c1908–9)	Op.18
1.7	"Múzsa csókja" (p1928, based on Schubert: Moments musicaux)	
1.8	"Szent Fáklya" (p1934, Galafrés, based on: Ruralia Hungarica, Op.32b & Szimfonikus percek, Op.36)	

2. SYMPHONIES

2.1	Symphony in F major (c ?1895–6, student work)	
2.2	Symphony No.1 in D minor (c1900–1)	Op.9
2.3	Symphony No.2 in E major (c1943–4, rewritten 1954–7)	Op.40

3. OTHER ORCHESTRAL WORKS

3.1	"Zrínyi Overture" (c ?1895–6, student work)	
3.2	"Suite," in F-sharp minor (c1908–9)	Op.19
3.3	"Ünnepi nyitány" (Festival overture) (c1923; d orch)	Op.31
3.4	"Ruralia Hungarica," 5 pieces (c1924)	Op.32b
3.5	"Szimfonikus percek" (Symphonic Minutes) (c1931)	Op.36
3.6	"Suite en valse" (c1942–3): No.1 "Valse symphonique"	Op.39
3.7	No.2 "Valse sentimentale"	
3.8	No.3 "Valse boiteuse"	
3.9	No.4 "Valse de fête"	
3.10	"American Rhapsody" (c1953)	Op.47

4. CONCERTOS, SOLO INSTR & ORCH

Pf & orch:

4.1	Piano Concerto No.1 in E minor (c1897–8)	Op.5
4.2	"Variations on a Nursery Song" (c1914, on song: Ah, vous dirai-je maman)	Op.25
4.3	Piano Concerto No.2 in B minor (c1946)	Op.42

Vn & orch:

4.4	Violin Concerto No.1 in D minor (c1914–5)	Op.27
4.5	Violin Concerto No.2 in C minor (c1948–9)	Op.43

Other:

4.6	"Koncertstück," in D major (c1903–4; vc & orch)	Op.12
4.7	"Concertino" (c1953; harp & chamber orch)	Op.45

5. STRING QUARTETS (Not listed juvenile pieces w/ out opus number)

5.1	String Quartet No.1 in A major (c1899)	Op.7
5.2	String Quartet No.2 in D-flat major (c1906)	Op.15
5.3	String Quartet No.3 in A minor (c1926)	Op.33

6. OTHER CHAMBER MUSIC (Not listed juvenile pieces w/ out opus number)

5 or more insts:

6.1	Piano Quintet No.1 in C minor (c1895)	Op.1
6.2	Piano Quintet No.2 in E-flat minor (c1914)	Op.26
6.3	Sextet in C major (c1935; cl, hn, str trio & pf)	Op.37

3 insts:

6.4	"Serenade," in C major (c1902; str trio)	Op.10

Vn & pf:

6.5	Violin Sonata in C-sharp minor (c1912)	Op.21
6.6	"Ruralia Hungarica," 3 pieces (c1924)	Op.32c

Vc & pf:

6.7	"Ruralia Hungarica," 1 piece (c1924; vc/vn & pf)	Op.32d
6.8	Cello Sonata in B-flat minor (c1899)	Op.8

Other 1–2 insts:

6.9	"Aria" (c1958; fl & pf)	(Op.48/1)
6.10	"Passacaglia" (c1959; fl, his last composition)	(Op.48/2)

7. PIANO (Not listed juvenile pieces w/ out opus number)

7.1	"4 Pieces" (c1896–7): No.1 "Scherzo," in C-sharp minor	Op.2
7.2	No.2 "Intermezzo," in A minor	
7.3	No.3 "Intermezzo," in F minor	
7.4	No.4 "Capriccio," in B-flat minor	
7.5	"Variations & Fugue on a Theme of E(mma) G(ruber)" (c1897)	Op.4
7.6	"Gavotte & Musette," in B-flat major (c1898)	
7.7	"Passacaglia," in E-flat minor (c1899)	Op.6
7.8	"4 Rhapsodies" (c1902–3): No.1 in G minor	Op.11
7.9	No.2 in F-sharp minor	
7.10	No.3 in C major	
7.11	No.4 in E-flat minor	
7.12	"Winterreigen," 10 bagatelles (c1905): No.1 "Dedication"	Op.13
7.13	No.2 "Marsch der lustigen Brüder"	
7.14	No.3 "To Ada"	
7.15	No.4 "Friend Victor's Mazurka"	
7.16	No.5 "Music of the Spheres"	
7.17	No.6 "Valse aimable"	
7.18	No.7 "At Midnight"	
7.19	No.8 "A Mad Party"	
7.20	No.9 "Dawn"	
7.21	No.10 "Postlude"	
7.22	"Humoresken" (in the Form of a Suite) (c1907): No.1 "March"	Op.17
7.23	No.2 "Toccata"	
7.24	No.3 "Pavane with Variations" (on a 16th cent theme: Gaudeamus Igitur)	
7.25	No.4 "Pastorale," canon	
7.26	No.5 "Introduction & Fugue"	
7.27	"3 Pieces" (c1912): No.1 "Aria"	Op.23
7.28	No.2 "Valse impromptu"	
7.29	No.3 "Capriccio"	
7.30	"Fugue," in D minor (c1913; left hand/2 hands)	
7.31	"Suite im alten Stil" (c1913): No.1 "Prelude"	Op.24
7.32	No.2 "Allemande"	
7.33	No.3 "Courante"	
7.34	No.4 "Sarabande"	
7.35	No.5 "Menuet"	
7.36	No.6 "Gigue"	
7.37	"6 Concert Etudes" (c1916): No.1 in A minor	Op.28
7.38	No.2 in D-flat major	
7.39	No.3 in E-flat minor	
7.40	No.4 in B-flat minor	
7.41	No.5 in E major	
7.42	No.6 in F minor (Capriccio)	
7.43	"Variations on a Hungarian Folksong" (c1917)	Op.29
7.44	"Pastorale: Hungarian Christmas Song" (c1921)	
7.45	"Ruralia Hungarica," 7 pieces (c1923, on Hungarian folk music): No.1 "Allegretto, molto tenero"	Op.32a
7.46	No.2 "Presto, ma non tanto"	
7.47	No.3 "Andante poco moto, rubato"	
7.48	No.4 "Vivace"	
7.49	No.5 "Allegretto grazioso"	
7.50	No.6 "Adagio non troppo" (Gypsy Andante)	
7.51	No.7 "Molto vivace"	
7.52	"Essential Finger Exercises" (c1933)	
7.53	"6 Pieces" (c1945): No.1 "Impromptu"	Op.41
7.54	No.2 "Scherzino"	
7.55	No.3 "Canzonetta"	
7.56	No.4 "Cascades"	
7.57	No.5 "Ländler"	

7.58	No.6 "Cloches"
7.59	"12 Short Studies for the Advanced Pianist" (c1951) ....
7.60	"3 Singular Pieces" (c1951): No.1 "Burletta" Op.44
7.61	No.2 "Nocturne" (Cats on the Roof)
7.62	No.3 "Perpetuum mobile"
7.63	"Daily Finger Exercises," 3 volumes (c by 1960) ....
7.64	Cadenzas to Beethoven's Piano Concertos Nos.1–4 (c1897–1915).............
7.65	Cadenzas to Mozart's Piano Concertos Nos.1–27 (c by 1941) ....

Pf duet:

7.66	"Waltz," in F-sharp minor (c1897)...	Op.3

2 Pf:

7.67	"Suite en valse" (c1945; orig for orch, Op.39): No.1 "Valse symphonique"	Op.39a
7.68	No.2 "Valse sentimentale"	
7.69	No.3 "Valse boiteuse"	
7.70	No.4 "Valse de fête"	

8. CHORAL WORKS

8.1	"Üdvözlö dal" (c1891; ch, pf, strings & harm)	
8.2	"Ave Maria" (c1891; vv, vn & strings)	
8.3	Mass in C major (c1892; vv, ch, strings & org)...........................	
8.4	"Pater noster" (c1892; ch)	
8.5	"O salutaris hostia et Ave verum," hymn (c1893; 4 m vv)	
8.6	"Veni Sancte Spiritus" (c1893; 4 m vv)	
8.7	"Psalm 6" (c1893; d ch)	
8.8	"Király hymnus" (c1893; ch)	
8.9	"Kyrie" (c1893)	
8.10	"Magyar Hiszekegy" (Hungarian Credo) (c1920; T, ch & orch)	
8.11	"Magyar Jövö" (c1921; ch & pf)	
8.12	"Himnusz Szent Imre" (Hymn to St Imre) (c1929)	
8.13	"Köszönto" (c1930; ch)	
8.14	"Szegedi Mise" (Missa in dedicatione ecclesiae) (Szeged Mass) (c1930, 4vv, ch of 8vv, orch & org) Op.35	
8.15	"Diádok dala" (c1931; ch)	
8.16	"Magyar induló" (Hungarian March) (c1932; ch/1v & pf/orch)	
8.17	"Cantus vitae," cantata (c1939–41, Madách; vv, ch, orch & org)	Op.38
8.18	"Stabat mater" (c1952–3; 3vv, boys' ch & orch)	Op.46

9. VOICE & ORCHESTRA

9.1	"3 Songs" (c1912, Gomoll; Bar & orch)	Op.22

10. SONGS (w/ pf)

10.1	"Zu deinen Füssen" (c1891)	
10.2	"Wiegenlied" (c1895)	
10.3	"6 Gedichte von Viktor Heindl" (c1905–6, Heindl; Bar & pf)	Op.14
10.4	"Im Lebenslenz," cycle (c1906–7, Gomoll): 1. "Fernes Klingen" (Forebodings)...................	Op.16
10.5	2. "Du silbernes Mondenlicht" (Haste, Silvery Moonbeams)	
10.6	3. "Grüsse zur Nacht" (Nocturne)	
10.7	4. "Im Traum" (Dream Vision)	
10.8	5. "Um deine Liebe" (To Win Thy Love)	
10.9	6. "Serenade"	
10.10	"Magyar népdalok" (Hungarian Folksongs) (c1922; 1v & pf)	
10.11	"Magyar karácsonyi énekek" (Hungarian Carols) (c1931)	

11. ARRANGEMENTS OF WORKS OF OTHERS (for pf)

11.1	Brahms: Waltzes (arr1921–2) ....
11.2	Brahms: "Rondo alla Zingarese" (arr1933)...........................
11.3	Cramer: Etudes (12 etudes transcr for the left hand) ....
11.4	Delibes: "Naila," waltz (arr1897) ....
11.5	Delibes: "Coppélia Waltz" (arr1925, from ballet) ....
11.6	Schubert: "Valses nobles," Op.77, D969 (arr1931, concert vers) ....
11.7	Strauss, J. Jr.: "Du und Du," waltz Op.367 (arr1930)...........................
11.8	Strauss, J. Jr.: "Treasure" (My Darling), waltz Op.418 (arr1930) ....

* * * * *

1. STAGE WORKS (operas)

1.1 "Il Pigmalione," 1 act scena drammatica (c1816) ....
1.2 "Olimpiade," opera seria (c1817, Metastasio, inc) ....
1.3 "L'ira d'Achille," 1 act (c1817) ....
1.4 "Enrico di Borgogna," 2 act semiseria (p1818, Merelli) ....
1.5 "Una follia" (?Il Ritratto parlante), 1 act farsa (p1818, Merelli) ....
1.6 "I piccioli virtuosi ambulanti," 1 act buffa, pasticcio (p1819, Merelli, inc) ....
1.7 "Il falegname di Livonia" (Pietro il Grande), 2 act buffa (p1819, Bevilacqua-Aldovrandini) ....
1.8 "Le nozze in villa" (I provinciali), 2 act buffa (p1820–1, Merelli) ....
1.9 "Zoraide di Granata," 2 act seria (p1822, Merelli) ....
1.10 "La zingara," 2 act semiseria (p1822, Tottola) ....
1.11 "La lettera anonima," 1 act farsa (p1822, Genoino) ....
1.12 "Chiara e Serafina" (I pirati), 2 act semiseria (p1822, Romani after Pixérécourt: La Cisterne) ....
1.13 "Alfredo il Grande," 2 act seria (p1823, Tottola) ....
1.14 "Il fortunato inganno," 2 act buffa (p1823, Tottola) ....
1.15 "L'ajo nell' imbarazzo" (Don Gregorio), 2 act buffa (p1824, Ferretti based on Giraud) ....
1.16 "Emilia di Liverpool" (L'eremitaggio di Liverpool), 2 act semiseria (p1824, Checcherini) ....
1.17 "Alahor in Granata," 2 act seria (p1826, M. A.) ....
1.18   *"Il castello degli invalidi," 1 act farsa (c ?1825–6, ?spur, lost)*
1.19 "Elvida," 1 act seria (p1826, Schmidt) ....
1.20 "Gabriella di Vergy," 3 act seria (c1826, Tottola; 2nd vers p1869) ....
1.21   *"La bella prigioniera," 1 act farsa (c1826, frags)*
1.22 "Olivo e Pasquale," 2 act buffa (p1827, Ferretti after Sografi) ....
1.23 "Otto mesi in due ore" (Gli esiliati in Siberia), 3 act romantica (p1827, Gilardoni) ....
1.24 "Il borgomastro di Saardam," 2 act buffa (p1827, Gilardoni) ....
1.25 "Le convenienze ed inconvenienze teatrali," 1 act farsa (p1827, Donizetti) ....
1.26 "L'esule di Roma" (Il proscritto / Settimio il Proscritto), 2 act seria (p1828, Gilardoni) ....
1.27 "Alina, regina di Golconda," 2 act semiseria (p1828, Romani after Boufflers) ....
1.28 "Gianni di Calais," 3 act semiseria (p1828, Gilardoni) ....
1.29 "Il giovedì grasso" (Il nuovo Pourceaugnac), 1 act farsa (p1828, Gilardoni) ....
1.30 "Il paria," 2 act seria (p1829, Gilardoni) ....
1.31 "Elisabetta al castello di Kenilworth" (Il castello di Kenilworth), 3 act seria (p1829, Tottola after Hugo) ....
1.32 "I pazzi per progetto," 1 act farsa (p1830, Gilardoni) ....
1.33 "Il diluvio universale," 3 act azione tragico-sacra (p1830, Gilardoni) ....
1.34 "Imelda de' Lambertazzi," 2 act seria (p1830, Tottola) ....
1.35 "Anna Bolena," 2 act seria (p1830, Romani) ....
1.36 "Francesca di Foix," 1 act semiseria (p1831, Gilardoni) ....
1.37 "La romanziera e l'uomo nero," 1 act buffa (p1831, Gilardoni) ....
1.38 "Fausta," 2 act seria (p1832, Gilardoni) ....
1.39 "Ugo, Conte di Parigi," 2 act opera seria (p1832, Romani) ....
1.40 "L'elisir d'amore" (The Elixir of Love), 2 act comica (p1832, Romani after Scribe) ....
1.41 "Sancia di Castiglia," 2 act seria (p1832, Salatino) ....
1.42 "Il furioso all' isola di San Domingo," 3 act semiseria (p1833, Ferretti) ....
1.43 "Parisina" (Parisina d'Este), 3 act seria (p1833, Romani after Byron) ....
1.44 "Torquato Tasso" (Sordello il trovatore), 3 act seria/semiseria (p1833, Ferretti) ....
1.45 "Lucrezia Borgia," 2 act seria (p1833, Romani after Hugo) ....
1.46 "Rosmonda d'Inghilterra," 2 act seria (p1834, Romani) ....
1.47 "Maria Stuarda," 3 act seria (c1834, Bardari after Schiller) ....
1.48 "Buondelmonte" (p1834, Salatino, new libretto to music of: Maria Stuarda) ....
1.49 "Gemma di Vergy," 2 act seria (p1834, Bidera after Dumas) ....
1.50   *"Adelaide," opera comica (c1834, never compl; partly used in: L'ange de Nisida)*
1.51 "Dalinda" (c1834, vers of: Lucrezia Borgia, characters: Dalinda, Ildamaro & Ugo) ....
1.52 "Marin Faliero," 3 act seria (p1835, Bidera after Byron) ....
1.53 "Lucia di Lammermoor," 3 act seria (p1835, Cammarano after Scott) ....
1.54 "Belisario," 3 act seria (p1836, Cammarano; p1837 w/ ballet: Il Corsaro, after Byron's The Corsair) ....
1.55 "Il campanello di notte," 1 act farsa (p1836, Donizetti after Brunswick, Troin & Lherie) ....
1.56 "Betly" (La Capanna Svizzera), 1 act giocosa (p1836, Donizetti after Scribe) ....
1.57 "L'assedio di Calais," 3 act seria (p1836, Cammarano) ....
1.58 "Pia de' Tolomei," 2 act seria (p1837, Cammarano) ....
1.59 "Roberto Devereux ossia Il Conte di Essex," 3 act seria (p1837, Cammarano after Ancelot) ....
1.60 "Maria di Rudenz," 3 act seria (p1838, Cammarano) ....
1.61 "Gianni di Parigi," 2 act comica (p1839, Romani after Saint-Just) ....
1.62 "Poliuto," 3 act seria (c1838, Cammarano after Corneille; r1840 as: Les martyrs) ....
1.63   *"L'ange de Nisida" (Silvia), 3 acts (c1839, Royer, inc; transformed into: La favorita)*
1.64 "Le duc d'Albe," 5 act grand (c1839, Scribe & Duveyrier; compl Salvi 1882, Zanardini) ....
1.65 "La fille du Régiment" (The Daughter of the Regiment), 2 act opéra comique (p1840, St Georges & Bayard)
1.66 "Les martyrs," 4 act grand opéra (p1840, Scribe, 2nd vers of: Poliuto) ....
1.67 "La favorita" (The Favorite), 4 act grand opéra (p1840, Royer & Vaëz, r vers of: L'ange de Nisida) ......
1.68 "Adelia" (La figlia dell'arciere), 2 act seria (p1841, Romani & Marini) ....
1.69 "Rita, ou Le mari battu" (Deux hommes et une femme), 1 act comique (c1841, p1860, Vaëz) ....
1.70 "Maria Padilla," 3 act seria (p1841, Rossi after Ancelot's play) ....
1.71 "Linda di Chamounix," 3 act semiseria (p1842, Rossi after D'Ennery & Lemoine) ....
1.72 "Don Pasquale," 3 act buffa (p1843, Ruffini & Donizetti after Anelli) ....
1.73 "Maria di Rohan" (Il Conte di Chalais), 3 act seria (p1843, Cammarano) ....

1.74   "Dom Sébastien, roi de Portugal," 5 act grand opéra (p1843, Scribe) ....
1.75   "Caterina Cornaro," 2 act seria (p1844, Sacchero) ....

Projects:

1.76   "Circe" (mentioned Saltus) ....
1.77   "La fidanzata," farsa (project, extant aria: Si, colpevol' son'io) ....
1.78   "Francesca da Rimini" (mentioned in letter of Donizetti to Prince of Palermo) ....
1.79   "Gli Illinesi" (1835, Romani, project) ....
1.80   "Gli innamorati" (project) ....
1.81   "Jeanne la folle" (1844, Scribe, project; later c by Clapisson) ....
1.82   "Lara" (1837, Pulle, project) ....
1.83   "Mlle de la Vallière" (project) ....
1.84   "Ne m' oubliez pas," 3 act opera-comique (c1842, St Georges, project, begun)........................
1.85   "Onore vince amore" (1845, Ruffini, project) ....
1.86   "Il pascià di Scutari," 3 act melodramma (p1832, ?spur) ....
1.87   "Ruy-Blas" (1842–3, Cammarano, project) ....
1.88   "Sganarelle" (1845, based on Molière: Sganarelle, project) ....
1.89   "L'ultima parte del comico," pasticcio (p1843, ?some numbers by Donizetti) ....

Numbers & sections from unidentified operas:

1.90   Chorus, scena & trio (2S, T, characters: Lesbia, Alpino & Pastore)..
1.91   "Scrivi, obbedisci, insano," duet (T, B, characters: James & Woender) ....
1.92   "Mi lasci ... come?," recit & duet for opera buffa (S, B w/ pf, characters: Deidamia & Don Achille) ....
1.93   "Che pensi, Enrico, riedi al campo," scena & cavatina (T & ch, character: Enrico) ....
1.94   "Gia dell'avita gloria," scena & cavatina (T & ch, character: Enrico) ....

1a. SELECTIONS FROM OPERAS (Nos. of sections in The Gramophone)

1a.35   "Anna Bolena," opera: ....
        excerpts: 1. "Overture"
        I: 2. "Nè venne il re"
                3. "Ella di me, sollecita"
                4a. "Si taciturna e mesta"
                4b. "Deh! non voler costringere"
                4c. "Come, innocente giovane"
                4d. "Non v'ha sguardo"
                5a. "Oh! qual parlar fu il suo!"
                5b. "Ecco il re"
                5c. "Tremate voi?"
                6a. "Chi veggo?"
                6b. "Da quel dì che, lei perduta"
                6c. "Ah! così nei ridenti"
                7a. "Desta sì tosto"
                7b. "Voi Regina"
                7c. "Io senti sulla mia mano"
                8a. "È sgombra il loco"
                8b. "Ah! parea che per incanto"
                9a. "Odo rumor"
                9b. "Basta, tropp'oltre vai"
                9c. "S'ei t'abborre"
                9d. "Ah! per pietà del mio spavento"
                10a. "Alcun potrai"
                10b. "In separato carcere"
        II: 11. "Dove mai ne andarono"
                12a. "Dio, che mi vedi in core"
                12b. "Sul suo capo aggravi un Dio"
                13a. "Ebben? dinanzi ai Giudici"
                13b. "Arresta Enrico"
                14a. "Sposa a Percy"
                14b. "Vieni, Seymor, tu sei Regina"
                15a. "Tu pur dannato a morte"
                15b. "Vivi tu, te ne scongiuro"
                16. "Chi può vederla"
                17a. "Piangete voi?"
                17b. "Al dolce guidami"
                17c. "Qual mesto suon?"
                17d. "Cielo, a' miei lunghi spasimi"
                17e. "Coppia iniqua, l'estrema vendetta"

1a.40   "L'elisir d'amore," opera: ....
        excepts: 1a. "Prelude"
        I: 1b. "Bel conforto"

35. "Madre, se ognor lontano"
36. "Era desso il figlio mio"

1a.53   "Lucia di Lammermoor," opera: ....
- I: 1a. "Percorrete le spiagge vicine"
- 1b. "Tu sei turbato"
- 1c. "Cruda, funesta smania"
- 1d. "La pietade in suo favore"
- 2a. "Ancor non giunse?" (2 vers)
- 2b. "Regnava nel silenzio"
- 2c. "Quando rapito in estasi"
- 3a. "Egli s'avanza"
- 3b. "Lucia perdona"
- 3c. "Sulla tomba"
- 3d. "Ah! Verrano a te"
- II: 4. "Lucia fra poco a te verrà"
- 5a. "Appressati, Lucia"
- 5b. "Il pallor funesto"
- 5c. "Soffriva nel pianto"
- 5d. "Se tradirmi"
- 6. "Ebben?... Di tua speranza"
- 7a. "Per te d'immenso giubilo"
- 7b. "Per poco fra le tenebre"
- 7c. "Dov'è Lucia?"
- 8. "Chi mi frena" (Sextet)
- 9. "T'allontana, sciagurato"
- III: 10. "Orrida è questa notte" (Wolf's Crag Scene)
- 11. "D'immenso giubilo"
- 12. "Dalle stanze"
- 13a. "Il dolce suono"
- 13b. "Ardon gl'incensi"
- 13c. "Alfin son tua"
- 13d. "Spargi d'amaro pianto" (Mad Scene)
- 14. "Si tragga altrove"
- 15a. "Tombe degl'avi miei"
- 15b. "Fra poco a me ricovero"
- 15c. "Giusto ciel, rispondete"
- 15d. "Tu che a Dio"
- 16b. "Perchè non ho del vento"

1a.59   "Roberto Devereux ossia Il Conte di Essex," opera: ....
- excerpts: 1. "Overture"
- I: 2. "All' afflitto è dolce il pianto"
- 3a. "Duchessa, alle fervide preci"
- 3b. "L'amor suo mi fe beata"
- 4a. "Ieri, taceva il giorno"
- 4b. "Forse in quel co sensible"
- 4c. "Qui ribelle"
- 5a. "Tutto è silenzio"
- 5b. "Dacchè tornasti, ahi misera!"
- 5c. "E quando fuggirai?"
- II: 8. "Un perfido, un vile, un mentitore tu sei"
- 9a. "Non venni mai sì vento"
- 9b. "Su lui non piombi il fulmine"
- 11. "Sì scellerata! Non sol che un nume vindice"
- III: 15a. "Ed ancor la tremenda porta"
- 15b. "Come un spirito angelico"
- 15c. "Odo un moment"
- 18b. "Vivi ingrato"
- 18c. "Qual sangue versato al cielo"

1a.65   "La fille du Régiment," opera: ....
- 1. "Overture"
- I: 2. "L'ennemi s'avance" (Armiamci in silenzio)
- 3. "Pour une femme de mon nom" (not in Italian vers)
- 4a. "Sacré nom" (Corpo di mille diavoli)
- 4b. "Au bruit de la guerre" (Apparvi alla luce sula campo guerrier)
- 5. "Quel bel jour" (Oh! che bel giorno)
- 6. "Allons, allons, march', march' " (Avanti, avanti)
- 7. "Chacun le sait" (Ciascun lo dice)
- 8a. "Dès que l'appel sonne" (É l'ora dell'appello)
- 8b. "Attention! en marche" (not in Italian vers)
- 9a. "Ils l'ont emmené brutalement" (L'hanno condotto)
- 9b. "Depuis l'instant" (Da quell'instante)
- 10. "Ah! mille z'Yeux!" (Lo dico con il cuore)

11. "Rataplan" (Rataplan)
12. "Ah! mes amis" (Miei buoni amiche)
13. "Pour mon âme" (Qual destino)
14a. "Je suis soldat" (Suo padre me l'ha data)
14b. "Il faut partir" (Convien partir)
15. "Ah! si vous nous quitter" (Ah se voi mi lascia)
II: 16. "Le jour naissant dans le bocage" (Sorge va il di bosco in seno)
17a. "C'en est donc fait" (Deciso è dunque!)
17b. "Par le rang et par l'opulance" (Le ricchezze ed il rango)
17c. "Pour ce contrat fatal" (Per questo imen fatal)
17d. "Qu'est-ce que c'est que t'entends" (Oh trasporto)
17e. "Salut à la France" (Salvezza alla Francia)
18. "Tonio! Marie!" (Tonio! Maria!)
19. "Tous les trois réunis" (Stretti insiem tutte tre)
20. "Entr'acte. Tyrolienne"
21. "Pour me rapprocher de Marie" (not in Italian vers)
22a. "Ah! c'est elle" (Eccola. Madre mia)
22b. "Au secours de notre fille" (Per giovar a nostra figlia)
22c. "Quand le destin" (Quando il destino)

1a.67   "La favorita," opera: ....
    excerpts: I: 1. "Bell'alba, foriera"
      2. "Quella preghiera non odi tu?"
      3. "Una vergine, un'angel di Dio"
      4. "Non sai tu"
      5. "Bei raggi lucenti"
      6a. "Messaggera gentile"
      6b. "Ah, mio bene!"
      7a. "Ah! Signora!"
      7b. "Sì, che un solo accento"
    II: 8a. "Ma de' malvagi invan"
      8b. "Vieni, amor / Leonora! A' piedi tuoi"
      8c. "De' nemici tuoi"
      9a. "Quando le soglie paterne"
      9b. "In questo suol a lusingar"
      9c. "Ah, l'alto ardor che nutro"
      10a. "Ah, Sire!"
      10b. "Qual tumulto!"
      11. "Il nome del Pastor"
    III: 12. "A lei son presso alfine!"
      13. "A tanto amor, Leonora"
      14a. "Fia dunque vero?"
      14b. "O mio Fernando"
      15. "Di già nella capella"
    IV: 16a. "Fratelli! andiam"
      16b. "Splendon più belle"
      17. "Figlio diletto, ascolta!"
      18a. "Favorita del re!"
      18b. "Spirto gentil"
      19a. "Fernando! Dove mai lo troverò?"
      19b. "Pietoso al par del Nume"
      20a. "Addio! Fuggir mi lascia!"
      20b. "Vieni, ah vien!"

1a.71   "Linda di Chamounix," opera: ....
    excerpts: I: 1. "Overture"
      2. "Ambo nati in questa valle"
      3a. "Ah! tardai troppo"
      3b. "O luce di quest'anima"
      4a. "Cari luoghi ov'io passai"
      4b. "Per sua madre andò una figlia"
      5a. "Linda! Linda!"
      5b. "Da quel dì che t'incontrai"
    II: 6a. "Già scorsero tre mesi"
      6b. "Al bel destin"
      7. "Se tanto in ira agli uomini"
      8. "Un buon servo del Visconte"
      9a. "Linda!... A che pensate?"
      9b. "A consolarmi affrettati"

1a.72   "Don Pasquale, roi de Portugal," opera: ....
    I: 1. "Overture"
      2. "Son nov'ore"
      3a. "E' permesso?"
      3b. "Bella siccome un angelo"

4. "Ah!... Un foco insolito"
5. "Prender moglie?"
6. "Sogno soave e casto"
7a. "Quel guardo il cavaliere"
7b. "So anch'io la virtù magica"
8a. "Buone nuove, Norina"
8b. "Pronto io son"
8c. "Vado, corro"
II: 9a. "Povero Ernesto!"
9b. "Chercherò lontana terra"
9c. "E se fia"
10a. "Quando avrete"
10b. "Via, da bravo"
11. "Fra da un parte etcetera"
12. "Pria di partir, signore"
13. "Siete marito e moglie"
III: 14. "I diamanti, presto"
15a. "Vediamo: alla modista"
15b. "Signorina, in tanta fretta"
15c. "E' finita, Don Pasquale"
16. "Che interminabile" (Servants' Chorus)
17a. "Siamo intesi"
17b. "Don Pasquale ... Cognato"
18a. "Cheti! cheti immantinente"
18b. "Aspetta, aspetta cara sposina"
19. "Com' è gentil"
20. "Tornami a dir" (Notturno)
21a. "Eccoli: attenti bene"
21b. "Eccomi ... A voi"

1a.73   "Maria di Rohan" (Il Conte di Chalais), opera: ....
excerpts: 1. "Overture"
I: 2. "Ed è cor"
3a. "Non seguite la caccia"
3b. "Quando il cor da lei piaggato"
4a. "Conte! Agitata siete!"
4b. "Cupa fatal mestizia"
5a. "Cavalieri! Che veggio!"
5b. "Per non istare in ozio"
6. "Gemea in tetro carcare"
7. "Sparve il nembo minaccioso"
II: 8a. "Nel fragor della festa"
8b. "Alma soave e cara"
8c. "Dorme un sonno affanoso!"
9. "Son leggero è ver d'amore"
10a. "T'aspettai finora"
10b. "Ah! no, tinganni"
11a. "Che mai potrà commuoverti?"
11b. "A morir incominicai"
III: 12a. "Ah, così santo affetto"
12b. "Voler d'iniquiasorte"
13. "Avvi un Dio che in sua clemenza"
14a. "Son ciffre di Riccardo"
14b. "Bella e di sol vestita"
14c. "Voce fatal di morte"
15. "So per prova il tuo bel core"
16. "Vivo non t'è concesso"

2. SINFONIAS

2.1   Sinfonia in C major (c1816) ....
2.2   "Sinfonia concertata," in D major (c1816) ....
2.3   Sinfonia in C major (c1816) ....
2.4   Sinfonia in D major (c1817) ....
2.5   Sinfonia in G minor (c1816; winds) ....
2.6   Sinfonia in D major, "Originale" (c1817) ....
2.7   Sinfonia, "La partenza" (c1817) ....
2.8   Sinfonia in D major (c1817) ....
2.9   Sinfonia in D minor (c1818, on death of A. Capuzzi) ....
2.10 Sinfonia, "L'incendio" (c1819, on text from an ode by Arrivabene) ....
2.11 Sinfonia in D major (c1832–3, inc) ....
2.12 Sinfonia (c1836, on themes by Bellini) ....
2.13 Sinfonia in D major (25 nonautograph parts in Museo Donizettiano in Bergamo)......................
2.14 "Adagio & Minuet" (from a symphony) ....

Other instr & pf:

Misc:

7. PIANO

Dated:

Undated:

Pf duet (dated):

Pf duet (undated / dated Zavadini 1813–21):

8. SACRED WORKS

Dated:

8.1	"Gloria in excelsis," in D major (c1814; S, T, B & small orch w/ org) ....
8.2	"Qui tollis," in F major (c1814; T & orch w/ cl obbl) ....
8.3	"Kyrie" (c1816; 4vv) ....
8.4	"In gloria Dei Patris," in C minor (c1816; 4vv, fugue) ....
8.5	"Tantum ergo" (c1816; 2T, B & orch) ....
8.6	"Cum Sancto Spiritu" (c1817; vv & orch) ....
8.7	"Cum Sancto Spiritu," in C major (c1817, 'for Giuseppe') ....
8.8	"Kyrie," in D major (c1817; 4vv) ....
8.9	"Kyrie," in D major (c1817; ch & orch, for the feast of St. Cecilia) ....
8.10	"Gloria in excelsis," in C major (c1818; 3/4vv & orch) ....
8.11	"Kyrie," in C minor (c1818; 3vv) ....
8.12	"Credo," in C major (c1819; 3vv & orch) ....
8.13	"Magnificat," in D major (c1819; 3vv & orch) ....
8.14	"De torrente," in F major (c1819; S, T & orch) ....
8.15	"Laudamus" & "Gratias," in G major (c1819; T/S & orch w/ ob/cl obbl) ....
8.16	"Qui tollis" & "Miserere" (c1819; 3vv & orch) ....
8.17	"Gloria in excelsis" (c1819; 3vv & orch) ....
8.18	"Salve Regina," in F major (c1819; T & orch) ....
8.19	"Iste confessor," hymn in C major (c1819; 3vv & orch) ....
8.20	"Sicut erat," in C major (c1819; 3vv, 'per campagna') ....
8.21	"Laudate pueri," in D major (c1819; 4vv & orch) ....
8.22	"Beatus vir," in F major (c1819; T & small orch) ....
8.23	"Cum Sancto Spiritu," in D major (c1819; 3/4vv & orch) ....
8.24	"Dixit," in C major (c1819; S, T, B & orch) ....
8.25	"Domine ad adjuvandum," in C major (S, T, B, winds & org) ....
8.26	"Domine ad adjuvandum" (breve), in C major (c1819; S, T, B & orch) .....
8.27	"Dominus a dextris," in D minor (c1819; B & orch) ....
8.28	"Oro supplex," in E major (c1819; B & orch w/ hn obbl, for funeral of G. Terzi) ...
8.29	"Tecum principium" (c1819; S/T & orch w/ ob/cl obbl) ....
8.30	"Miserere" (c1820; 4vv & ch) ....
8.31	"Motet" (c1820; T & small orch w/ cl obbl) ....
8.32	"Miserere" (c1820; 4vv, for 'filarmonici Grassi e Orlandini') ....
8.33	"Tibi solo peccavi," in F major (c1820; S & orch w/ bassett hn obbl) .....
8.34	"Tunc acceptabis," in D major (c1820; 4vv & orch) ....
8.35	"Asperges me," in B-flat major (c1820) ....
8.36	"Credo" (c1820; 3vv & orch) ....
8.37	"Domine Deus" (versetto), in E-flat major (c1820; B & orch w/ cl obbl) ...
8.38	"Gloria," in D major (c1820; 3/4vv & orch) ....
8.39	"Kyrie" (c1820; 4vv & orch) ....
8.40	"Qui tollis," in E-flat major (c1820; T, ch & orch) ....
8.41	"Gloria Patri," in F major (c1820; S & orch w/ vn obbl) ....
8.42	"Laudeamus te," in A major (c1820; 4vv & orch) ....
8.43	"Gratias agimus," in G major (c1820; S & orch w/ fl obbl) ....
8.44	"Dominus a dextris," in D minor (c1820; T & orch w/ vn obbl) ......
8.45	"Credo," in C major (c1820; S, T, B & orch) ....
8.46	"Libera me di sanguinibus," in A minor (c1820; S & orch w/ vn obbl) .....
8.47	"Ne proicias me," in E major (c1820; B & orch w/ hn obbl) ....
8.48	"Dixit Dominus," in C major (c1820) ....
8.49	"Tuba mirum," in E-flat major (c1821; B & orch) ....
8.50	"Kyrie" (c1821; 4vv) ....
8.51	"Kyrie," in F major (c1821; 4vv) ....
8.52	"Miserere," in C minor (c1822; 4vv & orch) ....
8.53	"Credo ," in D major (c1824; 4vv & orch) ....
8.54	"Parafrasi del Christus" (c1829, Gatti; S, A & strings) ....
8.55	"Requiem," in D minor (c1835; vv, ch & orch, for Bellini, unfin) .....
8.56	"Requiem" (c1837, for Zingarelli) ....
8.57	"Requiem" (c1837, for Fazzini) ....
8.58	"Messa di Gloria e Credo," in C minor (c1837; S, A, T, B, ch & large orch) ...
8.59	"Miserere" (c1841; 3m.vv, ch, strings & org (c1841, for Gregory XVI) ....
8.60	"Ave Maria," offertorio (c1842; 5vv, S, ch, 2vn, 2va, vc & bass) .....
8.61	"Miserere," offertorio (c1842; vv, ch & orch) ....
8.62	"Gloria Patri" (c1843; 4vv & orch) ....
8.63	"Ave Maria," offertorio (c1844, on lines by Dante; S, A & strings) .....
8.64	"Quoniam ad te," offertory (c1844; S & small orch) ....
8.65	"Sic transit gloria mundi" (c1844; 8vv & org) ....
8.66	"Domine, Dominus noster," offertory (c1845; B & orch) ....

Undated:

8.67	"Ave Maria," offertory in F major (2vv & pf) ....
8.68	"3 Canzoncine sacre" (2vv & pf): 1. "Questo cor, quest'alma mia" ....

8.69   2. "L'amor di Maria Santissima": "T'amo potessi adergere"
8.70   3. "Preghiera a Maria Vergine": "Fa che d'amarti impari"
8.71   "Christe" (?Christe eleison), in B-flat major (T & orch) ....
8.72   "Confitebor," in C major (S, T, B & org) ....
8.73   "Credidi," in D major (S, T, B & org) ....
8.74   "Credo," in E-flat major (4vv & orch) ....
8.75   "Credo ," in C major (4vv & orch) ....
8.76   *"Credo breve," in C major (vv & orch, vocal lost)* ....
8.77   *"Crucifixus," in F major (vv & orch, vocal lost)* ....
8.78   "Cum Sancto Spiritu," in C minor (4vv & orch) ....
8.79   *"Dies irae," in C minor (vv & orch, sketch)* ....
8.80   "Docebo," in D major (B & small orch w/ org) ....
8.81   "Domine Deus," in D major (B) ....
8.82   "Domine Deus," in D major (B & small orch) ....
8.83   "Et vitam," w/ fugue in C major (4vv) ....
8.84   "Gloria in excelsis," in C major (4vv & orch) ....
8.85   "Gloria in excelsis" (4vv & orch) ....
8.86   "Gloria Patri" & "Sicut erat," in C major (S, T, B & orch) ....
8.87   "In convertendo," in C major (B & orch) ....
8.88   "Inno" (to St Peter), in C major (T & small orch) ....
8.89   "Judica me Deus" (Psalm 42, versified vulgarization by S. Biava; 2 child vv & org ad lib) ....
8.90   "Kyrie," in C minor (3vv, 2ob, 2hn & org) ....
8.91   "Kyrie," in C minor (3vv, 2ob, 2hn & org) ....
8.92   "Kyrie," in C minor (3vv & small orch) ....
8.93   "Kyrie," in D minor (4vv, ch & orch) ....
8.94   *"Kyrie," in D minor (4vv & orch, part lost)* ....
8.95   "Kyrie—Christe—Kyrie," in E maj / G maj / E minor (vv & orch) ....
8.96   "Kyrie—Christe—Kyrie," in F maj / B-flat maj / F major (4vv & orch) ....
8.97   "Laudamus" & "Gratias," in F major (T & orch w/ cl obbl) ....
8.98   "Laudamus" & "Gratias," in G major (c1819; T/S & orch w/ ob/cl obbl) ....
8.99   "Laudamus" & "Gratias" (vv & orch w/ cl obbl) ....
8.100   "Laudamus" & "Gratias," in A major (4vv & orch w/ cl obbl) ....
8.101   "Laudate pueri," in C major (3vv & orch) ....
8.102   "Miserere" (2T, 2B, ch, org, 2va, 2vc & 2 basses) ....
8.103   "Miserere," in D minor (4vv & orch) ....
8.104   "Nisi Dominus," in D major (T & orch) ....
8.105   "Pange lingua," in F major (for a procession) ....
8.106   "Preces me," in E-flat major (T & ch) ....
8.107   "Qui sedes" & "Quoniam," in C major (T & orch w/ vn obbl) ....
8.108   "Qui sedes" & "Quoniam," in A minor (S & orch w/ vn obbl) ....
8.109   "Qui tollis," in E-flat major (3vv & orch) ....
8.110   "Qui tollis," in B-flat major (T & orch) ....
8.111   "Qui tollis," in E major (T & orch) ....
8.112   "Requiem" (w/ pf acc by Cottrau, benediction of the tomb of Alfonso della Valle di Casanova) ....
8.113   "Rex Christi" (in the library of the cathedral at Cracow, Poland) ....
8.114   "Salve regina," in F major (3vv & wind orch) ....
8.115   "Sicut erat," in C major (4vv & orch) ....
8.116   "Tantum ergo," in F major (T & orch) ....
8.117   "Tantum ergo," in D major (S & org) ....
8.118   "Tantum ergo," in E-flat major (T, winds & bass) ....
8.119   "Te Deum," in B-flat major (text = versified Latin by S. Biava; 2 child vv, B & org ad lib)................

         Oratorios:

8.120   *"Oratorio sacro" (p1841, arr by others from Donizetti's music)* ....
8.121   *"Le Sette Chiese" (p1842, Sernicoli, arr by others from Donizetti's music)* ....

9. CANTATAS & OCCASIONAL WORKS

9.1   "Il ritorno di primavera," cantata (p1818, Morando; 3vv & orch) ....
9.2   "Canto accompagnatorio" (p1819; 2S, T, B & orch, for funeral eulogies of Terzi)..
9.3   "Teresa e Gianfaldoni," cantata (p1821; mS, T & orch/pf)..
9.4   "Questo è il suolo, l'aura è questa," cantata (p1822; 2S & pf, for the birth of Maria Carolina Augusta) ....
9.5   "Angelica e Medoro," cantata (p1822, after Ariosto) ....
9.6   "L'assunzione di Maria Vergine," cantata (p1822, Rusi; 2T, B, ch & orch)..
9.7   "Aristea," 1 act azione pastorale (p1823, Schmidt; 3 fem vv, 3 m vv & orch)..
9.8   "A Silvio amante," little cantata (early work, but dated 1823; T & orch)..
9.9   "La fuga di Tisbe" (c1824; S & pf) ....
9.10   "I voti dei sudditi," 1 act azione pastorale (p1825, Schmidt; 4vv & orch) ....
9.11   "La partenza" (p1825; ch & orch, for departure of General Ugo delle Favare) ....
9.12   "Cantata for the birthday of the King of Naples" (Francesco I) (p1825; ch & orch) ....
9.13   "Licenza," cantata (p1825; ch & orch, for a gala at the Teatro Carolino)..
9.14   "Saffo," cantata (c before 1828; 1v, ch & orch; arr for 1v & pf)..
9.15   "Il Canto XXXIII della Divina Commedia" (p1828, Dante; B & pf)..

9.16 "Inno reale," hymn (p1828, Romani; vv & orch, for inauguration of Teatro Carlo Felice) ....
9.17 "Il genio dell'armonia," for Pius VIII (p1829, Visconti; 3vv, ch & ?orch) ....
9.18 "Il fausto ritorno o il ritorno desiderato," azione allegorico-melodrammatica (p1830, Gilardoni; 1v & orch) ...
9.19 "Cantata for wedding of Ferdinand of Austria" (p1831; ch & orch) ....
9.20 "Inno," hymn (p1832, for wedding of King Ferdinando II of Naples) ....
9.21 "Il fato," cantata (p1833, Ferretti, for the name day of Count A. Lozano) ....
9.22 "Cantata for name day of Anna Carnevali" (p1833) ....
9.23 "Cristoforo Colombo," cantata (p1834; Bar & orch) ....
9.24 "La preghiera di un popolo," hymn (p1837, N. C.; S, A, T, B & orch, for Ferdinand II) ....
9.25 "Cantata for royal birth" (p1838, Donizetti; ch & orch) ....
9.26 "Dalla Francia un saluto t'invia," cantata (p1841; vv & orch, for Simone Mayr's 78th birthday) ....
9.27 "Luge qui legis," funeral march (c1842; ch & orch, for P. Marchesi) ....
9.28 *"Aci e Galatea," cantata (mentioned Albinati)* ....
9.29 "Gloria a Dio di nostri padri," cantata (B & orch) ....
9.30 "Inno" (for the name day of P. Pangrati) ....
9.31 *"Niso e Violetta" (1v & orch, sketch)* ....
9.32 *"Per il nome di Francesco I" (mentioned Albinati, lost)* ....
9.33 "Sacro è il dolore," hymn (2vv & orch) ....
9.34 *"Uno sguardo," cantata (Romani, perf in Milan)* ....
9.35 "La pietade col nemico or mi sembra qui delitto" (B & orch) ....

10. VOCAL CHAMBER—PUBLISHED COLLECTIONS

10.1 "Tre canzonette" ....
10.2 "Collezione di canzonette," 5 songs, 3 duets & 1 quintet ....
10.3 "Donizetti per camera," 12 songs, 4 duets ....
10.4 "Nuits d'été à Pausilippe," 6 songs & 6 duets (nocturnes) (c1836) ....
10.5 "Soirées d'automne à l'Infrascata," 4 songs & 1 duet ....
10.6 "Un hiver à Paris," 4 songs, 1 duet ....
10.7 "Rêveries napolitaines" (r ed of: Un hiver à Paris w/ added: L'ultima notte & La dernière nuit) ....
10.8 "Matinées musicales," 6 songs, 2 songs, 6 duets, 2 quartets ....
10.9 "Inspirations viennoises," 5 songs, 2 duets ....
10.10 "Raccolta di (6) canzonette e (2) duettini" ....
10.11 "Dernières glânes musicales," 8 songs, 2 duets ....
10.12 "Fiori di sepolcro: melodie postume," 9 songs ....
10.13 "Tre melodie postume," 3 songs (also in: Fiori di sepolcro) ....
10.14 "Donizetti: Composizioni da camera" (p1961) ....
10.15 "Sei arie inedite" (p1974) ....

11. VOCAL CHAMBER—TRIOS, QUARTETS & QUINTETS

11.1 "Ah che il destino" (Metastasio; 2S, T or 2S) ....
11.2 "Cedè la mia costanza, Irene, al tuo rigor" (Metastasio; S, A, T, B w/ out acc) ....
11.3 "Clori infedel" (S, A, B) ....
11.4 "Di gioia, di pace la dolce speranza" (S, T, B) ....
11.5 "Finchè fedele tu mi sei stata," canzonetta (4vv) ....
11.6 "Io morrò, sonata è l'ora" (3vv w/ out acc) ....
11.7 "La campana" (La cloche): "Il sole discende" (2T, 2B; in: Matinées musicales) ....
11.8 "Lumi rei del mio martire," madrigale ....
11.9 "Qui sta il male" (3vv) ....
11.10 "Rataplan" (La partenza / Canto marciale): "Rataplan, rataplan, ecco grato" (in: Matinées musicales & Fiori di sepolcro) ....
11.11 "Se schiudi il labbro, o Fillide," divertimento (5vv; in: Donizetti per camera) ....
11.12 "Strofe di Byron" (S, T, 2B): 1. "Sien l'onde placide" ....
11.13 2. "Per noi la vita"
11.14 3. "Ma poi passati stragi e orror"

12. VOCAL CHAMBER—DUETS

12.1 "Ah, non lasciarmi, no" (Metastasio).........................
12.2 "Amor, voce del cielo": "Si t'amo, a te nascondere," notturno (Tarantini; in: Nuits d'été à Pausilippe) ....
12.3 "Armida e Rinaldo" (Tasso) ....
12.4 "Canzonetta con l'eco": "Per valli, per boschi, cercando vo Nice" (c1817) ....
12.5 "C'est le printemps": "On entend dans les brises," chansonette-valse (Plouvier) ....
12.6 "Che cangi tempra mai più non spero" (Metastasio; unacc) ....
12.7 "Che ciel sereno" ....
12.8 "Che vuoi di più? non splenda" (Guaita; in: Inspirations viennoises) ....
12.9 "Duettino" (2S, autograph in Naples) ....
12.10 Duet (2S, alla Marchesa Medici, in Paris) ....
12.11 Duet (c1822, for C. Carnevali and N. Cartoni) ....
12.12 "Godi diletta ingrata nell'ingannarmi tu," canzonetta ....
12.13 "Ha negli occhi un tale incanto" (Metastasio; in: Donizetti per camera) ....

12.14 "Héloïse et Abélard" (Quittons nous), duo historique (Crevel de Charlemagne) ....

12.15 "Ho perduto il mio tesoro" (Metastasio; in: Donizetti per camera) ....

12.16 "I bevitori": "Mesci, mesci e sperda il vento," notturno/brindisi (Tarantini; in: Nuits d'été) ....

12.17 "I due carcerati": "Via dimmi due parole" ....

12.18 "I fervidi desiri": "Da me che vuoi, che brami?" (in: Donizetti per camera) ....

12.19 "Il fiore": "Qui dove mercè negasti," duettino pastorale (in: Soirées d'automne à l'Infrascata)........................

12.20 "Il giuramento": "Tuo finche il sol rischiara," notturno (Palazzolo; in: Nuits d'été à Pausilippe).....................

12.21 "Io d'amor, o Dio, mi moro" (?Metastasio; in: Donizetti per camera) ....

12.22 "I sospiri": "Ti sento, sospiri" (Metastasio; in: Donizetti per camera) ....

12.23 "L'addio" (Le pelerinage): "Dunque addio, mio caro amore" (Romani; in: Un hiver a Paris) ....

12.24 "L'addio": "Io resto fra le lagrime" (Je reste abandonee) (in: Matinées musicales) ....

12.25 "La gelosia" (Querelle d'amour): "Non giova il sospirar," scherzo (in: Matinées & Donizetti per camera).........

12.26 "L'alito di Bice": "O profuno delicato," notturno (Puoti; in: Nuits d'été à Pausilippe) ....

12.27 "La passeggiata al lido": "Che bel mar, che bel sereno" (in: Dernières glânes musicales) ....

12.28 "L'aurora": "Vedi come in sul confine," notturno (Tarantini; in: Nuits d'été à Pausilippe)..............................

12.29 "La voce del core": "T'intendo, si mio cor" (Metastasio; in: Donizetti per camera) ....

12.30 "Les napolitains": "En main les mandolines," nocturne (Crevel de Charlemagne) ....

12.31 "L'incostanza di Irene": "Sara più fida Irene" (Metastasio; in: Soirées d'automne & Donizetti per camera) ...

12.32 "L'ultimo rimprovero": "O crudel che il mio pianto non vedi" (in: Dernières glânes musicales) ....

12.33 "Lumi rei del mio martire," canzonetta ....

12.34 "Non mi sprezzar licori" (Metastasio) ....

12.35 "Predestinazione": "Qual colomba che fugge" (Guaita; in: Inspirations viennoises) ....

12.36 "Quegli sguardi e quegli accenti" ....

12.37 "Se mal turbo il tuo riposo" (Metastasio) ....

12.38 "Sempre più t'amo, mio bel tesoro" ....

12.39 "Sempre sarò costante" (Metastasio) ....

12.40 "Se tu non vedi tutto il mio cor" (Metastasio) ....

12.41 "Si soffre una tiranna" (Metastasio) ....

12.42 "Sull'onda cheta e bruna," barcarola ....

12.43 "Uno sguardo ed una voce": "Uno sguardo di nera pupilla," notturno (Palazzolo; in: Nuits d'été) ....

12.44 "Une nuit sur l'eau": "L'air est pure" (French vers of: Uno sguardo ed una voce) ....

12.45 "Vedi là sulla collina" ....

12.46 "Vuoi casarti," duetto buffo ....

13. SOLO VOICE & PIANO

13.1 "Addio": "Ah! tu mi fuggi ... addio!," romanza (in: Reveries napolitanes & Dernières glânes musicales) ....

13.2 "Addio brunetta, son già lontano," allegretto scherzoso (in: Il Sibillo) ....

13.3 "Adieu, tu brise et pour jamais," romanze ....

13.4 "Ah, non lasciarmi, no, bel'idol mio," romanza (Metastasio) ....

13.5 "Ah, rammenta, o bella Irene," cavatina (Metastasio) ....

13.6 "Ah, si tu voulais, toi que j'aime," canzone ....

13.7 "Aimer ma Rose est la sorte de ma vie," romanze (in: Donizetti per camera) ....

13.8 "A mezzanotte": "Quando notte sara oscura," arietta (in: Nuits d'été à Pausilippe) ....

13.9 "Amiamo": "Or che l'eta ne invita," canzonetta ....

13.10 "Amis, courons chercher la gloire," canzone ....

13.11 "Ammore!," canzoneta napoletana ....

13.12 "Amor che a nulla amato," album leaf ....

13.13 "Amor corrisposto": "Bei labbri che amore formò" (Metastasio; in: Donizetti per camera) ....

13.14 "Amor marinaro": "Me voglio fà na casa," canzonetta napolitana (in: Soirées d'automne) ....

13.15 "Amore e morte": "Odi d'un uom che muore," arietta (Redaelli; in: Soirées d'automne) ....

13.16 "Amor tiranno": "Perchè due cori insieme," romanza (Puoti; in: Fiori di sepolcro) ....

13.17 "Amour jaloux": "Dans un salon si quelqu'um vous regarde," romanze ....

13.18 "Anch'io provai le tenere smanie," arietta ....

13.19 "Antonio Foscarini": "Quando da te lontano" (Niccolini) ....

13.20 "A piè del mesto salce," canzonetta ....

13.21 "Au Pied d'une croix": "Voyez-vous cette femme," romanze ....

13.22 "Au tic-tac des castagnettes," canzonetta/aria (in: Donizetti per camera) ....

13.23 "Che cangi tempra mai più non spero," andante (Metastasio) ....

13.24 "Che non mi disse un di," canzonetta (Metastasio; in: Il Sibillo) ....

13.25 "Combien la nuit est longue": "Helas, j'entend sonner une heure," romanza ....

13.26 "Come volgeste rapidi, giorni de' miei primi anni," romanza ....

13.27 "Dell' anno novello," canzonetta ....

13.28 "Del colle in sul pendio," canzonetta (in: Donizetti per camera) ....

13.29 "Doux souvenirs, vivez toujours," mélodie (Barateau) ....

13.30 "D'un genio che m'accende" (Metastasio; in: Donizetti per camera) ....

13.31 "Ella riposi alcuni istanti almeno," cavatina ....

13.32 "Elle n'existe plus," mélodie ....

13.33 "E morta!" (Morte! et pourtant hier): "Morta! e ieri ancor," scena (Guaita; in: Inspirations viennoises) ....

13.34 "E più dell'onda instabile," arietta ....

13.35 "Faut-il renfermer dans mon âme," mélodie ....

13.36 "Fra le belle Irene è quella," canzonetta (Metastasio) ....

13.111	"Le renégat": "J'ai renie ma foi" (Il Rinnegato: "Io rinnegai ma fe"), scène (p1835, Pacini)
13.112	"Les revenants": "Un soir a l'heure ou finit la veille," aria (Lacroix)
13.113	"Les yeux noirs et les yeux bleus": "Ah! quelle embarras extreme," romance (Monnier)
13.114	"L'étrangère," romance
13.115	"Le violon de Crémone": "Cet instrument silencieux renferme l'âme de ma fille," romance (Hoffmann)
13.116	"L'ora del ritorno": "Odi, Elisa, questa e l'ora," arietta (Guaita; in: Inspirations viennoises)
13.117	"Lu trademiento": "Aje, tradetore, tu m'haje lassata," canzone napoletana (in: Donizetti per camera)
13.118	"Malvina": "Dal di che un altro ti fu più bello" (Depuis qu'un autre), scéne dramatique (Vitali)
13.119	"Malvina la bella," romanza (in: Il Sibilo)
13.120	"Marie enfin quitte l'ouvrage," romance
13.121	"M'è Dio il tuo signore" (Ton Dieu est mon Dieu / Oh quanto in me tu puoi): "Il tuo pensiero e il mio"
13.122	"Mentre del caro lido," canzonetta
13.123	"Minvela": "Quando verrà sul colle," canzonetta/romanza (in: Donizetti per camera)
13.124	"Mon enfant, mon seul espoir": "Mon enfant, mon sang, ma vie," romance
13.125	"Morir per te!," arietta
13.126	"Nice, st'occhiuzzi càlali," canzonetta
13.127	"Noé, Scène du Déluge": "Dieu terrible, Dieu redoutable" (c1839, Boutellier)
13.128	"Non amerò che te," romanza (after Vitali)
13.129	"Non amo che te," romanza
13.130	"Non giova il sospirar," canzonetta veneziana (Metastasio)
13.131	"Non m'ami più" (L'ingratitude): "Tu n'aimes plus" (Guaita; in: Inspirations viennoises)
13.132	"Non v'è più barbaro di chi non sente," canzonetta (Metastasio)
13.133	"Non v'è nume, non v'è fato," romanza
13.134	"N'ornerà la bruna chioma," scena and cavatina (Romani)
13.135	"O anime affannate, venite a noi parlar" (Francesca da Rimini episode of the Divina commedia)
13.136	"Occhio nero incendiator," canzonetta (in: Donizetti per camera)
13.137	"O fille que l'ennui chagrine," romance
13.138	"Oh, Cloe, delizia di questo core," canzonetta
13.139	"Oh, je rêve d'une étrangere plus douce que l'enfant qui dort"
13.140	"On vous a peint l'amour," romance (Lacroix)
13.141	"Or che in cielo," barcarola
13.142	"Or che la notte invita," canzonetta
13.143	"Oui, je sais votre indifférence"
13.144	"Oui, ton dieu c'est le mien," romance (Michonne)
13.145	"Ov'è la voce magica," melodia
13.146	"Pace!," canzonetta
13.147	"Pas d'autre amour que toi," mélodie (Barateau)
13.148	"Perchè due cori," romanza
13.149	"Perchè mai, Nigella amata, insensibile tu sei?," romanza
13.150	"Perchè se mia tu sei," romanza (Metastasio)
13.151	"Philis plus avare que tendre," romance
13.152	"Più che non m'ama un angelo," romanza (also vers for duet: L'amor funesto)
13.153	"Plus ne m'est rien," romance
13.154	"Pourquoi me dire qu'il vous aime," romance
13.155	"Preghiera" (Una lagrima): "Dio! Dio! che col cenno moderi" (in: Matinées musicales)
13.156	"Quand un soupçon mortel," romance
13.157	"Quand je vis que j'étais trahie," scène religieuse (w/ pf & org)
13.158	"Quando il mio ben io rivedrò," canzonetta
13.159	"Quando morte coll'orrido artiglio," prayer
13.160	"Quanto mio ben t'adoro," canzonetta
13.161	"Quel nome se ascolto," romanza (Metastasio)
13.162	"Questo mio figlio è un fiorellin d'amore," berceuse
13.163	"Qui sospirò, là rise," aria
13.164	"Rendimi il core, o Barbara," canzonetta
13.165	"Rose che un di spiegaste," romanza
13.166	"Se a te d'intorno scherza," romanza (in:Il Sibillo)
13.167	"Se lontan, ben mio, tu sei," canzonetta (Metastasio)
13.168	"Se talor più nol rammento," cavatina
13.169	"Seul sur la terre, en vain j'espere," album leaf or romance
13.170	"Si o no": "Tutte le femmine fanno cosi," canzonetta giocosa (in: Dernières glânes musicales)
13.171	"Si tanto sospiri, ti lagni d'amore"
13.172	"Si tu m'as fait à ton image," romance
13.173	"Sorgesti alfin, aurora desiata," aria
13.174	"Sospiri, aneliti che m'opprimete," canzonetta
13.175	"Sovra il campo della vita, sono pianta abbandonata," larghetto
13.176	"Sovra il remo sta curvato," barcarola (Mira; in: Il Sibillo)
13.177	"Spunta il di, l'ombra spari," romanza
13.178	"Su l'onda tremula ride la luna" (in: Donizetti per camera)
13.179	"Su questi allor," canzonetta
13.180	"Taci invan, mia cara jole," romanza
13.181	"T'aspetto ancor": "Nel tuo cammin fugace," romanza (in: Dernières glânes musicales)
13.182	"Te dire adieu": "Tu pars, il faut te dire adieu," romanza (Vaëz)

13.183   "Te voglio bene assaje": "Io te voglio bene assaje e tu non pienze a me," canzone napoletana ....
13.184   "Tengo no n'namurato, faccia d'empiso," canzonetta napoletana (in: Donizetti per camera) ....
13.185   "Troppo vezzosa è la ninfa bella," canzone ....
13.186   "Trova un sol mia bella Clori" (Metastasio; S) ....
13.187   "Trova un sol mia bella Clori" (Metastasio; T, different music) ....
13.188   "Tu me chiedi se t'adoro," arietta ....

13.189   "Una prece sulla mia tomba": "Non priego mai ne piano le parche impietosi" (Redaelli) ....
13.190   "Una tortora innocente," romanza ....
13.191   "Una vergine donzella per amore sospiro," romanza ....
13.192   "Un bacio di speranza" (Un baiser pour espoir), romanza ....
13.193   "Un coeur pour abri": "Sur des bords inconnus," scène (Richomme) ....
13.194   "Un detto di speranza": "Abbandonar ogni speranza," romanza (in: Dernières glânes musicales) ....
13.195   "Uno sguardo": "Oh di quegli occhi teneri," romanza (Romani) ....

13.196   "V'era un di che il cor beato," romanza ....
13.197   "Vien ti conforta, o misera" ....
13.198   "Vision": "Quand descend la nuit sombre," mélodie (Plouvier) ....
13.199   "Viva il matrimonio": "Se tu giri tutto il mondo," cavatina buffa (p1843, Tarantini) ....

14. MISC WORKS

Misc vocal & student exercises:

14.1   "Ah! quel Guglielmo, qual sorpresa, o ciel, che miro" (c1812; 2S, 2T, 2B & orch) ....
14.2   "Ognun dice che le donne," aria (c1815; B & orch) ....
14.3   "Guarda che bianca luna," anacreontica (c1815, Vittorelli; 1v & orch) ....
14.4   "Perchè quell'alma ingrata" (c1816; S, T & small orch) ....
14.5   "Amor mio nume, eccomi a' piedi tuoi," aria (c1816, for exam at Bologna) ....
14.6   "Ti sovvenga amato bene, che fedel ti serbo il cor," aria (c1817; S & orch) ....
14.7   "Isabella ormai mi rendi" (c1818; 2T, B & orch) ....
14.8   "Se bramate che vi sposi" (2vv) ....
14.9   "Taci, tu cerchi invano" (2S & orch) ....
14.10   "Sposo lo so, lo so ... Da quel piano difendetemi, o Dei," recit & aria (S, B & small orch) ....
14.11   "Che avvenne che fu ... Solo per te sospiro," recit & romanza (T & small orch) ....
14.12   Aria for singer Carolina Magni (c1820; S & orch w/ hn obbl; added to Melara: Berengario) ....
14.13   "Pietosa all'amor mio," cabaletta (p1828) ....
14.14   "L'amor materno," recit & aria (c1844; 1v) ....

Other:

14.15   Fugue (4vv; in Naples Conservatory Library, Cat. No.63746) ....
14.16   Fugue (4vv; in Naples Conservatory Library, Cat. No.63861) ....
14.17   11 Fugues (4–6vv, student exercises; in Museo Donizettiano, Bergamo) ....
14.18   3 Fugues (4vv, student exercises; in Naples Conservatory Library, Cat. Nos.64003–5) ....
14.19   "Grande Offertorio" (org/pf; pubd in: Raccolta periodica) ....
14.20   Sketches of parts & scores (in Naples Conservatory Library, Cat. Nos.63855–7) ....
14.21   Sketches (in Naples Conservatory Library, Cat. No.63855–93) ....
14.22   Sketches & studies (in Naples Conservatory Library, Cat. Nos.63866–72) ....
14.23   Sketches & studies (in Naples Conservatory Library, Cat. Nos.63894–909) ....
14.24   Sketches & studies (in Naples Conservatory Library, Cat. Nos.63910–923) ....
14.25   Solfeggi (mS & pf, 32 pages in 2 notebooks) ....
14.26   Study in B-flat major (c1821; cl, for Benigni) ....
14.27   Studies in counterpoint and fugue (22 studies in counterpoint & 40 in fugue) ....
14.28   Vocalizzi or gorgheggi ....

*   *   *   *   *   •

1. STAGE WORKS (incid music)

1.1   "Le roi Lear" (c1954, Shakespeare transl Protopopescu; open-air production of 1954 incl music c by Massis) (also see incid music c by Balakirev, Debussy L109, Khachaturian & Shostakovich Op.58a, film score c by Shostakovich Op.137) ....

2. SYMPHONIES

2.1   Symphony in G minor (c1927; w/ org) Op.25

3. OTHER ORCHESTRAL WORKS

3.1   "Marche militaire" (c1915; orig for pf) Op.14
3.2   "Orientale" (c1916) Op.15

4. CONCERTOS, SOLO INSTR & ORCH

Org & orch:

4.1   "Cortège et litanie" (c1921; orig for pf, Op.19/2) .... (Op.19/2)
4.2   Organ Concerto in E minor (c1934) Op.31

Pf & orch:

4.3   "Fantaisie," in B minor (c1912) Op.8

Other:

4.4   "Verdun: Poème héroïque" (c1935; brass, field drum & org) Op.33

5. STRING QUARTETS

5.1   String Quartet (Allegro) (c1907, student work) ....

6. OTHER CHAMBER MUSIC

3 or more insts:

6.1   "Menuet" (c1898; vn, vc & pf, student work) ....
6.2   "Double Quatuor" (c1908, 1 movt, student work) ....

Vn & pf:

6.3   Violin Sonata in G minor (c1909) Op.5
6.4   "Berceuse enfantine" (c1916; vn/vc & pf) .... Op.13(/3)

Vc & pf:

6.5   "Deux pièces" (c1916): No.1 "Légende" Op.13
6.6   No.2 "Cantilène"

Other 2 insts:

6.7   "Deux pièces" (c1917; cl & pf) Op.10

W/ org:

6.8   "Résonances" (c1944; various insts & org) ....
6.9   Quartet (c1952; str trio & org) Op.52
6.10   Trio in F minor (c1955; vn, vc & org) Op.55
6.11   "Sonata," in A minor (c1960; vc & org) Op.60

7. PIANO

Student works:

7.1   "Marche des paysans" (c1898) ....
7.2   "Barcarolle" (c1899) ....
7.3   "Canon" (c1899) ....

7.4	"Danse du tambourin" (c1899)	
7.5	"Valse," in C-sharp minor (c1900)	
7.6	"Pièce caractéristique" (c1902)	
7.7	"Romance sans paroles" (c1907)	
7.8	"Fugue," in G major (c1910)	
7.9	"Impromptu," in B minor (c1910)	
7.10	2 Cadenzas for Beethoven: Piano Concerto No.1 in C major, Op.15 (c1910)	

Mature works:

7.11	"Six préludes" (c1916): No.1 in E-flat major	Op.12
7.12	No.2 in G-flat major	
7.13	No.3 in A major	
7.14	No.4 in D minor	
7.15	No.5 in F major	
7.16	No.6 in B-flat major	
7.17	"Quatre pièces" (c1921): No.1 "Étude," in E-flat minor	Op.19
7.18	No.2 "Cortège et litanie" (see arr for org & orch)	
7.19	No.3 "Chanson"	
7.20	No.4 "Air de ballet"	
7.21	"Variations," in C-sharp minor (c1924)	Op.22

8. ORGAN & PIANO

8.1	"Ballade" (c1932)	Op.30
8.2	"Variations on Two Themes" (c1937)	Op.35
8.3	"Sinfonia" (c1946)	Op.42

9. HARMONIUM

| 9.1 | "Élévation" (c1913) | Op.2 |

10. ORGAN

Student works:

10.1	"Fugue à trois voix," in C major (c1895)	
10.2	"Prière," in G major (c1895)	
10.3	"Fugue," in F major (c1900; ?org)	
10.4	"Fugue à quatre voix," in A minor (c1901)	
10.5	"Sonate en trio" (Allegro), in C major (c1901; ?org)	

Mature works:

10.6	"Trois préludes et fugues" (c1912): No.1 in B major (à la mémoire de René Vierne)	Op.7
10.7	No.2 in F minor (à la mémoire d'Augustin Barié)	
10.8	No.3 in G minor (à la mémoire de Joseph Boulnois)	
10.9	"Scherzo," in F minor (c1919)	Op.16
10.10	"15 Versets sur les Vêpres de la Vierge" (c1919): No.1 (While the King sitteth at His table)	Op.18
10.11	No.2 (His left hand is under my head, and His right hand doth embrace me)	
10.12	No.3 (I am black but comely, o ye daughters of Jerusalem)	
10.13	No.4 (Lo, the winter is past)	
10.14	No.5 (How fair and how pleasant art thou)	
10.15	"Hymne: Ave maris stella": No.1 (When the salutation Gabriel had spoken)	
10.16	No.2 (Jesus' tender Mother, make Thy supplication)	
10.17	No.3 (So now as we journey, aid our weak endeavour)	
10.18	No.4 (Amen) (Finale)	
10.19	"Magnificat": No.1 (My soul doth magnify the Lord)	
10.20	No.2 (For behold from henceforth all generations shall call me blessed)	
10.21	No.3 (And His mercy is on them that fear Him throughout all generations)	
10.22	No.4 "Cantilène" (He hath put down the mighty from their seat)	
10.23	No.5 (He rememb'ring His mercy hath holpen His servant Israel)	
10.24	No.6 "Final" (Gloria)	
10.25	"Cortège et litanie" (c1921)	Op.19/2
10.26	"Variations on an Old Noël" (c1922)	Op.20
10.27	"Suite bretonne" (c1923): No.1 "Berceuse"	Op.21
10.28	No.2 "Fileuse"	
10.29	No.3 "Les cloches de Perros-Guirec"	
10.30	"Symphonie-Passion" (c1924):	Op.23
	1. "Le monde dans l'attente du Sauveur"	
	2. "Nativité"	
	3. "Crucifixion"	

11. CHORAL WORKS

Student works:

11.1	"La songe de Jacob," cantata (c1901)	
11.2	"Acis et Galatée," cantata (c1911)	
11.3	"Aurore" (c1912; ch)	
11.4	"Cortège antique" (c1912; ch)	
11.5	"Crépuscule" (c1912; ch)	
11.6	"Danse orientale" (c1912; ch)	
11.7	"Tempête" (c1912; ch)	
11.8	"Yanitza," cantata (c1912)	
11.9	"Cantique de Racine" (c1913; ch)	
11.10	"Faust et Hélène," cantata (c1913)	
11.11	"Ismaël," cantata (c1913)	
11.12	"Soir sur la plaine" (c1913; ch)	
11.13	"Juin" (c1914; ch)	
11.14	"Selma," cantata (c1914)	

Mature works:

11.15	"Les normands" (c1911; ch & orch)	Op.1
11.16	"Psyché," cantata (c1914; ch & orch)	Op.4
11.17	"Quatre motets" (c1916; ch & org): 1. "O Salutaris"	Op.9
11.18	2. "Ave Maria"	
11.19	3. "Tantum ergo"	
11.20	4. "Laudate Dominum"	
11.21	"De profundis" (c1917; vv, ch, org & orch):	Op.17
	1. "De profundis clamavi ad te, Domine" (ch)	
	2. "Fiant aures tuoe intendentes" (S, T, B)	
	3. "Si iniquitates observaveris, Domine" (ch)	
	4. "Quia apud te propitiatio est" (T)	
	5. "Sustinuit anima mea in verbo ejus" (ch)	
	6. "A custodia matutina usque ad noctem" (S, B)	
	7. "Et ipse redimet Israël" (ch)	
	8. "Requiem aeternam dona eis" (S, T, B, ch)	
11.22	"La France au Calvaire," oratorio (c1953; vv, ch, org & orch)	Op.49
11.23	"Deux motets" (c1958; S & ch)	Op.53

12. VOICE & ORCHESTRA

12.1	"Agnus Dei" (c1915; Bar & orch)	
12.2	"Le glaive" (c1915; S & orch)	Op.3
12.3	"La tentation de Saint-Antoine" (c1915)	
12.4	"Ave Verum" (c1936; vv & strings)	Op.34/2

13. SONGS (w/ pf)

Student works:

13.1	"La fleur" (c1897)	
13.2	"Oudlette dans le puits" (c1898)	
13.3	"Le récif de corail" (c1905)	
13.4	"Le colibri" (c1907)	
13.5	"Lointain" (c1907)	
13.6	"Ton souvenir" (c1909)	
13.7	"Hantise" (c1910)	
13.8	"Pourquoi?" (c1912)	
13.9	"Sur les flots" (c1912)	
13.10	"Consolation" (c1917)	

Mature works:

13.11	"À l'amie perdue" (c1911, Angellier; orchd): 1. "Nos yeux seuls"	Op.11
13.12	2. "Quand je l'embrasserai"	
13.13	3. "Si mon amour"	
13.14	4. "Ah! les divins moments"	
13.15	5. "Je ne t'ai point connue"	
13.16	6. "Viens chercher sur mon coeur"	
13.17	7. "Une lueur au ciel"	
13.18	"Mélodies" (c1913, Louÿs; orchd): 1. "Marquise"	Op.6
13.19	2. "Les deux soeurs"	
13.20	3. "Chanson de Bilitis I"	

14. ARRANGEMENTS OF WORKS OF OTHERS

For org & orch:

For org:

Improvisations:

15. TEACHING WORKS

* * * * *

DVOŘÁK, Antonín (Leopold)
1841–1904

1. STAGE WORKS

Operas:

1.1	"Alfred," 3 act heroic (c1870, Körner; overture pubd as: Tragic, B16a)	B16
1.2	"Král a uhlíř" (King and Collier), 3 act comic opera (3 vers):	Op.14
	. Version 1 (c1871, Lobeský)	B21
	. Version 2 (c1874, Guldener)	B42
	. Version 3 (c1887, Guldener & Novotný, r of Version 2)	B151
1.3	"Tvrdé palice" (The Pig-headed Peasants / The Stubborn Lovers), 1 act comic (c1874, Štolba)	Op.17, B46
1.4	"Vanda," 5 act tragic (c1875, r1879,1883, Šumavský from Polish by Šurzycki)	Op.25, B55
1.5	"Šelma sedlák" (The Peasant a Rogue / The Cunning Peasant), 2 act comic (c1877, Veselý)	Op.37, B67
1.6	"Dimitri," 4 act historic opera (Červinková-Riegrová; 2 vers):	Op.64
	. Version 1 (c1881–2, r1885)	B127
	. Version 2 (c1894–5)	B186
1.7	"Jacobin" (The Jakobin), 3 acts (2 vers):	Op.84
	. Version 1 (c1887–8, Červinková-Riegrová)	B159
	. Version 2 (c1897, Červinková-Riegrová & Rieger)	B200
1.8	*"Hiawatha" (The Song of Hiawatha) (c1892–5, Longfellow, project)*	*B430*
1.9	*"Šárka" (c1878–80, 1897, Zeyer, project)*	*B436*
1.10	*"Vlasta's Death" (c ?1895–1902, Pippich, project)*	*B440*
1.11	"Čert a Káča" (The Devil and Kate), 3 act comic (c1898–9, Wenig)	Op.112, B201
1.12	"Rusalka" (The Water Nymph), 3 act lyric fairy tale (c1900, Kvapil)	Op.114, B203
1.13	"Armida," 4 acts (c1902–3, Vrchlický after Tasso)	Op.115, B206
1.14	*"Horymír" (c1903, Štárek, project)*	*B441*

Incid music:

1.15	"Josef Kajetán Tyl" (c1881–2, Šamberk; arr for pf duet p1882)	Op.62, B125

1a. SELECTIONS FROM OPERAS (Nos. of sections in The Gramophone)

1a.12	"Rusalka," opera:	Op.114, B203

excerpts: 1. "Overture"
- I: 2. "Ho, ho, ho!"
- 3. "Watersprite, my father dear"
- 4. "He comes here frequently"
- 5. "O, moon high up in the deep, deep sky" (O silver moon)
- 6. "Your ancient wisdom knows averything"
- 7. "Abracadabra"
- 8. "Here she appeared"
- 9. "The hunt is over, return home at once"
- 10. "I know you're but magic that will pass"
- II: 11. "Well then, well then"
- 12. "A week now do you dwell with me"
- 13. "Festival music: Ballet" (Polonaise)
- 14. "No one this world can give you"
- 16. "Rusalka, daughter, I am here"
- 17. "O, useless it is"
- 18. "Strange fire in your eyes is burning"
- III: 19. "Insensible water power" (God of the lake)
- 20. "Ah, ah! Already you have come back?"
- 21. "Only human blood can cleanse you"
- 22. "I'll rather suffer"
- 23. "Uprooted and banished"
- 24. "That you're afraid? Don't be silly"
- 25. "Who is noisy?"
- 26. "Hair, golden hair have I"
- 27. "Where are you, my white doe?"
- 28. "Do you still know me, lover?"

2. SYMPHONIES

2.1	Symphony No.1 in C minor, "The Bells of Zlonice" (c1865)	B9
2.2	Symphony No.2 in B-flat major (c1865, r1887)	Op.4, B12
2.3	Symphony No.3 in E-flat major (c1873)	Op.10, B34
2.4	Symphony No.4 in D minor (c1874)	Op.13, B41
2.5	Symphony No.5 in F major (c1875, r1887)	Op.76, B54
2.6	Symphony No.6 in D major (c1880)	Op.60, B112
2.7	Symphony No.7 in D minor (c1884–5)	Op.70, B141
2.8	Symphony No.8 in G major, "English" (c1889)	Op.88, B163
2.9	*Symphony in B minor (c1892, sketches)*	*B412*
2.10	Symphony No.9 in E min, "From the New World" (c1893; Largo used Fisher in: Goin' Home)	Op.95, B178

| 2.11 | *"Neptune" Symphony (c1893, sketches)* .... *B420* |
| 2.12 | *Symphony in A major (c1894, sketches)* .... *B431* |

3. OTHER ORCHESTRAL WORKS

3.1	*"Harfenice" (The Woman Harpist), polka (c ?1860, lost)* *B4*
3.2	*"Polka" & "Galop" (c1861 or 2, lost)* .... *B5 & B6*
3.3	"Interludes" (c1867): No.1 "Cappricio" B15
3.4	No.2 (w/ out tempo markings)
3.5	No.3 "Con molta espressione"
3.6	No.4 "Allegro con brio"
3.7	No.5 (w/ out tempo markings)
3.8	No.6 "Serenade"
3.9	No.7 "Allegro animato"
3.10	"Tragic Overture" (Dramatic Overture) (c1870, to opera: Alfred, B16) .... (Op.1), B16a
3.11	"Concert Overture," in F major (c1871, to 1st vers of opera: King & Collier, Op.14, B21).................B21a
3.12	"3 Nocturnes" (c1872, Nos.1 & 3 lost): No.2 "May Night" B31
3.13	*"Romeo and Juliet," overture (c1873, lost)* *B35*
3.14	"Symphonic Rapsody" (Symphonic Poem), in A minor (c1874) Op.14, B44
3.15	"Nocturne," in B major (c ?1875, r ?1882/3; strings, from: Str Qt No.4, B19 & Str Qnt, Op.77, B49) Op.40, B47
3.16	"Serenade," in E major (c1875; strings)..Op.22, B52
3.17	"Symphonic Variations" (c1877, on a theme from choral song: The Fiddler, B66/3) Op.78, B70
3.18	"Serenade," in D minor (c1878; 2ob, 2cl, 2bn, 2bn, 3hn, vc & d bass) Op.44, B77
3.19	"Slavonic Dances," I (c1878; orig for pf duet, Op.46, B78): No.1 in C major .... (Op.46), B83
3.20	No.2 in E minor
3.21	No.3 in A-flat major
3.22	No.4 in F major
3.23	No.5 in A major
3.24	No.6 in D major
3.25	No.7 in C minor
3.26	No.8 in G minor
3.27	"Slavonic Rhapsodies" (c1878): No.1 in D major Op.45, B86
3.28	No.2 in G minor
3.29	No.3 in A-flat minor
3.30	*"Serenade," in A major (c1879, sketch)* *B403*
3.31	"Festival March," in C major (c1879, for silver wedding of Franz Joseph & Elisabeth) B88
3.32	"Czech Suite," in D major (c1879): No.1 "Preludio" (Pastorale) Op.39, B93
3.33	No.2 "Polka"
3.34	No.3 "Sousedská" (Minuetto)
3.35	No.4 "Romanza"
3.36	No.5 "Finále" (Furiant)
3.37	"Vanda" Overture (c1879, no connection w/ opera) Op.25, B97
3.38	"Prague Waltzes," in D major (c1879) B99
3.39	"Polonaise," in E-flat major (c1879; arr for pf duet 1883) B100
3.40	"2 Waltzes" (c ?1880; strings): No.1 in A major (orig for pf, Op.54/1) .... (Op.54), B105
3.41	No.2 in D-flat minor (orig for pf, Op.54/4)
3.42	"Polka 'for Prague students,' " in B-flat major (c1880; arr for pf) Op.53a/1, B114
3.43	*"Galop," in E major (c1881, vers for orch lost; arr for pf extant)* *Op.53a/2, B119*
3.44	"Legends" (c1881; orig for pf duet, Op.59, B117): No.1 in D minor .... (Op.59), B122
3.45	No.2 in G major
3.46	No.3 in G minor
3.47	No.4 in C major
3.48	No.5 in A-flat major
3.49	No.6 in C-sharp minor
3.50	No.7 in A major
3.51	No.8 in F major
3.52	No.9 in D major
3.53	No.10 in B-flat minor
3.54	"My Home" Overture (arr1882 from incid music: Josef Kajetán Tyl, Op.62, B125) .... (Op.62), B125a
3.55	"Scherzo capriccioso," in D-flat major (c1883) Op.66, B131
3.56	"Husitská" Dramatic Overture (c1883) Op.67, B132
3.57	"Slavonic Dances," II (c1886–7; orig for pf duet, Op.72, B145): No.9 in B major .... (Op.72), B147
3.58	No.10 in E minor
3.59	No.11 in F major
3.60	No.12 in D-flat major
3.61	No.13 in B-flat minor
3.62	No.14 in B-flat major
3.63	No.15 in C major
3.64	No.16 in A-flat major
3.65	"Fanfares" (c1891; 4tpt & timp, for the opening of the Regional Exhibition in Prague) B167
3.66	"V přírodě" (In Nature's Realm) Concert Overture (c1891; = No.1 of: Nature, Life & Love) Op.91, B168
3.67	"Carnival" Concert Overture (c1891; = No.2 of: Nature, Life & Love) Op.92, B169
3.68	"Othello" Concert Overture (c1891–2; = No.3 of: Nature, Life & Love) Op.93, B174

4. CONCERTOS, SOLO INSTR & ORCH

Pf & orch:

Vn & orch:

Vc & orch:

Other:

5. STRING QUARTETS

6. OTHER CHAMBER MUSIC

6 or more insts:

5 insts:

4 insts:

Piano Trios:

Other 3 insts:

Vn & pf:

Vc & pf:

8.60	"Furiant," in G minor (c ?1884)	Op.12/2, B137
8.61	"Humoresque," in F-sharp major (c ?1884)	B138
8.62	"2 Little Pearls" (c1887): No.1 "In a ring"	B156
8.63	No.2 "Grandpa dances with Grandma"	
8.64	"Album leaf," in E-flat major (c1888)	B158
8.65	"Poetic Tone Pictures" (c1889): No.1 "Nocturnal route"	Op.85, B161
8.66	No.2 "Toying"	
8.67	No.3 "At the old castle"	
8.68	No.4 "Spring song"	
8.69	No.5 "Peasant ballad"	
8.70	No.6 "Reverie"	
8.71	No.7 "Furiant"	
8.72	No.8 "Goblins' dance"	
8.73	No.9 "Serenade"	
8.74	No.10 "Bacchanal"	
8.75	No.11 "Tittle-tattle"	
8.76	No.12 "At the hero's grave"	
8.77	No.13 "On the holy mountain"	
8.78	"Theme for Variations," in D minor (c ?1891)	B303
8.79	*"Piano Piece," in E minor (c1892, unfin)*	*B410*
8.80	*"Andante cantabile" (c1893, sketches)*	*B427*
8.81	"American Suite," in A major (c1894; also for orch, Op.98b, B190): No.1 "Moderato"	Op.98, B184
8.82	No.2 "Molto vivace"	
8.83	No.3 "Allegretto"	
8.84	No.4 "Andante"	
8.85	No.5 "Allegro"	
8.86	"Humoresques" (c1894): No.1 in E-flat minor	Op.101, B187
8.87	No.2 in B major	
8.88	No.3 in A-flat major	
8.89	No.4 in F major	
8.90	No.5 in A minor	
8.91	No.6 in B major	
8.92	No.7 in G-flat major	
8.93	No.8 in B-flat minor	
8.94	*"Piano Pieces" (c1894, sketches)*	*B433*
8.95	"2 Pieces" (c1894): No.1 "Berceuse," in G major	B188
8.96	No.2 "Capriccio," in G minor	
8.97	*"Wanda Mazurka" (p1912, from opera: Vanda, Op.25, B55)*	

Pf duet:

8.98	"Slavonic Dances," Set I (c1878; orchd, B83): No.1 in C major	Op.46, B78
8.99	No.2 in E minor	
8.100	No.3 in A-flat major	
8.101	No.4 in F major	
8.102	No.5 in A major	
8.103	No.6 in D major	
8.104	No.7 in C minor	
8.105	No.8 in G minor	
8.106	"Legends" (c1880–1; orchd, B122): No.1 in D minor	Op.59, B117
8.107	No.2 in G major	
8.108	No.3 in G minor	
8.109	No.4 in C major	
8.110	No.5 in A-flat major	
8.111	No.6 in C-sharp minor	
8.112	No.7 in A major	
8.113	No.8 in F major	
8.114	No.9 in D major	
8.115	No.10 in B-flat minor	
8.116	"Ze Šumavy" (From the Bohemian Forest) (c1883–4): No.1 "In the spinning-room"	Op.68, B133
8.117	No.2 "By the Black Lake"	
8.118	No.3 "Witches' Sabbath"	
8.119	No.4 "On the watch"	
8.120	No.5 "Silent woods"	
8.121	No.6 "In stormy times"	
8.122	"Slavonic Dances," Set II (c1886): No.9 in B major	Op.72, B145
8.123	No.10 in E minor	
8.124	No.11 in F major	
8.125	No.12 in D-flat major	
8.126	No.13 in B-flat minor	
8.127	No.14 in B-flat major	
8.128	No.15 in C major	
8.129	No.16 in A-flat major	

9. ORGAN

9.1 "Preludes & fugues" (c1859): No.1 in D major B302
9.2   No.2 in G major
9.3   No.3 in A minor
9.4   No.4 in B-flat major
9.5   No.5 in D major, "Prelude on a Given Theme"
9.6   . "Fughetta," in D major
9.7   . "Fugue," in D major
9.8   . "Fugue," in G minor

10. CHORAL WORKS

W/ orch:

10.1   *Mass in B-flat major (c ?1857–9, lost)* *B2*
10.2   "Patriotic Hymn" (The Heirs of the White Mountain) (Hálek; 3 vers): Op.30
        . Version 1 (c1872) B27
        . Version 2 (c1880) B102
        . Version 3 (c1884) B134
10.3   "Stabat Mater," oratorio (c1876–7, Todi; S, A, T, B, ch & orch): Op.58, B71
        1. "Stabat mater dolorosa" (qt, ch)
        2. "Quis est homo, qui non fleret" (qt)
        3. "Eia mater, fons amoris" (ch)
        4. "Fac, ut ardeat cor meum" (B, ch)
        5. "Tui nati vulnerati," chorus
        6. "Fac me vere tecum flere" (T, ch)
        7. "Virgo virginum praeclara," chorus
        8. "Fac, ut portem Christi mortem," duet (S, T)
        9. "Inflammatus et accensus" (A)
       10. "Quando corpus morietur" (qt, ch)
10.4   "Psalm 149": "Praise and sing," oratorio (c1879, Bible of Kralice; 2 vers): Op.79
        . Version 1 (c1879; m ch & orch) B91
        . Version 2 (c1887; ch & orch) B154
10.5   "The Spectre's Bride," cantata (c1884, on a ballad by Erben; S, T, Bar, ch & orch) Op.69, B135
10.6   "St Ludmila," oratorio (c1885–6, Vrchlický; S, A, T, B, ch & orch) Op.71, B144
10.7   "St Ludmila," recitatives for stage performance (c1901, Vrchlický & Novotný) .... (Op.71), B205
10.8   Mass in D major (2 vers): Op.86
        . Version 1 (c1887, Liturgy; S, A, T, B, ch & org) B153
        . Version 2 (c1892; S, A, T, B, ch & orch) B175
        1. "Kyrie"
        2. "Gloria"
        3. "Credo"
        4. "Sanctus"
        5. "Benedictus"
        6. "Agnus Dei"
10.9   "Requiem" (c1890, Liturgy; S, A, T, B, ch & orch): Op.89, B165
      I: 1. "Requiem aeternam" (vv, ch)
          2. "Requiem aeternam" (S, ch)
          3. "Dies irae" (ch)
          4. "Tuba mirum" (vv, ch)
          5. "Quid sum miser" (vv, ch)
          6. "Recordare" (T, str qt)
          7. "Confutatis maledictis" (ch)
          8. "Lacrimosa" (vv, ch)
      II: 9. "Offertorium" (vv, ch)
         10. "Hostias et preces" (vv, ch)
         11. "Sanctus" (vv, ch)
         12. "Pie Jesu" (vv, ch)
         13. "Agnus Dei" (vv, ch)
10.10   "Te Deum" (c1892, Liturgy; S, B, ch & orch): Op.103, B176
         1. "Te Deum laudamus"
         2. "Tu rex gloriae, Christe"
         3. "Aeterna fac cum sanctis"
         4. "Dignare Domine, die ista"
         5. "Benedicamus Patrem"
10.11   "The American Flag," cantata (c1892–3, Drake; A, T, B, ch & orch) Op.102, B177
10.12   *"Revelation of St. John": "Behold, he cometh with the clouds" (c1894, Bible, sketches)* *B422*
10.13   *"The Bridegroom's Arrival," oratorio (c1897, Zeyer, sketches)* *B437*
10.14   *"Job" (c ?1897, Bible of Kralice, sketches)* *B438*
10.15   *"Song of Songs," oratorio (c1897, Bible of Kralice, sketches)* *B439*
10.16   "Ode" (Festival Song) (c1900, Vrchlický; ch & orch) Op.113, B202

Unacc ch:

10.17	"4 Partsongs" (ca1876; ch): 1. "Evening's blessing" (Heyduk)	Op.29, B59
10.18	2. "Lullaby" (Heyduk)	
10.19	3. "I don't say it" (Moravian)	
10.20	4. "The forsaken one" (Moravian)	
10.21	"Choral Songs" (c1877; m ch): 1. "The ferryman" (trad Moravian)	B66
10.22	2. "The beloved as poison-mixer" (trad Moravian)	
10.23	3. "The fiddler" (Heyduk)	
10.24	"Bouquet of Czech folksongs" (c ?1877; m ch): 1. "The betrayed shepherd"	Op.41, B72
10.25	2. "The sweetheart's resolve"	
10.26	3. "The Guelder Rose"	
10.27	4. "The Czech Diogenes"	
10.28	"The song of a Czech" (c1877, Vacek-Kamenický; m ch, unfin)	B73
10.29	"From a bouquet of Slavonic folksongs" (c1878; m vv & pf; arr for pf duet): 1. "Sorrow"	Op.43, B76
10.30	2. "Miraculous water"	
10.31	3. "The girl in the woods"	
10.32	"5 Partsongs" (c1878, Lith transl Šelakovský; m vv): 1. "Village gossip": "With the dawn"	Op.27, B87
10.33	2. "Dwellers by the sea": "Laïma crieth, Laïma moaneth"	
10.34	3. "The promise of love": "Come my dearest lad"	
10.35	4. "The lost lamb": "Yestereve, as night was falling"	
10.36	5. "The sparrow's party": "Once a cock-sparrow did brew some strong cider"	
10.37	"Moravian Duets" (c1880; fem ch): 1. "Forsaken": "Lo, the dove from her" (= Op.32/2)	B107
10.38	2. "Omens": "Thrive and grow, thou" (= Op.32/5)	
10.39	3. "The wild rose": "Forth went a comely lass" (= Op.32/10)	
10.40	4. "Forsaken": "Lo, the dove from her" (= Op.32/2)	
10.41	5. "The slighted heart": "Oh, that now I held the sey the well sharpend" (= Op.29/3)	
10.42	"V přírodě" (In Nature's Realm) (c1882, Hálek; ch): 1. "A song went into my soul"	Op.63, B126
10.43	2. "Evening bells"	
10.44	3. "The rye field"	
10.45	4. "The silver birch"	
10.46	5. "With dance and song"	
10.47	"Hymn of the Czech Peasants" (c1885, Pippich; ch & orch; arr Zubatý w/ pf)	Op.28, B143

11. VOICE & ORCHESTRA

11.1	*"3 Modern Greek Poems" (c1878, transl Nebeský, lost except for oboe part)*	*(Op.50), B84a*
11.2	"Ballad of King Matthias" (c1880–1; Bar & orch, vers of ballad from opera: King & Collier, Op.14)	B115
11.3	"Two of the Evening Songs" (c1882, Hálek): 1. "I dreamt that you were dead" (= Op.3/2)	B128
11.4	2. "I am that knight of fairy tale" (= Op.3/3)	

12. VOICE & ORGAN

12.1	"Ave Maria" (c1877, Liturgy; A/Bar & org)	Op.19b, B68
12.2	"Hymnus ad laudes in festo Sanctae Trinitatis" (c1878, Liturgy; 1v & org)	B82
12.3	"Ave Maris Stella" (c1879, Sacred; 1v & org)	Op.19c, B95
12.4	"O Sanctissima dulcis Virgo Maria" (c1879, Sacred; A, Bar & org)	Op.19a, B95a
12.5	"O Sanctissima dulcis Virgo Maria" (c1890, Sacred; S, A & org)	Op.19a, B163a

13. VOCAL DUETS (w/ pf)

13.1	"Moravian Duets" (c1875; 2vv/ch & pf): 1. "Destined": "Vain all thy moaning"	Op.20, B50
13.2	2. "The parting": "Dance with me, my dearest maiden"	
13.3	3. "The silken band": "Is it lovely nightingale"	
13.4	4. "The last wish": "Šuhaj plow you follow"	
13.5	"Moravian Duets" (c1876; S, A & pf): 1. "The fugutive": "Where blue the Danube flows"	Op.29, B60
13.6	2. "Speed thee, birdie" (Fly, sweet songster)	
13.7	3. "The slighted heart": "Oh, that now I held the scythe well sharpened"	
13.8	4. "Parting without sorrow": "Gaily as I met thee"	
13.9	5. "The pledge of love": "Dost thou see the stars shining yonder?"	
13.10	"Moravian Duets" (c1876; S, A & pf; also for fem ch, B107): 1. "Sad of heart": "By the forest"	Op.32, B62
13.11	2. "Forsaken": "Lo, the dove from her"	
13.12	3. "The modest maid": "Sweeter than the violet"	
13.13	4. "The ring": "Let us sing today"	
13.14	5. "Omens": "Thrive and grow, thou"	
13.15	6. "The soldier's farewell": "Pod hájíčkem zelená se oves"	
13.16	7. "The last wish": "Šuhay plow you follow" (= Op.20/4, B50)	
13.17	8. "The maid imprisoned": "Maiden journeys forth"	
13.18	9. "Comfort": "Thou forest dear, fare well"	
13.19	10. "The wild rose": "Forth went a comely lass"	
13.20	"Moravian Duets" (c1877; S, A or ch & pf): 1. "Hoping in vain": "Plainting birdling"	Op.38, B69
13.21	2. "Greeting from afar": "Shine on, kindly, dearest star"	

14.68	3. "Downcast am I, so often with despair" (from B11/11)
14.69	4. "Everything's still in valley and mountain" (from B11/13)
14.70	*"The wild duck" (c1884, folksong, lost)* *B140*
14.71	"2 Songs" (c1885, Czech folk poems): 1. "Sleep, my baby, sleep" B142
14.72	2. "When I see you, my sweetheart"
14.73	"In Folk Tone" (Songs on Folk Poems) (c1886): 1. "Good night, my darling" (Slovak) Op.73, B146
14.74	2. "When a maiden was a-mowing" (Slovak)
14.75	3. "Nothing can change for me" (Czech)
14.76	4. "I have a faithful mare" (Slovak)
14.77	"4 Songs" (c1887–8, Malybrok-Stieler): 1. "Leave me alone in my fond dream" Op.82, B157
14.78	2. "Over her embroidery": "How great and good the blessing"
14.79	3. "Springtime": "When the earth the sunshine kisseth"
14.80	4. "At the brook": "Softly runs the brook and sighing"
14.81	"Love Songs" (c1888, r from cycle: Cypřiše, B11) 1. "Never will love lead us" (from B11/8) Op.83, B160
14.82	2. "Death reigns" (from B11/3)
14.83	3. "I wander oft" (from B11/9)
14.84	4. "I know that on my love" (from B11/6)
14.85	5. "Nature lies peaceful" (from B11/17)
14.86	6. "In deepest forest glade" (from B11/14)
14.87	7. "When thy sweet glances" (from B11/2)
14.88	8. "Thou only dear one" (from B11/4)
	"Biblical Songs" (Bible of Kralice; 2 vers): Op.99
	. Version 1 (c1894; 1v & pf) B185
	. Version 2 (arr Zemanek for 1v & orch 1895, p1929): B189
14.89	1. "Clouds and darkness" (from Psalm 97)
14.90	2. "Lord, Thou art my refuge" (from Psalm 119)
14.91	3. "Hear my prayer o God" (from Psalm 55)
14.92	4. "The Lord is my shepherd" (from Psalm 23)
14.93	5. "I will sing a new song" (from Psalm 144 & 145)
14.94	6. "Hear my prayer, O God" (from Psalm 61 & 63)
14.95	7. "By the waters of Babylon" (from Psalm 137)
14.96	8. "Turn Thee unto me" (from Psalm 25)
14.97	9. "I will lift up mine eyes" (from Psalm 121)
14.98	10. "O sing unto the Lord" (from Psalm 98 & 96)
14.99	"Lullaby" (c1895, Jelínek) B194
14.100	"Song from 'The Smith of Lešetín' ": "Glowing sparks are flashing" (c1901, S. Čech) B204

15. MISC WORKS

15.1	*Themes (c ?1889, some used later in Symphony No.8 in G major, Op.88, B163)* *B409*
15.2	*Various sketches (c1893–1900)* *B423*
15.3	*"The glow worm" (c1896, sketches)* *B435*

16. ARRANGEMENTS OF HIS OWN WORKS

For vc & pf:

16.1	Cello Concerto in B minor, Op.104, B191 (arr1895) B522

For pf:

16.2	"Festival March," in C major, B88 (arr ?1879) B507
16.3	"Prague Waltzes," in D major, B99 (arr ?1879) B508
16.4	"The Jacobin," opera, Op.84, B200 (revisions after the rehearsal, pf score 1897) B525
16.5	"Armida," opera, Op.115, B206 (arr1902–3) B532

For pf duet:

16.6	"Serenade," in E major, Op.22, B52 (arr1877) B504
16.7	"Slavonic Rhapsodies," Op.45, B86 (arr1878): No.1 in D major B506
16.8	No.2 in G minor
16.9	No.3 in A-flat minor
16.10	"Nocturne," in B major, Op.40, B47 (arr ?1882) B509
16.11	"Scherzo capriccioso," in D-flat major, Op.66, B131 (arr ?1883) B510
16.12	"Husitská" Dramatic Overture, Op.67, B132 (arr1883 or 4) B511
16.13	Symphony No.7 in D minor, Op.70, B141 (arr1885) B512
16.14	"Piano Pieces," Op.52, B110 (arr ?1887): No.1 "Impromptu," in G minor B513
16.15	No.2 "Intermezzo," in E-flat major
16.16	No.3 "Gigue," in B-flat major
16.17	No.4 "Eclogue," in G minor
16.18	No.5 "Allegro molto," in G minor
16.19	No.6 "Tempo di marcia," in E-flat major
16.20	"Symphonic Variations," Op.78, B70 (arr1887–8) B514

16.21	String Quartet No.8 in E major, Op.80, B57 (arr1887–8)	B515
16.22	"Concert Overture," in F major, B21a (arr1889)	B516
16.23	Symphony No.8 in G major, Op.88, B163 (arr1890)	B518
16.24	Piano Trio No.4 in E minor, "Dumky," Op.90, B166 (arr1893)	B520
16.25	Symphony No.9 in E minor, "From the New World," Op.95, B178 (arr1894)	B521
16.26	"Holoubek" (The Wild Dove), sym poem, Op.110, B198 (arr1897)	B524
16.27	"Hero's Song," sym poem, Op.111, B199 (arr1898)	B527

For 1v/vv & pf:

16.28	"Patriotic Hymn" (The Heirs of the White Mountain), Op.30, B27 (arr1873)	B501
16.29	"The Pig-headed Peasants" (The Stubborn Lovers), Op.17, B46 (arr ?1875)	B502
16.30	"Lenka's Song" (arr1875, from opera: The Pig-headed Peasants, Op.17, B46)	B503
16.31	"Song of the Prince" (arr1878, from opera: The Peasant a Rogue, Op.37, B67)	B505
16.32	"Requiem," Op.89, B165 (arr1890)	B517
16.33	"The American Flag," cantata, Op.102, B177 (arr1893)	B519
16.34	"Dimitrij," opera, Op.64, B186 (arr ?1895)	B523
16.35	*"Terinka's Song" (?sketch/vocal score, frags ?1897, from opera: The Jakobin, Op.84)*	*B526*
16.36	*"Dimitrij," opera, Op.64, B186 (frag 1898)*	*B528*
16.37	"Dimitrij," opera, Op.64, B186 (arr ?1898, unfin)	B529
16.38	"The Devil and Kate," opera, Op.112, B201 (arr1899)	B530
16.39	"King and Collier," opera, Op.14, B42 & B151 (arr1900)	B531

17. ARRANGEMENTS OF WORKS OF OTHERS

17.1	"2 Irish Songs" (arr1878): 1. "Oh my Connor"	B601
17.2	2. "Ho! adorn yourself with flowers"	
17.3	Brahms: "Hungarian Dances" (Nos.17–21) (arr1880; orch): No.17 in F-sharp minor	B602
17.4	No.18 in D major	
17.5	No.19 in B minor	
17.6	No.20 in E minor	
17.7	No.21 in E minor	
17.8	"16 Russian Songs" (arr1883; 2vv & pf, folksongs): 1. "Vïletala golubina"	B603
17.9	2. "Chem tebya ya ogorchila?"	
17.10	3. "Belolitsa, kruglolitsa"	
17.11	4. "Akh, chtozh tï, golubchik"	
17.12	5. "Tsveli, tsveli tsvetiki"	
17.13	6. "Akh, kak pal tuman"	
17.14	7. "Akh, rechenki, rechenki"	
17.15	8. "Molodka, molodaya"	
17.16	9. "Vniz po matushke po Volge"	
17.17	10. "Vo pole beryoza stoyala"	
17.18	11. "Vïydu ya na rechenku"	
17.19	12. "Kak u nas na ulitse"	
17.20	13. "Ya noseyal konopelku"	
17.21	14. "Akh, utushka lygovaya"	
17.22	15. "Gey, u poli vishnya"	
17.23	16. "Oy, kryache, chernenkiy voron"	
17.24	Lev: "Ah, that love" (arr ?1880–4; 1v & orch)	B604
17.25	Foster: "Old Folks at Home" (arr1893–4; S, B, ch & orch)	B605
17.26	Anon: "Vysoká polka" (arr1902; pf)	B606

* * * * *

B = Jarmil Burghauser: "Antonín Dvořák. Thematic Catalogue. Bibliography. Survey of Life and Work." Export Artia. Prague. Czechoslovakia, 1960.

1. STAGE WORKS

Operas:

1.1	*Opera in 3 acts (c1909, project)*	
1.2	"The Crown of India," 2 tableau imperial masque (c1911–2, Hamilton; A, B, ch & orch)	Op.66
1.3	"The Spanish Lady," 2 acts (c1932–3, Jackson from Jonson's The Devil is an Ass, inc)	Op.89

Ballets:

1.4   "Ballet Music" (c1879; fl, ob, cl, bn & strings, inc): ....
                1. "Ensemble" (from: Promenade No.1 for 2fl, ob, cl & bn of 1878)
                2. "Moderato" (used in: The Wand of Youth, Suite No.2, Op.1b/6)
                3. "Allegro"
1.5   *"Rabelais" (c1902–3, after Rabelais, frags)* ....
1.6   "The Sanguine Fan" (c1917, Lowther, based on Conder's Fan) Op.81
1.7   *Ballet Music (c1923, inc sketch)* ....

Incid music:

1.8   "Music for a Children's Play" (ca1867–71, used in: The Wand of Youth, Op.1) ....
1.9   "Grania & Diarmid" (c1901, Moore & Yeats) Op.42
1.10   "The Starlight Express" (c1915, from Blackwood's The Prisoner in Fairyland, collab Pearn) Op.78
1.11   "King Arthur" (c1923, Binyon) ....
1.12   "Beau Brummel" (c1928, Matthews) ....

1a. SELECTIONS FROM STAGE WORKS

1a.2   "The Crown of India," imperial masque: Op.66
           I. "The Cities of Ind": 1a. "Introduction"
                1b. "Sacred Measure"
                2. "Dance of Nautch Girls"
                2a. "India greets her cities"
                3. "Hail, Immemorial Ind!," song (A)
                3a. "Entrance of Calcutta"
                3b. "Entrance of Delhi"
                4a. "Introduction"
                4b. "March of the Mogul Emperors"
                5. "Entrance of 'John Company' "
                5a. "Entrance of St. George"
                6. "Rule of England," song (B)
                7. "Interlude"
          II. "Ave Imperator!": 8a. "Introduction"
                8b. "Warriors' Dance"
                9. "Cities of India"
                10. "March. The Crown of India"
                10a. "The Homage of Ind"
                11. "Crowning of Delhi"
                12. "Ave Imperator!"

1a.9   "Grania & Diarmid," incid music: Op.42
                1. "Incidental music"
                2. "Funeral March"
                3. "There are seven that pull the thread" (Spinning Song), song for Act I (Yeats)

1a.10   "The Starlight Express," incid music (Nos. of sections in The Gramophone): Op.78
           excerpts: 1. "Overture"
         I: 2. "O children, open your arms to me" (Organ-Grinder)
                3. "Scene 1"
                4a. "Interlude"
                4b. "Scene 2"
                5. "There is a fairy hides in the beautiful eyes" (Organ-Grinder)
         II: 6. "Interlude"
                7. "The sun has gone" (Curfew Song)
                8. "I'm everywhere" (Laughter)
                9a. "Wake up you little Night Winds"
                9b. "Entr'acte" (Sun Dance from 'The Wand of Youth')
                10a. "Oh stars, shine brightly" (Laughter)
                10b. "They'll listen to my song" (Laughter)
                11. "We shall meet the morning spiders" (Jane Anne's Dawn Song)
                12. "My Old Tunes" (Organ-Grinder)
         III: 13. "Dandelions, daffodils" (Jane Anne)
                14. "Waltz"
                15. "Laugh a little ev'ry day" (Laughter)

16. "They're all soft-shiny now" (Organ-Grinder)
17. "Oh, think beauty" (Jane Anne)
18. "Finale" (Dustman, Laughter, Tramp and busy Sweep)

2. SYMPHONIES

2.1   Symphony Movement in G minor (c1878, after Mozart: Sym No.40 in G minor, K550, inc) ....
2.2   Symphony No.1 in A-flat major (c1907–8).. Op.55
2.3   Symphony No.2 in E-flat major (c1909–11; motto from Shelley's Song: 'Rarely, rarely, comest thou') Op.63
2.4   Symphony No.3 (c1932–3, inc) Op.88

3. OTHER ORCHESTRAL WORKS

3.1   "Intonation No.2" (c1878; 2fl, 2ob, 2cl & strings, used in No.1 of: Harmony Music No.6) ....
3.2   "La brunette," 5 quadrilles (c1879, for Powick band) ....
3.3   "Die Junge Kokette," 5 quadrilles (or Caledonians) (c1879, for Powick band): No.1 in C major ....
3.4   No.2 in D major
3.5   No.3 in D major
3.6   No.4 in G major
3.7   No.5 in C major
3.8   "L'Assomoir," 5 quadrilles (c1879, for Powick band): No.1 in A minor ....
3.9   No.2 in D major
3.10   No.3 in A major
3.11   No.4 in D major
3.12   No.5 in A minor (= 6th movt of: Wand of Youth, Suite No.2, Op.1b)
3.13 "3 Quadrilles" (c1879, inc): No.1 in A major ....
3.14   No.2 in G major
3.15   No.3 in D major ('from an old set')
3.16 "Andantino," in G minor (c1879, inc; used in: 3 Characteristic Pieces, Op.10/2) ....
3.17 "Vivace," in F major (c1879, inc) ....
3.18 "Stars of Midnight" (c1879; fl, cl, cornet & strings, introduction to anon song) ....
3.19 "The Valentine," 5 lancers (c1880, for Powick band): No.1 in G major ....
3.20   No.2 in D major
3.21   No.3 in G major
3.22   No.4 in D major
3.23   No.5 in G major
3.24 "March Revaal" (c1880, inc) ....
3.25 "Maud," polka (c1880, for Powick band)...
3.26 "Paris," 5 quadrilles (c1880, for Powick band): No.1 "Châtelet" ....
3.27   No.2 "L'hippodrome"
3.28   No.3 "Alcazar d'été" (Champs Elysées)
3.29   No.4 "Là! Suzanne!"
3.30   No.5 "Café des ambassadeurs" (La femme d'emballeur)
3.31 "Pas redoublé No.2," in F-sharp minor (c1881; incl in opera: The Spanish Lady, Op.89) ....
3.32   Quadrille Fragments (c1881)...
3.33 "Nelly," polka (c1880, for Powick band) ....
3.34 "Air de ballet" (Pastourelle) (c ?1881; arr for pf; for 2vn & pf; for milit band) ....
3.35 "La blonde," polka (c1882, for Powick band) ....
3.36 March in D major (c1882; perf1888 as No.4 of: 3 Characteristic Pieces, Op.10).......................................
3.37   Overture Fragments (c1883, for project: ?Lakes Overture) ....
3.38 "Helcia," polka (c1883, for Powick band) ....
3.39 "Intermezzo mauresque" (c1883; see Op.10/2)..
3.40 "Blumine," polka (c1884, for Powick band)..
3.41   Overture Fragments (c1884–?5, for project: ?Scottish Overture)..
3.42   "3 Pieces" (c1888; strings, lost; ?r as: Serenade, Op.20): No.1 "Spring song" ....
3.43   No.2 "Elegy"
3.44   No.3 "Finale"
3.45 "The Wand of Youth," Suite No.1 (c1907, r vers of: Music for a Children's Play): No.1 "Overture" Op.1a
3.46   No.2 "Serenade"
3.47   No.3 "Minuet" (Old Style)
3.48   No.4 "Sun Dance" (theme used in incid music: The Starlight Express, Op.78)
3.49   No.5 "Fairy Pipers"
3.50   No.6 "Slumber Scene"
3.51   No.7 "Fairies and Giants"
3.52 "The Wand of Youth," Suite No.2 (c1908): No.1 "March" Op.1b
3.53   No.2 "The Little Bells" (melody used in incid music: The Starlight Express, Op.78)
3.54   No.3 "Moths and Butterflies" (melody used in incid music: The Starlight Express, Op.78)
3.55   No.4 "Fountain Dance"
3.56   No.5 "The Tame Bear"
3.57   No.6 "The Wild Bears" (from: Quadrille No.5 of: L'Assomoir of 1879)
3.58 "Cantique" (c1912; orch/org/pf, r & orchd from No.2 of: Harmony Music No.6) Op.3
3.59 "Sevillana" (Scène Espagnole) (c1884, r1889; arr for pf 1884; also for milit band p1904).................... Op.7
3.60 "3 Characteristic Pieces" (r1899 of: Suite in D major): No.1 "Mazurka" (c ?1883–4): Op.10

3.61 No.2 "Sérénade mauresque" (c1879; see perf as: Intermezzo mauresque of 1883)
3.62 No.3 "Contrasts: The Gavotte, A.D.1700 & 1900" (c ?1883):
3.63 "Sursum corda" (Elévation), in B-flat major (c1894; strings, brass, org & 2timp) Op.11
3.64 "Froissart," concert overture (c1890, r1901, inspired by Scott's Old Morality) Op.19
3.65 "Serenade," in E minor (c1892; strings, from: 3 Pieces for strings of 1888) Op.20
3.66 "3 Bavarian Dances" (c1896; see: Scenes from Bavarian Highlands, Op.27a): No.1 "The Dance" ... Op.27b
3.67 No.2 "Lullaby"
3.68 No.3 "The Marksman"
3.69 "Imperial March" (c1897): Op.32
3.70 "Enigma Variations" (Variations on an Original Theme) (c1898–9; orch & org, a series of portraits of
friends) (this work marks the beginning of the 'English Renaissance' in music): . "Theme" (Enigma)
(Elgar offers no explanation) Op.36
    1. "C.A.E." (C. Alice Elgar, composer's wife—romantic & delicate)
    2. "H.D.S.-P." (Hew David Steuart-Powell, pianist friend—diatonic run)
    3. "R.B.T." (Richard Baxter Townshend—low voice portrayed by bassoon)
    4. "W.N.B." (William Neath Baker, 'country squire,' gentleman, scholar)
    5. "R.P.A." (Richard Penrose Arnold, self-taught pianist)
    6. "Ysobel" (Isabel Fitton, viola player—pensive & romantic)
    7. "Troyte" (Arthur Troyte Griffith—saying the unexpected)
    8. "W.N." (Winifred Norbury—characteristic laugh)
    9. "Nimrod" (August J. Jaeger—discourse on Beethoven's 'Pathetique')
    10. "Dorabella" (Intermezzo) (Dora Penny—dancelike lightness)
    11. "G.R.S." (George Robert Sinclair—his dog falling into the river)
    12. "B.G.N." (Basil G. Nevinson, amateur cellist—cello solo)
    13. " * * * * " (Romanza) (Lady Mary Lygon on a sea voyage to Australia, throb of engines—throb
       of drums)
    14. "E.D.U." (Finale) (Edoo: Alice's pet name for composer—bold & vigorous)
3.71 "Sérénade lyrique" (c1899; small orch) ....
3.72 *"Welsh Overture" (c1901, sketch; used in: Introduction & Allegro, Op.47)* ....
3.73 "Pomp & Circumstance," milit marches: No.1 in D major, "Land of Hope and Glory" (c1901; arr Lemare
for org 1902) Op.39
3.74 No.2 in A minor (c1901)
3.75 No.3 in C minor (c1904)
3.76 No.4 in G major (c1907)
3.77 No.5 in C major (c1930)
3.78 *No.6 (c1930, frag)*
3.79 "Cockaigne Overture" (No.1) (In London Town), concert overture (c1900–1; w/ org) Op.40
3.80 "Dream Children" (c1902; small orch/pf, inspired by Lamb): No.1 "Andantino," in G minor Op.43
3.81 No.2 "Allegretto piacevole," in G major
3.82 *"Cockaigne Overture" No.2, concert overture (c1903, frag)* ....
3.83 "Introduction & Allegro" (c1905; str qt & strings, used sketch of: Welsh Overture of 1901) Op.47
3.84 "In the South" (Alassio), concert overture (c1904; also extract: In Moonlight of 1904) Op.50
3.85 *"Tuscan Fantastico," in A-flat maj / G major (c1909, frag)* ....
3.86 "Elegy" (c1909; strings) Op.58
3.87 "Coronation March" (c1911; w/ org, for King George V, incl parts of ballet: Rabelais) Op.65
3.88 "The Crown of India," suite (c1912): No.1 "Introduction Dance of Nautch Girls" .... (Op.66)
3.89 No.2 "Menuetto"
3.90 No.3 "Warriors' Dance"
3.91 No.4 "Intermezzo"
3.92 No.5 "Warriors' Dance"
3.93 No.6 "March of the Mogul Emperors"
3.94 "Falstaff, Symphonic Study" (w/ 2 Interludes in A minor), in C minor (c1913): Op.68
3.95 . "Interlude I—Jack Falstaff, Page to the Duke of Norfolk"
3.96 . "Interlude II—Gloucestershire, Shallow's Orchard"
3.97 "Carissima" (c1913; small orch/pf) ....
3.98 "Sospiri" (Adagio) (c1913–4; strings, harp & org) Op.70
3.99 "Symphonic Prelude: Polonia" (c1915) Op.76
3.100 "Rosemary" (That's for Remembrance—Douce Pensée) (c1915; orig: Menuetto & Trio of 1882) ....
3.101 "The British Empire March" (c1924; perf w/ Pageant of Empire; also see: March for pf trio of 1924) ....
3.102 "Civic Fanfare" (c1923; orch w/out vns & org, for opening service of Hereford Festival) ....
3.103 "Severn Suite" (c1930; brass; orchd): No.1 "Introduction" (Worcester Castle) Op.87
3.104 No.2 "Toccata" (Tournament)
3.105 No.3 "Fugue" (Cathedral)
3.106 No.4 "Minuet" (Commandery) (based on sketch of 1903)
3.107 No.5 "Coda"
3.108 "Nursery Suite" (c1930): No.1 "Aubade" (uses: Hymn Tune in F major 'Drakes Broughton' of 1878) ....
3.109 No.2 "The Serious Doll"
3.110 No.3 "Busy-ness!"
3.111 No.4 "The Sad Doll"
3.112 No.5 "The Waggon Passes"
3.113 No.6 "The Merry Doll"
3.114 No.7 "Dreaming"
3.115 No.8 "Envoy"
3.116 "Mina" (c1932–3) ....

3.117	"The Spanish Lady," suite (arr Young for strings 1956, from opera, Op.89): No.1 "Country Dance" ....
3.118	No.2 "Burlesco"
3.119	No.3 "Adagio"
3.120	No.4 "Sarabande" (arr Elkin for pf duet 1958)
3.121	No.5 "Bourrée" (arr Elkin for pf duet 1958)

4. CONCERTOS, SOLO INSTR & ORCH

Org & orch:

| 4.1 | Organ Concerto (c1879, frag) .... |

Pf & orch:

| 4.2 | "Scherzo" (c1909, frag) .... |
| 4.3 | Piano Concerto (c1913–32, frags; Poco andante arr for pf & strings) .... Op.90 |

Vn & orch:

| 4.4 | Violin Concerto (c1890, frag: extended incipit for slow movt) .... |
| 4.5 | Violin Concerto in B minor (c1909–10) .... Op.61 |

Vc & orch:

| 4.6 | Cello Concerto in E minor (c1919; arr Tertis as: Va Concerto p1933) .... Op.85 |

Other:

| 4.7 | "Romance" (c1910; bn & orch; arr for vc & pf ?1921) .... Op.62 |
| 4.8 | "Suite" (ca1930–1; ob & orch, inc; see: Soliloquy for ob & pf) .... |

5. STRING QUARTETS

5.1	"Imitation a Quattro Through all the Parts Alternately" (c1876, after Beethoven: Vn Sonata No.8, Op.30/3)
5.2	String Quartet Movement in B-flat major (c1878, inc) ....
5.3	String Quartet Movement in D minor (c1878, inc) ....
5.4	String Quartet in A minor (c1878, frag) ....
5.5	String Quartet in D major (c1878, frag) ....
5.6	String Quartet Movement in A minor (c1879, inc) ....
5.7	String Quartet in G major (c1879, frag) ....
5.8	String Quartet in E minor (c1880, frags) ....
5.9	String Quartet in D minor (ca1888, inc; 3rd movt arr as: Vesper Voluntaries for org, Op.14/3) ....
5.10	String Quartet in D major (c1907, frags) ....
5.11	String Quartet in E minor (c1918) Op.83

6. OTHER CHAMBER MUSIC

5 or more insts:

6.1	"2 Movements" (ca ?1875; ob & str qt): No.1 "Andante Sostenuto," in G major ....
6.2	No.2 "Allegro," in G minor
6.3	"Peckham March" (c1877; 2fl, ob, cl & bn) ....
6.4	"Harmony Music No.1" (Shed No.1) (c1878; 2fl, ob, cl & bn) ....
6.5	"Andante con variazione" (Evesham Andante) (c1878; 2fl, ob, cl & bn) ....
6.6	"Harmony Music No.2" (Shed No.2) (c1878; 2fl, ob, cl & bn) ....
6.7	"Harmony Music No.3" (Shed No.3) (c1878; 2fl, ob, cl & bn) ....
6.8	"Promenade No.1" (c1878; 2fl, ob, cl & bn) ....
6.9	"Promenade No.2, 'Mme Taussaud's' " (c1878; 2fl, ob, cl & bn) ....
6.10	"Promenade No.3" (c1878; 2fl, ob, cl & bn) ....
6.11	"Adagio Cantabile 'Mrs Winslow's Soothing Syrup' " (c1878; 2fl, ob, cl & bn) ....
6.12	"Promenade No.6, 'Hell and Tommy' " (c1878; 2fl, ob, cl & bn) ....
6.13	"Harmony Music No.4, 'The Farm Yard' " (Shed No.4) (c1878; 2fl, ob, cl & bn) ....
6.14	"Promenade No.4, 'Somniferous' " (c1878; 2fl, ob, cl, bn & vn) ....
6.15	"Largo cantabile: Theme and Variations" (c1878; 2fl, ob, cl & bn, inc) ....
6.16	"Promenade No.5, 'Skip' " (c1878; 2fl, ob, cl & bn) ....
6.17	"Promenade No.4a" (c1878; 2fl, ob, cl & bn, frag, replaced by Promenade No.4) ....
6.18	"Menuetto," in B-flat major (c1878; 2fl, ob, cl & bn) ....
6.19	"Andante," in G major (c1878; 2fl, 2ob, 2cl, ?bn & ?strings, inc) ....
6.20	"Harmony Music No.5" (c1879; 2fl, ob, cl & bn): No.1 "Allegro moderato" (The Mission) ....
6.21	No.2 "Minuetto and Trio"
6.22	No.3 "Andante" (Noah's Ark)
6.23	No.4 "Finale"

6.24 "Sarabande" (Largo) (c1879; 2fl, ob, cl & bn, recopied for opera: The Spanish Lady, Op.89) ....
6.25 "Alphonsa Gavotte" (c1879; 2fl, 2ob, cl & bn) ....
6.26 "Gigue" (c1879; 2fl, ob, cl & bn) ....
6.27 "5 Intermezzi" (c1879; 2fl, ob, cl & bn/vc): No.1 in A minor, "Nancy" ....
6.28   No.2 in E minor, "Mrs & Miss Howells"
6.29   No.3 in C major
6.30   No.4 in G major
6.31   No.5 in C major
6.32 "Harmony Music No.6" (c1879; 2fl, ob, cl & bn/vc): No.1 "Allegro molto" (from: Intonation No.2) ....
6.33   No.2 "Andante arioso" (used in: Cantique, Op.3)
6.34   No.3 "Menuet and trio"
6.35   No.4 "Finale"
6.36 "Harmony Music No.7" (c1881; 2fl, ob, cl, vn & vc): No.1 "Allegro" ....
6.37   No.2 "Scherzo and Trio"
6.38 Piano Quintet in A minor (c1918–9) Op.84

4 insts:

6.39   *"Allegro," in B-flat major (c1878; ob, vn, va & vc, inc movt; used in: The Wand of Youth, Op.1a/4)* ....

3 insts:

6.40   *String Trio Movement in C major (c1878, frags; used in: Harmony Music No.4)* ....
6.41 Trio in C major (c1879; fl, ob & ?cl, inc) ....
6.42   *String Trio in G major (c1879, frag)* ....
6.43 "Menuetto and Trio," in G major (c1882; pf trio) ....
6.44   *Fragments (ca ?1882; 2vn & pf)* ....
6.45 Piano Trio in D minor (c1886, inc) ....
6.46 "Andantino" (c1907; vn, mand & gui) ....

Vn & pf:

6.47 "Reminiscences" (c1877) ....
6.48   *Violin Sonata in C major (c1878, frag)* ....
6.49 "Fantasie" (c1878, inc) ....
6.50 "Romance" (c1878; orchd) Op.1
6.51 "Polonaise," in F major (c1879, inc) ....
6.52 "Polonaise," in D minor (c1879, inc) ....
6.53 "Fantasia on Irish Airs" (c1881, inc) ....
6.54 "3 Pieces" (c1884): No.1 "Une Idylle" Op.4
6.55   No.2 "Pastourelle"
6.56   No.3 "Virelai"
6.57 "Allegretto" (on 5 notes: G-E-D-G-E) (c1885, dedication: 'The Misses Gedge, Malvern') ....
6.58 "Gavotte" (Morceau de Salon) (c1885) ....
6.59 Violin Sonata (c1887, inc) Op.9
6.60 "Offertoire—Andante religioso" (c1893 & ?1902/3) Op.11
6.61 "Salut d'amour" (Liebesgrüss), in E major (c1888) Op.12
6.62 "2 Pieces" (c1889): No.1 "Mot d'amour" (Liebesahnung) Op.13
6.63   No.2 "Bizarrerie"
6.64 "2 Pieces" (c1897–9; also w/ orch 1901) No.1 "Chanson de nuit" (c1897) Op.15
6.65   No.2 "Chanson de matin" (r1899 from an earlier ?lost sketch)
6.66 "La capricieuse—morceau de genre" (c1891) Op.17
6.67 "Very Easy Melodious Exercises in the 1st Position" (c1892) Op.22
6.68 Violin Sonata in E minor (c1918) Op.82

Other 2 insts:

6.69 "Andante & Air" (c1881; ob & ?pf; used in opera: The Spanish Lady, Op.89) ....
6.70 "Fugue," in D minor (c1883; vn & ob) ....
6.71 Duet (c1887; trbn & d bass; ed Slatford 1970) ....
6.72 "Soliloquy" (c1930; ob & pf, for project: Suite for oboe & orch; orchd Jacob 1967).......................

Vn solo:

6.73 "Adagio," in C major (c1877) ....
6.74 "Arpeggio Studies" (ca1877): No.1 in E major ....
6.75   No.2 in A major
6.76 "Exercise for the Third Finger" (c1878; recopied in1920) ....
6.77 "Étude caprice" (c1878) ....
6.78   *(Chromatic Study) (ca1878, frags)* ....
6.79 "Study," in A minor (c1879) ....
6.80 "Second Study for Violin" (c1879) ....
6.81 "Caprice," in A minor (ca1879, inc) ....
6.82 "Study," in D minor (c1881) ....

8.6	No.4 "Allegretto piacevole. Intermezzo"
8.7	No.5 "Poco Lento"
8.8	No.6 "Moderato"
8.9	No.7 "Allegretto pensoso"
8.10	No.8 "Poco Allegro"
8.11	. "Coda"
8.12	*"Pastorale" (c1894, frag)* ....
8.13	Organ Sonata No.1 in G major (c1895, r1895) Op.28
8.14	Cadenza for C. H. Lloyd's Organ Concerto in F minor (c1904, placed towards the end of the Finale) ....
8.15	"For Dot's Nuns" (c1906) ....
8.16	*Organ Sonata No.2 in B-flat major (arr Atkins 1933 from: Severn Suite, Op.87)* *Op.87a*

9. CHORAL WORKS

W/ orch:

9.1	"Introduction Anonymous Anthem" (c1874; ch, strings & org) ....
9.2	"Introductory Overture & Song Arrs for Christy Minstrels" (c1878; vv, ch & orch): . "Overture" (inc) ....
9.3	1. "Shall I love thee"
9.4	2. "When the corn is waving"
9.5	3. "Roses underneath"
9.6	4. "Won't you buy my pretty flowers"
9.7	5. "They're a noddin' "
9.8	6. "Just look at him"
9.9	7. "Down by the riverside"
9.10	8. "Oh I'd like to be a devil"
9.11	9. "Medley Chorus"
9.12	10. "Runaway Mousketeers"
9.13	11. "Hushabye baby"
9.14	12. "Evangeline"
9.15	"Domine salvam fac reginam nostram victoriam," motet (c1878; ch, fl, ob, strings & org ad lib) ....
9.16	"Benedictus sit Deus Pater," offertory (c1882; ch, strings & org, inc) ....
9.17	"Spanish Serenade" (Stars of the Summer Night) (c1892, Longfellow; ch & orch) Op.23
9.18	"The Black Knight," cantata (c1888–9, 1892–3, r1898, Uhland transl Longfellow; ch & orch) Op.25
9.19	"The Light of Life" (Lux Christi), short oratorio (c1896, Capel-Cure; S, A, T, B, ch & orch): Op.29
	1. "Meditation"
	2. "Seek Him that maketh the seven stars"
	3. "As Jesus passed by"
	4. "Be not extreme, O Lord"
	5. "Neither hath this man sinned"
	6. "Light out of darkness"
	7. "And when He had thus spoken"
	8. "Doubt not thy Father's care!"
	9. "He went his way therefore"
	10. "As a spirit didst Thou pass before mine eyes"
	11. "They brought him to the Pharisees"
	12. "Thou only hast the words of life"
	13. "But the Jews did not believe"
	14. "Woe to the shepherds of the flock"
	15. "I am the Good Shepherd"
	16. "Light of the World, we know Thy praise"
9.20	"Scenes from the Saga of King Olaf," cantata (c1894–6, Longfellow; S, A, T, B, ch & orch): Op.30
	pubd separately: . "As torrents in summer"
	. "I am the God Thor"
	. "A Little Bird in the Air"
	. "The Wraith of Odin"
9.21	"The Banner of St. George," ballad (c1896–7, Wensley; ch, orch & org) Op.33
9.22	"Te Deum and Benedictus" (c1897; ch, orch & org; also w/ org alone) Op.34
9.23	"Caractacus," cantata (c1898, Acworth; S, T, Bar, B, ch, orch & org): Op.35
	1. "Sword Song": "Leap, leap to light"
	2. "Woodland Interlude"
	3. "Caractacus's Lament": "O my warriors"
	4. "Triumphal March"
9.24	"The Dream of Gerontius," oratorio (c by 1900, Newman; mS, T, B, ch, orch & org): Op.38
	I: 1. "Prelude"
	2. "Jesu Maria, I am near to death"
	3. "Kyrie eleison"
	4. "Rouse thee, my fainting soul"
	5. "Sanctus fortis"
	6. "I can no more"
	7. "Rescue him, O Lord"
	8. "Proficiscere, anima Christiana"
	9. "Go in the name of Angels"
	II: 10. "I went to sleep"

11. "It is a member of that family"
12a. "Low-born clods of brute earth" (Demons' Chorus)
12b. "Dispossessed, aside thrust"
13. "I see not those false spirits"
14. "Praise to the Holiest" (semi-ch)
15a. "But hark! a grand mysterious harmony"
15b. "Praise to the Holiest" (d ch)
16. "Thy judgement now is near"
17. "Jesu! by that shuddering dread"
18. "Take me away"
19. "Lord, Thou hast been our refuge"
20. "Softly and gently" (Angel's farewell)

9.25   "Coronation Ode" (c1901–2, Benson; S, A, T, B, ch, orch & org):... Op.44
1. "Crown the King with Life"
2. "Daughter of Ancient Kings"
3. "Britain, ask of thyself"
4. "Hark, upon the hallow'd air"
5. "Only let the heart be pure"
6. "Peace, gentle peace"
7. "Land of hope and glory" (Finale) (later pubd as a song)

9.26   "The Apostles," oratorio (c1901–3, Elgar from the Bible; S, A, T, 3B, semi-ch, ch, orch & org).......... Op.49
9.27   *"The Last Judgement," oratorio (c1903, 6, 9, 22, 26, 3rd part of trilogy, project)* ....
9.28   "The Kingdom," oratorio (c1905–6, Elgar from the Bible; S, A, T, B, semi-ch, ch, orch & org) Op.51
9.29   "Follow the Colours" (c1907–8, Stretton; unison ch & orch)..
9.30   *"Hymn to the Creator" (c ?1908, unknown; ch & orch, frag)* ....
9.31   "O Hearken Thou" (Intende voci orationis meae), offertory (c1911, Psalm 5; ch, orch & org) Op.64
9.32   "The Music Makers," ode (c by 1912, O'Shaughnessy; A, ch, orch & org) (also see Kodály: An Ode): Op.69
1. "Introduction"
2. "We are the music makers"
3. "With wonderful deathless ditties"
4. "We, in the ages lying"
5. "A breath of our inspiration"
6. "They had no vision amazing"
7. "And therefore today is thrilling"
8. "But we, with our dreaming and singing"
9. "For we afar with the dawning"
10. "Great hail! We cry to the comers"

9.33   "Psalm 29: Give unto the Lord," anthem (c1914, Psalm 29; B, ch, org & orch ad lib) Op.74
9.34   "The Spirit of England" (c1915, Binyon; S/T, ch, orch & org): Op.80
1. "The 4th of August": "Now in thy splendour go before us" (compl1917)
2. "To Women": "Your hearts are lifted up"
3. "For the Fallen": "With proud thanksgiving, a mother for her children"

9.35   "With Proud Thanksgiving" (c1920, Binyon; ch, orch & org, arr from No.3 of: For the Fallen, Op.80) ....
9.36   "Pageant of Empire: Songs" (c1924, Noyes; 1v/ch & orch): 1. "Shakespeare's Kingdom" ....
9.37   2. "The Islands: A Song of New Zealand"
9.38   3. "The Blue Mountains: A Song of Australia"
9.39   4. "The Heart of Canada"
9.40   5. "Sailing Westward"
9.41   6. "Merchant Adventurers"
9.42   7. "The Immortal Legions"
9.43   8. "A Song of Union" (ch)
9.44   "Queen Alexandra Memorial Ode": "So many true princesses who have gone" (c1932, Masefield; ch
       & milit band, for the unveiling of the memorial) ....

Sacred works w/ out orch:

9.45   "Credo on Themes from Beethoven Symphonies 5, 7, & 9" (c1873; S, A, T, B, ch & org)............................
9.46   "Salve Regina" (c1876; ch & org) ....
9.47   "Tantum Ergo" (c1876; ch & org) ....
9.48   "Credo," in E minor (c1877; ch & org) ....
9.49   Hymn Tune: "Now with the fast-departing light," in G major (c1878; No.89 in Leicester's collection) ....
9.50   *"Credo," in G major (c1878, frag)* ....
9.51   "Hear Thy children" (Drakes Broughton), hymn tune (c1878, Stanfield; used in No.1 of: Nursery Suite) ......
9.52   "Kyrie," in C minor (c1878; ch & org, inc) ....
9.53   "Magnificat," in G major (c1878, inc) ....
9.54   Hymn Tune: "Praise ye the Lord," in C major (c1878; No.63 in Leicester's collection) ....
9.55   "Brother, for thee He died," Easter anthem (c1878; 1v & pf, inc) ....
9.56   "Gloria," in C major (c1879; ch & ?org, inc) ....
9.57   "Kyrie," in D minor (ca1879; ch & org, inc) ....
9.58   "O Salutaris Hostia," in F major (ca1880; ch & org) ....
9.59   "O Salutaris Hostia," in E-flat major (ca1880; ch & org) ....
9.60   "Gloria" (c1880; S, A, T, B, ch & org, arr of Allegro from Mozart: Violin Sonata No.36 in F major, K547)......
9.61   "Hymn Tune": "O Salutaris Hostia," in E-flat major (ca1880, inc) ....
9.62   "Gloria," in D major (c1881; ch & org, inc) ....
9.63   "O Salutaris Hostia" (c1882; 1v & org) ....

9.64	"Stabat Mater" (c1886; ch)	
9.65	"4 Litanies of the Blessed Virgin Mary" (c1886; ch)	
9.66	"27 Litany Chants" (c1886; ch, No.8 = arr of Smith's hymn tune: Innocents)	
9.67	"3 Motets" (ca1887, r1907; ch & org): 1. "Ave verum" (r1902 w/ words: Jesu, word of God)	Op.2
9.68	2. "Ave Maria gratia plena" (r1907 w/ Eng words: Jesu, Lord of Life and Glory)	
9.69	3. "Ave maris stella" (r1907 w/ Eng words: Jesu, Meek and Lowly)	
9.70	"Laudate Dominum," chant in D-flat major (c1888; Psalm 117; unison ch & org)	
9.71	"Ecce sacerdos magnus," gradual (c1888; ch & org/orch)	
9.72	"O Mightiest of the Mighty," hymn (c1901, Childs Clarke; ch & org)	
9.73	"2 Single Chants for 'Venite' " (c1907; ch): 1. "Chant," in D major (Psalm 95)	
9.74	2. "Chant," in G major (Psalm 95)	
9.75	"2 Double Chants" (c1907; ch): 1. "Chant," in D major (Psalm 68)	
9.76	2. "Chant," in D major (Psalm 75)	
9.77	"A Christmas Greeting," carol (c1907, C. A. Elgar; T ad lib, B ad lib, ch, 2vn & pf)........................	Op.52
9.78	"Lo! Christ the Lord is Born," carol (c1908, Wensley; ch, music from: Grete Malverne)	
9.79	*"Choral Suite" (c1909, Landor; ch, project, only No.3 pubd): 1. "Introduction" ....*	
9.80	*2. "In a Vineyard"*	
9.81	*3. "The Angelus," partsong (from Tuscan dialect) ....*	Op.56/1
9.82	*4. "Dance"*	
9.83	*5. "Vintage"*	
9.84	*6. "Envoi"*	
9.85	"They are at rest," anthem (c1909, Newman; ch)	
9.86	"Psalm 48: Great is the Lord," anthem (c1910–2; ch & org; orchd1913)	Op.67
9.87	"Fear not O Land," harvest anthem (c1914, Book of Joel; ch & org)	
9.88	"I sing the birth," carol (c1928, Jonson; ch)	
9.89	"Good Morrow" (A simple Carol for His Majesty's happy recovery) (c1929, Gascoigne; ch)	

Secular works w/ out orch:

9.90	"3 Partsongs" (c1890; ch): 1. "O happy eyes, for you will see" (C. A. Elgar).......................	Op.18
9.91	2. "Love": "Like the rosy northern glow" (Macquarie, r1907)	
9.92	3. "Romance" (Lang's Romance): "My love dwelt in a northern land" (Lang)	
9.93	"2 Partsongs" (c ?1894, C. A. Elgar; ch, 2vn & pf; orchd1903): 1. "The Snow": "O snow, which sinks"	Op.26
9.94	2. "Fly, singing bird, fly"	
9.95	"Scenes from the Bavarian Highlands" (c1895; ch & pf; also see Op.27b): 1. "The Dance"	Op.27a
9.96	2. "False Love"	
9.97	3. "Lullaby"	
9.98	4. "Aspiration"	
9.99	5. "On the Alm"	
9.100	6. "The Marksman"	
9.101	"Grete Malverne on a rocke" (c1897; ch; music used in carol: Lo! Christ the Lord is born of 1908)	
9.102	"To her, beneath whose steadfast star" (c1899, Myers; ch)	
9.103	"From the Greek Anthology" (c1902; m ch): 1. "Yea, cast me from the heights" (transl Strettell)	Op.45
9.104	2. "Whether I find thee bright with fair" (transl Lang)	
9.105	3. "After many a dusty mile" (transl Goose)	
9.106	4. "It's oh! to be a wild wind" (transl Hardinge)	
9.107	5. "Feasting, I watch" (transl Garnett)	
9.108	"Weary Wind of the West" (c1902, from Brown's Old John and other Poems; ch)	
9.109	*"From the Greek Anthology" (c ?1902, inc): 1. "O Little Love" (transl Strettell, project) ....*	
9.110	*2. "Sea Dirge" (transl Lang, project)*	
9.111	*3. "Didyme's eyes" (transl Strettell, project)*	
9.112	*4. "Upon a small babe" (transl Rogers, project)*	
9.113	*5. "With courage seek the kingdom of the dead" (transl Merivale, project)*	
9.114	*6. "Eros, I pray thee" (transl Garnett)*	
9.115	*"From the Greek Anthology" (c ?1902, inc sketches): 1. "A pine, by tempests bruised" (transl Strettell) ....*	
9.116	*2. "A witching smile" (transl Garnett)*	
9.117	*3. "To Hermes" (transl Garnett)*	
9.118	*4. "Peace, wooded crags" (transl Garnett)*	
9.119	*5. "Now with the white iris blossoms" (transl Strettell)*	
9.120	*6. "Though I may know myself mortal" (transl Strettell)*	
9.121	"Evening scene": "The aspen leaflets scarcely stir," partsong (c1905, Patmore; ch)	
9.122	"April," partsong (c ?1905, Watson; 2S, 2vn & pf, inc)	
9.123	"How Calmly the Evening," partsong (c1907, from Lynch's The Rivulet; ch)	
9.124	"4 Part-Songs" (c1907; ch): 1. "There is sweet music here" (from Tennyson's The Lotos-Eaters)	Op.53
9.125	2. "Deep in my soul that tender secret dwells" (from Byron's The Corsair)	
9.126	3. "O Wild West Wind! Make me thy lyre, even as the forest is" (from Shelley's Ode)	
9.127	4. "Owls" (An Epitaph): "What is that? Nothing" (Elgar)	
9.128	"The Reveille": "Let me of my heart take counsel," partsong (c1907, Harte; m ch).............................	Op.54
9.129	"Go Song of Mine," partsong (c1909, Cavalcanti transl Rossetti; d ch).....................................	Op.57
9.130	*"Mild is the parting year," partsong (ca ?1909, Landor, frags) ....*	
9.131	*"Ballata of True and False Singing," partsong (ca ?1909, 13th cent Italian transl Rossetti, frags) ....*	
9.132	*"Night! Night!," partsong (ca ?1909, unknown, frag) ....*	
9.133	*"Darkest Music," partsong (ca ?1909, unknown, frag) ....*	
9.134	*"No star goes down," partsong (ca ?1909–14, from Massey's Long Expected, frag) ....*	

9.135   "2 Songs" (c1914, Vaughan; ch): 1. "The Shower": "(Cloud,) if, as thou dost melt" Op.71
9.136   2. "The Fountain": "The unthrift sun shot vital gold"
9.137   "Death on the Hills": "Why o'er the darkening hill-slopes" (c1914, Maikov transl Newmarch; ch) Op.72
9.138   "2 Songs" (c1914; ch): 1. "Love's Tempest": "Silent lay the sapphire ocean" (Maikov transl
                Newmarch) Op.73
9.139   2. "Serenade": "Dreams all too brief, dreams without grief" (Minsky transl Newmarch)
9.140   "The Birthright" (c ?1914, Stocks; unison boys' ch, bugles & drums) ....
9.141   "The Windlass Song": "Heave at the windlass!" (c1914, Allingham) ....
9.142   "Inside the Bar" (c1917, Parker; 4Bar; added as 5. to: The Fringes of the Fleet of 1917)...................
9.143   "Big Steamers": "Send out your big warships to watch your big waters" (c1918, Kipling; unison ch & pf) .....
9.144   "The Ballad of Brave Hector," hunting song (c1924, Anderson; 1v, ch & pf, inc) ....
9.145   "The Worcerstershire Squire," song (c1924, Anderson; 1v, ch & pf, inc) ....
9.146   "The Wanderer": "I wander through the woodlands," partsong (c1923, after: Wit & Drollery of 1661; ch) .....
9.147   "Zut! Zut! Zut!" (c1923, Elgar; ch) ....
9.148   "The Song of the Bull" (In May Week), revue song (c1924; m vv & pf) ....
9.149   "The Herald": "A grim old king whose blood leapt madly," partsong (c1925, Smith; m ch) ....
9.150   "The Prince of Sleep": "Dark in his pools clear visions lurk," partsong (c1925, de la Mare; ch)...........
9.151   "The Rapid Stream," unison / 2-part song (c1932, MacKay; ch & pf)...
9.152   "The Woodland Stream," unison / 2-part song (c1932, MacKay; ch & pf) ....
9.153   "When Swallows Fly," unison / 2-part song (c1931, MacKay; ch & pf)...

10. VOICE & ORCHESTRA

10.1   "Sea Pictures," cycle (c1897–9; A, orch & org): 1. "Sea Slumber-Song": "Sea-birds are
                asleep" (Noel) Op.37
10.2   2. "In Haven" (Capri): "Closely let me hold thy hand" (C. A. Elgar; orig w/ pf: Love alone will stay)
10.3   3. "A Sabbath Morning at Sea": "The ship went on with solemn face" (Browning)
10.4   4. "Where Corals Lie": "And see the land where corals lie" (Garnett)
10.5   5. "The Swimmer": "With short, sharp, violent lights made vivid" (Gordon)
10.6   "Callicles" I, scena (c1905, 13, 17, 26, Arnold: Empedocles on Etna, inc song for bass) ....
10.7   "Ozymandias" I, scena (c1905, Shelley; B, inc) ....
10.8   Song Cycle (c1909–10, Parker; Embers): *1. "Proem" (inc)* Op.59
10.9   2. "The Waking" (inc)
10.10   3. "Oh, soft was the song in my soul"
10.11   4. "There is an Orchard" (inc)
10.12   5. "Was it some golden star hot with romance?"
10.13   6. "Twilight": "Adieu!—and the sun goes a-wearily down"
10.14   "The Chariots of the Lord": "Where hands are weak" (c1914, trad transl Brownlie)...........................
10.15   "Soldier's Song: The Roll Call" (A War Song) (c1914, Begbie; 1v & orch/pf, withdrawn) ....
10.16   "Carillon": "Sing, Belgians" (c1914, Cammaerts; reciter, orch & org; text r by Binyon 1942) Op.75
                . Revised Version: "Over all this home-land of our fathers" (Binyon)
10.17   "Une voix dans le désert" (c1915, Cammaerts; reciter, S & orch): Op.77
10.18   . "Quand nos bourgeons se rouvriront," song (S)
10.19   "Le drapeau belge" (c1916, Cammaerts transl Curzon; reciter & orch).. Op.79
10.20   "Fight for Right": "When thou hearest the fool rejoicing" (c1916, Morris; 1v, ch & pf) ....
10.21   "The Fringes of the Fleet" (c1917, Kipling; Bar, 3Bar & orch): 1. "The Lowestoft Boat": "In Lowestoft
                a boat was laid" ....
10.22   2. "Fate's Discourtesy": "Then welcome Fate's discourtesy"
10.23   3. "Submarines": "The ships destroy us above"
10.24   4. "The Sweepers": "Boom after boom"
10.25   "Ozymandias" II (c ?1917, Shelley; mS & orch, inc) ....
10.26   "Humorous Sketch 'Kindly do not smoke in the Hall on Staircase' op.1001" (c1919; Bar & orch)................
10.27   "Tarantella": "Do you remember an Inn" (c1933, Belloc; Bar & orch, inc) ....

11. SONGS (w/ pf)

11.1   "The Language of Flowers": "In Eastern lands they talk in flow'rs" (c1872, Percival) ....
11.2   "The Self Banished" (ca1875, Waller) ....
11.3   "Archer's Song" (arr1878; 1v, pf & vn) ....
11.4   "Rondeau—Temple Bar": "If she loves me" (c1878, inc) ....
11.5   "A Soldier's Song" (c ?1884, Hayward) ....
11.6   "A Phylactery" (ca1885, Hay, used in opera: The Spanish Lady, Op.89)..
11.7   "Is she not passing fair?" (c1886, d'Orléans transl Costello) ....
11.8   "Queen Mary's Song": "Hapless doom of woman" (c1887, r1889, from Tennyson's Queen Mary)...............
11.9   "As I laye a-thinkynge" (c1887, Ingoldsby) ....
11.10   "The Wind at Dawn": "And the wind went out to meet with the sun" (c1888, Roberts; orchd1912)...............
11.11   "3 Songs": 1. "The Shepherd's Song" (c1892, from Pain's In a Canadian Canoe) Op.16
11.12   2. "Through the Long Days" (c1885, Hay)
11.13   3. "Rondel": "Love, what wilt thou with this heart of mine" (c1894, Froissart of 14th cent
                transl Longfellow)
11.14   "Ophelia's Song" (ca1892, Shakespeare) (also see Brahms WoO post 22, Castelnuovo-Tedesco
                Op.24/VII/1–2, Shostakovich Op.127/1 & R. Strauss Op.67) Op.21/1
11.15   "Like to the Damask Rose" (ca1887–?92, Wastell) ....

11.16	"The Poet's Life" (ca1887–?92, from Burroughs' The Common Chord) ....
11.17	"A Song of Autumn" (ca1887–?92, Gordon) ....
11.18	"A Spear, a Sword" (c1892, C. A. Elgar) ....
11.19	"The Millwheel Songs" (c1892, C. A. Elgar): 1. "Winter" ....
11.20	2. "May" (a rhapsody) ....
11.21	"Muleteer's Serenade" (c1894) ....
11.22	"The Wave" (c1894) ....
11.23	"2 Songs" (c1895): 1. "After": "A little time for laughter" (from Marston's Song-tide) Op.31
11.24	2. "A Song of Flight" (Arabian Serenade): "While we slumber and sleep" (Rossetti)
11.25	"Roundel": "The little eyes that never knew light" (p1897, Swinburne) ....
11.26	"Love alone will stay" (Lute Song) (c1897, C. A. Elgar; r as No.2 of: Sea Pictures, Op.37) ....
11.27	"The Pipes of Pan": "When the woods are gay in the time of June" (c1899, Ross; orchd1902) ....
11.28	"Dry those Fair, those Crystal Eyes" (c1899, from King's Poemes, Elegies, Paradoxes, And Sonets)..........
11.29	"Always and Everywhere" (c1901, Krasiński transl from Polish by Fortey) ....
11.30	"Come, gentle night" (c1901, Bingham: Lyrics without music) ....
11.31	"Land of Hope and Glory" (c1902, Benson, arr from: March, Op.39/1 & Coronation Ode, Op.44) ....
11.32	"2 Songs" (c1902, Benson): 1. "In the Dawn": "But to have loved her" Op.41
11.33	2. "Speak Music": "Song, take thy parable"
11.34	"Speak, my heart" (c1903, Benson) ....
11.35	"In Moonlight" (c1904, Shelley, arr of Canto popolare from overture: In the South, Op.50) ....
11.36	*"The Soul" (c ?1907, Davies, frag of song or ode) ....*
11.37	*"Nirvana" (c ?1907, Maquarie, frag) ....*
11.38	"I with the young wide Empire in my veins" (c ?1907, Maquarie: The Dance of Olives, inc) ....
11.39	*"In Memoriam: Silence and Sorrow" (c1908, frag)*
11.40	"Pleading": "Will you come homeward from the hills of Dreamland" (p1908, Salmon; orchd1908) ... Op.48/1
11.41	*"The Haven of Desire" (c ?1908, Salmon, frag) ....*
11.42	"Patriotic Song" (c1909, Elgar, inc)
11.43	"A Child Asleep": "Vision unto vision calleth" (c1909, from Browning's Albion Poets) ....
11.44	"2 Songs" (c1909–10, Elgar's paraphrases of East European folksongs; orchd1912): 1. "The Torch" Op.60
11.45	2. "The River": "River, mother of fighting men"
11.46	*3. "The Shrine" (project)*
11.47	*4. "The Bee" (project)*
11.48	*"Infant joy" (ca1909, ?Blake: Songs of Innocence, frag) ....*
11.49	*"The White Island" (ca1909, Herrick, frag) ....*
11.50	"The King's Way" (c1909, C. A. Elgar) ....
11.51	"Arabian Serenade" (c1914, from Lawrence's Songs of Childhood & Other Songs).........................
11.52	"The Brook," song for children (c1914, Soule) ....
11.53	"The Merry-go-round," song for children (c1914, Cox) ....
11.54	"Liebesweh" (ca1918, Wilcox) ....
11.55	"2 Songs" (ca ?1923, Drinkwater, inc): 1. "Moonlit Apples" ....
11.56	2. "Birthright"
11.57	"It isnae me" (c1930, Holmes) ....
11.58	"I gave my heart unto my love" (c1930, Elgar, inc) ....
11.59	*"Modest and Fair" (ed Young 1955, from opera: The Spanish Lady, Op.89) ....*
11.60	*"Still to be Neat" (ed Young 1955, from opera: The Spanish Lady, Op.89) ....*

12. MISC WORKS

12.1	" 'BACH' Motif" (c1866) ....
12.2	"Humoreske" (A Tune from Broadheath) (ca1867)..
12.3	*"Sketches for Original Compositions" (ca1875–6 & later): No.1 (Minuet) in G minor ....*
12.4	*No.2 "Menuetto Andante," in G major*
12.5	*No.3 "Overture," in A minor*
12.6	*No.4 "Trio," in A minor*
12.7	*No.5 "Andante," in A minor*
12.8	*No.6 "Trio," in G major*
12.9	*No.7 "Benedictus," in B-flat major*
12.10	*No.8 (Minuet frag?)*
12.11	*No.9 (Quadrille melody in D)*
12.12	*No.10 (Accompaniment in E-flat for Quadrille?)*
12.13	*No.11 (Allegro in D minor)*
12.14	*No.12 "Là Suzanne" (cornet solo)*
12.15	*No.13 "Psalm 83" (Vulgate), in A major (S solo)*
12.16	*No.14 "Eight Quadrille themes"*
12.17	*No.15 "Adagio," in E-flat major (Shed 7) (harmonised melody)*
12.18	*"Fugue," in A minor (c1878, frag) ....*
12.19	*"Fugue," in C major (c1878, frag) ....*
12.20	"Quadrille Melody," in D major (c1879, inc) ....
12.21	"Allegro Moderato," in A minor (ca ?1881) ....
12.22	"Fugue," in G major (c1882, inc) ....
12.23	"Fugue," in C major (c1887, inc)..
12.24	*"2 Fugal Sketches" (c1902, inc)*
12.25	"Loughborough Memorial Chime" (c1923; carillon; arr for org) ....
12.26	"Clock Chimes for Eaton Socon," peal of 8 bells in F major (c1931) ....

13. ARRANGEMENTS OF WORKS OF OTHERS

For orch:

13.1	Handel: 3rd movt of Overture to opera: Ariodante, HWV33 (arr1878; 2ob & strings) ....
13.2	Mozart: "Menuetto," from Symphony No.39 in E-flat major, K543 (arr1878 in D major) ....
13.3	Corelli: "Andante Largo," from Concerto Grosso, Op.6/10 (arr1878) ....
13.4	Haydn: Symphony No.102 in B-flat major, Hobl/102 (arr1879, parts for cls & hns) ....
13.5	Carafa: "Ognor più tenero," from: Masaniello (orchd1879; w/ fl solo) ....
13.6	Wagner: "Good Friday Music," from opera: Parcifal, WWV111 (arr1894; 3vn, vc, 2pf & org) ....
13.7	Mozart: "Epistle Sonatas," for 2vn, bass & org (added va parts 1901): No.15 in C major, K317c (K328) ......
13.8	No.17 in C major, K336d (K336)
13.9	Bach, J. S.: "Coda," of the Toccata in F major, BWV540 (orchd1908)...................................
13.10	Bach, J. S.: 2 Chorales from St Matthew Passion, BWV244 (arr1911; brass): No.1 "O Mensch"..............
13.11	No.2 "O Haupt voll Blut und Wunden"
13.12	Bach, J. S.: "Fantasia & Fugue," in C minor, BWV537 (transcr1921–2) Op.86
13.13	Handel: "Overture," in D minor, from: Chandos Anthem No.2, HWV247 (arr1923)......................
13.14	Chopin: "Funeral March," from Piano Sonata in B-flat minor, Op.35, B128 (arr1932)....................

For str qt:

13.15	*"Fugues etc and Original Sketches" (ca1875–6 & later, sketches): No.1 "Fugue 1," in C major (attr to Handel) ....*
13.16	*No.2 "Fugue 2," in C major (attr to Handel)*
13.17	*No.3 "Fugue 5," in D major (J. S. Bach: Das Wohltemperierte Klavier II/5)*
13.18	*No.4 "Fugue 6," in C major (attr to Handel)*
13.19	*No.5 "2nd Part of Overture" (Handel: Samson)*
13.20	*No.6 "Introduction," in D major (Rinck: Organ School Book III/5)*
13.21	*No.7 "Fugue," in G major (Rinck)*
13.22	*No.8 "Fugue in C major (Rinck: Organ School Book III/5)*
13.23	*No.9 "Prelude," in G major (Medelssohn, Op.37/2)*
13.24	*No.10 "Prelude," in C major (Rinck: Organ School Book III/8)*
13.25	*No.11 "Overture" (Handel: Messiah)*
13.26	*No.12 "Kraftig und feurig" (Mendelssohn: Charakteristische Stücke, Op.7/3)*
13.27	*No.13 "March," in D major (Handel: Hercules)*
13.28	*No.14 "Fugue," in C major (J. S. Bach: Das Wohltemperierte Klavier I/1)*
13.29	*No.15 "Fugue," in F major (Handel: Keyboard Suite No.2/ii, HWV427)*
13.30	*No.16 "Overture," in D minor (Handel: Chandos Anthem No.2 & Conc Grosso, Op.3/5)*
13.31	*No.17 "Larghetto," in G major (Geissler: Tonstücke für die Orgel, Op.97, Vol.2/12)*
13.32	*No.18 "Introduction," in D major (Geissler: Tonstücke für die Orgel, Op.97, Vol.2/11)*
13.33	*No.19 "Allegro moderato," in D major (attr to Handel)*
13.34	*No.20 "March" (Handel: Occasional Oratorio)*
13.35	*No.21 "Fugue," in C major (Geissler: Tonstücke für die Orgel, Op.97, Vol.2/2)*
13.36	*No.22 "Introduction & Fugue," in E minor (Geissler: Tonstücke für die Orgel, Op.97, Vol.1/7)*
13.37	*No.23 "Introduction & Fugue," in A major (Geissler: Tonstücke für die Orgel, Op.97, Vol.2/13)*
13.38	*No.23 "Larghetto," in A major (Geissler: Tonstücke für die Orgel, Op.97, Vol.1/2)*
13.39	*No.24 "Introduction & Fugue" (Hesse's Organ Book, ed Steggall, Vol.1, p62)*
13.40	*No.25 "Allegro non troppo," in G major (Mendelssohn: 6 Pieces, Op.72/1)*
13.41	*No.26 "Fugue," in G minor (J. S. Bach: Das Wohltemperierte Klavier I/16)*
13.42	*No.27 "Minuet," in B-flat major (Beethoven, deleted)*
13.43	*No.28 "Minuet," in B-flat major (Mozart: Piano Sonata No.4 in E-flat major, K189g /K282)*
13.44	*No.29 "Minuet" (Beethoven: Septet in E-flat major, Op.20)*
13.45	*No.30 "Scherzo," in G minor (Spohr: Str Qt, Op.4/2)*
13.46	*No.31 "Imitation a Quattro" (through all the parts alternately)*
13.47	*No.32 "Sketches for Quadrilles"*

For chamber ens:

13.48	Beethoven: Finale of Violin Sonata No.4 in A minor, Op.23 (arr1878; 2fl, ob, cl & bn) ....
13.49	Leybach: "Solemn March" (arr1878; 2fl, ob, cl & bn) ....
13.50	*Spohr: "Adagio," from Duet Op.39/1 (arr1878; 2vn & vc, frag) ....*
13.51	"Adeste Fideles" (arr1878; fl, ob, cl & bn, from: Hymns Ancient and Modern, 2nd edition of 1875) ....
13.52	Blackbourne (alias Berard): "Berceuse—petite reine," for pf (arr1886; vn & pf)........................

For fl & str qt:

13.53	"Christmas Pieces" (ca ?1875), Flute: No.1 "Allegro non troppo," in G major (Mendelssohn, Op.72/1) ....
13.54	No.2 "March," in D major (from Handel: Scipione, HWV20)
13.55	No.3 "Menuet," in A major (from Boccherini: Str Qnt in E major, G275)
13.56	No.4 "Adeste Fideles" (trad)
13.57	No.5 "Valse," in A minor (Chopin: Waltz No.3 in A minor, Op.34/2, B64)
13.58	Vn I (also parts as in Flute Book): No.6 "Adagio" (from Beethoven: Symphony No.9 in D minor, Op.125)
13.59	Vn II (also parts as in Flute Book): No.7 "Adagio" (from Beethoven: Symphony No.9 in D minor, Op.125)
13.60	No.8 "Allegretto" (from 1st movt of Mendelssohn: Sym No.2 in B-flat major, 'Lobegesang,' Op.52)
13.61	No.9 "Che farò senza Euridice" (from Gluck's opera: Orpheus, Wq30)
13.62	Va (all parts as in Vn II Book)

13.63	Vc (inc): No.10 "Allegro non troppo," in G major (from Mendelssohn: 6 Pieces, Op.72/1)
13.64	No.11 "March," in D major (from Handel: Scipione, HWV20)
13.65	No.12 "Menuet," in A major (from Boccherini: String Quintet in E major, G275)
13.66	No.13 "Adeste Fideles" (trad)
13.67	No.14 "Adagio" (from Beethoven: Symphony No.9 in D minor, Op.125)

For pf:

13.68	"National Anthem" (arr1879 in D major) ....
13.69	Schumann: "Scherzo," from: Overture, Scherzo & Finale, Op.52 (arr1883) ....
13.70	Wagner: "Entry of the Minstrels," from Act II of Tannhaüser, WWV70 (arr1883) ....

For org:

13.71	Handel: "Dead March," from oratorio: Saul, HWV53 (arr1878; cornet & org, inc) ....
13.72	Bach, J. S.: "Toccata," in D minor (arr Esser for org, add parts c by Elgar w/ orig end restored) ....

For ch & orch:

13.73	"The Holly and the Ivy" (arr1898; ch, semi-ch, orch & org) ....
13.74	Brewer: "Emmaus," cantata (arr1901; a biblical scene for S, T, ch & strings) ....
13.75	"God Save the King" (arr1902; S, ch, milit band, orch & org) ....
13.76	Bach, J. S.: "St Matthew Passion," BWV244 (performing edition 1911, collab Atkins) ....
13.77	Parry: "Jerusalem," hymn tune (orch acc added 1922) ....
13.78	Battishill: "O Lord look down from Heaven," motet (orch acc added 1923) ....
13.79	Wesley: "Let us lift up our Heart," motet (orch acc added 1923) ....
13.80	Atkins: "Abide with me," anthem (orchd1923) ....
13.81	Purcell: "Jehova, quam multi sunt hostes mei," motet (orch acc added 1929) ....

For 1v w/ acc:

13.82	Weber: "Oh, 'tis a glorious sight," recit & aria from Act II/5 of opera: Oberon, J306 (arr1878; T & strings)....
13.83	White: "Absent yet Present," song (arr1885; w/ vc obbl) ....
13.84	Dolby: "Out on the Rocks," song (arr1885; w/ vc obbl) ....
13.85	Buck: "Melody" (arr1885; w/ pf acc) ....
13.86	Tosti: "For Ever & for Ever," song (arr1885; w/ vc obbl) ....
13.87	"Clapham Town End," Yorkshire folksong (arr1885; 1v & pf) ....
13.88	Park: "Songs" (ca ?1920, revised edition): 1. "With the sunshine and the swallows" (Paton) ....
13.89	2. "The Saul's Songs" (Park)
13.90	3. "Tears, idle tears" (Tennyson)
13.91	4. "Her hair was dark as the raven's plume" (Park)
13.92	5. "The Miller's Daughter" (Tennyson)
13.93	6. "The Crusader's Return" (Scott)
13.94	7. "Still to thee and only thee" (Park)
13.95	8. "Jesu! bless our slender boat" (Wordsworth)
13.96	9. "I arise from dreams of thee" (Shelley)
13.97	10. "Midnight is brooding" (Park)
13.98	11. "I'll meet the fair lassie" (Park)
13.99	12. "Oh! Life and Youth" (Park)
13.100	13. "More fair than any mortal thing" (Park)
13.101	14. "Bright through scenes of beauty gliding" (Park)
13.102	15. "Sailor's song" (Park)
13.103	16. "Farewell to Northmaven" (Scott)
13.104	17. "Bishop Heber's prayer for his country" (Heber)
13.105	18. "In the grey dawn of the morning" (Park)
13.106	19. "Return, sweet sister Ellen" (Park)
13.107	20. "Under the greenwood tree" (Shakespeare)

* * * * *

1. STAGE WORKS

Opers:

1.1	*"El conde de Villamediana," puppet opera (c ?1891, Falla after Duque de Rivas, lost)*	*G1*
1.2	"La Juana y la Petra, o La Casa de Tócame Roque," 1 act zarzuela (c1900, Cruz)	G17
1.3	"Los Amores de la Inés," 1 act zarzuela (sainete lírico) (c1902, Dugi)	G26
1.4	*"Limosna de Amor," zarzuela (c1901–2, Veyán, lost)*	*G27*
1.5	*"El Cornetín de Órdenes," 3 act zarzuela (c1903, collab Vives, lost)*	*G31*
1.6	*"La Cruz de Malta," zarzuela (c1903, collab Vives, lost)*	*G32*
1.7	*"Prisionero de guerra," zarzuela (c1903–4, collab Vives, lost)*	*G33*
1.8	"La Vida breve" (The Short Life), lyric drama (Shaw; 2 vers):	
	. Version 1 (c1904–5, 1 act)	
	. Version 2 (c1913, French adapt by Milliet, 2 acts)	G39
1.9	*"La muerte de Carmen," 1 act opera (c1913–14, after Mérimée, project)*	
1.10	*"Barber of Seville" (c1913–4, after Beaumarchais: Le Mariage & Barbier de Séville, project)*	
1.11	"Fuego Fátuo" (Firefly), 3 acts (c1918, Martínez Sierra, on themes of Chopin, unfin):	G52

  quoted music of Chopin (orchd): I: 1a. Waltz No.8 in A-flat major, Op.64/3, B164/3
  1b. Scherzo No.2 in B-flat min / D-flat major, Op.31, B111
  2. Scherzo No.4 in E major, Op.54, B148 (central section)
  3. Mazurka No.15 in C major, Op.24/2, B89/2
  4. "Bolero," in C maj / A major, Op.19, B81
  5. Mazurka No.25 in B minor, Op.33/4, B115/4
  6. Scherzo No.2 in B-flat min / D-flat major, Op.31, B111
  II: 1. "Berceuse" (c by Falla, in the style of Chopin)
  2. Etude No.3 in E major, "Tristesse," Op.10/3, B74
  3. Mazurka No.8 in A-flat major, Op.7/4, B61/4
  4. Ballade No.1 in G minor, Op.23, B66
  5a. Waltz No.5 in A-flat major, "Grande valse," Op.42, B131
  5b. Mazurka No.51 in A minor, Op.posth, B140
  6. Etude No.12 in C minor, "Revolutionary," Op.10/12, B67
  III: 1. "Tarantelle," in A-flat major, Op.43, B139
  2. "Mazurka" (from Liszt's transcr of No.6 of: Songs, Op.74)
  3. "Berceuse," in D-flat major (Variantes), Op.57, B154
  4. Ballade No.4 in F minor, Op.52, B146
  5. "Barcarolle," in F-sharp major, Op.60, B158

1.12	*"La Gloria de don Ramiro" (ca1918–9, project, lost)*	
1.13	*"Cuadro flamenco," spectacle of song & dance (c1921, collab Lafita, arrs)*	
1.14	"El Retablo de Maese Pedro" (Master Peter's Puppet Show) (c1919–23, Falla from Cervantes)	G65
1.15	*"Lola la comédienne" (c1923, Lorca, project)*	
1.16	"Atlántida," scenic cantata (c1927–46, Falla after Verdaguer; compl Halffter 1961, r1976)	G102

Ballets:

1.17	"El Amor brujo" (Love the Magician), 1 act (Martínez Sierra; mS & orch; 3 vers):	
	. Version 1 (Gitaneria en un acto y dos cuadros) (c1915)	G44
	. Version 2 (c1916–7)	G68
	. *Version definitive (reconstr Gallego 1924)*	
1.18	"El Corregidor y la molinera," 2 scene pantomime (c1916–7, Martínez Sierra after Alarcón)	G50
1.19	"El Sombrero de Tres Picos" (The Three-Cornered Hat), 2 parts (c1917–9, expanded from: El Corregidor y la molinera, G50)	G53

Incid music:

1.20	"Soleá" (c1914, Martínez Sierra: La Pasión; 1v & gui)	G41
1.21	*"Amanecer" (c1915, Martínez Sierra, lost)*	*G43*
1.22	*"Otelo" (c1915, p1925, Shakespeare transl into Castilian by Martínez Sierra, lost)*	*G46*
1.23	*"2 Moorish Songs," interlude for: El Corazón ciego (c1919, Martínez Sierra, lost)*	*G54*
1.24	"Españoleta," for collab: La Niña que riega la albahaca (c1922, Lorca, mostly lost):	G63
	"La Niña que riega la albahaca": *1. "Serenata de la muñeca" (c by Debussy; pf)*	
	2. "La Vega de Granada" (c by Albéniz; pf, B46)	
	3. "Berceuse" (c by Ravel; vn & pf)	
	4. "Españoleta, Paso y medio" (anon 17th cent transcr Pedrell, arr Falla)	
1.25	"Misterio de los Reyes Magos" (c1922; hpd, vn, cl & lute, arr of 13th cent Spanish music):	G64
	1. "Cantiga 'Ave y Eva' " (Pedrell: Cancionero I/147)	
	2. Cantiga 65: "A creer debemos" (Pedrell: Cancionero III/5)	
	3. "Dos invitatorios del Llivre Vermell" (Pedrell: Cancionero III/8 & 8bis):	
	. "Laudemus Virginem"	
	. "Splendens ceptigera"	
	4. "Cançó de Nadal" (Antiguo villancico de los tres Reyes de Oriente)	
1.26	"El Gran Teatro del Mundo" (c1927, Barca; mS, ch, 2gui, winds & timp, part lost)	G73
1.27	"La Vuelta de Egipto" (The Flight from Egypt) (c1935, Calderón, inc):	G81
	extant: . "Fanfare"	
	. " 'Dresden' Amen"	
	. songs adapted from Pedrell's Cancionero	

1a. SELECTIONS FROM STAGE WORKS

1a.2   "La Juana y la Petra, o La Casa de Tócame Roque," zarzuela: G17
         1. "Coro inicial en la escena 1.a": "Para majas de rumbo"
         2. "Concertante en la escena 4.a": "Mira Petra que me tratas"
         3. "Dúo de Juana y Petra en la escena 13": "Si tienes que decirme"
         4. "Canción del ciego con el coro, en la escena 20": "La verbena de S. Pedro"
         5. "Bailable de la escena 22": "Es el amor un niño"

1a.3   "Los Amores de la Inés," zarzuela: G26
         . "Preludio"
         1. "Sequidillas de la corrida, en la escena 3": "Pasen las buenas mozas" (Inés, ch)
         2. "Carceleras, en la escena 7": "Cuando yo estaba en la cárcel" (Juan, ch)
         3. "Dúo de Inés y Juan, en la escena 9": "Mira tú si será grande," duet (Inés, Juan)
         4. "Intermedio instrumental"
         5. "Couplet, en la escena 14": "Guarde Dios al señor Lucas" (Lucas, ch)

1a.4   *"Limosna de Amor," zarzuela:* *G27*
         1. "Viva la orgía, viva el amor" (Pablo, ch)
         2. "Romanza de Elena": "Pablo me llama cuánto dolor"
         3. "Cuando el dolor nos roba paz y alegría," duet (Elena, Pablo)
         4. "Canciones y danzas de Asturias": "Desde Oviedo a Covadonga"
         5. "La noche tiende su negro manto," chorus

1a.8   "La Vida breve," lyric drama (Nos. of sections in The Gramophone): G39
         1. "Prelude, Act I"
         2. "Dance espagnole No.1"
         3. "Dance espagnole No.2"
         4. "Vivan los que rien!"
         5. "Alli está! Riendo"

1a.11   "Fuego Fátuo" (Firefly), opera-cómica: G52
       I: 1. "Dices que mi amor," duet (Clara, Leonardo)
            2. "Su amor es mío," aria (Leonardo)
            3. "El amor es una gansada," aria (Lord Tristán)
            4. "Ay, si yo supiera," aria (Lisa, ch)
            5. "Si el amor recuerda," trio (Lisa, Leonardo, Lord Tristán)
            6. "Ah! Dónde va mi amor?," aria (Clara)
       II: 1. "El amor promete," aria (Lisa)
            2. "Pobre de mí, que imaginé," aria (Leonardo)
            3. "Acércate un poquito a escuchar," duet (Lord Tristán, Marionetta)
            4. "Entonces es verdad?," duet (Leonardo, Lisa)
            5. "Aquí nos tienes!," quintet (Lisa, ch)
            6. "El corazón no me engañaba," aria (Leonardo)
       III: 1. "Tralá, la lá, la lá," chorus
            2. "La vida pasa, la ilusión va huyendo" (Lisa, ch)
            3. "Ah! Noche serena, noche piadosa," canción (Clara)
            4. "No me atreveré a acercarme a ti," duet (Clara, Leonardo)
            5. "Ah! Si la noche nos da su divina paz" (Lisa, Clara, Leonardo, ch)

1a.16   "Atlántida," scenic cantata (vers of 1961 p1962): G102
       Prologue: 1. "Atlantis submerged"
                  2. "Hymn to Spain"
       I: 3. "The burning of the Pyrenees"
            4. "Pyrene's aria"
            5. "Hymn to Barcelona"
            6. "Hercules and Geryon the three-headed"
            7. "Hymn to Atlantis"
       II: 8. "The garden of the Hesperides"
            9. "The games of the Pleiades"
           10. "Hercules and the dragon—lament of the Pleiades"
           11. "The Atlantides in the Temple of Neptune"
           12. "Hercules and the Atlantides"
           13. "Death of Geryon and Antaeus"
           14. "The straits of Hercules: Calpe"
           15. "The messenger voices"
           16. "The Voice of God"
           17. "The engulfment"
           18. "The Archangel"
           19. "The tower of the Titans"
           20. "The cataract"
           21. "No further"
       III: 22. "The pilgrim—prophetic chorus—Seneca's prophecy"
           23. "Isabella's dream"
           24. "The Caravels"

25. "The Salve at sea"
26. "The final night"
27. "Finale"

1a.17   "El Amor brujo" (Love the Magician), ballet: G44
Scene 1: 1. "Introducción y Escena"
     2. "Canción del amor dolido"
     3. "Sortilegio"
     4. "Danza del fin del día" (later: Danza del fuego)
     5. "Escena" (El amor vulgar) (later deleted)
     6. "Romance del pescador"
     7. "Intermedio" (later: Pantomima)
Scene 2: 8. "Introducción" (El fuego fátuo) (later deleted)
     9. "Escena" (El terror) (almost totally deleted)
    10. "Danza del fuego fátuo" (later: Danza del terror)
    11. "Interludio" (Alucinaciones)
    12. "Canción del fuego fátuo"
    13. "Conjuro para reconquistar el amor perdido" (deleted)
    14. "Escena" (El amor popular) (deleted)
    15. "Danza y canción de la bruja fingida" (later: Danza y canción del juego de amor)
    16. "Final" (Las campanas del amanecer)

1a.19   "El Sombrero de Tres Picos," ballet (Nos. of sections in The Gramophone): G53
     1. "Introduction—Afternoon"
     2. "Procession"
     3. "Dance of the Miller's Wife" (Fandango)
     4. "Corregidor"
     5. "Miller's Wife"
     6. "The Grapes"
     7. "Neighbour's Dance" (Seguidillas)
     8. "Miller's Dance" (Farruca)
     9. "The Miller's Arrest"
    10. "Dance of the Corregidor"
    11. "Final Dance" (Jota)

1a.26   "El Gran Teatro del Mundo," incid music (Nos. of sections in The Gramophone): G73
excerpts: 1. "Para empezar al auto"
     2. "Lento"
     3. "Alaben al Señor" (Cantigo de Alfonso X)
     4. "Ama al otro como a tí"
     5. "Rey de este caduco"
     6. "Toda la hermosura" (Canto de montañas)
     7. "Finale—Tantum ergo" (Victoria)

2. ORCHESTRAL WORKS

2.1   "El Amor brujo" (Version for small orch) (arr1917): No.1 "Introducción y Danza del fuego fátuo" G48
2.2   No.2 "Romance del pescador"
2.3   No.3 "Danza del fin del día" (later: Danza del fuego)
2.4   No.4 "Intermedio" (luego Pantomima)
2.5   No.5a "Danza de la bruja fingida" (later: Danza del juego de Amor)
2.6   No.5b "Final"
2.7   "El Sombrero de Tres Picos" Suite No.1 (c1921, from ballet G53): No.1 "Mediodía" G58
2.8   No.2 "Danza de la molinera" (Fandango)
2.9   No.3 "El Corregidor"
2.10   No.4 "Las uvas" (The Grapes)
2.11   "El Sombrero de Tres Picos" Suite No.2 (c1921, from ballet G53): No.1 "Los vecinos" G59
2.12   No.2 "Danza del molinero" (Farruca)
2.13   No.3 "Danza final" (Jota)
2.14   "El Amor brujo" (Suite del ballet) (arr1916–7, = G68 less Nos.2, 12 & instr changes) G69
2.15   "Fanfare sobre el nombre de E. F. Arbós" (c1934) G80
2.16   "Homenajes," suite (c1938–9): No.1 "Fanfare sobre el nombre de Arbós" (= G80) G86
2.17   No.2 "À Claude Debussy" (Elegia de la guitarra) (c1920, after guitar piece G56)
2.18   . "Rapel de la Fanfare" (c1941)
2.19   No.3 "À Paul Dukas" (Spes vitae) (c1939; orig for pf, G83)
2.20   No.4 "Pedrelliana" (c1938, from Pedrell's opera: La Celestina)
2.21   "Fuego Fátuo" (Firefly), suite (arr Ros Marbá p1976, from opera, G52) ....

3. CONCERTOS, SOLO INSTR & ORCH

3.1   "Nights in the Gardens of Spain," sym impressions (c1909–16; pf & orch): G49
     1. "En el Generalife"
     2. "Danza lejana"

3. "En los jardines de la Sierra de Córdoba"

3.2   Harpsichord Concerto (c1923–6; hpd/pf & fl, ob, cl, vn, vc) G71

4. STRING QUARTETS

4.1   Movement (c1903) G30

5. OTHER CHAMBER MUSIC

3 or more insts:

5.1   Piano Quartet in G major, "Cuarteto en sol" (c1898–9, Andante & Scherzo only) G8
5.2   "Mireya" (Fantasía) (c1899; fl & pf qt, after Part 5 of Mistral's poem Mireio; transcr for pf)...................... G9
5.3   "El Amor brujo" (Version for Sextet) (arr1915, r1926; 2vn, va, vc, d bass & pf): No.1 "Pantomima" G45
5.4   No.2 "Danza ritual del Fuego"
5.5   "Fanfare pour une fête" (c1921; 2hn & drums) G61

Vn & pf:

5.6   "Serenata andaluza" (c1899, not to be confused with the same title for pf) G12

Vc & pf:

5.7   "Melodia" (c1897, Falla's first acknowledged work) G4
5.8   "Romanza" (c1898) G6
5.9   "Piece," in C major (c1898) G7

1 instr:

5.10   "Homenaje pour 'Le Tombeau de Claude Debussy' " (c1920; gui; orchd in: Homenajes, G86) G56

6. PIANO

6.1   *"Gavotte & Musette" (c ?1892, after J. S. Bach, lost)* *G2*
6.2   "Nocturno" (c1896) G3
6.3   *"Scherzo," in C minor (c1898, frag)* *G5*
6.4   "Mireya" (Fantasía) (c1899; orig for fl & pf qt, G9).. G10
6.5   "Mazurka," in C minor (c1899) G11
6.6   "Serenata andaluza" (No.1) (c1900; transcr Velasco for gui) G13
6.7   "Canción" (c1900; pubd as No.1 of: 3 Obras Desconocidas) G14
6.8   "Vals Capricho" (c1900) G15
6.9   "Pasacalle torero" (c1900) G18
6.10   "Cortejo de gnomos" (c1901; pubd as: No.2 'Danza de gnomos' of: 3 Obras Desconocidas) G21
6.11   "Serenata" (c1901) G22
6.12   *"Serenata andaluza No.2" (c1901, lost)* *G23*
6.13   *"Suite fantástica" (c1901, lost)* *G24*
6.14   *Piece in E major (c1901, lost)* *G25*
6.15   "Allegro de concierto" (c1903–4, for a competition for a Conservatoire test piece)........................ G29
6.16   "4 Spanish Pieces" (c1906–9): No.1 "Aragonesa," jota G37
6.17   No.2 "Cubana"
6.18   No.3 "Montañesa" (Paysage)
6.19   No.4 "Andaluza"
6.20   "El Sombrero de Tres Picos" (3 Dances), suite (from ballet G53): No.1 "Danza de los vecinos" .... (G53)
6.21   No.2 "Danza del molinero"
6.22   No.3 "Danza de la molinera"
6.23   "Fantasía Baetica" (c1919, Baetica = Roman name of Andalusia; orchd Halffter)................................ G55
6.24   "Homenaje pour 'Le Tombeau de Claude Debussy' " (c1920; orig for gui, G56)................................ G57
6.25   "El Sombrero de Tres Picos" (c1921–6; pianola, from ballet G53).. G60
6.26   "Canto de los Remeros del Volga" (c1922; pubd as No.3 of: 3 Obras Desconocidas): G62
          . *Arr Stravinsky for winds & perc*
6.27   *"El Amor brujo" (Love the Magician), suite (transcr for pf, from ballet): No.1 "Pantomime"* .... *(G68)*
6.28   *No.2 "Scene"*
6.29   *No.3 "Song of the Will o' the Wisp"*
6.30   *No.4 "The Apparition"*
6.31   *No.5 "Dance of the Game of Love"*
6.32   *No.6 "The Magic Circle" (The Fisherman's Story)*
6.33   *No.7 "Midnight" (Witchcraft)*
6.34   *No.8 "Ritual Fire Dance"*
6.35   *No.9 "Dance of terror"*
6.36   "Pour le Tombeau de Paul Dukas" (c1935; orchd in: Homenajes, G86) G83

7. CHORAL WORKS

8. VOICE & ORCHESTRA

9. SONGS (w/ pf)

10. ARRANGEMENTS OF WORKS OF OTHERS

Choral arrs (Interpretaciones expresivas) of Spanish works of 15th, 16th & 17th cent:

* * * * *

G =   Antonio Gallego: "Catalogo de Obras de Manuel de Falla." Ministerio de Cultura. Dirección General
de Bellas Artes y Archivos. Madrid, 1987.

1. STAGE WORKS

Operas:

1.1	*"Barnabé," 1 act opéra comique (c1879, Moineaux, project)*	
1.2	"Prométhée," 3 act lyric tragedy (c1900, Lorrain & Hérold)	Op.82
1.3	"Pénélope," 3 act lyric drama (c1907–12, Fauchois)	
1.4	"Masques et bergamasques," 1 act musical comedy (c1919, Fauchois):	Op.112

    1. "Ouverture" (based on: Intermède symphonique for pf duet)
    2. "Pastorale" (c1919)
    3. "Madrigal" (= Op.35 w/ orch)
    4. "Le plus doux chemin" (= Op.87/1 w/ orch part by Samuel-Rousseau)
    5. "Menuet" (ca ?1869)
    6. "Clair de lune" (= Op.46/2 w/ orch)
    7. "Gavotte" (based on Gavotte for pf, orchd Samuel-Rousseau)
    8. "Pavane" (= Op.50 w/ ch)

Ballets:

1.5	"Dolly" (p1913, Laloy, = Suite for pf duet, Op.56 staged as a ballet)	(Op.56)

Incid music:

1.6	"Caligula" (c1888, Dumas père; fem ch & orch)	Op.52
1.7	"Shylock" (c1889, Haraucourt after Shakespeare; T & orch)	Op.57
1.8	"La Passion" (c1890, Haraucourt; ch & orch)	
1.9	"Le bourgeois gentilhomme" (c1893, Molière)	
1.10	"Pelléas et Mélisande" (c1898, Maeterlinck)	Op.80
1.11	"Le voile du bonheur" (c1901, Clemenceau)	Op.88
1.12	"Jules César" (c1905, Shakespeare transl Hugo, based on incid music: Caligula, Op.52)	Op.52bis

2. SYMPHONIES

2.1	"Suite d'orchestre" (Symphony in F) (c1865–74):	Op.20

    1. "Allegro" (see transcr Boëllmann for pf duet as: Allegro symphonique, Op.68)
    2. "Andante"
    3. "Gavotte" (orig: Gavotte for pf of 1869; reused in: Masques et bergamasques, Op.112/7)
    4. "Finale"

2.2	*Symphony in D minor (c1884, destroyed; reused in Vn Son No.2, Op.108 & Vc Son No.1, Op.109)*	*Op.40*

3. OTHER ORCHESTRAL WORKS

3.1	"Pavane" (c1887, Montesquiou; w/ ch ad lib; arr for S, A, T, B & pf)	Op.50
3.2	"Menuet," in F major (c ?1893, ?for incid music: Le bourgeois gentilhomme)	
3.3	"Pelléas et Mélisande," suite (orchd Koechlin; reorchd Fauré 1898): No.1 "Prélude"	(Op.80)
3.4	No.2 "Fileuse"	
3.5	No.3 "Sicilienne"	
3.6	No.4 "La mort de Mélisande"	
3.7	"Masques et bergamasques," suite (c1919, from stage work; also for pf duet): No.1 "Ouverture" ..	(Op.112)
3.8	No.2 "Menuet"	
3.9	No.3 "Gavotte"	
3.10	No.4 "Pastorale"	
3.11	"Chant funéraire" (c1921, for centenary of Napoleon's death; later incl in: Vc Sonata No.2, Op.117)	

4. CONCERTOS, SOLO INSTR & ORCH

Pf & orch:

4.1	"Fantaisie," in G major (c1918)	Op.111

Vn & orch:

4.2	Violin Concerto (c1878–9, unfin: 1st movt complete only):	Op.14

    1. "Allegro" (themes used in initial Allegro of: Str Qt in E minor, Op.121)
    2. "Andante" (perf w/ pf 1878, lost; ?used in: Andante, Op.75)
    3. "Finale" (sketches 1879, abandoned)

5. STRING QUARTETS

5.1	String Quartet in E minor (c1923–4)	Op.121

6. OTHER CHAMBER MUSIC

Piano Quintets:

6.1	Piano Quintet No.1 in D minor (c1890–4, 1903–5)	Op.89
6.2	Piano Quintet No.2 in C minor (c1919–21)	Op.115

Piano Quartets:

6.3	Piano Quartet No.1 in C minor (c1876–9, Finale r1883)	Op.15
6.4	Piano Quartet No.2 in G minor (c1885–6)	Op.45

Piano Trios:

6.5	Piano Trio in D minor (c1922–3)	Op.120

Vn & pf:

6.6	Violin Sonata No.1 in A major (c1875–6)	Op.13
6.7	"Berceuse" (c1879; orchd1880)	Op.16
6.8	"Romance," in B-flat major (c1877; orchd Gaubert 1919)	Op.28
6.9	"Andante," in B-flat major (c1897, ?themes from 2nd movt of: Vn Conc, Op.14)	Op.75
6.10	"Morceau de lecture" (Sight-reading piece) (c1903)	
6.11	Violin Sonata No.2 in E minor (c1916–7)	Op.108

Vc & pf:

6.12	"Elégie" (c1880; orchd1895)	Op.24
6.13	"Papillon" (c1884)	Op.77
6.14	*"Petite pièce," in G major (ca1888, lost)*	*Op.49*
6.15	"Romance" (Andante), in A major (c1894)	Op.69
6.16	"Sicilienne" (c1893, intended for incid music: Le bourgeois gentilhomme, arr for vc & pf 1898; orchd for incid music: Pelléas et Mélisande, Op.80)	Op.78
6.17	"Sérénade," in B minor (c1908)	Op.98
6.18	Cello Sonata No.1 in D minor (c1917)	Op.109
6.19	Cello Sonata No.2 in G minor (c1921)	Op.117

Other 2 insts:

6.20	"Morceau de lecture" (Sight-reading piece) (c1897; vc w/ 2nd vc acc)	
6.21	"Fantaisie" (c1898; fl & pf; orchd Aubert 1957)	Op.79
6.22	"Morceau de lecture" (Sight-reading piece) (c1898; fl & pf; arr & ed Hulme Brieff 1977)	
6.23	Piece for 2 double basses (c1905; 2 d basses, for the collection: Déchiffrage du manuscrit)	

Harp solo:

6.24	"Morceau de lecture" (Sight-reading piece) (c1904)	
6.25	"Impromptu" (c1904; see transcr Cortot for pf, Op.86bis)	Op.86
6.26	"Une châtelaine en sa tour" (c1918)	Op.110

7. PIANO

Ballades:

7.1	Ballade in F-sharp major (c1879; orchd1881)	Op.19

Barcarolles:

7.2	Barcarolle No.1 in A minor (c ?1881)	Op.26
7.3	Barcarolle No.2 in G major (c1885)	Op.41
7.4	Barcarolle No.3 in G-flat major (c1885)	Op.42
7.5	Barcarolle No.4 in A-flat major (c1886)	Op.44
7.6	Barcarolle No.5 in F-sharp minor (c1894)	Op.66
7.7	Barcarolle No.6 in E-flat major (c ?1895)	Op.70
7.8	Barcarolle No.7 in D minor (c1905)	Op.90
7.9	Barcarolle No.8 in D-flat major (c1906)	Op.96
7.10	Barcarolle No.9 in A minor (c1908–9)	Op.101
7.11	Barcarolle No.10 in A minor (c1913)	Op.104/2
7.12	Barcarolle No.11 in G minor (c1913–4)	Op.105/1
7.13	Barcarolle No.12 in E-flat major (c1915)	Op.105/2
7.14	Barcarolle No.13 in C major (c1921)	Op.116

Impromptus:

7.15	Impromptu No.1 in E-flat major (c1881)	Op.25
7.16	Impromptu No.2 in F minor (c1883)	Op.31
7.17	Impromptu No.3 in A-flat major (c1883)	Op.34
7.18	Impromptu No.4 in D-flat major (c1905)	Op.91
7.19	Impromptu No.5 in F-sharp minor (c1908–9)	Op.102
7.20	*Impromptu No.6 in D-flat major (c1904–13; transcr Cortot from Op.86 for harp)*	*Op.86bis*

Mazurkas:

7.21	Mazurka in B-flat major (c ?1875)	Op.32

Nocturnes:

7.22	Nocturne No.1 in E-flat minor (ca1875)	Op.33/1
7.23	Nocturne No.2 in B major (ca1881)	Op.33/2
7.24	Nocturne No.3 in A-flat major (c1883)	Op.33/3
7.25	Nocturne No.4 in E major (c1884)	Op.36
7.26	Nocturne No.5 in B-flat major (c1884)	Op.37
7.27	Nocturne No.6 in D-flat major (c1894)	Op.63
7.28	Nocturne No.7 in C-sharp minor (c1898)	Op.74
7.29	Nocturne No.8 in D-flat major (c1902; = No.8 of: 8 Pièces brèves, Op.84)	Op.84/8
7.30	Nocturne No.9 in B minor (c ?1908)	Op.97
7.31	Nocturne No.10 in E minor (c1908)	Op.99
7.32	Nocturne No.11 in F-sharp minor (c1913)	Op.104/1
7.33	Nocturne No.12 in E minor (c1915)	Op.107
7.34	Nocturne No.13 in B minor (c1921)	Op.119

Preludes:

7.35	"Prélude," in E minor (c1869)	
7.36	"Prélude," in C major (c1897, for Philipp's volume: Études d'octaves)	
7.37	"Préludes" (c1909–10): No.1 in D-flat major	Op.103
7.38	No.2 in C-sharp minor	
7.39	No.3 in G minor	
7.40	No.4 in F major	
7.41	No.5 in D minor	
7.42	No.6 in E-flat minor	
7.43	No.7 in A major	
7.44	No.8 in C minor	
7.45	No.9 in E minor	

Waltzes:

7.46	Valse-Caprice No.1 in A major (c ?1882)	Op.30
7.47	Valse-Caprice No.2 in D-flat major (c1884)	Op.38
7.48	Valse-Caprice No.3 in G-flat major (c1887–93)	Op.59
7.49	Valse-Caprice No.4 in A-flat major (c1893–4; arr Philipp for 2 pf 1902)	Op.62

Other:

7.50	*"Fugue à 3 parties" (ca1862, for the competition at the Ecole Niedermeyer, lost/=Op.84/3)*	
7.51	"Trois romances sans paroles" (c ?1863): No.1 in A-flat major (transcr for pf duet 1864)	Op.17
7.52	No.2 in A minor	
7.53	No.3 in A-flat major	
7.54	"Gavotte," in C-sharp minor (c1869; used in Op.20/3 & Op.112/7)	
7.55	"Thème et variations," in C-sharp minor (c1895)	Op.73
7.56	"Pièces brèves" (c1869–1902): No.1 "Capriccio," in E-flat major (c1899)	Op.84
7.57	No.2 "Fantasie," in A-flat major (c ?1902)	
7.58	No.3 "Petite fugue," in A minor (c1869, = ?Fugue ca1862)	
7.59	No.4 "Adagietto," in E minor (c1902)	
7.60	No.5 "Improvisation," in C-sharp minor (c1901)	
7.61	No.6 "Fugue," in E minor (c1869)	
7.62	No.7 "Allégresse," in C major (c1902)	
	No.8 "Nocturne No.8," in D-flat major (c1902)	

Cadenzas:

7.63	Cadenza for Beethoven: Piano Concerto No.3 in C minor, Op.37 (c1869)	
7.64	Cadenza for Mozart: Piano Concerto No.1 in F major, K37 (ca1875)	
7.65	Cadenza for Mozart: Piano Concerto No.24 in C minor, K491 (c1902)	Op.posth

Pf duet:

7.66   "La chanson dans le jardin" (c1864, r vers as: Berceuse, Op.56/1) ....
7.67   "Intermède symphonique," in F major (c1869; used as Ouverture in Op.112) ....
7.68   "Souvenirs de Bayreuth," fantaisie (c ?1888, on themes from Wagner's opera cycle: The Ring) ... Op.posth
7.69   "Dolly," suite (c1894–7; orchd Rabaud 1906): No.1 "Berceuse" (see orig: La chanson dans le jardin) Op.56
7.70   No.2 "Mi-a-ou" (c1894)
7.71   No.3 "Le jardin de Dolly" (c1895)
7.72   No.4 "Kitty-valse" (c1896, orig title: Ketty)
7.73   No.5 "Tendresse" (c1896)
7.74   No.6 "Le pas espagnol" (c1896)
7.75   *"Allegro symphonique" (transcr Boëllmann from Allegro of: Suite d'orchestre, Op.20)* *Op.68*

7.76   Transcr of works c by Saint-Saëns (pf duet, 2pf, 2pf 8hands) ....

8. ORGAN

8.1   "Impressions on a French Noel: Il est né le divin enfant" (ca1900) ....

9. CHURCH MUSIC

9.1   "Super flumina" (Psalmus 126) (c1863; ch & orch, for the competition at the École Niedermeyer) ....
9.2   *"Cantique à St Vincent de Paul" (c1868; 1v & org, lost)* ....
9.3   "Ave Maria" (c1871; ch & org) .... *Op.posth*
9.4   "Ave Maria," motet (c1877; 2S & org; used in: Ave Maria, Op.93) ....
9.5   *"O salutaris" (c1878; ?S & org, lost; ?used in Op.47/1)* ....
9.6   "Benedictus," in B-flat major (ca1880; ch, org & d bass) ....
9.7   "Messe des pêcheurs de Villerville" I (c1881; vv, fem ch, vn & harm, collab Messager): ....
        1. "Kyrie" (c by Messager)
        2. "Gloria"
        3. "Sanctus"
        4. "O salutaris" (c by Messager)
        5. "Agnus Dei"
9.8   "Messe des pêcheurs de Villerville" II (c1882; vv, fem ch & small orch, collab Messager): ....
        1. "Kyrie" (orchd Messager)
        2. "Gloria" (orchd Messager)
        3. "Sanctus" (orchd Messager)
        4. "O salutaris" (orchd Messager)
        5. "Agnus Dei" (orchd Fauré)
9.9   "Tu es Petrus" (ca1872; Bar, ch & org) ....
9.10   "2 Offertories": 1. "O salutaris," in B major (c1877–87; Bar & org; arr w/ insts) *Op.47*
9.11   2. "Maria Mater gratiae" (c1888; T, Bar & org)
9.12   "Requiem," in D minor (c1887–99; S, Bar, ch, orch & org): *Op.48*
        1. "Introitus et Kyrie" (c1887)
        2. "Offertorium" (c1889–91)
        3. "Sanctus" (c1888)
        4. "Pie Jesu" (c1887)
        5. "Agnus Dei" (c1888)
        6. "Libera me" (c1877; Bar & org ?1890; also for Bar, ch, orch & org p1892)
        7. "In Paradisum" (c1887)
9.13   "Ecce fidelis servus" (c1889; S, T, Bar & org) *Op.54*
9.14   "En prière": "Si la voix d'un enfant peut monter jusqu'à vous," canticle (c1890, Bordèse; 1v & org) ....
9.15   "Tantum ergo," in A major (c before 1891; T, ch, harp & org; also for T, ch & str qnt) *Op.55*
9.16   "2 Offertories" (c1894): 1. "Ave verum" (fem ch & org) *Op.65*
9.17   2. "Tantum ergo," in E major (3 child vv, vv, fem ch & org)
9.18   "Sancta mater" (c1894; T, ch & org) ....
9.19   "Ave Maria," in F major (c ?1894; T, Bar & org) ....
9.20   "2 Offertories": 1. "Salve Regina" (c1895; S & org) *Op.67*
9.21   2. "Ave Maria," in A-flat major (c1894–5; mS & org)
9.22   "Tantum ergo," in G-flat major (orig in F major) (c1904; S, ch & org; perf1904 w/ str qnt) ....
9.23   "Messe basse" (c1906; vv, fem ch & org, from: Messe des pêcheurs w/ out Messager's movts): ....
        1. "Kyrie" (new: c by Fauré)
        2. "Sanctus"
        3. "Benedictus" (on: Qui tollis, of the unpubd: Gloria)
        4. "Agnus Dei"
9.24   "Ave Maria," motet in B minor (c1906; 2S & org, uses: Ave Maria of 1877) *Op.93*

10. SECULAR CHORAL

10.1   "Cantique de Jean Racine" (c1865; ch & org) *Op.11*
10.2   "Les djinns" (c ?1875, Hugo; ch & orch) *Op.12*
10.3   "Le ruisseau" (c ?1881, anon; fem ch & pf) *Op.22*
10.4   "La naissance de Vénus," mythological scene (c1882, Collin; vv, ch & orch) *Op.29*

10.5	"Madrigal" (c1883, Silvestre; S, A, T, B & pf/orch) Op.35
10.6	"Caligula," concert version (c1888, Dumas père; fem ch & orch, from incid music Op.52): .... (Op.52)

      I. Prologue: 1. "Fanfare"
               2. "Marche"
               3. "Choeur des Heures"
      II. Act V: 1. "Choeur 'L'Hiver s'enfuit' "
               2. "Air de danse"
               3. "Mélodrame et choeur 'De roses vermeilles' "
               4. "Choeur final: 'César a fermé la paupière' "

10.8	"Il est né le divin enfant," harmonized carol (c1888; unison child ch, ob, vcs, d basses & org) ....
10.9	"Noël d'enfants": "Les anges dans nos campagnes" (ca1890; unison child ch & org) ....

11. VOICE & ORCHESTRA

11.1	"Shylock," concert version (c1890; T & orch, from incid music Op.57): .... (Op.57)

            1. "Chanson"
            2. "Entr'acte"
            3. "Madrigal"
            4. "Epithalame"
            5. "Nocturne"
            6. "Final"

11.2	"Hymne à Apollon" (c1894, trad Greek; 1v, fl, 2cl & harp; reconstr Reinach) Op.63bis

12. SONGS (w/ pf)

12.1	"2 Songs" (Hugo): 1. "Le papillon et la fleur": "La pauvre fleur disait au papillon" (c1861) Op.1
12.2	2. "Mai": "Puisque Mai tout en fleur" (c ?1862)
12.3	*"L'aube naît" (c ?1862, Hugo, lost)* ....
12.4	"Puisque j'ai mis ma lèvre" (c1862, Hugo) ....
12.5	"Tristesse d'Olympio" (ca1865, Hugo) ....
12.6	"2 Songs": 1. "Dans les ruines d'une abbaye": "Seuls, tous deux, ravis" (ca1866, Hugo) Op.2
12.7	2. "Les matelots": "Sur l'eau bleue et profonde" (ca1870, Gautier)
12.8	"L'aurore" (ca1870, Hugo) ....
12.9	"2 Songs": 1. "Seule!": "Dans un baiser l'onde au rivage" (c1871, Gautier) Op.3
12.10	2. "Sérénade toscane": "O toi que berce un rêve enchanteur" (c ?1878, anon transl Bussine)
12.11	"2 Songs": 1. "Chanson du pêcheur (Lamento): "Ma belle amie est morte" (c ?1872, Gautier) Op.4
12.12	2. "Lydia": "Lydia sur tes roses joues" (ca1870, Lisle)
12.13	"3 Songs": 1. "Chant d'automne": "Bientôt nous plongerons" (ca1871, Baudelaire) Op.5
12.14	2. "Rêve d'amour": "S'il est un charmant gazon" (c ?1862, Hugo)
12.15	3. "L'absent": "Sentiers où l'herbe se balance" (c1871, Hugo)
12.16	"2 Songs": 1. "Aubade": "L'oiseau dans le buisson" (ca1873, Pomey) Op.6
12.17	2. "Tristesse": "Avril est de retour" (ca1873, Gautier)
12.18	3. "Sylvie": "Si tu veux savoir ma belle" (c1878, Choudens)
12.19	"3 Songs": 1. "Après un rêve": "Dans un sommeil" (c ?1878, anon transl Bussine) Op.7
12.20	2. "Hymne": "A la très chère, à la très belle" (ca1870, Baudelaire)
12.21	3. "Barcarolle": "Gondolier du Rialto, mon château c'est la lagune" (c1873, Monnier)
12.22	"3 Songs": 1. "Au bord de l'eau": "S'asseoir tous deux au bord du flot" (c1875, Prudhomme) Op.8
12.23	2. "La rançon": "L'homme a, pour payer sa rançon" (c ?1871, Baudelaire)
12.24	3. "Ici-bas!": "Ici-bas tous les lilas meurent" (c ?1874, Prudhomme)
12.25	"2 Duets": 1. "Puisqu' ici-bas" (ca1863, r ca1873, Hugo; 2S & pf) Op.10
12.26	2. "Tarentelle" (ca1873, Monnier; 2S & pf)
12.27	"3 Songs" (c1878): 1. "Nell": "Ta rose de pourpre à ton clair soleil" (Lisle) Op.18
12.28	2. "Le voyageur": "Voyager, où vas-tu, marchant dans l'or vibrant" (Silvestre)
12.29	3. "Automne": "Automne au ciel brumeux, aux horizons navrants" (Silvestre)
12.30	"Poème d'un jour" (c1878, Grandmougin): 1. "Rencontre": "J'étais triste et pensif" Op.21
12.31	2. "Toujours": "Vous me demandez de me taire"
12.32	3. "Adieu": "Comme tout meurt vite, la rose déclose"
12.33	"3 Songs": 1. "Les berceaux" (c1879, Prudhomme) Op.23
12.34	2. "Notre amour": "Notre amour est chose légère" (ca1879, Silvestre)
12.35	3. "Le secret": "Je veux que le matin l'ignore le nom" (c1880–1, Silvestre)
12.36	"2 Songs" (c1882, Silvestre): 1. "Chanson d'amour": "J'aime tes yeux, j'aime ton front" Op.27
12.37	2. "La fée aux chansons": "Il était une Fée d'herbe folle coiffée"
12.38	"4 Songs" (c1884): 1. "Aurore": "Des jardins de la nuit s'envolent les étoiles" (Silvestre) Op.39
12.39	2. "Fleur jetée": "Emporte ma folie au gré du vent" (Silvestre)
12.40	3. "La pays des rêves": "Veux-tu qu'au beau pays des rêves" (Silvestre)
12.41	4. "Les roses d'Ispahan": "Les roses d'Ispahan dans leur gaine de mousse" (Lisle; orchd)
12.42	"2 Songs" (c1886): 1. "Noël": "La nuit descend du haut des cieux" (Wilder; w/ harm ad lib) Op.43
12.43	2. "Nocturne": "La nuit, sur le grand mystère" (Villiers de l'Isle-Adam)
12.44	"2 Songs" (c1887): 1. "Les présents": "Si tu demandes quelque soir" (Villiers de l'Isle Adam) Op.46
12.45	2. "Clair de lune": "Votre âme est un paysage choisi" (Verlaine; orchd1888)
12.46	"4 Songs" (c1888): 1. "Larmes": "Pleurons nos chagrins, chacun le nôtre" (Richepin) Op.51
12.47	2. "Au cimetière": "Heureux qui meurt ici" (Richepin)
12.48	3. "Spleen": "Il pleure dans mon coeur comme il pleut sur la ville" (Verlaine)

12.49	4. "La rose" (Ode Anacréontique): "Je dirai la Rose aux plis gracieux" (c1890, Lisle)
12.50	"Chanson & Madrigal" (c1889, Haraucourt, from incid music: Shylock, Op.57) ....
12.51	"Mélodies de Venise" (c1891, Verlaine): 1. "Mandoline": "Les donneurs de sérénades" Op.58
12.52	2. "En sourdine": "Calmes dans le demi-jour"
12.53	3. "Green": "Voici des fruits, des fleurs, des feuilles et des branches"
12.54	4. "À Clymène": "Mystiques barcarolles"
12.55	5. "C'est l'extase": "C'est l'extase langoureuse"
12.56	"Sérénade du bourgeois gentilhomme": "Je languis nuit et jour" (c1893, Molière) .... Op.posth
12.57	"La bonne chanson" (c1892–4, Verlaine; arr w/ str qnt & pf): 1. "Une sainte en son auréole" Op.61
12.58	2. "Puisque l'arbe grandit"
12.59	3. "La lune blanche luit dans les bois"
12.60	4. "J'allais par des chemins perfides"
12.61	5. "J'ai presque peur, en vérité"
12.62	6. "Avant que tu ne t'en ailles"
12.63	7. "Donc, ce sera par un clair jour d'été"
12.64	8. "N'est-ce pas?"
12.65	9. "L'hiver a cessé, la lumière est tiède"
12.66	"Pleurs d'or", duet (c1896, Samain; mS, Bar & pf) Op.72
12.67	"2 Songs" (c1897): 1. "Le parfum impérissable": "Quand la fleur du soleil" (Lisle) Op.76
12.68	2. "Arpège": "L'âme d'une flûte soupire" (Samain)
12.69	"2 Songs" (c1894): 1. "Prison": "Le ciel est, par dessus le toit" (Verlaine; orchd Schmitt) Op.83
12.70	2. "Soir": "Voici que les jardins de la nuit vont fleurir" (Samain; orchd Aubert)
12.71	"Mélisandre's song" (c1898, Maeterlinck transl Mackail, from incid music Op.80)........................ Op.posth
12.72	"3 Songs" (c1902): 1. "Dans la forêt de septembre": "Ramure aux rumeurs" (Mendès) Op.85
12.73	2. "La fleur qui va sur l'eau": "Sur la mer voilée" (Mendès)
12.74	3. "Accompagnement": "Tremble argenté tilleul, bouleau" (Samain)
12.75	*"Dans le ciel clair" (c1902, Lisle, sketches)* ....
12.76	"2 Madrigals" (c1904, Silvestre): 1. "Le plus doux chemin": "A mes pas le plus doux chemin" Op.87
12.77	2. "Le ramier": "Avec son chant doux et plaintif"
12.78	"Le don silencieux": "Je mettrai mes deux mains sur ma bouche" (c1906, Dominique) Op.92
12.79	"Chanson": "Que me fait toute la terre" (c1906, Régnier) Op.94
12.80	"Vocalise-étude" (c1906; transcr Doney for fl/ob/vn & pf as: Pièce 1920) ....
12.81	"La chanson d'Eve," cycle (c1906–10, Lerberghe): 1. "Paradis": "C'est le premier matin" Op.95
12.82	2. "Prima verba": "Comme elle chante dans ma voix"
12.83	3. "Roses ardentes": "Roses ardentes dans l'immobile nuit"
12.84	4. "Comme Dieu rayonne": "Comme Dieu rayonne aujourd'hui"
12.85	5. "L'aube blanche": "L'aube blanche dit à mon rêve"
12.86	6. "Eau vivante": "Que tu es simple et claire, eau vivante"
12.87	7. "Veilles-tu, ma senteur de soleil"
12.88	8. "Dans un parfum de roses blanches"
12.89	9. "Crépuscule": "Ce soir, à travers le bonheur"
12.90	10. "Ô mort, poussière d'étoiles"
12.91	"Le jardin clos" (c1914, Lerberghe): 1. "Exaucement": "Alors qu'en tes mains de lumière" Op.106
12.92	2. "Quand tu plonges tes yeux dans mes yeux"
12.93	3. "La messagère": "Avril, et c'est le point du jour"
12.94	4. "Je me poserai sur ton coeur"
12.95	5. "Dans la nymphée": "Quoique tes yeux ne la voient pas"
12.96	6. "Dans la pénombre": "A quoi, dans ce matin d'Avril"
12.97	7. "Il m'est cher, Amour, le bandeau"
12.98	8. "Inscription sur le sable": "Toute, avec sa robe et ses fleurs"
12.99	"Mirages" (c1919, Brimont): 1. "Cygne sur l'eau": "Ma pensée est un cygne harmonieux" Op.113
12.100	2. "Reflets dans l'eau": "Etendue au seuil du bassin"
12.101	3. "Jardin nocturne": "Nocturne jardin tout rempli de silence"
12.102	4. "Danseuse": "Soeur des Soeurs tisseuses de violettes"
12.103	"C'est la paix": "Pendant qu'ils étaient partis pour la guerre" (c1919, Debladis) Op.114
12.104	"L'horizon chimérique" (c1921, Mirmont) 1. "La mer est infinie et mes rêves sont fous".................. Op.118
12.105	2. "Je me suis embarqué sur un vaisseau qui danse"
12.106	3. "Diane, Séléné lune de beau métal"
12.107	4. "Vaisseaux, nous vous aurons aimés en pure perte"

* * * * *

1. STAGE WORKS (operas)

1.1	"Stradella," 3 acts (ca1844, Deschamps, vocal score only)	
1.2	"Le valet de ferme," 3 act opéra-comique (c1851–3, Royer & Vaëz)	
1.3	"Hulda," 4 acts (c1882–5, Grandmougin after Björnson, on a Scandinavian subject) M49	
1.4	"Ghisèle," 4 act lyric drama (c1888–90, Thierry, unfin: only Act I orchd Franck) M50	

2. SYMPHONIES

2.1   Symphony No.1 in G major (c1840) ....(op.13)
2.2   Symphony in D minor (c1886–8; arr for pf duet 1890; arr Adler for pf; arr for vn & pf) Op.48

3. OTHER ORCHESTRAL WORKS

3.1   "Variations brillantes sur l'Air du Pré aux clercs" (c1834; arr for pf) .... (op.5)
3.2   "Ce qu'on entend sur la montagne," sym poem (ca1845–7, after Hugo) ....
3.3   "Symphonic Interlude" (c1874, for r vers of: Redemption, M52) ....
3.3   "Les Éolides," sym poem (c1876, after Lisle's poem; arr for 2 pf 1892) M43
3.4   "Le chasseur maudit" (Accursed Huntsman), sym poem (c1882, on Bürger's ballad; arr for
      pf duet 1884) M44
3.5   "Psyché," sym poem (c1887–8, Sicard & Fourcaud; ch & orch; arr w/ pf duet 1893): M47
      I: . "Le sommeil de Psyché"
            . "Psyché enlevée par les zéphirs"
      II: . "Le jardin d'Éros"
            . "Amour! Amour! source de toute vie!" (ch)
            . "Psyché et Éros"
      III: . "Le châtiment": "Amour, Elle a connu ton nom. Malheur sur elle!"
            . "Souffrances et plaintes de Psyché"
            . "Apothéose": "Eros a pardonn'. Tressoillez, cieux et terre!"

4. PIANO CONCERTOS, PIANO & ORCH

4.1   "Variations brillantes sur la ronde favorite de Gustave III" (c1834–5) .... (op.8)
4.2   Piano Concerto No.2 in G minor (ca1835) ....(op.11)
4.3   "Les djinns," sym poem (c1884, after Hugo; arr for 2pf 1892) M45
4.4   "Variations symphoniques" (c1885; arr for 2pf 1892) M46

5. STRING QUARTETS

5.1   String Quartet in D major (c1889) M9

6. OTHER CHAMBER MUSIC

5 or more insts:

6.1   "Solo de piano" (c1843–4; pf & str qnt, on a theme from biblical eclogue: Ruth, M51, inc) Op.10
6.2   Piano Quintet in F minor (c1878–9) M7

Piano Trios:

6.3   "Grand trio" (c1834) .... (op.6)
6.4   "Trios concertants": No.1 in F-sharp minor (c1841) Op.1, M1
6.5   No.2 in B-flat major, "Trio de salon" (c1841) M2
6.6   No.3 in B minor (c1842) M3
6.7   "Trio concertant" No.4 in B minor (c1842) Op.2, M4

Vn & pf:

6.8   "Andantino quietoso," in E-flat major (c1843) Op.6, M5
6.9   "Duo concertant," in B-flat major (c1844, on motifs from Dalayrac: Gulistan) Op.14, M6
6.10 Violin Sonata in A major (c1886) M8
6.11 "Mélancolie" (p1911, transcr of a solfege lesson) ....Op.posth, M10

7. PIANO SONATAS

7.1   Piano Sonata No.1 (c1835) ....(op.10)
7.2   Piano Sonata No.2 (c before 1841) ....(op.18)

8. OTHER PIANO WORKS

Before 1841:

8.1 "Première grande fantaisie" .... (op.12)
8.2 "Deuxième fantaisie," in D major .... (op.14)
8.3 "Deux mélodies" .... (op.15)
8.4 "Troisième grande fantaisie" .... (op.19)
8.5 "Polka" ....

After 1841:

8.6 "Églogue" (Hirtengedicht) (c1842) Op.3, M11
8.7 "Grand caprice" No.1 (c1843) Op.5, M13
8.8 "Souvenir d'Aix-la-Chapelle" (c1843) Op.7, M14
8.9 "Deux mélodies: à Félicité" (ca1844) ....
8.10 "Quatre mélodies de Schubert" (transcr1844): No.1 "La jeune réligieuse" (Die junge Nonne,
            Op.43/1, D828) Op.8, M15
8.11   No.2 "La truite" (Die Forelle, Op.32, D550)
8.12   No.3 "Les plaintes de la jeune fille" (Des Mädchens Klage, Op.58/3, D191)
8.13   No.4 "La cloche des Agonisants" (Das Zügenglöcklein, Op.80/2, D871)
8.14 "Ballade" (c1844) Op.9
8.15 "1re grande fantaisie" (c1844, on themes from Dalayrac: Gulistan) Op.11, M16
8.16 "2e fantaisie" (c1844, on 'Le point du jour' from Dalayrac: Gulistan) Op.12, M17
8.17   "Fantaisie" (c ?1844, lost) Op.13
8.18 "Fantaisie" (c1845, on 2 Polish airs) Op.15, M18
8.19 "Trois petits riens" (c1845): No.1 "Duettino" Op.16
8.20   No.2 "Valse"
8.21   No.3 "Le Songe"
8.22 "Les plaintes d'une poupée" (c1865) M20
8.23 "Prélude, choral, et fugue" (c1884) M21
8.24 "Danse lente" (c1885) M22
8.25 "Prélude, aria et final" (c1886–7) M23

Pf duet:

8.26 "1er duo" (c1842, on: God Save the King) Op.4, M12
8.27 "2e duo" (c1846, on Grétry's opera: Lucille) Op.17, M19

2 Pf:

8.28 "Prélude, fugue et variations" (c ?1873; pf & harm or 2pf) Op.18, M30a

9. ORGAN (or harm)

9.1 "Grand choeur" (c before 1841; org) ....
9.2 "L'organiste" (Vol.2) (c1858–63; org/harm): No.1 "Sortie" M24
9.3   No.2 "Grand choeur"
9.4   No.3 "Élévation"
9.5   No.4 (w/ out tempo markings)
9.6   No.5 "Andantino"
9.7   No.6 "Marche"
9.8   No.7 "Allegretto"
9.9   No.8 "Amen"
9.10   No.9 "Offertoire"
9.11   No.10 "Quasi lento"
9.12   No.11 "Allegretto"
9.13   No.12 "Allegretto non troppo"
9.14   No.13 "Moderato"
9.15   No.14 "Moderato con moto"
9.16   No.15 "Andantino"
9.17   No.16 "Préludes pour l'Ave Maris Stella"
9.18   No.17 "Lent et trà soutenu"
9.19   No.18 (w/ out tempo markings)
9.20   No.19 "Lento"
9.21   No.20 "Andantino calmato"
9.22   No.21 "Kyrie de la Messe de Noël"
9.23   No.22 "Moderato"
9.24   No.23 "Moderato"
9.25   No.24 "Grand choeur"
9.26   No.25 "Offertoire pour la Messe de Minuit"
9.27   No.26 "Pièce Symphonique"
9.28   No.27 "Sortie"
9.29   No.28 "Grand choeur. Maestoso"

9.30	No.29 "Sortie"	
9.31	No.30 "Sortie"	
9.32	"Andantino," in G minor (c ?1858; org)	M25
9.33	"Cinq pièces" (ca1858; harm): No.1 "Offertoire"	M26
9.34	No.2 "Petit offertoire"	
9.35	No.3 "Verset" I (Andantino poco mosso), in F minor	
9.36	No.4 "Verset" II (Andante), in F minor	
9.37	No.5 "Communion"	
9.38	"Trois antiennes" (c1859; org): No.1 "Quasi lento"	M27
9.39	No.2 "Allegretto"	
9.40	No.3 "Lent et très soutenu"	
9.41	"Fantaisie," in C major (ca1860; org)	Op.16, M28
9.42	"Grande pièce symphonique," in F-sharp minor (c1863; org)	Op.17, M29
9.43	"Pastorale," in E major (c1863; org)	Op.19, M31
9.44	"Prière," in C-sharp minor (ca1860; org)	Op.20, M32
9.45	"Final," in B-flat major (ca1862; org)	Op.21, M33
9.46	"Quasi marcia" (c1862; harm)	Op.22, M34
9.47	"Offertoire sur un Noël bréton" (c1871; harm)	
9.48	"Trois pièces" (c1878; org): No.1 "Fantaisie," in A major	M35
9.49	No.2 "Cantabile," in B major	M36
9.50	No.3 "Pièce héroïque," in B minor	M37
9.51	"Andantino" (c1889; org, in d'Indy catalogue, = ?Andantino of 1858)	
9.52	"3 Chorals" (c1890; org): No.1 in E major	M38
9.53	No.2 in B minor	M39
9.54	No.3 in A minor	M40
9.55	"L'organiste" (Vol.1) (c1889–90; org/harm): No.1 "Poco allegretto," in C major	M41
9.56	No.2 "Andantino," in C major	
9.57	No.3 "Poco lento," in C major	
9.58	No.4 "Maestoso," in C minor	
9.59	No.5 "Poco lento," in C minor	
9.60	No.6 "Poco allegro," in C minor	
9.61	No.7 "Offertoire," in C major	
9.62	No.8 "Andante," in D-flat major	
9.63	No.9 "Andantino," in D-flat major	
9.64	No.10 "Poco andantino," in D-flat major	
9.65	No.11 "Poco allegro," in C-sharp minor	
9.66	No.12 "Lento," in C-sharp minor	
9.67	No.13 "Andantino poco mosso," in C-sharp minor	
9.68	No.14 "Andante," in D-flat major	
9.69	No.15 "Quasi allegro," in D major	
9.70	No.16 "Chant de la Creuse," in D minor	
9.71	No.17 "Quasi andante," in D major	
9.72	No.18 "Vieux Noël. Andantino," in D minor	
9.73	No.19 "Maestoso," in D major	
9.74	No.20 "Vieux Noël. Maestoso," in D minor	
9.75	No.21 "Sortie ou Offertoire," in D major	
9.76	No.22 "Andantino poco allegretto," in E-flat major	
9.77	No.23 "Quasi lento," in E-flat major	
9.78	No.24 "Molto moderato," in E-flat minor	
9.79	No.25 "Allegretto," in E-flat major	
9.80	No.26 "Poco allegro," in E-flat major	
9.81	No.27 "Andantino," in E-flat minor	
9.82	No.28 "Offertoire," in E-flat major	
9.83	No.29 "Andante quasi allegretto," in E minor	
9.84	No.30 "Moderato," in E minor	
9.85	No.31 "Prière," in E minor	
9.86	No.32 "Non troppo lento," in E major	
9.87	No.33 "Allegretto," in E major	
9.88	No.34 "Poco allegretto," in E major	
9.89	No.35 "Offertoire ou Communion," in E minor	
9.90	No.36 "Allegretto," in F major	
9.91	No.37 "Andantino," in F major	
9.92	No.38 "Lento," in F minor	
9.93	No.39 "Allegretto," in F minor	
9.94	No.40 "Allegretto," in F major	
9.95	No.41 "Poco lento," in F minor	
9.96	No.42 "Sortie," in F major	
9.97	No.43 "Air béarnais," in F-sharp minor	
9.98	No.44 "Chant béarnais," in G-flat major	
9.99	No.45 "Andantino," in F-sharp minor	
9.100	No.46 "Poco lento," in G-flat major	
9.101	No.47 "Poco allegro," in F-sharp minor	
9.102	No.48 "Poco allegretto," in G-flat major	
9.103	No.49 "Offertoire funèbre," in F-sharp minor	
9.104	No.50 "Poco allegretto," in G major	

9.105	No.51 "Poco lento," in G minor
9.106	No.52 "Noël angévin. Allegretto," in G major
9.107	No.53 "Quasi lento," in G major
9.108	No.54 "Quasi Allegro," in G minor
9.109	No.55 "Allegretto vivo," in G minor
9.110	No.56 "Sortie. Allegro," in G major
9.111	No.57 "Poco maestoso," in A-flat major
9.112	No.58 "Allegretto amabile," in A-flat major
9.113	No.59 "Andantino," in A-flat major
9.114	"Suite" (c1890; harm): No.1 "Andantino," in A major ....Op.posth, M42
9.115	No.2 "Lento," in A major
9.116	No.3 "Andantino quasi allegretto," in D-sharp minor
9.117	No.4 "Poco maestoso," in D-sharp minor
9.118	"Pièces posthumes" (c1858–63; org/harm): No.1 "Offertoire," in F minor ....
9.119	No.2 "Offertoire," in C minor
9.120	No.3 "Élévation," in A minor
9.121	No.4 "Magnificat," in D major
9.122	No.5 "Grand Choeur," in D major
9.123	No.6 "Andantino," in D major
9.124	No.7 "Quasi marcia," in D minor
9.125	No.8 "Allegretto," in D major
9.126	No.9 "Grand Choeur," in D major
9.127	No.10 "Amen," in D major
9.128	No.11 "Gloria Ppatri," in D major
9.129	No.12 "Offertoire," in A major
9.130	No.13 "Quasi lento," in F major
9.131	No.14 "Allegretto," in C minor
9.132	No.15 "Andantino," in C major
9.133	No.16 "Allegretto," in D minor
9.134	No.17 "Allegretto," in D major
9.135	No.18 "Magnificat," in E-flat major
9.136	No.19 "Magnificat," in E-flat major
9.137	No.20 "Grand Choeur," in E-flat major
9.138	No.21 "Moderato," in E-flat major
9.139	No.22 "Andantino," in E-flat major
9.140	No.23 "Allegretto," in E-flat major
9.141	No.24 "Gloria Patri," in E-flat major
9.142	No.25 "Gloria Patri," in E-flat major
9.143	No.26 "Amen," in E-flat major
9.144	No.27 "Gloria Patri," in E-flat major
9.145	No.28 "Prélude pour l'Ave maris stella," in D minor
9.146	No.29 "Prélude pour l'Ave maris stella," in D major
9.147	No.30 "Prélude pour l'Ave maris stella," in D minor
9.148	No.31 "Benedicamus," in C major
9.149	No.32 "Lento," in D minor
9.150	No.33 "Andantino," in A-flat major
9.151	No.34 "Grand Choeur" (Kyrie de la Messe de Noël), in C minor
9.152	No.35 "Moderato," in C minor
9.153	No.36 "Moderato," in C minor
9.154	No.37 "Grand choeur," in C minor
9.155	No.38 "Grand choeur," in C major
9.156	No.39 "Offertoire pour la Messe de minuit," in D minor
9.157	No.40 "Offertoire," in G minor
9.158	No.41 "Sortie," in D major
9.159	No.42 "Offertoire," in F-sharp minor
9.160	No.43 "Allegro moderato," in B-flat minor
9.161	No.44 "Offertoire," in B major

10. CHURCH MUSIC—LARGE WORKS

10.1	*"Notre-Dame des orages,"* cantata (ca1838, Pastouret; ?1v & pf, lost) ....
10.2	"Ruth," biblical eclogue (c1843–6, r1871; vv, ch & orch): M51

    I: 1. "Introduction"
          2. "Choeur des Moabites": "Elle s'en va"
          3. "Adieu, adieu, Ruth, Orpha, chères filles!," trio
          4. "Marche et choeur": "Quelle angoisse extrême"
          5. "Strophes": "Mes filles, le voile des veuves" (Noémi)
          6. "Récitatif et Air": "Moi, je vous suis" (Ruth)
          7. "Choeur": "Elles s'en vont"
          8. "Choeur de Bethléimistes et Strophes": "Elle descend la montagne"
    II: 9. "Choeur de Moissoneurs": "Tout ce que moissone L'heureux laboreur"
          10. "Récitatif et Duo": "Quelle est cette fille, Qui là, sans faucile" (Booz)
          11. "Le chant du crépuscule": "Flambeau des cieux, la fin de ta carrière"
    III. "L'aire de Booz": 12. "Récitatif et Duo": "Quelle est celle, qui sous ma tente" (Booz)

"La chaumière de Veuves": 13. "Récitatif et Air": "Soyez bénie, ô ma mère!"
"Les portes de Bethléem": 14. "Strophes et Choeur": "Avec bonheur, amis je vous l'annonce"
"Conclusion prophétique": 15. "Solo et Choeur": "Aller chercher la Moabite"

10.3 "Plainte des Israélites," cantata (ca ?1865; ch & orch) ....
10.4 "La tour de Babel," cantata (c1865; 1v, ch & orch) ....
10.5 "Rédemption" (c1871–2, Blau; S, fem ch, recit & orch): M52
    I: . "Introduction"
          . "Choeur terrestre": "Que le jour monte ou s'abaisse"
          . "Ah! malheur aux vaincus! Cette clameur s'élève," récit
          . "Nous venons du ciel" (Les Anges)
          . "Choeur, Récit et Air de l'Archange": "Où mènent vos chemins?"
          . "Choeur général": "Devant la joi nouvelle"
    II: . "Symphonie" (added 1874)
          . "Choeur d'hommes": "Où sommes nous!" (added 1874)
          . "L'Homme": "Toujours le chant moqueur! Toujours le cri sauvage!," récit
          . "Choeur des Anges": "Nous sommes au ciel bien loin"
          . "Air de l'Archange": "Le flot se lève"
          . "L'Homme": "Prier!—le pouvons-nous?—Par une loi fatale," récit
          . "Choeur général": "Seigneur, Seigneur, oublie"
10.6 "Les béatitudes," oratorio (c1869–79, Colomb; vv, ch & orch): M53
          . "Prologue": "En ce temps là, sur la terre" (T)
       1. "Poursui vous la richesse"
       2. "Le ciel est loin, la terre est sombre," chorus
       3. "Reine implacable, O douleur!" (B)
       4. "Puisque partout où nous entraîne" (T)
       5. "Comme le blé sur l'aire, Battu par les fléaux" (fem ch)
       6. "Les dieux qui parlaient à nos pères" (fem ch)
       7. "C'est moi, l'esprit du mal" (Satan)
       8. "A ma défaite. Mon pouvoir a survécu!" (B)
10.7 "Rébecca," scéne biblique (c1881, Collin; vv, ch & orch): M54
       1. "Introduction et Choeur": "Sous l'ombre fraîche despalmiers" (fem ch)
       2. "Air et Choeur": "Encore un jour qui fuit!," récit
       3. "Choeur des Chameliers": "Nous marchions avant que l'aurore. Eût chassé la nuit"
       4. "Air et Scène": "O Seigneur Dieu, qui protèges mon maître" (Eliézer)
       5. "Duo": "Seigneur, vous paraissez avoir fait longue route," duo
       6. "Final": "Dieu loin de nous tu vas partir" (Choeur de jeunne filles)
        . "Choeur Général": "En toi, mon Dieu, notre âme se confie"

11. CHURCH MUSIC—SMALLER WORKS

11.1 "O Salutaris" (c1835; ch & org) ....
11.2 "Justus ut palma florebit" (ca ?1840; B, ch & org) ....
11.3 "Gratias super gratiam" (ca ?1840; ch & org) ....
11.4 "Tunc oblati sunt" (ca ?1840; ch & org) ....
11.5 "Sinite parvulos" (ca ?1840; 1v & org) ....
11.6 "Laudate pueri" (ca ?1840; ch & org) ....
11.7 "Ave Maria" (c1845; ?ch) ....
11.8 "Sub tuum" (c1849; 2vv) ....
11.9 "O Gloriosa" (ca ?1850; 3vv) ....
11.10 "O Salutaris" (c1858; S & T or S, mS & org) M55
11.11 "Trois motets" (c1858): No.1 "O Salutaris" (S, ch & org) M56
11.12   No.2 "Ave Maria" (S, B & org) M57
11.13   No.3 "Tantum Ergo" (B, ch & org) M58
11.14 "Messe solennelle" (c1858; B & org) M59
11.15 "Tendre Marie," canticle (ca ?1858) ....
11.16 "Le garde d'honneur": "Divin Jésus, mon Sauveur," hymn (c1859; 1v, fem ch & pf) M60
11.17 "Cantique de Moïse": "Cantemus Domino" (ca1860; ch & pf) ....
11.18 "Messe solennelle" (c1860; S, T, B, ch, harp, vc & d bass & org): Op.12, M61
       1. "Kyrie"
       2. "Gloria"
       3. "Credo"
       4. "Sanctus"
       5. "Panis angelicus"
       6. "Agnus Dei"
11.19 "Ave Maria" (c1863; S, T, B & org) M62
11.20 "Trois offertoires" (c1871): 1. "Quae est ista" (vv, ch, org, harp & d bass) M63
11.21   2. "Domine Deus" (S, T, B, org & d bass) M64
11.22   3. "Dextera Domini" (vv, ch, org & d bass) M65
11.23 "Domine non secundum," offertory for Lent (c1871; S, T, B & org) M66
11.24 "Quasi fremuerunt gentes," offertory (c1871; ch, org & d bass) M67
11.25 "Panis angelicus" (c1872; T, org, harp, vc & d bass; interpolated in: Mass,Op.12, M61) ......
11.26 "Veni creator" (c1872; T, B & org) M68
11.27 "Psalm 150": "Louez le Dieu, caché dans ses saints tabernacles" (c1884; cl, ch, org & orch) M69

12. SECULAR CHORAL

12.1   "Marlborough" (c1869; ch, org, pf, vc, d bass & 4 obbl mirlitons) ....
12.2   "Le philistin mordra la poussière" (c1875; ch & pf) ....
12.3   "Premier sourire de mai" (c1888, Wilder; fem ch & pf) M90
12.4   "Hymne": "Source ineffable de lumière" (c1888, Racine; m ch & pf) M91
12.5   "Cantique" (c1888; ch & hn obbl) ....

13. VOICE & ORCHESTRA

13.1   "Hymne à la patrie" (c1848, inc) ....
13.2   "Paris": "Je suis Paris la reine des cités," patriotic ode (c1870; T & orch) M79
13.3   "Patria," patriotic ode (c1871, Hugo; also arr w/ pf) ....
13.4   "La procession": "Dieu s'avance à travers les champs!" (c1888, Brizeux; arr w/ pf) M88

14. MISC VOCAL

14.1   "6 Duos" (c1888; S, A & pf): 1. "L'ange gardien": "Veilez sur moi quand je m'éveille" (?Franck) M89
14.2   2. "Aux petits enfants": "Enfants d'un jour, ô nouveaux nés" (Daudet)
14.3   3. "La Vierge à la crèche": "Dans ses langes blancs fraîchement cousus" (Daudet)
14.4   4. "Les danses de Lormont": "Pour suivant les nuées" (Desbordes-Valmore)
14.5   5. "Soleil": "Incendiant les horizons" (Ropartz)
14.6   6. "La chanson du vannier": "Brins d'osier" (Theuriet)

15. SONGS (w/ pf)

15.1   *"Blond Phébus" (c1835, ?spur)* ....
15.2   "Souvenance": "Combien j'ai douce souvenance" (c1842–3, Chateaubriand) M70
15.3   "Ninon": "Ninon! Ninon! que fais tu de la vie?" (c1842–3, Musset) M71
15.4   "L'émir de Bengador": "Si tu savais que je t'adore" (c1842–3, Méry) M72
15.5   "Le sylphe": "Je suis un sylphe, une ombre un rien" (c1842–3, A. Dumas; w/ vc obbl) M73
15.6   "Robin Gray": "Quand les moutons sont dans la bergerie" (c1842–3, Florian) M74
15.7   "L'ange et l'enfant": "Un ange au radieux visage" (c1846, Reboul) M75
15.8   "Aimer": "J'entendais sa voix si touchante" (c1849, Méry) M76
15.9   "Les trois exilés": "Quand l'étranger en va" (Chant national) (c1849, Delfosse; Bar, B) M77
15.10   "S'il est un charmant gazon" (c1857, Hugo; 2 settings: in F major & in E-flat major) M78
15.11   "Le mariage des roses": "Mignonne, sais-tu" (c1871, David) M80
15.12   "Roses et papillons" (c1872, Hugo) M81
15.13   "Passez, passez toujours": "Duis que j'ai mis ma lèvre à ta coupe" (c1872, Hugo) M82
15.14   "Lied": "Pour moi sa main cueillait des roses" (c1873, Paté) M83
15.15   "Le vase brisé": "Le vase où meurt cette verveine" (c1879, Sully-Prudhomme) M84
15.16   "Nocturne": "O fraîche nuit, nuit transparente" (c1884, Fourcaud) M85
15.17   "Pour les victimes": "Sous les décombres entassés" (c1887) ....Op.posth, M86
15.18   "Les cloches du soir": "Quand les cloches du soir" (c1888, Desbordes-Valmore) M87

16. ARRANGEMENTS OF WORKS OF OTHERS

16.1   "Accompagnement d'orgue" & arr for vv of Gregorian services (restored Lambillotte) (c1858) M92
16.2   Duparc: "Lénore," sym poem (arr ca1875; pf duet) ....
16.3   Danican-Philidor: "Ernelinde," 3 act opera (vocal arr ca1880) M93
16.4   Danican-Philidor: "Tom Jones," 3 act opera (vocal arr ca1880) M94
16.5   Danican-Philidor: "Le bûcheron," 1 act opera (vocal arr ca1880) M95
16.6   Alkan: "Préludes et prières" (arr1889; org) M96
16.7   "Hymnes" (harmonizations for 3vv & org): 1. "Creator alme siderum" M97
16.8   2. "Sanctorum meritis"
16.9   3. "Iste confessor"

*   *   *   *   *

M = Wilhelm Mohr: Thematisches Werkverzeichnis in: "César Franck." Hans Schneider, Tutzing, 1969.

1. INSTRUMENTAL WORKS

1.1	36 "Basso canzoni per sonare" (c1608; w/ cont, 33 by others): No.1 "Canzon 13, a 4" A.1
1.2	No.2 "Canzon 21, a 5"
1.3	No.3 "Canzon 29, a 8"
1.4	"Fantasie a quattro," Vol.I (p1608): No.1 "Fantasia prima, sopra un soggietto" A.2
1.5	No.2 "Fantasia seconda, sopra un soggietto solo"
1.6	No.3 "Fantasia terza, sopra un soggietto solo"
1.7	No.4 "Fantasia quarta, sopra due soggietti"
1.8	No.5 "Fantasia quinta, sopra due soggietti"
1.9	No.6 "Fantasia sesta, sopra due soggietti"
1.10	No.7 "Fantasia settima, sopra tre soggietti"
1.11	No.8 "Fantasia ottaua, sopra tre soggietti"
1.12	No.9 "Fantasia nona, sopra tre soggietti"
1.13	No.10 "Fantasia decima, sopra quattro soggietti"
1.14	No.11 "Fantasia undecima, sopra quattro soggietti"
1.15	No.12 "Fantasia duodecima, sopra quattro soggietti"
1.16	"Toccate e partite d'intavolatura di cimbalo," Vol.I (p1615): No.1 "Toccata prima" A.3–A.4
1.17	No.2 "Toccata seconda"
1.18	No.3 "Toccata terza"
1.19	No.4 "Toccata quatra"
1.20	No.5 "Toccata quinta"
1.21	No.6 "Toccata sesta"
1.22	No.7 "Toccata settima"
1.23	No.8 "Toccata otava"
1.24	No.9 "Toccata nona"
1.25	No.10 "Toccata decima"
1.26	No.11 "Toccata undecima"
1.27	No.12 "Toccata duodecima"
1.28	No.13 "Partite sopra rugiero"
1.29	No.14 "Partite sopra la romanesca"
1.30	No.15 "Parte sopra lamonicha"
1.31	"Recercari, et canzoni franzese," Vol.I (p1615): No.1 "Recerca Primo" A.5
1.32	No.2 "Recercar Secondo"
1.33	No.3 "Recercar Terzo"
1.34	No.4 "Recercar Quatro. Obligo, mi, re, fa, mi"
1.35	No.5 "Recercar Quinto"
1.36	No.6 "Recercar Sesto. Obligo fa, fa, sol, la, fa"
1.37	No.7 "Recercar Settimo. Obligo sol, mi, fa, la, sol"
1.38	No.8 "Recercar Ottavo. Obligo di non mai di grado"
1.39	No.9 "Recercar Nono. Obligo di quattro soggetti"
1.40	No.10 "Recercar Decimo. Obligo la, fa, sol, la, fa, re"
1.41	No.11 "Canzon Prima. Primo Tono"
1.42	No.12 "Canzon Seconda. Primo Tono"
1.43	No.13 "Canzon Terza. Secondo Tono"
1.44	No.14 "Canzon Quarta. Sesto Tono"
1.45	No.15 "Canzon Quinta. Nono Tono"
1.46	"Capricci ... et arie," Vol.I (p1624): No.1 Capriccio "Primo ut, re, mi, fa, sol, la" A.6
1.47	No.2 "Capriccio Secondo la, sol, fa, mi, re ut"
1.48	No.3 "Capriccio Terzo sopra il Cucho"
1.49	No.4 "Capriccio Quarto la, sol, fa, re mi"
1.50	No.5 "Capriccio Quinto sopra la bassa fiammenga"
1.51	No.6 "Capriccio Sesto sopra la Spagnoletta"
1.52	No.7 "Capriccio Settimo sopra or che noi rimena"
1.53	No.8 "Capriccio Ottavo Cromatico di ligature al contrario"
1.54	No.9 "Capriccio Nono di durezze"
1.55	No.10 "Capriccio Decimo Obligo di cantare la quinta parte, senza toccarla ..."
1.56	No.11 "Capriccio Undecimo sopra un sogetto"
1.57	No.12 "Capriccio Duodecimo sopra l'Aria di Rugiero"
1.58	"Toccate, canzone ... di cimbalo et organo," Vol.II (p1627): No.1 "Toccata Prima" A.7
1.59	No.2 "Toccata Secoda"
1.60	No.3 "Toccata Terza. Per l'organo da sonarsi alla levatione"
1.61	No.4 "Toccata Quarta. Per l'organo da sonarsi alla levatione"
1.62	No.5 "Quinta Toccata sopra i pedali per l'organo, e senza"
1.63	No.6 "Toccata Sesta. Per l'organo sopra i pedali, e senza"
1.64	No.7 "Toccata Settima"
1.65	No.8 "VIII Toccata di durezze, e Ligature"
1.66	No.9 "Toccata Nona. Non senza fatiga si giunge al fine"
1.67	No.10 "Toccata Decima"
1.68	No.11 "Toccata Undecima"
1.69	No.12 "Ancidetemi pur d'Archadelt passaggiato"
1.70	No.13 "Canzona Prima"
1.71	No.14 "Canzona Seconda"
1.72	No.15 "Canzona Terza"
1.73	No.16 "Canzona Quarta"

1.74	No.17 "Canzona Quinta"
1.75	No.18 "Canzona Sesta"
1.76	No.19 "Hinno Della Domenica"
1.77	No.20 "Hinno Dell'Apostoli"
1.78	No.21 "Hinno iste confessor"
1.79	No.22 "Hinno Ave Maris stella"
1.80	No.23 "Magnificat Primi Toni"
1.81	No.24 "Magnificat Secundi Toni"
1.82	No.25 "Magnificat Sesti Toni"
1.83	No.26 "Aria detta Balletto"
1.84	No.27 "Gagliarda Prima"
1.85	No.28 "Gagliarda Seconda"
1.86	No.29 "Gagliarda Terza"
1.87	No.30 "Gagliarda Quarta"
1.88	No.31 "Gagliarda Quinta"
1.89	No.32 "Aria detta 'la Frescobalda' "
1.90	No.33 "Corrente Primo"
1.91	No.34 "Corrente Secondo"
1.92	No.35 "Corrente 2.a alio modo"
1.93	No.36 "Corrente Quarto"
1.94	No.37 "Corrente Quinto"
1.95	No.38 "Corrente Sesto"
1.96	No.39 "Partite Sopra Ciaccona"
1.97	No.40 "Partite Sopra Passacagli"
1.98	"Canzoni a 1–4," Vol.I (p1628), voci sole: No.1 "Canzon Prima, violino solo; over cornetto" A.8
1.99	No.2 "Canzon seconda, violino solo. over cornetto"
1.100	No.3 "Canzon terza, violino solo. over cornetto"
1.101	No.4 "Canzon quarta, violino solo"
1.102	No.5 "Canzon Prima, basso solo"
1.103	No.6 "Canzon seconda, basso solo"
1.104	No.7 "Canzon terza, basso solo"
1.105	No.8 "Canzon quarta, basso solo"
1.106	a due voci: No.9 "Canzon Prima, a due canti"
1.107	No.10 "Canzon seconda, a due canti"
1.108	No.11 "Canzon terza, a due canti"
1.109	No.12 "Canzon quarta, a due canti"
1.110	No.13 "Canzon quinta, a due canti"
1.111	No.14 "Canzon Prima, a due bassi"
1.112	No.15 "Canzon seconda, a due bassi"
1.113	No.16 "Canzon terza, a due bassi"
1.114	No.17 "Canzon quarta, a due bassi"
1.115	No.18 "Canzon Prima a due, canto, e basso"
1.116	No.19 "Canzon seconda a due, canto, e basso"
1.117	No.20 "Canzon terza a due, canto, e basso"
1.118	No.21 "Canzon quarta a due, canto, e basso"
1.119	No.22 "Canzon quinta a due, canto e basso"
1.120	No.23 "Canzon sesta a due, canto, e basso"
1.121	a tre voci: No.24 "Canzon Prima a 3, due bassi, e canto"
1.122	No.25 "Canzon seconda a 3. due bassi, e canto"
1.123	No.26 "Canzon terza a 3. due bassi, e canto"
1.124	No.27 "Canzon quarta a 3. due bassi, e canto"
1.125	No.28 "Canzon quinta a 3. due canti, e basso"
1.126	No.29 "Canzon sesta a 3. due canti, e basso"
1.127	a quattro voci: No.30 "Canzon Prima, due canti, e due bassi"
1.128	No.31 "Canzon seconda, due canti, e due bassi"
1.129	No.32 "Canzon terza, canto, alto, tenore & basso"
1.130	No.33 "Canzon quarta, due canti, e due bassi"
1.131	No.34 "Canzon quinta, due canti, e due bassi"
1.132	No.35 "Canzon sesta, a 4, canto, alto, tenore & basso"
1.133	"Canzoni a 1–4 voci" (p1628, 34 Nos. from A.8), canto solo: No.1 "detta la Bonuisia" A.9
1.134	No.2 "detta la Bernadina"
1.135	No.3 "detta la Lucchesina"
1.136	No.4 "detta la Donatina"
1.137	basso solo: No.5 "detta la Tromboncina"
1.138	No.6 "detta l'Altera"
1.139	No.7 "detta la Tuccina"
1.140	No.8 "detta l'Ambitiosa"
1.141	a due canti: No.9 "detta la Gualterina"
1.142	No.10 "detta l'Henricuccia"
1.143	No.11 "detta la Plettenberger"
1.144	No.12 "detta la Todeschina"
1.145	No.13 "detta la Bianchina"
1.146	a due bassi: No.14 "detta la Marina"
1.147	No.15 "detta la Licuoratta"
1.148	No.16 "detta la Samminiata"

1.149	No.17 "detta la Diodata"
1.150	canto e basso: No.18 "detta la Masotti"
1.151	No.19 "detta la Capriola"
1.152	No.20 "detta la Pipparella"
1.153	No.21 "detta la Tegrimuccia"
1.154	No.22 "detta la Nicolina"
1.155	No.23 "detta la Franciotta"
1.156	a tre. Due bassi, e canto: No.24 "detta la Nobile"
1.157	No.25 "detta la Garzoncina"
1.158	No.26 "detta la Moricona"
1.159	due canti, e basso: No.27 "detta la Lanciona"
1.160	No.28 "detta la Lanberta"
1.161	No.29 "detta la Boccellina"
1.162	a quattro. Due canti, e due bassi: No.30 "detta la Cittadellia"
1.163	No.31 "detta l'Arnolfinia"
1.164	No.32 "detta l'Altogradina"
1.165	No.33 "detta la Rouellina"
1.166	No.34 "detta la Sandoninia"
1.167	canto alto tenore, e basso: No.35 "detta l'Alessandrina"
1.168	No.36 "detta la Capponcina"
1.169	No.37 "detta la Sardina"
1.170	No.38 "Toccata per Spinettina, e Violino"
1.171	No.39 "Toccata per Spinettina sola"
1.172	No.40 "Canzona per Spinettina sola. detta la Vittoria"
1.173	"Canzoni a 1–4," I (p1634, 28 from A.8, 2 from A.9, 10 new), Canto solo: No.1 "Canzon prima" A.10
1.174	No.2 "Canzon seconda"
1.175	No.3 "Canzon Terza"
1.176	No.4 "Canzon quarta"
1.177	basso Solo: No.5 "Canzon prima"
1.178	No.6 "Canzon seconda"
1.179	No.7 "Canzon terza"
1.180	a due Bassi: No.8 "Canzon prima"
1.181	No.9 "Canzon seconda"
1.182	No.10 "Canzon terza"
1.183	No.11 "Canzon quarta"
1.184	a 2 Canto, e Basso: No.12 "Canzon prima"
1.185	No.13 "Canzon seconda"
1.186	No.14 "Canzon terza"
1.187	No.15 "Canzon quarta"
1.188	No.16 "Canzon quinta"
1.189	No.17 "Canzon sesta"
1.190	a 2 Canti: No.18 "Canzon prima"
1.191	No.19 "Canzon seconda"
1.192	No.20 "Canzon terza"
1.193	No.21 "Canzon quarta"
1.194	a 3. due Bassi, e Canto: No.22 "Canzon prima"
1.195	No.23 "Canzon seconda"
1.196	No.24 "Canzon terza"
1.197	No.25 "Canzon quarta"
1.198	due Canti, e Basso: No.26 "Canzon prima"
1.199	No.27 "Canzon seconda"
1.200	No.28 "Canzon terza"
1.201	No.29 "Canzon quarta"
1.202	No.30 "Canzon quinta"
1.203	a 4. due Canti, e due Bassi: No.31 "Canzon prima"
1.204	No.32 "Canzon seconda"
1.205	No.33 "Canzon terza"
1.206	No.34 "Canzon quarta"
1.207	canto Alto Tenor, e Basso: No.35 "Canzon prima sopra Rugier"
1.208	No.36 "Canzon seconda"
1.209	No.37 "Canzon terza"
1.210	No.38 "Canzon quarta"
1.211	No.39 "Canzon quinta"
1.212	No.40 "Canzon sesta"
1.213	"Fiori musicali," a 4 (p1635): No.1 "Tocata Avanti la Messa Della Domenica" A.11
1.214	No.2 "Kirie Della Domenica"
1.215	No.3 "kirie"
1.216	No.4 "Christe"
1.217	No.5 "Christe Alio modo"
1.218	No.6 "Christe Alio modo"
1.219	No.7 "Christe Alio modo"
1.220	No.8 "Kirie"
1.221	No.9 "kirie Alio modo"
1.222	No.10 "kirie Alio modo"
1.223	No.11 "kirie Ultimo"

1.224	No.12 "kirie Alio modo"
1.225	No.13 "kirie Alio modo"
1.226	No.14 "Canzon Dopo l'Epistola"
1.227	No.15 "Recercar Dopo il Credo"
1.228	No.16 "Tocata Cromaticha per l'Elevatione"
1.229	No.17 "Canzon post il Comune"
1.230	No.18 "Tocata Avanti la Messa Delli Apostoli"
1.231	No.19 "Kyrie delli Apostoli"
1.232	No.20 "Kyrie"
1.233	No.21 "Kirie
1.234	No.22 "Christe"
1.235	No.23 "Christe"
1.236	No.24 "Kirie"
1.237	No.25 "kirie"
1.238	No.26 "kirie"
1.239	No.27 "Canzon Dopo l'Epistola"
1.240	No.28 "Tocata Avanti il Recercar"
1.241	No.29 "Recercar Cromaticho post il Credo"
1.242	No.30 "Altro Recercar"
1.243	No.31 "Tocata per l'Elevatione"
1.244	No.32 "Recercar Con obligo del Basso come appare"
1.245	No.33 "Canzon quarti Toni Dopo il post Comune"
1.246	No.34 "Tocata Avanti la Messa della Madonna"
1.247	No.35 "Kyrie della Madonna"
1.248	No.36 "kirie"
1.249	No.37 "Christe"
1.250	No.38 "Christe"
1.251	No.39 "kirie"
1.252	No.40 "kirie"
1.253	No.41 "Canzon Dopo l'Epistola"
1.254	No.42 "Recercar Dopo il Credo"
1.255	No.43 "Tocata Avanti il Recercar"
1.256	No.44 "Recercar Con obligo di Cantare la Quinta parte senza Tocarla ..."
1.257	No.45 "Tocata per l'Elevatione"
1.258	No.46 "Bergamasca" (Chi questa Bergamasca sonara non pocho Imparera)
1.259	No.47 "Capricio sopra la Girolmeta"
1.260	"Toccate d'intavolatura di cimbalo et organo" (p1637): No.1 "Toccate dodeci" A.12
1.261	No.2 "Partite 14. sopra l'Aria di Romanesca"
1.262	No.3 "Partite 2. sopra l'Aria di Monicha"
1.263	No.4 "Partite 12. sopra l'Aria di Ruggiero"
1.264	No.5 "Partite 6. sopra l'Aria di Follia"
1.265	No.6 "Corente quattro"
1.266	No.7 "Balletto e Corrente"
1.267	No.8 "Passachagli e Balletto"
1.268	No.9 "Balletto e Corrente"
1.269	No.10 "Passachagli"
1.270	No.11 "Partite cento sopra il Passachagli"
1.271	No.12 "Corrente e Passachagli"
1.272	No.13 "Ciaccone e Passachagli"
1.273	No.14 "Capriccio Fra Jacopino sopra l'Aria di Ruggiero"
1.274	No.15 "Capriccio sopra la Battaglia"
1.275	No.16 "Balletto e Ciaccone"
1.276	No.17 "Corrente e Ciaccone"
1.277	No.18 "Capriccio fatto sopra la Pastorale"
1.278	"Canzoni alla francese," Vol.IV (p1645): No.1 "detta la Rovetta" A.13
1.279	No.2 "detta la Sabatina"
1.280	No.3 "detta la Crivelli"
1.281	No.4 "detta la Scacchi"
1.282	No.5 "detta la Bellerofonte"
1.283	No.6 "detta la Pesenti"
1.284	No.7 "detta la Tarditi"
1.285	No.8 "detta la Vincenti"
1.286	No.9 "detta la Querina"
1.287	No.10 "detta la Paulini"
1.288	No.11 "detta la Gardana"

2. SACRED VOCAL

2.1	"Liber II diversarum modulationum" (c1627;1–4vv & cont): 1. "Aspice Domine" (1v) B.1
2.2	2. "Ipsi sum desponsata" (1v)
2.3	3. "Deus noster refugium, & virtus" (1v)
2.4	4. "Exultavit cor meum" (T)
2.5	5. "O Iesu mi dulcissime" (T)
2.6	6. "Vidi speciosam sicut columbam" (2vv, inc)

3. SECULAR VOCAL

3.31	12. "Non me negate, ohimè," aria (1v)
3.32	13. "Di Licori un guardo solo," canto (1v; 2 settings)
3.33	14. "Voi partite mio Sole," aria (T)
3.34	15. "Se l'aura spira tutta vezzosa," aria (1v):
	. seconda parte: "A'balli, a'balli"
	. terza parte: "Suoi dolci versi"
3.35	16. "Cosi mi disprezzate," aria di Passacaglia (1v)
3.36	17. "Se m'amate io v'adoro," madrigale (2vv)
3.37	18. "Begli occhi io non provo," canto (2vv)
3.38	19. "Occhi che sete di voi pomposi," aria (2vv)
3.39	20. "Dove, dove ne vai pensiero," canzone (2vv)
3.40	21. "Eri gia tuta mia," canzona (2vv)
3.41	22. "Corilla danzando," canzona (2vv)
3.42	23. "Con dolcezza e pietate," canzona (A, T, B)
3.43	"Arie," Vol.II (p1630; 1–3vv, theorbo & hpd): 1. "Vanne, o carta amorosa" (1v) B.4
3.44	2. "Ben veggio donna homai," canto in stile recitativo (1v)
3.45	3. "Oscure selve," canto in stile recitativo (1v)
3.46	4. "Ohimè, che fur, che sono," sonetto spirituale in stile recitativo (1v)
3.47	5. "Dove, dove sparir," sonetto spirituale (1v)
3.48	6. "Ti lascio anima mia, Ruggieri" (1v):
	. seconda parte: "Io parto, ohimè convien ch'io mora"
	. terza parte: "Ah pur troppo e'l dolor ch'entro"
	. quarta parte: "Deh non languir, cor mio"
3.49	7. "Voi partite mio sole," aria (1v)
3.50	8. "La mia pallida faccia," aria (1v)
3.51	9. "A miei pianti al fine un di," aria (1v)
3.52	10. "O mio cor, dolce mia vita," aria (1v):
	. seconda parte: "Tu sai pur dolce mia vita"
3.53	11. "Son ferito, son morto," aria (1v)
3.54	12. "Voi partite" (Non vi partite), aria (2vv)
3.55	13. "Gioite o selve, o venti," canzona (2vv)
3.56	14. "Bella tiranna infida," madrigale (2T)
3.57	15. "Soffrir non posso," canzona (2T)
3.58	16. "Deh, volate oh miei voci dolenti," canzona (A, T, B)
3.59	17. "Quanto più sorda sete," madrigale (A, T, B)
3.60	18. "Deh, vien da me pastorella," ceccona (2T)
3.61	19. "Doloroso mio core," canzona (A, T, B)
3.62	20. "O dolore, o ferita," canzona (A, T, B)
3.63	"Alla gloria" (p1621; 1v & cont) ....
3.64	"Era l'anima mia" (p1622; 2vv & cont) ....
3.65	"O bell' occhi" (p1621; 1v & cont) ....

* * * * *

A = RISM (Répertoire International des Sources Musicales), Series A, "Einzeldrücke vor 1800" Vol.A/I/3.
B = RISM, Series B, "Recueils imprimés 16e–17e siècles" Vol.B/I/1.

1. STAGE WORKS

Operas:

1.1	"Blue Monday Blues," 1 act jazz opera (p1922, De Sylva; orchd Vodery; reorchd Grofé as: 135th Street) ...
1.2	"Porgy and Bess," 3 acts (p by Heyward 1935, lyrics DuBose Heyward & Ira Gershwin, libretto DuBose Heyward based on his play: Porgy) ....

Musicals & revues (also see Songs):

1.3	"The Passing Show of 1916" (p1916, Atteridge) ....
1.4	"Hitchy-Koo of 1918" (p1918) ....
1.5	"Ladies First" (p1918) ....
1.6	"Half Past Eight," revue (p by Perkins 1918, Caryll) ....
1.7	"Good Morning Judge" (p1919) ....
1.8	"The Lady in Red" (p1919) ....
1.9	"La-La-Lucille" (p by Aarons & Seitz 1919, lyrics Jackson & DeSylva, book Jackson, 1st full Broadway score) ....
1.10	"The Capitol Revue" (Demi-Tasse) (p1919) ....
1.11	"Morris Gest's Midnight Whirl" (p by Gest 1919, DeSylva & Mears) ....
1.12	"Dere Mable" (p1920) ....
1.13	"George White's Scandals of 1920" (p by White 1920, lyrics Jackson, book Rice & White) ....
1.14	"The Sweetheart Shop" (p1920) ....
1.15	"Broadway Brevities of 1920" (p1920) ....
1.16	"Picadilly to Broadway" (p1920) ....
1.17	"Blue Eyes" (p1921) ....
1.18	"A Dangerous Maid" (p by MacGregor 1921, lyrics Ira Gershwin, book Bell, George & Ira, first full score together) ....
1.19	"Selwyn's Snapshots of 1921" (p1921) ....
1.20	"George White's Scandals of 1921" (p by White 1921, lyrics Jackson, book 'Bugs' Baer & White) ....
1.21	"The Perfect Fool" (p1921) ....
1.22	"The French Doll" (p1922) ....
1.23	"For Goodness Sake" (p1922) ....
1.24	"George White's Scandals of 1922" (p by White 1922, lyrics DeSylva & Goetz, book White & Fields) ....
1.25	"Our Nell" (p by Davidov & LeMaire 1922, lyrics Hooker, book Thomas & Hooker, music collab Daly) ....
1.26	"The Dancing Girl" (p1923) ....
1.27	"The Rainbow" (p by Courville 1923, lyrics Grey, revue Courville, Wallace & Scott) ....
1.28	"G. White's Scandals of 1923" (p by White 1923, lyrics DeSylva, Goetz & MacDonald, book White & Wells)
1.29	"Little Miss Bluebeard" (p by 1923, Hopwood) ....
1.30	"Nifties of 1923" (p1923) ....
1.31	"Sweet Little Devil" (p by Schwab 1924, lyrics DeSylva, book Mandel & Schwab) ....
1.32	"George White's Scandals of 1924" (p by White 1924, lyrics DeSylva, book Wells & White) ....
1.33	"Primrose" (p by Grossmith & Malone 1924, lyrics Carter & Ira Gershwin, book Grossmith & Bolton) ....
1.34	"Lady, be Good" (p by Aarons & Freedley 1924, lyrics Ira Gershwin, book Bolton & Thompson) ....
1.35	"Tell Me More" (p by Aarons 1925, lyrics DeSylva & Ira Gershwin, book Thompson & Wells) ....
1.36	"Tip-Toes" (p by Aarons & Freedley 1925, lyrics Ira Gershwin, book Bolton & Thompson) ....
1.37	"Song of the Flame" (p by A. Hammerstein 1925, lyrics & book Harbach & O. Hammerstein II, music collab Stothart) ....
1.38	"Americana" (p1926, lyrics & book McEvoy, collab w/ others) ....
1.39	"Oh, Kay!" (p by Aarons & Freedley 1926, lyrics Ira Gershwin, book Bolton & Wodehouse) ....
1.40	"Strike Up the Band," I (p by Selwyn 1927, lyrics Ira Gershwin, book Kaufman) ....
1.41	"Funny Face" (p by Aarons & Freedley 1927, lyrics Ira Gershwin, book Thompson & Smith) ....
1.42	"Rosalie" (p by Ziegfeld 1928, Wodehouse & Ira Gershwin, book McGuire & Bolton, music collab Romberg)
1.43	"Treasure Girl" (p by Aarons & Freedley 1928, lyrics Ira Gershwin, book Thompson & Lawrence) ....
1.44	"Show Girl" (p by Ziegfeld 1929, lyrics Kahn & Ira Gershwin, book McGuire on McEvoy's novel) ....
1.45	*"East is West" (Ziegfeld, never produced)* ....
1.46	"Strike Up the Band" II (p by Selwyn 1930, lyrics Ira Gershwin, book Ryskind based on Kaufman's libretto)
1.47	"Nine-Fifteen Revue" (p1930) ....
1.48	"Girl Crazy" (p by Aarons & Freedley 1930, lyrics Ira Gershwin, book Bolton & McGowan; also 1st filmed vers 1932; 2nd filmed vers 1943) ....
1.49	"Of Thee I Sing" (p by Harris 1931, lyrics Ira Gershwin, book Kaufman & Ryskind) ....
1.50	"Pardon My English" (p by Aarons & Freedley 1933, lyrics Ira Gershwin, book Fields) ....
1.51	"Let 'Em Eat Cake" (p by Harris 1933, lyrics Ira Gershwin, book Kaufman & Ryskind) ....
1.52	"The Show Is On" (p1936, lyrics Ira Gershwin & others) ....
1.53	*"Crazy for You," pastiche (arr Ludwig & Ockrent p1993, after: Girl Crazy)* ....

Film:

1.54	"Delicious" (p by Sheehan, dir Butler 1931, lyrics Ira Gershwin, screenplay Bolton & Levien) ....
1.55	"Shall We Dance" (p by Berman, dir Sandrich 1937, lyrics Ira Gershwin, screenplay Scott & Pagano) ....
1.56	"A Damsel In Distress" (p by Berman, dir Stevens 1937, lyrics Ira Gerhwin, screenplay Wodehouse, Pagano & Lauren) ....
1.57	"The Goldwyn Follies" (p by Goldwyn, dir Marshall 1937, lyrics Ira Gershwin, screenplay Hecht, add music Duke) ....

1a. SELECTIONS FROM OPERAS

1a.2   "Porgy and Bess," opera: ....
  I/1:   . "Summertime"
          . (crap game) "Seems like these bones ..."
          . "I been sweatin' all day ..."
          . "Lord, I is tired this night ..."
          . "A woman is a sometime thing"
          . "Here come de Honey Man" (street cry)
          . "Evenin' ladies" (entrance of Porgy)
          . "They pass by singin' "
          . (crap game) "Yo mammy's gone ..."
          . "Crown cockeyed drunk ..."
          . "Oh, little stars ..." (Robbin's murder) (orch)
  I/2:   . "Gone, gone, gone"
          . "Overflow"
          . "My man's gone now"
          . "Leavin' fo' the Promis' Land" (Train song)
  II/1:   . "It take a long pull to get there"
          . "I got plenty o' nuttin' "
          . "I hates yo' struttin' style" (eliminated in Boston)
          . "Mornin', lawyer" (entrance of Frazier)
          . "Lord, Lord, listen what she say"
          . " 'Course I sells divorce"
          . "Woman to lady"
          . "Buzzard song" (eliminated in Boston)
          . "Bess, you is my woman now"
          . "Oh, I can't sit down"
  II/2:   . "Allegretto barbaro" (percussion)
          . "I ain't got no shame" (eliminated in Boston)
          . "It ain't necessarily so"
          . "Shame on all of you sinners"
          . "What you want with Bess?"
  II/3:   . "It take a long pull to get there" (reprise)
          . "De white folks put me in"
          . "Oh, Doctor Jesus" (time and time again)
          . "Street cries": "Strawberry Woman, Honey Man, Crab Man"
          . "I loves you, Porgy"
          . "Hurricane" (orch)
  II/4:   . "Prayers," for 6 voices (eliminated in Boston)
          . "Oh de Lord shake de heavens"
          . "Summertime" (reprise; orig for this spot: Lonely Boy, duet)
          . "Oh, dere's somebody knockin' at de do' "
          . "A red headed woman"
          . "Lawd, save us" (counterpoint to: A red headed woman)
          . "Prayers" (reprise)
  III/1:   . "Clara, Clara, don't you be downhearted"
          . "Summertime" (reprise by Bess)
          . "Fugue" (the death of Crown; orch)
  III/2:   . "Scene with detective": "Serena been very sick ..."
          . "We ain't seen nothin' Boss ..."
          . "You knows me, boss ..."
          . "There's a boat dat's leavin' soon for New York"
  III/3:   . "Moderato commodo" (occupational humoresque)
          . "Good mornin', sister" (eliminated in Boston)
          . "Sure to go to Heaven" (eliminated in Boston)
          . "How are you dis mornin" (eliminated in Boston)
          . "Thank Gawd, I's home again!" (return of Porgy)
          . "Here, boy look what I brought for you"
          . "Where's my Bess?"
          . "I'm on my way"
  Not used: . "Lonely boy"

2. ORCHESTRAL WORKS

2.1   "Rhapsody in Blue" (c1924; pf & jazz band; orchd Grofé 1926, r1942; arr for pf/2pf) ....

2.2   "Setting-up exercises" (c1928; see song: Rosalie) ....

2.3	"An American in Paris," tone poem (c1928) ....
2.4	"Mexican Dance" (c1930; see song: Girl Crazy) ....
2.5	"New York Rhapsody" (c1931, for film: Delicious) ....
2.6	"Cuban Overture" (Rhumba) (c1932) ....
2.7	"Catfish Row," suite (c1936, from opera: Porgy & Bess): No.1 "Catfish Row" ....
2.8	No.2 "Porgy sings"
2.9	No.3 "Fugue"
2.10	No.4 "Hurricane"
2.11	No.5 "Good morning, brother"

3. PIANO CONCERTOS, PIANO & ORCH

3.1	"Concerto in F" (c1925; arr for 2pf) ....
3.2	"Second Rhapsody" (c1932; expanded in: New York Rhapsody; arr for 2pf) ....
3.3	"Variations on 'I Got Rhythm' " (c1934; arr for 2pf) ....

4. STRING QUARTETS

| 4.1 | "Lullaby" (c1919, p1968) .... |

5. OTHER CHAMBER MUSIC

| 5.1 | "Piece for Four Strings" (c1920) .... |
| 5.2 | *"Short Story" (arr Dushkin for vn & pf 1925, from: 2 Novelettes / Preludes Nos.4–5 for pf, see 3 Preluds for pf)* .... |

6. PIANO

6.1	"Tango" (c1914) ....
6.2	"Rialto Ripples—piano rag" (c1917, collab Donaldson) ....
6.3	"3 Preludes" (c1926; Gershwin perf 6 preludes in 1927, Nos.4 & 5 arr Dushkin as: Short Story for vn & pf, No.6 remains in manuscript): No.1 in B-flat major ....
6.4	No.2 in C-sharp minor
6.5	No.3 in E-flat minor
6.6	"Merry Andrew" (c1928, p1974) ....
6.7	"Impromptu in Two Keys" (c1929; began as a song: Yellow blues) ....
6.8	"Gershwin Songbook," piano transcr of 18 songs (p1932): No.1 "Swanee" (from: Capitol Revue of 1919) ..
6.9	No.2 "Nobody but you" (from: La-La-Lucille of 1919)
6.10	No.3 "I'll build a stairway to paradise" (from: G. White's Scandals of 1922)
6.11	No.4 "Do it again" (from: The French Doll of 1922)
6.12	No.5 "Fascinating rhythm" (from: Lady, be Good of 1924)
6.13	No.6 "Oh, lady be good!" (from: Lady, be Good of 1924)
6.14	No.7 "Somebody loves me" (from: George White's Scandals of 1924)
6.15	No.8 "Sweet and low-down" (from: Tip-Toes of 1925)
6.16	No.9 "That certain feeling" (from: Tip-Toes of 1925)
6.17	No.10 "The man I love" (from: Lady, be Good of 1924)
6.18	No.11 "Clap yo' hands" (from: Oh, Kay! of 1926)
6.19	No.12 "Do-do-do" (from: Oh, Kay! of 1926)
6.20	No.13 "My one and only" (from: Funny Face of 1927)
6.21	No.14 " 's wonderful" (from: Funny Face of 1927)
6.22	No.15 "Strike-up the band" (from: Strike Up the Band I of 1927)
6.23	No.16 "Liza" (All the clouds'll roll away) (from: Show Girl of 1929)
6.24	No.17 "I got rhythm" (from: Girl Crazy of 1930)
6.25	No.18 "Who cares so long as you care for me?" (from: Of Thee I Sing of 1931)
6.26	"Mischa, Yascha ...," transcr of song of 1922 (c1932; incl in limited edition) ....
6.27	"2 Waltzes in C" (c1933, p1971, for: Pardon my English of 1933; arr for 2pf) ....
6.28	"Promenade" (c1937, arr of Walking the dog, from: Shall we dance of 1937; orchd) ....
6.29	"Three-Quarter Blues" (p1974) ....

7. SONGS

7.1	"Since I found you" (c1913, Praskins, first-known song) ....
7.2	"Ragging the Traumerei" (c1913, Praskins) ....
7.3	"When you want 'em, you can't get 'em ..." (c1916, Roth, first published song) ....

"The Passing Show of 1916" (p1916):

| 7.4 | used: . "Making of a girl" (Atteridge, music collab Romberg) .... |

7.5	"My runaway girl" (c1916, Roth) ....
7.6	"Good little tune" (c1916, Caesar) ....
7.7	"You are not the girl" (c1917, Ira Gershwin) ....

7.8 "We're six little nieces of Uncle Sam" (c1917, Paley)..
7.9 "A corner of heaven with you" (c1918, Paley) ....

"Hitchy-Koo of 1918" (p1918):

7.10 used: . "You-oo, just you" (Caesar) ....
7.11 . "When the armies disband" (c1918, Caesar) ....

"Ladies First" (p1918):

7.12 used: . "The real American folk song" (is a rag) (Ira Gershwin; pubd1959) ....
7.13 . "Some wonderful sort of someone" (Schuyler Greene)..........................

"Half Past Eight" (p1918):

7.14 used: . "There's magic in the air" (Ira Gershwin)...
7.15 . "Hong Kong" (Perkins) ....
7.16 . "Cupid" ....
7.17 . "Half past eight" ....
7.18 . "Little sunbeam" ....

"Good Morning Judge" (p1919):

7.19 used: . "I was so young, you were so beautiful" (Caesar & Al Bryan) ....
7.20 . "There's more to the kiss than X-X-X" (Caesar)....................................
7.21 . "O, land of mine, America" (O'Rourke) ....

"The Lady in Red" (p1919):

7.22 used: . "Something about love" (Paley; also see in: Lady, be Good of 1924) ....

"La-La-Lucille" (p1919, lyrics Jackson & DeSylva):

7.23 used: . "When you live in a furnished-flat"...
7.24 . "The best of everything" ....
7.25 . "From now on" ....
7.26 . "It's hard to tell" ....
7.27 . "Tee-oodle-um-bum-bo" ....
7.28 . "Nobody but you" (see pf transcr in: Gershwin Songbook) ....
7.29 . "It's great to be in love" ....
7.30 . "Somehow It seldom comes true" ....
7.31 . "The 10 commandments of love" (= There's magic in the air, in: Half Past Eight of 1918) ....
7.32 . "Oo, how I love to be loved by you" (Paley) ....
7.33 not used: . "The love of a wife" ....
7.34 . "Our little kitchenette" ....
7.35 . "Money, money, money!" ....
7.36 . "Kisses" ....

"The Capitol Revue" (Demi-Tasse) (p1919):

7.37 used: . "Swanee" (Caesar; see pf transcr in: Gershwin Songbook).......................
7.38 . "Come to the moon" (Wayburn & Paley) ....

"Morris Gest's Midnight Whirl" (p1919, lyrics DeSylva & Mears):

7.39 used: . "The League of Nations" ....
7.40 . "Doughnuts" ....
7.41 . "Poppyland" ....
7.42 . "I'll show you a wonderful world" ....
7.43 . "Limehouse nights" ....
7.44 . "Let cutie cut your cuticle" ....
7.45 . "Baby dolls" ....
7.46 . "Yan-Kee" (c1920, Caesar) ....

"Dere Mable" (p1920):

7.47 used: . "We're pals" (Caesar)..
7.48 . "Back home" (Arthur Francis—pseud of Ira Gershwin) ....
7.49 . "I don't know why" (Caesar) ....

7.50 "I want to be wanted by you" (Ira Gershwin) ....

"George White's Scandals of 1920" (p1920, lyrics Jackson):

7.51 used: . "My lady" ....
7.52 . "Everybody swat the profiteer" ....
7.53 . "On my mind the whole night long" ....
7.54 . "Turn on and tiss me" ....
7.55 . "Scandal walk" ....
7.56 . "The songs of long ago" ....
7.57 . "Idle dreams" ....

7.58   not used: . "Queen Isabella" ....

7.59   . "My old love is my new love" ....

"The Sweetheart Shop" (p1920):

7.60   used: . "Waiting for the sun to come out" (Arthur Francis—pseud of Ira Gershwin) ....

"Broadway Brevities of 1920" (p1920):

7.61   used: . "Spanish love" (Caesar) ....

7.62   . "Lu Lu" (Jackson) ....

7.63   . "Snow flakes" (Jackson) ....

"Picadilly to Broadway" (p1920):

7.64   used: . "On the brim of her old-fashioned bonnet" (Ray Goetz) ....

7.65   . "The Baby Blues" (Ray Goetz) ....

"Blue Eyes" (p1921):

7.66   used: . "Wanting you" (Caesar) ....

"A Dangerous Maid" (p1921, lyrics Ira Gershwin):

7.67   used: . "Just to know you are mine" ....

7.68   . "Boy wanted" ....

7.69   . "The simple life" ....

7.70   . "Dancing shoes" ....

7.71   . "True love" ....

7.72   . "Some rain must fall" ....

7.73   . "The sirens" ....

7.74   not used: . "Anything for you" ....

7.75   . "Pidgee woo" ....

7.76   . "Every girl has a way" ....

"Selwyn's Snapshots of 1921" (p1921):

7.77   used: . "Futuristic Melody" (Ray Goetz) ....

"George White's Scandals of 1921" (p1921, lyrics Jackson):

7.78   used: . "Mother Eve" ....

7.79   . "I love you" ....

7.80   . "South Sea isles" ....

7.81   . "Drifting along with the tide" ....

7.82   . "She's just a baby" ....

7.83   . "Where East meets West at Panama" ....

"The Perfect Fool" (p1921):

7.84   used: . "My log cabin home" (Caesar & DeSylva) ....

7.85   . "No one else but that girl of mine" (Caesar) ....

7.86   . "Tomale" (I'm hot for you) (DeSylva) ....

7.87   . "Dixie Rose" (Caesar & DeSylva; r as: Swanee Rose) ....

7.88   . "In the heart of the geisha" (Fisher) ....

7.89   . "Phoebe" (Ira Gershwin & Paley; r as: All the livelong day, in film: Kiss Me, Stupid of 1964) ....

"The French Doll" (p1922):

7.90   used: . "Do it again" (DeSylva; see pf transcr in: Gershwin Songbook) ....

"For Goodness Sake" (p1922):

7.91   used: . "All to myself" (Ira Gershwin) ....

7.92   . "Someone" (Arthur Francis—pseud of Ira Gershwin) ....

7.93   . "Tra-la-la" (Arthur Francis—pseud of Ira Gershwin) ....

7.94   "Mischa, Yascha, Toscha, Sascha" (c1922, p1932, Ira Gershwin) ....

"George White's Scandals of 1922" (p1922, lyrics DeSylva & Goetz):

7.95   used: . "Just a tiny cup of tea" ....

7.96   . "Oh, what she hangs out" (DeSylva) ....

7.97   . "Cinderelatives" (DeSylva) ....

7.98   . "I found a four leaf clover" (DeSylva) ....

7.99   . "I can't tell where they're from when they dance" ....

7.100   . "I'll build a stairway to paradise" (DeSylva & Arthur Francis—pseud of Ira Gershwin; see pf transcr in: Gershwin Songbook)

7.101   . "Across the Sea" ....

7.102   . "Argentina" (DeSylva) ....

7.103   . "Where is the man of my dreams?" ....

"Blue Monday Blues" (p1922):

7.104	used: . "Blue Monday blues" (DeSylva) ....
7.105	. "Has anyone seen my Joe?" ....
7.106	. "I'm going to see my mother" ....

"Our Nell" (p1922, lyrics Hooker):

7.107	used: . "Gol-Durn!" (music: collab Daly) ....
7.108	. "Innocent ingenue baby" ....
7.109	. "Names I love to hear" (music collab Daly) ....
7.110	. "By and by" ....
7.111	. "Madrigal" (music collab Daly) ....
7.112	. "We go to church on Sunday" ....
7.113	. "Walking home with Angeline" ....
7.114	. "Oh, you lady!" (music collab Daly) ....
7.115	. "Little villages" (music collab Daly) ....
7.116	not used: . "The custody of the child" ....

7.117	"The Yankee doodle blues" (c1922, Caesar & DeSylva) ....
7.118	"The flapper" (c1922, DeSylva) ....

"The Dancing Girl" (p1923):

7.119	used: . "That American boy of mine" (Caesar) ....

"The Rainbow" (p1923, lyrics Grey):

7.120	used: . "Sweetheart" (I'm so glad that I met you) ....
7.121	. "Good-night, my dear" ....
7.122	. "Any little tune" ....
7.123	. "Moonlight in Versailles" ....
7.124	. "In the rain" ....
7.125	. "Innocent lonesome blue baby" (Hooker & Grey, music collab Daly; r as: Innocent ingenue baby)
7.126	. "Beneath the Eastern moon" ....
7.127	. "Oh! Nina" ....
7.128	. "Strut lady with me" ....
7.129	. "Sunday in London town" ....
7.130	. "All over town" (melody = Come to the moon) ....
7.131	not used: . "Give me my mammy" ....

7.132	"The sunshine trail" (c1923, Arthur Francis—pseud of Ira Gershwin, theme song for film of the same title) .

"George White's Scandals of 1923" (p1923, lyrics DeSylva, Goetz & Ballard MacDonald):

7.133	used: . "Little scandal dolls" ....
7.134	. "You and I" ....
7.135	. "Katinka" ....
7.136	. "Lo-la-lo" (DeSylva) ....
7.137	. "There is nothing too good for you" (DeSylva & Goetz) ....
7.138	. "Throw her in high!" (DeSylva & Goetz) ....
7.139	. "Let's be lonesome together" (DeSylva & Goetz) ....
7.140	. "The life of a rose" (DeSylva) ....
7.141	. "Look in the looking glass" ....
7.142	. "Where is she?" (DeSylva) ....
7.143	. "Laugh your cares away" ....
7.144	. "(On the beach at) How've-you-been" (DeSylva) ....
7.145	. "Garden of love" ....

"Little Miss Bluebeard" (p1923):

7.146	used: . "I won't say I will and I won't say I won't" (DeSylva & Arthur Francis—pseud of Ira Gershwin) .....

"Nifties of 1923" (p1923):

7.147	used: . "At half past seven" (DeSylva) ....
7.148	. "Nashville nightingale" (Caesar) ....

"Sweet Little Devil" (p1924, lyrics DeSylva):

7.149	used: . "Strike, strike, strike" ....
7.150	. "Virginia" ....
7.151	. "Someone believes in you" ....
7.152	. "The Jijibo" ....
7.153	. "Under a one-man top" ....
7.154	. "The matrimonial handicap" ....
7.155	. "Just supposing" ....
7.156	. "Hey! Hey! Let 'er go!" ....
7.157	. "Hooray for the U.S.A." ....
7.158	. "Mah-Jongg" ....

7.159   . "Pepita" ....
7.160   not used: . "My little duckie" ....
7.161   . "Sweet little devil" ....
7.162   . "Be the life of the crowd" ....

"George White's Scandals of 1924" (p1924, lyrics DeSylva):

7.163   used: . "Just mised the opening chorus" ....
7.164   . "I need a garden"...
7.165   . "Night time in Araby" ....
7.166   . "I'm going back" ....
7.167   . "Year after year" ....
7.168   . "Somebody loves me" (DeSylva & Ballard MacDonald; see pf transcr in: Gershwin Songbook) ..
7.169   . "Tune in" (to station J.O.Y.) ....
                 . "Mah-Jongg" (see in: Sweet Little Devil of 1924)...
7.170   . "Lovers of art"...
7.171   . "Rose of Madrid" ....
7.172   . "I love you, my darling" ....
7.173   . "Kongo Kate" ....

"Primrose" (p1924, lyrics Carter & Ira Gershwin):

7.174   used: . "Leaving town while we may" (Carter)...
7.175   . "Till I meet someone like you" (Carter)...
7.176   . "Isn't it wonderful?" (Ira Gershwin & Carter) ....
7.177   . "This is the life for a man" (Carter) ....
7.178   . "When Toby is out of town" (Carter)..
7.179   . "Some far-away someone" (Ira Gershwin & DeSylva, melody = Half past seven) ....
7.180   . "The Mophams" (Carter) ....
7.181   . "Can we do anything?" (Ira Gershwin & Carter)..
7.182   . "Roses of France" (Carter) ....
7.183   . "Four little sirens" (Gershwin)...
7.184   . "Berkley Square and Kew" (Carter) ....
7.185   . "Boy wanted" (Ira Gershwin & Carter) ....
7.186   . "Wait a bit, Susie" (Ira Gershwin & Carter) ....
7.187   . "Isn't terrible what they did to Mary, Queen of Scots?" ....
7.188   . "I make hay while the moon shines" (Carter) ....
7.189   . "That new-fangled mother of mine" (Carter) ....
7.190   . "Beau Brummel" (Carter)..
7.191   not used: . "The live wire" (c1924, Carter) ....
7.192   . "Pep! Zip! and punch!" (c1924, Carter) ....

"Lady, be Good" (p1924, lyrics Ira Gershwin):

7.193   used: . "Hang on to me" ....
7.194   . "A wonderful party"..
7.195   . "The end of a string"...
7.196   . "We're here because" ....
7.197   . "Fascinating Rhythm" (see pf transcr in: Gershwin Songbook)..
7.198   . "So am I"..
7.199   . "Oh, lady be good!" (see pf transcr in: Gershwin Songbook) ....
7.200   . "The Robinson Hotel" ....
7.201   . "The half of it, dearie, blues" ....
7.202   . "Juanita" ....
7.203   . "Little jazz bird"..
7.204   . "Swiss miss" (Ira Gershwin & Jackson)..
7.205   not used: . "Seeing Dickie home"..
7.206   . "The man I love" (see pf transcr in: Gershwin Songbook; also in: Strike Up the Band I of 1927;
                 also in: Rosalie of 1928) ....
7.207   . "Will you remember me?"...
7.208   . "Singin' Pete"...
7.209   . "Evening star"...
7.210   . "The bad, bad men" ....
7.211   . "Weather man" ....
7.212   . "Rainy afternoon girls" ....
7.213   . "Laddie daddie" ....
7.214   . "Live it to love" ....
          added to London production of 1926: . "Something about love" (Paley; see: The Lady in Red of 1919) ...
7.215   . "I'd rather Charleston" (Carter)..
7.216   . "Buy a little button" (Carter) ....

"Tell Me More" (p1925, lyrics DeSylva & Ira Gershwin):

7.217   used: . "Tell me more" ....
7.218   . "Mr. and Mrs. Sipkin" ....
7.219   . "When the Debbies go by" ....
7.220   . "Three times a day" ....
7.221   . "Why do I love you" ....

7.222	. "How can I win you now?" ....
7.223	. "Kickin' the clouds away" ....
7.224	. "Love is in the air" ....
7.225	. "My fair lady" ....
7.226	. "In Sardinia" ....
7.227	. "Baby!" ....
7.228	. "The Poetry of Motion" ....
7.229	. "Ukulele Lorelei" ....
7.230	not used: . "Shop girls and mannikins" ....
7.231	. "Once" ....
7.232	. "I'm somethin' on Avenue A" ....
7.233	. "The he-man" ....
7.234	added to London production of 1925: . "Murderous Monty" (and Light-Fingered Jane) (Carter) ....
7.235	. "Love, I never knew" (Carter) ....

"Tip-Toes" (p1925, lyrics Ira Gershwin):

7.236	used: . "Waiting for the train" ....
7.237	. "Nice baby!" (Come to Papa!) ....
7.238	. "Looking for a boy" ....
7.239	. "Lady Luck" ....
7.240	. "When do we dance?" ....
7.241	. "These charming people" ....
7.242	. "That certain feeling" (see pf transcr in: Gershwin Songbook) ....
7.243	. "Sweet and low-down" (see pf transcr in: Gershwin Songbook) ....
7.244	. "Our little captain" ....
7.245	. "Harbor of Dreams" ....
7.246	. "Nightie-night" ....
7.247	. "Tip-toes" ....
7.248	not used: . "Harlem river chanty" ....
7.249	. "Gather ye rosebuds" ....
7.250	. "We" ....
7.251	. "Dancing hour" ....
7.252	. "Life's too short to be blue" ....
7.253	. "It's a great little world" ....

"Song of the Flame" (p1925, lyrics Harbach & O. Hammerstein II):

7.254	used: . "Midnight bells" ....
7.255	. "Far away" ....
7.256	. "Song of the flame" ....
7.257	. "Woman's work is never done" ....
7.258	. "The Signal" ....
7.259	. "Cossack love song" (Don't forget me) ....
7.260	. "Tar-tar" ....
7.261	. "You are you" ....
7.262	. "Vodka" ....

"Americana" (p1926):

7.263	used: . "That lost Barbershop chord" (Ira Gershwin) ....

"Oh, Kay!" (p1926, lyrics Ira Gershwin):

7.264	used: . "The woman's touch" ....
7.265	. "Don't ask!" ....
7.266	. "Dear little girl" (I hope you've missed me) (pubd1968) ....
7.267	. "Maybe" ....
7.268	. "Clap yo' hands" (see pf transcr in: Gershwin Songbook) ....
7.269	. "Bride and Groom" ....
7.270	. "Do-do-do" (see pf transcr in: Gershwin Songbook) ....
7.271	. "Someone to watch over me" ....
7.272	. "Fidgety feet" ....
7.273	. "Heaven on Earth" (Ira Gershwin & Dietz) ....
7.274	. "Oh!, Kay!" (Ira Gershwin & Dietz) ....
7.275	not used: . "Show me the town" ....
7.276	. "What's the use?" ....
7.277	. "When our ship comes sailing in" ....
7.278	. "The moon is on the sea" (The sun is on the sea) ....
7.279	. "Stepping with baby" ....
7.280	. "Guess who" (melody = Don't ask!) ....
7.281	. "Ain't it romantic" ....
7.282	. "Bring on the Ding Dong Dell" ....

"Strike Up the Band" I (p1927, lyrics Ira Gershwin):

7.283	used: . "Fletcher's American Cheese Choral Society" ....
7.284	. "Seventeen and twenty-one" ....

7.285	. "Meadow serenade" ....
7.286	. "The unofficial spokesman" (also see in: Strike Up the Band II of 1930) ....
7.287	. "Patriotic rally" ....
	. "The man I love" (The girl I love) (see in: Lady, be Good of 1924) ....
7.288	. "Yankee doodle rhythm" ....
7.289	. "Strike-up the band!" (see pf transcr in: Gershwin Songbook) ....
7.290	. "O, this is such a lovely war" (The knitting song) ....
7.291	. "Hoping that someday you'll care" ....
7.292	. "Military dancing dancing drill" ....
7.293	. "How about a man like me" ....
7.294	. "Homeward bound" ....
7.295	. "The war that ended war" ....

"Funny Face" (p1927, lyrics Ira Gershwin):

7.296	used: . "We're all a-worry, all agog" ....
7.297	. "When you're single" ....
7.298	. "Those eyes" ....
7.299	. "Birthday party" ....
7.300	. "High hat" ....
7.301	. "Let's kiss and make up" ....
7.302	. "Funny face" ....
7.303	. " 's wonderful" (see pf transcr in: Gershwin Songbook) ....
7.304	. "The world is mine" ....
7.305	. "Come along, let's gamble" ....
7.306	. "If you will take our tip" ....
7.307	. "He loves and she loves" ....
7.308	. "The finest of the finest" ....
7.309	. "My one and only" (What am I gonna do) (see pf transcr in: Gershwin Songbook) ....
7.310	. "Tell the doc" ....
7.311	. "Sing a little song" ....
7.312	. "In the swim" ....
7.313	. "The Babbitt and the Bromide" ....
7.314	. "Dance alone with you" ....
7.315	not used: . "How long has this been going on?" ....
7.316	. "Acrobats" ....
7.317	. "Once" ....
7.318	. "Aviator" ....
7.319	. "When you smile" ....
7.320	. "Dancing hour" ....
7.321	. "Blue hullabaloo" ....
7.322	added to London production of 1928: . "Look at the damn thing now" ....

"Rosalie" (p1928, lyrics Wodehouse & Ira Gershwin):

7.323	used: . "Show me the town" (Ira Gershwin) ....
7.324	. "Say so!" ....
7.325	. "Let me be a friend to you" (Ira Gershwin) ....
7.326	. "Oh gee! Oh joy!" ....
7.327	. "New York serenade" (Ira Gershwin) ....
7.328	. "Setting-up exercises," instrumental
	. "How long has this been going on?" (Ira Gershwin, see in: Funny Face of 1927) ....
7.329	. "Ev'rybody knows I love" (Ira Gershwin, melody = Dance alone with you) ....
7.330	not used: . "Rosalie" (Ira Gershwin) ....
7.331	. "Beautiful Gypsy" (Ira Gershwin, melody = Wait a bit, Susie) ....
7.332	. "Yankee doodle rhythm" (Ira Gershwin) ....
7.333	. "When cadets parade" (Ira Gershwin) ....
7.334	. "Follow the drum" (Ira Gershwin) ....
7.335	. "I forget what I started to say" (Ira Gershwin) ....
	. "The man I love" (Ira Gershwin, see in: Lady, be Good of 1924) ....
7.336	. "You know how it is" (Ira Gershwin) ....
7.337	. "True to them all" ....
7.338	. "When the right one comes along" ....

"Treasure Girl" (p1928, lyrics Ira Gershwin):

7.339	used: . "Skull and bones" ....
7.340	. "I've got a crush on you" (also see in: Strike Up the Band II of 1930) ....
7.341	. "Oh, so nice" ....
7.342	. "According to Mr. Grimes" ....
7.343	. "Place in the country" ....
7.344	. "K-ra-zy for you" ....
7.345	. "I don't think I'll fall in love today" ....
7.346	. "Got a rainbow" ....
7.347	. "Feeling I'm falling" ....
7.348	. "Where's the Boy? Here's the Girl!" ....
7.349	. "What causes that?" ....

7.350	not used: . "This particular party" ....
7.351	. "Treasure island" ....
7.352	. "Goodbye to the old love, hello to the new" ....
7.353	. "A-hunting we will go" ....
7.354	. "Dead men tell no tales" ....
7.355	. "I want to marry a marionette" ....

"Show Girl" (p1929, lyrics Kahn & Ira Gershwin):

7.356	used: . "Happy birthday" ....
7.357	. "My Sunday fella" ....
7.358	. "How could I forget" ....
7.359	. "Lolita" ....
7.360	. "Do what you do!" ....
7.361	. "One man" ....
7.362	. "So are you!" ....
7.363	. "I must be home by twelve o'clock" ....
7.364	. "Black and white" ....
7.365	. "Blues Ballet" (from tone poem: An American in Paris) ....
7.366	. "Home blues" ....
7.367	. "Follow the minstrel band" ....
7.368	. "Liza" (All the clouds'll roll away) (see pf transcr in: Gershwin Songbook) ....
7.369	. "Harlem serenade" ....
7.370	not used: . "Feeling Sentimental" ....
7.371	. "At Mrs. Simpkin's finishing school" ....
7.372	. "Adored one" ....
7.373	. "Tonight's the night" ....
7.374	. "I just looked at you" ....
7.375	. "I'm just a bundle of sunshine" ....
7.376	. "Minstrel show" ....
7.377	. "Somebody stole my heart away" ....
7.378	. "Someone's always calling a rehearsal" ....
7.379	. "I'm out for no good reason tonight" ....
7.380	. "Home lovin' gal" (man) ....

"East is West" (not produced):

7.381	written: . "Sing song girl" ....
7.382	. "Embraceable you" ....
7.383	. "We are visitors" ....
7.384	. "In the mandarin's orchid garden" ....
7.385	. "Yellow blues" (developed into: Impromptu in Two Keys for pf) ....
7.386	. "China girl" ....
7.387	. "Lady of the moon" (eventually: Blah, blah, blah) ....
7.388	. "Under the cinnamon tree" ....

"Strike Up the Band" II (p1930, lyrics Ira Gershwin):

7.389	used: . "Fletcher's American Chocolate Choral Society Workers" ....
7.390	. "I mean to say" ....
7.391	. "Soon" ....
7.392	. "A typical self-made American" ....
7.393	. "A man of high degree" ....
	. "The unofficial spokesman" (see in: Strike Up the Band I of 1927) ....
7.394	. "Three cheers for the Union!" ....
7.395	. "This could go on for years" ....
7.396	. "If I became the president" ....
7.397	. "Hangin' around with you" ....
7.398	. "He knows milk" (finaletto) ....
7.399	. "Strike up the band!" ....
7.400	. "In the rattle of the battle" (opening) ....
7.401	. "Military dancing drill" ....
7.402	. "Mademoiselle in New Rochelle" ....
	. "I've got a crush on you" (see in: Treasure Girl of 1928) ....
7.403	. "How about a boy like me?" ....
7.404	. "I want to be a war bride" ....
7.405	. "Unofficial march of general Holmes" ....
7.406	. "First there was Fletcher" (Official Resume) ....
7.407	. "Ding Dong" ....
7.408	not used: . "There was never such a charming war" ....

"Nine-Fifteen Revue" (p1930):

7.409	used: . "Toddlin' along" (melody = The world is mine) ....

"Girl Crazy" (p1930, lyrics Ira Gershwin):

7.410	used: . "The lonesome cowboy" ....

7.411	. "Bidin' my time" ....
7.412	. "Could you use me?" ....
7.413	. "Broncho busters" ....
7.414	. "Barbary coast" ....
	. "Embraceable you" (see in: East is West) ....
7.415	. "Goldfarb! That's I'm" ....
7.416	. "Sam and Delilah" ....
7.417	. "I got rhythm" (see: Variations for pf & orch; also see pf transcr in: Gershwin Songbook) ....
7.418	. "Land of the gay cabalerro" ....
7.419	. "Mexican Dance," instrumental ....
7.420	. "But not for me" ....
7.421	. "Treat me rough" ....
7.422	. "Boy! What love has done to me!" ....
7.423	. "When It's cactus time in Arizona" ....
7.424	not used: . "The gambler of the West" ....
7.425	. "And I have you" ....
7.426	. "You can't unscramble scrambled eggs" ....
7.427	. "Something peculiar" (Paley) ....
7.428	"Ask me again" ....

"Delicious," film (p1931, lyrics Ira Gershwin):

7.429	used: . "Delishious" ....
7.430	. "Welcome to the Melting Pot" (Dream Sequence) ....
7.431	. "Somebody from somewhere" ....
7.432	. "Katinkitschka" ....
7.433	. "Blah-blah-blah" (orig: Lady of the moon, see stage work: East is West) ....
7.434	. "New York Rhapsody" (insts) ....
7.435	. "You started it" ....
	not used: . "Mischa, Yascha, Toscha, Sascha" (see same song c1922) ....
7.436	. "Thanks to you" ....

"Of Thee I Sing" (p1931, lyrics Ira Gershwin):

7.437	used: . "Wintergreen for president" (also see in: Let 'Em Eat Cake of 1933) ....
7.438	. "Who is the lucky girl to be?" ....
7.439	. "The dimple on my knee" ....
7.440	. "Because, because" ....
7.441	. "Never was there a girl so fair" ....
7.442	. "Some girls can bake a pie" ....
7.443	. "Love is sweeping the country" ....
7.444	. "Of thee I sing" ....
7.445	. "Here's a kiss for Cinderella" ....
7.446	. "I was the most beautiful blossom" ....
7.447	. "Hello, good morning" ....
7.448	. "Who cares?" (see pf transcr in: Gershwin Songbook) ....
7.449	. "Garçon, s'il vous plait" ....
7.450	. "The illegitimate daughter" ....
7.451	. "The senatorial roll call" ....
7.452	. "Jilted" ....
7.453	. "I'm about to be a mother" ....
7.454	. "Posterity is just around the corner" ....
7.455	. "Trumpeter, blow your golden horn" ....
7.456	not used: . "Call me whate'er you will" ....

"Girl Crazy," 1st filmed vers (c1932):

7.457	used: . "You've got what gets me" ....

"Pardon My English" (p1933, lyrics Ira Gershwin):

7.458	used: . "In three quarter time" ....
7.459	. "Lorelei" ....
7.460	. "Pardon my English" ....
7.461	. "Dancing in the streets" ....
7.462	. "So what?" ....
7.463	. "Isn't it a pity?" ....
7.464	. "My cousin in Milwaukee" ....
7.465	. "Hail the happy couple" ....
7.466	. "The Dresden Northwest Mounted" ....
7.467	. "Luckiest man in the world" ....
7.468	. "What sort of wedding is this?" ....
7.469	. "Tonight" (also main theme of: 2 Waltzes in C) ....
7.470	. "Where you go I go" ....
7.471	. "I've got to be there" ....
7.472	. "He's not himself" ....
7.473	not used: . "Freud and Jung and Adler" ....

7.474	. "Together at last" ....
7.475	. "Bauer's house" ....
7.476	. "No tickee, no washee" ....
7.477	. "Poor Michael! Poor Golo!" ....
7.478	. "Fatherland, mother of the band" ....

"Let 'Em Eat Cake" (p1933, lyrics Ira Gershwin):

	used: . "Wintergreen for president" (see in: Of Thee I Sing of 1931) ....
7.479	. "Tweedledee, tweedleee" ....
7.480	. "Union Square: Our hearts are in communion" ....
7.481	. "Down with everything that's up" (pubd as: Interlude in: Union Square) ....
7.482	. "Orders, orders" ....
7.483	. "Comes the revolution" ....
7.484	. "Mine" ....
7.485	. "Climb up the social ladder" (The new D.A.R.) ....
7.486	. "Cloistered from the Noisy City" ....
7.487	. "The Union League" ....
7.488	. "On and on and on" ....
7.489	. "What more can a general do?" ....
7.490	. "What's this / Where's the general?" ....
7.491	. "The general's gone to a party" ....
7.492	. "All the mothers of the nation" ....
7.493	. "He's a bachelor" (melody = The Union League) ....
7.494	. "There's something we're worried about" ....
7.495	. "What's the proletariat?" ....
7.496	. "Let 'em eat cake" ....
7.497	. "Blue, blue, blue" ....
7.498	. "No one greater" ....
7.499	. "Who's the greatest?" ....
7.500	. "The welcome" ....
7.501	. "No comprenez, no capish, no versteh!" ....
7.502	. "Why speak of money?" ....
7.503	. "No better way to start a case" ....
7.504	. "Up and at 'em! On to vict'ry" ....
7.505	. "Oyez, oyez, oyez" ....
7.506	. "That's what he did" ....
7.507	. "I know a foul ball when I see one" ....
7.508	. "Throttle throttlebottom" ....
7.509	. "It isn't what you did but what you didn't" ....
7.510	. "We're in a hell of a jam" ....
7.511	. "I'm about to be a mother" ....
7.512	. "Hanging throttlebottom in the morning" ....
7.513	. "Let 'em eat caviar" ....
7.514	not used: . "First Lady and First Gent" ....
7.515	. "Till then" ....

7.516	"King of Swing" (c1936, Stillman) ....
7.517	"I won't give up till you give in to me" (c1936, Stillman).........
7.518	"Doubting Thomas" (c1936, Stillman) ....

"The Show Is On" (p1936):

7.519	used: . "By Strauss" (Ira Gershwin) ....

"Shall We Dance" (p1937, lyrics Ira Gershwin):

7.520	used: . "French ballet class" (orch) ....
7.521	. "Dance of the waves" (orch) ....
7.522	. "Ginger rhumba" (orch) ....
7.523	. "Graceful and elegant" (orch) ....
7.524	. "Slap that bass" ....
7.525	. "Walking the dog" (orch, pubd as: Promenade for pf) ....
7.526	. "I've got beginner's luck" ....
7.527	. "They all laughed" ....
7.528	. "Balloon ballet" (orch) ....
7.529	. "Let's call the whole thing off" ....
7.530	. "They can't take that away from me" ....
7.531	. "Hoctor's Ballet" (orch) ....
7.532	not used: . "Hi-ho! At last" (pubd1968) ....
7.533	. "Wake up, brother, and dance" ....

"A Damsel In Distress," film (p1937, lyrics Ira Gershwin):

7.534	used: . "I can't be bothered now" ....
7.535	. "The jolly Tar and the Milkmaid" ....
7.536	. "Put me to the test" (instrumental) ....
7.537	. "Stiff upper lip" ....

7.538	. "Things are looking up" ....
7.539	. "A foggy day" ....
7.540	. "Sling of Spring" ....
7.541	. "Nice work if you can get it" ....
7.542	not used: . "Pay some attention to me" ....

"The Goldwyn Follies," film (p1937, lyrics Ira Gershwin):

7.543	used: . "Love walked in" ....
7.544	. "I was doing all right" ....
7.545	. "I love to rhyme" ....
7.546	. "Love is here to stay" ....
7.547	not used: . "Just another rhumba" (pubd1959) ....

Posthumous:

7.548	"Dawn of a new day" (p1938, Ira Gershwin, song of the New York World's Fair of 1939) ....

"The Shocking Miss Pilgrim," film (p1946, lyrics Ira Gershwin, music adopted Swift & Ira Gershwin):

7.549	*used: . "Sweet Packard" ....*
7.550	*. "Stand up and fight" ....*
7.551	*. "Aren't you kind of glad we did?" ....*
7.552	*. "Changing my tune" ....*
7.553	*. "Back Bay Polka" ....*
7.554	*. "Demon rum" ....*
7.555	*. "One, two, three" ....*
7.556	*. "For you, for me, for evermore" ....*
7.557	*not used: . "Tour of the town" ....*
7.558	*. "Welcome song" ....*

"Kiss Me, Stupid," film (p1964, lyrics Ira Gershwin, music adopted Ira Gershwin & Previn):

7.559	*used: . "All the livelong day" (see orig: Phoebe in: The Perfect Fool of 1921) ....*
7.560	*. "I'm a poached egg" ....*
7.561	*. "Sophia" (based on: Wake up, brother, and dance, see: Shall We Dance of 1937) ....*

* * * * *

1. STAGE WORKS

Ballets:

1.1	"Raymonda," 3 acts (c1896–7, Pashkova & Petipa)	Op.57
1.2	"Les ruses d'amour," 1 act (c1898, Petipa)	Op.61
1.3	"The Seasons," 1 act 4 tableaux (c1898, Petipa)	Op.67

Incid music:

1.4	"Salomé" (Introduction & Dance of Salomé) (c1908, Wilde) (also see R. Strauss Op.54)	Op.90
1.5	"The King of the Jews" (c1913, Romanov; ch & orch)	Op.95
1.6	"Masquerade" (c1912–3, Lermontov)	

1a. SELECTIONS FROM STAGE WORKS (Nos. of sections in The Gramophone)

1a.1   "Raymonda," ballet" Op.57
        excerpts: I: 1a. "Introduction" (Moderato—Poco più mosso)
                1b. "Scène" (Lento maestoso)
                1c. "La Traditrice" (Moderato—Allegretto)
                1d. "Scène" (Moderato—Allegro agitato)
                1e. "Entrée de Raymonda" (Allegro)
                2a. "Grande Valse" (Allegro più sostenuto)
                2b. "Pizzicato" (Allegretto)
                3. "Scène" (Andante marcile)
                4. "Reprise de la Valse"
                5a. "Scène mimique" (Moderato—Allegro)
                5b. "Entrée des vasseux et des paysans" (Andante marciale)
                5c. "Scène: Pas de deux" (Andantino—Animato)
                6. "Prélude et La Romanesca" (Moderato)
                7. "Prélude et Variation" (Allegretto)
                8a. "Scène mimique" (Andante)
                8b. "Scène: Apparition de la Dame blanche"
                8c. "Grand Adagio"
                9. "Valse fantastique" (Allegro—Animato—Allegro)
                10. "Variation I" (Allegretto)
                11. "Variation II" (Allegretto)
                12. "Variation pour Raymonda" (Tempo di valse)
                13. "Coda" (Presto)
                14a. "Scène" (Moderato—Con moto—Animando—Appassionato)
                14b. "Scène" (Andante)
        II: 15a. "Marche" (Allegro moderato)
                15b. "Entrée d'Abérâme" (Moderato pesante—Più tranquillo)
                15c. "Grand pas d'action" (Andante—Grandioso)
                16a. "Variation I" (Moderato)
                16b. "Variation II" (Allegretto)
                17. "Variation pour Raymonda" (Allegretto)
                18. "Grand Coda" (Allegretto moderato—Poco più mosso—Allegro—Poco più mosso)
                19a. "Scène" (Moderato)
                20a. "Danse des garçons Arabes" (Vivace)
                20b. "Entrée des Sarrazins" (Presto)
                21. "Grand pas espagnol" (Andante—Allegro)
                22a. "Danse orientale" (Andante)
                22b. "Bacchanal" (Allegro—Animando)
                22c. "Scène" (Moderato maestoso—Agitato—Sostenuto)
                22d. "La combat" (Allegro assai—Moderato)
                22e. "Hymne"
        III: 23a. "Entr'acte" (Allegro moderato—Moderato)
                23b. "Le cortège hongrois" (Moderato maestoso)
                24. "Grand pas hongrois" (Moderato maestoso—Molto pesante—Presto)
                25. "Entrée" (Allegretto—Poco meno mosso)
                26. "Pas classique hongroise" (Adagio)
                27. "Variation" (Prestissimo)
                28. "Variation" (Moderato—Allegro)
                29. "Variation" (Adagio)
                30. "Variation" (Allegro moderato)
                31. "Coda" (Allegro—Vivo)
                32. "Galop" (Allegro assai—Vivo)
                33. "Apothéose" (Andante)

1a.2   "Les ruses d'amour," ballet: Op.61
        excerpts: 1. "Introduction"
                2. "Valse"
                3. "Ballabile"

2. SYMPHONIES

2.1   Symphony No.1 in E major, "Slavonic" (c1881–2, r1885 & 1929) Op.5
2.2   Symphony No.2 in F-sharp minor (c1886) Op.16
2.3   Symphony No.3 in D major (c1890) Op.33
2.4   Symphony No.4 in E-flat major (c1893) Op.48
2.5   Symphony No.5 in B-flat major, "Eroica" (c1895) Op.55
2.6   Symphony No.6 in C minor (c1896) Op.58
2.7   Symphony No.7 in F major, "Pastoral" (c1902) Op.77
2.8   Symphony No.8 in E-flat major (c1906) Op.83
2.9   Symphony No.9 in D major (c1910, unfin; orchd Yudin) ....

3. OTHER ORCHESTRAL WORKS

3.1   "Overture No.1 on 3 Greek Themes," in G minor (c1882) Op.3
3.2   "Overture No.2 on Greek Themes," in D major (c1883) Op.6
3.3   Serenade No.1 in A major (c1883) Op.7
3.4   "Elegy," in C-sharp min / D-flat major, "To the Memory of a Hero" (c1885) Op.8
3.5   "Suite caractéristique," in D major (c1881–5) Op.9
3.6   Serenade No.2 in F major (c1884; small orch; see orig vers: Serenade for hn & strings) Op.11
3.7   "Lyric Poem," in D-flat major (c1884–7) Op.12
3.8   "Stenka Razin," sym poem in B minor (c1885, to Borodin's memory) Op.13
3.9   "2 Pieces" (c1886–7): No.1 "Idylle," in D major (see orig vers: Idyll for hn & strings) Op.14
3.10   No.2 "Rêverie oriental," in A minor
3.11   "Mazurka," in G major (c1888) Op.18
3.12   "The Forest," fantasy in C-sharp minor (c1887) Op.19
3.13   "Wedding March" (Marche de Noces), in E-flat major (c1889) Op.21
3.14   "Slavonic Festival," sym sketch in G major (c1888, after Finale of: Str Qt No.3 in G major, Op.26) .. Op.26a
3.15   "The Sea," fantasy in E major (c1889) Op.28
3.16   "Oriental Rhapsody," in G major (c1889) Op.29
3.17   "2 Fanfares" (c1890, for Rimsky-Korsakov's Jubilee) ....
3.18   "The Kremlin," sym picture in C maj / E-flat major (c1890) Op.30
3.19   "Spring," musical picture in D major (c1891) Op.34
3.20   "Triumphal March," in E-flat major (c1892; orch & ch ad lib, for Chicago Exposition of 1893) Op.40
3.21   "Carnaval Overture," in F major (c1892) Op.45
3.22   "Chopiniana," suite (c1893) Op.46
3.23   Concert Waltz No.1 in D major (c1893) Op.47
3.24   "Cortège solennel," in D major (c1894) Op.50
3.25   Concert Waltz No.2 in F major (c1894) Op.51
3.26   "Scènes de ballet," suite in A major (c1894) Op.52
3.27   "From Darkness Into Light," fantasy in B min / C major (c1894) Op.53
3.28   "Oriental Suite" (c1895) ....
3.29   "Allegro vivo," in E-flat major (c1895) ....
3.30   "Raymonda Suite" (c1898, from ballet Op.57) Op.57a
3.31   "Variations on a Russian theme" (c1899, collab Lyadov, Rimsky-Korsakov & Vitols) ....
3.32   "Pas de caractère," in G major (c1899, insert for ballet: Raymonda, Op.57) Op.68
3.33   "Intermezzo romantico," in D major (c1900) Op.69
3.34   "Ouverture solennelle," in D major (c1900) Op.73
3.35   "March on a Russian Theme," in E-flat major (c1901) Op.76
3.36   "Valse lente," in F major (c1901) ....
3.37   "Ballade," in F major (c1902) Op.78
3.38   "From the Middle Ages," suite in E major (c1902): No.1 "Prelude" Op.79
3.39   No.2 "Scherzo"
3.40   No.3 "The Troubadour's Serenade"
3.41   No.4 "Finale: The Crusaders"
3.42   "Fortune-Telling & Dance," ballet scene in A major (c1904) Op.81
3.43   "Dramatic Overture," in D major, "The Song of Destiny" (c1908) Op.84
3.44   "2 Preludes": No.1 "In Memory of Stasoff," in A minor (c1906) Op.85
3.45   No.2 "In Memory of Rimsky-Korsakov," in E minor (c1908)
3.46   "Russian Fantasy," in A major (c1906; balalaika orch) Op.86
3.47   "Solemn Procession," in G major (c1907) ....
3.48   "In Memory of Gogol," sym prologue in C major (c1909) Op.87
3.49   "Finnish Fantasy," in C major (c1909) Op.88
3.50   "Petite suite de ballet" (c1910) ....
3.51   "Finnish Sketches" (c1912): No.1 "From the Kalevala," in E major Op.89
3.52   No.2 "Cortège solennel," in E major
3.53   "Cortège solennel," in B-flat major (c1910) Op.91
3.54   "Paraphrase on National Anthems of the Allies" (c1914) Op.96
3.55   "Theme & Variations," in G minor (c1917; strings; see orig for str qnt 1895) Op.97
3.56   "Karelian Legend," in A minor (c1916) Op.99
3.57   "Poème épique," in A minor (c1933–4) ....
3.58   "Fragment No.10" (found among composer's papers) ....

4. CONCERTOS, SOLO INSTR & ORCH

Pf & orch:

4.1	Piano Concerto No.1 in F minor (c1910–11)	Op.92
4.2	Piano Concerto No.2 in B major (c1917)	Op.100

Vn & orch:

4.3	Violin Concerto in A minor (c1904)	Op.82

Vc & orch:

4.4	"2 Pieces" (c1887–8; vc & orch/pf): No.1 "Mélodie," in D major	Op.20
4.5	No.2 "Spanish Serenade," in A major	
4.6	"Minstrel's Song," in F-sharp minor (c1900; vc & orch/pf)	Op.71
4.7	"Concerto-Ballata," in C major (c1930–1)	Op.108

Other:

4.8	"Idyll," in D major (c1884; hn & strings, orig vers of Op.14/1 for orch)	
4.9	"Serenade," in F major (c1884; hn & strings, orig vers of Op.11 for small orch)	
4.10	Saxophone Concerto in E-flat major (c1933; sax & strings, collab Petiot)	Op.109

5. STRING QUARTETS

5.1	"5 Pieces" (c1879–81): No.1 "Lento," in D major	
5.2	No.2 "Scherzo," in E major	
5.3	No.3 "Intermezzo," in D major	
5.4	No.4 "Scherzo," in C minor	
5.5	No.5 "Hungarian Scherzo," in A major	
5.6	String Quartet No.1 in D major (c1881–2)	Op.1
5.7	String Quartet No.2 in F major (c1884)	Op.10
5.8	"5 Novelettes" (c1886): No.1 "Allegretto alla spagnuola"	Op.15
5.9	No.2 "Orientale"	
5.10	No.3 "Interludium in modo antico"	
5.11	No.4 "Waltz"	
5.12	No.5 "Allegretto all'ungherese"	
5.13	"Finale," in B-flat major, for collab work: String Quartet, "B-la-F" (c1886, for the Name-day of Belayev):	
	String Quartet in B-flat major, "B-la-F" (Belayev): *1. "Sostenuto assai et Allegro" (c by Rimsky-Korsakov)*	
	2. "Scherzo" (c by Lyadov)	
	3. "Spanish Serenade" (c by Borodin)	
	4. "Finale" (c by Glazunov)	
5.14	"Carol-singers," for collab work: String Quartet, "Name-day" (Jour de fête) (c1888, ded to Belayev):	
	String Quartet in D major, "Name-day": 1. "Carol-singers" (c by Glazunov)	
	2. "Song of Praise" (c by Lyadov)	
	3. "Khorovod" (c by Rimsky-Korsakov)	
5.15	String Quartet No.3 in G major, "Quatuor slave" (Slav Quartet) (c1886–8)	Op.26
5.16	"Suite," in C major (c1887–91): No.1 "Andante—Fugue"	Op.35
5.17	No.2 "Scherzo"	
5.18	No.3 "Orientale"	
5.19	No.4 "Tema & Variazione"	
5.20	No.5 "Valse"	
5.21	"Variations on a popular Russian theme" (collab w/ others)	
5.22	3 Pieces for collab work: Fridays (Les vendredis) (c1895): . "Courante," in G major	
5.23	. "Polka," in D major (collab Lyadov & Sokolov)	
5.24	. "Prelude & Fugue," in D minor	
5.25	String Quartet No.4 in A major (c1894)	Op.64
5.26	String Quartet No.5 in D major (c1898)	Op.70
5.27	"2 Pieces" (c1902)	
5.28	"Elegy," in D minor (c1928, in memory of Belayev)	Op.105
5.29	String Quartet No.6 in B-flat major (c1920–1)	Op.106
5.30	String Quartet No.7 in C major, "Hommage to the Past" (c1930)	Op.107

6. OTHER CHAMBER MUSIC

4 or more insts:

6.1	Brass Quartet in E-flat major, "In modo religioso" (c1892; tpt, hn & 2tbn)	Op.38
6.2	String Quintet in A major (c1891–2; str qt & vc)	Op.39
6.3	"Theme & Variations," in G minor (c1895; str qnt; arr for strings, Op.97)	
6.4	Saxophone Quartet in B major (c1932)	Op.109

3 insts:

6.5   "Mélodie arabe" (c1884; vn, vc & pf) ....

Vn & pf:

6.6   "The Nightingale" (c1884) ....
6.7   "Méditation," in D major (c1891; vn & pf/orch) Op.32
6.8   "Mazurka-Oberek," in D major (c1917; vn & pf/orch) ....

Va & pf:

6.9   "Elegy," in G minor (c1893) Op.44

Vc & pf:

6.10   "Une pensée à Liszt," elegy in D-flat major (c1887) Op.17

Other instr & pf:

6.11   "Rêverie," in D-flat major (c1890; hn & pf) Op.24
6.12   "Albumleaf," in D-flat major (c1899; tpt & pf; orchd Rogal-Levitsky) ....

7. PIANO SONATAS

7.1   Piano Sonata No.1 in B-flat minor (c1901) Op.74
7.2   Piano Sonata No.2 in E major (c1901) Op.75

8. OTHER PIANO WORKS

8.1   "Suite on the name S-A-C-H-A" (c1883) Op.2
8.2   "2 Pieces" (c1889): No.1 "Barcarolle," in B-flat major Op.22
8.3   No.2 "Novelette," in D major
8.4   "Waltzes on the theme S-A-B-E-L-A" (c1890) Op.23
8.5   "3 Pieces" (c1888): No.1 "Prelude," in D major Op.25
8.6   No.2 "Mazurka," in F-sharp minor
8.7   No.3 "Mazurka," in D-flat major
8.8   "Trois études" (c1889–91): No.1 in C major Op.31
8.9   No.2 in E minor
8.10   No.3 in E major, "La nuit"
8.11   "Petite Valse" (c1891) Op.36
8.12   "Nocturne" (c1889) Op.37
8.13   "Grand Concert Waltz" (c1893) Op.41
8.14   "3 Miniatures" (c1893): No.1 "Pastorale," in D major Op.42
8.15   No.2 "Polka," in F major
8.16   No.3 "Waltz," in D major
8.17   "Valse de salon" (c1893) Op.43
8.18   "3 Pieces" (c1894): "Prelude," in D-flat major Op.49
8.19   No.2 "Caprice-Impromptu," in A major
8.20   No.3 "Gavotte," in D major
8.21   "2 Impromptus" (c1895): No.1 in D-flat major Op.54
8.22   No.2 in A-flat major
8.23   "4 Improvisations" (c1896, collab Arensky, Rachmaninov & Taneyev) ....
8.24   "Prelude & Fugue," in D minor (c1899; pf/org) Op.62
8.25   "Theme & Variations," in F-sharp minor (c1900) Op.72
8.26   "4 Preludes & Fugues" (c1918–23): No.1 in A minor Op.101
8.27   No.2 in C-sharp minor
8.28   No.3 in C minor
8.29   No.4 in C major
8.30   "Idylle," in F-sharp major (c1926) Op.103
8.31   "Prelude & fugue," in E minor (c1926; arr for org 1929) ....
8.32   "Minuet" (collab Arensky, Blumenfeld & others) ....

Pf duet:

8.33   "Pastourelle," for collab work: Joke Quadrille (c1890): ....
        "Joke Quadrille": *1. "Pantalon" (c by Artsybushev)*
            2. "Été" (c by Vitols)
            3. "Poule" (c by Lyadov)
            4. "Trénis" (c by Sokolov)
            5. "Pastourelle" (c by Glazunov)
            6. "Finale," in C major (c by Rimsky-Korsakov)

2 Pf:

8.34	"Fantasy," in F minor (c1919–20)	Op.104
8.35	"Fantasy" (c1929–30)	
8.36	"Badinage" (collab Withol, Sokolov & Rimsky-Korsakov)	

9. ORGAN

9.1	Prelude & Fugue No.1 in D major (c1906–7)	Op.93
9.2	Prelude & Fugue No.2 in D minor (c1914)	Op.98
9.3	"Fantasy," in G minor (c1934–5)	Op.110

10. CHORAL WORKS

10.1	"Coronation Cantata" (c1895; 4vv, ch & orch)	Op.56
10.2	"Festive Cantata for the 100th Anniversary of the Pavlovsk Institute" (c1898; vv, fem ch & 2pf)	Op.63
10.3	"Cantata for Pushkin's 100th Birthday" (c1899, Mashistov; vv, ch & orch)	Op.65
10.4	"Hymn to Pushkin" (c1899; fem ch & pf ad lib)	Op.66
10.5	"Cantata in Memory of Antokolsky" (c1903, Marshak; T, ch & orch, collab Lyadov)	
10.6	"Love," in F major (c1907, Shukovsky; ch)	Op.94
10.7	"Song of the Volga Boatmen" (arr1905; ch & orch)	
10.8	"Prelude-Cantata" (c1912, for the 50th anniv of the St Petersburg Conservatory)	
10.9	"Vniz po matushke po Volge," Russian folksong (c1921; ch)	
10.10	"Easter Hymn" (Exapostilarion) (ch)	

11. SONGS (w/ pf)

11.1	"A Song" (c1881, Heine/Nekrasov; mS & pf)	
11.2	"My Venomous Songs" (c1882, Heine)	
11.3	"5 Songs" (c1882–5): 1. "Romance" (Heine)	Op.4
11.4	2. "The Nightingale" (Koltsov)	
11.5	3. "Romance" (Heine)	
11.6	4. "Spanish Song"	
11.7	5. "Arabian Melody"	
11.8	"2 Songs" (c1888–90, Pushkin; orchd as Op.27bis): 1. "Chanson"	Op.27
11.9	2. "Oriental Romance"	
11.10	"From Hafiz" (c1889, Pushkin; Bar & pf)	
11.11	"The Beautiful" (c1890, Pushkin)	
11.12	"6 Songs" (c1898): 1. "The Muse" (Pushkin)	Op.59
11.13	2. "From Petrarch"	
11.14	3. "From Petrarch"	
11.15	4. "If You Will Love" (Petrarch)	
11.16	5. "Delia" (Pushkin)	
11.17	6. "The Silver-Shining Heaverns" (Maikov)	
11.18	"6 Songs" (c1898): 1. "Bacchic Song" (Pushkin)	Op.60
11.19	2. "A Wish" (Pushkin)	
11.20	3. "The Sea-Nymph" (Pushkin)	
11.21	4. "The Dream" (Pushkin)	
11.22	5. "Life Still Lies Before Me" (Maikov)	
11.23	6. "By the Majestic Towers of Venice" (Pushkin)	
11.24	"Song Without End": "Ekh ty, pesnya" (c1900, Seversky; S, A & pf)	Op.80
11.25	"Russian Song": "They Won't Let Masha" (arr1905)	
11.26	"Nina's Song" (c1912-3, Lermontov; mS & orch, from incid music: Masquerade)	Op.102

12. ARRANGEMENTS OF WORKS OF OTHERS

12.1	Arensky: "Variations," for str qt, Op.35 (orchd)	
12.2	Borodin: "Prince Igor," opera (Overture & Act III compl & orchd1888)	
12.3	Borodin: Symphony No.3 in A minor, "Unfinished" (2 movts orchd)	
12.4	Musorgsky: "King Saul," song (orchd)	
12.5	Works of Chopin, Cui, Dargomizhsky, Liszt, Schumann, Tchaikovsky	

* * * * *

1. STAGE WORKS

Operas:

1.1	*"Mathilda Rokeby" (c1824, after Scott, sketches for entr'acte only)* ....
1.2	*"Marina Roshcha" (Marina Grove) (c1834, after Zhukovsky, sketches only; used in: A Life for the Tsar)* ....
1.3	"A Life for the Tsar" (Ivan Susanin), 4 acts (c1834–6, Rosen, Zhukovsky & Kukolnik) ....
1.4	"Scene at the gates of the monastery," add scene to Act IV of: A Life for the Tsar (c1837, Kukolnik) ....
1.5	"Ruslan and Lyudmila," 5 acts (c1837–42, Shirkov & others after Pushkin) ....
1.6	*"The Bigamist" (The brigands of the Volga) (c1855, Petrov after Shakhovsky, sketches, lost)* ....

Incid music:

1.7	*"O God, by thy mighty right hand," prayer (c ?1827, frags)* ....
1.8	*"The Moldavian girl & the gypsy girl" (Gold & the dagger) (c1836, Bakhturin, only extant: aria for A & ch)* ....
1.9	"Prince Kholmsky" (c1840, Kukolnik) ....

Other:

1.10	"Tarantella," stage piece (c1841, Myatlev; reciter, ch & orch; arr for orch) ....

1a. SELECTIONS FROM STAGE WORKS (Nos. of sections in The Gramophone)

1a.5   "Ruslan and Lyudmila," opera: ....
       excerpts: 1. "Overture"
         I: 2. "There is a desert country" (The Bard's song)
               3. "Soon I must leave thee" (Lyudmila's cavatina)
        II: 5. "Introduction" (Entr'acte)
               8. "The happy day is gone" (Farlaf's rondo)
               9. "O say, ye fields!" (Ruslan's aria)
        III: 11. "The evening shadows" (Persian song)
              12. "O my Ratmir!" (Gorislava's romance and cavatina)
              13. "The wondrous dream of love" (Ratmir's aria)
              14. "Dances"
        IV: 19. "Chernomor's march"
              20. "Oriental dances"

2. SYMPHONIES

2.1	Symphony in B-flat major (ca1824, inc) ....
2.2	Symphony in D minor, "on two Russian themes" (c1834, inc) ....
2.3	*"Ukrainian Symphony: Taras Bulba" (c ?1848–52, 3 frags remembered Engelhardt & Balakirev)* ....

3. OTHER ORCHESTRAL WORKS

3.1	Overture in D major (ca1822–6) ....
3.2	Overture in G minor (ca1822–6) ....
3.3	"Andante cantabile" (ca1823) ....
3.4	"Rondo," in D minor (ca1823) ....
3.5	*French quadrille (c1825, lost)* ....
3.6	*"Cotillon" (c1827–8, frag: 1st vn part)* ....
3.7	*"La couventine," contredanse (c1839, lost; extant arr for pf)* ....
3.8	*"Grande valse," in G major (c1839, lost; extant arr for pf)* ....
3.9	*"Polonaise," in E major (c1839, lost; extant arr for pf)* ....
3.10	"Valse-fantaisie," in B minor (c1839–56; orig for pf, orchd1845 lost; reorchd1856) ....
3.11	*Waltz in B-flat major (c1840, lost)* ....
3.12	"Capricio brillante on the Jota aragonesa" (Spanish Overture No.1) (c1845) ....
3.13	*"Jaleo de Xeres" (c1845, lost)* ....
3.14	Spanish march theme (c1845 or 6; used Balakirev in: Overture on a Spanish march theme) ....
3.15	"Kamarinskaya" (Russian scherzo), fantasy (c1848; orig for pf 1840 lost; arr for pf duet 1856) ....
3.16	"Recuerdos de Castilla" (Recollections of Castille) (c1848) ....
3.17	*"Tarantella," fantasia (c1850, lost)* ....
3.18	"Recollection of a summer night in Madrid" (2nd Spanish Ov) (c1851, r vers of: Recuerdos de Castilla)......
3.19	"Polonaise on a Spanish bolero theme" (Solemn Polonaise), in F major (c1855) ....
3.20	*Concerto in E-flat major (frags)* ....

4. CONCERTOS, SOLO INSTR & ORCH

4.1	*"Rondo brillante" (c1834–5 or 1827–8; pf & orch, frags)* ....

5. STRING QUARTETS

5.1 String Quartet in D major (c1824, inc) ....
5.2 *"Rondo," in D major (c1827–8, frags)* ....
5.3 *String Quartet in C major (c1827 or 8 or 1830s, frags)* ....
5.4 *String Quartet in E-flat major (c ?1827–8, frags)* ....
5.5 String Quartet in F major (c1830; also for pf duet) ....

6. OTHER CHAMBER MUSIC

5 or more insts:

6.1 Septet in E-flat major (ca1823; ob, bn, hn, 2vn, vc & d bass, inc) ....
6.2 "Divertimento brillante," in A-flat major (c1832; pf, str qt & d bass, on Bellini's opera: La sonnambula) ....
6.3 "Serenade," in E-flat major (c1832; pf, harp, bn, hn, va, vc & d bass, on Donizetti's opera: Anna Bolena) ...
6.4 "Grand Sextet," in E-flat major (c1832; str qt & pf) ....

3 insts:

6.5 "Trio pathétique," in D minor (c1832; cl, bn & pf) ....

Va & pf:

6.6 Viola Sonata in D minor (c1825–8, inc: 2 movts only; compl Borisovsky) ....

7. PIANO

7.1 *"Variations on a theme from Weigl's The Swiss family," in C major (c1822; pf/harp, lost)* ....
7.2 *Waltz in F major (lost)* ....
7.3 "Variations on a theme from Mozart's Zauberflöte," in E-flat major (c1822; pf/harp) ....
7.4 "Variations on an original theme," in F major (ca1824) ....
7.5 *"Rondo," in G major (c1824–5, 2 frags)* ....
7.6 "Variations on the Russian song 'In the gentle valleys,' " in A minor (c1826) ....
7.7 "Variations on a theme from Cherubini's Faniska," in B-flat major (c1826 or 7) ....
7.8 "Variations on the romance 'Benedetta sia la madre,' " in E-flat major (c1826) ....
7.9 5 "Nouvelles quadrilles françaises" (c ?1826) ....
7.10 "Cotillon," in B-flat major (c by 1828) ....
7.11 "Mazurka," in G major (c by 1828) ....
7.12 4 "Nouvelles contredanses" (French quadrilles) (c by 1828) ....
7.13 "Nocturne," in E-flat major (c1828; pf/harp) ....
7.14 "13 Fugues" (c ?1828): No.1 in C major ....
7.15 No.2 in C major
7.16 No.3 in A minor
7.17 No.4 in A minor
7.18 No.5 in C major
7.19 No.6 in E-flat major
7.20 No.7 in F major
7.21 No.8 in D major
7.22 No.9 in B-flat major
7.23 No.10 in E major
7.24 No.11 in C major
7.25 No.12 in C major
7.26 No.13 in A minor
7.27 "Finnish Song," in D major (c1829) ....
7.28 "Farewell Waltz," in G major (c1831) ....
7.29 "Rondino brillante," in B-flat major (c1831, on a theme from Bellini's opera: I Capuleti ed i Montecchi) ....
7.30 "Variazioni brillanti," in A major (c1831, on a theme from Donizetti's opera: Anna Bolena) ....
7.31 "Variations on 2 themes from the ballet 'Chao-Kang,' " in D major (c1831) ....
7.32 "Variations on 'L'amo, l'amo,' " in C major (c1832, from Bellini's opera: I Capuleti ed i Montecchi) ....
7.33 "Variations on Alyabyev's romance 'The Nightingale,' " in E minor (c1833) ....
7.34 "3 Fugues" (c1833 or 4): No.1 in E-flat major (3-part) ....
7.35 No.2 in A minor (3-part)
7.36 No.3 in D major (4-part)
7.37 "Mazurka," in A-flat major (c1833 or 4) ....
7.38 "Mazurka," in F major (c1833–4) ....
7.39 "Motif de chant national" (c ?1834–6) ....
7.40 "Mazurka," in F major (c ?1835) ....
7.41 "5 Contredanses" (c1838) ....
7.42 "Waltz," in E-flat major (c1838) ....
7.43 "Waltz," in B-flat major (c ?1838) ....
7.44 "La couventine," contredanse (c1839; orig for orch lost) ....
7.45 "Grande valse," in G major (c1839; orig for orch lost) ....
7.46 "Polonaise," in E major (c1839; orig for orch lost) ....

7.47   "La séparation," nocturne in F minor (c1839) ....
7.48   *"Le regret," nocturne (c1839; lost; used in No.11 of: A Farewell to St Petersburg for 1v & pf)* ....
7.49   "Valse-fantaisie" (Melancholy Waltz), in B minor (c1839; orchd1845 lost; reorchd1856) ....
7.50   "Galopade," in E-flat major (c1838 or 9) ....
7.51   "Bolero," in D minor (c1840, arr from No.3 of: A Farewell to St Petersburg for 1v & pf) ....
7.52   "Tarantella," in A minor (c1843, on the Russian song: In the field there stood a little birch tree) ....
7.53   "Mazurka," in C minor (c ?1843) ....
7.54   "A Greeting to My Native Land" (c1847): No.1 "Recollection of a mazurka," in B-flat major ....
7.55   No.2 "Barcarolle," in G major
7.56   No.3 "Prayer," in A major (2nd vers for 1v, ch & pf 1855; 3rd vers w/ trbn obbl)
7.57   No.4 "Variations on a Scottish theme" (actually on Irish tune: The Last Rose of Summer)
7.58   "Polka," in D minor (c1849) ....
7.59   "Mazurka," in C major (c1852) ....
7.60   Excerpt from the Epilogue to opera: A Life for the Tsar (c1852) ....
7.61   Excerpt from Finn's Ballad in opera: Ruslan and Lyudmila (c1852) ....
7.62   Excerpt from Lyudmila's scene in Act IV of opera: Ruslan and Lyudmila (c1852) ....
7.63   "Children's polka," in B-flat major (c1854) ....
7.64   "Las Mollares," Andalusian dance in G major (transcr ?1855) ....
7.65   *"Mirror waltz" (c1856, lost)* ....
7.66   "Leggieramente," in E major (p1969) ....

        Pf duet:

7.67   "Trot de cavalerie," in G major (c1829 or 30) ....
7.68   "Trot de cavalerie," in C major (c1829 or 30) ....
7.69   "Impromptu en galop," in B-flat major (c1832, on barcarolle from Donizetti's opera: L'elisir d'amore) ....
7.70   "Capricio on Russian themes," in A major (c1834) ....
7.71   *"Kamarinskaya" (c1840; pf 3 hands, lost; also see for orch)* ....
7.72   "Polka" (Primary Polka), in B-flat major (c1840, written down 1852) ....

8. CHURCH MUSIC

8.1   *"We in this sacred cloister," canon (c1828, Golitsyn, lost)* ....
8.2   "Cherubims' Song," in C major (c1837, Biblical; ch) ....
8.3   "First litany" (c ?1856; ch) ....
8.4   "Let my prayer be fulfilled" (c1856; m ch) ....
8.5   "Resurrection hymn" (c1856 or 7; 2T, B) ....
8.6   *"Cum sancto spiritu," fugue (c?; ch, frags)* ....
8.7   *"Incline thine ear, O Lord, and hear me," fugue (c?; 4vv, frags)* ....
8.8   *"I shall invoke God," fugue for the concerto (c?; 4vv, frags)* ....
8.9   *"Who shall proclaim the strength of God?," subject for the fugue for the third concerto (c?)* ....

9. CHORAL WORKS

9.1   "Prologue on the death of Alexander I": "Pleurons sur la Russie" (c1826, Olidor in Fr; T, ch, pf & d bass) ...
9.2   *"Chorus in C minor on the Death of a Hero" (c1827, lost)* ....
9.3   *"Let us lift up all things unto the Tsar" (c1828; 4vv, frags)* ....
9.4   *"Lila in the black mantle," couplets w/ chorus (c1828, Golitsyn, lost)* ....
9.5   *"La notte omai s'appressa" (c1828; vv, ch & strings, frags)* ....
9.6   "Drinking Song": "Friends, friends" (c ?1829, Delvig; T, m ch & pf, inc) ....
9.7   "Not the frequent autumnal rains" (c1829, Delvig; T, m ch & pf) ....
9.8   "Comic canon a 4" (c1836, Pushkin & others, collab Odoyevsky) ....
9.9   "Great is our God": "What ecstasy, what joy," polonaise (c1837, Sollogub; ch & orch) ....
9.10   *"Chorus to Pavel Vasilyevich" (c1840, Kukolnik; T & ch, lost)* ....
9.11   "Farewell song for the students of the Ekaterinsky Institute" (c1840, Obodovsky; S, fem ch & orch) ....
9.12   "Toasting song": "Pije Kuba do Yakuba" (c1847; 1v & ch) ....
9.13   "Farewell song for the pupils of the Society of Genteel Maidens" (c1850, Timayev; fem ch & orch) ....
9.14   "Prayer: In a difficult moment of life" (arr1855, Lermontov; 1v, ch & orch; orig for pf) ....

10. VOICE & ORCHESTRA

10.1   *Aria in A-flat major (c1827; Bar, lost/?frag)* ....
10.2   *Recitative & duet in A major (c1827; T, B, lost)* ....
10.3   "A, ignobil core," aria (c1828 or 34; B, m ch & orch, inc) ....
10.4   "Come di gloria al nome" (c1828 or 9; S, A, T, B & strings, inc) ....
10.5   "Sogna chi crede d'esser felice" (c1828; A, 2T, B & strings) ....
10.6   "Prayer," in B-flat major (c1828; S, A, T, B & pf, inc) ....
10.7   *Aria to be included in Donizetti: Faust (c1832, lost)* ....
10.8   "Hymn to the Host," cantata (c1838, Markevich; T & orch, inc) ....

11. VOCAL STUDIES

11.1	"7 Studies" (c1829 or 30; A & pf, for Gedeonova) ....
11.2	"6 Studies" (c1833; S & pf, for Maria) ....
11.3	"Exercises for smoothing and perfecting the voice" (c1835 or 6) ....
11.4	"4 Exercises for voice" (c1840 or 1) ....
11.5	"A school of singing" (c1856 or 7; S, for Kashperova) ....

12. SONGS (w/ pf)

12.1	"My harp" (c1824, Scott transl Bakhturin, lost, written down from memory 1855) ....
12.2	"Do not tempt me needlessly" (c1825, Baratinsky; 1/2vv & pf) ....
12.3	"Ah, my sweetheart, thou art a beautiful maiden" (c1826, folksong) ....
12.4	"The singer": "O beautiful world," romance (c1826, Zhukovsky) ....
12.5	"Consolation": "The moon shines on the cemetary" (c1826, Uhland transl Zhukovsky) ....
12.6	"God, preserve our strength in days of distress" (c1827 or 8, Biblical; A, T, B & pf) ......
12.7	"Why do you cry, young beauty" (c1827, Delvig) ....
12.8	"Bitter, bitter it is for me," Russian song (c1827, A. Rimsky-Korsakov) ....
12.9	"Heart's memory," romance (c1827, Batyushkov) ....
12.10	"I love, you assured me" (Le baiser), romance (c1827, A. Rimsky-Korsakov; French text Golitsyn) ....
12.11	"Pour un moment" (Only for one moment), romance (c1827, Golitsyn; also w/ Russian text) ....
12.12	"Tell me, why?," romance (c1827 or 8, Golitsyn) ....
12.13	"Mio ben, ricordati" (I love the shady garden), aria (c1827 or 8; A, T/S & pf) ....
12.14	*"O mia dolce, mia carina," serenade (c1827 or 8, lost)* ....
12.15	*Aria in D major (c1828; A & pf, frags)* ....
12.16	"Due canzonette italiane" (c1828): 1. "Ah, rammenta, o bella Irene," in A major ....
12.17	2. "Alla cetra," in G minor
12.18	"Dovunque il guardo giro," aria (c1828; B & pf) ....
12.19	"Ho perduto il mio tesoro," aria (c1828; T & pf) ....
12.20	"Mi sento il cor trafiggere," aria (c1828; T & pf) ....
12.21	"O Dafni che di quest'anima amabile diletto" (c1828; S & pf) ....
12.22	"Pense che questo istante," aria (c1828; A & pf) ....
12.23	"Piangendo ancora rinascer suole," aria (c1828; S & pf) ....
12.24	"Pur nel sonno," aria (c1828; S & pf) ....
12.25	"Tu sei figlia," aria (c1828; S & pf) ....
12.26	"O thou black night" (c1828, Delvig) ....
12.27	"Grandfather, maids once told me" (c1828, Delvig) ....
12.28	"Sing not, thou beauty, in my presence," Georgian song (c1828, Pushkin) ....
12.29	"Disenchantment," romance (c1828, Golitsyn) ....
12.30	"Shall I forget?," romance (c1828, Golitsyn) ....
12.31	*"Barcarolle," in A-flat major (c1828; T & pf, lost)* ....
12.32	"A voice from the other world," romance (c1829, Schiller transl Zhukovsky) ....
12.33	"Beloved autumnal night," romance (c1829, A. Rimsky-Korsakov) ....
12.34	*"A hundred bright-eyed beauties," romance (c1832, frag: Bass part only)* ....
12.35	"Il desiderio" (Desire): "O if you had been with me," romance (c1832, Romani; Russ text ?Glinka) ....
12.36	"L'iniquo voto": "Pronto giunga il fatal momento" (c1832, Pini; S & pf, for Bellini's opera: Beatrice di Tenda)
12.37	"The conqueror" (Spanish Song) (c1832, Uhland transl Zhukovsky) ....
12.38	"Venetian night," romance (c1832, Kozlov) ....
12.39	"The leafy grove howls," romance (c1834, Schiller transl Zhukovsky) ....
12.40	"Say not that love will pass," romance (c1834, Delvig) ....
12.41	"Do not call her heavenly," romance (c1834, Pavlov; orchd) ....
12.42	"I had but recognized you," romance (c1834, Delvig) ....
12.43	"Spanish Romance": "I am here, Inezilla" (c1834, Pushkin after Cornwall) ....
12.44	*"Romance" (ca1835–44; S & pf, text lost, ?spur)* ....
12.45	"The night review," fantasy (c1836, Sedlitz transl Zhukovsky; orchd ca1836–40 & 1855) ......
12.46	"Where is our rose?," romance (c1837, Pushkin) ....
12.47	"Stanzas": "Here is the place of secret meeting" (c1837, Kukolnik) ....
12.48	"Adieu, petit (charmant) reduit" (c1837; 2vv & pf) ....
12.49	"The wind blows," Little Russian song (c1838, Zabella) ....
12.50	"Sing not, nightingale," Little Russian song (c1838, Zabella) ....
12.51	"Guadalquivir": "The night breeze sheds the air," romance (c1838, Pushkin) ....
12.52	"Doubt," dramatic romance (c1838, Kukolnik; A, harp & vn; also for 1v & pf) ....
12.53	"The fire of longing burns in my blood" (Always, everywhere you are with me) (c1838, Pushkin) ......
12.54	"You will not return again" (c1837 or 8, Glinka; 2S & pf) ....
12.55	"If I shall meet you," romance (c1839, Koltsov) ....
12.56	"Confession": "I love you, though I am furious," romance (c1839, Pushkin) ....
12.57	"The North Star" (Wedding Song): "There stands a wonderful tower," romance (c1839, Rostopchina) ....
12.58	"The bird-cherry tree is blossoming," romance (c1839, Rostopchina) ....
12.59	"How sweet for me to be with you" (c1840, Ryndin) ....
12.60	"A Farewell to St Petersburg" (c1840, Kukolnik): 1. "Romance": "Who is she" (from: David Rizzio) ....
12.61	2. "Hebrew song" (from: Prince Kholmsky)
12.62	3. "Bolero": "O my beautiful maid" (orig for pf; also orchd)
12.63	4. "Cavatina": "Long since have you blossomed gloriously like a rose"
12.64	5. "Lullaby": "Sleep, my angel, go to sleep" (arr Villebois for S, T & strings 1840)

12.65   6. "Travelling song" (The locomotive)
12.66   7. "Fantasy": "Stand, my true, tempestuous steed"
12.67   8. "Barcarolle"
12.68   9. "Virtus antiqua": "Farewell, the ship's sails have unfurled," romance of chivalry
12.69   10. "The Lark": "Between heaven and earth" (arr Villebois for S, T & pf 1840)
12.70   11. "To Molly": "Do not demand songs" (based on lost nocturne: Le regret for pf)
12.71   12. "Farewell Song": "Farewell, good friends" (1v, ch & pf)
12.72   "I recall the wonderful moment," romance (c1840, Pushkin) ....
12.73   *Vaudeville couplets for: The Hired Shot (c1842; 1v & pf, lost)* ....
12.74   "I love you, dear rose," romance (c1842, Samarin) ....
12.75   "To her": "When in a cheerful hour" (c1843, Mickiewicz transl Golitsyn) ....
12.76   "17 Spanish folksongs" (music noted down by Glinka 1845–6) ....
12.77   "Darling," romance (c1847, unknown) ....
12.78   "Soon you will forget me," romance (c1847, Zhadovskaya; orchd1855) ....
12.79   "Gretchen's song": "Meine Ruh' ist hin" (c1848, from Goethe's Faust, transl Huber) ....
12.80   "When I hear your voice," romance (c1848, Lermontov) ....
12.81   "The toasting cup," romance (c1848, Pushkin) ....
12.82   "Adele," romance (c1849, Pushkin) ....
12.83   "Mary," romance (c1849, Pushkin after Cornwall) ....
12.84   "Conversation": "O dear maid," romance (c1849, Mickiewicz) ....
12.85   "The Gulf of Finland" (Palermo) (c1850, Obodovsky) ....
12.86   "Say not that it grieves the heart" (c1856, Pavlov) ....
12.87   *"Funesti pensieri d'un alma dolente," aria (c?; S & pf, frags)* ....

13. ARRANGEMENTS OF WORKS BY OTHERS

13.1   Shterich: Waltz on a theme from Weber's opera: Oberon, J306 (orchd1829) ....
13.2   *Genishta: "The light of day has faded," elegy (orchd1838, Pushkin, sketch, lost)* ....
13.3   Yakovlev: "When, my soul, you asked," elegy (transcr1838, r1855, Delvig; A, B & pf) ....
13.4   *Halevy: Aria from: Guido e Ginerva (orchd1839, lost)* ....
13.5   *Labitsky: "Souvenir du Palais d'Anitshkoff," waltz (orchd1839, lost)* ....
13.6   Bulgakov: "The Scythe" (The Tress), gypsy song (arr1854, A. Rimsky-Korsakov; 1v, ch & orch) ....
13.7   Boikov: "John's couplets" (arr1854; pf)
13.8   Hummel: "Memory of Friendship," nocturne for pf, Op.99 (orchd1854) ....
13.9   Handel: Arias from oratorio: Jephtha, HWV70 (arr1854–5; 1v & pf): 1. "The smiling dawn of happy days" ..
13.10   2. "Tune the soft melodious lute," recit & aria
13.11   3. "Welcome as the cheerful light"
13.12   *Weber: "Invitation to the Dance," for pf, Op.65, J260 (orchd1854, lost)* ....
13.13   "Old gypsy song": "Oh, if I had known before" (arr1855; 1v & pf) ....
13.14   Dargomizhsky: "Fever," folksong (orchd1855) ....
13.15   Fedorov: "Forgive me, forgive," romance (transcr1855, Bulgakov; A, T & pf) ....
13.16   Gluck: Act IV Scene 2 of opera: Armide (arr1855; pf) ....
13.17   Gluck: "Sacrificial chorus," in Act III Scene 4 of opera: Iphigenie en Tauride (arr1855; pf) ....
13.18   Leonova: "The Tear," romance (arr1855, Vasilko-Petrov; 1v & pf) ....
13.19   Méhul: Duet from Act III of: Joseph (arr1856; pf) ....
13.20   Alyabyev: "The Nightingale," romance (orchd1856, Delvig) ....
13.21   Paer: Duet from Act I of: Sargino (arr for vv & pf) ....
13.22   Cherubini: "Romanza," from the opening of Act I of opera: Les deux journées (arr for 1v & pf) ....
13.23   Mozart: "Tamino's aria," from opera: Die Zauberflöte, K620 (arr for 1v & pf) ....

* * * * *

1. STAGE WORKS

Operas:

1.1	*"Artaserse," 3 act seria (p1741, Metastasio, frags)*	*Wq1*
1.2	*"Demetrio" (Cleonice), 3 act seria (p1742, Metastasio, frags)*	*Wq2*
1.3	"Demofoonte," 3 act seria (p1743, Metastasio)	Wq3
1.4	"Artamene" I, 3 act seria (p1743, Vanneschi after Vitturi; also see Wq11)	Wq4
1.5	*"Il Tigrane," 3 act seria (p1743, Silvani after Goldoni: La virtù trionfante, frags)*	
1.6	*"La Sofonisba," 3 act seria (p1744, Metastasio, recitatives by Silvani, frags)*	*Wq5*
1.7	"La finta schiava," 3 act pasticcio (p1744, Silvani, c by Manneri, only 2/3 arias c by Gluck)	Wq6
1.8	"Ipermestra," 3 act seria (p1744, Metastasio, inc)	Wq7
1.9	*"Poro" (Alessandro nell'Indie), 3 act seria (p1744, Metastasio, frags)*	*Wq8*
1.10	*"Ippolito," 3 act seria (p1745, Corio, frags)*	*Wq9*
1.11	"La caduta dei Giganti" (The Fall of Giants), 2 act pasticcio (p1746, Vanneschi)	Wq10
1.12	"Artamene" II, 3 act seria (p1746, Vanneschi after Vitturi; also see Wq4)	Wq11
1.13	"Le nozze d'Ercole e d'Ebe," 2 act seria (p1747, unknown)	Wq12
1.14	"La Semiramide riconosciuta," 3 act seria (p1748, Metastasio)	Wq13
1.15	"La contesa dei numi," 2 act festa teatrale (p1749, Metastasio)	Wq14
1.16	"Ezio," 3 act seria (p1750–1, Metastasio)	Wq15
1.17	"La clemenza di Tito," 3 act seria (p1752, Metastasio)	Wq16
1.18	*"Issipile," 3 act seria (p1752, Metastasio, frags)*	*Wq17*
1.19	"Le cinesi," 1 act azione teatrale (p1754, Metastasio)	Wq18
1.20	"La danza," 1 act componimento pastorale (p1755, Metastasio)	Wq19
1.21	"L'innocenza giustificata," 1 act festa teatrale (p1755, Durazzo & Metastasio)	Wq20
1.22	"Antigono," 3 act seria (p1756, Metastasio)	Wq21
1.23	"Il rè pastore," 3 act seria (p1756)	Wq22
1.24	"L'île de Merlin, ou Le monde renversé," 1 act opéra-comique (p1758, Anseaume after Le Sage & d'Orneval)	Wq23
1.25	"La fausse esclave," 1 act opéra-comique (p1758, Anseaume & Marcouville)	Wq24
1.26	"L'arbre enchanté" I, 1 act opéra-comique (p1759, Moline after Vadé; also see Wq42)	Wq25
1.27	"La Cythère assiégée" I, 1 act opéra-comique (p1759, after Favart & Fagan; also see Wq43)	Wq26
1.28	"Tetide," 2 act serenata (p1760, Migliavacca)	Wq27
1.29	"L'ivrogne corrigé" (Der bekehrte Trunkenbold), 2 act opéra-comique (p1760, Anseaume)	Wq28
1.30	"Le cadi dupé," 1 act opéra-comique (p1761, Lemonnier)	Wq29
1.31	"Orfeo ed Euridice," 3 act azione teatrale (p1762, Calzabigi, Italian vers; also see Wq41)	Wq30
1.32	*"Arianna," pasticcio (p1762, Migliavacca, lost)*	
1.33	"Il trionfo di Clelia," 3 act seria (p1763, Metastasio)	Wq31
1.34	"La rencontre imprévue," 3 act opéra-comique (p1764, Dancourt)	Wq32
1.35	"Il Parnaso confuso," 1 act serenata teatrale (p1765, Metastasio)	Wq33
1.36	"Telemacco nell'isola di Circè," 2 act seria (p1765, Capece & Coltellini)	Wq34
1.37	"La corona," 1 act azione teatrale (c1765, Metastasio)	Wq35
1.38	"Il prologo," 1 act (p1767, Rosso, for Traëtta: Ifigenia)	Wq36
1.39	"Alceste," 3 act seria (p1767, Calzabigi, Italian vers; also see Wq44)	Wq37
1.40	"Le feste d'Apollo," 3 act spectacle (p1769, Frugoni & Calzabigi):	Wq38
	"Prologo: Feste d'Apollo"	
	I. "Atto di Bauci e Filemone"	
	II. "Atto d'Aristeo"	
	III. "Atto d'Orfeo" (= Wq30)	
1.41	"Paride ed Elena," 5 act seria (p1770, Calzabigi)	Wq39
1.42	"Iphigénie en Aulide," 3 act tragédie-opéra (p1774, Roullet after Racine)	Wq40
1.43	"Orphée et Eurydice," 3 act drame héroïque (p1774, French vers; also see Wq30)	Wq41
1.44	"L'arbre enchanté" II, 1 act opéra-comique (p1775, Moline after Vadé; also see Wq25)	Wq42
1.45	"La Cythère assiégée" II, 1 act opéra-comique (p1775, after Favart & Fagan; also see Wq26)	Wq43
1.46	"Alceste," 3 act seria (p1776, Roullet after Calzabigi, French vers; also see Wq37)	Wq44
1.47	"Armide," 5 act drame héroïque (p1777, Quinault)	Wq45
1.48	"Iphigénie en Tauride," 4 act tragédie lyrique (p1779, Guillard)	Wq46
1.49	"Écho et Narcisse," 3 act drame lyrique (p1779, r1780, Tchoudy; r vers by Berton 1806)	Wq47

Ballets:

1.50	"Don Juan" (Le festin de pierre), pantomime (p1761, Angiolini & Calzabigi)	Wq(pp157–161)
1.51	"La Citera assediata," 3 acts (p1762, Angiolini, ballet vers of opera: La Cythère assiégée, Wq26)	
1.52	"Alessandro" (Les amours d'Alexandre et de Roxane) (p1764, Angiolini)	Wq(pp161–162)
1.53	"Semiramis," 1 act pantomime (p1765, Angiolini after Voltaire)	
1.54	*"Iphigénie," ballet tragique (p1765, Angiolini, lost)*	
1.55	*"L'orfano della China" (c1775, Angiolini after Voltaire, spur)*	*Wq(pp155–157)*

Spurious / dubious stage works:

1.56	*"Le déguisement pastoral," 1 act opéra-comique (p1745)*	*App.A1*
1.57	*"Les amours champêtres," pastorale (p1751, parody of 4th entrée of Rameau: Les Indes galantes)*	*App.A2*
1.58	*"Le chinois poli en France" (p1754, parody of Sellitti's 1 act intermezzo: Il cinese rimpatriato)*	*App.A3*
1.59	*"Le diable à quatre, ou La double métamorphose," 3 act opéra-comique (p1756)*	*App.A4*
1.60	*"On ne s'avise jamais de tout," opéra-comique (p ?1761)*	*App.A5*

1.61   *"Isabelle et Gertrude," 1 act comédie (p 1759, c by Blaise, 3 airs attributed to Gluck)* App.A6
1.62   *"Sulámitide," azione sacra (p1803)* .... App.B(1)
1.63   *"Il prodigio di misericordia a sia L'obbliazione del Divin Verbo," azione sacra (p1803)* .... App.B(2)
1.64   *"Semiramis," ballet (p ca1785, assembled from frags of Gluck's works)* .... App.C(1)
1.65   *"Ruggiero nell'Isola di Alcina," ballo eroico (p1792, in Argentina)* .... App.C(2)
1.66   *"Chansons choisies" ('une mélodie de Mr le Chevalier Gluck')* .... App.C(3)

1a. SELECTIONS FROM STAGE WORKS

1a.1   *"Artaserse," opera seria :* *Wq1*
        . *"Sinfonia" (music lost)*
        I: . *"Conservati fedele," aria (Mandane) (music lost)*
             . *"Frà cento affanni," aria (Arbace) (music lost)*
             . *"Sulle sponde del torbito Lete," aria (Artabano) (music lost)*
             . *"Per pietà, bell'idol mio," aria (Artaserse) (music lost)*
             . *"Bramar di perdere," aria (Semira) (music lost)*
             . *"Deh respirar lasciatemi," aria (Artaserse) (music lost)*
             . *"Non ti son padre," aria (Artabano) (music lost)*
             . *"Torna innocente," aria (Semira) (music lost)*
             . *"Dimmi che un empio sei," aria (Mandane) (music lost)*
             . *"Vò solcando un mar crudele," aria (Arbace) (music lost)*
        II: . *"Rendimi il caro amico," aria (Artaserse) (music lost)*
             . *"Mi scacci sdegnato," aria (Arbace) (music lost)*
             . *"Non temer ch'io mai ti dica," aria (Megabise) (music lost)*
             . *"Se d'un amor tiranno," aria (Mandane) (music lost)*
             . "Se del fiume altera l'onda," aria (Semira)
             . *"Per quel paterno amplesso," aria" (Arbace) (music lost)*
             . *"Va tra le selve ircane," aria (Mandane) (music lost)*
             . *"Per quell'affetto," aria (Semira) (music lost)*
             . *"Così stupisce e cade," aria (Artabano) (music lost)*
        III: . *"Perchè tarda è mai la morte," cavatina (Arbace) (music lost)*
             . *"Nuvoletta opposta al sole," aria (Artaserse) (music lost)*
             . *"Ardito ti renda," aria (Megabise) (music lost)*
             . *"Figlio se più non vivi," aria (Artabano) (music lost)*
             . *"Mi credi spietata?," aria (Mandane) (music lost)*
             . *"Non è ver che sia contendo," aria (Semira) (music lost)*
             . *"Tu vuoi ch'io viva, o cara," duet (Arbace, Mandane) (music lost)*
             . *"Giusto Rè, la Persia adora," final chorus (music lost)*
        Add aria: . "Da te s'io cerco amore," aria (Megabise) (for Act I/6, text not by Metastasio, music lost)

1a.2   *"Demetrio" (Cleonice), opera seria:* *Wq2*
        . *"Sinfonia" (music lost)*
        I: . "Misero non è tanto," aria (Barsene) (orig text by Metastasio: Misero tu non sei)
             . *"Se libera non sono," aria (Cleonice) (music lost)*
             . "Se fecondo e vigoroso," aria (Fenicio)
             . "Scherza il nocchier talora," aria (Alceste)
             . *"Saprò di quell'altero," aria (Olinto) (text not by Metastasio, music lost)*
             . "Dal suo gentil sembiante," aria (Alceste)
             . *"Vorrei da' lacci sciogliere," aria (Barsene) (music lost)*
        II: . *"Perfido in te punire," aria (Cleonice) (text not by Metastasio, music lost)*
             . *"Sò che per gioco," aria (Barsene) (music lost)*
             . *"Non fidi al mar che freme," aria (Olinto) (music lost)*
             . *"Non sò frenare il pianto," aria (Alceste) (music lost)*
             . *"Manca sollecita," aria (Cleonice) (music lost)*
             . *"Disperato in mare turbato," aria (Fenicio) (music lost)*
        III: . *"Io sò qual pena sia," aria (Cleonice) (music lost)*
             . "Quel labbro adorato," aria (Alceste)
             . *"Più non sembra ardito e fiero," aria (Olinto) (music lost)*
             . *"Giusti Dei, da voi non chiede," aria (Fenicio) (music lost)*
             . *"Quando scende in nobil petto," final chorus (music lost)*

1a.3   "Demofoonte," opera seria: Wq3
        . *"Sinfonia" (music lost)*
        I: . "O più tremar non voglio," aria (Matusio)
             . "In te spero, sposo amato," aria (Dircea)
             . "Per lei frà l'armi," aria (Demofoonte)
             . "Sperai vicino il lido," aria (Timante)
             . "T'intendo, ingrata," aria (Cherinto)
             . "Non curo l'affetto," aria (Creusa)
             . "Il suo leggiadro viso," aria (Cherinto)
             . "Padre, perdona ... oh pene!," aria (Dircea)
             . "Gemo in un punto e fremo," aria (Timante) (text from Metastasio: L'Olimpiade)
        II: . "Tu sai chi son," aria (Creusa)
             . "Non è ver che l'ira insegni," aria (Adrasto) (text from Metastasio: L'Asilo d'amore)

    . "Prudente mi chiedi?," aria (Timante)
    . "Se tronca un ramo," aria (Demofoonte)
    . "È soccorso d'incognita mano," aria (Matusio)
    . "Se tutti i mali miei," aria (Dircea)
    . "Nò, non chiedo, amate stelle," aria (Cherinto)
    . "Felice età dell'oro," aria (Creusa)
    . "Perfidi già che in vita," aria (Demofoonte)
    . "La destra ti chiedo," recit obbl & duet (Timante, Dircea)
    III: . "Non odi consiglio?," aria (Adrasto)
    . "Nel tuo dono veggo assai," aria (Cherinto)
    . "Ah che nè mal verace," aria (Matusio)
    . "Misero pargoletto," aria (Timante)
    . "Odo il suono de' queruli accenti," aria (Demofoonte)
    . "Che mai risponderti?," aria (Dircea)
    . "Non dura una sventura," aria (Creusa)
    . "Per maggiore ogni diletto," final chorus
   Add aria: . *"Tutti nemici e rei," aria (Timante) (for Act II/6, text from Metastasio: Adriano in Siria, music lost)*

1a.4   "Artamene," opera seria (libretto lost, arias & duet shown in alphabetical order): Wq4
    . "Care pupille amate," aria
    . "Colomba innamorata," aria
    . "Lungi da te, ben mio," duet
    . "Nero turbo il ciel imbruna," aria
    . "Padre ... rammenta ... oh Dio!," aria (parody of: Padre, perdona ... oh pene!, from: Demofoonte)
    . "Parto da te, mio bene," aria
    . "Perfido, traditore," aria
    . "Presso l'onda d'Acheronte," aria
    . "Priva del caro bene," aria
    . "Quando ruina con le sue," aria
    . "Rasserena il mesto ciglio," aria
    . "Se fido l'adorai," aria
    . "Se in grembo a lieta," aria
    . "Se spunta amica stella," aria
    . "Sì, ben mio, morrò se il vuoi," aria
    . "Sì, cadrà con grave scempio," aria
    . "Sparge al mar," aria
    . "Tema quell'alma audace," aria
    . "Troppo ad un alma è caro," aria
    . "Vezzi, lusinghe e sguardi," aria

1a.6   *"La Sofonisba," opera seria:* *Wq5*
    . *"Sinfonia" (music lost)*
    I: . *"Di che a sua voglia eleggere," aria (Siface) (music lost)*
    . "Nobil onda," aria (Siface)
    . "Se tanto piace," aria (Vermina) (text from Metastasio: Siface)
    . *"Tornate sereni, begli astri d'amore," aria (Massinissa) (text from Metastasio: Achille, music lost)*
    . *"Caro, tu sol, tu sei," aria (Sofonisba) (music lost)*
    . "Se in campo armato," aria (Siface)
    . *"Talor se il vento freme," aria (Massinissa) (music lost)*
    . "Non vi piacque, ingiusti Dei," aria (Janisbe)
    . "Tremo fra dubbi miei," aria (Sofonisba) (text from Metastasio: La clemenza di Tito)
    II: . *"Volgi un sol guardo in pace," aria (Scipione) (music lost)*
    . *"Fra sdegno ed amore," aria (Janisbe) (text from Metastasio: Siroe, music lost)*
    . *"Chi mai d'iniqua stella," aria (Vermina) (text from Metastasio: Temistocle, music lost)*
    . "Cara, dagl' occhi tuoi," aria (Siface)
    . "O frangi i lacci miei," aria (Sofonisba)
    . "È maggiore d'ogn'altro dolore," aria (Massinissa) (from Metastasio: Issipile)
    . "M'opprime, m'affanna," aria (Siface)
    . *"È sorta di tormento," aria (Janisbe) (text from Metastasio: Temistocle, music lost)*
    . *"Chi mai non vide fuggir le sponde," aria (Mezetulo) (text from Metastasio: Issipile, music lost)*
    . *"Non v'è perdono," finale (music lost)*
    III: . *"Scettro, corona e soglio," aria (Mezetulo) text from: Metastasio: Siface, music lost)*
    . *"Finchè un zeffiro soave," aria (Janisbe) (text from Metastasio: Orti Speridi, music lost)*
    . "Se fedel, cor mio, tu sei," recit obbl & duet (Siface, Sofonisba)
    . *"Contrasto assai più degno," aria (Scipione) (text from Metastasio: Temistocle, music lost)*
    . "Là sul margine di Lete," aria (Sofonisba)
    . *"Cedò alla sorte," aria (Vermina) (text from Metastasio: Achille, music lost)*
    . *"L'alma mia non è più quella," aria (Massinissa) (music lost)*
    . *"Quando un emulo l'imita," final chorus (text from Metastasio: Temistocle, music lost)*
   Add aria: . *"Dirò che il vincitor," aria (Mezetulo) (for Act I/9, music lost)*

1a.7   "La finta schiava," pasticcio: Wq6
    . "Troppo ad un alma è caro," aria (from: Artamene, Wq4)
    . "Ch'io mai vi possa lasciar d'amare," aria (text from Metastasio: Siroe)

1a.8   "Ipermestra," opera seria: Wq7
. "Sinfonia"
    I: . "Abbiam penato, è ver," aria (Elpinice)
. "Pensa che figlia sei," aria (Danao)
. "Ah non parlar d'amore," aria (Ipermestra)
. "Di pena si forte," aria (Linceo)
. "Solo effetto era d'amore," aria (Elpinice)
. "Ma rendi pur contento," aria (Plistene)
. "Più temer non posso ormai," aria (Adrasto)
. "Se pietà da voi non trovo," aria (Ipermestra)
. "Del suo dolor crudel," aria (Danao) (text not by Metastasio)
. "Io non pretendo, o stelle," aria (Linceo)
   II: . "Pria di lasciar la sponda," aria (Adrasto)
. "Non hai cor per un'impresa," aria (Danao)
. "Se il mio duol," aria (Ipermestra)
. "Gonfio tu vedi il fiume," aria (Linceo)
. "Belle d'amore, belle adorate," aria (Plistene) (text not by Metastasio)
. "Mai l'amor mio verace," aria (Elpinice)
. "Or del tuo ben la sorte," aria (Danao)
. "Ah se di te mi privi," duet (Ipermestra, Linceo)
. "Và, più non dirmi infida," aria (Ipermestra)
. "Tremo per l'idol mio," aria (Linceo)
. "Perdono al crudo acciaro," aria (Elpinice)
. "Alma eccelsa, accendi al trono," final chorus

1a.9   *"Poro" (Alessandro nell'Indie), opera seria:* *Wq8*
. "Sinfonia" (lost)
    I: *. "È prezzo leggiero," aria (Gandarte) (music lost)*
. "Vedrai con tuo periglio," aria (Poro) (music lost)
. "Vil trofeo d'un alma imbelle," aria (Alessandro) (music lost)
. "Chi vive amante sai che delira," aria (Erissena) (music lost)
. "O su gli estivi ardori," aria (Timagene) (music lost)
. "A tutti i nostri Dei lo giuro," arioso (Poro) (music lost)
. "Se mai turbo il mio riposo," aria (Cleofide) (music lost)
. "Compagni nell'amore," aria (Erissena) (music lost)
. "Voi che adorate il vanto," aria (Gandarte) (music lost)
. "Se amore a questo petto," aria (Alessandro) (music lost)
. "Se mai turbo il mio riposo," duet (Cleofide, Poro) (music lost)
   II: *. "Non sarei si sventurata," aria (Erissena) (music lost)*
. "Senza procella ancora," aria (Poro) (music lost)
. "Sommi Dei, se giusti siete," preghiera (Cleofide, Poro) (music lost)
. "D'un barbaro scortese," aria (Alessandro) (music lost)
. "Digli ch'io son fedele," aria (Cleofide) (music lost)
. "Destrier che all'armi usato," aria (Poro) (music lost)
. "È ver che all'amo intorno," aria (Timagene) (music lost)
. "Se il Ciel mi divide," aria (Cleofide) (music lost)
. "Se viver non poss'io," aria (Gandarte) (music lost)
. "Di rendermi la calma," aria (Erissena) (music lost)
   III: *. "Se troppo crede al ciglio," aria (Cleofide) (music lost)*
. "Serbati a grand'imprese," aria (Alessandro) (music lost)
. "Finchè rimango in vita," aria (Timagene) (music lost)
. "Dov'è? Si affretti," aria (Poro) (music lost)
. "Mio ben, ricordati," aria (Gandarte) (music lost)
. "Son confusa pastorella," aria (Erissena) (music lost)
. "Serva ad Eroe si grande," final chorus (music lost)

1a.10   *"Ippolito," opera seria:* *Wq9*
. "Sinfonia" (lost)
    I: *. "Se la tigre appena è nata," aria (Fedra) (music lost)*
. "Figlia dell'Erebo," aria (Fedra) (music lost)
. "Non luce stella," aria (Arbace) (music lost)
. "Varca il mar superba nave," aria (Ippolito)
. "Chi m'invola al mio rossore," aria (Fedra) (music lost)
. "Caro, nel tuo perglio," aria (Arsinoe) (music lost)
. "Men leone è di stragi bramoso," aria (Teseo) (music lost)
. "Se tu vedessi come vegg'io," aria (Ippolito)
. "Agitata non trovo riposo," aria (Arsinoe) (music lost)
   II: *. "Quando saprai tua sorte," aria (Fedra) (music lost)*
. "Quando ritorna la rondinella," aria (Licida) (music lost)
. "Chi vide mai d'un figlio," aria (Teseo) (music lost)
. "Questa è, crudel, la fede," trio (Arsinoe, Ippolito, Teseo) (music lost)
. "Se l'amico per la chioma," aria (Arbace) (music lost)
. "Non sò placar mio sdegno," aria (Arsinoe) (music lost)
. "Parto, ma un giorno Amore," aria (Ippolito)
. "Chi noto mi fa," aria (Teseo)

III: . *"Se a Timanto chiede,"* aria (Ippolito) *(music lost)*
. *"Conosco il tuo dolore,"* aria (Arbace) *(music lost)*
. *"Che affanni, che pene,"* aria (Arsinoe) *(music lost)*
. *"Digli che al fin del corso,"* aria (Fedra) *(music lost)*
. *"Tigre se vien sorpresa,"* aria *(Licida) (music lost)*
. "Ah m'ingannasti," duet (Arsinoe, Ippolito)
. "Ah già parmi che d'armi," aria (Teseo)
. *"Scenda il celeste lume,"* final aria (Teseo) *(music lost)*
Add arias: . *"Sovra la preda esangue,"* aria *(for Act I/13, music lost)*
. "Dirai all'idol mio," aria (for Act III/1)

1a.11   "La caduta dei Giganti" (The Fall of Giants), pasticcio: Wq10
. *"Sinfonia" (lost)*
. "Care pupille amate," aria (Signor Jozzi)
. "Vezzi, lusinghe e sguardi," aria (Signora Pompeati)
. "Ah m'ingannasti," duet (Signora Pompeati, Signor Monticelli)
. "Sì, ben mio, sarò se il vuoi," aria (Signor Monticelli)
. "È uguale ad un tormento," aria (Signor Monticelli)
. "Conserva a noi il contento," aria (Signor Jozzi)
. *"Pensa che il Ciel trema,"* aria (Signor Ciacchi) *(music lost)*
. *"Mai l'amor mio verace,"* aria (Signora Imer) *(music lost)*
. *"Volgo dubbioso,"* aria (Signora Pompeati) *(music lost)*

1a.12   "Artamene," opera seria: Wq11
. *"Sinfonia" (lost)*
. "Rasserena il mesto ciglio," aria (Signor Monticelli)
. "Pensa a serbarmi, o cara," aria (Signor Monticelli)
. "È maggiore d'ogn'altro dolore," aria (Signora Frasi)
. "Il suo leggiadro viso," aria (Signor Rozzi)
. "Se crudeli tanto siete," aria (Signora Pompeati)
. "Già presso al termine," aria (Signor Jozzi)

1a.13   "Le nozze d'Ercole e d'Ebe," opera seria: Wq12
. "Sinfonia"
Part I: . "Finchè l'aura increspa l'onda," aria (Ercole)
. "Chi di farsi altiero e grande," aria (Giove)
. "Quando nel suol figura," aria (Ercole)
. "Ben conosce maggior," aria (Giunone)
. "Passagiero va lieto frà l'onde," aria (Ebe)
. "Lasciami in pace," duet (Ercole, Giunone)
Part II: . "L'augellin," aria (Giunone)
. "Il piacer d'un dolce amore," aria (Ebe)
. "Se al troppo giubilo," aria (Ercole)
. "Saprò dalle procelle," aria (Giove)
. "Dell'allegrezza il nome," final chorus
Add aria: . "Così come s'accese," recit obbl & aria

1a.14   "La Semiramide riconosciuta," opera seria: Wq13
. "Sinfonia"
I: . "Non sò se più t'accendi," aria (Semiramide)
. "Vorrei spiegar l'affanno," aria (Scitalce)
. "Che quel cor, quel ciglio," aria (Tamiri)
. "Maggior follia non v'è," aria (Ircano)
. "Bel piacer saria d'un core," aria (Mirteo)
. "S'intende si poco," aria (Scitalce)
. "Ei d'amor quasi delira," aria (Tamiri)
. "Se amar volete," rondo (Semiramide) (text not by Metastasio)
. "Talor se il vento freme," aria (Ircano)
II: . "Il piacer, la gioia scenda," chorus
. "Voi che le mie vicende," aria (Scitalce)
. "Saper bramate," aria (Ircano)
. "Io veggo in lontananza," aria (Mirteo)
. "Il pastor se torna aprile," aria
. "Vieni che poi sereno," aria (Sibari)
. "Fiumicel che s'ode appena," aria (Mirteo)
. "Non sò se sdegno sia," aria (Tamiri)
. "Tradita, sprezzata," aria (Semiramide)
. "Non saprei qual doppia voce," aria (Scitalce)
III: . "Il Ciel mi vuole oppresso," aria (Ircano)
. "Torrente che ritegno," aria (Sibari)
. "Fuggi dagl'occhi miei," aria (Semiramide)
. "Odi quel fasto?," aria (Scitalce)
. "D'un genio che m'accende," aria (Tamiri)
. "Sentirsi dire," aria (Mirteo)
. "Di rabbia, di sdegno," aria (Ircano)

. "Viva lieta e sia Regina," final chorus
Add aria: . "Oscura il sol, le stelle," aria

1a.15   "La contesa dei numi," festa teatrale: Wq14
          Part I: . "Introduzione"
                  . "Oggi per me non sudi," recit obbl & aria (Giove)
                  . "Se la cura è a me negata," aria" (Apollo)
                  . "Per me la greggia errante," aria (La Pace)
                  . "Del mio scudo bellicoso," aria (Marte)
                  . "Con umil ciglio," aria (Astrea)
                  . "Perchè viva felice un regnante," aria (La Fortuna)
                  . "Del fiore nascente," chorus
          Part II: . "Introduzione"
                   . "Timido si scolora," recit obbl & aria (Marte)
                   . "Non meno risplende," aria (La Pace)
                   . "Se vorrà fidarsi all'onda," aria (La Fortuna)
                   . "Non si vedrà sublime," aria (Astrea)
                   . "Frà le memorie," aria (Apollo)
                   . "All'opre si volga," aria (Giove)
                   . "Accompagni della cuna," final chorus

1a.16   "Ezio," opera seria: Wq15
                  . "Sinfonia"
          I: . "Marcia"
                  . "Se tu la reggi al volo," aria (Valentiniano)
                  . "Pensa a serbarmi, o cara," aria (Ezio)
                  . "Caro padre, a me non dei," aria (Fulvia)
                  . "Se un bell'ardire," aria (Varo)
                  . "Quanto mai felici siete," aria (Onoria)
                  . "Se povero il ruscello," aria (Massimo)
                  . "Sò chi t'accese," aria (Valentiniano)
                  . "Se fedele mi brama," aria (Ezio)
                  . "Ancor non premi il soglio," aria (Onoria)
                  . "Finchè per te mi palpita," aria (Fulvia)
          II: . "Dubbioso amante," aria (Valentiniano)
                  . "Và dal furor portata," aria (Massimo)
                  . "Recagli quell'acciaro," aria (Ezio)
                  . "Quel fingere affetto," aria (Fulvia)
                  . "Nasce al bosco in rozza cuna," aria (Varo)
                  . "Finchè un zeffiro soave," aria (Onoria)
                  . "Ecco alle mie catene," aria (Ezio)
                  . "Passami il cor, tiranno!," trio (Fulvia, Valentiniano, Massimo)
          III: . "Peni tu per un'ingrata," aria (Onoria)
                  . "Per la memoria," aria (Ezio)
                  . "Per tutto il timore," aria (Valentiniano)
                  . "Tergi l'ingiuste lagrime," aria (Massimo)
                  . "Ah non son io che parlo," aria (Fulvia)
                  . "Della vita nel dubbio cammino," final chorus

1a.17   "La clemenza di Tito," opera seria: Wq16
                  . "Sinfonia"
          I: . "Deh se piacer mi vuoi," aria (Vitellia)
                  . "Io sento ch'in petto," aria (Annio)
                  . "Opprimete i contumaci," aria (Sesto)
                  . "Del più sublime soglio," aria (Tito)
                  . "Ah perdona al primo affetto," aria (Annio)
                  . "Amo te solo," aria (Servilia)
                  . "Ah se fosse intorno al trono," aria (Tito)
                  . "Parto; ma tu, ben mio," aria (Sesto)
                  . "Quando sarà quel dì," recit obbl & aria (Vitellia)
          II: . "Sia lontano ogni cimento," recit obbl & aria (Publio)
                  . "Almen se non poss'io," aria (Servilia)
                  . "Come potesti, oh Dio," aria (Vitellia)
                  . "Frà stupido e pensoso," aria (Sesto)
                  . "Tu, infedel, non hai difese," aria (Tito)
                  . "Ch'io parto reo, lo vedi," aria (Annio)
                  . "Se mai senti spirarti sul volto," aria (Sesto)
                  . "Tremo fra dubbi miei," aria (Vitellia)
          III: . "Tardi s'avvede d'un traditor," aria (Publio)
                  . "Pietà, Signor, per lui," arioso (Annio)
                  . "Vò disperato a morte," aria (Sesto)
                  . "Se all'impero, amici Dei," aria (Tito)
                  . "S'altro che lagrime," aria (Servilia)
                  . "Getta il nocchier talora," aria (Vitellia)
                  . "Che del Ciel, che degli Dei," final chorus

1a.18   *"Issipile," opera seria :* *Wq17*
- *"Sinfonia" (lost)*

I: . *"Sò che riduce a piangere," aria (Toante) (music lost)*
- . "Impallidisce in campo," aria (Issipile)
- . *"Non è ver, benchè si dica," aria (Eurinome) (music lost)*
- . *"Oh Dei piagato un core," aria (Rodope) (text not by Metastasio, music lost)*
- . *"Ritrova in quei detti," aria (Toante) (music lost)*
- . *"Chi mai non vide fuggir le sponde," aria (Giasone) (music lost)*
- . *"Ogni amante può dirsi guerriero," aria (Learce) (music lost)*
- . *"Sento d'intorno al core," aria (Giasone) (music lost)*
- . *"Crudo amore, oh Dio, ti sento," aria (Issipile) (music lost)*

II: . "Ombra diletta," aria (Eurinome)
- . *"Nell'istante fortunato," aria (Issipile) (music lost)*
- . *"Rendimi il figlio mio," aria (Eurinome) (music lost)*
- . *"Tu non sai che bel contendo," aria (Rodope) (music lost)*
- . *"Care selve, amato rio," aria (Giasone) (music lost)*
- . *"Parto, se vuoi così," aria (Issipile) (music lost)*
- . *"Ti vò cercando in volto," aria (Rodope) (music lost)*
- . "Io ti lascio, e questo addio," cavatina (Giasone)
- . *"Tortora che sorprende," aria (Toante) (music lost)*

III: . *"Guardami prima in volto," aria (Toante) (music lost)*
- . *"Care luci che regnate," duet (Issipile, Giasone) (music lost)*
- . *"Odia la pastorella," aria (Rodope) (music lost)*
- . *"Eccomi, non ferir," aria (Issipile) (music lost)*
- . *"È follia d'un alma stolta," final chorus (music lost)*

1a.19   "Le cinesi," azione teatrale: Wq18
- . "Sinfonia"
- . "Prenditi il figlio," recit obbl & aria (Lisinga)
- . "Son lungi e non mi brami," aria (Silango)
- . "Non sperar, non lusingarti," aria (Sivene)
- . "Ad un riso, ad un occhiata," aria (Tangia)
- . "Voli il piede in lieti giri," final chorus

1a.20   "La danza," componimento pastorale: Wq19
- . "Sinfonia"
- . "Va: della danza è l'ora," aria (Tirsi)
- . "Se tu non vedi," aria (Nice)
- . "Che ciascun per te sospiri," aria (Tirsi)
- . "Che chiedi, che brami?," aria (Nice)
- . "Mille volte, mio tesoro," final duet (Nice, Tirsi)

1a.21   "L'innocenza giustificata," festa teatrale: Wq20
- . "Sinfonia"
- . "D'atre nubi è il sol ravvolto," aria (Flavio)
- . "Sempre è maggior del vero," aria (Valerio)
- . "Guarda pria se in questa fronte," aria (Claudia)
- . "A' giorni suoi la sorte," aria (Flaminia)
- . "Và, ti consola, addio," duet (Claudia, Flavio)
- . "Fiamma ignota nell'alma," aria (Claudia)
- . "Quercia annosa sull'erte pendici," aria (Valerio)
- . "La meritata palma," aria (Claudia)
- . "Non è la mia speranza," aria (Flavio)
- . "Deh seconda, ospite Nume," chorus
- . "Noto è il reo," chorus
- . "Ah rivolgi, o casta Diva," preghiera (Claudia)
- . "Grazie al Ciel," final chorus

1a.22   "Antigono," opera seria: Wq21
- . "Sinfonia"

I: . "Di vantarsi hà ben ragione," aria (Ismene)
- . "A torto spergiuro," aria (Demetrio)
- . "È la beltà del cielo," aria (Antigono)
- . "Io non sò se amor tu sei," aria (Berenice)
- . "Marcia"
- . "Tu m'involasti un regno," aria (Antigono)
- . "Meglio rifletti al dono," aria (Alessandro)
- . "È pena troppo barbara," aria (Berenice)
- . "Contro il destin che freme," aria (Demetrio)

II: . "Di due ciglia," aria (Clearco)
- . "Sai qual ardor m'accende," aria (Alessandro)
- . "Basta così; ti cedo," aria (Berenice)
- . "Piango, è ver," aria (Demetrio)
- . "Perchè due cori insieme," aria (Ismene)
- . "Quercia annosa sull'erte pendici," aria (Antigono) (text from Metastasio: Sogno di Scipione)

. "Non temer, non son più amante," aria (Berenice, Demetrio)
III: . "Dì, che ricuso il trono," aria (Antigono)
. "Che pretendi, Amor tiranno?," aria (Ismene)
. "Guerrier che i colpi affretta," aria (Clearco)
. "Benchè giusto a vendicarmi," aria (Alessandro)
. "Già che morir degg'io," aria (Demetrio)
. "Perchè se tanti siete," recit obbl & aria (Berenice)
. "Doppo torbida procella," final chorus

1a.23   "Il rè pastore," opera seria: Wq22
I: . "Introduzione"
. "Intendo, amico rio," arioso (Aminta)
. "Alla selva, al prato," aria (Elisa)
. "Sò che pastor son io," aria (Aminta)
. "Sì spande al sole," aria (Alessandro)
. "Per me rispondete," aria (Agenore)
. "Di tante sue procelle," aria (Tamiri)
. "Vanne a regnar, ben mio," duet (Elisa, Aminta)
II: . "Al mio fedel dirai," aria (Tamiri)
. "Barbaro, oh Dio, mi vedi," aria (Elisa)
. "Ogn'altro affetto ormai," aria (Agenore)
. "Ah per voi la pianta umile," aria (Aminta)
. "Se vincendo vi rendo felice," aria (Alessandro)
. "Ah tu non sei più mio," quartet (Elisa, Aminta, Tamiri, Agenore)
III: . "L'amerò, sarò costante," aria (Aminta)
. "Io rimaner divisa," aria (Elisa)
. "Se tu di me fai dono," aria (Tamiri)
. "Sol può dir come si trova," aria (Agenore)
. "Voi che fausti ogn'or donate," aria (Alessandro)
. "Dalla selva e dall'ovile," final chorus

1a.24   "L'île de Merlin," opéra-comique: Wq23
. "Ouverture descriptive"
. "Ah! le bon pays, Scapin!," arietta (Pierrot)
. "Merlin nous dit que ce séjour," arietta (Scapin)
. "Bonjour, bonjour, belle nymphe," quartet (Argentine, Diamantine, Scapin, Pierrot)
. "Le mari tranquille," arietta (Argentine)
. "Pour repartir également," quartet (Argentine, Diamantine, Scapin, Pierrot)
. "Laisses faire, malgré leur colère," arietta (Pierrot)
. "Le vrai bonheur de la vie," couplets (Le Philosophe)
. "Heureux qui la nuit et le jour," ariette dialoguée (Le Philosophe, Scapin, Pierrot)
. "Fais-toi donc peintre ou poète," arietta (Scapin)
. "L'avocat, le procureur," couplets (La Candeur, Scapin)
. "Toujours amants sans avoir," arietta (La Candeur)
. "Qu'un mortel soit pulmonique," arietta w/ refrain (Hippocratine, Scapin, Pierrot)
. "Je voudrais que vous fussiez tous deux," trio dialogué (Argentine, Scapin, Pierrot)
. "Paix, paix! apprenez à me connaître," arietta (Le chevalier de Catonville)
. "Quoi, donc! un petit-maître," arietta (Pierrot)
. "Dieu, quel martyre!," arietta (Argentine)
. "Où sont-ils, ces rivaux maudits," aria (Hanif)
. "Renoncez à cet affreux projet," arietta (Diamantine)
. "Dans ce contrat," scene (Le Notaire)
. "Le sort ainsi l'ordonne," arietta (Diamantine)
. "Me voilà dans cette affaire," ariette dialoguée (Scapin)
. "Que les plaisirs, que l'allégresse," tutti

1a.25   "La fausse esclave," opéra-comique: Wq24
. *"Ouverture" (lost)*
. "Cours à ta belle, va!," arietta (Chrysante)
. "Est-ce donc un crime?," arietta (Valère)
. "Dans un temps contraire," arietta (Lisette)
. "Hé bien, cher époux," ariette dialoguée (Agathe, later Valère)
. "Je lui veux en ce jour," arietta (Agathe)
. "Oui, je vous aime," duet (Agathe, Valère)
. "Il faut donc vaincre ma faiblesse," arietta (Agathe)
. "Quelle folie extrême!," arietta (Chrysante)
. "Pour me punir d'être trop aimable," arietta (Agathe)
. "Tendre Agathe, quel aspoir," arietta (Agathe)
. "Pour héritage je n'eus," ariette dialoguée (Agathe, Chrysante)
. "L'hymen a plus d'un souci," arietta (Lisette)
. "Au doux plaisir livrons," tutti (Agathe, Lisette, Valère, Chrysante)

1a.26   "L'arbre enchanté" I, opéra-comique: Wq25
. *"Ouverture" (lost)*
. "Elle fixe mes désirs," arietta (Lubin)

. "On amorce le poisson," ariette dialoguée (Blaise, Lubin)
. "Du jeune objet que j'adore," arietta (Lubin)
. "Si l'amour était un crime," arietta (Claudine)
. "Est-il un plus cruel martyre?," duet (Claudine, Lubin)
. "Pour me plaire il faut qu'un amant," arietta (Lucette)
. "Je prétends que dans ce jour," arietta (Thomas)
. "Que l'objet qui m'enflamme," arietta (Claudine)
. "Pierrot ne se trompe pas," arietta (Claudine)
. "Ah, ah, ah, ah, Monsieur Thomas," arietta (Lubin)
. "L'aventure est très comique," arietta (Thomas)
. "Je me souviens de ma sottise," duet (Claudine, Lubin)
. "Ma soeur et ce garçon," arietta (Lucette)
. "Toujours par fillette franche," arietta (Blaise)
. "Jurons-nous, en ce jour," tutti

1a.27   "La Cythère assiégée" I, opéra-comique: Wq26
. "Ouverture" (lost)
. "Habitants de ce doux empire," duet (Daphné, Chloé)
. "Que tous les amants réunis," aria (Chloé)
. "Adonis est fait pour charmer," aria w/ dance (Doris)
. "Avec quelle ardeur Vénus," menuet w/ dance (Chloé)
. "Trio" (orch)
. "Sous un ormeau," aria (Carite)
. "Le barbare. Me déclare," aria (Carite)
. "Songeons à nous défendre," aria & chorus (Chloé, later ch)
. "De quoi, diable, nous mêlons-nous?," arioso (Barbarin)
. "Brontez, ce chef intrépide," aria (Olgar)
. "A moi, fiers soldats!," aria (Brontez)
. "Contre les objets les plus charmants," duet & chorus (Olgar, Brontez)
. "Pour nous emparer de ces murs," aria (Barbarin)
. "On s'arrache la victoire," aria (Carite)
. "D'où naît le transport," air dialoguée & chorus (Olgar, Daphné, later ch)
. "Nous soumettons le plus farouche," duo dialogué (Daphné, Olgar)
. "Méprisons ces perfides charmes," air dialogué & chorus (Olgar, Daphné, later ch)
. "Si l'on vous croit, c'est fait," aria & chorus (repeat) (Daphné, later ch)
. "Tu fais renaître en moi," aria (Olgar)
. "Les dieux dans leur grandeur," duet (Daphné, Olgar)
. "Enfants de la victoire," aria & chorus (Brontez, later ch)
. "Lorsque j'entends le bruit des armes," aria (Chloé)
. "Arrachez-moi de cet affreux séjour," duet (Chloé, Brontez)
. "Ce coeur si fier," air dialogué (Chloé, Brontez)
. "J'obtiens un doux retour," quartet (Daphné, Chloé, Olgar, Brontez)
. "La paix règne en ces asiles," aria & final chorus (Chloé)

1a.28   "Tetide," serenata: Wq27
. "Sinfonia"
Part I: . "A chi tu fidi, Achille," chorus
. "Stese all'acciar la mano," aria (Marte)
. "Quante volte a lui le impresse," aria (Apollo)
. "Ah tu del Ciel gran Nume," aria (Tetide)
. "Nò, nuovi oltraggi ormai," aria (Pallade)
. "Se de miei preghi altera," aria (Venere)
. "Stringa il plettro," aria (Pallade)
. "Alla virtude, amico," aria (Tetide)
. "Chi de' nemici sdegni," quartet (Pallade, Venere, Apollo, Marte)
Part II: . "Sotto si fausti rai," aria (Tetide)
. "Oggi Amor frà lacci miei," aria (Imeneo)
. "Ah tu affretta i dolci istanti," duet (Tetide, Apollo)
. "Vieni, Imeneo," final chorus

1a.29   "L'ivrogne corrigé" (Der bekehrte Trunkenbold), opéra-comique: Wq28
. "Ouverture"
I: . "Ça, compère Mathurin," arietta (Lucas)
. "Maudit ivrogne," trio (Mathurine, Mathurin, Lucas)
. "Sans soins, sans peine," arietta (Mathurine)
. "Non, non, jamais un tel époux," arietta (Colette)
. "Avec nous il prit naissance," aria (Cléon)
. "Ah! ah! ah! que j'ai bu de bon vin!," arietta (Mathurin)
II: . "Il est mort, le cher Mathurin," funeral chorus (Mathurin, Colette, Cléon, ch)
. "Ah! si j'empoigne ce maître ivrogne," duet (Furies)
. "Quels sont ces deux misérables?," air dialogué (Pluton, 2 Furies)
. "Vous n'aurez que la bastonnade," recit & aria (Pluton)
. "O puissant dieu que l'on révère," arietta (Mathurine)
. "Redez Mathurin à la vie," trio (Colette, Mathurine, Mathurin)
. "De vos tourments je suis confuse," arietta (Mathurine)

. "Allons, morbleu, plus de chagrin," arietta (Colas)
. "Que de plaisir l'Amour nous donne," final chorus (Colette, Mathurine, Cléon, Mathurin)

1a.30   "Le cadi dupé," opéra-comique: Wq29
     . *"Ouverture" (frag extant in hand written note by M. Aloys Fuchs)*
     . "Ah! que le sort d'une femme," arietta (Fatime)
     . "Si votre flamme est trahie," couplets (Nouradin)
     . "Mon destin est assez doux," ariette dialoguée (Zelmire, later Nouradin)
     . "Toi que mon coeur adore," arietta (Zelmire)
     . "Qu'en dites-vous, Monseigneur?," duo dialogué (Zelmire, le Cadi)
     . "Ah! quel heureux jour pour moi!," arietta (Le Cadi)
     . "Entre ma femme et la table," arietta (Omar)
     . "La pauvre créature," ariette dialoguée (Omar, le Cadi)
     . "Ah! rassurez mon esprit," ariette (Fatime)
     . "Perfide coeur volage," duet (Fatime, le Cadi)
     . "Regardez ces traits," arietta (Ali)
     . "Comment oses-tu te moquer," arietta (Le Cadi)
     . "Par votre propre artifice," ariette dialoguée (Zelmire, Nouradin)
     . "Adieu donc, mon cher poulet," arietta (Ali)
     . "C'est ainsi, toutes," arietta (Fatime)
     . "Jouissons désormais sans partage," final quartet

1a.31   "Orfeo ed Euridice," azione teatrale (Italian vers): Wq30
     . "Sinfonia"
     I: . "Ah se intorno a questa urna funesta," chorus
          . "Basta, basta, o compagni," recit (Orfeo)
          . "Ballo"
          . "Ah se intorno a quest'urna funesta," chorus
          . "Chiamo il mio ben così," strofe I (Orfeo)
          . "Cerco il mio ben così," strofe II (Orfeo)
          . "Piango il mio ben così," strofe III (Orfeo)
          . "Gli sguardi trattieni," aria (Amore)
     II: . "Ballo"
          . "Chi mai dell'Erebo," prelude & chorus
          . "Ballo"
          . "Chi mai dell'Erebo," chorus
          . "Ballo"
          . "Deh! placatevi con me," aria w/ chorus (Orfeo)
          . "Misero giovane!," chorus
          . "Mille pene, ombre moleste," arioso (Orfeo)
          . "Ah quale uncognito affetto," chorus
          . "Men tiranne, ah voi sareste," arioso (Orfeo)
          . "Ah quale incognito," chorus
          . "Ballo" (incl: Dance of the Blessed Spirits, w/ fl solo)
          . "Che puro ciel, che chiaro sol!," recit (Orfeo)
          . "Vieni a' regni del riposo," chorus
          . "Ballo"
          . "Anime avventurose," recit (Orfeo)
          . "Torna, o bella, al tuo consorte," chorus
          . "Vieni: appaga il tuo consorte," recit & duet (Euridice, Orfeo)
          . "Che fiero momento!," recit & aria (Euridice)
          . "Che farò senza Euridice!," recit & aria (Orfeo)
          . "Ma finisca; e per sempre Colla vita il dolor," recit (Orfeo)
          . "Ballo"
          . "Trionfi Amore," solo & final chorus (Orfeo)

1a.33   "Il trionfo di Clelia," opera seria: Wq31
     . "Sinfonia"
     I: . *"Sì, tacerò, se vuoi," aria (Tarquinio) (music lost)*
          . *"Ah celar la bella face," aria (Larissa) (music lost)*
          . *"Resta, o cara; e per timore," aria (Orazio) (music lost)*
          . *"Tempeste il mare minaccia," aria (Clelia) (music lost)*
          . *"Sai che piegar si vede," aria (Porsenna) (music lost)*
          . *"Saper ti basti, o cara," recit obbl & aria (Orazio) (music lost)*
          . *"Mille dubbi mi destano," aria (Clelia) (music lost)*
     II: . *"Dei di Roma, ah perdonate," aria (Orazio) (music lost)*
          . *"Sì, ti fido al tuo gran core," duet (Clelia, Orazio) (music lost)*
          . *"Sol del Tebro in su la sponda," aria (Porsenna) (music lost)*
          . *"Dico che ingiusto sei," aria (Larissa) (music lost)*
          . *"Vorrei che almen per gioco," aria (Manlio) (music lost)*
          . *"Marcia" (lost)*
          . *"Io nemica? a torto il dici," aria (Clelia) (music lost)*
          . *"Non speri onusto il pino" (Tarquinio) (music lost)*
          . *"Tanto esposta alle sventure," aria (Clelia) (music lost)*
          . *"Ah ritorna, età dell'oro," aria (Larissa) (music lost)*

. *"Spesso, sebben t'affretta," aria (Porsenna) (music lost)*
. *"In questa selva oscura," aria (Tarquinio) (music lost)*
. *"De' folgori di Giove," aria (Orazio) (music lost)*
. *"Oggi a te, gran Re toscano," final chorus (music lost)*

1a.34   "La rencontre imprévue," opéra-comique: Wq32
     I: . "Introduction"
       . "Heureux l'amant qui se dépêtre," aria (Osmin)
       . "Castagno, castagno, Pista fanache," air bouffe (Le Calender)
       . "Les hommes pieusement," aria (Le Calender)
       . "D'un céleste transport," aria (Vertigo)
       . "Il fait entendre sa sonnette," arietta (Le Calender)
       . "Je chérirai jusqu'au trépas," aria (Ali)
       . "Bel inconnu, qu'ici l'amour," aria (Balkis)
       . "Je suis touché des bontés," air dialogué (Balkis, Ali)
       . "Venez, venez vite voir cette maison!," final (Balkis, Ali, Osmin)
     II: . "J'ai fait un rêve des plus doux," arietta (Dardanée)
       . "Vous ressemblez à la rose," aria (Ali)
       . "A ma maîtresse j'avais promis," arietta (Dardanée)
       . "Je cherche à vous faire le sort," arietta (Amine)
       . "Jusqu'au moment qui m'ôtera," aria (Ali)
       . "J'ai perdu mon étalage," arietta (Amine)
       . "Oh, oh, oh! quel spectacle!," duet (Ali, Osmin)
       . "Que vois-je! ô ciel!," duet (Rézia, Ali)
       . "Dans l'espérance du retour," arietta (Rézia)
       . "Sans l'âme noire et mercenaire," arietta (Balkis)
       . "Ah! qu'il est doux de se revoir," aria (Rézia)
       . "Venez, venez, troupe brillante," arietta (Balkis)
       . "Ah! je suis en transe," final (Balkis)
     III: . "Mahomet, notre grand prophète," chanson (Le chef de la Caravane)
       . "D'une telle lâcheté," aria (Le Calender)
       . "Maître des coeurs, achève," aria (Rézia)
       . "Permettez que je vous embrasse," trio (Balkis, Osmin, Vertigo)
       . "Ouf! ouf! Oh! oh! Monsieur Vertigo!," trio (Balkis, Osmin, Vertigo)
       . "Est-ce un adagio?," trio dialogué (Balkis, Osmin, Vertigo)
       . "Des combats j'ai peint l'horreur," aria (Vertigo)
       . "C'est un torrent impétueux," aria (Verigo)
       . "Un ruisselet bien clair," aria (Vertigo)
       . "Qu'il est doux de partager tes chaînes," duet (Rézia, Ali)
       . "Après un tel outrage," final (le Sultan, ch)

1a.35   "Il Parnaso confuso," serenata teatrale: Wq33
       . "Sinfonia"
       . "In un mar che non ha sponde," aria (Melpomene)
       . "In fronte a voi risplende," aria (Apollo)
       . "Di questa cetra in seno," rondo (Erato)
       . "Fin là, dove l'aurora," aria (Euterpe)
       . "Sacre piante, amico rio," aria
       . "Vi scuseranno assai," aria (Apollo)
       . "Nel mirar solo i sembianti," final duet (Apollo, Melpomene)

1a.36   "Telemacco nell'isola di Circè," opera seria: Wq34
       . "Sinfonia"
     I: . "Ballo"
       . "La viva face accendi," chorus
       . "Ballo"
       . "La viva face accendi," chorus (repeat)
       . "Pietà chiedi," arioso (Oracolo)
       . "Ahi, che cielo sventurato," chorus
       . "In mezzo a un mar crudele," aria (Circe)
       . "Ch'io speri al cor mi dice," trio (merione, Asteria, Telemacco)
       . "Ah crudel, perchè ti piace," recit obbl & arioso (Merione)
       . "Non dirmi ch'io viva," aria (Telemacco)
       . "Ah l'hò presente ogn'or," recit obbl & aria (Asteria)
       . "Numi, che feci mai?," aria (Asteria)
       . "Ah non chiamarmi ingrato," aria (Ulisse)
       . "Quai tristi gemiti!," chorus
       . "Ah chi di voi m'addita," solo & chorus (Telemacco)
       . "Se per entro alla nera foresta," aria (Telemacco)
       . "Stringiti a questo seno," quartet (Circe, Merione, Telemacco, Ulisse)
       . "Oh come in un momento," quartet (Circe, Merione, Telemacco, Ulisse)
       . "Ah sventurati amici," arioso (Ulisse)
       . "Pietà degl'infelice," trio (Merione, Telemacco, Ulisse)
       . "Oh come è dolce il giorno," recit obbl
       . "Sempre così sereno," chorus (fem ch)

    II: . "Chi consola il tuo cor," aria (Merione)
          . "Doppo si lungi affanni," duet (Merione, Ulisse)
    Scena di Circe: . Recit obbl (Circe)
          . "Dall'orrido soggiorno," aria (Circe)
          . "Qual voce possente," chorus
          . "Larve nemiche al giorno," aria (Circe)
          . "Ah tremi l'indegno," chorus
          . "Notte fedel custode," aria (Circe)
    . "Perchè t'involi, oh Dio," arioso (Telemacco)
    . "Ah non turbi il mio riposo," recit obbl & aria (Telemacco)
    . "Freme gonfio di torbide spume," aria (Ulisse)
    . "Basta nel mio tormento," trio (Asteria, Merione, Telemacco)
    . "Se la nega a' tuoi martiri," aria (Merione)
    . "Pari a te, cangia in furore," aria (Asteria)
    . "Se a estinguer non bastate," aria (Circe)
    . "Perdo, oh Dio, l'amato bene," aria (Asteria)
    . "Al fin placavi, o Dei," quartet (Asteria, Merione, Telemacco, Ulisse)
    . "Al patrio lido facciam ritorno," chorus
    . "Vendicatemi, o fidi compagni," chorus & final scene (Circe)

1a.37   "La corona," azione teatrale: Wq35
    . "Sinfonia"
    . "Vacilla il mio coraggio," aria (Atalanta)
    . "Sol voi rese il Ciel cortese," aria (Meleagro)
    . "Anch'io mi sento in petto," aria (Asteria)
    . "Quel chiaro rio," aria (Atalanta)
    . "Benchè inesperto all'armi," aria (Climene)
    . "Fè germogliar il fato," aria (Meleagro)
    . "Deh l'accetta, ah giunga al fine," duet (Meleagro, Atalante)
    . "Sacro dover ci chiama," tutti (4S)

1a.38   "Il prologo": Wq36
    . "Introduzione"
    . "Non mai più lieto il mondo," chorus w/ soli:
          . "L'alta magion celeste," solo I (Giove)
          . "Non mai dal Ciel discesa," solo II (Giove)
          . "L'aureo gentil primiero," solo III (Soprano vv)
          . "Viva l'eccelsa prole," chorus
          . "Sul verdeggiante stelo," solo IV (Soprano vv)
    . "De' sublimi augusti eroi," recit obbl & aria (Giove)
    . "Lo splendor di si bel giorno," recit obbl & chorus

1a.39   "Alceste," opera seria (Italian vers) Wq37
    I: . "Intrada"
          . "Popoli che dolenti" (Banditore)
          . "Ah di questo afflitto regno," chorus
          . "Pantomimo"
          . "Misero Admeto!," chorus
          . "Io non chiedo, eterni Dei," recit (Alceste)
          . "Cari figli, ah non piangete!," aria (Alceste)
          . "Ah di questo afflitto regno," chorus (repeat)
          . "Ah per noi del Ciel lo sdegno," chorus
          . "Marcia"
          . "Che freme al trono," chorus
          . "I tuoi preghi, o Regina" (Scena del Gran Sacerdote con Coro) (Gran Sacerdote)
          . "Ombre, Larve," aria (Alceste)
          . "E non s'offerse alcuno?," recit & chorus (T)
          . "Chi serve e chi regna," chorus
    II: . "Parto ... ma senti ... oh Dio!," aria (Ismene)
          . "Mi fa tremare il core," aria (Ismene)
          . "Chi mi parla!... Che rispondo!," aria (Alceste)
          . "E vuoi morire, o misera," chorus (Numi infernali)
          . "Dunque vieni, la Morte t'accetta," aria (Nume)
          . "Non vi turbate, nò," arioso (Alceste)
          . "Pantomimo"
          . "Dal lieto soggiorno," chorus
          . "Ballo"
          . "Or che Morte il suo furore," aria (Evandro)
          . "Ballo"
          . "Ah perchè con quelle lagrime," duet (Alceste, Admeto)
          . "Nò, crudel, non posso vivere," aria (Admeto)
          . "Oh come rapida," chorus w/ soli (Ismene)
          . "Così bella, così giovane!," chorus w/ soli (Ismene, ina voce, altra voce)
          . "Vesta, tu che fosti e sei," arioso & chorus (Alceste)
          . "O casto, o caro nuzial mio letto," arioso & chorus (Alceste)

     . "Ah per questo già stanco," aria (Alceste)
   III: . "Misero! E che farò?," aria (Admeto)
     . "Cari figli ... Ah non piangete!," duet (Alceste, Admeto)
     . "Vieni, Alceste," scene (m ch)
     . "Fermatevi! udite!," arioso (Admeto)
     . "Non è più permesso," chorus (m ch)
     . "Piangi, o Patria!," scene (ch)
     . "Alceste è morta!" (Ismene)
     . "Piangi, o Patria!" (ch)
     . "Morte trionfa" (Evandro)
     . "Piangi, o Patria!" (ch)
     . "Ogni virtù più bella" (Ismene, Evandro)
     . "Piangi, o Patria!" (ch)
     . "Regna a noi con lieta sorte," final scene (ch)

1a.40 "Le feste d'Apollo," spectacle: Wq38
   "Prologo: Feste d'Apollo": . "Sinfonia"
     . "Ballo"
     . "Sorgi, possente Nume," chorus
     . "Del dì crescano le pompe," recit obbl & aria (Sacerdote)
     . "Le Grazie tenere," recit obbl & aria (Anfriso)
     . "Con tremito soave," recit obbl & aria (Aricinia)
   I. "Atto di Bauci e Filemone": . "Sinfonia"
     . "Mio tesor, che bel concento," duet (Bauci, Filemone)
     . "La fiamma dell mio petto," aria (Filemone)
     . "Il mio pastor tu sei," aria (Bauci)
     . "Di due bell'anime," chorus
     . "Lodi eterne al Re de' Numi," chorus
     . "Il mio Nume ha stanza degna," aria (Giove)
     . "Se tuo dono, o fausto Nume," duet (Bauci, Filemone)
     . "Non mai stato più beato," chorus
     . "Pe' gravi torti miei," aria (Giove)
     . "Tosto s'accenda il lampo," aria (Giove)
     . "Tempesta"
     . "Giove, pietà!," duet (Bauci, Filemone)
     . "Rè superno a cui si grata," final chorus
   II. "Atto d'Aristeo": . "Sinfonia"
     . "Quell'alma agitata," aria (Ati)
     . "Tu sei madre, e tu conosci," aria (Cidippe)
     . "Nocchier che in mezzo all'onde," aria (Cirene)
     . "Numi offesi, ombre sdegnate," cavatina (Aristeo)
     . "Ballo"
     . "Del figlio d'Apollo," chorus
     . "Cessate, fuggite," aria (Aristeo)
     . "Eccheggiar s'odano," chorus
     . "Fosti ognor l'amato bene," trio (Cidippe, Aristeo, Cirene)
     . "Accompagni la Coppia felice," final chorus
   III. "Atto d'Orfeo" (= Wq30)

1a.41 "Paride ed Elena," opera seria: Wq39
     . "Sinfonia"
   I: . "Non sdegnare, o bella Venere," chorus
     . "O del mio dolce ardor," aria (Paride)
     . "Dall'aurea sua stella," ballo & aria (una voce)
     . "Spiagge amate," aria (Paride)
     . "Ma ... chi sei? Ma come intendi," duet (Paride, Amare)
     . "Nell'idea ch'ei volge in mente," aria (Amore)
     . "Ballo"
   II: . "Forse più d'una beltà," aria (Elena)
     . "Le belle imagini d'un dolce amore," recit & aria (Paride)
   III: . "Introduzione"
     . "Dalla reggia rilucente," chorus (m ch)
     . "Negli strali, nell'arco possente," solo & later chorus
     . (Aria per i Atletti)
     . "Lodi al Nume nell'arco possente," chorus
     . "Quegli occhi belli," strofe I (Paride)
     . "È sua la luce," strofe II (Paride)
     . "Vi pose i chiari," strofe III (Paride)
     . "Chi guarda alquanto," strofe IV (Paride)
     . "Fingere più non sò," scena & duet (Elena, Paride)
     . "Mi fugge spietata?," aria (Paride)
     . "Ballo"
     . "Ciaccona e Gavotta"
   IV: . "Ah lo veggo! ad ingannarmi," trio (Amore, Elena, Paride)

     . "Non lontana esser già parmi," duet (Elena, Paride)
     . "Di te scordarmi," aria (Paride)
     . "Lo potrò! Mà fra tanto," aria (Elena)
    V: . "Donzelle semplici," rondo (Elena)
     . "Consolati, o Regina," recit (Amore)
     . (Scena III. Andante) "T'inganni" (Pallade)
     . "Và coll'amata in seno," scene w/ chorus (Pallade)
     . "Oh da quante eccelse vele," solo (Pallade)
     . "L'amo, l'adoro," duet (Elena, Paride)
     . "Sempre a te sarò fedele," trio (Amore, Elena, Paride)
     . "Ballo"
     . "Vieni al mar, tranquilla è l'onda," final chorus
     . "Altri mai da ignota sponda," solo (Amore)
     . "Vieni al mar, tranquilla è l'onda" (ch) (repeat)
     . "Presso fugge la Beltà," solo (Amore)
     . "Sempre a te sarò fedele" (Elena, Paride)
     . "Vieni al mar, tranquilla e l'onda" (ch) (repeat)

1a.42   "Iphigénie en Aulide," tragédie-opéra: Wq40
     . "Ouverture"
    I: . "Diane impitoyable ... Brillant auteur de la lumière," recit & aria (Agamemnon)
     . "C'est trop faire de résistance," chorus
     . "Tu veux que par ma main," arioso (Calchas)
     . "Nommez-nous la victime," chorus
     . "Peuvent-ils ordonner qu'un père," aria (Agamemnon)
     . "Clytemnestre et sa fille!... Au faîte des grandeurs," chorus & arioso (Calchas)
     . "Que d'attraits, que de majesté!," chorus
     . "Que j'aime à voir ces hommages," arioso (Clytemnestre)
     . "Air" (insts)
     . "Non, jamais aux regards," chorus
     . "Menuets"
     . "Les voeux dont ce peuple m'honore," arioso (Iphigénie)
     . "Passepied"
     . "Gigue"
     . "Armez-vous d'un noble courage," aria (Clytemnestre)
     . "Hélas, mon coeur sensible et tendre," aria (Iphigénie)
     . "Iphigénie, hélas, vous a trop fait," aria (Iphigénie)
     . "Cruelle, non, jamais," aria (Achille)
     . "Ne doutez jamais de ma flamme," duet (Iphigénie, Achille)
    II: . "Rassurez-vous, belle princesse," chorus
     . "Par la crainte et par l'espérance," aria (Iphigénie)
     . "Marche"
     . "Chantez, célébrez ... Chantons, célébrons notre Reine," solo & chorus (Achille)
     . "Danse"
     . "La Grèce à peine assemblait," chorus
     . "Son front est couronné," air gracieux (une Grecque)
     . "Passacaille et Gavotte"
     . "Jamais à tes autels," quartet w/ chorus (Iphigénie, Clytemnestre, Achille, Patrocle)
     . "Par son père cruel," aria (Clytemnestre)
     . "C'est mon père, Seigneur," trio (Iphigénie, Clytemnestre, Achille)
     . "Cours et dis-lui," arioso (Achille)
     . "De votre audace téméraire," duet (Achille, Agamemnon)
     . "Tu décides son sort!," monologue (Agamemnon)
    III: . "Non, non, nous ne souffrirons pas," chorus
     . "Il faut de mon destin," arioso (Iphigénie)
     . "Adieu! conservez dans votre âme," aria (Iphigénie)
     . "Calchas d'un trait mortel percé," aria (Achille)
     . "Vivez, vivez, pour Oreste, mon frère," arioso (Iphigénie)
     . "Ma fille!... Jupiter, lances ta foudre," scene & aria (Clytemnestre)
     . "Puissante déité, protège-nous," chorus
     . "Pour prix du sang que nous," chorus
     . "Fuyons, fuyons tous, d'Achille craignons," scene (Choeur des Grecs)
     . "Adorez la clémence ... Mon coeur ne saurait contenir," ensemble & quartet (Calchas; Iphigénie,
         Clytemnestre, Achille, Agamemnon)
     . "Les dieux ont eu pitié," quartet (Iphigénie, Clytemnestre, Achille, Agamamnon)
     . "Jusques aux voûtes éthérées," chorus
     . "Air pour les esclaves"
     . "Air"
     . "Tambourin"
     . "Menuet"
     . "Heureux guerriers, volez," aria
     . "Chaconne"
     . "Partons, volons à la victoire," final chorus

1a.43   "Orphée et Eurydice," drame héroïque (French vers of Wq30): Wq41
        . "Ouverture"
    I: . "Ah! dans ce bois tranquille," chorus
        . "Récitatif et Pantomime" (Orphée)
        . "Objet de mon amour," strophe
        . "Accablé de regrets," strophe
        . "Plein de trouble et d'effroi," strophe
        . "Divinités de l'Achéron," recit (Orphée)
        . "L'amour vient au secours ... Si les doux accords de ta lyre," recit & (1st) aria (L'Amour)
        . "Dieux! Je la reverrais!, recit (Orphée) & "Soumis au silence," (2nd) aria (L'Amour)
        . "Impitoyables Dieux!," recit & "L'espoir renaît dans mon âme," aria (Orphée)
    II: . "Quel est l'audacieux," introduction & chorus
        . "Air des Furies"
        . "Quel est l'audacieux," chorus (repeat)
        . "Laissez-vous toucher par mes pleurs," (1st) aria (Orphée)
        . "Qui t'amème en ces lieux?," chorus
        . "Ah! la flamme qui me dévore," (2nd) aria (Orphée)
        . "Par quels puissants accords," chorus
        . "La tendresse qui me presse," (3rd) aria
        . "Quels chants doux et touchants," chorus
        . "Air" (Danse des Furies)
        . "Solo de Flûte"
        . "Cet asile aimable et tranquille," solo w/ chorus (Eurydice)
        . "Quel nouveau ciel pare ces lieux!," aria (Orphée)
        . "Viens dans ce séjour paisible," chorus
        . "Ballet"
        . "Près du tendre objet qu'on aime," chorus
    III: . "Viens, viens, Eurydice," recit (Orphée)
        . "Viens, suis un époux," duet (Eurydice, Orphée)
        . "Mais d'où vient ... Fortune ennemie," recit & aria (Eurydice)
        . "Je goûtais les charmes," duet (Eurydice, Orphée)
        . "Fortune ennemie" (Eurydice)
        . "Quelle épreuve cruelle!... J'ai perdu mon Eurydice," recit & aria (Orphée)
        . "Ah! puisse ma douleur ... Arrête Orphée!," recit (Orphée, L'Amour)
        . "L'Amour triomphe," solo & chorus (Orphée)
        . "Gavotte"
        . "Air vif"
        . "Menuet gracieux"
        . "Tendre Amour, que tes chaînes," trio (L'Amour, Eurydice, Orphée)
        . "Quels transports et quel délire," duet
        . "Chaconne"

1a.44   "L'arbre enchanté" II, opéra-comique: Wq42
        . "Ouverture"
        . "Près de l'objet qui m'enflamme," arietta (Lubin)
        . "Elle fixe mes désirs," arietta (Lubin)
        . "On amorce le poisson," ariette dialoguée (Lubin, Blaise)
        . "Du jeune objet que j'adore," arietta (Lubin)
        . "Si l'amour était un crime," arietta (Claudine)
        . "Est-il un plus cruel martyre?," duet (Claudine, Lubin)
        . "Pour me plaire il faut qu'un amant Joigne," arietta (Lucette)
        . "Je prétends que dans ce jour," arietta (Thomas)
        . "Que l'objet qui m'engage," arietta (Claudine)
        . "Pierrot ne se trompe pas," arietta (Claudine)
        . "Ah! Monsieur Thomas," arietta (Pierrot)
        . "L'aventure est très comique," arietta (Thomas)
        . "Je me souviens de ma sottise," duet (Claudine, Lubin)
        . "Ma soeur et ce garçon," arietta (Lucette)
        . "Toujours par fillette franche," arietta (Blaise)
        . "Chantons tous en ce jour," ensemble

1a.45   "La Cythère assiégée" II, opéra-comique: Wq43
    I: . "Introduction"
        . "Habitants de se doux empire," solo et choeur dansé (Daphné)
        . "Airs de Ballet," I & II
        . "Que tous les amants réunis," aria (Chloé)
        . "Air de Ballet"
        . "Menuet"
        . "Adonis est fait pour charmer," aria (Doris)
        . "Air gracieux"
        . "Menuets," I & II
        . "Ah! quel bonheur d'aimer!," aria (Daphné)
        . "Air de Ballet"
        . "Sous un ormeau," aria (Carite)
        . "Le barbare me déclare," aria (Carite)

. "Dieu puissant, embrase," aria (Daphné)
. "Songeons, Songeons à nous défendre," trio (Chloé, Doris, Carite)
II: . "Cette injure n'est pas pour nous," arietta (Barbarin)
. "Brontez, ce chef intrépide," aria (Olgar)
. "Quelle était mon erreur!," aria (Olgar)
. "A moi, fiers soldats!," aria (Brontez)
. "Mars, ô Mars, dieu de la guerre," chorus (Scythes)
. "Marche"
. "Que tous nos guerriers," duet (Olgar, Brontez)
. "Quelle audace, soldats," aria (Daphné)
. "Mais des chefs tels que vous et moi," arioso (Barbarin)
. "On s'arrache la victoire," aria (Daphné)
. "D'où naît le transport," arioso (Olgar)
. "N'écoute rien que la vengeance," chorus
. "Nous soumettons le plus farouche," strophe (Doris)
. "Nous résistons à qui nous brave," strophe (Doris)
. "Méprisons ces perfides charmes," duet (Doris, Olgar)
. "Ah cruelle, infidèle!," duet (Doris, Olgar)
. "Quoi, déjà, tu sens des alarmes," duet (Doris, Olgar)
. "Triomphez, nymphes charmantes," chorus (Nymphes)
. "Je sens naître en mon coeur," aria (Olgar)
. "Enfants de la victoire," chorus (Brontez)
III: . "Pour ma gloire quel affront," aria (Brontez)
. "Mon coeur se plaît au bruit," aria (Chloé)
. "Arrachez-moi de ces affreux climats," duet (Chloé, Brontez)
. "Ce coeur si fier," duet (Chloé, Brontez)
. "Les dieux dans leur grandeur," quartet (Chloé, Doris, Olgar, Brontez)
. "Que le calme règne," recit (Daphné)
. "Air de Ballet"
. "Ici mille plaisirs," quartet & chorus
. "1re Entrée des Bergers. Gigue"
. "Nymphes, chantez victoire," aria (Daphné)
. "2e Entrée des Bergers"
. "L'aimable paix règne," aria (Chloé)
. "Passacaille (et Gavotte)"

1a.46   "Alceste," opera seria (French vers): Wq44
. "Ouverture"
. "Dieu rendez-nous notre Roi," chorus (& tpt)
. "Peuples, écoutez ... Ô dieux, qu'allons-nous devenir!," recit & chorus (Le héraut)
. "Ô malheureux Admète!," chorus
. "Grands Dieux! du destin," aria (Alceste)
. "Ô malheureux Admète!," chorus (repeat)
. "Ô dieux, qu'allons-nous devenir!," chorus (repeat)
. "Marche"
. "Dieu puissant, écarte du trône," chorus
. "Pantomime"
. "Apollon est sensible," scene (Le Grand-Prêtre)
. "Quel oracle funeste," scene (Basses, Sopranos)
. "Non, ce n'est point un sacrifice," aria (Alceste)
. "Déjà la mort s'apprête," aria (Le Grand-Prêtre)
. "Divinités du Styx," aria (Alceste)
II: . "Que les plus doux transports," chorus
. "Menuet"
. "Que les plus doux transports," chorus (repeat)
. "Vivez, aimez les jours," chorus
. "Livrons-nous à l'allégresse," chorus (w/ danse)
. "Parez vos fronts," chorus w/ dance
. "Bannis la crainte," aria (Admète)
. "Je n'ai jamais chéri la vie," aria (Alceste)
. "Ô malheureux Admète, que poursuis," chorus
. "Barbare, non, sans toi," aria (Admète)
. "Tant de grâces," chorus
. "Ah! malgré moi, mon faible coeur," final (Alceste)
. "O ciel, quel supplice" (Alceste)
. "Oh! que le songe," chorus
. "Ciel! quel supplice" (Alceste)
III: . "Nous ne pouvons trop ... Pleure, ô patrie," arioso & chorus (Evandre)
. "C'est en vain que l'enfer," aria (Hercule)
. "Grands Dieux! soutenez," scene (Alceste)
. "Malheureuse, où vas-tu?," chorus (Tenors, Basses)
. "Ah! divinités implacables," aria (Alceste)
. "Vis pour garder le souvenir," aria (Alceste)
. "Alceste, au nom des Dieux," aria (Admète)
. "Aux cris de la douleur," duet (Alceste, Admète)

. "Caron t'appelle," aria (Caron)
. "Alceste! Alceste!," chorus (Choeur d'hommes)
. "Ami, leur rage est vaine," aria (Hercule)
. "Notre fureur est vaine," chorus (Choeur d'hommes)
. "Reçois, Dieu bienfaisant," trio (Alceste, Admète, Hercule)
. "Qu'ils vivent à jamais," chorus
. "Marche"
. "Menuet"
. "Gavotte"
. "Chaconne"

1a.47   "Armide," drame héroïque: Wq45
. "Ouverture"
I: . "Dans un jour de triomphe," dialogue (Armide, Phénice, Sidonie)
. "Je ne triomphe pas," arioso (Armide)
. "Les enfers ont prédit cent fois," arioso (Armide)
. "Vous troublez-vous d'une image," arioso (Sidonie)
. "Je vois de près la mort," aria (Hidraot)
. "La chaîne de l'hymen," arioso (Armide)
. "Pour vous, quand il vous plait," arioso (Hidraot)
. "Si je dois m'engager un jour," arioso (Armide)
. "Armide est encor plus aimable ... Nos ennemis affaiblis et troublés," chorus w/ solo (Phénice)
. "Que la douceur d'un triomphe," solo & chorus (Sidonie)
. "Poursuivons jusqu'au trépas," recit & ensemble
II: . "Allez, allez remplir ma place," arioso (Renaud)
. "Le repos me fait violence," aria (Renaud)
. "Esprits de haine et de rage," recit & duet (Armide, Hidraot)
. "Plus j'observe ces lieux," aria (Renaud)
. "Au temps heureux où l'on sait plaire," arietta w/ dance (Un Naïde, 1er écho, 2e écho)
. "Ah! quelle erreur," chorus w/ dance
. "On s'étonnerait moins," arietta (Une Naïde)
. "Ah! quelle cruauté de lui ravir," recit & arioso (Armide)
. "Venez, secondez mes désirs," aria (Armide)
III: . "Ah! si la liberté me doit être ravie," aria (Armide)
. "Que ne peut point votre art," dialogue (Phénice)
. "Sur des bords séparés," dialogue (Sidonie)
. "De mes plus doux regards," aria (Armide)
. "Venez, venez, Haine implacable!," aria (Armide)
. "Plus on connaît l'Amour," aria w/ chorus (La Haine)
. "Amour, sors pour jamais," aria & chorus (La Haine)
. "Sors, sors du sein d'Armide," chorus (La Haine, Armide)
. "Suis l'Amour puisque tu le veux," aria w/ chorus (La Haine)
. "O ciel, quelle horrible menace!," recit (Armide)
IV: . "Nous ne voyons partout," duet (Le chevalier danois, Ubalde)
. "Redoublons nos soins," duet (Le chevalier danois, Ubalde)
. "Voici la charmante retraite," solo & chorus (Lucinde)
. "Musette"
. "Jamais dans ces beaux lieux," solo & chorus (Lucinde)
. "Enfin je vois l'amant," duet (Lucinde, le chevalier danois)
. "Je tourne en vain les yeux," duo dialogué (Le chevalier danois, Ubalde)
. "D'où vient que vous vous détournez," duet (Mélisse, Ubalde)
. "Fuyons les douceurs dangereuses," duet (Le chevalier danois, Ubalde)
V: . "Aimons-nous, tout nous y convie," duet (Armide, Benaud)
. "Chaconne"
. "Les Plaisirs ont choisi pour asile," solo & chorus
. "C'est l'Amour qui retient," solo & chorus
. "Sicilienne"
. "Jeunes coeurs, jeunes coeurs, tout vous est," solo & chorus
. "Allez, éloignez-vous de moi," aria (Renaud)
. "Notre général vous rappelle!," arioso (Ubalde)
. "Renaud! Ciel! ô mortelle peine!," final scene (Armide, Renaud)

1a.48   "Iphigénie en Tauride," tragédie lyrique: Wq46
I: . "Introduction" (Le Calme—Tempête)
. "Grands Dieux! soyez-nous secourables," solo & chorus (Iphigénie, Prêtresses)
. "Cette nuit j'ai revu le palais de mon père," monologue (Iphigénie)
. "Ô songe affreux!," chorus (Prêtresses)
. "Ô race de Pélops ... Ô toi qui prolongeas mes jours," recit & aria (Iphigénie)
. "Quand verrons-nous tarir," chorus (Prêtresses)
. "De noirs pressentiments," aria (Thoas)
. "Les dieux apaisent leur courroux," chorus (Scythes—Tenors & Basses)
. "Il nous fallait du sang," chorus (Scythes—Tenors & Basses)
II: . "Dieux qui me poursuivez," aria (Oreste)
. "Unis dès la plus tendre enfance," aria (Pylade)
. "Le calme rentre dans mon coeur," scene (Oreste)

    . "Vengeons et la nature," scene (Euménides)
    . "Patrie infortunée," chorus (Prêtresses)
    . "Ô malheureuse Iphigénie!," aria (Iphigénie)
    . "Contemplez ces tristes apprêts," chorus (Prêtresses)
III: . "D'une image, hélas!," arioso (Iphigénie)
    . "Je pourrais du tyran," trio (Iphigénie, Pylade, Oreste)
    . "Et tu prétends encore," duet (Pylade, Oreste)
    . "Ah! mon ami, j'implore," aria (Pylade)
    . "Quoi, toujours à mes voeux," arioso (Oreste)
    . "Divinités des grandes âmes," aria (Pylade)
IV: . "Je t'implore et je tremble," aria
    . "O Diane, sois nous propice," chorus (Prêtresses)
    . "Que ces regrets touchants," arioso (Oreste)
    . "Chaste fille de Latone," chorus (Prêtresses)
    . "Ah! laissons là ce souvenir," arioso (Iphigénie)
    . "Tremblez! tremblez, on sait tout," scene (Une femme grecque)
    . "Des tes forfaits la trame," trio (Iphigénie, Oreste, Thoas)
    . "Vengeons le sang de notre Roi!," chorus
    . "Dans cet objet touchant," arioso (Oreste)
    . "Les dieux, longtemps en courroux," chorus

1a.49   "Écho et Narcisse," drame lyrique: Wq47
    . "Ouverture"
Prologue: . "A l'ombre de ces bois épais," chorus (fem ch)
    . "Rien dans la nature," aria (L'Amour)
    . "Air de Ballet"
    . "Air des Peines"
    . "Aimables Plaisirs," arioso (L'Amour)
    . "Air de Ballet"
    . "Amusez, sachez plaire," aria (L'Amour)
    . "Air de Ballet"
    . "Contredanse"
    . "Vallons chéris par les amants," aria (L'Amour)
I: . "Nymphes des eaux ... L'Amour, ce dieu charmant," recit & arioso (Aglaë)
    . "Que la lumière est vive et pure!," choeur dansé
    . "Air de Ballet"
    . "Menuet"
    . "Air marqué"
    . "Écho par un charme innocent," air chanté et dansé (Églé)
    . "Pantomime"
    . "J'y cache, hélas," air dialogué (Écho, Cynire)
    . "Hélas, je n'ai pour moi," aria (Écho)
    . "Peut-être d'un injuste effroi," aria (Écho)
    . "Vous différez nos jeux," air dialoqué (Égle, Écho)
    . "Divinité des eaux," arioso (Narcisse)
    . "Lorsque je souriais," scene (Écho, Narcisse)
    . "Par mes ennuis" (Narcisse)
    . "Ah! s'il s'était laissé surprendre," arioso (Écho)
    . "Si votre amant," arioso (Cynire)
    . "D'une vie aussi malheureuse," arioso (L'Amour)
    . "L'espoir fuit de mon coeur," duet (Écho, Cynire)
II: . "Ton amitié vive et pressante," aria
    . "Ô chère et tendre amie," quartet (4 Nymphes)
    . "Ô mortelles alarmes!," chorus
    . "Quel coeur plus sensible," arioso (Écho)
    . "Dans ton temple immortel," arioso (Écho)
    . "Je ne puis m'ouvrir," aria (Narcisse)
    . "Sa voix plaintive et gémissante," aria (Cynire)
    . "Ô combats, o désordre extrême!," aria (Narcisse)
    . "Dieux qu'implorent," chorus (derrière le théâtre)
III: . "Chères compagnes," solo & chorus (Coryphée)
    . "Dissipe ce mortel effroi," aria (Cynire)
    . "Au reproche douloureux" (Narcisse)
    . "Beaux lieux, témoins," aria (Narcisse)
    . "Quel retour, ô dieux!," quartet (L'Amour, Écho, Narcisse, Cynire)
    . "Le dieu de Paphos," chorus
    . "Romanze"
    . "Air de Ballet final"

2. ORCHESTRAL WORKS

2.1   "March," in G major (c?, ?extracted from early stage work) .... Wq(p162)
2.2   "Ouvertures" (Sinfonie) of unidentified works (2ob, hns, bn & strings): No.1 in C major: ..... Wq(pp164–165)
    . "La Tempête"

	. "Le Calme"
	. "La Réjouissance"
2.3	No.2 in D major (strings)
2.4	No.3 in D major (2hn & strings)
2.5	No.4 in D major (2hn & strings)
2.6	No.5 in D major (2hn & strings)
2.7	No.6 in E major (strings)
2.8	No.7 in F major (2hn & strings)
2.9	No.8 in F major (2hn & strings)
2.10	No.9 in C major (strings)

3. CONCERTOS, SOLO INSTR & ORCH

3.1   *"Flute Concerto," in G major (spur: arr Scherchen)* ....

4. CHAMBER MUSIC

4.1	"6 Trio Sonatas" (p1746; 2vn & cont): No.1 in C major .... Wq(pp163–164)
4.2	No.2 in G minor
4.3	No.3 in A major
4.4	No.4 in B-flat major
4.5	No.5 in E-flat major
4.6	No.6 in F major
4.7	Trio Sonata No.7 in E major .... Wq(p164)
4.8	Trio Sonata No.8 in F major ....

5. SACRED VOCAL

5.1   *"Miserere" (p ?1744–5; ?8vv, lost)* ....

5.2   *"Psalm 8" (ca1753–8, lost)* ....

5.3   "Motets" (p before 1779; 1v & orch): 1. "Almae sedes" ....

5.4   2. "Voces cantate"

5.5   "De profundis" (p1787; vv & orch, perf at Gluck's funeral) .... Op.posth, Wq(p154)

6. SECULAR VOCAL

"Morceaux de chants détachés": .... Wq(pp151–152)

6.1	1. "Oh Dei, che dolce incanto," aria (S) (Metastasio: Temistocle) ....
6.2	2. "Per tutto il timore," aria (S) (Metastasio: Ezio) ....
6.3	3. "Benché copra al sole il volto," aria (c1749, Metastasio: l'Endimione)........................
6.4	4. "Và, ti sarò fedele," aria (text adapted from: Ipermestra) ....
6.5	5. "Pace, Amor, torniamo in pace" (Metastasio: l'Amor prigioniero) ....
6.6	6. "Che legge spietata" (Metastasio: Catone) ....
6.7	7. "Berenice, ove sei?," recit obbl & "Ombra che pallida," aria (on text from Zeno: Lucio Vero) ....
6.8	8. "Ah pietà, pietà se di me senti," duet (p1830; S, A & pf; ed Wollank) ....
6.9	9. "Nò, che non hà la sorte," recit & "Sì, vedrò quell' alma ingrata," aria ....

"Oden und Lieder" (p1785, Klopstock): .... Wq(pp153–154)

6.10	1. "Vaterlandslied": "Ich bin ein deutsches Mädchen" ....
6.11	2. "Wir und Sie": "Was that dir, Thor, dein Vaterland?" ....
6.12	3. "Schlachtgesang": "Wie erscholl der Gang des lauten Herrs" ....
6.13	4. "Der Jüngling": "Schweigend sahe der May die bekränzte" (2nd vers) ....
6.14	5. "Die Sommernacht": "Wenn der Schimmer von dem Monde" (1st vers) ....
6.15	6. "Die frühen Gräber": "Willkommen, o silbener Mond" (also see Schubert D290) ....
6.16	7. "Die Neigung": "Nein, ich wiederstrebe nicht mehr" ....

Other:

6.17	"Der Jüngling," song (p1775, 1st vers) ....
6.18	"Ode an den Tod": "O Anblick der Glanznacht" (c1783, Klopstock) ....
6.19	"Amour en ces lieux," arietta (ca1780) ....
6.20	"Quand la beauté lance," arietta (ca1780; 1v, 2vn & bass) ....
6.21	"Die Sommernacht": "Wenn der Schimmer von dem Monde" (p1785, Klopstock, 2nd vers) ....
6.22	"Minona lieblich und hold haucht reine Liebe," duet (p1795)..
6.23	"Siegsgesang für Freie": "Laut, wie des Stroms donnernder Sturz" (p1795, Matthisson) ....
6.24	"I lamenti d'amore," cantata (1v, arr from opera: Alceste, Wq37) ....

* * * * *

Wq = Alfred Wotquenne: "Catalogue Thématique des oevres de Chr. W. v. Gluck." Georg Olms
Hildesheim. Breitkopf & Härtel. Wiesbaden, 1967. **App.** = Appendix in Wotquenne's catalog.

1. STAGE WORKS

Operas:

1.1   "Morceaux de musique dramatique" (c1841, Envoi de Rome work) ....
1.2   "Romeo e Giulietta" (c1842, frags: Act II, Cantatrici villane, sextet; Envoi de Rome work) ....
1.3   "Sapho," 3 acts (p1851, Augier; r1884 in 4 acts) ....
1.4   "La nonne sanglante," 5 acts (p1854, Scribe & Delavigne after Lewis: The Monk) ....
1.5   "Le médecin malgré lui" (The Doctor in Spite of Himself), 3 acts (p1858, Barbier & Carré after Molière) ......
1.6   "Faust," 5 act opéra dialogué (p1859, Barbier & Carré after Goethe; ballet c1868) ....
1.7   "La colombe," 2 act opéra comique (p1860, Barbier & Carré after La Fontaine) ....
1.8   "Philémon et Baucis," 3 acts (p1860, Barbier & Carré after La Fontaine; r1876 in 2 acts) ....
1.9   "La reine de Carré after Nerval) ....
1.10   "Mireille," 5 act opéra dialogué (p1864, Carré after Mistral's poem: Mireio) ....
1.11   "Roméo et Juliette," 5 acts (p1867, Barbier & Carré after Shakespeare; r1888 w/ ballet) (also see ballet
          c by Prokofiev Op.64, incid music c by Kabalevsky, Milhaud Op.161 & R. Strauss AV86, film score
          c by Khachaturian, symphony c by Berlioz Op.17, H79)
1.12   "Cinq-Mars," 4 act opéra dialogué (p1877, Poirson & Gallet after novel by Vigny) ....
1.13   "Polyeucte," 5 acts (p1878, Barbier & Carré after Corneille) ....
1.14   "Le tribut de Zamora," 5 acts (p1881, Barbier & Carré) ....
1.15   "Maitre Pierre" (c begun 1877, Gallet on: Abelard & Heloïse, unfin) ....

Incid music:

1.16   "Ulysse," 5 act tragédie (p1852, Ponsard) ....
1.17   "Le bourgeois gentilhomme," comédie (p1857, Molière after Lully) ....
1.18   "Les deux reines de France," 4 act drama (p1872, Legouvé) ....
1.19   "Jeanne d'Arc," 5 act drama (p1873, Barbier) ....
1.20   "George Dandin," comedy (c1873, after Molière, unfin) ....
1.21   "Drames sacrés," 11 tableaux (p1893, Sylvestre & Morand) ....

1a. SELECTIONS FROM STAGE WORKS (Nos. of sections in The Gramophone)

1a.3   "Sapho," opera: ....
          excerpts: I: 1a. "Introduction and March"
                  1b. "O Jupiter"
                  2a. "Tu ne suis pas la multitude"
                  2b. "Puis-je oublier"
                  3. "Violà Sapho"
                  4a. "Quel entretien si doux"
                  4b. "Quand de choisir elle me presse"
                  5a. "Salut Alcée"
                  5b. "Les entrailles des victimes"
                  5c. "Les Dieux d'un oeil clément"
                  6. "O Liberté, déesse austère"
                  7. "Meure le tyrannie ... Sapho! Sapho! Sapho!"
                  8. "Héros sur la tour solitaire"
                  9. "Fille d'Apollon"
               II: 10a. "Gloire à Bachus"
                  10b. "Assez chante! Phaon, fais sortit"
                  11. "Oui, jourons tous"
                  12a. "Reste là! Pythéas"
                  12b. "Comprends-moi bien, ma bonne Phèdre"
                  13. "Ma vie en séjour"
                  14. "Glycère ici! Que cherche-t-elle"
                  15a. "Je viens sauver ta tête"
                  15b. "O Douleur qui m'oppresse"
               III: 15c. "Prélude"
                  16a. "J'arrive le premier"
                  16b. "O jours heureux"
                  17a. "Adieu Patrie"
                  17b. "La mer et la vaisseau"
                  17c. "Sois béni"
                  17d. "Adieu, adieu Patrie"
                  18. "Broutez le thym"
                  19a. "Où suis-je"
                  19b. "O ma lyre immortelle"

1a.6   "Faust," opera: ....
          excerpts: I: 1. "Introduction"
                  2a. "Rien! En vain j'interroge"
                  2b. "Salut! ô mon dernier matin"
                  3a. "Mais ce Dieu"
                  3b. "Me voici! D' où vient ta surprise?"

        6a. "Le nom de cette belle enfant?"
        6b. "Ange adorable"
        7a. "Quelqu'un!"
        7b. "Le voici"
II: 8a. "O nuit! sous tes ailes"
        8b. "L'amour, l'amour"
        8c. "Ah! lève-toi, soleil"
        9. "Hélas! moi, le haïr!"
        10a. "O nuit divine"
        10b. "Ah! ne fuis pas encore"
III: 11. "Mon père! Dieu vous garde!"
        12. "Dieu qui fit l'homme"
        13a. "Depuis hier je cherche en vain mon maître!"
        13b. "Que faites-tu, blance tourterelle"
        14. "Ah! voici nos gens!"
        15. "Eh quoi? toujours du sang?"
IV: 16a. "Va! Je t'ai pardonné"
        16b. "Nuit d'hyménée!"
        16c. "Non, ce n'est pas le jour"
        17a. "Quoi! ma fille"
        17b. "Que l'hymne nuptiale"
        18a. "Mon père! tout m'accable"
        18b. "Buvez donc ce breuvage"
        19. "Dieu! quel frisson court dans mes veines!"
        20. "Cortège nuptial"
        21. "Ma fille, cède aux voeux" (Finale)
V: 22. "Le sommeil de Juliette"
        23. "Salut! tombeau sombre"

2. SYMPHONIES

2.1   Symphony No.1 in D major (c1855; arr Bizet for pf duet 1855; arr Goria for pf 1856) ....
2.2   Symphony No.2 in E-flat major (c by 1856; red for pf 1856) ....

3. OTHER ORCHESTRAL WORKS

3.1   "Chant des compagnons" (c1865) ....
3.2   "Saltarello" (c1871) ....
3.3   "Marche pontificale" (Marche romaine) (c1872, for anniv of Pius IX) ....
3.4   "Marche-Fanfare," in E-flat major (p1876; brass band) ....
3.5   "Marche religieuse" (Marche festivale), in C major (p1878) ....
3.6   "Marche solennelle," in E-flat major (p1878) ....
3.7   "Wedding March" No.2 in A major (p1882, for wedding of Duke of Albany) (for No.1 see Chamber w/ org) .
3.8   *"Tempo di marcia" (c1893, frag)* ....

4. PIANO CONCERTOS, PIANO & ORCH

4.1   "Fantaisie sur l'hymne national russe" (p1886; pedal pf & orch) ....
4.2   "Le rendez-vous," valses in D major (p1887; orig for pf 1847) ....
4.3   "Suite concertante" (p1888; pedal pf & orch; arr Saint-Saëns for 2pf 1888; red Pierné for pf 1889).............

5. STRING QUARTETS

5.1   String Quartet No.3 in A minor (pubd posth1895) ....

6. OTHER CHAMBER MUSIC

5 or more insts:

6.1   Quintet (ca1840–2) ....
6.2   "Petite symphonie," in E-flat major (c1885; 2fl, 2ob, 2cl, 2hn & 2bn) ....

Vn & pf:

6.3   "Peacefully slumber" (Lullaby) (c1873) ....
6.4   "Cinq-Mars," fantaisie concertante (p1878) ....

Other 2 insts:

6.5   "Six mélodies" (p ca1840–8; hn & pf): No.1 in G minor ....

6.6	No.2 in E-flat major
6.7	No.3 in B-flat major
6.8	No.4 in C min / major
6.9	No.5 in F major
6.10	No.6 in B-flat major
6.11	"Petite étude-scherzo" (p1885; 2 d basses) ....
6.12	"Passacaille," sérénade (p1885; gui & vn ad lib, collab work: gui part c by Bosch, vn part c by Gounod) .....

W/ org (harm):

6.13	"Méditation sur le 1er prélude de piano de S. Bach" (c1852; pf, vn & org; arr for pf; also for 1v & pf) ....
6.14	"Meditation" (à son ami Gloria Heugel) (c1854; vn, pf & org ad lib; arr for pf 1857) ....
6.15	"La jeune religieuse" (c1856; vn, vc ad lib, pf & harm) ....
6.16	"Quintette" (arr1856; vn, vc, org & pf, from Mozart's opera: Cosi fan tutte, K588) ....
6.17	"Méditation sur Faust" (c1860; vn/vc, pf & org) ....
6.18	"Rêverie arabe" (arr1863; vn/vc & pf/org, from opera: La reine de Saba) ....
6.19	"Sérénade" (c1863; vn/vc & pf/org; also for pf & org) ....
6.20	"Hymne à Sainte-Cécile" (c1864; vn, org & pf; also vers for vn, harps, timp, winds & d bass) ....
6.21	"Méditation," in B-flat major (arr1873; vn/vc, pf & org, from: La nonne sanglante; also see: Le calme)........
6.22	"Wedding March" No.1 in C major (c1882; 3trbn & org) (for No.2 see Orchestral) ....
6.23	"Meditation on the 'The Arrow and the Song,' " in D major (p1886; pf, vn/cornet, vc & org) ....

7. PIANO

7.1	"Fugues" (c1837–9, for Concours du prix de Rome) ....
7.2	"Scherzo" (c1837) ....
7.3	"Marche militaire suisse" (c1840)
7.4	"Small pieces" (pour un album à M. et Mme Léon Vallès) (c1842) ....
7.5	"Canon" (c1843) ....
7.6	"Morceau instrumental" (c1843)
7.7	"Le rendez-vous," suite de valse in D major (c1847; pf; also for pf duet 1866; orchd1887) ....
7.8	"Valse" (c1854) ....
7.9	"Ouverture de l'opéra Le médecin malgré lui" (c1858) ....
7.10	"Valse caractéristique," in D major (c1860; pf/pf duet)
7.11	"Deux romances sans paroles" (c1861): No.1 "La pervenche," in B major ....
7.12	No.2 "Le ruisseau," in G-flat major
7.13	"Les pifferari" (Impromptu très facile), in F major (c1861) ....
7.14	"Royal-Menuet," in C major (c1863) ....
7.15	"Musette impromptu," in A minor (c1863) ....
7.16	"Sérénade" (c1863; also simplified vers)
7.17	"Le bal d'enfants," valse facile in C major (c1864) ....
7.18	"Mireille" (transcr1864; pf, from opera): . "Le berger de la Crau" ....
7.19	. "Choeur des Magnanarelles"
7.20	. "Valse-ariette de Mireille"
7.21	. "Heureux petit berger"
7.22	"Georgina," valse in D major (c1864; also see: Grand Waltz p1877) ....
7.23	"Six mélodies" (transcr1864; pf; simplified vers p1865): No.1 "Le premier jour de mai" ....
7.24	No.2 "O ma belle rebelle"
7.25	No.3 "Aubade"
7.26	No.4 "Chant d'automne"
7.27	No.5 "Le lever"
7.28	No.6 "Venise"
7.29	"Huit mélodies" (c1864): No.1 "Les champs" ....
7.30	No.2 "Chant du guerrier"
7.31	No.3 "Le vallon"
7.32	No.4 "Le juif-errant"
7.33	No.5 "Visions de Faust"
7.34	No.6 "Mon habit"
7.35	No.7 "L'ame d'un ange"
7.36	No.8 "Le chant d'Euryclée"
7.37	"Marche nuptiale," in F major (c1864) ....
7.38	"Le soir" (3e romance sans paroles) (c1864) ....
7.39	"Le calme" (4e romance sans paroles), in D-flat major (arr1864, from aria in opera: La nonne sanglante) ...
7.40	"Valse des fiancés," in D major (c1865; pf) ....
7.41	"Souvenances," nocturne in E-flat major (c1865) ....
7.42	"La chanson du printemps" (5e romance sans paroles) (c1866) ....
7.43	"Ivy" (Le lierre), in B-flat major (c1871) ....
7.44	"Dodelinette," lullaby in G major (c1873) ....
7.45	"Funeral March of a Marionette," in D minor (c1873; orchd1879) ....
7.46	"Maid of Athens" (transcr for pf 1873)
7.47	"La valse des sylphes," in A major (p1875) ....
7.48	"La veneziana," barcarolle in G minor (p1876) ....
7.49	"La fête de Jupiter" (grande marche processionnelle) (p1877) ....
7.50	"Sarabande de Cinq-Mars" (p1877)...

7.51	"Deux pièces" (p1877): No.1 "Invocation"	
7.52	No.2 "Prélude"	
7.53	"Deux pièces" (p1877): No.1 "Pastorale"	
7.54	No.2 "Sérénade"	
7.55	"Marche-fanfare" (pour le 12e husards) (c1877)	
7.56	"Grand Valse," in D major (p1877; orig: Georgina of 1864)	
7.57	"Méditation," in D-flat major (p1877)	
7.58	"Deux pièces" (p1878; pf/pf duet): No.1 "Saltarelle"	
7.59	No.2 "Marche religieuse"	
7.60	"Marche solennelle" (transcr1878; pf; also for harm & pf 1879)	
7.61	"Deux pièces" (p1879): No.1 "Invocation"	
7.62	No.2 "Prélude"	
7.63	"Valse caractéristique," in D major (p1881)	
7.64	"Wedding March" (No.1) (p1881)	
7.65	"Wedding March" (No.2) (p1882)	
7.66	"Matinée de mai" (p1896)	
7.67	"Six pièces" (p1907)	

Pf duet:

7.68	"Deux pièces" (c1858): No.1 "Menuet," in G minor	
7.69	No.2 "L'angélus" (petit morceau très facile), in C major	
7.70	"Ouverture de Cinq-Mars" (p1877; pf duet/pf)	
7.71	"Trois petits morceaux faciles" (p1879): No.1 "La nacelle," in C major	
7.72	No.2 "La rosière," in G major	
7.73	No.3 "Le page," in C major	

8. ORGAN

8.1	"Communion" (c1858)	
8.2	"Choix de chorals de J. S. Bach" (avec une préface par Ch. Gounod) (arr1869–70; org)	
8.3	"La melodia," romanza (c1871; org w/ pedal obbl; ed Spark 1871)	
8.4	"Offertorium" (p1876)	
8.5	"Cinq-Mars," marche religieuse (p1877; org w/ harps; transcr for pf duet)	
8.6	"Wedding March" (No.1) (p1882; org & 3trbn)	
8.7	"Méthode de cor à pistons" (p1885, pedagogical)	
8.8	"Préludes et fugues pour l'étude préparatoire au Clavecin ... de J. S. Bach" (p1895)	

9. MASSES

9.1	"Messe" (Eglise de Saint-Roch) (c1839)	
9.2	"Messe" (Rome) (c1840–1)	
9.3	"Messe de Requiem" (Vienna) (c1842)	
9.4	"Messe" (Vienna) (c1843)	
9.5	"Messe brève et salut" (À son ami Gabriel de Vendeuvre), in G major (c1846; 4 m vv)	
9.6	"Messe" (À l'Association des Sociétés chorales de Paris) (c1846; 4 m vv & org)	
9.7	"Messe à 3 voix hommes" (c1853; m ch)	
9.8	"Messe des Orphéonistes," in C min / major (p1853; m ch & 2S ad lib)	
9.9	"Messe solennelle de Sainte Cécile," in G major (c1855, S, T, B, ch, orch & org)	
9.10	"Messe brève," in C major (c1871; ch & org/harm)	
9.11	"Messe des anges gardiens," in C major (c1871; S, A, T, B, ch & org)	
9.12	"Messe brève pour les morts" (Requiem), in F major (c1873; vv, d ch & org/pf)	
9.13	"Messe du Sacré-Coeur de Jésus," in C major (p1877, S, A, T, B, ch & orch)	
9.14	"Messe no.3 aux communautés religieuses," in G major (c1883; ch & org ad lib)	
9.15	"Messe solennelle No.3 de Pâques," in E-flat major (c1883; ch & orch)	
9.16	"Messe funèbre," in F major (c1883; ch & org ad lib; arr Dormois)	
9.17	"Messe à la mémoire de Jeanne d'Arc" (w/ Prélude & Fanfare), in F major (c1887; S, A, T, B, ch & org)	
9.18	"Messe solennelle No.4," in G min / major (w/ Te Deum) (c1888; S, A, T, B, ch & org)	
9.19	"Messe No.6 aux cathédrales," in G major (c1890; vv, ch & org/pf)	
9.20	"Messe brève No.7 aux chapelles," in C major (c1890; vv, ch & org/pf)	
9.21	"Messe dite de Clovis, d'après le chant grégorien," in C major (c1890; ch & org)	
9.22	"Messe de St Jean, d'après le chant grégorien" (c1890; ch & org)	
9.23	"Requiem," in C major (c1893; S, A, T, B, ch & pf or S, A, T, B & pf/org or 2vv & pf/org; ed Busser 1895)...	

10. OTHER LITURGICAL

10.1	"Te Deum" (Envoi de Rome) (c1841; ch)	
10.2	"Offices de la Semaine Sainte sur la psalmodie rhythmée de l'Epistolier parisien" (p ?1846; ch)	
10.3	"Domine salvum fac" (p1853; ch)	
10.4	"Ave verum" (p1854; ch)	
10.5	"Sancta Maria" (p ?1854; ch)	
10.6	"Ecce panis" (p ?1854; ch)	

10.7   "O salutaris" (p1855; ch) ....
10.8   "Regina coeli" (p1855; ch) ....
10.9   "Ave verum" (p by 1856; ch) ....
10.10   "Virgo singularis" (p by 1856; ch) ....
10.11   "Ave verum" (p by 1856; ch) ....
10.12   "Sancta Maria" (p by 1856; ch) ....
10.13   "O salutaris" (p by 1856; ch) ....
10.14   "Ave regina" (p by 1856; ch) ....
10.15   "Da pacem" (p by 1856; ch) ....
10.16   "Da pacem," in F major (p1858; 3-part ch) ....
10.17   "Pater noster" (p1856; ch) ....
10.18   "Regina coeli" (p1856; 2 equal vv & pf/org) ....
10.19   "Laudate Dominum" (p1856; 2 equal vv & pf/org) ....
10.20   "O salutaris" (p1856; ch) ....
10.21   "Inviolata" (p1856; ch) ....
10.22   "Ave verum" (p1856; S/T & pf/org) ....
10.23   "Ave verum" (p1856; B/A & org) ....
10.24   "O salutaris" (p1856; mS/T & ch/org/orch & org; = 1. of: 4 Motets solennels) ....
10.25   "Inviolata" (p1860; 2 equal vv) ....
10.26   "Ave verum," in C major (p1860–1; 2S) ....
10.27   "Ave verum" (p1863; 4 equal vv) ....
10.28   "Ave verum," in E-flat major (p1863; ch & orch/org; = 2. of: 4 Motets solennels) ....
10.29   "Ave verum," in C major (p1864; S/T, ch & orch/org; = 3. of: 4 Motets solennels) ....
10.30   "Veni Creator Spiritus" (p1864; 4 m vv) ....
10.31   "O salutaris," in E-flat major (p1866; T/S, Bar/mS ad lib, org, harp, hns, vc & d bass; = 4. of: 4 Motets) .....
10.32   "Ave regina coelorum" (p1866; S, T & org; also w/ text: Ave Maria 1883) ....
10.33   "Trois jolis motets faciles" (p1868; 2 equal vv & org ad lib): No.1 "Ave verum" ....
10.34   No.2 "Tota pulchra es"
10.35   No.3 "Sub tuum"
10.36   "Ave verum" (c1868; ch; also ch & pf/org) ....
10.37   "Sicut cervus," motet (p1868; ch; also ch & org ad lib) ....
10.38   "Christus factus est," motet (p1871; 1v, pf, org & harm ad lib) ....
10.39   "De profundis" (p1871, Psalm 130; S, A, T, B, ch & orch) ....
10.40   "O salutaris," in A major (p1871; ch & kbd) ....
10.41   "O salutaris," in A-flat major (p1871; mS, T & org) ....
10.42   "O salutaris" (p ?1873; S/T & org) ....
10.43   "Vexilla Regis" (p1873; ch & org) ....
10.44   "Pater noster" (p1873; ch & org) ....
10.45   "Ave verum" (p ?1873; ch & org) ....
10.46   "60 Sacred Chants for Various Occasions," 3 vols (p1878, Latin; ch, incl many of the preceding) ......
10.47   "Laudate Dominum" (p1879; ch; pubd w/ Messe de Ste Cécile) ....
10.48   "Miserere" (c1880; 4vv, ch & org ad lib) ....
10.49   "O salutaris" (p1887; ch & pf/org) ....
10.50   "Quam dilecta tabernacula tua" (p1888; Bar & ?org) ....
10.51   "Te Deum" (p ?1888; 4vv/small ch, ch, harps & org) ....
10.52   "Pater noster" (p1893; 5vv, ch & org) ....
10.53   "O salutaris," in A major (p1898; 1v & pf/org) ....

11. OTHER SACRED & PIOUS CHORAL

11.1   "L'éternité" (p1855, Malory; ch; also w/ pf/org) ....
11.2   "Cieux, fondez-vous en pleurs," 17th century cantique (p1857; ch & pf/org) ....
11.3   "Les sept paroles du Christ sur la croix" (c1855; ch) ....
11.4   "Fixer ici ton sort," 17th century cantique (p1859; ch, pf & org) ....
11.5   "Dans cette étable," pastorale on an 18th century carol (c1855–6; ch & orch) ....
11.6   "Bethléem" (c1855–6, many arrs of 18th century carol; used in pastorale: Dans cette étable) ......
11.7   "Prière à Marie" (p1861, Bouscatel; ch & pf/org) ....
11.8   "Près du fleuve étranger" (p1861, Quételard, Psalm 137; ch & orch/pf/org) ....
11.9   "Tout l'univers est plein de sa magnificence" (p1862, Racine; 2ch) ....
11.10   "Le Vendredi-Saint" (p1866, Badou; ch; also w/ pf 1868) ....
11.11   "Prière du soir" (p1866, Manuel; ch or ch, pf & org; also solo song) ....
11.12   "Noël," chant des religieuses (p1866, Barbier after Uhland; S, A, fem ch & pf) ....
11.13   "Le crucifix" (p1867, Hugo; ch or ch & pf/org; also solo song) ....
11.14   "Stabat mater" (p1867, Abbé Castaing in French; ch & orch) ....
11.15   "D'un coeur qui t'aime" (c1851, from Racine: Athalie; 2 ch; also see Duets) ....
11.16   "Les martyrs," scène chorale (p1871, Quételard; m ch; also w/ pf) ....
11.17   "A New Morning Service" (p1872; ch & org): 1. "Te Deum" (English) ....
11.18   2. "Benedictus" (English)
11.19   "An Evening Service" (p1872; ch & org): 1. "Magnificat" (English) ....
11.20   2. "Nunc dimittis" (English)
11.21   "Omnipotent Lord," sacred psalm (p1872 or 3, Mason; ch & pf) ....
11.22   "Adam could find no solid peace" (p1872 or 3; ch & pf) ....
11.23   "Je te rends grâce, ô Dieu d'amour," cantique (p1892, Collin; ch & pf/org) ....
11.24   "Toujours à toi, Seigneur" (p1892, Collin; ch & pf/org; arr for 1–2vv & org) ....

12. ORATORIOS & CANTATAS

Oratorios:

12.1   "Tobie," petit oratorio (p1865, Lefèvre) ....
12.2   "Gallia," lamentation (c1871, Gounod; S, ch, orch & org, for London International Exhibition) ....
12.3   "Jésus sur le lac de Tibériade," scène biblique (p1878; 1v, ch & orch) ....
12.4   "La rédemption," sacred trilogy (p1882, Gounod; vv, ch & orch) ....
12.5   "Christus factus est" (c1883, words adapt Santley, music from sacred trilogy: La rédemption) ....
12.6   "Mors et vita," sacred trilogy (p1885, Gounod; vv, ch & orch): ....
        I. "Mors": 1. "Prologue"
                2. "Requiem"
        II: 3. "Somnus Mortuorum"
                4. "Resurrectio Mortuorum"
                5. "Judex"
                6. "Judicium electorum"
                7. "Judicium rejectaneorum"
        III. "Vita": 8. "Visio Sancti Joannis"
                9. "Jerusalem Coelestis"
               10. "Vox magna in Coelo"
               11. "Lacrymae, dolor, mors amplius non exstabunt"
               12. "Ecce, omnia novata!"

Cantatas:

12.7   "Le temple de l'harmonie," cantata (p1869, Barbier, Carré; S, mS, A, ch & pf/org) ....
12.8   "À la frontière," cantata (p1870, Frey; vv, ch & orch) ....

13. SECULAR CHORAL

13.1   "Hymne en français" (Envoi de Rome) (c1843; vv, ch & orch) ....
13.2   "Chantons, chantons de Dieu le pouvoir éternel" (p1852) ....
13.3   "Choeur de chasseurs: Où sommes-nous?" (p1855; ch; also w/ pf ad lib) ....
13.4   "Hymne à la France" (p ?1856, Baralle; ch; also w/ pf ad lib) ....
13.5   "L'enclume" (p1856, Barateau; ch; also w/ pf ad lib) ....
13.6   "Vive l'empéreur!," chant national (p1856, Lefranc; ch; also w/ pf ad lib) ....
13.7   "La cigale et la fourmi" (p1856, La Fontaine; ch; also w/ pf ad lib) ....
13.8   "God Save the Queen" (p ca1856; ch; also w/ pf ad lib) ....
13.9   "Le corbeau et le renard" (p1857, La Fontaine; ch; also w/ pf ad lib) ....
13.10   "Le retour des guerriers" (p1863; ch; also w/ pf ad lib) ....
13.11   "La chasse: Au fond des bois" (p1867; ch; also w/ pf ad lib) ....
13.12   "Le vin des gaulois et la danse de l'épée," légende bretonne (p1855, ch) ....
13.13   "Chant des compagnons" (p by 1858; ch & orch/pf) ....
13.14   "La nuit" (p1867, Crèvecoeur; ch) ....
13.15   "L'affût" (p1869, Ségur; ch; also w/ pf) ....
13.16   "Matinée dans la montagne" (p1869, Tourneux; vv, ch & pf) ....
13.17   "6 New Part Songs" (p1872 or 3; ch & pf): 1. "Omnipotent Lord" (Mason) ....
13.18   2. "Little Celandine" (Fleur des bois) (Wordsworth; orig for 2vv & pf)
13.19   3. "Gitanella" (Ashley)
13.20   4. "Bright Star of Eve"
13.21   5. "My true love hath my hearth" (Sydney)
13.22   6. "Take me, Mother Earth" (Mrs Jameson)
13.23   "6 New Part Songs" (p1872 or 3; ch & pf): 1. "The Farewell" (Hood) ....
13.24   2. "Go, lovely rose" (Waller)
13.25   3. "The Bell" (Bröchner)
13.26   4. "Far from my native mountains" (arr from solo song)
13.27   5. "Adam could find no solid peace"
13.28   6. "Le loup et l'agneau" (La Fontaine)
13.29   "En avant!," chanson militaire (p1875, Déroulède; vv, ch & pf/pf duet) ....
13.30   "Le ruisseau" (p1883, Quételard; 1v or 3 equal vv) ....

14. DUETS (w/ pf)

14.1   "Deux vieux amis," scène intime (p1856, Véron; T, Bar & pf) ....
14.2   "Les châteaux en Espagne" (p1858, Véron; T, Bar & pf) ....
14.3   "Par une belle nuit," nocturne (p1870, Ségur; S, A & pf) ....
14.4   "La siesta" (p1871, Anon Spanish; 2S & pf) ....
14.5   "The Message of the Breeze" (p1872, Palgrave; 2S & pf) ....
14.6   "Little Celandine" (p1872, Wordsworth; S, A & pf; also see arr for ch & pf as 2. of: 6 New Part Songs) ....
14.7   "Barcarola" (p1873, Zaffira transl Barbier; S, Bar & pf) ....
14.8   "Blessed is the man" (Bienheureux le coeur sincère) (p1875, Barbier after Psalm 1; S, A & pf) ....
14.9   "Sous le feuillage," duettino (p by 1876, Barbier; S, A & pf) ....
14.10   "D'un coeur qui t'aime" (p1882, from Racine: Athalie; S, A & pf, different from choral setting) ....
14.11   "Memorare" (p1883, Latin, St Bernard; S, A & pf/org) ....

15. SACRED & PIOUS SONGS (1v & pf/org)

15.1 "À la reine des apôtres" (Chant pour le départ des missionaires) (c ?1843, Gounod) ....
15.2 "Jésus de Nazareth," chant évangélique (p1856, Porte) ....
15.3 "Ave Maria," song adapted from J. S. Bach: Wohltemperirte Klavier, BWV846 (p1859; S & orch) ....
15.4 "Le ciel a visité la terre," cantique après la communion (p1869, Ségur) ....
15.5 "Prière pour l'empéreur et la familie imperiale" (p ?1869, Mme Baëlen) ....
15.6 "L'anniversaire des martyrs" (p1869, Dallet) ....
15.7 "Six cantiques" (p1870) ....
15.8 "There is a green hill far away," sacred song (p1871, Mrs Alexander)....................
15.9 "Thy will be done" (Que sa volonté soit faite!) (p1872, Elliot) ....
15.10 "Prière du soir" (p1872, Ligny) ....
15.11 "Entreat me not to leave thee" (Ruth's Song) (p1873)....................
15.12 "To God, ye choir above," sacred song (p1873, Skelton) ....
15.13 "Abraham's Request" (Prière d'Abraham) (p1873, Barbier) ....
15.14 "My beloved spake" (Song of Solomon) (p1873; also in French: Viens mon coeur) ....
15.15 "Cantique pour la première Communion" (p1874, Dulong de Rosnay) ....
15.16 "La salutation angélique" (p1877, Gounod; altern Latin text: Ave Maria) ....
15.17 "The King of Love my shepherd is" (Le roi d'amour est mon pasteur) (p1884, Baker) ....
15.18 "Quand l'enfant prie" (p1884, Boyer) ....
15.19 "Glory to Thee, my God, this night," evening song (c1872, Bishop Ken) ....
15.20 "Hymne à St Augustin" (p1885, Abbé Ribolet; unison ch & org) ....
15.21 "For ever with the Lord" (c1872, Montgomery) ....
15.22 "Ce qu'il faut à mon âme," cantique (p1887, Sédillot) ....
15.23 "The Holy Vision," sacred song (p1888, Weatherley) ....
15.24 "Hymne de la patrie. Notre Dame de France" (p1888, Boyer)....................
15.25 "Ave Maria" No.2, méditation on a 2nd Prelude of J. S. Bach (p1889) ....
15.26 "L'Ave Maria de l'enfant" (c ?1872 or 3, p1891) ....
15.27 "Ave Maria" (p1894, his last composition) ....
15.28 "Repentir" (O Divine Redeemer), scène sous forme de prière (p1894, Philips) ....
15.29 "L'Eucharistie," cantique (p1895, Frère Eucher) ....
15.30 "La paix de Dieu" (p1913, Hettich after M. Henry) ....

16. OTHER SONGS (w/ pf)

16.1 "Où voulez-vous aller?," barcarolle (p1839, Gautier; add vn/vc/fl/harm) ....
16.2 "Premier prélude de J. S. Bach" (p1852, Lamartine: Vers sur un album, 1st vers of: Ave Maria) ....
16.3 "Mon habit" (p1855, Béranger) ....
16.4 "Six mélodies" (c1842, p1855): 1. "Le premier jour de mai" (Passerat) ....
16.5 2. "O ma belle rebelle" (Baïf)
16.6 3. "Aubade" (Hugo)
16.7 4. "Chant d'automne" (Hugo)
16.8 5. "Le lever" (Musset)
16.9 6. "Venise" (Musset)
16.10 "Sérénade" (p1857, Hugo, add harm/vc ad lib) ....
16.11 "Chanson du printemps" (p1860, Tourneux; arr for pf as: 5e romance sans paroles)....................
16.12 "L'âme de la morte," mélodie (p1860, Banville) ....
16.13 "Le vallon," méditation poétique (c1840–2, p1861, Lamartine) ....
16.14 "Le juif errant" (p1861, Béranger) ....
16.15 "A une jeune grecque," épitaphe (p1862, Yvaren after Sappho) ....
16.16 "Vingt mélodies," 1er recueil (p1863) incl: . "Les champs" (Béranger) ....
16.17 . "Seul" (Lamartine: La pensée des morts)
16.18 . "Ni l'or ni la grandeur," cantilène (La Fontaine)
16.19 . "L'âme d'un ange," mélodie (Banville)
16.20 . "Le soir" (ca1840–2, Lamartine; arr for pf as: 3e romance sans paroles p1861)
16.21 "Medjé," chanson arabe (p1865, Barbier) ....
16.22 "Solitude," mélodie (p1865, Lamartine) ....
16.23 "Marguerite" (p1865, Pradère) ....
16.24 "Stances: si la mort est le but" (p1866, Bertin) ....
16.25 "Crépuscule," mélodie (p1866, Bertin) ....
16.26 "Tombez mes ailes!," romance (p1866, Legouvé) ....
16.27 "Au rosignol," harmonie poétique (p1867, Lamartine) ....
16.28 "Invocation" (p ?1867, Pradère) ....
16.29 "Primavera," mélodie (p1867, Gautier) ....
16.30 "Au printemps," mélodie (p1868, Barbier) ....
16.31 "Donne-moi cette fleur" (p1868, Gozlan) ....
16.32 "Ce que je suis sans toi" (p1868, Peyre) ....
16.33 "Hymne à la nuit" (p1868, Barbier) ....
16.34 "A une jeune fille" (p1869, Augier) ....
16.35 "Envoi de fleurs" (p1869, Augier) ....
16.36 "A une bourse," confidence (p1869, Augier) ....
16.37 "Départ," scène (p1869, Augier) ....
16.38 "Boire à l'ombre" (p1869, Augier) ....
16.39 "Hommage à Mme la comtesse Herminie de Leautaud" (p1869, Mme Baëlen) ....

16.114   "Mélancholie," rêverie (p1880, Coppée) ....
16.115   "Ring out, wild bells" (p1880, Tennyson) ....
16.116   "A Cécile," mélodie (p1881, Dubuffe) ....
16.117   "Funeral March of a Marionette" (p1882, Price & Ker Mary) ....
16.118   "Réponse de Medjé," mélodie (p1882, Barbier) ....
16.119   "Chant des sauveteurs bretons" (p1882, Ségalas) ....
16.120   "Pauvre Braga, charmant garçon!" (p1882, Nadaud) ....
16.121   "Elle sait!" (p1882, Boyer) ....
16.122   "Les deux pigeons" (p1883, La Fontaine) ....
16.123   "La chanson de la glu" (p1883, Richepin) ....
16.124   "Dernières volontés" (p1883, Veuillot) ....
16.125   "Vaguons sur les flots," barcarolle (p1884) ....
16.126   "Les adieux à la maison" (p1885) ....
16.127   "Blessures" (p1885, Turpin) ....
16.128   "Voix d'Alsace-Lorraine" (p1885, Rousseil) ....
16.129   "The Arrow and the Song" (p1885, Longfellow) ....
16.130   "Le temps des roses" (p1886, Roy) ....
16.131   "Vincenette," chanson provençale (p1887, Barbier) ....
16.132   "Passiflora" (p1888, Chambrun) ....
16.133   "A la nuit" (p1891, Gounod) ....
16.134   "Tout l'univers obéit à l'amour" (p1893, La Fontaine) ....
16.135   "L'aveu" (p1894, Rameau, Gounod's last mélodie) ....
16.136   "Chanson printanière" (p1895, Barbier) ....
16.137   "La chanson du pêcheur" (c1841, p1895, Gautier; 2nd setting as: Ma belle amie est morte) ....
16.138   "Soir d'automne" (p1896, Gounod) ....

17. CHILDREN'S SONGS & PARTSONGS

17.1   "La prière et l'étude" (L'emploi de la journée) (p ?1853–5, Turpin; 3–4 equal vv): 1. "L'arithmétique" ....
17.2   2. "La musique"
17.3   3. "La récréation"
17.4   4. "La géographie"
17.5   5. "L'écriture"
17.6   6. "La lecture"
17.7   7. "La grammaire"
17.8   8. "Le dessin"
17.9   9. "L'histoire de France"
17.10   10. "L'histoire sainte"
17.11   11. "La prière du matin"
17.12   12. "La prière du soir"
17.13   13. "La reine des cieux"
17.14   14. "L'action de grâce"
17.15   15. "Le catéchisme"
17.16   16. "Le Bénédicité"
17.17   17. "L'Angélus"
17.18   "Paraissez, roi des rois" (Chant de prix) (p1854; 3 equal vv) ....
17.19   "Le temps qui fuit et qui s'envole" (p1855; 3 equal vv; later for 1v & pf) ....
17.20   "Les pauvres du bon Dieu" (p1855; 3 equal vv; arr Morand for 1v & pf 1869) ....
17.21   "Les vacances" (p ?1855, Bigorie; 3 equal vv; later for 1v & pf) ....
17.22   "La distribution des prix" (p1855; 3 equal vv; later for 1v & pf) ....
17.23   "Le jour des prix" (c ?1855, Scribe; 3 equal vv) ....
17.24   "Un rêve" (p ?1855, Spenner; 4 equal vv; arr Morand for 1v & pf 1867) ....
17.25   "Le nid" (p ?1855, Quételard; 3 equal vv & pf; later for 1v & pf) ....
17.26   "Les couronnes" (p1856, Plouvier; 2 equal vv): 1. "Le travail béni" ....
17.27   2. "La fête des couronnes"
17.28   3. "Dieu partout"
17.29   "Cantate pour jeunes filles" (p1856, Turpin; 3 equal vv & pf) ....
17.30   "Fêtes des écoles" (p1856, Lefèvre; 3–4 equal vv) ....
17.31   "Aux amis de l'enfance" ....
17.32   "Le rosier blanc" (p1857, Spenner; 3 equal vv; later for 1v & pf) ....
17.33   "Bonjour, bon soir" (p1857, Spenner; 3 equal vv; later for 1v & pf) ....
17.34   "L'ange gardien" (p1858, Quételard; 4 equal vv; later for 1v & pf) ....
17.35   "Patte de velours" (p1858, Spenner; 3 equal vv; later for 1v & pf) ....
17.36   "La jeune fille et la fauvette" (p1860, E. de la Chauvinière; 3 equal vv; also for 1v & pf) ....
17.37   "Jésus à l'autel," souvenir de 1ère Communion (p ?1866; 2vv & pf) ....
17.38   "Livrons nos coeurs à l'espérance" (p before 1868; 3 equal vv) ....
17.39   "Enfants au doux visage" (p1868, E. de la Chauvinière; 1v & pf) ....
17.40   "Le mois de Marie" (Prière à la vierge), cantique (p1868; 1v/unison vv & pf/org) ....
17.41   "La charité" (p ?1883, E. de la Chauvinière; 3 equal vv) ....

* * * * *

GRANADOS (y Campiña), Enrique
1867–1916

1. STAGE WORKS

Lyric dramas:

2. SYMPHONIES

3. OTHER ORCHESTRAL WORKS

4. CONCERTOS, SOLO INSTR & ORCH

5. STRING QUARTETS

6. OTHER CHAMBER MUSIC

4 or more insts:

Vn & pf:

6.8	"Andante"	H9
6.9	*"Melodía" (p1903, lost)*	*H88*
6.10	"Romanza"	H115
6.11	Violin Sonata (c ?1910)	H127
6.12	"3 Preludes": No.1 "La góndola"	H135
6.13	No.2 "El toque de guerra"	
6.14	No.3 "Elevación"	

Vc & pf:

6.15	"Danza gallega" (arr of: Suite on Gallician Themes, H131/2)	H42
6.16	"Madrigal" (Danza XIII de las escenas gallegas) (p1915)	H80
6.17	Cello Sonata	H128
6.18	"Trova" (c1915, arr of No.2 of: Elisenda, H50)	H141

7. PIANO

7.1	*"A la antigua," bourée (c ?1885, sketch)*	*H1*
7.2	"A la cubana" (c ?1894)	Op.36, H2
7.3	"A la pradera" (c ?1908–9)	Op.35, H3
7.4	"Album. Paris, 1888," 40 pieces (written during stay in Paris, incl: En la aldea for pf duet, H52)	H4
7.5	"Allegro appassionato"	H5
7.6	"Allegro de concierto," in C major	Op.46 (also as Op.15), H6
7.7	"Allegro vivace" (part of: Album. Paris, 1888, H4)	H7
7.8	"El amor de la Virgen," melodía (inc)	H8
7.9	"Aparición"	H10
7.10	"Arabesca" (p1890)	H11
7.11	*"Balada" (perf1895, lost)*	*H13*
7.12	"Barcarola"	Op.45, H14
7.13	"Bocetos: Colección de obras fáciles" (c1900–5): No.1 "Despertar del cazador"	H16
7.14	No.2 "El hada y el niño"	
7.15	No.3 "Vals muy lento"	
7.16	No.4 "La campana de la tarde"	
7.17	No.5 "Palacio encantado en el mar" (Leyenda) (Países soñados No.1)	
7.18	"Canción árabe"	H20
7.19	"Canción y danza"	H21
7.20	"Canción morisca"	H22
7.21	"Capricho español" (c ?1886–7)	Op.39, H30
7.22	"Carezza" (Vals) (c ?1886–7)	Op.38, H31
7.23	"Cartas de amor" (Valses intimos) (c1887 or 1889–90): No.1 "Cadencioso"	H32
7.24	No.2 "Suspirante"	
7.25	No.3 "Dolente"	
7.26	No.4 "Appassionato"	
7.27	"Clothilde," mazurka (c ?1884–5)	H35
7.28	"Cuentos de la juventud" (c ?1900–6): No.1 "Dedicatoria" (arr Llobet for gui)	Op.1, H39
7.29	No.2 "La mendiga"	
7.30	No.3 "Canción de mayo"	
7.31	No.4 "Cuento viejo"	
7.32	No.5 "Viniendo de la fuente"	
7.33	No.6 (Lento con ternura)	
7.34	No.7 "Recuerdos de la infancia"	
7.35	No.8 "El fantasma"	
7.36	No.9 "La huérfana"	
7.37	No.10 "Marcha"	
7.38	"Danza característica"	H41
7.39	"Danza lenta"	H44
7.40	"Deux danses caractéristiques" (c ?1894): No.1 "Danza gitana"	H45
7.41	No.2 "Danza aragonesa" (arr ?1894, from incid music: Miel de la Alcarria, H91; orchd Ferrer)	
7.42	"Dolora" (apunte goyesca), in A minor	H48
7.43	"Elvira," mazurka (c ?1884–5)	H51
7.44	"Escenas infantiles": No.1 "Sueños de oro"	H54
7.45	No.2 "Niño que llora"	
7.46	No.3 "Otra melodía"	
7.47	No.4 "Hablando formal"	
7.48	No.5 "Recitado"	
7.49	No.6 "Pidiendo perdón"	
7.50	No.7 "El niño duerme"	
7.51	"Escenas poéticas" Series I (ca1905): No.1 "Berceuse"	H55
7.52	No.2 "Eva y Walter"	
7.53	No.3 "Danza de la Rosa"	
7.54	"Escenas poéticas" Series II: No.1 "Recuerdo de países lejanos"	H56
7.55	No.2 "El angel de los claustros"	

7.56	No.3 "Canción de Margarita"
7.57	No.4 "Sueños del poeta"
7.58	"Escenas románticas" (p1904): No.1 "Mazurka" H57
7.59	No.2 "Berceuse"
7.60	No.3 (Lento, con éxtasis) (pubd separately as: El poeta y el ruiseñor)
7.61	No.4 "Mazurka" (Allegretto)
7.62	No.5 (Allegro appassionato)
7.63	No.6 "Epílogo"
7.64	"Estudio" (Andantino espressivo) .... Op.posth, H58
7.65	"Exquise" (Vals tzigane) H59
7.66	"Goyescas" (Crepúsculo) (= ?Sérénade Goyesca) H63
7.67	"Goyescas" (Los majos enamorados), 2 books (c1909–11, inspired by paintings of Goya), I: No.1 "Los requiebros" H64
7.68	No.2 "Coloquio en la reja"
7.69	No.3 "El fandango de candil"
7.70	No.4 "Quejas, o La maja y el ruiseñor" (Lover and the Nightingale)
7.71	II: No.5 "El amor y la muerte" (Balada)
7.72	No.6 "Epílogo: Serenata del espectro"
7.73	"L'Himne dels morts" (c1897; arr Lopez-Chavarri for strings) H67
7.74	"Impresiones de viaje" (Hacia París, ante la tumba de Napoleón) (c ?1888)................... H68
7.75	"Impromptu" (Allegro assai) (p1895) Op.39, H69
7.76	"Impromptu" (Prestissimo) H70
7.77	"Intermezzo" (Goyescas) (c1916, arr from orch work H71) H72
7.78	"Jácara" (Danza para cantar y bailar)... Op.14, H74
7.79	"El jardí d'Elisenda" (arr of No.1 of suite: Elisenda, H50) H75
7.80	"Libro de horas" (p1913, subseries of: Escenas poeticas, H55): No.1 "En el jardín" H77
7.81	No.2 "El invierno" (La muerte del ruiseñor)
7.82	No.3 "Al suplicio"
7.83	"Marche militaire" (c ?1913, = ?No.2 of inc set of 6; 2 marches arr for pf duet) H82
7.84	"María del Carmen. Prelude" (unpubd but recorded, ?improvisation) H84
7.85	"Mazurka" (alla polacca) (c ?1888–90).. Op.2, H85
7.86	"Mazurka" (alla polacca) (p1985; pubd in La Ilustración Moderna) H86
7.87	"Mazurka," in E-flat major (c ?1888, from: Album. Paris, 1888, H4)............................... H87
7.88	"Minuetto" (c ?1886–7; pedal pf) H92
7.89	"Minuetto de la felicidad" H93
7.90	"Moresque y canción árabe," 2 pieces (p1910s) H95
7.91	"Ni así la distingue".. H97
7.92	"Obras fáciles para la educación del sentimiento" (Andantino espressivo) (inc) H99
7.93	"Oriental" (Canción variada, Intermedio y Final) H101
7.94	"Paisaje" (c by ?1912–3).. H104
7.95	"El pelele" (Goyesca) (c1913; arr Llongás for 2pf p1915) H106
7.96	*"Prelude," in D major (?lost)* *H110*
7.97	"Preludio," in F major (part of: Album. Paris, 1888, H4) H111
7.98	"Rapsodia aragonesa" (c1901) H113
7.99	"Reverie-Improvisation" (p1916, transcr from recording of improvisations perf by Granados)............ H114
7.100	"Romeo y Julieta" (also frag arr for 2pf subtitled: Poema) H116
7.101	"Sardana" (c by 1912–3) H118
7.102	*"Sérénade Goyesca" (lost/= Goyescas. Crepúsculo)* *H120*
7.103	*"Serenata española" (perf1890, lost)* *H121*
7.104	"La sirena" (Vals Mignone) (pubd in La Ilustración Moderna) H123
7.105	"6 Expressive Studies in the Form of Easy Pieces" (c1910s): No.1 "Theme, variations & finale" H124
7.106	No.2 (Allegro moderato)
7.107	No.3 "El caminante"
7.108	No.4 "Pastoral"
7.109	No.5 "La última pavana" (inspired by poem of Mestres: La condesa enferma)
7.110	No.6 "María" (Romanza sin palabras)
7.111	"6 Pieces on Spanish Folk Themes" (c ?1888–90): No.1 "Añoranza" (orchd Ferrer) H125
7.112	No.2 "Ecos de la parranda" (orchd Ferrer)
7.113	No.3 "Vascongada"
7.114	No.4 "Marcha Oriental"
7.115	No.5 "Zambra" (orchd Ferrer)
7.116	No.6 "Zapateado" (orchd Ferrer)
7.117	"Los soldados de cartón" (Marcha) H126
7.118	"Tango of the Green Eyes" (p1916, also sketches of orch score) H134
7.119	"12 Spanish Dances" (c1888–90), Vol I: No.1 "Galante" (Minuetto) Op.37, H142
7.120	No.2 "Oriéntale" (arr Kamins for vc/va & pf; orchd Grignon)
7.121	No.3 "Fandango" (Zarabando)
7.122	II: No.4 "Villanesca"
7.123	No.5 "Andaluza" (Playera) (arr w/ 1v, text Lorente; arr Kreisler for vn & pf; orchd Grignon)
7.124	No.6 "Rondalla aragonesa" (Jota) (arr Llobet for 2gui; orchd Grignon)
7.125	III: No.7 "Valenciana" (Calesera)
7.126	No.8 "Sardana" (Asturiana)
7.127	No.9 "Romántica" (Mazurca)
7.128	IV: No.10 "Melancólica" (Danza triste) (arr Llobet for 2gui)
7.129	No.11 "Arabesca"

7.130	No.12 "Bolero" (Zambra)	
7.131	"2 Impromptus" (p1912): No.1 "Vivo e appassionato"	H144
7.132	No.2 "Impromptu de la codorniz"	
7.133	"Vals de concert" (p1914)	Op.35, H146
7.134	"Valses poéticos" (c ?1886–7; orchd Ferrer for ballet: A tíempo romántico): "Introduction"	H147
7.135	No.1 "Melódico"	
7.136	No.2 "Tíempo de Vals noble"	
7.137	No.3 "Tíempo de Vals lento"	
7.138	No.4 "Allegro humorístico"	
7.139	No.5 "Allegretto" (Elegante)	
7.140	No.6 "Quasi ad libitum" (Sentimental)	
7.141	No.7 "Vivo. Presto"	
7.142	*"2 Gavotas" (p1973, spur: composer's copy from J. S. Bach : English Suite No.6 in D minor, BWV811)*	

Pf duet:

7.143	"En la aldea" (In the Village) (incl in: Album. Paris, 1888, H4), Part I: No.1 "Salida del sol. Maitines"	H52
7.144	No.2 "El cortejo" (Marcha nupcial)	
7.145	No.3 "La oración"	
7.146	No.4 "Regreso" (Marcha nupcial), "Canto" (recitado)	
7.147	II: No.1 "La siesta"	
7.148	No.2 "Danza pastoril"	
7.149	No.3 "Final"	
7.150	"2 Military Marches" (p1910): No.1 "Allegretto"	H145
7.151	No.2 "Lento marciale"	

8. CHORAL WORKS

8.1	"Cant de les estrelles" (c1910, Catalan transl of Heine; ch, pf & org)	H28
8.2	"L'Herba de amor" (Pregaria en estil gregoriá) (c1914, Catalan text; ch & org)	H66
8.3	"Salve regina" (c1896; 4vv & org)	

9. VOICE & ORCHESTRA

9.1	"Elisenda," suite (c1910, Mestres; 1v, pf, harp, str qnt, fl, ob & cl): 1. "El jardí d'Elisenda"	H50
9.2	2. "Trova" (see arr for vc & pf, H141)	
9.3	3. "Elisenda"	
9.4	4. "La tornada o Final"	
9.5	"Llegenda de la fada" (vv & orch, inc)	H79

10. SONGS (w/ pf)

10.1	"La boira" (c1900)	H17
10.2	"Canción del postillón"	H23
10.3	"Canciones amatorias" (orchd Ferrer): 1. "Descúbrase el pensamiento de mi secreto cuidado"	H24
10.4	2. "Mañanica era"	
10.5	3. "Llorad, corazón, que tenéis razón"	
10.6	4. "Mira que soy niña, amor, déjame!"	
10.7	5. "No lloréis ojuelos"	
10.8	6. "Iban al pinar" (Serranas de Cuenca)	
10.9	7. "Gracia mía" (Cantar)	
10.10	"Canso d'amor" (p1902, Roviralta, extracted from orch work: Boires baixes, H18/2)	H25
10.11	"Canso de Janer"	H26
10.12	"Cansonetta: El rey y el juglar"	H27
10.13	"Canto gitano"	H29
10.14	"La diosa en el jardín" (The Goddess in the Garden) (p1915)	H47
10.15	"Elegia eterna" (p1914, Mestres; also w/ orch p1915)	H49
10.16	"María de Carmen" (1v & pf, red from zarzuela, H83): 1. "Canción de la zagalica" (Act I/6)	
10.17	2. "Canción cartagenera" (Act II/2)	
10.18	3. "Murcianas, baile" (Act II/10)	
10.19	"L'ocell profeta" (Lied) (p1911, Castellà)	H100
10.20	"Si al Retiro me llevas" (Tonadilla) (anon 18th cent)	H122
10.21	"Tonadillas al estilo antiguo" (p1912, Periquet): 1. "Amor y odio" (orchd Ferrer)	H136
10.22	2. "Callejeo" (orchd Ferrer)	
10.23	3. "El majo discreto" (orchd Ferrer)	
10.24	4. "El majo olvidado"	
10.25	5. "El majo tímido" (orchd Ferrer)	
10.26	6. "El mirar de la maja" (orchd Ferrer)	
10.27	7. "El tra la la y el punteado" (orchd Ferrer)	
10.28	8. "La maja de Goya" (arr Llobet for gui)	
10.29	9. "La maja dolorosa" (3 pieces) (orchd Ferrer)	
10.30	10. "Las currutacas modestas" (2vv)	

12. ARRANGEMENTS OF WORKS OF OTHERS

11.1	Albéniz: "Azulejos" (Tiles / Mosaics) (compl Granados by 1910)	H12
11.2	Bach, J. S.: Chorale (transcr for strings)	H33
11.3	*Chopin: Piano Concerto No.2 in F minor, Op.21, B43 (reorchd, 1st movt only perf1900, lost)*	*H38*
11.4	Bach, J. S.: "Fugue," in C-sharp minor (p1900; strings, fl, ob, cl, bn, tpt & trbn)	H61
11.5	Noguéra i Balaguer: "Jota Aragonesa" (arr for pf; also for orch)	H76
11.6	Schubert: "Moment musical" (transcr for pf)	H94
11.7	Clementi: "Sonatinas," Op.36/1–4 (arr1891; str trio)	H129
11.8	Otaño: "Vuelta de la romería," 4th movt from: Suite vasca (arr for pf)	H132
11.9	Albéniz: "Triana," from: Iberia (arr1900–10; 2 pf)	H138
11.10	Scarlatti, D.: Keyboard Sonatas (p1905; transcr for pf): No.1 in G major, Kk520	H143
11.11	No.2 in G major, Kk521	
11.12	No.3 in G major, Kk522	
11.13	No.4 in F major, Kk518	
11.14	No.5 in F major, Kk541	
11.15	No.6 in F major, Kk540	
11.16	No.7 in G minor, Kk102	
11.17	No.8 in G minor, Kk546	
11.18	No.9 in B-flat major, Kk190	
11.19	No.10 in A minor, Kk110	
11.20	No.11 in D major, Kk534	
11.21	No.12 in D major, Kk535	
11.22	No.13 in D minor, Kk553	
11.23	No.14 in F minor, Kk555	
11.24	No.15 in F major, Kk554	
11.25	No.16 in G major, Kk547	
11.26	No.17 in A minor, Kk109	
11.27	No.18 in A major, Kk209	
11.28	No.19 in D minor, Kk552	
11.29	No.20 in A major, Kk537	
11.30	No.21 in B-flat major, Kk528	
11.31	No.22 in C minor, Kk139	
11.32	No.23 in C minor, Kk48	
11.33	No.24 in A major, Kk536	

12. PEDAGOGICAL WORKS

12.1	"Breves consideraciones sobre el ligado," booklet on producing legato on the piano	H19
12.2	"Dificultades especiales del piano," pedagogical work for piano (inc):	H46
	I. "Dificultades del cuarto y cinco dedo"	
	II. "Escalas y arpeggios con cambio del primero y quinto dedo"	
	III. "Elasticidad del cuarto y quinto dedo"	
12.3	"Método teórico práctico para el uso de los pedales del piano," manual on pedaling (p1954)	H90
12.4	"Ornamentos," pedagogical essay (inc)	H102
12.5	"El pedal," booklet on pedaling technique	H105

* * * * *

H = Carol A. Hess: "Enrique Granados. A Bio-Bibliography." Greenwood Press, 1991.

1. STAGE WORKS

Operas:

1.1	*"Arnljot Gelline" (c1872, Bjørnson, sketch, frag)* ....
1.2	"Olav Trygvason" (c1873, 1887–8, Bjørnson, unfin; r & orchd1889 as: Scenes from Olav Trygvason) Op.50

Incid music:

1.3	"Sigurd Jorsalfar" (p1872, Bjørnson)	Op.22
1.4	"Peer Gynt" (p1876, Ibsen; reorchd1886 & later)	Op.23

1a. SELECTIONS FROM STAGE WORKS (Nos. of sections in The Gramophone)

1a.2   "Olav Trygvason," opera: Op.50
      1. "Concealed in the many conjuring names"
      2. "You who from the well of Urd"
      3. "Evil man's evil spirits"
      4. "Tak! Tak!"
      5. "Toast the gods with delight and joy"
      6. "Elves and spirits"
      7. "Eternal Asatro"

1a.3   "Sigurd Jorsalfar," incid music: Op.22
      1. "Prelude"
      2. "Borghild's dream"
      3. "Trial of strength" (The matching game) (see orig: Gavotte for vn & pf)
      4. "Horn calls"
      5. "The northern people will wander" (Song)
      6. "Ceremonial march"
      7. "Interlude"
      8. "He who has dreamt of wandering" (The King's song)

1a.4   "Peer Gynt," incid music: Op.23
    I: 1. "Prelude" (In the wedding garden)
         2. "The bridal procession" (Wedding march) (= Op.19/2 for pf; orchd Halvorsen)
         3. "Norwegian dances" (Halling & Springdans) (solo vn off-stage)
    II: 4. "Prelude" (The abduction of the bride & Ingrid's lament)
         5. "Peer Gynt and the Saeter-Maidens"
         6. "Finale of the scene with the green-clad folk"
         7. "In the hall of the Mountain King" (ch & orch)
         8. "Dance of the Mountain King's daughter"
         9a. "Peer Gynt hunted by dwarfs"
         9b. "Scene with the hunchback"
    III: 10. "Prelude" (Deep in the coniferous forest)
         11. "Solvejg's song" (orch)
         12. "The death of Åse," scena (B & orch)
    IV: 13. "Prelude" (Morning mood)
         14. "Thieves and fences"
         15. "Arabian dance"
         16. "Anitra's dance"
         17. "Peer Gynt's serenade"
         18. "Solvejg's song"
    V: 19. "Prelude" (Peer Gynt's homecoming)
         20. "Solvejg's song in the hut" (unacc)
         21. "Night scene" (melodrama w/ ch)
         22. "The churchgoers' song" (chorale)
         23. "Solvejg's cradle song" (1v, strings & harp)

2. SYMPHONIES

2.1   Symphony in C minor (c1864; slow movt & Scherzo arr for pf duet, Op.14) ....

3. OTHER ORCHESTRAL WORKS

3.1	*Overture (c ?1862, inc, lost)* ....
3.2	"Im Herbst" (In Autumn), concert overture (c1866, r & orchd1887, pubd under the German title; see orig for pf duet) ....(Op.11)
3.3	"2 Elegiac Melodies" (c1881; strings; arr for pf): No.1 "The wounded heart" (from Op.33/3) Op.34
3.4	No.2 "Last Spring" (from Op.33/2)
3.5	"Peer Gynt" Suite No.1 (c1874–5, r1888, from incid music Op.23; arr for pf/pf duet): No.1 "Morning Mood" Op.46

4. PIANO CONCERTOS, PIANO & ORCH

5. STRING QUARTETS

6. OTHER CHAMBER MUSIC

3 or more insts:

Vn & pf:

Vc & pf:

7. PIANO SONATAS

8. OTHER PIANO WORKS

8.81	"6 Songs Transcriptions" (c1884): No.1 "Craddle song" (from Op.9/2)	Op.41
8.82	No.2 "Little Haakon" (from Op.15/1)	
8.83	No.3 "I love thee" (from Op.5/3)	
8.84	No.4 "When once she lay" (She is so white) (from Op.18/2)	
8.85	No.5 "The Princess" (from song of 1871)	
8.86	No.6 "To spring" (I give my song to the Spring) (from Op.21/3)	
8.87	"Lyric Pieces" Book III (p1886): No.1 "Butterfly"	Op.43
8.88	No.2 "Lone wanderer"	
8.89	No.3 "In my native land"	
8.90	No.4 "Little bird"	
8.91	No.5 "Erotik" (arr Spicker for strings & harp)	
8.92	No.6 "To the Spring"	
8.93	"Lyric Pieces" Book IV (p1888): No.1 "Waltz-Impromptu"	Op.47
8.94	No.2 "Albumleaf"	
8.95	No.3 "Melody"	
8.96	No.4 "Halling" (Norwegian dance)	
8.97	No.5 "Melancholy"	
8.98	No.6 "Spring dance"	
8.99	No.7 "Elegy"	
8.100	"6 Song Transcriptions" (c1891): No.1 "Mother's grief" (from Op.15/4)	Op.52
8.101	No.2 "First meeting" (from Op.21/1)	
8.102	No.3 "The poet's heart" (from Op.5/2)	
8.103	No.4 "Solvejg's song" (from incid music: Peer Gynt)	
8.104	No.5 "Love" (from Op.15/2)	
8.105	No.6 "The old mother" (from Op.33II/1)	
8.106	"Lyric Pieces" Book V (p1891): No.1 "Shepherd boy"	Op.54
8.107	No.2 "Norwegian rustic march" (Gangar)	
8.108	No.3 "March of the dwarfs" (Trolls' march)	
8.109	No.4 "Nocturne"	
8.110	No.5 "Scherzo"	
8.111	No.6 "Bell ringing"	
8.112	"Olav Trygvason," suite (p1893, arr from opera Op.50): No.1 "Prayer"	
8.113	No.2 "Temple Dance"	
8.114	"Lyric Pieces" Book VI (p1893): No.1 "Vanished days"	Op.57
8.115	No.2 "Gade"	
8.116	No.3 "Illusion"	
8.117	No.4 "Mystery" (Secrecy)	
8.118	No.5 "She dances"	
8.119	No.6 "Longing for home" (Home-sickness)	
8.120	"Lyric Pieces" Book VII (p1895): No.1 "Sylph"	Op.62
8.121	No.2 "Thanks" (Gratitude)	
8.122	No.3 "French Serenade"	
8.123	No.4 "Little brook"	
8.124	No.5 "Vision" (Phantom)	
8.125	No.6 "Homeward bound"	
8.126	"Lyric Pieces" Book VIII (p1897): No.1 "From days of youth"	Op.65
8.127	No.2 "Peasant's song"	
8.128	No.3 "Melancholy"	
8.129	No.4 "Salon"	
8.130	No.5 "In ballad style"	
8.131	No.6 "Wedding day at Troldhaugen" (also for pf duet)	
8.132	"19 previously unprinted Norwegian folksongs" (p1897): No.1 "Cattle call"	Op.66
8.133	No.2 "It is the greatest folly"	
8.134	No.3 "A king ruled in the East"	
8.135	No.4 "The song of Siri Dale"	
8.136	No.5 "It happened in my youth"	
8.137	No.6 "Call and cradle song"	
8.138	No.7 "Cradle song"	
8.139	No.8 "Call"	
8.140	No.9 "A little friend" (It was a little lad)	
8.141	No.10 "Tomorrow you shall marry"	
8.142	No.11 "There stood two girls"	
8.143	No.12 "Ranveig"	
8.144	No.13 "A little grey man"	
8.145	No.14 "In Ola valley, in Ola lake"	
8.146	No.15 "Craddle song"	
8.147	No.16 "Little Astrid"	
8.148	No.17 "Cradle song"	
8.149	No.18 "I wander deep in thought"	
8.150	No.19 "Gjendine's cradle song"	
8.151	"Lyric Pieces" Book IX (p1898): No.1 "Sailor's song"	Op.68
8.152	No.2 "Grandmother's minuet"	
8.153	No.3 "At your feet"	
8.154	No.4 "Evening in the mountains" (orchd as No.1 of: 2 Lyric Pieces)	
8.155	No.5 "Cradle song" (orchd as No.2 of: 2 Lyric Pieces)	

8.156	No.6 "Melancholy waltz"
8.157	"Lyric Pieces" Book X (p1901): No.1 "Once upon a time" Op.71
8.158	No.2 "Summer evening"
8.159	No.3 "Goblin" (Puck), in E-flat minor
8.160	No.4 "Silence of the woods"
8.161	No.5 "Halling" (Norwegian dance)
8.162	No.6 "Finished" (Gone)
8.163	No.7 "Remembrances" (Recollection)
8.164	"Slåtter" (Norwegian peasant dance-tunes) (p1903): No.1 "Giböen's bridal march" Op.72
8.165	No.2 "John Vaestafae's springdans"
8.166	No.3 "Bridal march from Telemark"
8.167	No.4 "Halling from the hills" (Tune from the Fairy Hill)
8.168	No.5 "Prillar from the churchplay Os" (Tune for the Goat-horn)
8.169	No.6 "Gangar"
8.170	No.7 "Rötnamsknut"
8.171	No.8 "Bridal march"
8.172	No.9 "Niels Rekve's halling"
8.173	No.10 "Knut Lurasen's halling" I
8.174	No.11 "Knut Lurasen's halling" II
8.175	No.12 "Spring dance"
8.176	No.13 "Havar Giböen's dream on the Oterholts bridge"
8.177	No.14 "The goblin's bridal procession at Vossevangen"
8.178	No.15 "The bride of Skuldal"
8.179	No.16 "The girls from Kivledal" (Spring dance)
8.180	No.17 "The girls from Kivledal" (Gangar)
8.181	"Stemninger" (Moods) (p1905): No.1 "Resignation" Op.73
8.182	No.2 "Scherzo-Impromptu"
8.183	No.3 "Night ride"
8.184	No.4 "Folk tune from Valders"
8.185	No.5 "Studie" (Hommage à Chopin)
8.186	No.6 "Studenternes serenade"
8.187	No.7 "Mountaineer's song"
8.188	"Piano Pieces" (p1908): No.1 "Wild dance" (c1891) .... Op.posth
8.189	No.2 "Gnomes' procession" (c1898)
8.190	No.3 "White clouds" (compl Röntgen 1908)

Pf duet:

8.191	"2 Symphonic Movements" (c1864, from: Sym in C min): No.1 "Adagio cantabile," in A-flat major Op.14
8.192	No.2 "Allegro energico," in C minor
8.193	"I Höst" (In Autumn), fantasy (c1866; see arr1887 as concert overture; also for 2pf 8 hands) Op.11
8.194	"Sigurd Jorsalfar," 3 pieces (p1874, arr from Op.22): No.1 "Borghild's dream"..............................
8.195	No.2 "Trial of strength" (The matching game)
8.196	No.3 "Triumphal march"
8.197	"2 Elegiac Melodies" (arr from Op.33; orchd): No.1 "The wounded heart" (from song Op.33/3) Op.34
8.198	No.2 "Last spring" (from song Op.33/2)
8.199	"4 Norwegian Dances" (c1881; also for pf/orch): No.1 in D minor Op.35
8.200	No.2 in A major
8.201	No.3 in G major
8.202	No.4 in D major
8.203	"2 Waltz Caprices" (c1883; arr for pf 1887): No.1 in C-sharp minor Op.37
8.204	No.2 in E minor
8.205	"The Bridal Procession passes by" (p1893, arr of pf piece Op.19/2)...

2 Pf:

| 8.206 | "Old Norwegian Romance w/ Variations" (c1891; orchd1904) .... Op.51 |

2nd pf acc for Mozart's Piano Sonatas:

8.207	Piano Sonata No.15 in F major, K533 (p1879) ....
8.208	"Fantasia," in C minor, K475 & Piano Sonata No.14 in C minor, K457 (p1880)................................
8.209	Piano Sonata No.16 in C major, "für Anfänger," K545 (p1880) ....
8.210	Piano Sonata No.5 in G major, K189h (K283) (p1880) ....

9. CHORAL WORKS

W/ orch:

9.1	"Cantata for Unveiling of the Christie monument" (c1868, m ch & milit band)...............................
9.2	"At a Southern Convent's Gate" (c1871, Bjørnson; S, A, fem ch & orch): Op.20
	1. "Who knocks so late?"
	2. "From guilt, from sin, to God come in"
9.3	"Land-sighting," cantata (c1872, r1881, Bjørnson; B, m ch, orch & org ad lib) Op.31

W/ pf:

9.4	*"Rückblick" (c1863; ch & pf, lost)* ....
9.5	"Danmark" (c1863–4, Andersen; ch & pf) ....
9.6	"Cantata for Hals Brothers piano firm's 25th anniversary" (c1874, Bjørnson; T, ch & pf) ....

Unacc m ch:

9.7	"4 Songs" (c1863–4; m ch, for Copenhagen students): 1. "Norwegian War Song" (Wergeland) ....
9.8	2. "Fredriksborg" (Richardt)
9.9	3. "Student life" (Richardt)
9.10	4. "The late rose" (Munch)
9.11	"The bear hunt" (c1867, Moe) ....
9.12	"Evening mood" (c1867, Moe) ....
9.13	"Election song: What are they saying about you" (c1868, Bjørnson) ....
9.14	"Stille nu!" (c1873, Moe, funeral song for J. S. Welhaven) ....
9.15	"Til Generalkonsul Tonsberg" (c1873, Bogh) ....
9.16	"Ballad for the Scandinavian freedom lovers" (c1874, Bjørnson) ....
9.17	"At Kjerulf's monument," cantata (c1874, Munch; T & m ch, for unveiling of the Kjerulf statue) ....
9.18	"Album," arrs of Norwegian folksongs (p1878; B & m ch): 1. "I lay down so late" Op.30
9.19	2. "Children's song"
9.20	3. "Little Torö"
9.21	4. "Kvalins halling"
9.22	5. "It is the greatest folly"
9.23	6. "Springdands: When I go out in the evening"
9.24	7. "Young Ole"
9.25	8. "Halling"
9.26	9. "The fairest of women"
9.27	10. "The great, white host"
9.28	11. "The gypsy lad"
9.29	12. "Rötnams knut"
9.30	"The Norwegian sailor" (c1868–70, Bjørnson) ....
9.31	"My finest thought" (c1881, Lofthus) ....
9.32	"Our watchword" (c1881, Lofthus) ....
9.33	"Trondhjem's greting to the singers" (c1883, Skavlan) ....
9.34	"Cantata for the Unveiling of the Holberg Memorial" (c1884, Rolfsen; Bar & m ch) ....
9.35	"Song of the Flag" (c1893, Brun) ....
9.36	"Westerly Wind" (c1896, Dahl) ....
9.37	"Greeting from Christiania's Singers" (c1896, Lie; Bar & m ch) ....
9.38	"4 Psalms" (c1906, Old Norwegian; Bar & ch): 1. "How fair thou art" (Laurentii) Op.74
9.39	2. "God's Son hath set me free" (Brorson)
9.40	3. "Jesus Christus is risen" (Thomissön)
9.41	4. "In heaven" (Brorson)

10. VOICE & ORCHESTRA

10.1	"The Mountain Thrall" (c1878, Old Norwegian ballad; Bar, 2hn & strings) Op.32
10.2	"Bergliot," melodrama (c1871, orchd1885, Bjørnson; recit & orch) Op.42
10.3	"6 Songs" (p1895–6): 1. "Solvejg's song" (c1891, Ibsen, from Op.23/18) ....
10.4	2. "Solvelg's cradle song" (c1891, Ibsen, from Op.23/23)
10.5	3. "From Monte Pincio" (c1894, Bjørnson, from Op.39/1)
10.6	4. "A swan" (c1894, Ibsen, from Op.25/2)
10.7	5. "Last spring" (c1894, Vinje, from Op.33/2)
10.8	6. "Henrik Wergeland" (c1894, Paulsen, from Op.58/3)

11. SONGS (w/ pf)

11.1	"The Singing Congregation" (c1860, Grundtvig) ....
11.2	"4 Songs" (c1861; A & pf): 1. "The Maid of the Mill" (Chamisso) Op.2
11.3	2. "Closely wrapt in misty billows" (Heine)
11.4	3. "I stood in gloomy musing" (Heine)
11.5	4. "What shall I say?" (Chamisso)
11.6	*"Ich denke dein" (c ?1862, Goethe, lost)*
11.7	"6 Songs" (c1863–4): 1. "The Orphan" (Chamisso) Op.4
11.8	2. "Morning Dew" (Chamisso)
11.9	3. "Farewell" (Heine)
11.10	4. "Hunting Song" (Uhland)
11.11	5. "The Old Song" (Heine)
11.12	6. "Where have they gone?" (Heine)
11.13	"She walked to the church" (c1864, Groth transl Feddersen) ....
11.14	"Melodies of the Heart" (c1863–4, Andersen): 1. "Two brown eyes" Op.5
11.15	2. "The Poet's Heart": "You grasp not the waves' eternal motion"
11.16	3. "I love thee"

11.17	4. "My thought is a mighty mountain"
11.18	"My little bird" (c1865, Andersen) ....
11.19	4 "Romances & Ballads" (p1866, Munch): 1. "The harp" Op.9
11.20	2. "Cradle song"
11.21	3. "Sunset" (c1863)
11.22	4. "Departure"
11.23	"Little lad" (c1866, Janson) ....
11.24	"4 Romances" (c1864, Winther): 1. "Gratitude" Op.10
11.25	2. "Woodland song"
11.26	3. "The flowers' message"
11.27	4. "Song on the mountain"
11.28	4 "Romances": 1. "Margaret's lullaby from 'The Pretenders' " (c1868, Ibsen) Op.15
11.29	2. "Love" (c1864, Andersen)
11.30	3. "Folk tune from Langeland" (c1864, Andersen)
11.31	4. "A mother's grief" (c1868, Richardt)
11.32	"Song of the Odalisque" (c1870, Bruun) ....
11.33	"Romances and Songs," Vol.I: 1. "Wandering in the woods" (c1869, Andersen) Op.18
11.34	2. "She is so white" (c1869, Andersen)
11.35	3. "A poet's last song" (c1869, Andersen)
11.36	4. "Autumn storms" (c1865, Richardt)
11.37	II: 5. "Poesy" (c1869, Andersen)
11.38	6. "The young birch tree" (c1869, Moe)
11.39	7. "The hut" (c1869, Andersen)
11.40	8. "The rosebud" (c1869, Andersen)
11.41	9. "Serenade to Welhaven" (c1868, Bjørnson; Bar & ch acc)
11.42	"The Princess" (c1871, Bjørnson) ....
11.43	"4 Songs" (from Bjørnson: The Fishermaiden): 1. "The first meeting" (c1870) Op.21
11.44	2. "Good morning" (c1870)
11.45	3. "I give my song to the spring" (c1872)
11.46	4. "Thanks for your advice" (c1872)
11.47	"6 Songs" (c1876, Ibsen): 1. "Minstrel" Op.25
11.48	2. "The swan"
11.49	3. "Album verse"
11.50	4. "With a waterlily"
11.51	5. "Departed!"
11.52	6. "A birdsong"
11.53	"5 Songs" (c1876, Paulsen): 1. "Hope" Op.26
11.54	2. "I wandered one lovely summer evening"
11.55	3. "The ambitious one"
11.56	4. "With a primrose"
11.57	5. "On a woodland path"
11.58	"12 Songs" (to poems by A. O. Vinje), Book I: 1. "The youth" (c1880) Op.33
11.59	2. "Spring" (c1880; orchd ?1894)
11.60	3. "The wounded heart" (c1880)
11.61	4. "The whortleberry" (c1880)
11.62	5. "Beside the stream" (c1877)
11.63	6. "A vision" (c1880)
11.64	II: 1. "Old mother" (c1873)
11.65	2. "The first thing" (c1880)
11.66	3. "At Rundarne" (c1880)
11.67	4. "A broken friendship" (c1880)
11.68	5. "Faith" (c1880)
11.69	6. "The goal" (c1880)
11.70	"Romances, old and new": 1. "From Monte Pincio" (c1870, Bjørnson; orchd1894) Op.39
11.71	2. "Hidden love" (c1872–3, Bjørnson)
11.72	3. "High on the grassy slope" (c1884, Lie)
11.73	4. "Among roses" (c1869, Janson)
11.74	5. "At the grave of a young wife" (c1873, Monrad)
11.75	6. "When I hear that song" (c1885, Rolfsen after Heine)
11.76	"Reminiscences from Mountain & Fjord" (c1886, Drachmann): 1. "Prologue" Op.44
11.77	2. "Johanne"
11.78	3. "Ragnhild"
11.79	4. "Ingeborg"
11.80	5. "Ragna"
11.81	6. "Epilogue"
11.82	"6 Songs" (c1889, from German transl Rolfsen): 1. "Greeting" (Heine) Op.48
11.83	2. "Some day, my thought" (Geibel)
11.84	3. "The way of the world" (Uhland)
11.85	4. "Silent nightingale" (Vogelweide)
11.86	5. "You wither, fair roses" (Goethe)
11.87	6. "A dream" (Bodenstedt)
11.88	"6 Poems" (c1889, Drachmann): 1. "Tell me now, did you see the lad?" Op.49
11.89	2. "Rock, o wave"
11.90	3. "Kind greetings, fair ladies"
11.91	4. "Now the evening is light and long"

11.92	5. "Christmas snow"
11.93	6. "Spring showers"
11.94	"Easter Song" (c1889, Böttger) ....
11.95	"Norway" (Norge), cycle (c1893–4, Paulsen): 1. "Homecoming" Op.58
11.96	2. "To Norway"
11.97	3. "Henrik Wergeland" (orchd1894)
11.98	4. "The tourist"
11.99	5. "The emigrant"
11.100	"Elegiac Poems" (c1893–4, Paulsen): 1. "When I wish to die" Op.59
11.101	2. "On Norway's bare mountains" (Heine's Ein Fichtenbaum)
11.102	3. "To the one" I
11.103	4. "To the one" II
11.104	5. "Farewell"
11.105	6. "Now you are resting in the earth"
11.106	"Poems by Vilhelm Krag" (c1893–4, Krag): 1. "Little Kirsten" Op.60
11.107	2. "The mother's lament: Gretchen lies in her coffin"
11.108	3. "While I wait"
11.109	4. "A bird cried out"
11.110	5. "And I will take a sweetheart"
11.111	"Children's Songs" (c1894–5, Rolfsen's Laesebog): 1. "The sea" Op.61
11.112	2. "Christmas tree song" (Krohn)
11.113	3. "Farmyard song" (Bjørnson)
11.114	4. "Fisherman's song" (Dass)
11.115	5. "Dobbin's good-night song"
11.116	6. "The Norwegian mountains"
11.117	7. "Fatherland's psalm" (Rolfsen after Runeberg)
11.118	"Haugtussa," cycle (c1895, Garborg; S & pf): 1. "The singing" Op.67
11.119	2. "Mountain girl" (Little maid)
11.120	3. "Bilberry slopes"
11.121	4. "Meeting"
11.122	5. "Love"
11.123	6. "Kids' dance"
11.124	7. "Evil day"
11.125	8. "At the brook"
11.126	"Ave Maris Stella" (c1899, Lange; arr for ch) ....
11.127	"5 Poems" (c1900, Benzon): 1. "A boat is rocking on the wave" Op.69
11.128	2. "To my little son"
11.129	3. "At mother's grave"
11.130	4. "Snail, snail, come out of your house"
11.131	5. "Dream"
11.132	"5 Poems" (c1900, Benzon): 1. "Eros" Op.70
11.133	2. "I live a life of longing"
11.134	3. "Lucent night"
11.135	4. "Beware when you choose your way"
11.136	5. "Poet's song"
11.137	"Posthumous Songs," Hansen Edition Book I: 1. "The fair-haired maiden" (c1867, Bjørnson) ....
11.138	2. "Thee I love!" (c1865, Caralis)
11.139	3. "Tears" (c1865, Andersen)
11.140	4. "The soldier" (c1865, Andersen)
11.141	II: 1. "On the ruins of Hamar' Cathedral" (c1880, Vinje)
11.142	2. "I loved him" (c1891, Bjørnson, frag from oratorio: Peace)
11.143	3. "A simple song" (c1889, Drachmann)
11.144	4. "Sigh" (c1873, Bjørnson)
11.145	5. "Christmas lullaby" (c1900, Langsted)
11.146	6. "The huntsman" (c1905, Schultz)

Unpubd:

11.147	"Clara's song from 'The Proposal at Helgoland' " (c1864, Feddersen) ....
11.148	"The old maid" (c1880, Vinje) ....
11.149	"The girl" (c1880, Vinje) ....
11.150	"8 Songs from Haugtussa" (c1895, Garborg): 1. "To the hills" ....
11.151	2. "The sparrow" (also for fem ch)
11.152	3. "Veslemøy's wandering"
11.153	4. "Veslemøy's longing"
11.154	5. "Veslemøy at the spinning wheel"
11.155	6. "Cow call"
11.156	7. "The haying"
11.157	8. "Condemned"

*   *   *   *   *

1. STAGE WORKS

Operas:

463

1a. SELECTIONS FROM STAGE WORKS

1a.1   "Der in Krohnen erlangte Glücks-Wechsel, oder Almira, Königin von Kastilien," opera: HWV1
. "Ouvertüre"
I: . "Durchlauchtigste, des Titans heller Schein," recit (Gonsalvo)
1. "Almire reggiere," aria (Consalvo)
. "Wohlan! entzündt den Blitz vom donnernden," recit (Consalvo)
2. "Viva Almira," chorus
3. "Chaconne"
4. "Saraband"
. "Die Nachwelt wird in Diamanten ätzen," recit (Almira, Consalvo, Osman, Fernando)
5. "Ach wiltu die Herzen auf ewig verbinden," aria (Osman)
. "Du hebst mich, grosse Königin," recit (Fernando, Almira)
6. "So ben che regnante più degna di te," aria (Fernando)
. "Durchlauchtigste, des Vaters letzten Willen," recit (Consalvo, Almira)
7. "Leset, ihr funkelnden Augen, mit Fleiss," aria (Consalvo)
. "Ach Schmerz! wie soll ich mich verbinden mit des Consalvo Haus?," recit (Almira)
8. "Chi più mi piace io voglio stretto legarmi al sen," aria (Almira)
. "Ritornello"
9. "Schönste Rosen," aria (Edilia)
. "Ist hier Edilia?," recit (Osman, Edilia)
10. "Du irrst dich, mein Licht," aria (Osman)
. "Ich bin versöhnt," recit (Edilia, Osman)
11. "Proverai di che fiere saette," aria (Edilia)
. "Schäum' immer Gift und Gallen!," recit (Osman)
12. "Zürne was hin!," aria (Osman)
. "Ritornello"
13. "Liebliche Wälder, schattige Felder," aria (Fernando)
. "Die Königin ist meiner Liebe Ziel," recit (Fernando)
14. "Vollkommene Hände, wie wollt ihr stets schneiden!," aria (Almira)
. "Ich liebe di wie, seh' ich nicht aufgehn mein Sonnenlicht?," recit (Fernando, Almira)
15. "Geloso tormento," aria (Almira)
. "Auf diesen angenehmen Wegen," recit (Consalvo, Edilia)
16. "Wer um Geld und Hoheit willen," aria (Consalvo)
. "Ich stimme solchen Worten bei," recit (Edilia)
17. "Più non vuo'tra sì e no ondeggiar sempre così," aria (Edilia)
. "Ritornello"
. "Weil es die Königin befohlen," recit (Tabarco)
18. "Am Hofe zu heissen galant," aria (Tabarco)
. "Ritornello"
. "Auf, auf, mein Herz!," recit (Fernando)
19. "Lass das Schicksal blitzen, wittern," aria (Fernando)
. "Dort wird sich Osman finden ein," recit (Fernando)
20. "Ich will euch verdammen," aria (Osman)
. "Nein, Amor, nein, du darfst nicht mehr gedenken," recit (Edilia, Osman)
21. "Ich will gar von nichtes wissen," duet (Edilia, Osman)
. "Ritornello"
. "Die Königin Almira lässt befehlen," recit (Consalvo, Edilia, Osman, Fernando, Bellante)
22. "Der Mund spricht zwar gezwungen: nein," aria (Bellante)
. "Sie wird mich in Verzweiflung stürzen," recit (Osman, Tabarco)
23. "Courante"
24. "Bourrée"
25. "Menuet"
26. "Rigaudon"
27. "Rondeau"
. "Wie, träum' ich oder nicht?," recit (Almira, Fernando, Edilia, Osman, Bellante, Consalvo)
28. "Ingrato, Spietato, Tosto rendi a me quel core," aria (Almira) (music lost)
II: . "Durchlauchtigste, aus Mauritanien," recit (Fernando, Almira)
. "Raymondo, der das Reich," recit (Raymondo, Consalvo, Almira, Fernando)
29. "Chi sa, mia speme," aria (Bellante)
. "Doch leerer Trost, der nur auf Hoffnung ruht," recit (Bellante, Consalvo, Tabarco)
30. "Lass ein sanftes Hände drükken nur entzükken," aria (Consalvo)
. "Verdruss und Unmut hält mich eingeschlossen," recit (Bellante, Consalvo, Tabarco)
31. "Alter schadt der Torheit nicht," aria (Tabarco)
. "Ritornello"
. "Ich muss allein in diesem Zimmer bleiben," recit (Fernando, Tabarco)
32. "Habbiate pazienza," aria (Tabarco)
. "Tabarco, lass ihn nur herein," recit (Fernando, Tabarco)
. "Es ist mir leid, dass ich dein' Arbeit störe," recit (Osman, Fernando)
33. "Sprich vor mir ein süsses Wort," aria (Osman)
. "Entzeuch das Blatt nur meinen Augen nicht," recit (Almira, Fernando)
34. "Schöne Flammen, fahret wohl," aria (Fernando)
. "Nein, nein, Fernando, nein!," recit (Almira, Osman, Fernando)
. "Durchlauchtigste, darf ich die Gnad' erbitten," recit (Consalvo)
35. "No, no, non voglio, no, che s'incaten ancor," aria (Almira)

. "Nein, Osman muss, was er versprochen," recit (Consalvo)
36. "Scepter und Kron'," aria (Osman)
. "Mein Vater wird zu den zerrissnen Banden," recit (Osman, Consalvo)
37. "Ritornello"
38. "Mi dà speranza al core," aria (Raymondo)
. "Almira kommt," recit (Raymondo, Almira)
39. "Zweier Augen Majestät," aria (Raymondo)
. "Und wo wird sich hie solche Schönheit zeigen?," recit (Almira, Raymondo)
40. "Ich kann nicht mehr," recit accompagnato (Almira)
41. "Move i passi alle ruine," aria (Almira)
. "Hilf, Himmel! Osman kommt," recit (Almira)
42. "Svenerò chi fa guerra a questo cor," aria (Osman)
. "Dort eben kommt mein Nebenbuhler her," recit (Osman, Fernando, Almira)
43. "Ob dein Mund wie Plutons Rachen," aria (Fernando)
. "Ritornello"
. "Beglückter Tag, daran ich meinem Leben," recit (Almira)
44. "Sanerà la piaga un dì," aria (Almira)
. "Raymondo hat mir seinen Fürstenstand entdeckt," recit (Almira, Consalvo)
. "Ich komme von Almirens Zimmer her," recit (Edilia, Osman)
45. "Der Himmel wird strafen," aria (Edilia)
. "Wie muss sich doch Tabarco stets," recit (Tabarco)
46. "Schürzchen mit dem Falbala," aria (Tabarco)
. "Ritornello"
. "Genug, genug; ich muss mit meinen Sachen," recit (Tabarco)
III: 47. "Entrée"
48. "Bücke dich, du Kreis der Welt," aria (Fernando)
49. "Meiner Pracht muss alles weichen," aria (Osman)
50. "Rigaudon"
51. "Du stolzer Erdenkreis!," aria (Consalvo)
52. "Saraband"
. "Gefällt ihr nicht der Africaner Lob?," recit (Raymondo, Almira, Edilia)
53. "Kommt, vermehrt der Torheit Ruhm," aria (Tabarco)
54. "Gigue"
55. "Quillt ihr überhäuften Zähren," aria (Edilia)
. "Was ist, das deinen Geist in Unmut setzt?," recit (Raymondo, Edilia)
56. "Gönne nach den Tränengüssen mir nur einen Gnadenblick," aria (Raymondo)
. "Entschliesse dich," recit (Consalvo, Edilia)
57. "Ja, Amor, deine Grausamkeit," recit accompagnato (Bellante)
58. "Blinder Schütz, brich die ungerechte Spitz deiner Pfeilen," aria (Bellante)
. "Und will dein Herz mich noch nicht lieben?," recit (Consalvo, Bellante)
59. "Unartige Schöne, wiltu mich verlassen," aria (Consalvo)
60. "Edele Sinnen schaffen von hinnen," aria (Fernando)
. "Fernando, gib mir deinen Degen," recit (Consalvo, Fernando)
61. "Was ist des Hofes Gunst?," aria (Fernando)
. "Geh, Unvorsichtiger, bedenke," recit (Consalvo)
. "Durchlauchtigste, Fernando liegt gefangen," recit (Consalvo, Almira)
62. "Vedrai, s'a tuo dispetto," aria (Almira)
. "Ritornello"
63. "Edilia, du bleibest mein," aria & recit (Raymondo, Edilia)
64. "Treuloser Mensch, ist mein Gemüt gleich zart," recit accompagnato (Almira)
65. "Kochet ihr Adern entzündete Rache," aria (Almira)
. "Durchlauchtigste, der Himmel muss verehren," recit (Osman, Almira, Tabarco)
66. "Werte Schrift, geliebte Zeilen," aria (Almira)
. "Entwich, verlasse mich," recit (Edilia, Osman)
67. "Quel Labro di coral," aria (Raymondo)
68. "Der kann im Blitz und Donner lachen," arioso (Fernando)
. "Was bringt Tabarco mir vor trost?," recit (Fernando, Tabarco)
69. "Verhängnis, wiltu denn nur mich," recit accompagnato (Fernando, Almira)
. "Fernando stirbet dein," aria (Fernando)
. "Fernando, fahre fort," recit (Almira)
70. "Spielet, ihr blitzenden Augen, mit mir," duet (Almira, Fernando)
. "Ritornello"
71. "Ich brenne zwar," aria (Bellante)
. "Glaub', Schöne, dass dein holder Mund," recit (Osman, Bellante)
72. "Mein Betrüben muss verschwinden," duet (Bellante, Osman)
. "Fernando hat sich zwar erklärt," recit (Almira, Consalvo, Bellante, Osman, Fernando)
73. "Anmuts Rosen streut. Hoffe," chorus
. "Durchlauchtigste, des Himmels hohe Gunst," recit (Raymondo & others)
. "Meine Lust, ich lege mich entzückt an deine Brust," recit (Almira & others)
74. "Wir hoffen, der Himmel wird nach dem Getümmel," chorus

. "Matelot" (Der Matrose)
. "Menuet I"
. "Bourée I"
. "Bourée II"
. "Menuet II"
. "Passacaille"

I: . *"Ah mostro, ah furia," recit (Florinda, Rodrigo) (music lost)*
1. *"Occhi neri, voi siete a pianger soli," aria (Rodrigo) (music lost)*
. *"petto col fulmine del cielo," recit (Florinda) (frag)*
2. "Pugneran con noi le stelle," aria (Florinda)
3. "Nasce il sol, e l'aura vola," aria (Esilena)
. "Reina, in si bel dì," recit (Fernando, Esilena)
4. "Agitata da fiato incostante," aria (Fernando)
. "Esilena! Mio Re!," recit (Rodrigo, Esilena)
5. "Dell' Iberia al soglio invito," aria (Giuliano)
. "Signor, questo reciso orribil teschio," recit (Giuliano, Rodrigo, Evanco, Esilena)
6. "Ti lascio a la pena," aria (Rodrigo)
. "Egregio Duce," recit (Esilena)
7. "In mano al mio sposo più vago sfavilla," aria (Esilena)
. "Evanco, armato in campo," recit (Giuliano, Evanco)
8. "Heroica fortezza," aria (Evanco)
. "Fra romori di Marte," recit (Giuliano, Florinda)
9. "Stragi, morti, sangue ed armi," aria (Giuliano)
. "Coronate mi, o sdegni!," recit (Florinda)
10. "Oh morte, vendetta," aria (Florinda)
. "Mentre di mie vittorie," recit (Rodrigo)
11. "Sommi Dei!," aria (Rodrigo)
. "Rodrigo, all' armi!," recit (Fernando, Esilena, Rodrigo)
. "Esilena, cotesto pur," recit (Rodrigo, Esilena)
12. "Vanne in campo," aria (Rodrigo)
. "Cor mio, non gir con fasto," recit (Esilena)
13. "Per dar pregio all'amor mio," aria (Esilena)

II: . "Campioni, una gran fede," recit (Giuliano, Evanco)
14. "Fra le spine offre gl'allori," aria (Giuliano)
. "Florinda, Amore è giusto," recit (Evanco, Florinda)
15. "Prestami, prestami un solo dardo," aria (Evanco)
. "Mi balza il core in petto," recit (Florindo, Esilena)
16. "Egliè tuo! nè mi riserbo altro più," aria (Esilena)
. "Chi esibisce, Esilena," recit (Florinda, Esilena)
17. "Parto, crudel, sì parto," aria (Esilena)
. "Baldanzosa pietà, quanto contrasto," recit (Florinda)
18. "Fredde ceneri d'amor," aria (Florinda)
19. "Siet' assai superbe, oh stelle," aria (Rodrigo)
. "Ma Rodrigo, si presto," recit (Rodrigo)
. "Signor, tutte rinchiuse son le nostre speranze," recit (Esilena, Rodrigo)
20. "Empio fato e fiera sorte," aria (Esilena)
. "Signor, non sempre cieca a l'ardir d'ogni destra," recit (Fernando, Rodrigo, Giuliano)
21. "Là ti sfido a fiera battaglia," aria (Giuliano)
. "Rodrigo, anco dell'Idra," recit (Esilena, Fernando, Rodrigo)
22. "Dopo i nembi e le procelle," aria (Fernando)
. "Amato sposo, e chi sa mai," recit (Esilena, Rodrigo)
23. "Dolce Amor, che mi consola e lusinga il cor," aria (Rodrigo)
. "Che più chiedi Esilena?," recit (Esilena)
24. "Si che lieta goderò e la pace troverò," aria (Esilena)
. "Qual' Democe mi scorta?," recit (Florinda, Evanco)
25. "Su! all'armi grida," aria (Evanco)
. "Ferma, Florinda," recit (Fernando, Giuliano, Florinda, Evanco)
26. "Alle glorie, alle palme, agli allori," aria (Florinda)

III: . *"Barbari Dei, son vinto," recit (Rodrigo) (music lost)*
27. "Qua rivolga gli orribili acciari," aria (Rodrigo)
. *"... fissi stan la fortuna e il fato," recit (Esilena, Rodrigo) (frag)*
. "Ah sommi Dei," recit (Esilena)
28. "Perchè viva il caro sposo," aria (Esilena)
. "Ritornello"
. "Abbiam vinto, o campioni!," recit (Giuliano)
29. "Spirti fieri," aria (Giuliano)
. "Non cederò. A me tu devi il sangue," recit (Rodrigo, Evanco, Giuliano)
. "German', t'arresta!," recit (Florinda)
. "Questi il difende," recit (Esilena, Rodrigo, Florinda)
30. "E tu, misero figlio," recit accompagnato (Esilena, Florinda, Evanco, Giuliano)
31. "Così m'alletti, così sei cara a me!," aria (Evanco)
. "Deciso ha di mia vita in voi pietade," recit (Rodrigo, Giuliano)
32. "Allor chè sorge astro lucente," aria (Giuliano)
. "Gran Donna, a cui oggi," recit (Evanco)
33. "Il dolce foco mio," aria (Evanco)

. "Dolcissima Esilena," recit (Rodrigo, Esilena)
34. "Prendi, l'alma, prendi il core," duet (Esilena, Rodrigo)
. "Signore, poich'è lo sdegno," recit (Florinda, Evanco)
35. "Begl'occhi del mio ben," aria (Florinda)
. "Mi son pur cari, oh bella, questi sensi d'amor," recit (Evanco)
36a. "Lucide stelle, gemelle d'amor," aria (Evanco)
36b. "Io son vostro, o luci belle," aria (Evanco)
. *"Tutti" (music lost)*
. *"Castiglia, anco su i so gli porta," recit (Rodrigo) (music lost)*
37. "L'amorosa Dea di Gnido," chorus
Anhang: *(14.) "Fra le spine offre gl'attori," aria (Giuliano) (frag)*

1a.6   "Agrippina," opera: HWV6
        . "Sinfonia"
      I: . "Nerone, amato figlio!," recit (Agrippina, Nerone)
1. "Con saggio tuo consiglio il trono ascenderò," aria (Nerone)
. "Per così grand impresa," recit (Agrippina)
. "A' cenni tuoi sovrani," recit (Pallante, Agrippina)
2. "La mia sorte fortunata," aria (Pallante)
. "Orche Pallante è vinto," recit (Agrippina)
. "Umile alle tue piante," recit (Narciso, Agrippina)
3. "Volo pronto, e lieto il core," aria (Narciso)
. "Quanto fa, quanto puole," recit (Agrippina)
4. "L'alma mia fra le tempeste," aria (Agrippina)
5. "Qual piacer a un cor pietoso," arioso (Nerone)
. "Amici, al sen vi stringo," recit (Nerone)
. "Ecco chi presto," recit (Narciso, Pallante, Nerone)
. "Questo è'l giorno fatal del mio destino," recit (Nerone, Narciso, Pallante)
. "Voi, che dell'alta Roma," recit (Agrippina)
6. "La tua prole merta sol scettro," quartet (Agrippina, Nerone, Narciso, Pallante)
. "Ma qual di liete trombe," recit (Agrippina)
7. "Allegrezza, allegrezza, allegrezza!," arietta (Lesbo)
. "Che sento! Crudo ciel!," recit (Pallante, Narciso, Agrippina, Nerone)
. "Evviva, Claudio, evviva!," chorus
. "Oh contenti perduti," recit (Narciso, Pallante, Nerone, Lesbo)
. "Vien la fiera cagion," recit (Agrippina, Nerone, Narciso, Pallante)
. "Ratto volo a poppea nunzio d'amore," recit (Lesbo)
. "Alle tue piante, oh Augusta," recit (Ottone, Agrippina, Narciso, Pallante, Nerone)
. "Augusta, amo Poppea," recit (Ottone, Agrippina)
8. "Tu ben degno sei dell'allor," aria (Agrippina)
. "L'ultima del gioir meta gradita," recit (Ottone)
9. "Lusinghiera mia speranza," aria (Ottone)
10. "Vaghe perle, eletti fiori," aria (Poppea)
. "Otton, Laudio, Nerone," recit (Poppea)
. "Signora, oh mia Signora!," recit (Lesbo, Poppea)
. "Di lieta nuova apportator," recit (Lesbo, Agrippina, Poppea)
. "Perchè in vece di Claudio," recit (Poppea)
11. "È un foco quel d'amore che penetra nel core," aria (Poppea)
. "Ma qui Agrippina viene," recit (Poppea, Agrippina)
12. "Ho un non so che nel cor," aria (Agrippina)
. "Cieli, quai strani casi," recit (Poppea)
13a. "Fa quanto vuoi, li scherni tuoi non soffrirò," aria (Poppea)
13b. "Per punir che m'ha ingannata saprò tessere un inganno," aria (Poppea)
. "Non veggo alcun," recit (Lesbo)
14. "Pur ritorno a rimirarvi, vaghe luci, stelle d'amor," aria (Claudio)
. "Ma, oh ciel, mesta e confusa," recit (Claudio, Poppea)
15. "Vieni, oh cara," arietta (Claudio)
. "Che mai farò!," recit (Poppea, Claudio)
. "Signor, Signor, presto fuggiamo!," recit (Lesbo, Claudio, Poppea)
16. "Quando vorrai!," trio (Poppea, Claudio, Lesbo)
. "Pur al fin si riandò," recit (Poppea)
. "Oh mia liberatrice," recit (Poppea, Agrippina)
17. "Non ho cor che per amarti," aria (Agrippina)
. "Se Ottone m'ingannò," recit (Poppea)
18a, b. "Se giunge un dispetto a' danni del cor," aria (Poppea)
     II: . "Dunque noi siam traditi?," recit (Pallante, Narciso)
. "A noi la destra sia pegno di fede," recit (Ottone, Pallante)
19. "Coronato il crin d'alloro io sarò," recit (Pallante, Narciso, Ottone)
. "Roma più ch'il trionfo," recit (Pallante, Narciso, Ottone)
20. "Prelude"
. "Ecco il superbo!," recit (Agrippina, Poppea, Nerone, Ottone, Narciso)
21. "Di timpani e trombe, Roma applauda," chorus
. "Nella Britannia vinta," recit (Claudio)
22. "Cade il mondo," aria (Claudio)
. "Signor, quanto il mio core," recit (Agrippina & others)

. "Giubila, oh core!," recit (Poppea, Ottone, Cladio)
23. "Nulla sperar da me," aria (Agrippina)
. "Ritornello"
. "E tu, Poppea, mio bene?," recit (Ottone)
24. "Tuo ben è'l trono," aria (Poppea)
. "Ritornello"
. "Soccori almen Nerone!," recit (Ottone)
25a, b. "Sotto il lauro che hai sul crine," aria (Nerone) (2 vers)
. "Scherzo son del destin," recit (Ottone, Narciso, Pallante, Lesbo)
26. "Otton, Otton, qual portentoso fulmine," recit accompagnato (Ottone)
27. "Voi che udite il mio lamento," aria (Ottone)
28. "Bella pur nel mio diletto," aria (Poppea)
. "Il tormento d'Ottone," recit (Poppea)
. "Par che amor sia cagion," recit (Poppea)
29. "Vaghe fonti, che mormorando," arioso (Ottone)
30. "Ma qui che veggo, oh cieli? ... Voi dormite," recit ed arioso (Ottone, Poppea)
. "Fantasme della mente," recit (Poppea, Ottone)
31. "Ti vo' giusta," aria (Ottone)
. "Ritornello"
. "Di quali ordite trame," recit (Poppea)
32. "Ingannata una sol volta esser posso," aria (Poppea)
. "Pur al fin ti ritrovo," recit (Lesbo, Poppea)
. "A non pochi perigli," recit (Poppea, Nerone)
. "Oh some amica sorte," recit (Poppea, Nerone)
33. "Col peso del tuo amor," aria (Poppea)
. "Qual bramato piacere," recit (Nerone)
34. "Quando invita la donna l'amante," aria (Nerone)
35. "Pensieri, voi mi tormentate," aria (Agrippina)
. "Ciel, soccorri, soccorri a miei di segni" (Tutti)
. "Quel ch'oprai è soggetto," recit (Agrippina)
36. "Pensieri, pensieri," aria (Agrippina)
. "Se ben nemica sorte," recit (Pallante, Agrippina)
37. "Col raggio placido della speranza," aria (Pallante)
. "Di giunger non dispero," recit (Agrippina)
. "Or è tempo, oh Narciso," recit (Agrippina, Narciso)
38. "Spererò, poichè mel dice," aria (Narciso)
. "Ritornello"
. "Per dar la pace al core," recit (Agrippina)
. "A vagheggiar io vengo," recit (Claudio, Agrippina)
. "Signor, Poppea ....," recit (Lesbo, Cladio, Agrippina)
39. "Basta che sol tu chieda," aria (Claudio)
. "Favorevol la sorte," recit (Agrippina)
40. "Ogni vento ch'al porto lo springa," aria (Agrippina)
III: . "Il caro Otton," recit (Poppea)
. "Ah mia Poppea! ti prego," recit (Ottone, Poppea)
41. "Tacerò, pur che fedele," aria (Ottone)
. "Attendo qui Nerone," recit (Poppea)
. "Anelante ti reco," recit (Nerone, Poppea, Ottone)
42. "Coll' ardor del tuo bel core," aria (Nerone)
. "Amico ciel," recit (Poppea)
. "Qui non v'è alcun, Signore," recit (Lesbo, Poppea, Claudio, Nerone, Ottone)
. "Temerario, insolente!," recit (Claudio, Nerone, Poppea, Ottone)
. "Ora, Claudio, che dici?," recit (Poppea, Claudio)
43. "Io di Roma il Giove sono," recit (Claudio)
. "Pur al fin se n'andò," recit (Poppea)
. "Ora, Ottone, che dici?," recit (Poppea, Ottone)
44. "Pur ch'io ti stringa al sen," aria (Ottone)
. "Piega pur del mio cor," recit (Poppea)
45. "Bel piacere è godere fido amor!," aria (Poppea)
. "Cotanto osò Poppea?," recit (Agrippina, Nerone)
46. "Come nube che fugge dal vento," aria (Nerone)
. "Evvi donna più empia?," recit (Pallante, Narciso)
. "Agrippina, Nerone," recit (Claudio, Pallante, Narciso)
. "Adorato mio sposo," recit (Agrippina, Claudio, Narciso, Pallante)
47. "Se vuoi pace, oh volto amato," aria (Agrippina)
. "Ecco la mia rivale," recit (Agrippina, Poppea, Nerone, Ottone, Claudio)
48. "Lieto il Tebro increspi l'onda," chorus
. "D'Ottone e di Poppea," recit (Giunone)
49. "V'accendano le tede i raggi della stelle," aria (Giunone)
Anhang: 1a. "Sarà qual vuoi a cenni tuoi," aria (Nerone)
39a. "Vagheggiar de tuoi bei lumi," aria (Claudio)
. "Vorrei della bellezza," recit (Agrippina, Claudio)
(42.) "Col valor del vostro brando," aria (Nerone)
44. "Esci, o mia vita, esci dal duolo," aria (Poppea)
44a. "No, no, ch'io non apprezzo," aria (Ottone)

44b. "Sì, sì, ch'il mio diletto," aria (Poppea)
44c. "No, no, ch'io non apprezzo che te ... Sì, sì, ch'il mio diletto," duet (Poppea, Ottone)
. "Sovra il core di Claudio," recit (Agrippina)

1a.7   "Rinaldo," opera (2nd vers): HWV7b
. "Ouverture"
. "Gigue"
I: . "Delle nostre fatiche," recit (Goffredo)
   1. "Sovra balze scoscesi e pungenti," aria (Goffredo)
    . "Signor, già dal tuo senno," recit (Rinaldo, Goffredo, Almirena)
   2. "Quel cor che mi donati," aria (Almirena)
    . "Questi saggi consigli," recit (Goffredo, Rinaldo)
   3. "Ogni indulgio," aria (Rinaldo)
    . "Signor, che delle stelle," recit (Araldo, Goffredo)
   4. "Sinfonia"
    . "Goffredo, se t'arrise," recit (Argante, Goffredo)
   5. "D'instabile fortuna," aria (Goffredo)
    . "Infra dubii di Marte," recit (Argante)
   6. "Furie terribili!," aria (Armida)
   7. "Come a tempo giungesti," recit accompagnato (Argente, Armida)
   8. "Sulla ruota di fortuna," aria (Argante)
    . "Ma fia la gloria," recit (Armida)
   9. "Combati da forte," aria (Armida)
  10. "Augelletti!," aria (Almirena)
    . "Adorato mio sposo," recit (Almirena, Rinaldo)
  11. "Scherzano sul tuo volto," duet (Almirena, Rinaldo)
    . "Al valor del mio brando," recit (Armida, Almirena)
  12. "Sinfonia"
  13. "Cara sposa," aria (Rinaldo)
    . "Ch'insolito stupore," recit (Goffredo, Rinaldo)
  14. "Cor ingrato, ti rammembri," aria (Rinaldo)
    . "Un mio giusto dolor," recit (Goffredo, Rinaldo)
  15. "Venti," aria (Rinaldo)
II: 16. "Siam prossimi al porto," aria (Goffredo)
    . "A quel sasso bramato," recit (Rinaldo, Goffredo)
    . "Per raccor d'Almirena," recit (Donna)
  17. "Il vostro maggio de'bei verdi anni," aria (Sirene)
    . "Qual incognita forza," recit (Rinaldo, Goffredo)
  18. "Il Tricerbero humilato," aria (Rinaldo)
    . "Numi! strano ardimento!," recit (Goffredo)
  19. "Mio cor, che mi sai dir!," aria (Goffredo)
    . "Armida dispietata!," recit (Almirena, Argante)
  20. "Lascia ch'io pianga mia cruda sorte," aria (Almirena)
    . "T'arresta, oh Dio!," recit (Argante)
  21. "Per salvarti, idolo mio," aria (Argante)
    . "Cingetemi d'alloro," recit (Armida, Rinaldo)
  22. "Fermati! Armida son fedel," duet (Armida, Rinaldo)
    . "Ah! Rinaldo crudel," recit (Voce: la Sirena, Rinaldo)
  23. "Abbruggio, avvampo e fremo," aria (Rinaldo)
  24. "Dunque i lacci d'un volto," recit accompagnato (Armida)
    . "Sembianze idolatrate," recit (Argante, Armida)
  25. "Arma lo sguardo d'un dolce dardo!," aria (Argante)
  26. "Ah! crudel," aria (Almirena)
    . "Rasserana i bei lumi, idolo mio," recit (Argante)
    . "Si lusinghi d'Argante l'amor tanto importuno," recit (Almirena)
  27. "Parolette, vezzi e sguardi," aria (Almirena)
III: 28. "Sinfonia"
    . "Quivi par che rubelle," recit (Goffredo)
    . "La causa che vi spinge," recit (Mago, Goffredo)
  29. "Sinfonia"
    . "Qui vomita cocito," recit (Goffredo, Mago)
  30. "Andate, o forti, fra stragie morti," aria (Mago)
    . "A fronte d'un sleal anco mi trovo?," recit (Armida, Argante)
  31a. "March"
  31b. "Di Sion nell alta sede," aria (Argante)
    . "Mori svenata! Oh! Numi!," recit (Armida, Almirena, Rinaldo)
    . "Nella guardata soglia," recit (Armida, Goffredo, Rinaldo, Almirena)
  32. "È un incendio fra due venti," aria (Rinaldo)
    . "Fremo nel mio furor contro l'inferno," recit (Goffredo, Almirena)
  33. "Al trionfo del nostro furore," duet (Almirena, Goffredo)
  34. "Orrori menzogneri, a voi ne vengo," recit accompagnato (Rinaldo)
    . "A voi de'miei trofei," recit (Rinaldo)
  35. "Vedrò più liete e belle," aria (Rinaldo)
    . "Ciel crudele! empia sorte!," recit (Argante, Armida)
  36. "Fatto è Giove un Dio d'inferno," aria (Armida)

37. "Sinfonia"
 . "Vompagni gloriosi," recit (Goffredo, Almirena, Rinaldo)
38. "Sì, caro, caro, sì," aria (Almirena)
 . "Chi vuol giunger di gloria a bei diletti," recit (Goffredo)
39. "Vinto è sol della virtù," chorus

1a.8b   "Terpsicore," prologo: HWV8b
 . "Ouverture"
1. "I nostri cori dobbiamo offrir," chorus
 . "Melodiosa Germana," recit (Apollo)
2. "Gran tonante," aria (Apollo)
 . "Ma, Terpsicore snella, dov'è?," recit (Apollo)
3. "Di Parnasso i dolci accenti," aria (Erato)
4. "Prelude"
 . "Ecco, sen vien," recit (Apollo)
5. "Chaconne"
6. "Col tuo piede brilla amor," duet (Erato, Apollo)
7. "Sarabanda"
 . "Pingi i transporti d'un amator," recit (Apollo)
8. "Gigue"
 . "La speme, e cura," recit (Erato)
9. "Tuoi passi son dardi," duet (Erato, Apollo)
 . "La gelosia, cieco il furor," recit (Apollo)
10. "Air"
 . "Dai, quando vuoi, gioja e dolor," recit (Erato, Apollo)
11. "Hai tanto rapido, leggiero il piè," aria (Apollo)
12. "Ballo"
13. "Vezzi più amabile chi puol veder?," duet (Erato, Apollo)
14. "Cantiamo lieti della virtù," chorus

1a.8   "Il pastor fido," opera: HWV8c
    A. "Ouverture"
    B. "Ouverture"
   I: 1a. "Fato crudo, Amor severo," arioso (Mirtillo)
       . "Ah! no, sia pur pietosa," recit (Mirtillo)
      2a. "Fra gelsomini, fra grati fiori," aria (Mirtillo)
       . "Ah! infelice mia patria," recit (Amarilli)
      1b. "Ah! infelice mia patria," recit accompagnato (Amarilli)
       . "Son di Mirtillo!," recit (Mirtillo, Amarilli)
      2b. "D'amor a fier contrasti," aria (Amarilli)
       . "Come viver poss'io," recit (Mirtillo)
       . "Ferma, Mirtillo! e qual dolor t'accora?," recit (Eurilla, Mirtillo)
      3a. "Lontan del mio tesoro," aria (Mirtillo)
      3b. "Sento brillar nel sen (cor)," aria (Mirtillo)
       . "Ah! che sperar mi resta," recit (Eurilla)
      4. "Frode, sol a te rivolta," aria (Eurilla)
       . "Tu sola, oh bella Diva," recit (Silvio, Amarilli)
      5. "Finchè un zeffiro soave," aria (Amarilli)
       . "Respira, anima mia!," recit (Dorinda, Silvio)
      6. "Quanto mai felici siete," aria (Dorinda) (= Ezio, HWV29/6)
      A. "Cintia, mia casta Dea," recit (Silvio)
      7a. "Quel Gelsomino che imperla il prato," aria (Silvio) (= Riccardo I, HWV23/14)
      B. "Cintia, mia casta Dea," recit (Silvio)
      7b. "Non vo' mai seguitar quel cieco Nume alato," aria (Silvio)
      8. "Oh, oh quanto bella gloria," chorus (= Il Parnasso in Fiesta, HWV72/17)
  Balli: 9. "March"
      10. "Pour les Chasseurs" (insts)
      11. (insts)
   II: 12. "Sinfonia" (= Ezio, HWV29/23)
       . "E ancor non giunge Eurilla," recit (Mirtillo)
      13. "Caro Amor, sol per momenti," aria (Mirtillo) (= Teseo, HWV9/27)
       . "Già fortuna m'arride," recit (Eurilla)
      14. "Ho un non so che nel cor," aria (Eurilla)
       . "E chi tenta rapirmi il bel tesoro?," recit (Mirtillo)
      15. "Torni pure un bel splendore," aria (Mirtillo) (= Il Parnasso in Fiesta, HWV72/15)
       . "Mi fian cari i tuoi voti," recit (Amarilli)
       . "Mia diletta, che pensi?," recit (Eurilla, Amarilli)
      16. "Finte labbra!," aria (Amarilli)
       . "Vanne lungi da me!," recit (Silvio, Dorinda)
      17. "Sol nel mezzo risona del core," aria (Silvio)
       . "Non mi fuggir, crudele," recit (Dorinda)
      18. "Se in ombre nascosto," aria (Dorinda)
       . "Ed è pur ver, mia fida amica al fine," recit (Mirtillo, Eurilla)
      19. "Sì, revedrò la sola mia speranza," aria (Mirtillo) (= Rodelinda, HWV19/23b)
       . "E tu stessa vedesti," recit (Amarilli, Eurilla)

20. "Scherza in mar la navicella," aria (Amarilli) (= Lotario, HWV26/12)
. "Ah! tepido amator, mira Amarilli," recit (Eurilla, Mirtillo)
21. "Accorrete, o voi Pastori," aria (Mirtillo) (= Il Parnasso in Fiesta, HWV72/30)
. "Accorriam de' vostri amori," chorus
Ballo di pastori e pastorelle: 22. "Ballo"
23. "Musette"
24. "Menuet"
25. "Menuet"
III: 26. "Sinfonia" (= Partenope, HWV27/31)
. "Sventurato mio amore!," recit (Dorinda)
. "Miei fidi, oggi v'accenda," recit (Silvio)
27. "Oh quanto bella gloria," chorus (= Il Parnasso in Fiesta, HWV72/19)
. "Ma veggio, o veder parmi," recit (Silvio)
. "Oh! dolce uscir di vita," recit (Dorinda, Silvio)
28. "Sento nel sen distruggersi fra," aria (Silvio)
. "Già Amarilli fu colta," recit (Eurilla)
. "Grazie alli Dei, mio caro," recit (Dorinda, Silvio, Eurilla)
29. "Secondaste al fine," aria (Eurilla)
30. "Sinfonia"
. "Oh! Mirtillo, Mirtillo!," recit accompagnato (Amarilli)
31. "Ah! non son io che parlo," aria (Amarilli) (= Ezio, HWV29/30)
. "Sciogliete quelle mani!," recit (Mirtillo, Amarilli)
32. "Per te, mio dolce bene," duet & chorus (Amarilli, Mirtillo)
. "S'unisce al tuo martir" (= Il Parnasso in Fiesta, HWV72/23)
33. "Dell'empia frode il velo," aria (Tirenio) (= Riccardo I, HWV72/23)
. "Cessate, omai, cessate," recit (Tirenio)
. "E ti stringo, mio ben!," recit (Mirtillo, Amarilli, Dorinda, Silvio)
34. "Caro, caro, ti dono in pegno il cor," duet (Amarilli, Mirtillo) (= Teseo, HWV9/32)
. "Chiedo, fedeli amanti," recit (Eurilla, Dorinda, Silvio, Amarilli, Mirtillo)
35. "Sciolga dunque al ballo, al canto," aria (Mirtillo) (= Il Parnasso in Fiesta, HWV72/11)
36. "Ballo"
37. "Gavotte"
38. "Ballo"
39. "Replicati al ballo, al canto," chorus (= Il Parnasso in Fiesta, HWV72/13)
Anhang: II: . "È felice chi puole amar," recit (Mirtillo)
III: . "Quell'ira che destai, inutile non è," recit (Sibari)

1a.9 "Teseo," opera: HWV9
. "Ouverture"
I: . "Sia qual' vuole il mio fato," recit (Agilea)
. "Clizia, son gli Atenensi," recit (Agilea, Clizia)
1. "È pur bello, è pur bello, in nobil core," aria (Agilea)
. "Ora svelaci Arcane," recit (Agilea, Arcane)
2. "Deh serbate, oh giusti Dei!," aria (Agilea)
. "Parte Agilea," recit (Clizia, Arcane)
3. "Ti credo, sì, ben mio," aria (Clizia)
. "Commanda dunque, oh bella," recit (Arcane, Clizia)
4. "Ah! cruda gelosia!," aria (Arcane)
. "Dunque all'affetto mio fede non presti?," recit (Clizia, Arcane)
5. "Addio! mio caro bene," duet (Clizia, Arcane)
. "Ritornello"
6. "Serenatevi, oh lucibelle!," aria (Egeo)
. "Or ch'affermato ho il soglio," recit (Egeo, Agilea)
7. "Ricordati, oh bella, che tu sol sei quella," aria (Egeo)
. "Ah! che sol per Teseo arde quest'alma!," recit (Agilea)
8. "M'adora l'idol mio, gode il mio core," aria (Agilea)
II: 9. "Dolce riposo!," arioso & recit (Medea)
. "L'infelice Medea!," recit (Medea)
10. "Quell'amor, ch'è nato a forza," aria (Medea)
. "Dell'armi nostre," recit (Egeo, Medea)
11. "Sì ti lascio," duet (Medea, Egeo)
. "Sire, tutto è in periglio!," recit (Arcane, Egeo)
12. "Ogn'un acclami," chorus
. "Amici, a bastanza mostrate," recit (Teseo)
. "Teseo, dove ten vai?," recit (Medea, Teseo)
13. "Quanto, quanto ch'ame sian care," aria (Teseo)
. "Ai vostri amori temo," recit (Medea, Teseo)
14. "Non so più che bramar, non so più che temer," aria (Teseo)
15. "Ira, sdegni, e furore," recit accompagnato (Medea)
16. "O stringerò nel sen," aria (Medea)
III: 17. "Le luci del mio bene sono per me due stelle," aria (Arcane)
. "Opportuna qui giunge," recit (Arcane, Clizia)
18. "Risplendete, amiche stelle," aria (Clizia)
. "Perdona omai, perdona," recit (Arcane, Clizia)
19. "Più non cerca libertà," aria (Arcane)

. "Quivi sarà fra poco Teseo," recit (Clizia, Agilea)
20. "Vieni, torna idolo mio," aria (Agilea)
. "Teseo qui giunge," recit (Clizia)
. "Pur ti riveggio al fine," recit (Teseo, Agilea)
21. "S'armi il fato, s'armi amore!," aria (Teseo)
. "Egeo di qui venir m'impose," recit (Arcane, Agilea, Clizia)
. "Tu ben sai, Principessa," recit (Medea, Agilea)
22. "Numi, chi ci soccorre!," recit accompagnato (Agilea, Clizia, Arcane)
. "Deh! dammi aita, Arcane," recit (Clizia, Arcane, Medea)
23. "Ombre, ombre, sortite dall'eterna notte!," recit accompagnato (Medea, Agilea)
24. "Sibillando, ululando," aria (Medea)
IV: . "Sire, come imponesti, ad Agilea portai," recit (Arcane, Egeo)
25. "Voglio stragi, voglio stragi, e voglio morte," aria (Egeo)
. "Amor per Agilea," recit (Arcane)
26. "Benchè tuoni e l'etra avvampi," aria (Arcane)
. "Cruda! ed ancor non vuoi," recit (Agilea, Medea)
. "Che mai veggio, oh Dio!," recit (Agilea)
27. "Deh! v'aprite, oh luci belle," aria (Agilea)
. "E ancor su gli acchi miei," recit (Medea)
28. "Dal cupo baratro venite, oh furie," aria (Medea)
. "S'arma contro di me tutto l'inferno?," recit (Agilea, Medea)
29. "Chi ritorna alla mia mente la perduta rimembranza," arioso (Teseo)
. "Mira, qual cura prendo, oh Teseo, per giovarti!," recit (Medea, Teseo)
. "Agilea, più non m'ama," recit (Teseo, Agilea)
30. "Qual tigre e qual Megera," aria (Teseo)
. "Tu piangi, e a me l'ascondi?," recit (Teseo, Agilea)
31. "Amarti sì vorrei, il ciel, il ciel lo sà," aria
. "Non vi lagnate più," recit (Medea, Agilea, Teseo)
. "Chi di mi più beato?," recit (Teseo, Agilea)
32. "Cara! cara, ti dono in pegno il cor," duet (Teseo, Agilea)
V: . "Dunque per vendicarmi," recit (Medea)
33. "Morirò, maventicata," aria (Medea)
. "Scoprii, ma non veduta," recit (Medea)
. "Questo va so, che miri, d'avelenato succo," recit (Medea)
34. "Non è da Re quel cor, che dominar non sà," aria (Egeo)
. "Ma de' popoli l'odio," recit (Medea, Egeo)
35. "Tengo in pugno l'idol mio," aria (Teseo)
. "Sire, a piedi tuoi Teseo s'inchina," recit (Teseo, Egeo)
36. "Giuro, giuro, per quest'acciaro," recit accompagnato (Teseo, Egeo)
. "Ah! perfida Medea!," recit (Arcane, Teseo)
37. "Sì, sì, t'amo, oh caro, quanto un dì t'amai," aria (Agilea)
. "Signore, in questo giorno," recit (Arcane, Egeo, Agilea)
38. "Unito, a un puro affetto," duet (Clizia, Arcane)
. "Ritornello"
. "Essenti del mio sdegno ancor non siete," recit (Medea)
. "Soccorrete, oh Numi!," recit (Agilea, Clizia, Egeo, Teseo)
39. "Il ciel già si compiace," recit accompagnato (Minerva)
40. "Goda ogn'alma in si bel giorno," chorus
Anhang: . "La crudele lontananza," aria (Teseo)
. "No, non piangete, no, che presto tornerò," aria (Teseo)

11. "È tempo, oh luci belle!," aria (Silla)
. "Ritornello"
. "Che se'l foco del mio amore" (unison vv)
. "Mio diletto, che pensi?," recit (Flavia, Lepido)
12. "Sol per te, bell' idol mio," duet (Lepido, Flavia)
. "Bella, lascia i sospiri!," recit (Claudio, Celia)
13. "Mi brilla nel seno un certo seren," aria (Claudio)
. "Mio bel nume, t'arresta!," recit (Silla, Metella)
14. "Hai due vaghe pupillette," aria (Metella)
. "Che miro? oh Dei!," recit (Flavia, Silla, Lepido)
. "Tanto ardisci? Il tuo tetto," recit (Lepido, Silla, Flavia)
15. "Ti lascio, idolo mio, ma teco resta il cor," duettino (Lepido, Flavia)
. "Anima mia! Mio caro!," recit (Claudio, Celia, Silla)
. "Scabro! Lepido sia," recit (Silla)
16. "La vendetta è un cibo al cor," aria (Silla)
. "Oh! perfido consorte!," recit (Metella)
17. "Se'l mio mal da voi dipende, perchè, oh Dei! non l'impedite?," arioso (Claudio)
. "Sì, questi son trofei," recit (Silla)
. "Deh! corri al tuo Signore!," recit (Metella, Silla)
. "T'affretta, oh Scabro," recit (Metella)
18. "Secondate, oh giusti Dei," aria (Metella)
III: . "Quanto devo, oh Metella," recit (Lepido, Metella)
. "Dunque partir," recit (Metella, Lepido)
19. "Io non ti chiedo più," aria (Metella)
. "Alla tua fedeltade," recit (Lepido)
20. "Già respira in petto il core," aria (Lepido)
. "Ritornello"
. "L'imper quanto è più vasto," recit (Silla)
. "Placasti, oh bella diva, il tuo rigore?," recit (Silla, Celia)
21. "Sei già morto, idolo mio," aria (Celia)
. "Rimembranze funeste," recit (Celia, Claudio)
22. "Luci belle, serene stelle," aria (Claudio)
23. "Stelle rubelle, a torto morirò," aria (Flavia)
. "Al fin del mio rigore," recit (Silla, Flavia)
. "Spirto adorato," recit (Flavia, Lepido)
. "Metella, oh Dio!," recit (Silla, Metella)
. "Propizio arrida il cielo," recit (Metella)
. "Pera la feritade!," recit (Lepido, Claudio)
. "De' miei falli pentito," recit (Silla, Lepido, Flavia, Celia, Claudio)
24. "Chi si trova tra procella," chorus

1a.11 "Amadigi di Gaula," opera: HWV11
. "Ouverture"
I: . "Or che di negro ammanto," recit (Amadigi, Dardano)
1a, b. "Pugnerò contro del fato," aria (Dardano) (2 vers)
2. "Oh notte! oh cara notte," recit accompagnato (Amadigi)
3. "Notte amica dei riposi," aria (Amadigi)
. "Ch'impedito è ogni passo," recit (Amadigi)
. "E tu cerchi fuggir?," recit (Melissa, Amadigi)
4. "Non sa temere questo mio petto," aria (Amadigi)
. "Il crudel m'abbandona, e mi detesta," recit (Melissa)
5. "Ah! spietato!," aria (Melissa)
. "Risveglian queste fiamme," recit (Amadigi, Dardano)
6. "Vado, vado, coro al mio tesoro," aria (Amadigi)
. "Deh! ferma, oh Dio!," recit (Dardano)
7. "Agitato il cor mi sento," aria (Dardano)
8. "Sinfonia"
. "Cieli, che fia?," recit (Oriana, Amadigi)
9. "Gioie, venite in sen" (Siciliana), aria (Oriana)
. "In questo istante io provo," recit (Amadigi, Oriana)
10. "È sì dolce il mio contento," aria (Amadigi)
. "Andiamo ora, mio ben," recit (Oriana, Amadigi)
11. "Oh caro mio tesor, deh! presto torna a me," aria (Oriana)
. "Cieli! Numi! che miro?," recit (Amadigi, Dardano, Melissa)
12a, b. "Io godo, scherzo e rido," aria (Melissa) (2 vers)
. "Ferma, deh! ferma, oh Dio!," recit (Amadigi)
13. "O rendetemi il mio bene," aria (Amadigi)
II: . "Io ramingo men vado," recit (Amadigi)
14. "Sussurrate, sussurrate," aria (Amadigi)
. "Numi! che veggio? io manco," recit (Amadigi)
. "Svenne Amadigi," recit (Melissa)
. "Cieli! che sarà mai?," recit (Oriana)
15. "S'estinto è l'idol mio," aria (Oriana)
. "Ma, qual scampo al mio affanno?," recit (Oriana, Amadigi)
16. "T'amai, quant'il mio cor già seppe amarti or che tu cangi amor," aria (Amadigi)

473

. "Chi mai creduto avria," recit (Oriana, Amadigi)
17. "Ti pentirai, crudel! d'avermi offesa un dì," aria (Oriana)
. "Dunque colei, da cui speravo ogni conforto," recit (Amadigi, Melissa)
18. "Crudel, tu non farai, ch'il tuo rigor giammai," duet (Melissa, Amadigi)
. "D'un sventurato amante," recit (Dardano)
19. "Pena tiranna io sento al core," aria (Dardano)
. "Arresta, oh Prence!," recit (Melissa, Dardano)
20. "Se tu brami di godere," aria (Melissa)
. "Ma, se questo non basta," recit (Dardano)
. "Amadigi, mio ben!," recit (Oriana, Dardano)
21. "Tu mia speranza, tu mio conforto," aria (Dardano)
. "Ma qui il rival!," recit (Dardano, Oriana)
. "Cieli! Numi! soccorso," recit (Melissa, Oriana)
22. "Ch'io lasci mai d'amare il caro mio tesoro," aria (Oriana)
. "Mi deride l'amante," recit (Melissa)
23. "Desterò dall'empia Dite," aria (Melissa)
III: . "Dove mi guida," recit (Oriana)
24. "Dolce vita del mio petto," aria (Oriana)
. "Sento, nè so che sia," recit (Melissa)
25. "Vanne lungi dal mio petto, vano amor," aria (Melissa)
. "Se t'offese Oriana," recit (Oriana, Amadigi)
26. "Cangia al fine il tuo rigore," duet (Oriana, Amadigi)
. "No, no! ho già risolto," recit (Melissa)
27. "Han penetrato i detti tuoi l'inferno, ei Numi," recit accompagnato (Dardano)
. "Cieli ingiusti, e inclementi!," recit (Melissa, Amadigi)
28. "Addio, crudo Amadigi!," recit accompagnato (Melissa)
. "Io già sento l'alma in sen," arioso (Melissa)
. "Che orrore!," recit (Oriana, Amadigi)
29. "Sinfonia"
. "Son finiti i tormenti," recit (Orgando, Amadigi, Oriana)
30. "Sento la gioia, ch'in sen mi brilla, e già scintilla," aria (Amadigi)
. "Godete omai felici," recit (Orgando)
31. "Godete, oh cori amanti," chorus (Oriana, Amadigi, ch)
32. "Ballo"
. "Trio"
Anhang: 1. "Affannami, tormentami, è vano il tuo rigor," aria (Oriana)
     2. "Torni la gioia in sen, scherzando col mio cor," aria (S)
     3. "Minacciami, non ho timor," aria (A)

1a.12   "Radamisto," opera: HWV12b
. "Ouverture"
I: 1. "Sommi Dei," arioso (Polissena)
. "Reina, in fausto avviso," recit (Tigrane, Polissena)
2. "Deh! fuggi un traditore!," aria (Tigrane)
3. "L'ingrato non amar, ma rendi a un fido cor," aria (Tigrane)
. "Ecco l'infido sposo," recit (Polissena, Tiridate)
4a, b. "Tu vuoi ch'io parta, io partò," aria (Polissena) (2 vers)
. "Il crudel odio tuo," recit (Farasmane, Tiridate)
5. "Con la strage de' nemici sono avvrezzo a trionfar," aria (Tiridate)
. "Ove seguirmi vuoi," recit (Radamisto, Zenobia)
6. "Cara sposa, amato bene," aria (Radamisto)
. "Ver le nemiche mura," recit (Fraarte/Tigrane, Zenobia, Radamisto, Farasmane)
7a. "Son contenta di morire," aria (Zenobia)
7b. "Deh! fuggi un traditore!," aria (Zenobia)
. "Seguila, oh figlio! E tu ...?," recit (Farasmane, Radamisto, Fraarte/Tigrane)
8. "Perfido! perfido, di a quell'empio tiranno," aria (Radamisto)
. "Fraarte/Tigrane, omai quel ferro," recit (Farasmane, Fraarte/Tigrane)
9. "Son lievi le catene," aria (Farasmane)
. "Coraggio, amici!," recit (Fraarte, Tigrane)
10a. "Sinfonia"
A. "Già, vint'è il nemico," recit (Tiridate, Tigrane, Polissena) (c1720)
B. "Misero Radamisto," recit (Polissena) (c1728)
10b. "Vieni pur amica spene," aria (Polissena)
. "Ferma i dove ti spinge," recit (Polissena, Tiridate)
. "Quento deggio, oh Tigrane," recit (Polissena, Tigrane)
11a, b. "Segni di crudeltà," aria (Tigrane) (2 vers)
. "Pur troppo è vero," recit (Polissena)
12. "Dopo l'orride procelle," aria (Polissena)
II: . "Sposo, vien meno il piè," recit (Zenobia, Radamisto)
13. "Quando mai spietata sorte," arioso (Zenobia)
. "Oh crudo ciel!," recit (Radamisto, Zenobia)
. "Ahimè! fermati!," recit (Radamisto, Tigrane)
. *"Di Polissena bella dal tiranno crudel già disprezzata," recit (Tigrane, Radamisto) (music lost)*
14. "Vuol ch'io serva, amor la bella, e salvo a quella," aria (Tigrane)
. *"Prencipe generoso, sieguo l'orme tue fide," recit (Radamisto) (music lost)*

15. "Ombra cara," aria (Radamisto)
  . "Mitiga il grave affanno," recit (Fraarte/Tigrane, Zenobia)
16. "Lascia pur amica spene le tue pene," aria (Fraarte/Tigrane)
  . "Oh senza esempio dispietata sorte," recit (Zenobia)
17. "Già che morir non posso," aria (Zenobia)
  . "Signor ... E che mi rechi?," recit (Tigrane, Tiridate)
  . "Eccomi a te davante," recit (Zenobia, Tiridate)
18. "Sì che ti renderai," aria (Tiridate)
  . "Nulla già di speranza," recit (Zenobia)
19a. "Fatemi, oh cieli almen saper dov'è il mio ben," aria (Zenobia)
19b. "Ferite, uccidete, oh numi del ciel!," aria (Zenobia)
  . "Questo vago giardin guida là dove," recit (Tigrane, Radamisto, Polissena)
20a, b. "La sorte, il ciel," aria (Tigrane) (2 vers)
  . "Adorato german," recit (Polissena, Radamisto)
21. "Vanne, sorella ingrata," aria (Radamisto)
  . "Tra il german, tra il sposo," recit (Polissena)
22. "Che farà quest'alma mia" (Polissena)
23. "Troppo sofferse," aria (Zenobia)
  . "Due seggi, olà!," recit (Tiridate, Zenobia, Tigrane)
  . "All'innocente frode," recit (Radamisto, Tiridate, Zenobia)
24. "Empio, empio, perverso cor!," arioso (Zenobia)
  . "Ascolta, Ismen: già che il suo sposo è morto," recit (Tiridate)
  . "Oh dì per me felice!," recit (Zenobia, Radamisto) (2 vers)
25a. "Se vive in te il mio cor," duet (Zenobia, Radamisto)
25b. "Parmi che giunta in porto," aria (Zenobia)
III: . "Stanco di più soffrir," recit (Tigrane, Fraarte) (c1720)
26a. "S'adopri il braccio armato," aria (Fraarte) (c1720)
26b. "Troppo sofferse già questo mio petto," aria (Polissena) (c1728)
  . "Reina, Tiridate," recit (Tigrane, Polissena) (c1728)
(27.) "Fatemi, oh cieli, almen," aria (Polissena) (c1728)
  . "So ben che nel mio Amore," recit (Tigrane) (c1720)
27a. "So che vana la speranza," aria (Tigrane) (c1720)
  . "Stanco di più soffrir Re si crudele," recit (Tigrane) (c1728)
27b. "So ch'e vana la speranza," aria (Tigrane) (c1728)
  . "Non temo, idolo mio," recit (Radamisto, Zenobia)
28. "Dolce bene di quest'alma," aria (Radamisto)
  . "O della Tracia, o dell'Armenia," recit (Tiridate, Zenobia, Radamisto, Polissena, Farasmane)
  . "Teco son io, e tu, perfido, mori," recit (Radamisto, Polissena, Farasmane, Tiridate)
29. "Vieni, d'empietà mostro crudele," recit accompagnato (Radamisto)
30. "Vile! se mi dai vita," aria (Radamisto)
  . "Mio Re, mio Tiridate," recit (Polissena, Tiridate)
31a, b. "Barbaro! partirò," aria (Polissena) (2 vers)
  . "Farasmane la segua," recit (Tiridate, Farasmane, Radamisto, Zenobia)
32a, b. "Alzo al volo di mia fama," aria (Tiridate) (2 vers)
  . "Di Radamisto il capo?," recit (Zenobia, Radamisto)
33. "Deggio dunque, oh Dio, lasciarti," aria (Zenobia)
  . "Oh Dio! parte Zenobia," recit (Radamisto)
34. "Qual nave smarrita," aria (Radamisto)
  . "In questo tempio," recit (Tiridate, Farasmane)
  . "Spavento mio? tua infamia," recit (Zenobia, Tiridate)
  . "Morrà Zenobia ancor?," recit (Radamisto, Zenobia, Polissena, Tiridate, Farasmane)
35. "O cedere o perir," quartet (Polissena, Zenobia, Radamisto, Tiridate)
  . "Arrestatevi, oh fidil," recit (Tigrane, Tiridate, Farasmane, Radamisto, Polissena, Zenobia)
36a. "Non ho più affanni no in braccio del mio bene," duet (Zenobia, Radamisto)
36b. "O scemami il diletto," aria (Zenobia)
  . "Festeggi omai la reggia," recit (Radamisto, Zenobia)
37. "Un dì più felice bramar si non lice," chorus
Anhang: (3.) "L'ingrato non amar, marendi a un fido cor," aria (Tigrane)

1a.13 "Muzio Scevola," opera: HWV13
  . "Ouverture"
III: . "Doppo l'arrivo degl'illustri ostaggi sicuro sì," recit (Porsenna, Clelia)
1. "Lungo pensar e dubitar," aria (Clelia)
2. "Eccessi di virtù," recit accompagnato (Porsenna, Muzio)
  . "Pensoso, a passo lento," recit (Clelia, Muzio)
3. "Pupille sdegnose! sareste pietose," aria (Muzio)
4. "Io d'altro regno," recit accompagnato (Clelia)
5. "Dimmi, crudele Amore," aria (Clelia)
  . "Chi mai più giusto sdegno," recit (Muzio, Porsenna)
6. "Volate più dei venti, momenti che scorrete," aria (Porsenna)
  . "Mio cor, pria ti ricorda," recit (Muzio)
7. "Il confine della vita," aria (Muzio)
  . "Patria della bellezza," recit (Fidalma, Irene)
8. "Non ti fidar, perchè il desire," aria (Fidalma)
  . "L'alto dovere alla mia patria," recit (Orazio, Irene)

9. "Come, se ti vedrò," aria (Orazio)
. "Oh, come passi al core," recit (Irene)
10. "Con lui volate, dolci pensieri," aria (Irene)
. "Già m'udiste, oh compagne," recit (Clelia, Porsenna, Muzio)
11. "Spera, che tra le care gioie di bella pace," aria (Muzio)
12a, b. "A chi vive di speranza," aria (Fidalma) (2 vers)
. "Ahi, che pur troppo è ver!," recit (Irene, Fidalma) (2 vers)
. "Fidalma, torni al Campo, o s'uccidà," recit (Tarquinio, Fidalma, Irene)
13. "Ah dolce nome!," aria (Irene)
14. "Sinfonia"
. "Lasciate d'inseguir," recit (Orazio, Irene)
15. "Vivo senza alma, oh bella, per ch'ella vive in te," duet (Orazio, Irene)
. "Piene di lor contento," recit (Muzio, Porsenna, Clelia)
16. "Ma come amar? ... Torna ad amar!," duet (Clelia, Muzio)
. "Dono d'alta fortuna," recit (Orazio, Irene, Porsenna)
17. "Su quell'ara fumante," recit accompagnato (Porsenna, Muzio)
. "Unica erede è del mio regno," recit (Porsenna, Orazio, Irene, Clelia, Muzio)
18. "Sì sarà più dolce amore con la cara liberta!," chorus

1a.14   "Floridante," opera: HWV14
. "Ouverture"
I: 1a, b. "Dimmi, oh spene!," aria (Elmira) (2 vers)
. "Oggi di Tracia," recit (Elmira, Rossane) (2 vers)
2a, b. "Godi, oh spene!," aria (Elmira) (2 vers)
. "Avventurosa Elmira!," recit (Rossane) (2 vers)
3a, b. "Ma un dolce mio pensiero, pensier d'amante cor," aria (Rossane) (2 vers)
3c. "Oh dolce mia sperance, no, non partir da me," aria (Rossane)
4a, b. "Marche" (2 vers)
. "Questo de'miei trionfi," recit (Floridante, Elmira)
5. "Alma mia, sì sol tu sei," aria (Floridante)
. "Giove, compensator," recit (Rossane, Floridante, Elmira, Timante)
. "Oronte, il Re de' Persi," recit (Coralbo, Floridante, Rossane, Elmira)
6. "Dopo l'ombre d'un fiero sospetto," aria (Rossane)
. "Ch'io parta? Ch'io ti perda?," recit (Floridante, Elmira)
7a, b. "Ma pria vedrò le stelle," aria (Elmira) (2 vers)
. "Fammi bersaglio pur," recit (Floridante (2 vers)
8. "Sventurato, godi, oh core abbandonato!," aria (Floridante)
. "Cinto d'allori Floridante torna," recit (Rossane, Oronte)
9. "Finchè lo strale non giunge al segno," aria (Oronte)
. "Novo aspetto di cose," recit (Rossane)
. "Ma viene il prigionier," recit (Rossane, Timante)
10a. "È un sospir che vien dal core," aria (Rossane)
10b, c. "Sospiro, è vero; ma se vuoi saper perchè," aria (Rossane) (2 vers)
. "Per quali vie lontane," recit (Timante) (2 vers)
11a, b, c. "Dopo il nembo e la precella," aria (Timante (3 vers)
. "Al primo cenno, Sire," recit (Floridante, Oronte)
. "Padre, Signor, frena lo sdegno," recit (Elmira, Oronte, Floridante)
12a, b. "Ah mia cara, ah mia cara, se tu resti," duet (Elmira, Floridante) (2 vers)
II: . "Ecco il vago mio sol," recit (Timante, Rossane)
13a, b, c. "Lascioti, oh bella, il volto d'un che vorrebbe ancor," aria (Timante) (3 vers)
. "O fortunati affetti miei," recit (Rossane)
14a, b. "Gode l'alma innamorata," aria (Rossane) (2 vers)
14c. "Oh quanto è caro amor," aria (Rossane)
. "Difficil cosa," recit (Timante, Floridante)
. "Fedele Elmira!," recit (Floridante, Elmira)
. "Glicon, se sei verace," recit (Rossane, Timante, Floridante, Elmira)
15. "Bramo te sola, non penso all'impero," aria (Floridante)
. "Oronte un messo invia," recit (Timante, Elmira, Rossane)
. "Questo è il tempo fatal," recit (Oronte, Elmira)
16a, b. "Barbaro! barbaro! t'odio a morte," aria (Elmira) (2 vers)
. "Convien lasciar libero il corso," recit (Oronte)
17. "Ma non s'aspetti, no," aria (Oronte)
. "Ormai tutta silenzio," recit (Rossane, Timante)
18. "Fuor di periglio di fiero artiglio," duet (Rossane, Timante)
19. "Notte cara, deh! riportami'l mio ben," arioso (Elmira)
. "Parmi ascoltare un lieve moto," recit (Elmira)
. "Oh facil porta," recit (Floridante, Elmira)
. "Qual buona sorte!," recit (Oronte, Elmira, Floridante)
20. "Tacerò, tacerò; ma non potrai," aria (Floridante)
. "Guardia a costei," recit (Oronte)
21. "Sorte nemica," recit accompagnato (Elmira)
. "Fatto ai l'estremo de' tuoi danni," recit (Elmira) (2 vers)
22. "Ma che vuoi più da me, sorte crudele e ria?," aria (Elmira)
III: . "Giunsi allor che fra guardie," recit (Timante, Rossane)
23a, b. "No, non piangete, pupille belle," aria (Timante) (2 vers)

. "Oh sventurati e vani," recit (Rossane, Elmira, Coralbo)
24. "Se risolvi abbandonarmi," aria (Rossane)
. "Or mi si svela," recit (Coralbo, Elmira)
25. "Non lasciar oppressa della sorte," aria (Coralbo)
. "Elmira, a te ritorno," recit (Oronte, Elmira)
. "Numi, che aspetto di dolor!," recit (Floridante, Oronte, Elmira)
26. "Se dolce m'era già viver, cor mio, con te," aria (Floridante)
. "Si mora, sì, vivere a voglia altrui," recit (Elmira)
27. "Vivere per penare, no, che non voglio, no," aria (Elmira)
. "Nella vasta città sparso è già pronto," aria (Elmira)
28a, b. "Vanne, segui'l mio desio!," aria (Rossane) (2 vers)
28c. "Oh cara spene del mio diletto," aria (Rossane)
. "Sevasi alla mia bella," recit (Timante)
29a, b. "Amor commanda, onore invita," aria (Timante) (2 vers)
30. "Questi ceppi, e quest'orrore non mi fanno già spavento," aria (Floridante)
. "Misera amato Prence!," recit (Elmira, Floridante)
. "Tale non era il cenno mio," recit (Oronte, Floridante, Elmira)
. "S'uccida, chi resiste a' nostr'armi," recit (Coralbo, Oronte, Timante, Elmira, Floridante)
31. "Sì, coronar vogl'io col nobil serto d'or," aria (Elmira)
. "Ah! traditor Coralbo," recit (Oronte)
32a, b. "Che veggio? che sento?," aria (Oronte) (2 vers)
33. "Sinfonia"
. "Fido e guerriero," recit (Elmira, Floridante, Rossane, Timante)
34. "Mia bella, godo che son per te," aria (Floridante)
. "La cittade, la reggia," recit (Elmira)
35. "Quando pena la costanza," chorus
Add songs: . "Parmi che giunta in porto," aria (Rossane)
(12.) "Amor ed impietà," aria (Floridante)
Anhang: (4.) "Sinfonia" (frag)
(14.) "Gode l'alma innamorata," aria (Rossane)

1a.15   "Ottone, Rè di Germania," opera: HWV15
. "Ouverture"
I: 1. "Pur che regni il figlio amato," arioso (Gismonda)
. "Chi più lieto è di me?," recit (Adelberto, Gismonda)
2a. "Giunt'in porto è la speranza," aria (Gismonda)
2b. "La speranza è giunta in porto," aria (Gismonda)
. "Vien di Romano inclita figlia," recit (Adelberto, Teofane)
3a. "Bel labbro, formato," aria (Adelberto)
. "E tale Otton?," recit (Teofane)
4. "Falsa imagine, m'ingannasti," aria (Teofane)
5. "Concerto"
. "Te, che assalir," recit (Ottone)
6. "Dal minacciar del vento," aria (Emireno)
. "Tutto a più piete cure," recit (Ottone, Matilda)
7a, b. "Io sperai, io sperai trovar riposo," aria (Ottone) (2 vers)
7c. "Ritorna, o dolce amore, conforta questo sen," aria (Ottone)
7d. "Cervo altier, poichè prostrò," aria (Ottone)
7e. "Vinto è l'Amor da sdegno e gelosia," aria (Matilda)
. "Anch'io sperai," recit (Matilda)
8. "Diresti poi così?," aria (Matilda)
. "Tu la madre d'Otton?," recit (Teofane, Gismonda)
9. "Pensa ad amare, che dal tuo cor," aria (Gismonda)
. "Adelaide, di cui con tanta lode," recit (Teofane, Adelberto, Gismonda)
. "Stendi la bianca mano," recit (Adelberto, Gismonda, Teofane)
. "Giunge Otton! e chi parte?," recit (Teofane)
10. "Affanni del pensier, un sol momento," aria (Teofane)
11. "Sinfonia"
. "Cede il ferro, o la vita!," recit (Ottone, Adelberto)
12. "Tu puoi straziarmi, puoi tormentarmi," aria (Adelberto)
. "È di più mio rival?," recit (Ottone)
13. "Dell'onda i fieri moti sottratto in porto il legno," aria (Ottone)
II: . "Per breve spazio," recit (Matilda, Adelberto, Gismonda)
. "Dove ... Al carcere, oh madre!," recit (Gismonda, Adelberto, Matilda)
14. "Lascia, che nel suo viso," aria (Adelberto)
. "Ah! che più non resisto!," recit (Matilda, Gismonda)
15a. "Pensa, pensa! spietata madre," aria (Matilda)
15b. "Ah! tu non sai, quant'il mio cor," aria (Matilda)
. "Ben a ragion Matilda," recit (Gismonda)
16. "Vieni, o figlio!," aria (Gismonda)
. "Quegli è certo il lio sposo," recit (Teofane, Ottone, Matilda)
17a. "All'orror d'un duolo eterno il mio amore tu condanni," aria (Matilda)
17b. "Spera sì, mi dice il core," aria (Teofane)
. "O illustre Teofane," recit (Ottone, Teofane)
18. "Alla fama, dimmi il vero," aria (Teofane)

. "Con gelosi sospetti," recit (Ottone)
19. "Dopo l'orrore d'un Ciel turbato," aria (Ottone)
20. "O grati orrori!," recit accompagnato (Teofane)
21a. "S'or mi dai pene, o Dio d'amore," aria (Teofane)
21b. "S'io dir potessi al mio crudele," aria (Teofane)
. "Del gran sasso alla mole," recit (Emireno, Adelberto)
22a, b. "Le profonde vie dell'onde," aria (Emireno) (2 vers)
. "Odo gente, dell'antro," recit (Adelberto, Matilda, Ottone, Teofane)
23. "Deh! non dir, che molle amante," aria (Ottone)
. "Già d'ogni intorno," recit (Emireno, Adalberto, Teofane)
. "Odo il suono dell'onda," recit (Gismonda, Matilda)
24a. "Notte cara! a te, a te si deve," duet (Gismonda, Matilda)
24b. "Di far le sue vendette," aria (Matilda)
24c. "Non tardate a festeggiar," duet (Gismonda, Matilda)
III: 25. "Dove sei? dove, sei, dolce mia vita!," aria (Ottone)
. "Già t'invola, tiranno," recit (Gismonda, Ottone)
26. "Trema, trema, tiranno," aria (Gismonda)
27a, b. "Io son tradito," recit accompagnato (Ottone)
28a. "Non a tempre per colpi si fieri," aria (Ottone)
28b. "Tanti affanni ho nel core," aria (Ottone)
28c, d. "Un disprezzato affetto," aria (Ottone) (2 vers)
. "Empi! al vostro attentato," recit (Teofane, Adelberto, Emireno)
29a. "D'inalzar i flutti al ciel," aria (Adelberto)
29b. "A te lascio, l'idol mio," arietta (Adelberto)
. "Perchè in vita tornai?," recit (Teofane, Emireno, Adelberto)
. "Temerario pirata," recit (Adelberto, Emireno, Teofane)
30a. "No, non temere," aria (Emireno)
30b. "Qual cervetta che cacciata," aria (Emireno)
. "Si me traete," recit (Teofante)
31a. "Dir li potessi vedi, crudele," aria (Teofane)
31b. "Ben chè mi sia crudele," aria (Teofane)
. "Deh! ti trattiene, o bella," recit (Emireno, Teofane)
32. "No, non temere, oh bella!," aria (Emireno)
. "Pur cangiasti alla fin," recit (Teofane)
33. "Gode l'alma consolata," aria (Teofane)
. "Uno de'servi miei anche mi disse," recit (Matilda, Ottone, Gismonda)
34a, b. "Nel suo sangue, e nel tuo pianto laverò del cor la colpa," aria (Matilda) (2 vers)
. "Matilda, arresta il piede," recit (Emireno, Adelberto, Gismonda, Matilda, Ottone)
. "Frena, crudel, la dispevata destra," recit (Teofane, Ottone)
35. "A' teneri affetti il cor s'abbandoni," duet (Teofane, Ottone)
. "Ma qual caso, qual Dio," recit (Ottone, Teofane, Emireno, Gismonda, Matilda, Adelberto)
36. "Faccia ritorno l'antica pace," chorus
Anhang: (3b.) "Cara, tu nel mio petto," aria (Adelberto)
(21.) "S'or mi dai pene, o Dio d'amore," aria (Teofane) (2 vers)
. "Sinfonia" (III/3)
(29.) "D'inalzar i flutti al ciel," aria (Adelberto) (frag)
(21c.) "Tra queste care ombre gradite," aria (Teofane)
. "Sinfonia" (II/1)

1a.16 "Flavio, Rè de' Langobardi," opera: HWV16
. "Ouverture"
I: . "Fra i ciechi orror notturni partirò," recit (Vitige, Teodata)
1. "Ricordati, mio ben," duet (Vitige, Teodata)
2. "Sinfonia"
. "Lotario, al sacro nodo," recit (Ugone, Lotario, Guido, Teodata)
. "Con l'alma riverente," recit (Emilia, Guido, Ugone, Lotario, Teodata)
3. "Quanto dolci, quanto care son le gioje nel mio sen," aria (Emilia)
. "Son pur felice al fine; ahi!," recit (Guido)
4. "Già la fama," aria (Guido)
. "Oh dell' Italo soglio eccelso Nume," recit (Ugone, Flavio, Teodata)
5. "Ah non posso nel mio core," aria (Teodata)
. "Della mia prole Emilia," recit (Lotario, Flavio, Vitige)
. "Di qual sovrano," recit (Ugone, Flavio, Lotario)
6. "Se a te vissi fedele, fedele ancor sarò," aria (Lotario)
. "Vitige. Mio Signore," recit (Flavio, Vitige)
7. "Di quel bel che m'innamora," aria (Flavio)
. "Io vo temendo, oh Dio," recit (Vitige)
8. "Che bel contento sarebbe amore," aria (Vitige)
. "Ah! Guido, Guido!," recit (Ugone, Guido)
A. "Guido, Lotario, Ugone," recit (Guido)
B. "Amor, Emilia, onore, Guido, Lotario," recit (Guido)
9a, b. "L'armelin vita non cura," aria (Guido) (2 vers)
. "Guido! consorte!," recit (Emilia, Guido)
. "Chi mai l'intende, oh Dio!," recit (Emilia)
10. "Amante stravagante," aria (Emilia)

II: . "Al tuo cenno Reale," recit (Teodata, Flavio)
. "Dove, dove mi celo?," recit (Ugone, Flavio, Teodata)
. "Ah Teodata, Teodata!," recit (Ugone, Teodata)
11a, b. "Fato tiranno e crudo," aria (Ugone) (2 vers)
. "Dunque per le mie nozze," recit (Emilia, Lotario)
12. "Vado; sorte crudele," aria (Lotario)
. "Che mai chiedete, oh stelle," recit (Emilia, Guido)
13. "Parto, sì, sì, ma non so poi," aria (Emilia)
. "Privarmi ancora," recit (Guido)
14. "Rompo i lacci, e frango i dardi," aria (Guido)
. "Di Teodata," recit (Flavio, Vitige)
15. "Chi può mirare e non amare," aria (Flavio)
. "Teodata! Vitige, ah," recit (Vitige, Teodata)
16. "Con un' vezzo, con un' riso fingerò d'innamorarmi," aria (Teodata)
. "Amo, e quel ben ch'adoro io condur deggio," recit (Vitige)
17. "Non credo instabile chi mi piagò," aria (Vitige)
. "Io deluso? Lotario?," recit (Lotario, Guido)
. "Ah misera! che veggio? ah!," recit (Emilia, Lotario)
18. "Ma chi punir desio? l'idolo del cor mio," aria (Emilia)
III: . "Alma, tu non l'intendi," recit (Flavio, Emilia, Ugone)
19. "Da te parto, da te parto," aria (Emilia)
. "Guido Lotario iccise?," recit (Flavio, Vitige, Teodata)
20. "Corrispondi a chi t'adora," arioso e recit (Vitige, Flavio, Teodata)
21. "Starvi a canto e non languire," aria (Flavio)
. "Barbara Teodata," recit (Vitige, Teodata)
22. "Che colpa è la mia, se Amor vuol così?," aria (Teodata)
. "Del niovo amante," recit (Vitige)
23. "Sirti, scogli, tempeste," aria (Vitige)
24. "Oh Guido! oh mio tiranno!," recit accompagnato (Emilia, Guido)
25. "Amor, nel mio penar," aria (Guido)
. "Vitige! Mia Reina!," recit (Teodata, Vitige, Flavio)
. "Signor, se il mio delitto," recit (Guido, Ugone, Flavio)
. "Al tuo piede, oh Regnante," recit (Emilia, Flavio, Ugone, Vitige, Guido)
26. "Deh! perdona, oh dolce bene," duet (Emilia, Guido)
. "E tu, Vitige, in pena," recit (Flavio, Vitige, Teodata, Ugone, Guido)
27. "Doni pace ad ogni core," chorus
Anhang: (9.) "Il suol che preme, l'aura che spira," aria (Guido)
(12a, b.) "Dille ch'il core tutto furore," aria (Lotario) (2 vers)

1a.17 "Giulio Cesare in Egitto," opera: HWV17
. "Ouverture"
I: 1. "Viva, viva il nostro Alcide!," chorus
2. "Presti omai l'Egizia terra," aria (Cesare)
. "Curio, Cesare viene," recit (Cesare, Curio)
. "Questa è Cornelia. Oh sorte!," recit (Cesare, Curio, Cornelia, Sesto)
. "La Reggia Tolomeo t'offre in albergo," recit (Achilla, Cesare, Sesto, Cornelia, Curio)
3. "Empio, dirò, tu sei, togliti a gli occhi miei," aria (Cesare)
. "Già torna in se," recit (Curio, Sesto, Cornelia)
4. "Priva son d'ogni conforto," aria (Cornelia)
. "Vani sono i lamenti," recit (Sesto)
5. "Svegliatevi nel core, furie d'un alma offesa," aria (Sesto)
A. "Regni Cleopatra," recit (Cleopatra, Nireno, Tolomeo)
6a. "Non disperar, non disperar; chi sa?," aria (Cleopatra)
B. "Reina, infausti eventi!," recit (Nireno, Cleopatra)
6b. "La speranza all'alma mia," aria (Nireno)
6c. "La speranza," aria (Nireno/Cleopatra)
. "Sire, Signor! Achilla," recit (Achilla, Tolomeo)
7. "L'empio, sleale, indegno," aria (Tolomeo)
8. "Alma del gran Pompeo," recit accompagnato (Cesare)
. "Due nobile donzelle," recit (Curio, Cesare, Cleopatra)
9. "Non è si vago e bello il fiornel prato," aria (Cesare)
. "Cleopatra, vincesti," recit (Nireno, Cleopatra)
10. "Tutto può donna vezzosa," aria (Cleopatra)
. "Ferma Cleopatra," recit (Nireno, Cleopatra)
11a. "Nel tuo seno," arioso (Cornelia)
11b. "La speranza all'alma mia," aria (Cornelia)
. "Ma che! vile e negletta," recit (Cornelia, Cleopatra, Sesto, Nireno)
12. "Cara speme, questo core," aria (Sesto)
. "Vegli pure il germano," recit (Cleopatra)
13. "Tu la mia stella sei," aria (Cleopatra)
. "Cesare, alla tua destra," recit (Tolomeo, Cesare, Achilla)
14. "Va tacito e nascosto, quand' avido è di preda," aria (Cesare)
. "Sire, con Sesto il figlio," recit (Achilla, Tolomeo, Cornelia, Sesto)
. "Cornelia, in quei tuoi lumi," recit (Achilla, Cornelia, Sesto)
15. "Tu sei il cor di questo core," aria (Achilla)

479

. "Madre! Mia vita!," recit (Sesto, Cornelia) (2 vers)
16a. "Son nata a lagrimar, e il dolce mio conforto," duet (Sesto, Cornelia)
16b. "S'armi a miei danni, l'empio tiranno non so temere sua crudeltà," aria (Sesto)
II: A. "Esegiusti, oh Niren," recit (Cleopatra, Nireno) (c1724)
    B. "Giunto è Cesare in corte?," recit (Cleopatra, Nireno) (c1725)
(17.) "Chi perde un momento d'un dolce contento," aria (Nireno) (c1725)
. "Da Cleopatra apprenda," recit (Nireno, Cesare)
17a. "Sinfonia"
17b. "Sinfonia"
. "Cieli, e qual delle sfere," recit (Cesare, Nireno)
18a. "Sinfonia"
18b. "Sinfonia"
. "Giulio, che miri?," recit (Cesare)
19. "V'adoro, pupille," aria (Cleopatra)
. "Non ha in cielo il Tonante," recit (Cesare)
. "Vola, vola, mio cor," recit (Cesare, Nireno)
20. "Se in fiorito ameno prato," aria (Cesare)
21. "Deh piangete, oh mesti lumi," arioso (Cornelia)
. "Bella, non lagrimare!," recit (Achilla, Cornelia)
. "Bella, placa lo sdegno!," recit (Tolomeo, Cornelia, Achilla)
22. "Se a me non sei crudelle," aria (Achilla)
. "Bella, cotanto abborri," recit (Tolomeo, Cornelia)
23. "Si spietata, il tuo rigore," aria (Tolomeo)
. "Su, che si tarda?," recit (Cornelia, Sesto)
. "Cornelia, infausto nove," recit (Nireno, Cornelia, Sesto)
24. "Cessa omai di sospirare!," aria (Cornelia)
. "Figlio non è," recit (Sesto)
25. "L'angue offeso mai riposa," aria (Sesto)
. "Esser qui deve in breve l'idolo mio sen," recit (Cleopatra)
26. "Venere bella, per un istante," aria (Cleopatra)
. "Che veggio, oh Numi?," recit (Cesare, Cleopatra)
. "Cesare, sei tradito," recit (Curio, Cesare, Cleopatra)
27. "Al lampo dell'armi quest'alma guerriera," aria & chorus (Cesare, Voci di congiurati)
28. "Che senot? oh Dio!," recit accompagnato (Cleopatra)
29. "Se pietà di me non senti," aria (Cleopatra)
30a. "Belle dee," arioso & recit (Tolomeo, Cornelia, Sesto)
. "Sire, prendi!," recit (Achilla, Tolomeo, Sesto, Cornelia)
30b. "Dal mio brando si veda umiliata," aria (Tolomeo)
. "Ecco in tutto perduta," recit (Sesto, Cornelia)
31a. "L'aure che spira," aria (Sesto)
31b. "Scorta siate a passi miei," aria (Sesto)
31c. "L'aure che spira tiranno e fiero," aria (Cornelia)
III: . "In tal modi si premia," recit (Achilla)
32. "Dal fulgor di questa spada," aria (Achilla)
33. "Sinfonia"
. "Vinta cadesti," recit (Tolomeo, Cleopatra)
34a. "Domerò la tua fierezza," aria (Tolomeo)
34b. "Dal mio brando si veda umiliata," aria (Tolomeo)
. "E pur così in un giorno," recit (Cleopatra)
35. "Piangerò, piangerò la sorte mia," aria (Cleopatra)
36. "Dall'ondoso periglio ... Aure, aure, deh, per pietà," recit accompagnato & aria (Cesare)
. "Cerco in van Tolomeo," recit (Sesto, Achilla, Cesare, Nireno)
. "Lascia questo sigillo. Oh Dei!," recit (Cesare, Sesto)
37. "Quel torrente, che cade dal monte," aria (Cesare)
  A. "Tutto lice sperar," recit (Sesto, Nireno)
  B. "Tutto lice sperar," recit (Sesto)
38a. "La giustizia ha già sull'arco pronto strale," aria (Sesto)
38b. "Sperai ne m'ingannai," aria (Sesto)
39. "Voi, che mie fide ancelle," recit accompagnato (Cleopatra)
. "Forzai l'ingresso," recit (Cesare, Cleopatra)
40. "Da tempeste il legno infranto," aria (Cleopatra)
. "Cornelia, è tempo omai," recit (Tolomeo, Cornelia)
. "T'arresta, oh genitrice!," recit (Sesto, Tolomeo, Cornelia)
41. "Non ha più che temere," aria (Cornelia)
42a. "Sinfonia"
42b. "La Marche"
. "Qui Curio vincitor," recit (Nireno, Cesare, Sesto, Cornelia, Cleopatra)
43. "Caro! più amabile beltà," duet (Cleopatra, Cesare)
. "Goda pur or l'Egitto," recit (Cesare)
44. "Ritorni omai nel nostro core," chorus
Add songs (c1730): (10.) "Parolette, vezzi e sguardi," aria (Cleopatra)
(35.) "Io vo' di duolo in duolo," aria (Cleopatra)
Anhang: (30a.) "Presti omai l'Egizia terra," aria (Cesare)
(16.) "Son nato a sospirar," duet (Cornelia, Sesto)
(10.) "Tutto può donna vezosa," aria (Berenice)

(6.) "Non di sperar, chi sa, se al Regno non avrai," aria (Cleopatra)
(13.) "Di te compagna fida," aria (Berenice)
(9.) "Non è si vago e bello il fior nel prato," aria (Cesare)
(11./39.) "Nel tuo seno, amico sasso," aria (Cornelia)
(13.) "Speranza mi dice che questo mio petto," aria (Cleopatra)
(14.) "Questo core incatenato," aria (Cesare)
(4.) "Priva son d'ogni conforto," aria (Cornelia)
(23.) "Nobil cor non può mirare," aria (Berenice)
(26.) "Venere bella, per un istante, deh! mi concedi," aria (Cleopatra)
(38a.) "Per dar vita all'idol mio corro ardita," aria (Cleopatra)
(35.) "Troppo crudeli siete affanni del mio seno," aria (Cleopatra)
(35.) "Piangerò la sorte mia, si crudele e tanto ria," aria (Cleopatra)

1a.18   "Tamerlano," opera: HWV18
. "Ouverture"
I: 1. "Introduzione"
. "Esci, esci, oh Signore!," recit (Andronico)
2. (insts)
. "Prence, lo so, ti devo," recit (Bajazet, Andronico)
3. "Forte e lieto a morte andrei," aria (Bajazet)
. "Non si perda di vista," recit (Andronico, Tamerlano)
4. "Vo' dar pace a un alma altiera," aria (Tamerlano)
. "Il Tartaro ama Asteria," recit (Andronico)
5. "Bella Asteria, bella Asteria, il tuo cor mi difenda," aria (Andronico)
. "Il fortunato Andronico," recit (Asteria, Tamerlano)
6. "Dammi pace, oh volto amato," aria (Tamerlano)
. "Serve Asteria di prezzo," recit (Asteria)
7. "Se non mi vuol amar, almeno il traditor," aria (Asteria)
. "Non ascolto più nulla," recit (Bajazet, Andronico, Asteria)
8. "Ciel e terra armi di sdegno," aria (Bajazet)
. "Asteria, non parlate?," recit (Andronico, Asteria)
9. "Deh! Lasciatemi il nemico," aria (Asteria)
. "Così la sposa," recit (Irene, Leone, Andronico)
10a, b. "Dal crudel che m'ha tradita," aria (Irene) (2 vers)
11. "Chi vide mai," recit accompagnato (Andronico)
12. "Benche mi sprezzi l'idol che adoro," aria (Andronico)
II: . "Amico, tengo," recit (Tamerlano, Andronico)
13. "Bella gara che faranno," aria (Tamerlano)
. "Qui l'infedel! cogliamo," recit (Asteria, Andronico)
14. "Non è più tempo, no," aria (Asteria)
15. "Ah no! dove trascorri," recit accompagnato (Andronico)
16. "Cerco in vano di placare," aria (Andronico)
. "Signor, vergine illustre chiede accostarvi," recit (Leone, Tamerlano, Irene)
. "Senti, chiunque tu sia," recit (Asteria, Irene)
. "Gran cose espone Asteria"
17a, b. "Par che mi nasca in seno," aria (Irene) (2 vers)
18. "Amor dà guerra e pace," aria (Leone)
. "Dov'è mia figlia," recit (Bajazet, Andronico)
19. "A suoi piedi padre esangue," aria (Bajazet)
. "Se Asteria mi tradisce," recit (Andronico)
20. "Più d'una tigre altero e perfido e severo," aria (Andronico)
. "Al soglio, al soglio," recit (Tamerlano, Asteria, Bajazet, Andronico)
21. "E per lei vengo," recit accompagnato (Irene, Asteria, Tamerlano, Bajazet, Andronico)
22. "Voglio stragi," trio (Asteria, Tamerlano, Bajazet)
. "Padre, dimmi," recit (Asteria (2 vers)
23. "No, no, il tuo sdegno," aria (Bajazet)
. "Andronico, son più l'infida amante?," recit (Asteria) (2 vers)
24. "No, che del tuo gran cor io sono l'offensor," aria (Andronico)
. "Amica, son quella superba donna?," recit (Asteria) (3 vers)
25. "No, che sei tanto costante," aria (Irene) (2 vers)
. "Sì, sì, son vendicata," recit (Asteria) (2 vers)
26. "Se potessi un dì placare," aria (Asteria)
III: . "Figlia, siam rei," recit (Bajazet, Asteria)
27. "Cor di padre, e cor d'amante," aria (Asteria)
. "Andronico, il mio amore," recit (Tamerlano, Andronico, Asteria)
. "Come? Asteria, tu a piè del Tamerlano?," recit (Bajazet, Tamerlano, Andronico)
28. "A dispetto d'un volto ingrato," aria (Tamerlano)
. "Figlia, con atto vil," recit (Bajazet, Asteria, Andronico)
. "Asteria, allor che andaste," recit (Andronico, Asteria, Leone)
29. "Vivo in te, mio caro bene!," duet (Asteria, Andronico)
. "Reina, è vuoto," recit (Leone, Irene)
30. "Crudel più non son io, amarlo è dover mio," aria (Irene)
. "Se Irene al trono ascende," recit (Leone)
31. "Se ad un costante core tu non dai pace, Amore," aria (Leone)
. "Eccoti Bajazete, dall'angusto ritiro," recit (Tamerlano, Bajazet, Andronico)

32. "Se non mi rendi il mio tesoro," aria (Andronico)
. "Eccomi, che si chiede?," recit (Asteria, Tamerlano, Andronico, Bajazet)
33. "Padre, amante," recit accompagnato (Asteria)
34. "Folle sei, folle sei lo consenti!," arioso & recit (Asteria, Andronico, Bajazet, Tamerlano)
35. "E il soffrirete, d'onestade, oh Numi?," recit accompagnato (Bajazet)
36. "Empio, empio, per farti guerra," aria (Bajazet)
. "Signor, fra tante cure," recit (Irene, Tamerlano)
37. "Vedrò ch'un dì si cangerà del mio penar la crudeltà," duet (Irene, Tamerlano)
. "Vieni, Asteria, e saprai quanto m'impose," recit (Leone, Andronico, Tamerlano, Asteria)
. "Oh per me lieto, avventuroso giorno!," recit (Bajazet, Tamerlano)
38. "Fremi, mi naccia!," recit accompagnato (Bajazet, Asteria)
39. "Figlia mia, non pianger, no," arioso, Bajazet)
40. "Tu, spietato, il vedrai," recit accompagnato (Bajazet)
41. "Barbaro! al fin sei sazio ancor?," recit accompagnato (Andronico, Asteria)
42. "Padre amato, in me riposa," aria (Asteria)
A. "Seguitela, miei fidi," recit (Irene, Andronico, Tamerlano)
B. "A me convien seguir," recit (Andronico, Tamerlano, Irene)
C. "Barbaro! or manca solo," recit (Asteria, Tamerlano, Andronico)
43. "Coronata di giglie di rose," duet (Andronico, Tamerlano)
. "Ora invita regina," recit (Tamerlano, Irene)
44. "D'atra notte già mirasi a scorno d'un bel giorno," chorus (Irene, ch)
Anhang: I: . "Prence, dunque vi devo questi di liberta brievi respiri," recit (Bajazet, Andronico)
  (1a.) "Lacci, ferri," arioso (Bajazet)
. "Sciol gansi, o-là, quei nodi!," recit (Andronico, Bajazet)
  (2a.) "Conservate per mia figlia," aria (Bajazet)
  (1b.) "Esci, esci, oh Signore!," recit accompagnato (Andronico, Bajazet)
  (14a.) "Non è più tempo, no," aria (Asteria)
  (16a.) "Cerco in vano di placare," aria (Andronico) (frag)
  (24a.) "No, che del tuo gran cor, io sono l'offensor," aria (Andronico) (frag)
III: . "Figlia, siam rei io di schernito sdegno," recit (Bajazet, Asteria)
  (27a.) "Su la sponda del pigro Lete," aria (Bajazet)
  (28a.) "Fiero, mi rivedrete," aria (Tamerlano)
. "Principessa infelice," recit (Leone)
  (31a.) "Nel mondo e nell' abisso io non pavento," aria (Leone)
. "Hai vinto, hai vinto omai," recit (Andronico, Asteria, Irene, Tamerlano, Leone)
. "Sì, Bajazette è morto, raccogli pur," recit accompagnato (Asteria)

1a.19   "Rodelinda, Regina de' Langobardi," opera: HWV19
. "Overture"
I: 1. "Ho perduto il caro sposo," aria (Rodelinda)
. "Regina? Grimoaldo," recit (Grimoaldo, Rodelinda)
  2. "L'empio rigor del fato," aria (Rodelinda)
. "Duca, vedesti mai," recit (Grimoaldo, Garibaldo)
. "E tanto da che sei Re," recit (Eduige, Grimoaldo)
  3. "Io già t'amai," aria (Grimoaldo)
. "E tu dice d'amarmi?," recit (Eduige, Garibaldo)
  4. "Lo farò; lo farò, dirò spietato," aria (Eduige)
. "Eduige, t'inganni," recit (Garibaldo)
  5. "Di Cupido impiego i vani," aria (Garibaldo)
  6. "Sinfonia"
. "Pompe vane di morte!," recit accompagnato (Bertarido)
  7a, b. "Dove sei? amato bene!," aria (Bertarido)
. "Ma giunge Unulfo: oh Dio! deh! mio fedel," recit (Bertarido, Unulfo)
  8. "Ombre, piante, urne funeste!," recit (Rodelinda)
  9. "Ombra del mio bel sol," recit accompagnato (Bertarido, Unulfo)
. "Baci inutili e vani," recit (Garibaldo, Bertarido, Unulfo, Rodelinda)
  10. "Morrai sì, l'empia tua testa," aria (Rodelinda)
. "E ben, Duca, poss'io all ardor del cor mio," recit (Grimoaldo, Garibaldo)
  11. "Se per te giiungo a godere," aria (Grimoaldo)
. "Unulfo, oh Dio!," recit (Bertarido, Unulfo)
  12a, b. "Sono i colpi della sorte per un alma invita e forte," aria (Unulfo) (2 vers)
  13. "Sì, l'infida consorte," recit accompagnato (Bertarido)
  14. "Confusa si miri l'infida consorte," aria (Bertarido)
II: . "Già perdesti, oh Signora, il nome di Regina," recit (Garibaldo, Eduige)
. "Rodelinda, si mestra ritorni," recit (Eduige, Rodelinda)
  15. "De' miei scherni per far le vendete," aria (Eduige)
. "Rodelinda, è pur ver ...?," recit (Grimoaldo, Rodelinda, Unulfo, Garibaldo)
  16. "Spietati, io vi giurai, se al mio figlio il cor," aria (Rodelinda)
. "Unulfo, Garibaldo," recit (Grimoaldo, Unulfo, Garibaldo)
  17a. "Prigioniera ho l'alma in pena," aria (Grimoaldo)
  17b. "Non pensi quell'altera," aria (Grimoaldo)
. "Massime così indegne," recit (Unulfo, Garibaldo)
  18. "Tirannia gli diede il regno gli e'l conservi crudeltà," aria (Garibaldo)
. "Sì, sì, fellon t'intendo," recit (Unulfo)
  19. "Fra tempeste funeste a quest'alma," aria (Unulfo)

20. "Con rauco mormorio piangono al pianto mio," aria (Bertarido)
. "Dell'estinto germano," recit (Eduige)
. "Ah, no; che non m'inganna," recit (Eduige, Bertarido, Unulfo)
21. "Scacciata dal suo nido sen vola in altro lido," aria (Bertarido)
. "Vive il mio sposo?, recit (Rodelinda, Unulfo)
22. "Ritorna, oh caro e dolce mio tesoro!," aria (Rodelinda)
. "Ah! sì, ecco lo sposo," recit (Rodelinda, Bertarido, Grimoaldo)
23a. "Tuo drudo è mio rivale," aria (Grimoaldo)
23b. "Sì, rivedrò la sola mia speranza," aria (Bertarido)
. "Non ti bastò, consorte," recit (Rodelinda, Bertarido)
24a. "Io t'abbraccio, e più che morte aspro e forte," duet (Rodelinda, Bertarido)
24b. "Se il cor si perde, oh caro!," duet (Rodelinda, Bertarido) (= Tolomeo, HWV25/19)
III: . "Del german nel periglio," recit (Eduige, Unulfo)
25. "Un zeffiro spirò che sereno quest'alma," aria (Unulfo)
. "Con opra giusta," recit (Eduige)
26. "Quanto più fiera tempesta freme," aria (Eduige)
. "Oh, falso è Bertarido," recit (Garibaldo, Grimoaldo)
27. "Tra sospetti, affetti, e timori," aria (Grimoaldo)
28. "Chi di voi fu più infedele," arioso (Bertarido)
29. "Ma non che so dal remoto balcon," recit accompagnato (Bertarido, Unulfo)
. "Non temere Signore?," recit (Eduige, Rodelinda)
30a. "Se'l mio duol non è si forte," aria (Rodelinda)
30b. "Ahi perchè, giusto ciel, tanta pena a questo cor?," aria (Rodelinda)
. "Amico! ah! che a me duole," recit (Bertarido, Unulfo)
31. "Se fiera belva ha cinto fra le catene il piede," aria (Bertarido)
32. "Fatto inferno è il mio petto," recit accompagnato (Grimoaldo)
32a. "Pastorello d'un povero armento pur dorme contento," aria (Grimoaldo)
33b. "Vi sento, sì, vi sento rimorsi entrò al mio cor," aria (Grimoaldo) (= Lotario, HWV26/27)
. "Che miro? amica sorte," recit (Garibaldo, Grimoaldo)
. "To morrai, traditor!," recit (Bertarido, Grimoaldo, Rodelinda)
(34.) "Vivi tiranno, vivi tiranno," aria (Bertarido)
. "Ecco ti innanzi il Reo," recit (Unulfo, Eduige, Grimoaldo, Bertarido, Rodelinda)
34a. "Mio caro bene! caro, caro!," aria (Rodelinda)
. "Sposa, figlio, sorella," recit (Bertarido)
(34b.) "D'ogni crudel martir il torbido pensier," duet (Rodelinda, Bertarido)
35. "Dopo la notte oscura più lucido, più chiaro," chorus
Anhang: (8b.) "Ombre piante, urne funeste," arioso (Rodelinda)
(16./21b.) "Ben spesso in vago prato un aspide e celato," aria (Rodelinda)
(31.) "Verrete a consolarmi se torno a rimirarvi," aria (Bertarido)

1a.20 "Publio Cornelio Scipione," opera: HWV20
. "Ouverture"
I: 1. "Marche"
2. "Abbiam vinto e Iberia doma," arioso (Scipione)
. "A Tiberio io, e a Sesto," recit (Scipione, Lelio, Berenice, Armira)
3. "Scaccia, oh bella, dal seno il timore!," arioso (Scipione)
. "Oh Lucejo! E qual nome con dolor proferisti?," recit (Berenice, Lelio, Armira)
4. "Un caro amante, gentil costante, mi diede Amor," aria (Berenice)
. "Quando vengo," recit (Lucejo)
5. "Lamentandomi corro a volo," aria (Lucejo)
. "Oh quante grazie Amore," recit (Scipione, Lelio)
. "Armira, e perchè mesta?," recit (Lelio, Armira)
6. "Libera chi non è i lacci del suo piè," aria (Armira)
. "Indegna è in ver," recit (Lelio)
. "Del vincitore, oh bella," recit (Lelio, Berenice)
7. "No, non sì teme d'incerto affanno," aria (Lelio)
8. "Oh sventurato," recit accompagnato (Berenice)
9. "Dolci aurette che spirate," aria (Berenice)
. "Molli aurette, v'arrestate!... E che ascolto! che veggio?," arioso & recit (Lucejo, Berenice)
10. "Dimmi, cara, dimmi: 'tu dei morir,' " aria (Lucejo)
. "Ah, t'ascondi! non lunge," recit (Berenice, Lucejo)
. "Guardin gli Dei Scipione!," recit (Berenice, Scipione, Lucejo)
11. "Vanne! Vanne, parti, audace, altiero," aria (Berenice)
. "Giunsi a tempo; si salvi," recit (Lelio, Lucejo, Scipione)
12. "Figlia di reo timor, fredo velen," aria (Lucejo)
II: 13. "Sinfonia"
. "Mercè del vincitor," recit (Ernando, Lelio)
14. "Braccio si valoroso," aria (Ernando)
15. "Tutta raccolta ancor nel palpitante cor," arioso (Berenice)
. "Di libertade il dono," recit (Scipione, Berenice)
16a. "So gli altri debellar," aria (Scipione)
16b. "Pensa, oh bella, alla mia speme," aria (Scipione)
. "Ecco, oh Prence," recit (Lelio, Lucejo, Berenice)
17. "Parto, parto, fuggo; resta, e godi," aria (Lucejo)
. "Seguilo, oh duce!," recit (Berenice, Lelio)

18. "Come onda incalza altr'onda," aria (Berenice)
. "Importuno tu sei," recit (Armira, Lelio)
19. "Temo che lusinghiero," aria (Lelio)
. "Lusingarlo mi giova," recit (Armira)
20. "Voglio contenta allor," aria (Armira)
. "Qui torno, e qui," recit (Lucejo, Armira)
. " 'Bella! mi conforti,' " recit (Berenice, Lucejo, Armira)
. "Tanto s'ardisce ancora," recit (Scipione, Lucejo, Berenice)
. "Numi, lo difendete!," recit (Berenice, Scipione, Lelio, Lucejo)
21. "Cedo a Roma, e cedo a te," aria (Lucejo)
. "Signor, del tuo fisso pensar," recit (Berenice, Scipione)
22. "Scoglio d'immota fronte nel torbido elemento," aria (Berenice)
III: . "Miseri affeti mieil," recit (Scipione)
. "Scipione, a privata udienza Ernando vedi," recit (Lelio, Ernando, Scipione)
23. "Tutta rea la vita umana," aria (Ernando)
. "Degni amici di Roma," recit (Scipione, Lelio)
24. "Il poter quelche brami," recit accompagnato (Scipione)
. "In questo luogo, oh Prence," recit (Lelio, Berenice, Lucejo)
25. "Se mormora rivo o fronda," aria (Lucejo)
. "Più resister non posso," recit (Lelio)
26. "Ah! Scipion, dove sei?," recit accompagnato (Berenice)
. "Tenerezza del cor, cedo," recit accompagnato (Scipione)
27a. "Il fulgido seren d'un rapido balen già l'ombre dileguò," aria (Berenice)
27b. "Già cessata è la procella e la calma," aria (Berenice)
28a. "Sinfonia"
28b. "Sinfonia"
. "All'invito," recit (Ernando, Scipione, Berenice)
. "Oh dolce figlia!" (Ernando)
29. "Gioja sì speri, sì," aria (Scipione)
. "Tu, d'indibile Figlia," recit (Lelio, Armira)
30. "Nell' amor nella speranza," aria (Armira)
. "Prence, il rigor," recit (Lelio, Lucejo)
31. "Del debella la gloria e il bel piacer d'amor," aria (Lelio)
. "Dove, oh Prencipe amato?," recit (Berenice, Lucejo)
32. "Bella notte senza stelle," aria (Berenice)
. "Squarciasi'l fosco vel," recit (Lucejo)
33. "Come al nazio boschetto," aria (Lucejo)
. "Quanto timor costate," recit (Lucejo)
34. "Son pellegrino che d'alto vede," aria (Lucejo)
35. "Dopo il nemico oppresso," arioso (Scipione)
. "Venga Lucejo!," recit (Scipione, Lelio, Ernando, Lucejo, Berenice)
36. "In testimon io chiamo," recit accompagnato (Lucejo)
37. "Sì fuggano i tormenti," duet (Berenice, Lucejo)
. "Marte riposi," recit (Scipione)
38. "Faranno gioja intera vittoria, pace e amor," chorus
Production of 1730/1: I: . "Ascrivo a mia gran sorte Donna o Dea," recit (Lelio, Armira)
5. "Lusinghe più care," aria (Armira) (= Alessandro, HWV21/6)
. "Oh quante grazie Amore," recit (Scipione, Lelio)
. "Tra speranze, affetti e timore," aria (Scipione) (= Rodelinda, HWV19/27)
. "Generoso Scipione!," recit (Lelio)
. "Armira, e perchè mesta?," recit (Lelio, Armira)
6. "Libera chi non è i lacci del suo piè," aria (Armira)
7. "No, non sì teme d'incerto affanno," aria (Lelio)
III: . "Inquieti miei pensieri," recit (Lelio)
. "Lelio: a Ernando richiesi," recit (Scipione, lelio)
29. "Pregi son d'un alma grande," aria (Scipione)
35. "Dopo il nemico opresso voglio esser di me stesso," arioso (Scipione)
. "Venga Lucejo," recit (Scipione)
Anhang: . "Sì, tutto del seren," recit (Ernando, Berenice)
. "T'aspetta fuor dell'onde," aria (Rosalba/Ernando) (= Partenope, HWV27/8)
. "No, l'intero diletto," recit (Berenice)
. *"Mi par sognar," aria (Berenice) (frag)*
. "O sommi Dei," recit (Rosalba)
. "Nulla temer," recit (Rosalba)
. "Generoso chi sol brama," aria (Rosalba)

4. "Che vidi! Che mirai?," recit accompagnato (Lisaura, Rossane)
  . "Ecco Tassile," recit (Lisaura, Rossane, Tassile)
5. "Quanto dolce amor saria," aria (Lisaura)
  . "Ne'trofei d'Alessandro," recit (Rossane)
6. "Lusinghe più care," aria (Rossane)
  . "Sventurato ch'io sono!," recit (Tassile)
7. "Vibra, cortese Amor, un'altro strale del mio rivale al cor," aria (Tassile)
8. "Fra le guerre e le vittorie," solo & chorus (Alessandro, Leonato, Cleone, Tassile, Clito)
  . "Apprestasti, oh Cleone," recit (Alessandro, Cleone)
  . "Dalla vittoria alla bellezza in braccio," recit (Alessandro, Cleone, Lisaura, Rossane, Tassile)
9. "No, più soffrir non voglio, è troppa infedelta," aria (Lisaura)
10. "Vilipese bellezze, lusinghe," recit accompagnato (Rossane
  . "Pur ti ritrovo; e perchè mai partisti?," recit (Alessandro, Rossane)
11. "Men fedele, e men costante," aria (Alessandro)
  . "Sì, lusingando ei parla," recit (Rossane)
12. "Un lusinghiero dolce pensiero," aria (Rossane)
  . "Tu, che Rossane adori," recit (Clito, Cleone)
13. "Spesso suol bella tiranna," aria (Cleone)
  . "Amico Leonato," recit (Clito, Leonato)
14a, b. "Pregi son d'un alma grande," aria (Leonato) (2 vers)
  . "Sempre del suo valor," recit (Clito)
15. "A sprone, a fren leggiero un nobile destriero," aria (Clito)
16. "Sinfonia"
  . "Al magnanimo, al forte," recit (Cleone)
17. "Sinfonia"
  . "Primo motor delle superne sfere," recit accompagnato (Alessandro)
  . "Figlio del Re degl'immortali Numi," recit (Tassile, Cleone, Clito, Alessandro, Rossane, Lisaura)
18. "Placa l'alma, quieta il petto!," duet (Lisaura, Rossane)
  . "Fra gli uomini e fra i Numi," recit (Alessandro)
19. "Da un breve riposo di stato amoroso," aria (Alessandro)
II: 20. "Solitudini amate, Aure, fonti, ombre gradite," recit accompagnato & arioso (Rossane)
  . "Eccola in preda al sonno," recit & arioso (Alessandro, Lisaura, Rossane)
  . "Permettete ch'io vi baci," arioso (Alessandro)
  . "Più non vuol gelosia," recit (Lisaura, Alessandro, Rossane)
  . "Superbette luci amate," arioso (Alessandro)
  . "Permettete ch'io vi baci," arioso (Lisaura (2 vers)
  . "Lasciandomi qui sol," recit (Alessandro)
  . "Superbette luci amate," arioso (Rossane)
  . "Ch onor si rende," recit (Alessandro)
21. "Vano amore, lusinga, diletto," aria (Alessandro)
22. "Tiranna passion," arioso & recit (Lisaura)
  . "Deh, Lisaura crudele, Se ti credessi io cangerei pensiero," recit (Tassile, Lisaura)
  . "Amo, Spero, ne so perchè. L'amor mio non è gradito," duettino (Tassile, Lisaura)
23a, b. "Sempre fido e disprezzato," aria (Tassile) (2 vers)
  . "Pur troppo veggio," recit (Lisaura)
24. "Che tirannia d'Amor! fuggir chi siegue ed ama," aria (Lisaura)
  . "Qui aspetto l'incostante," recit (Rossane, Alessandro)
25. "Alla sua gabbia d'oro suol ritornar talor," aria (Rossane)
  . "Vince al fin la beltà," recit (Alessandro)
  . "Vincitor generoso!," recit (Lisaura, Alessandro)
26. "No! Risolvo abbandonar la bella che mi sprezza," aria (Alessandro)
  . "Finto sereno," recit (Lisaura)
27. "La cervetta nei lacci avvolta," aria (Lisaura)
28. "Sinfonia"
  . "Dopo il sublime onor," recit (Alessandro, Clito, Tassile, Cleone)
  . "Oh Dei! che infausta nuova!," recit (Rossane, Alessandro)
  . "Sire, il popol già vinto l'armi ripiglia," recit (Leonato, Alessandro, Rossane)
29. "Il cor mio, ch'è già per te," aria (Alessandro)
  . "Svanisci, oh reo timore," recit (Rossane)
30. "Dica il falso, dica il vero," aria (Rossane)
III: 31. "Sfortunato è il mio valore, è perchè?," arioso (Clito)
  . "L'adulator s'appressa," recit (Clito, Cleone)
  . "Renditi o mori! E quale ardir?," recit (Leonato, Cleone, Clito)
32. "Sarò qual vento," aria (Cleone)
  . "La resa libertà dunque, oh Rossane," recit (Lisaura, Rossane)
33. "Sì, m'è caro imitar quel bel fiore," aria (Lisaura)
  . "Sento un'interno," recit (Rossane)
34a. "Brilla nell'alma un non inteso ancor," aria (Rossane)
34b. "Si dolce lusingar," aria (Rossane)
  . "Qual tormento crudel," recit (Lisaura, Alessandro)
35. "L'amor, che per te sento," aria (Lisaura)
  . "Si generoso affetto," recit (Alessandro)
  . "E qual fisso pensier," recit (Tassile, Alessandro, Rossane)
36. "Pupille amate, voi m'insegnate a trionfar," aria (Alessandro)
  . "Numi eterni," recit (Rossane)

37. "Tempesta e calma sento nell'alma," aria (Rossane)
38. "D'un fiero tiranno," chorus
. "Chi oserà traditore," recit (Alessandro, Leonato, Clito, Tassile)
39. "Prove sono di grandezza," aria (Alessandro)
40. "Spegni, oh supremo Regnator de' Numi," recit accompagnato (Rossane, Lisaura)
. "Al primo sguardo," recit (Tassile)
41. "Oh sommo Giove," recit accompagnato (Rossane, Lisaura)
. "Si festigi il bel giorno," recit (Alessandro, Rossane, Tassile, Lisaura) (2 vers)
42. "In generoso onor," duet & chorus (Lisaura, Alessandro)
. "Cara, cara, la tua beltà," duet (Rossane, Alessandro)
. "Amico arrida il ciel, e questo ogn'or sarà," chorus
Add song: . "L'armi implora dal tuo figlio al mio labbro ed al mio ciglio," aria (Rossane)
Anhang: II: 28. "Symfonia" (= Scipione, HWV20/13)

1a.22   "Admeto, Rè di Tessaglia," opera: HWV22
. "Ouverture"
I: 1. "Introduzione"
2. "Orride larve," recit accompagnato (Admeto)
. "Chiudetevi, miei lumi, chiudetevi," arioso (Admeto)
. "Sire, l'invitto Alcide," recit (Orindo, Admeto)
. "A bastanza onorato nella tua Regia fui," recit (Ercole, Admeto)
3. "La gloria sola, che ogn'or bramai," aria (Ercole)
. "Consolati, Signor!," recit (Orindo, Admeto, Alceste)
4. "La Statua parla: Risanarti non puoi," recit accompagnato (Statua)
. "Stravagante portento!," recit (Admeto, Alceste, Orindo)
5. "Luci care, addio, posate!," aria (Alceste)
6. "Sinfonia"
. "Admeto, traditor, A che chiedermi al padre," recit (Antigona, Meraspe)
7. "Spera allor, che in mar turbato," aria (Antigona)
. "Non lagrimate," recit (Alceste)
8. "Farò così più bella," aria (Alceste)
9. "Cangio d'aspetto il crudo fato," aria (Admeto)
. "Quanto io goda, Admeto," recit (Ercole, Admeto, Voce di dentro, Orindo)
. "Oh, come spesso è, Sire," recit (Orindo, Admeto, Ercole)
10. "Un lampo è la speranza, fa lume, è ver, mai poi," aria (Admeto)
. "Meraspe ancor dalla città non torna," recit (Antigona, Meraspe)
11. "Sinfonia"
. "Cara Antigona amata, dal pennello animata," recit (Trasimede, Meraspe, Antigona)
12. "Se l'arco avessi e i strali," aria (Trasimede)
. "Non potrà meglio il fato," recit (Antigona, Meraspe)
13. "Se'n vola lo sparvier per ogni estraneo lido, spiando in ogni nido," aria (Antigona)
II: 14. "Ouverture"
15. "In vanti scuoti, in vano," recit accompagnato (Ercole, Alceste)
16. "Sinfonia"
. "Ecco, Alceste spezzati," recit (Ercole, Alceste)
17a. "Quanto godrà, allor che mi vedrà," aria (Alceste)
. "E che sperar poss'io," recit (Antigona, Orindo)
18a. "Bella, non t'adirar!," aria (Orindo)
. "Godo, oh bella," recit (Trasimede, Antigona, Orindo)
19. "Da te più tosto partir vogl'io," aria (Trasimede)
. "Per me si strugge trasimede, oh Dio!," recit (Antigona)
20. "E per monti e per piano e per selve," aria (Antigona)
. "Sire, da che bramasti," recit (Orindo, Admeto)
21. "Sparite, oh pensieri, se solo volete," aria (Admeto)
. "Ecco chi tanto adoro," recit (Antigona, Meraspe, trasimede)
22. "Da tanti affanni oppressa talor dico a me stessa: vivere tu non puoi," aria (Antigona)
. "A qual fine, oh Regina," recit (Ercole, Alceste)
23. "Gelosia, spietata Aletto," aria (Alceste)
24. "Quivi tra questi solitarii orrori," recit accompagnato (Admeto)
25. "Ah, sì, morrò; e allor potrò dividere quel cor," aria (Admeto)
. "Lasciatemi, oh felloni!," recit (Antigona, Trasimede)
. "Questo dunque è il ritratto," recit (Trasimede)
26. "Chi è nato alle sventure non può mai ritrovar," aria (Trasimede)
. "Il ritratto d'Admeto," recit (Antigona, Alceste)
27. "La sorte mia vacilla," aria (Antigona)
. "Quest'è dunque la fede," recit (Alceste)
28. "Vedrò fra poco, se l'idol mio," aria (Alceste)
III: 29. "A languir ed a penar m'ha destinato Amor," arioso (Admeto)
. "Ah Sire, imploro," recit (Meraspe, Admeto, Orindo)
30a. "Signor, lo credi a me: ti serba amore e fè," aria (Meraspe)
. "Amor, qual nuova fiamma," recit (Admeto)
31. "La tigre arde di sdegno," aria (Admeto)
. "Dalla Regia dell'ombre," recit (Ercole, Admeto)
32. "Amor è un tiranno, che ai sensi fa guerra," aria (Ercole)
. "Oh Dio! non formo passo," recit (Antigona)

. "Sì ti bacio, oh bella imago," arioso & recit (Antigona, Alceste)
. "Olà, soldati, ecco qui," recit (Orindo, Alceste, Antigona)
33. "Io ti bacio, oh bella imago," aria (Antigona)
. "Che veggio, oh ciel, che veggio?," recit (Ercole, Orindo, Alceste)
34. "Là dove gli occhi io giro, e l'erbe e i fiori rimiro," aria (Alceste)
. "Prence, meco gioisci!," recit (Meraspe, Trasimede, Antigone)
35. "E che ci posso far, se non ti posso amar," aria (Antigona)
. "Mie speranze abbattute," recit (Trasimede)
36. "Armati, oh core, di cieco sdegno!," aria (Trasimede)
. "Ma giunge il Re," recit (Trasimede)
. "Vieni, Antigona mia," recit (Admeto, Alceste, Antigona, Trasimede)
37. "Alma mia! io ti stringo," duet (Antigona, Admeto)
. "Muori! Fermati, iniquo!," recit (Trasimede, Alceste, Admeto)
. "Signore ...? Sia arrestato costui!," recit (Orindo, Admeto, Antigona, Alceste)
. "Opportuno qui giungo. Ombra, oh Re," recit (Ercole, Alceste, Admeto)
. "No, no, Signor, son qui," recit (Trasimede, Admeto, Alceste, Antigona)
38. "Sì, caro, caro, sì," aria (Alceste)
. "Ad Alceste la vita, a te l'onore," recit (Admeto)
39. "Se un core è contento, se un core è contento, non sa più bramar," chorus
Add songs: 5b. "Spera, sì, mio caro bene," aria (Alceste)
17b. "Mostratevi serene a questo amante cor, pupille care!," aria (Alceste)
18b. "Io son qual Fenice risorta dal foco," aria (Alceste: 1728 / Antigona: 1731)
18c. "Dolce riso, dolci sguardi," aria (Orindo (c1728)
34b. "Sento primo le procelle," aria (Alceste: 1731)
. "Amor ed impietà, amor ed inpietà voi pur voreste il cor," aria (Admeto)
(9.) "Spirti fieri, spirti fieri dell'alme guerrieri, dell'alme guerrieri," aria (Ercole) (= Rodrigo, HWV5/29)
. "Amor con sola, e affanna," recit (Admeto)
III: 30b. "Signor, lo credi a me," aria (Meraspe) (2 vers)

1a.23   "Riccardo Primo, Rè d'Inghilterra," opera: HWV23
. "Ouverture"
I: 1. "Lascia, Berardo, lasciami!," recit accompagnato (Costanza, Berardo)
2. "Se perì l'amato bene," aria (Costanza)
. "Se la vergin Regale," recit (Pulcheria, Isacio, Berardo, Costanza, Oronte)
3. "Vado per obedirti," aria (Pulcheria)
. "T'arresta, Oronte, ascolta," recit (Isacio, Oronte)
4. "V'adoro, oh luci belle," aria (Oronte)
. "Torni la gioja," recit (Riccardo)
5. "Calmate le tempeste, risorge il mio contento," aria (Riccardo)
. "Cortese a noi si mostra," recit (Costanza, Berardo, Oronte, Pulcheria)
6. "Bella, teco non ho," aria (Pulcheria)
. "Oronte! Sire! Parti," recit (Isacio, Oronte, Costanza, Berardo)
7. "Lascia la pace all'alma!," aria (Costanza)
. "Isacio, il cui gran merto," recit (Riccardo, Isacio)
8. "Agitato da fiere tempeste," aria (Riccardo)
II: 9. "Se m'è contrario il Cielo," arioso (Costanza)
. "Seco Isacio mi volle," recit (Berardo, Costanza)
10. "Dell'empia frode il velo," aria (Berardo)
. "Riccardo sospirato," recit (Costanza, Isacio)
11. "Di notte il pellegrino, se perde il suo camino, non sa dove guidar," aria (Costanza)
. "Quanto saresti insano cuor d'Isacio," recit (Isacio)
. "All'affetto di padre supplichevole io vengo," recit (Pulcheria, Isacio)
12. "Ti vedrò regnar sul trono," aria (Isacio)
13. "Ah, padre! ah, Cielo!," recit accompagnato (Pulcheria)
14. "Quel gelsomino, che imperla il prato," aria (Pulcheria)
. "Prencipe, ogn'or compagna," recit (Costanza, Oronte, Berardo)
15. "Caro, vieni a me," aria (Costanza)
16. "Quanto tarda, quanto tarda il caro bene," arioso (Riccardo)
. "Ma, vedo corteggiata," recit (Riccardo)
17. "Sì, già vedo il mio bel sole," arioso (Riccardo)
. "Vieni, bell'idol mio," recit (Riccardo, Pulcheria, Oronte)
18. "Ai guardi tuoi son pur vaga," aria (Pulcheria)
. "Sì, sforzi alla ragion questo tiranno," recit (Oronte, Riccardo)
19. "O vendicarmi saprò con l'armi," aria (Riccardo)
. "Che mai pensa tentar l'alma guerriera!," recit (Oronte)
20. "Dell'onor di giuste imprese," aria (Oronte)
. "Ah! scampo dagli qguati Oronte," recit (Isacio, Berardo, Riccardo)
. "T'inganni. Mira e da saggio," recit (Riccardo, Pulcheria, Isacio)
21. "Nube, che il sole adombra," aria (Riccardo)
22. "Se m'è contrario il Cielo," arioso (Costanza)
. "Mesta e pensosa è ancor Costanza?," recit (Pulcheria, Costanza, Riccardo)
23. "L'aqui la altera conosce i figli," aria (Pulcheria)
. "Tut'i passati affanni," recit (Riccardo, Costanza)
24. "T'amo, sì! t'amo, sì, sarai tu quella solo cara, solo bella," duet (Riccardo, Costanza)
III: 25. "Perfido Isacio! traditor! tiranno!," recit accompagnato (Riccardo, Oronte)

26. "Per mia vendetta ancor punito si vedrà," aria (Oronte)
27. "Oh voi, che meco del Tamigi in riva," recit accompagnato (Riccardo)
28. "All'orror delle procelle," aria (Riccardo)
29. "Morte, vieni, ma in van ti chiamo, oh morte," arioso (Costanza)
   . "A me nel mio Rossore," recit (Pulcheria, Costanza)
30. "Quell'innocente afflitto core fedele amore gentil beltà," aria (Pulcheria)
31. "Alto immenso poter," recit accompagnato (Costanza)
   . "Ingiustizia e furore," recit (Isacio, Costanza)
   . "Dall'alta rocca avvicinar si vede a tue mura," recit (Berardo, Isacio)
32. "Nel mondo e nell'abisso io non pavento," aria (Isacio)
   . "Pulcheria vuol, che seco a Riccardo io men vado," recit (Berardo, Costanza)
33. "Bacia per me la mano del caro idolo mio," aria (Costanza)
34a, b. "Atterato il muro cada," aria (Riccardo)
   . "Arrestati, Riccardo," recit (Isacio, Riccardo)
   . "Sire, in vendetta me uccidi ancora," recit (Pulcheria, Isacio, Riccardo, Costanza)
   . "Empio, perisci tu!," recit (Oronte, Isacio, Riccardo, Pulcheria)
35. "Alla vittoria, alla vittoria!," chorus & sinfonia
   . "Dal passato spavento ancor non ponno," recit (Costanza, Berardo, Pulcheria)
36. "Il volo così fido al dolce amato nido," aria (Costanza)
   . "Pietoso Ciel, tu m'ispirasti sempre," recit (Pulcheria)
   . "Liete nuove, idol mio!," recit (Oronte, Pulcheria)
37. "Tutta brillanti rai per lungo scintillar," aria (Pulcheria)
38. "Marche"
   . "Generosa Pulcheria! fu la vita d'Isacio," recit (Riccardo, Pulcheria, Costanza, Oronte)
39. "Volgete ogni desir," aria (Riccardo)
   . "Spargansi pur d'oblio," recit (Oronte)
40. "La memoria dei tormenti," chorus
Anhang: I: 1. "Che tenti Real Costanza?," recit accompagnato (Berardo, Costanza)
   2. "Se perì l'amato bene," aria (Castanza)
   . "Di qui non lungi, vedi popolo che a poi viene," recit (Berardo, Costanza)
   . "Se la vergine Augusta," recit (Pulcheria, Isacio, Oronte, Costanza, Berardo)
   3. "Vado per obedirti," aria (Pulcheria)
   . "T'arresta, Oronte," recit (Isacio, oronte)
   4. "Per due begl'occhi avvampo," aria (Oronte)
   . "Mio fido o qual tu rechi," recit (Riccardo, Corrado)
   5. "Fra poco spero, che tornerai," aria (Corrado)
   . "Beltà, che mai non vidi," recit (Riccardo)
   6. "Calmate le tempeste," aria (Riccardo)
   . "Grata ver noi si mostra," recit (Costanza, Berardo, Oronte, Pulcheria)
   7. "Bella, teco non ho," aria (Pulcheria)
   . "Oronte, Sire. Parti," recit (Isacio, oronte, Costanza, Berardo)
   . "Sire, il monarca Britanno," recit (Oronte, Isacio, Costanza)
   8. "Lascia la pace a;;'alma!," aria (Costanza)
   . "Isacio, a cui tributo," recit (Riccardo, Isacio)
   9. *"Agitata da fiere tempeste," aria (Riccardo) (frag)*
   . "Riccardo sospirato," recit (Costanza, Isacio)
   10. "Perch'io goda il bel d'un viso," aria (Isacio)
   . "Signor; fin ora intema stessi per te," recit (Corrado, Riccardo)
   11. "Nube, che il sole adombra," aria (Riccardo)
   . "Servitù amica sorte, apensier miei," recit (Isacio, Pulcheria)
   12. "Ah, padre! ah, cielo!," recit accompagnato (Pulcheria)
   13. "Quel gelsomino, che imperla il prato," aria (Pulcheria)
   . "Gran Duce, ogn' or compagna," recit (Costanza, Oronte, Berardo)
   14. "Bella già il cor s'accende," aria (Oronte)
   . "Berardo, l'una all'altra per me," recit (Costanza, Berardo)
   15. "Caro, torna a me," aria (Costanza)
   16. "Quando vieni, quando vieni, o mio conforto," arioso (Riccardo)
   "Signor, in comitiva," recit (Corrado, Pulcheria, Riccardo) (frag)
   . "Colà, da cento spade," recit (Oronte, Pulcheria, Riccardo, Corrado)
   17. "Io più soffrir non sò e adesso impiegherò," aria (Riccardo)
   . "Ah, crudo Oronte!," recit (Pulcheria, Oronte)
   18. "L'aquila altera conosce i figli," aria (Pulcheria)
III: 19. "Numi, soccorso; ohime!," recit accompagnato (Costanza, Isacio, Corrado)
   20. "Del cielo e nell'abisso io," aria (Isacio)
   . "E stringon, mia Regina, quel piè," recit (Berardo, Costanza)
   21. "Bacia per me la mano," aria (Costanza)
   . "Chi di me più infelice?," recit (Riccardo)
   22. "Son qual colombo amante che attorno alla sua cara," aria (Riccardo)
   . "Pulcheria. Gran Guerriero," recit (Corrado, Pulcheria, Oronte)
   23. "A chi? misera: dove ricorro supplicante," recit accompagnato (Pulcheria)
   24. "Nubiloso fra tempeste," aria (Pulcheria)
   . "Subiti, formidabili, frequenti," recit (Riccardo, Oronte, Corrado)
   . "Riccardo. Che mai veggio!," recit (Isacio, Riccardo, Corrado)
   . "Ah! Padre, cessa da furor tuoi," recit (Pulcheria, Isacio, Riccardo, Corrado)
   25. "Sinfonia"

. "Come lo scampo avesti," recit (Berardo, Costanza)
26. "Or mi perdo di speranza," aria (Costanza)
27. "Sinfonia"
. "Isacio, tu sei vinto," recit (Riccardo, Isacio, Pulcheria)
28. "Di me non ti lagnar," aria (Riccardo)
. "A che sei giunta," recit (Pulcheria)
29. "Quando non vedo la cara madre quell'agnellina gemendo và," aria (Pulcheria)
. "A noi si guidi," recit (Riccardo, Costanza)
30. "Quanto goda l'alma mia," duet (Costanza, Riccardo)
31. "Spira grata l'aura e il vento," chorus

1a.24   "Siroe, Rè di Persia," opera: HWV24
. "Ouverture"
I: . "Introduzione"
1. "Figli, di vuoi non meno," recit accompagnato (Cosroe, Siroe, Medarse)
2. "Se il mio paterno amore sdegna il tuo core," aria (Cosroe)
. "E puoi senza arrossirti," recit (Siroe, Medarse)
. "Perchè di tanto sdegno," recit (Emira, Medarse)
. "Bella Emira adorata," recit (Siroe, Emira)
. "Al fin giungesti a consolar Laodice," recit (Emira, Laodice, Siroe)
3. "D'ogni amator la fede è sempre mal sicura?," aria (Emira)
. "Siroe, non parla?," recit (Laodice, Siroe)
4. "Se il labbro amor ti giura," aria (Siroe)
. "Di te, germana, in traccia," recit (Arasse, Laodice)
5. "O placido il mare lusinga la sponda," aria (Laodice)
. "Dall'insidie d'Emira," recit (Siroe)
. "Che da un superbo figlio," recit (Cosroe, Laodice, Siroe)
. "Padre, io ti miro cangiato in volto," recit (Medarse, Cosroe, Laodice, Siroe)
. "Chi tradisce il mio Re," recit (Emira, Siroe, Cosroe, Laodice, Medarse)
6. "La sorte mia tiranna farmi di più non può," aria (Siroe)
. "Olà, s'osservi il Prence," recit (Cosroe, Emira, Medarse, Laodice)
7. "Vedeste mai sul prato cader la pioggia estiva?," aria (Emira)
. "Gran mistero in que'detti," recit (Laodice, Medarse)
8. "Chi è più fedele ritrova pene," aria (Medarse)
. "Non credo che sian finti," recit (Laodice)
9. "Or mi perdo di speranza," aria (Laodice)
II: 10. "Deh! voi mi dite, o Numi! se quale il mio fumai," arioso (Siroe)
. "Ma qui Laodice!," recit (Siroe, Laodice)
11. "Mi lagnerò tacendo del mio destino avaro," aria (Laodice)
. "Come quel di Laodice," recit (Siroe, Emira)
. "Che fai, superbo?," recit (Cosroe, Emira, Siroe)
12. "Mi credi infedele; sol questo m'affanna," aria (Siroe)
. "Pensoso, è il Re!," recit (Emira, Cosroe, Medarse)
13. "Sgombra dell' anima tutto il timor," aria (Emira)
. "Signor, per tua salvezza," recit (Medarse, Cosroe)
14. "Fra l'orror della tempesta," aria (Medarse)
. "Qui da Cosroe richiesto," recit (Siroe, Cosroe, Emira)
. "Eccomi a'cenni tuoi," recit (Laodice, Cosroe)
15. "Tu di pietà mi spogli," aria (Cosroe)
. "Che risolver deggio?," recit (Siroe, Emira, Laodice)
16. "Fra dubbi affetti miei risolvere non so," aria (Siroe)
. "A costei che dirò?," recit (Emira, Laodice)
17. "L'aura non sempre spira a favore," aria (Laodice)
. "Sì diversi sembianti per odio," recit (Emira)
18. "Non vi piacque ingiusti Dei, ch'io nascessi pastorella," aria (Emira)
III: 19. "Sinfonia"
. "No. no; voglio che mora," recit (Cosroe)
. "Mio Re, che fai?," recit (Laodice, Cosroe)
20. "Se il caro figlio vede in periglio," aria (Laodice)
. "Rendi, o Signor, il Prence," recit (Emira, Cosroe)
. "Arasse! oh ciel!," recit (Emira, Cosroe)
21. "Gelido, in ogni vena scorrer mi sento il sangue," aria (Cosroe)
. "Che vuoi, d'un empio Re," recit (Emira, Arasse)
. "Tutto è in tumulto, Idaspe," recit (Medarse, Emira)
22. "Benchè tinta del sangue fraterno," aria (Medarse)
23. "Son stanco, ingiusti Numi," recit accompagnato (Siroe)
24. "Deggio morire, o stelle, nè all'innocenza mia," aria (Siroe)
. "Arasse non mentì," recit (Emira, Siroe)
. "Non temete, o miei fidi," recit (Medarse, Emira, Siroe)
. "Vieni, Siroe. Ah! difendi, Arasse," recit (Arasse, Medarse)
. "Numi! ogn' un m'abbandona," recit (Medarse, Emira, Siroe)
25. "Ch'io mai vi possa lasciar d'amare," aria (Emira)
. "Siroe, già so qual sorte sovrasti," recit (Medarse, Siroe)
26. "Se l'amor tuo mi rendi, se più fedel sarai," aria (Siroe)
. "Ah con mio dano imparo," recit (Medarse, Laodice)

27. "Torrente cresciuto per torbida piena," aria (Laodice)
28. "Sinfonia"
. "Vinto ancor non son io," recit (Cosroe, Emira, Siroe, Arasse, Medarse, Laodice)
. "Padre. Signor. Del mio fallir," recit (Medarse, Laodice, Cosroe, Siroe, Emira)
29. "La mia speranza diceva al core, soffri le pene," aria (Emira)
. "Ecco, Persia, il tuo Re," recit (Cosroe)
30. "Dolcissimo amore ogn'alma, ogni core," chorus
Anhang: (3b.) "Son come un arbocello, che da due venti è scosso," aria (Emira)
(7a.) "Vedeste mai sul prato cader la pioggia estiva?," aria (Emira) (frag)

1a.25   "Tolomeo, Rè di Egitto," opera: HWV25
. "Ouverture"
I: 1. "Orgoglioso elemento," recit accompagnato (Tolomeo)
. "Numi, pietà! Qual mesta voce ascolto?," recit (Alessandro, Tolomeo)
2. "Cielo ingiusto, potrai fulminarmi," aria (Tolomeo)
. "Ahi! Elisa infelice," recit (Elisa, Alessandro)
3. "Non lo dirò col labbro, che tanto ardir non ha," aria (Alessandro)
. "Veggio che m'ama il Prence," recit (Elisa)
4. "Quell'onda, che si frange, mormora insieme e piange," aria (Elisa)
. "Quest'è pur Cipro, e queste," recit (Seleuce, Araspe)
5. "Mi arresto ad ogni fronda, m'arresto al suon dell'onda," aria (Seleuce)
. "O cari a gli occhi miei rustici alberghi," recit (Elisa, Tolomeo)
6. "Sa talor miri un fior che non può germogliar," aria (Elisa)
. "Conosco ben," recit (Tolomeo)
7. "Tiranni miei pensieri, datemi di riposo," arioso (Tolomeo)
. "E dove, e dove mai," recit (Seleuce)
8. "Fonti amiche, aure leggiere," aria (Seleuce)
. "Ma! quel pastor che dorme sarà?," recit (Seleuce)
. "Delia ad un pastor che dorme s'avvicina?," recit (Araspe, Seleuce, Tolomeo)
9. "Respira almen un poco, oh misero mio core," aria (Araspe)
. "V'è ancor qualche martire, vi sono più tormenti," recit (Tolomeo)
10. "Torna sol per un momento," aria (Tolomeo)
II: 11. "Voi dolci aurette al cor," arioso (Elisa)
. "Dov'è chi la mia morte richiede?," recit (Tolomeo, Elisa)
. "Osmin, Osmino! e come ha i tanto ardire," recit (Araspe, Tolomeo, Elisa)
12. "Quanto è felice quell'augelletto," aria (Elisa)
. "S'io potessi sperare," recit (Seleuce)
13a. "Aure, portate a' caro bene," aria (Seleuce)
. "Delia, attendi un momento," recit (Elisa, Tolomeo, Seleuce)
14. "Se un solo è quel core ch'io chiudo nel petto," aria (Tolomeo)
. "Disperato e schernito," recit (Elisa)
. "Signora, la mia sorte," recit (Alessandro, Elisa)
15. "Il mio core non apprezza," aria (Elisa)
. "Affetto che ragione," recit (Alessandro)
16. "Pur sento, oh Dio, che l'alma in calma ancor non sta," aria (Alessandro)
17. "Dite, che fa, dov'è l'idolo mio?, aria à 2 (Seleuce, Tolomeo)
. "Dove sei, caro sposo?, recit (Seleuce, Tolomeo)
. "Dite dov'è, che fa," arioso (Tolomeo)
. "Io ti cerco per tutto," recit (Seleuce)
. "Delia, per queste si remote selve," recit (Araspe, Seleuce, Tolomeo)
18. "Piangi pur, ma non sperare," aria (Araspe)
. "Seleuce! Tolomeo! Tu vivi," recit (Tolomeo, Seleuce)
19. "Se il cor ti perde, oh cara," duet (Seleuce, Tolomeo)
III: 20. "Madre, pagasti al fine," recit accompagnato (Alessandro)
. "Signor, se non t'è noto," recit (Araspe, Alessandro)
21. "Se l'interno pur vedonno i Numi," aria (Alessandro)
. "Se non era il pensiero," recit (Araspe)
22. "Sarò giusto e non tiranno," aria (Araspe)
. "Elisa, che ricerchi," recit (Seleuce, Elisa)
23. "Voglio amore o pur vendetta da chi l'alma acceso m'ha," aria (Elisa)
. "Eccolo appunto!," recit (Seleuce)
. "Bella, già men severe," recit (Tolomeo, Seleuce)
24. "Senza il suo bene la tortorella," aria (Seleuce)
. "Al fin che si risolve," recit (Elisa, Tolomeo)
25. "Ti pentirai, crudel, d'aver offeso," aria (Elisa)
. "Olà! che più si tarda," recit (Tolomeo)
26. "Son qual rocca percossa dall'onde," aria (Tolomeo)
. "In questa più remota parte del bosco imposi," recit (Alessandro, Seleuce)
27a. "Torni omai la pace all'alma," aria (Seleuce)
. "Che più si tarda omai," recit (Tolomeo)
28. "Inumano fratel," recit accompagnato (Tolomeo)
29. "Stille amare, già vi sento," arioso (Tolomeo)
. "Eccoti, oh Prence, il tuo germano!," recit (Araspe, Alessandro, Elisa, Tolomeo, Seleuce)
30. "Tutto contento or gode quest'alma innamorata," duet (Seleuce, Tolomeo)
. "Lascia, oh fratel, che nel mio sen t'abbraccio!," recit (Alessandro, Tolomeo)

31. "Applauda ogn'uno il nostro fato!," chorus
Anhang: (6b.) "Se talor miri un fior," aria (Elisa)
    (6c.) "Osmino, addio," aria (Elisa)
    . "S'io potessi sperare," recit (Seleuce)
    (13b.) "Io vo' di duolo in duolo," aria (Seleuce)
    (13c./15.) "Il mio core non apprezza," aria (Seleuce)
    (27b.) "Parmi che giunta in porto," aria (Elisa)

1a.26   "Lotario," opera: HWV26
    . "Ouverture"
   I: 1. "Grave è'l fasto di regnar," arioso (Berengario)
       . "Signor, vuole il mio fato," recit (Idelberto, Berengario)
       . "Alto Signor, dall'Alpi, scese della Germania," recit (Clodomiro, Berengario, Idelberto)
       . "Sposo! Regina!," recit (Matilde, Berengario, Idelberto)
      2. "Non pensi quell'altera di vincermi d'orgoglio," aria (Berengario)
       . "Madre, e Reina!," recit (Idelberto, Matilde)
      3. "Vanne a colei che adori, seco d'amor favella," aria (Matilde)
       . "Fin ch'io non chiuda," recit (Idelberto)
      4. "Per salvarti, idolo mio," aria (Idelberto)
      5. "Soglie, degliavi miei," recit accompagnato (Adelaide)
       . "Attenta ogni mio cenno osservi," recit (Adelaide)
       . "Bella Reina: il cielo," recit (Lotario, Adelaide)
      6. "Rammentati, rammentati, cor mio," aria (Lotario)
       . "Or venga il messagiero," recit (Adelaide)
       . "Regina, anche fra l'armi," recit (Clodomiro, Adelaide)
      7. "Se il mar promete calma," aria (Clodomiro)
       . "Nel Ciel sì speri, e poi," recit (Adelaide, Lotario)
      8. "Quel cor che mi donasti," aria (Adelaide)
       . "O del mio caro ben," recit (Lotario)
      9. "Già mi sembra al carro avvinto," aria (Lotario)
      10. "Viva, viva, viva e regni fortunato," chorus
       . "Popoli generosi," recit (Berengario, Matilde)
       . "Dell'altrui felonia," recit (Adelaide, Berengario, Clodomiro, Matilde, Idelberto)
      11. "Orgogliosetto va l'augelletto," aria (Matilde)
       . "Quanto più fien tenacci," recit (Adelaide)
      12. "Scherza in mar la navicella," aria (Adelaide)
   II: 13. "Sinfonia"
       . "Son vinto, o Ciel, son vinto!," recit accompagnato (Berengario)
       . "Sei priggioniero! Stelle!," recit (Lotario, Berengario)
      14. "Regno e grandezza, vassalli e trono," aria (Berengario)
       . "Se del fiero tiranno trionfò," recit (Lotario)
      15. "Tiranna, ma bella, m'uccide, e m'alletta," aria (Lotario)
      16. "Menti eterne, menti eterne che reggete," aria (Adelaide)
       . "Con due doni, Adelaide," recit (Clodomiro, Adelaide)
      17. "Non t'inganni la speranza," aria (Clodomiro)
       . "Adelaide che pensi?," recit (Adelaide, Matilde)
       . "Hai tanto ardir? nè ti sovvien," recit (Matilde, Idelberto, Adelaide)
       . "Reina, in fausti avvisi," recit (Clodomiro, Idelberto, Matilde, Adelaide)
      18. "Arma lo sguardo d'un dolce dardo," aria (Matilde)
       . "Di miglio genitor," recit (Adelaide, Idelberto)
      19. "Bella, bella, non mi negar," aria (Idelberto)
      20. "Sommo Rettor del Cielo, i tuoi consigli," recit accompagnato (Adelaide)
      21. "D'una torbida sorgente," aria (Adelaide)
      22. "Quanto, quanto più forte è il valor," arioso (Lotario)
       . "Pressi gli ostaggi, or ora," recit (Lotario, Matilde)
       . "Ecco la prigioniera," recit (Clodomiro, Lotario, Adelaide, Matilde)
       . "No, no, colla mia vita," recit (Idelberta, Adelaide, Matilde, Lotario)
       . "Berengario, rifletti," recit (Lotario, Berengario, Idelberto)
      23. "D'instabile fortuna non sempre in tuo favore," aria (Berengario)
       . "Alla tenda Reale vada Idelberto," recit (Lotario)
      24. "Non disperi peregrino se nel dubbio suo camino," aria (Lotario)
   III: 25. "Sinfonia"
       . "Sciolta dalle catene," recit (Matilde, Berengario)
       . "Vieni, o bella Adelaide," recit (Berengario, Matilde, Adelaide)
      26. "Non sempre invendicata io resterò così," aria (Adelaide)
       . "Ben conosce Adelaide," recit (Berengario, Matilde)
      27. "Vi sento, sì, vi sento, rimorsi entro al mio sen," aria (Berengario)
       . "Non mi tradir speranza," recit (Matilde)
      28. "Quel superbo già si crede," aria (Matilde)
       . "Berengario al mio campo," recit (Lotario)
      29. "Sinfonia"
       . "Misero me! che veggio?," recit (Lotario)
       . "Ah! Signor, se la vita," recit (Idelberto, Lotario)
       . "A tempo qui giungesti," recit (Lotario, Idelberto, Berengario)
       . "Alla Regal mia tenda," recit (Lotario, Berengario)

. "Ah! fortuna incostante!," recit (Cldomiro, Lotario)
30. "Alza il Ciel pianta orgogliosa," aria (Clodomiro)
. " 'Inclito Re, Pavia,' " recit (Lotario)
31. "Vedrò, vedrò più liete e belle," aria (Lotario)
. "Lasciami, iniquo figlio!," recit (Matilde, Idelberto)
32. "Impara, codardo, ch'un anima forte," aria (Matilde)
. "Omai non v'è più speme," recit (Clodomiro, Matilde, Idelberto)
33. "S'è delitto trar da' lacci un innocente," aria (Idelberto)
34. "Furie del crudo averno, e dove siete?, recit accompagnato (Matilde)
. "Ecco la cruda; olà," recit (Lotario, Matilde)
. "Matilde, e qual furore?," recit (Berengario)
. "Lascia, mio Re, mio difensor," recit (Adelaide, Lotario)
. "Deh! mia Reina, salva," recit (Idelberto, Adelaide, Lotario, Matilde, Berengario)
35. "Sì, bel sembiante, tu m'hai ferito," duet (Adelaide, Lotario)
. "Cessi di Marte," recit (Lotario)
36. "Gioje e serto dona al merto," chorus
Anhang: *(9a.) "Già mi sembra al carro avvinto," aria (Lotario) (frag)*
(23a.) "D'instabile fortuna non sempre in tuo favore," aria (Berengario)
. "Inclito Re, Pavia mossa a pietade," recit (Lotario)
(31a.) "Vedrò più liete e belle o vago mio tesor," aria (Lotario) (frag)
Add scene: . "Ombre di vil timore," recit (Adelaide)
. *"Io vedo, sì, non più torbida la face," aria (Adelaide) (= Partenope, HWV27/45a, frag)*

1a.27   "Partenope," opera: HWV27
. "Ouverture"
I: 1. "Viva, viva!, viva, viva, Partenope, viva," chorus
. "Miei fidi, arride il Cielo," recit (Partenope)
. "Arsace, Armindo. Osserva!," recit (Armindo, Arsace, Partenope, Rosmira)
. "Regina, in folte schiere il popolo Cumano," recit (Ormonte & others)
2. "L'amor ed il destin combatterà per me," aria (Partenope)
3. "O Eurimene ha l'idea di Rosmira," aria (Arsace)
. "Cavalier, se gli Dei," recit (Rosmira, Armindo)
4. "Se non ti sai spiegar," aria (Rosmira)
. "Armindo, ardisci," recit (Armindo) (2 vers)
5a, b. "Voglio dire al mio tesoro," aria (Armindo) (2 vers)
A. "Ah! che un volto fatal," recit (Arsace, Rosmira)
B. "Ah, ingannator! Vaneggio?," recit (Rosmira, Arsace)
6. "Un altra volta ancor mi promettesti amor," aria (Rosmira)
. "Rosmira, oh Dio! Rosmira," recit (Arsace)
7. "Sento amor con novi dardi," aria (Arsace)
A. "Stan pronti i miei guerrier," recit (Partenope, Ormonte)
B. "Se guerra Emilio vuol'," recit (Partenope, Ormonte)
8a, b. "T'appresta forse amore," aria (Ormonte) (2 vers)
. "Signora! Armindo," recit (Armindo, Partenope)
. "E di che reo son io?," recit (Arsace, Partenope)
9. "Ed io per amato bene," duet & recit (Partenope, Arsace)
. "E se giunge Eurimene?," recit (Partenope, Arsace, Rosmira)
10. "Sei mia gioja, sei mio bene," aria (Partenope)
. "I novelli amor tuoi io stessa udii," recit (Rosmira, Arsace)
11. "Dimmi, pietoso Ciel," aria (Arsace)
. "Ecco Emilio! Reina," recit (Ormonte, Emilio, Partenope, Armindo, Rosmira)
12. "Ach'io pugnar saprò, armato di valor," aria (Emilio)
. "Arsace, tu sarai," recit (Partenope, Armindo, Rosmira, Arsace, Ormonte)
13. "Io ti levo dell'armi, non l'impero dell'anima mia," aria (Partenope)
. "Lascia, deh! lascia, o Prence, i cimenti!," recit (Arsace, Rosmira, Armindo)
14. "E figlio il mio timore d'amor e di pietà," aria (Arsace)
. "Prence, di te mi lagno," recit (Armindo, Rosmira)
15. "Io seguo sol fiero tra boschi le belve," aria (Rosmira)
II: 16. "Sinfonia"
. "Forti miei schiere, alla vicina impresa," recit (Emilio) (2 vers)
17. "Marche"
. "Ma le nemiche squadre," recit (Emilio, Partenope)
18. "Con valoroso mano. L'esercito Cumano gl'eroi Partenopei," chorus
19. "Sinfonia"
. "Soccorso! Armindo è teco," recit (Partenope, Armindo)
. "Renditi, o pure estinto," recit (Emilio, Arsace, Rosmira, Partenope)
20. "Vi circondi la gloria d'allori!," recit (Partenope, ...)
21. "Contro un pudico amor cotanto sdegno," recit accompagnato (Emilio)
22. "Barbaro fato, sì, la speme mi tradì," aria (Emilio)
23. "Care mura, care mura, in si bel giorno," arioso (Partenope)
. "Emilio! Alta Regina," recit (Partenope, Emilio, Rosmira, Arsace, Ormonte, Armindo)
24. "Voglio amare insin ch'io moro," aria (Partenope)
. "Ti bramo amico," recit (Arsace, Emilio, Armindo, Rosmira)
25. "E vuoi, con dure tempre," duet (Arsace, Rosmira)
. "Non può darsi in un petto," recit (Emilio, Armindo, Rosmira)

. "Che tumulto d'affetti," recit (Rosmira)
26. "Furie son dell'alma mia gelosia," aria (Rosmira)
. "A pro di chi t'offese," recit (Partenope, Arsace)
27. "Poterti dir vorrei l'affanno del mio cor," aria (Arsace)
. "Regina! Armindo, ancora tu mi devi," recit (Armindo, Partenope)
28a, b. "Non chiedo, oh luci vaghe," aria (Armindo) (2 vers)
. "Più d'ogn'altro sarebbe," recit (Partenope)
29. "Qual farfalletta gira a quel lume," aria (Partenope)
. "Quanto godo, Eurimene," recit (Armindo, Rosmira)
. "Rosmira mia, mio bene!," recit (Arsace, Rosmira)
30a, b. "Furibondo spira il vento," aria (Arsace) (2 vers)
III: 31. "Sinfonia"
. "Regina, ti compiace," recit (Armindo, Partenope, Arsace, Emilio)
32. "Non è incauto il mio consiglio," quartet (Partenope, Arsace, Armindo, Emilio)
. "Partenope, Eurimene," recit (Rosmira, Partenope, Arsace, Armindo, Emilio)
33. "Arsace, oh Dio, così infido l'inganno," arioso (Rosmira)
. "Che m'apre i lumi," recit (Partenope, Emilio, Armindo)
34. "Spera e godi, oh mio tesoro," aria (Partenope)
. "Prencipe, ardir! Quanto ti devo!," recit (Emilio, Armindo, Rosmira, Arsace)
35. "La speme ti consoli, ti rasserena il cor," aria (Emilio)
. "Rosmira, ove ti guida," recit (Arsace, Rosmira)
36. "Ch'io parta? sì, crudele, parto, ma senza cor," aria (Arsace)
. "Oh Dio! perchè dal petto," recit (Rosmira)
37. "Quel volto mi piace, ma temo quel core," aria (Rosmira)
. "Ormonte, ti destino," recit (Partenope, Ormonte, Armindo)
38. "Nobil core che ben ama," aria (Armindo)
. "Non chiedo, oh miei tormenti," recit (Arsace)
39. "Ma quai note di mesti lamenti," arioso (Arsace)
40. "Cieli! che miro? abbandonato e solo," recit accompagnato (Rosmira)
. "Ma Partenope vien," recit (Rosmira, Partenope, Arsace)
41. "Un cor infedele si deve punir," trio (Partenope, Arsace, Rosmira)
. "Passo di duolo in duolo," recit (Arsace)
42. "Fatto è Amor un Dio d'inferno," aria (Arsace)
. "Di bel desire avvampo," recit (Emilio)
43. "La gloria in nobil alma," aria (Emilio)
44. "Sinfonia"
. "Regina, in queste arene," recit (Ormonte, Partenope, Emilio, Rosmira, Armindo, Arsace)
45a. "Sì, scherza, sì, sempre Amor con doppia face," aria (Partenope)
45b. "Amanti voi ch'andate spesso cangiando amor," aria (Arsace)
A. "Armindo sia mio sposo," recit (Partenope, Armindo, Arsace, Rosmira)
B. "Tu vanne in libertate," recit (Partenope)
46. "D'Imeneo le belle Tede splendon fauste in questo dì," chorus
Anhang: (11a.) "Io son ferito da doppio strale," aria (Arsace) (= Scipione, HWV20/34)
(26.) "Qual farfalletta gira a quel lume," aria (Emilio)

1a.28   "Poro, Rè dell'Indie," opera: HWV28
. "Ouverture"
I: 1. "Fermatevi, compagni," recit accompagnato (Poro)
. "Mio Re, che fai!," recit (Gandarte, Poro)
2. "È prezzo leggiero d'un suddito il sangue," aria (Gandarte)
. "Guerrier, t'arresta, e cedi," recit (Timagene, Poro, Alessandro)
3. "Vedrai, vedrai con tuo periglio di questa spada il lampo," aria (Poro)
. "Oh sublime ardimento!," recit (Alessandro, Timagene, Erissena)
4. "Vil trofeo d'un alma imbelle," aria (Alessandro)
. "Questo è Alessandro?," recit (Erissena, Timagene)
5. "Chi vive amante sai che delira," aria (Erissena)
. "Perfidi! ite di Poro," recit (Cleofide, Poro)
6. "Se mai più sarò geloso," arioso (Poro)
. "Erissena, che veggo?," recit (Cleofide, Poro, Erissena)
7a, b. "Se mai turbo il tuo riposo," aria (Cleofide) (2 vers)
. "Cleofide, va al campo," recit (Poro, Erissena, Gandarte)
8. "Se possono tanto due luci vezzose," aria (Poro)
. "Dimmi: vedesti," recit (Erissena, Gandarte)
9. "Compagni nell'amore se tolerar non sai," aria (Erissena)
. "Ecco, vien la cagion," recit (Alessandro)
10. "Sinfonia"
. "Ciò che t'offro, Alessandro," recit (Cleofide, Alessandro)
. "Monarca, impaziente il Duce Asbite," recit (Timagene, Alessandro)
. "Eccola; oh gelosia!," recit (Poro, Cleofude, Alessandro)
11. "Se amor a questo petto," aria (Alessandro)
. "Lode a gli Dei!," recit (Poro, Cleofide)
12. "Se mai turbo il tuo riposo," duet (Poro, Cleofide)
II: 13. "Sinfonia"
. "Signor, l'India festiva esulta meco al tuo gradito arrivo," recit (Cleofide, Alessandro, Timagene)
. "Seguitemi, oh compagni!," recit (Gandarte)

. "Mio ben! Lasciami!," recit (Cleofide, Poro)
14. "Caro amico amplesso!," duet (Cleofide, Poro)
. "Ah Ciel! viene il nemico," recit (Cleofide, Poro)
. "Crudel, t'arresta!," recit (Alessandro, Cleofide, Poro)
. "Pronto le Greche schiere," recit (Timagene, Poro, Cleofide, Alessandro)
15. "D'un barbaro scortese non rammentar l'offese," aria (Alessandro)
. "Macedoni, alla Reggia," recit (Timagene, Cleofide, Poro)
16. "Digli, ch'io son fedele," aria (Cleofide)
. "Tenerezze ingegnose!," recit (Poro, Timagene)
17. "Senza procelle ancora si perde quel nocchiero," aria (Poro)
. "E tentò di svenarti?," recit (Gandarte, Cleofide)
. "Per salvarti, oh Regina," recit (Alessandro, Cleofide, Gandarte)
. "Quanto dobbiamo a' tuoi pietosi inganni!," recit (Cleofide, Gandarte, Erissena)
18. "Se il Ciel mi diride dal caro mio sposo," aria (Cleofide)
. "Adorata Erissena," recit (Gandarte, Erissena)
19. "Se viver non poss'io lungi da te, mio bene," aria (Gandarte)
. "E pur, chi'l crederia?," recit (Erissena)
20. "Di rendermi la calma prometti, oh speme infida," aria (Erissena)
III: 21. "Sinfonia"
. "Erissena! Che miro? Poro, tu vivi?," recit (Poro, Erissena)
22. "Risveglia lo sdegno, rammenta l'offesa," aria (Poro)
. "Ah! funesto commando!," recit (Erissena, Cleofide)
. "Reina, è dunque vero," recit (Alessandro, Cleofide, Erissena)
. "Cleofide, si presto io non credea," recit (Erissena, Cleofide)
23. "Se troppo crede al ciglio colui che va per l'onde," aria (Cleofide)
. "Giunge Alessandro; oh Dei!," recit (Erissena, Alessandro)
24. "Come il candore d'intatta neve," aria (Erissena)
. "Per qual via non pensata," recit (Alessandro, Timagene)
25. "Serbati a grandi imprese," aria (Alessandro)
. "Ecco spezzato il solo filo," recit (Poro, Gandarte)
. "Fermati! Oh Ciel, che fai?," recit (Erissena, Poro, Gandarte)
26. "Dov'è? s'affretti per me la morte," aria (Poro)
. "Gandarte, in questo stato," recit (Erissena, Gandarte) (2 vers)
27a, b. "Mio ben, ricordati, se avvien ch'io mora," aria (Gandarte) (2 vers)
. "D'inaspettati eventi," recit (Erissena)
28. "Son confusa pastorella," aria (Erissena)
. "Tu mi contrasti in vano," recit (Poro)
29. "Sinfonia"
. "Nella odorata pira si destino le fiamme!," recit (Cleofide, Alessandro, Poro)
30. "Spirto amato, spirto amato dell'idol mio," arioso (Cleofide)
. "Come! Poro? Ed è vero?," recit (Cleofide, Alessandro, Poro, Erissena, Gandarte, Timagene)
31. "Caro, vieni al mio seno," duet (Cleofide, Poro)
32. "Dopo tanto penare è più grato il piacer," chorus
Add in 1736: II: . "Torrente cresciuto per torbida piena," aria (Alessandro) (= Siroe, HWV24/27)
. "Come il candore d'intatta neve," aria (?Alessandro)
25. "Dopo notte atra e funesta," aria (Alessandro) (= Ariodante, HWV33/47)

1a.29   "Ezio," opera: HWV29
. "Ouverture"
I: 1. "La Marche"
. "Signor, vincemmo. Attila fugitivo," recit (Ezio, Valentiniano)
2. "Se tu la reggi al volo," aria (Valentiniano)
. "Lascia, ch'al senti stringa," recit (Massimo, Ezio, Fulvia)
3. "Pensa a serbarmi, oh cara, i dolci affetti tuoi," aria (Ezio)
. "È tempo, oh genitore," recit (Fulvia, Massimo)
4. "Caro padre, a me non dei," aria (Fulvia)
. "Un oltraggiato amore," recit (Massimo)
5. "Il nocchier, che si figura," aria (Massimo)
. "Del vincitor ti chiedo," recit (Onoria, Varo)
6. "Quanto mai felice siete," aria (Onoria)
. "Perchè tanto tormento?," recit (Varo)
7. "Se un bell'ardire può innamorarti," aria (Varo)
. "Olà? Ezio qui venga?," recit (Valentiniano, Massimo)
8. "Se povero il ruscello," aria (Massimo)
. "Signor! Duce, un momento," recit (Ezio, Valentiniano)
9. "So chi t'accese: basta per ora," aria (Valentiniano)
. "Ezio, ti leggo in volto l'ire del cor," recit (Fulvia, Ezio)
. "Ezio, vole il germano avvilir la mia mano," recit (Onoria, Ezio, Fulvia)
10. "Se fedele mi brama il regnante," aria (Ezio)
. "A Cesare nascondi," recit (Fulvia, Onoria)
. "Via, per mio danno ad una," recit (Fulvia)
11. "Finchè un zeffiro soave," aria (Fulvia)
II: 12a. "Symfonia"
A. "Avrà punito Emilio," recit (Massimo, Fulvia)
12b. "Sinfonia"

. "Qual silenzio è mai questo!," recit accompagnato (Massimo)
B. "Ah! genitor! Figlia, che porti?," recit (Fulvia, Massimo)
. "Ogni via custodite, ed ogni ingresso," recit (Valentiniano, Massimo, Fulvia)
. "Cesare, in vano il traditor cercai," recit (Varo, Valentiniano, Massimo)
13. "Vi fida lo sposo, vi fida il regnante," aria (Valentiniano)
. "E puoi d'un tuo delitto," recit (Fulvia, Massimo)
14. "Va! va, dal furor portate," aria (Massimo)
15. "Che fo? dove mi volgo?," recit accompagnato (Fulvia)
. "Ah, qual consiglio mai ...," recit (Fulvia, Ezio)
. "Cesare a te m'invia," recit (Varo, Ezio, Fulvia)
16. "Recagli quell'acciaro, che gli diffese il trono," aria (Ezio)
. "Varo, se amasti mai," recit (Fulvia, Varo)
17. "Quel finger affento allorche non s'ama," aria (Fulvia)
18. "Folle è colui, che al tuo favor si fida," recit accompagnato (Varo)
19. "Nasce al bosco in rozza cuna," aria (Varo)
. "Massimo, ach'io lo veggo," recit (Onoria, Massimo)
. "Onoria, non partir," recit (Valentiniano, Onoria, Massimo)
20. "Finchè per te mi palpita timido in petto il cor," aria (Onoria)
. "Olà! qui si conduca," recit (Valentiniano, Fulvia, Massimo)
. "Stelle! che mirol," recit (Ezio, Fulvia, Valentiniano, Massimo)
21. "La mia costanza non si sgomenta," aria (Fulvia)
. "Ah! ingrata!," recit (Valentiniano, Ezio, Massimo)
. "Chi di me più felice?," recit (Ezio)
22. "Ecco alle mie catene, ecco a morir m'invio," aria (Ezio)
III: 23. "Sinfonia"
. "Ezio qui venga, il suo fatal periglio," recit (Onoria, Ezio)
24. "Guarda pria se in questa fronte, se in questa fronte," aria (Ezio)
. "Eh ben, da quel superbo," recit (Valentiniano, Onoria)
25. "Peni tu per un ingrata," aria (Onoria)
. "Olà! Varo si chiami," recit (Valentiniano, Varo)
. "Signor, tutto sedai," recit (Massimo)
. "Ezio, qui tra di noi d'odio più non si parli," recit (Valentiniano, Massimo, Ezio)
. "Vedi qual dono. Fulvia!," recit (Valentiniano, Ezio, Massimo, Fulvia)
26. "Se la mia vita dono è d'Augusto," aria (Ezio)
. "Che mai sarà?," recit (Massimo, Fulvia, Valentiniano)
. "Eseguito è il tuo cenno: Ezio morì," recit (Varo, Fulvia, Massimo)
. "Liete novelle, Augusto," recit (Onoria, Valentiniano, Massimo, Fulvia)
. "Massimo, di scolparti," recit (Valentiniano, Fulvia, Massimo)
27. "Per tutto il timore perigli m'addita," aria (Valentiniano)
. "Cara figlia, per te vivo," recit (Massimo, Fulvia)
28. "Tergi l'ingiuste lagrime, dilegua il tuo lartiro," aria (Massimo)
29. "Misera, dove son!," recit accompagnato (Fulvia)
30. "Ah! non son io che parlo," aria (Fulvia)
. "Inorridisci, o Roma," recit (Massimo, Varo)
31. "Gia risonar d'intorno," aria (Varo)
. "Ah traditori! Amico," recit (Valentiniano, Massimo, Fulvia)
. "Cesare viva! Ezio! Che veggo!," recit (Ezio, Varo, Fulvia, Valentiniano, Massimo, Onoria)
32. "Stringo al fine il mio contento," aria (Ezio)
33. "Sulle sponde di cocito," aria (Fulvia)
34. "Cangia sorte di ripente," aria (Onoria)
35. "Un gran cor non dà ricetto," aria (Varo)
36. "È più bella quella fede," chorus

1a.30 "Sosarme, Rè di Media," opera: HWV30
. "Ouverture"
I: . "Di mio padre al furore," recit (Argone)
1. "Voi miei fidi compagni ora mirate," recit accompagnato (Argone)
2. "Alla stragge, alla morte!," choro militare
. "Madre, e Regina. Elmira. E tanta fede," recit (Elmira, Erenice)
3. "Rasserena Erenice il mesto ciglio," recit accompagnato (Erenice, Elmira)
4. "Rendi'l sereno al ciglio, madre, non pianger più," aria (Elmira)
. "Giusti Numi, conforto," recit (Erenice, Elmira)
. "Così un figlio ribelle," recit (Erenice)
5. "Forte inciampo al suo furore," aria (Erenice)
. "Melo, mio prence, soffri ch'io nipote t'appelli," recit (Altomaro, Melo)
6. "Fra l'ombre e gl'orrori farfalla confusa," aria (Altomaro)
. "Come più dell'usato," recit (Sosarme, Melo)
7. "Sì, sì, sì, sì, mi naccia, e vinta," aria (Melo)
. "Il cesar dagli assalti," recit (Haliate, Sosarme)
8. "Il mio valore ch'albergo in petto," aria (Sosarme)
. "Così dunque sospiran," recit (Haliate)
9. "La turba adulatrice da me ritiri'l piè," aria (Haliate)
. "Amici, troppo oscuro," recit (Argone)
. "Ferma, o figlio, ove vai?," recit (Erenice, Elmira, Argone)
. "Ma chi ritorna in vita," recit (Argone, Erenice)

    10. "Due parti del core tra'l figlio e'l consorte," aria (Erenice)
    . "Oh Diva Hecate," recit (Elmira)
    11. "Dite pace, e fulminante," aria (Elmira)
II: 12. "Padre, germano, e sposo di voi chi vincerà," arioso (Elmira)
    . "E ben dall'alta torre, di, che sorgesti, oh figlia?," recit (Erenice, Elmira)
    13. "Sinfonia"
    . "Ma, oh Dei! ritorna il figlio," recit (Erenice)
    . "Madre, Germana ...," recit (Argone, Erenice, Elmira)
    14. "E udir potrei? direi che sei un spietato, un traditor," duet (Erenice, Argone)
    . "Mio Re l'ultimo sforzo," recit (Altomaro, Haliate)
    . "Padre, Signor! Che fia?," recit (Melo, Haliate, Altomaro)
    15. "Se discordia ci disciolse," aria (Haliate)
    . "E così tu disprezzi," recit (Altomaro, Melo)
    16. "So ch'il Ciel ben spesso gode," aria (Melo)
    . "Quanto più Melo ha sdegno," recit (Altomaro)
    17. "Sento il cor che lieto gode," aria (Altomaro)
    . "Grazie al Cielo, Signor," recit (Elmira, Sosarme)
    18. "Per le porte del tormento passan l'anime a gioir," duet (Elmira, Sosarme)
    . "Signor, tuo reggio sangue," recit (Erenice, Sosarme, Elmira)
    19. "Alle sfere della gloria," aria (Sosarme)
    . "Son tuo congiunto," recit (Sosarme, Argone)
    . "A queste voci, io riconosco il figlio," recit (Erenice, Elmira, Sosarme, Argone, Altomaro)
    . "Oh Dei! pria che succeda," recit (Erenice, Sosarme, Elmira)
    20. "Vado, vado al campo, a combater col pianto," aria (Erenice)
    . "Mio sposo, ahi qual orror," recit (Elmira, Sosarme)
    21. "In mille dolci modi al senti stringerò," aria (Sosarme)
    . "Parmi ch'un dolce ragio di bella speme," recit (Elmira)
    22. "Vola l'augello del caro nido," aria (Elmira)
III: 23. "Sinfonia"
    . "Mi sigue la Regina, ajuto, o frodi!," recit (Altomaro, Haliate, Melo)
    . "Ella giunge. Consorte ....," recit (Altomaro, Erenice, Haliate)
    24. "S'io cadrò per tuo consiglio," aria (Haliate)
    . "Melo dov'è'l tuo zelo?," recit (Erenice, Melo)
    25. "Cuor di madre, e cuor di moglie," aria (Erenice)
    . "A deluder le frodi," recit (Melo)
    26. "Sincero affetto dolce preghiere," aria (Melo)
    . "Per la segreta porta," recit (Argone)
    . "E amor di figlio? Un padre reo l'estinse," recit (Elmira, Argone, Sosarme)
    . "Fermati, ingrato! Ah! mostro," recit (Elmira, Sosarme)
    27. "M'opporrò da generoso," aria (Sosarme)
    . "Correte pur a fiumi," recit (Elmira)
    28. "Vorrei, ne pur saprei che la spene nel mio core," aria (Elmira)
    . "Altomaro si renda libero lo steccato," recit (Haliate, Altomaro)
    29. "Tiene Giove in mano il folgore gl'empi sol per fulminar," aria (Altomaro)
    . "Ah padre! eccoti al piede," recit (Melo, Haliate)
    . "Signor qui giunge Argone," recit (Altomaro, Argone, Haliate)
    . "Oh! padre! Ah! figlio mio!," recit (Melo, Erenice, Haliate, Argone, Altomaro)
    . "Io fui presente. Io testimon ne sono," recit (Elmira, Sosarme, Argone, Haliate, Enerice)
    30. "Tu caro, caro sei il dolce mio tesoro," duet (Elmiro, Sosarme)
    . "Fugga da questo suol," recit (Sosarme)
    31. "Dopo l'ire si funeste," chorus
Anhang: (1.) "Voi miei fidi compagni valerosi guerrier," recit accompagnato (Argone)
    (16./17.) "So ch'il ciel ben spesso gode," aria (Sancio) (frag)
    (21.) aria (Sosarme) (frag)

    . "Ouverture"
I: 1. "Gieroglifici eterni," accompagnato & recit (Zoroastro)
    2. "Stimulato dalla gloria," arioso (Orlando)
    . "Purgalo ormai da effeminati sensi!," recit (Zoroastro, Orlando)
    3. "Sinfonia"
    . "Mira, e prendi l'esempio!," recit (Zoroastro)
    4. "Lascia Amor, e siegui Marte, va! combatti," aria (Zoroastro)
    5. "Imagini funeste," recit accompagnato (Orlando)
    6. "Non fu già men forte Alcide," aria (Orlando)
    7. "Quanto diletto avea tra questi boschi!," recit accompagnato (Dorinda)
    . "Io non so che sian questi moti," recit (Dorinda)
    8. "Itene pur fremendo," accompagnato & recit (Orlando, Dorinda)
    9. "Ho un certo rossore, di dir quel che sento," aria (Dorinda)
    . "M'hai vinto al fin," recit (Angelica)
    10. "Ritornava al suo bel viso, fatto già bianco e vermiglio," duet arioso (Angelica, Medoro)
    . "Spera, mio ben, che presto," recit (Angelica, Medoro)
    11. "Chi possessore è del mio core," aria (Angelica)
    . "Ecco Dorinda," recit (Medoro, Dorinda)
    12. "Se'l cor mai ti dirà, ch'io mi scordi di te," aria (Medoro)

. "Povera me!," recit (Dorinda)
13. "O care parolette, o dolci sguardi!," aria (Dorinda)
. "Noti a me sono," recit (Zoroastro, Angelica, Orlando)
14. "Se fedel vuoi ch'io ti creda, fa'che veda," aria (Angelica)
. "T'ubbidirò, crudele," recit (Orlando)
15. "Fammi combattere mostri e tifei," aria (Orlando)
. "Angelica, deh! lascia ...," recit (Medoro, Angelica)
. "O Angelica, o Medoro!," recit (Dorinda, Angelica, Medoro)
16. "Consolati, o bella," trio (Angelica, Dorinda, Medoro)
II: 17. "Quando spieghi i tuoi tormenti," arioso (Dorinda)
. "Perchè, gentil Dorinda," recit (Orlando, Dorinda)
18. "Se mi rivolgo al prato, veder Medoro mio," aria (Dorinda)
. "È questa la mercede, Angelica spietata!," recit (Orlando)
19. "Cielo! se tu il consenti," aria (Orlando)
. "A qual rischio vi espone," recit (Zoroastro, Angelica, Medoro)
20. "Tra caligini profonde," aria (Zoroastro)
. "Da queste amiche piante," recit (Angelica, Medoro)
21. "Verdi allori, sempre unito," aria (Medoro)
. "Dopo tanti perigli," recit (Angelica)
22. "Non potrà, non potrà dirmi ingrata, no, no, no, no," aria (Angelica)
. "Dove, dove guidate," recit (Orlando)
. "Tutto a poter partire ha già disposto," recit (Angelica)
23. "Verdi piante," aria (Angelica)
. "Ah! perfida, qui sei!," recit (Orlando, Angelica)
. "Ohime! che miro?," recit (Medoro)
. "Amor, caro Amore!," recit (Angelica, Orlando)
24. "Ah! stigie larve," recit accompagnato (Orlando)
III: 25. "Sinfonia"
. "Di Dorinda alle mura," recit (Medoro, Dorinda)
26. "Vorrei poterti amar, il cor ti vorrei dar," aria (Medoro)
. "Più abbligata gli sono," recit (Dorinda)
. "Pur ti trovo, o mio bene," recit (Orlando, Dorinda)
27. "Unisca amor in noi gli miei gl'affetti tuoi," duet arioso & recit (Dorinda, Orlando)
28. "Già lo stringo, già l'abbraccio con la forza del mio braccio," aria (Orlando)
. "Di Dorinda all'albergo," recit (Angelica, Dorinda)
29. "Così giusta è questa speme," aria (Angelica)
. "S'è corrisposto un core," recit (Dorinda)
30. "Amor è qual vento, che gira il cervello," aria (Dorinda)
. "Impari ogn'un da Orlando," recit (Zoroastro)
31. "O voi, del mio poter ministri eletti," recit accompagnato (Zoroastro)
. "Là al furor dell'eroe siatene attenti," recit (Zoroastro)
32. "Sorge infausta una lrocella," aria (Zoroastro)
. "Dorinda, e perchè piangi?," recit (Angelica, Dorinda, Orlando)
. "Più non fuggir potrai," recit (Orlando, Angelica)
33. "Finchè prendi ancora il sangue," duet (Angelica, Orlando)
. "Vieni!... Vanne precipitando," recit (Orlando, Angelica)
34. "Già per la man d'Orlando d'ogni mostro più rio," recit accompagnato (Orlando)
35. "Già l'ebro mio ciglio quel dolce liquore," aria (Orlando)
. "Ecco il tempo prefisso!," recit (Zoroastro)
36. "Tu, che del gran Tonante coll'artiglio celeste," recit accompagnato (Zoroastro)
37. "Sinfonia"
. "Ah! che fate, Signor?," recit (Dorinda, Zoroastro)
. "Dormo ancora, o son desto?," recit (Orlando, Dorinda)
38. "Per far, mia diletta, per te la vendetta," ariso (Orlando, Angelica)
. "Che vedo, oh Dei! Angelica, tu vivi?," recit (Orlando, Angelica, Medoro, Zoroastro)
39. "Vinse in canti, battaglie," recit accompagnato (Orlando, Angelica, Dorinda, Medoro, Zoroastro)
40. "Trionfa oggi'l mio cor, e da si bell'aurora" (Orlando)
. "Con un diverso ardor, giacchè ciascun è pago," chorus
Anhang: *(3.) "Sinfonia" (frag)*
. "Vaga, mia Dea, che con pietosa mano," recit (Medoro, Angelica)
(25.) "Sinfonia"

1a.32 "Arianna in Creta," opera: HWV32
. "Ouverture"
I: . "Egeo, mio genitor," recit (Teseo, Minos, Arianna, Carilda, Tauride)
1. "Sinfonia"
. "Qual presagio funesto!," recit (Minos, Teseo, Arianna, Carilda, Tauride)
. "Pensa, oh Carilda," recit (Tauride, Teseo)
2a. "Mirami, altero in volto," aria (Tauride)
2b. "Del labbro tuo l'accenti portan per l'aria i venti," aria (Tauride)
. "Non si disperi," recit (Teseo, Arianna, Carilda)
3. "Dille, che nel mio seno," aria (Carilda)
. "Pur siam soli, idol mio," recit (Tseo, Arianna)
4. "Deh! lascia un tal desio ti prego idolo mio!," aria (Arianna)
. "Ma, non è questi Alceste?," recit (Teseo, Alceste)

5a, b. "Nel pugnar," aria (Teseo) (2 vers)
  . "Speriam; ma non si attenda," recit (Alceste)
6. "Tal' or d'oscuro velo ricopre il bel sereno," aria (Alceste)
  . "Non più, non più che l'amor tuo m'offende?," recit (Carilda, Tauride)
  . "Son le vittime pronte?," recit (Minos, Tauride, Alceste, Carilda, Teseo, Arianna)
  . "Perdona, Alceste," recit (Carilda)
7. "Quel cor che adora vago sembiante," aria (Carilda)
  . "Della patria e de' miseri il soccorso," recit (Teseo, Minos, Arianna)
  . "Volesti, al fin volesti nel tuo rischio," recit (Arianna, Teseo)
8. "Sdegnata sei con me, mi credi ingannator," aria (Teseo)
  . "E mi lascio il crudele?," recit (Arianna)
9. "Sdegno, amore, fanno guerra a questo core," aria (Arianna)
II: 10. "Oh patria! oh cittadini!," recit accompagnato & arioso (Teseo)
  . "Disseratevi, o porte," recit accompagnato (Il Sonno)
  . "Io ti tengo, o mostro infame!," arioso (Teseo)
  . "Ah! che pur sogno ancor!," recit (Teseo)
  . "Per Carilda, e per me dunque in periglio," recit (Alceste, Teseo)
11. "Salda quercia inerta balza," aria (Teseo)
  . "Alceste è qui, si tenti," recit (Arianna, Alceste)
12. "Non ha diffesa, non ha consiglio un core," aria (Alceste)
  . "Il soccorrer Carilda," recit (Arianna)
13. "So che non è più mio, m'abbandonò l'ingrato," aria (Arianna)
  . "Pensa, che di Carilda il gran campion è forte," recit (Minos, Tauride, Arianna)
14. "Qual Leon, che fere irato," aria (Tauride)
  . "Eh! la speme l'inganna, vieni!," recit (Tauride, Carilda, Arianna)
  . "Me rispettate," recit (Arianna, Carilda)
15. "Narrar gli allor saprai, allor saprai," aria (Carilda)
  . "Idolo mio! Va, perfido," recit (Teseo, Arianna)
A. "Ti saresti ingannato," recit (Teseo)
B. "Nelli sdegni d'Arianna vuol scherzar," recit (Teseo)
16a, b. "Al fine amore," aria (Teseo) (2 vers)
  . "Fuggiam, fuggiam! Vieni mia sposa in Lenno!," recit (Tauride, Carilda)
17. "Che se fiera poi mi nieghi," aria (Tauride)
  . "Numi, e voi lo soffrite!," recit (Carilda, Alceste)
18. "Son qual stanco pellegrino," aria (Alceste)
  . "Perdon ti chiedo ...," recit (Teseo, Arianna)
  . "Ov'è Carilda?," recit (Tauride, Arianna, Teseo, Minos)
19. "Se ti condanno," aria (Minos)
  . "Ah! silenzio spietato!," recit (Arianna, Teseo)
20. "Bell'idolo amato, rasciuga quel pianto," duet (Arianna, Teseo)
  . "Quel crudele di me pietà non sente," recit (Arianna)
21. "Se nel bosco resta solo rusignolo col suo canto," aria (Arianna)
III: 22. "Sinfonia"
  . "Vorrai dunque, oh Carilda?," recit (Alceste, Carilda)
23. "Un tenero pensiero mi parla al cor per te," aria (Carilda)
  . "Questa sola speranza," recit (Alceste)
24. "Lusinghiera nel mio seno bella sorge la speranza," aria (Alceste)
25a, b. "Ove son, qual orrore?," recit accompagnato (Teseo) (2 vers)
26a, b. "Qui ti sfido, o mostro infame!," aria (Teseo) (2 vers)
  . "Ho vinto! Grazie ai Numi, salva," recit (Teseo) (2 vers)
  . "Arianna! Che miro?," recit (Teseo, Arianna)
27. "Turbato il mar si vede con subita procella," aria (Arianna)
  . "Se il Minotauro ei vinse, non ho men forte il core" recit (Tauride)
28. "In mar tempestoso s'affanna il nocchiero," aria (Tauride)
  . "Di te in traccia nè vengo," recit (Teseo, Tauride)
  . "Vincesti; tanto basti," recit (Minos, Teseo, Arianna)
29. "Mira adesso questo seno più sereno," duet (Arianna, Teseo)
  . "Meta del mio gior," recit (Teseo, Arianna, Alceste, Carilda, Minos) (2 vers)
30a, b. "Bella sorge la speranza," aria (Teseo) (2 vers)
31a, b. "Bella sorge la speranza," chorus
32. "Gavotta"
33. "Menuetto"
34. "Gavotta"
35. "Musette"
36. "Menuetto"
Anhang: III: . "Bella, tu vivi. Intendo," recit (Alceste, Carilda)
  . "Ch'il crederia? pur doppo tante pene," recit (Alceste)

1a.33 "Ariodante," opera: HWV33
  . "Ouverture"
I: 1. "Vezzi, lusinge, e brio rendano il volto mio," arioso (Ginevra)
  . "Ami dunque, oh Signora?," recit (Dalinda, Ginevra)
  . "Ginevra? Tanto ardire?," recit (Polinesso, Ginevra)
2. "Orrida a gl'occhi miei," aria (Ginevra)
  . "Orgogliosa beltade!," recit (Polinesso, Dalinda)

3a, b. "Apri le luci, e mira gli ascosi altrui martiri," aria (Dalinda)
. "Mie speranze, che fate?," recit (Polinesso)
4. "Coperta la frode di lana servile," aria (Polinesso)
5. "Qui d'amor nel suo linguaggio parla il rio," arioso (Ariodante)
. "T'amerò dunque sempre," recit (Ariodante, Ginevra)
6. "Prendi, prendi da questa mano," duet (Ginevra, Ariodante)
. "Non vi turbate, bell'alme innamorate!," recit (Il Re di Scozia, Ginevra, Ariodante)
7. "Volate, amori, di due bei cori," aria (Ginevra)
. "Vanne pronto, Odoardo," recit (Il Re, Odoardo)
8. "Voli colla sua tromba," aria (Il Re)
. "Oh, felice mio core!," recit (Ariodante)
9. "Con l'ali di costanza alza il suo volo amor," aria (Ariodante)
. "Conosco il merto tuo," recit (Polinesso, Dalinda)
10. "Spero, spero per voi, sì, sì, begli occhi in questo dì," aria (Polinesso)
. "Dalinda, in occidente," recit (Lurcanio, Dalinda)
11. "Del mio sol vezzosi rai," aria (Lurcanio)
. "Ah! che quest'alma amante," recit (Dalinda)
12. "Il primo ardor, il primo ardor è così caro a questo core," aria (Dalinda)
. "Pare, ovunque mi aggiri," recit (Ariodante)
. "E qual propizia stella," recit (Ginevra, Ariodante)
13. "Sinfonia"
14. "Se rinasce nel mio cor, bella gioja, bella speme," duet (Ginevra, Ariodante)
15. "Si godete al vostro amor," soli & chorus (Ginevra, Ariodante)
Ballo: 16. "Gavotte"
17. "Musette"
18. "Musette"
19. (Allegro)
II: 20. "Sinfonia"
. "Di Dalinda l'amore," recit (Polinesso)
. "Eccolo, o amico, e come qui ti ritrovo?, recit (Polinesso, Ariodante)
21. "Tu preparati a morire," aria (Ariodante)
. "Ginevra? O mio Signore!," recit (Polinesso, Dalinda, Lurcanio, Ariodante)
22. "Tu vivi, vivi e punito rimanga l'eccesso," aria (Lurcanio)
. "E vivo ancora?," recit (Ariodante)
23. "Scherza infida!," aria (Ariodante)
. "Lo stral feri nel segno," recit (Polinesso, Dalinda)
24a, b. "Se tanto piace al cor il volto tuo Signor," aria (Polinesso) (2 vers)
. "Felice fu il mio inganno," recit (Polinesso)
25. "Se l'inganno sortisce felice," aria (Polinesso)
. "Andiam, fidi, al consiglio," recit (Il Re, Odoardo)
26a. "Invida sorte avara, misero in questo dì!," aria (Il Re)
26b. "Più contento e più felice," aria (Il Re)
27. "Mi palpita il core nè intendo perchè," aria (Ginevra)
. "Sta lieta, oh Principessa," recit (Dalinda, Il Re, Ginevra)
. "Mio Re. Lurcanio, oh! Dei!," recit (Lurcanio, Il Re)
28. "Il tuo sangue, ed il tuo zelo, per la figlia e per astrea," aria (Lurcanio)
. "Quante sventure un giorno sol ne Iorta!," recit (Odoardo, Dalinda, Ginevra, Il Re)
29. "A me impudica? Oh Ciel, che intesi!," recit accompagnato (Ginerva, Dalinda)
. "Si rischiara la mente," recit (Dalinda, Ginevra)
30. "Il mio crudel martoro crescer non può di più," aria (Ginevra)
31. "Entrée des Songes agréables"
32. "Entrée des Songes funestes"
33. (Allegro)
34. "Entrée des Songes agréables effrayés"
35. "Le combat des Songes funestes et agréables"
36. "Che vivi? oh Dei! misera me! non ponno," recit accompagnato (Ginevra)
37. "Entrée de' Mori"
38. "Rondeau"
III: 39. "Sinfonia"
. "Numi! lasciar mi vivere per darmi mille morti," arioso (Ariodante)
. "Perfidi! io son tradita! Ah, Duca iniquo!," recit (Dalinda, Ariodante)
40. "Cieca notte, infidi sguardi, spoglie infauste, insano core," aria (Ariodante)
. "Ingrato Polinesso," recit (Dalinda) (2 vers)
41a, b. "Neghittosi or voi che fate?," aria (Dalinda) (2 vers)
. "Sire; deh! non negare a figlia supplicante," recit (Odoardo, Il Re, Polinesso)
42. "Dover, giustizia, amor m'accendono nel cor," aria (Polinesso)
. "Or venga a me la figlia," recit (Il Re)
. "Eccola figlia; ahi vista!," recit (Il Re, Ginevra)
43. "Io ti bacio, o mano augusta, dolce a me benchè severa," aria (Ginevra)
. "Figlia, da dubbia sorte," recit (Il Re, Ginevra)
44. "Al sen ti stringo e parto," aria (Il Re)
. "Così mi lascia il padre?," recit (Ginevra)
45. "Sì, morrò; ma l'onor mio meco, oh Dio! morir dovrà?," aria (Ginevra)
46. "Sinfonia"
. "Arrida il Cielo alla giustizia," recit (Lurcanio, Polinesso, Odoardo, Il Re)

. "Ferma, Signor, non manca difesa," recit (Ariodante, Il Re, Lurcanio)
. "E Dalinda, dov'è? Ti è presente," recit (Il Re, Dalinda, Odoardo)
47. "Dopo notte, atra e funesta," aria (Ariodante)
. "Dalinda! ecco risorge," recit (Lurcanio, Dalinda)
48. "Dite spera, e son contento," duet (Dalinda, Lurcanio)
. "Da dubbia infausta sorte," recit (Ginevra)
49. "Manca, oh Dei! la mia costanza," arioso (Ginevra)
50. "Sinfonia"
. "Figlia, innocente figlia!," recit (Il Re, Ariodante, Dalinda, Lurcanio, Ginevra)
51. "Bramo haver mille vite," duet (Ariodante, Ginevra)
52. "Ogn'uno acclami," chorus
53. "Gavotte"
54a, b. "Rondeau" (2 vers)
55. (w/ out tempo markings)
56. "Andante allegro"
57. "Sa trionfar ogn' or virtute in ogni cor," chorus
Anhang: *31a. "Entrée des Songes agréables" (frag)*

1a.34   "Alcina," opera: HWV34
. "Ouverture"
I: . "Oh Dei! quivi non scorgo," recit (Bradamante, Melisso, Morgana)
1. "O s'apre al riso, o parla, o tace," aria (Morgana)
2a, b. "Questo è cielo di contenti," chorus (2 vers)
3. "Gavotte"
4. "Sarabande"
5. "Menuet"
6. "Gavotte"
. "Ecco l'infido," recit (Bradamante, Melisso, Alcina)
7. "Di', cor mio, quanto t'amai," aria (Alcina)
. "Generosi guerrier, deh! per pietade," recit (Oberto, Melisso, Bradamante)
8. "Chi m'insegna il caro padre? chi mi rende il genitor," aria (Oberto)
. "Mi ravisi Ruggier, dimmi?," recit (Bradamante, Ruggiero, Melisso)
9. "Di te mi rido, semplice stolto," aria (Ruggiero)
. "Qua dunque ne veniste," recit (Oronte, Bradamante)
. "Io sono tua diffesa," recit (Morgana, Bradamante)
10. "È gelosia, forza è d'amore," aria (Bradamante)
. "Io dunque ... Audace Oronte, in te ritorna," recit (Oronte, Morgana)
. "Vo cercando la bella cagion," recit (Ruggiero)
11. "Bramo di trionfar," aria (Ruggiero)
. "La cerco in vano," recit (Ruggiero, Oronte)
12. "Semplicetto! a donna credi?," aria (Oronte)
. "Ah! infedele," recit (Ruggiero, Alcina)
. "Regina; il tuo soggiorno," recit (Bradamante, Alcina, Ruggiero)
13. "Sì: son quella! non più bella," aria (Alcina)
. "Se nemico mi fossi," recit (Bradamante, Ruggiero)
. "Bradamante favella?," recit (Ruggiero, Melisso, Bradamante)
14. "La bocca vaga, quell' occhio nero," aria (Ruggiero)
. "A quai strani perigli," recit (Melisso, Bradamante)
. "Fuggi, cor mio, ti affretta!," recit (Morgana, Bradamante)
. "Tiranna gelosia," recit (Alcina)
15. "Tornami a vagheggiar, te solo vuol' amar," aria (Morgana/Alcina)
II: 16. "Col celarvi, a chi v'ama un momento," arioso & recit (Ruggiero, Melisso)
. "Taci, taci, codardo," recit (Melisso)
17. "Qual portento, qual portento mi richiama," cavata arioso (Ruggiero)
. "Atlante, dove sei?," recit (Ruggiero, Melisso)
18. "Pensa a chi geme d'amor piagata," aria (Melisso)
. "Qual' odio ingiusto contro me?," recit (Bradamante, Ruggiero)
19. "Vorrei vendicarmi del perfido cor," aria (Bradamante)
. "Chi scopre al mio pensiero," recit (Ruggiero)
20. "Mi lusinga il dolce affetto con l'aspetto del mio bene," aria (Ruggiero)
. "S'acquieti il rio sospetto," recit (Alcina, Morgana)
. "È la tua pace, con tanta crudeltà," recit (Morgana, Alcina, Ruggiero)
21. "Ama, sospira, ma non ti offende," aria (Morgana)
. "Non scorgo nel tuo viso," recit (Alcina, Ruggiero)
22. "Mio bel tesoro, fedel son io," aria (Ruggiero)
. "Regina; io cerco in vano," recit (Oberto, Alcina)
23. "Tra speme timore mi palpita il core," aria (Oberto)
. "Reina, sei tradita," recit (Oronte, Alcina)
24. "Ah! mio cor! schernito sei!," aria (Alcina)
. "Or, che dici, Morgana?," recit (Oronte, Morgana)
. "All'offesa il disprezzo giunge l'ingata?," recit (Oronte)
25. "È un folle; è un vile affetto, non è la sua beltà," aria (Oronte)
. "Ed è ver che mi narri?," recit (Oberto, Bradamante)
. "Eccomi a' piedi tuoi," recit (Ruggiero, Bradamante, Morgana)
26. "Verdi prati, selve amene, perderete labeltà," aria (Ruggiero)

27. "Ah! Ruggiero crudel, tu non mi amasti!," recit accompagnato (Alcina)
28. "Ombre pallide, lo so, mi udite," aria (Alcina)
III: 29. "Sinfonia"
. "Voglio amar e disamar," recit (Oronte, Morgana)
30. "Credete al mio dolore, luci tiranne e care!," aria (Morgana)
. "M'inganna me n'avveggo, e pur ancor l'adoro ...," recit (Oronte)
31. "Un momento di contento dolce rende a un fido amante," aria (Oronte)
. "Molestissimo incontro!," recit (Ruggiero, Alcina)
32. "Ma quando tornerai di lacci avvinto il piè," aria (Alcina)
. "Tutta d'armate squadre l'isola è cinta," recit (Melisso, Ruggiero, Bradamante)
33. "Sta nell'Ircana pietrosa tana," aria (Ruggiero)
. "Vanne tu seco ancora; dove fa seno il mare," recit (Melisso, Bradamante)
34. "All'alma fedel amore placato," aria (Bradamante)
. "Niuna forza lo arrsta. Vinse Ruggiero," recit (Oronte, Alcina)
35. "Mi restano le lagrime, direi dell'alma i voti," aria (Alcina)
36. "Sin per le vie del sole una gloriosa prole," chorus
. "Già vicino è'l momento," recit (Oberto, Alcina)
37. "Barbara! barbara; io ben lo so, è quello il genitor," aria (Oberto)
. "Le lusighe, gl'inganni, non udir più," recit (Bradamante, Alcina, Ruggiero)
38. "Non è amor, ne gelosia," trio (Alcina, Bradamante, Ruggiero)
. "Prendi, e vivi," recit (Ruggiero, Oronte)
. "Ah mio Ruggier, che tenti?," recit (Alcina, Ruggiero, Bradamante)
. "Misera, ah, no!... Per quella vita," recit (Alcina, Morgana)
. "A che tardi?," recit (Melisso, Ruggiero, Oronte, Bradamante, Alcina, Morgana)
39. "Dall'orror di notte cieca," chorus
40. "Entrée"
41. "Tamburino"
42. "Doppo tante amare pene già proviam conforto all'alma," chorus
Changes in 1736 production: I: 1. "O s'apre al riso," aria (Morgana)
9. "Di te mi rido," aria (Ruggiero)
14. "La bocca vaga," aria (Ruggiero)
II: 16. "Col celarvi, a chi v'ama un momento," ariso (Ruggiero)
20. "Mi lusinga il dolce affetto," aria (Ruggiero)
21. "In mar tempestoso s'affanna il nocchiero," aria (Morgana) (= Arianna in Creta, HWV32/28)
22. "Mio bel tesoro," aria (Ruggiero)
26. "Verdi prati, selve amene," aria (Ruggiero)
III: 30. "Vedrò fra poco, se l'idol mio," aria (Morgana) (= Admeto, HWV22/28)
33. "Sta nell'Ircana pietrosa tana," aria (Ruggiero)

1a.35   "Atalanta," opera: HWV35
. "Ouverture"
I: 1. "Care selve, care, care selve," arioso (Meleagro)
. "Sempre ti lagni, oh Tirsi?," recit (Aminta, Meleagro)
. "Ecco Aminta! agli inganni," recit (Irene, Aminta, Meleagro)
2. "Lascia ch'io parta solo, e tu rimanti, oh bella," aria (Meleagro)
. "Ch'io rimanga con te?," recit (Irene, Aminta)
3. "S'è tuo piacer, ch'io mora, vado a morir, Irene," aria (Aminta)
. "Perchè sospesa, oh figlia," recit (Nicandro, Irene)
4. "Impara, ingrata, impara," aria (Nocandro)
. "Ah! che pur troppo adoro il caro Aminta," recit (Irene)
5. "Come alla tortorella," aria (Irene)
6. "Al varco, oh pastori! vicina è la fera," arioso (Atalanta)
. "Tirsi, e tu che per fama," recit (Atalanta, Meleagro)
. "Cerchi in vano la morte," recit (Irene, Aminta)
7. "Sinfonia"
. "Trattenetolo, oh fidi," recit (Atalanta, Meleagro)
8. "Riportai gloriosa palma," aria (Atalanta)
. "Ah! che tu sei la fera," recit (Meleagro)
9. "Non sarà poco, se il mio gran foco," aria (Meleagro)
II: 10. "Oggi rimbombano di feste, e giubilo," chorus
. "Sei pur sola una volta," recit (Atalanta, Meleagro)
11. "Lassa! ch'io t'ho perduta," aria (Atalanta)
. "Amarili? Amarili?," recit (Meleagro, Atalanta)
12. "Oh Dei, che vuoi?," duet (Atalanta, Meleagro)
. "Ah! ch'io ancora l'intendo!," recit (Meleagro, Irene)
13. "Sì, sì, mel raccorderò, sì, mel raccorderò," aria (Meleagro)
. "Il mio caro pastore," recit (Irene, Aminta)
14. "Soffri in pace il tuo dolore, se il mio amor tu disprezzasti," aria (Irene)
. "È non moro d'affanno?," recit (Aminta, Atalanta)
15. "Di' ad Irene, tiranna, infedele," aria (Aminta)
. "Ma giunge il caro mio vago pastore," recit (Atalanta, Meleagro)
16. "M'allontano, sdegnose pupille," aria (Meleagro)
. "Poveri affetti miei!," recit (Atalanta)
17. "Se nasce un rivoletto," aria (Atalanta)
III: 18. "Sinfonia"

. "È dalla man di Tirsi," recit (Atalanta, Irene)
19. "Bech'io non sappia ancor intender il mio fato," aria (Atalanta)
. "Sono Irene? oppur sogno?," recit (Irene, Aminta)
20. "Diedi il core ad altra Ninfa," aria (Aminta)
. "Ohimè! che pene!," recit (Irene, Meleagro, Aminta)
21. "Ben'io sento l'ingrato, spietata," aria (Irene)
. "Oh! del crudo mio bene," recit (Meleagro)
. "Quanto più ti contemplo," recit (Atalanta, Meleagro)
22. "Custodite, o dolci sogni," arioso (Atalanta, Meleagro)
. "Io vo' morir," recit (Meleagro)
. "Re Meleagro, e tu gran Principessa," recit (Nicandro)
23. "Or trionfar ti fanno," aria (Nicandro)
. "Oh forza del destin!," recit (Atalanta, Meleagro, Irene, Aminta)
24a. "Tu solcasti il mare infido," aria (Meleagro)
24b. "Cara! Cara, cara, nel tuo bel volto," duet (Atalanta, Meleagro)
25. "Sinfonia"
. "Del supremo Tonante messagiero fedel qui corro a volo," recit accompagnato (Mercurio)
. "Contento sol promete Amor," recit (Mercurio)
26a, b. "Sol prova contenti," aria (Mercurio) (2 vers)
27. "Dalla stirpe degli Eroi," chorus
. "Con voce giuliva gridiam tutti," recit (Mercurio)
28. "Gridiam, gridiam, gridiam tutti," chorus
29. "Sinfonia"
30. "Viva la face, viva l'amor! Viva, su, festeggiate!," chorus
31. "Gavotta"
32. "Con voce giuliva gridiam, gridiam tutti," chorus

1a.36 "Arminio," opera: HWV36
. "Ouverture"
I: . "Fuggi, fuggi, mio bene," recit (Tusnelda, Arminio)
1. "Il fuggir, cara mia vita, non è tema, nè viltà," duet (Tusnelda, Arminio)
. "Signor, è in tuo potere," recit (Tullio, Varo)
2. "Non deve Roman petto dar all'amor ricetto," aria (Tullio)
. "Ah! che un vero valore," recit (Varo)
3. "Al lume di due rai più fiero io pugnerò," aria (Varo)
. "Colla spada d'Arminio, Signore," recit (Segeste, Varo, Arminio, Tusnelda)
4. "Scaglian amore e sangue," aria (Tusnelda)
. "Arminio, al tuo furore," recit (Segeste, Arminio, Varo)
5. "Al par della mia sorte," aria (Arminio)
. "Se Arminio oggi non piega a ricever da Roma," recit (Segeste)
6. "Fiaccherò quel fiero orgoglio," aria (Segeste)
7. "Non son sempre vane larve," aria (Sigismondo)
. "Ramise, oh Dei!... Quali infelici avvisi," recit (Tusnelda, Ramise, Sigismondo)
8. "Sento il cor per ogni lato circondato di spavento," aria (Ramise)
. "Oime! parte Ramise," recit (Sigismondo, Tusnelda)
9. "È vil segno d'un debole amore," aria (Tusnelda)
. "Cruda sorella! oh Dei!," recit (Sigismondo)
. "Figio? Padre Signor ...," recit (Segeste, Sigismondo)
10. "Posso morir, posso morir, ma vivere, vivere, e non amare," aria (Sigismondo)
II: 11. "Sinfonia"
. "Come, Signor, vorrai?," recit (Tullio, Segeste)
12. "Con quel sangue di pinta vedrai forriera," aria (Tullio)
. "Questo è, Signor, di Cesare il volere ...," recit (Varo, Segeste)
13. "Duri lacci! voi non siete," aria (Arminio)
. "Arminio, inquesti accenti," recit (Segeste, Arminio)
14. "Sì, cadrò! Sì, cadrò, ma sorgerà," aria (Arminio)
. "Figlia, son vani i pianti," recit (Segeste, Tusnelda)
15. "Al furor che ti consiglia ad Augusto," aria (Tusnelda)
. "Prencipe senza fede!," recit (Ramise, Segeste)
. "Ah! Ramise! Ah! destino!," recit (Sigismondo, Ramise, Segeste)
16. "Niente spero, tutto credo," aria (Ramise)
. "O Ramise, o Segeste!," recit (Sigismondo)
17. "Quella fiamma," aria (Sigismondo)
. "Olà! Custodi, alcun di voi," recit (Arminio, Tusnelda, Varo)
18. "Vado, vado a morir," aria (Arminio)
. "Tusnelda, io son confuso!," recit (Varo, Tusnelda)
19. "Rendimi, rendimi il dolce sposo due vire io ti dovrò," aria (Tusnelda)
III: 20. "Sinfonia"
. "Fier teatro di morte!," recit accompagnato (Arminio)
. "Ministri, alla mia morte," recit (Arminio, Varo, Segeste)
21. "Ritorno alle ritorte; sorte, che vuoi da me?," aria (Arminio)
. "Del castello in diffesa," recit (Varo, Segeste)
22. "Mira il Ciel, vedrai d'Alcide e le guerriere armi omicide," aria (Varo)
23. "Ho veleno e ferro avanti," arioso (Tusnelda)
. "Ti stringo, o il lustre acciaro," recit (Tusnelda, Ramise)

28. "O fiero e rio sospetto, taci per poco ancora," aria (Anastasio)
III: 29. "Sinfonia"
. "Amici, tutto devo," recit (Vitaliano)
30. "Il piacer dello vendetta già mi chiama, e già m'alletta," aria (Vitaliano)
. "Generoso Giustino, oh! quanto ammiro," recit (Arianna, Giustino, Amanzio)
31. "Zeffiretto, che scorre nel prato," aria (Giustino)
. "E fia ver, che infedele," recit (Anastasio, Amanzio, Giustino, Arianna, Leocasta)
32. "Di Re sdegnato l'ira tremenda," aria (Anastasio)
. "Quale infernal veleno," recit (Arianna, Leocasta)
33. "Il mio cor già più non sa raffrenar sospiri e affanni," aria (Arianna)
. "Giustino, anima mia!," recit (Leocasta)
34. "Augelletti garruletti," aria (Leocasta)
. "Riusci il bel disegno," recit (Amanzio)
35. "Dall'occaso in oriente ogni gente," aria (Amanzio)
36. "Fortuna! m'hai tradita! dove son li tesor," recit accompagnato (Giustino)
. "Prima che splenda in oriente il sole," recit (Vitaliano)
37. "Trattien l'acciar! Contro il fraterno sangue," recit accompagnato (Voce dentro al sepolcro)
. "Qual voce ascolto?," recit (Vitaliano, Giustino)
38. "Sollevar il mondo oppresso," aria (Giustino)
39. "Or che cinto ho il crin d'alloro," arioso (Amanzio)
. "E dove mi traete," recit (Anastasio, Amanzio)
40. "Sinfonia"
. "Qual marzial fragor d'onde deriva?," recit (Amanzio, Voci di dentro, Arianna & others)
. "Olà? Renditi a me! Fra duri lacci," recit (Giustino, Arianna, Anastasio)
41. "Ti rendo questo cor, che ti serbò l'amor," aria (Arianna)
. "Signor, se vile intercessor non sono," recit (Giustino, Anastasio, Vitaliano)
42. "In braccio a te la calma," chorus

1a.38   "Berenice, Regina d'Egitto," opera: HWV38
. "Ouverture"
I: . "Aristobolo, a noi venga," recit (Berenice)
. "Berenice, al tuo soglio quella stessa amistà," recit (Fabio, Alessandro, Berenice)
1. "No. no. no. no. che servire altrui, no, quest'anima non sa," aria (Berenice)
. "Fabio, vedesti mai più bell'orgoglio?," recit (Alessandro, Fabio)
2. "Vedi l'ape, vedi l'ape ch'ingegnosa," aria (Fabio)
. "Io di Selene? io d'altri," recit (Alessandro)
3. "Che sarà quando amante accarezza," aria (Alessandro)
. "Cara, non sospirar!," recit (Demetrio, Selene)
4. "No, soffrir non può il mio amore, che non regni tua beltà," aria (Demetrio)
. "Selene, oh Dei! dov'è Demetrio?," recit (Aristobolo, Selene)
5. "Gelo, avvampo, considero, e sento," aria (Selene)
. "Alla quiete d'Egitto," recit (Aristobolo)
6. "Con gli strali d'amor cangia morte talor," aria (Aristobolo)
. "Roma, sì, sì, t'intendo a Selene," recit (Berenice, Arsace)
. "Oh Dei! sorella, oh Dei!," recit (Berenice, Selene, Arsace)
7. "Dice amor, quel bel vermiglio, che raccolto su quel volto," aria (Berenice)
. "Principessa, ed è ver?," recit (Arsace, Selene)
8. "Senza nudrice alcuna, qual pargoletto in cuna," aria (Arsace)
. "Alessandro, che pensi?," recit (Alessandro)
. "Nè pur le regie porte," recit (Demetrio, Alessandro, Berenice, Fabio, Aristobolo)
9. "Quell'aggetto, ch'e caro a chi adoro," aria (Alessandro)
. "Che valor! Che finezza!," recit (Demetrio, Berenice)
10. "Se il mio amor fu il tuo delitto, tua vendetta ancor sarà," duet (Berenice, Demetrio)
II: 11. "Se non ho l'idol mio scetro e corona, addio!," arioso (Demetrio)
. "Demetrio, anima mia," recit (Berenice, Demetrio)
. "Già che per tuo consorte," recit (Fabio, Demetrio, Berenice)
12. "Guerra, e pace Egizia terra," arietta (Fabio)
. "Molto afflitto, Demetrio, ancor paventi?," recit (Berenice, Demetrio)
13. "Sempre dolci, ed amorose non vi voglio," aria (Berenice)
14. "Selene, infida ... spergiurato amore ...," recit accompagnato (Demetrio)
15. "Su, Megera, Tesifone, Aletto!," aria (Demetrio)
16a, b. "Mio bel sol, dove t'aggiri?," arioso (Alessandro)
. "Prence Alessandro, e quale maligna stella," recit (Arsace, Alessandro)
. "Oh Dei! Fabio minaccia," recit (Aristobolo, Alessandro, Arsace)
17. "La bella mano, che mi pigò," aria (Alessandro)
. "Aristobolo, oh Dei!," recit (Arsace, Aristobolo)
18. "Amore contro amor combatte nel mio cor," aria (Arsace)
. "Tiranna degli affetti," recit (Aristobolo)
19. "Senza te sarebbe il mondo," aria (Aristobolo)
. "E qual furor geloso," recit (Selene, Demetrio, Berenice)
. "Perfida ... A me fedel? Ingrato core!," recit (Demetrio, Selene, Berenice)
20. "Traditore, traditore!," aria (Berenice)
. "Empia, tu piangi?," recit (Demetrio, Selene)
. "Prencipessa, t'arresta; e tu, felon," recit (Berenice, Selene, Demetrio, Arsace)
. "A me nè fè il rifiuto," recit (Fabio, Selene, Alessandro, Berenice, Demetrio)

21a, b. "Sì, tra i ceppi, e le ritorte," aria (Demetrio) (2 vers)
. "È questo l'amor tuo?," recit (Arsace)
22. "Si poco è forte dunque tua fede," aria (Selene)
III: 23. "Sinfonia"
. "Olà! tra lacci suoi," recit (Berenice, Aristobolo)
. "Eccomi, o Berenice," recit (Demetrio, Berenice, Aristobolo)
24. "Per si bella cagion," aria (Demetrio)
. "Mia Regina ... Fa pronto," recit (Aristobolo, Berenice)
. "Regina, addio," recit (Fabio, Berenice)
25. "Chi t'intende? o cieca instabile!," aria (Berenice)
26. "Tortorella, che rimira presa al laccio la compagna," arioso (Selene)
. "Qui dove il mio tesoro," recit (Selene, Arsace)
27. "Questa qual sia beltà," aria (Selene)
. "Qual arduo impegno, o Arsace!," aria (Selene)
28. "Le dirai ... Dirò, che amore come il cor ti lega il piè," duet (Alessandro, Arsace)
. "Prence, d'Iside al tempio," recit (Fabio, Alessandro)
29. "In quella, sola in quella candida mano e bella," aria (Alessandro)
. "De'satrapi è adunata l'assemblea," recit (Aristobolo, Berenice)
30. "Avvertite mie pupille, non tradite l'onor mio," aria (Berenice)
31. "Sinfonia"
. "Gran Nume tutelar di questo Regno," recit (Berenice, Selene, Arsace, Alessandro)
32. "Quel bel labbro, quel vezzo, quel sguardo," duet (Berenice, Alessandro)
. "Ora Selene è mia ...," recit (Arsace, Selene, Demetrio, Alessandro, Berenice)
33. "Le vicende della sorte hanno sempre un novo aspetto," aria (Demetrio)
34. "Con verace dolce pace brilli ogn'alma ed ogni cor," chorus

1a.39 "Faramondo," opera: HWV39
. "Ouverture"
I: . "Popolo, figlio, in basse note e meste," recit (Gustavo, Adolfo)
1. "Ascolta dagli Elisi, ombra di Sveno," recit accompagnato (Gustavo)
2. "Pera, pera, pera, pera! l'alma fiera," chorus
. "Mio Re, pronta qui vedo l'orrida pompa," recit (Teobaldo, Gustavo, Adolfo, Clotilde)
3. "Viva, sì, che nel mio seno venir meno," aria (Gustavo)
. "Siam pur fiori, o mia cara," recit (Adolfo, Clotilde)
4. "Conoscerò, se brami ch'io t'ami," aria (Clotilde)
. "Perdoni all'amor mio," recit (Adolfo)
5. "Chi ben ama, og'n altro affetto," aria (Adolfo)
. "Finchè avrò spirto, e vita, del mio sen farò scudo," recit (Childerico, Rosimonda, Faramondo)
6. "Vanne, che più ti miro, più cresce il mio dolor," aria (Rosimonda)
. "Faramondo infelice!," recit (Faramondo Gernando)
7. "Rival ti sono," aria (Faramondo)
. "Va pur; prevenirò gli empii di segni," recit (Gernando)
8. "Voglio che mora, sì, sì," aria (Gernando)
. "S'è giusto l'odio mio," recit (Rosimonda)
. "Proncipessa, in vedermi," recit (Gernando, Rosimonda)
. "Sino ad ora, Gernando)
. "Rosimonda, tu sei libera," recit (Faramondo, Rosimonda)
9. "Sì, tornero à morir, non a placarti," arietta (Faramonda)
. "Qual nemico m'ha andato," recit (Rosimonda)
10. "Sento, che un giusto sdegno mi sprona a vendicarmi," aria (Rosimonda)
. "Sì, Clotilde, il mio seno," recit (Gustavo, Clotilde)
. "Faramondo, Signor, solo ed in erme," recit (Teobaldo, Gustavo)
11. "Vado a recar la morte all'empio traditor," aria (Teobaldo)
. "Dalla citade, e solo," recit (Clotilde, Adolfo)
12. "Mi parto lieta sulla tua fede," aria (Clotilde)
. "Fra quest'ombre selvagge," recit (Faramondo, Gustavo, Adolfo)
. "Vuò stancare il destin," recit (Faramondo)
13. "Se ben mi lusinga l'infida speranza," aria (Faramondo)
II: 14. "Sinfonia"
. "Già udisti i sensi miei," recit (Gustavo, Rosimonda, Childerico, Gernando)
. "Principessa, a tuoi lumi tu devi," recit (Gernando, Rosimonda)
15. "Sì l'intendesti, sì è questa la mercè," aria (Rosimonda)
. "Sì, sdegna Rosimonda," recit (Gernando)
16. "Non ingannarmi, nò, conforto del mio sen," aria (Gernando)
. "Faramondo, e pur salvo," recit (Clotilde, Faramondo)
. "Benchè di Faramondo tu sii germana," recit (Rosimonda, Clotilde)
. "E mora! Misero, e qual tuo fato," recit (Faramondo, Rosimonda)
. "E dal mio brando questa morte avrai," recit (Teobaldo, Rosimonda, Clotilde, Childerico)
17. "Poi che pria di morire," aria (Faramondo)
. "Rosimonda, il suo duolo non basta," recit (Clotilde, Rosimonda)
18. "Combattuta da due venti," aria (Clotilde)
. "Faramondo è in catene, e morir deve," recit (Gustavo, Adolfo)
19. "Se a'piedi tuoi morrò, la destra bacierò," aria (Adolfo)
. "Signor, umil ti chiedo," recit (Clotilde, Gustavo)
20. "Sol la brama di vendetta," aria (Gustavo)

     A. "Quanto di Faramonto," recit (Childerico, Teobaldo)
     B. "Tentai d'aver l'ingresso," recit (Gernando)
     . "Aprimi quelle porte," recit (Gernando, Childerico)
    21. "Nella terra, in ciel, nell'onda," aria (Gernando)
     . "Childerico? I tuoi cenni," recit (Rosimonda, Childerico)
     . "Tu non sei, Faramondo, prigione," recit (Rosimonda, Faramondo)
    22. "Vado e vivo con la speranza," duet (Faramondo, Rosimonda)
  III: 23. "Sinfonia"
     . "Mi tradiscono i figli, il nemico mi fugge!," recit (Gustavo, Clotilde, Adolfo)
     A. "Quai mi straziano l'alma dubbii pensieri," recit (Childerico, Clotilde, Adolfo)
     B. "Del destin non mi lagno"
    24. "Caro, caro, tu mi accendi nel mio core," duet (Clotilde, Adolfo)
     . "Signor, non t'inoltrar," recit (Teobaldo, Gernando, Faramondo)
    25. "Così suole a rio vicina" (Gernando)
     A. "A me viene Teobaldo?," recit (Faramondo, Teobaldo)
     B. "Ritorna pur, ritorna al tuo Signor crudel, mostro, non padre," recit (Faramondo)
     . "Andiam, fidi guerrieri," recit (Faramondo)
    26. "Voglio che sia l'indegno," aria (Faramondo)
     . "D'un oltraggiato Re," recit (Gustavo, Teobaldo)
     . "Padre ... Tu Adolfo in libertà?," recit (Adolfo, Gustavo, Teobaldo)
     . "Disarmato è gia il Re," recit (Teobaldo, Gustavo)
     . "Ecco gl'iniqui. Su, ferite gli empii," recit (Adolfo, Faramondo, Teobaldo, Gustavo)
    27. "Se ria procella sorge nell'onde," aria (Adolfo)
     . "Non isdegnar, Gustavo," recit (Faramondo, Gustavo, Rosimonda, Clotilde)
    28. "Sappi, crudel, io t'amo, e per tua pena ancor!," aria (Rosimonda)
     . "Or vo'lieto alla morte!," recit (Faramondo, Clotilde, Gustavo, Gernando, Adolfo)
     . "Misera! ei corre a morte, ed io resto a goder?," recit (Clotilde, Adolfo)
    29. "Un'aura placida e lusinghiera," aria (Clotilde)
     . "Reggi il mio braccio già impotente," recit (Gustavo, Childerico)
     . "Ohime! tradito io sono!," recit (Teobaldo, Gustavo & others)
     . "Figlia, di Faramondo ... lo su la sorte; per ciò voglio morir," recit (Gustavo, Rosimonda, others)
    30. "Virtù che rende si forte un core," aria (Faramondo)
    31. "Virtù che rende si forte un core," chorus
  Anhang: (6a.) "Vanne, vanne, che più ti miro," aria (Rosimonda)
     (6b.) "Vanne, che più ti miro," aria (Rosimonda) (frag)
    25a. "Così suole a rio vicina umil pianta alzare i rami," aria (Gernando)

1a.40   "Serse," opera: HWV40
     . "Ouverture"
    I: 1. "Frondi tenere e belle," recit accompagnato (Serse)
      2. "Ombra mai fù di vegetabile," recit accompagnato (Serse)
      . "Siam giunti, Elviro ...," recit (Arsamene, Elviro)
      3. "Sinfonia"
      . "Sento un soave concente," recit (Arsamene, Elviro)
      4. "O voi. Questa è Romilda. O voi che penate!," arioso e recit (Romilda, Arsamene, Elviro, Serse)
      . "Un Serse mirate, un Serse mirate" (Romilda)
      . "Arsamene. Mio Sire? Udite?, recit (Serse, Arsamene)
      5. "Va godendo vezzoso e bello," aria (Romilda)
      . "Quel canto a un bel amor," recit (Serse, Arsamene)
      6. "Io le dirò che l'amo / Tu le dirai che l'ami," aria (Serse / Asamene)
      . "Arsamene! Romilda, oh Dei, pavento," recit (Romilda, Arsamene, Atalanta)
      7. "Sì, sì, sì, sì, sì, sì, mio ben, sì, sì," aria (Atalanta)
      . "Presto, Signor, vien Serse," recit (Elviro, Arsamene)
      . "Come, qui, Principessa," recit (Serse, Romilda, Arsamene, Elviro)
      8. "Meglio in voi col mio partire," aria (Arsamene)
      . "Bellissima Romilda, eh! non celate," recit (Serse)
      9. "Di tacere e di schernirmi, ah! crudel," aria (Serse)
      . "Aspide sono," recit (Romilda)
     10. "Nè men con l'ombre d'infedeltà," aria (Romilda)
     11. "Se cangio spoglia, non cangio core," aria (Amastre)
      . "Pugnammo, amici," recit (Ariodante, Amasre)
     12. "Già la tromba, che chiamò," chorus
      . "Ecco Serse, o che volto," recit (Amastre, Serse, Ariodante)
     13. "Soggetto al mio volere, gl'astri non voglio, no," aria (Ariodante)
      . "Queste vittorie, io credo," recit (Serse, Amastre)
     14. "Più che penso alle fiamme del core," aria (Serse)
      . "Eccoti il foglio Elviro," recit (Arsamene, Elviro)
     15. "Signor, Signor, lasciate far a me," arietta (Elviro)
     16. "Non so se sia la speme, che mi sostiene in vita," aria (Arsamene)
      . "Tradir di reggia sposa," recit (Amastre)
     17. "Saprà delle mie offese ben vendicarsi il cor," aria (Amastre)
      . "Al fin sarete sposa," recit (Atalanta, Romilda)
     18. "Se l'idol mio rapir mi vuoi," aria (Romilda)
      . "Per rapir quel tesoro," recit (Atalanta)
     19. "Un cenno leggiadretto, un riso vezzosetto," aria (Atalanta)

II: 20. "Speranze mie fermate, non mi lasciate ancor," arioso (Amastre)
    21. "Ah! chi voler fiora di bella giardina," arietta (Elviro)
     . "E chi di rebbe mai, ch'io sono Elviro?," recit (Elviro, Amastre)
    22. "Or che siete speranze tradite," aria (Amastre)
     . "Quel curioso è partito," recit (Elviro)
    23. "A piangere ogn'ora Amor mi destinà," arioso e recit (Atalanta, Elviro)
    24. "Ah! tigre infedele, cerasta crudele cerasta," arietta (Elviro)
     . "Parti; il Re s'avvicina. Ah! chi voler fiori," recit (Atalanta, Elviro)
     . "Conquesto foglio mi farò contenta," recit (Atalanta)
    25. "È tormento troppo fiero," arioso (Serse)
     . "Di quel foglio, Atalanta," recit (Serse, Atalanta)
    26. "Dirà che amor per me piagato il cor non gli ha," aria (Atalanta)
     . "Voi quel foglio lasciate a me per prova," recit (Serse, Atalanta)
     . "Ingannata Romilda," recit (Serse, Romilda)
    27. "L'amerete? L'amerò," duet (Romilda, Serse)
    28. "Se bramate d'amar, chi vi sdegna," aria (Serse)
    29. "L'amerò? non fia vero," recit accompagnato (Romilda)
    30. "E gelosia quella tiranna," aria (Romilda)
     . "Già che il duol non m'uccide," recit (Amastre, Elviro)
    31. "Anima infida, tradita io sono, vien tu m'uccida," aria (Amastre)
     . "È pazzo affè! Elviro," recit (Elviro, Arsamene)
    32. "Quella che tutta fè per me languia d'amore," aria (Arsamene)
    33. "La virtute sol potea," chorus
     . "Ariodate! Signore. Del mare ad onta," recit (Serse, Ariodate)
    34. "Per dar fine alla mia pena, chi mi svena, per lietà!," arioso (Arsamene)
     . "Arsamene, ove andate?," recit (Serse, Arsamene)
    35. "Sì, la voglio e la otterò," aria (Arsamene)
     . "V'inchino, eccelso Re," recit (Atalanta, Serse)
    36. "Voi mi dite che non l'ami, che non l'ami," aria (Atalanta)
     . "Saria lieve ogni doglia," recit (Serse)
    37. "Il core spera e teme penando ogn'or così," aria (Serse)
    38. "Me infelice, ho smarrito il mio padrone!," recit accompagnato (Elviro)
    39. "Del mio caro baco amabile," aria (Elviro)
    40. "Gran pena è gelosia per altri io son sprezzato," duet (Serse, Amastre)
     . "Aspra sorte! Empie stelle!," recit (Serse, Amastre)
     . "Romilda, e sarà ver," recit (Serse)
    41. "Val più contento core," arietta (Romilda)
     . "Vuò, ch'abbian fine," recit (Serse, Romilda, Amastre)
     . "La fortuna la vita, e l'esser mio," recit (Amastre, Romilda)
    42. "Chi cede al furore di stelle rubelle amante non è," aria (Romilda)
III: 43. "Sinfonia"
     . "Sono vani i pretesti," recit (Arsamene, Romilda)
     . "Ahi! Scoperto è l'inganno!," recit (Atalanta, Elviro, Arsamene, Romilda)
    44. "No, no, se tu mi sprezzi, morir non vuò," arietta (Atalanta)
     . "Ecco in segno di fè la destra amica!," recit (Romilda, Elviro, Arsamene, Serse)
    45. "Per rendermi beato parto, vezzose stelle," aria (Serse)
     . "Ubbidirò al mio Re?," recit (Arsamene, Romilda)
    46. "Amor, tiranno Amor, per me non hai pietà," aria (Arsamene)
     . "Come già vi accennammo," recit (Serse, Ariodate)
    47. "Del Ciel d'amore sorte si bella," aria (Ariodate)
     . "Il suo serto rifiuto," recit (Romilda)
     . "Fermatevi, mia Sposa," recit (Serse, Romilda)
     . "Prode guerrier ... Signora ... A me venite!," recit (Romilda, Amastre)
    48. "Cagion son io del mio dolore," aria (Amastre)
     . "Romilda infida, e di me pensa ancora?," recit (Arsamene, Romilda)
    49. "Troppo oltraggi la mia fede, alma fiera, core ingrato," duet (Romilda, Arsamene)
    50. "Ciò che Giove, ciò che Giove destinò," chorus
     . "Ecco lo sposo!," recit (Ariodante, Arsamene, Romilda)
     . "Chi infelice, chi infelice si trovò," chorus
     . "Sene viene Ariodante," recit (Serse, Ariodante)
    51. "Crude furie degl'orridi abissi, aspergetemi," aria (Serse)
     . "Perfidi! e ancor osate," recit (Serse, Ariodate, Arsamene, Romilda, Amastre, Elviro, Atalanta)
    52. "Caro voi siete all'alma," aria (Romilda)
    53. "Ritorna a noi la calma, riede la gioja al cor," chorus
Anhang: 21a. "Ah! chi voler fiora di bella giardina," arietta (Elviro)
    23a. "A piangere ogn'ora," aria (Atalanta)
    30a. "È gelosia quella tiranna," aria (Romilda) (frag)
    32a. "Quella che tutta fè per me languia d'amore," aria (Arsamene)
    35a. "Sì, la voglio, la voglio e l'otterò," aria (Arsamene) (frag)

1a.41   "Imeneo" (Hymen), opera: HWV41
    . "Ouverture"
  I: 1. "La mia bella, perduta Rosmene," arioso (Tirinto)
  A, B. "Tirinto! Argenio. O barbara fortunata!," recit (Argenio, Tirinto)
    2a. "La mia bella, perduta Rosmene," ariso (Tirinto)

2b. "Se potessero i sospir' miei," aria (Tirinto)
C. "Dal dì ch'io la perdei," recit (Tirinto)
D. "Tirinto. Argenio. O barbara fortuna!," recit (Argenio, Tirinto)
. "Cerere onnipotente," recit (Argenio)
3. "Vien Imeneo fra voi, viene fra voi," chorus
. "Argenio, addio," recit (Tirinto, Argenio, Imeneo)
4. "Vien Imeneo fra voi," chorus
. "Valoroso Imeneo!," recit (Tirinto, Argenio, Imeneo, Clomiri, Rosmene)
5a. "La beltà che innamora," aria (Argenio)
5b. "Di cieca notte allor, che l'ombra il monte ingombra," aria (Imeneo)
5c. "Di cieca notte allor, che l'ombra," aria (Argenio)
. "Rosmene, al fin dovresti," recit (Imeneo)
6. "Ingrata mai non fui, non ho di sasso il cor," aria (Rosmene)
. "Se non era il mio braccio," recit (Imeneo, Tirinto) (3 vers)
7a. "Mi chiederesti meno, se mi chiedessi il core," aria (Tirinto)
7b. "D'amor nei primi istanti facili son gli amanti," aria (Tirinto) (= Deidamia, HWV42/16)
. "Se non era il tuo braccio mi troverei," recit (Clomiri, Imeneo)
8a. "V'è un infelice, che per te muore," aria (Clomiri) (3 vers)
. "Paventar non degg'io, che non venga Rosmene," recit (Imeneo)
9a, b. "Esser mia dovrà la bella tortorella," aria (Imeneo) (2 vers)
9c. "Vado e vivo colla speranza," duet (Rosmene, Tirinto) (= Faramondo, HWV39/22)
10. "Vien Imeneo frà voi," chorus
II: 11. "Deh! m'ajutate, oh Dei!," arioso (Rosmene)
. "Vogliono i tuoi maggiori," recit (Argenio, Rosmene)
12. "Su l'arena di barbara scena," aria (Argenio)
. "La mia mente or confusa vorria ...," recit (Rosmene, Clomiri)
13. "Semplicetta, la saetta," aria (Rosmene)
. "Tirinto, era poc'anzi meco Rosmene," recit (Clomiri, Tirinio)
14a, b. "Sorge nell'alma mia," aria (Tirinto) (2 vers)
. "Imeneo, lieto in viso," recit (Clomiri, Imeneo) (4 vers)
15a, b, c, d. "È si vaga del tuo bene, che al suo mal non penserà," aria (Clomiri / Tirinto) (4 vers)
. "Sembra un fanciullo, amore, innocente," recit (Imeneo / Tirinto) (3 vers)
16a, b. "Chi scherza colle rose un dì si pungerà," aria (Imeneo)
. "Udisti già, che ad Imeneo concesso," recit (Argenio, Tirinio, Imeneo, Rosmene) (2 vers)
17. "Consolami, mio bene, pria che il dolor m'uccida," trio (Rosmene, Tirinto, Imeneo)
18. "È troppo bel trofeo della bellezza il cor," chorus
III: 19. "Sinfonia"
. "Al fin decidi," recit (Tirinto, Imeneo, Rosmene)
20. "In mezzo a voi dui qui lascio il mio core," aria (Rosmene)
. "Se tua sarà Rosmene," recit (Imeneo, Tirinto)
21a, b. "Pieno il core di timore palpitar," aria (Tirinto) (2 vers)
. "Sarei lieta ancor io," recit (Clomiri, Imeneo)
22a, b. "Se ricordar t'en vuoi, già che di lei non puoi," aria (Clomiri) (2 vers)
. "Perdonami, Clomiri," recit (Imeneo)
. "Fiero destino," recit (Rosmene)
. "Rosmene, a che sospendi," recit (Imeneo, Rosmene)
23. "Se la mia pace a me vuoi togliere," arioso (Imeneo)
. "Sospirata Rosmene, Rosmene, anima mia," recit (Tirinto, Rosmene)
24a, b. "Se la mia pace a me vuoi togliere," arioso (Tirinto)
24c. "Un guardo solo, pulille amate," aria (Tirinto) (= Deidamia, HWV42/14)
. "Scorgesti, che Rosmene più non sembra in se stessa?," recit (Clomiri, Argenio, Rosmene)
25. "Se la mia pace a me vuoi togliere," duettino (Imeneo, Tirinto)
. "La vita? Eh, che la donna venne qua giù," recit (Rosmene, Tirinto, Imeneo, Argenio, Clomiri)
26. "Miratela, che arriva," recit accompagnato (Rosmene)
. "Misera! Sventurata!," recit (Imeneo, Tirinto, Clomiri, Argenio, Rosmene)
27. "Al voler di tua fortuna già Rosmene acconsentì," arioso (Rosmene)
. "Disse appunto così," recit (Rosmene, Argenio, Clomiri, Imeneo, Tirinto)
28. "Io son quella navicella, che veniva a questa sponda," aria (Rosmene)
. "Non vuol ch'io più ritorni," recit (Rosmene, Imeneo)
29. "Per le porte del tormento," duet (Tirinto, Rosmene) (= Sosarme, HWV30/18)
30. "Se consulta il suo dover," chorus
Anhang: . "Ouverture"
3. "Vien Imeneo fra voi, viene fra voi," chorus (frag)
(5.) "Se d'amore amanti siete," aria (Clomiri)
(22.) "Se ricordar t'en vuoi già che di lei non puoi, ricordati di me," aria (Clomiri)

1a.42 "Deidamia," opera: HWV42
. "Ouverture"
I: 1. "Marche"
. "Per vendicar di Menelaò l'offesa," recit (Ulisse, Lycomede, Fenice)
2. "Grecia tu offendi, Troja diffendi," aria (Ulisse)
. "Falsa è la voce che in mia regia," recit (Lycomede, Fenice)
3. "Al tardar della vendetta," aria (Fenice)
. "O d'amicizia sante leggi," recit (Lycomede)
4. "Nelle nubi intorno al Fato," aria (Lycomede)

5. "Due bell'alme innamorate, care, fide," arioso e recit (Deidamia, Nerea)
6a, b. "Di lusinghe, di dolcezza non fatica non asprezza," aria (Nerea)
. "Ecco il mio ben," recit (Deidamia)
7. "Seguir di selva in selva la fuggitiva belva diletto egual non ha," aria (Achille)
. "E sempre fisse vi ritrovo a questo opre d'ozio," recit (Achille, Deidamia)
8. "Quando accenderan quel petto," aria (Deidamia)
. "Alla delizia del cor mio," recit (Achille)
9. "Se pensi amor tu solo per vezzoe per beltà," aria (Achille)
. "L'uno è Fenice d'Argo," recit (Nerea, Deidamia)
10a, b. "Sì, che desio quel che tu brami," aria (Nerea) (2 vers)
. "In vano, o principessa," recit (Ulisse, Deidamia)
11. "Perdere il bene amato che il fato e amor ti diè," aria (Ulisse)
. "Da questi scaltri ospiti Greci è d'uopo," recit (Deidamia)
12. "Nasconde l'usignol' in alti rami il nido," aria (Deidamia)
II: 13. "Sinfonia" (= Imeneo, HWV41/19)
. "Deidamia qui veggo appressarsi," recit (Achille)
. "Esser non può mortale," recit (Ulisse, Deidamia)
14. "Un guardo solo, pupille amate," aria (Ulisse) (= Imeneo, HWV41/24c)
. "Oh! che importuni affetti!," recit (Deidamia, Achille)
15. "Lasciami! Tu sei fedele? Vatene," arioso (Achille)
. "Se l'ira del mio bene," recit (Deidamia)
. "Il Real Lycomede," recit (Nerea, Deidamia)
16. "D'amor nei primi istanti facili son gli amanti," aria (Nerea) (= Imeneo, HWV41/7b)
. "Lusinghe allettatrici," recit (Deidamia)
17. "Se il timore il ver mi dice infelice," aria (Deidamia)
. "Della caccia i diporti," recit (Lycomede, Ulisse)
18. "Nel riposo e nel contento," aria (Lycomede)
19. "Della guerra la caccia ha sembianza," chorus (Ulisse, Deidamia)
. "In seguito da' veltri rapido cervo," recit (Fenice, Nerea)
20. "Non ti credo, non mi fido, maggior prova al ver si vuole," aria (Nerea)
. "Ninfa, da noi non vista ancor," recit (Ulisse, Fenice)
21. "Presso ad occhi esperti già nei ministri dell'amor," aria (Fenice)
. "Pochi momenti a me, ninfa vezzosa," recit (Ulisse, Achille)
. "Ma più amar ben poss' io," recit (Ulisse, Achille)
22. "No, no, no, quella beltà non amo," aria (Ulisse)
. "Questa è la caccia ch'ami tanto?," recit (Deidamia, Achille)
23. "Va, perfido! quel cor mi tradirà," aria (Deidamia)
. "Placar tosto saprò," recit (Achille, Fenice)
24. "Sì, m'appaga, sì, m'alletta," aria (Achille)
. "No, che ninfa non è," recit (Fenice)
. "Al ritorno chiama già l'oricalco i cacciatori," recit (Fenice)
25. "L'alto Giove al travaglio penoso per seguace il riposo formò," chorus
III: 26. "Sinfonia"
27. "Degno più di tua beltà, questo cor ritornerà," arioso (Fenice)
. "Molto dagli altri amanti," recit (Nerea)
28. "Quanto ingannato è quella, mal consigliata bella," aria (Nerea)
. "Tutto è già pronto," recit (Fenice, Ulisse, Achille, Deidamia)
29. "Ai Greci questa spada sovra i nemici estinti," aria (Achille)
. "Che più giova celarlo," recit (Deidamia, Ulisse)
30. "M'ai resa infelice; che vanto n'avrai?," aria (Deidamia)
. "Verso al gran fine," recit (Ulisse)
31. "Come all'urto aggressor d'un torrente," aria (Ulisse)
. "Dal destino dipendono gli eventi," recit (Lycomede, Deidamia, Achille, Ulisse)
. "Tacita, mesta, sospirosa ....," recit (Achille, Deidamia)
. "Antiloco, opportuno or più giungesti," recit (Achille, Ulisse)
32. "Or pensate, amanti cori, che le gioje più soavi," aria (Ulisse)
. "Sprone ad affetti," recit (Achille, Deidamia)
33. "Consolarmi se brami, ch'io viva in te, mio ben," aria (Deidamia)
. "Scoperte son le mire," recit (Nerea, Fenice)
34a, b. "Non vuò perdere l'istante," aria (Nerea) (2 vers)
. "Itaco Prence, testimon sarai, che all'amistà," recit (Lycomede, Ulisse)
35. "Ama, ama nell'armi, e nell'amar," duet (Deidamia, Ulisse)
36. "Non trascurate amante, gl'istanti del piacer volan per non tornar," chorus

1a.57   "The Alchemist," incid music: HWV43
1. "Ouverture"
2. "Air"
3. "Minuet I"
4. "Saraband"
5. "Boree"
6. "Aire"
7. "Minuet II"
8. "Aire"
9. "Jigg"

2. ORCHESTRAL WORKS

2.34   No.21 (flauto piccolo & vn I)
2.35   No.22 (vn I & bn)

2.36   "Music for the Royal Fireworks," in D major (c1749; 3ob, 2bn, 3tpt, 3hn
             & 3timp): No.1 "Ouverture" HWV351
2.37   No.2 "Bourée"
2.38   No.3 "La paix"
2.39   No.4 "La Réjouissance"
2.40   No.5 "Menuet I"
2.41   No.6 "Menuet II"
2.42   Suite in B-flat major (c1705–6; 2ob, bn, 2vn & cont, from: Die verwandelte
             Daphne, HWV4):No.1 "Coro" (Amor, Amor, deine Tükke stiften dieses Ungelükke) HWV352
2.43   No.2 "Bourrée" (Dispensa il Dio d'amor le gioie ad ogni cor che soffre)
2.44   No.3 "Allemande"
2.45   No.4 "Rigaudon à deux Hautbois"
2.46   Suite in G major (c1705–6; 2ob, bn, 2vn, va & cont, from: Die verwandelte
             Daphne, HWV4): No.1 "Allemande" HWV353
2.47   No.2 "Bourrée à deux Hautbois"
2.48   No.3 "Menuet"
2.49   No.4 "Allemande"
2.50   Suite in B-flat major (c1705–6; 2vn, va & cont, from: Der beglückte
             Florindo, HWV3): No.1 "Menuet" HWV354
2.51   No.2 "Coro" (Ihr muthigen Hörner, verdoppelt den Schall)
2.52   No.3 "Sarabande"
2.53   No.4 "Gavotte"
2.54   "Aria" (Hornpipe), in C minor (ca1710–2; strings & cont) HWV355
2.55   "Hornpipe," in D major (ca1740; vns, vas & cont, for the Concert at Vauxhall in 1740) HWV356

3. CONCERTI GROSSI (HWV312–HWV330: '&' separates concertino from ripieno insts)

3.1   "Concerti Grossi" (c1716–20): No.1 in B-flat maj (2rec, 2ob, 2bn, vn & 2vn, 2va, vc, cont) Op.3/1, HWV312
3.2   No.2 in B-flat major (2ob, 2vc & 2vn, va, 2vc, cont) Op.3/2, HWV313
3.3   No.3 in G major (fl/ob, 2vn & strings, cont) Op.3/3, HWV314
3.4   No.4 in F major (Orchestra Concerto) (2ob, bn & strings, cont) Op.3/4, HWV315
3.5   No.5 in D minor (2ob, strings & cont) Op.3/5, HWV316
3.6   No.6 in D maj / minor (org/hpd, 2ob, bn & strings, cont) Op.3/6, HWV317
3.7   Concerto Grosso in C major, "Alexander's Feast" (c1736; 2vn, vc & 2ob, strings, cont) HWV318
3.8   "12 Concerti Grossi" (c1739): No.1 in G major (2vn, bc & strings, cont) Op.6/1, HWV319
3.9   No.2 in F major (2vn, vc & strings, cont) Op.6/2, HWV320
3.10   No.3 in E minor (2vn, vc & strings, cont) Op.6/3, HWV321
3.11   No.4 in A minor (2vn, vc & strings, cont) Op.6/4, HWV322
3.12   No.5 in D major (2vn, vc & strings, cont) Op.6/5, HWV323
3.13   No.6 in G minor (2vn, vc & strings, cont) Op.6/6, HWV324
3.14   No.7 in B-flat major, "Hornpipe" (2vn, vc & strings, cont) Op.6/7, HWV325
3.15   No.8 in C minor (2vn, vc & strings, cont) Op.6/8, HWV326
3.16   No.9 in F major (2vn, vc & strings, cont) Op.6/9, HWV327
3.17   No.10 in D minor (2vn, vc & strings, cont) Op.6/10, HWV328
3.18   No.11 in A major (2vn, vc & strings, cont) Op.6/11, HWV329
3.19   No.12 in B major (2vn, vc & strings, cont) Op.6/12, HWV330
3.20   "Concerto," in F major (ca1722; brass, wind & strings; orig for Suite No.3 of: Water Music) HWV331
3.21   "Concerto" (for Trumpets & French Horns), in D major (ca1746–7; orig for: Fireworks Music) HWV335a
3.22   "Concerto," in F major (ca1746–7; brass, wind & strings; orig for: Fireworks Music) HWV335b

4. ORGAN CONCERTOS

4.1   "6 Organ Concertos," I (c1735–6; org/harp, ob & strings) : No.1 in G minor Op.4/1, HWV289
4.2   No.2 in B-flat major Op.4/2, HWV290
4.3   No.3 in G minor Op.4/3, HWV291
4.4   No.4 in F major (arr from: Recorder Sonata No.5, Op.1/11, HWV369) Op.4/4, HWV292
4.5   No.5 in F major Op.4/5, HWV293
4.6   No.6 in B-flat major (Harp Concerto) Op.4/6, HWV294
4.7   "6 Organ Concertos," III (c1740–51; w/ ob & strings): No.7 in B-flat major Op.7/1, HWV306
4.8   No.8 in A major Op.7/2, HWV307
4.9   No.9 in B-flat major, "Hallelujah" Op.7/3, HWV308
4.10   No.10 in D minor Op.7/4, HWV309
4.11   No.11 in G minor Op.7/5, HWV310
4.12   No.12 in B-flat major Op.7/6, HWV311
4.13   "6 Organ Concertos," II (c1739; w/ obs & strings): No.13 in F major, "Cuckoo & the Nightingale" .. HWV295
4.14   No.14 in A major HWV296a
4.15   No.15 in D minor (arr from: Conc Grosso, Op.6/10, HWV328) HWV297
4.16   No.16 in G major (arr from: Conc Grosso, Op.6/1, HWV319) HWV298
4.17   No.17 in D major (arr from: Conc Grosso, Op.6/5, HWV323) HWV299
4.18   No.18 in G minor (arr from: Conc Grosso, Op.6/6, HWV324) HWV300

4.19	Organ Concerto No.19 in D minor (ca1746)	HWV304
4.20	Organ Concerto No.20 in F major (ca1748, arr of: Conc No.3 a due cori, HWV334)	HWV305a
4.21	Organ Concerto in A major (c1743; pastiche concerto from: Organ Concertos Nos.8, 6,14)	HWV296b
4.22	Double Organ Concerto in D minor (ca1737–9)	HWV303
4.23	Organ Concerto in F major, "Judas Maccabaeus" (c1747, in oratorio HWV63)	HWV305b

5. OTHER CONCERTOS, SOLO INSTR & ORCH

Oboe Concertos:

5.1	Oboe Concerto No.1 in B-flat major (ca1718; ob, strings & cont)	HWV302a
5.2	Oboe Concerto No.2 in B-flat major (c1706–10; ob, strings & cont)	HWV301
5.3	Oboe Concerto No.3 in G minor (c ?1703–5; ob, strings & cont)	HWV287

"Concerti a due cori" (coro I: 2ob & bn, coro II: 2ob & bn, strings & cont):

5.4	Concerto No.1 in B-flat major (ca1746–7)	HWV332
5.5	Concerto No.2 in F major (ca1746–7)	HWV333
5.6	Concerto No.3 in F major (c1747, in oratorio: Judas Maccabaeus, HWV63)	HWV334

Other:

| 5.7 | "Sonata à 5" (Concerto), in B-flat major (ca1706–7; vn & 2ob, strings, cont) | HWV288 |
| 5.8 | "Suite de Pièces" (Konzertsatz), in F major (ca1737–8; 2ob, 2hn, strings & cont) | HWV302b |

6. TRIO SONATAS

6.1	"6 Trio Sonatas" (Oboe Trios) (ca1700–5; ob, vn & hpd, ?spur): No.1 in B-flat major	HWV380
6.2	No.2 in D minor	HWV381
6.3	No.3 in E-flat major	HWV382
6.4	No.4 in F major	HWV383
6.5	No.5 in G major	HWV384
6.6	No.6 in D major	HWV385
6.7	Trio Sonata in C minor (ca1718; rec/fl, vn & cont, orig vers of Op.2/1, HWV386b)	H386a
6.8	"6 Trio Sonatas": No.1 in B minor (ca1726–32; fl/vn, vn & cont)	Op.2/1, HWV386b
6.9	No.2 in G minor (ca1700; 2vn & cont)	Op.2/2, HWV387
6.10	No.3 in B-flat major (ca1718; 2vn & cont)	Op.2/3, HWV388
6.11	No.4 in F major (ca1718; fl/rec/vn, vn & cont)	Op.2/4, HWV389
6.12	No.5 in G minor (ca1730; 2vn & cont)	Op.2/5, HWV390b
6.13	No.6 in G minor (ca1707–10; 2vn & cont)	Op.2/6, HWV391
6.14	"3 Trio Sonatas" (Dresden) (2vn & cont): No.1 in F major (ca1706–9)	Op.2/7, HWV392
6.15	No.2 in G minor (ca1720)	Op.2/8, HWV393
6.16	No.3 in E major (ca1730)	Op.2/9, HWV394
6.17	Trio Sonata in E minor (ca1720–30; 2fl & cont)	HWV395
6.18	"7 Trio Sonatas" (c1737–8; 2vn & cont): No.1 in A major	Op.5/1, HWV396
6.19	No.2 in D major	Op.5/2, HWV397
6.20	No.3 in E minor	Op.5/3, HWV398
6.21	No.4 in G major	Op.5/4, HWV399
6.22	No.5 in G minor	Op.5/5, HWV400
6.23	No.6 in F major	Op.5/6, HWV401
6.24	No.7 in B-flat major	Op.5/7, HWV402
6.25	Trio Sonata in C major (ca1738; 2vn & cont)	HWV403
6.26	Trio Sonata in G minor (ca1718–20; ob/vn, vn & cont)	HWV404
6.27	Trio Sonata in F major (ca1707–9; 2rec & cont)	HWV405

7. MISC INSTRUMENTAL

7.1	"Adagio—Allegro," in A major (ca1751; vn, strings & cont)	HWV406
7.2	"Allegro," in G major (c1738; vn)	HWV407
7.3	"Allegro," in C minor (ca1724–6; vn & cont)	HWV408
7.4	"Andante," in D minor (ca1725–6; rec & cont)	HWV409
7.5	"Aria," in F major (ca1725; 2ob, 2hn & bn)	HWV410
7.6	"Aria," in F major (ca1725; 2ob/2vn, 2hn & bn, frag)	HWV411
7.7	"Andante," in A minor (ca1724–5; vn & cont)	HWV412
7.8	"Gigue," in B-flat major (ca1736–7)	HWV413
7.9	"Marche for the Fife," in C major (ca1747; querpfeife & cont)	HWV415
7.10	"Marche allegro" (Dragoon's March), in D major (ca1734; 2ob, tromba & bn)	HWV416
7.11	"La marche," in D major (ca1746–7; 2hn/2ob & bn)	HWV417a, b
7.12	"Marche," in G major (ca1741; 2ob/2vn & bn)	HWV418
7.13	"6 Marches" (ca1710–20; fl/ob/vn & cont): No.1 in G major (March in Ptolomy)	HWV419
7.14	No.2 in G major, "Loudon's March"	
7.15	No.3 in G major, "Admiral Boscowin's March"	

7.16	No.4 in F major
7.17	No.5 in C major
7.18	No.6 in C major, "Handel's March"
7.19	"Menuet," in D major (ca1743; vn & cont) HWV420
7.20	"Menuet," in D major (ca1744; vn & cont) HWV421
7.21	"Menuet," in G major (ca1746–7; 2ob, 2hn & bn) HWV422
7.22	"Menuet," in G major (ca1746–7; 2ob, 2hnt & bn) HWV423
7.23	"Ouverture," in D major (ca1740–1; 2cl & corno da caccia) HWV424
7.24	"Air" (Sarabande), in E major (ca1750; vn & cont) HWV425

37 Menuets arranged from operatic arias, etc (1 instr & cont):

7.25	Menuet No.1 in E minor (6th movt of Ouverture to: Il pastor fido, HWV8a)..............A15/1
7.26	Menuet No.2 in G major (Would you gain the tender creature, in: Acis and Galatea, HWV49a/14) A15/2
7.27	Menuet No.3 in G major (Segni di crudeltà, in: Radamisto, HWV12b/11).....................A15/3
7.28	Menuet No.4 in D major (Alzo al volo, in: Radamisto, HWV12a/28) A15/4
7.29	Menuet No.5 in G major (A chi vive di speranza, in: Muzio Scevola, HWV13/12a) A15/5
7.30	Menuet No.6 in E minor (Finchè lo strale, in: Floridante, HWV14/9) A15/6
7.31	Menuet No.7 in A major (No, non piangete, in: Floridante, HWV14/15)........................A15/7
7.32	Menuet No.8 in A minor (Se risolvi abbandonarmi, in: Floridante, HWV14/24)...............A15/8
7.33	Menuet No.9 in E-flat major (O cara speme, in: Floridante, HWV14/28c) (2nd vers in G major) ....A15/9a, b
7.34	Menuet No.10 in G major (Alla fama, dimmi il vero, in: Ottone, HWV15/18)...................A15/10
7.35	Menuet No.11 in B minor (Benchè mi sia crudele, in: Ottone, HWV15/31b)...................A15/11
7.36	Menuet No.12 in G major (Gode l'alma consolata, in: Ottone, HWV15/33)....................A15/12
7.37	Menuet No.13 in G major (Che bel contento sarebbe amore, in: Flavio, HWV16/8) A15/13
7.38	Menuet No.14 in A minor (Chi può mirare, Flavio, in: HWV16/15).............................A15/14
7.39	Menuet No.15 in G major (Non credi instabile, Flavio, in: HWV16/17) A15/15
7.40	Menuet No.16 in G major (Venere bella, per un istanta, in: Giulio Cesare in Egitto, HWV17/26) A15/16
7.41	Menuet No.17 in B minor (Lamentandomi corro a volo, in: Scipione, HWV20/5)..............A15/17
7.42	Menuet No.18 in G major (Dimmi, cara, dimmi: tu dei morir, in: Scipione, HWV20/10) A15/18
7.43	Menuet No.19 in G major (Pensa, oh bella, alla mia speme in:, Scipione, HWV20/16b) A15/19
7.44	Menuet No.20 in A major (Già cessate è la procella, in: Scipione, HWV20/27b) A15/20
7.45	Menuet No.21 in D major (Gioia sì speri, Scipione, HWV20/29)..................................A15/21
7.46	Menuet No.22 in A major (Dica il falso, dica il vero, in: Alessandro, HWV21/30) A15/22
7.47	Menuet No.23 in G major (Sì, caro, sì, in: Admeto, HWV22/38)..................................A15/23
7.48	Menuet No.24 in G minor (Spera, sì, mio caro bene, in: Admeto, HWV22/5b) A15/24
7.49	Menuet No.25 in G major (Caro, vieni a me, in: Riccardo I, HWV23/15) A15/25
7.50	Menuet No.26 in A minor (Sgombra dell'anima, in: Siroe, HWV24/13) A15/26
7.51	Menuet No.27 in A major (Se il caro figlio vede in periglio, in: Siroe, HWV24/20) A15/27
7.52	Menuet No.28 in G minor (Il mio core non apprezza, in: Tolomeo, HWV25/15) A15/28
7.53	Menuet No.29 in E minor (Orgogliosetto và l'augelletto in: Lotario, HWV26/11) A15/29
7.54	Menuet No.30 in D major (Sei mia gioia, in: Partenope, HWV27/10).............................A15/30
7.55	Menuet No.31 in G major (Sì, scherza, sì, in: Partenope, HWV27/45a) A15/31
7.56	Menuet No.32 in G major (Sollevar il mondo appresso, in: Giustino, HWV37/38) A15/32
7.57	Menuet No.33 in D major (Mi parto lieta, in: Faramondo, HWV39/12) A15/33
7.58	Menuet No.34 in D major (Vado e vivo con la speranza, in: Faramondo, HWV39/22) A15/34
7.59	Menuet No.35 in D major (Va godendo vezzoso e bello, in: Serse, HWV40/5) A15/35
7.60	Menuet No.36 in E minor (Se l'idol mio, Serse, in: HWV40/18)...................................A15/36
7.61	Menuet No.37 in D major (Quanto ingannata è quella, in: Deidamia, HWV42/28) A15/37

8. SOLO SONATAS (w/ cont)

Violin Sonatas:

8.1	Violin Sonata No.1 in G major (ca1707–9) HWV358
8.2	Violin Sonata No.2 in D minor (ca1724, = Fl Son in E minor, Op.1/1b, HWV359b) HWV359a
8.3	Violin Sonata No.3 in A major (ca1725–6) Op.1/3, HWV361
8.4	Violin Sonata No.4 in G minor (ca1724, = Ob Son No.3 in G minor, Op.1/6, HWV364a) . Op.1/6, HWV364a
8.5	Violin Sonata No.5 in G minor (ca1730) Op.1/10, HWV368
8.6	Violin Sonata No.6 in F major (ca1730)... Op.1/12, HWV370
8.7	Violin Sonata No.7 in D major (ca1750, inc) Op.1/13, HWV371
8.8	Violin Sonata No.8 in A major (ca1725–6) Op.1/14, HWV372
8.9	Violin Sonata No.9 in E major (ca1725–6) Op.1/15, HWV373
8.10	*Violin Sonata in A major (?sketch for orch movt)*..

Viola da Gamba Sonatas:

8.11	Viola da Gamba Sonata in G minor (ca1724, arr of: Vn Son No.4 in G min, Op.1/6, HWV364a) ..HWV364b

Flute Sonatas:

8.12	Flute Sonata No.1 in E minor (ca1726–32; orig: Vn Son in D minor, HWV359a) Op.1/1b, HWV359b
8.13	Flute Sonata No.2 in G major (ca1726–32, = Ob Son in F major, HWV363a) Op.1/5, HWV363b
8.14	Flute Sonata No.3 in B minor (ca1726–32, = Rec Son in D minor, HWV367a)................ Op.1/9, HWV367b

9. HARPSICHORD

"8 Suites of Pieces for Harpsichord," I:

"9 Suites of Pieces for Harpsichord," II:

9.116	Suite in D minor (ca1705): No.1 "Prélude"	HWV449
9.117	No.2 "Allemande"	
9.118	No.3 "Courante"	
9.119	No.4 "Sarabande"	
9.120	No.5 "Aria con (7) Variazioni"	
9.121	No.6 "Giga"	
9.122	No.7 "Menuett"	
9.123	"Partita" (Suite), in G major (ca1700–5): No.1 "Preludio"	HWV450
9.124	No.2 "Allemande"	
9.125	No.3 "Courante"	
9.126	No.4 "Sarabande"	
9.127	No.5 "Gigue"	
9.128	No.6 "Menuet"	
9.129	Suite in G minor (ca1703–6): No.1 "Allemande"	HWV451
9.130	No.2 "Courante"	
9.131	Suite in G minor (ca1738–9, for Princess Louisa): No.1 "Allemande"	HWV452
9.132	No.2 "Courante"	
9.133	No.3 "Sarabande"	
9.134	No.4 "Gigue"	
9.135	Suite in G minor (ca1705–6): No.1 "Ouverture"	HWV453
9.136	No.2 "Entrée"	
9.137	No.3 "Menuet," I	
9.138	No.3 "Menuet," II	
9.139	No.4 "Chaconne"	
9.140	"Partita" (Suite), in A major (ca1703–6): No.1 "Allemande"	HWV454
9.141	No.2 "Courante"	
9.142	No.3 "Sarabande"	
9.143	No.4 "Gigue"	
9.144	Suite in B-flat major (c1706): No.1 "Ouverture"	HWV455
9.145	No.2 "Sarabande"	
9.146	No.3 "Gavotte"	
9.147	No.4 "Menuet"	

Arrs from operatic overtures:

9.148	No.1 "Ouverture," in D minor (ca1725, to: Il pastor fido, HWV8a,1st vers)	HWV456/1
9.149	No.2 "Ouverture," in C minor (ca1725, to: Amadigi, HWV11)	HWV456/2
9.150	No.3 "Ouverture," in G minor (ca1723, to: Flavio, HWV16)	HWV456/3
9.151	No.4 "Ouverture," in C major (ca1725, to: Rodelinda, HWV19)	HWV456/4
9.152	No.5 "Ouverture," in D major (ca1727, to: Riccardo I, HWV23)	HWV456/5

Airs:

9.153	"Air," in C major (ca1720–1)	HWV457
9.154	"Air," in C minor (ca1710–20)	HWV458
9.155	"Aria," in C minor (ca1710–20)	HWV459
9.156	"Air" (March), in D major (ca1720)	HWV460
9.157	"Air" (Hornpipe), in D minor (ca1717–18)	HWV461
9.158	(Air en) "Menuet," in D minor (ca1724–6)	HWV462
9.159	"Air," in F major (ca1707–9)	HWV463
9.160	"Air," in F major (ca1725–6)	HWV464
9.161	"Air and 2 Doubles," in F major (ca1710–20): No.1 "Air"	HWV465
9.162	No.2 "Double," I	
9.163	No.3 "Double," II	
9.164	"Air" (for 2-manual harpsichord), in G minor (ca1710–20)	HWV466
9.165	"Air," in G major (ca1710–20)	HWV467
9.166	"Air," in A major (ca1727–8)	HWV468
9.167	"Air," in B-flat major (ca1738–9)	HWV469
9.168	"Air" (for 2-manual harpsichord), in B-flat major (ca1710–20)	HWV470
9.169	"Air," in B-flat major (ca1710–20)	HWV471
9.170	"Allegro," in C major (ca1705)	HWV472
9.171	"Air," in G major (ca1736–8, from oratorio: Acis and Galatea, HWV49a)	HWV474
9.172	"Allegro," in D minor (ca1710–20)	HWV475

Other:

9.173	"Allemande," in F major (ca1730–5)	HWV476
9.174	"Allemande," in A major (ca1724–6)	HWV477
9.175	"Allemande," in A minor (ca1705)	HWV478
9.176	"Allemande," in B minor (ca1721–2)	HWV479
9.177	"Choral: Jesu meine Freude," in G minor (arr ca1736–40)	HWV480
9.178	"Capriccio pour le Clavecin," in F major (ca1703–6)	HWV481

Arrs from operatic arias:

9.179 "Molto voglio," in C major (ca1725, from: Rinaldo, HWV7a/10) HWV482/1
9.180 "Sventurato, godi," in E-flat major (ca1721–2, from: Floridante, HWV14/8) HWV482/2
9.181 "Ombra cara di mia sposa," in G minor (ca1720, from: Radamisto, HWV12a/13) HWV482/3
9.182 "Pupille sdegnose!," in F major (ca1721, from: Muzio Scevola, HWV13/Act III/3) HWV482/4
9.183 "Come, se ti vedrò," in G major (caca1721, from: Muzio Scevola, HWV13/Act III/9) HWV482/5

Other:

9.184 "Capriccio," in G minor (ca1720) HWV483
9.185 "Chaconne" (w/ 49 variations), in C major (ca1700–5)..HWV484
9.186 "Chaconne" (for 2-manual harpsichord), in F major (ca1705) HWV485
9.187 "Chaconne," in G minor (ca1705) HWV486
9.188 "Concerto," in G major (ca1710–20)...HWV487
9.189 "Allegro" (Courante), in F major (ca1717–8) HWV488
9.190 "Courante," in B minor (ca1720) HWV489
9.191 "Fantaisie pour le clavecin," in C major (ca1703–6) HWV490
9.192 "Gavotte," in G major (ca1705)..HWV491
9.193 "Gigue," in F major (ca1726)..HWV492
9.194 "Gigue," in G minor (ca1704–5; 2 vers) ....HWV493a, b
9.195 "Impertinence" (Bourée), in G minor (ca1705)..HWV494
9.196 "Lesson" (Gigue), in D minor (ca1705–10) ....HWV495a, b
9.197 "Lesson," in A minor (ca1715–20) HWV496

Menuets:

9.198 "Menuet," in C major (ca1725, from Overture to: Rodelinda, HWV19)..HWV497
9.199 "Menuet," in C major (ca1710–20)...HWV498
9.200 "Menuet," in C minor (ca1724, from Overture to: Tamerlano, HWV18) HWV499
9.201 "Menuet," in D major (ca1717–20)...HWV500
9.202 "Menuet," in D major (ca1717–20)..HWV501
9.203 "Menuet," in D major (ca1705–6, arr of HWV344, orig from: Der beglückte Florindo, HWV3) HWV502
9.204 "Menuet," in D major (ca1710–17; used in No.13 of Suite No.2 of: The Water Music, HWV349) HWV503
9.205 "Menuet," in D major (ca1720, from Final Chorus of: Radamisto, HWV12a) HWV504
9.206 "Menuet," in D major (ca1710–20)...HWV505
9.207 "Menuet," in D maj (ca1710–20; used in Eng song: As on a sunshine summer's day, HWV228/3) HWV506
9.208 "Menuet," in D major (ca1710–20; 2 vers) ....HWV507a, b
9.209 "Menuet," in D minor (ca1724, from Ah, non posso, in: Flavio, HWV16/5; 2nd vers in E min)... HWV508a, b
9.210 "Menuet," in F major (ca1710–20) HWV509
9.211 "Menuet," in F major (ca1721, from Vanne sequi'l mio desio, in: Floridante, HWV14/28a).............HWV510
9.212 "Menuet," in F major (ca1710–17, vers of No.7 in Suite No.1 of: The Water Music, HWV347) HWV511
9.213 "Menuet," in F major (ca1728, from Dolcissimo amore, in: Siroe, HWV24/30) HWV512
9.214 "Menuet," in F major (ca1710–20; 2nd vers in G major) ....HWV513a, b
9.215 "Menuet," in F major (ca1710–12; 2nd vers in G major) ....HWV514a, b
9.216 "Menuet," in F major (ca1710–20; 2nd vers in G major) ....HWV515a, b
9.217 "Menuet," in F major (ca1710–20; 3 vers) HWV516a–c
9.218 "Menuet," in F major (ca1710–20) HWV517
9.219 "Menuet," in F major (ca1710–20) HWV518
9.220 "Menuet," in F major (ca1710–20) HWV519
9.221 "Menuet," in F major (ca1710–20) HWV520
9.222 "Menuet," in G major (ca1710–20) HWV521
9.223 "Menuet," in G major (ca1710–20) HWV522
9.224 "Menuet," in G major (ca1710–20) HWV523
9.225 "Menuet," in G major (ca1710–20) HWV524
9.226 "Menuet," in G major (ca1710–20) HWV525
9.227 "Menuet," in G major (ca1710–20) HWV521
9.228 "Menuet," in G major (ca1710–20) HWV522
9.229 "Menuet," in G major (ca1710–20) HWV523
9.230 "Menuet," in G major (ca1710–20) HWV524
9.231 "Menuet," in G major (ca1710–20) HWV525
9.232 "Menuet," in G major (ca1710–20) HWV526
9.233 "Menuet," in G major (ca1710–20) HWV527
9.234 "Menuet," in G major (ca1710–20) HWV528
9.235 "Menuet," in G major (ca1710–20) HWV529
9.236 "Menuet," in G maj (ca1710–20; used in Eng song: Bacchus one day gayly striding, HWV228/4) ..HWV530
9.237 "Menuet," in G major (ca1710–20) HWV531
9.238 "Menuet," in G minor (ca1750; used in Menuet of the Overture to: Japhta, HWV70) HWV532
9.239 "Menuet," in G minor (ca1750, vers of In gentle murmurs, in: Jephtha, HWV70/5).......................HWV533
9.240 "Menuet," in G minor (ca1710–20; 2 vers) ....HWV534a, b
9.241 "Menuet" (The Princess Sophia's favourite Minuet), in G minor (ca1710–20) ....HWV535a, b
9.242 "Menuet," in G minor (ca1710–20) HWV536
9.243 "Menuet," in G minor (ca1710–20; 2 vers)..HWV537a, b
9.244 "Menuet," in G minor (ca1710–17; 2 vers, used in Eng song: Love's a dear deceitful Juwel)....HWV538a, b
9.245 "Menuet," in G minor (ca1710–20; 2 vers) ....HWV539a, b

9.246   "Menuet," in G minor (ca1704–5; 2 vers)...HWV540a, b
9.247   "Menuet," in G minor (ca1710–20) HWV541
9.248   "Menuet," in G minor (ca1710–20) HWV542
9.249   "Menuet," in G minor (ca1710–20; used in Eng song: When I survey, HWV228/20) HWV543
9.250   "Menuet," in A major (ca1710–20) HWV544
9.251   "Menuet," in A major (ca1710–20; used in Eng song: Phillis be kind and hear me, HWV228/16) ... HWV545
9.252   "Menuet," in A major (ca1710–17) HWV546
9.253   "Menuet," in A minor (ca1710–17) HWV547
9.254   "Menuet," in A minor (ca1710–20) HWV548
9.255   "Menuet," in A minor (ca1710–20) HWV549
9.256   "Menuet," in B-flat major (ca1705–6, from: Der beglückte Florindo, HWV3) HWV550
9.257   "Menuet," in B-flat major (ca1710–20) HWV551
9.258   "Menuet," in B-flat major (ca1710–20) HWV5527
9.259   "Menuet," in B-flat major (ca1710–20) HWV553
9.260   "Menuet," in B-flat major (ca1710–20) HWV554
9.261   "Menuet," in B-flat major (ca1710–20; 2 vers) ....HWV555a, b
9.262   "Menuet," in B-flat major (ca1710–20) HWV556
9.263   "Menuet," in B-flat major (ca1710–20) HWV557
9.264   "Menuet," in B minor (ca1707–8, from: Poro, HWV28/31–32)...HWV558

Passepieds:

9.265   "Passepied," in C major (ca1721–2).. HWV559
9.266   "Passepied," in A major (ca1705) HWV560

Preludes:

9.267   "Prélude," in D minor (ca1705–6) HWV561
9.268   "Prélude" (Harpeggio), in D minor (ca1711–12) HWV562
9.269   "Préludio," in D minor (ca1700–3) HWV563
9.270   "Preludio," in D minor (ca1705) HWV564
9.271   "Prélude," in D minor (ca1710–20) HWV565
9.272   "Preludio," in E major (ca1710–20) HWV566
9.273   "Preludium," in F major (ca1710–20) HWV567
9.274   "Preludium," in F minor (ca1710–20) HWV568
9.275   "Preludium" (Arpeggio del Cook), in F minor (ca1710–20) HWV569
9.276   "Prélude" (Harpeggio), in F-sharp minor (ca1717–8) HWV570
9.277   "Prélude e Capriccio," in G major (ca1703–6) HWV571
9.278   "Prélude," in G minor (ca1710–17) HWV572
9.279   "Prélude" (Harpeggio), in G minor (ca1705) HWV573
9.280   "Preludio ed Allegro (Sonata) pour le Clavecin," in G minor (ca1705) HWV574
9.281   "Prélude" (Harpeggio), in A minor (ca1717–8) HWV575
9.282   "Preludio ed Allegro," in A minor (ca1705–6) HWV576

Sonatas:

9.283   "Sonata" (Fantaisie) pour le Clavecin," in C major (ca1703–5) HWV577
9.284   "Sonata" (for 2-manual harpsichord), in G major (ca1707–9) HWV579
9.285   "Sonata," in G minor (ca1707–9) HWV580
9.286   "Sonatina," in D minor (ca1705) HWV581
9.287   "Sonatina" (Fuga), in G major (ca1722)..HWV582
9.288   "Sonatina," in G minor (ca1722) HWV583
9.289   "Sonatina," in A minor (ca1706–8) HWV584
9.290   "Sonatina," in B-flat major (ca1722)...HWV585
9.291   "Toccata," in G minor (ca1710–20) HWV586

10. ORGAN (or hpd)

10.1   Fugue No.1 in G minor (ca1711–6, from HWV54/7) HWV605
10.2   Fugue No.2 in G major (ca1715–7, from HWV314/3) HWV606
10.3   Fugue No.3 in B-flat major (ca1717–8, from Sinfonia of HWV48 & HWV313/3) HWV607
10.4   Fugue No.4 in B minor (ca1717–8) HWV608
10.5   Fugue No.5 in A minor (ca1717–8, from HWV54/2)..HWV609
10.6   Fugue No.6 in C minor (ca1711–6, from HWV400/2) HWV610
10.7   "Fugue," in F major (ca1705) HWV611
10.8   "Fugue," in E major (ca1748–50)...HWV612

11. MUSICAL CLOCK

11.1   "Allegro," in C major (c1738) HWV473
11.2   "Sonata con Trio e Gavotta," in C major (ca1750): No.1 "Sonata," in C major HWV578
11.3   No.2 "Trio," in C major
11.4   No.3 "Gavotte," in C major

"11 Pieces for Musical Clock," Set I (ca1730–40):

"7 Pieces for Musical Clock," Set II (ca1730–40):

12. ORATORIOS

2a. SELECTIONS FROM ORATORIOS

    . "Sonata dell'Overtura"

    I: 1. "Fido specchio! Fido specchio, in te vagheggio, in te vagheggio," aria (Bellezza)
    . "Il, che sono il Piacere, giuro che sempre sarai bella," recit (Piacere, Bellezza)
    2. "Fosco genio, e nero dolo, mai non vien per esser solo," aria (Piacere)
    . "Ed io, che il Tempo sono," recit (Tempo, Disinganno)
    3. "Se la Bellezza perde vaghezza," aria (Disinganno)
    . "Dunque si prendam l'armi, e si vedrà," recit (Piacere, Bellezza, Tempo, Disganno)
    4. "Una schiera di piaceri," aria (Bellezza)
    . "I colossi del sole per me cadderò a terra," recit (Tempo)
    5. "Urne voi, urne voi! che racchiudete tante belle," aria (Tempo)
    . "Sono troppo crudeli i tuoi consigli," recit (Piacere)
    6. "Il voler nel fior degl'anni fra gl'affanni passar l'ore è vanità," duet (Bellezza, Piacere)
    . "Della vita mortale scorre un guardo," recit (Disganno, Bellezza)
    7. "Un pensiero nemico di pace," aria (Bellezza)

. "Folle tu nieghi il Tempo," recit (Disganno, Piacere, Bellezza)
8. "Nasce l'uomo ma nasce bambino," aria (Tempo)
9. "L'uomo sempre se stesso distrugge," aria (Disganno)
. "Questa è la reggia mia, vegheggiami," recit (Piacere) (2 vers)
10. "Sonatina"
. "Taci, qual suono ascolto!," recit (Bellezza)
11. "Un leggiadro giovinetto," aria (Piacere)
. "Ha nella destra l'ali," recit (Bellezza)
12. "Venga il Tempo, e con l'ali funeste," aria (Bellezza)
13. "Crede l'uom ch'egli riposi," aria (Disganno)
. "Tu credi che sia lungi," recit (Tempo, Bellezza)
14. "Folle, folle dunque, tu sola presumi," aria (Tempo)
. "La reggia del Piacer vedesti," recit (Disganno, Tempo)
15. "Se non sei più ministro di pene," aria à 4 (Bellezza, Piacere, Disinganno, Tempo)
II: . "Se del falso Piacere vedesti già," recit (Tempo)
16. "Chiudi, chiudi, chiudi, chiudi i vaghi rai," aria (Piacere)
. "In tre parti divise," recit (Tempo)
17. "Io sperai trovar nel vero il piacer," aria (Bellezza)
. "Tu vivi in van dolente," recit (Piacere)
18. "Tu giurasti di mai non lasciarmi, o il dolore che sia tua mercede," aria (Piacere)
. "Sguardo, che infermo ai rai del sol si volge," recit (Tempo)
19. "Io vorrei due cori in seno, un per darlo al pentimento," arioso & recit (Bellezza, Disganno)
. "Io giurerei, che tu chiudesti i lumi," recit (Disganno, Bellezza)
20. "Più non cura valle oscura chi dal monte saggio vede," aria (Disganno)
. "È un ostinato orrore," recit (Tempo)
21. "È ben folle quel nocchier che non vuol cangiar sentier," aria (Tempo)
. "Dicesti il verro, e benchè tardi, intesi," recit (Bellezza)
22. "Voglio Tempo," quartet (Bellezza, Piacere, Disganno, Tempo)
. "Presso la reggia ove il piacer risiede," recit (Bellezza, Disganno)
23. "Lascia la spina cogli la rosa," aria (Piacere)
. "Con troppo chiare note la vertà mi chiama," recit (Bellezza, Disganno)
24. "Voglio cangiar desio, e voglio dir, mi pento," aria (Bellezza)
. "Or che tiene la destra," recit (Bellezza, Piacere, Disganno)
25. "Chi già fudel biondo crine consigliero, al suol cadrà," recit (Bellezza, Piacere, Disganno)
. "Mà che veggio, che miro?," recit (Bellezza)
26. "Ricco pino, nel cammino, getta al mare e gemme ed oro," aria (Bellezza)
27. "Sì, bella penitenza, mentre io spargo pentita amaro pianto," recit accompagnato (Bellezza)
28. "Il bel pianto dell'aurora, che s'indora," duet (Disganno, Tempo)
. "Ritornello"
. "Piacer, che meco già vivesti," recit (Bellezza)
29. "Come nembo che fugge col vento," aria (Piacere)
30. "Pure del cielo intelligenze eterne," recit accompagnato (Bellazza)
31. "Tu del ciel mini stro eletto, non vedrai più nel mio petto," aria (Bellezza)

12a.3   "La Resurrezione," oratorio: HWV47
I: . "Sonata"
. "A dispetto de'Cieli ho vinto, ho vinto," recit (Lucifero)
1. "Caddi, è ver, caddi, è ver, ma nel cadere," aria (Lucifero)
2a. "Ma che insoli ta luce squarcia le tende"
2b. "Qual insolita luce squarcia le tende," recit accompagnato (Lucifero)
3. "Disseratevi, oh porte d'averno!," aria (Angelo)
4. "Ma che veggio? di spirti a me nemici," recit accompagnato (Lucifero, Angelo)
. "Chi sei? chi è questo re," recit (Lucifero, Angelo)
5. "D'amor fu consiglio," aria (Angelo)
. "E ben, questo tuo Nume," recit (Lucifero, Angelo)
6. "O voi dell' Erebo potenze orribili," aria (Lucifero)
7. "Notte, notte funesta, che del divino sole," recit accompagnato (Maddalena)
8. "Ferma l'ali, ferma l'ali, e sù i miei lumi," aria (Maddalena)
. "Concedi, o Maddalena," recit (Cleofe, Maddalena)
9. "Piangete, sì, piangete," aria (Cleofe)
. "Ahi dolce mio Signore," recit (Maddalena, Cleofe)
10. "Dolci, chiodi, amate spine," duet (Maddalena, Cleofe)
. "O Cleofe, o Maddalena," recit (S. Giovanni, Maddalena)
11. "Quando è parto dell'affetto, il dolore in nobil petto," aria (S. Giovanni)
. "Ma dimmi, e sarà vero," recit (Cleofe, S. Giovanni, Maddalena)
12. "Naufragando va per l'onde," aria (Cleofe)
. "Itene pure, o fide amiche donne," recit (S. Giovanni, Maddalena)
13. "Così la tortorella talor piange e si lagna," aria (S. Giovanni)
. "Se Maria dunque spera," recit (Maddalena)
14. "Ho un non so che nel cor, che invece di dolor," aria (Maddalena)
. "Uscite pur, uscite," recit (Angelo)
15. "Il Nume vincitor trionfi, regni e viva!," chorus
II: 16. "Introduzione"
. "Di quai nuovi portenti," recit (S. Giovanni)
17. "Ecco il sol ch'esce dal mare," aria (S. Giovanni)

. "Ma ove Maria dimora," recit (S. Giovanni)
18. "Risorga il mondo lieto e giocondo," aria (Angelo)
19. "Di rabbia indarno freme," recit accompagnato (Angelo)
. "Misero! ho pure udito!," recit (Lucifero, Angelo)
20. "Per celare il nuovo scorno," aria (Lucifero)
. "Oh come cieco il tuo furor delira!," recit (Angelo)
21. "Duro, duro è il cimento," duet (Angelo, Lucifero)
. "Amica, troppo tardo," recit (Maddalena, Cleofe)
22. "Per me già di morire," aria (Maddalena)
. "Ahi abborrito nome, ahi," recit (Lucifero)
23. "Vedo il ciel che più sereno," aria (Cleofe)
. "Cleofe, siam giunte al luogo," recit (Maddalena, Cleofe)
24. "Se per colpa di donna infelice all'uomo nel seno il crudo veleno la morte sgorgò," aria (Angelo)
. "Ritornello"
. "Mio Giesù, mio Signore," recit (Maddalena)
25. "Del ciglio dolente l'ondosa procella," aria (Maddalena)
. "Sì, sì, cerchiamo pure l'orme del nostro amor," recit (Cleofe)
26. "Augelletti, ruscelletti," aria (Cleofe)
. "Dove si frettolosi, Cleofe," recit (S. Giovanni, Cleofe)
27. "Caro figlio!," aria (S.Giovanni)
. "Ritornello"
. "Cleofe, Giovanni, udite," recit (Maddalena, S. Giovanni, Cleofe)
28. "Se impassibile, immortale sei risorto, o Sole amato," aria (Maddalena)
. "Sì, sì, col Redentore sorga il mondo redento," recit (S. Giovanni, Cleofe, Maddalena)
29. "Dia si lode in cielo, in terra a chi regna in terra, in ciel!," chorus
Anhang: (15.) "Viva e trionfi quel Dio così grande, che i cieli spande, che dà luce al sol," chorus

12a.4   "Der für die Sünde der Welt gemarterte und sterbende Jesus" (Brockes Passion), oratorio: HWV48
. "Sinfonia" (Allegro = 3rd movt of Concerto Grosso in B-flat major, Op.3/2, HWV313)
1. "Mich vom Stricke meiner Sünden zu entbinden," soli & chorus
. "Als Jesus nun zu Tische sasse," recit (Evangelist)
2. "Das ist mein Leib: kommt, nehmet, esset," recit accompagnato (Jesus)
3. "Der Gott, dem alle Himmelskreise," aria (Tochter Zion)
. "Und bald hernach nahm er den Kelch," recit (Evangelist)
4. "Das ist mein Blut im neuen Testament," recit accompagnato (Jesus)
5. "Ach, wie hungert mein Gemüte," chorus
. "Drauf sagten sie dem Höchsten Dank," recit (Evangelist, Jesus)
6a, b. "Wir wollen alle eh' erblassen," chorus (2 vers)
. "Es ist gewiss, denn also steht geschrieben," recit (Jesus)
7. "Weil ich den Hirten schlagen werde," aria (Jesus)
. "Auf's wenigste will ich, trotz allen Unglücksfällen," recit (Petrus, Jesus)
8. "Mein Vater, mein Vater! Schau, wie ich mich quäle," aria (Jesus)
. "Mich drückt der Sünden Zentnerlast," recit (Jesus)
9. "Sünder, schaut mit Furcht und Zagen eurer Sünden Scheusal an," arioso (Tochter Zion)
. "Die Pein vermehrte sich mit grausamem Erschüttern," recit (Evangelist)
10. "Brich, mein Herz, zerfliess in Tränen," aria (Tochter Zion)
. "Ein Engel aber kam von den gestirnten Bühnen," recit (Evangelist)
11. "Erwachet doch!," arioso (Johannes, Jakobus, Petrus, Jesus)
. "Und eh' die Rede noch geendigt war," recit (Evangelist)
12. "Greift zu, schlagt tot, schlagt tot," chorus
. "Und der Verräter hatte dieses ihnen zum Zeichen lassen dienen," recit (Evangelist, Judas)
13. "Er soll uns nicht entlaufen," chorus
. "Nimm, Rabbi, diesen Kuss von mir," recit (Judas, Jesus)
14. "Gift und Glut, Strahl und Flut, Gift und Glut," aria (Petrus)
. "Steck nur das Schwert an seinen Ort," recit (Jesus)
15. "O weh, sie binden ihn mit Strick und Ketten!," chorus
. "Wo flieht ihr hin? Verzagte, bleibt!," recit (Petrus)
16. "Nehmt mich mit, verzagte Scharen, hier ist Petrus ohne Schwert!," aria (Petrus)
. "Und Jesus ward zum Palast Caiphas'," recit (Evangelist, Caiphas, Jesus, Kriegsknecht)
17. "Was Bärentatzen Löwenklauen trotz ihrer Wut sich nicht getrauen," aria (Tochter Zion)
. "Dies sahe Petrus an," recit (Evangelist, 1. Magd, Petrus, 2. Magd, 3. Magd)
18. "Ich will versinken und vergehn, mich stürz' des Wetters Blitz und Strahl," arioso (Petrus)
. "Drauf krähete der Hahn," recit (Evangelist, Petrus)
19. "Heul, du (Fluch! Schaum!) heul, du (Fluch, Schaum) der Menschenkinder!," aria (Petrus)
. "Doch wie, will ich verzweifelnd untergehn?," recit (Petrus)
20. "Schau, ich fall'in strenger Busse, Sündenbüsser, dir zu Fusse," aria (Petrus)
21. "Ach Gott und Herr, wie gross und schwer," chorus
. "Als Jesus nun, wie hart man ihn verklagte," recit (Evangelist, Caiphas, Jesus)
22. "Er hat den Tod verdient," chorus
23. "Erwäg, erwäg, erwäg, ergrimmte Natternbrut, was deine Wut und Rachgier tut," aria (T)
. "Die Nacht war kaum vorbei," recit (Evangelist, Tochter Zion)
24. "Meine Laster sind die Stricke," aria (Tochter Zion)
. "O, was hab' ich verfluchter Mensch getan!," recit (Judas)
25. "Lasst diese Tat nicht ungerochen!," aria (Judas)
. "Unsäglich ist mein Schmerz," recit (Judas)

26. "Die ihr Gottes Gnad'versäumet und mit Sünden Sünden häuft," aria (Tochter Zion)
. "Wie nun Pilatus Jesum fragt, ob er der Juden König wär," recit (Evangelist, Jesus)
27. "Bestrafe diesen Übeltäter," chorus
. "Hast du denn kein Gehör?," recit (Pilatus, Evangelist)
28. "Sprichst du denn auf dies Verklagen und dies spöttische Befragen," duet (Tochter Zion, Jesus)
. "Pilatus wunderte sich sehr," recit (Evangelist)
29. "Nein, diesen nicht, nein, diesen nicht, den Barrabas gib frei," chorus
. "Was fang ich denn mit eurem sogenannten König an?," recit (Pilatus)
30. "Weg, weg, weg! Lass ihn kreuzigen!," chorus
. "Was hat er denn getan?," recit (Pilatus)
31. "Weg, weg, weg! Lass ihn kreuzigen," chorus
. "Wie er nun sah, dass dies Getümmel nicht zu stillen," recit (Evangelist)
32. "Besinne dich, Pilatus, schweig, halt ein!," arioso (Tochter Zion)
. "Drauf zerreten die Kriegsknecht ihn hinein," recit (Evangelist)
33. "Ich seh' an einen Stein gebunden den Eckstein," arioso (Gläubige Seele)
. "Drum, Seele, schau mit ängstlichem Vergnügen," recit (Gläubuge Seele)
34. "Dem Himmel gleicht sein buntgefärbter Rücken," aria (Gläubige Seele)
. "Wie nun das Blut in Strömen von ihm rann," recit (Evangelist)
35. "Die Rosen krönen sonst der rauhen Dornen Spitzen," aria (Tochter Zion)
. "Verwegner Dorn, barbar'sche Spitzen!," recit (Tochter Zion)
36. "Lass doch diese herbe Schmerzen, frecher Sünder, dir zu Herzen," aria (Tochter Zion)
. "Die zarten Schläfen sind bis ans Gehirne durchlöchert," recit (Tochter Zion)
37. "Jesu! Jesu, dich mit unsern Seelen zu vermählen," aria (Tochter Zion)
. "Drauf beugten sie aus Spott vor ihm die Kniee," recit (Evangelist)
38. "Gegrüsset seist du, Judenkönig!," chorus
. "Ja, scheuten sich nicht, ihm ins Gesicht zu speien," recit (Evangelist)
39. "Schäumest du, du Schaum der Welt," aria (Tochter Zion)
. "Worauf sie mit dem Rohr, das seine Hände trugen," recit (Evangelist)
. "Bestürzter Sünder, nimm in acht des Heilands Schmerzen!," recit (Tochter Zion)
40. "Heil der Welt, dein schmerzlich Leiden schreckt die Seel'," aria (Tochter Zion)
. "Wie man ihm nun genug Verspottung, Qual und Schmach hatt' angetan," recit (Evangelist)
41. "Eilt, ihr angefochten Seelen," solo & chorus (Tochter Zion)
. "Ach Gott, ach Gott! Mein Sohn wird fortgeschleppt," recit (Maria)
42. "Soll mein Kind, mein Leben sterben," duet (Maria, Jesus)
. "Und er trug selbst sein Kreuz," recit (Evangelist, Tochter Zion)
43. "Es scheint, da den zerkerbten Rücken," aria (T)
. "Wie sie nun an die Stätte, Golgatha mit Namen," recit (Evangelist)
44. "Hier erstarrt mein Herz und Blut, hier erstaunen Seel' und Sinnen!," aria (Gläubige Seele)
. "O Anblick, o entsetzliches Gesicht!," recit (Gläubige Seele)
45. "O Menschenkind, nur deine Sünd' hat dieses angerichtet," chorus
. "Sobald er nun gekreuzigt war, da losete die Schar," recit (Evangelist)
46. "Pfui! Pfui, pfui! Pfui seht mir doch den neuen König an!," chorus
. "Und eine dikke Finsternis," recit (Evangelist)
47. "Was Wunder, dass der Sonnen Pracht," aria (Gläubige Seele)
. "Dies war zur neunten Stund'," recit (Evangelist)
48. "Mein Heiland, mein Heiland, Herr und Fürst!," arioso (Gläubige Seele)
. "Drauf lief ein Kriegsknecht hin, der einen Schwamm, mit Essig," recit (Evangelist)
49. "O Donnerwort! O schrecklich Schreien!," trio (S, A, B)
. "O selig, wer dies glaubt," recit (Gläubige Seele)
50. "Sind meiner Seele tiefe Wunden durch deine Wunden," duet (Tochter Zion, Gläubige Seele)
. "O Grossmut! O erbarmendes Gemüt!," recit (Tochter Zion, Evangelist)
51. "Brich, brüllender Abgrund," aria (Gläubige Seele)
. "Ja, ja, es brüllet schon in unterird'schen Grüften," recit (Gläubige Seele, Hauptmann)
52. "Wie kommt's, dass da der Himmel weint, da seine Klüfte zeigt," aria (Gläubige Seele)
53. "Bei Jesus' Tod und Leiden leidet des Himmels Kreis," recit accompagnato (Gläubige Seele)
54. "Mein Sünd' mich werden kränken sehr," chorus
55. "Wisch ab der Tränen scharfe Lauge, steh', sel'ge Seele, nun in Ruh'," aria (Tochter Zion)
56. "Ich bin ein Glied an deinem Leib," chorus

12a.5   "Acis & Galatea," oratorio: HWV49a
    I: 1. "Sinfonia"
        2. "Oh the pleasure of the plains!," chorus
        3. "Ye verdant plains and woody mountains," accompagnato (Galatea)
        4. "Hush, hush, ye pretty warbling quire!," air (Galatea)
        5. "Where shall I seek the charming fair?," air (Acis)
        . "Stay, shepherd, stay!," recit (Damon)
        6. "Shepherd, what art thou pursuing?," air (Damon)
        . "Lo! Here my love!," recit (Acis)
        7. "Love in her eyes sits playing," air (Acis)
        . "Oh! Didst thou know the pains of absent love," recit (Galatea)
        8. "As when the dove laments her love," recit (Galatea)
        9a. "Happy, happy, happy, happy, happy we! What joys I feel," duet (Galatea, Acis)
        9b, c. "Happy, happy, happy, happy, happy we!," chorus (1st vers w/ carillon)
    II: 10. "Wretched lovers! Fate has past this sad decree," chorus
        11. "I rage I rage, I melt, I burn!," accompagnato (Polypheme)

12. "O ruddier than the cherry, o sweeter than the berry," air (Polypheme)
. "Whither, fairest, art thou running," recit (Polypheme, Galatea)
13. "Cease to beauty to be suing," air (Polypheme)
14. "Would you gain the tender creature," air (Damon)
. "His hideous love provokes my rage," recit (Acis)
15. "Love sounds th'alarm," air (Acis)
16. "Consider, fond shepherd, how fleeting's the pleasure," air (Damon)
. "Cease, oh cease, thou gentle youth," recit (Galatea)
17. "The flocks shall leave the mountain, the woods the turtle dove," trio (Galatea, Acis, Polypheme)
18. "Help, Galatea! help, ye parent gods!," accompagnato (Acis)
19. "Mourn, all ye muses! the gentle Acis is no more!," chorus
20a. "Must I my Acis still bemoan," solo & chorus (Galatea)
20b. "Cease, Galatea, cease to grieve, bewail not whom thou can'st relieve," recit (Damon)
. " 'Tis done; thus I exert my pow'r divine," recit (Galatea)
21. "Heart, the seat of soft delight," air (Galatea)
22. "Galatea, dry thy tears, Acis now a god appears!," chorus

12a.8 "Esther," oratorio: HWV50b
. "Ouverture"
I: 1. "Breathe soft, ye gales," arioso (Israelite Woman)
2a, b. "Watchful, angels, let her share," air (Israelite Woman) (1st p1832, = HWV47/8, 2nd 1751,7)
. "O King of Kings, celestial Lord!," recit (Esther) (2 vers)
3. "Alleluja, alleluja," air (Esther) (= No.6 in motet: Silete venti, HWV242)
. "O King of Kings, celestial Lord," recit (Esther)
. "With transport, lovely Queen, I see," recit (Mordecai)
4. "So much beauty, sweetly blooming," air (Mordecai)
5. "My heart inditing," chorus (= Coronation Anthem No.4, HWV261)
6. "Kings' daughters were among thy honorable women," ch (= Coronation Anthem No.4, HWV261)
7. "Upon thy right hand," chorus (= Coronation Anthem No.4, HWV261)
8. "Kings, Kings shall be thy nursing fathers," chorus (= Coronation Anthem No.4, HWV261)
A. "Let me with freedom thy petition know," recit (Ahasverus, Haman)
B. "O King, for ever live!," recit (Haman, Ahasverus) (p1751)
9a, b. "Endless fame, thy days adorning," air (Ahasverus) (2 vers)
. " 'Tis greater far to spare, than to destroy," recit (Harbonah, Haman)
10. "Pluck root and branch from out the Land," air (Haman) (= Esther, HWV50a/1)
11. "Shall we the God of Israel fear," chorus
. "Jerusalem no more shall mourn," recit (Israelite Woman)
12a, b. "Tune, tune your harps to cheerful strains," air (Israelite Woman) (2nd vers p1757)
(13.) "Shall we of servitude complain," chorus (p1751, 1757)
13a. "Praise the Lord with cheerful noise," air (Israelite Woman)
. "Thus pleas'd is th'Almighty to dispense," recit (Esther) (p1751)
13b. "No, no, no more, no more disconsolate," air (Esther) (p1751, = Deborah, HWV51/26)
. "How have our sins provok'd the Lord!," recit (Mordecai)
14a. "O Jordan, Jordan, sacred tide!," aria (Mordecai)
. "Now persecution shall lay by her iron rod," recit (Priest Israelite) (p1751)
(14.) "Me thinks I see each stately tow'r of Salem rise," accompagnato (Priest Israelite) (p1751)
14b. "Sacred raptures cheer my breast," air (Priest Israelite) (p1751, = Solomon, HWV67/6)
15. "Ye sons of Israel, mourn," chorus
II: 16. "Tyrants may awhile presume they never shall," chorus (= Esther, HWV50a/16)
. "Why sits that sorrow on thy brow?," recit (Esther, Mordecai)
17a, b. "Dread not, righteous Queen, the danger! Love will pacify his anger," air (Mordecai) (2 vers)
. "Haste to the King, his mercy crave," recit (Priest Israelite) (p1751, 1757)
. "O Heav'n, protect her with thy tender care," recit (Israelite Woman)
18. "Blessings, descend on downy wings!," duet (Israelite Woman, Mordecai)
. "I go the pow'r of grief to prove," recit (Esther) (2 vers)
19a, b. "Tears assist me, pity moving," air (Esther) (2 vers)
20. "Save us, o Lord, save us, o Lord," chorus
. "O heav'n, protect her with thy tender care," recit (Mordecai)
(20.) "Hope, a pure and lasting treasure," air (Mordecai) (p1751, = No.3 in: Silete venti, HWV242)
. "Who dares intrude into our presence," recit (Ahasverus, Esther) (2 vers)
21. "Who calls my parting soul from death?," duet (Esther, Ahasverus)
22. "O beauteous Queen, un close those eyes!," air (Ahasverus)
. "If I find favour in thy sight," recit (Esther)
23. "How can I stay, when love invites?," air (Ahasverus)
. "With inward joy his visage glows," recit (Priest Israelite)
23a. "Virtue, truth, and innocence shall ever be her sure defence," air (Israelite) (p1751,= HWV67/16)
23b. "Sion now her head shall raise," duet & chorus (Israelite Woman, Israelite Man) (p1757; ch)
23c. "May thy beauty, sweetly, smiling," air (Mordecai) (p1757)
. "With inward joy his visage glows," recit (Priest Israelite)
24. "Heaven o lend me every charm," air (Israelite Woman)
. "The King will listen to his royal fair," recit (Priest Israelite)
25. "God is our hope, and he will shew the King," chorus (= Coronation Anthem No.1, HWV258)
(25.) "Blessed, blessed are all they, all they that fear the Lord," chorus (p1751)
III: 26. "Jehovah crown'd with glory bright" (The Invocation), arioso (Mordecai)
27. "He comes to end our woes," chorus

. "Now, O Queen, thy suit declare," recit (Ahasverus, Esther)
. "Permit me, Queen, with duteous address," recit (Israelite Woman)
. "How sweet the rose in vernal bloom delighting," air (Israelite Woman)
28. "Turn not, O Queen, thy face away," arioso (Haman)
29. "Flatt'ring tongue, no more I hear thee!," air (Esther)
. "Guards, seize the traitor, bear him hence!," recit (Ahasverus)
30a. "Thro' the nation he shall be," air (Ahasverus) (= No.5 of Birthday Ode, HWV74)
30b. "All applauding crowds around," chorus
. "By thee, great Prince, we now again are freed," recit (Esther) (p1757)
. "This glorious deed defending will ever thee commending," air (Esther) (p1757)
31. "How art thou fall'n from thy height! Tremble, ambition," air (Haman)
32. "I'll proclaim the wond'rous story," duet (Esther, Israelite Woman)
33a, b. "The Lord our enemy has slain," chorus (2 vers)
Anhang: Add airs (p1737): . "Tua bellezza, tua dolcezza vincerà del Rege il cor," aria (S)
. "Angelico splendor rischiari il nobil cor," aria (S)
. "Cor fedele, cor fedele, spera sempre," aria (S) (= No.3 in motet: Silete venti, HWV242)
. "Bianco giglio in tutto fiore," aria (S) (= No.5 in motet: Silete venti, HWV242)

12a.9   "Deborah," oratorio: HWV51
. "Ouverture" (Poco allegro = No.8 in Chandos Anthem No.10, HWV255)
I: 1. "Immortal Lord of earth and skies," d chorus
. "O Barak, favour'd of the skies!," recit (Deborah, Barak)
2. "Where do thy ardours raise me!," duet (Deborah, Barak)
3. "Forbear thy doubts! to arms!," chorus (= No.12 in: Brockes Passion, HWV48)
. "Since Heav'n has thus his will express'd," recit (Barak)
4. "For ever to the voice of pray'r," chorus
5. "By that adorable decree, that Chaos cloath'd with symmetry," accompagnato (Deborah)
6. "O hear thy lowly servants' pray'r," d chorus
. "Ye sons of Israel, cease your fears," recit (Deborah)
7. "O blast with thy tremendous brow," chorus
. "To whom so e'er his fate the tyrant owes," recit (Barak)
8. "How lovely is the blooming fair," air (Barak)
. "O Deborah, where'er I turn my eyes," recit (Jael, Deborah)
9. "Choirs of angels all around thee," air (Deborah)
. "My transports are too great to tell," recit (Jael)
10. "To joy he brightens my despair," air (Jael)
. "Barak, my son, the joyful sound of acclamation," recit (Abinoam)
11. "Awake the ardour of thy breast," air (Abinoam)
. "I go, where Heav'n and duty call," recit (Barak) (2 vers)
12. "All danger all danger disdaining, for battle I glow," recit (Barak)
13. "Let thy deeds be glorious," chorus
. "My charge is to declare from Sisera," recit (Herald, Barak)
. "Let him approach pacific, or in rage," recit (Deborah)
14. "Despair all around them shall swiftly confound," chorus (= Coronation Anthem No.2, HWV259)
II: 15. "See, see! see, the proud chief advances now," chorus
. "That here rebelious arms I see," recit (Sisera: A/T) (2 vers)
16a, b. "At my feet extended low," aria (Sisera: A/T) (2 vers)
. "Go, frown, Barbarian, where thou art fear'd!," recit (Deborah)
17. "In Jehovah's awful sight, haughty tyrants are but dust," air (Deborah)
. "Yes, how your God in wonders can excel," recit (Sisera) (2 vers: A/T)
18a, b. "Whilst you boast the wond'rous story," air (Sisera) (2 vers: A/T)
19. "Impious mortal, cease to brave us! Jehovah soon will save us," air (Barak)
. "Behold the nations all around," recit (Chief Priest of Baal) (2 vers)
20. "Baal! O Baal, o Baal! monarch of the skies!," chorus (Baal's Priests)
. "No more! ye infidels, no more! false is the God whom ye adore," recit (Chief Priest of Israelites)
21. "Lord of eternity! who hast in store plagues for the proud," chorus
22. "Plead thy just cause, Avenge thy servants," chorus
. "By his great name, and His alone," recit (Deborah, Sisera)
23. "All your boast will end in woe," solo & d chorus (Deborah, Sisera, Barak, Baal's Priest)
. "Great prophetess! my soul's on fire," recit (Barak)
24. "In the battle fame pursuing," air (Barak)
. "Thy ardours warm the winter of my age," recit (Abinoam)
25. "Swift inundation of desolation," air (Abinoam) (= Aci, Galatea e Poliferno, HWV72/9)
. "Oh Judah, with what joy I see," recit (Israelite Woman / Jael)
26. "No, no, no more! no more disconsolate I'll mourn," air (Israelite Woman / Jael)
. "Now, Jael, to thy tent retire," recit (Deborah)
27. "O the pleasure my soul is possessing," air (Jael) (= Il trionfo, HWV46a/18)
. "Barak, we now to battle go," recit (Deborah)
28. "Smiling freedom, lovely guest," duet (Deborah, Barak)
29. "The great King of Kings will us aid today," chorus (= Coronation Athem No.3, HWV260)
III: 30. "Now the proud insulting foe," chorus (Israelites)
. "The haughty foe, whose pride to Heav'n did soar, is fall'n," recit (Israelite Woman / Deborah)
31. "Now sweetly smiling Peace," air (Israelite Woman) (= No.6 in: Chandos Anthem No.9, HWV254)
. "My pray'rs are heard, the blessings of this day," recit (Abinoam, Barak)
32. "Tears, tears such as tender fathers shed," air (Abinoam)

. "O Deborah! my fears are o'er," recit (Jael)
33. "Doleful tidings, doleful tidings, doleful tidings, how ye wound!," chorus (Baal's Priests)
34. "Our fears are now for ever fled," air (Israelite Woman) (= No.3 in: Chandos Anthem No.9)
. "I saw the tyrant breathless in her tent," recit (Barak)
. "When from the battle that proud captain fled," recit (Jael)
35. "Tyrant, now no more we dread thee," air (Jael)
. "If, Jael, I aright divine," recit (Deborah)
36. "The glorious sun shall cease to shed," air (Deborah)
. "May Heav'n with kind profusion shed its chosen joys on Jael's head!," recit (Barak)
37. "Low at her feet, low at her feet he bow'd," air (Barak)
38. "O great Jehovah! may thy foes thus perish," accompagnato (Deborah)
39. "Let our glad songs to Heav'n ascend," chorus
. "O celebrate his sacred name, with gratitude his praise," chorus
. "Alleluja, alleluja," chorus (= Coronation Anthem No.3, HWV260)
Later changes: I: . "Me thinks I hear the mother's groans," accompagnato (A) (= Esther, HWV50a/7)
(10.) "O Jordan, Jordan, sacred tide!," air (A) (= Esther, HWV50a/9)
(10.) "Flowing joys do now surround me," air (Jael) (= Esther, HWV50a/20)
(10.) "To joy he brightens my despair," air (Jael) (= Siroe, HWV24/13)
. "My vengeance awakes me, compassion forsakes me," air (Herald) (= Athalia, HWV52/21a)
. "Hateful man, thy raptur'd mind," air (Barak) (= Tolomeo, HWV25/18)
. "Let him approach pacific or in rage," recit (Deborah)
. "Alleluja," chorus (= Athalia, HWV52/16)
(14.) "Cease, o Judah, cease thy mourning," air (Deborah) (= Athalia, HWV52/18b)
(23.) "Hence I hasten, then fear thy danger," air (Sisera) (= Athalia, HWV52/21b)
. "Away, unhallow'd slaves, away!," recit (Chief Priest of Israel)
(26.) "Watchful angels, watchful angels, let her share," air (Jael) (= Esther, HWV50b/2)
. "Rejoice, o Judah, this triumphant day," recit (Barak) (= Athalia, HWV52/36)
(29.) "The mighty pow'r," chorus (= Athalia, HWV52/17)
(34.) "Our fears are now for ever fled," air (Israelite Woman) (= Alessandro, HWV21/36)
(34.) "All his mercies I review," air (Jael) (= Athalia, HWV52/23)
(38a.) "I'll proclaim the wond'rous story of the mercies," duet (Deborah, Jael) (= Esther, HWV50b/32)

12a.10 "Athalia," oratorio: HWV52
A. "Symphony" (Allegro I = 1st movt of: Trio Son, Op.5/4, HWV399; Allegro II = 2nd movt of same)
B. "Ouverture" (= 2nd movt of Trio Sonata , Op.5/4, HWV399)
I: 1. "Blooming virgins, blooming virgins, blooming virgins, spotless train," air (Josabeth)
2. "The rising world Jehovah crown'd," chorus
3. "Tyrants would in impious throngs," solo & chorus (Josabeth)
. "When He is in his wrath reveal'd," recit (Abner)
4. "When storms the proud to terrors doom," solo & chorus (Abner)
. "Your sacred songs awhile forbear," recit (Joad)
5. "Oh Judah, Judah! chosen seed! to what distress," accompagnato (Joad)
6a, b. "Oh, Lord, oh, Lord, whom we adore, shall Judah rise no more?," solo & ch (Joad) (2 vers)
7. "What scenes of horrors round me rise!," accompagnato (Athalia)
. "Oh Mathan, aid me to control," recit (Athalia, Mathan)
8. "Oh Athalia, tremble at thy fate!," accompagnato (Athalia)
9a. "The gods, who chosen blessings shed," chorus
9b. "The gods, who chosen blessings shed," air (Mathan) (= HWV48/34)
. "Her form at this began to fade," recit (Athalia)
10. "Cheer her, O Baal, with a soft serene," chorus
. "Amidst these horrors that my soul dismay'd," recit (Athalia, Mathan)
11 "Gentle airs, melodious strains!," air (Mathan)
12. "Softest sounds no more can ease me," air (Athalia)
. "Swift to the temple let us fly to know," recit (Mathan, Abner)
13. "The traitor if you there descry, oh let him by the altar die," chorus
. "My Josabeth! the greatlful time appears," recit (Joad, Josabeth, Abner)
14. "Faithful cares in vain extended, lovely hopes for ever ended," air (Josabeth)
. "O cease, fair princess, to indulge your woe," recit (Abner, Joad)
15. "Gloomy tyrants, gloomy tyrants! we disdain," air (Joad)
16. "Alleluja, alleluja," chorus
II: 17. "The mighty pow'r, in whom we trust," chorus
18a, b. "Through the land, so lovely blooming," air (Josabeth) (2 vers)
. "Ah! were this land from proud oppression freed," recit (Abner, Joad)
19. "Ah, canst thou but prove me! to vengeance I spring," air (Abner)
. "Thou dost the ardour that I wish display," recit (Joad)
A. "Confusion to my thoughts!," recit (Athalia, Josabeth, Joas)
B. "What can the faithful fear for Judah's foes," recit (Joas) (p1743)
20. "Will Good, whose mercies ever flow, expose his children's youth to woe?," air (Joas)
. " 'Tis my intention, lovely youth, that you a scene," recit (Athalia, Joas)
21a. "My vengeance awakes me, compassion forsakes me," air (Athalia)
21b. "Hence I hasten, then fear for thy danger!," air (Athalia) (p1743, = Il trionfo, HWV46b/33)
. "O Queen, now let your pow'r be known," recit (Mathan) (p1743)
(21.) "My vengeance awakes me," air (Mathan) (p1743)
22. "My spirits fail, faint, I die," duet (Josabeth, Joas)
. "Dear Josabeth, I trembled whilst thy woe," recit (Joad)

23. "Cease thy anguish, smile once more," duet (Joad, Josabeth)
  . "Joad, ere day has ended half its race," recit (Abner)
24. "The clouded scene begins to clear," chorus (Young Virgins)
  . "When crimes aloud for vengeance call," chorus (Priests & Levites)
  . "Rejoice, oh Judah, in thy God!," chorus
III: 25. "What sacred horrors shake my breast! Ah!," accompagnato (Joad)
26. "Unfold, great seer, what heav'n imparts," chorus"
27a. "Let harmony breathe soft around," accompagnato (Joad)
27b. "Cor fedele, spera sempre," aria (Joad) (p1735, = 3. of motet: Silete Venti, HWV242)
28. "Jerusalem, thou shalt no more," solo & chorus (Joad)
  . "Eliakim! My father! Let me know," recit (Joad, Joas, Josabeth)
29. "With firm united hearts, we all will conquer," chorus
  . "O princess, I approach thee to declare," recit (Mathan, Josabeth)
30a. "Soothing tyrant, falsely smiling," air (Josabeth)
30b. "Happy Judah, in every blessing," air (Josabeth) (p1756, = Il Parnasso in Festa, HWV73/16)
  . "Apostate priest! how canst thou dare to violate," recit (Joad, Mathan)
  . "O bold seducer, art thou there?," recit (Athalia, Joad)
31. "Around let acclamations ring," solo & chorus (Joad)
  . "Oh treason, treason! impious scene!," recit (Athalia, Joad, Abner)
32. "Oppression, no longer I dread thee," air (Abner)
  . "Where am I? furies, wild despair!," recit (Athalia, Mathan)
33. "Hark, hark, hark! His thunders round me roll," arioso (Mathan)
  . "Yes, proud apostate, thou shalt fall," recit (Joad, Athalia)
34. "To darkness eternal and horrors infernal," air (Athalia)
  . "Now, Josabeth, thy fears are o'er," recit (Joad, Josabeth)
35a. "Joys, in gentle trains appearing, heav'n does to my fair impart," duet (Joad, Josabeth)
35b. "Angelico splendor," air (Josabeth (p?1743, = Esther, HWV50b)
  . "Rejoice, oh Judah, this triumphant day!," recit (Abner)
36. "Give glory, give glory to his awful name," chorus
Anhang: (15.) "When storms the proud to terrors doom," duet & d chorus

12a.11 "Saul," oratorio: HWV53
  . "Symfonia"
I: 1. "How excellent, how excellent thy name, o Lord," chorus
2. "An infant rais'd by thy command," air (S)
3. "Along the Monster Atheist strode with more than human pride," trio (A, T, B)
4. "The youth inspir'd by thee, o Lord," chorus
5. "How excellent," chorus
6. "He comes, he comes!," recit (Michal)
7. "O godlike youth! by all confess'd, of human race," air (Michal)
8. "Behold, o King, the brave victorious youth," recit (Abner, Saul, David)
9. "O King, your favours with delight I take," air (David)
10. "O early piety," recit (Jonathan)
11a, b. "What abject thoughts," air (Merab) (2nd vers p after 1759, = Siroe, HWV24/27)
12. "Yet think, on whom this honour you bestow," recit (Merab)
13. "Birth and fortune I despise!," air (Jonathan)
14. "Go on, illustrious pair! Your great example," recit (High Priest)
15. "While yet thy tide of blood runs high," air (High Priest)
16. "Thou, Merab, first in birth, be first in honour," recit (Saul, Merab)
17. "My soul rejects the thoughts with scorn," air (Merab)
18. "See, see, with what a scornful air," air (Michal)
19. "Ah! lovely youth! Ah! lovely youth! wast thou design'd," air (Michal)
20. "Sinfonie pour les Carillons"
21. "Already see, the daughters of the land," recit (Michal) (also vers for carillons)
22. "Welcome, welcome, mighty king!," chorus
23. "What do I hear? Am I then sunk so low," accompagnato (Saul)
24. "David his ten Thousands slew, ten Thousands praises," chorus
25. "To him ten Thousands! and to me but Thousands?," accompagnato (Saul)
26. "With rage I shall burst his praises to hear!," air (Saul)
27. "Imprudent women! Your ill tim'd comparisons," recit (Jonathan, Michal)
28. "Fell rage and black despair possest," air (Michal)
29. "This but the smallest part of harmony," recit (High Priest)
30. "By thee this universal frame," accompagnato (High Priest)
31. "Rack'd with infernal pains ev'n now the king comes forth," recit (Abner)
32a, b. "O Lord, whose mercies numberless," air (Michal) (2 vers)
33. "Symphony"
34. " 'Tis all in vain, his fury still continues," recit (Jonathan)
35. "A serpent in my bosom warm'd would sting me to the heart," air (Saul)
36. "Has he escap'd my rage?," recit (Saul)
37. "Capricious man, in humour lost," air (Merab)
38. "O filial piety! O sacred friendship!," accompagnato (Jonathan)
39. "No, no, cruel father, no," air (Jonathan)
40. "O Lord, whose providence ever wakes for their defence," air (High Priest)
41. "Preserve him for the glory of thy name, thy people's safety, and the heathen's shame," chorus

II: 42. "Envy! Envy!," chorus
     43. "Ah, dearest friend, undone by too much virtue," recit (Jonathan)
     44. "But sooner Jordan's stream, I swear," air (Jonathan)
     45. "O strange vicissitude!," recit (David, Jonathan)
     46. "Such haughty beauties rather move aversion, than engage our love," air (David)
     47. "My father comes. Retire, my friend," recit (Jonathan)
     48. "Hast thou obey'd my orders," recit (Saul, Jonathan)
     49. "Sin not, o King, against the youth," air (Jonathan)
     50. "As great Jehovah lives, I swear, the youth shall not be slain," air (Saul)
     51. "From cities storm'd, and battles won," air (Jonathan)
     52. "Appear, my friend. No more imagine danger," recit (Jonathan, Saul)
     53. "Your words, o King, my loyal heart," air (David)
     54. "Yes, he shall wed my daughter," recit (Saul)
     55. "A father's will has authoriz'd my love," recit (Michal)
     56. "O fairest of ten thousand fair," duet (Michal, David)
     57. "Is there a man, who all his ways directs, his god alone to please?," chorus
     58a. "Symphony"
     58b. "Gavotte" (p1750)
     59. "Thy father is as cruel, and as false," recit (David)
     60. "At persecution I can laugh; no fear my soul can move," duet (Michal, David)
     61. "Whom dost thou seek? And who has sent thee hither?," recit (Michal, Doeg—a Messenger)
     62. "No, no, let the guilty, the guilty tremble," air (Michal)
     63. "Mean as he was, he is my brother now," recit (Merab)
     64. "Author of peace, who canst cotrol ev'ry passion of the soul," air (Merab)
     65. "Sinfonia"
     66a, b. "The time at length is come, when I shall take my full revenge," accompagnato (Saul)
     67. "Where is the son of Jesse? Comes he not," recit (Saul, Jonathan)
     68. "O fatal consequence of rage, by reason uncontroll'd," chorus
III: 69. "Wretch that I am! of my own ruin author!," accompagnato (Saul)
     70. " 'Tis said, here lives a woman, close familiar," recit (Saul)
        . "Yet, o hard fate; my self am now reduc'd," accompagnato (Saul)
     71. "With me what would'st thou?," recit (Witch, Saul)
     72. "Infernal spirits, by whose pow'r," air (Witch)
     73. "Why hast thou forc'd me from the realms of peace," accompagnato (Samuel, Saul)
        . "Hath God forsaken thee?," recit (Samuel)
        . "Thou and thy sons shall be with me tomorrow," accompagnato (Samuel)
     74. "Sinfonia"
     75. "Whence comest thou? Out of the camp of Israel," recit (David, Amalekite)
     76. "Impious wretch, of race accurst," air (David)
     77a. "Elegy"
     77b. "La Marche"
     78. "Mourn, Israel, mourn, thy beauty lost!," chorus (Elegy on the Death of Saul and Jonathan)
     79. "O let it not in Gath be heard," air (T)
     80. "From this unhappy day," air (S)
     81. "Brave Jonathan his bow ne'er drew, but wing'd with death," air (A)
     82. "Eagles were not so swift as they, nor lions with so strong a grasp," chorus
     83. "In sweetest harmony they liv'd," air (S)
     84. "O fatal day! How low the mighty lie!," solo & chorus (David)
     85a. "Ye men of Judah, weep no more," recit (High Priest / Abner)
     85b. "Ye men of Judah, weep no more," air (Abner)
     86. "Gird on thy sword, gird on thy sword thou man of might," chorus
Anhang: (3.) "Along the monster Atheist strode," chorus
     (10b.) "Wise, valiant, good, above thy tender years endu'd," air (Jonathan)
     (12.) "Yet think, with whom you stoop to link yourself," recit (Merab)
     (32.) "Fly, fly, malicious spirit, fly," air (David)
     (59.) "Let all the enemies of my Lord the King," recit (David, Saul)
     (37.) "Capricious man, in humour lost," air (Merab)
        . *"What words can tell how happy they," chorus (frag)*
        . "What words can tell how happy they," air (S)
        . "Love from such a parent sprung," air (Michal)
     (58.) "Symphony"
     (76.) "Impious wretch, of race accurst!," air (David)
        . "O Jonathan, o Jonathan, thou wast slain," accompagnato (David)
        . "Saul and Jonathan were lovely and pleasant in their lives," recit (S)
     (81.) "Brave Jonathan his bow ne'er drew, but wing'd with death," air (S)

12a.12   "Israel in Egypt," oratorio: HWV54
         I. "The Lamentation of the Israelites for the death of Joseph" (= The ways of Zion do mourn, HWV264)
         II. "Exodus": 1. "And the children of Israel sigh'd," d chorus
            . "Then sent He Moses, His servant, and Aaron, whom He had chosen," recit (T)
            2. "They loathed to drink of the river," chorus
            3. "Their land brought forth frogs," air (A)
            4. "He spake the word: And there came all manner of flies," d chorus
            5. "He gave them hailstones for rain," d chorus
            6. "He sent a thick darkness over all the land," chorus

7. "He smote all the firstborn in Egypt," chorus
8. "But as for His people, but as for His people, He led, He led them forth like sheep," chorus
9a. "Egypt was glad when they departed," chorus
9b. "Through the land so lovely blooming," air (S) (= HWV52/18b)
10. "He rebuked the Red Sea, and it was dried up," d chorus
11. "He led them through the deep," d chorus
12. "But the waters overwhelmed their enemies," chorus
  . "Angelico splendor," air (S) (p1739, = Esther, HWV50b/add air of 1737)
13. "And Israel saw that great work that the Lord did upon th' Egyptians," d chorus
  . "Hope, hope, a pure and lasting treasure," add air (S) (p1756, = Esther, HWV50b/20 add air)
14. "And believed the Lord and his servant Moses," chorus
III. "Moses Song": 15. Introitus: "Moses and the children of Israel sung this song unto the Lord," d ch
16. "The Lord is my strength and my song," duet (2S)
17. "He is my God, and I will prepare him an habitation," d chorus
18. "The Lord is a man of war," duet (2B)
19. "The depths have cover'd them," d chorus
  . "Cor fedele," air (S) (= Esther, HWV50b/add air of 1737)
  . "Thou sentest forth thy wrath, which consumed them as stubble," d chorus
20. "And with the blast of thy nostrils the waters were gathered together," chorus
21. "The enemy said: I will pursue, I will overtake," air (T)
22. "Thou didst blow, thou didst blow with the wind," air (S)
23. "Who is like unto Thee, oh Lord, among the Gods?," d chorus
  . "The earth swallow'd them," d chorus
24. "Thou in thy mercy hast led forth thy people," duet (A, T)
25a. "The people shall hear, and be afraid," d chorus
25b. "La speranza, la costanza," air (S) (= Esther, HWV50b/add air of 1737)
26. "Thou shalt bring them in," air (A)
27. "The Lord shall reign for ever and ever," d chorus
  . "For the horse of Pharaoh went in with his chariots," recit (T)
  . Repeatur: 27. "The Lord shall reign," d chorus
  . "And Miriam the prophetess, the sister of Aaron, took a timbrel in her hand," recit (T)
28. "Sing ye to the Lord, for he hath triumphed gloriously!," d chorus & solo (S)
Anhang: *(1.) "And the children of Israel sigh'd," chorus (frag)*
  . "And the children of Israel sigh'd," recit (T)

12a.13   "L'Allegro, il Penseroso ed il Moderato," oratorio: HWV55
    I: 1. "Hence, loathed Melancholy, of Cerberus and blackest midnight born," accompagnato (L'Allegro)
        2a, b. "Hence, vain deluding Joys," accompagnato (Il Penseroso) (2 vers: S/A)
        3. "Come, come, thou goddess fair and free," air (L'Allegro)
        4a, b. "Come, rather, goddess, sage and holy," air (Il Penseroso) (2 vers: S/A)
        5. "Haste thee, nymph," air & chorus (L'Allegro)
        6. "Come, and trip it as you go," air & chorus (T)
        7. "Come, pensive Nun, devout and pure," accompagnato (Il Penseroso)
        8. "Come, come, come, but keep thy wonted state," arioso (S)
        9a, b. "There held in holy passion still," accompagnato (2 vers: S/A)
        . "Join with thee calm Peace and Quiet," chorus
        . "Hence, loathed melancholy!," recit (L'Allegro)
        10. "Mirth, admit me of thy crew," air (S)
        11. "First and chief, on golden wing," accompagnato (Il Pensieroso)
        12. "Sweet bird, sweet bird, that shun'st the noise of folly," air (S)
        . "If I give thee honour due," recit (L'Allegro)
        13. "Mirth, admit me of thy crew," air (B)
        14. "Oft, on a plot of rising ground," air (Il Pensieroso)
        15. "Far from all resort of mirth," air (S)
        . "If I give thee honour due," recit (L'Allegro)
        16. "Let me wander not unseen, by hedgerow elms on hillocks green," air (T)
        17. "Straight mine eye hath caught new pleasures," air (S)
        18a, b, c. "Mountains, on whose barren breast," accompagnato (3 vers: S/A/B)
        19a, b. "Or let the merry bells ring round," air (S) (2 vers)
        . "And young and old come forth to play," chorus (2 vers)
    II: 20a, b. "Hence, vain deluding Joys, the brood of Folly," accompagnato (Il Penseroso) (2 vers: S/A)
        21a, b. "Sometimes let gorgeous Tragedy," air (2 vers: S/A)
        22. "But oh! Sad virgin that thy pow'r might raise," air (S)
        . "Thus, Night, oft see me in thy pale career," recit (S)
        23. "Populous cities please me," solo & chorus (L'Allegro)
        24. "There let Hymen oft appear," air (T)
        25a. "Me, when the sun begins to fling," accompagnato (A)
        26b. "Hide me from day's garish eye," air (A)
        27. "I'll to the well-trod stage anon," air (L'Allegro)
        28. "And ever against eating cares," air (S)
        29a, b. "Orpheus self may heave his head," air (2 vers: S/B)
        30. "These delights if thou canst give," air & chorus (T)
        . "But let my due feet never fail," recit (Il Penseroso)
        31. "There let the pealing organ blow," chorus
        32a, b. "May at last my weary age," air (2 vers: S/A)

33. "These pleasures, Melancholy, give," solo & chorus (S)
III: 34. "Hence, boast not ye profane," accompagnato (B)
    35. "Come, with native lustre shine, Moderation, grace divine," air (B)
    36. "Sweet Temp'rance in thy right hand bear," accompagnato (B)
    . "All this company serene," chorus
    37. "Come, with gentle hand restrain," air (S)
    . "No more short life they then will spend," recit (T)
    38. "Each action will derive new grace," air (T)
    39. "As steals the morn upon the night," duet (S, T)
    . "L'insaziabil, fantasia risvegli stravaganti desiri," accompagnato (S)
    . "Troppo audace umano stuolo," aria (S)
    40. "Thy pleasures, Moderation, give, in them alone we truly live," chorus

12a.14   "Messiah," oratorio: HWV56
    I: 1. "Sinfony"
      2. "Comfort ye, comfort ye my people," accompagnato (T)
      3. "Ev'ry valley, ev'ry valley shall be exalted," air (T)
      4. "And the glory, the glory of the Lord," chorus
      5. "Thus saith the Lord, the Lord of Hosts," accompagnato (B)
      6a, b, c. "But who may abide the day of His coming?" (B) (2nd vers p1742; 3rd vers p1750)
      7. "And He shall purify, and He shall purify the sons of Levi," chorus
      . "Behold, a virgin shall conceive, and bear a son," recit (A)
      8. "O thou that tellest good tidings to Zion," air (A)
      . "O thou that tellest good tidings to Zion," chorus
      9. "For behold, darkness shall cover the earth," accompagnato (B)
      10. "The people that walked in darkness," air (B)
      11. "For unto us a Child is born, unto us a Son is given," chorus
      12. "Pastoral Symphony"
      . "There were shepherds abiding in the field," recit (S)
      13a. "And lo, the angel of the Lord came upon them," accompagnato (S)
      13b. "And lo, the angel of the Lord came upon them," arioso (S) (p1743)
      . "And the angel said unto them: Fear not," recit (S)
      14. "And suddenly there was with the angel a multitude," accompagnato (S)
      15. "Glory to God, glory to God in the highest, and peace on earth," chorus
      16a, b. "Rejoice, rejoice, rejoice greatly, o daughter of Zion," air (S) (2nd vers p1745)
      . "Then shall the eyes of the blind be open'd" (S/A) (2nd vers p1742, 1749)
      17a, b. "He shall feed His flock like a shepherd," air (S/A) (2nd vers p1742, 1749)
      17c. "He shall feed His flock like a shepherd," duet (S, A)
      18. "His yoke is easy, His burden is light," chorus
    II: 19. "Behold the Lamb of God," chorus
      20. "He was despised, despised and rejected," air (A)
      21. "Surely, surely, He hath borne our griefs and carried our sorrows," chorus
      22. "And with His stripes we are healed," chorus
      23. "All we like sheep, all we like sheep, have gone astray," chorus
      24. "All they that see Him, laugh Him to scorn," accompagnato (T)
      25. "He trusted in God that He would deliver Him," chorus
      26. "Thy rebuke hath broken His heart," accompagnato (T)
      27. "Behold, and see, behold and see if there be any sorrow," arioso (T)
      28. "He was cut off out of the land of the living," accompagnato (T)
      29. "But Thou didst not leave His soul in hell," air (T)
      30. "Lift up your heads, O ye gates," chorus
      . "Unto which of the angels said He at any time," recit (T)
      31. "Let all the angels of God worship Him," chorus
      32a, b, c, d. "Thou art gone up on high," air (B/A/A/S) (2nd vers p1743, 1749; 3rd 1750; 4th in G min)
      33. "The Lord gave the word," chorus
      34a, c, d. "How beautiful are the feet of them that preach," air (S/S/A) (2nd vers p1745; 3rd 1751)
      34b. "How beautiful are the feet of Him that bringeth glad tidings," duet & chorus (S, A)
      35a. "Their sound is gone out, their sound is gone out into all lands," arioso (T) (p1743)
      35b. "Their sound is gone out into all lands," chorus (p1745)
      36a. "Why do the nations so furiously rage together," air (B)
      36b. "The Kings of the earth rise up," air (B) (p1742)
      37. "Let us break their bonds asunder," chorus
      . "He that dwelleth in heaven shall laugh them to scorn," recit (T)
      38a. "Thou shall break them," aria (T)
      38b. "Thou shall break them," recit (T) (p1742)
      39. "Hallelujah" (Hallelujah Chorus), chorus
    III: 40. "I know that my Redeemer liveth," air (S)
      41. "Since by man came death," chorus
      . "By man came also the resurrection of the dead," chorus
      . "For as in Adam all die," chorus
      . "Even so in Christ shall all be made alive," chorus
      42. "Behold, I tell you a mystery," accompagnato (B)
      43a, b. "The trumpet shall sound, and the dead shall be rais'd," air (B) (2 vers)
      . "Then shall be brought to pass the saying that is written," recit (A)
      44a, b. "O death, o death, where, where is thy sting?," duet (A, T) (2 vers)

45. "But thanks, but thanks, thanks, thanks be to God," chorus
46a. "If God is for us who can be against us," air (S)
47. "Worthy is the Lamb that was slain and hath redeemed us to God by His blood," chorus
48. "Amen," chorus
Anhang: (5.) "Thus saith the Lord, the Lord of Hosts," accompagnato (B)

12a.15   "Samson," oratorio: HWV57
    . "Symfony"
I: . "This day, a solemn feast to Dagon held," recit (Samson)
1. "Awake the trumpeter's lofty sound!," chorus (Philistines)
2. "Ye men of Gaza, hither bring," air (Philistine Woman)
3. "Awake the trumpet's lofty sound!," chorus (Philistines)
4. "Loud as the thunder's awful voice," air (Philistine)
5. "Then free from sorrow, free from thrall," air (Philistine Woman)
  . "Why by an angel was my birth foretold," recit (Samson)
6. "Torments, alas! are not confined," air (Samson)
  . "O change beyond report," recit (Micah)
7. "O miror of our fickle state," air (Micah)
  . "Whom have I to complain of," recit (Samson, Micah)
8. "Total eclipse! no sun, no moon, all dark," air (Samson)
9. "Since light so necessary is to life," accompagnato (Micah)
10. "O first created beam!," chorus (Israelites)
  . "Ye see, my friends, how woes enclose me round," recit (Samson, Micah)
  . "Brethren, and men of Dan, say, where is my son," recit (Manoa, Micah)
11. "Oh miserable change! is this the man," accompagnato (Manoa)
  . "Oh ever failing trust in mortal strength!," recit (Micah) (2 vers)
12a, b. "God of our fathers," air (Micah) (2 vers)
13. "Oft He that's most exalted high," chorus (Israelites)
14. "The good we wish for, often proves our bane," accompagnato (Manoa)
15. "Thy glorious deeds inspir'd my tongue," air (Manoa)
  . "Justly these evils have befall'n thy son," recit (Samson, Manoa)
16. "My griefs for this forbid mine eyes to close," accompagnato (Samson)
17. "Why does the God of Israel sleep?," air (Samson)
  . "There lies our hope! true prophet may'st thou be," recit (Micah)
18. "Then shall they know, that He whose name Jehovah is alone," chorus (Israelites)
  . "For thee, my dearest son," recit (Manoa, Samson)
19. "My genial spirits droop, my hopes are flat," accompagnato (Samson)
20. "Then long eternity shall greet," air (Micah)
21. "Then round about the starry throne and triumph over Death," chorus (Israelites)
II: . "Despair not thus! you once were God's delight," recit (Manoa, Samson)
22. "Just are the ways of God to man," air (Manoa)
  . "My evils hopeless are!," recit (Samson, Micah)
23. "Return, return, oh God of hosts!," air (Micah)
24. "To dust his glory they would tread," solo & chorus (Micah, Israelites)
  . "But who is this? so bedeck'd and gay," recit (Micah, Samson, Dalila) (2 vers)
25a, b. "With plaintive notes and am'rous moan," air (Virgin of Dalila)
  . "Alas! th'event was worse," recit (Dalila)
  . "Did love constrain thee? no!," recit (Samson)
26. "Your charms to ruin led the way," air (Samson)
  . "Forgive what's done, nor think of what's past cure," recit (Dalila)
27. "My faith and truth, oh Samson, prove," duet (Dalila, Virgin)
28. "Her faith and truth, oh Samson, prove," chorus (Virgins)
29. "To fleeting pleasures make your court," air (Dalila)
  . "Ne'er think of That! I know thy warbling charms," recit (Samson, Dalila)
30. "Traitor to love! I'll sue no more for pardon scorn'd," duet (Dalila, Samson)
  . "She's gone! a serpent manifest," recit (Micah, Samson)
31a. "It is not virtue, valour, wit, or comeliness of grace," air (Micah)
31b. "Fly from the cleaving mischief, fly," air (Micah) (p1745)
  . "Favour'd of heav'n is he," recit (Samson)
32. "To man God's universal law," chorus (Israelites)
  . "No words of peace, no voice enchanting fear," recit (Micah, Harapha, Samson)
33. "Honour and arms scorn such a foe," air (Harapha)
A. "Who could withstand me, single and unarm'd?," recit (Samson)
B. "Put on your arms, then take for spear," recit (Samson)
34. "My strength is from the living God," air (Samson)
A. "Thy God regards thee not," recit (Harapha, Samson)
B. "Cam'st thou for this, vain boaster? Yet take heels," recit (Samson, Harapha)
C. "With thee! a man condemn'd," recit (Harapha, Samson)
35. "Go, baffled coward, go," duet (Samson, Harapha)
  . "Here lie the proof: if Dagon be thy God," recit (Micah)
36. "Hear, Jacob's God," chorus (Israelites)
  . "Dagon, arise! attend thy sacred feast!," recit (Harapha)
37a. "To song and dance we give the day," air (Philistine)
37b. "To song and dance, to song and dance we give the day," chorus (Philistines)
38. "Fix'd in his everlasting seat, Jehovah," chorus (Israelites & Philistines, Dalila, Samson)

III: (39.) "How great and many perils do enfold," air (Micah) (p1754, = Occasional Oratorio, HWV61/21a)
. "More trouble is behind," recit (Micah, Samson, Harapha)
39. "Presuming slave, presuming slave, to move their wrath!," air (Harapha)
. "Reflect then, Samson, matters now are strain'd," recit (Micah, Samson)
40. "With thunder arm'd, with thunder arm'd, great God, arise!," chorus (Israelites)
. "Be of good courage," recit (Samson, Micah, Harapha)
41. "Then shall I make Jehovah's glory known!," accompagnato (Samson)
42. "Thus when the sun from's wat'ry bed," air (Samson)
43. "With might endued above the sons of men," accompagnato (Micah)
44. "The Holy One of Israel be thy guide," air (Micah)
45. "To fame, to fame immortal go," chorus (Israelites)
. "Old Manoa, with youthful steps, makes haste," recit (Micah, Manoa)
46. "Great Dagon has subdued our foe," air (Philistine)
47. "Great Dagon has subdued our foe," chorus (Philistines)
. "What noise of joy was that?," recit (Manoa, Micah)
48. "How willing my paternal love," air (Manoa)
. "Your hopes of his deliv'ry seem not vain," recit (Micah, Manoa)
49. "Symphony"
. "Heav'n! what noise!," recit (Manoa)
50. "Hear us, our God, hear us!," chorus (Philistines)
. "Noise call you this? an universal groan," recit (Micah, Manoa)
. "Where shall I run, or which way fly," recit (Messenger, Micah, Manoa)
51. "Ye sons of Israel, now lament," air (Micah)
52. "Weep, Israel, weep," chorus (Israelites)
. "Proceed we hence to find this body soak'd," recit (Manoa)
53a, b. "A Dead March" (2nd vers p1749, = Saul, HWV53/77b)
. "The body comes; we'll meet it on the way," recit (Micah, Manoa)
54. "Glorious hero, may thy grave," soli & chorus (Manoa, Israelite Woman, Israelites)
. "The virgins too shall on their feastful days," accompagnato (Israelite Woman)
. "Bring the laurels, bring the bays," chorus (Virgins)
. "May ev'ry hero fall like thee" (Israelite Woman)
. "Bring the laurels, bring the bays," chorus (Virgins)
. "Glorious hero, may thy grave," chorus (Israelites)
. "Come, come! no time for lamentation now," recit (Manoa, Micah)
55. "Let the bright Seraphim in burning row," air (Israelite Woman)
56. "Let their celestial concerts all unite," chorus (Israelites)
Anhang: (7a.) "O mirror of our fickle state," chorus (Israelites)
(24a.) "To dust his glory they would tread," chorus (Israelites)
(34a.) "My strength is from the living God," air (Samson) (frag)

12a.16 "Semele," oratorio: HWV58
. "Ouverture"
I: 1. "Behold! auspicious flashes rise," accompagnato (Priest)
2. "Lucky omens, lucky omens bless our rites," chorus
3. "Daughter, obey, hear and obey!," recit & arioso (Cadmus, Athamas)
4. "Ah me, ah me! what refuge," accompagnato (Semele)
5. "Oh Jove! in pity," air (Semele)
6. "The morning lark to mine accords his note," air (Semele)
. "See, she blushing turns her eyes," recit (Athamas)
7. "Hymn haste! Hymne, haste! thy torch prepare!," air (Athamas)
. "Alas! she yield, and has undone me!," recit (Ino, Athamas, Semele)
8. "Why dost thou thus untimely grieve," quartet (Semele, Ino, Athamas, Cadmus)
9. "Avert these omens, all ye pow'rs," chorus
10. "Again auspicious flashes rise," accompagnato (Cadmus)
. "Thy aid, pronubial Juno," recit (Athamas)
11. "Cease, cease your vow's, 'tis impious to proceed," chorus
. "Oh Athamas, what torture hast thou borne!," recit (Athamas)
12. "Turn, hopeless lover, turn thy eyes," air (Ino)
. "She weeps! the gentle maid," recit (Athamas)
13. "Your tuneful voice my tale would tell," air (Athamas)
. "Too well I see, thou wilt not," recit (Ino, Athamas)
14. "You've undone me, look not on me," duet (Ino, Athamas)
. "Ah, wretched prince, doom'd to disastrous love!," recit (Cadmus, Athamas)
15. "Wing'd with our fears, and pious haste, from Juno's fane we fled," accompagnato (Cadmus)
. "Oh prodigy, to me of dire portent!," recit (Athamas, Ino)
. "See, see! Jove's Priest and holy Augurs come," recit (Cadmus)
16. "Hail hail, hail, Cadmus hail," chorus
17. "Endless pleasure, endless pleasure, endless love Semele enjoys above," air (Semele)
18. "Endles pleasure, endless love," chorus
II: 19. "Symphony"
. "Iris, impatient of thy stay," recit (Juno, Iris)
20. "There, from mortal cares retiring," air (Iris)
. "No more! I'll hear no more!," recit (Juno)
21. "Awake, Saturnia, from thy lethargy!," accompagnato (Juno, Iris)
22. "Hence, hence, Iris hence away," air (Juno)

23. "Oh sleep, oh sleep, why dost thou leave me?," air (Semele)
. "Let me not another moment," recit (Semele)
24. "Lay your doubts and fear aside," air (Jupiter)
. "You are mortal," recit (Jupiter)
25. "With fond desiring, with bliss expiring," air (Semele)
26. "How engaging, how endearing," chorus
. "Ah me! Why sighs my Semele?," recit (Semele, Jupiter)
27. "I must with speed amuse her, lest she too much explain," air (Jupiter)
28. "Now Love that everlasting boy," chorus
. "By my command now at this instant," recit (Jupiter, Semele)
29. "Where'er you walk, cool gales shall fan the glade," air (Jupiter)
. "Dear sister, how was your passage hither?," recit (Semele, Ino)
30. "But hark! the heav'nly sphere turns round," air (Ino)
31. "Prepare, prepare then, ye," duet (Semele, Ino)
32. "Bless the glad earth with heav'nly lays," chorus
III: 33. "Symphony"
34. "Somnus, awake! raise thy reclining head!," accompagnato (Juno, Iris)
35. "Leave me, leave me, loathsome light!," air (Somnus)
. "Dull God, canst thou attend," recit (Juno, Somnus)
36. "More sweet is that name than a soft purling stream," air (Somnus)
. "My will obey," recit (Juno, Somnus)
37. "Obey my will, thy rod resign," duet (Juno, Somnus)
38. "My racking thoughts by no kind slumbers freed," air (Semele)
. "Thus shap'd like Ino," recit (Juno, Semele)
. "O ecstasy of happiness," recit (Semele) (2 vers)
39a, b. "Myself I shall adore, if I persist in gazing," air (Semele) (2 vers)
. "Be wise, as you are beautiful," recit (Juno, Semele)
40. "Conjure him by his oath not to approach your bed," accompagnato (Juno)
41. "Thus let my thanks be pay'd, thus let my arms embrace thee," air (Semele)
. "Rich odours fill the fragrant air," recit (Juno, Semele)
42. "Come to my arms, my lovely fair," air (Jupiter)
. "Oh Semele! why art thou thus insensible?," recit (Jupiter)
43. "I ever am granting, you always complain," air (Semele)
. "Speak, speak your desire," recit (Jupiter, Semele)
44. "By that tremendous flood, I swear," accompagnato (Jupiter)
. "You'll grant what I require?," recit (Semele, Jupiter)
45. "Then cast off this human shape," accompagnato (Semele)
46. "Ah! take heed what you press!," air (Jupiter)
47. "I'll be pleas'd with no less, than my wish in excess," air (Semele)
48. "Ah, wither is she gone! unhappy fair!," accompagnato (Jupiter)
49. "Above measure is the pleasure," air (Juno)
50. "Ah me! too late I now repent," arioso (Semele)
. "Of my ill-boding dream," recit (Ino)
51. "Oh terror, oh terror and astonishment," chorus
. "How I was hence remov'd," recit (Ino, Cadmus, Athamas)
52. "Despair no more shall wound me," air (Athamas)
. "See from above the bellying clouds descend," recit (Cadmus)
53. "Sinfonia"
54. "Apollo comes, to relieve your care," accompagnato (Apollo)
55. "Happy, happy! Happy, happy, happy, happy shall we be, and free from care," chorus
Anhang: I/1: (1.) "Behold! auspicious flashes rise," accompagnato (Priest / Cadmus)
(3.) "Daughter, obey," recit & arioso (Cadmus, Athamas)
(6a.) "See, she blushing turns her Eyes," air (Ino)
(7.) *"Hymen, haste, Hymen haste, thy torch prepare," air (Athamas) (frag)*
(12.) "Turn, hopeless lover, turn your Eyes," recit (Ino)
(23.) "Come Zephyrs, come, while Cupid sings," air (Cupid)
(32.) *"Bless the glad earth with heav'nly lays," chorus (frag)*
. "Behold in this miror," air (Juno)
(55.) *"Then Mortals be merry and scorn the blind Boy," chorus (frag)*

12a.17 "Joseph and his Brethren," oratorio: HWV59
. "Symphony"
I: 1a, b. "Be firm, my soul! nor faint beneath," air (Joseph)
2a, b. "But wherefore thus? whence Heav'n these bitter bonds?," accompagnato (Joseph)
. "Be firm, my soul!," air (Joseph)
. "Joseph, thy fame has reach'd great Pharaoh's ear," recit (Phanor, Joseph) (also vers p1757)
3. "Come, divine inspirer, come," air (Joseph) (also vers p1768)
. "Pardon, that I so long forgot thee, Joseph!," recit (Phanor, Joseph) (also vers p1757)
4a, b, c. "Ingratitude's the queen of crimes," air (Phanor) (2nd vers p1751; 3rd p1757)
. "Thus, stranger, I have laid my troubled thoughts," recit (Pharaoh, Joseph)
5. "O God of Joseph, gracious shed thy spirit," chorus (Egyptians)
6a. "Pharaoh, thy dreams are one," accompagnato (Joseph)
B. "Pharaoh, thy dreams are one," recit (Joseph) (p1747)
6b. "The seven fat cattle, and full ears of corn," accompagnato (Joseph)
. "Divine interpreter! What oracle," recit (Pharaoh, Joseph)

7. "O lovely youth, with wisdom crown'd, where ev'ry charm has place!," air (Asenath)
. "Ritornello"
. "Wear, worthy man, this Royal signet wear," recit (Pharaoh)
8. "Joyful sounds, melodious strains! Health to Egypt is the theme," chorus
. "Whence this unwonted ardour in my breast?," recit (Asenath)
9. "I feel a spreading flame," air (Asenath)
. "Fair Asenath, I've ask'd thee of thy father," recit (Joseph)
. "Zaphnath, I grant thy," recit (Pharaoh, Potiphera—High Priest, Joseph)
10. "Celestial virgin! Godlike youth," duet (Asenath, Joseph)
. "Now Potiphera, instant to the temple," recit (Pharaoh)
11. "March"
. " 'Tis done, the sacred Knot is tied," recit (High Priest)
12. "Pow'rful guardians of all nature," air (High Priest) (p1751, = Alexander Balus, HWV65/27)
13. "Immortal pleasures crown this pair," chorus
. "Glorious and happy is thy lot," recit (Pharaoh)
14. "Since the race of time begun," air (Pharaoh)
15. "Swift our numbers, swiftly roll," chorus
II: 16. "Hail hail, thou youth, by Heav'n belov'd," chorus (Egyptians)
. "How vast a theme has Egypt for applause!," recit (Phanor, Asenath) (2 vers)
17a, b. "Our fruits, whilst yet in blossom die," air (Asenath) (b: Phanor p1757)
. "He's Egypt's common parent, gives her bread," recit (Phanor) (2 vers)
18. "Blest be the man, blest be the man by pow'r unstain'd," chorus
. "Phanor, we mention not his highest glory!, recit (Asenath, Phanor)
19. "Together, lovely innocents, grow up," recit (Asenath, Phanor)
. "He then is silent, then again exclaims," recit (Asenath)
20. "Where are these Brethren," accompagnato (Simeon)
21. "Remorse, confusion, horror," arioso (Simeon)
. "This Hebrew prisoner ... Hither bring him, Phanor," recit (Phanor, Joseph)
22. "Ye departed hours, what happier moments have I seen!," accompagnato (Joseph)
23. "The peasant tastes the sweets of life," air (Joseph)
. "But Simeon comes—Treacherous, bloodthirsty brother!," recit (Joseph, Simeon)
. "I tremble at his presence!," recit (Simeon, Joseph)
24. "Impostor! Ah! my foul offence," air (Simeon)
. "Whence, Asenath, this grief that hangs upon thee," recit (Joseph, Asenath)
25. "The silver stream, that all its way," air (Asenath)
. "Tell me, o tell me thy heart's malady," recit (Asenath, Joseph)
. "Fear not, peace be unto you," recit (Phanor, Judah)
26. "To keep afar from all offence, and conscious of its innocence," air (Judah)
27. "Thus one with ev'ry virtue crown'd, for ev'ry vice may be renown'd," chorus (The Brethren)
. "Once more, o pious Zaphnath, at thy feet," recit (Reuben)
28. "Our reverend Sire intreats thee to accept," accompagnato (Judah)
. "This kiss, my gracious Lord, comes wash'd with tears," recit (Benjamin, Joseph, Judah)
29. "Thou deign'st to call thy servant son," arioso (Benjamin)
. "Sweet innocence! divine simplicity!," recit (Joseph, Benjamin, Reuben, Judah)
30. "O God, who in thy heav'nly hand," chorus
III: 31. "Symphony"
. "What say'st thou, Phanor? Prove these strangers then," recit (Asenath, Phanor)
32a. "The wanton favours of the great are like the scatter'd seed when sown," air (Phanor)
32b. "Though on rapid whirlwind's wing," air (Phanor) (p1751, = Susanna, HWV66/27)
32c. "The wanton favours of the great," air (Phanor) (p1757)
. "Whence so disturb'd, my Lord?," recit (Asenath, Joseph)
33. "Ah Jealousy, thou pelican!," air (Asenath)
. "O wrong me not! thy Zaphnath never harbour'd," recit (Joseph, Asenath)
34a, b. "The people's favour, and the smiles of pow'r," air (Joseph)
. "Art thou not Zaphnath?," recit (Asenath)
35. "Prophetic raptures swell," air (Asenath)
. "They come, and indignation in their looks," recit (Joseph)
. "Whence this vile treatment! these injorious chains?," recit (Simeon, Phanor, Joseph)
. "At length the cup is found. Where?," recit (Joseph, Benjamin)
36a, b, c. "What, without me? Ah, how return in peace!," accompagnato (Benjamin) (3 vers)
37a, b. "O pity!... Ah! I must not hear," duet (Benjamin, Joseph) (2 vers)
. "To prison with him!," recit (Joseph, Simeon, Reuben)
38. "The man who flies the wretched, nor will hear them," accompagnato (Simeon, Reuben)
. "What counsel can we take?, recit (Reuben)
39. "O gracious God, we merit well this scourge," arioso (Simeon)
40. "Eternal monarch of the sky," chorus
. "But peace, Zaphnath returns," recit (Simeon)
. "How not departed? Ye insolent," recit (Joseph, Simeon, Judah)
41. "Thou had'st, my Lord, a father once," arioso (Simeon)
. "Give, give him up the lad," recit (Simeon)
42. "Lay all on me, imprisonment, chains," accompagnato (Simeon)
. "I can no longer Phanor," recit (Joseph, Benjamin, Simeon, Judah, Reuben)
. "Joseph! O Heav'n! Joseph! wretched we!," recit (Benjamin, Joseph, Simeon, Judah, Reuben)
. "Whilst the Nile and Memphis," recit (Asenath, Joseph)
43a. "What's sweeter than the newblown rose," duet (Asenath, Joseph)

43b. "What's sweeter than the newborn rose," air (Asenath) (p1744)
  . "With songs of ardent gratitude and praise," recit (Joseph) (2 vers)
44. "We will rejoice," chorus (= Dettingen Anthem, HWV265)
Anhang: . "Menuet" (= Menuet in D major, HWV420)
  . "Whence this unwonted ardour in my breast?," recit (Asenath)
  (9.) "I feel a preading flame," air (Asenath) (frag)
(17.) "Our fruits, whilst yet in blossom, die," air (Phanor) (frag of 1st vers; 2nd vers p1751)
  . "Be gone away thou'rt baneful to my eye," recit (Joseph)
(32.) "The wanton favours of the great," air (Phanor)

12a.18 "Hercules," oratorio: HWV60
  . "Ouverture"
I: 1. "See, with what sad dejection in her looks," accompagnato (Lichas)
    2. "No longer, fate, relentless frown," air (Lichas)
    3. "Oh Hercules! why art thou absent from me?," accompagnato (Dejanira)
    4. "The world, when day's career is run," air (Dejanira)
    . "Princess! be comforted, and hope the best," recit (Lichas, Dejanira)
    . "My son! dear image of thy absent sire!," recit (Dejanira, Hyllus, Lichas)
    5. "I feel, I feel the god," air (Hyllus)
    . "He said: the sacred fury left his breast," recit (Hyllus, Dejanira)
    6a, b. "There, there in myrtle shades reclin'd to streams," air (Dejanira) (2 vers)
    . "Despair not; but let rising hope," recit (Hyllus)
    7. "Where congeal'd the northern streams, bound in icy fetters," air (Hyllus)
    8. "Oh filial piety! oh gen'rous love!," chorus
    . "Banish your fears! Alcmena's godlike son lives," recit (Lichas, Dejanira)
    9. "Begone, my fears, fly, hence, away, like clouds," air (Dejanira)
    . "A train of captives, red with honest wounds," recit (Lichas, Hyllus, Dejanira)
    10. "The smiling hours, a joyful train," air (Lichas)
    11. "Let none despair, let none despair, relief may come though late," chorus
    . "Ye faithful followers of the wretched Iole," recit (Iole, 1st Oechalian)
    12. "Daughter of gods, bright liberty! with thee a thousand graces reign," air (Iole)
    . "But hark! the victor comes," recit (Iole)
    13. "March"
    . "Thanks to the pow'rs above, but chief to thee," recit (Hercules)
    . "Oechalia's fall is added to my titles," recit (Hercules, Iole)
    14. "My father! ah! methinks I see the sword inflict the deadly wound," air (Iole)
    . "Now farewell, arms! from hence the tide of time," recit (Hercules)
    15. "The god of battle quits the bloody field," air (Hercules)
    16. "Crown with festal pomp the day, crown," chorus
II: 17. "Symfonie"
    . "Why was I born a princess rais'd on high," recit (Iole)
    18. "How blest the maid ordain'd to dwell," air (Iole)
    . "It must be so! fame speaks aloud my wrongs," recit (Dejanira, Iole)
    19. "When beauty sorrow's liv'ry wears, our passions take the fair one's part," air (Dejanira)
    . "Whence this unjust suspicion?," recit (Iole, Dejanira)
    20. "Ah! ah! think what ills the jealous prove: adieu to peace," air (Iole)
    . "It is too sure, that Hercules is false," recit (Dejanira)
    . "My godlike master? is a traitor," recit (Lichas, Dejanira)
    21. "As stars, that rise and disappear, still in the same bright circle move," air (Lichas)
    . "In vain you strive his falsehood to disguise!," recit (Dejanira, Lichas)
    22. "Jealousy! jealousy! infernal pest, infernal pest," chorus
    . "She knows my passion, and has heard my breath," recit (Hyllus, Iole)
    23. "Banish love from thy breast, 'tis a womanish guest," air (Iole)
    . "Forgive a passion, which resistless sways," recit (Hyllus)
    24. "From coelestial seats descending, joys divine awhile suspending," air (Hyllus)
    25. "Wanton god of amorous fires," chorus
    . "Yes, I congratulate your titles," recit (Dejanira, Hercules)
    26. "Alcides' name in latest story shall with brightest lustre shine," air (Hercules)
    . "Oh glorious pattern of heroic deeds!," recit (Dejanira)
    27. "Resign thy club and lion's spoils, and fly from war to female toils," air (Dejanira)
    . "You are deceived! some villain has bely'd," recit (Hercules, Dejanira)
    28. "Cease, ruler of the day, to rise," air (Dejanira)
    . "Some kinder pow'r inspire me, to regain," recit (Dejanira, Lichas)
    29. "Constant lovers, never roving," air (Lichas)
    . "But see, the princess Iole!—Retire!," recit (Dejanira)
    . "Forgive me, princess, if my jealous frenzy too roughly greeted you!," recit (Dejanira, Iole)
    30. "Joys, joys of freedom," duet (Iole, Dejanira)
    . "Father of Hercules, great Jove, succeed," recit (Dejanira)
    31. "Love and Hymen, hand in hand, come, restore the nuptial band!," chorus
III: 32. "Symfony"
    . "Ye sons of Trachin, mourn your valiant chief," recit (Lichas, 1st Trachinian)
    33. "Oh scene, oh scene of unexampled woe," air (Lichas)
    . "Oh fatal jealousy! Oh cruel recompence of virtue," recit (1st Trachinian)
    34. "Tyrants now no more shall dread on necks of vanquish'd slaves to tread," chorus
    35. "Oh Jove! what land is this," accompagnato (Hercules)

. "Great Jove! relieve his pains!," recit (Hyllus)
36. "Was it for this unnumber'd toils I bore?," accompagnato (Hercules, Hyllus)
37. "Let not fame the tidings spread," air (Hyllus)
38. "Where shall I fly! where hide this guilty head?," accompagnato (Dejanira)
. "Lo! the fair, fatal cause of all this ruin!," recit (Dejanira, Iole)
39. "My breast with tender pity swells," air (Iole)
. "Princess, rejoice! whose heav'n directed hand," recit (Priest of Jupiter, Dejanira)
40. "His mortal part by eating fires consum'd," accompagnato (Priest of Jupiter)
41. "He, who for Atlas prop'd the sky, now sees the sphere beneath him lie," air (Lichas)
42. "Words are too faint to speak the warring passions," recit (Dejanira, Priest of Jupiter)
. "Hymen with purest joys of love shall crown," accompagnato (Dejanira, Priest of Jupiter)
. "How blest is Hyllus, if the lovely Iole consenting," recit (Hyllus, Iole)
43. "Oh prince, whose virtues all admire," duet (Iole, Hyllus)
. "Ye sons of freedom, now, in ev'ry clime," recit (Priest of Jupiter)
44. "To him your grateful notes of praise belong," chorus
Anhang: II/2: . "Alas! What mean you? Well dissembled ignorance!," recit (Iole, Dejanira)

12a.19   "Belshazzar," oratorio: HWV61
. "Ouverture"
I: 1a. "Vain, fluctuating state of human empire!," accompagnato & arioso (Nitocris)
1b. "Vain, fluctuating state of human empire!," recit (Nitocris) (p1758)
2. "Thou, God most high, and Thou alone," air (Nitrocris)
. "The fate of Babylon, I fear, is nigh," recit (Nitrocris)
. "O much belov'd of God and man!," recit (Nitocris, Daniel)
3. "Lament not thus, oh Queen, in vain!," air (Daniel)
4. "Behold, behold, by Persia's hero made," chorus (Babylonians)
. "Well may they laugh, from meagre famine safe," recit (Gobrias, Cyrus)
5. "Oh memory, still bitter to my soul!," accompagnato (Gobrias)"
6a, b, c. "Oppres'd with never-ceasing grief," air (Gobrias) (2nd vers p1745; 3rd p1751)
7. "Dry those unavailing tears," air (Cyrus)
. "Be comforted: safe though the tyrant seem within the walls," recit (Cyrus)
8. "Methought, as on the bank of deep Euphrates I stood revolving," accompagnato (Cyrus)
. "Now tell me, Gobrias, does not this Euphrates," recit (Cyrus, Gobrias)
9. "Behold the monstrous human beast," air (Gobrias) (Cyrus in 1745)
. "Can you then think it strange, if drown'd in wine," recit (Cyrus) (2 vers)
10. "Great God! who, yet but darkly known," air (Cyrus)
. "My friends, be confident, and boldly enter," recit (Cyrus)
11. "All empires upon God depend," chorus
12. "Oh sacred, sacred oracles of truth!," arioso (Daniel)
13. "Rejoice, my countrymen: the time draws near," accompagnato (Daniel)
. "For long ago, whole ages ere this Cyrus yet was born," recit (Daniel)
14. "Thus saith the Lord to Cyrus his anoited," accompagnato (Daniel)
15. "Sing, sing, sing, oh ye heav'ns," chorus
16. "Let festal joy triumphant reign!," air (Belsazzar)
. "For you, my friends, the nobles of my court," recit (Belsazzar, Nitocris)
17a, b. "The leafy honours of the field," air (Nitocris) (2nd vers p1751)
. "It is the custom, I may say, the law," recit (Belshazzar, Nitocris)
18. "Recall, oh King! thy rash command," chorus (Jews)
. "They tell you true; nor can you be to learn," recit (Nitocris, Belshazzar)
19. "Oh dearer than my life, forbear!," duet (Nitocris, Belshazzar)
20. "By slow degrees the wrath of God," chorus (Jews)
II: 21. "See, see, see, from post Euphrates flies!," chorus
22. "Why, faithless river, dost thou leave," semi-chorus I
23. "Euphrates has his task fullfill'd," semi-chorus II
24. "Of things on earth, proud man must own," chorus
. "You see, my friends, a path into the city lies open," recit (Cyrus)
25. "Amaz'd to find the foe so near," air (Cyrus)
26. "To arms, to arms, to arms, to arms!," chorus (Persians)
27. "Ye tutelar Gods of our empire, look down," chorus (Babylonians)
28. "Let the deep bowl thy praise confess!," air (Belshazzar)
29. "Where is the God of Judah's boasted pow'r?," accompagnato (Belshazzar, Chorus)
. "Call all my Wise Men, Sorcerers, Chaldeans," recit (Belshazzar)
30. "Symphonie" (Allegro Postillions) (p1745)
. "Ye sages! welcome always to your King," recit (Belshazzar)
31. "Alas! too hard a task the King imposes," trio (Wise Men)
32. "Oh misery! oh terror! hopeless grief!," chorus
A. "Oh King, live for ever!," recit (Nitocris)
B. "Though all thy wise men fail thee," recit (Nitocris)
C. "O King, live forever, let not thine heart," recit (Nitocris) (p1758)
32a. "Wise men flatt'ring may deceive you with their vain mysterious art," air (Nitocris) (p1758)
. "Art thou that Daniel of the Jewish captives?," recit (Belshazzar)
33. "No! to thyself thy trifles be," air (Daniel)
34. "Yet, to obey his dread command, who vindicates his honour now," accompagnato (Daniel)
35. "The most high God, o King, gave to thy Grand Sire a Kingdom," accompagnato (Daniel)
36. "Thou, o King, hast lifted up thyself," accompagnato (Daniel)

. "Oh sentence too severe! and yet too sure!," recit (Nitocris)
37. "Regard, oh son, my flowing tears, proofs of maternal love," air (Nitocris)
38. "Oh God of truth! oh faithful guide!," air (Cyrus)
. "You, Gobrias, lead directly to the palace," recit (Cyrus)
39a, b. "Oh glorious prince, oh glorious prince, oh glorious prince!," chorus (2 vers)
III: 40a, b. "Alternate hopes and fears distract my mind," air (Nitocris) (2nd vers p1751)
. "Fain would I hope," recit (Nitocris, Daniel)
40c. "Fain would I know if virtue confessing," air (Nitocris) (p1758)
41. "Can the black Aethiop change his skin?," air (Daniel)
. "My hopes revive—here Arioch comes," recit (Nitocris, Arioch, Messenger)
42. "Bel boweth down! Nebo stoopeth! how is Sesach taken!," chorus (Jews)
43. "I thank thee, Sesach," air (Belshazzar)
44. "Symphony" (A Martial Symphony)
45a, c. "To pow'r immortal my first thanks are due," air (Gobrias) (3rd vers p1751)
45b. "To pow'r immortal my first thanks are due," recit (Gobrias) (p1745)
. "Be it thy care, good Gobrias," recit (Cyrus)
46. "Destructive War, thy limits know," air (Cyrus)
47a, b. "Great victor, at your feet I bow," duet (Nitocris, Cyrus) (2nd vers p1751)
. "Say, venerable prophet, is there aught in Cyrus' pow'r," recit (Cyrus, Daniel)
48. "Tell it, tell it out among the heathen, that the Lord is King!," chorus
49a, b. "Yes, I will build thy city, God of Israel!," accompagnato (Cyrus) (2nd vers p1751)
50. "I will magnify thee, oh God my King," soli & chorus (= HWV250b)

12a.20 "Occasional Oratorio," oratorio: HWV62
. "Ouverture"
I: 1. "Why do the gentiles tumult," recit accompanied (B)
2. "Let us break off by strength of hand," chorus
3a. "O Lord, how many are my foes!," air (T)
3b. "O Lord, how many are my foes!," accompagnato (T)
4. "Him or his God we not fear!," chorus
5. "Jehovah, Jehovah, to my words give ear," air (T)
6. "Him or his God we scorn to fear," chorus
. "The Highest who in Heav'n doth dwell," recit (B)
7. "God has his mansion fix'd on high," air (S) (= Comus, HWV44/5)
. "The Lord shall speak to them in his wrath," recit (B)
8a, b. "O who shall pour into my swollen eyes," air (S) (2 vers)
8c. "Jehovah, Lord! how great, how wond'rous great," accompagnato (S) (p after 1759)
8d. "Lord, God of Hosts, to whom the pray'r," air (S) (p after 1759, = Alcina, HWV34/20)
9a, b. "Fly from the threatning vengeance, fly," air (S) (2 vers, = Samson, HWV57/31b)
10. "Humbled with fear and awful reverence," accompagnato (B)
11. "His sceptre is the rod of righteousness," air (B)
12. "Be wise, be wise at length, ye Kings," air (S)
13. "Be wise, be wise at length," chorus
. "Of many millions the populous rout," recit (T)
14. "Jehovah is my shield, my glory," air (T)
. "Fools or madmen stand not within thy sight," recit (B) (2nd vers p after 1759)
15a. "God found them guilty," chorus
15b. "Sing unto God, ye Kingdoms of the earth" (p after 1759, = Wedding Anthem, HWV263)
II: 16a. "O libery, thou choicest treasure, seat of virtue," air (S) (= Judas Maccabaeus, HWV63/9)
16b. "O liberty! thou goddess bright," air (S) (p after 1759, = Rodelinda, HWV19/10)
A. "Who trusts in God, should ne'er despair," recit (S)
B. "Methinks, prophetic visions from above," recit (S) (p after 1759)
17a. "Prophetic visions strike my eye," air (S)
17b. "War with sullen steps retiring," air (S) (p after 1759, = Lotario, HWV26/12)
18a, b. "May God, from whom all mercies spring," chorus & solo
. "The Lord hath heard my pray'r," recit (T)
19a. "Then will I Jehovah's praise," air (T) (= Comus, HWV44/1)
19b. "God is my strength, my treasure," air (S/T) (p after 1759, = Atalanta, HWV35/3)
20. "All his mercies shall endure," chorus (= Comus, HWV44/2)
21a. "How great and many perils do enfold the righteous man," air (S)
21b. "Why, ah why do Mortals erring," air (S) (p after 1759, = Alcina, HWV34/7)
22. "After long storms, after long storms, and tempest overblown," duet (2S)
23. "To God, our strength, sing loud and clear," solo & chorus (B)
24a. "He has his mansion," air (T) (= HWV62/7)
24b. "Tell me, tell me, tell me, ye starry host," air (S) (p after 1759, = Scipione, HWV20/10)
25. "Hallelujah, hallelujah," chorus
III: 26. "Sinfonia" (= Concerto Grosso in G major, Op.6/1, HWV319)
27. "Musette" (= 3rd movt of: Concerto Grosso in G minor, Op.6/6, HWV324)
28. "I will sing unto the Lord, for he hath triumphed gloriously," d ch (= Israel in Egypt, HWV54/15)
29a. "Thou shalt bring them in," air (S) (p1747, = Israel in Egypt, HWV54/26)
29b. "The Lord doth great and mighty things," air (S) (p after 1759, = Alessandro, HWV21/34b)
30. "Who is like unto Thee, oh Lord, among the Gods?," d chorus (= Israel in Egypt, HWV54/23)
31. "He gave them hailstones for rain," d chorus (= Israel in Egypt, HWV54/5)
32. "When warlike ensigns wave on high," air (S)
A. "The enemy said: I will pursue," recit (T)

B. "And see, the mystic essence now descends, spirit of peace," recit (T) (p after 1759)
33a. "The enemy said: 'I will pursue," air (T) (= Israel in Egypt, HWV54/21)
33b. "Glorious victors who subduing," air (S) (p after 1759, = Ottone, HWV15/18)
34. "The sword that's drawn in virtue's cause," air (B)
35. "Millions unborn shall bless the hand that gave, that gave deliv'rance to the land," chorus
. "When Israel, like the bounteous Nile," recit (S)
36. "When Israel, like the bounteous Nile," air (S)
37. "Tyrants, tyrants, whom no cov'nants bind," air (T)
38. "May balmy peace, and wreath'd renown," accompagnato (S)
39a. "May balmy peace, and wreath'd renown," air (S) (= Comus, HWV44/3)
39b. "Calm peace appearing, each prospect clearing," air (S) (= Alcina, HWV34/15)
40. "Blessed are all they," chorus (= Esther, HWV50b/25, Coronation Anthem No.1, HWV258)
Anhang: (23a.) *"To God, our strength, sing loud and clear," air (B) (frag)*
. "The Highest, who in Heav'n doth dwell, shall laugh to scorn the enemies," recit (B)
(32.) "When warlike ensigns wave on high," air (S)

12a.21   "Judas Maccabaeus," oratorio: HWV63
. "Ouverture"
I: 1. "Mourn, mourn, mourn, ye afflicted children," chorus
. "Well may your sorrows, brethren, flow," recit (Israelite Man, Israelite Woman)
2. "From this dread scene, these, adverse pow'rs," duet (Israelite Woman, Israelite Man)
3. "For Sion lamentation make," chorus
A. "Not vain is all this storm of grief," recit (Simon)
4a. "Pious orgies, pious airs, decent sorrow," air (Simon)
B, C. "Not vain is all this storm of grief," recit (Israelite Man)
4b, c. "Pious orgies, pious airs," air (Israelite Woman) (2 vers)
5. "Oh Father, whose almighty pow'r," chorus
6. "I feel, I feel the Deity within," accompagnato (Simon)
7. "Arm, arm ye brave!," solo & chorus (Simon)
. " 'Tis well, my friends," recit (Judas Maccabaeus)
8. "Call forth thy pow'rs, my soul, and dare," air (Judas Maccabaeus)
. "To Heav'ns Almighty King we kneel," recit (Israelite Woman)
9. "Oh liberty, thou choicest treasure," air (Israelite Woman) (= HWV62/16)
10. "Come, ever smiling liberty," air (Israelite Woman)
. "Oh Judas, may these noble views," recit (Israelite Man)
11. " 'Tis liberty, dear liberty alone," air (Israelite Man)
12. "Come, ever smiling liberty, come," duet (Israelite Woman, Israelite Man)
13. "Lead on, lead on, lead on, lead on! Judah disdains the galling load of hostile chains," chorus
14. "So will'd my father, now at rest," recit & accompagnato (Judas Maccabaeus)
15. "Disdainful of danger, we'll rush on the foe," semi-chorus
. "Ambition! if e'er honour was thine aim," recit (Judas Maccabaeus)
16. "No, no unhallow'd desire our breasts shall inspire," air (Judas Maccabaeus)
. "Oh Judas, may thy just pursuits," recit (Israelite Man) (p1750)
(16a.) "May balmy peace," air (Israelite Man) (p1750, = Occasional Oratorio, HWV62/39a)
(16b.) "Far brighter than the morning thy glorious name adoring," air (Israelite Woman) (p1758)
. "Haste we, my brethren, haste we to the field," recit (Israelite Man) (p1750)
17. "Hear us, oh Lord, oh Lord, oh Thee we call," chorus
II: 18. "Fall'n is the foe, fall'n is the foe; so fall Thy foes," chorus
. "Victorious hero! Fame shall tell," recit (Israelite Man)
19. "So rapid thy course is," air (Israelite Man)
A. "Well may we hope our freedom to receive," recit (Israelite Man) (p1750)
20a. "Flowing joys do now surround me," aria (Israelite Man) (p1750, = Esther, HWV50b/4)
B. "Well may we hope our freedom to receive," recit (Israelite Man) (p1758)
20b. "Sion now her head," duet & chorus (Israelite Woman, Man) (p1758, = Esther, HWV50b/23b)
. "Oh let eternal honours crown his name," recit (Israelite Woman)
21. "From mighty Kings he took the spoil," air (Israelite Woman)
22. "Hail, hail, hail, Judea, happy land," duet & chorus (Israelite Woman, Israelite Man)
. "Thanks to my brethren; but look," recit (Judas Maccabaeus)
23. "How vain is man, who boasts in fight," air (Judas Maccabaeus)
(23.) "Great in wisdom, great in glory," air (Israelite Woman) (p1758)
. "Oh Judas, oh my brethren!," recit (Israelite Messenger)
24. "Ah! wretched, wretched Israel!," solo & chorus (Israelite Woman)
. "Be comforted," recit (Simon)
25. "The Lord worketh wonders," air (Simon)
. "My arms! against this Gorgias," recit (Judas Maccabaeus)
26. "Sound an alarm! your silver trumpets sound," solo & chorus (Judas Maccabaeus)
A. "Enough! To Heav'n we leave the rest," recit (Simon)
27a. "With pious hearts, and brave as pious," air (Simon)
B. "Ye worshippers of God," recit (Israelite Man, Israelite Woman)
27b. "Wise men, flatt'ring may deceive," air (Israelite Woman) (p1758, = Belshazzar, HWV61/add air)
28. "Oh! never, never bow we down," duet & chorus (Israelite Woman, Man)
III: 29. "Father of Heav'n! from thy eternal throne," air (Israelite Man / Priest)
30. "See, see yon flames, that from the altar broke," accompagnato (Israelite Man)
. "Oh grant it, Heav'n, that our long woes may cease," recit (Israelite Woman)
31. "So shall the lute and harp awake, and sprightly voice sweet descant run," air (Israelite Woman)

. "From Capharsalama, on eagle wings I fly," recit (Israelite Messenger)
A. "Pow'rful guardians of all nature," air (Israelite Messenger) (p1748) (= A. Balus, HWV65/27)
B. "All his mercies I review," air (Israelite Messenger) (p1750, = Athalia, HWV52/23)
. "Happy, oh, thrice happy we," air (Israelite Woman) (p1748, = Joshua, HWV64/30)
(A, B.) "Yet more, Nicanor lies with thousands slain," recit (Messenger) (2nd vers p1750)
(C.) "But lo! the conqueror comes," recit (Messenger)
A, B, C. "See the conqu'ring hero comes!," chorus (2nd vers: duet; 3rd: ch; = Joshua, HWV64/35–37)
32a. "March" (p1750)
32b. "March" (w/ side drum)
33. "Sing unto God, and high affections raise," chorus
. "Sweet flow the strains, that strike my feasted ear," recit (Judas Maccabaeus)
34. "With honour let desert be crown'd," air (Judas Maccabaeus)
. "Peace to my countrymen," recit (Eupolemus)
. "Oh! had I Jubal's lyre," air (Israelite Woman) (p1748, = Joshua, HWV64/38)
35. "To our great God be all the honour giv'n," chorus
. "Again to earth let gratitude descend," recit (Israelite Woman)
36a, b. "Oh lovely peace, with plenty crown'd," air (Israelite Woman) (2nd vers: duet)
37. "Rejoice, oh Judah! and, in songs divine," solo & chorus (Simon)
Anhang: *(4.) "Dead March" (frag)*

12a.22   "Joshua," oratorio: HWV64
I: . "Introduzione a tempo di Ouverture"
1. "Ye sons of Israel," chorus
. "Behold, my friends, what vast rewards are giv'n," recit (Joshua, Caleb)
2. "Oh first in wisdom, first in pow'r," air (Caleb)
. "Matrons, and virgins, with unweary'd pray'r," recit (Achsah)
3. "Oh! who can tell, oh! who can hear of Egypt," air (Achsah)
. "Caleb, attend to all I now prescribe," recit (Joshua)
4. "To long posterity we here record," solo & chorus (Joshua)
5. "So long the memory shall last," accompagnato
6. "While Kedron's brook to Jordan's stream its silver tribute pays," air (Joshua)
. "But who is He?... tremendous to behold!," recit (Othniel)
7. "Awful, pleasing being, say," air (Othniel)
. "Joshua, I come commission'd from on high," recit (Angel, Joshua)
8. "Leader of Israel, 'tis the Lord's decree," accompagnato (Angel)
. "To give command, prerogative is thine," recit (Joshua)
9. "Haste, Israel, haste," air (Joshua)
10. "The Lord commands, and Joshua leads," chorus
11. "In these blest scenes, where constant pleasure reigns," accompagnato (Othniel, Achsah)
. " 'Tis Achsah's voice! who but that heav'nly fair," recit (Othniel, Achsah)
12. "Hail, lovely virgin of this blissful bow'r!," arioso (Othniel, Achsah)
13. "Hark, hark! 'tis the linnet and the thrush," air (Achsah)
. "Oh Achsah! form'd for ev'ry chaste delight," recit (Othniel)
14. "Our limpid streams with freedom flow," duet (Achsah, Othniel)
. "The trumpet calls," recit (Othniel)
15. "May all the host of heav'n attend him round," chorus
II: . " 'Tis well; six times the Lord hath been obey'd," recit (Joshua)
16. "March" (Solemn March during the Circumvection of the Ark of the Covenant)
17. "Glory to God," solo & chorus (Joshua)
. "The walls are levell'd," recit (Caleb)
18. "See, the raging flames arise," air (Caleb)
19. "To vanity and earthly pride," air (Achsah)
. "Let all the seed of Abrah'm now prepare" (The Passover), recit (Joshua)
20. "Almighty ruler of the skies!," solo & chorus (Joshua)
. "Joshua, the men, dispatch'd," recit (Caleb)
21. "How soon, how soon our tow'ring hopes are cross'd!," chorus
. "Whence this dejection?," recit (Joshua)
22. "With redoubled rage return," air (Joshua)
23. "We with redoubled rage return," chorus
. "Now give the army breath," recit (Othniel)
24. "Indulgent Heav'n hath heard," recit (Achsah)
25. "As cheers the sun, as cheers the tender flow'r," air (Achsah)
. "Sure I'm deceiv'd! with sorrow," recit (Caleb, Othniel)
26. "Nations, who in future story would recorded be with glory," air (Othniel)
. "Brethren and friends, what joy this scene imparts," recit (Joshua)
27. "Sinfonia"
. "Thus far our cause is favour'd," recit (Caleb)
28. "Oh! thou bright orb," solo & chorus (Joshua)
III: 29. "Hail! hail, mighty Joshua, Our children's children shall rehearse thy deeds," chorus
30. "Happy, oh, thrice happy we," air (Achsah)
. "Caleb, for holy Eleazer send," recit (Joshua, Caleb)
31. "Shall I in Mamre's fertile plain," air (Caleb)
32. "For all these mercies we will sing," chorus
. "Oh Caleb, fear'd by foes," recit (Othniel, Caleb)
33. "Place danger around me, the storm I'll despise," air (Othniel)

34. "Father of mercy, hear the pray'r we make," chorus
. "In bloom of youth, this stripling hath achiev'd," recit (Joshua)
35. "See, the conqu'ring hero comes!," chorus (Youths)
36. "See, the godlike youth advance!," duet (2S)
37. "See, the conqu'ring hero comes!," chorus
. "Welcome, my son! my Othniel, good and great!," recit (Caleb, Othniel, Achsah)
38. "Oh! had I Jubal's lyre, or Miriam's tuneful voice," aria (Achsah)
. "While life shall last, each moment we'll improve," recit (Othniel)
39. "Oh peerless maid, with beauty blest," duet (Achsah, Othniel)
. "While lawless tyrants," recit (Caleb)
40. "The great Jehovah is our awful theme, sublime in majesty," chorus

12a.23   "Alexander Balus," oratorio: HWV65
. "Ouverture"
I: 1. "Flush'd with conquest, fir'd by Mithra," chorus (Asiatics)
. "Thus far, ye glorious partners of the war," recit (Alexander Balus, Jonathan)
2. "Great author of this harmony," air (Jonathan)
. "And thus let happy Egypt's King," recit (Ptolomee)
3. "Thrice happy the monarch, whom nations contend," air (Ptolomee)
. "Congratulation to our father's friend," recit (Cleopatra)
4. "Hark, hark, hark! he strikes the golden lyre," air (Cleopatra)
. "Be it my chief ambition there to rise," recit (Alexander Balus)
5. "Fair virtue shall charm me," air (Alexander Balus) (= La Resurrezione, HWV47/5)
6. "Ye happy nations round," chorus (Asiatics)
. "My Jonathan, didst thou mark well her graces?," recit (Alexander Balus) (2nd vers p1751/4)
7a, b. "Oh, what resistless charms are giv'n," air (Alexander Balus) (2nd vers p1751/4)
8. "Subtle love, with fancy viewing, rapt'rous joys on joys ensuing," air (Alexander Balus)
. "Aspasia, I know not what to call this interview," recit (Cleopatra)
9. "How happy should we mortals prove," air (Cleopatra)
. "Check not the pleasing accents of thy tongue," recit (Aspasia) (2 vers)
10. "So shall the sweet attractive smile, winning graces," air (Aspasia)
. "How blissful state! That blissful state be yours!," recit (Cleopatra, Aspasia)
11. "O, what pleasures, past expressing," duet (Cleopatra, Aspasia)
. "Why hangs this heavy gloom," recit (Jonathan, Alexander Balus) (2 vers)
12. "Heroes may boast their mighty deeds, and talk of conquest," air (Alexander Balus)
13. "Mighty love now calls to arm," air (Alexander Balus) (= La Resurrezione, HWV47/3)
. "Ye sons of Judah, with high festival proclaim," recit (Jonathan)
14. "Great god, from whom all blessings spring," air & chorus (Jonathan)
II: 15. "Kind hope, thou universal friend," air (Alexander Balus)
. "Long, long and happy live the King!," recit (Jonathan, Alexander Balus)
16. "O Mithra, with thy brightest beams," air (Alexander Balus)
. "Stay, my dread sovereign," recit (A sycophant Courtier, Alexander Balus, Jonathan) (2 vers)
17. "Hateful man! thy sland'rous tongue throws in vain the poison'd dart," air (Jonathan)
18. "O calumny, on virtue waiting," chorus (Israelites)
. "Ah! whence these dire forebodings of the mind?," recit (Cleopatra)
19. "Tost from thought to thought I rove," air (Cleopatra)
. "Give to the winds," recit (Aspasia) (2nd vers p1751/4)
20. "Love, glory, ambition, whate'er can inspire a flame that is lasting," air (Aspasia)
. "Thus far my wishes thrive," recit (Ptolomee)
21. "Virtue, thou ideal name, all thy honours I disclaim," air (Ptolomee)
. "Ye happy people," accompagnato (Jonathan) (p1751/4, = Alceste, HWV45/2)
. "Triumph Hymen in the pair," soli & chorus (p1751/4, = HWV45/3)
. "Glad time, at length, hath reach'd the happy point," recit (Alexander Balus, Cleopatra)
22. "Hail, hail, hail wedded love," duet (Alexander Balus, Cleopatra)
23. "Hymen, fair Urania's son, show'r thy choicest blessings down," chorus (Asiatics)
III: 24. "Sinfonia"
. " 'Tis true, instinctive nature seldom points," recit (Cleopatra)
25. "Here amid the shady woods, fragrant flow'rs and crystal floods," air (Cleopatra)
26. "The gods and Ptolomee have otherwise ordain'd!," quintet (Cleopatra, Ruffians)
. "Ah! was it not my Cleopatra's voice?," recit (Alexander Balus)
27. "Pow'rful guardians of all nature," air (Alexander Balus)
. "Treach'ry, o King, unheard of treachery," recit (Jonathan, Alexander Balus, Aspasia)
28. "Fury, fury, with red sparkling eyes," air (Alexander Balus)
. "Gods! can there be a more afflicting sight," recit (Aspasia)
29. "Strange reverse of human fate," air (Aspasia)
. "May he return with laurel'd victory," recit (Jonathan) (2 vers)
(29a.) "Guardian angels as ye fly," air (Jonathan) (p1751/4, = HWV45/5)
. "But oh! I fear, the Gods," recit (Jonathan) (p1751/4)
30. "To God, who made the radiant sun," air (Jonathan)
31. "Sun, moon, and stars, and all ye host of heav'n," chorus (Israelites)
. "Yes—he was false, my daughter, false to you," recit (Ptolomee, Cleopatra)
32. "Ungrateful child, by ev'ry sacred pow'r," accompagnato (Ptolomee)
33. "O sword, and thou, all-daring hand," air (Ptolomee)
34. "Shall Cleopatra ever smile again?," accompagnato (Cleopatra)
. "Ungrateful tidings to the royal ear," recit (Messenger)

35. "O take me from this hateful light," arioso (Cleopatra)
. "Forgive, o Queen, the messenger of ill!," recit (Another Messenger, Cleopatra)
36. "Calm thou my soul, kind Isis, with a noble scorn of life," accompagnato (Cleopatra)
37. "Convey me to some peaceful shore," air (Cleopatra)
. "Mysterious are thy ways, o providence!," recit (Jonathan)
38. "Ye servants of th'eternal King," solo & chorus (Jonathan, Israelites)
Anhang: (13.) "that revenge may give some ease," air (Alexander Balus)

12a.24   "Susanna," oratorio: HWV66
. "Overture"
I: 1. "How long, oh Lord! shall Israel groan," chorus (Israelites)
. "Our crimes repeated have provok'd his rage," recit (Joacim)
2. "Clouds o'ertake the brightest day," air (Joacim)
. "Oh Joacim! when thou art by," recit (Susanna)
3. "When thou art nigh, my pulse beats high and raptures swell my breast," duet (Susanna, Joacim)
. "Lives there in Babylon so bless'd a pair?," recit (Chelsias)
4. "Who fears the Lord, may dare all foes," air (Chelsias)
. "A flame like mine, so faithful and so pure," recit (Joacim)
5. "When first I saw my lovely maid, beneath the citron's shade," air (Joacim)
. "Let me contess, I hear my praises sung," recit (Susanna)
6. "Would custom bid the melting fair," air (Susanna)
. "Down my old cheeks the tears of transport roll," recit (Chelsias)
7. "Peace, peace crown'd with roses on your slumbers wait," air (Chelsias)
. "Oh pious Chelsias! thy paternal care," recit (Susanna)
8. "Without the swain's assiduous care, how soon the sickly flow'r," air (Susanna)
. "Source of each joy, thou comfort of my life," recit (Joacim, Susanna)
9. "The parent bird in search of food awhile deserts her callow brood," air (Joacim)
. "On Joacim may ev'ry joy attend," recit (Susanna)
10. "What means this weight that in my bosoms lies," accompagnato (Susanna)
11. "Bending to the throne of glory," air (Susanna)
12. "Virtue shall never long," chorus
13a, b. "Tyranic love! feel thy cruel dart," accompagnato (Elder 1)
14. "Ye verdant hills, ye balmy vales, bear witness of my pain," air (Elder 1)
. "Say is it fit that age should drop his pride," recit (Elder 2, Elder 1)
15. "The oak that for a thousand years," air (Elder 2)
. "Ye winged gales, convey these whisp'ring sighs," recit (Elder 1, Elder 2)
16. "When the trumpet sounds to arms," air (Elder 1)
17. "Rifhteous Heav'n beholds their guile," chorus
II: . "Frost nips the flow'rs, that would the fields adorn," recit (Joacim)
18. "On fair Euphrates' verdant side, where nodding osiers play," air (Joacim)
. "Lead me, oh lead me to some cool retreat," recit (Susanna)
. "Soon will the Lord the Joacim return," recit (Attendant, Susanna)
19. "Crystal streams in murmurs flowing," air (Susanna)
. "Too lovely youth, for whom these sorrows flow," recit (Susanna, Attendant)
20. "Ask if yon damask rose be sweet that scents the ambient air?," air (Attendant)
. "In vain you try to cure my rising grief," recit (Susanna, Attendant)
21. "Beneath the cypress gloomy shade where silver lilies paint the glade," air (Attendant)
. "Thy plaintive strains my inmost sorrows move," recit (Susanna, Attendant)
22. "Blooming as the face of spring," air (Elder 1)
. "We long have languish'd, and now mean to prove," recit (Elder 2, Susanna)
23. "The torrent that sweeps in its course," air (Elder 2)
. "Deceitful wolves! who left in truth's defence," recit (Susanna, Elder 2)
24. "Away, away! ye tempt me both in vain!," trio (Susanna, Elder 1, Elder 2)
. "Alas! I find the fatal toils are set," recit (Susanna, Elder 2, Elder 1)
25. "If guiltless blood be your intent, I here resign it all," air (Susanna)
. "Quick to her fate the loose adult'ress bear," recit (Elder 2)
26. "Let justice reign and flourish thro' the land," chorus
. "Is fair Susanna false? it ne'er can be," recit (Joacim)
27. "On the rapid whirlwind's wing, see, I fly to seek the fair," air (Joacim)
28. "Oh Joacim! thy wedded truth, thy wedded truth is warranted of heav'n," chorus
III: 29. "The cause is decided, Susanna is guilty," chorus
. "I hear my doom, nor yet the laws accuse," recit (Susanna)
30. "Faith displays her rosy wing," air (Susanna)
. "Permit me, fair, to mourn thy fate severe," recit (Elder 1)
31. "Round thy urn my tears shall flow," air (Elder 1)
. " 'Tis thus the crocodile his grief displays," recit (Susanna)
32. "But you, who see me on the verge of life," accompagnato (Susanna)
. "The sentence now is past: the wretch convey to instant death," recit (Elder 2, Daniel, Elder 1)
33. " 'Tis not age's sullen face, wrinkl'd front and solemn pace," air (Daniel)
. "Oh wond'rous youth! rejudge the cause," recit (A Judge, Daniel)
34. "Impartial heav'n! impartial heav'n! whose hand shall never cease," chorus
. "Thou artful wretch! in vice's practice grey," recit (Daniel, Elder 1, Elder 2) (2 vers)
35. "Righteous Daniel, matchless youth," chorus
. "Instant conduct them to their fate," recit (Daniel) (2 vers)
36. "Chastity thou Cherub bright, gentle as the dawn of light," air (Daniel)

. "But see! my Lord, my Joacim appears," recit (Susanna)
37. "Gold within the furnace try'd, shall the sharp essay abide," air (Joacin)
. "The joyful news of chaste Susanna's truth," recit (Chelsias, Susanna) (2nd vers p1759)
(38.) "Endless pleasure, endless pleasure," solo & chorus (Attendant) (p1759, = Semele, HWV58/17)
38a, b. "Raise your voice to sounds of joy," air (Chelsias) (2 vers)
39. "Bless'd be the day that gave Susanna birth," chorus
. "Hence ev'ry pang, which late my soul oppress'd," recit (Susanna)
40. "Guiult trembling spoke my doom," air (Susanna)
. "Sweet are the accents of thy tuneful tongue," recit (Joacim, Susanna)
41. "To my chaste Susanna's praise I'll the swelling note prolong," duet (Susanna, Joacim)
42. "A virtuous wife shall soften fortune's frown, she's far more precious than a golden crown," ch
Anhang: *. "Ouverture" (frag)*
(2.) *"Heartfelt sorrow, constant woe, from our streaming eyes shall flow," air (Joacim)*
(6.) *"Would custom bid the melting fair, the purpose of her soul declare," air (Susanna) (frag)*
(9.) *"The parent bird in search of food," air (Joacim) (frag)*
(20a, b.) "Ask if yon damask rose be sweet," air (Attendant) (2 vers)
(28.) "O piety, unfading light, thou eldest born of Heav'n," chorus

12a.25 "Solomon," oratorio: HWV67
. "Ouverture"
I: 1. "Your harps and cymbals sound," chorus
2. "Praise ye the Lord for all his mercies past," air (Levite)
3. "With pious heart, and holy tongue," chorus
4. "Almighty pow'r! who rul'st the earth and skies," accompagnato (Solomon)
. "Imperial Solomon, thy pray'rs are heard," recit (Zadok)
5. "See! from the op'ning skies descending flames," accompagnato (Zadok)
6. "Sacred raptures cheer my breast," air (Zadok)
7. "Throughout the land Jehovah's praise record," chorus
. "Blest be the Lord, who look'd with gracious eyes," recit (Solomon)
8. "What though I trace each herb and flow'r," air (Solomon)
. "And see my Queen, my wedded love," recit (Solomon)
9. "Bles'd the day when first my eyes," air (Queen)
. "Thou fair inhabitant of Nile," recit (Solomon, Queen)
10. "Welcome as the dawn of day to the pilgrim on his way," duet (Queen, Solomon)
. "Vain are the transient beauties of the face," recit (Zadok)
11. "Indulge thy faith and wedded truth," air (Zadok)
. "My blooming fair, come, come away," recit (Solomon)
12. "Haste, haste to the cedar grove," air (Solomon)
. "When thou art absent from my sight," recit (Queen)
13. "With thee th' unshelter'd moor I'd tread," air (Queen)
. "Search round the world," recit (Zadok)
14. "May no rash intruder disturb their soft hours," chorus
II: 15. "From the censer curling rise grateful incense," chorus
. "Prais'd be the Lord," recit (Solomon)
16. "When the sun o'er yonder hills pours in tides the golden day," air (Solomon)
. "Great prince, thy resolution's just," recit (Levite)
17. "Thrice bless'd that wise discerning King, who can each passion tame," air (Levite)
. "My sovereign liege, two women stand," recit (Attendant, Solomon)
. "Thou son of David, hear a mother's grief," recit (1st Harlot)
18. "Words are weak to paint my fears," trio (1st Harlot, 2nd Harlot, Salomon)
. "What says the other," recit (Solomon, 2nd Harlot)
19. "Thy sentence, great King, is prudent and wise," air (2nd Harlot)
. "Withhold, withhold the executing hand!," recit (1st Harlot)
20. "Can I see my infant gor'd," air (1st Harlot)
21. "Israel, attend to what your King shall say," accompagnato (Solomon)
22. "Thrice bless'd be the King," duet (1st Harlot, Solomon)
23. "From the East unto the West, who so wise as Solomon?," chorus
. "From morn to eve I could enraptur'd sing," recit (Zadok)
24. "See the tall Palm that lifts the head," air (Zadok)
A. "The shepherd shall hail him," recit (1st Harlot)
B. "No more shall armed bands," recit (1st Harlot)
25. "Beneath the vine, or figtree's shade," air (1st Harlot)
26. "Swell, swell, swell the full chorus to Solomon's praise," chorus
III: 27. "Sinfonia" (Arrival of the Queen of Sheba)
. "From Arabia's spicy shores," recit (Queen of Sheba, Solomon)
28. "Ev'ry sight these eyes behold," air (Queen of Sheba)
. "Sweep, sweep the string, to sooth the royal fair," recit (Solomon)
29. "Music, spread thy voice around," solo & chorus (Solomon)
30. "Now a diff'rent measure try," air & chorus (Solomon)
. "Then at once from rage remove," recit (Solomon)
31. "Draw the tear from hopeless love," chorus
. "Next the tortur'd soul release," recit (Solomon)
32. "Thus rolling surges rise," solo & chorus (Solomon)
. "Thy harmony's divine, great king," recit (Queen of Sheba)
33. "Pious king, and virtuous queen," air (Levite)

. "Thrice happy king, to have achiev'd," recit (Zadok)
34. "Golden columns, fair and bright," air (Zadok)
35. "Praise the Lord with harp and tongue!," chorus
. "Gold now is common on our happy shore," recit (Solomon)
36. "How green our fertile pastures look!," air (Solomon)
37a, b. "Will the sun forget to streak eastern skies with amber ray," air (Queen of Sheba)
. "Adieu, fair queen," recit (Solomon)
38. "Ev'ry joy that wisdom knows," duet (Queen of Sheba, Solomon)
39. "The name of the wicked shall quickly be past," chorus
Changes in 1759 production: I: . "Sinfony"
. "Prais'd be the Lord, from whom all wisdom springs," recit (Solomon)
(2.) "When the sun gives brightest day," air (Solomon)
(4.) "Wise, great, and good," air (Zadok)
II: . "From Arabia's spicy shores," recit (Zadok)
(11.) "To view the wonders of thy throne," air (Zadok)
. "Sad solemn sounds, o ease my breast," recit (2nd Woman)
(16.) "Sad solemn sounds, o ease my breast," air (2nd Woman)
. "Next the tortur'd soul release," recit (Solomon)
17. "Beneath the vine or figtree's shade ev'ry shepherd sings the maid," air & chorus
. "Love from such a parent sprung," recit (Zadok)
(18.) "Love from such a parent sprung," air (Zadok)
. "Love from such a parent sprung," chorus
III: . "Ages to come shall hail these happy days," recit (Solomon)
(22.) "This music is divine, o King," air (Queen of Sheba)
(23.) "But when the Temple I behold," accompagnato (Queen of Sheba)
(27.) "How green our fertile pastures look," air (Solomon)
Anhang: . "Sweep, sweep the string, to sooth the blooming fair," recit (Solomon)
. "Indulge thy faith and wedded truth," recit (Zadok)
(26.) "Swell, swell," chorus
(27.) "Symfony"
. *"Well, my fair Queen, in converse sweet," recit (Solomon) (frag)*
(35./37.) "Will the sun forget to streak eastern skies with amber ray," air (Zadok) (frag)
(37.) "Will the sun forget to stream," air (Queen of Sheba) (frag)

12a.26   "Theodora," oratorio: HWV68
. "Ouverture"
I: . " 'Tis Dioclesian's natal day," recit (Valens)
1a. "Go, my faithful soldier, go," air (Valens)
1b. "Go, my faithful soldier, go," recit (Valens)
2. "And draw a blessing down on his imperial crown, who rules the world," chorus (Heathens)
. "Vouchsafe, dread Sir, a gracious ear," recit (Didymus, Valens)
3. "Racks, gibbets, sword, and fire shall speak my vengeful ire," air (Valens)
4. "For ever thus stands fix'd the doom," chorus (Heathens)
. "Most cruel edict!," recit (Didymus)
5. "The raptur'd soul, the raptur'd soul defies the sword," air (Didymus)
. "I know thy virtues, and ask not thy faith," recit (Septimius)
6. "Descend, kind Pity, heav'nly guest," air (Septimius)
. "Though hard, my friends," recit (Theodora)
7. "Fond flatt'ring world, adieu!," air (Theodora)
. "O bright example of all goodness!," recit (Irene)
8. "Bane of virtue, nurse of passions, soother of vile inclinations," air (Irene)
9. "Come, mighty Father, mighty Lord," chorus (Christians)
. "Fly, fly, my brethren! heathen rage," recit (Messenger)
. "Ah! whither should we fly?," recit (Irene)
10. "As with rosy steps the morn advancing, drives the shades of night," air (Irene)
11. "All pow'r in heaven above, or earth beneath," chorus (Christians)
. "Mistaken wretches! why thus blind to fate," recit (Septimius)
12. "Dread the fruits of christian folly," air (Septimius)
. "Deluded mortal!," recit (Theodora, Septimius) (2 vers)
13. "Oh worse than death indeed! Lead me, ye guards, lead me," accompagnato (Theodora)
14. "Angels, ever bright and fair," air (Theodora)
. "Unhappy, happy crew!," recit (Didymus, Irene) (2 vers)
15. "Kind Heav'n, kind Heav'n if virtue be thy care," air (Didymus)
. "Oh love, how great thy pow'r!," recit (Irene)
16. "Go, gen'rous pious youth, May all the pow'rs above reward," chorus (Christians)
II: . "Ye men of Antioch, with solemn pomp," recit (Valens)
17. "Queen of summer, queen of love," chorus (Heathens)
18. "Wide spread his name," air (Valens)
. "Return, Septimius," recit (Valens) (2 vers)
19. "Venus laughing from the skies," chorus (Heathens)
20. "Sinfonia"
. "Oh thou bright sun! how sweet thy rays," recit (Theodora)
21. "With darkness deep, as is my woe," air (Theodora)
21b. "Air" (Sinfonia)
21c. "Sinfonia"

. "But why art thou disquieted, my soul?," recit (Theodora)
22. "Oh that I on wings could rise," air (Theodora)
. "Long have I known thy friendly social soul," recit (Didymus, Septimius) (2 vers)
23. "Though the honours that Flora and Venus receive from the Romans," air (Septimius)
. "Oh save her then, or give me pow'r to save," recit (Didymus, Septimius)
24. "Deeds of kindness to display," air (Didymus)
. "The clouds begin to veil the hemisphere," recit (Irene)
25a, b. "Defend her, Heav'n let angels spread," air (Irene) (2nd vers p1759, = Siroe, HWV24/25)
. "Or lull'd with grief, or rapt her soul to Heav'n," recit (Didymus)
26. "Sweet rose and lily, flow'ry forml," air (Didymus)
. "O save me, Heav'n, in this my perilous hourl," recit (Theodora, Didymus)
27. "The pilgrim's home, the sick man's health, the captive's ransom," air (Theodora)
28. "Forbid it, Heav'n! shall I destroy the life I came to save?," accompagnato (Didymus)
. "Or, say, what Right have I to take," recit (Didymus)
. "Ah! what is liberty or life to me," recit (Theodora, Didymus) (2 vers)
29. "To thee, to thee, thou glorious son of worth," duet (Theodora, Didymus)
. " 'Tis night: but night's sweet blessing is denied," recit (Irene)
30. "He saw the lovely youth," chorus (Christians)
III: 31. "Lord, to thee each night and day," air (Irene)
. "But see, the good, the virtuous Didymusl," recit (Irene, Theodora) (2 vers)
32a. "When sunk in anguish and despair," air (Theodora)
32b. "Blessed be the pow'r who gave us," solo & chorus (Theodora) (p1755)
33. "Blest be the hand, and blest the pow'r," solo & chorus (Theodora, Christians)
. "Undaunted in the court stands Didymus," recit (Messenger, Irene)
34. "Oh my Irene, heav'n is kind and Valens too is kind," accompagnato (Theodora)
. "Stay me not, my friend," recit (Theodora)
35. "Whither, princess, do you fly?," duet (Theodora, Irene)
. "She's gone! disdaining liberty and life," recit (Irene)
36. "New scenes of joy come crowding on," air (Irene)
. "Is it a Christian virtue then," recit (Valens, Didymus) (3 vers)
. "Be that my dooml," recit (Theodora, Septimius) (2nd vers p1750; 3rd vers p1755)
37a, b. "From virtue springs," air (Septimius) (2nd vers p after 1759, = Admeto, HWV22/13)
38a, b. "Cease, ye slaves," air (Valens) (2nd vers p after 1759, = Tolomeo, HWV25/18)
. " 'Tis kind, my friends; but kinder still," recit (Didymus, Theodora) (2 vers)
38c. "Lost in anguish quite despairing, Heav'n alone for virtue caring," air (Theodora) (p after 1759)
39. "How strange their ends and yet how glorious!," chorus (Christians)
. "On me your frowns, your utmost rage exert," recit (Didymus, Theodora, Valens)
40a. "Ye ministers of justice," air (Valens)
(40b.) "Ye ministers of justice, lead them hence," recit (Valens)
. "And must such beauty suffer?," recit (Didymus, Theodora, Septimius)
41. "Streams of pleasure ever flowing," air & duet (Didymius, Theodora)
. "Ere this their doom is past," recit (Irene)
42. "Oh Love divine, thou source of fame," chorus (Christians)

12a.27   "The Choice of Hercules," oratorio (used as: Act III of Alexander's Feast, HWV75): HWV69
1. "Symphony" (= Alceste, HWV45/12)
2. "See, Hercules! how smiles yon myrtle plain," accompagnato (Pleasure) (= Alceste, HWV45/14)
3. "Come, blooming boy, with me repair," air (Pleasure) (= Alceste, HWV45/9)
4. "There the brisk sparkling nectar drain," air (Pleasure)
5. "While for thy arms," solo & chorus (Pleasure, Attendants on Pleasure) (= Alceste, HWV45/9)
. "Away, mistaken wretch, away!," recit (Virtue)
6. "This manly youth's exalted mind," air (Virtue) (= Alceste, HWV45/7a)
. "Rise, youth! exalt thyself and me," recit (Virtue)
7. "Go, assert thy heav'nly race," air (Virtue)
. "In peace, in war, pursue thy country's good," recit (Virtue)
8. "So shalt thou gain immortal praise," solo & ch (Virtue, Attendants) (= Alceste, HWV45/6)
. "Hearst thou, what dangers then thou must engage?," recit (Pleasure)
9. "Turn thee, youth," solo & chorus (Pleasure, Attendants on Pleasure) (= Alceste, HWV45/4)
. "Short is my way, fair, easy, smooth, and plain," recit (Pleasure, Hercules)
10. "Yet, can I hear that dulcet lay," air (Hercules) (= Alceste, HWV45/7b)
11. "Enjoy the sweet Elysian grove," air (An Attendant on Pleasure) (= Alceste, HWV45/10)
. "Oh! whither, Reason, dost thou fly?," recit (Hercules)
12. "Where shall I go?," trio (Pleasure, Virtue, Hercules)
13. "Mount, mount the steep ascentl," accompagnato (Virtue)
14. "Mount, mount the steep ascent, mount," air (Virtue)
15. "Arise, arise! Mount, mount the steep ascent," chorus (= Alceste, HWV45/13)
. "The sounds breathe fire celestial," recit (Hercules)
16. "Lead, Goddess, lead the way," air (Hercules) (= Alceste, HWV45/8)
17. "Virtue will place thee in that blest abode," chorus (Attendants on Virtue)

12a.28   "Jephtha," oratorio: HWV70
. "Ouverture"
I: 1. "It must be so or these vile Ammonites," accompagnato (Zebul)
2. "Pour forth no more unheeded pray'rs," air (Zebul)
3. "No more to Ammon's god and King," chorus

. "But Jephtha comes.—Kind Heav'n, assist our plea," recit (Zebul, Jephtha)
4. "Virtue my soul shall still embrace," air (Jephtha)
. " 'Twill be a painful separation," recit (Storgè)
5a, b. "In gentle murmurs will I mourn," air (Storgè) (2nd vers p1756)
. "Happy this embassy, my charming Iphis," recit (Hamor)
6. "Dull delay, in piercing anguish, bids thy faithful lover languish," air (Hamor)
. "Ill suits the voice of love when glory calls," recit (Iphis)
7. "Take the heart you fondly gave," air (Iphis)
. "I go; my soul, inspir'd by thy command," recit (Hamor)
8. "These labours past, how happy we!," duet (Iphis, Hamor)
. "What mean these doubtful fancies of the brain?," recit (Jephtha)
9. "If, Lord sustain'd by thy almighty pow'r, Ammon I drive," accompagnato (Jephtha)
. " 'tis said. Attend, ye chiefs," recit (Jephtha)
10. "O God, behold our sore distress," chorus
. "Some dire event hangs o'er our heads," recit (Storgè)
11. "Scenes of horror, scenes of horror, scenes of woe," air (Storgè)
. "Say, my dear mother, whence these piercing cries," recit (Iphis, Storgè)
12. "The smiling dawn of happy days presents a prospect clear," air (Iphis)
. "Such, Jephtha, was the haughty King's reply," recit (Zebul, Jephtha)
13. "When loud his voice in thunder spoke," chorus
II: . "Glad tidings of great joy to thee, dear Iphis," recit (Hamor)
14. "Cherub and Seraphim, unbodied forms," chorus
15. "Up the dreadful steep ascending," air (Hamor)
. " 'Tis well.—Haste, haste, ye maidens," recit (Iphis)
16. "Tune the soft melodious lute," air (Iphis)
A. "Heav'n smiles once more on his repentant people," recit (Jephtha)
B. "Again Heav'n smiles on his repentant people," recit (Zebul) (p1753)
17. "Freedom now once more possessing," air (Zebul) (p1753, = Agrippina, HWV6/2)
. "Zebul, thy deeds were valiant," recit (Jephtha)
18. "His mighty arm, with sudden blow, dispers'd," air (Jephtha)
19. "In glory high, in might serene, he sees, moves all," chorus
20. "Symphony"
. "Hail, glorious conqueror!," recit (Iphis)
21. "Welcome, as the cheerful light," solo & chorus (Iphis)
. "Horror! confusion! harsh this music grates," recit (Jephtha)
22. "Open thy marble jaws, o tomb, and hide me, earth," air (Jephtha)
. "Why is my brother thus afflicted?," recit (Zebul, Jephtha)
23. "First perish thou and perish all the world!," accompagnato & arioso (Storgè)
. "If such thy cruel purpose; lo!," recit (Hamor)
24. "On me, on me let blind mistaken zeal," air (Hamor)
25. "Spare my child! O spare your daughter!," quartet (Storgè, Hamor, Jephtha, Zebul)
. "Such news flies swift; I've heard the mournful cause," recit (Iphis)
26. "For joys so vast, too little is the price," accompagnato (Iphis)
27. "Happy they! this vital breath with content I shall resign," air (Iphis)
28. "Deeper and deeper still, thy goodness, child," accompagnato (Jephtha)
29. "How dark, how dark o Lord, are thy decrees!," chorus
III: 30. "Hide thou thy hated beams, o sun, in clouds," arioso (Jephtha)
31. "A father, off'ring up his only child," accompagnato (Jephtha)
32. "Waft her, angels, through the skies," air (Jephtha)
33. "Ye sacred priests, whose hands ne'er yet ere stain'd with human blood," accompagnato (Iphis)
34. "Farewell, farewell, ye limpid springs and floods," air (Iphis)
35. "Doubtful fear, doubtful fear, and reverend awe," chorus (Piests)
36. "Symphony"
. "Rise, Jephtha. And ye reverend priests," recit (Angel)
37. "Happy, Iphis, shalt thou live," air (Angel)
38. "For ever blessed be thy holy name," arioso (Jephtha)
39. "Theme sublime of endless praise," chorus
. "Let me congratulate this happy turn," recit (Zebul)
40a, b. "Laud her, all ye virgin train," air (Zebul) (2 vers)
. "O let me fold thee in a mother's arms," recit (Storgè)
41a, b. "Sweet as sight to the blind, or freedom to the slave," air (Storgè) (2nd vers p1756)
. "With transport, Iphis, I behold thy safety," recit (Hamor)
42. " 'Tis heaven's all-ruling pow'r," air (Hamor)
. "My faithful Hamor, may that Providence," recit (Iphis)
43a. "Freely I to Heav'n resign," air (Iphis)
43b. "All that is in Hamor mine, freely I," quintet (Iphis, Hamor, Storgè, Jephtha, Zebul) (p1753)
44. "Ye house of Gilead, with one voice, in blessings manifold rejoice," chorus
Anhang: . "Ouverture"
(26./27.) "For joys so vast, too little is the price of one poor life," air (Iphis)
(27.) "Happy they; this vital Breath with content I shall resign," air (Iphis) (frag)

12a.29 "The Triumph of Time and Truth," oratorio: HWV71
. "Ouverture"
I: 1. "Time is supreme, Time is a mighty pow'r!," chorus (= Sing unto God, HWV263/1)
. "How happy could I fix but here," recit (Beauty)

2. "Faithful mirror!," air (Beauty)
. "Fear not! I, Pleasure, swear," recit (Pleasure, Beauty)
3. "Pensive sorrow, deep possessing," air (Pleasure) (= Sing unto God, HWV263/2)
A. "Despise old Time; if short his stay," recit (Deceit)
(3.) B. "Sorrow darkens ev'ry feature," air (Deceit) (p1758, = chamber cantatas: HWV107/1 & 145/1)
4. "Come, come! live with Pleasure, taste in Youth life's only joy," air & chorus (Beauty, The Boys)
. "Come, come! live with Pleasure," chorus
. "Turn, look on me! Behold old Time," recit (Time, Counsel)
5. "The Beauty, smiling, and sweet beguiling," air (Counsel)
. "Our different pow'rs we'll try," recit (Pleasure, Beauty, Time, Counsel)
6. "Ever flowing tides of Pleasure," air (Beauty)
. "The hand of Time pulls down the great colossus of the sun," recit (Time)
7. "Loathsome urns, disclose your treasure," air (Time)
8. "Strengthen us, oh Time, with all thy lore," chorus
. "Too rigid the reproof you give," recit (Deceit)
(8a.) "Happy Beauty, who Fortune now smiling," air (Deceit) (p1758, = Agrippina, HWV6/40)
9. "Happy, if still they reign in pleasure," solo & chorus (Deceit)
. "Youth is not rich in Time; it may be poor," recit (Counsel, Time, Pleasure)
10. "Like the shadow, life ever is flying," air & chorus (Time)
II: 11. "Pleasure submits to pain, as day recedes to night," chorus (= Acis and Galatea, HWV49b/21)
. "Here Pleasure keeps her splendid court," recit (Pleasure)
. "Flourish of horns"
. "Hark! what sounds are these I hear?," recit (Beauty)
12. "Oh, how great the glory," chorus (= Il Parnasso in Festa, HWV72/17)
13. "Dryads, Sylvans, with fair Flora," air & chorus (Pleasure) (= Il Parnasso in Festa, HWV72/30)
(13a.) "No more complaining, no more disdaining," air (Deceit) (p1758, = Rodrigo, HWV5/32)
(13b.) "Pleasure's gentle Zephyr's playing," air (Deceit) (p1758, = Agrippina, HWV6/3)
(13c.) "Pleasure's gentle Zephyr's playing," air (Deceit) (p after 1758)
14. "Come, oh Time, and thy broad wings displaying," air (Beauty)
15. "Mortals think, that Time is sleeping," air (Counsel)
. "You hop'd to call in vain, but see me here," recit (Time)
16. "False destructive ways of Pleasure leave," air (Time)
. "Too long deluded you have been," recit (Counsel, Time)
17. "Lovely Beauty," air (Pleasure)
. "Seek not to know what known will prove," recit (Deceit)
18a, b. "Melancholy is a folly," air (Deceit) (2 vers)
. "What is the present hour?," recit (Time, Beauty)
19. "Fain would I, two hearts enjoying, this in penitence employing," air (Beauty)
. "Vain the delights of age, or youth," recot (Counsel)
20. "On the valleys, dark and cheerless," air (Counsel)
. "Not venial error this, but stubborn pride," recit (Time, Beauty)
. "Hear the tale of Truth and Duty," recit (Counsel)
21. "Ere to dust is chang'd that beauty, change the heart, and good pursue," chorus (= HWV263/4)
III: 22. "Sinfonia"
. "Beauty once more I thee address," recit (Deceit)
23a. "Sharp thorns despising, cull fragrant roses," air (Deceit)
. "Once more I thee address, regardful of thy happiness," recit (Deceit) (p1758)
(23.) "Charming Beauty, stop the starting tear from flowing," air (Deceit) (p1758)
. "Tempt me no more: your words give no relief," recit (Beauty) (p1758)
23b. "Sharp thorns despising, cull fragrant roses," air (Deceit) (p1758)
. "Regard her not. Unvalued here, such tears may fall," recit (Counsel, Beauty)
24. "Pleasure! my former ways resigning, to Virtue's cause inclining," air (Beauty)
25. "Comfort them, oh Lord, when they are sick," chorus (= anthem: HWV268/5)
. "Since the immortal mirror I possess," recit (Beauty, Pleasure, Counsel)
26. "Thus to ground, thou false, delusive," air (Counsel)
. "Oh mighty Truth! thy pow'r I see," recit (Beauty)
27. "Adieu, vain world! In search of greater good I'll pass my days," accompagnato (Beauty)
28. "From the heart that feels my warning," air (Time)
. "Pleasure, too long associates we have been," recit (Beauty)
. "As with error long have been dwelling," recit (Pleasure)
29. "Like clouds, stormy winds them impelling," air (Pleasure) (Andante = Athalia, HWV52/33)
. "She's gone; and Truth, descending from the sky," recit (Beauty)
30. "Oh, thither let me cast my longing eye," accompagnato
31. "Guardian angels, oh, protect me, and in Virtue's path direct me," air (Beauty)
32. "Alleluja, alleluja," chorus

13. ODES & SERENATAS

13a. SELECTIONS FROM ODES & SERENATAS

13a.1   "Aci, Galatea e Polifemo," serenata: HWV72
        1. "Sorge il dì e tranquillo," duet (Aci, Galatea)
        . "Vanti, o cara, il ruscello," recit (Aci, Galatea)
        2. "Sforzano a piangere con più dolor," aria (Galatea)
        . "E qual nuova sventura," recit (Aci, Galatea)
        3. "Che non può la gelosia quando un core arde d'amore," aria (Aci)
        4. "Ma qual orrido suono mi ferisce l'udito?," recit accompagnato (Galatea, Aci)
        5. "Sibilar l'angui d'Aletto," aria (Polifemo)
        . "Deh lascia, oh Polifemo," recit (Galatea, Polifemo)
        6. "Benchè tuoni e l'etra avvampi," aria (Galatea)
        . "Cadrai depressa e vinta," recit (Polifemo, Galatea)
        7. "Non sempre, no, crudele, mi parlerai così," aria (Polifemo)
        . "Ritornello"
        . "Folle quanto mi rido," recit (Galatea, Polifemo, Aci)
        8. "Dell'aquila l'artigli se non paventa un angue," aria (Aci)
        . "Megli spiega i tuoi sensi," recit (Polifemo, Aci)
        9. "Precipitoso nel marche freme più corre il fiume che stretto fù," aria (Polifemo)
        . "Si t'intendo inumano," recit (Galatea)
      10. "S'agità in mezzo all'onde," aria (Galatea)
        . "So che le cinosure," recit (Polifemo, Aci)
      11. "Proverà lo sdegno mio chi da me non chiede amor," trio (Aci, Galatea, Polifemo)
        . "Ingrata se mi nieghi," recit (Polifemo, Galatea, Aci)
      12. "Fra l'ombre e gl'orrori," aria (Galatea)
        . "Ma che? non andrà inulta," recit (Polifemo, Aci)
      13. "Qui l'augel da pianta in pianta lieto vola," aria (Aci)
        . "Giunsi al fin mio tesoro," recit (Galatea, Aci)
      14. "Se m'ami, oh caro! se mi sei fido," aria (Galatea)
        . "Quì su l'alto del monte," recit (Polifemo, Aci, Galatea)
      15. "Dolce amico amplesso," trio (Aci, Galatea, Polifemo)
        . "Or poichè sordi sono," recit (Polifemo, Aci)
      16. "Verso già l'alma col sangue," aria (Aci)
        . "Misera, e dove sono?," recit (Galatea)
      17. "Impara, ingrata," aria (Polifemo)
        . "Ah tiranno inhumano!," recit (Galatea, Polifemo)
      18. "Del mar fra l'onde per non mirarti," aria (Galatea)
      19. "Ferma, ma già nel mare," recit accompagnato (Polifemo)
      20. "Chi ben ama ha per oggetti fido amor," trio (Aci, Galatea, Polifemo)
    Anhang: (7.) "Non sempre, no, crudele, mi parlerai così," aria (Polifemo)

13a.2   "Il Parnasso in festa," serenata: HWV73
        . "Ouverture" (= 2nd & 3rd movts of: Trio Sonata in G major, Op.5/4, HWV399)
    I: 1. "Verginette dotte e belle," aria (Clio)
        2. "Corriamo pronti ad ubbidir," chorus
        . "Germane, figlio amato," recit (Apollo, Clio, Calliope, Orfeo, Cloride, Eurilla, Proteo)
        3. "Deh! cantate un bell'amor," chorus
        . "Ma prima che s'avanzi," recit (Apollo)
        4. "Spira al sen celeste ardo re," aria (Orfeo/Clio)
        5. "Gran Tonante," aria (Apollo)
        6. "Già vien da lui il nostro ben," chorus
        . "Spetacolo gradito era quel," recit (Clio)
        7. "Con un vezzo lusinghiero," aria (Clio)
        . "Rimembranza gradita!," recit (Apollo)
        8. "Sin le Grazie nel bel volto hanno in te novo splendor," duet (Clio, Apollo)
        . "Ma di si belle fiamme, ah," recit (Clio)
        9. "Quanto breve è il godimento se la gioja," aria (Clio)
        . "Vada in oblio," recit (Apollo)
      10. "Cantiamo a Bacco in sì lieto dì," chorus
      11. "Del Nume Lieo quel sacro liquor," aria (Proteo)
      12. "Sciolga dunque al ballo, al canto," aria (Apollo/Clio)
      13. "S'accenda purdi festa il cor," soli & chorus (Clio, Orfeo)
      14. "Replicati al ballo, al canto," chorus
    II: 15. "Nel petto sento un certo ardor," soli & chorus (Cloride, Eurilla, Clio)
        . (Concerto: Bassoon)
        . "Qual tetra nube, Orfeo," recit (Apollo)
      16. "Torni pure un bel splendore," aria (Apollo)
        . "Ogn'uno siegua, e goli," recit (Clio)
      17. "Nel spiegar sua voce al canto," aria (Clio)
        . "E non s'udiran mai," recit (Cloride/Silvio)
      18. "Oh, oh quanto bella gloria," chorus
      19. "Tra sentier di amene selve fo guerra colle belve," aria (Cloride)
      20. "Oh quanto bella gloria," chorus
        . (Concerto per l'Hautbois)
        . "Che mai facesti, Orfeo?," recit (Calliope/Clio)

21. "Già, già, già le furie vedo ancor," arioso (Calliope/Clio)
22. "Dopo d'aver perduto il caro bene," recit accompagnato (Orfeo)
23. "Ho perso il caro ben," aria (Orfeo)
   . "S'unosce al tuo martir, al tuo martir pietà," chorus
   . "Figlio, diletto Orfeo," recit (Apollo)
24. "Cangia in gioja il tuo dolor," duet (Clio, Apollo)
   . "Di Nettuno seguaci," recit (Apollo)
25. "Coralli e perle vogliamo offrir," chorus
III: 26. "Sinfonia"
   . "Io, che degli avi eccelsi," recit (Marte)
27. "Si parli ancor di trionfar," soli & chorus (B)
   . "Oh! stirpe gloriosa," recit (Orfeo/Clio)
28a, b. "Da sorgente rilucente un bel rio trae lo splendor," aria (Orfeo/Clio) (1st vers p1737)
   . "Dall'opre illustri dei genitor," recit (Calliope/Silvio)
29. "Sempre aspira," aria (Calliope)
   . "Delle dotti germane," recit (Apollo)
30. "Non tardate, Fauni ancora," aria & chorus (Apollo)
   . "Sia degli accelsi sposi," recit (Clio)
31. "Circonda in lor vite le grazie fiorite," aria (Clio)
   . "Con un spirto divoto," recit (Euterpe)
32. "Han mente eroica, han volto amabile," aria (Euterpe)
   . "Di virtù, di valor," recit (Apollo)
33. "Lunga seria d'altri eroi," solo & chorus (Apollo)

13.3   "Eternal source of light divine," serenata/ode: HWV74
1. "Eternal source," solo (A)
2. "The day that gave great Anna birth, who fix'd lasting peace on earth," solo & chorus (A)
3. "Let all the winged race with joy," solo & chorus (S)
4a. "Let flocks and herds their fear forget," soli & chorus (S, A)
4b. "Let flocks and herds their fear forget," solo (T)
5. "Let rolling, rolling, streams," duet & chorus (A, B)
6. "Kind Health descends on downy wings, angels conduct," duet (S, A)
7. "The day that gave great Anna birth," duet & chorus (S, A)
8. "Let Envy then conceal her head," solo & chorus (B)
9. "United nations shall combine," solo & d chorus (A)

13a.4   "Alexander's Feast," ode: HWV75
I: 1. "Overture"
   . " 'Twas at the royal feast," recit (T)
1. "Happy, happy, happy pair!," air (T)
2. "Happy, happy, happy pair!," chorus
   . "Timotheus, plac'd on high," recit (T)
3. "The song began from Jove," accompagnato (S)
4. "The list'ning crowd admire the lofty sound," chorus
5. "With ravish'd ears the monarch hears," air (S)
   . "The praise of Bacchus then the sweet musician sung," recit (B/T)
6. "Bacchus, ever fair and young," air & chorus (B)
   . "Sooth'd with the sound," recit (T)
7a, b. "He chose a mournful Muse," accompagnato (S/A)
8a, b. "He sung Darius, great and good," air (S/A)
9a, b. "With downcast looks the joyless victor sate," accompagnato (S/A)
10. "Behold Darius great and good," chorus
   . "The mighty master smil'd to see," recit (T/A) (2 vers)
11. "Softly sweet in Lydian measures soon he sooth'd the soul to pleasures," arioso (S) (3 vers)
12. "War, he sung, is toil and trouble, Honour but an empty bubble," air (S)
13. "The many rend the skies with loud applause," chorus
14. "The Prince, unable to conceal his pain"
II: 15. "Now strike the golden Lyre again!," accompagnato & chorus (T)
16a, b. "Revenge, revenge, revenge, Timotheus cries," air (B/A)
17. "Give the vengeance due to the valiant crew," accompagnato (T)
18. "The princes applaud with furious joy," air (T)
19. "Thais led the way," air & chorus (S)
20. "Thus, long ago, ere heaving Bellows learn'd to blow," accompagnato & chorus (T)
   . "At last divine Cecilia came," chorus
   . "Let old Timotheus yield the prize," recit (T, B)
21. "Let old Timotheus yield the prize," chorus
Add movts (p1742–51): . "Your voices tune, and raise them high," recit (A) (p1751)
   (22.) "Let's imitate her notes above," duet (S, A) (p1742–51)
   (23.) "Your voices tune, and raise them high," chorus (p1736)
Anhang: (20.) "Thus long ago ere heaving Bellows learn'd to blow," accompagnato (T)
   (21.) "Let old Timotheus yield the prize," duet (2B)
   . "Tune ev'ry string, your voices raise," recit (S)
   (22.) "Your voices tune and raise them high," air (S)

13a.5   "From Harmony, from heav'nly Harmony," ode: HWV76
        . "Ouverture" (= Concerto Grosso in D major, Op.6/5, HWV323)
        . "From Harmony, from heav'nly Harmony," recit (T)
        1. "Nature underneath a heap of jarring atoms lay," accompagnato (T)
        2. "From Harmony, from heav'nly Harmony," chorus
        3. "What passion cannot Music raise and quell!," air (S)
        4. "The Trumpet's loud clangor excites us to arms," solo & chorus (T)
        5. "La Marche"
        6a. "The soft complaining Flute," air (S)
        7. "Sharp Violins proclaim their jealous pangs," air (T)
        8. "But oh! what art can teach," air (S)
        9. "Orpheus could lead," air (S)
        10. "But bright Cecilia rais'd the wonder high'r," accompagnato (S)
        11. "As from the pow'r of sacred lays," chorus
      Anhang: 6b. "The soft complaining flute," air (A) (p1742)

14. CHURCH MUSIC

"7 hallesche Kirchenkantaten" (ca1700–3, lost):

14.1	*1. "Das gantze Haupt ist krank"*	*HWV229/1*
14.2	*2. "Es ist der alte Bund"*	*HWV229/2*
14.3	*3. "Fürwahr, er trug unsere Krankheit"*	*HWV229/3*
14.4	*4. "Thue Rechnung von deinem Hausshalten"*	*HWV229/4*
14.5	*5. "Victoria. Der Tod ist verschlungen"*	*HWV229/5*
14.6	*6. "Was werden wir essen"*	*HWV229/6*
14.7	*7. "Wer ist der, so von Edom kömmt"*	*HWV229/7*

Latin & Italian:

14.8	"Ah, che troppo ineguali," cantata for BVM (c1708; S, strings & cont)	HWV230
14.9	"Coelestis dum spirat aura," motet in D/G major (c1707; S, 2vn & cont)	HWV231
14.10	"Dixit Dominus Domino meo," in G minor (c1707, Psalm 109; S, A, ch, 2vn, 2va & cont)	HWV232
14.11	"Donna, che in ciel," cantata (c1707; S, ch, 2vn, va & cont, for anniv of Rome's earhquake)..........	HWV233
14.12	*Il pianto di Maria: "Giunta l'ora fatal," cantata (c1709; S, strings & cont, ?spur)*	*HWV234*
14.13	"Haec est Regina virginum," antiphon (c1707; S, strings & org)	HWV235
14.14	"Laudate pueri Dominum," in F major (c1703–6, Psalm 112; S, 2vn & cont)	HWV236
14.15	"Laudate pueri Dominum," in D major (c1707, Psalm 112; S, ch, 2ob, 2vn, 2va & cont)	HWV237
14.16	"Nisi Dominus" (Gloria patri), in G major (c1707, Psalm 126; A, T, B, d ch, strings & cont)	HWV238
14.17	"O qualis de coelo sonus," motet in G major (c1707; S, 2vn & cont)	HWV239
14.18	"Saeviat tellus inter rigores," motet in D major (c1707; S, 2ob, strings & cont)	HWV240
14.19	"Salve Regina," antiphon in G minor (c1707, Vehringen; S, 2vn, vc & org)	HWV241
14.20	"Silete venti," motet in B-flat major (ca1724; S, 2ob, 2bn, strings & cont)	HWV242
14.21	*"Te decus virginum," antiphon (c1707–8; A, strings & cont, music lost)*	*HWV243*
14.22	"Kyrie eleison" (ca1740; S, A, T, B, strings & cont)	HWV244
14.23	"Gloria in excelsis Deo" (ca1740; 5–6vv, ob, tromba, 2vn, 2va, org & cont)	HWV245

"Chandos" Anthems (vv, ch, insts & cont, for Duke of Chandos):

14.24	1. "O be joyful in the Lord" (ca1717, Psalm 100, arr from: Utrecht Jubilate, HWV279)	HWV246
14.25	2. "In the Lord put I my trust" (ca1717, Psalm 9)	HWV247
14.26	3. "Have mercy upon me, O God" (ca1717, Psalm 51)	HWV248
14.27	4. "O sing unto the Lord a new song" (c1714, Psalm 96; 2nd vers ca1717, Psalm 96, 93)	HWV249a–b
14.28	5. "I will magnify Thee, O God" (ca1717, Ps 145,144; 2nd vers after 1718, Ps 145, 96, 89)....	HWV250a–b
14.29	6. "As pants the Hart" (c1714, Psalm 42; 2nd vers ca1717; 3rd after 1720; 4th ca1721).........	HWV251a–d
14.30	7. "My song shall be alway" (ca1717, Psalm 89)	HWV252
14.31	8. "O come let us sing unto the Lord" (ca1718, Psalm 95, 96, 97, 99, 103)	HWV253
14.32	9. "O praise the Lord with one consent" (ca1718, Psalm 117, 135, 148)......................................	HWV254
14.33	10. "The Lord is my Light" (ca1718, Psalm 27, 18, 20, 34, 28, 29, 30 & 45)	HWV255
14.34	11. "Let God arise" (ca1717, Psalm 68, 76; 2nd vers ca1720, Psalm 68)	HWV256a–b
14.35	*12. "O praise the Lord, ye angels of his" (c ?1723, Psalms 103, 115 & 145, ?spur)*	*HWV257*

Coronation Anthems (c1727; ch, insts & org, for George II):

14.36	1. "Zadok the priest" (Book of Kings)	HWV258
14.37	2. "Let thy hand be strengthened" (Psalm 89)	HWV259
14.38	3. "The King shall rejoice" (Psalm 21)...	HWV260
14.39	4. "My heart is inditing" (Psalm 45, Jesaja 49)	HWV261

Occasional anthems (vv, ch, insts & org):

14.40	"This is the day which the Lord has made," wedding (c1734, for Anne & William)	HWV262
14.41	"Sing unto God, ye kingdoms of the earth," wedding (c1736, Frederick & Augusta).......................	HWV263
14.42	"The ways of Zion do mourn," funeral (c1737, for Queen Caroline)	HWV264

15. CHAMBER CANTATAS (most ca1707–10 during Handel's Italian sojourn)

15.41 "Hendel, non può mia Musa" (c1708, Pamphilj; S & cont)..HWV117
15.42 "Ho fuggito Amore anch'io" (c after 1720; A & cont)...HWV118
15.43 "Echeggiate, festeggiate, Numi eterni" (Io languisco) (c1710; 3S, A, B, fl, 2ob, strings & cont) HWV119
15.44 "Irene, idolo mio" (c1707–9; S & cont; 2nd vers for A & cont after 1710) HWV120a–b
15.45 "L'aure grate, il fresco rio" (La Solitudine) (ca1721–3; A & cont, frag; 2nd vers ca1718)...........HWV121a–b
15.46 "La terra è liberata" (Apollo e Dafne) (c1706–9; S, B, fl, 2ob, bn, vn, va, strings & cont)................HWV122
15.47 "Languia di bocca lusinghiera" (c1707–9; S, ob, vn & cont, frag) HWV123
15.48 "Look down, harmonious Saint" (The Praise of Harmony) (ca1736, Hamilton; T, strings & cont) HWV124
15.49 "Lungi da me, pensier tiranno" (c1707–9; S & cont; 2nd vers for A & cont after 1710) HWV125a–b
15.50 "Lungi da voi, che siete poli" (c1708; S & cont; 2nd vers 1708; 3rd for A & cont after 1710) HWV126a–c
15.51 "Lungi dal mio bel Nume" (c1708; S & cont; 2nd vers for A & cont after 1710; 3rd ca1724–7) ..HWV127a–c
15.52 "Lungi n'andò Fileno" (c1708; S & cont)..HWV128
15.53 "Manca pur quanto sai" (c1708; S & cont) HWV129
15.54 "Mentre il tutto è in furore" (c1708; S & cont) HWV130
15.55 "Menzognere speranze" (c1707; S & cont) HWV131
15.56 "Mi palpita il cor" (c after 1710; S & cont, vers of HWV106; 2nd vers w/ ob; 3rd w/ fl; 4th w/ ob) HWV132a–d
15.57 "Ne' tuoi lumi, o bella Clori" (c1707; S & cont)..HWV133
15.58 "Nel dolce dell'oblio" (Pensieri notturni di Filli) (c1707–8; S, rec & cont) HWV134
15.59 "Nel dolce tempo" (c1708; S & cont; 2nd vers for A & cont after 1710)..................................HWV135
15.60 "Nell'africane selve" (c1708; B & cont; 2nd vers for B & cont after 1710) HWV136a–b
15.61 "Nella stagion che di viole e rose" (c1707; S & cont)..HWV137
15.62 "Nice, che fa? che pensa?" (c1707–9; S & cont) HWV138
15.63 "Ninfe e pastori" (c1707–9; S & cont; 2nd vers for A & cont after 1710; 3rd: S & different acc). HWV139a–c
15.64 "Nò se emenderà jamás" (Cantata spagnuola) (c1707; S, gui & cont) HWV140
15.65 "Non sospirar, non piangere" (c1707; S & cont) HWV141
15.66 "Notte placida e cheta" (c1707–8; S, 2vn & cont)..HWV142
15.67 "Oh come chiare e belle" (Olinto pastore, Tebro fiume, Gloria) (c1708; 2S, A, tpt, strings & cont) ..HWV143
15.68 "O lucenti, o sereni occhi" (c1707–9; S & cont) HWV144
15.69 "Oh Numi eterni" (La Lucrezia) (c1706–7; S & cont) HWV145
15.70 "Occhi miei, che faceste?" (c1707–8; S & cont) HWV146
15.71 "Partì l'idolo mio" (c after 1710; S & cont) HWV147
15.72 "Poichè giuraro Amore" (c1707; S & cont) HWV148
15.73 "Qual sento io non conosciuto" (c1706–7; S & cont) HWV149
15.74 "Qual tu riveggio, oh Dio" (Ero e Leandro) (c1707, ?Ottoboni; S, 2ob, strings & cont) HWV150
15.75 "Qualor crudele, sì, mia vaga Dori" (c after 1710; A & cont) HWV151
15.76 "Qualor l'egre pupille" (c1707; S & cont) HWV152
15.77 "Quando sperasti, o core" (c1708; S & cont) HWV153
15.78 "Quel fior che all'alba ride" (ca1738–40; S & cont; see duet HWV192 & trio HWV200)..................HWV154
15.79 "Sans y penser," chanson (c1707; S & cont) HWV155
15.80 "Sarai contenta un dì" (c1706–7; S & cont) HWV156
15.81 "Sarei troppo felice" (c1707, Pamphilj; S & cont) HWV157
15.82 "Se pari è la tua fè" (c1708; S & cont; 2nd vers after 1710; 3rd vers ca1724–7) HWV158a–c
15.83 "Se per fatal destino" (c1707; S & cont) HWV159
15.84 "Sei pur bella, pur vezzosa" (La bianca Rosa) (c1707; S & cont; 2nd & 3rd vers ca1724–30) ..HWV160a–c
15.85 "Sento là che ristretto" (c1708–9; S & cont; 2nd vers for A & cont 1708; 3rd vers ca1717–20) . HWV161a–c
15.86 "Siete rose ruggiadose" (ca1711–2; A & cont) HWV162
15.87 "Solitudini care, amata libertà" (c after 1710; S & cont) HWV163
15.88 "Son gelsomino" (Il gelsomino) (ca1720–7, Rolli; S & cont; 2nd vers for A & cont after 1717–8) HWV164a–b
15.89 "Spande ancor al mio dispetto" (c1707–8; B, 2vn & cont) HWV165
15.90 "Splenda l'alba in oriente" (ca1711–2; A, 2fl, ob, strings & cont)..HWV166
15.91 "Stanco di più soffrire" (c1707–8; A & cont; 2nd vers for S & cont 1708) HWV167
15.92 "Stelle, perfide stelle" (Partenza di G. B.) (c1707; S & cont) HWV168
15.93 "Torna il core al suo diletto" (c1707–8; S & cont) HWV169
15.94 "Tra le fiamme" (Il consiglio) (c1707–8, Pamphilj; S, 2rec, 2vn, va da gamba & cont)....................HWV170
15.95 "Tu fedel? tu costante?" (c1706–7; S, 2vn & cont) HWV171
15.96 "Udite il mio consiglio" (c1706–7; S & cont) HWV172
15.97 "Un alma innamorata" (c1707; S, vn & cont) HWV173
15.98 "Un sospir a chi si muore" (c1707; S & cont) HWV174
15.99 "Vedendo Amor" (c1707–8; A & cont) HWV175
15.100 "Venne voglia ad Amore" (Amore uccellatore) (c1707–8; A & cont) HWV176
15.101 "Zeffiretto, arresta il volo" (c1707–9; S & cont) HWV177

Duets:

15.102 "A mirarvi io son intento" (c1710–2, ?Mauro; S, A & cont) HWV178
15.103 "Ahi, nelle sorti umane" (c1745; 2S & cont) HWV179
15.104 "Amor, gioie mi porge" (c1707–9; 2S & cont) HWV180
15.105 "Beato in ver chi può" (c1742, after Horace: Beatus ille; S, A & cont) HWV181
15.106 "Caro autor di mia doglia" (ca1707; S, T & cont; 2nd vers for 2A & cont ca1740–3) HWV182a–b
15.107 "Caro autor di mia doglia" (ca1710–2; 2S & cont) HWV183
15.108 "Che vai pensando, folle pensier" (c1707–9, ?Mauro; S, B & cont) HWV184
15.109 "Conservate, raddoppiate" (c1710–2, ?Mauro; S, A & cont) HWV185
15.110 "Fronda leggiera e mobile" (ca1740–5; S, A & cont) HWV186
15.111 "Giù nei Tartarei regni" (ca1707; S, B & cont) HWV187
15.112 "Langue, geme e sospira" (ca1722–4, Totis; S, A & cont)..HWV188

16. SONGS & ARIAS

"9 German Arias" (c1724–7, Brockes from: Irdisches Vergnügen in Gott; S, 1 instr obbl & cont):

Italian arias:

"24 English Songs" (S & cont):

. Version w/ different text: "Molly Mogg": "Says my uncle I pray you discover"

16.42	16. "Phillis be kind and hear" (ca1730, Paratt)	HWV228/16
16.43	17. "Phillis Advised": "Phyllis the lovely, turn to your swain" (ca1739)	HWV228/17
16.44	18. "A Song for Volunteers of London": "Stand round, my brave boys" (p1745)	HWV228/18
16.45	19. "The faithful Maid" (Melancholy Nymph): " 'Twas when the seas were roaring" (ca1725, Gay)	HWV228/19
16.46	20. "Matchless Clarinda": "When I survey Clarinda's charms" (ca1725):	HWV228/20
	. Version w/ different text: "The Rapture": "Venus now leaves her Paphian dwelling"	
16.47	21. "The Death of the Stag": "When Phoebus the tops of the Hills does adorn" (ca1740)	HWV228/21
16.48	22. "Who to win a Woman's favour" (ca1746)	HWV228/22
16.49	23. "An Answer to Collin's Complaint": "Ye winds to whom Collin complains" (ca1716)	HWV228/23
16.50	24. "The 'Je ne sa quoi' ": "Yes, I'm in love" (ca1740, Whitehead)	HWV228/24

17. MISC WORKS

17.1	"6 Songs": 1. "Son d'Egitto"
17.2	2. "Aure, più non bacciate"
17.3	3. "Porta la braccia al seno"
17.4	4. "Gran guerrier di tua virtù"
17.5	5. "Quanto dolci, quanto cari"
17.6	6. "Non posso dir di più"
17.7	"Di godere la speranza" (p ca1719)
17.8	"È troppo bella, troppo amorosa" (La bella pastorella) (from: Ho fuggito amore)
17.9	"Airs François de G. F. Hendel" (ca1707–9): 1. "Sans y penser," chanson (= HWV155)
17.10	2. "S'il ne falloit que bien aimer," recit
17.11	3. "Petite fleur brunette," air
17.12	4. "Vous, qui m'aviez procuré une amour eternelle," recit
17.13	5. "Nos plaisirs seront peu durables," air
17.14	6. "Vous ne scauriez-flatter ma peine," recit
17.15	7. "Non, je ne puis plus souffrir," air
17.16	"2 Songs" (autograph sold at Sotheby in 1954): 1. "Sans y penser," chanson (= HWV155)
17.17	2. "Quand on suit l'amoureuse loix," chanson
17.18	"Der Mund spricht zwar gezwungen Nein" (vers of aria from: Almira, HWV1)
17.19	"Dizente mis oyos"

* * * * *

HWV = Bernd Baselt: "Thematisch-systematisches Verzeichnis." Händel-Handbuch. Band 1–4, VEB Deutscher Verlag für Musik. Leipzig, 1986.
A = Anhang (Appendix) in Baselt's catalog.

1. STAGE WORKS

Operas:

1.1	"Acide e Galatea," 1 act festa teatrale (c1762, Migliavacca, inc; 2nd vers 1773)	HobXXVIII/1
1.2	"La canterina," 2 act intermezo (c1766)	HobXXVIII/2
1.3	"Lo speziale" (Der Apotheker), 3 act dramma giocoso (c1768, Goldoni)	HobXXVIII/3
1.4	"Le pescatrici," 3 act dramma giocoso (c1769, Goldoni)	HobXXVIII/4
1.5	"L'infedeltà delusa," 2 act burletta (c1773, Coltellini)	HobXXVIII/5
1.6	"L'incontro improvviso," 3 act dramma giocoso (c1775, Friberth)	HobXXVIII/6
1.7	"Il mondo della luna," 3 act dramma giocoso (c1777, after Goldoni's Lustspiel)	HobXXVIII/7
1.8	"La vera costanza," 3 act dramma giocoso (c by 1779, Travaglia after Puttini, partly lost)	HobXXVIII/8
1.9	"Laurette," 3 act comedia (c1791, in French, arr from: La vera Costanza, HobXXVIII/8)	HobXXVIII/8a
1.10	"L'isola disabitata," 2 part azione teatrale (c1779, Metastasio)	HobXXVIII/9
1.11	"La fedeltà premiata," 3 act dramma giocoso (c1780, after Lorenzi: l'infedeltà fedele)	HobXXVIII/10
1.12	"Orlando paladino," 3 act dramma eroicomico (c1782, Porta)	HobXXVIII/11
1.13	"Armida," 3 act dramma eroico (c1783, Durandi)	HobXXVIII/12
1.14	"L'anima del filosofo" (Orfeo ed Euridice), 4 act dramma per musica (c1791, Badini)	HobXXVIII/13

Marionette operas:

1.15	"Philemon und Baucis," 1 act (c1773, Pfeffel)	HobXXIXa/1
1.16	*Vorspiel to: Philemon und Baucis, HobXXiXa/1 (music lost)*	*HobXXIXa/1a*
1.17	*"Hexenschabbas" (c1773, lost)*	*HobXXIXa/2*
1.18	*"Didone abbandonata" (Dido) (c1776, Bader, music lost)*	*HobXXIXa/3*
1.19	*"Opéra comique vom abgebrannten Haus" (ca ?1773–9, lost)*	*HobXXIXa/4*
1.20	*"Genovevens vierter Theil" (c1777, Pauersbach, music lost)*	*HobXXIXa/5*

Singspiels:

1.21	*"Der krumme Teufel" (c ?1751, Kurz-Bernadon, music lost)*	*HobXXIXb/1a*
1.22	*"Der neue krumme Teufel" (ca ?1758, Kurz-Bernadon, music lost)*	*HobXXIXb/1b*
1.23	"Philemon und Baucis" (after marionette opera, HobXXIXa/1)	HobXXIXb/2
1.24	*"Die bestrafte Rachbegierde," 3 acts (c1779, Bader, music lost)*	*HobXXIXb/3*
1.25	"Die Feuerbrunst," 2 acts (c ?1775–8)	HobXXIXb/A
1.26	*"Le glorieux" (Der Grosssprecher) (c1778–9, lost)*	*HobXXIXb/B*
1.27	*"Die Hochzeit auf der Alm" (c1768, spur: c by Michael Haydn)*	*HobXXIXb/C*
1.28	*"L'isola di Calypso abbandonata" (c1783, spur: c by Luigi Bologna)*	*HobXXIXb/D*

Incid music:

1.29	"Comedia la Marchesa Ne(s)pola" (c1762, inc)	HobXXX/1
1.30	*"Die Feuersbrunst" (c1774, ?Grossmann, music lost)*	*HobXXX/2*
1.31	*"Der Zerstreute" (c1774, after Regnard: Le distrait, music lost; used in: Sym No.60)*	*HobXXX/3*
1.32	(Unknown comedy) (c before 1793):	HobXXX/4
	1. "Fatal amour," accompagnato	
	2. "L'Objet, l'objet qui regna," aria	
	3. "Si jamais je prends un époux, je veux que l'amour me le donne," chanson	
1.33	"Alfred oder der patriotische König" (c1796, Cowmeadow):	HobXXX/5
1.34	1. "Triumph, Triumph, Triumph dir Haldane," chorus (Dänen)	HobXXX/5a
1.35	2. "Ausgesandt vom Strahlenthrone," aria (Schutzgeistes)	HobXXX/5b
1.36	3. "Der Morgen graut, es ruft der Hahn," duet (Alfred, Odun)	HobXXX/5c
1.37	*"King Lear" (c by 1806, Shakespeare, ?spur/lost; see extant: Ouvertüre, HobIa/9)*	*HobXXX/A*
1.38	*"Hamlet" (ca ?1774–6, Shakespeare, ?spur/lost)*	*HobXXX/B*
1.39	*"Götz von Berlichigen" (c by ?1776, Goethe, ?spur/lost)*	*HobXXX/C*
1.40	*"Soliman II" (ca ?1777, after Favart: Les trois Sultanes, ?spur/lost)*	*HobXXX/D*

Pasticcios:

1.41	"La Circe ossia L'isola incantata," dramma (p1789, arr from Naumann: Ipocondriaco):	HobXXXII/1
	. "Son due ore che giro," accompagnato	
	. "Son pietosa, son bonina," aria (Lindora)	
	. "Levatevi presto," trio (Teodora, Brunoro, Corrado)	
1.42	*"Der Freybrief," 2 act Singspiel (p1788, 1797, music lost)*	*HobXXXII/2*
1.43	"Allesandro il Grande," 3 act opera seria (p1790 or later; arr Schellinger)	HobXXXII/3
1.44	*"Der Äpfeldieb," 1 act Singspiel (p1791; arr Bretzner, music lost)*	*HobXXXII/4*

1a. SELECTIONS FROM STAGE WORKS

1a.1	"Acide e Galatea," opera:	HobXXVIII/1
	extant: 1. "La beltà che m'innamore," aira (Acide)	
	2. "Perchè stupisci tanto," aria (Glauce)	
	3. "Se men gentile l'aspetto ostento," aria (Polyfemo)	
	4. "Misero! che ascolto," accompagnato (Acide)	

 5. "Tergi vezzosi rai," aria (Tetide)
 6. "Ah vedrai, bell'idol mio," quartet (Galatea, Glauce, Tetide, Acide)
Alternate vers: 7. "Ouvertüre" (= Hobla/5)
 8. *"Se nol turbasse crudel timor," aria (Galatea) (frag)*
 9. "Il caro tuo tesoro," accompagnato (Glauce)
 10. "Tergi i vezzosi rai," aria (Nettuno)

1a.2   "La canterina," opera: HobXXVIII/2
 I: 1. "Che visino delicato," aria & rect (Apollonia, Gasperina, Don Ettore)
     2. "Che mai far deggio?," accompagnato (Don Pelagio)
     3. "Io sposar l'empio tiranno," aria (Don Pelagio)
     4. "Che mai far deggio?," accompagnato (Don Pelagio, Gasperina, Apollonia, Don Ettore)
     5. "Scellerata, mancatrice," quartet (Gasperina, Don Ettore, Apollonia, Don Pelagio)
 II: 6. "Signor mio l'afficio suo," aria (Don Pelagio)
     7. "Non v'è chi mi ajuta," aria (Gasperina)
     8. "O stelle, ajuto!," accompagnato, Don Pelagio, Gasperina, Don Ettore, Apollonia)
     9. "Apri pur, mia dea terrestre," chorus/quartet (Don Pelagio, Apollonia, Don Ettore, Gasparina)

1a.3   "Lo speziale" (Der Apotheker), opera: HobXXVIII/3
    . "Ouvertüre" (= Hobla/10)
 I: 1. "Tutto il giorno," aria (Mengone)
     2. "Questa è un'altra novità," aria (Sempronio)
     3. "Per quel che ha mal di stomaco," aria (Mengone)
     4. "Caro Volpino amabile," aria (Grilletta) (2 vers)
     5. "Amore nel mio petto," aria (Volpino)
     6. "Quanti son di questa polvere," finale/trio (Mengone, Grilletta, Sempronio)
 II: 7. "Un certo tutore in Francia vi fu," aria (Volpino)
     8. "Ragazzaccie, che senza cervello," aria (Sempronio)
     9. "A fatti tuoi bador tu puoi," aria (Grilletta)
     10. "Colla presenta scrittura privata," finale/quartet (Sempronio, Volpino, Mengone, Grilletta)
 III: . *(scene 1–3 & beginning of scene 4: music lost)*
     11. "Salamelica," aria (Volpino)
     . *(scene 5 & beginning of scene 6: music lost)*
     12. "Signor Sempronio," finale (Mengone, Grilletta, Volpino, Sempronio)

1a.4   "Le pescatrici," opera: HobXXVIII/4
 I: 1. "Tira, Tira viene, viene, viene," chorus
     2. "Tra tuoni, lampi e fulmini," aria (Burlotto)
     3. "So far la simplicetta," aria (Nerina)
     4. "Fra cetre e cembali ti sposerò," aria (Frisellino)
     5. "Voglio amar e vuò scherzare," cavatina (Lesbina)
     6. *"Voglio goder contente," aria (Eurilda) (frag)*
     7. *"detto, detto, detto e si va di tetto in tetto," aria (Mastricco) (frag)*
     8. *"Varca il mar di sponda in sponda," aria (Lindoro) (frag)*
     9. *"Mi ferisce, ferisce qui," aria (Lesbina) (frag)*
     10. "Bell' ombra gradita, bell' aura diletta," chorus
     11a. "Udite, or son tre lustri," accompagnato (Lindoro)
     11b. "Fiera stragge dell'indegno," tutti
     12. "Principessa a voi mi prostro," finale (Lesbina, Nerina, Burlotto, Frisellino)
 II: 13. "Ha gl'occhi brilanti che pajon diamanti," aria (Frisellino)
     14. "Vi cerca il fratello vi deve parlar," aria (Burlotto)
     15. "Son vecchio, son furbo," aria (Mastriccio)
     16a. "Chi vi par," accompagnato (Lesbina)
     16b. "Son Maestosa," aria (Lesbina)
     17. "Già si vede i vezzi e vanti," aria (Lesbina)
     18. *"Pescatori, Pescatrice," aria (Nerina) (frag)*
     19. "Burlottino, mio carino," finale (Lesbina, Nerina, Burlotto, Frisellino)
 III: 20. "Nume che al maro sovrano imperi," chorus
     21. "Questa mano e questa cuore," aria (Eurilda)
     22. "Favorisco la sua bella mano," quartet (Lesbina, Nerina, Frisellino, Burlotto)
     23. "Soavi zeffiri al mar c'invitano," chorus
     24. "Discendi amor pietoso," finale (Nerina, Lesbina, Burlotto, Frisellino)

1a.5   "L'infedeltà delusa," opera: HobXXVIII/5
    . "Sinfonia" (= Hobla/1)
 I: 1. "Bella sera ed aure grate," quartet (Vespina, Nencio, Filippo, Nanni)
     1a. "Ah Padre, che tale mi siete e m'amate" (Sandrina)
     2. "Quando viene far l'amore," aria (Filippo)
     3. "Che imbroglio è questo? Che vuoi che ti dica?," aria (Sandrina)
     4. "Come piglia si bene la mira," aria (Vespina)
     6. "Son disparato," duet (Nanni, Vespina)
     7. "Chi s'impiccia di moglie citadina," aria (Nencio)
     8. "O piglia questa. Infedel, cosi tradirmi?," finale (Vespina, Nanni, Nencio, Sandrina, Filippo)
 II: 9. "Ho un tumore in un ginocchio," aria (Vespina)
     10. "Tu, tu sposarti," aria (Filippo)

11. "Triche Vaine allegramente," aria (Vespina)
12. "Oh che gusto!," aria (Nencio)
13. "Ho tesa la rete, ho messo il zimbello," aria (Vespina)
14. "È la pompa un grand' imbroglio," aria (Sandrina)
15. "Nel mille settecento," finale

1a.6   "L'incontro improvviso," opera: HobXXVIII/6
       . "Sinfonia" (= HobIa/6)
   I: 1. "Che bevanda, che liquore," introduzione (Alle Calandri)
         2. "L'amore è un gran briccone," canzonetta (Osmin)
         3. "Castagno, castagna," aria (Calandro)
         4. "Noi pariamo Santarelli," aria (Calandro)
         5a. "Lo trovasti?," accompagnato (Rezia, Balkis, Dardane) (frag)
         5b. "Quanto affetto mi sorprende!," aria (Rezia)
         6. "Mi sembra un sogno che diletta," trio (Rezia, Balkis, Dardane)
         7a. "Indarno m'affanno di veder Osmin," accompagnato (Ali)
         7b. "Deh! se in ciel pietade avete," aria (Ali)
         8. "Castagno, castagna," duet (Calandro, Osmin)
         9. "Che sian i Calandri filosofi pazzi," aria (Osmin)
         10. "Siam femine buonine," aria (Balkis)
         11. "Sangue d'un ginoccio storto," finale (Osmin, Ali)
   II: 12. "Quivi in un seren gentile," canzonetta (Ali, Osmin)
         13. "Ho promesso oprar destrezza," aria (Dardane)
         14. "Non piangete, putte care, chè nissuna morirà," canzonetta (Rezia)
         15. "Or vicina a te mio cuore," aria (Rezia)
         16. "Il guerrier con armi, avvolto," aria (Ali)
         17. "Ad acquistar già volo," aria (Balkis)
         18. "Il Profeta Maometo non avea cervello netto," canzonetta (Calandro)
         19. "Senti, al buio pian, pianino," aria (Osmin)
         20. "Son quest' occhi un stral d'amore," duet (Ali, Rezia)
         21. "È in ordine la festa," finale (Balkis, Ali, Rezia, Calandro, Osmin, Dardane)
   III: 22. "S'ègli è vero, che dagli astri," canzonetta (Rezia)
         23. "Ecco un splendido banchetto," aria (Ali)
         24. "Straniero! Voi gia siete tutti scoperti," recit (Ufficiale)
         25. "Marcia"
         26. "Ah signor," accompagnato (Rezia, Ali, Sultan)
         27. "Or gli affanni son svaniti," finale/chorus

1a.7   "Il mondo della luna," opera: HobXXVIII/7
       . "Sinfonia"
   I: 1. "O Luna lucente" (Ecclitico, 4 Schüler)
         1bis. "Prendiamo fratelli" (4 Schüler)
         2. "Servitor, obbligato" (Buonafede, Schüler, Ecclitico)
         3a. "Intermezzo" I
         3b. "Ho veduto una ragazza," cavatina (Buonafede)
         3a. "Intermezzo" II
         3b. "Ho veduto un buon marito," cavatina (Buonafede)
         3a. "Intermezzo" III
         3b. "Ho veduto d'all amante," cavatina (Buonafede)
         4. "La ragazza con vecchione," aria (Buonafede)
         5. "Un poco di denaro," aria (Ecclitico)
         6. "Begli occhi vezzosi," aria (Ernesto) (2 vers)
         7. "Mi fanno ridere," aria (Cecco)
         8. "Ragion nell'alma siede," aria (Flamina)
         9. "Son fanciulla da marito," aria (Clarice)
         10. "Una donna come me," aria (Lisetta)
         11a. "Mondo mondaccio rio," accompagnato (Buonafede, Ecclitico)
         11b. "Vado, vado," finale (Ecclitico, Buonafede)
   II: 12. "Sinfonia"
         13. "Balletto"
         14. "Balletto"
         15. "Uomo felice," chorus
         16. "Voi lo sapete come son fatte," aria (Ecclitico)
         17. "Marcia" (= HobVIII/5)
         18. "Un avaro suda e pena suda e pena," aria (Cecco)
         19. "Qualche volte non fa male," aria (Ernesto)
         20. "Che Mondo amabile," aria (Buonefede)
         21. "Non aver di me sospetto," duet (Buonafede, Lisetta)
         22a. "Lei è mio," accompagnato (Lisetta, Cecco)
         22b. "Se lo commanda," aria (Lisetta)
         23. "Balletto"
         24. "Se la mia stella," aria (Flaminia)
         25. "Quanta gente che sospira," aria (Clarice)
         26. "Al comando tuo lunatico," finale
   III: 27. "Vorspiel" (= HobIa/12)

28. "Un certo ruscelletto," duet (Ecclitico, Clarice)
29. "Il Mondo della Luna," finale

1a.8   "La vera costanza," opera: HobXXVIII/8
. "Sinfonia" (= HobIa/15)
I: 1. "Che burasca," introduzione (Rosina, Masino, Baronessa, Lisetta, Ernesto)
        2. "Non s'inalza non stride sdegnosa," aria (Baronessa)
        3. "So che una bestia sei," aria (Masino)
        4. "Con un tenero sospiro," aria (Rosina)
        5. "Non sperate mi didisco," aria (Villotto)
        6. "Io son poverina, nè ricca nè bella," aria (Lisetta)
        7a. "Mira il Campo all'intorno de sen giace in riposo," accompagnato (Conte)
        7b. "Al trionfar," aria (Conte)
        8. "Ah che devenni stupida," finale
II: 9. "Masima filosofica," duet (Masino, Villotto)
        10. "Per pietà vezzosi rai," aria (Ernesto)
        11. "Va pettegola insolente comprendo il tuo disegno," couplet (Rosina, Baronessa)
        12a. "Misera, chi m'aiuta," accompagnato (Rosina)
        12b. "Dove fuggo, ove m'ascondo," aria (Rosina)
        13. "Gia la morte in mante nero," aria (Villotto)
        14a. "Mi quale ascolto oh Dei," accompagnato (Conte)
        14b. "Andantino"
        . "Or che torna il vago aprile," recit (Conte)
        14c. "Ma che miro? non e quello?," aria (Conte)
        15a. "Eccomi giunta al colmo," accompagnato (Rosina)
        15b. "Care spiagge, selve, addio," aria (Rosina)
        . "Caro figlio, partiamo," recit (Rosina)
        16. "Animo risoluto," finale
III: 17. "Rosina vezzosina," duet (Conte, Rosina)
        18. "Ben chè gema un alma oppressa," chorus
        A. "Que l'amour lui cause d'alarme"

1a.9   "Laurette," opera: HobXXVIII/8a
. "Ouvertüre"
I: 1. "Quel vacarme," introduzione (Laurette)
        2. "Oui Medemoiselle" (Le Bailli)
        3. "Une flamme parait" (Laurette)
        4. "Ou je crois encore l'entendre" (Laurette)
        5. "On peut rester sage" (Lisette)
        6. "Un peu devant l'aurore" (Comte)
        . "Pour voler aux Cambats"
        7. "Certes vous voulez rire" (Gervais)
        8. "C'est trop de peine prendre" (Gervais)
II: 9. "Objet de ma tendresse," duet (Comte, Laurette)
        10. "Ah, souffrez que je repète" (Comte)
        11. "Mon père pour la sagesse" (Baronne)
        12. "Laissez faire par adresse" (Thibaudin)
        13. "Juste Ciel, quel peine" (Laurette)
        . "Quelle asile et quelle terre"
        14. "Que venez vous donc faire," finale (Laurette)
III: 15. "Que l'amour lui cause d'alarme" (Gervais)
        16. "Je crois voir la mort en face" (Thibaudin)
        17. "A quelle extrémité" (Laurelle)
        . "Bois, rochers, triste retraite"
        18. "On m'a dit qu'en lieux" (Comte)
        . "Aux doux son d'une Musette"
        19. "Ah je sens un trouble extrème," finale (Comte)
        20. "Dans l'excès de la souffrance," tutti

1a.10   "L'isola disabitata," opera: HobXXVIII/9
. "Sinfonia" (= HobIa/13)
I: 1. "Qual contrasto non vince," accompagnato (Costanza, Silvia)
        2. "Se non piange un infelice," aria (Costanza)
        3. "Che ostinato dolor," accompagnato (Silvia)
        4. "Chi nel camin d'onore," aria (Enrico)
        5a. "Che fù mai quel ch'io vidi," accompagnato (Silvia)
        5b. "Fra un dolce deliro," aria (Silvia)
II: 6. "Ah presaga fù l'Alma di sue sventure," accompagnato (Gernando, Enrico)
        7. "Non turbar quand'io mi lagna," aria (Gernando)
        8. "Non s'irriti fra primi impeti il suo dolor," accompagnato (Enrico, Silvia)
        9. "Come il vapor s'accende," aria (Silvia)
        10. "Ah, che invan, ah, che invan per me pietoso," aria (Costanza)
        11. "Giacche da me lontana," accompagnato (Costanza)
        12. "Giacche il pietoso amico," arietta & recit (Gernando, Costanza, Enrico, Silvia)
        13. "Sono contente appieno," quartet (Costanza, Gernando, Silvia, Enrico)

1a.11   "La fedeltà premiata," opera: HobXXVIII/10
. "Sinfonia" (= Hobl/11)

    I: 1. "Bella Dea," introduzione (Nerina, Lindoro, Melibeo, Amaranta)
           2. "Già mi sembra di sentire," aria (Lindoro)
           3. "Per te m'accese amore," aria (Amaranta)
           4. "Salva, salva ajuto, ajuto," aria (Perrucchetto) (2 vers)
           5. "Mi dica il mio signore," aria (Melibeo)
           6. "Dove oh Dio, dove oh Dio rivolgo il piede," aria (Fileno)
           7. "È amore di natura," aria (Nerina)
           8. "Placidi ruscelletti," aria (Celia)
           9. "Miseri affetto miei," aria (Fileno)
          10. "Vanne, fuggi, traditore," aria (Amaranta)
          11. "Deh soccorri un infelice e di più," aria (Celia)
          12. "Coll' amoroso foco," aria (Perrucchetto)
          13. "Questi torti questi affronti," finale I (Amaranta, Lindoro, Melibeo)
    II: 14. "Non vi sdegnate mia signorina," aria (Lindoro)
          15. "Sappi che la bellezza," aria (Melibeo)
          16. "Se da' begli occhi tuoi," aria (Fileno)
          17. "Volgi pure ad altr'oggetto," aria (Nerina)
          18. "Più la belva nel bosco non freme," chorus (Cacciatori) (2 vers)
          19. "Di questo audace ferro," aria (Perrucchetto)
         20a. "Bastano, bastano i pianti," accompagnato (Fileno)
         20b. "Recida il ferro istesso," aria (Fileno)
         21a. "Ah come il core mi palpita nel seno," accompagnato (Celia)
         21b. "Ombra del caro bene," aria (Celia) (2 vers)
         22a. "Barbaro Conte," accompagnato (Amaranta)
         22b. "Dell' amor mio fedele," aria (Amaranta)
         23. "Quel silenzio, e quelli pianti," finale II (Fileno)
    III: 24. "Ah se tu vuoi, ch'io viva," duet (Celia, Filene)
         25. "Misero mei," accompagnato (Melibeo, Amaranta, Perrucchetto, Celia, Fileno, Lindoro, Diana)
         26. "Quanto più diletta e pace," chorus

1a.12   "Orlando paladino," opera: HobXXVIII/11
. "Sinfonia" (= Hobla/16)

    I: 1. "Il lavorar l'è pur la brutta cosa," introduzione (Eurilla, Licone, Rodomonte)
           2. "Ah se dire io vi potesse," aria (Eurilla)
           3. "Temerario," aria (Rodomonte)
           4. "Palpita ad ogni istante," aria (Angelica)
           5. "Auftritt" (insts)
           6. "A un mio accento a un guardo solo," aria (Alcina)
           7. "Parto, ma oh Dio! non posso," aria (Medoro)
           8. "La mia bella diceva di no," cavatina (Pasquale)
           9. "Ho viaggiato in Francia, in Spagna," aria (Pasquale)
        11a. "Angelica mio ben," accompagnato (Orlando)
        11b. "D'Angelica il nome," aria (Orlando)
         12. "Presto risponde in degno," finale I
    II: 13. "Mille lampi d'accese faville," aria (Rodomonte)
          14. "Delle ch'un infelice," aria (Medoro)
          15. "Vittoria, Vittoria," Auftritt & aria (Pasquale)
          16. "Quel tuo visetto amabile," duet (Eurilla, Pasquale)
          17. "Aure chete. Verdi allore," aria (Angelica)
         18a. "Fra queste selve," accompagnato (Angelica, Medoro)
         18b. "Qual contento," duet (Medoro, Angelica)
         19a. "Oime qual tetro ogetto," accompagnato (Orlando)
         19b. "Cosa vedo, cosa sento," aria (Orlando)
         20. "Ecco spiano," aria (Pasquale)
         21. "Nel solitario specchio," finale II
    III: 22. "Ombre in sepolte," aria (Caronte)
         23a. "Sogno, veglio," accompagnato (Orlando)
         23b. "Miei pensieri dove siete," aria (Orlando)
         24. "Combatimento"
         25a. "Implacabili Numi," accompagnato (Angelica)
         25b. "Dell' estreme sue voci dolenti," aria (Angelica)
         26. "Son confuso e stupe fatto," chorus
    Add sections: A. "A un mio accento a un guardia solo," aria (Alcina)
              B1. "In odio al mio bel Nume," recit (Medoro)
              B1. "Angelica mio ben, mio sol, mia vita," accompagnato (Orlando)
              B2. "D'Angelica il nome? Ma quando? Ma come?," aria (Orlando)
              C. "Disperata invan m'affanno," aria (Angelica)
              D. "Sinfonia"
              E. "Implacabili Numi," accompagnato (Angelica)
              F. "Fra tiranni i naqui al soglio"
         10bis. "Non partir mia bella face" (Fliehe nicht, o mein Geliebster), aria (Angelica)
         13bis. "Mille colpi in un baleno," aria (Rodomonte)
          14bis. "Che smania oh Dio che affanno," aria (Medoro)

19bis. "Voi di notte tenebrosa," aria (Orlando)

1a.13 "Armida," opera: HobXXVIII/12
. "Ouvertüre" (= Hobla/14)
I: 1. "Vado a pugnar contento," aria (Rinaldo)
2. "Se dal suo braccio oppresso," aria (Rinaldo)
3a. "Parti, Rinaldo," accompagnato (Armida)
3b. "Se pietade avete, o Numi," aria (Armida)
4. "Marcia"
5a. "Valorosi compagni," accompagnato (Ubaldo)
5b. "Dove son! Che miro intorno," aria (Ubaldo)
. "Qual turbamento ignoto," accompagnato (Ubaldo)
6. "Se tu seguir mi vuoi," aria (Zelmira)
7a. "Oh amico," accompagnato (Rinaldo, Armida)
7b. "Cara, sarò fedele," duet (Rinaldo, Armida)
II: 8. "Tu mi sprezzi, e mi derindi," aria (Zelmira)
9. "Ah si plachi il fiero Nume," aria (Clotarco)
10. "Teco lo guido al campo," aria (Idreno)
11a. "Armida," accompagnato (Rinaldo, Ubaldo, Armida)
11b. "Cara e vero," aria (Rinaldo)
12a. "Barbaro, e ardisci ancor," accompagnato (Armida)
12b. "Odio, furor, dispetto, dolor," aria (Armida)
13. "Prence amato in questo amplesso," aria (Ubaldo)
14. "Partirò, ma pensa ingrato," finale/trio (Armida, Rinaldo, Ubaldo)
III: 15. "Questa dunque e la selva?," accompagnato (Rinaldo)
16. "Torna pure al caro bene," aria (Zelmira)
. "Qual tumulto d'idee," accompagnato (Rinaldo)
. "Ah non ferir," accompagnato (Armida)
17. "Ah non ferir ... t'arresta ... Passami prima il core," aria (Armida)
. "Che inopportuno incontro," accompagnato (Rinaldo, Armida)
18. "Dei pietosi! In tal cimento," aria (Rinaldo)
19. "Astri che in ciel splendete," finale

1a.14 "L'anima del filosofo" (Orfeo ed Euridice), opera: HobXXVIII/13
. "Ouvertüre" (= Hobla/3)
I: 1a. "Sventurata che fo," accompagnato (Euridice)
1b. "Ferma, ferma il piede principessa," chorus (Euridice)
2a. "Che Chiedate da me," accompagnato (Euridice)
2b. "Filomena abbandonata," aria (Euridice)
. "Cieli! Soccorso! Aiuta," recit (2 Coriste, Euridice, Orfeo)
3a. "Rendete a questo seno," accompagnato (Orfeo)
3b. "Cara speme," aria (Orfeo)
. "O Prodigio, o stupor," recit (Corista, Euridice, Orfeo)
4. "O poter dell'armonica," chorus
. "Ah chi sa dirmi," recit (Creonte, Corista)
5. "Il pensier sta negli oggetti," aria (Creonte)
. "Grazie agli Dei," recit (Orfeo, Euridice, Creonte)
6. "Come il foco allo splendore," duet (Orfeo, Euridice)
II: 7. "Finchè circola il vigore, finchè sei nell'età bionda," chorus (Amorini)
. "Adorata consorte," recit (Orfeo, Euridice)
7bis. "Finchè circola il vigore," chorus (Amorini, Orfeo, Euridice)
. "Numi, che ascolto," accompagnato (Euridice, Orfeo)
. "Ecco Signor," recit (Corista, Euridice)
8a. "Dov'è," accompagnato (Euridice)
8b. "Del mio core il voto estremo," aria (Euridice)
. "Con Euridice," recit (Corista, Creonte)
9a. "Dov'è quell'alma audace," accompagnato (Orfeo)
9b. "In un mar d'acerbe pene," aria (Orfeo)
. "Euridice signor," recit (Corista, Creonte)
10. "Mai non fa inulto," aria (Creonte)
III: 11. "Ah sposa infelice," chorus (Virgini, Uomini) (2 vers)
. "Al ciele te ne voli, anima bella," recit (Orfeo, Creonte)
. "Che sarà mai d'Orfeo," recit (Creonte, Coriste)
12. "Chi spira e non spera d'amar e gioira," aria (Creonte)
. "Venerata Sibilla," recit (Orfeo, Genio)
13. "Al tuo seno fortunato," aria (Genio)
. "Costanza a me si chiede?," recit (Orfeo)
14. "La giustizia in cor regina," chorus
. "Dove me guide?," recit (Orfeo, Genio)
IV: 15. "Infelice ombre dolenti, cento lustri varcar dobbiamo," chorus
. "Che ascolto, oh Numi," recit (Orfeo, Genio)
16. "Urli or rendi disperati," chorus (Furie)
. "O Signor, che all'ombre inperi," recit (Orfeo)
17. "Trionfi oggi pieta ne compe inferni," chorus
. "O della Reggia mia," recit (Pluto, Orfeo, Genio)

18. "Balletto"
  . "Quai dolce e care note ascolto," recit (Orfeo, Genio)
19. "Son finite le tue pene," chorus
  . "Sovvengati la legge," recit (Genio, Euridice, Orfeo)
20a. "Perduto un altro volta," accompagnato (Orfeo)
20b. "Mi sento languire, morire mi sento," aria (Orfeo)
  . "Barbaro infido amore," recit (Orfeo)
21. "Vieni, vieni amato Orfeo," chorus (Baccanti)
  . "Perfido non turbati di più il mio afflitto core," recit (Orfeo, Baccante)
22. "Bevi, bevi in questa tazza," finale/chorus

2. SYMPHONIES

3. OVERTURES

3.8	"Sinfonia" (Overture), in F major (c1773, to marionette opera: Philemon und Baucis, HobXXIXa/1) Hobla/8
3.9	"Sinfonia" (Overture), in E-flat major (c?, to incid music: King Lear, HobXXX/A) Hobla/9
3.10	"Sinfonia" (Overture), in G major (c before 1782, to opera: "Lo speziale, HobXXVIII/3) Hobla/10
3.11	"Sinfonia" (Overture), in G major (c1780, to opera: La fedeltà premiata, HobXXVIII/10) Hobla/11
3.12	"Sinfonia" (Overture), in G minor (c1777, to Act III of opera: Il mondo della luna, HobXXVIII/7) Hobla/12
3.13	"Sinfonia" (Overture), in G minor (c1779, to opera: L'isola disabitata, HobXXVIII/9) Hobla/13
3.14	"Sinfonia" (Overture), in G minor (c1783, to opera: Armida, HobXXVIII/12) Hobla/14
3.15	"Sinfonia" (Overture), in B-flat major (c1777, to opera: La vera costanza, HobXXVIII/8) Hobla/15
3.16	"Sinfonia" (Overture), in G minor (c1782, to opera: Orlando paladino, HobXXVIII/11) Hobla/16

4. DIVERTIMENTOS (orch/instr ens)

4.1	Divertimento in G major (c before 1766; fl, ob, 2vn, vc & bass) HobII/1
4.2	Divertimento in G major (c by 1754; 2vn, 2va & bass) HobII/2
4.3	*Divertimento in G major (c by 1766, lost) HobII/3*
4.4	*Divertimento in F major (ca ?1765; 2cl, bn & 2hn, lost) HobII/4*
4.5	*Divertimento in F major (ca ?1765; 2cl, 2hn, lost) HobII/5*
	Divertimento (String Quartet No.0), in E-flat major (c1765; 2vn, va & bass; see: String Quartets) HobII/6
4.6	Divertimento in C major (c by 1765; 2ob, 2bn & 2hn) HobII/7
4.7	Divertimento in B minor (c1767; 2fl, 2hn, 2vn & bass) HobII/8
4.8	Divertimento in G major (c by 1764; 2ob, 2hn, 2vn, 2va & bass) HobII/9
4.9	*Divertimento in D major, "Der verliebte Schulmeister" (c before 1766, lost) HobII/10*
4.10	Divertimento in C major, "Mann und Weib" / "Birthday" (c by 1765; fl, ob, 2vn, vc & bass) HobII/11
4.11	*Divertimento in E-flat major (c?, lost) HobII/12*
4.12	*Divertimento in D major (c?, lost) HobII/13*
4.13	Divertimento in C major (c by 1761; 2cl, 2hn & ?2insts) HobII/14
4.14	Divertimento in F major (c1760; 2ob, 2bn & 2hn) HobII/15
4.15	Divertimento in F major (c before 1760; 2vn, 2 Eng hn, 2bn & 2hn) HobII/16
4.16	Divertimento in C major (c before 1766; 2ob/cl, 2hn, 2vn, 2va & bass) HobII/17
4.17	*"Notturno" (Divertimento), in D major (c?, spur: c by ?Vanhal, lost) HobII/18*
4.18	*"Notturno" (Divertimento), in G major (c?, spur: c by ?Vanhal, lost) HobII/19*
4.19	Divertimento in F major (c before 1763; 2ob, 2hn, 2vn, 2va & bass) HobII/20
4.20	*Divertimento in A major (ca by ?1765, lost) HobII/20bis*
4.21	Divertimento in E-flat major, "Eine Abendmusik" (c by 1763; 2hn, 2vn, va & bass) HobII/21
4.22	Divertimento in D major (c before 1765; 2hn, 2vn, va & bass) HobII/22
4.23	Divertimento in F major (c after ?1775; 2ob, 2bn & 2hn) HobII/23
4.24	Divertimento (5 Var on a minuet), in E-flat major (c before 1775; 11 insts, ?movt of larger work) HobII/24
4.25	*"Minuet with variations," in D major (c?, lost) HobII/24a*
4.26	*"Minuet with variations," in A major (c?, lost) HobII/24b*

"8 Notturni" (c before 1790; 2cl, 2hn, 2 lyre organizate, 2va & bass):

4.27	Notturno (Divertimento) No.1 in C major HobII/25
4.28	Notturno (Divertimento) No.2 in F major HobII/26
4.29	Notturno (Divertimento) No.3 in G major HobII/27
4.30	Notturno (Divertimento) No.4 in F major HobII/28
4.31	Notturno (Divertimento) No.5 in C major HobII/29
4.32	Notturno (Divertimento) No.6 in G maj / C major HobII/30
4.33	Notturno (Divertimento) No.7 in C major HobII/31
4.34	Notturno (Divertimento) No.8 in C major HobII/32

"6 Scherzandi" (c by 1765; fl, 2ob, 2hn, 2vn & bass):

4.35	Scherzando (Divertimento) No.1 in F major HobII/33
4.36	Scherzando (Divertimento) No.2 in C major HobII/34
4.37	Scherzando (Divertimento) No.3 in D major HobII/35
4.38	Scherzando (Divertimento) No.4 in G major HobII/36
4.39	Scherzando (Divertimento) No.5 in E major HobII/37
4.40	Scherzando (Divertimento) No.6 in A major HobII/38

Other:

4.41	*"Sextet" (Divertimento), in E-flat major, "Echo" (c ?1761; 2vn, bass & 2vn & bass, ?spur)..................... HobII/39*
4.42	*"Sextet" (Divertimento), in E-flat major (c before 1781; ob, bn, hn, vn, va & bass, ?spur) HobII/40*
4.43	*"Fieldparthie" (Divertimento) in E-flat major (c?; 2ob, 2cl, 2bn & 2hn/2tpt, ?spur) HobII/41*
4.44	*"Fieldparthie" (Divertimento), in B-flat major (c?; 2ob, 2cl, 2bn & 2hn/2tpt, ?spur) HobII/42*
4.45	*"Fieldparthie" (Divertimento), in B-flat major (c?; 2ob, 2cl, 2bn & 2hn/2tpt, ?spur) HobII/43*
4.46	*"Fieldparthie" (Divertimento), in F major c?; 2ob, 2bn obbl, bn ripieno, serpent & 2hn, ?spur) HobII/44*
4.47	*"Fieldparthie" (Divertimento), in F major (c?; 2ob, 2bn obbl, bn ripieno, serpent & 2hn, ?spur) HobII/45*
4.48	*"Fieldparthie" (Divertimento), in B-flat major, "St. Anthony" (c?; 2ob, 2bn obbl, bn ripieno, serpent, 2hn,*
	?spur): HobII/46
	quoted: "Chorale St. Antoni" (the old Austrian pilgrim's song)
4.49	*"Toy Symphony," in C major/ G major (c by 1786; 2vn, bass & 7 children insts, ?spur; various vers) HobII/47*

Attributed to Haydn (various degrees of possible authenticity):

4.50	"Notturno," in C major (fl, 2hn, 2vn, va & bass)	HobII/C1
4.51	"Quintetto," in C major (2vn, 2va & bass)	HobII/C2
4.52	"Cassation," in C major (2ob, 2bn, 2hn, 2vn & bass)	HobII/C3
4.53	"Concertino," in C major (2hn, 2vn, va & bass)	HobII/C4
4.54	"Divertimento," in C major (2vn, va, vc & bass)	HobII/C5
4.55	"Cassatio," in C major (2ob, 2hn, 2vn, 2va & bass)	HobII/C6
4.56	"Quintetto," in C major (2vn, 2vc, bass & 2hn ad lib)	HobII/C7
4.57	"Quartetto," in C major (fl, vn, va & vc)	HobII/C8
4.58	"Quintetto Concertant," in C major (2vn, 2va & bass)	HobII/C9
4.59	"Cassatio," in C major (strings & 2tpt ad lib)	HobII/C10
4.60	"Divertimento," in C major (2vn, va & cont)	HobII/C11
4.61	"Allegro molto," in C major (2ob, 2bn & 2hn)	HobII/C12
4.62	"Cassatio," in D major (2hn, vn, va & bass)	HobII/D1
4.63	"Cassatio," in D major (2hn, vn, va & vc)	HobII/D2
4.64	"Serenade," in D major (2fl, 2hn, 2vn, va & bass)	HobII/D3
4.65	"Cassatio," in D major (fl, 2hn, vn, va & bass)	HobII/D4
4.66	"Quartetto," in D major (2fl & 2hn)	HobII/D5
4.67	"Divertimento," in D major (fl, vn concertante, va & bass, c by ?Hoffmann)	HobII/D6
4.68	"Cassatio," in D major (2fl, 2hn, 2va & bass)	HobII/D7
4.69	"Divertimento," in D major (fl/2fl, 2vn & va)	HobII/D8
4.70	"Quartetto concertante," in D major (fl, vn, va & bass)	HobII/D9
4.71	"Quartetto concertante," in D major (fl, vn, va & bass)	HobII/D10
4.72	"Quartetto concertante," in D major (fl, vn, va & bass)	HobII/D11
4.73	"Quintetto," in D major (2vn, 2va, bass & 2hn ad lib)	HobII/D12
4.74	"Concertino," in D major (ob, 2hn, 2vn, va, vc & bass)	HobII/D13
4.75	"Concertino," in D major (ob, 2hn, 2vn, va, vc obbl & bass)	HobII/D14
4.76	"Concertino," in D major (fl, 2hn, 2vn, va, vc & bass)	HobII/D15
4.77	"Quartetto," in D major (fl, vn, va & vc)	HobII/D16
4.78	"Cassation," in D major (3/4 insts)	HobII/D17
4.79	"Quintette," in D major (2hn, 2vn & 2va)	HobII/D18
4.80	"Quintette," in D major (ob, 2vn, va & bass)	HobII/D19
4.81	"Nocturno," in D major (2hn, 2vn, 2va & vc)	HobII/D20
4.82	"Cassatio," in D major (2vn, 2va & cont)	HobII/D21
4.83	"Cassatio," in D major (4hn, vn, va & bass)	HobII/D22
4.84	"Divertimento," in D major (2ob, 2bn & 2hn)	HobII/D23
4.85	"Cassation," in E-flat major (va solo, 2 Eng hn, hn, tpt & bass)	HobII/Es1
4.86	"Cassation," in E-flat major (va solo, 2 Eng hn, hn, tpt & cont)	HobII/Es2
4.87	"Cassation," in E-flat major (ob, Eng hn, 2hn, vn, va & bass)	HobII/Es3
4.88	"Sinfonia o Cassatione," in E-flat major (2fl, 2hn, 2vn, 2va & bass)	HobII/Es4
4.89	"Notturno," in E-flat major (2hn, 2vn, 2va & bass)	HobII/Es5
4.90	"Serenade," in E-flat major (2hn, 2vn, va & bass)	HobII/Es6
4.91	"Cassation," in E-flat major (Eng hn, 2hn, bn, 2va & bass)	HobII/Es7
4.92	"Notturno," in E-flat major (2vn, 2va & vc)	HobII/Es8
4.93	"Quintetto," in E-flat major (2hn, vn, va & bass)	HobII/Es9
4.94	"Quintetto," in E-flat major (2hn, 2vn, 2va & bass)	HobII/Es10
4.95	"Concertante," in E-flat major (2cl, bn, 2hn, 2vn, va & bass)	HobII/Es11
4.96	"Parthia," in E-flat major (2ob, 2cl, 2bn & 2hn)	HobII/Es12
4.97	"Allegro," in E-flat major (2ob, 2cl, 2bn & 2hn)	HobII/Es13
4.98	"Parthia," in E-flat major (2ob, 2cl, 2bn & 2hn)	HobII/Es14
4.99	"Quartetto," in E-flat major (fl, vn, va & vc)	HobII/Es15
4.100	"Parthia," in E-flat major (2cl, 2ob, 2bn & 2hn)	HobII/Es16
4.101	"Suite a 6," in E-flat major (2cl, 2bn & 2hn)	HobII/Es17
4.102	"Divertimento," in F major (2hn, 2vn, va & bass)	HobII/F1
4.103	"Cassatio," in F major (ob, bn, 2hn, vn, va & bass)	HobII/F2
4.104	"Cassatio," in F major (2hn, 2vn, 2va & bass)	HobII/F3
4.105	"Cassatio," in F major (2hn, vn, va & bass)	HobII/F4
4.106	"Quintetto," in F major (2hn, vn, va & bass)	HobII/F5
4.107	"Concertino," in F major (2hn, 2vn, va & bass)	HobII/F6
4.108	"Parthia," in F major (2ob, 2cl, 2bn & 2hn, c by ?Wranitzky)	HobII/F7
4.109	"Synfonia," in F major (2ob, 2hn, 2vn, va & bass)	HobII/F8
4.110	"Concertante," in F major (ob, bn, hn, 2vn, va, vc & violone)	HobII/F9
4.111	"Quartetto," in F major (3vn & vc, c by ?Ferandini)	HobII/F10
4.112	"Serenata," in F major (2hn, 2vn, 2va & bass)	HobII/F11
4.113	"Divertimento," in F major (2ob, bn & 2hn)	HobII/F12
4.114	"Quintetto," in F minor (2vn, 2va, bass & 2hn ad lib)	HobII/f1
4.115	"Cassatio," in G major (2ob, 2hn, 2vn, 2va & bass)	HobII/G1
4.116	"Cassatio," in G major (2hn, 2vn, 2va & bass)	HobII/G2
4.117	"Divertimento," in G major (fl, 2hn, 2vn, 2va & bass, vers of 5th, 3rd & 2nd movt of G2)	HobII/G2bis
4.118	"Parthia," in G major (2vn, 2va & bass)	HobII/G3
4.119	"Quartetto," in G major (fl, vn, va & bass)	HobII/G4
4.120	"Quintetto," in G major (2vn, 2va, bass & 2hn ad lib)	HobII/G5
4.121	"Quartetto Concertant," in G major (fl, vn, va & vc)	HobII/G6
4.122	"Cassatio," in G major (2vn, va, vc & bass)	HobII/G7

5. MARCHES (orch/instr ens)

6. DANCES (orch/instr ens)

6.118	No.6 in D major
6.119	No.7 in E-flat major
6.120	No.8 in C major
6.121	No.9 in E-flat major
6.122	No.10 in B-flat major
6.123	No.11 in D major
6.124	No.12 in G major
6.125	No.13 in A major
6.126	No.14 in E major
6.127	No.15 in C major
6.128	No.16 in G major
6.129	No.17 in B-flat major
6.130	No.18 in D major
6.131	No.19 in A major
6.132	No.20 in C major
6.133	No.21 in E-flat major
6.134	No.22 in F major
6.135	No.23 in B-flat major
6.136	No.24 in A major
6.137	*"17 Deutsche Tänze" (c?, lost)* *HobIX/17*
6.138	*"9 Menuette" (c?, lost/unknown)* *HobIX/18*
6.139	"13 Menuetti" (c?; 2vn & bass): No.1 in C major (w/ Trio) HobIX/19
6.140	No.2 in F major
6.141	No.3 in B-flat major
6.142	No.4 in D major
6.143	No.5 in G major
6.144	No.6 in C major (w/ Trio)
6.145	No.7 in A major
6.146	No.8 in D major
6.147	No.9 in G major (w/ Trio)
6.148	No.10 in E-flat major
6.149	No.11 in C major (w/Trio)
6.150	No.12 in E major
6.151	No.13 in A major
6.152	"Menuett" (w/ Trio), in G major (ca1762–7; 2fl, 2hn, 2vn & bass) HobIX/23
6.153	"Menuett" (w/ Trio), in C major (c ?1792; 2vn & bass) HobIX/24
6.154	"Menuett," in F major (c?; 2vn, va & bass, ?movt of spur sym/str qt) HobIX/25
6.155	*"Unos 24 minués y otras. .." (c by 1789, for Duchess of Osuna in Madrid, lost/unidentified)* ....

7. OTHER ORCHESTRAL WORKS

7.1   "Die sieben letzten Worte unseres Erlösers am Kreuze" (The Seven Last Words of Jesus Christ on the Cross) (c1785; arr for str qt HobIII/50–6; also oratorio HobXX/2): HobXX/1a
      . "Introduzione" (Maestoso ed adagio)
      . "Sonata I: Pater Pater dimitte illis, quia nesciunt, quid faciunt" (Largo)
      . "Sonata II: Amen dico tibi, hodie mecum, eris in Paradiso" (Grave e cantabile)
      . "Sonata III: Mulier, ecce filius tuus, et tu, ecce mater tua" (Grave)
      . "Sonata IV: Deus meus, Deus meus, utquid dereliquisti me?" (Largo)
      . "Sonata V: Sitio" (Adagio)
      . "Sonata VI: Consumatum est" (Lento)
      . "Sonata VII: In Manus tuas Domine, commendo Spiritum meum" (Largo)
      . "Il Terremoto" (Presto et con tutta la forza)

8. KEYBOARD CONCERTOS

8.1	Keyboard Concerto in C major (c1756) HobXVIII/1
8.2	Keyboard Concerto in D major (c before 1767) HobXVIII/2
8.3	Keyboard Concerto in F major (ca1765) HobXVIII/3
8.4	Keyboard Concerto in G major (c before 1782)..HobXVIII/4
8.5	Keyboard Concerto in C major (c before 1763)...HobXVIII/5
8.6	Keyboard Concerto in F major (c before 1766; w/ vn solo) HobXVIII/6
8.7	*Keyboard Concerto in F major (c before 1766, ?spur)* *HobXVIII/7*
8.8	Keyboard Concerto in C major (c before 1766) HobXVIII/8
8.9	*Keyboard Concerto in G major (c before 1767, ?spur)* *HobXVIII/9*
8.10	Keyboard Concertino in C major (c before 1771) HobXVIII/10
8.11	Keyboard Concerto in D major (c before 1784) HobXVIII/11

Divertimentos (Concertos) w/ clavier:

8.12	Divertimento in E-flat major (c before 1766; hpd, 2hn, vn & bass) HobXIV/1
8.13	*Divertimento in F major (c before 1769; hpd, 2vn & baryton; lost)* *HobXIV/2*
8.14	Divertimento in C major (ca1767; hpd, 2vn & vc) HobXIV/3
8.15	Divertimento in C major (c1764; hpd, 2vn & vc) HobXIV/4

8.16	*Divertimento in D major (c before 1766; hpd, ?2vn & ?vc, frag for hpd only; see: Kbd Son No.28)*	........HobXIV/5
8.17	*Divertimento in G major (c before 1767; hpd, ?2vn & ?vc, ?spur: arr from: Kbd Sonata No.13)*	...........HobXIV/6
8.18	Divertimento in C major (ca before1767; hpd, 2vn & vc)	.................HobXIV/7
8.19	Divertimento in C major (c before 1766; hpd, 2vn & vc)	..................HobXIV/8
8.20	Divertimento in F major (c before 1766; hpd, 2vn & vc)	..................HobXIV/9
8.21	Divertimento in C major, "con violini" (ca ?1764–7; hpd, ?2vn & ?bass)	.............HobXIV/10
8.22	Divertimento in C major (c1760; hpd, 2vn & bass)	...........................HobXIV/11
8.23	"Concerto" (Partita), in C major (c before 1772; hpd, 2vn & bass)	.................HobXIV/12
8.24	"Concerto," in G major (c before ?1767; hpd, 2vn & bass)	........................HobXIV/13

9. STRING / WIND CONCERTOS

Vn & orch:

9.1	Violin Concerto No.1 in C major (c before 1769, for Luigi Tomasini)	.... HobVIIa/1
9.2	*Violin Concerto No.2 in D major (c before ?1765, lost)*	.... *HobVIIa/2*
9.3	Violin Concerto No.3 in A major, "Melker Konzert" (c before 1770, discovered in monastery in Melk)	.... HobVIIa/3
9.4	Violin Concerto No.4 in G major (c before 1769)	.... HobVIIa/4

Vc & orch:

9.5	Cello Concerto No.1 in C major (c before ?1765)	.... HobVIIb/1
9.6	Cello Concerto No.2 in D major (c1783)	.... Op.101, HobVIIb/2
9.7	*Cello Concerto No.3 in C major (c ?1761–5, lost/=HobVIIb/1)*	.... *HobVIIb/3*
9.8	*Cello Concerto in D major (c by 1772, spur: c by ?Costanzi)*	.... *HobVIIb/4*
9.9	*Cello Concerto in C major (ca1769, spur: c by Popper ?from Haydn's sketch never found)*	.... *HobVIIb/5*
9.10	*"Concerto per il violone" (contraviolone) (ca ?1761–5, lost)*	.... *HobVIIc/1*

Hn & orch:

9.11	*Horn Concerto (Concerto per il corno di caccia), in D major (c before ?1765, lost)*	.... *HobVIId/1*
9.12	*"Concerto a 2 corni," in E-flat major (c before ?1784, lost)*	.... *HobVIId/2*
9.13	Horn Concerto No.1 (per il corno di caccia), in D major (c1762)	.... HobVIId/3
9.14	*Horn Concerto No.2 (Concerto per il corno di caccia), in D major (c before 1781, ?spur)*	.... *HobVIId/4*

Other wind instr & orch:

9.15	*Flute Concerto in D major (ca ?1761–5, lost)*	.... *HobVIIf/1*
9.16	Trumpet Concerto (Concerto per il clarino), in E-flat major (c1796)	.... HobVIIe/1
9.17	Oboe Concerto in C major (ca ?1800; 2ob, 2hn, 2tpt, strings & timp)	.... HobVIIg/C1
9.18	*"Concert für Fagott" (c?, lost)*	.... *Hob.i,facs,V*

Other:

9.19	"Concerti" (c1786; 2 lire organizzate, 2hn, 2vn, 2va & vc): No.1 in C major	.... HobVIIh/1
9.20	No.2 in F major	.... HobVIIh/4
9.21	No.3 in G major	.... HobVIIh/2
9.22	No.4 in F major	.... HobVIIh/5
9.23	No.5 in G major	.... HobVIIh/3
9.24	*"Concerti per il pariton" (baryton): No.1 in D major (ca ?1765–70, lost)*	.... *HobXIII/1*
9.25	*No.2 in D major (ca ?1765–70, lost)*	.... *HobXIII/2*
9.26	*"Concerto per 2 pariton," in D major (ca ?1765–70, lost)*	.... *HobXIII/3*

10. STRING QUARTETS (Not listed—spur quartets unnumbered by Hoboken but attributed to Haydn)

10.1	"Divertimento" (String Quartet No.0), in E-flat major (c before 1765)	.... "Op.0," HobII/6
10.2	"Divertimentos": No.1 in B-flat major, "La chasse" (c before 1762)	....................Op.1, HobIII/1
10.3	No.2 in E-flat major (c before 1762)	.... HobIII/2
10.4	No.3 in D major (c before 1762)	.... HobIII/3
10.5	No.4 in G major (c before 1764)	.... HobIII/4
10.6	*No.5 Arr of Symphony in B-flat major, HobI/107 (c before 1770–1, spur)*	.... *HobIII/5*
10.7	No.6 in C major (c before 1762)	.... HobIII/6
10.8	"Divertimentos": No.1 in A major (c before 1763)	.... Op.2, HobIII/7
10.9	No.2 in E major (c before 1765)	.... HobIII/8
10.10	*No.3 Arr of Divertimento in B-flat major, HobII/43 (c before 1766, spur)*	.... *HobIII/9*
10.11	No.4 in F major (c before 1762)	.... HobIII/10
10.12	*No.5 Arr of Divertimento in F major, HobII/44 (c before 1766, spur)*	.... *HobIII/11*
10.13	No.6 in B-flat major (c before 1762)	.... HobIII/12
10.14	*"6 String Quartets" (c before 1777, spur: c by ?Hofstetter): No.1 in E major*	.... *Op.3, HobII/13*
10.15	*No.2 in C major*	.... *HobIII/14*
10.16	*No.3 in G major*	.... *HobIII/15*
10.17	*No.4 in B-flat major*	.... *HobIII/16*

Arr for str qt:

10.79   "Quartetti: La vera costanza" (c before 1799, 16 pieces from opera, HobXXVIII/8) ....
10.80   "Quartetti: Armida" (c before 1799, 18 pieces from opera, HobXXVIII/12) ....

11. STRING TRIOS (DIVERTIMENTOS) (2vn & vc/bass)

11.1   String Trio No.1 in E major (c before 1767) HobV/1
11.2   String Trio No.2 in F major (c before 1767) HobV/2
11.3   String Trio No.3 in B minor (c before 1767) HobV/3
11.4   String Trio No.4 in E-flat major (c before 1767) HobV/4
11.5   *String Trio No.5 in B major (c before ?1765, ?lost)* *HobV/5*
11.6   String Trio No.6 in E-flat major (c before ?1765) HobV/6
11.7   String Trio No.7 in A major (c before 1766) HobV/7
11.8   String Trio No.8 in B-flat major (c before 1765; vn, va & vc) HobV/8
11.9   *String Trio No.9 in E-flat major (c before ?1765, lost)* *HobV/9*
11.10   String Trio No.10 in F major (c before 1767) HobV/10
11.11   String Trio No.11 in E-flat major (c by 1765) HobV/11
11.12   String Trio No.12 in E major (c before 1767) HobV/12
11.13   String Trio No.13 in B-flat major (c before ?1765) HobV/13
11.14   *String Trio No.14 in B minor (c before ?1765, lost)* *HobV/14*
11.15   String Trio No.15 in D major (c by 1762) HobV/15
11.16   String Trio No.16 in C major (c by 1766) HobV/16
11.17   String Trio No.17 in E-flat major (c by 1766) HobV/17
11.18   String Trio No.18 in B-flat major (c by 1765) HobV/18
11.19   String Trio No.19 in E major (c by 1765) HobV/19
11.20   String Trio No.20 in G major (c by 1766) HobV/20
11.21   String Trio No.21 in D major (c before 1768) HobV/21

Attributed to Haydn (2vn & bass, various degrees of possible authenticity):

11.22   *String Trio in C major* *HobV/C1*
11.23   *String Trio in C major* *HobV/C2*
11.24   *String Trio in C major* *HobV/C3*
11.25   *"Weinzierler" Trio No.1 in C major (2vn & bass / vn, va & bass)* *HobV/C4*
11.26   *String Trio in C major* *HobV/C5*
11.27   *String Trio in C major* *HobV/C6*
11.28   *"Eisenstädter" Trio No.3, in C major* *HobV/C7*
11.29   *String Trio in C major* *HobV/C8*
11.30   *String Trio in C major (lost)* *HobV/C9*
11.31   *String Trio in D major* *HobV/D1*
11.32   *String Trio in D major (c by ?M. Haydn)* *HobV/D2*
11.33   *"Weinzierler" Trio No.2 in D major* *HobV/D3*
11.34   *"Weinzierler" Trio No.5, in D major* *HobV/D4*
11.35   *String Trio in D major (vn, vc & bass, lost)* *HobV/D5*
11.36   *String Trio in D major (vn, va & bass, lost)* *HobV/D6*
11.37   *String Trio in E-flat major (vn, va & vc, c by M. Haydn)* *HobV/Es1*
11.38   *String Trio in E-flat major* *HobV/Es2*
11.39   *String Trio in E-flat major* *HobV/Es3*
11.40   *String Trio in E-flat major* *HobV/Es4*
11.41   *String Trio in E-flat major (5 movts, 2 mots pubd1938)* *HobV/Es5*
11.42   *String Trio in E-flat major (lost)* *HobV/Es6*
11.43   *String Trio in E-flat major (c by ?Gasparini)* *HobV/Es7*
11.44   *String Trio in E-flat major (lost)* *HobV/Es8*
11.45   *"Weinzierler" Trio No.6 in E-flat major (c by ?Hoffmann)* *HobV/Es9*
11.46   *String Trio in E-flat major (c by ?Asplmayr)* *HobV/Es10*
11.47   *String Trio in E-flat major* *HobV/Es11*
11.48   *String Trio in E-flat major (c by Kammel)* *HobV/Es12*
11.49   *String Trio in E-flat major (c by ?Auffmann, lost)* *HobV/Es13*
11.50   *String Trio in E major (c by ?M. Haydn)* *HobV/E1*
11.51   *String Trio in E major* *HobV/E2*
11.52   *String Trio in E major (lost)* *HobV/E3*
11.53   *String Trio in F major* *HobV/F1*
11.54   *String Trio in F major (c by ?Kammel)* *HobV/F2*
11.55   *String Trio in F major (c by ?Asplmayr/Ivanschiz)* *HobV/F3*
11.56   *String Trio in F major (c by ?J. Ch. Bach)* *HobV/F4*
11.57   *String Trio in F major (lost)* *HobV/F5*
11.58   *String Trio in F major (c by ?Kammel)* *HobV/F6*
11.59   *String Trio in F major* *HobV/F7*
11.60   *String Trio in F major (lost)* *HobV/F8*
11.61   *String Trio in G major* *HobV/G1*
11.62   *String Trio in G major (c by M. Haydn)* *HobV/G2*
11.63   *String Trio in G major* *HobV/G3*
11.64   *String Trio in G major* *HobV/G4*

11.65	*String Trio in G major*	*HobV/G5*
11.66	*String Trio in G major (lost)*	*HobV/G6*
11.67	*String Trio in G major (lost)*	*HobV/G7*
11.68	*String Trio in A major (c by M. Haydn)*	*HobV/A1*
11.69	*String Trio in A major*	*HobV/A2*
11.70	*String Trio in A major*	*HobV/A3*
11.71	*String Trio in A major (lost)*	*HobV/A4*
11.72	*String Trio in A major, "Sonata Pastorella" (c by ?Enderle)*	*HobV/A5*
11.73	*String Trio in A major (c by ?Filtz)*	*HobV/A6*
11.74	*String Trio in A major (c by ?Hoffmann)*	*HobV/A7*
11.75	*String Trio in B-flat major*	*HobV/B1*
11.76	*String Trio in B-flat major (c by ?M. Haydn)*	*HobV/B2*
11.77	*String Trio in B-flat major*	*HobV/B3*
11.78	*String Trio in B-flat major*	*HobV/B4*
11.79	*String Trio in B-flat major (c by ?Chiesa)*	*HobV/B5*
11.80	*String Trio in B-flat major (lost)*	*HobV/B6*

12. BARYTON TRIOS (DIVERTIMENTOS) (baryton, va/violone & bass)

ca1765–6:

12.1	Baryton Trio No.1 in A major (p1926)	HobXI/1
12.2	Baryton Trio No.2 in A major (2 vers)	HobXI/2
12.3	Baryton Trio No.3 in A major (c by 1770)	HobXI/3
12.4	Baryton Trio No.4 in A major (2 vers)	HobXI/4
12.5	*Baryton Trio No.5 in A major (inc, reconstruction, 2 movts)*	*HobXI/5*
12.6	Baryton Trio No.6 in A major (c by 1769)	HobXI/6
12.7	Baryton Trio No.7 in A major (c by 1769)	HobXI/7
12.8	Baryton Trio No.8 in A major	HobXI/8
12.9	Baryton Trio No.9 in A major (c by 1770)	HobXI/9
12.10	Baryton Trio No.10 in A major (c by 1772)	HobXI/10
12.11	Baryton Trio No.11 in D major (c by 1772)	HobXI/11
12.12	Baryton Trio No.12 in A major (p ca1804)	HobXI/12
12.13	Baryton Trio No.13 in A major (p ca1804)	HobXI/13
12.14	Baryton Trio No.14 in D major (p ca1803/4)	HobXI/14
12.15	Baryton Trio No.15 in A major (p ca1803)	HobXI/15
12.16	Baryton Trio No.16 in A major (c by 1772)	HobXI/16
12.17	Baryton Trio No.17 in D major (c by 1772)	HobXI/17
12.18	*Baryton Trio No.18 in A major (c by 1772, lost/unidentified)*	*HobXI/18*
12.19	Baryton Trio No.19 in A major	HobXI/19
12.20	Baryton Trio No.20 in D major	HobXI/20
12.21	Baryton Trio No.21 in A major (c by 1771)	HobXI/21
12.22	Baryton Trio No.22 in A major	HobXI/22
12.23	*Baryton Trio No.23 in D major (lost/unidentified)*	*HobXI/23*
12.24	Baryton Trio No.24 in D major (c1766)	HobXI/24

ca1766–7:

12.25	Baryton Trio No.25 in A major	HobXI/25
12.26	Baryton Trio No.26 in G major	HobXI/26
12.27	Baryton Trio No.27 in D major	HobXI/27
12.28	Baryton Trio No.28 in D major	HobXI/28
12.29	Baryton Trio No.29 in A major	HobXI/29
12.30	Baryton Trio No.30 in G major	HobXI/30
12.31	Baryton Trio No.31 in D major	HobXI/31
12.32	Baryton Trio No.32 in G major	HobXI/32
12.33	Baryton Trio No.33 in A major	HobXI/33
12.34	Baryton Trio No.34 in D major (c by 1776)	HobXI/34
12.35	Baryton Trio No.35 in A major (c by 1771)	HobXI/35
12.36	Baryton Trio No.36 in D major (c by 1776)	HobXI/36
12.37	Baryton Trio No.37 in G major (c by 1776)	HobXI/37
12.38	Baryton Trio No.38 in A major (c by 1776)	HobXI/38
12.39	Baryton Trio No.39 in D major (c by 1776)	HobXI/39
12.40	Baryton Trio No.40 in D major	HobXI/40
12.41	Baryton Trio No.41 in D major	HobXI/41
12.42	Baryton Trio No.42 in D major (c1767)	HobXI/42
12.43	Baryton Trio No.43 in D major	HobXI/43
12.44	Baryton Trio No.44 in D major	HobXI/44
12.45	Baryton Trio No.45 in D major	HobXI/45
12.46	Baryton Trio No.46 in A major	HobXI/46
12.47	Baryton Trio No.47 in G major	HobXI/47
12.48	Baryton Trio No.48 in D major	HobXI/48

ca1767–8:

12.49	Baryton Trio No.49 in G major	HobXI/49

12.50	Baryton Trio No.50 in D major	HobXI/50
12.51	Baryton Trio No.51 in A major	HobXI/51
12.52	Baryton Trio No.52 in D min / major (Minuet & Trio based on movt in: Sym No.58, HobI/58)	HobXI/52
12.53	Baryton Trio No.53 in G major (c1767)	HobXI/53
12.54	Baryton Trio No.54 in D major	HobXI/54
12.55	Baryton Trio No.55 in G major	HobXI/55
12.56	Baryton Trio No.56 in D major	HobXI/56
12.57	Baryton Trio No.57 in A major (c1768)	HobXI/57
12.58	Baryton Trio No.58 in D major	HobXI/58
12.59	Baryton Trio No.59 in G major	HobXI/59
12.60	Baryton Trio No.60 in A major	HobXI/60
12.61	Baryton Trio No.61 in D major	HobXI/61
12.62	Baryton Trio No.62 in G major	HobXI/62
12.63	Baryton Trio No.63 in D major	HobXI/63
12.64	Baryton Trio No.64 in D major (uses Alleluia theme of: Sym No.30 in C major, HobI/30)	HobXI/64
12.65	Baryton Trio No.65 in G major	HobXI/65
12.66	Baryton Trio No.66 in A major	HobXI/66
12.67	Baryton Trio No.67 in G major	HobXI/67
12.68	Baryton Trio No.68 in A major	HobXI/68
12.69	Baryton Trio No.69 in D major	HobXI/69
12.70	Baryton Trio No.70 in G major	HobXI/70
12.71	Baryton Trio No.71 in A major	HobXI/71
12.72	Baryton Trio No.72 in D major	HobXI/72

c by 1771:

12.73	Baryton Trio No.73 in G major (c by 1772)	HobXI/73
12.74	Baryton Trio No.74 in D major	HobXI/74
12.75	Baryton Trio No.75 in A major	HobXI/75
12.76	Baryton Trio No.76 in C major (c by 1772)	HobXI/76
12.77	Baryton Trio No.77 in G major	HobXI/77
12.78	Baryton Trio No.78 in D major	HobXI/78
12.79	Baryton Trio No.79 in D major (c1769)	HobXI/79
12.80	Baryton Trio No.80 in G major	HobXI/80
12.81	Baryton Trio No.81 in D major	HobXI/81
12.82	Baryton Trio No.82 in C major	HobXI/82
12.83	Baryton Trio No.83 in F major	HobXI/83
12.84	Baryton Trio No.84 in D major	HobXI/84
12.85	Baryton Trio No.85 in D major	HobXI/85
12.86	Baryton Trio No.86 in A major	HobXI/86
12.87	Baryton Trio No.87 in A minor	HobXI/87
12.88	Baryton Trio No.88 in A major	HobXI/88
12.89	Baryton Trio No.89 in G major (vn instead of va)	HobXI/89
12.90	Baryton Trio No.90 in C major (vn instead of va)	HobXI/90
12.91	Baryton Trio No.91 in D major (vn instead of va)	HobXI/91
12.92	Baryton Trio No.92 in G major	HobXI/92
12.93	Baryton Trio No.93 in C major	HobXI/93
12.94	Baryton Trio No.94 in A major (c by 1774)	HobXI/94
12.95	Baryton Trio No.95 in D major	HobXI/95
12.96	Baryton Trio No.96 in B minor	HobXI/96

c before 1778:

12.97	Baryton Trio No.97 in D major (c by ?1766)	HobXI/97
12.98	Baryton Trio No.98 in D major	HobXI/98
12.99	*Baryton Trio No.99 in G major (lost)*	*HobXI/99*
12.100	Baryton Trio No.100 in F major	HobXI/100
12.101	Baryton Trio No.101 in C major	HobXI/101
12.102	Baryton Trio No.102 in G major	HobXI/102
12.103	Baryton Trio No.103 in A major (based on: Divertimento in F major for pf, HobXIV/2)	HobXI/103
12.104	Baryton Trio No.104 in D major	HobXI/104
12.105	Baryton Trio No.105 in G major	HobXI/105
12.106	Baryton Trio No.106 in D major	HobXI/106
12.107	Baryton Trio No.107 in D major	HobXI/107
12.108	Baryton Trio No.108 in A major	HobXI/108
12.109	Baryton Trio No.109 in C major	HobXI/109
12.110	Baryton Trio No.110 in C major (movts 1–2 based on: Divertimento in C maj for pf, HobXIV/8)	HobXI/110
12.111	Baryton Trio No.111 in G major	HobXI/111
12.112	Baryton Trio No.112 in D major	HobXI/112
12.113	Baryton Trio No.113 in D major	HobXI/113
12.114	Baryton Trio No.114 in D major	HobXI/114
12.115	Baryton Trio No.115 in D major	HobXI/115
12.116	Baryton Trio No.116 in G major	HobXI/116
12.117	Baryton Trio No.117 in F major	HobXI/117
12.118	Baryton Trio No.118 in D major	HobXI/118
12.119	Baryton Trio No.119 in G major (part lost: only baryton part extant)	HobXI/119

Attributed to Haydn (1 str instr = ?baryton, various degrees of possible authenticity):

13. WORKS WITH 1–2 BARYTONS

14. KEYBOARD TRIOS

Attributed to Haydn (various degrees of possible authenticity):

15. OTHER CHAMBER MUSIC (2–3 string/wind insts)

Attributed to Haydn (various degrees of possible authenticity):

16. KEYBOARD SONATAS (hpd; Nos.1–62: in Christa Landon Edition, Vienna 1964–6)

16.47   Keyboard Sonata No.47 (Divertimento) in B minor (c before 1776) Op.14/6, HobXVI/32
16.48   Keyboard Sonata No.48 in C major (c by 1780; hpd/pf).. Op.30/1, HobXVI/35
16.49   Keyboard Sonata No.49 in C-sharp minor (c by 1780; hpd/pf) Op.30/2, HobXVI/36
16.50   Keyboard Sonata No.50 in D major (c by 1780; hpd/pf).. Op.30/3, HobXVI/37
16.51   Keyboard Sonata No.51 in E-flat major (c by 1780; hpd/pf) Op.30/4, HobXVI/38
16.52   Keyboard Sonata No.52 in G major (c by 1780; hpd/pf) Op.30/5, HobXVI/39
16.53   Keyboard Sonata No.53 in E minor (c by 1780; hpd/pf) HobXVI/34
16.54   Keyboard Sonata No.54 in G major (c by 1784; pf).. HobXVI/40
16.55   Keyboard Sonata No.55 in B-flat major (c by 1784; pf) HobXVI/41
16.56   Keyboard Sonata No.56 in D major (c by 1784; pf) HobXVI/42
16.57   Keyboard Sonata No.57 in F maj (c by 1788; hpd/pf, from orig vers: Kbd Son No.19, Hobi/771). HobXVI/47
16.58   Keyboard Sonata No.58 in C major (c1789, hpd) HobXVI/48
16.59   Keyboard Sonata No.59 in E-flat major (c1789; pf) HobXVI/49
16.60   Keyboard Sonata No.60 in C major (ca1794–5; pf).. HobXVI/50
16.61   Keyboard Sonata No.61 in D major (ca ?1794–5; pf) HobXVI/51
16.62   Keyboard Sonata No.62 in E-flat major (c1794; pf) HobXVI/52

Attributed to Haydn (various degrees of possible authenticity):

16.63   Keyboard Sonata in C major (c by 1785; arr of Divertimento, HobII/11) HobXVI/15
16.64   "Divertimento," in E-flat major (ca ?1750–5, ?spur) HobXVI/16
16.65   Keyboard Sonata in B-flat major (c by 1768, c by ?Schwanenberger) HobXVI/17
16.66   Keyboard Sonata in C major (c?) HobXVI/C1
16.67   "Sonata militaire" (The conquest of Oczakow) in D major (c1788–9, c by Kauer) HobXVI/D1
16.68   "Sonata" (Die Belagerung Pelgrads), in E-flat major (ca1789–93, arr of XXXII/1c) XVI/Es1
16.69   Keyboard Sonata in B-flat major (c?) HobXVI/B1
16.70   Keyboard Sonata in E-flat major (c by 1789; w/ vn ad lib) Hobi/731
16.71   "Caprices" (Fantasie et variations), in G major (c?, pubd before 1800) HobXVII/G2
16.72   3 "Göttweiger Sonaten," in C major, A major, D major (c?, c by Hoffmeister) Hobi/733
16.73   Keyboard Sonata in C major (1 movt only, in Feder: Probleme einer Neuordnung) ....
16.74   "Children's Concerto" (Concerto de bebe), in C major (c by ?1876, forgery) ....

17. KEYBOARD DANCES

17.1   "16 (?12) Menuette" (c before 1767, from lost orig for orch, 12 known): No.1 in D major (w/ Trio) ... HobIX/3
17.2   No.2 in G major
17.3   No.3 in B-flat major
17.4   No.4 in F major (w/ Trio)
17.5   No.5 in D major (w/ Trio)
17.6   No.6 in B-flat major
17.7   No.7 in E-flat major
17.8   No.8 in G major
17.9   No.9 in C major
17.10   No.10 in F major
17.11   No.11 in C major
17.12   No.12 in D major
17.13   "6 Minuetti für Cembalo" (w/ Trios) (c1769, falsely attrib to Mozart, K61f/ K105): No.1 in D maj HobIX/4a
17.14   No.2 in D major
17.15   No.3 in D major
17.16   No.4 in G major
17.17   No.5 in G major
17.18   No.6 in G major
17.19   "12 Menuette" (c by 1785, from lost orig for orch): No.1 in C major (w/ Trio), "Rococo" HobIX/8
17.20   No.2 in G major
17.21   No.3 in B-flat major
17.22   No.4 in F major (w/ Trio)
17.23   No.5 in D major (w/ Trio)
17.24   No.6 in A major
17.25   No.7 in D major (w/ Trio)
17.26   No.8 in G major
17.27   No.9 in E major
17.28   No.10 in C major (w/ Trio)
17.29   No.11 in G major (w/ Trio)
17.30   No.12 in F major
17.31   "6 Minuetti ridotti per Cembalo Solo" (c by 1787, lost) HobIX/9a
17.32   "12 Deutsche Tänze" (c before 1793, arr from Martin y Soler: L'arbore di Diana): No.1 in D maj... HobIX/10
17.33   No.2 in G major
17.34   No.3 in C major
17.35   No.4 in F major
17.36   No.5 in B-flat major
17.37   No.6 in E-flat major
17.38   No.7 in G major
17.39   No.8 in E major
17.40   No.9 in A major

17.41	No.10 in D major
17.42	No.11 in D major
17.43	No.12 in D major
17.44	"12 Deutsche Tänze" (aus dem K. K. Redoutensale) (c1792): No.1 in D major (w/ Trio) HobIX/13
17.45	No.2 in G major
17.46	No.3 in F major (w/ Trio)
17.47	No.4 in C major
17.48	No.5 in A major
17.49	No.6 in F major (w/ Trio)
17.50	No.7 in D major
17.51	No.8 in D major (w/ Trio)
17.52	No.9 in G major
17.53	No.10 in D major
17.54	No.11 in A major
17.55	No.12 in D major
17.56	"18 Menuette" (c?): No.1 in D major (w/ Trio) HobIX/20
17.57	No.2 in G major
17.58	No.3 in B-flat major (w/ Trio)
17.59	No.4 in G major
17.60	No.5 in E major
17.61	No.6 in C major (w/ Trio)
17.62	No.7 in A major
17.63	No.8 in F major (w/ Trio)
17.64	No.9 in D major
17.65	No.10 in C major (w/ Trio)
17.66	No.11 in A major (w/ Trio)
17.67	No.12 in E major
17.68	No.13 in A major
17.69	No.14 in F major
17.70	No.15 in D major
17.71	No.16 in G major
17.72	No.17 in C major (w/ Trio)
17.73	No.18 in D major
17.74	"12 Menuette" (de la Redoute) (c?): No.1 in C major (w/ Trio) HobIX/21
17.75	No.2 in F major
17.76	No.3 in A major
17.77	No.4 in D major (w/ Trio)
17.78	No.5 in B-flat major
17.79	No.6 in F major (w/ Trio)
17.80	No.7 in A major
17.81	No.8 in D major
17.82	No.9 in G major
17.83	No.10 in C major (w/ Trio)
17.84	No.11 in C major (w/ Trio)
17.85	No.12 in E-flat major
17.86	"10 Deutsche Tänze" (Ballo Tedesco) (c?): No.1 in D major HobIX/22
17.87	No.2 in D major
17.88	No.3 in G major
17.89	No.4 in E-flat major
17.90	No.5 in B-flat major
17.91	No.6 in G major
17.92	No.7 in D major
17.93	No.8 in A major
17.94	No.9 in E major
17.95	No.10 in A major
17.96	"Minuetto," in F-sharp major (c before 1785, ?movt of pf sonata) HobIX/26
17.97	"Ochsenmenuett" (w/ Trio), in C major (ca1805) HobIX/27
17.98	"8 Zingarese" (c before 1799): No.1 in C major (w/ Trio) HobIX/28
17.99	No.2 in G major (w/ Trio)
17.100	No.3 in B-flat major
17.101	No.4 in F major
17.102	No.5 in D major
17.103	No.6 in F major
17.104	No.7 in D major
17.105	No.8 in F major
17.106	"5 Contratänze und 1 Quadrille" (c?): No.1 in F major HobIX/29
17.107	No.2 in B-flat major
17.108	No.3 in C major
17.109	No.4 in G major
17.110	No.5 in E-flat major
17.111	. "Quadrille," in C major
17.112	"Englischer Tanz," in B-flat major (c?) HobIX/30

18. MISC KEYBOARD WORKS

18.1   "Capriccio: Acht Sauschneider müssen seyn," in G major (c1765; hpd) HobXVII/1
18.2   "20 Variazioni," in A major (c before 1771; hpd; arr for 1v & hpd) HobXVII/2
18.3   "12 Variations" (Menuetto con Var), in E-flat major (c before 1774; hpd, theme from HobII/20) HobXVII/3
18.4   "Fantasia" (Capriccio), in C major (c1789; pf) HobXVII/4
18.5   "6 Easy Variations" (Sonatina), in C major (c1790; pf) HobXVII/5
18.6   "Andante with Variations," in F minor (c1793; pf; arr for str qt) HobXVII/6
18.7   Piece in D major (c ?1791–5; ?pf, w/ song: The Ladies Looking-Glass, HobXXXIc/17) HobXXXIc/17b
18.8   "Divertimento," in F major, "Il maestro e lo scolare" (c by 1778; hpd duet) HobXVIIa/1

Attributed to Haydn (various degrees of possible authenticity):

18.9   "5 Variations," in D major (c before 1766; hpd) HobXVII/7
18.10   "Variations," in D major (c?, spur arr from: Baryton Trio, HobXI/2bis) HobXVII/8
18.11   "Adagio," in F major (c by 1786; hpd/pf) HobXVII/9
18.12   "Allegretto," in G major (c by 1794, spur arr of HobXIX/27) HobXVII/10
18.13   "Andante," in C major (c before 1807; hpd) HobXVII/11
18.14   "Andante con variazioni," in B-flat major (c by 1807; pf) HobXVII/12
18.15   "Mahlbarough," in C major HobXVII/C1
18.16   "3 Praeambeln" (org) HobXVII/C2
18.17   "Präludium & Fuga" (No.1 of: 3 Präludien und Fugen) (in the library of Lüneburg) HobXVII/C3
18.18   "Variazioni," in D major HobXVII/D1
18.19   "Allegro molto" (No.3 of: 5 Einzelsätze) HobXVII/D2
18.20   "Aria," in F major HobXVII/F1
18.21   "Andante," in F major HobXVII/F2
18.22   "Sonata ... la Bataille de Rossbach," in F major (spur: c by C. P. E. Bach, Wq272) HobXVII/F3
18.23   "Präludium & Fuga" (No.3 of: 3 Präludien und Fugen, in the library of Lüneburg) HobXVII/F4
18.24   "Pieces pour le Clavecin," No.1 in G major HobXVII/G1
18.25   "Caprices" (Adagio, Allegro moderato, Andantino), in G major HobXVII/G2
18.26   "Präludium & Fuga" (No.2 of: 3 Präludien und Fugen) (in the library of Lüneburg) HobXVII/G3
18.27   "Variationes," in A major HobXVII/A1
18.28   "Tema con Variazione," in A major HobXVII/A2
18.29   "Variazioni," in A major HobXVII/A3

19. FLUTE-CLOCK

19.1   "Allegretto," in F major (c by ?1796, uses aria 4. from: Il mondo della luna, HobXXVIII/7) HobXIX/1
19.2   "Vivace," in F major (c by ?1796, source unknown) HobXIX/2
19.3   "Andantino," in F major (c by ?1796, uses 2nd movt of: Sym No.53 in D maj, 'Imperial,' HobI/53) .HobXIX/3
19.4   "Der Dudelsack" (The Bagpipes), in C major (c by ?1796, spur arrs) HobXIX/4
19.5   "Menuett," in F major (c by ?1796, from 3rd movt of: Baryton Trio No.82 in C major, HobXI/82) ...HobXIX/5
19.6   "Der Kaffeeklatsch" (Gossip at the Coffee Table), in F major (c by ?1796, from 3rd movt of:
    Baryton Trio No.76 in C major, HobXI/76) HobXIX/6
19.7   "Menuet," in C major (c by 1792, source unknown) HobXIX/7
19.8   "Der Wachtelschlag" (The Call of the Quail), in C major (c by 1792, source unknown) HobXIX/8
19.9   "Menuet," in C major (c1788–92, uses 3rd movt of: Str Qt in C major, Op.54/2, HobIII/57) HobXIX/9
19.10   "Andante," in C major (c before 1792) HobXIX/10
19.11   "Allegretto," in C major (c by 1793, r ?1793) HobXIX/11
19.12   "Andante," in C major (c before 1793, r ?1793) HobXIX/12
19.13   "Vivace," in C major (c ?1789, r ?1793) HobXIX/13
19.14   "Menuet," in C major (c ?1789) HobXIX/14
19.15   "Allegro ma non troppo," in C major (c ?1789, r ?1793) HobXIX/15
19.16   "Fuga," in C major (c1789, r ?1793) HobXIX/16
19.17   "Allegro moderato," in C major (c before 1792) HobXIX/17
19.18   "Presto," in C major (c before 1792) HobXIX/18
19.19   "Andante," in C major (c by 1792, adaptation, source unknown) HobXIX/19
19.20   "Menuett," in C major (c by 1792, uses 3rd movt of: Sym No.85 in B-flat, 'La reine,' HobI/85) HobXIX/20
19.21   "Allegretto," in G major (c by 1792, source unknown) HobXIX/21
19.22   "Allegro moderato," in C major (c by 1792, spur arrs) HobXIX/22
19.23   "Vivace," in C major (c by 1792, spur arrs) HobXIX/23
19.24   "Presto," in C major (c by 1792, source unknown) HobXIX/24
19.25   "Marche," in D major (c by 1793, from: Marcia in E-flat major, HobVIII/6) HobXIX/25
19.26   "Andante, Allegro," in E major (c by 1793, spur arrs) HobXIX/26
19.27   "Allegretto," in G major (c ?1793) HobXIX/27
19.28   "Allegro," in C major (c1793, from 4th movt of: Str Qt in D major, Op.71/2, Hob.III/70) HobXIX/28
19.29   "Menuet," in C major (c1793, from 3rd movt of: Sym No.101 in D major, 'Clock,' Hob.I/101) HobXIX/29
19.30   "Presto," in G major (c1790–3, from 4th movt of: Str Qt in D major, 'Lark,' Op.64/5, HobIII/63) ...HobXIX/30
19.31   "Presto," in C major (c before ?1794/5) HobXIX/31
19.32   "Allegro," in F major (c1793 or after, from 4th movt of: Sym No.99 in E-flat major, HobI/99) HobXIX/32

20. ORATORIOS

20a. SELECTIONS FROM ORATORIOS

15b. "Dunque, oh Dio, quando sperai," duet (Tobia, Anna)
16a. "Qui di morir si parla," accompagnato (Alle)
16b. "Io non oso alzar le ciglia," quartet (Sara, Anna, Tobia, Tobit)
16c. "Otterrem gloria maggiore e maggior felicità," chorus (fuga)

20a.4   "Die Schöpfung," oratorio: HobXXI/2
    I: 1a. "Introduction"
          1b. "Im Anfange schuf Gott," recit (Raphael)
          1c. "Und der Geist Gottes schwebte auf der Fläche der Wasser," chorus
          2a. "Nun schwanden vor dem heiligen Strahle," aria (Uriel)
          2b. "Verzweiflung, Wut und Schrecken," chorus
          3a. "Und Gott machte das Firmament," recit (Raphael)
          3b. "Da tobten brausend heftige Stürme," recit (Raphael)
          4a. "Mit Staunen sieht das Wunderwerk," solo (Gabriel)
          4b. "Und laut ertönt aus ihren Kehlen," chorus
          5a. "Und Gott sprach," recit (Raphael)
          5b. "Rollend in schäumenden Wellen," aria (Raphael)
          6a. "Und Gott sprach," recit (Gabriel)
          6b. "Nun beut die Flur das frische Grün," aria (Gabriel)
          7a. "Und die himmlischen Heerscharen," recit (Uriel)
          7b. "Stimmt an die Saiten," chorus
          7c. "Denn er hat Himmel und Erde bekleidet in herrlicher Pracht," chorus
          8a. "Und Gott sprach," recit (Uriel)
          8b. "In vollem Glanze," accompagnato (Uriel)
          8c. "Die Himmel erzählen die Ehre Gottes" (Heavens are telling), chorus & trio
    II: 9a. "Und Gott sprach," recit (Gabriel)
          9b. "Auf starken Fittige schwinget sich der Adler stolz," aria (Gabriel)
          10. "Und Gott schuf grosse Walfische und ein jedes," recit (Raphael)
          10b. "seid fruchtbar alle," accompagnato (Raphael)
          11. "Und die Engel" (Raphael)
          11b. "In holder Anmut stehn," trio
          . "Der Herr ist gross in seiner Macht," chorus
          12a. "Und Gott sprach," recit (Raphael)
          12b. "Gleich öffnet sich der Erde Schoss," accompagnato (Raphael)
          12c. "Nun scheint in vollem Glanze der Himmel," aria (Raphael)
          13a. "Und Gott schuf den Menchen," recit (Uriel)
          13b. "Mit Würd' und Hoheit angetan," aria (Uriel)
          14a. "Und Gott sah jedes Ding," recit (Raphael)
          14b. "Vollendet ist das grosse Werk," chorus
          14c. "Zu dir, o Herr, blickt alles auf," trio
          . "Vollendet ist das grosse Werk," chorus
          14d. "Alles lobe seinen Namen," fuge
    III: 15a. "Aus Rosenwolken bricht, geweckt," recit (Uriel)
          15b. "Von deiner Güt', o Herr und Gott" (Eva)
          15c. "Der Sterne hellster, o wie schön" (Adam)
          15d. "Heil dir, o Gott!," chorus
          16a. "Nun ist die erste Pflicht erfüllt," recit (Adam)
          16b. "Holde Gattin!," duet
          16c. "Der thauende Morgen, o wie ermuntert er!" (Adam)
          17a. "O glücklich Paar," recit (Uriel)
          17b. "Singt dem Herren alle Stimmen!," chorus
          . "Des Herren Ruhm, er bleibt in Ewigkeit," fugue

20a.5   "Die Jahreszeiten," oratorio: HobXXI/3
    "Der Frühling": 1. "Introduction"
          . "Seht, wie der strenge Winter flieht," recit (Simon)
          2. "Kom, holder Lenz! des Himmels Gabe, komm!," chorus (Landvolks)
          3a. "Vom Widder strahlet jetzt," recit (Simon)
          3b. "Schon eilet froh der Ackermann zur Arbeit auf das Feld," aria (Simon)
          4a. "Der Landman hat sein Werk vollbracht," recit (Lucas)
          4b. "Sei uns gnädig, milder Himmel!" (Bittgesang), trio & chorus
          5a. "Erhört ist unser Fleh'n," recit (Hanne)
          5b. "O wie lieblich ist der Anblick" (Freuden-lied), chorus (Jugend)
          5c. "Ewiger, mächtiger, gütiger Gott!," chorus
          5d. "Von deinem Segensmahle," trio (Hanne, Lucas, Simon)
          5e. "Ehre, Lob und Preis sei dir," fuge
    "Der Sommer": 6a. "In grauem Schleier," introduction & recit (Lucas)
          6b. "Der munt're Hirt versammelt nun," aria
          6c. "Die Morgenröte bricht hervor," recit (Hanne)
          7a. "Sie steigt herauf die Sonne" (Hanne)
          7b. "Heil! O Sonne, Heil!" (Lobgesang), chorus
          7c. "Dir danken wir, was uns ergötzt" (Hanne)
          . "Heil! O Sonne, Heil!" (Lobgesang), chorus
          8a. "Nun regt und bewegt sich alles umher," recit (Simon)
          8b. "Die Mittagssonne brennet jetzt," accompagnato (Lucas)

8c. "Cavatina"
. "Dem Druck' erlieget die Natur" (Lucas)
9a. "Willkommen jetzt, o dunkler Hain," accompagnato (Hanne)
9b. "Welche Labung für die Sinne," aria (Hanne)
9c. "Die Seele wachet auf" (Hanne)
10a. "O seht, es steiget in der schwülen Luft," recit (Simon)
10b. "Ach! das Ungewitter naht!," chorus
10c. "Erschüttert wankt die Erde bis in des Meeres Grund"
11a. "Die düstren Wolken trennen sich" (Lucas)
11b. "Von oben winkt der helle Stern," trio & chorus (Hanne, Lucas, Simon)
"Der Herbst": 12. "Introduction"
. "Was durch seine Blüte der Lenz zuerst verschprach," recit (Hanne)
13a. "So lohnet die Natur den Fleiss" (Simon)
13b. "O Fleiss, o edler Fleiss, von dir kommt alles Heil" (Fuge), chorus
14a. "Seht, wie zum Hasel busche dort," recit (Hanne)
14b. "Ihn Schönen aus der Stadt" (Lucas)
14c. "welch ein Glück, welch ein Glück" (Hanne, Lucas)
14d. "Lieben und geliebet werden" (Hanne, Lucas)
15a. "Nun zeiget das entblösste Feld," recit (Simon)
15b. "Seht auf die breiten Wiesen hin!," aria (Simon)
16a. "Hier treibt ein dichter Kreis," recit (Lucas)
16b. "Hört! Hört! hört das laute Getön!," chorus
17a. "Am Rebenstocke blinket jetzt," recit (Hanne)
17b. "Juhe, juhhe! der Wein ist da," chorus
17c. "Nun tönen die Pfeifen, und wirbelt die Trommel," chorus
"Der Winter": 18. "Introduction"
. "Nun senket sich das blasse Jahr," recit (Simon)
. "Licht und Leben sind geschwächet" (Cavatine) (Hanne)
19a. "Gefesselt steht der breite See," recit (Lucas)
19b. "Hier steht der Wandrer nun," aria (Lucas)
19c. "Da lebt er wieder auf" (Lucas)
20a. "So wie er naht't," recit (Lucas)
20b. "Am Rokken spinnen die Mütter" (Simon)
20c. "Knurre, schnurre, knurre," Lied with chorus
21a. "Abgesponnen ist der Flachs," recit (Lucas)
21b. "Ein Mädchen, das auf Ehre hielt," Lied with chorus (Hanne)
22a. "Vom dürren Osten dringt," recit (Simon)
22b. "Erblikke hier, betörter Mensch," aria & recit (Simon)
22c. "Wo sind sie nun die hoh'n Entwürte" (Simon)
22d. "sie bleibt allein," recit (Simon)
23a. "Dann bricht der grosse Morgen an," trio & d chorus (Simon)
23b. "Uns leite deine Hand, o Gott!" (Fuge), chorus

21. MASSES

22. MISC SACRED

Graduals, offertories & motets:

22.5	*"Ad aras convolate," gradual (c before 1794; ch, orch & org, ?spur)*	*HobXXIIIa/5*
22.6	*"Salus et Gloria," offertory motet (c before 1779; ch, 2tpt, 2vn, timp & org, ?spur)*	*HobXXIIIa/6*
22.7	*"Super flumina Babylonis," motet (c before 17772; A, S, T, B, 2tpt, 2vn, va, timp & org, ?spur)*	*HobXXIIIa/7*
22.8	*"Ardentes seraphini," offertory (c before 1765; 2S, A, 2vn & bass, ?spur)*	*HobXXIIIa/8*

Antiphons:

22.9	"Salve Regina," in E major (c ?1756; S, ch, 2vn, bass & org)	HobXXIIIb/1
22.10	"Salve Regina" (Salve Organo solo), in G minor (c1771; S, A, T, B, 2vn, va obbl, bass & org) ..	HobXXIIIb/2
22.11	"Ave Regina," in A major (ca ?1763; S, ch, 2vn & org)	HobXXIIIb/3
22.12	"Salve Regina" (in 1 movt), in E-flat major (c before 1770; S, A, T, B, strings & org)	HobXXIIIb/4
22.13	*"Salve regina" (c before ?1766; S, A, 2vn, bass & org, ?spur)*	*HobXXIIIb/5*
22.14	*"Ave regina" (c by 1782; ch, 2tpt, 2vn, bass, timp & org, ?spur)*	*HobXXIIIb/6*

Te Deum & misc choruses:

22.15	"Te Deum," in C major (c by 1765; ch, 2tpt, timp, 2vn, bass & org)	HobXXIIIc/1
22.16	"Grosses Te Deum," in C major (c before 1800; ch, fl, 2ob, 2bn, 2hn, 3tpt, timp, strings & org).	HobXXIIIc/2
22.17	"Alleluia," in G major (c1768–71; ch, strings & org)	HobXXIIIc/3
22.18	"Lauda Sion" (ca ?1765–9; S, A, T, B, 2hn, 2vn, bass & org; 4 vers: B-flat / D min / A / E-flat) ..	HobXXIIIc/4
22.19	"Lauda Sion," motetto (c1760s; 4vv, 2ob, 2tpt, strings & org)	HobXXIIIc/5
22.20	*"Lauda Sion" (Aria de Venera) (c1760s, ?spur)*	*HobXXIIIc/6*

Arias:

22.21	"Ein Magd, ein' Dienerin" (Cantilena pro adventu), in A major (ca ?1770–5; S, strings & org) ...	HobXXIIId/1
22.22	"Mutter Gottes, mir erlaube" (Cantilena/Aria pro adventu), in G maj (ca ?1775; SA, 2vn & org).	HobXXIIId/2
22.23	"Herst Nachbä" (Cantilena pro adventu), in D major (ca ?1768; S, ?2hn, strings & org)	HobXXIIId/3

22.24	"6 English Psalms" (c1794–5, Merrick; 2S, B): 1. "How oft, instinct with warmth" (Psalm 26.5–8) .	Hobii/181
22.25	2. "Blest be the name of Jacob's God" (Psalm 31.21–24)	
22.26	3. "Maker of all! be Thou my guard" (Psalm 41.12–16)	
22.27	4. "The Lord, th' almighty Monarch, spake" (Psalm 50.1–6)	
22.28	5. "Long life shall Israel's king behold" (Psalm 61.6–8)	
22.29	6. "O let me in th' accepted hour" (Psalm 69.13–17, uses: Pleasing Pain, HobXXVIa/29)	

Attributed to Haydn (various degrees of possible authenticity):

22.30	*"O tremenda Majestatis," offertorium in C major*	*HobXXIIIa/C1*
22.31	*"Coelestis urbs Jerusalem," graduale in C major*	*HobXXIIIa/C2*
22.32	*"Venite gentes," offertorium in C major*	*HobXXIIIa/C3*
22.33	*"Exsultate Deo," offertorium in C major*	*HobXXIIIa/C4*
22.34	*"Offertorium de Venerabili": "Sit laus plena," in C major*	*HobXXIIIa/C5*
22.35	*"Vidi civitatem sanctam," motette in C major*	*HobXXIIIa/C6*
22.36	*"Magna coeli Domina," motette in C major*	*HobXXIIIa/C7*
22.37	*"Dulcis quies qua felix anima," motette in C major*	*HobXXIIIa/C8*
22.38	*"Tanta in solemnitate," offertorium in C major*	*HobXXIIIa/C9*
22.39	*"Laudate dominum," motetto in C major*	*HobXXIIIa/C10*
22.40	*"Fons vivos et origo," offertorium in C major*	*HobXXIIIa/C11*
22.41	*"Latetur ecclesia," chorus in C major*	*HobXXIIIa/C12*
22.42	*"Florete flores quasi lilium," motette in C major*	*HobXXIIIa/C13*
22.43	*"Eja cantate et jubilate," offertorium in C major*	*HobXXIIIa/C14*
22.44	*"Tu es Deus," graduale in C major*	*HobXXIIIa/C15*
22.45	*"Mane nobiscum domine," offertorium in D major*	*HobXXIIIa/D1*
22.46	*"Huc omnes volate nobiscum exultate," offertorium in D major*	*HobXXIIIa/D2*
22.47	*"Benedicta et venerabilis," motetto in D major*	*HobXXIIIa/D3*
22.48	*"Pastores loquebantur," offertorium in D major*	*HobXXIIIa/D4*
22.49	*"Te Deum reges," offertorium in D major*	*HobXXIIIa/D5*
22.50	*"Ubi sunt misericordiae," graduale in D minor*	*HobXXIIIa/d1*
22.51	*"Laudate Dominum," offertorium in D minor*	*HobXXIIIa/d2*
22.52	*"Non me ad te avertit amor," offertorium in E-flat major*	*HobXXIIIa/Es1*
22.53	*"Quis sicut Dominus," offertorium in E-flat major*	*HobXXIIIa/Es2*
22.54	*"Veni sancte Spiritus," offertorium in E-flat major*	*HobXXIIIa/Es3*
22.55	*"Inimici circumcederunt nos," motetto in E-flat major*	*HobXXIIIa/Es4*
22.56	*"Alma Dei creatorisr," motetto in E-flat major*	*HobXXIIIa/Es5*
22.57	*"Salve o verum speculum," offertorium in E-flat major*	*HobXXIIIa/Es6*
22.58	*"Oratorium ad Sepulchrum Domini": "Auf Abraham. Wer ruft?," in E-flat major*	*HobXXIIIa/Es7*
22.59	*"Oratorium de Passione": "Erbarmungsreicher Gott," in E-flat major*	*HobXXIIIa/Es8*
22.60	*"O sacrum convivium," offertorium in F major*	*HobXXIIIa/F1*
22.61	*"Ad festum gaudiorum," motette in F major*	*HobXXIIIa/F2*
22.62	*"Offertorium de Venerabili": "Caro cibus" & "A sumente," in F major*	*HobXXIIIa/F3*
22.63	*"Confitemini Domino," offertorium in G major*	*HobXXIIIa/G1*
22.64	*"Veni Sancte Spiritus," motette in G major*	*HobXXIIIa/G2*
22.65	*"Te adoro latens Deus," motetto in G major*	*HobXXIIIa/G3*
22.66	*"Exaudi me tu Domine," motetto in G major*	*HobXXIIIa/G4*

23. CANTATAS & CHORUSES (w/ orch)

      1. "Quae metamorphosis," accompagnato (Prudentia, Temperantia, Justitia, Fortitudo)
      1a. "Virtus inter ardua," aria à quatro
      2. "Supersedete admirationi," recit (Theologia)
      2a. "Non chymaeras somniatis," aria (Theologia)
      3. "Ergone securae sunt meae deliciae," recit (Prudentia, Theologia, Temperantia, Justitia)
      3a. "Dictamina mea," aria à duo (Prudentia, Temperantia)
      3b. "Haec studia tollunt ad gradis honoris"
      4. "Et ego, o sorores!," recit (Justitia, Temperantia, Fortitudo)
      4a. "O pii Patres Patriae," aria (Justitia)
      5. "Consolationes plenus sum," recit (Fortitudo, Temperantia, Prudentia)
      5a. "Si obstrudat," aria (Fortitudo)
      6. "Prima fueram aedificii," recit (Temperantia, Prudentia, Theologia)
      6a. "Rerum quas perpendimus," aria (Temperantia)
      7. "Jubilaea est incolatus nostri magnificentia," recit (Prudentia, Theologia, Justitia)
      7a. "O beatus incolatus," aria (Justitia)
      7b. "Juste nobis vendicatur"
      8. "Ad vos, ad vos convertimur," recit (Prudentia, Justitia, Temperantia, Fortitudo, Theologia)
      8a. "O Coelites vos invocamus," chorus

      1. "Nor can I think my suit is vain," aria (Neptune)
      2. "Thy great endeavours to increase the marine power," chorus

24. ARIAS (w/ orch)

24.1	*"Costretta piangere dolente" (c by 1762, frag)*	*HobXXIVb/1*
24.2	"D'una sposa meschinella" (c ?1777, for Paisiello: La Frascatana)	HobXXIVb/2
24.3	"Quando la rosa" (c1779, for Anfossi: La Metilde Ritrovata)	HobXXIVb/3
24.4	*"Il cor nel seno balzar mi sento" (c1780, for Salieri: La scuola de'Gelosi, inc, ?spur)*	*HobXXIVb/4*
24.5	"Dice benissimo chi si marita" (c1780, for Salieri: La scuola de' gelosi)	HobXXIVb/5
24.6	*"Mora l'infido ... Mi sento nel seno," recit & aria (c1781, for Righini: Il convitato, inc, ?spur)*	*HobXXIVb/6*
24.7	"Signor, voi sapete" (c1785, for Anfossi: Il matrimonio per inganno)	HobXXIV/7
24.8	"Dica pure chi vuol dire" (c ?1785, for Anfossi: Il geloso in cimento)	HobXXIVb/8
24.9	"Sono Alcina e sono ancora," cavatina (c1786, for Gazzaniga: L'isola d'Alcina)	HobXXIVb/9
24.10	"Ah, tu non senti, amico ... Qual destra omicida," recit & aria (c1786, for Traëtta: Ifigenia)	HobXXIVb/10
24.11	"Un cor si tenero" (c1787, for Bianchi: Il disertore)	HobXXIVb/11
24.12	"Vada adagio, Signorina" (c1787, for Guglielmi: La Quakera spiritosa)	HobXXIVb/12
24.13	"Chi vive amante" (c1787, for Bianchi: Alessandro nell'Indie)	HobXXIVb/13
24.14	"Se tu mi sprezzi, ingrata" (c1788, for Sarti: I finti eredi)	HobXXIVb/14
24.15	"Infelice sventurata" (c1789, for Cimarosa: I due supposti conti)	HobXXIVb/15
24.16	"Da che penso a maritarmi" (c1790, for Gassmann: L'amore artigiano)	HobXXIVb/16
24.17	"Il meglio mio carattere" (c1790, for Cimarosa: L'impresario in angustie)	HobXXIVb/17
24.18	"La moglie quando è buona" (c1790, for Cimarosa: Giannina e Bernardone)	HobXXIVb/18
24.19	"La mia pace, oh Dio" (c1790, for Gassmann: L'amore artigiano)	HobXXIVb/19
24.20	"Solo e pensoso" (c1798, sonetto from Petrarch: Canzoniere)	HobXXIVb/20
24.21	*?Aria of Giannina (c1788, for Sarti: I finti Eredi, vocal part lost, ?spur)*	*HobXXIVb/21*
24.22	"Tornate pur mia bella" (ca ?1785–95)	HobXXIVb/22
24.23	"Via siate bonino" (ca ?1785–95)	HobXXIVb/23

25. MISC VOCAL (2–4vv & acc)

"2 Duetti of Nisa & Tirsi" (c1796, Badini; S, T & hpd):

25.1	1. "Guarda qui, che lo vedrai"	HobXXVa/1
25.2	2. "Saper vorrei se m'ami"	HobXXVa/2

"Aus des Ramlers Lyrischer Blumenlese" (c1796; 3–4vv & cont):

25.3	1. "Der Augenblick": "Inbrunst, Zärtlichkeit, Verstand" (Ramler)	HobXXVc/1
25.4	2. "Die Harmonie in der Ehe": "O, wunderbare Harmonie" (Götz)	HobXXVc/2
25.5	3. "Alles hat seine Zeit": "Lebe, liebe, trinke, lärme" (Athenaeus transl Ebert)	HobXXVc/3
25.6	4. "Die Beredsamkeit": "Freunde, Wasser machet stumm" (Lessing)	HobXXVc/4
25.7	5. "Der Greis": "Hin ist alle meine Kraft" (Gleim)	HobXXVc/5
25.8	6. "An den Vetter": "Ja, Vetter, ja" (Ramler)	HobXXVb/2
25.9	7. "Daphnens einziger Fehler": "Sie hat das Auge" (Götz)	HobXXVb/2
25.10	8. "Die Warnung" (Athenaeus transl Ebert)	HobXXVc/6
25.11	9. "Betrachtung des Todes": "Der Jüngling hofft der Greises Ziel" (Gellert)	HobXXVb/3
25.12	10. "Wider den Übermut": "Was ist mein Stand, mein Glück" (Gellert; w/ hpd obbl)	HobXXVc/7
25.13	11. "An die Frauen": "Natur gab Stieren Hörner" (Anakreon transl Bürger; w/ hpd obbl)	HobXXVb/4
25.14	12. "Aus dem Danklied zu Gott": "Du Du bist's dem Ruhm" (Gellert; w/ hpd obbl)	HobXXVc/8
25.15	13. "Abendlied zu Gott": "Herr! Herr! Der du mir das Leben" (Gellertt; w/ hpd obbl)	HobXXVc/9
25.16	"Pietà di me, benigni Dei," trio (c?)	HobXXVb/5

Arrangements:

25.17	"12 Catches & Glees" (c1795; 3vv & harp/pf): 1. "Know then this truth"	HobXXXIc/16
25.18	2. "O say what is, that thing call'd light"	
25.19	3. "Hail to the myrtle shade"	
25.20	4. "Love free as air"	
25.21	5. "Ah no lasciarmi no"	
25.22	6. "O ever beauteous"	
25.23	7. "Where shall the hapless Lover find"	
25.24	8. "Ye little loves that round her wait"	
25.25	9. "Some kind angel gently flying"	
25.26	10. "I fruitless mourn to her who cannot hear"	
25.27	11. "Farewell my flocks once tender care"	
25.28	12. "The envious snow comes down in haste"	
25.29	"The Lady's Looking-glass": "Trust not too much to that chanting face" (ca1791–5)	HobXXXIc/17
25.30	"6 Admired Scotch Airs" (c1801–3; 1v, vn, vc & pf): 1. "The blue bell of Scotland"	Hobii/533
25.31	2. "My love she's but a lassie yet" (Macneill)	
25.32	3. "Bannocks o' barley meal" (?Boswell)	
25.33	4. "Saw ye my father?" (Burns)	
25.34	5. "Maggy Lauder"	
25.35	6. "Killicrankie" (?Grant/?Burns)	

26. SONGS (w/ kbd)

26.1   "12 Lieder," I (c by 1781): 1. "Das strickende Mädchen": "Und hörst du" (Sedley tr Herder) HobXXVIa/1–12
26.2   2. "Cupido": "Weisst Du mein kleines Mägdelein" (Leon)
26.3   3. "Der erste Kuss": "Leiser nannt ich deinen Namen" (Jacobi)
26.4   4. "Eine sehr gewöhnliche Geschichte": "Philint stand jüngst vor Baucis Thür" (Weisse)
26.5   5. "Die Verlassene": "Hör' auf mein armes Herz so bang zu schlagen"
26.6   6. "Der Gleichsinn": "Sollt' ich voller Sorg' und Pein um ein schönes Mädchen sein?" (Wither)
26.7   7. "An Iris": "Ein Liedchen vom Lieben verlangst du von mir?" (Weppen)
26.8   8. "An Thyrsis": "Eilt ihr Schäfer aus den Gründen" (Ziegler)
26.9   9. "Trost unglücklicher Liebe": "Ihr missvergnügten Stunden"
26.10   10. "Die Landlust": "Entfernt von Gram und Sorgen" (Stahl)
26.11   11. "Liebeslied": "So lang, ach! schon so lang erfüllt" (Leon)
26.12   12. "Die zu späte Ankunft der Mutter": "Beschattet von blühenden Ästen" (Weisse)
26.13   "12 Lieder," II (c1781): 13. "Jeder meint, der Gegenstand" (?Bader) HobXXVIa/13–24
26.14   14. "Lachet nicht, Mädchen"
26.15   15. "O liebes Mädchen, höre mich"
26.16   16. "Gegenliebe": "Wüsst' ich, wüsst' ich, dass Du mich" (Bürger)
26.17   17. "Geistliches Lied": "Dir nah ich mich"
26.18   18. "Auch die Sprödeste der Schönen" (Gotter)
26.19   19. "O fliess, ja wallend fliess"
26.20   20. "Zufriedenheit": "Ich bin vergnügt, will ich was mehr?" (Gleim)
26.21   21. "Das Leben ist ein Traum" (Gleim)
26.22   22. "Lob der Faulheit": "Faulheit, endlich muss ich dir" (Lessing)
26.23   23. "Minna": "Schon fesselt Lieb' und Ehre mich" (Engel)
26.24   24. "Auf meines Vaters Grab": "Hier sein Grab bei diesen stillen Hügeln"
26.25   "English Canzonettas," I (c by 1794, Hunter): 25. "Mermaid's Song": "Now the dancing" .. HobXXVIa/25–30
26.26   26. "Recollection": "The season comes when first we met"
26.27   27. "A Pastoral Song": "My mother bids me bind my hair"
26.28   28. "Despair": "The anguish of my bursting heart"
26.29   29. "Pleasing Pain": "Far from this throbbing besom haste"
26.30   30. "Fidelity": "While hollow burst the rushing winds"
26.31   "English Canzonettas," II (c1794–5): 31. "Sailor's Song": "High on the giddy bending mast" HobXXVIa/31–36
26.32   32. "The Wanderer": "To wander alone" (Hunter)
26.33   33. "Sympathy": "In thee I bear so dear a part" (Metastasio transl into English)
26.34   34. "She never told her love" (Shakespeare)
26.35   35. "Piercing Eyes": "Why asks my fair one if I love?"
26.36   36. "Content": "Ah me how scanty is my store"
26.37   "Beim Schmerz, der dieses Herz durchwühlet" (ca ?1765–75) HobXXVIa/37
26.38   "Der schlaue Pudel": "Die ganze Welt will glücklich sein" (ca1780) HobXXVIa/38
26.39   "Trachten will ich nicht auf Erden" (c1790) HobXXVIa/39
26.40   *"Der Feldzug" (c?, lost/?unidentified)* *HobXXVIa/40*
26.41   "The Spirit's Song": "Hark! Hark! what I tell to thee" (c before 1800, Hunter) HobXXVIa/41
26.42   "O tuneful Voice" (ca ?1795, Hunter) HobXXVIa/42
26.43   "Das Kaiserlied": "Gott, erhalte Franz den Kaiser!," national anthem (c1797, Haschka) HobXXVIa/43
26.44   "Als einst mit Weibes Schönheit" (ca ?1796–1800) HobXXVIa/44
26.45   "Ein kleines Haus" (c1801) HobXXVIa/45
26.46   "Vergiss mein nicht" (Antwort auf die Frage eines Mädchens): "Denkst du auch" (c ?1796) ... HobXXVIa/46
26.47   *"Bald wehen uns des Frühlings Lüfte" (c?, lost)* *HobXXVIa/47*
26.48   *"4 German Songs" (c?, arr of popular tunes, lost): a. "Ich liebe, du liebest, er liebet"* *HobXXVIa/48a–d*
26.49   *b. "Dürre, Staub, vermorschte Knochen"*
26.50   *c. "Sag'n allweil vom Staatsleb'n"*
26.51   *d. "Kein besseres Leben ist ja auf der Welt"*

Misc cantatas:

26.52   "Deutschlands Klage auf den Tod des ... Friedrichs Borussens König" (c1786; 1v & barytons) HobXXVIb/1
26.53   "Arianna a Naxos": "Teseo mio ben," cantata (c by 1789; S & hpd/pf) HobXXVIb/2
26.54   "Dr. Har(r)ingtons Compliment": "What Art expresses" (ca ?1794; S, ch & pf, var on a song) .. HobXXVIb/3
26.55   "The Battle of the Nile" (Nelson's aria): "Ausonia, trembling" (c ?1800, Knight; 1v & hpd/pf) HobXXVIb/4

27. CANONS

27.1   "Die heiligen zehn Gebote" (The 10 Commandments) (ca1791–5): 1. "Du sollst an einen Gott
              glauben" HobXXVIIa/1–10
27.2   2. "Du sollst den Namen Gottes nicht eitel nennen"
27.3   3. "Du sollst Sonn- und Feiertag heiligen"
27.4   4. "Du sollst Vater und Mutter verehren"
27.5   5. "Du sollst nicht töten" (2 vers)
27.6   6. "Du sollst nicht Unkeuschheit treiben"
27.7   7. "Du sollst nicht stehlen"
27.8   8. "Du sollst kein falsch Zeugnis geben"
27.9   9. "Du sollst nicht begehren deines Nächsten Weib"
27.10   10. "Du sollst nicht begehren deines Nächsten Gut"

27.11   "40 (47) Sinngedichte" (ca1791–9): 1. "Hilar an Narzis": "O stelle dich, Narciss" (Hagedorn) HobXXVIIb/1–47
27.12   2. "Auf einen adeligen Dummkopf": "Das nenn' ich einen Edelmann" (Lessing)
27.13   3. "Der Schuster bleib bei seinem Leist": "Ein jeder bleib bey seinem Stand" (Eckartshausen)
27.14   4. "Herr von Gänsewitz zu seinem Kammerdiener": "Befehlt doch draussen" (Bürger)
27.15   5. "An den Marull": "Gross willst du und auch artig sein?" (Lessing)
27.16   6. "Die Mutter an ihr Kind in der Wiege": "Höre, Mädchen, meine Bitte!"
27.17   7. "Der Menschenfreund": "O wollte doch der Mensch des Menschen Schutzgeist sein" (Gellert)
27.18   8. "Gottes Macht und Vorsehung": "Ist Gott mein Schutz" (Gellert)
27.19   9. "An Dorilis": "Wie grausam, Dorilis, bestrafst du meinen Scherz!" (Kretschmann)
27.20   10. "Vixi": "Ille potens sui laetusque deget" (Horace)
27.21   11. "Der Kobold": "Du, merke dir die Lehre" (Lichtwer)
27.22   12. "Der Fuchs und der Marder": "Wer Schwache leiten will, der sei" (Lichtwer)
27.23   13. "Abschied": "Kenne Gott, die Welt und dich"
27.24   14. "Die Hofstellungen": "Es stekket Ja im linken" (Logau)
27.25   15. "Aus Nichts wird Nichts": "Nackt ward' ich zur Welt geboren" (Blumauer after Richey)
27.26   16. "Cacatum non est pictum": "Beherzigt doch das Dictum" (Bürger)
27.27   17. "Tre cose": "Aspettare e non venire" (Federico)
27.28   18. "Vergebliches Glück": "Es ist umsonst" (Tscherning from Arabic)
27.29   19. "Grabschrift": "Hier liegt Hans Lau mit seiner Frau" (Hensler)
27.30   20. "Das Reitpferd": "Wie manche schliefen hier mit Ehren" (Lichtwer)
27.31   21. "Tod und Schlaf": "Tod ist ein langer Schlaf" (Logau)
27.32   22. "An einen Geizigen": "Ich dich beneiden? Tor!" (Lessing)
27.33   23. & 23bis. "Das böse Weib": "Ein einzig böses Weib lebt höchstens in der Welt" (Lessing; 2 vers)
27.34   24. "Der Verlust": "Alles ging für mich verloren, als ich Sylvien verlor" (Lessing)
27.35   25. "Der Freigeist": "Fliehe, fliehe, wenn dein Wohl dir heilig ist"
27.36   26. "Die Liebe der Feinde": "Nie will ich dem zu schaden suchen" (Gellert)
27.37   27. "Der Furchtsame": "Kaum seh ich den Donner die Himmel umziehen" (Lessing)
27.38   28. "Die Gewissheit": "Ob ich morgen leben werde, weiss ich freilich nicht" (Lessing)
27.39   29. "Phöbus und sein Sohn": "Zwichen Gott und unsern Sinnen" (Lichtwer)
27.40   30. "Die Tulipane": "So war der Mensch zu allen Zeiten" (Lichtwer)
27.41   31. "Das Grösste Gut": "Ein weises Herz und guter Mut"
27.42   32. "Der Hirsch": "Jeder prüfe seine Stärke!" (Lichtwer)
27.43   33. "Überschrift eines Weinhauses": "Wein, Bad und Liebe" (Opitz from Latin)
27.44   34. "Der Esel und die Dohle": "Ein Narr trifft allemal noch einen grössern an" (Lichtwer)
27.45   35. "Schalksnarren": "Ein Herr, der Narren hält" (Logau)
27.46   36. "Zweierlei Feinde": "Dein kleiner Feind ist der" (Tscherning from Arabic)
27.47   37. "Der Bäcker und die Maus": "Wer leichtlich zürnt, wird leicht berückt" (Lichtwer)
27.48   38. "Die Flinte und der Hase": "Was hilft Gesetz, was helfen Strafen" (Lichtwer)
27.49   39. "Der Nachbar": "Sehr nützlich ist uns oft ein Feind" (Lichtwer)
27.50   40. "Liebe zur Kunst": "Wer Lust zu lernen hat, dem mangelt immer was" (Logau)
27.51   41. "Frag und Antwort zweier Fuhrleute; Die Welt": "Geh sag mir nur, was ist die Welt?"
27.52   42. "Der Fuchs und der Adler": "Je höher Stand, je mehr Gefahr" (Lichtwer)
27.53   43. "Wunsch": "Langweiliger Besuch macht Zeit und Zimmer enger" (Hagedorn)
27.54   44. "Gott im Herzen, ein gut Weibchen im Arm" (cancelled; incl in: Mass, HobXXII/10)
27.55   45. "Turk was a faithful dog" (Rauzzini)
27.56   46. "Thy voice, o Harmony, is divine" (arr of HobXXVIIa/1)
27.57   *47. (w/ out text), in G major*

Attributed to Haydn (various degrees of possible authenticity):

27.58   *"Meine Herren lasst uns jetzt eine Sinfonie aufführen"* *HobXXVIIb/C1*
27.59   *"O wie schmecket mir die Ruh"* *HobXXVIIb/F1*
27.60   *"Narm san mar alle"* *HobXXVIIb/G1*
27.61   *"Mein Glass": "Mich freut ein blinkend Glas"* *HobXXVIIb/A1*
27.62   *"Vom Glück sey alles Dir beschert"* *HobXXVIIb/B1*

28. FOLKSONG ARRANGEMENTS (1v & acc)

(HobXXXIa = Scottish, HobXXXIb = Welsh):

    "Adieu to Llangollen" (= Happiness lost)
28.1   "Ae fond kiss" (c1795, ?Celtic air; w/ vn & cont) HobXXXIa/131
    "Age & youth" (= What can a young lassie do)
    "Aileen a roon" (= Robin Adair)
    "Alas! Yat I came o'er the moor" (= Last time I came o'er the muir)
28.2   "Allurement of love, The" (c1804; w/ vn, vc & pf) HobXXXIb/48
    "Anna" (= Shepherds, I have lost by love)
    "Answer, The" (= My mither's ay glowran)
28.3   "An thou wert mine ain thing" (c1800; w/ vn, vc & pf) HobXXXIa/164
28.4   "An thou wert mine ain thing" (c ?1804; w/ vn, vc & pf) HobXXXIa/164bis
    "An ye had been where I hae been" (= Killicrankie)
    "Argyll is my name" (= Bannocks o' barley meal)
28.5   "Ar hyd y nos", duet (c1803; w/ vn, vc & pf) HobXXXIb/9
28.6   "Aria di guerra e vittoria" (c1804; w/ vn, vc & pf) HobXXXIb/55

28.7	"As I cam down by yon castle wa' " (c1795, w/ vn & cont)	HobXXXIa/114
	"As I came o'er the Cairney mount" (= Old highland laddie)	
	"As Sylvia in a forest lay" (= Maid's complaint)	
28.8	"Auld gudeman, The" (c1801; w/ vn, vc & pf)	HobXXXIa/184
28.9	"Auld lang syne" (c1802/3; w/ vn, vc & pf)	HobXXXIa/218
28.10	"Auld Robin Gray" (c1800; w/ vn, vc & hpd)	HobXXXIa/168
28.11	"Auld Rob Morris," duet (c1801; w/ vn, vc & hpd)	HobXXXIa/192
28.12	"Auld wife ayont the fire, The" (c1801; w/ vn, vc & pf)	HobXXXIa/195
28.13	"Ay waking, O!," duet (c1800; w/ vn, vc & hpd)	HobXXXIa/157
	"Banks of Banna, The" (= Shepherds, I have lost my love)	
28.14	"Banks of Spey, The" (c by 1792; w/ vn & cont)	HobXXXIa/57
	"Banks of the Dee, The" (= Langolee)	
28.15	"Bannocks o' barley meal" (c1801; w/ vn, vc & pf)	HobXXXIa/171
28.16	"Barbara Allen" (c by 1792; w/ vn & cont)	HobXXXIa/11
28.17	"Barbara Allen" (c1800; w/ vn, vc & hpd)	HobXXXIa/11bis
	"Bashful lover, The" (= On a bank of flowers)	
28.18	"Be kind to the young thing" (c by 1792; vn & cont)	HobXXXIa/54
28.19	"Bend of the horse shoe, The" (c1804; w/ vn, vc & pf)	HobXXXIa/56
28.20	"Bess and her spinning wheel" (c1795; w/ vn & cont)	HobXXXIa/147
28.21	"Bessy Bell and Mary Gray" (c1800; w/ vn vc & pf)	HobXXXIa/178
28.22	"Bessy Bell and Mary Gray" (c ?1804; w/ vn vc & pf)	HobXXXIa/178bis
28.23	"Bid me not forget" (c1795; w/ vn & cont)	HobXXXIa/126
28.24	"Birks of Abergeldie, The" (c by 1792; w/ vn & cont)	HobXXXIa/58
28.25	"Birks of Abergeldie, The" (c1801; w/ vn, vc & hpd)	HobXXXIa/58bis
28.26	"Birks of Invermay, The" (c1801; w/ vn, vc & pf)	HobXXXIa/187
28.27	"Birks of Invermay, The" (c1802/3; w/ vn, vc & pf)	HobXXXIa/187bis
	"Black cock, The" (= Ton y ceiliog du)	
28.28	"Black eagle, The" (c by 1792; w/ vn & cont)	HobXXXIa/66
28.29	"Blathrie o't, The" (c1800; w/ vn, vc & hpd)	HobXXXIa/162
28.30	"Blink o'er the burn, sweet Betty" (c by 1792; w/ vn & cont)	HobXXXIa/68
28.31	"Blithsome bridal, The" (c by 1792; w/ vn & cont)	HobXXXIa/20
28.32	"Blithsome bridal, The" (c1801; w/ vn, vc & pf)	HobXXXIa/20bis
28.33	"Blodau Llundain," duet (c1804; w/ vn, vc & pf)	HobXXXIb/23
28.34	"Blodau'r drain" (c1803; w/ vn, vc & pf)	HobXXXIb/35
28.35	"Blodau'r grug" (c1803; w/ vn, vc & pf)	HobXXXIb/30
28.36	"Blossom of the honey suckle, The" (c1804; w/ vn, vc & pf)	HobXXXIb/54
	"Blossom of the raspberry, The" (= My jo Janet)	
28.37	"Blue bell(s) of Scotland, The" (c1801/2; w/ vn, vc & pf/hpd)	HobXXXIa/176
28.38	"Blue bonnets" (c by 1792; w/ vn & cont)	HobXXXIa/39
28.39	"Boatman, The" (c1801; w/ vn, vc & pf/hpd)	HobXXXIa/246
28.40	"Bonnie gray ey'd morn, The" (c1795; w/ vn & cont)	HobXXXIa/101
28.41	"Bonnie gray ey'd morn, The" (c1801; w/ vn, vc & pf)	HobXXXIa/101bis
	"Bonnie laddie, highland laddie" (= Jingling Jonnie)	
28.42	"Bonniest lass in a' the warld, The" (c by 1792; w/ vn & cont)	HobXXXIa/25
28.43	"Bonnie wee thing" (c1795; w/ vn & cont) (also see Beethoven WoO 158c/4)	HobXXXIa/102
28.44	"Bonnie wee thing" (c ?1802/3; w/ vn, vc & pf) (also see Beethoven WoO 158c/4)	HobXXXIa/102bis
28.45	"Bonnie wee thing" (c1801; w/ vn, vc & pf) (also see Beethoven WoO 158c/4)	HobXXXIa/102ter
	"Bonny Anne" (= If a body meet a body)	
	"Bonny Barbara Allan" (= Barbara Allen)	
	"Bonny black eagle," The (= Black eagle)	
28.46	"Bonny brucket lassie," The (c by 1792; w/ vn & cont)	HobXXXIa/59
28.47	"Bonny Jean" (c1800; w/ vn, vc & pf)	HobXXXIa/172
	"Bonny Jean" (= Willie was a wanton wag)	
28.48	"Bonny Kate of Edinburgh" (c by 1792; w/ vn & cont)	HobXXXIa/94
	"Bonny, roaring Willie" (= Rattling roaring Willy)	
	"Bonny Scot-man, The" (= Boatman)	
28.49	"Braes of Ballenden, The" (c1801; w/ vn, vc & pf)	HobXXXIa/200
28.50	"Braes of Ballenden, The" (c1802/3; w/ vn, vc & pf)	HobXXXIa/200bis
28.51	"Braes of Yarrow, The" (c1802/3; w/ vn, vc & pf)	HobXXXIa/207
	"Braw lads of Galla water" (= Galla water)	
	"Bridegroom greets when the sun gangs down, The" (Auld Robin Gray)	
	"Bride's song, The" (= Blithsome bridal)	
28.52	"Brisk young lad, The" (c by 1792; w/ vn & cont)	HobXXXIa/46
28.53	"Brisk young lad, The" (c by 1801; w/ vn, vc & hpd)	HobXXXIa/46bis
28.54	"Britons, The" (c1804; w/ vn, vc & pf)	HobXXXIb/51
28.55	"Broom of Cowdenknows, The" (c1800; w/ chorus & vn, vc, hpd)	HobXXXIa/170
	"Broom, the bonny broom" (= Broom of Cowdenknows)	
28.56	"Bush aboon Traquair, The," duet (c1802,3; w/ vn, vc & pf)	HobXXXIa/204
	"Busk ye, busk ye" (= Braes of Yarrow)	
	"Butcher boy, The" (= My Godess woman)	
	"By the stream so cool and clear" (= St Kilda song)	
	"Captain Cook's death" (= Highland Mary)	
28.57	"Captain O' Kain" (c ?1802/3, ?Irish air; w/ vn, vc & pf)	HobXXXIa/224
	"Captain's lady, The" (= Mount your baggage)	

28.108	"Frae the friends and land I love" (c1795; w/ vn & cont)	HobXXXIa/105
28.109	"Fy! gar rub her o'er wi' strae" (c by 1792; w/ vn & cont)	HobXXXIa/7
28.110	"Fy! gar rub her o'er wi' strae," duet (c1801; w/ vn, vc & pf)	HobXXXIa/7bis
	"Gaberlunzie" (Gaberlunyie) man, The" (= Brisk young lad)	
28.111	"Galashiels" (c1800; w/ vn, vc & hpd)	HobXXXIa/179
28.112	"Galla water" (c by 1792; w/ vn & cont)	HobXXXIa/15
28.113	"Galla water" (c ?1802/3; w/ vn, vc & pf)	HobXXXIa/15bis
28.114	"Galla water" (c1803; w/ vn, vc & pf)	HobXXXIa/15ter
	"Gardener's march, The" (= Gard'ner wi' his paidle)	
28.115	"Gard'ner wi' his paidle, The" (c by 1792; w/ vn & cont)	HobXXXIa/45
	"Gentle swain, The" (= Johnny's gray breeks)	
28.116	"Gilderoy," duet (c ?1802/3; w/ vn, vc & pf)	HobXXXIa/225
28.117	"Gil Morris (Morrice)" (c1801; w/ vn, vc & hpd)	HobXXXIa/196
	"Gin you meet a bonny lassie" (= Fy! gar rub her o'er wi' strae)	
28.118	"Glancing of her apron, The" (c by 1792; w/ vn & cont)	HobXXXIa/88
	"Gordons has (had) the guiding o't, The" (= Strephon and Lydia)	
28.119	"Gorhoffedd gwyr Harlech" (c1803; w/ vn, vc & pf)	HobXXXIb/2
	"Go to the ew-bughts, Marion" (= Ewe-bughts)	
28.120	"Gramachree" (Irish air) (c by 1792; w/ vn & cont)	HobXXXIa/13
28.121	"Gramachree" (Irish air) (c1801; w/ vn, vc & pf)	HobXXXIa/13bis
28.122	"Gramachree" (Irish air) (c ?1802/3; w/ vn, vc & pf)	HobXXXIa/13ter
28.123	"Green grow the rashes" (c by 1792; w/ vn & cont)	HobXXXIa/8
28.124	"Green grow the rashes" (c by 1792; w/ chorus & vn, vc & pf)	HobXXXIa/8bis
28.125	"Green sleeves" (c1795; w/ vn & cont)	HobXXXIa/112
28.126	"Green sleeves" (c1801; w/ vn, vc & pf)	HobXXXIa/112bis
28.127	"Grisiel ground," duet (c1803; w/ vn, vc & pf)	HobXXXIb/15
	"Had awa frae me, Donald" (= Thou'rt gane awa')	
28.128	"Hallow ev'n" (c by 1792; w/ vn & cont)	HobXXXIa/63
28.129	"Happiness lost" (c1804; w/ vn, vc & pf)	HobXXXIb/42
	"Happiness lost" (= Tears that must ever fall)	
28.130	"Happy topers, The" (c1801; w/ chorus & vn, vc & pf)	HobXXXIa/243
28.131	"Hela'r ysgyfarnog" (c1804; w/ vn, vc & pf)	HobXXXIb/33
	"Hellvellyn" (= Erin-go-bragh)	
	"Hemp-dresser, The" (= Looking glass)	
28.132	"Her absence will not alter me" (c by 1792; w/ vn & cont)	HobXXXIa/100
28.133	"Here awa', there awa' " (c ?1802/3; w/ vn, vc & pf)	HobXXXIa/257
28.134	"Here's a health to my true love" (c by 1792; w/ vn & cont)	HobXXXIa/49
	"He's far away" (= Weary pund o' tow)	
	"He who presum'd to guide the sun" (= Maid's complaint)	
	"Hey now the day dawes" (= Hey tutti taiti)	
28.135	"Hey tutti taiti" (c1801; w/ vn, vc & hpd)	HobXXXIa/174
	"Highland air" (= Lone vale)	
	"Highland lamentation" (= Young Damon)	
	"Highland lassie (laddie), The" (= Old highland laddie)	
28.136	"Highland Mary" (c1800; w/ vn, vc & pf)	HobXXXIa/159
	"Highway to Edinburgh, The" (= Black eagle)	
28.137	"Hob y deri dando" (c1803; w/ vn, vc & pf)	HobXXXIb/11
28.138	"Hob y deri danno" (c1804; w/ vn, vc & pf)	HobXXXIb/16
28.139	"Hoffedd Hywel ab Owen Gwynedd" (c1804; w/ vn, vc & pf)	HobXXXIb/28
	"Hold away from me, Donald" (= Thou'rt gane awa')	
28.140	"Holly and fairly" (c1801; w/ vn, vc & hpd)	HobXXXIa/237
	"House of Glams" (= Roslin Castle)	
28.141	"How can I be sad on my wedding day" (c by 1792; w/ vn & cont)	HobXXXIa/36
28.142	"How long and dreary is the night" (Gaelic) (c by 1792; w/ vn & cont)	HobXXXIa/67
	"How sweet is the scene" (= Humours o' glen)	
	"How sweet this lone vale" (= Lone vale)	
28.143	"Hughie Graham" (c1795; w. vn & cont)	HobXXXIa/141
28.144	"Humours o' glen, The" (?Irish air) (c ?1802/3; w/ vn, vc & pf)	HobXXXIa/256
28.145	"I canna come ilke day to woo" (c1795; w/ vn & cont)	HobXXXIa/140
28.146	"I canna come ilke day to woo" (c1801; w/ vn, vc & hpd)	HobXXXIa/140bis
28.147	"I do confess thou art sae fair" (c1795; w/ vn & cont)	HobXXXIa/110
28.148	"I dream'd I lay" (c by 1792; w/ vn & cont)	HobXXXIa/87
28.149	"If a body meet a body" (c by 1792; w/ vn & cont)	HobXXXIa/80
28.150	"If a body meet a body" (c1801; w/ vn, vc & pf)	HobXXXIa/80bis
28.151	"If e'er ye do well it's a wonder" (c by 1792; w/ vn & cont)	HobXXXIa/95
28.152	"I had a horse" (c by 1792; w/ vn & cont)	HobXXXIa/17
28.153	"I had a horse" (c ?1804; w/ vn, vc & pf)	HobXXXIa/17bis
28.154	"I'll never leave thee" (c1802/3; w/ vn, vc & pf)	HobXXXIa/205
28.155	"I love my love in secret" (c1795; w/ vn & cont)	HobXXXIa/3
28.156	"I'm o'er young to marry yet" (c by 1792; w/ vn & cont)	HobXXXIa/30
28.157	"I wish my love were in a myre" (c1800; w/ vn, vc & hpd)	HobXXXIa/177
28.158	"Jacobite air," duet (c1801; w/ vn, vc & pf)	HobXXXIa/231
28.159	"Jamie, come try me" (c by 1792; w/ vn & cont)	HobXXXIa/79
28.160	"Jenny drinks nae water" (c1795; w/ vn & cont)	HobXXXIa/132

"Margret's ghost" (= William and Margaret)
28.216   "Marsh of Rhuddlan, The" (c1804; w/ vn, vc & pf) HobXXXIb/49
28.217   "Mary's dream" (c by 1792; w/ vn & cont) HobXXXIa/1
28.218   "Mary's dream" (c1801; w/ vn, vc & hpd) HobXXXIa/1bis
     "McFarsence's testament" (= Macpherson's farewell)
28.219   "McGrigor of Rora's lament" (Celtic air) (c by 1792; w/ vn & cont) HobXXXIa/81
     "McPherson's rant" (= Macpherson's farewell)
28.220   "Mentra Gwen," duet (c1803; w/ vn, vc & pf) HobXXXIb/6
28.221   "Merry may the maid be" (c by 1792; w/ vn & cont) HobXXXIa/50
28.222   "Merry may the maid be" (c ?1804; w/ vn, vc & pf) HobXXXIa/50bis
     "Miller, The" (= Merry may the maid be)
     "Miller's daughter, The" (= If a body meet a body)
     "Miller's wedding, The" (= Auld lang syne)
28.223   "Mill, mill O!, The" (c by 1792; w/ vn & cont) HobXXXIa/92
28.224   "Mill, mill O!, The" (c ?1802/3; w/ vn, vc & pf) HobXXXIa/92bis
28.225   "Minstrel, The" (c1795; w/ vn & cont) HobXXXIa/115
28.226   "Minstrel, The" (c1801; w/ vn, vc & hpd) HobXXXIa/115bis
     "Miss Admiral Gordon's strathspey" (= Poet's ain Jean)
     "Miss Farquharson's reel" (= My love she's but a lassie yet)
     "Miss Hamilton's delight" (= My jo Janet)
28.227   "Morag" (Celtic air) (c1795; w/ vn & cont) HobXXXIa/143
28.228   "Morag" (Celtic air) (c1801; w/ vn, vc & pf) HobXXXIa/143bis
     "Moudiewart, The" (= O, for ane-and-twenty Tam!)
28.229   "Mount your baggage" (c by 1792; w/ vn & cont) HobXXXIa/42
28.230   "Mucking of Geordie's byer, The" (c by 1792; w/ vn & cont) HobXXXIa/51
28.231   "Mucking of Geordie's byer, The" (c1801; w/ vn, vc & pf) HobXXXIa/51bis
28.232   "Muirland Willy" (c1801; w/ chorus & vn, vc, pf) HobXXXIa/242
     "Musket salute, The" (= My heart's in the highlands)
28.233   "Mwynen Cynwyd" (c1804; w/ vn, vc & pf) HobXXXIb/31
     "My ain fireside" (= Todlen hame)
     "My ain kind deary" (= Lea-rig)
28.234   "My apron deary" (c1801; w/ vn, vc & pf) HobXXXIa/189
28.235   "My apron deary" (c ?1802/3; w/ vn, vc & pf) HobXXXIa/189bis
28.236   "My boy, Tammy" (c by 1792; w/ vn & cont) HobXXXIa/18
28.237   "My dearie if thou die" (c1800; w/ vn, vc & pf) HobXXXIa/166
28.238   "My Goddess woman" (c1795; w/ vn & cont) HobXXXIa/120
28.239   "My heart's in the highlands" (Celtic air) (c by 1792; w/ vn & cont) HobXXXIa/77
     "My Jockey was the blythest lad" (= Flowers of Edinburgh)
28.240   "My jo Janet" (c ?1804; w/ vn, vc & pf) HobXXXIa/258
28.241   "My lodging is on the cold ground" (?Irish) (c ?1802/3; w/ vn, vc & pf) HobXXXIa/262
     "My love's bonny when she smiles on me" (= Flowers of Edinburgh)
28.242   "My love she's but a lassie yet" (c1801; w/ vn, vc & pf) HobXXXIa/194
     "My love's in Germanie" (= Wish)
     "My Mary dear, departed shade" (= Highland Mary)
28.243   "My mither's ay glowran o'er me" (c by 1792; w/ vn & cont) HobXXXIa/70
28.244   "My mither's ay glowran o'er me" (c1800; w/ vn, vc & pf) HobXXXIa/70bis
28.245   "My Nanie, O" (c by 1792; w/ vn & cont) HobXXXIa/37
28.246   "My Nanie, O" (c1802/3; w/ vn, vc & pf) HobXXXIa/37bis
28.247   "My Nanie, O" (c1803; w/ vn, vc & pf) HobXXXIa/37ter
28.248   "My Nanie, O" (c1801; w/ vn, vc & pf) HobXXXIa/37quater
     "My plaid away" (= O'er the hills and far away)

     "Nancy's to the green-wood gane" (= Scornfu' Nancy)
     "Nanny, O" (= My Nanie, O)
     "Nelly's dream" (= Marg'ret's ghost)
     "New hilland laddie" (= Lass of Livingston)
28.249   "New year's gift, The" (c1804; w/ vn, vc & pf) HobXXXIb/60
     "Nine pint cogie" (= Collier's bonny lassie)
28.250   "Nithsdall's welcome home" (c1795; w/ vn & cont) HobXXXIa/125
28.251   "Nos galan" (c1803; w/ vn, vc & pf) HobXXXIb/29
28.252   "Now westlin winds" (c1795; w/ vn & cont) HobXXXIa/111
28.253   "O bonny lass" (?Irish air) (c by 1792; w/ vn & cont) HobXXXIa/89
     "O can ye labor lea" (= Auld lang syne)
28.254   "O can you sew cushions" (c by 1792; w/ vn & cont) HobXXXIa/48
28.255   "O'er bogie" (c by 1792; w/ vn & cont) HobXXXIa/16
28.256   "O'er bogie" (c1801; w/ vn,vc & pf) HobXXXIa/16bis
28.257   "O'er the hills and far away" (c1795; w/ vn & cont) HobXXXIa/149
28.258   "O'er the hills and far away" (c1801; w/ chorus & vn, vc, pf) HobXXXIa/149bis
28.259   "O'er the moor amang the heather" (c1795; w/ vn & cont) HobXXXIa/122
28.260   "O'er the moor amang the heather" (c ?1802/3; w/ vn, vc & pf) HobXXXIa/122ter
     "Of a' the airts" (= Poet's ain Jean)
     "Of noble race was Shenkin" (= Y gadly's)
28.261   "O, for ane-and-twenty Tam!" (c1795; w/ vn & cont) HobXXXIa/108
28.262   "Oh, onochrie (Oh! ono Chrio)" (Irish air) (c by 1792; w/ vn & cont) HobXXXIa/85
     "Oh, open the door, Lord Gregory" (= Lass of Lochroyan)

28.263	"Old highland laddie (lassie), The" (c1801; w/ vn, vc & pf)	HobXXXIa/248
	"Old man, The" (= My jo Janet)	
	"O let me in this ae night" (= Let me in this ae night)	
28.264	"On a bank of flowers" (c1795; w/ vn & cont)	HobXXXIa/142
28.265	"On Ettrick banks" (c1800; w/ vn, vc & hpd)	HobXXXIa/151
	"On the death of Delia's linnet" (= Death of the linnet)	
28.266	"Oonagh (Oonagh waterfall)" (Irish air) (c1801; w/ vn, vc & pf)	HobXXXIa/249
28.267	"Open the door" (?Irish air) (c ?1804; w/ vn, vc & pf)	HobXXXIa/255
	"O poortith cauld" (= I had a horse)	
28.268	"Oran gaoil," duet (Gallic air) (c1801; w/ vn, vc & pf)	HobXXXIa/228
	"O steer her up and had her gaun" (= Steer her up)	
	"Palmer, The" (= Open the door)	
28.269	"Pant corlant yr wyn: neu, Dafydd or Garreg-las," duet (c1804; w/ vn,vc & pf)	HobXXXIb/22
28.270	"Pat & Kate," duet (Irish air) (c1803; w/ vn, vc & pf)	HobXXXIa/241
28.271	"Peggy, I must love thee," duet (c1801; w/ vn, vc & hpd)	HobXXXIa/167
28.272	"Peggy in devotion" (c by 1792; w/ vn & cont)	HobXXXIa/96
28.273	"Pentland Hills" (c by 1792; w/ vn & cont)	HobXXXIa/33
	"Phely & Willy" (= Jacobite air)	
	"Phoebe" (= Yon wild mossy mauntains)	
28.274	"Pinkie House" (c1800; w/ vn, vc & pf)	HobXXXIa/183
28.275	"Ploughman, The" (c by 1792; w/ vn & cont)	HobXXXIa/10
28.276	"Poet's ain Jean, The" (c1801; w/ vn, vc & pf)	HobXXXIa/230
28.277	"Poet's ain Jean, The," duet (c ?1804; w/ vn, vc & pf)	HobXXXIa/230bis
28.278	"Polwarth on the green," duet (c1801; w/ vn, vc & hpd)	HobXXXIa/265
28.279	"Poor pedlar, The" (c1804; w/ vn, vc & pf)	HobXXXIb/53
28.280	"Posie, The" (c1795; w/ vn & cont)	HobXXXIa/113
28.281	"Pursuit of love, The" (c1804; w/ vn, vc & pf)	HobXXXIb/52
28.282	"Queen Mary's lamentation" (c1800; w/ vn, vc & pf)	HobXXXIa/161
	"Ranting highlandman, The" (= White cockade)	
	"Ranting, roving Willie" (= Rattling roaring Willy)	
28.283	"Rattling roaring Willy" (c1801; w/ vn, vc & pf/hpd)	HobXXXIa/227
	"Raving winds" (= McGrigor of Rora's lament)	
28.284	"Reged" (c1804; w/ vn, vc & pf)	HobXXXIb/38
28.285	"Rhyfelgyrch Cadpen Morgan" (c1803; w/ vn, vc & pf)	HobXXXIb/8
28.286	"Robin Adair," duet (?Irish air) (c1801; w/ vn, vc & pf) (also see Beethoven WoO 157/7)	HobXXXIa/202
	"Robin is my only jo" (= Robin, quo' she)	
28.287	"Robin, quo' she" (c by 1792; w/ vn & cont)	HobXXXIa/72
28.288	"Robin, quo' she" (c ?1804; w/ vn, vc & pf)	HobXXXIa/72bis
	"Roger's farewell" (= Auld lang syne)	
	"Rory Dall's port" (= Ae fond kiss)	
28.289	"Rose bud, The" (c1795; w/ vn & cont)	HobXXXIa/135
28.290	"Roslin Castle" (Roslane Castle) (c1801; w/ vn, vc & pf)	HobXXXIa/191
28.291	"Roslin Castle" (Roslane Castle) (c1802/3; w/ vn, vc & pf)	HobXXXIa/191bis
28.292	"Rothiemurche's rant" (c1800; w/ vn, vc & pf)	HobXXXIa/165
	"Row saftly, thou stream" (= Captain O'Kain)	
28.293	"Roy's wife of Alldivaloch" (c1795; w/ vn & cont)	HobXXXIa/103
28.294	"Sae merry as we ha'e been" (c1802/3; w/ vn, vc & pf)	HobXXXIa/223
	"Sandie and Jockie" (= Jockie and Sandy)	
	"Sawney will never be my love again" (= Corn riggs)	
	"Sawnie's pipe" (= Colonel Gardner)	
	"Saw ye Johnnie cummin? quo' she" (= Fee him, father)	
28.295	"Saw ye my father?" (c by 1792; c/ vn & cont)	HobXXXIa/5
28.296	"Saw ye my father?" (c1800; w/ vn, vc & hpd)	HobXXXIa/5bis
28.297	"Saw ye my father?" (c ?1804; c/ vn, vc & pf)	HobXXXIa/5ter
28.298	"Saw ye nae my Peggy?" (c by 1792; w/ vn & cont)	HobXXXIa/56
28.299	"Scornfu' Nancy" (c1800; w/ vn, vc & pf)	HobXXXIa/185
28.300	"Scornfu' Nancy" (c ?1804; w/ vn, vc & pf)	HobXXXIa/185bis
	"Scots Jenny" (= Jenny was fair)	
28.301	"Sensibility" (c1800; w/ vn, vc & pf)	HobXXXIa/173
	"Seventh of November" (= Day returns)	
	"She grip'd at the greatest on't" (= East Neuk o' Fife)	
28.302	"Shepherd Adonis, The" (c by 1792; w/ vn & cont)	HobXXXIa/21
28.303	"Shepherds, I have lost my love" (c by 1792; w/ vn & cont)	HobXXXIa/93
28.304	"Shepherds, I have lost my love" (c ?1802/3; w/ vn, vc & pf)	HobXXXIa/93bis
28.305	"Shepherd's son, The" (c1795; w/ vn & cont)	HobXXXIa/106
28.306	"Shepherd's son, The" (c ?1802/3; w/ vn, vc & pf)	HobXXXIa/106bis
28.307	"Shepherd's son, The" (c1804, 2 vers; w/ vn, vc & pf)	HobXXXIa/106ter
28.308	"Shepherd's wife, The" (c1795; w/ vn & cont)	HobXXXIa/128
28.309	"Shepherd's wife, The" (c1801; w/ vn, vc & pf)	HobXXXIa/128bis
28.310	"She rose and loot me in" (c ?1802/3; w/ vn, vc & pf)	HobXXXIa/219
28.311	"She rose and loot me in" (c1801; w/ vn, vc & pf)	HobXXXIa/219bis
	"She says she lo'es me best of a' " (= Oonagh)	
28.312	"She's fair and fause" (c1795; w/ vn & cont)	HobXXXIa/121
28.313	"Silken snood, The" (c1802/3; w/ vn, vc & pf)	HobXXXIa/208

28.314 "Siller crown, The" (c ?1804; w/ vn, vc & pf) HobXXXIa/260
"Sir Alex. Don" (= Auld lang syne)
28.315 "Sir Patrick Spence" (c1803; w/ vn, vc & pf) HobXXXIa/250
28.316 "Slave's lament, The" (c1795; w/ vn & cont) HobXXXIa/137
28.317 "Sleepy bodie" (c by 1792; w/ vn & cont) HobXXXIa/44
"So for seven years" (= Tho' for sev'n years)
28.318 "Soger laddie, The" (c by 1792; w/ vn & cont) HobXXXIa/60
28.319 "Soger laddie, The" (c1801; w/ vn, vc & pf) HobXXXIa/60bis
"Soldier laddie, The" (= Soger laddie)
"Soldier's dream, The" (= Captain O'Kain)
"Soldier's return, The" (= Mill, mill O!)
28.320 "Steer her up, and had ger gawin" (c by 1792; w/ vn & cont) HobXXXIa/78
28.321 "St Kilda song" (c by 1792; w/ vn & cont) HobXXXIa/19
28.322 "Strathallan's lament" (c1795; w/ vn & cont) HobXXXIa/145
28.323 "Strathallan's lament" (c1801; w/ vn, vc & pf) HobXXXIa/145bis
28.324 "Strephon and Lydia" (c1795; w/ vn & cont) HobXXXIa/150
"Sun had loos'd his weary team, The" (= Looking glass)
28.325 "Sutor's daughter, The," duet (c1801; w/ vn, vc & pf) HobXXXIa/198
28.326 "Sweet Annie" (c?1802/3; w/ vn, vc & pf) HobXXXIa/261
28.327 "Sweet melody of north Wales, The" (c1803; w/ vn, vc & pf) HobXXXIb/44
"Sweet's the lass that loves me" (= Bess and her spinning wheel)
28.328 "Tak' your auld cloak about ye" (c1800; w/ vn, vc & pf) HobXXXIa/180
28.329 "Tak' your auld cloak about ye" (c ?1804; w/ vn, vc & pf) HobXXXIa/180bis
"Tarry woo' " (= Lewie Gordon)
28.330 "Tears I shed, The" (c1795; w/ vn & cont) HobXXXIa/123
28.331 "Tears of Caledonia, The" (c1801; w/ vn, vc & pf) HobXXXIa/201
28.332 "Tears that must ever fall" (c1801; w/ vn, vc & pf) HobXXXIa/186
"Their groves o' sweet myrtle" (= Humours o' glen)
28.333 "This is no mine ain house" (c by 1792; w/ vn & cont) HobXXXIa/14
28.334 "This is no mine ain house" (c ?1802/3; w/ vn, vc & pf) HobXXXIa/14bis
28.335 "Tho' for sev'n years and mair" (c1795; w/ vn & cont) HobXXXIa/146
28.336 "Thou'rt gane awa' " (c by 1792; w/ vn & cont) HobXXXIa/12
28.337 "Thou'rt gane awa' " (c ?1802/3; w/ vn, vc & pf) HobXXXIa/12bis
28.338 "Three captains, The" (Irish air) (c1803; w/ vn, vc & pf) HobXXXIa/264
28.339 "Thro' the wood, laddie" (c1800; w/ vn, vc & hpd) HobXXXIa/181
28.340 "Tibby Fowler" (c by 1792; w/ vn & cont) HobXXXIa/52
" 'Tis woman" (= Bonnie gray ey'd morn)
28.341 "Tither morn, The" (c1795; w/ vn & cont) HobXXXIa/130
28.342 "To daunton me" (c by 1792; w/ vn & cont) HobXXXIa/98
28.343 "Todlen hame" (c by 1792; w/ vn & cont) HobXXXIa/6
28.344 "Todlen hame" (c ?1802/3; w/ vn, vc & pf) HobXXXIa/6bis
28.345 "Ton y ceiliog du," duet (c1804; w/ vn, vc & pf) HobXXXIb/18
28.346 "Torriad y dydd" (c1803; w/ vn, vc & pf) HobXXXIb/3
"To the rose bud" (= Rose bud)
"Tranent Muir" (= Killicrankie)
28.347 "Troiad y droell," duet (c1804; w/ vn, vc & pf) HobXXXIb/41
28.348 "Tros y garrer" (c1804; w/ vn, vc & pf) HobXXXIb/17
28.349 "Tweedside," duet (c1802/3; w/ vn, vc & pf) HobXXXIb/206
28.350 "Twll yn ei boch" (c1803; w/ vn, vc & pf) HobXXXIb/10
28.351 "Up and war them a' Willy" (c1801; w/ vn, vc & pf) HobXXXIa/233
28.352 "Up in the morning early" (c by 1792; w/ vn & cont) HobXXXIa/28
28.353 "Up in the morning early" (c ?1802/3; w/ vn, vc & pf) HobXXXIa/28bis
28.354 "Up in the morning early" (c1801; w/ vn, vc & pf) HobXXXIa/28ter
28.355 "Vain pursuit, The" (c1795; w/ vn & cont) HobXXXIa/133
28.356 "Waefu' heart, The" (c by 1792; w/ vn & cont) HobXXXIa/9
28.357 "Waefu' heart, The" (c ?1802/3; w/ vn, vc & pf) HobXXXIa/9bis
28.358 "Waly, waly" (c1802/3; w/ vn, vc & pf) HobXXXIa/214
28.359 "Waly, waly" (c1801; w/ vn, vc & pf) HobXXXIa/214bis
"Wandering Willie" (= Here awa')
"Wap at the widow, my laddie" (see Widow)
28.360 "Wat ye wha I met yestreen?" (c by 1792; w/ vn & cont) HobXXXIa/69
28.361 "Wat ye wha I met yestreen?" (c1801; w/ vn, vc & pf) HobXXXIa/69bis
28.362 "Wawking of the fauld, The" (c by 1792; w/ vn & cont) HobXXXIa/40
28.363 "Weary pund o' tow, The" (c1795; w/ vn & cont) HobXXXIa/129
28.364 "Weary pund o' tow, The" (c1801; w/ vn, vc & hpd) HobXXXIa/129bis
28.365 "Wee wee man, The" (c1795; w/ vn & cont) HobXXXIa/124
28.366 "Wee wee man, The" (c1801; w/ vn, vc & pf) HobXXXIa/124bis
"Welcome home, old Rowley" (= Thou'rt gane awa')
28.367 "What ails this heart of mine," duet (c1804; w/ vn, vc & pf) HobXXXIa/244
28.368 "What can a young lassie do" (c1795; w/ vn & cont) HobXXXIa/134
28.369 "What can a young lassie do" (c1801; w/ chorus & vn, vc & pf) HobXXXIa/134bis
"What shall I do with an auld man" (= What can a young lassie do)
28.370 "When she came ben she bobbit" (c by 1792; w/ vn & cont) HobXXXIa/62
"Where Helen lies" (= Fair Helen of Kirkconnell)

28.371	"While hopeless" (c1795; w/ vn & cont)	HobXXXIa/104
28.372	"Whistle o'er the lave o't" (c by 1792; w/ vn & cont)	HobXXXIa/76
28.373	"Whistle o'er the lave o't" (c1801; w/ vn, vc & pf/hpd)	HobXXXIa/76bis
28.374	"White cockade, The" (c by 1792; w/ vn & cont)	HobXXXIa/22
28.375	"Widow, The" (c1795; w/ vn & cont)	HobXXXIa/118
28.376	"Widow, are ye waking?" (c by 1792; w/ vn & cont)	HobXXXIa/75
28.377	"Widow, are ye waking?" (c ?1804; w/ vn, vc & pf)	HobXXXIa/75bis
28.378	"William and Margaret" (c1800; w/ vn, vc & hpd)	HobXXXIa/153
	"Willie brew'd a peck o' maut" (= Happy topers)	
28.379	"Willie was a wanton wag" (c by 1792; w/ vn & cont)	HobXXXIa/4
28.380	"Willie was a wanton wag" (c1801; w/ vn, vc & pf)	HobXXXIa/4bis
28.381	"Willow hymn, The" (c1803; w/ vn, vc & pf)	HobXXXIb/47
	"Will ye go to Flanders" (= Gramachree)	
28.382	"Willy's rare" (c1792; w/ vn & cont)	HobXXXIa/82
	"Wilt thou be my dearie" (= Sutor's daughter)	
28.383	"Winifreda," duet (c1803; w/ vn, vc & pf)	HobXXXIb/46
28.384	"Wish, The" (c1801; w/ vn, vc & pf)	HobXXXIa/245
	"Wo betyd thy wearie bodie" (= Bonnie wee thing)	
28.385	"Woes my heart that we shou'd sunder," duet (c1800; w/vn, vc & hpd)	HobXXXIa/155
	"Women's work will never be done" (= Black eagle)	
28.386	"Woo'd and married and a' " (c by 1792; w/ vn & cont)	HobXXXIa/38
28.387	"Woo'd and married and a' " (c1801; w/ chorus & vn, vc & pf)	HobXXXIa/38bis
28.388	"Wyres Ned Puw" (c1804; w/ vn, vc & pf)	HobXXXIb/19
28.389	"Y bardd yn ei awen" (c1804; w/ vn, vc & pf)	HobXXXIb/25
28.390	"Y Cymry dedwydd" (c1804; w/ vn, vc & pf)	HobXXXIb/32
28.391	"Ye Gods! was Strephon's picture blest" (c by 1792; w/ vn & cont)	HobXXXIa/43
28.392	"Yellow hair'd laddie, The," duet (c1802/3; w/ vn, vc & pf)	HobXXXIa/221
28.393	"Y gadly's," duet (c1803; w/ vn, vc & pf)	HobXXXIb/24
28.394	"Yon wild mossy mountains" (c1795; w/ vn & cont)	HobXXXIa/119
28.395	"Young Damon" (c by 1792; w/ vn & cont)	HobXXXIa/71
	"Young highland rover, The" (= Morag)	
28.396	"Young Jockey was the blythest lad" (c1792; w/ vn & cont)	HobXXXIa/64
28.397	"Young Jockey was the blythest lad" (c1801; w/ vn, vc & pf)	HobXXXIa/64bis
	"Young laird and Edinburgh Katy, The" (= Wat ye wha I met)	
	"Young Peggy blooms" (= Boatman)	
28.398	"Yr hen erddigan" (c1803; w/ vn, vc & pf)	HobXXXIb/37

Spurious:

28.399	*"Bonnie wee thing" (c?; w/ pf)*	*HobXXXIa/102quater*
28.400	*"Border widow's lament, The" (c by Neukomm 1803; w/ vn, vc & pf)*	*HobXXXIa/232*
28.401	*"Braes of Ballochmyle, The" (c by Neukomm 1803; w/ vn, vc & pf)*	*HobXXXIa/226*
28.402	*"Captain O'Kain" (?Irish) (c by Neukomm 1803; w/ vn, vc & pf)*	*HobXXXIa/224bis*
	"Colin to Flora" (= Rock and a wee pickle tow)	
	"Come under my plaidy" (= Johny MacGill)	
28.403	*"Cro Challin" (c by Neukomm 1803; w/ vn, vc & pf)*	*HobXXXIa/253A*
28.404	*"Erin-go-bragh" (c by Neukomm 1803; w/ vn, vc & pf)*	*HobXXXIa/203*
	"Exile of Erin, The" (= Erin-go-bragh)	
	"Get up and bar the door" (= Rise up and bar the door)	
	"Good night, & God be with you" (= Good night & joy be wi' ye a'	
28.405	*"Good night & joy be wi' ye a' " (c by Neukomm 1803; w/ vn,vc & pf)*	*HobXXXIa/254*
28.406	*"Hallow ev'n" (c by Neukomm 1803; w/ vn, vc & pf)*	*HobXXXIa/63bis*
28.407	*"Happy Dick Dawson" (c by Neukomm 1803; w/ vn, vc & pf)*	*HobXXXIa/247*
28.408	*"Here awa', there awa'," duet (c by ?Neukomm 1803; w/vn, vc & pf)*	*HobXXXIa/257bis*
	"I loe na a laddie but ane" (= Happy Dick Dawson)	
	"Jenny beguil'd the webster" (= Jenny dang the weaver)	
28.409	*"Jenny dang the weaver" (c by Neukomm 1803; w/ vn, vc & pf)*	*HobXXXIa/240*
28.410	*"Johny Faw" (c by ?Neukomm 1804; w/ vn, vc & pf)*	*HobXXXIa/251*
28.411	*"Johny MacGill" (?Irish air) (c by Neukomm 1803; w/ vn, vc & pf)*	*HobXXXIa/238*
28.412	*"Kelvin grove" (c?; w/ pf, ?spur)*	*HobXXXIa/269*
28.413	*"Lochaber" (c by Neukomm 1803; w/ vn, vc & pf)*	*HobXXXIa/190*
28.414	*"McGrigor of Rora's lament" (c by Neukomm 1803; w/ vn, vc & pf)*	*HobXXXIa/81bis*
28.415	*"My love's a wanton wee thing" (c by Neukomm 1803; w/vn, vc & pf)*	*HobXXXIa/268*
	"My silly auld man" (= Johny MacGill)	
	"My wife's a wanton, wee thing" (= My love's a wanton wee thing)	
28.416	*"O bonny lass" (c by Neukomm 1803; w/ vn, vc & pf)*	*HobXXXIa/89bis*
28.417	*"O'er the moor" (c by Neukomm 1803; w/ vn, vc & pf)*	*HobXXXIa/122bis*
28.418	*"O gin my love were yon red rose" (c1804; w/ vn, vc & pf)*	*HobXXXIa/273*
28.419	*"Over the water to Charlie" (c by Neukomm 1803; w/ vn, vc & pf)*	*HobXXXIa/267*
28.420	*"O were my love yon lilac fair" (c?; w/ pf, ?spur)*	*HobXXXIa/271*
28.421	*"Parson boasts of mild ale, The" (Irish) (c by Neukomm 1803; w/vn, vc & pf)*	*HobXXXIb/61*
28.422	*"Rise up and bar the door" (c by Neukomm 1803; w/ vn, vc & pf)*	*HobXXXIa/197*
28.423	*"Rock and a wee pickle tow, The" (c by Neukomm 1803; w/vn, vc & pf)*	*HobXXXIa/253B*
28.424	*"Sailor's lady, The" (c?; w/ pf, ?spur)*	*HobXXXIa/266*
	"Savourna deligh" (Irish air) (= Erin-go-bragh)	

28.425	*"Shelah O' Neal" (c by Neukomm 1803; w/ vn, vc & pf)*	*HobXXXIa/239*
	"Tibbie Dunbar" (= Johny MacGill)	
28.426	*"Tibby Fowler" (c by Neukomm 1803; w/ vn, vc & pf)*	*HobXXXIa/52bis*
28.427	*"Tullochgorum" (c by Neukomm 1803; w/ vn, vc & pf)*	*HobXXXIa/270*
	"Waes me for Prince Charlie" (= Johny Faw)	
28.428	*"Waly, waly" (c?, ?spur duet arr for w/ vn, vc & pf)*	*HobXXXIa/214ter*
28.429	*"When she came ben she bobbit" (c by Neukomm 1803; w/vn, vc & pf)*	*HobXXXIa/62bis*
28.430	*"White cockade, The" (c by Neukomm 1803; w/ vn, vc & pf)*	*HobXXXIa/22bis*

*   *   *   *   *

Hob =   Anthony van Hoboken: "Joseph Haydn. Thematisch-bibliographisches Werkverzeichnis."
B. Schott's Söhne, Mainz. 1957 (Band I), 1971 (Band II), 1978 (Band III).

1. STAGE WORKS

Operas:

1.1	"Mörder, Hoffnung der Frauen" (Murder, the Hope of Women), 1 act (c1919, after Kokoschka's play) Op.12
1.2	"Das Nusch-Nuschi," 1 act ballet opera for Burmese marionettes (c1920, Blei, parody of Wagner's Tristan und Isolde) Op.20
1.3	"Sancta Susanna," 1 act (c1921, Stramm) Op.21
1.4	*"Zwischenaktmusik zu einer grotesken Oper" (c ?1922; va & orch, frags)* ....
1.5	"Cardillac," 3 acts (c1925–6, Lion after Hoffmann; r vers in 4 acts 1948–52, Hindemith after Lion): ... Op.39
1.6	. "Duet" (No.16), for Act II of r vers of opera: Cardillac, Op.39 (c1961)
1.7	"Hin und Zurück" (There and Back), 1 act musical sketch (c1927, Schiffer) Op.45a
1.8	"Neues vom Tage" (News of the Day), 3-part comic opera (c1928–9, Schiffer; r vers in 2 acts 1953–4) ......
1.9	*"Kinderoper" (c ?1930; 1v & instr, frag)* ....
1.10	"Mathis der Maler" (Mathias the Painter), 7 scenes (c1934–5, Hindemith; Eng text Ducloux 1966) ....
1.11	"Die Harmonie der Welt" (The Music of the Spheres), 5 acts (c1956–7, some c1951, Hindemith; used in symphony) ....
1.12	"Das lange Weihnachtsmahl" (The Long Christmas Dinner), 1 act (c1960–1, Wilder; Ger transl Hindemith)

Ballets:

1.13	"Der Dämon" (The Demon), 2 scene dance-pantomime (c1922, Krell) Op.28
1.14	"Nobilissima Visione," 6 scene dance legend (c1938, Hindemith & Massine, on the life of St. Francis) ....
1.15	"Thema mit vier Variationen. Die vier Temperamente" (The Four Temperaments) (c1940; pf & strings) ......
1.16	"Hérodiade" (An orchestral recitation) (c1944, after Mallarmé) ....

Incid music for marionette plays:

1.17	"Kasperls Heldentaten" (c ?1915, Pocci; vc) ....
1.18	"Das Glück ist blind" (c ?1915, Pocci; pf) ....
1.19	"Lohengrin," parody (c ?1915, Huch; pf) ....
1.20	"Kasperl unter den Wilden" (c ?1915, Pocci; child tpt, other insts & vc) ....
1.21	"Die Zaubergeige" (c1916, Pocci; 1v & pf) ....
1.22	"Die Zaubergeige" (c ?1916, Pocci; vc) ....

Other incid music:

1.23	"Tuttifäntchen," 3 scene Christmas fairy tale (c1922, Michel & Becker) ....
1.24	"Lehrstück," 1 scene stage work (c1929, Brecht; 3 m vv, narrator, 3 clowns, audience, orch & band) ....

Sing- und Spielmusik (also called 'Gebrauchsmusik'—music for use):

1.25	*"Der Vetter auf Besuch" (The Cousin's Visit), Singspiel (c1912–3, Busch, student work, lost)* ....
1.26	"Spielmusik" (c1927; 2fl, 2ob & strings) Op.43/1
1.27	"Lieder für Singkreise" (c1927; ch) Op.43/2
1.28	"Schulwerk für Instrumental-Zusammenspiel" (c1927) Op.44
1.29	"Sing und Spielmusik für Liebhaber und Musikfreunde" (c1928–9) Op.45
1.30	"Wir bauen eine Stadt" (Let's Build a City), play for children (c1930, Seitz) ....
1.31	"Plöner Musiktag" (A Day of Music in Plön) (c1932) ....

Radio:

1.32	"Der Lindbergflug" (Lindbergh's Flight) (c1929, Brecht, collab: 4 pieces c by Hindemith, other c by Weill) ...
1.33	"Sabinchen," radio play (c1930, Seitz) ....

Film:

1.34	"In Sturm und Eis" (c1921; small orch) ....
1.35	*"Vormittagsspuk" (Morning Ghost), surrealist film (c1928; mech pf, lost)* ....
1.36	*"Musik zu einem Trickfilm" (c1931; pf, lost)* ....
1.37	*"Musik zu einem abstrakten Fischinger-Film" (c1931; str trio, lost)* ....
1.38	*"Reklamefilm Clermont de Fouet" (c1931; str trio, lost)* ....
1.39	*"Film musik für Violine solo zu einem Fischinger-Film" (c1932, lost)* ....

1a. SELECTIONS FROM STAGE WORKS

1a.13	"Der Dämon," ballet: Op.28
	I: 1. "Tanz des Dämons"
	2. "Tanz der bunten Bander"
	3. "Tanz der geangsteten Schwalben"
	4. "Tanz des Giftes"
	5. "Tanz der Schmerzen"
	6. "Tanz des Dämons" (Passacaglia)
	7. "Tanz der Trauer und der Sehnsucht"

II: 8. "Einleitung"
    9. "4 Tänze des Werbens": a. "Tanz des Kindes"
          b. "Tanz des weilen Gewandes"
          c. "Tanz der ganz erschlossenen Orchidee"
          d. "Tanz der roten Raserei"
    10. "Tanz der Brutalität"
    11. "Tanz des geschlagenen Tieres"
    12. "Finale: Tanz des Damon"

1a.14   "Nobilissima Visione," ballet: ....
        1. "Einleitung und Lied des Troubadours"
        2. "Tuchkäufer und Bettler"
        3. "Der Ritter"
        4. "Marsch"
        5. "Erscheinung der drei Frauen"
        6. "Festmusic"
        7. "Schluss des Festes"
        8. "Meditation"
        9. "Geigenspiel. Der Wolf"
      10. "Kärgliche Hochzeit"
      11. "Incipiunt Laudes creaturarum"

1a.15   "The Four Temperaments: Theme with 4 Variations," ballet: ....
       . "Theme"
        1. "Melancholic"
        2. "Sanguinic"
        3. "Phlegmatic"
        4. "Choleric"

1a.24   "Lehrstück," incid music: ....
        1. "Bericht vom Fliegen"
        2. "Ob der Mensch dem Menchen hilft"
        3. "Der Chor spricht zum Abgestürzten"
        4. "Betrachtet den Tod"
        5. "Belehrung"
        6. "Zweite Untersuchung: Ob der Mensch dem Menschen hilft" (Clowns)
        7. "Examen"

1a.26   "Spielmusik": Op.43/1
        1. "Mässig bewegte Halbe"
        2. "Langsam schreitende Viertel"
        3. "Schnelle Halbe"

1a.27   "Lieder für Singkreise" : Op.43/2
        1. "Ein jedes Band" (Platen)
        3. "O Herr, gib jedem seinen eignen Tod" (Rilke)
        4. "Man weiss oft grade denn am meisten" (Claudius)
        5. "Was meinst du, Kunz, wie gross die Sonne sei" (Claudius)

1a.28   "Schulwerk für Instrumental-Zusammenspiel": Op.44
      I. "9 Pieces in First Position" (2vn)
      II. "8 Canons in First Position" (2vn & vn/va)
     III. "8 Pieces in First Position" (str qt & d bass): 1. "Mässig schnell"
        2. "Schnell"
        3. "Mässig schnell"
        4. "Lustig, Mässig schnell"
        5. "Schnell"
        6. "Mässig schnell"
        7. "Lebhaft"
        8. "Mässig schnell, Munter"
     IV. "5 Pieces in First Position" (strings): 1. "Langsam"
        2. "Langsam, Schnell"
        3. "Lebhaft"
        4. "Sehr langsam"
        5. "Schnell"

1a.29   "Sing und Spielmusik für Liebhaber und Musikfreunde": Op.45
      I. "Frau Musica" (c1928, r1943, Luther): 1. (w/ out title)
        2. "Pastorale-Musette"
        3. (w/ out title)
        4. "Trio"
      II. "8 Canons" (c1928; ch & str qt): 1. "Hie kann nit sein ein böser Mut" (Old Proverb)
        2. "Wer sich die Musik erkiest" (Luther)
        3. "Die wir dem Licht in Liebe dienen" (Goering)
        4. "Auf a folgt b" (Morgenstern)

5. "Niemals wieder will ich eines Menschen Antlitz verlachen" (Werfel)
6. "Das weiss ich und hab' ich erlebt" (Kneip)
7. "Mund und Augen wissen ihre Pflicht" (Claudius)
8. "Erde, die uns dies gebracht" (Morgenstern)
III. "Ein Jäger aus Kurpfalz, der reitet durch den grünen Wald" (c1928; orch): 1. "Breit. Majestätisch"
2. "Munter"
IV. "Kleine Klaviermusik" (12 easy 5-note piano pieces) (c1928; pf)
V. "Martin's Song": "Was haben doch die Gänse getan" (c1929, Olorinus; 1v/unison ch & 3 str/wind)

1a.31　　"Plöner Musiktag" (A Day of Music in Plön): ....
I. "Morning Music" (brass in a tower): 1. "Mässig bewegt"
2. "Lied"
3. "Bewegt"
II. "Luncheon Music" (fl, tpt/cl & strings): 1. "March"
2. "Intermezzo"
3. "String Trio"
4. "Waltz"
III. "Advice to Youth to Apply itself to Music," cantata (Agricola of 16th cent; vv, ch & orch)
IV. "Evening Concert": 1. "Prelude" (orch)
2. "Flute solo" (w/ strings)
3. "2 Duets" (vn & cl)
4. "Variations" (cl & strings)
5. "Trio" (3 recorders)
6. "Quodlibet" (orch)

2. SYMPHONIES

2.1　　"Mathis der Maler" Symphony (c1934, from opera, inspired by Grünewald's paintings): ....
1. "Angelic Concert" (inspired by painting for Isenheim Altar)
2. "Entombment" (inspired by painting of interment of Jesus)
3. "Temptation of Saint Anthony"
2.2　　Symphony in E-flat major (c1940) ....
2.3　　"Symphonia Serena" (c1946) ....
2.4　　Symphony, "Die Harmonie der Welt" (The Music of the Spheres) (c1951): ....
1. "Musica Instrumentalis"
2. "Musica Humana"
3. "Musica Mundana"
2.5　　Symphony in B-flat major (c1951; concert band) ....
2.6　　"Pittsburgh Symphony" (c1958) ....

3. OTHER ORCHESTRAL WORKS

3.1　　"Lustige Sinfonietta" (c1916; small orch) Op.4
3.2　　"Rag Time" (well-tempered) (c1921) ....
3.3　　"Nusch-Nuschi Tänze," suite (arr1921, from ballet opera Op.20) .... (Op.20)
3.4　　"Der Dämon," concert suite (arr1923, from ballet Op.28) .... (Op.28)
3.5　　"Concerto for Orchestra" (c1925) Op.38
3.6　　"Konzertmusik für Blasorchester" (c1926; wind band): Op.41
1. "Overture"
2. "Six Variations" (on song: Prince Eugen, the Noble Knight)
3. "March"
3.7　　"Neues vom Tage," overture (c1930, from opera, w/ concert ending) ....
3.8　　"Konzertmusik" (c1930; brass & strings) Op.50
3.9　　"Philharmonic Concerto: Variations for Orchestra" (c1932, theme & 6 variations) ....
3.10　　*"Übungsstück für das Räuberorchester in der Hochschule" (c1932, frag, lost)* ....
3.11　　"Symphonic Dances" (c1937): No.1 "Langsam" ....
3.12　　　　No.2 "Lebhaft"
3.13　　　　No.3 "Sehr langsam"
3.14　　　　No.4 "Mässig bewegt, mit Kraft"
3.15　　"Nobilissima Visione," suite (c1938, from ballet, enlarged instrumentation): No.1 "Einleitung und Rondo" ...
3.16　　　　No.2 "Marsch und Pastorale"
3.17　　　　No.3 "Passacaglia"
3.18　　　　*"Poor Lazarus and the rich man" (A Virginian Ballad for Orchestra) (c1941, frags)* ....
3.19　　"Amor & Psyche" (Farnesina), overture to a ballet (c1943; chamber orch) ....
3.20　　"Symphonic Metamorphosis of Themes by Carl Maria von Weber" (c1943): ....
1. "Allegro"
2. "Turandot" (Scherzo)
3. "Andantino"
4. "Marsch"
3.21　　"The Lilacs Requiem," orch prelude (c1946; also see Choral: When lilacs last in the dooryard bloom'd) ......
3.22　　"Sinfonietta," in E major (c1949) ....
3.23　　"Marsch über den alten 'Schweizerton' " (c1960, for the 500th anniv of the University of Basel) ....

4. CONCERTOS, SOLO INSTR & ORCH

Org & orch:

4.1	"Kammermusik No.7" (Organ Concerto) (c1927)	Op.46/2
4.2	Organ Concerto (c1962–3, for the dedication of Lincoln Center for the Performing Arts):..........................	

       1. "Crescendo"
       2. "Allegro assai"
       3. "Canzonetta in triads and two Ritornelli"
       4. "Phantasy on Veni Creator spiritus"

Pf & orch:

4.3	"Piano Concerto for the Left Hand" (c1923)	Op.29
4.4	"Kammermusik No.2" (Piano Concerto) (c1924; pf & 12 insts)	Op.36/1
4.5	"Konzertmusik" (c1930; pf, 10 brass insts & 2 harps)	Op.49
4.6	Piano Concerto (c1945)..	

Vn & orch:

4.7	"Tuttifäntchen," suite (p1969, from incid music): No.1 "Vorspiel"	
4.8	No.2 "Lied"	
4.9	No.3 "Intermezzo"	
4.10	No.4 "Lied"	
4.11	No.5 "Marsch"	
4.12	No.6 "Musik zum Kaspertheater"	
4.13	No.7 "Tanz der Holzpuppen"	
4.14	No.8 "Lied"	
4.15	No.9 "Melodram"	
4.16	No.10 "Wiegenlied"	
4.17	No.11 "Schlusslied"	
4.18	"Kammermusik No.4" (Violin Concerto) (c1925)	Op.36/3
4.19	Violin Concerto (c1939)	

Va & orch:

4.20	"Kammermusik No.5" (Viola Concerto) (c1927)	Op.36/4
4.21	"Kammermusik No.6" (Viola d'amore Concerto) (c1927; va d'amore & chamber orch)	Op.46/1
4.22	"Konzertmusik" (c1930; va & large chamber orch)	Op.48
4.23	"Der Schwanendreher" (Viola Concerto) (c1935; va & small orch, after old German folksongs):	

       1. "Zwischen Berg und tiefem Tal"
       2. "Nun laube, Lindlein laube"
      . "Der Gutzgauch auf dem Zaune sass" (Fugato)
       3. "Seid ihr nicht der Schwanendreher" (Variations)

4.24	"Trauermusik" (c1936; va/vn/vc & strings, on death of George V of England)	

Vc & orch:

4.25	Cello Concerto in E-flat major (c1915–6; red w/ pf)...	Op.3
4.26	"Kammermusik No.3" (Cello Concerto) (c1925; vc & 10 insts)...	Op.36/2
4.27	Cello Concerto (c1940)	

Other:

4.28	"Konzertmusik" (c1931; trautonium & strings) ....
4.29	"5 Folksongs" (arr1936; cl & strings) ....
4.30	Clarinet (in A) Concerto (c1947) ....
4.31	"Concerto" (c1949; fl, ob, cl, bn, harp & orch) ....
4.32	Horn Concerto (c1949) ....
4.33	"Concerto" (c1949–52; tpt, bn & strings) ....

5. STRING QUARTETS

5.1	String Quartet No.1 in C major (c1914–5, student work)...	Op.2
5.2	String Quartet No.2 in F minor (c1918)	Op.10
5.3	String Quartet No.3 in C major (c1920)	Op.16
5.4	String Quartet No.4 (c1921)	Op.22
5.5	String Quartet No.5 (c1923)	Op.32
5.6	String Quartet No.6 in E-flat major (c1943)	
5.7	String Quartet No.7 (c1945)	

6. OTHER CHAMBER MUSIC

6 or more insts:

6.1   *"Sonata for 10 Instruments" (c1917; fl, 2cl, hn, bn & str qnt, frags)* ....
6.2   "Kammermusik" No.1 (c1922; 12 solo insts, Finale c1921) Op.24/1
6.3   "Septet for Wind Instruments" (c1948; fl, ob, cl, b cl, bn, hn & tpt) ....
6.4   "Octet" (c1958; cl, bn, hn, vn, 2va, vc & d bass) ....

5 insts:

6.5   *Piano Quintet in E minor (c1917, lost)* *Op.7*
6.6   "Kleine Kammermusik" (c1922; woodwind qnt) Op.24/2
6.7   Clarinet Quintet (c1923/54; cl & str qt) Op.30
6.8   "3 Pieces for 5 Instruments" (3 Anecdotes) (c1925; cl, tpt, vn, d bass & pf): No.1 "Scherzando" ....
6.9   No.2 "Langsame Achtel"
6.10   No.3 "Sehr lebhafte Halbe"

4 insts:

6.11   "Quartet" (c1938; cl & pf trio) ....
6.12   "Sonata" (c1952; 4hn) ....

3 insts:

6.13   *"Andante & Scherzo" (c1914; cl, hn & pf, student work, lost: sketches exist)* *Op.1*
6.14   String Trio No.1 (c1924) Op.34
6.15   *"2 Very Easy Trios" (c1927; fl, cl & d bass, lost)* ....
6.16   "Trio" (c1928; heckelphone/t sax, va & pf)... Op.47
6.17   "Rondo" (c1930; 3gui) ....
6.18   String Trio No.2 (c1933) ....
6.19   *"Entertainment Music" (c1934; 3cl, composition class project, lost): No.1 "3 Märsche"* ....
6.20   *No.2 "Foxtrot"*
6.21   *No.3 "Walzer"*
6.22   *No.4 "Polka"*
6.23   *No.5 "Paso doble"*
6.24   *No.6 "Tango"*
6.25   "Recorder Trio" (c ?1942):
           1. "Dixie"
           2. "Old Folks at Home"
           3. "Auld Lang Syne"

Vn & pf:

6.26   *Violin Sonata in D minor (c1913, student work, frags)* ....
6.27   Violin Sonata in E-flat major (c1918) Op.11/1
6.28   Violin Sonata in D major (c1918) Op.11/2
6.29   Violin Sonata in E major (c1935) ....
6.30   Violin Sonata in C major (c1939) ....

Va & pf:

6.31   Viola Sonata in F major (c1919) Op.11/4
6.32   "Little Sonata" (c1922; va d'amore & pf)... Op.25/2
6.33   Viola Sonata (c1922) Op.25/4
6.34   Viola Sonata in C major (c1939) ....

Vc & pf:

6.35   "3 Pieces" (c1917): No.1 "Capriccio," in A major Op.8
6.36   No.2 "Phantasiestück," in B major
6.37   No.3 "Scherzo," in C minor
6.38   Cello Sonata (c1919, r1921) Op.11/3
6.39   "3 Easy Pieces" (c1938): No.1 "Mässig, schnell, munter" ....
6.40   No.2 "Langsam"
6.41   No.3 "Lebhaft"
6.42   "A Frog He Went A-Courtin'," 13 variations (c1941, on an Old Eng nursery song) ....
6.43   "Little Sonata" (c1942)
6.44   Cello Sonata (c1948) ....

Other instr & pf:

6.45   *"Grosses Rondo," in B-flat major (c1913; cl & pf, student work, lost)* ....
6.46   "8 Pieces" (c1927; fl & pf) ....
6.47   Flute Sonata (c1936) ....

6.48   "Meditation" (c1938; vn/va/vc & pf, from ballet: Nobilissima visione) ....
6.49   Bassoon Sonata (c1938) ....
6.50   Oboe Sonata (c1938) ....
6.51   Clarinet Sonata in B-flat major (c1939) ....
6.52   Horn Sonata (c1939) ....
6.53   Trumpet Sonata (c1939) ....
6.54   Eng Horn Sonata (c1941) ....
6.55   Trombone Sonata (c1941) ....
6.56   "Echo" (arr for fl & pf 1942, from 24. of: 25 Songs of 1942) ....
6.57   Saxophone Sonata (c1943; alto hn/hn/alto sax & pf) ....
6.58   Double Bass Sonata (c1949) ....
6.59   Tuba Sonata (c1955) ....

        Other 2 insts:

6.60   "Canonic Sonatina" (c1923; 2fl) Op.31/3
6.61   "9 Pieces" (c1927; cl & d bass) ....
6.62   "2 Canonic Duets" (c1929; 2vn): No.1 "Canonic Recital Piece" ....
6.63   No.2 "Canonic Variations"
6.64   "18 Canonic Pieces" (c1931; 2vn) ....
6.65   "Konzertstück" (c1933; 2 alto sax) ....
6.66   "Duett" (c ?1935; bn & d bass, 2 pieces w/ out titles) ....
6.67   "Duet" (Scherzo) (c1934; va & vc) ....
6.68   "4 Pieces" (c1941; vc & bn): No.1 "Mässig schnell" ....
6.69   No.2 "Fuge"
6.70   No.3 "Lebhaft"
6.71   No.4 "Variationen"
6.72   "6 Light Pieces" (ca1942; bn & d bass) ....
6.73   "Gay" (ca1942; 2vc) ....
6.74   "Ludus minor" (c1944; cl & vc): ....
           1. "Fuga prima ex C"
           2. "Interludium"
           3. "Fuga secunda ex G"
           4. "Interludium"
           5. "Fuga tertia ex F"

        Vn solo:

6.75   *"Studien" (c ?1916, frags): No.1 (w/ out title)* ....
6.76   *No.2 "Praeludium"*
6.77   "Sonata," in G minor (c1917) Op.11/6
6.78   "Sonata" (c1924) Op.31/1
6.79   "Sonata" (c1924) Op.31/2
6.80   *Sonata fragments (c ?1925, frags): No.1 "Presto"* ....
6.81   *No.2 (w/ out title)*
6.82   "Übungen" (c1926): No.1 "Ohne Lagenwechsel durch die Lagen" ....
6.83   No.2 "Gewandtheit des Bogens bei rhythmischem Wechsel"
6.84   No.3 "Saitenwechsel"
6.85   No.4 "Gebrochene Akkorde"
6.86   Cadenzas for Mozart's Violin Concertos (c1933–4): No.1 Two Cadenzas for spurious: Violin Concerto
           in D major, "Adelaide", KC14.05 (App.294a) ....
6.87   No.2 Two Cadenzas for: Violin Concerto No.3 in G major, K216
6.88   No.3 Four Cadenzas for: Violin Concerto No.4 in D major, K218

        Va solo:

6.89   "Sonata" (c1919) Op.11/5
6.93   "Sonata" (c1922) Op.25/1
6.94   "Sonata" (c1923) Op.31/4
6.95   "Sonata" (c1937) ....

        Vc solo:

6.96   "Sonata" (c1922) Op.25/3

        Other 1 instr:

6.97   "8 Pieces" (c1927; fl): No.1 "Gemächlich, leicht bewegt" ....
6.98   No.2 "Scherzando"
6.99   No.3 "Sehr langsam, frei im Zeitmass"
6.100   No.4 "Gemächlich"
6.101   No.5 "Sehr lebhaft"
6.102   No.6 "Lied, leicht bewegt"
6.103   No.7 "Rezitativ"
6.104   No.8 "Finale"

6.105   Harp Sonata (c1939) ....

    7. "Interludium" (Scherzando)
    8. "Fuga 4," in A major (With energy)
    9. "Interludium" (Fast)
  10. "Fuga 5," in E major (Fast)
  11. "Interludium" (Moderato)
  12. "Fuga 6," in E-flat major (Quiet)
  13. "Interludium" (March)
  14. "Fuga 7," in A-flat major (Moderato)
  15. "Interludium" (Very broad)
  16. "Fuga 8," in D major (With strength)
  17. "Interludium" (Very fast)
  18. "Fuga 9," in B-flat major (Moderato)
  19. "Interludium" (Very quiet)
  20. "Fuga 10," in D-flat major (Moderately fast)
  21. "Interludium" (Allegro pesante)
  22. "Fuga 11," in B major (Slow)
  23. "Interludium" (Valse)
  24. "Fuga 12," in F-sharp major (Very quiet)
  25. "Postludium"

Pf duet:

8.57	"7 Waltzes" (3 Beautiful Maidens in the Black Forest) (c1916, inc): No.1 "Langsames Walzertempo" .. Op.6
8.58	No.2 "Mässig schnell"
8.59	No.3 "Lebhaft" (ma non troppo!)
8.60	No.4 "Mässig schnell"
8.61	No.5 "Munter"
8.62	No.6 "Langsam"
8.63	No.7 "Langsam" (etwas sentimental vorzutragen), "Zum Beschluss" (Im Zeitmass des ersten Walzers)
8.64	*"March," in F minor (c1916, destroyed)* ....
8.65	"Sonata" (c1938) ....

2 Pf:

8.66	"Sonata" (c1942) ....

9. MECH & ELECTRONIC INSTRUMENTS

9.1	*"Music for mech insts" (c1926, frags): No.1 "Toccata für mechanisches Klavier" (Welte-Mignon)* *Op.40*
9.2	*No.2 "Das triadische Ballett"*
9.3	*"Music for mech insts" (c1927, frags): No.1 "Felix the Cat at the Circus," cartoon film score (mech pf)* ....
9.4	*No.2 "Suite" (mech org, arr of part I of: Das triadische Ballett)*
9.5	"Experiments on 2 gramophone discs" (c1930) ....
9.6	"7 Pieces" (c1930; 3 trautoniums): No.1 "Langsam" ....
9.7	No.2 "Langsam"
9.8	No.3 "Mässig bewegt"
9.9	No.4 "Breit"
9.10	No.5 "Mässig schnelle Achtel"
9.11	No.6 "Lebhaft"
9.12	No.7 "Langsam"
9.13	*"Slow Piece & Rondo" (c1935; trautonium; reconstr Sala)* ....

10. ORGAN

10.1	*"2 Pieces" (c1918, destroyed)* ....
10.2	Organ Sonata No.1 (c1937) ....
10.3	Organ Sonata No.2 (c1937) ....
10.4	Organ Sonata No.3 (c1940, on old folksongs): ....
	1. "Ach Gott, wem soll ich's klagen"
	2. "Wach auf, mein Hort"
	3. "So wünsch ich ihr"

11. CHORAL WORKS

W/ acc:

11.1	"Lügenlied" (c1928; ch, wind & strings ad lib) ....
11.2	"Das Unaufhörliche," oratorio (c1931, Benn; S, T, Bar, B, ch, child ch & orch) ....
11.3	*"Cantata for an Outing" (c1934; 1v, ch & 4cl, composition class project, lost)* ....
11.4	"A Song of Music" (As Donkeys Bray and Robins Sing) (c1940, Tyler; ch & pf/strings) ....
11.5	"The Harp that Once thro' Tara's Halls" (Old Irish Air) (c1940; ch & pf/harp w/ strings; also in German) ......

11.6 "When lilacs last in the dooryard bloom'd" (Requiem for those we Love / The Lilacs Requiem) (c1946, Whitman; mS, Bar, ch & orch; Ger transl Hindemith): ....
. "Prelude"
1. "When lilacs last in the door-yard bloom'd" (Als Flieder jüngst) (Bar, ch)
2. "In the swamp, in secluded recesses" (Aus dem Ried), arioso (mS)
3. "Over the breast of the spring" (Über die Hügel im Lenz), march (ch, Bar)
4. "O western orb, sailing the heaven!" (O Westgestirn) (Bar & ch)
5. "Sing on, there in the swamp!" (Sing weiter, du im Ried), arioso (mS)
6. "O how shall I warble myself for the dead one there I loved?" (O wie werd' ich), song (Bar, ch)
7. "With the fresh herbage ... Lo! body and soul!" (Schau, Sinn und Verstand), introd & fugue (ch)
8. "Sing on! Sing on, you gray-brown bird!" (Sing mehr, du Vogel dort) (mS, Bar: soli & duet)
9. "Death Carol": "Come, lovely and soothing Death" (Komm lieber und sanfter Tod) (ch)
10. "To the tally of my soul" (Wie ein Gleichklang meiner Seel') (Bar & ch)
11. "Passing the visions" (Schwinden die Bilder), finale (mS, Bar, ch)
11.7 "Apparebit repentina dies" (c1947, medieval Latin; ch & 10 brass insts): ....
1. "Apparebit repentina dies"
2. "Hujus omnes ad electi colligentur dexteram"
3. "Retro ruent tunc injusti ignes in perpetuos"
4. "Ydri fraudes ergo cave"
11.8 "Ite angeli veloces," cantata (c1953–5, Claudel; vv, ch, orch & brass, for UNESCO): ....
1. "David's Song of Triumph" (c1955; w/ A, T)
2. "Custos, quid de nocte" (c1955; w/ T)
3. "Canticle to Hope" (c1953; w/ mS)
11.9 "Mainz Procession" (c1962, Zuckmayer & Hindemith; S, T, Bar, ch & orch, for 2000th anniv of Mainz): ......
1. "Chor" (w/ solo vv)
2. "Terzett"
3. "Bariton Solo und Dialog"
4. "Couplet, die Schwarzwaldkinder"
5. "Ariette"
6. "Bariton-solo"
7. "Variationen"
8. "Quodlibet"
9. "Schluss, Soli und Chor"

W/ out acc:

11.10 "Songs on Old Texts" (c1923): 1. "Vom Hausregiment": "Es ist gewiss" (Luther, r1937; 3 vers) Op.33
11.11 2. "Frauenklage": "Nun heissen sie mich meiden" (Burggraf zu Regensburg, r1937; 2 vers)
11.12 3. "Art lässt nicht von Art": "Ein Wolf, den Sündenangst bewog" (Spervogel, r1937; 3 vers)
11.13 4. "Der Liebe Schrein": "Wüsst ich, ob es auch blieb verschwiegen fein" (Morungen; 2 vers)
11.14 5. "Heimliches Glück": "Mir kommt zuweilen wohl ein Tag" (Reinmar)
11.15 6. "Landsknechtstrinklied": "Tummel dich, tummel dich, guts Weinlein" (anon, r1937; 2 vers)
11.16 7. "Der Guguck": "Ein Guguck auf dem Birnbaum sass"
11.17 "Spruch eines Fahrenden": "Das Gott all die berate" (c1928, 14th cent; fem/child ch) ....
11.18 "Über das Frühjahr": "Lange bevor wir uns stürzten auf Erdöl" (c1929, Brecht; m ch) ....
11.19 "Eine lichte Mitternacht": "Dies ist deine Stunde, o Seele" (c1929, Whitman transl Schlaf; m ch) ....
11.20 "3 Choruses" (c1930, Benn; m ch): 1. "Du musst dir alles geben" ....
11.21 2. "Fürst Kraft": "Fürst Kraft ist—liest man—gestorben"
11.22 3. "Vision des Mannes": "Vision des Mannes, der stumm und namenlos"
11.23 "4 Choruses for Boys" (c1930, Schnog): 1. "Bastellied": "Lasst uns alleine machen" ....
11.24 2. "Lied des Musterknaben": "Meine Eltern zeigen die Zensuren"
11.25 3. "Angst vorm Schwimmunterricht": "Vorher denk ich immer"
11.26 4. "Schundromane lesen": "Das ist das Schönste"
11.27 "Der Tod": "Er erschreckt uns, unser Retter" (c1931, Hölderlin) ....
11.28 "5 Songs on Old Texts" (c1937): 1. "True Love": "Tristan, Tristan musste ohne Dank" (Veldeke tr Mendel)
11.29 2. "Lady's Lament": "Nun heissen sie mich meiden" (after Op.33/2, transl Strunk, Jr.)
11.30 3. "Of Household Rule": "Es ist gewiss ein frommer Mann" (after Op.33/1, transl Strunk, Jr.)
11.31 4. "Trooper's Drinking Song": "Tummel dich, guts Weinlein" (after Op.33/6, transl Strunk, Jr.)
11.32 5. "The Devil a Monk would be": "Ein Wolf, den Sündenangst bewog" (after Op.33/3, tr Strunk, Jr.)
11.33 "3 Choruses" (c1939; m ch): 1. "Das verfluchte Geld": "Ei, dass dich doch Potz Velten!" (Old German) ......
11.34 2. "Nun, da der Tag des Tages müde ward" (Nietzsche)
11.35 3. "Die Stiefmutter": "Kind, wo bist du hingewesen?" (Old German)
11.36 "6 Chansons" (c1939, French poems by Rilke, Engl transl Sinçay): 1. "La biche" (The Doe): "O la biche" ...
11.37 2. "Un cygne" (A Swan): "Un cygne avance sur l'eau"
11.38 3. "Puisque tout passe" (Since all is passing)
11.39 4. "Printemps" (Springtime): "O mélodie de la sève"
11.40 5. "En hiver" (In Winter): "En hiver, la mort meurtière"
11.41 6. "Verger" (Orchard): "Jamais la terre n'est plus"
11.42 "Erster Schnee": "Wie nun alles stirbt und endet" (c1939, Keller; m ch) ....
11.43 "Variations on an Old Dance Song": "Das jung und auch das alte" (c1939, anon; m ch) ....
11.44 "Oh, Threats of Hell," canon (c1945, from Rubáiyát of Omar Khayyám transl FitzGerald) ....
11.45 "The Demon of the Gibbet" (Das Galgenritt): "Die Heide wüst" (c1949, O'Brien transl Hindemith; m ch)......
11.46 "Musika divinas laudes" (Coolidge Canon) (c1949, Old Proverb; child/fem vv) ....
11.47 "12 Madrigals" (c1958, Weinheber): 1. "Mitwelt": "Besser als der Rattenschwanz" ....
11.48 2. "Eines Narren, eines Künstlers Leben": "Vor dem dunklen"

11.49	3. "Tauche deine Furcht in schwarzen Wein"
11.50	4. "Trink aus!": "Schenk ein, Kamerad!"
11.51	5. "An eine Tote": "Stille Blume"
11.52	6. "Frühling": "Frühling lässt sein blaues Band"
11.53	7. "An einen Schmetterling": "Du, leicht und schön"
11.54	8. "Judaskuss": "Ihr seht nur das verfluchte Geld"
11.55	9. "Magisches Rezept": "Nimm einen alten Suppentopf"
11.56	10. "Es bleibt wohl, was gesagt wird"
11.57	11. "Kraft fand zu Form"
11.58	12. "Du Zweifel an dem Sinn der Welt"
11.59	"Mass" (c1963; fem ch & m ch, his last completed composition) ....

12. MISC CANONS

12.1	Canon (c1928; 4-part) ....
12.2	Canon: "O Sönnlein geh nicht fort" (c ?1936; 2-part) ....
12.3	"Geburtstagskanon" (c1941; 5-part, for Donavan)..
12.4	"Canon à 4" (Weihnachtskanon) (c1942) ....
12.5	"Canon à 4" (c1943, Abaelard, birthday canon for Ansermet) ....
12.6	"Sine musica nulla disciplina," canon (c1946, Hrabanus Maurus; 3-part) ....
12.7	"Canon à 4" (c1945, Rubayat) ....
12.8	"Birthday Canon for Mrs. Elisabeth Sprague Coolidge" (c1949; 3vv & insts) ....
12.9	Canon (c1949, Arezzo; 3-part, for 50th birthday of Preussner) ....
12.10	Canon (c1952; 5-part, for 70th birthday of Strecker) ....
12.11	Canon (c1952; 6-part) ....
12.12	Canon (c1953; 3-part) ....
12.13	"Canon à 3" (c1954, for Amigos de la Musica in Buenos Aires)..
12.14	"Kanon à 11" (c1954, for Ansermet) ....
12.15	Canon (c1955; 4-part, for Vienna State Opera) ....
12.16	Canon (c1956; 3-part, for 40th anniv of Wiener Konzerthausgesellschaft) ....
12.17	Canon (c1956; 4-part, for 70th birthday of Schoeck) ....
12.18	Canon (c1956; 3-part, for 70th birthday of Tiessen) ....
12.19	Canon (c1957; 3-part, for 75th birthday of Stravinsky) ....
12.20	Canon (c1958; 3-part, for 100th anniv.of Wiener Singsakademie) ....
12.21	Canon (c1958; 3-part, for 75th birthday of Praetorius) ....
12.22	Canon (c1958; 4-part) ....
12.23	Canon (c1958; 7-part) ....
12.24	Canon (c1958; 9-part) ....
12.25	Canon (c1959; 4-part, for 80th birthday of Haas) ....
12.26	"Festmarsch," canon (c1959; m ch & tuba) ....
12.27	Canon: "Wollt ich allen brieflich danken" (c1960; 3-part)..
12.28	2 Canons: "Hoch leb' der Jubilar" (c1962; 3-part) ....
12.29	Canon (c1962, Muris; 5-part, for 80th birthday of Strecker) ....
12.30	Canon (c1963; 4-part) ....

13. VOICE & ORCHESTRA (also 1v & insts)

13.1	"3 Songs" (c1917; S & orch): 1. "Meine Nächte sind heiser zerschrien" (Lotz) Op.9
13.2	2. "Weltende": "Es ist ein Weinen in der Welt" (Lasker-Schüler)
13.3	3. "Aufbruch der Jugend": "Die flammenden Gärten des Sommers" (Lotz)
13.4	"Wie es wär', wenn's anders wär' " (c1918, Miris; S, fl, ob, bn & str qt)
13.5	"Melancholie" (c1917–9, Morgenstern; S & str qt): 1. "Die Primeln blühn und grüssen" (c1919) Op.13
13.6	2. "Nebelweben": "Der Nebelweber webt im Wald ein weisses Hemd für sein Gemahl" (c1918)
13.7	3. "Dunkler Tropfe": "Dunkler Tropfe, der mit heut in den Becher fiel" (c1919)
13.8	4. "Traumwald": "Des Vogels Aug verschleiert sich" (c1917)
13.9	*"Eine Kammermusik" (c ?1920; 1v, fl, harp, pf & str qt, frags): 1. "Einleitung: Sehr langsam"* ....
13.10	"Des Todes Tod" (c1922, Reinacher; mS, 2va & 2vc): 1. "Gesicht von Tod & Elend": "In einer Dämmrung" Op.23a
13.11	2. "Gottes Tod": "Seid still, ihr Vögelein In dem dunkeln Wald!"
13.12	3. "Des Todes Tod": "Der Tod ist müde worden"
13.13	"Die junge Magd," cycle (c1922, Trakl; A, fl, cl & str qt): 1. "Oft am Brunnen" Op.23b
13.14	2. "Stille schafft sie in der Kammer"
13.15	3. "Nächtens überm kahlen Anger"
13.16	4. "In der Schmiede dröhnt der Hammer"
13.17	5. "Schmächtig hingestreckt im Bette"
13.18	6. "Abends schweben blutige Linnen"
13.19	"Die Serenaden," little cantata (c1925; S, ob, va & vc): Op.35
	I: 1. "Barcarole": "Treibe, treibe, Schifflein" (Licht)
	2. "An Phylis: Toccata (vc) & Corrente": "Phyllis, unter diesen Buchen" (Gleim)
	3. "Nur Mut": "Aus Wolken fällt die frohe Stunde" (Tieck)
	II: 4. "Duet" (va & vc)
	5. "Der Abend": "Schweigt der Menschen laute Lust" (Eichendorff)
	6. "Der Wurm am Meer": "Wie dies Gewürm" (Meinhold)

III: 7. "Trio" (ob, va & vc)
       8. "Gute Nacht": "Gute Nacht! Liebchen sieh" (Meinhold)

Arias & Lieder from operas & oratorios:

13.20	"Mag Sonne leuchten," aria (c1926; Bar & orch, from opera: Cardillac, Op.39) ....
13.21	"Die Zeit vergeht," Lied (c1926; S & orch, from opera: Cardillac, Op.39) ....
13.22	"Es trägt die Nacht," aria (c1931; S & orch, from oratorio: Das Unaufhörliche of 1931) ....
13.23	"Ein Wille treibt mich," aria (c1952; Bar & orch, from r vers of opera: Cardillac, Op.39) ....
13.24	"Was gabst du mir," Lied (c1952; S & orch, from r vers of opera: Cardillac, Op.39) ....

14. SONGS (w/ pf)

14.1	"7 Lieder" (c1808–9; S/T & pf, juvenilia): 1. "Nachtlied" (Hebbel) ....
14.2	2. "Die Rosen" (Hebbel)
14.3	3. "Sommerbild" (Hebbel)
14.4	4. "Mein Sterben" (Hodel)
14.5	5. "Heimatklänge" (Matt)
14.6	6. "Frühlingstraum" (Ott)
14.7	7. "Georgslied" (Goethe)
14.8	"Nähe des Geliebten" (c1914, Goethe, student work) ....
14.9	"7 Merry Songs in the Aargau Dialect" (c1914–6): 1. "Schössli bschnyde" (Hämmerli-Marti; 2 vers) Op.5
14.10	2. "Zur Unzeit" (Frey)
14.11	3. "Die Hexe" (Frey)
14.12	4. "Da liess ig y!" (Reinhart)
14.13	5. "Kindchen" (Frey)
14.14	6. "Erwachen" (Reinhart)
14.15	7. "Tanzliedli" (Reinhart)
14.16	"2 Lieder" (c1917; A & pf): 1. "Ich bin so allein" (Lasker-Schüler) ....
14.17	2. "Schlaflied" (Gezelle)
14.18	"3 Hymns of Walt Whitman" (c1919, transl Schlaf; Bar & pf): 1. "Der ich, in Zwischenträumen" Op.14
14.19	2. "O, nun hab du an, dort in deinem Moor"
14.20	3. "Schlagt! Schlagt! Trommeln!"
14.21	"8 Songs" (c1920; S & pf): 1. "Die trunkene Tänzerin": "Sieh, an letzten Himmels Saum" (Bock) Op.18
14.22	2. "Wie Sankt Franciscus schweb' ich in der Luft" (Morgenstern)
14.23	3. "Traum": "Der Schlaf entführte mich" (Lasker-Schüler)
14.24	4. "Auf der Treppe sitzen meine Öhrchen" (Morgenstern)
14.25	5. "Vor dir schein' ich aufgewacht" (Morgenstern)
14.26	6. "Du machst mich traurig—hör' ": "Bin so müde" (Lasker-Schüler)
14.27	7. "Durch die abendlichen Gärten" (Schilling)
14.28	8. "Trompeten": "Unter verschnittenen Weiden" (Trakl)
14.29	"Das Kind" (c1922, Hagedorn; S & pf) ....
14.30	"Das Marienleben" (c1922–3, Rilke; S & pf, r1935–48): 1. "Geburt Mariä": "O was muss es die Engel gekostet haben" (orchd1939) Op.27
14.31	2. "Die Darstellung Mariä im Tempel": "Um zu begreifen, wie sie damals war"
14.32	3. "Mariä Verkündigung": "Nicht dass ein Engel eintrat"
14.33	4. "Mariä Heimsuchung": "Noch erging sie's leicht im Anbeginne"
14.34	5. "Argwohn Josephs": "Und der Engel sprach und gab sich Müh" (orchd1939)
14.35	6. "Verkündigung über die Hirten": "Seht auf, ihr Männer. Männer dort am Feuer"
14.36	7. "Geburt Christi": "Hättest du der Einfalt nicht" (orchd1939)
14.37	8. "Rast auf der Flucht nach Ägypten": "Diese, die noch eben atemlos" (orchd1939)
14.38	9. "Von der Hochzeit zu Kana": "Konnte sie denn anders"
14.39	10. "Vor der Passion": "O hast du dies gewohllt" (orchd1959)
14.40	11. "Pietà": "Jetzt wird mein Elend voll"
14.41	12. "Stillung Mariä mit dem Auferstandenen": "Was sie damals empfanden"
14.42	13. "Vom Tode Mariä" I: "Derselbe grosse Engel"
14.43	14. "Vom Tode Mariä" II (Thema mit Variationen): "Wer hat bedacht"
14.44	15. "Vom Tode Mariä" III: "Doch vor dem Apostel Thomas" (orchd1959)
14.45	"2 Lieder" (c1927; 3vv): 1. "Geh unter, schöne Sonne" (Hölderlin) ....
14.46	2. "Wenn schlechte Leute zanken" (Keller)
14.47	"3 Songs" (c1933, Claudius): *1. "Es ist etwas im Menschen" (lost)* ....
14.48	2. "Der Tod ist 'n eigener Mann"
14.49	*3. "Ein gutes Gewissen im Menschen" (lost)*
14.50	*4. "Wenn du Paul den Peter loben hörst" (lost)*
14.51	"4 Songs" (c1933, Rückert): *1. "Mitternacht" (lost)* ....
14.52	*2. "Ein Obdach gegen Sturm und Regen" (lost)*
14.53	3. "Das Ganze, nicht das Einzelne"
14.54	*4. "Was du getan" (lost)*
14.55	"4 Songs" (c1933, Novalis): 1. "Hymne" ....
14.56	2. "Das Lied der Toten"
14.57	3. "Gesang"
14.58	4. "Ich will nicht klagen mehr"
14.59	*"3 Songs" (c1933, Busch, lost): 1. "Schein und Sein"* ....
14.60	*2. "Verfrüht"*

14.61	*3. "Es sass ein Fuchs"*
14.62	"6 Songs" (c1933–5, Hölderlin; T/Bar & pf): 1. "An die Parzen": "Nur einen Sommer gönnt, ihr Gewaltigen" (c1935) ....
14.63	2. "Sonnenuntergang" (c1933, r1935; 2 vers)
14.64	3. "Ehmals und jetzt" (c1933, r1935; 2 vers)
14.65	4. "Des Morgens" (c1935)
14.66	5. "Fragment" (c1933)
14.67	6. "Abendphantasie" (c1933)
14.68	"4 Songs" (c1935, Silesius): 1. "Weg, weg, ihr Seraphim" ....
14.69	2. "Es kann in Ewigkeit"
14.70	3. "Du sprichst, das Grosse kann nicht"
14.71	4. "Du sprichst versetze dich"
14.72	"2 Songs" (c1936, Brentano): 1. "Singet leise" ....
14.73	2. "Brautgesang"
14.74	"Das Köhlerweib ist trunken" (c1936, Keller) ....
14.75	"Der Einsiedler" (c1939, Cruz transl Vossler) ....
14.76	"2 Songs" (c1939, Nietzsche): 1. "Unter Feinden" ....
14.77	2. "Die Sonne sinkt"
14.78	"14 Motetten" (c1940–60, from Bible; S/T & pf): 1. "Exit edictum" (c1940, r1960) ....
14.79	2. "Cum natus esset" (c1941)
14.80	3. "In principio erat verbum" (c1941)
14.81	4. "Ascendente Jesu in naviculam" (c1943)
14.82	5. "Pastores loquebantur" (c1944)
14.83	6. "Nuptiae facta sunt" (c1944)
14.84	7. "Angelus Domini apparunt" (c1958)
14.85	8. "Defuncto Herode" (c1958)
14.86	9. "Dicebat Jesus scribis et pharisaeis" (c1959)
14.87	10. "Dixit Jesus Petro" (c1959)
14.88	11. "Erat Joseph et Maria" (c1959)
14.89	12. "Vidit Joannes Jesum venientem" (c1959)
14.90	13. "Cum factus esset Jesus annorum duodecim" (c1959)
14.91	14. "Cum descendisset Jesus de monte" (c1960)
14.92	25 "Songs" (c1942; S & pf): 1. "Frauenklage" (Burggraf zu Regensburg) ....
14.93	2. "On arrange et on compose" (Rilke)
14.94	3. "To a Snowflake" (Thompson)
14.95	4. "Zum Abschiede meiner Tochter" (Eichendorff)
14.96	5. "Nach einer alten Skizze" (Meyer)
14.97	6. "Abendständchen" (Brentano)
14.98	7. "La cigale et la fourmi" (Lafontaine)
14.99	8. "Lampe du Soir" (Rilke)
14.100	9. "Ranae ad Solem" (Phaedrus)
14.101	10. "Tränenkrüglein" (Rilke)
14.102	11. "Trübes Wetter" (Keller)
14.103	12. "Ich will Trauern lassen stehen" (anon)
14.104	13. "Abendwolke" (Meyer)
14.105	14. "O Grille sing" (Dauthenday)
14.106	15. "Wer wüsste je das Leben recht zu fassen" (Platen)
14.107	16. "Eau qui se presse" (Rilke)
14.108	17. "The Moon": "And like a dying lady" (Shelley) (also see Castelnuovo-Tedesco's choral work)
14.109	18. "On a Fly Drinking Out of His Cup": "Busy, curious, thirsty fly" (Oldys)
14.110	19. "The Wild Flower's song": "As I wander'd the forest" (Blake)
14.111	20. "C'est de la côte d'Adam" (Rilke)
14.112	21. "Envoy": "Go, songs, for ended is our brief, sweet play" (Thompson)
14.113	22. "La belle dame sans merci" (Ballad No.1): "O what can ail thee, knight-at-arms" (Keats)
14.114	23. "On Hearing 'The Last Rose of Summer' ": "That strain again" (Wolfe)
14.115	24. "Echo": "How sweet the answer Echo makes" (Moore; see arr for fl & pf 1942) (also see Sullivan's 4. of: 7 Partsongs)
14.116	25. "The Whistlin' Thief": "When Pat came o'er the hill" (Lover)
14.117	"Levis exsurgit Zephyrus" (c1943, anon) ....
14.118	"Sing On There In The Swamp" (c1943, Whitman) ....
14.119	"Bal des Pendus" (Ballad No.2): "On the black gallows" (c1944, Rimbaud, in Eng Hindemith; Ger transl Bartlett) ....
14.120	"Sainte" (c1944, Mallarme) ....
14.121	"Le revenant" (c1944, Baudelaire) ....
14.122	"To Music, to Becalm his Fever": "Charm me asleep" (c1944, Herrick) ....
14.123	"2 Songs" (c1955, Cox): 1. "Image" ....
14.124	2. "Beauty touch me"
14.125	*"Credo" (c1963; 1v & instr, frag)* ....

15. PARODIES

15.1	*"Das Grab ist meine Freude" (Festmarsch) (c ?1917; pf, fl, 2vn, vc & d bass, lost)* ....
15.2	*"Gut Zid" (Valse lente) (c ?1917; pf, fl, 2vn, vc & d bass, lost)* ....
15.3	*"Musik für 6 Instrumente und einen Umwender," march (c ?1917; pf, fl, 2vn, vc & d bass, lost)* ....

17.3 "9 Songs for an American School Songbook" (c1938, only 6 were used): ....
    1. "The Spider's Web": "Spider! Spider! What are you spinning?" (Cole; unison ch & pf)
    2. "Romance": "Round the next corner and in the next street" (Grach; 2-part ch & pf)
    3. "Prayer for a Pilot" (ch)
    4. "April Rain" (2S, A)
    5. "Thrush Song": "Hark to the song of the thrush" (2-part ch & pf)
    6. "A Rain Song": "Don't you love to lie and listen, Listen to the rain" (Scollard; unison ch & pf)
    7. "The Sea Gypsy" (Hovey; 2-part ch & pf)
    8. "Young and Old": "When all the world is young, lad" (ch a capella)
    9. "Rain": "The spring rain helps the bushes bud" (McCullough; unison ch & pf)
17.4 "A Concentrated Course in Traditional Harmony," a book (c1942–3) ....
17.5 "Elementary Training for Musicians" (c1945–6) ....
17.6 "A Composer's World" (Komponist in seiner Welt) (c1950; German vers p1953) ....
17.7 "J. S. Bach—Heritage and Obligation" (c1950) ....

18. ARRANGEMENTS OF WORKS OF OTHERS

18.1   *Popper: "Serenade," for cello (arr1919; winds, lost)* ....
18.2   *"Ausländischer Lieder" (arr1936; str qnt & cl, lost)* ....
18.3 Schumann: Violin Concerto in D minor, WoO23 (arr1937) ....
18.4 Monteverdi: "Orfeo" (ed1943, an attempt at reconstruction of original score) ....
18.5 Reger: "Psalm 100," Op.16 (ed1955; ch & orch, thinning of choral & instr scoring)...................
18.6 "Suite of French Dances" (arr1948; small orch, from 16th cent): No.1 "Pavane & Gaillarde" ....
18.7   No.2 "Tourdion"
18.8   No.3 "Bransle simple"
18.9   No.4 "Bransle de Bourgogne"
18.10   No.5 "Bransle simple"
18.11   No.6 "Bransle d'Escosse"
18.12   No.7 "Pavane" (as in No.1)

* * * * *

1. STAGE WORKS

Operas & operettas:

1.1	"Lansdown Castle, or The Sorcerer of Tewkesbury," 2 act operetta (c1892, Cunningham)	App.I/21
1.2	*"Ianthe," romantic operetta for children (c ?1894, lost, see orch work App.I/42a)*	*App.I/42*
1.3	"The Revoke," 1 act (c1895, Hart)	Op.1, H7
1.4	*"4 Sketches for Unidentified Stage Works" (c1896, inc sketches):*	*App.II/11*
	1. "Adagio quasi andante" (orch)	
	2. "Allegretto" (orch)	
	3. "Tempo di Valse" (pf)	
	4. "Fragment of a ballet" (pf)	
1.5	*"The Magic Mirror," 1 act opera (c1896, sketches for Scene 1 only)*	*App.II/12*
1.6	"The Idea," 2 act children's operetta (c ?1896, Hart)	H21
1.7	"Cinderella," fairy pantomime for children (ca1901–2) (also see operas c by Massenet & Rossini, ballet c by Prokofiev)	
1.8	"The Youth's Choice," 1 act musical idyll (c1902, Holst)	Op.11, H60
1.9	"Sita," 3 acts (c1900–6, Holst from the Ramayana)	Op.23, H89
1.10	"Sávitri" (An Episode from the Mahábharata), 1 act chamber opera (c1908–9, Holst)	Op.25, H96
1.11	*"Opera as She is Wrote," parody (c1917–8, frags)*	*App.II/15*
1.12	"The Perfect Fool," 1 act (c1920–2, Holst, ballet music c1918)	Op.39, H150
1.13	"At the Boar's Head," 1 act interlude (c1924, Holst after Shakespeare's tavern scenes from Henry IV Part I & II, Sonnets 12 & 19, Old English melodies)	Op.42, H156
1.14	"The Wandering Scholar," 1 act chamber opera (c1929–30, Bax after Waddell)	Op.50, H176

Ballets:

1.15	"A Magic Hour" (ca1902)	
1.16	"The Lure, or the Moth and the Flame" (c1921, Barney; arr for pf)	H149
1.17	"The Golden Goose," choral ballet (c1926, Joseph, based on tale of Grimm)	Op.45/1, H163
1.18	"The Morning of the Year," choral ballet (c1926–7, Wilson)	Op.45/2, H164

Incid music:

1.19	*"Nabou, or Kings in Babylon" (ca ?1906, Buckton, lost except for sketches):*	*H94*
	extant sketches: 1. "Entrance and Dance"	
	2. "Psalm 137": "By the waters of Babylon"	
	3. "Dance"	
1.20	"The Vision of Dame Christian," masque (c1909, Gray; ch & orch):	Op.27a, H101
	1. "Prelude"	
	2. "Knowest thou not the warning?," first chorus	
	3. "Oh let us render thanks to God above," hymn	
	4. "How shall we tell of him?," choral dance	
	5. "Oh let us render thanks to God above!," finale (unison vv)	
1.21	*"Stepney Children's Pageant" (c1909, Menzies, lost except for H102a & H103):*	*Op.27b, H102*
	extant: . "A Song of London": "Grey the streets and grey the sky" (unison vv & pf)	H102a
	. "O England my Country": "What heroes thou hast bred" (unison ch & orch/pf)	H103
1.22	"The Pageant of London" (Part I, Scene 4 only) (c ?1910–11; unison vv & milit band):	H114
	1. "Trumpet Calls"	
	2. "First Battle Music"	
	3. "The Raven": "The Raven has flapped his wings"	
	4. "Biarkamal": "Day is come up"	
	5. "Second Battle Music"	
	6. "The Praise of King Olaf": "Bold is the battle"	
1.23	*"Philip the King" (c1914, Masefield, lost)*	*H122*
1.24	*"The Sneezing Charm" (c1918, Bax, lost; used in ballet of opera: The Perfect Fool, Op.39, H150):*	*H143*
	extant frag sketches: 1. "Prelude"	
	2. "Song" (w/ mS)	
	3. "Ballet"	
1.25	"7 Choruses from Alcestis of Euripides" (c1920, transl Murray; unison vv, 3fl & harp):	H146
	1."O Paian wise!"	
	2. "Daughter of Pelias, fare thee well"	
	3. "Oh, a House that loves the stranger"	
	4. "Ah me! Farewell"	
	5. "Advance, advance"	
	6. "I have sojourned in the Muses' land"	
	7. "There be many shapes of mystery"	
1.26	"The Coming of Christ," mystery play (c1927, Masefield; S, T, Bar, B, ch, tpt, org, pf & strings ad lib): H170	
	1. "First Song of the Host of Heaven": "Men say Prometheus stole the holy fire"	
	2. "Song of the Four Angels": "As, after thunder, the stormclouds sunder"	
	3. "Second Song of the Host of Heaven": "O sing, as thrushes in the winter"	
	4. "First Song of the Kings": "Man was dark, yet he made himself light"	
	5. "Second Song of the Kings": "The days are past when rocks and streams"	
	6. "The Antiphonal": "Glory to God in the highest"	
	7. "The Song of the Coming of Christ": "By weary stages the old world ages"	

1.27 "The Passing of the Essenes" (c1930, Moore; unison m vv): H180
      1. "In the Lord put I my trust"
      2. "All the powers of the Lord"
1.28   *"The Song of Solomon" (c1933–4, for a Hollywood pageant, inc: frags & sketches) App.II/17*

Film:

1.29   *"The Bells" (c1931, Dand adapted from Irving's Le juif polonais, lost) H184*

2. SYMPHONIES

2.1   Symphony in C minor (c1892) App.I/14
2.2   Symphony in F major, "The Cotswolds" (c1899–1900, 2nd movt 'Elegy—In Memoriam William
      Morris'; arr for 2pf) Op.8, H47
2.3   *"Unfinished Symphony: Fragments" (c1933–4, frags & sketches, Scherzo: completed) App.II/18*

3. OTHER ORCHESTRAL WORKS

3.1   "Intermezzo" (c1891; fl, cl & strings) App.I/12
3.2   "Scherzo" (c1891; small orch) App.I/13
3.3   *"Wedding March" (c ?1891–2, from Finale of Act II of an unidentified stage work, inc) App.II/2*
3.4   *"Funeral March" (c ?1891–2, from Finale of Act II of an unidentified stage work, inc) App.II/3*
3.5   "Bolero" (c1893) App.I/24
3.6   "2 Dances from Ianthe" (arr1894 from operetta App.I/42): No.1 "Ländler" App.I/42a
3.7   No.2 "Storm Dance" (arr for pf duet)
3.8   *"Children's Suite" (c1895; small orch, inc, only No.1 composed): No.1 "Nursery Tale" App.II/8*
3.9   *"2 Pieces" (c1896–7, inc sketches): No.1 "Andante con moto" App.II/10*
3.10   *No.2 "Allegretto"*
3.11   "A Winter Idyll" (c1897) H31
3.12   *"Suite," in G minor (c1898; strings, lost; Berceuse & Dance perf1899) H41*
3.13   "Walt Whitman: Overture" (c1899; arr for 2pf) Op.7, H42
3.14   "Suite de ballet," in E-flat major (c1899, r1912): No.1 "Danse rustique," in E-flat major Op.10, H43
3.15   No.2 "Valse," in E-flat major
3.16   No.3 "Scène de nuit," in G major
3.17   No.4 "Carnival," in E-flat major
3.18   "Greeting" (ca1901–2, from No.3 of: 6 Solos for vn & pf) H53
3.19   "Indra," sym poem (c1903) Op.13, H66
3.20   "Songs of the West" (c1906, rewritten 1907): Op.21/1, H86
      folk tunes used: . "Hal-an-tow"
          . "Henry Martin"
          . "Cicely Sweet"
          . "As I walked out"
          . "Old Adam was a poacher"
          . "Death and the Lady"
          . "The Marigold"
3.21   "A Somerset Rhapsody" (c1906, rewritten 1907): Op.21/2, H87
      folk tunes used: . "The Sheep Shearing Song"
          . "High Germany"
          . "O Polly, love"
          . "The Lovers Farewell"
3.22   "2 Songs without Words" (c1906; chamber orch): No.1 "Country Song" (arr for pf p1907) Op.22, H88
3.23   No.2 "Marching Song" (arr for milit band 1911)
3.24   Suite No.1 in E-flat major (c1909; milit band): No.1 "Chaconne" Op.28/1, H105
3.25   No.2 "Intermezzo"
3.26   No.3 "March"
3.27   Suite No.2 in F major (c1911; milit band): No.1 "March" Op.28/2, H106
3.28   No.2 "Song without words: I'll love my love"
3.29   No.3 "Song of the Blacksmith"
3.30   No.4 "Fantasia on the Dargason"
3.31   "3 Folk Tunes" (c?; milit band, played without a break): H106a
      folk tunes used: . "Glorishears"
          . "He-back, she-back"
          . "Sons of Levi"
3.32   "Beni Mora: Oriental Suite" (c1909–10; arr for pf): No.1 "First Dance" (Oriental Dance) Op.29/1, H107
3.33   No.2 "Second Dance"
3.34   No.3 "Finale: In the street of the Ouled Naïls"
3.35   "Phantastes," suite in F major (c1911): No.1 "Prelude" H108
3.36   No.2 "March"
3.37   No.3 "Sleep"
3.38   No.4 "Dance"
3.39   "St Paul's Suite" (c1912–3; strings): No.1 "Jig" Op.29/2, H118
3.40   No.2 "Ostinato"
3.41   No.3 "Intermezzo"

3.42	No.4 "Finale: The Dargason" (adapted from No.4 of: Suite No.2 in F major, H106)
3.43	"The Planets," suite (c1914–6; arr for 2pf): No.1 "Mars, the Bringer of War" Op.32, H125
3.44	No.2 "Venus, the Bringer of Peace"
3.45	No.3 "Mercury, the Winged Messenger"
3.46	No.4 "Jupiter, the Bringer of Jollity" (tune used in choral song: I vow to The, my country, H148)
3.47	No.5 "Saturn, the Bringer of Old Age"
3.48	No.6 "Uranus, the Magician"
3.49	No.7 "Neptune, the Mystic" (w/ hidden 8-part fem ch; arr for org)
3.50	"Japanese Suite" (c1915): No.1 "Prelude: Song of the Fisherman" Op.33, H126
3.51	No.2 "Dance of the Marionette"
3.52	No.3 "Interlude: Song of the Fisherman"
3.53	No.4 "Finale: Dance of the Wolves"
3.54	Ballet music from opera: The Perfect Fool, Op.39, H150 (c1918–22; arr for pf) ....
3.55	"A Fugal Overture" (c1922, to opera: The Perfect Fool, Op.39, H150) Op.40/1, H151
3.56	"Egdon Heath: Homage to Thomas Hardy" (c1927).. Op.47, H172
3.57	"A Moorside Suite" (c1928; brass band): No.1 "Scherzo" H173
3.58	No.2 "Nocturne" (arr for strings 1928)
3.59	No.3 "March"
3.60	"Hammersmith" (c1930; milit band; orchd1931): No.1 "Prelude"................................Op.52, H178
3.61	No.2 "Scherzo"
3.62	"Mr. Shilkret's Maggot" (Jazz-band Piece) (c1932; ed I. Holst as: Capriccio for orch 1967) H185
3.63	"Brook Green Suite" (c1933; strings & woodwinds ad lib): No.1 "Prelude" H190
3.64	No.2 "Air"
3.65	No.3 "Dance"
3.66	"Gavotte" (c1933; strings & woodwinds ad lib; intended for: Brook Green Suite, H190) H190a
3.67	"Scherzo" (c1933–4).. H192

4. CONCERTOS, SOLO INSTR & ORCH

4.1	"A Song of the Night" (c1905; vn & orch)...Op.19/1, H74
4.2	"Invocation" (c1911; vc & orch) Op.19/2, H75
4.3	"A Fugal Concerto" (c1923; fl, ob & strings; also for: 2vn & strings) Op.40/2, H152
4.4	Double Violin Concerto (c1929) Op.49, H175
4.5	"Lyric Movement" (c1933; va & chamber orch) H191

5. STRING QUARTETS

5.1	"Theme and Variations" (c1893) App.I/29
5.2	String Quartet No.1 (c1893) App.I/30
5.3	*"Fragment of an Allegro" (Allegro con brio) (ca ?1893–6, inc)* *App.II/6*
5.4	*"Fragment of a Scherzo" (Scherzando) (ca ?1893–6, inc)* *App.II/7*
5.5	"Phantasy on British Folk Songs" (c1916): H135
	Hampshire folk tunes used: . "Eggs in her basket"
	. "The female farmer"
	. "The outlandish Knight"
	. "Claudy Banks"

6. OTHER CHAMBER MUSIC

4 or more insts:

6.1	"Air and Variations" (c1894; pf & str qt) App.I/32
6.2	*"Fragment of an Allegro" (Allegro con brio) (c1896; wind septet, inc)* *App.II/9*
6.3	"Fantasiestücke" (c1896; ob & str qt, 1st vers of: 3 Pieces, H8a): No.1 "Air & Variations," in G maj Op.2, H8
6.4	No.2 "Tempo di Marcia," in G major (inc)
6.5	"3 Pieces" (c1910; ob & str qt, 2nd vers of: Fantasiestücke, Op.2, H8): No.1 "March," in G maj... Op.2, H8a
6.6	No.2 "Minuet," in G major
6.7	No.3 "Scherzo," in C major
6.8	"Variations" (c1896; ob, cl, bn, vn, va & vc) H9
6.9	Sextet in E minor (ca1896; ob, cl, bn, vn, va & vc)... H10
6.10	Quintet in A minor (c1896; pf, ob, cl, hn & bn)...Op.3, H11
6.11	"Scherzo" (c1897; str sextet) H23
6.12	Wind Quintet in A-flat major (c1903; fl, ob, cl, hn & bn)..Op.14, H67
6.13	"7 Scottish Airs" (arr1907; pf & strings): H93
	tunes used: . "The women are a'gane wud"
	. "My love's in Germany"
	. "O how could ye gang, lassie"
	. "Stu mo run"
	. "We will take the good old way"
	. "O gin I were where Gowdie rins"
	. "Auld Lang Syne"
6.14	"Gavotte" (arr1933; recorder qt, discarded from: Brook Green Suite, H190) ....

3 insts:

6.15	"Short Trio," in E major (c1894; str trio)	App.I/33
6.16	String Trio in G minor (c1894)	App.I/34
6.17	"Terzetto" (c1925; fl, ob & va)	H158

Vn & pf:

6.18	"6 Solos" (ca ?1901–2): No.1 "Song Without Words" (p1902)	H51
6.19	No.2 "A Spring Song" (p1903; vn/vc & pf)	H52
6.20	No.3 "Greeting" (p1903; arr for small orch)	H54
6.21	No.4 "Maya: Romance" (p1904)	H55
6.22	No.5 "Valse-Etude" (p1904f)	H56
6.23	No.6 "Ländler" (p1903; 2vn & pf; arr from Ländler in operetta: Ianthe, App.I/42)	H53

Other 2 insts:

6.24	"Duet" (c1894; trbn & org)	App.I/31

7. PIANO

7.1	"Arpeggio Study" (c1892)	App.I/17
7.2	"Deux pièces" (ca1901): No.1 "Fancine"	H50
7.3	No.2 "Lucille"	
7.4	*"Tender Bars" (c1920s, frag)*	
7.5	"Toccata" (c1924, based on the Northumbrian pipe-tune: Newburn Lads)	H153
7.6	"A Piece for Yvonne" (c1924)	H154
7.7	"Chrissemas Day in the Morning" (c1926, tune from: North Countrie Ballads)	Op.46/1, H165
7.8	"2 Folk Song Frags" (c1927, from: North Countrie Ballads): No.1 "O I hae seen the roses"	Op.46/2, H166
7.9	No.2 "The Schoemaker"	
7.10	"2 Pieces": No.1 "Nocturne" (c1930)	H179
7.11	No.2 "Jig" (c1932)	

Pf duet:

7.12	"Introduction and Bolero" (c1893)	App.I/23
7.13	2 "Dances" (c1895): No.1 "Allegretto," in A major	H5
7.14	No.2 "Ländler," in E-flat major	

2 Pf:

7.15	"Duet" (c before 1899)	H6

8. ORGAN

8.1	"4 Voluntaries" (c1891): No.1 "March," in C major	App.I/8
8.2	No.2 "Allegretto Pastorale"	App.I/9
8.3	No.3 "Postlude," in C major	App.I/10
8.4	No.4 "Funeral March," in G minor	App.I/11
8.5	"A Duet For 3 Hands And No Feet" (extract, arr from: Terzetto, H158)	

9. CHORAL WORKS

Mixed ch & orch:

9.1	*"Horatius" (c ?1887, Macaulay, inc)*	*App.II/1*
9.2	"Clear and Cool" (The Song of the River): "Clear and cool, clear and cool" (c1897, Kingsley)	Op.5, H30
9.3	"King Estmere": "Hearken to me" (c1903, Percy's Reliques of Ancient English Poetry)	Op.17, H70
9.4	"Choral Hymns from Rigveda," I (transl Holst): 1. "Battle Hymn": "King of the earth" (c1908–9) Op.26/1, H97	
9.5	2. "To the Unknown God": "He, the Primal one" (c1910)	
9.6	3. "Funeral Hymn": "Away O Death, thy work is ended now" (c1908–9)	
9.7	"Christmas Day" (Choral Fantasy on old carols): "Good Christian men rejoice" (c1910, trad)	H109
9.8	"The Cloud Messenger": "Oh thou who com'st" (c1909–10, r1912, Kalidasa transl Holst)	Op.30, H111
9.9	"2 Psalms" (c1912; ch, strings & org): 1. "Psalm 86": "To my humble supplication" (Bryan from Bible) H117	
9.10	2. "Psalm 148": "Lord, who hast made us for thine own" (Gray; arr for fem ch)	
9.11	"Festival Choruses" (c1916): 1. "Let all mortal flesh" (Liturgy tr Moultrie, tune: trad Fr carol) ..Op.36a, H134	
9.12	2. "Turn back, O Man" (Bax, tune: 'old 124th Psalm' from Genevan Psalter)	
9.13	3. "A Festival Chime": "In town and in village our church-bells today" (Bax, tune: St. Denio)	
9.14	"The Hymn of Jesus" (c1917, Apocryphal Acts of St John):	Op.37, H140
	. "Prelude": "Vexilla regis prodeunt" (based on plainsong hymns: Pange lingua & Vexilla regis)	
	. "Hymn": "Glory to Thee, Father!"	
9.15	"Ode to Death": "Come, lovely and soothing death" (c1919, Whitman)	Op.38, H144

9.16   "Short Festival Te Deum": "We praise thee, O God" (c1919, Book of Common Prayer) H145
9.17   "First Choral Symphony" (c1923–4, Keats; S, ch & orch) (also see Castelnuovo-Tedesco's
       choral work: Endymion): Op.41, H155
       . "Prelude" (Invocation to Pan): "O Thou, whose mighty palace roof doth hang" (from Endymion)
       1. "Song and Bacchanal": "Beneath my palm trees, by the river side" (from Endymion)
       2. "Ode on a Grecian Urn": "Thou still unravish'd bride of quietness"
       3. "Scherzo" (Fancy): "Ever let the Fancy roam"
       . "Folly's Song": "When wedding fiddlers are a-playing"
       4. "Finale": "Spirit here that reignest"
9.18   *"Second Choral Symphony" (c1926–31; 1v, ch & orch, frags)* *App.II/16*
9.19   *"Christ hath a garden" (c?, Watts adapt Bridges, frags)* *H167*
9.20   "A Choral Fantasia": "Man born of desire" (c1930, Bridges; S, ch, org, strings, brass & perc) ..Op.51, H177

M ch & orch:

9.21   *"Sailors' Chorus" (c?1891–2, inc: words not indicated)* *App.II/4*
9.22   "Ode to the North East Wind" (c1892, Kingsley): App.I/20
       1. "Overture"
       2. "Welcome, wild North-easter!," chorus
9.23   "Choral Hymns from Rigveda," IV (c1912, transl Holst): 1. "Hymn to Agni": "I praise thee" Op.26/4, H100
9.24   2. "Hymn to Soma" (the juice of a herb): "The thoughts of men are manifold"
9.25   3. "Hymn to Manas" (... the spirit of a dying man): "O thou who hast fled away"
9.26   4. "Hymn to Indra" (... god of heaven, storm and battle): "Who is he of lofty pow'r"
9.27   "A Dirge for 2 Veterans": "The last sunbeam lightly falls" (c1914, Whitman; m ch, brass & perc) H121
9.28   "6 Choruses" (c1931–2, Waddell; m ch & strings/org/pf): 1. "Intercession": "Set free" Op.53, H186
9.29   2. "Good Friday": "Alone to sacrifice Thou goest, Lord"
9.30   3. "Drinking Song": "To you, consummate drinkers"
9.31   4. "A Love Song": "Noblest, I pray thee," canon
9.32   5. "How mighty are the Sabbaths" (m ch & orch; also vers for unison ch, strings & org)
9.33   6. "Before Sleep": "The toil of the day is ebbing"
9.34   *"On the Battle which was fought at Fontenoy": "When the Dawn" (c1931; intended for Op.53, frag)* *H186a*

Fem ch & orch:

9.35   "Choral Hymns from Rigveda," II (c1909, transl Holst): 1. "To Varuna": "O Varuna, we offer" .Op.26/2, H98
9.36   2. "To Agni" (God of Fire): "Burn up our sin, fierce flaming Agni"
9.37   3. "Funeral Chant": "To those for whom the meath is poured"
9.38   "Hecuba's Lament": "Lo, I have seen" (c1911, Euripides transl Murray; A, fem ch & orch) Op.31/1, H115
9.39   "Hymn to Dionysus": "Oh, blessed he" (c1913, Euripides transl Murray; A, fem ch & orch) ...Op.31/2, H116
9.40   "A Dream of Christmas": "The other night I saw a sight" (c1917, anon 15th cent; fem ch & strings/pf) H139
9.41   "7 Partsongs" (c1925–6, Bridges; S, fem ch & strings): 1. "Say who is this?" Op.44, H162
9.42   2. "O Love, I complain"
9.43   3. "Angel spirits of sleep"
9.44   4. "When first we met we did not guess"
9.45   5. "Sorrow and joy, two sisters coy"
9.46   6. "Love on my heart from heaven fell"
9.47   7. "Assemble, all ye maidens, at the door"

Unison ch & orch:

9.48   "7 Folksongs" (arr ?1904–19): 1. "On the Banks of the Nile": "O hearken, I hear the drums" (= H84/8) . H85
9.49   2. "The Willow Tree": "O take me to your arms, Love" (variant of H83/6)
9.50   3. "Our ship she lies in harbour" (= H83/16)
9.51   4. "I'll love my love": "Abroad as I was walking" (= H84/6)
9.52   5. "Claudy Banks": "As I roamed out one evening" (= H84/7)
9.53   6. "John Barleycorn": "There were three Kings came from the North" (= H83/9)
9.54   7. "Spanish ladies": "Farewell and adieu" (arr1919)
9.55   "3 Carols" (c1916–7, Morris; also w/ pf): 1. "I saw three ships come sailing in" (trad) H133
9.56   2. "Christmas Song": "On this day earth shall ring" (Latin transl Joseph)
9.57   3. "Masters in this Hall" (old French carol transl Morris)
9.58   "I vow to Thee, my country" (c?1921, Spring-Rice, tune from: The Planets, Op.32/4, H125/4; pubd in
       Songs of Praise as a hymn: Thaxed) H148

Mixed ch & pf/org/insts:

9.59   "Christmas Carol": "The silver bells ring out across the snow" (ca ?1890; ch & pf) App.I/7
9.60   "The Listening Angels": "Blue against the bluer Heavens" (c1891; A, hidden ch & pf, inc) App.I/5
9.61   "New Year Chorus": "Here we bring new water" (c1892, trad; ch & pf) App.I/16
9.62   "Not Unto Us, O Lord," anthem (ca ?1893–6, Psalm 115; ch & org) H22
9.63   "4 Old English Carols" (c1907, anon 15th cent; ch & pf): 1. "A Babe is born" Op.20b, H82
9.64   2. "Now let us sing"
9.65   3. "Jesu, Thou the Virgin-born": "Jesu of a maiden Thou wast born" (unacc)
9.66   4. "The Saviour of the world is born": "In Bethlehem that noble place"
9.67   "2 Carols" (anon 15th cent; ch, ob & vc): 1. "A Welcome Song": "Proface, welcome" (c before 1909) ... H91
9.68   2. "Terly terlow": "About the field they piped full right" (c1916)

9.69   "2 Anthems" (c1927, Bridges): 1. "Man born to toil, in his labour rejoiceth" (ch, org & bells ad lib; also see hymn: Gird on thy sword) H168
9.70   2. "Eternal father, Who didst all create" (S, ch, org & bells ad lib) H169

Fem ch & pf/harp:

9.71   "Choral Hymns from Rigveda," III (c1910, transl Holst): 1. "To the Dawn": "Hear our hymn" ... Op.26/3, H99
9.72   2. "To the Waters": "Flowing from the firmament"
9.73   3. "To Vena" (the Sun rising through the mist): "Vena comes, born of light"
9.74   4. "Hymn of the Travellers": "Go thou on before us"
9.75   "2 Eastern Pictures" (c1911, Kalidasa transl Holst): 1. "Spring": "Spring the warrior hither comes" H112
9.76   2. "Summer": "The fierce glaring day is gone"
9.77   "Dirge and Hymeneal": "Woe, woe, this is death's hour" (c1915, Beddoes) H124

Children's ch & pf:

9.78   "Clouds o'er the summer sky," canon (c before ?1900, Hart) H40
9.79   "4 Partsongs" (c1910, Whittier): 1. "Song of the Ship-builders": "Hark! roars the bellows" H110
9.80   2. "Song of the Shoemakers": "Ho! workers of the old-time" (arr for unison ch & pf)
9.81   3. "Song of the Fishermen": "Hurrah! the seaward breezes"
9.82   4. "Song of the Drovers": "Through heat and cold"
9.83   "2 Partsongs" (c1917, Whittier): 1. "The Corn Song": "Through vales of grass and meads of flowers" H138
9.84   2. "Song of the Lumbermen": "Not for us the measured ringing"

Unison ch & pf/org:

9.85   "The Strain Upraise," anthem (ca ?1891–2, Clowes; 1 tr v, unison ch & org) App.I/4
9.86   "Advent Litany" (ca ?1891–2; unison vv & org): App.I/6
         1. "Death"
         2. "Judgement"
         3. "Hell"
         4. "Hymn 463 A and M"
9.87   "Sanctus": "Holy, holy, holy Lord God of Hosts" (c1892; unison vv & org) App.I/15
9.88   "In Loyal Bonds United" (Coronation / An Empire Day Song) (c1911, Wensley; unison ch & pf) H113
9.89   "Playground Song": "With joyful hearts our song we raise" (c before ?1914; unison ch & pf) H118a
9.90   "Roadways": "One road leads to London" (c ?1931, Masefield; unison ch & pf) H181

Unacc mixed ch:

9.91   "Winter and the Birds" II: "Winter doth come at the close of the year" (arr?, from App.I/40:1) App.I/40:2
9.92   "Love wakes and weeps" (c1894, from Scott's The Pirate) App.I/41
9.93   "The autumn is old" (c1895, Hood) H1
9.94   "The stars are with the voyager" (c1890s, Hood; 2nd setting 1895) H2
9.95   "Spring it is cheery" (c1895, Hood) H3
9.96   "O lady, leave that silken threat" (c1895, Hood; see 2nd setting for 1v & pf 1897) H4/1
9.97   "The Kiss": "Oh! that joy so soon should waste!" (c1896, from Jonson's Cynthia's Revels, inc) H16
9.98   "Ah Tyrant Love": "Ah tyrant Love, Megaera's serpent bearing" (c1890s, Kingsley's Frank Leigh's Song A.D.1586) H18
9.99   "Light leaves whisper" (c ?1896, Hart) H20
9.100   "There's a voice in the wind" (c1896) H15
9.101   "5 Partsongs" (c1897–1900): 1. "Love is Enough": "Love is enough: ho ye who seek saving" (c1897, Morris) Op.9a, H48
9.102   2. "To Sylvia": "O Spring's little children" (c1899, Thompson, orig for unacc fem ch, H24)
9.103   3a, b. "Autumn Song": "Fair is the world, now autumn's wearing" (c1899, Morris; 2 vers)
9.104   4. "Come away, death," madrigal (c1900, Shakespeare) (also see Brahms Op.17/2, Castelnuovo-Tedesco Op.24/I/1 & Vaughan Williams' partsong of 1899)
9.105   5. "A Love Song": "Dawn talks to Day" (c1900, Morris)
9.106   "Thou didst delight my eyes" (ca ?1903, Bridges) H58
9.107   "It was a lover and his lass" (c ?1890s, from Shakespeare's As You Like It) (also see Castelnuovo-Tedesco Op.24/II/3, Delius RTv/30/1, Sullivan's partsong of 1857 & Vaughan Williams' partsong of 1922) H59
9.108   "5 Partsongs" (c1902–3): 1. "Dream Tryst": "The breaths of kissing night and day" (Thompson) Op.12, H61
9.109   2. "Ye little birds" (from Heywood's The Fair Maid of the Exchange)
9.110   3. "Her eyes the glow-worm lend thee" (Herrick's Hesperides: The Night-Piece, to Julia)
9.111   4. "Now is the month of Maying" (anon 16th cent; 2 vers)
9.112   5. "Come to me": "Come, come to me in the silence of the night" (Rossetti)
9.113   "In Youth is Pleasure": "In arbor green asleep I lay" (c by 1908, Wever) H76
9.114   "Now rest thee from all care" (c by 1908, ?adapted from Mabbe's poem; also song H77) H78
9.115   "I love thee" (ca ?1912, Hood) H57
9.116   "Nunc dimittis" (c1915, Liturgy) H127
9.117   "This have I done for my true love": "Tomorrow shall be my dancing day" (c1916, trad) Op.34/1, H128
9.118   "Lullay my liking," carol (c1916, anon 15th cent; S & ch) Op.34/2, H129
9.119   "Of one that is so fair and bright" (c ?1916, anon 15th cent; S, A, T, B & ch) Op.34/3, H130
9.120   "Bring us in good ale": "Bring us in no brown bread," carol (c1916, anon 15th cent) Op.34/4, H131

9.121	"6 Choral Folk Songs" (c1916): 1. "I sowed the seeds of love" (arr for m ch 1924) Op.36b, H136
9.122	2. "There was a tree"
9.123	3. "Matthew, Mark, Luke and John" (arr for m ch 1924)
9.124	4. "The Song of the Blacksmith": "For the blacksmith courted me" (arr for m ch 1924)
9.125	5. "I love my love": "Abroad as I was walking" (arr for m ch 1924)
9.126	6. "Swansea Town": "Oh! farewell to you my Nancy" (arr for m ch 1924)
9.127	"Diverus and Lazarus": "As it fell out upon one day" (c?, p1918, trad) H137
9.128	"2 Motets": 1. "The Evening-Watch": "Farewell! I go to sleep" (c1924, Vaughan) Op.43/1, H159
9.129	2. "Sing me the men ere this" (c1925, Dolben; d ch) Op.43/2, H160
9.130	"Ode to C.K.S. and the Oriana": "Fair Oriana's feast proclaim," round with comments (c1925) H157
9.131	"Wassail Song": "The wassail, the wassail throughout all the town" (ca1928–31, trad) H182
9.132	"12 Welsh Folksongs" (c1930–1, trad transl Wilson): 1. "Lisa Lan": "I've loved you truly" H183
9.133	2. "Green Grass": "Stretching where lush grasses quiver"
9.134	3. "The Dove": "Down by the wood one morning early"
9.135	4. "Awake, awake": "Awake, awake, before daybreak"
9.136	5. "The Nightingale and Linnet": "O nightingale and linnet"
9.137	6. "The mother-in-law": "Hear my husband's mother screeching"
9.138	7. "The First Love": "Eden's garden knew no posies"
9.139	8. "O 'twas on a Monday morning"
9.140	9. "My sweetheart's like Venus"
9.141	10. "White summer rose": "If we are going to part for ever"
9.142	11. "The Lively Pair": "O my sweetheart, let's get married"
9.143	12. "The lover's complaint": "O light of Gwyneth shining clearly"
9.144	"O spiritual pilgrim" (c1933, Flecker; S & ch) H188

Unacc m ch:

9.145	"The Homecoming": "Gruffly growled the wind" (c1913, Hardy) H120

Unacc fem ch:

9.146	"Ave Maria, maiden mild" (c1894, from Scott's The Lady of the Lake) (also see Rossini's opera: La donna del lago & Schubert's song: Ellens Gesang' III, Op.52/6, D839) App.I/35
9.147	"Fathoms deep beneath the wave" (c1894, from Scott: The Pirate) App.I/36
9.148	"Now Winter's winds are banished" (c ?1894, Meleager transl Harding) App.I/37
9.149	"Summer's welcome": "On the wings of the swallows" (c1894, Hart) App.I/39
9.150	"There is dew for the flow'ret" II (c1894, Hood) (also see Gounod's song of 1871) App.I/38:2
9.151	"Winter and the birds" I: "Winter doth come at the close of the year" (c1894, Hart) App.I/40:1
9.152	"All night I waited by the spring" (c1890s) H12
9.153	"3 Short Partsongs" (c1896): 1. "In the forest moonbeam-brightened" H13
9.154	2. "All the nests with song are ringing"
9.155	3. "Soft and gently through my soul"
9.156	"O Spring's Little Children" (c1897, Thompson; also see arr as: To Sylvia, Op.9a/2, H48/2) H24
9.157	"Ave Maria" (c1900, Liturgy) Op.9b, H49
9.158	"Songs from 'The Princess' " (c1905, Tennyson): 1. "Sweet and low, sweet and low" Op.20a, H80
9.159	2. "The splendour falls on castle walls" (also see Britten Op.31/2, Delius RTiv/6, Sullivan's opera: Princess Ida & Vaughan Williams' song of 1905)
9.160	3. "Tears, idle tears, I know not what they mean"
9.161	4. "O swallow, swallow, flying, flying South"
9.162	5. "Now sleeps the crimson petal, now the white"
9.163	"Home they brought her warrior dead" (c1905, from Tennyson's The Princess; orig in Op.20a, H80) ... H81
9.164	"A Song of Fairies": "In the moonlit forest" (c ?1908–9) H104
9.165	"Pastoral": "Early as I rose up in the morn" (ca1909, trad adapt ?Holst) H92
9.166	"The swallow leaves her nest" (c?, p1914, Beddoes) H119
9.167	"Here is joy for every age" (c?, Ecce novum gaudium, transl Neale, tune: Piae Cantiones 1582) H142

Equal voices:

9.168	"Canterbury Bells," 2 rounds (c1928, Jones): 1. "Within this place all beauty dwells" H171
9.169	2. "To Bother Missis Bell"
9.170	"8 Canons" (c1932, Waddell from Medieval Latin): 1. "If you love songs" H187
9.171	2. "Lovely Venus": "Lovely Venus, what's to do"
9.172	3. "The fields of sorrow": "They wander in deep woods"
9.173	4. "David's lament for Jonathan": "Low in thy grave with thee"
9.174	5. "O strong of heart"
9.175	6. "Truth of all Truth"
9.176	7. "Evening on the Moselle": "What colour are they now, thy quiet waters?" (ch & pf)
9.177	8. "If 'twere the time of lilies" (ch & pf)
9.178	"Come live with me" (c1933, Marlowe) H189

Hymns (unison or harmonized):

9.179	"3 Hymns for the English Hymnal" (c1904–5): 1. "In the bleak mid-winter" (25.) (Rossetti, tune: Cranham) (also see Britten Op.3/5) H73
9.180	2. "From glory to glory advancing" (310.) (Liturgy of St. James transl Humpreys, tune: Sheen)
9.181	3. "Holy Ghost, come down upon thy children" (571.) (Faber, tune: Bossiney)

9.182   "God is love, his the care" (arr ca1925 from 1. of: 3 Carols, H133) ....
9.183   "4 Hymns for Songs of Praise" (c ?1925): 1. "O valiant hearts" (Arkwright, tune: Valiant hearts) H161
9.184   2. "In this world, the Isle of Dreams" (Herrick, tune: Brookend)
9.185   3. "Onward, Christian soldiers!" (Baring-Gould, tune: Prince Rupert)
9.186   4. "I sought thee round about, O Thou my God" (Heywood adapt Dearmer, tune: Monk Street)
9.187   "By weary stages" (arr from The Song of the Coming of Christ in: The Coming of Christ, H170) ....
9.188   "Gird on thy sword / Lift up your hearts" (arr from anthem: Man born to toil, H168, tune: Chilswell) ....

10. VOICE & ORCHESTRA

10.1   *"Duet: Herald and Tom" (c ?1891–2; T, B & orch, inc: words not indicated) App.II/5*
10.2   "Örnulf's Drapa," scena (c1898, from Ibsen's Vikings at Helgeland, transl Archer; Bar & orch) Op.6, H34
10.3   "The Mystic Trumpeter": "Hark, some wild trumpeter" (c1904, r1912, Whitman; S & orch) Op.18, H71
10.4   "Song of the Valkyrs": "The clash and the clang" (c1893, Adkin; 2S, A, tpt & d strings) App.I/22

11. SONGS (w/ pf)

11.1   "The Harper": "On the green banks of Shannon" (c1891, Campbell) App.I/1
11.2   "The Exile of Erin": "There came to the beach a poor Exile of Erin" (c ?1890s, Campbell; B & pf) App.I/2
11.3   "Die Spröde" (The Coquette): "An dem reinsten Frühlingsmorgen" (c?, p1891, Goethe) App.I/3
11.4   "I come from haunts of coot and hern" (c1892, Tennyson) App.I/18
11.5   "Sing Heigh-Ho" I: "There sits a bird on ev'ry tree" (c1892, Kingsley) App.I/19
11.6   "A lake and a fairy boat" I (c1893, Hood) App.I/25
11.7   "There sits a bird on yonder tree" (c1893, Ingoldsby) App.I/26
11.8   "Anna-Marie": "Anna-Marie, love, up is the sun" (c1893, from Scott's Ivanhoe) App.I/27
11.9   "The white lady's farewell": "Fare thee well" (c1893, from Scott's The Monastery) App.I/28
11.10   "There is dew for the flow'ret" I (ca ?1891–2, Hood) App.I/38:1
11.11   "O lady, leave that silken thread" (c1897, Hood; see 1st setting for: ch,1895)..................................H4/2
11.12   "4 Songs" (c1896–8): 1. "Slumber-Song": "Soft, soft wind, from out the sweet south sliding" (c1896,
                 from Kingsley's Water-Babies) Op.4, H14
11.13   2. "Margrete's Cradle-Song": "Now roof and rafters blend" (c1896, Ibsen transl Archer)
11.14   3. "Soft and gently": "Soft and gently through my soul" (c1897, Heine)
11.15   4. "Awake, my heart": "Awake my heart to be loved" (c1898, Bridges)
11.16   "Song to the sleeping lady": "Rest is now fill'd full of beauty" (c1897, from Macdonald's Phantastes) ... H17
11.17   "The ballade of prince Eric": "Gaily laughed the summer wind" (c before ?1902, Hart) H19
11.18   "A lake and a fairy boat" II (c1897, Hood) H25
11.19   "Sing heigh-ho" II: "There sits a bird on ev'ry tree" (c1897, Kingsley) H26
11.20   "Airly Beacon": "Airly Beacon, Airly Beacon, Oh the pleasant sight to see" (c1897, Kingsley) H27
11.21   "Twin stars aloft" (c ?1890s, Kingsley) H28
11.22   "The Day of the Lord": "Day of the Lord is at hand" (c ?1890s, Kingsley) H29
11.23   "Not a sound but echoing in me" (c1897, Macdonald) H32
11.24   "Whether we die or we live" (c1898, Meredith) H33
11.25   "Autumn Song": "The birds that sing on autumn eves" (c ?1890s, Bridges) H35
11.26   "My joy": "My spirit sang all day" (c1898, Bridges) H36
11.27   "Draw not away thy hands, my love" (c ?1890s, Morris) H37
11.28   "I scann'd her picture" (c ?1896–1900) H38
11.29   "Two brown eyes" (p1898, lost) H39
11.30   "Bhanavar's lament": "Take me to thee!" (c1898–9, Meredith) H44
11.31   "Ah, come, fair mistress": "Ah come with me, fair mistress" (c ?1890s, Grogan) H45
11.32   "She who is dear to me" (c before ?1900, Grogan) H46
11.33   "A prayer for light": "Oh give me light today or let me die" (c1903, Mackay) H62
11.34   "Dewy roses": "Sleep, for the twilight scattereth her dews" (c?, p1904, Hyatt) H63
11.35   "Song of the woods": "Woods, Springtime Woods" (c before 1904, Hyatt) H64
11.36   "To a wild rose": "Little flow'r so sweet and fragrant" (c?, Hyatt) H65
11.37   "6 Songs" (c1902–3; Bar & pf): 1. "Invocation to the Dawn": "Light hath come" (Rigveda) Op.15, H68
11.38   2. "Fain would I change that note" (anon 16th cent)
11.39   3. "The Sergeant's Song": "When lawyers strive to heal a breach" (from Hardy's The Trumpet
                 Major)
11.40   4. "In a Wood": "Pale beech and pine tree blue" (from Hardy's The Woodlanders)
11.41   5. "Between us now and here" (Hardy)
11.42   6. "I will not let thee go" (Bridges)
11.43   "6 Songs" (c1903–4; S & pf): 1. "Calm is the morn" (from Tennyson's In Memoriam) Op.16, H69
11.44   2. "My true love hath my heart" (Sidney)
11.45   3. "Weep you no more, sad fountains!" (anon 16th cent)
11.46   4. "Lovely kind and kindly loving" (Breton)
11.47   5. "Cradle song": "Sweet dreams form a shade" (Blake) (also see Vaughan Williams: Blake's
                 Cradle Song)
11.48   6. "Peace": "The toil of day is done" (Hyatt)
11.49   "Darest thou now, o soul" (c ?1905, from Whitman's Whispers of Heavenly Death) H72
11.50   "Now sleep and take thy rest" (c ?1890s, Fernando de Rojas transl Mabbe) H77
11.51   "To Hope": "Child of heav'n who shinest ever" (c1900s, adapted from: To a wild rose, H65) H79

11.52	"Hymns from the Rig Veda" (c1907–8, Sanskrit transl Holst), I: 1. "Ushas" (Dawn): "Behold the Dawn" Op.24, H90
11.53	2. "Varuna I" (Sky): "Oh thou great judge, Varuna"
11.54	3. "Maruts" (Stormclouds): "Mighty Warriors, Children of Thunder"
11.55	II: 4. "Indra" (God of Storm & Battle): "Noblest of songs for the noblest of Gods!" (orchd)
11.56	5. "Varuna II" (The Waters): " 'Fore mine eyes" (orchd)
11.57	6. "Song of the Frogs": "Throughout the summer"
11.58	7. "Vac" (Speech): "I, the queen of all"
11.59	8. "Creation": "Then, Life was not!" (orchd)
11.60	9. "Faith": "By Thee the fire doth shine"
11.61	*. "Battle Song" (Indra and Maruts) (lost/?used in: Battle Hymn, Op.26/1, H97)*
11.62	*. "Manas" (lost/?used in: Hymn to Manas, Op.26/4, H100/3)*
11.63	*. "Funeral Hymn" (lost/?used in: Funeral Chant, Op.26/2, H98/3)*
11.64	"Ratri" (Night) (c1907, Sanskrit transl Holst, discarded from Op.24, H90) H90a
11.65	"The Heart Worships": "Silence in Heav'n" (c1907, Buckton) H95
11.66	*"Glory of the West" (c?, sketch of unfin arr)*...*App.II/14*
11.67	"A Vigil of Pentecost": "Listen! The shores of other climes" (c before ?1914, Buckton) H123
11.68	"4 Songs" (c1916–7, anon 15th cent; S/T & vn): 1. "Jesu Sweet, now will I sing" Op.35, H132
11.69	2. "My soul has nought but fire and ice"
11.70	3. "I sing of a maiden that matchless is"
11.71	4. "My Leman is so true"
11.72	"May Day Carol": "The moon shines bright" (c?, p1918, trad; 1v & 2vn) H141
11.73	"The Ballad of Hunting Knowe": "Why dost thou tremble so my Burd?" (c after 1918, Ramsden) H147
11.74	"He-back She-Back" (arr ca1920s)..
11.75	"12 Songs" (c1929, Wolfe): 1. "Persephone": "Come back Persephone!" Op.48, H174
11.80	2. "Things lovelier": "You cannot dream things lovelier"
11.77	3. "Now in these Fairylands": "Now in these fairylands"
11.78	4. "A Little Music": "Since it is evening let us invent"
11.79	5. "The Thought": "I will not write a poem for you"
11.86	6. "The Floral Bandit": "Beyond the town—oh far!"
11.82	7. "Envoi": "When the spark that glittered flakes into ash"
11.83	8. "The Dream-City": "On a dream-hill we'll build our city"
11.76	9. "Journey's End": "What will they give me, when journey's done?"
11.81	10. "In the Street of Lost Time": "Rest and have ease"
11.84	11. "Rhyme": "Rhyme in your clear chime we hear ringing"
11.85	12. "Betelgeuse": "On Betelgeuse the gold leaves hang"
11.87	"Epilogue": "I lay these lilies, goddess" (c1929, Wolfe, discarded from Op.48, H174, ?inc)........... H174a

12. FOLKSONG ARRANGEMENTS (1v & pf)

12.1	"Folksongs from Hampshire" (c ?1906–8): 1. "Abroad as I was walking" H83
12.2	2. "Lord Dunwaters": "The King he wrote a long letter"
12.3	3. "The Irish Girl": "Abroad as I was walking"
12.4	4. "Young Reilly": "Young Reilly is my true Love's name"
12.5	5. "The New-mown Hay": "As I walked forth one summer's morn' "
12.6	6. "The Willow Tree": "O take me to your arms, Love"
12.7	7. "Beautiful Nancy": "As beautiful Nancy was a-walking one day"
12.8	8. "Sing ivy": "My father gave me an acre of land"
12.9	9. "John Barleycorn": "There were three Kings came from the North"
12.10	10. "Bedlam City": "Down by the side of Bedlam City"
12.11	11. "The Scolding Wife": "Some men they do delight in hounds"
12.12	12. "The Squire and the Thresher": "A nobleman lived in a village"
12.13	13. "The Happy Stranger": "As I was a-walking one morning in spring"
12.14	14. "Young Edwin in the Lowlands low": "Come all you wild young people"
12.15	15. "Yonder sits a fair young damsel"
12.16	16. "Our ship she lies in harbour"
12.17	"9 Folksongs" (c ?1906–14): 1. "Sovay": "The fair Sovay on a certain day" H84
12.18	2. "The Seeds of Love": "I sowed the seeds of love"
12.19	3. "The Female Farmer": "A famous farmer, as you shall hear"
12.20	4. "Thorneyfield Woods": "In Thorneyfield woods, in Nottinghamshire"
12.21	5. "Moorfields": " 'Twas through Moorfields I rambled"
12.22	6. "I'll love my love": "Abroad as I was walking"
12.23	7. "Claudy Banks": "As I roamed out one evening"
12.24	8. "On the Banks of the Nile": "O hearken, I hear the drums beat"
12.25	9. "Here's Adieu": "Here's adieu my lovely Nancy"
12.26	"Stu Mo Run": "Oh my bonnie highland laddie" (c ?1906–7, Scottish folksong) H84a
12.27	*"4 Folksongs" (c ?1906–8 or 1909–11, sketches): 1. "On Monday morning"*...*App.II/13*
12.28	*2. "Pretty Nancy"*
12.29	*3. "Jocky and Jenny"*
12.30	*4. "Swansea" (Town)*

13. ARRANGEMENTS OF WORKS OF OTHERS

13.1	Vaughan Williams: "Pan's Anniversary," masque (dances arr1905; orch)	App.III/1
13.1	Macfarren: "Bourée" (arr ?1906; pf & str qt)	App.III/2
13.2	Tours: "March" (arr ?1906; pf & str qt)	App.III/3
13.3	Tours: "Dreaming" (orchd ?1906)	App.III/4
13.4	Cowen: "Minuet d'Amour" (orchd ?1906; arr for vn/str qt & pf ?1906)	App.III/5
13.5	Lemare: "Andantino" (arr ?1908; small orch; also for pf & strings ?1908)	App.III/6
13.6	East: "How merrily we live," madrigal (ed for fem ch, p1908)	App.III/7
13.7	Byrd: "Benedictus" (ed ca1908, w/ Eng words; fem ch)	App.III/8
13.8	Arne: "Help me, O Lord," canon (ed before 1908; fem ch)	App.III/9
13.9	Orlando di Lasso: "Adoramus Te Christe" (ed ?1908; fem ch)	App.III/10
13.10	Purcell: 2 duets from ambigue: King Arthur, Z628 (arr ?1910; 2S & orch): 1. "Shepherd, shepherd, leave your labours" (Z628/16b)	App.III/11
13.11	2. "The Stream Daughters" (Z628/29)	
13.12	"Morris Dance Tunes," 2 sets (collected Sharp) (arr1910; small orch; for milit band 1911): I: No.1 "Bean Setting"	App.III/12
13.13	No.2 "Laudnum Bunches"	
13.14	No.3 "Country Gardens"	
13.15	No.4 "Constant Billy"	
13.16	No.5 "Trunkles"	
13.17	No.6 "Morris Off"	
13.18	II: No.1 "Rigs o' Marlow"	
13.19	No.2 "Bluff King Hal"	
13.20	No.3 "How d'ye do, sir?"	
13.21	No.4 "Shepherd's Hey"	
13.22	No.5 "The Blue-eyed Stranger"	
13.23	No.6 "Morris Off"	
13.24	"Sacred Rounds and Canons," 3 sets (17th & 18th cent composers, ed ca1910; equal vv): I: 1. "Glory be to God on high," round (c by Boyce)	App.III/13
13.25	2. "Allelujah," round (c by Boyce)	
13.26	3. "As pants the hart," canon (anon)	
13.27	4. "Who can express the noble works of God?," canon (c by Webbe)	
13.28	II: 1. "I will magnify thee, O God," canon (c by Webbe)	
13.29	2. "From everlasting to everlasting thou art God," canon (c by Webbe)	
13.30	3. "Let the words of my mouth," canon (c by Woodward)	
13.31	4. "Hallelujah, Amen," canon (c by Norris)	
13.32	III: 1. "Young men and maidens," canon (anon)	
13.33	2. "I said, I will take heed unto my ways," canon (c by Norris)	
13.34	3. "Glory be to the Father," canon (c by Webbe)	
13.35	4. "Alleluia," round (c by Hayes)	
13.36	Gardiner: "News from Whydah" (arr of acc for small orch ?1912)	App.III/14
13.37	West: "Light's glittering morn" (orchd ?1913)	App.III/15
13.38	"Old Airs and Glees" (17th & 18th cent composers, arr ?1913–6; fem ch): 1. "Once in England's age of old" (c by Baildon)	App.III/16
13.39	2. "Nothing fairer have I seen" (anon)	
13.40	3. "The Captive Lover": "If my mistress fix her eye" (c by Lawes)	
13.41	3a. "A measure to pleasure your leisure": "With rhymes that are witty and pretty" (c by Martini)	
13.42	4. "Beside a lake of lilies" (c by Arne)	
13.43	5. "Cherry-Stones": "Tinker, tailor, soldier, sailor" (c by Spencer-Churchill)	
13.44	unpubd: . "Come forth you ladies"	
13.45	. "Fallen Summer"	
13.46	. "In the Bay"	
13.47	. "The Picnic"	
13.48	"All people that on earth do dwell" (arr ?1916–9; ch & orch)	App.III/17
13.49	Purcell: 2 suites from incid music "The Gordian Knot Untied," Z597 (arr ca1916–8; strings & ad lib: winds, perc): I (Z597/1–5): No.1 "Overture"	App.III/18
13.50	No.2 "Air"	
13.51	No.3 "Rondeau Minuet"	
13.52	No.4 "Air"	
13.53	No.5 "Jig"	
13.54	II (Z597/6–8): No.1 "Chaconne"	
13.55	No.2 "Air"	
13.56	No.3 "Minuet"	
13.57	Purcell: suite from incid music "The Virtuous Wife," Z611 (arr ca1916–8; strings & ad lib: winds, perc): No.1 "Overture"	App.III/19
13.58	No.2 "Slow Air"	
13.59	No.3 "Hornpipe"	
13.60	No.4 "Minuet I"	
13.61	No.5 "Minuet II"	
13.62	No.6 "Allegro"	
13.63	Purcell: "The Married Beau," Z603, suite (arr ca1916–8; strings & ad lib: winds, perc): No.1 "Overture"	App.III/20
13.64	No.2 "Hornpipe"	
13.65	No.3 "Slow Air"	

13.66	No.4 "Trumpet Air"
13.67	No.5 "Jig"
13.68	No.6 "Hornpipe"
13.69	No.7 "March"
13.70	No.8 "Hornpipe on a Ground"
13.71	*Purcell: "The Old Bachelor," Z607, suite (arr ca1916–8; strings & ad lib: winds & perc, project)* ....
13.72	Byrd: "Short Communion Service" (arr1916; equal vv) App.III/21
13.73	"St Martin-In-The-Fields Pageant," incid music (arr1921, words arr Housman; ch & orch) App.III/22
13.74	"Morley's pupils: Morley Rounds," 2 sets (ed ca1916–24; equal vv): I: 1. "Hushabye Baby"
	(c by Spink) App.III/23
13.75	2. "There was an old man who said 'How' " (c by Joseph)
13.76	3. "How many miles to Babylon?" (c by Joseph)
13.77	4. "As I rode out this enderes night" (c by Jones)
13.78	5. "There was a young man of Calcutta" (c by Palmer)
13.79	6. "Alleluia" (c by Cox)
13.80	II: 7. "Agnus Dei" (c by Joseph)
13.81	8. "Ave Maris stella" (c by Joseph)
13.82	9. "Fair Daffodils" (c by Harrison)
13.83	10. "Kyrie eleison" (c by Cox)
13.84	11. "Christe eleison" (c by Cox)
13.85	12. "Let dogs delight to bark and bite" (c by Gandy)
13.86	Byrd: "O Magnum Mysterium" (ed1927; ch) App.III/24
13.87	Bach, J. S.: "Fugue à la gigue," BWV577 (arr1928; milit band/orch; 2 vers) App.III/25

* * * * *

H = Imogen Holst: "A Thematic Catalogue of Gustav Holst's Music." Faber Music Limited. London, 1974.
App. = Appendix in I. Holst's Catalog.

1. STAGE WORKS

Operas:

1.1 "Philippa," 3 acts (c1903, Honegger, juvenilia) .... Hi
1.2 "Sigismond" (ca1904, juvenilia, lost) .... *Hii*
1.3 "La Esmeralda" (c1907, after Hugo: Notre-Dame de Paris, juvenilia, project) .... *Hiii*
1.4 "La mort de sainte Alméenne," 1 act (c1918, Jacob; 1v & pf, not orchd; see: Interlude, H20a) H20
1.5 "Judith," 3 act opéra sérieux (c1925, Morax, r vers of drame biblique H57a; see choral works).......... H57b
1.6 "Antigone," 3 act lyric tragedy (c1924–7, Cocteau after Sophocles) H65
1.7 "L'aiglon," 5 act drame musical (c1936–7, Cain after Rostand, collab Ibert): H108
    I. *"Les ailes qui s'ouvrent" (c by Ibert)*
    II. "Les ailes qui battent" (c by Honegger)
    III. "Les ailes meurtries" (c by Honegger)
    IV. "Les ailes brisées" (c by Honegger)
    V. *"Les ailes fermées" (c by Ibert)*

Operettas:

1.8 "Les aventures du roi Pausole," 3 acts (c1930, Willemetz after novel by Louÿs) H76
1.9 "La belle de Moudon," 5 acts (c1931, Morax) H78
1.10 "Les petites Cardinal," 2 acts (c1937, Willemetz & Brach after novel by Halévy, collab Ibert) H128

Ballets:

1.11 "Le dit des jeux du monde," ballet / incid music (c1918, Méral; chamber orch) H19
1.12 "Vérité? Mensonge?," ballet de marionettes (c1920, Hellé) H34
1.13 "Marche funèbre," in collab work: Les mariés de la tour Eiffel (c1921, Cocteau, music c by 'Les Six'):.. H35
    "Les mariés de la tour Eiffel": *1. "Ouverture" (Le 14 juillet) (c by Auric)*
    2. "Marche nuptiale" (c by Milhaud)
    3. "Discours du général" (Polka pour deux cornets à pistons) (c by Poulenc)
    4. "La baigneuse de Trouville" (Carte postale en couleurs) (c by Poulenc)
    5. "Fugue du massacre" (c by Milhaud)
    6. "Valse des dépêches" (c by Tailleferre)
    7. "Marche funèbre sur la mort du général" (c by Honegger)
    8. "Quadrille" (Pantalon—Été—Poule—Pastourelle—Final) (c by Tailleferre)
    9. "Ritournelles" (c by Auric)
    10. "Sortie de la noce" (c by Milhaud)
1.14 "Skating Rink" (Symphonie chorégraphique) (c1921–2, Canudo) H40
1.15 "Fantasio" (Sketch en trois images), ballet-pantomime (c1922, Wague) H46
1.16 "Sous-marine," scène mimée (c1924, Carina Ari) H56
1.17 "Roses de métal" (c1928, Grammont, lost except for: Blues, H66) *H66*
1.18 "Les noces d'Amour et de Psyché" (c1930, I. Rubinstein, orchd from J. S. Bach: Eng & Fr Suites)...... H68
1.19 "Amphion," mélodrame (ballet) (c1929, Valéry) H71
1.20 "Sémiramis," 3 act ballet-mélodrame (c1933–4, Valéry) H85
1.21 "Icare" (c1935, Lifar) H96
1.22 "Un oiseau blanc s'est envolé" (c1937, Guitry; incorp in film: Mermoz, H167).................................. H113
1.23 "Le cantique des cantiques" (c1937, Boissy based on Song of Solomon, rhythms Lifar) H123
1.24 "La naissance des couleurs" (c1940, Klausz & Morax) H142
1.25 "Le mangeur de rêves" (c1941, Lenormand, lost) *H154*
1.26 "L'appel de la montagne" (c1943–5, Favre Le Bret) H174
1.27 "Chota Roustaveli" (c1945, Lifar, collab work: Tableau 2 & 3 c by Tcherepnine & Harsányi) H180
1.28 "Sortilèges" (c1946, Bederkhan; 4 ondes martenot, lost) *H189*
1.29 "De la musique" (c1950, Wild, lost) *H200*

Incid music:

1.30 "La danse macabre" (c1919, Larronde, lost except for 2 pieces): H21
    extant: 1. "Danse aux charniers"
    2. "Foire sur la place"
1.31 "Saül" (c1922, Gide, inc) H41
1.32 "La tempête" (c1923, Shakespeare transl Pourtalès, inc) (also see semi-opera c by Purcell Z631,
    incid music c by Sibelius Op.109 & Sullivan Op.1) H48
1.33 "Liluli" (c1923, Rolland) H49
1.34 "L'impératrice aux rochers" (c1925, from Bouhélier's Un miracle de Notre-Dame) H60
1.35 "Phaedre" (c1926, D'Annunzio transl Doderet) H61
1.36 "Prélude: Marche sur la Bastille," in collab work: Le 14 Juillet (c1936, Rolland): H104
    "Le 14 Juillet," I: *1. "Ouverture" (c by Ibert)*
    2. "Palais-Royal" (c by Auric)
    3. "Introduction et Marche funèbre de la Liberté" (c by Milhaud)
    II: *4. "Prélude: La nuit du grand soir" (c by Roussel)*
    5. "Choeur: Liberté, dans ce beau jour" (c by Koechlin)
    6. "Prélude: Marche sur la Bastille" (c by Honegger)
    7. "Final—Interlude—Fête populaire de la Liberté" (c by Lazarus)
1.37 "La mandragore" (c1941, Machiavelli) H146

1a. SELECTIONS FROM STAGE WORKS

1a.6   "Antigone," opera: H65
  I/1. "Exposition du drame: les deux soeurs": 1. "Introduction"
    2. "Dialogue des deux soeurs"
    3. "L'Amour fraternel"
    4. "Reprise de l'altercation"
    5. "Épilogue"
  I/2. "Glorification de la victoire thébaine," chorus
  I/3. "L'action se noue": 1. "Créon approuvé par les coryphées serviles"
    2. "Récit du Garde"
    3. "Colère de Créon"
    4. "Transition orchestrale vers l'Interlude"
  II/4. "Le premier conflit: Créon et Antigone": 1."Introduction"
    2. "Récit du Garde"
    3. "Monologue d'Antigone"
    4. "Altercation entre Créon et Antigone"
  II/5. "Suite et développement du conflit": 1. "Créon interroge Ismène"
    2. "Ismène tente de se solidariser avec Antigone"
    3. "Dialogue entre Créon et Ismène"
    4. "Interlude"
    5. "Le Coryphée" (S)
  II/6. "Le deuxième conflit: Créon et Hémon": 1. "Créon tente de convainxre Hémon"
    2. "Plaidoyer d'Hémon"
    3. "Altercation entre Créon et Hémon"
  II/7. "La Sentence": 1. "Sentence de Créon"
    2. "Interlude": "Amour qui saisis les uns et les autres" (Coryphée / A)
  II/8. "Les Adieux d'Antigone": 1. "Introduction"
    2. "Marche au supplice, premier palier"
    3. "Marche au supplice, deuxième palier"
    4. "Marche au supplice, troisième palier"
    5. "Marche au supplice, quatrième palier"
    6. "Quatuor des Coryphées"
  II/9. "L'Avertissement de Tirésias à Créon": 1. "Entrevue de Créon et de Tirésias"
    2. "Créon, ébranlé, consulte les Coryphées"
  "Interlude": 1. "Hymne à Bacchus": "Tu fais danser les étoiles et chanter la nuit"
    2. "Interlude" (orch)
  III/10. "Apparition de la reine Euridice": 1. "Le Messager annonce la mort d'Antigone et d'Hémon"
    2. "Brève et unique intervention de la reine Euridice"
    3. "Récit du Messager"
    4. "Dialogue du Messager et du coryphée basse"
  III/11. "La Tragédie finale de Créon": 1. "Créon portant son fils mort"
    2. "Désespoir de Créon"
    3. "Conclusion"

1a.8   "Les aventures du roi Pausole," operetta: H76
  I: . "Ouverture"
    1. "Choeur de la Sieste" (les Reines)
    2. "Sortie des Reines"
    3. "J'ai fait, pourquoi le taire, tous les métiers," air (Taxis)
    4. "Papa veut toujours, seule, hélas! que je m'amuse," air (Aline)
    5. "Ballet"
    6. "Entrée des bois de justice" (Pausole, ch)
    7. "J'ai l'honneur d'être votre page," air (Giglio)
    8. "Septuor des sept avis différents" (les Reines)
    9. "Final" (les Reines, Taxis, Pausole, Giglio, ch)
  II: . "Prélude"
    10. "Frottons, époussetons," chorus (les Fermières & le Métayer)
    11. "Duo du Travesti": "Êtes-vous un homme? êtes-vous une femme?" (Aline et Mirabelle)
    12. "Ritournelle de la mule" (music = Prélude)
    13. "Cantate": "Vive le Roi Pausole" (le Métayer, Thierrette, les Fermiéres)
    14. "Air de la coupe de Thulé": "Descendant du Roi de Thulé" (Pausole)
    15. "Sortie américaine du Roi"
    16. "Vos joues sont d'exquises pêches," trio (Aline, Mirabelle, Giglio)
    17. "Pardon, mon papa que j'adore," air (Aline)
    18. "Si vous saviez combien c'est long d'attendre," air (Diane)
    19. "Duetto de la révolte" (Taxis, Perchuque, ch)
    20. "Final" (Pausole, Giglio, Taxis, Diane, le Métayer, le Brigadier, ch w/ soloists)
  III: 21. "Choeur des Soubrettes": "Chut! pas de bruit le Roi sommeille" (Les Caméristes)
    22. "Duo du rêve": "j'ai fait un rêve merveilleux" (Diane, Giglio)
    23. "Entrée du chocolat espagnol" (Thierrette, ch)
    24. "Ah! mon Dieu, qu'ai-je vu," air (Taxis)
    25. "Duo du téléphone": "Allô, le Roi?" (Aline, Pausole)
    26. "L'amour, c'est comme la musique," air (Giglio)
    27. "Les Adieux de Pausole": "Adieu, mon peuple aimé" (Pausole, Aline)

28. "Final" (all except Pausole)

1a.9   "La belle de Moudon," operetta: H78
    I: 1. "Ouverture"
        2. "Romance de la Pâquerette" (Isabelle)
        3. "Avec le battoir," chorus (Laveuses)
        4. "Il est bientôt midi," chorus (Laveuses)
        5. "Choeur de la diligence," chorus
    II: 6. "C'est l'heure où tout repose," chorus
        7. "Valse"
        8. "Chanson de Petit Jean" (Gizèle)
    III: . "Introduction"
        9. "Ombre et silence," chorus
      10. "Voix de la Forêt": "Allez devant les vers luisants" (child ch, ch)
    IV: 11. "Introduction"
      12. "Tu fuis, ingrat, qui me juras ta foi," air (Isabelle)
      13. "Barcarolle": "Viens avec moi mon ami" (m ch)
      14. "Entrée de la fanfare"
      15. "Polka"
    V: 16. "Un an se passe," chorus
      17. "Couplet final": "Je suis heureuse" (Isabelle, ch)

1a.10 "Les petites Cardinal," operetta: H128
    I: 1. "Introduction"
        2. "Scène du berger"
        3. "Y'a quelqu'chose à faire" (c by Ibert)
        4. "Entrée des petites Cardinal"
        5. "Interlude" (c by Ibert)
        6. "Couplets de Monsieur Cardinal" (c by Ibert)
        7. "Couplets de la tour de Nesle" (c by Ibert)
        8. "Interlude" (c by Ibert)
        9. "De la Madeleine à l'Opéra"
      10. "Interlude"
      11. "Quatuor des jeunes gens" (c by Ibert)
      12. "Couplets (Conseils) du bon diable"
      13. "Final"
    II: 14. "Entr'acte"
      14bis. "Choeur des petits Ponts"
      15. "Trio de la migraine"
      16. "Finaletto—Revue" (c by Ibert)
      17. "C'est le charme de Florence" (c by Ibert)
      18. "Musique de scène" (c by Ibert)
      19. "Une lionne à la gare de Lyon" (c by Ibert)
      20. "Musique de scène" (c by Ibert)
      21. "Air de la Calomnie"
      22. "Interlude"
      23. "Interlude"
      24. "L'utile et l'agréable" (c by Ibert)
      25. "Si nous avions un Colonel" (c by Ibert)
      26. "Musique de scène" (c by Ibert)
      27. "Couplet Final" (c by Ibert)
      28. "Sortie du public" (c by Ibert)

1a.11 "Le dit des jeux du monde," ballet: H19
        1. "Le Soleil et la fleur" (Dance 1)
        2. "La Montagne et les pierres" (Dance 2)
        3. "L'enfant et la mer" (Dance 3)
        4. "L'Homme tournant sur le sol" (Dance 4)
        5. "L'Homme fou" (Interlude 1)
        6. "Les Hommes et le village" (Dance 5)
        7. "Les Hommes et la terre" (Dance 6)
        8. "L'Homme et la femme" (Dance 7)
        9. "L'Homme qui lutte et conduit" (Interlude 2)
      10. "L'Homme et l'ombre" (Dance 8)
      11. "Le rat et la mort" (Dance 9)
      12. "L'Homme et la mer" (Dance 10)
      13. "Épilogue"

1a.12 "Vérité? Mensonge?," ballet: H34
        1. "Prologue"
        2. "Refrain des Appariteurs"
        3. "1er tableau"
        4. "2ème tableau"

2. "Les Noirs"
3. "Le plus fort"
4. "Discipline"
5. "Couronnement"
6. "Cortège de l'or"
7. "Danse de l'enfant"
8. "Les Bleus"
9. "Choeur angélique"
10. "Le Rouge"
11. "Révolte"
12. "Hymne vermeil"
13. "Complot des Noirs"
14. "L'Arc-en-ciel"
15. "Hymne blanc"

1a.26 "L'appel de la montagne," ballet: H174
    I: 1. "Introduction et ensemble"
           2. "Danse des filles des cantons"
           3. "Entrée de MacGuire"
           4. "Entrée d'Haecky et des bergers"
           5. "Danse générale"
           6. "Variation de MacGuire"
           7. "Variation de Saesli"
           8. "Appel aux jeux"
           9. "Lancement des pierres"
          10. "Luttes"
          11. "Distribution des prix et sortie"
          12. "Alpenglüe" (Coucher de soleil)
    II: 13. "Introduction, ascension et chute de MacGuire" (passacaille)
    III: 14. "Apparition des déesses"
          15. "Ronde des déesses"
          16. "Entrée des dieux maléfiques"
          17. "Apparition de la Jungfrau"
          18. "Tuba sur la scène"

1a.27 "Chota Roustaveli," ballet: H180
    I: . "Prélude"
           1. "Oiseaux"
           2. "Entrée du léopard"
           3. "Passage des oiseaux"
           4. "Entrée et danse de Chota"
           5. "Passage des oiseaux"
           6. "Combat avec le léopard"
           7. "Apparition et Danse de Tzetzkly"
           8. "Poème récité" (w/ out music)
           9. "Apparition de Thamar"
    II: (music c by Tcherepnine)
    III: (music c by Harsányi)
    IV: 1. "Chota et Tzetzkly"
           2. "Oiseaux" (from: Tableau I)
           3. "Danse guerrière de Chota"
           4. "Danse de Tzetzkly"
           5. "Chota—Tzetzkly—Thamar"
           6. "Final et apparition de saint Georges"

1a.32 "La tempête," incid music: H48
           1. "Prélude"
           2. "Le Manteau magique"
           3. "Motif pour les entrées" (Motif d'Ariel)
           4. "Ritournelle de Caliban"
           5. "Chant d'Ariel": "Venez jusqu'à ces sables d'or"
           6. "Enchantement"
           7. "Final"
           8. "Ritournelle de Stefano"
           9. "Ariel joue du pipeau"
          10. "Ariel en Harpie" (Scherzo)
          11. "La Grotte de Prospero"
          12. "Danse de l'acte IV"
          13. "Chant d'Ariel": "Où butine l'abeille"

1a.33 "Liluli," incid music: H49
           1. "Choeur des Ouvriers": "Ah Joseph dites-nous"
           2. "Laïra"

1a.34 "L'impératrice aux rochers," incid music: H60
　　　　　　1. "Prologue" (w/ reciter)
　　　　I:　2. "Introduction" (Prélude)
　　　　　　2b. "La Chasse de l'empereur. Fanfares de chasse sur la scène"
　　　　　　3. "Interlude"
　　　　　　4. "Interlude" (la Salle du conseil)
　　　　　　5. "Entrée du pape"
　　　　　　6. "Sortie de l'empereur" (w/ ch)
　　　　II:　7. "Prélude" (La Neige sur Rome)
　　　　　　8. "Interlude"
　　　　　　9. "Interlude" (La Tour)
　　　　　　10. "Postlude"
　　　　III: 11. "Prélude" (Les Jardins du palais)
　　　　　　12. "Concert champêtre"
　　　　　　13. "Postlude"
　　　　　　14. "Interlude" (Le Retour de l'empereur) (from Finale of: Partita, H139)
　　　　　　15. "Cortège de l'impératrice"
　　　　　　16. "Interlude" (L'Orage)
　　　　IV: 17. "Introduction: L'Orgie au palais" (Prélude)
　　　　　　18. "Musique de fête"
　　　　　　19. "Vocalise" (S)
　　　　　　20. "Interlude" (Le Rocher)
　　　　　　21. "Apparition" (ch)
　　　　　　22. (Calme) (ch)
　　　　　　23. (Lent) (ch)
　　　　V:　24. "Introduction: Les Ruines du temple" (Prélude)
　　　　　　25. "Interlude" (Le Parvis de la cathédrale)
　　　　　　26. "Choeur final"

1a.35 "Phoèdre," incid music: H61
　　　　I:　1. "Prélude"
　　　　　　2. "Cortège des suppliantes"
　　　　II:　3. "Prélude"
　　　　　　4. "Le Baiser"
　　　　　　5. "Imprécation de Thésée"
　　　　III: 6. "Prélude"
　　　　　　7. "Lamentation d'Aethra"
　　　　　　8. "Choeur des prêtresses d'Aphrodite"
　　　　　　9. "Mort de Phaèdre"

1a.37 "La mandragore," incid music: H146
　　　　　　1. "Prologue—1bis Cloches—Rirournelle I—Ritournelle II"
　　　　　　2. "Reprise des Cloches et Ritournelle I"
　　　　　　3. "Ritournelle III"
　　　　　　4. (Andante)
　　　　　　5. "Reprise de (No.4) à la lettre 'A' puisqu'à la fin enchaîner Coda"
　　　　　　6. (Allegro)
　　　　　　7. (Moderato)
　　　　　　8. "Nocturne"
　　　　　　9. "Ritournelle IV enchaîner les Cloches"

1a.38 "L'ombre de la Ravine," incid music: H147
　　　　　　1. "Prélude"
　　　　　　2. "Postlude"

1a.39 "Les suppliantes," incid music: H149
　　　　　　1. "Prélude"
　　　　　　2. "Mélodrame 1. Fanfare por les suppliantes"
　　　　　　3. "Choeur I": "Mais d'abord" (w/ Danse panique)
　　　　　　4. "Salutation aux dieux"
　　　　　　5. "Choeur II": "O fils de Palaichton"
　　　　　　6. "Choeur III": "Seigneur des Seigneurs"
　　　　　　7. "Mélodrame 2"
　　　　　　8. "Choeur IV": "Voici l'heure pour les Dieux"
　　　　　　9. "Entrée des Égyptiens"
　　　　　　10. "Choeur V"
　　　　　　11. "Choeur VI"
　　　　　　12. "Mélodrame 3" (Sortie du Roi)
　　　　　　13. "Choeur VII": "Que la cité prospère"

1a.41 "La ligne d'horizon," incid music: H151
　　　　I:　1. "Le port de Cannes" (Le Départ)
　　　　　　2. "Au large" (Destination inconnue)
　　　　　　3. "En vue de Syracuse" (Faits divers) (T)
　　　　　　4. "Samos" (Une minute)

5. "Pondichéry" (Les Jeux sont faits) (T)
II: 6. "Shanghaï" (la Prison habitude)
7. "Hiva Hoha" (Arrêt facultatif)
8. "Honolulu" (une Retraite)
9. "Demain" (La Vie recommence) (unison m ch)

1a.42 "Le soulier de satin," incid music: H165
1. "Mouvement de Rumba"
2. "La Mer—Plénitude de la Mer"
3. "La Vierge"
4. (w/ out title)
5. "Rumba de Jobarbara" (S)
6. "L'Ange Gardien"
7. "Scène XIV 1ère Journée" (melodic fragments): a. "Don Balthazar"
b. "Don Balthazar"
c. "Le Chinois"
c.bis "La Négresse"
d. "Don Balthazar"
e. "Voix de Musique"
8. (Lent)
9. "Prélude pour la 2ème Journée"
10a, b, c. "Choeur de l'Epreuve" (S, Bar, ch)
11. "Saint Jacques" (Interlude)
12. "Thème de Dona Musique—Forêt vierge—Ruisseaux"
13. "La Mer—Sonate au clair de lune"
14. "Sicile (Interlude)—Cors siciliens"
15. "L'Ombre double" (S, Bar)
16. "La Lune"
17. "Dona Musique à Prague"
18. (w/ out title)
19a.–g. "Petit orchestre sur scène" (melodic fragments: Dona Isabel)
20. "Rhythme"
21. "Mort de Prouhèze"
22. "Marche funèbre"
23a–g. "Scène finale"

1a.44 "Charles le téméraire," incid music: H175
Prologue: 1. "Choeur I": "Victoire au duc, victoire au Téméraire ..."
II: 2. "Choeur II": "La Nation que Dieu protège"
3. "Choeur III": "Les Taons ont réveillé le taureau sur l'alpage" (m ch)
III: 4. "Choeur IV"
5. "Choeur V": "Charlot le Téméraire va partir pour la guerre"
6. "Fanfare I"
7. "Fanfare II"
8. "Marche"
IV: 9. "Rythme I / Choeur VI": "Salva nos Domine vigilantes" (fem ch, superimposed on Rythme)
10. "Rythme II / Choeur VII": "Il est venu le jour de la colère" (superimposed on Rythme)
11. "Choeur VIII" "La Pauvre âme immortelle—Requiem aeternam"
12. "Marche des Suisses"

1a.45 "Prométhée," incid music: H187
1. "Prélude"
2. "Entrée des Océanides"
3. "Interlude"
4. "Entrée du char de l'océan"
5. "Choeur des Océanides"
6. "Choeur des Océanides"
7. "Interlude" (repeat of 3.)
8. "Choeur des Océanides"
9. "Sortie d'Io"
10. "Choeur des Océanides"
11. "Final"

1a.46 "Hamlet," incid music: H190
"Fanfares pour Hamlet": 1. "Introduction"
2. "Fanfares du Réveil"
3. "Entrée et Sortie du Roi"
3b. "Fanfare du Banquet"
4. "Trompettes de Fortimbras"
5. "Fanfares du Duel"
6. "Arrivée de Fortimbras"
7. "Cortège funèbre"
"Hamlet": a. "Monologue"
b. "Interlude"
c. "Pantomime"

         d. "Mélodrame"
         e. "Entrée de Lucianus"
         e.bis "Sommeil du Roi"
         f. "Entre la Fanfare 6 et la Fanfare 7"
    "Chant" (Ophélie): a. "Comment puis-je entre tant d'amours reconnaître le seul fidèle?"
         b. "Chantons tire lire"
         c. "S'il n'est pas déjà de retour"
    "Chanson de route des Comédiens"
    "Chanson du Fossoyeur"

1a.47   "Oedipe," incid music: H194
         1. "Prélude"
         2. "Fanfares"
         3. "Choeur 1"
         4. "Choeur 2"
         5. "Choeur 2bis"
         6. "Choeur 3"
         7. "Entrée de Jocaste"
         8. "Choeur 4"
         9. "Choeur 5"
        10. "Interlude"
        11. "Mélodrame"
        12. "Sortie d'Oedipe"
        13. "Rideau final"

1a.50   "Oedipe-roi," incid music: H210
         1. "Ouverture et Scène I"
         2. "Entrée de Créon"
         3. "Sortie d'Oedipe"
         4. "Entrée du peuple et ritournelle pendant le choeur no.1"
         5. "Entrée de Tirésias"
         6. "Ritournelle pendant le choeur no.2"
         7. "Ritournelle pendant le choeur no.3"
         8. "Entrée de Jocaste"
         8bis. "Cris de Jocaste"
         9. "Ritournelle pendant le choeur no.4"
        10. "Ritournelle pendant le choeur no.5"
        11. "Mélodrame" (Oedipe et le Choeur)
        12. "Finale"

1a.51   "Les douze coups de minuit," radio: H84
         1. "Cortège"
         2. "Danse"
         3. "La Pierre"
         3a. "Le Bois"
         3b. "Le Métal"
         3c. "Le Verre"
         4. "Cascade des métaux"
         5. "Cloche de Fer"
         6. "Cloche d'Airain"
         7. "Chanson des Ivrognes"
         8. (Très lent)
         9. "Chorus": "Avec la règle et le compas"
         9b. "Disque de Jazz"
        10. "Les Aviateurs"
        11. "Chorus": "Ouvrez les yeux"

1a.52   "Christophe Colomb," radio: H140
      I. 1. "Prologue"
     II. "Le palais de l'Alhambra": 2. "Évocation"
         3. "Sacre burlesque"
         4. "Sortie du roi"
    III. "La Chapelle de la Rabida": 5. "Fin de la messe"
         6. "Procession" (Choeur des marins)
    IV. "Palos": 7. "Lamentations des femmes de Palos"
         8. "Départ de Christophe Colomb"
     V. "La Traversée": 9. "Rythme du temps"
        10. "Prière des moussess"
        11. "Miracle du vent"
        12. "Mélopée" (used in: Derrière Murcie en fleurs, H184)
        13. "Prière de Christophe Colomb"
        14. "Te Deum"
    VI. "Le Retour" (w/ out music)
    VII. "La Mort de la reine Isabelle": 15. "Prière des morts"
        16. (w/ out title)

      17. "Final"

1a.54   "Saint François d'Assise," radio: H197
        1. "Prelude" (Allegretto)
        2. "Le Bateleur"
        3. (w/ out title)
        4. "Musique de banquet" (instruments anciens)
        5. "Chanson de troubadour" (T & instruments anciens)
        6.–9. (w/ out title)
        10. "Reconstruction de l'église"
        11.–12. (w/ out titles)
        13. "Plain chant"
        14. "Fondation des Clarisses"
        15. (w/ out title)
        16. "La Prédication aux oiseaux"
        17. (w/ out title)
        18. "Les Stigmates"
        19. (w/ out title)
        20. "Le Feu"
        21.–23. (w/ out title)
        24. "Cantique du Soleil"
        25. "Agonie et mort de François"
        26.–27. "Finale"

1a.56   "Tête d'or," radio: H199
        1. (Largamente)
        2. "Les Champs à la fin de l'hiver"
        3. "Ils marchent ..."
        4. "Deux arbres et toute la nuit dernière"
    "Tête d'or—2ème partie": 5. "La Nuit dans le Palais"
        6. "Mesure du temps" (60)
        7. "Le Rossignol" (A and B)
        8. "Entrée et Pantomime de la Princesse"
        9. "Le Rêve éveillé"
        . "Entrée rapide du Messager"
        . "Récit de la Bataille"
    "Tête d'or—Suite 2ème partie": . "Entrée de Tête d'Or": a. "Je ne le précède que de peu"
        b. "... la voix de trompette"
        . "Marche de Cébès"
        . "Mort du Roi"
        . "Final 2ème partie"
    "Tête d'or—3ème partie": . "Le Caucase"
        . "Crucifixion"
        . "Fond sonore de la Déroute"
        . "Tête d'Or blessé"

1a.57   "La rédemption de François Villon," radio: H209
        1. "Neige"
        2. "Pluie et Vent"
        3. "1er Tableau: Chanson de la Grosse Margot"
        4. "2ème Tableau: Trompe"
        5. "En me quittant Robin Robinet"

1a.60   "Rapt" (La séparation des races), film: H86
        1. "Procession"
        2. "Danse paysanne—au matin"
        3. "Chanson d'Eloi": "Frühlings Nacht, Märchen Nacht" (Kessel)

1a.61   "L'idée," animated: H87
        1. "Générique"
        2. "Arbres et idées"
        3. "Facteur"
        4. "Tribunal"
        5. "Usine"
        6. "Cortège funèbre"
        7. "Savant"
        8. "La Rotation"
        9. "Cortège ouvriers-soldats"
        10. "Coda"

1a.62   "Les misérables," film: H88
      I: 1. "Prélude I" (Générique)
         2. "Jean Valjean sur la route—Passeport—Place du Village" (Place de Bigne)
         3. (Evocation des) "Forçats"
         3b. "Passeport déchiré"

    4. "Jean Valjean avec la carte"
    5. "Fantine—La Route, nuit"
    6. "Fantine à l'infirmerie—Javert"
    6b. "Chant de Fantine—Mort de Fantine"
    7. "Fuite de Jean Valjean"
II: 8. "Prélude II" (Cosette et Marius)
    9. "Musique de la Foire lointaine—Cosette dans la forêt—Jean Valjean et Cosette"
    9b. "Transition" (Le Gâteau)
    10. "Sortie de l'Église"
    11. (Le) "Luxemburg—prévenir la Police"
    12. "Le Jardin de la rue Plumet"
III: 13. "Prélude III" (L'Emeute)
    14. "La Tour St. Jacques"
    15. "Après la chute de Mabeuf" (Emeute) (Mort de Mabeuf)
    16. "Emeute" (Mort de Gavroche)
    17. "Emeute" (Mort d'Eporire—Eporire et Marius—Jean Valjean et Javert—Mort d'Eporire)
    18. "Emeute" (Après le parlementaire) (l'Assaut)
    18b. (w/ out title)
    19. "Transition" (Matin sur Notre-Dame)
    20. "Dans les Egouts"
    21. "Musique (de fête) chez Gillenormand"
    22. "Solitude de Jean Valjean"
    23. "Mort de Jean Valjean"

1a.63   "Cessez le feu," film: H90
    1. "Chanson du cul-de-jatte" (Zimmer)
    2. "Valse de Lagasse"
    3. (La Marseillaise)
    4. "Fox-trot"
    5. "Tango, major and minor"
    6. "Signal"
    7. "Chanson de l'escadrille" (Kessel)
    8. "Valse musette"

1a.64   "Le roi de la Camargue," film: H91
    1. "Poursuite et bataille"
    2. "L'Église"
    3. "Fanfare"
    4. "Nuit devant la Cabane"
    5. "Final"
    6a. "Chanson I": "Ma plaine finit vers l'occident" (Cuel)
    6b. "Chanson II": "En Camarque, les filles sont belles" (Cuel)

1a.65   "Le démon de l'Himalaya," film: H93
    1. "Générique chanté": "Om mani pad me hum"
    2. "Rumba"
    3. "La lettre"
    4. "Voyage"
    5. "Szynagai"
    6. "Les Jardins de Moghul"
    7. "Défilé de la caravane"
    8. "Danse des lamas" (song)
    9. "Vision"
    10. "Caravane des Kulis" (ch)
    11. "Chant nocturne des Kulis" (ch)
    12. "Récit de la femme"
    13. "Himalaya"
    14. "Montée de la Caravane"
    15. "Tempête de neige"
    16. "Batailles des Kulis"
    17. "Chant de joie" (song)
    18. "Final chanté"

1a.67   "L'équipage," film: H98
    1. "Chanson du Lapin" (Kessel)
    2. "Premier Vol."

1a.67   "Mayerling," film: H101
    1. "Générique"
    2. "Dans le Fiacre"
    3. "Dans les Couloirs"
    4. "Jardins"
    5. "Scène finale"

1a.70   "Nitchevo" (L'agonie du sous-marin), film: H106
        1. "De l'Atlantique au Pacifique": "Nous n'avons jamais de chagin," song (Féline)
        2. "Dans le sous-marin"
        3. "Explosion"
        4. "Tramonto"
        5. "Après l'attentat"
        6. "Souks"
        7. "Jardins à Bizerte"
        8. "Canot Sarak"
        9. "De l'Atlantique au Pacifique"
       10. "Valse-Nitchevo": "Triste est mon coeur"

1a.71   "Mademoiselle Doctor" (Salonique nid d'espions), film: H109
        1. "Ouverture"
        2. "Hôtel à Berne"
        3. "Café Turc"
        4. "Port de Salonique"
        5. "Départ en auto"
        6. "Villa abandonnée"
        7. "Micro dans la nuit" (Préludes I & II)
        8. "Réveil"
        9. "Dans le Beuglant"
      10. "Bristol-Valse"
      11. "Maison de Passe"
      12. "Dans la ferme"
      13. "Blues"
      14. "La Soirée: tango"
      15. "Poursuite"
      16. "Final"

1a.72   "Marthe Richard au service de la France," film: H110
        1. "Générique"
        2. "Entrée des Allemands"
        3. "Village en flammes"
        4. "Chanteur espagnol"
        5. "Musique de gitane" (Valses I & II)
        6. "Tango de Mata-Hari"
        7. "Ludow au piano"
        8. "Marthe et Ludow"
        9. "Combat naval"
      10. "Annonce du Torpillage"
      11. "Tango de Charlotte"
      12. "Sur la falaise"
      13. "Sonnerie au phono"
      14. "Orgue dans l'église" (= H110a)
      15. "Banquet"
      16. "Mobilisation américaine"
      17. "Attaque des avions"
      18. "Final de l'Armistice"

1a.75   "Regain," film: H117
        1. "Générique"
        2. "Hiver et Printemps"
        3. "Refrain de Gédémus"
        4. "Nuit dans la grange"
        5. "Printemps ... Été"
        6. "Mort de Mamèche"
        7. "Nocturne"
        8. "Le Soc"
        9. "Panturle"
      10. "Panturle abat des arbres"
      11. "Foire à Manosque"

1a.77   "Miarka ou la fille à l'ourse," film: H124
        1. "Générique" (c by Honneger)
        2. "Chanson de la route" (c by Honneger)
        3. "Chanson de l'eau" (c by Honneger)
        4. "Après le baptême" (c by Harsányi)
        5. "Tétée" (c by Harsányi)
        6. "Ruisseau petit jardin" (c by Harsányi)
        7. "Rythme du Chaudron" (c by Harsányi)
        8. "Danse petite Miarka" (c by Honneger)
        9. "Scène de la prédiction et Final" (c by Harsányi)
       10. "Scène des oeufs" (c by Harsányi)
      11. "Scène des abeilles" (c by Harsányi)

12. *"Scène de l'ours" (c by Harsányi)*
13. *"Scène des confitures" (c by Harsányi)*
14. "Chanson sans paroles" (c by Honneger)
15. "Signal Radio" (c by Honneger)
16. *"Conférence" (c by Harsányi)*
17. *"Sortie de la conférence" (c by Harsányi)*
18. *"Danse estrade" (c by Harsányi)*
19. *"Danse" (c by Harsányi)*
20. *"Incendie" (c by Harsányi)*
21. *"Danse de Miarka" (suite) (c by Harsányi)*
22. *"Mort de Sarah" (c by Harsányi)*
23. *"Miarka triste" (c by Harsányi)*
24. *"Viol" (c by Harsányi)*
25. *"Disque et montée à la tour" (c by Harsányi)*
26. "Valse de l'Escalier" (c by Honneger)
27. "L'Innocent et l'Oiseau" (c by Honneger)

1a.78   "Passeurs d'hommes," film: H125
      1. "Cabarets"
      2. "Piano mécanique"
      3. "Ivresse"
      4. "Le Mat"

1a.81   "L'or dans la montagne" (Faux monnayeurs), film: H130
      1. "Générique"
      2. "Brume du matin"
      3. "La Mort: final"

1a.83   "Cavalcade d'amour," film: H136
      1. "Projet"
      2. "Rencontre"
      3. "Marche nuptiale"
      4. "Messe de Mariage: Kyrie, O Salutaris"
      5. "Final"

1a.84   "Le journal tombe à 5 heures," film: H156
      1. "Machines"
      2. "Blues"
      3. "Tango"
      4. "Sandetti"
      5. "Villa Rabaud"
      6. "En perdition"
      7. "Expédition"
      8. "La Bateau-phare"
      9. "Final"

1a.85   "Huit hommes dans un château," film: H157
      1. "Aurore"
      2. "Hallucination"
      3. "Fantôme"
      4. "Enigme"
      5. "Victoire"

1a.86   "Les antiquités de l'Asie occidentale," documentary: H158
      1. "Générique"
      2. "Vase Our Nina"
      3. "Tête de Taureau"
      4. "Gudea-Apis"
      5. "Code Hamourabi"
      6. "Grande Salle"
      7. "Transport et Tributaires"
      8. "Cheval et Char de guerre"
      9. "Cylindres"
      10. "Frise des Archers"
      11. "Chapiteaux"
      12. "Bas-relief hittite"
      13. "La Dame d'Elcké"

1a.88   "La boxe en France," documentary: H160
      1. "Hymne au Sport": "Soyons unis! Amples poitrines" (c by Honnegger, words Bruyr)
      2. *"Générique Boxe en France" (c by Jolivet)*
      3. *"Gravures sur Boxe de l'Antiquité" (c by Jolivet)*
      4. *"La Foire" (c by Jolivet)*
      5. *"Arrivée des Boxeurs" (c by Jolivet, based on 1. + acc)*

1a.89   "Secrets," film: H161
             1. "Générique"
             2. "Claire"
             3. "René et Michel"
             4. "Au pigeonnier"
             5. "Amadou"
             6. "Réveil"
             7. "Michel et Marie-Thérèse"
             8. "La Bassin"
             9. "Jalousie"
             10. "Amour"
             11. Song: "Le ciel a caché ses nuages" (Solar)
             12. "Colère"
             13. "Réconciliation"
             14. "Adieu de Michel"

1.91   "Le capitaine Fracasse," film: H166
             1. "Générique"
             2. "Orage"
             3. "Sigognac"
             4. "Guitare"
             5. "Les Comédiens"
             6. "Banquet des comédiens"
             7. "Guitare"
             8. "Attaque des comédiens"
             9. "Recherches des comédiens"
             10. "Requiem"
             11. (Le) "Capitaine Fracasse"
             12. "Duel dans le Cimetière"
             13. "Musique de théâtre"
             14. "Scène d'amour"
             15. "Faux enterrement"
             16. "Bataille (de) Brigands"
             17. "Poursuite de carosse"
             18. "Duel chez les Valombreuses"
             19. "Sigognac mourant"
             20. "Ariette": "Si mon coeur parlait, Lysandre" (Badet)
             21. "Chanson du chariot de Thespis": "Portant le rire et le drame" (Badet)
             22. "Chanson pour Isabelle": "Avant que la journée de notre âge qui fuit ..." (arr Honneger)

1a.92   "Mermoz," film: H167
             1. "Mermoz"
             2. "Misère"
             3. "L'Officine"
             4. "Départ du Courrier"
             5. "Le Poème d'Icare"
             6. "La Ligne"
             7. "Amérique du Sud"
             8. "Nocturne à Rio"
             9. "L'Envoi"
             10. "Sur les Andes"
             11. "Le Vent se lève"
             12. "Lever du jour"
             13. "Réparation de l'avion"
             14. "Traversée de l'Atlantique"
             15. "Montmartre"
             16. "Conseil d'Administration / Ricanement"
             17. "Attente"
             18. "Evocation des Morts"
             19. "Final"

1a.94   "Un seul amour," film: H171
             1. "Générique"
             2. "La Sylphide"
             3. "En voyage"
             4. "Couloirs de l'Opéra"
             5. "Dans la loge"
             6. "Mort de Clara"
             7. "Le Château"
             8. "Petit Déjeuner"
             9. "Les Lettres"
             10a. "Quand tu verras les hirondelles," song (Zimmer)
             10b. "Si le mal d'amour," song (Zimmer)
             11. "Appréhension"
             12. "L'Inquiétude"

4. OTHER ORCHESTRAL WORKS

636

6.4 String Quartet No.3 in E (c1936–7) H114

7. OTHER CHAMBER MUSIC

4 or more insts:

7.1	"Musiques (Pièces) d'ameublement" (c1919; fl, cl, tpt, str qt & pf): No.1 "Vif" (w/ out str qt)	H22
7.2	No.2 "Lent" (w/ out tpt)	
7.3	No.3 "Modéré (w/ out 2nd vn & va)	
7.4	"Hymne," in B minor (c1920; 10 strings)	H33
7.5	"Trois contrepoints" (c1922; fl, Eng hn, vn & vc): No.1 "Prélude"	H43
7.6	No.2 "Chorale"	
7.7	No.3 "Canon sur basse obstinée"	
7.8	*"Prélude et blues" (c ?1925; 4 harps, lost)*	*H56*
7.9	"Berceuses pour la Bobcisco" (c1929; vn, fl/2nd vn, tpt/va, vc & pf)	H73
7.10	"Pasiphaé" (Petit décor musical), 3 miniatures (c1943, Montherlant; 2ob, 2cl, 2sax & 2bn)	H163
7.11	"Andante" (c1943; 4 ondes martenot, short illustration for documentary film on ondes Martenot)	H215
7.12	"Colloque" (c?; fl, celesta, vn & va, for ?Générique of unknown film)	H216
7.13	"Introduction et Danse" (c?; fl, harp/pf ad lib, vn, va & vc)	H217

3 insts:

7.14	"Ouverture to Philippa" (arr for 2vn & pf 1907, from opera Hi, juvenilia)	Hib
7.15	"Ouverture to Esmeralda" (arr for 2vn & pf 1907, from opera Hiii, juvenilia)	Hiiib
7.16	Piano Trio (Allegro vivace), in F minor (c1914, 1st movt only)	H6
7.17	"Rapsodie," in F major (c1917; 2fl, cl & pf or 2vn, va & pf)	H13

Vn & pf:

7.18	"6 Violin Sonatas" (c1908, juvenilia): No.1 in C minor	Hvi
7.19	No.2 in F major	
7.20	No.3 in C major	
7.21	No.4 in B minor	
7.22	No.5 in A minor	
7.23	No.6 in G major	
7.24	*"Adagio" (c ?1910, lost)*	*H2*
7.25	Violin Sonata (No.0) in D minor (c1912)	H3
7.26	Violin Sonata No.1 in C-sharp minor (c1916–8)	H17
7.27	Violin Sonata No.2 in B (c1919)	H24
7.28	"Morceau de concours" (c1945)	H179
7.29	"Arioso" (c late ?1920s)	H214

Va & pf:

7.30	Viola Sonata (c1920)	H28

Vc & pf:

7.31	*Cello Sonata (ca1912 or 3, lost)*	*H4*
7.32	Cello Sonata in D minor (c1920)	H32

Other 2 insts:

7.33	"Sonatine," in G major (c1920; 2vn)	H29
7.34	"Sonatine" (c1921–2; cl & pf)	H42
7.35	"Antigone" (c1922; ob/Eng hn & harp, for Jean Cocteau)	H45
7.36	"Hommage du trombone exprimant la tristesse de l'auteur absent" (c1925; trbn & pf)	H59
7.37	"Prélude," in C major (c1932; d bass & pf)	H79
7.38	"Sonatine," in E minor (c1932; vn & vc)	H80
7.39	"Petite suite" (c1934): No.1 (1 tr instr & pf; recorded for sax & pf)	H89
7.40	No.2 (2 tr insts; recorded for 2fl)	
7.41	No.3 (2 tr insts & pf; recorded for vn, cl & pf)	
7.42	"Intrada," in B-flat major (c1947; tpt & pf, for Concours international d'exécution musicale in Geneva)	H193
7.43	"Romance" (c1952 or 3; fl & pf, ?last composition of Honegger)	H211

1 instr:

7.44	"Cadence" (c1920; vn, for: Cinéma-Fantaisie for vn & pf, after Milhaud: Le boeuf sur le toit, Op.58)	H36
7.45	"Danse de la chèvre" (c ?1921; fl, for Sacha Derek: La mauvaise pensée)	H39
7.46	"Sonate," in D minor (c1940; vn)	H143
7.47	"Paduana," in G major (c1945; vc)	H181

8. PIANO

8.1   "Trois pièces" (c1909–10): No.1 "Scherzo" H1
8.2   No.2 "Humoresque"
8.3   No.3 "Adagio espressivo"
8.4   "Toccata & Variations" (c1916) H8
8.5   "Trois pièces": No.1 "Prélude" (c1919) H23
8.6   No.2 "Hommage à Ravel" (c1915)
8.7   No.3 "Danse" (c1919)
8.8   "Sept pièces brèves" (c1919–20): No.1 "Souplement" (À Rose Martin-Lafon) H25
8.9   No.2 "Vif" (À Mina Vaurabourg)
8.10   No.3 "Très lent" (À Andrée Vaurabourg)
8.11   No.4 "Légèrement" (À Marcelle Meyer)
8.12   No.5 "Lent" (À Mytyl Fraggi)
8.13   No.6 "Rythmique" (À Mme E. Alleaume)
8.14   No.7 "Violent" (À Robert Casadesus)
8.15   "Sarabande," for collab work: Album des Six (c1920): H26
        "Album des Six": *No.1 "Prélude" (c by Auric)*
        No.2 "Sarabande" (c by Honegger)
        No.3 "Romanze sans paroles" (c by Durey)
        No.4 "Mazurka" (c by Milhaud)
        No.5 "Valse" (c by Poulenc)
        No.6 "Pastorale" (c by Tailleferre)
8.16   "Le cahier romand" (c1921–3): No.1 "À Alice Ecoffey" H52
8.17   No.2 "À Jacqueline Ansermet"
8.18   No.3 "À Miquette Wagner-Rieder"
8.19   No.4 "À Paul Boepple"
8.20   No.5 "À René Morax"
8.21   "La neige sur Rome" (c1925, from incid music: L'impératrice aux rochers, H60/7) H60b
8.22   "Sur le nom d'Albert Roussel," for collab work: Hommage à Albert Roussel (c1928): H69
        "Hommage à Albert Roussel," other Nos: . *"Pièce brève sur le nom d'Albert Roussel" (c by Poulenc)*
        . *"Berceuse" (c by Tansman)*
        . *"Toccata sur le nom d'Albert Roussel" (c by Ibert)*
        . *"Fox-trot" (c by Beck)*
        . *"Fanfare" (c by Hoérée)*
        . *"A Roussel," song (c by Delage)*
        . *"Quatrain," song (c by Milhaud)*
8.23   "Les aventures du Roi Pausole," suite (c1931, from operetta H76): No.1 "Ouverture" (= 1.) H76a
8.24   No.2 "Ritournelle de la mule" (= 12.)
8.25   No.3 "Les adieux de Pausole" (= 25.)
8.26   No.4 "Air d'Aline" (= 17.)
8.27   No.5 "Le chocolat espagnol" (= 23.)
8.28   "Prélude, arioso et fughette sur le nom de BACH," for collab work: Hommage à Bach (c1932): H81
        "Hommage à Bach": *No.1 "Piece" (c by Roussel)*
        No.2 "Ricercare sul nome Bach" (c by Casella)
        No.3 "Valse—Improvisation" (c by Poulenc)
        No.4 "Prélude à une fugue imaginaire" (c by Malipiero)
        No.5 "Prélude, arioso et fughetta" (c by Honegger)
8.29   "Berceuse," in F-sharp major, for collab work: Bal des Petits Lits blancs (c1935) H95
8.30   "Scenic Railway," for collab work: Parc d'Attractions—Expo 1937 (c1937): H115
        "Parc d'Attractions—Expo 1937," other Nos: . *"Autour des Montagnes russes" (c by Tcherepnine):*
            a. "Le guichet"
            b. "Les 'On dit' "
            c. "Le 'swing' "
            d. "Et voilà"
        . *"Le train hanté" (c by Martinu)*
        . *"Souvenirs de l'Exposition" (c by Mompou):*
            a. "Tableaux de statistiques"
            b. "Le planétaire"
            c. "Pavillon de l'élégance"
        . *"La danseuse aux lions" (c by Rieti)*
        . *"L'espagnolade" (c by Halffter)*
        . *"Le géant" (c by Tansman)*
        . *"Un danseur roumain" (c by Mihalovici)*
        . *"Le tourbillon mécanique" (c by Harsányi)*
8.31   "Petits airs sur une basse célèbre" (c1941) H145
8.32   "Trois pièces" (c1943, from film: Le Captaine Fracasse, H166): No.1 "Matamore" H166b
8.33   No.2 "Isabelle"
8.34   No.3 "Danse de Scapin"
8.35   "Deux esquisses" (c1943–4, in Obouhow's simplified notation): No.1 "Large et rapsodique" H173
8.36   No.2 "Allegretto malinconico"
8.37   "Trois pièces" (c1945, from film: Un ami viendra ce soir, H183): No.1 "Souvenir de Chopin" H183a
8.38   No.2 "Jacques au piano"
8.39   No.3 "Prélude à la mort"
8.40   "Très modéré" (c?) H213

Pf duet:

8.41 "Trois contrepoints," suite (c?, orig for: fl, ob/Eng hn, vn & vc, H43): No.1 "À Maurice Jaubert" H43a
8.42   No.2 "À Jacques Brillouin"
8.43   No.3 "À Marcel Delannoy"

2 Pf:

8.44 "Suite" (Partita) (c1929, arr from 4., 12., 25. & 14. of incid music: L'impératrice aux rochers, H60) H60c
8.45 "Partita" (c1940) H139

9. ORGAN

9.1 "Deux pièces" (c1917): No.1 "Fugue" H14
9.2   No.2 "Choral"
9.3 "Orgue dans l'église" (c1910–1, used in film: Marthe Richard, H110/14).. H110a

10. CHORAL WORKS

10.1   *"Calvaire," oratorio (c1907, juvenilia, lost)* .... *Hiv*
10.2 "Cantique de Pâques" (c1918, orchd1922, Honegger; vv, fem ch & orch)..................................... H18
10.3 "Le roi David" (Psaume symphonique), 3 parts (c1923 after Morax; 3 vers):..................................... H37
    . Version 1: drame biblique (c1921, Morax)
    . Version 2: psaume symphonique (c1923, Reinhart in German; Agate in English, w/ reciter)
    . Version 3 (reorchd for large orch 1923)
10.4 "Chanson de Fagus" (c ?1923, Fagus; 1v, ch & pf) H50
10.5 "Judith," oratorio (c1926, Morax; reciter, vv, ch & orch; 3 vers): H57
    . Version 1: drame biblique (c1924–5, Morax)
    . Version 2: opéra sérieux (see opera H57b)
    . Version 3: oratorio (revised & elongated 1927)
10.6 "Cris du monde," oratorio (c1930–1, R. Bizet; vv, ch & orch, inspired by Keats: l'Hymne à la Solitude). H77
10.7 "Jeanne d'Arc au bûcher," oratorio dramatica (c1935, Claudel; also film by Rossellini 1956) H99
10.8 "Les mille et une nuits," spectacle (c1937, Mardrus, for Exposition des Arts et Techniques) H107
10.9 "Armistice" (c1937, Kerdyk, unison ch & pf) H122
10.10 "La danse des morts," oratorio (c1938, Claudel) H131
10.11 *"L'alarme" (c1938; 1v, ch & orch, lost)* *H132*
10.12 "Nicolas de Flue" (Légende dramatique), 3 act dramatic oratorio (c1938–9, Rougemont) H135
10.13 "Possèdes-tu, pauvre pécheur," cantique (c1939; unison ch & harm/pf) H137
10.14 *"Chant de libération," cantata (c1942, Zimmer; Bar, unison ch & orch, lost)* *H155*
10.15 *"Das Selzacher Passionspiel," 2 parts (c1938–44, frags & sketches)* *H177*
10.16 "Cantate de Noël" (c1952–3; Bar, ch, child ch & org, based on: Das Selzacher Passionsspiel, H177) H212

10a. SELECTIONS FROM CHORAL WORKS

10a.3 "Le roi David" (Psaume symphonique): H37
    I. "David berger, chef et conducteur d'armée": 1. "Introduction"
      2. "Cantique du berger" (A)
      3. "Psaume" (unison ch)
      3bis. "Fanfare"
      4. "Chant de Victoire," chorus
      5. "Cortège" (insts)
      6. "Psaume" (T)
      7. "Psaume" (S)
      8. "Cantique des Prophètes" (m ch)
      9. "Psaume" (T)
      10. "Le camp de Saül"
      11. "Psaume" (ch)
      12. "Incantation" (reciter)
      13. "Marche des Philistins"
      14. "Lamentations de Guilboa" (reciter, S, A, fem ch)
    II. "David, roi": 15. "Cantique de Féte" (S, fem ch)
      16. "La Danse devant l'Arche" (reciter, S, ch)
    III. "David, roi et prophète": 17. "Cantique" (unison ch)
      18. "Chant de la Servante" (A)
      19. "Psaume de pénitence" (ch)
      20. "Psaume" (ch)
      21. "Psaume" (T)
      22. "La Chanson d'Éphraïm" (S, fem ch)
      23. "Marche des Hébreux"
      24. "Psaume" (ch)
      25. "Psaume" (unison ch)
      26. "Couronnement de Salomon" (reciter)

                27. "La mort de David" (reciter—S, ch)

10a.5   "Judith," oratorio: H57
       I: 1. "Lamentations" (Judith, fem ch)
           2. "La Trompe d'alarme" (Judith, la Servante)
           3. "Peière de Judith" (Judith)
           4. "Cantique funèbre" (S, fem ch)
           5. "Invocation" (fem ch)
      II: 6. "Fanfare"
           7. "Incantation" (m ch)
           8. "Scène à la source" (Judith, la Servante)
           9. "Musique de Fête"
           9bis. "Mort d'Holopherne" (la Servante, Judith, une Sentinelle) (c for oratorio)
      III: 10. "Nocturne"
           10bis. "Retour de Judith" (Judith, un Soldat, une Voix, ch) (c for oratorio)
           11. "Cantique de la bataille" (ch)
           11bis. "Interlude" (c.for oratorio)
           12. "Cantique des vierges" (S, fem ch)
           13. "Cantique de victoire" (Judith, ch)

10a.6   "Cris du monde," oratorio: H77
           1. "Introduction"
           2. "Voix du Matin—Voix des autres"
           3. "Voix de la Mer et de la Montagne"
           4. "Voix des Espaces"
           5. "Voix des Villes inconnues"
           6. "Voix de Femme"
           7. "Voix de la Nuit"

10a.7   "Jeanne d'Arc au bûcher," stage oratorio: H99
          . "Prologue" (c1944, added 1947)
           1. "Les Voix du ciel"
           2. "Le Livre"
           3. "Les Voix de la terre"
           4. "Jeanne livrée aux bêtes"
           5. "Jeanne au poteau"
           6. "Les rois, ou l'invention du jeu de cartes"
           7. "Catherine et Marguerite"
           8. "Le Roi qui va-t-à Rheims"
           9. "L'Épée de Jeanne"
           10. "Trimazo"
           11. "Jeanne d'Arc en flammes"

10a.8   "Les mille et une nuits," spectacle: H107
          . "Prelude: Les Contes—Les Nuits"
           1. "Le Roi Schahrian"
           2. "Schéhérazade"
           3. "Les Palais"
           4. "Les Jardins"
           5. "Schahrian et Schéhérazade"
           6. "La Lampe d'Aladin"
           7. "Ali Baba"
           8. "Sindbad le Marin"
           9. "Combat des Génies"
           10. "La Ville d'Airain"
           11. "Schahrian et Schéhérazade—Apothéose"

10a.10   "La danse des morts," oratorio: H131
           1. "Introduction et Dialogue" (reciter, ch)
           2. "Danse des Morts" (reciter, ch)
           3. "Lamento" (Bar)
           4. "Sanglots" (ch)
           5. "La Réponse de Dieu" (reciter)
           6. "Espérance dans la Croix" (S, A, Bar, ch)
           7. "Affirmation" (S, ch)

10a.12   "Nicolas de Flue" (Légende dramatique), dramatic oratorio: H135
       I: 1. "Prologue"
           2. "Chanson des Enfants"
           3. "Fanfare"
           4. "Choeur": "Souviens-toi!"
           5. "Choral": "Il s'en va" (1ère et 2ème strophe)
           6. "Choeur céleste": "Solitaire, solitaire!"
           7. "La prière de Nicolas" (Gebetlein)
           8. "Récitatif": "Dure est la peine"

        9. "Choral": "Il s'en va" (3ème strophe)
      10. "La Montée au Ranft"
II: 11. "Chant des Pèlerins"
      12. "Double Choeur": "Étoile du matin"
      13. "Récital du Guetteur"
      14. "Choeur céleste": "Dieu l'a voulu"
      15. "Cortèges"
      16. "Récitatif et choral": "Ainsi les affaires du monde"
      17. "Récitatif et choral": "Tout un peuple a prété l'oreille"
      18. "Choeur des Puissances"
      19. "Choeur": "Victoire et Malheur!"
III: 20. "Marche des Ambassadeurs"
      21. "Les Compagnons de la Follevie"
      22. "Fanfare de la Diète"
      23. "Récitatif": "Demain la guerre!"
      24. "Choral": "Nicolas, souviens-toi!"
      25. "Récitatif": "Parmi nous, peuple, parmi nous"
      26. "Choeur céleste": "Solitaire, solitaire!"
      27. "Choral": "Il descend"
      28. "Choeur céleste": "Terre et cieux, prêtez l'oreille!"
      29. "Récitatif": "Écoute-moi, mon peuple!"
      30. "Récitatif des Cloches et choeur final"

10a.15   *"Das Selzacher Passionspiel" (unfin):* *H177*
     A. "Première partie: La Création du Monde": 1. "Prélude à l'orgue avec récitant"
       2. "Récitant et orchestre"
       3. "Choeur": "Gloria in excelsis Deo"
     B. "Première partie: Adam et Ève; le Paradis terrestre": 1. "Récitant avec orchestre"
       2. "Larghetto" (orch)
       3. "Satan et les Démons" (orch)
       4. "L'Archange Michaël"
       5. "Choeur et orchestre" (w/ out words, then: De profundis)
     D. "Fin de la première partie: Job": 1. "Choeur et orchestre": "Lobet den Herrn"
       2. "Ténor solo (Job) et orchestre"
       3. "Choeur sur le Psaume 150"
       4. "Choeur et orchestre" (Mimaamaquim)
       5. "Cortège des malades et des mendiants" (orch)
       6. "Orchestre avec récit parlé de Job"
     C. "Début de la deuxième partie: Annonce de la venue du Christ": 1. "Récitant et orgue"
       2. "Choeur a capella" (Benedictus—Jesus Christus—Agnus Dei—Hosanna)
       3. "Choral": "Nieder Herr die Himmel neige"
       4. "Récit avec orchestre"
       5. "Musique funèbre de la fille de Jaïre"
       6. "Choral": "O Haupt voll Blut und Wunden"
       7. "Adagio dialogué" (Agnus Dei)
     E. "Deuxième partie: La Nativité": 1. "Choeur avec orchestre": "O Komm o komm Emmanuel"
       2. "Chants de Noël" (orch)
       3. "Crescendo d'orchestre seul"
       4. "Choeur et orchestre" (Laudate Dominum)
       5. "Épilogue pour orchestre seul" (Largo)

10a.17   "Cantate de Noël": H212
       1. "Introduction et De profundis"
       2. "O Komm o komm Emmanuel," chorus
       3. "Interlude I" (Bar)
       3. "Quodlibet des Noël"
       4. "Interlude II" (Bar)
       5. "Laudate Dominum"
       6. "Épilogue" (2e quodlibet des noëls)

11. VOICE & ORCHESTRA

11.1   "Chanson de Ronsard" (c1925; 1v, fl & strings; see orig w/ pf, H54) .... (H54)
11.2   "Pour le cantique de Salomon" (c1926; reciter & chamber orch) H62
11.3   "La petite sirène" (c1926, Morax on Andersen; 1v, fl & str qt; also 1v & pf): 1. "Chanson des sirènes" .. H63
11.4   2. "Berceuse de la sirène"
11.5   3. "Chanson de la poire"
11.6   *"Céline" (c1943, Aubry; 1v, fl, harp & str trio, lost)* *H158*
11.7   "La nuit est si profonde" (c before 1920) H222

12. SONGS DERIVED FROM FILMS

12.1	"Cesez le feu," 2 songs: 1. "Chanson de l'escadrille" (Kessel) H90a
12.2	2. "Chanson du cul-de-jatte" (Zimmer)
12.3	3. "Valse (Rengaine) de Lagasse"
12.4	*"Le roi de la Camargue," 2 songs (lost): 1. "Ma plaine finit vers l'occident"* *H91a*
12.5	*2. "En Camarque les filles sont belles"*
12.6	"Le démon de l'Himalaya," 3 songs: 1. "Chant de la caravane" H93a
12.7	2. "Les trois petits moutons"
12.8	*3. "Le Cocu du désert" (?spur)*
12.9	"L'équipage," 2 songs: *1. "Chanson du lapin" (lost)* H98a
12.10	2. "Quand par hasard le noir cafard"
12.11	"Les mutinés de l'Elseneur," 2 songs: 1. "L'Elseneur est un voilier à vaches" H100a
12.12	*2. (lost)*
12.13	"Nitchevo," 2 songs: 1. "De l'Atlantique au Pacifique": "Nous n'avons jamais de chagin" (Féline) H106a
12.14	2. "Triste est mon coeur" (Féline)
12.15	"Miarka ou la fille à l'ourse," 2 songs: 1. "Chanson de la route" (Richepin) H124a
12.16	2. "Chanson de l'eau" (Richepin)
12.17	"Les bâtisseurs," 1 song: . "Hymne au Bâtiment" H126a
12.18	"La boxe en France," 1 song: . "Hymne au sport": "Soyons unis! Amples poitrines" (Bruyr) H160a
12.19	"Le capitaine Fracasse," 4 songs: *1. "Sérénade de Scapin" (lost)* H166a
12.20	2. "Si mon coeur parlait, Lysandre," arietta (Badet)
12.21	3. "Chanson du chariot de Thespis": "Portant le rire et le drame" (Badet; 2 vers)
12.22	4. "Chanson pour Isabelle": "Avant que la journée de notre âge qui fuit" (arr Honneger)
12.23	"Un seul amour" (2 romances sentimentales) (from H171): 1. "Quand tu verras les hirondelles" (Zimmer)
12.24	2. "Si le mal d'amour" (Zimmer)
12.25	"Un ami viendra ce soir," 1 song (from H183): . "Chant de la délivrance": "Nous sommes cent" (Bruyr) ......

13. OTHER SONGS (w/ pf)

13.1	*"3 Mélodies de jeunesse" (ca1906–8, Moréas, Hérold, Guillard, juvenilia, lost)* .... *Hv*
13.2	*"2 Mélodies" (Barcarolle & 'une autre') (c ?1913–4, lost)* *H5*
13.3	"Quatre poèmes" (c1914–6): 1. "Sur le basalte" (Fontaines) H7
13.4	2. "Petite chapelle" (Laforgue)
13.5	3. "Prière" (Jammes)
13.6	4. "La mort passe" (Tchobanian)
13.7	"Trois poèmes de Paul Fort" (c1916): 1. "Le chasseur perdu en forêt" H9
13.8	2. "Cloche du soir"
13.9	3. "Chanson de fol"
13.10	"Nature morte" (c1917, Vanderpyl) H11
13.11	"Six poèmes d'Apollinaire" (c1915–7, from Alcools): 1. "À la santé" (orchd Hoérée 1930) H12
13.12	2. "Clothilde"
13.13	3. "Automne" (orchd Hoérée 1930)
13.14	4. "Saltimbanques" (orchd Hoérée 1930)
13.15	5. "L'adieu" (orchd Hoérée 1930)
13.16	6. "Les cloches" (orchd Hoérée 1930)
13.17	"Pâques à New York" (c1920, Cendrars: Du Monde entier; mS & str qt/pf): 1. "C'est à cette heure-ci" . H30
13.18	2. "Faîtes, Seigneur"
13.19	3. "Dic nobis Maria"
13.20	"Deux chants d'Ariel" (c1923, Shakespeare, from: La tempête, H48): 1. "Venez jusqu'à ces sables d'or" H48b
13.21	2. "Où butine l'abeille"
13.22	"Six poésies de Jean Cocteau" (c1920–3; arr Hoérée w/ str qt 1930): 1. "Le nègre" (from Températures) H51
13.23	2. "Locutions"
13.24	3. "Souvenirs d'enfance"
13.25	4. "Ex-voto"
13.26	5. "Une danseuse"
13.27	6. "Madame"
13.28	"Chanson de Ronsard" (c1924; see vers for 1v, fl & strings of 1925) H54
13.29	"Vocalise-étude" (c1929) H70
13.30	"Le grand étang" (Chanson du XVe) (c1932, Tranchand) H82
13.31	"Fièvre jaune," chanson (c1936, Nino) H97
13.32	"Tuet' weh?, chanson de cabaret (c1937, after Lesch) H118
13.33	"2 Songs for spectacle 'La construction d'une cité' " (c1937, Bloch): 1. "Chanson des quatre" H119a
13.34	2. "Chanson de l'émigrant"
13.35	"Jeunesse": "En avant jeunesse de France" (c1937, Vaillant-Couturier) H120
13.36	"Trois chansons" (c1935–7, Kerdyk): 1. "On est heureux" H127
13.37	2. "Chanson de la route"
13.38	3. "Le naturaliste"
13.39	"Hommage au travail" (c1938, Senart) H133
13.40	"O Salutaris" (c1939; 1v & org/pf/harp, from film: Cavalcade d'amour, H136) H136a
13.41	"Trois poèmes de Claudel" (c1939–40, Claudel): 1. "Sieste" H138
13.42	2. "Le delphinium"

14. ARRANGEMENTS OF WORKS OF OTHERS

* * * * *

H = Harry Halbreich: "Arthur Honegger. Un musicien dans la cité des hommes." Fayard / Sacem, 1992.

1. STAGE WORKS

Operas:

1.1	*"Il viaggiator ridicolo" (c1797, sketch)*	*WoO 30, S25*
1.2	"Dankgefühl einer Geretteten," monodrama (c1799)	S29
1.3	*"Demagorgon," comic opera (ca1800, frag; used in: Don Anchise)*	*S41*
1.4	"Don Anchise Campione," 2 act buffa (ca ?1800, Lorenzi, inc)	S42
1.5	"Le vicende d'Amore," 2 act buffa (c1804; r1806 as: Die vereitelten Ränke, WoO 27)	WoO 26, S56
1.6	*"Die beyden Genies," Lustspiel (c1805, lost)*	*S65*
1.7	"Die Messenier," 3 act grosse heroische Oper (ca ?1805–10)	WoO 29, S61
1.8	"Pimmalione," azione teatrale (ca ?1805–15, after Rousseau)	WoO 33, S62
1.9	"Die vereitelten Ränke" (c1806, r vers of: Le vicende d'Amore, WoO 26)	WoO 27, S71
1.10	"Mathilde von Guise," 3 act opera (c1809–10, r1821, Mercier-Dupary)	Op.100
1.11	"Stadt und Land," Singspiel (ca1810, inc)	S85
1.12	"Dies Haus ist zu verkaufen," Singspiel (p1812, Klebe after Duval: Maison à vendre)	WoO 28, S90
1.13	"Aria in Fünf sind Zwey" (p1813, Posse, Castelli)	S95
1.14	"Der Junker in der Mühle," Singspiel (p1813, ?Schmidt)	S97
1.15	"Die Eselshaut, oder Die blaue Insel," Feenspiel (p1814, Geway)	Op.60, S101
1.16	Overture in Singspiel: Die gute Nachricht (p ca1814, w/ music by others; also see: Overture, S148)	Op.61, S103
1.17	"Die Rückfahrt des Kaisers," Singspiel (p1814, Veith; pubd for pf 1814)	Op.69
1.18	Duet & Quartet for Isouard's opera: Jeannot et Colin (p1815): . "Lass uns in Trauer scheiden," duet . "Ich will das Leben froh geniessen," aria & quartet	Op.72
1.19	*"Atilla," opera (ca1825–7, Juoy, lost)*	*S163*
1.20	March for Weigl's opera: Hadrian (c1820)	Op.106c
1.21	Epilogue to Gluck's opera: Armide (p1832)	S198
1.22	*Finale to Act III of Hérold: Zampa (c1833, lost)*	*S200*
1.23	Finale for Act V of Auber: Gustave III (p1836, Seidel)	S204

Ballets & pantomimes:

1.24	"Helene und Paris," ballet (p1807)	Op.26
1.25	"Das belebte Gemälde," ballet (c1809; arr for pf ca1810)	Op.33
1.26	"Quintuor des nègres," in ballet: Paul et Virginie (ca1809; arr for pf p ca1810)	Op.41
1.27	3 Nos. for a ballet or pantomime (ca1810)	S84
1.28	"Der Zauberring oder Harlekin als Spinne," 2 scene pantomime (p1811, Angiolini; p1812 for pf)	Op.46
1.29	4 Nos. in: Das Zauberschloss, 2 scene ballet (p1814, Vigano)	WoO 32, S88
1.30	"Der Zauberkampf," 2 scene pantomime (p1812, Kees)	WoO 34, S92
1.31	"Sappho von Mitilene oder die Rache der Venus," 6 scene ballet (p1812, Vigano; p ca1814 for pf)	Op.68
1.32	Add Nos. for Auffenberg: Der Löwe von Kurdistan (c1834, r vers of ballet Op.68 & new music)	S201
1.33	Finale (Ballet) for Hérold: Das Zauberglöckchen (La clochette) (p1837)	WoO 31, S206

Incid music:

1.34	"Marpha" (ca1800–10)	S31
1.35	Overture in D minor to Weissenthurn: Johann von Finnland (ca ?1812; arr for pf duet)	Op.43
1.36	"Der Löwe von Kurdistan" (c1812, Auffenberg)	WoO35, S99
1.37	Romanza in the play: Angelica (ca1814)	S100
1.38	Prelude & chorus for Grillparzer: Die Ahnfrau (p1817)	S105

1a. SELECTIONS FROM STAGE WORKS

1a.10   "Mathilde von Guise," opera: Op.100
. "Ouvertüre"
I: 1. "O wie mächtig ist der Reiz," recit (Beaufort)
. "Mathilde! ach! diese reitzende Natur!," aria (Beaufort)
2. "Ja ich muss mit ihm allein," terzettino (Baronesse, Beaufort, Nicolo)
3. "Heil! Heil! Heil der Edlen, Heil und Glück!," pezzo concertato con coro (Soprano-ch)
4. "So bin ich denn geliebt!," terzetto (Matilda, Beaufort, Valentino)
5. "Gott, ein König!" (Matilda, Baronessa, Il Duca, Claudina, Valentino, C. te Leszensky, Nicolo, ch)
II: 6. "Was hab ich vernommen?," recit (Matilda)
. "Ach mildre meine Qualen, o Liebe, reich an Macht," aria (Matilda)
7. "Wir wollen hier nicht schwärmen," terzetto (Duca, Matilda, Beaufort)
8. "Gelungen ist mein Plan," recit (Duca)
. "Ach, es folgt dir in die Ferne, Theure!," aria (Duca)
9. "Wie mir die Pulse schlagen," terzetto (Matilda, Baronesse, Beaufort)
. "Pastorale sul Palco"
10. "Heil dem Herzog! Heil dem Besten," finale
III: 11. "Nur mir nach, Leutchen!," vaudeville con coro (Nicolo)
12. "Geheimnisvolle Nacht," romanza (Mathilda)
13. "O Gott! Wie kann ich wiederstreben?," duetto (Beaufort, Matilda)
14. "Blikke freundlich, blikke mild"

2. ORCHESTRAL WORKS

3. CONCERTOS, SOLO INSTR & ORCH

Pf & orch:

3.1   Piano Concerto in A major (c1790s) .... WoO 24, S4
3.2   Piano Concerto in A major (ca ?1790s, different from WoO 24) .... WoO 24a, S5
3.3   "Variations," in F major (p ca1798, from Vogler: Castor et Pollux) Op.6
3.4   Piano Concerto in C major (p ca1811) (pubd w/ 2 different opus numbers) .... Op.34a / Op.36
3.5   "Rondo brillant," in A major (p ca1814) Op.56
3.6   "Concertino," in G major (p ca1816; pf & small orch, arr of: Mand Concerto, S28) Op.73
3.7   Piano Concerto in A minor (ca1816) Op.85
3.8   Piano Concerto in B minor (c1819) Op.89
3.9   "Variations," in F major (ca1820; pf & small orch, ?r vers of earlier work) Op.97
3.10   "Rondo brillant," in B-flat major (c1822, on Russian theme) Op.98
3.11   Piano Concerto in E major, "Les adieux" (p1814) Op.110
3.12   Piano Concerto in A-flat major (c1827) Op.113
3.13   "Variations," in B-flat major (c1830, from 'local' Singspiel: Das Fest der Handwerker) Op.115
3.14   "Oberons Zauberhorn," fantasy (c1829) Op.116
3.15   "Gesellschafts-Rondo," in D major (c1829) Op.117
3.16   "Le retour de Londres," rondo brillant in F major (c1830) Op.127
3.17   Piano Concerto in F major (c1833) .... Op.posth 1

Other:

3.18   Mandolin Concerto in G major (c1799; r as: Concertino, Op.73) S28
3.19   Trumpet Concerto in E-flat major (c1803) .... WoO 1, S49
3.20   Bassoon Concerto in F major (ca1805) .... WoO 23, S63
3.21   Double Concerto in G major (p ca1805; pf, vn & orch) Op.17
3.22   "Potpourri," in G minor (c1820; va & orch; arr for vc & orch, Op.95) Op.94
3.23   "Potpourri," in G minor (c1820; vc & orch; orig for va & orch, Op.94) Op.95
3.24   "Variations," in F major (c1822; ob & orch, arr of: Nocturne for pf duet, Op.99) Op.102

4. STRING QUARTETS

4.1   "3 String Quartets" (c before 1804): No.1 in C major Op.30
4.2   No.2 in G major
4.3   No.3 in E-flat major

5. OTHER CHAMBER MUSIC

5 or more insts:

5.1   "Parthia" (Octet-Partita), in E-flat major (c1803; 2cl, 2ob, 2hn & 2bn) S48
5.2   "Sérénade en potpourri," in G major (p ca1814–5; pf, vn, gui, cl/fl & bn/vc) Op.63
5.3   Sérénade No.2 (p ca1814–5; vn, gui, cl/fl, bn/vc & pf) Op.66
5.4   Septet in D minor (p ca1816; pf, fl, ob, hn, va, vc & d bass; also for pf qnt) Op.74
5.5   Piano Quintet in E-flat maj / minor (c1802; pf, vn, va, vc & d bass) Op.87
5.6   "Septett militaire," in C major (c1829; pf, fl, vn, cl, vc, tpt & d bass; also for pf qnt) Op.114

4 insts:

5.7   Piano Quartet in D major (c1790s; vn, va, vc & hpd/pf) S3
5.8   Clarinet Quartet in E-flat major (c1808; cl, vn, va & vc) .... WoO 5, S78
5.9   *Piano Quartet (p ca ?1900, not sufficient info/?lost)* .... *WoO 6*
5.10   Piano Quartet in G major (p ca1839, inc: 2 movts only) .... Op.posth 4

3 insts:

5.11   Trio in B-flat major (p1792; fl/vn, vc & pf/hpd) Op.2a/1
5.12   Piano Trio in F major (c1799) Op.22
5.13   String Trio in E-flat major (c1799; va/vn, va & vc) .... WoO 3, S30
5.14   String Trio in G major (c1801; va/vn, va & vc) .... WoO 4, S46
5.15   Piano Trio in E-flat major (p ca1803) Op.12
5.16   Piano Trio in G major (p1811) Op.35
5.17   Piano Trio in G major (p ca1814–5) Op.65
5.18   "Adagio, Variations & Rondo on 'Schöne Minka,' " in A min (p ca1818; fl, vc & pf, on Russian theme) Op.78
5.19   Piano Trio in E major (p1819) Op.83
5.20   Piano Trio in E-flat major (c1821, r vers of a work from the 1790s) Op.93
5.21   Piano Trio in E-flat major (ca1821, ?r vers of an earlier work) Op.96

Vn & pf:

5.22   Violin Sonata in G major (p1792; vn/fl & pf/hpd) Op.2a/2

5.23 "3 Sonatas" (p ca1798): No.1 Violin Sonata in B-flat major Op.5
5.24   No.2 Violin Sonata in F major
5.25   No.3 Viola Sonata in E-flat major
5.26 "Variations," in G major (p ca1803; fl/vn & pf, on a romance c by Méhul) Op.14
5.27 "Sonata," in C minor (p ca1810; mand/vn & hpd/pf) Op.37a
5.28 Violin Sonata in D major (p ca1810–4; vn/fl & pf) Op.50
5.29 "Sonata," in A major (p ca1814–5; vn/fl & pf) Op.64
5.30 "Amusement" (Sonatine), in F major (c1825) Op.108
5.31 "Rondo brillant," in G major (c1834; vn/fl & pf) Op.126
5.32 "Introduction & Variations on a German song," in F major (ca1839; vn/fl & pf) .... Op.posth 2

Other 2 insts:

5.33 "Potpourri," in G minor (p ca1810–4; gui & pf) Op.53
5.34 "Variations," in D minor (p ca1810–4) Op.54
5.35 "Grand potpourri national" (p ca1818; gui & pf, collab Giuliani) Op.79
5.36 "Rondoletto," in E-flat major (p ca ?1820s; harp & pf) S146
5.37 Cello Sonata in A major (c1824) Op.104

1 instr:

5.38 Piece in G major (c ?1820s; fl) S147

6. PIANO SONATAS

6.1 Piano Sonata in F minor (c1790s, 1st movt = vers of Op.20, 3rd movt = vers of Op.7/1) S23
6.2 Piano Sonata No.1 in C major (p1792) Op.2a/3
6.3 Piano Sonata No.2 in E-flat major (p ca1805) Op.13
6.4 Piano Sonata No.3 in F minor (p ca1807) Op.20
6.5 Piano Sonata No.4 in C major (p ca1808) Op.38
6.6 Piano Sonata No.5 in F-sharp minor (p1891) Op.81
6.7 Piano Sonata No.6 in D major (c1824) Op.106

7. OTHER PIANO WORKS

7.1 "Variations," in A major (ca ?1789; hpd/pf) S1
7.2 "Variations on 'Malborouck,' " in C major (c ?1790s) S2
7.3 "Variations" (p1791, same themes in Op.119): No.1 "The Plough Boy," in C major Op.1
7.4   No.2 "A German Air," in G major
7.5   No.3 "La belle Cathérine," in C major
7.6 "Variations" (c1791): No.1 "The Lass of Richmond Hill," in G major Op.2
7.7   No.2 "Jem of Aberdeen," in G major
7.8 "Variations" (p ?1794): No.1 "Air écossais," in G major (= Op.2/2) Op.3
7.9   No.2 "Air anglais," in G major (= Op.2/1)
7.10   No.3 "Air allemand," in G major
7.11 Cadenzas to 7 Mozart piano concertos Op.4
7.12 "3 Fugues" (c after 1793; pf/hpd): No.1 in D minor.. Op.7
7.13   No.2 in E-flat major
7.14   No.3 in F-sharp minor
7.15 "Variations on theme by Count von Brühl," in B-flat major (c ?1791–3) S16
7.16 "Variations," in D major (ca ?1794) S18
7.17 "Variations," in C major (ca ?1794) S19
7.18 "Fantasia," in C minor (ca1799, on themes by Haydn, Mozart & ?) S20
7.19 "Fantasia," in A-flat major (ca1799) S27
7.20 Piece in G major (ca1800, inc) S39
7.21 "3 Pieces for Orfica" (ca1800, inc) S40
7.22 "Variations on an 'oberländische Melodie,' " in G major (p ca1801) Op.8
7.23 "Variations," in E major (p ca1802, from Cherubini's opera: Les deux journées) Op.9
7.24 "Variations on 'God Save the King,' " in D major (p ca1804) Op.10
7.25 "Rondo," in E-flat major (p ca1804) Op.11
7.26 "Variations," in A minor (p ca1804, from Dalayrac's opera: Les deux savoyards) Op.15
7.27 "Fantasie," in E-flat major (p ca1805) Op.18
7.28 "Rondo quasi una fantasia," in E major (p ca1806) Op.19
7.29 "Variations on a 'Chanson hollandaise,' " in B-flat major (p ca1806) Op.21
7.30 "Variations" (p ca1810): No.1 "La sentinelle," in C major Op.34
7.31   No.2 "Partant pour la Syrie," in D major
7.32   No.3 "Vivat Bacchus" (Mozart), in C major
7.33 "Choix des plus beaux morceaux de musique," 8 pieces (ca1811): No.1 "Larghetto" Op.37
7.34   No.2 "Adagio"
7.35   No.3 "Allegretto"
7.36   No.4 "Allegretto"
7.37   No.5 "Allegretto"
7.38   No.6 "Andante"

7.114   "Les charmes de Londres," 3 sets of variations (c1831): No.1 "The Plough-Boy" (theme = Op.1/1) . Op.119
7.115   No.2 "Thême allemand" (theme = Op.1/2)
7.116   No.3 "La belle Cathérine" (theme = Op.1/3)
7.117   "La galante," rondo in E major (c1831; also pubd as Op.121) Op.120
7.118   "Villageois," rondo in C major (c1831) Op.122
7.119   "Recollections of Paganini," fantasia in C major (c1831) .... WoO 8, S190
7.120   "Étude," in B-flat major (c1831, for Fétis: Méthode des méthodes) S191
7.121   "Fantasie," in G minor (c1833, on themes of Neukomm & Hummel) Op.123
7.122   "Fantasina," in G minor (c1833, from Mozart's opera: Le nozze di Figaro, K492) Op.124
7.123   "24 Etudes" (1833): No.1 "Allegro" Op.125
7.124   No.2 "Allegro ma non troppo"
7.125   No.3 "Tempo di Polacca"
7.126   No.4 "Grave non troppo"
7.127   No.5 "Allegro con brio"
7.128   No.6 "Fughette. Allegro moderato"
7.129   No.7 "Andante cantabile"
7.130   No.8 "Vivace"
7.131   No.9 "Allegro"
7.132   No.10 "Allegro comodo"
7.133   No.11 "Allegro ma cantabile"
7.134   No.12 "Allegro moderato assai"
7.135   No.13 "Allegro moderato"
7.136   No.14 "Allegro con fuoco"
7.137   No.15 "Allegro moderato"
7.138   No.16 "Adagio sostenuto"
7.139   No.17 "Allegro brillante"
7.140   No.18 "Allegretto"
7.141   No.19 "Allegro"
7.142   No.20 "Allegro moderato"
7.143   No.21 "Allegro"
7.144   No.22 "Adagio"
7.145   No.23 "Vivace"
7.146   No.24 "Un poco Adagio"
7.147   "Impromptu," in F major (c1831) S194
7.148   "Scotch Country-Dance-Rondo" (p1839) .... Op.posth 3
7.149   "Capriccio," in E-flat minor (p1839) .... Op.posth 6
7.150   "6 Pieces" (p1839): No.1 "Capriccio abrupto" .... Op.posth 9
7.151   No.2 "Capriccio"
7.152   No.3 "Impromptu"
7.153   No.4 "Ex abrupto"
7.154   No.5 "Rondoletto"
7.155   No.6 "Rondino"

Pf duet:

7.156   "Sonata," in E-flat major (p ca1811–5) Op.51
7.157   "Sonata," in A-flat major (c1820) Op.92
7.158   "Nocturne," in F major (c1822; w/ 2hn ad lib) Op.99

2 Pf:

7.159   "Impromptu," in C major (c1836) S205
7.160   "Introduction & Rondo," in E-flat major (p ca1839) .... Op.posth 5

8. ORGAN

8.1   "Prelude & 2 Fugues" (p ca1839; org) .... Op.posth 7
8.2   "Ricercare," in G major (p1839; org; arr for pf) .... Op.posth 8

9. SACRED WORKS

9.1   "Der Durchzug durchs rote Meer," oratorio (ca ?1800–10) .... WoO 11, S33
9.2   Mass No.1 in B-flat major (ca1804–10; ch, orch & org; 2 text vers: Latin & German) Op.77
9.3   Mass No.2 in E-flat major (c1804; 4vv, ch & orch; 2 text vers: Latin & German) Op.80
9.4   "Dominus Deo," mass section (ca1804–10; ch) .... WoO 14, S50
9.5   "Sub tuum praesidium," antiphon in B-flat major (ca1804–10) S53
9.6   "Salve regina," offertory in G major (ca1804–10) S54
9.7   "Plus non timet," recitative (ca1804–10; S, T, 2vn, va & bass) S55
9.8   "Kyrie" (Litania lauretana), in A minor (ca1804–10) .... WoO 17, S51
9.9   "Pro te respiro," duet-offertory in E major (ca1804–10; S & T) .... WoO 22, S52
9.10   "Alma virgo," offertory (c1805; S, ch, orch & org) Op.89a
9.13   "Ja der Himmel," recitative (ca1805; T, vc & d bass) S64
9.11   "Alma virgo mater Dei," offertory in F major (c1805; A/?S) .... WoO 21, S66

14. ARRANGEMENTS OF WORKS OF OTHERS

* * * * *

Op.posth & **WoO** = Dieter Zimmerschied: "Thematisches Verzeichnis der Werke von Johann Nepomuk
        Hummel." Musikverlag Friedrich Hofmeister. Hofheim am Taunus, 1971.
S =   Suppl. Nos. from Joel Sachs (Notes, XXX/4, June, 1974, 732-53).
        Opus numbers 32, 90 & 121 not used.

1. SYMPHONIES

1.1	Symphony No.1 (c1895–8)	Kv8
1.2	Symphony No.2 (c1900–2)	Kv11
1.3	Symphony No.3, "The Camp Meeting" (c1904; small orch)	Kv15
1.4	Symphony No.4 (c1909–16)	Kv39
1.5	*"Universe Symphony" (c1911–28, unfin, inc):*	*Kv43*

. Section A "Past: Formation of the waters and mountains"
. Section B "Present: Earth, evolution in nature and humanity"
. Section C "Future: Heaven, the rise of all to the Spiritual"

1a. MUSIC QUOTED IN SYMPHONIES

1a.1   Symphony No.1: Kv8
    1. "Allegro" (from early sketch of Kz51a):
        quoted: . "Shining Shore" (vn) H54
    2. "Adagio molto"
    3. "Scherzo: Vivace"
    4. "Allegro molto"

1a.2   Symphony No.2: Kv11
    1. "Andante moderato" (from lost: Org Sonata & lost: Down East Overture):
        quoted: . "Massa's in de Cold, Cold Ground" (vn) H121
              . "Pig Town Fling" (vn) H167
              . "Columbia, the Gem of the Ocean" (hns) H75
    2. "Allegro" (from lost overture: In These United States):
        quoted: . "Wake Nicodemus" (fl) H144
              . "Bringing in the Sheaves" (vn) H10
              . "Where, O Where, Are the Pea-Green Freshmen?" (fl) H157
              . "Massa's in de Cold, Cold Ground" (vn) H121
              . (unknown) (vn) H192
              . "Hamburg" (trbn) H26
              . "Naomi" (trbn) H40
              . Brahms: Symphony No.3 in F major, Op.90 (vn) H177
    3. "Adagio cantabile" (from lost: Org Prelude & rejected 2nd movt of: Sym No.1, Kv8):
        quoted: . "Beulah Land" (vn) H8
              . "Materna" (vn) H36
              . "There is a Happy Land" (vn) H57
              . Brahms: Symphony No.1 in C minor, Op.68 (fl) H175
              . Wagner: Prelude to Act III of opera: Tristan and Isolde, WWV90 (fl) H191
              . Wagner: Prelude to Act II of opera: Tristan and Isolde, WWV90 (vn) H190
              . "Missionary Chant" (hns) H37
              . "Nettleton" (hns) H42
              . "Massa's in de Cold, Cold Ground" (fl) H121
              . "America" (fl) H69
    4. "Lento maestoso" (from lost overture: Town, Gown & State of 1896):
        quoted: . "Columbia, the Gem of the Ocean" (trbn) H75
              . "Pig Town Fling" (fl) H167
    5. "Allegro molto vivace" (from lost overture: The American Woods of 1889):
        quoted: . "De Camptown Races" (vn) H100
              . "The Kerry Dance" (vn) H165
              . "Columbia, the Gem of the Ocean" (bn) H75
              . "Turkey in the Straw" (vn) H169
              . "Pig Town Fling" (vn) H167
              . "Long, Long Ago" (fl) H119
              . "Where, O Where, Are the Pea-Green Freshmen?" (vn) H157
              . "Wake Nicodemus" (vn) H144
              . "Massa's in de Cold, Cold Ground" (fl) H121
              . "Reveille" (tpt) H83

1a.3   Symphony No.3, "The Camp Meeting": Kv15
    1. "Andante: Old Folks Gatherin" (from lost: Org Prelude of 1901):
        quoted: . "Erie" (vn) H17
              . "Azmon" (vn) H5
              . "Woodworth" (hns) H67
    2. "Allegro: Children's Day" (from lost: Org Postlude of 1901):
        quoted: . "Naomi" (hn) H40
              . "Fountain" (vn) H23
              . "There Is a Happy Land" (fl) H57
              . "There's Music in the Air" (fl) H142
              . "Blessed Assurance" (vn) H9
    3. "Largo: Communion" (from lost: Communion of 1901 for org; used in Kz88):
        quoted: . "Woodworth" (vc) H67
              . "Azmon" (vn) H5

. "Erie" (fl) H17
4. Rejected 4th movt:
 quoted: . "The Beautiful River" *H6*

1a.4 Symphony No.4: Kv39
 1. "Prelude: Maestoso" (from Kw16/3):
  quoted: . "Bethany" (2vn) H7
  . "In the Sweet Bye and Bye" (vc) H29
  . "Proprior Deo" (fl) H49
  . "Watchman" (vv) H61
  . "Something for Thee" (fl) H55
  . "Westminster Chimes" (vc) H170
  . "Welcome Voice" (fl) H63
 2. "Allegretto" (from Kv14 & Kx19/2; used in Kx23):
  quoted: . "Martyn" (pf) H35
  . "Home! Sweet Home!" (vn) H108
  . "Massa's in de Cold, Cold Ground" (fl) H121
  . (unknown) (vn) H200
  . "Throw Out the Life-Line" (vc) H59
  . "In the Sweet Bye and Bye" (vn) H29
  . "Nettleton" (vn) H42
  . "Marching Through Georgia" (pf) H79
  . "Welcome Voice" (tpt) H63
  . "Blow the Man Down" (piccolo) H159
  . "Turkey in the Straw" (vn) H169
  . (unknown) (orch) H201
  . "De Camptown Races" (cl) H100
  . (unknown) (high bells) H202
  . "Battle Hymn of the Republic" (tpt) H72
  . "Old Black Joe" (pf) H128
  . "There Is a Happy Land" (fl) H57
  . "Westminster Chimes" (celesta) H170
  . "Columbia, the Gem of the Ocean" (tpt) H75
  . "Hello! Ma Baby" (pf) H107
  . "The Beautiful River" (bells) H6
  . (unknown) (pf) H203
  . "Pig Town Fling" (bn) H167
  . "Long, Long Ago" (orch) H119
  . "On the Banks of the Wabash, Far Away" (tpt) H130
  . "Beulah Land" (trbn) H8
  . "Yankee Doodle" (piccolo) H92
  . "Saint Patrick's Day" (bn) H168
  . "Garryowen" (vn) H163
  . "Reveille" (piccolo) H83
  . "Irish Washerwoman" (vn) H164
  . Bugle Call Derivative (piccolo) H74
 3. "Fugue: Andante moderato" (from Kw1/1): H38
  quoted: . "Missionary Hymn" (vc)
  . "Christmas" (vn) H12
  . "Coronation" (fl) H13
  . "Welcome Voice" (cl) H63
  . "Antioch" (trbn) H3
 4. "Largo maestoso" (from lost: Memorial Slow March of 1901 for org):
  quoted: . "Bethany" (vns) H7
  . "Dorrnance" (vn) H15
  . (unknown) (fl) H204
  . "Martyn" (cl) H35
  . (unknown) (vns) H205
  . "Missionary Chant" (fl) H37
  . "Westminster Chimes" (bell) H170
  . "Antioch" (bn) H3
  . "Nettleton" (celesta) H42
  . "St. Hilda" (hn) H51
  . "There Is a Happy Land" (ob) H57
  . "Proprior Deo" (ob) H49
  . "Something for Thee" (ob) H55

2. OTHER ORCHESTRAL WORKS

2.1 "Holiday Quickstep" (c1887; piccolo, 2 cornets, 2vn & pf; arr for band lost; ed Sinclair 1975) Kv1
2.2 *"The American Woods," overture (c ?1889, lost; used in Symphony No.2, Kv11)* *K1C2*
2.3 "March No.2" (c1892, from Kx4; used in Kz29; ed Singleton 1977) Kv2
2.4 "March No.3" (c1892, from lost pf vers; ed Singleton 1975) Kv3
2.5 "March 'Intercollegiate' " (c1892; band, from Kx6; ed Brion 1973) Kv4

2.77	*"Set No.6": No.1 "The Ruined River" (from Kv27/3)* ....
2.78	*No.2 "Largo, 'The Indians' " (from Kv32/1)*
2.79	*No.3 "Ann Street": "Quaint name, Ann Street" (from Kz137)*
2.80	*"Three Poets and Human Nature": No.1 "Paracelsus": "For God is glorified in man" (from Kz136)* ....
2.81	*No.2 "Walt Whitman": "Who goes there?" (from Ky34)*
2.82	*No.3 "West London": "Crouch'd on the pavement" (from Kz127)*
2.83	*"The Other Side of Pioneering": No.1 "The Ruined River" (from Kv27/3)* ....
2.84	*No.2 "Largo, 'The Indians' " (from Kv32/1)*
2.85	*No.3 "Charlie Rutlage": "Another good cow-puncher" (from Kz119)*
2.86	*No.4 "Ann Street": "Quaint name, Ann Street" (from Kz137)*
2.87	*"From the Side Hill": No.1 "Requiem": "Under the wide and starry sky" (from Kz86)* ....
2.88	*No.2 "The Rainbow": "So May It Be!" (from Kv35)*
2.89	*No.3 "Afterglow": "At the quiet close of day" (from Kz111)*
2.90	*No.4 "Evening": "Now came still evening on" (from Kz144)*
2.91	*"Water Colours": No.1 "Adagio sostenuto, 'At Sea' " (from Kv40/1)* ....
2.92	*No.2 "Swimmers": "Then the swift plunge" (from Kz100)*
2.93	*No.3 "The Pond" (from Kv21)*
2.94	*No.4 "A Sea Dirge": "Full fathom five thy father lies" (from Kz150)*
2.95	*"Three Outdoor Scenes" (c ?1949): No.1 "Halloween" (from Kw11)* ....
2.96	*No.2 "The Pond" (from Kv21)*
2.97	*No.3 "Central Park in the Dark" (from Kv23/2)*

2a. MUSIC QUOTED IN OTHER ORCHESTRAL WORKS

2a.2	*"The American Woods," overture:*		.... K1C2
	quoted:	*. "Columbia, the Gem of the Ocean" (vn & pf)*	.... H75
		. "De Camptown Races" (pf)	.... H100
2a.3	"March No.2":		....Kv2
	quoted:	. "The Son of a Gambolier" (cornet)	.... H135
2a.4	"March No.3":		....Kv3
	quoted:	. "My Old Kentucky Home" (cornet)	.... H123
2a.5	"March 'Intercollegiate' ":		....Kv4
	quoted:	. "Annie Lisle" (trbn)	.... H95
2a.6	"March 'The Circus Band' ":		....K1C8
	quoted:	. "Marching Through Georgia" (hn)	.... H79
		. "Jolly Dogs" (hn)	.... H154
		. "Reuben and Rachel" (piccolo)	.... H131
2a.9	"March in F & C":		....Kv7
	quoted:	. "Omega Lambda Chi" (basses)	.... H156
2a.10	"Fugue in 4 keys on 'The Shining Shore' ":		..............................Kv9
	quoted:	. "Shining Shore" (vc)	.... H54
		. "Azmon" (vn)	.... H5
2a.11	"Yale-Princeton Football Game":		....Kv10
	quoted:	. "Bright College Years"	.... H149
		. "Harvard Has Blue Stocking Girls"	.... H151
		. "Hold the Fort"	.... H152
		. "Hy-can nuck a no"	.... H153
		. "Old Nassau"	.... H155
		. "Second Regiment Connecticut National Guard March"	.... H84
2a.12	*"Skit for Danbury Fair":*		....K1C13
	quoted:	*. "Happy Day"*	.... H27
		. "Bringing in the Sheaves"	.... H10
2a.13	"Ragtime Dances" Nos.1–4:		....Kv12
	quoted:	. "Happy Day"	.... H27
		. "Bringing in the Sheaves"	.... H10
		. "Welcome Voice"	.... H63
2a.14	"Overture and March '1776' ":		....Kv13
	quoted:	. "Hail! Columbia" (ob)	.... H77
		. "The British Grenadiers" (fl)	.... H73
		. Bugle Call Derivative (fl)	.... H74
		. "Battle Hymn of the Republic" (cl)	.... H72
		. "Columbia, the Gem of the Ocean" (cornet)	.... H75
		. "Saint Patrick's Day" (vn)	.... H168
		. "Tramp, Tramp, Tramp" (fl)	.... H89

  . "The Campbells Are Comin" (fl) H160
  . "Washington Post" March" (pf) H90

2a.30 "Cartoons" (Take-offs) (inc: Nos.7 & 8 only): No.7 "Mike Donlin-Johny Evers": Kv24
    quoted: . "Ta-ra-ra Boom-de-ay!" (winds) H140
    . "When Johnny Comes Marching Home" (winds) H91

2a.31 No.8 "Willy Keeler at the Bat"

2a.32 "Emerson" Overture / Pf Conc: Kv25
    quoted: . Beethoven: Symphony No.5 in C minor, Op.67 .... H173
    . (?) "Missionary Chant" H37
    . (?) "Parah" H48

2a.33 "Washington's Birthday": Kv26
    quoted: . "Home! Sweet Home!" (vn) H108
    . "Old Folks at Home" (hn) H129
    . "Turkey in the Straw" (fl) H169
    . (unknown) (vn) H197
    . "College Hornpipe" (fl) H161
    . "De Camptown Races" (fl) H100
    . "For He's a Jolly Good Fellow" (fl) H101
    . "The White Cockade" (vn) H171
    . "Massa's in de Cold, Cold Ground" (fl) H121
    . "Irish Washerwoman" (hn) H164
    . "The Campbells Are Comin' " (hn) H160
    . "Garryowen" (hn) H163
    . "Fisher's Hornpipe" (piccolo) H162
    . "Saint Patrick's Day" (hn) H168
    . "Money Musk" (piccolo) H166
    . "Pig Town Fling" (vn) H167
    . (unknown) (vn) H198
    . "Goodnight, Ladies" (fl) H104

2a.34 "Set No.1": No.1 "The See'r" Kv27
2a.35 No.2 "A Lecture"
2a.36 No.3 "The Ruined River":
    quoted: . "Tammany" (piccolo) H139
    . "Ta-ra-ra Boom-de-ay!" (cornet) H140
2a.37 No.4 "Like a Sick Eagle"
2a.38 No.5 "Calcium Light Night":
    quoted: . "Few Days" (trbn) H150
    . "Jolly Dogs" (piccolo) H154
    . "A Band of Brothers in DKE" (cl) H146
    . "Tramp, Tramp, Tramp" (cl) H89
    . "Marching Through Georgia" (cl) H79
2a.39 No.6 "When the Moon" (Allegretto sombreoso)
2a.40 No.6a "Yale-Princeton Football Game"

2a.41 "The Gong on the Hook & Lader" (Firemen's Parade on Main Street): Kv28
    quoted: . "Oh, My Darling Clementine" (fl) H126
    . "Marching Through Georgia" (tpt) H79

2a.43 "3 Places in New England" (Orch Set No.1): No.1 "The 'St. Gaudens' in Boston Common": Kv30
    quoted: . "Old Black Joe" (fl) H128
    . "The Battle Cry of Freedom" (fl) H71
    . "Marching Through Georgia" (vn) H79
    . Bugle Call Derivative (hn) H74
    . "Deep River" (hn) H14
    . "Massa's in de Cold, Cold Ground" (vn) H121
2a.44 No.2 "Putnam's Camp, Redding, Connecticut":
    quoted: . "Happy Day" (bn) H27
    . "The British Grenadiers" (fl) H73
    . Bugle Call Derivative (bn) H74
    . "Arkansas Traveller" (cl) H158
    . "Liberty Bell" March (pf) H78
    . "Semper Fideles" (trbn) H85
    . "Massa's in de Cold, Cold Ground" (fl) H121
    . "Marching Through Georgia" (pf) H79
    . "The Battle Cry of Freedom" (tpt) H71
    . "Yankee Doodle" (vn) H92
    . "Hail! Columbia" (vn) H77
    . "The Star Spangled Banner" (ob) H86
2a.45 No.3 "The Housatonic at Stockbridge":
    quoted: . "Dorrnance" (vc) H15
    . "Missionary Chant" (hn) H37

2a.46	"Decoration Day":	Kv31
	quoted: . "Adeste Fideles" (vn)	H1
	. "Lambeth" (vns)	H32
	. "Over There" (tpt)	H82
	. "The Battle Cry of Freedom" (fl)	H71
	. "Marching Through Georgia" (hns)	H79
	. "Nelly Bly" (fl)	H124
	. "Tenting on the Old Camp Ground" (vn)	H88
	. "Taps" (tpt)	H87
	. "Bethany" (vns)	
	. "Second Regiment Connecticut National Guard March" (piccolo)	H84
	. "Battle Hymn of the Republic" (cl)	H72
2a.47	"Set No.2": No.1 "Largo, 'The Indians' "	Kv32
2a.48	No.2 "Gyp the Blood or Hearst!? Which is Worst?!"	
2a.49	No.3 "Andante, 'The Last Reader' ":	
	quoted: . "Cherith" (cornet)	H11
	. "Manoah" (cornet)	H34
2a.51	"The Fourth of July":	Kv34
	quoted: . "Columbia, the Gem of the Ocean" (vn)	H75
	. "Assembly" (hn)	H70
	. "The Battle Cry of Freedom" (vc)	H71
	. "Marching Through Georgia" (tpt)	H79
	. (unknown) (fl)	H199
	. "College Hornpipe" (ob)	H161
	. "Fisher's Hornpipe" (piccolo)	H162
	. "Battle Hymn of the Republic" (vn)	H72
	. "Reveille" (hn)	H83
	. "Hail! Columbia" (cl)	H77
	. "London Bridge" (piccolo)	H118
	. "Tramp, Tramp, Tramp" (piccolo)	H89
	. "The Girl I Left Behind Me" (piccolo)	H102
	. "Garryowen" (pf)	H163
	. "Saint Patrick's Day" (pf)	H168
	. "Irish Washerwoman" (hn)	H164
	. "Katy Darling" (piccolo)	H113
	. "Yankee Doodle" (xylophone)	H92
	. "Dixie's Land" (piccolo)	H76
	. "Kingdom Coming" (piccolo)	H114
2a.56	"The Rainbow" (So May It Be!):	Kv35
	quoted: . "Serenity" (Eng hn)	H53
2a.58	"Second Orchestral Set": No.1 "An Elegy to our Forefathers":	Kv37
	quoted: . "Old Black Joe" (zither)	H128
	. "Oh, Nobody Knows de Trouble I've Seen" (tpt)	H43
	. "Reveille" (fl)	H83
	. "Jesus Loves Me" (tpt)	H30
	. "Nettleton" (zither)	H42
	. "Massa's in de Cold, Cold Ground" (fl)	H121
2a.59	No.2 "The Rockstrewn Hills Join in the People's Outdoor Meeting":	
	quoted: . "Bringing in the Sheaves" (vn)	H10
	. "The Girl I Left Behind Me" (tpt)	H102
	. "Rock-a-bye Baby" (fl)	H132
	. "Welcome Voice" (vn)	H63
	. "Massa's in de Cold, Cold Ground" (tpt)	H121
2a.60	No.3 "From Hanover Square North, at the End of a Tragic Day":	
	quoted: . "In the Sweet Bye and Bye" (cl)	H29
	. "Massa's in de Cold, Cold Ground" (va)	H121
2a.61	"Tone Roads et al" (c1909–15): No.1 "Fast, 'All Roads Lead to the Centre' "	Kv38
2a.62	*No.2 "Slow"*	
2a.63	No.3 "Slow and fast, 'Rondo rapid transit' ":	
	quoted: . "On the Banks of the Wabash, Far Away"	H130
2a.68	"Third Orchestral Set": No.1 (Hymn-tune movement):	Kv42
	quoted: . "Old Hundredth"	H44
	. "Hebron"	H28
	. "The Beautiful River"	H6
	. "Dormnance"	H15
	. "Shining Shore"	H54
2a.69	No.2 "Comedy of Danbury reminiscence":	
	quoted: . "Azmon"	H5
	. "Materna"	H36

. "Kingdom Coming" H114
. "Silver Threads Among the Gold" H134
. "Little Brown Jug" H116
. "Has Anybody Here Seen Kelly?" H106
. "In the Sweet Bye and Bye" H29
. "Shining Shore" H54
. "Alexander" H94
. "Battle Hymn of the Republic" H72
. "Columbia, the Gem of the Ocean" H75
. "Reveille" H83
. "The Girl I Left Behind Me" H102
. "Windsor" H66
. "Greenwood" H25
. "Grandfather's Clock" H105
. "Sweet Rosie O'Grady" H138
. "Jingle, Bells" H110
. "My Old Kentucky Home" H123
. "I've Been Working on the Railroad" H109

2a.70   No.3 (Hymn-tune movement)

2a.71   *"Set No.4": No.1 "Andante cantabile, 'The Last Reader' ":* *K1C36*
         quoted: . "Cherith" (cornet) *H11*
         . *"Manoah" (cornet)* *H34*

2a.72   *No.2 "The See'r"*
2a.73   *No.3 "The Unanswered Question"*

3. STRING QUARTETS

3.1   String Quartet No.1, "From the Salvation Army" (c1896) Kw1
3.2   "Intermezzo" (c ?1898, = Ky23/4) ....
3.3   *"Pre-Second String Quartet" (c1904–5, unfin, lost; used in Kw15/1, Kz146 & Kz151)* *Kw8*
3.4   String Quartet No.2 (c1907–13) Kw19

3a. MUSIC QUOTED IN STRING QUARTETS

3a.1   String Quartet No.1, "From the Salvation Army": Kw1
        1. "Chorale" (from lost: Org Fugue; used in Kv39/3):
            quoted: . "Missionary Hymn" (vc) H38
            . "Christmas" (va) H12
            . "Coronation" (vns) H13
        2. "Prelude" (?from lost: Org Prelude):
            quoted: . (unknown) (vn) H206
            . "Beulah Land" (vn) H8
            . "Azmon" (vn) H5
            . "Bringing in the Sheaves" (vc) H10
            . (unknown) (vn) H207
            . (unknown) (vn) H208
            . (unknown) (vn) H209
        3. "Offertory" (?from lost: Org Prelude/Offertory):
            quoted: . "Nettleton" (vn) H42
            . (unknown) (vn) H210
            . (unknown) (vn) H211
        4. "Postlude" (from lost: Org Postlude of 1896):
            quoted: . (unknown) (vn) H212
            . "Webb" (vn) H62
            . (unknown) (vn) H213

3a.4   String Quartet No.2: Kw19
        1. "Discussions":
            quoted: . Wagner: Prelude to Act I of opera: Tristan and Isolde, WWV90 (va) H189
            . "Columbia, the Gem of the Ocean" (vn) H75
            . "Dixie's Land" (va) H76
            . "Marching Through Georgia" (vn) H79
            . "Turkey in the Straw" (va) H169
            . "Hail! Columbia" (vn) H77
            . "Taps" (vn) H87
        2. "Arguments":
            quoted: . "Columbia, the Gem of the Ocean" (va) H75
            . "Hail! Columbia" (vn) H77
            . Tchaikovsky: 3rd movt of Sym No.6 in B minor, "Pathétique," Op.74 (vc) H188
            . Brahms: Symphony No.2 in D major, Op.73 (vn) H176
            . Beethoven: Symphony No.9 in D minor, "Choral," Op.125 (vn) H174
            . "Marching Through Georgia" (vn) H79

. "Massa's in de Cold, Cold Ground" (vn) H121
3. "The Call of the Mountains":
   quoted: . "Nettleton" (vns) H42
       . "Bethany" (vn) H7
       . "Westminster Chimes" (va) H170

4. OTHER CHAMBER MUSIC

3 or more insts:

4. MUSIC QUOTED IN OTHER CHAMBER MUSIC

    . "Reuben and Rachel" (vc) H131
    . (unknown) (pf) H216
    . "Fountain" (pf) H23
  3. "Moderato con moto" (from Kz34):
    quoted: . (unknown) (pf) H217
    . (unknown) (vn) H218
    . "Toplady" (vc) H60

4a.14   "A Set of 3 Short Pieces": No.1 "Largo cantabile: Hymn": Kw15
    quoted: . "More Love to Thee" (vn) H39
    . (unknown) (vc) H219

4a.15   No.2 "Scherzo: Holding Your Own":
    quoted: . "Bringing in the Sheaves" (vc) H10
    . "Massa's in de Cold, Cold Ground" (vc) H121
    . "My Old Kentucky Home" (vc) H123
    . "College Hornpipe" (vn) H161
    . "Streets of Cairo" (vns) H137

4a.16   No.3 "Adagio cantabile: The Innate"

4a.19   "Pre-First Violin Sonata": Kw4
  1. "Allegretto moderato" (used in Kw17/2):
    quoted: . "God Be with You" (vn) H24
    . "The Battle Cry of Freedom" (vn) H71
  2. "Largo," in D major (used in Kw16/2):
    quoted: . "Araby's Daughter" (vn) H96
  2a. rejected "Largo," in G major (used in Kw5; ed Zukofsky 1967)
  3. "Adagio—Allegro" (used in Kw4/2a):
    quoted: . "Autumn" (vn) H4
  3a. rejected "Scherzo" (unfin; used in Kw17/2):
    quoted: . "College Hornpipe" (vn) H161
    . "Money Musk" (vn) H166
    . "The White Cockade" (pf) H171

4a.20   Violin Sonata No.1: Kw16
  1. "Andante—Allegro":
    quoted: . "Shining Shore" (pf) H54
    . "Bringing in the Sheaves" (vn) H10
    . "Araby's Daughter" (vn) H96
  2. "Largo cantabile" (from Kw4/2):
    quoted: . "Araby's Daughter" (vn) H96
    . "Tramp, Tramp, Tramp" (pf) H89
    . "Work Song" (vn) H68
  3. "Allegro" (from lost sacred song: Watchman; used in Kv39/1, Kz90):
    quoted: . "Work Song" (pf) H68
    . "Watchman" (vn) H61

4a.21   Violin Sonata No.2: Kw17
  1. "Autumn" (from Kw4/3; used in Kz89):
    quoted: . "Autumn" (pf) H4
    . "Oh! Susanna" (vn) H127
  2. "In the Barn" (from Kw4/1 & Kw4/3a):
    quoted: . "College Hornpipe" (vn) H161
    . "Money Musk" (vn) H166
    . "The White Cockade" (pf) H171
    . "Turkey in the Straw" (vn) H169
    . "The Battle Cry of Freedom" (vn) H71
  3. "The Revival" (from Kw22/3a):
    quoted: . "Nettleton" (vn) H42

4a.22   "Decoration Day": Kw18
    quoted: . "Adeste Fideles" (pf) H1
    . (unknown) (vn) H220

4a.23   Violin Sonata No.3: Kw21
  1. "Adagio" (from lost: Org Prelude of 1901):
    quoted: . "Need" (vn) H41
    . "Beulah Land" (vn) H8
  2. "Allegro" (from lost: Ragtime Piece of 1902–3):
    quoted: . "There'll Be No Dark Valley" (vn) H58
  3. "Adagio cantabile" (from lost: Org Prelude of 1901):
    quoted: . "Need" (pf) H41
    . "Happy Day" (pf) H27

4a.24   Violin Sonata No.4, "Children's Day at the Camp Meeting": Kw22
  1. "Allegro" (from: Fugue in B-flat major & lost Sonata for tpt & org):

```
                    quoted: . "Old, Old Story" (vn) ....................................................................... H45
                           . "Fourth Fugue in B-flat" (c by Ives; pf) ................................................. H184
              2. "Largo":
                    quoted: . "Jesus Loves Me" (pf) ...................................................................... H30
              3. "Allegro" (from sketch of 1905; used in Kz101):
                    quoted: . "The Beautiful River" (pf) ................................................................ H6
              3a. "Adagio—Faster" (rejected, used in Kw17/3):
                    quoted: . "Nettleton" (vn) ............................................................................. H42
```

5. PIANO SONATAS

5.1	Piano Sonata No.1 (c1901–9, from Kv12)	Kx17
5.2	Piano Sonata No.2, "Concord, Mass., 1840–60" (c1910–15)	Kx19

5. MUSIC QUOTED IN PIANO SONATAS

```
5a.1    Piano Sonata No.1: ......................................................................................................... Kx17
              1. "Adagio con moto":
                    quoted: . "Lebanon" ..................................................................................... H33
                           . "Where Is My Wandering Boy?" ........................................................ H64
              2a. "Allegro moderato" (from Kx13):
                    quoted: . "Happy Day" .................................................................................. H27
                           . "Bringing in the Sheaves" ............................................................... H10
                           . "Welcome Voice" ............................................................................. H63
              2b. "In the Inn" (Allegro) (from Kx13; used in Kv22/2):
              3. "Largo—Allegro—Largo":
                    quoted: . "Erie" ............................................................................................ H17
                           . "Lebanon" ...................................................................................... H33
              4a. (Allegro):
                    quoted: . "Bringing in the Sheaves" ............................................................... H10
                           . "Welcome Voice" ............................................................................. H63
              4b. "Allegro" (from Kx13):
                    quoted: . "Bringing in the Sheaves" ............................................................... H10
                           . "Welcome Voice" ............................................................................. H63
              5. "Andante maestoso—Adagio cantabile—Allegro—Andante" (from/used in Kx15/4):
                    quoted: . "Lebanon" ..................................................................................... H33

5a.2    Piano Sonata No.2, "Concord, Mass., 1840–60": ........................................................... Kx19
              1. "Emerson" (from Kv25; used in Kx20):
                    quoted: . Beethoven: Symphony No.5 in C minor, Op.67 ......................... H173
              2. "Hawthorne" (from Kv14; used in Kv39/2 & Kx23):
                    quoted: . Beethoven: Symphony No.5 in C minor, Op.67 ......................... H173
                           . "Martyn" ......................................................................................... H35
                           . "Columbia, the Gem of the Ocean" ................................................ H75
              3. "The Alcotts" (from lost: Orchard House Overture of 1904):
                    quoted: . "Missionary Chant" ........................................................................ H37
                           . Beethoven: Symphony No.5 in C minor, Op.67 ............................ H173
                           . "Stop That Knocking at My Door" .................................................... H136
              4. "Thoreau" (w/ fl obbl; used in Kz99):
                    quoted: . "Massa's in de Cold, Cold Ground" ........................................... H121
                           . Beethoven: Symphony No.5 in C minor, Op.67 ............................ H173
```

6. OTHER PIANO WORKS

6.1	"March No.1, with 'The Year of Jubilee' " (c ?1890; lost arr for band & lost arr for orch)	Kx2
6.2	"March (No.2), with 'The Son of a Gambolier' " (c ?1892, inc; used in Kv2 & Kz29)	Kx4
6.3	"March No.3, with 'Omega Lambda Chi' " (c ?1892; used in Kv7)	Kx5
6.4	"March No.5, with 'Annie Lisle' " (c1892; used in Kv4)	Kx6
6.5	"March No.6, with 'Here's to Good Old Yale' " (c1892–?7; 3 vers; lost arr for band/orch)	Kx7
6.6	"March in G and C, with 'See the conquering hero comes' " (c1893)	Kx9
6.7	"March: The Circus Band" (c ?1894)	Kx10
6.8	"Invention," in D major (c ?1896)	Kx11
6.9	"Ragtime Pieces" (c1902–4, from/used in Kv12; used in Kx17/2a, Kx17/2b & Kx17/4b)	Kx13
6.10	"Three-Page Sonata" (c1905; ed Cowell 1949; r ed Kirkpatrick 1975)	Kx14
6.11	"Set of Five Take-offs" (c1906–7; ed Kirkpatrick): No.1 "The Seen and Unseen"	Kx15
6.12	No.2 "Rough and Ready et al and/or The Jumping Frog"	
6.13	No.3 "Song Without (Good) Words" (Melody in F and F-flat)	
6.14	No.4 "Scene Episode" (from/used in Kx17/5):	
6.15	No.5 "Bad Resolutions and Good One"	
6.16	"Studies" (c1907–?8, inc): No.1 ?"Allegro" (inc)	Kx16
6.17	No.2 "Andante moderato—Allegro molto" (from cadenza for Kv25)	
6.18	*No.3 (lost)*	

6.19	No.4 ?"Allegro moderato" (inc)
6.20	No.5 "Moderato (con) anima"
6.21	No.6 "Andante" (renumbered No.14)
6.22	No.7 "Andante cantabile" (renumbered No.15)
6.23	No.8 "Trio: Allegro moderato—Presto"
6.24	No.9 "The Anti-Abolitionist Riots" (from cadenza for Kv25; ed Cowell 1949)
6.25	*No.10–18 (unidentified/?lost)*
6.26	. "Allegro moderato" (renumbered No.15)
6.27	. "Andante cantabile" (inc, renumbered No.16)
6.28	*No.19 (untitled, amorphous sketch) (Study in major and minor intensities)*
6.29	No.20 "March: Slow allegro or Fast andante"
6.30	No.21 "Some South-Paw Pitching" (c ?1909; ed Cowell 1949; r ed Kirkpatrick 1975)
6.31	No.22 "Andante maestoso—Allegro vivace" (c ?1909; ed Cowell 1949; r ed Kirkpatrick)
6.32	(?No.23) "Allegro" (c ?1909)
6.33	"Waltz-Rondo" (c1911; ed Kirkpatrick & Cox 1977) Kx18
6.34	"4 Transcriptions from Emerson" (c ?1917–22, from Kv25 & Kx19/1): No.1 "Slowly" Kx20
6.35	No.2 "Moderato"
6.36	No.3 "Largo"
6.37	No.4 "Allegro agitato—Broadly"
6.38	"Varied Air and Variations" (c ?1923, inc; ed Kirkpatrick & Clarke 1972) Kx21
6.39	"The Celestial Railroad" (c ?1924–?5, from Kv14, Kx19/2 & Kv39/2) Kx23

Pf duet:

6.40	"Drum Corps or Scuffle" (c before 1902) K3C2

2 Pf:

6.41	"3 Quarter-tone Pieces" (c1923–4; ed Pappastavrou 1968): No.1 "Largo" Kx22
6.42	No.2 "Allegro" (from Kv27/1)
6.43	No.3 "Chorale" (from Kv36)

6a. MUSIC QUOTED IN OTHER PIANO WORKS

6a.1	"March No.1, with 'The Year of Jubilee' ": Kx2
	quoted: . "Year of Jubilee" H145
	. "That Old Cabin Home upon the Hill" H141
6a.2	"March (No.2), with 'The Son of a Gambolier' ": Kx4
	quoted: . "The Son of a Gambolier" H135
6a.3	"March No.3, with 'Omega Lambda Chi' ":..Kx5
	quoted: . "Omega Lambda Chi" H156
6a.4	"March No.5, with 'Annie Lisle' ": Kx6
	quoted: . "Annie Lisle" H95
6a.5	"March No.6, with 'Here's to Good Old Yale' ":...Kx7
	quoted: . "Bingo" H148
6a.6	"March in G and C, with 'See the conquering hero comes' ": Kx9
	quoted: . Handel's oratorio: Judas Maccabeus, HWV63 ....H181
6a.8	"Invention," in D major: Kx11
	quoted: . Bach: Sinfonia in A minor H172
6a.10	"Three-Page Sonata":...Kx14
	quoted: . "Proprior Deo" H49
	. "Westminster Chimes" H170
6a.11	"Set of Five Take-offs" (c1906–7; ed Kirkpatrick): No.1 "The Seen and Unseen" Kx15
6a.12	No.2 "Rough and Ready et al and/or The Jumping Frog"
6a.13	No.3 "Song Without (Good) Words" (Melody in F and F-flat)
6a.14	No.4 "Scene Episode":
	quoted: . "Happy Day" H27
6a.15	No.5 "Bad Resolutions and Good One"
6a.16	"Studies": No.1 ?"Allegro"...Kx16
6a.17	No.2 "Andante moderato—Allegro molto"
6a.18	*No.3 (lost)*
6a.19	No.4 ?"Allegro moderato"
6a.20	No.5 "Moderato (con) anima"
6a.21	No.6 "Andante"
6a.22	No.7 "Andante cantabile"

6a.23   No.8 "Trio: Allegro moderato—Presto"

6a.24   No.9 "The Anti-Abolitionist Riots"

6a.25   *No.10–18 (unidentified/?lost)*

6a.26   . "Allegro moderato"

6a.27   . "Andante cantabile":
                  quoted: . "Home! Sweet Home!" H108

6a.28   *No.19 (untitled, amorphous sketch) (Study in major and minor intensities):*
                  quoted: . "Even Me" *H18*

6a.29   No.20 "March: Slow allegro or Fast andante":
                  quoted: . "Battle Hymn of the Republic" H72
                  . "I've Been Working on the Railroad" H109
                  . "The Girl I Left Behind Me" H102
                  . "Turkey in the Straw" H169
                  . "Alexander" H94

6a.30   No.21 "Some South-Paw Pitching":
                  quoted: . "Massa's in de Cold, Cold Ground" H121
                  . "Antioch" H3

6a.31   No.22 "Andante maestoso—Allegro vivace"

6a.32   (?No.23) "Allegro"

6a.33   "Waltz-Rondo": Kx18
                  quoted: . "Columbia, the Gem of the Ocean" H75
                  . "Turkey in the Straw" H169
                  . "College Hornpipe" H161
                  . "The White Cockade" H171
                  . "Fisher's Hornpipe" H162
                  . "Marching Through Georgia" H79

6a.34   "4 Transcriptions from Emerson": No.1 "Slowly": Kx20
                  quoted: . Beethoven: Symphony No.5 in C minor, Op.67 .... H173

6a.35   No.2 "Moderato"

6a.36   No.3 "Largo"

6a.37   No.4 "Allegro agitato—Broadly"

6a.39   "The Celestial Railroad": Kx23
                  quoted: . "Tramp, Tramp, Tramp" H89
                  . (unknown) H201
                  . "Massa's in the Cold, Cold Ground" H121
                  . "Columbia, the Gem of the Ocean" H75
                  . Beethoven: Symphony No.5 in C minor, Op.67 .... H173
                  . "Hello! Ma Baby" H107
                  . "Martyn" H35
                  . "Beulah Land" H8
                  . (?) "The Battle Cry of Freedom" H71

6a.40   "Drum Corps or Scuffle": K3C2
                  quoted: . "Happy Day" (or ?Bringing in the Sheaves, H10) H27

6a.41   "3 Quarter-tone Pieces": No.1 "Largo" Kx22

6a.42   No.2 "Allegro" (from Kv27/1):
                  quoted: . "The Battle Cry of Freedom" H71
                  . "Happy Day" H27

6a.43   No.3 "Chorale" (from Kv36):
                  quoted: . "America" H69
                  . "La Marseillaise" H80

7. ORGAN

7.1   "Variations on 'Jerusalem the Golden' " (c ?1888; lost arr for band) Kx1

7.2   "Variations on a National Hymn (America)" (c ?1891) Kx3

7.3   "Interludes for Hymns" (c ?1892): No.1 "Interlude for 'Nettleton' " K3D6

7.4   No.2 "Interlude for 'Bethany' "

7.5   No.3 (Interlude)

7.6   No.4 "Interlude for 'Woodworth' "

7.7   "Canzonetta," in F major (c ?1893) Kx8

7.8   "Prelude on 'Adeste fideles' " (c1897) Kx12

7.9   *"Prelude for Thanksgiving Service" (c1897, lost; used in: Thanksgiving, Kv17)* *K3D17*

7.10   *"Prelude for Thanksgiving Service" (c1897, lost; used in: Thanksgiving, Kv17)* *K3D18*

7.11   *"Prelude" (c1901, lost; used in: Vn Sonata No.3, Kw21/3)* *K3D24*

7.12   *"Piece for Communion Service" (c1901, lost; used in: Symphony No.3, Kv15/3)* *K3D26*

7a. MUSIC QUOTED IN ORGAN WORKS

7a.1   "Variations on Jerusalem the Golden": Kx1
        quoted: . "Ewing" H20
7a.2   "Variations on America": Kx3
        quoted: . "America" H69

7a.3   "Interludes for Hymns": No.1 "Interlude for 'Nettleton' ": K3D6
        quoted: . "Nettleton" H42
7a.4   No.2 "Interlude for 'Bethany' ":
        quoted: . "Bethany" H7
7a.5   No.3 (Interlude)
7a.6   No.4 "Interlude for 'Woodworth' ":
        quoted: . "Woodworth" H67

7a.8   "Prelude on 'Adeste fideles' ": Kx12
        quoted: . "Adeste Fideles" H1

7a.9   *"Prelude for Thanksgiving Service":* *K3D17*
        quoted: *. "Shining Shore"* *H54*

7a.10   *"Prelude for Thanksgiving Service":* *K3D18*
        quoted: *. "Federal Street"* *H22*
                      . "Shining Shore" *H54*

7a.11   *"Prelude":* *K3D24*
        quoted: *. "Need"* *H41*

7a.12   *"Piece for Communion Service":* *K3D26*
        quoted: *. "Woodworth"* *H67*

8. CHORAL WORKS

8.1   "Psalm 42": "As pants the hart" (c ?1888; ch & org) Ky1
8.2   "The year's at the spring" (c ?1889, Browning; ch) (also see Beach Op.44/1, B17/1 & Vaughan
        Williams' 440. of: The Songs of Praise p1925) Ky2
8.3   "I think of Thee, my God" (c ?1889, Monsell; ch; used in Kz11) Ky3
8.4   "Benedictus": "Blessed be the Lord," in E major (c ?1890; ch & org) Ky4
8.5   "Turn Ye, Turn Ye" (c ?1890, Hopkins: ch & org, org part lost; ed Kirkpatrick 1973) Ky5
8.6   "Crossing the Bar": "Sunset and evening star" (c ?1890, Tennyson; ch & org, org part lost;
        ed Kirkpatrick 1974) (also see Vaughan Williams' song of 1892) Ky6
8.7   "Communion Service" (c1891; ch & org, org part lost) Ky7
8.8   "Serenade": "Stars of the summer night" (c ?1891, Longfellow; ch) Ky8
8.9   "Bread of the World" (c ?1891, Heber; unison fem ch & org, unfin) Ky9
8.10   "God of my life" (c ?1892, Elliott; ch & org, org part lost) Ky10
8.11   "Easter Carol": "Wake, wake, earth" (c1892, r ?1901; S, A, T, B, ch & org) Ky11
8.12   "Lord God, Thy sea" (c ?1893; ch & org, org part lost) Ky12
8.13   "Psalm 150": "Praise ye the Lord" (c ?1894; boys' ch, ch & org; ed Kirkpatrick & Smith 1972) Ky13
8.14   "Psalm 67": "God be merciful unto us" (c ?1894, ch) Ky14
8.15   "Psalm 54": "Save me, O God" (c ?1894; ch; ed Kirkpatrick & Smith 1973) Ky15
8.16   "Psalm 24": "The earth is the Lord's" (c ?1894; ch) Ky16
8.17   "The Light that is Felt" (c ?1895, Whittier; 1v, ch & org; used in Kz74) Ky17
8.18   "For you and Me!" (c ?1895–6; ch) Ky18
8.19   "A Song of Mory's" (c ?1896, Merrill; ch) Ky19
8.20   "The Bells of Yale, or Chapel Chimes" (c1897–?8, Mason; Bar, ch & vc/pf; 3 vers) Ky20
8.21   "O Maiden fair" (c1897–?8; 1v, ch & pf) Ky21
8.22   "All-forgiving, look on me" (c ?1898, Palmer; ch & ?org, org part lost) Ky22
8.23   "The Celestial Country" (c1898–9; vv, ch, insts & org, org part lost; ed Kirkpatrick 1978): Ky23
                1. "Far o'er yon horizon," prelude, trio & chorus
                2. "Naught that country needeth" (= 98. of: 114 Songs)
                3. "Seek the things before us"
                4. "Intermezzo"
                5. "Glories on glories"
                6. "Forward, flock of Jesus" (= 99. of: 114 Songs)
                7. "To the Eternal Father," chorale & finale
8.24   "Psalm 100": "Make a joyful noise" (c1898–?9; boys' ch, ch & bells ad lib; ed Kirkpatrick 1979) Ky24
8.25   "Psalm 14": "The fool hath said" (c ?1899; 2ch & org, org part lost) Ky25
8.26   "Psalm 25": "Unto thee O God" (c1899–?1901; ch & org; ed Kirkpatrick & Smith 1979) Ky26
8.27   "Psalm 135" (Anthem-Processional) (c ?1900; ch, timp & org; ed Kirkpatrick) Ky27
8.28   "3 Harvest Home Chorales" (ch, brass & org; r ed Echols): 1. "Harvest Home" (c ?1898) Ky28
8.29   2. "Lord of the Harvest" (c ?1901)
8.30   3. "Harvest Home": "Come, ye thankful people" (c ?1901)
8.31   "Processional: Let there be light" (c1901, Ellerton; ch or ch & org/brass) Ky29
8.32   *"Hymn-Anthem" (c before 1902, lost; used in: In the Night, Kv22/3)* *K5C39*

8a. MUSIC QUOTED IN CHORAL WORKS

8a.44   "They are There!": Ky38b
        quoted: . "Columbia, the Gem of the Ocean" (ch) H75
                . "Dixie's Land" (fl).. H76
                . "Battle Hymn of the Republic" (trbn) H72
                . "Marching Through Georgia" (fl) H79
                . "Tramp, Tramp, Tramp" (ch) H89
                . "Yankee Doodle" (fl) H92
                . "Over There" (fl) H82
                . "Maryland, My Maryland" (fl) H81
                . "La Marseillaise" (fl) H80
                . "Tenting on the Old Camp Ground" (ch) H88
                . "The Battle Cry of Freedom" (fl)... H71
                . "The Star Spangled Banner" (fl) H86
                . "Reveille" (fl) H83

8a.45   "An Election": Ky39
        quoted: . "Over There" (vv) H82
                . "The Star Spangled Banner" (vn) H86

8a.46   "Psalm 90": "Lord, thou hast been": Ky40
        quoted: . "The Last Hope" (T) H180

8a.47   "Johny Poe: When fell the gloom": Ky41
        quoted: . "Old Nassau" (B) H155

9. SONGS (w/ pf; first collection: 114 Songs p1922)

(letters 'b' and 'c' following Kirkpatrick's catalog numbers identify songs which are later revisions
and adaptations to new words)

9.1   "Slow March": "One evening just at sunset" (c ?1887, r1921, Brewster, = 114. of: 114 Songs) Kz1
9.2   "Hear my Prayer, O Lord": "O have mercy, Lord, on me" (c ?1888, Tate, Brady) Kz2a
9.3   "When the waves softly sigh" (c ?1892, ?Ives)..Kz2b
9.4   "A Song for Anything": "Yale farewell! we must part" (c ?1898, Ives, = 89. of: 114 Songs) Kz2c
9.5   "At Parting": "The sweetest flow'r that blows" (c ?1889, Peterson) Kz3
9.6   "Abide with me" (c ?1890, Lyte, new acc later) Kz4
9.7   "Far from my heav'nly home" (c ?1890, Lyte) Kz5
9.8   "Country Celestial": "For thee, o dear, dear country" (c ?1891, Neale after Bernard of Cluny) Kz6a
9.9   "Du bist wie eine Blume" (c ?1897, Heine) Kz6b
9.10 "When stars are in the quiet skies" (c ?1898, Bulwer-Lytton, = 113. of: 114 Songs) Kz6c
9.11 "Rock of Ages": "Rock of ages, cleft for me" (c ?1891, Toplady; w/ org)..Kz7
9.12 "My Lou Jeninne": "Has she need of monarch's swaying wand" (c ?1891) Kz8
9.13 "In Autumn": "The skies seemed true above thee" (c ?1892)...Kz9
9.14 "A Perfect Day": "Bland air and leagues of immemorial blue" (c ?1892) Kz10
9.15 "Through Night and Day": "I dream of thee, my love" (c ?1892, ?Ives, from Ky3) Kz11
9.16 "Minnelied": "Holder klingt der Vogelsang" (c ?1892, Hölty) Kz12a
9.17 "Nature's Way": "When the distant evening bell" (c1908, Ives, = 61. of: 114 Songs) Kz12b
9.18 "Friendship": "All love that has not friendship for its base" (c1892) Kz13
9.19 "Her Eyes": "Her eyes are like unfathomable lakes" (c ?1892) Kz14a
9.20 "Mirage": "The hope I dreamed of was a dream" (c1902, Rossetti, = 70. of: 114 Songs) Kz14b
9.21 "Canon": "Not only in my lady's eyes" (c1903) Kz15a
9.22 "Canon": "Oh! the days are gone, when Beauty bright" (c ?1894, Moore, = 111. of: 114 Songs) Kz15b
9.23 "There is a certain garden" (c1893) Kz16
9.24 "Song for Harvest Season": "Summer ended" (c1893, Phillimore; w/ org; also w/ tpt, trbn & tuba) Kz17
9.25 "Song": "She is not fair to outward view" (c ?1893, Coleridge) (also see Sullivan's song of 1866) Kz18
9.26 "Waltz": "Round and round the old dance ground" (c ?1894) (see 98. of: 114 Songs) Kz19
9.27 "The Circus Band": "All summer long we boys" (c ?1894, Ives, from Kx10, = 56. of: 114 Songs) Kz20
9.28 "The Old Mother" I: "Oh dearest mother" (c ?1894, Corder after Vinje, see Kz66) Kz21
9.29 "Far in the Wood": "Far in the wood where pine trees" (c ?1894) Kz22a
9.30 "A Night Song": "The young May moon is beaming, love" (c1895, Moore, = 88. of: 114 Songs) Kz22b
9.31 "A Christmas Carol": "Little star of Bethlehem" (c1894, Ives, = 100. of: 114 Songs) Kz23
9.32 "Rosamunde": "Der Vollmond strahlt" (c ?1895, Chézy) Kz24a
9.33 "Rosamunde": "J'attends, hélas, dans la douleur" (c1898, Bélanger, = 79. of: 114 Songs) Kz24b
9.34 "Ein Ton": "Mir klingt ein Ton" (c ?1895, Cornelius) Kz25a
9.35 "Night of Frost in May": "There was the lyre" (c1899, Meredith, = 84. of: 114 Songs) Kz25b
9.36 "Songs my mother taught me" (c1895, Macfarren after Heyduk; used in Kw7, = 108. of: 114 Songs) ..Kz26
9.37 "In April-tide": "Be ye in love with April-tide" (c ?1895, Scollard) Kz27a
9.38 "Amphion": "The mountain stirred its bushy crown" (c1896, Tennyson, = 106. of: 114 Songs) Kz27b
9.39 "My Native Land" (Un rêve) I (c ?1895, after Heine; also see Kz69, = 101. of: 114 Songs) Kz28
9.40 "A Son of a Gambolier" (c1895, ?after the Irish, from Kx4, = 54. of: 114 Songs)...............................Kz29
9.41 "Kären" (Little Kären): "Do'st remember, child" (c ?1895, Kappey after Ploug, = 91. of: 114 Songs) Kz30
9.42 "Gruss": "Leise zieht durch mein Gemüth" (c ?1895, Heine)...Kz31a
9.43 "The World's Wanderers": "Tell me, star" (c ?1895, Shelley, = 110. of: 114 Songs) Kz31b
9.44 "Die Lotosblume" (c ?1895, Heine) Kz32a

667

9.45   "The South Wind": "When gently blows" (c1908, Twichell, = 97. of: 114 Songs) Kz32b
9.46   "In my Beloved's Eyes": "I looked into the midnight deep" (c ?1895, r ?1899, Chauvenet) Kz33a
9.47   "A Night Thought": "How oft a cloud, with envious veil" (c ?1903, Moore, = 107. of: 114 Songs) Kz33b
9.48   "The All-enduring": "Man passes" (c1896, from/used in lost ch vers) Kz34
9.49   "Marie": "Marie, am Fenster sitzest du" (c1896, Gottschall) Kz35a
9.50   "Marie": "Marie, I see thee, fairest one" (c1896, Gottschall transl Rücker, altered Ives,
       = 92. of: 114 Songs) Kz35b
9.51   "An Old Flame" (A Retrospect): "When dreams enfold me" (c1896, Ives, = 87. of: 114 Songs) Kz36
9.52   "In the Alley": "On my way to work" (c1896, Ives, = 53. of: 114 Songs) Kz37
9.53   "William Will": "What we want is honest money" (c1896, Hill) Kz38
9.54   "A Scotch Lullaby": "Blaw! skirlin' win' " (c1896, Merrill) Kz39
9.55   "Frühlingslied": "Die blaue Frühlingsaugen" (c1896, Heine) Kz40a
9.56   "I travelled among unknown men" (c1901, Wordsworth, = 75. of: 114 Songs) Kz40b
9.57   "God Bless and Keep Thee": "I know not if thy love" (c ?1897) Kz41
9.58   "Dreams": "When twilight comes" (c1897, after Baroness Porteous, = 85. of: 114 Songs) Kz42
9.59   "Qu'il m'irait bien" (c ?1897, ?after M. Delano, = 76. of: 114 Songs) Kz43
9.60   "Her gown was of vermilion silk" (c1897, Ives) Kz44
9.61   "Memories": "We're sitting" (c1897, Ives, = 102. of: 114 Songs) Kz45
9.62   "Widmung": "O danke nicht für diese Lieder" (c ?1897, Müller) Kz46a
9.63   "There is a lane" (c1902, Ives, = 71. of: 114 Songs) Kz46b
9.64   "Feldeinsamkeit": "Ich ruhe still" (c1897, Almers, = 82. of: 114 Songs) Kz47a
9.65   "In Summer Fields": "Quite still I lie" (c1897, Chapman) Kz47b
9.66   "No More": "They walked beside the summer sea" (c1897, Winter) Kz48a
9.67   "Hymn of Trust": "O Love divine" (c ?1898, Holmes) Kz48b
9.68   "Ich grolle nicht" (c1898, Heine, = 83. of: 114 Songs) Kz49a
9.69   "I'll not complain" (c1898, Dwight) Kz49b
9.70   "Chanson de Florian": "Ah s'il est dans votre village" (c ?1898, Florian, = 78. of: 114 Songs) Kz50
9.71   "On Judges' Walk": "That night on Judges' Walk" (c1893–?8, Symons; used in Kv8/1) Kz51a
9.72   "Rough Wind": "Rough wind, that moanest loud" (c1902, Shelley, = 69. of: 114 Songs) (also see
       Respighi P108/2) Kz51b
9.73   "The Only Son": "The lark will make her hymn" (c ?1898, Kipling) Kz52a
9.74   "Harpalus": "Oh Harpalus! thus would he say" (c1902, from Percy's Reliques, = 73. of: 114 Songs) .. Kz52b
9.75   "Wie Melodien zieht es mir" (c ?1898, Groth) Kz53a
9.76   "Evidence": "There comes o'er the valley a shadow" (c1910, Ives, = 58. of: 114 Songs) Kz53b
9.77   "The Love Song": "Alone upon the housetops to the North" (c ?1898, Kipling) Kz54
9.78   "Tarrant Moss": "I closed and drew for my love's sake" (c ?1898, Kipling, = 72. of: 114 Songs) Kz55a
9.79   "Slugging a Vampire": "I closed and drew, but not a gun" (c1902, Ives) Kz55b
9.80   "Hear now the song of the dead" (c ?1898, Kipling) Kz56a
9.81   "The Ending Year": "Frail autumn lights" (c1902) Kz56b
9.82   "The Waiting Soul": "Breathe from the gentle south" (c1908, Cowper, = 62. of: 114 Songs) Kz56c
9.83   "Because of you": "What have you done for me, dear one" (c1898) Kz57
9.84   "I knew and loved a maid" (c ?1898) Kz58
9.85   "Flag Song": "Accept you these emblems" (c1898, Durand, from lost song) Kz59
9.86   "Because thou art": "My life has grown so dear to me" (c ?1899) Kz60
9.87   "Grace": "Sweetheart, sweetheart" (c ?1899) Kz61a
9.88   "Where the eagle" (c1906, Turnbull, = 94. of: 114 Songs) Kz61b
9.89   "Omens and Oracles": "Phantoms of the future" (c1899, = 86. of: 114 Songs) Kz62
9.90   "Sehnsucht": "Ich konnte heute nicht schlafen" (c ?1899, Lobedanz after Winther) Kz63a
9.91   "Rosenzweige": "Wohl manchen Rosenzweig" (c ?1899, Stieler) Kz63b
9.92   "Allegro": "By morning's brightest beams" (c1900, Ives, = 95. of: 114 Songs) Kz63c
9.93   "Romanzo di Central Park": "Grove, rove, night, delight" (c1900, Hunt, = 96. of: 114 Songs) Kz64
9.94   "Wiegenlied": "Guten Abend" (c ?1900, from Des Knaben Wunderhorn) Kz65a
9.95   "Berceuse": "O'er the mountain towards the west" (c ?1903, Ives, = 93. of: 114 Songs) Kz65b
9.96   "The Old Mother" II: "Du alte Mutter" (c1900, Lobedanz after Vinje, = 81. of: 114 Songs) Kz66a
9.97   "My dear old mother" (c1900, Corder after Vinje) Kz66b
9.98   "The Children's Hour": "Between the dark and daylight" (c1901, Longfellow, = 74. of: 114 Songs) Kz67
9.99   "Elégie": "O doux printemps d'autrefois" (c1901, Gallet, = 77. of: 114 Songs) Kz68
9.100   "My Native Land" II (c?1901, after Heine; also see Kz28) Kz69
9.101   "Ilmenau": "Über allen Gipfeln ist Ruh' " (c1901, Goethe, = 68. of: 114 Songs) Kz70
9.102   "Weil' auf mir" (c ?1901, Lenau, = 48. of: 114 Songs) Kz71
9.103   "Watchman" (c1901, Bowring, lost) K6B39
9.104   "Walking": "A big October morning" (c1900–?2, Ives, from lost anthem of 1898, = 67. of: 114 Songs) .. Kz72
9.105   "The Sea of Sleep": "Good night, my care and my sorrow" (c1903) Kz73a
9.106   "Those Evening Bells" (c1907, Moore, = 63. of: 114 Songs) Kz73b
9.107   "The Light that is felt" (c1903, Whittier, from Ky17, = 66. of: 114 Songs) Kz74
9.108   "The Cage": "A leopard went" (c1906, Ives, from/used in Kv22/1, = 64. of: 114 Songs) Kz75
9.109   "Pictures": "The ripe corn bends low" (c1906, Turnbull) Kz76
9.110   "The World's Highway": "For long I wandered happily" (c1906, Twichell, = 90. of: 114 Songs) Kz77
9.111   "Spring Song": "Across the hill" (c1907, Twichell, from lost song, = 65. of: 114 Songs) Kz78
9.112   "Soliloquy": "When a man is sitting before the fire" (c1907, Ives) Kz79
9.113   "Autumn": "Earth rests" (c1907, Twichell, from lost song of ?1902, = 60. of: 114 Songs) Kz80
9.114   "Runaway Horse on Main Street": "So long, Harris" (c ?1909, Ives, inc, from Kv19; used in Kz119) Kz81
9.115   "Tolerance": "How can I turn from any fire" (c ?1909, Kipling, from Kv27/2, = 59. of: 114 Songs) Kz82
9.116   "A Farewell to Land": "Adieu, adieu! my native shore" (c1909, Byron) Kz83
9.117   "Mists": "Low lie the mists" (c1910, H. T. Ives, = 57. of: 114 Songs) Kz84

9.118   "Religion": "There is no unbelief" (c ?1910, Case, from lost anthem of 1902, = 16. of: 114 Songs) Kz85

9.119   "Requiem": "Under the wide and starry sky" (c1911, Stevenson) Kz86

9.120   "Vote for Names" (c1912, Ives, unfin) Kz87

9.121   "The Camp Meeting" (c1912, Ives after Elliot, from Kv15/3, = 47. of: 114 Songs) Kz88

9.122   "His Exaltation": "For the grandeur" (c1913, Robinson, from Kw17/1, = 46. of: 114 Songs) Kz89

9.123   "Watchman" (c1913, Bowring, from Kw16/3, = 44. of: 114 Songs) Kz90

9.124   "The New River": "Down the river comes a noise" (c1913, Ives, from Kv27/3, = 6. of: 114 Songs).......Kz91

9.125   "The See'r": "An old man with a straw" (c ?1913, Ives, from Kv27/1, = 29. of: 114 Songs) Kz92

9.126   "December": "Last for December" (c ?1913, Rossetti after Folgore, from Ky32, = 37. of: 114 Songs) ..Kz93

9.127   "Like a Sick Eagle": "The spirit is too weak" (c ?1913, Keats, from Kv27/4, = 26. of: 114 Songs) Kz94

9.128   "Luck and Work": "While one will search" (c ?1913, Johnson, from Kv40/2, = 21. of: 114 Songs) Kz95

9.129   "Lincoln, the Great Commoner": "And so he came from the prairie cabin" (c ?1913, Markham,
from Ky31, = 11. of: 114 Songs) Kz96

9.130   "Old Home Day": "Go, my songs" (c ?1913, Ives after Virgil; w/ fife, vn & fl obbl, = 52. of: 114 Songs) Kz97

9.131   "General William Booth Enters into Heaven": "Booth led boldly" (c1914, Lindsay; used in Ky35) Kz98

9.132   "Thoreau": "He grew in those seasons" (c1915, Ives after Thoreau, from Kx19/4, =48. of: 114 Songs) Kz99

9.133   "Swimmers": "Then the swift plunge" (c1915, r1921, Untermeyer, = 27. of: 114 Songs) Kz100

9.134   "At the River": "Shall we gather" (c ?1916, Lowry, from Kw22/3, = 45. of: 114 Songs).......................Kz101

9.135   "The Innate": "Voices live in every finite being" (c1916, Ives, from Kw15/3, = 40. of: 114 Songs) Kz102

9.136   "In Flanders Fields" (c1917, McCrae, = 49. of: 114 Songs) Kz103

9.137   "He is There!": "Fifteen years ago today" (c1917, Ives; used in Ky38a, = 50. of: 114 Songs) Kz104a

9.138   "They Are There!": "There's a time in every life" (c1942, Ives; used in Ky38b) Kz104b

9.139   "The Things Our Fathers Loved": "I think there must be a place" (c1917, Ives, = 43. of: 114 Songs) .Kz105

9.140   "Tom Sails Away": "Scenes from my childhood" (c1917, Ives, = 51. of: 114 Songs) Kz106

9.141   "To Edith": "So like a flower" (c1919, H. T. Ives, from lost song of 1892, = 112. of: 114 Songs) Kz107

9.142   "Down East": "Songs! visions" (c1919, Ives, from lost: Down East Overture, = 55. of: 114 Songs) Kz108

9.143   "Serenity": "O Sabbath rest of Galilee" (c1919, Whittier, from lost earlier vers, = 42. of: 114 Songs)..Kz109

9.144   "Cradle Song": "Hush thee, dear child" (c1919, A. Ives, = 33. of: 114 Songs) Kz110

9.145   "Afterglow": "At the quiet close of day" (c1919, Cooper, = 39. of: 114 Songs)...................................Kz111

9.146   "The Collection": "Now help us Lord" (c1920, Kingsley, ?from lost early anthem, = 38. of:
114 Songs)..Kz112

9.147   "Granchester": "Just now the lilac" (c1920, Brooke, = 17. of: 114 Songs) Kz113

9.148   "La fède" (c1920, Ariosto, = 34. of: 114 Songs) Kz114

9.149   "August": "For August, be your dwelling thirty towers" (c1920, Rossetti after Folgore da San
Geminiano, = 35. of: 114 Songs) Kz115

9.150   "September": "And in September, O what keen delight" (c1920, Rossetti after Folgor da San
Geminiano, = 36. of: 114 Songs) Kz116

9.151   "On the Counter": "Tunes we heard in 'ninety-two' " (c1920, Ives, =28. of: 114 Songs) Kz117

9.152   "Maple leaves": "October turned my maple's leaves to gold" (c1920, Aldrich, = 23. of: 114 Songs) Kz118

9.153   "Charlie Rutlage": "Another good cow-puncher" (c1920–1, D. J. O'Malley, from Kv19 & Kz81,
= 10. of: 114 Songs) Kz119

9.154   "At Sea": "Some things are undivined" (c1921, Johnson, from Kv40/1, = 4. of: 114 Songs)................Kz120

9.155   "Hymn": "Thou hidden love of God" (c1921, Wesley after Tersteegen, from Kw15/1,
= 20. of: 114 Songs) Kz121

9.156   "Remembrance": "A sound of a distant horn" (c1921, Ives, from Kv21, = 12. of: 114 Songs) Kz122

9.157   "Incantation": "When the moon is on the wave" (c1921, from Byron's Manfred, Act I/1, from Kv27/6,
= 18. of: 114 Songs) (also see Schumann's incid music: Manfred, Op.115 & Tchaikovsky:
'Manfred Symphony,' in B minor, Op.58) Kz123

9.158   "The Last Reader": "I sometimes sit beneath a tree" (c1921, Holmes, from Kv32/3,
= 3. of: 114 Songs)..Kz124

9.159   "The Housatonic at Stockbridge": "Contented river" (c1921, Johnson, from Kv30/3,
= 15. of: 114 Songs) Kz125

9.160   "The Indians": "Alas for them, their day is o'er" (c1921, Sprague, from Kv32/4, = 14. of: 114 Songs).Kz126

9.161   "West London": "Crouch'd on the pavement" (c1921, Arnold, from Kv33, = 105. of: 114 Songs) Kz127

9.162   "2 Slants, or Christian and Pagan" (c1921, from Ky33, = 9. of: 114 Songs): 1. "Duty": "So nigh is
grandeur to our dust" (Emerson) Kz128
             2. "Vita": "Nascentes morimur finisque ab origine pendet" (Manlius)

9.164   "Walt Whitman": "Who goes there?" (c1921, Whitman, from Ky34, =31. of: 114 Songs) Kz129

9.165   "The Rainbow": "My heart leaps up" (c1921, Wordsworth, from Kv35, = 8. of: 114 Songs) Kz130

9.166   "Majority": "The masses have toiled" (c1921, Ives, from Ky37, = 1. of: 114 Songs) Kz131

9.167   "Premonitions": "There's a shadow on the grass" (c1921, Johnson, from Kv40/3,
= 24. of: 114 Songs)..Kz132

9.168   "Nov. 2, 1920": "It strikes me that" (c1921, Ives, from Ky39, = 22. of: 114 Songs) Kz133

9.169   "The Side Show": "Is that Mister Riley" (c1921, Ives after Rooney, from lost sketch of 1896,
= 32. of: 114 Songs) Kz134

9.170   "1, 2, 3": "Why doesn't one, two, three" (c1921, Ives, from Kw10, = 41. of: 114 Songs) Kz135

9.171   "Paracelsus": "For God is glorified in man" (c1921, Browning, from Kv29, = 30. of: 114 Songs) Kz136

9.172   "Ann Street": "Quaint name, Ann Street" (c1921, Morris, = 25. of: 114 Songs) Kz137

9.173   "Immortality": "Who dares to say the spring is dead" (c1921, Ives, = 5. of: 114 Songs) Kz138

9.174   "Two Little Flowers": "On sunny days" (c1921, Ives & H. T. Ives, = 104. of: 114 Songs) Kz139

9.175   "The Greatest Man": "My teacher said" (c1921, Collins, = 19. of: 114 Songs)..................................Kz140

9.176   "Resolution": "Walking stronger under distant skies" (c1921, Ives, = 13. of: 114 Songs) Kz141

9.177   "Disclosure": "Thoughts which deeply rest at evening" (c1921, Ives, = 7. of: 114 Songs) Kz142

9.178   "The White Gulls" (c1921, Morris after the Russian, = 103. of: 114 Songs)......................................Kz143

9.179   "Evening": "Now came still evening on" (c1921, Milton, = 2. of: 114 Songs) Kz144

9.180	"On the Antipodes": "Nature's relentless" (c1915–23, Ives)	Kz145
9.181	"Aeschylus & Sophocles": "We also have our pest" (c1922, Landor, from Kw8)	Kz146
9.182	"The One Way": "Here are things you've heard" (c1923, Ives)	Kz147
9.183	"Peaks": "Quiet faces that look in faith" (c1923, Bellamann)	Kz148
9.184	"Yellow Leaves": "Heart-shaped yellow leaves" (c1923, Bellamann)	Kz149
9.185	"A Sea Dirge": "Full fathom five thy father lies" (c1925, Shakespeare)	Kz150
9.186	"Sunrise": "A light low in the east" (c1926, Ives; w/ instr obbl, from Kw8)	Kz151
9.187	*Song (c ?1926, ?unfin/lost)*	*K6B77a*

9a. MUSIC QUOTED IN SONGS

9a.1	"Slow March": "One evening just at sunset":	Kz1
	quoted: . "Dead March," from Handel's oratorio: Saul, HWV53 (pf)	H182
9a.11	"Rock of Ages": "Rock of ages, cleft for me":	Kz7
	quoted: . "Toplady" (1v)	H60
9a.26	"Waltz": "Round and round the old dance ground":	Kz19
	quoted: . "Little Annie Rooney" (pf)	H115
9a.40	"A Son of a Gambolier":	Kz29
	quoted: . "The Son of a Gambolier" (pf)	H135
9a.103	*"Watchman":*	*K6B39*
	quoted: . "Watchman" (1v)	*H61*
9a.118	"Religion": "There is no unbelief":	Kz85
	quoted: . "Shining Shore" (1v)	H54
	. "Azmon" (pf)	H5
	. "Bethany" (pf)	H7
9a.119	"Requiem": "Under the wide and starry sky":	Kz86
	quoted: . "Taps" (1v)	H87
9a.121	"The Camp Meeting":	Kz88
	quoted: . "Azmon" (pf)	H5
	. "Woodworth" (1v)	H67
9a.122	"His Exaltation": "For the grandeur":	Kz89
	quoted: . "Autumn" (1v)	H4
9a.123	"Watchman":	Kz90
	quoted: . "Watchman" (1v)	H61
9a.129	"Lincoln, the Great Commoner": "And so he came from the prairie cabin":	Kz96
	quoted: . "Battle Hymn of the Republic" (pf)	H72
	. "Hail! Columbia" (1v)	H77
	. "Columbia, the Gem of the Ocean" (pf)	H75
	. "The Star Spangled Banner" (pf/1v)	H86
	. "America" (1v)	H69
	. "The Battle Cry of Freedom" (1v)	H71
9a.130	"Old Home Day": "Go, my songs":	Kz97
	quoted: . "Battle Hymn of the Republic" (1v)	H72
	. (unknown) (1v)	H221
	. "Arkansas Traveller" (obbl)	H158
	. "The Girl I Left Behind Me" (obbl)	H102
	. "Garryowen" (obbl)	H163
	. "Saint Patrick's Day" (obbl)	H168
	. "Annie Lisle" (1v)	H95
	. "Auld Lang Syne" (obbl)	H98
	. "Assembly" (obbl)	H70
9a.131	"General William Booth Enters into Heaven": "Booth led boldly":	Kz98
	quoted: . "Fountain" (1v)	H23
	. "Oh, Dem Golden Slippers" (pf)	H125
	. "Reveille" (1v)	H83
	. "Onward, Upward" (1v)	H47
9a.132	"Thoreau": "He grew in those seasons":	Kz99
	quoted: . "Massa's in de Cold, Cold Ground" (pf)	H121
9a.134	"At the River": "Shall we gather":	Kz101
	quoted: . "The Beautiful River" (1v)	H6

9a.135   "The Innate": "Voices live in every finite being": Kz102
          quoted: . "Nettleton" (1v) H42

9a.136   "In Flanders Fields": Kz103
          quoted: . "Columbia, the Gem of the Ocean" (pf) H75
                   . "The Battle Cry of Freedom" (pf) H71
                   . "America" (1v) H69
                   . "Taps" (pf) H87
                   . "Reveille" (pf) H83
                   . "All Saints New" (1v) H2
                   . "La Marseillaise" (1v) H80

9a.137   "He is There!": "Fifteen years ago today": Kz104a
          quoted: . "Marching Through Georgia" (1v) H79
                   . "Columbia, the Gem of the Ocean" (1v) H75
                   . "Dixie's Land" (obbl) H76
                   . "Tramp, Tramp, Tramp" (1v) H89
                   . "Yankee Doodle" (obbl) H92
                   . "Over There" (1v) H82
                   . "Reveille" (obbl) H83
                   . "Maryland, My Maryland" (obbl) H81
                   . "La Marseillaise" (obbl) H80
                   . "Tenting on the Old Camp Ground" (pf) H88
                   . "The Battle Cry of Freedom" (1v) H71
                   . "The Star Spangled Banner" (obbl) H86
                   . *"Just Before the Battle, Mother" (obbl, in sketches; later: Over There, H82)* *H111*

9a.138   "They Are There!": "There's a time in every life": Kz104b
          quoted: . "Marching Through Georgia" (1v) H79
                   . "Columbia, the Gem of the Ocean" (1v) H75
                   . "Dixie's Land" (obbl) H76
                   . "Battle Hymn of the Republic" (1v) H72
                   . "Tramp, Tramp, Tramp" (1v) H89
                   . "Yankee Doodle" (obbl) H92
                   . "Over There" (1v) H82
                   . "Reveille" (obbl) H83
                   . "Maryland, My Maryland" (obbl) H81
                   . "La Marseillaise" (obbl) H80
                   . "Tenting on the Old Camp Ground" (1v) H88
                   . "The Battle Cry of Freedom" (obbl) H71
                   . "The Star Spangled Banner" (obbl) H86

9a.139   "The Things Our Fathers Loved": "I think there must be": Kz105
          quoted: . "Dixie's Land" (1v) H76
                   . "My Old Kentucky Home (1v) H123
                   . "On the Banks of the Wabash, Far Away" (1v) H130
                   . "Nettleton" (1v) H42
                   . "The Battle Cry of Freedom" (pf) H71
                   . "In the Sweet Bye and Bye" (1v) H29

9a.140   "Tom Sails Away": "Scenes from my childhood": Kz106
          quoted: . "Araby's Daughter" (1v) H96
                   . "Columbia, the Gem of the Ocean" (1v) H75
                   . "Over There" (1v) H82

9a.142   "Down East": "Songs! visions": Kz108
          quoted: . (unknown) (1v) H222
                   . "Bethany" (1v) H7

9a.143   "Serenity": "O Sabbath rest of Galilee": Kz109
          quoted: . "Serenity" (1v) H53

9a.146   "The Collection": "Now help us Lord": Kz112
          quoted: . "Tappan" (1v) H56

9a.147   "Granchester": "Just now the lilac": Kz113
          quoted: . Debussy: "Prelude to The Afternoon of a Faun," L86 (pf) H178

9a.151   "On the Counter": "Tunes we heard in 'ninety-two' ": Kz117
          quoted: . "Narcissus" (1v) H185
                   . "Auld Land Syne" (pf) H98

9a.153   "Charlie Rutlage": "Another good cow-puncher": Kz119
          quoted: . "Git Along Little Dogies" (pf) H103

9a.155	"Hymn": "Thou hidden love of God":	Kz121
	quoted: . "More Love to Thee" (1v)	H39
	. (unknown) (1v)	H219
	. "Olivet" (1v)	H46
9a.156	"Remembrance": "A sound of a distant horn":	Kz122
	quoted: . "Kathleen Mavourneen" (1v)	H112
	. "Taps" (pf)	H87
9a.158	"The Last Reader": "I sometimes sit beneath a tree":	Kz124
	quoted: . "Cherith" (1v)	H11
	. "Manoah" (1v)	H34
9a.159	"The Housatonic at Stockbridge": "Contented river":	Kz125
	quoted: . "Missionary Chant" (1v)	H37
	. "Dorrnance" (1v)	H15
9a.161	"West London": "Crouch'd on the pavement":	Kz127
	quoted: . (unknown) (1v)	H223
	. (unknown) (1v)	H224
	. "Fountain" (pf)	H23
9a.165	"The Rainbow": "My heart leaps up":	Kz130
	quoted: . "Serenity" (1v)	H53
9a.168	"Nov. 2, 1920": "It strikes me that":	Kz133
	quoted: . "Over There" (1v)	H82
	. "The Star Spangled Banner" (1v)	H86
9a.169	"The Side Show": "Is that Mister Riley":	Kz134
	quoted: . "Are You the O'Reilly" (1v)	H97
	. Tchaikovsky: 2nd movt of Sym No.6 in B minor, "Pathétique," Op.74 (1v)	H187
9a.173	"Immortality": "Who dares to say the spring is dead":	Kz138
	quoted: . "St. Peter" (1v)	H52
9a.174	"Two Little Flowers": "On sunny days":	Kz139
	quoted: . "St. Peter" (1v)	H52
9a.175	"The Greatest Man": "My teacher said":	Kz140
	quoted: . "I've Been Working on the Railroad" (1v)	H109
	. Rossini: Overture to opera: William Tell (1v)	H186
9a.179	"Evening": "Now came still evening on":	Kz144
	quoted: . "Bethany" (1v)	H7
9a.187	*Song:*	*K6B77a*
	quoted: . *"In the Sweet Bye and Bye" (1v)*	*H29*
	. *"Reveille" (pf)*	*H83*
	. *"Shining Shore" (1v)*	*H54*

10. ARRANGEMENTS OF WORKS OF OTHERS

10.1	Beethoven: "Adagio," from Piano Sonata No.1 in F minor, Op.2/1 (arr ?1899; str qt)	
10.2	Schubert: "March," in D major, Op.51/1, D733/1 (arr ?1891; orch)	
10.3	Schubert: "Impromptu," in C minor, Op.90/1, D899/1 (arr1892; orch, inc)	
10.4	Schumann: "Préambule" & "Valse noble," from Carnaval, Op.6 (arr1892–?3; orch)	
10.5	Ives, E.: "Christmas Carol" (arr1924; unison fem ch, pf/org & bells)	
10.6	Negro spiritual: "Give me Jesus" (arr1929; 1v & pf)	
10.7	*"Search me, O God," response (S, T & pf, ?spur arr)*	
10.8	*"Love does not die" (S, T & pf, ?spur arr)*	

* * * * *

Kv, Kw, Kx, Ky, Kz = John Kirkpatrick: "A Temporary Mimeographed Catalogue of the Music Manuscripts
and Related Materials of Charles Edward Ives." New Haven, 1960. (Kv = orch
& band, Kw = chamber music, Kx = keyboard, Ky = choral & partsongs, Kz = songs)

H = Clayton W. Henderson: "The Charles Ives Tunebook." Harmonie Park Press. Michigan, 1990.

1. STAGE WORKS

Operas:

1.1	*"Smrt" (Death), melodrama (p1876, Lermontov's Death of a Poet; reciter & orch, on Pushkin's death, lost)* ....
1.2	"Šárka," 3 acts (c1887–8, r1818–9 & 1824–5, after Zeyer's libretto about mythic woman warrior) ....
1.3	"Počátek románu" (The Beginning of a Romance), 1 acts (c1891, Tichý after Preissová's story inspired by Věšín's painting) ....
1.4	"Jenůfa," 3 acts (c1894–1904, r before 1908, Janáček after Preissová's drama: Její pastorkyňa) ....
1.5	"Osud" (Fate), 3 acts (c1903–5, r1906–7, story outline Janáček, dialog versified Bartošová) ....

"Výlety Páně Broučkovy" (The Excursions of Mr. Brouček), opera in 2 parts:

1.6	Part I. "Mr. Brouček's Excursion to the Moon," 2 acts (c1908–17, Janáček after Čech's novel, add text by others, orig epilogue discarded when 2nd Excursion added) ....
1.7	Part II. "Mr. Brouček's Excursion to the 15th Century," 2 acts (c1917, Procházka after Čech's novel) ....

1.8	"Káťa Kabanová," 3 acts (c1919–21, Janáček after Ostrowsky's play: The Thunderstorm, transl Červinka)
1.9	"Příhody Lišky Bystroušky" (The Cunning Little Vixen), 3 acts (c1921–3, Janáček after Těsnohlídek's story)

1.10	"Věc Makropulos" (The Makropulos Affair), 3 acts (c1923–5, Janáček after Čapek's comedy) ....
1.11	"Z Mrtvého Domu" (From the House of the Dead), 3 acts (c1927–8, Janáček after Dostojevsky's novel) ....

Projected operas:

1.12	*"The Adventures of the Last of the Abencerages" (c1885–6, after Chateaubriand)* ....
1.13	*"The Angel Sonata" (c1903, after Merhaut)* ....
1.14	*"The Housewife" (c1904, r1907, after Preissová)* ....
1.15	*"The Song of Spring," 1 act (c1904, Preissová)* ....
1.16	*"John the Hero" (c1905, after Dostál-Lutinov)* ....
1.17	*"The Mintmaster's Wife" (c1906–7, Stroupežnický)* ....
1.18	*"Anna Karenina" (c1907, after Tolstoy)* ....
1.19	*"The Living Corpse" (c1916, Tolstoy)* ....
1.20	*"Ondras" (c1916–20, Chamrad, project)* ....
1.21	*"Tomboy" (c1920, after Krylov)* ....
1.22	*"The Child" (c1923, after Šalda)* ....

Ballets:

1.23	*"At the foot of Radhošť Mountain" (c1888–9, project)* ....
1.24	*"Valachian Dances," 1 scene romance (c1889, Kosmák, project)* ....
1.25	"Rákós Rákóczy" (folk dances & songs), 1 act (c1891, Herben, 41 pieces, incl 1–3, 5–6 of: Lachian Dances)

Incid music:

1.26	*"Schluk und Jau" (c1928, Hauptmann, frags: sketches of introd & 3 movts only)* ....

2. ORCHESTRAL WORKS

2.1	"Suite" (ca1877; strings; in brackets—abandoned titles of sections): No.1 (Prelude) ....
2.2	No.2 "Adagio" (Allemande)
2.3	No.3 (Saraband)
2.4	No.4 (Scherzo)
2.5	No.5 "Adagio" (Air)
2.6	No.6 "Andante"
2.7	"Idyll" (c1878; strings; ed Štědroň 1958) ....
2.8	*"Scherzo for a Symphony" (c1880, lost)*
2.9	"Lachian Dances" (c1889–90; used in ballet: Rákós Rákóczy; arr Máslo for pf): No.1 "Starodávny I" ....
2.10	No.2 "Požehnaný" (The Blessed One)
2.11	No.3 "Dymák" (Smoke dance / Blacksmith's dance)
2.12	No.4 "Starodávny II"
2.13	No.5 "Čeladenský" (from the village of Čeladná)
2.14	No.6 "Pilky" (Saw dance)
2.15	"Suite" (Serenade) (c1891, material from opera: The Beginning of a Romance): No.1 "Con moto" Op.3
2.16	No.2 "Adagio," in C minor
2.17	No.3 "Allegretto" (material from No.2 of: Lachian Dances)
2.18	No.4 "Allegro"
2.19	"Adagio" (ca1891) ....
2.20	"Jealousy," overture (c1894; orig to opera: Jenůfa; arr for pf duet) ....
2.21	"Kozáček" (The Cossack Dance) (c1899) ....
2.22	"Serbian Reel" (Serbian Circle Dance) (ca1899) ....
2.23	*"Moderato" (ca1904, lost)* ....
2.24	"Šumařovo dítě" (The Fiddler's Child; Ballad), sym poem (c1912, r before 1914, after Čech's poem) ....
2.25	"Taraš Bulba—Rhapsody for Orchestra" (c1915–8, after Gogol; arr for pf duet): ....
	1. "Death of Andryj"

2. "Death of Ostap"
3. "Prophecy and Death of Taraš Bulba"

2.26   "Ballad of Blanik," sym poem (c1920, after Vrchlický's poem) ....
2.27   *"The Cunning Little Vixen," suite (from opera; 3 vers: arr Jílek, Talich & Talich's r by Smetácek)* ....
2.28   "Sinfonietta" (Military sinfonietta) (c1926) ....
2.29   "The Danube," sym poem (c1923–8; S & orch; compl Chlubna 1948; also compl Faltus, Štědroň & Trhlik) .
2.30   "From the House of the Dead," overture (c1927–8, for opera, music from: Vn Conc)...........................

3. CONCERTOS, SOLO INSTR & ORCH

Pf & orch:

3.1   "Concertino" (c1925; pf & chamber ens: 2vn, va, cl, hn & bn; orig: The Spring, suite for pf) ....
3.2   "Capriccio 'Defiance' " (c1926, pf left hand & chamber ens: fl/pic, 2tpt, 3trbn & tuba) ....

Vn & orch:

3.3   Violin Concerto, "Pilgrimage of the Soul" (c1927–8, reconstr from sketches)...............................

4. STRING QUARTETS

4.1   "Sarabande" (p1878; str qt, lost) ....
4.2   String Quartet (c1880, lost) ....
4.3   String Quartet No.1, "Kreutzer" (c1923, inspired by Tolstoy's Kreutzer Sonata; also see lost Pf Trio) ....
4.4   String Quartet No.2, "Intimate Letters" (c1928, r1947) ....

5. OTHER CHAMBER MUSIC

3 or more insts:

5.1   "Sonnet for 4 Violins" (c1875; 4vn; theme used in Scherzo of: Idyll for strings) ....
5.2   "Sounds in memory of A. Förchtgott-Tovačovský" (ca1875; 3vn, va, vc & d bass) ....
5.3   Piano Trio (ca1908, r1909, inspired by Tolstoy's Kreutzer Sonata, lost; used in: Str Qt No.1) ....
5.4   "Mládí" (Youth) (Wind Sextet), suite (c1924; fl/pic, ob, cl, b cl, hn & bn) ....

Vn & pf:

5.5   "Dumka" (c1875) ....
5.6   "Romance," in E major (c1879; No.4 of: 7 Romances, Nos.1–3, 5–7 lost) ....
5.7   Violin Sonata No.1 (c1880, lost) ....
5.8   Violin Sonata No.2 (c1880, lost) ....
5.9   "Ballad" (c1912; became 2nd movt of: Vn Sonata No.3) ....
5.10   Violin Sonata No.3 (c1914 & 21; 4 vers) ....
5.11   "The Mosquito" (sketch)...

Other 2 insts:

5.12   "Minuet and Scherzo" (ca1880; cl & pf, lost) ....
5.13   "Fairy Tale" (The Story of Tzar Berendjey) (c1910, r1923; vc & pf, after Zhukovsky) ....
5.14   "Presto" (ca1910; vc & pf) ....
5.15   "March of the Blue Boys" (c1924; piccolo & carillon/tambourine/pf; used in 3rd movt of suite: Youth) ....
5.16   "2 Short Pieces" (p1924, in feuilleton Berlin in: Lidové noviny): No.1 "Sans-Souci" (fl & spinet) ....
5.17   No.2 "Berlin" (piccolo, bells & drum)

1 instr:

5.18   "A Blown-away Leaf" (arr Štědroň for vn; arr Miloš Sádlo for vc, from: On an Overgrown Path).....................
5.19   "The Madonna of Frydek" (arr Miloš Sádlo for vc, from: On an Overgrown Path) ....

6. PIANO SONATAS

6.1   Piano Sonata No.1 in E-flat major (c1879, lost) ....
6.2   Piano Sonata, "Sonata 1.X.1905, From the Street" (c1905, 2 movts only, 3rd destr by composer) ....

7. OTHER PIANO WORKS

7.1   "Rondo" (c1877, mostly lost) ....
7.2   "Dumka" (c1879, lost)...
7.3   "Nocturne" (c1879, lost) ....
7.4   "Funeral march" (c1879, lost) ....

10. CHORAL WORKS

Cantatas:

10.1	"Amarus" (ca1897, r1901–6, Vrchlický; S, T, Bar, ch & orch) ....
10.2	"Otčenáš" (Moravian 'Our Father') (c1901, r1906; T, ch & pf, to paintings by Krzecz-Mecina) ....
10.3	"Elegy on the death of my daughter Olga" (c1903, r1904, Veverica) ....
10.4	"Na Soláni Čarták" (Čarták on the Soláň) (c1911, Kurt; T, ch & orch) ....
10.5	"Věčné Evangelium" (The Eternal Gospel) (c1914, r1924, Vrchlický; S, T, ch & orch) (title borrowed from the name: Evangelium aeternum, given to the writings of Abbot Joachim di Fiore of 12th cent, interpreter of biblical prophesies) ....
10.6	"Mša Glagolskaja" (Glagolitic Mass) (c1926, Old Slavonic text arr Weingart; S, A, T, B, ch, orch & org): ....

    1. "Urod" (Prelude)
    2. "Gospodi pomiluy" (Kyrie)
    3. "Slava" (Gloria)
    4. "Véruju" (Credo)
    5. "Svet" (Sanctus)
    6. "Agneoe Bozij" (Agnus Dei)
    7. (org solo)
    8. "Intrada" (Postlude)

Choruses:

10.7	*"The Forced Bridegroom" (c1873, trad, lost: mentioned in the magazine Dalibor as arr of a Serbian folk song)* ....
10.8	"Ploughing": "Bonny lad, why aren't you ploughing?" (c1873, trad) ....
10.9	"Válečná" (War song) (c1873, anon; ch, tpt, 3trbn & pf) ....
10.10	"Nestálost lásky" (The fickleness of love): "Bonny lad on a black horse" (c1873, trad) ....
10.11	"Alone without comfort" (c1874, r1898, 1925, trad, reminiscent of a folksong: Dawn no longer breaks) ....
10.12	"True love" (c1876, trad) ....
10.13	"A drowned wreath": "Before the gate a golden stone and a white lily" (ca1875–6, trad from Príbor) ....
10.14	"If you no longer want me, what is left?" (c1876, Čelakovský) ....
10.15	"Choral elegy" (c1876, Čelakovský; ch & pf) ....
10.16	"How strange my lover is" (c1876) ....
10.17	"Festive Chorus" (c1877, Kucera; 4 m vv, ch & pf) ....
10.18	"You will not escape fate" (c1878; m ch, a setting of a Serbian folk poem) ....
10.19	"Two pigeons sit on a Fir tree" (c1878–80, trad Moravian: Love and Envy) ....
10.20	"Autumn Song" (c1880, Vrchlický) ....
10.21	"Ave Maria" (c1883, Byron's Don Juan Canto III, transl Durdík) ....
10.22	"On the ferry" (c1883–5, trad Slovak folk ballad) ....
10.23	"4 Male Choruses" (c1885, trad): 1. "The threat" (words from East Moravian: Listen to me, my lad) ....
10.24	2. "Oh, love"
10.25	3. "Alas the war" (The soldier's lot) (words from Moravian-Slovak)
10.26	4. "Your lovely eyes" (Tichý)
10.27	"The wild duck" (ca1885, trad) ....
10.28	"3 Male Choruses" (c1888): 1. "Parting" (Krásnohorská) ....
10.29	2. "The little dove" (Krásnohorská)
10.30	3. "The jealous one" (trad Moravian)
10.31	"Our song" (c1890, = 16. of opera: The Beginning of a Romance; used in: The grey falcon flew away) ....
10.32	"Green I sowed, red I shall reap" (ca1892, trad; ch & orch, arr of: Ej, danaj for pf) ....
10.33	"Our birch tree" (c1893, Krásnohorská) ....
10.34	"Vínek" (The Garland) (ca1893) ....
10.35	"The sun has risen over that hill" (c1894, trad; Bar, ch & pf) ....
10.36	"Festive Chorus" (Chorus to St Joseph) (c1897, Šťastný) ....
10.37	"4 Moravian Male-voice Choruses" (ca1904): 1. "If you only knew" (Přikryl) ....
10.38	2. "Mosquitoes" (trad)
10.39	3. "The evening witch" (Přikryl)
10.40	4. "Parting" (trad)
10.41	"Kantor Halfar" (Schoolmaster Halfar) (c1906, r1917, Bezruč) ....
10.42	"Maryčka Magdónová" (c1906 & 1907, Bezruč; 2 vers) ....
10.43	"Sedmdesát tisíc" (The 70,000) (c1909, r1913, Bezruč) ....
10.44	"Perina" (The Eiderdown / The Featherbed) (c ?1914) ....
10.45	"Vlčí stopa" (The Wolf's Trail) (c1916, Vrchlický; S, ch & pf) ....
10.46	"Songs of Hradčany" (c1916, Procházka): 1. "The Golden Alley" ....
10.47	2. "The Weeping Fountain" (S, fl & ch)
10.48	3. "Belvedere" (S, harp & ch)
10.49	"Kašpar Rucký," ballad (c1916, Procházka; S & fem ch) ....
10.50	"The Diary of One Who Disappeared," cycle (c1917–9, anon; mS, T, fem ch & pf) ....
10.51	"The Czech Legion" (c1918, Horák) ....
10.52	"Potulný šílenec" (The Wandering Madman) (c1922, Tagore transl Balej; S & ch) ....
10.53	"Nursery Rhymes," 8 songs (c1925; 3 fem vv, cl & pf; see r vers of 1927) ....
10.54	"Our Flag" (c1925–6, Procházka; 2S & ch) ....
10.55	"Chorus for laying of the foundation stone of the Masaryk University in Brno" (c1928, Trýb) ....
10.56	"Nursery Rhymes," 18 songs w/ introd & epilogue (c1927; 2S, 2A, 3T, 2B & 10 insts, r from vers of 1925) ..

11. SONGS (1v & pf)

11.1	*"Die Abendschoppen," song cycle (c1879, Mayer, lost)* ....
11.2	*"Song for Grill" (c1879, lost)* ....
11.3	*"Spring Songs," song cycle (c1880, Zusner, lost)* ....
11.4	*Songs (perf1899, lost)* ....
11.5	"Spring song" (c1897, r1905, Tichy) ....
11.6	"Singers' training Manual," 28 vocal exercises (c1899) ....

12. FOLKSONG ARRANGEMENTS

Folksongs:

12.1	"Královničky" (Little Queens), 10 folksongs (c1889; 1v & pf, from the village of Hrozenkov, collab Bakeš) ..
12.2	21 "National Dances of Moravia" (p1891–3; 12 for pf/pf duet, 9 for 1v & pf) ....
12.3	"Mariage of mosquitos" (arr of Moravian folksong for ch & orch/pf 1892) ....
12.4	"Folk Poetry Of Hukvaldy in Songs," 13 songs (arr1898; 1v & pf) ....
12.5	6 "Songs from Hukvaldy" (c1899; ch; ed Štědroň 1949) ....
12.6	"26 Folk ballads," 4 vols: I. "6 Folksongs which Eva Gabelová sang" (c1909; 1v & pf)............
12.7	II. 7 "Folk nocturnes" (c1906; 2 fem vv & pf)
12.8	III. 8 "Brigand Songs from Detva" (c1916) ....
12.9	IV. "5 Folksongs" (c1916–7; T, ch & pf/harm)
12.10	"Come, dear, come" (c1911; 1v & pf)
12.11	"Krajcpolka" (c1912; 1v & pf) ....
12.12	10 "Silesian songs" (c1918, from Salichová's collection; arr Bakala 1951 w/ fl, vn, va & vc) ....
12.13	15 "Moravian folksongs" (c1921; pf w/ text added; ed Štědroň 1949)
12.14	"Mayor Smolnik" (pubd in Lidové noviny 1923): . "Rejoice all of you" (1v & vn)............
12.15	. "Sklenov border country" (1v & 1 instr)
12.16	. "Come along, girls" (1v & triad acc)
12.17	7 "Folksongs" (c?, p1978; 1v & pf): 1. "The Hukvaldy chapel" ....
12.18	2. "Sawrnaker's song"
12.19	3. "Oh women"
12.20	4. "Ballada"
12.21	5. "The mayor's Kacanka"
12.22	6. "The oaks"
12.23	7. "I have a family"
12.24	"A prisoner sat" (c?; 1v & pf) ....

Folkdances:

12.25	12 "Valachian Dances" (arr for ch & orch 1889–90) ....
12.26	10 "Dances from Haná" (arr for pf / pf duet / orch / ch & orch 1889–90): No.1 "Tetka" ....
12.27	No.2 "Holubička"
12.28	No.3 "Sekerečka"
12.29	No.4 "Kalamajka"
12.30	No.5 "Konope" (Courava)
12.31	No.6 "Troják"
12.32	No.7 "Rožek"
12.33	No.8 "Silnice"
12.34	No.9 "Kukačka"
12.35	No.10 "Trojky"
12.36	5 "Moravian Dances" (arr for orch p1958; ed Burghauser) ....
12.37	2 "Moravian Dances" (arr for pf 1904): No.1 "Čeladenský" ....
12.38	No.2 "Pilky"

Editions of folksongs:

12.39	"A Bouquet of Moravian Folk Songs," 174 songs (ed1890, w/ out acc, collected w/ Bartoš)............
12.40	"Folk Songs of Moravia Newly Collected," 2,057 songs w/ introduction (ed1901, collab Bartoš) ....
12.41	"Love Songs of Moravia," 150 groups of folksong variants (p1930, collab Váša) ....

13. ARRANGEMENTS OF WORKS OF OTHERS

13.1	Dvořák: "Moravian Duets" (arr ca1877 & 1884; ch & pf) ....
13.2	Liszt: "Messe pour orgue," S264 (arr1901; ch & org) ....
13.3	Grieg: "Taking Land," from opera: Olav Trygvason (arr ca1902 as part of cantata for vv, ch & orch)...........
13.4	Czech folk carol: "Christ the Lord is born" (ca1909; pf acc) ....
13.5	Komenský: "Lullaby" (p1920; pf acc)
13.6	Haydn: Austrian National Anthem (God Save the King), HobXXVIa/43 (arr for 1v & org)............

* * * * *

KABALEVSKY, Dmitri Borisovich
1904–1987

1. STAGE WORKS

Operas:

1.1	"Colas Breugnon," 3 acts (c1936–8, Bragin after Rolland; r1969 as Op.90)	Op.24 / Op.90
1.2	"Into the Fire," 4 acts (c1942, Soldar)	Op.37
1.3	"The Taras family," 4 acts (c1947, r1950, Tsenin after Gorbatov)	Op.47
1.4	"Nikita Vershinin" (c1954–5, Tsenin after Ivanov)	Op.53
1.5	"In the Magic Forest," scenes for children (c1958; narrator, ch & pf)	Op.62
1.6	"The Sisters," 3 act lyrical opera (c1967; also see film)	Op.83

Operettas:

1.7	"Spring Sings," 3 acts (c1957)	Op.58

Ballets:

1.8	"Golden Ears of Corn," 3 scenes (c1939–40, unfin)	Op.28

Incid music:

1.9	"Earth and Heaven" (c1932)
1.10	"Mstislav Udaloy" (c1932, Prut)
1.11	"The Jesters" (The Comedians) (c1933, Ostrovsky)
1.12	"The Destruction of the Squadron" (c1934, Korneychuk)
1.13	"Road of Flowers" (c1934, Korneychuk)
1.14	"Eastern Battalion" (c1934)
1.15	"Glory" (c1935, Ghusev)
1.16	"Measure for Measure" (c1938, Shakespeare)
1.17	"Friendship" (c1938, Ghusev)
1.18	"Inventor and Comedian" (c1938, Danyel)
1.19	"Devil's Bridge" (c1939, Tolstoy)
1.20	"The School for Scandal" (c1939, Sheridan transl Lozinsky)
1.21	"Madame Bovary" (c1939, Koonen after Flaubert)
1.22	"A City of the Masters" (c1940, Gabbe)
1.23	"The Barber of Seville" (c1940, Beaumarchais transl Lyubimov)
1.24	"Dombey and Son" (c1949, Venkstern after Dickens)
1.25	"Romeo and Juliet" (c1956, Shakespeare transl Pasternak) (also see opera c by Gounod, ballet c by Prokofiev Op.64, incid music c by Milhaud Op.161 & R. Strauss AV86, film score c by Khachaturian, symphony c by Berlioz Op.17, H79)

Radio:

1.26	"As You Like It" (c1935, Shakespeare) (also see overture c by Castelnuovo-Tedesco Op.166)
1.27	"William Tell" (c1937, after Schiller)
1.28	"Don Quixote" (c1944, Boghomazov after Cervantes)
1.29	"Feasts of the Wise Crocodile" (c1954, Barto & Zelenaya)
1.30	"Club of the Celebrated Captains" (c1955)

Film:

1.31	"Petersburg Night" (c1933, Roshal & Stroevoy)
1.32	"Aerograd" (c1935, Dovzhenko)
1.33	"Shchors" (c1937–8, Dovzhenko)
1.34	"Anton Ivanovich is Angry" (c1940, Ivanovsky)
1.35	"First Class Girl" (c1946, Frez)
1.36	"Academician Ivan Pavlov" (c1946, Roshal)
1.37	"Musorgsky" (c1950, Roshal)
1.38	"Unfriendly Winds" (c1953, Kalatozov)
1.39	"Freemen" (c1955, Roshal after Ghladkov's novel)
1.40	"The Sisters" (c1959, Roshal after Tolstoy; also see opera)
1.41	"The Year '18" (c1959, Roshal after Tolstoy)
1.42	"The Gloomy Morning" (c1959, Roshal after Tolstoy)

2. SYMPHONIES

2.1	Symphony No.1 in C-sharp minor (c1932)	Op.18
2.2	Symphony No.2 in C minor (c1934)	Op.19
2.3	Symphony No.3 in B-flat minor, "Requiem" (c1933, Aseyev; w/ ch)	Op.22
2.4	Symphony No.4 in C minor (c1956)	Op.54

3. OTHER ORCHESTRAL WORKS

4. CONCERTOS, SOLO INSTR & ORCH

Pf & orch:

Vn & orch:

Vc & orch:

5. STRING QUARTETS

6. OTHER CHAMBER MUSIC

Vn & pf:

Vc & pf:

Vc solo:

7. PIANO SONATAS

8. OTHER PIANO WORKS

8.74	No.8 "Song," in D minor	
8.75	No.9 "A Little Dance"	
8.76	No.10 "March"	
8.77	No.11 "Song of Autumn," in B minor	
8.78	No.12 "Scherzo," in C major	
8.79	No.13 "Waltz," in C major	
8.80	No.14 "A Fable," in A major	
8.81	No.15 "Jumping," in C major	
8.82	No.16 "A Sad Story," in E minor	
8.83	No.17 "Folk Dance," in D major	
8.84	No.18 "Galop," in C major	
8.85	No.19 "Prelude," in G minor	
8.86	No.20 "Clowns" (The Clown)	
8.87	No.21 "Improvisation," in D minor	
8.88	No.22 "A Short Story," in A minor	
8.89	No.23 "Slow Waltz," in A minor	
8.90	No.24 "A Happy Outing," in E major	
8.91	"Rondo," in A minor (c1952)	Op.59
8.92	"4 Rondos" (c1959): No.1 "March"	Op.60
8.93	No.2 "Dance"	
8.94	No.3 "Song"	
8.95	No.4 "Toccata"	
8.96	"6 Preludes & Fugues" (c1958–9, for children): No.1 "2-Voice Fugue"	Op.61
8.97	No.2 "2-Voice Fugue"	
8.98	No.3 "3-Voice Fugue"	
8.99	No.4 "3-Voice Fugue"	
8.100	No.5 "3-Voice Fugue"	
8.101	No.6 "4-Voice Fugue"	
8.102	"Recitative and Rondo" (for children)	Op.84
8.103	10 "Variations" (for children), Book I. (on American themes)	Op.85
8.104	II. (on French themes)	
8.105	III. (on Japanese themes)	

Collections:

8.106	"Piano Music for Children and Youth," 13 Vols (p1970–3, collection of pieces c1927–1971)	

9. CHORAL WORKS

9.1	"Poem of Struggle" (c1930, Zharov; ch & orch)	Op.12
9.2	"Parade of Youth" (c1941, child ch & orch)	Op.31
9.3	"The Mighty Homeland," cantata (c1941–2, various authors; 2vv, ch & orch)	Op.35
9.4	"The People's Avengers," suite (c1942, Dolmatovsky; ch & orch)	Op.36
9.5	"Song of Morning, Spring & Peace," cantata (c1957–8, Solodar; child ch & orch)	Op.57
9.6	"Leninists" (c1959, Dolmatovsky; child ch, youth ch & adult ch)	Op.63
9.7	"Requiem" (c1962, Rozhdzhestvensky; mS, Bar, d ch & orch)	Op.72
9.8	"Of the Homeland," cantata (c1965, Solodar; child ch & orch)	Op.82
9.9	"Letter to the 30th Century," oratorio (c1972; vv, ch & orch, inc)	Op.93

10. SONGS (w/ pf)

10.1	"3 Poems" (c1927, Blok)	Op.4
10.2	"8 Comic Songs" (c1929–30, Katayev)	Op.11
10.3	"8 Songs" (c1932; child ch & pf)	Op.17
10.4	"3 Vocal Monologues" (c1941, Kobynyev)	Op.33
10.5	"7 Merry Songs," settings of English nursery rhymes (c1944–5)	Op.41
10.6	"10 Sonnets" (c1953–4, Shakespeare transl Marshak) (also see Castelnuovo-Tedesco Op.125, Britten Op.60/8 & Shostakovich Op.62/5): 1. "Sonnet 8": "Music to hear, why hear'st thou music sadly"	Op.52
10.7	2. "Sonnet 13": "O that you were yourself! but, love, you are"	
10.8	3. "Sonnet 27": "Weary with toil, I haste me to my bed"	
10.9	4. "Sonnet 30": "When to the sessions of sweet silent thought"	
10.10	5. "Sonnet 71": "No longer mourn for me" (also see Vaughan Williams' choral work of 1896)	
10.11	6. "Sonnet 76": "Why is my verse so barren of new pride?"	
10.12	7. "Sonnet 81": "Or I shall live your epitaph to make"	
10.13	8. "Sonnet 90": "Then hate me when thou wilt, if ever, now"	
10.14	9. "Sonnet 102": "My love is strength'ned, though more weak in seeming"	
10.15	10. "Sonnet 153": "Cupid laid by his brand and fell asleep"	
10.16	"Camp of Friendship," 6 pioneer songs (c1961)	Op.66
10.17	"3 Songs of the Cuban Revolution" (c1963)	Op.73
10.18	"5 Romances" (c1963–4, Gamzatov transl Ghrebnev)	Op.76

* * * * *

1. STAGE WORKS

Operas:

1.1   *Operetta (c1887, for Ukrainian group of Kropivnitzky, lost)* ....

1.2   *"Princess Mara" (ca1894, Fofanov, project, extant frag of: Sbirajte podruzhky for fem ch & pf)* ....

1.3   "In 1812" (c1899–1900, Mamontov, inc): ....
   1. "Prologue"
   2. *(pf sketches)*
   3. "Romance"
   4. "Spanish Song" (Ramon's Song) (1v & ch)

Incid music:

1.4   "Tsar Boris" (c1898, Tolstoy; arr for pf duet): ....
         . "Overture"
         . "Act II—Entr'acte"
         . "Act III—Entr'acte"
         . "Act IV—Entr'acte"
         . "Act V—Entr'acte"
         . "Fanfare" I & II

2. SYMPHONIES

2.1   Symphony No.1 in G minor (c1894–5) ....

2.2   Symphony No.2 in A major (c1895–7) ....

3. OTHER ORCHESTRAL WORKS

3.1   "Fugue" (Allegro moderato), in D minor (c1889) ....

3.2   "Fugue" (Moderato), in D minor (c1889) ....

3.3   "The Nymphs," sym picture (c1889, after Turgenev) ....

3.4   "Serenade" (c1891; strings; arr for pf duet 1952) ....

3.5   "Suite," 4 movts (c1891–2; arr for pf duet 1901) ....

3.6   "Bilina" (Epic poem), overture (c ?1892; arr for pf duet 1952) ....

3.7   "Overture," in D minor (c1894; arr for pf duet 1894) ....

3.8   "Intermezzo" No.1 in F-sharp minor (c1896) ....

3.9   "Intermezzo" No.2 in G major (c1897) ....

3.10 "The Cedar and the Palm," sym picture (c1897–8, after Heine, sketches from 1894) ....

4. STRING QUARTETS

4.1   *Pieces for str qt (lost)* ....

5. PIANO

5.1   *"Sadness" (c1884, lost; also see: Chanson triste of 1892–3)* ....

5.2   "Scherzo," in F major (c1888–9) ....

5.3   "Chanson triste," in G minor (c1892–3, = ?r vers of: Sadness of 1884) ....

5.4   "Russian intermezzo," in F minor (c1894) ....

5.5   "Minuet," in E major (c1894) ....

5.6   "Waltz," in A major (c1894) ....

5.7   "Nocturne," in F-sharp minor (c1894) ....

5.8   "Elegy," in B-flat minor (c1894) ....

5.9   "Moderato," in E-flat minor (p1950) ....

Pf duet:

5.10 "Polonaise," in B-flat major (on a theme from: Sym No.1 in G minor) ....

6. CHORAL WORKS

6.1   *"Cherubic hymn" No.1 (c1885; ch, lost)* ....

6.2   *"Cherubic hymn" No.2 (c1886; ch, lost)* ....

6.3   *"Little chorus" (c1887; ch, lost)* ....

6.4   *"The mountain tops" (c1887, Lermontov; ch, lost)* ....

6.5   *"Lord, our Lord," 4-voice fugue in D major (c1888–9; ch)* ....

6.6   "Christe eleison," double 4-voice fugue (c ?1889; ch) ....

6.7   *"Ioann Damaskin," cantata (c1890, Tolstoy; vv, ch & orch, lost; pf arr extant)* ....

6.8   "A beautiful girl sits on the sea" (c1894, Lermontov; fem ch & orch) ....

6.9   "The Triumph of Lilliput" (c?; ch & pf) ....

7. MISC VOCAL

7.1   "Come to me" (Koltsov; S, A, B & pf) ....

8. SONGS (w/ pf)

8.1   "When life is weighed down with suffering" (c1887, Polivanov)...
8.2   "On your lovely little shoulder dear" (c1887, Heine transl Fyodorov) ....
8.3   "On the old burial mound" (c1887, Nikitin) ....
8.4   "The gentle stars shone down on us" (c1894, Pleshcheyev)..
8.5   "Bright stars" (c1894, Fofanov) ....
8.6   "There was an old king" (c1894, Pleshcheyev) ....
8.7   16 "Musical Letters" (c1892–9)...
8.8   "Prayer" (c1900, Pleshcheyev) ....
8.9   "Bells" (c1900) ....
8.10   "A present for 1 January 1900"..

8.11   "Do not ask why I smile in thought" (c?, p1916, Pushkin) ....
8.12   "I am yours, my darling" (c?, Heine transl Fyodorov) ....
8.13   "I would like to make my songs into wonderful flowers" (c?, Heine transl Fyodorov) ....

9. ARRANGEMENTS OF WORKS OF OTHERS

9.1   *Musorgsky: Scene from opera Khovanshchina (orchd1897, lost)* ....
9.2   *Schumann: Nos.3 & 4 of: Bilder aus Osten, Op.66 (orchd, lost)* ....

* * * * *

1. STAGE WORKS

Ballets:

1.1   "Happiness," 3 acts, 6 scenes (c1939, Ovanesian-Kimik) ....

1.2   "Gayaneh," 4 acts (c1942, Derzhavin, incl music from ballet: Happiness; 2nd vers 1952; 3rd 1957) ....

1.3   "Spartacus," 4 acts, 9 scenes (c1950–4, Volkov): ....

       I: 1. "Triumph of Rome"

           2. "Slave market"

           3. "Circus"

       II: 4. "Barracks of gladiators"

           5. "Appian Way"

           6. "Banquet at Crassus's"

       III: 7. "Spartacus's tent"

           8. "Crassus's tent"

       IV: 9. "Death of Spartacus" (Epilogue)

Incid music:

1.4   "Ruined Hearth" (ca1929–32, Sundukian) ....

1.5   "Khatabala" (ca1929–32, Sundukian)...

1.6   "Dentist from the East" (ca1929–32, Paronian) ....

1.7   "Macbeth" (c1954, Shakespeare transl Masiian & Akhumian; 2nd setting 1955) (also see operas c by
Bloch & Verdi, incid music c by Bacewicz, Milhaud Op.175, Spohr WoO 55 & Sullivan) ....

1.8   "The Valencian Widow" (c1940, Vega)...

1.9   "Masquerade" (c1941, Lermontov) ....

1.10   "The Kremlin Chimes" (c1942, Pogodin) ....

1.11   "Deep Prospecting" (c1943, Kron) ....

1.12   "Tale of Truth" (c1946, Aliger) ....

1.13   "Ilya Golovin" (c1949, Mikhalkov) ....

1.14   "The Two Gentlemen of Verona" (c1952, Shakespeare) (also see incid music c by Rodrigo).....................

1.15   "Guardian Angel from Nebraska" (c1953, Yakovtzon) ....

1.16   "Lermontov" (c1954, Lavrenev) ....

1.17   "The Merry Wives of Windsor" (c1957, Shakespeare) (also see opera c by Vaughan Williams: Sir John
in Love, incid music c by Sullivan & Vaughan Williams) ....

1.18   "King Lear" (c1958, Shakespeare) (also see incid music c by Balakirev, Debussy L109, Dupré &
Shostakovich Op.58a, film score c by Shostakovich Op.137) ....

Film:

1.19   "Pepo" (c1934–5, Bek-Nazarov, after Sundukian's play) ....

1.20   "Zangezur," documentary (c1937–8, Bek-Nazarov) ....

1.21   "Orchard" (c1938, Dostal, 1st artistic film made in Tadzhikistan) ....

1.22   "Salavat Ulayev," documentary (c1939, Protazanov) ....

1.23   "Prisoner No.217," anti-Nazi film (c1944–5, Romm) ....

1.24   "The Russian Question" (c1947, Romm, after Simonov) ....

1.25   "They have their Motherland" (c1948, Legoshtchin & Feinzimmer) ....

1.26   "Vladimir Ilyich Lenin," documentary (c1948, Romm) ....

1.27   "The Battle of Stalingrad," 2 series (c1949) ....

1.28   "The Secret Mission" (c1950, Romm) ....

1.29   "Admiral Ushakov" (c1953, Romm) ....

1.30   "Ships storm bastions" (c1953, Romm, sequel to film: Admiral Ushakov)...

1.31   "Sultanate" (c1955, Brozhovskiy & Riskulov) ....

1.32   "Othello" (c1955, Utkevitch after Shakespeare) (also see operas c by Rossini & Verdi) ....

1.33   "Romeo and Juliet" (c1956) (also see opera c by Gounod, ballet c by Prokofiev Op.64, incid music c by
Kabalevsky, Milhaud Op.161 & R. Strauss AV86, symphony c by Berlioz Op.17, H79) ....

1.34   "The Duel" (c1957, Petrov) ....

1a. SELECTIONS FROM STAGE WORKS (Nos. of sections in The Gramophone)

1a.2   "Gayaneh," ballet: ....

       1. "Sabre Dance"

       2. "Ayesha's Dance"

       3. "Dance of the Rose Maidens"

       4. "Dance of the Kurds"

       5. "Lullaby"

       6. "Dance of the Young Kurds"

       7. "Armen's Variation"

       8. "Lexghinka"

       9. "Gopak"

      10. "Introduction" (Andante)

      11. "Gayaneh's adagio"

      12. "Fire"

      13. "Lyrical duo"

3. ORCHESTRAL SUITES

3.1	"Dance Suite" (c1932–3): No.1 "Armenian-Azerbaidzhanian Dance" (Allegretto) ....
3.2	No.2 "Armenian circular dance" (Allegretto ma non troppo)
3.3	No.3 "Uzbek dance" (Largo—Andante—Allegro—Largo)
3.4	No.4 "Uzbek march" (Allegro ma non troppo)
3.5	No.5 "Lezghinka" (Dance) (Presto)
3.6	"Gayaneh" Suite No.1 (c1943, from ballet): No.1 "Entrance" (Andante) ....
3.7	No.2 "Dance of the girls"
3.8	No.3 "Awakening and dance of Aisha"
3.9	No.4 "Mountaineers' dance"
3.10	No.5 "Lullaby"
3.11	No.6 "Scena: Gayaneh & Ghiko"
3.12	No.7 "Adagio of Gayaneh"
3.13	No.8 "Lezghinka" (Dance)
3.14	"Gayaneh" Suite No.2 (c1943, from ballet): No.1 "Welcome dance" ....
3.15	No.2 "Lyrical duet"
3.16	No.3 "Russian dance"
3.17	No.4 "Variations of Nune"
3.18	No.5 "Dance of the old man and the carpet-maker"
3.19	No.6 "Dramatic scene"
3.20	"Gayaneh" Suite No.3 (c1943, from ballet): No.1 "Cotton harvest" ....
3.21	No.2 "Dance of the young Kurds"
3.22	No.3 "Entrance and dance of the old men"
3.23	No.4 "Scene of the carpet-makers"
3.24	No.5 "Dance with swords"
3.25	No.6 "Hopák" (Ukrainian folk dance)
3.26	"Masquerade," suite (c1943, from incid music): No.1 "Waltz" ....
3.27	No.2 "Nocturne"
3.28	No.3 "Mazurka"
3.29	No.4 "Romance"
3.30	No.5 "Galop"
3.31	"The Battle on the River Volga" (The Battle of Stalingrad), suite (c1950): No.1 "City on the river Volga" ......
3.32	No.2 "Invasion"
3.33	No.3 "City on fire"
3.34	No.4 "The enemy is doomed"
3.35	No.5 "Into the battle for the Motherland!"
3.36	No.6 "Eternal Glory to the Heroes"
3.37	No.7 "Forward to Victory"
3.38	No.8 "There is a rock on the river Volga"
3.39	"The Valencian Widow," suite (c1953, from incid music) ....
3.40	"Spartacus" Suite No.1 (c1955–7, from ballet): No.1 "Entrance and dance of nymphs" ....
3.41	No.2 "Entrance, Adagio of Eghina and Gharmodya (Harmondius)"
3.42	No.3 "Variation of Eghina and bacchanalia"
3.43	No.4 "Scene and dance"
3.44	No.5 "Dance"
3.45	No.6 "Spartacus's victory"
3.46	"Spartacus" Suite No.2 (c1955–7, from ballet): No.1 "Adagio of Spartacus and Phrygia" ....
3.47	No.2 "Entrance of merchants, dance of Roman courtesan, danceuse"
3.48	No.3 "Entrance of Spartacus, quarrel scene, betrayal of Gharmodya (Harmondius)"
3.49	No.4 "Dance of pirates"
3.50	"Spartacus" Suite No.3 (c1955–7, from ballet): No.1 "Town Square" ....
3.51	No.2 "Dance of the Greek slave"
3.52	No.3 "Egyptian danceuse"
3.53	No.4 "Phrigia's dance and farewell scene"
3.54	No.5 "Dance of the young Thracians with swords"
3.55	"Lermontov Suite" (c1955): No.1 "Entrance" ....
3.56	No.2 "Waltz"
3.57	No.3 "Mazurka"
3.58	No.4 "Intermezzo and Finale"
3.59	"Othello," suite (c1956, after film): No.1 "Prologue and Introduction" ....
3.60	No.2 "Desdemona's Arioso"
3.61	No.3 "Vineyards"
3.62	No.4 "Venice" (Nocturne)
3.63	No.5 "Nocturnal Murder" (Rodrigo's Death)
3.64	No.6 "Othello's Despair"
3.65	No.7 "A fit of Jealousy"
3.66	No.8 "Othello's arrival"
3.67	No.9 "The Striking of Desdemona"
3.68	No.10 "Othello's Farewell"
3.69	No.11 "Finale"

4. OTHER ORCHESTRAL WORKS

4.1   "Choreographic Waltz" (c1944; also see for pf) ....

4.2   "Russian Fantasy" (c1945, from ballet: Happiness) ....

4.3   "Ode in Memory of Lenin" (c1949, from film: Vladimir Ilyich Lenin) ....

4.4   "Triumphal (Solemn) Poem" (c1952) ....

4.5   "Greetings Overture" (c1959) ....

Milit or brass bands:

4.6   March No.1 (c1929; orchd Ivanov-Radkevich) ....

4.7   March No.2 (c1930, for the 10th anniversary of Armenian S.S.R.) ....

4.8   "2 Pieces" (c1933, after Armenian folksongs): No.1 "Dancing piece" ....

4.9   No.2 "Dance"

4.10   "2 Pieces" (c1933, after Uzbek folksongs) ....

4.11   "Zangezurian March" (No.5) (c1938, from film: Zangezur) ....

4.12   "To the Heroes of the World War II," march (c1942) ....

5. CONCERTOS, SOLO INSTR & ORCH

Pf & orch:

5.1   Piano Concerto in D-flat major (c1936) ....

Vn & orch:

5.2   Violin Concerto in D minor (c1940; transcr Rampal for fl & orch) ....

5.3   "Concerto-Rhapsody" (c1961) ....

Vc & orch:

5.4   Cello Concerto (c1946) ....

5.5   "Concerto-Rhapsody" (c1963) ....

6. STRING QUARTETS

6.1   "Double Fugue" (c1932; r1967 as: Recitative and Fugue) ....

7. OTHER CHAMBER MUSIC

3 insts:

7.1   Trio in G minor (c1932; vn, cl & pf) ....

Vn & pf:

7.2   "Dance," in B-flat major (c1926) Op.1

7.3   "Song-Poem" (c1929) ....

7.4   "Allegretto" (c1929) ....

7.5   Violin Sonata in D major (c1932) ....

8. PIANO SONATAS

8.1   Piano Sonata (c1961, revised later) ....

9. OTHER PIANO MUSIC

9.1   "Waltz-Caprice" (c1926) ....

9.2   "Poem," in C-sharp minor (c1927) ....

9.3   "6 Fugues" (c1929) ....

9.4   "Toccata" (c1932) ....

9.5   "Round dance" (c1932, on a theme from Davidenko's song) ....

9.6   "Choreographic Waltz" (c1944; also see for orch) ....

9.7   "Masquerade Suite" (c1945, from incid music): No.1 "Waltz" (transcr Khachaturian 1953) ....

9.8   *No.2 "Nocturne" (transcr Dolukhanian)*

9.9   *No.3 "Mazurka" (transcr Dolukhanian)*

9.10   *No.4 "Romance" (transcr Dolukhanian)*

9.11   *No.5 "Gallop" (transcr Dolukhanian)*

9.12   "Children's Album" (No.1) (c1926–47): No.1 "Andantino" (c1926) ....

9.13   No.2 "It is not allowed to play today"

9.14	No.3 "Lyado seriously hurt"
9.15	No.4 "Birthday"
9.16	No.5 "Etude"
9.17	No.6 "Musical Picture"
9.18	No.7 "Cavalry"
9.19	No.8 "Invention" (Adagio from ballet: Gayaneh)
9.20	No.9 "Imitating people"
9.21	No.10 "Fugue"
9.22	"Selections from film score Othello" (p1956, transcr Khachaturian): No.1 "Prologue" ....
9.23	No.2 "Desdemone's vocalise" (also see Songs)
9.24	No.3 "Scene in the vineyard"
9.25	No.4 "Soldier's song" (also see Choral works)
9.26	No.5 "Venice" (Nocturne)
9.27	No.6 "Song for Sallow" (also see Songs)
9.28	No.7 "Othello's Despair"
9.29	"Selections from Macbeth," 4 pieces (c1955, from incid music) ....
9.30	"Sonatina," in C major (c1959) ....
9.31	"Children's Album No.2" (c1965): No.1 "Skipping rope" ....
9.32	No.2 "An evening tale"
9.33	No.3 "Oriental dance"
9.34	No.4 "Barsik on the swings"
9.35	No.5 "Playing the tambourine"
9.36	No.6 "Two funny aunties quarrelling"
9.37	No.7 "Funeral procession"
9.38	No.8 "Rhythmic gymnastics"
9.39	No.9 "Toccata"
9.40	No.10 "Fugue"

2 Pf:

9.41	"Piano Suite" (c1944, in 3 parts) ....

10. CHORAL WORKS

10.1	"Song of the Black Sea Fleet" (c1931, Steinberg; m ch) ....
10.2	"Comsomol-miners' Song" (c1932, Sitkovskoy; ch & pf) ....
10.3	"3 Songs of Young Pioneers" (c1933, Vladimirskoy & Mikhalkov; child ch & pf) ....
10.4	"Poem about Stalin" (c1938; ch & orch) ....
10.5	"Guards' March" (c1942, Lebedev-Kumatch) ....
10.6	"Glory to our Motherland" (c1943, Lebedev-Kumatch; 1v, ch & pf) ....
10.7	"What children dream about" (c1949, Vinnikov; child ch & pf) ....
10.8	"March Song" (c1953, Surkov; m ch, from film: Admiral Ushakov) ....
10.9	"Song of Russian Sailors" (c1953, Surkov; m ch, from film: Ships storm bastions) ....
10.10	"Soldier's Song" (c1955, from film: Othello) ....
10.11	"Ode of Joy" (c1956; mS, ch, 10 harps, vns & orch) ....
10.12	Compilations of folksongs (Armenian, Uzbek, Tadzhik, Turkmenian, Tatar, Bashkir & other) ......

11. VOICE & ORCHESTRA

11.1	"3 Concert Arias" (c1944–6, Armenian poets): 1. "Poem" ....
11.2	2. "Legend"
11.3	3. "Dithyramb"
11.4	"Ballade about the Fatherland" (c1961, Garnakeryan; B & orch) ....

12. SONGS (w/ pf)

12.1	"Our future" (c1931, Burunov) ....
12.2	"New song" (c1931, Tcharenetz) ....
12.3	"An ear started to ripen" (c1932, Gidash) ....
12.4	"Pepo's song" (c1934, Tcharenetz, from film: Pepo) ....
12.5	"On the Gogol's Boulevard" (c1935, Mikhalkov) ....
12.6	"Into the battle" (c1936, Smolyan) ....
12.7	"My dear orchard" (c1936, Lebedev-Kumatch, from film: Orchard) ....
12.8	"Daughters of Iran" (c1939, Lakhuta) ....
12.9	"In the rain" (c1939, Rodyonov) ....
12.10	"Nina's romance" (c1941, from incid music: Masquerade) ....
12.11	"Captain Gastello" (c1941, Lughin) ....
12.12	"Baltic Sea" (c1941, Rodyonov) ....
12.13	"Formidable Ural Mountains" (c1942, Barto) ....
12.14	"A maid of the Ural Mountains" (c1942, Slavin) ....
12.15	"Men of the Ural Mountains fight well" (c1942, Barto) ....
12.16	"I need you" (c1943, Slavin) ....

* * * * *

KODÁLY, Zoltán
1882–1967

1. STAGE WORKS

Operas:

1.1   "Háry János," 5 scene Singspiel (c1925–7, Paulini & Harsányi; in Hung & Ger) Op.15
1.2   "Czinka Panna," 3 act Singspiel (c1946–8, Balázs) ....

Ballet:

1.3   "Kuruc Tale" (p1935, Harsányi, music = Dances of Marosszék & Dances of Galánta) ....

Incid music:

1.4   *"The Hunchback of the Notre Dame," parody (c1902; small orch, lost)* ....
1.5   *"Le Cid," parody (c1903; small orch, lost)* ....
1.6   "A nagybácsi" (The Uncle) (c1904; small orch) ....
1.7   "Pacsirtaszó" (The Song of the Lark) (c1917, Móricz; 1v & small orch) ....
1.8   "Székely Fonó" (The Transylvanian Spinning Room), 1 act lyrical play (c1924–32; in Hung, Ger, Eng & It).

Film:

1.9   "Kádár Kata" (Mother, listen) (c1943; mS & small orch) ....

2. SYMPHONIES

2.1   Symphony in C major (c1930s–61) ....

3. OTHER ORCHESTRAL WORKS

3.1   *Overture in D minor (c1897, lost)* ....
3.2   "Summer Evening" (c1906, r1929–30) ....
3.3   "Old Hungarian Soldier's Songs" (c1917; arr as: Hungarian Rondo for vc & pf) ....
3.4   "Ballet Music" (c1925; intended for opera: Háry János, Op.15; arr Földes for pf) ....
3.5   "Háry János," suite (c1927; arr for brass; arr Szatmári & Földes for pf; arr Szigeti for vn & pf): No.1 "Prelude: A Fairy Tale Begins" ....
3.6   No.2 "Viennese Musical Clock"
3.7   No.3 "Song"
3.8   No.4 "The Battle and Defeat of Napoleon"
3.9   No.5 "Intermezzo"
3.10   No.6 "Entrance of the Emperor and His Court"
3.11   "Theatre Overture" (c1927; 2 vers; orig for opera: Háry János, Op.15) ....
3.12   "Dances of Marosszék" (c1930, after pf work; arr for ballet in: Kuruc Tale) ....
3.13   "Dances of Galánta" (c1933; arr for ballet in: Kuruc Tale; red Kenessey for pf 1935) ....
3.14   "Felszállott a Páva" (Peacock Variations) (c1938–9, on a Hung folksong: The Peacock) ....
3.15   "Concerto for Orchestra" (c1939–40) ....
3.16   "Honvéd Parad March" (c1948; brass band, from opera: Háry János, Op.15) ....
3.17   "Minuetto Serio" (c1948–53, enlarged from opera: Czinka Panna) ....

4. STRING QUARTETS

4.1   String Quartet No.1 (c1908–9) Op.2
4.2   String Quartet No.2 (c1916–8) Op.10

5. OTHER CHAMBER MUSIC

4 insts:

5.1   Wind Quartet (ca1960) ....

3 insts:

5.2   Trio in E-flat major (c1899; 2vn & va) ....
5.3   "Intermezzo" (c1905; str trio) ....
5.4   "Serenade" (c1919–20; 2vn & va) Op.12

Vn & pf:

5.5   "Adagio" (c1905; vn/va/vc & pf; orchd Frid; arr Kresz for vn & chamber orch; arr Por for chamber orch) ......
5.6   "Feigin" (c1958, arr of song: Kálló double dance of 1937) ....

Vc & pf:

5.7 "Romance lyrique" (c1898) ....
5.8 Cello Sonata (c1909–10) Op.4
5.9 "Hungarian Rondo" (c1917; orig for orch: Old Hungarian Soldier's Songs) ....
5.10 "Sonatina" (c1921–2) ....

Other 2 insts:

5.11 Duo (c1914; vn & vc) Op.7

1 instr:

5.12 "Sonata" (c1915; vc) Op.8
5.13 "Capriccio" (c1915; vc) ....
5.14 "Calling to Campfire" (c1930; cl) ....
5.15 "Exercise" (c1942; vn, for Vásárhelyi-Gábriel: Violin Method) ....

6. PIANO

6.1 Piano pieces (c before 1900) ....
6.2 "Valsette" (c1907; arr Telmanyi for vn & pf) ....
6.3 "Méditation sur un motif de Claude Debussy" (c1907) ....
6.4 "9 Piano Pieces" (c1905–9): No.1 "Lento" Op.3
6.5 No.2 "Andante poco rubato"
6.6 No.3 "Lento"
6.7 No.4 "Allegretto scherzoso"
6.8 No.5 "V. (quos ego ...) Furioso"
6.9 No.6 "Moderato triste"
6.10 No.7 "Allegro giocoso"
6.11 No.8 "Allegretto grazioso"
6.12 No.9 "Allegro commodo, burlesco"
6.13 "7 Piano Pieces" (c1910–8; orchd Ránki): No.1 "Lento" Op.11
6.14 No.2 "Székely Lament. Rubato, parlando"
6.15 No.3 "... il pleure dans mon coeur, comme il pleut sur la ville. Allegretto malinconico"
6.16 No.4 "Epitaph. Rubato"
6.17 No.5 "Tranquillo"
6.18 No.6 "Székely Tune. Poco rubato"
6.19 No.7 "Rubato"
6.20 "Dances of Marosszék" (rondo w/ 3 interludes & coda) (c1927) ....
6.21 "Gyermektáncok" (Children's Dances) (c1945) ....
6.22 "24 Little Canons on the Black Keys" (c1945, educational work) ....

7. ORGAN

7.1 "Prelude" (c1931; orig for: Pange lingua) ....
7.2 "Csendes mise orgonára" (Organ Mass) (c1940–2; r1966 as: Organoedia) ....

8. CHORAL WORKS (w/ acc)

W/ orch:

8.1 "Assumpta est," offertorium (c1901; Bar, ch & orch) ....
8.2 "Psalmus Hungaricus" (c1923, Vég from Psalm 55; T, ch, child ch ad lib, orch & org; in Hung, Ger, Eng, Fr & It) Op.13
8.3 "Te Deum of Budavár" (c1936, Latin text; S, A, T, B, ch, orch & org) ....
8.4 "Missa brevis" (c1944, Latin text; ch & org or 3S, A, T, B, ch, orch & org ad lib) ....
8.5 "At the grave of the Martyrs" (c1945; ch & orch) ....
8.6 "Kálló double dance" (c1950; ch & folk-music orch) ....
8.7 "An Ode" (The Music Makers) (c1964, O'Shaughnessy; ch & orch; in Hung & Ger) (also see Elgar Op.69)

W/ insts:

8.8 *Mass (c before 1897; ch & org, lost)* ....
8.9 "Ave Maria" (c before 1900; ch & org) ....
8.10 5 "Tantum Ergo" (c1928; child ch & org) ....
8.11 "Pange lingua" (c1929; ch/child ch & org) ....
8.12 "Katonadal" (Soldiers' Song) (c1934; m ch, tpt & drum) ....
8.13 "Angyalok és Pásztorok" (Shepherds' Christmas Dance) (c1935, d child ch & recorder; in Hung, Ger & Eng)
8.14 "Hymn to King Saint Stephen" (c1938; ch & org; also for unacc ch / m ch / fem ch / child ch) ....
8.15 "Vejnemöjnen's Music" (c1944; high vv ch & harp/pf) ....
8.16 "Geneva Psalm 114" (c1952, transl Molnár; ch & org) ....

8.17 "Intermezzo" (c1956; ch & pf, from opera: Háry János, Op.15)..

8.18 "Magyar mise" (Hungarian Mass) (c1966; unison ch & org)..

8.19 "Laudes organi" (c1966; ch & org)..

9. CHORAL WORKS (w/ out acc)

Mixed ch:

9.1   "Miserere" (Psalm 51) (c1903; d ch)..

9.2   "Este" (Evening) (c1904, Gyulai; S & ch; in Hung, Ger & Eng)..

9.3   "Mátrai Képek" (Mátra Pictures) (c1931; in Hung, Ger & Eng)..

9.4   "Nagyszalontai Köszöntő" (A Birthday Greeting) (c1931; in Hung, Ger & Eng)..............................

9.5   "Öregek" (The Aged) (c1933, Weöres; in Hung, Ger & Eng)..

9.6   "Székely Keserves" (Transylvanian Lament) (c1934; in Hung, Ger & Eng).....................................

9.7   "Jézus és a Kufárok" (Jesus and the Traders) (c1934, Weöres after Bible; in Hung, Ger & Eng).........

9.8   "Akik Mindig Elkésnek" (Too Late) (c1934, Ady; in Hung, Ger & Eng)...

9.9   "Horatii Carmen II.10" (Rectius vives) (c1934)...

9.10 "Liszt Ferenchez" (Ode to Franz Liszt) (c1936, Vörösmarty; in Hung, Ger & Eng)........................

9.11 "Molnár Anna" (c1936; in Hung, Ger & Eng)...

9.12 "A Magyarokhoz" (Song of Faith), 4-part canon (c1936, Berzsenyi)..

9.13 "Esti Dal" (Evening Song) (c1938; also for child ch /m ch)...

9.14 "Norvég Lányok" (Norwegian Girls) (c1940, Weöres)...

9.15 "Balassi Bálint Elfelejtett Éneke" (The Forgotten Song of Bálint Balassi) (c1942, Gazdag)...............

9.16 "Első Áldozás" (The First Holy Communion) (c1942, Szedő; also see song).................................

9.17 "Szép könyörgés" (Invocation) (c1943, Balassa)...

9.18 "A Székelyekhez" (To the Magyars) (c1943, Petőfi; also for child ch)..

9.19 "A 121. Genfi Zsoltár" (The Geneva Psalm 121) (c1943)...

9.20 "Song at Advent" (O come, Emmanuel) (c1943, 18th cent French missal; also see song).................

9.21 "Cohors Generosa" (Hungarian students' greeting of 1777) (c1943, Latin text).............................

9.22 "Song from Gömör" (c1943)...

9.23 "Csatadal" (Battle Song) (c1943, Petőfi; d ch)..

9.24 "Sirató Ének" (Dirge) (c1947, Bodrogh)...

9.25 "A Magyar Nemzet" (The Hungarian Nation) (c1947, Petőfi)...

9.26 "A Szabadság Himnusza" (La marseillaise) (c1948, transl Jankovich; also for m ch / fem ch).........

9.27 "Naphimnusz" (Adoration) (c1948, Jewish Folk Choruses, collected Fraknoi).................................

9.28 "Jelige" (Epigraph / Motto) (c1948, Jankovich; also for m ch / child ch)...

9.29 "Az 50. Genfi Zsoltár" (The Geneva Psalm No.50) (c1948; also for child ch)...................................

9.30 "Békességóhajtás—1801" (Wish for Peace—The Year 1801) (c1953, Virág)..................................

9.31 "Zrínyi Szózata" (Hymn of Zrínyi / Zrínyi's Appeal) (c1954, Zrínyi; Bar & ch; in Hung & Eng)..........

9.32 "Magyarország Cimere" (The Code of Arms of Hungary) (c1956, Vörösmarty)................................

9.33 "I Will Look for Death" (c1959, Masefield transl Kistétényi)...

9.34 "Sik Sándor's Te Deum" (c1961)...

9.35 "Media vita in morte sumus" (c1961, for death of M. Seiber)...

9.36 "Jövel, Szentlélek Uristen" (Come, Holy Ghost) (ca1961, Batizi)..

9.37 "An Ode for Music" (c1963, Collins, Shakespeare) ....

9.38 "Mohács" (c1965, Kisfaludy)..

M ch:

9.39 "Stabat Mater" (c1898) ....

9.40 "2 Drinking Songs" (c1913–7, Kölcsey, anon 17th cent; in Hung, Ger & Eng): 1. "Bordal" ....
9.41   2. "Mulató Gajd"

9.42 "Jesus Appears" (c1927) ....

9.43 "Canticum nuptiale" (c1928) ....

9.44 "Karádi Nóták" (Songs from Karád) (c1934)..

9.45 "Kit Kéne Élvenni" (The Bachelor / Whom to Marry?) (c1934; in Hung & Eng)...............................

9.46 "Horatius: Justum et Tenacem" (c1935, Horace) ....

9.47 "Huszt" (The Ruins) (c1936, Kölcsey; in Hung & Ger)...

9.48 "Felszállott a Páva" (The Peacock) (c1937, Ady; also for mixed ch)..

9.49 "Semmit ne Bánkódjál" (Cease your Bitter Weeping) (c1939, Szkhárosi Horvát; also for fem ch).......

9.50 "Rab Hazának" (The Son of an Enslaved Country) (c1944, Petőfi)...

9.51 "Isten Csodája" (God's Miracle): "Still, by a miracle, our country stands" (c1944, Petőfi) ....

9.52 "Élet vagy Halál" (To Live or Die) (c1947, Petőfi)..

9.53 "Hey, Bandi Büngözsdi" (c1947, Petőfi)...

9.54 "Nemzeti Dal" (National Song) (c1955, Petőfi) ....

9.55 "In András Fáy's Album" (c1956, Vörösmarty)...

9.56 "A Nándori Toronyőr" (The Watchman of Nándor) (c1956, Vörösmarty) ....

9.57 "A Franciaországi Változásokra" (To the Changes in France) (c1963, Batsányi) ....

Fem ch:

9.58 "2 Folksongs from Zobor" (c1908; 3S, 3A & ch; in Hung, Ger & Eng) ....

9.59 "Hegyi Éjszakák" (Mountain Nights) (c1923, r1955–6 & 1962; textless) ....

9.60 "4 Italian Madrigals" (c1932; Italian text) ....

9.61   "Ave Maria" (c1935; Latin text) ....
9.62   "Árva Vagyok" (Orphan Am I) (c1953) ....
9.63   "Meghalok, Meghalok" (Woe Is Me) (c1957; S, 3A & ch) ....

Children's ch / high vv ch:

9.64   "Villő" (The Straw Guy) (c1925; in Hung, Ger, Eng & Fr) ....
9.65   "Túrót Eszik a Cigány" (See, the Gypsy Munching Cheese) (c1925; in Hung, Ger, Eng & Fr) ....
9.66   "Gergelyjárás" (St. Gregory's Day) (c1926; in Hung, Ger, Eng & Fr) ....
9.67   "Lengyel László" (King László's Men) (c1927; in Hung, Ger, Eng & Fr) ....
9.68   "Jelenti Magát Jézus" (Jesus Appears) (c1927; arr for m ch 1944) ....
9.69   "A juhász" (The Shepherd) (c1928) ....
9.70   "A süket Sógor" (The Deaf Boatman) (c1928; in Hung, Ger, Eng & Fr) ....
9.71   "Cigánysirató" (Gypsy Lament) (c1928; in Hung, Ger, Eng & Fr) ....
9.72   "Isten kovácsa" (God's Blacksmith) (c1928; in Hung, Ger, Eng & Fr) ....
9.73   "Gólyanóta" (The Swallow's Wooing) (c1929; in Hung, Ger, Eng & Fr) ....
9.74   "Pünkösdölő" (Whitsuntide) (c1929; in Hung, Ger, Eng & Fr) ....
9.75   "Táncnóta" (Dancing Song) (c1929; in Hung, Ger, Eng & Fr) ....
9.76   "New Year's Greeting" (c1929; in Hung, Ger, Eng & Fr) ....
9.77   "Vszkereszt" (Epiphany) (c1933, Sik; in Hung, Ger & Eng) ....
9.78   "Nyulacska" (The Leveret) (c1934) ....
9.79   "Rorate" (c1935; child ch & fem ch) ....
9.80   "7 Easy children's choruses and 6 humorous canons" (c1936) ....
9.81   "Psalm 150" (de Theodore de Béze) (c1936, Béze; also for fem ch) ....
9.82   "The Bells" (c1937; d ch) ....
9.83   "Garden of Angels," 5 plays (c1937; child ch) ....
9.84   "Hajnövesztö" (Grow, tresses), children's song (c1937) ....
9.85   "Katalinka" (Ladybird) (c1937) ....
9.86   "3 Folksongs from Gömör" (c1937) ....
9.87   "The Filly" (c1937) ....
9.88   "Egyedem—begyedem" (Hippity, hoppity), children's song (c1938) ....
9.89   "Cú fől, lovam" (Gee-up, My Horse) (c1938) ....
9.90   "Csalfa sugár" (False spring) (c1938, Arany) ....
9.91   "Greeting on St John's Day" (c1939; boys' ch) ....
9.92   "Solmization Canon" (c1942) ....
9.93   "Singing Youth: Hungarian against Hungarian," canon (c1944) ....
9.94   "Singing Youth: Saint Agnes' Day" (c1945, Sik) ....
9.95   "Hymn of Liberty" (c1948; 2 arrs of: La marseillaise) ....
9.96   "Békedal" (Song of Peace) (c1952, Weöres) ....
9.97   "Ürgeöntés" (Gopher-flooding), children's song (c1954) ....
9.98   "Arany szabadság" (Golden Freedom), canon (c1957; in Hung text Jankovich & Latin text Kontra) ....
9.99   "Házasodik a vakond" (Mole marriage), children's song (c1958) ....
9.100 "Méz, méz, méz" (Honey, Honey, Honey) (c1958) ....
9.101 "Tell me where is fancy bred" (c1959, from Shakespeare's The Merchants of Venice) (also see songs
          c by Castelnuovo-Tedesco Op.24/I/2 & Poulenc, choral work c by Britten) ....
9.102 "Harasztosi legénynek" (The Lad of Harasztos) (c1961) ....
9.103 "Az éneklő ifjusághoz" (To the Singing Youth) (c1962, Vargha) ....

10. VOICE & ORCHESTRA

10.1   "Ave Maria" (ca1897; 1v & strings, lost) ....
10.2   "My heart is aching" (c1917, Móricz; Bar & gypsy orch; used as 4. in incid music: The Song of the Lark) ....
10.3   "Molnár Anna" (c1943, r1956; 1v & small orch) ....
10.4   "5 Songs of Bela Bartók" (c1962, = Bartók's Op.15 orchd) ....

11. SONGS (w/ pf)

11.1   "Ave Maria" (ca1897; 1v & org, lost) ....
11.2   "A wilderness is the world" (c before 1900, Petőfi) ....
11.3   "I should like to leave this bright world" (c1905, Petőfi) ....
11.4   "20 Hungarian Folksongs" (c1906, collab Bartók: 1.–10. c by Bartók, 11.–20. c by Kodály) ....
11.5   "4 Songs" (1.–3.: c1907, Arany, Bálint, Móricz, 4. = My heart is aching c1917; in Hung, Ger & Eng) ....
11.6   "16 Songs" (c1907–9; English words Cecil Grey; in Hung & Eng) Op.1
11.7   "Himfy song" (c1915, Kisfaludy) ....
11.8   "2 Songs" (c1913–6, Berzsenyi, Ady; Bar & pf/orch) Op.5
11.9   "Late melodies," 7 songs (c1912–6, Berzsenyi, Kölcsey, Csokonai; in Hung & Ger) Op.6
11.10 "Kádár István" (c1917; included as 37. of: Hungarian Folk Music) ....
11.11 "My heart is aching" (c1917, Móricz; incl as 4. of: 4 Songs; see orig w/ orch) ....
11.12 "5 Songs" (c1915–8, Ady, Balázs; in Hung & Ger) Op.9
11.13 "3 Songs" (c1924–9, Balassi, anon; 1v & pf/orch; in Hung, Ger & Eng) Op.14
11.14 "Hungarian Folk Music," Vol.I–X, 57 folksong transcriptions (c1917–32; in Hung, Ger & Eng) ....
11.15 "Kálló double dance" (c1937; 1v & pf; also see choral work) ....
11.16 "The First Holy Communion" (c1942, Szedő; 1v & org; also see choral work) ....

11.17 "Song at Advent" (O come, Emmanuel) (c1943; 1v & org) ....
11.18 "Jesus and the Children" (c1947, Szedő; 1 child's v & org) ....
11.19 "8 Small Duets" (c1953; S, T & pf, after: Bicinia Hungarica) ....
11.20 "Epigrams," 9 vocalises w/ out words (c1954; 1v & instr) ....
11.21 "Epigrams" (c1958, Kistetenyi; 1v & instr) ....
11.22 "5 Songs of the mountain Tcheremis" (c1960) ....
11.23 "Hungarian Folk Music," Vol.XI, 5 folksong transcriptions (c1964) ....
11.24 "Epitaphium Joannis Hunyadi" (c1965) ....

12. ARRANGEMENTS OF WORKS OF OTHERS

12.1 Haydn: Rondo of Vn Son No.5, HobXVI:43bis (arr of Kbd Son No.35, HobXVI/43) (arr ca1900; strings) .....
12.2 Bach, J. S.: "Chorale Preludes," BWV743, 762, 747 (arr1924; vc & pf; arr Dubensky for strings) ....
12.3 Bach, J. S.: "Chromatic Fantasy," BWV903 (arr1950; va solo; ed Primrose) ....
12.4 Bach, J. S.: "Prelude & fugue," in E-flat major, BWV853 (arr1951; vc & pf) ....
12.5 Bach, J. S.: "Lute Prelude," in C minor, BWV999 (arr1959; vn & pf) ....

13. EDUCATIONAL WORKS

13.1 "15 Two-Part Exercises" (c1941; wordless) ....
13.2 "Let Us Sing Correctly," 107 intonation exercises (c1941; wordless) ....
13.3 "Bicinia Hungarica," 180 progressive 2-part songs in 4 books (c1937–42) ....
13.4 "333 Elementary Exercises in Sight-Singing" (An Introduction to the Folk Music of Hungary) (c1943).........
13.5 "Songs for Schools," 2 vols (c1943–4, ed w/ Kerenyi) ....
13.6 "Ötfoku zene" (Pentatonic Music), 440 melodies in 4 books (c1942–7) ....
13.7 "Szo-mi" (SOL-MI), 8 books for children (c1944–7, ed w/ Ádám) ....
13.8 "Songbook for Primary Schools," 4 vols (c1947–8, ed w/ Ádám) ....
13.9 "33 Two-Part Exercises" (c1954) ....
13.10 "44 Two-Part Exercises" (c1954) ....
13.11 "55 Two-Part Exercises" (c1954) ....
13.12 "Tricina," 29 progressive 3-part songs (c1954) ....
13.13 "50 nursery rhymes" (c1961) ....
13.14 "66 Two-Part Exercises" (c1962) ....
13.15 "22 Two-Part Exercises" (c1964) ....
13.16 "77 Two-Part Exercises" (c1966) ....

* * * * *

1. STAGE WORKS

Operas:

1.1   "Fiesque," 3 acts (c1866–7, Beauquier after Schiller) ....
1.2   "Le roi d'Y's" (The King of Ys), 3 acts (c1875–88, Blau) ....
1.3   "La jacquerie," 4 acts (c1891–2, Blau & Arnaud; compl Coquard) ....

Ballets:

1.4   "Namouna," 2 acts (c1881–2, Nuitter, de Bury & Petipa) ....
1.5   "Néron," 3 act pantomime (c1891, Milliet, w/ ch, from opera: Fiesque) ....

1a. SELECTIONS FROM STAGE WORKS (Nos. of sections in The Gramophone)

1a.2   "Le roi d'Y's," opera: ....
       excerpts: I: 1. "Ouverture"
              2. "Noël!"
              3. "Margared, ô ma soeur!"
              4. "Vainement j'ai parlé"
              5. "Désireux d'accomplir"
       II: 6. "De tous côtes j'aperçois"
              7. "Hélas, pourrais-je en mes alarmes"
              8. "Tais-toi, Margared!"
              9. "Victorie!"
            10. "Perdu!"
       III: 11. "Vous qui venez ici"
            12a. "Puisqu'on ne peut fléchir"
            12b. "Vainement, ma bien-aimée!" (Aubade)
            13. "Voici l'heure"
            14. "Salut á l'époux"
            15. "Ces rumeurs, ces cris d'alarm"
            16. "Ô Puissance infinie!"

1a.4   "Namouna," ballet: ....
       excerpts: Prologue: 1. "Prélude"
              2. "Scene du Balcon"
       I: 3. "Allegro vivace"
              4. "Pas des Cymbales"
              5. "Valse de la Cigarette"
              6. "Tambourin"
              7. "Danse Marocaine"
              8. "La Gitane"
              9. "Parades de Foire"
            10. "Danse de Namouna"
            11. "Fête Foraine"
       II: 12. "La Sieste"
            13. "Mazurka"
            14. "Presto: Danse de toutes les Esclaves"
            15. "Théme varié"
            16. "Bacchanale"

2. SYMPHONIES

2.1   *2 Symphonies (c early, destr Lalo)* ....
2.2   "Symphonie espagnole" (c1874; vn & orch) Op.21
2.3   Symphony in G minor (c1886) ....

3. OTHER ORCHESTRAL WORKS

3.1   "2 Aubades" (c1872; 10 insts/small orch, from opera: Fiesque): No.1 "Allegretto" ....
3.2   No.2 "Andantino"
3.3   "Divertissement" (c1872, ballet music & 2 aubades from opera: Fiesque)...
3.4   "Rapsodie norvégienne" (c1878, portions arr from: Fantaisie norvégienne for vn & orch)...
3.5   "Namouna" Suite No.1 (c1881–2, from ballet): No.1 "Prélude" ....
3.6   No.2 "Sérénade"
3.7   No.3 "Thème varié"
3.8   No.4 "Parade de foire"
3.9   No.5 "Fête foraine"
3.10   "Namouna" Suite No.2 (c1881–2, from ballet): No.1 "Danse marocaine" ....
3.11   No.2 "Mazurka"
3.12   No.3 "La sieste"

Pf duet:

7.2	"La mère et l'enfant," 2 morceaux (c1873): No.1 "Romance" ....
7.3	No.2 "Sérénade"

8. CHURCH MUSIC

8.1	"Litanies de la sainte Vierge" (p1876; ch & org/pf) ....
8.2	"O salutaris" (p1884; 3 fem vv & org) Op.34
8.3	"Veni, Creator" (d'après un thème bohème) (A & pf/org) ....

9. SONGS (w/ pf)

9.1	"Adieux au désert" (p1848, Flobert) ....
9.2	"L'ombre de Dieu" (p ?1848, Lehugeur) ....
9.3	"Six romances populaires" (p1849, Béranger): 1. "La pauvre femme" ....
9.4	2. "Beaucoup d'amour"
9.5	3. "Le suicide"
9.6	4. "Si j'étais petit oiseau"
9.7	5. "Les petits coups"
9.8	6. "Le vieux vagabond"
9.9	"Le novice" (p1849, Stupuy) Op.5
9.10	"Six mélodies" (p1856, Hugo): 1. "Guitare" Op.17
9.11	2. "Puisqu'ici-bas toute âme"
9.12	3. "L'aube naît et ta porte est close"
9.13	4. "Dieu qui sourit et qui donne"
9.14	5. "Oh! quand je dors"
9.15	6. "Chanson à boire" (2 settings)
9.16	"Ballade à la lune" (p1860, Musset) ....
9.17	"Humoresque" (p ?1867, Beauquier) ....
9.18	"Trois mélodies" (p ca ?1870, Musset): 1. "A une fleur" ....
9.19	2. "Chanson de Barberine"
9.20	3. "La Zuecca"
9.21	"Aubade" (p1872, Wilder) ....
9.22	"5 Lieder" (p1879): 1. "Prière de l'enfant à son réveil" (Lamartine) ....
9.23	2. "A celle qui part" (Silvestre)
9.24	3. "Tristesse" (Silvestre)
9.25	4. "Viens!" (Lamartine)
9.26	5. "La chanson de l'alouette" (Laprade)
9.27	"Chant breton" (p1884, Delpit; w/ fl/ob) Op.31
9.28	"Marine" (p1884, Theuriet) Op.33
9.29	"Dansons," duet (p1884, S & mS, arr from ballet: Namouna) Op.35
9.30	"Trois mélodies" (p1887): 1. "La fenaison" (Stella) ....
9.31	2. "L'esclave" (Gautier)
9.32	3. "Souvenir" (Hugo)
9.33	"Au fond des halliers," duet (p1887, Theuriet; S & T, arr from opera: Fiesque) ....
9.34	"Le rouge-gorge" (p1887, Theuriet) ....

* * * * *

1. STAGE WORKS

Operas:

1.1   "Der Kürassier" (c1891–2, Ruther, inc) ....
1.2   "Rodrigo," 1 act (c1893, Mlčoch, inc) ....
1.3   "Kukuška," 3 acts (p1896, orig vers of: Tatjana of 1905) ....
1.4   "Tatjana," 3 acts (p1905, Falzari & Kalbeck, r vers of opera: Kukuška of 1896) ....
1.5   "Frasquita," 3 acts comic opera (p1933, Willner.& Reichert, r vers of operetta of 1922) ....
1.6   "Giuditta," 5 acts (p1934, Knepler & Löhner; Eng transl Carstairs) ....
1.7   "Garabonciás diák," 3 acts (p1943, Ernő, r vers of operetta: Zigeunerliebe of 1910) ....

Operettas:

1.8   "Das Club-Baby" (c1901, Léon, inc) ....
1.9   "Arabella, die Kubanerin" (c1901, Schmidt, inc) ....
1.10   "Wiener Frauen," 3 acts (p1902, Tann-Bergler & Norini; r as: Der Schlüssel zum Paradies 1906) ....
1.11   "Der Rastelbinder," 2 acts (p1902, Léon) ....
1.12   "Der Göttergatte," 3 acts (p1904, Léon & Stein) ....
1.13   "Die Juxheirat," 3 acts (p1904, Bauer) ....
1.14   "Die lustige Witwe" (The Merry Widow) (p1905, Léon & Stein after Meilhac's comedy: L'attaché
         d'ambassade; Eng transl Hassall) ....
1.15   "Der Mann mit den drei Frauen," 3 acts (p1908, Bauer; Eng transl Atteridge & Potter) ....
1.16   "Das Fürstenkind" (Maids of Athens), 2 acts (p1909, r1932, Léon; Eng transl Wells) ....
1.17   "Der Graf von Luxemburg," 3 acts (p1909, Willner & Bodanzky; Eng transl Maschwitz) ....
1.18   "Zigeunerliebe" (Gypsy Love), 3 acts (p1910, Willner & Bodanzky; Eng transl Carstairs) ....
1.19   "Eva" (Das Fabriksmädel), 3 acts (p1911, Willner, Bodanzky & Spero; Eng transl Carstairs) ......
1.20   "Die ideale Gattin," 3 acts (p1913, Brammer & Grünwald, r of operetta: Der Göttergatte of 1904) ....
1.21   "Endlich Allein" (Alone at Last), 3 acts (p1914, Willner & Bodanzky; Eng transl Woodward & Herbert) ....
1.22   "Der Sterngucker," 3 acts (p1916, Löhner & Willner) ....
1.23   "Wo die Lerche singt" (Where the Lark Sings), 3 acts (p1918, Willner & Reichert after Martos; Eng transl
         Taylor) ....
1.24   "Die blaue Mazur" (The Blue Mazurka), 2 acts (p1920, Stein & Jenbach; Eng transl Graham) ....
1.25   "Die Tangokönigin," 3 acts (p1921, Brammer & Grünwald, r vers of: Die Ideale Gattin of 1913) ....
1.26   "Frühlingsmädel" (Frühling), 3 acts (p1922, Eger; orig: Frühling in 1 act) ....
1.27   "Frasquita," 3 acts (p1922, Willner & Reichert; Eng transl Arkell; also see comic opera of 1933) ....
1.28   "Libellentanz" (The Three Graces), 3 acts (p1922, Lombardo & Willner; Eng transl Travers) ....
1.29   "Die gelbe Jacke," 3 acts (p1923, Léon) ....
1.30   "Cloclo" (Lolotte), 3 acts (p1924, Jenbach after Engel & Horst: Der Schrei nach dem Kinde) ....
1.31   "Paganini," 3 acts (p1925, Knepler & Jenbach) ....
1.32   "Gigolette," 3 acts (p1926, Lombardo & Forzano, r vers of operetta: Der Sterngucker of 1916) ....
1.33   "Der Zarewitsch" (The Czarevitch), 3 acts (p1927, Reichert & Jenbach after Zapolska; Eng transl
         Carstairs) ....
1.34   "Friederike" (Frederica), 3 acts (p1928, Herzer & Löhner; Eng transl Pepper) ....
1.35   "Das Land des Lächelns" (The Land of Smiles), 3 acts (p1929, Herzer & Löhner, r of: Die gelbe Jacke;
         Eng transl Graham) ....
1.36   "Schön ist die Welt," 3 acts (p1930, Herzer & Löhner, r vers of: Endlich Allein; Eng transl Carstairs) ....

Other stage works:

1.37   "Fräulein Leutnant," 1 act Schauspiel (p1901, Kolhapp) ....
1.38   "Peter und Paul im Schlaraffenland," 1 act children's operetta (p1906, Bodanzky & Grünbaum) ....
1.39   "Mitislaw der Moderne," 1 act parody (p1907, Grünbaum & Bodanzky) ....
1.40   "Rosenstock und Edelweiss," 1 act Singspiel (p1910, Bauer) ....
1.41   "Die Spieluhr," 1 act musical comedy (p1911, Zasche) ....
1.42   "Komm' deutscher Bruder!," Volksstück (p1914, collab Eysler) ....
1.43   "Walzer" (Walzermusik), comedy (p1917, Ruttkay) ....
1.44   "Rose de Noël" (Vincy) ....

Radio:

1.45   "Die Gefährten des Odysseus" (p1937) ....

Film:

1.46   "Die grosse Attraktion" (c1931) ....
1.47   "Es war einmal ein Walzer" (c1932) ....
1.48   "Grossfürstin Alexandra" (c1934) ....
1.49   "Die ganze Welt dreht sich um Liebe" (c1936) ....
1.50   "Une nuit à Vienne" (c1937) ....

1a. SELECTIONS FROM STAGE WORKS

(Nos. of musical themes in: "Franz Lehár. Thematic Index." Glocken Verlag Ltd. London, 1985)

1a.4   "Tatjana," opera: ....
1. "Scheidend von den goldbeglänzten Höhen schmilzt dahin der letzte Schnee!," chorus
2. "Der heilige Georg schreitet, die Wolga weihend entlang"
3. "Ich denke dein, seh ich die Schwalben ziehn" (Alexis, Tatjana)
4. "Da schaut, hier kommt ein Hase mit Stummelschwanz und mit gespaltner Nase!" (Pimen)
5. (Bauerntänze), in F major
6. (Bauerntänze), in C major
7. "Gütiger Gott, einmal giebst du unserer Noth Frieden und Ruh!" (Bauern, Bäuerinnen, Soldaten)
8. "Was weinst du, Steppenkind? da alles blüht" (Raisa)
9. "In meinen Adern sprüht es, in meinem Herzen glüht es"

1a.6   "Giuditta," opera: ....
  I: 1. "Du meine schwarze Donna Antonia" (Strassensänger)
2. "Ein brauner Bursch, ein braunes Mädel" (Pierrino, Anita)
3. "Uns ist alles einerlei"
4. "Alle Tag' nichts, als Müh' und Plag', wenig Geld und Sorgen dazu" (Manuele)
5. "Freunde, das Leben ist lebenswert!" (Octavio)
6. "O Signora, o Signorina! hört man flüstern und liebkosen!" (Octavio, ch)
7. "Wohin, wohin will es mich treiben" (Giuditta)
8. "Liebestraum, du ewiger Liebestraum"
9. "In einem Meer von Liebe" (Octavio, Giuditta)
10. "Schönste der Frau'n, wenn alle Sterne glühen" (Octavio)
11. "Weit übers Meer mit dir möcht' ich zieh'n," chorus (Soldaten)
12. "Herr Kapitän, der Weg ist weit von hier bis Navarra"
  II: 13. "Keine Angst, lieber Schatz, weisst du was: läuten wir an!" (Pierrino)
14. "Zwei, die sich lieben, vergessen die Welt" (Pierrino, Anita)
15. "Schön, wie die blaue Sommernacht" (Giuditta, Octavio)
16. "Sag', ist die Welt nicht so zauberhaft schön für uns allein?"
  III: 17. "Uns're Heimat ist die Wüste," chorus (Soldaten)
18. "Du bist meine Sonne" (Octavio)
19. "Wer kennt mein Weh, wie schwer brennt mein Weh, mein Herz" (Giuditta)
20. "Ich bin nicht schön, das weiss ich" (Martini)
21. "Ja, die Liebe ist so wie ein Schaukelbrett"
22. "Komm, komm wir wollen fort von hier!" (Anita, Pierrino)
23. "Ich weiss es selber nicht" (Giuditta)
24. "Meine Lippen, sie küssen so heiss"
  IV: 25. "Komme doch zurück zu mir" (Giuditta)

1a.7   "Garabonciás diák," opera: ....
1. "Utam muzsikálva járom" (Diák)
2. "Hová merült el szép szemed világa?" (Drághy, Sárika)
3. "Zúg az erdö zúg a mezö" (Diák)
4. "Sietve jöttem, nagy út mögöttem" (Karolin)
5. "A fátylas estben utat keresve"
6. "Ide libbenj, oda lebbenj egyre szebben, kecsebben!" (Sárika)
7. "Öreg asszony vagyok én már! nem kell bál!" (Borcsa)
8. "Különben, ki tudja, jöhet még nyár!," duet (Karolin, Drághy)
9. "Sorsomon egyszer átsuhant könny ű selyem ruhája" (Drághy)
10. "Mindhiábe vártam lestem én szertefoszlott minden szépremény" (Sárika)
11. "Árva magyarokra nehéz próbát mért az örök Magasság!" (Férfikar)
12. "Kösdjet azt a pántlikát kis galambom, t űz mellé bukétát" (Férfikar)
13. "Bár sohase tudtam volna mi a szerelem" (Sárika)
14. "Öreg ember nem vén ember, Boriskám!," duet (Borcsa, István)
15. "Deres már a határ"
16. "Valami gyújt itt bent" (Diák)
17. "Amerre csak jártak zúgatták a zivatart!"

1a.10   "Wiener Frauen," operetta: ....
1. "Wunderbar ist für wahr dieses Nest für's junge Paar," chorus (Confectioneusen)
2. "Spitzengeweb' und Seide, schimmernde Augenweide!"
3. "Der Herrin bin ich treu ergeben" (Jeanette)
4. "Jeder Mann pocht auf das Vorrecht des Geschlechts" (Philippe)
5. "Zwei müssen sein! lehrt schon ein Bibelwort"
6. "Die Frauenfrage, wie ihr wisst" (Fleurette, Georgette, Sylvette)
7. "Ja den jede Mutter hat mit Rat und Tat"
8. "Die Häuser bau'n sie himmelhoch, erst der zweite Stock heisst Hochparterre" (Claire)
9. "Schreit' ich durch die eig'nen Räume ach so feierlich im Hochzeitskleid"
10. "Aber trotz Ach und Wehe sonderbar"
11. "Liebe Tochter, hör auf mich junge Frau braucht manchen Kniff" (Claire, Mme Brionne)
12. "So muss die Frau bei Zeiten pfiffig vorbereiten ihren Sieg"
13. "Denkt nicht mehr an Widerstand"

14. "Num zum Schluss wie zum Beginn nehmt unsern Glückwunsch freundlich hin" (Brautchor)
15. "O ich denk' zurück so gerne an die Zeit" (Nechledil)
16. "Wo die Moldau majestätisch rauscht"
17. "Man will ja gern versöhnlich sein" (Claire, Philippe)
18. "Durch die Nacht mit Siegermiene zieht der kecke Ritters mann" (Claire)
19. "Schöne Rose, schöne Rose, lieblich edle Frauenblüte"
20. "Wenn ich mit meinem Tambourstab bin an der Tête marschiert" (Nechledil)
21. "Nechledil, Du schöner Mann, Du hast es allen angethan"
22. "Ich seh' jetzt mein Unrecht ein" (Claire)
III: 23. "Ein hohes und frohes begeistertes Lied" (Philippe)
24. "Schöne Frauen blond und braun, Edelsteine sonder Zahl"
25. "Aber es geht nicht" (Casimir, Claire) (orig in: Der Schüssel zum Paradies)
26. "Ich begreif', dass Sie sich kränken, Mir geht nah' Ihr Ungemach" (Claire, Casimir)

1a.11   "Der Rastelbinder," operetta: ....
Vorspiel: 1. "Der Slovak, der Slovak rackert sich den ganzen Tag," chorus
2. "Es lebte einst in der Slovakei ein weiser Slovak!" (Milosch)
3. "Spanem bohem! Spanem bohem! Heut' geht's in die Welt, juchhei!" (Janku, Suza, child ch)
4. "O boze, boze, boze, mir thut das Herz so weh"
5. "Ä jeder Mensch, was handeln thut, der sucht sich ein Artikel" (Pfefferkorn)
6. "Ich handel' nur mit Zweifel, es geht mir gor nix gut"
7. "Pass' auf, mein Sohn, so spricht zu Dir der Wolf Bär Pfefferkorn" (Pfefferkorn)
8. "Das is a einfache Rechnung, mei Kind, mei Kind, vergess' die nit!"
I: 9. "Ohne Küssen wär' die Lieb' " (Mizzi)
10. "Freund, kann dir's gar nicht sagen, bin ja so kreuzfidel" (Janku, Milosch)
11. "Hab' einmal ein Herz gehabt, jetzt hab' ich's nimmer mehr"
12. "Ach endlich, endlich heut' erfüllt sich mir mein Wunsch nach jahrelanger Zeit" (Suza)
13. "Er schrieb mir manches Brieflein, der liebe gute Mann"
14. "Es war in eurem Heimatsdorf, in einer kleinen Hütt'n" (Pfefferkorn)
15. "Und Suzinka hat gleich gemacht für ihren Bräut'gam Schulden"
16. "Mei' Schatz, mei' Braut, hat mir vertraut ganz leis; net laut" (Janku)
17. "Ich bin ein Wiener Kind, so wie's im Büchel steht"
18. "Denk' ich zurück, drei Jahre sind's grad' " (Milosch, Suza)
19. "Wenn zwei sich lieben, so steht's geschrieben, sind sie ein Herz, da sind sie ein Sinn!"
20. "Hauptsach' is beim Ball nobles Benehmen in dem Tanzsaal!" (Pfefferkorn, Suza)
21. "Das Tanzen sehr erhitzt! Die schöne Tänz'rin schwitzt"
22. "Eins, zwei, drei! 'S geht gut die Tanzerei"
23. "Tanz' weiter schnell, ich kann nicht steh'n auf einer Stell'!" (Pfefferkorn)
24. "Jetzt nehm Deine Füsse in die Hände"
25. "Hast es net g'sehn beim Hausthor dort stehn" (Janku, Mizzi)
26. "Dui du du du, weanerische Hölzelweis' "
27. "Ihr Gesindel, so ein Schwindel war im Leben" (Glöppler, Janku, Milosch, Mizzi, ch)
28. "Milosch, ich kann nichts dafür" (Janku, Mizzi, Pfefferkorn, ch)
II: 29. "Ein Infant'rist von Numm'ro vier und ein Husar von acht" (Janku)
30. "Kamerad von Numm'ro vier, Kamerad von acht"
31. "Die Männerkleider, ach, sie passen leider nicht recht" (Mizzi, Suza)
32. "Zwar jeder Schritt und Tritt sieht hübscher aus!"

1a.12   "Der Göttergatte," operetta: ....
I: 1. "Wir armen Musen, man hat uns boykottiert" (Introduction) (Ensemble)
2. "Leugne nicht, dir schoss jetzt etwas durch den Kopf" (Juno, Jupiter)
3. "Sieh' mich doch nur an, du Bösewicht"
4. "Vorwärts! Auf zur Erdenfahrt," finale (Jupiter, 9 Musen, ch)
II: 5. "Heute Nacht ist es besonders finster" (Sosias, Mercur)
6. "Süsseste Charis, ein Vierteljahr is"
7. "Muss denn alles auf der Welt" (Juno, Jupiter)
8. "Du hast mich doch betrogen!" (Charis, Mercur, Sosias)
9. "Der Klügere gibt, vielleicht auch hast du recht?"
10. "Man hält mich für den grössten aller Götter" (Jupiter)
11. "Cupido, do loser Spötter Cupido"
12. "Wachst du, Liebchen? Wachst du, sag', es mir!" (Amphitryon)
13. "Was ich längst erträumte, was ich bang versäumte"
14. "Ja, so geht's, es kommt anders" (Amphitryon, Juno, Sosias)
15. "Hoch der Held Amphitryon, vor dem die Feinde sind entfloh'n," chorus (Krieger, Männer)
16. "Ruft ihn das Vaterland, dann stürmt er kühn voran," chorus (Kinder, Frauen, Krieger, Männer)
III: 17. "Jeder Mann glaubt, seine Frau, sie sei, schau, schau, mehr dumm, als schlau!" (Juno)
18. "Wer ein Trinklied singt, der ist unbedingt nicht modern," trio (Charis, Juno, Sosias)

1a.13   "Die Juxheirat," operetta: ....
I: 1. "Ich bin ein armer Milliardär" (Brockwiller)
2. "Tag und Nacht Geschäfte über Menschen kräfte!"
3. "Ein Mann erzählt dort eine Anekdote" (Edith, Euphrasia, Juliane, Phoebe, Selma)
4. "Los vom Mann! So laute die Parole"
5. "Also hier das Revier und ihr Schloss, schön und gross" (Harold)
6. "Ermutigend ist es wohl nicht"

  7. "Sie also, mein süssestes Herrchen, Sie sind der gewaltige Held" (Selma)
  8. "Nein, das ist wirklich zu komisch" (Juliane, Phoebe, Selma)
  9. "Ein Rennen wurde arrangiert" (Philly)
 10. "Nur eins bereitet mir viel Verdruss"
 11. "O du Böser, weg die Hände, meinen Zweifeln mach ein Ende" (Philly, Phoebe)
 12. "Mit dir bald Hochzeit feiern ist mein einzig Ziel" (Philly)
 13. "Ich sah mal in der alten Welt. Wo war es nur?" (Selma, Philly)
 14. "Ja und sehen Sie, sehen Sie, just so einen Jux" (ensemble)
II: 15. "Es gibt heute Frau'n, die sagen uns: 'trau'n wir wollen vom Manne nichts wissen!' " (Arthur)
 16. "Immer Er und Sie, immer und Sie, s'ist nicht anders zu treiben" (Arthur, Juliane, Phoebe)
 17. "Ich bin wie eine Harfensaite, kaum angerührt, so schwirre ich" (Brockwiller, Edith)
 18. "Sie können's doch vierhändig spielen" (Philly)
 19. "Ich sage nicht, dass Sie die schönste sind von allen Rosen, die im Garten steh'n"
 20. "Was könnte man ersinnen zur Strafe für den Hohn?" (Edith, Euphrasia, Phoebe, Selma)
 21. "So wär' es wahr, die Dichter sin gen's allesammt" (Arthur)
 22. "Herz, du bist bewegt! Neue Wonnen dich durchbeben"
 23. "Einen Kuss auf diese kleine Hand werden Sie wohl noch leisten können?" (Selma, ch)
 24. "Bei Gott, ich wollte weder sie noch dich in böser Absicht kränken" (Philly)
 25. "Wie rücksichts los war doch der Mann, ein Philosoph, und Grobian" (Euphrasia, Phoebe)
 26. "Hei, das war ein Fahren durch die Pande frei," chorus
 27. "Wie soll ich, Freunde, euch beschreiben" (Harold, Edith, Euphrasia, Philly, Phoebe, ch)
III: 28. "Ich stutze und putze den Nagelrand rundum, rundum, rundum" (Philly, Phoebe)
 29. "Wozu den Mann bekämpfen? Er folgt uns auf den Pfiff," ariette (Phoebe)
 30. "Ging ein Knab' im Mondenschein mit dem süssen Mägdelein," couplet (Philly)
 31. "Tiefes Schweigen in der Runde, abendlich die Wälder ruh'n" (Arthur, Juliane, Philly, Phoebe)

1a.14   "Die lustige Witwe," operetta: ....
  I: 1. "Bin Landesvater per procura" (Baron Zeta, ensemble)
       2. "Ich bin eine anständ'ge Frau" (Valencienne)
       3. "Bitte, meine Herr'n!" (Entrance song) (Hanna, ensemble)
       4. "Hab' in Paris mich noch nicht ganz" (Hanna)
       5. "Gar oft hab' ich's gehört" (Hanna)
       6. "Oh Vaterland du machst bei Tag" (Danilo)
       7. "Da geh' ich zu Maxim"
       8. "Ja was? Ein trautes Zimmerlein" (Zauber der Häuslichkeit) (Camille, Valencienne)
       9. "Das ist der Zauber der stillen Häuslichkeit!" (Camille, Valencienne)
      10. "Ja, wenn man es so recht betrachtet" (Valencienne)
      11. "Damenwahl! Hört man rufen rings im Saal!" (m ch)
      12. "Es gibt keine gröss're Beleidigung" (Cascada)
      13. "Wie die Blumen im Lenze erblüh'n" (Danilo)
      14. "O kommet doch, o kommt, Ihr Ballsirenen" (ensemble)
      15. "Der junge Mann tanzt Polka, ich hab' es ausprobiert" (Valencienne)
  II: 16. "Ach," chorus
      17. "Mi velimo dase dase Veslimo!," chorus
      18. "Es lebt' eine Vilja, ein Waldmägdelein" (Vilja-Lied) (Hanna)
      19. "Vilja, o Vilja, du Waldmägdelein" (Hanna, ch)
      20. "Heia, Mädel, aufgeschaut" (Hanna)
      21. "Dummer, dummer Reitersmann" (Hanna, Danilo)
      22. "Wie die Weiber Wie die Weiber? Man behandelt? Hört ihn an!" (Danilo, Zeta, ensemble)
      23. "Ja, das Studium der Weiber ist schwer"
      24. "Wie eine Rosenknospe im Maienlicht erblüht" (Camille)
      25. "Sieh dort den kleinen Pavillon"
      26. "Ein flotter Ehestand soll's sein: 'Ganz nach Pariser Art!' " (Hanna)
      27. "Das hat Rrrrass, 'so' trallalalalala" (Hanna, ensemble)
      28. "Es waren zwei Königskinder" (Danilo)
      29. "Ja, wir sind es, die Grisetten von Pariser Cabaretten!" (Grisettes)
      30. "Auf dem Boulevard am Abend" (Valencienne)
      31. "Ritantouri tantirette Eh voilà les belles Grisettes"
      32. "We are the dear little butterflies that hover," chorus (English: Ross)
      33. "I was born by cruel fate, in a little Balkan state" (Njegus) (English: Tracey)
      34. "For I am quite Parisian, A most distinguished man"
      35. "Lippen schweigen, 's flüstern Geigen: Hab' mich lieb!" (Danilo)
      36. "Bei jedem Walzerschritt tanzt auch die Seele mit" (Hanna)

1a.15   "Der Mann mit den drei Frauen," operetta: ....
  I: 1. "Ach, der Mann kommt leicht zu Falle" (Hans)
       2. "Ich mache den Hof auf Bällen"
       3. "Strohwitwe sein" (Lori)
       4. "Nicht weinen, lieber Schatz!" (Hans, Butzi, Lori)
       5. "Ich liebe meine Häuslichkeit bei meiner kleinen, süssen Frau" (Hans)
       6. "Bienchen, summt nicht mehr, Käfer, brummt nicht mehr!" (Lori)
       7. "Entschuld'gen Sie, wo ist denn meine Frau?" (Baron, Lori, Wendelin)
       8. "Rächen, rächen will ich mich rächen, rächen will ich mich fürchterlich!" (Baron, Lori, Wendelin)
       9. "Böser Mann, hör' mal an" (Hans, Lori)
      10. "Rote Mühle, rote Mühle" (ensemble)

11. "Es wachen tolle Geister auf" (Major, ensemble)
II: 12. "Die armen, die armen Kadetten!" (Kadetten, Pensionärinnen)
13. "Er war Kapitän der chasseurs d'afrique" (Coralie)
14. "Ach, Rosen ohne Zahl" (Coralie, Kadetten, Mädchen)
15. "Wahrlich wie ein Troubadour" (Coralie, Major)
16. "Liebchen! Komm und öffne dein Stübchen"
17. "Ich bin eine Frau von Temp'rament" (Lori, Coralie, Hans)
18. "Ach, vielleicht, wer kann es wissen"
19. "Es wär' so schön im Menschenleben" (Hans)
20. "Klinge, klinge, kleines Instrument" (Hans, Lori)
21. "Schillernder Falter du sollst nicht immer kosen mit den fremden Rosen" (Tanz-Duett) (Lori, Hans)
22. "Ich denke mir mir scheint mich deucht" (Lori)
23. "Bitte schön, bitte schön der Armen wieder ihre Ruh'!"
24. "Drum brauch' dein rotes Mündchen" (Hans)
25. "Es wird in Liebesdingen mit Schreiben nichts erreicht" (Hans)
26. "Seh'n Sie, meine Jungen, sind sie nicht gelungen Jeder so galant, wie brav!" (Major, ensemble)
III: 27. "Halloh, halloh, halloh! Wer dort?" (Telephon-Lied) (Olivia)
28. "Drei Minuten für Himmel und Hölle"
29. "Nach altem Brauche pflanzt sich fort der Mensch in Land und Stadt" (Hans)
30. "So wird halt jede Nation selig nach ihrer Façon!"
31. "Kenne gar viele Damen, nenne nicht ihre Namen" (Coralie, Major)

1a.16   "Das Fürstenkind," operetta: ....
I: 1. "Papa, ich bin verliebt, du ahnst nicht, wie!" (Photini, Harris)
2. "Mutter ging schlafen, Vater ging schlafen" (Photini)
3. "Lange Jahre, bange Jahre musste ich mein Kind entbehren" (Pallikarenlied) (Stavros)
4. "O du herrlicher, bester Mann der Welt!," finale (Photini)
5. "Ich denke ach Sie verzeih'n, das kann nicht richtig sein" (Harris)
II: 6. "Holioh! Holioh, holala! Holala!" (Mary-Ann)
7. "Ich bin doch wirklich ein schlimmes Kind"
8. " 'Kindchen, sei hübsch brav', immer predigt das Mama"
9. "Doch heia! und tausendmal heia!" (Stavros)
10. "Ich diene so gerne den Damen" (Mary-Ann, Stavros)
11. "Wüsset du, Mädchen, wie wohl das tut" (Stavros)
12. "Es lebe hoch, es lebe hoch der Hadschi Stavros" (Perikles, Räuber, Stavros, Gendarmen)
13. "Wie umkost so mild mich dein Hauch!," finale (Mary-Ann, Stavros)
14. "Ich kann ja nichts dafür"
15. "Schweig', zagendes Herz, zitternde Sehnsucht, schweig' still!" (Stavros)
III: 16. "Nur ein Lächeln ich sehen doch mocht' " (Doktor, Gwendolyne, Harris, Mary-Ann, Photini)
17. "Walzer, sage mir, wer hat dich wohl erdacht?"
18. "Einst traf der Herbst den Frühling: Viel schönen, guten Tag" (Mary-Ann, Stavros)
19. "Alt und Jung und Jung und Alt können sich nicht finden"

1a.17   "Der Graf von Luxemburg," operetta: ....
I: 1. "Karneval!, Ja du allerschönste Zeit" (Introduction), chorus
2. "Wer kein Philister ist, mit uns marschiert"
3. "Hoch der Graf von Luxemburg, des Faschings toller König"
4. "Mein Ahnherr war der Luxemburg" (René)
5. "So liri, liri, lari, das ganze Moos ging tschari"
6. "Ein Stübchen so klein, grad zwei geh'n hinein, just Frau und Mann!," duet (Juliette, Brissard)
7. "Wir bummeln durchs Leben, was schert uns das Ziel?"
8. "Leichtsinn ist die Parole," chorus
9. "Pierre, der schreibt an klein Fleurette Abends heut' um zehn" (Juliette)
10. "Denn doppelt schmeckt's dem Bübchen, wenn selber Du kaufst ein"
11. "Ich bin verliebt, ich muss es ja gestehen" (Basil)
12. "Ein Scheck auf die englische Bank!," quintet (Basil, Pawlowitsch, Mentschikoff, Pelegrin, René)
13. "Unbekannt, deshalb nicht minder int'ressant" (Angèle)
14. "Sie geht links, er geht rechts, Mann und Frau, jeder möcht's" (René)
15. "Bist Du's, lachendes Glück" (Angèle, René)
II: 16. "Hoch, Evöe, Angèle Didier," chorus
17. "Soll ich? Soll ich nicht?" (Angèle)
18. "Lieber Freund, man greift nicht nach den Sternen," duet (Angèle, René)
19. "Schau'n Sie freundlichst mich an," duet (Brissard, Juliette)
20. "Mädel klein, Mädel fein, gib Dich drein, sag' nicht Nein!"
21. "Ein Löwe war ich im Salon" (Polkatänzer) (Basil, Juliette)
22. "Polkatänzer, Polkatänzer war ich comme il faut"
23. "Kam ein Falter leicht geflattert" (Basil)
III: 24. "Was ist das für'ne Zeit, liebe Leute?," couplet (Kokozow)
25. "Alles mit Ruhe geniessen"
26. "Packt die Liebe einen alten justament beim Schopf," march-trio (Juliette, Brissard, Basil)
27. "Liebe, ach du Sonnenschein"
28. "Es duftet nach Trèfle incarnat" (Renè)
29. "Hoch das Brautpaar, hoch das junge Liebespaar!," chorus

1a.18   "Zigeunerliebe," operetta: ....
    I: 1. "Willst du das Wunderland je erseh'n," duet (Zorika, Józsi)
          2. "Trägst den Zweig in deinen Händen rosigzart" (Jonel)
          3. "Willst mich bezaubern wohl durch dein Fleh'n" (Zorika)
          4. "Wie sie hier verwundert steh'n" (Ilona)
          5. "Will die Männer ich berükken, mach' ich's so!" (Ilona)
          6. "Zuerst sucht man Gelegenheit" (Ilona)
          7. "Füllt den Becher, wack're Zecher, immer voll!" (m ch)
          8. "Glück hat als Gast nie lange Rast" (Józsi)
    II: 9. "Weisst ja doch, ich bin Zigeuner, den es nirgends lange hält" (Józsi)
        10. "Endlich, Józsi, endlich, Józsi, bist Du hier!," chorus
        11. "Deiner Fiedel Klängen lauschen wir doch alle ja alle!" (Zorika, Józsi, Mihály, ch)
        12. "War einst ein Mädel" (Zorika)
        13. "Gib mir dort vom Himmelszelt" (Ilona, Dragotin)
        14. "Ich weiss ein Rezept"
        15. "Durch's Leben da klingt eine Melodie" (Ilona)
        16. "Nur die Liebe macht uns jung"
        17. "Liebes Männchen, folge mir" (Jolán, Kajetán)
        18. "Zeige, Schätzchen, zeige schnell"
        19. "Zorika, Zorika, kehre zurück" (Zorika, Jonel)
        20. "Ich bin ein Zigeunerkind" (Józsi)
    III: 21. "Gib mir das Zweiglein, o gib es mir" (Jonel)
        22. "Lieber Onkel, hör mich nur an" (Jolán)
        23. "Schöne Tage, wo ich ein Springsfeld!" (Dragotin)
        24. "Hör' ich Cymbalklänge, wird ums Herz mir enge" (Ilona)
        25. "Macht nichts! Hol's der Teufel!"
        26. "Will nicht ohne Küsse leben, nein, nein!"

1a.19   "Eva" (Das Fabriksmädel), operetta: ....
    I: 1. "Im heimlichen Dämmer der silbernen Ampel" (Eva)
          2. "Reich flutend gleich gesponnenem Gold, duftig und schwer"
          3. "Wär' es auch nichts als ein Augenblick"
          4. "Glück und Glas, klingelinge, linge ling," scene & duet (Octave)
          5. "Pipsi, holde Pipsi" (Dagobert, Pipsi)
          6. "Um Zwölfe in der Nacht" (Octave, Pipsi)
    II: 7. "Fräulein Frau, das klingt doch nicht gewöhnlich" (Pipsi)
        8. "Hat man das erste Stiefelpaar vertreten in Paris" (Octave)
        9. "Und wie sie aussehn, diese süssen Dinger" (ensemble)
        10. "O du Pariser Pflaster, o, du Pariser Luft"
        11. "Und wenn auch der Philister den Stab darüber bricht"
        12. "Rechts das Männchen meiner Wahl" (Pipsi)
        13. "Geschieden muss sein, so heisst es im Lied" (Dagobert, Pipsi)
        14. "Nur das eine Wort sprich es aus!" (Octave)
        15. "Schwül aus tiefen Kelchen lockt dich ein Duft" (Eva, Octave)
        16. "Octave, gesteh' dir's ein, du bist verliebt!" (Octave)
        17. "Ziehe hin zu deinem Vater als ein pflichtgetreuer Sohn," duet (Pipsi, Dagobert)
        18. "Sei nicht bös, nicht nervös!"
        19. "Mädel! Mein süsses Aschenbrödel du" (Octave)
        20. "Kannst du die Sonne entbehren" (Octave, Eva)
    III: 21. "Wenn die Pariserin spazieren fährt," duet (Eva, Pipsi)
        22. "Manches diskret man zeigt"
        23. "Dort springt er lustig um die Eck', heraus, heraus aus dem Versteck!" (Lied) (Eva)
        24. "Es braust dahin wie Frühlingssturm und Flügel kriegt der Erdenwurm"
        25. "Herrgott, lass mir doch meinen Leichtsinn nur" (Eva, Freddy, Teddy, ch)

1a.20   "Die ideale Gattin," operetta: ....
    I: 1. "Mein Kind, du weisst, wie du mir teuer" (Pablo)
          2. "Mein Kind, du wirst ironisch, bitte, lass das sein" (Elvira, Pablo)
          3. "Mündlich bin ich schüchtern sehr" (Don Gil)
          4. "Mein Gesang klingt nicht wie Cello"
          5. "Denkst du noch, mein Freund, an jenen Tag" (Elvira, Pablo)
          6. "Tausend rote Rosen schmeichelnd dich umkosen"
          7. "Du weisst, ich bete meine Gattin an" (Pablo)
          8. "Süsse Lieblingsmelodie, du Lied der idealen Gattin!" (Don Gil, Pablo)
          9. "Im Lande der süssen Kastanien da liebt man mit doppelter Glut" (Carmen, Don Gil, Pablo)
        10. "Nur in Spanien darfst Du den Männern vertrau'n!"
        11. "So hab' ich's gelernt im Pensionat, das ist mein Erziehungsresultat" (Carmen, Don Gil, Pablo)
        12. "Was man träumt in Frühlingsnächten süsser Mädchentraum" (Carmen, Elvira)
        13. "Sie luden Herr Vicond' uns ein zu einem Klubdiner," chorus
        14. "Doch nun zum Diner! Darf ich bitten die Damen und Herr'n" (Pablo, ch)
    II: 15. "Es jauchzen und jubeln die Geigen" (Ensemble, ch)
        16. "Vor allem will so fort ich proklamieren" (Carmen)
        17. "Ich regier' mein lustiges Reich im Dreivierteltakt"
        18. "Ein kleines Stükkerl Walzer bei schmeichelnder Musik"
        19. "Oh, la la, 'Paris' das dasciniert, wie das kleine Wort allein elektrisiert" (Carola, ensemble)

20. "Willst du mein süsser, kleiner, braver Hampelmann sein" (Carmen, Don Gil)
21. "Kinder, heut' geht's mir famos" (Pablo, Carmen, Don Gil, Fiorella, Manolito, Mara, 4 Damen)
22. "Die Frau Gemahlin ist auf kurze Zeit verreist" (Pablo)
23. "Also bitte, hören Sie das 'wo' und 'wann' und 'wie' " (Sartrewski)
24. "Als ich Sie vor mir geseh'n so reizend und so schön"
25. "Komm den Frauen zart entgegen" (Pablo, Carmen & others)
26. "Zigarette in den Zähnen, schief den kekken Hut" (Carola, Don Gil)
27. "An Bolettchen ihm gefiel das kokette Mienenspiel"
28. "Wenn meine Gattin so küssen könnt', wie Du, mein Schätzchen, wie Du" (Carola, Pablo)
29. "War einst im schönen Polenland ein Musikant!" (Sartrewski)
30. "Nur mit Dir, mit Dir allein" (Carola, Pablo)
III: 31. "Küsse mich, so tönt es leise" (Carola)
32. "Schau mich an Kind und sag' mir dann" (Carmen, Don Gil)
33. "Wie seid ihr Männer alle doch so leicht zu fangen" (Carola)

1a.21   "Endlich Allein," operetta: ....
I: 1. "Gibst eine Hochzeiterei, da gehts immer lustig her dabei," chorus
2. "You fickle men! It is a shame the way that you are acting" (Dolly, ch)
3. "O, ich gib fein acht, ich weiss schon wie man's macht" (Bräutigam, ch)
4. "Nur wer je verliebt war, kanns verstehn, dass ich beinah schon verrückt!" (Frank)
5. "Ist man jung so wie ich, stramm gewachsen, frisches Blut" (Tilly, Willy)
6. "Hätt' man das, was meistens fehlt, hätt' man das, was üb'rall zählt"
7. "Da war der blonde Fritze" (Tilly, Willy)
8. "Süsse kleine Tilly, Engel der Pension, glaube mir dein Willy" (Tilly)
9. "Wenn ich die leuchtenden Gletscher seh' " (Dolly)
10. "Erst geht man, dann steigt man," trio (Dolly, Splenningen, Willy)
11. "Sport, und immer Sport, so heisst das grosse Zauberwort"
12. "Wann und wo man Walzer tanzt" (Tilly)
13. "Du, du! so tönt es leise, lockt dich, zieht dich, gibt keine Ruh"
II: 14. "Sag' Du mein Sternchen, sag', stets allein zu sein," scene & Lied (Dolly)
15. "Hell wie die Sonne aus wolkigem Flor," finale (Dolly, Frank)
III: 16. "Ja, komm', gehn wir durch" (Tilly, Willy)
17. "Männchen, komm' fahr mit mir doch Ringelspiel" (Dolly, Frank)
18. "Wir zu Zwei'n so ganz so ganz allein, im Mondenschein" (Dolly)
Themes which appear also in operetta: Schön ist die Welt: . "Willst du's verstehn" (1.)
. "Dort wo im dämmrigen" (11.)
. "Schön ist die Welt" (8.)
. "Es steht vom lieben" (12.)
. "In luftiger Höh' im ewigen Schnee" (2.)
. "Die Berge stehn im Silberlicht" (15.)
. "Ja man flüstert überall" (16.)

1a.22   "Der Sterngucker," operetta: ....
I: 1. "Kosend schweben wir dahin, lokken, lachen und entfliehn" (Kitty, Lilly, Lizzi, Isolde)
2. "Ich grüsste Sie einst auf den Stiegen" (Kitty, Paul)
3. "Fräulein, ich kann es nicht sagen"
4. "Ich möchte einen Mann mit einem Profil!" (Lilly, Franz)
5. "Kaum vor einer Stund, hatt' ich's einst geträumt"
II: 6. "Liebster komme, o Liebster komme, ich harre dein" (Kitty)
7. "Die Jahre gleiten flüchtig hin, man lebt und lebt ganz ohne Sinn" (Kitty, Paul)
8. "Ja, Franze, wer war denn jetzt hier?" (Kitty, Franz, Nepomuk)
9. "Wie geht es dir, du dikker Bär?" (Lilly)
10. "Lieber guter Theddy Bär"
11. "Gib acht! es lockt und lacht bei Tag und Nacht der Frauen Macht" (Lilly, Mizzi, Isolde, Franz)
12. "Sterngucker, Sterngucker, nimm dich in acht!" (Lilly, Franz)
13. "Nur wie im Traum wusst' von Liebe und Leben ich kaum"
14. "Mein Schwesterlein und ich, wir zwei, wir liebten beide uns so treu!"
15. "Als ich heute morgens bin erwacht, Josefin, Josefin" (Nepomuk)
16. "Meist ist entzückt doch der Bräutigam" (Lilly, Franz, Nepomuk)
17. "Kann es wohl im Leben, je was Schön'res geben" (Kitty, Lilly, Paul, Franz)
Themes which appear also in operetta: Libellentanz: . "Lange schon spürt ich" (1.)
. "Ja das jetzt die Dinge steh'n" (2.)
. "Mein Herz ist wie der junge Mai" (5.)
. "Du, du, du, überstrahlst" (14.)
. "So nur so, so müsste mein Liebster sein" (7.)
. "Nur dir, dir will ich Alles sein" (13.)
. "Muss denn jeder gleich ein Eh'mann sein?" (12.)
. "Bitte sich nur zu bedienen" (17.)
. "Ja, das war die wunderwunder Schöne" (19.)

1a.23   "Wo die Lerche singt," operetta: ....
I: 1. "Es rötelt im Laube, es duftet das Heu," chorus
2. "Hat man's Grün der Sommerwiesen satt" (Rezsó, ch)
3. "Was geh'n mich an die Leute in grosser Welt?" (Pál)
4. "Ein Hauch, wie von Blüten, so süss, so schwer" (Vilma)

5. "Wenn die Liebe ruft kaum erwacht liegt was in der Luft das uns glücklich macht" (Vilma, Arpád)
6. "Durch die weiten Felder, durch die dunklen Wälder" (Margit)
7. "Wo die Lerche singt, wo die Sichel klingt"
8. "Schöne Mergit, kleine Lerche, komm und werde mein" (Margit, Sándor)
9. "Auf dem Bankerl vor dem Haus sitzt es sich gemütlich" (Margit, Pál, Vilma)
10. "Kein Theater und kein Kino, nie ein eleganter Ball" (Pál, Vilma)
11. "Ja auf dem Land, da ist das Leben g'sund!" (Vilma)
12. "Kommen gradewegs vom Schnitt" (Margit, Pista, ch)
II: 13. "Sonntag kommt mein Schatz und tanzt mit mir" (Margit)
14. "Bin ich erst der grosse Mann, pass' auf, dann geht es an!" (Margit, Sándor)
15. "Wer ist denn der Mann mit der schönen Frau? Das ist der berühmteste Maler" (Margit, Sándor)
16. "Pali, sagt' mir einst die Mutter, wie ich jung noch war" (Pál)
17. "Palikám, Palikám, schöner Mann, komm nur ja recht bald wiederum her!"
18. "Fern wie aus vergang'nen Tagen seh' ich dein Bild!" (Sándor)
19. "Die Rosen hörens nur allein" (Sándor, Vilma)
20. "Dich hat das Glück zu mir gesandt! Was ich bin dank' ich dir!" (Margit, Sándor)
21. "Jancsi hat ein braunes Rökkel, geht er auf die Weide" (Margit, Sándor)
III: 22. "Heut' hab' ich das Glück beim Schopf gepackt ich hab's gewagt, bin am Ziel!" (Sándor)
23. "Was ist nur gescheh'n, ich kann's nicht versteh'n" (Margit)

1a.24 "Die blaue Mazur," operetta: ....
I/1: 1. "Lasst uns Blumen streu'n dem neuvermählten Paar" (Introduction)
2. "Freuet Euch, ihr lieben Leut', denn unser Pan hält Hochzeit heut'," chorus (behind the scene)
3. "Dieses kleine Medaillon" (Blanka)
4. "Komm, ich sag' dir was ins Ohr" (Juljan)
5. "Komm, mein Herz, und tanz mit mir in die Eh' hinein" (Blanka, Juljan)
6. "Seit Bestand der Weltgeschichte" (Adolar)
7. "Drum soll sich keine ewig binden" (Gretl)
8. "Ich bin zum letztenmal verliebt" (Gretl)
9. "Ja, ja, bei Tag da bin ich nicht zu seh'n" (Adolar)
10. "Jetzt hätt' ich grade Zeit für meine kleine Maid"
11. "Ich darf nur Eine lieben" (Juljan)
12. "Nun kommt das grosse Abschied nehmen"
13. "Was sich ein Mädchen erträumt" (Blanka, Juljan, ensemble)
14. "Hochzeitsnacht, die hold hernieder lacht" (Blanka)
I/2: 15. "Verrauscht sind längst der Jugendzeiten" (Reiger)
16. "Lokkend erwartet mich das Leben" (Blanka)
17. "O du lachende, hold erwachende"
18. "Oj, Tak teskno mi za toba duszko ma" (Juljan)
II: 19. "Klinge du süsse Musik, sing' ein Lied mir vom Glück!" (Gretl)
20. "Tanzt de Pole die Mazur" (Blanka, Juljan)
21. "Heimlich süsse Händedrücke"
22. "Nur mit Einer tanzt der Pole die blaue Mazur, mit ...'"
23. "Lumperl, Lumperl, einmal muss es sein" (Gretl, Adolar)
24. "Mäderl, mein süsses Grederl geh', schlag' dir das aus deinem Schäderl" (Adolar)
25. "Lieben will ich dich treu und wahr" (Gretl, Adolar)
26. "Wer die Liebe kennt, weiss allein wie die Sehnsucht brennt" (Juljan)

1a.25 "Die Tangokönigin," operetta: ....
I: 1. "Mein Kind, du wirst ironisch" (Leandro, Manolita)
2. "Mündlich bin ich schüchtern sehr" (Don Gil)
3. "Mein Gesang klingt nicht wie Cello"
4. "War's der Frühling der unsre Herzen verband?" (Leandro, Manolita)
5. "Der Walzer und die Liebe die waren schuld daran" (Manolita)
6. "Was uns Männer intressiert ist das gewissewisse Etwas!" (Leandro)
7. "Geh'n sie doch, mein Herr, sie sind ja Ehemann" (Coletta)
8. "Ich will es tun, ich hab' ihn lieb" (Manolita)
9. "Don Kamiro di Padilla werde ich genannt" (Coletta, Don Gil)
10. "Braunes Mädel von Madrid, sei nicht dumm und geh' doch mit" (Don Gil)
11. "Er ist grad heut' so froh bewegt" (Coletta, Columbus, Don Gil, Leandro, ensemble)
12. "Die Frau Gemahlin ist auf kurze Zeit verreist" (Leandro)
13. "Kinder, heut' geht's uns famos" (Coletta, Columbus, Don Gil, Leandro, ch)
II: 14. "Es jauchzen und jubeln die Geigen, man tanzt, man schwebt im Reigen" (ensemble)
15. "Vor allem will so fort ich proklamieren" (Coletta)
16. "Bitte, sehen Sie selbst mich an, bitte sagen Sie selber dann" (Manoletta)
17. "Oh, du mein Weltbijou" (Manoletta)
18. "Oh, la la 'Paris' das fasciniert, fasciniert" (Manoletta, ensemble)
19. "Heissgeliebteste Coletta" (Don Gil)
20. "Willst du mein süsser, kleiner braver Hampelmann sein" (Coletta)
21. "Schau mich an Kind und sag' mir dann" (Don Gil)
22. "Als ich Sie vor mir geseh'n so reizend und so schön" (Manoletta, Sartrewski)
23. "Wer ein Frauenmündchen sieht" (Coletta, Manoletta, Mara, Florella, Pepita, fem ch)
24. "Bei Valparaiso in der Schenke von Durango" (Tango) (Manoletta)
25. "Wenn du so schwebst durch den Raum" (Leandro)
26. "Ach, was liegt denn dran, Herr Graf, ach wissen" (Manoletta)

27. "War einst im schönen Polenland ein Musikant!" (Sartrewski)
28. "Hören Sie den Walzer er ruft uns und wirbt" (Don Gil)
29. "Des abends werden wach der Liebe Gluten" (Manoletta)
30. "Küsse mich, so tönt es leise"

1a.26   "Frühlingsmädel" (Frühling), operetta: ....
1. "Hemdchen, Strumpf und Leibchen winken sanft mir zu" (Ewald, Lorenz)
2. "Nur ein Stückchen Batist, das man nie mehr vergisst"
3. "Jeden Abend so um acht, wenn die Läden zugemacht" (Die freundin, Ewald)
4. "O ich bin so verliebt in die Liebe"
5. "Ich denk' sie mir so recht zum Liebgewinnen" (Lorenz)
6. "Schuhchen, ihr kleinen, zu welch' Stelldicheinen habt ihr eure Herrin gebracht?"
7. "Wer verliebt ist, muss es zeigen" (Lorenz, das Mädchen)
8. "Blüht im Frühling der Flieder"
9. "Mäntel und Roben, immer nur proben ist mein Los" (Freundin, Mädchen)
10. "Ein Muff aus Zobel und ein Hut aus Tüll"
11. "Ich kenne ein heimliches Plätzchen" (Lorenz, das Mädchen)
12. "Bei seinem ersten Stelldichein sagt jedes kleine Mädel: nein"

1a.27   "Frasquita," operetta: ....
I: 1. "Gib mit dem Fächer ein Zeichen mir" (Juan, ch)
2. "Wer hat das gesagt?" (Frasquita)
3. "Nimm mich, nimm mich so, wie ich bin"
4. "Hört, es klingt ein Lied" (Sebastiano, ch)
5. "Sag mir, sag' mir, bist du die Frau" (Armand)
6. "Einem Kavalier, der so wie dieser ein Erzpariser" (Armand, Dolly)
7. "Wenn ganz sacht über Nacht"
8. "Fragst mich, was Liebe ist?" (Frasquita)
9. "Tanzen, das ist jetzt die grosse Mode" (Dolly, Girot, Hippolyt)
10. "Darum Mädel suchst du einen Mann"
11. "Du siehst auf jedem kleinen Blatt," finale (Armand, Frasquita)
12. "Wenn eine Rose ich schenke" (Frasquita)
II: 13. "Schwärmerisch sprach Don Rodrigo" (Inez, Lola, ch)
14. "Geh' mit mir in die Alhambra"
15. "War in einem Städtchen einst ein armes Mädchen in der Fabrik" (Frasquita)
16. "Wüsst' ich, wer morgen mein Liebster ist"
17. "Weisst Du nicht, was ein Herz voller Sehnsucht begehrt?" (Armand, Frasquita)
18. "Amelie, die gute Tante gab den Rat mir immer" (Dolly, Hippolyte)
19. "Ich gäb' was d'rum"
20. "Schatz, ich bitt' dich, komm heut' Nacht!" (Armand)
21. "Ein Glück dir winkt so wie noch nie"
22. "Kinder, heute fühl' ich mich wie zwanzig Jahr" (Girot)
23. "Ja! Jung ist Jeder, der jung sich noch fühlt" (Girot, Inez, Lola, fem ch)
24. "Lasst den Tage seine Sonne," finale (Frasquita)
III: 25. "Oh, glaub' mir, mein Freund" (Frasquita)
26. "Wo du weilst, was du immer tust"
27. "Kinder! Kinder! Heut' ist Karneval!," chorus
28. "Wenn zwei sich immer küssen" (Dolly, Hippolyte)
29. "Du, küss' mich immerzu"
30. "Träumen möcht' ich für mich hin von vergang'nen," finale (Armand)

1a.28   "Libellentanz," operetta: ....
I: 1. "Töricht ist jeder, der heut' beim Ofen hockt," chorus
2. "Mit dem Schlittschuh' ritz' ich ein Geheimnis ein"
3. "Ob du willst oder nicht, du musst mit" (Helene)
4. "Wenn mir, auch Geld und Gut entglitt" (Charles)
5. "Ja die, die einst vielleicht mir blüht"
6. "Es schmeichelt mir sehr, dass ein Mann wie Sie aus Sympathie" (Helene, Charles)
7. "Frühlingswind sonnigen Südens Kind"
8. "Ich ward geboren, ich weiss nicht wie" (Toutou)
9. "Wenn ich lieb', lieb' ich enorm, ganz tigerhaft!"
10. "Hochbegabt bin ich, man sieht mir's an" (Bouquet, Toutou)
11. "Beim Kino möcht' ich sein"
II: 12. "Schminke, Puder sind das Arsenal" (Charlotte, fem ch)
13. "Nur er ist meiner Wünsche Traum" (Helene)
14. "Du, Du, Du, überstrahlst alle Sterne an Glanz" (Charles)
15. "Draussen weit im Meer betten" (Charles, Charlotte, Helene, Toutou)
16. "Ein mal war verliebt ich im Monat Mai" (Bouquet, Toutou)
17. "Bambolina, geh' durch, geh' durch mit mir!"
18. "Bitte Madame, bitte, treten in Ihre Gard'robe Sie ein!" (Helene, Charles)
19. "Spielt man eine Rolle, die verliebt gefährlich ist"
20. "Schon hat die Nacht" (Bouquet, Toutou)
21. " 'Komm' sei heut' mein Liebchen, sei nett!' sagt der Apach' zu Gigolett' "
III: 22. "Herz, mein Herz, flieg' nicht himmelwärts!" (Helene)
23. "Gib Acht, dass nicht ein kekkes Irrlicht nur Dich narrt"

24. "Höchst romantisch ist der Mond" (Bouquet, Toutou)
25. "Lieber, guter Mond schau' weg"

1a.29   "Die gelbe Jacke," operetta: ....
1. "Meine Damen, meine Herrn! Viel zu reden liegt mir fern" (Claudius)
2. "Ich bin verliebt, weiss gar nicht wie"
3. " 'Ich konnte nicht kommen' und fragt man warum?" (Sou-Chong)
4. "Schau, Claudi, sei doch g'scheit, lass' dir doch zum Ehemann noch Zeit!" (Wimpach)
5. "Vater, such mir eine Braut, schön und jung und fesch gebaut" (Claudius)
6. "Na, endlich kann ich Sie begrüssen! Wie geht's! Wie steht's?," finale (Lea)
7. "Hier in China blast fast jedas Mädchen" (Mi)
8. "Blas', blas', du kleines Mädchen, du" (Claudius, Mi, Miao, Sou-Chong)
9. "Wien, du mein Wien, ach, zu dir zieht's mich hin" (Lea)
10. "Ach, ach, wär ich zuhaus', flög' ich zu dir jubelnd hinaus"
11. "Schau, mir kommen Tränen und ums Herz wird's mir warm und weich" (Mi)
12. "Wärst du jetzt bei mir, was wollt' mit dir ich alles tun" (Lea)
13. "Moderne Frau'n heisst der Roman, den jetzt man liest" (Lea, Mi)
14. "S'hängt der Himmel voller Geigen und die Stimmung ist da"
Themes which appear also in operetta: Das Land des Lächelns: . "Freunderl mach' dir nichts draus" (4.)
. "Immer nur lächeln" (5.)
. "Von Apfelblüten einen Kranz" (9.)
. "Zig, zig, zig" (19.)
. "Ich möcht' wieder einmal den Prater" (15.)
. "Als Gott die Welt erschuf" (12.)

1a.30   "Cloclo" (Lolotte), operetta: ....
I: 1. "Wir sind die berühmte Garde, die Garde Cloclos" (Tricolet, Rasolin, Pipere, Flipeur, m ch)
2. "Tanzende Puppe, Liebling der Truppe, fliegend, siegend" (Cloclo)
3. "Ich suche einen Mann der sehr veliebt sein kann"
4. "So weint am Nil das Krokodil!" (Severin)
5. "Geh' schön nach Haus zu deiner Frau" (Cloclo)
6. "Bedenk, du bist ein ält'rer Herr"
7. "Komm', du alter Jubelgreis stell' dich in der Jugend Kreis" (Tricolet, Rasolin, Pipère, Flipeur, ch)
8. "Wenn man über fünfzig ist, dann erst lebt man und geniesst!" (Severin)
9. "Lass mich zu dir in dein heimliches Liebesrevier" (Cloclo, Maxime)
10. "Nur ein einziges Stündchen und einen Kuss, so klein"
11. "Hei! Juhei! Ich geh' aufs Land hinaus" (Cloclo)
II: 12. "Glokken klingen leise durch das Tal in uns're Herzen dringt ihr süsser Schall" (fem ch)
13. "Liebes Kind, hör' die Mama und schau' auf die Lampe da" (Melousine)
14. "Die Lampe der Familie!" (Cloclo)
15. "Ferne her, übers Meer, dringt ein wonniger Klang" (Severin, ch)
16. "Feurige Tänzer tanzen nur noch Java allein"
17. "Babette! Babette! Ach, wenn ich dich hätte" (Chablis, Cloclo)
18. "Komm', lass' dir ein Geheimnis sagen" (Cloclo)
19. "Wenn ich heute schlafen geh, dann denk' ich dein"
20. "Droben im Himmel, bei Amors Thron" (Cloclo, Maxime)
21. "Kinder, es ist keine Sünde wenn man liebt"
22. "Ich war nie eine Messalina, ich war nie eine Pompadour" (Melousine)
23. "Ich habe 'La Garçonne' gelesen, mein Busen hat heut' Platz für zehn!"
24. "Junggesellin sein, wie wär das so fein, das hat was für sich!"
III: 25. "Seht die schaurige, seht die traurige arme Kleine!," chorus
26. "Olé, olá, olé ich bin da!" (Severin, Tricolet, Rasolin, Pipière & ch w/ Flipeur)
27. "Zu jeder Zeit gab's Narren auf der Welt" (Severin)
28. "Sag', Liebster, wie gefall' ich dir?" (Cloclo)
29. "Gehen die Mädchen zu Bette, denken sie mancherlei" (Maxine)

1a.31   "Paganini," operetta: ....
I: 1. "Mein lieber Freund, ich halte viel auf Etikette" (Anna Elisa)
2. "Schönes Italien, erst gedenk' ich dein" (Paganini)
3. "Der Töne holde Welt nenn' ich mein"
4. "Was ich denke, was ich fühle, höchstes Glück und tiefstes Leid" (Paganini)
5. "Feuersglut lodert heiss in meinem Blut" (Anna Elisa)
6. "So ein Mann ist eine Sünde wert"
7. "Niemals habe ich mich int'ressiert für Kunst und Literatur" (Pimpinelli, Bella)
8. "Mit den Frau'n auf du und du"
9. "Die Fürstin Anna Elisa, des Reiches höchste Zier," chorus (Landleute)
10. "Töne, süsses Zauberlied" (Anna Elisa)
II: 11. "Wenn keine Liebe wär' " (Bella)
12. "Glück im Spiel war einst mein höchstes Ziel" (Paganini)
13. "Gern hab' ich die Frau'n geküsst" (Paganini)
14. "Ich kenn der wahrhaften Liebe Glut"
15. "Deinen süssen Rosenmund" (Paganini)
16. "Launisch sind alle Frau'n" (Bella, Pimpinelli)
17. "Einmal möcht' ich was Närrisches tun"
18. "Sag' mir, wieviel süsse rote Lippen hast Du schon geküsst?" (Anna Elisa)

19. "Niemand liebt Dich so wie" (Anna Elisa, Paganini)
20. "Ich kann es nicht fassen" (Anna Elisa)
21. "Liebe, du Himmel auf Erden, ewig besteh'!"
22. "Man sprach von dem Künstler" (Pimpinelli, ch)
23. "Spiel', kleine Silberflöte die Melodei" (Bella)
III: 24. "Liegen um Mitternacht alle Bürger schnarchend im Schlaf," chorus
25. "O, wie schön ist es nichts zu tun"
26. "Wenn man das letzte Geld verlumpt" (Foletto)
27. "Jetzt beginnt ein neues Leben" (Bella, Pimpinelli)
28. "Wir gehen ins Theater, dann führst Du mich aus"
29. "Wo meine Wiege stand ich weiss es nicht!" (Anna Elisa)
30. "Wer will heut Nacht mein Liebster sein?"
31. "Du darfst keiner Frau gehören, die im Arm Dich liebend hält" (Anna Elisa)

1a.33   "Der Zarewitsch," operetta: ....
I: 1. "Hell erklingt ein liebliches frohed Heimatlied," chorus (Tscherkessen)
2. "Dich nur-allein nenne ich mein" (Iwan)
3. "Schaukle, Liebchen, schaukle"
4. "Einer wird kommen, der wird mich begehren" (Sonja)
5. "Mir ist so bang als hielt mich ein Traum befangen"
6. "Es steht ein Soldat am Wolgastrand" (Zarewitsch)
7. "Hast du dort oben vergessen auf mich?"
8. "Jag' mich nicht fort!" (Sonja)
9. "Ich fürchte das grosse Geheimnis, das alle Frau'n umgibt" (Zarewitsch)
10. "Trinkt man auf Du und Du, muss man in's Aug' sich seh'n" (Sonja)
II: 11. "Sag, liegt das Glück nur in Ruhm und Glanz und Pracht?" (Zarewitsch)
12. "Stosset an! lacht und trinkt und singt!" (Zarewitsch, ch)
13. "Bleib' bei mir, wie die Blumen hier, blüh' für mich!" (Zarewitsch)
14. "Was ich hab' und bin, das sei dein, will mit frohem Sinn, dir mich weih'n!" (Sonja)
15. "Hab' nur dich allein" (Sonja, Zarewitsch)
16. "Heute hab' ich meinen schönsten Tag" (Napolitana) (Zarewitsch)
17. "O komm, es hat der Frühling ach nur einen Mai"
18. "Was mir einst an dir gefiel, war dein Balalaikaspiel" (Mascha, Iwan)
19. "Heute Abend komm' ich zu dir"
20. "Bin ein glückseliges Menschenkind, ich jauchze, ich juble, ich singe" (Sonja)
21. "Das Leben ruft, es lockt der Liebe Macht, der Tag ist schön"
22. "Liebe mich, küsse mich, bist ja doch mein" (Zarewitsch)
23. "Deine Glut berauscht die Sinne mir" (Sonja, Zarewitsch)
24. "Wir Tscherkessen brauchen weder Gut noch Geld, nur ein Mädel her zum Tanz," chorus
25. "Ich bin verliebt und wär' ich es nicht, so möcht ich's sein" (Zarewitsch)
III: 26. "Kosende Wellen, ihr fröhlich tanzende Gesellen" (Zarewitsch)
27. "Mädel, wonniges Mädel, wie hast du das gemacht" (Zarewitsch)
28. "Küss' mich, küss' mich, küss' mich, küss' mich, Oh wie ich dich liebe!" (Zarewitsch, Sonja)
29. "Komm' an meine Brust, ans stille Plätzchen, wo immer du lagst" (Mascha, Iwan)
30. "Wenn dein zartes Herz nach Liebe schreit" (Iwan)

1a.34   "Friederike," operetta: ....
I: 1. "Gott gab einen schönen Tag" (Friederike)
2. "Kleine Blumen, kleine Blätter" (Friederike)
3. "Mit Mädchen sich vertragen," chorus (Students)
4. "Bravo! So hab' ich die Männer gern!" (Salomea)
5. "Tralalalala! Tralalalala! Die Mädels sind nur zum Küssen da!" (Salomea, Students)
6. "O, wie schön, wie wunderschön!" (Goethe)
7. "Blikke ich auf deine Hände" (Goethe)
8. "Du bist so sanft, du bist so zart, mein Lämmchen" (Lenz)
9. "Lämmchen brav, Lämmchen brav, später wirst du doch ein Schaf"
10. "Sah ein Knab' ein Röslein steh'n" (Goethe)
11. "Was kümmert mich die ganze Welt? Ich liebe ihn!," finale (Friederike)
12. "Es spielen die Geigen zum lieblichen Reigen"
II: 13. "Bin ich wirklich schön, wie der junge Mai" (Salomea)
14. "Elsässer Kind, du mein süsses Elsässer Kind" (Lenz)
15. "All'mein Fühlen, all'mein Sehnen" (Friederike, Goethe)
16. "O Mädchen, mein Mädchen, wie lieb' ich dich!" (Goethe)
17. "Warum hast du mich wachgeküsst?" (Friederike)
III: 18. "Riekchen, komm mit uns zum Tanz" (Malchen, fem vv)
19. "Meine Lieben, hört, was ich euch sage, eh' die Reue naht!" (Friederike)
20. "Heute tanzen wir den Pfälzertanz!" (Lenz, Salomea)
21. "Stolz wie eine kleine Königin schreitet hin die holde Tänzerin" (Salomea)
22. "Ein Herz, wie Gold so rein" (Goethe)

1a.35   "Das Land des Lächelns," operetta: ....
I: 1. "Flirten, bisschen flirten" (Lisa)
2. "Gern, gern, wär' ich verliebt"
3. "Es ist nicht das erste Mal" (Lisa, Gustl)
4. "Freunderl, mach' dir nix d'raus, 's war ja nicht so bös gemeint"

5. "Immer nur lächeln und immer vergnügt" (Sou-Chong)
6. "Ach, trinken Sie vielleicht mit mir ein Tässchen Tee?" (Lisa, Sou-Chong)
7. "Bei einem Tee à deux" (Sou-Chong)
8. "Von Apfelblüten einen Kranz" (Sou-Chong)
II: 9. "Prelude"
10. "Wer hat die Liebe uns ins Herz gesenkt" (Sou-Chong)
11. "Im Salon zur blau'n Pagode" (Mi)
12. "Als Gott die Welt erschuf, war'n alle Menschen gleich" (Gustl)
13. "Meine Liebe, deine Liebe, die sind beide gleich" (Gustl, Mi)
14. "Dein ist mein ganzes Herz" (You are my heart's delight) (Sou-Chong)
15. "Ich möcht' wieder einmal die Heimat seh'n" (Lisa)
16. (Chinesischer Hochzeitszug)
17. "Kann es möglich sein" (Sou-Chong)
III: 18. "Liebe besiegt, Liebe durchfliegt Zeiten und Raum" (Sklavinnen)
19. "Zig, zig, zig, zig, ih!" (Mi)
20. "Wenn die Chrysanthemen blüh'n am Paiho"
21. "Du bist so lieb, du bist so schön" (Gustl)

1a.36   "Schön ist die Welt," operetta: ....
1. "Lieber Direktor, ich bitte sehr" (Direktor, Oberhofmeister)
2. "Wie seltsam bewegt das Herz mir heut schlägt!" (Elisabeth)
3. "Sag', armes Herzchen, sag', wird dir nicht der Tag und die Nacht oft zu lange"
4. "Herzogin Marie, Herzogin Marie, keine war so reizend, entzükkend wie Sie" (König)
5. "Nur ein Viertelstündchen vor der Schlafengeh'n möcht' ich dich" (Sascha)
6. "Nur ein Viertelstündchen oben auf dem Gang" (Mercedes, Sascha)
7. "Bruder Leichtsinn, so werd' ich genannt" (Georg)
8. "Schön ist die Welt"
9. "Frei und jung dabei" (Elisabeth, Georg)
10. "Rio de Janeiro, Märchenstadt voll Sonnenglut!" (Mercedes, ch)
11. "Dort, wo im dämmrigen Schein" (Georg)
II: 12. "Es steht vom Lieben so oft geschrieben" (Elisabeth, Georg)
13. "Liebste, glaub' an mich, denn ich liebe dich!" (Georg)
14. "Hell wie die Sonne aus wolkigem Flor strahlt die göttliche Liebe hervor!" (Georg)
15. "Die Berge steh'n im Silberlicht und Wölkchen ziehen sacht"
III: 16. "Ja, die Liebe ist brutal" (Mercedes, Sascha)
17. "Dort in der kleinen Tanzbar" (Mercedes)
18. "In der kleinen Bar"
19. "Bin verliebt bin so verliebt, masslos verliebt so wie ein kleines Mädel!" (Elisabeth)
20. "Warum bin ich so froh?"
21. "Heimlich, wie in der Nacht die Diebe schleicht sich dir in das Herz die Liebe" (Sascha)
22. "Schön sind lachende Frau'n, doch sei auf der Hut"

1a.38   "Peter und Paul im Schlaraffenland," children's operetta: ....
1. "Trala la und trala la, ich der Schlendrian bin da" (Schlendrianus)
2. "Schuster der hat niemals Ruh', Abends spät und morgens früh" (Kneipp)
3. "Sum, sum, sum, sum, sum wenn die Sonne schlafen geht" (Meisterin)
4. "Spielt auf Musikanten wir dreh'n uns im Tanz," chorus
5. "Wir wandern, wir wandern jetzt in's Schlaraffenland" (Peter, Paul)
6. "Wir sind bitte die Minister hier in dem Schlaraffenland" (8 Minister)
7. "Ich nehm' den Säbel in die Hand" (Peter, Paul)
8. "Stramm aufmarschiert, Flott exerziert"
9. "Hab' die Ehre und mein Compliment" (Ferkel)
10. "Ei die kleinen Wichte jeder kennt" (Tanzerinnen, Tänzer, ch)
11. "Der Müller der hat eine Kuh, die ist so dumm und schreit muh, muh" (child ch)
12. "Ich hab' ein schönes Schaukelpferd mit Sattel und mit Bügel" (Karlchen)
13. "Ein Sternlein ist gekommen in einer stillen Nacht" (Apotheose), chorus

1a.39   "Mitislaw der Moderne," parody: ....
1. "Ich bin sehr schwach, ich bin nicht stark!" (Graf Jerzabinka)
2. "Man sagte mir, als ich noch klein: 'Du bist bestimmt zum Throne!' " (Mitislaw)
3. "Mon cher Papa ist mächtig, ein Kavalier mit Geld" (Amaranthe)
4. "Das knistert und rauscht von verborg'ner Seide"
5. "Viele Frauen legen leider viel zu grossen Wert auf Kleider" (Amaranthe, Tina)
6. "Wollt' ihr Frau'n bei Männern reüssier'n"
7. "Ich schaff' mir einen Musterstaat, wo man modern regiert" (Mitislaw)
8. "Sei modern, mein Sohn" (ensemble)
9. "Ich pfeife auf die Tugend immerdar" (Amaranthe)
10. "Zwei sind da hineingegangen, ach, ich sah's mit Neid und grau'n" (Amaranthe)
11. "O du kleines Schlüsselloch, sei nicht so indiskret!"

1a.40   "Rosenstock und Edelweiss," Singspiel: ....
1. "I hab' amol mei Muatta g'fragt, was d'Liab bedeut' im Leb'n" (Everl)
2. "Herrgott, wie prächtig is die Natur" (Rosenstock)
3. "Sie ham noch nie gesehn ä Kohn? das is auf Ehre schad" (Everl, Rosenstock)
4. "O dieses Evchen ist ein liebes Schäfchen, Gott"

709

5. "Jetzt wass i was d'Liab is und was sie uns macht" (Everl)
6. "Die Liab is die Sunn, sie tut brennen und glüh'n"
7. "Wer kommt heut' in jedem Theaterstück vor? Ä Jud!" (Rosenstock)
8. "Das sieht die ganze Welt jetzt ein, woraus sich klar ergibt"
9. "Naturschauspiel' könnens betrachten hier gnau," duet (Everl, Rosenstock)

1a.44   "Rose de Noël": ....
    I: 1. "Pour un rendezvous d'amour" (Michel)
          2. "Un sourire, un soupir, un regard. Peuvent, soudain"
          3. "Mais je vois s'avancer Le Mair, bien aimé, De notre Cité" (Promenade dominicale) (les Choeurs)
          4. "Dimanche est le plus beau jour de repos" (les Choeurs)
          5. "Ça manque d'horizon Un' petit' vill' de garnison" (Un Officier)
          6. "La semaine terminée, Qu'il fait bon se promener" (les Choeurs)
          7. "Toujours, sur tout' la terre" (Popelka)
          8. "Y'a de l'amour dans la giberne"
          9. "Mad'moiselle, Vous êtes si belle" (Totsi, les Choeurs-Hommes)
        10. "Parpitié, décidez-vous!"
        11. "Chantons, chantons en choeur" (les Choeurs)
        12. "Tant que je vivrai" (Michel, Vilma)
        13. "Tout est en effervescence" (Ludovica)
        14. "On dit, on dit Que le Gou le Gouverneur est gentil" (Ludovica, Mme Schmilputner, Sofia)
        15. "Mon beau ciel bleu, c'est le bleu de tes yeux" (Michel)
        16. "Chaque soir, Je cueillais, au long du chemin"
        17. "Ma chanson vous dira" (Vilma)
        18. "Pour vous j'aurais voulu"
        19. "Papa, mon petit papa, Je n'oublierai pas" (Le Colonel, Vilma)
        20. "Pour les p'tits soldats Qui marchent au pas" (Colonel, Popelka, Totsi)
        21. "Quand les soldats s'en vont au pas" (Colonel, Popelka, Totsi, les Choeurs)
        22. "Mais sitôt qu'une fille apparait au tournant" (Totsi, les Femmes)
        23. "La Rose de Noël" (Michel)
        24. "On dit qu'autrefois La fille d'un roi"
        25. "La Rose de Noël" (Michel, Vilma)
        26. "Cette fleur tardive, Tendre et naïve"
        27. "Vous livrez un assaut à ma vertu" (Totsi)
        28. "Le soleil qui brille" (Michel)
        29. "Ah! qu'il est joli le temps" (Michel, les Choeurs)
        30. "Jamais les belles Ne sont rebelles"
    II: 31. "Quand on a le bonheur" (Totsi, les Dames de la Bourgeosie)
        32. "A vos pieds, Monsieur le Gouverneur, Je me précipite" (Totsi)
        33. "Quand on est si jolie modiste" (Sandor)
        34. "Dans ce vieux château hanté" (Mathias, Popelka, Sandor, le Gardien)
        35. "Avec un peu de musique"
        36. "Chante, Tzigane, sur le chemin" (Choeur tzigane)
        37. "Les dernières fleurs vont se faner" (Michel)

2. ORCHESTRAL / INSTRUMENTAL

2.1	"Ach! wie herzig," polka-française	Op.71, NV1
2.2	"Adria-Walzer" (Klänge aus Pola / La belle Polesane) (p1895)	Op.24, NV3
2.3	"Altwiener-Liebeswalzer" (Rund um die Liebe) (p1911): No.1 in G major	NV9
2.4	No.2 in C major	
2.5	No.3 in F major	
2.6	"An der grauen Donau," waltz (p1921)	NV12
2.7	"Angelica-Walzer" (p1901): No.1 in B-flat major	NV14
2.8	No.2 in G major	
2.9	No.3 in G major	
2.10	No.4 in G major	
2.11	"Asklepius-Walzer" (p1901, incl waltz: Pikanterien)	Op.73, NV21
2.12	"Bessie" (Valse Boston)	NV24
2.13	"Buntes aus der Tonwelt" (large orch)	NV26
2.14	"Burleske" (ballet music added to opera: Giuditta)	NV38
2.15	"Caprice-valse" (p1909; pf)	NV41
2.16	"Chinesen-Marsch" (p1917)	NV44
2.17	"Chinesische Ballet-Suite" (p1938)	NV46
2.18	"Concertino" (vn & orch)	NV52
2.19	"Concordia-Walzer" (p1901): No.1 in F major	Op.71, NV55
2.20	No.2 in C major	
2.21	No.3 in G major	
2.22	No.4 in D major	
2.23	"Danse exotique" (p1909; pf)	NV60
2.24	"Do-Re-La!" (Mia cara, mia bella Dorela! Du gehst am blauen Meer), waltz (p1921)	NV62
2.25	"Elfentanz," concert waltz (p1892)	NV64
2.26	"En Autocar" (from film: Une nuit à Vienne)	NV68
2.27	"Fantasie" (pf)	Op.7, NV70

2.103	"Sternennächte-Walzer"	NV247
2.104	"Suite de danse" (p1936; orch)	NV249
2.105	"Sylphiden-Gavotte" (p1893)	Op.15, NV252
2.106	"Triumph-Marsch" (p1898)	NV254
2.107	"Türkischer Marsch" (p1916)	NV257
2.108	"Valse américaine" (p1909; pf)	NV259
2.109	"Valse des fleurs" (p1909; pf)	NV261
2.110	"Vásárhelyi induló," march (p1893)	Op.14, NV263
2.111	"Eine Vision" (Meine Jugend) (Huldigungs-Ouvertüre) (p1907)	NV265
2.112	"Wiener Landsturm-Marsch" (p1917)	NV267
2.113	"Wiener Lebenslust," waltzes (p1892; arr for pf duet): No.1 in A major	Op.11, NV268
2.114	No.2 in D major	
2.115	No.3 in G major	
2.116	No.4 in D major	
2.117	"Wiener Zugvögel-Marsch" (p1892)	Op.4, NV277
2.118	"Wilde Rosen" (Valse Boston) (p1921)	NV281
2.119	"Zigeunerfest," balletszene (p1912; orch)	NV283

3. PIANO SONATAS

| 3.1 | Piano Sonata in D minor | Op.29, NV216 |
| 3.2 | Piano Sonata in F major | NV224 |

4. VOCAL (non-operatic)

4.1	"Am Klavier": "Ach, am Klavier, sass ich mit ihr," gavotte-polka (p1907, Merkt)	Op.65, V1
4.2	"Amours" (p1923, Dunan): 1. "Sans phrase": "Nous nous aimerons très longtemps"	V3
4.3	2. "Fruit défendu": "Elle affectait d'être très farouche"	V4
4.4	3. "À Versailles": "Versailles s'en dort au clair de la lune"	V6
4.5	"An der Saar und am Rhein": "Saarland, du mein herrliches, deutsches Saarland" (p1939, Welisch)	V7
4.6	"Anú elmúlt"	V9
4.7	"Aus eiserner Zeit" (p1915): 1. "Trutzlied": "Es tönen die Hörner Tag um Tag" (Löhner)	V10
4.8	2. "Ich hab' ein Hüglein im Polenland" (Zwerger)	V12
4.9	3. "Nur einer ...": "Es reisst der Wind vom Baum ein Blatt" (Oestéren)	V13
4.10	4. "Reiterlied 1914": "Drüben am Wiesenrand hocken zwei Dohlen" (Zuckermann)	V15
4.11	5. "Fieber": "Sie wird mit mir sein," sym poem (Weill; 1v & orch)	V16
4.12	"Aus längst vergang'ner Zeit!": "Sieh' jenes Weib, gebeugt, zerrissen" (p1891, Baronesse Fries)	V20
4.13	"Bukowiner Helden-Marsch": "Wir sind Bukowiner in Treue bewährt" (Norst)	V22
4.14	"Les compagnons d'Ulysse" (Mauprey & Geiringer): 1. "Sur le ch'min creux"	V24
4.15	2. "La chanson d'Angelica": "Je n'ai jamais dit t'aimer"	V26
4.16	3. "L'amour ne peut se tromper"	V28
4.17	4. "Ma rose blanche"	V30
4.18	5. "Je lis dans tes regards surpris"	V31
4.19	6. "Chant et danse d'Arequipa" (Tango d'amour): "Ne refuse plus de me voir"	V33
4.20	"Devasthymne": "Wenn aus düstern Wolkenmassen" (Seehund)	V35
4.21	"Die du mein Alles bist": "Du weisst es wohl" (p1891, Komtesse Rosa Cebrian)	V37
4.22	"Dir sing' ich mein Lied," English waltz (p1932, Herz)	V38
4.23	"Erre, Arra Jártam"	V40
4.24	"Erste Liebe": "Du bist meine erste, grosse Liebe!" (Valse Boston) (p1923, Löhner)	V41
4.25	"Es ist zu schön, um wahr zu sein!" (Si troppo bello essere vero) (p1926, Herz)	V43
4.26	"Gendarmenlied": "Wir sind die Gendarmen im Buchenland" (p1916, Horst)	V45
4.27	"Das gold'ne Ringlein": "Der gold'nen Treue hohes Lied" (c1905, Bruckner)	V46
4.28	"Ha megéhülök"	V48
4.29	"Hie und da sagt eine Frau zu allem 'Ja'!": "Schwer ist es," English waltz (p1936, Herz)	V49
4.30	"Hogyha a lány mosolyog"	V51
4.31	"Horthy induló": "Horthy Miklós hadja" (Gyula)	V52
4.32	"Ich fühl's, dass ich tief innen kränke"	V54
4.33	"Ich hol' dir vom Himmel das Blau!": "Nichts auf der Welt" (p1928, Schanzer & Welisch, = 20. & 21. of operetta: Libellentanz)	V55
4.34	"Ich liebe dich!": "Chérie das süsse Wort vergess' ich nie!" (p1936, Löhner)	V57
4.35	"Im Boudoir": "Es ist die kleine Leontine" (p1906, Merkt)	Op.67, V59
4.36	"Jetzt geht's los!": "Das Schönste ist auf dieser Erde," humoristic march (p1898, Markenau)	Op.17, V61
4.37	"Karpathen-Wacht": "Jung-Österreich-Ungarns stolze Wacht" (p1914, Schnitzer, after: Vater Radetzky ruft, V129; in Hung Zsolt)	V63
4.38	"Karst-Lieder" (p1894, Falzari): 1. "Schicksalsahnung": "Ein wogendes Gedränge geht"	Op.26, V64
4.39	2. "Erfüllung": "Ich weiss dir nichts zu sagen"	V65
4.40	3. "Was streift mein Blick"	V66
4.41	4. "Ich drücke deine liebe Hand": "Ein leichter Windhauch zieht durch's Land"	V67
4.42	5. "Es duften die Blüten": "Es zieht ein kühlendes Wehen vom silberglänzenden Meer"	V68
4.43	6. "Mein Traumschloss-versunken": "Das ewige Lied vom Scheiden erklingt"	V69
4.44	7. "Verzaubert": "Es hebt und senkt sich, glänzt und gleisst"	V70
4.45	"Kiss me, my darling": "Claire war fals Backfisch fabelhaft praktisch" (p1925, Vallas)	V71
4.46	"Komm zu mir zum Tee!": "Wenn die Lichter glühn" (Paso doble) (p1925, Herz)	V73

*   *   *   *   *

NV (non-vocal), **V** (vocal non-operatic) = "Franz Lehár. Thematic Index." Glocken Verlag Ltd. London, 1985.

Some opus numbers were given to more than one composition.

1. STAGE WORKS

Operas:

1.1	"Chatterton," 4 act melodramma (ca1876, Leoncavallo after Vigny's play: Chatterton) ....
1.2	"Pagliacci" (The Strolling Players), 2 act dramma (p1892, Leoncavallo)..
1.3	"Crepusculum," poema epico in forma di trilogia storica: I. "I Medici," 4 acts (p1893) ....
1.4	II. "Savonarola" (not composed)
1.5	III. "Cesare Borgia" (not composed)
1.6	"La bohème" (The Bohemians), 4 act commedia lirica (p1897, Leoncavallo, r as: Mimì Pinson p1913) (also see famous opera c by Puccini) ....
1.7	"Zazà," 4 act commedia lirica" (p1900, Leoncavallo after Berton & Simon) ....
1.8	"Der Roland von Berlin," 4 act historisches Drama (p1904, after Alexis) ....
1.9	"Majà," 3 act dramma lirico (p1910, Nessi after Choudens) ....
1.10	"Zingari," 2 act dramma lirico (p1912, Cavacchioli & Emanuel after Pushkin) ....
1.11	"Edipo re," 1 act grand opera (p1920, Forzano after Sophocles) ....
1.12	"Prometeo" (not perf, unpubd) ....
1.13	"Ave Maria" (abandoned in 1915, Illica & Cavacchioli)...
1.14	"Tormenta," 3 acts (Belvederi, inc) ....

Operettas:

1.15	"La jeunesse de Figaro" (p1906, after Sardou: Les premières armes de Figaro) ....
1.16	"Malbruck," 3 act fantasia comica medioevale (p1910, Nessi) ....
1.17	"La reginetta delle rose," 3 acts (p1912, Forzano) ....
1.18	"Are you there?," 3 act farce (p1913, Courville & Wallace) ....
1.19	"La candidata," 3 acts (p1915, Forzano) ....
1.20	"Prestami tua moglie," 3 acts (p1916, Corradi) ....
1.21	"Goffredo Mameli," 3 acts (p1916, Belvederi) ....
1.22	"A chi la giarrettiera?," 3 acts (p1919) ....
1.23	"Il primo baccio," 1 act (p1923, Bonelli) ....
1.24	"La maschera nuda," 3 acts (p1925, Bonelli & Paolieri; compl Allegri) ....

Ballet:

1.25	"La vita di una marionetta" (ca1900) ....

1a. SELECTIONS FROM STAGE WORKS (Nos. of sections in The Gramophone)

1a.2 "Pagliacci," opera: ....
        1. "Si può?" (Prologue)
    I: 2. "Son qua!"
        3. "Un grande spettacolo"
        4. "Un tal gioco"
        5a. "I zampognari!"
        5b. "Din, don" (Bell Chorus)
        6a. "Qual fiamma avea nel guardo!"
        6b. "Oh! Che volo d'augelli"
        6c. "Stridono lassù"
        7a. "Sei là!"
        7b. "So ben che difforme"
        8a. "Silvio! A quest'ora"
        8b. "Decidi il mio destin"
        8c. "E allor perchè"
        9a. "Recitar!"
        9b. "Vesti la giubba" (On with the motley)
        10. "Intermezzo"
    II: 11. "Presto, affrettiamoci"
        12a. "Pagliaccio, mio marito"
        12b. "O Colombina" (Serenade)
        12c. "È dessa!"
        13a. "Versa il filtro"
        13b. "No, Pagliaccio non son"
        14a. "Ebben, se mi giudichi"
        14b. "No, per mia madre!"

1a.7 "Zazà," opera: ....
    excerpts: I: 1. "A voi, su presto"
           2. "Salute a tutti"
           3. "Lo sai tu che vuol dire"
           4. "Augusto, buona sera"
           5. "Ah, ah, là, là"
           6. "Signor, entrate"
    II: 7. "È deciso, tu parti"

8. "Or lasciarmi andare!"
9. "Ecco gli stivaletti"
10. "Toh, o che quadretto"
11. "Buona Zazà del mio buon tempo"
12. "Hai ragione"
III: 13. "O mio piccolo tavolo"
14. "Eccomi pronta"
15a. "Mama usciva di casa"
15b. "Dir che ci sono al mondo"
IV: 16. "Dunque nessuna nuova"
17. "Zazà, piccola zingara"
18. "Che non vorresti farlo"
19. "Tu non m'amavi più"
20. "Ed ora io mi domando"

2. ORCHESTRAL WORKS

2.1 "Séraphitus—Séraphita," sym poem (c1894, after Balzac) ....

3. PIANO

3.1 "Pantins vivants," danse de caractère (p ?1898) ....
3.2 "La joyeuse," waltz (p ?1898) ....
3.3 "Valse mélancolique" (p1901) ....
3.4 "Cortége de Pulcinella," petite marche humoristique (p1903) ....
3.5 "Flirt-Walzer" (p1905) ....
3.6 "Papillon," scherzo (p1906) ....
3.7 "Sarabande," danse ancienne (p1906)..
3.8 "Viva l'America," march (p1906) ....
3.9 "Airs des ballets espagnols" (p ?1904): No.1 "Sevillana" ....
3.10   No.2 "Gitana-tango"
3.11   No.3 "Playeras ancienne"
3.12   No.4 "Granadinas"
3.13 "Nights of Italy," intermezzo (p1914) ....

W/ out date:

3.14 "Romanesca," morceau de style ancien ....
3.15 "Sous les palmiers"..
3.16 "Valse coquette" ....
3.17 "Valse mignonne" ....
3.18 "Serenata d'Arlecchino" ....
3.19 "Tarantella" ....

4. CHORAL WORKS (w/ orch)

4.1 "Nuit de mai" (ca1895) ....
4.2 "Requiem" (c1900, for Umberto I) ....
4.3 "Inno alla Croce rossa" (p1901) ....
4.4 "Inno della Lega nazionale" (p1913)...
4.5 "Inno franco-italiana" (France-Italie) (p1915) ....

5. SONGS (w/ pf)

5.1 "Album Stecchetti" (p1880, Guerrini: Postuma): 1. "October," fantasia ....
5.2   2. "Un organetto suona per la via," pensiero
5.3   3. "Donna vorrei morir," melodia
5.4   4. "Era d'inverno," pensiero
5.5 "At Peace" (p1884, Roberts) ....
5.6 "Lost Love" (p1884, Roberts) ....
5.7 "10 Songs" (p1893, Leoncavallo): 1. "Dietro le nubi" ....
5.8   2. "Addio"
5.9   3. "Nulla so"
5.10   4. "Suzon, adieu Suzon!"
5.11   5. "Un sogno"
5.12   6. "Non dirmi chi sei"
5.13   7. "October" (= 1. in: Album Stecchetti)
5.14   8. "Un organetto suona per la via" (= 2. in: Album Stecchetti)
5.15   9. "Donna vorrei morir" (= 3. in: Album Stecchetti)
5.16   10. "Chitaretta"
5.17 "Déclaration" (p1893, Silvestre) ....

* * * * *

PART I: ORIGINAL COMPOSITIONS

1. STAGE WORKS

1.1   "Don Sanche, ou Le château d'amour," 1 act opera (c1824–5, Théaulon & Rancé after Florian) S1

2. SYMPHONIES

2.1   "Eine Faust-Symphonie in drei Charakterbildern" (Faust Symphony) (c1854–7; T, ch & orch; arr
       for 2pf, S647): S108
         1. "Faust"
         2. "Gretchen" (arr for pf, S513)
         3. "Mephistopheles" and "Final Chorus"
2.2   "Eine Symphonie zu Dantes Divina commedia" (Dante Symphony) (c1855–6; arr for 2pf, S648): S109
         1. "Inferno"
         2. "Purgatorio" & "Magnificat" (w/ ch)

3. SYMPHONIC POEMS

3.1   No.1 "Bergsymphonie" (Ce qu'on entend sur la montagne) (c1848–9, after Hugo; 3 vers): S95
         . *Orig Version (c1848–9; orchd Raff)*
         . Version 2 (c1850)
         . Version 3 (c1854)
3.2   No.2 "Tasso, Lamento e trionfo" (c1849, after Byron; also see S112/3 & S159; 3 vers): S96
         . *Orig Version (c1849; orchd Conradi)*
         . *Version 2 (c1850–1; orchd Raff)*
         . Version 3 (c1854)
3.3   No.3 "Les préludes" (d'après Lamartine) (c1848, r by 1854; also see S80, S142 & S304) S97
3.4   No.4 "Orpheus" (c1853–4; arr for pf duet, S592; arr for 2pf, S638) S98
3.5   *No.5 "Prometheus" (c1850; orchd Raff, r1859; arr for 2pf , S639; also see S69 & S121)* *S99*
3.6   No.6 "Mazeppa" (c1851, after Hugo, r by 1854, from S139/4; arr for pf duet, S595; for 2pf, S640) S100
3.7   No.7 "Festklänge" (c1853; arr for pf duet, S595; for 2pf, S641) S101
3.8   *No.8 "Héroïde funèbre" (c1849–50; orchd Raff, r1854, from 1 movt of S690; arr for 2pf, S642)* *S102*
3.9   No.9 "Hungaria" (c1854, from S231; arr for pf duet, S596; for 2pf, S643) S103
3.10   No.10 "Hamlet" (c1858; arr for pf duet, S597; for 2pf, S644) S104
3.11   No.11 "Hunnenschlacht" (Battle of the Huns) (c1857, after Kaulbach; arr for 2pf, S645) S105
3.12   No.12 "Die Ideale" (c1857, after Schiller; arr for 2pf, S646) S106
3.13   No.13 "Von der Wiege bis zum Grabe—Du berceau jusqu'à la tombe" (From the Cradle to the Grave)
         (c1881–2, from S198; arr for pf, S512; for pf duet, S598) S107

4. OTHER ORCHESTRAL WORKS

4.1   "2 Episodes from Lenau's Faust" (c1861; arr for pf duet, S599): No.1 "Der nächtliche Zug" S110
4.2   No.2 "Der Tanz in der Dorfschenke" (Mephisto Waltz No.1) (arr for pf, S514)
4.3   "Mephisto Waltz" No.2 (c1880–1; arr for pf, S515; for pf duet, S600) S111
4.4   "Trois odes funèbres": No.1 "Les morts" (c1860–6, Lamennais; w/ m ch; arrs: S516, S601 & S268/2) S112
4.5   No.2 "La notte" (c1863–4, after Michelangelo; arrs: S699, S602 & S377a)
4.6   No.3 "Le triomphe funèbre du Tasse" (c1866, epilogue to S96; arrs: S517 & S603)
4.7   "Salve Polonia" (c1863; used as Interlude for S688; arr for pf, S518; for pf duet, S604) S113
4.8   "Kunstlerfestzug zur Schillerfeier 1859" (c1857, from S70 & S106; arr for pf, S521; for pf duet, S605) S114
4.9   *"Goethe Festmarsch" (c1849; orchd Conradi, r by Raff 1857; arr for pf, S520; pf duet, S606)* *S115*
4.10   "Festmarsch" (c1859, from Gotha: Diana von Solange; arr for pf, S522; for pf duet, S607) S116
4.11   "Rákóczy March" (c1865, from S242/13,15; arr for pf, S244/15; for pf duet, S608) S117
4.12   "Ungarischer Marsch" (c1870; arr for pf, S523; for pf duet, S609) S118
4.13   "Ungarischer Sturmmarsch" (c1875, r from S232; arr for pf, S524; for pf duet, S610)......................... S119

5. PIANO CONCERTOS, PIANO & ORCH

5.1   "Grande Fantasie symphonique" (c1834, on themes from Berlioz: Lélio, Op.14bis, H55a) S120
5.2   "Malédiction" (c1839–40; pf & strings; also see S99 & S108) S121
5.3   "Fantasia" (c1848–52, from Beethoven: Ruins of Athens, Op.113; arr for pf, S388, 9; for 2pf, S649) ... S122
5.4   "Hungarian Fantasia" (c1852, on Hungarian folk tunes, from S244/14) S123
5.5   Piano Concerto No.1 in E-flat major, "Triangle" (c by 1849, collab Raff, r1853, 56; arr for 2pf, S650) ..S124
5.6   Piano Concerto No.2 in A major (c1839, r1849–61; arr for 2pf, S651) S125
5.7   "Totentanz" (Paraphrase on the Dies irae) (c1849, r1853, 59; arr for pf, S525; for 2pf, S652) S126
5.8   *Piano Concerto in E-flat major (c1836–9, ed Rosenblatt)* .... *Op.posth*

6. STRING QUARTETS

6.1   "Am Grabe Richard Wagners" (c1883; str qt & harp ad lib; arr for pf, S202; for org, S267) S135

7. OTHER CHAMBER MUSIC

4 insts:

7.1   (Erste) "Elegie" (c1874; vc, pf, harp & harm or vc/vn & pf; arr for pf, S196; for pf duet, S612) S130
7.2   "Die Wiege" (c1881; 4vn) S133

Vn & pf:

7.3   Duo (Violin Sonata) (ca1851, on Chopin: Mazurka No.2 in C-sharp minor, Op.6/2, B60/2) S127
7.4   "Grand duo concertant sur la romance de M. Lafont 'Le marin' " (ca1837, r1849) S128
7.5   "Epithalam zu E. Reményis Vermählungsfeier" (c1872; arr for pf, S526; for pf duet, S611) S129
7.6   "Zweite Elegie" (c1877; vn/vc & pf; arr for pf, S197) S131
7.7   "Romance oubliée" (c1880; vn/va/vc & pf; arr for pf, S527) S132
7.8   "La lugubre gondola" (c1882; vn/vc & pf; arr for pf, S200) S134

8. PIANO SONATAS

8.1   Piano Sonata in B minor (c1852–3) S178

9. PIANO—STUDIES & EXERCISES

9.1   "Étude en 48 exercises dans tous les tons" (c1826, only 12 composed; used in S137) S136
9.2   "Vingt-quatre grandes études" (c1837, from S136, only 12 composed, 1st vers of S139)................... S137
9.3   "Mazeppa" (c1840, from S137/4; used in S139/4)...S138
9.4   "Études d'exécution transcendante" (Transcendental Etudes) (c1851, from S137): No.1 "Preludio" S139
9.5   No.2 "Fusées"
9.6   No.3 "Paysage"
9.7   No.4 "Mazeppa" (from S138)
9.8   No.5 "Feux follets"
9.9   No.6 "Vision"
9.10   No.7 "Eroica"
9.11   No.8 "Wilde Jagd"
9.12   No.9 "Ricordanza"
9.13   No.10 "Appassionata"
9.14   No.11 "Harmonies du soir"
9.15   No.12 "Chasse-neige"
9.16   "Études d'exécution transcendante d'après Paganini" (Transcendental Etudes after Paganini) (c1838; used in S141): No.1 "Tremolo," in G minor S140
9.17   No.2 "Scale and Octave," in E-flat major
9.18   No.3 "La campanella" (after Rondo of Paganini: Vn Concerto No.2 in B minor, Op.7, MS48)
9.19   No.4 "Arpeggio," in E major
9.20   No.5 "La chasse"
9.21   No.6 "Theme and variations," in A minor
9.22   "Grandes études de Paganini" (c1851, from S140): No.1 "Preludio" & "Étude" S141
9.23   No.2 "Andante"
9.24   No.3 "La campanella"
9.25   No.4 "Vivo"
9.26   No.5 "Allegretto"
9.27   No.6 "Quasi presto"
9.28   "Morceau de salon, étude de perfectionnement" (c1840, for Fetis: Méthode; used in S143) S142
9.29   "Ab-irato, étude de perfectionnement de la Méthode des méthodes" (c1852, from S142) S143
9.30   "Trois études de concert" (ca1848): No.1 "Il lamento," in A-flat major S144
9.31   No.2 "La leggierezza," in F minor
9.32   No.3 "Un sospiro," in D-flat major
9.33   "2 Konzertetüden" (c1862–3): No.1 "Waldesrauschen"..S145
9.34   No.2 "Gnomenreigen"
9.35   "Technical Studies," 12 books (c1868–ca1880) S146
9.36   "Variation on a Waltz by Diabelli" (c1882) S147
9.37   "Huit variations" (ca1824) S148
9.38   "Sept variations brillantes sur un thème de Rossini" (ca1824, from opera: La donna del lago) S149
9.39   "Impromptu brillant sur des thèmes de Rossini et Spontini" (c1824) S150
9.40   "Allegro di bravura" (c1824) S151
9.41   "Rondo di bravura" (c1824) S152
9.42   "Scherzo," in G minor (c1827) S153

10. PIANO—DANCES

11. PIANO—WORKS ON NATIONAL THEMES

11.35	"Hungarian Rhapsodies": No.1 "Lento, quasi Recitativo," in C-sharp minor (c1846) S244
11.36	No.2 "Lento a capriccio," in C-sharp minor (c1847)
11.37	No.3 "Andante," in B-flat major (p1853, from S242/11)
11.38	No.4 "Quasi Adagio," in E-flat major (p1853, from S242/7)
11.39	No.5 "Lento con duolo," E min (Héroïde-élégiaque) (p1853, from S242/12; also see S359/5 & S621)
11.40	No.6 "Tempo giusto," in D-flat major (p1853, from S242/4,5,11,20; also see S245 & S359)
11.41	No.7 "Lento," in D minor (p1853, from S242/15)
11.42	No.8 "Lento a capriccio," in F-sharp minor (p1853, from S242/19)
11.43	No.9 "Moderato," in E-flat major, "Pester Karneval" (p1848,53; also see S359/6, S621/6 & S379)
11.44	No.10 in E major (Preludio) (p1853, from S242/16)
11.45	No.11 "Lento a capriccio," in A minor (p1853, from S242/14)
11.46	No.12 "Mesto," in C-sharp minor (p1853, from S242/18,20)
11.47	No.13 "Andante Sostenuto," in A minor (p1853, from S242/17)
11.48	No.14 "Lento quasi marcia funèbre," in F min (p1853, from S242/21; orchd as S123; also see S359)
11.49	No.15 "Allegro animato," in A minor, "The Rákóczy March" (based on Barna's march of early 1700):
	. Version 1 (from S242/10,13)
	. Version 2 (p1871, from S117)
	. Simplified Version (p1852, from 1st vers)
11.50	No.16 "Allegro," in A minor (c1882; also see S622)
11.51	No.17 "Lento," in D minor (p1882)
11.52	No.18 "Lento," in C-sharp minor (c1885; also see S623)
11.53	No.19 "Lento," in D minor (c1885, from: Abrányi's Csárdás nobles)
11.54	*No.20 "Allegro vivace," in G minor ('Rumanian' Rhapsody) (ed Busoni; also see S242/20)*
11.55	"Hungarian Folk Songs" (c1873; also arr Abrányi): No.1 "Csak titokban akartalak szeretni" (Lassan) ..S245
11.56	No.2 "Jaj beh szennyes az a maga kendője" (Mérsékelve)
11.57	No.3 "Beh szomorú ez az élet én nékem" (Lassan)
11.58	No.4 "Beh! sok falut, beh! sok várost bejártam" (Kissé élénken)
11.59	No.5 "Erdő, erdő, s űrű erdő árnyában" (Búsongva)
11.60	"Puszta—Wehmut. A Puszta Keserve" (c after 1880, after Lenau's poem; also see S379a) S246
11.61	(Renumbered as S252a) S247
11.62	"Canzone napolitana" (c1842) S248
11.63	"Glanes de Woronince" (c1847–8): No.1 "Ballade d'Ukraine" (Dumka) S249
11.64	No.2 "Mélodies polonaises" (Chopin's song: Maiden's wish, Op.74/1, B33; also see S480/1)
11.65	No.3 "Complainte" (Dumka)
11.66	"Deux mélodies russes. Arabesques" (c1842): No.1 "Le rossignol" (on Alabyev's song) S250
11.67	No.2 "Chanson bohémienne" (on Bulakhov's song)
11.68	"Abschied. Russisches Volkslied" (c1885) S251
11.69	"Rondeau fantastique sur un thème espagnol" (c1836, on Garcia's song) S252
11.70	"La romanesca" (c1839) S252a
11.71	"Grosse Konzertfantasie über spanische Weisen" (c1845) S253
11.72	"Rhapsodie espagnole" (Folies d'Espagne et Jota aragonese) (ca1863) S254

12. PIANO—MISCELLANEOUS

12.1	"Harmonies poétiques et réligieuses" (c1834; used in S173): No.1 "Invocation" S154
12.2	No.2 "Ave Maria"
12.3	No.3 "Bénédiction de Dieu dans la solitude"
12.4	No.4 "Pensée des morts"
12.5	No.5 "Pater noster"
12.6	No.6 "Hymne de l'enfant à son réveil"
12.7	No.7 "Funérailles"
12.8	No.8 "Miserere, d'après Palestrina"
12.9	No.9 (Andante lagrimoso)
12.10	No.10 "Cantique d'amour"
12.11	"Apparitions" (c1834): No.1 "Senza lentezza quasi allegretto" S155
12.12	No.2 "Vivamente"
12.13	No.3 "Molto agitato ed appassionato"
12.14	"Album d'un voyageur" (c1835–6; also see S157 & S160), I. "Impressions et poésies": No.1 "Lyon" ... S156
12.15	No.2a "Le lac de Wallenstadt"
12.16	No.2b "Au bord d'une source"
12.17	No.3 "Les cloches de G..."
12.18	No.4 "Vallée d'Obermann"
12.19	No.5 "La chapelle de Guillaume Tell"
12.20	No.6 "Psaume"
12.21	II. "Fleurs mélodiques des Alpes": No.7a "Allegro," in C major
12.22	No.7b "Lento," in E min / G major
12.23	No.7c "Allegro pastorale," in G major
12.24	No.8a "Andante con sentimento," in G major
12.25	No.8b "Andante molto espressivo," in G minor
12.26	No.8c "Allegro moderato," in E-flat major
12.27	No.9a "Allegretto," in A-flat major
12.28	No.9b "Allegretto," in D-flat major
12.29	No.9c "Andantino con molto sentimento," in G major
12.30	III. "Paraphrases": No.10 "Improvisata sur le ranz de vaches de Ferd. Huber"

12.31	No.11 "Un soir dans les montagnes" (Nocturne sur le chant montagnard d'Ernest Knop)	
12.32	No.12 "Rondeau sur le ranz de chèvres de Ferd. Huber"	
12.33	"Fantaisie romantique sur deux mélodies suisses" (c1836; also see S156/7b)	S157
12.34	"3 Petrarch Sonnets" (c ?1839–46, orig vers, from S270/1; also see S161/4–6): No.1 "Sonetto 47"	S158
12.35	No.2 "Sonetto 104"	
12.36	No.3 "Sonetto 123"	
12.37	"Venezia e Napoli" (ca1840, orig vers; also see S96; used in S162): No.1 "Lento"	S159
12.38	No.2 "Allegro"	
12.39	No.3 "Andante placido"	
12.40	No.4 "Tarantelles napolitaines"	
12.41	"Années de pèlerinage," 1e année, "Suisse" (c1848–54, from S156): No.1 "Chapelle de G. Tell"	S160
12.42	No.2 "Au lac de Wallenstadt" (from S156/2a)	
12.43	No.3 "Pastorale" (from S156/7c)	
12.44	No.4 "Au bord d'une source" (from S156/2b)	
12.45	No.5 "Orage"	
12.46	No.6 "Vallée d'Obermann" (from S156/4)	
12.47	No.7 "Églogue"	
12.48	No.8 "Le mal du pays" (from S156/7b)	
12.49	No.9 "Les cloches de Genève" (from S156/3)	
12.50	"Annes de pèlerinage," 2e année, "Italie" (c1837–49): No.1 "Sposalizio"	S161
12.51	No.2 "Il penseroso"	
12.52	No.3 "Canzonetta del Salvator Rosa"	
12.53	No.4 "Sonetto 47 del Petrarca" (from S158/1)	
12.54	No.5 "Sonetto 104 del Petrarca" (from S158/2)	
12.55	No.6 "Sonetto 123 del Petrarca" (from S158/3)	
12.56	No.7 "Après une lecture du Dante" (Dante Sonata), fantasia quasi sonata	
12.57	"Venezia e Napoli" (c1859, r vers of S159): No.1 "Gondoliera"	S162
12.58	No.2 "Canzone"	
12.59	No.3 "Tarantelle"	
12.60	"Années de pèlerinage," 3e année (c1867–77): No.1 "Angelus! Prière aux anges gardiens"	S163
12.61	No.2 "Aux cyprès de la Villa d'Este, thrénodie I"	
12.62	No.3 "Aux cyprès de la Villa d'Este, thrénodie II"	
12.63	No.4 "Les jeux d'eau à la Villa d'Este"	
12.64	No.5 "Sunt lacrymae rerum, en mode hongrois"	
12.65	No.6 "Marche funèbre"	
12.66	No.7 "Sursum corda"	
12.67	"Albumblatt," in E major (c1841, from S210)	S164
12.68	"Feuilles d'album," in A-flat major (c1841)	S165
12.69	"Albumblatt in form of a waltz," in A major (c1842; also see S212)	S166
12.70	"Feuille d'album," in A minor (ca1843, from S274/1)	S167
12.71	"Ruhig" (unpubd)	S167a
12.72	"Élégie sur des motifs du Prince Louis Ferdinand de Prusse" (c1842)	S168
12.73	"Andante amoroso" (p1847)	S168a
12.74	"Romance" (c1848, from S301a; arr for vn/va/vc & pf, S132)	S169
12.75	Ballade No.1 in D-flat major (c1845–8)	S170
12.76	Ballade No.2 in B minor (c1853)	S171
12.77	"Madrigal" (c1845, early vers of S172/5)	S171a
12.78	"6 Consolations" (c1849–50): No.1 "Andante con moto"	S172
12.79	No.2 "Un poco più mosso"	
12.80	No.3 "Lento placido"	
12.81	No.4 "Quasi adagio"	
12.82	No.5 "Andantino"	
12.83	No.6 "Allegretto sempre cantabile"	
12.84	"Harmonies poétiques et réligieuses" (c1845–52; also see S154): No.1 "Invocation"	S173
12.85	No.2 "Ave Maria" (from S20)	
12.86	No.3 "Bénédiction de Dieu dans la solitude"	
12.87	No.4 "Pensée des morts" (from S154 & S691)	
12.88	No.5 "Pater noster" (from S21)	
12.89	No.6 "Hymne de l'enfant à son réveil" (from S19)	
12.90	No.7 "Funérailles"	
12.91	No.8 "Miserere, d'après Palestrina"	
12.92	No.9 "Andante lagrimoso"	
12.93	No.10 "Cantique d'amour"	
12.94	"Hymne de la nuit; Hymne du matin" (c1847, intended w/ S173)	S173a
12.95	"Berceuse" (c1854 & 1862; 2 vers)	S174
12.96	"Légendes" (c1863): No.1 "St Francis of Assisi preaching to the birds"	S175
12.97	No.2 "St Francis of Paule walking on the water"	
12.98	"Grosses Konzertsolo" (c ?1849; arr for 2pf, S258; for pf & orch, S365)	S176
12.99	"Scherzo and March" (c1851)	S177
12.100	"Weinen, Klagen, Sorgen, Zagen," prelude (c1859, after J. S. Bach, BWV12; also see S180)	S179
12.101	"Variations on a theme of Bach" (c1862, on bass line of BWV12/1; arr for org, S673)	S180
12.102	"Sarabande and Chaconne" (c1879, from Handel's opera: Almira, HWV1)	S181
12.103	"Ave Maria" (The Bells of Rome) (c1862, for the piano school of Lebert & Stark)	S182
12.104	"Alleluja et Ave Maria" (c1862, d'Arcadelt)	S183
12.105	"Urbi et orbi. Bénédiction papale" (c1864)	S184

13. PIANO DUET & 2 PIANOS

Pf duet:

2 Pf:

14. ORGAN

15. SACRED CHORAL

15.1 "Die Legende von der heiligen Elisabeth," oratorio (c1857–62, Roquette; vv, ch, orch & org): S2
  I: . "Einleitung"
    1. "Ankunft der Elisabeth auf Wartburg"
    2. "Ludwig"
    3. "Die Kreuzritter"
    . "Marsch des Kreuzzugs"
  II: 4. "Landgräfin Sophie"
    5. "Elisabeth"
    6. "Feierliche Bestattung der Elisabeth"
15.2 "Christus," oratorio (c1862–7, Bible & Catholic liturgy; vv, ch, org & orch): S3
  I. "Christmas Oratorio": 1. "Introduction"
    2. "Pastorale and Annunciation"
    3. "Stabat mater speciosa"
    4. "Shepherd's song at the manger" (arr for pf duet, S579/1)
    5. "The three holy kings" (March) (arr for pf duet, S579/2)
  II. "After Epiphany": 6. "The Beatitudes"
    7. "Pater noster"
    8. "The foundation of the Church" (arr for org, S664; for ch & org, S36)
    9. "The Miracle"
    10. "The Entry into Jerusalem"
  III. "Passion and Ressurection": 11. "Tristis est anima mea"
    12. "Stabat mater dolorosa"
    13. "O filii et filiae"
    14. "Resurrexit"
15.3 "Cantico del sol di San Francesco d'Assisi" (c1862, r1880–1; Bar, m ch, orch & org; arr for pf, S499) S4
15.4 "Die heilige Cäcilia," legend (c1874, Girardin; mS, ch ad lib & orch/pf; earlier settings lost) S5
15.5 "Die Glocken des Strassburger Münsters" (c1874, Longfellow; mS, Bar, ch & orch): S6
    1. "Vorspiel: Excelsior!" (arr for pf, S500; for pf duet, S580)
    2. "Die Glocken"
15.6 "Cantantibus organis," antiphon (c1879; vv, ch & orch, for a Palestrina festival in Rome) S7
15.7 "Missa quattor vocum" (Szekszárd) (c1848, r1859; m ch & org; 2nd vers 1869; also see S264) S8
15.8 "Missa solennis zur Einweihung der Basilika in Gran" (c1855, r1857–8; vv, ch & orch) S9
15.9 "Missa choralis" (c1865; S, A, T, B, ch & org) S10
15.10 "Hungarian Coronation Mass" (c1867; S, A, T, B, ch & orch): S11
    Arrs: . "Benedictus & Offertorium" (arr for pf, S501; pf duet, S581; vn & org, S678; vn & pf, S381)
      . "Benedictus" (arr for vn & orch, S362)
      . "Offertorium" (arr for org, S667)
15.11 "Requiem" (c1867–8; 2T, 2B, m ch, org & brass ad lib; used in S266) S12
15.12 "Psalm 13": "Lord, how long?" (c1855, r1859; T, ch & orch) S13
15.13 "Psalm 18": "Coeli enarrant" (c1860; m ch & orch/org/winds) S14
15.14 "Psalm 23": "The Lord is my shepherd" (c1859, r1862; T/S, harp/pf & org/harm; vers w/ m ch ad lib) S15
15.15 "Psalm 116": "Laudate Dominum" (c1869; m ch & pf; added to S11 as: Gradual 1869) S15a
15.16 "Psalm 129": "De Profundis" (c1881; Bar, m ch & org; 2nd vers for: B/A & org, added to S688) S16
15.17 "Psalm 137": "By the waters of Babylon" (c1859, r1862; S, fem ch, vn, harp & org) S17
15.18 "5 Choruses with French texts" (c1840s): 1. "Qui m'a donné" (3 equal vv) S18
15.19   2. "L'Éternel est son nom" (Racine; ch)
15.20   3. "Chantons, chantons l'auteur" (ch)
15.21   4. in A major (w/ out text; ch)
15.22   5. "Combien j'ai douce souvenance" (Chateaubriand; ch, melody Chateaubriand)
15.23 "Hymne de l'enfant à son réveil" (ca1845, r1862, 74, Lamartine; ch, harm/pf & harp ad lib; arr for pf,
      S173/6) S19
15.24 "Ave Maria" I, in B-flat major (c1846; ch & org; vers in A maj ca1852; arr for pf, S173/2; org, S264) S20
15.25 "Pater noster" II (c1846; m ch; 2nd vers for 4 equal vv & org ca1848) S21
15.26 "Pater noster" IV (c1850; ch & org) S22
15.27 "Domine salvum fac regem" (c1853; T, m ch & org; orchd Raff) S23
15.28 "Te Deum" II (c?1853; m ch & org) S24
15.29 "Die Seligkeiten" (c1855–9; Bar, ch & org ad lib; added to oratorio: Christus, S3) S25
15.30 "Festgang zur Eröffnung" (c1858, Fallersleben; m ch & org ad lib) S26
15.31 "Te Deum" I (c?1859; ch, org, brass & drums ad lib) S27
15.32 "An den heiligen Franziskus von Paula" (c1861, r74; m vv, m ch, harm/org & 3trbn; also see S175/2) ..S28
15.33 "Pater noster" I (c before1861, r1874; ch & org; added to oratorio: Christus, S3) S29
15.34 "Responses and Antiphons" (c1860; ch & org) S30
15.35 "Christus ist geboren" I, carol (c?1863, Landmesser; ch/m ch & org; 2 vers) S31
15.36 "Christus ist geboren" II (c?1863, Landmesser; ch & org / m ch w/ org postlude / ch; 3 vers; also
      see S502) S32
15.37 "Slavno Slavno Slaveni!" (c1863, Pucić; m ch & org; arr for pf, S503; for org, S668) S33
15.38 "Ave maris stella" (c?1865–6; ch & org; 2nd vers for m ch & org/harm 1868) S34
15.39 "Crux!," sailors hymn (c1865, Grandpont; m ch; 2nd vers for fem/child ch & pf) S35
15.40 "Dall' alma Roma" (c after 1867; ch & org, from oratorio: Christus, S3/8) S36
15.41 "Mihi autem adhaerere" (c1868, from Psalm 73; m ch & org) S37
15.42 "Ave Maria" II (c1869; ch & org; arr for pf/harm, S504; for 1v & org/harm, S681) S38
15.43 "Inno a Maria Vergine" (c1869; ch, harp or org/pf duet & harm) S39
15.44 "O salutaris hostia" I (ca1869; fem ch & org) S40

15.45	"Pater noster" III, in F major (c1869; ch & org/pf; 2nd vers in B-flat major for m ch & org/harm/pf)	S41
15.46	"Tantum ergo" (c1869; m ch & org; 2 vers for fem ch & org)	S42
15.47	"O salutaris hostia" II (ca ?1870; ch & org)	S43
15.48	"Ave verum corpus" (c1871; ch & org ad lib)	S44
15.49	"Libera me" (c1871; m ch & org; added to S12)	S45
15.50	"Anima Christi, sanctifica me" (c1874; m ch & org; 2 vers)	S46
15.51	"Sankt Christoph," legend (c after 1874; Bar, fem ch, pf, harm & harp ad lib)	S47
15.52	"Der Herr bewahret die Seelen seiner Heiligen," Festgesang (c1875; ch, org & wind)	S48
15.53	"O heilige Nacht," Christmas song (c after 1876; T, fem ch & org/harm, from S186/2)	S49
15.54	"12 alte deutsche geistliche Weisen," chorales (c ?1878–9): 1. "Es seqne uns Gott" (ch & org)	S50
15.55	2. "Gott sei uns gnädig" (Meine Seel' erhebet) (ch & org; used in S51)	
15.56	3. "Nun ruhen alle Wälder" (ch/pf)	
15.57	4. "O Haupt voll Blut" (ch/pf, added to S53)	
15.58	5. "O Lamm Gottes" (ch/pf; arr for pf duet, S582)	
15.59	6. "Was Gott tut" (ch)	
15.60	7. "Wer nur den lieben Gott" (ch)	
15.61	8. "Vexilla regis" (ch, added to S53)	
15.62	9. "Crux benedicta" (ch, added to S53)	
15.63	10. "O Traurigkeit" (ch, added to S53)	
15.64	11. "Nun danket alle Gott" (ch; used in S61)	
15.65	12. "Jesu Christe" (Die fünf Wunden) (ch)	
15.66	"Gott sei uns gnädig und barmherzig" (Kirchensegen) (c1878; ch & org, from S50/2)	S51
15.67	"Septem sacramenta," responsories (c1878; mS, Bar, ch & org): 1. "Baptisma"	S52
15.68	2. "Confirmatio"	
15.69	3. "Eucharistia"	
15.70	4. "Poenitentia"	
15.71	5. "Extrema unctio"	
15.72	6. "Ordo"	
15.73	7. "Matrimonium"	
15.74	"Via crucis. Les 14 Stations de la Croix" (c1878–9; vv, ch & org/pf; arr for pf duet, S583)	S53
15.75	"O Roma nobilis" (c1879; ch & org ad lib; also for1v & org)	S54
15.76	"Ossa arida" (c1879; unison m ch & org duet/pf duet)	S55
15.77	"Rosario" (c1879; 1.–3. arr for org, S670): 1. "Mysteria gaudiosa" (ch & org/harm)	S56
15.78	2. "Mysteria dolorosa" (ch & org/harm)	
15.79	3. "Mysteria gloriosa" (ch & org/harm)	
15.80	4. "Pater noster" (Bar/unison m ch & org/harm)	
15.81	"In domum Domini ibimus" (c1880s; ch, org, brass & drums; Prelude arr for pf, S505 & org, S671)	S57
15.82	"O sacrum convivium," litany (c1880s; A, fem ch ad lib & org/harm)	S58
15.83	"Pro Papa" (ca1880): 1. "Dominus conservet eum" (ch & org)	S59
15.84	2. "Tu es Petrus" (unison m ch & org)	
15.85	"Zur Trauung" (Ave Maria III) (c1883; org/harm & unison fem ch ad lib, from S161/1)	S60
15.86	"Nun danket alle Gott" (c1883; m ch/ch, org, brass & drums ad lib)	S61
15.87	"Mariengarten" (Quasi cedrus) (c by 1884; ch & org)	S62
15.88	"Qui seminant in lacrimis" (c1884; ch & org)	S63
15.89	"Pax vobiscum!" (c1885; m ch & org ad lib)	S64
15.90	"Qui Mariam absolvisti" (c1885; Bar & unison ch)	S65
15.91	"Salve Regina" (c1885; ch)	S66

16. SECULAR CHORAL

16.1	"Enthüllung des Beethoven-Denkmals in Bonn" (Beethoven Cantata), cantata (c1845, Wolff, Part 2 includes arr of Adagio from Beethoven: Trio in B-flat major, Op.97; arr for pf duet, S584):	S67
16.2	"Zur Säkularfeier Beethovens" (Beethoven Cantata No.2) (c1869–70, Stern; vv, d ch & orch, Introduction = orchd Adagio from Beethoven: Trio in B-flat major, Op.97):	S68
16.3	"Chöre zu Herders Entfesseltem Prometheus" (c1850; vv, d ch & orch): 1. "Chor der Oceaniden"	S69
16.4	2. "Chor der Tritonen"	
16.5	3. "Chor der Dryaden"	
16.6	4. "Chor der Schnitter"	
16.7	5. "Chor der Winzer"	
16.8	6. "Chor der Unterirdischen"	
16.9	7. "Chor der Unsichtbaren"	
16.10	8. "Schluss-Chor" (Chor der Musen)	
16.11	"An die Künstler" (c1853, 1853 & 1869, Schiller; 2T, 2B, m ch & orch; 3 vers)	S70
16.12	"Gaudeamus igitur" (1869; vv ad lib, m ch/ch & orch; arr for pf, S509; for pf duet, S586)	S71
16.13	"4-Part Male Choruses" (c1841): 1. "Rheinweinlied" (Herwegh; m ch & pf)	S72
16.14	2. "Studentenlied aus Goethes Faust" (m ch)	
16.15	3. "Reiterlied" (Herwegh; m ch & pf, 1st vers)	
16.16	4. "Reiterlied" (Herwegh; m ch, 2nd vers)	
16.17	"Es war einmal ein König" (from Goethe: Faust; B, m ch & pf)	S73
16.18	"Das deutsche Vaterland" (c1841, Arndt; m ch; 2 vers: 2nd not traced)	S74
16.19	"Über allen Gipfeln ist Ruh" (c1842, Goethe; m ch; also for m ch & 2hn 1849)	S75
16.20	"Das düstre Meer umrauscht mich" (c1842; m ch & pf)	S76
16.21	"Die lustige Legion" (c1846, Buchheim; m ch & pf ad lib)	S77
16.22	"Trinkspruch" (c1843; m ch & pf)	S78

17. SONGS (w/ pf)

PART II: ARRANGEMENTS, TRANSCRIPTIONS, PARAPHRASES, ETC

18. ORCHESTRAL (arrs)

Bülow:
18.1   "Mazurka-fantasie," Op.13 (c1865) S351

Cornelius:
18.2   "2nd Overture to The Barber of Bagdad" (c1877, compl Liszt from sketches of Cornelius) S352

Egressy & Erkel:
18.3   "2 Patriotic songs" (c1870–3): No.1 "Szózat" S353
18.4   No.2 "Ungarischer Hymnus"

Liszt:
18.5   "2 Legends," S175 (c1863): No.1 "San Francesco d'Asisi" S354
18.6   No.2 "San Francisco di Paola"
18.7   "Vexilla Regis prodeunt," S185 (c1864).. S355
18.8   "Festvorspiel," S226 (c1857) S356
18.9   "Huldigungsmarsch," S228 & S87 (c1857) S357
18.10   "Vom Fels zum Meer. Deutscher Siegesmarsch," S229 (c1860) S358
18.11   (6) "Hungarian Rhapsodies," S244/14, 12, 6, 2, 5, 9 (collab Doppler) S359
18.12   "À la Chapelle Sixtine," S461 .... S360
18.13   "Der Papsthymnus," S261 .... S361
18.14   "Benedictus," from: Hungarian Coronation Mass, S11 (c1875) S362

Schubert:
18.15   "4 Marches," from pf arrangement, S526 (c1859) S363

Zarembski:
18.16   "Dances galiciennes" (c1881).. S364

19. PIANO CONCERTOS, PIANO & ORCH (arrs)

Liszt:
19.1   "Grand solo de concert," S176, S258 (ca1850) S365

Schubert:
19.2   "Wandererfantasie," D760 (c1851) S366

Weber:
19.3   "Polonaise brillante," from Weber's Polacca brillante, Op.72, J268 (ca1851) S367

20. CHAMBER MUSIC (arrs)

Liszt:
20.1   "La notte," S112/2 (c1864–6; vn & pf) S377a
20.2   "Angelus," S163/1 (c1877; harm) S378/1
20.3   "Angelus," S163/1 (c1880; str qt)... S378/2
20.4   "Pester Karneval," S244/9 (c?; pf trio) S379
20.5   "Puszta-Wehmut," S246 (vn & pf) S379a
20.6   "Benedictus & Offertorium," from: Hungarian Coronation Mass, S11 (c1869; vn & pf) S381
20.7   "Die Zelle in Nonnenwerth," S274/2 (vn/vc & pf) S382
20.8   "Die drei Zigeuner," S320 (c1864; vn & pf)... S383

Wagner:
20.9   "O du mein holder," from opera: Tannhäuser, WWV70 (c1852; vc & pf)................................ S380

21. PIANO (arrs; also see separate heading for piano scores, transcriptions, etc)

Ábrányi:
21.1   Elaboration on: Virág dal (c1881) S383a

Alabieff:
21.2   "Mazurka pour piano composée par un amateur de St. Pétersbourg" (c1842) S384

Anon:

21.3 Variations on: Tiszántuli szép leány (c1846) S384a

Auber:

21.4 "Grande fantaisie sur la Tyrolienne," from opera: La fiancée (c1829) S385
21.5 "Tyrolean Melody" (c1856, from theme of S385; also see S733) S385a
21.6 "Tarantelle di bravura," from: La muette de Portici (c1846) S386
21.7 "3 Pieces" (unpubd): Nos.1 & 2 (on themes from opera: La muette de Portici) S387
    No.3 (on: Berceuse)

Beethoven:

21.8 "Capriccio alla turca," from incid music: The Ruins of Athens, Op.113 (c1846, from S122) S388
21.9 "Fantasia on Ruins of Athens" (c1865, from S122) S389

Bellini:

21.10 "Réminiscences des Puritains" (c1836) S390
21.11 "Introduction et polonaise," from opera: I puritani (c1840, from S390) S391
21.12 "Hexaméron, morceau de concert," variations on March from: I puritani (c1837, collab w/ others) S392
21.13 "Fantasie sur des motifs favoris de l'opéra La sonnambula" (c1839, r1840–1) S393
21.14 "Réminiscences de Norma" (c1841) S394

Berlioz:

21.15 "L'idée fixe. Andante amoroso," on a theme from: Symphonie fantastique, Op.14, H48 (c1833) S395
21.16 "Bénédiction et Serment," from: Benvenuto Cellini, Op.23, H76a (c1852) S396

Donizetti:

21.17 "Réminiscences de Lucia di Lammermoor" (c1835–6) S397
21.18 "Marche et cavatine de Lucie de Lammermoor" (c1835–6, intended as part of S397) S398
21.19 "Nuits d'été à Pausilippe" (c1838): No.1 "Il Barcajuolo," barcarola S399
21.20   No.2 "L'alito di Bice," notturno
21.21   No.3 "La torre di Biasone," canzone napolitana
21.22 "Réminiscences de Lucrezia Borgia" (c1840): No.1 "Trio" (from Act II) S400
21.23   No.2 "Fantasia on themes from the opera: Chanson à boire (Orgie)—Duo—Finale"
21.24 "Valse à capriccio," from: Lucia et Parisina (c1842) S401
21.25 "Marche funèbre de Dom Sébastien" (c1844) S402
21.26 "Grande paraphrase de la marche ... pour Sa Majesté le sultan Abdul Medjid-Khan" (c1847) S403

Duke Ernst of Saxe-Coburg-Gotha:

21.27 "Halloh! Jagdchor & Steyrer," from opera: Tony (c1849) S404

Erkel:

21.28 "Schwanengesang & March," from: Hunyadi László (c1847) S405

Festetics:

21.29 "Variations on Pásztor Lakodalmas" (c1858) S405a

Glinka:

21.30 "Tscherkessenmarsch," from opera: Ruslan & Lyudmila (c1843) S406

Gounod:

21.31 "Valse de l'opéra Faust" (c1861) S407
21.32 "Les sabéennes," berceuse from opera: La reine de Saba (c1865) S408
21.33 "Les adieux," rêverie from opera: Roméo et Juliette (c1867) S409

Halévy:

21.34 "Réminiscences de La juive" (c1835) S409a

Mendelssohn:

21.35 "Wedding March & Dance of the Elves," from: A Midsummer Night's Dream, Op.61 (c1849–50) S410

Mercadante:

21.36 "Soirées italiennes. 6 Amusements sur des motifs de Mercadante" (c1838): No.1 "La primavera" S411
21.37   No.2 "Il galop"
21.38   No.3 "Il pastore svizzero," tirolese
21.39   No.4 "La serenata del marinaro"
21.40   No.5 "Il brindisi," rondoletto
21.41   No.6 "La zingarella spagnola," bolero

Wagner:

21.87	"Phantasiestück," on themes from opera: Rienzi, WWV49 (c1859)	S439
21.88	"Spinning Chorus," from opera: Der fliegende Holländer, WWV63 (c1860)	S440
21.89	"Ballad," from opera: Der fliegende Holländer, WWV63 (c1872)	S441
21.90	"Overture to Tannhäuser" (c1848)	S442
21.91	"Pilgrims' Chorus," from opera: Tannhäuser, WWV70 (ca1861 & 1862; 2 vers)	S443
21.92	"O du mein holder Abendstern," from opera: Tannhäuser, WWV70 (c1849; arr for vc & pf, S380)	S444
21.93	"2 Pieces" (c1852): No.1 "Entry of the Guests on the Wartburg," from opera: Tannhäuser, WWV70	S445
21.94	No.2 "Elsa's Bridal Procession to the Minster," from opera: Lohengrin, WWV75	
21.95	"2 Pieces," from opera: Lohengrin, WWV75 (c1854): No.1 "Festival & Bridal Song"	S446
21.96	No.2 "Elsa's Dream and Lohengrin's Rebuke"	
21.97	"Isolda's Liebestod," from opera: Tristan & Isolde, WWV90 (c1867)	S447
21.98	"Am stillen Herd," from opera: Die Meistersinger, WWV96 (c1871)	S448
21.99	"Valhalla," from opera cycle: The Ring of the Nibelung, WWV86 (c1878–80)	S449
21.100	"Solemn march to the Holy Grail," from opera: Parsifal, WWV111 (c1882)	S450

Weber:

21.101	"Freischütz Fantasy," on themes from opera: Der Freischütz, J277 (c1840–1)	S451
21.102	"Leyer und Schwert" (c1846–7)	S452
21.103	"Einsam bin ich, nicht alleine," from incid music: La Preciosa, J279 (c1848)	S453
21.104	"Schlummerlied von C. M. von Weber mit Arabesken" (c1848)	S454
21.105	"Polonaise brillante" (ca1851, from S367)	S455

Zichy:

21.106	"Valse d'Adèle," for left hand (ca1877)	S456

Other arrangements:

21.107	(Renumbered as S431a)	S457
21.108	Piece on Italian operatic melodies	S458
21.109	(Deleted, same as S387)	S459
21.110	"Kavallerie-Geschwindmarsch" (c1883)	S460

22. PIANO SCORES, TRANSCRIPTIONS, ETC (also see separate heading for piano arrangements)

Allegri & Mozart:

22.1	"À la Chapelle Sixtine. Miserere d'Allegri et Ave verum corpus de Mozart" (c1862)	S461

Bach, J. S.:

22.2	"6 Preludes & fugues," for organ (c1842–50): No.1 in A minor	S462
22.3	No.2 in C major	
22.4	No.3 in C minor	
22.5	No.4 in C major	
22.6	No.5 in E minor	
22.7	No.6 in B minor	
22.8	"Organ Fantasia & Fugue," in G minor, BWV542 (p1863)	S463

Beethoven:

22.9	"Symphonies de Beethoven": No.1 in C major, Op.21 (c1863–64)	S464
22.10	No.2 in D major, Op.36 (c1863–4)	
22.11	No.3 in E-flat major, "Eroica," Op.55 (c1863–4, Marcia funèbre movt c1843)	
22.12	No.4 in B-flat major, Op.60 (c1863–4)	
22.13	No.5 in C minor, Op.67 (c1837)	
22.14	No.6 in F major, Op.68, "Pastorale" (c1837)	
22.15	No.7 in A major, Op.92 (c1837)	
22.16	No.8 in F major, Op.93 (c1863–4)	
22.17	No.9 in D minor, Op.125, "Choral" (c1863–64; arr for 2pf, S657)	
22.18	"Grand Septuor," Op.20 (c1841; arr for pf duet, S634)	S465
22.19	"Adélaïde de Beethoven," song, Op.46 (c1839)	S466
22.20	"6 Geistliche Lieder," Op.48 (c1840, Gellert): No.1 "Gottes Macht und Versehung"	S467
22.21	No.2 "Bitten"	
22.22	No.3 "Busslied"	
22.23	No.4 "Vom Tode"	
22.24	No.5 "Die Liebe des Nächsten"	
22.25	No.6 "Die Ehre Gottes aus der Natur"	
22.26	"Beethoven's Lieder von Goethe" (c before 1849): No.1 "Mignon" (from Op.75)	S478
22.27	No.2 "Mit einem gemalten Bande" (from Op.83)	
22.28	No.3 "Freudvoll und leidvoll" (from Op.84)	
22.29	No.4 "Es war einmal ein König" (from Op.75)	
22.30	No.5 "Wonne der Wehmut" (from Op.83)	
22.31	No.6 "Die Trommel gerühret" (from Op.84)	

Dessauer:

22.83 "3 Lieder" (c1846): No.1 "Lockung" S485
22.84   No.2 "Zwei Wege"
22.85   No.3 "Spanisches Lied"

Draeseke:

22.86 "Der Schwur am Rütli," cantata (c1870) S485a

Egressy & Erkel:

22.87 "Szózat und Ungarischer Hymnus" (c after1870, from S353) S486

Festetics:

22.88 "Spanisches Ständchen" (c1846) S487

Franz:

22.89 "Er ist gekommen in Sturm und Regen" (c1848) S488
22.90 "12 Lieder" (c1848) I. "Schilflieder," Op.2: No.1 "Auf geheimen Waldespfade" S489
22.91   No.2 "Drüben geht die Sonne scheiden"
22.92   No.3 "Trübe wird's, die Wolken jagen"
22.93   No.4 "Sonnenuntergang"
22.94   No.5 "Auf dem Teich, dem regungslosen"
22.95   II: No.6 "Der Schalk" (from Op.3)
22.96   No.7 "Der Bote" (from Op.8)
22.97   No.8 "Meeresstille" (from Op.8)
22.98   III: No.9 "Treibt der Sommer seine Rosen" (from Op.8)
22.99   No.10 "Gewitternacht" (from Op.8)
22.100   No.11 "Das ist ein Brausen und Heulen" (from Op.8)
22.101   No.12 "Frühlung und Liebe" (from Op.3)

Goldschmidt:

22.102 "Liebesscene und Fortunas Kugel," from: Die sieben Todsünden (c1880) S490

Gounod:

22.103 "Hymne à Sainte Cécile" (c1866) S491

Herbeck:

22.104 "Tanzmomente" (c1869) S492

Hummel:

22.105 "Septet," Op.74 (c1848) S493

Lassen:

22.106 "Löse, Himmel, meine Seele" (c1861) S494
22.107 "Ich weil' in tiefer Einsamkeit" (c1872) S495
22.108 "From Hebbel's Nibelungen & Goethe's Faust" (c1878–9), I : No.1 "Hagen und Krunhild" S496
22.109   No.2 "Bachlarn"
22.110   II: No.1 "Osterhymne"
22.111   No.2 "Hoffest. Marsch und Polonaise"
22.112 "Sym Intermezzo for Calderon's Über allen Zauber Liebe" (c1882) S497

Lessmann:

22.113 "3 Songs from Wolff's Tannhäuser" (ca1882): No.1 "Der Lenz ist gekommen" S498
22.114   No.2 "Trinklied"
22.115   No.3 "Du schaust mich an"

Liszt:

22.116 "Cantico del sol di San Francesco," S4 (c1881) S499
22.117 "Excelsior! Prelude to Die des Strassburger Münsters," S6 (ca1875) S500
22.118 "2 Pieces from Hungarian Coronation Mass," S11 (c1867): No.1 "Benedictus" S501
22.119   No.2 "Offertorium"
22.120 "Weihnachtslied" II, S32/1 (ca1864) S502
22.121 "Slavimo Slavno Slaveni!," S33 (ca1863) S503
22.122 "Ave Maria" II, S38 (ca1870 & ca1872; 2 vers) S504
22.123 "Via crucis" S504a
22.124 "Zum Haus des Herrn ziehen wir" (Prelude to S57), S671 (c?) S505
22.125 "Ave maris stella," S34/2 (ca1868) S506
22.126 "Fragment (70 bars) on themes from the first Beethoven Cantata," S67 (ca1847) S507
22.127 "Pastorale. Schnitterchor aus dem Entfesselten Prometheus," S69 (c1861) S508
22.128 "Gaudeamus igitur. Humoreske," S71 (ca1870) S509
22.129 "Marche héroïque," S82 (ca1848) S510

22.191	No.2 "Der Asra" (p1884)	
22.192	"Introduction to Study," in C major	S554a

Saint-Saëns:

22.193	"Danse macabre," Op.40 (c1876)	S555

Schubert:

22.194	"Die Rose" (Heidenröslein), D745 (c1833)	S556
22.195	"Lob der Thränen," Op.13/2, D711 (c1838)	S557
22.196	"12 Lieder" (c1837–8): No.1 "Sei mir gegrüsst"	S558
22.197	No.2 "Auf dem Wasser zu singen"	
22.198	No.3 "Du bist die Ruh"	
22.199	No.4 "Erlkönig"	
22.200	No.5 "Meeresstille"	
22.201	No.6 "Die junge Nonne"	
22.202	No.7 "Frühlingsglaube"	
22.203	No.8 "Gretchen am Spinnrade"	
22.204	No.9 "Ständchen" (Horch, horch! die Lerch)	
22.205	No.10 "Rastlose Liebe"	
22.206	No.11 "Der Wanderer" (Ich komme vom Gebirge her)	
22.207	No.12 "Ave Maria," III	
22.208	"Gondelfahrer," D809 (1838)	S559
22.209	"Schwanengesang," D957 (c1838–9): No.1 "Die Stadt"	S560
22.210	No.2 "Das Fischermädchen"	
22.211	No.3 "Aufenthalt"	
22.212	No.4 "Am Meer"	
22.213	No.5 "Abschied"	
22.214	No.6 "In der Ferne"	
22.215	No.7 "Ständchen" (Leise flehen)	
22.216	No.8 "Ihr Bild"	
22.217	No.9 "Frühlingssehnsucht"	
22.218	No.10 "Liebesbotschaft"	
22.219	No.11 "Der Atlas"	
22.220	No.12 "Der Doppelgänger"	
22.221	No.13 "Die Taubenpost"	
22.222	No.14 "Kriegers Ahnung"	
22.223	"Winterreise," Op.89, D911 (c1839): No.1 "Gute Nacht"	S561
22.224	No.2 "Die Nebensonnen"	
22.225	No.3 "Mut"	
22.226	No.4 "Die Post"	
22.227	No.5 "Erstarrung"	
22.228	No.6 "Wasserfluth"	
22.229	No.7 "Der Lindenbaum"	
22.230	No.8 "Der Leyermann"	
22.231	No.9 "Täuschung"	
22.232	No.10 "Das Wirthshaus"	
22.233	No.11 "Der stürmische Morgen"	
22.234	No.12 "Im Dorfe"	
22.235	"Geistliche Lieder" (c1840): No.1 "Am tage Aller Seelen" (Litaney), D343	S562
22.236	No.2 "Himmelsfunken," D651	
22.237	No.3 "Die Gestirne," D444	
22.238	No.4 "Dem Unendlichen" (Hymne), D291	
22.239	"6 Melodien" (c1846): No.1 "Lebewohl"	S563
22.240	No.2 "Des Mädchens Klage"	
22.241	No.3 "Das Zügenglöcklein," Op.80/2	
22.242	No.4 "Trock'ne Blumen," Op.25/18	
22.243	No.5 "Ungeduld" (1st vers), Op.25/7	
22.244	No.6 "Die Forelle" (1st vers), D550	
22.245	"Die Forelle," Op.32, D550 (c1846, 2nd vers)	S564
22.246	"Müllerlieder" (c1846): No.1 "Das Wandern," Op.25/1	S565
22.247	No.2 "Der Müller und der Bach," Op.25/19	
22.248	No.3 "Der Jäger," Op.25/14	
22.249	No.4 "Die böse Farbe," Op.25/17	
22.250	No.5 "Wohin?," Op.25/2	
22.251	No.6 "Ungeduld" (2nd vers), Op.25/7	

Schumann:

22.252	"Liebelied" (Widmung), Op.25/1 (c1848)	S566
22.253	"2 Songs" (c1861): No.1 "An den Sonnenschein," Op.36/4	S567
22.254	No.2 "Dem roten Röslein," Op.27/2	
22.255	"Frühlingsnacht" (Überm Garten durch die Lüfte), Op.39/12 (c1872)	S568
22.256	"Lieder by Robert & Clara Schumann," Robert: No.1 "Weihnachtslied," Op.79/16	S569
22.257	No.2 "Die wandelne Glocke," Op.79/17	
22.258	No.3 "Frühlings Ankunft," Op.79/19	

25. ORGAN (arrs)

26. ORGAN WITH OTHER INSTS (arrs)

27. VOICE & ORCHESTRA (arrs)

PART III: DOUBTFUL OR LOST WORKS

30. ORCHESTRAL (doubtful/lost)

30.1	*(Renumbered as S113)*	*S709*
30.2	*"Funeral march"*	*S710*
30.3	*Arr of "Csárdás macabre," S224*	*S711*
30.4	*Arr of "Romance oubliée," S132 (arr for va & orch, spur)*	*S712*
30.5	*2 Piano Concertos (c1821, lost)*	*S713*
30.6	*"Piano Concerto in the Hungarian Style"*	*S714*
30.7	*"Piano Concerto in the Italian Style"*	*S715*
30.8	*"Grande fantaisie symphonique," in A minor*	*S716*

31. CHAMBER MUSIC (doubtful/lost)

31.1	*Trio (c1825, lost)*	*S717*
31.2	*Quintet (c1825, lost)*	*S718*
31.3	*(Renumbered as S692a)*	*S719*
31.4	*"Allegro moderato," in E major (vn & pf)*	*S720*
31.5	*Prélude (vn)*	*S721*
31.6	*(Renumbered as S377a)*	*S722*
31.7	*"Tristia," from: Vallée d'Obermann, S160/6 (arr for pf trio)*	*S723*

32. PIANO (doubtful/lost)

32.1	*"Rondo & Fantasia" (c1824, lost)*	*S724*
32.2	*"3 Sonatas" (c1825, lost)*	*S725*
32.3	*"Study," in C major*	*S726*
32.4	*"Valse," in E major*	*S726a*
32.5	*"Prélude omnitonique"*	*S727*
32.6	*(Renumbered as S192/5)*	*S728*
32.7	*(Renumbered as S42)*	*S729*
32.8	*(Renumbered as S195)*	*S730*
32.9	*"Valse élégiaque" (c?)*	*S731*
32.10	*(Renumbered as S215/4)*	*S732*
32.11	*(Renumbered as S233b)*	*S733*
32.12	*"Ländler," in D major*	*S734*
32.13	*"Air cosaque"*	*S735*
32.14	*"Kerepesi csárdás" (?spur)*	*S736*
32.15	*"3 Morceau en style de danse ancien hongrois" (p1850, spur): No.1 "Maestoso"*	*S737*
32.16	*No.2 "Tempo di Werbung"*	
32.17	*No.3 "Andante ritmico"*	
32.18	*Spanish folksong arrs (ca1850)*	*S738*
32.19	*Beethoven: "Coriolan" Overture, Op.62 (arr, ?lost)*	*S739*
32.20	*Beethoven: "Egmont" Overture, Op.84 (arr)*	*S740*
32.21	*Berlioz: "Le carnival romain" Overture, Op.9, H95 (arr)*	*S741*
32.22	*Donizetti: "Duettino" (arr, ?same as S399)*	*S742*
32.23	*Gounod: "Soldiers' Chorus," from: Faust (?lost)*	*S743*
32.24	*Halévy: "Guitarero," fantasia*	*S743a*
32.25	*Kullak: "Dom Sébastien," paraphrase of Act IV*	*S744*
32.26	*"Funeral March" (?same as S173/7)*	*S745*
32.27	*"Andante maestoso"*	*S746*
32.28	*"Poco adagio," from: Missa solemnis, S9*	*S747*
32.29	*Mozart: "The Magic Flute" Overture (arr)*	*S748*
32.30	*Radovsky: "Preussischer Armeemarsch No.120"*	*S749*
32.31	*(Renumbered as S421a)*	*S750*
32.32	*"Nonetto e Mose," fantasia on themes by Rosini*	*S751*
32.33	*Rubinstein: "Gelb rollt" (arr)*	*S752*
32.34	*Schubert: Act I of opera: Alfonso und Estrella, Op.69, D732 (c1850–1, pf score, ?lost)*	*S753*
32.35	*(Renumbered as S573a)*	*S754*

33. OTHER INSTRUMENTAL WORKS (doubtful/lost)

33.1	*"Sonata" (c1825; pf duet, lost)*	*S755*
33.2	*Arr of "Mosonyis Grabgeleit" (arr for pf duet)*	*S756*
33.3	*Arr of "Le triomphe funèbre du Tasse," S112/3 (arr for 2 pf)*	*S757*
33.4	*"The Organ," sym poem (after Herder; org)*	*S758*
33.5	*Arr of "Consolation in D major," S172/4 (pubd as: Adagio, ?spur)*	*S759*
33.6	*Arr of "Cantico del sol," S4 (arr for org)*	*S760*
33.7	*Chopin: "Marche funèbre," from Op.35, B128 (arr for org, vc & pf)*	*S761*

34. CHORAL WORKS (doubtful/lost)

34.1	*"Tantum ergo" (c1882, lost)*	S702
34.2	*"Psalm 2" (c1851; T, ch & orch, ?part of S690)*	S703
34.3	*"Requiem on the death of Emperor Maximilian of Mexico" (?)*	S704
34.4	*"The Creation" (?)*	S705
34.5	*"Benedictus" (p1939, ch & pf, ?spur)*	S706
34.6	*Arr of Excelsior!, prelude to S6 (mS/Bar, m ch & pf, spur)*	S707
34.7	*"Rinaldo" (ca1848, Goethe; T, m ch & pf, spur; orchd Conradi)*	S708
34.8	*(Renumbered as S81a)*	S708a
34.9	*Piece (c ?1843–4; 4 m vv, companion-piece to S78)*	S708b

35. VOCAL (doubtful/lost)

35.1	*"Air de Chateaubriand" (1v & pf)*	S762
35.2	*"Strophes de Herlossohn" (1v & pf)*	S763
35.3	*"Kränze pour chant" (1v & pf)*	S764
35.4	*"Glöckchen" (Müller; 1v & pf, ?companion-piece to S316/1–2)*	S765
35.5	*"L'aube naît" (c1842, Hugo, lost)*	S765a
35.6	*Arr of "Der Papsthymnus," S261 (arr for S/T & pf, ?spur)*	S766
35.7	*Arr of "Excelsior!," prelude to S6 (arr for 1v & org, ?spur)*	S767
35.8	*"Der ewige Jude," recitation (Schubart; w/pf acc)*	S768

36. WORKS PLANNED

Operas:

36.1	*"Le corsaire" (c1842)*
36.2	*"La Divina commedia," stage vers (c1845, Autran)*
36.3	*2 Italian operas (c1846)*
36.4	*Opera on Faust (c1846–54)*
36.5	*"Richard en Palestine" (based on Scott's novel)*
36.6	*"Spartacus" (c1848)*
36.7	*Hungarian opera (János or Jankó) (c1856–8)*
36.8	*"Jeanne d'Arc"*

Orch:

36.9	*Music to: The Tempest (c1853)*
36.10	*"The History of the World in Sound and Picture" (after pictures by Kaulbach):*
	. *"The Tower of Babel"*
	. *"Nimrod"*
	. *"Jerusalem"*
	. *"The Glory of Greece"*
36.11	*Continuation to: Hungaria, S103 (c1865)*
36.12	*Arr of 2 works of Chopin (incl: Fantasy, Op.49) (c1871; pf & orch)*
36.13	*Arr of "Ungarische Bildnisse," S205 (c1885; orch)*

Pf:

36.14	*Arr of Schubert's Symphony No.6 in C major (c1850)*
36.15	*"Polonaise martiale" (c1860)*
36.16	*Transcription of Beethoven's Quartets (c1863)*
36.17	*New edition of Mendelssohn's Songs Without Words*
36.18	*Arr of Bach's Chaconne (c1880)*
36.19	*Piano score of Rousseau's Devin du village (c1883)*
36.20	*"Fantasia on Mackenzie's The Troubadour" (c1886)*
36.21	*"Somogyi Csárdás" (c1886)*

Choral:

36.22	*"Les laboureurs, Les matelots, Les soldats" (c1845, Lamennais, additions to S81)*
36.23	*Oratorio (c1849, Wagner after Byron's Heaven and Earth)*
36.24	*2 Masses (c1856)*
36.25	*"Liturgie catholique, Liturgie romaine" (c1860–1)*
36.26	*"Manfred" (c1862)*
36.27	*"St. Etienne, roi d'Hongrie, or Fire and Water" (c1869)*
36.28	*"Longfellow's Golden Legend," recitation (c1874)*

* * * * *

S = H. Searle: "Liszt, Ferencz" Grove 5. ("The New Grove Dictionary of Music and Musicians." Vol.11, ed Stanley Sadie. Macmillan Publishers Limited. 1980.)

1. STAGE WORKS

Operas (5 act tragédies lyriques):

1.1	"Cadmus et Hermione" (c1673, Quinault)	LWV49
1.2	"Alceste ou Le triomphe d'Alcide" (c1674, Quinault)	LWV50
1.3	"Thésée" (c1675, Quinault)	LWV51
1.4	"Atys" (c1676, Quinault)	LWV53
1.5	"Isis" (c1677, Quinault)	LWV54
1.6	"Psyché" (c1678, Corneille, Quinault & Fontenelle)	LWV56
1.7	"Bellérophon" (c1679, Corneille, Fontenelle & Boileau-Despréaux)	LWV57
1.8	"Proserpine" (c1680, Quinault)	LWV58
1.9	"Persée" (c1682, Quinault)	LWV60
1.10	"Phaëton" (c1683, Quinault)	LWV61
1.11	"Amadis de Gaule" (c1684, Quinault)	LWV63
1.12	"Roland" (c1685, Quinault)	LWV65
1.13	"Armide et Renaud" (c1686, Quinault)	LWV71
1.14	"Achille et Polyxène" (c1687, Campistron, unfin; compl Collasse)	LWV74

Ballets, mascarades, intermèdes—collab w/ others (c1653–8, Lully assisted writing the music):

1.15	"La nuit," pastorale héroïque (c1653, Benserade)	
1.16	*"Les proverbes" (c1654, Benserade, music lost)*	
1.17	"Les noces de Pélée et de Thétis," intermèdes (c1654, Benserade, intermèdes for Caproli's opera)	
1.18	"Ballet du Temps," ballet (c1654, Benserade)	LWV1
1.19	"Ballet des Plaisirs," ballet (c1655, Benserade)	LWV2
1.20	"Ballet des Bienvenus," ballet (c1655, Benserade)	LWV4
1.21	*"Psyché et la puissance de l'amour," ballet (c1656, Benserade, lost)*	*LWV6*
1.22	*"La galanterie du temps," mascarade (c1656, anon, music lost)*	*LWV7*
1.23	"Ballet de L'amour malade," ballet (c1657, L'abbé Buti, for opera c by Marazzoli)	LWV8
1.24	*"Les plaisirs troublés" (c1657, music lost)*	

Ballets, mascarades, intermèdes:

1.25	"Ballet de La revente des habits," ballet (c1655 or 61, Benserade)	LWV5
1.26	"Ballet d'Alcidiane," ballet (c1658, Benserade)	LWV9
1.27	"Ballet de La raillerie," ballet (c1659, Benserade)	LWV11
1.28	"Xersès," 6 intermèdes / comédie en musique (c1660, Benserade, for Cavalli's opera: Serse)	LWV12
1.29	"Ballet de Toulouse" (au mariage du Roy), ballet (c1660, text lost)	LWV13
1.30	"Ballet de L'impatience," ballet (c1661, L'abbé Buti)	LWV14
1.31	"Ballet des Saisons," ballet (c1661, Benserade)	LWV15
1.32	"Hercule amoureux & Ballet des Sept planètes," ballet (c1662, Buti, for Cavalli: Ercole)	LWV17
1.33	"Ballet des Arts," ballet (c1663, Benserade)	LWV18
1.34	"Les noces de village," mascarade ridicule (c1663, Benserade)	LWV19
1.35	"Les amours désguisés," ballet (c1664, Périgny)	LWV21
1.36	"Oedipe," entr'actes (c1664, for Corneille's tragedy)	LWV23
1.37	"Petit ballet de Fontainebleau" (c1664, music = Oedipe, LWV23)	
1.38	*"Mascarade du capitaine ou L'impromptu," masquerade (c1664 or 5, anon, music lost)*	*LWV24*
1.39	"Ballet de La naissance de Vénus," ballet (c1665, Benserade)	LWV27
1.40	"Ballet des Gardes ou Les délices de la campagne," ballet (c1665, anon)	LWV28
1.41	"Le triomphe de Bacchus dans les Indes," mascarade (c1666, anon, parts c by Lully)	LWV30
1.42	"Ballet des Muses," ballet (c1666, Benserade)	LWV32
1.43	"Le carnaval ou Mascarade de Versailles," mascarade (c1668, Benserade, 1st vers)	LWV36
1.44	"Ballet de Flore," ballet (c1669, Benserade)	LWV40
1.45	"La jeunesse," ballet (c1669)	
1.46	"Les jeux pythiens," ballet (c1670)	
1.47	"Ballet des ballets," (pastiche) ballet (c1671, Quinault, for Molière: La Comtesse d'Escarbagnas)	LWV46
1.48	"Le carnaval mascarade," mascarade (c1675, Molière, Benserade, 2nd version of LWV36)	LWV52
1.49	"Le triomphe de l'amour," ballet (c1681, Quinault & Benserade)	LWV59
1.50	"Le temple de la paix," ballet (c1685, Quinault)	LWV69
1.51	*"Fragments de Monsieur de Lully," ballet (arr Campra, text Danchet p1702)*	*LWV79*
1.52	"Pourceaugnac," divertissement comique	LWV80

Comédies-ballets, tragédies-ballets, pastorales, idylles, eglogues:

1.53	"Les fâcheux," comédie (c1661, Molière, only courante c by Lully, rest c by Beauchamp)	LWV16
1.54	"L'impromptu de Versailles," 1 act comedy (c1663, Molière)	
1.55	"Le mariage forcé," ballet (c1664, Molière)	LWV20
1.56	"Les plaisirs de l'ile enchantée," 5 act grande fête royale (c1664, Benserade & Molière)	LWV22
1.57	"La Princesse d'Elide" (c1664, Molière; inserted in LWV22)	
1.58	"L'Amour médecin," 3 act comédie (c1665, Molière)	LWV29
1.59	"Pastorale comique," 1 act pastorale (c1667, Molière)	LWV33
1.60	"Le Sicilien, ou L'Amour peintre," 1 act comédie (c1667, Molière)	LWV34
1.61	"Le Grand Divertissement Royal de Versailles," divertissement / comédie (c1668)	LWV38
1.62	"George Dandin" (c1668, Molière; incl in LWV38)	

1a. SELECTIONS FROM STAGE WORKS

1a.1   "Cadmus et Hermione," opera: LWV49
               1. "Ouverture"
          Prologue: 2. "Hâtez vous, hâtez-vous, Pasteurs, accourez, accourez" (Pales, Melisse)
               3. "Que l'astre qui nous luit" (Pales, Melisse)
               4. "Admirons, admirons, admirons l'astre qui nous éclaire" (Choeur)
               5. "Rondeau" (Premier Air des Faunes / Ritournelle du Dieu Pan)
               6. "Que chacun se ressente De la douceur charmante" (Pan)
               7. "Quel desordre soudain, Quel bruit affreux redouble" (Choeur)
               8. "Entrée de l'Envie" (Air des vents. Les furies)
               9. "Osons, osons tous obscurcir ses clartés les plus" (Violons; l'Envie)
             10. "Gavotte"
             11. "Chassons, chassons la crainte qui nous presse" (Pales)
             12. "Ce n'est point par l'éclat d'un pompeux sacrifice" (Ritournelle; Le Soleil)
             13. "Profitons des beaux jours, profitons" (Choeur)
             14. "Heureux qui peut plaire, Heureux les amants!" (Pales, Melisse, Pan)
             15. "Peut-on mieux faire, Quand on sçait plaire" (Archas; Menuet)
         I: 16. "Quoy, Cadmus, fils d'un Roy qui tient sous sa puissance" (Premier Prince tirien)
             17. "Ces grands hommes pleins de chimères, sont d'un raisonnement" (Arbas)
             18. "Non, non, nous n'aurons point de bruit ni d'embarras" (Arbas)
             19. "Cet aimable séjour si paisible" (Ritournelle; Hermione)
             20. "On a beau fuir l'amour, On ne peut l'éviter" (Aglante)
             21. "La peine d'aimer est charmante" (Charite)
             22. "Chaconne" (La Chaconne des Africains / La feste africaine)
             23. "Suivons, suivons l'amour laissons nous enflâmer" (Premier et Second Africain, Arbas)
             24. "Il faut que vôtre destinée suive l'ordre du Dieu" (Le Géant)
        II: 25. "Charité, il est trop vray, Cadmus veut entreprendre" (Ritournelle; Arbas)
             26. "Puisqu'enfin pour te satisfaire" (Charite)
             27. "C'est trop railler de mon martire le dépit" (Arbas)
             28. "Guery-toy si tu peux" (Charite)
             29. "Croy-moy, modère l'éclat de ta colère" (Charite)
             30. "Je suis jeune, je le confesse" (Charite)
             31. "Je vais partir, belle Hermione" (Ritournelle; Cadmus)
             32. "Amour, voy quels maux" (Ritournelle; Hermione)
             33. "Calme tes déplaisirs" (Ritournelle; L'Amour)
             34. "Air des Statues"
             35. "Cessez de vous plaindre de souffrir" (L'Amour)
             36. "Second Air pour les Statues"
        III: 37. "Que maudit soit l'amour funeste" (Arbas)
             38. "Gardons-nous bien d'avoir envie" (Premier, second Prince, Arbas)
             39. "Il ne faut plus que je diffère" (Arbas se cache et Cadmus contre le Dragon)
             40. "Quoy! l'épée à la main" (Ritournelle; Premier Prince)
             41. "Tous ces chagrins et ces regrets, Sont des soins" (Arbas)
             42. "Marche des Sacrificateurs"
             43. "O Mars, o toy qui peux dechaîner, quand tu veux" (Le grand Sacrificateur)
             44. "Les Sacrificateurs"
             45. "Mars redoutable, Mars indomptable" (Le grand Sacrificateur, Choeur)
        IV: 46. "Voicy le champ de Mars" (Ritournelle; Cadmus)
             47. "Air pour les Combattans"
             48. "Ma Princesse quel bonheur ... Cadmus quelle gloire" (Ritournelle; Cadmus, Hermione)
             49. "Dieu! Je ne vois plus Hermione!" (Ritournelle; Cadmus)
             50. "Belle Hermione Hélas!" (Ritournelle; Cadmus)
             51. "Que ce qui suit les loix du maître du Tonnerre" (Prélude pour la Nopce de Cadmus)
             52. "Apres un sort si rigoureux" (Choeur)
             53. "Venez, Dieu des festins, aimables jeux" (L'Hymen)
             54. "Air pour Comus et sa suite" (Entrée du Basque)
             55. "Serons-nous dans le silence, quand on rit" (La Nourrice, Arbas; Gavotte)
             56. "Amants, aimez vos chaînes" (Charite)
             57. "Menuet"

1a.2   "Alceste ou Le triomphe d'Alcide," opera: LWV50
           1. "Ouverture"
      Prologue: 2. "Le Héros que j'attens" (La Nymphe de la Seine)
           3. "Quel bruit de guerre m'épouvante" (Bruit de Trompettes; La Nymphe)
           4. "La Gloire paroist au milieu d'un Palais brillant" (La descente de la Gloire) (insts)
           5. "Hélas! superbe Gloire, Hélas!" (La Nymphe)
           6. "On ne voit plus icy paroître" (La Nymphe)
           7. "Qu'il est doux d'accorder" (La Gloire, la Nymphe)
           8. "L'art d'accord avec la nature" (Ritournelle; La Nymphe des Tuileries)
           9. "Menuet. Les Divinitez des fleuves"
         10. "L'onde se presse d'aller sans cesse" (La Nymphe de la Marne; Ritournelle)
         11. "La Loure. Les Divinitez et les Nymphes"
         12. "Que tout retentisse" (Ritournelle; La Gloire)
         13. "Que tout retentisse" (Ritournelle; Choeur)
         14. "Menuet. Les Divinitez de fleuves et les Nymphes forment une danse generale"
         15. "Quel coeur sauvage, Icy ne s'engage" (Choeur)
      I: 16. "Vivez, vivez, heureux Epoux, Vivez, vivez" (Choeur des Thessaliens)
         17. "Ce n'est point avec toi que je prétens me taire" (Alcide)
         18. "L'Amour a bien des maux" (Lycas, Alcide, Straton)
         19. "Je prétens rire" (Lycas)
         20. "Le mépris d'un coeur volage doit" (Straton)
         21. "Dans ce beau jour" (Cephise, Straton)
         22. "Si je change d'amant Qu'y trouves-tu" (Cephise)
         23. "Essaye un peu de l'inconstance" (Cephise)
         24. "Il faut changer toûjours" (Cephise, Straton)
         25. "Straton, donne ordre Enfin grâce au dépit je goûte la douceur" (Licomede, Straton, Cephise)
         26. "Qu'aisément le dépit dégage" (Licomede)
         27. "Il n'est pas sûr toûjours de croire" (Cephise)
         28. "Quand on est sans espérance on est bientôt" (Licomede)
         29. "Loure pour les Pêcheurs" (Air pour les Matelots) (insts)
         30. "Malgré tant d'orages" (Deux Tritons)
         31. "Jeunes coeurs, laissez-vous prendre" (Cephise)
         32. "Rondeau" (Rondeau pour la Fête Marine)
         33. "Dieux, le pont s'abîme dans l'eau" (Prélude; Admete, Alcide)
         34. "Les Vents"
         35. "Le Ciel protège les Héros" (Ritournelle; Eole)
         36. "Et laissez règner" (Eole)
     II: 37. "Alceste ne vient point" (Ritournelle; Cephise)
         38. "Un rival n'est pas inutile" (Cephise)
         39. "Un hymen qui peut plaire" (Straton)
         40. "Puisque je perds toute espérance" (Licomede)
         41. "Les Combattans, la Marche" (La Marche du siège)
         42. "A l'assaut, à l'assaut, aux armes" (Admete, Alcide, Choeur)
         43. "Marche" (Les Combattans)
         44. "Achevons d'emporter la place" (Les Assiégeants)
         45. "Courage, courage enfants, je suis à vous" (Phères)
         46. "Que la vieillesse est lente" (Phères)
         47. "Rendez à vostre fils" (Ritournelle; Alcide)
         48. "O Dieux! quel spectacle funeste" (Ritournelle; Alceste)
         49. "Admete, vous mourez, vous mourez" (Alceste, Admete)
         50. "La lumière aujourd'huy" (Ritournelle; Apollon)
    III: 51. "Ah! pourquoi nous séparez-vous?" (Ritournelle; Alceste)
         52. "Plus vostre époux mourant voit d'amour" (Cephise, Phères)
         53. "De tant d'amis qu'avoit Admete" (Cephise, Alceste, Phères)
         54. "O trop heureux Admete" (Ritournelle; Choeur)
         55. "Alceste est morte" (Cephise, Choeur)
         56. "Prélude pour la Pompe funebre" (Marche funèbre)
         57. "La mort, la mort barbare" (Ritournelle; une Femme affligée)
         58. "Alceste si jeune et si belle" (Ritournelle; un Homme desolé)
         59. "Tant de beauté, tant de vertus" (Ritournelle; une Femme affligée)
         60. "Rompons, brisons, rompons, brisons" (Choeur)
         61. "Symphonie" (Les Affligez)
         62. "Que nos pleurs, que nos cris" (Prélude, Choeur)
         63. "Sans Alceste, sans ces appas" (Ritournelle; Admete)
         64. "Allez, allez ne tardez pas" (Cephise, Phères, Cleante)
         65. "Le dieu dont tu tiens la naissance" (Ritournelle; Diane)
         66. "Il faut passer tôt ou tard" (Ritournelle; Charon)
         67. "Hélas Charon, hélas! hélas! Crie hélas" (Charon)
    IV: 68. "Reçois le juste prix" (la barque de Caron) (Prélude; Pluton)
         69. "La Fête infernale, premier Air" (Les Démons) (insts)
         70. "Tout mortel doit icy paroître" (Choeur)
         71. Chacun vient icy bas prendre place" (Choeur)
         72. "Chacun vient ici bas prendre" (Les Démons; Choeur)
     V: 73. "Alcide est vainqueur du trépas" (Prélude; Admete, Choeur)
         74. "Qu'on ne porte point d'autres fers" (Straton, Lycas)

75. "Je n'ai point de choix à faire" (Cephise)
76. "L'hymen détruit la tendresse" (Cephise, Lycas, Straton)
77. "Pour une si belle victoire" (Prélude; Alcide)
78. "Ah! Ah! que ne fait-on pas" (Alceste, Admete)
79. "Les Muses et les Jeux s'empressent" (Prélude; Apollon)
80. "Chantons, chantons, faisons entendre" (Choeur des Thessaliens)
81. "Premier Air pour les Pastres"
82. "Deuxiesme Air pour les Pastres"
83. "A quoy bon tant de raison" (Straton)
84. "Troisiesme Air pour les Pastres, Menuet"
85. "C'est la saison d'aimer" (Cephise)
86. "Triomphez, triomphez généreux" (Les Choeurs)

1a.3   "Thésée," opera: LWV51
1. "Ouverture"
Prologue: 2. "Les Jeux et les Amours Ne regnent" (Choeur)
3. "Ah quelles peines" (Choeur)
4. "Revenez, revenez Amours" (Ritournelle; Vénus)
5. "Trompettes" (La descente de Mars)
6. "Que rien ne trouble icy" (Mars)
7. "Hautbois" (Menuet)
8. "Partez, allez, volez" (Mars)
9. "Inéxorable Mars, pourquoi" (Vénus)
10. "Qu'il passe au gré de ses désirs" (Vénus, Mars)
11. "Meslons aux chants de victoire" (Choeur)
12. "Premier Air"
13. "Trop heureux qui moissonne" (Cérès)
14. "Second Air"
15. "Pour les plus Fortunez" (Bacchus)
I: 16. "Avançons, avançons que rien ne nous estonne" (Choeur)
17. "Il n'est rien de si beau que les noeuds" (Cleone, Aeglé)
18. "Prétens-tu que je sois un Amant" (Arcas)
19. "La valeur à mes yeux a des charmes" (Cleone)
20. "Prions, prions la Déesse" (La Prêtresse)
21. "Mourez, mourez, perfides coeurs, mourez" (Choeur)
22. "O Minerve! arrestez la cruelle" (Ritournelle; la Prêtresse)
23. "Liberté, liberté, liberté" (Choeur)
24. "Les Mutins sont vaincus" (Prélude; Aegée)
25. "Cessez, charmante Aeglé de répandre des larmes" (Le Roy)
26. "Faites grâce à mon âge faveur" (Le Roy)
27. "Cet Empire puissant" (Le Sacrifice, Prélude; la Prêtresse)
28. "Il faut profiter du bonheur" (La Prêtresse)
29. "Chantez tous en paix" (Choeur)
30. "La Marche" (Marche du sacrifice)
31. "Animez nos coeurs et nos bras" (Choeur)
32. "Entrée des Combattans"
II: 33. "Doux repos, innocente paix" (Ritournelle; Medée)
34. "Le dépit veut que l'on s'engage" (Dorine)
35. "Un tendre engagement va plus loin" (Medée)
36. "Quand on suit une amour nouvelle" (Medée)
37. "Heureux deux amants inconstans" (Medée, le Roy)
38. "N'aimons jamais ou n'aimons guère" (Dorine)
39. "Premier Air pour l'Entrée triomphante de Thesée" (Marche du Triomphe de Thesée)
40. "Que l'on doit estre content d'avoir" (Choeur)
41. "Second Air" (Air des vieillards)
42. "Pour le peu de bon temps qui nous reste" (Les Vieillards)
43. "Dépit mortel, transport jaloux" (Ritournelle; Medée)
III: 44. "Vous allez voir bientost vostre amant" (Ritournelle; Cleone)
45. "La Gloire n'est que trop pressante" (Cleone, Aeglé)
46. "Lorsque par le feu du bel âge" (Arcas)
47. "Il n'est point de grandeur charmante" (Aeglé, Cleone, Arcas)
48. "Princesse, sçavez-vous ce que peut ma colère" (Medée)
49. "J'avois toûjours bravé l'Amour" (Aeglé)
50. "Dieux! Dieux! où sommes nous, où sommes nous" (Prélude; Aeglé, Cleone, Arcas)
51. "Non, non, je le ... Non, non, je le promets" (Cleone, Arcas)
52. "Sortez, Ombres, sortez" (Invocation, Ritournelle; Medée)
53. "Premier Air" (Les Démons)
54. "On nous tourmente sans cesse" (Les Ombres)
55. "Second Air"
IV: 56. "Cruelle, ne voulez-vous pas" (Ritournelle; Aeglé)
57. "Quel spectacle vient me surprendre" (Ritournelle; Aeglé)
58. "Voyez ce que j'ay soin de faire" (Ritournelle; Medée)
59. "De quoy ne vient point à bout Un Roy" (Medée)
60. "Aeglé ne m'ayme plus" (Thesée)
61. "Espargnez ce que j'ayme, C'est moy" (Aeglé, Thesée)

62. "Quel bonheur surprenant pour nos coeurs" (Thesée, Aeglé et Thesée)
63. "Gardez vos tendres amours" (Medée, Aeglé, Thesée)
64. "Que nos prairies Seront fleuries!" (Habitants de l'Isle enchantée, Flûtes, deux Bergers)
65. "Aimons, aimons, tout nous y convie" (Flûtes; Habitants de l'Isle enchantée, deux Bergers)
66. "Quel plaisir d'aimer sans contrainte" (Un Berger, Choeur)
67. "L'Amour plaist malgré ses peines" (Un Berger, Choeur)
V: 68. "Ah! Ah! faut-il me vanger" (Ritournelle; Medée)
69. "Que la vengeance a d'attraits" (Medée, le Roy)
70. "Nostre parfait bonheur" (Thesée)
71. "Que l'hymen prépare des noeuds" (Le Roy)
72. "Soyez unis à jamais, à jamais" (Choeur)
73. "Les plus belles chaisnes" (Aeglé, Thesée)
74. "Vous n'estes pas encor délivrez" (Ritournelle; Medée)
75. "Secourez-nous, justes Dieux" (Choeur)
76. "Prélude, Minerve"
77. "Vivez, vivez contents dans ces aymables" (Choeur)
78. "Premier Air pour la dernière Entrée" (Entré de Beauchamps)
79. "Second Air" (Chaconne)
80. "Le plus sage s'enflamme et s'engage" (Arcas, Cleone)

1a.4   "Atys," opera: LWV53
      1. "Ouverture"
   Prologue: 2. "En vain j'ay respecté" (Le Temps)
      3. "Ses justes loix ses grands exploits" (Choeur)
      4. "Air pour les Nymphes de Flore"
      5. "La saison des frimats peut-elle" (Le Temps)
      6. "Quand j'attens les beaux jours" (Flore)
      7. "Les Plaisirs à ses yeux ont beau se" (Flore, le Temps)
      8. "Rien ne peut l'arrester" (Choeur)
      9. "Air pour la suite de Flore, Gavotte"
     10. "Le Printemps quelquefois est moins doux" (Un Zéphir)
     11. "Retirez-vous, cessez" (Prélude pour Melpomène; Melpomène)
     12. "Air pour la suite de Melpomène"
     13. "Cibele veut que Flore aujourd'huy" (Ritournelle; Iris)
     14. "Préparez de nouvelles Festes, Profitez" (Choeur)
     15. "Menuet"
   I: 16. "Allons, allons, accourez tous" (Ritournelle; Atys, Atys et Idas)
     17. "Le Soleil peint nos champs des plus vives" (Atys)
     18. "Vous veillez lorsque tout sommeille" (Idas)
     19. "Mon coeur veut fuir toûjours" (Atys)
     20. "Tost ou tard l'Amour est vainqueur" (Idas)
     21. "Amans qui vous plaignez" (Idas)
     22. "Allons, allons, accourez tous, Cybele" (Sangaride, Doris)
     23. "Escoutons les oyseaux de ces bois" (Sangaride)
     24. "L'Amour fait trop verser de pleurs" (Atys)
     25. "Quand le peril est agréable" (Sangaride)
     26. "Peut-on estre insensible aux plus charmans" (Sangaride)
     27. "Atys est trop heureux, Souverain" (Sangaride)
     28. "C'est le commun deffaut des Belles" (Doris)
     29. "Un amour malheureux dont le devoir" (Doris, Atys)
     30. "Sangaride, ce jour est un grand jour pour vous" (Atys)
     31. "Si l'Hymen unissoit mon destin" (Sangaride, Atys)
     32. "Aimons un bien plus durable" (Atys)
     33. "Commençons, commençons de célébrer" (Sangaride, Atys, Choeur)
     34. "Entrée des Phrygiens"
     35. "Second Air des Phrygiens"
     36. "Venez tous dans mon Temple" (Prélude; Cybelle)
     37 "Vous devez vous animer d'une ardeur" (Cybelle)
     38. "Nous devons nous animer d'une ardeur" (La descente de Cybelle) (Choeur)
   II: 39. "N'avancez pas plus loin" (Ritournelle; Celenus)
     40. "Qu'un indifférent est heureux!" (Celenus)
     41. "Quand on aime bien tendrement" (Atys)
     42. "Je veux joindre en ces lieux" (Prélude; Cybelle)
     43. "Je sens un plaisir extrême" (Cybele)
     44. "Vous méprisiez trop l'amour" (Melisse)
     45. "Célébrons la gloire immortelle" (Choeur des Nations)
     46. "Entrée des Nations"
     47. "Entrée des Zéphirs"
     48. "Que devant vous tout s'abaisse et tout tremble" (Choeurs)
  III: 49. "Que servent les faveurs" (Ritournelle; Atys)
     50. "Dans l'Empire amoureux le Devoir" (Doris, Idas)
     51. "En vain, un coeur, incertain de son choix" (Doris, Atys, Idas)
     52. "Nous pouvons nous flater" (Ritournelle; Atys)
     53. "Laisse mon coeur en paix, impuissante vertu" (Atys)
     54. "Dormons, dormons tous" (Prélude; le Sommeil)

55. "Ne vous faites point violence" (Photebor)
56. "Dormons, dormons tous, Ah!" (Morphée, Phantase, Photebor)
57. "Que l'Amour a d'attraits" (Morphée)
58. "Entrée des Songes agréables"
59. "Gouste en paix chaque jour une douceur" (Photebor)
60. "Entrée des Songes funestes"
61. "L'Amour qu'on outrage se transforme en rage" (Choeur des Songes funestes)
62. "Second Air"
63. "Qu'Atys dans ses respects mesle d'indifférence" (Cybele)
64. "Ce n'est pas un si grand crime" (Melisse)
65. "Espoir si cher et si doux Ah!" (Ritournelle; Cybele)
IV: 66. "Quoy, vous pleurez? D'où vient vostre peine" (Ritournelle; Doris, Idas)
67. "Peut-on changer sitost quand l'amour" (Doris, Idas)
68. "Une infidélité cruelle N'efface" (Doris, Idas)
69. "Qu'une première amour est belle!" (Sangaride, Doris, Idas)
70. "Belle Nymphe, l'Hymen va suivre" (Prélude; Celaenus)
71. "Qu'il sçait peu son malheur!" (Ritournelle; Atys)
72. "Pourquoy m'abandonner pour une amour nouvelle" (Sangaride, Atys)
73. "O vous! qui prenez part" (Prélude; le Fleuve Dangaride)
74. "Que l'on chante que l'on dance" (Le Fleuve Sangar, Choeur)
75. "La beauté la plus sévère prend pitié" (Flûtes; Choeur)
76. "L'Hymen seul ne sçauroit plaire" (Flûtes; Choeur)
77. "Menuet"
78. "D'une constance extrême" (Choeur)
79. "Gavotte"
80. "Un grand calme est trop fascheux" (Choeur)
V: 81. "Vous m'ostez Sangaride, inhumaine" (Ritournelle; Celaenus)
82. "Ciel! quelle vapeur m'environne" (Prélude; Atys)
83. "Que je viens d'immoler une grande victime" (Atys)
84. "Venez, furieux Corybantes" (Ritournelle; Cybele)
85. "Entrée des Nymphes" (Air pour les flûtes)
86. "Première Entrée des Coribantes"
87. "Seconde Entrée"
88. "Que tout sente icy bas l'horreur" (Choeur)
89. "Passepied"

1a.5   "Isis," opera: LWV54
1. "Ouverture"
Prologue: 2. "Publions en tous lieux Du plus grand" (Choeur)
3. "Heureux l'Empire Qui suit ses loix" (Choeur)
4. "C'est le Dieu des Eaux qui va paroître" (Air des Tritons; les deux Tritons)
5. "Second Air des Tritons"
6. "Mon Empire a servi de théâtre à la guerre" (Neptune)
7. "Célébrez son grand nom sur la terre" (La Renommée, Neptune, Choeur)
8. "Cessez, cessez pour quelque temps" (Prélude des Muses; Calliope)
9. "Ne troublez point les charmes" (Calliope, Thalie, Apollon)
10. "Premier Air pour les Muses"
11. "Second Air pour les Muses"
12. "Air" (Marche / Air pour les Trompettes)
13. "Hâtez-vous, Plaisirs, hâtez-vous" (La Renommée, Choeur)
I: 14. "Cessons, cessons d'aimer" (Ritournelle; Hierax)
15. "Revenez, revenez liberté charmante" (Hierax)
16. "L'Inconstance n'a plus l'empressement extrême" (Hierax)
17. "Vous juriez autrefois que cette Onde" (Hierax)
18. "Je cherche en vain l'heureux amant" (Hierax)
19. "Echos retentissant, echos retentissant dans ces lieux" (Choeur)
20. "Que tout l'univers separe, Que tout la terre partage" (Mercure, Choeur)
21. "Premier Air pour les Divinitez de la Terre"
22. "Second Air" (Menuet)
23. "Les armes que je tiens protegent l'innocence" (Jupiter)
24. "Jupiter vient sur La terre" (Jupiter, Choeur)
II: 25. "Où suis-je, d'où vient ce Nuage" (Ritournelle; Isis)
26. "Un coeur fidèle" (Mercure)
27. "Promettez-moy de constantes amours" (Isis, Mercure)
28. "Gardez pour quelqu'autre Vôtre amour" (Isis, Mercure)
29. "J'ai cherché vainement la fille" (Prélude; Isis)
30. "L'Amour, cet amour infidelle" (Junon)
31. "Entrée pour la Jeunesse"
32. "Les Plaisirs les plus doux" (Hebé, Choeur)
33. "Premier Air" (Air des Plaisirs)
34. "Aimez, profitez, profitez du temps" (Deux Nymphes)
35. "Second Air" (Bourée)
36. "Que ces lieux ont d'attraits" (Choeur)
37. "Tout plaît et tout rit" (Isis, Mercure)

III: 38. "Dans ce solitaire séjour" (Ritournelle; Argus)
    39. "Dégagez-vous d'un amour si fatal" (Argus)
    40. "Heureux, heureux qui peut briser" (Argus, Hierax et Argus)
    41. "Liberté, Liberté, Liberté" (Choeur des Nymphes; Ritournelle)
    42. "Air des Sylvains et des Satyres"
    43. "Marche, Violons, Musettes et Hautbois"
    44. "Quel bien devez-vous attendre" (Second Air; deux Bergers)
    45. "Troisième Air" (Menuet)
    46. "Je n'auray pas de peine A m'engager" (Pan)
    47. "Courons à la chasse à la chasse" (Choeur des Nymphes; la chasse)
    48. "Hélas! Hélas!" (Plainte de Dieu Pan)
    49. "Les yeux qui m'ont charmé" (Pan)
    50. "Sors, barbare Erinnis, sors du fond des enfers" (Junon)
    51. "Des Peuples paroissent transis de froid" (Les glacez)
    52. "L'hyver qui nous tourmente" (Choeur des Peuples des Climats glacés)
IV: 53. "Tôt tôt tôt tôt tôt tôt, Que le feu des forges" (Choeur des Chalytes)
    54. "Entrée des Forgerons"
    55. "Exécutons l'Arrest du sort" (Choeur)
    56. "Premier Air des Parques" (Les Maladies furieuses)
    57. "Second Air des Parques" (Les Malades lentes)
    58. "Le fil de la vie" (Ritournelle; le trois Parques)
V: 59. "Terminez mes tourments, puisant" (Ritournelle, Rondeau, gravement; Io)
    60. "Il ne m'est pas permis de finir" (Prélude; Jupiter)
    61. "J'abandonneray ma vengeance" (Junon, Jupiter)
    62. "Noires Ondes du Stix, c'est pour vous" (Jupiter)
    63. "Apres un rigoureux supplice" (La Furie)
    64. "Isis est immortelle" (Junon, Jupiter, Choeur)
    65. "Rondeau, Canaries" (Rondeau pour les Egyptiens)
    66. "Second et dernier Air"

1a.6   "Psyché," opera: LWV56
    1.–7. (= Psyché, LWV45/1–7)
    8. "Pourquoy du Ciel m'obliger à descendre" (Vénus)
    9. "Mon fils si tu plains mes malheurs" (Prélude pour la descente de l'Amour; Vénus)
I: 10. "Enfin ma soeur le Ciel est appaisé" (Ritournelle; Aglaure)
    11. "Aprés un temps plein d'orage" (Aglaure)
    12. "Ah qu'il est dangereux de trouver" (Aglaure, Cidippe)
    13.–15. (= Psyché, LWV45/8–10)
II: 16. "Cyclopes achevez ce superbe palais" (Prélude; Vulcain)
    17.–18. (= Psyché, LWV45/11–12)
    19. "Pressez-vous ce travail que l'amour vous demande?" (Zéphire)
    20.–21. (= Psyche, LWV45/13–14)
    22. "Quoy vous vous employez pour la fière Psyché" (Ritournelle; Vénus)
    23. "Où suis-je, quel spectacle est offert" (Prélude; Psyché)
    24. "Quels agréables sons ont frappé" (Symphonie cachée; Vénus)
    25. "Aimez, aimez, il n'est de beaux airs" (Vénus, la Nymphe)
    26. "Et bien Psyché des cruautez du sort" (Ritournelle; l'Amour)
    27. "Ah qu'en amour le plaisir" (Psyché, l'Amour)
    28.–30. (= Psyché, LWV45/15–17)
III: 31. "Pompe que ce Palais de tous côtés" (Ritournelle; Vénus)
    32. "Que fais-tu, montre-moy" (Ritournelle; Psyché)
    33. "Vous me demandez donc" (Ritournelle; Psyché)
IV: 34. "Par quels noirs et fâcheux passages" (Ritournelle; Psyché)
    35. "Où penses-tu porter tes pas" (Prélude; les trois Furies)
    36. (= Psyché, LWV45/18)
    37. "Venez, venez, nymphes" (Prélude; les trois Furies)
    38. "Ah que mes peines sont charmantes" (Une Nymphe)
    39. "L'amour anime l'univers tout cede" (Deux Nymphes)
    40. "Si je fais vanité" (Ritournelle; Psyché)
    41. "Vénus veut-elle resister" (Prélude; Jupiter)
    42.–60. (= Psyché, LWV45/19–37)

1a.7   "Bellérophon," opera: LWV57
    1. "Ouverture"
Prologue: 2. "Muses, preparons nos concerts" (Apollon)
    3. "Apres avoir chanté les fureurs" (Choeur)
    4. "Marche pour l'Entrée de Bacchus et de Pan"
    5. "Du fameux bord de l'Inde où toûjours la victoire" (Bacchus, Pan)
    6. "Chantons, chantons le plus grand des mortels" (Choeur)
    7. "Pourquoy n'avoir pas le coeur tendre" (Choeur; Menuet)
    8. "Entrée des Aegipans et Menades"
    9. "Menuet pour les Bergers"
    10. "Tout est paisible sur la terre" (Pan)
    11. "Quittez, quittez de si vaines chansons" (Apollon)
    12. "Pour ce grand Roy redoublons nos efforts" (Choeur)

I: 13. "Non, les soulevements d'une ville rebelle" (Stenobée)
14. "Malgré tous mes malheurs" (Stenobée)
15. "En vain quand l'amour est extrême" (Stenobée)
16. "Qu'il est doux de trouver dans un amant qu'on aime" (Philonoé)
17. "Un coeur qui paraît invincible peut être un" (Argie)
18. "Contre Bellérophon j'ay fait" (Prélude; le Roy)
19. "Trompettes"
20. "Venez, venez goûter les doux fruits de la gloire" (Le Roy)
21. "Un héros que la Gloire éleve n'est qu'à demy" (Le Roy)
22. "Quand un vainqueur est tout brillant" (Prélude; Choeur des Amazones et des Solymes)
23. "Premier Air"
24. "Second Air"
25. "Faisons cesser nos allarmes Goûtons les" (Choeur)
II: 26. "Amour, mes voeux sont satisfaits" (Ritournelle; Philonoé)
27. "Chantez, chantez la valeur éclattante" (Philonoé et Choeur)
28. "Princesse tout conspire à couronner ma" (Prélude; Bellérophon)
29. "Que tout parle a l'envy de notre amour" (Bellérophon, Philonoé)
30. "Vous me jurez sans cesse une amour éternelle" (Ritournelle; Stenobée)
31. "Lorsque l'Amour vous asservit mon âme" (Amisodar)
32. "Hâtez-vous, hâtez-vous de servir" (Stenobée)
33. "Que ce jardin se change un un Desert" (Prélude; Amisodar)
34. "Premier Air"
35. "Parle, nous voilà prêts, tout nous sera possible" (Les Magiciens)
36. "Second Air"
37. "La terre nous ouvre ses gouffres" (Les Magiciens)
III: 38. "Que vous faites couler et de sang et de larmes" (Ritournelle; Argie)
39. "Impuissante vengeance inutile secours!" (Stenobée)
40. "Que de malheurs accablent la Luci-e" (Prélude; Le Roy)
41. "La Marche du Sacrifice"
42. "Le malheur qui nous accable demande un Dieu" (Choeur de Peuple; Gavotte)
43. "Dieux! qui connoissez nos malheurs" (Violons/Symphonie 1715; Choeur de Peuple)
44. "Apres un augure si doux, tâchons" (Choeur)
45. "Montrons notre allégresse, ne parlons plus" (Choeur de Peuple)
46. "Tout m'apprend qu'Apollon dans nos voeux" (Ritournelle; le Sacrificateur)
47. "Assez de pleurs ont suivy nos malheurs" (Choeur)
48. "Gardez tous un silence extrême" (Prélude; La Pythie)
49. "Dans quel accablement cet Oracle me laisse" (Ritournelle; Bellérophon et Philonoé)
IV: 50. "Quel spectacle charmant pour mon coeur" (Ritournelle; Amisodar)
51. "Quand on obtient ce qu'on aime Qu'importe" (Amisodar)
52. "Tout est perdu, le monstre avance" (Voix derrière le Théâtre)
53. "Plaignons, plaignons les maux" (Flûtes; Dryade, Napée)
54. "Les forets sont en feu, le ravage s'augmente" (Ritournelle; Dieu des bois)
55. "Heureuse mort, tu vas me secourir" (Ritournelle; Bellérophon)
56. "Espère en ta valeur, Belérophon" (Prélude; Pallas)
57. "Quelle horreur! quel affreux ravage" (Choeur de Peuple)
58. "Menuet"
V: 59. "Préparez vos chants d'allegresse" (Prélude; Le Roy)
60. "Viens, digne sang des Dieux jouir de ta victoire" (Choeur de Peuple)
61. "Pour tout vaincre il suffit qu'un héros" (Philonoé)
62. "O jour! O jour pour la Lycie" (Choeur de Peuple)
63. "Venez-vous partager l'allegresse publique" (Le Roy)
64. "Trompettes, Tymbales et Violons, Pallas"
65. "Enfin je vous revoy Princesse" (Bellérophon, Philonoé)
66. "Jouissez des douceurs que l'hymen" (Le Roy)
67. "Le plus grand des héros rend le calme" (Trompettes; Choeur de Peuple)
68. "Premier Air"
69. "Second Air, Trompettes, Fanfare"
70. "Les Plaisirs nous preparent leurs charmes, ne songeons" (Choeur de Peuple)

1a.8   "Proserpine," opera: LWV58
1. "Ouverture"
Prologue: 2. "Héros dont la valeur estonne l'univers" (La Paix, Suite de la Paix)
3. "Air" (Entrée des Furies)
4. "Bruit de Trompettes" (Bruit de guerre)
5. "Air pour les trompettes"
6. "Venez aimable paix, le vainqueur" (La Victoire; la Victoire et sa suite)
7. "Apres avoir vaincu mille peuples" (La suite de la Victoire et de la Paix)
8. "Le vainqueur est comblé de gloire" (Prélude; la Victoire et la Paix, Choeur)
9. "Gavotte"
10. "Menuet"
11. "Il est temps que l'amour nous enchaîne" (La Félicité et l'Abondance)
12. "On a quitté les armes" (Prélude; la Paix, Choeur)
13. "Menuet"
14. "Que l'amour est doux à suivre!" (La Félicité)

I: 15. "Goustons, goustons dans ces aymables" (Cérès; Cérès, Cyane, Crinise)
16. "Mercure, quel dessein vous fait icy" (Ritournelle pour Mercure pendant qu'il vole; Cérès)
17. "L'Amour qui pour luy m'anime" (Cérès)
18. "Je quitte une paix profonde" (Cérès)
19. Les soins d'un amour extresme" (Cérès)
20. "Pour fuir l'amour qui vous appelle" (Cérès)
21. "Vaine fierté, foible rigeur" (Ritournelle; Arethuse)
22. "Je vois Alphée, ô Dieux" (Ritournelle; Arethuse)
23. "Cérès va vous oster sa divine présence" (Prélude; Proserpine)
24. "Vous, qui voulez pour moy signaler vostre zele" (Ritournelle; Cérès)
25. "Célebrons la victoire" (Proserpine, Choeur)
26. "Premier Air" (Les Siciliens)
27. "Second Air" (Menuet)
28. "Le Palais va tomber, ô Dieux" (Prélude; Proserpine)
29. "Jupiter lance le tonnerre" (Choeur)
II: 30. "Jupiter a dompté les Géants pour jamais" (Ritournelle; Crinise)
31. "La paix dans ces beaux lieux m'offre en vain" (Alphée)
32. "Heureux, heureux qui peut estre inconstant" (Alphée)
33. "Qu'il couste cher d'estre fidèle!" (Crinise, Alphée)
34. "Les flames amoureuses Descendent-elles" (Alphée)
35. "L'Astre brillant qui vous luit" (Ascalaphe)
36. "Amants qui n'estes point jaloux" (Ritournelle; Alphée)
37. "Ingrate, écoutez-moy, je ne veux" (Ritournelle; Alphée)
38. "Faut-il que vostre coeur à l'amour" (Alphée)
39. "C'est une autre que moy qui règne" (Alphée, Arethuse)
40. "En luy donnant la préference" (Ascalaphe)
41. "J'ai peine à concevoir" (Ritournelle; Pluton, Ascalaphe)
42. "L'Amour comblé de gloire Triomphe" (Pluton, Ascalaphe)
43. "Les beaux jours et la paix sont revenus" (Choeur des Nymphes)
44. "Premier Air"
45. "Que nostre vie Doit faire envie" (Proserpine, Choeur des Nymphes)
46. "Belles fleurs, charmant ombrage, Il ne faut" (Proserpine)
47. "Second Air"
48. "Voyons qui sçait le mieux assortir" (Choeur; Hautbois)
III: 49. "Proserpine, Proserpine" (Vioilons; Choeur)
50. "J'ay sans cesse suivy vos pas" (Alphée)
51. "Que l'absence de ce qu'on aime" (Alphée)
52. "Cérès revient, ah! quelle peine!" (Violons; Choeur)
53. "Je vais revoir ma fille" (Prélude; Cérès)
54. "J'ay rendu les humains heureux" (Ritournelle; Cérès)
55. "O malheureuse mère" (Ritournelle; Cérès, Choeur)
56. "Ah quelle injustice cruelle O Dieux!" (Ritournelle; Cérès)
57. "Apres un si sensible outrage" (Ritournelle; Cérès)
58. "Air" (La Colère de Céres)
59. "Que tout se ressente de la fureur que je sens" (Cérès, Choeur)
60. "Les Ombres heureuses forment un Concert. Flûtes et Violons"
61. "Loin d'icy, loin de nous, Tristes ennuis" (Les Ombres heureuses)
62. "Ah! que ces demeures sont belles!" (Ritournelle; les Ombres heureuses)
63. "Dans ces beaux lieux tout nous enchanté" (Les Ombres)
64. "O bienheureuse vie! Vous ne nous serez" (Ombres heureuses)
IV: 65. "Ma chère liberté" (Prélude; Proserpine)
66. "Aimez qui vous aime rien n'est" (Asalaphe)
67. "Rien n'est impossible à l'amour constant" (Alphée, Arethuse)
68. "Je ne verray jamais la lumière" (Proserpine)
69. "Venez-vous contre moy défendre" (Prélude; Proserpine)
70. "Rendons hommage à vostre Reine" (Pluton, Choeur)
71. "Premier Air" (Air des Divinitez)
72. "C'est assez, c'est assez de regrets" (Second Air; Choeur)
73. "Dans les enfers tout rit tout chante" (Choeur)
V: 74. "Vous qui reconnoissez ma suprême puissance" (Prélude; Pluton)
75. "C'est la première fois que j'aime" (Pluton)
76. "Nous avons pour nous en ce jour" (Pluton)
77. "Renversons, renversons toute la nature" (Choeur)
78. "Desserts écartez, sombres lieux" (Prélude; Cérès)
79. "Quel coeur se peut asseurer" (Arethuse, Aphée)
80. "Tous les Dieux sont d'accord" (Ritournelle; Mercure)
81. "Apres une peine extresme" (Cérès)
82. "Prélude, Trompettes, Tymballes, Jupiter"
83. "Que l'on enchaîne pour jamais" (Jupiter, Choeur)
84. "Premier Air"
85. "Second Air"
86a. "Gigue de Proserpine"
86b. "Marche des Silvains"

1a.9   "Persée," opera: LWV60
            1. "Ouverture"
      Prologue: 2. "La vertu veut choisir ce lieu" (Phronime et Megatyme)
            3. "Suivons, suivons par tout ses pas" (Phronime et Megatyme)
            4. "O vertu charmante! Vostre empire" (Choeur de suivants et suivantes de la Vertu)
            5. "La grandeur brillante" (Air pour les hautbois. Passepied; Megatyme, Phronime)
            6. "Marche pour les suivants de la Fortune"
            7. "Sans cesse combattons" (La Fortune, la Vertu)
            8. "Les Dieux ne l'ont donné que pour le bien" (Choeur des suivants de la Vertu)
            9. "Mille nouveaux concerts viennent se faire" (La Fortune, la Vertu)
            10. "Air" (Chaconne en rondeau)
            11. "Quel heureux jour pour nous" (Menuet; la Fortune et la Vertu)
            12. "Heureuse inteligence" (Choeur)
      I: 13. "Je crains que Junon ne refuse" (Cephée)
            14. "Par un crudel chastiment, les Dieux" (Cassiope)
            15. "Les Dieux punissent la fierté" (Cephée)
            16. "O Dieux! O Dieux qui punissez l'audace" (Cassiope, Merope, Cephée)
            17. "Je goûtois une paix heureuse" (Merope)
            18. "Mon vainqueur encore aujourd'huy" (Merope)
            19. "Le temps seul peut guérir les maux" (Cassiope, Merope)
            20. "Ah! je garderay bien mon coeur" (Ritournelle; Merope)
            21. "Croyez-moy, croyez-moy" (Ritournelle; Andromede, Phinée)
            22. "Vous estes tous deux aymables" (Merope)
            23. "Non, non je ne puis souffrir qu'il partage" (Phinée)
            24. "Vous suivez à regret la gloire" (Phinée)
            25. "Ah que l'amour cause d'allarmes!" (Merope, Andromede, Phinée)
            26. "Jeux Junoniens, premier Air"
            27. "O Junon! puissante Déesse" (Ritournelle; Cassiope)
            28. "Laisez calmer vostre colère" (Choeur de spectateurs)
            29. "Second Air"
            30. "Troisième Air"
            31. "Fuyons, fuyons nos voeux sont vains" (Prélude; trois Ethiopiens)
      II: 32. "Faut-il que contre nous tout le ciel" (Ritournelle; Cassiope)
            33. "Briserez-vous des noeuds, Que vous avez formés" (Merope)
            34. "L'espoir dans nos coeurs doit renaistre" (Cephée)
            35. "Le fils de Jupiter va combattre" (Merope, Cassiope, Cephée)
            36. "Hélas! il va périr, dois-je en trembler" (Ritournelle; Merope)
            37. "Infortunez qu'un monstre affreux" (Prélude, Andromede)
            38. "Il ne m'ayme que trop" (Andromede)
            39. "Vous l'aymez, vous l'aymez, vous l'aymez, Ah!" (Andromede, Merope)
            40. "L'Amour qu'il a pour moy l'engage" (Andromede)
            41. "Ce héros s'expose pour nous" (Andromede, Merope)
            42. "Belle Princesse enfin vous souffrez ma presence" (Persée)
            43. "Ah vostre peril est extrême!" (Andromede, Persée)
            44. "Entrée des Cyclopes"
            45. "Entrée des Nymphes guerrieres"
            46. "Que la Valeur et la Prudence" (Une nymphe guerrière)
            47. "Entrée des divinitez infernales"
            48. "Ce don misterieux doit aprendre" (Une Divinité infernale)
            49. "Que l'Enfer la Terre et les Cieux" (Mercure, Choeur)
      III: 50. "J'ay perdu la beauté" (Prélude; Meduse)
            51. "O le doux employ pour la rage" (Euriale, Meduse, Stenone)
            52. "Dans ce triste séjour qui peut" (Euriale, Meduse, Stenone)
            53. "Mon terrible secours vous est-il necessaire?" (Meduse)
            54. "O tranquile sommeil" (Mercure)
            55. "Non, non, non, non ce n'est que pour la colère" (Euriale, Meduse, Stenone)
            56. "Le Monde est delivré" (Prélude; Persée)
            57. "Entrée des Fantosmes"
            58. "Monstres cherchez vostre victime, Vengez" (Euriale, Stenone)
      IV: 59. "Courons, courons tous admirer le vainqueur" (Choeur)
            60. "Nous ressentons mesmes douleurs" (Phinée, Merope)
            61. "Que le ciel pour Persée est prodigue en miracles" (Phinée)
            62. "Les vents impetueux" (La Tempeste) (Gay, Phinée)
            63. "O ciel inéxorable! O malheur" (Prélude; deux Ethiopiens, Idas)
            64. "O sort inéxorable! O malheur" (L'Ethiopien, Phinée, Idas)
            65. "L'amour meurt dans mon coeur, la rage" (Phinée)
            66. "Dieux! qui me destinez une mort" (Ritournelle; Andromede)
            67. "Le monstre approche de ces lieux" (Choeur d'Ethiopiens)
            68. "Temeraire Persée arrestez" (Choeur)
            69. "Descendons sous les ondes" (Choeur)
            70. "Le monstre est mort, Persée" (Gay, Choeur)
            71. "Gigue"
            72. "Nostre espoir alloit faire naufrage" (Menuet; un Ethiopien)
            73. "Que n'aimez-vous coeurs insensible?" (Rondeau; un Ethiopien, Choeur)
            74. "Honorons à jamais" (Cephée, Choeur)

V: 75. "O mort! venez finir mon destin" (Prélude; Merope)
76. "Hymen, ô doux hymen" (Prélude; le grand Prestre, Choeur)
77. "Air pour les Sacrificateurs"
78. "Persée, il faut perir" (Violons; Phinée)
79. "Le soin de vous deffendre" (Violons; Cephée)
80. "Qu'il n'eschape pas, qu'il périsse" (Choeur)
81. "Cessons de redouter la fortune cruelle" (Prélude; Persée, Choeur)
82. "Passacaille"
83. "Héros victorieux Andromède" (Choeur)
84. "Air"

1a.10 "Phaëton," opera: LWV61
1. "Ouverture"
Prologue: 2. "Troupe de Compagnes d'Astrée dansante, Menuet"
3. "Cherchons la paix dans cet azile" (Troupe de Compagnes d'Astrée chantante)
4. "Dans cette paisible retraite" (Ritournelle; Astrée)
5. "La douceur de l'espérance doit flatter" (Astrée)
6. "Troupe d'Astrée dansante, Menuet"
7. "Dans ces lieux, tout rit sans cesse" (Troupe de Compagnes d'Astrée chantante)
8. "Que les mortels se réjouissent" (Prélude; Choeur)
9. "Un héros qui mérite une gloire immortelle" (Saturne)
10. "Les Muses vont lui faire entendre" (Saturne)
11. "L'envie en vain frémit de voir" (Ritournelle; Saturne)
12. "Suivons ce héros, suivez-nous" (Astrée)
13. "Jeux innocens, rassemblez-vous" (Choeur)
14. "Air pour les suivants de Saturne"
15. "Air pour les suivants d'Astrée et de Saturne"
16. "Plaisirs, venez sans crainte" (Choeur des suivantes d'Astrée)
17. "On a veu ce héros terrible" (Saturne, Astrée, Choeur)
I: 18. "Heureuse une âme indifférente" (Prélude; Lybie)
19. "Je ne vous croyois pas Dans un lieux" (Ritournelle; Theone)
20. "J'aime, c'est mon destin d'aimer" (Theone)
21. "Ah! qu'il est difficile de bien aimer" (Lybie et Theone)
22. "Je m'aperçois sans cesse" (Theone)
23. "Heureux qui peut voir du rivage" (Protée et sa suite, Protée)
24. "Prenez soin sur ces hords des troupeaux" (Prélude; Protée)
25. "Air" (Air des Tritons)
26. "Que Protée avec nous partage" (Triton)
27. "Rondeau"
28. "Le plaisir est nécessaire. La sagesse" (Triton)
29. "C'est un secret qu'il faut" (Prélude; Triton)
30. "Le sort de Phaëton se découvre" (Prélude; Protée)
II: 31. "Protée en a trop dit" (Ritournelle; Clymène)
32. "Il me fuit, l'inconstant" (Ritournelle; Theone)
33. "Que l'incertitude Est un rigoureux" (Ritournelle; Lybie)
34. "Mon sort étoit digne d'envie" (Lybie)
35. "Amour, cruel vainqueur, Ah!" (Theone, Lybie)
36. "Quel malheur! Dieux! quelle tristesse" (Epaphus, Lybie)
37. "Prélude" (Marche de Merops)
38. "Roys, qui pour souverain" (Merops)
39. "Que de tous côtez on entende le nom" (Merops, Choeur)
40. "Chaconne"
41. "Gay. Petit Air pour les mesmes"
III: 42. "Ah! Phaëton, est-il possible" (Ritournelle; Theone)
43. "Je plains ses malheurs, Je m'attendris" (Phaëton)
44. "Songez-vous qu'Isis est ma mère?" (Epaphus)
45. "Mon père est le Dieu redoutable" (Epaphus)
46. "Non, non rien n'est comparable" (Phaëton, Epaphus)
47. "Marche" (Marche des sacrificateurs)
48. "Rondeau. Menuet"
49. "O vous! Pour qui l'amour" (Merops)
50. "Entrée des Furies"
51. "Vous êtes son Fils, Je le jure" (Clymène)
52. "Le Dieu semble aprouver le serment" (Prélude; Clymène)
IV: 53. "Sans le Dieu qui nous éclaire" (Ritournelle; Choeur des Heures du jour)
54. "O Dieu de la clarté! Vous réglez" (Une des Heures du jour)
55. "Sans le Dieu qui nous éclaire" (Choeur des heures du jour)
56. "C'est par vous, ô Soleil! Que le Ciel" (L'Automne)
57. "Premier Air. Le Printemps et sa suite"
58. "Second Air" (Menuet)
59. "Dans ce Palais bravez l'Envie" (Une des Heures, Choeur)
60. "Dans cette demeure charmante" (CHoeur)
61. "Allez répandre la Lumière" (Choeur)
V: 62. "Assemblez-vous, habitans" (Ritournelle; Clymène)
63. "Dieu qui vous déclarez mon Père" (Epaphus)

64. "O rigoureux martyre" (Lybie)
65. "Hélas une chaîne si belle" (Lybie, Epaphus)
66. "Que l'on chante, que tout réponde" (Prélude; Merops, Clymène, Choeur)
67. "Bourrée pour les Egyptiens"
68. "Second Air"
69. "Ce beau jour ne permet qu'à l'Aurore" (Une Bergère égyptienne)
70. "Dieux! quel feu vient par tout s'étendre" (Choeur)
71. "C'est vôtre secours que j'implore" (La Déesse de la terre)
72. "O Dieu qui lancez le Tonnerre" (Choeur)

1a.11   "Amadis de Gaule," opera: LWV63
1. "Ouverture"
Prologue: 2. "Ah j'entends un bruit qui nous presse" (Prélude; Urgande)
3. "Esprits empressés à nous plaire" (Urgande, Alquif, Choeur)
4. "Premier Air"
5. "Second Air. Gigue"
6. "Les Plaisirs nous suivent désormais" (Une des suivantes d'Urgande)
7. "Lors qu'Amadis périt une douleur profonde" (Urgande)
8. "C'est à lui d'enseigner aux maîtres" (Urgande, Alquif)
9. "Nous ne sçaurions choisir de demeure" (Alquif)
10. "Tout l'univers admire ses exploits" (Urgande, Alquif, Choeur)
11. "Les Suivants d'Alquif et d'Urgande témoignent leur joie en chantant et en dansant"
12. "Suivons l'amour, C'est lui qui nous mène" (Choeur)
13. "Volez tendres amours" (Urgande, Alquif)
I: 14. "Je reviens dans ces lieux pour y voir ce que j'aime" (Amadis)
15. "Ah! que l'amour paraît charmant!" (Amadis)
16. "Fut-il jamais amant plus fidèle" (Amadis)
17. "Quand on est aimé comme on aime" (Florestan)
18. "Florestan ... Corisande! O bienheureux" (Ritournelle; Corisande, Florestan)
19. "Que ne puis-je arrêter l'ardeur qui vous porte" (Corisande)
20. "Amadis punit les ingrats" (Florestan)
21. "Trop heureux qui peut s'engager" (Corisande, Oriane, Florestan)
22. "Marche pour le Combat de la Barrière"
23. "Premier Air des Combattants"
24. "Second Air"
25. "Belle Princesse Que vos charmes" (Choeur)
II: 26. "Amour que veux-tu de moi?" (Prélude; Arcabonne)
27. "L'amour n'est qu'une vaine erreur" (Arcalaus)
28. "Irritons notre barbarie" (Arcabonne, Arcalaus)
29. "Dans un piège fatal son mauvais sort" (Symphonie pour Arcalaus; Arcalaus)
30. "Bois épais redouble ton ombre" (Prélude; Amadis)
31. "O fortune cruelle" (Ritournelle; Corisande)
32. "Esprits infernaux il est temps" (Amadis combat contre Arcalaus; Arcalaus)
33. "Air pour les Démons et les Monstres"
34. "Non, non pour être invincible" (Prélude; Choeur)
35. "Aimez, soupirez, soupirez, coeurs" (Deux Bergers)
36. "Vous ne devez plus attendre" (Choeur)
37. "Est-ce vous Oriane? O Ciel" (Amadis)
III: 38. "Ciel finissez nos peines" (Prélude; Choeur de Captifs et de Geôliers)
39. "Tel s'empresse d'appeler la mort" (Un Geôlier)
40. "O mort que vous êtes lente" (Choeur de Captifs et Captives)
41. "Il est temps de finir" (Prélude; Arcabone)
42. "Contentez-vous des maux" (Prélude; Choeur)
43. "Consolez-vous, consolez-vous dans vos tourments" (Arcabonne)
44. "Toi qui dans ce tombeau n'es plus" (Prélude; Arcabonne)
45. "Ah! tu me trahis malheureuse" (Prélude; L'Ombre d'Ardan)
46. "Non, rien n'arrêtera la fureur" (Prélude; Arcabonne)
47. "Vivez, quittez vos fers" (Ritournelle; Arcabonne)
48. "Sortons, sortons d'esclavage" (Prélude; Choeur)
49. "Premier Air"
50. "Second Air"
IV: 51. "Par mes enchantemens" (Ritournelle; Arcalaus)
52. "Ne permettons pas qu'elle ignore" (Arcalaus)
53. "Je veux haïr toujours un amant" (Oriane)
54. "Quel plaisir quel plaisir de voir" (Ritournelle; Arcabonne, Arcalaus)
55. "Je soumets à mes loix l'Enfer" (Prélude; Urgande)
56. "Tremblez, tremblez" (Urgande, deux suivantes d'Urgande)
57. "Menuet pour les suivantes d'Urgande"
58. "Coeurs accablez de rigueurs inhumaines" (Deux suivantes d'Urgande)
59. "Démons soumis à nos loix" (Prélude; Arcalaus)
V: 60. "Apollidon par un pouvoir magique" (Prélude; Urgande)
61. "Fermez-vous pour jamais" (Oriane)
62. "Ma douleur eut été nortelle, hélas" (Oriane, Amadis)
63. "Je vous promets de n'éteindre" (Amadis, Amadis et Oriane)
64. "Il est temps de vous arrêter" (Symphonie; Urgande)

65. "Fidèles coeurs" (Prélude; une des Héroines)
66. "A la fin l'amour couronne" (Choeur)
67. "Chaconne"
68. "Chantons tous en ce jour la gloire" (Le grand Choeur)

1a.12 "Roland," opera: LWV65
1. "Ouverture"
Prologue: 2. "Le Ciel qui m'a fait vôtre Roy" (Demogorgon)
3. "On n'entend plus le bruit des armes" (La principale Fée et Demogorgon)
4. "Première Entrée. Menuet"
5. "Second Menuet"
6. "Que la guerre est effroyable!" (Choeur des Fées)
7. "Au millieu d'une paix profonde" (Prélude; la principale Fée)
8. "Du célèbre Roland renouvellons l'histoire" (Demogorgon)
9. "Allons, allons faire entendre nos voix" (Demophon, première Fée)
10. "Il avoit aux fers la Discorde" (Demogorgon)
11. "Seconde Entrée. Les Genies et les Fées font un essay de Danses"
12. "Gavotte"
13. "C'est l'amour qui nous menace" (Une Fée chante, Choeurs des Genies et des Fées)
14. "Le vainqueur a contraint" (La principale Fée, Demogorgon, Choeur)
I: 15. "Ah! que mon coeur est agité" (Prélude; Angelique)
16. "Vous avez peu d'impatience" (Ritournelle; Angelique, Temire)
17. "Aymez, aymez Roland à vôtre tour" (Temire)
18. "Ah! quel tourment de garder" (Prélude; Médor)
19. "Je ne verray plus ce que j'ayme" (Angelique, Temire)
20. "Le secours de l'absence" (Temire)
21. "Ziliante. Troupe d'Insulaires Orientaux. Marche"
22. "Au genereux Roland je dois ma délivrance" (Ziliante portant un brasselet à Angelique)
23. "Triomphez, charmante reine" (Ziliante, Choeur)
24. "Air"
25. "Dans nos climats sans chagrin" (Deux Insulaires, Chanson)
II: 26. "Un charme dangereux dans ces bois" (Ritournelle; Temire)
27. "C'est la fontaine de la haine" (Angelique)
28. "Non, non, non, non, on ne peut trop plaindre" (Temire, une Suivante, un Suivant)
29. "Belle Angelique Enfin je vous trouve" (Roland)
30. "Quelle cruauté! quel mépris!" (Roland)
31. "Peut-on vous mepriser sans crime!" (Temire)
32. "Le dépit éteint ma flâme Heureuse" (Roland)
33. "C'est l'amour qui prend soin luy-même" (Angelique)
34. "Agréables retraites" (Ritournelle; Médor)
35. "Fontaine, qui d'une eau si pure" (Médor)
36. "Je vivray si c'est vôtre envie" (Médor)
37. "Ma gloire murmure en ce jour" (Angelique)
38. "Témoins du désespoir dont mon coeur" (Médor)
39. "Aimez, aimez-vous. Aimons, aimons-nous" (Angelique, Médor)
40. "Entrée, Gavotte"
41. "Qui goûte de ces eaux ne peut plus" (Deux Amantes contentes)
42. "Second Air"
43. "Que pour jamais un noeud charmant" (Choeur)
III: 44. "Non, je n'entends vos conseils" (Ritournelle; Médor, Temire)
45. "S'il faut que ma félicité" (Médor)
46. "Je n'osois pas espérer le bien" (Médor)
47. "Faut-il encore que je vous aime?" (Prélude; Roland)
48. "J'abandonne ma gloire et la laisse ternir" (Roland)
49. "Peut-être un soûpir si tendre" (Roland)
50. "En des lieux écartez dans une paix" (Roland)
51. "Médor, je tremble pour nos jours" (Angelique)
52. "Je ne veux que vôtre coeur, C'est l'unique" (Angelique, Médor)
53. "Vous me quittez, Et je demeure" (Médor, Angelique)
54. "Vivons, l'amour nous y convie" (Angelique, Médor)
55. "Les Peuples de Catay rendent hommage à Médor, Air"
56. "Chaconne, gay"
57. "C'est Médor qu'une Reyne si belle" (Choeur)
58. "Angelique n'est plus insensible" (Un Suivant)
59. "Aimez, regnez en depit de l'envie" (Choeur)
IV: 60. "Va, ton soin m'importune" (Ritournelle; Roland)
61. "Ah! J'attendray longtemps" (Prélude; Roland)
62. "Ce que je lis m'apprend" (Roland)
63. "Hautbois"
64. "J'entends un bruit de Musique" (Roland)
65. "Quand on vient dans ce boccage" (Une Nôce de Village. Le Marié. Marche; Choeur)
66. "Menuet"
67. "Entrée de Pastres, de Pastourelles, de Bergers et de Bergères"
68. "Vivez en paix, Vivez en paix, Amants" (Une Pastre et une Pastourelle)
69. "J'aymerai toûjours ma bergère" (Hautbois; Coridon)

70. "Angélique est Reine elle est belle" (Coridon)
71. "Quand des riches pays arrosez" (Belise)
72. "Allez, allez, laissez-nous" (Tersandre)
73. "Dans les climats les plus heureux" (Tersandre)
74. "Je suis trahi! Ciel!" (Roland)
75. "Ah! Je suis descendu" (Prélude; Roland)
V: 76. "Sage et divine fée" (Prélude; Astolfe)
77. "Je puis des éléments interrompre" (Logistille)
78. "Par le secours d'une douce" (Symphonie; Logistille)
79. "O vous dont le nom plein de gloire" (Prélude; Logistille)
80. "Roland, courez aux armes" (Prélude; Logistille, Roland)
81. "Sortez pour jamais en ce jour" (Choeur)
82. "Air. Rondeau"
83. "Second Air"
84. "La Gloire vous appelle" (Choeur)

1a.13   "Armide et Renaud," opera: LWV71
1. "Ouverture"
Prologue: 2. "Tout doit céder dans l'Univers" (La Gloire)
3. "Chantons, chantons la doucer" (Choeur)
4. "D'une esgale tendresse, Nous aimons" (La Gloire et la Sagesse)
5. "Disputons seulement à qui sçait mieux" (La Gloire, la Sagesse)
6. "Dès qu'on le voit paroistre" (Choeur)
7. "Entrée"
8. "Menuet"
9. "Rondeau"
10. "Suivons nostre héros" (Prélude; La Sagesse)
11. "Que l'éclat de son nom s'estende" (Choeur)
12. "Entrée"
13. "Menuet"
14. "Menuet"
15. "Que dans le temple de memoire" (La Sagesse, la Gloire, Choeur)
I: 16. "Dans un jour de triomphe au milieu" (Ritournelle; Phenice)
17. "Quel sort a plus d'appas Et qui peut estre heureux" (Phenice, Sidonie)
18. "Je ne triomphe pas du plus vaillant de tous" (Armide)
19. "Un songe affreux m'inspire une fureur" (Prélude; Armide)
20. "Armide que le sang qui m'unit avec vous" (Hidraot)
21. "La chaîne de l'hymen" (Armide)
22. "Pour vous, quand il vous plaît tout l'Enfer" (Hidraot)
23. "Bornez-vous vos desirs à la gloire crudele" (Hidraot)
24. "Air"
25. "Armide est encor" (Hidraot)
26. "Rondeau"
27. "Suivons Armide et chantons sa victoire" (Phenice, Choeur)
28. "Sarabande. Rondeau"
29. "Que la douceur d'un triomphe" (Sidonie, Choeur)
30. "Poursuivons, poursuivons jusqu'au trépas l'ennemy" (Armide, Hidraot, Choeur)
II: 31. "Invincible Héros, c'est par vostre courage" (Artémidore)
32. "Fuyez les lieux où regne Artémide" (Artémire)
33. "Arrestons-nous icy" (Prélude; Hidraot)
34. "Esprits de haine et de rage" (Prélude; Armide, Hidraot)
35. "Plus j'observe ces lieux" (Prélude, Sourdines; Renaud)
36. "Au temps heureux où l'on sçait plaire" (La nymphe)
37. "Ah! quelle erreur!" (Prélude, Sourdines; Choeur)
38. "Premier Air, Sourdines"
39. "Second Air, Gravement, Sourdines"
40. "Enfin il est en ma puissance" (Prélude; Armide)
41. "Venez, venez seconder mes desirs" (Prélude; Armide)
III: 42. "Ah! si la liberté" (Prélude; Armide)
43. "Venez, venez, Haine implacable" (Viste, Armide)
44. "Je respons à tes voeux" (Prélude; la Haine)
45. "Plus on connoît l'Amour" (Prélude; la Haine, Choeur)
46. "Entrée de la Haine"
47. "Amour, sors pour jamais" (La Haine, Choeur)
48. "Air" (Air des Démons / Air pour la suite de la Haine)
49. "Sors, sors du sein d'Armide Amour" (Armide)
IV: 50. "Nous ne trouvons partout que des gouffres" (Prélude; Ubalde, le Chevalier Danois)
51. "Air" (Les Démons)
52. "Voicy la charmante retraite" (Lucinde, Choeur)
53. "Gavotte" (Les Habitants Champêtres)
54. "Canaries"
55. "Jouissons d'un bonheur extrême" (Lucinde, le Chevalier)
56. "Je tourne en vain les yeux" (Prélude; le Chevalier)
57. "Ce que l'amour a de charmant" (Ubalde)
58. "Non, je n'ai point gardé mon coeur" (Ubalde)

V: 59. "Armide, vous m'allez quitter" (Ritournelle; Renaud, Armide)
   60. "Aimons-nous, aimons-nous, tout nous y convie" (Armicide, Renaud)
   61. "Passacaille"
   62. "Les plaisirs ont choisi pour azile" (Un Amant fortuné, Choeur)
   63. "C'est l'amour qui retient" (Flûtes; un Amant fortuné, Choeur)
   64. "Allez, allez, éloignez-vous de moy" (Renaud)
   65. "Il est seul profitons d'un temps" (Prélude; Ubalde)
   66. "Renaud? Ciel! ô mortelle peine!" (Armide)
   67. "Le perfide Renaud me fuit" (Prélude; Armide)
   68. "Traistre, attends, je le tiens" (Prélude; Armide)
   69. "Prélude"

1a.14 "Achille et Polyxène," opera: LWV74
   1. "Ouverture"
   2. "Non, je ne sçaurois plus me taire" (Patrocle)
   3. "Je cours assûrer ma mémoire, J'ay tous" (Patrocle)
   4. "Patrocle va combattre?" (Prélude; Achille)
   5. "J'abandonne les Cieux" (Prélude; Vénus)
   6. "Chaconne"
   7. "Vous, Divinitez aimables" (Vénus)
   8. "Vénus et les grâces, Air"
   9. "Passacaille" (Passacaille d'Achille / dernière Pièce de M. de Lully)
  10. "Grand Héros, Le Ciel vous est propice" (Une Grâce)
  11. "Quel mortel osa jamais prétendre" (Deux Grâces et un Plaisir)
  12. "Manes de ce guerrier dont je pleure le sort" (Prélude; Achille)

1a.19 "Ballet des Plaisirs," ballet: LWV2
   1. "Ière Partie, VI. Entrée, Gavotte"
   2. "Entrée, Sarabande"
   3. (IIe. Partie, VI. Entrée, Sérénade): "Peutestre dormez-vous adorable inhumaine" (un Amoureux)
   4. "Entrée, six Filous"
   5. "Gavotte pour les Suisses"
   6. "Bourée pour les Courtisans"

1a.23 "Ballet de L'amour malade," ballet: LWV8
   1. "Ouverture"
   2. "Ritournelle"
   3. "Ritournelle"
   4. "Ritournelle"
   5. "Ouverture pour le premier Divertissement"
   6. "I. Entrée, le Divertissement"
   7. "Second Air, Sarabande"
   8. "Ritournelle"
   9. "Troisième Air pour le Concert du Divertissement"
  10. "II. Entrée, deux Astrologues poursuivis chacun par son propre malheur"
  11. "Second Air pour les mêmes, le Bonheur et le Malheur"
  12. "Ritournelle"
  13. "III. Entrée, deux Chercheurs de Trésors"
  14. "III. Entrée, deux Esprits follets"
  15. "Air pour les mêmes battus par quatre Démons"
  16. "Ritournelle"
  17. "IV. Entrée de quatre Galants braves, de deux Coquettes et de Jaloux, de Pages et de Laquais"
  18. "Ritournelle"
  19. "Que les jaloux sont importuns" (Ritournelle; Chanson contre les Jaloux)
  20. "E che sarebbe amor senza" (Ritournelle; le Damigelle delle cochette)
  21. "Second Air, les Braves et les Jaloux"
  22. "V. Entrée, onze Docteurs reçoivent un Docteur en asnérie"
  23. "Ritournelle"
  24. "Second Air pour un Docteur portant une teste d'Asne"
  25. "Troisième Air pour Scaramouche"
  26. "VI. Entrée, huit Chasseurs vont à la chasse avec des tambours"
  27. "Ritournelle"
  28. "VII. Entrée, deux Alchimistes"
  29. "Ritournelle"
  30. "Second Air, six Mercures"
  31. "Ritournelle"
  32. "VIII. Entrée, six Indiens et six Indiennes basannez portent des parasols"
  33. "Ritournelle"
  34. "IX. Entrée, Jean Doucet et son Frère"
  35. "Second Air pour les mêmes"
  36. "Ritournelle"
  37. "Troisième Air pour les quatre Bohémiennes"
  38. "Une nopce de Village, Concert champêtre"
  39. "Gavotte pour le Marié et la Mariée"
  40. "Sarabande pour le Père et la Mère du Marié"

41. "Ritournelle"
42. "Gavotte pour les Parents de la Mariée"
43. "Second Air pour les Parents de la Mariée"
44. "Gaillarde pour les Parents et Amis des Mariés"
45. "Sarabande et dernier Air"
46. "Ritournelle"
47a, b, c. "Ritournelle" I, II, III

1a.25 "Ballet de La revente des habits," ballet: LWV5
1. "Ouverture"
2. "Je ne viens point en qualité de nymphe" (Symphonie, la Revente des Habits; une Revendeuse)
I: 3. "I. Entrée, une Fripière couverte d'habits de Masques"
4. "II. Entrée, les Vieillards"
5. "Quatre Vieillards et quatre Enfants"
6. "III. Entrée, les Contre-faiseurs"
7. "Les Contre-faiseurs"
8. "IV. Entrée, deux Amants, & deux Servantes desguisés en Damoiselles"
9. "Deux Amants et deux Servantes desguisés en Damoiselles"
10. "V. Entrée, trois Yvrognes"
11. "Trois Sobres et trois Yvrognes"
II: 12. "Récit Turquesque, I. Entrée, les Paysans et Docteurs"
13. "Trois Paysans et trois Docteurs"
14. "II. Entrée, les Adroits et Maladroits"
15. "Les Adroits et Maladroits"
16. "III. Entrée, Soldats et Notaires"
17. "Quatre Soldats et deux Notaires"
18. "IV. Entrée, Poltrons et Braves"
19. "Deux Poltrons et deux Braves"
20. "V. et dernière Entré, deux Vieillards espousent deux jeunes filles ..."
21. "Deux Vieillards qui espousent deux jeunes filles. On leur fait le Charivari"
22. "Chaconne"

1a.26 "Ballet d'Alcidiane," ballet: LWV9
1. "Ouverture"
2. "Amiam dunque in fin ch'e lecito" (Ritournelle; Récit italien)
2a. "Ritournelle"
3. "Ritournelle pour le Concert du Roy"
4. "Symphonie pour le Concert du Roy"
5. "Que votre empire, Amour" (Ritournelle; Récit)
5a. (w/ out title) (Ritournelle)
6. "Suivons de si douces loix" (Récit)
7. "I. Entrée, premier Air de la Haine"
8. "Second Air"
9. "Le Roy représentant la Haine"
10. "Entrée de six autres Passions"
11. "II. Entrée, l'Innocence"
12. "L'Innocence"
13. "Second Air"
14. "III. Entrée, les Pêcheurs de perles"
15. "Les Pêcheurs de perles"
16. "IV. Entrée, les Baladins ridicules"
17. "Second Air"
18. "Un Baladin"
19. "Second Air"
20. "V. Entrée, six Galants amis et rivaux"
21. "Les Galants amis"
22. "VI. Entrée, huit meilleurs Danseurs de la Court d'Alcidiane"
23. "Les Baladins serieux"
24. "VII. Entrée, un Combat de plaisir" (La petite guerre)
25. "Autre Assemblée"
26. "Marche italienne"
27. "L'Exercise des Mousquetaires"
28. "Marche françoise"
29. "La Charge"
30. "Le Retraite"
31. "L'Attaque du fort"
32. "Le Combat"
33. "Dernière Entrée, la Victoire"
II: 34. "Ouverture"
34a. "Ouverture"
35. "Bien que je sois fière et crudele" (Récit de Bellone)
36. "I. Entrée, Eole"
37. "Second Air, les Vents"
38. "Troisième Air pour Eole et les quatre Vents"
39. "Quatrième Air pour les mêmes"

40. "Le Roy représentant Eole"
41. "II. Entrée, un Pilote et six Mariniers"
42. "Un Pilote et les mariniers"
43. "III. Entrée, Zelmatide et Chevaliers de la suite"
44. "Second Air"
44a. "Zelmatide"
45. "IV. Entrée, six Géants et autant de Nains"
46. "V. Entrée, quatre des principaux Corsaires de Bajazet vaincus sur Mer par Polexandre ..."
47. "Second Air"
48. "Quatre Corsaires de Bajazet"
49. "Les mesmes pour plusieurs autres Corsaires"
50. "Troisième Air pour les mesmes"
51. "VI. Entrée, huit Démons envoyez par la Magicienne Zelopa"
52. "Huit Démons"
53. "VII. Entrée, Pallante, Chef des illustres Esclaves d'Alcidiane et de quatre de ses Compagnes"
54. "Second Air"
55. "Pallante"
56. "Bourrée pour les mesmes"
III: 57. "Ouverture"
58. "Que d'esclaves soûmis" (Ritournello; Récit de la Fortune)
58a. "Ritournelle"
59. "I. Entrée, Polexandre triomphant et suivi des principaux des siens, arrivant en l'Isle inaccessible"
60. "Second Air, Polexandre"
61. "Troixième Air, Chevaliers de Polexandre"
62. "Quatrième Air, la suite de Polexandre"
63. "Polexandre"
64. "II. Entrée, trois Bergers et autant de Bergers de cette heureuse Contrée, Rondeau"
65. "Second Air"
66. "Troisième Air, Gavotte"
67. "Trois Bergers et trois Bergères"
68. "III. Entrée, quelques Courtisans se réjoüissent de la satisfaction de leur Roy"
69. "Six Courtisans"
70. "IV. Entrée, Course de Faquin"
71. "Second Air"
72. "Troisième Air"
73. "Quatrième Air"
74. "V. Entrée, les Saisons, le Printemps"
75. "VI. "Entrée, les Plaisirs"
76. "Petite Chaconne"
77. "Cede al vostro valore Ogni Deità" (VII. et dernière Entrée, Récit italien)
78. "Sorte ch'ognh'or leggiera Volubil" (Air chanté alternativement)
79. "Chaconne des Maures"

1a.27   "Ballet de La raillerie," ballet: LWV11
1. "Ouverture
2. "Je descends, je descends" (Rirournelle; la Poësie)
3. "Ouverture"
4. "L'un del altro ogn'un si burla" (Ritournelle; la Beffa, la Saviezza, la Pazzia)
5. "Cosi a me sola e dato" (La Beffa)
6. "E di non ridère com'è possibile" (La Saviezza e la Pazzia)
7. "Che colei solo pondo" (La Pazzia)
8. "Sapete che sia amor" (La Beffa, la Saviezza, la Pazzia)
9. "Sarabande"
10. "I. Entrée, le Ris accompagné d'un Choeur d'instrumens"
11. "Sarabande pour le concert du Roy"
12. "Gavotte pour le Roy"
13. "Le Roy représentant le Ris"
14. "Bourée"
15. "II. Entrée, quatre Vieillards et quatre Enfants"
16. "Quatre Vieillards et quatre Enfants"
17. "III. Entrée, les Sçavans et les Ignorans" (Les Docteurs et quatre Paysans)
18. "Un Docteur et quatre Paysans"
19. "IV. Entrée, un Poltron et deux Braves"
20. "Un Poltron et deux Braves"
21. "V. Entrée, le Bonheur de l'Esprit et de l'Argent"
22. "Second Air pour les mêmes"
23. "Le Bonheur de l'esprit et de l'argent"
24. "VI. Entrée, les Sobres et les Yvrognes"
25. "Entrée des Sobres et des Yvrognes"
26. "Gentil Musica francese il mio" (Intermedio, Ritournelle)
26a. "Ritournelle"
27. "VII. Entrée, les Filles de Cour et les Filles de Village"
28. "Les Filles de la Cour et les Filles de Village"
29. "Vos beaux yeux embrassent mon coeur" (VIII. Entrée, les Contrefaiseurs, des Gens ...)
30. "Enfin je vous revois, charmante Cour" (Second Air, Sarabande; des Gens ...)

     31. "Troisième Air, les Cotrefaiseurs"
     32. "Air des Cotrefaiseurs"
     33. "IX. Entrée, la Farse et ses Soldats, la Raison"
     34. "Second Air pour les Soldats"
     35. "La Farce, quatre Soldats"
     36. "La Raison et quatre Notaires"
     37. "X. Entrée, quatre Amants et quatre Maîtresses"
     38. "Bourée pour les mêmes"
     39. "Quatre Amants et quatre Maîtresses"
     40. "XI. Entrée, les Adroits et Maladroits"
     41. "Rondeau pour les Droits et Maldroits"
     42. "Bourée pour les mêmes"
     43. "Entrée"
     44. "Ritournelle"
     45. "La Louchie" (Chaconne)

1a.28   "Xersès," 6 intermèdes: LWV12
     1. "Ouverture"
    Prologue: 2. "I. Entrée, les Basques moitiée François, moitié Espagnols"
     3. "Rondeau pour les mêmes"
    I/9: 4. "II. Entrée, des Paysans et Paysannes, chantans et dansans à l'Espagnole"
    end of Act II: 5. "III. Entrée, Scaramouche au milieu de deux Docteurs deguisez"
     6. "Second Air, Les Docteurs, Trivelins et Scaramouches"
     7. "Troisième Air, Trivelins et Polichinels"
    end of Act III: 8. "IV. Entrée, un Poltron de vaisseau les Esclaves portans des singes ..."
     9. "Second Air, les Matelots jouans des trompettes marines" (Les Matassins)
     10. "Troisième Air, les mêmes"
    end of Act IV: 11. "V. Entrée, les Matassins"
     12. "Second Air pour les mêmes"
    end of Act V: 13. "Bacchues accompagné de Sylvains, Bacchantes, Satyres ..."
     14. "Gavotte en Rondeau pour les mêmes"

1a.29   "Ballet de Toulouse" (au mariage du Roy) ballet: LWV13
     1. "Ouverture"
     2. "Gigue"

1a.30   "Ballet de L'impatience," ballet: LWV14
     1. "Ouverture"
     2. "Sommes-nous pas trop heureux belle Iris" (I. Entrée, Sérénade; six Seigneurs)
     3. "II. Entrée, deux Alchimistes et six Enfants"
     4. "Les Alchimistes"
     5. "Les Enfans"
     6. "Second Air pour les six Enfans"
     7. "III. Entrée, seux Maistres à danser s'impatientent en montrant la Courante à des Moscovites"
     8. "Courante pour les Nations"
     9. "IV. Entrée pour les Plaideurs"
    II: 10. "Courons où tendent nos desirs" (Ritournelle; Récit de l'Impatience)
     11. "I. Entrée, six Portefaix et six Nains"
     12. "Second Air"
     13. "II. Entrée, des Oyseleurs à la Choüette"
     14. "Second Air"
     15. "Six Oyseleurs"
     16. "III. Entrée, deux Jeunes Desbauchez"
     17. "Second Air"
     18. "Bourée pour le Père et les Vallets des Desbauchez"
     19. "Deux jeunes desbauchez"
     20. "IV. Entrée, Jupiter"
     21. "Jupiter"
     22. "Le Roy représentant Jupiter"
     23. "O ch'immensa impatianza di cantar" (Récit des Preneurs de Tabac)
     24. "Se non canto io pur mi strozzo" (Choro)
     25. "Altro è da quel fu" (Ritournelle, Air italien)
     26. "Oh che concerto harmonico s'unisce" (Choro)
     27. "Air pour les Paysans"
     28. "Entrée de six Goguenards"
    III: 29. "I. Entrée, les Gourmands"
     30. "Entrée des Gourmands voyant leur soupe"
     31. "Second Air"
     32. "II. Entrée, les Créanciers"
     33. "Quatre Créanciers impatients"
     34. "Bourée, second Air pour le Débiteur"
     35. "Bourée pour les Débiteurs"
     36. "Seconde Bourée"
     37. "Air pour les Archers et Sergents"
     38. "III. Entrée, huit Chevaliers"

39. "IV. Entrée, quatre Marchands Mores"
40. "Quatre Marchands mores impatients de l'arrivée de leur vaisseau"
IV: 41. "Venez vous ranger sous mes loix" (Ritournelle; Récit de la Loterie)
42. "I. Entrée, les Suisses"
43. "Les Florentins"
44. II. Entrée, les Amoureux"
45. "Quatre Galants et quatre Maîtresses impatients de voir leurs Amants"
46. "Second Air pour les Amoureux et deux Servantes"
47. "III. Entrée, dix Aveugles"
48. "Dix Aveugles impatients de sortir"
49. "Apres la clarté perdue, qui nous fut" (Récit des Aveugles)
50. "Second Air pour les Aveugles jouant de la Vielle"
51. "Deux Amants qui enlevent leurs Maîstresses"
52. "Second Air, Sarabande pour le mêmes"
53. "Dernier Air pour les Démons et les Vents"
54. "Menuet et dernier Air"

1a.31   "Ballet des Saisons," ballet: LWV15
1. "Ouverture"
2. "Qui dans la nuit rameine le soleil" (Choeur)
3. "Bois, ruisseaux, aimable verdure" (Ritournelle; Récit de la Nymphe de Fontainbleau)
4. "I. Entrée, six Faunes"
5. "II. Entrée, Diane et ses Nymphes"
6. "Second Air"
7. "Bourée"
8. "III. Entrée, Flore suivi de quatre Jardiniers"
9. "Entrée, Cérès suivie de huit Moissonneurs"
10. "V. Entrée, l'Automne, quatre Vendangeurs et quatre Vendangeuses"
11. "L'Automne"
12. "Second Air"
13. "VI. Entrée, un Hyver, six Gallands"
14. "Une Bohemienne et six Masques"
15. "Menuet"
16. "VII. Entrée, sept Masques"
17. "Objets charmants et rares" (Ritournelle; Récit des Masques)
18. "Second Air"
19. "Ritournelle pour le Concert du Printemps"
20. "VIII. Entrée, le Printemps suivi du Jeu, du Ris, de la Joye, et de l'Abondance"
21. "Bourée pour le Jeu, le Ris, la Joye et l'Abondance"
22. "IX. et dernière Entrée, les neuf Muses guidées par Apollon, et par l'Amour"
23. "Menuet et dernier Air"

1a.32   "Hercule amoureux & Ballet des Sept planètes": LWV17
1. "I. Entrée, le Roy représentant la Maison de France"
2. "II. Entrée, le Roy, la Maison de France, la Reine, la Maison d'Autriche"
3. "III. Entrée Des Foudres et Tempestes"
4. "IV. Entrée Des Songes"
5. "V. Entrée des Statues"
6. "Second Air"
7. "Les Statues"
8. "VI. Entrée des Zéphirs"
9. "VII. Entrée des Fantosmes & Demoiselles"
10. "Entrée des Fantosmes et Demoisells" (Les Influences de la Lune)
11. "Les Fantosmes"
12. *"VIII. Entrée, Pluton & Proserpine, avec douze Furies" (lost)*
13. "Les diverses Influances des sept Planettes ... Ouverture"
14. "Concert des Trompettes"
15. "IX. Entrée, Mars suivy d'Alexandre, Jules Cesar, Marc Antoine, Pompée, & autres ..."
16. "Quatre Combattants jouant des Enseignes"
17. "Pour les Combattants romains"
18. "Le Combat"
19. "X. Entrée, Influances de la Lune, & Pellerins"
20. "Saturne, Dieu des enchantements"
21. "Pour les Pellerins jouant de la vieille"
22. "XI. Entrée, Influances de Mercure, & Charlatans"
23. "Mercure, Dieu des Charlatans"
24. "Mercure, Dieu des Charlatans"
25. "Air pour les Charlatans"
26. "XII. Entrée, Influances de Jupiter, accompagnée de quatre Monarques & de quatre Nations"
27. "Rondeau pour les quatre Nations"
28. "XIII. Entrée, Vénus & les Plaisirs. Concert de Vénus & des Plaisirs"
29. "Plaisirs, plaisirs, venez en foule" (Récit de Vénus)
30. "Les Plaisirs et la suite de Vénus"
31. "XIV. Entrée, Influances de Saturne, qui produit plusieurs enchantemens"
32. "Saturne, Dieu des enchantemens"

33. "Second Air avec des échos et des enchantemens"
34. "Influances du Soleil, accompagné des 24 Heures, de l'Aurore & des Estoilles"
35. "XV. Entrée, les douze Heures de la Nuit"
36. "XVI. Entrée, l'Aurore"
37. "Air pour le Roy, septième Influence"
38. "XVII. Entrée, le Soleil & les douze Heures du Jour"
39. "XVIII. et dernière Entrée, des Estoilles"
40. "Sarabande pour les mêmes"
41. "Gaillarde pour les Etoilles"

1a.33   "Ballet des Arts," ballet: LWV18
1. "Ouverture"
2a. "Ritournelle"
2b. "Douce felicité, ne quittons" (Ritournelle; Bergers et Bergères)
3. "L'Agriculture, cet Art est representé par des Bergers et des Bergères, I. Entrée"
4. "Second Air"
5. "Troisième Air"
6. "Quatrième Air, Bourée"
7. "Seconde Bourée"
8. "Ne craignez point le naufrage" (La Navigation, Ritournelle; Récit de Thetis)
9. "Entrée, un Corsaire et quatre Pirates"
10. "Second Air"
11. "Je repands sur les humains" (L'Orfevrerie, Ritournelle; Récit de Junon sur les Richesses)
12. "III. Entrée, Courtisans chargez d'Orfevrerie"
13. "Second Air"
14. "Ma Vénus a charmé les hommes" (La Peinture, Ritournelle; Dialogue d'Appelle et de Zeuxis)
15. "IV. Entrée, Peintres, Dames, Valets"
16. "Second Air, les Peintres"
17. "Les Peintres et quatre Dames ridicules"
18. "Amour se glisse dans nos bois" (Ritournelle; Récit de Diane)
19. "V. Entrée, Chasseurs"
20. "Cephale et six Chasseurs"
21. "Bel art, qui retardez" (La Chirurgie, Ritournelle; Récit d'Esculape sur la Médicine)
22. "VI. Entrée, un Chirurgien"
23. "Quatre Docteurs"
24. "Huit Estropiez"
25. "Quoi? jamais plus de sang?" (La Guerre, Ritournelle; Dialogue de Mars et de Bellone)
26. "VII. et dernière Entrée, Vertus, Pallas et Amazones, Concert des Amazones"
27. "Second Air, Pallas et quatre Amazones"
28. "Troisième Air"
29. "Dernier Air, les Verus"

1a.34   "Les noces de village," mascarade ridicule: LWV19
1. "Ouverture"
2. "A mon habit, à mon visage" (Ritournelle; Récit de l'Hymen vêtu à la mode de village)
3. "I. Entrée, le Marié et la Mariée" (= Ballet des Plaisirs, LWV2/4)
4. "II. Entrée, six Vieillards" (= Ballet des Saisons, LWV15/4)
5. "III. Entrée, le Patissier, sa Servante, et son Garçon"
6. "IV. Entrée, quatre Valets de la feste"
7. "V. Entrée, le Seigneur du village"
8. "VI. Entré, les Importans du village"
9. "Le Bailly"
10. "VII. Entrée, les quatre Messieurs"
11. "Bourée"
12. "Son dottor per occasion" (Deuxième Récit, le Maistre d'Escole un peu Poëte, et Compositeur ...)
13. "Bona sera Barbacola Bona sera" (Choro)
14. "Air pour Barbacola"
15. "VIII. Entrée, trois Filles de Village"
16. "IX. Entrée, six bons Bourgeois"
17. *"X. Entrée, quatre Offociers" (lost)*
18. "XI. Entrée, la Sage-Femme"
19. "XII. Entrée, un Operateur suivy d'un Arracheur de dens et de deux Valets"
20. "XIII. et dernière Entrée, une troupe de Bohesmiens et de Bohesmiennes"

1a.35   "Les amours désguisés," ballet: LWV21
1. "Ouverture"
2. "Concertans des Arts et Vertus, qui suivent Pallas. Concertans des Grâces ... Vénus"
3. "I. Entrée, Amours déguisées en Forgerons"
4. "Second Air pour les Forgerons forgeant sur l'enclume"
5. "II. Entrée, le Gouverneur d'Egypte"
6. "Second Air"
7. "Doutez-vous de mon feu" (Ritournelle; Dialogue de Marc-Antoine et de Cléopatre)
8. "III. Entrée, Amours déguisés en Rameurs"
9. "IV. Entrée, Proserpine (la Reine)"
10. "Second Air, Sarabande"

11. "Troisième Air, Bourée"
12. "V. Entrée, Amours déguisés en Jardiniers de Cerés"
13. "Pluton enlevant Proserpine"
14. "Les Démons"
15. "Guerriers, il ne faut pas faire" (Concert de Bergers; Récit Champestre)
16. "VII. Entrée, le Roy représentant Regnaut"
17. "Second Air pour la Gloire et la Renommée"
18. "VIII. Entrée, Flore et ses Nymphes"
19. "Second Menuet"
20. "Ah Rinaldo E dove sei?" (Ritournelle; Récit d'Armide)
21. "Ahi che senvola lungi" (Ritournelle; Armide)
22. "A' che spargo indarno gridi" (Ritournelle; Armide)
23. "IX. Entrée, Troupe de petits Amours"
24. "Second Air, Concert de flûtes pour les Amours"
25. "Troisième Air, Sarabande pour les mêmes"
26. "X. Entrée des Sauvages de la Colchide"
27. "Second Air"
28. "Amours deguisés en Dieux Marins et Nymphes Maritimes"
29. "Second Air, Nymphes Maritimes"
30. "Troisième Air"
31. "Quatrième Air, Bourée"
32. "XII. Entrée, Combat des Grecs et des Troyens"
33. "Combat des Grecs et Troyens"
34. "Troisième Air, les Grecs vainqueurs des Troyens"
35. "Quatrième Air"
36. "A qui sçait bien aymer l'Amour" (Ritournelle; Junon)
37. "XIII. Entrée, Goujats, Soldats"
38. "XIV. Entrée, les Amours déguisés en Grecs apres avoir exterminé les restes des Troyens"

1a.36   "Oedipe," entr'actes: LWV23
1. "Ouverture"
2. "Premier Air, les Cavaliers"
3. "Second Air" (Vallets de pied et Ecuyers)
4. "Troisième Air" (Les Médecins)
5. "Quatrième Air" (Les Thebains)
6. "Cinquième Air" (Menuet)

1a.39   "Ballet de La naissance de Vénus," ballet: LWV27
1. "Ouverture"
I: 2. "Taisez-vous, taisez-vous, flots" (Ritournelle; Récit de Neptune, de Thetis et des Tritons)
3. "Quelle gloire pour la mer" (Choeur)
4. "I. Entrée, Vénus et ses Nereïdes"
5. "Estoille du point du jour"
6. "Les Heures"
7. "Menuet pour les mêmes"
8. "II. Entrée, Dieux et Déesses Maritimes"
9. "Petite Bourée pour les Dieux"
10. "III. Entrée, Eole et les quatre Vents"
11. "Second Air des Vents"
12. "Troisième Air pour Eole, Dieu des Vents"
13. "IV. Entrée, Castor et Pollux"
14. "Bourée pour les mêmes"
15. "IV. Entrée, Casor et Pollux, Capitaines des Vaisseaux, deux Marchands et deux Mariniers"
16. "Second Air pour les mêmes"
17. "V. Entrée, les Ris, Les Jeux et les Zéphirs"
18. "VI. Entrée, Lore, Pales, trois Bergers et trois Bergères"
19. "Second Air pour Flore et Pales"
20. "Air pour les Bergers et Bergères"
21. "Menuet des Bergers"
II: 22. "Admirons notre jeune et charmante" (Ritournelle; Récit des trois Grâces)
23. "I. Entrée, Europe et six Nymphes"
24. "Second Air"
25. "Menuet pour les mêmes"
26. "II. Entrée, Apollon, Daphne et Cupidon"
27. "Entrée de Cupidon"
28. "Troisième Air pour Apollon, Daphne et Cupidon"
29. "III. Entrée, Bacchus, Ariadne, deux Indiens, deux Indiennes et quatre Faunes"
30. "Second Air, les Faunes, Indiens et Indiennes"
31. "Sarabande pour les mêmes"
32. "Rochers vous estes sourds" (Ritournelle; Plainte d'Ariadne)
33. "IV. Entrée, Sacrificateurs et Philosophes"
34. "Les Philosophes"
35. "Second Air"
36. "V. Entrée, six Poëtes"
37. "Dernière Entrée, Alexandre, Achille, Hercule, Jason, Roxane, Briseis, Omphale, Medée ..."

38. "Bourée pour les héros et héroïnes"
39. "Les Sacrificateurs"
40. "Menuet pour les mêmes"
41. "Dieu des Enfers, hélas, voyez mes peines" (Concert pour Orphée; Récit d'Orphée)
42. "Pluton et Proserpine"
43. "Bourée pour Orphée et Euridice"
44. "Huit Ombres enlevant Euridice"
45. "Les mêmes"

1a.40   "Ballet des Gardes ou Les délices de la campagne," ballet: LWV28
1. "Premier Air pour les Exempts et gardes"
2. "Second Air, Gavotte pour les Pages"
3. "Troisième Air, Canaries"
4. "Quatrième Air, Rondeau pour les Paysans"
5. "Courante de Jean le Blanc"

1a.41   "Le triomphe de Bacchus dans les Indes," mascarade: LWV30
1. "Ouverture"
2. "C'est dans ces climats écartez" (Récit de Silène)
3. "I. Entrée, les Cobales ou Esprits folets"
4. "Interrompez vos badinages" (Récit de Silène)
5. "II. Entrée, Bacchus couronné de Pampre"
6. "III. Entrée, Indiens et Indiennes"
7. "IV. Entrée, les Silvains et Bacchantes"
8. "V. Entrée, les Indiens avec des Bacchantes et Silvains"

1a.42   "Ballet des Muses," ballet: LWV32
1. "Ouverture"
2. "Enfin, apres tant de hasards" (Dialogue, Mnémosine)
3. "Rangeons-nous sous ses lois; Il est beau" (Choeur)
4. "Vivant sous sa conduite, Muses" (Mnémosine)
5. "Première Entrée pour les Astres et les Planettes"
6. "II. Entrée, Pirasme et Thisbé"
7. "Vous savez l'amour extrême" (IV. Entrée, Chanson sur un Air de Gavotte, un Berger, Choeur)
8. "Vivons heureux, aimons-nous" (Chanson sur un Air de Menuet, un Berger, Choeur)
9. "V. Entré, Alexandre et Porus, cinq Grecs, cinq Indiens"
10. "Marche des Grecs"
11. "Marche des Indiens"
12. "Le Combat"
13. "VI. Entrée, cinq Poëtes"
14. "Mascarade Espagnole, les Espagnols"
15. "Ay que padesco de amor" (Première Femme)
16. "Second Air"
17. "Les Basques"
18. "Canaries"
19. "Trop indiscret amour" (VII. Entrée, Concert et Récit d'Orphée)
20. "Orphée"
21. "VIII. Entrée, trois Amants et trois Amantes"
22. "Rondeau pour le Roy"
23. "X. Entrée, Les Faunes et Femmes rustiques"
24. "Le soin de gouster la vie est icy" (Récit du Satyre; Les Faunes et Sauvages)
25. "XI. Entrée, Les Muses et Pierides"
26. "XII. Entrée, trois Nymphes juges de combat"
27. "Les mêmes"
28. "XIII. Entrée, Jupiter"

1a.43   "Le carnaval ou Mascarade de Versailles," mascarade: LWV36
1. "Ouverture"
2. "Je reviens enfin à mon tour" (Récit du Carnaval)
3. "Profitons du temps qu'il donne" (Choeur des Jeux et des Plaisirs)
4. "I. Entrée, les Plaisirs"
5. "Aimez, cherchez à plaire" (Chanson des Plaisirs; second Air des Plaisirs)
6. "II. Entrée, les Joueurs"
7. "III. Entrée, les Gens de bonne chère"
8. "Nous n'avons jamais de chagrin" (Chanson à boire)
9. "IV. Entrée, les Maîtres à danser"
10. "Canaries"
11. "V. Entrée, Masques ridicules"
12. "VI. Entrée, Masques serieux"
13. "Soyez fidèle, Le soin d'un amant" (Chanson de la Galanterie)
14. "VII. Entrée, le Carnaval"
15. "Corrigeons de l'hyver la rigueur" (Dialogue du Carnaval et de la Galanterie)
16. "Chantons et dansons et dansons" (Choeur)
17. "Gavotte pour les mêmes"

1a.44   "Ballet de Flore," ballet: LWV40
        1. "Ouverture"
        2. "Entourez de glaçons" (Récit de l'Hyver)
        3. "Célébrons en tous lieux" (Choeur des glaçons)
        4. "I. Entrée, Sa Majesté représentant le Soleil"
        5. "II. Entrée, Flore"
        6. "III. Entrée, les Nymphes"
        7. "Bourée pour les mêmes"
        8. "IV. Entrée, le Printemps"
        9. "V. Entrée, les Jardiniers"
      10. "VI. Entrée, les Galants, les Galantes"
      11. "Menuet pour les mêmes"
      12. "VII. Entrée, quatre Esclaves"
      13. "VIII. Entrée, les Debauchez"
      14. "Menuet pour les mêmes"
      15. "Sérénade pour les nouveaux Mariez"
      16. "Si vous aimez bien tous deux" (Un Musicien)
      17. "Amour veut qu'on suive ses loix" (Première Musicienne)
      18. "IX. Entrée, le Marié et la Mariée"
      19. "Amants que l'hymen a joints" (Une Musicienne)
      20. "X. Entrée, l'Aurore"
      21. "XI. Entrée, les Heures"
      22. "XII. Entrée, Vertumne"
      23. "Ah! quelle cruauté" (Ritournelle; Plainte de Vénus sur la mort d'Adonis)
      24. "Cher Adonis que ton sort est funeste" (Ritournelle; Vénus)
      25. "XIII. Entrée, Proserpine avec deux Compagnes"
      26. "Pluton"
      27. "Douze Démons"
      28. "XIV. Entrée, six Héros"
      29. "Second Air"
      30. "Jusqu'au plus haut des cieux quel bruit" (Jupiter)
      31. "Pleurs qui fustes jadis des héros" (Le Destin)
      32. "Jeunes lis qui semblez ne faire que" (Jupiter et le Destin)
      33. "XV. Entrée, deux Trompettes, Marche à la tête de quatre Quadrilles"
      34. "Amour n'est-ce point vous" (Prélude les quatre Parties du Monde)
      35. "Pour le Roy Européen"
      36. "Venez, venez, peuples" (Choeur des quatre Parties du Monde) (Grande Musique)
      37. "Charmons icy toute la Terre" (Second Choeur des quatre Parties du Monde) (Grande Musique)
      38. "Canaries"
      39. "Menuet"

1a.47   "Ballet des ballets," pastiche ballet: LWV46
        1.–3. (= Oedipe, LWV23/1, 2, 6)
        4. "Prologue" (= Le divertissement Royal, LWV42/2)
        6.–11. (= Psyché, LWV45/2–7)
      12. "Premier acte de la Comédie"
      13.–15. (= Psyché, LWV45/8–10)
      16. "Second acte de la Comédie"
      17.–20. (= Pastorale comique, LWV33/1–4)
      21. "Troisième acte de la Comédie"
      22.–29. (= Le Grand Divertissement Royal de Versailles, LWV38/7–14)
      30. "Quatrième acte de la Comédie"
      31.–32. (= Pastorale comique, LWV33/12–13)
      33.–35. (= Psyché, LWV45/12–14)
      36. "Cinquième acte de la Comédie"
      37.–45. (= Le bourgeois gentilhomme, LWV43/14–22)
      46. "Sixième acte de la Comédie"
      47.–58. (= Le bourgeois gentilhomme, LWV43/33–36, 25–32)
      59.–61. (= Oedipe, LWV23/3–5)
      62.–81. (= Psyché, LWV45/19–38)

1a.48   "Le carnaval mascarade," mascarade: LWV52
        1.–3. (= Le carnaval ou Mascarade de Versailles, LWV36/1–3)
        4.–11. (= Le bourgeois gentilhomme, LWV43/25–32)
      12. "Giustizia, giustizia" (Pourceaugnac)
      13. "I Signor avocato, che sete il ben trovato" (Pourceaugnac)
      14.–15. (= Divertissement de Chambord, LWV41/14–15)
      16. "Gia soche chi due Volte" (Pourceaugnac)
      17. "Facio la reverenza" (Pourceaugnac)
      18. "Tinque, tinque, tinque, tinque" (Pourceaugnac)
      19. "Amor, crudel amor" (Pourceaugnac)
      20.–23. (= Divertissement de Chambord, LWV41/9–12)
      24.–26. (= Le Sicilien, ou L'Amour peintre, LWV34/1–3)
      27. (= Pastorale comique, LWV33/8)
      28.–31. (= Le bourgeois gentilhomme, LWV43/33–36)

32.–43. (= Divertissement de Chambord, LWV41/20, 16–19, 2–8)
44.–47. (= Ballet de Flore, LWV40/15–18)
48.–55. (= Le bourgeois gentilhomme, LWV43/14–21)
56.–58. (= Le carnaval ou Mascarade de Versailles, LWV36/12–14)
59. "Air pour le Carnaval et la Galanterie"
60.–61. (= Le carnaval ou Mascarade de Versailles, LWV36/15–16)

1a.49   "Le triomphe de l'amour," ballet: LWV59
1. "Ouverture"
2. "Un héros que le ciel fit naître" (Vénus)
3. "Tranquiles coeurs, preparez-vous" (Ritournelle; Vénus)
4. "Nymphes des caux, Nymphes de ce boccage" (Ritournelle; Vénus)
5. "Première Entrée des Grâces, des Driades & des Nayades"
6. "Menuet pour les Mesmes"
7. "Sy quelquefois l'amour cause des peines" (Deuxiesme Menuet pour les Mesmes; Vénus)
8. "Entrée des Plaisirs. Premier Air"
9. "Un coeur toûjours en paix sans amour" (Deux Plaisirs)
10. "Menuet pour les Plaisirs"
11. "Non, non il n'est pas possible" (Prélude pour Vénus et les Plaisirs; Vénus)
12. "Entrée de Mars et de Guerriers. Air"
13. "Air pour les Amours et les Guerriers"
14. "Entrée de Mars et des Amours. Air"
15. "Fierté, sévère honneur vous déffendez" (Ritournelle pour Amphitrite; Amphitrite)
16. "Cedez, belle Amphitrite à mes soins amoureux" (Neptune)
17. "Ah! qu'un fidelle Amant est redoutable" (Amphitrite)
18. "Malgré moy vostre amour vainqueur Me réduit" (Amphitrite)
19. "Il faut aimer, c'est un fatal destin" (Amphitrite et Neptune)
20. "Entrée des Dieux Marins et des Nereides"
21. "C'est en vain qu'à l'amour on se veut opposer" (Amphitrite, Neptune)
22. "Menuet pour les Mesmes"
23. "Troisiesme Air pour les Mesmes"
24. "Un coeur qui veut estre volage" (Amphitrite)
25. "Air pour l'entrée de Borée et des quatre Vents"
26. "Gavotte pour Orithie et ses Nymphes"
27. (w/ out title) (Sarabande)
28. "Air pour Borée & quatre Vents qui enlevent Orithie & les Nymphes" (Bourrée)
29. "Va dangereux amour, va fuis loins" (Ritournelle pour Diane; Diane)
30. "Entrée des Nymphes de Diane"
31. "Un coeur maistre de luy mesme" (Diane)
32. "Deuxiesme Air pour les Nymphes de Diane"
33. "Dans ces forests venez suivre nos pas" (Diane)
34. "Entrée d'Endimion, Premier Air"
35. "Deuxiesme Air pour Endimion"
36. "Voicy le favorable temps" (Prélude pour la Nuit; la Nuit)
37. "Il est des nuits charmantes qui valent" (La Nuit)
38. "Je ne puis plus braver l'amour" (Prélude pour Diane; Diane)
39. "Nuit charmante et paisible, Tu rends le calme" (Diane)
40. "Vous qui fuyez la lumière et le bruit" (Prélude pour la Nuit; la Nuit)
41. "Entrée des Songes"
42. "Que de Fantômes vains errent de toutes parts" (Entré des Cariens)
43. "Ouvrez, ouvrez les yeux, voyez cet Astre" (La Nuit)
44. "Tout doit se ressentir du trouble de nos coeurs" (Choeur des Cariens)
45. "Diane dissipez nos craintes" (Choeur des Cariens)
46. "Entrée des Cariens"
47. "Bacchus revient vainqueur des climats" (Prélude pour un Indien)
48. "Bacchus n'a triomphé du monde qu'avec peine" (Un Indien)
49. "Non, non la plus fière liberté contre l'amour" (Deux Indiennes de la suite de Bacchus)
50. "Tout ressent les feux de l'amour" (L'Indien, Choeur)
51. "Entrée de Bacchus, d'Indiens, d'Ariane et de Dames Grecques. Premier Air"
52. "Menuet pour les Mesmes"
53. "Chaconne pour les Mesmes"
54. "Pourquoi tant se contraindre" (Choeur d'Indiens)
55. "Ah cedons, rendons-nous" (Deux Indiennes et l'Indien)
56. "D'une affreuse fureur Mars n'est plus" (Prélude pour Mercure; Mercure)
57. "Suivons l'amour, portons sa chaisne" (Ritournelle; Mercure)
58. "Entrée d'Apollon et de quatre Bergers héroyques"
59. "Deuxiesme Air pour les Mesmes"
60. "Entrée de Pan, d'Arcas et de Silvains; Ritournelle pour les hautbois"
61. "Que l'empire amoureux Est un charmant" (Arcas, Choeur)
62. "Entrée de Pan et des quatre Silvains. Premier Air"
63. "Il faut qu'un amant persévère" (Chanson pour Arcas)
64. "Second Air pour les Mesmes"
65. "Entrée de Flore, de Zéphire, de Nymphes de Flore, et des Zéphires. Premier Air"
66. (w/ out title) (Bourrée)
67. "Que de fleurs vont esclore. Le Zéphire aime" (Air chanté par une Nymphe de Flore)

68. "Tout ce que j'attaque se rend Tout cède" (Prélude pour l'Amour; l'Amour)
69. "Premier Air pour la Jeunesse"
70. "Ne troublez pas nos jeux importune raison" (La Jeunesse)
71. "Deuxiesme Air pour les Mesmes"
72. "Triomphez, triomphez amour victorieux" (Prélude pour Jupiter; Choeur)

1a.50   "Le temple de la paix," ballet: LWV69
1. "Ouverture"
2. "Préparons-nous pour la feste nouvelle" (Climène)
3. "D'un Roy toujours vainqueur la vertu" (Silvandre)
4. "La prompte renommée a publié la Feste" (Silvandre)
5. "Sans crainte dans nos prairies" (Silvie)
6. "Entrée de Bergers et Bergères"
7. "Rondeau"
8. "Charmant repos d'une vie" (Deux Bergers)
9. "Le Prince qui poursuit" (Prélude; Alcipe)
10. "Que ce Roy vainqueur a de gloire" (Amyntas, Choeur)
11. "Pour rendre son Empire heureux" (Prélude; Silvie)
12. "Entre les autres roys ce roy victorieux" (Alcimedon)
13. "Gigue"
14. "Menuet"
15. "Menuet"
16. (w/ out title)
17. "La gloire où ce vainqueur aspire" (Daphnis, Choeur)
18. "On conteroit plustost les Espices" (Silvie)
19. "Sans cesse benissons ce vainqueur" (Prélude; Climène)
20. "Jouissons sous ses loix d'un sort digne" (Choeur)
21. "Trop heureux. Malheureux, malheureux" (Prélude; Silvandre, Daphnis)
22. "La paix regne dans ce bocage" (Philène)
23. "Il est doux d'estre amant d'une bergère" (Choeurs)
24. "Entrée des Basques"
25. "Suivons l'aimable paix qui nous appelle" (Un Biscayen et une Biscayenne)
26. "Canaries"
27. "Canaries"
28. "Qu'estes-vous devenu doux" (Prélude; Silvie)
29. "Heureux les tendres coeurs où l'amour" (Silvie, Daphnis, Choeur)
30. "Entrée de Bretons et bretonnes, Passepied"
31. "Pasepied, hautbois"
32. "Menuet"
33. "La paix revient dans cet azile" (Deux Bretonnes)
34. "Menuet, hautbois"
35. "Lorsqu'un amour fidelle et tendre" (Climène)
36. "Ainsi qu'apres l'orage le céleste" (Silvandre, Climène, Silvie, Choeur)
37. "Rondeau: Entrée des Sauvages de l'Amérique"
38. "Nous avons traversé le vaste sein" (Un Sauvage)
39. "Second Air des Américains"
40. "Dans ces lieux il faut que tout ressente" (Choeur des Américains)
41. "Douce paix qui dans ces retraites" (Prélude; Licidas)
42. "Te plaindras-tu toûjours de l'amour tendre" (Alcipe)
43. "Quel bonheur pour la France" (Prélude; un Africain)
44. "Chantons tous sa valeur triomphante" (Choeur)
45. "Chaconne"

1a.51   *"Fragments de Monsieur de Lully," ballet (arr Campra, text Danchet p1702)* LWV79
1. (= Le Divertissement Royal, LWV42/1)
2.–9. (= Les fêtes de l'Amour et de Bacchus, LWV47/4–11)
10. (= Ballet de Flore, LWV40/35)
11. "Menuet"
12. "Joignons aux plus aimables chants les danses" (Choeur)
13.–14. (= Le bourgeois gentilhomme, LWV43/4–5)
15. "Prélude"
16. (= Le Divertissement Royal, LWV42/4)
17. (= Le Divertissement Royal, LWV42/2)
18. (= Ballet des Muses, LWV32/14)
19.–20. (= Pastorale comique, LWV/33, 28)
21. (= Le triomphe de Bacchus dans les Indes, LWV30/3)
22. (= Ballet des Muses, LWV32/24)
23. (= Le Divertissement Royal, LWV42/21)
24. (= Ballet des Arts, LWV18/26)
25.–26. (= Ballet des Muses, LWV32/6, 8)
27.–29. (= Ballet d'Alcidiane, LWV9/54–56)
30.–32. (= Les amours désguisés, LWV21/20–22)
33. (= Ballet des Muses, LWV32/27)
34.–35. (= Pastorale comique, LWV33/5–6)
36. "Iris paroît dans ce boccage" (Philène)

37. (= *Ballet de La naissance de Vénus, LWV27/32*)
38. 40. (= *Pastorale comique, LWV33/9–11*)
41.–42. (= *Le bourgeois gentilhomme, LWV43/37–38*)
43. (= *Ballet de Flore, LWV40/39*)
44. (= *Les plaisirs de l'île enchantée, LWV22/21*)
45. (= *Le carnaval ou Mascarade de Versailles, LWV36/4*)
46. (= *Ballet de La naissance de Vénus, LWV27/5*)
47. (= *Les plaisirs de l'île enchantée, LWV22/5*)
48.–49. (= *Le Grand Divertissement Royal de Versailles, LWV38/2–3*)
50. (= *Le bourgeois gentilhomme, LWV43/39*)
51. (= *Ballet de Flore, LWV40/39*)
52. (= *Ballet des Muses, LWV32/19*)
53. *"Nos tendres soins et ma langueur" (Un Bohémien et une Bohémienne)*
54. (= *Ballet d'Alcidiane, LWV9/4*)
55. *"Je ne dois plus me contraindre" (La Bohemienne)*
56. (= *Ballet des Muses, LWV32/16*)
57.–58. (= *Pastorale comique, LWV33/12–13*)
59. (= *Ballet des Muses, LWV32/13*)
60. (= *Menuet from: Trios de la chambre du Roi, LWV35/3*)
61. *"Dans les chans, dans les jeux, passons notre jeunesse" (Choeur)*
62. (= *Ballet de La naissance de Vénus, LWV27/20*)
63. *"Perche, perche crudo Amore" (Cariselli) (c by Campra)*
64. *"Bondi Cariselli" (Les trois Pantalons) (c by Cambert)*
65. *"Dalla baretta" (Les trois Pantalons) (c by Campra)*
66. (= *Les Plaisirs de l'Île enchantée, LWV22/27*)
67. (= *L'Amour médecin, LWV29/1*)
68. *"Voi sete il ristoro Di questa" (Vafrina) (c by Campra)*
69. (= *Ballet des Muses, LWV32/18*)
70. *"Air des Scaramouches" (c by ?Campra)*

1a.52   "Pourceaugnac," divertissement comique: LWV80
      1.–12. (= Le carnaval mascarade, LWV52/12–23)

1a.55   "Le mariage forcé," ballet: LWV20
      1. "Ouverture"
      2. "Si l'amour vous soumet à ses loix" (Rirournelle; Récit de la Beauté)
      3. "Première Entré: la Jalousie, les Chagrins et les Soupçons"
      4. "Seconde Entrée, quatre Plaisants, ou Goguenards"
      5. "Troisième Entrée, seux Egyptiens, & quatre Egyptiennes"
      6. "Second Air pour les mêmes"
      7. "Hola! qui va là? Dismoy viste quel soucy" (Récit d'un Magicien)
      8. "Quatrième Entrée, un Magicien qui fait sortir quatre Démons"
      9. "Cinquième Entrée, un Maître à danser"
      10. "Second Air, un Maître à danser vient d'enseigner une Courante à Sganarelle"
      11. "Sixième Entrée, Ritournelle"
      12. "Deux Espagnols et deux Espagnoles"
      13. "Septième Entrée, Rondeau pour le Charivary crotesque"
      14. "Second Air pour les mesmes"
      15. "Huitième et dernière Entrée, Gavotte pour quatre Galants cajolant la femme de Sganarelle"
      16. "Bourée pour les mesmes"

1a.56   "Les plaisirs de l'île enchantée," grande fête royale: LWV22
      1. "Ouverture"
      "1re Journée": 2. "Les quatre Saisons, les douze signes de Zodiaque et les douze Heures"
      3. "Marche de hautbois pour le Dieu Pan et sa suite" (Concert de Pan)
      4. "Rondeau pour les flûtes et les violons allant à la table du Roi"
      "2e Journée": 5. "Quand l'Amour à vos yeux offre un choix" (1er Intermède, Ritournelle; Récit de l'Aurore)
      6. "Holà! Debout, debout. Pour la chasse ordonnée il faut" (Valets de chiens et Musiciens)
      7. "Premier Air les Valets de chiens endormis"
      8. "Second Air des Valets de chiens et des Chasseurs avec des cors de chasse"
      9. "Troisième Air pour les Valets de chiens éveillés" (Gavotte)
      10. "Deuxième Intermède, premier Air des chasseurs et paysans avec des bâtons"
      11. "Second Air pour les Chasseurs et Paysans" (Gavotte)
      12. "Je le veux, mais auparavant" (Troisième Intermède; Satyre)
      13. "Dans vos chants si doux, Chantez" (Seconde Chanson de Satyre)
      14. "Ritournelle et Entrée pour les postures des Satyres"
      15a. "Loure unsuitte" (one line notation only)
      15. "Gigue en suite" (one line notation only)
      16. "Tu m'écoutes, hélas!" (Quatrième Intermède; Tircis)
      17. "Arbres épais, et vous prés émailés" (Tircis)
      18. "Ton extrême rigeur s'acharne" (Moron)
      19. "Ah! quelle douceur extrême" (Tircis)
      20. "Chère Philis, dis-moi" (Cinquième Intermède, Ritournelle; Clymène)
      21. "Usez mieux, o beautés fières du pouvoir" (Sixième Intermède; Choeur)
      22. "Les Bergers et les Faunes"

"3e Journée": 23. "I. Entrée, quatre Géants et quatre Nains"
24. "II. Entrée, les Maures"
25. "III. Entrée, six Chevaliers et six Monstres"
26. "IV. Entrée, Démons agiles"
27. "V. Entrée, Démons sauteurs"
28. "VI. et dernière Entrée, Alcine, Melisse, Roger et des Chevaliers"
29. "Bourée"

1a.58   "L'Amour médecin," comédie: LWV29
1. "Ouverture, Chaconne"
2. "Quittons, quittons notre vaine" (Ritournelle; la Comédie)
3. "Ritournelle pour donner du plaisir"
4. "Premier Entr'acte, première Entrée, Champagne heurtant aux portes de quatre Médicins"
5. "Seconde Entrée, pour les quatre Médicins"
6. "L'or de tous les climats" (L'Opérateur chantant)
7. "Deuxième Entr'acte, Entrée pour les Trivelins et Scaramouches"
8. "Sans nous tous les hommes deviendroient" (La Comédie, la Musique, le Ballet)
9. "Bourée"

1a.59   "Pastorale comique," pastorale: LWV33
1. "Première Entrée, les Magiciens"
2. "Déesse des appas, Ne nous refuse pas" (Trois Magiciens)
3. "Seconde Entrée, la Chaconne des Magiciens"
4. "Ah qu'il est beau le jouvenceau!" (Trois Magiciens)
5. "Paissez, chères grebis" (Scène III., Ritournelle; Filène)
6. "Iris charme mon ame; Iris" (Filène)
7. "Scène VIII., les Paysans combattent avec les bâtons"
8. "Scène IX., quatrième Entrée, les Paysans reconciliés"
9. "N'attendez pas qu'ici je me vante" (Scène XI.; Filène)
10. "Hélas! peut-on sentir" (Scène XIII.; Filène)
11. "Ha! quelle folie! Ha!" (Scène XIV., Ritournelle; un Berger enjoué)
12. "D'un pauvre coeur soulagez" (Scène XV., une Egyptienne; Air pour les Egyptiens, Egyptiennes)
13. "Croyez-moi, hâtons-nous ma Silvie" (Sixième et dernière Entrée, une Egyptienne, second
        Air: Ballet des Ballets: Gigue)

1a.60   "Le Sicilien, ou L'Amour peintre," comédie: LWV34
1. "Si du triste récit" (Scène III., Ritournelle; premier Musicien, représentant Philène)
2. "Les oiseaux réjouis" (Ritournelle; second Musicien, représentant Tircis)
3. "Pauvres amants, quelle erreur D'adorer" (Troisième Musicien, représentant un pâtre)
4. "Scène VIII., Les Esclaves"
5. "D'un coeur ardent, en tous lieux Un amant" (Hali)
6. "Savez vous mes drôles, Que cette chanson" (Dom Pèdre)
7. "Scène XX., Les Maures"
8. "Second Air"

1a.61   "Le Grand Divertissement Royal de Versailles," divertissement / comédie: LWV38
1. "Ouverture"
2. "Air pour les Bergers"
3. "L'autre jour d'Annette j'entends" (Climène et Cloris; les flûtes et les violons)
4. "Laissez-nous en repos Philène" (Dialogue, Cloris, Climène)
5. "Ah! mortelles douleurs!" (Ritournelle; Cloris)
6. "Entrée de Bateliers"
7. "Rondeau pour les Bergers"
8. "Ici l'ombre des ormeaux" (Tircis)
9. "Ah! qu'il est doux, belle Sylvie" (Ritournelle; Climène)
10. "Chantons tous de l'Amour le pouvoir" (Choeur)
11. "Nous suivons, nous suivons de Bacchus" (Choeur de Bacchus)
12. "Le soleil chasse les ombres" (Un Suivant de Bacchus)
13. "Bacchus est réveré sur la terre" (Choeur de Bacchus, les deux Choeurs)
14. "Entrée"

1a.63   "La grotte de Versailles," églogue: LWV39
1. "Ouverture"
2. "Allons, allons, Bergers, entrons" (Silvandre)
3. "Cessons, cessons de porter" (Choeur)
4. "Dans ces charmantes retraites" (Choeur)
5. "Goutons bien les plaisirs, Bergère" (Ritournelle; Iris, Caliste)
6. "Sortons, sortons de ces déserts" (Menalque)
7. "Voyons tous deux en aimant" (Menalque et Corridon)
8. "Venez prés de ces fontaines" (Daphnis, Choeur)
9. "Menuet"
10. "Les oyseaux vivent sans contrainte" (Ritournelle; Iris et Caliste)
11. "Dans ces deserts paisibles" (Ritournelle; Iris)
12. "Chantons tous en ce jour" (Choeur)
13. "Air des échos"

1a.64   "Le divertissement de Chambord," divertissement / comédie: LWV41
       1. "Ouverture"
       2. "Répands, charmante nuit" (Sérénade, Ritournelle; première Voix)
       3. "Que soupirer d'amour Est une douce" (Deuxième Voix)
       4. "Tout ce qu'à nos voeux on oppose" (Troixième Voix)
       5. "Aimons-nous donc d'une ardeur éternelle" (Le trois Voix)
       6. "Les Maîtres à danser"
       7. "Les Combattants"
       8. "Les Combattants reconciliés"
       9. "Buon di, buon di" (Deux Musiciens italiens)
      10. "Altro non e pa pazzia. Allegramente, allegramente" (Premier Musicien, les deux)
      11. "Les Matasins"
      12. "Piglialo sù, Signor monsù" (Les deux Musiciens)
      13. "Deux Avocats musiciens, deux Procureurs et deux Sergents"
      14. "La polygamie. Vostre fait est clair et net" (L'Avocat, traînant ses paroles, l'Avocat, bredouilleur)
      15. "Tous les peuples policés et bien sensés" (Les deux Avocats)
      16. "Sortez, sortez de ces lieux" (Une Egyptienne)
      17. "Ne songeons qu'à nous réjouir" (Choeur des Musiciens)
      18. "A me suivre tous ici. Votre ardeur" (L'Egyptienne, L'Egyptien, Double)
      19. "Sus, sus, chantons, sus, sus" (Choeur)
      20. "Les Sauvages et les Biscayens"
      21. "Bourée; les Tropmpettes"
      22. "Bourée"
      23. "Menuet"

1a.66   "Le divertissement Royal," divertissement: LWV42
       1. "Ouverture"
       2. "Vents qui troublez les plus beaux jours" (Premier Intermède; Récit d'Eole)
       3. "Allons, allons, tous au devant" (Tous les Tritons)
       4. "Les Pêcheurs de corail"
       5. "Redoublons nos concerts" (Choeur)
       6. "Air de Neptune"
       7. "Les Suivants de Neptune"
       8. "Second Intermède, trois Pantomimes"
       9. "Venez grande Princesse" (Troisième Intermède, Prologue, Ritournelle; la Nymphe de Tempé)
      10. "Vous chantez sous ces feuillages" (Scène première, Ritournelle; Tircis)
      11. "Ah! que sur notre coeur" (Scène troisième, Ritournelle pour les flûtes; Caliste)
      12. "Dormez, dormez, beaux yeux" (Scène quatrième, Ritournelle; Tircis, Lycaste, Menandre)
      13. "Soit amour, soit pitié" (Lycaste, Ménandre)
      14. "Aux amants qu'on pousse à bout" (Scène cinquième; premier Satyre)
      15. "Champêtres divinités" (Tous)
      16. "Six Dryades et six Faunes"
      17. "Quand je plaisois à tes yeux" (Depit amoureux; Philinte)
      18. "Ah! Ah! plus que jamais aimons" (Climène, Philinte)
      19. "Amants que vos querelles" (Tous les acteurs de la comédie)
      20. "Menuet pour les Faunes et les Dryades"
      21. "Jouissons, jouissons des plaisirs" (Ritournelle, Rondeau; les Bergers et les Bergères)
      22. "Quatrième Intermède, Symphonie des Plaisirs"
      23. "Air des Statues"
      24. "Cinquième Intermède, Air des Pantomimes"
      25. "Second Air des Pantomimes"
      26. "Chantez peuples, chantez" (Sixième Intermède qui est la solennité des Jeux Pythiens,
          Prélude des Sacrificateurs; la Prêtresse)
      27. "Poussons à sa memoire des concerts si touchants" (Choeur des grecs)
      28. "Les Porteurs de haches"
      29. "Les Voltigeurs"
      30. "Les Esclaves"
      31. "Les Hommes et Femmes armés"
      32. "Prélude de Trompettes"
      33. "Ouvrons tous nos yeux" (Choeur)
      34. "Entrée d'Apollon"
      35. "Menuet des Trompettes"

1a.68   "Le bourgeois gentilhomme," comédie-ballet: LWV43
       1. "Ouverture"
       2. "Je languis. Je languis nuit et jour" (L'Elève de musique, la Musicienne)
       3. "Je croyois Jeanneton" (M. Jourdin)
       4. "Un coeur dans l'amoureux empire" (Dialogue en musique, Ritournelle; une Musicienne)
       5. "Aimable ardeur Franchise heureuse" (Ritournelle; la Musicienne, deux Musiciens)
       6. "Quatre Danseurs, gravement, plus vite, mouvement de Sarabande, Bourée, Gaillarde"
       7. "Canaries"
       9. "Les six Garçons tailleurs"
      10. "Second Air, la Gavotte"
      11. "Un petit doigt, Philis pour commencer" (Premier Chanson à boire)
      12. "Buvons, chers amis, buvons" (Seconde Chanson à boire)

13. "Sus, sus, du vin, du vin, partout" (Tous ensemble)
14. "Marche pour la Cérémonie turque"
15. "Seti sabir. Ti respondir" (Le Mufti)
16. "Mahameta, per Giourdina" (Le Mufti)
17. "Star bon Turca Giourdina? Hei valla" (Le Mufti, Choeur)
18. "Second Air"
19. "Troisième Air pour les Turcs portant le Turban"
20. "Ti star nobile, non star fabola" (Le Mufti, Choeur)
21. "Quatrième Air"
22. "Non tener honta, non tener" (Le Mufti, Choeur)
"Ballet des Nations": 23. "A moy, Monsieur, à moy de grâce" (I. Entrée; Dialoque)
24. "II. Entrée, Les trois Importuns"
25. "Sé que me muero me muero" (III. Entrée, Ritournelle; trois Espagnols)
26. "Ay! que locura con tanto rigor" (Le second Espagnol)
27. "Premier Air des Espagnols"
28. "El dolor solicita" (Un Espagnol)
29. "Dulce muerte es el amor" (Deux Espagnols)
30. "Second Air des Espagnols"
31. "Alefresse enamorado" (Un Espagnol)
32. "Vaya, vaya, de fiestas vaya" (Trois Espagnols)
33. "Di rigori armata il seno" (IV. Entrée, Italiens, Ritournelle; une Musicienne italienne)
34. "Entrée des Scaramouches, Trivelins et un Arlequin représentant une nuit"
35. "Bel tempo che vola Rapis" (Les Musiciens italien)
36. "Chaconne des Scaramouches, Trivelins)
37. "Ah qu'il fait beau dans ces boccages" (V. Entrée. François, Menuet; premier Musicien poitevin)
38. "Vois ma Climène, Vois sous ce chêne" (Second Menuet; deux Musiciens poitevins)
39. "Quels spectacles charmants, quels plaisirs" (Choeur)
40. (Pieces w/ out title in Philidor's copy)
41. "Dieu du vin, Dieu du vin, c'est à toi" (Duo à boire)

1a.70   "Psyché," tragédie-ballet: LWV45
1. "Ouverture"
2. "Ce n'est plus le temps de la guerre" (Flore)
3. "Nous goûtons une paix profonde" (Choeur)
4. "Pour les Nayades, Silvains, Fleuves et Driades"
5. "Rendez-vous beautez cruelles" (Vertumne)
6. "Menuet"
7. "Est-on sage dans le bel age" (Flore) (Menuet)
8. "Deh piangete al pianto mio" (Premier Intermède, Plainte en italien, Prélude; Femme désolée)
9. "Ahi dolore, ahi martire cruda" (Deux Hommes affligés)
10. "Entrée de Ballet de huit Personnes affligées"
11. "Second Intermède. Entrée des Cyclopes et des Fées"
12. "Six Cyclopes"
13. "Dépéchez, préparez ces lieux" (Vulcain)
14. "L'amour ne veut point qu'on diffère" (Vulcain)
15. "Troisième Intermède, Entrée de Ballet de quatre Amours et quatre Zéphirs, Menuet"
16. "Aimable jeunesse, suivez" (Première Nymphe)
17. "Chacun est obligé d'aimer" (Deux Nymphes)
18. "Quatriesme Intermède. Entrée des Furies et des Lutins"
19. "Unissons-nous, troupe immortelle" (Prélude; Récit d'Apollon)
20. "Célébrons, célébrons ce grand jour" (Choeur)
21. "Si quelquefois suivant nos douces loix" (Prélude; Bacchus)
22. "Je cherche à médire sur la terre" (Récit de Mome)
23. "Mes plus fiers ennemis vaincus" (Mars)
24. "Chantons les plaisirs charmans" (Choeur)
25. "Le Dieu qui nous engage à luy" (Entrée de la suite d'Apollon, Bergers galants, Apollon)
26. "Second Air"
27. "Gardez-vous beautés sévères" (Deux Muses)
28. "Entrée de la suite de Bacchus"
29. "Admirons le jus de la treille" (Récit de Bacchus)
30. "Second Air"
31. "Bacchus veut qu'on boive à longs traits" (Silène)
32. "Voulez-vous des douceurs parfaites" (Silène et deux Satyrs)
33. "Entrée de la suite de Mome. Les Polichinels, Matassins et Esprits follets"
34. "Folâtrons, folâtrons, divertissons" (Mome)
35. "Laissons en paix toute la terre" (Entrée de la suite de Mars; Mars)
36. "Quatre Hommes portant des enseignes"
37. "Dernier Air"
38. "Mome et Polichinel"

1a.71   "Les fêtes de l'Amour et de Bacchus," (pastiche) pastorale: LWV47
1. (= Le bourgeois gentilhomme, LWV43/1)
Prologue: 2. (= Le bourgeois gentilhomme, LWV43/23)
3. "Le Donneur de Livres et les quatre Importuns forment la première Entrée"
4. "Elevez, élevez vos concerts" (Ritournelle; Polymnie)

     5. "Joignez à mes chants magnifiques" (Symphonie; Melpomène)
     6. "C'est à moy, c'est à moy de prétendre à luy" (Melpomène et Euterpe)
     7. "C'est un doux amusement" (Euterpe)
     8. "Que nôtre accord est doux" (Le trois Muses ensemble)
     9. "II. Entrée, Premier Air"
    10. "Joignons nos soins et nos voix" (Les trois Muses ensemble, Choeur)
    11. "Faisons tout retentir du bruit" (Symphonie pour les Hautbois et les Musettes; Melpomène, ch)
  I: 12. (= Le divertissement Royal, LWV42/10)
    13. "Viens dans notre village" (Climène)
    14. "Tu devrois bien plutôt songer" (Climène)
    15.–20. (= Le divertissement Royal, LWV42/11–16)
    21.–22. (= Ballet de Flore, LWV40/18, 14)
  II: 23. "Je ne puis souffrir l'outrage" (Florestan)
    24. "Caliste aura beau se deffendre" (Florestan)
    25.–28. (= Pastorale comique, LWV33/1–4)
    29. "Qu'un beau visage. A davantage" (Florestan)
    30. "Il est bien doux de boire" (Florestan)
    31. "Ah qu'il est beau! Ho, ho, ho, ho, ho" (Silvandre)
    32. "Amy, me veux-tu croire" (Silvestre)
    33. "C'est pour servir Cloris" (Damon)
    34. "Ma volage s'avance. Vengeons-nous, vengeons-nous" (Climène, Damon)
    35.–37. (= Le Divertissement Royal, LWV42/17–19)
    38. "Venez, que rien ne vous arrête" (Arcas)
    39. "Les plaisirs où l'Amour convie" (Tous ensemble)
    40. "Les Suivants de l'Amour, Gigue"
  III: 41.–48. (= Le Grand Divertissement Royal de Versailles, LWV38/7–14)

1a.72   "Idylle sur la paix," idylle: LWV68
     1. "Ouverture"
     2. "Un plein repos favorise" (Licidas)
     3. "Tu pares nos jardins d'une grâce" (Licidas, Amarillis)
     4. "Menuet"
     5. "Déja grondoient les horribles tonnerres" (Prélude; Silvandre)
     6. "Divine Paix apprends-nous" (Ritournelle; Philis)
     7. "Un Héros, des mortels l'amour" (Choeur)
     8. "Son bras est craint du Couchant" (Silvandre)
     9. "Gavotte"
    10. "Chantons Bergers, et nous réjouissons" (Astrée, Choeur)
    11. "Loure"
    12. "De ces lieux l'éclat et les attraits" (Celimène)
    13. "Il veut bien quelquefois visiter" (Cloris, Choeur)
    14. "Menuet"
    15. "O Ciel! ô saintes destinées!" (Prélude; Flore, Choeur)
    16. "Qu'il règne, qu'il règne" (Gay, Choeur)

1a.73   "Acis et Galatée," pastorale héroïque: LWV73
     1. "Ouverture"
  Prologue: 2. "Qu'avec plaisir je reviens" (Diane)
     3. "Nous avons preparé pour luy les festes" (Prélude; un Silvain)
     4. "Suivez les mouvements" (Diane, Choeur)
     5. "Première Entrée. Menuet"
     6. "Première Rigaudon"
     7. "Air gay. Second Rigaudon"
     8. "Marche de Comus"
     9. "Dans les jours de réjouissance" (L'Abondance)
    10. "Unissons nos efforts et qu'une ardeur" (L'Abondance, Diane, Comus, Choeur)
    11. "Air" (Gigue)
    12. "Apollon en ce jour aprouve vostre" (Prélude; Apollon)
    13. "Apollon flatte nos voeux d'un succés" (Comus, Choeur)
    14. "Air"
    15. "Menuet"
  I: 16. "C'est en vain qu'en ces lieux" (Prélude; Acis)
    17. "La charmante Scylla, l'honneur" (Teleme)
    18. "Faudrat'il encor vous attendre" (Prélude; Acis)
    19. "J'ay crû trouver icy la Nimphe" (Ritournelle; Galatée)
    20. "Ah! qu'un amant dont la plainte" (Galatée)
    21. "Mais quels concerts se font entendre" (Flûtes; Scylla)
    22. "Que l'amour qui nous enchaîne" (Aminte)
    23. "L'Amour dans ces beaux lieux" (Aminte, Choeur)
    24. "Premier Air"
    25. "Que les plus galantes fêtes" (Aminte, Choeur)
    26. "Air" (Gigue)
    27. "Marche pour l'entrée de Polipheme"
    28. "Tout ce que vous voyez reconnoist mon pouvoir" (Polipheme)
    29. "Je suis au comble de mes voeux" (Polipheme)

II: 30. "Quoy vous avez promis" (Ritournelle; Acis)
    31. "Immortels habitans des Cieux" (Acis)
    32. "Chaconne"
    33. "Qu'une injuste fierté nous cause" (Galatée)
    34. "Marche"
    35. "Qu'à l'envy chacun se presse" (Poliphème, Choeur)
    36. "Connoy puissant Amour ta dernière victoire" (Poliphème)
    37. "O vous adorable immortelle, Escoutez" (Choeur)
    38. "Second Air, Entrée des Ciclopes"
    39. "Pour hâter mon bonheur je vais tout entreprendre" (Poliphème)
III: 40. "Vous qui dans ces lieux solitaires" (Symphonie; le Prestre)
    41. "Puissent-ils prés de nous trouver un sûr" (Choeur)
    42. "Quel chemin ont-ils pris ces amans" (Prélude; Poliphème)
    43. "Il est mort l'insolent, j'ay trompé" (Poliphème)
    44. "Enfin j'ay dissipé la crainte" (Prélude; Galatée)
    45. "Que ne puis-je expirer aprés ce coup" (Prélude; Galatée)
    46. "Je sors de mes grottes profondes" (Prélude; Neptune)
    47. "Nous accourons au seul bruit de ta voix" (Choeur)
    48. "Que votre sang se change" (Prélude; Neptune)
    49. "Air"
    50. "Passacaille"
    51. "Sous ses loix l'amour veut qu'on jouisse" (Une Nayade, Choeur)
    52. "Vous qui croyez l'Amour une foiblesse" (Flûtes; une Nayade)
    53. "Tendres coeurs conservez l'espérance" (Violons; première Nayade, Choeur)
    54. "Désormais on doit aimer sans crainte" (Flûtes; seconde Nayade)

2. INSTRUMENTAL WORKS

Marches:

3. SACRED WORKS

Motets:

3.19	11. "O sapientia in misterio" ....
3.20	12. "Regina coeli" ....
3.21	13. "Salve Regina" ....
3.22	14. "Domine salvum fac regem" (Grand Motet) ....
3.23	15. "Exaudiat te Dominus" (Grand Motet) ....
3.24	16. "Jubilate Deo omnis terra" (Grand Motet) ....
3.25	17. "Natus in Judea Deus" (Grand Motet) ....
3.26	*18. "Il faut périr, pécheur," aria (music lost)* ....

4. SECULAR VOCAL

4.1	*"Un charmant Dialogue de la Guerre avecque la Paix," dialogue (p1655, anon, lost)* **LWV3**

Misc secular vocal (w/ out date): **LWV76**

4.2	1. "Ritournelle": "Ingratte bergère, dimoy, dismoy" (Le Président de Périgny) ....
4.3	2. "Ritournelle, Air espagnol": "Aunque prodigoas monstrais del oro" ....
4.4	3. "Ritournelle": "Scoca per tutti tuoi strali" ....
4.5	4. "Chanson de Baptiste": "A la fin pétit Desfarges vous" ....
4.6	5. "D'un beau pêcheur la pêche malheureuse" (Vaudeville) ....
4.7	6. "Canon à cinq parties de Monsieur de Lully": "Un tendre coeur, rempli d'ardeur" ....
4.8	7. "Courage, Amour, la paix est faite" (Benserade) ....
4.9	*8. "Italienische Arie": "Non vi è più bel piacer" (music lost)* ....
4.10	*9. "Menuet": "Le Printemps, aimable Silvie" (music lost)* ....
4.11	10. "Air": "Tous les jours cent jeunes Bergères" ....
4.12	*11. "Menuet": "Viens, mon aymable Bergère, sur la fougère" (music lost)* ....
4.13	12. "Qui les sçaura, mes secrettes amours?" (Perrin) ....
4.14	13. "Air": "Où estes-vous allez, mes belles amourettes" ....
4.15	14. "Air à boire": "Nous meslons toute nostre gloire" ....
4.16	15. "Air": "Pendant que ces flambeaux de lumière immortelle" ....
4.17	*16. "La Langueur des beaux yeux De la jeune Silvie" (music lost)* ....
4.18	*17. "On dit que vos yeux sont trompeurs" (M. le Président de Périgny, music lost)* ....
4.19	*18. "Que vous connoissez peu trop aimable Climène" (Quinault, music lost)* ....
4.20	*19. "Si je n'ay parlé de ma flamme" (S. M., music lost)* ....
4.21	*20. "En ces lieux je ne voy que des promenades" (Lully, music lost)* ....
4.22	*21. "Ah qu'il est doux de se rendre" (Quinault, music lost)* ....
4.23	*22. "J'ai fait serment, cruelle. De suivre une autre loy" (Quinault, music lost)* ....
4.24	*23. "Le Printemps ramène la verdure" (M. M., music lost)* ....
4.25	*24. "Depuis que l'on soûpire Sous l'amoureux empire" (Quinault, music lost)* ....
4.26	*25. "Sans mentir on est bien misérable" (anon, music lost)* ....
4.27	26. "Air à boire": "Venerabilis barba capucinorum" ....

Works presumably c by Lully: **LWV78**

4.28	1. "Adieu de Mademoiselle" ....
4.29	2. "Marche des Fanatiques" ....
4.30	3. "Amarillis," sarabande ....
4.31	4. "Sarabande" ....
4.32	5. "Sarabande" ....
4.33	6. "La Niert," sarabande ....
4.34	7. "Gigue" ....
4.35	8. "Gigue" ....
4.36	9. "Air" ....
4.37	10. "Menuet en trio" ....
4.38	11. "Ouverture de la convalescence du Roy" ....
4.39	12. "Entrée" ....
4.40	13. "Menuet" ....
4.41	14. "Petite chaconne italienne" ....
4.42	15. "L'Allarme" ....
4.43	16. "Croissez, croissez, jeunes raisins" ....

* * * * *

LWV = Hans Schneider: "Chronologisch-thematisches Verzeichnis. Sämtlicher Werke von Jean-Baptiste Lully." Verlag Bei Hans Schneider. Tutzing, 1981.

1. STAGE WORKS

1.1   Incid music for stage & radio (c1945–60, no artistic importance to composer) ....

Film:

1.2   "Attention!" (c1935–6) ....
1.3   "Contraction" (c1935–6) ....
1.4   "Fire" (c1935–6) ....
1.5   "To the Baltic on the Oder" (c1946) ....
1.6   "Warsaw Suite" (ca1947) ....

2. SYMPHONIES

2.1   Symphony No.1 (c1941–7) ....
2.2   Symphony No.2 (c1966–7) ....
2.3   Symphony No.3 (c1972–3) ....
2.4   Symphony No.4 (c1993) ....

3. OTHER ORCHESTRAL WORKS

3.1   *"Scherzo" (c1930, lost)* ....
3.2   "Haroun al Rashid" (c1931, reorchd ballet music for Makarczyk's play) ....
3.3   "Double Fugue" (c1936) ....
3.4   "Symphonic Variations" (c1936–8) ....
3.5   "5 Folk Songs" (c1952; strings, transcr from: Folksongs of 1947): No.1 "Oh, my Johnny" (Lowickian) ....
3.6   No.2 "Hey, I come from Cracow" (Cracovian)
3.7   No.3 "The grove" (Silesian)
3.8   No.4 "The gander" (Silesian)
3.9   No.5 "The schoolmaster" (Silesian)
3.10   "Overture for Strings" (c1949) ....
3.11   "Little Suite" (c1950, chamber orch; r & reorchd for full orch 1951): No.1 "Fife" ....
3.12   No.2 "Hurra polka"
3.13   No.3 "Song"
3.14   No.4 "Dance"
3.15   "10 Polish Dances" (c1953; chamber orch, on folktunes of Silesia & Kashubia) ....
3.16   "Concerto for Orchestra" (c1950–4) ....
3.17   "Dandelions" (c1954, based on Polish folk dances) ....
3.18   "Muzyka żałobna" (Musique funèbre) (c1954–8; strings, for 10th anniv of Bartok's death) ....
3.19   "3 Postludes" (c1958–60, r1963) ....
3.20   "Gry weneckie" (Venetian Games) (c1960–1; chamber orch) ....
3.21   "Livre pour orchestre" (c1968): No.1 "1er chapitre" ....
3.22   No.2 "1er intermède"
3.23   No.3 "2me chapitre"
3.24   No.4 "2me intermède"
3.25   No.5 "3me chapitre"
3.26   No.6 "3me intermède et chapitre final"
3.27   "Preludes & Fugue" (c1970–2; 13 strings: 7vn, 3va, 2vc & d bass): No.1 "Prelude 1" ....
3.28   No.2 "Prelude 2"
3.29   No.3 "Prelude 3"
3.30   No.4 "Prelude 4"
3.31   No.5 "Prelude 5"
3.32   No.6 "Prelude 6"
3.33   No.7 "Prelude 7"
3.34   No.8 "Fugue"
3.35   "Mi-Parti" (c1975–6) ....
3.36   "Novelette" (c1978–9) ....
3.37   "Łańcuch 1" (Chain 1) (c1983; chamber orch) ....
3.38   "Łańcuch 3" (Chain 3) (c1986) ....
3.39   "Przeźrocza" (Slides) (c1988; chamber orch of 11 soloists) ....
3.40   "Interlude" (c1990) ....

4. CONCERTOS, SOLO INSTR & ORCH

Pf & orch:

4.1   "Variations on a theme of Paganini" (c1977–8; orig for 2 pf 1941) ....
4.2   Piano Concerto (c1987) ....

Vn & orch:

4.3   "Łańcuch 2" (Chain 2) (Dialogue for Violin and Orchestra) (c1984) ....

4.4   "Partita" (c1985; w/ pf obbl, r vers of: Partita for vn & pf) ....

Other:

4.5   5 "Dance Preludes" (c1955; cl solo, harp, pf, perc & strings; orig for cl & pf 1954) ....
4.6   Cello Concerto (c1969–70) ....
4.7   Double Concerto (c1980; ob, harp & chamber orch) ....

5. STRING QUARTETS

5.1   String Quartet (c1964) ....

6. OTHER CHAMBER MUSIC

5 insts:

6.1   "Mini Overture" (c1978; brass qnt) ....

4 insts:

6.2   "4 Silesian Melodies" (c1954; 4vn, transcr from songs) ....

2–3 wind insts:

6.3   "30 Pieces for woodwinds" (c1943–4): ....
            . 10 Canons (2cl)
            . 10 Canons (3cl)
            . 10 Pieces (ob & bn)
6.4   Trio (c1944–5; ob, cl & bn) ....
6.5   "4 Fanfares" (c1954, for 2nd festival of Polish Music) ....
6.6   "6 Christmas Carols" (c1959; 3 recorders) ....

Vn & pf:

6.7   "2 Violin Sonatas" (c1927, lost) ....
6.8   "Recitativo e arioso" (c1951) ....
6.9   "Partita" (c1984; also see w/ orch 1988) ....

Other 2 insts:

6.10   "Bukoliki" (Bucolics) (c1962; va & vc; orig for pf) ....
6.11   "Dance Preludes" (c1954; cl & pf; also vers for 9 insts 1959): No.1 "Allegro molto" ....
6.12   No.2 "Andantino"
6.13   No.3 "Allegro giocoso"
6.14   No.4 "Andante"
6.15   No.5 "Allegro molto"
6.16   "Epitaph" (c1979; ob & pf) ....
6.17   "Grave" (c1981; vc & pf; orchd1982 w/ strings) ....

1 instr:

6.18   "Sacher Variation" (c1975; vc) ....

7. PIANO SONATAS

7.1   Piano Sonata (c1934)..

8. OTHER PIANO WORKS

8.1   Juvenilia: small pieces for piano (c1922–30, lost) ....
8.2   "Prelude" (c1922)..
8.3   "Poème" (c1930) ....
8.4   "Dance of the Chimera" (c1930, lost) ....
8.5   "Prelude & aria" (c1936, lost) ....
8.6   "2 Etudes" (c1940–1): No.1 "Allegro" ....
8.7   No.2 "Non troppo allegro"
8.8   "Folk Melodies," 12 easy pieces (c1945; also see: Folk Songs of 1947): No.1 "Oh, my Johnny" (Lowickian)
8.9   No.2 "Hey, I come from Cracow" (Cracovian)
8.10   No.3 "There is a path, there is" (Podlasian)
8.11   No.4 "The shepherd girl" (Podlasian)
8.12   No.5 "An apple hangs on the apple tree" (from Sieradz)

8.13	No.6 "A river flows from Sieradz" (from Sieradz)
8.14	No.7 "Master Michael" (Kurpian waltz)
8.15	No.8 "The linden in the field" (from Mazury)
8.16	No.9 "Flirting" (Silesian)
8.17	No.10 "The grove" (Silesian)
8.18	No.11 "The gander" (Silesian)
8.19	No.12 "The schoolmaster" (Silesian)
8.20	"Bucolics," 5 pieces (c1952, based on Kurpian folk melodies, from Skierkowski) ....
8.21	"3 Pieces for Young Pianists" (c1953): No.1 "Four-finger exercise" ....
8.22	No.2 "Melody"
8.23	No.3 "March"
8.24	"Invention" (c1968) ....

2 Pf:

8.25	"Variations on a Theme of Paganini" (c1941; also see chamber work) ....
8.26	"An overheard tune" (c1957) ....
8.27	"Miniature" (c1979) ....

9. CHORAL WORKS

9.1	"2 Fragments of a Requiem" (c1937): *1. "Requiem aeternam" (ch & orch, lost)* ....
9.2	2. "Lacrimosa" (S & orch; transcr for S & org)
9.3	"3 Carols" (c1945, Maliszewski; vv, unison ch & chamber ens) ....
9.4	"6 Children's Songs" (c1952/3; child ch/mS & orch; orig for 1v & pf) ....
9.5	"10 Soldiers' Songs" (c1951; m ch): 1. "A black field near Cracow" ....
9.6	2. "No tear will be shed"
9.7	3. "And in Warsaw"
9.8	4. "The sun is setting"
9.9	5. "Oh! and in the field a lake"
9.10	6. "I broke the guelder-rose"
9.11	7. "Where are you going, Jack?"
9.12	8. "And on that mountain"
9.13	9. "The seventh year passes already"
9.14	10. "Maggie"
9.15	"I would marry" (c1951; ch; orig for 1v & pf) ....
9.16	"Service to Poland" (c1951; m ch & pf; orig for 1v & pf) ....
9.17	"Iron march" (c1951; ch; orig for 1v & pf) ....
9.18	"We are going forward" (c1951; ch; orig for 1v & pf) ....
9.19	"Trois poèmes d'Henri Michaux" (c1961–3; ch/20vv, strings & perc): 1. "Pensées" ....
9.20	2. "Le grand combat"
9.21	3. "Repos dans le malheur"

10. VOICE & ORCHESTRA

10.1	"Tryptyk Śląski" (Silesian Triptych) (c1951, Mroczkowski after trad; S & orch, collab Bystroń; in Eng Mroczkowski; in Fr Konopka; in Russ Żytomirski): 1. "Allegro non troppo" ....
10.2	2. "Andante quieto"
10.3	3. "Allegro vivace"
10.4	"Słomkowy Łańcuszek" (Little Chain of Straw), children's song cycle (c1950–1, Krzemieniecka, Porazińska, Lenartowicz & others; S, mS, fl, ob, 2cl & bn): 1. "Introduction" (insts) ....
10.5	2. "Low hut" (duet)
10.6	3. "There was an old woman" (mS)
10.7	4. "What went boom in the woods?" (S)
10.8	5. "A pear tree stood in the field" (mS)
10.9	6. "A guelder-rose grew" (S)
10.10	7. "Sophie wanted some berries" (S)
10.11	8. "Chain of straw" (theme & variations):
10.12	a. "Children" (duet)
10.13	b. "The well" (S)
10.14	c. "The rosebush" (mS)
10.15	d. "The dog" (mS)
10.16	e. "Flower" (S)
10.17	f. "The cow" (mS)
10.18	g. "Finale" (duet)
10.19	"Spring," children's song cycle (c1951; mS & chamber orch): 1. "Spring is here" (Domeradzki) ....
10.20	2. "Song of the golden leaf" (Korczakowska)
10.21	3. "Like a Warsaw driver" (Januszewska)
10.22	4. "May night" (Krzemieniecka)
10.23	"Jesień" (Autumn), 4 children's songs (c1951, Krzemieniecka; mS & chamber orch) ....
10.24	"Sleep, sleep," children's song (c1952, Krzemieniecka; S & chamber orch) ....
10.25	"Night is falling," children's song (c1952, Osińska; S & chamber orch) ....

10.26	"2 Children's Songs" (c1954, Tuwim; 1v & chamber orch): 1. "Vegetables" ....
10.27	2. "Hard arithmetic"
10.28	"5 Songs" (c1958, Iłłakowicz; mS & chamber orch; orig for mS & pf): 1. "The sea" ....
10.29	2. "The wind"
10.30	3. "Winter"
10.31	4. "Knights"
10.32	5. "Church bells"
10.33	"Paroles tissées" (Woven words) (c1965, Chabrun, in French; T & 20 solo insts) ....
10.34	"Les espaces du sommeil" (The Spaces of Sleep) (c1975, Desnos: Corps et biens, in French; Bar & orch)
10.35	"Chantefleurs et Chantefables" (c1991, Desnos, in French; S & orch) ....

11. SONGS (w/ pf)

11.1	"2 Songs" (c1934, Iłłakowicz): 1. "Water Sprite" ....
11.2	*2. "Lullaby of the Linden" (lost)*
11.3	"Pieśni walki podziemnej" (Songs of the Underground Struggle) (c1939–45): 1. "Iron march" (Dobrowolski)
11.4	2. "To arms" (Maliszewski)
11.5	3. "An open stretch before us" (Zawadzka)
11.6	4. "One word, one sign" (Zawadzka)
11.7	5. "The merry platoon" (anon)
11.8	"Folk Songs" (p1947, collab Olszewski; also see Folk Melodies for pf): 1. "Oh, my Johnny" (Lowickian) .....
11.9	2. "Hey, I come from Cracow" (Cracovian)
11.10	3. "There is a path, there is" (Podlasian)
11.11	4. "The shepherd girl" (Podlasian)
11.12	5. "An apple hangs on the apple tree" (from Sieradz)
11.13	6. "A river flows from Sieradz" (from Sieradz)
11.14	7. "Master Michael" (Kurpian waltz)
11.15	8. "The linden in the field" (from Mazury)
11.16	9. "Flirting" (Silesian dance)
11.17	10. "The grove" (Silesian dance)
11.18	11. "The gander" (Silesian dance)
11.19	12. "The schoolmaster" (Silesian dance)
11.20	"20 Polish Carols" (c1946, trad; orchd1985 w/ small fem ch): 1. "The angel said to the shepherds" ....
11.21	2. "When Christ was born"
11.22	3. "They hurried to Bethlehem"
11.23	4. "Tiny Jesus"
11.24	5. "God is born"
11.25	6. "He is lying in a manger"
11.26	7. "It was already midnight"
11.27	8. "Heigh, we rejoice"
11.28	9. "When the lovely maiden"
11.29	10. "Sleep, little Jesus"
11.30	11. "We shepherds too"
11.31	12. "Heigh, on the day of the Nativity"
11.32	13. "Hola, hola, shepherds from the fields"
11.33	14. "Jesus, lovely flower"
11.34	15. "Of the Lord's birth"
11.35	16. "The gentle shepherds"
11.36	17. "And what with this child"
11.37	18. "The little babe"
11.38	19. "Heigh, heigh, thou lily Virgin Mary"
11.39	20. "The most blessed maiden walked on earth"
11.40	"6 Children's Songs" (c1947; 1 fem v & pf/chamber orch; also for child ch & orch): 1. "Dance" ....
11.41	2. "Year and trouble"
11.42	3. "Kitten"
11.43	4. "Here comes Greg"
11.44	5. "River"
11.45	6. "Birds' gossip"
11.46	"2 Children's Songs" (c1948, Tuwim; 1v & pf/orch): 1. "Belated nightingale" ....
11.47	2. "About Mr Tralaliński"
11.48	"The Snowslide" (c1949, Pushkin: Obval; S & pf) ....
11.49	"2 Songs" (c1952, Korczakowska & Krzemieniecka; mS & pf; orig w/ chamber orch): 1. "Song of the
	golden leaf" ....
11.50	2. "May night"
11.51	"7 Songs" (c1950–2; 1v/unison ch & pf): 1. "The road of victory" (Urgacz) ....
11.52	2. "I would marry" (Lewin; arr for ch)
11.53	3. "The City of Nowa Huta" (Wygodzki)
11.54	4. "Service to Poland" (Wygodzki; arr for m ch & pf)
11.55	5. "Iron march" (= 1. of: Songs of the Underground; arr for ch)
11.56	6. "The most beautiful dream" (Urgacz)
11.57	7. "We are going forward" (Brzechwa; arr for ch)
11.58	"2 Children's Songs" (c1952, Barto; orchd1953): 1. "Silver window-pane" ....
11.59	2. "Little seashell"
11.60	"Little Feather," children's song (c1953, Osińska; orchd) ....

*   *   *   *   *

MAHLER, Gustav

1. STAGE WORKS

Operas:

1.1   *"Herzog Ernst von Schwaben" (c before 1875, Steiner after Uhland, project, lost)* ....
1.2   *"Die Argonauten" (c1879–80, Mahler or Steiner after Grillparzer, project, lost)* ....
1.3   *"Rübezahl" (c1880–90, Mahler, music lost/not composed)* ....
1.4   *Opera (c1887–8, lost, cited Bauer-Lechner as collab work w/ Weber)* ....

Incid music:

1.5   "Der Trompeter von Säkkingen" (c ?1884, Scheffel, part lost, cited la Grange): ....
         extant: . "Ein Ständchen am Rhein"
                  . "Die erste Begegnung"
                  . "Das Maifest am Bergsee"
                  . "Trompeten-Unterricht in der Geissblattlaube"
                  . "Der Überfall im Schlossgarten"
                  . "Liebesglück"
                  . "Wiedersehen in Rom"
1.6   "Das Volkslied" (c ?1885, part lost, cited la Grange) ....

2. SYMPHONIES

2.1   *Symphony (c1876–8, rehearsed at Vienna Conservatory, lost)* ....
2.2   *Symphony in A minor (c1876–8, lost, cited Bauer-Lechner)* ....
2.3   Symphony No.1 in D major, "Titan" (c ?1884–8, r1893–6): ....
         Abandoned orig titles of movts: I. "From the Days of Youth": 1. "Spring without End"
                                         2. "Flora" (Blumine) (c1888, discarded in final revision; see Other Orchestral)
                                         2. "Under Full Sail"
                                       II. "Human Comedy": 3. "Funeral March in the Manner of Callot" (reference to Callot's etching: The Hunter's
                                                  Funeral Procession)
                                         4. "From Inferno to Paradise"
2.4   Symphony No.2 in C minor, "Resurrection" (c1888–94, r1903; w/ S, A & ch) ....
2.5   Symphony No.3 in D minor (c1893–6, r1906, Nietzsche; w/ A, fem ch & boys' ch): ....
         Programmatic info suppressed by composer: 1. "Summer Marches in"
                                         2. "What the Wild Flowers Tell Me"
                                         3. "What the Animals in the Forest Tell Me"
                                         4. "What the Night Tells Me"
                                         5. "What the Morning Bells Tell Me"
                                         6. "What Love Tells Me"
2.6   Symphony No.4 in G major, "Ode to Heavenly Joy" (c1899–1900, Finale c1892, r1901–10): ....
         . (4th movt words from the famous collection of German folk poetry Des Knaben Wunderhorn;
            w/ S—see song: Wir geniessen die himmlischen Freuden)
2.7   Symphony No.5 in C-sharp minor, "The Giant" / "Riesen-Symphonie" (c1901–2, repeatedly revised) ....
2.8   Symphony No.6 in A minor, "Tragic" (c1903–4, r1906, repeatedly revised) ....
2.9   Symphony No.7 in E minor, "Song of the Night" (c1904–5, repeatedly revised) ....
2.10   Symphony No.8 in E-flat major, "Of a Thousand" (c1906; w/ solo vv & 2 ch): ....
         Part I. (based on: Veni Creator Spiritus," Latin hymn)
         Part II. (based on: Final Scene from Goethe's Faust Part II)
2.11   Symphony No.9 in D major (c1908–9) ....
2.12   "Das Lied von der Erde" (The Song of the Earth) (c1908–9; w/ A, T, from Bethge's The Chinese Flute):.....
         1. "Das Trinklied vom Jammer der Erde" (The Drinking Song of Earth's Sorrows): "Schon winkt
            der Wein im goldnen Pokale"
         2. "Der Einsame im Herbst" (The Solitary in Autumn): "Herbstnebel wallen bläulich überm See"
         3. "Von der Jugend" (Of Youth): "Mitten in dem kleinen Teiche"
         4. "Von der Schönheit" (Of Beauty): "Junge Mädchen pflücken Blumen"
         5. "Der Trunkene im Frühling" (The Drunkard in Spring): "Wenn nur ein Traum das Leben ist"
         6. "Der Abschied" (The Farewell): "Die Sonne scheidet hinter dem Gebirge"
2.13   *Symphony No.10 in F-sharp minor (c1910, unfin; compl Cooke 1960, r until 1976)* ....

3. OTHER ORCHESTRAL WORKS

3.1   "Flora" (Blumine) (c1888, orig 2nd movt of: Sym No.1 in D major, 'Titan,' discarded in final revision) ....
3.2   "Totenfeier," sym poem (c1888, orig vers of 2nd movt of: Sym No.2 in C minor, 'Resurrection') ....
3.3   "Scherzo," in C minor (ca1900, inc) ....
3.4   "Presto," in F major (ca1900) ....
3.5   *"Sinfonisches Präludium" (theorized to be an early work, but proved by R. Stephan not to be by Mahler)* ....

4. STRING QUARTETS

4.1   *String Quartet (ca1880, ?not composed/lost, cited Alma Mahler-Werfel)* ....

5. OTHER CHAMBER MUSIC

Piano Quintets:

5.1   *Piano Quintet in A minor (c1876, 1st movt awarded prize at Vienna Conservatory in 1876, lost)* ....
5.2   *Piano Quintet (Scherzo) (c1878, lost, cited Bauer-Lechner)* ....

Piano Quartets:

5.3   *Piano Quartet in A minor (c1876, frags):* ....
       . *"Nicht zu schnell," in A minor*
       . *"Scherzo," in G minor*
5.4   *Piano Quartet (?Quintet) (c1878, lost, cited Bauer-Lechner as sent to Russia for competition & lost)* ....

Vc & pf:

5.5   *"Nocturne" (c ?1876–8, lost, cited Bauer-Lechner)* ....

6. PIANO

6.1   *"Polka with Introductory Funeral March" (c1867, lost, cited Bauer-Lechner)* ....
6.2   *"Pieces for Piano" (c before 1875, lost/not written down, cited la Grange)* ....
6.3   *"Suite" (c ?1875–8, lost, cited Bauer-Lechner)* ....

7. CHORAL WORKS

7.1   "Das klagende Lied," cantata (c1880, r1888, 1892–3 & 1898–9, after Grimm; S, A, T, B, ch & orch): ....
       1. "Waldmärchen" (deleted from r vers of 1888)
       2. "Der Spielmann"
       3. "Hochzeitsstück"

8. SONGS (w/ pf/orch)

8.1   *"Die Türken haben schöne Tochter" (ca1867, Lessing, lost, cited Bauer-Lechner)* ....
8.2   *Song (c ?1875–8, lost, cited Karpath as written for a competition at the Conservatory in Vienna)* ....
8.3   "2 Lieder" (c ?1875–80, Heine, inc, cited Bauer-Lechner): 1. "Es fiel ein Reif in der Frühlingsnacht" ....
8.4   2. "Im wunderschönen Monat Mai"
8.5   "3 Songs" (c1880, Mahler; T & pf; projected set of 5): 1. "Im Lenz": "Sag' an, du Träumer am lichten Tag" .
8.6   2. "Winterlied": "Über Berg und Tal mit lautem Schall"
8.7   3. "Maitanz im Grünen": "Ringel, ringel Reih'n!" (early vers of Hans & Grethe in: Aus der Jugendzeit)
8.8   "Aus der Jugendzeit", Vol.I (c1880–3): 1. "Frühlingsmorgen": "Es klopft an die Scheiben" (Leander) ....
8.9   2. "Erinnerung": "Es wecket meine Liebe" (Leander)
8.10   3. "Hans und Grethe", r vers of: Maitanz im Grünen)
8.11   4. "Serenade aus 'Don Juan' ": "Ist's dein Wille, süsse Maid" (Molina transl Braunfels)
8.12   5. "Phantasie aus 'Don Juan' ": "Das Mägdlein trat aus dem Fischerhaus" (Molina transl Braunfels)
8.13   II (c1887–90, from Des Knaben Wunderhorn): 6. "Um schlimme Kinder artig zu machen": "Es kam
       ein Herr"
8.14   7. "Ich ging mit Lust durch einen grünen Wald"
8.15   8. "Aus! Aus!": "Heute marschieren wir!"
8.16   9. "Starke Einbildungskraft": "Hast gesagt, du willst mich nehmen"
8.17   III (c1887–90, from Des Knaben Wunderhorn): 10. "Zu Strassburg auf der Schanz"
8.18   11. "Ablösung im Sommer": "Kuckuck hat sich zu Tod gefallen"
8.19   12. "Scheiden und Meiden": "Es ritten drei Reiter zum Tor hinaus"
8.20   13. "Nicht wiedersehen!": "Nun ade mein allerherzliebster Schatz"
8.21   14. "Selbstgefühl": "Ich weiss nicht, wie mir's ist"
8.22   "Lieder eines fahrenden Gesellen," cycle (c1883–5, r1891, 6): 1. "Wenn mein Schatz Hochzeit macht" ......
8.23   2. "Ging heut' Morgen übers Feld"
8.24   3. "Ich hab' ein glühend' Messer, ein Messer in meiner Brust"
8.25   4. "Die zwei blauen Augen von meinem Schatz"
8.26   "Lieder aus Des Knaben Wunderhorn": 1. "Der Schildwache Nachtlied": "Ich kann" (c1892) ....
8.27   2. "Verlorne Müh' ": "Büble, wir wollen ausse gehe" (c1892)
8.28   3. "Trost im Unglück": "Wohlan, die Zeit ist kommen" (c1892)
8.29   4. "Wer hat dies Liedlein erdacht?": "Dort oben am Berg in dem hohen Haus" (c1892)
8.30   5. "Das irdische Leben": "Mutter, ach Mutter! es hungert mich," Phrygian (c1892–3)
8.31   6. "Des Antonius von Padua Fischpredigt": "Antonius zur Predigt die Kirche findt ledig!" (c1893)
8.32   7. "Rheinlegendchen": "Bald gras' ich am Neckar, bald gras' ich am Rhein" (c1893)
8.33   8. "Lied des Verfolgten im Turm": "Die Gedanken sind frei" (c1895)
8.34   9. "Wo die schönen Trompeten blasen": "Wer ist denn draussen und wer klopft an" (c1895)
8.35   10. "Lob des hohen Verstandes": "Einsmals in einem tiefen Tal" (c1896)
8.36   11. "Es sungen drei Engel": "Es sungen drei Engel einen süssen Gesang" (c1895; incl in: Sym No.3)
8.37   12. "Urlicht": "O Röschen rot" (c1892–4; incl in: Sym No.2 in C minor, 'Resurrection')

8.38	"Wir geniessen die himmlischen Freuden" (c1892, from Des Knaben Wunderhorn; S & orch; incl in: Sym No.4 in G major) ....
8.39	"O Mensch, gib acht!" (c1896, Nietzsche; A & orch; incl in: Sym No.3 in D minor) ....
8.40	"Revelge": "Des Morgens zwischen drein und vieren" (c1899, from Des Knaben Wunderhorn) ....
8.41	"Der Tambourgesell": "Ich armer Tambourgesell" (c1901, from Des Knaben Wunderhorn) ....
8.42	"Kindertotenlieder," cycle (p1905, Rückert): 1. "Nun will die Sonn' so hell aufgehn" (c1901) ....
8.43	2. "Nun seh' ich wohl, warum so dunkle Flammen" (c1901)
8.44	3. "Wenn dein Mütterlein tritt zur Tür herein" (c1901)
8.45	4. "Oft denk' ich, sie sind nur ausgegangen!" (c1904)
8.46	5. "In diesem Wetter, in diesem Braus" (c1904)
8.47	"5 Rückert-Lieder" (p1905, Rückert): 1. "Ich atmet' einen linden Duft" (c1901) ....
8.48	2. "Liebst du um Schönheit": "Liebst du um Schönheit, o nicht mich liebe!" (c1902) (also see Schumann Op.37/4)
8.49	3. "Blicke mir nicht in die Lieder!" (c1901)
8.50	4. "Ich bin der Welt abhanden gekommen" (c1901)
8.51	5. "Um Mitternacht": "Um Mitternacht hab' ich gewacht" (c1901)

9. ARRANGEMENTS OF WORKS OF OTHERS

Bach, J. S.:

9.1	"Suite from works by Bach" (arr1910; orch, hpd & org): No.1 "Ouverture," in B minor (from BWV1067) ....
9.2	No.2 "Rondeau und Badinerie," in B minor (from BWV1067)
9.3	No.3 "Air," in D major (from BWV1068)
9.4	No.4 "Gavottes I & II," in D major (from BWV1068)

Beethoven:

9.5	Symphonies (rescored): . Symphony No.5 in C minor, Op.67 ....
9.6	. Symphony No.9 in D minor, "Choral," Op.125 (rescored 1895)
9.7	Overtures (reorchd): . "Coriolan," Op.62 (rescored 1898) ....
9.8	. "Egmont," Op.84
9.9	. "Die Weihe des Hauses," Op.124 (rescored 1899)
9.10	. "Leonore No.2," Op.72a
9.11	String Quartet No.11 in F minor, "Serioso," Op.95 (rescored for strings 1899) ....

Bruckner:

9.12	Symphony No.5 in B-flat major, WAB105 (arr1878; pf duet) ....

Mozart:

9.13	"The Marriage of Figaro," opera, K492, recitatives for judgement scene (c1906, collab Kalbeck) ....

Schubert:

9.14	Symphony No.9 in C major, "Great," D944 (rescored) ....
9.15	String Quartet No.14 in D minor, "Death and the Maiden," D810 (arr1894; strings) ....

Schumann:

9.16	Symphonies (rescored): . Symphony No.1 in B-flat major, "Spring," Op.38 ....
9.17	. Symphony No.2 in C major, Op.61
9.18	. Symphony No.3 in E-flat major, "Rhenish," Op.97
9.19	. Symphony No.4 in D minor, Op.120
9.20	"Manfred" Overture, in E-flat major, Op.115 (rescored, perf1900) ....

Weber:

9.21	"Die drei Pintos," opera, Anh.5 (reconstruction p1888) ....
9.22	"Euryanthe," opera, J291 (new libretto 1903–4) ....
9.23	"Oberon, König der Elfen," opera, J306 (new libretto 1919) ....

* * * * *

1. STAGE WORKS

Operas:

3.100   "Paraboly" (The Parables) (c1957–8, after Saint-Exupéry & Neveux): No.1 "Andante pastorale" (The
         Parable of a Sculpture) H367
3.101   No.2 "Poco moderato" (The Parable of a Garden)
3.102   No.3 "Poco allegro—Moderato—Poco allegro" (The Parable of a Navire)
3.103   "Rytiny" (Estampes), 3 pieces (c1958): No.1 "Andante" H369
3.104   No.2 "Adagio—Allegretto—Tempo Imo"
3.105   No.3 "Poco allegro"

4. CONCERTOS, SOLO INSTR & ORCH

Pf & orch:

4.1   Piano Concerto No.1 (c1925; w/ chamber orch) H149
4.2   "Concertino" (Divertimento) (c1926, r1928; pf left hand & chamber orch) H173
4.3   "Inventions" (c1934): No.1 "Allegro moderato" H234
4.4   No.2 "Andante moderato"
4.5   No.3 "Poco allegro"
4.6   Piano Concerto No.2 (c1934, r1944) H237
4.7   "Concertino" (c1938) H269
4.8   "Sinfonietta giocosa" (c1940, r1941; w/ small orch) H282
4.9   Piano Concerto No.3 (c1948) H316
4.10   "Sinfonietta 'La jolla' " (c1950; w/ chamber orch) H328
4.11   Piano Concerto No.4, "Incantations" (c1955–6) H358
4.12   Piano Concerto No.5, "Fantasia concertante" (c1957) H366

Hpd & orch:

4.13   Harpsichord Concerto (c1935; hpd & chamber orch) H246

Vn & orch:

4.14   Nocturne No.1 in F-sharp minor (c1914–5) H91
4.15   Violin Concerto No.1 (c1933, r1955) H232bis
4.16   "Suite concertante" (c1939 & 1945; 2 vers): No.1 "Toccata" (Allegro un poco moderato) H276
4.17   No.2 "Aria" (Andantino)
4.18   No.3 "Scherzo" (Allegretto scherzando)
4.19   No.4 "Rondo" (Poco allegro)
4.20   Violin Concerto No.2 (c1943) H293

Va & orch:

4.21   "Rhapsody-Concerto" (c1952) H337

Vc & orch:

4.22   "Concertino" (c1924; vc, wind, pf & perc) H143
4.23   Cello Concerto No.1 (c1930, r1939 & 1955) H196
4.24   "Sonata da Camera" (c1940; vc & small orch) H283
4.25   Cello Concerto No.2 (c1944–5) H304

Other instr & orch:

4.26   "Candlemass" (Village Wake) (c1907; fl & strings) H2
4.27   Oboe Concerto (c1955; ob & small orch) H353

2 or more insts & orch:

4.28   "Concerto" (c1931; str qt & orch) H207
4.29   "Divertimento" (Serenade No.4) (c1932; vn, va & chamber orch) H215
4.30   "Concerto" (c1933; pf trio & strings) H231
4.31   "Concertino" (c1933; pf trio & strings) H232
4.32   "Concerto" (c1936; fl, vn & orch) H252
4.33   "Concerto Grosso" (c1937; 2pf & chamber orch) H263
4.34   "Duo concertant" (Double Violin Concerto No.1) (c1937; 2vn & orch) H264
4.35   Double Concerto (c1938; d strings, pf & timp) H271
4.36   "Concerto da camera" (c1941; vn, pf, perc & strings) H285
4.37   Double Piano Concerto (c1943) H292
4.38   "Sinfonia concertante" (No.2) (c1949; ob, bn, vn, vc & chamber orch) H322
4.39   Double Violin Concerto (No.2) (c1950) H329
4.40   "Concerto" (c1953; vn, pf & orch) H342

5. STRING QUARTETS

6. OTHER CHAMBER MUSIC

9 insts:

7 insts:

6 insts:

5 insts:

4 insts:

3 insts:

7. PIANO SONATAS

8. OTHER PIANO WORKS

8.165	No.3 "Andante"
8.166	No.4 "Allegro"
8.167	No.5 "Andante"
8.168	No.6 "Allegro"
8.169	"2 Dances from ballet Špaliček" (c1931–2): No.1 "Waltz. Allegro moderato" H214c
8.170	No.2 "Polka. Moderato"
8.171	"Esquisses de dances," 5 pieces (c1932): No.1 "Allegro moderato" H220
8.172	No.2 "Poco andantino. Allegretto"
8.173	No.3 "Allegro vivo"
8.174	No.4 "Tempo di valse"
8.175	No.5 "Allegro"
8.176	"Children's Pieces" (c1932): No.1 "Allegro" H221
8.177	No.2 "Moderato"
8.178	No.3 "Andante moderato"
8.179	No.4 "Little waltz"
8.180	Piano piece (c1932, pubd1932 in Album des auteurs modernes) H222
8.181	"Les ritournelles," 6 pieces (c1932): No.1 "Andante. Poco allegro" H227
8.182	No.2 "Andante moderato"
8.183	No.3 "Intermezzo I. Andantino"
8.184	No.4 "Andante. Poco allegro"
8.185	No.5 "Intermezzo II. Andante"
8.186	No.6 "Allegro vivo"
8.187	"Albumleaf" (c1935) H241
8.188	"Piece for Little Eva" (c1935) H242
8.189	Dumka No.1 (c1936, ded to Roudnická) H249
8.190	Dumka No.2 (c1936, ded to Kubínová) H250
8.191	*"Fourths and Octaves," small pieces (c1937, unpubd, autograph missing)* *H257*
8.192	"Le train hanté" (c1937) H258
8.193	"Window on to the Garden," 4 pieces (c1938): No.1 "Poco andante" H270
8.194	No.2 "Allegro moderato"
8.195	No.3 "Moderato"
8.196	No.4 "Allegretto"
8.197	*"Fairy-tales" (c1939, unpubd, autograph missing)* *H272*
8.198	"Fantaisie and Toccata" (c1940): No.1 "Fantaisie: Andante—Moderato—Poco allegro—Andante" H281
8.199	No.2 "Toccata. Allegro"
8.200	"Mazurka" (Hommage to Paderewski) (c1941) H284
8.201	Dumka No.3 (c1941, ded to Rybka) H285bis
8.202	"Etudes and Polkas," 16 pieces in 3 vols (c1945), I: No.1 "Etude. Allegro," in D major H308
8.203	No.2 "Polka. Poco allegro," in D major
8.204	No.3 "Etude. Vivo," in A major
8.205	No.4 "Polka. Poco allegro," in A major
8.206	No.5 "Pastorale. Moderato"
8.207	No.6 "Etude. Poco allegro"
8.208	II: No.7 "Etude. Allegro," in C major
8.209	No.8 "Polka. Poco allegro," in F major
8.210	No.9 "Danse-Etude. Allegretto"
8.211	No.10 "Polka. Allegro moderato," in E major
8.212	No.11 "Etude. Allegro," in F major
8.213	III: No.12 "Etude. Moderato," in A major
8.214	No.13 "Polka. Poco allegro," in A major
8.215	No.14 "Etude. Allegro," in F major
8.216	No.15 "Polka. Moderato," in A major
8.217	No.16 "Etude. Allegro," in F major
8.218	"The Fifth Day of the Fifth Moon" (c1948, inspired by Lin Yutang's book: The Gay Genius, page 148) H318
8.219	"Les bouquinistes du quai Malaquais" (c1948) H319
8.220	"Salute to the 'Sokol' Festival" (Ceremonial Fanfare) (ca1948) ....
8.221	"Morceau facile" (Bagatela) (c1949) H323
8.222	"Barcarolle" (c1949) H326
8.223	"Improvisation" (c1951) H333
8.224	"Adagio. Memories" (In memoriam Václav Kaprál and Vitulka) (c1957) H362

2 Pf:

8.225	"La fantaisie" (c1929) H180
8.226	"3 Czech Dances" (c1949): No.1 "Allegro" H324
8.227	No.2 "Andante moderato"
8.228	No.3 "Allegro (non troppo)"
8.229	"Impromptu" (c1956) H359

9. HARPSICHORD

9.1	"2 Pieces" (c1935): No.1 "Lente" H244
9.2	No.2 "Allegro con brio"
9.3	Harpsichord Sonata (c1958, 1 movt in 3 parts) H368

9.4 "2 Impromptus" (c1959): No.1 "Allegretto" H381
9.5   No.2 (w/ out tempo markings)

10. ORGAN

10.1 "Vigilie" (c1959; compl Janáček) H382

11. CHURCH MUSIC

11.1   "Offertorium" (c1912; S & org, unpubd, autograph missing) *H58*
11.2   "Ave Maria" (c1912; S & org, unpubd, autograph missing) *H59*

12. CHORAL WORKS

W/ orch:

12.1   "Česká rapsódie" (Czech Rhapsody), cantata (c1918, Psalm 23, Vrchlický's poem: Čechy &
       St. Wenceslas chorale; Bar, ch, orch & org) H118
12.2   "Kytice" (Bouquet of Flowers), cycle (c1937, trad; vv, ch, child ch & orch), I: 1. "Předehra" H260
12.3   2. "Sestra trávička"
12.4   3. "Selánka"
12.5   4. "Kravárky"
12.6   5. "Intráda"
12.7   6. "Milá nad rodinou"
12.8   II: 7. "Koleda"
12.9   8. "Člověk a smrt" "
12.10 "3 Fragments from opera Juliette" (c1939; vv, ch & orch): 1. "Scène des Souvenirs" H253a
12.11   2. "Scène de la forêt"
12.12   3. "Finale"
12.13 "Field Mass," cantata (c1939, Mucha, Psalms; Bar, m ch, winds, harm & perc, 1 movt in 5 sections): H279
              a. "Úvod" (orch)
              b. "Otčenáš" (ch)
              c. "Mezihra" (orch)
              d. "Bože náš" (ch)
              e. "Kyrie eleison" (Bar & ch)
12.14 ""Gilgameš" (The Epic of Gilgamesh), oratorio (c1954–5, Martinů after Thompson; vv, ch & orch): H351
              1. "Gilgameš"
              2. "Smrt" Enkiduova"
              3. "Zaklínání" (Invokace)

W/ other acc:

12.15 "3 Legends" (c1952, trad Czech; fem ch & vn; Eng transl Bush): 1. "The Birth of Our Lord" H339
12.16   2. "The Ascension"
12.17   3. "The Way to Paradise"
12.18 "Hymn to St. Jacob," cantata (c1954, Daněk; vv, ch, hn, strings & org) H347
12.19 "Primrose," 5 pieces (c1954, trad Moravian; fem ch, vn & pf; Eng transl Finlayson-Samsour; Ger transl
       Langer): 1. "Klobouk novej" H348
12.20   2. "Nade dvorem"
12.21   3. "Žaloba"
12.22   4. "Malované dřevo"
12.23   5. "Poledně"
12.24 "Mount of Three Lights," cantata (c1954, Morton, trad Czech, Bible, in Eng; vv, speaker, m ch & org) H349
12.25 "The Opening of the Wells," cantata (c1955, Bureš; S, A, Bar, speaker, fem ch, strings & pf) H354
12.26 "Legend of the Smoke from Potato Fires," cantata (c1956; S, A, Bar, ch & insts; Eng transl Urwin;
       Ger transl Honolka) H360
12.27 "Mikeš of the Mountains," chamber cantata (c1959, Bureš; S, T, ch, strings & pf; Ger transl Honolka) H375
12.28 "The Bird Feast" (c1959, Třeboň Manuscript; 2–3vv, child ch, va & tpt) H379
12.29 "The Prophecy of Isaiah," cantata (c1959, Bible, in Eng, Ger & Hebrew; vv, m ch, tpt, va, pf & timp) .. H383
12.30   "The Burden of Moab," cantata (c1959, Bible; m ch & pf, inc sketch, continuation of H383) *H383a*

Unacc ch:

12.31 "2 Male Choruses" (c1919, trad Lithuanian): 1. "Moonshine" H121
12.32   2. "The Dancer"
12.33 "Old Czech Nursery Rhymes," 6 pieces (c1930–1; fem ch), I: 1. "Konečná smrt" " H209
12.34   2. "Zavírání lesa"
12.35   3. "Hlásání pasaček" I
12.36   II: 4. "Mořena, Mořena"
12.37   5. "Hlásání pasaček" II
12.38   6. "Vynášení smrti"

12.39   "4 Songs of Mary" (c1934, trad Moravian): 1. "Zvěstování" H235
12.40   2. "Sen"
12.41   3. "Snídaní panny Marie"
12.42   4. "Obraz panny Marie"
12.43   "8 Czech Madrigals" (c1939, trad Moravian), I: 1. "Aj, stupaj můj koníčku na most" H278
12.44   2. "Půjdeme, chodnička nevíme"
12.45   3. "Daj mi Bože vědět"
12.46   4. "Hej! Máme na prodej"
12.47   II: 5. "Hlavěnka mne bolí"
12.48   6. "Chceme my se chceme, ale potajem ně"
12.49   7. "Jak je mně, tak je mně"
12.50   8. "Ešče jednů"
12.51   "5 Czech Madrigals" (c1948, trad Czech; Eng transl Bush): 1. "Vzkázání pro holuběnku" H321
12.52   2. "Bolavá hlavěnka"
12.53   3. "Husičky na vodě"
12.54   4. "Cestou k milé"
12.55   5. "Čarování a pomluvy"
12.56   "3 Part-Songs" (c1952, trad Czech; fem ch, unfin; Eng transl Bush): 1. "Chudá děvčica" H338
12.57   2. "Bolavé srdéčko"
12.58   3. "Hlásání pasaček"
12.59   "2 Choruses" (c after 1955, ?intended w/ org): 1. "Kyrie" ....
12.60   2. (w/ out title)
12.61   "The Brigand Songs" (c1957, trad Moravian & Slovak; m ch), I: 1. "Valaši" H361
12.62   2. "Hody"
12.63   3. "Stavajú"
12.64   4. "Jede Jánošek"
12.65   5. "V zeleném boři"
12.66   II: 1. "Čie sa to ovečky"
12.67   2. "Pijú chlapci"
12.68   3. "Na horách"
12.69   4. "Ej, Janík"
12.70   5. "U tej Bílej hory"
12.71   "Romance of the Dandelions," chamber cantata (c1957, Bureš; S & d ch; Ger transl Honolka) H364
12.72   "3 Songs for Children's Choir" (c1959, trad Czech; Ger transl Sieber): 1. "Velikonoční" H373
12.73   2. "Kováříček"
12.74   3. "Dětské hádanky"
12.75   "Madrigals" (c1959, trad Czech; ch): 1. "Tam s tej strany Dunaja" H380
12.76   2. "Ej, jeden hájek"
12.77   3. "Na tom světě nic stálého"
12.78   4. "A ty si myslíš"
12.79   "A Greeting" (c1959, trad Czech; child vv, inc) H384

13. MISC VOCAL (reciter & acc)

13.1   "3 Melodramas" (c1913, French & Czech texts): 1. "Večer" (Evening) (Samain; reciter & harp) H82
13.2   2. "Vážka" (The Dragonfly) (d'Orange; reciter, vn, harp & pf) H83
13.3   3. "Tanečnice z Jávy" (Danseuses from Java) (Symons; reciter, va, harp & pf) H84

14. VOICE & ORCHESTRA

14.1   "Niponari," 7 songs (c1912, Japanese; 1 fem v & small orch): 1. "Modrá hodina" H68
14.2   2. "Vzpomínka"
14.3   3. "Stopy ve sněhu" (2 vers, 2nd vers w/ title: Na hoře Miosyna)
14.4   4. "Stáří"
14.5   5. "Prosněný život"
14.6   6. "Pohled nazpět"
14.7   7. "U posvátného jezera" (2 vers)
14.8   "3 Songs" (c1913, unknown, French words): 1. "Le sapin de Noël" H88
14.9   2. "Le petit oiseau"
14.10   3. "Le soir"
14.11   "Magic Nights" (c1918, Chinese texts by Li Tai Po & Tschang Jo Su; S & orch): 1. "V cizině" H119
14.12   2. "Jarem nedotčená"
14.13   3. "Tajemná flétna"

15. SONGS (w/ pf)

15.1   "Before you know" (c1910, Červenka) H6
15.2   "In Nature" (c1910, Hálek, unpubd, autograph missing) H7
15.3   "Pastel" (c1910, Kaminský) H8
15.4   "The drowned maiden" (c1910, Sládek, unpubd, autograph missing) H9
15.5   "When we are old" (c1910, Klášterský) H10

15.80	*8. "Grabschrift" (from Des Knaben Wunderhorn)*	
15.81	*"3 Songs" (c1918, Háfiz, unpubd, autograph missing): 1. "Sweet death"*	*H115*
15.82	*2. "A long pilgrimage"*	
15.83	*3. "The recovery"*	
15.84	*A Song (I Wreathed Flowers) (ca1919, on Russian poetry, sketch)*	
15.85	"The New Slovak Songs" (c1920, trad Slovak): 1. "Máť moja, máť moja"	H126
15.86	2. "Ej horo, horo, zelenáhoro"	
15.87	3. "Hore hájom, dolu hájom"	
15.88	4. "Povedz, že mi povedz"	
15.89	5. "Čo robíš, Hanka?"	
15.90	6. "Od Oravy dášť ide"	
15.91	7. "Povedz mi, môj najmilejší"	
15.92	8. "Ještě jednu sestru mám"	
15.93	9. "Mala som já rukávce"	
15.94	10. "Vysoko zornička"	
15.95	11. "Ej poznať, je to poznať "	
15.96	12. "Oženil som sa ja"	
15.97	13. "Zjedzte ma, vľčky"	
15.98	14. "Stojí dievča u šentýsa"	
15.99	15. "Hore Hronom"	
15.100	16. "Trenčianskej kasárny"	
15.101	17. "Bože, bože, čo mám robiť "	
15.102	18. "Hanuljenka, Hanuljenka"	
15.103	19. "Čie sa to ovečky"	
15.104	20. "Chlapovi je dobre"	
15.105	21. "Never, že mu never"	
15.106	22. "Kopala studěnku"	
15.107	23. "Sedmdesiat sukieň mala"	
15.108	24. "Ej lúka, lúka"	
15.109	25. "Ej mal som frajerku"	
15.110	26. "Holubienka bielá"	
15.111	27. "Zpoza čiernej hory"	
15.112	28. "Povídajú ludé"	
15.113	29. "Budzil som sa"	
15.114	30. "Dievča z Bielej hory"	
15.115	"3 Songs from the cabaret 'Červená Sedma' " (c1921): 1. "Balada letní" (Herold)	H129
15.116	2. "Bar" (Dréman)	
15.117	3. "Havířská" (Gellner)	
15.118	*A Song (Nightingale mine ...) (c1922, Kolcov, on Russian poetry, sketch)*	
15.119	"The Months," 3 songs" (c1922, Toman): 1. "Leden" (also French transl Martinů)	H135
15.120	2. "Září" (also French transl Martinů)	
15.121	3. "Thou, who dwellest in heaven"	
15.122	*"Children's Songs," 2 vols (c1925, unpubd, autograph missing): I (ded to the Osusky Children)*	*H146*
15.123	*II (ded to the Children of Fernand Couget)*	
15.124	*"Chinese Songs" (c1925, unpubd, autograph missing)*	*H147*
15.125	"3 Children's Christmas Songs" (c1929, in French & Czech): 1. "La poule a couvé" (Aicard)	H184bis
15.126	2. "Le poulet" (Gramont)	
15.127	3. "Le petit chat" (Xaurov)	
15.128	"Vocalise-Étude" (c1930; 1 middle v & pf)	H188
15.129	"3 Songs" (c1930, Apollinaire, French text; Czech transl Nezval): 1. "White snow"	H197
15.130	2. "The farewell"	
15.131	3. "Comedians"	
15.132	*"3 Songs for Children" (c1931, unpubd, autograph missing): 1. "Tatínkova písnička"*	*H210*
15.133	*2. "Píseň Soničce"*	
15.134	*3. "Píseň Rozánkova"*	
15.135	"4 Songs and Nursery Rhymes for Children" (c1932)	H225
15.136	"2 Songs on Negro folk-poetry" (c1932): 1. "Berceuse"	H226
15.137	2. "Touha"	
15.138	"Automne malade" (c1932, Apollinaire)	
15.139	"Fleur de pêcher" (c1932, modified from orch cycle: Magic Nights, H119/2; French transl Pátková)	
15.140	"2 Ballades" (c1932, trad Czech): 1. "Putovali hudci"	H228
15.141	2. "Sirota"	
15.142	"Easter Song" (c1933, Erben from trad Czech)	H230
15.143	*"Let's Repose" (c1936, trad Slovak, unpubd, autograph missing)*	
15.144	"A Love Carol" (c1937, trad Moravian)	H259
15.145	"I know of a grove" (c1939, trad Moravian)	H273
15.146	*"Best Wishes for Mummy" (c1939, Mucha, ded to R. (Rudy) Kundera's mother, unpubd, autograph missing)*	
15.147	"New Špaliček," cycle (c1942, trad Moravian): 1. "Bohatá milá"	H288
15.148	2. "Opuštěný milý"	
15.149	3. "Touha"	
15.150	4. "Zvědavé dievča"	
15.151	5. "Veselé dievča"	
15.152	6. "Smutný milý"	
15.153	7. "Prosba"	
15.154	8. "Vysoká veža"	

15.155	"Songs on One Page," cycle (c1943, trad Moravian; Eng transl Thomsen): 1. "Dew" H294
15.156	2. "Unlocking with a word"
15.157	3. "Going to my love"
15.158	4. "The Path"
15.159	5. "At Mother's"
15.160	6. "The Virgin Mary's Dream"
15.161	7. "Rosemary"
15.162	"Songs on Two Pages," cycle (c1944, trad Moravian; Eng transl Thomsen): 1. "Děvče z Moravy" H302
15.163	2. "Súsedova stajňa"
15.164	3. "Náděje"
15.165	4. "Hlásný"
15.166	5. "Tajná láska"
15.167	6. "Boží muka"
15.168	7. "Zvolenovcí chlapci"
15.169	*"Ah, Let me Know" (w/ out date, sketch)* ....

* * * * *

H =   Harry Halbreich: "Bohuslav Martinů, Werkverzeichnis, Dokumentation und Biographie." Zurich,
Atlantis Verlag, 1968.

1. STAGE WORKS

Operas:

1.1	*"Les deux boursiers," 1 act operetta (ca1859, ?lost)*	....
1.2	*"Noureddin," opéra-comique (ca1865, sketches)*	....
1.3	*"Valéria," Italian opera (ca1865, sketches)*	....
1.4	*"Esmeralda" (ca1865, after Hugo, lost)*	
1.5	"La coupe du roi de Thulé," 3 acts (ca1866, Gallet & Blau, for Paris Opéra competition of 1867, not perf; Act II music used in Act III of opera: Le Roi de Lahore)	....
1.6	"Le florentin," opéra-comique (c1867–8, Vernoy & Saint-Georges, for Paris Opéra-Comique competition of 1867, not perf)	
1.7	"La grande-tante," 1 act opéra-comique (p1867, Adénis & Granvallet, pf-vocal score only, full score lost)	...
1.8	"Manfred" (ca1869, Ruelle after Byron, inc)	
1.9	"Méduse," 3 acts (c1870, Carré père, not perf)	....
1.10	"Don César de Bazan," 4 act opéra-comique (c1872, d'Ennery after Hugo; 2nd vers 1888)	....
1.11	*"Les templiers" (inc, destroyed)*	
1.12	*"L'adorable bel'-boul'," 1 act operetta (p1873, Gallet, lost)*	....
1.13	*"Bérangère et Anatole," 1 act sainète (p1876, Meilhac & Poirson, destroyed)*	....
1.14	"Le roi de Lahore," 5 acts (p1877, Gallet, 3 vers)	....
1.15	*"Robert de France," drama lyrique (ca1880, lost)*	
1.16	*"Les Girondins" (c1881, lost)*	....
1.17	"Hérodiade," 4 acts (p1881, Milliet, Grémont & Zamadini after Flaubert)	....
1.18	"Manon," 5 act opéra-comique (p1884, Meilhac & Gille)	....
1.19	"Le Cid," 4 acts (p1885, d'Ennery, Blau & Gallet after Corneille)	....
1.20	"Esclarmonde," 4 act opéra romanesque (p1889, Gallet & Gramont)	....
1.21	"Le mage," 5 acts (p1891, Richepin)	....
1.22	"Werther," 4 act drame lyrique (p1892, Blau, Milliet & Hartmann after Goethe)	....
1.23	"Thaïs," 3 act comédie lyrique (p1894, Gallet after A. France)	....
1.24	"Le portrait de Manon," 1 act opéra-comique (p1894, Boyer)	....
1.25	"La navarraise" (The Girl from Navarre), 2 act épisode lyrique (p1894, Claretie & Cain)	....
1.26	"Amadis," 4 act opéra légendaire (ca1895, Claretie)	....
1.27	"Sapho," 5 act pièce lyrique (p1897, Cain & Bernède after Daudet; 2 vers)	....
1.28	"Cendrillon" (Cinderella), 4 act opéra féerique (p1899, Cain after Perrault's La belle au bois dormant) (also see operas c by Holst, Rossini & ballet c by Prokofiev)	....
1.29	"Grisélidis," 3 act conte lyrique (p1901, Silvestre & Morand)	....
1.30	"Le jongleur de Notre-Dame" (Our Lady's Tumbler), 3 act miracle (p1902, Léna)	....
1.31	"Chérubin," 3 act comédie chantée (p1903, Croisset & Cain)	....
1.32	"Ariane," 5 acts (p1906, Mendès)	....
1.33	"Thérèse," 2 act drame musical (p1907, Claretie)	....
1.34	"Bacchus," 4 acts (p1909, Mendès)	....
1.35	"Don Quichotte," 5 act comédie héroïque (p1910, Cain after Le Lorrain)	....
1.36	"Roma," 5 act opéra tragique (p1912, Cain after Parodi: Rome vaincue)	....
1.37	"Panurge," 3 act farce (p1913, Boukay & Spitzmüller after Rabelais)	....
1.38	"Cléopâtre," 4 acts (p1914, Payen)	....
1.39	*"Montalte" (w/ out date, lost)*	....

Sacred & profane dramas:

1.40	"Les érinnyes," 2 act tragédie antique (p1873, Lisle)	....
1.41	"Marie-Magdeleine," 3 act drame sacré (p1873, r1904, Gallet)	....
1.42	"Ève," 3 act mystère (p1875, Gallet)	....
1.43	"Narcisse," idylle antique (p1878, Collin)	....
1.44	"La Vierge," 4 act légende sacrée (p1880, Grandmougin)	....
1.45	"Biblis," scène païenne (p1887, Boyer after Ovid's Metamorphoses)	....
1.46	"La terre promise," 3 part oratorio (p1900, Bible)	....

Ballets:

1.47	"Le carillon," 1 act légende mimée et dansée (p1892, Roddaz & van Dyck)	....
1.48	"Les rosati" (Divertissement des roses), 1 act (p1901, Mme Mariquita, pubd as Divertissement for orch)	....
1.49	"Le cigale," 2 act divertissement-ballet (p1904, Cain)	....
1.50	"Espada," 1 act ballet (p1908, Baron H. de Rothschild)	....

Incid music:

1.51	*"Un drame sous Philippe II" (p1875, Porto-Riche, lost except: Sarabande espagnnole for pf)*	....
1.52	"La vie de Bohème" (p1876, Barrière & Mürger after Mürger's novel)	....
1.53	"L'Hetman" (p1877, Déroulède)	....
1.54	"Notre-Dame de Paris" (c1879, Foucher after Hugo)	....
1.55	"Michel Strogoff" (p1880, d'Ennery & Verne)	....
1.56	"Nana-Sahib" (p1883, Richepin)	....
1.57	"Théodora" (p1884, Sardou)	....
1.58	"Le crocodile" (p1886, Sardou)	....
1.59	"Phèdre" (p1900, Racine)	....

1.60   "Le grillon du foyer" (p1904, Francmesnil after Dickens) ....
1.61   "Le manteau du roi" (p1907, Aicard) ....
1.62   "Perce-Neige et les sept gnômes" (p1909, Dortzal after Grimm brothers) ....
1.63   "Jérusalem" (p1914, Rivollet) ....

1a. SELECTIONS FROM STAGE WORKS (Nos. of sections in The Gramophone)

1a.17   "Hérodiade," opera: ....
       excerpts: 1. "Prélude"
       I: 2a. "Ah! Salomé! dans ce palais"
             2b. "Il est doux, il est bon"
             3a. "Venge-moi d'une suprême offense!"
             3b. "Hérod! Ne me refuse pas"
             4. "Calmez donc vos fureurs"
       II: 5a. "Ce breuvage pourrait me donner un tel rêve!"
             5b. "Vision fugitive"
       III: 6a. "Dors, ô cité perverse"
             6b. "Astres étincelants"
             6c. "Ah! Phanuel!"
             6d. "L'horizon devient menaçant"
             7a. "Je souffre!"
             7b. "Charme des jours passés"
             8a. "C'en est fait!"
             8b. "Demande au prisonnier"
             8c. "Que m'oses-tu dire?"
       IV: 9a. "Ne pouvant réprimer les élans de la foi"
             9b. "Adieu donc, vains objets"
             10. "Quand nos jours s'éteindront"
             11. "Ballet music"

1a.18   "Manon," opera: ....
       I: 1. "Prélude"
             2a. "Holà! Hé! Monsieur l'Hôtelier?"
             2b. "Hors d'oeuvre de choix"
             3a. "C'est très bien le diner!"
             3b. "Entendez-vous la cloche"
             3c. "C'est bon!"
             4. "Les voilà! les voilà!"
             5a. "Voyez cette jeune fille!"
             5b. "Je suis encore tout étourdie"
             6a. "Partez! On sonne!"
             6b. "Revenez, Guillot, revenez!"
             7a. "Il vous parlait, Manon?"
             7b. "Regardez-moi"
             7c. "Ne bronchez pas"
             8a. "Restons ici"
             8b. "Voyons, Manon!"
             9a. "J'ai marqué l'heure du départ"
             9b. "Et je sais votre nom"
             9c. "Non! Je ne veux pas croire"
             10a. "Par aventure"
             10b. "Nous vivrons à Paris"
             11. "Ce sont elles"
       II: 12a. "Introduction"
             12b. "J'écris à mon père"
             12c. "On l'appelle Manon"
             12d. "Tu le veux?"
             13a. "Enfin, les amoureux"
             13b. "Venir ici sous un déguisement?"
             14a. "Allons! Il le faut pour lui-même"
             14b. "Adieu, notre petite table"
             15a. "C'est vrai"
             15b. "Instant charmant"
             15c. "En ferment les yeux"
             15d. "C'est un rêve"
       III: 16a. "Entr'acte"
             16b. "Voyez mules à fleurettes!"
             17a. "A quoi bon l'économie"
             17b. "O Rosalinde"
             18. "Voici les élégantes!"
             19a. "Suis-je gentille ainsi?"
             19b. "Je marche sur tous les chemins"
             19c. "Obéissons quand leur voix appelle" (Gavotte)
             20a. "Voici les élégantes!"

                    20b. "Elle est charmante"
                    21a. "L'Opéra! voici l'Opéra!"
                    21b. "Ballet"
                    22. "Quelle éloquence!"
                    23a. "Les grands mots que voilà!"
                    23b. "Épouse quelque brave fille"
                    24a. "Je suis seul!"
                    24b. "Ah! fuyez, douce image"
                    25a. "Toi! Vous!"
                    25b. "N'est-ce plus ma main"
              IV: 26a. "Le jouer sans prudence"
                    26b. "J'enfourche aussi Pégase"
               V: 27a. "Manon! Pauvre Manon!"
                    27b. "Capitaine, ô gué"
                    28. "Ah! Des Grieux!"
                    29. "Oui, dans les bois ... Fabliau" (Alternative aria to replace Gavotte)

1a.19   "Le Cid," opera: ....
         excerpts: I: 1. "O noble lame éticelante"
         II (ballet): 2a. "Castillane"
                    2b. "Andalouse"
                    2c. "Aragonaise"
                    2d. "Aubade"
                    2e. "Catalane"
                    2f. "Madrilène"
                    2g. "Navarraise"
              III: 3a. "De cet affreux combat"
                    3b. "Pleurez, mes yeux"
                    4a. "Ah! tout est bien fini"
                    4b. "O souverain, ô juge, ô père"
              IV: 5. "Il a fait noblement"

1a.22   "Werther," opera: ....
              I: 1. "Prélude"
                    2. "Assez! Assez!"
                    3a. "Je ne sais si je veille"
                    3b. "O nature, pleine de grâce"
                    4. "Jésus vient de naître!"
                    5. "O spectacle idéal d'amour"
                    6. "Sophie! Albert!"
                    7a. "Elle m'aime"
                    7b. "Interlude" (Clair de lune)
                    7c. "Il faut nous séparer"
                    7d. "Si vous l'aviez connue!"
              II: 8a. "Prélude"
                    8b. "Vivat Bacchus!"
                    9. "Trois mois!"
                    10a. "Un autre est son époux!"
                    10b. "J'aurais sur ma poitrine"
                    11a. "Au bonheur!"
                    11b. "Je vous sais un coeur loyal et fort"
                    12a. "Frère, voyez le beau bouquet!"
                    12b. "Du gai soleil, plein de flamme"
                    12c. "Va porter ton bouquet"
                    13a. "Ah! qu'il est loin ce jour"
                    13b. "N'est-il donc pas d'autre femme"
                    14. "Lorsque l'enfant revient d'un voyage"
              III: 15a. "Werther! Qui m'aurait dit la place"
                    15b. "Des cris joyeux"
                    16. "Bonjour, grande soeur!"
                    17. "Ah! le rire est béni"
                    18a. "Va! Laisse couler"
                    18b. "Les larmes qu'on ne pleure pas"
                    19. "Ah! mon courage m'abandonne"
                    20. "Oui, c'est moi!"
                    21a. "Traduire"
                    21b. "Pourquoi me réveiller?"
                    22. "N'achevez pas!"
                    23. "Werther est de retour"
              IV: 24a. "Prélude" (Le nuit de Noël)
                    24b. "Werther!... Rien!... Dieu! Ah! du sang!"
                    25. "Noël! Noël!"
                    26. "Là-bas, au fond du cimetière"
                    27. "Finale"

1a.23   "Thaïs," opera: ....
    excerpts: I: 1a. "Hélas! enfant encore"
          1b. "Toi qui mis la pitié"
          2a. "Va mendiant!"
          2b. "Voilà donc la terrible cité"
       II: 3a. "Ah! je suis seule"
          3b. "Dis-moi que je suis belle"
          4a. "Étranger, te voila"
          4b. "Ah! pitié"
          5. "Méditation"
          6. "L'amour est une vertu rare"
       III: 7a. "L'ardent soleil"
          7b. "O messager de Dieu"
          7c. "Baigne d'eau"
          8. "Que te fait si sévère"
          9. "Te souvient-il"

1a.25   "La navarraise," opera: ....
    excerpts: 1. "Ouverture"
       I: 2. "L'ssaut a coûté cher"
          3. "Vierge très bonne, Marie"
          4. "Je ne pensais qu'à toi"
          5. "Araquil! mon père"
          6. "Deux mille duros!"
          7. "Étes-vous de la compagnie"
          8. "Général! Qu'est-ce encore?"
          9. "Grénelons les maisons"
          10. "Ô bienaimée, pourquoi n'es-tu pas la?"
          11. "Anita! La Navarraise?"
          12. "Á moi, á moi"
          13. "Interlude"
       II: 14. "Alerte! On attaque!"
          15. "Le bonheur! Araquil"
          16. "Blessé, mourant, j'espère"
          17. "Mon fils! Père!"

1a.30   "Le jongleur de Notre-Dame," opera: ....
    excerpts: 1. "Ouverture"
       I: 2. "Pour Notre-Dame des cieux"
          3. "Attention! avancez"
          4. "Pardonnez-moi, Sainte Vierge Marie"
          5. "C'est le Prieur! Fuyons!"
          6. "Il pleure"
          7a. "Dame des cieux"
          7b. "Liberté!"
          8. "Pour la Vierge d'abord"
          10. "Prélude"
       II: 11. "Ave coeleste lilium"
          12. "Mes frères, c'est très bien"
          13. "Mes frères, je connaise ma triste indignité"
          14. "Jongleur, piteux métier"
          15. "Seul, je n'offre rien à Marie"
          16. "La Vierge entend fort bien"
          17. "La sauge et en effet précieuse en cuisine"
          18. "Prélude"
       III: 19. "Un regard, le dernier"
          20. "Personne ... Allons, courage!"
          21. "Mais ce vacarme ... Belle Doètte"
          22. "Et maintenant voulez-vous des tours"
          23. "Arrière tous"
          24. "C'est le Prieur!"
          25. "Spectacle radieux"

1a.44   "La Vierge," légende sacrée: ....
    Scene I: 1. "Prélude"
          2. "Le sommeil n'a pas quitté notre maison"
          3. "Les Messager du Roi des Pois paraît"
          4. "Je viens te saleur"
       II: 5. "Buvons! ah! quel sumptueux festin"
          6. "Danse galileenne"
          7. "Miracle! O prodige! J'en frémis encore!"
          8a. "O mons fils! on t'acclame et la foule r'envire!"
          8b. "Gloire au Maître des cités!"
       III: 9. "Là-bas du côté du prétoire"

IV: 10. "Le dernier sommeil de la Vierge" (Last Sleep of the Virgin)
    11. "Dans nos choeurs quelle douleur profonde!"
    12. "Marie! Viens! éveille toi du grand sommeil"
    13. "Rêve infini! divine extase"
    14. "Magnificat anima mea Dominum ... Gloire à Dieu ... Consolez-vous"

2. SYMPHONIES

3. OTHER ORCHESTRAL WORKS

4. CONCERTOS, SOLO INSTR & ORCH

5. CHAMBER MUSIC

5.1	*String Quintet (c1864, mentioned in a letter to A. Thomas, ?lost)* ....
5.2	*Piano Trio No.1 (?not composed/?lost)* ....
5.3	*Piano Trio No.2 ('second trio' described in 2 letters of 1865, lost)* ....
5.4	"Deux pièces" (c before ?1866; vc & pf; see arr for pf duet as Nos.1 & 2 of: Trois pièces, Op.11): No.1 "Andante" ....
5.5	No.2 (w/ out title)
5.6	"Introduction et variations" (p 1872; fl, ob, cl, hn, bn, str qt & d bass) ....
5.7	"Les Grands Violons du Roy Louis XV" (p 1899) ....

6. PIANO

6.1	"Grande fantaisie de concert" (c1861, on Meyerbeer's opera: Dinorah ou Le pardon de Ploërmel) ....
6.2	"Dix pièces de genre" (p1867): No.1 "Nocturne" Op.10
6.3	No.2 "Marche"
6.4	No.3 "Barcarolle"
6.5	No.4 "Rigodon"
6.6	No.5 "Mélodie: Élégie des Érinnyes"
6.7	No.6 "Saltarello"
6.8	No.7 "Vieille chanson"
6.9	No.8 "Légende"
6.10	No.9 "Fughetta"
6.11	No.10 "Carillon"
6.12	"Le roman d'Arlequin" (p1871 w/ strophes by Silvestre & etchings by Heyer): No.1 "Ouverture—gigue" ......
6.13	No.2 "Entrée d'Arlequin"
6.14	No.3 "Rêverie de Colombine"
6.15	No.4 "Sérénade d'Arlequin à Colombine"
6.16	No.5 "Duo—finale"
6.17	"Ma cousine," pantomime (undated) ....
6.18	"Improvisations" (p1874): No.1 "Andantino" ....
6.19	No.2 "Allegretto"
6.20	No.3 "Triste et très lent"
6.21	No.4 "Allegretto scherzando"
6.22	No.5 "Andante cantabile espressivo"
6.23	No.6 "Allegro deciso"
6.24	No.7 "Allegretto"
6.25	"Toccata," in B-flat major (p1892) ....
6.26	"Deux impromptus" (p1896): No.1 "Eau dormante" ....
6.27	No.2 "Eau courante"
6.28	"Un momento musicale" (p1897) ....
6.29	"Valse folle" (p1898) ....
6.30	"Valse très lente" (p1901) ....
6.31	"Musique pour bercer les petits enfants" (p1902) ....
6.32	"Deux pièces" (p1907): No.1 "Papillons noir" ....
6.33	No.2 "Papillons blanc"

Pf duet:

6.34	"Trois pièces" (p1867): No.1 "Andante" (orig for vc & pf) Op.11
6.35	No.2 "Allegretto quasi allegro" (orig for vc & pf)
6.36	No.3 "Andante"
6.37	"Six danses" (c1869–70) ....
6.38	"Trois marches" (c1870) ....
6.39	"Deux berceuses" (c1870) ....
6.40	"Scènes de bal" (c ?1863; arr Bizet for pf) Op.17
6.41	"Année passée" (Suite de pièces en 4 livres) (p1897), I. "Après-midi d'été": No.1 "À l'ombre" ....
6.42	No.2 "Dans les blés"
6.43	No.3 "Grand soleil"
6.44	II. "Jours d'automne": No.1 "Feuilles jaunies"
6.45	No.2 "Deux novembre"
6.46	No.3 "Joyeuse chasse"
6.47	III. "Soirs d'hiver": No.1 "Noël"
6.48	No.2 "En songeant"
6.49	No.3 "On valsait"
6.50	IV. "Matins de printemps": No.1 "Les premiers nids"
6.51	No.2 "Lilas"
6.52	No.3 "Pâques—Sortie de grand' messe"

7. CHURCH MUSIC

7.1	"Messe de Requiem" (ca1863; 4vv, ch, vcs, d bass & org, part of envoi de Rome 1864) ....
7.2	"Ave Maris Stella," motet (c1880; 2vv & vc ad lib) ....

7.3   "Alleluja": "Sous un épais manteau de neige" (c1866, Chouquet; ch, won competition of the City of Paris) .
7.4   "Souvenez-vous, Vierge Marie: Prière de St. Bernard" (c1880, Boyer; S, ch & orch, = 20 Mélodies Vol.II/12)
7.5   "Pie Jésu" (p1893; 1v & vc ad lib; also for 1v & org 1884) ....
7.6   "O Salutaris" (p1894; S, ch, harp & org) ....
7.7   "Panis angelicus" (p1910; 3vv/1v, ch & org) ....

8. SECULAR CHORAL

8.1   *"Louise de Mézières," cantata (c1862, Monnais, for Prix de Rome—honorable mention, ?lost)* ....
8.2   "David Rizzio," cantata (c1863, Chouquet, won Grand Prix de Rome; also see song: Ballade de D. Rizzio)
8.3   "Prométhée," cantata (c1867, not perf) ....
8.4   "Deux fantaisies" (c1864, Chouquet; ch & orch): 1. "Noces flamandes" ....
8.5   2. "Le retour de la caravane"
8.6   *"Paix et liberté," cantata (p1867, destroyed in the fire of 1887)* ....
8.7   "Cantate en l'honneur du Bienheureux Jean-Gabriel Perboyre" (c ?1879; B, m ch & org ad lib) ....
8.8   "La fédérale" (Marche de la Fédération des sociétés musicales de France): "Au nom de la patrie et de la
             liberté" (c1890, Boyer; unison ch) ....
8.9   "Épithalame": "Calliope blanche et seulette," duet & unison chorus (p1891, Silvestre; w/ hpd) ....
8.10   "Les bluets" (p1899, Chaffotte; vv, fem ch & pf duet) ....
8.11   "À la jeunesse" (p1904, Combarieu; fem ch) ....
8.12   *"La Nef triomphale" (p1910, Aicard; ch & orch, ?lost)* ....
8.13   "Suite parnassienne" (p1913, Léna; speaker, d ch & orch): 1. "Uranie (l'Astronomie), Rêverie" ....
8.14   2. "Clio (L'Histoire), Visions antiques"
8.15   3. "Euterpe (la Musique), Double choeur"
8.16   "Suite théâtrale" (p1913, Léna; speaker, 1v & orch): 1. "La tragédie" ....
8.17   2. "La comédie"
8.18   3. "La danse"

9. PART-SONGS (4-part m ch)

9.1   "1812": "Salut, Moscau! Salut ville sainte!" (c1860) ....
9.2   "La caravane perdue," scène chorale (c ?1867) ....
9.3   "Le moulin": "Lorsque notre moulin tourne plein" (p1868, Chouquet) ....
9.4   "Villanelle" (c ?1872, Ruelle) ....
9.5   "Moines et Forbans": "La nuit va couvrir de son voile" (c1877, Chouquet) ....
9.6   "Le sylphe" (c1879, Bernier) ....
9.7   "Amour" (c1880, Milliet) ....
9.8   "Alerte" (ca1880–6, Massiat) ....
9.9   "Donnons" (c ?1886, Boyer) ....
9.10   "Chant de concorde" (c ?1893, Salmona) ....
9.11   "Mort à Néron!" (p1913, Galerne) ....

10. VOICE & ORCHESTRA

10.1   "Apollon aux Muses" (Apollo's Invocation), ode (c1884–5; T & orch, Collin, used for mystic scene of Act III
             in opera: Le Mage) ....

11. VOCAL DUETS, TRIOS & QUARTETS

11.1   "3 Songs" (c1868, Distel; 2–3 fem vv): 1. "Marine": "Viens, la voile mutine avec le vent," duettino ....
11.2   2. "Joie": "Un oiselet sautille et chante," duet (2S)
11.3   3. "Matinée d'été": "Le beau matin vient de luire," trio
11.4   "Le soir," duet (c1870, Baillet; 2 fem vv) ....
11.5   "Au large," duet (c1871, Seiffert; mS, Bar & pf) ....
11.6   "Dialogue nocturne," duet (c1871, Silvestre; S, T & pf) ....
11.7   "Rêvons, c'est l'heure," duet (c1871, Verlaine; S, T & pf) ....
11.8   "Salut, printemps," duet (c1872, Baillet; 2 equal vv) ....
11.9   "Horace et Lydie," duet (c1886, Musset after Horace; S, Bar & pf; = Mélodies, Vol.IV/19) ....
11.10   "Lui et elle," duet (p1891, Maquet; 2vv & pf) ....
11.11   "Aux étoiles," duet (p1891, Maquet; 2 fem vv/fem ch) ....
11.12   "Les fleurs," duet (p1894, Normand; S, Bar & pf; orchd; = Mélodies, Vol.IV/20) ....
11.13   "Noël," scène chorale (p1895; 1v, 2-part fem ch & pf) ....
11.14   "La chevrière," petit conte rustique (p1895, Noël; 2 fem vv & pf; also vers w/ orch 1901) ....
11.15   "Chansons des bois d'Amaranthe" (c1900, Legrand after Redwitz; 4vv & pf): 1. "O bon printemps," trio.....
11.16   2. "Oiseau de bois," duet
11.17   3. "Chères fleurs," quartet
11.18   4. "O ruisseau," trio
11.19   5. "Chantez!," quartet
11.20   "Poème des fleurs" (p1908, Allievo transl Gaspuy; 2S, A & pf): 1. "Prélude" (2S, A) ....
11.21   2. "L'Hymne des fleurs" (A)
11.22   3. "La danse des rameaux" (2S)

11.23	4. "Chanson de mai" (chorus of 3 fem vv)
11.24	"Le temps et l'amour," duet (p1907, Ludana; T, Bar & pf) ....
11.25	"L'heure solitaire," duet (p1908, Ader; S, A & pf) ....
11.26	"L'immortalité": "Pour le juste, la vie n'est point ici-bas," canon (p1909, Combarieu; 2vv)......
11.27	"La gavotte de Puyjoli": "La marquise a dit: 'Mon bon Puyjoli,' " gavotte chantée et dansée (c1909, Noël; S & Bar; = Mélodies, Vol.VII/10)
11.28	"La chanson du ruisseau" (p1912, Lugnier, vv & 2-part fem ch) ....
11.29	"La vision de Loti," poème mélodique (p1912, Noël; S, A, T & Bar).................................

12. SONGS (w/ pf)

c1867–9:

12.1	"Ballade de David Rizzio": "Le pâtre, à l'écho des montagnes" (Chouquet, extract from cantata) ....
12.2	"L'improvisatore: rimembranza del Trastevere" (Zaffira; also see: Mélodies, Vol.I/20) ....
12.3	"Nouvelle chanson sur un vieil air" (Hugo) ....
12.4	"Souvenir de Venise" (Musset; arr for 2vv & pf as: À la Zuecca, chanson vénitienne; = Vol.I/16) ....
12.5	"Je crains des baisers, ô vierge charmante" (Chouquet after Shelley; = 1. of: Chants intimes; = Vol.II/15) ..
12.6	"Poème d'avril" (Silvestre): 1. "Prélude": "Une rose frileuse" (recitation)................... Op.14
12.7	2. "Sonnet matinal": "Les étoiles effarouchées" (= Mélodies, Vol.III/20)
12.8	3. "Voici que les grands lys"
12.9	4. "Riez-vous?" (recitation)
12.10	5. "Vous aimerez demain": "Le doux printemps a bu" (= Mélodies, Vol.I/5)
12.11	6. "Que l'heure est donc brève" (= Mélodies, Vol.II/11)
12.12	7. "Sur la source elle se pencha"
12.13	8. "Complainte": "Nous nous sommes aimés trois jours"
12.14	"Poème du souvenir" (Silvestre): 1. "À la trépassée": "Lève-toi, chère ensevelie!" (= Mélodies, Vol.I/8) ....
12.15	2. "L'air du soir emportait"
12.16	3. "Un souffle de parfums"
12.17	4. "Dans l'air plein de fils de soie"
12.18	5. "Pour qu'à l'espérance"
12.19	6. "Epitaphe": "Souvenir éternel"
12.20	"Quatre mélodies": 1. "L'esclave": "Captive et peut-être oubliée" (Gautier) Op.12
12.21	2. "Sérénade aux mariés": "Voici l'heure du mystère" (Ruelle)
12.22	3. "La vie d'une rose": "Par un beau matin" (Ruelle)
12.23	4. "Le portrait d'un enfant": "Quand je vois tant de couleurs" (Ronsard)
12.24	"Sous les branches": "En avril sous les branches" (Silvestre; = Mélodies, Vol.I/10) ....
12.25	"Trois mélodies" (Distel; 2–3vv): 1. "Bonne nuit": "La terre dort au ciel pur" Op.2
12.26	2. "Les bois des pins, souvenir de Douarnenez": "L'ombre descend de leurs rameaux"
12.27	3. "Le verger, ancienne chansonnette": "Oh! combien j'aime le verger"
12.28	"Chants intimes" (Chouquet): 1. "Déclaration": "Je crains tes baisers" (after Shelley; = Mélodies, Vol.II/15)
12.29	2. "À Mignonne": "Pour qui sera, Mignonne" (= Mélodies, Vol.II/18)
12.30	3. "Berceuse": "Enfant rose, fleur éclose" (= Mélodies, Vol.III/11)
12.31	"Sérénade de Zanetto" (Sérénade du Passant): "Mignonne, voici l'avril" (text from Coppée's comedy: Le passant; = Mélodies, Vol.I/9) ....
12.32	"Sonnet": "Les grands bois s'éveillaient" (Pradel; = Mélodies, Vol.II/5) ....

c1871–5:

12.33	"Poème pastoral" (F. & A. Silvestre): 1. "Pastorale": "Voici venir le doux printemps" (ch) ....
12.34	2. "Musette": "L'autre jour sous l'ombrage" (orchd; = Mélodies, Vol.III/6)
12.35	3. "Aurore": "Cocorico, le coq chante" (orchd)
12.36	4. "Paysage": "Arbre charmant qui me rapelle"
12.37	5. "Crépuscule": "Comme un rideau sous le blancheur" (= Mélodies, Vol.I/15)
12.38	6. "Adieux à la prairie": "Adieu! adieu! bergère chérie" (1v & ch; orchd)
12.39	"Nuit d'Espagne" (L'heure d'amour / Guitare): "L'air est embaumé" (Gallet; = Mélodies, Vol.I/6) ....

"Mélodies," Vol.I (p ca1875):

12.40	1. "Elégie": "O doux printemps d'autrefois" (Gallet) ....
12.41	2. "À Colombine" (Sérénade d'Arlequin): "Colombine charmante" (Gallet) ....
12.42	3. "Les femmes de Magdala": "Le soleil effleure la plaine" (Gallet) ....
12.43	4. "Stances de Gilbert": "Au banquet de la vie, infortuné" (Gilbert) ....
12.44	5. "Vous aimerez demain": "Le doux printemps a bu" (Silvestre) ....
12.45	6. "Nuit d'Espagne": "L'air est embaumé" (Gallet) ....
12.46	7. "Chant provençal": "Mireille ne sais pas encore" (Carré; orchd)
12.47	8. "À la trépassée": "Lève-toi, chère ensevelie!" (Silvestre)
12.48	9. "Sérénade du passant": "Mignonne, voici l'avril" (Coppée; orchd) ....
12.49	10. "Sous les branches": "En avril sous les branches" (Silvestre) ....
12.50	11. "Dors, ami, dors et que les songes" (Chantepie)
12.51	12. "Il pleuvait": "Il pleuvait, l'épaisseur des mousses," impromptu-mélodie (Silvestre) ....
12.52	13. "Chanson de Capri": "Connaissez-vous qui m'a charmé" (Gallet) ....
12.53	14. "Un adieu": "Sur ta bouche avec le désir" (Silvestre) ....
12.54	15. "Crépuscule": "Comme un rideau sous le blancheur" (Silvestre) ....
12.55	16. "Souvenir de Venise": "À Saint Blaise, à la Zuecca" (Musset) ....
12.56	17. "Sonnet païen": "Rosa, Rosa, l'air est plus doux" (Silvestre) ....

12.57	18. "Sérénade d'automne": "Non! tu n'as pas fini d'aimer" (Blanchecotte) ....
12.58	19. "Madrigal": "Le soir frissonne au coeur des roses" (Silvestre) ....
12.59	20. "L'improvisateur": "Vois-tu là-bas sur le chemin" (Zaffira transl Bussine jeune) ....

c1876–81

12.60	"Poème d'octobre" (Collin): . "Prélude": "Qu'il est doux d'éveiller" ....
12.61	1. "Profitons bien des jours d'automne" (= Mélodies, Vol.III/13)
12.62	2. "Hélas! les marronniers"
12.63	3. "Qu'importe que l'hiver éteigne les clartés"
12.64	4. "Belles frileuses qui sont nées" (= Mélodies, Vol.II/16)
12.65	5. "Pareils à des oiseaux que leur aile meurtrie"
12.66	"Poème d'amour" (Robiquet): 1. "Je me suis plaint aux tourterelles" ....
12.67	2. "La nuit, sans doute, était trop belle"
12.68	3. "Ouvre tes yeux bleus" (= Mélodies, Vol.III/12)
12.69	4. "Puisqu'elle a pris ma vie" (= Mélodies, Vol.II/19)
12.70	5. "Pourquoi pleures-tu?"
12.71	6. "Oh! ne finis jamais, nuit clémente," duet
12.72	"Sérénade de Molière" (Musique du temps): "C'est un amant, ouvrez la porte" (= Mélodies, Vol.II/2) ....
12.73	"Anniversaire" (Devant la maison de Th. Gautier, Octobre, 1880): "Le poète dort: l'oiseau chante" (Silvestre) (Gautier died on October 23rd, 1872 at 32 Rue de Longchamps in Paris; = Mélodies, Vol.II/6) ....
12.74	"Come into the garden, Maud" (Tennyson) (also see Delius RTiii/3) ....
12.75	"Les enfants": "On ne devrait faire aux enfants" (Boyer; orchd; = Mélodies, Vol.III/1) ....

"Mélodies," Vol.II (p ca1881):

12.76	1. "Si tu veux, Mignonne" (Boyer; orchd) ....
12.77	2. "Sérénade de Molière": "C'est un amant, ouvrez la porte" ....
12.78	3. "Les oiselets": "Sous le brouillard léger que soulève l'aurore" (Normand) ....
12.79	4. "Loin de moi ta lèvre qui ment" (Aicard) ....
12.80	5. "Sonnet": "Les grands bois s'éveillaient" (Pradel) ....
12.81	6. "Anniversaire": "Le poète dort: l'oiseau chante" (Silvestre) ....
12.82	7. "Aubade": "Le jour parait à l'horizon" (Prévost) ....
12.83	8. "Le sentier perdu": "J'ai voulu le revoir ce sentier sous les bois," idylle (Choudens) ....
12.84	9. "Las alcyons": "Vos destins sont pour l'homme un étrange mystère" (Autran) ....
12.85	10. "Narcisse à la fontaine": "Enfin, elles s'en vont" (Collin) ....
12.86	11. "Que l'heure est donc brève" (Silvestre) ....
12.87	12. "Souvenez-vous, Vierge Marie" (Boyer) ....
12.88	13. "Souhait": "Si vous étiez fleur, ô ma bien aimée" (Normand) ....
12.89	14. "Néére": "Au détour du chemin, ma Néére fidèle" (Carré, from tragédie antique: Les Érinnyes) ....
12.90	15. "Déclaration": "Je crains tes baisers, ô vierge charmante" (Chouquet after Shelley) ....
12.91	16. "Roses d'octobre": "Belles frileuses qui sont nées" (Collin) ....
12.92	17. "Le sais-tu?": "N'as-tu pas vu l'hirondelle?" (Bordèse) ....
12.93	18. "À Mignonne": "Pour qui sera, Mignonne" (Chouquet) ....
12.94	19. "Puisqu'elle a pris ma vie" (Robiquet) ....
12.95	20. "La veillée du petit Jésus": "Il est minuit, l'étable est sombre" ....

c1882–91:

12.96	"Poème d'hiver" (Silvestre): 1. "C'est au temps de la chrysanthème" ....
12.97	2. "Mon coeur est plein de toi"
12.98	3. "Noël! en voyant dans ses langes"
12.99	4. "Tu l'as bien dit: je ne sais pas t'aimer"
12.100	5. "Mon coeur l'a bien mérité"
12.101	"Où qui s'envole" (Bourguignat) ....
12.102	"Pensée d'automne": "L'an fuit vers son déclin" (Silvestre; orchd; = Mélodies, Vol.III/17) ....
12.103	"Fleurs cueilles": "Vous avez pris un jour une fleur, ô ma belle" (Bricourt) ....
12.104	"Enchantement": "Comme un rayon qui luit" (Ruelle, on air from opera: Hérodiade) ....
12.105	"Rien n'est que de France": "Où sont, sous les matins en pleurs" (Silvestre; w/ harp/hpd) ....
12.106	"L'âme des fleurs": "Gardez les fleurs que je vous ai données" (Delair) ....
12.107	"Les mères": "Celle qui devient mère, a comme une auréole" (Boyer; 2 vers) ....

"Mélodies," Vol.III (p1891):

12.108	1. "Les enfants": "On ne devrait faire aux enfants" (Boyer) ....
12.109	2. "Enchantement" (Ruelle) ....
12.110	3. "Septembre": "Que les premiers jours de Septembre" (Vacaresco) ....
12.111	4. "Dans le sentier parmi les roses" (Bertheroy) ....
12.112	5. "Guitare": "Comment, disaient-ils, avec nos nacelles" (Hugo) ....
12.113	6. "Musette": "L'autre jour, sous l'ombrage" (Florian) ....
12.114	7. "Printemps dernier" (Gille) ....
12.115	8. "Marquise": "Vous en souvenez-vous, Marquise?," menuet pour chant (Silvestre) ....
12.116	9. "Les belles de nuit": "Joyeux et clair, le soleil luit" (Maquet) ....
12.117	10. "Je cours après le bonheur" (Maupassant) ....
12.118	11. "Berceuse": "Enfant rose, fleur éclose" (Chouquet) ....
12.119	12. "Ouvre tes yeux bleus" (Robiquet) ....
12.120	13. "Automne": "Profitons bien des jours d'automne" (Collin) ....
12.121	14. "Le poète et le fantôme": "Qui donc es-tu, forme légère?" (unknown; orchd) ....

12.122   15. "Beaux yeux que j'aime": "Il est des étoiles aux cieux" (Maquet) ....
12.123   16. "Noël païen": "Noël! Noël! sous le ciel étonné" (Silvestre) ....
12.124   17. "Pensée d'automne": "L'an fuit vers son déclin" (Silvestre) ....
12.125   18. "Royauté": "Le poète est roi" (Boyer) ....
12.126   19. "Quend on aime": "Quand on aime, on est tout léger," sérénade (Manuel) ....
12.127   20. "Sonnet matinal": "Les étoiles effarouchées" (Silvestre) ....

c1892–96:

12.128   "Mienne!": "De ce soir, je serai joyeux" (Laroche) ....
12.129   "Soir de printemps: déclamatorium" (Martin) ....
12.130   "Tristesse": "Marcher dans un sentier de pierres et de roses" (Carrier) ....
12.131   "Poème d'un soir" (Vanor): 1. "Antienne": "Tes yeux aux lueurs fières" ....
12.132   2. "Fleuramye": "J'ai bu tout le printemps sur la fleur de ton rire"
12.133   3. "Defuncta nascuntur": "Les roses se sont fermées"

"Mélodies," Vol.IV (p1896):

12.134   1. "L'âme des oiseaux": "Le printemps a jeté sa lyre" (Vacaresco) ....
12.135   2. "Pensée de printemps": "C'est l'espoir des beaux jours" (Silvestre; orchd) ....
12.136   3. "Je t'aime": "J'ai cherché dans mon coeur" (Bozzani; orchd) ....
12.137   4. "Chanson andalouse": "Pourquoi chanter l'amoureuse ivresse?" (Ruelle, on air from opera: Cid) ....
12.138   5. "Ave Maria": "Ave Maria, gratia plena" (on Méditation, from opera: Thaïs) ....
12.139   6. "Hymne d'amour": "Comme un lierre grimpant s'enlace" (Desachy; orchd) ....
12.140   7. "Devant l'infini": "Les feuilles dans les airs tourbillonnent" (Troillet) ....
12.141   8. "Ne donne pas ton coeur aux roses du chemin" (Mariéton) ....
12.142   9. "Plus vite": "Lorsque le vent du soir l'agite" (Vacaresco) ....
12.143   10. "Chant de guerre cosaque": "Vierge, tes cheveux noirs dépassent ta ceinture" (Vacaresco) ....
12.144   11. "Sévillana": "À Séville, belles Señoras" (on Entr'acte from opera: Don César de Bazan) ....
12.145   12. "Fourvières": "Dans la brume rêveuse" (Léna) ....
12.146   13. "L'éventail": "Aimable bijou de famille, éventail léger," vieille chanson française (Morel-Retz) ....
12.147   14. "Séparation": "Puisque tu ne veux pas m'attendre" (Mariéton) ....
12.148   15. "Elle s'en est allée": "Là-bas, sous d'autres cieux" (Solvay) ....
12.149   16. "Larmes maternelles": "La guerre a fait une voctime" (Delines after Necrasov; orchd) ....
12.150   17. "Jour de noces": "Il fait beau, le ciel nous protège" (Bordèse) ....
12.151   18. "Départ": "Puisque pour moi le temps a sonné" (Guérin-Catelain; orchd) ....
12.152   19. "Horace et Lydie": "Du temps où tu m'aimais, Lydie," duet (Musset) ....
12.153   20. "Les fleurs": "Jetant leur fantaisie exquise de couleurs," duet (Normand) ....

c1897–1900:

12.154   "Souvenance": "J'ai vu tous les yeux qu'on aime en ce monde" (Mariéton) ....
12.155   "Éternité": "L'éternité! je l'ai comprise" (Girard) ....
12.156   "Passionnément": "Tout recevoir de toi me charme" (Fuster) ....

"Mélodies," Vol.V (p1900):

12.157   1. "Chanson pour bercer la misère humaine": "Le petit Jésus, en habits de neige" (Boyer) ....
12.158   2. "Amoureuse": "Tu voudrais lire dans mon âme" (Morel-Retz) ....
12.159   3. "Première danse": "Des bons vieux airs connus" (Normand; orchd) ....
12.160   4. "Regard d'enfant": "Petit enfant, fragile et beau" (Pélissier) ....
12.161   5. "Petite Mireille": "Lorsque vous dormez" (Beissier) ....
12.162   6. "Pour Antoinette": "Quand je m'en vais par les sentiers" (Chabaleyret) ....
12.163   7. "Les mains": "Lorsque je regarde mes mains" (Bazan) ....
12.164   8. "Ce sont les petits que je veux chanter" (Grieumard) ....
12.165   9. "Les âmes": "Dites-moi ce que sont les âmes" (Demouth) ....
12.166   10. "La dernière chanson": "Si désormais vivre ensemble" (Lefèbvre) ....
12.167   11. "Premiers fils d'argent": "Le soir, quand pour dormir" (Valandré) ....
12.168   12. "Coupe d'ivresse": "Jusqu'à ta bouche, j'ai levé la coupe" (Simoni) ....
12.169   13. "Vieilles lettres": "Quand chauffant nos pieds aux tisons" (Normand) ....
12.170   14. "Vous qui passez": "O vous qui passez, solitaire" (Chabaleyret) ....
12.171   15. "Amours bénis": "Une aube fraîche et printanière" (Alexandre) ....
12.172   16. "Pitchounette": "Pitchounette, entends-tu pas," farandole pour chant (Normand; orchd) ....
12.173   17. "À deux pleurer": "Comme vous dormiez" (Croze) ....
12.174   18. "Chanson pour elle": "Pour toi j'écris cette chanson" (Maigrot) ....
12.175   19. "Le nid": "Si j'étais le bon Dieu" (Demouth) ....
12.176   20. "Avril est là, chantant" (Ferrant) ....

c1901–3:

12.177   "On dit": "On dit beaucoup de choses" (Roux; see arr for small orch as: Simple phrase) ....
12.178   "Quelques chansons mauves" (Lebey): 1. "En même temps que ton amour" ....
12.179   2. "Quand nous nous sommes vus pour la première fois"
12.180   3. "Jamais un tel bonheur"
12.181   "Trois poèmes chastes": 1. "Le pauv' petit": "Il était un petit enfant," légende (Boyer) ....
12.182   2. "Vers Béthléem": "Ils cheminent depuis longtemps" (Le Moyne)
12.183   3. "La légende du baiser": "Un jour de fête au Paradis" (Villeurs)

"Mélodies," Vol.VI (p1903):

12.184	1. "Je m'en suis allé vers l'amour": "Pleins d'un concert de fraîches voix" (Maurer)...........................
12.185	2. "Ce que disent les cloches": "Les cloches tintent dans l'air triste" (Vingtrie) ....
12.186	3. "Poésie de Mytis": "Losque nous serons seuls" ....
12.187	4. "Sainte Thérèse prie": "Je le possède" (Sylvestre; orchd) ....
12.188	5. "L'heure volée": "Sonneur qui sonnes l'heure et l'heure" (Mendès) ....
12.189	6. "Extase printanière": "O je t'implore à genoux" (Alexandre) ....
12.190	7. "L'heureuse souffrance": "Coeur, va vite, pauvre coeur" (Dubor) ....
12.191	8. "Voix de femmes": "Voix des mamans, voix câlineuses" (Pierre d'Amor) ....
12.192	9. "Mousmé": "Au jardin de ma fantaisie, fleur du Japon, Mousmé jolie" (Alexandre) ....
12.193	10. "Avec toi!": "Avec toi courir dans les plaines" (Gruaz) ....
12.194	11. "Les amoureuses sont des folles" (Duc de Tarente) ....
12.195	12. "Ave Margarita, prière d'amour": "Je te salue, ô Marguerite" (Noël) ....
12.196	13. "On dit": "On dit beaucoup de choses" (Roux) ....
12.197	14. "Le printemps visite la terre" (Chaffotte) ....
12.198	15. "Rondel de la belle au bois": "Ouvrez vos tendres yeux" (Gruaz) ....
12.199	16. "Sur une poésie de Van Hasselt, L'attente": "L'azur si pur des cieux joyeux" ....
12.200	17. "Soeur d'élection": "O ma soeur d'idéal" (Troillet; see arr for small orch as: Cantique) ....
12.201	18. "Mon page": "J'ai pour page un bel escholier" (Théus) ....
12.202	19. "Amoureux appel": "Viens, ô le désiré, viens chanter avec moi" (Dubor) ....
12.203	20. "La rivière": "Ah! la rivière chantait ainsi" (Bruno; orchd) ....

c1904–12:

12.204	"Avant la bataille (de Reichshofen)" (Villeurs) ....
12.205	"Dors, Magda, si blanche et si rose" (Silvestre) ....
12.206	"Chanson juanesque": "Toujours! et, demain, plus jamais!" (Champsaur; = Mélodies Vo.VIII/14) ....
12.207	"Tes cheveux": "Tels que les brins de paille fin" (Bruno) ....
12.208	"Chant de nourrice": "Dors, mon petit enfant, dors," chant et déclamation (Aicard; A—female voice offstage & 'the Poet' at the piano)
12.209	"La mélodie des baisers": "Toujours les lilas fleuriront" (Alexandre) ....
12.210	"En chantant": "Dans la familiale demeure" (Boyer) ....
12.211	"C'est le printemps": "L'azur sourit, le vent tiédit" (Gillouin) ....
12.212	"L'heure douce": "Ainsi qu'un fier guerrier" (Chabroux) ....
12.213	"Dormons par les lys": "C'est toi qui me diras les saisons infinies" (Picard) ....
12.214	"La gavotte de Puyjoli": "La marquise a dit: Mon bon Puyjoli" (Noël, = Mélodies, Vol.VII/10) ....
12.215	"Ton souvenir": "Mon coeur n'est pas dépossédé" (Feillet) ....
12.216	"Dieu créa le désert" (Grain) ....
12.217	"Toujours" (Max) ....
12.218	"Retour de oiseau" (Stuart) ....
12.219	"Effusion": "C'est toi que j'aime en la nature" (Allorge) ....

"Mélodies," Vol.VII (p1912):

12.220	1. "La mort de la cigale" (M. Faure) ....
12.221	2. "Oh! si les fleurs avaient des yeux" (Buchillot; extract from opera: Chérubin) ....
12.222	3. "Au très aimé" (Duer) ....
12.223	4. "C'est l'amour": "Oh oui! ta terre est belle" (Hugo) ....
12.224	5. "Chanson désespérée" (Teulet) ....
12.225	6. "La marchande des rêves": "Pour faire mes heures plus brèves" (Silvestre) ....
12.226	7. "La lettre": "Je mets sur le papier luisant" (Mendès) ....
12.227	8. "Le Noël des humbles": "L'enfant est nu" (Aicard) ....
12.228	9. "Orphelines": "Elles marchent deux par deux" (Ludana) ....
12.229	10. "La gavotte de Puyjoli": "La marquise a dit: Mon bon Puyjoli" (Noël) ....
12.230	11. "Rêverie sentimentale": "Si tu m'aimes" (Peyre) ....
12.231	12. "Rien ne passe" (Monrousseau) ....
12.232	13. "Tout passe" (Bruno) ....
12.233	14. "Si tu l'oses" (Mansilla) ....
12.234	15. "Les youx clos" (Buchillot) ....
12.235	16. "Si vous vouliez bien me le dire" (Ludana) ....
12.236	17. "Avril est amoureux": "Avril dort sous la lune blanche" (d'Halmont; orchd) ....
12.237	18. "Âmes obscures": "Tout, dans l'immuable nature" (A. France) ....
12.238	19. "Heure vécue": "Une nuit brune d'un soir d'hiver" (Jacquet) ....
12.239	20. "Menteuse chérie": "Menteuse chérie, lorsque tu m'as dit" (Ludana) ....

"Expressions lyriques" (avec déclamation rythmée) (pubd posth1913):

12.240	1. "Dialogue": "Pourquoi donc ne dis-tu plus rien?" (Varenne) ....
12.241	2. "Les nuages": "Les voyez-vous passer sous le ciel monotone?" (Louvencourt) ....
12.242	3. "En voyage": "Où donc allez-vous, Madame, sans postillon ni piqueur?" (Maurer) ....
12.243	4. "Battements d'ailes": "Les soirs d'été si doux, voilés de crêpes bleus" (Dortzal) ....
12.244	5. "La dernière lettre de Werther à Charlotte": "Il faut nous séparer" (Biron) ....
12.245	6. "Comme autrefois": "J'ai revêtu, ce soir, son large manteau noir" (Dortzal) ....
12.246	7. "Nocturne": "Il était minuit, la bonne odeur du bois" (Dortzal) ....
12.247	8. "Mélancolie": "Sur les flots de la vie, suivant ce qui me tient" (anon) ....
12.248	9. "Rose de mai": "Ce n'est pas ta beauté qui m'attire" (Poirson) ....
12.249	10. "Feux follets d'amour": "Mes soeurs! dans cette nuit d'étoiles" (Grain) ....

"Mélodies," Vol.VIII (pubd posth1914):

12.250	1. "Aube païenne": "Quand de mon tertre en fleur" (Rocha) ....
12.251	2. "La nuit": "Parfois, losque tout dort" (Hugo) ....
12.252	3. "Les extases": "Des chants, des fleurs et du soleil" (Dessierier) ....
12.253	4. "L'amour pleure, romance de jadis": "La pauvre Amour est tout en larmes" (Postel) ....
12.254	5. "Dites-lui que je l'aime": "Dites-lui que les fleurs ont ouvert leur calice" (Fleury-Daunizeau) ....
12.255	6. "Soleil couchant": "Le soleil s'est couché ce soir" (Hugo) ....
12.256	7. "Jamais plus": "Dans un nuage d'or" (Sarmento) ....
12.257	8. "Soir de rêve": "Au bosquet de ta lèvre" (Lugnier) ....
12.258	9. "La chanson des lèvres": "Lèvres, ô mères du baiser" (Lahor) ....
12.259	10. "Voix suprême": "O murmure du vent qui monte" (Lafaix-Gontié) ....
12.260	11. "Si tu m'aimes": "Si tu m'aimes, dis-le ce mot qui fait ma vie" (Girard-Duverne) ....
12.261	12. "L'ange et l'enfant": "L' ange Amabed a cueilli des roses" (Barbier) ....
12.262	13. "Au delà du rêve": "Où n'atteindrai-je pas?" (Hirsch) ....
12.263	14. "Chanson juanesque": "Toujours! et, demain, plus jamais!" (Champsaur) ....
12.264	15. "Et puis ...": "Vous aurez la fleur d'oranger," rondel (Chassang) ....
12.265	16. "Être aimé": "Être aimé! tout est là, vois-tu" (Hugo) ....
12.266	17. "Ivre d'amour": "Je suis ivre d'amour" (after Akhtamar) ....
12.267	18. "Noël des fleurs": "Il pleut des iris, des jasmins, des roses" (Schneider) ....
12.268	19. "Ma petite mère a pleuré" (Gravollet) ....
12.269	20. "Éveil": "La vierge étoile est effacée" (Gassier) ....

W/ out date:

12.270	"L'oiseau de paradis" (Princet) ....
12.271	"Parfums" (Dortzal) ....
12.272	"Le coffret d'ébène" (Jannet) ....
12.273	"Je mourrai plus que toi" (Verlaine) ....
12.274	"La verdadera vida, coplas": "La la la! La vie a mal guidé mes pas" (Saix, collab Berthomieu).......

13. ARRANGEMENTS OF WORKS OF OTHERS

13.1	Baldi: "Marche napolitaine" (p1903; 1v & pf, text Barbier) ....
13.2	Boccherini: "Sicilienne" (transcr for pf) ....
13.3	Delibes: "Kassya," opera (compl & orchd1893) ....
13.4	Lalo: "Divertissement pour orchestre," from opera: Fiesque (red1872; pf) ....
13.5	Schubert: "La mer" (arr1891; hn & orch) ....

* * * * *

1. STAGE WORKS

Operas:

1.1 "Ich, J. Mendelssohn ...," 3 act Lustspiel (c1820, Mendelssohn) ....
1.2 "Die Soldatenliebschaft," 1 act comic opera (c1820, Caspar) ....
1.3 "Die beiden Pädagogen," 1 act Singspiel (c1821, Caspar after Scribe) ....
1.4 *"Die wandernden Komödianten," 1 act comic opera (c1822, words lost)* ....
1.5 *"Der Onkel aus Boston oder die beiden Neffen," 2 act comic opera (c1823, Klingemann, words lost)* ....
1.6 "Die Hochzeit des Camacho" (The Wedding of Camacho), 2 act comic (c1825, after Cervantes) Op.10
1.7 "Die Heimkehr aus der Fremde" (Son and Stranger), 1 act operetta (c1829, Klingemann) Op.89
1.8 *"Trala. A frischer Bua bin I," Schnadahüpferl (c1833, East-Bavarian Alpine folk song/dance)* ....
1.9 *"Lorelei," 3 acts (c1847, Geibel, unfin, frags):* *Op.98*
    1. Finale of Act I: "Woher, woher am dunkeln," chorus
    2. "Ave Maria": "Horch der Abendglocke Ton!" (S & fem ch)
    3. "Vintage Song": "Wir han geschnitzt das lange" (m ch)

Incid music:

1.10 "Der standhafte Prinz" (The Steadfast Prince) (c1833, Calderón) ....
1.11 "Ruy Blas: Romance" (c1839, Hugo) Op.94
1.12 "Antigone" (c1841, Sophocles) Op.55
1.13 "Ein Sommernachtstraum" (A Midsummer Night's Dream) (c1842, Shakespeare; also see: Overture in E major, Op.21) (also see Britten's opera Op.64, Castelnuovo-Tedesco's overture Op.108, Orff's music drama, Purcell's semi-opera: The Fairy Queen, Z629 & Satie's incid music: 5 Grimaces) Op.61
1.14 "Athalie" (c1845, Racine) Op.74
1.15 "Oedipus in Kolonos" (Oedipus at Colonos) (c1845, Sophocles) Op.93

1a. SELECTIONS FROM STAGE WORKS

1a.6 "Die Hochzeit des Camacho," comic opera: Op.10
    . "Ouverture"
  I: 1. "Beglücktes Jugendleben, von Liebe geschmückt," duet
       2. "Wie? ihr wagt es hier vermessen," trio
       3. "So kehrest du wieder, Geliebter, mir treu?," duet
       4. "Nur frischer Muth und klares Blut," Lied
       5. "Viva Camacho," chorus
       6. "Lasst mich, o lasst mich noch einmal be," ensemble
       7. "Viva Camacho, Viva Quiteria," chorus & aria
       8. "Fricassiren" (Camacho, 1.ter Vetternchor)
       9. "Wer klopft so leise an die Thür?," aria
      10. "Dem sollen die Knochen im Leibe" (Carrasco, 2.ter Vetternchor)
      11. "Lasset euch winden," finale
  II: 12. "Frisch die Hände nun gerührt," chorus & aria
      13. "Die schönste Braut im ganzen Land," Lied
      14. "Richtend mag das Spiel entscheiden," chorus & ballet
      15. "Was sollen mir die räthselhaften Worte?," trio
      16. "Nun zündet an geweihte Kerzen," chorus
      17. "Welche Stimme, welche Störung," ensemble
      18. "Wie? betrogen! Was? belogen!," finale

1a.7 "Die Heimkehr aus der Fremde," operetta: Op.89
    . "Ouverture"
       1. "Es sass vor langer, grauer Zeit" (Spinnlied), romance
       2. "Man geht und kommt und fragt," duet (S, A)
       3. "So Mancher zog in's Weite," Lied (S)
       4. "Ich bin ein viel gereister Mann," Lied (B)
       5. "Wenn die Abendglocken läuten," Lied (T)
       6. "O wie verschweig' ich, verberg' ich," trio (S, T, B)
       7. "Ihr wollt uns hier mit List verwirren," trio (A, 2B)
       8. "Es steigt das Geisterreich herauf," Lied (T)
       9. "Hört ihr Herrn und lasst euch sagen," Lied (B)
      10. "Heraus! zu Hilf! Verrath und Mord!," duet (T, B)
      11. "Nachtmusik"
      12. "Die Blumenglocken mit hellem Schein," Lied (S)
      13. "Wir kommen, wir nahen," chorus
      14. "O lasst ihn, Vater! alles Streiten geht," finale

1a.12 "Antigone," incid music: Op.55
    . "Introduction"
       1. "Strahl des Helios schönstes Licht"
       2. "Vieles Gewaltige lebt"
       3. "Ihr Seligen, deren Geschick"
       4. "O Eros, Allsieger im Kampf"

    5. "Noch toset des Sturmes Gewalt," recit & "Auch der Danaë Reiz," chorus
    6. "Vielnamiger! Wonn' und Stolz," chorus I & II
    7. "Hier kommt er ja selbst," chorus I & II

1a.13   "A Midsummer Night's Dream," incid music (Nos. of sections in The Gramophone): Op.61
        1. "Overture" (= Op.21)
        2. "Scherzo" (Entr'acte to Act II)
    II: 3. "Over hill, over dale," melodrama
     . "March of the Elves"
        4. "Ye spotted snakes," song w/ chorus
        5. "The Spells," melodrama
        6. "Entr'acte/Intermezzo" (Hermia seeks Lysander, Entry of the Rustics)
    III: 7. "What hempen homespuns," melodrama
        8. "Nocturne"
    IV: 9. "The Removal of the Spells," melodrama
      10. "Wedding march" (Entr'acte to Act V)
    V: 11. "Fanfare and Funeral March"
      12. "Bergomask" (Dance of the Rustics)
      13. "Wedding March," reprise
      14. "Through this house give glimm'ring light," finale

1a.14   "Athalie," incid music: Op.74
     . "Ouverture"
        1. "Herr, durch die ganze Welt," chorus
        2. "O seht, welch ein Stern uns erschienen!"
        3. "Lasst uns dem heil'gen Wort," d chorus
        4. "Ist es Glück, ist es Leid," chorus
     . "Kriegsmarsch der Priester"
        5. "So geht, so geht, ihr Kinder Aron's, geht!"
        6. "Ja durch die ganze Welt," chorus

1a.15   "Oedipus in Kolonos," incid music: Op.93
     . "Introduction"
        1. "O schau! Er entfloh" (T)
        2. "Grausam ist es, o Freund, wecken ein Leid" (T, B)
        3. "Allegro tranquillo"
        4. "Weh mir!" (Oedipus)
        5. "Ach, wär' ich, wo bald die" (T)
        6. "Andante"
        7. "Auf uns bricht von dem blinden" (B)
        8. "Ist es verstattet, dich" (T, B)
        9. "Sostenuto assai"

2. SYMPHONIES

Early sinfonias (strings):

2.1   Sinfonia No.1 in C major (c1821) ....
2.2   Sinfonia No.2 in D major (c1821) ....
2.3   Sinfonia No.3 in E minor (c1821) ....
2.4   Sinfonia No.4 in C minor (c1821) ....
2.5   Sinfonia No.5 in B-flat major (c1821) ....
2.6   Sinfonia No.6 in E-flat major (c1821) ....
2.7   Sinfonia No.7 in D minor (c1821–2) ....
2.8   Sinfonia No.8 in D major (c1822; arr for orch 1822) ....
2.9   Sinfonia No.9 in C major (c1823) ....
2.10   Sinfonia No.10 in B minor (c1823) ....
2.11   Sinfonia No.11 in F major (c1823) ....
2.12   Sinfonia No.12 in G minor (c1823) ....
2.13   Sinfonia No.13 in C minor (c1823, 1 movt only) ....

Symphonies (orch):

2.14   Symphony No.1 in C minor (c1824) Op.11
2.15   Symphony No.2 in B-flat major, "Lobgesang" / "Hymn of Praise" (c1840; w/ vv, ch & org): Op.52
        1. "Sinfonie"
        2. "Alles, alles," chorus
        3. "Saget es, die ihr erlöst seid durch den Herrn," recit & "Er zählet unsre Thränen," aria
        4. "Sagt es, die ihr erlöset seid," chorus
        5. "Ich harrete des Herrn," duet (2S & ch)
        6. "Stricke des Todes hatten uns" (T)
        7. "Die Nacht ist" (T, Bs)
        8. "Nun danket alle Gott," choral
        9. "Drum sing' ich mit meinem Liede ewig dein Lob" (T)

10. "Ihr Völker, bringet her dem Herrn," final chorus

2.16	Symphony No.3 in A minor, "Scottish" (c1841–2)	Op.56
2.17	Symphony No.4 in A major, "Italian" (c1833)	Op.90
2.18	Symphony No.5 in D minor, "Reformation" (c1830–2):	Op.107

. (1st–3rd movts derived from: Dresden Amen, religious motive—a symbol of the Holy Ghost)
. (4th movt based on: A Mighty Fortress is Our God, hymn c by Luther)

3. OTHER ORCHESTRAL WORKS

Overtures:

3.1	Overture in E major, "A Midsummer Night's Dream" (c1826, for incid music Op.61)	Op.21
3.2	Overture in C major (c1824; winds)	Op.24
3.3	Overture in B minor, "The Hebrides" (Fingal's cave) (c1830, final vers 1832)	Op.26
3.4	Overture in D major, "Calm Sea & Prosperous Voyage" (c1828)	Op.27
3.5	Overture in E major, "Fair Melusina" (c1833, after Grillparzer)	Op.32
3.6	Overture in C minor, "Ruy Blas" (c1839, after Hugo, for incid music Op.94)	Op.95
3.7	Overture in C major, "Trumpet" (c1826, r1833)	Op.101

Marches:

3.8	"Trauermarsch," in A minor (c1836; milit band, in memory of N. Burgmüller)	Op.103
3.9	"March," in D major (c1841, to celebrate Cornelius's visit to Dresden)	Op.108

4. CONCERTOS, SOLO INSTR & ORCH

Pf & orch:

4.1	Piano Concerto in A minor (c1822; pf & strings)	
4.2	"Capriccio brillant," in B minor (c ?1825–6)	Op.22
4.3	Piano Concerto No.1 in G minor (c1830–1)	Op.25
4.4	"Rondo brillant," in E-flat major (c1834)	Op.29
4.5	Piano Concerto No.2 in D minor (c1837)	Op.40
4.6	"Serenade & Allegro gioioso," in B minor (c1838)	Op.43

Vn & orch:

4.7	Violin Concerto in D minor (c1822; vn & strings)	
4.8	Violin Concerto in E minor (c1844)	Op.64

Other:

4.9	Double Concerto in D minor (c1823; vn, pf & strings)	
4.10	Double Piano Concerto in E major (c1823)	
4.11	Double Piano Concerto in A-flat major (c1824)	

5. STRING QUARTETS

5.1	"15 Fugues" (c1821)	
5.2	String Quartet in E-flat major (c1823)	
5.3	String Quartet No.1 in E-flat major (c1829)	Op.12
5.4	String Quartet No.2 in A minor (c1827)	Op.13
5.5	"Fugue," in E-flat major (c1827)	
5.6	String Quartet No.3 in D major (c1838)	Op.44/1
5.7	String Quartet No.4 in E minor (c1838)	Op.44/2
5.8	String Quartet No.5 in E-flat major (c1838)	Op.44/3
5.9	String Quartet No.6 in F minor (c1847)	Op.80
5.10	"4 Pieces": No.1 "Andante," in E major (c1847)	Op.81
5.11	No.2 "Scherzo," in A minor (c1847)	
5.12	No.3 "Capriccio," in E minor (c1843)	
5.13	No.4 "Fugue," in E-flat major (c1827)	

6. OTHER CHAMBER MUSIC

6 or more insts:

6.1	String Octet in E-flat major (c1825; 4vn, 2va & 2vc)	Op.20
6.2	String Quintet No.1 in A major (c1826, r1832; 2vn, 2va & vc)	Op.18
6.3	String Quintet No.2 in B-flat major (c1845)	Op.87
6.4	Piano Sextet in D major (c1824; vn, 2va, vc, d bass & pf)	Op.110

Piano Quartets:

Piano Trios:

Other 3 insts:

Vn & pf:

Va & pf:

Vc & pf:

Other instr & pf:

7. PIANO SONATAS

8. OTHER PIANO WORKS

10. ORATORIOS

10a. SELECTIONS FROM ORATORIOS

10a.2   "Elias," oratorio: Op.70
        . "Introduction" (Elias)
        . "Overture"
      I: 1. "Help, Lord!," chorus
           . "The deep affords no water"
           2. "Lord! bow Thine ear," duet & chorus
           3. "Ye people, rend your hearts," recit
           4. "If with all your hearts," aria
           5. "Yet doth the Lord see it not," chorus
           6. "Elijah! get thee hence," recit (A)
           7a. "For He shall give his angels," d quartet
           7b. "Now Cherith's brook is dried up"
           8. "What have I to do with thee?," recit
           9. "Blessed are the men that fear Him," chorus
           10. "As God the Lord," recit
           11. "Baal, we cry to thee," chorus
           12. "Call him louder," recit
           . "Hear our cry, O Baal"
           13. "Call him louder!," recit
           . "Hear and answer, Baal!"
           14. "Lord God of Abraham," aria
           15. "Cast thy burden upon the Lord"
           16. "O Thou, who makest Thine angels spirits," recit (Elias)
           17. "Is not his word like a fire?," aria
           18. "Woe unto them," arioso
           19. "O man of God," recit
           . "O Lord, Thou hast overthrown"
           20. "Thanks be to God!," chorus
      II: 21. "Hear ye, Israel," aria
           22. "Be not afraid," chorus
           23. "The Lord hath exalted thee," recit & chorus
           24. "Woe to him," chorus
           25. "Man of God," recit
           26. "It is enough," aria
           27. "See, now he sleepeth," recit
           28. "Lift thine eyes," trio
           29. "He, watching over Israel," chorus
           30. "Arise, Elijah," recit
           31. "O rest in the Lord," aria
           32. "He that shall endure to the end," chorus
           33. "Night falleth round me," recit
           34. "Behold! God the Lord passeth by!," chorus
           35. "Above Him stood the Seraphim," recit
           36. "Go, return upon thy way!," chorus/recit
           . "I go on my way"
           37. "For the mountains shall depart," aria
           38. "Then did Elijah," chorus
           39. "Then shall the righteous shine forth," aria
           40. "Behold, God hath sent Elijah"
           41. "But the Lord," chorus
           . "O come everyone that thristeth"
           42. "And then shall your light break forth," final chorus

10a.3   "Christus," oratorio: Op.97
        I. "Geburt Christi": "Da Jesus geboren ward zu Bethlehem," recit
          . "Wo ist der neugeborne König" (T, 2B)
          . "Es wird ein Stern aus Jacob aufgehen," chorus
        II. "Leiden Christi": "Und der ganze Haufe stand auf," recit (T)
          . "Diesen finden wir," chorus
          . "Da überantwortete er ihn," recit
          . "Ihr Töchter Zions, weint über euch selbst," chorus
          . "Er nimmt auf seinen Rücken die Lasten," choral

11. PSALMS & SACRED CANTATAS

11.1   "Psalm 66" (c1822; d fem ch & cont) ....
11.2   "Magnificat" (c1822, ch & orch) ....
11.3   "Salve regina" (c ?1824; S & strings)...
11.4   "2 Sacred pieces" (c1824; ch): 1. "Wie gross ist des Allmächt'gen Güte" ....
11.5   2. "Allein Gott in der Höh' sey Ehr"
11.6   "Te Deum" (c1826; d ch & cont) ....
11.7   "Jesu, meine Freude," chorale cantata (d ch & strings)..
11.8   "Psalm115": "Non nobis, Domine" (c1830, 1v, ch & orch) Op.31
11.9   "Verleih' uns Frieden," prayer (c1831; ch & orch) ....

14.43 "6 Lieder" (ch): 1. "Neujahrslied": "Mit der Freude zieht der Schmerz" (c1844, Hebel) Op.88
14.44   2. "Der Glückliche": "Ich hab' ein Liebchen recht lieb von" (c1843, Eichendorff)
14.45   3. "Hirtenlied": "Winter, schlimmer Winter" (c1839, Uhland)
14.46   4. "Die Waldvögelein": "Kommt, lasst uns gehn spazieren durch" (c1843, Schütz)
14.47   5. "Deutschland": "Durch tiefe Nacht ein Brausen zieht" (c ?1839–43, Geibel)
14.48   6. "Der wandernde Musikant": "Durch Feld und Buchenhallen" (c1840, Eichendorff)
14.49 "4 Lieder" (ch): 1. "Andenken": "Die Bäume grünen überall" (c1844) Op.100
14.50   2. "Lob des Frühlings": "Saatengrün, Veilchenduft" (c1843, Uhland)
14.51   3. "Frühlingslied": "Berg und Thal will ich durchstreifen" (c ?1843–4)
14.52   4. "Im Wald": "O Wald, du kühlender Bronnen" (c1839)
14.53 "Sahst du ihn hernieder schweben," funeral song (c1845) Op.116
14.54 "Der Sänger" (c1845, Schiller) ....
14.55 "4 Lieder" (m ch): 1. "Jagdlied": "Auf, ihr Herrn und Damen schön!" (c1837, Scott) (also see
                Beethoven WoO 155/12) Op.120
14.56   2. "Morgengruss des Thüringischen Sängerbundes": "Seid gegrüsset, traute Brüder" (c1847)
14.57   3. "Im Süden": "Süsse Düfte, milde Lüfte"
14.58   4. "Zigeunerlied": "Im Nebelgeriesel" (Goethe)
14.59 "Lob der Trunkenheit": "Trunken müssen wir alle sein" (m ch) ....
14.60 "Musikantenprügelei": "Seht doch diese Fiedlerbanden" (m ch) ....

Canons:

14.61 "Der weise Diogenes" (c1833; m ch) ....
14.62 "Und ob du mich züchtigst" (c1835; ch) ....
14.63 2-Part Canon in B minor (c1837; pf) ....
14.64 2-Part Canon in C minor (c1838; pf) ....
14.65 3-Part Canon (c1839) ....
14.66 2-Part Canon (c1840, solution by Möhring) ....
14.67 2-Part Canon (c1841, ded to Lepsius) ....
14.68 2-Part Canon (c1841, ded to Carus) ....
14.69 Canon in F-sharp minor (c1844, ded to Lallemant) ....

15. VOICE & ORCHESTRA

15.1 Concert aria: "Che vuoi mio cor?" (mS & strings) ....
15.2 Concert aria: "Infelice," recit & "Ah! ritorna," aria (c1834, r1843; S & orch) Op.94

16. VOCAL DUETS (w/ pf)

16.1 "Ein Tag sagt es dem andern" (c1821) ....
16.2 "6 Duets" (p1845): 1. "Ich wollt' meine Lieb' ergrösse sich" (c1836, Heine) Op.63
16.3   2. "Abschiedslied der Zugvögel": "Wie war so schön doch" (Fallersleben)
16.4   3. "Gruss": "Wohin ich geh' " (Eichendorff)
16.5   4. "Herbstlied": "Ach wie so bald" (Klingemann)
16.6   5. "Volkslied": "O säh' ich auf der Heide dort im" (c1842, Burns) (also see Shostakovich Op.62/2)
16.7   6. "Maiglöckchen und die Blümelein": "Maiglöckchen läufet in dem Thal" (c1844, Fallersleben)
16.8 "3 Duets" (p1848): 1. "Sonntagsmorgen": "Das ist der Tag des Herrn" (c1836, Uhland) Op.77
16.9   2. "Das Aehrenfeld": "Ein Leben war's im Aehrenfeld" (c1847, Fallersleben)
16.10   3. "Lied aus Ruy Blas": "Wozu der Vöglein Chöre" (c1839, Hugo)
16.11 "3 Folksongs": 1. "Wie kann ich froh und lustig sein?" (Kaufmann) ....
16.12   2. "Abendlied": "Wenn ich auf dem Lager" (Heine)
16.13   3. "Wasserfahrt": "Ich stand gelehnet" (Heine)

17. SONGS (w/ pf)

17.1 "Ave Maria" (c1820) ....
17.2 "Raste Krieger, Krieg ist aus" (c1820) ....
17.3 "Die Nachtigall": "Da ging ich hin" (c ?1821–2) ....
17.4 "Der Verlassene": "Nacht ist um mich her" (c ?1821–2) ....
17.5 "Von allen deinen zarten Gaben" (c1822) ....
17.6 "Wiegenlied": "Schlummre sanft" (c1822) ....
17.7 "Sanft weh'n im Hausch der Abendluft" (c1822) ....
17.8 "Der Wasserfall": "Rieselt hernieder" (c ?1823) ....
17.9 "12 Songs" (p1828): 1. "Minnelied im Mai": "Holder klingt der Vogelsang" (Hölty) (also see
                Brahms Op.71/5 & Schubert D429) Op.8
17.10   2. "Das Heimweh": "Was ist's, das mir den Athem hemmet" (Robert) (c by Fanny Mendelssohn)
17.11   3. "Italien": "Schöner und schöner schmückt" (Grillparzer) (c by Fanny Mendelssohn)
17.12   4. "Erntelied": "Es ist ein Schnitter, der heisst Tod" (trad)
17.13   5. "Pilgerspruch": "Lass dich nur nichts nicht" (Flemming)
17.14   6. "Frühlingslied": "Jetzt komt der Frühling, der Himmel isch blau" (c1824, Robert)
17.15   7. "Maienlied": "Man soll hören süsses Singen" (Warte)
17.16   8. "Andres Maienlied" (Hexenlied): "Die Schwalbe fliegt" (Hölty)

17.17	9. "Abendlied": "Das Tage Werk ist" (Voss)
17.18	10. "Romanze": "Einmal aus seinen Blicken" (from Spanish)
17.19	11. "Im Grünen": "Willkommen im Grünen" (Voss)
17.20	*12. "Suleika und Hatem": "An des lust'gen Brunnens" (Goethe; 2vv) (c by Fanny Mendelssohn)*
17.21	"The Garland" (Der Blumenkranz): "By Celia's arbour all the night" (c1829, Moore) ....
17.22	"12 Lieder" (p1830): 1. "Frage": "Ist es wahr?" (Voss) Op.9
17.23	2. "Geständnis": "Kennst du nicht das Gluthwer"
17.24	3. "Wartend": "Sie trug einen Falken auf ihrer Hand," romance (anon)
17.25	4. "Im Frühling": "Ihr frühlings" (c1829)
17.26	5. "Im Herbst": "Ach wie schnell die Tage fliehen" (Klingemann)
17.27	6. "Scheidelied" (Voss)
17.28	*7. "Sehnsucht": "Fern und ferner" (Droysen) (c by Fanny Mendelssohn)*
17.29	8. "Frühlingsglaube": "Die linden Lüfte sind erwacht" (c1830, Uhland) (also see
	Schubert Op.20/2, D686)
17.30	9. "Ferne": "In weite Ferne will ich träumen" (Droysen)
17.31	*10. "Verlust": "Und wüssten's die Blumen" (Heine) (c by Fanny Mendelssohn) (also see Schumann Op.48/8)*
17.32	11. "Entsagung": "Herr, zu dir will ich mich" (Droysen)
17.33	*12. "Die Nonne": "Im stillen Kloster" (Uhland) (c by Fanny Mendelssohn)*
17.34	"4 Songs" (c1830): 1. "Der Tag": "Sanft entschwanden mir" ....
17.35	2. "Reiterlied": "Immer fort"
17.36	3. "Abschied": "Leb wohl mein Lieb"
17.37	4. "Der Bettler": "Ich danke Gott dir"
17.38	"Seemanns Scheidelied": "Es freut sich Alles" (c1831, Fallersleben) ....
17.39	"Weihnachtslied": "Auf schicke dich recht feierlich" (c1832; 2 vers) ....
17.40	"6 Songs" (p1834): 1. "Frühlingslied": "In dem Walde" (c1830, Lichtenstein) Op.19a
17.41	2. "Das erste Veilchen": "Als ich das" (Ebert)
17.42	3. "Winterlied": "Mein Sohn, wo willst du hin so spät?" (from Swedish)
17.43	4. "Neue Liebe": "In dem Mondenschein" (Heine)
17.44	5. "Gruss": "Leise zieht durch mein Gemüt" (Heine)
17.45	6. "Reiselied": "Bringet des" (c1830, Ebert)
17.46	"Mailied": "Ich weiss mir'n Mädchen" (c1834) ....
17.47	"2 Romances" (Byron): 1. "Keine von der Erde Schönen" (There be none of Beauty's daughters) (c1833)
	(also see Wolf's 4. of: 4 Poems of Heine, Shakespeare & Byron)
17.48	2. "Schlafloser Augen Leuchte" (Sun of the sleepless) (c1834) (also see Rimsky-Korsakov Op.41/1,
	Schumann Op.95/2 & Wolf's 3. of: 4 Poems of Heine, Shakespeare & Byron)
17.49	"2 Songs" (c1835, Eichendorff): 1. "Das Waldschloss": "Wo noch kein Wandrer" ....
17.50	2. "Pagenlied": "Wenn die Sonne lieblich"
17.51	"6 Songs" (p1836): 1. "Minnelied": "Leucht't heller" (c1834, Old German) Op.34
17.52	2. "Auf Flügeln des Gesanges": "Auf Flügeln des Gesanges, Herzliebchen, trag' ich
	dich fort" (Heine)
17.53	3. "Frühlingslied": "Es brechen im" (Klingemann)
17.54	4. "Suleika": "Ach, um deine feuchten Schwingen" (from Goethe's West-östlicher Divan) (also
	see Schubert Op.31, D717)
17.55	5. "Sonntagslied": "Ringsum erschalt in Wald und Flur viel" (c1834, Klingemann)
17.56	6. "Reiselied": "Der Herbstwind" (Heine)
17.57	"Lied einer Freundin": "Zarter Blumen leicht Gewinde" (c1837, Goethe) ....
17.58	"Im Kahn" (c1837, Heine) ....
17.59	"O lönnt ich zu dir fliegen" (c1838)
17.60	"6 Songs" (p ?1840): 1. "Minnelied": "Wie der Quell so lieblich" (Tieck) Op.47
17.61	2. "Morgengruss": "Über die Berge steigt" (Heine)
17.62	3. "Frühlingslied": "Durch den Wald, den dunkeln" (c1839, Lenau)
17.63	4. "Volkslied": "Es ist bestimmt in Gottes Rath" (c1839, Feuchtersleben)
17.64	5. "Der Blumenstrauss": "Sie wandelt im" (c1832, Klingemann)
17.65	6. "Bei der Wiege": "Schlumme! Schlummre und träume von kommender Zeit" (Klingemann)
17.66	"2 Songs": 1. "Ich hör ein Vöglein" (c1841, Böttger) ....
17.67	2. "Todeslied der Bojaren": "Leg' in den Sarg" (c before 1841, Immermann)
17.68	"6 Lieder" (p1843): 1. "Altdeutsches Lied": "Es ist in den Wald" (Schreiber) Op.57
17.69	2. "Hirtenlied": "O Winter, schlimmer" (c1839, Uhland)
17.70	3. "Suleika": "Was bedeutet die Bewegung" (Goethe)
17.71	4. "O Jugend, schöne Rosenzeit": "Von allen schönen Kindern" (Rhenish folksong)
17.72	5. "Venezianisches Gondellied": "Wenn durch die Piazzetta die Abendluft weht" (c1845, Moore
	transl Freiligrath) (also see Schumann Op.25/18)
17.73	6. "Wanderlied": "Laue Luft kommt" (c1841, Eichendorff)
17.74	"6 Lieder" (p ?1847): 1. "Tröstung": "Werde heiter" (c1845, Fallersleben) Op.71
17.75	2. "Frühlingslied": "Der Frühling nacht mit" (c1845, Klingemann)
17.76	3. "An die Entfernte": "Diese Rose pflück' ich dir" (c1847, Lenau)
17.77	4. "Schilflied": "Auf dem Teich, dem regungslosen" (c1842, Lenau)
17.78	5. "Auf der Wanderschaft": "Ich wandre fort in's ferne Land" (c1847, Lenau)
17.79	6. "Nachtlied": "Vergangen ist der lichte Tag" (c1847, Eichendorff)
17.80	"3 Lieder" (p1850): 1. "Da lieg' ich unter den Bäumen" (c1831) Op.84
17.81	2. "Herbstlied": "Im Walde rauschen dürre" (c1839, Klingemann)
17.82	3. "Jagdlied": "Mit Lust thät ich ausreiten" (c1834, from Des Knaben Wunderhorn)
17.83	"6 Songs" (p1851): 1. "Es lauschte das Laub" (Klingemann) Op.86
17.84	2. "Morgenlied": "Erwacht in neuer"

17.85	3. "Die Liebende schreibt": "Ein Blick von deinen Augen in die meinen" (c1831, Goethe) (also see Brahms Op.47/5 & Schubert Op.posth 165/1, D673)
17.86	4. "Allnächtlich im Traume seh' ich dich" (Heine) (also see Schumann Op.48/14)
17.87	5. "Der Mond": "Mein Herz ist wie die dunkle Nacht" (Geibel)
17.88	6. "Altdeutsches Frühlingslied": "Der trübe Winter ist vorbei" (Spee)
17.89	"6 Songs": 1. "Erster Verlust": "Ach wer bringt die schönen Tage" (Goethe) (also see Schubert Op.5/4, D226) Op.99
17.90	2. "Die Sterne schau'n in stiller Nacht" (Schlippenbach)
17.91	3. "Lieblingsplätzchen": "Wisst ihr, wo ich gerne weil' " (from Des Knaben Wunderhorn)
17.92	4. "Das Schifflein": "Ein Schifflein ziehet leise den Strom hin" (Uhland)
17.93	5. "Wenn sich zwei Herzen scheiden" (Geibel)
17.94	6. "Es weiss und räth es doch keiner" (Eichendorff) (also see Schumann Op.39/4)
17.95	"2 Sacred Songs": 1. "Doch der Herr, er leitet die Irrenden recht," arioso (T & pf) Op.112
17.96	2. "Der du die Menschen lässest sterben," aria (S & pf, intended for oratorio: Paulus, Op.36)
17.97	"Des Mädchens Klage": "Der Eichwald" (Schiller) ....
17.98	"Warnung vor dem Rhein": "An den Rhein, an den Rhein, zieh' nicht an den Rhein" (Simrock) ....
17.99	"Der Abendsegen" (The Evening Service): "Lord! have mercy upon us" ....
17.100	"Gretchen": "Meine Ruh ist hin" (Goethe) ....
17.101	"Lieben und Schweigen": "Ich flocht ein Kränzlein" (Tischendorf) ....
17.102	"Es rauscht der Wald" ....
17.103	"Vier trübe Monden sind entfloh'n" ....
17.104	"Weinend seh' ich in die Nacht" ....
17.105	"Weiter, rastlos atemlos vorüber" ....
17.106	*"Erwartung": "Bist auf ewig du gegangen" (frag)* ....

18. ARRANGEMENTS OF WORKS OF OTHERS

Bach, J. S.:

18.1	"Organ Compositions on Chorales," I–IV (p1845–6) ....
18.2	"44 kleine Choralvorspiele für die Orgel" (p1845) ....
18.3	"15 grosse Choral-Vorspiele für die Orgel" (p1846) ....
18.4	"6 Variations on the Chorale: Christ der du bist der helle Tag," BWV766 (p1846) ....
18.5	"11 Variations on the Chorale: Sei gegrüsset, Jesu gütig," BWV768 (ed from manuscript p1846) ....
18.6	"Chaconne," in D minor for vn solo (arr w/ pf acc p1847) ....
18.7	"Suite," in D major for orch (perf edition p1866) ....

Handel:

18.8	"Israel in Egypt," oratorio, HWV54 (org part p1846) ....
18.9	"Dettingen Te Deum," HWV283 (add acc) ....
18.10	"Acis and Galatea," oratorio, HWV49a (add acc) ....
18.11	"Solomon," oratorio, HWV67 (org parts arr1834) ....
18.12	"Messiah," oratorio, HWV56, 2 choruses ....

Other:

18.13	"6 schottische National-Lieder," German & orig English texts (p1839; ed Elvers 1977) ....

* * * * *

Opus numbers after Op.72 were given to works posthumously published.

1. STAGE WORKS

1.1   "Saint François d'Assise," 3 act opera (c1975–9, orchd1979–83; 7vv, ch & orch): ....
        I: Scene 1. "La Croix"
                2. "Les laudes"
                3. "Le baiser au lépreux"
        II: 4. "L'ange voyageur"
                5. "L'ange musicien"
                6. "Le prêche aux oiseaux"
        III: 7. "Les stigmates"
                8. "La mort et la nouvelle vie"

2. SYMPHONIES

2.1   "Turangalîla-symphonie" (c1946–8; pf, ondes martenot & orch): ....
                1. "Introduction"
                2. "Chant d'amour I"
                3. "Turangalîla I"
                4. "Chant d'amour II"
                5. "Joie du sang des étoiles"
                6. "Jardin du sommeil d'amour"
                7. "Turangalîla II"
                8. "Développement de l'amour"
                9. "Turangalîla III"
                10. "Final"

3. OTHER ORCHESTRAL WORKS

3.1   "Fugue," in D minor (c1928) ....
3.2   "Le banquet eucharistique" (c1928) ....
3.3   "Simple chant d'une âme" (c1930) ....
3.4   "Les offrandes oubliées" (Méditation symphonique) (c1930; arr for pf): ....
                1. "La Croix"
                2. "Le Péché"
                3. "L'Eucharistie"
3.5   "Le tombeau resplendissant" (c1931) ....
3.6   "Hymne au Saint Sacrement" (c1932) ....
3.7   "L'Ascension" (Quatre méditations) (c1932–3): No.1 "Majesté du Christ demandant sa gloire à son Père" ..
3.8   No.2 "Alléluias sereins d'une âme qui désire le ciel"
3.9   No.3 "Alléluia sur la trompette, alléluia sur la cymbale"
3.10   No.4 "Prière du Christ montant vers son Père"
3.11   "Chronochromie" (c1960): ....
                1. "Introduction"
                2. "Strophe I"
                3. "Antistrophe" I"
                4. "Strophe II"
                5. "Antistrophe II"
                6. "Epode"
                7. "Coda"
3.12   "Et exspecto resurrectionem mortuorum" (c1964): ....
                1. "Des profondeurs de l'abîme, je cris vers toi, Seigneur: Seigneur, écoute ma voix!"
                2. "Le Christ, ressuscité des morts, ne meurt plus; la mort n'a plus sur lui d'empire"
                3. "L'heure vient où les morts entendront la voix du fils de Dieu"
                4. "Ils ressusciteront, glorieux, avec un nom nouveau"
                5. "Et j'entendis la voix d'une foule immense"
3.13   "Un sourire" (c1991) ....
3.14   "Éclairs sur l'au-delà ..." (Flash Visions of the Beyond), 11 pictures (of paradise) (c1987–91, his last
        completed composition): No.1 "Apparition du Christ glorieux" ....
3.15   No.2 "La Constellation du Sagittaire"
3.16   No.3 "L'Oiseau-Lyre et la Ville-Fiancée"
3.17   No.4 "Les élus marqués du sceau"
3.18   No.5 "Demeurer dans l'Amour ..."
3.19   No.6 "Les sept Anges aux sept trompettes"
3.20   No.7 "Et Dieu essuiera toute larme de leurs yeux ..."
3.21   No.8 "Les Étoiles et la Gloire"
3.22   No.9 "Plusiers oiseaux des arbes de Vie"
3.23   No.10 "Le Chemin de l'Invisible"
3.24   No.11 "Le Christ, lumière du Paradis"

4. PIANO CONCERTOS, PIANO & ORCH

4.1   "Réveil des oiseaux" (c1953) ....

5. CHAMBER MUSIC, TAPE

Ondes martenot / tape:

4 insts:

Vn & pf:

Other 2 insts:

1 instr:

6. PIANO

10. "Adoptionem filiorum perfectam"
11. "Récit évangélique"
12. "Terribilis est locus iste"
13. "Tota Trinitas apparuit"
14. "Choral de la lumière de gloire"

9. SONGS (w/ pf)

9.1   "Deux ballades de Villon" (c1921): 1. "Epître à ses amis" ....
9.2   2. "Ballade des pendus"
9.3   "Trois mélodies" (c1930; S & pf): 1. "Pourquoi?" (Sauvage) ....
9.4   2. "Le sourire" (Messiaen)
9.5   3. "La fiancée perdue" (Messiaen)
9.6   "La mort du nombre" (c1930, Messiaen; S, T, vn & pf) ....
9.7   "Vocalise" (c1935; S & pf) ....
9.8   "Poèmes pour Mi" (c1936, Messiaen; S & pf; orchd1937), Book I: 1. "Action des grâces" ....
9.9   2. "Paysage"
9.10   3. "La maison"
9.11   4. "Epouvante"
9.12   II: 5. "L'épouse"
9.13   6. "Ta voix"
9.14   7. "Les deux guerriers"
9.15   8. "Le collier"
9.16   9. "Prière exaucée"
9.17   "Chants de terre et de ciel" (c1938, Messiaen; S & pf): 1. "Bail avec Mi" (pour ma femme) ....
9.18   2. "Antienne du silence" (pour le jour des Anges gardiens)
9.19   3. "Danse du bébé Pilule" (pour mon petit Pascal)
9.20   4. "Arc-en-ciel d'innocence" (pour mon petit Pascal)
9.21   5. "Minuit pile et face" (pour la mort)
9.22   6. "Résurrection" (pour le jour de Pâques)
9.23   "Harawi, chant d'amour et de mort" (c1945, Messiaen; S & pf): 1. "La ville qui dormait, toi" ....
9.24   2. "Bonjour toi, colombe verte"
9.25   3. "Montagnes"
9.26   4. "Doundou tchil"
9.27   5. "L'amour de Piroutcha"
9.28   6. "Répétition planétaire"
9.29   7. "Adieu"
9.30   8. "Syllabes"
9.31   9. "L'escalier redit, gestes du soleil"
9.32   10. "Amour oiseau d'étoile"
9.33   11. "Katchikatchi les étoiles"
9.34   12. "Dans le noir"

* * * * *

1. STAGE WORKS

Operas:

1.1	"Jephtas Gelübde," 3 acts (p1812, Schreiber) ....
1.2	"Wirth und Gast oder Aus Scherz Ernst," 2 act Lustspiel (p1813, Wohlbrück) ....
1.3	"Romilda e Costanza," 2 act melodramma semiserio (p1817, Rossi) ....
1.4	"Semiramide riconosciuta," 2 act dramma per musica (p1819, Rossi after Metastasio) ....
1.5	"Emma di Resburgo" (Emma di Leicester), 2 act melodramma eroico (p1891, Rossi) ....
1.6	"Margherita d'Anjou," 2 act melodramma semiserio (p1820, Romani based on Pixérécourt) ....
1.7	"L'esule di Granata," 2 act melodramma eroico (p1822, Romani) ....
1.8	"Il crociato in Egitto," 2 act melodramma eroico (p1824, r1825, Rossi) ....
1.9	"Robert le diable" (Robert the Devil), 5 act grand opéra (p1831, Scribe & Delavigne) ....
1.10	"Les Huguenots," 5 act grand opéra (p1836, Scribe & Deschamps) ....
1.11	"Ein Feldlager in Schlesien," 3 act Singspiel (p1844, Scribe & Rellstab) ....
1.12	"Le prophète" (The Prophet), 5 act grand opéra (p1849, Scribe) ....
1.13	"L'étoile du Nord," 3 act opéra comique (p1854, Scribe, based on ballet: La cantinière) ....
1.14	"Dinorah ou Le pardon de Ploërmel," 3 act opéra comique (p1859, Barbier & Carré) ....
1.15	"L'africaine" (The African Maid), 5 act grand opéra (p1865, Scribe; final vers words Fétis) ....

Opera frags & projects:

1.16	*"Abu Hassan," 2 act Singspiel (c1810, ?Hiemer, not perf)* ....
1.17	*"Der Admiral" (Der verlorene Prozess) (c1811, not perf)* ....
1.18	*"Le bachelier de Salamanque" (c ?1815, sketches)* ....
1.19	*"L'Almanzore" (c1821, Rossi, not perf)* ....
1.20	*"Ines de Castro," melodramma tragico (c1824, Rossi, outline)* ....
1.21	*"Malek Adel," melodramma (c1824, Rossi, outline)* ....
1.22	*"La nymphe de Danube," pasticcio (c1826–9, Sauvage, outline)* ....
1.23	*"Le portefaix," opéra-comique (c1831, Scribe, outline)* ....
1.24	*"Les brigands" (c1832, Dumas, outline)* ....
1.25	*"Cinq Mars" (c1837, Saint-Georges & Planard after Vigny, sketches)* ....
1.26	*"Noëma ou le repentir" (L'ange au exil) (c1846, Scribe & Saint-Georges, outline)* ....
1.27	*"Die Drei Pintos" (c1826–52, sketches & frags, based on sketches by C. M. von Weber)* ....
1.28	*"Judith" (c1854, Scribe, inc)* ....

Other dramatic:

1.29	"Der Fischer und das Milchmädchen," divertissement (p1810, Lauchery) ....
1.30	"Das Brandenburger Tor," lyrical drama (c1814, Veith, not perf?) ....
1.31	"Gli amori di Teolinda," dramatic cantata (p1816, Rossi; S, cl, ch & orch) ....
1.32	"Das Hoffest von Ferrara," masque (p1843, Raupach after Tasso) ....

Incid music:

1.33	"Struensee" (p1846, Beer) ....
1.34	Ballade in the play: Murillo, ou La corde du pendu (c1853, Langlois) ....
1.35	*"La jeunesse de Goethe" (c1860–2, Bury, not perf?, lost)* ....

1a. SELECTIONS FROM STAGE WORKS

1a.9   "Robert le diable," opera: ....
      I: 1. "Ouverture"
          . "Versez à tasses pleines," choeur (Buveurs)
          . "Jadis régnait en Normandie," ballade (Raimbaud)
          . "C'en est trop! qu'on arrête un vassal insolent," suite et fin de l'introduction
          2. "Ô mon Prince! ô mon maître!," récit (Alice)
          . "Va! va! va! dit elle, va, mon enfant," ballade (Alice)
          . "Je n'ai pu fermer sa paupière!," récit (Robert)
          3. "Le Duc de Normandie," choeur et sicilienne (Bertram)
          . "J'ai perdu!... ma revanche!," scène du jeu (Robert)
      II: 4. "Entr'acte"
          . "Que je hais la grandeur dont l'éclat m'environne!," récit (Isabelle)
          . "En vain j'espère," air (Isabelle)
          5. "Courage! Allons montrez vous à ses yeux," récit (Alice)
          . "Avec bonté voyez ma peine," duo (Robert, Isabelle)
          6. "Accourez au devant d'elle," choeur dansé
          7. "Pas de cinq"
          8. "Quand tous nos chevaliers; pour la gloire et leur dame," récit (un Maître des cérémonies)
      III: 9. "Entr'acte"
          . "Du rendez-vous voici l'heureux instant!," récit (Raimbaud)
          . "Ah! l'honnête homme!," duo bouffe (Raimbaud, Bertram)
          . "Encore un de gagné, glorieuse conquête," récit (Bertram)
          10. "Noirs démons, fantômes," la valse infernale (Choeur des Démons invisibles)

. "Raimbaud! Raimbaud! dans ce lieu solitaire," récit (Alice)
11. "Quand je quittai la Normandie," couplets et scène (Alice)
12. "Mais Alice, qu'as-tu donc?," duo et scéne (Alice, Bertram)
13. "Fatal moment, cruel mystère!," trio sans accompagnement (Alice, Robert, Bertram)
. "Qu'a-t-elle donc?... Qui sait? l'amour, la jalousie," récit (Robert, Bertram)
14. "Des chevaliers de ma patrie," duo (Robert, Bertram)
15a. "Voici donc les débris du monastère antique," scène (Bertram)
. "Nonnes qui reposez sous cette froide pierre," évocation (Bertram)
. "Procession des nonnes"
15b. "Bacchanale"
15c. "Voici ce lieu témoin d'un terrible mystère!," récit (Robert)
15d. "1er Air de Ballet" (Séduction par l'ivresse)
15e. "2me Air de Ballet" (Séduction par le jeu)
15f. "3me Air de Ballet" (Séduction par l'amour)
15g. "Il est à nous!," choeur dansé
IV: 16. "Entr'acte"
. "Noble et belle Isabelle," choeur de femmes dansé
. "Mais n'est-ce pas cette jeune étrangère," récit (Isabelle)
17. "Frappez les airs, chants d'allégresse," choeur
18a. "Du magique rameau qui s'abaisse sur eux," scène (Robert)
. "Ah! qu'elle est belle!... qu'elle est belle!," cavatine (Robert)
18b. "Grand Dieu! grand Dieu toi qui vois mes alarmes," duo (Isabelle, Robert)
18c. "Robert, Robert, toi que j'aime et qui reçus, qui reçus ma foi," cavatine (Isabelle)
18d. "Quelle aventure? quel prestige?," morceau d'ensemble
V: 19. "Entr'acte"
. "Malheureux, malheureux ou coupable," choeur des moines
20. "Gloire à la providence!," choeur (prière)
21. "Dans ce lieu pourquoi me forcer à te suivre?," scène et duo avec choeur (reprise de la prière)
. "Je conçois que ces chants puissent troubler ton âme," récit (Bertram)
22. "Je t'ai trompé, je fus coupable," air (Bertram)
. "L'arrêt est prononcé l'enfer est le plus fort!," récit (Robert)
23. "À tes lois, à tes lois je souscris d'avance!," grand trio (Alice, Robert, Bertram)
24. "Ah! chantez, troupe immortelle," choeur final
Supplément (Scène et Prière): . "Où me cacher? quelle horreur! quel supplice!," récit (Robert)
. "Oh! ma mère, ombre si tendre," prière

1a.10   "Les Huguenots," opera (Nos. of sections in The Gramophone): ....
I: 1. "Ouverture"
2. "Des beaux jours"
3a. "De ces lieux enchanteurs"
3b. "Sous le beau ciel de Touraine"
4. "Bonheur de la table"
5a. "Non loin des vieilles tours"
5b. "Ah! quel spectacle"
5c. "Plus blanche que la blanche hermine"
6a. "Quelle étrange figure"
6b. "Seigneur, rempart et seul"
7. "Eh! mais-plus je le vois"
8. "Piff paff, piff paff"
9. "Au maître de ces lieux"
10. "L'aventure est singulière"
11. "Honneur au conquérant"
12a. "Nobles seigneurs"
12b. "Une dame noble et sage"
13a. "Trop de mérite aussi"
13b. "Vous savez si je suis un ami"
13c. "Les plaisirs, les honneurs"
II: 14. "Entr'acte"
15a. "O beau pays de la Touraine"
15b. "Belle forêt"
15c. "Sombre chimère"
15d. "A cet mot seul s'aime"
16. "Jeunes beautés"
17. "Non, non, non, vous n'avez jamais"
18a. "Le voici, du silence"
18b. "Pareille loyauté"
19a. "Beauté divine"
19b. "Preux doit vivre"
19c. "Si j'étais coquette"
19d. "A vous et me vie et mon âme"
20. "Allons! toujours le page"
21. "Par l'honneur, par le nom"
22a. "Et maintenant je dois offrir"
22b. "O transport"
III: 23. "Entr'acte"

24. "C'est le jour de dimanche"
25a. "Rataplan"
25b. "Prenant son sabre de batailles"
26. "Vierge Marie"
27. "Profanes, impies"
28a. "Gypsy Round"
28b. "Gypsy Dance"
29. "Pour rempir un voeu solennel"
30. "Rentrez, habitants de Paris"
31a. "O terreur! Je tressaille"
31b. "Dans la nuit"
31c. "Ah! l'ingrat"
31d. "Ah! tu ne peux"
32. "Un danger le menace"
33. "En mon bon droit j'ai confiance"
34. "Nous voila! félons, arrière"
35a. "Ma fille"
35b. "Au banquet"
IV: 36. "Entr'acte"
37a. "Je suis seule"
37b. "Parmi les pleurs"
38. "Juste ciel! est-ce lui"
39a. "Des troubles renaissants"
39b. "Qu'en ce riche quartier"
40. "Gloire au grand Dieu vengeur"
41a. "O ciel! Où courez vous"
41b. "Tu l'as dit"
V: 42. "Entr'acte"
43a. "Aux armes!"
43b. "A la lueur de leurs torches"
44. "C'est toi"
45. "Dieu Seigneur, rempart et seul soutien"
46. "Savez-vous qu'en joignant vos mains"
47. "Abjurez, hugenots!"
48. "Ah! voyez, le ciel s'ouvre"
49. "Par le fer et par l'incende"

1a.12   "Le prophète," opera (Nos. of sections in The Gramophone): ....
        excerpts: I: 1. "Prélude, 'La brise est muette' "
                2. "Mon coeur est muette"
                3. "Fidès, ma bonne mère"
                4. "Ad nos salutarem undam"
                5. "Ainsi ces beaux châteaux?"
                6. "O roi des cieux"
                7. "Le Comte d'Oberthal"
                8. "Un jour, dans les flots"
                9. "Eh quoi! tant de candeur"
            II: 10. "Valsons toulours"
                11. "Ami, quel nuage"
                12. "Pour Berthe moi je souspire"
                13. "Ils partent, grâce au ciel"
                14. "Ah! mon fils, sois béni!"
                15. "O fureur! le ciel"
                16. "Gémissant sous le joug"
                17. "Ne sais-tu pas qu'en France"
                18. "Et la couronne"
           III: 19. "Entr'acte, 'Du sang!' "
                20. "Aussi nombreux que les étoiles"
                21. "Voici la fin du jour"
                22. "Voici les fermières"
                23. "Ballet"
                24. "Livrez-vous au repos, frères"
                25. "Sous votre bannière"
                26. "Pour prendre Munster"
                27. "Mais pourquoi dans l'ombre"
                28. "Qu'on le mène au supplice"
                29. "Par toi Munster nous fut promis"
                30. "Qui vous a sans mon ordre"
                31. "Éternel, Dieu sauveur"
                32. "Grand prophète"
                33. "Roi du ciel et des anges"
            IV: 34. "Entr'acte, 'Courbons notre tête' "
                35. "Donnez, donnez pour une pauvre âme"
                36. "C'est l'heure!... On nous attend"
                37. "Un pauvre pèlerin"

38a. "Dernier espoir"
38b. "Non, plus d'espoir"
39. "Un matin je trouvai"
40. "Coronation March"
41. "Domine, salvum fac regem nostrum"
42. "Le voilà, le Roi Prophète"
43. "Qui je suis?"
44. "Arrêtez!... Il prend ma défense!"
45. "Tu chérissais ce fils"
V: 46. "Entr'acte, 'Ainsi vous l'attestez?' "
47. "O prêtres de Baal"
48. "O toi qui m'abandonnes"
49. "Comme un éclair"
50. "Ma mère!"
51a. "Eh bien! si le remords"
51b. "À la voix de ta mère"
52. "Voici le souterrain"
53. "Loin de la ville"
54. "O spectre, ô spectre épouvantable!"
55. "Hourra! gloire!"
56. "Versez! que tout respire"

1a.14   "Dinorah ou Le pardon de Ploërmel," opera: ....
     I: . "Ouverture"
         1. "Le jour radieux—Se voile à nos yeux," choeur villageois
         2. "Bellah, ma chèvre chérie!," récit (Dinorah)
         . "Dors, petite, dors tranquille," berceuse (Dinorah)
         2bis. "Air de cornemuse"
         3. "Dieu nous donne à chacun en partage," couplets (Corentin)
         4. "Encor, encor, encor!... "Sonne, sonne, gai sonneur," duo (Dinorah, Corentin)
         5. "O puissante magie," grand air (Hoël)
         6. "Si tu crois revoir ton père expirant," scène et conjutation (Hoël, Corentin)
         7. "Un trésor, bois encor," duo bouffe (Hoël, Corentin)
         8. "Ce tintement que l'on entend," terzettino de la clochette (Dinorah, Corentin, Hoël)
     II: . "Entr'acte"
         9. "Qu'il est bon, le vin," choeur (le Retour du cabaret)
         10. "Me voici, Hoël doit m'attendre ici," récit (Dinorah)
         . "Le vieux sorcier de la montagne," romance (Dinorah)
         11. "Allons vite, prends ta leçon," scène
         . "Ombre légère qui suis mes pas," air (Dinorah)
         12. "Ah! que j'ai froid! ah! que j'ai peur!," chanson (Corentin)
         13. "Sombre destinée, âme condamnée," légende (Dinorah)
         14. "Quand l'heure sonnera," duo (Hoël, Corentin)
         15. "Taisez-vous!—Pauvre victime," grand trio final (Dinorah, Hoël, Corentin)
     III: . "Entr'acte"
         16. "En chasse, piqueurs adroits," chant (Chasseur)
         . "Le jour est levé"
         17. "Les blés sont bons à faucher," chant (Faucheur)
         18. "Sous les genévriers," villanelle (Deux Patres)
         19. "Bonjour, bergers," scène (à quatre voix)
         . "Mon Dieu, notre père," Pater Noster
         20. "Comment, encor vivante!," mélodrame (Hoël)
         . "Ah! mon remords te venge," romance (Hoël)
         21a. "Un songe, ô Dieu!," récit et duo (Dinorah, Hoël)
         21b. "Sainte Marie," choeur du pardon
         21c. "Morceau d'ensemble"

1a.15   "L'africaine," opera (Nos. of sections in The Gramophone): ....
     I: 1. "Ouverture"
         2. "Adieu, mon doux rivage"
     II: 3. "Sur mes genoux"
         4. "Fille des rois"
         5. "Combien tu m'es chère"
     III: 6. "Holà! Matelots"
         7. "Adamastor, roi des vagues"
     IV: 8. "Prelude"
         9a. "Pays merveilleux"
         9b. "O Paradis"
         9c. "Conduisez-moi"
         10. "L'avoir tant adorée" (Averla tanto amata)
     V: 11. "Erreur fatal"

2. SYMPHONIES

2.1   Symphony in E-flat major (c1811) ....

3. OTHER ORCHESTRAL WORKS

3.1   Orch pieces (c1809; small orch)...
3.2   "4 Fackeltänze" (4 Torch Dances) (milit band, for Prussian royal wedding): No.1 in B-flat major (c1844).....
3.3   No.2 in E-flat major (c1850)
3.4   No.3 in C minor (c1853)
3.5   No.4 in C major (c1858, with: God save the King)
3.6   "Festival March" (c1859, for centenary of Schiller's birth) ....
3.7   "Coronation March" (c1861; 2 orch, for coronation of Wilhelm I)..
3.8   "Festival Overture in March Style" (c1862, for London World Exhibition) ....
3.9   *"Les patineurs," ballet suite (arr Lambert 1937)*...

4. CONCERTOS, SOLO INSTR & ORCH

Pf & orch:

4.1   Piano Concerto (c1811)..
4.2   Concert piece (c early)..
4.3   "Variations" (c1807, on march from B. A. Weber: Weihe der Kraft) ....

Other:

4.4   Bassoon Concerto (c1812)..
4.5   Double Concerto (c1812; pf, vn & orch) ....

5. CHAMBER MUSIC

5.1   "Ouvertüre" (c1810; vn & pf)..
5.2   Quintet in E-flat major (c1813; cl & str qt) ....

6. PIANO SONATAS

6.1   Piano Sonata (c1803)..
6.2   Piano Sonata in E-flat major (c1812)...

7. OTHER PIANO WORKS

7.1   "Fandango" (c1811) ....
7.2   "Divertimento" (c1812) ....
7.3   "Fugue," in A minor (c1812)...
7.4   "Rondò," in G major (c1812)...
7.5   "Variations," in D major (c1812)...
7.6   "Variations," in F major (c1812) ....

8. ORGAN (or harm)

8.1   "Offertoire" (org)..
8.2   "Prière" (harm) ....

9. SACRED VOCAL

9.1   "Psalm 98" (c1811; ch) ....
9.2   "Gott und die Natur" (God and Nature), oratorio (c1811, Schreiber; vv & ch) ....
9.3   "7 Spiritual Songs" (ca1811, p1841, Klopstock; S, A, T, B & pf ad lib): 1. "Morning Song" ....
9.4   2. "To the Holy Trinity"
9.5   3. "Preparation for the Service"
9.6   4. "Song of Thanks"
9.7   5. "After the Lord's Supper"
9.8   6. "Awake, my Heart"
9.9   7. "Dearest Jesus, We are Here"
9.10   "The Lord is My Shepherd," psalm (c1813; vv & d ch) ....
9.11   "Hallelujah," small cantata (c1815, Kley; 4vv & org ad lib) ....
9.12   "To God," hymn (c1814, Gubitz; S, A, T, B & pf ad lib) ....
9.13   "Children's Prayer": "The Almighty Lord" (c1839; 3 fem vv) ....

9.14 "2 Religious Poems" (c1853, Neuss; 2S, A & org ad lib): 1. "Glory to the Highest" ....
9.15   2. "Hallelujah, the Lord is here"
9.16 "Psalm 91": "Comfort in the face of death" (c1853; S, A, T, B & d ch) ....
9.17 "Pater noster," offertory (p1857; ch) ....
9.18 "Busslied" (Penitential Hymn): "Qui sequitur me" (c1859, Corneille & Rellstab; B & ch) ....
9.19 "Prière du matin" (Morning Prayer) (c1864, Deschamps; d ch & pf ad lib)...............................

10. OCCASIONAL & CHORAL WORKS

10.1 "Zur Feier des 15ten Juni 1810" (c1810; vv, ch & pf, for Vogler's birthday) ....
10.2 "Bavarian Riflemen's March," cantata (c1829, King Ludwig I of Bavaria; 4vv, m ch & winds) ....
10.3 "Festival Song" (c1834, Rosenberg; 2T, 2B, ch & pf ad lib, unveiling of Gutenberg monument in Mainz) ....
10.4 "Kindergebet" (p1839; ch) ....
10.5 "Friendship" (c1842, Deschamps; m ch, founding of the Berlin Singakademie) ....
10.6 "To the Fatherland" (c1842; m ch) ....
10.7 "The Joyous Hunters" (m ch) ....
10.8 "A Song for the Master of German Song" (c1845; m ch, for the reception of Louis Spohr)...........................
10.9 "The Wanderer and the Spirits at Beethoven's Grave" (c1845, Brown; B & ch) ....
10.10 "Festival Hymn": "Thou, Thou throughout time and space" (c1848, Winkler; vv, ch & pf ad lib) ....
10.11 "Blood and Life for such a King" (c1851, Rellstab) ....
10.12 "Ode to Rauch": "Stand up and receive with festive song" (p1851, Kopisch; vv, ch & orch) ....
10.13   "Hymn of Sacrifice to Zeus" (Variant of: Ode to Rauch, new text Rellstab) ....
10.14 "Maria & Her Guardian Spirit": "The joyous day has come" (c1852, Goldtammer; S, T, ch & pf) ....
10.15 "Bridal Procession from the Homeland," serenade (c1856, Rellstab; ch) ....
10.16 "Choeur des sybarites" (c1857) ....
10.17 "Nice à Stephanie" (c1857, Pillet; S, ch & pf) ....
10.18 "You were born unto us, you have never died" (c1859, Pfau; S, A, T, B, ch & orch) ....
10.19 "Song of the Union" (Bundeslied) (c1861; m ch & pf ad lib, based on: God save the King)...........................
10.20 "Festive Hymn" (c1861, Köster; 6vv, ch & orch)...
10.21 "The Song of the Blind Hessian": "Ich weiss ein theuerwerthes Land" (c1862, Altmüller; T & m ch) ....

11. VOCAL DUETS (w/ pf)

11.1 "Le ranz-des-vâches d'Appenzell," chanson suisse (c1828, Scribe) ....
11.2 "La mère grand," nocturne (c1830, Betourné) ....

12. SONGS (w/ pf)

12.1 "6 canzonettes italiennes" (c1810, Metastasio) ....
12.2 "Der Traumgeist" (c1824, Robert) ....
12.3 "Ballade de la reine Marguerite de Valois" (c1829) ....
12.4 "La barque légère" (p1829, Naudet) ....
12.5 "Le voeu pendant l'orage" (p1830, Betourné) ....
12.6 "Au revoir" (c ?1833) ....
12.7 "L'absence" (c1833, Desbordes-Valmore) ....
12.8 "Le miroir magique" (c1833) ....
12.9 "Soave l'istante" (c1833) ....
12.10 "Le ricordanze" (c1833) ....
12.11 "L'enlèvement" (c1834) ....
12.12 "Le moine" (c1834, Pacini) ....
12.13 "Rachel à Nephtali" (c1834, Deschamps) ....
12.14 "Sie und ich" (c1835, Rückert) ....
12.15 "Le poète mourant," élégie (c1836, Millevoye) ....
12.16 "Fantaisie" (c1836, Blaze) ....
12.17 "Hör ich das Liedchen klingen" (De ma première amie) (c1837, Heine) ....
12.18 "Komm du schönes Fischermädchen" (Guide au bord) (c1837, Heine) ....
12.19 "La fille de l'air" (c1837, Méry) ....
12.20 "La folle de St Joseph" (c1837, Custine) ....
12.21 "Scirocco" (c1837, Beer) ....
12.22 "Lied des venezianischen Gondoliers" (c ?1837, Beer) ....
12.23 "Chant de mai" (c1837, Blaze) ....
12.24 "Menschenfeindlich" (c1837, Beer) ....
12.25 "La Marguerite du poète" (c1837, Blaze) ....
12.26 "Die Rose, die Lilie, die Taube, die Sonne" (C'est elle) (c1838, Heine) (also see Schumann Op.48/3) ....
12.27 "Die Rosenblätter" (p1838, Müller) ....
12.28 "Chant des moissoneurs vendéens" (c1839, Blaze) ....
12.29 "Nella," chansonette (ca1839, Deschamps) ....
12.30 "Suleika" (c1838, Goethe) ....
12.31 "Der Garten des Herzens" (c1839, Müller) ....
12.32 "Le baptême" (c1839, Flassan) ....
12.33 "La chanson de Maître Floh" (c1839 or 40, Blaze de Bury)...
12.34 "A une jeune mère" (c by 1839, Durand) ....

* * * * *

1. STAGE WORKS

Operas:

1.1	"La brebis égarée," 3 acts (c1910–14, Jammes)	Op.4
1.2	"Les malheurs d'Orphée," 3 acts (c1924, Lunel)	Op.85
1.3	"Esther de Carpentras," 2 act comic opera (c1925, Lunel)	Op.89
1.4	"Le pauvre matelot" (The Poor Sailor), 3 acts (c1926, Cocteau)	Op.92
1.5	"Trois Opèra-Minutes" (c1927, Hoppenot from Greek mythology): I. "L'enlèvement d'Europe," 1 act	Op.94
1.6	II. "L'abandon d'Ariane," 1 act	Op.98
1.7	III. "Le délivrance de Thésée," 1 act	Op.99
1.8	"Christophe Colomb" (Christopher Columbus), 2 parts, 27 tableaux (c1928, Claudel)	Op.102
1.9	"Maximilien," 3 acts, 9 tableaux (c1930, Werfel, Hoffmann & Lunel)	Op.110
1.10	"Médée," 1 act (c1938, M. Milhaud)	Op.191
1.11	"Bolivar," 3 acts (c1943, M. Milhaud & Supervielle)	Op.236
1.12	"David," 5 acts (c1952–3, Lunel)	Op.320
1.13	"Fiesta," 1 act (c1958, Vian)	Op.370
1.14	"La mère coupable," 3 acts (c1964–5, M. Milhaud after Beaumarchais)	Op.412
1.15	"Saint Louis, roi de France," 2 part opera-oratorio (c1970, Claudel & Doublier)	Op.434

Misc dramatic:

1.16	"Les récitatifs pour 'Une éducation manquée' de Chabrier" (c1923)	Op.82
1.17	"Fête de la musique" (Celestial ballet), spectacle (c1936–7, Claudel; S, 4vv, pf & orch)	Op.159

Plays for children:

1.18   "À propos de bottes" (c1932, Chalupt; 1v & pf/vns, vcs): Op.118
       1. "Chanson du savetier et de la pie"
       2. "Chanson de Babolin, le livreur"
       3. "Chanson d'Alfred"
       4. "Chanson d'Alfred et de la pie"
       5. "Chanson du fantôme"
       6. "Chanson des anthropophages"
       7. "Chanson du chinois"
       8. "Chanson du cinéaste, chanson d'Alfred et de la Star"
       9. "Chanson de l'ogre. Chanson finale"

1.19   "Un petit peu de musique" (c1932, Lunel; 1v & pf/vns, vcs): Op.119
       1. "Le petit examen"
       2. "Pour sauter à la corde"
       3. "La lecture enfantine"
       4. "Pour tirer au sort"
       5. "Mademoiselle Lunette"
       6. "Mea culpa"
       7. "Le maître pion Jujube"
       8. "Un éloge mérité"
       9. "La dispute"
       10. "L'orchestre des bons élèves"
       11. "L'orchestre des mauvais élèves"
       12. "Choeur final en l'honneur de la radio"

1.20   "Un petit peu d'exercice" (c1934, Lunel; 1v & pf/vns, vcs): Op.133
       1. "Chant du départ"
       2. "Repos hebdomadaire"
       3. "Tohu-bohu des sportifs—Farniente des débonnaires"
       4. "La culture physique"
       5. "Le sportif paisible"
       6. "Natation"
       7. "Le vélo"
       8. "La raquette"
       9. "Le jeune homme studieux"
       10. "Le chant du skieur"
       11. "Jeunes filles 1900"
       12. "Choeur final de réconciliation"

Ballets:

1.21	"L'homme et son désir" (c1918, Claudel; 4vv, 12 solo insts & 15 perc)	Op.48
1.22	"Le boeuf sur le toit" (c1919, Cocteau; also see: Cinéma Fantaisie, Op.58b; red for pf duet)	Op.58
1.23	Nos.2, 5 & 10 for collab work: Les mariés de la tour Eiffel (c1921, Cocteau, music c by 'Le Six'):	Op.70

       "Les mariés de la tour Eiffel": *1. "Ouverture" (Le 14 juillet) (c by Auric)*
       2. "Marche nuptiale" (c by Milhaud)
       3. "Discours du général" (Polka pour deux cornets à pistons) (c by Poulenc)
       4. "La baigneuse de Trouville" (Carte postale en couleurs) (c by Poulenc)
       5. "Fugue du massacre" (c by Milhaud)
       6. "Valse des dépêches" (c by Tailleferre)

Radio:

Film:

2. SYMPHONIES

3. OTHER ORCHESTRAL WORKS

3.97	"Suite française" (c1944; arr for orch, Op.248b; also for pf duet): No.1 "Normandie"	Op.248
3.98	No.2 "Bretagne"	
3.99	No.3 "Ile-de-France"	
3.100	No.4 "Alsace-Lorraine"	
3.101	No.5 "Provence"	
3.102	"2 Marches" (c1945; orig for orch, Op.260): No.1 "In Memoriam" (Pearl Harbour)	Op.260b
3.103	No.2 "Gloria Victoribus"	
3.104	"West Point Suite" (c1951): No.1 "Introduction"	Op.313
3.105	No.2 "Récitatif"	
3.106	No.3 "Fanfare"	
3.107	"Musique de Théâtre" (c1954–70, after incid music to: Saül, Op.334): No.1 "Prélude et Fugue"	Op.334b
3.108	No.2 "Triomphe"	
3.109	No.3 "Interlude"	
3.110	No.4 "Funèbre et Choral"	
3.111	"Fanfare" (c1962; 4hn, 3tpt, 3trbn & tuba)	Op.396
3.112	"Fanfare" (c1962; 2tpt & 2trbn)	Op.400

4. CONCERTOS, SOLO INSTR & ORCH

Pf & orch:

4.1	"Poème sur un cantique de Camargue" (c1913)	Op.13
4.2	"Ballade" (c1920; red for 2pf)	Op.61
4.3	"Cinq études" (c1920): No.1 "Vif"	Op.63
4.4	No.2 "Doucement"	
4.5	No.3 "Fugues"	
4.6	No.4 "Sombre"	
4.7	No.5 "Romantique"	
4.8	"Le carnaval d'Aix," suite (c1926, after ballet: Salade, Op.83; red for 2pf): No.1 "Le Corso"	Op.83b
4.9	No.2 "Tartaglia"	
4.10	No.3 "Isabella"	
4.11	No.4 "Rosetta"	
4.12	No.5 "Le bon et le mauvais tuteur"	
4.13	No.6 "Coviello"	
4.14	No.7 "Polichinelle"	
4.15	No.8 "Polka"	
4.16	No.9 "Cinzio"	
4.17	No.10 "Souvenir de Rio"	
4.18	No.11 "Final"	
4.19	Piano Concerto No.1 (c1933; red for 2pf)	Op.127
4.20	"Fantaisie pastorale" (c1938; red for 2pf)	Op.188
4.21	Piano Concerto No.2 (c1941; red for 2pf)	Op.225
4.22	Piano Concerto No.3 (c1946; red for 2pf)	Op.270
4.23	"Suite concertante" (c1952, after: Concerto Marimba, Op.278)	Op.278b
4.24	Piano Concerto No.4 (c1949; red for 2pf)	Op.295
4.25	Piano Concerto No.5 (c1955; red for 2pf)	Op.346

2 Pf & orch:

4.26	Double Piano Concerto No.1 (c1941; red for 3pf)	Op.228
4.27	"Suite Opus 300" (c1950): No.1 "Entrée"	Op.300
4.28	No.2 "Nocturne"	
4.29	No.3 "Java fuguée"	
4.30	No.4 "Mouvement perpétuel"	
4.31	No.5 "Final"	
4.32	"Concertino d'automne" (c1951; 2pf & 8 insts)	Op.309
4.33	Double Piano Concerto No.2 (c1961; 2pf & 4perc)	Op.394

Vn & orch:

4.34	"Cinema-Fantaisie" (p1921, from ballet: Le boeuf, Op.58; also see: Le boeuf for vn & pf, Op.58b) ..	Op.58b
4.35	Violin Concerto No.1 (c1927)	Op.93
4.36	"Concertino de printemps" (c1934; vn & chamber orch; red w/ pf)	Op.135
4.37	"Suite anglaise" (c1942; orig for harmonica & orch, Op.234; red w/ pf)	Op.234b
4.38	Violin Concerto No.2 (c1946; red w/ pf)	Op.263
4.39	Violin Concerto No.3, "Concert Royal" (c1958; red w/ pf)	Op.373
4.40	"Music for Boston" (c1965; red w/ pf)	Op.414

Va & orch:

4.41	Viola Concerto No.1 (c1929; red w/ pf)	Op.108
4.42	"Air de la sonate" (c1944)	Op.242
4.43	"Concertino d'été" (c1950; va & chamber orch; red w/ pf)	Op.311
4.44	Viola Concerto No.2 (c1954–5; red w/ pf)	Op.340

Vc & orch:

4.45	Cello Concerto No.1 (c1934; red w/ pf)	Op.136
4.46	Cello Concerto No.2 (c1945; red w/ pf)	Op.255
4.47	"Suite cisalpine" (sur des airs populaires piémontais) (c1954; red w/ pf): No.1 "Vif"	Op.332
4.48	No.2 "Modéré"	
4.49	No.3 "Très animé"	

Other instr & orch:

4.50	"Concerto" (Percussion Concerto) (c1929–30; perc & chamber orch; red w/ pf)	Op.109
4.51	"Scaramouche," suite (c1939; sax & orch, after incid music: Le médecin volant, Op.165; red w/ pf)	Op.165c
4.52	"Scaramouche," suite (c1939; cl & orch, after incid music: Le médecin volant, Op.165; red w/ pf)	Op.165d
4.53	"Concerto" (c1939; fl, vn & orch; red w/ pf)	Op.197
4.54	Clarinet Concerto (c1941)	Op.230
4.55	"Suite anglaise" (c1942; harmonica & orch; arr for vn/accordion & orch; red w/ pf): No.1 "Gigue"	Op.234
4.56	No.2 "Sailor's Song"	
4.57	No.3 "Hornpipe"	
4.58	"Concerto Marimba" (c1947; marimba, vibraphone & orch; arr for pf & orch, Op.278b; red w/ pf)	Op.278
4.59	Harp Concerto (c1953; red w/ pf)	Op.323
4.60	"Concertino d'hiver" (c1953; trbn & strings; red w/ pf)	Op.327
4.61	Oboe Concerto (c1957; red w/ pf)	Op.365
4.62	"Symphonie concertante" (c1959; tpt, hn, bn, d bass & orch)	Op.376
4.63	Harpsichord Concerto (c1964; red w/ pf)	Op.407
4.64	"Stanford Serenade" (c1969; ob & 11 insts; red w/ pf)	Op.430

5. STRING QUARTETS

5.1	String Quartet No.1 (c1912)	Op.5
5.2	String Quartet No.2 (c1914–5)	Op.16
5.3	String Quartet No.3 (c1916, Latil; 1v & str qt, in memory of Léo Latil)	Op.32
5.4	String Quartet No.4 (c1918)	Op.46
5.5	String Quartet No.5 (c1920)	Op.64
5.6	String Quartet No.6 (c1922)	Op.77
5.7	String Quartet No.7 (c1925)	Op.87
5.8	String Quartet No.8 (c1932)	Op.121
5.9	String Quartet No.9 (c1935)	Op.140
5.10	"La reine de Saba" (c1939, after Palestinian song)	Op.207
5.11	String Quartet No.10, "Birthday Quartet" (c1940)	Op.218
5.12	String Quartet No.11 (c1942)	Op.232
5.13	String Quartet No.12 (c1945)	Op.252
5.14	String Quartet No.13 (c1946)	Op.268
5.15	String Quartet No.14 (c1948–9, playable together w/ No.15 as octet)	Op.291/1
5.16	String Quartet No.15 (c1948–9, playable together w/ No.14 as octet)	Op.291/2
5.17	String Quartet No.16 (c1950)	Op.303
5.18	String Quartet No.17 (c1950)	Op.307
5.19	String Quartet No.18 (c1950–1)	Op.308
5.20	"Hommage à Igor Stravinsky" (c1971)	Op.435
5.21	"Études" (sur des thèmes liturgiques du Comtat Venaissin) (c1973): No.1 "Modéré"	Op.442
5.22	No.2 "Animé"	
5.23	No.3 "Modéré"	

6. OTHER CHAMBER MUSIC

6 or more insts:

6.1	String Sextet (c1958; 2vn, 2va & 2vc)	Op.368
6.2	String Septet (c1964; 2vn, 2va, 2vc & d bass)	Op.408

5 insts:

6.3	"La création du monde," concert suite (c1926; str qt & pf, from ballet Op.81)	Op.81b
6.4	"La cheminée du Roi René," suite (c1939; wind qnt, after film: Cavalcade, Op.204): No.1 "Cortège"	Op.205
6.5	No.2 "Aubade"	
6.6	No.3 "Jongleurs"	
6.7	No.4 "La Moussinglade"	
6.8	No.5 "Joutes sur l'Arc"	
6.9	No.6 "Chasse à Valabre"	
6.10	No.7 "Madrigal nocturne"	
6.11	"Eglogue Madrigal" (arr1941; wind qnt, from: Quatre esquisses for pf, Op.227)	(Op.227)
6.12	"Les rêves de Jacob," dance suite (c1949; ob, str trio & d bass): No.1 "L'oreiller de Jacob"	Op.294
6.13	No.2 "Premier rêve" (l'echelle de Jacob)	
6.14	No.3 "Prophétie"	

6.15	No.4 "Deuxième rêve" (Lutte avec l'ange et Bénédiction)	
6.16	No.5 "Israël" (Hymne)	
6.17	"Divertissement" (c1958; wind qnt, from film: Gauguin, Op.299): No.1 "Balancé"	Op.299b
6.18	No.2 "Dramatique"	
6.19	No.3 "Joyeux"	
6.20	Quintet No.1 (c1951; pf qnt)	Op.312
6.21	Quintet No.2 (c1952; str qt & d bass)	Op.316
6.22	Quintet No.3 (c1953; va & str qt)	Op.325
6.23	Quintet No.4 (c1956; vc & str qt)	Op.350
6.24	Wind Quintet (c1973; fl, ob, cl, hn & bn)	Op.443

4 insts:

6.25	"Sonate" (c1918; pf, fl, cl & ob)	Op.47
6.26	Piano Quartet (c1966)	Op.417

3 insts:

6.27	"Sonate" (c1914; 2vn & pf)	Op.15
6.28	"Pastorale" (c1935; ob, cl & bn)	Op.147
6.29	"Le voyageur sans bagages," suite (c1936; vn, cl & pf, from incid music Op.157)	Op.157b
6.30	"Suite d'après Corrette" (c1937; ob, cl & bn, from incid music Op.161): No.1 "Entrée et Rondeau"	Op.161b
6.31	No.2 "Tambourin"	
6.32	No.3 "Musette"	
6.33	No.4 "Sérénade"	
6.34	No.5 "Fanfare"	
6.35	No.6 "Rondeau"	
6.36	No.7 "Menuet"	
6.37	No.8 "Le Coucou"	
6.38	"Sonatine à trois" (c1940; str trio)	Op.221b
6.39	String Trio (c1947)	Op.274
6.40	Piano Trio (c1968)	Op.428

Vn & pf (hpd):

6.41	Violin Sonata No.1 (c1911)	Op.3
6.42	"Le printemps" (c1914)	Op.18
6.43	Violin Sonata No.2 (c1917)	Op.40
6.44	"Le boeuf sur le toit" (c1919, from ballet Op.58)	Op.58b
6.45	"Impromptu" (c1926)	Op.91
6.46	"Trois caprices de Paganini" (c1927)	Op.97
6.47	"Dixième sonate de Baptiste Anet (1729)," in D major (c1935, free transcr)	Op.144
6.48	"Danses de Jacaremirim" (c1945): No.1 "Chorinho"	Op.256
6.49	No.2 "Tanguinho"	
6.50	No.3 "Sambinha"	
6.51	"Sonate" (c1945; vn & hpd)	Op.257
6.52	"Farandoleurs" (c1946)	Op.262

Va & pf:

6.53	"Quatre visages" (c1943): No.1 "La californienne"	Op.238
6.54	No.2 "La wisconsinian"	
6.55	No.3 "La bruxelloise"	
6.56	No.4 "La parisienne"	
6.57	Viola Sonata No.1 (c1944)	Op.240
6.58	Viola Sonata No.2 (c1944)	Op.244

Vc & pf:

6.59	"Élégie" (c1945)	Op.251
6.60	Cello Sonata (c1959)	Op.377

Other 2 insts:

6.61	"Sonatine" (c1922; fl & pf)	Op.76
6.62	"Sonatine" (c1927; cl & pf)	Op.100
6.63	"Suite" (c1932; ondes martenot & pf, from incid music: Le château, Op.120): No.1 "Choral"	Op.120c
6.64	No.2 "Sérénade"	
6.65	No.3 "Impromptu"	
6.66	No.4 "Étude"	
6.67	No.5 "Elégie"	
6.68	"Exercice musical" (c1934; pipe & pf)	Op.134
6.69	"Sonatine" (c1940; 2vn; also see: Sonatine à Trois, Op.221b)	Op.221
6.70	"Sonatine" (c1941; vn & va)	Op.226
6.71	"Eglogue Madrigal" (arr1941; cl & pf, from: Quatre esquisses for pf, Op.227)	Op.227c

8.45	No.13 "Promenade"
8.46	No.14 "Pensée"
8.47	No.15 "Chagrin"
8.48	No.16 "Barcarolle"
8.49	No.17 "Dernier feuillet"
8.50	"Trois valses" (c1933, from film: Madame Bovary, Op.128) Op.128c
8.51	"Quatre romances sans paroles" (c1933) Op.129
8.52	"Le tour de l'Exposition," for collab work: À l'Exposition (c1937, for World's Fair in Paris 1937): Op.162

        "À l'Exposition," other Nos: . *"La Seine, un matin ..." (c by Auric)*
                . *"Dîner sur l'eau" (c by Delannoy)*
                . *"L'espiègle du village de Lilliput" (c by Ibert)*
                . *"Bourrée au Pavillon d'Auvergne" (c by Poulenc)*
                . *"Nuit coloniale sur les bords de la Seine" (c by Sauguet)*
                . *"La retardée" (c by Schmitt)*
                . *"Au pavillon d'Alsace" (c by Tailleferre)*

8.53	"Touches noirs, Touches blanches" (Black Keys, White Keys), for children (c1941) Op.222
8.54	"Choral" (c1941, for collab work: Hommage à Paderewski) ....
8.55	"Quatre esquisses" (c1941; also see arr for chamber orch; for cl & pf; for wind qnt): No.1 "Eglogue" Op.227
8.56	No.2 "Madrigal"
8.57	No.3 "Sobre la Loma"
8.58	No.4 "Alameda"
8.59	"La libertadora," dance suite (c1943, from opera: Bolivar, Op.236; also for 2pf, Op.236b) Op.236b
8.60	"La muse ménagère" (c1944; pf; also for chamber orch, Op.245b): No.1 "La mienne" (dédicace) Op.245
8.61	No.2 "Le réveil"
8.62	No.3 "Les soins du ménage"
8.63	No.4 "La poésie"
8.64	No.5 "La cuisine"
8.65	No.6 "Les fleurs dans la maison"
8.66	No.7 "La lessive"
8.67	No.8 "Musique ensemble"
8.68	No.9 "Le fils peintre"
8.69	No.10 "Le chat"
8.70	No.11 "Cartomancie"
8.71	No.12 "Les soins au malade"
8.72	No.13 "La douceur des soirées"
8.73	No.14 "Lectures nocturnes"
8.74	No.15 "Reconnaissance à la Muse"
8.75	"Une journée" (c1946): No.1 "L'aube" Op.269
8.76	No.2 "La matinée"
8.77	No.3 "Midi"
8.78	No.4 "L'après-midi"
8.79	No.5 "Le crépuscule"
8.80	"Méditation" (c1947) Op.277
8.81	"L'enfant aimé" (c1948): No.1 "Les fleurs" Op.289
8.82	No.2 "Les bonbons"
8.83	No.3 "Les jouets"
8.84	No.4 "Sa mère"
8.85	No.5 "La vie"
8.86	"Jeu" (c1950, for collab album: Les contemporains) Op.302
8.87	"Candélabre à sept branches" (c1951): No.1 "Le premier jour de l'an" Op.315
8.88	No.2 "Jour de pénitence"
8.89	No.3 "Fête des cabanes"
8.90	No.4 "La résistance des Macchabées"
8.91	No.5 "Fête de la reine Esther"
8.92	No.6 "Fête de la Pâque"
8.93	No.7 "Fête de la Pentecôte"
8.94	"Accueil amical," for children (c1944–7) Op.326
8.95	"Hymne de glorification" (c1953–4) Op.331
8.96	"La couronne de Marguerite" (Valse en forme de rondo) (c1956; orchd) Op.353
8.97	"Sonatine" (c1956) Op.354
8.98	"Le globe-trotter" (c1956–7; orchd): No.1 "France" Op.358
8.99	No.2 "Portugal"
8.100	No.3 "Italie"
8.101	No.4 "Etats-Unis"
8.102	No.5 "Mexique"
8.103	No.6 "Brésil"
8.104	"Les charmes de la vie" (Hommage à Watteau) (c1957; orchd): No.1 "Pastorale" Op.360
8.105	No.2 "L'indifférent"
8.106	No.3 "Plaisirs champêtres"
8.107	No.4 "Sérénade"
8.108	No.5 "Musette"
8.109	No.6 "Mascarade"

Pf duet:

8.110 "Enfantines" (arr of songs: Trois poèmes de Jean Cocteau, Op.59) ....

2 Pf:

8.111 "Scaramouche," suite (c1937, from: Le médecin volant, Op.165; also for sax/cl & orch): No.1 "Vif" Op.165b
8.112   No.2 "Modéré"
8.113   No.3 "Brazileira"
8.114 "La libertadora," dance suite (c1943, from opera: Bolivar, Op.236; also for pf, Op.236b) Op.236b
8.115 "Les songes," suite (c1943, from ballet: Les songes, Op.124) Op.237b
8.116 "Le bal martiniquais" (c1944; orchd as Op.249b): No.1 "Chanson créole" Op.249
8.117   No.2 "Béguine"
8.118 "Carnaval à la Nouvelle-Orléans" (c1947): No.1 "Mardi Gras! Chic à la paille!" Op.275
8.119   No.2 "Domino noir de Cajun"
8.120   No.3 "On danse chez Monsieur Degas"
8.121   No.4 "Les mille cents coups"
8.122 "Kentuckiana" (c1948; orchd as Op.287b) Op.287
8.123 "Six danses en trois mouvements" (c1969–70): No.1 "Tarentelle—Bourée" Op.433
8.124   No.2 "Sarabande—Pavane"
8.125   No.3 "Gigue—Rumba"

4 Pf:

8.126 "Paris," suite (c1948; 4pf; orchd as Op.284b): No.1 "Montmartre" Op.284
8.127   No.2 "L'Ile Saint Louis"
8.128   No.3 "Montparnasse"
8.129   No.4 "Bateaux-mouches"
8.130   No.5 "Longchamps"
8.131   No.6 "La tour Eiffel"

9. ORGAN

9.1 "Sonate" (c1931) Op.112
9.2 "Pastorale" (c1941) Op.229
9.3 "Neuf préludes" (c1942, after incid music: L'annonce faite à Marie, Op.231) Op.231b
9.4 "Petite suite" (c1955): No.1 "Entrée" Op.348
9.5   No.2 "Romance"
9.6   No.3 "Gigue"

10. CHORAL WORKS

10.1 "Deux poèmes" (c1916–9; ch/4vv): 1. "Enfance" (c1916, Léger) Op.39
10.2   2. "Le Brick" (c1919, Chalupt)
10.3 "Psalm 136" (c1919, transl Claudel; Bar, ch & orch) Op.53
10.4 "Psalm 126" (c1921, transl Claudel; m ch) Op.72
10.5 "Cantate pour Louer le Seigneur" (c1928; ch, child ch, org & orch) Op.103
10.6 "Deux poèmes de Cendrars" (c1932; ch/4vv): 1. "La danse des animaux" Op.113
10.7   2. "Le chant de la mort"
10.8 "Deux élégies romaines" (c1932, Goethe; fem ch/4vv): 1. "Eclaire donc, gamin" Op.114
10.9   2. "Pourquoi donc?"
10.10 "La mort du tyran" (c1932, Lampride, Diderot; ch, piccolo, cl, tuba & perc) Op.116
10.11 "Devant sa main nue" (c1933, Raval; fem ch/4vv) Op.122
10.12 "Les amours de Ronsard" (c1934; ch/4vv & small orch): 1. "La rose" Op.132
10.13   2. "La tourterelle"
10.14   3. "L'aubépine"
10.15   4. "Le rossignol"
10.16 "La sagesse," stage spectacle (c1935, Claudel; 4vv, ch & orch) Op.141
10.17 "Cantique du Rhône" (c1936, Claudel; ch/4vv): Op.155
    1. "Qu'il est beau ..."
    2. "Ah! qu'il la prenne déracinée ..."
    3. "Et le bonheur ..."
    4. "Il faut bien des montagnes ..."
10.18 "Cantate de la paix" (c1937, Claudel; m ch & child ch) Op.166
10.19 "Main tendue à tous" (c1937, Vildrac; ch) Op.169
10.20 "Les deux cités," cantata (c1937, Claudel; ch) Op.170
10.21 "4 Popular Songs of Provence" (c1938; ch & orch): 1. "Magali" Op.194
10.22   2. "Se canto"
10.23   3. "L'Antoni"
10.24   4. "Le Mal d'amour"
10.25 "Incantations" (Poèmes aztèques) (c1939, Carpentier; m ch): 1. "Invocation du pêcheur à son filet" Op.201
10.26   2. "Invocation pour conjurer la fureur des abeilles"
10.27   3. "Invocation pour vaincre les ennemis"

. "Prélude III"
3. "Rejection"
10.75 "Cantate de l'initiation" (Bar Mitzvah Israël 1948–1961) (c1960, Liturgy; ch & orch/org): Op.388
    1. "Hymne"
    2. "L'Appel" (Aliyah)
    3. "Lecture de la Thorah" (Extrait de Ki Tabo)
    4. "Bénédiction après la Torah"
    5. "Bénédiction précédant la Haphtarah"
    6. "Lecture de la Haphtarah"
10.76 "Traversée" (c1961, Verlaine; ch) Op.393
10.77 "Invocation à l'ange Raphael," cantata (c1962, Claudel; d fem ch & orch) Op.395
10.78 "Caroles," cantata (c1963, d'Orléans: in Eng & Fr; 4 solo groups & ch) Op.402
10.79 "Pacem in Terris," choral symphony (c1963, from Pope John XXIII: Encyclique; Bar, ch & orch) Op.404
10.80 "Cantata from Job" (c1965–6; Bar, ch & org) Op.413
10.81 "Promesse de Dieu" (c1971–2, Bible; ch) Op.438
10.82 "Les momies d'Egypte," choral comedy (c1972, Régnard; ch) Op.439
10.83 "Ani maamin, un chant perdu et retrouvé," cantata (c1972, Wiesel; S, 4 reciters, ch & orch) Op.441

11. VOICE & ORCHESTRA, MISC VOCAL

11.1   "Notre Dame de Sarrance," hymn (c1915, Jammes; 1v only) Op.29
11.2   "Deux poèmes du 'Gardener' " (c1916–7, Tagore; 2vv & pf): 1. "Ne gardez pas" Op.35
11.3   2. "Ayez pitié de votre serviteur"
11.4   "No.34 de L'église habillée de feuilles" (c1916, Jammes; 4vv & pf 6h) Op.38
11.5   "Le retour de l'enfant prodigue," cantata (c1917, Gide; 5vv & 21 insts) Op.42
11.6   "Deux poèmes tupis" (c1918, Indian texts; 4 fem vv & hand-clapping): 1. "Caïné" Op.52
11.7   2. "Catiti"
11.8   "Psalm 129" (c1919, transl Claudel; Bar & orch) ....
11.9   "Machines agricoles" (Pastorales) (c1919, texts from catalogues of farm machinery; 1v
       & 7 insts): 1. "La moissonneuse Espigadora" Op.56
11.10 2. "La faucheuse"
11.11 3. "La lieuse"
11.12 4. "La déchaumeuse-semeuse-enfouisseuse"
11.13 5. "La fouilleuse-draineuse"
11.14 6. "La faneuse"
11.15 "Caramel Mou" (Shimmy) (c1920; 1v/sax & jazz band; orig for pf, Op.68) Op.68b
11.16 "Cocktail" (c1921, Larsen; 1v & 3cl) Op.69
11.17 "Quatre poèmes de Catulle" (c1923; 1v & vn) Op.80
11.18 "Adages," 16 settings of poems (c1932, Richaud; 4vv & insts/pf) Op.120b
11.19 "Pan et la Syrinx," cantata (c1934, Claudel; S, Bar, 4vv & 5 insts): Op.130
    1. "Nocturne"
    2. "Pan et Syrinx"
    3. "Nocturne"
    4. "L'invention de la gamme"
    5. "Nocturne"
    6. "Danse de Pan"
11.20 "Cantate pour l'Inauguration du Musée de l'Homme" (c1937, Desnos; 4vv, recit & 6 insts) Op.164
11.21 "Cantate nuptiale," 4 numbers (c1937, after: Song of Songs; 1v & orch) Op.168
11.22 "Prends cette rose" (c1937, Ronsard; S, T & orch) Op.183
11.23 "Cantate de l'enfant et de la mère" (c1938, Carême; speaker, str qt & pf) Op.185
11.24 "Les quatre éléments," cantata (c1956, Desnos; S, T/S & orch, from orig of 1938 w/ pf, Op.189) .. Op.189b
11.25 "Trois élégies" (c1939, Jammes; S, T & strings): 1. "Dis-moi, dis-moi" Op.199
11.26 2. "Sur le sable des allées"
11.27 3. "Mon amour, disais-tu"
11.28 "Couronne de gloire," cantata (c1940, Hebrew transl Lunel; 1v, fl, tp & str qt): Op.211
    1. "Couronne de gloire"
    2. "Prière pour les âmes des persécutées"
    3. "Couronne de gloire"
    4. "Prière pour le pape"
    5. "Couronne de gloire"
    6. "Chant pour le jour de réclusion"
    7. "Couronne de gloire"
    8. "Prière pour la paix"
11.29 "Sornettes," for children (c1940, Provençal folk poems transl Mistral; 2 child vv) Op.214
11.30 "Cours de solfège—Papillon, Papillonette," for children (c1940, Fluchère; child vv & pf) Op.217
11.31 "Cinq prières" (c1942, Latin Liturgy; 1v & org, after incid music: L'announce faite à Marie, Op.231) Op.231c
11.32 "Cain et Abel," for collab cantata: Genesis (c1942, Bible; reciter & orch) Op.241
       "Genesis": *1. "Prelude" (c by Schoenberg)*
       2. "Creation" (c by Schilkret)
       3. "Fall of man" (c by Tansman)
       4. "Cain and Abel" (c by Milhaud)
       5. "Flood" (c by Castelnuovo-Tedesco)
       6. "Covenant" (c by Toch)
       7. "Babel" (c by Stravinsky)

12.114	"Trois poèmes de Jean Cocteau" (c1920; also see arr as: Enfantines for pf duet): 1. "Fumée" Op.59
12.115	2. "Fête de Bordeaux"
12.116	3. "Fête de Montmartre"
12.117	"Catalogue de fleurs" (c1920, Daudet—texts from catalogues of flowers, also see: Machines agricoles, Op.56; arr for 1v & 7insts p1932): 1. "La violette" Op.60
12.118	2. "Le bégonia"
12.119	3. "Les fritillaires"
12.120	4. "Les jacinthes"
12.121	5. "Les crocus"
12.122	6. "Le brachycome"
12.123	7. "L'eremurus"
12.124	"Feuilles de température" (c1920, Morand): 1. "Don Juan" Op.65
12.125	2. "Révérence"
12.126	3. "Étrennes"
12.127	"Poème" (du journal intime de Léo Latil) (c1921) Op.73
12.128	"Six chants populaires hébraïque" (c1925, trad; also w/ orch): 1. "La séparation" Op.86
12.129	2. "Le chant du veilleur"
12.130	3. "Chant de déliverance"
12.131	4. "Berceuse"
12.132	5. "Gloire à Dieu"
12.133	6. "Chant hassidique"
12.134	"Deux hymnes" (c1925; arr for orch, Op.88b): 1. "Hymne de Sion" Op.88
12.135	2. "Israël est vivant"
12.136	"Piece de circonstance" (c1926, Cocteau) Op.90
12.137	"Prières journalières à l'usage des juifs du Comtat Venaissin" (c1927): 1. "Prière du matin" Op.96
12.138	2. "Prière de l'après-midi"
12.139	3. "Prière du soir"
12.140	"Vocalise" (c1928, wordless) Op.105
12.141	"Quatrain," for collab work: Hommage à Albert Roussel (c1929, Jammes): Op.106
	"Hommage à Albert Roussel," other Nos: . *"Pièce brève sur le nom d'Albert Roussel" (c by Poulenc)*
	. *"Sur le nom d'Albert Roussel" (c by Honegger)*
	. *"Berceuse" (c by Tansman)*
	. *"Toccata sur le nom d'Albert Roussel" (c by Ibert)*
	. *"Fox-trot" (c by Beck)*
	. *"Fanfare" (c by Hoérée)*
	. *"A Roussel," song (c by Delage)*
12.142	"A flower given to my child" (c1930, Joyce) ....
12.143	"Le funeste retour: chanson de marin" (c1933, 17th cent Canadian) Op.123
12.144	"Liturgie comtadine: 5 chants de Rosch Haschanah" (c1933; also w/ chamber orch) Op.125
12.145	"Deux chansons" (c1933, Flaubert, from film: Madame Bovary, Op.128): 1. "Chanson de l'aveugle" Op.128d
12.146	2. "Chanson du printemps"
12.147	"Le cygne" (c1935, Claudel; 2 settings) Op.142
12.148	"Quatrain" (c1935, Flament) Op.143
12.149	"Trois chansons de négresse" (c1935–6, Supervielle, from incid music: Bolivar, Op.148): 1. "Mon histoire" Op.148b
12.150	2. "Abandonnée"
12.151	3. "Sans feu ni lieu"
12.152	"Six chansons de théâtre" (c1936): Op.151b
	from incid music: . "La folle du ciel," Op.149
	. "Tu ne m'echapperas jamais," Op.151
	. "La première famille," Op.193
12.153	"Trois chansons de troubadour" (c1936, Baisse, from incid music: Bertran de Born, Op.152) Op.152b
12.154	"Cinq chansons" (c1936–7, Vildrac; also w/ chamber orch): 1. "Les quatre petits lions" Op.167
12.155	2. "La pomme et l'escargot"
12.156	3. "Le malpropre"
12.157	4. "Poupette et Patata"
12.158	5. "Le jardinier impatient"
12.159	"2 Songs" (c1937, Bloch, from incid music: Naissance, Op.173): 1. "Chanson du Capitaine" Op.173b
12.160	2. "Java de la Femme"
12.161	"Rondeau" (c1937, Corneille) Op.178
12.162	"Holem Tsaudi—Gam Hayom" (c1937, 2 popular Palestine folksongs): 1. "Holem tsaudi" Op.179
12.163	2. "Gam hayom"
12.164	"Quatrain" (c1937, Mallarmé) Op.180
12.165	"Les quatre éléments" (c1938, Desnos; also see r vers w/ orch, Op.189b): 1. "L'eau" Op.189
12.166	2. "La terre"
12.167	3. "Le feu"
12.168	4. "L'air"
12.169	"Recréation," 4 songs for children (c1938, Krieger): 1. "Pas bien grand" Op.195
12.170	2. "Haut comme trois pommes"
12.171	3. "La tortue naine"
12.172	4. "Il faut obéir"
12.173	"Le voyage d'été," suite (c1940, Paliard): 1. "Modestes vacances" Op.216
12.174	2. "Les deux hôtels"
12.175	3. "Le boulanger"

12.246	19. "Les lilas qui avaient fleuri"
12.247	20. "Deux ancolies se balançaient"
12.248	21. "Parce que j'ai souffert"
12.249	22. "Venez sous la tonnelle"
12.250	23. "Venez, ma bien-aimée"
12.251	24. "Demain fera un an"
12.252	"Le chat" (c1956, for 80th birthday of Marya Freund) ....
12.253	"Préparatif à la mort et allégorie maritime" (c1963, d'Aubigné) Op.403
12.254	"L'amour chante" (c1964): 1. "Le vrai amour" (Bellay) Op.409
12.255	2. "J'aime" (Musset)
12.256	3. "Sonnet" (Labbé)
12.257	4. "De sa peine et des beautés de sa Dame" (Bellay)
12.258	5. "Moins je la vois" (Scève)
12.259	6. "Nevermore" (Verlaine)
12.260	7. "Veillées" (Rimbaud)
12.261	8. "Plusieurs de leurs corps dénués" (Ronsard)
12.262	9. "Le lai du chèvrefeuille" (Marie de France)

13. ARRANGEMENTS OF WORKS OF OTHERS

13.1	Auric: "Adieu New York" (arr for pf duet) ....
13.2	Poulenc: Finale of Piano Sonata of 1918 for pf duet (orchd as: Ouverture) ....
13.3	Satie: "Cinq grimaces," for incid music: Midsummer Night's Dream (arr for pf) ....
13.4	Satie: "Gymnopédie" (arr for pf duet) ....
13.5	Satie: "Jack-in-the-Box," pantomime of 1899–1900 for pf (orchd1929) ....
13.6	Satie: "Cinéma: Entr'acte symphonique de Relâche" (arr1926; pf duet) ....
13.7	Satie: "Trois morceaux en forme de poire," for pf duet (arr for vn & pf as: Suite) ....

* * * * *

1. STAGE WORKS

Operas:

1.1 "Halka," 2 acts (c1846–7, p1848, Wolski on Wójcicki's story: Góralka; 2nd vers in 4 acts p1858) ....
1.2 "Bettly," 2 act comic opera (c1852, Scribe & Mélesville's Le chalet, transl Schober) ....
1.3 "Flis" (The Raftsman), 1 act (c1858, Bogusławski) ....
1.4 "Rokiczana," 3 acts (c1858–9, Korzeniowski; Bar, ch & orch, inc) ....
1.5 "Hrabina" (The Countess), 3 acts (c1859, Wolski) ....
1.6 "Verbum Nobile," 1 act (c1860, Chęciński) ....
1.7 "Straszny dwór" (The Haunted Manor), 4 acts (c1861–4, p1865, Chęciński) ......
1.8 "Paria," 3 acts (c1859–69, Chęciński after Delavigne) ....
1.9 "Beata" (c1870–1, Chęciński) ....
1.10 "Trea," 2 acts (c1872, Jasiński, inc) ....

Operettas:

1.11 "Biuraliści" (The Bureaucrats), 1 act comic opera (c1834, Skarbek) ....
1.12 *"Cudowna woda" (Water of Life), 2 act comic opera (lost except for overture)* ....
1.13 *"Sen wieszcza" (The Seer's Dream) (c1841, Leuven: Le songe d'une nuit d'été, transl Syrokomla, lost)* ...
1.14 "Nocleg w Apeninach" (A Night's Lodging in the Apennines) (c1838, Fredro) ....
1.15 "Ideał czyli Nowa Precjoza" (Ideal or The New Preciosa) (c1841, Milewski) ......
1.16 "Karmaniol czyli Francuzi lubią żartować" (Carmagnole or The French Like Joking) (c1841, Milewski after Forges) ....
1.17 *"Żółta szlafmyca" (The Yellow Nightcap) (c1841, Zabłocki; 4vv, lost except for: Kolęda)* ....
1.18 "Nowy Don Kiszot czyli Sto szaleństw" (The New Don Quichote or 100 Follies) (c1841, Fredro) ....
1.19 "Loteria" (The Lottery) (c1843, Milewski) ....
1.20 "Nowy dziedzic" (The New Landlord) (c1841, Radziszewski) ......
1.21 *"Walka muzyków" (The musicians' struggle) (c1841, Marcinkiewicz, lost)* ......
1.22 *"Pobór rekrutów" (The Conscription) (c1842, Marcinkiewicz, lost: song extant)* ......
1.23 *"Sielanka" (Idyll), 2 acts (c ?1848, Marcinkiewicz, lost)* ......
1.24 "Cyganie" (The Gypsies) (c1850, p1852, Kniaźnin; r1860 as operetta: Jawnuta) ......
1.25 "Jawnuta" (p1860, w/ popular krakowiak: Wesół i szczęśliwy, r vers of operetta: Cyganie) ......

Ballets:

1.26 "Monte Christo" (c1866, after Dumas) ....
1.27 "Na kwaterunku" (In the Quarters) (c1868) ......
1.28 "Figle szatana" (The Devil's Jests) (c1870, collab Münchheimer) ....

Incid music:

1.29 "Kupiec wenecki" (The Merchant of Venice) (c1870–1, Shakespeare transl Jeske) (also see opera c by Castelnuovo-Tedesco Op.181, incid music c by Sullivan & overture c by Castelnuovo-Tedesco Op.76) ..
1.30 "Zbójcy" (The Robbers) (c1870–1, Schiller) ....
1.31 "Hamlet" (c1871, Shakespeare) (also see incid music c by Honegger H190, Milhaud Op.200, Prokofiev Op.77, Shostakovich Op.32 & Tchaikovsky Op.67a) ......
1.32 Music to 11 other plays ......

2. ORCHESTRAL WORKS

2.1 "Bajka" (Winter's tale), sym poem (c1848) ......
2.2 "Kain," overture (c1856) ......
2.3 "Polonaise de concert" (p1866; arr for pf) ......
2.4 "Uwertura wojenna" (Military Overture) (c1857) ......

3. STRING QUARTETS

3.1 String Quartet No.1 in D minor (c1839) ......
3.2 String Quartet No.2 in F minor (c before 1840) ......

4. PIANO

4.1 "Polkas" (ca1945) ......
4.2 "6 Polonaises" (c before 1858) ......
4.3 "Adieu" ......
4.4 "Air à carillons tiré du 'Manoir hanté' " (p1877) ......
4.5 "3 Bagatelles": No.1 in G major ......
4.6 No.2 in A major
4.7 No.3 in C major
4.8 "Chanson d'automne" ......
4.9 "Chansons sans paroles" ......

4.10   "Mazurka" ....
4.11   "La valse bambochade" ....
4.12   "Valse," in A-flat major ....
4.13   "Valse," in E-flat major (p1873) ....

Pf duet:

4.14   "La chanson du vagabond" ....
4.15   "4 Contredanses" (c1863) ....
4.16   "Danses montagnardes de 'Halka' " (p1857) ....
4.17   "La fileuse" ....
4.18   "Mazurka des noces" (p1873) ....
4.19   "Polonaise concertante," in A major (p1866) ....
4.20   "Polonaise," in D major (p1898) ....
4.21   "Valse" ....

5. SACRED

Masses:

5.1   Mass No.1 in D minor, "Funeral" (c1850) ....
5.2   Mass No.2 in E minor (c1855; child ch & org) ....
5.3   Mass No.3 in E-flat major (c1865) ....
5.4   Mass No.4 in A minor (p1870) ....
5.5   Mass No.5 in B-flat major, "Piotrovin Mass" (c1872) ....
5.6   Mass No.6 in G minor, "Funeral" (c1873) ....
5.7   Mass No.7 in D-flat major (p1874) ....

Other:

5.8   "Litania Ostrobramska" (Ostra Brama Litany / Litany to the Virgin Mary at Ostra Brama,
       Wilno) No.1 (c1843; vv, ch & orch): ....
          1. "Kyrie"
          2. "Sancta Maria"
          3. "Salus infirmorum"
          4. "Agnus"
5.9   "Litania Ostrobramska" (Ostra Brama Litany) No.2 (c1849; vv, ch & orch) ....
5.10 "Litania Ostrobramska" (Ostra Brama Litany) No.3 (c before 1854; vv, ch & orch) ....
5.11 "Litania Ostrobramska" (Ostra Brama Litany) No.4 (c1855; vv, ch & orch) ....
5.12 "Ecce lignum crucis," motet (c1872; Bar, ch & org) ....
5.13 "Requiem aeternam" (p1890; vv, ch & orch) ....

6. SECULAR CHORAL

6.1   "Milda," cantata (c1848, after Kraszewski's Witolorauda; vv, ch & orch).....................
6.2   "Nijoła," cantata (c1852, after Kraszewski's Witolorauda) ....
6.3   "Madonna" (c1856, Petrarch: Sonnets; B, ch & orch) ....
6.4   "Ballada o Florianie Szarym" (Ballad of Florian the Grey) (c1858–9, Korzeniowski; Bar, ch & orch,
       from opera: Rokiczana) ....
6.5   "Widma" (Phantoms), cantata (c before 1859, after fantastic drama of Mickiewicz: Dziady; vv, ch & orch) ..
6.6   "Sonety krymskie" (The Crimean Sonnets), cantata (c1867, Mickiewicz; vv, ch & orch) ....
6.7   "Pani Twardowska," ballad (c1869, Mickiewicz; vv, ch & orch) ....
6.8   4 other cantatas ....

7. VOICE & ORCHESTRA (Nos. in Dzieła Stanisława Moniuszki, ed Rudziński, P.W.M. 1965–74)

Secular songs w/ orch (Vol.V of Dzieła Stanisława Moniuszki):

7.1   26. "Trzech Budrysów": "Stary Budrys trzech synów, tęgich jak sam Litwinów" (Mickiewicz) ....
7.2   27. "Żal dziewczyny": "W zimny grób ją położyli" (Stürmer) ....
7.3   28. "Czaty": "Z ogrodowej altany wojewoda zdyszany bieży w zamek" (Mickiewicz) ....
7.4   29. "Koszykarz": "Oj da dana! oj dana! rokicino kochana!" (Pług—pseud of Pietkiewicz) ....
7.5   30. "Księżyc i rzeczka": "Księżyc krąży wśród chmur fali" (Sowa—pseud of Żeligowski).............
7.6   31. "Prząśniczka": "U prząśniczki siedzą jak anioł dzieweczki" (Czeczot) ....

Sacred songs & duets w/ org/orch. Organ arrs of sacred songs (Vol.VI of Dzieła Stanisława Moniuszki):

7.7   1. "Modlitwa—O władco świata" I: "O władco świata, wiekuisty Boże" ....
7.8   2. "Modlitwa—O władco świata" II: "O władco świata, wiekuisty Boże" ....
7.9   3. "Modlitwa—O władco świata" III: "O władco świata, wiekuisty Boże" ....
7.10   4. "Zwiastowanie": "Lśni Gabriel promienną ozdobą" (Czajkowski) ....
7.11   5. "Modlitwa do Boga Rodzicy": "Głos mój podnoszę do Boga Rodzicy" ....
7.12   6. "Pieśń pokutna": "Powszedni chleb łzami obmywam" ....

7.13   7. "Modlitwa Pańska—W ciężkiej niedoli": "W ciężkiej niedoli, którą dziś ponoszę" (Moroz) ....

7.14   8. "Ad te Domine": "Ad te Domine levavi animam meam" (Psałterz Dawida) ....

7.15   9. "Boże, zbawco mój" (Psałterz Dawida) ....

7.16   10. "Domine, ne in furore tuo" (Wszechmocny Boże nasz, nie karz mię w gniewie Twoim) (Psałterz Dawida) ....

7.17   11. "Modlitwa—O Mario, bądź pozdrowiona": "O Mario, bądź pozdrowiona, o matko boskiego Syna" ....

7.18   12. "Pieśń pokutna" (Miserere mei): "O Panie! co losy ludzkości dzierżysz w dłoni swej" (Radziszewski) ....

7.19   13. "Modlitwa—Na skrzydłach pieśni" I: "Na skrzydłach pieśni z duszy czcią przejętej" (Radziszewski) ....

7.20   14. "Modlitwa—Na skrzydłach pieśni" II: "Na skrzydłach pieśni z duszy czcią przejętej" (Radziszewski) ......

7.21   15. "Modlitwa Pańska—Ojcze nasz": "Ojcze nasz, któryś jest w niebie" (St Matthew) ....

7.22   16. "Hymn do Pana Jezusa": "Z Ojcem przedwiecznym stolicę dzieli" (Syrokomla—pseud of Kondratowicz)

7.23   17. "Psalm I" (Beatus vir) I: "Szczęśliwy, który nie postał w radzie" (Psałterz Dawida) ....

7.24   18. "Psalm I" (Beatus vir) II: "Szczęśliwy, który nie postał w radzie" (Psałterz Dawida) ....

7.25   19. "Inclina aurem tuam" (Psałterz Dawida) ....

7.26   20. "Modlitwa—Do Ciebie, Panie": "Do Ciebie, Panie, wznosim nasze modły" (Zaleski) ....

7.27   21. "Modlitwa—W poświstach wichru losu": "W poświstach wichru losu" (Wasilewski) ....

7.28   22. "Intende voci": "Intende voci, intende voci orationis meae" (Psałterz Dawida) ....

7.29   23. "Laudate Dominum": "Laudate Dominum quoniam bonus est psalmus" (Psałterz Dawida) ....

7.30   24. "Hymn do Matki Boskiej": "O Królowo pełna łaski, racz wysłuchać dzieci Twe!" (F. S.) ....

7.31   25. "Exaudi Deus": "O! racz wysłuchać, wiekuisty Boże, tych próśb" (Psałterz Dawida) ....

7.32   26. "Sub tuum praesidium" I: "Sub tuum praesidium confugimus, Sancta Dei Genitrix" ....

7.33   27. "Sub tuum praesidium" II: "Sub tuum praesidium confugimus, Sancta Dei Genitrix" ....

7.34   28. "Boga Rodzico" ....

7.35   29. "Hejnały krakowskie—Królowo Polski": "Hejnał wszyscy zaśpiewajmy" ....

7.36   30. "Anioł pasterzom mówił" ....

7.37   31. "Gorzkie żale" ....

7.38   32. "Ojcze, Boże wszechmogący" ....

7.39   33. "Rozmowa duszy" ....

7.40   34. "Zawitaj ukrzyżowany" ....

7.41   35. "Przez Twoje święte zmartwychwstanie" ....

7.42   36. "Wesoły nam dziś dzień nastał" ....

7.43   37. "Idzie, idzie Bóg prawdziwy" ....

7.44   38. "U drzwi Twoich" ....

7.45   39. "Pod Twoją obronę" ....

7.46   40. "Kto się w opiekę" ....

7.47   41. "Za umarłych" ....

7.48   42. "Głos wdzięczny" ....

7.49   43. "Nieszpory" ....

7.50   44. "Witaj święta" ....

8. SONGS (w/ pf)

(267 songs originally pubd in Śpiewnik domowy /Songbook for Home Use/, Vol.I–VI in Vilnus 1843-59 & Vol.VII–XII in Warsaw 1877–1910)

(Nos. in Dzieła Stanisława Moniuszki, ed Rudziński, P.W.M. 1965–74)

c1837–1844 (Vol.I of Dzieła Stanisława Moniuszki):

8.1   1. "Sen": "Chociaż zmuszona będziesz mnie porzucić" (Mickiewicz) ....

8.2   2. "Niepewność": "Gdy cię nie widzę, nie wzdycham" (Mickiewicz) ....

8.3   3. "Pieszczotka": "Moja pieszczotka gdy w wesołej chwili" (Mickiewicz) ....

8.4   4. "Świtezianka": "Jakiż to chłopiec piękny i młody? jaka to obok dziewica?" (Mickiewcz; also see 64.) .....

8.5   5. "Śpiew masek": "Ach! na tym świecie śmierć wszystko zmiecie" (Malczewski) ....

8.6   6. "Barkarola": "Po dolinie Brenta płynie" (Korsak) ....

8.7   7. "Kochać": "Kochać, kochać śpiesz, dziewczyno!" (Korsak) ....

8.8   8. "Pielgrzym": "Pielgrzym idący w zimny kraj północny" (Korsak) ....

8.9   9. "Morel": "Morel podajesz mi z drzewa" (Chodźko) ....

8.10   10. "Pieśń żeglarzy": "Wesoło żeglujmy, wesoło!" (Wasilewski) ....

8.11   11. "Triolet": "Komu ślubny splatasz wieniec z róż" (Zan) ....

8.12   12. "Panicz i dziewczyna": "W gaiku zielonym dziewczę rwie jagody" (Odyniec & Mickiewicz) ....

8.13   13. "Żal dziewczyny": "W zimny grób go położyli" (Stürmer) ....

8.14   14. "Dalibógże": "Dalibógże, powiem mamie, on co złego zrobić gotów" (Massalski) ....

8.15   15. "Przyczyna": "Mówię ci grzecznie i skromnie" (Witwicki) ....

8.16   16. "Zawód": "Ach, dzieweczko, zmilujże się" (Witwicki) ....

8.17   17. "Kukulka": "Dąbrową szła matka i niosła, gdzie chatka" (Witwicki) ....

8.18   18. "Ach, daleko za mąż matka mię oddała" (Czeczot; = 1. of: Piosnki wieśniacze) ....

8.19   19. "Co to za kwiatek": "Co to za kwiatek, zawsze zielony" (Czeczot; = 2. of: Piosnki wieśniacze) ....

8.20   20. "Latem brzózka mała z liściem rozmawiała" (Czeczot; = 3. of: Piosnki wieśniacze) ....

8.21   21. "Dziad i baba": "Był sobie Dziad i Baba, bardzo starzy oboje" (Kraszewski) ....

8.22   22. "Niemen i Wilja do Litwinek": "Jam jest Niemen! Jam Wilja! bóstwa waszych rzek," duet (Odyniec) ...

8.23   23. "Dziadek i babka": "Jeśli nie zaśnie dziadunio kochany" (John of Dycalp—pseud of Jankowski) ....

8.24   24. "Książę Magnus i Trolla": "Magnus okienkiem patrzył z wieżycy" (Siemieński) ....

8.25   25. "Wyjazd z Ukrainy": "A dokąd jedziesz, panie namiestniku" (Tarsza Edward—pseud of Grabowski) ......

8.26   26. "Kum i kuma": "Kuma sobie siedziała, motek nici zwijała" (Czeczot) ....

8.27   27. "Czy powróci": "Matuleńku, on nie wróci" (Kraszewski; also see 65. & 66.) ....

W/ out date (Vol.V of Dzieła Stanisława Moniuszki):

Incomplete (Vol.V of Dzieła Stanisława Moniuszki):

9. PEDAGOGICAL WORKS

* * * * *

1. STAGE WORKS

Operas:

1.1	"La favola d'Orfeo" (The Legend of Orpheus), favola in musica (p1607, Striggio)	Mxi1, SV318
1.2	*"L'Arianna," opera (p1608, Rinuccini, music lost except for: Lamento d'Arianna, Mvi1, SV107)*	*SV291*
1.3	*"Prologue to Guarini: L'Idropica," comedy w/ music (p1608, Chiabrera, music lost)*	
1.4	*"Le nozze di Tetide," favola marittima (c begun 1616, not compl, lost)*	
1.5	"La Maddalena," aria w/ ritornello only: Su le penne de' venti (p1617, Andreini)	SV333
1.6	*"Andromeda," opera (c begun 1618–20, Marigliani, lost)*	
1.7	*"Apollo," dramatic cantata (not compl, lost)*	
1.8	"Il combattimento di Tancredi e Clorinda" (The Fight between Tancredi and Clorinda) (p1624, Tasso; also in: Madrigals, Book VIII)	Mviii132, SV153
1.9	*"La finta pazza Licori" (c1627, Strozzi, not perf, music lost)*	
1.10	*"Gli amori di Diana e di Endimione" (p1628, Pio, music lost)*	
1.11	*"Proserpina rapita," opera (p1630, Strozzi, music lost except for trio: Come dolce hoggi)*	*SV323*
1.12	"Il ritorno d'Ulisse in patria" (Ulysses' Return Home), 3 acts (p1641, Badoaro)	Mxii, SV325
1.13	*"Le nozze d'Enea con Lavinia," opera (p1641, Badoaro, music lost)*	
1.14	"L'incoronazione di Poppea" (The Coronation of Poppea), 3 acts (p1642, Busenello)	Mxiii, SV308

Ballets:

1.15	"Il ballo delle ingrate" (p1608, Rinuccini; also in: Madrigals, Book VIII)	Mviii314, SV167
1.16	"Tirsi e Clori" (p1616, Striggio; also in: Madrigals, Book VII)	Mvii191, SV145
1.17	*"Mercurio e Marte, Torneo" (p1628, Achillini, music lost)*	
1.18	"Volgendo il ciel per l'immortal sentiero" (p ?1636, Rinuccini; vv, ch & orch)	Mviii157, SV145/2
1.19	*"La vittoria d'amore" (p1641, Morando, music lost)*	

2. SACRED VOCAL—COLLECTIONS

"Sacrae cantiunculae tribus vocibus," Book I (p1582):

2.1	"Lapidabant Stephanum"	Mxiv1, SV207
2.2	"Veni in hortum meum"	Mxiv3, SV208
2.3	"Ego sum pastor bonus"	Mxiv6, SV209
2.4	"Surge propera, amica mea"	Mxiv8, SV210
2.5	"Ubi duo vel tres congregati fuerint"	Mxiv11, SV211
2.6	"Quam pulchra es"	Mxiv13, SV212
2.7	"Ave Maria, gratia plena"	Mxiv15, SV213
2.8	"Domine Pater et Deus vitae meae"	Mxiv17, SV214
2.9	"Tu es pastor ovium":	Mxiv19, SV215
	1. "Tu es pastor ovium"	
	2. "Tu es Petrus"	
2.10	"O magnum pietatis opus":	Mxiv22, SV216
	1. "O magnum pietatis opus"	
	2. "Eli clamans"	
2.11	"O crux benedicta"	Mxiv25, SV217
2.12	"Hodie Christus natus est"	Mxiv26, SV218
2.13	"O Domine Jesu Christe":	Mxiv29, SV219
	1. "O Domine Jesu Christe," part 1	
	2. "O Domine Jesu Christe," part 2	
2.14	"Pater, venit hora"	Mxiv33, SV220
2.15	"In tua patientia"	Mxiv34, SV221
2.16	"Angelus ad pastores ait"	Mxiv36, SV222
2.17	"Salve, crux pretiosa"	Mxiv38, SV223
2.18	"Quia vidisti me, Thoma, credidisti"	Mxiv40, SV224
2.19	"Lauda, Sion, salvatorem"	Mxiv42, SV225
2.20	"O bone Jesu, illumina oculos meos"	Mxiv44, SV226
2.21	"Surgens Jesus, Dominus noster"	Mxiv46, SV227
2.22	"Qui vult venire post me"	Mxiv48, SV228
2.23	"Iusti tulerunt spolia impiorum"	Mxiv50, SV229

"Madrigali spirituali à 4 voci" (p1583, only bass part extant):

2.24	"Sacrosanta di Dio verace imago"	SV179
2.25	"Laura del ciel sempre feconda":	SV180
	1. "Laura del ciel sempre feconda"	
	2. "Poi che benigno il novo cant' attende"	
2.26	"Aventurosa notte":	SV181
	1. "Aventurosa notte"	
	2. "Serpe crudel"	
2.27	"D'empi martiri":	SV182
	1. "D'empi martiri"	
	2. "Ond'in ogni pensier"	

3. SACRED VOCAL—IN ANTHOLOGIES

3.14   "Venite, venite siccientes ad aquas Domini" (2vv) Mxvi467, SV335

        "Sacri affetti ... raccolti da Francesco Sammaruco" (p1625):

3.15   "Ego dormio et cor meum vigilat" (2vv) Mxvi481, SV300

        "Ghirlanda sacra ... Libro primo opera seconda per Leonardo Simonetti" (p1625; 1v):

3.16   "Currite populi, psallite timpanis" (T) Mxvi491, SV297
3.17   "Ecce sacrum paratum convivium" Mxvi497, SV299
3.18   "O quam pulchra es, amica mea" Mxvi486, SV317
3.19   "Salve regina" Mxvi502, SV327

        "Psalmi de vespere à 4 voci del Cavalier D. Gio. Maria Sabino da Turi" (p1627):

3.20   "Confitebor tibi, Domine" Mo45, SV295

        "Quarta raccolta de sacri canti ... fatta da Don Lorenzo Calvi" (p1629):

3.21   "Salve regina" III (3vv; also in: Salve morale e spirituale of 1640) Mxv741, SV285
3.22   "Exulta, filia Sion" (1v) Mxvii8, SV303
3.23   "Exultent caeli et gaudeant angeli" (5v) Mxvii15, SV304

        "Motetti à voce sola de diversi eccellentissimi autori ... Libro primo" (p1645):

3.24   "Venite, videte martyrem quam sit carus" (1v) Mxvii25, SV336

        "Raccolta di motetti à 1. 2. 3. voci di Gaspro Casati ..." (p1651):

3.25   "En gratulemur hodie" (1v & 2vn) Mxvi517, SV302

4. SACRED VOCAL—CONTRAFACTA (w/ spiritual words to secular music)

        "Musica tolta da i madrigali ... e fatta spirituale da Aquilino Coppini" (p1607; 5vv):

4.1   "Felle amaro" (= Cruda Amarilli) SV94.k
4.2   "Stabat virgo" (= Era l'anima mia) SV96.k
4.3   "Qui pependit" (= Ecco Silvio) SV97/1.k
4.4   "Maria, quid ploras?" (= Dorinda, ah dirò mia) SV97/3.k
4.5   "Te, Jesu Christe" (= Ecco piegando) SV97/4.k
4.6   "Pulchrae sunt" (= Ferir quel petto) SV97/5.k
4.7   "Sancta Maria" (= Deh, bella e cara) SV98/2.k
4.8   "Spernit Deus" (= Ma tu più che mai dura) SV98/3.k
4.9   "Vives in corde" (= Ahi, com'a un vago sol) SV101.k
4.10   "Ure me Domine" (= Troppo ben può questo tiranno amore) SV102.k
4.11   "Gloria tua" (= T'amo, mia vita) SV104.k

        "Il secondo libro della musica di Monteverde ... fatta spirituale da Coppini" (p1608; 5vv):

4.12   "Florea serta" (= La giovinetta pianta) SV60.k
4.13   "O dies infelices" (= O come è gran martire) SV61.k
4.14   "Praecipitantur, Jesu Christe" (= O primavera) SV68.k
4.15   "O infelix recessus" (= Ah dolente partita) SV75.k
4.16   "O mi Fili" (= O Mirtillo) SV95.k
4.17   "Te sequar, Jesu" (= Ch'io t'ami) SV98/1.k
4.18   "Qui regnas" (= Che dar più vi poss'io?) SV99.k
4.19   "Animas eruit" (= M'è più dolce il penar) SV100.k

        "Il terzo libro della musica di Monteverde ... fatta spirituale da Coppini" (p1609; 5vv):

4.20   "Jesu, dum te" (= Cor mio, mentre vi miro) SV76.k
4.21   "Jesu, tu obis" (= Cor mio, non mori?) SV77.k
4.22   "O stellae" (= Sfogava con le stelle) SV78.k
4.23   "Ardebat igne" (= Volgea l'anima mea) SV79.k
4.24   "Domine Deus" (= Anima mia, perdona) SV80/1.k
4.25   "O gloriose martyr" (= Che se tu se'il cor mio) SV80/2.k
4.26   "Luce serena" (= Luci serene e chiare) SV81.k
4.27   "Plagas tuas" (= La piaga c'ho nel core) SV82.k
4.28   "Tu vis a me" (= Voi pur da me partite) SV83.k
4.29   "Cantemus" (= A un giro sol) SV84.k
4.30   "Rutilante in nocte" (= Io mi son giovinetta) SV86.k
4.31   "Qui laudes" (= Duel augellin che canta) SV87.k
4.32   "O Jesu, mea vita" (= Si ch'io vorrei morire) SV89.k
4.33   "Anima miseranda" (= Anima dolorosa) SV90.k
4.34   "Anima quam dilexi" (= Anima del cor mio) SV91.k
4.35   "Longe a te" (= Longe da te, cor mio) SV92.k
4.36   "Plorat amare" (= Piagne e sospira) SV93.k
4.37   "Qui pietate" (= Ma se con la pieta) SV97/2.k
4.38   "Amemus te" (= Amor, se giusto sei) SV103.k
4.39   "Una es" (= Una donna fra l'altre) SV109.k

"Concerti sacri ... libro secondo ... del P. Pietro Lappi" (p1623):

4.40   "Ave regina mundi" (= Vaga su spina ascosa) (3vv) SV134.k1

"Erster Theil geistlicher Concerten und Harmonien ... durch Ambrosium Profium" (p1641):

4.41   "Jesum viri senesque" (= Vaga su spina ascosa) (3vv) SV134.k2

"Ander Theil geistlicher Concerten und Harmonien ... durch Ambrosium Profium" (p1641; 6vv):

4.42   "Ergo gaude, laetare" (= Due belli occhi) SV155/2.k1
4.43   "Pascha concelebranda" (= Altri canti di Marte) SV155/1.k1
4.44   "Lauda, anima mea" (= Due belli occhi) SV155/2.k2

"Dritter Theil geistlicher Concerten und Harmonien ... durch Ambrosium Profium" (p1642):

4.45   "Heus, bone vir" (= Armato il cor) (2vv) SV150.k
4.46   "Spera in Domino" (= Io che armato sin hor) (1v) SV249/2.k
4.47   "Haec dicit Deus" (= Voi ch'ascoltate in rime sparse) (5vv) SV253.k

"Corollarium geistlicher collectaneorum ... gewähret von Ambrosio Profio" (p1649):

4.48   "Longe, mi Jesu" (= Parlo, miser'o taccio?) (3vv) SV136.k1
4.49   "O Jesu, lindere meinen Schmertzen" (= Tu dormi?) (4vv) SV137.k
4.50   "O rex supreme" (= Al lume delle stelle) (4vv) SV138.k
4.51   "O du mächtiger Herr" (= Hor ch'el ciel e la terra) (6vv) SV147/1.k
4.52   "Dein allein ist ja" (= Così sol d'una chiara) (6vv) SV147/2.k
4.53   "Alleluja, kommet, jauchzet" (= Ardo, avvampo) (8vv) SV152.k1
4.54   "Freude, kommet lasset uns gehen" (= Ardo, avvampo) (8vv) SV152.k2
4.55   "Resurrexit de sepulcro" (= Vago augelletto) (6–7vv) SV156.k1
4.56   "Veni, veni, soror mea" (= Vago augelletto) (6–7vv) SV156.k2

5. SACRED VOCAL—IN MANUSCRIPT

5.1   "Fuggi fuggi, cor, fuggi a tutte l'or" SV306
5.2   "Gloria in excelsis Deo" (8vv) Mo65, SV307
5.3   "Se d'un angel il bel viso" SV330

6. SECULAR VOCAL—COLLECTIONS

"Canzonette à 3 voci," Book I (p1584):

6.1   "Qual si può dir maggiore" Mx2, SV1
6.2   "Canzonette d'amore che m'uscite del cuore" Mx3, SV2
6.3   "La fiera vista e'l velenoso sguardo" Mx4, SV3
6.4   "Raggi, dov'è il mio bene non mi date più pene" Mx6, SV4
6.5   "Vita de l'alma mia, cara mia vita" Mx8, SV5
6.6   "Il mio martir tengo celat'al cuore" Mx9, SV6
6.7   "Son questi i crespi crini e questo il viso" Mx11, SV7
6.8   "Io mi vivea com'Aquila mirando" (Guarini) Mx11, SV8
6.9   "Su su, su che'l giorno è fore, su pastori uscite" Mx12, SV9
6.10 "Quando sperai del mio servir mercede" Mx13, SV10
6.11 "Come farò, cuor mio quando mi parto" Mx14, SV11
6.12 "Corse a la morte il povero Narciso" Mx15, SV12
6.13 "Tu ridi sempre mai per darmi pene" Mx16, SV13
6.14 "Chi vuol veder d'inverno un dolc'aprile" Mx17, SV14
6.15 "Già mi credev'un sol esser in cielo" Mx18, SV15
6.16 "Godi pur del bel sen felice pulce" Mx19, SV16
6.17 "Giù lì a quel petto giace un bel giardino" Mx20, SV17
6.18 "Sì come crescon alla terra i fiori" Mx21, SV18
6.19 "Io son Fenice e voi sete la fiamma" Mx22, SV19
6.20 "Chi vuol veder un bosco folto e spesso" Mx23, SV20
6.21 "Hor, care canzonette sicuramente andrete" Mx24, SV21

"Madrigali à 5 voci," Book I (p1587):

6.22 "Ch'io ami la vita mia nel tuo bel nome" Mi1, SV23
6.23 "Se per havervi oimè donato il core" Mi5, SV24
6.24 "A che tormi il ben mio" (Strozzi) Mi8, SV25
6.25 "Amor per tua mercè vatene a quella" (Bonardo) Mi11, SV26
6.26 "Baci soavi e cari" (Guarini) Mi14, SV27
6.27 "Se pur non mi consenti" (Groto) Mi18, SV28
6.28 "Filli cara e amata" (Parma) Mi21, SV29
6.29 "Poi che del mio dolore" Mi24, SV30
6.30 "Fumia la pastorella" (Allegretti): Mi27, SV31
        1. "Fumia la pastorella"
        2. "Almo divino raggio"

"Madrigali à 1. 2. 3. 4. & 6 voci," Book VII (p1619; w/ insts & cont):

"Canti amorosi":

6.179 "Altri canti di Marte" (Marino; 6vv & 2vn): Mviii181, SV155
    1. "Altri canti di Marte"
    2. "Due belli occhi fur l'armi"
6.180 "Vago augelletto" (Petrarch; 6–7vv, 2vn & d bass).. Mviii222, SV156
6.181 "Mentre vaga Angioletta ogn'anima gentil cantando" (Guarini; 2vv) Mviii246, SV157
6.182 "Ardo, e scoprir, ahi lasso, io non ardisco" (2vv; also in: Madrigals, Book IX)...................Mix32, SV158
6.183 "O sia tranquillo il mare" (2vv; also in: Madrigals, Book IX) Mix36, SV159
6.184 "Ninfa che scalza il piede" (1–3vv): Mviii259, SV160
    1. "Ninfa che scalza il piede"
    2. "Qui, deh, meco t'arresta"
    3. "Dell'usate mie corde al suon"
6.185 "Dolcissimo uscignolo" (Guarini; 5vv) Mviii271, SV161
6.186 "Chi vol haver felice e lieto il core" (c1638, Guarini; 5vv) Mviii280, SV162
6.187 "Lamento della Ninfa" (Rinuccini; 1–4vv): Mviii286, SV163
    1. "Non havea Febo ancore"
    2. "Lamento della Ninfa: Amor, dicea"
    3. "Si tra sdegnosi pianti"
6.188 "Perchè t'en fuggi, o Fillide?" (3vv).. Mviii295, SV164
6.189 "Non partir, ritrosetta" (3vv) Mviii305, SV165
6.190 "Su su, su pastorelli vezzosi" (3vv)... Mviii310, SV166
6.191 "Ballo delle ingrate" (Rinuccini; also see operas) Mviii314, SV167

"Madrigali e canzonette à 2, e 3 voci," Book IX (p1651):

6.192 "Se vittorie si belle" (Testi; 2vv; also in: Madrigals, Book VIII).............................Mix21, SV149
6.193 "Armato il cor d'adamantina fede" (Rinuccini; 2vv; also in: Scherzi of 1632) Mix27, SV150
6.194 "Ardo, e scoprir, ahi lasso, io non ardisco" (2vv; also in: Madrigals, Book VIII).....................Mix32, SV158
6.195 "O sia tranquillo il mare" (2vv; also in: Madrigals, Book VIII) Mix36, SV159
6.196 "Bel pastor dal cui bel guardo" (dialogo di ninfa e pastore) (Rinuccini; 2vv) Mix1, SV168
6.197 "Alcun non mi consigli" (3vv) Mix42, SV169
6.198 "Di far sempre gioire amor speranza dà" (3vv)...Mix50, SV170
6.199 "Quando dentro al tuo seno" (3vv)...Mix56, SV171
6.200 "Non voglio amare per non penare" (3vv) Mix58, SV172
6.201 "Come dolci hoggi l'auretta spira" (Strozzi: Proserpina rapita; 3vv) Mix60, SV173
6.202 "Alle danze, alle gioie" (3vv)..Mix68, SV174
6.203 "Perchè se m'odiavi" (3vv)..Mix79, SV175
6.204 "Si si ch'io v'amo, occhi vaghi, occhi belli" (3vv) Mix82, SV176
6.205 "O mio bene, o mia vita" (3vv) Mix95, SV178
6.206 "Zefiro torna," ciacona a 2 (Rinuccini; 2vv; also in: Scherzi of 1632) Mix9, SV251

7. SECULAR VOCAL—IN ANTHOLOGIES

"Canzonette à 3 voci di A. Morsolino (& others)," Book I (p1594):

7.1 "Io ardo, sì, ma'l fuoco di tal sorte" Mxvii1, SV309
7.2 "Occhi miei, se mirar, più non debb'io" Mxvii2, SV314
7.3 "Quante son stelle in ciel" (Cerreto)... Mxvii3, SV324
7.4 "Se non mi date aita" Mxvii4, SV331

"I Nuovi Fioretti Musicali à 3 voci d'Amante Franzoni Mantovano" (p1605):

7.5 "Prima vedrò ch'in questi prati" Mxvii5, SV322

"Lamento d'Arianna ... et con due lettere amorose in genere representativo" (p1623; 1v):

7.6 "Lasciatemi morire" (Rinuccini; also in: Madrigals, Book VI) Mxi159, SV22/1
7.7 "Se i languidi miei squardi" (Achillini; also in: Madrigals, Book VII) Mvii160, SV141
7.8 "Se pur destina e vole il cielo" (also in: Madrigals, Book VII) Mvii167, SV142

"Madrigali del signor cavaliere Anselmi" (p1624, Anselmi; 2–5vv & cont):

7.9 "O come vaghi, o come cari" (2vv) Mix102, SV315
7.10 "Taci, Armelin, deh taci" (3vv) Mix106, SV334

"Quarto Scherzo delle ariose vaghezze" (p1624, Milanuzi; 1v):

7.11 "La mia turca che d'amor" Mix117, SV310
7.12 "Ohimè ch'io cado, ohimè ch'inciampo" Mix111, SV316
7.13 "Si dolce è'l tormento" Mix119, SV332

"Arie de diversi raccolte da Alessandro Vincenti" (p1634; 1v):

7.14 "Perchè, se m'odiavi" Mxvii24, SV320
7.15 "Più lieto il guardo"... Mxvii22, SV321

8. SECULAR VOCAL—IN MANUSCRIPT

8.1   "Ahi, che si partì il mio bel sol adorno" (3vv) Mxvii38, SV290

8.2   "Lamento d'Olimpia" (p1620; 1v): Mo10, SVA2
         1. "Voglio morir: van'è'l conforto tuo"
         2. "Anzi che non amarmi"
         3. "Ma perchè, o ciel, invendicate lassi"

8.3   "Voglio di vita uscir" (p1630, ?Ferrari; 1v) Mo18, SV337

*   *   *   *   *

M =   Malipiero, G. F., ed.: "C. Monteverdi: Tutte le opere." Asolo, 1926–42, rev. 2/1954; w/ added
       Vol.XVII / suppl. /, 1966.

SV =   Manfred H. Stattkus: "Claudio Monteverdi Verzeichnis der erhaltenen Werke." Musikverlag Stattkus
       Bergkamen, 1985.

1. STAGE WORKS

Operas:

1.1	"Die Schuldigkeit des ersten Gebots," sacred drama (c1767, Weiser, part I only, II–III c by others)	K35
1.2	"Apollo et Hyacinthus," 3 part Latin intermezzo (p1767, Widl)	K38
1.3	"Bastien und Bastienne," 1 act Singspiel (p1768, Weiskern & Schachtner after Rousseau)	K46b (K50)
1.4	"La finta semplice," 3 act opera buffa (p1769, Coltellini after Goldoni)	K46a (K51)
1.5	"Mitridate, rè di Ponto," 3 act opera seria (p1770, Cigna-Santi after Parini & Racine)	K74a (K87)
1.6	"Ascanio in Alba," 2 act serenata teatrale (p1771, Parini)	K111
1.7	"Il sogno di Scipione," 1 act serenata drammatica (p1772, Metastasio)	K126
1.8	"Lucio Silla," 3 act dramma per musica (p1772, Gamerra)	K135
1.9	"La finta giardiniera," 3 act opera buffa (p1775, ?Calzabigi r by Coltellini)	K196
1.10	"Il rè pastore," 2 act dramma per musica (p1775, after Metastasio)	K208
1.11	*"Semiramis," duodrama (p ?1778, Gemmingen, lost)*	*K315e (App11)*
1.12	"Zaide," 2 act Singspiel (p1779–80, Schachtner after Sebastiani: Das Serail, unfin)	K336b (K344)
1.13	"Idomeneo, rè di Creta" (Ilia ed Idamante), 3 acts (p1781, Varesco after Danchet, w/ ballet K367)	K366
1.14	"Die Entführung aus dem Serail" (The Abduction from the Seraglio), 3 act komisches Singspiel (p1782, J. Gottlieb Stephanie Jr. after Bretzner's play: Belmonte und Constanze)	K384
1.15	"L'oca del Cairo," 2 act dramma giocoso (c1783, Varesco, unfin)	K422
1.16	"Lo sposo deluso," 2 act opera buffa (c1783, ?Da Ponte, unfin)	K424a (K430)
1.17	"Der Schauspieldirektor," 1 act Singspiel (p1786, J. Gottlieb Stephanie Jr.)	K486
1.18	"Le nozze di Figaro" (The Marriage of Figaro), 4 act opera buffa (p1786, Da Ponte after Beaumarchais: Le mariage de Figaro)	K492
1.19	"Don Giovanni" (Il dissoluto punito ossia il Don Giovanni), 2 act dramma giocoso (p1787, Da Ponte)	K527
1.20	"Così fan tutte, o sia la scuola degli amanti" (They All Do It), 2 act opera buffa (p1790, Da Ponte)	K588
1.21	"Die Zauberflöte" (The Magic Flute), 2 act Deutsche Oper (p1791, Schikaneder)	K620
1.22	"La clemenza di Tito" (The Clemency of Titus), 2 act opera seria (p1791, Mazzolà after Metastasio)	K621

Ballets:

1.23	*"Ascanio in Alba" (c1771, inc; arr for pf):*	*KC27.06 (App207)*
	"9 Stücke für Klavier" (arr from ballet): No.1 in D major	
	No.2 in E-flat major	
	No.3 in C major	
	No.4 in E-flat major	
	No.5 "Gavotte," in B-flat major	
	No.6 in F major	
	No.7 in G major	
	No.8 in C major	
	No.9 "Maggiore," in D major	
1.24	*"Le gelosie del Serraglio" (c1772, for: Lucio Silla, K135, sketches)*	*K135a (App109)*
1.25	"Les petits riens," pantomime (p1778, after Piccinni: Le finte gemelle):	K299b (App10)
1.26	*. "La chasse" (p1778, frag)*	*K299d (App103)*
1.27	. "Gavotte," in B-flat major (p1778, ?discarded movt of: Les petits riens, K299b)	K300
1.28	Ballet music for opera: Idomeneo, K366 (c1781)	K367
1.29	Pantomime (p1783, only 5 Nos. extant)	K416d (K446)
1.30	*Sketches for a ballet (c1778)*	*K299c*

Incid music:

1.31	"Thamos, König in Ägypten" (p ?1776–9, Gebler)	K336a (K345)

1a. SELECTIONS FROM STAGE WORKS

1a.1	"Die Schuldigkeit des ersten Gebots," sacred drama:	K35

    . "Sinfonia"
1. "Mit Jammer muss ich schauen," aria (Christgeist)
2. "Ein ergrimmter Löwe brüllet," aria (Barmherzigkeit)
3. "Erwache, erwache," aria (Gerechtigkeit)
4. "Hat der Schöpfer dieses Leben," aria (Weltgeist)
   . "Dass Träume Träume sind, gesteh' ich willig ein," recit (Christ)
5. "Jener Donnerworte Kraft," aria (Christ)
6. "Schildre einen Philosophen," aria (Weltgeist)
7. "Manches Übel will zuweilen," aria (Christgeist)
8. "Lasst mir eurer Gnade Schein," trio (Barmherzigkeit, Gerechtigkeit, Christgeist)

1a.2	"Apollo et Hyacinthus," Latin intermezzo:	K38

    . "Prologus"
1. "Numen o Latonium!," chorus
2. "Saepe terrent Numina," aria (Hyacinthus)
3. "Iam pastor Apollo," aria (Apollo)
4. "Laetari," chorus Imus, aria (Melia)
5. "En! duos conspicis: amantem et nocentem," aria (Zephirus)

6. "Discede crudelis!," duet (Melia, Apollo)
7. "Ut navis in aequore luxuriante," chorus IIdus, aria (Oebalus)
8. "Natus cadit, atque Deus," duet (Melia, Oebalus)
9. "Tandem post turbida fulmina, nubila," trio (Melia, Apollo, Oebalus)

1a.3   "Bastien und Bastienne," Singspiel: K46b (K50)
. "Intrada"
1. "Mein liebster Freund hat mich verlassen," aria (Bastienne)
2. "Ich geh' jetzt auf die Weide," aria (Bastienne)
3. (insts)
4. "Befraget mich ein zartes Kind," aria (Colas)
5. "Wenn mein Bastien im Scherze," aria (Bastienne)
6. "Würd' ich auch, wie manche Buhlerinnen," aria (Bastienne)
7. "Auf den Rat, den ich gegeben," duet (Bastienne, Colas)
8. "Grossen Dank dir abzustatten," aria (Bastien)
9. "Geh', du sagst mir eine Fabel," aria (Bastien)
10. "Diggi, daggi, churry, murry," aria (Colas)
11. "Meiner Liebsten schöne Wangen," aria (Bastien)
12. "Er war mir sonst treu und ergeben," aria (Bastienne)
13. "Geh' hin! geh' hin!," aria (Bastien, Bastienne)
14. "Dein Trotz vermehrt sich durch mein Leiden?," recit (Bastien, Bastienne)
15. "Geh'! geh'! geh'! Herz von Flandern," duet (Bastien, Bastienne)
16. "Kinder! Kinder! seht, nach Sturm und Regen," trio (Colas, Bastien, Bastienne)

1a.4   "La finta semplice," opera buffa: K46a (K51)
. "Sinfonia"
I: 1. "Bella cosa è far l'amore," quartet (Ninetta, Giacinta, Fracasso, Simone)
2. "Troppa briga a prender moglie," aria (Simone)
3. "Marito io vorrei, ma senza fatica," aria (Giacinta)
4. "Non c'è al mondo altro che donne," aria (Cassandro)
5. "Guarda la Donna in viso," aria (Fracasso)
6. "Colla bocca e non col core," aria (Rosina)
7. "Cosa ha mai la donna indosso," aria (Polidoro)
8. "Ella vuole ed io torrei," aria (Cassandro)
9. "Senti l'eco ove t'aggiri," aria (Rosina)
10. "Chi mi vuol bene presto mel' dica," aria (Ninetta)
11. "Dove avete la creanza?," finale
II: 12. "Un marito, donne care," aria (Ninetta)
13. "Con certe persone," aria (Simone)
14. "Se a maritarmi arrivo," aria (Giacinta)
15. "Amoretti," aria (Rosina)
16. "Ubbriaco non son io, non, nò," aria (Cassandro)
17. "Sposa cara, sposa bella," aria (Polidoro)
18. "Ho sentito a dir di tutte le più belle," aria (Rosina)
19. "Cospetton, cospettonaccio mi credete," duet (Fracasso, Cassandro)
20. "In voi belle è leggiadria," aria (Fracasso)
21. "T'ho detto, buffone, se parli con lei," finale (Ninetta, Polidoro, Fracasso, Cassandro)
III: 22. "Vieni, vieni, o mia Ninetta," aria (Simone)
23. "Sono in amore, voglio marito," aria (Ninetta)
24. "Che scompiglio, che flagello," aria (Giacinta)
25. "Nelle guerre d'amore," aria (Fracasso)
26. "Se le pupille io giro," finale

1a.5   "Mitridate, rè di Ponto," opera seria: K74a (K87)
. "Ouverture"
I: 1. "Al destin, che la minaccia," aria (Aspasia)
2. "Soffre il mio cor con pace," aria (Sifare)
3. "L'odio nel cor frenate," aria (Arbate)
4. "Nel sen mi palpita dolente il core," aria (Aspasia)
5. "Parto: nel gran cimento," aria (Sifare)
6. "Venga pur, minacci," aria (Farnace)
7. "Se di lauri il crine adorno," aria (Mitridate)
8. "In faccia all'oggetto," aria (Ismene)
. "Respira al fin, respira," recit (Mitridate)
9. "Quel ribelle e quell' ingrato," aria (Mitridate)
II: 10. "Va, va, l'error mio palesa," aria (Farnace)
11. "Tu, che fedel mi sei," aria (Mitridate)
12. "Lungi da te, mio bene," aria (Sifare)
13. "Nel grave tormento," aria (Aspasia)
14. "So, quanto a te dispiace," aria (Ismene)
15. "Son reo, l'error confesso," aria (Farnace)
16. "Già di pietà mi spoglio," aria (Mitridate)
17. "Se viver non degg' io," duet (Aspasia, Sifare)
III: 18. "Tu sai per chi m'accese," aria (Ismene)
19. "Vado incontro al fato," aria (Mitridate)

20. "Se il rigor d'ingrata sorte," aria (Sifare)
21. "Se di regnar sei vago," aria (Marzio)
22. "Già dagli occhi il velo è tolto," aria (Farnace)
23. "Non si ceda al Campidoglio," quintet (Aspasia, Ismene, Sifare, Arbate, Farnace)

1a.6   "Ascanio in Alba," serenata teatrale: K111
. "Ouverture"
I: 1. Andante grazioso" (che ballano le Grazie)
2. "Di te più amabile nè Dea maggiore" (cantano e ballano), chorus (Geni, Grazie)
3. "L'ombra de' rami tuoi," aria (Venere)
4. (repeat of 2.)
5. "Cara," aria (Ascanio)
6. "Venga, venga de' sommi eroi," chorus (Pastori)
7. (repeat of 6.)
8. "Se il labbro più non dice," aria (Fauno)
9. "Hai di Diana il core," chorus (Pastori, Pastorelle, Ninfe)
10. (repeat of 6.)
11. (repeat of 6.)
12. "Per la gioia in questo seno," aria (Aceste)
13. "Si, si, si, ma d'un altro amore," cavatina (Silvia)
14. "Come è felice stato," aria (Silvia)
15. (repeat of 6.)
16. "Ah, di sì nobil alma," aria (Ascanio)
17. "Al chiaror di que' bei rai," aria (Venere)
18. "Di te più amabile, nè Dea maggiore," chorus (Geni, Grazie)
II: 19. "Spiega il desio," aria (Silvia)
20. "Già l'ore sen volano," chorus (Pastorelle)
. "Numi? che fo...? m'appresso?," recit (Silvia, Ascanio)
21. "Dal tuo gentil sembiante," aria (Fauno)
22. "Al mio ben mi veggio avanti," aria (Ascanio)
23. "Infelici affetti miei," aria (Silvia)
24. "Che strano evento turba la Vergine in questo dì!," chorus (Pastorelle)
25. "Torna mio bene ascolta," aria (Ascanio)
26. (repeat of 6.)
27. "Sento, che il cor mi dice," aria (Aceste)
28. "Scendi, celeste Venere," chorus (Pastori, Ninfe/Pastorelle)
29. "No, non possiamo vivere," chorus (Pastori, Pastorelle)
30. (repeat of 28.)
31. "Ah caro sposo, oh Dio!," trio (Silvia, Ascanio, Aceste)
32. "Che bel piacere io sento" (Ascanio) (small part of 31.)
33. "Alma Dea tutto il mondo," final chorus (Geni, Grazie, Pastori, Ninfe)

1a.7   "Il sogno di Scipione," serenata drammatica: K126
. "Ouverture"
1. "Risolver non osa confusa," aria (Scipione)
2. "Lieve sono al par del vento," aria (Fortuna)
3. "Ciglio, che al sol si gira," aria (Costanza)
4. "Germe di cento Eroi," chorus
5. "Se vuoi, che te raccolgano," aria (Publio)
6. "Voi colagiù ridete," aria (Emilio)
7. "Quercia annosa su l'erte pendici," aria (Publio)
8. "A chi serena io giro," aria (Fortuna)
9. "Biancheggia in mar lo scoglio," aria (Costanza)
10. "Di che sei l'arbitra del mondo in tero," aria (Scipione)
. "E ben, provami avversa," recit (Fortuna, Scipione)
11a, b. "Ah perchè cercar degg' io," aria (Licenza) (2 vers)
12. "Cento volte con lieto sembiante," chorus

1a.8   "Lucio Silla," dramma per musica: K135
. "Ouverture"
I: 1. "Vieni, vieni ov'amor t'invita," aria (Cinna)
2. "Il tenero," aria (Cecilio)
3. "Se lusinghiera speme," aria (Celia)
4. "Dalla sponda tenebrosa," aria (Giunia)
. "Mi piace?," recit (Silla)
5. "Il desio di vendetta," aria (Silla)
. "Morte, morte fatal," recit (Cecilio)
6. "Fuor di queste urne," chorus
7. "D'Eliso in sen m'attendi," duet (Giunia, Cecilio)
II: 8. "Guerrier, che d'un acciaro," aria (Aufidio)
. "Ah corri, vola," recit (Cecilio)
9. "Quest' improviso tremito," aria (Cecilio)
10. "Se il labbro timido scoprir non osa," aria (Celia)
. "vanne," recit (Giunia)
11. "Ah se il crudel, se il crudel periglio," aria (Giunia)

　　　　. "Ah si, scuotasi omai," recit (Cinna)
　　　12. "Nel fortunato istante," aria (Cinna)
　　　13. "Dogni pietà mi spoglio perfida," aria (Silla)
　　　14. "Ah se a morir mi chiama," aria (Cecilio)
　　　15. "Quando sugl'arsi campi," aria (Celia)
　　　　. "In un istante," recit (Giunia)
　　　16. "Parto, m'affretto," aria (Giunia)
　　　17. "Se gloria il crin ti cinse," chorus
　　　18. "Quell' orgoglioso sdegno," trio (Giunia, Cecilio, Silla)
　III:　19. "Strider sento la procella," aria (Celia)
　　　20. "De' più superbi il core," aria (Cinna)
　　　21. "Pupille amate non lagrimate," aria (Cecilio)
　　　　. "Sposo ... mia vita ... Ah dove. Dove vai?," recit (Giunia)
　　　22. "Frà i pensier più funesti," aria (Giunia)
　　　23. "Il gran Silla che a Roma in seno" (Finale), chorus

1a.9　"La finta giardiniera," opera buffa: K196
　　　　. "Ouverture"
　　　I:　1. "Che lieto giorno, che contentezza," introduzione (Sandrina, Serpetta, Ramiro, Podestà, Nardo)
　　　2. "De l'augellin sen fugge," aria (Ramiro)
　　　3. "Dentro il mio petto il sento," aria (Podestà)
　　　4. "Noi donne poverine," aria (Sandrina)
　　　5. "A forza di martelli," aria (Nardo)
　　　6. "Che beltà, che leggiadrìa," aria (Contino)
　　　7. "Si promette facilmente Dagl'amanti," aria (Arminda)
　　　8. "Da scirocco a tramontana," aria (Contino)
　　　9a, b. "Un marito oh Dio! vorrei," arietta (Serpetta) (2nd vers sung by Nardo/B)
　　　10. "Appena mi vendon Chi cade chi sviene," aria (Serpetta)
　　　11. "Geme la Tortorella," aria (Sandrina)
　　　12. "Numi! Che incanto," septet (Sandrina, Serpetta, Arminda, Ramiro, Contino, Podestà, Nardo)
　　　II:　13. "Vorrei punirti indegno," aria (Arminda)
　　　14. "Con un vezzo all'italiana," aria (Nardo)
　　　15. "Care pupille, pupille belle," aria (Contino)
　　　16. "Una voce sento al core," aria (Sandrina)
　　　17. "Una damina una nipote," aria (Podestà)
　　　18. "Dolce d'amor compagna," aria (Ramiro)
　　　19. "Ah non partir m'ascolta," recit (Contino)
　　　20. "Chi vuol godere il mondo," aria (Serpetta)
　　　21. "Crudeli fermate," aria (Sandrina)
　　　22. "Ah dal pianto, dal singhiozzo," cavatina (Sandrina)
　　　23. "Frà quest'ombre," septet (Sandrina, Serpetta, Arminda, Ramiro, Contino, Podestà, Nardo)
　III:　24. "Mirate, che contrasto" (Sandrina, Contino, Nardo)
　　　25. "Mio Padrone, io dir volevo," aria (Podestà)
　　　26. "Và pure ad altri in braccio," aria (Ramiro)
　　　27. "Dove mai son! Dove son mai!," recit (Sandrina, Contino)
　　　　. "Tu mi lasci? o fiero istante," duet (Sandrina, Contino)
　　　28. "Viva pur la giardiniera" (Finale), chorus

1a.10　"Il rè pastore," dramma per musica: K208
　　　　. "Ouverture"
　　　I:　1. "Intendo, amico rio," aria (Aminta)
　　　2. "Alla selva, al prato, al fonte," aria (Elisa)
　　　3. "Aer tranquillo e di sereni," aria (Aminta)
　　　4. "Si spande al Sole in faccia," aria (Alessandro)
　　　5. "Per me rispondete begl'astri d'amore," aria (Agenore)
　　　6. "Di tante sue procelle," aria (Tamiri)
　　　7. "Vanne, vanne à regnar, ben mio," duet (Elisa, Aminta)
　　　II:　8. "Barbaro, oh Dio! mi vedi," aria (Elisa)
　　　9. "Se vincendo vi rendo felici," aria (Alessandro)
　　　10. "L'amerò, sarò costante," aria (Aminta)
　　　11. "Se tu di me fai dono," aria (Tamiri)
　　　12. "Sol può dir, come si trova," aria (Agenore)
　　　13. "Voi che fausti ognor donate," aria (Alessandro)
　　　14. "Viva! Viva l'invitto duce!" (Finale), quintet (Elisa, Tamiri, Aminta, Agenore, Alessandro)

1a.12　"Zaide," Singspiel: K336b (K344)
　　　I:　1. "Brüder, lasst uns lustig sein," chorus (ein Vorsinger und 3 andere)
　　　2. "Melodram" (Gomatz)
　　　3. "Ruhe sanft, mein holdes Leben," aria (Zaide)
　　　4. "Rase, Schicksal, wüte immer," aria (Gomatz)
　　　5. "Meine Seele hüpft vor Freuden," duet (Zaide, Gomatz)
　　　6. "Herr und Freund, wie dank' ich dir," aria (Gomatz)
　　　7. "Nur mutig, mein Herze," aria (Allazim)
　　　8. "O selige Wonne! Die glänzende Sonne steigt," trio (Zaide, Gomatz, Allazim)
　　　II:　9. "Melodram" (Sultan Soliman, Zaram, Oberster der Leibwache)

. "Der stolze Löw' lässt sich zwar zähmen," aria (Soliman)
10. "Wer hungrig bei der Tafel sitzt," aria (Osmin)
11. "Ich bin so bös' als gut," aria (Soliman)
12. "Trostlos schluchzet Philomele," aria (Zaide)
13. "Tiger! Wetze nurdie Klauen," aria (Zaide)
14. "Ihr Mächtigen seht ungerührt," aria (Allazim)
15. "Freundin, stille deine Tränen," quartet (Zaide, Gomatz, Soliman, Allazim)

1a.13   "Idomeneo, rè di Creta" (Ilia ed Idamante), opera seria: K366
. "Ouverture"
I: . "Quando avran fine omai," recit (Ilia)
1. "Padre, Germani, addio!," aria (Ilia)
2. "Non ho colpa, e mi condanni," aria (Idamante)
3. "Godiam la pace, trionfi Amore," chorus (Trojani, Cretesi)
4. "Tutte nel cor vi sento," aria (Elettra)
5. "Pietà! Numi pietà!," chorus
6. "Vedrommi intorno," aria (Idomeneo)
. "Spietatissimi Dei!," recit (Idamante, Idomeneo)
7. "Il padre adorato," aria (Idamante)
8. "March"
9. "Nettuno s'onori!," chorus
II: 10. "Se il tuo duol, se il mio desio," aria (Arbace) (also see recit & rondo, K490)
11. "Se il padre perdei," aria (Ilia)
12. "Fuor del mar ho un mar in seno," aria (Idomeneo) (2 vers)
13. "Idol mio, se ritroso," aria (Elettra)
14. "Odo da lunge armonioso suono," march (Elettra)
15. "Placido è il mar, andiamo," chorus
16. "Pria di partir, o Dio!," trio (Elettra, Idamante, Idomeneo)
17. "Qual nuovo terrore!," chorus
18. "Corriamo, fuggiamo quel mostro spietato," chorus
III: 19. "Zefiretti lunsinghieri," aria (Ilia)
20. "S'io non moro a questi accenti," duet (Ilia, Idamante) (see 2nd vers K489)
21. "Andrò ramingo e solo," quartet (Ilia, Elettra, Idamante, Idomeneo)
22. "Se colà ne' fati è scritto," aria (Arbace)
23. "Volgi intorno lo sguardo, o Sire," recit (Gran Sacerdote)
24. "O, o voto tremendo!," chorus
25. "March"
26. "Accogli, o rè del mar," aria (Idomeneo, Sacerdoti)
27. "No, la morte, la morte io non pavento," aria (Idamante)
28. "Ha vinto amore ... a Idomeneo perdona" (La voce) (3 vers)
29. "D'Oreste, d'Ajace," aria (Elettra)
30. "Popoli! a voi l'ultima legge," recit (Idomeneo)
31. "Torna la pace al core," aria (Idomeneo)
32. "Scenda Amor, scenda Imeneo," chorus

1a.14   "Die Entführung aus dem Serail," komisches Singspiel: K384
. "Ouverture"
I: 1. "Hier soll ich dich denn sehen, Constanze!," aria (Belmonte)
2. "Wer ein Liebchen hat gefunden," Lied & duet (Belmonte, Osmin)
3. "Solche hergelauf'ne Laffen," aria (Osmin)
4. "Constanze! Constanze! O wie ängstlich, o wie feurig," aria (Belmonte)
5. "Singt dem grossen Bassa Lieder," chorus (der Janitscharen)
6. "Ach ich liebte, war so glücklich," aria (Constanze)
7. "Marsch, marsch, marsch! trollt euch fort," trio (Belmonte, Pedrillo, Osmin)
II: 8. "Durch Zärtlichkeit und Schmeicheln," aria (Blonde)
9. "Ich gehe, doch rate ich dir," duet (Blonde, Osmin)
10. "Welcher Wechsel herrscht in meiner Seele," recit (Constanze)
. "Traurigkeit ward mir zum Lose," aria (Costanze)
11. "Martern aller Arten," aria (Constanze)
12. "Welche Wonne, welche Lust herrscht nun mehr in meiner Brust," aria (Blonde)
13. "Frisch zum Kampfe!," aria (Pedrillo)
14. "Vivat Bacchus, Bacchus lebe," duet (Pedrillo, Osmin)
15. "Wenn der Freude Tränen fliessen," aria (Belmonte)
16. "Ach, Belmonte! ach, mein Leben!," quartet (Constanze, Blonde, Belmonte, Pedrillo)
III: 17. "Ich baue ganz auf deine Stärke," aria (Belmonte)
18. "In Mohrenland gefangen war ein Mädel hübsch und fein," romance (Pedrillo)
19. "Ha, wie will ich triumphieren," aria (Osmin)
20. "Welch ein Geschick! o Qual der Seele!," recit & duet (Constanze, Belmonte)
. "Meinetwegen soll't du sterben," duet
21. "Nie werd' ich deine Huld verkennen," vaudeville (Constanze, Blonde, Belmonte, Pedrillo, Osmin)

1a.15   "L'oca del Cairo," dramma giocoso: K422
1. "Cosi si fa: Due paroline," duet (Auretta, Chichibio)
2. "Se fosse, qui nascoso," aria (Auretta)
3. "Ogni momento dicon le Donne," aria (Chichibio)

4. "Ho un pensiero nel cervello," duet (Auretta, Chichibio)
  . "O pazzo, o pazzo, o pazzo, pazzissimo Biondello!," recit (Don Pippo)
5. "Siano pronte alle gran nozze," aria (Don Pippo)
6. "S'oggi, oh Dei, sperar mi fate," quartet (Celidora, Lavina, Biondello, Calandrino)
7. "Su via putti," finale (Celidora, Lavina, Auretta, Biondello, Calandrino, Don Pippo, Chichibio)

1a.16   "Lo sposo deluso," opera buffa: K424a (K430)
  . "Ouverture"
1. "Ah, ah, ah, ah, ah, che ridere!," quartet (Bettina, Don Asdrubale, Pulcherio, Bocconio)
2. "Nacqui all'aura trionfale," aria (Eugenia)
3. "Dove mai trovar quel ciglio?," aria (Pulcherio)
4. "Che accidenti," trio (Eugenia, Don Asdrubale, Bocconio)

1a.17   "Der Schauspieldirektor," Singspiel: K486
  . "Sinfonia"
1. "Da schlägt die Abschiedsstunde," arietta (Madame Herz)
2. "Bester Jüngling! mit Entzükken!," rondò (Mademoiselle Silberklang)
3. "Ich bin die erste Sängerin," trio (Herz, Silberklang, Monsieur Vogelsang)
4. "Jeder Künstler strebt nach Ehre," Schlussgesang (Herz, Silberklang, Vogelsang)

1a.18   "Le nozze di Figaro," opera buffa: K492
  . "Ouverture"
   I: 1. "Cinque dieci," duettino (Susanna, Figaro)
       2. "Se a caso madama," duettino (Susanna, Figaro)
       3. "Se vuol ballare, signor contino," cavatina (Figaro)
       4. "La vendetta," aria (Bartolo)
       5. "Via, resti servita," duettino (Susanna, Marcellina)
       6. "Non sò più cosa son," aria (Cherubino)
       7. "Cosa sento! tosto andate," trio (Susanna, Basilio, Il Conte)
       8. "Giovani liete, fiori spargete," chorus
       9. "Non più andrai farfalone amoroso," aria (Figaro)
   II: 10. "Porgi amor qualche ristoro," cavatina (La Contessa)
      11. "Voi, che sapete che cosa è amor," arietta (Cherubino)
      12. "Venite inginocchiatevi," aria (Susanna)
      13. "Susanna or via sortite," trio (Susanna, La Contessa, Il Conte)
      14. "Aprite presto, aprite," duettino (Susanna, Cherubino)
      15. "Esci, omai, garzon malnato," finale (Il Conte)
   III: 16. "Crudel! perchè finora," duet (Susanna, Il Conte)
      17. "Hai già vinta la causa!," recit & aria (Il Conte)
       . "Vedrò mentr'io sospiro"
      18. "Riconosci in questo amplesso," sextet
      19. "E Susanna non vien!," recit & aria (La Contessa)
       . "Dove sono i bei momenti"
      20. "Sull' aria ... che soave zefiretto," duettino (Susanna, La Contessa)
      21. "Ricevete, o padroncina," chorus
      22. "Ecco la marcia, andiamo!" (Wedding March) (Figaro)
       . "Amanti costanti, seguaci d'onor," chorus (Due donne)
   IV: 23. "L'ho perduta ... me meschina!," cavatina (Barbarina)
      24. "Il capro e la capretta," aria (Marcellina)
      25. "In quegl' anni, in cui val poco," aria (Basilio)
      26. "Tutto è disposto," recit & aria (Figaro)
       . "Aprite un po' quelgl' occhi," aria
      27. "Giunse alfin il momento," recit & aria (Rondo) (Susanna)
       . "Deh vieni, non tardar, o gioja bella"
      28. "Pian, pianin le andrò più presso," finale

1a.19   "Don Giovanni" (Il dissoluto punito ossia il Don Giovanni), dramma giocoso: K527
  . "Ouverture"
   I: 1. "Notte e giorno faticar," introduzione (D. Anna, D. Giovanni, Leporello, Commendatore)
       2. "Mà qual mai s'offre, oh Dei," recit (D. Anna, D. Ottavio)
       . "Fuggi, crudele, fuggi," duet (D. Anna, D. Ottavio)
       3. "Ah! chi mi dice mai," aria (D. Elvira, D. Giovanni, Leporello)
       4. "Madamina! Il catalogo è questo," aria (Catalog Song) (Leporello)
       5. "Giovinette, che fate all' amore" (Zerlina, Masetto, ch)
       6. "Hò capito, Signor, sì," aria (Masetto)
       7. "Là ci darem la mano, là mi dirai di si," duettino (Zerlina, D. Giovanni)
       8. "Ah, fuggi il traditor," aria (D. Elvira)
       9. "Non ti fidar, o misera," quartet (D. Anna, D. Elvira, D. Ottavio, D. Giovanni)
      10. "Don Ottavio, son morta!," recit (D. Anna, D. Ottavio)
       . "Or sai chi l'onore," aria (D. Anna)
      11. "Dalla sua pace la mia dipende," aria (D. Ottavio) (added later, K540a)
      12. "Finch' han dal vino calda la testa," aria (Champagne Aria) (D. Giovanni)
      13. "Batti, batti, o bel Masetto," aria (Zerlina)
      14. "Presto, presto! pria ch'ei venga, por mi vo'," finale (Masetto)
   II: 15. "Eh via, buffone," duet (D. Giovanni, Leporello)

16. "Ah, taci ingiusto core," trio (D. Elvira, D. Giovanni, Leporello)
17. "Deh! vieni alla finestra," canzonetta (D. Giovanni)
18. "Metà di voi quà vadano," aria (D. Giovanni)
19. "Vedrai, carino, se sei buonino," aria (Zerlina)
20. "Sola, sola in buio loco palpitar," sextet
21. "Ah, pietà, signori miei!," aria (Leporello)
22. "Il mio tesoro intanto," aria (D. Ottavio)
. "Per queste tue manine," duet (Zerlina, Leporello) (added later, K540b)
23. "In quali eccessi, o Numi," recit (D. Elvira) (added later, K540c)
. "Mi tradì quell' alma ingrata," aria (D. Elvira) (added later, K540c)
24. "O statua gentilissima," duet (D. Giovanni, Leporello)
25. "Crudele! Ah nò, mio bene," recit & aria (D. Anna, D. Ottavio)
. "Non mi dir, bell' idol mio," rondò
26. "Già la mensa è preparata," finale (D. Giovanni)

1a.20   "Così fan tutte, o sia la scuola degli amanti," opera buffa: K588
. "Ouverture"
   I: 1. "La mia Dorabella capace non è," trio (Ferrando, Don Alfonso, Guglielmo)
        2. "È la fede delle femine come l'araba fenice," trio (Ferrando, Don Alfonso, Guglielmo)
        3. "Una bella serenata," trio (Ferrando, Don Alfonso, Guglielmo)
        4. "Ah guarda, sorella," duet (Fiordiligi, Dorabella)
        5. "Vorrei dir, e cor non hò," aria (Don Alfonso)
        6. "Sento o Dio, che questo piede," quintet (Fiordiligi, Dorabella, Ferrando, Don Alfonso, Guglielmo)
        7. "Al fato dan legge quegli occhi vezzosi," duettino (Ferrando, Guglielmo)
        8. "Bella vita militar," chorus
        9. "Di scrivermi ogni giorno!," quintet (Fiordiligi, Dorabella, Ferrando, Guglielmo, Don Alfonso)
       10. "Soave sia il vento," terzettino (Fiordiligi, Dorabella, Don Alfonso)
       11. "Smanie implacabili," aria (Dorabella)
       12. "In uomini, in soldati," aria (Despina)
       13. "Alla bella Despinetta," sextet (Fiordiligi, Dorabella, Despina, Ferrando, Don Alfonso, Guglielmo)
       14. "Come scoglio," aria (Fiordiligi)
       15. "Non siate ritrosi," aria (Guglielmo)
       16. "E voi ridete?," trio (Ferrando, Guglielmo, Don Alfonso)
       17. "Un' aura amorosa," aria (Ferrando)
       18. "Ah che tutta in un momento," finale (Dorabella)
   II: 19. "Una donna a quindici anni," aria (Despina)
       20. "Prenderò quel brunettino," duet (Fiordiligi, Dorabella)
       21. "Secondate, aurette amiche," duet w/ chorus (Ferrando, Guglielmo)
       22. "La mano a me date," quartet (Despina, Ferrando, Don Alfonso, Guglielmo)
       23. "Il core vi dono, bell' idolo mio!," duet (Dorabella, Guglielmo)
       24. "Ah! Io veggio, quell'anima bella al mio pianto resister non sà," aria (Ferrando)
       25. "Per pietà, ben mio, perdona, all' error," rondo (Fiordiligi)
       26. "Donne mie, la fate a tanti," aria (Guglielmo)
       27. "Tradito, schernito dal perfido cor," cavatina (Ferrando)
       28. "È Amore un ladroncello," aria (Dorabella)
       29. "Fra gli amplessi in pochi istanti," duet (Fiordiligi, Ferrando)
       30. "Tutti accusan le donne" (Don Alfonso)
       31. "Fate presto, o cari amici," finale

1a.21   "Die Zauberflöte," Deutsche Oper: K620
. "Ouverture"
   I: 1. "Zu Hilfe! zu Hilfe! sonst bin ich verloren!," introduction (Tamino)
        2. "Der Vogelfänger bin ich ja," aria (Papageno)
        3. "Dies Bildnis ist bezaubernd schön," aria (Tamino)
        4. "O zitt're nicht, mein lieber Sohn," recit (Königin der Nacht)
        . "Zum Leiden bin ich auserkoren," aria (Königin der Nacht)
        5. "Hm! hm! hm!," quintet (3 Damen, Tamino, Papageno)
        6. "Du feines Täubchen, nur herein!," trio (Pamina, Papageno, Monostatos)
        7. "Bei Männern, welche Liebe fühlen," duet (Pamina, Papageno)
        8. "Zum Ziele führt dich diese Bahn," finale
   II: 9. "Marsch der Priester"
        9a. "Adagio"
       10. "O, Isis und Osiris," aria & chorus
       11. "Bewahret euch vor Weibertükken," duet (2 Priester)
       12. "Wie? Wie? Wie? Ihr an diesem Schrekkensort?," quintet (3 Damen, Tamino, Papageno)
       13. "Alles fühlt der Liebe Freuden," aria (Monostatos)
       14. "Der Hölle Rache kocht in meinem Herzen," aria (Königin der Nacht)
       15. "In diesen heil'gen Hallen," aria (Sarastro)
       16. "Seid uns zum zweiten Mal willkommen," trio (3 Knaben)
       17. "Ach, ich fühl's, es ist verschwunden," aria (Pamina)
       18. "O, Isis und Osiris, welche Wonne!," chorus (Priester)
       19. "Soll ich dich, Teurer, nicht mehr sehen?," trio (Pamina, Tamino, Sarastro)
       20. "Ein Mädchen oder Weibchen wünscht Papageno sich," aria (Papageno)
       21. "Bald prangt, den Morgen zu verkünden," finale

877

1a.22   "La clemenza di Tito," opera seria: K621
    . "Ouverture"
    I: 1. "Come ti piace, imponi," duet (Vitellia, Sesto)
        2. "Deh se piacer mi vuoi," aria (Vitellia)
        3. "Deh prendi un dolce amplesso, amico mio fedel," duettino (Sesto, Annio)
        4. "Marcia"
        5. "Serbate, o Dei custodi," chorus
        6. "Del più sublime soglio," aria (Tito)
        7. "Ah, perdona al primo affetto," duet (Servilia, Annio)
        8. "Ah, se fosse intorno al trono," aria (Tito)
        9. "Parto, parto, ma tu ben mio," aria (Sesto)
      10. "Vengo ... aspettate," trio (Vitellia, Annio, Publio)
      11. "Ah Dei, che smania è questa," recit (Sesto)
      12. "Deh conservate, oh Dei!," quintet w/ ch (Sesto, Annio, Sevilia, Vitellia, Publio)
    II: 13. "Torna di Tito a lato," aria (Annio)
      14. "Se al volto mai ti senti," trio (Vitellia, Sesto, Publio)
      15. "Ah grazie si rendano," chorus
      16. "Tardi s'avvede d'un tradimento," aria (Publio)
      17. "Tu fosti tradito," aria (Annio)
      . "Che orror! Che tradimento! Che nera infedeltà!," scena VIII (Tito)
      18. "Quello di Tito è il volto," trio (Sesto, Tito, Publio)
      19. "Deh, per questo istante solo," rondò (Sesto)
      20. "Se all' impero, amici Dei," aria (Tito)
      21. "S'altro che lagrime," aria (Servilia)
      22. "Ecco il punto, oh Vitellia," recit (Vitellia)
      23. "Non, più di fiori vaghe catene," rondò (Vitellia)
      24. "Che del ciel, che degli Dei," chorus
      25. "Ma, che giorno è mai questo?," recit (Tito)
      26. "Tu, è ver, m'assolvi, Augusto?," sextet w/ ch (Vitellia, Servilia, Sesto, Annio, Tito, Publio)

1a.25   "Les petits riens," pantomime: K299b (App10)
    . "Ouverture"
    1. "Largo"
    2. "Gavotte"
    3. "Andantino"
    4. "Allegro"
    5. "Larghetto"
    6. "Gavotte joyeuse"
    7. "Adagio"
    8. (w/ out tempo markings)
    9. "Gavotte gracieuse"
   10. "Pantomime"
   11. "Passepied"
   12. "Gavotte"
   13. "Andante"

1a.28   Ballet music for opera: Idomeneo, K366: K367
    1. "Chaconne"
    2. "Pas seul"
    3. "Passepied"
    4. "Gavotte"
    5. "Passacaille"

1a.31   "Thamos, König in Ägypten," incid music: K336a (K345)
    1. "Schon weichet dir, Sonne," chorus (2 vers)
    2. "Nach dem Ersten Akt"
    3. "Nach dem 2 ten Akt"
    4. "Nach dem 3 ten Akt"
    5. "Nach dem 4 ten Akt
    6. "Gottheit, Gottheit, über alle," chorus (2 vers)
    7a. "Nach dem 5. und letzten Akt"
    7b. "Ihr Kinder des Staubes, erzittert und bebet" (Der Oberpriester)

2. SYMPHONIES

2.1   Symphony No.1 in E-flat major (c1764 or 5) K16
2.2   *Symphony in A min / ?major (c1765, lost)* .... *K16a (App220)*
2.3   *Symphony No.2 in B-flat major (spur)* .... *KC11.02 (K17)*
2.4   *Symphony No.3 in E-flat major (spur: c by Abel)* .... *KA51 (K18)*
2.5   Symphony No.4 in D major (c1765) K19
2.6   *Symphony in F major (c1765, frag)* .... *K19a (App223)*
2.7   *Symphony in C major (c1765, lost)* .... *K19b (App222)*
2.8   Symphony No.5 in B-flat major (c1765) K22
2.9   *Symphony in D major (c1766, = Overture to: Galimathias Musicum, K32)* ....

3. SINFONIAS CONCERTANTES

4. SERENADES (orch)

4.1	Serenade No.1 in D major (c1769, w/ March, K62)	K62a (K100)
4.2	Serenade No.2 in F major, "Contredanse" (c1776, conflation of 4 Contredances)	K101
4.3	Serenade No.3 in D major (c1773, w/ March, K167b)	K167a (K185)
4.4	Serenade No.4 in D major (c1774, w/ March, K189c)	K189b (K203)
4.5	Serenade No.5 in D major (c1775, w/ March, K213b)	K213a (K204)
4.6	Serenade No.6 in D major, "Serenata notturna" (c1776)	K239
4.7	Serenade No.7 in D major, "Haffner" (c1776; vn & orch, w/ March, K249)	K248b (K250)
4.8	Serenade No.8 in D major, "Notturno" (c1776–7, 4 groups, each: 2hn & strings)	K269a (K286)
4.9	Serenade No.9 in D major, "Posthorn" (c1779, w/ 2 Marches, K320a; see: Sinfonia conc, K320)	K320
4.10	Serenade No.10 in B-flat major, "Gran Partita" (c1781–4; 13 wind insts)	K370a (K361)
4.11	Serenade No.11 in E-flat major (c1781; winds; obs added in 2nd vers of 1782)	K375
4.12	Serenade No.12 in C minor, "Nacht Musique" (c1782 or 3; winds; arr as: Ob Qnt, K406)	K384a (K388)
4.13	Serenade No.13 in G major, "Eine kleine Nachtmusik" (c1787; strings, orig 5 movts, 2nd lost)	K525

5. DIVERTIMENTOS (orch)

5.1	*"6 Divertimenti" (c1767, lost)*	*K41a*
5.2	Divertimento No.1 in E-flat major (c1771, r1773)	K113
5.3	Divertimento No.2 in D major (c1772)	K131
5.4	*Divertimento (c1772–3; vn, va, vc & 2hn, frag)*	*K246b*
5.5	Divertimento No.3 in E-flat major (c1773; winds)	K159d (K166)
5.6	Divertimento No.4 in B-flat major (c1773; winds)	K159b (K186)
5.7	*Divertimento No.5 in C major (c1773; winds, spur: arr L. Mozart of: Dances c by Starzer & Gluck)*	*K187*
5.8	Divertimento No.6 in C major (c1773; winds)	K240b (K188)
5.9	Divertimento No.7 in D major (c?1773, w/ March, K167AB)	K167A (K205)
5.10	Divertimento No.8 in F major (c1775; winds)	K213
5.11	*Divertimento in E-flat major (c1775; wind octet, ?spur)*	*KC71.01 (App226)*
5.12	*Divertimento in B-flat major (c1775; wind octet, ?spur)*	*KC17.02 (App227)*
5.13	Divertimento No.9 in B-flat major (c1776; winds)	K240
5.14	Divertimento No.10 in F major (c1776, w/ March, K248)	K247
5.15	Divertimento No.11 in D major (c1776)	K251
5.16	Divertimento No.12 in E-flat major (c1776; winds)	K240a (K252)
5.17	Divertimento No.13 in F major (c1776; 2ob, 2hn & 2bn)	K253
5.18	Divertimento No.14 in B-flat major (c1777; winds)	K270
5.19	Divertimento No.15 in B-flat major (c1777)	K271H (K287)
5.20	*Divertimento in F major (c1777; vn, va, vc & 2hn, frag)*	*K246c (K288)*
5.21	Divertimento No.16 in E-flat major (c1777; 2ob, 2hn & 2bn)	K271g (K289)
5.22	Divertimento No.17 in D major (c1779–80, w/ March, K320c)	K320b (K334)
5.23	"5 Divertimenti," in B-flat major (c ?1783; 3 basset hn)	K439b (App229)

6. CASSATIONS (orch)

6.1	Cassation No.1 in G major (c1769)	K63
6.2	Cassation No.2 in B-flat major (c1769)	K63a (K99)
6.3	Cassation (March) (No.3) in D major (c1769)	K62
6.4	*Cassation in C major (c1769, lost)*	

7. MARCHES (orch)

7.1	*March (c1767; lost)*	*K41c*
7.2	March (Cassation) in D major (c1769, = Cassation No.3, K62)	K62
7.3	March in D major (c1773, w/ Serenade No.3 in D major, K167a)	K167b (K189)
7.4	March in D major (c1774; later used in: Idomeneo, K366)	K206
7.5	March in C major (c1775)	K214
7.6	March in D major (c1775, w/ Serenade No.5 in D major, K213a)	K213b (K215)
7.7	March in D major (c1774, w/ Serenade No.4 in D major, K189b)	K189c (K237)
7.8	March in F major (c1776, w/ Divertimento No.10 in F major, K247)	K248
7.9	March in D major, "Haffner" (c1776, w/ Serenade No.7 in D major, 'Haffner,' K248b)	K249
7.10	March in D major (c1773, w/ Divertimento No.7 in D major, K167A)	K167AB (K290)
7.11	2 "Marches," in D maj (c1779, w/ Serenade No.9 in D maj, 'Posthorn,' K320): No.1 (w/ ob)	K320a (K335)
7.12	No.2 "Maestoso assai" (w/ fl)	
7.13	March (c1780; later used in opera: Idomeneo, K366)	K362
7.14	"3 Marches" (c1782): No.1 in C major	K383e (K408/1)
7.15	No.2 in D major	K385a (K408/2)
7.16	No.3 in C major	K383F (K408/3)
7.17	March in D major (c1779, w/ Divertimento No.17 in D major, K320b)	K320c (K445)
7.18	"Masonic Funeral Music," in C minor (c1785)	K479a (K477)
7.19	*"Kleiner Marsch," in D major (c1788, lost)*	*K544*

8. MINUETS (orch)

8.1	*Minuet in C major (spur: c by ?Beethoven)* *K25a*
8.2	*Minuet (c1767, lost)* *K41d*
8.3	*"2 Minuets" (c1770; 2fl & strings): No.1 in A major (w/ out Trio, ?spur)* *K61g*
8.4	*No.2 in C major (lost; see extant transcr for kbd)*
8.5	*"6 Minuets" (c1769, ?spur): No.1 in C major* *K61h*
8.6	*No.2 in A major (w/ out Trio)*
8.7	*No.3 in D major (w/ out Trio)*
8.8	*No.4 in B-flat major*
8.9	*No.5 in G major*
8.10	*No.6 in C major*
8.11	*Minuet in D major (spur: c by ?L. Mozart)* *K64*
8.12	"7 Minuets" (c1769; 2vn & bass): No.1 in G major K61b (K65a)
8.13	No.2 in D major
8.14	No.3 in A major
8.15	No.4 in F major
8.16	No.5 in C major
8.17	No.6 in G major
8.18	No.7 in D major
8.19	"19 Minuets" (c1772; orig 20 Minuets, rearranged Mozart): No.1 in C major K61d (K103)
8.20	No.2 in G major
8.21	No.3 in D major
8.22	No.4 in F major
8.23	No.5 in C major
8.24	No.6 in A major (w/ out Trio)
8.25	No.7 in D major
8.26	No.8 in F major
8.27	No.9 in C major
8.28	No.10 in G major
8.29	No.11 in F major
8.30	No.12 in C major
8.31	No.13 in G major
8.32	No.14 in B-flat major
8.33	No.15 in E-flat major
8.34	No.16 in E major (w/ out Trio)
8.35	No.17 in A major (w/ out Trio)
8.36	No.18 in D major
8.37	No.19 in G major (w/ out Trio)
8.38	"6 Minuets" (c1770–1): No.1 in C major (arr from M. Haydn, P79/1) K61e (K104)
8.39	No.2 in F major (arr from M. Haydn, P79/3)
8.40	No.3 in C major
8.41	No.4 in A major (w/ out Trio)
8.42	No.5 in G major
8.43	No.6 in G major
8.44	*"6 Minuets" (c1769, spur: c by Haydn, HobIX/4a): No.1 in D major* .... *K61f (K105)*
8.45	*No.2 in D major*
8.46	*No.3 in D major*
8.47	*No.4 in G major*
8.48	*No.5 in G major*
8.49	*No.6 in G major*
8.50	Minuet in E-flat major (c1770, w/ out Trio) K73t (K122)
8.51	"6 Minuets" (c1772): No.1 in D major K130a (K164)
8.52	No.2 in D major
8.53	No.3 in D major
8.54	No.4 in G major
8.55	No.5 in G major
8.56	No.6 in G major
8.57	"16 Minuets" (c1773): No.1 in C major K176
8.58	No.2 in D major
8.59	No.3 in E-flat major (w/ out Trio)
8.60	No.4 in B-flat major (w/ out Trio)
8.61	No.5 in F major
8.62	No.6 in D major
8.63	No.7 in A major
8.64	No.8 in C major
8.65	No.9 in G major
8.66	No.10 in B-flat major (w/ out Trio)
8.67	No.11 in F major
8.68	No.12 in D major
8.69	No.13 in G major
8.70	No.14 in C major
8.71	No.15 in F major
8.72	No.16 in D major

9. GERMAN DANCES (LÄNDLER) (orch)

9.24	No.6 in D major	
9.25	"12 German Dances" (c1789): No.1 in C major	K586
9.26	No.2 in G major	
9.27	No.3 in B-flat major	
9.28	No.4 in F major	
9.29	No.5 in A major	
9.30	No.6 in D major	
9.31	No.7 in G major	
9.32	No.8 in E-flat major	
9.33	No.9 in B-flat major	
9.34	No.10 in F major	
9.35	No.11 in A major	
9.36	No.12 in C major	
9.37	"6 German Dances" (c1791): No.1 in C major	K600
9.38	No.2 in F major	
9.39	No.3 in B-flat major	
9.40	No.4 in E-flat major	
9.41	No.5 in G major	
9.42	No.6 in D major	
9.43	"4 German Dances" (c1791, w/ Minuets, K601): No.1 in B-flat major	K602
9.44	No.2 in F major	
9.45	No.3 in C major (= K611)	
9.46	No.4 in A major	
9.47	"3 German Dances" (c1791, w/ Minuets, K604): No.1 in D major	K605
9.48	No.2 in G major	
9.49	No.3 in C major, "Die Schlittenfahrt"	
9.50	"6 German Dances" (c1791, orig incl also: Contredance, K605a): No.1 in B-flat major	K606
9.51	No.2 in B-flat major	
9.52	No.3 in B-flat major	
9.53	No.4 in B-flat major	
9.54	No.5 in B-flat major	
9.55	No.6 in B-flat major	
9.56	German Dance in C major, "Die Leyerer" (c1791, = K602/3)	K611

10. CONTREDANSES (orch)

10.1	"4 Contredanses" (c1776): No.1 in F major	K250a (K101)
10.2	No.2 in G major	
10.3	No.3 in D major	
10.4	No.4 in F major	
10.5	*"12 Contredanses" (c1776; extant: Nos.1, 2, 3, 12 in kbd reduction only): No.1 in G major*	*K269b*
10.6	*No.2 in G major (= K101/2)*	
10.7	*No.3 in C major*	
10.8	*No.12 in D major (= K101/3)*	
10.9	"Overture & 3 Contredances" (c1790): "Overture," in D major	K588a (K106)
10.10	No.1 in D major	
10.11	No.2 in A major·	
10.12	No.3 in B-flat major	
10.13	Contredance in B-flat major (c1770)	K73g (K123)
10.14	"4 Contredanses" (c1777): No.1 in G major	K271c (K267)
10.15	No.2 in E-flat major	
10.16	No.3 in A major	
10.17	No.4 in D major	
10.18	"6 Contredanses" (c1784): No.1 in C major	K448b (K462)
10.19	No.2 in E-flat major	
10.20	No.3 in B-flat major	
10.21	No.4 in D major	
10.22	No.5 in B-flat major	
10.23	No.6 in F major	
10.24	"2 Contredances" (c1784, each preceded by a Minuet): No.1 in F major	K448c (K463)
10.25	No.2 in B-flat major	
10.26	*"9 Contredances" (c1787, ?spur): No.1 in D major*	*KC13.02 (K510)*
10.27	*No.2 in D major*	
10.28	*No.3 in D major*	
10.29	*No.4 in B-flat major*	
10.30	*No.5 in D major*	
10.31	*No.6 in D major*	
10.32	*No.7 in F major*	
10.33	*No.8 in B-flat major*	
10.34	*No.9 in C major*	
10.35	*Contredance in D major, "Das Donnerwetter" (c1788; pf red only)*	*K534*
10.36	Contredance in C major, "La bataille" / "The Siege of Belgrade" (c1788)	K535
10.37	*"3 Contredances" (c1788; pf vers only): No.1 in C major*	*K535a*
10.38	*No.2 in G major*	

11. OTHER ORCHESTRAL WORKS

12. PIANO CONCERTOS, PIANO & ORCH (also Double & Triple Pf Concs)

12.31 Piano Concerto No.26 in D major, "Coronation" (c1788) K537
12.32 Piano Concerto No.27 in B-flat major (c1788?–91, w/ cadenzas K626a/K624/62–64) K595

13. VIOLIN CONCERTOS, VIOLIN & ORCH

13.1 Violin Concerto No.1 in B-flat major (c1775) K207
13.2 Violin Concerto No.2 in D major (c1775) K211
13.3 Violin Concerto No.3 in G major (c1775) K216
13.4 Violin Concerto No.4 in D major, "Strassburg Concerto" (c1775) K218
13.5 Violin Concerto No.5 in A major, "Turkish" (c1775, w/ Turkish March in Finale) K219
13.6 "Adagio," in E major (c1776; intended for: Vn Conc No.5 in A major, K219)............................K261
13.7 *Violin Concerto No.6 in E-flat major (c1780, spur)* *K268*
13.8 "Rondo concertante," in B-flat maj (c1776; intended for: Vn Conc No.1 in B-flat maj, K207) ... K261a (K269)
13.9 *Violin Concerto in D major, "Adelaide" (spur: c by ?Casadesus)*..*KC14.05 (App294a)*
13.10 *Violin Concerto No.7 in D major (c1777, spur)* ....*K271a (K271i)*
13.11 "Rondo," in C major (c1781) K373
13.12 *"Andante," in A major (c1785, ?for Vn Concerto, lost)* *K470*
13.13 *"Andante," in F major (vn & orch; transcr Saint-Saëns from: Pf Conc No.21 in C major, K467)* ....

14. OTHER CONCERTOS, OTHER INSTR & ORCH

Fl & orch:

14.1 Flute & Harp Concerto in C major (c1778) K297c (K299)
14.2 Flute Concerto No.1 in G major (c1778) K285c (K313)
14.3 Flute (Oboe?) Concerto No.2 in D majo(c1778; possibly = lost Ob Conc, 'Ferlendis,' K271k) K285d (K314)
14.4 "Andante," in C major (c1779–80) K285e (K315)
14.5 *"Rondo," in D major (?spur)* *App184*

Ob & orch:

14.6 *Oboe Concerto, "Ferlendis-Konzert" (c1777, ?lost / = Fl Conc No.2 in D major, K285d/K314)* *K271k*
14.7 *Oboe Concerto in F major (c1783, frag)* ....*K416f (K293)*

Cl & orch:

14.8 *Clarinet Concerto in A major (c1789; orig for basset hn lost; ed1791 for cl; orig reconstr1974)* *K622*

Tpt & orch:

14.9 *Trumpet Concerto (c1768, lost)* *K47c*

Hn & orch:

14.10 *"Concerto Movement," in E-flat major (frag: reconstr Jeurissen)*...*K370b*
14.11 *"Concert Rondo," in E-flat major (c1781, frag)* *K371*
14.12 Horn Concerto No.1 in D major (c1791, 2nd movt inc, Rondo c by Süssmayer) .... K386b (K412 + K514)
14.13 Horn Concerto No.2 in E-flat major (c1783) K417
14.14 Horn Concerto No.3 in E-flat major (c ?1786–7, slow movt c1784) K447
14.15 *"Concerto Movement," in E major (frag)* ....*K494a (App98a)*
14.16 Horn Concerto No.4 in E-flat major (c1786) K495
14.17 "Rondo," in D major (c1782, inc; orig intended for: Horn Conc No.1, K386b) K514

Bn & orch:

14.18 Bassoon Concerto in B-flat major (c1774)..K186e (K191)

Other:

14.19 *"Concerto for Piano & Violin," in D major (vn, kbd & orch, frag)* ....*K315f (App56)*
14.20 "Concertone," in C major (c1774; 2vn, ob, vc & orch) K186E (K190)

15. STRING QUINTETS (2vn, 2va & vc)

15.1 *String Quintet in B-flat major (?spur arr of: Serenade No.10 in B-flat major, K370a)* *K46*
15.2 *"3 Preludes & Fugues" (c1782, ?spur): No.1 in D minor (Fugue = arr of J. S. Bach, BWV849)*..........................
15.3 *No.2 in A minor (Fugue = arr of J. S. Bach, BWV867)*
15.4 *No.3 in C minor (Fugue = arr of J. S. Bach, BWV546)*
15.5 String/Flute Quintet .... (App177)
15.6 String Quintet No.1 in B-flat major (c1773) K174
15.7 String Quintet No.2 in C minor (c1787, arr from: Serenade No.12 in C minor, K384a) K516b (K406)
15.8 String Quintet No.3 in C major (c1787) K515

21.32   No.9 "Menuetto" (w/ Trio)
21.33   No.10 "Andante"
21.34   No.11 "Menuetto" (w/ Trio)
21.35   No.12 "Allegro"

22. PIANO SONATAS

22.1	*Piano Sonata in G major (c1766, lost)*	*K33d (App199)*
22.2	*Piano Sonata in B-flat major (c1766, lost)*	*K33e (App200)*
22.3	*Piano Sonata in C major (c1766, lost)*	*K33f (App201)*
22.4	*Piano Sonata in F major (c1766, lost)*	*K33g (App202)*
22.5	Piano Sonata No.1 in C major (c1775)	K189d (K279)
22.6	Piano Sonata No.2 in F major (c1775)	K189e (K280)
22.7	Piano Sonata No.3 in B-flat major (c1775)	K189f (K281)
22.8	Piano Sonata No.4 in E-flat major (c1775)	K189g (K282)
22.9	Piano Sonata No.5 in G major (c1775)	K189h (K283)
22.10	Piano Sonata No.6 in D major, "Dürnitz" (c1775)	K205b (K284)
22.11	Piano Sonata No.7 in C major (c1777)	K284b (K309)
22.12	Piano Sonata No.8 in A minor (c1778)	K300d (K310)
22.13	Piano Sonata No.9 in D major (c1777)	K284c (K311)
22.14	Piano Sonata No.10 in C major (c1781–3)	K300h (K330)
22.15	Piano Sonata No.11 in A major, "Alla Turca" (c1781–3, 3rd movt = Rondo alla turca)	K300i (K331)
22.16	Piano Sonata No.12 in F major (c1781–3)	K300k (K332)
22.17	Piano Sonata No.13 in B-flat major (c1783–4)	K315c (K333)
22.18	Piano Sonata No.14 in C minor (c1784)	K457
22.19	Piano Sonata No.15 (w/ out No.) in F major (c1786, = Allegro & Andante + r vers of: Rondo, K494)	K533
22.20	Piano Sonata No.16 (15) in C major, "für Anfänger" (c1788)	K545
22.21	*Piano Sonata in F major (c1788, ?spur, modified Finale of: Pf Son No.16 in C major, K545)*	*K547a (App135)*
22.22	Piano Sonata No.17 (16) in B-flat major (c1789, also known as Vn Sonata: vn part not by Mozart)	K570
22.23	Piano Sonata No.18 (17) in D major, "Trumpet" (c1789, fanfare-like opening theme)	K576

Pf duet:

22.24	Piano Sonata in C major (c1765)	K19d
22.25	*"Allegro & Andante," in G major (c1786, both unfin)*	*K497a + 500a (K357)*
22.26	Piano Sonata in B-flat major (c1773–4)	K186c (K358)
22.27	Piano Sonata in D major (c1772)	K123a (K381)
22.28	Piano Sonata in F major (c1786)	K497
22.29	Piano Sonata in C major (c1787)	K521

2 Pf:

22.30	Piano Sonata in D major (c1781)	K375a (K448)

23. PIANO VARIATIONS

23.1	*"Variations" (c1765, lost)*	*K21a (App206)*
23.2	8 "Variations on Dutch song by Graaf 'Laat ons juichen,' " in G major (c1766)	K24
23.3	7 "Variations on Dutch national song 'Willem van Nassau,' " in D major (c1766)	K25
23.4	6 "Variations on an Allegretto," in F major (c1788; reused in: Vn Son No.36 in F major, K547)	K547b (K54)
23.5	12 "Variations on a Minuet," in C major (c1774, Minuet = Finale of Fischer: Ob Conc No.1)	K189a (K179)
23.6	6 "Variations on 'Mio caro Adone,' " in G major (c1773, from Salieri: La fiera di Venezia)	K173c (K180)
23.7	"Andantino," in E-flat maj (c1790, theme from aria Non vi turbate, in Gluck: Alceste, Wq37)	K588b (K236)
23.8	9 "Variations on 'Lison dormait,' " in C major (c1778, from Dezède: Julie)	K315d (K264)
23.9	12 "Variations on French song 'Ah, vous dirai-je, Maman,' " in C major (c1781–2)	K300e (K265)
23.10	8 "Variations on 'Dieu d'amour,' " in F major (c1781, from Grétry: Les mariages samnites)	K374c (K352)
23.11	12 "Variations on French song 'La belle françoise,' " in E-flat major (c1781–2)	K300f (K353)
23.12	12 "Var on 'Je suis Lindor,' " in E-flat maj (c1778, from Beaumarchais: Le barbier de Séville)	K299a (K354)
23.13	6 "Var on 'Salve tu, Domine,' " in F major (c1783, from Paisiello: I filosofi immaginarii)	K416e (K398)
23.14	10 "Var on 'Unser dummer Pöbel,' " in G major (c1784, from Gluck: La recontre imprévue, Wq32)	K455
23.15	8 "Variations on 'Come un agnello,' " in A maj (c1784, from Sarti's opera: Fra i due litiganti)	K454a (K460)
23.16	12 "Variations on an Allegretto," in B-flat major (c1786)	K500
23.17	9 "Variations on Minuet," in D major (c1789, Minuet from Duport: Vc Sonata, Op.4/6)	K573
23.18	8 "Variations on Schack or Gerl 'Ein Weib ist das herrlichste Ding,' " in F major (c1791)	K613

Pf duet:

23.19	"Andante & 5 Variations," in G major (c1786)	K501

24. OTHER PIANO WORKS

24.1	"Andante," in C major (c1761)	K1a

25. MISC WORKS

26. CHURCH SONATAS (EPISTLE SONATAS) (2vn, bass & org)

27. MASSES & MASS SECTIONS

    1. "Kyrie"
    2. "Gloria"
    3. "Laudamus te"
    4. "Gratias"
    5. "Domine"
    6. "Qui tollis"
    7. "Quoniam"
    8. "Jesu Christe"
    9. "Cum sancto spiritu"
    10. "Sanctus"
    11. "Osanna"
    12. "Benedictus"
    13. "Credo" (frag)
    14. "Et incarnatus est" (frag)

15. "Benedicimus te" (frag)

27.39   Mass No.19 (Requiem) in D minor (c1791; S, A, T, B, ch, orch & org; compl Süssmayr): K626
        1. "Requiem" (completely c by Mozart)
        2. "Dies irae" (draft by Mozart, lack of final orchestration)
        3. "Tuba mirum" (draft by Mozart, lack of final orchestration)
        4. "Rex tremendae" (draft by Mozart, lack of final orchestration)
        5. "Recordare" (draft by Mozart, lack of final orchestration)
        6. "Confutatis" (draft by Mozart, lack of final orchestration)
        7. "Lacrimosa" (draft of first 8 measures by Mozart, lack of final orchestration)
        8. "Domine Deus" (draft by Mozart, lack of final orchestration)
        9. "Hostias" (draft by Mozart, lack of final orchestration)
       10. "Sanctus" (c by Süssmayr, Mozart's sketches not found—some scholars believe they existed)
       11. "Benedictus" (c by Süssmayr, Mozart's sketches not found—some scholars believe they existed)
       12. "Agnus Dei" (c by Süssmayr, Mozart's sketches not found—some scholars believe they existed)

28. LITANIES, VESPERS & VESPER PSALMS

28.1   "Litaniae de B.M.V." (Lauretanae), in B-flat major (c1771; S, A, T, B, ch, 2vn, bass & org) K74e (K109)
28.2   "Litaniae de venerabili altaris sacramento," in B-flat major (c1772; S, A, T, B, ch, orch & org).............. K125
28.3   "Dixit" & "Magnificat," in C major (c1774; S, T, ch, insts & org) K186g (K193)
28.4   "Litaniae Lauretanae," in D major (c1774; S, A, T, B, ch, orch & org) K186d (K195)
28.5   "Litaniae de venerabili altaris sacramento," in E-flat major (c1776; S, A, T, B, ch, orch & org).............. K243
28.6   "Vesperae de Dominica," in C major (c1779; S, A, T, B, ch, insts & org) K321
28.7   "Vesperae solennes de confessore," in C major (c1780; S, A, T, B, ch, insts & org) K339

28a. SELECTIONS FROM LITANIES, VESPERS & VESPER PSALMS

28a.1   "Litaniae de B.M.V." (Lauretanae): K74e (K109)
        1. "Kyrie"
        2. "Sancta Maria"
        3. "Salus infirmorum"
        4. "Regina angelorum"
        5. "Agnus Dei"

28a.2   "Litaniae de venerabili altaris sacramento": K125
        1. "Kyrie"
        2. "Panis vivus"
        3. "Verbum caro factum"
        4. "Hostia sancta"
        5. "Tremendum"
        6. "Panis omnipotentia"
        7. "Viaticum"
        8. "Pignus"
        9. "Agnus Dei"

28a.4   "Litaniae Lauretanae": K186d (K195)
        1. "Kyrie"
        2. "Sancta Maria"
        3. "Salus infirmorum"
        4. "Regina angelorum"
        5. "Agnus Dei"

28a.5   "Litaniae de venerabili altaris sacramento": K243
        1. "Kyrie"
        2. "Panis vivus"
        3. "Verbum caro factum"
        4. "Hostia sancta"
        5. "Tremendum"
        6. "Dulcissimum convivium"
        7. "Viaticum"
        8. "Pignus"
        9. "Agnus Dei"
       10. "Miserere nobis"

28a.6   "Vesperae de Dominica": K321
        1. "Dixit"
        2. "Confitebor"
        3. "Beatus vir"
        4. "Laudate pueri"
        5. "Laudate Dominum"
        6. "Magnificat"

28a.7   "Vesperae solennes de confessore": K339
       1. "Dixit"
       2. "Confitebor"
       3. "Beatus vir"
       4. "Laudate pueri"
       5. "Laudate Dominum"
       6. "Magnificat"

29. SHORT SACRED WORKS

29.1   "God is our Refuge," motet in G minor (c1765; S, A, T, B)..K20
29.2   *"Stabat mater" (c1766; ch, lost)* *K33c*
29.3   "Scande coeli," offertory in C major (c1767; S, ch, insts & org)...K34
29.4   *"Cibavit eos," antiphon in A minor (c1770; ch & org, ?spur)* ....*K73u (K44)*
29.5   "Veni Sancte," in C major (c1768; S, A, T, B, ch & insts) K47
29.6   "Inter natos mulierum," offertory in G major (c1771; ch, 2vn/2tpt, bass/strings & org) K74f (K72)
29.7   "Miserere," in A minor (c1770; ch & bass)..K73s (K85)
29.8   "Quaerite primum regnum Dei," antiphon in D minor (c1770; ch) K73v (K86)
29.9   "Regina Coeli," in C major (c1771; S, ch, orch & org) K74d (K108)
29.10   "Benedictus sit Deus, Introibo & Jubilate," offertory in C major (c1769; S, ch, orch & org) K66a (K117)
29.11   "Regina Coeli," in B-flat major (c1772; S, ch, orch & org) K127
29.12   "Te Deum," in C major (c1769; ch, 4tpt, 2vn, bass & org) K66b (K141)
29.13   "Ergo interest" & "Quaere superna," motet in G major (c1773; S, strings & org) K73a (K143)
29.14   "Kommet her, ihr frechen Sünder" (Passionslied), aria in B-flat maj (c1779; S, strings & org) K317b (K146)
29.15   "Exsultate, jubilate," motet in F major (c1773; S, orch & org)..K158a (K165)
29.16   *"Tantum ergo," in D major (c1774; ch, orch & org, ?spur)* ....*KC3.05 (K197)*
29.17   *"Sub tuum praesidium," offertory in F major (c1774; S, T, strings & org, ?spur)* ....*KC3.08 (K198)*
29.18   "Misericordias Domini," offertory in D minor (c1775; ch, 2vn, bass & org) K205a (K222)
29.19   "Venite, populi," offertory in D major (c1776; d ch, 2vn ad lib, bass & org) K248a (K260)
29.20   "Sancta Maria, mater Dei," gradual in F major (c1777; ch, strings & org) K273
29.21   "Regina Coeli," in C major (c1779; S, A, T, B, ch, insts & org)..K321b (K276)
29.22   "Alma Dei creatoris," offertory in F major (c1777; S, A, T, B, ch, 2vn, bass & org) K272a (K277)
29.23   *"8 Pieces for Holzbauer: Miserere" (c1778; ch & orch, lost)* ....*K297a (App1)*
29.24   "2 German Sacred Songs" (c1787; S & bass): 1. "O Gottes Lamm," in F major K336c (K343)
29.25   2. "Als aus Ägypten," in C major
29.26   "Ave verum Corpus," motet in D major (c1791; ch, strings & org) K618

30. ORATORIOS & CANTATAS (v/vv, ch & orch)

30.1   "Grabmusik" (Passion Cantata), cantata (ca1767, additions ca1773) K35a (K42)
30.2   "La Betulia liberata," 2-part oratorio (c1771, Metastasio) K74c (K118)
30.3   "Dir, Seele des Weltalls," cantata (c1785, Haschka, inc; part Stadler)...................................K468a (K429)
30.4   "Davidde penitente," oratorio (c1785, Ponte; vv, ch & orch, music from: Mass, K427) ......,............K469
30.5   "Die Maurerfreude": "Sehen, wie dem starren Forscherauge," small cantata (c1785, Petran) K471
30.6   "Die ihr des unermesslichen Weltalls Schöpfer ehrt," small cantata (c1791, Ziegenhagen; S & pf) K619
30.7   "Freimaurerkantate," cantata (1791, Schikaneder; 2T, B & orch) K623

30a. SELECTIONS FROM ORATORIOS & CANTATAS

30a.1   "Grabmusik," cantata: K35a (K42)
      . "Wo bin ich? bittrer Schmerz!," recit (Die Seele)
      1. "Felsen spaltet euren Rachen," aria (Die Seele)
      . "Geliebte Seel', was redest du?," recit (Der Engel)
      2. "Betracht dies Herz und frage mich," aria (Der Engel)
      . "O Himmel! Was ein traurig Licht," recit (Die Seele)
      3. "Jesu, was hab ich getan?," duet (Der Engel, Die Seele)
      . "O lobenswerter Sinn!," recit
      . "Jesu, Jesu, Jesu," chorus

30a.2   "La Betulia liberata," oratorio: K74c (K118)
      . "Overtura"
    I: 1. "D'ogni colpa," aria (Ozia)
        2. "Ma qual virtù non cede," aria (Cabri)
        3. "Non hai cor, se in mezzo a questi," aria (Amital)
        4. "Pietà se irato sei" (Ozia & chorus)
        5. "Del pari infeconda," aria (Giuditta)
        6. "Terribile d'aspetto," aria (Achior)
        7. "Parto," aria (Giuditta)
        8. "Oh prodigio!," chorus
    II: 9. "Se Dio veder tu vuoi," aria (Ozia)
        10. "Quel nocchier, che in gran procella," aria (Amital)
        11. "Prigionier, che fa ritorno," aria (Giuditta)

12. "Te solo adoro," aria (Achiore)
13. "Con troppa rea viltà," aria (Amital)
14. "Quei moti, che senti," aria (Carmi)
15. "Lodi al gran Dio, che oppresse gli empi nemici suoi" (Giuditta & chorus)

30a.3   "Dir, Seele des Weltalls," cantata: K468a (K429)
     1. "Dir, Seele des Weltalls, o Sonne"
     2. "Dir danken wir die Freude"
     3. "Die Lichter, die zu Tausenden"
30a.4   "Davidde penitente," oratorio: K469
     1. "Alzai le flebili voci al Signor," chorus
     2. "Cantiam," chorus
     3. "Lungi le cure ingrate," aria (S)
     4. "Si-i pur sempre benigno," chorus
     5. "Sorgi, o Signore, e spargi," duet
     6. "A te, frantati affanni," aria
     7. "Se vuoi, se vuoi puniscimi," chorus
     8. "Fra l'oscure ombre funeste," aria (S)
     9. "Tutte, tutte le mie, le mie speranze," trio
    10. "Chi in Dio sol spera," chorus
    11. "di tai pericoli non ha timor"

30a.7   "Freimaurerkantate," cantata: K623
     1. "Laut verkünde unsre Freude," chorus
     . "Zum ersten Male, edle Brüder, schliesst uns dieser neue Sitz der Weisheit," recit
     2. "Dieser Gottheit Allmacht ruhet," aria
     . "Wohlan, ihr Brüder, überlasst euch ganz der Seligkeit eurer Empfindungen," recit
     3. "Lange sollen diese Mauern," duet
     4. "Laut verkünde unsre Freude," chorus

31. VOCAL ENSEMBLES

W/ orch:

31.1   *"Welch ängstliches Beben," duet (c1782, Bretzner; 2T & orch, frag) .... K384A (K389)*
31.2   "Dite almeno in che mancai?" (c1785, Bertati; S, T, 2B & orch, for Bianchi: La villanella rapita) K479
31.3   "Mandina amabile" (c1785, Bertati; S, T, B & orch, for Bianchi: La villanella rapita) K480
31.4   *"Del gran regno delle amazoni" (c1785, Petrosellini; T, 2B & orch, frag) .... K480b (K434)*
31.5   "Spiegarti non poss' io" (c1786; S, T & orch, for: Idomeneo, K366) K489
31.6   "Per queste due manine" (c1788, Da Ponte; S, B & orch, for: Don Giovanni, K527) K540b
31.7   *"Viviamo felici in dolce contento" (c1791, Grandi: Le gelosie villane; S, B & orch, lost) K615*

W/ pf/insts:

31.8   *"Ach, was müssen wir erfahren" (c1767, 2S & pf, frag) .... K43a (App24a)*
31.9   "Luci care, luci belle," notturno (c1783–6, Metastasio; 2S, B & 3 basset hn) K439a (K346)
31.10   "Ecco quel fiero istante" (c1783–6, Metastasio: Canzonette; 2S, B & 3 basset hn) K436
31.11   "Mi lagnerò tacendo," notturno (c1783–6, Metastasio: Siroe; 2S, B & 2cl & basset hn) K437
31.12   "Se lontan, ben mio, tu sei" (c1783–6, Metastasio: Strofe per musica; 2S, B & 2cl & basset hn) K438
31.13   "Due pupille amabili," notturno (c1783–6, Metastasio; 2S, B & 3 basset hn) K439
31.14   "Das Bandel": "Liebes Mandel, wo is's Bandel?" (c ?1783, ?Mozart; S, T, B & strings) K441
31.15 *"Liebes Mädchen" (2S, B, ?spur) K441c*
31.16 *"Grazie agl'inganni tuoi" (c1787, Metastasio: La liberta di Nice; S, T, B & 7insts, frag) K532*
31.17   "Più non si trovano," notturno (c1788, Metastasio: L'Olimpiade; 2S, B & 3 basset hn) K549
31.18 *"Caro mio Druck und Schluck" (c1789, Mozart; S, 2T, B & ?pf, frag) .... K571a (App5)*

32. ARIAS & SCENES (1v & orch)

Soprano:

32.1   "Conservati fedele" (c1765, Metastasio: Artaserse) K23
32.2   "A Berenice," recit & "Sol nascente," aria (c1766) K61c (K70)
32.3   *"Per quel paterno amplesso" (ca1766, Metastasio: Artaserse, frag) K73D*
32.4   "Non curo l'affetto" (c1771, Metastasio: Demofoonte) K74b
32.5   "Misero me," recit & "Misero pargoletto," aria (c1770, Metastasio: Demofoonte) K73e (K77)
32.6   "Per pietà, bell' idol mio" (ca1766, Metastasio: Artaserse) K73b (K78)
32.7   "Cara se le mie pene" (ca1769; w/ 2hn, vn, va & bass) ....
32.8   *"Misero tu non sei" (c1770, Metastasio: Demetrio, lost) .... K73A (App2)*
32.9   "O temerario Arbace," recit & "Per quel paterno," aria (ca1766, Metastasio: Artaserse) K73d (K79)
32.10   "Fra cento affanni" (c1770, Metastasio: Artaserse) K73c (K88)
32.11   "Se ardire, e speranza" (c1770, Metastasio: Demofoonte) K73o (K82)
32.12   "Se tutti i mali miei" (c1770, Metastasio: Demofoonte; 2 vers) K73p (K83)
32.13   "Der Liebe himmlisches Gefühl" (c1782, acc in kbd reduction only) K382h (K119)

32.14 "Ah, spiegarti, o Dio" (c1783, Anfossi: Il curioso indiscreto, acc in kbd reduction only) K417e (K178)
32.15 "Voi avete un cor fedele" (c1775, after Goldoni: Le nozze di Dorina) K217
32.16 "Ah, lo previdi," recit & "Ah, t'invola agl'occhi miei," aria (c1777, Cigna-Santi: Andromeda) K272
32.17 "Alcandro, lo confesso," recit & "Non sò d'onde viene," aria (c1778, Metastasio: L'Olimpiade)........... K294
32.18 "Popoli di Tessaglia," recit & "Io non chiedo," aria (c1779, Calzabigi, in Gluck: Alceste,
Wq37)..K300b (K316)
32.19 "Scena" (c1778, for castrato Tenducci, lost) K315b (App3)
32.20 "Warum, o Liebe," recit & "Zittre, töricht Herz," aria (c1780, Werther, lost) K365a (App11a)
32.21 "Ma che vi fece," recit & "Sperai vicino il lido," aria (c1781, Metastasio: Demofoonte) K368
32.22 "Misera, dove son!," scena & "Ah, non son' io che parlo," aria (c1781, Metastasio: Ezio) K369
32.23 "A questo seno deh vieni," recit & "Or che il cielo a me," aria (c1781, Gamerra: Sismano nel Mogol) ..K374
32.24 "Nehmt meinen Dank, ihr holden Gönner!" (c1782, anon) K383
32.25 "Mia speranza adorata," scena & "Ah, non sai, qual pena," aria (c1783, Sertor: Zemira) K416
32.26 "Vorrei spiegarti, oh Dio," "Ah conte, partite" (c1783, Anfossi: Il curioso indiscreto) K418
32.27 "No, no, che non sei capace" (c1783, Anfossi: Il curioso indiscreto) K419
32.28 "In te spero, o sposo amato" (Metastasio: Demofoonte, frag) K383h (K440)
32.29 "Basta, vincesti," recit & "Ah, non lasciarmi," aria (c1778, Metastasio: Didone) K295a (K486a)
32.30 "Non più, tutto ascoltai," scena & "Non temer, amato bene," rondo (c1786, Ponte, in: Idomeneo).......K490
32.31 "Ch' io mi scordi di te?," scena & "Non temer, amato bene," rondo (c1786, add to: Idomeneo, K490)..K505
32.32 "Bella mia fiamma," scena & "Resta, o cara," aria (c1787, Scarcone: Cerere placata)...............K528
32.33 "Ah se in ciel, benigne stelle" (c1788, Metastasio: L'eroe cinese)...................................K538
32.34 "In quali eccessi" & "Mi tradì quell' alma ingrata" (c1788, Da Ponte, add to: Don Giovanni, K527/23) K540c
32.35 "Ohne Zwang, aus eignem Triebe" (Eine teutsche Aria) (c1789, lost) K569
32.36 "Al desio di chi t'adora," rondo (c1789, ?Da Ponte, add to: Le nozze di Figaro, K492)....................K577
32.37 "Alma grande e nobil core" (c1789, Palomba, insertion in Cimarosa: I due baroni) K578
32.38 "Un moto di gioia mi sento" (c1789, ?Da Ponte, add to: Le nozze di Figaro, K492) K579
32.39 "Schon lacht der holde Frühling" (c1789, German vers of Paisiello: Il barbiere di Siviglia) K580
32.40 "Chi sà, chi sà, qual sia" (c1789, ?Da Ponte, in Soler: Il burbero di buon cuore)......................K582
32.41 "Vado, ma dove?—oh Dei!" (c1789, ?Da Ponte, in Soler: Il burbero di buon cuore)...........................K583

Alto:

32.42 "Ombra felice," recit & "Io ti lascio," aria (c1776, Mortellari: Arsace) K255

Tenor:

32.43 "Va, dal furor portata" (c1765, Metastasio: Ezio; 2 vers) K19c (K21)
32.44 "Or che il dover," recit & "Tali e cotanti sono," aria (c1766) K33i (K36)
32.45 "Ah, più tremar non voglio" (c1769–70, Metastasio: Demofoonte, frag) K71
32.46 "Si mostra la sorte" (c1775) K209
32.47 "Con ossequio, con rispetto" (c1775) K210
32.48 "Clarice cara mia sposa" (c1776) K256
32.49 "Se al labbro mio non credi" & "Il cor dolente" (c1778, ?Pasquini, in Hasse: Artaserse; 2 vers)...........K295
32.50 "Per pietà, non ricercate" (c1783, Anfossi: Il curioso indiscreto) K420
32.51 "Misero! o sogno!," recit & "Aura, che intorno spiri," aria (c1783) K425b (K431)
32.52 "Müsst' ich auch durch tausend Drachen" (c1783, frag) K416b (K435)
32.53 "Dalla sua pace" (c1788, Da Ponte, add to: Don Giovanni, K527/11) K540a

Bass:

32.54 "Un dente guasto e gelato" (c1772, frag) K209a
32.55 "Così dunque tradisci," recit & "Aspri rimorsi atroci," aria (c1783, Metastasio: Temistocle) K421a (K432)
32.56 "Männer suchen stets zu naschen" (c ?1783, frag: orch part sketched only) K416c (K433)
32.57 "Alcandro, lo confesso," recit & "Non so, d'onde viene," aria (c1787, Metastasio: L'Olimpiade) K512
32.58 "Mentre ti lascio, o figlia" (c1787, Morbilli, in Paisiello: La disfatta di Dario) K513
32.59 "Ich möchte wohl der Kaiser sein," German warsong (c1788, Gleim) K539
32.60 "Un bacio di mano," arietta (c1788, ?Da Ponte, in Anfossi: Le gelosie fortunate) K541
32.61 "Rivolgete a lui lo sguardo" (c1789, Da Ponte, for: Così fan tutte, K588) K584
32.62 "Per questa bella mano" (c1791) K612
32.63 "Io ti lascio, o cara, addio" (c1791, only vn parts by Mozart, rest c by Jacquin) K621a (App245)

33. SONGS (w/ pf)

33.1 "Daphne deine Rosenwangen" (spur: arr Leopold Mozart) K46c (K52)
33.2 "An die Freude": "Freude, Königin der Weisen" (c1768, Uz) K47e (K53)
33.3 "Wie unglücklich bin ich nit" (c ?1775–6, anon) K125g (K147)
33.4 "Lobegesang auf die feierliche Johannisloge": "O heiliges Band" (c1775–6, Lenz) K125h (K148)
33.5 "Die grossmütige Gelassenheit": "Ich hab' es längst gesagt" (spur) K125d (K149)
33.6 "Geheime Liebe": "Was ich in Gedanken küsse" (c1772, Günther, spur) K125e (K150)
33.7 "Die Zufriedenheit im niedrigen Sande": "Ich trachte nicht nach solchen Dingen" (spur) K125f (K151)
33.8 "Ridente la calma," canzonetta (arr of aria c by Myslivecek, ?spur) K210a (K152)
33.9 "Oiseaux, si tous les ans," ariette (c1777–8, Ferrand) K284d (K307)
33.10 "Dans un bois": "Dans un bois solitaire et sombre," ariette (c1777–8, Motte) K295b (K308)

33.11   "Die Zufriedenheit": "Was frag ich viel nach Geld und Gut" (c1780–1, Miller; also
      vers w/ mand) K367a (K349)
33.12   *"Wiegenlied" (spur: c by Flies)* *K350*
33.13   "Komm, liebe Zither, komm" (c1780–1, anon; w/ mand) K367b (K351)
33.14   "An die Hoffnung": "Ich würd' auf meinem Pfad" (c1781–2, from Hermes: Sophiens Reisen) . K340c (K390)
33.15   "An die Einsamkeit": "Sei du mein Trost" (c1781–2, from Hermes: Sophiens Reisen) K340b (K391)
33.16   "Verdankt sei es dem Glanz der Grossen" (c1781–2, from Hermes: Sophiens Reisen) K340a (K392)
33.17   *"Gibraltar": "O Calpe! dir donnerts am Fusse" (c1782, Denis, frag: only pf part sketched)* ....*K386d (App25)*
33.18   "Gesellenreise": "Die ihr einem neuen Grade" (c1785, Ratschky) K468
33.19   "Der Zauberer": "Ihr Mädchen flieht Damöten ja!" (c1785, Weisse) K472
33.20   "Die Zufriedenheit": "Wie sanft, wie ruhig fühl' ich hier" (c1785, Weisse) K473
33.21   "Die betrogene Welt": "Der reiche Tor, mit Gold geschmücket" (c1785, Weisse) K474
33.22   *"Einsam bin ich meine Liebe" (c1785, frag)* .... *K475a (App26)*
33.23   "Das Veilchen": "Ein Veilchen auf der Wiese stand" (c1785, Goethe) K476
33.24   "Zerfliesset heut', geliebte Brüder," masonic song (c1785; w/ m ch & org) K483
33.25   "Ihr unsre neuen Leiter," masonic song (c1785, Schlittersberg; w/ m ch & org) K484
33.26   "Lied der Freiheit": "Wer unter eines Mädchens Hand" (c1785, Blumauer) K506
33.27   "Die Alte": "Zu meiner Zeit" (c1787, Hagedorn) K517
33.28   "Der Verschweigung": "Sobald Dämotas Chloen sieht" (c1787, Weisse) K518
33.29   "Das Lied der Trennung": "Die Engel Gottes weinen" (c1787, Schmidt) K519
33.30   "Als Luise die Briefe ihres ungetreuen Liebhabers verbrannte": "Erzeugt von heisser Phantasie"
      (c1787, Baumberg) K520
33.31   "Abendempfindung an Laura": "Abend ist's, die Sonne ist verschwunden" (c1787, ?Campe)...............K523
33.32   "An Chloe": "Wenn die Lieb aus deinen blauen, hellen, offnen Augen sieht" (c1787, Jacobi) K524
33.33   "Des kleinen Friedrichs Geburtstag": "Es war einmal, ihr Leutchen" (c1787, Schall) K529
33.34   "Das Traumbild": "Wo bist du, Bild" (c1787, Hölty) K530
33.35   "Die kleine Spinnerin": "Was spinnst du" (c1787) K531
33.36   "Beim Auszug in das Feld": "Dem hohen Kaiser-Worte treu" (c1788) K552
33.37   "Sehnsucht nach dem Frühling": "Komm, lieber Mai" (c1791, Overbeck) K596
33.38   "Im Frühlingsanfang": "Erwacht zum neuen Leben" (c1791, Sturm) K597
33.39   "Das Kinderspiel": "Wir Kinder, wir schmecken" (c1791, Overbeck) K598

34. CANONS

34.1   "Canon 4 in 1," in A major (c1772) K73i (K89al)
34.2   "4 Rätselkanons" (c1772): 1. "Incipe menalios meum," 3 in 1, in F major K73r (K89all)
34.3   2. "Cantate Domino omnis," 8 in 1, in G major
34.4   3. "Confitebor tibi Domine," 2 in 1 (+1), in C major
34.5   4. "Tebana bella cantus," 6 in 2, in B-flat major
34.6   "14 Canonic Studies" (c177; vv): 1. "Kyrie eleison" (3 ch) K73x (App109d)
34.7   2. (d canon)
34.8   3. (w/ out text)
34.9   4. "Cantate Domino omnis terra" (d canon)
34.10   5. "Regna terrae cantate" (d canon)
34.11   6. "Jovi patri" (Krebskanon)
34.12   7. "Cantemus Domino"
34.13   8. (Canon ad Unissonum) (4 ch)
34.14   9. "Laudabo nomen Dei cum cantico"
34.15   10. "introite portas ejus in confessione"
34.16   11. "Jovi patri canendo oblectant"
34.17   12. "Hymnus canunt demulcentque"
34.18   13. "A Musis Heliconiadibus"
34.19   14. "Incipe Menalios"
34.20   "Canon 8 in 1," in A minor (c1770–1) ....
34.21   "Sie ist dahin," canon 3 in 1, in C minor (ca1782, Hölty) K382a (K229)
34.22   "Selig, selig," canon 2 in 1, in C minor (ca1782, Hölty) K382b (K230)
34.23   "Leck mich im Arsch" (Lasst froh uns sein), 6 in 1, in B-flat major (ca1782, Mozart) K382c (K231)
34.24   "Lieber Freistädtler, lieber Gaulimauli," 4 in 1, in G major (c1787, Mozart) K509a (K232)
34.25   "Leck mir den Arsch" (Nichts labt mich mehr), 3 in 1, in B-flat major (ca1782, Mozart) K382d (K233)
34.26   "Bei der Hitz im Sommer ess ich" (Essen, Trinken), 3 in 1, in G major (ca1782, Mozart) K382e (K234)
34.27   "2 Canons" (c1787): 1. "Doppelkanon" (für 4 Singstimmen), in F major K515b (K228)
34.28   2. "Doppelkanon": "Ach! zu kurz ist unsers Lebens Lauf," in E-flat major (Härtel)
34.29   "Lasst uns ziehn, wo die volle Beere schwillt," canon 6 in 1, in D major (ca1782) K382f (K347)
34.30   "V'amo di core teneramente," 12 in 3, in A major (ca1782) K382g (K348)
34.31   "Heiterkeit und leichtes Blut," canon 3 in 1, in F major (c1786) K507
34.32   "Auf das Wohl aller Freunde," canon 3 in 1, in F major (c1786)..K508
34.33   "Canon 3 in 1," in C major (c1786) K508A
34.34   "8 Canons, in F major (c1786): 1. "Canone a tre soprani" (Canone perpetuo) K508a
34.35   2. "Kanon für 3 Stimmen" (S, A, B)
34.36   3. "Kanon für 2 Soprane" (in seconda)
34.37   4. "Kanon für 2 Soprane" (in terza)
34.38   5. "Kanon für 2 Soprane" (in quarta)
34.39   6. "Kanon für 2 Soprane" (in quinta)
34.40   7. "Kanon für 2 Soprane" (in sesta)

35. ARRANGEMENTS OF WORKS OF OTHERS

* * * * *

K = Dr. Ludwig Ritter von Köchel: "Chronologisch-thematisches Verzeichnis sämtlicher Tonwerke Wolfgang Amadé Mozarts." Sechste Auflage bearbeitet von Franz Giegling, Zürich, Alexander Weinmann, Wien, Gerd Sievers, Wiesbaden. Breitkopf & Härtel, Wiesbaden, 1964.
(Nos. in brackets: Köchel, 1862.)
App = Appendix in Köchel's catalog.

1. STAGE WORKS (operas)

1.1   *"Han d'Islande" (c1856, after Hugo's novel, project)* ....

1.2   "Salambo" (The Libyan), 4 acts (c1863–6, after Flaubert's novel: Salammbô, inc): ....
    extant: . "Song of the Balearic Islander"
          . 2nd Scene of Act II
          . "Salambo's Prayer" (1st Scene of the 2nd Tableau of Act II) (orchd Senilov 1915)
          . 1st Scene of Act III
          . 1st Scene of Act IV
          . "The Priestesses comfort Salambo and robe her in wedding garments" (fem ch, Act IV)

1.3   "The Marriage," comic opera (c1868, Gogol, Act I only; scored Hauk; also Ravel) ....

1.4   "Boris Godunov," 4 acts (c1868–9, r until 1872, Musorgsky after Pushkin & Karamzin; 7 vers): ....
          . Version of 1868–9
          . Version of 1871–2 (broader, longer, more varied)
          . Alterations in the 1874 vocal score of Version of 1871–2 (substantial cuts)
          . *Rimsky-Korsakov's Version 1 (p1896, based on 1874 vocal score, drastically cut)*
          . *Rimsky-Korsakov's Version 2 (p1908, based on 1874 vocal score)*
          . *Shostakovich's Orchestration (orchd1939–40, p1963)*
          . *Rathaus's Version (unpubd, perf1952–3 at Metropolitan Opera, restored 1874 cuts)*

1.5   *"The Tramp" (The landless peasant) (c1870, after Spielhagen, project; used in opera: Khovanshchina)* ....

1.6   "Mlada," opera-ballet (c1872, Krylov after scenario by Gedeonov, collab Rimsky-Korsakov, Borodin, Cui):.
    used: . "St John's Night on the Bare Mountain," sym poem
          . "Salambo," opera
          . "Oedipus in Athens," incid music
    new: . "Procession of Slav Princes" (c1872; see orchd1880 as: Turkish March)

1.7   "Khovanshchina" (The Princess Khovansky), 5 acts (c1872–80, Musorgsky; compl Rimsky-Korsakov 1886)

1.8   "Sorochinsky Fair," comic opera (c1874–80 after Gogol; compl Cui p1917) ....

1.9   *"Pugachovshchina" (c1877, after Pushkin, project)* ....

Incid music:

1.10   *"Oedipus in Athens" (c1860–1, Ozerov after Sophocles, only chorus extant)* ....

1a. SELECTIONS FROM STAGE WORKS (Nos. of sections in The Gramophone)

1a.4   "Boris Godunov," opera: ....
    Prologue: 1a. "To whom are you abandoning us"
             1b. "Mityukha, what are we bawling about?"
             1c. "True Believers"
             1d. "The Angel of the Lord spake to the world"
             2a. "Like to the red sun"
             2b. "I am sick at heart" (Coronation Scene)
        I: 3a. "Yet one last tale" (Pimen's monologue)
             3b. "You have been writing"
             4a. "I caught a dove-coloured drake"
             4b. "For the building of a church"
             4c. "Once in the town of Kazan" (Varlaam's Song)
             4d. "How he rides ... Hostess, where does this road lead?"
             4e. "Why, from here, for instance"
             5. "Who are you? Eh?"
        II: 6a. "Where are you, my bridegroom?"
             6b. "Once a gnat was sawing wood" (Song of the Gnat)
             6c. "A tale of this and that" (Clapping game)
             7a. "And you, my son, what are you busy with?"
             7b. "I have attained the highest power" (Monologue)
             7c. "Our poll parrot was sitting with the nannies" (Song of the Parrot)
             7d. "Your Majesty, I make obeisance"
             7e. "Ugh, it's oppressive" (Clock Scene)
       III: 8a. "On the banks of the azure Vistula," chorus
             8b. "Enough! The beauteous lady is grateful"
             8c. "Marina's bored"
             8d. "Oh, it's you, father"
             9a. "At midnight in the garden"
             9b. "Tsarevich!... At my heels again"
             9c. "I don't believe in your passion"
             9d. "The crafty Jesuit squeezed me hard"
             9e. "Oh tsarevich, I implore"
       IV: 10a. "Is the mass over, then?"
             10b. "Trrrr Tin hat"
             10c. "The moon is going"
             10d. "What is he crying for?"
            10e. "Gush forth, bitter tears"
             11a. "Well, let's put it to the vote," chorus
             11b. "Your pardon, my lords"

11c. "One day at the hour of vespers"
11d. "Farewell, my son, I am dying"
12a. "Bring him down here"
12b. "No falcon flies across the skies"
12c. "The sun and moon have gone dark"
12d. "Unleashed, raging our might has been"
12e. "Oh Lord, save the king"
12f. "Hail to thee, tsarevich"
12g. "Gush forth, bitter tears"

1a.7   "Khovanshchina," opera: ....
1. "Prelude" (Dawn over the Moscow River)
14b. "Mysterious forces" (Marfa's divination)
21a. "I walked all through the meadows," aria
24. "The lair of the Streltsy is sunk in sleep," aria
34. "Dance of the Persian Slave Girls"
36. "Prelude"
41. "Here on this spot," aria
46. "Intermezzo"
47. "Golitsyn's journey"

2. SYMPHONIES

2.1   *Symphony in D major (c1861–2, project)* ....

3. OTHER ORCHESTRAL WORKS

3.1   "Scherzo," in B-flat major (c1858; orig for pf; ed Rimsky-Korsakov) ....
3.2   "Alla marcia notturna" (c1861) ....
3.3   "St John's Night on the Bare Mountain," sym poem (c1867; pf & orch; used in opera-ballet: Mlada) ....
3.4   *"A Night on the Bare Mountain" (arr & reorchd Rimsky-Korsakov 1886, from: St John's Night of 1867)* ....
3.5   "Intermezzo in modo classico," in B minor (orchd1867 w/ new Trio; orig for pf 1860–1) ....
3.6   *"Podebrad of Bohemia," sym poem (c1867, project)* ....
3.7   *"Turkish March" (c1880; orchd Rimsky-Korsakov from Procession of Slav Princes in opera-ballet: Mlada)* ....
3.8   "The Capture of Kars," tableau vivant (c1880, w/ Turkish March as accompaniment) ....
3.9   *"Transcaucasian Suite" (c1880; orch w/ harps & pf, project)* ....
3.10   *"Pictures at an Exhibition," suite (orchd Ravel 1922; see orig for pf 1874): . "Promenade" (Prelude)* ....
3.11   *No.1 "The Gnome"*
3.12   *. "Promenade" (Interlude)*
3.13   *No.2 "The Old Castle"*
3.14   *. "Promenade" (Interlude)*
3.15   *No.3 "Tuileries"*
3.16   *. "Promenade" (Interlude)*
3.17   *No.4 "Bydlo"*
3.18   *. "Promenade" (Interlude)*
3.19   *No.5 "Unhatched Chickens"*
3.20   *No.6 "Samuel Goldenberg and Schmuyle"*
3.21   *No.7 "The Market Place at Limoges"*
3.22   *No.8 "Catacombes"*
3.23   *No.9 "Baba-jaga" (La cabane sur des pattes de poules)*
3.24   *No.10 "Great Gate of Kiev"*

4. PIANO SONATAS

4.1   *"2 Piano Sonatas" (c1858, lost): No.1 in E-flat major* ....
4.2   *No.2 in F-sharp minor*

5. OTHER PIANO WORKS

5.1   *"Porte-Enseigne Polka" (Ensign's Polka) (c1852, lost)* ....
5.2   "Souvenir d'enfance" (c1857) ....
5.3   "Scherzo," in C-sharp minor (c1858; orchd Senilov 1917) ....
5.4   "Scherzo," in B-flat major (c1858; orchd) ....
5.5   "Impromptu passionné" (c1859) ....
5.6   "A Child's Jest" (Ein Kinderscherz), scherzo (c1859, r1860) ....
5.7   *"Preludio in modo classico" (c1860, lost)* ....
5.8   "Intermezzo in modo classico" (c1860–1; see orchd 1867; rearr for pf 1867) ....
5.9   *"Menuet monstre" (c1861, lost)* ....
5.10   *"Scherzo of a Sonata in D" (c1862, lost, = ?Scherzo of the projected Symphony in D major)* ....
5.11   "From memories of childhood" (Souvenirs d'enfance) (c1865): No.1 "Nanny and I" ....
5.12   No.2 "First punishment: Nanny shuts me in a dark room" (ed Karatigin)

5.13	"Duma" (Rêverie) (c1865, on a theme of V. A. Loginov) ....
5.14	"La capricieuse" (c1865, on a theme of L. Heyden) ....
5.15	"The Seamstress," scherzino (c1871) ....
5.16	"Pictures at an Exhibition," suite (c1874, based on Hartmann's drawings; orchd Ravel 1922): . "Promenade"
5.17	No.1 "Gnomus"
5.18	. "Promenade"
5.19	No.2 "Il Vecchio Castello"
5.20	. "Promenade"
5.21	No.3 "Tuileries"
5.22	No.4 "Bydlo"
5.23	. "Promenade"
5.24	No.5 "Ballet of the Unhatched Chicks"
5.25	No.6 "Samuel Goldenberg and Schmuyle"
5.26	No.7 "Limoges: The Market"
5.27	No.8 "Catacombs—Sepulchrum Romanum"
5.28	. "Cum Mortuis in Lingua Mortua"
5.29	. "The Little Hut on Chicken's Legs"
5.30	. "The Great Gate of Kiev"
5.31	*"Storm on the Black Sea," fantasy (c1879, lost)* ....
5.32	"On the South Coast of the Crimea," 2 pieces (c1879): No.1 "Goursouf" ....
5.33	No.2 "Capriccio"
5.34	"Méditation," albumleaf (c1880) ....
5.35	"Une larme" (A Tear) (c1880) ....
5.36	"Au village," quasi fantasia (c ?1880) ....
5.37	"Fair Scene and Hopak" (arr1880, from opera: Sorochinsky Fair) ....

Pf duet:

5.38	"Allegro & Scherzo," in C major (c1860, for a sonata, 2nd piece from: Scherzo in C-sharp of 1858) ....

6. CHORAL WORKS

6.1	"Shamyl's March" (c1859; T, B, ch & orch) ....
6.2	"The Destruction of Sennacherib" (c1866–7, r1873–4, from Byron's Hebrew Melodies; ch & orch; also Eng transl Cox, Fr transl Ruelle) ....
6.3	"Jesus Navinus" (Joshua) (c1874–7; mS, Bar, ch & orch, from: Salambo; orchd Rimsky-Korsakov 1883) ...
6.4	"5 Russian Folksongs" (c1880; arr for m ch): 1. "Skazi, devitsa milaya" ....
6.5	2. "Ti vzoydi, solntse krasnoye"
6.6	3. "U vorot, vorot batyshkinikh"
6.7	4. "Uzh ti, volya, moya volya" (w/ 2T)
6.8	*5. (Incompl)*
6.9	"3 Vocalises" (c1880; 3 fem vv) ....

7. SONGS (w/ pf)

7.1	"Where are thou, little star?" (c1857, Grekov; orchd1858) ....
7.2	"Meines Herzens Sehnsucht" (c1858) ....
7.3	"Tell me why, o maiden" (c1858, ?Pushkin) ....
7.4	"A Happy Hour" (Capriccio) (c1858, Koltsov; 2 vers) ....
7.5	"Sadly rustle the leaves" (a musical story) (c1858, after Pleshcheyev's poem) ....
7.6	"What are words of love to you?" (c1860, Ammosov) ....
7.7	"I have many palaces and gardens" (c1860, Koltsov) ....
7.8	"The Harper's Song" (Old man's song) (c1863, from Goethe's Wilhelm Meister, transl unknown) ....
7.9	"King Saul" (c1863, p1871, from: Byron's Hebrew Melodies, transl Kozlov; orchd Glazunov): ....
7.10	"King Saul Before the Battle" (c1863, p1923, from: Byron's Hebrew Melodies, Fr transl Laloy, music not related to setting p1871)
7.11	"We parted coldly": "But if I could meet thee again" (c1863, Kurochkin) ....
7.12	"The wild winds blow" (c1864, Koltsov) ....
7.13	"Kalistratushka" (Kallistrat) (c1864, Nekrasov; 2nd vers: Kallistrat 1864) ....
7.14	"Night," fantasy (c1864, after Pushkin; orchd1868; 2nd vers orchd Rimsky-Korsakov) ....
7.15	"Prayer" (c1865, Lermontov) ....
7.16	"The Outcast Woman" (The Lost Soul), essay in recitative (c1865, Holz-Miller) ....
7.17	"Lullaby" (c1865, from Ostrovsky's drama: Voyevoda; 2nd vers: Sleep, peasant son) ....
7.18	"Darling Sávishna" (c1865, Musorgsky) ....
7.19	"Dear one, why are thine eyes sometimes so cold?" (c1866, Pleshcheyev) ....
7.20	"Ich wollt' meine Schmerzen ergösse sich" (c1866, Heine) ....
7.21	"From my tears" (c1866, Heine transl Mikhaylov) ....
7.22	"You drunken sot!" (c1866, Musorgsky from: Adventures of Pakhomitch; A & pf) ....
7.23	"Hopak" (c1866, from Shevchenko's play: The Haidamaks, transl Mey; orchd1868) ....
7.24	*"Yarema's song" (c1866, from Shevchenko's play: The Haidamaks, transl Mey, lost; see: On the Dnieper)* ....
7.25	"Hebrew song" (c1867, Mey) ....
7.26	"The Magpie," a musical jest (c1867, on 2 poems by Pushkin) ....

7.27   "The Seminarist" (c1867, Musorgsky) ....
7.28   "Gathering Mushrooms" (c1867, Mey; orchd Rimsky-Korsakov) ....
7.29   "The Feast" (The Banquet) (c1867, Koltsov) ....
7.30   "The Ragamuffin" (The street urchin) (c1867, Musorgsky) ....
7.31   "The Goat: a worldly story" (c1867, Musorgsky) ....
7.32   "The Classicist" (a musical pamphlet) (c1867, Musorgsky) ....
7.33   "The Garden by the Don" (c1867, Koltsov) ....
7.34   "The Orphan" (c1868, Musorgsky) ....
7.35   "Yeremushka's lullaby" (c1868, Nekrasov) ....
7.36   "Child's song" (c1868, Mey) ....
7.37   "The Nursery," cycle (Musorgsky): 1. "With nurse" (Nanny and I) (c1868) ....
7.38   2. "In the corner" (c1870)
7.39   3. "The beetle" (c1870)
7.40   4. "With the doll" (c1870)
7.41   5. "Going to sleep" (c1870)
7.42   6. "On the hobby-horse" (c1872)
7.43   7. "The cat Sailor" (Naughty Puss) (c1872)
7.44   "The Peepshow" (The Penny Gaff), musical satire (c1870, Musorgsky) ....
7.45   "Evening Song" (c1871, ?Pleshcheyev) ....
7.46   "Without Sunlight," cycle (c1874, Golenishchev-Kutuzov): 1. "Between four walls" ......
7.47   2. "Thou didst not know me in the crowd"
7.48   3. "The idle, noisy day is ended"
7.49   4. "Boredom"
7.50   5. "Elegy"
7.51   6. "On the river"
7.52   "Forgotten" (Ballad) (c1874, Golenishchev-Kutuzov) ....
7.53   "The Mound of Nettles" (The Crab) (c1874, Musorgsky, inc) ....
7.54   "Songs & Dances of Death," cycle (c1875–7, Golenishchev-Kutuzov): 1. "Trepak" (orchd Glazunov) ....
7.55   2. "Death's craddle-song" (orchd Glazunov)
7.56   3. "Serenade" (orchd Rimsky-Korsakov)
7.57   4. "Field-Marshall Death" (orchd Rimsky-Korsakov)
7.58   "Cruel Death: An Epitaph" (c1875, Musorgsky; compl Karatigin) ....
7.59   "The Sphinx" (c1875, Musorgsky) ....
7.60   "Not like thunder from heaven, trouble struck" (Misfortune) (c1877, Tolstoy) ......
7.61   "Softly the spirit flew up to heaven" (The Spirit in Heaven) (c1877, Tolstoy) ......
7.62   "Arrogance" (Master Haughty) (c1877, Tolstoy) ....
7.63   "Is spinning man's work?" (c1877, Tolstoy) ....
7.64   "It scatters and breaks" (c1877, Tolstoy) ....
7.65   "The Vision" (c1877, Golenishchev-Kutuzov) ....
7.66   "The Wanderer" (c1878, Rückert transl Pleshcheyev) ....
7.67   "The Song of the Flea" (Mephisto's song) (c1879, Goethe transl Strugovshchikov) (also see Beethoven
     Op.75/3 & Busoni K278) ....
7.68   "On the Dnieper" (c1879, from Shevchenko's play: The Haidamaks, new vers of lost: Yarema's Song) ....

8. ARRANGEMENTS OF WORKS OF OTHERS

8.1   Gordigiani: "Ogni sabbato avrete il lume acceso" (canto popolare toscano) (arr1864; mS, Bar) ....

    Beethoven: String Quartets (arr1867; pf, for the 'Opotchinin Saturdays'):

8.2   "Andante," from Str Qt No.9 in C major, Op.59/3 ....
8.3   "Scherzo," from Str Qt No.16 in F major, Op.135 ....
8.4   "Andante" (Lento), from Str Qt No.16 in F major, Op.135 ....
8.5   "Scherzo," from Str Qt No.8 in E minor, Op.59/2 ....
8.6   Fragments from Str Qt No.14 in C-sharp minor, Op.131 ....

*   *   *   *   *

1. STAGE WORKS

Operas:

1.1	"Saul and David," 4 acts (c1898–1901, Christiansen)	FS25
1.2	"Maskarade" (Masquerade), comic opera (c1904–6, Andersen after Holberg)	FS39

Melodramas:

1.3	"Snefrid," melodrama (c1893, r1899, Drachmann)	FS17

Incid music:

1.4	"En Aften paa Giske," Prelude & Final Chorus (c1889, Munch)	FS9
1.5	"Atalanta," song: Gudhjæp (c1901, Wied & Petersen)	FS30
1.6	"Hr. Oluf han rider" (Master Oluf Rides) (c1906, Drachmann)	FS37
1.7	"Tove" (c1906–8, Holstein)	FS43
1.8	"Willemoes" (c1907–8, Nielsen)	FS44
1.9	"Forældre" (c1908, Benzon)	FS45
1.10	"Ulvens søn" (The Son of the Wolf) (c1909, Aakjær)	FS50
1.11	"Habarth and Signe" (c1910, Oehlenschlæger):	FS57
	incl: . "My helmet is too shiny and too heavy"	
1.12	"Sankt Hansaftenspil" (A Midsummer Eve Play) (c1913, Oelenschlæger)	FS65
1.13	"Fædreland" (c1915, Christiansen)	FS71
1.14	"Løgneren" (The Liar) (c1918, Sigurjonsson):	FS88
	incl: . "The Bard's Lay"	
1.15	"Aladdin," 5 act fairy tale drama (c1918–9, Oehlenschlæger)	Op.34, FS89
1.16	"Moderen" (The Mother) (c1920, Rode)	Op.41, FS94
1.17	"Cosmus" (c1921–2, Christiansen):	FS98
	incl: . "The sun springs out like a rose"	
1.18	"Ebbe Skammelsen" (c1925, Bergstedt)	FS117
1.19	"Amor og Digteren" (Amor and the Poet) (c1930, Michaëlis)	FS150
1.20	"Paaskeaften" (c1931, Grundtvig)	FS156

1a. SELECTIONS FROM STAGE WORKS

1a.8	"Willemoes," incid music:	FS44

1. "Fædreland"
2. "Ja, tag os, vor Moder"
3. "Følger hvo som følge kan"
4. "Vibekes Sang" (Vieke's song)
5. "Havets Sang" (Song of the Sea)

1a.10	"The Son of the Wolf," incid music:	FS50

1. "Gamle Anders Røgters Sang": "There stands a stunted tree"
2. "Are you coming soon, you cottagers"

1a.16	"The Mother," incid music:	Op.41, FS94

1. "The storm wages over the dark waters"
2. "My girl is fair as amber"
3. "The day the eagle was ready to fly"
4. "A mother was told at the feast"
5. "The thistle crop looks promising"
6. "Once when death was awaited"
7. "So bitter was my heart"
8. "Like a venturous fleet at anchor"
9. "The fog is lifting"
10. "The children are playing"

1a.19	"Amor and the Poet," incid music:	Op.54, FS150

1. "Italian Pastorale": "In un boschetto trovai pastorella" (Cavalcanti of 13th cent; S & pf)
2. "We love you, our lofty North" (Michaëlis)
3. "Allegretto con brio"

2. SYMPHONIES

2.1	Symphony No.1 in G minor (c1891–2)	Op.7, FS16
2.2	Symphony No.2, "De fire temperamenter" (The Four Temperaments) (c1901–2)	Op.16, FS29
2.3	Symphony No.3, "Sinfonia espansiva" (c1910–1, w/ S, Bar)	Op.27, FS60
2.4	Symphony No.4, "Det uudslukkelige" (Inextinguishable) (c1915–6)	Op.29, FS76
2.5	Symphony No.5 (c1921–2)	Op.50, FS97
2.6	Symphony No.6, "Sinfonia semplice" (c1924–5)	FS116

3. OTHER ORCHESTRAL WORKS

3.1	"Little Suite," in A minor (c1888, r1889; strings; arr Koppel for pf): No.1 "Prelude" Op.1, FS6
3.2	No.2 "Intermezzo"
3.3	No.3 "Finale"
3.4	"Symphonic Rhapsody," in F major (c1888) FS7
3.5	"Saul and David. Prelude to the Act II" (c1900, for opera: Saul and David, FS25) ....
3.6	"Helios," concert overture (c1903) Op.17, FS32
3.7	"Masquerade—Overture" (c1906, to opera FS39) ....
3.8	"Masquerade. Prelude to Act II" (c1905, for opera FS39) ....
3.9	"Masquerade. Dance of Cocks" (c1905, for opera FS39; arr for pf) ....
3.10	"Aladdin," suite (c1918, from Op.34, FS89): No.1 "Oriental Festival March" (also for small orch/pf) . (Op.34)
3.11	No.2 "Aladdin's Dream and Dance of the Morning Mists" (also for small orch)
3.12	No.3 "Hindoo Dance" (also for small orch)
3.13	No.4 "Chinese Dance" (also for small orch)
3.14	No.5 "The Market-Place at Ispahan"
3.15	No.6 "Prisoners' Dance"
3.16	No.7 "Negro Dance" (also for small orch)
3.17	"Saga-Drøm" (The Dream of Gunnar), tone poem (c1907–8) Op.39, FS46
3.18	"Prelude to the 7th Picture of 'The Mother' " (c1920, for incid music Op.41, FS94) ....
3.19	"Paraphrase on: Nearer my God to Thee" (c1912; winds) FS63
3.20	"Pan and Syrinx," a nature scene (c1917–8) Op.49, FS87
3.21	"Rhapsodic Overture: An imaginary journey to the Faeroe Islands" (c1927) FS123
3.22	"Bohemian-Danish Folk Tone," paraphrase (c1928; strings) FS130

4. CONCERTOS, SOLO INSTR & ORCH

4.1	Violin Concerto (c1911) Op.33, FS61
4.2	Flute Concerto (c1926) FS119
4.3	Clarinet Concerto (c1928) Op.57, FS129

5. STRING QUARTETS

5.1	"Movements" (c1883–7): No.1 "Andante," in B-flat major FS3c
5.2	No.2 "Minuet," in G minor
5.3	No.3 "Allegro," in F major
5.4	No.4 "Scherzo," in D minor
5.5	No.5 "Andante," in F-sharp minor FS3d
5.6	String Quartet in D minor (c1882–3) Op.13, FS4
5.7	String Quartet No.1 in G minor (c1887–8, r1897–8) Op.5, FS11
5.8	String Quartet No.2 in F minor (c1890) Op.14, FS23
5.9	String Quartet No.3 in E-flat major (c1897–8) Op.14, FS23
5.10	String Quartet No.4 in F major, "Piacevolezza" (c1906, r1919) Op.44

6. OTHER CHAMBER MUSIC

5 insts:

6.1	String Quintet in G major (c1888; 2vn, 2va & vc) FS5
6.2	"Ved en ung kunstners baare" (At the Bier of a Young Artist) (c1910; str qt & d bass, for the funeral of the painter O. Hartmann) FS58
6.3	"Serenata in vano" (c1914; cl, bn, hn, vc & d bass) FS68
6.4	Wind Quintet (c1922; fl, ob/Eng hn, cl, hn & bn) Op.43, FS100

3 insts:

6.5	Piano Trio in G major (c1883) FS3i

Violin Sonatas:

6.6	Violin Sonata in G major (c1881–2) FS3b
6.7	Violin Sonata No.1 in A major (c1895) Op.9, FS20
6.8	Violin Sonata No.2 in G minor (c1912) Op.35, FS64

Other 2 insts:

6.9	Duet in A major (c1882–3; 2vn) FS3e
6.10	"Fantasy Piece," in G minor (ca1885; cl & pf) FS3h
6.11	"Fantasy Pieces" (1889; ob & pf): No.1 "Romance" (arr Sitt for vn & orch) Op.2, FS8
6.12	No.2 "Humoresque"
6.13	"The Fog is lifting" (c1921, r1959; fl & pf/harp, from incid music: The Mother, Op.41, FS94) ....
6.14	"Faith and Hope Are Playing," duet (c1921, r1959; fl & va, from incid music: The Mother, Op.41, FS94) .....

6.15	"Canto serioso" (c1928–30; hn/vc & pf)	FS132
6.16	"Allegretto," in F major (c1931, 2 recorders)	FS157

1 instr:

6.17	"Polka" (c1874; vn)	FS1
6.18	"3 Pieces for Langeleg" (c1918; langleik—Danish folk instr): No.1 "Naar Solen skinner"	FS77
6.19	No.2 "Det tunge Budskab"	
6.20	No.3 "Sorn Fisken i Vandet"	
6.21	"The Children Are Playing" (c1921, r1959; fl, from incid music: The Mother, Op.41, FS94)	
6.22	"Prelude & Theme with Variations" (c1923; vn)	Op.48, FS104
6.23	"Preludio e Presto" (c1927–8; vn)	Op.52, FS128

7. PIANO

7.1	"Cobbler's Wedding Waltz" (c1878)	FS2
7.2	"2 Character Pieces" (c1882–3)	FS3f
7.3	"5 Pieces" (c1890): No.1 "Folk-Tune"	Op.3, FS10
7.4	No.2 "Humoreske"	
7.5	No.3 "Arabeske"	
7.6	No.4 "Mignon"	
7.7	No.5 "Elf-Dance"	
7.8	"Symphonic Suite for Piano" (c1894): No.1 "Intonation. Maestoso"	Op.8, FS19
7.9	No.2 "Quasi allegretto"	
7.10	No.3 "Andante"	
7.11	No.4 "Finale. Allegro"	
7.12	"Humoresque-Bagatelles" (c1894–7; orchd Roikjer): No.1 "Goddag! Goddag!" (Hallo, Hallo!)	Op.11, FS22
7.13	No.2 "Snurretoppen" (The Spinning Top)	
7.14	No.3 "En lille langsom Vals" (A Short Slow Waltz)	
7.15	No.4 "Spræellemanden" (Jumping Jack)	
7.16	No.5 "Dukke-Marsch" (Doll's March)	
7.17	No.6 "Spilleværket" (The Musical Clock)	
7.18	"Festpraeludium ved Aarhundredskiftet" (Festival Prelude to the New Century) (c1900)	FS24
7.19	"Drømmen om 'Glade Jul' " (The Dream of a 'Merry Christmas') (c1905)	FS34
7.20	"Chaconne" (c1916)	Op.32, FS79
7.21	"Theme with Variations" (c1916–7)	Op.40, FS81
7.22	"Suite 'Den Luciferiske' " (Luciferian Suite) (c1919–20): No.1 "Allegretto un pochettino"	Op.45, FS91
7.23	No.2 "Poco moderato"	
7.24	No.3 "Molto adagio e patetico"	
7.25	No.4 "Allegretto innocente"	
7.26	No.5 "Allegretto vivo"	
7.27	No.6 "Allegro non troppo ma vigoroso"	
7.28	"3 Pieces" (c1928): No.1 "Impromptu" (Allegro fluente)	Op.59, FS131
7.29	No.2 "Molto adagio"	
7.30	No.3 "Allegro non troppo"	
7.31	"Piano Music for Young and Old" (24 Short 5-Tone Pieces in all Keys), 2 vols (c1930)	Op.53, FS148
7.32	"Piece," in C major (c1931)	FS159

8. ORGAN

8.1	"29 Short Preludes" (c1929)	Op.51, FS136
8.2	"2 Preludes" (c1930)	FS137
8.3	"Commotio" (c1930–1)	Op.58, FS155

9. CHORAL WORKS

W/ orch:

9.1	"Hymnus amoris" (c1896–7, Olrik, Latin transl Heiberg; S, T, Bar, B, child ch, ch, m ch & orch)	Op.12, FS21
9.2	"Cantata for the Lorens Frølich Festival" (c1900, Olrik; reciter & pf)	FS26
9.3	"Cantata for the Students' Association" (c1901, Drachmann)	FS31
9.4	"Søvnen" (The Sleep) (c1903–4, Jørgensen)	Op.18, FS33
9.5	"Cantata for the Anniversary of Copenhagen University" (c1908, Møller)	Op.24, FS47
9.6	"Cantata for the Commemoration of 11 Feb 1659" (c1909, L. C. Nielsen)	FS49
9.7	"Cantata for the National Exhibition at Aarhus" (c1909, L. C. Nielsen, collab Bangert)	FS54
9.8	"Cantata for the Commemoration of P. S. Krøyer" (c1909, L. C. Nielsen)	FS56
9.9	"Hymn to Denmark": "Danmark i tusend Aar" (c1917, Rørdam, 100th anniv of the Merchants' Guild)	FS86
9.10	"Fynsk foraar" (Springtime in Funen), lyric humoresque (c1921, Berntsen; S, T, B/Bar, ch, child ch & orch)	Op.42, FS96
9.11	"Hyldest til Holberg" (Hommage to Holberg) (c1922, Pedersen; vv, ch & orch)	FS102
9.12	"Cantata for the Centenary of the Polytechnic High School" (c1929, Pedersen)	FS140
9.13	"Hymne til kunsten" (Hymn to Art) (c1929, Michaëlis; S, T, ch & winds)	FS141

11.102	3. "Alt oprejst Maanen staar"
11.103	"Christianshavn" (c1918, Bauditz) FS90
11.104	"2 Sacred Songs" (c1917–8): 1. "Den store Mester kommer" FS92
11.105	2. "Udrundne er de gamle Dage"
11.106	"Dawn" (c1919–20, Lorenzen) FS93
11.107	"20 Popular Melodies" (c1917–21) incl: 1. "Gone are the days of Old" FS95
11.108	2. "On the ground"
11.109	3. "That tiny lark"
11.110	4. "The noble nature-lover"
11.111	5. "A Fisherman sat so pensive"
11.112	6. "I only looked back"
11.113	7. "Like the deepest well"
11.114	8. "Freedom is the purest gold"
11.115	9. "The barques meet"
11.116	10. "Heavy, sombre clouds of night"
11.117	11. "The great Master comes"
11.118	12. "Our eyes may rejoice"
11.119	13. "When Summer's song is sung"
11.120	14. "Earth in whose embrace"
11.121	15. "See my fragile web"
11.122	"Den milde Dag er lys og lang" (c1921, Berntsen, from choral work: Springtime in Funen, Op.42, FS96) ....
11.123	"To my little friend Sonja Helleberg" (c1922) FS99
11.124	"4 Popular Melodies" (c1922): 1. "Now shall it be revealed" (Richardt).......... FS101
11.125	2. "The song casts light" (Björnson)
11.126	3. "Of what you are singing?" (Hostrup)
11.127	4. "Teach me, o stars of night" (Grundtvig)
11.128	"Danish worksong" (c1923, Rørdam) FS105
11.129	"Christmas song": "Heaven darkens, great and silent" (c1923, Falck) FS106
11.130	"Kom Jul til Jord" (Come Yule to Earth), carol (c1923)................................. FS107
11.131	"Hjemlige Jul," carol (c1923) FS108
11.132	"The Ballad of the Bear" (c1923, Berntsen) Op.47, FS109
11.133	"Danmark," songbook (c1924, collab Andersen) FS111
11.134	"Det vi end, at siden Slangens Gift" (c1923–4, Hostrup) FS112
11.135	"10 Little Danish Songs" (c1923–4): 1. "I know a lark's nest" (Bergstedt) FS114
11.136	2. "The sun is so red, Mother" (Bergstedt)
11.137	3. "As quietly as the stream runs in the meadow" (Rode)
11.138	4. "The sparrow sits in silence behind the gable" (Aakjaer)
11.139	5. "The fiddler is playing his fiddle" (Damm)
11.140	6. "When children whimper at Eventide" (Dabelsteen)
11.141	7. "Green is the hedge in Spring" (Møller)
11.142	8. "I settle down to sleep so snugly" (Winther)
11.143	9. "O, today I am so happy" (Rosing)
11.144	10. "The Danish Song" (Hoffmann)
11.145	"Jutish Songs" (c1924–5, Berntsen): 1. "Jens Madsen to An-Sofi": "Jens Madsen wa en Feskermand"... FS115
11.146	2. "Our daughter": "Hun ae sa møj en hwalle Piig"
11.147	3. "One and the Other": "Den jenn ska studier"
11.148	4. "The Haypole": "Mi Hasbond wa en piiwon Rad"
11.149	"New melodies for Johan Borup's Songbook" (c1926) FS120
11.150	"It is Autumn" (c1929, Rogberg)... FS121
11.151	"Danish Weather" (c1927, Rode)... FS122
11.152	"Vocalise-étude" (c1927) FS124
11.153	"Den trænger ud til hvert et Sted" (c1927, Hostrup) FS126
11.154	"The Golden River" (c1927, Ingemann) FS127
11.155	"Velkommen, Lærkelil" (c1928, Richardt) FS133
11.156	"Hjemstavn" (c1929, Poulsen) FS142
11.157	"Der gaar et stille Tog" (c1929, Balslev & Hansen) FS143
11.158	"The Land of the Future" (Bjørnson)... FS145
11.159	"Danmark, now sleeps the Light Night" (c1929, Larsen) FS146
11.160	"Vi Jyder" (c1929, Vilhelm's song from Bartrumsen: Fra Rold til Rebild) FS147
11.161	"Reunion" (c1930, Paludon-Müller) FS151

* * * * *

FS = Dan Fog and Torben Schousboe: "Carl Nielsen kompositioner: en bibliografi." København: Nyt Nordisk Forlag—Arnold Busck, 1965.

1. STAGE WORKS

Operettas & opéras comiques:

1.1	"L'alcôve" (Marielle), 1 act opéra-comique (p1847, Forges & Leuven) .....
1.2	"Le trésor à Mathurin," 1 act opéra-comique (p1853, Battu; see r1857 as: Le mariage aux lanternes) ....
1.3	"Pépito" (Das Mädchen von Elizondo), 1 act opéra-comique (p1853, Moinaux & Battu; 2 vers) .....
1.4	"Luc et Lucette," 1 act (p1854, Forges & Roche) .....
1.5	"Oyayaye ou La reine des îles," 1 act antropophagie musicale (p1855, Moinaux) .....
1.6	"Entrez, messieurs, mesdames," prologue for: Opening for Bouffes (p1855, Méry & Halévy) .....
1.7	"Les deux aveugles" (The Blind Beggars), 1 act 'bouffonérie musicale' (p1855, Moinaux) .....
1.8	"Une nuit blanche," 1 act opéra-comique (p1855, Plouvier) .....
1.9	"Le rêve d'une nuit d'été," 1 act saynète (p1855, Tréfeu) .....
1.10	"Le violoneux" (Die Zaubergeige), 1 act légende brétonne (p1855, Mestépès & Chevalet) .....
1.11	"Madame Papillon," 1 act bouffonérie (p1855, Halévy) .....
1.12	"Périnette" (Paimpol et Périnette), 1 act saynète lyrique (p1855, Forges, r1871, Ernst) .....
1.13	"Ba-ta-clan" (Tschin-Tschin), 1 act chinoiserie musicale (p1855, Halévy) .....
1.14	"Élodie ou Le forfait nocturne," 1 act bouffonérie (p1856, Battu & Crémieux) .....
1.15	"Le postillon en gage," 1 act bouffonérie (p1856, Plouvier & Adenis) .....
1.16	"Tromb-al-Cazar ou Les criminels dramatiques," 1 act bouffonérie (p1856, Dupeuty & Bourget) .....
1.17	"La rose de Saint-Fleur" (The Rose of Auvergne), 1 act opérette (p1856, Carré) .....
1.18	"Les dragées du baptême," 1 act (p1856, Dupeuty & Bourget) .....
1.19	"Le '66' " (Die beiden Savoyarden), 1 act opérette (p1856, Forges & Laurencin) .....
1.20	"Le savetier et le financier," 1 act opérette bouffe (p1856, Crémieux after La Fontaine) .....
1.21	"La bonne d'enfants," 1 act opérette bouffe (p1856, Bercioux) .....
1.22	"Aimons Notre Prochain," 1 act parable (c1857, Méry, adapted from: Entrez, messieurs, mesdames) .....
1.23	"Les trois baisers du diable," 1 act opérette fantastique (p1857, Mestépès) .....
1.24	"Croquefer ou Le dernier des paladins" (Ritter Eisenfrass), 1 act opérette bouffe (p1857, Jaime & Tréfeu) .
1.25	"Dragonette," 1 act opérette bouffe (p1857, Jaime & Mestépès) .....
1.26	"Vent du soir ou L'horrible festin" (Abendwind), 1 act opérette bouffe (p1857, Gille) .....
1.27	"Une demoiselle en lôterie" (Die Kunstreiterin),1 act opérette bouffe (p1857, Jaime & Crémieux) .....
1.28	"Le mariage aux lanternes," 1 act opérette (p1857, Carré & Battu, r vers of: Le trésor à Mathurin of 1853) .
1.29	"Les deux pêcheurs," 1 act bouffonérie musicale (p1857, Dupeuty & Bourget) .....
1.30	"Mesdames de la Halle" (Die Damen von Strand), 1 act opérette bouffe (p1858, Lapointe) .....
1.31	"La chatte métamorphosée en femme," 1 act opérette (p1858, Scribe & Mélesville) .....
1.32	"Orphée aux enfers" (Orpheus in the Underworld), 2 act opéra bouffon (p1858, Crémieux & Halévy, r1874 in 4 acts) .....
1.33	"Un mari à la porte" (Ein Ehemann vor der Tür), 1 act opérette (p1859, Delacour & Morand) .....
1.34	"Les vivandières de la grande armée," 1 act pièce d'occasion (p1859, Jaime & Forges) .....
1.35	"Geneviève de Brabant" (Genovefa), 2/3/5 act opéra (p1859, r1867 & 1875, Jaime & Tréfeu) .....
1.36	"Le carnaval des revues," revue (p1860, Grangé, Gille & Halévy) .....
1.37	"Daphnis et Chloé" (Daphnis und Cloë), 1 act opérette (p1860, Clairville & Cordier) .....
1.38	"Barkouf," 3 act opéra-comique (p1860, Scribe & Boisseaux) .....
1.39	"La chanson de Fortunio" (The Magic Melody), 1 act opérette (p1861, Crémieux & Halévy) .....
1.40	"Le pont des soupirs" (The Bridge of Sighs), 2 act bouffe (p1861, r1868, Crémieux & Halévy) .....
1.41	"Monsieur Choufleury restera chez lui le ...," 1 act opéra bouffe (p1861, Saint-Rémy & others) .....
1.42	"Apothicaire et perruquier" (The Barber of Bath), 1 act opérette (p1861, Frébault) .....
1.43	"Le roman comique," 3 act opéra bouffe (p1861, Crémieux & Halévy) .....
1.44	"Monsieur et Madame Denis," 1 act opéra bouffe (p1862, Delaporte & Laurencin) .....
1.45	"Le voyage de MM. Dunanan, père et fils," 3 act opéra bouffe (p1862, Siraudin & Moinaux) .....
1.46	"Les bavards," 2 act opéra bouffe (p1862, Nuitter based on Cervantes: Los habladores) .....
1.47	"Jacqueline" (Dorothéa), 1 act opérette (p1862, Crémieux & Halévy) .....
1.48	"Il signor Fagotto," 1 act opéra bouffe (p1863, Nuitter & Tréfeu) .....
1.49	"Lischen et Fritzchen," 1 act conversation alsacienne (p1863, Boisselot & Nuitter) .....
1.50	"L'amour chanteur," 1 act opérette (p1864, Nuitter & L'Épine) .....
1.51	"Die Rheinnixen" (Les fées du Rhin) 3 act romantic opera (p1864, Wolzogen after Nuitter) .....
1.52	"Les géorgiennes" (Feroza), 3 act opéra bouffe (p1864, Moinaux) .....
1.53	"Jeanne qui pleure et Jean qui rit," 1 act opérette (p1864, Nuitter & Tréfeu) .....
1.54	"Le fifre enchanté ou Le soldat magicien," 1 act opérette (p1864, Nuitter & Tréfeu) .....
1.55	"La belle Hélène," 3 act opéra bouffe (p1864, Meilhac & Halévy) .....
1.56	"Coscoletto ou Le lazzarone," 2 act opéra-comique (p1865, Nuitter & Tréfeu) .....
1.57	"Les refrains des bouffes," 1 act revue (p1865, various) .....
1.58	"Les bergers" (Die Schäfer), 3 act opéra-comique (p1865, Crémieux & Gille) .....
1.59	"Barbe-bleue" (Bluebeard), 3 act opéra bouffe (p1866, Meilhac & Halévy) .....
1.60	"La vie parisienne," 5 act opéra-bouffe (p1866, Meilhac & Halévy; r1873 in 4 acts) .....
1.61	"La Grande-Duchesse de Gérolstein," 3 act opéra bouffe (p1867, Meilhac & Halévy) .....
1.62	"La permission de dix heures," 1 act opérette (p1867, Mélesville & Carmouche) .....
1.63	"La leçon de chant" (Do-re-mi-fa), 1 act bouffonérie (p1867, Bourget) .....
1.64	"Robinson Crusoé," 3 act opéra-comique (p1867, Cormon & Crémieux after Defoe) .....
1.65	"Die Kindsmädchen," 1 act opérette (p1867, Juin) .....
1.66	"Le château à Toto," 3 act opéra bouffe (p1868, Meilhac & Halévy) .....
1.67	"L'île de Tulipatan" (Die Insel Tulipatan), 1 act bouffonérie (p1868, Chivot & Duru) .....
1.68	"La Périchole," 2 act opéra bouffe (p1868, r1874, Meilhac & Halévy) .....
1.69	"Vert-vert" (Kakadu), 3 act opéra-comique (p1869, Meilhac & Nuitter) .....
1.70	"La diva," 3 act opéra bouffe (p1869, Meilhac & Halévy) .....

1.71 "La princesse de Trébizonde," 2/3 act opéra bouffe (p1869, Nuitter & Tréfeu) ....
1.72 "Les brigands" (Falsacappa), 3 act opéra bouffe (p1869, Meilhac & Halévy) ....
1.73 "La romance de la rose," 1 act opérette (p1869, Tréfeu & Prével) ....
1.74 "Boule-de-neige," 3 act opéra bouffe (p1871, Nuitter & Tréfeu, r vers of opéra-comique: Barkouf) ....
1.75 "Le Roi Carotte," 4 act opéra-bouffe-féerie (p1872, Sardou after Hoffmann) ....
1.76 "Fantasio," 3 act opéra-comique (p1872, Paul de Musset after book by Alfred de Musset) ....
1.77 "Fleurette, oder Näherin und Trompeter," 1 act opérette (p1872, Hopp & Zell after Forges & Laurencin).....
1.78 "Psychic Force," 1 act musical sketch (p1872, for J. L. Toole's benefit) ....
1.79 "Der schwarze Korsar," 3 act opéra-comique (p1872, Offenbach & Genée)...........................
1.80 "Les braconniers" (Die Wilddiebe), 3 act opéra bouffe (p1873, Chivot & Duru) ....
1.81 "Pomme d'api" (Onkel hat's gesagt), 1 act opérette (p1873, Halévy & Busnach) ....
1.82 "La jolie parfumeuse" (Schönröschen), 3 act opéra-comique (p1873, Crémieux & Blum) ....
1.83 "Bagatelle," 1 act opérette (p1874, Crémieux & Blum) ....
1.84 "Madame l'archiduc" (Marietta), 3 act opéra bouffe (p1874, Meilhac & Halévy) ....
1.85 "Les hannetons," 3 act revue (p1875, Grangé & Meilhac) ....
1.86 "La boulangère à des écus," 3 act opéra bouffe (p1875, Meilhac & Halévy) ....
1.87 "La créole" (The Commodore), 3 act opéra-comique (p1875, Meilhac, Meilhac & Halévy)...............
1.88 "Le voyage dans la lune," 4 act opéra-féerie (p1875, Vanloo, Leterrier & Mortier) ....
1.89 "Tarte à la crème," 1 act opérette (p1875, Meilhac, 1 number only c by Offenbach: a waltz) ....
1.90 "Pierette et Jacquot," 1 act opérette (p1876, Noriac & Gille) ....
1.91 "La boîte au lait," 4 act opérette (p1876, Grangé & Noriac) ....
1.92 "Cigarette," operetta (p1876, D'Arcy) ....
1.93 "Le Docteur Ox," 3 act opéra bouffe (p1877, Mortier & Gille after Verne) ....
1.94 "La Foire Saint-Laurent," 3 act opéra bouffe (p1877, Crémieux & Saint-Albin) ....
1.95 "Maître Péronilla," 3 act opéra bouffe (p1878, Offenbach, Nuitter & Ferrier) ....
1.96 "Madame Favart," 3 act opéra-comique (p1878, Chivot & Duru) ....
1.97 "La marocaine" (Fatime), 3 act opéra-comique (p1879, Blum, Blau & Toché)...........................
1.98 "La fille du tambour-major," 3 act opéra-comique (p1879, Chivot & Duru)...........................
1.99 "Belle Lurette," 3 act opéra bouffe (p1880, Ferrier & Halévy) ....
1.100 "Les contes d'Hoffmann" (The Tales of Hoffmann), 4 act opéra fantastique (p posth1881, Barbier; compl Guiraud) ....
1.101 "Mam'zelle Moucheron," 1 act opérette (p posth1881, Leterrier & Vanloo; ed Delibes)...............

Ballets:

1.102 "Arlequin barbier," 1 scene pantomime (p1855, after Rossini: The Barber of Seville) ....
1.103 "Pierrot clown," 1 scene pantomime (p1855, Jackson) ....
1.104 "Polichinelle dans le monde," 1 scene pantomime (p1855, Busnach & Servières—pseud of Halévy) ....
1.105 "Les bergers de Watteau," 1 scene (tableau vivant) (p1856, Mathieu & Placet) ....
1.106 "Le papillon," 3 acts (p1860, Taglioni & Saint-Georges) ....
1.107 "Whittington" (Dick Whittington and His Cat) (Le chat du diable), 4 act féerie (ballet-pantomime) (p1874, Nuitter & Tréfeu) ....

Vaudevilles & incid music:

1.108 "Pascal et Chambord," incid music to 2 act comedy (p1839, Bourgeois & Brisebarre) ....
1.109 "Le brésilien" (Fürst Acapulco), 1 act comédie (p1863, Meilhac & Halévy) ....
1.110 "Le gascon," incid music (p1973, Barrière) ....
1.111 "La haine," 5 act drama (p1874, Sardou) ....

Incid music for the Comédie-Française:

1.112 "Le bonhomme jadis," overture ....
1.113 "Le barbier de Séville," fantasy ....
1.114 "Mademoiselle de La Seiglière," overture ....
1.115 "Le mariage de Figaro," incid music ....

Projects:

1.116 "La Duchesse d'Alba," opéra-comique (c1848, St. Georges) ....
1.117 "Le testament de Sganarelle," opéretta (c1860, Nérée-Désarbres & Nuitter)...........................
1.118 "Féodéa" (La baguette), opéra-comique (c1862, Meilhac & Halévy) ....
1.119 "La jeunesse de Don Juan," opérette (Crémieux & Gille) ....
1.120 "La belle Aurore," opérette (c1863, Fee Rosa) ....
1.121 "Friquette," 1 act (c1863–4) ....
1.122 "Le bourgeois gentilhomme" (c1865) ....
1.123 "Le jockey" (c1866) ....
1.124 "Le zéphir," opérette (c1877, Nuitter) ....
1.125 "Don Quichotte," opéra-bouffe-féerie (c1875, Sardou & Nuitter after Sardou's play) ....
1.126 "Le cabaret des lilas" (c1880, Blum & Toché) ....

Fragments:

1.127 "Phénice" ....
1.128 "Léonard"...........................

1.129	*"Scapin et Mazetta"* ....
1.130	*"Le mur"* ....

Stage works based on compilations of Offenbach's music:

1.131	*"Malala!," 2 act African extravaganza (arr1871)* ....
1.132	*"Nemesis," extravaganza (arr Fitzgerald 1873, Farnie, music of various composers)* ....
1.133	*"La poule aux oeufs d'or," 3 act féerie (arr1878, Dennery & Clairville, various composers)* ....
1.134	*"Gaîté parisienne," ballet (arr Rosenthal 1893)* ....
1.135	*"The Homecoming of Odysseus" (arr Schmiedt p1917, Ettlinger & Motz)* ....
1.136	*"The Happy Island" (arr Schmidt 1918)* ....
1.137	*"The Goldsmith of Toledo" (arr Stern & Zamara 1919, based on Hoffmann's story)* ....
1.138	*"Fürstin Tanagra," 3 act opéra-comique (arr Lafite 1924, Friedmann)* ....
1.139	*"The Queen's Chemise" (arr Rössler & Feuchtwanger 1929)* ....
1.140	*"Der König ihres Herzens," 3 act opérette (arr Drachenthal 1930, Sterk)* ....
1.141	*"The Happiest Girl in the World," musical comedy (p1961, Saidy, Myers & Harburg)* ....
1.142	*"Not in Front of the Waiter" (adapted Graham, orchd Tausky 1965, Tunnard)* ....
1.143	*"Christopher Columbus" (arr Schmid 1976, White)* ....
1.144	*"Bon Voyage" (arr Brodsky Lawrence 1977, Mabley)* ....

1a. SELECTIONS FROM STAGE WORKS (Nos. of sections in The Gramophone)

1a.32   "Orphée aux enfers," opéra bouffon: ....
     excerpts: 1. "Ouverture"
          1a. "Can-can"
      I: 3. "La femme dont le coeur"
          4. "Ah! c'est ainsi!"
          5. "Ballet pastoral"
          6a. "Moi, je suis Aristée"
          6b. "Voici le tendre Aristée"
          6c. "Mélodrame"
          7a. "La mort m'apparaît"
          7b. "Violà une plume," mélodrame
          8. "Libre! ô bonheur"
      II: 9. "Entr'acte and Chorus of Sleep"
          10. "Je suis Vénus!"
          11. "Tzing, tzing, tzing"
          12. "Par Saturne!"
          13a. "Eh hop! Eh hop!"
          13b. "Entry of Pluto"
          14. "Comme il me regarde!"
          15. "Aux armes, dieux et demi-dieux!"
          16. "Pour séduire Alcmène ..."
          17. "Il approche! Il s'avance ... Le violà, c'est bien lui!"
          18. "Entr'acte"
      III: 19. "Ah! quelle triste destinée"
          20a. "Quand j'étais roi de Béotie"
          20b. "Ah! tenez, Madame," mélodrame
          21. "Ah! mon bras!," mélodrame
          22. "Nez au vent, oeil au guet"
          23. "Allons, mes fins limiers"
          24. "Le beau bourdon que voilà"
          25. "Il m'a semblé sur mon épaule"
          26a. "Si j'étais roi de Béotie"
          26b. "Galop"
      IV: 27. "Vive le vin! Vive Pluton!"
          28. "J'ai vu le Dieu Bacchus"
          29. "Maintenant, je veux, moi qui" (Menuet et Galop infernal)
          30. "Elle est assez bonne!," mélodrame
          31. "Ne regarde pas en arrière!," finale

1a.55   "La belle Hélène," opéra bouffe: ....
          1a. "Ouverture" (prepared Haensch)
      I: 1b. "Vers tes autels, Jupin" (chorus)
          1c. "C'est le devoir des jeunes filles" (Chorus of girls)
          2a. "Amours divins!" (Helen)
          2b. "Entrez, vite, Grande Reine!" (Calchas, Hélène)
          3a. "Au cabaret du labyrinthe" (Oreste, Calchas, ch)
          3b. "Tzing la la" (Oreste, ch)
          4. "Quoi?... Là-bas dans l'azur," mélodrame
          5. "Homme de 20 anns," mélodrame
          6. "Au mont Ida" (Paris)
          7a. "Voici les rois de la Grèce," chorus
          7b. "Ces rois remplis de vaillance" (Kings)

7c. "Nous commençons" (ensemble)
7d. "Fanfare!" (Hélène, ch)
8. "Gloire," finale
II: 9. "Entr'acte"
10. "O Reine, en ce jour" (Hélène, Bacchus, ch)
11. "On me nomme Hélène la Blonde" (Hélène)
12. "Le voici le Roi des Rois" (March of the goose)
13. "Vous le voyez" (Gambling Scene)
14. "En couronnes, tressons les roses" (Hélène, Paris, ch)
15. "C'est le ciel qui m'envoie" (Hélène, Paris)
16. "A moi! Rois de la Grèce," finale (ensemble)
III: 17. "Entr'acte"
18a. "Dansons, buvons" (Oreste, ch)
18b. "Vénus au fond de notre âme" (Oreste, ch)
18c. "Oh mais alors ce n'était pas un rêve," mélodrame
19. "Là vrai, je ne suis pas coupable" (Hélène)
20. "Lorsque le Grèce" (Menelaus, Calchas, Agamemnon)
21a. "La galère de Cythère," chorus
21b. "Et tout d'abord, ô vile multitude" (Paris, ch)
22. "Elle vient, c'est elle," finale (ensemble)

1a.61 "La Grande-Duchesse de Gérolstein," opéra bouffe: ....
excerpts: 1. "Ouverture"
I: 2. "Tournons et valsons?"
3a. "O mon Fritz"
3b. "Allez, jeunes filles"
4. "Pif, Paf, Pouf"
5. "Me voici! me voici!"
6. "Portez armes"
7a. "Vous aimez le danger"
7b. "Ah! Que j'aime les militaires"
8. "Ah! c'est un fameux régiment"
9. "Pour epouser une princesse" (Chronique de la Gazette de Hollande)
9a. "Ils vont tous partir"
9b. "Voici le sabre de mon père"
II: 10a. "Enfin la guerre est terminée"
10b. "Je t'ai sur mon coeur"
10c. "Ah! lettre adorée"
11. "Après le victoire"
12. "En très bon ordre"
13a. "Oui, Général"
13b. "Dites-lui qu'on l'a remarqué distigué"
14a. "Ne devinez-vous pas"
14b. "Max étais soldat de fortune"
15. "Logeons-la donc"
III: 16. "Ce qu'on a fait"
17. "Sortez, sortez"
18a. "Nous amenons la jeune femme"
18b. "Bonne nuit, monsieur"
19a. "On peut être aimable"
19b. "Ouvrez, ouvrez"
19c. "À cheval, à cheval"
19d. "Notre auguste maîtresse"
20. "Au repas comme à la Bataille"
21. "Il était un de mes aïeux" (Légende du Verre)
22. "Voici revenir"
23. "Enfin j'ai repris la panache"

1a.68 "La Périchole," opéra bouffe: ....
excerpts: 1a. "Ouverture"
I: 1b. "Du vice-roi c'est aujourd'hui la fête"
1c. "Promptes à servir la pratique"
1d. "Ah! Qu'on y fait gaîment glouglou"
2. "C'est lui, c'est notre vice-roi!"
3. "Dis-moi, Piquillo?" (Marche indienne)
4. "Le conquérant dir à la jeune indienne"
5. "Vous a-t-on dit souvent" (Seguidille)
6. "Levez-vous et prenez vos rangs"
7. "O mon cher amant, je te jure"
8a. "Ah! mon Dieu!," mélodrame
8b. "Holà! hé!... holà! de là-bas"
8c. "Et prenez les bras de vos clercs!"
8d. "Ah! quel diner je viens de faire!"
8e. "C'est un ange, messieurs!"
8f. "Ah! les autres"

8g. "Pourrais-je vous prier"
8h. "Mon Dieu!... que de cérémonie"
8i. "Et maintenant, séparez-les"
II: 9. "Entr'acte"
10. "Cher seigneur, revenez à vous"
11. "On vante partout son sourire"
12. "Quel marché sa bassesse"
13a. "Et là, maintenant que que nous sommes seuls"
13b. "Est-ce bientôt cette présentation?"
13c. "Son Altesse à l'heure ordinaire"
14a. "Nous allons donc voir un mari"
14b. "Que veulent dire ces colères"
14c. "C'est vrai, j'ai tort de m'emporter"
14d. "Sautez dessus!"
14e. "Conduisez-le, bons courtisans"
III: 15. "Les maris courbaient le tête" (Boléro)
16. "On me proposait d'être infâme"
17a. "Qui va là?"
17b. "Dans ces couloirs obscurs"
17c. "Tu n'es pas beau, tu n'es pas riche"
17d. "Je t'adore, brigand, j'ai honte à l'avour"
18. "Je suis le joli geôlier"
19. "Roi pas plus haut qu'une botte!"
20a. "Tais-toi!"
20b. "Elle m'adore"
21a. "En avant! en avant soldat!"
21b. "Pauvres gens, où sont-ils?"
22. "Écoutez, peup d'Amérique"
23. "Tous deux, au temps de peine et de misère"

1a.100 "Les contes d'Hoffmann," opéra fantastique: ....
Prologue: 1. "Prélude"
2. "Glou! glou! glou!"
3a. "Le conseilleur Lindorf, morbleu!"
3b. "Dans les rôles d'amoureux langoureux"
4. "Deux heures devant moi"
5. "Drig, drig, drig"
6. "Il était une fois à la cour d'Eisenach" (Legend of Kleinsach)
7. "Peuh! cette bière est détestable"
I: 8. "Entr'acte"
9. "Là! dors en paix"
10a. "Allons! courage et confiance"
10b. "C'est elle!"
10c. "Ah! vivre deux!"
11a. "C'est moi, Coppélius" (Je me nomme Coppélius)
11b. "J'ai des veux"
12. "Non aucun hôte vraiment"
13. "Les oiseaux dans la charmille" (Doll's Song)
14a. "Le souper vous attend"
14b. "Ils se sont éloignés enfin!"
15. "Voici les valseurs" (Waltz)
II: 16. "Belle nuit, ô nuit d'amour" (Barcarolle)
17a. "Et moi, ce n'est pa là"
17b. "Que d'un brûler désir"
18a. "Scintille diamant!"
18b. "Cher ange!"
19a. "Malheureux!"
19b. "O Dieu! de quelle ivresse"
20. "Helas! mon coeur s'égare encore!"
21. "Ecoutez, messieurs!"
III: 22. "Elle a fui, la tourterelle"
23. "Jour et nuit"
24a. "C'est une chanson d'amour"
24b. "J'ai le bonheur dans l'âme"
25. "Qu'as-tu donc?"
26. "Pour conjurer le danger"
27a. "Ne chanteras plus?"
27b. "Écoute! Antonia! Dieu, ma mère"
28. "Mon enfant! ma fille! Antonia!" (Finale)
29. "Entr'acte"
Épilogue: 30. "Voilà quelle fut l'histoire"
31. "Vidons les tonneaux"
32a. "Et moi?"
32b. "O Dieu! de quelle ivresse"
33. "Non, ivre mort"

34. "Barcarolle" (orch vers)

1a.134   *"Gaîté parisienne," ballet:* ....
       1. "Ouverture" (from: La vie parisienne)
       2. "Allegro moderato" (from: Mesdames de la Halle)
       3. "Polka" (from: Le voyage dans la lune)
       4. "Ländler" (from: Lieschen et Fritzchen)
       5. "Mazurka" (from: La vie parisienne)
       6. "Valse" (from: La vie parisienne)
       7. "Entrée du Brésilien" (from: La vie parisienne)
       8. "Polka" (from: La belle Hélène)
       9. "Valse" (from: Orpheus in the Underworld)
      10. "Marche" (from: Tromb-al-Cazar)
      11. "Valse" (from: La vie parisienne)
      12. "Entrée du Brésilien" (from: La vie parisienne)
      13. "Valse" (from: Les contes d'Hoffmann)
      14. "Duel" (c by Rosenthal)
      15. "Valse" (from: La Périchole)
      16. "Prélude au Can-Can" (c by Rosenthal)
      17. "Can-Can Scène 1" (from: Orpheus in the Underworld, Robinson Crusoe)
      18. "Can-Can Scène 2—Polka" (from: Orpheus in the Underworld)
      19. "Can-Can Scène 3" (potpourri)

2. ORCHESTRAL WORKS

2.1   "Les jeunes filles," suite of waltzes (p1836) ....
2.2   "Fleurs d'hiver," suite of waltzes (p1836) ....
2.3   "Les Amazones," suite of waltzes (p1836) ....
2.4   "Rébecca," suite of waltzes (p1837, on hebraic motifs of 15th cent) ....
2.5   "Brunes et blondes," suite of waltzes (p1837) ....
2.6   "Les trois Grâces," suite of waltzes (p1838) ....
2.7   "Overture to a Grand Orchestra" (c1843) ....
2.8   "Le désert," oratorio parody (c1846) ....
2.9   "Entr'actes et Mélodrame," for Langlé: Murillo (c1853) ....
2.10 "Zwischenakte," for Dumas: Romulus (c1854) ....
2.11 "Le chanson de ceux qui n'aiment plus" (c1859) ....
2.12 "Abendblätter," waltzes (c1864) ....
2.13 "Pariser Mädchen," waltz (c1875) ....
2.14 "Madeleine," polka ....
2.15 "Réminiscences de la Lucie" ....
2.16   *"Nuits d'Espagne" (frags)* ....

3. CELLO CONCERTOS, CELLO & ORCH

3.1   "Grande scène espagnole" (c1840; vc & str sextet/orch): Op.22
       1. "Introduction"
       2. "Prayer"
       3. "Zambada"
       4. "Serenade"
       5. "Boléro"
3.2   "Musette—Air de ballet du 17me siècle" (p1843) Op.24
3.3   "Hommage à Rossini" (grosse Concert-Fantasie) (c1843, on themes from: W. Tell, Moses, etc) ....
3.4   "Le sylphe" (grosse Konzert-Fantasie) (c1845) Op.30
3.5   "Concerto militaire" (Militärkonzert), in G major (c1848) ....
3.6   "Phantasie on Bellini's La sonnambula" (c1848) Op.32
3.7   "Concertino" (c1851) ....

4. CHAMBER MUSIC

Vn & pf:

4.1   "Six études brillantes" (c1844; vn & pf ad lib) Op.1

Vc solo & w/ acc:

4.2   "Divertimento über Schweizerlieder" (c1833; vc & 2vn, va, d bass) ....
4.3   "Rêveries" (p1839; vc & pf, collab Flotow): No.1 "La harpe éolienne" ....
4.4   No.2 "Scherzo"
4.5   No.3 "Polka de salon"
4.6   No.4 "Chanson d'autrefois"
4.7   No.5 "Les larmes"
4.8   No.6 "Rédowa brillante"

4.9   "Chants du soir" (Serenades) (p1839; vc & pf, collab Flotow): No.1 "Au bord de la mer" ....
4.10   No.2 "Souvenir de bal"
4.11   No.3 "La prière du soir"
4.12   No.4 "La retraite"
4.13   No.5 "Ballade du pâtre"
4.14   No.6 "Danse norvégienne"
4.15   "Introduction et Valse mélancolique" (p1839; vc & pf) Op.14
4.16   "Caprice on Proch's Le Cor des Alpes" (c1841; vc) Op.15
4.17   "École du violoncelle" (p1839–46; 2vc) Opp.19–21, 34
4.18   "Prière et Boléro" (also see: Grande scène espagnole for vc & orch, Op.22) .... (Op.22)
4.19   "Deux âmes au ciel" (Élégie) (c1843; vc & pf) Op.25
4.20   "Quatrième mazurka" Op.26
4.21   "Caprice on the Romance from Méhul's Joseph in Egypt" (c1843; vc solo) Op.27
4.22   "Chants du crépuscule" (p1846; vc & pf): No.1 "Souvenir du bal" Op.29
4.23   No.2 "Sérénade"
4.24   No.3 "Ballade"
4.25   No.4 "Le retour"
4.26   No.5 "L'adieu"
4.27   No.6 "Pas villageois"
4.28   "Adagio et Scherzo" (c1845; 4vc) ....
4.29   "Caprice on Bellini's I puritani" (vc solo) Op.33
4.30   3 "Grands duos concertants" (2vc) Op.43
4.31   "Marche chinoise" (c1846) ....
4.32   "Las campanillas" (c1847; vc & bells) ....
4.33   "Cours méthodique de duos" (p1847–8; 2vc) Opp.49–54
4.34   "Rêverie au bord de la mer" (p1849; vc & pf) ....
4.35   "La course en traîneau," étude-caprice (p1849; vc & pf) ....
4.36   "Arie aus 'Les mariniers galants' " (by Rameau) (c1851) ....
4.37   "Fantasy on Meyerbeer's Robert le diable" (p1852; 7vc) ....
4.38   "Harmonies du soir" (c1852; vc solo) Op.68
4.39   "Fantasy on Grétry's Richard Coeur-de-Lion" (c1853; vc solo) Op.69
4.40   "Fantasy on Boïeldieu's Jean de Paris" (c1853; vc solo) Op.70
4.41   "Fantasy on Rossini's Le barbier de Séville" (c1853; vc solo) Op.71
4.42   "Fantasy on Mozart's Les noces de Figaro" (c1853; vc solo) Op.72
4.43   "Fantasy on Bellini's Norma" (c1853; vc solo) Op.73
4.44   "Fantaisie facile et brillante sur différents motifs" (c1853; vc solo) Op.74
4.45   "Fantasy-caprice on Donizetti's L'elisir d'amore" (c1853; vc solo) ....
4.46   "Fantasy-caprice on Donizetti's Parisina" (c1853; vc solo) ....
4.47   "Fantasy-caprice on Donizetti's Anne dè Bolène" (c1853; vc solo) ....
4.48   "Fantasy-caprice on Bellini's Béatrice di Tenda" (c1853; vc solo) ....
4.49   "Fantasy-caprice on Boïeldieu's La dame blanche" (vc solo) ....
4.50   "Gaietés champêtres" (c1853) ....
4.51   "Harmonies des bois" (c1853; vc solo): No.1 "Le soir," élégie Op.75
4.52   No.2 "La chanson de Berthe"
4.53   No.3 "Les larmes de Jacqueline"
4.54   "Vingt petites études" (p1855; vc w/ d bass acc) Op.77
4.55   "Douze études" (p1855; vc & d bass) Op.78

5. PIANO (dances)

Pubd:

5.1   "Décameron dramatique" (p1854): No.1 "Rachel," grand waltz ....
5.2   No.2 "Émilie," polka-mazurka
5.3   No.3 "Madeleine," village polka
5.4   No.4 "Delphine," rédowa
5.5   No.5 "Augustine," Scottish dance
5.6   No.6 "Louise," grand waltz
5.7   No.7 "Maria," polka-mazurka
5.8   No.8 "Élisa," polka-trilby
5.9   No.9 "Nathalie," Scottish dance
5.10   No.10 "Clarisse," varsoviana
5.11   "Herminie," waltz (p ca1850–76) ....
5.12   "Berthe," suite of waltzes ....
5.13   "The Times," grand waltz (p ca1850–76) ....
5.14   "Les feuilles du soir," waltzes (p1864) ....
5.15   "Jacqueline," suite of waltzes (p1865) ....
5.16   "Valse favorite" ....
5.17   "Les roses du Bengale," 6 waltzes ....
5.18   "Offenbach-valse" (p1876) ....
5.19   "La fleuve d'or," suite de valses (p1876) ....
5.20   "Les belles américaines," suite de valses (p1876) ....
5.21   "Souvenir d'Aix-les-Bains," waltz ....
5.22   "Polka des singes" ....

5.23	"Polka du mendiant" ....
5.24	"Polka burlesque" (p1876) ....
5.25	"Kissi-Kissi," polka ....
5.26	"Sum-Sum," polka ....
5.27	"Schüler polka" ....
5.28	"Taxopholite," polka-mazurka (p1876) ....
5.29	"Quatrième mazurka de salon" ....
5.30	"Postillon-galop" ....
5.31	"Cachucha" ....
5.32	"Parade militaire" ....

Unpubd:

5.33	"Valse triomphale du château de Digoenne" ....
5.34	"Valse à quatre mains" ....
5.35	"Plaintes de la châtelaine" ....
5.36	"Les cinq soeurs," suite of waltzes (c1855): No.1 "Anna la sévère" ...
5.37	No.2 "Clotilde la coquette"
5.38	No.3 "Cécile la mélancolique"
5.39	No.4 "Élise la villageoise"
5.40	No.5 "Caroline la sautillante"
5.41	"Polka des mirlitons" (pf, tpt & 3 kazoos) ....
5.42	"Polka," in E major ....
5.43	"La 'Chabrillan' polka" ....
5.44	"Polka," in C major ....
5.45	"Scottish" ....

6. CHURCH MUSIC

6.1	"Ave Maria" (1v & org) ....
6.2	"Agnus Dei" (1v & org) ....
6.3	"Le cantique a l'Esprit-Saint" ....
6.4	"Espoir en Dieu" ....
6.5	"Près du Très-Haut" ....
6.6	"Gloire à Dieu" ....
6.7	"La prière de Moïse" (2vn, pf & org) ....

7. CHORAL WORKS

7.1	"Introduction et Ballade" (c1846, for: Les Moissonneurs) ....
7.2	"Valse du bal" (c1846) ....
7.3	"Venise," barcarolle (Latte) ....
7.4	"Vive la Suisse" ....

8. MISC VOCAL (patriotic songs)

8.1	"Marche et Prière" ....
8.2	"Hymne" ....
8.3	"Dieu sauve la France," hymne patriotique ....

9. FRENCH SONGS (1v & pf)

Pubd:

9.1	"Le sylphe," romance (p1838, Laube) ....
9.2	"Le pauvre prisonnier," romance (p1838, Laube) ....
9.3	"Ronde tyrolienne" (p1838, Catelin; 1v, ob & pf) ....
9.4	"Jalousie!," romance dramatique (p1839, Gourdin) ....
9.5	"J'aime la rêverie," romance (p1839, Vaux) ....
9.6	"L'attente," romance (p1840) ....
9.7	"L'aveu du page," romance (p1842, Plouvier) ....
9.8	"Six fables de LaFontaine" (p1842): 1. "La cigale et la fourmi" ...
9.9	2. "Le renard et le corbeau"
9.10	3. "Le loup et l'agneau"
9.11	4. "Le savetier et le financier"
9.12	5. "Le rat de ville et le rat des champs"
9.13	5. "La laitière et le pot au lait"
9.14	"L'arabe a son coursier," chant (p1843, Réboul de Nismes) ....
9.15	"La croix de ma mère," chansonette (p1843, Armand) ....
9.16	"Dors mon enfant," mélodie (p1843, Armand) ....
9.17	"Doux ménéstrel," romance (p1843, Saudeur) ....

10. GERMAN SONGS (1v & pf)

Pubd:

Unpubd:

11. ARRANGEMENTS OF WORKS BY OTHERS

Schubert melodies (orchd):

* * * * *

1. STAGE WORKS

Juvenilia:

1.1   "Gisei, das Opfer" (c1913, after Florenz: Terakoya) op.20
1.2   "Aglavaine et Sélysette" (c1914, sketches, destroyed) ....
1.3   "Der Tod de Tintagile" (c1914, Maeterlinck, sketches, destroyed) ....
1.4   "Traumspiel" (c1914, Strindberg, sketches, destroyed) ....

Early works:

1.5   "Leonce und Lena," incid music (c1918, Büchner) ....

Mature works—Monteverdi realisations:

1.6   "Orpheus" (p1925, r1931, 1940, Günther, free adapt of Monteverdi: La favola d'Orfeo, Mxi1, SV318) ....
1.7   "Tanz der Spröden" (p1925, r1940, Günther, free adapt of Monteverdi's ballet: Il ballo delle
       ingrate, Mviii314, SV167) ....
1.8   "Klage der Ariadne" (p1925, r1940, Orff, free adapt of Lamento d'Arianna, Mvi1, SV107 from
       Monteverdi's opera: L'Arianna, SV291) ....

Other mature works:

1.9   "Der Mond" (Ein kleines Welttheater) (c1937–8, Orff after Grimm brothers) ....
1.10   "Die Kluge" (Die Geschichte von dem König und der klugen Frau) (The Clever Girl) (c1941–2, Orff after
       Grimm brothers) ....
1.11   "Ein Sommernachtstraum," music drama (c1917, 27, 38, 43, 52, 62, Shakespeare transl Schlegel; 6 vers)
       (also see Britten's opera Op.64, Castelnuovo-Tedesco's overture Op.108, Purcell's semi-opera:
       The Fairy Queen, Z629, Mendelssohn's incid music Op.61 & Satie's incid music: 5 Grimaces) ....
1.12   "Die Bernauerin" (Ein bairisches Stück) (c1944–5, Orff) ....
1.13   "Astutuli" (Eine bairische Komödie) (c1945–6, Orff) ....
1.14   "Antigonae" (Ein Trauerspiel des Sophocles von Friedrich Hölderlin) (c1947–8, Sophocles transl Hölderlin)
1.15   "Trionfo di Afrodite" (Concerto scenico) (c1950–1, Latin & Greek text)..
1.16   "Trionfi" (p1953, = Carmina burana + Catulli carmina + Trionfo di Afrodite) ....
1.17   "Comoedia de Christi Resurrectione" (Osterspiel) (c1955, Orff) ....
1.18   "Lamenti" (Trittico teatrale) (p1958, = Klage der Ariadne + Orpheus + Tanz der Spröden) ....
1.19   "Oedipus der Tyrann" (Ein Trauerspiel des Sophocles von Friedrich Hölderlin) (c1957–9, Sophocles
       transl Hölderlin) ....
1.20   "Ludus de nato Infante mirificus," a Christmas play (c1960, Orff) ....
1.21   "Prometheus" (c1963–7, after Aeschylus) ....
1.22   "De Temporum fine Comoedia," Bühnenspiel (c1962–72, Orff; vv, ch & orch) ....

2. ORCHESTRAL WORKS

Juvenilia:

2.1   "Tanzende Faune" (ein Orchesterspiel) (c1914) op.21

Early works:

2.2   "Entrata," festival overture (c1928–41; 5 orch groups & org, after Byrd: The Bells)....................................

3. CONCERTOS, SOLO INSTR & ORCH

Early works:

3.1   "Kleines Konzert" (c1927; hpd & winds, based on 16th cent lute pieces) ....

4. STRING QUARTETS

Juvenilia:

4.1   2 String Quartets (ca1914) ....

5. CHORAL WORKS

Juvenilia:

5.1   "Also sprach Zarathustra" (c1912, after Nietzsche; Bar, 3ch, orch & org):.. op.14
          1. "Nachtlied"
          2. "Mitternacht"

3. "Vor Sonnenaufgang"
5.2   "Treibhauslieder" (c1914, Maeterlinck, unfin, destroyed except for sketches) ....
5.3   "Monna Vanna," sym poem (c1914, Maeterlinck, unfin, destroyed) ....

Early works:

5.4   "Des Turmes Auferstehung," cantata (c1920, Werfel; 2ch, orch & org) ....

"Das Werkbuch I," cantatas (c1929–30, Werfel; ch, 3pf & perc, arr of early 'Werfel Songs'):

5.5   1. "Veni creator spiritus": ....
       1. "Litanei"
       2. "Nachts"
       3. "Veni creator spiritus"
5.6   2. "Der gute Mensch": ....
       1. "Lächeln, Atmen, Schreiten"
       2. "Liebeslied"
       3. "Der gute Mensch"
5.7   3. "Fremde sind wir": ....
       1. "Aufruf"
       2. "Fremde sind wir"
       3. "Hymnus"

"Das Werkbuch II," cantatas (c1930, Brecht):

5.8   1. "Von der Freundlichkeit der Welt" (ch & strings, unpubd) ....
5.9   2. "Vom Frühjahr, Öltank und vom Fliegen": ....
       1. "Über das Frühjahr" (m ch)
       2. "Siebenhundert Intellektuelle beten einen Öltank an" (m ch, large percussion orchestra)

"Catulli Carmina I" (c1930, Latin texts; ch, 4pf, 4timp, 2 castanets & add perc for 10–12 players):

5.10   1. "Odi et amo" ....
5.11   2. "Vivamus, mea Lesbia" ....
5.12   3. "Lugete, o Veneres" ....
5.13   4. "Ille mihi paresse deo videtur" ....
5.14   5. "Ammiana" ....
5.15   6. "Miser Catulle" ....
5.16   7. "Nulla potest mulier" ....

"Catulli Carmina II" (c1931; ch, 4pf, 4timp, 2castanets & add perc for 10–12 players):

5.17   1. "Jam ver egelidos" ....
5.18   2. "Multas per gentes" ....
5.19   3. "Sirmio" ....

Mature works:

5.20   "Carmina Burana" (Cantiones profanae cantoribus et choris cantandae comitantibus instrumentis atque
       imaginibus magicis) (Songs of Beuren), scenic cantata (c1935–6, medieval Latin; S, T, Bar, ch & orch)
       (Benediktbeuern—a monastery in the Bavarian Alps where a Latin codex of 13th cent songs of jesters
       and minstrels was found, p1847, Orff used 1935 edition): ....
       "Fortuna imperatrix mundi": 1. "O Fortuna" (ch)
       2. "O Fortune plango vulnera" (ch)
       Part I "Primo vere": 3. "Veris leta facies" (semi-ch)
       4. "Omnia Sol temperat" (Bar)
       5. "Ecce gratium" (ch)
       "Uf dem Anger": 6. "Tanz"
       7. "Floret silva" (ch & semi-ch)
       8. "Chramer, gip die varwe mir" (ch & semi-ch)
       9. "Reie" (round dance)
       10. "Swaz hie gat umbe—Chume, chum geselle min" (ch)
       11. "Were diu werit alle min" (ch)
       Part II. "In taberna": 12. "Estuans interius" (Bar)
       13. "Olim lacus colueram" (cT & m ch)
       14. "Ego sum abbas" (Bar & m ch)
       15. "In taberna quando sumus" (m ch)
       Part III. "Cours d'Amour": 16. "Amor volat undique" (S & boys' ch)
       17. "Dies, nox et omnia" (Bar)
       18. "Stetit puella" (S)
       19. "Circa mea pectora" (Bar & ch)
       20. "Si puer cum puellula" (Bar & m ch)
       21. "Veni, veni, venias" (ch)
       22. "In trutina" (S)
       23. "Tempus est iocundum" (S, Bar, ch & choirboys)
       24. "Dulcissime" (S)
       "Blanziflor et Helena": 25. "Ave formosissima" (ch)
       "Fortuna imperatrix mundi": 26. "O Fortuna" (repeat of 1.) (ch)

6. VOICE & ORCHESTRA

7. SONGS (w/ pf)

Juvenilia:

Early works:

8. MISC WORKS

"Musik für Kinder" (Orff-Schulwerk) (early vers by1935 withdrawn, p1950–4 ed Orff & Keetman), 5 vols:

"Jugendmusik" (subsidiary collection, incl pieces from 1st vers of: Musik für Kinder):

* * * * *

1. STAGE WORKS

1.1 "Manru," 3 act opera (c1900, Nossig after Kraszewski's novel: Chata za wsią) Op.20

2. SYMPHONIES

2.1 Symphony in B minor, "Polonia" (c1907) Op.24

3. OTHER ORCHESTRAL WORKS

3.1 "Suite" (unfin) ....

4. CONCERTOS, SOLO INSTR & ORCH

Pf & orch:

4.1 Piano Concerto in A minor (c1888) Op.17
4.2 "Fantazja polska" (Polish Fantasia on Original Themes) (c1893; pf & orch) Op.19

Vn & orch:

4.3 Violin Concerto (unfin) ....

5. CHAMBER MUSIC

5.1 Violin Sonata in A minor (c1880) Op.13

6. PIANO SONATAS

6.1 Piano Sonata in E-flat minor (c1903) Op.21

7. OTHER PIANO WORKS

7.1 "Valse mignonne" (c1876) ....
7.2 "2 Pieces" (c1876): No.1 "Prélude à capriccio" Op.1
7.3   No.2 "Minuet," in G minor
7.4 "Impromptu," in F major (c1878) ....
7.5 "3 Pieces" (c1879): No.1 "Gavotte," in E minor Op.2
7.6   No.2 "Mélodie," in C major
7.7   No.3 "Valse mélancolique," in A major
7.8 "2 Intermezzos" (c1879): No.1 in G minor ....
7.9   No.2 in C minor
7.10 "2 Canons" (c1882) ....
7.11 "Chants du voyageur" (c1882): No.1 "Allegro agitato," in B-flat major Op.8
7.12   No.2 "Andantino melancolico," in A minor
7.13   No.3 "Andantino gracioso," in B major (pf duet)
7.14   No.4 "Andantino mistico," in B minor
7.15   No.5 "Allegro giocoso," in A major
7.16 "Variations & fugue," in A minor (c1882) Op.11
7.17 "Krakowiak" (c1884) Op.3
7.18 "Élégie" (c1884) Op.4
7.19 "Polish Dances" (c1884; arr for pf duet ca1892): No.1 "Krakowiak," in E major Op.5
7.20   No.2 "Mazurek," in C minor
7.21   No.3 "Krakowiak," in B-flat minor
7.22 "Powódź (The Flood) (c1884) Op.9
7.23 "Polish Dances" (c1884), Book I: No.1 "Krakowiak," in F major ....
7.24   No.2 "Mazurek," in A minor
7.25   No.3 "Mazurek," in A major
7.26 II: No.4 "Mazurek," in B-flat major
7.27   No.5 "Krakowiak," in A major
7.28   No.6 "Polonaise," in B major
7.29 "Album de mai: Scènes romantiques" (c1884): No.1 "Au soir" Op.10
7.30   No.2 "Chant d'amour"
7.31   No.3 "Scherzino"
7.32   No.4 "Barcarolle"
7.33   No.5 "Caprice" (Valse)
7.34 "Tatra Album" (c1884; arr for pf duet) Op.12
7.35 "Humoresques de concert" (c1884), I. (à l'antique): No.1 "Menuet célèbre," in G major Op.14
7.36   No.2 "Sarabande"

8. CHORAL WORKS

9. SONGS (w/ pf)

* * * * *

1. VIOLIN CONCERTOS

1.1 Violin Concerto No.1 in E-flat maj (c1815–6, usually played in D major; red w/ pf) . Op.6, ms5560–2, MS21
1.2 Violin Concerto No.2 in B minor, "La campanella" (c1826) Op.7, ms5563–5, MS48
1.3 Violin Concerto No.3 in E major (c1826) ms5647, MS50
1.4 Violin Concerto No.4 in D minor (c1829–30) ms5648, ms5565, MS60
1.5 Violin Concerto No.5 in A minor (c?, orch part lost: indicated on vn part only) ms5649, MS78
1.6 Violin Concerto No.6 in E minor (c early, orch part lost; added by Mompellio) MS75
1.7 Violin Concerto (lost: mentioned in letter of 1823 to L. G. Germi) MSivN4
1.8 Violin Concerto in F-sharp minor (lost: mentioned in letter of 1830 to L. G. Germi) MSivN10

2. OTHER WORKS FOR VIOLIN & ORCH

2.1 "Napoléon," in E-flat major (c1805–8; w/ gui/orch; red w/ pf) ms5577–8, MS5
2.2 "Polacca con variazioni," in A major (ca1810; arr for vn & pf p1952) ms5580, MS18
2.3 "Le streghe," variations in E-flat major (c1813, from Süssmayr: Il noce di Benevento;
red w/ pf) Op.8, ms5566–7, MS19
2.4 "Non più mesta," var in E-flat major (c1817–9, from Rossini: La cenerentola) Op.12, ms5570–1, MS22
2.5 "Sonata a preghiera," in F minor (ca1819, on: Dal tuo stellato, from Rossini: Mosè, vn partlost) ms5573, MS23
2.6 "Pot-Pourri" (c1819, vn part lost) ms5581, MS24
2.7 "Sonata militare," in E-flat major (c1824, on: Non più andrai, from Mozart: Le nozze di Figaro, K492,
vn part lost) ms5588, MS46
2.8 "Suonata con variazioni," in E major (c1824, on: Pria ch'io l'impegno, from Weigl: L'amor;
red w/ pf) ms5591–2, MS47
2.9 "Adagio," in E major (c1826, orch part: sketches) ms5564, MS49
2.10 "Maestosa suonata sentimentale" (c1828, on Austrian national hymn; red w/ pf): ms5585–6, MS51
quoted: . Haydn: "Gott, erhalte Franz den Kaiser!" (Das Kaiserlied), HobXXVIa/43
2.11 "La tempesta" (La Grande Sonata drammatica), 2 variations (c1828, collab Panny) ms5595–7, MS52
2.12 "Sonatina e Polacchetta," in B-flat major (c before 1829, vn part inc) ms5594, MS55
2.13 "Suonata Varsavia," 7 variations in E major (c1829, on Mazurka c by Elsner, orch part lost) ms5593, MS57
2.14 "Suonata Appassionata" (c1829, vn part lost) ms5584, MS58
2.15 "O mamma, mamma ca(ra)" (Il carnevale di Venezia), in A major (c1829) . Op.10, ms5647, ms5669, MS59
2.16 "Sonata amorosa galante," in A-flat major (c1830, on theme of Rossini, vn part lost) ms5583, MS61
2.17 "St Patrick's Day," variations in E major (c1831, on the Irish folktune, vn part lost) ms5579, MS64
2.18 "Sonata movimento perpetuo," in B-flat major (c1831–2; 2 vers): MS66
. Version A ms5635, ms5590
. Version B in B-flat major (red w/ pf) ms5594, ms5635, ms5594, ms5589
2.19 "La primavera" (Sonata w/ variations), in A major (ca1838, orch part lost; arr w/ pf) ms5582, MS73
2.20 "Balletto campestre," 49 variations in A major (c1838; red Dacci w/ pf 1952) ms5574, MS74
2.21 "Tarantella," in A minor (c?; red Bulatov w/ pf 1978) MS76
2.22 "I palpiti" (Introduction & Variations), in B-flat major (c?, from Rossini: Tancredi) Op.13, ms5572, MS77
2.23 "Maria Luisa" (Sonata con variazioni), in E major (c?, orch part lost; arr w/ gui) ms5587, MS79
2.24 "Tema con variazioni," in D major (dubious, orch part lost) MSvN4
2.25 "Polonoise concertante" (spur: c by Sołtyk in Warsaw 1929, ded to Paganini) MSviN3

3. OTHER ORCHESTRAL WORKS

3.1 "Niccolò Paganini a Mr. Henry" (c1831; hn, bn & orch, ded to A. N. Henry) ms5642, MS65
3.2 "Sonata per la Grand Viola," in C minor (c1834; large va & orch) ms5598, MS70

4. STRING QUARTETS

4.1 "3 String Quartets" (c1815): No.1 in D minor ms5602, MS20
4.2 No.2 in E-flat major
4.3 No.3 in A minor

5. GUITAR QUARTETS (vn, va, gui & vc)

5.1 Guitar Quartet No.1 in A minor (c1813, compl by 1818 p1820, ded to his sister Nicoletta) Op.4/1, MS28
5.2 Guitar Quartet No.2 in C major (c1813, compl by 1818 p1820) Op.4/2, MS29
5.3 Guitar Quartet No.3 in A major (c1813, compl by 1818 p1820) Op.4/3, MS30
5.4 Guitar Quartet No.4 in D major (c by 1818 p1820) Op.5/1, MS31
5.5 Guitar Quartet No.5 in C major (c by 1818 p1820) Op.5/2, MS32
5.6 Guitar Quartet No.6 in D minor (c by 1818 p1820) Op.5/3, MS33
5.7 Guitar Quartet No.7 in E major (c1817–18, ded to marchesa Pallavicini) ms5637, MS34
5.8 Guitar Quartet No.8 in A major (ca1817–18, ded to marchese Carrega) ms5632, (ms19236), MS35
5.9 Guitar Quartet No.9 in D major (c1818, ded to L. G. Germi) ms5638, MS36
5.10 Guitar Quartet No.10 in A major (c1818, ded to L. G. Germi) ms5633–4, MS37
5.11 Guitar Quartet No.11 in B major (c1819, ded to L. G. Germi) ms5639, MS38
5.12 Guitar Quartet No.12 in A minor (c1819, ded to L. G. Germi) ms6530, ms6540, MS39

5.13	Guitar Quartet No.13 in F major (c1819, ded to L. G. Germi)	ms5641, MS40
5.14	Guitar Quartet No.14 in A major (c1819, ded to L. G. Germi)	ms5635, MS41
5.15	Guitar Quartet No.15 in A minor (c1820, ded to marchese Crosa)	ms5636, MS42
5.16	*"6 Cantabili con Minuetti a Valtz" (c?; vn solo, gui, va & vc, lost)*	*MSivN5*

6. OTHER CHAMBER MUSIC

5 insts:

6.1	*"Variazioni per violino" (vn solo, 2vn, va, vc, spur)*	*MSviN6*

String Trios:

6.2	"Divertimenti carnevaleschi" (c1803–5; 2vn & bass, ded to gen. Milhaud): "Minuetto," in E-flat major	MS4
6.3	"6 Alessandrine con trio e minore": No.1 in E-flat major	
6.4	No.2 in A major	
6.5	No.3 in D major	
6.6	No.4 in C major	
6.7	No.5 in B-flat major	
6.8	No.6 in E-flat major	
6.9	"2 Perigordini": No.1 in B-flat major	
6.10	No.2 in A major	
6.11	"4 Valzer": No.1 in B-flat major	
6.12	No.2 in A major	
6.13	No.3 in C major	
6.14	No.4 in A major	
6.15	"Scozzese," in F major	
6.16	"6 Inglesi": No.1 in C major	
6.17	No.2 in C major	
6.18	No.3 in A major	
6.19	No.4 in F major	
6.20	No.5 in F major	
6.21	No.6 in C major	
6.22	"3 Ritornelli" (c?; 2vn & bass): No.1 in A major	ms5601, MS113
6.23	No.2 in C major	
6.24	No.3 in C major	
6.25	"In cuor più non mi sento," in A major (c?; vn solo, vn & vc, from Paisiello's opera: La Molinara)	MS117
6.26	"Sonata a violino scordato" (c?; vn solo & 2vn)	MS118
6.27	*"Sonata," in A major (vn solo, vn & vc, dubious)*	*MSvN5*
6.28	*"Sei preludi" (vn solo, vn & vc, vn part only, dubious)*	*MSvN12*

Trios w/ gui:

6.29	"Serenata," in C major (ca1808; va, vc & gui, ded to his sister Dominica)	ms5628, MS17
6.30	"Terzetto," in D major (c1833; vn, vc & gui)	ms5631, MS69
6.31	"Terzetto concertante," in D major (c?; va, gui & vc, perf1833)	ms5629, MS114
6.32	"Serenata," in F major (c?; 2vn & gui)	ms5631, MS115
6.33	"Terzetto," in A minor (c?; 2vn & gui)	ms5631, MS116

Vn & pf:

6.34	"4 Notturni a quartetto" (c1805–8): No.1 in E major	MS15
6.35	No.2 in D minor	
6.36	No.3 in D major	
6.37	No.4 in E minor	
6.38	"Cantabile," in D major (c?)	ms5599, MS109
6.39	*"Trois airs variés" (dubious)*	*MSvN3*
6.40	*"Tema napolitana" (c1829, pf part only, dubious)*	*MSvN11*
6.41	*"Divertimenti concertanti" (spur)*	*MSviN4*
6.42	*"Le charme de Padoue" (spur)*	*MSviN5*

Vn & va:

6.43	"Sonata a violino e viola" (c?)	MS108

Vn & vc:

6.44	"Rondò," in A major (c1831, ded to De Begnis)	MS63
6.45	"3 Duetti concertanti" (c?): No.1 in E-flat major	ms5601, MS107
6.46	No.2 in G minor	
6.47	No.3 in A major	

Vn & gui:

6.48	"Carmagnola con (14) variazioni," in A major (ca1795–1800) MS1	
6.49	*"3 Sonate" (c1805–8, ded to princess E. Bonaparte Baciocchi, vn part lost): No.1 in A minor ....(ms19226), MS7*	
6.50	*No.2 in D minor*	
6.51	*No.3 in E minor*	
6.52	"Entrata d'Adone nella reggia di Venere," in C major (c1805–8) .... (ms19228), MS8	
6.53	"6 Sonate" (c1805–8, ded to Madame Frassinet): No.1 in C major .... (ms19229), MS9	
6.54	No.2 in G major	
6.55	No.3 in D major	
6.56	No.4 in C major	
6.57	No.5 in A major	
6.58	No.6 in E major	
6.59	"6 Sonate" (c1805–8, ded to Madame Frassinet): No.1 in A major .... (ms19230), MS10	
6.60	No.2 in C major	
6.61	No.3 in F major	
6.62	No.4 in A minor	
6.63	No.5 in E minor	
6.64	No.6 in E minor	
6.65	"6 Sonate" (c1805–8, ded to prince Felice I of Lucca e Piombino): No.1 in G major .... (ms19225–7), MS11	
6.66	No.2 in C major	
6.67	No.3 in A minor	
6.68	No.4 in C major	
6.69	No.5 in D major	
6.70	No.6 in A minor	
6.71	"6 Sonate" (c1805–8): No.1 in E minor... (ms19232), MS12	
6.72	No.2 in C major	
6.73	No.3 in A minor	
6.74	No.4 in D minor	
6.75	No.5 in A major	
6.76	No.6 in G major	
6.77	"6 Sonate" (p1985, ded to La Principessina Napoleone): No.1 in G major .... (ms19233), MS13	
6.78	No.2 in C major	
6.79	No.3 in A minor	
6.80	No.4 in F major	
6.81	No.5 in D major	
6.82	No.6 in E minor	
6.83	"6 Sonate" (c1805–8, compl by 1818, p1820, ded to Agostino Dellepiane): No.1 in A major Op.2, MS26	
6.84	No.2 in C major	
6.85	No.3 in D minor	
6.86	No.4 in A major	
6.87	No.5 in D major	
6.88	No.6 in A minor	
6.89	"6 Sonate" (c1805–8, compl by 1818, p1820, ded to Eleonora Quilici): No.1 in A major Op.3, MS27	
6.90	No.2 in G major	
6.91	No.3 in D major	
6.92	No.4 in A minor	
6.93	No.5 in A major	
6.94	No.6 in E minor	
6.95	"Cantabile & Waltz," in E major (ca1823, ded to Camillo Sivori) ms5622, MS45	
6.96	60 "Variazioni sul Barucabà" (c1835, on Genoese air, ded to L. G. Germi) Op.14, ms5627, MS71	
6.97	"Allegro vivace a movimento perpetuo," in C major (c1835; orchd Toscanini) Op.11, MS72	
6.98	"6 Duetti" (c?; arr for vn & pf 1952): No.1 in E minor ms5623, MS110	
6.99	No.2 in A major	
6.100	No.3 in A minor	
6.101	No.4 in F major	
6.102	No.5 in D minor	
6.103	No.6 in G major	
6.104	"Duetto amoroso," in C major (c?; arr for vn & pf 1952) ms5623, MS111	
6.105	"Centone di sonate," 18 sonatas (c after ?1828), "Lettera A": No.1 in A minor ms5626, MS112	
6.106	No.2 in D major	
6.107	No.3 in C major	
6.108	No.4 in A major	
6.109	No.5 in E major	
6.110	No.6 in A major	
6.111	"Lettera B": No.1 in F major	
6.112	No.2 in G major	
6.113	No.3 in A major	
6.114	No.4 in C major	
6.115	No.5 in A minor	
6.116	No.6 in D major	
6.117	"Lettera C": No.1 in E major	
6.118	No.2 in G major	
6.119	No.3 in A major	
6.120	No.4 in E major	

6.121	No.5 in A major
6.122	No.6 in C major
6.123	"Duetto" (c?) MS122
6.124	*"11 Cantabili e Valtz" (lost) MSivN6*
6.125	*"Sonata con variazioni" (lost) MSivN8*
6.126	*"Sonatine" (for gen. Pino, lost) MSivN9*
6.127	*"Variazioni di bravura sopra un tema originale" (vn & gui/pf, spur arr of: Capriccio No.24)...................MSviN7*

Gui & vn:

6.128	"Sonata concertata," in A major (c1803, ded to Emilia Di Negro) ms5624, MS2
6.129	"Grand sonata," in A major (ca1803) ms5625, MS3

Mand & gui:

6.130	"Sonata per Rovene," in E minor (c1805–8)...MS14
6.131	"Serenata," in G major (c1805–8)..MS16

7. VIOLIN (solo)

7.1	"Sonata a violino solo," in C major (c1805–8, ded to princess Elisa Bonaparte Baciocchi) ms5600, MS6
7.2	"24 Caprices" (c by 1817, p1820): No.1 "Andante," in E major Op.1, MS25
7.3	No.2 "Moderato," in B minor
7.4	No.3 "Sostenuto—Presto—Sostenuto," in E minor
7.5	No.4 "Maestoso," in C minor
7.6	No.5 "Agitato," in A minor
7.7	No.6 "Lento," in G minor
7.8	No.7 "Posato," in A minor
7.9	No.8 "Maestoso," in E-flat major
7.10	No.9 "Allegretto," in E major, "The Hunt"
7.11	No.10 "Vivace," in G minor
7.12	No.11 "Andante—Presto—Tempo I," in C major
7.13	No.12 "Allegro," in A-flat major
7.14	No.13 "Allegro," in B-flat major, "The Devil's Chucle"
7.15	No.14 "Moderato," in E-flat major
7.16	No.15 "Posato," in E minor
7.17	No.16 "Presto," in G minor
7.18	No.17 "Sostenuto—Andante," in E-flat major
7.19	No.18 "Corrente—Allegro," in C major
7.20	No.19 "Lento—Allegro assai," in E-flat major
7.21	No.20 "Allegretto," in D major
7.22	No.21 "Amoroso—Presto," in A major
7.23	No.22 "Marcato," in F major
7.24	No.23 "Posato," in E-flat major
7.25	No.24 "Tema—Quasi presto—(11) Variazioni—Finale," in A minor
7.26	"Capriccio a violino solo 'Nel cor più non mi sento,' " in G major (c1821, from Paisiello: La molinara) .MS44
7.27	"Capriccio" (c1828, ded to Maurizio Dietrichstein; ed Bulatov 1977) MS54
7.28	"God Save the King," 6 variations in E-flat major (c1829, on English hymn)............... Op.9, ms5568, MS56
7.29	"Caprice d'adieu" (c1833, ded to Eduard Eliason)...MS68
7.30	Untitled (Waltz) (c?) MS80
7.31	"Inno patriotico" (Allegro & 6 variations), in A major (c?) MS81
7.32	"Tema variato" (Theme & 7 variations), in A major (c?) MS82
7.33	"Sonata a violin solo," in A major (c?, 3rd movt: Polonoise w/ 7 variations) MS83
7.34	*"Allegro assai" (sketch)...MSiiiN1*
7.35	*"Cadenza" (sketch) MSiiiN2*
7.36	*"Preludio" (c1829, sketch)..MSiiiN3*
7.37	*"Andante" (ded to Szymanowska, sketch) MSiiiN4*
7.38	*"Minuetto—Allegretto e Trio" (sketch) ms5630, MSiiiN5*
7.39	*"Polacca" (sketch) ms5645/1, MSiiiN6*
7.40	*"Canone" (sketch)..ms5645/2, MSiiiN7*
7.41	*"Canone" (sketch) ms5645/3, MSiiiN8*
7.42	*"Ghiribizzo" (sketch) ms5645/3, MSiiiN9*
7.43	*"Minore" (sketch) ms5603/3, MSiiiN10*
7.44	*"4 Valtz" (sketch) ms5603/14, MSiiiN11*
7.45	*"Valtz" (sketch) ms5603/16, MSiiiN12*
7.46	*"Trio" (& Minore) (sketch) MSiiiN13*
7.47	*"Finale" (sketch) ms5576/5–8, MSiiiN14*
7.48	*"Fandango" (lost) ms5577, MSivN1*
7.49	*"Capriccio sul tema 'Là ci darem la mano' " (from Mozart's opera: Don Giovanni, K527, lost) MSivN2*
7.50	*"Due adagi a doppie corde" (lost) MSivN3*
7.51	*"Fantasia" (lost) MSivN7*
7.52	*"Sinfonia della Lodowiska" (perf1800 in Modena, lost; see arr for gui, MS98) MSivN11*
7.53	*"Pastorale" (perf1813 in Milan, lost) MSivN12*
7.54	*"Concerto," in D minor (perf1814 in Genova, lost) MSivN13*

8. GUITAR (solo)

9. MANDOLIN (solo)

10. MISC INSTRUMENTAL

11. CHORAL WORKS

4. "L'aurora" (orch)
5. "Maestoso" (m ch & insts/orch)
6. "Rondò" (vn & orch)

11.3   *"Inno all'armonia" (perf1820 in Milan, lost)* *MSivN14*

12. MISC VOCAL

12.1   *"Ghiribizzo vocale": "Da voi cari Lumi," in B major (c?; 1v & orch; orch part in pf red only)* *ms5643, MS120*
12.2   *"Bella pace ormai discendi" (3vv, dubious)* *MSvN6*
12.3   *"Scena e aria 'L'Andromaca infelice' " (dubious)* *MSvN7*
12.4   *"Gratias" (S, dubious)* *MSvN10*
12.5   *"Dolci d'amor parole" (spur)* *MSviN2*

13. SONGS (w/ pf)

13.1   "É pur amabile," canzonetta (c1828, Paganini, ded to contessa Wimpffen) MS53
13.2   "Sul margine d'un rio" (c?) MS119
13.3   "Canzonetta," in C major (c?; w/ gui) ms5645, MS121
13.4   *"La farfaletta": "Come la farfaletta" (dubious)* *MSvN8*
13.5   *"Canto spianato" (dubious)* *MSvN9*
13.6   *"Romance de Beauplan" (spur)* *ms5644, MSviN1*

* * * * *

MS =   "Catalogo Tematico delle Musiche di Niccolò Paganini." Edited by Maria Rosa Moretti & Anna
             Sorrento. Comune de Genova, 1982.
ms =   manuscript number in Biblioteca Casanatense, Rome.
(ms) =   manuscript number in Bibliothèque Nationale, Paris.

1. STAGE WORKS

Operas:

1.1	"Diably z Loudun" (Die Teufel von Loudun) (The Devils of Loudun), 3 acts (c1968–69, Penderecki after Whiting's dramatization of Huxley's The Devils of Loudun; Ger transl Fried) ....
1.2	"Paradise Lost" (Das verlorene Paradies), 2 act sacra rappresentazione (c1976–8, Fry after Milton; Ger transl Wollschläger) ....
1.3	"The Black Mask," 1 act (c1984–6, after Hauptman's play: Die schwarze Maske) ....
1.4	"Ubu roi" (after Jarry) ....

Incid music & film:

1.5	Ca 50 scores (incl film: Manuscript found in Saragossa) ....

2. SYMPHONIES

2.1	Symphony No.1 (c1973) ....
2.2	Symphony No.2, "Christmas Symphony" (c1979–80) ....

3. OTHER ORCHESTRAL WORKS

3.1	"Emanacje" (Emanations) (c1958; 2 string orch) ....
3.2	"Epitaph Artur Malawski in memoriam" (c1958; strings & kettle-drums) ....
3.3	"Anaklasis" (c1959–60; strings & perc) ....
3.4	"Tren Ofiarom Hiroszimy" (Threnody for the Victims of Hiroshima) (c1959–61; 52 strings) ....
3.5	"Polymorphia" (c1961; 48 strings) ....
3.6	"Fluorescencje" (Fluorescences) (c1961–2) ....
3.7	"Canon" (c1962; strings & 2 tape recorders) ....
3.8	"3 Pieces in the Antique Style" (c1963): No.1 "Aria" ....
3.9	No.2 "Minuet I"
3.10	No.3 "Minuet II"
3.11	"De Natura Sonoris" I (c1966) ....
3.12	"Uwertura pittsburska" (Pittsburgh Overture) (c1967; woodwinds & kettle-drums) ....
3.13	"De Natura Sonoris" II (c1971) ....
3.14	"Prelude" (c1971; woodwinds, perc & d basses) ....
3.15	"Actions" (c1971; 14 jazz insts) ....
3.16	"Partita" (c1971; hpd, electric gui, bass gui, d bass & chamber orch) ....
3.17	"Intermezzo" (c1973; 24 strings) ....
3.18	"The Awakening of Jacob" (c1974) ....
3.19	"Adagietto" (c1979, from stage work: Paradise Lost) ....
3.20	"Passacaglia and Rondo" (c1988) ....
3.21	"Adagio" (c1989) ....

4. CONCERTOS, SOLO INSTR & ORCH

Vn & orch:

4.1	Violin Concerto (c1963) ....
4.2	"Capriccio" (c1967) ....
4.3	Violin Concerto (c1976–7) ....

Va & orch:

4.4	Viola Concerto (c1983; red vers 1985) ....

Vc & orch:

4.5	"Sonata" (c1964) ....
4.6	Cello Concerto No.1 (c1972; orig: Concerto for Violino Grande) ....
4.7	Cello Concerto No.2 (c1982) ....

Other:

4.8	"Fonogrammi" (c1961; fl & chamber orch) ....
4.9	"Capriccio" (c1965; ob & 11 strings) ....

5. STRING QUARTETS

5.1	String Quartet No.1 (c1960) ....
5.2	String Quartet No.2 (c1968) ....

5.3   "Der unterbrochene Gedanke" (c1988) ....

6. OTHER CHAMBER MUSIC

3 or more insts:

6.1   String Trio (c1990–1) ....
6.2   "Quartet" (c1993; cl & str trio) ....

Vn & pf:

6.3   Violin Sonata (c1953) ....
6.4   3 "Miniatures" (c1959) ....

Other 2 insts:

6.5   3 "Miniatures" (c1956; cl & pf) ....

1 instr:

6.6   "Capriccio for Siegfried Palm" (c1968; vc, commissioned S. Palm) ....
6.7   "Capriccio" (c1980; tuba) ....
6.8   "Cadenza" (c1984; va; arr Edinger for vn 1986) ....
6.9   "Per slava" (c1985–6; vc) ....
6.10   "Prelude" (c1987; B-flat cl) ....

7. PIANO

2 Pf:

7.1   "Mensura sortis" (c1963) ....

8. ELECTRONIC TAPE

8.1   "Psalmus 1961" (c1961; 2 tape recorders) ....
8.2   "Brygada śmierci" (Brigade of Death) (c1963, Weliczker; electronic tape) ....
8.3   "Ekecheira" (c1972; electronic tape, for Olympic Games in Monaco) ....

9. CHORAL WORKS

9.1   "Psalmy Dawida" (Psalms of David) (c1958, Kochanowski; ch & perc) ....
9.2   "Wymiary czasu i ciszy" (Dimensions of time and silence) (c1959–60; ch, strings & perc) ....
9.3   "Stabat mater" (c1962; 3ch) ....
9.4   "Cantata in honorem Almae Matris Universitatis Iagellonicae" (c1964; 2ch & orch) ....
9.5   "Pieśń żałobna ku czci B. Rutkowskiego" (Funeral song in memory of Rutkowski) (c1964; ch) ....
9.6   "St. Luke Passion" (c1965–6; 3vv, speaker, 3ch, boys' ch & orch): ....
          I: 1. "O crux ave" (Hymn to the Cross) (Roman Breviary, hymn: Vexilla regis prodeunt; ch)
                    2. "Et egressus ibat" (Christ on the Mount of Olives) (St. Luke 22: 39–44)
                    3. "Deus meus, Deus meus" (Christ's Aria) (Psalm 21: 1–2)
                    4. "Domine, quis habitabit in tabernaculo tuo" (Soprano Aria) (Psalm 9: 16)
                    5. "Adhuc eo loquente" (Capture) (St. Luke 22: 47–53)
                    6. "Jerusalem, Jerusalem" (Lamentation I) (Roman Breviary: Jeremiah's Threnody; ch)
                    7. "Ut quid, Domine, recessisti longe" (Chorus a capella) (Psalm 10: 1)
                    8. "Comprehendentes autem eum" (Peter's Triple Denial) (St. Luke 22: 54–59)
                    9. "Judica me, Deus" (Peter's Aria) (Psalm 43: 1)
                 10. "Et viri, qui tenebant" (Flagellation) (St. Luke 22: 63–70)
                 11. "Jerusalem, Jerusalem" (Lamentation II) (Roman Breviary: Jeremiah's Threnody; S)
                 12. "Miserere mei" (Psalm 56; ch)
                 13. "Et surgens omnis multitudo" (Jesus before Pilate) (St. Luke 23: 1–22; ch)
          II: 14. "Et bajulans sibi crucem" (The Way of the Cross) (St. John 19, Missal & Breviary)
                 15. "Ibi crucifixerunt eum" (The Crucifixion) (St. Luke 23: 33)
                 16. "Crux fidelis" (Soprano Aria) (Hymn: Pangue lingua, Roman Breviary, Good Friday)
                 17. "Dividentes vero vestimenta eius" (St. Luke 23: 34)
                 18. "In pulverem mortis deduxisti me" (Psalm 22: 16–19; ch)
                 19. "Et stabat populus spectans" (... and Mocked Him) (St. Luke 23: 35–37; ch)
                 20. "Unus autem de his" (Christ speaks to the Malefactors) (St. Luke 23: 39–43; ch)
                 21. "Stabant autem juxta crucem" (Christ speaks to His Mother & to St. John) (St. John 19: 25–27)
                 22. "Stabat mater dolorosa" (The Sequence) (ch)
                 23. "Erat autem fere hora sexta" (The Death of Jesus) (St. Luke 23: 44–46)
                 24. "In te, Domine, speravi" (Finale) (Psalm 31; ch)
9.7   "Dies Irae" (Oratorio to the Memory of Those Murdered at Auschwitz) (c1967; S, T, B, ch & orch) ....

9.8   "Utrenia" (Jutrznia), I: "Złożenie do grobu" (The Entombment of Christ) (c1969–70, Orthodox church; 5vv, 2ch & orch) ....

9.9   "Kosmogonia" (Cosmogony) (c1970, words from Copernicus, da Vinci, Sophocles & Genesis; 4vv, ch & orch) ....

9.10   "Utrenia" (Jutrznia), II: "Zmartwychwstanie" (The Resurrection of Christ) (c1970–1, Orthodox church; 5vv, 2ch, boys' ch & orch) ....

9.11   "Ecloga VIII" (c1972, Virgil: Bucolica; 6 m vv) ....

9.12   "Canticum canticorum Salomonis" (c1970–3, from Bible's Song of Songs; ch & chamber orch)..................

9.13   "Magnificat" (c1974; B, 7 m vv, boys' ch, ch & orch) ....

9.14   "Prologue, Visions & Finale" (c1979; 6vv, ch & orch, from stage work: Paradise Lost) ....

9.15   "Te Deum" (c1979–80; S, A, T, B, 2 ch & orch)...

9.16   "Lacrymosa" (c1980; S, ch & orch, intended as part of: Polish Requiem) ....

9.17   "Agnus Dei" (c1981; ch)..

9.20   "Polish Requiem" (c1980–4; S, A, T, B, ch & orch) ....

9.21   "Song of Cherubim" (c1986; ch) ....

9.22   "Veni creator" (Hymnus) (c1989, Hrabanus Maurus; ch & orch) ....

10. VOICE & ORCHESTRA

10.1   "Strofy" (Strophes) (c1959; S, reciter & 10 insts): ....
         text: 1. "What a beautiful being is man, when he is man" (Menander, in Greek)
                2. "The dependence of our lives should frighten" (Sophocles: Oedipus Rex, in Greek)
                3. "Woe unto them that call evil good, and good evil" (Isaiah V, 20–21, in Hebrew)
                4. "The heart is deceitful above all things" (Jeremiah XVII, 9, in Hebrew)
                5. (Impossibility of penetrating the mystery of death) (A Persian verse by ?Omar Chajjam)

* * * * *

1. STAGE WORKS

Operas:

1.1 "Les mamelles de Tirésias" (The Breasts of Tiresias), 2 act comic opera (c1944, based on surrealist play by Apollinaire) ....

1.2 "Dialogues des Carmélites," 3 acts (c1953–6, Bernanos) ....

1.3 "La voix humaine," 1 act lyric tragedy (c1958, Cocteau; 1 character only—a young woman on the phone)..

1.4 Recitatives for Gounod's opera: La colombe (c1923, Barbier & Carré after La Fontaine) ....

1.5 "L'histoire de Babar, le petit éléphant," melodrama (c1940–5, Brunhoff; recit & pf; orchd Françaix) ....

Ballets:

1.6 Nos.3 & 4 for collab work: Les mariés de la tour Eiffel (c1921, Cocteau, music c by 'Le Six'): ....
"Les mariés de la tour Eiffel": *1. "Ouverture" (Le 14 juillet) (c by Auric)*
2. "Marche nuptiale" (c by Milhaud)
3. "Le discours du Général" (Polka pour deux cornets à pistons) (c by Poulenc)
4. "La baigneuse de Trouville" (Carte postale en couleurs) (c by Poulenc)
5. "Fugue du massacre" (c by Milhaud)
6. "Valse des dépêches" (c by Tailleferre)
7. "Marche funèbre sur la mort du général" (c by Honegger)
8. "Quadrille" (Pantalon—Eté—Poule—Pastourelle—Final) (c by Tailleferre)
9. "Ritournelles" (c by Auric)
10. "Sortie de la noce" (c by Milhaud)

1.7 "Les biches," 1 act (c1923, 17th cent text; w/ ch; see transcr for pf) ....

1.8 "Pastourelle," for collab work: L'éventail de Jeanne (c1927; see arr for pf p1929) ....

1.9 "Aubade," choreographic concerto (c1929; pf & 18 insts; red for pf; also for 2pf) ....

1.10 "Les animaux modèles," 1 act (c1940–1, after La Fontaine's Fables) ....

Incid music:

1.11 "Le gendarme incompris" (c1921, Cocteau & Radiguet) ....

1.12 "Esquisse d'un fanfare," overture for Act V of Shakespeare: Roméo & Juliette (c1921) ....

1.13 "Intermezzo" (c1933, Giraudoux) ....

1.14 "La reine Margot" (c1935, Bourdet, collab Auric; pubd as: Suite française; see song: A sa guitar) .....

1.15 "Léocadia" (c1940, Anouilh; see song: Les chemins de l'amour) ....

1.16 "La fille du jardinier" (c1941, Exbrayat) ....

1.17 "Le voyageur sans bagages" (c1944, Anouilh) ....

1.18 "La nuit de la Saint-Jean" (c1944, Barrie) ....

1.19 "Le soldat et la sorcière" (c1945, Salacrou) ....

1.20 "L'invitation au château" (c1947, Cocteau) ....

1.21 "Amphitryon" (c1947, Molière) ....

1.22 "Renaud et Armide" (c1962, Cocteau) ....

Film:

1.23 "La belle au bois dormant" (c1935, Alexeyev) ....

1.24 "La duchesse de Langeais" (c1942, Baroncelli) ....

1.25 "Le voyageur sans bagages" (c1944, Anouilh) ....

1.26 "Ce siècle a 50 ans" (c1950, collab Auric) ....

1.27 "Le voyage en Amérique" (c1951, Lavorelle; 2pf) ....

1a. SELECTIONS FROM STAGE WORKS (Nos. of sections in The Gramophone)

1a.7 "Les biches," ballet: ....
1. "Ouverture"
2. "Rondeau"
3. "Chanson dansée": "Qu'est-ce qu'amour"
4. "Adagietto"
5. "Jeu"
6. "Rag-mazurka"
7. "Andantino"
8. "Petite chanson dansée": "J'ai un joli laurier"
9. "Final"

1a.10 "Les animaux modèles," ballet: ....
1. "Le petit jour"
2. "L'ours et les deux compagnons"
3. "La cigale et la fourmi"
4. "Le lion amoureux"
5. "L'homme entre deux âges et ses deux maîtresses"
6. "La mort et le bûcheron"
7. "Les deux coqs"
8. "Les repas de midi"

2. ORCHESTRAL WORKS

2.1	"Le gendarme incompris," suite (c1921, from incid music): No.1 "Overture" ....
2.2	No.2 "Madrigal"
2.3	No.3 "Finale"
2.4	"Suite française: d'après Claude Gervaise" (c1935; winds, perc & hpd): No.1 "Bransle de Bourgogne" ....
2.5	No.2 "Pavane"
2.6	No.3 "Petite marche militaire"
2.7	No.4 "Complainte"
2.8	No.5 "Bransle de Champagne"
2.9	No.6 "Sicilienne"
2.10	No.7 "Carillon"
2.11	"Deux marches et un intermède" (c1937; chamber orch, for Paris Exhibition of 1937): No.1 "Marche 1889"
2.12	No.2 "Intermède champêtre"
2.13	No.3 "Marche 1937"
2.14	"Les biches," suite (c1939–40; reorchd from ballet; also see for pf): No.1 "Rondeau" ....
2.15	No.2 "Adagietto"
2.16	No.3 "Rag-mazurka"
2.17	No.4 "Andantino"
2.18	No.5 "Final"
2.19	"Les animaux modèles," suite (c1942, from ballet): No.1 "Le petit jour" ....
2.20	No.2 "Le lion amoureux"
2.21	No.3 "L'momme entre deux âges et ses deux maîtresses"
2.22	No.4 "La mort et le bûcheron"
2.23	No.5 "Les deux coqs"
2.24	No.6 "Le repas de midi"
2.25	"Sinfonietta" (c1947) ....
2.26	"Matelote provençale," for collab work: La guirlande de Campra (c1952): ....
	"La guirlande de Campra," other Nos: . *"Écossaise" (c by Auric)*
	. *"Toccata sur un thème de Campra" (c by Honegger)*
	. *"Sarabande et Farandole" (c by Daniel-Lesur)*
	. *"Canarie" (c by Roland-Manuel)*
	. *"Variation" (c by Sauguet)*
	. *"Sarabande Campra" (c by Tailleferre)*
2.27	"Bucolique," for collab work: Variations sur le nom de Marguérite Long (c1954) ....

3. CONCERTOS, SOLO INSTR & ORCH

3.1	"Concert champêtre" (c1927–8; hpd & orch; vers for pf & orch p1934) ....
3.2	Double Piano Concerto in D minor (c1932)
3.3	Organ Concerto in G minor (c1938; org, strings & timp) ....
3.4	Piano Concerto in C-sharp minor (c1949) ....

4. CHAMBER MUSIC

3 or more insts:

4.1	"Sonata" (c1922, r1945; hn, tpt & trbn; red for pf 1925) ....
4.2	Trio (c1926; ob, bn & pf) ....
4.3	Sextet (c1932–9; pf & wind qnt) ....

Violin Sonatas:

4.4	Violin Sonata (c1942–3, r1949, to the memory of F. Garcia Lorca) ....

Other 2 insts:

4.5	"Sonata" (c1918, r1945; 2cl; red for pf) ....
4.6	"Sonata" (c1922, r1945; cl & bn; red for pf 1925) ....
4.7	"Villanelle" (c1934; pipe/fl & pf) ....
4.8	Cello Sonata (c1948) ....
4.9	Flute Sonata (c1956) ....
4.10	"Élégie" (c1957; hn & pf) ....
4.11	Clarinet Sonata (c1962) ....
4.12	Oboe Sonata (c1962) ....

1 instr:

4.13	"Sarabande" (c1960; gui) ....

5. PIANO

Improvisations:

Nocturnes:

Other:

5.94   "Capriccio" (p1952, after Finale of cantata: Le bal masqué; also see: Caprice for pf) ....
5.95   "Sonata" (c1952–3) ....
5.96   "Élégie" (en accords alternés) (c1959) ....

6. CHURCH MUSIC

6.1   "Litanies à la Vierge noire" (c1936; fem ch/child ch & org; vers for ch & orch) ....
6.2   Mass in G major (c1937; ch) ....
6.3   "Quatre motets pour un temps de pénitence" (ch): 1. "Timor et tremor" (c1939) ....
6.4   2. "Vinea mea electa" (c1938)
6.5   3. "Tenebrae factae sunt" (c1938)
6.6   4. "Tristis est anima mea" (c1938)
6.7   "Exultate Deo," motet pour les fêtes solennelles (c1941; ch) ....
6.8   "Salve Regina" (c1941; ch) ....
6.9   "Quatre petites prières de Saint François d'Assise" (c1948; m ch): 1. "Salut, Dame Sainte" ....
6.10   2. "Tout puissant, très saint"
6.11   3. "Seigneur, je vous en prie"
6.12   4. "O mes très chers frères" (w/ T)
6.13   "Stabat Mater" (c1950; S, ch & orch) ....
6.14   "Quatre motets pour le temps de Noël" (ch): 1. "O magnum mysterium" (c1952) ....
6.15   2. "Quem vidistis pastores" (c1951)
6.16   3. "Videntes stellam" (c1951)
6.17   4. "Hodie Christus natus est" (c1952)
6.18   "Ave Verum Corpus," motet (c1952; S, mS, A) ....
6.19   "Laudes de Saint Antoine de Padoue" (m ch): 1. "O Jésu" (c1957) ....
6.20   2. "O Proles" (c1958)
6.21   3. "Laus Regi" (c1959)
6.22   4. "Si quaeris" (c1959)
6.23   "Gloria" (c1959; S, ch & orch): ....
        1. "Gloria in excelsis Deo"
        2. "Laudamus te"
        3. "Domine Deus"
        4. "Domine Fili unigenite"
        5. "Domine Deus, Agnus Dei"
        6. "Qui sedes ad dexteram Patris"
6.24   "Sept répons des ténèbres" (c1961; child S, m & child ch & orch): 1. "Una hora non potuistis vigilare mecum"
6.25   2. "Judas, mercator pessimus"
6.26   3. "Jesum tradidit"
6.27   4. "Caligaverunt oculi mei"
6.28   5. "Tenebrae factae sunt"
6.29   6. "Sepulto Domino"
6.30   7. "Ecce quomodo moritur justus"

7. OTHER CHORAL WORKS

7.1   "Chanson à boire" (c1922, 17th cent text; m ch, for Harvard Glee Club) ....
7.2   "Sept chansons" (c1936; ch): 1. "Blanche neige" (Apollinaire) ....
7.3   2. "A peine défigurée" (Éluard)
7.4   3. "Pour une nuit nouvelle" (Éluard)
7.5   4. "Tous les droits" (Éluard)
7.6   5. "Belle et ressemblante" (Éluard)
7.7   6. "Marie" (Apollinaire)
7.8   7. "Luire" (Éluard)
7.9   . "La reine de Saba" (Legrand) (incl in 1st performance, replaced with: Blanche neige)
7.10   "Petites voix" (c1936, Ley; child ch): 1. "La petite fille sage" ....
7.11   2. "Le chien perdu"
7.12   3. "En rentrant de l'école"
7.13   4. "Le petit garçon malade"
7.14   5. "Le hérisson"
7.15   "Sécheresses," cantata (c1937, James; ch & orch): ....
        1. "Les sauterelles"
        2. "Le village abandonné"
        3. "Le faux avenir"
        4. "Le squelette de la mer"
7.16   "Figure humaine," cantata (c1943, Éluard; d ch): ....
        1. "De tous les printemps du monde"
        2. "En chantant, les servantes s'élancent"
        3. "Aussi bas que le silence"
        4. "Toi, ma patiente"
        5. "Riant du ciel et des planètes"
        6. "Le jour m'étonne et la nuit me fait peur"
        7. "La menace sous le ciel rouge"
        8. "Liberté" (Éluard)

7.17   "Un soir de neige," chamber cantata (c1944, Éluard; 6vv/ch): ....
                         1. "De grands cuillers de neige"
                         2. "La bonne neige"
                         3. "Bois meurti"
                         4. "La nuit, le froid, le solitude"
7.18   "Chansons françaises" (ch): 1. "Margoton va-t-a-l'iau" (c1945) ....
7.19   2. "La belle se siet au pied de la tour" (c1945)
7.20   3. "Pilons l'orge" (c1945)
7.21   4. "Clic-clac, dansez sabots" (c1945)
7.22   5. "C'est la petit' fille du prince" (c1946)
7.23   6. "La belle si nous étions" (c1946)
7.24   7. "Ah! Mon beau laboureur" (c1945)
7.25   8. "Les tisserands" (c1946)

8. VOICE & ORCHESTRA

8.1   "Rapsodie nègre" (c1917, r1933, 'Makoko Kangourou'; Bar, fl, cl, str qt & pf): ....
                         1. "Prélude"
                         2. "Ronde"
                         3. "Honoloulou" (intermède; 1v & pf)
                         4. "Pastorale"
                         5. "Final"
8.2   "Le bal masqué," cantata (c1932, Jacob; Bar/mS & small orch): ....
                         1. "Préambule et air de bravoure"
                         2. "Intermède"
                         3. "Malvina"
                         4. "Bagatelle"
                         5. "La dame aveugle"
                         6. "Finale"
8.3   "La dame de Monte Carlo," monologue lyrique (c1961, Cocteau; S & orch) ....

9. SONGS (w/ pf)

9.1   "Toréador" (chanson hispano-italienne) (c1918, r1932, Cocteau) ....
9.2   "Le bestiaire au cortège d'Orphée" (c1919, Apollinaire; orchd): 1. "Le dromadaire": "Avec ses quatre" ....
9.3   2. "La chèvre du Thibet": "Les poils de cette chèvre"
9.4   3. "La sauterelle": "Voici la fine sauterelle"
9.5   4. "Le dauphin": "Dauphins vous jouez dans la mer"
9.6   5. "L'écrevisse": "Incertitude o! mes délices"
9.7   6. "La carpe": "Dans vos viviers dans vos étangs"
9.8   "Cocardes" (c1919, Cocteau; also w/ ens): 1. "Miel de Narbonne": "Use ton coeur" ....
9.9   2. "Bonne d'enfant": "Técla: notre âge d'or, Pipe, Carnot, Joffre"
9.10   3. "Enfant de trouppe": "Morceau pour piston seul, polka"
9.11   "Poèmes de Ronsard" (c1924–5; orchd vers perf1934): 1. "Attributs": "Les épis sont à Cérès" (c1924) ....
9.12   2. "Le tombeau": "Quand le ciel et mon heure" (c1924)
9.13   3. "Ballet": "Le soir qu'Amour vous fit en la salle descendre" (c1924)
9.14   4. "Je n'ai plus que les os" (c1925)
9.15   5. "A son page": "Fais rafraîchir mon vin de sorte" (c1925)
9.16   "Chansons gaillardes" (c1925–6, anon 17th cent): 1. "La maîtresse volage": "Ma maîtresse volage" ....
9.17   2. "Chanson à boire": "Les rois d'Egypte et de Syrie"
9.18   3. "Madrigal": "Vous êtes belle comme un ange"
9.19   4. "Invocation aux Parques": "Je jure, tant que je vivrai"
9.20   5. "Couplets bachiques": "Je suis tant que dure le jour"
9.21   6. "L'offrande": "Au dieu d'Amour une pucelle"
9.22   7. "La belle jeunesse": "Il faut s'aimer toujours"
9.23   8. "Sérénade": "Avec une si belle main"
9.24   "Vocalise" (c1927) ....
9.25   "Airs chantés" (c1927–8, Moréas; orchd): 1. "Air romantique": "J'allais dans la campagne avec le vent" .....
9.26   2. "Air champêtre": "Belle source, je veux me rappeler sans cesse"
9.27   3. "Air grave": "Ah! fuyez à présent, malheureuses pensées!"
9.28   4. "Air vif": "Le trésor du verger et le jardin en fête"
9.29   "Épitaphe": "Belle âme qui fus mon flambeau" (c1930, Malherbe) ....
9.30   "Trois poèmes de L. Lalanne" (c1931): 1. "Le présent": "Si tu veux je te donnerai" (Lalanne—pseud of
                                Apollinaire)
9.31   2. "Chanson": "Les myrtilles sont pour la dame" (Laurencin)
9.32   3. "Hier": "Hier, c'est ce chapeau fané" (Laurencin)
9.33   "Quatre poèmes" (c1931, Apollinaire): 1. "L'anguille": "Jeanne Houhou la très gentille" ....
9.34   2. "Carte postale": "L'ombre de la très douce est évoquée ici"
9.35   3. "Avant le cinéma": "Et puis ce soir on s'en ira au cinéma"
9.36   4. "1904": "A Strasbourg en 1904"
9.37   "Cinq poèmes" (c1931, Jacob): 1. "Chanson bretonne": "J'ai perdu ma poulette" ....
9.38   2. "Cimetière": "Si mon marin vous le chassez"
9.39   3. "La petite servante": "Préservez-nous du feu et du tonnerre"

9.40   4. "Berceuse": "Ton père est à la messe"
9.41   5. "Souric et Mouric": "Souric et Mouric, rat blanc, souris noire"
9.42   "Huit chansons polonaises" (c1934): 1. "La couronne" (Wianek) ....
9.43   2. "Le départ" (Odjazd)
9.44   3. "Les gars polonais" (Polska młodzież)
9.45   4. "Le dernier mazour" (Ostatni mazur)
9.46   5. "L'adieu" (Pożegnanie)
9.47   6. "Le drapeau blanc" (Biała chorągiewka)
9.48   7. "La Vistule" (Wisła)
9.49   8. "Le lac" (Jezioro)
9.50   "Quatre chansons pour enfants" (c1934): 1. "Nous voulons une petite soeur" (Nohain) ....
9.51   2. "La tragique histoire du petit René" (Jaboune)
9.52   3. "Le petit garçon trop bien portant" (Jaboune)
9.53   4. "Monsieur sans souci" (Jaboune)
9.54   "Cinq poèmes" (c1935, Éluard): 1. "Peut-il se reposer?" ....
9.55   2. "Il la prend dans ses bras"
9.56   3. "Plume d'eau claire"
9.57   4. "Rôdeuse au front de verre"
9.58   5. "Amoureuses": "Elles ont les épaules hautes et l'air malin"
9.59   "A sa guitare": "Ma guitare, je te chante" (c1935, Ronsard; w/ gui/harp; from: La reine Margot; orchd) ....
9.60   "Tel jour, telle nuit," cycle (Éluard): 1. "Bonne journée": "Bonne journée j'ai revu je n'oublie pas" (c1937) ...
9.61   2. "Une ruine coquille vide" (c1936)
9.62   3. "Le front comme un drapeau perdu" (c1937)
9.63   4. "Une roulotte couverte en tuiles" (c1936)
9.64   5. "A toutes brides" (c1937)
9.65   6. "Une herbe pauvre" (c1936)
9.66   7. "Je n'ai envie que de t'aimer" (c1936)
9.67   8. "Figure de force brûlante et farouche" (c1937)
9.68   9. "Nous avons fait la nuit" (c1937)
9.69   "Trois poèmes" (c1937, Vilmorin): 1. "Le garçon de Liège": "Un garçon de conte de fée" ....
9.70   2. "Au-delà": "Eau-de-vie! Au-delà! A l'heure du plaisir"
9.71   3. "Aux officiers de la garde blanche": "Officiers de la Garde Blanche"
9.72   "Trois poèmes" (c1938, Apollinaire): 1. "Dans le jardin d'Anna": "Certes si nous avions vécu" ....
9.73   2. "Allons plus vite": "Et le soir vient"
9.74   "Miroirs brûlants" (Éluard): 1. "Tu vois le feu du soir" (c1938) ....
9.75   2. "Je nominerai ton front" (c1939)
9.76   "Le portrait": "Belle, méchante, menteuse, injuste" (c1938, Colette) ....
9.77   "La grenouillère": "Au bord de l'île on voit" (c1938, Apollinaire) ....
9.78   "Priez pour paix": "Priez pour paix, douce Vierge Marie" (c1938, d'Orléans) ....
9.79   "Ce doux petit visage": "Rien que ce doux petit visage" (c1939, Éluard) ....
9.80   "Bleuet": "Jeune homme de vingt ans" (c1939, Apollinaire) ....
9.81   "Fiançailles pour rire" (c1939, Vilmorin): 1. "La dame d'André": "André ne connaît pas la dame" ....
9.82   2. "Dans l'herbe": "Je ne peux plus rien dire"
9.83   3. "Il vole": "En allant se coucher le soleil"
9.84   4. "Mon cadavre est doux comme un gant"
9.85   5. "Violon": "Couple amoureux aux accents méconnus"
9.86   6. "Fleurs": "Fleurs promises, fleurs tenues dans tes bras"
9.87   "Banalités" (c1940, Apollinaire): 1. "Chanson d'Orkenise": "Par les portes d'Orkenise" ....
9.88   2. "Hôtel": "Ma chambre a la forme d'une cage"
9.89   3. "Fagnes de Wallonie": "Tant de tristesses plénières"
9.90   4. "Voyage à Paris": "Ah! la charmante chose"
9.91   5. "Sanglots": "Notre amour est réglé par les calmes étoiles"
9.92   "Les chemins de l'amour": "Les chemins qui vont" (c1940, Anouilh, = Valse chantée from: Léocadia; orchd)
9.93   "Colloque," duet (c1940, Valéry; S, Bar & pf) ....
9.94   "Chansons villageoises" (c1942, Fombeure; orchd p1943): 1. "Chanson du clair tamis": "Où le bedeau" ....
9.95   2. "Les gars qui vont à la fête"
9.96   3. "C'est le joli printemps"
9.97   4. "Le mendiant": "Jean Martin prit sa besace"
9.98   5. "Chanson de la fille frivole": "Ah dit la fille frivole"
9.99   6. "Le retour du sergent": "Le sergent s'en revient de guerre"
9.100   "Métamorphoses" (c1943, Vilmorin): 1. "Reine des mouettes": "Reine des mouettes, mon orpheline" ....
9.101   2. "C'est ainsi que tu es": "Ta chair, d'âme mêlée"
9.102   3. "Paganini": "Violon hippocampe et sirène"
9.103   "Deux poèmes" (c1943, Aragon): 1. "C": "J'ai traversé les ponts de Cé" ....
9.104   2. "Fêtes galantes": "On voit des marquis sur des bicyclettes"
9.105   "Montparnasse": "O porte de l'hôtel avec deux plantes vertes" (c1941–5, Apollinaire) ....
9.106   "Hyde Park": "Les faiseurs de religion" (c1945, Apollinaire) ....
9.107   "Deux mélodies" (c1946, Apollinaire): 1. "Le pont": "Deux dames le long du fleuve" ....
9.108   2. "Un poème": "Il est entré Il s'est assis"
9.109   "Paul et Virginie": "Ciel! les colonies" (c1946, Radiguet) ....
9.110   "Trois Chansons de F. Garcia Lorca" (c1947): 1. "L'enfant muet": "L'enfant cherche sa voix" ....
9.111   2. "Adelina à la promenade": "La mer n'a pas d'oranges"
9.112   3. "Chansons de l'oranger sec": "Bûcheron abat mon ombre"
9.113   "... mais mourir": "Mains agitées aux grimaces nouées" (c1947, Éluard) ....
9.114   "Hymne": "Sombre nuit, aveugles ténèbres" (c1947, Racine from Roman Breviary) ....

9.115   "Le disparu": "Je n'aime plus la rue St Martin" (c1947, Desnos) ....
9.116   "Main dominée par le coeur" (c1947, Éluard) ....
9.117   "Calligrammes," cycle (c1948, Apollinaire): 1. "L'espionne": "Pâle espionne de l'Amour" ....
9.118   2. "Mutation": "Une femme qui pleurait"
9.119   3. "Vers le sud": "Zénith Tous ces regrets"
9.120   4. "Il pleut": "Il pleut des voix de femmes"
9.121   5. "La grâce exilée": "Va-t'en va-t'en mon arc-en-ciel"
9.122   6. "Aussi bien que les cigales": "Gens du midi gens du midi vous n'aves donc pas regardé
         les cigales"
9.123   7. "Voyage": "Adieu amour nuage qui fuit"
9.124   "Les bijoux aux poitrines," mazurka for collab: Mouvements du coeur (c1949, Vilmorin, ded to Chopin): .....
         "Mouvements du coeur," other Nos: . *"Prélude et Postlude: polonaise" (c by Sauguet)*
                                          . *"Valse" (c by Auric)*
                                          . *"Scherzo impromptu" (c by Françaix)*
                                          . *"Étude" (c by Preger)*
                                          . *"Ballade nocturne," Op.296 (c by Milhaud)*
9.125   "La fraîcheur et le feu" (c1950, Éluard): 1. "Rayon des yeux" ....
9.126   2. "Le matin les branches attisent"
9.127   3. "Tout disparut"
9.128   4. "Dans les ténèbres du jardin"
9.129   5. "Unis la fraîcheur et le feu"
9.130   6. "Homme au sourire tendre"
9.131   7. "La grande rivière qui va"
9.132   "Parisiana" (c1954, Jacob): 1. "Jouer du bugle": "Les trois dames qui jouaient du bugle" ....
9.133   2. "Vous n'écrivez plus?": "M'as-tu connu marchand d'journaux"
9.134   "Rosemonde": "Longtemps au pied du perron" (c1954, Apollinaire) ....
9.135   "Le travail du peintre" (c1956, Éluard): 1. "Pablo Picasso": "Entoure ce citron de blanc d'oeuf informe" ......
9.136   2. "Marc Chagall": "Ane ou vache coq ou cheval"
9.137   3. "Georges Braque": "Un oiseau s'envole"
9.138   4. "Juan Gris": "De jour merci de nuit prends garde"
9.139   5. "Paul Klee": "Sur la pente fatale le voyageur profite"
9.140   6. "Joan Miró": "Soleil de proie prisonnier de ma tête"
9.141   7. "Jacques Villon": "Irrémédiable vie"
9.142   "Deux mélodies 1956" (c1956): 1. "La souris": "Belles journées, souris du temps" (Apollinaire) ....
9.143   2. "Nuage": "J'ai vu reluire en un coin de mes âges" (Beylié)
9.144   "Dernier poème": "J'ai rêvé tellement fort de toi" (c1956, Desnos) ....
9.145   "Une chanson de porcelaine" (c1958, Éluard) ....
9.146   "La courte paille" (c1960, Carême): 1. "Le sommeil": "Le sommeil est en voyage" ....
9.147   2. "Quelle aventure!": "Une puce, dans sa voiture"
9.148   3. "La reine de coeur": "Mollement accoudée a ses vitres de lune"
9.149   4. "Ba, be, bi, bo, bu ...": "Ba, be, bi, bo, bu, bé! Le chat a mis ses bottes"
9.150   5. "Les anges musiciens": "Sur les fils de la pluie"
9.151   6. "Le carafon": "Pourquoi, se plaignait la carafe"
9.152   7. "Lune d'avril": "Lune, belle lune, lune d'avril"
9.153   "Fancy": "Tell me where is fancy bred" (c1962, from Shakespeare's The Merchant of Venice,
         for Classical Songs for Children) (also see song c by Castelnuovo-Tedesco Op.24/I/2 & choral
         works c by Britten & Kodály) ....

10. ARRANGEMENTS OF WORKS OF OTHERS

10.1   Satie: 3 works for pf (orchd1939 as: Deux préludes posthumes et 3e gnossienne): No.1 "Fête donnée
         par des chevaliers normands en l'honneur d'une jeune demoiselle" ....
         No.2 "1er prélude du Nazaréen"
         No.3 "3ème gnossienne"

* * * * *

1. STAGE WORKS

Operas:

1.1	"The Giant," 3 acts (c1900)	
1.2	"Desert Islands" (c1900–2, inc, extant: Overture & 3 scenes of Act I)................................	
1.3	"A Feast in Time of Plague," 1 act (c1903, r1908–9, after Pushkin)	
1.4	"Undina," 4 acts (c1904–7, Kilstett after Motte Fouqué)...	
1.5	"Maddalena," 1 act (c1911–13, Lieven, inc; Scenes 2–4 orchd Downes) Op.13
1.6	"The Gambler," 4 acts (c1915–17, r1927–8, Prokofiev after Dostoyevsky)....................... Op.24
1.7	"The Love for Three Oranges," 4 acts (c1919, Prokofiev after Gozzi)............................. Op.33
1.8	"The Fiery Angel" (L'ange de feu), 5 acts (c1919–23, r1927, Prokofiev after Bryusov) Op.37
1.9	"Semyon Kotko," 5 acts (c1939, Katayev & Prokofiev after Katayev's story) Op.81
1.10	"Betrothal in a Monastery" (The Duenna), 4 acts (c1940, Prokofiev after Sheridan's play) Op.86
1.11	"Khan Buzay" (c from 1942, inc) ....
1.12	"War & Peace," 5 acts (c1941–3, Prokofiev & M. Mendelson-Prokofiev after Tolstoy; 2nd vers 1955) Op.91
1.13	"The Story of a Real Man," 4 acts (c1947–8, M. Mendelson-Prokofiev after Polevoy's novel) Op.117
1.14	"Distant Seas," comic opera (c from 1948, after Dikhovichniy, inc) ....

Ballets:

1.15	*"Ala and Lolli" (c1914–15, withdrawn)* ....
1.16	"Chout" (The Tale of the Buffoon), 6 scenes (c1915, r1920, Prokofiev after Afanasyev)............ Op.21
1.17	"Trapeze," 1 scene (c1924; used in: Quintet in G minor, Op.39).....................................
1.18	"The Steel Step" (Le pas d'acier), 2 scenes (c1925–6, Prokofiev & Yakulov) Op.41
1.19	"The Prodigal Son," 3 scenes (c1928–9, Kokhno)... Op.46
1.20	"On the Dnieper" (Sur le Borysthène), 2 scenes (c1930–1, Lifar & Prokofiev)...................... Op.51
1.21	"Romeo and Juliet," 4 acts (c1935–6, r1939 & 1946, Radlov & others after Shakespeare; filmed 1955)
	(also see opera c by Gounod, incid music c by Kabalevsky, Milhaud Op.161 & R. Strauss AV86,
	film score c by Khachaturian, symphony c by Berlioz Op.17, H79) Op.64
1.22	"Cinderella," 3 acts (c1940–4, Volkov) (also see operas c by Holst, Massenet & Rossini) Op.87
1.23	"The Tale of the Stone Flower," 4 acts (c1948–53, Lavrovsky, M. Mendelson-Prokofiev after
	Bazhov).. Op.118

Incid music:

1.24	"Egyptian Nights" (c1934, Pushkin, Shakespeare, Shaw) ....
1.25	"Boris Godunov" (c1936, Pushkin) Op.70bis
1.26	"Eugene Onegin" (c1936, Pushkin) Op.71
1.27	"Hamlet" (c1937–8, Shakespeare) (also see incid music c by Honegger H190, Milhaud Op.200,
	Moniuszko, Shostakovich Op.32 & Tchaikovsky Op.67a) Op.77

Film:

1.28	*"Lieutenant Kijé" (The Czar Wants to Sleep) (c1933, unrealized; see orch suite Op.60)* ....
1.29	*"The Queen of Spades" (c1936, after Pushkin, unrealized)* *Op.70*
1.30	"Alexander Nevsky" (c1938, Eisenstein; see cantata Op.78 & songs Op.78bis)...................
1.31	"Lermontov" (c1941; see orch work Op.110/3 & pf works Op.96/2,3) ....
1.32	"Kotovsky" (c1942) ....
1.33	"The Partisans in the Ukrainian Steppes" (c1942)..
1.34	*"Tonya" (c1942, unrealized)* ....
1.35	"Ivan the Terrible," 2 parts (c1942–5, Eisenstein; see arr as oratorio 1961) Op.116

1a. SELECTIONS FROM STAGE WORKS (Nos. of sections in The Gramophone)

1a.21   "Romeo and Juliet," ballet:... Op.64

I: 1. "Introduction"
2. "Romeo"
3. "The street awakens"
4. "Morning Dance"
5. "The Quarrel"
6. "The Fight"
7. "The Prince gives his order"
8. "Interlude"
9. "Preparing for the Ball" (Juliet and the Nurse)
10. "Juliet as a young girl"
11. "Arrival of the guests" (Minuet)
12. "Masks"
13. "Dance of the Knights"
14. "Juliet's Variation"
15. "Mercutio"
16. "Madrigal"
17. "Tybalt recognizes Romeo"
18. "Departure of the guests" (Gavotte)

19. "Balcony scene"
20. "Romeo's Variation"
21. "Love Dance"
II: 22. "Folk Dance"
23. "Romeo and Mercutio"
24. "Dance of the five couples"
25. "Dance with the five mandolins"
26. "The Nurse"
27. "The Nurse gives Romeo the note from Juliet"
28. "Romeo with Friar Laurence"
29. "Juliet with Friar Laurence"
30. "The people continue to make merry"
31. "A Folk Dance again"
32. "Tybalt meets Mercutio"
33. "Tybalt and Mercutio fight"
34. "Mercutio dies"
35. "Romeo decides to avenge Mercutio's death"
36. "Finale"
III: 37. "Introduction"
38. "Romeo and Juliet" (Juliet's bedroom)
39. "The last farewell"
40. "The Nurse"
41. "Juliet refuses to marry Paris"
42. "Juliet alone"
43. "Interlude"
44. "At Friar Laurence's"
45. "Interlude"
46. "Again in Juliet's bedroom"
47. "Juliet alone"
48. "Morning Serenade"
49. "Dance of the girls with the lilies"
50. "At Juliet's bedside"
Epilogue: 51. "Juliet's funeral"
52. "Death of Juliet"

1a.22   "Cinderella," ballet: Op.87
I: 1. "Introduction"
2. "Pas de châle"
3. "Cinderella"
4. "The Father"
5. "The Fairy Godmother"
6. "The Sisters' new clothes"
7. "The Dancing Lesson"
8. "Departure for the Ball"
9. "Cinderella dreams of the Ball"
10. "Gavotte"
11. "Fairy Godmother returns"
12. "Spring Fairy"
13. "Summer Fairy"
14. "Grasshoppers and Dragonflies"
15. "Autumn Fairy"
16. "Winter Fairy"
17. "Interrupted departure"
18. "Clock Scene"
19. "Cinderella's departure for the Ball"
II: 20. "Dance of the Courtiers"
21. "Court Dance" (Passepied)
22. "Cavaliers' Dance"
23. "Skinny's variation"
24. "Dumpy's variation"
25. "Court Dance" (repeat)
26. "Mazurka and Entrance of the Prince"
27. "Dance of the Prince's Companion"
28. "Mazurka"
29. "Cinderella's arrival at the Ball"
30. "Grand Waltz"
31. "Promenade"
32. "Cinderella's variation"
33. "The Prince's variation"
34. "Refreshments for the Guests"
35. "Duet of the Sisters with their Oranges"
36. "Duet of the Prince and Cinderella"
37. "Waltz-Coda"
38. "Midnight"

III: 39. "The Prince and the Shoemakers"
       40. "First Galop"
       41. "Temptation"
       42. "Second Galop"
       43. "Oriental Dance"
       44. "Third Galop"
       45. "Cinderella awakes"
       46. "The Morning after the Ball"
       47. "The Prince's visit"
       48. "The Prince finds Cinderella"
       49. "Slow Waltz"
       50. "Amoroso"

2. SYMPHONIES

2.1	Symphony in G major (c1902, juvenilia)	
2.2	Symphony in E minor (c1908, juvenilia; used in: Piano Sonata No.4 in C minor, Op.29)	
2.3	Symphony No.1 in D major, "Classical" (c1916–7)	Op.25
2.4	Symphony No.2 in D minor (c1924–5)	Op.40
2.5	Symphony No.3 in C minor (c1928, from opera: The Fiery Angel, Op.37)	Op.44
2.6	Symphony No.4 in C major (c1929–30, from ballet: The Prodigal Son, Op.46)	Op.47
2.7	Symphony No.5 in B-flat major (c1944)	Op.100
2.8	Symphony No.6 in E-flat minor (c1944–7)	Op.111
2.9	2nd Version of Sym No.4 in C major, Op.47 (c1947)	Op.112
2.10	Symphony No.7 in C-sharp minor (c1951–2; arr for pf duet 1954)	Op.131
2.11	*2nd Version of Sym No.2 in D minor, Op.40 (unrealized)*	*Op.136*

3. ORCHESTRAL SUITES

3.1	"Scythian Suite" (revised from ballet: Ala and Lolli): No.1 "The Adoration of Veles and Ala"	Op.20
3.2	No.2 "The Enemy God and the Dance of the Black Spirits Night"	
3.3	No.3 "The Glorious Departure of Lolli and the Procession of the Sun"	
3.4	"Chout" (The Tale of the Buffoon), suite (c1920, from ballet): No.1 "Le bouffon et sa bouffonne"	Op.21bis
3.5	No.2 "Danse des bouffonnes"	
3.6	No.3 "Les bouffons tuent leurs bouffonnes" (fugue)	
3.7	No.4 "Le bouffon travesti en jeune femme"	
3.8	No.5 "3ième entr'acte"	
3.9	No.6 "Danse des filles des bouffons"	
3.10	No.7 "L'arrivée du marchand, la danse des révérences et le choix de la fiancée"	
3.11	No.8 "Dans la chambre à coucher du marchand"	
3.12	No.9 "La jeune femme est devenue chèvre"	
3.13	No.10 "5ième entr'acte et l'enterrement de la chèvre"	
3.14	No.11 "La querelle du bouffon avec la marchand"	
3.15	No.12 "Danse finale"	
3.16	"The Love for Three Oranges," suite (c1919, r1924, from opera Op.33): No.1 "Ridiculous fellows"	Op.33bis
3.17	No.2 "Magician Celio and Fata Morgana play cards" (Infernal scene)	
3.18	No.3 "March"	
3.19	No.4 "Scherzo"	
3.20	No.5 "The Prince and the Princess"	
3.21	No.6 "Flight"	
3.22	"The Steel Step" (Le pas d'acier), suite (c1926, from ballet Op.41)	Op.41bis
3.23	"The Prodigal Son," suite (c1929, from ballet Op.46)	Op.46bis
3.24	"Quatre portraits & dénouement," suite (c1931, from opera: The Gambler, Op.24): No.1 "Alexis"	Op.49
3.25	No.2 "La grand'mère"	
3.26	No.3 "Le général"	
3.27	No.4 "Pauline"	
3.28	No.5 "Dénouement"	
3.29	"On the Dnieper," suite (c1933, from ballet Op.51): No.1 "Prelude"	Op.51bis
3.30	No.2 "Variation of the First Dancer"	
3.31	No.3 "The Betrothal"	
3.32	No.4 "The Quarrel"	
3.33	No.5 "Scene"	
3.34	No.6 "Epilogue"	
3.35	"Lieutenant Kijé," suite (c1934; w/ Bar ad lib, based on film): No.1 "Birth of Kijé"	Op.60
3.36	No.2 "Romance"	
3.37	No.3 "Kijé's Wedding"	
3.38	No.4 "Troika"	
3.39	No.5 "Burial of Kijé"	
3.40	"Egyptian Nights," suite (c1934, from incid music)	Op.61
3.41	"Romeo and Juliet" Suite No.1 (c1936, from ballet Op.64): No.1 "Folk Dance"	Op.64bis
3.42	No.2 "Scene" (The Street Awakens)	
3.43	No.3 "Madrigal"	
3.44	No.4 "Minuet" (The Arrival of the Guests)	

3.45	No.5 "Masks" (Romeo and Mercutio masked)
3.46	No.6 "Balcony Scene" (Romeo and Juliet)
3.47	No.7 "Death of Tybalt" (Funeral cortège of Tybalt's corpse)
3.48	"Romeo and Juliet" Suite No.2 (c1936, from ballet Op.64): No.1 "Montagues and Capulets" Op.64ter
3.49	No.2 "The Young Juliet"
3.50	No.3 "Friar Laurence"
3.51	No.4 "Dance"
3.52	No.5 "Romeo and Juliet Before Parting"
3.53	No.6 "Dance of the Maids with Lilies" (Dance of the Antilese girls)
3.54	No.7 "Romeo at Juliet's Grave"
3.55	"Summer Day," suite (c1941; small orch, arr from: Music for children, Op.65): No.1 "Morning" Op.65bis
3.56	No.2 "Tag"
3.57	No.3 "Waltz"
3.58	No.4 "Repentance"
3.59	No.5 "March"
3.60	No.6 "Evening"
3.61	No.7 "The Moon Sails O'er the Meadows"
3.62	"Semyon Kotko," suite (c1941, from opera Op.81): No.1 "Introduction" Op.81bis
3.63	No.2 "Semyon and His Mother"
3.64	No.3 "The Betrothal"
3.65	No.4 "The Southern Night"
3.66	No.5 "Execution"
3.67	No.6 "The Village is Burning"
3.68	No.7 "Funeral"
3.69	No.8 "Ours Have Come"
3.70	"The Year 1941," suite (c1941): No.1 "In Battle" Op.90
3.71	No.2 "Night"
3.72	No.3 "For the Brotherhood of Nations"
3.73	"Romeo and Juliet" Suite No.3 (c1946, from ballet Op.64): No.1 "Romeo at the Fountain" Op.101
3.74	No.2 "Morning Dance"
3.75	No.3 "Juliet Prepares for the Ball"
3.76	No.4 "The Nurse"
3.77	No.5 "Aubade"
3.78	No.6 "The Death of Juliet"
3.79	"Cinderella" Suite No.1 (c1946, from ballet Op.87): No.1 "Introduction" Op.107
3.80	No.2 "Pas de Chat"
3.81	No.3 "Quarrel"
3.82	No.4 "Fairy Godmother and Fairy Winter"
3.83	No.5 "Mazurka"
3.84	No.6 "Cinderella Goes to the Ball"
3.85	No.7 "Cinderella's Waltz"
3.86	No.8 "Midnight"
3.87	"Cinderella" Suite No.2 (c1946, from ballet Op.87): No.1 "Dancing Lesson and Gavotte" Op.108
3.88	No.2 "Spring Fairy"
3.89	No.3 "Cinderella at the Castle"
3.90	"Cinderella" Suite No.3 (c1946, from ballet Op.87): No.1 "Pavane" Op.109
3.91	No.2 "Cinderella and the Prince" (Adagio)
3.92	No.3 "The Three Oranges" (from opera: The Love for 3 Oranges, Op.33)
3.93	No.4 "Fantasy"
3.94	No.5 "Orientalia"
3.95	No.6 "The Prince Finds his Cinderella"
3.96	No.7 "Lingering Waltz"
3.97	No.8 "Amoroso"
3.98	"Waltz Suite" (c1946): No.1 "Since We Met" (from opera: War & Peace, Op.91) Op.110
3.99	No.2 "Cinderella in the Palace" (from ballet: Cinderella, Op.87)
3.100	No.3 "Mephisto Waltz" (from film: Lermontov)
3.101	No.4 "End of the Fairy Tale" (from ballet: Cinderella, Op.87)
3.102	No.5 "Waltz for the New Year's Ball" (from opera: War & Peace, Op.91)
3.103	No.6 "Happiness" (from ballet: Cinderella, Op.87)
3.104	"Summer Night," suite (c1950, from opera: The Duenna, Op.86): No.1 "Introduction" Op.123
3.105	No.2 "Serenade"
3.106	No.3 "Minuet" (ed Blok)
3.107	No.4 "Dreams"
3.108	No.5 "Dance"
3.109	"Wedding Suite" (c1951, from ballet: The Stone Flower, Op.118): No.1 "Amorous Dance" Op.126
3.110	No.2 "Dance of the Fiancée's Girl-friends"
3.111	No.3 "Maidens' Dance"
3.112	No.4 "Ceremonial Dance"
3.113	No.5 "Wedding Dance"
3.114	*"The Mistress of Copper Mountain," suite (from ballet: The Stone Flower, Op.118, project)* *Op.129*

4. OTHER ORCHESTRAL WORKS

4.1	"Sinfonietta," in A major (c1909, r1914–15; r1929 as Op.48) Op.5

4.2	"Dreams," sym poem (c1910)	Op.6
4.3	"Autumnal Sketch" (c1910, r1915,1934; small orch)	Op.8
4.4	"Andante" (c1934, from: Pf Sonata No.4 in C minor, Op.29)	Op.29bis
4.5	"Overture on Hebrew Themes" (c1934, after chamber work)	Op.34bis
4.6	"Overture," in B-flat major, "American" (c1926; 17 insts; see r vers for full orch, Op.42bis)	Op.42
4.7	"Overture," in B-flat major, "American" (= Op.42 r for full orch 1928)	Op.42bis
4.8	"Divertissement" (c1925–9; also see Op.43bis for pf)	Op.43
4.9	Revision of "Sinfonietta," in A major, Op.5 (r1929; used in pf music Op.5/6)	Op.48
4.10	"Andante" (c1930; strings, from: Str Qt No.1 in B minor, Op.50)	Op.50bis
4.11	"Symphonic Song" (c1933)	Op.57
4.12	"4 Marches" (c1935–7; brass band)	Op.69
4.13	"Russian Overture" (c1936, r1937)	Op.72
4.14	"Symphonic March," in B-flat major (c1941)	Op.88
4.15	"March," in A-flat major (c ?1941; milit band, after song Op.79/7)	Op.89b
4.16	"March," in B-flat major (c1943–4; milit band)	Op.99
4.17	"Ode to the End of the War," in C major (c1945; 8 harps, 4pf, brass, perc & d basses)	Op.105
4.18	"Thirty Years" (Festive Poem for the 30th Anniversary of October 1917) (c1947)	Op.113
4.19	"Pushkin Waltzes" (c1949): No.1 "Allegro espressivo," in F major	Op.120
4.20	No.2 "Allegro meditativo," in C-sharp minor	
4.21	"Gypsy Fantasy" (c1951, from ballet: The Stone Flower, Op.118)	Op.127
4.22	"Urals Rhapsody" (c1951, from ballet: The Stone Flower, Op.118)	Op.128
4.23	"The Volga Meets the Don," festive poem (c1951)	Op.130

5. CONCERTOS, SOLO INSTR & ORCH

Piano Concertos:

5.1	Piano Concerto No.1 in D-flat major (c1911–2, 1 movt)	Op.10
5.2	Piano Concerto No.2 in G minor (c1912–3, r1923; arr for 2pf)	Op.16
5.3	Piano Concerto No.3 in C major (c1917–21)	Op.26
5.4	Piano Concerto No.4 in B-flat major (c1931, for left hand)	Op.53
5.5	Piano Concerto No.5 in G major (c1931–2)	Op.55
5.6	Piano Concerto No.6 in D minor (c1952; 2pf & strings, inc)	Op.133

Violin Concertos:

5.7	Violin Concerto No.1 in D major (c1916–7)	Op.19
5.8	Violin Concerto No.2 in G minor (c1935)	Op.63

Vc & orch:

5.9	Cello Concerto in E minor (c1933–8; also see: Sinfonia Concertante, Op.125)	Op.58
5.10	"Sinfonia Concertante," in E minor (c1950–1, r1952, after: Vc Conc No.2, Op.58)	Op.125
5.11	*Cello Concertino in G minor (c1952; compl Rostropovich & orchd Kabalevsky)*	*Op.132*

6. STRING QUARTETS

6.1	String Quartet No.1 in B minor (c1930; see orch work Op.50b & pf work Op.52/5)	Op.50
6.2	String Quartet No.2 in F major, "Kabardinian" (c1941, on Kabardinian themes)	Op.92

7. OTHER CHAMBER MUSIC

4 or more insts:

7.1	"Humoresque Scherzo" (p1915; 4bn, after pf work Op.12/9)	Op.12bis
7.2	"Overture on Hebrew Themes," in C minor (c1919; cl, str qt & pf; also see Op.34b)	Op.34
7.3	"Quintet," in G minor (c1924; ob, cl, vn, va & d bass, after music from ballet: Trapeze)	Op.39

Vn & pf:

7.4	Juvenilia	
7.5	Violin Sonata in C minor (c1903, juvenilia)	
7.6	"Little Song," in D minor (c1903, juvenilia)	
7.7	"Little Song" (No.2), in C minor (c1904, juvenilia)	
7.8	"5 Mélodies" (c1925, arr of: Songs without Words, Op.35): No.1 "Andante"	Op.35bis
7.9	No.2 "Lento ma non troppo"	
7.10	No.3 "Animato, ma non allegro"	
7.11	No.4 "Andantino, un poco scherzando"	
7.12	No.5 "Andante non troppo"	
7.13	Violin Sonata No.1 in F minor (c1938–46)	Op.80
7.14	Violin Sonata No.2 in D major (c1944, arr from: Fl Sonata in D major, Op.94)	Op.94bis

Vc & pf:

7.15	"Ballade," in C minor (c1912)	Op.15
7.16	"Adagio" (c1944, arr from ballet: Cinderella, Op.87)	Op.97bis
7.17	Cello Sonata in C major (c1949)	Op.119

Other 2 insts:

7.18	"Sonata," in C major (c1932; 2vn)	Op.56
7.19	Flute Sonata in D major (c1943; arr for vn & pf, Op.94bis)	Op.94

Vc solo:

7.20	"Sonata," in D major (c1947; unison vns/vn)	Op.115
7.21	"Sonata," in C-sharp minor (compl Blok)	Op.134

8. PIANO SONATAS

Juvenilia:

8.1	Piano Sonata in B-flat major (c1903–4)
8.2	Piano Sonata No.2 in F minor (c1907; reworked in: Pf Sonata No.1 in F minor, Op.1)
8.3	Piano Sonata No.3 in A minor (c1907; reworked in: Pf Sonata No.3 in A minor, Op.28)
8.4	*Piano Sonata No.4 (c ?1907–8, lost)*
8.5	Piano Sonata No.5 (c1908; reworked in: Pf Sonata No.4 in C minor, Op.29)
8.6	*Piano Sonata No.6 (c ?1908–9, lost)*

Mature:

8.7	Piano Sonata No.1 in F minor (r1909 of Pf Son No.2 of 1907, see Juvenilia)	Op.1
8.8	Piano Sonata No.2 in D minor (c1912)	Op.14
8.9	Piano Sonata No.3 in A minor (r1917 of Pf Son No.3 of 1907, see Juvenilia)	Op.28
8.10	Piano Sonata No.4 in C minor, "From Old Notebooks" (r1917 of Pf Son No.5 of 1908, see Juvenilia)	Op.29
8.11	Piano Sonata No.5 in C major (c1923; see r vers Op.135)	Op.38
8.12	Piano Sonata No.6 in A major, "War Sonata 1" (c1939–40)	Op.82
8.13	Piano Sonata No.7 in B-flat major, "War Sonata 2" / "Stalingrad" (c1939–42, Stalin Prize 1st time)	Op.83
8.14	Piano Sonata No.8 in B-flat major, War Sonata 3" (c1939–44)	Op.84
8.15	Piano Sonata No.9 in C major (c1947)	Op.103
8.16	2nd Version of Pf Sonata No.5 in C major, Op.38 (c1952–3)	Op.135
8.17	Piano Sonata No.10 in C minor (inc)	Op.137
8.18	*Piano Sonata No.11 (project)*	*Op.138*

9. OTHER PIANO WORKS

Juvenilia:

9.1	"Indian Galop," in F major (c1896)
9.2	"March," in C major (c1896)
9.3	"Waltz," in C major (c1896)
9.4	"Rondo," in C major (c1896)
9.5	"March," in B min / D major (c1897)
9.6	"Polka," in G major (c1899)
9.7	"Waltz," in G major (c1899)
9.8	"Waltz," in C maj / G major (c1899)
9.9	"March" (c1900)
9.10	"7 Pieces" (c1901)
9.11	"12 Little Songs," 1st series (c1902)
9.12	"12 Pieces" (c1902)
9.13	"Bagatelle No.2," in A minor (c1902)
9.14	"12 Little Songs," 2nd series (c1903)
9.15	"12 Little Songs," 3rd series (c1903–4)
9.16	"Variations" (c1904, on: Chizhika)
9.17	"12 Little Songs," 4th series (c1905)
9.18	"Polka mélancolique," in F-sharp minor (c1905)
9.19	"12 Little Songs," 5th series (c1906)
9.20	"Songs without words," in D-flat major (c1907)
9.21	"Intermezzo," in A major (c1907)
9.22	"Humoresque," in F minor (c1907)
9.23	Untitled work in B-flat minor (c1907)
9.24	"Oriental piece," in G minor (c1907)
9.25	Untitled piece in C minor (c1907)
9.26	"4 Pieces" (c1907–8; see r vers in Op.3)
9.27	"4 Pieces" (c1908; see r vers in Op.4)

9.100	No.6 "Scherzo" (from: Sinfonietta in A major, Op.48)	
9.101	"2 Sonatinas" (c1931–2): No.1 in E minor	Op.54
9.102	No.2 in G major	
9.103	"3 Pieces" (c1933–4) No.1 "Promenade"	Op.59
9.104	No.2 "Landscape"	
9.105	No.3 "Pastoral Sonatina," in C major	
9.106	"Thoughts" (c1933–4): No.1 "Adagio pensieroso. Moderato"	Op.62
9.107	No.2 "Lento"	
9.108	No.3 "Andante"	
9.109	"Music for children," 12 easy pieces (c1935; arr as: Summer Day for orch, Op.65bis): No.1 "Morning" Op.65	
9.110	No.2 "Walk"	
9.111	No.3 "Fairy Tale"	
9.112	No.4 "Tarantella"	
9.113	No.5 "Repentence" (Regrets)	
9.114	No.6 "Waltz"	
9.115	No.7 "Grasshoppers' Parade"	
9.116	No.8 "Rain and Rainbow"	
9.117	No.9 "Playing Tag"	
9.118	No.10 "March"	
9.119	No.11 "Evening"	
9.120	No.12 "The moon sails o'er the meadows"	
9.121	"Music for gymnastic exercises" (c ?1936, inc)	
9.122	"Romeo & Juliet," 10 pieces (c1937, arr from ballet, Op.64): No.1 "National Dance"	Op.75
9.123	No.2 "The Street Wakens" (Scena)	
9.124	No.3 "The Arrival of the Guests," minuet	
9.125	No.4 "Juliet as a Young Girl"	
9.126	No.5 "Masks"	
9.127	No.6 "Montagues and Capulets"	
9.128	No.7 "Friar Laurence"	
9.129	No.8 "Mercutio"	
9.130	No.9 "Dance of the Girls with the Lilies"	
9.131	No.10 "Romeo and Juliet Before Parting"	
9.132	"Gavotte" (c1938, from incid music: Hamlet, Op.77/4)	Op.77bis
9.133	"3 Pieces" (c1942, from ballet: Cinderella, Op.87): No.1 "Printemps" (Intermezzo)	Op.95
9.134	No.2 "Gavotte"	
9.135	No.3 "Valse lente"	
9.136	"3 Pieces" (c1941–2): No.1 "Waltz" (from opera: War & Peace, Op.91)	Op.96
9.137	No.2 "Contredanse" (from film: Lermotov)	
9.138	No.3 "Mephisto-waltz" (from film: Lermotov)	
9.139	"10 Pieces" (c1943, from ballet: Cinderella, Op.87): No.1 "Spring Fairy"	Op.97
9.140	No.2 "Summer Fairy"	
9.141	No.3 "Autumn Fairy"	
9.142	No.4 "Winter Fairy"	
9.143	No.5 "Grasshoppers and Dragonflies"	
9.144	No.6 "Orientalia"	
9.145	No.7 "Passepied"	
9.146	No.8 "Capriccio"	
9.147	No.9 "Bourrée"	
9.148	No.10 "Adagio"	
9.149	"6 Pieces" (c1944, from ballet: Cinderella, Op.87)	Op.102

Pf duet (juvenilia):

9.150	"March," in C major (c1897)	
9.151	"March," in C major (c1899)	
9.152	"March," in F major (c1899)	
9.153	Piece in F major (c1899)	
9.154	Piece in D minor (c1900)	
9.155	Piece (c1900; w/ zither, inc)	
9.156	"Bagatelle No.1," in C minor (c1901)	

10. CHORAL WORKS

W/ orch:

10.1	"2 Poems" (c1909–10, Balmont; fem ch & orch): 1. "The White Swan"	Op.7
10.2	2. "The Wave"	
10.3	"Seven, They Are Seven," cantata (c1917–8, r1933, after Balmont; T, ch & orch)	Op.30
10.4	"Cantata for the 20th Anniv of the October Revolution" (c1936–7; 2ch, accordions & orch)	Op.74
10.5	"Songs of Our Times" (c1937; mS, Bar, ch & orch): 1. "March"	Op.76
10.6	2. "Over the Bridge" (Prishelts)	
10.7	3. "Good Luck" (Rusak)	
10.8	4. "Golden Ukraine" (trad)	
10.9	5. "Brother for Brother" (Lebedev-Kumach)	

10.10	6. "Maidens" (Prishelts)
10.11	7. "The 20-year-old" (Marshak)
10.12	8. "Lullaby" (Lebedev-Kumach)
10.13	9. "From Shore to Shore" (October Flag) (Dolmatovsky)
10.14	"Alexander Nevsky," cantata (c1938–9, Lugorsky; mS, ch & orch, from film): Op.78

    1. "Russia under the Mongolian Yoke"
    2. "Song about Alexander Nevsky"
    3. "The Crusaders in Pskov"
    4. "Arise, ye Russian People"
    5. "The Battle on Ice"
    6. "Field of the Dead"
    7. "Alexander's Entry in Pskov"

10.15	"Hail to Stalin," cantata (c1939, on folk texts; ch & orch) Op.85
10.16	"Ballad of an Unknown Boy," cantata (c1942–3, Antokolsky; S, T, ch & orch) Op.93
10.17	"Flourish, Mighty Homeland," cantata (c1947, Dolmatovsky; ch & orch) Op.114
10.18	*"Ivan the Terrible," oratorio (arr Stasevich 1961, from film Op.116) .... (Op.116)*
10.19	"Winter Bonfire," suite (c1949–50, Marshak; narrator, boys' ch & orch): 1. "Departure" Op.122
10.20	2. "Snow on the Window"
10.21	3. "Waltz on the Ice"
10.22	4. "The Bonfire"
10.23	5. "Assembly of the Pioneers"
10.24	6. "Winter Evening"
10.25	7. "March of the Pioneers"
10.26	8. "The Return"
10.27	"On Guard of Peace," oratorio (c1950, Marshak; narrator, mS, ch, boys' ch & orch) Op.124

W/ pf:

10.28	"2 Choruses" (c1935): 1. "Partisan Zheleznyak" (Golodny) Op.66a
10.29	2. "Anyutka" (trad)
10.30	"4 Songs" (c1935): 1. "The fatherland Awakens" (Afinogenov) Op.66b
10.31	2. "Through Snow and Fog" (Afinogenov)
10.32	3. "Beyond the Hills" (trad)
10.33	4. "Song of Voroshilov" (Sikorskaya)
10.34	"7 Songs" (c1941–2): 1. "Song" Op.89
10.35	2. "Song of the Brave"
10.36	3. "The Tankman's Vow"
10.37	4. "Son of Kabarda"
10.38	5. "The Soldier's Sweetheart"
10.39	6. "Fritz"
10.40	7. "Love of War"
10.41	*National Anthem of Soviet Union & Anthem of Russian Republic (c1946, sketches) Op.98*
10.42	"Soldiers' Marching Song" (c1950, Lugovskoy) Op.121

11. VOICE & ORCHESTRA

11.1	"Mélodie" (c ?1920, from: 5 Songs, Op.35/2) Op.35b
11.2	"The Fiery Angel," suite (c1923, from opera Op.37, inc) Op.37b
11.3	"Peter and the Wolf," tale for children (c1936, Prokofiev; narrator & orch; arr for pf 1940) Op.67

12. MISC VOCAL

| 12.1 | "12 Russian Folksongs," 2 vols (c1944, arrs) .... Op.104 |
| 12.2 | "2 Duets," arrs of Russian folksong (c1945, texts written down by Hippius; T, B & pf) .... Op.106 |

13. SONGS (w/ pf)

13.1	Juvenilia: 1. "Tell me" (c1903, Lermontov) ....
13.2	2. "O no, not Figner" (c1903)
13.3	3. "Look, the down" (c1903, Prokofiev)
13.4	4. "I am no longer the same" (c1903, Pushkin)
13.5	5. "Ancient, gnarled oaks" (c1906–7, Maykov)
13.6	"2 Poems" (c1910–1): 1. "There are other planets" (Balmont) Op.9
13.7	2. "The drifting boat" (Apukhtin)
13.8	"The Ugly Duckling" (c1914, after Andersen; orchd) Op.18
13.9	"5 Poems" (c1915, Balmont): 1. "Under the roof" Op.23
13.10	2, "The little grey dress"
13.11	3. "Follow me"
13.12	4. "In my garden"
13.13	5. "The prophet"
13.14	"5 Poems" (c1916, Akhmatova): 1. "The sun has filled my room" Op.27
13.15	2. "True tenderness"

949

13.16   3. "Memory of the sun"
13.17   4. "Greetings"
13.18   5. "The king with grey eyes"
13.19 "Songs without Words" (c1920; see for vn & pf, Op.35bis; for pf, Op.52/4): 1. "Andante" Op.35
13.20   2. "Lento ma non troppo"
13.21   3. "Animato, ma non allegro"
13.22   4. "Andantino, un poco scherzando"
13.23   5. "Andante non troppo"
13.24 "5 Poems" (c1921, Balmont): 1. "Incantation of water & fire" Op.36
13.25   2. "Birdsong"
13.26   3. "The butterfly"
13.27   4. "Remember me"
13.28   5. "The pylons"
13.29 "5 Kazakh Popular Songs" (1927) ....
13.30 "2 Songs" (c1934, from film: Lieutenant Kijé): 1. "Moans the little grey dove" Op.60bis
13.31   2. "Troika"
13.32 "3 Children's Songs" (c1936): 1. "Chatterbox" Op.68
13.33   2. "Sweet song"
13.34   3. "The little pig"
13.35 "3 Romances" (c1936, Pushkin): 1. "Pine trees" Op.73
13.36   2. "With a blush"
13.37   3. "In your brightness"
13.38 "3 Songs" (c1939, Lugovsky, from film: Alexander Nevsky): 1. "Arise, men of Russia" Op.78bis
13.39   2. "Mark, ye bright falcons"
13.40   3. "And it happened on the Neva banks"
13.41 "7 Songs" (c1939): 1. "Song about the fatherland" Op.79
13.42   2. "Stakhanovka"
13.43   3. "On the polar sea"
13.44   4. "Send-off"
13.45   5. "Bravely forward"
13.46   6. "Through the village came a Cossack"
13.47   7. "Hey, to the road" (also see orch work Op.89b)
13.48 "About sheatfish": "Broad & deep the river flows" (Mikhalkov, inc) ....

14. ARRANGEMENTS OF WORKS OF OTHERS

14.1   Buxtehude: "Organ Prelude & Fugue," in D minor, B240 (transcr1920; pf) ....
14.2   Schubert: Waltzes (transcr1920; pf; also for 2pf 1923) ....

* * * * *

1. STAGE WORKS (operas)

1.1   "Le villi," 1 act opera-ballo (p1884, Fontana; r1884 in 2 acts) ....
1.2   "Edgar," 4 act dramma lirico (p1889, Fontana after Musset: La coupe et les lèvres; r1892 in 3 acts) ....
1.3   "Manon Lescaut," 4 act dramma lirico (p1893, Leoncavallo & others after Prévost's novel) ....
1.4   "La bohème" (The Bohemians), 4 part 'scene' (p1896, Giacosa & Illica after Mürger's novel: La vie de
      bohème) (also see opera c by Leoncavallo) ....
1.5   "Tosca," 3 act melodramma (p1900, Giacosa & Illica after Sardou's drama)...
1.6   "Madama Butterfly," 2 act tragedia giapponese (p1904, Giacosa & Illica after Belasco's tale; r1904 in 3 acts)
1.7   "La fanciulla del West" (The Girl of the Golden West), 3 act (p1910, Civinini & Zangarini after Belasco) ....
1.8   "La rondine" (The Swallow), 3 act commedia lirica (p1917, Adami after Ger libretto of Willner & Reichert) ..
1.9   "Il Trittico" (p1918): I. "Il tabarro" (The Cloak), 1 act dramma (Adami after Gold: La houppelande) ....
1.10   II. "Suor Angelica" (Sister Angelica), 1 act dramma (Forzano)
1.11   III. "Gianni Schicchi," 1 act (Forzano from Dante's Inferno)
1.12 "Turandot," 3 act dramma lirico (p1926, Adami & Simoni after Gozzi's play) ....

1a. SELECTIONS FROM STAGE WORKS (Nos. of sections in The Gramophone)

1a.1   "Le villi," opera: ....
       excerpts: I: 1. "Prelude"
                    2. "Evviva! Evviva!"
                    3. "Se come voi piccina io fossi"
                    4. "Non esser, Anna mia"
                    5. "Presto! Presto in vaggio"
                 II: 6. "L'Abbandono"
                    7. "La Tregenda"
                    8. "No, possibil non è"
                    9a. "Ecco la casa"
                    9b. "Torna ai felice"
                    10. "Roberto!"

1a.3   "Manon Lescaut," opera: ....
                 I: 1. "Ave, sera gentile"
                    2a. "No, non ancora"
                    2b. "Tra voi, belle"
                    3a. "Cortese damigella"
                    3b. "Manon Lescaut mi chiamo"
                    4. "Donna non vidi mai"
                    5. "La sua ventura"
                    6. "Vedete? Io son fedele"
                 II: 7a. "Dispettosetto questo riccio!"
                    7b. "Buon giorno"
                    8. "In quelle trine morbide"
                    9. "Sulla vetta" (Madrigal)
                    10. "L'ora, o Tirsi"
                    11a. "Tu, tu, amore? Tu?"
                    11b. "O tentatrice!"
                    12. "Ah! Manon, mi tradisce"
                    13. "Intermezzo"
                 III: 14. "Ansia, eterna, crudel!
                    15a. "Ah! non v'avvicinate!"
                    15b. "No!... No!... pazzo son"
                 IV: 16. "Prelude"
                    17a. "Tutta su me ti posa"
                    17b. "Manon ..."
                    18. "Sola, perduta, abbandonata"
                    19. "Nulla rinvenni"

1a.4   "La bohème," opera: ....
                 I: 1a."Questo Mar Rosso"
                    1b. "Nei cieli bigi" (Rudolph)
                    1c. "Pensier profondo! Giusto color!"
                    1d. "Legna! Sigari! Bordo!"
                    1e. "Si può? Chi è là? Benoit!"
                    1f. "Io resto per terminar l'articolo"
                    1g. "Non sono in vena. Chi è là!"
                    1h. "Si sente meglio? Sì. Qui cè tanto freddo"
                    2. "Che gelida manina"
                    3. "Sì. Mi chiamano Mimì"
                    4. "O soave fanciulla"
                 II: 5. "Aranci, datteri!"
                    6a. "Chi guardi?"
                    6b. "Eccoci qui!"
                    7a. "Come un facchino"

7b. "Quando me'n vo' soletta la via" (Musetta's Waltz Song)
III: 8. "Ohè, là, le guardie"
9. "Mimì?!... Speravo di trovarvi"
10a. "Marcello ... Finalmente"
10b. "Mimì è una civetta"
11. "Donde lieta uscì" (Mimì's Farewell)
12. "Addio dolce svegliare"
IV: 13a. "In un coupè?"
13b. "O Mimì, tu più non torni"
14. "Che ora sia?"
15. "Musetta!... C'è Mimì"
16. "Vecchia zimarra" (Coat song)
17a. "Sono andati?"
17b. "Tornò al nido"
17c. "Oh Dio! Mimì!"

1a.5 "Tosca," opera: ....
I: 1a. "Ah! Finalmente!"
1b. "E sempre lava!"
1c. "Sante ampolle!"
2. "Recondita armonia"
3a. "Mario! Mario! Mario!"
3b. "Perchè chiuso?"
3c. "Ora stammi a sentir"
3d. "Non la sospiri"
3e. "Or lasciami al lavoro"
3f. "Ah, quegli occhi!"
4. "È buona la mia Tosca"
5. "Sommo giubilo"
6a. "Un tal baccano in chiesa!"
6b. "Fu grave sbaglio"
7a. "Or tutto è chiaro"
7b. "Tosca divina"
7c. "O che v'offende"
8. "Tre sbirri" (Te Deum)
II: 9a. "Tosca è un buon falco"
9b. "Ella verrà"
10a. "Sale, ascende ... A te quest'inno" (Cantata)
10b. "Mario, tu qui?"
11a. "La povera mia cena"
11b. "Già, mi dicon venal"
11c. "Se la giurata"
12. "Vissi d'arte"
13a. "Sei troppo bella"
13b. "Tosca, finalmente mia!"
III: 14. "Prelude"
15a. "Io de' sospiri"
15b. "Mario Cavaradossi?"
16. "E lucevan le stelle"
17a. "Franchigia a Floria Tosca"
17b. "O dolci mani"
17c. "Senti, l'ora è vicina"
18a. "Amaro sol per te"
18b. "Trionfa!... Di nova speme"
19a. "Son pronto"
19b. "Com'è lunga l'attesa!"

1a.6 "Madama Butterfly," opera: ....
I: 1a. "E soffitto"
1b. "Questa è la cameriera"
2. "Dovunque al mondo"
3a. "Ed è bella la sposa?"
3b. "Amore o grillo"
4a. "Ah! ah! quanto cielo!"
4b. "Ancora un passo"
5a. "Gran ventura"
5b. "L'Imperial Commissario"
6. "Vieni, amor mio!"
7a. "Ieri son salita tutta sola"
7b. "Ed eccoci in famiglia"
8a. "Viene la sera"
8b. "Bimba, dagli occhi"
8c. "Vogliatemi bene"
8d. "Un po' di vero c'è"
II: 9. "E Izaghi e Izanami"

10. "Un bel dì vedremo"
11a. "C'è. Entrate"
11b. "Ora a noi"
11c. "Ebbene, che fareste"
11d. "E questo?"
12. "Che tua madre"
13a. "Il cannone del porto!"
13b. "Scuoti quella fronda di ciliego"
13c. "Tutti i fior"
13d. "Or vienmi ad adornar"
14. "Humming Chorus"
15. "Intermezzo"
16. "Già il sole!"
17a. "Povera Butterfly"
17b. "Ve lo dissi?"
17c. "Io so che alle sue pene"
18a. "Non ve l'avevo detto?"
18b. "Addio, fiorito asil"
18c. "Glielo dirai?"
19a. "Che vuol da me"
19b. "Come una mosca prigioniera"
20a. "Con onor muore chi non puo serbar vita con onore"
20b. "Tu? tu? piccolo iddio"

1a.7   "La fanciulla del West," opera: ....
      I: 1. "Che faranno i vecchi miei"
            2. "Jim, perchè piangi?"
            3a. "Dove eravamo?"
            3b. "Lavami e sarò bianco"
            4a. "Ti voglio bene, Minnie"
            4b. "Minnie, dalla mia casa"
            5. "Laggiù nel Soledad"
            6a. "Mister Johnson siete rimasto"
            6b. "Non so, non so"
      II: 7. "Oh, se sapeste"
            8a. "Sì! Tanto!"
            8b. "Perchè questa parola?"
            9a. "Una parola sola!"
            9b. "Sono Ramerrez"
            9c. "Or son sei messi"
            10. "Che c'è di nuovo, Jack?"
            11. "Siete pronto?"
     III: 12. "Ch'ella mi creda libero"
            13a. "Ah!... Ah!"
            13b. "Non vi fu mai chi disse"

1a.8   "La rondine," opera: ....
      excerpts: 1. "Chi il bel sogno di Doretta"
              2. "Ore dolci e divine"

1a.9   "Il tabarro," opera: ....
      excerpts: 1. "Hai ben ragione"
             2a. "È ben altro il mio sogno!"
             2b. "Ma chi lascia il sobborgo"
             2c. "O Luigi!"
             2d. "Folle di gelosia!"
             3. "Perchè non m'ami più"
             4a. "Scorri, fiume eterno" (orig vers of Michelè's aria)
             4b. "Nulla! Silenzio!" (replacement vers of Michelè's aria)

1a.10   "Suor Angelica," opera: ....
      excerpts: 1. "Tutto ho offerto"
             2. "Intermezzo"
             3. "Senza mamma, O bimbo tu sei morto"
             4. "Amici fiori che nel"

1a.11   "Gianni Schicchi," opera: ....
            1. "Firenze è come un albero fiorito"
             2. "O mio babbino caro"
             3. "Lauretta mia"

1a.12   "Turandot," opera: ....
      I: 1. "Popolo di Pekino!"
             2. "Gira la cote!"
             3. "Perchè tarda la luna?"

    4. "O giovinetto!"
    5. "Principessa! Pietà!"
    6. "Fermo! che fai?"
    7. "Non indugiare!"
    8. "Signore, ascolta!"
    9. "Non piangere, Liù!"
    10. "Ah! per l'ultima volta!"
II: 11a. "Olà, Pang! Olà, Pong!"
    11b. "O China"
    11c. "Ho una casa"
    11d. "Vi ricordare il principe regal"
    11e. "Addio, amore"
    12a. "Gravi, enormi"
    12b. "Un giuramento"
    12c. "Popolo di Pekino!"
    13a. "In questa Reggia"
    13b. "O Principe, che a lunghe carovane"
    14. "Straniero, ascolta!"
    15. "Tre enigmi"
III: 16. "Così comanda Turandot"
    17. "Nessun dorma!"
    18. "Tu che guardi le stelle"
    19. "Principessa divina!"
    20. "Tanto amore"
    21. "Tu, che di gel sei cinta"
    22. "Liù!"
    23. "Principessa di morte"
    24a. "Del primo pianto"
    24b. "Diecimila anni al nostro Imperatore!"

2. ORCHESTRAL WORKS

2.1	"Preludio sinfonico," in A major (c1876)	
2.2	"Adagietto" (c1883)	
2.3	"Capriccio sinfonico" (c1883; arr for pf duet 1884)	
2.4	"Scozza elettrica," march (c1896)	

3. STRING QUARTETS

3.1	"Scherzo," in A minor (ca1880–3)	
3.2	String Quartet in D major (ca1880–3)	
3.3	"Fugues" (c1882–3)	
3.4	"3 Minuets" (p1890; arr for strings): No.1 "Moderato," in C minor (r1898)	
3.5	No.2 "Allegretto," in A major	
3.6	No.3 "Assai mosso," in A major (r1898)	
3.7	"Crisantemi," elegy (p1890)	

4. OTHER CHAMBER MUSIC

4.1	"La sconsolata" (c1883; vn & pf)	
4.2	*?Piano Trio (2vn & pf, frag)*	

5. PIANO

5.1	"Foglio d'album" (c ?1907)	
5.2	"Piccolo tango" (c ?1907)	
5.3	"Calmo e molto lento" (c1916)	

6. ORGAN

6.1	Several juvenile pieces (c before 1880)	

7. CHURCH MUSIC

7.1	"Vexilla Regis prodeunt," hymn (c1878, Fortunatus; m ch & org)	
7.2	"Motet et Credo" (c1878, in honour of San Paolino)	
7.3	"Messa di Gloria," in A-flat major (c1880; T, Bar, B; ch & orch, includes: Motet et Credo of 1878)	
7.4	"Salve del ciel regina" (c before 1880, Ghislanzoni; S & harm)	
7.5	"Requiem" (c1905; S, T, B & org/harm, in memory of G. Verdi)	

8. CHORAL WORKS

8.1   "I figli d'Italia bella," cantata (c1877; vv & orch) ....

8.2   "Cantata a Giove" (p1897) ....

9. SONGS (w/ pf)

9.1   "A Te": "O quanto è vano" (c ?1875, unknown) ....

9.2   "Melanconia": "Allor ch'io sarò morto" (c1881, Ghislanzoni, lost; 2nd vers w/ strings extant) ....

9.3   *"Ah! se potese" (c ?1882; T & pf, lost)* ....

9.4   *"Ad una morta!": "Spirito gentil" (c ?1882,; Bar & pf/orch Ghislanzoni, frags)* ....

9.5   "Mentì l'avviso," romanza (c1883, Romani) ....

9.6   Storiella d'amore": "Noi leggeramo" (c1883, Ghislanzoni) ....

9.7   "Sole e amore": "Il sole allegramente batte ai tuoi vetri," mattinata (c1888, ?Puccini) ....

9.8   *"Solfeggi" (c1888, lost)* ....

9.9   "Avanti, Urania!": "Io non ho l'ali" (p1896, Fucini) ....

9.10   "Inno a Diana": "Gloria a te, se alle notti silenti" (p1897, Abeniacar) ....

9.11   "E l'uccellino" (Ninna-Nanna) (p1899, Fucini) ....

9.12   "Terra e mare": "I pioppi, curvati dal vento" (p1902, Panzacchi, 2 vers) ....

9.13   "Canto d'anime": "Fuggon gli anni, gli inganni e le chimere," albumleaf (c1904, Illica) ....

9.14   "Casa mia, casa mia" (c1908) ....

9.15   "Morire?" (p ca1917–8, Adami, for album Croce Rossa Italiana) ....

9.16   "Inno di Roma": "Roma divina" (p1923, Salvatori; arr Rixner as: Hymne an Rom for ch & orch, words
       Siegel p1942) ....

*   *   *   *   *

1. STAGE WORKS

Operas:

1.1	"Dido and Aeneas," opera (c ?1689, Tate after Virgil, inc)	Z626

Ambigues (semi-operas):

1.2	"The Prophetess, or The History of Dioclesian" (c1690, ?Betterton or ?Dryden from Fletcher & Massinger, dances Priest, inc)	Z627
1.3	"King Arthur, or The British Worthy" (c1691, Dryden, dances Priest, inc)	Z628
1.4	"The Fairy Queen" (c1692, r1693, ?Settle from Shakespeare: Midsummer-Night's Dream) (also see Britten's opera Op.64, Castelnuovo-Tedesco's overture Op.108, Mendelssohn's incid music Op.61, Orff's music drama & Satie's incid music: 5 Grimaces)	Z629
1.5	"The Indian Queen" (c ?1695, Dryden & Howard)	Z630
1.6	"The Tempest, or The Enchanted Isle" (c ?1695, Shadwell from Shakespeare or anon after D'Avenant & Dryden's adaptation) (also see incid music c by Honegger H48, Sibelius Op.109 & Sullivan Op.1)	Z631

Masques:

1.7	"Timon of Athens, the Man-Hater" (c ?1694, Shadwell, addition to Shakespeare's play) (also see incid music c by Britten & overture c by Sullivan)	Z632

Incid music:

1.8	"Abdelazer, or the Moor's Revenge" (c1695, Behn from: Lust's Dominion of 1657; S, 2vn, va & cont)	Z570
1.9	"A Fool's Preferment, or The Three Dukes of Dunstable" (c1695, D'Urfey from Fletcher's Noble Gentleman; T, ?S & cont)	Z571
1.10	"Amphitryon, or the Two Sosias" (c1690, Dryden after Plautus & Molière; S, B, ch, 2vn, va & cont)	Z572
1.11	"Aureng-Zebe, or the Great Mogul" (c ?1692–4, Dryden; S & cont)	Z573
1.12	"Bonduca, or the British Heroine" (c1695, after Fletcher; 2S, A, T, B, ch, 2fl, 2ob, tpt, 2vn, va & cont)	Z574
1.13	"Circe" (c1685, D'Avenant; S, A, T, B, ch, 2vn, va & cont)	Z575
1.14	"Cleomenes, the Spartan Hero" (c1692, Dryden & Southerne; S & cont)	Z576
1.15	"Distressed Innocence, or the Princess of Persia" (c1690, Settle & Mountfort; 2vn, va & cont)	Z577
1.16	"Don Quixote, (The Comical History of)," 3 parts (Part I & II c1694, Part III c1695, D'Urfey after Cervantes; S, A, T, B, ch, 2vn, va, cont & tpt)	Z578
1.17	"Epsom Wells" (c1693, Shadwell; S, B & cont)	Z579
1.18	"Henry II, King of England" (c1692, ?Mountforr & ?Bancroft; S & cont)	Z580
1.19	"King Richard II, or the History of the Sicilian Usurper" (c1680, Tate after Shakespeare; S/T & cont)	Z581
1.20	"Love Triumphant, or Nature Will Prevail" (c1693, Dryden, words of song Congreve; S & cont)	Z582
1.21	"Oedipus" (c1692, Dryden & Lee; A, T, B, ch, 2vn & cont)	Z583
1.22	"Oroonolo" (c1695, Coutherne; 2S & cont)	Z584
1.23	"Pausanias, the betrayer of His Country" (c1695, Norton; S, T & cont)	Z585
1.24	"Regulus, or the Faction of Carthage" (c1692, Crowne; S & cont)	Z586
1.25	"Rule a Wife and Have a Wife" (c1693, Fletcher; S & cont)	Z587
1.26	"Sir Anthony Love, or the Rambling Lady" (c1690, Southerne, song Sackville; S, B, 2vn & cont)	Z588
1.27	"Sir Barnaby Whigg, or No Wit Like a Woman's" (c1681, D'Urfey; S, A, ch & cont)	Z589
1.28	"Sophonisba, or Hannibal's Overthrow" (c ?1685, Lee; S & cont)	Z590
1.29	"The Canterbury Guests, or A Bargain Broken" (c1694, Ravenscroft; 2S, A, B & cont)	Z591
1.30	"The Double Dealer" (c1693, Congreve; S, 2vn, va & cont)	Z592
1.31	"The Double Marriage" (c ?1682–5, Fletcher & Massinger; ?2vn, ?va & cont)	Z593
1.32	"The English Lawyer" (ca ?1685, Ravenscroft from a Ruggle's Latin Comedy: Ignoramus; 3vv)	Z594
1.33	"The Fatal Marriage, or the Innocent Adultery" (c1694, Southerne; S & cont)	Z595
1.34	"The Female Virtuosos" (c1693, Wright from Molière's Les femmes savantes, words of song Anne, Countess of Winchelsea: On love; 2S & cont)	Z596
1.35	"The Gordian Knot Unty'd" (c1691, anon; 2vn, va & cont)	Z597
1.36	"The Indian Emperor, or The Conquest of Mexico" (c1691, Dryden & Howard; S & cont)	Z598
1.37	"The Knight of Malta" (c ?1691, Beaumont & Fletcher; 3B)	Z599
1.38	"The Libertine, or the Libertine Destroyed" (c ?1692, Shadweil; S, A, B, ch, tpts, 2vn, va & cont)	Z600
1.39	"The Maid's Last Prayer, or Any Rather than Fail" (c1693, Southerne; 2S & cont)	Z601
1.40	"The Marriage-Hater Match'd" (c1692, D'Urfey; S, B & cont)	Z602
1.41	"The Married Beau, or the Curious Impertinent" (c1694, Crowne; S, 2vn, va & cont)	Z603
1.42	"The Massacre of Paris" (c1689, Lee; S/B & cont)	Z604
1.43	"The Mock Marriage" (c1695, Scott; S & cont)	Z605
1.44	"Theodosius, or the Force of Love" (c1680, Lee; S, A, T, B, ch, 2fl & cont)	Z606
1.45	"The Old Bachelor" (c1691, Congreve; S, B, 2vn, va & cont)	Z607
1.46	"The Richmond Heiress, or A Woman Once in the Right" (c1693, D'Urfey; S, B & cont)	Z608
1.47	"The Rival Sisters, or the Violence of Love" (c1695, Gould; S, 2vn, va & cont)	Z609
1.48	"The Spanish Friar, or the Double Discovery" (c ?1694, Dryden; S & cont)	Z610
1.49	"The Stairre Case Overture"	ZN614
1.50	"The Virtuous Wife, or Good Luck at Last" (c1694, D'Urfey)	Z611
1.51	"The Wives' Excuse, or Cuckolds Make Themselves" (c1691, Southerne; S & cont)	Z612
1.52	"Tyrannic Love, or the Royal Martyr" (c1695, Dryden; S, B & cont)	Z613
1.53	*"?Neglected Virtue, or the Unhappy Conqueror" (c before ?1695, Hopkins, doubtful)*	*ZD200*
1.54	*Unidentified Play (When Night her purple veil, for B & cont, w/ Prelude for 2vn, doubtful)*	*ZD201*

1a. SELECTIONS FROM STAGE WORKS

1a.1   "Dido and Aeneas," opera: Z626
Prologue (lost/not composed)
I: 1. "Ouverture": a. (Grave)
        b. (Canzona)
        2a. "Shake the cloud from off your brow" (Belinda)
        2b. "Banish sorrow" (ch)
        3a. "Ah! Belinda, I am prest" (Dido)
        3b. "Ritornello"
        4. "Grief increases by concealing" (Belinda, Dido)
        5. "When monarchs unite" (ch)
        6. "Whence could so much virtue spring?" (Dido)
        7a, b. "Fear no danger" (Belinda, Second Woman, later ch)
        8. "See, your royal guest appears" (Belinda)
        9. "Cupid only throws the dart" (ch)
        10. "If not for mine, for empire's sake" (Aeneas)
        11a. "Prelude"
        11b. "Pursue thy conquest, Love" (Belinda)
        12. "To the hills and the vales" (ch)
        13. "Triumphing dance"
        14a. "Prelude"
        14b. "Wayward sisters, you that fright" (Sorceress)
        15. "Harm's our delight" (ch)
        16. "The Queen of Carthage, whom we hate" (Sorceress)
        17. "Ho, ho, ho" (ch)
        18. "Ruin'd ere the set of sun?" (First Witch, Second Witch)
        19. (= 17.) (in F major)
        20. "But ere we this perform" (First Witch, Second Witch)
        21. "In our deep vaulted cell" (ch)
        22. "Echo Dance of Furies"
II: 23. "Ritornello"
        24a, b. "Thanks to these lonesome vales" (Belinda, later ch)
        25a. "Oft she visits this lone mountain" (Second Woman)
        25b. "Ritornello"
        26. "Behold, upon my bended spear" (T)
        27. "Haste, haste to town" (Belinda, later ch)
        28a. "Stay, prince! and hear great Jove's command" (Spirit)
        28b. "The Sorceress and Witches"; chorus: "Then since our charms have sped"
        28c. "The Groves' Dance"
III: 29a. "Prelude"
        29b, c. "Come away, fellow sailors" (Sailor, later ch)
        30. "The sailor's dance"
        31. "See the flags and streamers" (Sorceress)
        32. "Our next motion must be" (Sorceress)
        33. "Destruction's our delight" (ch)
        34a. "The witches' dance"
        34b. (strings)
        34c. (strings)
        35a. "Your counsel all is urg'd in vain" (Dido)
        35b. "But Death, alas!" (Dido)
        36. "Great minds against themselves conspire" (ch)
        37. "Thy hand, Belinda" (Dido)
        38a. "Ground" (cont)
        38b. "When I am laid in earth" (Dido's Lament)
        38c. "Ritornello"
        39. "With drooping wings" (ch)
        Epilogue: 40. "All that we know the angels do above"

1a.2   "The Prophetess, or The History of Dioclesian," ambigue: Z627
        1a. "First music"
        1b. (insts)
        2a. "Second music"
        2b. "Trumpet tune"
        3. "Overture": a. (Grave)
           b. (Canzona)
           c. (Adagio)
I: 4. "First Act tune: Hornpipe" (adapted as a mock-song: O how happy's he, Z403)
II: 5a. "Prelude"
        5b. "Great Diocles the boar has killed" (B)
        5c. "Sing Io's" (ch)
        5d. "Praise the thund'ring Jove" (ch)
        6a. "Prelude" (2fl)
        6b. "Charon the peaceful shade invites" (Second song, by a woman)
        7a. "Sound all your instruments" (S)

  7b. "Symphony"
  7c. (Canzona)
  8a. "Let all mankind the pleasures share" (S, B)
  8b. "Sound all your instruments" (unacc ch)
  8c. "Flourish" ('with all instruments in C fa ut key')
  8d. (= 8a.) (ch)
  9a. "Prelude" (A, ob)
  9b. "Let the soldiers rejoice" (A)
  9c. "Rejoice with a general voice" (ch)
  10. "Ritornello" (between the verses of 9.)
  11. "To Mars let 'em raise" (A, T, B) (tune = 9b.)
  12. (= 9b.)
  13a. "Prelude" (2fl)
  13b. "Since the toils and the hazards of war" (A, also S, A, T, B, later ch)
  13c. "With dances and songs" ('Song on a ground') (A, 2fl)
  13d. "Ritornello" (2fl)
  13e. "Let the priests with processions" (ch)
  14a. "Prelude"
  14b. "Dance of the Furies"
  15. "Second Act tune"
III: 16. "Chaconne" (2fl)
  17. "Chair dance"
  18a. "Prelude" (2ob)
  18b. "What shall I do?" (S, 2ob)
  18c. (= 18a.)
  18d. "Since gods themselves" (tune = 18b.)
IV: 19. "Third Act tune"
  20a. (= 14a.)
  20b. "Butterfly dance"
  21. "Trumpet tune" (2tpt)
  22. "Sound, Fame, thy brazen trumpet" (A, tpt)
  23a. "Let all rehearse" (ch)
  23b. "All sing his story" (ch)
  24. "Fourth Act tune" (= 21. arr for strings)
V: 25. "Country dance"
The Masque: 26a. "Prelude"
  26b. "Call the nymphs and the fauns" (S, later ch)
  26c. "Let the Graces and Pleasures" (S)
  27. "Come away, no delay" (2B)
  28a. "Prelude"
  28b. "Behold, O mightiest of gods" (ch)
  29. "Paspe" (2tpt, strings)
  30. "O, the sweet delights of love" (2S)
  31. "Let monarchs fight" (S, later ch)
  32a. "Prelude" (2ob)
  32b. "Make room for the great god of wine" (Baccanales—2B, 2ob)
  32c. "I'm here with my jolly crew" (Bacchus, later ch)
  32d. "Dance of Baccanals"
  33a. "Still I'm wishing" (Cupid's follower—S)
  33b. "Ritornello"
  33c. "Can Drusilla give no more" (tune = 33a.)
  34. "Canaries" (strings)
  35a. "Tell me why, my charming fair" (Shepherd—B, S)
  35b. "O Mirtillo! you're above me" (Shepherdess—S)
  35c. "Could this lovely charming" (Shepherd—B)
  35d. "O, how gladly we believe" (S)
  35e. (= 35d.) (S, B)
  36. "Dance"
  37a. "All our days and our nights" (T)
  37b. "Begone, importunate reason" (ch)
  37c. "Wisdom and counsel" (ch)
  37d. "Dance"
  38a. "Triumph, victorious Love" (A, T, B, later ch)
  38b. "Ritornello"
  38c. (= 38a.)
  38d. "Thou hast tam'd almighty Jove" (A, T, B)
  38e. "Ritornello"
  38f. "Prelude"
  38g. (= 38a.)
  38h. "Ritornello"
  39. "Then all rehearse in lofty verse" (ch)
  App.1 "When first I saw the bright Aurelia's eyes" (S)
  App.2 "Since from my dear Astrea's sight" (S)
  App.3 "Let us dance" (S)

1a.3   "King Arthur, or The British Worthy," ambigue: Z628
              1. "First Music" (used in ode: Sound the trumpet, Z335/7a, b): a. "Chaconne"
                b. (Chaconne)
              2. "Second Music": a. "Overture" (Grave)
                b. (Canzona)
              3. "Air"
              4a. "Overture" (Grave) (used in birthday song: Arise my muse, Z320/1a, b)
              4b. "Canzona"
I/2:   5a. "Prelude"
              5b. "Woden, first to thee" (Grimbald—B, T, ch)
              6a. "The white horse neigh'd" (A, T)
              6b. "To Woden thanks we render" (A, T)
              6c. (= 6b.) (ch)
              7a. "The lot is cast" (S, later ch)
              7b. "Brave souls" (ch)
              8. "Die and reap" (ch)
              9a. "I call you all to Woden's hall" (A)
              9b. "To Woden's hall" (ch)
              10a. "Symphony"
              10a, b, c. "Come if you dare" (T, later ch)
              10d, e. "Now they charge on amain" (T, later ch)
              10f. "Ritornello" (2tpt, 2ob)
              10g. "The fainting Saxons" (T, later ch)
              10h. "Now the victory's won" (T, later ch)
              11. "First Act tune" (Air)
II: 12a. "Prelude"
              12b, c. "Hither this way" (S, later ch)
              13a. "Let not a moon-born elf" (B)
              13b. "Ritornello"
              14a, b, c. "Come follow me" (2S, A, T, B, later ch)
              14d. "Ritornello"
              14e, f. "We brethren of air" (2S, A, later ch)
              15a. "Dance"
              15b. "How blest are shepherds" (T)
              15c. (= 15b.) (ch)
              15d. (= 15b.)
              16a. "Symphony" (2fl, 2ob)
              16b. "Shepherd, leave decoying" (2S, 2fl, 2ob)
              17a. "Come, shepherds, lead up a lively measure" (ch)
              17b. "Hornpipe"
              18. "Second Act tune"
III/2: 19a. "Prelude to 'Frost scene' "
              19b. "What ho! thou genius of this isle" (S)
              20a. "Prelude while the Cold Genius rises"
              20b. "What pow'r art thou" (Cold Genius—B)
              21. "Thou doting fool, forbear" (Cupid—S)
              22. "Great Love, I know thee now" (Cold Genius—B)
              23. "No part of my dominion" Cupid—S)
              24a. "Prelude"
              24b. "See, we assemble" (ch)
              24c. "Dance"
              25a. " 'Tis I that have warmed ye" (Cupid—S)
              25b. "Ritornello"
              25c. " 'Tis Love that has warmed us" (Cold People—ch)
              26a. "Prelude"
              26b. "Sound a parley" (Cupid—S, Cold Genius—B)
              27a. (= 25a.)
              27b. (= 25b.)
              27c. (= 25c.)
              27d. (= 25b.)
              28. "Third Act tune"
IV/2: 29. "Two daughters of this aged stream" (Two Sirens—2S)
              30a. "Passacaglia"
              30b, c. "How happy the lover" (A, Nymphs and Sylvans—ch)
              30d. "Ritornello"
              30e, f. "For love ev'ry creature is form'd" (S, B, later ch)
              30g. "In vain are our graces" (3S)
              30h. "Then use the sweet blessing" (A, T, B)
              30i. "No, no joys are above" (3S, ch)
              31. "Fourth Act tune" (Trumpet tune)
V/2: 32a. "Prelude"
              32b. "Ye blust'ring brethren" (Aeolus—B)
              32c. "Serene and calm" (B, 2fl)
              33. "Symphony"
              34a, b. "Round thy coasts, fair nymph" (Nereid—S, B, later ch)

35a. "You say 'tis Love" (She—S, B)
35b. " 'Tis not my passion" (He—B)
35c. "Love has a thousand" (She—S)
35d. "But one soft moment" (He—B)
35e. "Let us love"
36. "For folded flocks" (Nereid—S, Pan—B)
37a, b. "Your hay it is mow'd" (Comus—T, later ch)
38. "Fairest isle" (Venus—S)
39a. "St. George, the patron of our isle" (Honour—S)
39b. "Our natives not alone appear" (ch)
40. "Fifth act tune" (Trumpet tune)
App.1 "Song tune: Come if you dare"
App.2 "Song tune: Round thy coasts"
App.3 "Song tune: Fairest isle"
App.4 "St. George the patron" (Honour—S, 2tpt)

1a.4   "The Fairy Queen," ambigue: Z629
1a. "First music: Prelude"
1b. "Hornpipe" (tune used in: There's not a swain, Z587)
2a. "Second music: Air" (also in ambigue: The Indian Queen, Z630/12)
2b. "Rondeau"
I: 3. "Overture" (also vers for hpd, ZT692): a. (Grave)
b. (Canzona)
4a. "Prelude"
4b. "Come let us leave the town" (S, B)
5a. "Prelude"
5b. "Fill up the bowl" (2S, Drunken Poet—B, later ch)
5c, d. "Trip it in a ring" (First Fairy—S, later ch)
5e. "Enough, enough: we must play" (B)
5f. "About him go" (S, later ch)
5g. "Hold, you damned tormenting punk" (B)
5h. "I'm drunk" (B)
5i. "If you will know it" (B)
5j. "Pinch him for his crimes" (ch)
5k. "I confess" (B)
5l. "Drive 'em hence" (ch)
6. "First Act tune: Jig"
II: 7a. "Prelude"
7b. "Come all ye songsters" (A)
8a. "Prelude"
8b. "May the god of wit inspire" (A, T, B)
8c. "Echo" (tpt, ob)
9. "Now join your warbling" (ch)
10a, b. "Sing while we trip it" (S, later ch)
10c. (= 10b.) (For 'A Dance of Fairies')
11a. "Prelude"
11b. "See, even Night herself is here" (Night—S)
12. "I am come to lock all fast" (Mystery—S)
13a. "Prelude" (2fl)
13b. "One charming night" (Secrecy—A, 2fl)
14a, b. "Hush no more" (Silence—B, later ch)
15. "Dance for the followers of Night"
16. "Second Act tune"
III: 17a. "Prelude"
17b, c. "If love's a sweet passion" (S, later ch)
18. "Symphony" (while the swans come forward): a. (Grave)
b. (Canzona)
19. "Dance for the fairies"
20. "Dance for the Green Men"
21a. "Ye gentle spirits of the air" (S)
21b. "Catch and repeat" (S)
22a. "Prelude"
22b. "Now the maids and the men": a. (Mr. Reading)
b. (Mr. Pate), "Dialogue between Corydon and Mopsa"
22c. "Nay, what do you mean?" (A, B)
23. "When I have often heard" (Mrs. Butler—S)
24a. "Dance for the haymakers" (vn)
24b. "Dance for a Clown" (missing)
25a, b. "A thousand ways we'll find" (A, later ch)
26. "Third Act tune: Hornpipe"
IV: 27. "Sonata while the sun rises": a. (Grave)
b. (Canzona)
c. (Largo)
d. (Allegro)
e. (Adagio)

28a. "Now the night is chas'd away" (S)
28b. "All salute the rising sun" (ch)
28c. "Ritornello"
29. "Let the fifes and the clarions" (2A)
30. "Entry of Phoebus"
31a. "Prelude"
31b. "When a cruel long winter" (Phoebus—T)
31c. " 'Tis I who give life" (T)
32a. "Hail, great parent" (ch)
32b. "Light and comfort" (ch)
32c. (= 32a.)
32d. "Thou who giv'st all" (ch)
33a. "Prelude"
33b. "Thus the ever grateful spring" (Mrs. Butler) (Spring—S)
34a. "Prelude" (2ob)
34b. "Here's the summer sprightly gay" (Mr. Pate) (Summer—A)
35a. "Prelude"
35b. "See my many colour'd fields" (Autumn—T)
36a. "Prelude"
36b. "Next, winter comes slowly" (Winter—B)
37. (= 32.)
38. "Fourth Act tune, Air"
V: 39a. "Prelude to Juno's song"
39b. "Thrice happy lovers" (Epithalamium) (Juno—S)
39c. "Be to one another true" (S)
40a, b. "O let me weep" ('the Plaint') (S, vn obbl)
41. "Entry dance"
42a. "Symphony"
42b. (Symphony)
42c. (= 42a.)
43. "Thus the gloomy world at first began to shine" (A)
44a. "Prelude"
44b, c. "Thus happy and free" (Mrs. Ayliff) (Chinese Woman—S, later ch)
45a. "Ground" (cont)
45b. "Yes Daphne (Xansi), in your looks I find" (Chinese Man—A)
46a. "Monkey's dance"
46b. (= 46a.)
47a. "Prelude"
47b. "Hark how all things in one sound agree" (First Woman—A)
48a. "Prelude" (tpt)
48b, c. "Hark! the ech'ing air" (Second Woman—S, later ch)
49a. "Sure the dull god of marriage" (2S)
49b. "Hymen! appear" (2S)
49c. (= 49b.) (ch)
49d. "Our Queen of Night" (2S)
49e. (= 49d.) (ch)
50a. "Prelude"
50b. "See, I obey" (Hymen—B)
50c. "Turn, then thine eyes" (First Woman—S, Second Woman—S)
50d. "My torch indeed will from such brightness shine" (Hymen—B)
50e, f. "They shall be as happy" (2S, B, later ch)
51. "Dance for the Chinese Man and Woman: Chaconne"
App.1 (= 8b.) (ch)
App.2 (= 36a.) (vers)
App.3 (= 41.)
App.4 "Entry Dance"

1a.5   "The Indian Queen," ambigue: Z630
1a. "First music: Air"
1b. "Second Air"
2a. "Second music: Hornpipe"
2b. "Hornpipe"
3. "Overture" (transcr for kbd, ZT690): a. (Grave)
b. (Canzona)
Prologue: 4a. "Trumpet tune" (transcr for kbd, ZT698)
4b. "Wake, Quivera" (Boy—A)
4c. "Prelude"
4d. "Why should men quarrel" (Quivera—S)
4e. "By ancient prophecies" (A)
4f. "If these be they" (S, A)
4g. "Their looks are such" (A)
4h. "If so, your goodness may your pow'r express" (S, A)
4i. (= 4a.)
4j. (= 4a.)

II: 5. "Symphony" (a, b, c used in: Come ye sons of art, Z323/1): a. (Grave)
        b. (Canzona)
        c. (Adagio)
        d. (Allegro)
6a. "I come to sing great Zempoalla's story" (Fame—A)
6b. "We come to sing great Zempoalla's story" (ch)
7a, b. "What flatt'ring noise is this" (A, T, Envy—B)
7c. "Scorn'd Envy, here's nothing" (Fame—A)
7d. "I fly from the place" (B)
7e. (= part of 7a, b.)
7f. "Begone, curst fiends of Hell" (A)
8. "First Act tune" (= 4a.)
9a. "Symphony" (tune = 6.)
9b, c. (= 6a, b.)
10. "Dance" (vn)
11. "Second Act tune: Trumpet tune" (= 9a.)
III: 12. "Dance" (?vn) (= Second Music in ambigue: The Fairy Queen, Z629/2a)
13a. "Ye twice ten-hundred deities" (Ismeron—B)
13b. "By the croaking of the toad" (Ismeron—B)
13c. "While bubbling springs" (B)
14. "Symphony" (2ob)
15. "Seek not to know" (God of Dreams—S, ob)
16. "Trumpet Overture": a. (Grave)
        b. (Canzona)
        c. (Adagio)
17a. "Ah! how happy are we" (First Aerial Spirit—A, Second Aerial Spirit—T)
17b, c. "We, the spirits of the air" (2S, later ch)
17d. "Greatness clogg'd with scorn" (2S)
17e. (= 17c.)
17f. "Cease to languish" (2S)
17g. (= 17c.)
17h. "I attempt from Love's sickness to fly" (Mrs. Cross—S)
17i. (= 17c.)
17j. (= 17d.)
17k. (= 17e.)
17l. (= 17f.)
17m. (= 17g.)
18. "Third Act tune" (also for kbd, ZT677 & ZD217)
IV: 19. "They tell us that you mighty powers" (Mrs. Cross—S)
20. "Fourth Act tune"
V: 21a. "Prelude"
21b. "While thus we bow" (ch)
21c. "You who at the altar" (High Priest—B, ch)
21d. "Prelude"
21e. "All dismal sounds" (ch)
22. "Air"

1a.6   "The Tempest, or The Enchanted Isle," ambigue: Z631
1. "Overture": a. (Grave)
        b. (Canzona)
II: 2a. "Where doth the black fiend Ambition reside?" (First Devil—B, Second Devil—B)
2b. "In Hell, with flames" (ch)
2c. "Who are the pillars" (2B)
2d. "Care, their minds when they wake" (ch)
2e. "Around we pace" (ch)
3a. "Prelude"
3b. "Arise, ye subterranean winds" (B)
4. "Dance" (vn)
III: 5a, b. "Come unto these yellow sands" (Ariel—S)
5c. "Hark the watch-dogs bark" (ch)
6a. "Prelude" (cont)
6b. "Full fathom five" (Ariel—S)
6c. "Sea-nymphs hourly" (ch)
7a. "Dry those eyes" (Ariel—S)
7b. "Ritornello"
8a. "Prelude"
8b. "Kind Fortune smiles" (S)
IV: 9. "Dance of Devils" (vn)
10. "Dear pretty youth" (Miss Cross) (A)
V: 11a. "Great Neptune" (Amphitrite—S)
11b. "My dear, my Amphitrite" (Neptune—B)
11c. "Fair and serene" (Neptune—B)
11d. "Ritornello"
13. "Aeolus, you must appear" (Neptune—B)
14a. "Your awful voice I hear" (Aeolus—A)

14b. "Air"
14c. "Come down my blusterers" (Aeolus—A)
14d. "To your prisons below" (Aeolus—A)
15a. "Prelude"
15b. "Halcyon days" (Amphitrite—S)
16a. "Prelude"
16b. "See the heavens smile" (Neptune—B)
17a, b. "No stars again shall hurt you" (Amphitrite—S, Neptune—B, later ch)

1a.7 "Timon of Athens, the Man-Hater," masque: Z632
      1. "Overture" (= Z342/1; also transcr for kbd, ZT691/1): a. (Grave)
        b. (Canzona)
        c. (Adagio)
        d. (= a.)
      2. "Air"
      3. "Jig"
      4. "Air"
      5. "Minuet"
      6a. "Air"
      6b. "Air"
      7. "Minuet"
      8. "Scotch tune"
      9. "Hornpipe"
      10a. "Prelude" (2fl)
      10b. "Hark! how the songsters" (George—S, Jacob—S, 2fl)
      11a. "Love in their little veins" (George—S)
      11b. "Ritornello" (2fl)
      12. "But ah! how much are our delights" (2S, B)
      13a. "Prelude" (2ob)
      13b. "Hence with your trifling deity" (Bacchus—B, 2ob)
      13c. "But over us no griefs prevail" (ch)
      14a. "Prelude"
      14b. "Come all to me! make haste" (Cupid—S)
      15. "Who can resist such mighty charms?" (ch)
      16a. "Prelude"
      16b. "Return, revolting rebels" (Bacchus—B)
      16c. "To grief and to care" (B)
      16d, e. (= 16a, b.)
      17. "The cares of lovers" (George—A)
      18a. "Prelude" (2ob)
      18b. "Love quickly is pall'd" (George—A, 2ob)
      19a, b. "Come let us agree" (Cupid—S, Bacchus—B, ch)
      20. "Curtain tune" (transcr for kbd, ZT680; also as: Chaconne for hpd, Z649)

1a.8 "Abdelazer, or the Moor's Revenge," incid music: Z570
      1. "Overture": a. (Grave)
        b. (Canzona: Allegro)
      2. "Rondeau" (transcr for hpd, ZT684)
      3. "Air"
      4. "Air"
      5. "Minuet"
      6. "Air" (transcr for kbd, ZT693/2)
      7. "Jig" (transcr for kbd, ZT686)
      8. "Hornpipe"
      9. "Air"
      10. "Lucinda is bewitching fair" (S & cont)

1a.9 "A Fool's Preferment, or The Three Dukes of Dunstable," incid music: Z571
      1a. "I sigh'd and I pin'd" (T)
      1b. "But now I'm a thing" (T)
      2. "There's nothing so fatal as woman" (T)
      3. "Fled is my love" (T)
      4. " 'Tis Death alone can give me ease" (T)
      5. "I'll mount to yon blue coelum" (T)
      6. "I'll sail upon the dog-star" (T)
      7. "Jenny, 'gin you can love" (Jockey—S/T)
      8. "If thou wilt give me back my love" (?Lyonel—T)
      9. "Here's a health to the king" (doubtful)

1a.10 "Amphitryon, or the Two Sosias," incid music: Z572
      1. "Overture": a. (Grave)
        b. (Canzona): "Allegro"
        c. (Adagio)
      2. "Saraband"
      3. "Hornpipe"

                    4. "Scotch tune"
                    5. "Air"
                    6. "Minuet"
                    7. "Hornpipe"
                    8. "Bourée"
        III: 9a. "Celia, that I once was blest" (S)
                    9b. "Ritornello"
                    10a. "Symphony"
        IV: 10b. "For Iris I sigh" (S)
                    11a. "Fair Iris and her swain" (S, B)
                    11b. "Thus at the height we love" Thyrsis, Iris)
                    N12. (Song tune)

1a.11   "Aureng-Zebe, or the Great Mogul," incid music: Z573
                    1a. "Ground"
                    1b. "I see she flies me" (S)
                    1c. "Were she but kind" (S)

1a.12   "Bonduca, or the British Heroine," incid music: Z574
                    1. "Overture": a. (Grave)
                            b. (Canzona)
                            c. (Adagio)
                    2. "Song-tune"
                    3. "Song-tune"
                    4. "Air" (= Minuet, Slow Air, Z592/6)
                    5. "Hornpipe"
                    6. "Air"
                    7. "Hornpipe"
                    8. "Air"
                    9. "Minuet"
                    10. "Jack, thou'rt a toper" (Soldiers—3vv)
                    11a. "Prelude"
                    11b. "Hear us, great Rugwith" (S, A, T, B, ch)
                    12. "Hear, ye gods of Britain" (Druid—B)
                    13a. "Symphony" (2fl & cont)
                    13b. "Sing ye Druids all" (2S, ch)
                    13c. "Sing divine Andate's praise" (Druids—ch)
                    14. "Divine Andate" (Druid—T)
                    15a. "Symphony" (tpt) (tune = 2.)
                    15b. "To arms, your ensigns straight display" (First Druid—A, Third Druid—B, later ?ch)
                    16a. "Prelude" (tpt, 2ob) (tune = 2.)
                    16b. "Britons strike home" (First Druid—A, later ch)
                    17a. "O lead me to some peaceful gloom" (Bonduca—S)
                    17b. "There let me soothe" (S)

1a.13   "Circe," incid music: Z575
        I/4:   1a. "Prelude"
                    1b. "We must assemble" (B, ch)
                    2a. "Their necessary aid you use" (T, B)
                    2b. "The air with music gently wound" (Third Priest—A, later ch)
                    3a. "Come ev'ry demon" (First Priest—T)
                    3b. "Circe the daughter of the sun" (T, later ch)
                    3c. "You who hatch factions" (First priest—T)
                    3d. (= 3b.) (ch)
                    4a. "Lovers who to their first embraces go" (First Woman—S)
                    4b. "In speed you can outdo" (S)
                    4c. "Behold, quick as thy thought" (A)
                    4d. "Great minister of fate" (ch)
                    4e. "At your dread word" (Second Woman—A)
                    4f. (= 4d.)
                    5. "Magician's dance" (also in incid music: The Married Beau, Z603/2)
                    6. "Pluto, arise!" (Third Priest—B)

1a.14   "Cleomenes, the Spartan Hero," incid music:.. Z576
        II: . "No, no, poor suff'ring heart" (S)

1a.15   "Distressed Innocence, or the Princess of Persia," incid music: Z577
                    1. "Overture": a. (Grave)
                            b. (Canzona)
                    2. "Air"
                    3. "Slow air"
                    4. "Air"
                    5. "Hornpipe"
                    6. "Rondeau"
                    7. (Second Music)

8. "Minuet" (also as Z770/3)

1a.16 "Don Quixote, (The Comical History of)," incid music: Z578
  Part I: 1a. "Sing all ye muses" (A, B)
    1b. "When a soldier's the story" (A, B)
    1c. "Yet see how they seem" (A, B)
    1d. "They scale the high wall" (A, B)
    1e. "Though death's underfoot" (A, B)
    1f. " 'Til fate claps her wings" (A, B)
    1g. "Then happy's she whose face" (A, B)
    2. "When the world first knew" (Galley slave—B)
    3a. "Let the dreadful engines" (Mad song) (Cardenio—B)
    3b. "Or let the frozen North" (B)
    3c. "Can nothing warm me" (B)
    3d. "Ye powers, I did but use her name" (B)
    3e. "Ah! where are now those flow'ry groves" (B)
    3f. "Why must I burn?" (B)
    3g. "Cool it then and rail" (B)
    3h. "When a woman love pretends" (B)
    3i. "And so I fairly bid 'em" (B)
    4a. "Prelude"
    4b. "With this sacred charming wand" (Montesmo—B)
    4c. "I from the clouds" (S)
    4d. "I, when I please" (S)
    4e. "Groves with eternal sweets" (ch)
    4f. "I can give beauty" (S)
    4g. "Nature restore and life when spent" (S)
    4h. "Art all can do, why then will mortals" (2S, B)
    4i. "See there a wretch" (B)
    4j. "I've a little spirit yonder" (S)
    4k. "No, that fate's too high" (ch)
    5a. "Appear ye fat fiends" (Montesmo—B, later ch)
  Part II: 6a. "Since times are so bad" ('A song sung by a clown and his wife') (S, B)
    6b. "Ambition's a trade" (Clown's wife—S, Clown—B)
    7a. "Prelude" (tpt)
    7b. "Genius of England" (Saint George—T, tpt)
    7c. "Then follow brave boys" (T, tpt)
    8. "Lads and lasses, blithe and gay" (S)
  Part III: 9. "From rosy bow'rs" (Mad song) (Altisidora—S): a. (Love): "From rosy bow'rs"
    b. (Mirthfully mad): "Or if more influencing"
    c. (Slow melancholy): "Ah! 'tis in vain"
    d. (Passion): "Bleak winds in tempests"
    e. (Swift frenzy): "No, I'll straight run mad"

1a.17 "Epsom Wells," incid music: Z579
  . "Leave these useless arts in loving" (S, B) (also for 1v & cont, Z389)

1a.18 "Henry II, King of England," incid music: Z580
  1a. "In vain 'gainst Love I strove" (S)
  1b. "Yet love more strong" (S)
  2. "Hornpipe"

1a.19 "King Richard II, or the History of the Sicilian Usurper," incid music: Z581
  . "Retir'd from any mortal's sight" ('Song for the prison scene in the last Act') (S)

1a.20 "Love Triumphant, or Nature Will Prevail," incid music: Z582
  V: . "How happy's the husband"

1a.21 "Oedipus," incid music: Z583
  III/1: 1a. "Prelude"
    1b. "Hear, ye sullen powers below" (A, T, B)
    1c. "Till they drown" (A, T, B)
    1d. "Ritornello"
    2. "Music for a while" (A)
    3a. "Come away, do not stay" (B)
    3b. (= 3a.) (ch)
    4. "Laius, hear!" (A, T, B)

1a.22 "Oroonolo," incid music: Z584
  . "Celemene, pray tell me" (2S)

1a.23 "Pausanias, the betrayer of His Country," incid music: Z585
  III/1: 1. "Sweeter than roses" (Pandora—S)
    2. "My dearest, my fairest" (S, T)

1a.24   "Regulus, or the Faction of Carthage," incid music: Z586
        II: . "Ah me! to many deaths decreed" (S)

1a.25   "Rule a Wife and Have a Wife," incid music: Z587
        . "There's not a swain on the plain" (S) (also in ambigue: The Fairy Queen, Z629/1b second part)

1a.26   "Sir Anthony Love, or the Rambling Lady," incid music: Z588
            1. "Overture": a. (Grave)
                b. (Canzona)
                c. (Adagio)
        II: 2a. "Prelude"
                2b. "Pursuing beauty men descry" (S)
                2c. "Be wise and do not try" (S)
        IV: 3. "No more, Sir, no more" (S, B)
        V: 4. "In vain, Clemene, you bestow" (S)
                5. "Ground"

1a.27   "Sir Barnaby Whigg, or No Wit Like a Woman's," incid music: Z589
        I/1: 1a. "Blow, Boreas, blow" (A)
              1b. "Then cheer my heart" (S)
              1c. "Hey! how she tosses up" (S)
              1d. "With them we'll live" (S)
              1e. "The flashes of lighting" (ch)

1a.28   "Sophonisba, or Hannibal's Overthrow," incid music: Z590
              1a. "Beneath the poplar's shadow" (Mad song) (Cumana—S)
              1b. "I swell and am bigger" (S)
              1c. "I cannot, I will not" (S)

1a.29   "The Canterbury Guests, or A Bargain Broken," incid music: Z591
        III/5:   . "Good neighbour, why do you look awry?" (2S, A, B)

1a.30   "The Double Dealer," incid music: Z592
            1. "Overture": a. (Grave)
                b. (Canzona)
                c. (Adagio)
            2. "Hornpipe"
            3. "Minuet" (transcr for kbd, Z669/4)
            4. "Air"
            5. "Hornpipe"
            6. "Minuet" (Slow Air) (also in incid music: Bonduca, Z574/4 as an air in C minor)
            7. "Minuet" (transcr for kbd, ZT676)
            8. "Air"
            9. "Air"
        II/1: 10a. "Cynthia frowns whene'er I woo her" (S)
              10b. "Prithee, Cynthia, look" (S)

1a.31   "The Double Marriage," incid music: Z593
            1. (First Music)
            2. (First Music)
            3. (Second Music)
            4. (Second Music: Minuet)
            5. "Overture": a. (Grave)
                b. (Canzona)
                c. (Adagio)
            6. "Jig"
            7. "Rondo"
            8. (Minuet)
            9. (Minuet)

1a.32   "The English Lawyer," incid music: Z594
        . "My wife has a tongue" (The Scolding Wife)

1a.33   "The Fatal Marriage, or the Innocent Adultery," incid music: Z595
        III/2: 1. "The danger is over" (S)
              2a. "I sigh'd and owned my love" (S)
              2b. "But, oh! her change" (S)
              2c. "But while she strives" (S)

1a.34   "The Female Virtuosos," incid music: Z596
        V: . "Love, thou art best of human joys" (2S)

1a.35   "The Gordian Knot Unty'd," incid music: Z597
            1. "Overture": a. (Grave)
                b. (Canzona)

      c. (Adagio)
      2. "Air" (also in welcome song: What shall be done, Z341/4b)
      3. "Rondeau Minuet" (also in ode: Why are all the muses mute, Z343/9)
      4. "Air" (pubd as part of: Overture in G major, Z770/1c)
      5. "Jig"
      6. "Chaconne"
      7. "Air"
      8. "Minuet" (also as Ritornello in song: From hardy climes, Z325/7)

1a.36   "The Indian Emperor, or The Conquest of Mexico," incid music: Z598
      . "I look'd and saw within the book of Fate" (Kalib—S)

1a.37   "The Knight of Malta," incid music: Z599
      . "At the close of the ev'ning"

1a.38   "The Libertine, or the Libertine Destroyed," incid music: Z600
      IV: 1a. "Prelude"
            1b. "Nymphs and shepherds, come away" (S)
            1c. "We come" (ch)
            1d. "In these delightful, pleasant groves" (ch)
      V: 2a. "Prelude" (flatt tpts)
            2b, c. "Prepare, prepare, new guests draw near" (S, A, B, later ch) (reused in funeral music Z851)
            2d. "Let 'em come" (ch)
            2e. "In mischief they've all" (A, later B, S)
            2f. (= 2c.) (in E-flat major)
            2g. (= 2d.)
            3a. "Prelude" (tpt)
            3b. "To arms, heroic prince" (S, tpt)
            3c. "But battles" (S, tpt)

1a.39   "The Maid's Last Prayer, or Any Rather than Fail," incid music: Z601
      IV: 1. "Though you make no return to my passion" (S)
            2a. "No, resistance is but vain" (2S) (c by Anthony Henly)
            2b. "A thousand ways" (2S)
            2c. "Sometimes he sighs" (S)
            2d. "The fierce with fierceness" (S)
            2e. "The soft with tenderness" (2S)
            2f. "The weak with pain" (2S)
            2g. (= 2a.)
      V/1: 3. "Tell me no more I am deceiv'd" (S)

1a.40   "The Marriage-Hater Match'd," incid music: Z602
      V: 1a. "As soon as the chaos was made" (S, B)
            1b. "They quickly did join" (S, B)
            1c. "For never, my friends" (S, B)
            2. "How vile are the sordid intrigues of the town" (S) (= Z608/3)

1a.41   "The Married Beau, or the Curious Impertinent," incid music: Z603
            1. "Overture": a. (Grave)
               b. (Canzona)
            2. "Slow Air" (also in incid music: Circe, Z575/5)
            3. "Hornpipe" (transcr for hpd, Z668/3)
            4. "Air"
            5. "Hornpipe"
            6. "Jig"
            7. "Trumpet Air"
            8. "March" (transcr for hpd, ZT687)
            9. "Hornpipe on a ground"
      V: 10. "See where repenting Celia lies" (S & cont)

1a.42   "The Massacre of Paris," incid music: Z604
      V/1: (A) a. "Thy genius, lo!" (Genius—B)
               b. "And swift as thought" (B)
               c. "She told thy story" (B)
               d. "But Charles, beware" (B)
         (B) . "Thy genius, lo!" (S)

1a.43   "The Mock Marriage," incid music: Z605
      II: 1. "Oh! how you protest and solemnly lie" (S)
      III: 2. " 'Twas within a furlong of Edinboro' town" (S)
            3. "Man is for the woman made" (S)

1a.44   "Theodosius, or the Force of Love," incid music: Z606
      I/1: 1. "Prepare, the rites begin" (Atticus—B, later ch)
            2a. "Can'st thou, Marina, leave" (A, T, B)

2b. "Say, votaries, can this" (ch)
3a. "The gate to bliss" (Marina—S)
3b. "Haste then" (2S)
4a. "Prelude" (2fl)
4b. "Hark, behold the heavenly choir" (Atticus—B, 2fl)
4c. "To the powers divine" (ch)
After I: 5. "Now the fight's done" (S)
After II: 6a. "Sad as death at dead of night" (S)
6b. "Curse the night" (B)
7. "Dream no more of pleasures past" (S, later S, A)
After III: 8. "Hail to the myrtle shade" (A, later S, A)
After IV: 9. "Ah! cruel, bloody fate" (S)

1a.45   "The Old Bachelor," incid music: Z607
         1. "Overture": a. (Grave)
            b. (Canzona)
            c. (Adagio)
         2. "Hornpipe"
         3. "Slow Air"
         4. "Hornpipe" (transcr for hpd, ZT685)
         5. "Rondeau"
         6. "Minuet"
         7. "Boree"
         8. "March"
         9. "Jig"
         10. "Thus to a ripe consenting maid" (Music Master—S)
         11. "As Amoret and Thyrsis"

1a.46   "The Richmond Heiress, or A Woman Once in the Right," incid music: Z608
         II: 1a. "Behold the man that with gigantic might" (Mad Man—B, Mad Woman—S)
            1b. "Come on, ye fighting fools" (B)
            1c. "Who's he that talks" (S)
            1d. "When I appear" (S)
            1e. "Ha! ha! now we mount" (B)
            1f. "Drive 'em o'er" (B)
            1g. "By this disjointed" (S)
            1h. "Then mad, very mad" (S, B)
            1i. "My face has heav'n enchanted" (S)
            1j. (= 1h.)
            1k. "I found Apollo singing" (S)
            1l. (= 1h.)
            1m. " 'Tis true, my dear Alcides" (S)
            1n. (= 1h.)
            2. "Bring the bowl and cool Nantz" (3vv) (= catch Z243)
            3. "How vile are the sordid intrigues" (S) (from incid music: The Marriage-Hater Match'd, Z602/2)

1a.47   "The Rival Sisters, or the Violence of Love," incid music: Z609
         1. "Overture" (= Z331/1): a. (Grave)
            b. (Canzona)
            c. (Adagio)
          2. "Air"
         3. "Jig"
         4. "Air"
         5. "Jig"
         6. "Air"
         7. "Minuet"
         8. "Air"
         9. "Air"
    II/1: 10a. "Celia has a thousand charms" (S)
            10b. "But while the nymph" (S)
    IV/1: 11. "Take not a woman's anger ill" (T)
            12. "How happy is she that early" (S)

1a.48   "The Spanish Friar, or the Double Discovery," incid music: Z610
    V/1:   1a. "Whilst I with grief did on you look" (S)
            1b. "Marcella, then your lover prize" (S)

1a.50   "The Virtuous Wife, or Good Luck at Last," incid music: Z611
         1. "Overture" (also for kbd, ZT693/1a, b): a. (Grave)
            b. (Canzona)
         2. "Song tune" (from incid music: Tyrannic Love, Z613/2)
         3. "Slow Air"
         4. "Air"
         5. "Preludio"
         6. "Hornpipe"

7. "Minuet"
8. "Minuet" (Trumpet minuet)
9. (?1st Act Tune)

1a.51   "The Wives' Excuse, or Cuckolds Make Themselves," incid music: Z612
 I/2:   1. "Ingrateful Love! thus ev'ry hour to punish me" (S)
 IV/1: 2. "Say, cruel Amoret, how long in billet-doux?" (T)
        3. "Corinna, I excuse thy face" (S)
 IV/3: 4. "Hang this whining way of wooing" (S)

1a.52   "Tyrannic Love, or the Royal Martyr," incid music: Z613
 IV: 1a. "Hark my Damilcar" (Nakar—B)
        1b. "Let us go" (S, B)
        1c. "Merry we go" (S, B)
        1d. "But now the sun's down" (B)
        1e. "For you need not to fear 'em" (S, later B)
        1f. "So ready and quick" (S, B)
        2. "Ah! how sweet it is to love" (Damilcar—S) (based on song tune in: The Virtuous Wife, Z611/2)

2. INSTRUMENTAL WORKS

String Fantasias & related forms:

2.1	"Chacony" (à 4), in G minor	Z730
2.2	"Fantasia" (3 parts upon a ground) (c before ?1680; 3fl/vn & cont)	Z731
2.3	"Fantasia" (à 3), in D minor (ca1678–80)	Z732
2.4	"Fantasia" (à 3), in F major (ca1678–80)	Z733
2.5	"Fantasia" (à 3), in G minor (c before ?1680)	Z734
2.6	"Fantasia" (à 4), in G minor (c1680)	Z735
2.7	"Fantasia" (à 4), in B-flat major (c1680)	Z736
2.8	"Fantasia" (à 4), in F major (c1680)	Z737
2.9	"Fantasia" (à 4), in C minor (c1680)	Z738
2.10	"Fantasia" (à 4), in D minor (c1680)	Z739
2.11	"Fantasia" (à 4), in A minor (c1680)	Z740
2.12	"Fantasia" (à 4), in E minor (c1680)	Z741
2.13	"Fantasia" (à 4), in G major (c1680)	Z742
2.14	"Fantasia" (à 4), in D minor (c1680)	Z743
2.15	"Fantasia" (à 4), in A minor (c1680)	Z744
2.16	"Fantasia upon one note" (à 5), in F major (c before ?1680)	Z745
2.17	"In nomine" (à 6), in G minor (c before ?1680)	Z746
2.18	"In nomine" (à 7), in G minor (c before ?1680)	Z747
2.19	"Pavan" (à 3), in A major (c before ?1680)	Z748
2.20	"Pavan" (à 3), in A-re flat (c before ?1680)	Z749
2.21	"Pavan" (à 3), in B-flat major (c before ?1680)	Z750
2.22	"Pavan" (à 3), in Gamut (c before ?1680)	Z751
2.23	"Pavan" (à 4), in G minor (ca ?1677)	Z752
2.24	"Pavan" (à 4), in F minor	ZN755
2.25	"Pavan," in F minor	ZN756

String Sonatas & related forms:

2.26	"Overture and Suite fragment," in G major (2vn, va & cont): No.1 "Overture": a. (Grave)	Z770
	b. (Canzona)	
	c. (Adagio)	
2.27	No.2 (Air)	
2.28	No.3 (Minuet)	
2.29	No.4 "Jigg"	
2.30	"Overture," in D minor (2vn, va & cont): a. (Grave)	Z771
	b. (Canzona)	
	c. (Adagio)	
2.31	"Overture à 5," in G minor (c ?1680; 2vn, 2va & cont): a. (Grave)	Z772
	b. (Canzona)	
	c. (Adagio)	
2.32	"Prelude for solo violin," in G minor	ZN773
2.33	"Mr. Purcell's Jig" (c1687)	ZN774
2.34	"Overture à 4," in C major	ZN775
2.35	"Overture," in C major	ZN776
2.36	"Sonata," in G minor (vn, ?b viol obbl & cont): 1a. (Grave)	Z780
	1b. (Canzona)	
	2. (Largo)	
	3. (Vivace)	

String Sonatas of three parts (2vn, b viol & cont):

2.37	Sonata No.1 in G minor (c1683)	Z790
2.38	Sonata No.2 in B-flat majorr (c1683)	Z791
2.39	Sonata No.3 in D minor (c1683)	Z792
2.40	Sonata No.4 in F major (c1683)	Z793
2.41	Sonata No.5 in A minor (c1683)	Z794
2.42	Sonata No.6 in C major (c1683)	Z795
2.43	Sonata No.7 in E minor (c1683)	Z796
2.44	Sonata No.8 in G major (c1683)	Z797
2.45	Sonata No.9 in C minor (c1683)	Z798
2.46	Sonata No.10 in A major (c1683)	Z799
2.47	Sonata No.11 in F minor (c1683)	Z800
2.48	Sonata No.12 in D major (c1683)	Z801

String Sonatas of four parts (2vn, b viol & cont):

2.49	Sonata No.1 in B minor	Z802
2.50	Sonata No.2 in E-flat major	Z803
2.51	Sonata No.3 in A minor	Z804
2.52	Sonata No.4 in D minor	Z805
2.53	Sonata No.5 in G minor	Z806
2.54	Sonata No.6 in G minor	Z807
2.55	Sonata No.7 in C major	Z808
2.56	Sonata No.8 in G minor	Z809
2.57	Sonata No.9 in F major, "The Golden Sonata"	Z810
2.58	Sonata No.10 in D major	Z811

Tpt & strings:

2.59	"Sonata," in D major (c ?1694; tpt, 2vn, va & cont)	Z850

Wind consort:

2.60	"March and Canzona" (c1692; 4 flatt tpt—slide tpts & trbn & ?kettledrum): No.1 "March"	Z860
2.61	No.2 "Canzona"	

Doubtful:

2.62	*"Fantasia" (à 4), in C major*	*ZD250*
2.63	*"Sonata Fragment," in C minor*	*ZD251*
2.64	*Sonata fragment in C minor*	*ZD252*
2.65	*"Tinker's Dance"*	*ZD253*
2.66	*"Mr. Mountfort's Farewell"*	*ZD254*
2.67	*?"Jig"*	*ZD255*
2.68	*?"Jig"*	*ZD256*
2.69	*(?Jig)*	*ZD257*

3. HARPSICHORD

3.1	"Air," in G major	Z641
3.2	"Almand," in A minor	Z642/1
3.3	"Corant," in A minor	Z642/2
3.4	"Almand" (with divisions) in G major	Z643
3.5	"Corant," in G major	Z644
3.6	"Ground in Gamut" (same bass for the first bars of Aria in J. S. Bach: Goldberg Variations, BWV988)	Z645
3.7	"Lilliburlero. A New Irish tune" (c1689)	Z646
3.8	"March," in C major (c1689)	Z647
3.9	"March," in C major (c1689)	Z648
3.10	"Minuet," in A minor (c1689)	Z649
3.11	"Minuet," in A minor (c1689)	Z650
3.12	"Minuet," in G major	Z651
3.13	"Prelude," in A minor	Z652
3.14	"Rigadoon," in C major (c1689)	Z653
3.15	"Saraband with division," in A minor	Z654
3.16	"Scotch tune" (A New Scotch tune), in G major (c1687)	Z655
3.17	"Sefauchi's farewell" (c1689)	

Harpsichord Suites:

3.18	Harpsichord Suite in G major: No.1 "Prelude"	Z660
3.19	No.2 "Almand"	
3.20	No.3 "Corant"	
3.21	No.4 "Saraband"	

Doubtful:

4. ORGAN

Doubtful:

5. ANTHEMS—SACRED VOCAL

5.1   "Awake, put on thy strength" (ca1683, Isaiah 51: 9–11; 2A, B, ch, 2vn, va & cont, inc: ch part lost): Z1
            1. "Symphony": a. (Grave)
                 b. (Canzona)
            2. "Awake, put on thy strength" (B)
            3. "Ritornello"
            4. "Therefore the redeem'd" (2A, B)
            5. (= 1b.)
            6. "Alleluia" (2A, B)
            7. "Ritornello"
            8. (ch, lost, also no indication of further sections)

5.2   "Behold, I bring you glad tidings" (c by 1687, Luke 2: 10–11, 14; A, T, B, ch, 2vn, va & cont): Z2
            1. "Symphony": a. (Grave)
                 b. (Canzona)
            2a. "Behold, I bring you" (A, T, B)
            2b. "Glad tidings" (A, T, B, ch)
            2c. "Ritornello"
            2d. "Glory to God" (2A, T, B, ch)
            3a. "And on earth peace" (A, T, B)
            3b. "Ritornello"
            3c. (= 2d.)
            3d. (= 3a.)
            3e. (= 2d.)
            3f. "Ritornello"
            4. "Alleluia" (A, T, B)
            5. (= 2d.) (ch)

5.3   "Behold, now praise the Lord" (ca1680, Psalm 134: 1–3, w/ Doxology; A, T, B, ch, 2vn, va & cont): Z3
            1. "Symphony": a. (Grave)
                 b. (Canzona)
            2. "Behold, now praise" (A, T, B)
            3. "Ritornello"
            4. "Lift up your hands" (A, T, B)
            5. "Ritornello"
            6. "Glory be to the Father" (A, T, B, ch)

5.4   "Be merciful unto me" (c by 1687, Psalm 56: 1–7, 10–11; A, T, B, ch & cont): Z4
                1. "Be merciful unto me" (A, T, B)
                2. "Mine enemies are daily" (B)
                3a. "I will praise" (A, T, B)
                3b. (= 3a.) (ch)
                4. "They daily mistake" (T)
                5. "They hold all together" (A, T, B)
                6. "In God's word" (A, T, B)
                7. "Alleluia" (ch)

5.5   "Blessed are they that fear the Lord" (c by 1688, Psalm 128: 1–3, 5, 6, 4; 2S, A, B, ch, 2vn, va & cont): .Z5
                1. "Symphony": a. (Grave)
                  b. (Canzona)
                2. "Blessed are they" (2S, A, B)
                3. "Ritornello"
                4a. "For thou shalt eat the labour" (B)
                4b. "O well is Thee" (2S, A, B)
                5a. "The Lord thy God" (B)
                5b. (= 4b.)
                6. "Yea, thou shalt see" (A)
                7a. "O well is Thee" (2S, A, B)
                7b. "Lo, thus shall the man" (2S, A, B)
                7c. "Ritornello"
                7d. (= 7b.) (2S, A, B)
                8. "Alleluia" (2S, A, B)
                9. "Alleluia" (ch)

5.6   "Blessed be the Lord, my strength" (c before 1683, Psalm 144: 1–8; A, T, B, ch & cont): Z6
                1. "Blessed be the Lord, my strength" (B)
                2a. "Lord, what is man?" (A, T, B)
                2b. "Man is like a thing" (A, T, B)
                3. "His time passeth away" (ch)
                4. "Bow Thy heav'ns, O Lord" (A, T, B)
                5. "Send down Thine hand" (ch)

5.7   "Blessed is he that considereth the poor" (ca1688, Psalm 41: 1–3, w/ Doxology; A, T. B, ch & cont): Z7
                1. "Blessed is he" (A, T, B)
                2. "The Lord preserve him" (A)
                3. "The Lord comfort him" (A, T, B)
                4. "Make Thou all" (A, T, B)
                5. "Glory be to the Father" (A, T, B)
                6. "Alleluia" (ch)

5.8   "Blessed is he whose unrighteousness ..." (ca1680–2, Psalm 32: 1–7, 10, 11; 2S, A, 2T, B, ch & cont): .Z8
                1. "Blessed is he whose unrighteousness is forgiv'n" (2S, A, 2T, B)
                2a. "For while I held my tongue" (B)
                2b. (= 3.) (B)
                3. "I will acknowledge my sin" (ch)
                4. "I said, I will" (A, T, B)
                5a. "Thou art a place" (T)
                5b. (= 6.) (T)
                6. "Thou shalt compass" (ch)
                7. "Great plagues remain" (2S)
                8. "Be glad, O ye righteous" (2S, A, 2T, B)
                9. "Alleluia" (ch)

5.9   "Blessed is the man that feareth the Lord" (ca1688, Psalm 112: 1–5, 9; A, T, B, ch & cont): Z9
                1. "Symphony"
                2. "Blessed is the man" (A, T, B)
                3. "His seed shall be" (A, T, B)
                4. "Riches and plenteousness" (A, T, B)
                5. "Unto the Godly" (A, T, B)
                6a. "Alleluia" (A, T, B)
                6b. (= 6a.) (ch)

5.10   "Blow up the trumpet in Sion" (ca1681, Joel 2: 15–17; vv, ch & cont): Z10
                1. "Blow up the trumpet" (cantoris: S, A & decani: 2S, A, T, B)
                2. "Sanctify a fast" (cantoris: S, A & decani: 2S, A, T, B)
                3. (= 1.) (ch: cantoris & decani)
                4. "Assemble the elders" (cantoris: S, A & decani: 2S, A, T, B)
                5a. "Let them weep" (cantoris: S, A & decani: 2S, A, T, B)
                5b. "And let them say" (cantoris: S, A & decani: 2S, A, T, B)
                5c. (= 6.) (cantoris: S, A & decani: 2S, A, T, B)
                6. "Spare Thy people" (d ch)
                7. "Wherefore should they" (cantoris: S, A & decani: 2S, A, T, B)
                8. (= 7.) (d ch)

5.11   "Bow down Thine ear, O Lord" (ca1680–2, Psalm 86: 1, 3–5, 8, 10–12; S, A, T, B, ch & cont)...............Z11
                1a. "Prelude"
                1b. "Bow down Thine ear" (S, A, T, B)
                2. "Be merciful unto me" (T)
                3a. "For Thou, Lord" (A, T, B)

3a. "Jerusalem is built" (A, T, B)
3b. "Ritornello"
3c. "For there is the seat" (T)
4. "Symphony"
5. "O pray for the peace" (A, T, B)
6. "Peace be within" (ch)
7. "For my brethen" (A, T, B)

5.23   "I will give thanks unto Thee, O Lord" (ca1685, Psalm 138: 1–8; 2S, A, T, B, ch, 2vn, va & cont): Z20
1. "Symphony": a. (Grave)
   b. (Canzona)
2a. "I will give thanks" (2S, A, T, B)
2b. "Ritornello"
3. "I will worship" (S)
4. "When I called" (2S, A, T, B)
5. "Ritornello"
6. (= 2.) (ch)
7. (= 1a, b.)
8. "All the kings" (A, T, B)
9. "Ritornello"
10. "For though the Lord" (B)
11. "The Lord shall" (2S, A, T, B, ch)

5.24   "I will give thanks unto the Lord" (c ?1685, Psalm 111: 1–4, 6–9; T, 2B, ch, 2vn & cont): Z21
1a. "Prelude"
1b. "I will give thanks" (T, 2B)
2. "Symphony"
3a. "The works of the Lord" (B)
3b. "Ritornello"
3c. "His work is worthy" (T, 2B)
4a. "The merciful and gracious" (ch)
4b. (= 4a.) (2T, B)
4c. (= 4a.)
5. (= 2.)
6. "He hath shewed" (T)
7. "They stand fast" (T, 2B)
8. "Holy and reverend" (T, 2B)

5.25   "I will love Thee, O Lord" (ca ?1679, Psalm 18: 1–6, 16–18; B, ch & cont, discovered Zimmerman): .. ZN67
1. "I will love Thee" (B)
2. "I will call upon the Lord" (B)
3. "They prevented me" (ch)
4. "The sorrows of death" (B)
5. "So shall He hear" (B)
6. "He shall send down" (B)

5.26   *"I will love Thee, O Lord" (frag)* *ZN70*
5.27   "I will sing unto the Lord" (c before 1683, Psalm 104: 33–5; 2S, A, T, B & ch): Z22
1. "I will sing" (ch)
2. "My joy shall be" (ch)
3a. "As for sinners" (2S, A, T, B)
3b. (= 3a.) (ch)
4. "And the ungodly" (2S, A, T, B)
5. "But praise ye the Lord" (ch)

5.28   "Let God arise" (c after 1683, Psalm 68: 1–3, 7–8; 2T, ch & cont): Z23
1. "Let God arise" (2T)
2. "But let the righteous" (ch)
3. "O God, when Thou" (2T)
4. "Ev'n as Mount Sinai also" (ch)

5.29   "Let mine eyes run down with tears" (c ?1682, Jeremiah 14: 17–22; 2S, A, T, B, ch & cont): Z24
1a. "Let mine eyes" (2S, A, T, B)
1b. "If I go forth" (B)
2. "We acknowledge" (ch)
3. "Do not abhor us" (2S, A, T, B)
4. "Therefore will we wait" (2S, A, T, B)

5.30   "Lord, how long wilt Thou be angry" (ca1680–2, Psalm 79: 5, 8, 9, 13; A, T, B, ch & cont): Z25
1. "Lord, how long" (ch)
2. "O remember not" (A, T, B)
3. "Help us, O God" (ch)
4. "So we that are" (ch)

5.31   "Lord, who can tell how oft he offendeth?" (ca1678, Psalm 19: 12–14, w/ Doxology; 2T, B, ch & cont):.. Z26
1a. "Prelude"
1b. "Lord who can tell" (2T, B)
2. "Keep Thy servant" (2T, B)
3. "Let the words" (2T, B)
4. "Glory be to the Father" (ch)

5.32   "Man that is born of a woman" (ca1680–2, Job 14: 1–2 & Funeral Sentences from The Book of Common
Prayer of 1660; S, A, T, B, ch & cont): Z27
1a. "Man that is born" (S, A, T, B)

        1b. "He fleeth as it were" (ch)
        2. "In the midst of life" (S, A, T, B)
        3. "Yet, O Lord" (S, A, T, B)
        4a. "Thou knowest, Lord" (ch)
        4b. "But spare us, Lord" (ch)
        5. "Suffer us not" (S, A, T, B, ch)

5.33   "My beloved spake" (c before 1683, The Song of Solomon 2: 10–13, 16; A, T, 2B, ch, 2vn, va & cont): Z28
        1. "Symphony"
        2a. "My beloved spake" (A, T, 2B)
        2b. "Ritornello"
        3a. "For lo! the winter" (A, T, 2B)
        3b. "Ritornello"
        4. "The flow'r appear" (A, T, 2B)
        5a. "And the time" (ch)
        5b. "Ritornello"
        5c. (= 5a.) (A, T, 2B)
        5d. "Alleluia" (A, T, 2B)
        5e. "Ritornello"
        6. "And the voice" (A, T, 2B)
        7. (= 1.)
        8a. "The fig tree" (T)
        8b. (= 2b.)
        9. "My beloved is mine" (A, T, 2B)
        10. "Ritornello"
        11. "Alleluia" (A, T, 2B)
        12. "Ritornello"
        13a. (= opening of 9.) (ch)
        13b. "Alleluia" (A, T, B)

5.34   "My heart is fixed, O God" (ca1684, Psalm 57: 7–11; A, T, B, ch, 2vn, va & cont): Z29
        1. "My heart is fixed" (A, T, B)
        2a. "Awake up my glory" (A, T, B)
        2b. "I myself will awake" (A, T, B)
        3. "Ritornello"
        4. "I will give thanks" (A, T, B)
        5. (= 3.)
        6a. "Set up Thyself" (A, T, B)
        6b. "Ritornello"
        6c. (= 6a.)
        6d. "Ritornello"
        7a. "Alleluia" (A, T, B)
        7b. "Ritornello"
        7c. "Alleluia" (ch)

5.35   "My heart is inditing" (c1685, Psalm 45: 1, 9b, 14, 15, 10, 17, Isaiah 49: 23; 2S, 2A, 2T, 2B, d ch, 2vn,
    va & cont): Z30
        1. "Symphony": a. (Grave)
          b. (Canzona)
        2a. "My heart is inditing" (d ch)
        2b. "Ritornello"
        3. "At his right hand" (d ch)
        4a. "She shall be brought" (2S, 2A, T, B)
        4b. "With joy and gladness" (2S, 2A, T, 2B)
        5. (= 1a, b.)
        6a. "Hearken, O daughter" (2S, 2A, 2T, 2B)
        6b. "Ritornello"
        7a. "Praise the Lord" (d ch)
        7b. "Ritornello"
        7a. "Praise the Lord" (d ch)
        7b. "Ritornello"
        8. "Alleluia, Amen" (d ch)

5.36   "My song shall be alway" (c ?1688, Psalm 89: 1, 5–9, 13–15; B/S, ch, 2vn, va & cont): Z31
        1. "Symphony": a. (Grave)
          b. (Canzona)
        2. "My song shall be" (B/S)
        3. "O Lord, the very heav'ns" (B/S)
        4a. "Prelude" (= 4b.)
        4b. "For who is he" (B/S)
        5. "God is very greatly" (B/S)
        6. "Alleluia" (ch)
        7. (= 1.)
        8a. "O Lord God of hosts" (B/S)
        8b. "Thou rulest the raging" (B/S)
        8c. "Ritornello"
        9. "Thou hast a mighty arm" (B/S)
        10. "Mercy and truth" (B/S)
        11. "Alleluia" (B/S)

8. "O Lord, our Governor" (2B)
9. "Glory be to the Father" (ch)

5.45   "O Lord, rebuke me not" (Psalm 6: 1–7; 2S, ch & cont): Z40
1a. "O Lord, rebuke me not" (2S)
1b. "Ritornello"
1c. "Have mercy upon me" (2S)
2. "Turn Thee, O Lord" (2S)
3. (= 2.) (ch)
4. "For in death" (2S)

5.46   "O Lord, Thou art my God" (ca1680–2, Isaiah 25: 1, 4, 7–9; A, T, B, ch & cont): Z41
1. "O Lord, Thou art my God" (B)
2. "For Thou hast been" (A, T)
3. "And He will destroy" (B)
4. "He will swallow up death" (A, T, B)
5. "O Lord, Thou art my God" (ch)
6. "And it shall be said" (A, T, B)
7. "Alleluia" (A, T, B)
8. "Alleluia" (ch)

5.47   "O praise God in His holiness" (ca1683, Psalm 150: 1–6; A, T, 2B, ch, 2vn, va & cont):.........................Z42
1. "Symphony": a. (Grave)
      b. (Canzona)
2a. "O praise God" (A, T, B)
2b. "Praise Him in the firmament" (A, T, B)
3. "Ritornello"
4a "Praise Him in His noble acts" (A, T, 2B)
4b. "Praise Him according" (A, T, B)
5. "Ritornello"
6. "Praise Him in the sound" (A, T, 2B w/ vn obbl)
7. "Praise Him in the cymbals" (A)
8. (= 1b.)
9a. "Praise Him on the well-tuned cymbals" (B)
9b. "Ritornello"
10. "Let ev'rything that hath breath" (A, T, 2B, ch)

5.48   "O praise the Lord, all ye heathen" (ca1682, Psalm 117: 1–2, w/ Doxology; 2T, ch & cont): Z43
1. "O praise the Lord" (2T)
2. "Alleluia" (ch)
3. "Glory be to the Father" (2T)

5.49   "O sing unto the Lord" (c1688, Psalm 96: 1–3, 6, 4, 5, 9, 10; S, A, T, 2B, ch, 2vn, va & cont): Z44
1. "Symphony": a. (Grave)
      b. (Canzona)
2a. "O sing unto the Lord" (B)
2b. "Alleluia" (ch)
2c. "Sing unto the Lord all the whole earth" (B)
2d. "Alleluia" (ch)
2e. "Ritornello"
2f. "Sing unto the Lord" (S, A, T, B)
3a. "Declare His honour" (B)
3b. "Glory and worship" (ch)
4. "The Lord is great" (S, A)
5. "Ritornello"
6. "O worship the Lord" (S, A, T, 2B)
7a. "Tell it out" (B, ch)
7b. "The Lord is King" (ch)
7c. "And that it is He" (B)
7d. " 'Tis He who hath made" (ch)
7e. "And how that He shall" (B)
7f. "He shall judge" (ch)
8. "Alleluia" (S, A, 2B, later ch)

5.50   "Out of the deep have I called" (ca1680, Psalm 130: 1–7; S, A, B, ch & cont): Z45
1. "Out of the deep" (S, A, B)
2. "But there is mercy" (S, A, B, later ch)
3. "I look for the Lord" (B)
4. "O! Israel, trust in the Lord" (S, A, B, later ch)

5.51   "Praise the Lord, O Jerusalem" (ca1688, Psalm 147: 12, w/ Isaiah 49: 23, Psalm 48: 8, Psalm 21: 13;
     2S, A, T, B, ch, 2vn, va & cont): Z46
1. "Symphony": a. (Grave)
      b. (Canzona)
2a. "Praise the Lord" (2S, A, T, B)
2b. "Ritornello"
2c. "For Kings shall be" (ch)
3a. "Prelude"
3b. "As we have heard" (A, T, B, later ch)
4a. "Ritornello"
4b. "Be Thou exalted" (2S, A, T, B, ch)
5. "Alleluia" (ch)

5.60　"The Lord is King, be the people never so impatient" (c after ?1690, Psalm 99: 1–3, 5, w/ Doxology;
　　　　2S, ch & cont): Z53
　　　　　1. "The Lord is King" (2S)
　　　　　2. "The Lord is great" (2S)
　　　　　3. "O magnify" (ch)
　　　　　4. "Glory be to the Father" (2S)
　　　　　5. "Alleluia" (ch)
5.61　"The Lord is King, the earth may be glad" (c1688, Psalm 97: 1–6, 10–12; B, ch & cont): Z54
　　　　　1. "Prelude"
　　　　　2. "The Lord is King" (B)
　　　　　3. "Clouds of darkness" (B)
　　　　　4. "There shall go before Him" (B)
　　　　　5. "The hills melted" (B)
　　　　　6. "The heav'ns have declared" (ch)
　　　　　7. "O ye that love" (B)
　　　　　8. "There is sprung up a light" (B)
　　　　　9. "Rejoice in the Lord" (B)
　　　　　10. "Alleluia" (ch)
　　　　　11. "Rejoice and give thanks" (B)
　　　　　12. (= 9.)
5.62　"The Lord is my light" (ca1683–4, Psalm 27: 1, 3–6; A, T, B, ch, 2vn, va & cont): Z55
　　　　　1. "Symphony": a. (Grave)
　　　　　　　b. (Canzona)
　　　　　2a. "The Lord is my light" (A, T, B)
　　　　　2b. "Ritornello"
　　　　　3a. "Though an host" (B)
　　　　　3b. "Ritornello"
　　　　　3c. "For in the time of trouble" (A, T, B)
　　　　　4. (= 1b.)
　　　　　5a. "And now shall He lift" (A)
　　　　　5b. "Ritornello"
　　　　　6. "Therefore will I offer" (A, T, B)
　　　　　7a. "Alleluia" (A, T, B)
　　　　　7b. "Ritornello"
　　　　　7c. "Alleluia" (ch)
5.63　"The way of God is an undefiled way" (c1694, Psalm 18: 30–32, 34, 38–42, 49–51; 2A, B, ch & cont): .Z56
　　　　　1. "Prelude"
　　　　　2. "The way of God" (2A, B)
　　　　　3a. "It is God that girdeth me" (2A, B)
　　　　　3b. "He teacheth my hands" (2A, B)
　　　　　3c. "Thou hast girded me" (B)
　　　　　4. "For this cause will I" (2A)
　　　　　5. "Alleluia" (2A, B)
　　　　　6. "Thou hast made mine enemies" (B)
　　　　　7. "They shall cry" (2A)
　　　　　8. "The Lord liveth" (B)
　　　　　9. "Great prosperity" (2A, B)
　　　　　10. "It is He that hath" (B)
　　　　　11. "Great prosperity" (2A, B)
　　　　　12. (= 5.) (2A, B, ch)
5.64　"They that go down to the sea" (c1685, Psalm 107: 23–32; A, B, ch, 2vn & cont): Z57
　　　　　1. "Symphony": a. (Grave)
　　　　　　　b. (Canzona)
　　　　　2. "They that go down" (B)
　　　　　3. "Ritornello"
　　　　　4. "So when they cry" (A, B)
　　　　　5. "Ritornello"
　　　　　6. "Then are they glad" (A, B)
　　　　　7. "Ritornello"
　　　　　8. "O that men would therefore" (A, B)
　　　　　9. "Ritornello"
　　　　　10. "O, praise the Lord" (ch)
5.65　"Thou know'st, Lord, the secrets of our hearts" I (1st vers of 1st setting) (c before 1683, The Book of
　　　　　Common Prayer of 1660; ch & cont): Z58A
　　　　　1. "Thou know'st Lord" (ch)
　　　　　2. "But spare us, Lord" (ch)
　　　　　3. "Suffer us not" (ch)
5.66　"Thou know'st, Lord, the secrets of our hearts" I (2nd vers of 1st setting) (ca1683, The Book of
　　　　　Common Prayer of 1660; S, A, T, B, ch & cont): Z58B
　　　　　1. "Thou knowest, Lord" (S, A, T, B)
　　　　　2. "But spare us" (S, A, T, B)
　　　　　3. "Suffer us not" (S, A, T, B)
5.67　"Thou know'st, Lord, the secrets of our hearts" II (2nd setting) (ca1683, The Book of Common Prayer
　　　　　of 1660; ch, flatt tpts & cont): Z58C
　　　　　1. "Thou knowest, Lord" (ch)

9c. "Blessed are all they" (A, T, B)
9d. "Ritornello"
10. "Blessed are they" (ch)
11. "Alleluia" (ch)

Doubtful:

6. CANONS—SACRED VOCAL (ch)

Doubtful:

7. CHANTS—SACRED VOCAL (ch)

Doubtful:

8. HYMNS, PSALMS & PART-SONGS—SACRED VOCAL

8.1   "Ah! few and full of sorrows," hymn (c1680, G. Sandys after Job 14: 1; T, B, ch & cont): Z130
        1. "Ah! few and full of sorrows" (ch)
        2. "Wilt thou thine eyes" (T)
        3. "O! that thou would'st" (B)
        4. "I will expect until my change" (ch)
8.2   "Beati omnes qui timent Dominum," Latin hymn (c1680, Vulgate: Psalm 127: 1–4; S, B, ch & cont): ... Z131
        1. "Beati omnes qui timent Dominum" (ch)
        2a. "Labores manuum tuarum" (ch)
        2b. "Uxor tua sicut vitis" (B)
        2c. "Filii tui sicut novellae olivarum" (S)
        3. "Ecce, sic benedicitum homo" (ch)
        4. "Alleluia" (ch)

9. SONGS & DUETS—SACRED VOCAL

10. SERVICES—SACRED VOCAL

10.1   Service (in B-flat major) (Morning, Communion and Evening Services) (c1682): Z230
        "Morning Service" (in B-flat major):
           1. "Te Deum laudamus" (The Song of St. Ambrose) (Eng transl of Latin hymn by ?Nicetas,
              Bishop of Remesiana of ca 400 A.D.; vv, ch & cont):
              a. "We praise Thee, O God" (ch)
              b. "To Thee all angels cry" (decani & cantoris: 2S, A, T, B)
              c. "Holy, holy, holy" (ch: decani & cantoris)
              d. "The Father of an infinite majesty" (decani & cantoris: 2S, A, T, B)
              e. "When Thou took'st upon Thee" (decani & cantoris: 2S, A, T, B)
              f. "Thou sittest at the right hand of God" (ch)
              g. "Make them to be numbered" (decani: S, A, T, B & cantoris: S, A)
              h. "Day by day we magnify Thee" (ch)
              i. "Vouchsafe, O Lord" (Canon 4 in 2) (decani & cantoris: S, A, B)
              j. "O Lord, let Thy mercy" (decani: S, A & cantoris: S)
              k. "O Lord, in Thee" (ch: decani & cantoris)
           2. "Benedictus" (Luke 1: 68, The Song of Zacharias; vv, ch & cont):
              a. "Blessed be the Lord of Israel" (ch)
              b. "As He spake" (decani & cantoris: 2S, 2A, T, B)
              c. "To perform the mercy" (ch: decani & cantoris)
              d. "And thou, child, shalt be called the prophet" (Canon 4 in 1) (ch)
              e. "To give knowledge" (decani & cantoris: 2S, 2A, T, B)
              f. "Glory be to the Father" (Canon 2 in 1 by inversion) (ch: decani & cantoris)
           3. "Benedicite omnia opera" (Daniel 3: 52–58, The song of the Three Children; vv, ch & cont):
              a. "O all ye works of the Lord" (B)
              b. "Bless ye the Lord" (ch)
              c. "O ye sun and moon" (decani & cantoris: 2S, A, T, B)
              d. "O ye fire and heat" (ch: decani & cantoris)
              e. "O ye nights and days" (decani & cantoris: 2S, A, T, B)

      f. "O let the earth bless the Lord" (ch)

      g. "O ye mountains and hills" (ch: decani & cantoris)

      h. "O ye seas and floods" (decani & cantoris: 2S, A, T, B)

      i. "O ye priests of the Lord" (decani & cantoris: 2S, A, T, B)

      j. "Glory be to the Father" (Canon 2 in 1) (ch)

    4. "Jubilate Deo" (Psalm 100: 1–5; vv, ch & cont):

      a. "O be joyful in the Lord" (ch)

      b. "Be ye sure that the Lord" (ch)

      c. "O go your way into His gates" (Canon 4 in 2 per arsin et thesin) (decani: S, A, T, B)

      d. "For the Lord is gracious" (cantoris: A, T, B)

      e. "Glory be to the Father" (ch)

"Communion Service" (in B-flat major):

    5. "Kyrie eleison: Lord have mercy upon us" (ch: decani & cantoris)

    6. "Nicene creed" (vv, ch & cont):

      a. "I believe in one God"

      b. "The Father almighty" (ch)

      c. "And in one Lord" (decani: S, A, T, B & cantoris: S, T)

      d. "Very God of very God" (ch)

      e. "Who for us men" (decani: S, A, T, B & cantoris: S, A)

      f. "And ascended into Heav'n" (Canon 4 in 1) (ch: decani & cantoris)

      g. "And I believe in the Holy Ghost" (decani: S, A, T, B & cantoris: S, A)

      h. "And I believe in one Catholic and Apostolic" (decani: S, A, T, B & cantoris: S, A)

      i. "And I look for the Resurrection" (ch: decani & cantoris)

"Evening Service" (in B-flat major):

    7. "Magnificat" (Luke 1: 46–55, The Song of Blessed Marie; vv, ch & cont):

      a. "My soul doth magnify the Lord" (ch)

      b. "For He hath regarded" (cantoris: S, A & decani: S, A, T, B)

      c. "And His mercy is on them" (ch: decani & cantoris)

      d. "He hath shewed strength" (cantoris: S, A & decani: S, A, T, B)

      e. "He rememb'ring His mercy" (ch: decani & cantoris)

      f. "As He promised" (decani: A & cantoris: A, T, B)

      g. "Glory be to the Father" (Canon 3 in 1) (ch: decani & cantoris)

    8. "Nunc dimittis" (Luke 2: 29–32, The Song of Simeon; vv, ch & cont):

      a. "Lord, now lettest Thou Thy servant depart in peace" (ch)

      b. "For mine eyes have seen" (decani: S, A, T, B & cantoris: S, A)

      c. "Glory be to the Father" (Canon 4 in 2) (ch)

    9. "Cantate Domino" (Psalm 98: 1–8; vv, ch & cont):

      a. "O sing unto the Lord a new song" (ch)

      b. "The Lord declared His salvation" (decani: S, A, T, B & cantoris: S, A)

      c. "O shew yourselves joyful" (ch: decani & cantoris)

      d. "Praise the Lord upon the harp" (cantoris: A, T, B & ch)

      e. "With trumpets also" (ch)

      f. "Let the sea make a noise" (ch)

      g. "Let the floods clap their hands" (decani: S, A & cantoris: A)

      h. "With righteousness shall He judge" (decani: A, T, B & cantoris: A)

      i. "Glory be to the Father" (Canon 3 in 1 by inversion) (ch)

    10. "Deus misereatur" (Psalm 67: 1–7; vv, ch & cont):

      a. "God be merciful unto us" (ch)

      b. "That Thy way may be known" (decani: S, A & cantoris: S)

      c. "Let the people praise Thee" (ch: decani & cantoris)

      d. "O let the nations rejoice" (cantoris: A, T, B)

      e. (= c. except for opening) (ch)

      f. "Then shall the earth" (decani: S, A & cantoris: S)

      g. "God shall bless us" (decani: A, T, B & cantoris: A)

      h. "Glory be to the Father" (Canon 4 in 1 by inversion) (ch)

10.2   "Evening Service" (in G minor): Z231

    1. "Magnificat" (Luke 1: 46–55, The Song of Blessed Marie; vv, ch & cont):

      a. "My soul doth magnify the Lord" (ch)

      b. "For behold, He hath regarded" (cantoris: A, T, B & decani: 2S, A)

      c. "Holy is His name" (ch)

      d. "And His mercy is on them" (cantoris: A, T, B & decani: 2S, A)

      e. "He hath put down the mighty" (cantoris: A, T, B & 'full')

      f. "He rememb'ring His mercy" (cantoris: A, T, B & decani: 2S, A)

      g. "Glory be to the Father" (ch)

    2. "Nunc dimittis" (Luke 2: 29–32, The Song of Simeon; S, A, T, B, ch & cont):

      a. "Lord now lettest Thou Thy sevant depart" (ch)

      b. "For mine eyes have seen" (decani: 2S, A & cantoris: A, T, B)

      c. "Glory be to the Father" (Canon 4 in 2, inc) (S, A, T, B)

      d. "As it was in the beginning" (B, ch)

10.3   "Te Deum and Jubilate" (in D major) (Morning Service) (c1694) Z232

    1. "Te Deum laudamus" (The Song of St. Ambrose) (Eng transl of Latin hymn by ?Nicetas,
       Bishop of Remesiana of ca 400 A.D.; vv, ch, 2tpt, 2vn, va & cont):

      a. "Prelude"

      b. "We praise Thee, O God" (A, T, B)

      c. "To Thee Cherubin and Seraphin" (2S, ch)

        d. "The glorious company of the Apostles" (A, T, B)
        e. "The Father of an infinite Majesty" (2S, 2A)
        f. "Thou art the King of Glory" (ch)
        g. "When Thou took'st upon Thee" (A, B)
        h. "Thou sittest at the right hand" (2S, A, T, B)
        i. "O Lord save Thy people" (A, T, B)
        j. "Day by day we magnify Thee" (ch)
        k. "Vouchsafe, O Lord, to keep us this day" (A)
        l. "O Lord, in Thee have I trusted" (ch)
    2. "Jubilate Deo" (Psalm 100: 1–5):
        a. "Prelude"
        b. "O be joyful in the Lord" (A)
        c. "O be joyful" (ch)
        d. "Be ye sure that the Lord He is God" (S, A)
        e. "O go your way into His gates" (Canon 4 in 1) (ch)
        f. "For the Lord is gracious" (A, B)
        g. "Glory be to the Father" (ch)

Doubtful:

10.4	*"Sanctus"*	*ZD90*
10.5	*"Te Deum," in C major*	*ZD91*

11. CATCHES—SECULAR VOCAL

11.1	"A health to the nut-brown lass" (c before 1685; 3vv)	Z240
11.2	"An ape, a lion, a fox and an ass" (c1686; 3vv)	Z241
11.3	"As Roger last night" (Roger and Jenny) (3vv)	Z242
11.4	"Bring the bowl and cool Nantz" (A Punch Catch) (c1693–4; 3vv; used in incid music Z608/2)	Z243
11.5	"Call for the reck'ning" (The Careless Drawer) (3vv)	Z244
11.6	"Come, let us drink" (3vv)	Z245
11.7	"Come, my hearts, play your parts" (A Loyal Catch) (c1685; 3vv)	Z246
11.8	"Down with Bacchus" (c1693; 3vv)	Z247
11.9	"Drink on, till night be spent" (c1686; 3vv)	Z248
11.10	"Full bags, a brisk bottle" (c1686, Colonel Jacob Allistree; 3vv)	Z249
11.11	"God save our sov'reign Charles" (c1685; 3vv)	Z250
11.12	"Great Apollo and Bacchus" (ca1682–90; 3vv)	Z251
11.13	"Here's a health, pray let it pass" (4vv)	Z252
11.14	"Here's that will challenge all the Fair" (Bartholomew Fair) (c1673; 3vv)	Z253
11.15	"He that drinks is immortal" (c1686; 3vv)	Z254
11.16	"If all be true that I do think" (c1689, ?Dean Aldrich after epigram of Jean Sirmond; 3vv)	Z255
11.17	"I gave her cakes and I gave her ale" (c1690; 3vv)	Z256
11.18	"Is Charleroi's siege come too?" (A catch upon Charleroy) (c1692; 3vv)	Z257
11.19	"Let the grave folks go preach" (The Jovial Drinker) (c1685; 3vv)	Z258
11.20	"Let us drink to the blades" (c ?1691; 3vv)	Z259
11.21	"My lady's coachman John" (c1687; 3vv)	Z260
11.22	"Now England's great council" ('A catch made in time of Parliament, 1676') (c1676; 3vv)	Z261
11.23	"Now we are met and humours agree" (c1687; 3vv)	Z262
11.24	"Of all the instruments that are" ('A catch for three voices in commendation of the viol') (c1693; 3vv)	Z263
11.25	"Once in our lives let us drink to our wives" (c ?1680, anon: A Farewell to Wives; 3vv)	Z264
11.26	"Once, twice, thrice I Julia tried" (3vv)	Z265
11.27	"One industrious insect" (3vv, also in Latin)	Z266
11.28	"Pale faces, stand by" (c1688; 3vv)	Z267
11.29	"Pox on you for a fop" (3vv)	Z268
11.30	"Prithee ben't so sad and serious" (3vv)	Z269
11.31	"Room for th' express" ('Written on the fall of Limerick, July, 1694') (c1694; 3vv)	Z270
11.32	"Since the Duke is return'd" (On the Duke's return) (c ?1682; 3vv)	Z271
11.33	"Since time so kind to us does prove" (ca1682–90; 3vv)	Z272
11.34	"Sir Walter enjoying his damsel" (3vv)	Z273
11.35	"Soldier, take off thy wine" (4vv)	Z274
11.36	"Sum up all the delights" (c1687; 3vv)	Z275
11.37	"The Macedon youth left behind" (c1686; 4vv)	Z276
11.38	"The miller's daughter riding to the fair" (c1686; 3vv)	Z277
11.39	"The surrender of Lim'rick" (c1691; 3vv)	Z278
11.40	" 'Tis easy to force" (A catch on a horse) (c ?1681; 4vv)	Z279
11.41	" 'Tis too late for a coach" (c1686; 3vv)	Z280
11.42	" 'Tis women makes us love" (c1685 or ca ?1681; 4vv)	Z281
11.43	"To all lovers of music" (A catch by way of epistle) (c1687, Carr; 3vv)	Z282
11.44	"To thee and to a maid" (c1685; 3vv)	Z283
11.45	"True Englishmen drink a good health" ('Song with music on the 7 Bishops') (ca1689; 3vv)	Z284
11.46	"Under a green (great) elm lies Luke Shepherd's helm" (c1686; 4vv)	Z285
11.47	"Under this stone lies Gabriel John" (An old epitaph) (c1686; 3vv)	Z286
11.48	"When V and I together meet" (c1686; 3vv)	Z287
11.49	"Who comes there? Stand!" (c1685; 3vv)	Z288

11.50   "Wine in a morning makes us frolic" (c1686, Tom Brown; 3vv) Z289
11.51   "Would you know how we meet" (c1685, ?Thomas Otway; 3vv) Z290
11.52   "Young Collin cleaving of a beam" (c1691, Thomas D'Urfey from Latin of G. Buchanan; 3vv) Z291
11.53   "Young John the gard'ner" (c1683; 4vv) Z292

Doubtful:

11.54   *"Fie, nay prithee John" (A scolding catch) (c1685, anon)* *ZD100*
11.55   *"Hail happy words, abodes of peace" (A round)* *ZD101*
11.56   *"Say, good master Bacchus"* *ZD103*
11.57   *"Since women so false and so jiltish are grown"* *ZD104*
11.58   *"The glass was just tim'd"* *ZD105*
11.59   *"Tom, making a mantua for a lass" (Tom the Tailor)* *ZD106*
11.60   *"Well rung, Tom boy"* *ZD107*

12. ODES, BIRTHDAY SONGS, WELCOME SONGS, ETC—SECULAR VOCAL

12.1   "Arise, my muse" (Birthday song for Queen Mary) (c1690, D'Urfey; 2A, T, B, ch, 2fl, 2ob, 2tpt, 2vn,
            2va & cont): Z320
                         1. "Symphony": a. (Grave)
                              b. (Canzona)
                         2a. "Arise, my muse" (A)
                         2b. "Ritornello"
                         3a. "Ye sons of music" (ch)
                         3b. "Ritornello"
                         4a. "Then sound your instruments" (T, B)
                         4b. (= 4a.) (ch)
                         5. "See how the glitt'ring ruler" (A)
                         6a. "Hail, gracious Gloriana, hail" (2A)
                         6b. "All hail, Gloriana" (ch)
                         6c. "Ritornello"
                         7a. "And since the time's distress" (B)
                         7b. "Only to rise" (B)
                         8a. "Prelude"
                         8b. "To quell his country's foes" (A, T, B)
                         9a. "But ah! I see Eusebia" (A)
                         9b. "Ah! wretched me" (A)
                         9c. "But Glory cries" (B)
                         9d. (= 9c.) (ch)
                         9e. (= 9c.)
                         9f. "No Fate must some meaner force" (A)
                         9g. (= 9c.) (ch)
12.2   "Celebrate this festival" (Birthday song for Queen Mary) (c1693, Tate; 2S, A, T, B, d ch, 2ob, 2tpt,
            2vn, va & cont): Z321
                         1. "Symphony": a. (Grave)
                              b. (Canzona)
                         2a. "Celebrate this festival" (2S, A, T, B)
                         2b. (= 2a.) (ch)
                         3. "Britain now thy cares beguile" (2S)
                         4a. "Prelude" (2ob)
                         4b. (= 2b.)
                         5. " 'Tis sacred, bid the trumpet" (S, tpt, later ch)
                         6a. "Prelude" (2vn)
                         6b. "Let sullen discord smile" (S)
                         6c. "Devote this day to Peace" (ch)
                         7. "Crown the altar, deck the shrine" (A)
                         8a. "Prelude" (2vn)
                         8b. "Expected Spring at last" (B, 2vn)
                         8c. "She waited for Maria's day" (ch)
                         9a. "April, who till now" (A)
                         9b. "Ritornello"
                         10a. "Departing thus" (A)
                         10b. "I envy not the pride of May" (A)
                         11a. "Ritornello"
                         11b. "Happy realm" (A, T, B)
                         12a. "While for a righteous cause" (B, tpt)
                         12b. "Let guilty monarchs shun" (B, tpt)
                         13a. "Prelude"
                         13b. "Return, fond muse" (A)
                         13c. "Repeat Maria's name" (A, d ch)
                         14a. "Kindly treat Maria's day" (S)
                         14b. (= 14a.) (ch)
12.3   "Celestial music did the gods inspire" (c1689; S, A, T, B, ch, 2fl, 2vn, va & cont): Z322
                         1. "Symphony": a. (Grave)

b. (Canzona)
2. "Celestial music" (B)
2b. "Ritornello"
2c. "Hence he by right the God of wit" (ch)
3a. "Her charming strains" (A, 2fl)
3b. "Ritornello" (2fl)
4. "Thus Virgil's genius lov'd the country best" (S)
5a. "Whilst Music did improve Amphion's song" (A, B)
5b. "Ritornello"
6. "When Orpheus sang all nature did rejoice" (A)
7a. "Let Phillis by her voice" (A, T, B)
7b. (= 7a.) (ch)

12.4   "Come ye sons of art away" (Birthday song for Queen Mary) (c1694; S, 2A, B, ch, 2ob, tpt, kettledrum, 2vn, va & cont): Z323
1. "Symphony": a. (Grave)
b. (Canzona)
2a. "Prelude"
2b. "Come ye sons of art" (A)
2c. (= 2b.) (ch)
3. "Sound the trumpet 'till around" (2A)
4a. (= 2a.)
4b. (= 2c.)
5a. "Strike the viol, touch the lute" (A, 2fl)
5b. "Ritornello"
6a. "Prelude"
6b. "The day that such a blessing" (B)
6c. (= 6b.) (ch)
7. "Bid the Virtues, bid the Graces" (S, ob)
8. "These are the sacred charms" (B)
9a. "See Nature, rejoicing, has shown us" (S, B)
9b. (= 9a.) (ch)

12.5   "Fly bold rebellion" (The Welcome Song) (c1683; 2S, 2A, T, 2B, d ch, 2vn, va & cont): Z324
1. "Symphony": a. (Grave)
b. (Canzona)
2a. "Fly bold rebellion" (2A, T, 2B)
2b. "Ritornello"
2c. "The plot is displayed" (B)
3. "Then with heart and with voice" (ch)
4. "Ritornello"
5a. "Rivers from their channels" (A)
5b. "Ritornello"
6. "For Majesty moves" (ch)
7. "If then we've found" (B)
8a. "But kings, like the sun" (T)
8b. "Ritornello"
9a. "But heaven has now dispelled those fears" (2S, A)
9b. "Ritornello"
10a. "Come then, change your notes" (A, T, B)
10b. "But with heart and with voice" (ch)
11a. "Be welcome then, great Sir" (A)
11b. "Ritornello"
12. "Welcome to all those wishes" (2S, 2A, T, 2B)
13. "Thus let united duty pray" (d ch)

12.6   "From hardy climes" (A Song ... to Prince George upon his Marriage with the Lady Ann) (c1683; B, ch, 2vn, va & hpd): Z325
1. "Symphony": a. (Grave)
b. (Canzona)
2. "From hardy climes" (B)
3a. "Hail, welcome Prince" (B)
3b. (= 3a.) (ch)
3c. "Ritornello"
4a. "Prelude" (hpd)
4b. "As Fame, great Sir" (A)
5a. "For since Heaven pleas'd" (2S)
5b. "Ritornello"
6a. "Wake then my muse" (B)
6b. "To celebrate the joys" (vn, ch)
7. "Ritornello"
8a. "The sparrow and the gentle dove" (T)
8b. "Ritornello"
9a. "So all the boons" (A, T, B)
9b. "Ritornello"
10a. "Hence without scheme or figure" (S)
10b. "(= 10a.) (ch)
10c. "Do we foretell" (S)

12.7   "From those serene and rapturous joys" (On the King's Return to White-hall) (c1684; 2S, A, T, B, ch, 2vn ,va & cont): Z326

         1. "Symphony": a. (Grave)
            b. (Canzona)
         2a. "From those serene and rapturous joys" (A)
         2b. "Ritornello"
         3a. "Behold, th'indulgent Prince" (B, 2vn)
         3b. "Ritornello"
         4. "Welcome home" (ch, 2vn)
         5. "Not with an helmet" (2S)
         6. "Ritornello"
         7. "Welcome as soft refreshing showers" (B)
         8. "Welcome home" (ch, 2vn)
         9a. "Welcome, more welcome does he come" (T)
         9b. "Ritornello"
       10a. "Nor does the sun more comforts bring" (A, B)
       10b. "Ritornello"
       11a. "Ritornello"
       11b. "With trumpets and shouts" (A)
       11c. (= 11a.)
       11d. (= 11b.) (ch, 2vn)

12.8   "Great parent, hail" (Commemoration Ode) (c1694, Tate; S, A, T, B, ch, 2fl, 2vn, va & cont): Z327

         1. "Symphony": a. (Grave)
            b. (Canzona)
         2a. "Great parent, hail" (A, T, B)
         2b. "All hail to thee" (ch)
         2c. "Who hast thro' last distress" (ch)
         2d. "To see this joyful year" (ch)
         3. "Another century commencing" (A)
         4a. "Ritornello"
         4b. "After war's alarms" (A, T)
         5. "Awful Matron, take thy seat" (B)
         6a. "She was the first who did inspire" (T, ch)
         6b. "Whose deathless memory the soul" (T)
         7. "Succeeding Princes next recite" (A, B)
         8. "But chiefly recommend to fame" (ch)
         9a. "Symphony" (2fl, va)
         9b. "The royal Patron's sung" (S, 2fl)
        10. "Then a second Ormond's story" (S)
        11. "With themes like these" (ch)

12.9   "Hail, bright Cecilia" (A Song for St. Cecilia's Day) (c1692, Brady; S, 2A, T, 2B, ch, 2fl, b fl, 2ob, 2tpt, kettledrum, 2vn, va & cont): Z328

         1. "Symphony": a. (Grave)
            b. (Canzona)
            c. "Adagio"
            d. "Allegro"
            e. "Adagio"
         2a. "Hail, bright Cecilia" (B)
         2b. "Hail, bright Cecilia" (ch)
         2c. "Fill ev'ry heart" (ch)
         2d. "That thine and music's sacred love" (A, T, ch)
         2e. "Ritornello"
         3a. "Prelude"
         3b. "Hark each tree its silence breaks" (A, T)
         4. " 'Tis Nature's voice" (A)
         5. "Soul of the world" (ch)
         6a. "Symphony" (2ob)
         6b. "Thou tun'st this world" (S, 2ob)
         6c. (= 6b.) (ch)
         7. "With that sublime celestial lay" (2A, B)
         8a. "Prelude" (2ob)
         8b. "Wond'rous machine" (B, 2ob)
         9. "The airy violin and lofty viol" (A, 2vn)
       10a. "Prelude" (2fl)
       10b. "In vain the am'rous flute" (A, T)
       11a. "Prelude" (2tpt, kettledrum)
       11b. "The fife and all the harmony" (A, 2tpt, kettledrum)
       12. "Let these among themselves contest" (2B)
       13. "Hail, bright Cecilia" (ch)
       14. "With rapture of delight" (2A, T, B)

12.10   "Laudate Ceciliam" (A Latin Song made upon St. Cecilia) (c1683; A, T, B, ?ch, 2vn & cont): Z329

         1. "Symphony": a. (Grave)
            b. (Canzona)
         2. "Laudate Ceciliam" (A, T, B)
         3a. "Modulemini psalmum novum" (A, T, B)

3b. "Ritornello"
4. "Quia preceptum est in Ecclesia sanctorum" (B)
5. (= 2.)
6. (=1.)
7. "Dicite Virgini, canite martyri" (A, T)
8a. "Adeste Caelites" (A, T, B)
8b. "Nobiscum martyri alternate" (A, T, B)
9. (= 2.)

          1. "Symphony": a. (Grave)
             b. (Canzona)
             c. (Adagio)
          2a. "Love's goddess sure" (A)
          2b. "Ritornello"
          3a. "Those eyes, that form" (B)
          3b. "Ritornello"
          4. "Sweetness of Nature" (2A, 2fl)
          5a. "Long may she reign" (S)
          5b. (= 5a.) (ch)
          6a. "Ostinato" (cont)
          6b. "May her blest example chase" (S)
          6c. "Ritornello"
          7a. "Many such days may she behold" (2A)
          7b. "Ritornello"
          8. "May she to heaven late return" (ch)
          9a. "As much as we below shall mourn" (A, T, B)
          9b. "Our short but their eternal choice" (ch)
          1. "Symphony": a. (Grave)
             b. (Canzona)
          2a. "Now doth the glorious day appear" (ch)
          2b. "Ritornello"
          3. "Not anyone such joy could bring" (T, B)
          4a. "This does our fertile isle" (T)
          4b. "Ritornello"
          5. (= 2a, b.)
          6. "It was a work of full as great" (B)
          7a. "By beauteous softness" (A)
          7b. "Ritornello"
          8. "Her Hero to whose conduct" (2B)
          9. "Our dear religion" (S, A, T)
          10. "No more shall we the great Eliza" (T)
          11. "Symphony"
          12a. "Now with one united voice" (ch)
          12b. "Io Tiumphe"
          1. "Symphony": a. (Grave)
             b. (Canzona)
          2. "Of old when heroes" (B, 2vn)
          3a. "Ritornello"
          3b. "Brigantium, honour'd with a race divine" (A, B)
          4a. "Prelude" (2fl)
          4b. "The bashful Thames" (T, 2fl)
          5. (= 4b.) (ch)
          6a. "Ritornello"
          6b. "The pale and the purple Rose" (A)
          7a, b. "And in each tract of glory" (T, B, later ch)
          8. (= 1.)
          9a. "And now when the renown'd Nassau" (2A, 2tpt)
          9b. "Ritornello" (2tpt)
          10. "They did no storms nor threat'nings fear" (2B)
          11a. "Prelude"
          11b. "So when the glitt'ring Queen of night" (T)
          12. "Let music join in a chorus" (ch)
          13a. "Sound, trumpet, sound, beat every drum" (A)
          13b. "Ritornello"
          14a. "Sound all to him" (ch)
          14b. "Long flourish the city and county of York" (ch)
          1. "Symphony": a. (Grave)
             b. (Canzona)

2a. "Raise, raise the voice" (B/T)
2b. (= 2a.) (ch)
3. "Ritornello"
4. "The god himself says" (S)
5a. "Crown the day with harmony" (S, T, B, ch)
5b. "And let every generous heart" (ch)
6. "Ritornello"
7a. "Mark how readily each pliant string" (S)
7b. "Then altogether all in one" (ch)
7c. "Symphony"
8. "Come raise your voices" (ch)

12.16   "Sound the trumpet, beat the drum" (Birthday Song for King James) (c1687; 2A, 2T, 2B, ch, 2vn, va
      & cont): Z335
          1. "Symphony": a. (Grave)
            b. (Canzona)
          2a. "Sound the trumpet" (A, B, ch)
          2b. "Ritornello"
          2c. "Caesar and Urania come" (ch)
          2d. "Ritornello"
          2e. (= 2c.) (ch)
          2f. "Bid the Muses haste" (B)
          2g. (= 2a.) (ch)
          3. "Crown the year and crown the day" (T)
          4. "To Caesar all hail" (ch)
          5a. "Let Caesar and Urania live" (2A)
          5b. "Ritornello"
          6a. "What greater bliss can Fate bestow" (T, B)
          6b. "With plenty surrounding" (ch)
          7. "Chaconne"
          8a. "While Caesar, like the morning star" (B)
          8b. "His fame like incense mounts" (B)
          9a. "To Urania and Caesar delights without measure" (A, T, B)
          9b. (= 9a.) (ch)

12.17   "Swifter, Isis, swifter flow" (A Welcome Song ... For the King) (Charles II) (c1681; 2S, A, T, B, ch, 2fl,
      ob, 3vn, va & cont): Z336
          1. "Symphony": a. (Grave)
            b. (Canzona)
          2a. "Swifter, Isis" (A)
          2b. (= 2a.) (ch)
          2c. "Ritornello"
          3a. "Charles, the mighty sov'reign" (ch)
          3b. "Ritornello"
          4a. "Prelude" (2fl)
          4b. "Land him safely on her shore" (B, 2fl)
          4c. "He with joy her walls" (B)
          5a. "Prelude"
          5b. "Hark! just now my list'ning ears" (A)
          5c. "Ritornello"
          6a, b. "Welcome, dread Sir" (A, T, B, later ch)
          6c, d. "Though causeless jealousy" (A, T, B, later ch)
          7. "But with as great devotion" (B)
          8a, b. "Your Augusta he charms" (T, later ch)
          8c. "Ritornello"
          9. "The king, whose presence like the spring" (2S)
         10a. "Then since, Sir" (ch)
         10b. "May no harsher sounds" (S)
         10c. "No trumpet be heard" (ch)

12.18   "The summer's absence unconcerned we bear" (A Welcome Song) (c1682; 2S, 2A, T, 2B, ch, 2vn, va
      & cont): Z337
          1. "Symphony": a. (Grave)
            b. (Canzona)
            c. (Adagio)
          2. "The summer's absence" (B)
          3. "Shine thus for many years" (A, T, B, later ch)
          4. "Ritornello"
          5a. "And when late from your throne" (A)
          5b. "Let no sham pretences" (A, later ch)
          5c. "Ritornello"
          6. "Ah! had we, Sir, the pow'r" (B)
          7a. "All hearts should smile" (2S)
          7b. "Then would we conclude" (ch)
          8a. "Prelude" (cont)
          8b. "Happy while all her neighbours bled" (2A, 2B)
          8c. "Ritornello"
          9. "So happily still you your counsels" (T)

10a. "These had by their ill usage" (A)
10b. "Ritornello"
11. "But those no more shall dare" (T)
12. "Britannia shall now" (ch)

12.19 "Welcome, glorious morn" (Birthday song for Queen Mary) (c1691; S, A, T, 2B, ch, 2ob, 2tpt, 2vn, va & cont): Z338
1. "Symphony": a. (Grave)
b. (Canzona)
2a. "Welcome, glorious morn" (A, 2ob)
2b. (= 2a.) (ch)
3a. "At thy return the joyful earth" (A, B)
3b. "Ritornello" (2ob)
4. (= 2b.)
5. "Welcome as when three happy kingdoms strove" (A, B)
6a. "Prelude"
6b. "The mighty goddess of this wealthy isle" (T)
7a. "Full of wonder and delight" (A, T, B)
7b. (= 7a.) (ch)
8. "Ritornello"
9a. "And lo! a sacred fury" (B)
9b. "To lofty strains" (B)
9c. (= 9b.) (ch)
10a. "My pray'rs are heard" (S)
10b. "I see the round years" (S)
10c. "Then our sad Albion" (ch)
11. "He to the field by honour call'd" (2B)
12. "Whilst undisturb'd his happy Consort" (T)
13a. "Sound all ye spheres" (T, 2tpt)
13b. (= 13a.) (ch)

12.20 "Welcome to all the pleasures" (A song for St. Cecilia's Day) (c1683, Fishburn; 2S, A, T, B, ch, 2vn, va & cont): Z339
1. "Symphony": a. (Grave)
b. (Canzona)
2a. "Welcome to all the pleasures" (A, T, B)
2b. "Hail, great assembly" (ch)
2c. "Ritornello"
3a, b. "Here the Deities approve" (A)
3c. "Ritornello"
4a. "While joys celestial" (S, A, T)
4b. "Ritornello"
5. "Then lift up your voices" (B)
6. (= 5.) (ch)
7. "Symphony" (cont)
8a. "Beauty, thou scene of love" (T)
8b. "Ritornello"
9a. "In a consort of voices" (T)
9b. (= 9a.) (ch)

12.21 "Welcome, Vicegerent of the mighty King" (Welcome song for Charles II) (c1680; 2S, A, T, B, ch, 2vn, va & cont): Z340
1. "Symphony": a. (Grave)
b. (Canzona)
2. "Welcome, Vicegerent" (ch)
3a. "Ah! mighty Sir" (A, B)
3b. "Ritornello"
4. "But your blest presence" (ch)
5. "Ritornello"
6. "Your influous approach" (T, later ch)
7. "Ritornello"
8. "When the summer in his glory" (2S)
9. "All loyalty and honour" (ch)
10a. "Music, the food of love" (T)
10b. (= 10a.) (ch)
10c. "Touch with a joyful sound" (T)
10d. (= 10c.) (ch)
10e. "Ritornello" (cont)
10f. "Ritornello"
11. "His absence was Autumn" (A, B, ch)
12. "Then all that have voices" (A, B, ch)

12.22 "What shall be done in behalf of the man" (A Welcome Song) (c1682; 2S, A, T, B, ch, 2fl, 2vn, va & cont): Z341
1. "Symphony": a. (Grave)
b. (Canzona)
2. "What shall be done" (B, 2fl)
3a. "His foes shall all tremble" (A, T, B)
3b. "And the mobilé crowd" (T)

3c. "And now ev'ry tongue" (A, T, B)
3d. (= 3c.) (ch)
3e. "Ritornello"
4a. "All the grandeur he possesses" (A)
4b. "Ritornello"
5. "Let us sing the praises" (ch)
6. "Mighty Charles, though joined" (B)
7. "But thanks be to Heaven" (ch)
8. "Long live great Charles" (S, A, T, B, ch)
9. (= 3e.)
10a. "May all factious troubles" (S, A)
10b. (= 10a.) (ch)

12.23   "Who can from joy refrain?" (A Birthday song for the Duke of Gloucester) (c1695, Tate; 2S, 2A, B, ch, 2ob, ?t ob, tpt, 2vn, va & cont): Z342
1. "Symphony": a. (Grave)
    b. (Canzona)
    c. (Adagio)
2a. "Prelude" (cont)
2b. "Who can from joy" (A)
2c. "Wond'rous day" (A, T, B, ch)
2d. (= 2b.)
2e. "For tho' the sun" (A, B)
3a. "A Prince of glorious race" (A)
3b. "Ritornello"
4a. "Prelude" (2vn)
4b. "The father brave as e'er was Dane" (B, 2vn)
5a. "Prelude" (2ob)
5b. "The graces in his mother shine" (S, 2ob)
6. "Sound the trumpet, beat the warlike drum" (A, tpt)
7. "Chaconne"
8a. "If now he burns" (2S)
8b. "Ritornello"
8c. "From pole to pole" (2S)
8d. "Ritornello"
8e. "Then Thames shall be Queen" (2S, 2A, B)
8f. "Ritornello"
8g. (= 8e.) (ch)

12.24   "Why, why are all the muses mute?" (Welcome Song ... King James) (c1685; 2S, A, T, 2B, ch, 2vn, va & cont): Z343
1a. "Why, why are all the muses mute?" (S)
1b. "Awake, 'tis Caesar" (A, ch)
2. "Symphony": a. (Grave)
    b. (Canzona)
3a. "When should each soul" (T)
3b. "Caesar, Earth's greatest good" (T)
4a. "For Caesar's welcome we prepare" (ch, vn)
4b. "Ritornello"
5a. "Britain, thou now art great" (A)
5b. "Ritornello"
6a. "Look up, and to our isle" (A, T, B)
6b. "Great Caesar's reign with conquest" (A, T, B, later ch, vn)
7a. "Accursed rebellion reared his head" (B, 2vn)
7b. "Prelude"
7c. "But when Caesar from on high" (B)
8. "So Jove scarce settled" (2S)
9. "Ritornello"
10a. "Caesar for milder virtues" (A, B, vn)
10b. "Secured by his victorious arms" (A, B, vn)
11. "The many-headed beast is quelled" (T, later ch)
12. "In the equal balance laid" (2B)
13a. "O how blest is the isle" (A)
13b. "Symphony"
13c. (= 13a.) (ch)

12.25   "Ye tuneful muses, raise your heads" (Birthday Song for King James II) (c ?1686; 2S, A, T, B, ch, 2fl, ?kettledrum, 2vn, va & cont): Z344
1. "Symphony": a. (Grave)
    b. (Canzona)
2. "Ye tuneful muses" (2B)
3. "Ritornello"
4. "This point of time ends all your grief" (A, ch, vn)
5a. "Be lively, then and gay" (A)
5b. (= 5a.) (ch, vn)
5c. "Ritornello"
6. "In his just praise your noblest song" (B, 2vn)
7a. "Try ev'ry strain" (ch, vn)

7b. "Tune all your strings" (ch, vn)
7c. "To celebrate his so much wish'd return" (ch, vn)
8. "Ritornello"
9a. "Prelude"
9b. "Ritornello"
9c. "From the ratt'ling of drums" (T)
9d. (= 9c.) (ch, vn)
9e. "The best protectors" (2S, B)
9f. (= 9d.)
9g. "By which he glory first" (A, T, B)
9h. (= 9d.)
9i. (= 9b.)
9j. (= 9d.)
9k. "Ritornello"
10. "To music's softer but yet kind" (2A, B, 2fl)
11a. "With him he brings the partner" (A)
11b. "Ritornello"
12. "Happy in a mutual love" (2S)
13. "Whilst in music and verse" (T, later ch)

Doubtful:

12.26   *"Address of the Children of the Chapel Royal to the King, and their master, Capt. Cooke, on his Majesty's birthday, A.D. 1670, composed by master Purcell, one of the children of the said chapel"* ZD120

13. THREE- AND FOUR-PART SONGS & LARGER VOCAL WORKS—SECULAR

13.1   "Hark, Damon, hark" (ca1683; S, B, ch, 2fl, 2vn & cont): Z541
    1. "Symphony": a. (Grave)
      b. (Canzona)
    2. "Hark, Damon, hark" (S)
    3a. "Orpheus perhaps is from the shades" (B)
    3b. "Come, shepherds, come" (B)
    4. "Ritornello" (2fl)
    5. "I'll warrant you, boys" (ch)

13.2   "Hark how the wild musicians sing" (ca1683; 2T, B, ch, 2vn & cont): Z542
    1. "Hark how the wild musicians sing" (2T, B)
    2a. "Prelude"
    2b. "Look how the fields" (T)
    2c. "Ritornello"
    2d. "See, fairest, see" (T)
    2e. "Pleas'd Nature thus drest up" (ch)
    3a. "Prelude"
    3b. "Then why, Dorinda" (B)
    3c. "Ritornello"
    3d. "We'll freely feast" (2T, B)
    3e. "Ritornello"
    4. "Though now your eyes" (T)
    5. "Then let us not waste" (ch)

13.3   "How pleasant is this flow'ry plain" (ca1683, Cowley; S, T, ch, 2fl & cont): Z543
    1. "Symphony": a. (Grave)
      b. (Canzona)
    2a. "How pleasant is this flow'ry plain" (T)
    2b. "The happy swain in these enamelled fields" (S)
    2c. "No fears, no storms" (S, T)
    2d. "Oft to the silent groves he does" (S)
    3a. "Prelude"
    3b. "Ah, happy life" (S, T)
    4. "No guilty remorse" (ch)

13.4   "If ever I more riches did desire" (ca1686–7, Cowley; 2S, T, B, ch, 2vn & cont): Z544
    1. "Symphony": a. (Grave)
      b. (Canzona)
    2a. "If ever I more riches" (S)
    2b. (= 2a.) (ch)
    3a. "Upon the slippery tops" (B)
    3b. "Ritornello"
    4. "Me, O ye gods" (2S)
    5a. "Here let my life with as much silence slide" (T)
    5b. "An old plebeian let me die" (T)
    5c. "An old plebeian let me die" (ch)
    5d. "Ritornello"
    6a, b. "To him, alas, to him I fear" (S, later ch)

13.5   "In a deep vision's intellectual scene" (ca1683, Cowley: The Complaint; 2S, B, ch & cont): Z545
    1. "In a deep vision's intellectual scene" (B)

2. "She touch'd him with her harp" (ch)
3a. "Art thou return'd" (S)
3b. "But when I meant" (S)
3c. "When I resolv'd" (S)
3d. "Go, renegado, cast up" (S)
3e. "Go on, twice the muse" (ch)
3f. "But think how likely" (S)
4. "Thus spake the muse" (ch)
5a. "Ah, wanton foe" (B)
5b. "To all the ports" (B)
5c. "Whoever this world's happiness" (B)
5d. "Teach me not, then" (B)
6. "However, of all princes" (ch)

13.6   " 'Tis wine was made to rule the day" (A drinking song with chorus for three voices) (S, ch & cont): Z546
1. " 'Tis wine was made to rule the day" (S)
2. "Wine is th' amazement of the old" (S)
3. "Let my Queen live forever" (ch)
4. "Infus'd in wine, let's sink" (S) (melody = 1.)
5. (= 3.)
6. "O! lull me, couch'd in soft repose" (S)

13.7   "We reap all the pleasures" (ca1683; ?vv, ch, 2fl & cont, inc): Z547
1. "Symphony": a. (Grave)
       b. (Canzona)
2. "We reap all the pleasures" (ch)

Doubtful:

13.8   *"A poor blind woman that has no sight at all" (The Blind Beggar's Song) (2S & B)* ZD171
13.9   *"When the cock begins to crow"* ZD172

14. TWO-PART SONGS—SECULAR (S, B & cont)

14.1	"Above the tumults of a busy state" (ca1683)	Z480
14.2	"A grasshopper and a fly" (c1686, D'Urfey: A allegory)	Z481
14.3	"Alas, how barbarous are we" (Philips)	Z482
14.4	"Come, dear companions of th' Arcadian fields" (c1686)	Z483
14.5	"Come, lay by all care" (Adieu to his mistress) (c1685)	Z484
14.6	"Dulcibella, whene'er I sue for a kiss" (c1694, Henly)	Z485
14.7	"Fair Cloe my breast so alarms" (c1692, Glanville)	Z486
14.8	"Fill the bowl with rosy wine" (c1687, Cowley: The Epicure)	Z487
14.9	"For love ev'ry creature is form'd" (c1691, Dryden, vers of duet & ch, from: King Arthur, Z628/30e, f)	Z488
14.10	"Go tell Amynta (Amintor), gentle swain" (ca1684, Dryden)	Z489

14.11 "Haste, gentle Charon" (A dialogue between Charon and Orpheus) (ca1683; 2B & cont): Z490
1. "Haste, gentle Charon" (B)
2. "Be still" (2B)

14.12	"Has yet your breast no pity learn'd?" (A dialogue between Strephon and Dorinda) (c1688)	Z491
14.13	"Hence, fond deceiver" (Love and Despair: A Dialogue) (c1687)	Z492
14.14	"Here's to thee, Dick" (ca1685, Cowley)	Z493
14.15	"How great are the blessings" (c1685, Tate: A health to King James)	Z494
14.16	"How sweet is the air and refreshing" (c1687)	Z495
14.17	"In all our Cynthia's shining sphere" (Settle: A dialogue in The World in the Moon of 1697)	Z496
14.18	"In some kind dream" (ca1685, Etherege)	Z497
14.19	"I saw fair Cloris all alone" (c1686, Strode)	Z498
14.20	"I spy Celia, Celia eyes me"	Z499
14.21	"Julia, your unjust disdain"	Z500
14.22	"Let Hector, Achilles, and each brave commander" (c1689, text: On Celia's Charms)	Z501
14.23	"Lost is my quiet forever" (c1691)	Z502
14.24	"Nestor, who did to thirice man's age attain" (c1689)	Z503

14.25 "O dive Custos Auriacae domus" (c1694/5, Parker: Elegy on the death of Queen Mary; 2S & cont): .. Z504
1. "O dive Custos" (2S)
2. "Seu te fluentem" (2S)
3. "Maria musis flebilis" (2S)

14.26	"Oft am I by the women told" (c1687, Cowley; S, B & cont)	Z505

14.27 "O! what a scene does entertain my sight" (ca1683–4; S, B, ch, vn & cont): Z506
1. "Symphony": a. (Grave)
       b. (Canzona)
2a. "O what a scene" (S)
2b. "How my senses all are courted" (S)
2c. (= 2b.) (ch)
3a. "All creatures now are in a merry vein" (S)
3b. "The wanton lambs" (S)
3c. "Come, then let's strike up" (S, B)

14.28	"Saccharissa's grown old" (c1686)	Z507

14.29   "See where she sits" (Cowley; S, B, ch, 2vn & cont): Z508
           1a. "Prelude"
           1b. "See where she sits" (S, B)
           2a. "Prelude"
           2b. "As stars reflect on waters" (S)
           3a. "Ne'er yet did I behold" (B)
           3b. "Ah! mighty love" (B)
14.30   "Sit down, my dear Sylvia" (c1685, D'Urfey: A dialogue betwixt Alexis and Sylvia) Z509
14.31   "Soft notes and gently rais'd accent" (ca1683–4, Howe: A serenading song; S, B, ch, 2fl & cont): Z510
           1. "Symphony": a. (Grave)
              b. (Canzona)
           2. "Soft notes and gently" (S)
           3. (= 1b.)
           4. "Thus feeble man" (S)
           5. "Ten thousand raptures" (ch)
14.32   "Sylvia, thou brighter eye of night" (A serenading song) (ca1683–4): Z511
           1. "Sylvia, thou brighter eye" (S, B)
           2. "Remember, remember" (S, B)
           3. "Did we the happy time" (S, B)
14.33   "Sylvia, 'tis true you're fair" (A serenading song) (c1686) Z512
14.34   "There ne'er was so wretched a lover" (Congreve) Z513
14.35   "Though my mistress be fair" (c1683–4) Z514
14.36   "To this place we're now come" ZN526
14.37   "Trip it in a ring" (A song for two voices) (arr from solo song in: Fairy Queen, Z629/5c, d) Z515
14.38   "Underneath this myrtle shade" (ca1683, Cowley: The Epicure; S, B, ch & cont): Z516
           1. "Underneath this myrtle shade"
           2. "In this more than kingly state"
           3. "Why do we precious ointments"
           4. "Crown me with roses"
14.39   "Were I to choose the greatest bliss" (c1689) Z517
14.40   "What can we poor females do?" (c ?1694; also solo vers Z430) Z518
14.41   "When gay Philander left the plain" (c1684) Z519
14.42   "When, lovely Phyllis, thou art kind" (c1685) Z520
14.43   "When Myra sings" (c ?1695, Granville) Z521
14.44   "When Teucer from his father fled" (ca1685, Kenrick: Teucer's Voyage from Horace: Odes, I/7): Z522
           1. "When Teucer from his father" (S, B)
           2. "Cheer up my hearts" (S, B)
           3. "Let us drink" (S, B)
14.45   "While bolts and bars my days control" Z523
14.46   "While you for me alone had charms" (ca1683, Oldham, imitation of the 9th Ode of Horace, a dialogue
         of love and jealousy between Horace and Lydia): Z524
           1. "While you for me alone" (B, later S)
           2. "Then cease all jealousies" (S, B)
14.47   "Why, my Daphne, why complaining?" (A dialogue between Thyrsis and Daphne) (c1691) Z525

15. SOLO SONGS WITH CHORUS—SECULAR (S, ch & cont)

15.1   "Beneath a dark and melancholy grove" (ca1681) Z461
15.2   "Draw near, you lovers" (ca1683, Stanley: The Exequies) Z462
15.3   "Farewell, ye rocks, ye seas, ye sands" (c1685, D'Urfey: The Storm) Z463
15.4   "Gentle shepherds, you that know" (c1687, Tate: A Pastoral elegy on the death of Mr. John Playford) Z464
15.5   "High on a throne of glitt'ring ore" (c1690, D'Urfey: An Ode to the Queen) Z465
15.6   "Let us, kind Lesbia, give away in soft embraces" (c1684) Z466
15.7   "Musing on cares of human fate" (c1685, D'Urfey: Cynthia and Endimion) Z467
15.8   "No, to what purpose should I speak?" (ca1683, Cowley: The Concealment) Z468
15.9   "Scarce had the rising sun appear'd" (c1679) Z469
15.10   "See, how the fading glories of the year" (c1689) Z470
15.11   "Since the pox or the plague" (c1679) Z471
15.12   "What hope for us remains now he is gone?" (c1677, on the death on Matthew Lock) Z472
15.13   "Young Thyrsis' fate the hills and groves deplore" (c1690, ?Tate, on the death of Thomas Farmer) Z473

16. SOLO SONGS—SECULAR (S & cont)

16.1   "Aaron thus propos'd to Moses" (c1688) Z351
16.2   "Ah! cruel nymph! you give despair" Z352
16.3   "Ah! how pleasant 'tis to love" (c1688) Z353
16.4   "Ah! what pains, what racking thoughts" (Congreve; inc: voice part only) Z354
16.5   "Amidst the shades and cool refreshing streams" (c1683) Z355
16.6   "Amintas, to my grief I see" (c1679) Z356
16.7   "Amintor, heedless of his flocks" (c1681) Z357
16.8   "Ask me to love no more" (c1694, Hammond) Z358
16.9   "A thousand sev'ral ways I tried" (ca1681) Z359
16.10   "Bacchus is a pow'r divine" Z360

17. DIDACTIC EXAMPLES

17.1 "Counterpoint and Canon" (c1694): Z870
    A. "Examples in two parts": 1. "Fuge in the fourth below"
        2. "Imitation or reports"
        3. "Double fuge"
        4. "Per Arsin et Thesin"
        5. "Per Augmentation"
        6. "Recte et Retro"
        7a. "Double Descant"
        7b. "Reply"
        8. "Canon in the 8th or 15th"
    B. "Examples in three parts": 1. "Plain fugeing"
        2. "Double fugeing"
        3. "Per Arsin & Thesin"
        4. "Per Augmentation"
        5. "Recte & Retro"
        6. "Double Descant"
        7. "Triple fuge"
    C. "Examples in four parts": 1. "Plain fugeing"
        2. "Double fugeing"
        3. "Per Arsin & Thesin"
        4. "Per Augmentation"
        5. "Recte & Retro"
        6. "Four fugues carried on, interchanging one with another"
    D. "Canons on Sacred Texts": 1. "Gloria Patri" (A Canon Three Parts in One)
        2. "Miserere mei" (A Canon, Four in Two)
        3. "Glory be to the Father" (A Canon, Four in One) Z871
17.2 "Miscellaneous Exercises": ......
        1. "Several Examples of taking Discords elegantly": a. "... taking of Ninths and Sevenths"
          b. "... taking the lesser Fourth"
          c. "... taking the Greater Fourth"
          d. "... taking two Sevenths in two Parts"
        2. "Counterpoint or bass to Tunes or Songs"
        3. "Composition of Three Parts"
        4. "Tune with Second Treble"
        5. "Four parts Counterpoint"
        6. "Elegant (Italianate) Passages": a. "Sharp and Flat Seventh"
          b. "Flat sixth before a Close"
          c. "Third and Fourth Together"
          d. (Pedal point)

18. SPURIOUS WORKS

Sacred vocal:

18.1	*"By the waters of Babylon," anthem (c by Humfrey)*	ZS1
18.2	*"Christ is risen" (c by White)*	ZS2
18.3	*"Come, honest Sexton" (c by Locke)*	ZS3
18.4	*"God sheweth me His goodness" (c by Norris, Psalm 59: 10–12, 16, 17; A, T, B & ?cont)*	ZS4
18.5	*"Great is the Lord," hymn (c by ?Loosemore, tune = ZS6)*	ZS5
18.6	*"Hosannah to the Prince of light," hymn (c by ?Loosemore, tune = ZS5)*	ZS6
18.7	*"How pleasant is Thy dwelling place," hymn (c by Carey, Psalm 84, setting = ZS18)*	ZS7
18.8	*"I am the Resurrection" (Wanless's Funeral Service) (c by Weldon)*	ZS8
18.9	*"I heard a voice from Heav'n" (c by Croft; ch & cont)*	ZS9
18.10	*"My heart rejoiceth in the Lord" (c by Norris, I Samuel 2: 1–4, 6–8, 10; S, A, T, B, ch & cont)*	ZS10
18.11	*"O come, loud anthems" (c by Cooke)*	ZS11
18.12	*"O God, wherefor art Thou" (c by Blow)*	ZS12
18.13	*"O Lord God of my salvation" (c by Richardson, Psalm 88: 1, 2, 3, 4, 13; ch)*	ZS13
18.14	*"O Lord, rebuke me not," sacred song (c by Weldon)*	ZS14
18.15	*"O miserable man," sacred song (c by Daniel Purcell)*	ZS15
18.16	*"O that mine eyes would melt into a flood" (An Hymn for Good Friday) (c by Loosemore; S, B, ch & cont)*	ZS16
18.17	*"The Lord my pasture shall prepare," hymn (c by Carey)*	ZS17
18.18	*"To celebrate Thy praise, O Lord," psalm (c by Carey, setting = ZS7)*	ZS18
18.19	*"Turn Thou us, O good Lord" (c by Jeffries, Psalm 80; A, 2T, B & ch)*	ZS19

Secular vocal:

18.20	*"A lass there lives upon the green" (c by Courteville; S & cont)*	ZS50
18.21	*"Cease the rovers" (c by Daniel Purcell; S, B)*	ZS51
18.22	*"Come pull away boys" (c by Holmes; 3vv)*	ZS52
18.23	*"Fill all the glasses" (c by Eccles; 2vv)*	ZS53
18.24	*"Had she not care enough" (c by Savile; 3vv)*	ZS54
18.25	*"Hang sorrow" (c by Lawes; 3vv)*	ZS55
18.26	*"Hark the bonny Christ Church bells" (c by Aldrich; 3vv)*	ZS56
18.27	*"How happy are they" (c by Marsh; S & cont)*	ZS57
18.28	*"How well doth this harmonious meeting prove" (c by Bond; S, 2vn, va & cont)*	ZS58
18.29	*"Lightly tread, 'tis hallow'd ground" (c by Wise; 2S, B)*	ZS59
18.30	*"Ode to an expiring frog" (c by Hutchings; S & kbd)*	ZS60
18.31	*"Old Chiron thus preached" (c by Wise; S, B & cont)*	ZS61
18.32	*"Say what you please" (c by Turner; 3vv)*	ZS62
18.33	*"Since Cloris the pow'rs" (c by ?; 3vv)*	ZS63
18.34	*"The owl is abroad" (c by Smith; S, A, B & kbd)*	ZS64
18.35	*"Was ever Nymph like Rosamund?" (c by Arne; S & cont)*	ZS65
18.36	*"Why does the morn" (c by Blow)*	ZS66
18.37	*"Hark, Harry, 'tis late" (c by Eccles)*	ZS67
18.38	*"Forth from ye dark and dismal cell" (Tom of Bedlam) (c by ?1661)*	ZS68
18.39	*"Sweet Tyranness, I now resign" (c by Henry Purcell, Sr.; 2S, B; also see ZS70)*	ZS69
18.40	*"Sweet Tyranness, I now resign" (c by Henry Purcell, Sr.; S & cont; red vers of ZS69)*	ZS70

Stage works:

18.41	*"Macbeth" (c by Leveridge; S, ch, 2vn & cont)*	ZS100

Instrumental:

18.42	*"Air," in D major (c by Clarke)*	ZS120
18.43	*"Cibell" (c by Lully)*	ZS121
18.44	*"Purcell's ground, or the 'Welsh Ground' "*	ZS122
18.45	*"Jig" (c by Morgan, = ZT693/3)*	ZS123
18.46	*"Trumpet Tune" (c by Clarke)*	ZS124
18.47	*"Trumpet Voluntary" (c by Clarke)*	ZS125
18.48	*"Verse in the Phrygian mode" (c by Lebègue)*	ZS126

* * * * *

Z = Franklin B. Zimmerman: "Henry Purcell. 1659–1695. An analytical catalogue of his music." Macmillan & Co Ltd. London. St Martin's Press. New York, 1963.
ZN = newly-discovered or at present doubtfully ascribed to Purcell, **ZT** = transcriptions,
ZD = doubtful works, **ZS** = spurious ascriptions to Purcell.

1. STAGE WORKS

Operas:

1.1	"Aleko," 1 act (c1892, Nemirovich-Danchenko after Pushkin's poem: The Gypsies)	TNii/70
1.2	"The Miserly Knight," 3 scenes (c1903–5, after Pushkin's play):	Op.24

      1. "Introduction. Scene with Albert and the servant"
      2. "In the vaults. The Baron's monologue"
      3. "At the court"

1.3	"Francesca da Rimini," 2 scenes (c1900–5, M. Tchaikovsky after Dante's Inferno, Canto V):	Op.25

      1. "Prologue"
      2. "Scene I"
      3. "Scene II"
      4. "Epilogue"

1.4	*"Monna Vanna" (c1906–8, Slonov after Maeterlinck, inc pf score; Act I orchd Buketoff)*	*TNii/71*

Misc dramatic:

1.5	*"Mazepa," quartet (Mazeppa, Kochubey, Lyubov and Maria) (c?, on Pushkin's Poltava; 4vv & pf, frag)*	*TNii/82*

Monologues:

1.6	"2 Monologues from Pushkin's drama 'Boris Godunov' " (c ?1891):	TNii/80

      1. "Boris's Monologue: Thou, father patriarch" (3 vers)
      2. "Pimen's Monologue: One last story" (2 vers)

1.7	"Arbenin's Monologue from Lermontov's drama 'Masquerade' " (c ?1891)	TNii/81

Operatic & dramatic projects:

1.8	*"Esmeralda" (c1888, after Hugo: Notre Dame de Paris, frags in pf score):*	*TNii/72a*

    . *"Introduction" (to Act I)*
    . *"Entr'acte"*
    . *Act III (frags)*

1.9	*"Undine" (c1893, M. Tchaikovsky after Zhukovsky)*	*TNii/72b*
1.10	*"Richard II" (M. Tchaikovsky on Shakespeare's play)*	*TNii/72c*
1.11	*"Salammbô," 7 scenes (c1906, Slonov after Flaubert, scenario only)*	*TNii/72d*

1a. SELECTIONS FROM STAGE WORKS

1a.1	"Aleko," opera:	TNii/70

      1. "Introduction"
      2. "Gypsy chorus"
      3. "Old Gypsy's story"
      4. "Scena and chorus"
      5. "Gypsy Girls' dance"
      6. "Men's dance"
      7. "Chorus"
      8. "Duet"
      9. "Zemfira's song"
      10. "Aleko's cavatina"
      11. "Young Gypsy's song"
      12. "Duet and finale"

2. SYMPHONIES

2.1	*Symphony in D minor, "Youth Symphony" (c1891, part lost: 1st movt survives)*	*TNii/43*
2.2	*Symphony No.1 in D minor (c1895, lost; reconstr from pf duet vers & orch frags)*	*Op.13*
2.3	*Symphony (c1897, abandoned sketches only)*	*Op.27*
2.4	Symphony No.2 in E minor (c1906–7)	Op.27
2.5	Symphony No.3 in A minor (c1935–6, r1938)	Op.44

3. OTHER ORCHESTRAL WORKS

3.1	"Scherzo," in D minor (c1887)	TNii/40
3.2	*"Manfred," sym poem (c1890, unfin, lost, = lost ?Suite for orch)*	*TNii/42*
3.3	"Prince Rostislav," sym poem (c1891, after Tolstoy's ballad)	TNii/44
3.4	"The Rock," sym poem (c1893, after Lermontov's The Rock & Chekhov; arr for pf duet 1894)	Op.7
3.5	"Capriccio on Gypsy Themes" (Caprice bohémien), in E min / major (c1892,4; arr for pf duet 1892)	Op.12
3.6	*"2 Episodes à la Liszt" (c1894, unfin, lost): No.1 "Don Juan"*	*TNii/45*
3.7	*No.2 "Don Juan and Haidée; Lambro; and the death of Haidée"*	
3.8	"The Isle of the Dead," sym poem in A minor (c1909, inspired by painting of Böcklin)	Op.29

3.9   "Symphonic Dances" (c1940; arr for 2pf p1942): No.1 "Non allegro—Lento—Tempo I," in C minor ... Op.45
3.10   No.2 "Andante con moto" (Tempo di valse), in G minor
3.11   No.3 "Lento assai—Allegro vivace," in D minor

4. PIANO CONCERTOS, PIANO & ORCH

4.1   *Piano Concerto in C minor (c1889, unfin 1st movt only)* *TNii/41*
4.2   Piano Concerto No.1 in F-sharp minor (c1890–1, r1917; pf & orch/pf) Op.1
4.3   Piano Concerto No.2 in C minor (c1900–1; pf & orch/pf) Op.18
4.4   Piano Concerto No.3 in D minor (c1909) Op.30
4.5   Piano Concerto No.4 in G minor (c1926, r1927 & 1941) Op.40
4.6   "Rhapsody on a Theme of Paganini" (Introduction & 24 Variations), in A minor (c1934): Op.43
        quoted: . Caprice No.24 of Paganini, Op.1/24
            . "Dies irae," ancient death chant (Day of Judgment—part of the Catholic Requiem)

5. STRING QUARTETS

5.1   String Quartet (c1889, part lost: 2 movts only; arr for strings 1890): TNii/30
        1. (lost)
        2. "Romance," in G minor
        3. "Scherzo," in D major
        4. (lost)
5.2   String Quartet (c ?1896 or 1910–13, unfin: 2 movts only): TNii/35
        1. "Allegro moderato," in G minor
        2. "Andante molto sostenuto," in C minor
        3. (not composed)
        4. (not composed)

6. OTHER CHAMBER MUSIC

3 or more insts:

6.1   *?String Quintet (lost)* ....
6.2   "Trio élégiaque," in G minor (c1892, pf trio) TNii/34
6.3   "Trio élégiaque," in D minor (c1893, r1907, 1917; pf trio) Op.9

Vn & pf:

6.4   "Romance," in A minor (c1880s) TNii/31
6.5   "2 Pieces" (c1893): No.1 "Romance," in D minor Op.6
6.6   No.2 "Hungarian Dance," in D minor

Vc & pf:

6.7   "Lied" (Romance), in F minor (c1890) TNii/32
6.8   "Melodie on a Theme by S. Rachmaninov," in D major (c1890; vc/vn & pf) TNii/33
6.9   "2 Pieces" (c1892): No.1 "Prelude," in F major (from: Prelude for pf of 1891) Op.2
6.10   No.2 "Oriental Dance," in A minor
6.11   Cello Sonata in G minor (c1901) Op.19

7. PIANO SONATAS

7.1   Piano Sonata No.1 in D minor (c1907) Op.28
7.2   Piano Sonata No.2 in B-flat minor (c1913, r1931) Op.36

8. OTHER PIANO WORKS

8.1   *(Study), in F-sharp major (c ?1886, ?lost)* *TNii/10*
8.2   "Lento," in D minor (c ?1887, one surviving of possible 10: Songs without Words) TNii/11
8.3   "4 Pieces" (c1887): No.1 "Romance," in F-sharp minor TNii/12
8.4   No.2 "Prélude," in E-flat minor
8.5   No.3 "Mélodie," in E major
8.6   No.4 "Gavotte," in D major
8.7   "3 Nocturnes": No.1 "Andante cantabile," in F-sharp minor (c1887) TNii/13
8.8   No.2 "Andante maestoso—Allegro assai," in F major (c1887)
8.9   No.3 "Andante," in C minor (c1887–8)
8.10   "Piano Piece" (Canon), in D minor (c1890–1 or 1884) TNii/14
8.11   "Prélude," in F major (c1891; arr1892 as: Prélude for vc & pf, Op.2/1) TNii/15
8.12   "Cinq morceaux de fantaisie" (c1892): No.1 "Elégie," in E-flat minor Op.3
        No.2 "Prélude" (Prelude No.1), in C-sharp minor, "The Bells of Moscow" (arr for 2pf 1938)

8.85   "Six morceaux" (6 Duets) (c1894): No.1 "Barcarolle," in G minor Op.11
8.86   No.2 "Scherzo," in D major
8.87   No.3 "Russian song," in B minor
8.88   No.4 "Valse," in A major
8.89   No.5 "Romance," in C minor
8.90   No.6 "Glory," in C major
8.91   "Polka italienne," in E-flat min / major (c1906; 2 vers) TNii/21

2 Pf:

8.92   "2 Pieces" (6 hands): No.1 "Waltz," in A major (c1890) TNii/22
8.93   No.2 "Romance," in A major (c1891)
8.94   "Russian Rhapsody," in E minor (c1891) TNii/23
8.95   Suite No.1 (Fantaisie-tableaux) (c1893): No.1 "Barcarolle," in G minor Op.5
8.96   No.2 "Oh night, oh love," in D major
8.97   No.3 "Tears," in G minor
8.98   No.4 "Easter," in G minor
8.99   Suite No.2 (c1900–1): No.1 "Introduction," in C major Op.17
8.100   No.2 "Valse," in G major
8.101   No.3 "Romance," in A-flat major
8.102   No.4 "Tarantella," in C minor

9. CHORAL WORKS

9.1   "Deus meus" (canon), motet (c1890; ch) TNii/60
9.2   "O Mother of God vigilantly praying" (Sacred Concerto), motet (c1893; ch) TNii/61
9.3   "Don Juan" (c ?1894, from Tolstoy's poem: Don Juan): 1. "Chorus of Spirits" (ch) TNii/62
9.4   2. "Song of the Nightingale" (ch & pf)
9.5   "6 Choruses" (c1895–6; fem/child ch & pf): 1. "Be praised" (Glorious forever) (Nekrasov) Op.15
9.6   2. "The night" (Ladyzhensky)
9.7   3. "The pine tree" (The lonely Pine) (Lermontov)
9.8   4. "The waves slumbered" (Dreaming waves) (Romanov)
9.9   5. "Captivity" (Tsyganov)
9.10   6. "The angel" (Lermontov)
9.11   "Panteley the Healer" (c1901, Tolstoy; ch) TNii/63
9.12   "The Spring," cantata (c1902, from Nekrasov's The verdant noise; Bar, ch & orch) Op.20
9.13   "Liturgy of St John Chrysostom" (c1910; ch; adapted Henderson w/ Eng text 1915): Op.31
            1. "The Great Ektenya"
            2. "Praise the Lord, O my soul"
            3. "The only-begotten"
            4a. "In Thy Kingdom" (d ch)
            4b. "In Thy Kingdom" (ch)
            5. "Come, bow"
            6. "Lord, save the faithful, and Holy God"
            7. "The two-fold and following Ektenii"
            8. "Which Cherubim"
            9. "The suppliant Ektenya"
            10. "I believe" (Credo)
            11. "The grace at peace"
            12. "We sing to thee"
            13. "It is right for all men and all things"
            14. "Our Father" (d ch)
            15. "One Church"
            16. "Praise God in the Heavens" (Communion)
            17. "Blessed be the hosts, and We see the true light"
            18. "And our faith shall show forth"
            19. "Cry the name of the Lord" (d ch)
            20. "Praise the Father and the Faithful"
9.14   "The Bells" (Choral Symphony) (c1913, Poe transl Balmont; S, T, Bar, ch & orch) Op.35
9.15   "Vespers" (All-Night Vigil) (c1915; A, T & ch; ed Douglas w/ Eng text 1920): Op.37
            1. "O come, let us worship" (Venite adoremus)
            2. "Praise the Lord, O my soul" (Benedic anima mea)
            3. "Blessed is the man" (Beatus vir)
            4. "Gladsome Radiance"
            5. "Nunc dimittis"
            6. "Ave Maria"
            7. "Glory be to God" (6 psalms)
            8. "Praise the name of the Lord" (Laudate Dominum)
            9. "Blessed be the Lord"
            10. "The Veneration of the Cross" (Christ's resurrection witnessed)
            11. "Magnificat"
            12. "Gloria in Excelsis"
            13. "The day of salvation"
            14. "Christ is risen"

* * * * *

TN =   Robert Threlfall and Geoffrey Norris: "A Catalogue of the Compositions of S. Rachmaninoff."
          Scolar Press. London, 1982.

1. STAGE WORKS

Operas & opera-ballets:

1.1	*"Samson," 5 act tragédie-lyrique (c1733, Voltaire, unpubd, lost)* ....
1.2	"Hippolyte et Aricie," 5 act tragédie-lyrique (p1733, Pellegrin) ....
1.3	"Les Indes galantes," 4 entrée opéra-ballet (p1735, Fuzelier): ....

    I. "Le turc généreux"
    II. "Les Incas du Pérou"
    III. "Les fleurs"
    IV. "Les sauvages"

1.4	"Castor et Pollux," 5 act tragédie-lyrique (p1737, Bernard) ....
1.5	"Les fêtes d'Hébé ou Les talents lyriques," 3 entrée opéra-ballet (p1739, Montdorge): ....

    I. "La poésie"
    II. "La musique"
    III. "La danse"

1.6	"Dardanus," 5 act tragédie-lyrique (p1739, Bruyère) ....
1.7	*"Pandore," 5 act opéra (c1740, Voltaire, lost)* ....
1.8	"La princesse de Navarre," 3 act comédie-ballet (p1745, Voltaire; see r1745 as: Les fêtes de Ramire) ....
1.9	"Platée," 3 act comédie-lyrique (p1745, Autreau & Le Valois d'Orville) ....
1.10	"Les fêtes de Polymnie," 3 entrée opéra-ballet (p1745, Cahusac): ....

    Prologue. "Le Temple de mémoire"
    I. "La fable"
    II. "L'histoire"
    III. "La féerie"

1.11	"Le temple de la gloire," 5 act opéra-ballet (p1745, Voltaire) ....
1.12	"Les fêtes de Ramire," 1 act comédie-ballet (r1745 of: La princesse de Navarre of 1745) ....
1.13	"Les fêtes de l'Hymen et de l'Amour, ou Les Dieux d'Egypte," 3 entrée ballet-heroïque (p1748, Cahusac): .

    I. "Osiris"
    II. "Canope"
    III. "Aruéris ou Les Isies"

1.14	"Zaïs," 4 act ballet héroïque (p1748, Cahusac) ....
1.15	"Pygmalion," (1) acte de ballet (p1748, de Savot after La Monte) ....
1.16	"Les surprises de l'amour," 2 act divertissement (p1748, Bernard): ....

    . "Le retour d'Astrée"
    I. "La lyre enchantée"
    II. "L'enlèvement d'Adonis"

1.17	"Naïs," 3 act pastorale-héroïque (p1749, Cahusac) ....
1.18	"Zoroastre," 5 act tragédie-lyrique (p1749, Cahusac) ....
1.19	*"Linus," 3 act tragédie-lyrique (c1752, de la Bruyère, most lost)*
1.20	"La guirlande, ou Les fleurs enchantées," 1 act ballet (p1751, Marmontel) ....
1.21	"Acante et Céphise, ou La sympathie," 3 act pastorale-héroïque (p1751, Marmontel) ....
1.22	"Daphnis et Eglé," 1 act pastorale-héroïque (p1753, Collé) ....
1.23	*"Lysis et Délie," 1 act pastorale (c1753, unperf, music lost)* ....
1.24	"Les sybarites," (1) acte de ballet (p1753, Marmontel) ....
1.25	"La naissance d'Osiris" (p1754, Cahusac) ....
1.26	"Anacréon" I, 1 act ballet-héroïque (p1754, Cahusac) ....
1.27	*"Zéphire," (1) acte de ballet (c ?1754, unperf)* ....
1.28	"Anacréon" II, (1) acte de ballet (p1757, Bernard, for: Les surprises de l'Amour of 1748) ....
1.29	*"Le procureur dupé sans le savoir," opéra-comique en vaudevilles (p1758/9, lost)* ....
1.30	"Les Paladins," 3 act comédie-ballet (p1760, Monticourt) ....
1.31	"Abaris ou Les Boréades," 5 act tragédie-lyrique (c1764, Cahusac, unperf) ....
1.32	*"Jo," (1) acte de ballet (unperf, inc)* ....
1.33	*"Nélée et Myrthis," (1) acte de ballet (unperf)* ....

Other stage works:

1.34	"Aruéris," 1 act intermède (p1762, Choisy-le Roi) ....
1.35	"La cornemuse," ballet-pantomime (Sodi) ....
1.36	*"Les jardinières et les ciseaux," ballet-pantomime (lost)* ....

Incid music:

1.37	*"L'Endriague," 3 act comedy (p1723, Piron, lost)* ....
1.38	*"L'enrôlement d'Arlequin," 1 act comedy (p1726, Piron, lost)* ....
1.39	*"La robe de dissension, ou La faux prodigue," 2 act comedy (p1726, Piron, lost)* ....
1.40	*"Les courses de tempé," 1 act pastorale (p1734, vocal part of airs extant)* ....
1.41	*"Les jardins de l'Hymen ou La rose," 1 act pastorale (p1744, lost)* ....

1a. SELECTIONS FROM STAGE WORKS (Nos. of sections in The Gramophone)

1a.4	"Castor et Pollux," opera: ....

    excerpts: 1. "Ouverture"
    Prologue: 2. "Vénus, ô Vénus"

3. "Symphonie"
4. "Je vous revois, belle Désse"
5a. "Gavottes"
5b. "Renais, plus brillante"
6a. "Premier Menuet & Tambourin"
6b. "Naissez, dons de Flore"
7a. "Deuxième Menuet & Tambourin"
7b. "D'un spectacle nouveau"
I: 8. "Que tout gémisse"
9. "Où courez-vous?"
10. "Tristes apprêts, pâles flambeaux"
11a. "Symphonie guerière"
11b. "D'où partent ces cris nouveaux?"
11c. "Eclatez, fières trompettes" (Premier Air des Athlètes)
12. "Deuxième et Troisième Airs des Athlètes"
13. "Je remets à vos pieds"
II: 14. "Nature, Amour, qui partagez mon coeur"
15. "Le souverain des Dieux"
16. "Ma voix, puissant maître du monde"
17. "Connaissez notre puissance"
18. "Qu'Hébé de fleurs"
19. "Voici des Dieux"
III: 20. "Rassemblez-vous, peuples"
21. "Son char a reculé"
22. "Sortez d'esclavage"
23. "Brisons tous nos fers"
24. "Tout cède à ce héros vainqueur"
IV: 25. "Séjour de l'éternelle paix"
26. "Qu'il soit heureux comme nous"
27. "Ici se lève l'aurore"
28a. "Gavotte"
28b. "Sur les Ombres fugitives"
29a. "Passepieds"
29b. "Autant d'amours que de fleurs"
30. "Fuyez, Ombres légères"
31. "Rassurez-vous, habitants fortunés"
32. "Mais, qui s'offre à mes yeux"
33. "Revenez sur les rivages sombres"
V: 34. "Castor revoit le jour"
35. "Le Ciel est donc touché"
36. "Vivez, heureux époux"
37. "Peuples, éloignez-vous"
38. "Eh quoi! tous ces objets"
39. "Qu'ai-je entendu!"
40. "Les Destins sont contents"
41. "Mon trère ... ô Ciel!"
42. "Palais de ma grandeur"
43. "Tant de vertus doivent prétendre"
44. "Entrée des Astres" (Gigue)
45a. "Ariette"
45b. "Brillez, Astres nouveaux"
46a. "Chaconne"
46b. "Que les Cieux"

2. CHAMBER MUSIC

"Pièces de clavecin en concerts" (p1741; hpd, vn/fl & viol/vn):

2.1	"Premier concert": No.1 "La Coulicam," in E-flat major ....
2.2	No.2 "La Livri," in C minor
2.3	No.3 "Le Vézinet," in C major
2.4	"Deuxième concert": No.1 "La Laborde," in G major ....
2.5	No.2 "La Boucon," in G minor
2.6	No.3 "L'agaçante," in G major
2.7	No.4 "1er menuet," in G major
2.8	No.5 "2e menuet," in G minor
2.9	"Troisième concert": No.1 "La Poplinière," in A major ....
2.10	No.2 "La timide: 1er rondeau gracieux," in A major
2.11	No.3 "La timide: 2e rondeau gracieux," in A major
2.12	No.4 "1er tambourin," in A major
2.13	No.5 "2e tambourin en rondeau," in A minor
2.14	"Quatrième concert": No.1 "La pantomime," in B-flat major ....
2.15	No.2 "L'indiscrète," in B-flat major
2.16	No.3 "La Rameau," in B-flat major

3. HARPSICHORD

3.60	No.3 "La timide," 1er rondeau in A minor
3.61	No.4 "La timide," 2e rondeau in A major
3.62	No.5 "L'indiscrète," in B-flat major
3.63	"La Dauphine," in G minor (c1747, for wedding of the Dauphin w/ Maria-Josepha) ....

4. SACRED VOCAL

4.1	"Deus noster refugium" (c1716, Psalm 46; vv, ch, 2ob, vn, va & cont/org) ....
4.2	"In convertendo" (c1718, Psalm 126; vv, ch, 2fl, 2hn, 2vn, va & cont) ....
4.3	"Quam dilecta tabernacula tua" (ca1720, Psalm 133; vv, ch, 2fl, 2vn, va & cont/org) ....
4.4	*"Exultet caelum laudibus" (ca1720, lost)* ....
4.5	"Laboravi" (ca1722, part of Psalm 69; ch & cont) ....
4.6	*"Diligam te" (part of Psalm 69) (spur)* ....
4.7	*"Inclina Domine" (spur: c by François Martin)* ....

5. SECULAR VOCAL

5.1	"Duo paysan," duet (p1707; Bar, B) ....
5.2	"Avec du vin," canon (p1719) ....
5.3	"Les amants trahis," cantata (ca1721; S, B, viol & cont) ....
5.4	"Orphée," cantata (ca1721; S, vn, viol & cont) ....
5.5	"L'impatience," cantata (c1715–22; S, viol & cont) ....
5.6	"Ah! loin de rire," canon (p1722; 2S, Bar, B) ....
5.7	"Aquilon et Orinthie," cantata (c1727; B, vn & cont) ....
5.8	"Thétis," cantata (ca1727; B, vn & cont) ....
5.9	"Le berger fidèle," cantata (c1728; T, 2vn & cont) ....
5.10	"Cantate pour la fête de Saint Louis" (c1740 or later; S, tr instr & cont) ....
5.11	"Un Bourbon ouvre sa carrière," ariette (c ?1751; Haute-contre, 2vn & cont) ....
5.12	*"Medée," cantata (ca ?1720, lost)* ....
5.13	*"L'absence," cantata (ca ?1720, lost)* ....
5.14	*"La musette," cantata (B & cont, spur: c by ?de la Garde)* ....
5.15	*"Diane et Actéon," cantata (S, vn & cont, spur: c by Boismortier)* ....

*   *   *   *   *

1. STAGE WORKS

Operas:

1.1	*"Interieur" (c early, Maeterlinck, started 1890, sketches)* ....
1.2	*"La cloche engloutie" (c early, Hauptmann, started 1906, sketches)* ....
1.3	"L'heure espagnole" (The Spanish Hour), 1 act comédie musicale (c1907–9, Franc-Nohain) ....
1.4	"L'enfant et les sortilèges" (The Child and the Magic), 2 part fantaisie lyrique (c1920–5, Colette) ....

Ballets:

1.5	"Ma mère l'oye" (c1911, Ravel & Perrault, after suite for pf duet, w/ add movts & interludes) ....
1.6	"Daphnis et Chloé" (choreographic symphony in 3 scenes), ballet (c1909–12, Fokine after Longus) ....
1.7	"Adélaïde ou Le langage des fleurs" (c1912, Ravel, based on: Valses nobles et sentimentales)................
1.8	"Le tombeau de Couperin" (c1919, from orch suite; orig for pf) ....
1.9	"Fanfare," opening number for collab work: L'éventail de Jeanne (c1927; arr for pf duet)..........................
1.10	"La valse," choreographic poem (p1929; also as orch work) ....
1.11	"Boléro" (c1928; also see as orch work) ....

1a. SELECTIONS FROM STAGE WORKS

1a.5	"Ma mère l'oye," ballet: ....
	1. "Prélude et Danse du Rouet" (orch, new music)
	2. "Pavane de la Belle au Bois dormant"
	3. "Les Entretiens de la Belle et de la Bête"
	4. "Petit Poucet"
	5. "Laideronnette, Impératrice des Pagodes"
	6. "Le Jardin féerique"

2. ORCHESTRAL WORKS

2.1	"Shéhérazade—Fairy Overture" (c1898) ....
2.2	"Une barque sur l'océan" (c1906, r1926; orig No.3 of: Miroirs for pf) ....
2.3	"Rapsodie espagnole" (c1907–8; arr for 2pf): No.1 "Prélude à la nuit" ....
2.4	No.2 "Malagueña"
2.5	No.3 "Habanera" (orig for pf)
2.6	No.4 "Feria"
2.7	"Pavane pour une infante défunte" (c1910; orig for pf 1899) ....
2.8	"Ma mère l'oye," suite (c1911; orig for pf duet): No.1 "Pavane de la Belle au Bois dormant" ....
2.9	No.2 "Petit Poucet"
2.10	No.3 "Laideronnette, Impératrice des Pagodes"
2.11	No.4 "Les entretiens de la Belle et de la Bête"
2.12	No.5 "Le jardin féerique"
2.13	"Daphnis et Chloé" Suite No.1 (c1911, from ballet): No.1 "Nocturne" ....
2.14	No.2 "Interlude"
2.15	No.3 "Danse guerrière" (w/ ch)
2.16	"Valses nobles et sentimentales" (c1912; orig for pf; used in ballet: Adélaïde) ....
2.17	"Daphnis et Chloé" Suite No.2 (c1913, from ballet): No.1 "Lever de jour"..............................
2.18	No.2 "Pantomime"
2.19	No.3 "Danse générale"
2.20	"Alborada del gracioso" (c1918; orig No.4 of: Miroirs for pf) ....
2.21	"Le tombeau de Couperin" (c1919, from suite for pf; used for ballet): No.1 "Prélude" ....
2.22	No.2 "Forlane"
2.23	No.3 "Menuet"
2.24	No.4 "Rigaudon"
2.25	"La valse," poème chorégraphique (c1919–20; orig for ballet)..
2.26	"Boléro" (c1928; orig ballet; arr for 2pf 1930) ....
2.27	"Menuet antique" (c1929; orig for pf 1895) ....

3. CONCERTOS, SOLO INSTR & ORCH

Pf & orch:

3.1	*Piano Concerto on Basque themes, "Zaspiak-Bat" (c from 1906, sketches)* ....
3.2	Piano Concerto for the left hand (c1929–31) ....
3.3	Piano Concerto in G major (c1929–31) ....

Vn & orch:

3.4	"Tzigane," rapsodie de concert (c1924; orig for vn & pf) ....

4. STRING QUARTETS

4.1   String Quartet in F major (c1902–3) ....

5. OTHER CHAMBER MUSIC

3 or more insts:

5.1   "Introduction & Allegro" (c1905; harp & fl, cl, str qt; transcr for 2pf) ....
5.2   Piano Trio in A minor (c1914) ....

Vn & pf:

5.3   Violin Sonata in G major (c1897) ....
5.4   "Berceuse sur le nom de Gabriel Fauré" (c1922) ....
5.5   "Tzigane" (Rapsodie de concert) (c1924; orchd) ....
5.6   Violin Sonata (c1923–7) ....

Vn & vc:

5.7   "Le tombeau de Claude Debussy" (p1920) ....
5.8   "Sonata" (en duo) (c1920–22) ....

6. PIANO

6.1   "Sérénade grotesque" (ca1893) ....
6.2   "Menuet antique" (c1895; orchd1929) ....
6.3   "Pavane pour une infante défunte" (c1899; also see orchd1910) ....
6.4   "Jeux d'eau" (c1901) ....
6.5   "Sonatine" (c1903–5) ....
6.6   "Miroirs" (c1904–5): No.1 "Noctuelles" ....
6.7   No.2 "Oiseaux tristes"
6.8   No.3 "Une barque sur l'océan" (also see orchd1906 & 1926)
6.9   No.4 "Alborada del gracioso" (also see orchd1918)
6.10   No.5 "La vallée des cloches"
6.11   "Gaspard de la nuit" (c1908): No.1 "Ondine" ....
6.12   No.2 "Le gibet"
6.13   No.3 "Scarbo"
6.14   "Menuet sur le nom d'Haydn" (c1909) ....
6.15   "Valses nobles et sentimentales" (c1911): No.1 "Modère" ....
6.16   No.2 "Assez lent"
6.17   No.3 "Modère"
6.18   No.4 "Anime"
6.19   No.5 "Presque lent"
6.20   No.6 "Assez vif"
6.21   No.7 "Moins vif"
6.22   No.8 "Epilogue; Lent"
6.23   "Prélude" (c1913, for the piano competition at the Conservatoire de Paris) ....
6.24   "À la manière de ..." (c1913): No.1 "Borodine" (Valse) ....
6.25   No.2 "Chabrier" (Paraphrase sur un air de Gounod, Faust, 2e acte)
6.26   "Le tombeau de Couperin" (c1914–17; also see orchd): No.1 "Prélude" ....
6.27   No.2 "Fugue"
6.28   No.3 "Forlane"
6.29   No.4 "Rigaudon"
6.30   No.5 "Menuet"
6.31   No.6 "Toccata"
6.32   "La valse" (arr1921; orig for orch) ....
6.33   "Extraits de Daphnis et Chloé" (from ballet): No.1 "Danse gracieuse et légère" ....
6.34   No.2 "Nocturne, Interlude et Danse guerrière"
6.35   No.3 "Scène de Daphnis et Chloé"
6.36   "Extraits de L'enfant et les sortilèges" (from opera): No.1 "Five o'clock Fox-trot" ....
6.37   No.2 "Danse des Libellules et des Sphinx"
6.38   No.3 "Danse des Rainettes"

Pf duet:

6.39   "Ma mère l'oye" (c1908–10): No.1 "Pavane de la Belle au Bois dormant" ....
6.40   No.2 "Petit Poucet"
6.41   No.3 "Laideronnette, Impératrice des Pagodes"
6.42   No.4 "Les entretiens de la Belle et de la Bête"
6.43   No.5 "Le jardin féerique"

2 Pf:

6.44	"Sites auriculaires" (c1895–7): No.1 "Habanera" ....
6.45	No.2 "Entre cloches"
6.46	"Frontispiece" (c1918; 2pf 5 hands) ....
6.47	"La Valse" (p1921; 2pf; orig for orch) ....
6.48	"Boléro" (arr1930, from ballet) ....

7. CHORAL WORKS

7.1	"Trois chansons" (c1914–15, Ravel; 4vv & ch): 1. "Nicolette" ....
7.2	2. "Trois beaux oiseaux du paradis"
7.3	3. "Ronde"

8. VOICE & ORCHESTRA (or ensemble)

8.1	"Myrrha," cantata (c1901, Beissier; 3vv & orch, entry for the Prix de Rome) ....
8.2	"Alcyone," cantata (c1902, E. & E. Adénis; 3vv & orch, entry for the Prix de Rome) ....
8.3	"Alyssa," cantata (c1903, Coiffier; 3vv & orch, entry for the Prix de Rome) ....
8.4	"Manteau de fleurs" (c1903, Gravollet; 1v & orch; orig w/ pf) ....
8.5	"Shéhérezade" (c1903, Klingsor; mS & orch; also w/ pf, see Songs): 1. "Asie" ....
8.6	2. "La flûte enchantée"
8.7	3. "L'indifférent"
8.8	"Noël des jouets" (c1905, Ravel; 1v & orch; orig w/ pf; 2nd vers 1913) ....
8.9	"Trois poèmes de Stéphane Mallarmé" (c1913; 1v, piccolo, fl, cl, bass cl, pf & str qt): 1. "Soupir" ....
8.10	2. "Placet futile"
8.11	3. "Surgi de la croupe et du bond"
8.12	"Chanson hébraïque" (c1923–4; 1v & orch, after 4. of: Chants populaires of 1910) ....
8.13	"Chansons madécasses" (c1925–6, Parny; 1v, fl, pf & vc; also see w/ pf): 1. "Nahandove" ....
8.14	2. "Aoua"
8.15	3. "Il est doux de se coucher"
8.16	"Don Quichotte à Dulcinée" (c1932–3, Morand; also w/ pf): 1. "Chanson romanesque": "Si vous me disiez"
8.17	2. "Chanson épique": "Bon Saint Michel qui me donnez loisir"
8.18	3. "Chanson à boire": "Foin du bâtard, illustre Dame"
8.19	"Ronsard à son âme" (c1935; 1v & orch; orig w/ pf) ....

9. SONGS (w/ pf)

9.1	"Ballade de la reine morte d'aimer" (ca1893, Marès) ....
9.2	"Un grand sommeil noir" (c1895, Verlaine) ....
9.3	"Sainte" (c1896, Mallarmé) ....
9.4	"Chanson du rouet" (c1898, Lisle) ....
9.5	"Si morne!" (c1898, Verhaeren) ....
9.6	"Deux épigrammes de Clément Marot" (c1896–9): 1. "D'Anne qui me jecta de la neige" ....
9.7	2. "D'Anne jouant de l'espinette"
9.8	"Manteau de fleurs" (c1903, Gravollet: Les Frissons; also see orchd) ....
9.9	"Shéhérazade," song cycle (c1903, Klingsor; orig w/ orch; arr for pf duet): 1. "Asie": "Asie, Asie, Asie" ....
9.10	2. "La flûte enchantée": "L'ombre est douce et mon maître dort"
9.11	3. "L'indifférent": "Tes yeux sont doux comme ceux d'une fille"
9.12	"Noël des jouets" (c1905, Ravel; also see orchd) ....
9.13	"Cinq mélodies populaires grecques" (c1904–6, transl Calvocoressi): 1. "Le réveil de la mariée" (orchd) ....
9.14	2. "Là-bas, vers l'église" (orchd Rosenthal)
9.15	3. "Quel galant m'est comparable" (orchd Rosenthal)
9.16	4. "Chanson des cueilleuses de lentisques": "O joie de mon âme" (orchd Rosenthal)
9.17	5. "Tout gail": "Tout gai, ha, tout gai" (orchd)
9.18	*. "A vous, oiseaux des plaines" (lost)*
9.19	*. "Chanson de pâtre épirote" (lost)*
9.20	*. "Mon mouchoir, hélas, est perdu" (lost)*
9.21	"Histoires naturelles" (c1906, Renard): 1. "Le paon": "Il va sûrement se marier aujourd'hui" ....
9.22	2. "Le grillon": "C'est l'heure où, las d'errer, l'insecte nègre revient de promenade"
9.23	3. "Le cygne": "Il glisse sur le bassin, comme un traîneau blanc"
9.24	4. "Le martin-pêcheur": "Ça n'a pas mordu ce soir, mais je rapporte une rare émotion"
9.25	5. "La pintade": "C'est la bossue de ma cour"
9.26	"Vocalise-étude" (en forme de habanera) (c1907) ....
9.27	"Les grands vents venus d'outre-mer" (c1907, Régnier) ....
9.28	"Sur l'herbe" (c1907, Verlaine) ....
9.29	"Extraits de L'heure espagnole" (from opera): 1. "Duo de Gonzalve et Concepcion" (T, S & pf) ....
9.30	2. "Air de Concepcion": "Oh! la pitoyable aventure"
9.31	3. "Air de Gonzalve": "Adieu cellule"
9.32	4. "Quintette final" (S, 2T, Bar, B & pf)
9.33	"Tripatos," chanson populaire grecque (c1909, transl Calvocoressi) ....
9.34	"Chants populaires" (c1910): 1. "Chanson espagnole" ....

9.35	2. "Chanson française" (Limousin)
9.36	3. "Chanson italienne" (Romaine)
9.37	4. "Chanson hébraïque" (also see orchd)
9.38	5. "Chanson écossaise" (Burns)
9.39	*. "Chanson flamande" (lost)*
9.40	*. "Chanson russe" (lost)*
9.41	"Trois poèmes de Stéphane Mallarmé" (c1913, after songs w/ ens): 1. "Soupir" ....
9.42	2. "Placet futile"
9.43	3. "Surgi de la croupe et du bond"
9.44	"Deux mélodies hébraïques" (c1914): 1. "Kaddisch" ....
9.45	2. "L'énigme éternelle"
9.46	"Trois chansons" (c1914–15, Ravel, after choral work): 1. "Nicolette" ....
9.47	2. "Trois beaux oiseaux du paradis"
9.48	3. "Ronde"
9.49	"Ronsard à son âme" (c1923–4, Ronsard) ....
9.50	"Extraits de L'enfant et les sortilèges" (from opera): 1. "Air de l'Horloge" ....
9.51	2. "Air du Feu"
9.52	3. "Choeur des Pâtres" (S, A & pf)
9.53	4. "Duo de la Théière et de la Tasse" (mS, T & pf)
9.54	5. "Air de l'Enfant"
9.55	"Chansons madécasses" (c1925–6, Parny, after songs w/ ens): 1. "Nahandove" ....
9.56	2. "Aoua!"
9.57	3. "Il est doux de se coucher"
9.58	"Rêves" (c1927, Fargue) ....
9.59	"Don Quichotte à Dulcinée" (c1932–3, Morand; orig w/ orch): 1. "Chanson romanesque": "Si vous me disiez"
9.60	2. "Chanson épique": "Bon Saint Michel qui me donnez loisir"
9.61	3. "Chanson à boire": "Foin du bâtard, illustre Dame"

10. ARRANGEMENTS OF WORKS OF OTHERS

Orchestrations:

10.1	*Rimsky-Korsakov: "Antar" (frags partly reorchd ca1910 for use as incid music)* ....
10.2	*Musorgsky: "Khovanshchina," opera (reorchd ca1913, collab Stravinsky, lost)* ....
10.3	Satie: "Prélude," to incid music: Le fils des étoiles (orchd1913) ....
10.4	Schumann: "Carnaval," Op.9 (orchd ca1914 for use as ballet, other Nos. lost): . "Préambule" ....
10.5	. "Valse allemande"
10.6	. "Paganini"
10.7	. "Marche des 'Davidsbündler' contre les philistins"
10.8	Chabrier: "Menuet pompeux," No.9 of: Dix pièces pittoresques (orchd1918 for use as ballet) ....
10.9	*(Chopiniana) "Les sylphides," ballet based on music c by Chopin (orchd1914, collab work, lost)* ....
10.10	Debussy: "Sarabande," from: Pour le piano, L95/2 (orchd1922) ....
10.11	Debussy: "Tarantelle styrienne," L69 (orchd1922 as: Danse) ....
10.12	Musorgsky: "Tableaux d'une exposition" (orchd1922): . "Promenade" (Prelude) ....
10.13	No.1 "Gnomus"
10.14	. "Promenade" (Interlude)
10.15	No.2 "Il vecchio Castello"
10.16	. "Promenade" (Interlude)
10.17	No.3 "Tuileries"
10.18	. "Promenade" (Interlude)
10.19	No.4 "Bydlo"
10.20	. "Promenade" (Interlude)
10.21	No.5 "Ballet des Poussins dans leur coque"
10.22	No.6 "Samuel Goldenberg et Schmuyle"
10.23	No.7 "Limoges. Le Marché"
10.24	No.8 "Catacombes"
10.25	No.9 "La Cabane sur des pattes de poules"
10.26	No.10 "La grande Porte de Kiev"

Pf reductions:

10.27	Delius: "Margot la rouge," opera RTi/7 (vocal score 1902) ....
10.28	Debussy: "Nocturnes," L91 (arr1909; 2pf) ....
10.29	Debussy: "Prélude à L'après-midi d'un faune," L86 (arr1910; pf duet) ....

Editions:

10.30	Mendelssohn: Complete works for piano solo and piano concertos (ed1915–17) ....

* * * * *

1. STAGE WORKS

Operas:

1.1	"Re Enzo," 3 act comic opera (c1905, Donini)	P055
1.2	"Al mulino," 2 acts (c1908, Donini)	P076
1.2	"Semirâma," 3 act poema tragico (c1910, Ceré)	P094
1.3	"Marie-Victoire," 4 acts (c1913–4, Guiraud)	P100
1.4	"La bella addormentata nel bosco," 3 act fiaba musicale (c1921, Bistolfi)	P134
1.5	"Belfagor," 2 act commedia lirica (c1921–2, Guastalla after Morselli; arr for pf & small orch)	P137
1.6	"La campana sommersa," 4 acts (c1923–7, Guastalla after Hauptmann)	P152
1.7	"Maria Egiziaca," mistero (c1931, Guastalla; arr Cecco as: Due fantasie for pf & small orch)	P170
1.8	"La fiamma," 3 act melodramma (c1933, Guastalla after Jenssen's The Witch)	P175
1.9	"La bella dormente nel bosco," 3 act fiabba (c1933, Bistolfi; r by E. Respighi & Tocchi)	P176
1.10	"Lucrezia" (c1935, Guastalla after Shakespeare & Titus Livius; compl E. Respighi 1936)	P180

Ballets:

1.11	"La boutique fantasque" (c1918, from music c by Rossini; arr Carr, Godfrey; suite arr Sargent)	P120
1.12	"La pentola magica," ballet (c1920, on Russian melodies)	P129
1.13	"Scherzo veneziano" (Le astuzie di Colobina) (c1920, Leonidov)	P130
1.14	"Belkis, regina di Saba" (c1931, Guastalla; see orch suite, P177):	P171

　　　. "Quadro I"
　　　. "Quadro II: danze uccelli, dell'offerta, dei venti del sud, dell'araba fenice"
　　　. "Quadro III: danze dell'aurora, passo del gallo, dei sette profumi, le lacrime"
　　　. "Quadro IV"
　　　. "Quadro V: danza guerresca, sullo specchio d'acqua"
　　　. "Quadro VI: danze delle vesti, mistica, cerchio d'amore"
　　　. "Quadro VII: danza delle anfore, sul tamburo, orgiastica"

1a. SELECTIONS FROM STAGE WORKS

1a.11	"La boutique fantasque," ballet (Nos. of sections in The Gramophone):	P120

　　　excerpts: 1. "Overture"
　　　　　　2. "Scene"
　　　　　　3. "Vivo"
　　　　　　4. "Tarantella"
　　　　　　5. "Mazurka"
　　　　　　6. "Scene"
　　　　　　7. "Cossack Dance"
　　　　　　8. "Valse brillante"
　　　　　　9. "Can-Can"
　　　　　　10. "Andantino mosso"
　　　　　　11. "Valse lente"
　　　　　　12. "Scene"
　　　　　　13. "Nocturne"
　　　　　　14. "Galop"
　　　　　　15. "Finale"

1a.12	"La pentola magica," ballet:	P129

　　　　　1. "Preludio" (arr of music c by Grecianninov)
　　　　　2. "Canzone armena"
　　　　　2a. "Danza"
　　　　　3. "Entrata dello Tzar coi fidanzati" (arr of music c by Arenski)
　　　　　4. "Scena dello Tzarewich" (arr of music c by Paciulski)
　　　　　5. "Danza degli arceri tartari" (arr of music c by Rubinstein)
　　　　　6. "Introduzione e danza"
　　　　　7. "Danza cosacca" (arr of music c by Kosaciok)
　　　　　8. "Danza della seduzione"
　　　　　9. "Scena dei baci e arrivo dello Tzar"
　　　　　10. "Finale" (arr of music c by Rabikov)

2. SYMPHONIES

2.1	"Sinfonia drammatica" (c1914)	P102

3. OTHER ORCHESTRAL WORKS

3.1	"Piccola ouverture" (c1893)	P001
3.2	"Preludio" (c1894)	P002
3.3	"Compito di armonia" (c1894, school work)	P003
3.4	"Compito di armonia" (c1895, school work)	P004

13. ARRANGEMENTS OF WORKS OF OTHERS

* * * * *

P = Potito Pedarra: "Catalogo delle composizioni di Ottorino Respighi." 1985.

1. STAGE WORKS

Operas:

1.1 "The Maid of Pskov," 4 acts (Rimsky-Korsakov after Mey; 3 vers; also see incid music of the same title): ...
. Version 1 (c1868–72, p1873)
. Version 2 (c1868–77, unperf)
. Version 3 (c1891–2, p1895, Final Chorus & new aria for Act III 1898)
1.2 "Mlada," 4 act opera-ballet (c1872, Krylov after Gedeonov, collab Borodin, Cui, Musorgsky & Minkus, unfin)
1.3 "A May Night," 3 acts (c1878–9, Rimsky-Korsakov after Gogol's story) ....
1.4 "The Snow Maiden" (Spring fairy-tale), 4 acts (c1880–1, Rimsky-Korsakov after Ostrovsky; r vers ca1895)
1.5 "Mlada," 4 act magical opera-ballet (c1889–90, Rimsky-Korsakov after Krylov; also see collab
opera-ballet: Mlada of 1872) ....
1.6 "Christmas Eve," 4 acts (c1894–5, Rimsky-Korsakov after Gogol's story)..
1.7 "The Barber of Baghdad," 1 act (c1895, Rimsky-Korsakov, sketches) ....
1.8 "Sadko," 7 scenes (c1895–6, Rimsky-Korsakov & Belsky on epic ballad: Sadko the rich Merchant) ....
1.9 "Mozart and Salieri," 1 act (c1897, on Pushkin's play, Intermezzo unfin) Op.48
1.10 "Boyarina Vera Sheloga," prologue (c1898, Rimsky-Korsakov & Tyumenev, composed as Prologue
to 1898 performance of 2nd vers of opera: The Maid of Pskov) Op.54
1.11 "The Tsar's Bride," 4 acts (c1898, Rimsky-Korsakov after Mey; new aria for Act III 1899) ....
1.12 "The Tale of Tsar Saltan, of his son the famous and mighty hero Prince Gvidon Saltanovich and of the
beautiful Swan Princess," 4 acts (c1899–1900, Belsky after Pushkin) ....
1.13 "Servilia," 5 acts (c1900–1, Rimsky-Korsakov after Mey) ....
1.14 "Kashchei the Immortal," 1 act (c1901–2, Rimsky-Korsakov after Petrovsky; Conclusion r1906) ....
1.15 "Pan Voyevoda," 4 acts (c1902–3, Tyumenev, in memory of Chopin) Op.59
1.16 "The Legend of the Invisible City of Kitezh and the Maiden Fevroniya," 4 acts (c1903–5, Belsky) ....
1.17 "Heaven and Earth" (c1905, Belsky after Byron, sketches) ....
1.18 "Sten'ka Razin" (c1906, Belsky, sketches) ....
1.19 "The Golden Cockerel" (Le coq d'or), 3 acts (c1906–7, Belsky after Pushkin) ....

Operatic projects:

1.20 "Dobrynya Nitkitich" ....
1.21 "Nausicaä" (based on Homer) ....
1.22 "Ilya Muromets" ....
1.23 "The Tempest" (scenario only) ....
1.24 "Saul and David" (scenario only) ....

Incid music:

1.25 "The Maid of Pskov" (c1877, Mey; 2nd vers 1882; also see opera of the same title):....................................
1. "Overture befor the Prologue"
2. "Entr'acte before Act I"
3. "Entr'acte before Act II"
4. "Entr'acte before Act III"
5. "Entr'acte before Act IV"

1a. SELECTIONS FROM STAGE WORKS (Nos. of sections in The Gramophone)

1a.8 "Sadko," opera:..
1. "Greetings, ye merchants of Novgorod"
2. "O you dark forests" (Sadko's aria)
3. "O fearful crags" (Song of the Viking Guest)
4. "Song of the Indian Guest"
5. "Song of the Venetian Guest"
6. "Farewell, my friends" (Sadko's aria)
7. "Sleep went along the river" (Berceuse)
8. "Songs of the Venetian Merchant"
8a. "The paragon of cities"
8b. "Beautiful city!"

1a.12 "The Tale of Tsar Saltan," opera: ....
1. "Tsar's farewell and departure"
2. "Tsarina in a barrel at sea"
3. "Flight of the bumble-bee"
4. "The three wonders"
5. "March"

1a.19 "The Golden Cockerel," opera: ....
1. "King Dondon in his palace"
2. "King Dondon on the battlefield"
3. "King Dondon as the guest of Queen Shemakha"
4. "The marriage feast and lamentable end of Dondon"

2. SYMPHONIES

2.1	Symphony No.1 in E-flat minor (c1861–5; 2nd vers in E minor 1884)	Op.1
2.2	*Symphony in B minor (c1866–9, sketches)*	
2.3	Symphony No.2, "Antar" (subtitled after the name of the hero of Senkowsky's Arabian tale):	Op.9
	. Version 1 (c1868)	
	. Version 2 (c1875, r1903)	
	. Version 3 (Definitive) (c1897 as: Symphonic Suite)	
	. Version 4 (c1903, r of 2nd vers)	
2.4	Symphony No.3 in C major (c1866–73; 2nd vers 1886)	Op.32
2.5	*Symphony No.4 (c1884, pf sketches for Scherzo in D minor only)*	

3. ORCHESTRAL SUITES FROM OPERAS

3.1	"The Maid of Pskov," suite (c1877, r1882, from incid music): No.1 "Overture before Prologue"	
3.2	No.2 "Entr'acte before Act I"	
3.3	No.3 "Entr'acte before Act II"	
3.4	No.4 "Entr'acte before Act III"	
3.5	No.5 "Entr'acte before Act IV"	
3.6	"The Snow Maiden," suite (ca1890): No.1 "Introduction"	
3.7	No.2 "Dance of the Birds"	
3.8	No.3 "Procession"	
3.9	No.4 "Dance of the Buffoons"	
3.10	"Mlada," suite (c1903): No.1 "Introduction"	
3.11	No.2 "Redova"	
3.12	No.3 "Lithuanian Dance"	
3.13	No.4 "Indian Dance"	
3.14	No.5 "Procession of the Nobles"	
3.15	"Christmas Eve," suite (c1903; ch ad lib): No.1 "Introduction: A late frosty evening in Dikanka"	
3.16	No.2 "The ethereal space," sym picture	
3.17	"Episodes from Act III" (Nos.3–7): No.3 "Devilish Kolyadka"	
3.18	No.4 "Polonaise"	
3.19	No.5 "Scene: Vacula's return journey"	
3.20	No.6 "Dawn," musical picture	
3.21	No.7 "Views of the village of Dikanka"	
3.22	"Tsar Saltan," suite (c1900): No.1 "Introduction to Act I"	(Op.57)
3.23	No.2 "Introduction to Act II"	
3.24	No.3 "Introduction to Act IV, Scene 2" (The Three Wonders):	
	. "The learned squirrel"	
	. "The legendary knights"	
	. "The beautiful Swan-Princess"	
3.25	"Pan Voyevoda," suite (c1903–4): No.1 "Introduction"	(Op.59)
3.26	No.2 "Krakowiak"	
3.27	No.3 "Nocturne"	
3.28	No.4 "Mazurka"	
3.29	No.5 "Polonaise"	
3.30	"The Tale of the Invisible City of Kitezh," suite (ca1907): No.1 "Prelude: A hymn to nature"	
3.31	No.2 "Wedding procession"	
3.32	No.3 "Tartar invasion and Battle of Kerzhenets"	
3.33	No.4 "Death of Fevronya and apotheosis of the Invisible City"	

4. OTHER ORCHESTRAL WORKS

4.1	"Sadko," musical picture (c1867; 2nd vers 1869; 3rd vers 1891–2)	Op.5
4.2	"Fantasia on Serbian Themes," in B minor (c1867; 2nd vers 1886–7; 1st vers arr for pf duet ca1870).	Op.6
4.3	"Overture on Three Russian Themes" (c1866; 2nd vers 1879–80; arr for pf duet 1882):	Op.28
	quoted folksongs: . "Slava" (Glory)	
	. "At the gate, the gates"	
	. "Ivan has a big coat on"	
4.4	"Fairy Tale" (Baba-Yaga), in D min / major (c1879–80; arr for pf duet ca1880)	Op.29
4.5	"Sinfonietta on Russian Themes," in A min (c1879–84, from: Str Qt on Russian Themes of 1878–9)	Op.31
4.6	"Capriccio espagnol," in A major (c1887; arr for pf duet 1887):	Op.34
	1. "Alborada," in A major	
	2. "Variazioni," in F major	
	3. "Alborada," in B-flat major	
	4. "Scena e canto gitano," in D minor	
	5. "Fandango asturiano," in A major	
4.7	*"Little Russian Fantasia" (c1887, pf sketches only)*	
4.8	"Sheherazade" (Sym suite after: 1001 Nights) (c1888): No.1 "The Sea and Sinbad's ship," in E maj.	Op.35
4.9	No.2 "The story of Kalender Prince," in B minor	
4.10	No.3 "The Young Princess and the young Princess," in G major	
4.11	No.4 "Festival at Baghdad—The Sea," in E major	
4.12	"Russian Easter Overture," in D major (c1888, based on liturgical themes)	Op.36

4.13   "A Night on Mount Triglav," in B minor (c1899–1901, arr of Act III of 2nd vers of collab opera: Mlada) ....

4.14   "Theme & Variation No.4," in F major (c1901, for: Variations on a Russian theme, collab w/ others): ....
       quoted tune: . "O my field"

4.15   "At the Grave. Prelude," in B-flat minor (c1904, in memory of Belayev; arr for pf duet ca1904) Op.61

4.16   "Dubinushka" (The little oak stick), in B-flat minor (arr of Russian folksong 1905; see vers w/ ch) ....

4.17   "Toast to A. K. Glazunov," in E-flat major (c1907, for Glazunov's jubilee in 1907) ....

4.18   "Neapolitan Song," in C major (c1907, on Denza: Funiculi, funicula; arr for pf duet ca1907) Op.63

4.19   "The Golden Cockerel" (c1907, concert arr of: Introduction & Wedding March from opera) ....

4.20   "Tale of the Fisherman and the Fish," sym poem (c1907, after Pushkin, sketches) ....

5. CONCERTOS, SOLO INSTR & ORCH

Pf & orch:

5.1   Piano Concerto in C-sharp minor (c1882–3) Op.30

Vn & orch:

5.2   "Concert-fantasia on Russian Themes," in B minor (c1886–7): Op.33
       quoted folksongs: . "I am tired of the nights"
              . "A young girl was walking in the forest"

5.3   "Mazurka on Polish Themes" (c1888; used in Mazurka in opera: Pan Voyevoda, Op.59) ....

Vc & orch:

5.4   "Serenade," in B-flat major (c1903, arr of: Serenade for vc & pf of 1893) Op.37

Wind instr & milit band:

5.5   "Concerto," in B-flat major (c1877; trbn & milit band) ....

5.6   "Variations," in G minor (c1878; ob & milit band, on Glinka's song: Why do you cry, young beauty) ....

5.7   "Concerto," in E-flat major (c1878; cl & milit band) ....

6. STRING QUARTETS

6.1   String Quartet in F major (c1875) Op.12

6.2   "String Quartet on Russian Themes" (c1878–9; first 3 movts used in: Sinfonietta, Op.31): ....
       1. "In the field"
       2. "At the wedding-eve party"
       3. "In a khorovod" (round-dance)
       4. "In the monastery" (fugue) (see arr for pf duet as: In Church 1879)

6.3   "4 Variations on a Chorale," in G minor (c1885) ....

6.4   1st movt for collab: String Quartet, "B-la-F" (c1886, for the Name-day of Belayev; arr for pf duet 1887)
       (Belayev—publisher & friend of Balakirev, Borodin, Cui, Musorgsky & Rimsky-Korsakov, a group
       known as The Mighty Five / The Russian Five / The Mighty Fistful / The Cabinet): ....
       String Quartet in B-flat major, "B-la-F" (Belayev): 1. "Sostenuto assai et Allegro" (c by Rimsky-Korsakov)
          2. "Scherzo" (c by Lyadov)
          3. "Spanish Serenade" (c by Borodin)
          4. "Finale" (c by Glazunov)

6.5   "Khorovod" (Finale) for collab: String Quartet, "Name-day" (Jour de Fête) (c1887, ded to Belayev): ....
       String Quartet in D major, "Name-day": *1. "Carol-singers" (c by Glazunov)*
          2. "Song of Praise" (c by Lyadov)
       3. "Khorovod" (c by Rimsky-Korsakov)

6.6   String Quartet in G major (c1897) ....

6.7   "Theme & Variation No.4," in G major, for collab work: Variations on a Russian Theme (c1898): ....
       quoted folksong: . "I am tired of the nights"

6.8   1st movt (Allegro), in B-flat major, for collab work: Les Vendredis (c1899) ....

7. OTHER CHAMBER MUSIC

4 or more insts:

7.1   String Sextet in A major (c1876; 2vn, 2va & 2vc) ....

7.2   Quintet in B-flat major (c1876; fl, cl, hn, bn & pf) ....

7.3   "Nocturne," in F major (ca1888; 4hn) ....

3 insts:

7.4   Piano Trio in C minor (c1897; compl Shteynberg 1936–9) ....

Vn & pf:

7.5   "Mazurka on 3 Polish Themes" (arr1893, from orig for vn & orch of 1888) ....

Vc & pf:

7.6   "Serenade," in B-flat major (c1893; orchd1903 as Op.37)...

Other 2 insts:

7.7   "2 Duets," in F major (ca1883–94; 2hn)..
7.8   "Canzonetta," in A minor & "Tarantella," in A-flat major (c ?1883–94; 2cl) ....

8. PIANO

8.1	*"Overture" (ca1855, unfin)*	
8.2	"Allegro," in D minor (c1859–60)	
8.3	"Variations on a Russian Theme" (c1859–60)	
8.4	"Nocturne," in B-flat minor ((ca1860)	
8.5	"Funeral March," in D minor (ca1860)	
8.6	"4-Part Fugue," in C major (c1875; arr for pf duet)	
8.7	"Two 3-Part Fugues" (c1875): No.1 in G major	
8.8	No.2 in F major	
8.9	"Three 3-Part Fugues" (c1875): No.1 in E major	
8.10	No.2 in A major	
8.11	No.3 in D minor	
8.12	"3-Part Fugue," in D major (c1875; 2 vers)...	
8.13	"3 Fughettas on Russian Themes" (c1875): No.1 in G minor (4-part, theme: Mother it's dusty in the field) ..	
8.14	No.2 in D minor (4-part, theme: There was no wind)	
8.15	No.3 in G minor (3-part, theme: How in the garden)	
8.16	"4-Part Fugues" (c1875): No.1 in C major	
8.17	No.2 in E minor (double fugue)	
8.18	No.3 in G minor (double fugue on B-A-C-H)	
8.19	"6 Fugues" (c1875): No.1 in D minor	Op.17
8.20	No.2 in F major	
8.21	No.3 in C major	
8.22	No.4 in E minor	
8.23	No.5 in A major	
8.24	No.6 in E minor	
8.25	"3 Pieces" (c1875–6): No.1 "Valse," in C-sharp major	Op.15
8.26	No.2 "Romance," in A-flat major	
8.27	No.3 "Fugue," in C-sharp minor	
8.28	"3-Part Fugue," in G minor (c1876)	
8.29	"4 Pieces" (c1876–7): No.1 "Impromptu," in B major........................	Op.11
8.30	No.2 "Novellette," in B min / major	
8.31	No.3 "Scherzino," in A major	
8.32	No.4 "Etude," in D-flat major	
8.33	"6 Variations on B-A-C-H" (c1878): No.1 "Valse," in B-flat major	Op.10
8.34	No.2 "Intermezzo," in B-flat major	
8.35	No.3 "Scherzo," in F major	
8.36	No.4 "Nocturne," in B-flat major	
8.37	No.5 "Prelude," in B minor	
8.38	No.6 "Fugue on a theme of J. S. Bach," in G minor	
8.39	"Chopsticks Paraphrases" (24 Variations & 15 small pieces on theme 'Chopsticks') (c1878, collab work)	

       (Chopsticks—a quick waltz tune for pf duet. A hand held flat & perpendicular to the keyboard 'chops'
       the melody with the side of the little finger): No.1 "24 Variations & Finale" (c by Rimsky-Korsakov:
             Variation 1, 2, 6, 11, 12, 13, 16 & 19; other variations c by Cui & Lyadov) ....

         No.2 "Polka" (c by Borodin)
         No.3 "Marche funèbre" (c by Borodin)
         No.4 "Valse" (c by Lyadov)

8.40   No.5 "Berceuse," in C maj (on children's song: There goes a goat with horns) (c by Rimsky-Korsakov)
         No.6 "Galop" (c by Lyadov)
         No.7 "Gigue" (c by Lyadov)

8.41   No.8 "Little Fugue on B-A-C-H," in C major (c by Rimsky-Korsakov)
8.42   No.9 "Tarantella," in C major (c by Rimsky-Korsakov)
8.43   No.10 "Minuet," in C major (c by Rimsky-Korsakov)
         No.11 "Valse" (c by Cui)
         No.12 "Requiem" (c by Borodin)

8.44   No.13 "Carillon," in C major (c by Rimsky-Korsakov)
         No.14 "Mazurka" (c by Borodin)

8.45   No.15. "Comic Fugue," in C major (c by Rimsky-Korsakov)
       Added later: *No.16 "Cortège triomphal" (c by Lyadov, added 1893)*
         No.17 "Bigarrures. Petit supplement" (c by Shcherbachev, added 1893)

8.46   "Musical Letter" (a postcard to Lyadov) (c1878; used in Variation 16 of No.1 of: Chopsticks Paraphrases) .

8.47	"Finale," for collab work: Joke Quadrille (c1890): ....
	"Joke Quadrille": *1. "Pantalon" (c by Artsybushev)*
	2. "Été" (c by Vitols)
	3. "Poule" (c by Lyadov)
	4. "Trénis" (c by Sokolov)
	5. "Pastourelle" (c by Glazunov)
	6. "Finale," in C major (c by Rimsky-Korsakov)
8.48	"Allegretto," in C major (c1895) ....
8.49	"Prelude," in G major (c1896) ....
	2 Pieces for collab work: Album russe (c1896–7, for Bessel's 25th jubilee): Op.38
	"Album russe": *No.1 "Mazurka" (c by Artsybushev)*
	No.2 "Impromptu-caprice" (c by Cui)
	No.3 "Barcarolle" (c by Glazunov)
	No.4 "Prélude-Pastorale" (c by Lyadov)
8.50	No.5 "Prélude-Impromptu," in A-flat major (c by Rimsky-Korsakov)
8.51	No.5a "Mazurka," in F-sharp minor (c by Rimsky-Korsakov, added ?1897)
	No.6 "Prélude" (c by Sokolov)
8.52	"Variations on a Russian Theme" (c1899, Theme & Variation 1 in A major only, collab work): ....
	quoted theme: . "Little boy" (from Abramychev's folksong collection)
8.53	"Song" (in the Dorian mode) (c1901, melody Tears, incl as No.3 of: Armenian collection) ....

Pf duet:

8.54	"Scherzo," in C minor (ca1860) ....
8.55	"In Church" (In the Monastery) (c1879, arr of last movt of: Str Qt on Russian Themes of 1878–9) ....
8.56	"Variations on a Theme by Misha," in C major (c1879, theme by eldest son Mikhail) ....
8.57	"Intermezzo-fughetta," in G minor (ca1897, arr from unfin Intermezzo for opera: Mozart & Salieri) ....
8.58	"Dubinushka" (The little oak stick), in B-flat minor (arr1906–7; see orig for orch; arr for pf duet) ....

9. CHURCH MUSIC

9.1	"We praise Thee, O God" (c1883, from the 'Greek chant'; d ch) ....
9.2	"8 Settings from the Liturgy of St John Chrysostom" (c1883; ch): 1. "Song of the Cherubim" I Op.22
9.3	2. "Song of the Cherubim" II
9.4	3. "The Creed" (I Believe)
9.5	4. "Mercy of peace"
9.6	5. "We praise Thee" I
9.7	6. "It is truly meet" I
9.8	7. "Our Father"
9.9	8. "Praise the Lord from the Heavens" (Sunday Communion hymn)
9.10	"Collection of Sacred-Musical Arrangements" (c1884; ch): 1. "Song of the Cherubim" III Op.22b
9.11	2. "Let all mortal flesh keep silent"
9.12	3. "Sunday Communion hymn"
9.13	4. "See the Bridegroom comes"
9.14	5. "I enter Thy mansion, my Saviour"
9.15	6. "Psalm: By the waters of Babylon"
9.16	"Collection of Sacred-Musical Compositions & Arrs" (c1883–4; ch; ed Azeyev): 1. "Who is the King of
	Glory?" ....
9.17	2. "Before Thy Cross" (arr)
9.18	3. "Song of the Cherubim" IV
9.19	4. "Song of the Cherubim" V
9.20	5. "Song of the Cherubim" VI
9.21	6. "We praise Thee" II
9.22	7. "We praise Thee" III
9.23	8. "We praise Thee" IV
9.24	9. "We praise Thee" V (arr)
9.25	10. "We praise Thee" VI (arr)
9.26	11. "It is truly meet" II
9.27	12. "Praise the Lord from the Heavens" (d ch)
9.28	13a. "Praise the Lord from the Heavens" I (arr)
9.29	13b. "Praise the Lord from the Heavens" II (Communion hymn No.1 for Sunday) (arr)
9.30	14. "Angelic host" (Communion hymn No.2 for Monday) (arr)
9.31	15. "The memory of the Righteous" (Communion hymn No.3 for Tuesday) (arr)
9.32	16. "The Chalice of Salvation" (Communion hymn No.4 for Wednesday) (arr)
9.33	17. "To all the Earth" (Communion hymn No.5 for Thursday) (arr)
9.34	18. "You have created Salvation" (Communion hymn No.6 for Friday) (arr)
9.35	19a. "Rejoice the Righteous" I (Communion hymn No.7 for Saturday) (arr)
9.36	19b. "Rejoice the Righteous" II (Communion hymn No.7 for Saturday) (arr)
9.37	20. "Bestow on us the Light of your Countenance" (Communion—Exaltation of the Cross) (arr)
9.38	21. "Arise O God" (Communion—the Ascension of our Lord)
9.39	22. "Dogmatik of the First Mode: Glory to the whole World" (arr)
9.40	23. "Irmos of the Canon for Matins on Easter Saturday: By the waves of the sea"

10. CHORAL WORKS

10.1	"2 Choruses" (c1874, Lermontov; fem ch): 1. "Heavenly clouds"	Op.13
10.2	2. "The golden cloud had gone to rest"	
10.3	"4 Variations & Fughetta on a Russian song 'I am tired of the nights' " (c1875; fem ch)	Op.14
10.4	"6 Choruses" (c1875–6; ch & pf/harm ad lib), I: 1. "In the wild North" (Lermontov)	Op.16
10.5	2. "Bacchic song" (Pushkin; m ch)	
10.6	3. "Old song": "From the dense northern forests" (Koltsov)	
10.7	II: 4. "The moon sails quietly and peacefully" (Lermontov)	
10.8	5. "The last cloud of the storm" (Pushkin; fem ch)	
10.9	6. "Prayer": "Ruler of my days" (Pushkin)	
10.10	"2 Choruses" (c1876; ch): 1. "Before the Cross" (Fugue in the Mixolydian mode) (Koltsov)	Op.18
10.11	2. "The Tatar captivity" (Variations on a Russian theme. In the Mixolydian mode)	
10.12	"15 Russian folksongs" (c1879), I (fem ch): 1. "From the forest, the dark forest"	Op.19
10.13	2. "Wedding song": "As at evening"	
10.14	3. "The leaves are thick on the birch tree"	
10.15	4. "Wedding song": "Green is the pear-tree in the garden"	
10.16	5. "Ceremonial": "Beyond the river"	
10.17	II (m ch): 1. "Khorovod": "In the meadows"	
10.18	2. "Drawling song": "When you waved my light brown curls"	
10.19	3. "Drawling song": "Begone, begone bad weather"	
10.20	4. "Drawling song": "Oh, my good fortune"	
10.21	5. "Robbers' song": "Rise, rise, red sun"	
10.22	III (mix ch): 1. "Khorovod": "Rise, O sun, not low but high"	
10.23	2. "Trinity khorovod": "In the field there is a lime-tree"	
10.24	3. "Spring khorovod": "Plait the wattle fencing"	
10.25	4. "Khorovod": "Just see, good people"	
10.26	5. "Khorovod": "With a youth I go"	
10.27	"Poem about Alexei, the man of God" (c1878, trad; ch & orch)	Op.20
10.28	"Be Praised" (Slava) (c1879–80, trad; ch & orch, on folk theme: Near the dish):	Op.21
	quoted: . "Near the dish," Russian peasant song used in folk divination ceremonies (also quoted Beethoven in Str Qt No.8 in E minor, 'Rasumovsky 2,' Op.59/2 & Musorgsky in Prologue to opera: Boris Godunov)	
10.29	"2 Choruses" (c1884, trad; child ch): 1. "The Turnip" (ca1884)	
10.30	2. "The Kitten"	
10.31	"Robbers' Song": "Rise, rise, red sun" (ca1884, trad; m ch; also see Op.19/10)	
10.32	"4 Choruses" (c1876; m ch & pf ad lib): 1. "The peasant feast" (Koltsov)	Op.23
10.33	2. "Raven flies to raven" (Pushkin)	
10.34	3. "Enslaved by the rose, the nightingale" (Eastern Song) (Koltsov)	
10.35	4. "Pass the goblets" (Koltsev)	
10.36	"Świtezianka," cantata (c1897, Mey after Mickiewicz; S, T, ch & orch, based on song Op.7/3)	Op.44
10.37	"Song of Oleg the Wise" (c1899, Pushkin; T, B, m ch & orch)	Op.58
10.38	"From Homer," prelude cantata (c1901, from Homer's Odyssey; S, mS, A, fem ch & orch)	Op.60
10.39	"Dubinushka" (The little oak stick) (arr1906; ch & orch, from orig for orch)	Op.62

11. VOCAL DUETS & TRIOS

11.1	"The Butterfly," duet (c1855, children's words)	
11.2	"2 Duets" (c1897; mS, Bar / S, T; also S, T & orch 1897–1905): 1. "Pan" (Maykov)	Op.47
11.3	2. "The Song of Songs" (Mey after Bible)	
11.4	"2 Duets" (Maykov): 1. "The mountain spring" (c1897; S, mS or T, Bar; arr for S, mS, A & orch, Op.52b)	Op.52
11.5	2. "Angel and demon" (c1898; S, Bar or T, mS)	
11.6	"Dragonflies" (c1897, Tolstoy; 2S, mS; orchd w/ fem ch ad lib 1897)	Op.53

12. SONGS (w/ pf)

12.1	"Come out to me, signora" (c1861)	
12.2	*"My blood burns" (In the blood burns the fire of desire) (c1865, Pushkin, ?lost)*	
12.3	"4 Songs" (c1865–6): 1. "Lean thy cheek to mine" (Heine transl Mikhailov, pf part c by Musorgsky)	Op.2
12.4	2. "Eastern song": "Enslaved by the rose, the nightingale" (Koltsov)	
12.5	3. "Lullaby" (Mey; later used in 2nd vers of opera: The Maid of Pskov & in: Boyarina Vera Sheloga)	
12.6	4. "From my tears" (Heine transl Mikhailov)	
12.7	*"You will soon forget me" (c1866, lost)*	
12.8	"4 Songs" (c1866): 1. "The pine-tree and the palm" (Heine transl Mikhailov; 3 vers):	Op.3
	. Version 1: "On the northern bare cliff" (c1866)	
	. Version 2: "The pine-tree and the palm. A musical picture" (c1889; w/ orch)	
	. Version 3: "The pine-tree and the palm" (= Version 2 arr w/ pf p1946)	
12.9	2. "Southern night" (Shcherbina)	
12.10	3. "The golden cloud has slept" (Lermontov)	
12.11	4. "On the hills of Georgia" (Pushkin)	
12.12	"4 Songs" (c1866): 1. "What is my name to thee?" (Pushkin)	Op.4
12.13	2. "The messenger" (from Heine's Die Botschaft, transl Mikhailov)	

12.14	3. "In the dark grove the nightingale is silent" (Nikitin; orchd1891)
12.15	4. "Quietly evening falls" (Fet; orchd1891)
12.16	"4 Songs" (c1867): 1. "My voice for thee is sweet and languid" (Pushkin) Op.7
12.17	2. "Hebrew song" (Mey)
12.18	3. "Świtezianka" (Mickiewicz transl Mey; used in cantata Op.44)
12.19	4. "Thy glance is radiant as the heavens" (Lermontov)
12.20	"6 Songs": 1. "Where art thou, my thought flies there" (c1870) Op.8
12.21	2. "Night" (c1868, Pleshcheyev; orchd1891)
12.22	3. "The Secret" (c1868, after Chamisso)
12.23	4. "Arise, come down! Long the dawn" (c1870, Mey)
12.24	5. "To the kingdom of roses and wine—come!" (c1870, Fet)
12.25	6. "I believe I'm in love" (c1870, Pushkin)
12.26	"2 Songs" (Heine transl Mikailov): 1. "To my song" (c1870, from Heine's Traumbilder) Op.25
12.27	2. "When I gaze into thy eyes" (c1876)
12.28	"4 Songs" (c1882): 1. "In moment to delight devoted" (Byron transl Kozlov; also Fr transl Ruelle
	titled: Élan de Tendresse; pubd in Eng titled: In One Sweet Rush of Tender Feeling) ... Op.26
12.29	2. "Evocation" (Pushkin)
12.30	3. "For the shores of thy far native land" (Pushkin)
12.31	4. "Zuleika's song" (from Byron's The Bride of Abydos, transl Kozlov)
12.32	"4 Songs" (c1883): 1. "Softly the soul flew up to Heaven" (Tolstoy) Op.27
12.33	2. "Echo" (Coppée transl Andreyevsky)
12.34	3. "Thou and you" (Pushkin)
12.35	4. "Forgive! Remember not these tearful days" (Nekrasov)
12.36	"4 Songs" (c1897, Tolstoy; 2 vers: medium & high v): 1. "Oh, if thou couldst for one moment" Op.39
12.37	2. "The West dies out in pallid rose"
12.38	3. "Silence descends on the golden cornfields"
12.39	4. "Sleep, my poor friend"
12.40	"4 Songs" (c1897; 2 vers: medium & high v): 1. "When the golden cornfield waves" (Lermontov) Op.40
12.41	2. "Across the midnight sky" (Lermontov)
12.42	3. "Of what I dream in the quiet night" (Elegy) (Maykov)
12.43	4. "I waited for thee in the grotto at the appointed hour" (Maykov)
12.44	"4 Songs" (c1897; 2 vers: medium & high v): 1. "Sun of the sleepless, sad star" (Tolstoy after Byron)
	(also see Mendelssohn's 2. of: 2 Romances of 1834, Schumann Op.95/2 & Wolf's 3. of:
	4 Poems of Heine, Shakespeare & Byron) Op.41
12.45	2. "I am unhappy" (Lermontov)
12.46	3. "I love thee, moon" (Melody from the banks of the Ganges) (Maykov)
12.47	4. "Look in thy garden" (From the Eastern World) (Maykov)
12.48	"4 Songs" (c1897; 2 vers: medium & high v): 1. "A whisper, a gentle breath" (Fet) Op.42
12.49	2. "I have come to greet thee" (Fet)
12.50	3. "The clouds begin to scatter" (Elegy) (Pushkin)
12.51	4. "My spoiled darling" (Mickiewicz transl Mey)
12.52	"In Spring" (c1897; 2 vers: medium & high v): 1. "The lark sings louder" (Tolstoy) Op.43
12.53	2. "Not the wind, blowing from the heights" (Tolstoy)
12.54	3. "Cool and fragrant is thy garland" (Fet)
12.55	4. "It was in early spring" (Tolstoy)
12.56	"To the Poet" (2 vers: medium & high v): 1. "The echo" (c1897, Pushkin) Op.45
12.57	2. "Art" (c1897, Maykov)
12.58	3. "The Octave" (c1897, Maykov)
12.59	4. "Doubt" (c1897, Maykov)
12.60	"The Poet" (c1899, Pushkin; 2 vers: medium & high v) ....
12.61	"By the Sea" (c1897, Tolstoy, 2 vers: medium & high v): 1. "The waves break into spray" Op.46
12.62	2. "The sea does not foam"
12.63	3. "The sea is tossing, wave after wave"
12.64	4. "Do not believe me, friend"
12.65	5. "The waves rise up like mountains"
12.66	"2 Songs" (Pushkin; B): 1. "The Upas-tree, Tree of Death" (c1882, r1897; orchd1906) Op.49
12.67	2. "The Prophet" (c1897; B & pf; orchd w/ m ch ad lib 1899; orchd vers red for 1v & pf 1899)
12.68	"4 Songs" (Maykov after Greek poems; 2 vers: medium & high v): 1. "The maiden & the sun" (c1897) Op.50
12.69	2. "The singer" (c1897)
12.70	3. "Quiet is the blue sea" (c1897)
12.71	4. "I am still filled, dear friend" (c1898)
12.72	"5 Songs" (c1897, Pushkin; 2 vers: medium & high v): 1. "Slowly drag my days" Op.51
12.73	2. "Do not sing to me, o lovely one"
12.74	3. "Withered flower"
12.75	4. "The Beauty"
12.76	5. "A rainy day has waned"
12.77	"4 Songs": 1. "Awakening" (c1897, Pushkin) Op.55
12.78	2. "To a Grecian girl" (c1898, Pushkin)
12.79	3. "The Dream" (c1898, Pushkin)
12.80	4. "I died from happiness" (c1898, Uhland transl Zhukovsky)
12.81	"2 Songs" (c1898, Maykov): 1. "The Nymph" (orchd1905) Op.56
12.82	2. "Summer night's dream" (orchd1906, ed Steinberg 1910)

13. FOLKSONG COLLECTIONS

13.1   "Collection of Russian Folksongs" (c1875–6, 100 songs in 5 genres): Op.24
            I. "Byliny and Narrative Songs"
            II. "Lyrical Songs"
            III. "Dance Songs"
            IV. "Game Songs"
            V. "Ritual Songs"
13.2   "40 Folksongs" (c1875–82, collected Filippov, harmonized Rimsky-Korsakov): ....
            incl.   . 6 "Spiritual Verses"

14. ARRANGEMENTS OF WORKS OF OTHERS

For orch:

14.1   Borodin: Final chorus of opera: Prince Igor (orchd1879)...
14.2   Borodin: Prologue & Act I scene 1 of opera: Prince Igor (r1885) ....
14.3   Borodin: "Prince Igor," opera (compl & orchd1887–8 p1896, collab Glazunov) ....
14.4   Borodin: "Nocturne," from String Quartet No.2 (arr1887; vn & orch) ....
14.5   Borodin: Symphony No.1 in E-flat major (revised, collab Glazunov) ....
14.6   Borodin: Symphony No.2 in B minor (revised, collab Glazunov) ....
14.7   Borodin: Finale to Act IV of collab ballet-opera: Mlada (orchd1890) ....
14.8   Borodin: "The Sleeping Princes," song (orchd1897) ....
14.9   Borodin: "The Sea," song (orchd1906) ....

14.10   Cui: "Wedding chorus" & "Blessing scene," from opera: William Ratcliff (orchd1868) ....
14.11   Cui: Introduction to Act I & Entr'acte to Act III of opera: William Ratcliff (reorchd1894) ....

14.12   Dargomizhsky: "The Stone Guest," opera (orchd1869–70, scene 1: reorchd ca1899, parts rewritten 1902)
14.13   Dargomizhsky: "Chorus of Maidens," from opera: Rogdana (orchd1873) ....

14.14   Glinka: Music for stage band in opera: Ruslan and Lyudmila (arr1876) ....
14.15   Glinka: "A Life for the Tsar," opera (ed1878–81, collab Balakirev & Lyadov; new ed p1907, collab Glazunov)
14.16   Glinka: "Ruslan and Lyudmila," opera (ed1878–81, collab Balakirev & Lyadov).............................
14.17   Glinka: Excerpts from operas (arr1884; str qt) ....
14.18   Glinka: "Prince Kholmsky," incid music (ed1902, collab Glazunov) ....
14.19   Glinka: Orchestral works (arr & ed) ....

14.20   Handel: 7 Numbers from oratorio: Samson, HWV57 (orchd1875–6, collab Conservatory students)............

14.21   Musorgsky: 2nd vers of trio of choral work: The Destruction of Sennacherib (orchd1874) ....
14.22   Musorgsky: "Persian Dances," from opera: Khovanshchina (ed & orchd1881–3).............................
14.23   Musorgsky: Various orch, choral works & songs (ed & orchd1881–3) ....
14.24   Musorgsky: "Khovanshchina," opera (rewritten, compl & orchd1886) ....
14.25   Musorgsky: "Dream Intermezzo," from opera: Sorochintsy Fair (arr1886 as: Night on the Bare Mountain) ..
14.26   Musorgsky: "Polonaise," from opera: Boris Godunov (reorchd1892–6) ....
14.27   Musorgsky: "Coronation scene," from opera: Boris Godunov (reorchd1892) ....
14.28   Musorgsky: "Boris Godunov," opera (cut, rewritten & reorchd1892–6) ....
14.29   Musorgsky: "Boris Godunov," opera (rewriten, reorchd, cuts restored 1906) ....
14.30   Musorgsky: "The Marriage," comic opera (revised & partly orchd1906) ....
14.31   Musorgsky: Songs (orchd1906): . "Hopak" ....
14.32   . "Gathering Mushrooms"
14.33   . "Yeremushka's lullaby"
14.34   Musorgsky: 2 add passages for the Coronation Scene of opera: Boris Godunov (c1907, for Diaghilev) ......
14.35   Musorgsky: "With Nurse," song from cycle: The Nursery (free arr1908) ....
14.36   Musorgsky: Songs (orchd1908): . "Night," 2nd vers (Pushkin words restored) ....
14.37   . "Serenade" (No.3 of: Songs & Dances of Death)
14.38   . "The Field Marshal Death" (No.4 of: Songs & Dances of Death)

14.39   Schubert: "March for the Coronation of Nicholas I," D885 (orchd1868) ....
14.40   Schumann: 2 Numbers from pf work: Carnaval, Op.9 (orchd1902): . "Florestan" (No.6) ....
14.41   . "Promenade" (No.19)

For milit band (arr1873–83):

14.42   Beethoven: "Egmont" Overture, Op.84...
14.43   Glinka: Finale from opera: A Life for the Tsar ....
14.44   Meyer, L. de: Berlioz's version of: Marche marocaine ....
14.45   Mendelssohn: "Nocturne" & "Wedding March," from incid music: Midsummer Night's Dream, Op.61 ....
14.46   Meyerbeer: "Isabella's aria," from opera: Robert le diable (cl & milit band)................................
14.47   Meyerbeer: "Conspiracy Scene," from opera: Les Huguenots ....
14.48   Meyerbeer: "Coronation March," from opera: Le prophète..
14.49   Schubert: "March," in B minor ....
14.50   Wagner: Prelude to opera: Lohengrin, WWV75 ....

* * * * *

1. STAGE WORKS

Operas:

1.1	"El Hijo fingido," zarzuela (c1954, p1964, Valverde after Vega) ....
1.2	"La azucena de Quito," opera (c1965, Valverde) ....

Ballets:

1.3	"Pavana real" (c1955, Kamhi) ....
1.4	"Juana y los caldereros" (c1956) ....

Incid music:

1.5	"La vida es sueño di Calderón" (c1954) ....
1.6	"Cyrano de Bergerac" (c1955, Rostand) ....
1.7	"Oedip" (c1956, Sophocles)...
1.8	"Tieste" (c1957, Seneca) ....
1.9	"The Two Gentlemen of Verona" (c1978, Shakespeare) (also see incid music c by Khachaturian) ....

2. ORCHESTRAL WORKS

2.1	"Juglares" (c1923) ....
2.2	"5 Piezas infantiles" (c1924; also for 2 pf): No.1 "Son chicos que pasan"................................
2.3	No.2 "Mazurca"
2.4	No.3 "Después de un cuento"
2.5	No.4 "Plegaria"
2.6	No.5 "Gritería final"
2.7	"Preludio para un poema a la Alhambra" (c1926) ....
2.8	"Zarabanda lejana y Villancico" (c1923–8; strings) ....
2.9	"3 viejos aires de danza" (c1926–9): No.1 "Pastoral" ....
2.10	No.2 "Minueto"
2.11	No.3 "Giga"
2.12	"Por la Flor del Lliri Blau," sym poem (c1934) ....
2.13	"2 Berceuses" (c1935; see orig for pf) ....
2.14	"Homenaje a la Tempranica" (c1939)..
2.15	"2 Piezas caballerescas" (Homenaje a R. Casanx) (c1945; orch of vcs): No.1 "Madrigal" ....
2.16	No.2 "Danza de cortesía"
2.17	"Soleriana" (c1953)...
2.18	"Música para un jardín" (c1957) ....
2.19	"A la busca del más allá" (In Search of the Beyond) (c1976–7) ....
2.20	"Palillos y panderetas" (2 danzas de España) (c1982) ....

3. CONCERTOS, SOLO INSTR & ORCH

Pf & orch:

3.1	"Concierto heróico" (c1941–2) ....

Vn & orch:

3.2	"Canzoneta" (c1923) ....
3.3	"Concierto de Estío" (Summer Concerto) (c1943) ....

Vc & orch:

3.4	"Concierto en modo galante" (c1949)...
3.5	"Concierto como un divertimiento" (c1981–2) ....

Gui & orch:

3.6	"Concierto de Aranjuéz" (c1939; 2nd movt arr1968 for pf/gui as: Aranjuéz, ma pensée) ....
3.7	"Fantasía para un gentilhombre" (c1954): ....
	1. "Villano y Ricercare"
	2. "Españoleta"
	3. "Fanfare de la Caballeria de Nápoles"
	4. "Danza de las Hachas"
	5. "Canario"
3.8	"Concierto para una fiesta" (c1982) ....
3.9	"Concierto andaluz" (c1967; 4gui & orch)..
3.10	"Concierto-Madrigal" (c1965–8; 2gui & orch) ....

Harp & orch:

3.11   "Concierto-Serenata" (c1952) ....
3.12   "Sones en la Giralda" (Fantasia sevillana) (c1963; harp & chamber orch) ....

Other:

3.13   "Concierto pastoral" (c1978; fl & orch) ....

4. CHAMBER MUSIC

Vn & pf:

4.1   "2 Esbozos" (c1923): No.1 "La enamorada junto al pequeño surtidor" Op.1
4.2   No.2 "Pequeña ronda"
4.3   "Rumaniana" (c1943) ....
4.4   "Capricho" (c1944) ....
4.5   "Sonata pimpante" (c1966) ....
4.6   "Serenata al Alba del Dia" (c1982; vn/fl & pf/gui) ....
4.7   "6 Cançons valencianes" (c1981–4) ....

Vc & pf

4.8   "Siciliana" (c1929) ....
4.9   "Sonata alla breve" (c1976–8) ....

Other 2 insts:

4.10   "Serenata para el alba del día" (c1982–3; fl & gui) ....

1 instr:

4.11   "Impromptu" (c1943; harp) ....
4.12   "Capricho" (c1944; vn) ....
4.13   "Como una fantasia" (c1980; vc) ....

5. GUITAR

5.1   "Zarabanda lejana" (Homenaje a Luis de Milán) (c1923; arr for gui, pf & strings)............
5.2   "Por los campos de España": No.1 "En los trigales" (c1939) ....
5.3   No.2 "Entre olivares" (c1942)
5.4   "Tiento antiguo" (c1942) ....
5.5   "Bajando de la meseta" (c1954) ....
5.6   "Junto al Generalife" (c1954) ....
5.7   "3 Piezas españolas" (c1954): No.1 "Fandango" ....
5.8   No.2 "Passacaglia"
5.9   No.3 "Zapateado"
5.10   "Romance de Durandarte" (transcr from ballet: Pavana real of 1955) ....
5.11   "Sonata giocosa" (c1961) ....
5.12   "Invocación y danza" (Homage to M. de Falla) (c1961) ....
5.13   "Tonadilla" (c1960; 2gui) ....
5.14   "Pastoral" (c1965) ....
5.15   "Sonata a la española" (c1969) ....
5.16   "Elogio de la guitarra" (c1971) ....
5.17   "3 Pequeñas piezas" (c1971): No.1 "Ya se van los pastores" ....
5.18   No.2 "Por Caminos de Santiago"
5.19   No.3 "Pequeña Sevillana"
5.20   "Pájaros de primavera" (c1972) ....
5.21   "Por tierras de Jerez" (antologia) (c1972) ....
5.22   "Ya se van los pastores" ....
5.23   "2 Preludes" (c1977): No.1 "Adagio" ....
5.24   No.2 "Allegro"
5.25   "Triptic" (c1979): No.1 "Preludio" (Allegro aperto) ....
5.26   No.2 "Nocturno"
5.27   No.3 "Scherzino" (Allegro vivace)
5.28   "Un tiempo fue Itálica famosa" (c1981) ....
5.29   "Ecos de Sefarad" (c1987) ....
5.30   "Que buen caminito!" (c1987) ....

6. PIANO

6.1   "Homenaje a un viejo clavicordio" (c1922) ....

6.2	"Lied" (c1923) ....
6.3	"Sus manos" (c1923) ....
6.4	"Suite" (c1923): No.1 "Preludio" ....
6.5	No.2 "Siciliana"
6.6	No.3 "Bourrée"
6.7	No.4 "Minué"
6.8	No.5 "Rigodón"
6.9	"Berceuse de Otoño" (c1923) ....
6.10	"Bagatela" (c1926) ....
6.11	"Balada de añoranza" (c1926) ....
6.12	"Pastoral" (c1926) ....
6.13	"Preludio al gallo mañanero" (c1926) ....
6.14	"Zarabanda lejana" (c1926, transcription) ....
6.15	"Berceuse de primavera" (c1928) ....
6.16	"Air de ballet sur le nome d'une jeune fille" (c1930) ....
6.17	"Serenata española" (c1931) ....
6.18	"Sonata de adiós" (Homenaje à Paul Dukas) (c1935) ....
6.19	"5 Piezas del siglo XVI" (c1937): No.1 "Diferencias sobre el Canto del Caballero" (Cabezón) ....
6.20	No.2 "Pavana" (Milán)
6.21	No.3 "Pavana" (Milán)
6.22	No.4 "Pavana" (Valderrábano)
6.23	No.5 "Fantasía" (Mudarra)
6.24	"Danzas de España," first sketch-book (c1938): No.1 "Danza valenciana" ....
6.25	No.2 "Plegaria de la Infanta de Castilla"
6.26	No.3 "Fandango del ventorrillo"
6.27	No.4 "Caleseras" (Homenaje a Chuecca)
6.28	"Danzas de España," second sketch-book (c1941): No.1 "Rústica" ....
6.29	No.2 "Danza de las tres doncellas"
6.30	No.3 "Serrana"
6.31	"Gran Marcha de los Subsecretarios" (c1941; arr Tovar & Rubio for pf duet) ....
6.32	"El album de mimina" (c1942) ....
6.33	"A l'ombre de Torre Bermeja" (Homenaje a Ricardo Viñes) (c1945) ....
6.34	"Música para un despertador" (c1946, for the left hand) ....
6.35	"El album de Cecilia" (6 Piezas para manos pequeñas) (c1948): No.1 "María de los Reyes" ....
6.36	No.2 "A la jota—Jota de las Palomas"
6.37	No.3 "Canción del hada rubia"
6.38	No.4 "Canción del hada morena"
6.39	No.5 "El negrito Pepo"
6.40	No.6 "Borriquillos a Belén"
6.41	"4 Estampas andaluzas" (c1946–54) ....
6.42	"5 Sonatas de Castilla con toccata a modo de pregón" (c1950–1): No.1 "Sonata" ....
6.43	No.2 "Sonata en Fa sostenido menor"
6.44	No.3 "Sonata en Re"
6.45	No.4 "Sonata como un tiento"
6.46	No.5 "Sonata en La"
6.47	"Danza de la amapola" (c1972) ....
6.48	"3 Evocaciones" (c1980–2): No.1 "Tarde en el parque" ....
6.49	No.2 "Noche en el Guaralquivir"
6.50	No.3 "Mañana en Triana"
6.51	"Preludio de Añoranza" (c1987) ....

Pf duet:

| 6.52 | "Atardecer" (c1976) .... |
| 6.53 | "Sonatina para dos muñecas" (c1977) .... |

2 Pf:

| 6.54 | "5 Piezas infantiles" (c1924) .... |

7. CHURCH MUSIC

| 7.1 | "Ave María" (c1923; 1v & org) .... |
| 7.2 | "Agnus" (c1939; ch) .... |

8. CHORAL WORKS

W/ orch:

8.1	"Yo tengo un burro," canción popular valenciana (c1933) ....
8.2	"Ausencias de Dulcinea" (c1948, inspired by Cervantes and his vision of Dulcinea) ....
8.3	"Villancicos y canciones de Navidad" (c1952; S, ch & orch) ....
8.4	"Música para un códice salmantino," cantata (c1953; B, ch & 11 insts) ....

8.5 "Himnos de los neófitos de Qumran" (c1965; 3 fem vv, m ch & small orch) ....
8.6 "Cántico de San Francisco de Asis" (c1981) ....

Unacc ch:

8.7 "Triste estaba el rey David" (c1950) ....
8.8 "2 Canciones sefardíes del siglo XV" (c1951) ....

9. VOICE & ORCHESTRA

9.1 "Tríptic de Mosén Cinto" (c1935, Verdagner): 1. "L'harpa sagrada" ....
9.2   2. "Lo violi de San Francesch"
9.3   3. "San Francesch i la cigala"
9.4 "Cancíones sobre textos catalanes" (c1936): 1. "El arpa sagrada" ....
9.5   2. "Le violi de San Francesch"
9.6   3. "San Francech i la Sigala"
9.7   4. "Brollador gentil"
9.8   5. "Inquietud primaveral de la doncella"
9.9   6. "Canticel"
9.10 "Romance del Comendador de Ocaña" (c1947, Vega) ....
9.11 "Ausencias de Dulcinea" (c1948; Bar, 4S & orch) ....
9.12 "Rosalina" (c1965) ....
9.13 "Cantos de amor y de guerra" (c1968) ....
9.14 "Líricas castellanas" (c1981; S & period insts) ....

10. SONGS (w/ pf or gui)

10.1 "Soliloquio" (c1922, Mallarino) ....
10.2 "Cantiga": "Muy graciosa es la doncella" (c1925, Vicente) ....
10.3 "Schiffenlied Liedchen" (c1926, Camhi) ....
10.4 "Romance de la Infantina de Francia" (c1928) ....
10.5 "Serranilla" (c1928, Santillana) ....
10.6 "Cántico espiritual" (c1934, Cruz) ....
10.7 "Estribillo" (c1934, Medina) ....
10.8 "Soneto" (c1934, Meso) ....
10.9 "Cántico de la esposa" (c1934, S. J. de la Cruz; 1v & pf/orch) ....
10.10 "Esta níña se lleva la flor" (c1934, Fuigueroa) ....
10.11 "Coplas del pastor enamorado" (c1935, Vega) ....
10.12 "Fino cristal" (c1935, Pintos) ....
10.13 "Canción del cucú" (c1937, Camhi) ....
10.14 "Canción del grumete" (c1939, trad) ....
10.15 "Trovadoresca" (c1939, Diego after trad) ....
10.16 "4 Madrigales amatorios" (Four Love Songs) (c1947; 1v/vn & pf/orch): 1. "Y con que la lavaré?" ....
10.17   2. "Vos me matasteis"
10.18   3. "De dónde venís, amores?"
10.19   4. "De los álamos vengo, madre"
10.20 "12 Canciones populares españolas" (c1951, trad): 1. "Viva la novia y el novio" ....
10.21   2. "De ronda"
10.22   3. "Una palomita blanca"
10.23   4. "Canción de baile con pandero"
10.24   5. "Porque toco el pandero"
10.25   6. "Tararán"
10.26   7. "En las montañas de Asturias"
10.27   8. "Estando yo en mi majada"
10.28   9. "Adela"
10.29   10. "En Jerez de la Frontera"
10.30   11. "San José y María"
10.31   12. "Canción de cuna"
10.32 "3 Villancicos" (c1952; S & pf/orch): 1. "Pastorcito Santo" (Vega) ....
10.33   2. "Copillas de Belén" (Kamhi)
10.34   3. "Aire y donaire" (anon)
10.35 "2 Poemas de J. R. Jiménez" (c1961, Jiménez; 1v & fl/pf) ....
10.36 "Homenaje a Debussy: 'La grotte' " (c1962) ....
10.37 "4 Canciones sefardíes" (c1963) ....
10.38 "Con Antonio Machado" (c1970) ....
10.39 "2 Canciones para cantar a los niños" (c1973) ....

* * * * *

1. STAGE WORKS

Operas:

1.1 "Demetrio e Polibio," 2 act, seria (c before 1808, p1812, Viganò-Mombelli after Metastasio's Demetrio) .....

1.2 "La cambiale di matrimonio," 1 act farsa comica (p1810, Rossi after Federici's La cambiale of1790) ....

1.3 "L'equivoco stravagante," 2 act dramma giocoso (p1811, Gasparri) ....

1.4 "L'inganno felice," 1 act farsa (p1812, Foppa after Palomba's libretto for Paisiello's L'inganno of1798).......

1.5 "Ciro in Babilonia, ossia La caduta di Baldassare," 2 act dramma con cori (p1812, Aventi) ....

1.6 "La scala di seta," 1 act farsa comica (p1812, Foppa after Planard's libretto for Gaveaux: L'échelle de soie)

1.7 "La pietra del paragone," 2 act melodramma giocoso (p1812, Romanelli) ....

1.8 "L'occasione fa il ladro, ossia Il cambio della valigia," 1 act burletta (p1812, Prividali) ....

1.9 "Il signor Bruschino, ossia Il filglio per azzardo," 1 act farsa (p1813, Foppa after Chazet & Ourry: Le fils par hazard of 1809) ....

1.10 "Tancredi," 2 act melodramma eroico (p1813, Rossi after Tasso: Gerusalemme & Voltaire: Tancrede).......

1.11 "L'italiana in Algeri," 2 act dramma giocoso (p1813, Anelli r own libretto for Mosca: L'italiana of 1808) ....

1.12 "Aureliano in Palmira," 2 act dramma serio (p1813, Romanelli).......

1.13 "Il turco in Italia," 2 act dramma buffo (p1814, Romani from Mazzola's libretto for Seydelmann) ....

1.14 "Sigismondo," 2 act dramma (p1814, Foppa) ....

1.15 "Elisabetta, regina d'Inghilterra," 2 act dramma (p1815, Schmidt after Federici's play of 1814) ....

1.16 "Torvaldo e Dorliska," 2 act dramma semiserio (p1815, Sterbini) ....

1.17 "Il Barbiere di Siviglia" (orig title: Almaviva, ossia L'inutile precauzione), 2 act commedia (p1816, Sterbini after Beaumarchais)....

1.18 "La Gazzetta," 2 act buffa (p1816, Palomba after Goldoni: Il matrimonio per concorso of 1763) ....

1.19 "Otello, ossia Il moro di Venezia," 3 act dramma (p1816, Berio on Ducis' adaptation of Shakespeare) (also see opera c by Verdi & film score c by Khachaturian) ....

1.20 "La Cenerentola ossia La bontà in trionfo" (Cinderella), 2 act dramma giocoso (p1817, Ferretti after Perrault's La belle au bois dormant) (also see operas c by Holst & Massenet, ballet c by Prokofiev)....

1.21 "La gazza ladra" (The Thieving Magpie), 2 act melodramma (p1817, Gherardini after d'Aubigny & Caigniez: La Pie voleuse 1815) ....

1.22 "Armida," 3 act dramma (p1817, Schmidt after Tasso: Gerusalemme liberata) ....

1.23 "Adelaide di Borgogna, ossia Ottone, re d'Italia," 2 act dramma (p1817, Schmidt) ....

1.24 "Mosè in Egitto," 3 act azione tragico-sacra (p1818, Tottola after Ringhieri: Sara in Egitto of 1747)....

1.25 "Adina, ovvero Il Califfo di Bagdad," 1 act farsa (c1818, p1826, Bevilacqua-Aldobrandini from Romani)......

1.26 "Ricciardo e Zoraide," 2 act dramma (p1818, Salsa after Forteguerri: Ricciardetto) ....

1.27 "Ermione," 2 act azione tragica (p1819, Tottola after Racine's Andromaque of 1667) ....

1.28 "Edoardo e Cristina," 2 act dramma (p1819, after Schmidt's libretto for Pavesi: Odoardo e Cristina of 1810)

1.29 "La donna del lago," 2 act melodramma (p1819, Tottola after Scott's The Lady of the Lake of 1810) (also see Holst's choral work: Ave Maria maiden mild, App.I/35 & Schubert's song Ellens Gesang III, Op.52/6, D839) ....

1.30 "Bianca e Falliero," 2 act melodramma (p1819, Romani after Arnhault's Blanche et Montcassin of 1798) ...

1.31 "Maometto II," 2 act dramma (p1820, Valle after Voltaire's Mahomet) ....

1.32 "Matilde (di) Shabran," 2 act opera melodramma giocoso (p1821, Ferretti after Hoffmann) ....

1.33 "Zelmira," 2 act dramma (p1822, Tottola after Belloy: Zelmire of 1762) ....

1.34 "Semiramide," 2 act melodramma tragico (p1823, Rossi after Voltaire's Sémiramis of 1748) ....

1.35 "Il viaggio a Reims, ossia L'albergo del giglio d'oro," 1 act cantata scenica (p1825, Balocchi) ....

1.36 "Le siège de Corinthe," 3 act grand opéra (p1826, Balocchi, Soumet, r of Ventignano's libretto: Maometto II)

1.37 "Moïse et Pharaon, ou Le passage de la Mer Rouge," 4 acts (p1827, Balocchi & Jouy, r of: Mosè in Egitto)

1.38 "Le Comte Ory," 2 act opéra-comique (p1828, Scribe & Delestre-Poirson after their play of 1817) ....

1.39 "Guillaume Tell," 4 act grand opéra (p1829, Jouy, Bis & others after Schiller's Wilhelm Tell of 1804) ....

Adaptations from Rossini's operas (w/ Rossini's participation):

1.40 *"Ivanhoé," 3 act opera seria (p1826, Deschamps & Wailly after Scott, adapt Pacini from Rossini's operas)* ....

1.41 *"Robert Bruce," 3 acts (p1846, Royer & Vaëz, adapt Niedermeyer from: La donna del lago & other)* ....

Adaptations from Rossini's operas (w/ out Rossini's participation):

1.42 *"La fausse Agnès," 3 act opéra-bouffon (p1826, Castil-Blaze)* ....

1.43 *"Le neveu de Monseigneur," 2 act opéra-bouffe (p1826, Bayard, Romieu & Sauvage)* ....

1.44 *"Le Testament," 2 acts (p1827, Saur & Saint-Géniès)* ....

1.45 *"Monsieur de Pourceaugnac," 3 act opéra-bouffon (p1827, ?Castil-Blaze from Rossini & Weber)* ....

1.46 *"Cinderella, or The Fairy & the Little Glass Slipper," 2 acts (p1830, Lacy from: La Cenerentola)* ....

1.47 *"Andremo a Parigi?," 2 act comica (p1848, Balocchi & Dupin from: Il viaggio a Reims)* ....

1.48 *"Un Curioso accidente," 2 act buffa (p1859, Berettoni)* ....

Ballets:

1.49 *"La boutique fantasque" (arr1918 Respighi, P120, from misc pieces of Rossini)* ....

Incid music:

1.50 "Edipo a Colonno" (c before 1817, Sophocles: Oedipus at Colonus, transl Giusti; B, ch & orch) ....

1a. SELECTIONS FROM STAGE WORKS (Nos. of sections in The Gramophone)

1a.2   "La cambiale di matrimonio," opera: ....
         excerpts: 1. "Overture"
                   2. "Non c'è il vecchio sussurrone"
                   3. "Chi mai trova il dritto, il fondo"
                   4. "Ecco un lettera per voi, signore"
                   5a. "Ma, signore, questa lettera"
                   5b. "Isacchetto!"
                   5c. "Signor et caetera et caetera"
                   5d. "Povera Miss Fanny!"
                   6. "Tornami a dir che m'ami"
                   7a. "Sì cara mia, speriam"
                   7b. "Avete voi veduto"
                   8. "Presto, presto"
                   9. "Grazie ... grazie ..."
                   10. "Sicchè, dunque, istruitemi"
                   11a. "Servo! proprio in Europa"
                   11b. "Volea dirlo ... sicchè dunque saprete"
                   12. "Darei per sì'bel fondo"
                   13. "Quell'amabile visino"
                   14a. "Non si farà"
                   14b. "Anch'io son giovine"
                   15. "Eccolo appunto"
                   16. "Ipotecato!—Diavolo!—Madama"
                   17. "Dite presto, dove sta questa gran difficoltà"
                   18. "Venite, sono andati"
                   19a. "Bravi! Bravi!"
                   19b. "Ragazzi miei"
                   20a. "Come tacer"
                   20b. "Vorrei spiegarvi"
                   21. "Eppur lo cred'anch'io che il far del bene"
                   22a. "Metti là tutto, e parti"
                   22b. "Porterò così il cappello"
                   23. "Qual'ira, oh ciel"
                   24. "Vi prego un momento, signore"

1a.4   "L'inganno felice," opera: ....
         excerpts: 1. "Overture"
                   2a. "Cosa dite! ma cosa dite!"
                   2b. "Ebben, che ascendi"
                   3a. "Qual tenero diletto"
                   3b. "Né posson due lustri"
                   4. "Ebben, che tenta"
                   5. "Chi mi chiama?"
                   6a. "Prima d'andar"
                   6b. "Una voce m'ha colpito"
                   7. "Egli restò indeciso"
                   8. "Ciel protettor"
                   9a. "Oh, Cielo"
                   9b. "Quel sembiante, quello sguardo"
                   10. "Oh, l'impressione è fatta"
                   11a. "Quale inchiesta!"
                   11b. "Tu mi conosci, e sai che"
                   12a. "Mel pagherà tua vita!"
                   12b. "Va taluno mormorando"
                   13. "È deciso!"
                   14a. "Al nuovo dì col mio fedele"
                   14b. "Al più dolce e caro oggetto"
                   15. "Son fuor di me!"
                   16. "Oarmi tutto disposto"
                   17. "Tacita notte amica, deh," finale

1a.6   "La scala di seta," opera: ....
         excerpts: 1. "Overture"
                   2. "Va' sciocco, non seccarmi"
                   3. "Siamo sicuri. Uscite!"
                   4. "Egli è sceso ..."
                   5a. "Signor padron"
                   5b. "Io so ch'hai buon core"
                   6. "Oh senza ceremonia ..."
                   7a. "E che? tutti mariti?"
                   7b. "Va lesto"
                   7c. "Vedrò qual sommo incanto"
                   8a. "Io non so conquistare un cor di donna?"

6a. "Oh patria!"
6b. "Di tanti palpiti"
7. "E voi nella gran piazza"
8a. "Andante, al gran tempi"
8b. "Pensa, pensa che sei mia figlia"
9a. "Che feci! incauta!"
9b. "L'aura che intorno spiri"
10. "Amori scendete"
11. "Alla gloria, al trionfo"
11e. "Si, la patria si difenda"
12. "Amici, Cavalieri"
13a. "E morte infame"
13b. "Ciel! che feci!"
13c. "Ah! se giusto, o ciel"

II: 14. "Vedesti? L'indegna!"
15a. "Io padre più non sono"
15b. "Oh Dio! Crudel!
15c. "Ah! segnar invano"
16a. "Trionfa, esulta"
16b. "Tu che i miseri"
17a. "Di mia vita infelice"
17b. "No, che il morir non è"
18. "Di già l'ora"
19. "Fermate!"
20a. "M'abbraccia, Argirio"
20b. "Ah! se de' mali"
20c. "Ecco le trome"
21. "Ov'è ... dov'è?"
22a. "Gran Dio! Deh! tu proteggi"
22b. "Giusto Dio"
23. "Plaudite, o popoli"
24a. "T'arresta"
24b. "Lasciami, non t'ascolto"
24c. "Ah! come mai quell'anima"
24d. "Dunque?... Addio"
25. "Infelice Tancredi!"
26a. "S'avverassero pure"
26b. "Torni alfin"
27a. "Dove son io?"
27b. "Ah! che scordar"
27c. "Regna il terror"
28a. "Ecco, amici"
28b. "Perchè turbar"
28c. "Traditrice"
29. "Quanti tormenti"
30a. "Gran Dio!"
30b. "Muore il prode"
30c. "Oh Dio ... lasciarti"
30d. "Amenaide ... serbami"
Replacement arias: 31a. "A sospirato lido!"
31b. "Dolci d'amor parole"
31c. "Voce, che tenera"
32a. "Qual suon? che miro?"
32b. "Solamir d'Amenaide"
32c. "Va, palese è troppo omai"
32d. "E' questa la fede"
32e. "Si, la patria si difenda"

I: 2. "Serenate il mesto ciglio"
3. "Il mio schiavo italian"
4. "Languir per una bella"
5a. "Ah, quando fia"
5b. "Se inclinassi a prender moglie"
6a. "Quanta roba!"
6b. "Cruda sorte!"
7. "Misericordia"
8a. "Ah! Isabella"
8b. "Ai capricci della sorte"
9a. "E ricusar potresti"
9b. "Ascoltami, italiano"
9c. "Dunque degg'io lasciarvi?"
10. "Già d'insolito"
11a. "Viva, viva"

17b. "Ombra del caro sposo"
17c. "Vieni a giurar"
18a. "Sia compiuto il mio fato"
18b. "Essa corre al trionfo"
18c. "Di, che vedesti piangere"
19a. "Il voglia il Ciel"
19b. "Amata, l'amai"
20a. "Ma che ascolto?"
20b. "Un'empia mel rapi"
21. "Il tuo dolor ei affretta"
22a. "Ah! qual sovrasta a Pirro"
22b. "A così triste immagine"
23a. "Che feci? dove son?"
23b. "Parmi, che ad ogn'istante"
25. "Ah! ti rinvenni!"

1a.29   "La donna del lago," opera: ....
         excerpts: 1. "Overture"
    I: 2. "O, mattutini albori"
           3. "Qual suon!"
           4. "Uberto! Ah! Dove t'ascondi?"
           5. "Sei già nel tetto mio"
           6. "D'Inibaca Donzella"
           7. "Sei già sposa?"
           8. "Quali accenti!"
           9. "Ma son sorpreso"
           10. "Mura felici"
           11. "Elena! o tu, che chiamo!"
           12. "O quante lacrime"
           13. "Figlia! È così"
           14. "Taci, lo voglio"
           15. "E nel fatal conflitto"
           16. "Vivere io non potrò"
           17. "Qual rapido torrente"
           18. "Eccomi a voi"
           19. "Ma dov'è colei"
           20. "Se a'miei voti"
           21. "Alfin mi è dato"
           22. "Vieni, o stella"
           23. "Quanto a quest'alma"
           24. "La mia spada"
           25. "Quest'amplesso"
           26. "Crudele sospetto"
           27. "Sul colle a Morve"
           28. "Già un raggio"
           29. "Su ... amici!"
    II: 30. "O fiamma soave"
           31. "Va, non temer"
           32. "Alla ragion deh rieda"
           33. "Numi, se a'miei sospiri"
           34. "Vincesti!... Addio!"
           35. "Qual pena in me"
           36. "Parla ... che sei?"
           37. "Io son la misera"
           38. "Quante sciagure"
           39. "Ah! Si pera"
           40. "Douglas! Douglas! Ti salva!"
           41. "Che sento!"
           42. "Attendi: Il Re fra poco"
           43. "Che sento! Qual soave armonia!"
           44. "Stelle! Sembra egli stesso!"
           45. "Eccolo! Amica sorte"
           46. "Impogna il Re"
           47. "Ah! Che vedo!"
           48. "Tanti affetti"
           49. "Fra il padre"

1a.31   "Maometto II," opera: ....
         excerpts: 1. "Overture"
    I: 2. "Al tou cenno, Erisso"
           3. "Risponda a te primiero"
           4. "Sì, giuriam!"
           5. "Ah! che invan su questo ciglio"
           6. "Petoso ciel"
           7a. "No, tacer non deggio"

1a.34 "Semiramide," opera: ....
   excerpts: 1. "Overture"
   I: 2. "Sì ... gran Nume ... t'intesi"
     3. "Suoni festevoli"
     4. "Là dal Gange a te primiero"
     5. "Di plausi qual clamor"
     6. "Di tanti regi e populi"
     7. "Ah! già il sacro foco è spento"
     8. "Eccomi alfine in Babilonia"
     9. "Ah! quel giorno ognor rammento"
    10. "Io t'attendeva, Arsace"
    11. "Bella imago"
    12. "Serena i vaghi rai"
    13a. "Bel raggio lusinghier"
    13b. "Dolce pensiero"
    13c. "Mitrane! E che rechi?"
    14. "Serbami ognor sì fido"
    15. "Alle più calde immagini"
    16. "March"
    17. "Ergi omai la fronte altera"
    18. "I vostri voti omai"
    19. "L'alto eroe"
    20. "Qual mesto gemito"
    21. "D'un semidio che adoro"
    22. "Ah! Sconvolta nell'ordine eterno"
   II: 23. "Assur, i cenni miei"
    24. "Se la vita"
    25. "Quekka, ricordati"
    26. "La forza primiera"
    27. "Ebben, compiasi omai"
    28. "In sì barbara sciagura"
    29. "Su, ti scuoti"
    30. "No: non ti lascio"
    31. "Ebben ... a tei, ferisci"
    32. "Giorno d'orrore!"
    33. "Madre—addio"
    34. "La speranza più soave"
    35. "Sì, sperar voglio contento"
    36. "Il dì già cade"
    37. "Deh! ti ferma"
    38. "Que' numi furenti"
    39. "Qual densa notte!"
    40. "Al mio pregar t'arrendi"
    41. "Dei! qual sospiro!"
    42. "Ninia, ferisci!"

1a.35 "Il viaggio a Reims, ossia L'albergo del giglio d'oro," opera: ....
   excerpts: 1. "Overture"
     2a. "Presto, presto, su coraggio"
     2b. "Benché grazie al mio talento"
     3. "Di vaghi raggi adorno"
     4a. "Partire io pur vorrei"
     4b. "Amabil Contessina"
     4c. "Che accede"
     5a. "Ahimè! sta in gran pericolo"
     5b. "Partir, oh cieli desio"
     5c. "Che miro! ah! qual sorpressa"
     5d. "Eh! senti, mastro Antonio"
     6a. "Sì, di matti una gabbia"
     6b. "La mia quota a voi consegno"
     6c. "Donna ingrata"
     6d. "Naturale è l'impazienza"
     7. "Non pavento alcun periglio"
     8. "Arpa gentil"
     9. "Zitti. Non canta più"
    10a. "Ah! perchè la conobbi?"
    10b. "Invan strappar dal core"
    11. "Milord, una parola"
    12a. "Sola ritrovo alfin la bella Dea"
    12b. "Nel suo divin sembiante"
    12c. "Bravo il signor Ganimede!"
    13a. "Medaglie incomparabili"
    13b. "Vedeste il Cavaliere?"
    14a. "Ah! A tal colpo inaspettato"
    14b. "Signor, acco una lettera"

1a.39   "Guillaume Tell," opera: ....
      excerpts: 1. "Overture"
      I: 2a. "Quel jour serein le ciel présage" (È il ciel seren)
            2b. "Accours dans ma nacelle" (Il piccol legno ascendi)
            3a. "On entend des montagnes" (Oh! quale alta d'intorno)
            3b. "Près des torrents qui grondent" (Al fremer del torrente)
            4a. "Où vas tu?" (Arresta!)
            4b. "Ah! Mathilde, idole de mon âme" (Ah! Matilde, io t'amo)
            5. "Bridal Procession"
            6a. "Ciel, qui du monde" (Ciel che del monde)
            6b. "Hymenée, ta journée" (Cinto il crine) (Dance)
            7. "Pas de Six"
            8. "Dieu de bonté" (Nume opaca)
            9a. "Ils s'éloignent enfin" (S'allontanano alfine!)
            9b. "Sombre forêt" (Selva opaca)
            10. "Ma présence pour vous est peut-être un outrage?" (Se il mio giunger)
            11a. "Quand l'Helvétie" (Allor che scorre de' forti il sangue)
            11b. "Ses jours" (Troncar suoi di)
            12. "Scène de la conjuration"
      III: 13a. "Pas de trois"
            13b. "À nos chants" (Tyrolienne)
            13c. "Allegretto et Maestoso"
            14. "Soldiers' March"
            15a. "Je te bénis" (Ti benedico)
            15b. "Sois immobile" (Resta immobile)
      IV: 16a. "Ne m'abandonne pas" (Non mi lasciare)
            16b. "Asile héréditaire" (O muto asil)
            16c. "Amis, amis, secondez ma venegance" (Corriam, voliam)
            17. "Finale"

1a.49   *"La boutique fantasque," ballet:* ....
      excerpts: 1. "Overture"
            2. "Scene"
            3. "Vivo"
            4. "Tarantella"
            5. "Mazurka"
            6. "Scene"
            7. "Cossack Dance"
            8. "Valse brillante"
            9. "Can-Can"
            10. "Andantino mosso"
            11. "Valse lente"
            12. "Scene"
            13. "Nocturne"
            14. & 15. "Galop" & "Finale"

2. ORCHESTRAL WORKS

2.1   "Overture al conventello," in D major (ca1806; 1st theme reused in opera: Il signor Bruschino) ....
2.2   Sinfonia / Overture in D major (c1808; 2nd theme reused in opera: L'inganno felice) QRviii,1
2.3   Sinfonia / Overture in E-flat major (c1809; reused in opera: La cambiale di matrimonio; r vers in: Adelaide)
2.4   "Overture obbligata a contrabasso," in D major (ca1807–10) ....
2.5   *"Passo doppio" (c1822; milit band, lost; reused in Overture to opera: Guillaume Tell)* ....
2.6   "Mariage du Duc d'Orléans," 3 milit marches (c1837; milit band): No.1 in G major ....
2.7   No.2 in E-flat major
2.8   No.3 in E-flat major
2.9   "March" (Pas-redoublé), in C major (c1852; milit band) ....
2.10   "La corona d'Italia," in E-flat major (c1868; milit band) ....

3. CONCERTOS, SOLO INSTR & ORCH

3.1   "Variazioni di clarinetto," in C major (c1809; cl & orch) QRvi,57
3.2   "Rendez-vous de chasse," in D major (c1828; 4 corni da caccia & orch) QRix,45

4. STRING QUARTETS

4.1   "Sonate a quattro" (ca1804; 2vn, vc & d bass): No.1 in G major QRi,1
4.2   No.2 in A major
4.3   No.3 in C major
4.4   No.4 in B-flat major
4.5   No.5 in E-flat major
4.6   No.6 in D major

5. OTHER CHAMBER MUSIC (also see: Péchés de vieillesse)

4 or more insts:

5.1   "Variazioni a più istrumenti obbligati," in F major (c1809; 2vn, va, vc & B-flat cl) QRix,1
5.2   "Andante e tema con variazioni," in F major (c1812; fl, cl, hn & bn).. QRvi,18
5.3   "Serenata," in E-flat major (c1823; 2vn, va, vc, fl, ob & Eng hn) QRvi,31

Vn & pf:

5.4   "Theme, Variations & Polacca di Giovacchino Giovacchini," in A major (c1845) ....

Other 2 insts:

5.5   "Duets" (ca1806; 2hn): No.1 in E-flat major ....
5.6   No.2 in E-flat major
5.7   No.3 in B-flat major
5.8   No.4 in E-flat major
5.9   No.5 in E-flat major
5.10   "Andante e tema con variazioni," in F major (ca1820; va & harp, on Di tanti palpiti, from: Tancredi) . QRvi,1
5.11   "Duetto," in D major (c1824; vc & d bass) ....
5.12   "Fantasie," in E-flat major (c1829; cl & pf) ....
5.13   "Thème de Rossini suivi de 2 variations et coda par Moscheles Père," in E-flat major (c1860; hn & pf) ....

6. PIANO (also see: Péchés de vieillesse & Other late works)

6.1   "Waltz," in E-flat major (c ?1823) ....
6.2   "Scherzo," in A minor (c1843, r1850) ....

7. SACRED WORKS

c early (1802–9):

7.1   "Kyrie a tre voci" (2T, B & orch) ....
7.2   "Gloria" (A, T, B, m ch & orch) ....
7.3   "Laudamus" (A & orch) ....
7.4   "Gratias" (T, m ch & orch)..
7.5   "Domine Deus" (2B & orch) ....
7.6   "Qui tollis" (T & orch) ....
7.7   "Laudamus and Qui tollis" (T & orch)..
7.8   "Quoniam" (T & orch)..
7.9   "Crucifixus" (S, A & orch) ....
7.10   "Dixit" (2T, B & orch)..
7.11   "De torrente" (B & orch) ....
7.12   "Gloria Patri" ....
7.13   "Sicut erat" (2T, B & orch) ....
7.14   "Magnificat" (2T, B & orch) ....

c1808 and after:

7.15   "Messa di Bologna" (c1808, other sections c by students): ....
       1. "Christe eleison" (2T, B & orch)
       2. "Benedicta et venerabilis," graduale (2T, B & orch)
       3. "Qui tollis, Qui sedes" (S, hn & orch)
7.16   "Messa di Ravenna" (c1808; m vv, m ch & orch): ....
       1. "Gloria"
       2. "Laudamus te"
       3. "Gratias agimus"
       4. "Domine te"
       5. "Qui tollis"
       6. "Quoniam"
       7. "Cum sancto"
7.17   "Messa" (c?; m vv, m ch & orch):..
       1. "Kyrie"
       2. "Gloria"
       3. "Credo"
7.18   "Messa di Rimini" (c1809; S, A, T, B & orch): ....
       1. "Kyrie"
       2. "Gloria"
       3. "Laudamus te"
       4. "Gratias"
       5. "Domine Deus"
       6. "Qui tollis"
       7. "Qui sedes"

8. CHORAL WORKS

Cantatas:

Choruses & hymns:

9. MISC VOCAL (also see: Péchés de vieillesse & Other late works)

9.1	"Se il vuol la marinara," arietta buffa (c1801, r?; S & pf) ....
9.2	"Dolce aurette che spirate," cavatina (c1810; T & orch) ....
9.3	"La mia pace io già perdei" (c1812; T & orch) ....
9.4	"Qual voce, quai note" (c1813; S & pf) ....
9.5	"Alla voce della gloria," scena & aria (c1813; B & orch) ....
9.6	"Amore mi assisti" (ca1814; S, T & pf) ....
9.7	For Niccolini: Quinto Fabio (c1817): 1. "Cara Patria, invitta Roma," coro e cavatina (S, ch & orch) ....
9.8	2. "Guida Marte i nostri passi," aria (T, ch & orch)
9.9	3. "Ah! per pieta t'arresta," duet (2S & orch)
9.10	"Il trovatore": "Chi m'ascolta il canto usato" (c1818; T & pf) ....
9.11	"Il carnevale di Venezia": "Siamo ciechi" (c1821, Rossini, Paganini, d'Azeglio, Lipparini; 2T, 2B & pf)........
9.12	"Beltà crudele": "Amori scendete propizi al mio core" (c1821, Santo-Magno; S & pf) ....
9.13	"La pastorella": "Odia la pastorella" (ca1821, Santo-Magno; S & pf) ....
9.14	"Canzonetta spagnuola": "En medio a mis dolores" (Piangea un di pensando) (c1821; S & pf) ....
9.15	"Infelice ch'io son" (c1821; S & pf, based on theme from opera: Maometto II) ....
9.16	"Addio ai viennesi": "Da voi parto, amate sponde" (c1822; T & pf) ....
9.17	"Dall'oriente l'astro del giorno" (c1824; S, 2T, B & pf, from chorus in opera: Ermione) ....
9.18	"Ridiamo, cantiamo, che tutto sen va" (c1824; S, 2T, B & pf, from chorus in opera: Armida) ....
9.19	"In giorno sì bello," nocturne (c1824; 2S, T & pf) ....
9.20	"3 quartetti da camera" (c1827): *1. (Unidentified)* ....
9.21	2. "In giorno sì bello" (2S, T, B & pf)
9.22	3. "Oh giorno sereno" (S, A, T, B & pf)
9.23	"Les adieux à Rome": "Rome pour la dernière fois" (c1827, Delavigne; T & pf/harp) ....
9.24	"Orage et beau temps": "Sur les flots inconstans" (ca1829–30, Betourne; T, B & pf) ....
9.25	"La passeggiata" (Anacreontica): "Or che di fiori adorno" (c1831; S & pf) ....
9.26	"La dichiarazione" (La promessa): "Ch'io mai vi possa lasciar d'amare" (ca1834, Metastasio; S & pf) ....
9.27	"Soirées musicales" (ca1830–5): 1. "La promessa": "Ch'io mai vi possa" (Metastasio; S & pf) ....
9.28	2. "Il rimprovero": "Mi lagnerò tacendo" (Metastasio; S & pf)
9.29	3. "La partenza": "Ecco quel fiero istante" (Metastasio; S & pf)
9.30	4. "L'orgia": "Amiamo, cantiamo" (Pepoli; S & pf)
9.31	5. "L'invito": "Vieni o Ruggiero" (Pepoli; S & pf)
9.32	6. "La pastorella dell'Alpi": "Son bella pastorella" (Pepoli; S & pf)
9.33	7. "La gita in gondola": "Voli l'agile barchetta" (Pepoli; S & pf)
9.34	8. "La danza": "Già la luna è in mezzo al mare" (Pepoli; T & pf)
9.35	9. "La regata veneziana": "Voga o Tonio benedetto" (Pepoli; 2S & pf)
9.36	10. "La pesca": "Già la notte s'avvicina" (Metastasio; 2S & pf)
9.37	11. "La serenata": "Mira, la bianca luna" (Pepoli; S, T & pf)
9.38	12. "Li marinari": "Marinaro in guardia sta" (Pepoli; T, B & pf)
9.39	"Deux nocturnes" (c1836, Ch. de Charlemagne; S, T & pf): 1. "Adieu à l'Italie": "Je te quitte, belle Italie" ....
9.40	2. "Le départ": "Il faut partir"
9.41	"Nizza": "Nizza, je puis sans peine" (Mi lagnerò tacendo) (c1836, Metastasio & Deschamps; S & pf) ....
9.42	"L'âme délaissée" (L'âme du Purgatoire): "Mon bien aimé" (ca1844, Delavigne; S & pf): ....
	. Version in Italian: "L'abbandonata": "Mio dolce amor"
9.43	"Recitativo rimato" (Francesca da Rimini): "Farò come colui che piange e dice" (c1848, Dante; S & pf) ......
9.44	"Mi lagnerò tacendo" (c1835–50, Metastasio; S & pf, many versions as albumleafs) ....
9.45	"La separazione": "Muto rimase il labbro" (ca1858, Uccelli; S & pf) ....
9.46	"Deux nouvelles compositions" (ca1860, Pacini; S & pf): 1. "À Grenade": "La nuit règne" QRv,90
9.47	2. "La veuve andalouse": "Toi pour jamais"

10. "PÉCHÉS DE VIEILLESSE" (SINS OF OLD AGE) (c1857–68)

Vol.I "Album italiano":

10.1	1. "I gondolieri," quartettino (S, A, T, B & pf) QRvii,1
10.2	2. "La lontananza," arietta (Torre; T & pf) QRvii,12
10.3	3. "Tirana alla spagnola" (Rossinizzata), bolero (Metastasio; S & pf, music = QRxi,3) QRiv,30
10.4	4. "L'ultimo ricordo," elegia (Redaelli; Bar & pf) QRiv,19
10.5	5. "La fioraia fiorentina," arietta (S & pf, theme first used for: Mi lagnerò tacendo) QRiv,5
10.6	6. "Le gittane": "Il suon, le danze, il canto son nostro sol tesoro," duetto (Torre; S, A & pf) ....
10.7	7. "Ave Maria su due sole note": "A te, che benedetta fra tutte sei, Maria" (A & pf) QRiv,51
10.8	8. "Anzoleta avanti la regata": "La su la machina" (mS & pf; = 1. of: La regata veneziana) ....
10.9	9. "Anzoleta co passa la regata": "Ixe qua vardeli povereti" (mS & pf; = 2. of: La regata veneziana) ....
10.10	10. "Anzoleta dopo la regata": "Ciapa un baso" (mS & pf; = 3. of: La regata veneziana) ....
10.11	11. "Il fanciullo smarrito": "Oh! chi avesse trovato," arietta (Sonetto) (Castellani; T & pf) ....
10.12	12. "La passeggiata," quartettino (S, A, T, B & pf) QRvii,16

Vol.II "Album français" (Pacini):

10.13	1. "Toast pour le nouvel an": "En ce jour si doux," ottettino (2S, 2A, 2T, 2B) QRvii,50
10.14	2. "Roméo": "Juliette chère idole" (T & pf) ....
10.15	3. "Pompadour, la grande coquette": "La Perle des coquettes" (S & pf, from: Mi lagnerò tacendo)............
10.16	4. "Un sou. Complainte à deux voix": "Pitie pour la misere" (T, Bar & pf) QRv,58
10.17	5. "Chanson de Zora" (La petite bohémienne): "Gens de la plaine" (Deschamps; mS & pf) QRv,49

11. OTHER LATE WORKS

12. MISC WORKS

13. WORKS NOT TRACED (or of uncertain authenticity)

* * * * *

QR = "Quaderni Rossiniani," a cura della Fondazione Rossini. (Pesaro, 1954–)

1. STAGE WORKS

Operas:

1.1	*Opera on a North American Indian legend (ca1892, Blanchon, unfin, lost, extant one song):*	
	extant: . "Ici tu dors, ô Nemissa," song (1v & pf)	
1.2	*"Le roi Tobol" (ca1911–4, Beaunier, unfin, destroyed)*	
1.3	"Padmâvatî," 2 act opéra-ballet (c1914–8, Laloy; arr for vv & pf)	Op.18
1.4	"Le testament de la tante Caroline," 3 act opéra-bouffe (c1932–3, Nino)	
1.5	*"Charles le téméraire" (c1937, Weterings, project)*	

Ballets:

1.6	"Le festin de l'araignée" (The Spider's Feast), 1 act ballet-pantomime (c1912–3, Voisins after Fabre: Souvenirs; arr for pf)	Op.17
1.7	"Sarabande," for collab work: L'éventail de Jeanne (c1927; orch; transcr for pf duet; also for pf)	
1.8	"Bacchus et Ariane," 2 acts (c1930, Hermant; orch; red for pf 1931)	Op.43
1.9	"Aenéas," 1 act (c1935, Weterings; ch & orch)	Op.54

Incid music:

1.10	"Le marchand de sable qui passe," 1 act 'conte lyrique' (c1908, Jean-Aubry)	Op.13
1.11	"La naissance de la lyre," 1 act 'conte lyrique' (c1922–4, Reinach after Sophocles)	Op.24
1.12	"Prélude," to Act II of collab work: Le Quatorze juillet (c1936, Rolland; winds & perc)	

Radio:

1.13	"Elpénor," poème radiophonique (c?, p1947, Weterings after Odyssey; fl & str qt)	Op.59

Film:

1.14	*Music for a film (c?, destroyed)*	

1a. SELECTIONS FROM STAGE WORKS

1a.6	"Le festin de l'araignée," ballet-pantomime:	Op.17

    1. "Prélude"
    2. "Entrée des fourmis"
    3. "Danse du papillon"
    4. "Danse de l'araignée"
    5. "Éclosion de éphémère"
    6. "Danse de l'éphémère"
    7. "Funérailles de l'éphémère"

1a.8	"Bacchus et Ariane," ballet:	Op.43

    I: 1. "Prélude"
         2. "Jeux des Éphèbes et des Vierges"
         3. "Danse du labyrinthe"
         4. "Danse de Bacchus"
    II: 5. "Prélude: Le sommeil d'Ariane"
         6. "Réveil d'Ariane"
         7. "Bacchus danse seul"
         8. "Le baiser"
         9. "Danse d'Ariane"
       10. "Danse d'Ariane et de Bacchus"
       11. "Bacchanale"

1a.9	"Aenéas," 1 act (c1935, Weterings; ch & orch)	Op.54

    1. "Prélude"
    2. "Introduction—Danse des ombres"
    3. "Les épreuves d'Aeneas—La solitude"
    4. "Apparition de la Sibylle"
    5. "Les Joies funestes"
    6. "Danse de Didon—Les amours tragiques"
    7. "Danse guerrière—Le passé"
    8. "Danse d'Enée"
    9. "Hymne final": "Les freins, les chaînes"

2. SYMPHONIES

2.1	Symphony No.1 in D minor, "Le poème de la forêt" (c1904–6; red for pf duet 1909):	Op.7

    1. "Forêt d'hiver"
    2. "Renouveau"

6.17   No.4 "Monsieur de la Péjaudie"
6.18   Duo (c1925; bn & d bass/vc, on themes from: Naissance de la lyre, Op.24) ....
6.19   "Andante & Scherzo" (c1934; fl & pf) Op.51
6.20   "Pipe in D major" (c1934; flageolet & pf) ....

        1 instr:

6.21   "Impromptu" (c1919; harp) Op.21
6.22   "Ségovia" (c1925; gui; transcr for pf) Op.29

7. PIANO

7.1   *"Valse lente" (ca1895, lost)* ....
7.2   "Badinage" (c before 1897) ....
7.3   "Fugue" (ca1898) ....
7.4   "Des heures passent," suite (c1898): No.1 "Graves, légères ..." Op.1
7.5   No.2 "Joyeuses ..."
7.6   No.3 "Tragiques ..."
7.7   No.4 "Champêtres ..."
7.8   "Conte à la poupée" (c1904) ....
7.9   "Rustiques," suite (c1904–6): No.1 "Danse au bord de l'eau" Op.5
7.10   No.2 "Promenade sentimentale en forêt"
7.11   No.3 "Retour de fête"
7.12   "Suite," in F-sharp minor (c1909–10): No.1 "Prélude" Op.14
7.13   No.2 "Sicilienne"
7.14   No.3 "Bourrée"
7.15   No.4 "Ronde"
7.16   "Petit canon perpétuel" (c1912) ....
7.17   "Sonatine" (c1912) Op.16
7.18   "Doute" (c1919) ....
7.19   "L'accueil des muses" (c1920, to the memory of Claude Debussy) ....
7.20   "Prelude et Fugue" (c1932–4): No.1 "Prélude" (c1934) Op.46
7.21   No.2 "Fugue" (sur le nom de Bach) (c1932)
7.22   "Trois pièces" (c1933): No.1 "Allegro con brio" Op.49
7.23   No.2 "Allegro grazioso"
7.24   No.3 "Allegro con spirito"

8. ORGAN

8.1   "Marche nuptiale" (c1893) ....
8.2   *"Allegro symphonique" (ca1899, lost)* ....
8.3   "Prelude and Fughetta" (c1929; arr Goldbeck for strings) Op.41

9. CHORAL WORKS

9.1   "Deux madrigaux à quatre voix" (c1897, trad 15th cent; ch): 1. "Chanson ancienne du XVe siècle. La
        cloche lentement tinte sur la colline": "Et où vas-tu? Petit souspir" ....
9.2   2. "Le Soucy. Chanson ancienne du XVe siècle": "Ne pouvant vous donner ni sceptre ni couronne"
9.3   "Evocations" (c1910–1, Calvocoressi; vv, ch & orch; red for 2pf; arr Roques for pf duet): 1. "Les Dieux
        dans l'ombre des cavernes" Op.15
9.4   2. "La Ville rose"
9.5   3. "Aux bords du fleuve sacré"
9.6   "Madrigal aux muses": "Souffrez les amours sur vos traces" (c1923, Bernard; fem ch) Op.25
9.7   "Le bardit des Francs": "Pharamond" (c1926, Chateaubriand; m ch, brass & perc ad lib)............................
9.8   "Psalm 80" (c1928, Bible; T, ch & orch) Op.37

10. SONGS (w/ pf)

10.1   "Les rêves": "Les heures d'aimer passent brèves" (ca1898–1900, Silvestre) ....
10.2   "Pendant l'attente": "C'était entre les deux allées" (ca1898–1900, Mendès) ....
10.3   "Tristesse au jardin": "Le doux rêve que tu nias" (c before 1897, Tailhade) ....
10.4   "Quatre poèmes" (c1903, Régnier): 1. "Le départ": "Je n'emporte avec moi" Op.3
10.5   2. "Voeu": "Je voudrais"
10.6   3. "Le jardin mouillé": "La croisée est ouverte"
10.7   4. "Madrigal lyrique": "Vous êtes"
10.8   "Quatre poèmes" (c1907, Régnier): 1. "Adieux": "Il est de doux adieux" (orchd1907) Op.8
10.9   2. "Invocation": "Pour que la nuit soit douce"
10.10   3. "Nuit d'automne": "Le couchant est si beau"
10.11   4. "Odelette": "J'aurais pu dire mon amour"
10.12   "La ménace": "Vous aimerez un jour peut-être" (In years to come perchance you'll learn) (c1908,
        Régnier; 1v & pf/orch; Eng transl Newmarch) Op.9

10.13	"Flammes": "Je suis près de la porte" (c1908, Jean-Aubry) Op.10
10.14	"Deux poèmes chinois" (c1907–8, Roché after Giles; Eng transl Newmarch): 1. "Ode à un jeune
	gentilhomme": "N'entrez pas, Monsieur" (Don't come in, good Sir) Op.12
10.15	2. "Amoureux séparés" (Lovers divided): "Dans le royaume de Yen" (Fu-Mi)
10.16	"Deux mélodies" (c1918; also Fr vers): 1. "Light": "In vain tears have been shed" (Des larmes ont coulé)
	(Jean-Aubry) Op.19
10.17	2. "A Farewell": "If thou insist" (Si tu l'exiges) (Oliphant)
10.18	"Deux mélodies" (c1919, Chalupt; 1v & pf/orch; Eng transl Newmarch): 1. "Le bachelier de
	Salamanque": "Où vas-tu" (Passer-by) Op.20
10.19	2. "Sarabande": "Les jets d'eau" (Fountain spray)
10.20	"Deux poèmes de Ronsard" (c1924; S & fl): 1. "Rossignol, mon mignon" Op.26
10.21	2. "Ciel, aer et vens"
10.22	"Odes anacréontiques" (c1926, transl Lisle): 1. "Ode XVI: Sur lui-même": "Tu chantes les" (orchd) .. Op.31
10.23	2. "Ode XIX: Qu'il faut boire": "La noire terre"
10.24	3. "Ode XX: Sur une jeune fille": "La fille de Tantalos"
10.25	"Odes anacréontiques" (c1926, transl Lisle): 1. "Ode XXVI: Sur lui-même": "Dès que
	Bakkhos" (orchd) Op.32
10.26	2. "Ode XXXIV: Sur une jeune fille": "Ne me fuis pas" (orchd)
10.27	3. "Ode XLIV: Sur un songe": "Il me semblait"
10.28	"Deux poèmes chinois" (c1927, Roché after Giles): 1. "Des fleurs font une broderie" (Li-Ho) Op.35
10.29	2. "Réponse d'une épouse sage" (Chang-Chi; orchd ca1927)
10.30	Vocalise No.1 (c1927) ....
10.31	"Ô bon vin, où as-tu crû?" (c1928, chanson de terroir from Champagne collected Dévignes) ....
10.32	Vocalise No.2 (c1928; orchd Hoérée 1930; arr Hoérée as: Aria for fl/ob/cl/va/vc & pf/orch) ....
10.33	"Jazz dans la nuit": "Le bal sur le parc incendié" (The lamps from the ball in the park) (c1928,
	Dommange; Eng transl Newmarch; orchd Vellones) Op.38
10.34	"Deux idylles" (c1931): 1. "Le kérioklépte": "Une cruelle" (Theocritus transl Lisle) Op.44
10.35	2. "Pan aimait Ekhô" (Moskhos transl Lisle)
10.36	"A Flower Given to My Daughter": "Frail the white rose" (Rose frêle) (c1931, Joyce; Fr transl Myers) Op.44
10.37	"Deux poèmes chinois" (c1932, Roché after Giles): 1. "Favorite abandonnée": "Sous la lune" Op.47
10.38	2. "Vois, de belles filles"
10.39	"Deux mélodies" (c1933–4, Chalupt): 1. "L'heure de retour": "Une bise aigre et monotone" Op.50
10.40	2. "Coeur en péril": "Que m'importe"
10.41	"Deux mélodies" (c1935, Ville): 1. "Vieilles cartes, vieilles mains" Op.55
10.42	2. "Si quelquefois tu pleures"

11. ARRANGEMENTS OF WORKS OF OTHERS

Mendelssohn's works revised for publication in 1920:

11.1	Piano Trio No.1 in D minor, Op.49 ....
11.2	Piano Trio No.2 in C minor, Op.66 ....
11.3	Violin Sonata in F minor, Op.4 ....
11.4	"Variations concertantes," in D major, for vc & pf, Op.17 ....
11.5	Cello Sonata No.1 in B-flat major, Op.45 ....
11.6	Cello Sonata No.2 in D major, Op.58 ....

* * * * *

Opus number 44 used for two different works.

1. STAGE WORKS

Operas:

1.1   "La princesse jaune," 1 act opéra-comique (c1872, Gallet) Op.30
1.2   "Le timbre d'argent," 4 act drame lyrique (c1877, Barbier & Carré) ....
1.3   "Samson et Dalila," 3 acts (c1877, Lemaire) Op.47
1.4   *Finale of: Nina Zombie, opéra bouffe (c1878, ?spur)* ....
1.5   "Étienne Marcel," 4 acts (c1879, Gallet) ....
1.6   "Henry VIII," 4 acts (c1883, Détroyat & Silvestre from Calderón's play: La Cisma in Inglaterra) ....
1.7   *Sketch for Gabrieli di Vergi, lyric drama (c1885, ?spur)* ....
1.8   "Proserpine," 4 act drame lyrique (c1887, Gallet after Vacquerie) ....
1.9   "Ascanio," 5 acts (c1890, Gallet after Meurice) ....
1.10   "Phryné," 2 act opéra-comique (c1893, Augé de Lassus) ....
1.11   "Frédégonde," 5 act drame lyrique (c1895, Gallet, collab Guiraud) ....
1.12   "Les barbares," 3 act tragédie lyrique (c1901, Sardou & Gheusi) ....
1.13   "Hélène," 1 act poème lyrique (c1903, Saint-Saëns) ....
1.14   "L'ancêtre," 3 act drame lyrique (c1906, Augé de Lassus)...............................
1.15   "Déjanire," 4 act drame lyrique (c1911, Saint-Saëns after Gallet; also see incid music)...........................

Ballets:

1.16   "Javotte," 1 scene (c1896, Croze) ....

Incid music:

1.17   *"Le sicilien, ou L'amour peintre" (c1892, Molière, ?spur)* ....
1.18   "Déjanire," 4 acts (c1892, Gallet)..
1.19   "Antigone" (c1894, Meurice & Vacquerie after Sophocles) ....
1.20   "Parysatis," 3 acts (c1902, Dieulafoy) ....
1.21   "Andromaque," 4 acts (c1903, Racine) ....
1.22   "La foi" (c1909, Brieux) Op.130
1.23   *"La fille du tourneur d'ivoire" (c1909, Ferrare after Bertheroy's novel, ?spur)* ....
1.24   "On ne badine pas avec l'amour" (c1917, Musset) ....

Film:

1.25   "L'assassinat du Duc de Guise" (c1908, Lavedan) Op.128

1a. SELECTIONS FROM STAGE WORKS (Nos. of sections in The Gramophone)

1a.3   "Samson et Dalila," opera: Op.47
       I: 1. "Dieu d'Israël!"
            2. "Arrêtez, ô mes frères"
            3. "Qui donc élève ici la voix?"
            4. "Que vois-je!"
            5. "Maudite à jamais"
            6. "Hymne de joie"
            7. "Je viens célébrer la victoire"
            8. "Danse des prêtresses de Dagon"
            9. "Printemps qui commence"
       II: 10. "Prelude"
            11a. "Samson, recherchant"
            11b. "Amour! viens aider ma faiblesse!"
            12a. "J'ai gravi la montagne"
            12b. "La victoire facile"
            13a. "En ces lieux, malgré moi"
            13b. "Mon coeur s'ouvre à ta voix"
       III: 14. "Voix ma misère"
            15. "L'aube qui blanchit"
            16. "Bacchanale"
            17. "Gloire à Dagon"

2. SYMPHONIES

2.1   *Symphony in B-flat major (ca1848, frag)* ....
2.2   *Symphony in D major (ca1850, frag)* ....
2.3   Symphony in A major (ca1850) ....
2.4   Symphony No.1 in E-flat major (c1853)... Op.2
2.5   *Symphony in C minor (c1854, frag)* ....
2.6   Symphony in F major, "Urbs Roma" (c1856) ....
2.7   Symphony No.2 in A minor (c1859) Op.55
2.8   Symphony No.3 in C minor, "Organ" (c1886) Op.78

3. OTHER ORCHESTRAL WORKS

3.1	Comic opera overture in E minor (ca1850)	
3.2	"Scherzo," in A major (ca1850; small orch)	
3.3	"Ouverture d'un opéra comique inachevé," in G major (c1854)	Op.140
3.4	"Suite," in D major (c1863): No.1 "Prélude"	Op.49
3.5	No.2 "Sarabande"	
3.6	No.3 "Gavotte"	
3.7	No.4 "Romance"	
3.8	No.5 "Final"	
3.9	"Spartacus Overture," in E-flat major (c1863)	
3.10	"Marche héroïque," in E-flat major (c1871)	Op.34
3.11	"Le rouet d'Omphale," sym poem in A major (c1872)	Op.31
3.12	"Phaéton," sym poem in C major (c1873)	Op.39
3.13	"Danse macabre," sym poem in G minor (c1874; orig a song)	Op.40
3.14	"La jeunesse d'Hercule," sym poem in E-flat major (c1877)	Op.50
3.15	*"Rêverie orientale" (c1879; orch, ?spur)*	
3.16	"Suite algérienne," in C major (c1880): No.1 "Prélude"	Op.60
3.17	No.2 "Rapsodie mauresque"	
3.18	No.3 "Rêverie du soir"	
3.19	No.4 "Marche militaire française"	
3.20	"Une nuit à Lisbonne," barcarolle in E-flat major (c1880)	Op.63
3.21	"Jota aragonese," in A major (c1880)	Op.64
3.22	"Rapsodie bretonne," in F major (c1891)	Op.7bis
3.23	"Hymne à Victor Hugo" (w/ ch ad lib)	Op.69
3.24	"Sarabande et Rigaudon," in E major (c1892; strings)	Op.93
3.25	"Marche du couronnement" (Coronation March), in C major (ca1902)	Op.117
3.26	"Trois tableaux symphoniques d'aprés La foi" (c1908)	Op.130
3.27	"Ouverture de fête," in F major (c1910)	Op.133

Milit band:

3.28	"Orient et occident" (c1869; orchd)	Op.25
3.29	"Hymne franco-espagnol" (c1900)	
3.30	"Sur les bords du Nil" (c?)	Op.125

4. CONCERTOS, SOLO INSTR & ORCH

Pf & orch:

4.1	Piano Concerto No.1 in D major (c1858)	Op.17
4.2	Piano Concerto No.2 in G minor (c1868)	Op.22
4.3	Piano Concerto No.3 in E-flat major (c1869)	Op.29
4.4	Piano Concerto No.4 in C minor (c1875)	Op.44
4.5	"Allegro appassionato" (c1884)	Op.70
4.6	"Rhapsodie d'Auvergne" (c1884)	Op.73
4.7	"Wedding Cake," caprice-valse in A-flat major (c1885; pf & strings)	Op.76
4.8	"Africa," fantaisie in G minor (c1891)	Op.89
4.9	Piano Concerto No.5 in F major, "Egyptian" (c1896)	Op.103

Vn & orch:

4.10	Violin Concerto No.1 in A minor (c1859)	Op.20
4.11	"Introduction and Rondo capriccioso," in A minor (c1863)	Op.28
4.12	"Romance," in C major (c1874)	Op.48
4.13	Violin Concerto No.2 in C major (c1858)	Op.58
4.14	Violin Concerto No.3 in B minor (c1880)	Op.61
4.15	"Morceau de concert," in G major (c1880)	Op.62
4.16	"Caprice andalous," in G major (c1904)	Op.122

Vc & orch:

4.17	Cello Concerto No.1 in A minor (c1872)	Op.33
4.18	"Romance," in F major (c1874; hn/vc & orch/pf)	Op.36
4.19	Cello Concerto No.2 in D minor (c1902)	Op.119

Other:

4.20	"Tarantelle," in A minor (c1857; fl, cl & orch)	Op.6
4.21	"Romance," in D-flat major (c1871; fl/vn & orch/pf)	Op.37
4.22	"Morceau de concert," in F minor (c1887; hn & orch)	Op.94
4.23	"Morceau de concert," in G major (c1918–9; harp & orch)	Op.154
4.24	"Cyprès et Lauriers" (c1919; org & orch)	Op.156
4.25	"Odelette," in D major (c1920; fl & orch/pf)	Op.162

5. STRING QUARTETS

6. OTHER CHAMBER MUSIC

5 or more insts:

4 insts:

3 insts:

Vn & pf:

Vc & pf:

Other 2 insts:

6.50	"Andante" (ca1854; hn & org)	
6.51	"Romance," in E major (c1885; hn & pf, from: Suite for vc & pf, Op.16)	Op.67
6.52	"Fantaisie," in A major (c1907; vn & harp)	Op.124
6.53	"Cavatine" (c1915; trbn & pf)	Op.144
6.54	"Prière" (c1919; vn/vc & org)	Op.158
6.55	Oboe Sonata in D major (c1921)	Op.166
6.56	Clarinet Sonata in E-flat major (c1921)	Op.167
6.57	Bassoon Sonata in G major (c1921)	Op.168
6.58	"Adagio," in E-flat major (hn & pf)	

1 instr:

6.59	"Fantaisie," in A minor (c1893; harp)	Op.95
6.60	Cadenza for Beethoven: Vn Conc in D major, Op.61 (c1900)	

7. PIANO

7.1	"Valse" (ca1843)	
7.2	"Six bagatelles" (c1855)	Op.3
7.3	Mazurka No.1 in G minor (c1862)	Op.21
7.4	"Gavotte," in C minor (c1871; orchd)	Op.23
7.5	Mazurka No.2 in G minor (c1871)	Op.24
7.6	"Romance sans paroles," in B minor (c1871)	
7.7	"Allegro appassionato," in C-sharp minor (c1874; w/ orch ad lib)	Op.70
7.8	"Six études" (c1877): No.1 "Prélude"	Op.52
7.9	No.2 "Pour l'indépendance des doigts"	
7.10	No.3 "Prélude et fugue"	
7.11	No.4 "Étude de rythme"	
7.12	No.5 "Prélude et fugue"	
7.13	No.6 "En forme de valse" (transcr Ysaÿe as: Caprice for vn)	
7.14	"Menuet et valse" (c1878)	Op.56
7.15	Mazurka No.3 in B minor (c1882)	Op.66
7.16	"Album" (c1884): No.1 "Prélude"	Op.72
7.17	No.2 "Carillon"	
7.18	No.3 "Toccata"	
7.19	No.4 "Valse"	
7.20	No.5 "Chanson napolitaine"	
7.21	No.6 "Final"	
7.22	"Andantino" (c1884)	
7.23	"Improvisation" (c1885)	
7.24	"Souvenir d'Italie," in G major (c1887)	Op.80
7.25	"Les cloches du soir," in E-flat major (c1889)	Op.85
7.26	"Valse canariote," in A minor (c1890)	Op.88
7.27	"Suite," in F major (c1891): No.1 "Prélude et fugue"	Op.90
7.28	No.2 "Menuet"	
7.29	No.3 "Gavotte"	
7.30	No.4 "Gigue"	
7.31	"Thème varié" (c1894)	Op.97
7.32	"Souvenir d'Ismailia" (c1895)	Op.100
7.33	"Valse mignonne," in E-flat major (c1886)	Op.104
7.34	"Valse nonchalante," in D-flat major (c1898; orchd)	Op.110
7.35	"Quatre morceaux" (ca1898)	
7.36	"Six études" (c1899): No.1 "Tierces majeures et mineures"	Op.111
7.37	No.2 "Traits chromatiques"	
7.38	No.3 "Prélude et fugue"	
7.39	No.4 "Les cloches de Las Palmas"	
7.40	No.5 "Tierces majeures chromatiques"	
7.41	No.6 "Toccata"	
7.42	"Valse langoureuse" (c1903)	Op.120
7.43	"Feuillet d'album" (c1909, in Musée de Dieppe)	
7.44	"Six études" (c1912, for left hand)	Op.135
7.45	"Valse gaie" (c1913)	Op.139
7.46	"Six fugues" (c1920)	Op.161
7.47	"Feuillets d'album" (c1921)	Op.169
7.48	"Les heurs" (w/ narrator, in Musée de Dieppe)	
7.49	*"Fantaisie on Lvov's Russian National Anthem" (pf, ?spur)*	
7.50	Cadenza for Beethoven: Pf Conc No.4 in G major, Op.58 (ca1878)	
7.51	Cadenza for Mozart: Pf Conc No.22 in E-flat major, K482	
7.52	Cadenza for Mozart: Pf Conc No.24 in C minor, K491	

Pf duet:

7.53	"Duettino," in G major (c1855)	Op.11
7.54	"König Harald Harfagar" (c1880, after Heine's ballade)	Op.59
7.55	"Feuillet d'album," in B-flat major (c1887)	Op.81
7.56	"Pas redoublé," in B-flat major (c1887)	Op.86
7.57	"Berceuse," in E major (c1896)	Op.105
7.58	"Vers la victoire" (c ?1918)	Op.152
7.59	"Marche interalliée" (c1918)	Op.155
7.60	"Marche dédiée aux étudiants d'Alger" (c1921; w/ ch ad lib)	Op.163

2 Pf:

7.61	"Variations on a Theme of Beethoven" (c1874)	Op.35
7.62	"Caprice arabe" (c1884)	Op.96
7.63	"Polonaise," in F minor (c1886)	Op.77
7.64	"Scherzo" (c1889)	Op.87
7.65	"Duos" (c1898)	Op.8bis
7.66	"Caprice héroïque" (c1898)	Op.106
7.67	*Cadenza for Mozart: Double Pf Concerto No.10 in E-flat major, K365 (K316a) (2pf, ?spur)*	

8. ORGAN (or harm)

8.1	"Trois morceaux" (c1852; harm): No.1 "Méditation"	Op.1
8.2	No.2 "Barcarolle"	
8.3	No.3 "Prière"	
8.4	"Deux pièces" (ca1853)	
8.5	Fantaisie No.1 in E-flat major (c1857)	
8.6	"Bénédiction nuptiale," in F major (c1859)	Op.9
8.7	"Elévation, ou Communion" (c1865; org/harm)	Op.13
8.8	"3 Rhapsodies on Breton themes" (c1866): No.1 in E major	Op.7
8.9	No.2 in D major	
8.10	No.3 in F major	
8.11	"Trois préludes et fugues" (c1894): No.1 in B major	Op.99
8.12	No.2 in E major	
8.13	No.3 in E-flat major	
8.14	Fantaisie No.2 in D-flat major (c1895)	Op.101
8.15	"Marche religieuse," in F major (c1897)	Op.107
8.16	"Trois préludes et fugues" (c1898): No.1 in D minor	Op.109
8.17	No.2 in G minor	
8.18	No.3 in C major	
8.19	"7 Improvisations" (c1916–7): No.1 in E major	Op.150
8.20	No.2 in B minor	
8.21	No.3 in B-flat major	
8.22	No.4 in A major	
8.23	No.5 in G minor	
8.24	No.6 in B minor	
8.25	No.7 in A minor	
8.26	Fantaisie No.3 in C major (c1919)	Op.157
8.27	"Cinq morceaux" (org/harm)	
8.28	"Morceau"	
8.29	"Prélude"	
8.30	"Six duos" (c1858; harm & pf)	Op.8

9. SACRED WORKS

9.1	"Moïse sauvé des eux" (ca1851)	
9.2	"Messe solennelle" (c1855; vv, ch, orch & org)	Op.4
9.3	"Tantum ergo" (c1856; ch & org)	Op.5
9.4	"Oratorio de Noël" (c1858; vv, ch, str qt, harp & org)	Op.12
9.5	"Veni Creator," in C major (c1858; ch & org ad lib)	
9.6	"O salutaris," in B-flat major (c1858; S, A, Bar & org)	
9.7	"Ave Maria," in B-flat major (ca1859; S & org)	
9.8	"Ave Maria," in E major (ca1859; Bar & org)	
9.9	"Ave Maria," in A major (ca1860; 2A & org)	
9.10	"Ave verum," in E-flat major (ca1860; S, A, T, B & org)	
9.11	"O salutaris," in A major (ca1860; A & org)	
9.12	"Sub tuum," in F minor (ca1860; S, A & org)	
9.13	"Tantum ergo," in E-flat major (ca1860; 2S, A, org & ch ad lib)	
9.14	"Ave verum," in B minor (ca1863; S, A & org)	
9.15	"Coeli enarrant" (Psalm 18) (c1865; vv, ch & orch)	Op.42
9.16	"Ave Maria," in A major (c1865; S/T & org)	

9.17   "Inviolata," in D major (c1865; A & org) ....
9.18   "O salutaris," in A-flat major (c1869; S, A, Bar & org) ....
9.19   "La déluge" (The Flood), oratorio (c1875, Gallet; vv, ch & orch) Op.45
9.20   "O salutaris," in E major (c1875; S & org) ....
9.21   *"Tecum principium," motet (c1876, ?spur)* ....
9.22   "Requiem" (c1878; vv, ch & orch) Op.54
9.23   "O salutaris," in E major (c1884; T, Bar & org) ....
9.24   "O salutaris," in E-flat major (c1884; A & org) ....
9.25   "Deus Abraham," in F major (c1885; A & org) ....
9.26   "Pie Jesu," in C minor (c1885; B & org) ....
9.27   "Panis angelicus," in F major (c1898; T/S & str qnt/org) ....
9.28   "Offertoire pour la Toussaint," in F major (c1904; ch & org, ad lib: vc, d bass) ....
9.29   "Praise ye the Lord" (Psalm 150) (p1908; d ch, orch & org) Op.127
9.30   "The Promised Land," oratorio (c1913, Klein; vv, ch & orch) ....
9.31   "Ave Maria" (c1914; ch) Op.145
9.32   "Tu es Petrus" (c1914; 4 m vv & org) Op.147
9.33   "Quam dilecta" (1v & org) Op.148
9.34   "Laudate Dominum" (c1916; ch) Op.149
9.35   "Litanies à la Sainte Vierge" (c1917; 1v & org) ....

9.36   "Ave verum," in D major (4 fem vv, org & hn obbl) ....
9.37   "Six choeurs religieux" ....
9.38   "Neuf chants religieux latins" (w/ acc) ....
9.39   "Super flumina Babylonis" (Psalm 136) (ch) ....

Canticles:

9.40   "À Saint Joseph" (ca1844) ....
9.41   "Dans ce beau moi" (ca1844) ....
9.42   "Nous qu'en ces lieux" (ca1844) ....
9.43   "Reçois mes hommages" (ca1844) ....
9.44   "La madonna col bambino," in F major (ca1855; A/ch & pf) ....
9.45   "Heureux qui du coeur de Marie," in A major (ca1860; A/ch & pf) ....
9.46   "O Saint Autel," in D major (ca1860; 3A, ch & pf) ....
9.47   "Pour vous bénir, Seigneur," in E major (ca1860, Cuinet; 3A, ch & pf) ....
9.48   "Reine des cieux," in A-flat major (ca1860; A/ch & pf) ....

10. SECULAR CHORAL WORKS

10.1   "Imagine," cantata (ca1848) ....
10.2   *"Les Israélites sur la montagne d'Oreb," oratorio (ca1848, frag)* ....
10.3   "Télétille," cantata (ca1848) ....
10.4   Cantata (ca1849, Tastu) ....
10.5   "Antigone," prolog (ca1950; vv, ch & orch) ....
10.6   *"Les Dijinns" (ca1850, Hugo, frag)* ....
10.7   "La rose" (ca1850) ....
10.8   Cantata (c1852; ch & orch) ....
10.9   "Les cloches," symphonic ode (c1852) ....
10.10   "Fugue & chorus" (c1852) ....
10.11   "Ode à Sainte-Cécile" (c1852; 1v, ch & orch) ....
10.12   "Le retour de Virginie" (c1852) ....
10.13   "Toilette de la Marquise de Présalé," grande scène lyrique (c1857) ....
10.14   "Macbeth," scène (c1858; ch & orch) ....
10.15   *"Ivanhoé," cantata (c1864, Roussy, ?spur)* ....
10.16   "Les noces de Prométhée," cantata (c1867, Cornut; vv, ch & orch) Op.19
10.17   "Sérénade d'hiver" (c1867, Cazalis; 4 m vv) ....
10.18   *"Pour le centenaire de Hoche," cantata (c1868, ?spur, ?lost)* ....
10.19   *"Les chants de guerre" (c1870; 2vv, ch & orch, ?spur)* ....
10.20   "Le nuage" (c1875) ....
10.21   "Les soldats de Gédéon" (c1876, Gallet; d m ch) Op.46
10.22   "Deux choeurs" (c1878, Hugo): 1. "Chanson de grand-père" (w/ 2 fem vv) Op.53
10.23   2. "Chanson d'ancêtre" (w/ Bar)
10.24   "La lyre et la harpe" (c1879, Hugo; vv, ch & orch) Op.57
10.25   "Hymne à Victor Hugo" (c1881; orch & ch ad lib) Op.69
10.26   "Deux choeurs" (c1882; w/ pf ad lib): 1. "Calme des nuits" Op.68
10.27   2. "Les fleurs et les arbres"
10.28   "Deux choeurs" (c1884, Saint-Felix): 1. "Les marins de Kermor" Op.71
10.29   2. "Les Titans"
10.30   "Saltarelle" (c1885, Deschamps; m ch) Op.74
10.31   "Les guerriers" (c1888, Audigier; m ch) Op.84
10.32   "Nuit persane" (c1891, Renaud; vv, ch & orch) Op.26bis
10.33   "Chant d'automne" (c1899, Sicard; m ch) Op.113
10.34   "La nuit," cantata (c1900, Audigier; S, fem ch & orch) Op.114
10.35   "La feu céleste," cantata (c1900, Silvestre; narrator, S, ch, orch & org) Op.115
10.36   "À la France," choral ode (c1903, Combarieu; m ch & ch ad lib) Op.121

10.37	"Ode d'Horace" (c1905, transl Saint-Saëns; m ch)	
10.38	"La gloire de Corneille," cantata (c1906, Lecomte)	Op.126
10.39	*"Hommage des enfants à Victor Hugo," cantata (c1907, Carminet, ?spur)*	
10.40	"Le matin" (m ch)	Op.129
10.41	"La gloire," cantata (c1911; vv, ch & pf)	Op.131
10.42	"Aux aviateurs" (c1911, Bonnerot; m ch)	Op.134
10.43	"Aux mineurs" (c1912; m ch)	Op.137
10.44	"Hymne au printemps" (c1912)	Op.138
10.45	"Deux choeurs" (c1913): 1. "Des pas dans l'allée"	Op.141
10.46	2. "Trinquons" (Béranger)	
10.47	"Hymne au travail" (c1914; m ch)	Op.142
10.48	"Hail California" (c1915; w/ orch & org)	
10.49	"Trois choeurs" (c1917; fem ch): 1. "Chanson des aiguilles" (Bonnerot)	Op.151
10.50	2. "Salut au chevalier" (Fournier)	
10.51	3. "Le sourire" (Mirval)	
10.52	"Aux conquérants de l'air"	Op.164
10.53	"Le printemps"	Op.165
10.54	"Hymne à Jeanne d'Arc" (c1920; ch & org)	
10.55	Canon (fem ch)	

11. MISC VOCAL

11.1	"Antwort" (Uhland)	
11.2	"Chanson de Fortunio" (Musset)	
11.3	"La cigale et la fourmi": "La cigale ayant chanté tout l'été" (p1958, Lafontaine)	
11.4	"L'écho de la harpe"	
11.5	"God Save the King" (French transl; w/ pf)	
11.6	"Primavera" (d'Orléans)	
11.7	"Sérénade" (p ca1866, Mangeot; w/ orch)	
11.8	"Toi" (p ca1856, St Chaffray)	
11.9	"Pastorelle" (c1855, Destouches; 2vv)	
11.10	"Viens" (ca1855, Hugo; 2vv)	
11.11	"Le soir descend sur la colline" (c1857; 2vv)	
11.12	"Scène d'Horace" (c1860, Corneille; 2vv & orch)	Op.10
11.13	"El desdichado" (c1871; 2vv & orch)	
11.14	"Les cygnes" (c1891, Renaud; 2vv & orch & ch ad lib, from Op.26bis)	
11.15	"Vénus" (c1896, Saint-Saëns; 2vv)	
11.16	"Romance du soir" (c1902, Croze; S, A, T, B)	Op.118

12. SONGS (w/ pf)

12.1	"Ariel" (c1841)	
12.2	"Le soir" (c1841, Desbordes-Valmore)	
12.3	"La maman" (ca1841, Tastu)	
12.4	"Tandis que sur vos ans" (c1844)	
12.5	"Le golfe de Baya" (ca1847, Lamartine)	
12.6	"Télesille" (c1849, Tastu)	
12.7	"Bergeronnette" (c1850, Lombard)	
12.8	"Lamento" (c1850, Gautier)	
12.9	"Le lac" (c1850, Lamartine)	
12.10	"Guitare" (c1851, Hugo)	
12.11	"La poète mourant" (c1851, Lamartine)	
12.12	"Le rendezvous" (c1851, Fiéffé)	
12.13	"Rêverie" (c1851, Hugo; w/ orch)	
12.14	"Idylle" (c1852, Deschoulières)	
12.15	"L'automne" (ca1852, Lamartine)	
12.16	"Le pas d'armes du Roi Jean" (c1852, Hugo; w/ orch)	
12.17	"Mélodie" (c1852, Lamartine; w/ orch)	
12.18	"Le feuille de peuplier" (c1853, Tastu; w/ orch)	
12.19	"Ruhethal" (c1854, Uhland)	
12.20	*"La chasse du burgrave" (ca1854, ?lost)*	
12.21	"La porta dell'inferno" (ca1854, Dante)	
12.22	"La cloche": "Seule en ta sombre tour aux faîtes dentelés" (ca1855, Hugo)	
12.23	"L'attente": "Monte, écureuil, monte au grand chêne" (ca1855, Hugo; w/ orch)	
12.24	"Le lever de la lune" (c1855, Ossian)	
12.25	"Le sommeil des fleurs" (c1855, Penmarch)	
12.26	"Plainte" (ca1855, Tastu; w/ orch)	
12.27	"À la lune" (c1856)	
12.28	"La mort d'Ophélie" (ca1857, Legouvé)	
12.29	"Pourquoi t'exiler" (ca1858)	
12.30	"Souvenences" (ca1858, Lemaire)	
12.31	"Alla riva del Tebro" (ca1860)	
12.32	"Etoil du matin" (ca1860, Distel)	

12.108	5. "Pâques"
12.109	6. "Jour de pluie"
12.110	7. "Amoroso"
12.111	8. "Mai"
12.112	9. "Petite main"
12.113	10. "Reviens"
12.114	"Les sapins" (c1914, Martin) ....
12.115	"Vive la France" (c1914, Fournier) ....
12.116	"La française" (c1915, Zamacoïs, in: Le petit parisien) ....
12.117	"Ne l'oubliez pas" (ca1915, Regnault) ....
12.118	"S'il est un charmant gazon" (c1915, Hugo) ....
12.119	"Honneur à l'Amérique" (c1917, Fournier) ....
12.120	"Angélus" (c1918, Aguétant; w/ orch) ....
12.121	"Où nous avons aimé" (c1918, Aguétant; w/ orch) ....
12.122	"Papillons" (c1918, Leche; w/ orch) ....
12.123	"Victoire" (c1918, Fournier) ....
12.124	"Hymne à la paix" (c1919, Faure) Op.159
12.125	"Cinq poèmes de Ronsard" (c1921, Ronsard): 1. "L'amour oyseau" ....
12.126	2. "L'amour blessé"
12.127	3. "À Saint-Blaise"
12.128	4. "Grasselette et Maigrelette"
12.129	5. "L'amant malheureux"
12.130	"Vieilles chansons" (c1921): 1. "Temps nouveau" (d'Orléans) ....
12.131	2. "Avril" (Belleau)
12.132	3. "Villanelle" (Fresnaye)

13. ARRANGEMENTS OF WORKS OF OTHERS

13.1	Bach, J. S.: "6 Transcriptions," Set I ....
13.2	Bach, J. S.: "6 Transcriptions," Set II ....
13.3	Bach, J. S.: "Prelude," of Violin Sonata No.6 (pf acc) ....
13.4	Bach, J. S.: "Sarabande" (vn & pf/orch) ....
13.5	Beethoven: "Chorus of Dervishes," from incid music: The Ruins of Athens, Op.113/3 (arr for pf) ....
13.6	Beethoven: "3 Transcriptions from the Quartets" (transcr for pf) ....
13.7	Beethoven: "Points d'orgue pour le concerto de piano en Sol" ....
13.8	Berlioz: "Easter hymn," from cantata: Damnation de Faust, Op.24, H111/5a (transcr for pf)
13.9	Berlioz: "Lélio," mélologue, Op.14bis, H55a (arr for 1v & pf)
13.10	Bizet: "Scherzo," from: Les pêcheurs de perles (transcr for pf) ....
13.11	Chopin: Piano Sonata No.2 in B-flat minor, Op.35, B128 (arr for 2pf)
13.12	Duparc: "Leonore," sym poem (arr for 2pf)
13.13	Durand: "Chanson des Maucroix" (transcr for pf) ....
13.14	Gluck: "Caprice sur les airs de ballet d'Alceste" (pf) ....
13.15	Gluck: "Menuet," from: Orphée (transcr for pf) ....
13.16	Gounod: "Kermesse," from opera: Faust (transcr for pf) ....
13.17	Gounod: "Valse," from opera: Faust (transcr for pf) ....
13.18	Gounod: "Gallia," lamentation (paraphrased for pf) ....
13.19	Gounod: "Suite concertante," for pedal pf & orch (arr for 2pf) ....
13.20	Haydn: "Andante," from: Symphony No.36 in E-flat major, Hobl/36 (transcr for pf) ....
13.21	Liszt: "Beethoven Cantata," S67 (Improvisation for piano) ....
13.22	Liszt: "Orphée," sym poem, S98 (arr for pf, vn & vc) ....
13.23	Liszt: "La prédication aux oiseaux," legend, S175/1 (transcr for org) ....
13.24	Massenet: "Thais" (Concert Paraphrase) ....
13.25	Mendelssohn: "Scherzo," from incid music: Midsummer Night's Dream, Op.61 (transcr for pf) .....
13.26	Milan de Valence, L. (16th cent Spain): "2 Fantasias for the lute" (transcr for pf) ....
13.27	Mozart: "Andante" (transcr for vn & pf/orch) ....
13.28	Paladilhe: "La mandolinata" (Paraphrase for piano) ....
13.29	Paladilhe: "La Islena" (Paraphrase for piano) ....
13.30	Reber, H.: 4 Symphonies (arr for pf duet) ....
13.31	Schumann: "Night Song" (arr for orch/pf) ....
13.32	Wagner: "Marche religieuse," from opera: Lohengrin, WWV75 (transcr for pf, vn & org) ....

* * * * *

1. VIOLIN & ORCHESTRA

1.1 "La chasse" (p1901) Op.44
1.2 "Nocturne-sérénade" (p1901) Op.45

2. CONCERT FANTASIES ON THEMES FROM OPERAS (vn & orch/pf)

2.1 Bizet: "Carmen" (p ?1883) Op.25
2.2 Weber: "Der Freischütz," J277 (p1874) ....
2.3 Mozart: "Don Giovanni," K527 (p1874) ....
2.4 Gounod: "Faust" (p1874) ....
2.5 Verdi: "La forza del destino" (p1876) ....
2.6 Flotow: "Martha" (p1876) ....
2.7 Gounod: "Mireille" ....
2.8 Gounod: "Roméo et Juliette" ....
2.9 Hérold: "Zampa" ....

3. VIOLIN & PIANO

3.1 "Réverie" Op.4
3.2 "Confidence" Op.7
3.3 "Les adieux" Op.9
3.4 "Sérénade andalouse" Op.10
3.5 "Le sommeil" Op.11
3.6 "Prière et berceuse" (p1870) Op.17
3.7 "Zigeunerweisen" (p1878; orchd) Op.20
3.8 "Danzas españolas" (p1878–82): No.1 "Malagueña" Opp.21, 22, 23, 26
3.9 No.2 "Habanera"
3.10 No.3 "Romanza andaluza"
3.11 No.4 "Jota Navarra"
3.12 No.5 "Playera"
3.13 No.6 "Zapateado"
3.14 No.7 "Dance," in C major
3.15 No.8 "Dance," in C major
3.16 "Caprice basque" (p1881) Op.24
3.17 "Jota aragonesa" (p1883) Op.27
3.18 "Sérénade andalouse" (p1883) Op.28
3.19 "El canto del ruiseñor" (p1885) Op.29
3.20 "Bolero" (p1885) Op.30
3.21 "Muiñera" (p1885) Op.32
3.22 "Navarra" (p1889; 2vn & pf) Op.33
3.23 "Airs écossais" (p1892) Op.34
3.24 "Peteneras" (p1894; orchd) Op.35
3.25 "Jota de San Fermín" (p1894) Op.36
3.26 "Adiós montañas mias" (p1896) Op.37
3.27 "Viva Sevilla!" (p1896) Op.38
3.28 "Zortzico" (p1898) Op.39
3.29 "Introduction et fandango" (p1898) Op.40
3.30 "Introduction et caprice-jota" (p1899) Op.41
3.31 "Miramar-Zortzico" (p1899) Op.42
3.32 "Introduction et tarantelle" (p1899; orchd) Op.43
3.33 "Barcarolle vénitienne" (ca1902) Op.46
3.34 "Mélodie roumaine" (p1901) Op.47
3.35 "L'esprit follet" Op.48
3.36 "Chansons russes" Op.49
3.37 "Jota de Pamplona" (p1904) Op.50
3.38 "Jota de Pablo" Op.52
3.39 "Rêve" (p1909) Op.53

* * * * *

1. STAGE WORKS

Operas:

1.1	"Geneviève de Brabant," 3 act miniature marionette opera (ca1900, Latour; vv, ch & pf) ....
1.2	*"Pousse l'amour" (Coco chéri), operetta (c1905, collab Feraudy & Kolb, frags)* ....
1.3	"Le piège de Méduse" (Medusa's Trap), 1 act lyric comedy (c1913, p1921 w/ illustrations by G. Braque)....
1.4	"Socrate," sym drama (c1917–18, Plato's dialogues transl Cousin; 1v/vv & orch; arr Cage for 2pf): ....
	1. "Portrait de Socrate" (from Symposium)
	2. "Les Bords de l'Illissus" (from Phaedrus)
	3. "Mort de Socrate" (from Phaedo)
1.5	Recitatives for Gounod's opera: Le Médecin malgré lui (The Doctor in Spite of Himself) (c1923)................

Ballet:

1.6	"Uspud" (Christian ballet in 3 scenes) (c1892, Latour; pf; orchd Caby 1970) ....
1.7	"Jack in the Box," pantomime (c1899–1900, Depaquit; pf; orchd Milhaud 1929)................................
1.8	"Parade" ('realistic ballet in 1 scene') (c1916–7, story Cocteau, choreography Massine, sets Picasso; orch)
1.9	"Mercure" ('plastic poses in 3 tableaux') (c1924, choreography Massine, sets Picasso) ....
1.10	"Relâche" (No Performance Today) (c1924, w/ Picabia & Börlin; orch; red for pf 1926) ....

Incid music:

1.11	"Le fils des étoiles" (c1891, Péladan: Chaldean Pastoral; pf; orig for fls & harps) ....
1.12	"Hymne pour le Salut Drapeau" (c1891, Péladan: Le prince de Byzance; 1v & pf; orchd Caby 1968) ....
1.13	"Le Nazaréen" (c1892, Mazel; pf; see Nos.3 & 4 of: 4 Préludes of 1892) ....
1.14	"Prélude de La Porte héroïque du ciel" (Prelude to 'The Heroic Gate of Heaven'), for Bois: La Porte
	héroïque du ciel (c1894; pf; orchd1912) ....
1.15	"The Dreamy Fish" (Le poisson rêveur), esquisse (c1901, Latour; pf; arr Caby for pf & orch 1970).............
1.16	"5 Grimaces for 'Midsummer Night's Dream' " (c1915, Cocteau after Shakespeare; orch) (also see
	Britten's opera Op.64, Castelnuovo-Tedesco's overture Op.108, Mendelssohn's incid music
	Op.61, Orff's music drama & Purcell's semi-opera: The Fairy Queen, Z629) ....

1a. SELECTIONS FROM STAGE WORKS

1a.1	"Geneviève de Brabant," opera: ....
	1. "Prélude"
	I: 2. "Choeur"
	3. "Entrée des soldats"
	II: 4. "Entr'acte"
	5. "Air de Geneviève"
	6. "Sonnerie de cor"
	7. "Entrée des soldats"
	III: 8. "Entr'acte"
	9. "Choeur"
	10. "Air de Golo"
	11. "Entrée des soldats"
	12. "Cortège"
	13. "Entrée des soldats"
	14. "Petit air de Geneviève"
	15. "Choeur final"

1a.7	"Jack in the Box," pantomime: ....
	1. "Prélude"
	2. "Entr'acte"
	3. "Final"

1a.8	"Parade," ballet: ....
	1. "Choral-Prélude du rideau rouge—Prestidigitateur chinois" (arr for pf duet 1917)
	2. "Petite fille américaine" (extracted Ourdine for pf as: Rag-Time Parade 1919; also orchd)
	3. "Acrobates"
	4. "Final—Suite au Prélude du rideau rouge"

1a.9	"Mercure," ballet: ....
	1. "Marche Ouverture"
	I: 2. "La Nuit"
	3. "Danse de tendresse"
	4. "Signes du Zodiaque"
	5. "Entrée de Mercure"
	II: 6. "Danses des Grâces"
	7. "Bain des Grâces"
	8. "Fuite de Mercure"
	9. "Colère de Cerbère"
	III: 10. "Polka des Lettres"

11. "Nouvelle Danse"
12. "Le Chaos"
13. "Rapt de Proserpine"

1a.10   "Relâche," ballet: ....
1. "Ouverture"
2. "Projection—Rideau"
I: 3. "Entrée de la Femme"
4. "Musique entre l'entrée de la Femme et sa 'Danse sans musique' "
5. "Entrée de l'Homme"
6. "Danse de la Porte tournante" (Dance of the Revolving Door)
7. "Entrée des Hommes"
8. "Danse des Hommes"
9. "Danse de la Femme"
10. "Final"
II: 11. "Musique de Rentrée"
12. "Rentrée des Hommes"
13. "Rentrée de la Femme"
14. "Les Hommes se dévêtissent"
15. "Danse de l'Homme et de la Femme"
16. "Les Hommes regagnent leur place et retrouvent leurs pardessus"
17. "Danse de la Brouette" (Dance of the Wheelbarrow)
18. "Danse de la Couronne" (Dance of the Coronet)
19. "Le Danseur dépose la Couronne sur la tête d'une spectatrice"
20. "La Femme rejoit son fauteuil"
21. "Petite Danse Finale; La Queue du Chien" (The Dog's Tail)

1a.16   "5 Grimaces for 'Midsummer Night's Dream,' " incid music: ....
1. "Préambule" (Preamble)
2. "Coquecigrue" (Fiddle-faddle)
3. "Chasse" (Chase)
4. "Fanfaronnade" (Bluster)
5. "Pour sortir" (For Exit)

2. ORCHESTRAL WORKS

2.1   "Danse" (c1890; used in: 3 Morceaux en forme de poire) ....
2.2   "Trois petites pièces montées" (3 Little Stuffed Pieces) (c1919): No.1 "De l'enfance de Pantagruel; Rêverie" ....
2.3   No.2 "Marche de Cocagne; Démarche"
2.4   No.3 "Jeux de Gargantua; Coin de Polka"
2.5   "La belle excentrique" (The Eccentric Belle), 'serious fantasy' (c1920; arr for pf duet): No.1 "Grande ritournelle" (Grand Ritornello) ....
2.6   No.2 "Marche franco-lunaire" (Franco-Lunar March)
2.7   No.3 "Valse du mystérieux baiser dans l'oeil" (Waltz of the Mysterious Kiss in the Eye)
2.8   No.4 "Cancan Grand-Mondain" (High-Society Cancan)
2.9   "Musique d'ameublement" (Furniture Music) (c1920, collab Milhaud): No.1 "Chez un Bistrot" ....
2.10   No.2 "Un salon"
2.11   "Musique d'ameublement" (Furniture Music) (c1923): No.1 "Tenture de cabinet préfectoral" (Wall Hanging for a Prefectural Office) ....
2.12   No.2 "Tapisserie en fer forgé" (Forged Iron Tapestry) (c1917–23)
2.13   No.3 "Carrelage phonique" (Phonic Floor Tiles) (c1917–23)
2.14   "Cinéma: Entr'acte symphonique de Relâche" (c1924; arr Milhaud for pf duet 1926; arr for pf): No.1 "Cheminées, ballons qui explosent" (Chimneys, exploding balloons) ....
2.15   No.2 "Gants de boxe et allumettes" (Boxing gloves and matches)
2.16   No.3 "Prises d'air, jeux d'échecs et bateaux sur les toits"
2.17   No.4 "La danseuse, et figures dans l'eau"
2.18   No.5 "Chasseur, et début de l'enterrement"
2.19   No.6 "Marche funèbre"
2.20   No.7 "Cortège au ralenti"
2.21   No.8 "La poursuite"
2.22   No.9 "Chûte du cerceuil et sortie de Börlin"
2.23   No.10 "Final; écran crevé et fin"

3. STRING QUARTETS

Arr Caby for str qt:

3.1   *"Quatuor intime et secret," 16 pieces (p1979): No.1 "Choral" (No.6 of: Douze petits chorals)* ....
No.2 "Désespoir agréable" (No.1 of: Six pièces de la période 1906–13)
No.3 "Nostalgie" (No.1 of: Musiques intimes et secrètes)
No.4 "Poésie" (No.3 of: Six pièces de la période 1906–13)
No.5 "Songerie vers 'Jack' " (No.10 of: Carnet d'esquisses et de croquis)

No.6 *"Nostalgie" (transposed vers of No.3)*
No.7 *"Songe-creux" (No.6 of: Six pièces de la période 1906–13)*
No.8 *"Fâcheux exemple" (No.3 of: Musiques intimes et secrètes)*
No.9 *"Profondeur" (No.5 of: Six pièces de la période 1906–13)*
No.10 *"Froide songerie" (No.2 of: Musiques intimes et secrètes)*
No.11 *"Rêverie du pauvre"*
No.12 *"Harmonies delectables" (No.9 of: Carnet d'esquissese & No.3 of: Pages mystiques)*
No.13 *"Songe-creux" (repeat of No.7)*
No.14 *"Mouvement de Polka" (No.4 of: Carnet d'esquisses et de croquis)*
No.15 *"Le grand singe" (No.6 of: Carnet d'esquisses et de croquis)*
No.16 *"Petite danse" (No.17 of: Carnets d'esquisses et de croquis)*

4. OTHER CHAMBER MUSIC

4.1   "Choses vues à droite et à gauche; sans lunettes" (Things Seen to Right and Left; without Glasses)
        (c1914; vn & pf): No.1 "Choral hypocrite" (Hipocritical Chorale) ....
4.2   No.2 "Fugue à tâtons" (Groping Fugue)
4.3   No.3 "Fantaisie musculaire" (Muscular Fantasy)
4.4   "Sonnerie pour réveiller le bon gros Roi des Singes; lequel ne dort toujours que d'un oeil" (Fanfare for
        Waking Up the Big Fat King of the Monkeys; Who Always Sleeps with One Eye Open) (c1921; 2tpt) ......

5. PIANO

5.1   "Allegro" (c1884, sketch) ....
5.2   "Valse-ballet" (c1885; p1975 as No.1 of: Deux Oeuvres de jeunesse) ....
5.3   "Fantaisie-valse" (c1885; p1975 as No.2 of: Deux Oeuvres de jeunesse) ....
5.4   4 "Ogives" (4 Nose Cones) (c1886) ....
5.5   "Trois sarabandes" (c1887; orchd Caby 1968; arr by others for 2gui, brass qnt): No.1 (in F minor) ....
5.6   No.2 "à Maurice Ravel"
5.7   No.3 (in B-flat minor)
5.8   "Trois gymnopédies" (c1888): No.1 "Lent et douloureux" (orchd Debussy 1898) ....
5.9   No.2 "Lent et triste" (orchd Murrill & Roland-Manuel)
5.10   No.3 "Lent et grave" (orchd Debussy 1898)
5.11   "Gnossienne" (No.5) (c1889; orchd Caby 1968) ....
5.12   "Chanson hongroise" (c1889, unfin sketch)
5.13   "Trois gnossiennes" (c1890; orchd by others; instr arrs by others): No.1 "Lent" ....
5.14   No.2 "Avec étonnement"
5.15   No.3 "Lent"
5.16   "Gnossienne" (No.4) (c1891; orchd Caby 1968; also instr arrs by others) ....
5.17   "Première pensée Rose + Croix" (c1891; orchd Caby 1968) ....
5.18   "Le fils des étoiles," préludes (c1891, for a play of the same title, for 'Rose + Croix'—French branch
        of the Rosicrucian Brotherhood, a mystical religious sect he joined in 1891): No.1 "Act I. La vocation"
        (The Calling; Chaldean Night) (orchd Roland-Manuel 1962) ....
5.19   No.2 "Act II. L'initiation" (The Initiation; The Lower Room of the Grand Temple)
5.20   No.3 "Act III. L'incantation" (The Incantation; The Terrace of Patesi—Priest-King, Goudea's Palace)
                (orchd Roland-Manuel 1962)
5.21   "Leit-Motif du Panthée" (c1891, in Péladin's novel: Le Panthée) ....
5.22   "Sonneries de la Rose + Croix" (c1892): No.1 "Air de l'Ordre" ....
5.23   No.2 "Air du grand Maitre"
5.24   No.3 "Air du Grand Prieur"
5.25   "Quatre préludes" (c1892; orchd by others): No.1 "Fête donnée par des Chevaliers Normands" (c ?1884) .
5.26   No.2 "Prélude d'Eginhard" (c ?1893)
5.27   No.3 "Premier prélude du Nazaréen" (from incid music for Mazel: Le Nazaréen)
5.28   No.4 "Deuxième prélude du Nazaréen" (from incid music for Mazel: Le Nazaréen)
5.29   "Danses gothiques" (Neuvaine pour le plus grand calme et la forte tranquillité de mon Âme) (Novena for
        the greatest calm and tranquility of my soul) (c1893): No.1 "A l'occasion d'une grande peine" (On the
        occasion of a great sorrow) ....
5.30   No.2 "Dans laquelle les Pères de la Très Véritable et très Sainte Eglise sont invoqués"
5.31   No.3 "En faveur d'un malheureux" (On behalf of a poor wretch)
5.32   No.4 "A propos de Saint Bernard et de Sainte Lucie"
5.33   No.5 "Pour les pauvres trépassés"
5.34   No.6 "Où il est question du pardon des injures reçues" (Where there is question of forgiveness
                for insults received)
5.35   No.7 "Par pitié pour les ivrognes, honteux, débauchés, imparfaits, désagréables, et faussaires ..."
5.36   No.8 "En le haut honneur du vénéré Saint Michel, le gracieux Archange"
5.37   No.9 "Après avoir obtenu la remise de ses fautes"
5.38   "Pages mystiques" (c1893–5): No.1 "Prière" ....
5.39   No.2 "Vexation"
5.40   No.3 "Harmonies" (ca1905–8?)
5.41   "Gnossienne" (No.6) (c1897; orchd Caby 1968; arr Kraus for 2gui) ....
5.42   "Danse de travers" (c1897)
5.43   "Pièces froides" (Cold Pieces) (c1897, arr Kraus for 2gui): No.1 "Airs à faire fuir" (Tunes to Make You
        Run Away), 3 pieces ....

5.44	No.2 "Danses de travers" (Crooked Dances), 3 pieces
5.45	"Caresse" (ca1897) ....
5.46	"Poudre d'or" (Gold Dust) (ca1900; orchd1978) ....
5.47	"Le Piccadilly" (ca1900–4; orchd1907) ....
5.48	"Rêverie du pauvre" (c1900) ....
5.49	"Petite ouverture à danser" (ca1900; orchd Caby 1968; arr Kleynjans for gui 1982) ....
5.50	"Petite musique de clown triste" (c1900) ....
5.51	"Verset laïque et sompteux" (c1900) ....
5.52	"Passacaille" (c1906; orchd Diamond 1950) ....
5.53	"Prélude en tapisserie" (Tapestry Prelude) (c1906) ....
5.54	"Douze petits chorals" (Twelve Little Chorales) (c1906–8) ....
5.55	"Musiques intimes et secrètes" (Intimate and Secret Musics) (c1906–13; arr Laniau for 10-string gui 1982): No.1 "Nostalgie" ....
5.56	No.2 "Froide songerie" (Cold Musing)
5.57	No.3 "Fâcheux exemple" (Peevish Example)
5.58	"Six pièces de la période 1906–1913" (c1906–13): No.1 "Désespoir agréable" (Plesant Despair) (c1908) ..
5.59	No.2 "Effronterie"
5.60	No.3 "Poésie" (ca1913)
5.61	No.4 "Prélude canin" (Doggy Prelude) (ca1910; orchd Caby 1968)
5.62	No.5 "Profondeur"
5.63	No.6 "Songe-creux" (arr Kraus for 2gui 1968)
5.64	"Nouvelles Pièces froides" (New Cold Pieces) (c1910–11; arr Kraus for 2gui 1968): No.1 "Sur un mur" (On a Wall) ....
5.65	No.2 "Sur un arbre" (On a Tree)
5.66	No.3 "Sur un pont" (On a Bridge)
5.67	"Deux rêveries nocturnes" (Two Nocturnal Reveries) (c1910–11; arr Kraus for 2gui 1968): No.1 "Pas vite"
5.68	No.2 "Très modérément"
5.69	"Carnet d'esquisses et de croquis" (Notebook of Sketches and Rough Drafts) (c1897–1914): No.1 "Air" (c1914) ....
5.70	No.2 "Essais"
5.71	No.3 "Notes"
5.72	No.4 "Notes"
5.73	No.5 "Le Prisonnier maussade"
5.74	No.6 "Esquisses; Le Grand Singe"
5.75	No.7 "Exercices"
5.76	No.8 "Notes"
5.77	No.9 "Harmonies"
5.78	No.10 "Songerie vers 'Jack' " (c1897)
5.79	No.11 "Bribes"
5.80	No.12 "Choral"
5.81	No.13 "Exercices"
5.82	No.14 "Exercices"
5.83	No.15 "Exercices"
5.84	No.16 "Exercices"
5.85	No.17 "Esquisse & Sketch Montmartrois 1 & 2"
5.86	No.18 "Essais; Arrière-Propos"
5.87	No.19 "Petite Danse"
5.88	"Préludes flasques; pour un chien" (Flabby Preludes; for a Dog) (c1912): No.1 "Voix d'intérieur" ....
5.89	No.2 "Idylle cynique"
5.90	No.3 "Chanson canine"
5.91	No.4 "Avec camaraderie"
5.92	"Véritable préludes flasques; pour un chien" (True Flabby Preludes; for a Dog) (c1912): No.1 "Sévère réprimande" ....
5.93	No.2 "Seul à la maison"
5.94	No.3 "On joue"
5.95	"Le piège de Méduse" (Medusa's Trap), dances (c1913; pf; p1968 for cl, tpt, trbn, vn, vc, d bass & perc): No.1 "Quadrille" ....
5.96	No.2 "Valse"
5.97	No.3 "Pas vite"
5.98	No.4 "Mazurka"
5.99	No.5 "Un peu vif"
5.100	No.6 "Polka"
5.101	No.7 "Quadrille"
5.102	"Descriptions automatiques" (Automatic Descriptions) (c1913): No.1 "Sur un vaisseau" (On a Ship) ....
5.103	No.2 "Sur une lanterne" (On a Streetlamp)
5.104	No.3 "Sur un casque" (On a Helmet)
5.105	"Embryons desséchés" (Dried-up Embryos) (c1913; orchd): No.1 "d'Holothurie" ....
5.106	No.2 "d'Edriophthalma"
5.107	No.3 "de Podophthalma"
5.108	"Croquis et agaceries d'un gros bonhomme en bois" (Sketches and Exasperations of a Big Wooden Fellow) (c1913): No.1 "Tyrolienne turque" (Turkish Yodeling) ....
5.109	No.2 "Danse maigre; à la manière de ces messsieurs" (Meager Dance; in the manner of these gentlemen)
5.110	No.3 "Españaña"

5.111	"Chapitres tournés en tous sens" (Chapters Turned Every Which Way) (c1913): No.1 "Celle qui parle trop" (She Who Talks Too Much) ....
5.112	No.2 "Le porteur de grosses pierres" (The Hauler of Big Stones)
5.113	No.3 "Regret des Enfermés; Jonas et Latude" (Lament of the Confined)
5.114	"Vieux sequins et vieilles cuirasses" (Old Sequins and Armor) (c1913): No.1 "Chez le marchand d'or; Venise XIIIe Siècle" (At the Gold Merchant's) ....
5.115	No.2 "Danse cuirassée; Période grecque" (Armor-plated Dance)
5.116	No.3 "La défaite des cimbres; Cauchemar" (The Defeat of the Cimbri)
5.117	"Enfantines" (Children's Pieces) (c1913), I. "Menus propos enfantins" (Childish Chatter): No.1 "Chant guerrrier du roi des haricots" ....
5.118	No.2 "Ce qui dit la petite princesse des Tulipes"
5.119	No.3 "Valse du Chocolat aux amandes"
5.120	II. "Enfantillages pittoresques" (Picturesque Childishness): No.1 "Petit prélude à la journée"
5.121	No.2 "Berceuse"
5.122	No.3 "Marche du grand escalier"
5.123	III. "Peccadilles importunes" (Tiresome Peccadilloes): No.1 "Être jaloux de son camarde qui à une grosse tête"
5.124	No.2 "Lui manger sa tartine"
5.125	No.3 "Profiter de ce qu'il à des cors aux pieds pour lui prendre son cerceau"
5.126	"Trois nouvelles enfantines" (Three New Children's Pieces) (c1913): No.1 "Le Vilain petit vaurien" ....
5.127	No.2 "Berceuse"
5.128	No.3 "La Gentille toute petite fille"
5.129	"Les pantins dansent" (The Puppets are Dancing) (c1913; orchd1967; arr Laniau for 10-string gui 1983) ...
5.130	"Sports et divertissements" (Sports and Diversions) (c1914; p1924 w/ illustrations by Ch. Martin; Nos.1–7 arr Davidson for 3cl & bass cl 1975): No.1 "Choral inappétissant" (Unappetizing Choral) ....
5.131	No.2 "La balançoire" (The Seesaw)
5.132	No.3 "La chasse"
5.133	No.4 "La comédie italienne"
5.134	No.5 "Le réveil de la mariée" (The Bride's Awakening)
5.135	No.6 "Colin-Maillard"
5.136	No.7 "La pêche" (Fishing)
5.137	No.8 "Le yachting"
5.138	No.9 "Le bain de mer" (Sea Bathing)
5.139	No.10 "Le carnaval"
5.140	No.11 "Le golf"
5.141	No.12 "La pieuvre"
5.142	No.13 "Les courses" (The Races)
5.143	No.14 "Les quatres coins"
5.144	No.15 "Le pique-nique"
5.145	No.16 "Le water-chute"
5.146	No.17 "Le tango perpétuel"
5.147	No.18 "Le traîneau"
5.148	No.19 "Le flirt"
5.149	No.20 "Feu d'artifice"
5.150	No.21 "Le tennis"
5.151	"Heures séculaires et instantanées" (Age-old and Instantaneous Hours) (c1914): No.1 "Obstacles venimeux" (Venomous Obstacles) ....
5.152	No.2 "Crépuscule matinal; de midi" (Morning Twilight; Noon)
5.153	No.3 "Affolements granitiques" (Granitic Distractions)
5.154	"Les trois valses distinguées du précieux dégoûté" (Three Distinguished Waltzes of a Disgusted Dandy) (c1914): No.1 "Sa taille" (His Waist) ....
5.155	No.2 "Son binocle" (His Spectacles)
5.156	No.3 "Ses jambes" (His Legs)
5.157	"Avant-dernières pensées" (Next-to-last Thoughts) (c1915): No.1 "Idylle" ....
5.158	No.2 "Aubade"
5.159	No.3 "Méditation"
5.160	"Sonatine bureaucratique" (Bureaucratic Sonatina) (c1916–17, satiric paraphrase of M. Clementi's music)
5.161	"Nocturnes" (c1919): No.1 "Doux et calme" ....
5.162	No.2 "Simplement"
5.163	No.3 "Un peu mouvemente"
5.164	No.4 (w/ out title)
5.165	No.5 (w/ out title)
5.166	"Premier menuet" (c1920) ....
	Pf duet:
5.167	"Trois morceaux en forme de poire" (Three Pieces in the Shape of a Pear) (c1903; orchd1950): . "Manière de commencement" (A Manner of Commencement) ....
5.168	. "Prolongation de même" (A Prolongation of the Same)
5.169	No.1 "Lentement"
5.170	No.2 "Enlevé"
5.171	No.3 "Brutal"
5.172	. "En plus" (A Little More)
5.173	. "Redite" (Repetition)

5.174   "Aperçus désagréables" (Unpleasant Glimpses) (c1908–12): No.1 "Pastorale" (c1912) ....
5.175   No.2 "Choral" (c1908)
5.176   No.3 "Fugue" (c1908)
5.177   "En habit de cheval" (In Riding Habit) (c1911; orchd1912): No.1 "Chorale" ....
5.178   No.2 "Fugue litanique" (Litanical Fugue)
5.179   No.3 "Autre chorale"
5.180   No.4 "Fugue de papier" (Paper Fugue)

6. SACRED WORKS

6.1   "Messe des pauvres" (Mass for the Poor) (c1892?–5; pf/org & ch ad lib; orchd Diamond 1950):..................
      1. "Kyrie eleison"
      2. "Dixit Domine"
      3. "Prière des orgues" (Organ's Prayer)
      4. "Commune qui mundi nefas"
      5. "Chant ecclésiastique" (Ecclesiastical Chant)
      6. "Prière pour les voyageurs et les marins en danger de mort ..." (Prayer for travellers and
          sailors in danger of death, to the very good and august Virgin Mary, mother of Jesus)
      7. "Prière pour le salut de mon âme" (Prayer for the salvation of my soul)

7. SONGS (w/ pf)

7.1   "Trois mélodies de 1886" (c1886, Latour; orchd Caby 1968): 1. "Les anges" ....
7.2   2. "Élégie"
7.3   3. "Sylvie"
7.4   "Les fleurs" (c1886, Latour; orchd Caby 1968) ....
7.5   "Chanson" (c1887, Latour) ....
7.6   "Je te veux" (I Want You), café-concert song (c1897, Pacory; arr by others for insts)...............................
7.7   "L'omnibus automobile" (ca1900–6, Hyspa)
7.8   "Un dîner à l'Élysée" (A Dinner at the Élysée) (ca1900, Hyspa) ....
7.9   "Le veuf" (The Widower) (c1900–2, Hyspa, unpubd; version used in: Trois morceaux en forme de poire) ...
7.10   *"Légende californienne" (ca1900, Latour, words lost)* ....
7.11   *"Imperial-Oxford" (ca1900–5, Latour, words lost)* ....
7.12   "Tendrement" (Tenderly), valse chantée (ca1902, Hyspa; arr as: Illusion for orch 1979) ....
7.13   "La diva de l'Empire," café-concert song (c1904, Bonnaud & Bles, from revue: Devidons la bobine) ....
7.14   "Trois mélodies sans paroles" (ca1905; 1v & pf): 1. "Rambouillet" ....
7.15   2. "Les oiseaux"
7.16   3. "Marienbad"
7.17   "Chez le docteur" (At the Doctor's) (ca1905–6, Hyspa)...
7.18   "Allons-y chochotte," café-concert song (c1905–6, Durante) ....
7.19   "Chanson médiévale" (Medieval Song) (c1906, Mendès; orchd Caby 1968)..
7.20   "Trois poèmes d'amour" (Three Love Poems) (c1914, Satie): 1. "Ne suis que grain de sable" (Am Only
      a Grain of Sand)
7.21   2. "Suis chauve de naissance" (Am Bald from Birth)
7.22   3. "Ta parure est secrète" (Your Attire is Discreet)
7.23   "Trois mélodies" (c1916; orchd Caby 1968): 1. "La statue de bronze" (The Bronze Statue): "La grenouille
      du jeu de tonneau" (Fargue) ....
7.24   2. "Daphénéo": "Dis-moi, Daphénéo, quel est donc cet arbre dont les fruits" (Godebska)
7.25   3. "Le chapelier" (The Hatter): "Le chapelier s'étonne" (Chalput after Lewis Carroll's Alice in
      Wonderland)
7.26   "Quatre petites mélodies" (c1920): 1. "Élégie" (Lamartine) ....
7.27   2. "Danseuse" (Cocteau)
7.28   3. "Chanson" (anon 18th cent)
7.29   4. "Adieu" (Radiguet)
7.30   "Ludions" (Bottle Imps) (c1923, Fargue): 1. "Air du rat" (Rat's Tune) ....
7.31   2. "Spleen"
7.32   3. "La grenouille américaine" (The American Frog)
7.33   4. "Air du poète" (Poet's Tune)
7.34   5. "Chanson du chat" (Cat's Song)

8. ARRANGEMENTS OF WORKS BY OTHERS

8.1   Verley: "Pastels sonores" (arr for ?pf): No.1 "Cloches dans la vallée" ....
8.2   No.2 "L'aurore aux doigts de rose" (transcr1916; pf duet; orchd, unpubd)

* * * * *

1. STAGE WORKS

Operas (3 acts):

1.1 "Gli equivoci nel sembiante" (L'errore innocente, L'amor non vuol inganni) (opera I) (p1679, Contini) ....
1.2 "L'onestà negli amori," dramma (p1680, Parnasso) ....
1.3 "Tutto il mal non vien per nuocère" (Dal male il bene), commedia (p1681, Totis) ....
1.4 *"Il Lisimaco," dramma (p1681, Sinibaldi, ?spur)* ....
1.5 "Il Pompeo," dramma (p1683, Minato) ....
1.6 "L'Aldimiro o vero Favore per favore," dramma (p1683, Totis) ....
1.7 "La Psiche o vero Amore innamorato," commedia (p1683, Totis, inc) ....
1.8 *"Il Fetonte," dramma (p1685, Totis, ?spur)* ....
1.9 "Olimpia vendicata," dramma (p1685, Aureli) ....
1.10 *"L'Etio," dramma (p1686, Morselli, frags, ?spur)* ....
1.11 "Rosmene o vero L'infedeltà fedele," melodramma (p1686, Totis) ....
1.12 "Clearco in Negroponte," dramma (p1686, Arcoleo) ....
1.13 "La santa Dinna," commedia (p1686, Pamphilj, collab w/ others: Act III c by Scarlatti) ....
1.14 "Il Flavio," dramma (p1688, Noris) ....
1.15 "L'Anacreonte tiranno," melodramma (p1689, Bussani, inc) ....
1.16 *"La Serva favorita," dramma (p1689, Villifranchi, ?spur)* ....
1.17 "L'Amazone corsara o vero L'Alvida," dramma (p1689, Corradi) ....
1.18 "La Statira," dramma (p1690, Ottoboni) ....
1.19 "La Rosaura" (Gli equivoci in amore o vero La Rosaura), melodramma (p1690, Lucini) ......
1.20 *"L'umanità nelle fiere ovvero Il Lucullo," dramma (p1691, music lost)* ....
1.21 "La Teodora Augusta," dramma (p1692, Morselli) ....
1.22 "Gerone tiranno di Siracusa," dramma (p1692, Aureli) ....
1.23 *"L'Amante doppio o vero Il Ceccobimbi," melodramma (p1693, music lost)* ....
1.24 "Il Pirro e Demetrio" (La forza della fedeltà), dramma (p1694, Morselli) ....
1.25 "Il Bassiano o vero Il maggior impossibile," melodramma (p1694, Noris) ....
1.26 "La santa Genuinda," dramma sacro (p1694, Pamphilj, collab w/ others: Act II c by Scarlatti) ......
1.27 "Le nozze con l'inimico ovvero L'Analinda," melodramma (p1695) ....
1.28 "Nerone fatto Cesare," melodramma (p1695, Noris, inc) ....
1.29 "Massimo Puppieno," melodramma (p1695, Aureli) ....
1.30 "Penelope la casta" (opera LX), dramma (p1696, Noris) ....
1.31 "Il Flavio Cuniberto," dramma (p1696, Noris) ....
1.32 "La Didone delirante," opera drammatica (p1696, Paglia after Franceschi) ....
1.33 *"Comodo Antonino," dramma (p1696, Paglia after Bussani, ?spur)* ....
1.34 "L'Emireno o vero Il consiglio dell'ombra," opera drammatica" (p1697, Paglia) ....
1.35 "La caduta de' Decemviri," dramma (p1697, Stampiglia) ....
1.36 *"Mutio Scevola," dramma (p1698, ?spur)* ....
1.37 "La donna ancora è fedele," dramma (p1698, Contini) ....
1.38 "Il prigioniero fortunato," dramma (p1698, Paglia) ....
1.39 "Gl'inganni felici" (L'Agarista), dramma (p1699, Zeno) ....
1.40 "L'Eraclea," dramma (p1700, Stampiglia, inc) ....
1.41 "Odoardo," dramma with intermezzi: Adolfo e Lesbina (p1700, Zeno, inc) ....
1.42 "Dafni" (L'amore non viene dal caso), favola boschereccia (p1700, Paglia after Manfredi) ......
1.43 "Laodicea e Berenice," dramma (p1701, adapted by Noris) ....
1.44 "Il pastore di Corinto," favola boschereccia (p1701, Paglia) ....
1.45 "Tito Sempronio Gracco," dramma with intermezzi: Bireno e Dorilla (p1702, Stampiglia, inc) ......
1.46 "Tiberio imperatore d'Oriente," dramma (p1702, Pallavicino, inc) ....
1.47 "Arminio," dramma (p1703, Salvi, inc) ....
1.48 "Turno Aricino," dramma (p1704, Salvi, inc) ....
1.49 "Lucio Manlio, L'imperioso" (opera LXXXVIII) (p1705, Stampiglia) ....
1.50 *"Il Gran Tamerlano" (opera XC), dramma (p1706, Salvi after Pradon, music lost)* ....
1.51 "Il Mitridate Eupatore," 5 act tragedia (p1707, Frigimelica Roberti) ....
1.52 "Il trionfo della libertà," 5 act tragedia (p1707, Frigimelica Roberti) ....
1.53 "Il figlio delle Selve" (p1708, Capeci) ....
1.54 *"Teodosio," dramma (p1709, ?Grimani, music lost)* ....
1.55 "L'amor volubile e tiranno" (La Dorisbe), dramma (p1709, Pioli & Papis) ....
1.56 "La principessa fedele," dramma (p1710, Piovene) ....
1.57 "La fede riconosciuta" (opera C), dramma pastorale (p1710, ?Marcello) ....
1.58 "Giunio Bruto" (La caduta dei Tarquini), dramma (p1712, ?Sinibaldi, collab w/ others: Act III c by Scarlatti) ......
1.59 "Il Ciro," dramma (p1712, Ottoboni) ....
1.60 "Scipione nelle Spagne," dramma with intermezzi: Pericca e Varrone (p1714, Zeno & Serino) ......
1.61 "L'amor generoso," dramma with intermezzi: Despina e Niso (p1714, Papis & Stampiglia) ......
1.62 "Il Tigrane o vero L'egual impegno d'amore e di fede" (opera CVI), dramma (p1715, Lalli) ......
1.63 "Carlo re d'Allemagna," dramma with intermezzi: Palandrana e Zamberlucco (p1716, Silvani) ......
1.64 "La virtù trionfante dell'odio e dell'amore," dramma (p1716, Silvani) ....
1.65 "Telemaco" (opera CIX), dramma (p1718, Capece) ....
1.66 "Il trionfo dell'onore" (opera CX), commedia (p1718, Tullio) ....
1.67 "Il Cambise" (opera CXI), dramma (p1719, Lalli) ....
1.68 "Marco Attilo Regolo" (opera CXII), dramma with intermezzi: Leonzio e Eurilla (p1719) ......
1.69 "La Griselda" (opera CXIV), dramma (p1721, after Zeno) ....

Intermezzi:

1.70   "Pericca e Varrone," scene buffe for opera: Scipione nelle Spagne (p1714, Salvi, later p as: La Dama spagnola e il Cavalier romano) ....
1.71   "Vespetta e Milo," intermezzi I & II for Lotti's opera: Giove in Argo (p1717; intermezzo III c by Conti) ....

Collaborations:

1.72   *"La Santa Dinna," 3 act commedia (p1687, Pamphilj, lost):* ....
        I. (c by Melani)
        II. (c by Pasquini)
        III. (c by A. Scarlatti)
1.73   "La Santa Genuinda, o vero L'innocenza difesa dall'inganno," 3 act dramma sacro (p1694; Pamphilj): ....
        I. (c by Lulier)
        II. (c by A. Scarlatti)
        III. (c by Cesarini or Pollaroli)
1.74   "Giunio Bruto o vero La caduta dei Tarquini," 3 act dramma (p ?1709, Sinibaldi) ....
        I. (c by Cesarini)
        II. (c by Caldara)
        III. (c by A. Scarlatti)

Operas c by others w/ contributions by Scarlatti:

1.75   Pasquini: "L'Idalma o vero Chi la dura la vince," dramma (p1682, Totis, reworked Act I) ....
1.76   Legrenzi: "Il Giustino," dramma (p1684, Beregan, contributed prologue) ....
1.77   Cesti: "La Dori," dramma (p1689, Apolloni, added prologue & arias) ....
1.78   Varischino: "L'Odoacre," dramma (p1694, Bonis, contributed arias) ....
1.79   Valtolina & others: "L'Arione," dramma (p1694, Arles, contributed aria: Mio povero core) ....
1.80   Lonati: "L'Aiace," dramma (p1697, d'Averara, added 38 arias & 1 duet) ....
1.81   Pollaroli: "Tito Manlio" (p1698, Noris, revisions & additions) ....
1.82   Bani: "Il figlio delle Selve," dramma (p1698, Capeci, added arias) ....
1.83   Pollaroli & others: "La forza della Virtù" (Creonte), dramma (p before 1699, Noris, added arias) ....
1.84   Perti, Magni & Ballarotti: "L'Ariovisto," dramma (p1702, Vangelisti, added arias) ....
1.85   Cesarini, Lulier & Giovanni: "La pastorella" (Love's Triumph), opera pastorale (p1705, added arias) ....
1.86   "Thomyris Queen of Scythia," pasticcio (p1707, Motteux, incl arias) ....
1.87   Conti: "La Clotilda," dramma (p1709, incl arias) ....
1.88   Scarlatti, Francesco: "Lo Petrachio scremmetore," opera comica (p1711, Capis, incl arias) ....
1.89   Lotti: "Il Porsenna," dramma (p1713, Piovene, added arias) ....

1a. SELECTIONS FROM STAGE WORKS (Nos. of sections in The Gramophone)

1a.5   "Il Pompeo," opera: ....
        excerpts: 1. "O cessate di piagarmi"
                  2. "Toglietemi la vita ancor"
                  3. "Già il sole dal Gange"

1a.37 "La donna ancora è fedele," opera: ....
        excerpts: 1. "Son tutta duolo"
                  2. "Se Florindo è fedele"

1a.69 "La Griselda," opera: ....
        excerpts: 1. "In voler ciò che tu brami"
                  2. "Nell'aspro mio dolor"
                  3. "Mi rivedi, o selva ombrosa"
                  4. "Figlio! Tiranno!"
                  5. "Finirá, barbara sorte"

2. ORCHESTRAL WORKS

2.1   "12 Sinfonie di concerto grosso" (c from 1715, 2vn, va, vc, fl & cont): No.1 in F major (+ 2nd fl) ....
2.2   No.2 in D major (+ tpt)
2.3   No.3 in D minor
2.4   No.4 in E minor (+ ob/vn)
2.5   No.5 in D minor (+ 2nd fl)
2.6   No.6 in A minor
2.7   No.7 in G minor
2.8   No.8 in G major
2.9   No.9 in G minor
2.10   No.10 in A minor
2.11   No.11 in C major
2.12   No.12 in C minor, "La Geniale"
2.13   "6 Concerti Grossi" (p ca1740; concertino: 2 solo vn, vc & ripieno: 2vn, va, cont): No.1 in F minor ....
2.14   No.2 in C minor

2.15	No.3 in F major
2.16	No.4 in G minor
2.17	No.5 in D minor
2.18	No.6 in E major

3. KEYBOARD CONCERTOS

3.1	*"6 Concertos for Keyboard and Orchestra" (?spur): No.1 in C major* ....
3.2	*No.2 in A major*
3.3	*No.3 in E minor*
3.4	*No.4 in C minor*
3.5	*No.5 in G major*
3.6	*No.6 in E-flat major*

4. STRING QUARTETS

4.1	"Quattro sonate a quattro" (2vn, va & vc): No.1 in F minor ....
4.2	No.2 in C minor
4.3	No.3 in G minor
4.4	No.4 in D minor

5. OTHER CHAMBER MUSIC

5.1	"Sette sonate per flauto e archi" (c1725; fl, 2vn, vc & cont): No.1 in D major ....
5.2	No.2 in A minor
5.3	No.3 in C minor
5.4	No.4 in A minor
5.5	No.5 in A major
5.6	No.6 in C major
5.7	No.7 in G minor
5.8	"Sonata," in F major (fl, 2vn & cont) ....
5.9	*"Sonata," in D major (fl, 2vn & cont, ?spur)* ....
5.10	"Sonata," in A major (2fl, 2vn & cont) ....
5.11	"Sonata," in F major (3fl & cont) ....
5.12	"Suite," in F major (c1699; fl & cont) ....
5.13	"Suite," in G major (c1799; fl & cont) ....

6. KEYBOARD

6.1	"Toccate per cembalo" ....
6.2	"Dieci partite sopra Basso obbligato" (c1716) ....
6.3	"Primo e Secondo Libro di Toccate": No.1 in G major ....
6.4	No.2 in A minor
6.5	No.3 in G major
6.6	No.4 in A minor
6.7	No.5 in G major
6.8	No.6 in D minor
6.9	No.7 in D minor
6.10	No.8 in A minor
6.11	No.9 in G major
6.12	No.10 in F major
6.13	"Due Sinfonie per cembalo" (c1699) ....
6.14	"Toccata per studio di cembalo" (c1716) ....
6.15	"Toccata d'intavolatura per Cembalo ò pure per organo d'ottava stesa" (c1729) ....
6.16	"Tre Toccate, ognuna seguita da Fuga e Minuetto" (p1716) ....
6.17	"Variations on 'La Follia' " (c1715) ....
6.18	"Toccate e altre composizioni per cembalo" ....

7. MASSES, MASS SECTIONS

7.1	"Missa Clementina" I (c1705; ch) ....
7.2	"Messa a quattro voci" (c1706; ch, for Cardinal Ottoboni) ....
7.3	"Messa per il natale di Nostro Signore Gesù Cristo" (c1707; 2ch, 2vn & cont) ....
7.4	"Missa Clementina" II (c1716; ch) ....
7.5	"Missa pro defunctis" (Requiem) (c1717; ch) ....
7.6	"Messa di Santa Cecilia," in A major (c1720; 2S, A, T, B, ch, 2vn, va & cont; ed Steele 1968) ....
7.7	"Missa ad usum Cappellae Pontificiae" (c1721; ch, for Innocent XIII) ....
7.8	"Missa ad canonem" (ch) ....
7.9	"Mass in E minor, in IV. tono" (ch & org) ....
7.10	"Messa tutta in canone di diverse specie" (ch) ....

7.11	"Credo," in B-flat major (S, A, T, B, ch, 2ob, 2hn, strings & org, ?spur) ....
7.12	"Credo breve" (ch, 2vn & cont, ?spur) ....
7.13	"Gloria a 4 voci" (ch, 2vn, va, 2ob, 2hn & cont, ?spur) ....

8. ORATORIOS & LARGE SACRED CANTATAS

8.1	?Latin oratorio (p1679) ....
8.2	?Latin oratorio (p1680) ....
8.3	"St John Passion" (ca1680, Bible; A, B, ch, strings & cont)...
8.4	?Latin oratorio (p1682) ....
8.5	"Agar et Ismaele esiliati" (Il sacrificio di Abramo) (p1683, Totis; 3S, A, B, strings & cont) ....
8.6	"Santa Maria Maddalena" (La conversione di S. Maria Maddalena) (p1685, Pamphilj; 2S, A, strings & cont)
8.7	"Il martirio di Santa Teodosia" (p1685; S, A, T, B, strings & cont) ....
8.8	"I dolori di Maria sempre Vergine" (La Concettione della Beata Vergine) (p1693; S, A, T, B, strings & cont)
8.9	"La Giuditta" I (p1693, Pamphilj; 2S, A, T, B, strings, tpt, trbns, 2fl & cont).............................
8.10	"Samson vindicatus" (Latin oratorio) (p1695, Pamphilj, lost) ....
8.11	"Cantata per la notte di Natale" (p1695, ?Ottoboni, lost) ....
8.12	"Il martirio di Sant' Orsola" (ca1695–1700; 2S, A, T, B, strings, tpt, lute & cont)........................
8.13	"Davidis pugna et victoria" (Latin oratorio) (p1700; 2S, A, T, B, 2ch, strings & cont) ....
8.14	"La Giuditta" II (p1700, Ottoboni; S, A, T, strings & cont) ....
8.15	"L'Assunzione della Beata Vergine Maria" (p1703, Ottoboni; 2S, 2A, strings & cont) ....
8.16	"Sancti Michaelis Arcangelis cum Lucifer pugna et victoria" (Latin oratorio) (p1705, ?Pullioni, lost) ....
8.17	"San Casimiro, re di Polonia" (p1705; 3S, A, T, strings & cont) ....
8.18	"Santa Maria Maddalena de' pazzi" (p1705, Pamphilj, music lost)..
8.19	"San Filippo Neri" (p1705; S, 2A, T, strings, tpt, lute & cont) ....
8.20	"Tirsi e Fileno": "Qual di lieti concenti" (Christmas cantata) (p ca1705) ....
8.21	"Il Sedecia, re di Gerusalemme" (p1705, Fabbri; 2S, A, T, B, ch, strings, 2ob, 2tpt, timp, lute & cont)..........
8.22	"Abramo il tuo sembiante" (Christmas cantata) (p1705; 2S, A, T, B, ch, strings, 2ob & cont) ....
8.23	"San Francesco di Paola " (p1706, ed1745) ....
8.24	"Humanità e Lucifero" (p ?1706; S, T, strings, tpt, piccolo & cont) ....
8.25	"Il trionfo della Ss Vergine assunta in cielo" (p1706, Ottoboni; 2S, 2A, strings, fl, 2ob, tpt, lute & cont) ......
8.26	"Il martirio di Santa Susanna" (p1706, Stampiglia, music lost) ....
8.27	"Alcone, ove per queste" (Christmas cantata) (p1706, Fabbri; ch & ?insts, music lost) ....
8.28	"Cain overo il primo omicidio" (p1707; 2S, 2A, T, B, strings & cont) ....
8.29	"Il giardino di rose: La Ss Vergine del Rosario" (p1707; 2S, A, T, B, strings, 2tpt, 2fl, 2ob, bn, lute & cont) ..
8.30	"Serafini al nostro canto" (Christmas cantata) (p1707, Mirandolano; ch & ?insts) ....
8.31	"Il martirio di Santa Cecilia" (p1708, music lost) ....
8.32	"Oratorio per la Passione di Nostro Signore Gesù Cristo": "Fosco orrore il tutto ingombra" (p1708, Ottoboni; 2S, A, strings, 4tpt, trbn, timp & cont) ....
8.33	"La vittoria della fede" (p1708, Capeci, music lost) ....
8.34	"Il trionfo del valore" (p1709; 5vv & ?insts, lost) ....
8.35	"La Giuditta 'di Cambridge' " (ca1705–10; 3vv & insts) ....
8.36	"La Santissima Annunziata" (ca1710; 3S, A, T, strings & cont)...
8.37	"La Santissima Trinità" (p1715) ....
8.38	"La Vergine addolorata" (p1717; 2S, A, T, strings, fl, ob, tpt & cont) ....
8.39	"La gloriosa gara tra la Santità e la Sapienza" (Cantata spirituale) (p1720; 3vv) ....

Arias in pasticcio oratorios:

8.40	"I trionfi di Giosuè" (Giosue in Gabaon) (p1703, Berzini) ....
8.41	"Sara in Egitto" (p1708, Canavese) ....

9. MOTETS, PSALMS, HYMNS & OTHER SACRED

9.1	"Ad amantem cordis," motet (S, 2vn & cont) ....
9.2	"Ad Dominum dum tribularer," motet (c ?1708; ch) ....
9.3	"Adorna thalamum tuum Sion," antiphon (c1708; ch).....................................
9.4	"Ad te Domine levavi," motet (c ?1708; ch) ....
9.5	"Audi filia, et inclina aurem," gradual (c1720; ch, ob, 2vn, va & org; ed Steele 1968) ....
9.6	"Ave Maris stella," hymn (ch & cont) ....
9.7	"Ave Regina coelorum," motet (2S & cont) ....
9.8	"Beatus Vir qui timet Dominum" (Psalm 111; ch & org) ....
9.9	"Benedicta et venerabilis es," graduale (c1720; S, ch, 2vn, va & cont) ....
9.10	"Cantantibus organis Cecilia," antiphon (c1720; S, ob, 2vn, va & cont) ....
9.11	"Caro mea requiescet," antiphon (c1707; ch & org) ....
9.12	"Confitebor tibi Domine" (Psalm 110; ch & org) ....
9.13	"Constitues eos principes," gradual (c1716; ch & org) ....
9.14	"Date sonum, date cantum," motet (c1705; S & cont) ....
9.15	"De tenebroso lacu" (A, 2vn, va & cont) ....
9.16	"Dextera Domini fecit virtutem," offertory (c1715; ch & org) ....
9.17	"Diffusa est gratia," gradual (2S & org) ....
9.18	"Diligam te" (ch, 2vn & cont; = 7. of: Concerti sacri p1702) ....
9.19	"Dixit Dominus" I (Psalm 109; ch & org) ....

9.20	"Dixit Dominus" II (Psalm 109; ch, ob, 2vn, va & cont) ....
9.21	"Dixit Dominus" III (Psalm 109; ch & org) ....
9.22	"Dixit Dominus" IV (S, A, T, B, ch, 3vn & cont) ....
9.23	"Domine in auxilium meum," motet offertory (c ?1708; ch) ....
9.24	"Domine refugium factus es nobis," gradual (ch) ....
9.25	"Domine vivifica me," motet (c ?1708; ch) ....
9.26	"Egli è ver che mi consolo," motet (c1705; A & cont) ....
9.27	"Est dies trophei" (ch, 2vn & cont; = 9. of: Concerti sacri p1702) ....
9.28	"Exaltabo te Domine quoniam," motet (c ?1708; ch) ....
9.29	"Exultate Deo adjutori nostro" (Psalm 130; ch) ....
9.30	"Exurge Domine non prevaleat," motet gradual (c ?1708; ch).......................................
9.31	"Infirmata, vulnerata" (c1702; A, 2vn & cont; = 3. of: Concerti sacri p1702) ....
9.32	"In hoc mundo inconstante," motet (c1705; S, 2vn & cont) ....
9.33	"Inni e Improperi per la Missa Praesanctificatorum della Parasceve" (c ?1708; S, A, ch, 2vn
9.34	& cont): 1. "Vexilla regis prodeunt," hymn (even-numbered verses) (ch, 2vn & cont) ....
9.35	2. "Popule meus" (S, A, ch, 2vn & cont)
9.36	3. "Crux fidelis—Pange lingua gloriosi" (ch, 2vn & cont)
9.37	4. "Vexilla regis prodeunt," hymn (odd-numbered verses) (ch, 2vn & cont)
9.38	"Intellige clamorem meum," motet (c ?1708; ch) ....
9.39	"Iste est panis," motet (ch, inc) ....
9.40	"Jam sole clarior" (S, 2vn & cont; = 2. of: Concerti sacri p1702) ....
9.41	"Jesu corona Virginum," hymn (c1720; S, A, T, ch, 2vn, va & cont) ....
9.42	"Justitiae Domini rectae," motet (c ?1708; ch) ....
9.43	"Laetatus sum" I (Psalm 121; ch) ....
9.44	"Laetatus sum" II (Psalm 121; ch, inc) ....
9.45	"Laetatus sum" III (c1688, Psalm 121; ch, 2vn & cont) ....
9.46	"Laetatus sum" IV (c1721, Psalm 121; ch, 2vn, va & cont) ....
9.47	"Lamentazioni per la Settimana Santa" (c1706): 1. "Incipit lamentatio Jeremiae" (S, 2vn, va & cont) ....
9.48	2. "Jod-Manum suam misit hostis" (S, 2vn, va & cont)
9.49	3. "De lamentatione Jeremiae Prophetae" (S, 2vn, va & cont)
9.50	4. "Lamed-Matribus suis dixerunt" (S, 2vn, va & cont)
9.51	5. "De lamentatione Jeremiae Prophetae" (S, 2vn & cont)
9.52	6. "Aleph-Quomodo obscuratum est" (T, 2vn & cont)
9.53	"Lauda Jerusalem Dominum," offertory (ch & org) ....
9.54	"Laudate Dominum omnes gentes" (Psalm 116; ch, 2vn, 2va, vc & cont) ....
9.55	"Laudate Dominum quia benignus," offertory (ch & org) ....
9.56	"Laudate pueri Dominum" I, gradual (ch & cont) ....
9.57	"Laudate pueri Dominum" II (Psalm 112; S, ch, 2vn & cont, inc)...................................
9.58	"Magnificat" I (primo tono), offertory (ch & org) ....
9.59	"Magnificat" II, offertory in D major (ch & insts) ....
9.60	"Memento, Domine David" (Psalm 131; ch) ....
9.61	"Miserere mei Deus, miserere," motet (ch)...
9.62	"Miserere mei Deus, secundum" I (c1680, Psalm 50; d ch) ....
9.63	"Miserere mei Deus, secundum" II, in E minor (c1705, Psalm 50; S, ch, 2vn, va & cont) ....
9.64	"Miserere mei Deus, secundum" III, in C minor (c ?1715, Psalm 50; S, ch, 2vn, va & cont) ....
9.65	*"Miserere mei Deus, secundum" IV, in A minor (c1721; ch & cont, ?spur)*...............................
9.66	"Mortales non auditis" (S, A, 2vn & cont; = 5. of: Concerti sacri p1702) ....
9.67	"Nisi Dominus aedificaverit" I (Psalm 126; S, A, ch, 2vn & cont) ....
9.68	"Nisi Dominus aedificaverit" II (Psalm 126; ch & org) ....
9.69	"O magnum mysterium," motet (c1707; d ch) ....
9.70	"Properate fideles" (ch, 2vn & cont; = 8. of: Concerti sacri p1702) ....
9.71	"Quae est ista" (ch, 2vn & cont; = 6. of: Concerti sacri p1702) ....
9.72	"Responsori per la Settimana Santa" (c ?1708; S, A, T, B, ch & cont): 1. "Aestimatus sum" ....
9.73	2. "Amicus meus"
9.74	3. "Animam meam dilectam"
9.75	4. "Astiterunt reges terrae"
9.76	5. "Caligaverunt oculi mei"
9.77	6. "Ecce quomodo moritur"
9.78	7. "Ecce vidimus eum"
9.79	8. "Eram quasi agnus"
9.80	9. "Jerusalem surge"
9.81	10. "In Monte Oliveti"
9.82	11. "Jesum tradidit impius"
9.83	12. "Judas mercator pessimus"
9.84	13. "Omnes amici mei"
9.85	14. "O vos omnes"
9.86	15. "Plange quasi virgo"
9.87	16. "Recessit pastor noster"
9.88	17. "Seniores populi"
9.89	18. "Sepulto Domino"
9.90	19. "Sicut ovis"
9.91	20. "Tamquam ad latronem"
9.92	21. "Tenebrae factae sunt"
9.93	22. "Tradiderunt me"
9.94	23. "Tristis est anima mea"

9.95	24. "Una hora"
9.96	25. "Unus ex discipulis"
9.97	26. "Velum templi"
9.98	27. "Vinea mea electa"
9.99	"Rorate coeli dulcem" (S, 2vn & cont; = 1. of: Concerti sacri p1702) ....
9.100	"Sacerdotes Domini incensum et panes," offertorio (ch & org) ....
9.101	"Salve regina" I, antiphon (ch, 2vn & cont; = 10. of: Concerti sacri p1702) ....
9.102	"Salve regina" II, antiphon (c1703; ch) ....
9.103	"Salve regina" III, antiphon (S, 3vn & cont) ....
9.104	"Salve regina" IV (ch, 2vn & cont) ....
9.105	"Salve regina" V (S, 2vn, va & cont) ....
9.106	"Salvum fac populum tuum," motet (c ?1708; ch) ....
9.107	"Sancti et justi in Domino gaudete," motet (d ch, inc) ....
9.108	"Spirate, aure, spirate," motet (A, 2vn & cont) ....
9.109	"Stabat Mater," hymn (ch, 2vn & cont) ....
9.110	"Super solium gemmis ornatum," motet (S, 2vn & cont) ....
9.111	"Te Deum" (ch, 2ob, 2vn, va & cont) ....
9.112	"Totus amore languens" (A, 2vn & cont; = 4. of: Concerti sacri p1702) ....
9.113	"Tu es Petrus" (d ch & org) ....
9.114	"Tui sunt caeli et terra" (ch & org) ....
9.115	"Unam petii a Domino," motet (c ?1708; ch) ....
9.116	"Valerianus in cubiculo. Caeciliam," antiphon (A, ob, 2vn, va & cont) ....
9.117	*"Veritas mea et misericordia" (ch, ?spur)* ....
9.118	"Vexilla regis prodeunt," hymn (ch, 2vn & cont) ....
9.119	"Volo Pater ut ubi ego sum," antiphon (d ch & org) ....

10. MADRIGALS (ch)

10.1	"Arsi un tempo e l'ardore" ....
10.2	"Cor mio, deh!, non languire" (Tasso) ....
10.3	"Intenerite voi, lacrime mie" (Rinuccini) ....
10.4	"Mori, mi dici" ....
10.5	"O morte, a gli altri fosca, a me serena" ....
10.6	"Or che da te, mio bene" ....
10.7	"O selce, o tigre, o ninfa" ....
10.8	"Sdegno la fiamma estinse" ....

11. SERENATAS (w/ insts)

11.1	"Diana ed Endimione": "Voi solitarie piante" (p ca1680–5; 2vv) ....
11.2	*"Serenata in honour of James II of England" (p1688, lost)* ....
11.3	"Il genio di Partenope, la gloria del Sebeto, il piacere di Mergellina": "Venticelli soavi che con ali" (p1696)..
11.4	"Venere, Adone ed Amore": "Dal giardin del piacere" (c1696, r1706, Paglia; 3vv) ....
11.5	*"Il trionfo delle stagioni" (p1696, Paglia, lost)* ....
11.6	"Venere ed Amore": "Del mar Tirreno in su l'amena sponda" (p ca1695–1700; 2vv) ....
11.7	"Clori, Lidia e Filli": "Già compito il suo giro" (p ca1700; 3vv) ....
11.8	"Clori, Dorino ed Amore": "Cari lidi, amene sponde" (p1702; 3vv) ....
11.9	"Venere e Adone: Il giardino d'Amore": "Care selve, amati orrori" (p ca1700–5; 2vv) ....
11.10	"Endimione e Cintia": "Sento un'aura che dolce" (p1705; 2vv) ....
11.11	"Amore e virtù ossia Il trionfo della virtù": "No, che non voglio più" (p1706; 2vv) ....
11.12	"Clori e Zeffiro": "Vaga, auretta soave" (p1706; 2vv) ....
11.13	"Fileno, Niso e Doralbo: Serenata a Filli": "Tacete, aure, tacete" (p1706; 3vv) ....
11.14	"Sole, Urania e Clio. Le muse Urania e Clio lodano le bellezze di Filli": "O mie figlie canore" (p1706; 3vv) ..
11.15	"Venere, Amore e Ragione. Il ballo delle Ninfe": "Cerco Amore, Amor che fa?" (p1706, Stampiglia; 3vv) ....
11.16	"Cupido e Onestà. Il trionfo dell'Onestà": "Puote si poco!" (p1706; 2vv) ....
11.17	*"Le glorie della bellezza del Corpo e dell'Anima" (p1709, Papis; 4vv, for Queen Elisabeth of Spain, lost)* ....
11.18	"Pace, Amore e Provvidenza": "Al fragor di lieta tromba" (p1711, Papis; 3vv, 4ch) ....
11.19	*"Il genio austriaco" (p1712, lost)* ....
11.20	*"Il genio austriaco, Zefiro, Flora, il Sole, Partenope e il Sebeto" (p1713, Papis, lost)* ....
11.21	*"Serenata in honour of the vicereine, Donna Barbara d'Erbenstein" (p1715, lost)* ....
11.22	"La gloria di Primavera. Primavera, Estate, Autunno, Inverno e Giove": "Nato è già l'Austriaco Sole" (p1716, Giovo; 5vv, ch) ....
11.23	"Partenope, Teti, Nettuno, Proteo e Glauco": "Chi al vasto ondoso" (p1716) ....
11.24	"Filli, Clori e Tirsi": "Dalle fiorite arene" (p ?1718) ....
11.25	"La virtù negli amori. La Notte, il Sole, Lanso, Lisa, Toante e Agave": "Dolce sonno, oblo dei mali," 2 act pastorale (p1721, Lamer) ....
11.26	"Erminia, Tancredi, Polidoro e Pastore": "Ove smarrita e sola" (p1723; 4vv) ....

12. CHAMBER CANTATAS (incl cantatas of uncertain authorship)

12.1	"A battaglia, pensieri, a battaglia" (c1699; S, A, 2vn, vc, d bass, tpt, mandola & cont, uncertain) ....
12.2	"Abbandonar Fileno dovea" (S/A & cont) ....

12.153	"Correa nel seno amato" (c before 1694; S, 2vn & cont) ....
12.154	"Cruda Filli spietata" (S & cont) ....
12.155	*"Crudelissimo amore" (A & cont, ?spur: c by ?Albinoni)* ....
12.156	*"Crudel, mira quest'occhi" (S & cont, ?spur)* ....
12.157	"Crudel, perché privarmi?" (2S & cont) ....
12.158	"Crudo Amor, che vuoi da me?" (S & cont) ....
12.159	"Crudo Amor, empie stelle, iniqua sorte" (c before 1702; S & cont) ....
12.160	"Crudo Amor, empie stelle, Irene ingrata" (S & cont) ....
12.161	"Crudo Amor, saper vorrei" (S & cont) ....
12.162	"Da che Tirsi mirai" (S & cont) ....
12.163	"Dagli strali d'Amore vivea lieto" (c1701; S & cont) ....
12.164	*"Da l'arco d'un bel ciglio" (A & cont, ?spur: pubd1702 in Albinoni's Op.4)* ......
12.165	"Dal bel volto d'Irene" (c1705; S & cont) ....
12.166	"Dal colle al pian discesa" (S & cont) ....
12.167	*"Dal crudele Daliso" (S & cont, ?spur: pubd1682 in Basani's Op.3)* ....
12.168	"Dal dì ch'Amor m'accese" (S & cont) ....
12.169	"Dal dì che l'empio Fato" (S & cont) ....
12.170	*"Dal giorno fortunato ch'io vidi" (Paglia; S & cont, ?spur)* ....
12.171	"Dal grato mormorio" (S & cont) ....
12.172	*"Dalisa, e come mai?" (A & cont, ?spur)* ....
12.173	"Dalla fida compagna abbandonata" (S & cont) ....
12.174	"Dalla nativa sfera scese" (c1704; S & cont) ....
12.175	"Dalla speme deluso" (Paglia; S & cont) ....
12.176	"Dalle pene amorose" (S & cont, uncertain) ....
12.177	"Dalle tirrene sponde partì Filli" (S & cont, uncertain) ....
12.178	"Dall'oscura magion dell'arsa Dite" (L'Orfeo) (S, 2vn & cont) ....
12.179	"Dammi, Amore, un altro cor" (S & cont) ....
12.180	"Da qual parte celeste" (c1701; S & cont) ....
12.181	"Da quel dì che Mitilde" (S & cont) ....
12.182	"Da quell'hora fatale" I (S & cont) ....
12.183	"Da quell'hora fatale" II (c1716; S & cont) ....
12.184	"Da sventura a sventura" (c ?1690; S & cont) ....
12.185	"Da turbini di pene" (S & cont) ....
12.186	*"Da voi parto amati rai" (B & cont, ?spur)* ....
12.187	*"Deh, per mercè l'ignudo Dio" (S & cont, ?spur)* ....
12.188	"Deh! torna, amico sonno" (Il sonno) (c1716; S & cont) ....
12.189	"Del faretrato Nume Amor tiranno" (S & cont) ....
12.190	"Del lacrimoso lido" (Euridice dall'Inferno. L'Euridice) (c1699; S & cont) ......
12.191	"Della spietata Irene fur l'accese pupille" (S & cont) ....
12.192	"Delle patrie contrade" (S & cont, uncertain) ....
12.193	"Del mio seno la constanza" (S/A & cont) ....
12.194	"Del Tebro in su le sponde" (S & cont) ....
12.195	"Del Tirreno a le sponde" (Cantata di lontananza) (S & cont) ....
12.196	"Del Tirreno sul lido" (c1697; A & cont) ....
12.197	"Dentro il sen della mia Irene" (S & cont) ....
12.198	"Dentro un orrido speco" (S & cont, uncertain) ....
12.199	*"Di che havete paura?" (S & cont, ?spur)* ....
12.200	"Di cipresso funesto" (Querele e morto di Tirsi per Clori ingrata) (c before 1694; S & cont) ....
12.201	*"Di colore de' cieli" (Occhi azurri) (S & cont, ?spur)* ....
12.202	*"Di due vaghe pupille nere" (S & cont, ?spur)* ....
12.203	"Diedi a Fileno il core" (Amor corrisposto) (c1705; A/S & cont) ....
12.204	"Di me che sarà?" (S & cont) ....
12.205	"Dimmi che pensi, o Amore" (c before 1702; S & cont) ....
12.206	"Dimmi, Clori superba" (Clori superba) (c1704; S/A & cont) ....
12.207	*"Dimmi, crudel, e quando" (S, A & cont, ?spur)* ....
12.208	"Dimmi, mio ben, perché" ....
12.209	"Dipende da te solo la pace" (1v & cont) ....
12.210	"Di pensiero in pensier" (A & cont) ....
12.211	"Disperate pupille, hor, sì, piangete" (Disperatione amorosa) (S, B & cont, uncertain) ....
12.212	"Dispettoso pensiero" (S & cont) ....
12.213	*"Dolci istinti d'amore" (S & cont, ?spur)* ....
12.214	"Doppo lungo penar" (B & cont) ....
12.215	"Doppo lungo penar" (S & cont, uncertain) ....
12.216	"Dorisbe i miei lamenti" (Eurillo sdegnato) (S & cont) ....
12.217	"Dormono l'aure estive" (c1705; S/A & cont) ....
12.218	"Dove alfin mi traeste?" (L'Arianna) (S & cont) ....
12.219	"Dov'è, Filli, dov'è?" (S & cont) ....
12.220	"Dove fuggi, o bella Clori?, I (Lidio e Clori) (S, A & cont) ....
12.221	"Dove fuggi, o bella Clori?" II (Lidio e Clori) (S, A, 2vn & cont) ....
12.222	"Dove fuggo, a che penso?" (S, vn & cont) ....
12.223	"Dove l'eneta Dori alla reggia" (S & cont, uncertain) ....
12.224	"Dove una quercia annosa" (Beltà bruna) (Paglia; S & cont) ....
12.225	*"Dove xestu, cor mio?" (S & cont, lost)* ....
12.226	"Dov'io mi volga o vada" (S & cont) ....
12.227	"Due nemici tiranni" (c1722; S & cont) ....

12.228   "D'un platano frondoso" (S & cont, uncertain) ....

12.229   "Dunque ingrato spergiuro" (S/A & cont) ....

12.230   "Dunque perché lontano" (S & cont) ....

12.231   "Dunque sperar non lice" (S & cont) ....

12.232   "Ebra d'amor fuggia" (L'Arianna) (S, 2vn & cont) ....

12.233   "Ecco ch'a voi ritorno" (after Lemene; S & cont; 2 vers, uncertain) ....

12.234   "E come, oh Dio, lontana" (c before 1707; S & cont) ....

12.235   "E come, o Dio, tacito e fido?" (S & cont, ?spur) ....

12.236   "E come, ohimè, poss'io?" (c1714; S & cont) ....

12.237   "E con qual core, oh Dio" I (S & cont, uncertain) ....

12.238   "E con qual core, oh Dio" II (S & cont, ?spur) ....

12.239   "E con qual core, oh Dio" III (S, 2vn & cont, uncertain) ....

12.240   "È'l gran pena l'amare" (S & cont, ?spur) ....

12.241   "È la speme un desio tormentoso" (c1704; S & cont) ....

12.242   "Elitropio d'amor sempre m'aggiro" (c1694; S/mS & cont) ....

12.243   "E lungi dal mio bene" (S & cont) ....

12.244   "Entro a più foschi horrori" (S & cont, uncertain) ....

12.245   "Entro romito speco" (S & cont) ....

12.246   "E penar deggio ancora" (S/A & cont) ....

12.247   "È pure il gran tormento" (S/A & cont) ....

12.248   "E pur è vero che alletti" (S & cont, ?spur) ....

12.249   "E pur odo e non moro" (S & cont, uncertain) ....

12.250   "E pur tenti il ritorno" (Monaci; S & cont) ....

12.251   "E pur vuole il cielo e amore" (c before 1706, Benigni; S, A & cont) ....

12.252   "E quando, ingrata Nice?" (S & cont) ....

12.253   "E quando mai cessate?" (S & cont) ....

12.254   "Era già l'alba e in cielo" (Europa rapita da Giove in forma di toro) (S & cont, uncertain) ....

12.255   "Era giunta quell'ora" (c1704; S & cont) ....

12.256   "Era l'oscura notte e d'ogni intorno di fosco ammanto" (S, 2vn & cont, uncertain) ....

12.257   "Era l'oscura notte e d'ogni intorno le tremolanti stelle" (S & cont) ....

12.258   "E satio ancor non sei" (S & cont) ....

12.259   "E sia (fia) pur vero" (S/A & cont) ....

12.260   "E sino a quando, Amor?" (S & cont) ....

12.261   "E sino a quando, o stelle?" (S & cont) ....

12.262   "Essere innamorato e non poterlo dir" (S & cont, ?spur) ....

12.263   "Eurilla all'or che sei cinta" (S & cont) ....

12.264   "Eurilla, amata Eurilla" (c before 1698; S & cont) ....

12.265   "Eurilla, io parto, addio" (S & cont, uncertain) ....

12.266   "Eurilla, oh Dio, nel seno palpita" (S & cont, uncertain) ....

12.267   "È viva al diletto la mia rimembranza" (S & cont, ?spur) ....

12.268   "Facile sembra a un core l'amar" (S & cont) ....

12.269   "Farfalla che s'aggira" (La Pazzia, ovvero La Stravaganza) (c1706; S & cont) ....

12.270   "Farfalletta innocente se correndo" (S & cont) ....

12.271   "Fatto d'Amor seguace" (S/A & cont) ....

12.272   "Ferma omai, fugace e bella" (c1724; A, 2vn, va & cont) ....

12.273   "Fiamma ch'avvampa" (S & cont) ....

12.274   "Fida compagna, del tuo alato amante" (Lontananza) (S, 2vn & cont) ....

12.275   "Fiero acerbo destin dell'alma mia" (S & cont) ....

12.276   "Filen, mio caro bene" (Filli che esprime la sua fede a Fileno) (A, 2vn, fl & cont) ....

12.277   "Fileno, oh Dio! Fileno, di quest'anima amante" (S, 2vn & cont, uncertain) ....

12.278   "Fileno, ove t'en vai?" (Clori abbandonata, Fileno abbandona Clori) (c1704; S & cont) ....

12.279   "Fileno, quel Fileno, tutto fe' " (S, 2vn & cont) ....

12.280   "Fille, dolente Fille" (S & cont) ....

12.281   "Fille, mia cara Fille" (c1704; S & cont) ....

12.282   "Fille, tu parti, oh Dio" (c1722; S/A & cont, uncertain) ....

12.283   "Filli adorata, ah ben comprendo" (Chiese Fileno come stasse in gratia di Filli) (S & cont, uncertain) ....

12.284   "Filli adorata e cara, Filli che fosti" (c1705; S & cont) ....

12.285   "Filli adorata e cara, io parto" (Partenza. Fileno giura fedeltà a Filli) (c1706; S & cont) ....

12.286   "Filli altera e spietata" (S & cont) ....

12.287   "Filli che del mio core" (c1700; S & cont, ?spur) ....

12.288   "Filli che fra gl'orrori" (Cantata ... notturna) (c1706; S, 2vn & cont) ....

12.289   "Filli crudel, dunque tu parti?" (S & cont) ....

12.290   "Filli, di questo cor parte più cara" (S & cont) ....

12.291   "Filli, già volge l'anno" (S & cont) ....

12.292   "Filli, la lontananza homicida" (c1695; S & cont, ?spur) ....

12.293   "Filli, la tua bellezza" (c1702; S & cont) ....

12.294   "Filli mia, Filli cara" (Descrittore di bella donna) (c1702; S & cont) ....

12.295   "Filli mia, perché piangi?" (S & cont) ....

12.296   "Filli mia, tu mi consoli" (S & cont, uncertain) ....

12.297   "Filli, mio ben, mia vita" (c1704; S & cont) ....

12.298   "Filli, sei bella, è ver" (S & cont, ?spur) ....

12.299   "Filli, tu sai s'io t'amo" (Sconsolato Rusignolo) (c1701; S, 2fl & cont, uncertain) ....

12.300   "Fiumicel che del mio pianto" (S & cont, uncertain) ....

12.301   "Fiumicel cui l'onde chiare" (A & cont, ?spur) ....

12.302   "Flagellava nel cielo" (Il Narciso) (S & cont, ?spur) ....

12.303 "Fonte d'ogni dolcezza" (c1709; S & cont) ....

12.304 "Fonti amiche, erbe care" (S & cont) ....

12.305 "Forse di Sirio ardente" (S & cont) ....

12.306 "Fra liete danze" (S & cont) ....

12.307 "Fra mille semplicetti augei canori" (c ?1701; S & cont) ....

12.308 "Frangi l'arco e lo stral" (c1706; S & cont) ....

12.309 "Fra tante pene e tante" (c1706; S & cont) ....

12.310 "Fu d'oro il primo dardo" (S & cont) ....

12.311   "Fuori di sua capanna" (S, vn/fl & cont, ?spur) ....

12.312 "Giacea d'un mirto all'ombra" (S & cont, uncertain) ....

12.313 "Giacea presso alla sponda" (S & cont, uncertain) ....

12.314 "Già di trionfi onusto" (Il Germanico) (c1691, Pamphilj; S & cont) ....

12.315 "Già per lunga stagion bersaglio" (Lo strale d'Amore) (S & cont) ....

12.316 "Già sepolto è fra l'onda" (S, 2vn, va, va da gamba & cont) ....

12.317 "Già sorge l'alba" (Dorisbe cacciatrice) (S & cont) ....

12.318 "Già sul carro dorato" (Occhi neri) (S & cont) ....

12.319 "Già vicina è quell'ora" (c1699; S/A cont) ....

12.320 "Giù di Vulcan nella fucina eterna" (c1698; A & cont, uncertain) ....

12.321 "Giunto è il fatal momento" (Partenza) (c1705; S & cont) ....

12.322 "Goderai sempre crudele" (c1695; S & cont, inc, uncertain) ....

12.323 "Ha l'umore stravagante" (S & cont) ....

12.324 "Ho una pena intorno al core" (S & cont) ....

12.325   "I celesti zaffiri" (c1701; S & cont, lost) ....

12.326 "Il centro del mio core" (S & cont) ....

12.327 "Il cielo seren, le fresche aurette" (La primavera: Clori e Lisa compagne) (2S & cont) ....

12.328   "Il cor che vive oppresso" (S & cont, ?spur)..

12.329 "Il fulgido splendor d'un ciglio arciero" (c1705; S & cont) ....

12.330 "Il genio di Mitilde mente non sia" (S/A & cont) ....

12.331 "Il mio sol non è più meco" (c1704; S & cont) ....

12.332 "Il più misero amante" (A & cont, uncertain) ....

12.333 "Il rosignuolo se scioglie il volo" I, in F major (c1698; A/S & cont) ....

12.334 "Il rosignuolo se scioglie il volo" II, in F minor (c1700; A/S & cont) ....

12.335 "Il timido mio core" (Immagini d'orrore) (S & cont) ....

12.336 "Imagini d'orrore" (c1710; B, 2vn & cont) ....

12.337 "In amorosi ardori" (S & cont) ....

12.338 "In bel sonno profondo" (S & cont) ....

12.339 "In che giammai t'offesi?" (c1706; S & cont) ....

12.340 "In due vaghe pupille" (S & cont) ....

12.341 "Infelice mio core, che ti valse?" (S & cont, uncertain) ....

12.342 "Infelice mio core! giunse alfin" (S & cont) ....

12.343   "In fra notturni orrori" (S & cont, ?spur: pubd1708 in Marcello's 12 cantate a voce sola) ....

12.344 "Ingiustissimo Amor, tu che sovvente" (S & cont) ....

12.345 "In placida sembianza" (S & cont) ....

12.346 "In questa lacrimosa orrida valle" (Tantalo sitibondo) (S & cont) ....

12.347 "In solitaria soglia" (S & cont) ....

12.348   "In traccia del suo bene" (S & cont, ?spur: pubd1680 in Bassani's Op.2)..........................

12.349 "In vano, Amor tiranno tenta" (S & cont) ....

12.350 "Io ben so che siete arciere" (c1704; S & cont) ....

12.351 "Io che ad un tronco" (S & cont) ....

12.352   "Io che con aurea luce" (S & cont, ?spur) ....

12.353 "Io che dal cor di Fille" (S/A & cont) ....

12.354 "Io credei che felice" (S & cont, uncertain) ....

12.355 "Io m'accendo a poco a poco" (S & cont) ....

12.356 "Io morirei contento" (S & cont) ....

12.357 "Io non v'intendo, o stelle" (S & cont) ....

12.358   "Io per Dori mi struggo" (c before 1694; S & cont, ?spur) ....

12.359 "Io son Neron l'imperator del mondo" (Il Nerone) (c1698; S & cont) ....

12.360 "Io son pur solo" (S & cont) ....

12.361   "Io t'amerò e nel mio petto" (S & cont, ?spur) ....

12.362 "Io ti vuò dir, Dorisbe" (c1700; S & cont) ....

12.363 "Io vengo, o Filli" (c1706; S & cont) ....

12.364 "Irene, idolo mio, in questo a me" (c1705; S & cont) ....

12.365 "Irene, idolo mio, se per te vivo" (S & cont) ....

12.366 "La beltà ch'io sospiro" (c1688 or 1701, Pamphilj; S & cont) ....

12.367 "La cagion delle mie pene" (S & cont) ....

12.368 "Là dell'Arno sull'onda" (S & cont) ....

12.369   "Là dove al sonno in braccio" (Paglia; 1v & insts, lost) ....

12.370 "Là dove al vivo argento" (S & cont) ....

12.371 "Là dove a Mergellina" (c1725; S & cont) ....

12.372 "La face d'Amor ch'il core m'ardé" (c before 1710, Ottoboni; S & cont) ....

12.373 "La Fortuna di Roma" (Il Coriolano) (c ?1694, Pamphilj; S/A & cont) ....

12.374 "La gran madre d'Amore" (Innamoramento di Venere et Adone) (S & cont) ....

12.375 "La gratia, la sembianza della tua pastorella" (c1702; S & cont) ....

12.376   "Lagrime dolorose dagl'occhi miei" (T, 2vn & cont, ?spur) ....

12.377   "Là. nel bel sen della regal Sirena" (S & cont) ....

12.378   "Là nel campo de fiori" (S & cont, inc) ....

12.379   "Là nell'arcadie spiagie" (c1700; S & cont, uncertain) ....

12.380   "Langue Clori vezzosa" (S & cont) ....

12.381   "Langue, geme e sospira" (S, A & cont, uncertain) ....

12.382   "L'armi crudeli e fiere" (A & cont) ....

12.383   "Lascia, deh lascia al fine" (S & cont) ....

12.384   "Lascia di tormentarmi, Amor tiranno!" (c1709; S & cont) ....

12.385   "Lasciami alquanto piangere" (c1716; S & cont) ....

12.386   "Lasciami sospirar, io voglio piangere" (Dorindo e Fileno) (S, B & cont) ....

12.387   "Lascia omai di tormentarmi, o memoria" (S & cont) ....

12.388   "Lascia più di tormentarmi, rimembranza" (c1688; S & cont) ....

12.389   "Lasciate ch'io v'adori" (Preghiera amorosa) (c1705; S & cont) ....

12.390   "Lasciate, homai lasciate di tormentarmi (d'impotrunarmi) più" (S & cont) ....

12.391   "Lasciato havea l'adultero superbo" (La Lucretia romana) (c before 1691, Pamphilj; S & cont) ....

12.392   "La speranza che lusinga" (Colombi; S & cont, uncertain) ....

12.393   *"L'augellin che scioglie il volo" (A & cont, ?spur)* ....

12.394   "La vezzosa Celinda" (S & cont) ....

12.395   "Leandro, anima mia" (Ero e Leandro) (A/S & cont) ....

12.396   *"Leggi, de' leggi, o Clori" (A & cont, ?spur)* ....

12.397   "L'empio mio destin brama la morte" (2vv & cont) ....

12.398   "La vaghe tue pupille" (Bella donna crudele) (S & cont) ....

12.399   "Libertà del mio cor" (S & cont) ....

12.400   "Lidia, in van mi condanni" (Bella donna rimproverata) (S & cont) ....

12.401   "Liete, placide e belle acque" (c1709; S & cont) ....

12.402   "Lieti boschi, ombre amiche" (c1704; A/S & cont) ....

12.403   *"Lilla, mi parto, addio" (S/A & cont, ?spur)* ....

12.404   "Lisa, del foco mio" (Clori e Lisa compagne) (c1706; 2S & cont) ....

12.405   "Lontananza, che fai?" (c1701; S & cont) ....

12.406   "Lontananza crudele, dehl, perché?" (Lontananza) (c1713; S & cont) ....

12.407   "Lontananza crudele, tu mi trafiggi" (c before 1694; S & cont) ....

12.408   "Lontananza non risana" (A & cont) ....

12.409   "Lontananza tiranna che da te mi divide" (S & cont) ....

12.410   "Lontan da la sua Clori" (S & cont) ....

12.411   "Lontan dal Idol mio" (c1699, S/A & cont) ....

12.412   "Lontan dal suo tesor" (S & cont, uncertain) ....

12.413   "Lontan dal tuo bel viso" (Paglia; S/A & cont) ....

12.414   "Lontano dal suo bene" (S & cont) ....

12.415   *"Lo sa il cielo, o Lidio caro" (S & cont, ?spur: c by ?Mancini)* ....

12.416   "Lo sa il ciel, sallo Amore" (S & cont) ....

12.417   "Lo so ben io" (S & cont) ....

12.418   "Luci care al mondo sole" (S & cont) ....

12.419   *"Luci, siete per quelle" (S/A & cont, ?spur)* ....

12.420   "Lumi ch'in fronte al mio bel sole" (Ama e non spera godere) (c1703; S & cont) ....

12.421   "Lumi, dolenti lumi, chiudetevi" (S/A & cont) ....

12.422   "Lunga stagion dolente" (c1706; S & cont) ....

12.423   "Lungi dal ben ch'adoro" (S & cont) ....

12.424   "Lungi dalla cagion per cui sospiro" (Lontananza) (c1704; S & cont) ....

12.425   "Lungi dall'idol mio" (A & cont) ....

12.426   *"L'uom (L'huom) che segue una speranza" (Tormento della Speranza e della Fortuna) (A & cont, ?spur)* ....

12.427   *"Mal fondati sospetti" (c1685; S & cont, ?spur)* ....

12.428   "Mal sicuro è il fior nel prato" (c before 1710, Ottoboni) ....

12.429   "Mentre affidan al mar di Cupido" (S & cont, uncertain) ....

12.430   "Mentre al sonno chiudea" (S & cont) ....

12.431   *"Mentre Clori la bella presso un ruscel sedea" (S, 2vn & cont, ?spur)* ....

12.432   "Mentre Clori la bella sotto l'ombre d'un mirto" (S, 2fl & cont) ....

12.433   "Mentre da questo monte" (S & cont) ....

12.434   "Mentre Eurillo fedele (infelice)" (c before 1694; S & cont) ....

12.435   *"Mentre in un dolce oblio" (S & cont, ?spur)* ....

12.436   "Mentre mesto e piangente" (A & cont) ....

12.437   "Mentre sul carro aurato" (Clori e Mirtillo) (S, A & cont) ....

12.438   "Mentre un zeffiro altero" (S & cont) ....

12.439   "Mentre un zeffiro arguto" (c ?before 1694; S/B, 2vn & cont) ....

12.440   "Mesto, lasso e ramingo" (c1704; S & cont) ....

12.441   "M'ha diviso il cor dal core" (c before 1710, Ottoboni; A & cont) ....

12.442   *"Mia bella Clori, ascolta" (S & cont, ?spur)* ....

12.443   "Mia bellissima Clori, quando i lumi" (S & cont) ....

12.444   "Mia Climene adorata, se mai occhio" (c1710; S & cont) ....

12.445   "Mia Dorinda, mia vita" (c1706; S, vn & cont, uncertain) ....

12.446   *"Mi contento così" (T, 2vn & cont, ?spur)* ....

12.447   "Mie speranze fallaci" (S & cont) ....

12.448   "Mi nasce un sospetto" (Amante insospettito) (S & cont) ....

12.449   *"Mio cor, dov'è la bella libertà?" (A, vn & cont, ?spur)* ....

12.450   "Mi parto, Eurilla, addio" (A & cont) ....

12.451   "Mira, o Filli, quella rosa" (La Rosa) (S & cont) ....

12.452	"Mirtillo, anima mia, già che parti" (Partenza) (S, 2vn & cont)	......
12.453	"Mitilde addio, poiché di nuovo amante" (S & cont)	......
12.454	"Mitilde, alma (anima) mia, se udiste mai" (c1720; S & cont)	......
12.455	"Mitilde, anima mia, conforto di mie pene" (S & cont)	......
12.456	"Mitilde, mio tesor, così veloce" (S & cont)	......
12.457	"Mitilde, mio tesoro, e dove sei?" (Mitilde; S & cont)	......
12.458	"Mitilde, oh quanto dolce e lusinghiero" (S & cont, uncertain)	......
12.459	"Mi tormenta il pensiero" I (c1701; S & cont)	......
12.460	"Mi tormenta il pensiero" II (Amante parlando con il pensiero) (A/B & cont)	......
12.461	*"Mondo, non più" (S & cont, lost)*	
12.462	"Morirei disperato se credessi" (c before 1694, Paglia; S & cont)	......
12.463	*"Mostri, deh!, non temete" (S & cont, ?spur)*	......
12.464	"Nacqui a' sospiri e al pianto" (c before ?1693; S, 2vn & cont, uncertain)	......
12.465	"Nei languidi respiri" (S & cont)	......
12.466	"Nei tuoi lumi, o bella Clori" (Begli occhi) (c1704; S & cont)	......
12.467	"Nel centro oscuro di spelonca" (S & cont)	......
12.468	"Nel dolce tempo in cui ritorno" (c1712; S & cont)	......
12.469	"Nella stagione appunto che il pianeta" (Paglia; S, 2vn & cont)	......
12.470	"Nella tomba di Gnido" (Paglia; S, 2vn & cont)	......
12.471	"Nelle arene del Tago" (c1698; A & cont)	......
12.472	"Nell'estiva stagione" (S & cont)	......
12.473	"Nel mar che bagna al bel Sebeto il piede" (B & cont)	......
12.474	"Nel mar che bagna a Mergellina il piede" (S & cont)	......
12.475	"Nel profondo del mio core" (S & cont)	......
12.476	"Nel sen degl'antri" (S & cont)	......
12.477	"Nel silentio commune" (S, 2vn, va & cont)	......
12.478	"Nel suo fido caro nido" (S & cont)	......
12.479	"Nice mia, un solo istante" (S & cont)	......
12.480	"Ninfa crudel, deh!, vieni" (A & cont)	......
12.481	"Non è come si dice" (c ?1701; S & cont)	......
12.482	"Non è facile ad un core" (La Catena d'Amore) (c1704; S & cont)	......
12.483	*"Non mi credi, deh!, perché?" (S & cont, ?spur)*	......
12.484	"No, non deggio, è troppo cara" (c1709; S & cont)	......
12.485	"No, non è ver ch'altro amore" (c1706; S & cont)	......
12.486	"No, non lasciar, canora e bella" (c1704; S & cont)	......
12.487	"No, non posso fingere di non amar" (c before 1710, Ottoboni; S & cont)	......
12.488	"No, non ti voglio, Cupido" (S, A & cont)	......
12.489	"No, non vorrei vivere fra le catene" (S & cont)	......
12.490	"Non per pioggia del cielo" (c1720; S & cont)	......
12.491	"Non più contrasti (contese), nò" (Amore e rispetto) (c1721; S & cont)	......
12.492	"Non posso già, né voglio" (S & cont)	......
12.493	"Non sdegnar, bella Clori" (S & cont)	......
12.494	*"Non si parli di ventura" (S & cont, ?spur)*	......
12.495	"Non so qual più m'ingombra" (Cantata pastorale) (c1716; S, 2vn & cont)	......
12.496	*"Non temo disastri" (S & cont, ?spur)*	......
12.497	*"Non v'è simile al mio core" (Paglia; 1v & insts, lost)*	......
12.498	"Notte cara à un cor che langue" (c1705; S & cont)	......
12.499	"Notte cara, ombre beate" (c before 1694; S & cont)	......
12.500	"Notte ch'in carro d'ombre" (S, 2vn & cont)	......
12.501	"Notte placida e lieta" (c1706; S & cont)	......
12.502	"Occhi miei ch'al pianto avvezzi" (A & cont, uncertain)	......
12.503	"Occhi miei che pagaste" (Cantata spirituale) (c1705; S & cont)	......
12.504	"O che mostro, o che furia" (c1709, Ottoboni; S & cont)	......
12.505	"O che pena è la mia" (Fedeltà non creduta) (c1704; S/A & cont)	......
12.506	*"O chi ridir potrebbe?" (S & cont, ?spur)*	......
12.507	"O Clori, ahi!, bella Clori" (S & cont)	......
12.508	"O come bello, con onde chiare" (Tirsi e Clori) (c before 1702; 2S & cont)	......
12.509	"O de' pastori diletto stuolo" (L'Agnellino) (S & cont)	......
12.510	"O de' regni di Dite, Eumenidi spietate" (S & cont, uncertain)	......
12.511	"O di fere e d'augelli che ricetti" (S & cont)	......
12.512	"Oh Dio, che viene Amore" (S & cont)	......
12.513	"O dolce servitù" (S & cont)	......
12.514	*"O Fileno, Filen, crudele ingrato" (S & cont, ?spur)*	......
12.515	"O generoso eroe" (c1702; S & cont)	......
12.516	"Ogni affanno crudele" (S & cont)	......
12.517	"Oh di Betlemme altera povertà" (Cantata pastorale per la nascità) (S, 2vn, va, vc & lute)	......
12.518	*"Omai dal cielo al più sublime punto" (S & cont, ?spur)*	......
12.519	"Ombre romite e solitarie piante" (S, A & cont)	......
12.520	"Ombre tacite e sole" (c1716; S, 2vn, va & cont)	......
12.521	"O Mitilde, fosti meco tiranna" (c1711; S & cont)	......
12.522	"O Mitilde, o del core" (c1708; S & cont)	......
12.523	*"Onde della mia Nera" (A/S & cont, ?spur: c by ?D. Scarlatti)*	......
12.524	"O pace del mio cor" I (S/A & cont)	......
12.525	"O pace del mio cor" II (S & cont)	......

12.526	*"O penosa lontananza—o felice lontananza" (S, B & cont, ?spur)* ....
12.527	"Ora che 'l verno riede" (A & cont, uncertain) ....
12.528	"Or che a me ritornasti" (S/A & cont) ....
12.529	*"Or che barbara sorte" (S & cont, ?spur)* ....
12.530	*"Or che disciolto è il nodo" (S & cont, ?spur)* ....
12.531	"Or che di te son privo" (S & cont) ....
12.532	"Or che di Teti in seno" (S & cont) ....
12.533	"Or (Hor) che di Febo ascosi" (c1704; S, 2vn & cont) ....
12.534	"Or (Hor) che graditi orrori copron del dì" I (S & cont) ....
12.535	"Or (Hor) che graditi orrori copron del dì" II (S & cont) ....
12.536	"Or (Hor) che l'aurato Nume" (S, 2vn & cont) ....
12.537	"Or (Hor) che lungi son io" (S & cont; 2 vers) ....
12.538	"Or che su legno aurato" (S & cont, uncertain) ....
12.539	"Or ch'in petto d'Eurilla" (Eurilla placata) (S & cont) ....
12.540	"Or per pietà del mio crudel destino" (S, A & cont, inc, uncertain) ....
12.541	"O sol degl'occhi miei" (c1704, Ottoboni; S & cont) ....
12.542	"O sventurata Olimpia" (S & cont, uncertain) ....
12.543	"Ove al Sebeto in riva" (S & cont) ....
12.544	"Ove fuor del mio seno" (Il sospiro) (S & cont) ....
12.545	"Ove il fiorito impero mostra" (S & cont) ....
12.546	"Ove in grembo alla pace" (Desio di solitudine) (S & cont) ....
12.547	"Ove placido e cheto" (S & cont, uncertain) ....
12.548	*"O v'ingannate a fe' " (S & cont, ?spur)* ....
12.549	"O voi di queste selve habitatrici" (c1717; S/A & cont) ....
12.550	"Parla mia pena omai" (S/A & cont) ....
12.551	"Parte da me Cupido" (S & cont, uncertain) ....
12.552	*"Pastor d'Arcadia, è morta Clori" (S & cont, ?spur)* ....
12.553	"Pastorella innamorata" (S & cont) ....
12.554	"Pastori amici, amiche pastorelle" (S & cont) ....
12.555	"Peno, e del mio penar" (Costanza) (c1705; S & cont) ....
12.556	"Pensier che in ogni parte" (S/A & cont) ....
12.557	"Pensier che sei inflessibile" (c1702; S & cont) ....
12.558	"Pensieri, oh Dio!, qual pena" (S & cont) ....
12.559	"Penso che non ho core" (Piange la lontananza della sua donna/bella) (c ?1705; S & cont) ....
12.560	*"Per celeste bellezza arde il mio cor" (S & cont, ?spur)* ....
12.561	"Perché mai, luci amorose?" (c1700; S & cont) ....
12.562	"Perché sospiri, o Niso?" (Doralba e Niso) (S, A & cont, uncertain) ....
12.563	"Perché, perché tacete regolati concenti?" (A, 2vn & cont) ....
12.564	"Perde al vostro confronto" (c ?before 1696; S, 2vn & cont) ....
12.565	*"Per destin d'ingrat' amore" (T & cont, ?spur)* ....
12.566	"Perdono, Amor, perdono" I (c ?1702; A & cont) ....
12.567	"Perdono, Amor, perdono" II (c1704; S & cont) ....
12.568	"Per farmi amar da tutte" (c before 1710, Ottoboni; S & cont) ....
12.569	"Perfida Filli ingrata" (Constanza) (c1705; S & cont) ....
12.570	*"Per formare la bella che adoro" (Ritratto di Clori) (S & cont, ?spur)* ....
12.571	*"Per l'ondoso sentiero" (S, 2vn & cont, ?spur)* ....
12.572	"Per prova di mia fede" (A & cont) ....
12.573	"Per queste dell'antica Alba famosa" (S & cont) ....
12.574	"Per saettar un seno" I (S & cont) ....
12.575	"Per saettar un seno" II (S & cont) ....
12.576	"Per te, Florida bella" (c1708; S & cont, uncertain) ....
12.577	"Per tormentarmi il core" (S & cont) ....
12.578	"Per un momento solo" (Lo Sfortunato) (S/A & cont) ....
12.579	"Per un vago desire" (La lezione di musica) (S & cont) ....
12.580	*"Per un volto di gigli e di rose" (S & cont, ?spur: c by ?Albinoni)* ....
12.581	"Piagge fiorite, ameni prati" (S & cont) ....
12.582	"Piagge fiorite e amene, io parto" (c1716; S & cont) ....
12.583	*"Piangea, un dì piangea Fileno" (S/A & cont, ?spur)* ....
12.584	*"Piangete o mie pupille" (S, 2vn & cont, ?spur)* ....
12.585	"Piangi la tua sventura" (c1706; S & cont) ....
12.586	"Piango ogn'ora del mio core" (S & cont) ....
12.587	"Piango, sospiro e peno: servo" I (S & cont) ....
12.588	"Piango, sospiro e peno: servo" II (c before 1693; A, 2vn & cont) ....
12.589	"Più che penso all'Idol mio" (S & cont) ....
12.590	"Più non risplende" (c before 1696; 2S, strings & cont) ....
12.591	"Più non si puote amar" (S & cont) ....
12.592	"Più veggio Lidia mia" (S & cont) ....
12.593	"Poi che a Tirsi infelice" (S & cont) ....
12.594	"Poi che cessano (cessaro) al fin" (S & cont) ....
12.595	"Poi che la bella Clori" (Amante schernito) (c ?1699; S & cont) ....
12.596	*"Poi che legge fatal" (S & cont, ?spur)* ....
12.597	"Poi che l'Ercole argivo" (Lisimaco, re di Traccia) (S & cont, uncertain) ....
12.598	"Poi che riseppe Orfeo" (S & cont, uncertain) ....
12.599	*"Porto il cor incantato" (S & cont, ?spur)* ....
12.600	*"Potesse almen" (c before 1696; 1v, vn & cont, lost)* ....

12.601   "Preparati, o mio core" (A & cont) ....

12.602   "Presso a un limpido fonte" (Fileno disingannato) (c1706; S & cont) ....

12.603   "Presso il balcon dell'incostante Nisa" (c1699; S & cont) ....

12.604   *"Pria che desto ai nitriti spaventati dal ciel" (S & cont, ?spur)* ....

12.605   "Prima d'esservi infedele" (Clori fedele) (S, 2vn & cont) ....

12.606   "Primavera, sei gentile" (S & cont) ....

12.607   "Pur al fine la vincesti" (S & cont) ....

12.608   "Qual bellezza divina?" (S & cont) ....

12.609   "Quale al gelo s'adugge" (c1705; S & cont) ....

12.610   "Qualora io veggio la vezzosa Irene" (S, 2vn & cont) ....

12.611   *"Qualor io vi passeggio" (S & cont, ?spur)* ....

12.612   "Qualor l'egre pupille" (S & cont) ....

12.613   "Qualor miro la bella" (S & cont) ....

12.614   "Qualor tento scoprire" (after Lemene; A/B & cont, uncertain) ....

12.615   "Quando Amor vuol ferirmi" (S & cont) ....

12.616   "Quando che ti vedrò" (S & cont, uncertain) ....

12.617   "Quando credeva il core" (c ?1701; S & cont) ....

12.618   *"Quando Lidia amorosa" (S & cont, ?spur)* ....

12.619   "Quando l'umide ninfe" (c1704; S & cont) ....

12.620   "Quando mai troverò d'Amor nel regno?" (c1705; S & cont) ....

12.621   "Quando satia sarai?" (S & cont, uncertain) ....

12.622   "Quando stanche dal pianto" (S & cont) ....

12.623   "Quando un Eroe che s'ama" (2S & cont, uncertain) ....

12.624   "Quando veggio un gelsomino" (S & cont, uncertain) ....

12.625   "Quante le grazie son" (c1703; A & cont) ....

12.626   "Quanti affanni ad un core" (Pene amorose per lontananza / Lontananza in amore) (S/A & cont) ......

12.627   "Quanto io v'ami o luci" (A & cont) ....

12.628   *"Quanto mi sdegni più" (S & cont, ?spur)* ....

12.629   "Quanto, o Filli, t'inganni?" (c1701; S & cont) ....

12.630   "Quanto piace agl'occhi miei" (S & cont) ....

12.631   "Quanto vezzosa e quanto adorna" (S & cont) ....

12.632   "Quel cor ch'a te già diede" (S & cont, uncertain) ....

12.633   "Quel Fileno infelice" (c1705; S & cont) ....

12.634   "Quella che chiudo in seno fiamma amorosa" (c1705; S & cont) ....

12.635   "Quella pace gradita" (S, fl, vn, vc & cont) ....

12.636   "Quel pastor sì gentile" (S, 2vn & cont, inc) ....

12.637   "Quel piacer che nell'amarti" (c1704; S & cont) ....

12.638   "Quel ruscelletto, o Clori" (S & cont) ....

12.639   "Questa, quest'è la selva" (S/A & cont) ....

12.640   "Questa vermiglia rosa" (c1705; S & cont) ....

12.641   "Quest'è il giardin felice" (S & cont) ....

12.642   "Queste torbide e meste onde" (c1717; S & cont) ....

12.643   "Questo di bei giacinti serto" (S/A & cont) ....

12.644   "Questo silenzio ombroso" (Il Sonno) (c1707; S, A & cont; 2nd vers 2S & cont) ....

12.645   "Qui, dove alfin m'assido" (Il rosignuolo al genio di Mitilde sola) (S & cont) ....

12.646   "Qui, dove a piè d'un colle" (S & cont) ....

12.647   "Qui, dove aure ed augelli" (c1705; S & cont) ....

12.648   *"Qui dove in aspre balze" (A & cont, ?spur)* ....

12.649   "Qui vieni, ingrata Fille" (S & cont) ....

12.650   *"Radamisto, è portento che Zenobia" (S & cont, ?spur)* ....

12.651   "Regie soglie, alte moli" (c1720; S & cont) ....

12.652   *"Ritardati momenti, egre dimore" (S & cont, ?spur: pubd1682 in Bassani's Op.3)* ....

12.653   "Rondinella torna al lido (nido)" I (c1701; S & cont) ....

12.654   "Rondinella torna al lido" II (S & cont, uncertain) ....

12.655   "S'accinge Eurillo al canto" (S & cont) ....

12.656   "Sanno, o Filli adorata" (c1716; S & cont) ....

12.657   "Sarà pur vero, o stelle?" (S & cont) ....

12.658   "Sarei troppo felice" (c ?1701, Pamphilj; S & cont) ....

12.659   "Sazio di più soffrire" (S/B & cont) ....

12.660   *"Scherza col onda del caro lido" (S & cont, ?spur)* ....

12.661   "Sciolgo in lagrime amare" (S & cont) ....

12.662   "Sciolta da freddi amplessi" (Marito vecchio, sposa giovane) (c1704; S & cont) ....

12.663   "Scompagnata tortorella" (La tortorella) (S & cont) ....

12.664   "Scorgo il fiume e scorgo il rio" (La Primavera) (c1704; S/A & cont) ....

12.665   "Scuote di fronte all'Appennin" (S & cont, uncertain) ....

12.666   *"Sdegno fiero ed amore" (S & cont, ?spur)* ....

12.667   "Se a goder torna il mio core" (S & cont) ....

12.668   "Se amassi da dovere" (L'infedeltà) (S & cont) ....

12.669   "Se amor con un contento" (S & cont) ....

12.670   "Se a quel fiero dolor" (L'amante non corrisposto lascia d'amare) (S/A & cont) ....

12.671   *"Se credete all'amor mio" (S & cont, ?spur)* ....

12.672   *"Sa dalla cruda Irene" (A/S & cont, ?spur)* ....

12.673   "Se d'Elisa spietata il bel sembiante" (S & cont) ....

12.674   "Sedeva Eurillo un giorno" (Esagerationi d'Eurilla) (Paglia; S & cont) ....

12.675	"Se mai Clori gentile" (S & cont)	
12.676	*"Se nell'amar Coriste" (S & cont, ?spur)*	
12.677	"Senti, bella crudele" (S & cont)	
12.678	"Senti, bell'Idol mio" (Bella donna prega ad essere amata) (c1705; S & cont)	
12.679	*"Sentite, o tronchi, o sassi" (c1715; S/A & cont, ?spur)*	
12.680	"Sento nel core certo dolore" (S'allontana per non innamorarsi / La lontananza) (S/A & cont)	
12.681	"Senz'alma, senza cor" (S & cont)	
12.682	*"Se per amor quest'alma" (S & cont, ?spur)*	
12.683	"Serba il mio cor costante" (S & cont, uncertain)	
12.684	*"Se tu parti io morirò" (L'Armida) (S & cont, ?spur: pubd1680 in Bassani's Op.2)*	
12.685	"Se vagheggio nel mattino" (c1709; S & cont)	
12.686	"Siamo in contesa, la Bellezza ed io" (c ?1701, Pamphilj; S & cont)	
12.687	"Sì, conosco, o Mitilde" (S & cont)	
12.688	"Siete uniti a tormentarmi" (A, 2vn & cont)	
12.689	"Silentio, aure volanti" (S, 2vn & cont)	
12.690	"S'io t'amo, s'io t'adoro" (c1704; S & cont, uncertain)	
12.691	"Sì, t'intendo, tu vuoi ch'io non pensi" (Non può scordarsi della sua dama) (S/A & cont)	
12.692	*"So che non lice" (c before 1696; 1v & cont, lost)*	
12.693	"Solitudini amene, apriche collinette" (S, fl & cont, uncertain)	
12.694	"Solitudini amene, bersaglio d'empia sorte" (c1705; S & cont)	
12.695	"Solitudini care, in voi spera" (S & cont)	
12.696	"Son contenta di soffrire" (S & cont)	
12.697	"Son io, barbara donna" (A & cont)	
12.698	"Son le nere pupillette (pupille)" (c1702; A & cont)	
12.699	"Sono amante e m'arde il core" (c before 1694; A & cont)	
12.700	"Sono un alma tormentata" (S & cont, uncertain)	
12.701	*"Son pur care le catene" (S, A & cont, ?spur)*	
12.702	"Son quest'ultimi momenti" (Cantata di lontananza) (c before 1714; S/A & cont)	
12.703	"Sopra le verdi sponde che la Brenta" (c1694; S & cont)	
12.704	"Sopra le verdi sponde del Sebeto" (c1712; S & cont)	
12.705	"Sorge l'alba" (S & cont)	
12.706	"Sorta fin da le piume" (c1702; S & cont)	
12.707	"Sotto l'ombra d'un faggio, piangente e sospirante" (B, vn & cont)	
12.708	"Sotto l'ombra d'un faggio, sul margine d'un rivo" (Paglia; S, 2vn & cont)	
12.709	"Sovente Amor mi chiama" (A & cont)	
12.710	"Sovra carro stellato" (S, 2vn & cont, uncertain)	
12.711	"Sovra il margine erboso" (S & cont)	
12.712	"Sovra questi fecondi ameni colli" (c1704; S & cont)	
12.713	"Speranze mie, addio" (c1694; mS & cont)	
12.714	"Spero ch'avrò (ch'havrò) la pace" (c before 1710, Ottoboni; S & cont)	
12.715	*"Spesso suol l'alma mia" (Amore e Gelosia) (S & cont, ?spur)*	
12.716	"Spiega l'ali il mio pensiero" (La lontananza) (c ?1702; S & cont)	
12.717	"Splendeano in bel sembiante" (B & cont)	
12.718	*"Stanca l'afflitta Clori" (S/A & cont, ?spur)*	
12.719	"Stanco di più soffrire a voi ritorno" (S & cont, uncertain)	
12.720	"Sta presente il mio tesoro" (S & cont)	
12.721	"Strali, facelle, Amore" (A & cont)	
12.722	"Stravagante è l'amor" (Fileno amante di Clori, Irene, e Nice) (c1720; S & cont)	
12.723	"Stravagante non è l'Amor" (c1720; S & cont)	
12.724	*"Stravaganza d'amore accade in noi" (Paglia; S & cont, ?spur)*	
12.725	"Su bel seggio di fiori" (c1705; S & cont)	
12.726	*"Su la morbida erbetta" (S & cont, lost)*	
12.727	"Su la sponda del mare" (L'Olimpia) (S, 2vn, va & cont)	
12.728	"Su la sponda fiorita d'un rio pargoleggiante" (L'Adone) (S & cont)	
12.729	"Su le rive dell'Elba" (S & cont, uncertain)	
12.730	"Su le sponde del Reno" (S & cont, uncertain)	
12.731	"Su le sponde d'Abbido" (Il Leandro) (c1693; S & cont)	
12.732	"Su le fiorite sponde di un vago ruscelletto" (c1712; S & cont)	
12.733	*"Sulla sponda fiorita d'un limpido ruscello" (c ?1718; S & cont, ?spur)*	
12.734	"Su le sponde del Tebro" (S, 2vn, tpt & cont)	
12.735	"Sul margine d'un rio dove l'onde fugaci" (Elpino tradito) (S/A & cont)	
12.736	"Sul margine d'un rivo cui facevan ricamo" (S, 2vn & cont)	
12.737	"Sul margine fiorito d'un limpido (tumido) ruscello" (c1704; S & cont)	
12.738	*"Sul margine fiorito d'un placido torrente" (S & cont, ?spur)*	
12.739	"Su l'ora appunto che col carro d'oro" (La Fenice) (c1703; S, 2vn & cont)	
12.740	"Sventurati miei pensieri" (S & cont)	
12.741	"Taccio e tacendo io moro" (A & cont, uncertain)	
12.742	"Taci, infedele (infelice) Amore" (c1720; S & cont)	
12.743	"Talor per suo diletto" (c ?1718; S & cont, incl: La libertà perduta, inc)	
12.744	"Tanti affanni e tante pene" (S & cont)	
12.745	"Tanto strano è l'amor mio" (c1697; S & cont)	
12.746	"Temo d'amarti poco" (S & cont)	
12.747	"Tenebrose foreste, erme" (S & cont)	
12.748	*"The Beautious Melissa" (S & cont, ?spur)*	
12.749	"Tiranna ingrata, che far dovrò?" (B, 2vn & cont)	

12.750   *"Tiranna di mia fè" (S & cont, ?spur)* ....
12.751   *"Tirsi, mentr'io dormiva" (S & cont, ?spur)* ....
12.752   "Tirsi pastore amante" (Pastorello innamorato che va in traccia della sua ninfa) (S, 2vn & cont) ....
12.753   "Ti vorrei credere speranza" (S & cont) ....
12.754   "Tormentatemi pur, furie d'amore" (S/A & cont) ....
12.755   "Torna al sen dolce mia pace" (S & cont, uncertain) ....
12.756   *"Torna il giorno fatale" (Anniversario amoroso) (c1710, ?Pamphilj; ?S & cont, lost)* ....
12.757   "Tra le pompe fiorite" (A & cont, uncertain) ....
12.758   *"Tra l'ombre più secrette" (S & cont, ?spur)* ....
12.759   "Tra queste ombrose piagge" (c1709; S & cont) ....
12.760   "Tra solitarie balze" (S & cont) ....
12.761   "Tra speranza e timore" (B, vn & cont) ....
12.762   "Tra verdi piante ombrose" (S & cont, uncertain) ....
12.763   "Troppo care, troppo belle" (Amante contento) (S & cont) ....
12.764   "Troppo ingrata Amaranta" (S & cont) ....
12.765   "Troppo oppresso dal sonno" (S & cont) ....
12.766   "Tu, che una dea rassembri" (S, 2vn & cont) ....
12.767   "Tu mi chiedi s'io t'amo" (c1709; S & cont) ....
12.768   "Tu mi lasciasti, o bella" (c1698; S & cont) ....
12.769   "Tu parti, idolo amato" I (Cantata di lontananza) (c1702; S/A & cont) ....
12.770   "Tu parti, idolo amato" II (Amante che parte a bella donna che resta) (c1706; S & cont) ......
12.771   "Tu resti, o mio bel nume" I (B, 2vn & cont) ....
12.772   "Tu resti, o mio bel nume" II (Bella donna che parte al suo amante che resta) (c1706; S & cont) ......
12.773   "Tu sei quella che al nome" (Bella dama di nome Santa) (A, 2vn, fl & cont) ....
12.774   *"Tutto acceso d'Amore" (S/A & cont, ?spur)* ....

12.775   "Udite, o selve, o fiumi" (S & cont, uncertain) ....
12.776   "Una beltà ch'eguale" (Amante sventurato) (S & cont) ....
12.777   "Un cervello frenetico ch'amò" (S & cont, uncertain) ....
12.778   "Un di Tirsi l'amante" (S & cont) ....
12.779   "Un giorno Amor la benda si disciolse" (c1709; S & cont, uncertain) ....
12.780   "Un'incredula speranza" (S & cont) ....
12.781   "Un sol guardo di Clori" (A & cont, uncertain) ....
12.782   "Un sospiro d'un Amante" (La Lucioletta) (Pamphilj; S & cont) ....
12.783   "Un spietato destino" (A & cont) ....
12.784   "Un Tantalo assetato" (S & cont) ....

12.785   "Vaga Elisa, la tua rimembranza" (c1708; S & cont, uncertain) ....
12.786   "Vaghe fonti di luce" (Occhi neri) (S & cont) ....
12.787   "Vaghe selve beate" (Mitilde ritirata in solitudine) (S & cont) ....
12.788   "Vaghe tende adorate" (S & cont) ....
12.789   "Vago il ciel non saria" (S & cont) ....
12.790   "Va pur lungi da me" (c1704; S & cont) ....
12.791   "Vedi, Eurilla, quel fior" (Cantata per camera per l'Ecc. mo Duca di Maddaloni) (c1725; S, 2vn, va & cont) .
12.792   "Vedi, Fille, quel sasso" (S & cont) ....
12.793   "Veggio l'Idolo mio" (S & cont) ....
12.794   "Venite, amici, e con ghirlande" (Ansaldi; S & cont) ....
12.795   "Venne ad'Amor desio" (c1705; S & cont) ....
12.796   *"(...) ver per un diletto ma senza Amor" (S & cont, frag)* ....
12.797   "Vi comanda un cenno solo" (c before 1710, Ottoboni; S & cont) ....
12.798   *"Vidi un giorno un fiumicello" (S & cont, ?spur)* ....
12.799   "Vieni, o caro Mirtillo" (c1708; A & cont, uncertain) ....
12.800   *"Viva, viva mia libertà" (2S & cont, ?spur)* ....
12.801   "Voi ben sapete, o di romito bosco" (S & cont) ....
12.802   *"Voi che dell'alma mia havete il vanto" (S & cont, ?spur, lost)* ....
12.803   "Voi dell'idolo mio care treccie" (A & cont, uncertain) ....
12.804   "Voi giungeste, o vaghi fiori" (I fiori) (A & cont) ....
12.805   *"Voi mi dite, tu sei bella" (S & cont, ?spur)* ....
12.806   "Vola, Cupido, dal cor mio fido" (c before ?1696; S & cont) ....
12.807   *"Vo narrando a quel ruscello" (?spur)* ....
12.808   "Vorrei, Filli adorata, farti palese" (c1705; S/A & cont) ....
12.809   *"Vuoi che mora incenerito" (S & cont, ?spur)* ....
12.810   "Vuoi ch'io spiri, tra i sospiri" (Amante desideroso di morire per liberarsi dall'amore) (c1699; S & cont, ...
12.811   "Vuoi più, Filli crudele?" (A & cont, uncertain) ....

12.812   *"Zeffiretti che spirate" (A & cont, ?spur)* ....
12.813   "Zeffiretto che indrizzi il tuo volo" (c1702; S & cont) ....

13. THEORETICAL & PEDAGOGICAL

13.1   "Regole per principianti" (ca1715) ....
13.2   "Varie partite obligate al basso" (kbd) ....
13.3   "Varie introduttioni per sonare e mettersi in tono delle compositioni" (c ?1715; kbd) ....
13.4   "Tenta la fuga ma la tenta invano," canon ....
13.5   "2 Canons à 2" ....

* * * * *

1. STAGE WORKS (operas)

1.1	"L'Ottavia ristituita al trono," melodramma (p1703, Convò, extant 31 arias & 2 duets) ....
1.2	"Il Giustino" (p1703, Convò after Beregani, collab Legrenzi, extant 21 arias & 3 duets) ....
1.3	"L'Irene" (p1704, ?Convò, extant 33 arias, r of Pollarolo's setting of 1695)......................................
1.4	*"La Silvia," dramma pastorale (p1710, Capece, music lost) ....*
1.5	"Tolomeo e Alessandro, ovvero La corona disprezzata" (p1711, Capece, Act I extant only) ....
1.6	*"L'Orlando, ovvero La gelosa pazzia" (p1711, Capece after Ariosto, music lost) ....*
1.7	"Tetide in Sciro" (p1712, Capece) ....
1.8	*"Ifigenia in Aulide" (p1713, Capece after Euripides, music lost) ....*
1.9	*"Ifigenia in Tauri" (p1713, Capece after Euripides, music lost) ....*
1.10	"Amor d'un'ombra e gelosia d'un'aura" (p1714, Capece, r by Rolli as: Narcisso p1720) ....
1.11	"Ambleto" (p1715, Zeno, extant Scene 8 of Act I) ....
1.12	*"La Dirindina," farsetta per musica (intermezzo for Ambleto) (Gigli, unperf, lost)................*
1.13	*"Intermedi pastorali," intermezzo in Ambleto (p1715, lost) ....*
1.14	*"Berenice, regina d'Egitto" (p1718, Salvi, collab Porpora, lost) ....*
1.15	*"Didone abbandonata" (p1724, Metastasio, ?spur: c by ?Sarro, lost).............................*

2. ORCHESTRAL WORKS (orch/ens)

2.1	Sinfonia No.1 in A major (strings & cont) ....
2.2	Sinfonia No.2 in G major (fl, ob, strings & cont) ....
2.3	Sinfonia No.3 in G major (strings & cont) ....
2.4	Sinfonia No.4 in D major (ob, strings & cont) ....
2.5	Sinfonia No.5 in A minor (2vn & cont) ....
2.6	Sinfonia No.6 in D major (ob, 2vn & cont) ....
2.7	Sinfonia No.7 in C major (strings & cont) ....
2.8	Sinfonia No.8 in B-flat major (ob, strings & cont) ....
2.9	Sinfonia No.9 in D minor (ob, strings & cont) ....
2.10	Sinfonia No.10 in G major (ob, strings & cont) ....
2.11	Sinfonia No.11 in C major (ob, strings & cont) ....
2.12	Sinfonia No.12 in G major (ob, strings & cont; = Overture to: Amor d'un ombra) .....
2.13	Sinfonia No.13 in B-flat major (ob, strings & cont; = Overture to: Tolomeo et Alessandro)..........
2.14	Sinfonia No.14 in G major (fl, ob, strings & cont) ....
2.15	Sinfonia No.15 in B-flat major (ob, strings & cont) ....
2.16	Sinfonia No.16 in A major (ob, strings & cont; = Overture to: Tetide in Sciro, 1st movt inc) ....
2.17	Sinfonia No.17 in C major (ob, strings & cont, doubtful) ....

3. HARPSICHORD CONCERTOS

3.1	*Harpsichord Concerto in F major (hpd, 2fl, 2hn, 2vn, va & cont, ?spur: c by ?G. Scarlatti) ....*

4. KEYBOARD

4.1	Sonata in D minor (Allegro)	Kk1
4.2	Sonata in G major (Presto)	Kk2
4.3	Sonata in A minor (Presto)	Kk3
4.4	Sonata in G minor (Allegro)	Kk4
4.5	Sonata in D minor (Allegro)	Kk5
4.6	Sonata in F major (Allegro)	Kk6
4.7	Sonata in A minor (Presto)	Kk7
4.8	Sonata in G minor (Allegro), "Bucolic"	Kk8
4.9	Sonata in D major (Allegro)	Kk9
4.10	Sonata in D minor (Presto)	Kk10
4.11	Sonata in D minor...	Kk11
4.12	Sonata in G minor (Presto)	Kk12
4.13	Sonata in G major (Presto)	Kk13
4.14	Sonata in G major (Presto)	Kk14
4.15	Sonata in E minor (Allegro)	Kk15
4.16	Sonata in B-flat major (Presto)	Kk16
4.17	Sonata in F major (Presto)	Kk17
4.18	Sonata in D minor (Presto)	Kk18
4.19	Sonata in F minor (Allegro)	Kk19
4.20	Sonata in E major (Presto), "Capriccio"	Kk20
4.21	Sonata in D major (Allegro)	Kk21
4.22	Sonata in C minor (Allegro)	Kk22
4.23	Sonata in D major (Allegro)	Kk23
4.24	Sonata in A major (Presto)	Kk24
4.25	Sonata in F-sharp minor (Allegro)	Kk25
4.26	Sonata in A major (Presto)	Kk26
4.27	Sonata in B minor (Allegro)	Kk27
4.28	Sonata in E major (Presto)	Kk28

4.554	Sonata in F major (Allegretto)	Kk554
4.555	Sonata in F minor (Allegro)	Kk555

Not included in Kirkpatrick's catalogue:

4.556	*Sonata in A major (Allegro; Spiritoso) (?spur)*	
4.557	*Sonata in A major (?spur; ed Baciero 1978)*	
4.558	*Sonata in A major (?spur)*	
4.559	*Sonata in C major (Presto) (?spur)*	
4.560	*Sonata in C major (Prestissimo) (?spur)*	
4.561	*Sonata in C major (Andantino) (?spur)*	
4.562	*Sonata in D major (?spur)*	
4.563	*Sonata in D minor (?spur; ed Baciero 1978)*	
4.564	Sonata in D minor (ed Martinez 1984)	
4.565	*Sonata in E major (?spur; ed E. Granados 1905; ed Baciero 1978)*	
4.566	*Sonata in G major (?spur; ed Baciero 1978)*	
4.567	*Sonata in G minor (?spur)*	

5. SACRED MUSIC

5.1	(Capriccio fugato a dodici) (d ch, strings & cont, no text; ed Winter 1969)	
5.2	"Cibavit nos Dominus" (ca1708; ch)	
5.3	*"Dixit Dominus" (lost)*	
5.4	"Iste confessor," in G major (S, ch & org)	
5.5	"Laetatus sum" (S, A, ch & org)	
5.6	*"Lauda Jerusalem" (lost)*	
5.7	"Laudate pueri" (d ch & cont, not confirmed)	
5.8	*"Magnificat," in D minor (ch, lost)*	
5.9	"Memento Domine David" (ch, not confirmed: c by ?A. Scarlatti)	
5.10	"Miserere," in E minor (d ch)	
5.11	"Miserere," in G minor (d ch)	
5.12	"Missa," in D major (d ch, 2ob, 2hn, 2tpt, timp, 2vn & org)	
5.13	"Missa," in A minor, "La stella" (ca1708; ch & org)	
5.14	"Missa quatuor vocum," in G minor (ch)	
5.15	"Nisi quia Dominus" (c ?1708; ch & org)	
5.16	"Pangue lingua" (ca1708; ch, inc: T part lost)	
5.17	"Salve Regina," in A major (c1756–7; S, strings & cont; ed Ewerhart 1960)	
5.18	"Salve Regina," in A minor (S, A & org; ed Hautus 1971)	
5.19	"Stabat Mater," in C minor (2ch & cont; ed Jürgens 1973)	
5.20	"Te Deum," in C major (c ?1721; d ch & org)	
5.21	"Te gloriosus" (mottetto per l'Ognissanti) (ch & cont)	

6. ORATORIOS

| 6.1 | "La conversione di Clodoveo, re di Francia," oratorio (p1709, Capece) | |
| 6.2 | "Cantata da recitarsi ... la notte del Ss.mo Natale" (p1714, Gasparri) | |

7. SERENATAS

7.1	*"Il consilio degli dei" (p1704, Riccio, music lost)*	
7.2	*(Unidentified) Serenata for Prince Vaini (p1712, Zappi, lost)*	
7.3	*"Applauso devoto al nome di Maria Santissima" (p1712, Capece, music lost)*	
7.4	*"Applauso genetliaco" (p1712 & 1714, music lost)*	
7.5	"Contessa delle stagioni" (p1720; 2S, A, T, ch, fl, 2tpt, 2hn, strings & cont, part 1 extant)	
7.6	*"Cantata pastorale" (p1720, music lost)*	
7.7	*(Unidentified) Serenata (p1722 in Lisbon, lost)*	
7.8	*"Le nozze di Baco e d'Arianna" (p1722, music lost)*	
7.9	*"Festeggio armonico" (p1728, music lost)*	

8. CHAMBER CANTATAS (w/ cont)

8.1	"A chi nacque infelice" (A)	
8.2	"Ah, sei troppo infelice" (c1705; S)	
8.3	"Al fin diviene amante" (S/A)	
8.4	"Alla caccia di tiranna beltà" (A)	
8.5	*"Alme dilette, e care" (La virtù in trionfo) (c1711, Bonis; S & insts, music lost)*	
8.6	"Amare e tacere, temere e sperar" (S)	
8.7	"Amenissimi prati, fiorite piagge" (B)	
8.8	"Avrei ben folle il core" (S)	
8.9	"Bella rosa adorata" (S)	
8.10	*"Belle pulille care" (c1702; S, 2vn, ?spur: c by ?Fr. Scarlatti)*	

8.11	"Cara qualor lontano" (S) ....
8.12	"Care pupille belle" (c1702; S, 2vn) ....
8.13	*"Che, che pretendi, ò tiranna" (S, spur: c by A. Scarlatti)* ....
8.14	"Che si peni in amore" (A) ....
8.15	"Che vidi, o ciel" (S, 2vn) ....
8.16	"Chi in catene ha il mio core" (S) ....
8.17	"Con qual cor mi chiede pace" (S) ....
8.18	*"Dal bel volto d'Irene" (S, ?spur)* ....
8.19	"Deh che fate o mie pulille" (S) ....
8.20	"Di Fille vendicarmi vorrei" (S) ....
8.21	"Dir vorrei, ah m'arrossisco" (S, 2vn) ....
8.22	"Dopo lungo servire" (c1702; A, 2vn) ....
8.23	*"Dorme la rosa, aurette grate" (Pamphilj; S/A, ?spur)* ....
8.24	"E pur per mia sventura" (S) ....
8.25	"E temerario ardire" (S) ....
8.26	"Fille già più non parlo" (S) ....
8.27	Già che al partir t'astringe" (S) ....
8.28	"In questa lacrimosa orrida valle" (Tantalo sitibondo) (S, ?spur: c by ?A. Scarlatti) ....
8.29	"La cagion delle mie pene" (S, ?spur: c by ?A. Scarlatti) ....
8.30	"Mi tormenta il pensiero" (c1701; S) ....
8.31	"Ninfe belle e voi pastori" (S) ....
8.32	"No, non fuggire o Nice" (S) ....
8.33	"Ogni core innamorato" (c1724; S) ....
8.34	"Onde della mia Nera" (A/S, ?spur) ....
8.35	"O qual meco Nice cangiata" (S, 2vn) ....
8.36	"Pende la vita mia" (S) ....
8.37	"Perché vedi ch'io t'amo" (c1703 or 5; S) ....
8.38	"Piangete, occhi dolenti" (S, 2vn) ....
8.39	"Piango ogn'ora del mio core" (c1703; S) ....
8.40	"Povero cor fedele" (S) ....
8.41	"Pur nel sonno almen tal'ora" (Metastasio; S, 2vn) ....
8.42	"Qual pensier" (S) ....
8.43	"Quando miro il vostro foco" (A) ....
8.44	"Quando penso a Daliso" (S) ....
8.45	"Qui dove a pie' d'un colle" (S) ....
8.46	"Rimirai la rosa un dì" (A) ....
8.47	"Scritte con falso inganno" (S, 2vn) ....
8.48	"Se dicessi ch'io t'amo" (S) ....
8.49	"Se fedele tu m'adori" (S, 2vn) ....
8.50	"Se la sorte crudele mi divise" (S) ....
8.51	"Selve, caverne e monti" (S) ....
8.52	"Se per un sol momento" (2S) ....
8.53	"Se sai qual sia la pena" (S) ....
8.54	"Se ti dicesse un core" (S) ....
8.55	"Sono un alma tormentata" (S) ....
8.56	"Sospendi o man per poco" (S) ....
8.57	"Su la sponda fiorita di limpido ruscello" (c ?1718; S) ....
8.58	"T'amai, Clori, t'amai" (S) ....
8.59	"Tinte a note di sangue" (S, 2vn) ....
8.60	"Ti ricorda o bella Irene" (S) ....
8.61	"Tirsi caro—Amata Fille" (2S) ....
8.62	"Tirsi, mentr'io dormiva" (S) ....
8.63	"Tu mi chiedi o mio ben" (S) ....
8.64	"V'adoro o luci belle" (c ?1699; S) ....
8.65	"Vago il ciel non saria" (S) ....
8.66	"Vuoi ch'io spiri tra i sospiri" (Amante desideroso di morire per libberarsi dall'amore) (S) ....

* * * * *

Kk = Ralph Kirkpatrick: "Domenico Scarlatti." Princeton University Press. Princeton, New Jersey, 1953.

SCHOENBERG (SCHÖNBERG), Arnold (Franz Walter)
1874–1951

1. STAGE WORKS

1.1	*"Und Pippa tanzt," prelude & recit (c1906–7, Hauptmann, short score only: 68 bars)* ....
1.2	"Erwartung" (Expectation), 1 act monodrama (c1909, Pappenheim; S & orch; arr Steuermann for pf) Op.17
1.3	"Die glückliche Hand" (The Lucky Hand / The Hand of Fate), 1 act drama (c1910–3; arr Steuermann for pf) Op.18
1.4	"Pierrot lunaire" (Moonstruck Pierrot), melodrama (c1912, Guiraud transl Hartleben; speaker & insts) Op.21
1.5	"Von Heute auf Morgen" (From One Day to the Next), 1 act opera (c1928–29, G. Schoenberg) Op.32
1.6	"Moses und Aaron," 3 act biblical drama (12-tone method) (c1930–2, Schoenberg, inc: Act III in sketches):

    I. Scene 1. "The Calling of Moses"
          2. "Moses meets Aaron in the Wasteland"
          3. & 4. "Moses and Aaron bring God's Message to the people"
          . "Interlude"
    II. Scene 1. & 2. "Aaron and the 70 Elders before the Mountain of Revelation"
          3. "The Golden Calf and the Altar"
          4. (Moses descending from the mountain)
          5. "Moses and Aaron"
    III. "Aaron's Death"

1a. SELECTIONS FROM STAGE WORKS

1a.4	"Pierrot lunaire," melodrama: Op.21

    I: 1. "Mondestrunken"
        2. "Colombine"
        3. "Dandy"
        4. "Die blasse Wäscherin"
        5. "Valse de Chopin"
        6. "Madonna"
        7. "Der kranke Mond"
    II: 8. "Nacht"
        9. "Gebet an Pierrot"
      10. "Raub"
      11. "Rote Messe"
      12. "Galgenlied"
      13. "Enthauptung"
      14. "Kreuze"
    III: 15. "Heimweh"
      16. "Gemeinheit"
      17. "Parodie"
      18. "Mondfleck"
      19. "Serenade"
      20. "Heimfahrt"
      21. "O alter Duft"

2. SYMPHONIES

2.1	*Symphony in G minor (c1900, frag)* ....
2.2	*Chamber Symphony in A minor (c ?before Op.9, frag: 22 bars)* ....
2.3	Chamber Symphony No.1 in E major (c1906; 15 insts; r vers for full orch 1922; r as Op.9b 1935) Op.9
2.4	Chamber Symphony No.2 in E-flat minor (c1906–16, 39; vers for 2pf, Op.38b) Op.38
2.5	*Symphony with choral movts (c1912–4, sketches)* ....
2.6	*Symphony (c1937, short score: 30–50 bars of each of the 4 movts)* ....

3. OTHER ORCHESTRAL WORKS

3.1	*"Waltz" (c early; strings, frag: 10 sections)* ....
3.2	"Serenade," in D major (c1896; small orch, 2nd & 3rd movts inc) ....
3.3	"Gavotte and Musette" (in Olden Style) (c1897; strings) ....
3.4	*"Frühlings Tod," sym poem (c1898, after Lenau, frag)* ....
3.5	"Verklärte Nacht" (Transfigured Night) (c1917, r1943; strings, , arr from Str Sextet, Op.4) .... (Op.4)
3.6	"Pelleas und Melisande," sym poem (c1902–3, after Maeterlinck's drama) Op.5
3.7	"5 Orchestral Pieces" (atonal) (c1909, r1922, 1949; small orch): No.1 "Premonitions" Op.16
3.8	No.2 "The Past"
3.9	No.3 "Chord-Colours"
3.10	No.4 "Peripetie" (Turning Point)
3.11	No.5 "The Obbligato Recitative"
3.12	3 "Little Pieces for Chamber Orchestra" (c1910): No.1 (ob, cl, hn & solo str qnt) ....
3.13	No.2 (fl, ob, cl, bn, hn & solo str qnt)
3.14	*No.3 (fl, ob, cl, bn, hn, org/harm, celesta & solo str qnt, frag)*
3.15	*"Passacaglia" (c1920, sketches)* ....
3.16	"Variations for Orchestra" (c1926–8) Op.31
3.17	"Accompaniment to a Film-Scene" (c1929–30) Op.34

3.18	"Suite," in G major (c1934; strings, first tonal work since Str Qt No.2 in F-sharp minor, Op.10)	
3.19	"Theme and Variations," in G minor (c1943; band):	Op.43a
	Version for full orch (c1944)	Op.43b
3.20	*Untitled work (c1946, frag)*	
3.21	*Untitled work (c1948, frag)*	

4. CONCERTOS, SOLO INSTR & ORCH

4.1	"Adagio," in A-flat major (c early; harp & strings)	
4.2	Cello Concerto (c1932–33, after Monn: Harpsichord Concerto in D major of 1746; also for vc & pf)	
4.3	"Concerto" (c1933; str qt & orch, after Handel: Concerto Grosso No.7 in B-flat major, Op.6/7, HWV325)	
4.4	Violin Concerto (12-tone method) (c1935–6)	Op.36
4.5	Piano Concerto (12-tone method) (c1942)	Op.42

5. STRING QUARTETS (also see: Canons)

5.1	*String Quartet in C major (c early, frag: 41 bars)*	
5.2	"Presto," in C major (c early)	
5.3	String Quartet in D major (c1897)	
5.4	"Scherzo," in F major & "Trio," in A minor (c1897, ?rejected 2nd movt of Str Qt of 1897)	
5.5	*"Fugue," in D minor (c1904, frag: 80 bars)*	
5.6	String Quartet No.1 in D minor (c1904–5)	Op.7
5.7	String Quartet No.2 in F-sharp minor (c1907–8, George; w/ S in movts 3 & 4; arr for S & strings)	Op.10
5.8	String Quartet No.3 (c1927)	Op.30
5.9	String Quartet No.4 (12-tone method) (c1936)	Op.37
5.10	*String Quartet (c1949, started: openings of all 4 movts: total of 36 bars)*	

6. OTHER CHAMBER MUSIC

6 or more insts:

6.1	*"Toter Winkel" (c early; 2vn, 2va & 2vc, after G. Falke: Dead Corner, frag: 31 bars)*	
6.2	String Sextet, "Verklärte Nacht" (Transfigured Night) (c1899, after Dehmel's poem; arr for strings)	Op.4
6.3	*String Septet (c1918, frag: 25 bars)*	
6.4	*"Tempo zwischen langsamem Walzer und Polacca" (c1920, intended for Op.24, frag: 40 bars)*	
6.5	"Serenade" (c1920–3, Petrarch transl Förster; cl, b cl, mand, gui, vn, va, vc & B in 4th movt)	Op.24
6.6	"Suite" (Septet) (c1925–6; E-flat cl/fl, cl, b cl/bn, vn, va & vc & pf): No.1 "Ouverture" (Allegretto)	Op.29
6.7	No.2 "Tanzschritte" (Moderato)	
6.8	No.3 "Thema mit Variationen"	
6.9	No.4 "Gigue"	

5 insts:

6.10	*Clarinet Quintet in D minor (c early, frag: 28 bars)*	
6.11	*String Quintet in D major (c1904–5, frag: 25bars)*	
6.12	*"Ein Stelldichein" (c1905; ob, cl, pf, vn & vc, after Dehmel, frag: 90 bars; compl Cerha)*	
6.13	"Die eiserne Brigade," march (c1916; pf qnt)	
6.14	"Weihnachtsmusik" (c1921; 2vn, vc, pf & harm)	
6.15	"Gerpa" (Theme & variations), in F major (c1922; hn, pf, 1st vn, 2nd vn & harm, theme & 3 var complete)..	
6.16	Wind Quintet (c1923–4; arr Greissle as: Vn/Cl Sonata)	Op.26

3 insts:

6.17	String Trio (12-tone method) (c1946)	Op.45

Vn & pf:

6.18	Untitled work in D minor (c early)	
6.19	*Violin Sonata (c1928, frag: 43 bars)*	
6.20	"Phantasy" (12-tone method) (c1949; vn w/ pf acc)	Op.47

2 Vn:

6.21	"Alliance Walzer" (c early)	
6.22	"Sonnenschein Polka schnell" (c early)	
6.23	"3 Songs without Words" (c early)	

7. PIANO

7.1	"6 Ländler" (c early)	
7.2	"Song without Words" (Nocturne) (c early)	

8. ORGAN

9. MISC CANONS (vv or insts)

9.23   Puzzle canon by augmentation and diminution, 4-part (c1934) ....
9.24   Puzzle canon, 4-part (c1934) ....
9.25   "Es ist so dumm," 4-part puzzle canon (c1934, for Ganz) ....
9.26   Canon (c1935, Schoenberg, for Alban Berg on his 50th birthday) ....
9.27   Mirror canon, 4-part (c1935, for Dieterle) ....
9.28   Mirror canon, 4-part (c1936) ....
9.29   Double canon, 4-part (c1938) ....
9.30   "Mr Saunders I owe you thanks," 4-part (c1939, Schoenberg) ....
9.31   Mirror canon, 4-part (c1943) ....
9.32   "I am almost sure, when your nurse will change your diapers," 4-part (c1945, for Rodzinsky) ....
9.33   Double canon, 4-part (c1945, for Thomas Mann on his 70th birthday) ....
9.34   "Gravitationszentrum eigenen Sonnensystems," 4-part (c1949, Schoenberg) ....

10. CHORAL WORKS

10.1   "Ei du Lütte," partsong (c early, Groth; m ch) ....
10.2   "Friedlicher Abend senkt sich aufs Gefilde," partsong in canon (c early; ch) ....
10.3   "Viel tausend Blümlein auf der Au," partsong (c early; ch) ....
10.4   *"Wenn weder Mond noch Stern am Himmel stehn" (c1897, Pfau; m ch, winds, frag: 54 bars)* ....
10.5   "Gurrelieder" (Songs of Gurre), oratorio (c1900–1, Jacobsen transl Arnold; S, A, T, Bar, B, recit, ch & orch;
        orchd1901–3 & 1910–11) ....
10.6   *"Darthulas Grabgesang" (c1903, Goethe; ch & orch, frag: 65 bars)* ....
10.7   "Peace on Earth" (c1907, Meyer; ch & insts ad lib; acc added 1911) Op.13
10.8   "Der Deutsche Michel," war-song (c1914 or 5, Kernstock; m ch) ....
10.9   "Die Jakobsleiter" (Jacob's Ladder), oratorio (c1917–22, Schoenberg; vv, ch & orch; r from1944 unfin) ......
10.10   "4 Pieces" (c1925; ch): 1. "Inescapable" (Schoenberg) Op.27
10.11   2. "Thou shall not, Thou must!" (Schoenberg)
10.12   3. "Moon & Mankind" (Tschan-Jo-Su in Bethge's Die chinesische Flöte)
10.13   4. "The Lover's Wish" (Hung-So-Fan in Bethge's Die chinesische Flöte; w/ cl, mand, vn & vc)
10.14   "3 Satires" (c1925, Schoenberg; ch): 1. "At the Crossroads" Op.28
10.15   2. "Versality"
10.16   3. "The New Classicism," small cantata (ch, va, vc & pf)
10.17   App.1 "Ein Spruch und zwei Variationen über ihn: O glaubet nicht," 4-part (c1925–6)
10.18   App.2 "Canon" (c1926; str qt)
10.19   App.3 "Legitimation als Canon: Wer Ehr erweist," 6-part (c1926)
10.20   "3 Folksongs" (c1929; ch): 1. "Es gingen zwei Gespielen gut" ....
10.21   2. "Herzlieblich Lieb, durch Scheiden"
10.22   3. "Schein uns, du liebe Sonne"
10.23   "6 Pieces" (c1929–30, Schoenberg; m ch): 1. "Restraint" Op.35
10.24   2. "The Law"
10.25   3. "Means of Expression"
10.26   4. "Happiness"
10.27   5. "Yeomen"
10.28   6. "Obligation"
10.29   "Kol Nidre," Jewish liturgy in English (tonal) (c1938; speaker, ch & orch) Op.39
10.30   "Prelude," to collab cantata: Genesis (Creation) (c1945, wordless; ch & orch) Op.44
               "Genesis": 1. "Prelude" (c by Schoenberg)
               2. "Creation" (c by Schilkret)
               3. "Fall of man" (c by Tansman)
               4. "Cain and Abel" (c by Milhaud)
               5. "Flood" (c by Castelnuovo-Tedesco)
               6. "Covenant" (c by Toch)
               7. "Babel" (c by Stravinsky)
10.31   "A Survivor from Warsaw" (12-tone method) (c1947, Schoenberg; speaker, m ch & orch) Op.46
10.32   "3 Folksongs" (tonal) (c1948; ch): 1. "Es gingen zwei Gespielen gut" (Two comely maidens) Op.49
10.33   2. "Der Mai tritt ein mit Freuden" (Now May has come with gladness)
10.34   3. "Mein Herz in steten Treuen" (To her I shall be faithful)
10.35   *"Israel Exists Again" (c1949, Schoenberg; ch & orch, short score only: 55 bars)* ....
10.36   "Dreimal tausend Jahre" (12-tone method) (c1949, Runes; ch) Op.50a
10.37   "De Profundis" (12-tone method) (c1950, Psalm 130 in Hebrew; ch) Op.50b
10.38   "Modern Psalm" (Der erste Psalm), (12-tone method) (c1950, Schoenberg; speaker, ch & orch) Op.50c

11. VOICE & ORCHESTRA

11.1   *"Gethsemane" (c1899, Dehmel; 1 m v & orch, frag: 88 bars)* ....
11.2   "6 Orchestral Songs": 1. "Nature" (c1903–4, Hart) Op.8
11.3   2. "The Coat-of-Arms" (c19033–4, from Des Knaben Wunderhorn)
11.4   3. "Longing" (c1905, from Des Knaben Wunderhorn)
11.5   4. "Ne'er, mistress, did I weary" (c1904, Petrarch transl Förster)
11.6   5. "Filled with that sweetness" (c1904, Petrarch transl Förster)
11.7   6. "When little birds complain" (c1904, Petrarch transl Förster)
11.8   "4 Orchestral Songs": 1. "Seraphita": "Come not before me now, O visionary face!" (c1913, Dowson
               transl George) Op.22

11.9	2. "All that seek Thee" (c1914, Rilke)
11.10	3. "Make me Thy guardian" (c1914–5, Rilke)
11.11	4. "Premonition" (c1916, Rilke)
11.12	"String Quartet No.2" (arr1919; S & strings, from: Str Qt, Op.10) .... (Op.10)
11.13	"Allein Gott in der Höh' sei Ehr' " (ca1918–25, Hovesch; A, vn, vc & pf, arr of chorale) ....
11.14	"Lied der Waldtaube" (arr1922; mS & 17 insts, from choral work: Gurrelieder of 1900–1) ....
11.15	"Ode to Napoleon Buonaparte": " 'Tis done—but yesterday a King!" (12-tone method) (c1942, from Byron; reciter, pf & str qt/ strings) Op.41

12. SONGS (w/ pf)

Undated (c before 1900):

12.1	"Dass gestern eine Wepe Dich" ....
12.2	"Dass schon die Maienzeit vorüber" (Christen) ....
12.3	"Der Pflanze, die dort über dem Abgrund" (Pfau) ....
12.4	"Schilflied": "Drüben geht die Sonne scheiden" (Lenau) ....
12.5	"Du kehrst mir den Rücken" (Pfau) ....
12.6	"Mannesbangen": "Du musst nicht meinen" (Dehmel) ....
12.7	"Eclogue": "Duftreich ist die Erde" ....
12.8	"Einsam bin ich und alleine" (Pfau) ....
12.9	"Einst hat vor deines Vaters Haus" ....
12.10	"Es ist ein Flüstern in der Nacht" (T & str qt) ....
12.11	"Gedenken": "Es steht sein Bild noch immer da" ....
12.12	"Gott grüss dich Marie" (Pfau) ....
12.13	"Ich grüne wie die Weide grünt" (Wackernagel) ....
12.14	"Das zerbrochene Krüglein": "Ich hab' zum Brunnen ein Krüglein gebracht" (Greif) ....
12.15	"Im Fliederbusch ein Vöglein sass" (Reinick) ....
12.16	"Juble, schöne junge Rose" ....
12.17	"Klein Vögelein, du zwitscherst fein" ....
12.18	"Könnt' ich je zu dir mein Licht" (Pfau) ....
12.19	"Lied der Schnitterin": "Lass deine Sichel rauschen" (Pfau) ....
12.20	"Nicht doch!": "Mädel, lass das Stricken" (Dehmel) ....
12.21	"Mein Herz das ist ein tiefer Schacht" ....
12.22	"Mein Schatz ist wie ein Schneck" (Pfau) ....
12.23	"Nur das thut mir so bitter weh" (Redwitz) ....
12.24	"Mädchenlied": "Sang ein Bettlerpärlein am Schenkentor" (Heyse) ....
12.25	"Waldesnacht": "Waldesnacht, du wunderkühle" (Heyse) ....
12.26	"Warum bist Du aufgewacht" ....

Dated:

12.27	"In hellen Träumen hab ich Dich oft gesehen" (c1893, Gold) ....
12.28	"Zweiffler": "Du kleine bist so lieb und hold" (c ?1895, Pfau) ....
12.29	"Vergissmeinnicht": "War ein Blümlein wunderfein" (c ?1895, Pfau) ....
12.30	"Mädchenlied": "In meinem Garten die Nelken" (c ?1896, Geibel) ....
12.31	"Sehnsucht": "Als mein Auge sie fand" (c ?1896, Zedlitz) ....
12.32	"Mädchenfrühling": "Aprilwind, alle Knospen" (c1897, Dehmel) ....
12.33	"2 Songs" (c ?1898, Levetzow; Bar & pf): 1. "Thanks" Op.1
12.34	2. "Farewell"
12.35	"Die Beiden": "Sie trug den Becher in der Hand" (c1899, Hofmannsthal) ....
12.36	"4 Songs" (c1899): 1. "Expectation" (Dehmel) Op.2
12.37	2. "Give me thy golden comb" (Dehmel)
12.38	3. "Exaltation" (Dehmel)
12.39	4. "The forest sun" (Schlaf)
12.40	"Gruss in die Ferne": "Dunkelnd über den See" (c1900, Lingg) ....
12.41	"Cabaret songs" (Brettellieder) (c1901, for cabaret 'Bunte Bühne'): 1. "Der genügsame Liebhaber" (Salus)
12.42	2. "Einfältiges Lied" (Salus)
12.43	3. "Nachtwandler" (Falke; S, piccolo, tpt, side drum & pf)
12.44	4. "Jedem das Seine" (Colly)
12.45	5. "Mahnung" (Hochstetter)
12.46	6. "Galathea" (Wedekind)
12.47	7. "Gigerlette" (Bierbaum)
12.48	8. "Seit ich so viele Weiber sah" (from Schikaneder's Mirror of Arcadia)
12.49	"Deinem Blick zu mich bequemen" (c1903, from Goethe's West-östlicher Divan) ....
12.50	"6 Songs" (mS/Bar & pf): 1. "How Georg von Frundsberg sang about himself" (c1903, from Des Knaben Wunderhorn) Op.3
12.51	2. "The excited ones" (c1903, Keller)
12.52	3. "Warning" (c1899, Dehmel)
12.53	4. "Wedding song" (c ?1900, Jacobsen transl Arnold)
12.54	5. "The experienced heart" (c1903, Keller)
12.55	6. "Free and fair" (c1900, Lingg)
12.56	"8 Songs": 1. "Dream life" (c1903, Hart) Op.6
12.57	2. "Everything" (c1905, Dehmel)

12.58	3. "Maiden's song" (c1905, Remer)
12.59	4. "Forsaken" (c1903, Conradi)
12.60	5. "Ghasel" (c1904, Keller)
12.61	6. "By the wayside" (c1905, Mackay)
12.62	7. "Temptation" (c1905, Aram)
12.63	8. "The Wanderer" (c1905, Nietzsche)
12.64	"2 Ballads" (c1907): 1. "Jane Grey" (Ammann) Op.12
12.65	2. "The lost battalion" (Klemperer)
12.66	*"Jeduch," ballad (c1907, Löns, frag: 82 bars, intended for Op.12)* ....
12.67	*"Mignon": "Kennst du das Land" (c1907, Goethe, frag: 54 bars)* ....
12.68	"2 Songs": 1. "I dare not thank thee" (c1907, George) Op.14
12.69	2. "In diesen Wintertagen" (In these winter days) (c1908, Henckel) (also see R. Strauss Op.48/4)
12.70	"Fünfzehn Gedichte aus 'Das Buch der hängenden Gärten' " (The Book of the Hanging Gardens), cycle
	(c1908–9, George): 1. "Unterm Schutz von dichten blättergründen" Op.15
12.71	2. "Hain in diesen Paradiesen"
12.72	3. "Als Neuling trat ich ein in dein Gehege"
12.73	4. "Da meine Lippen reglos sind und brennen"
12.74	5. "Saget mir, auf welchem Pfade"
12.75	6. "Jedem Werke bin ich fürder tot"
12.76	7. "Angst und Hoffen wechselnd mich beklemmen"
12.77	8. "Wenn ich heut nicht deinen Leib berühre"
12.78	9. "Streng ist uns das Glück und Spröde"
12.79	10. "Das schöne Beet beträcht ich mir im Harren"
12.80	11. "Als wir hinter dem beblümten Tore"
12.81	12. "Wenn sich bei heiliger Ruh in tiefen Matten"
12.82	13. "Du lehnest wider eine Silberweide"
12.83	14. "Sprich nicht immer von dem Laub"
12.84	15. "Wir bevölkerten die abend-düstern Lauben"
12.85	*"Friedensabend" (c1908, George, frag: 27 bars; intended for Op.15)* ....
12.86	"Am Strande" (c1909, Rilke)
12.87	"Herzegewächse" (c1911, Maeterlinck transl Ammer & Oppeln; S, celesta, harp & harm) Op.20
12.88	"4 Folksong Arrangements" (c1929): 1. "Der Mai tritt ein mit Freuden" ....
12.89	2. "Es gingen zwei Gespielen gut"
12.90	3. "Mein Herz in steten Treuen"
12.91	4. "Mein Herz ist mir gemenget"
12.92	"3 Songs" (12-tone method) (c1933, Haringer; A/B & pf): 1. "Weary of Summer" Op.48
12.93	2. "Dead"
12.94	3. "Maiden's Song"

13. ARRANGEMENTS OF WORKS OF OTHERS

13.1	Susaneck: "Irmen Walzer" (arr early; 2vn) ....
13.2	Waldman: "So wie du" (arr early; 2vn) ....
13.3	"Wiener Fiakerlied" (arr early; 2vn) ....
13.4	Zemlinsky, A. von: "Sarema," opera (vocal score 1897) ....
13.5	Schenker, H.: "4 syrische Tänze," for pf duet (orchd1903) ....
13.6	Monn, G. M.: Cello Concerto in G minor (arr1913; vc & pf, incl cadenza) ....
13.7	Zemlinsky, A. von: String Quartet No.2, Op.15 (arr1915; pf duet) ....
13.8	Bach, J. S.: "Chorale Prelude: Komm, Gott, Schöpfer, heiliger Geist," BWV631 (orchd1922) ....
13.9	Bach, J. S.: "Chorale Prelude: Schmücke dich, O liebe Seele," BWV654 (orchd1922) ....
13.10	Strauss, J. Jr.: "Kaiserwalzer," Op.437 (arr1925; fl, cl & pf qnt) ....
13.11	Bach, J. S.: "Prelude and fugue," in E-flat major, "St.Anne," BWV552 (arr1928; large orch) ....
13.12	Brahms: Pf Quartet No.1 in G minor, Op.25 (arr1937; orch, Schoenberg called it: 'Brahms's Fifth') ....

Hack-work, scoring of 6000 pages of works by others, incl:

13.13	Eyken, H. van: "Lied der Walküre" (arr1901; 1v & orch) ....
13.14	Zepler, B.: "Mädchenreigen" (arr1902; 3vv & orch) ....
13.15	Lortzing: "Der Waffenschmied von Worms" (arr ?1904; pf duet) ....
13.16	Rossini: "Il Barbiere di Siviglia," opera (Overture & 15 Nos.) (arr p1903; pf duet) ....
13.17	Schubert: "Rosamunde," incid music, Op.26, D797 (Overture, Entr'actes & Ballet) (arr ?1903; pf duet) ......

Editions (realization of figured basses 1911–2):

13.18	Monn, G. M.: "Sinfonia a 4," in A major ....
13.19	Monn, G. M.: Cello Concerto in G minor ....
13.20	Monn, G. M.: Harpsichord Concerto in D major (used in: Cello Concerto of 1932–3) ....
13.21	Monn, J. C.: "Divertimento," in D major (Denkmäler der Tonkunst in Österreich) ....
13.22	Tuma, F.: "Sinfonia a 4," in E minor ....
13.23	Tuma, F.: "Partita a 3," in A major ....
13.24	Tuma, F.: "Partita a 3," in C minor ....
13.25	Tuma, F.: "Partita a 3," in G major ....

Songs orchd for Julia Culp (arr1912; 1v & orch):

13.26 Beethoven: "Adelaide," Op.46 ....
13.27 Löwe, C.: "Der Nöck" (The Water-Sprite), Op.129/2 ....
13.28   Schubert: 3 Songs (titles unknown, lost) ....

Arrs for the Society for Private Musical Performances:

13.29 Busoni, F.: "Berceuse élégiaque" (arr1919–21; fl, cl, harm, pf qnt) ....
13.30 Strauss, J. Jr.: "Roses from the South," Op.388 (arr1921; pf qnt & harm) ....
13.31 Strauss, J. Jr.: "Lagunenwalzer," Op.411 (arr1921; pf qnt & harm)....................................

Instrumentation exercises for teaching (arr1921):

13.32   Schubert: "Der Lindenbaum": "Am Brunnen vor dem Tore," D911/5 (arr for large orch, frag)...........................
13.33 Schubert: "Ständchen": "Horch, horch! die Lerch," D889 (arr for cl, bn, mand, gui & str qt) ....
13.34 Denza: "Funiculi, funiculà" (arr for cl, mand, gui & str trio) ....
13.35 Untitled polka (w/ Trio in waltz-time) (arr / ?c by Schoenberg; cl, mand, gui & str trio) ....

* * * * *

12-tone method—a system of music organization based on a composer's chosen 'series' or 'row' of
12 pitches of the chromatic scale. (Schoenberg—the author of the 12-tone method, Webern & Berg are
known as the Second Viennese School.) The method is indicated in the text for some more representative
compositions only.

1. STAGE WORKS

Operas:

1.1	"Die Bürgschaft," 3 acts (c1816, unfin)	D435
1.2	*"Sakuntala," 3 acts (c1820, Neumann after Kalidasa, sketches)*	*D701*
1.3	"Alfonso und Estrella," 3 acts (c1821–2, Schober)	Op.69, D732
1.4	*"Rüdiger" (c1823, ?Mosel, sketches)*	*D791*
1.5	"Fierabras," 3 acts (c1823, Kupelwieser)	Op.76, D796
1.6	"Der Graf von Gleichen," 2 acts (c1827, Bauernfeld, unfin)	D918
1.7	*Sketches for opera (c after 1820, sketches for 3 Nos. only)*	*D982*

Singspiels:

1.8	"Der Spiegelritter," 3 act Singspiel (c1811–2, Kotzebue, unfin)	D11
1.9	"Das Teufels Lustschloss" (The Devil's Pleasure Palace), 3 act Singspiel (c1813–4, Kotzebue; 2 vers)	D84
1.10	"Adrast," 2 acts (c ?1817–9, Mayrhofer, unfin)	D137
1.11	"Der vierjährige Posten," 1 act Singspiel (c1815, Körner)	D190
1.12	"Fernando," 1 act Singspiel (c1815, Stadler)	D220
1.13	"Claudine von Villa Bella," 3 act Singspiel (c1815, Goethe, unfin)	D239
1.14	"Die Freunde von Salamanka," 2 act Singspiel (c1815, Mayrhofer)	D326
1.15	"Die Zwillingsbrüder," 1 act Singspiel (c1819, Hofmann)	D647
1.16	"Die Verschworenen," 1 act Singspiel (c1823, Castelli after Aristophanes: Lysistrata)	D787
1.17	*"Der Minnesänger," Singspiel (unfin, lost)*	*D981*

Melodramas & incid music:

1.18	"Die Zauberharfe" (The Magic Harp), 3 act melodrama (c1820, Hofmann)	D644
1.19	Add music (duet & aria) to Hérold's La clochette (c1821, Lambert transl Treitsche):	D723
	. "Nein, nein, nein, nein, das ist zu viel," duet (Zedit, Bedur)	
	. "Der tag entflieht, der Abend glüht," aria (Azolin)	
1.20	"Rosamunde, Fürstin von Zypern," incid music to romantic play (c1823, Chézy)	Op.26, D797

1a. SELECTIONS FROM STAGE WORKS

1a.1	"Die Bürgschaft," opera:	D435

   I: 1. "Hülfe! Rettung!," chorus
        2. "Muss ich fühlen," aria (Möros)
        3. "Wie dürstet der Ätna, der heisse Koloss," chorus
        4. "Es lebe, es lebe der meutrische Tor," chorus
        5. "Diese Gnade dank ich dir," aria (Möros)
        6. "Ob er wohl wiederkehrt?," aria (Dionys)
        7. "Die Mutter sucht ihr liebes Kind," romance (Anna, Ismene, Julus)
        8. "Wir bringen dir die Kette hier," duet (Ismene, Julus)
        9. "Du gehst in Kerker, du?," finale (Anna, Ismene, Julus, Theages, Chor der Wache)
   II: 10. "O Götter! O, Dank euch!," entr'acte & aria (Möros)
       11. "Welche Nacht hab ich erlebt," aria (Anna)
       12. "Horch die Seufzer unsrer Mutter," ensemble (Anna, Ismene, Julus, Philostratus)
       13. "Hinter Büschen, hinterm Laub, sitzt der Vogel, lauscht der Raub," quartet (4 Räuber)
       14. "O göttliche Ruhe!," scene & aria (Möros)
   III: 15. "Entr'acte"
       16. "Der Abend rückt heran," ensemble (Theages, chorus)

1a.2	*"Sakuntala," opera (sketches):*	*D701*

   I: 1. "Das holde Licht des Tages," introduction (Sakuntala, Gautomi, Kanna, ch)
        2. "Du hoffest im Arme des Gatten," aria (Durwasas)
        3. "Wie fühl ich, ihr Götter, mein Innres erschüttert," aria (Sakuntala)
        4. "Wie du wandelst atme dir Freudenluft entgegen," chorus (Waldnymphen)
        5. "Noch schläft die goldne Sonne," aria (Madhavia)
        6. "Sieg, Sieg deinen Fahnen," finale
   II: 7. "Komm nur Dieb!," trio (Häscher/T, Häscher/B, Fischer)
        8. "Rosenzeit der Freuden," quartet (Sakuntala, Menaka, 2 Mädchen)
        9. "Mit lieben dem Verlangen sieht er dem Bild entgegen," septet
       10. (not listed in Deutsch's catalog)
       11. "Trauet auf Götter trauet," aria (Kanna)
        . "Hier liegen wir, im Staub gebeget," quintet (Anusuya, Priyamwada, Durwasas, 2 Dämonen)

1a.3	"Alfonso und Estrella," opera:	Op.69, D732

        . "Ouvertüre"
   I: 1. "Still noch decket uns die Nacht," introduction (Landleute)
        2. "Sei mir gegrüsst, o Sonne," aria (Troila)
        3. "Versammelt euch, Brüder," chorus & ensemble (Mädchen, Jüngling, Troila, ch)
        4. "Geschmückt von Glanz und Siegen," duet (Alfonso, Troila)
        5. "Es ist dein streng Gebot ... Schon, wenn es beginnt zu tagen," recit & aria (Alfonso)

      6. "Du rührst mich, Teurer, sehr ... Schon schleichen meine Späher," recit & duet (Alfonso, Troila)
      7. "Zur Jagd, zur Jagd!... Es schmückt die weiten Säle," chorus & aria (Estrella)
      8. "Verweile, o Prinzessin ... Doch im Getümmel der Schlacht," recit & aria (Estrella, Adolfo)
      9. "Ja gib, vernimm mein Flehen," duet (Estrella, Adolfo)
     10. "Glänzende Waffe den Krieger erfreut," finale (Estrella, Mauregato, Adolfo, Frauen, Krieger)
II: 11. "Der Jäger ruhte hingegossen," recit & aria (Alfonso, Troila) (Troila's aria = D683)
     12. "Wie rührt mich dein herrlicher Gesang," recit & duet (Estrella, Alfonso, Troila)
     13. "Wer bist du, holdes Wesen?... Wenn ich dich Holde sehe," recit & aria (Estrella, Alfonso)
     14. "Freundlich bist du mir erschienen," duet (Estrella, Alfonso)
     15. "Könnt ich ewig hier verweilen," aria (Estrella)
     16. "Lass dir als Erinnrungszeichen," duet (Estrella, Alfonso)
     17. "Stille, Freunde, seht euch vor ... Ja, meine Rache," chorus & aria (Adolfo, Verschworene)
     18. "Wo ist sie, was kommt ihr zu künden?," chorus & aria (Mauregato, ch)
     19. "Die Prinzessin ist erschienen!," ensemble (Estrella, Mauregato, ch)
     20. "Darf dich dein Kind umarmen?," duet & chorus (Estrella, Mauregato, ch)
     21. "Herrlich auf des Berges Höhen," aria (Estrella)
     22. "Sag, wo ist er hingekommen," finale
III: 23. "Introduction"
     24. "Hörst du rufen?," duet & chorus
     25. "Du wirst mir nicht entrinnen!," duet (Estrella, Adolfo)
     26. "Hülfe! Welche Stimme!," trio & chorus (Estrella, Alfonso, Adolfo, Jäger)
     27. "Doch nun werde deinem Retter," duet (Estrella, Alfonso)
     28. "Ja ich, ich bin gerettet," recit & duet (Estrella, Alfonso)
     29. "Wehe, wehe," duet w/ chorus (Estrella, Alfonso, Krieger)
     30. "Sie haben das Rufen vernommen," ensemble (Alfonso, Krieger, Jäger)
     31. "Was geht hier vor," recit & ensemble (Estrella, Alfonso, Troila, Krieger & Jäger)
     32. "Wo find ich nur den Ort," aria (Mauregato)
     33. "Kein Geist, ich bin am Leben," duet (Mauregato, Troilla)
     34. "Empfange nun aus meiner Hand," trio (Estrella, Mauregato, Troila)
     35. "Die Schwerter hoch geschwungen ... Liebe hat den Friedensbogen," finale

1a.4   *"Rüdiger," opera (sketches):* *D791*
      1. "Durch der Ostsee wilde Wogen," introduction (Rüdiger, Ritter, Reisigen)
      2. "Ja, sie war's, der Frauen Krone," duet (Rüdiger, Balderon)

1a.5   "Fierabras," opera: Op.76, D796
     . "Ouvertüre"
  I: 1. "Der runde Silberfaden," introduction (Emma, Jungfrauen)
     2. "O mög auf froher Hoffnung Schwingen," duet (Emma, Eginhard)
     3. "Zu hohen Ruhmespforten," march & chorus
     4. "Die Beute lass, o Herr," ensemble (Emma, Fierabras, Ogier, Eginhard, Roland, Karl, ch)
     5. "Lass uns mutvoll hoffen," duet (Fierabrass, Roland)
     6. "Der Abend sinkt auf stiller Flur," finale (Emma, Eginhard, Fierabras, Karl, ch)
  II: 7. "Im jungen Morgenstrahle," Lied w/ chorus (Eginhard, Roland, Ritter)
     8. "Beschlossen ist's, ich löse seine Ketten!," ensemble
     9. "Weit über Glanz und Erdenschimmer," duet (Florinda, Maragond)
    10. "Verderben denn und Fluch," quintet (Florinda, Maragond, Eginhard, Der Fürst, Brutamonte)
    11. "Lasst Friede in die Hallen des Fürstensitzes ziehn," chorus
    12. "Im Tode sollt ihr büssen," trio w/ ch (Florinda, Roland, Der Fürst, Ritter, Mauren)
    13. "Die Brust gebeugt von Sorgen," aria (Florinda)
    14. "O teures Vaterland!," chorus (Ritter)
    15. "Selbst an des Grabes Rande," melodram & ensemble (Florinda, Roland, Ritter, Ogier, Olivier)
    16. "Der Hoffnung Strahl, den du gegeben," ensemble & melodram (Ogier, Roland, Ritter)
    17. "Uns führt der Vorsicht weise," finale (Florinda, Eginhard, Roland, Ritter)
 III: 18. "Bald tönet der Reigen," chorus (Emma, ch)
    19. "Bald, bald, bald wird es klar," quartet (Emma, Fierabras, Eginhard, Karl)
    20. "Wenn hoch im Wolkensitze der Götter Grimm erwacht," trio (Emma, Eginhard, Fierabras)
    21. "Des Jammers herbe Qualen," aria w/ chorus (Florinda, Ritter)
    . "Marcia funebre"
    22. "Der Rache Opfer fallen," chorus w/ ensemble (Florinda, Roland, Der Fürst, Mauren, Ritter)
    23. "Er ist mein Vater, halte ein!," finale

1a.6   "Der Graf von Gleichen," opera: D918
  I: 1. "Es funkelt der Morgen wie Perlen und Glut," introduction (indischen Sklaven, Frauen)
     2. "O Himmel! kannst du mir so freundlich lächeln?... Mein Weib, o Gott," recit & cavatina (Graf)
     3. "Wart, nur wart!, trio (Fatime, Kurt, Hassan)
     4. "Ein Schiff? ein Schiff?," duet (Kurt, Graf)
    5a. "Ihr Blumen, ihr Bäume, sagt," aria (Suleika)
    5b. "Suleika! Mein Herr und Freund!," recit & duet (Suleika, Graf)
    5c. "Ha! was ist das?," march & chorus (Graf, Inder) (chorus not composed)
     6. "Ihr geht und bringt die holde Tochter uns," recit & aria (Sultan)
     7. "Wie Mondlicht durch die Wolken glänzt," quintet (Suleika, 3 Fürsten, Sultan)
     8. "Himmel! Was musst' ich hören?," recit & aria (Suleika)
     9. "Tausend Frauen konnt' ich schauen," Lied (Kurt)
    10. "Ob ich verstehe?," duet (Fatime, Kurt)

11. "Finale": "Scheiden, scheiden," duet
. "Sieh die Purpurblume," recit
. "Lass das befreiende," duet
. "Hurrah! Hurrah! Die Segel gespannt," chorus (Matrosen)
II: 12. "Lasst uns nicht feiern," chorus (Schnitterinnen, Schnitter)
13. "Trocknet nicht, trocknet nicht, Tränen der ewigen Liebe," aria (Gräfin)
14. "Vaterland Vaterland nimm uns auf in deinen Arm," chorus (Kreuzfahrer)
15. "Burg meiner Väter ... O Vater der Güte," recit & aria (Graf)
16a. "Wo ist er? Wo ist er?... Lass ab, lass ab!," recit & duet (Gräfin, Graf)
16b. "Doch sprich, wo ist mein süsser Knabe?," scene & chorus (Gräfin, Graf, Burgleute)
17a. "Das Zeichen war's, das er versprach," trio (Suleika, Fatime, Kurt)
17b. "O sieh, sie kommt, der ich die Freiheit danke," quintet (Suleika, Gräfin, Fatime, Kurt, Graf)
18. "Vor allem müsst ihr wissen," Lied w/ chorus (Kurt)
19. "Gratuliere! Gratuliere! nun ich habe nichts dagegen," quartet (Susanne, Fatime, Kurt, Vogt)
20a. "Sie schläft, lass uns ihre Ruhe nicht stören," recit & aria (Gräfin, Graf)
20b. "Wohl-an! sprich zu dem frommen Kinde," duet (Gräfin, Graf)
20c. "Guter Gott, guter Gott, nimm aus dem Herzen," aria (Gräfin)
20d. "Angelika! Schlage nicht die Augen nieder," recit & duet (Suleika, Gräfin)
20e. "Ihr seid bewegt, was ist geschehen?," trio (Suleika, Gräfin, Graf)
20f. "Es geht schon im Kreise," quintet (Suleika, Fatime, Gräfin, Kurt, Graf)
21. *"Von der Eh' hat jedes so eigene Gedanken," duet (Kurt, Fatime) (not composed)*
22. *"Ich dank' euch, Freunde," finale (not composed)*

1a.7   Sketches for opera: D982
1. *"O lang ersehnte Seligkeit," quartet (Sophie, Louise, Bretone, Belville)*
2. *"Philomele, Philomele," arietta (Sophie)*
3. *"Wir giessen die Nelken," trio (Sophie, Louise, Beliville)*

1a.8   "Der Spiegelritter," Singspiel: D11
. "Ouvertüre"
1. "Heil Euch, Herr Ritter," introduction & chorus (ch, König)
2. *"Wohlan! Lasst die rüstigen Gesellen," scene (ch, Prinz, 3 Knappen, Schmurzo) (frag)*
3. *"Der Sonne Strahl ist warm," aria (König) (frag) (also frag of orch interlude, D966)*
4. "Wir gratulieren!," quintet (4 Damen, Schmurzo)
5. "Ach! es ist schön, fremde Länder zu sehn," aria & trio (Prinz, Königin, König)
6. "Ein Sinnbild auf den blanken Schild," scene w/ chorus
7. "Halte graues Haar in Ehren," aria (Prinz)
8. "So nimm, du junger Held," scene w/ chorus

1a.9   "Das Teufels Lustschloss," Singspiel: D84
. "Ouvertüre"
I: 1. "Hülfe! Hülfe, hier ist Gefahr!," scene w/ ch (Luitgarde, Oswald, Robert, 2 Bediente, Bauern)
2. "Was kümmert mich ein sumpfig Land," Lied (Robert)
3. "Ja morgen, wenn die Sonne sinkt," duet (Luitgarde, Oswald)
4. "Wohin zwei Liebende sich retten," aria (Luitgarde)
5. "Kaum hundert Schritt von dieser Schenke," quartet (Wirtin, Oswald, Robert, ein Bauer)
6. "Fort! will ich, fort!," trio (Wirtin, Oswald, Robert)
7. "Welcher Frevel, so sind die Menschen," aria (Wirtin)
8. "Gesundheit ist mit Mut verschwistert," aria (Oswald)
9. "Herr Ritter, zu Hülfe!," duet (Oswald, Robert)
10. "Trauermusik"
11. "Ach, nun ist der Teufel los!," finale (Amazone, Oswald, Robert, 4 Statuen)
II: 12. "Ich lebe noch und glaub es kaum," recit & duet (Luitgarde, Robert) (2nd vers lost)
13. "Nie bebte vor dem nahen Tode," aria (Oswald) (2nd vers lost)
14. "Melodram" (Oswald) (2nd vers lost)
15. "Hast du vergessen, kannst du ermessen," scene w/ chorus (2nd vers lost)
16. "Auf, es ist Zeit!," scene w/ ch (Oswald, Knappe, Jungfrauen, Männer) (2nd vers lost)
17. "Die Schöne, die dich hergesandt," finale (Oswald, Knappe, alter Sklave, Männer) (2nd vers lost)
III: 18. "Ihr unsichtbaren Geister!," aria (Luitgarde) (1st vers lost)
19. "O wär ich fern!," duet (Luitgarde, Robert) (1st vers lost)
20. "Ha! Die Mörder meines Gatten!," scene w/ chorus (1st vers lost)
21. "Hab ich dich wieder!," trio (Luitgarde, Oswald, Robert) (2nd vers: duet of Luitgarde & Robert)
22. "Ich lach, ich weine, ich wein," trio (Luitgarde, Oswald, Robert) (1st vers incorp in 21.)
23. "Heil! Heil! dem mächt'gen Triebe," finale (chorus)
. Orch frag from ?Act III

1a.10   "Adrast," Singspiel: D137
1. "Introduction" (Chor der Hirten, Adrast)
2. "War einer je der Sterblichen beglückt," recit & aria (Krösus)
3. "Dem König Heil, dem König Heil!," scene w/ ch (Chor der Myser, Krösus)
4. "Trauermarsch"
5. "Wie liegst du starr und bleich, mein Sohn," recit & duet (Adrast, Krösus)
6. "Meine Seele, die dich liebt," aria (Adrast)
7. "Ein schlafend Kind!," recit & aria (Adrast)
8. "Introduction"

9. *"Erheitre dich, der Lenz entbreitet,"* duet *(Arianys, Krösus) (frag)*
10. *"Aus den Fluten winket Gold,"* chorus *(Goldfischer) (sketch)*
11. *"Die Lyder sind ein reiches Volk,"* recit & duet *(Atys, Adrast) (sketch)*
12. *"Aus den Memnaden bin denn ich alleinverdammt,"* recit & duet *(Ariany, Atys) (sketch)*

1a.11   "Der vierjährige Posten," Singspiel: D190
 . "Ouvertüre"
1. "Heiter strahlt der neue Morgen," introduction (Käthe, Duval, Walther, Bäuern & Bäuerinnen)
2. "Du guter Heinrich! Du süsses Kind!," duet (Käthe, Duval)
3. "Mag dich die Hoffnung nicht betrügen!," trio (Käthe, Duval, Walther)
4. "Freund, eilet euch zu retten!," quartet (Käthe, Duval, Veit, Walther)
5. "Gott! Gott! Höre meine Stimme," aria (Käthe)
6. "Lustig in den Kampf," march & chorus (Soldaten)
7. "Um Gottes willen," scene w/ ch (Käthe, Hauptmann, Duval, Veit, Walther, Bauern, Soldaten)
8. "Schöne Stunde die uns blendet," finale

1a.12   "Fernando," Singspiel: D220
1. "Mutter! Mutter! Wo bist du?," introduction (Philipp)
2. "Lässt mich mein Verbrechen nicht schlafen?," aria (Fernando)
3. "Als einst schon hinter blauer Berge Rücken," romanze (Philipp)
4. "Wärst du mir auf immer nicht entrissen," duet (Philip, Fernando)
5. "Nicht der Erde Schätze lohnen," aria (Eleonore)
6. "Vergessen sei, was uns getrennt," duet (Eleonore, Fernando)
7. "Auf dich träufle Taues Regen," finale (Eleonore, Philipp, Fernando, Köhler, Jäger, chorus)

1a.13   "Claudine von Villa Bella," Singspiel: D239
 . "Ouvertüre"
I: 1. "Das hast du wohl bereitet," introduction (Lucinde, Pedro, Alonzo)
    2. "Fröhlicher, seliger, herrlicher Tag!" (Lucinde, Claudine, ein Kind, Pedro, Alonzo, Landleute)
    3. "Hin und wieder fliegen die Pfeile," arietta (Lucinde)
    4. "Alle Freuden, alle Gaben," aria (Claudine)
    5. "Es erhebt sich eine Stimme," aria (Pedro)
    6. "Liebe schwärmt auf allen Wegen," arietta (Claudine)
    7. "Mit Mädeln sich vertragen" (Räuberlied) (Rugantino, Vagabunden)
    8. "Deinem Willen nachzugeben" (Finale I) (Rugantino, Basco, Vagabunden)
II: 9. "Liebliches Kind, kannst du mir sagen," arietta (Pedro)
III: 10. "Mich umfängt ein banger Schauer," duet (Claudine, Pedro)

1a.14   "Die Freunde von Salamanka," Singspiel: D326
 . "Ouvertüre"
I: 1. "Die Sonne zieht in goldnen Strahlen," introduction (Alonso, Diego, Fidelio)
    2. "Man is so glücklich und so frei," aria (Fidelio)
    3. "Morgen, wenn des Hahnes Ruf erschallt," quartet (Tormes, Alonso, Diego, Fidelio)
    4. "Einsam schleich ich durch die Zimmer," aria (Olivia)
    5. "Lebensmut und frische Kühlung," trio (Olivia, Eusebia, Laura)
    6. "Freund, wie wird die Sache enden," trio (Alonso, Diego, Fidelio)
    7. "Mild senkt sich der Abend nieder," finale (Eusebia, Olivia, Alonso, Diego, Fidelio, Alkade, ch)
II: 8. "Lasst nur alles leichtfertige Wesen," introduction (Manuel, Winzerinnen, Winzer)
    9. "Guerillas zieht durch Feld und Wald," Lied (2 Guerillas)
    10. "Aus Blumen deuten die Damen gern," aria (Tormes)
    11. "Ein wackres Tier, das müsst Ihr sagen," duet (Diego, Xilo)
    12. "Gelagert unterm hellen Dach," duet (Laura, Diego)
    13. "Wo ich weile, wo ich gehe," aria (Olivia)
    14. "Von tausend Schlangenbisen," duet (Olivia, Alonso)
    15. "Es murmeln die Quellen, es leuchtet der Stern," romanze (Diego)
    16. "Nichte, Don Diego da," trio (Laura, Diego, Alkade)
    17. "Traurig geht der Geliebte von dannen," aria (Laura)
    18. "Gnäd'ge Frau, ich hab die Ehre," finale

1a.15   "Die Zwillingsbrüder," Singspiel: D647
 . "Ouvertüre"
1. "Verglühet sind die Sterne," introduction (Anton, Landleute)
2. "Vor dem Busen möge blühen," duet (Lieschen, Anton)
3. "Der Vater mag wohl immer Kind mich nennen," aria (Lieschen)
4. "Mag es stürmen, donnern, blitzen," aria (Franz)
5. "Zu rechter Zeit bin ich gekommen," quartet (Lieschen, Anton, Franz, Schulze)
6. "Liebe teure Muttererde," aria (Friedrich)
7. "Nur dir will ich gehören," duet (Lieschen, Anton)
8. "Wagen Sie, Ihr Wort zu brechen?," trio (Lieschen, Anton, Franz)
9. "Packt ihn, führt ihn vor Gericht," quintet (Lieschen, Anton, Franz, Schulze, Amtmann)
10. "Die Brüder haben sich gefunden," final chorus

1a.16   "Die Verschworenen," Singspiel: D787
 . "Ouvertüre"
1. "Sie ist's! Er ist's!," duet (Isella, Udolin) (2 vers)

2. "Ich schleiche gang und still herum," romanze (Helene)
3. "Ihr habt auf Eure Burg entboten," ensemble (Gräfin, Isella, Udolin, Helene, Luitgarde, ch)
4. "Ja, wir schwören" (Verschwörungschor, Gräfin)
5. "Vorüber ist die Zeit," march & chorus
6. "Verräterei hab ich entdeckt," ensemble (Udolin, Graf, Ritter)
7. "Willkommen, schön willkommen," chorus (Ritter, Frauen)
8. "Ich muss sie finden," duet (Helene, Astolf)
9. "Ich habe gewagt und habe gestritten," arietta (Graf)
10. "Gesetzt, Ihr habt wirklich gewagt und gestritten," arietta (Gräfin)
11. "Wie? darf ich meinen Augen traun?," finale

1a.18   "Die Zauberharfe," melodrama: D644
         . "Ouvertüre"
         I: 1. "Harfentöne lasst erklingen," chorus (Palmerin, Troubadoure)
               2. "Zum Saal, der goldne Becher blinkt," chorus (Troubadoure, Ritter)
               3. "Melodram" (Sutur, melinde, Ida)
               4. "Ida! Ida, gib ein Zeichen," finale (Ritter, Knappen)
         II: 5. "Leben lasst den goldnen Wein," chorus (Palmerin, Troubadoure, Ritter)
               6. "Furie bebe!," melodram (Arnulf, Melinde)
               7. "Die Zauberin lasst uns betrügen," chorus (Ritter)
               8. "Da ziehn sie hin ...," melodram (Ida)
               9. "Was belebt die schöne Welt?," romanze (Palmerin)
               . "Schlafe, Liebliche, denn dein Sehnen wird erfüllt," chorus (Genien)
         III: . "Ouvertüre" (to Act III)
               10. "Melodram" (Folko, Ryno, Arnulf, Melinde)
               11. "Melodram hinter den Kulissen" (Melinde)
               12. "Melodram" (Melinde, Arnulf, Ida, Sutur, Palmerin, 3 Ritter, Folko, Ryno, Alf, Geister)
               13. "Durch der Töne Zaubermacht schönes Werk, bist du vollbracht," finale (ch)

1a.20   "Rosamunde, Fürstin von Zypern," incid music: Op.26, D797
         . "Ouvertüre," D644 (c1820 for melodrama: The Magic Harp, D644)
         1. "Entr'acte," in B minor
         2. "Ballet," in B minor
         3. "Entr'acte," in D major
         3b. "Romanze": "Der Vollmond strahlt auf Bergeshöhn" (Axa)
         4. "Geisterchor": "In der Tiefe wohnt das Licht"
         5. "Entr'acte," in B-flat major
         6. "Hirtenmelodien"
         7. "Hirtenchor": "Hier auf den Fluren mit rosigen Wangen"
         8. "Jägerchor": "Wie lebt sich's so fröhlich im Grünen"
         9. "Ballet," in G major

2. SYMPHONIES

3. OTHER ORCHESTRAL WORKS

6.14	Piano Quintet in A major, "Die Forelle" (Trout) (c1819; pf, vn, va, vc, d bass)	Op.posth114, D667
6.15	String Quintet in C major (c1828; 2vn, va & 2vc)	Op.posth163, D956

4 insts:

6.16	Quartet in G major (c1814; fl, va, gui & vc; add to Schubert's arr of Matiegka's Notturno, Op.21)	D96
6.17	"Adagio & Rondo concertante," in F major (c1816; pf qt)	D487

String Trios:

6.18	*String Trio in B-flat major (c1814, ?sketch for D112, frag, lost)* *D111a*
6.19	String Trio in B-flat major (c1816, inc: 1st movt & frag of 2nd)	D471
6.20	String Trio in B-flat major (c1817)	D581

Piano Trios:

6.21	Piano Trio (Sonata in 1 movt) in B-flat major (c1812)	D28
6.22	Piano Trio in E-flat major, "Notturno" (c ?1828)	Op.posth148, D897
6.23	Piano Trio No.1 in B-flat major (c1827)	Op.posth99, D898
6.24	Piano Trio No.2 in E-flat major (c1827) Op.100, D929

Vn & pf:

6.25	Violin Sonata (Sonatina), in D major (c1816)	Op.posth137/1, D384
6.26	Violin Sonata (Sonatina), in A minor (c1816)	Op.posth137/2, D385
6.27	Violin Sonata (Sonatina), in G minor (c1816)	Op.posth137/3, D408
6.28	Violin Sonata (Grand Duo), in A major (c1817)	Op.posth162, D574
6.29	"Rondo brillant," in B minor (c1826) Op.70, D895
6.30	"Fantasie," in C major (c1827)	Op.posth159, D934

Other 2 insts:

6.31	*"Duo," in D major (c1816; 2vn, spur)* *Anh.I/6*
6.32	"4 komische Ländler," in D major (c1816; 2vn)	D354
6.33	"Variations on song 'Trockne Blumen,' " in E min / major (c1824; fl & pf, from Op.25, D795)	Op.posth160, D802
6.34	Sonata in A minor, "Arpeggione" (c1824; arpeggione/vc & pf)	D821

1 instr:

6.35	8 "Ländler," in F-sharp minor (c1816; ?vn)	D355
6.36	9 "Ländler," in D major (c1816; ?vn)	D370
6.37	11 "Ländler," in B-flat major (c1816; vn)	D374
6.38	*"Variations," in A major (c1817; vn, sketch, lost)* *D597a*
6.39	*"Generalbassübungen" (?spur)* ....*Anh.I/31 (D598a)*

7. PIANO SONATAS

7.1	*Piano Sonata in F major (c1815, lost)* *Anh.I/8*
7.2	Piano Sonata No.1 in E major (c1815, 3 movts only)	D157
7.3	Piano Sonata No.2 in C major (c1815, Minuet = D277a w/ altern Trio, Finale = ?Allegretto, D346)	D279
7.4	*Piano Sonata in F major (c1816, lost)* *Anh.I/9*
7.5	Piano Sonata No.3 in E major (c1816, = Nos.1 & 2 of: 5 Klavierstücke, D459a, inc)	D459
7.6	Piano Sonata No.4 in A minor (c1817)	Op.posth164, D537
7.7	Piano Sonata No.5 in A-flat major (c1817)	D557
7.8	Piano Sonata No.6 in E minor (c1817, ?Finale = Rondo in E major, D506)	D566
7.9	*Piano Sonata in D-flat major (c1817, inc, 1st vers of: Pf Sonata No.7 in E-flat major, D568)* *D567*
7.10	Piano Sonata No.7 in E-flat major (c1817)	Op.posth122, D568
7.11	*Piano Sonata No.8 in F-sharp major (c1817, frag of 1st movt only, + ?D604 + ?D570)* *D571*
7.12	Piano Sonata No.9 in B major (c1817)	Op.posth147, D575
7.13	Piano Sonata No.10 in C major (c1818, inc: 2 movts only, ?slow movt = Adagio in E major, D612)	D613
7.14	Piano Sonata No.11 in F minor (c1818, inc: 2 movts only, slow movt = Adagio in D-flat major, D505)	D625
7.15	*Piano Sonata No.12 in C-sharp minor (c1819, frag of 1st movt only)* *D655*
7.16	Piano Sonata No.13 in A major (c1819 or 1825)	Op.posth120, D664
7.17	*Piano Sonata in E minor (ca1823, frag of 1st movt)* .... *D769a (D994)*
7.18	Piano Sonata No.14 in A minor, "Grande Sonate" (c1823)	Op.posth143, D784
7.19	Piano Sonata No.15 in C major, "Relique" / "Unfinished" (c1825, inc movts 3 & 4)	D840
7.20	Piano Sonata No.16 in A minor (c1825)	Op.42, D845
7.21	Piano Sonata No.17 in D major (c1825)	Op.53, D850
7.22	Piano Sonata No.18 in G major, "Fantasy" (c1826)	Op.78, D894
7.23	Piano Sonata No.19 in C minor (c1828)	D958
7.24	Piano Sonata No.20 in A major (c1828)	D959
7.25	Piano Sonata No.21 in B-flat major (c1828)	D960

8. DANCES FOR PIANO

8.74	No.5 in B major (= Ecossaise in A-flat major, D421/1)
8.75	No.6 in A-flat major (= Ecossaise, D697/5)
8.76	No.7 in B major
8.77	No.8 in B minor (2 vers)
8.78	No.9 in G major
8.79	IV. "Atzenbrugger Tänze" (Nos.1–3)
8.80	"20 Waltzes" (c1815 & 23): No.1 in D maj / G major Op.posth127, D146
8.81	No.2 in A major
8.82	No.3 in E maj / A major (= Deutscher in E major, D135 w/ new Trio)
8.83	No.4 in A major
8.84	No.5 in A maj / A-flat major
8.85	No.6 in D major
8.86	No.7 in B minor
8.87	No.8 in G maj / D major
8.88	No.9 in C major
8.89	No.10 in F maj / B major
8.90	No.11 in B major
8.91	No.12 in G minor
8.92	No.13 in C major
8.93	No.14 in G major
8.94	No.15 in G minor
8.95	No.16 in F major
8.96	No.17 in B major
8.97	No.18 in B major
8.98	No.19 in F major
8.99	No.20 in D maj / G major
8.100	"Ecossaise," in D min / F major (c1815) D158
8.101	"Minuet" (w/ Trio), in A minor (c1815; used in: Pf Sonata No.2 in C major, D279) D277a
8.102	"12 Ecossaises" (c1815): No.1 in A-flat major (= D145/1) D299
8.103	No.2 in E-flat major
8.104	No.3 in E major
8.105	No.4 in A major
8.106	No.5 in D-flat major
8.107	No.6 in A-flat major
8.108	No.7 in E major
8.109	No.8 in C major
8.110	No.9 in F major
8.111	No.10 in B-flat major
8.112	No.11 in A-flat major
8.113	No.12 in A-flat major
8.114	"Minuet" (w/ Trio in E), in A major (ca1815) D334
8.115	"Minuet" (w/ 2 Trios), in E major (ca1813) D335
8.116	*"Minuet" (w/ Trio), in D major (c?, ?spur)* ....*Anh.I/15 (D336)*
8.117	"36 Originaltänze" (Erste Walzer) (c1816–21): No.1 in A-flat major Op.9, D365
8.118	No.2 in A-flat major, "Trauerwalzer"
8.119	No.3 in A-flat major
8.120	No.4 in A-flat major
8.121	No.5 in A-flat major
8.122	No.6 in A-flat major
8.123	No.7 in A-flat major
8.124	No.8 in A-flat major
8.125	No.9 in A-flat major
8.126	No.10 in A-flat major
8.127	No.11 in A-flat major
8.128	No.12 in A-flat major
8.129	No.13 in A-flat major
8.130	No.14 in D-flat major
8.131	No.15 in D-flat major
8.132	No.16 in A major
8.133	No.17 in A major
8.134	No.18 in A major
8.135	No.19 in G major
8.136	No.20 in G major
8.137	No.21 in G major
8.138	No.22 in B major
8.139	No.23 in B major
8.140	No.24 in B major
8.141	No.25 in E major
8.142	No.26 in E major
8.143	No.27 in C-sharp minor
8.144	No.28 in A major
8.145	No.29 in D major
8.146	No.30 in A major
8.147	No.31 in C major
8.148	No.32 in F major

8.149	No.33 in F major	
8.150	No.34 in F major	
8.151	No.35 in F major	
8.152	No.36 in F major	
8.153	"17 Ländler" (c1816–24): No.1 in A major	D366
8.154	No.2 in A major	
8.155	No.3 in C major	
8.156	No.4 in C major	
8.157	No.5 in C major	
8.158	No.6 in C major	
8.159	No.7 in G major	
8.160	No.8 in D major	
8.161	No.9 in B major	
8.162	No.10 in D major	
8.163	No.11 in B major	
8.164	No.12 in G-flat major	
8.165	No.13 in D-flat major	
8.166	No.14 in D-flat major	
8.167	No.15 in D-flat major	
8.168	No.16 in A-flat major	
8.169	No.17 in E-flat major (arr from pf duet, D814/1)	
8.170	"8 Ländler," in B-flat major (c1816)	D378
8.171	"3 Minuets" (each w/ 2 Trios) (c1816): No.1 in E major	D380
8.172	No.2 in A major	
8.173	No.3 in C major (2nd Trio lost)	
8.174	"12 Deutsche" (c1816): No.1 in D major	D420
8.175	No.2 in A major	
8.176	No.3 in D major	
8.177	No.4 in A major	
8.178	No.5 in D major	
8.179	No.6 in A major	
8.180	No.7 in E major	
8.181	No.8 in A major	
8.182	No.9 in D major	
8.183	No.10 in A major	
8.184	No.11 in D major	
8.185	No.12 in A major	
8.186	. "Coda," in D major	
8.187	"6 Ecossaises" (c1816): No.1 in A-flat major (= D145/5)	D421
8.188	No.2 in F minor	
8.189	No.3 in E-flat major	
8.190	No.4 in B-flat major	
8.191	No.5 in E-flat major	
8.192	No.6 in A-flat major	
8.193	"Ecossaise," in E-flat major (ca1817)	D511
8.194	"8 Ecossaises" (c1817): No.1 in D major	D529
8.195	No.2 in D major	
8.196	No.3 in G major	
8.197	No.4 in D major	
8.198	No.5 in D major	
8.199	No.6 in D major	
8.200	No.7 in D major	
8.201	No.8 in D major (after folksong)	
8.202	"Minuet," in C-sharp minor (c ?1814, ?Trio = D610)	D600
8.203	"Trio," in E major (c1818, for ?Minuet, D600)	D610
8.204	"2 Dances" (c1819): No.1 "Deutscher," in C-sharp minor	
8.205	No.2 "Ecossaise," in D-flat major	
8.206	"12 Ländlers" (ca1815, Nos.1–4 lost): No.5 in E-flat major	D681
8.207	No.6 in B-flat major	
8.208	No.7 in E-flat major	
8.209	No.8 in A-flat major	
8.210	No.9 in A-flat major	
8.211	No.10 in A-flat major	
8.212	No.11 in E-flat major	
8.213	No.12 in B-flat major	
8.214	"6 Ecossaises," in A-flat major (c1820, No.5 = D145/6)	D697
8.215	"Deutscher," in G-flat major (c1821)	D722
8.216	*"Ecossaise de Vienne," in A-flat major (c ?1821, spur: c by ?Hüttenbrenner)*	*Anh.I/16*
8.217	"16 Ländler & 2 Ecossaises" (Wiener-Damen Ländler) (ca1822): No.1 in G major	Op.67, D734
8.218	No.2 in D major	
8.219	No.3 in G major	
8.220	No.4 in G major	
8.221	No.5 in D major	
8.222	No.6 in A major	
8.223	No.7 in E major	

8.224	No.8 in C major
8.225	No.9 in G major
8.226	No.10 in C major
8.227	No.11 in G major
8.228	No.12 in B-flat major
8.229	No.13 in G major
8.230	No.14 in B major
8.231	No.15 in G major
8.232	No.16 in G major
8.233	"Ecossaisen": No.1 in C major
8.234	No.2 in A major
8.235	"Galop & 8 Ecossaises" (ca1822): "Galop," in G major Op.49, D735
8.236	"Ecossaisen": No.1 in G major
8.237	No.2 in G major
8.238	No.3 in D major
8.239	No.4 in B-flat major
8.240	No.5 in E-flat major
8.241	No.6 in E-flat major
8.242	No.7 in E-flat major
8.243	No.8 in A-flat major
8.244	"2 Deutsche": No.1 in A major (c1824) D769
8.245	No.2 in D major (c1823)
8.246	"Valses sentimentales" (ca1823): No.1 in C major Op.50, D779
8.247	No.2 in C major
8.248	No.3 in G major
8.249	No.4 in G major
8.250	No.5 in B major
8.251	No.6 in B major
8.252	No.7 in G minor
8.253	No.8 in D major
8.254	No.9 in D major
8.255	No.10 in G major
8.256	No.11 in G major
8.257	No.12 in D major
8.258	No.13 in A major
8.259	No.14 in D major
8.260	No.15 in F major
8.261	No.16 in C major
8.262	No.17 in C major
8.263	No.18 in A-flat major
8.264	No.19 in E-flat major
8.265	No.20 in E-flat major
8.266	No.21 in E-flat major
8.267	No.22 in E-flat major
8.268	No.23 in E-flat major
8.269	No.24 in G major
8.270	No.25 in G major
8.271	No.26 in C major
8.272	No.27 in E-flat major
8.273	No.28 in E-flat major
8.274	No.29 in E-flat major
8.275	No.30 in C major
8.276	No.31 in A minor
8.277	No.32 in C major
8.278	No.33 in A-flat major
8.279	No.34 in A-flat major
8.280	"12 Ecossaises" (c1823): No.1 in D major (= D783/2) D781
8.281	No.2 in G-flat major
8.282	No.3 in D major
8.283	No.4 in G-flat major
8.284	No.5 in E-flat major
8.285	No.6 in A-flat major
8.286	No.7 in E-flat minor
8.287	No.8 in B minor
8.288	No.9 in D major
8.289	No.10 in B major
8.290	No.11 in G-sharp minor
8.291	No.12 in B minor
8.292	"Ecossaise," in D major (ca1823) D782
8.293	"16 Deutsche & 2 Ecossaises" (c1823–4), Deutsches: No.1 in A major Op.33, D783
8.294	No.2 in D major (= D781/1)
8.295	No.3 in B major
8.296	No.4 in G major
8.297	No.5 in B minor
8.298	No.6 in B major

8.299	No.7 in B major	
8.300	No.8 in E-flat major	
8.301	No.9 in C major	
8.302	No.10 in A minor	
8.303	No.11 in E minor	
8.304	No.12 in C major	
8.305	No.13 in C major	
8.306	No.14 in F minor	
8.307	No.15 in F minor	
8.308	No.16 in F major	
8.309	Ecosaissen: No.1 in D major	
8.310	No.2 in D major	
8.311	"12 Deutsche" (Ländler) (c1823): No.1 in D major	Op.posth171, D790
8.312	No.2 in A major	
8.313	No.3 in D major	
8.314	No.4 in D major	
8.315	No.5 in B minor	
8.316	No.6 in G-sharp minor	
8.317	No.7 in A-flat major	
8.318	No.8 in A-flat minor	
8.319	No.9 in B major	
8.320	No.10 in B major	
8.321	No.11 in A-flat major	
8.322	No.12 in E major	
8.323	"3 Ecossaises" (c1824): No.1 in D major	D816
8.324	No.2 in D major	
8.325	No.3 in B-flat major	
8.326	"6 Deutsche" (c1824; orchd Webern): No.1 in A-flat major	D820
8.327	No.2 in A-flat major	
8.328	No.3 in A-flat major	
8.329	No.4 in B-flat major	
8.330	No.5 in B-flat major	
8.331	No.6 in B-flat major	
8.332	"2 Deutsche" (c1825): No.1 in F major	D841
8.333	No.2 in G major	
8.334	"Waltz" (Albumblatt), in G major (c1825)	D844
8.335	"12 Grazer Walzer" (c1827): No.1 in E major	Op.91, D924
8.336	No.2 in E major	
8.337	No.3 in E major	
8.338	No.4 in A major	
8.339	No.5 in A major	
8.340	No.6 in A major	
8.341	No.7 in C major	
8.342	No.8 in A major	
8.343	No.9 in C major	
8.344	No.10 in A major	
8.345	No.11 in G major	
8.346	No.12 in E major	
8.347	"Grazer Galopp," in C major (c1827)	D925
8.348	*"Deutscher" (c1828, lost)*	*D944a*
8.349	"Valses nobles" (c1826): No1. in C major	Op.77, D969
8.350	No.2 in A major	
8.351	No.3 in C major	
8.352	No.4 in G major	
8.353	No.5 in A minor	
8.354	No.6 in C major	
8.355	No.7 in E major	
8.356	No.8 in A major	
8.357	No.9 in C major	
8.358	No.10 in F major	
8.359	No.11 in C major	
8.360	No.12 in C major	
8.361	"6 Ländler" (c?): No.1 in E-flat major	D970
8.362	No.2 in E-flat major (= D145/7)	
8.363	No.3 in A-flat major	
8.364	No.4 in A-flat major	
8.365	No.5 in D-flat major	
8.366	No.6 in D-flat major	
8.367	"3 Deutsche" (c1822): No.1 in A minor	D971
8.368	No.2 in A major	
8.369	No.3 in E major	
8.370	"3 Deutsche" (c?): No.1 in D-flat major	D972
8.371	No.2 in A-flat major	
8.372	No.3 in A major	
8.373	"3 Deutsche" (c?): No.1 in E major	D973

8.374	No.2 in E major
8.375	No.3 in A-flat major
8.376	"2 Deutsche," in D-flat major (c?) D974
8.377	"Deutscher," in D major (c?) D975
8.378	"Cotillon," in E-flat major (c1825) D976
8.379	"8 Ecossaises" (c?): No.1 in D-flat major D977
8.380	No.2 in D-flat major
8.381	No.3 in A-flat major
8.382	No.4 in B major
8.383	No.5 in D major
8.384	No.6 in D major
8.385	No.7 in B-flat major
8.386	No.8 in F major
8.387	"Waltz," in A-flat major (c1825) D978
8.388	"Waltz," in G major (c1826) D979
8.389	"2 Waltzes" (c1826): No.1 in G major D980
8.390	No.2 in B minor
8.391	*"Kupelwieser-Walzer" (c1826, ?spur) Anh.I/14*
8.392	*"2 Dances" (c?, sketches): No.1 in A major .... D980a (D640)*
8.393	*No.2 in E major*
8.394	"2 Ländler," in E-flat major (c?) D980b (D679)
8.395	*"2 Ländler," in D-flat major (c?, frags) .... D980c (D680)*
8.396	"Waltz," in C major (c1827) D980d
8.397	*"2 Dances" (c?, sketches): No.1 in G minor D980e*
8.398	*No.2 in F major*

9. OTHER WORKS FOR PIANO

9.1	*"7 leichte Variationen," in G major (c ?1810, ?spur) Anh.I/12*
9.2	"Fantasie," in C minor (c1811) D2e (D993)
9.3	"Fugue," in D minor (ca1812) D13
9.4	*"Overture" (ca1812, sketch, lost) D14*
9.5	*"6 Variations," in E-flat major (c1812, lost).. D21*
9.6	*"7 Variations," in F major (c1812, frag, lost) D24*
9.7	"Fugue," in C major (c1812; pf/?org) D24a
9.8	"Fugue," in G major (c1812; pf/?org) D24b
9.9	"Fugue," in D minor (c1812; pf/?org) D24c
9.10	*"Fugue," in C major (c1812, frag) D24d*
9.11	*"Fugue," in F major (c1812, frag)..D25c*
9.12	"Andante," in C major (c1812, arr of: Str Qt No.3, D36) D29
9.13	*Fugal sketches in B-flat major (c ?1813) .... D37a (D967)*
9.14	*"Fugue," in E minor (c1813, frag).. D41a*
9.15	*"Fugue," in E minor (c1813, frag) D71b*
9.16	*"Allegro," in E major (c1815, sketch of D157)...D154*
9.17	"10 Variations," in F major (c1815) D156
9.18	"Adagio," in G major (c1815; also frag of 2nd vers) D178
9.19	*"Allegretto," in C major (c ?1816, frag, ?Finale of D279) D346*
9.20	*"Allegretto moderato," in C major (c ?1813, frag) D347*
9.21	*"Andantino," in C major (c ?1816, frag) D348*
9.22	*"Adagio," in C major (c ?1816, frag) D349*
9.23	"5 Klavierstücke" (c ?1816, Nos.1 & 2 = Piano Sonata No.3 in E major, D459): No.3 in C major D459a
9.24	No.4 in A major
9.25	No.5 in F major
9.26	"Adagio," in D-flat major (c1818; orig slow movt of: Pf Sonata No.11 in F minor, D625) D505
9.27	"Rondo," in E major (c1817, = ?Finale of: Pf Sonata No.6 in E minor, D566) D506
9.28	"Scherzo," in D maj & "Allegro," in F-sharp min (c1817, ?intend as movts 3–4 of: Pf Son No.8, D571) D570
9.29	"13 Variations on a Theme by Anselm Hüttenbrenner," in A minor (c1817).......................... D576
9.30	"2 Scherzos" (c1817): No.1 in B-flat major D593
9.31	No.2 in D-flat major
9.32	"Klavierstück," in A major (c1816 or 7, ?slow movt of: Pf Sonata No.8 in F-sharp minor, D570/571) ... D604
9.33	*"Fantasie," in C major (c1821–3, frag)... D605*
9.34	"Grazer Fantasie," in C major (c ?1818) D605a
9.35	"March," in E major (c ?1818) D606
9.36	"Adagio," in E major (c1818, ?slow movt of D613) D612
9.37	"Variation on a waltz by Diabelli," in C minor (c1821) D718
9.38	"Overture to opera Alfonso and Estrella," in D major (c1822, arr from opera D732) Op.69, D759a
9.39	"Wanderer-Fantasie," in C major (c1822).. Op.15, D760
9.40	*"Fantasie," in E-flat major (c ?1825, lost) Anh.I/10*
9.41	"6 Moments musicaux" (c1823–8): No.1 in C major Op.94, D780
9.42	No.2 in A-flat major
9.43	No.3 in F minor
9.44	No.4 in C-sharp minor
9.45	No.5 in F minor
9.46	No.6 in A-flat major

9.47	"Ungarische Melodie," in B minor (c1824, ?1st vers of pf duet, D818)	D817
9.48	"4 Impromptus" (c1827): No.1 in C minor	Op.90, D899
9.49	No.2 in E-flat major	
9.50	No.3 in G-flat major	
9.51	No.4 in A-flat major	
9.52	*"Allegretto," in C minor (c after ?1820, frag)*	*D900*
9.53	"Allegretto," in C minor (c1827)	D915
9.54	*Piano piece in C major (c1827, sketch)*	*D916b*
9.55	*Piano piece in C minor (c1827, sketch)*	*D916c*
9.56	"4 Impromptus" (c1827): No.1 in F minor	Op.posth142, D935
9.57	No.2 in A-flat major	
9.58	No.3 in B-flat major (Thema & 5 Variations)	
9.59	No.4 in F minor	
9.60	"3 Klavierstücke" (Impromptus) (c1828): No.1 in E-flat minor	D946
9.61	No.2 in E-flat major	
9.62	No.3 in C major	
9.63	"March," in G major (c?)	D980f
9.64	*"Allegro," in G major & "Menuet" (Trio: lost), in C major (c?, spur)*	*Anh.I/11*

10. PIANO DUET

10.1	"Fantasie," in G major (c1810)	D1
10.2	*"Fantasie," in G major (c1810 or 11, frag)*	*D1b*
10.3	*Sonata in F major (c1810 or 11, frag, 1st movt only)*	*D1c*
10.4	"Fantasie," in G minor (c1811)	D9
10.5	"Fantasie" (Grande Sonate), in C minor (c1813; 2 vers: 1st w/ out Finale)	D48
10.6	"Overture im italienischen Stile," in D major (c1817, arr of: Overture, D590)	D592
10.7	"Overture im italienischen Stile," in C major (c1817, arr of: Overture, D591)	D597
10.8	"4 Polonaises" (c1818): No.1 in D minor	Op.75, D599
10.9	No.2 in B-flat major	
10.10	No.3 in E major	
10.11	No.4 in F major	
10.12	"Marches héroïques" (c1818 or 24): No.1 in B minor	Op.27, D602
10.13	No.2 in C major	
10.14	No.3 in D major	
10.15	"Rondo," in D major (c1818; 2nd vers w/ subtitle: Notre amitié est invariable)	Op.posth138, D608
10.16	"Sonata," in B-flat major (c1818)	Op.30, D617
10.17	"Deutscher" (w/ 2 Trios), in G major & 2 "Landler," in E major (c1818)	D618
10.18	*"Polonaise" (w/ Trio) (c1818, sketch; Trio used in: Polonaise, D599)*	*D618a*
10.19	"8 Variations on a French song," in E minor (c1818, on song: Le bon Chevalier)	Op.10, D624
10.20	"Overture," in G minor (c1819)	D668
10.21	"Overture," in F major (c ?1819)	Op.34, D675
10.22	"Marches militaires" (c1818): No.1 in D major (arr as: Marche militaire for pf)	Op.51, D733
10.23	No.2 in G major	
10.24	No.3 in E-flat major	
10.25	"Overture to Alfonso und Estrella" (c1823, arr from opera D732)	D773
10.26	"Overture to Fierabras" (c1823, arr from opera D796)	D798
10.27	"Grand Duo," sonata in C major (c1824)	Op.posth140, D812
10.28	"8 Variatons on a Original Theme," in A-flat major (c1824)	Op.35, D813
10.29	"4 Ländler" (c1824): No.1 in E-flat major (arr for pf, D366/17)	D814
10.30	No.2 in A-flat major	
10.31	No.3 in C minor	
10.32	No.4 in C major	
10.33	"Divertisement à l'hongroise," in G minor (c1824)	Op.54, D818
10.34	"6 Grandes Marches" (c1824): No.1 in E-flat major	Op.40, D819
10.35	No.2 in G minor	
10.36	No.3 in B minor	
10.37	No.4 in D major	
10.38	No.5 in E-flat major	
10.39	No.6 in E major	
10.40	"Divertissement on French themes," in E major (ca1825): No.1 "Marche brillante"	Op.63/1, D823/1
10.41	No.2 "Andantino varié"	Op.84/1, D823/2
10.42	No.3 "Rondo brillant"	Op.84/2, D823/3
10.43	"6 Polonaises" (c1826): No.1 in D minor	Op.61, D824
10.44	No.2 in F major	
10.45	No.3 in B-flat major	
10.46	No.4 in D major	
10.47	No.5 in A major	
10.48	No.6 in E major	
10.49	*"March" (c1825; 2pf 8 hands, lost)*	*Anh.I/7 (D858)*
10.50	"Grande marche funèbre," in C minor (c1825, for the death of Alexander I of Russia)	Op.55, D859
10.51	"Grande marche héroïque," in A minor (c1826, for the coronation of Nicholas I of Russia)	D885
10.52	"8 Variations on a Theme from Hérold's Marie," in C major (c1827)	Op.82/1, D908
10.53	"March" (Kindermarsch), in G major (c1827)	D928

11. MASSES

                1. "Zum Eingang": "Bei des Entschlafnen Trauerbahre"
                2. "Nach der Epistel": "Der Tod rückt Seelen vors Gericht"
                3. "Zum Evangelium": "Wie tröstlich ist, was Jesus lehrt"
                4. "Zum Offertorium": " Dir Vater! weihen wir hier Gaben"
                5. "Zum Sanctus": "Droben nur ist wahres Leben!"
                6. "Zur Wandlung": "Jesu! dir leb ich; Jesu! dir sterb ich"
                7. "Zum Memento für die Abgestorbenen": "Der Frommen abgeschiedne Seelen"
                8. "Zum Agnus Dei": "Lamm Gottes! Guade, Heil und Leben"
                9. "Zur Kommunion": "O hohes Glück, vor dir zu stehn!"
                10. "Am Ende der Messe": "Euch, die von uns geschieden"
                1. "Zum Eingang": "Wohin soll ich mich wenden"
                2. "Zum Gloria": "Ehre, Ehre sei Gott in der Höhe!"
                3. "Zum Evangelium und Credo": "Noch lag die Schöpfung formlos da"
                4. "Zum Offertorium": "Du gabst, o Herr, mir Sein und Leben"
                5. "Zum Sanctus": "Heilig, heilig, heilig, heilig ist der Herr!"
                6. "Nach der Wandlung": "Betrachtend Deine Huld und Güte"
                7. "Zum Agnus Dei": "Mein Heiland, Herr und Meister!"
                8. "Schlussgesang": "Herr, Du hast mein Flehn vernommen"
            Anhang: "Das Gebet des Herrn": "Anbetend Deine Macht"

12. OTHER CHURCH MUSIC

                1. "Jesus Christus schwebt am Kreuze!," chorus
                2. "Bei des Mittlers Kreuze standen bang," aria (S)
                3. "Liebend neiget er sein Antlitz," chorus
                4. "Engel freuten sich der Wonne," duet (S, T)
                5. "Wer wird Zähren sanften Mitleids," chorus
                6. "Ach, was hätten wir empfunden," aria (T)
                7. "Erben sollen sie am Throne," chorus
                8. "Sohn des Vaters, aber leiden, leiden müssen deine Brüder," aria (B)
                9. "O du herrlicher, du herrlicher Vollender," chorus
                10. "Erdenfreuden und ihr Elend," trio (S, T, B)
                11. "Dass dereinst wir, wenn im Tode," trio (S, T, B) w/ chorus
                12. "Amen, amen, amen," chorus

12.20   "Magnificat," in C major (c1815; S, A, T, B, ch, orch & org) D486
12.21   "Auguste jam coelestium," in G major (c1816; S, T & orch) D488
12.22   "Evangelium Johannis 6, Vers 55–58," in E major (c1818; 1v & cont) D607
12.23   "Salve Regina," offertorium in A major (c1819; S & strings) Op.posth153, D676
12.24   "6 Antiphones" (c1820; ch, for Palm Sunday): 1. "Hosanna filio David" Op.113, D696
12.25   2. "In monte Oliveti"
12.26   3. "Sanctus, sanctus, sanctus"
12.27   4. "Pueri hebraeorum"
12.28   5. "Cum angelis et pueris"
12.29   6. "In grediente Domino"
12.30   "Tantum ergo," in B-flat major (c1821; S, A, T, B, ch, orch & org) D730
12.31   "Tantum ergo," in C major (c1814; ch, orch & org) Op.45, D739
12.32   "Tantum ergo," in D major (c1822; ch, orch & org) D750
12.33   "Kyrie," in A minor (c1822; S, A, T, B, ch, strings & org, sketch) D755
12.34   "Salve Regina," quartet in C major (c1824; 2T, 2B) Op.posth149, D811
12.35   "Benedictus," in A min (c1828; S, A, T, B, ch, orch & org, altern movt for: Mass No.4 in C maj, D452) D961
12.36   "Tantum ergo," in E-flat major (c1828; S, A, T, B, ch & orch) D962
12.37   "Intende voci" (Offertorium), aria w/ ch in B-flat major (c1828; T, ch & orch) D963
12.38   "Wer wird sich nicht innig freuen" (sketches for: Stabat mater, D383) D992
12.39   "Tantum ergo," in B-flat major (c?, frag: S part only, ?spur) Anh.I/17

13. CHORAL WORKS

W/ orch:

13.1   "Wer ist gross?" (c1814; B, m ch & orch) D110
13.2   "Namensfeier für Franz Michael Vierthaler" (Gratulations Kantate) (c1815; S, T, B, ch & orch) D294
13.3   "Prometheus," cantata (c1816, Dräxler von Carin; S, B, ch & orch, lost) D451
13.4   "Kantate auf den Vater" (c1816, lost) Anh.I/24
13.5   "Kantate zu Ehren von Josef Spendou" (c1816, Hoheisel; 2S, B, ch & orch): Op.posth128, D472
             1. "Da liegt er," recit & aria w/ chorus (Witwe, B, Waisen)
             2. "Gottes Bild ist Fürst und Staat," recit & duet (Witwe—S, Waise—S, B)
             3. "Ein Punkt nur ist der Mensch," recit & chorus (B, Witwen)
             4. "Die Sonne sticht," recit & quartet w/ chorus (Witwe—S, Waise—S, T, B, ch)
13.6   "Drum Schwester und Brüder" (c1819, unknown; 1v, ch & insts, frag) Anh.I/25
13.7   "Lazarus" (Der Feier der Auferstehung), oratorio (c1820, Niemeyer; 3S, 2T, B, ch & orch, unfin): D689
         I: . "Hier lasst mich ruhn die letzte Stunde" (Lazarus)
              . "Trübe nicht mit Klagen seine Seele" (Maria)
              . "Steh im letzten Kampf dem Müden," aria
              . "Voll Friede, ja voll Fried ist die Seele" (Lazarus)
              . "Wenn ich ihm nachgerungen habe," aria (Nathanael)
              . "Nathanael, bewundern kann ich dich" (Martha)
              . "Der Trost begleite dich hinüber in das Reich des Lichts" (Maria)
              . "Gottes Liebe, du bist seine Zuversicht," aria (Maria)
              . "Ach, so find ich ihn noch" (Jemina)
              . "Viel selige Stunden gab der Freundschaft Wonne" (Lazarus)
              . "So schlummert auf Rosen" (Jemina)
              . "Allgnädiger, heile du unsrer Seelen Wunde!," chorus (Freunde)
         II: . "Largo—Allegretto"
              . "Wo bin ich?," recit (Simon)
              . "O könnt ich, Allgewaltiger," aria (Simon)
              . "Wes ist der Klage Stimme," recit (Nathanael)
              . "Sanft und still schläft unser Freund," chorus (Freunde des Lazarus)
              . "So legt ihn in die Blumen," recit (Nathanael)
              . "Hebt mich der Stürme Flügel empor vom Totenhügel" (Martha)
13.8   "Am Geburtstage des Kaisers," cantata (c1822, Deinhardstein; S, A, T, B, ch & orch) .. Op.posth157, D748
13.9   "Glaube, Hoffnung und Liebe": "Gott, lass die Glocke," quartet (c1828, Reil; 2T, 2B, ch & winds/pf) ... D954
13.10   "3 Choruses" (c?, unknown; ch, 2hn & 2bn, frag, spur): 1. "Lieblich ist, wenn sanftes Grau" Anh.I/27
13.11   2. "Leb wohl, geliebte Freundin"
13.12   3. "O Zeit, wie manchen herben Schmerz"

W/ pf:

13.13   "Dithyrambe" (Der Besuch): "Nimmer, das glaubt mir" (c1813, Schiller; T, B, ch & pf, frags) D47
13.14   "Trinklied": "Freunde, sammelt euch im Kreise" (c1813, Schäffer; B, ch & pf) D75
13.15   "Trinklied": "Brüder! unser Erdenwallen" (c1815, Castelli; T, ch & pf) Op.posth131/2, D148
13.16   "Nun lasst uns den Leib begraben" (Begräbnislied): "Begrabt den Leib" (c1815, Klopstock; ch & pf) .. D168
13.17   "Jesus Christus unser Heiland": "Überwunden hat der Herr" (c1815, Klopstock; ch & pf) D168a (D987)
13.18   "Trinklied vor der Schlacht": "Schlacht, du brichst an!," in C major (c1815, Körner; 2 unison ch & pf) . D169
13.19   "Schwertlied": " Du Schwert an meiner Linken," in C major (c1815, Körner; 1v, unison ch & pf) D170
13.20   "Trinklied": "Ihr Freunde und du gold'ner Wein," in G major (Zettler; 1v, unison ch & pf) D183
13.21   "An die Freude": "Freude, schöner Götterfunken," in E major (Schiller; 1v, unison ch & pf) (also see
             Beethoven: Sym No.9 in D min, Op.125 & Tchaikovsky's cantata: Ode to Joy) Op.posth111/1, D189
13.22   "Trinklied": "Funkelnd im Becher so helle so hold" (c1816; 1v, m ch & pf, pf part lost) D356

13.23	"Das Grab III": "Das Grab ist tief und stille" (c1816, Salis-Seewis; m ch & pf) D377
13.24	*"Die Schlacht" II: "Schwer und dumpfig" (c1816, Schiller; vv, ch & pf, sketch) D387*
13.25	"Das grosse Halleluja": "Ehre sei dem Hoherhebnen" (c1816, Klopstock; 1v/ch & pf) D442
13.26	"Schlachtlied" I: "Mit unserm Arm ist nichts getan" (c1816, Klopstock; 1v/ch & pf) D443
13.27	"Das Grab" IV: "Das Grab ist tief und stille," in C-sharp minor (Salis-Seewis; unison m ch & pf) D569
13.28	"Lied eines Kriegers": "Des stolzen Männerlebens," in A maj (c1824, unknown; B, unison m ch & pf) .. D822
13.29	"Coronach" (Totengesang): "Er ist uns geschieden" (c1825, Scott transl Storck; ch & pf) Op.52/4, D836
13.30	"Widerspruch": "Wenn ich durch Busch," in D maj (Seidl; m ch & pf; 2nd vers for 1v & pf) ..Op.105/1, D865
13.31	"Zur guten Nacht": "Horcht auf! Es schlägt die Stunde" (c1827, Rochlitz; Bar, ch & pf) Op.81/3, D903
13.32	"Ständchen" I: "Zögernd, leise" (c1827, Grillparzer; A, m/fem ch & pf; 2 vers) ... Op.posth135, D920 (D921)
13.33	"Kantate für Irene Kiesewetter": "Al par del ruscelletto" (c1827, anon Italian; 2T, 2B, ch & pf duet) D936
13.34	"Mirjams Siegesgesang": "Rührt die Zimbel," cantata (c1828, Grillparzer; S, ch & pf) ... Op.posth136, D942

W/ out acc:

13.35	*"Das Grab" I: "Das Grab ist tief und stille," canon (c1815, Salis-Seewis; ch, sketch) D329a*
13.36	"Chor der Engel": "Christ ist erstanden!" (c1816, from Goethe's Faust; ch) D440
13.37	"Schlachtlied" II: "Mit unserm Arm ist nichts getan" (c1827, Klopstock; d ch) Op.posth151, D912
13.38	"Hymnus an den Heiligen Geist" (c1828, Schmidl; 2T, 2B & ch; also w/ winds) . Op.posth154, D948 (D964)
13.39	"Psalm 92: Lied für den Sabbath": "tôw l'hôdôs ladônoj" (c1828, in Hebrew; Bar, vocal qt SATB & ch) D953

14. VOCAL DUETS, TRIOS & QUARTETS

Mixed vv & acc:

14.1	"Hymne an den Unendlichen": "Zwischen Himmel und Erd" (c1815, Schiller; 4vv & acc) Op.112/3, D232
14.2	"Das Abendrot": "Der Abend blüht, der Westen glüht" (c1815, Kosegarten; 2S, B & pf) D236
14.3	"Das Grab" II: "Das Grab ist tief und stille" (c1815, Salis-Seewis; vv & pf; also see Lied, D330) D330
14.4	"Licht und Liebe" (Nachtgesang): "Liebe ist ein süsses Licht," in G major (Collin; S, T & pf) D352
14.5	"An die Sonne": "O Sonne, Königin der Welt" (c1816, Uz; S, A, T, B & pf) D439
14.6	"Die Geselligkeit" (Lebenslust): "Wer Lebenslust fühlet" (c1818, Unger; S, A T B & pf) D609
14.7	"Viel tausend Sterne prangen am Himmel" (c ?1812, Eberhard; S, A, T, B & pf) D642
14.8	"Im traulichen Kreise" (part of vocal qt D609) D665
14.9	"Kantate zum Geburtstag des Sängers Johann Michael Vogl," cantata (c1819, Stadler; S, T, B & pf): D666
	. Variant pubd w/ different text titled: Der Frühlingsmorgen Op.posth158
14.10	"Gesang der Geister" IV (c1820, Goethe; 4T, 4B, 2va, 2vc & d bass; 2 vers, frag of 1st) Op.posth167, D714
14.11	"Des Tages Weihe": "Schicksalslenker, blickenieder" (c1822, unknown; S, A, T, B) Op.posth146, D763
14.12	"Gebet": "Du Urquell aller Güte" (c1824, Motte Fouqué; S, A, T, B & pf) Op.posth139, D815
14.13	"Der Tanz": "Es redet und träumet die Jugend so viel" (c1828, ?Meerau; S, A, T, B & pf) D826
14.14	*"Die Allmacht" II: "Gross ist Jehova der Herr!" (c1826, Pyrker von Felsö-Eör, sketch) D875a*
14.15	"Nachtgesang im Walde": "Sei uns stets gegrüsst" (c1827, Seidl; 2T, 2B & 4hn) Op.posth139B, D913
14.16	"Der Hochzeitsbraten": "Ach liebes Herz, ach Theobald" (c1827, Schober; S, T, B & pf) Op.104, D930
14.17	"Gott im Ungewitter": "Du Schrecklicher" (c ?1827, Uz; S, A, T, B & pf) Op.posth112/1, D985
14.18	"Gott der Weltschöpfer": "Zu Gott flieg auf" (c ?1827, Uz; S, A, T, B & pf) Op.posth112/2, D986
14.19	*Piano acc in B-flat major (c after ?1820) D988a*

M vv & acc:

14.20	"Die Advokaten": "Mein Herr, ich komm mich anzufragen" (c1812, Engelhart; 2T, B & pf) Op.72, D37
14.21	"Zur Namensfeier meines Vaters": "Ertöne Leier, zur Festesfeier" (c1813, Schubert; 2T, B & gui) D80
14.22	"Klage um Ali Bey" I: "Lasst mich! lasst mich! Ich will klagen" (c1815, Claudius; 2T, B & ?pf) D140
14.23	"Trinklied": "Auf! Jeder sei nun froh" (c1815; 2T, B) D267
14.24	"Bergknappenlied": "Hinab, ihr Brüder, in den Schacht!" (c1815; 2T, 2B) D268
14.25	"Das Leben": "Das Leben ist ein Traum" (c1815, Wannovius; T, 2B; also see D269/2) D269/1
14.26	"Punschlied": "Vier Elemente, innig gesellt" (c1815, Schiller; 2T, B) D277
14.27	"Beitrag zur fünfzig jährigen Jubelfeier des Herrn von Salieri" (c1816, Schubert): D407/1
	1. "Gütigster, Bester! Weisester Grösster!" (2T, 2B; also for 2T, B & pf, D441)
	2. "So Güt als Weisheit strömen mild," aria (T & pf)
	3. "Unser aller Grosspapa bleibe noch recht lange da," canon w/ coda (3vv)
14.28	"Naturgenuss" II: "Im Abendschimmer wallt der Quell" (c ?1822, Matthisson; 2T, 2B & pf) Op.16/2, D422
14.29	"La pastorella al prato" I (c ?1817, Goldoni; 2T, 2B & pf) D513
14.30	"Das Dörfchen" II: "Ich rühme mir mein Dörfchen hier" (c1818, Bürger; 2T, 2B; 2 vers) Op.11/1, D598
14.31	*"Gesang der Geister über den Wassern" III: "Des Menschen Seele" (c1820, Goethe; 2T, 2B & pf, sketch) D705*
14.32	"Im Gegenwärtigen Vergangenes": "Ros und Lilie morgentaulich" (c1821, Goethe; 2T, 2B) D710
14.33	"Die Nachtigall": "Bescheiden verborgen" (c1821, Unger; 2T, 2B & pf) Op.11/2, D724
14.34	"Frühlingsgesang" II: "Schmücket die Locken" (c1822, Schober; 2T, 2B & pf) Op.16/1, D740
14.35	"Geist der Liebe" II: "Der Abend schleiert Flur und Hain" (c1822, Matthisson; 2T, 2B & pf) ...Op.11/3, D747
14.36	"Gondelfahrer" II: "Es tanzen Mond und Sterne" (c1824, Mayrhofer; 2T, 2B & pf) Op.28, D809
14.37	"Bootsgesang": "Triumph, erm Hail, Heil" (c1825, Scott transl Storck; 2T, 2B & pf) Op.52/3, D835
14.38	"Mondenschein": "Des Mondes Zauberblume lacht" (c1826, Schober; 2T, 3B & pf) Op.102, D875
14.39	"Nachthelle": "Die Nacht ist heiter und ist rein" (c1826, Seidl; T, vocal qt 2T2B & pf) Op.134, D892
14.40	"Der Wintertag": "In schöner heller Winterzeit" (c?, unknown; 2T, 2B & lost pf acc) Op.posth169, D984

Fem vv & acc:

14.41	"Das Leben": "Das Leben ist ein Traum" (c1815, Wannovius; 2S, A & pf; also see D269/1)	D269/2
14.42	"Psalm 23": "Gott ist mein Hirt" (c1820, Bible transl M. Mendelssohn; 2S, 2A & pf)	Op.132, D706
14.43	"Gott in der Natur": "Gross ist der Herr" (c1822, Kleist; 2S, 2A & pf)	D757

Unacc mixed/unspecified vv:

14.44	"Quell' innocente figlio" III–IX (ca1812, Metastasio; III, V, VI for S, A, T; IV, VII–IX for S, A, T, B)	D17
14.45	"Entra l'uomo allor che nasce" III–VI (c1812, Metastasio; III for S, A, T; IV–VI for S, A, T, B)	D33
14.46	"Te solo adoro" (c1812, Metastasio: Betulia liberata; S, A, T, B)	D34
14.47	"Serbate, o dei custodi" (c1812, Metastasio: La clemenza di Tito; 1st vers for S, A, T, B; 2nd for ch)	D35
14.48	"Ein jugendlicher Maienschwung," canon (c1813, from Schiller's Der Triumph der Liebe; 3vv)	D61
14.49	"Dreifach ist der Schritt der Zeit" (Spruch des Konfuzius) II, canon (c1813, Schiller; 3vv)	D69
14.50	"Der Schnee zerrinnt" I, canon (c ?1815, Hölty; 3vv)	D130
14.51	"Lacrimoso son io," canon (c1815; 3vv; 2 vers)	D131
14.52	"Mailied" II: "Grüner wird die Au" (c1815, Hölty; 2vv/2hn)	D199
14.53	"Mailied" II: "Der Schnee zerrinnt" (c1815, Hölty; 2vv/2hn)	D202
14.54	"Der Morgenstern" II: "Stern der Liebe, Glanzgebilde" (c1815, Körner; 2vv/2hn)	D203
14.55	"Jägerlied": "Frisch auf, ihr Jäger, frei und flink!" (c1815, Körner; 2vv/2hn)	D204
14.56	"Lützows wilde Jagd": "Was glänzt dort vom Walde im Sonnenschein?" (c1815, Körner; 2vv/2hn)	D205
14.57	"Willkommen, lieber schöner Mai," canon (c1815, from Hölty's Mailied; 3vv; 2 parts/2 vers)	D244
14.58	"Punschlied. Im Norden zu singen": "Auf der Berge" (c1815, Schiller; 2vv; also see D253/1)	D253/2
14.59	"Goldner Schein deckt den Hain," canon (c1816, from Matthisson's Abendlandschaft; 3vv)	D357
14.60	"Das Grab" V: "Das Grab ist tief und stille" (c1819, Salis-Seewis; S, A, T, B)	D643a
14.61	*Canon in A minor (c1826, sketch w/ out text)*	*D873*
14.62	"Liebe säuseln die Blätter," canon (c ?1815, Hölty; 3vv)	D988
14.63	*"Sturmbeschwörung": "Nirgends Rettung, nirgends Land" (c?, unknown, frag)*	*Anh.I/26*

Unacc m vv:

14.64	"Totengräberlied" I: "Grabe, Spaden, grabe, alles, was ich habe" (c ?1813, Hölty; 2T, B)	D38
14.65	"Dreifach ist der Schritt der Zeit" (Spruch des Konfuzius) I (c1813, Schiller; 2T, B)	D43
14.66	"Unendliche Freude durchwallet das Herz" I (c1813, from Schiller's Elysium; 2T, B)	D51
14.67	"Vorüber die stöhnende Klage" (c1813, from Schiller's Elysium; 2T, B)	D53
14.68	"Unendliche Freude durchwallet das Herz" II, canon (c1813, from Schiller's Elysium; 3 m vv)	D54
14.69	"Selig durch die Liebe" (c1813, from Schiller's Der Triumph der Liebe; 2T, B)	D55
14.70	"Hier strecket der wallende Pilger" (c1813, from Schiller's Elysium; 2T, B)	D57
14.71	"Dessen Fahne Donnerstürme wallte" (c1813, from Schiller's Elysium; 2T, B)	D58
14.72	"Hier umarmen sich getreue Gatten" (c1813, from Schiller's Elysium; 2T, B)	D60
14.73	"Thronend auf erhabnem Sitz" (c1813, from Schiller's Der Triumph der Liebe; 2T, B)	D62
14.74	"Wer die steile Sternenbahn" (c1813, from Schiller's Der Triumph der Liebe; 2T, B)	D63
14.75	"Majestätsche Sonnenrosse" (c1813, from Schiller's Der Triumph der Liebe; 2T, B)	D64
14.76	*"Schmerz verzerret ihr Gesicht," canon (c1813, from Schiller's Gruppe aus dem Tartarus; 2T, B, sketch)*	*D65*
14.77	"Frisch atmet des Morgens lebendiger Hauch" (c1813, from Schiller's Der Flüchtling; 2T, B)	D67
14.78	*"Dreifach ist der Schritt der Zeit" (Spruch des Konfuzius) III, canon (c1813, Schiller; 2T, B, frag)*	*D70*
14.79	"Die zwei Tugendwege": "Zwei sind der Wege" (c1813, Schiller; 2T, B)	D71
14.80	"Verschwunden sind die Schmerzen," canon (c1813; 2T, B)	D88
14.81	"Mailied" I: "Grüner wird die Au," trio (c ?1815, Hölty; 2T, B)	D129
14.82	*"Lied beim Rundetanz": "Auf, es dunkelt" (c1815 or 6, Salis-Seewis, frag)*	*Anh.I/18 (D132)*
14.83	*"Lied im Freien": "Wie schön ist's im Freien" (c1815 or 6, Salis-Seewis, frag)*	*Anh.I/19 (D133)*
14.84	"Bardengesang": "Rolle, du strömigter Carun" (c1816, from Ossian's Comola, transl Harold; 2T, B)	D147
14.85	"Trinklied im Winter": "Das Glas gefüllt! der Nordwind brüllt" (c1815, Hölty; 2T, B)	D242
14.86	"Frühlingslied" I: "Die Luft ist blau, das Tal ist grün" (c1815, Hölty; 2T, B)	D243
14.87	"Der Entfernten" I: "Wohl denk ich allenthalben" (ca1816, Salis-Seewis; 2T, 2B)	D331
14.88	"Die Einsiedelei" I (Lob der Einsamkeit): "Es rieselt klar und wehend" (ca1816, Salis-Seewis; 2T, 2B)	D337
14.89	"An den Frühling" II: "Willkommen schöner Jüngling" (c1816, Schiller; 2T, 2B)	D338
14.90	*"Amors Macht": "Wo Amors Flügel weben" (c1815 or 6, Matthisson, frag)*	*Anh.I/20 (D339)*
14.91	*"Badelied": "Zur Elbe, zur Elbe" (c1815 or 6, Matthisson, frag)*	*Anh.I/21 (D340)*
14.92	*"Sylphen": "Was unterm Monde gleicht" (c1815 or 6, Matthisson, frag)*	*Anh.I/22 (D341)*
14.93	*"Lebenslied": "Kommen und scheiden" (c1815 or 16, Matthisson, frag)*	*Anh.I/23*
14.94	"Fischerlied" II: "Das Fischergewerbe gibt rüstigen Mut!" (c ?1816–7, Salis-Seewis; 2T, 2B)	D364
14.95	"Beitrag zur fünfzig jährigen Jubelfeier des Herrn von Salieri," canon (c1816, Schubert; 3vv)	D407/3
14.96	"Andenken" II: "Ich denke dein, wenn durch den Hain" (c1816, Matthisson; 2T, B)	D423
14.97	"Erinnerungen" II: "Am Seegestad, in lauen Vollmondnächten" (c1816, Matthisson; 2T, B)	D424
14.98	*"Lebensbild" (c1816; 2T, B, lost)*	*D425*
14.99	*"Trinklied": "Herr Bacchus ist ein braver Mann" (c1816; 2T, B, lost)*	*D426*
14.100	"Trinklied im Mai": "Bekränzet die Tonnen und zapfet mir Wein" (c1816, Hölty; 2T, B)	D427
14.101	"Widerhall": "Auf ewig dein, wenn Berg und Meere trennen" (c1816, Matthisson; 2T, B)	D428
14.102	"Der Geistertanz" IV: "Die bretterne Kammer der Toten erbebt" (c1816, Matthisson; 2T, 3B)	D494
14.103	"Gesang der Geister über den Wassern" II: "Des Menschen Seele" (c1817, Goethe; 2T, 2B)	D538
14.104	"Lied im Freien": "Wie schön ist's im Freien" (c1817, Salis-Seewis; 2T, 2B)	D572
14.105	"Leise, leise lasst uns singen" (c1819, unknown; 2T, 2B)	D635
14.106	"Sehnsucht" IV: "Nur wer die Sehnsucht kennt" (c1819, from Goethe's Wilhelm Meister; 2T, 3B)	D656
14.107	"Ruhe, schönstes Glück der Erde" (c1819, unknown; 2T, 2B)	D657

14.108 "Frühlingsgesang" I: "Schmücket die Locken" (c before 1822, Schober; 2T, 2B) D709
14.109 "Ich hab in mich gesogen" (c ?1823, Rückert; 2T, 2B, sketch) D778b
14.110 "Wehmut": "Die Abendglocke tönt" (c1826, Hüttenbrenner; 2T, 2B) Op.64/1, D825
14.111 "Ewige Liebe": "Ertönet, ihr Saiten, in nächtlicher Ruh" (c1826, Schulze; 2T, 2B) Op.64/2, D825a
14.112 "Flucht": "In der Freie will ich leben" (c1825, Lappe; 2T, 2B) Op.64/3, D825b
14.113 "Trinklied aus dem 16 Jahrhundert": "Edit Nonna" (c1825, Gräffer; 2T, 2B) Op.posth155, D847
14.114 "Nachtmusik": "Wir stimmen dir mit Flötensang" (c1825, Seckendorf; 2T, 2B) Op.156, D848
14.115 "Nachtklänge" (c1826; 2T, 2B, sketch w/ out text) D873a
14.116 "Grab und Mond": "Silberblauer Mondenschein fällt herab" (c1826, Seidl; 2T, 2B) D893
14.117 "Wein und Liebe": "Liebchen und der Saft der Reben" (c1827, Haug; 2T, 2B) D901
14.118 "Fruhlingslied" I: "Geöffnet sind des Winters Riegel" (c1827, Pollak; 2T, 2B) D914
14.119 "Das stille Lied": "Schweige nur" (c1827, Seegemund; 2T, 2B, sketch) D916
14.120 "Jünglingswonne": "So lang im deutschen Eichentale" (c ?1822, Matthisson; 2T, 2B) Op.17/1, D983
14.121 "Liebe": "Liebe rauscht der Silberbach" (c ?1822, Schiller; 2T, 2B) Op.17/2, D983a
14.122 "Zum Rundetanz": "Auf! es dunkelt; silbern funkelt" (c ?1822, Salis-Seewis; 2T, 2B) Op.17/3, D983b
14.123 "Die Nacht": "Wie schön bist du" (c ?1822, ?Krummacher; 2T, 2B) Op.17/4, D983c

Unacc fem vv:

14.124 "Quell' innocente figlio" II (ca1812, Metastasio; 2S) D17
14.125 "Entra l'uomo allor che nasce" II (c1812, Metastasio; S, A) D33

15. SONG CYCLES

15.1 "Die schöne Müllerin," cycle (c1823, Müller): 1. "Das Wandern": "Das Wandern ist
   des Müllers Lust, das Wandern!," in B-flat major Op.25, D795
15.2 2. "Wohin?": "Ich hört' ein Bächlein rauschen," in G major
15.3 3. "Halt!": "Eine Mühle seh ich blinken," in C major
15.4 4. "Danksagung an den Bach": "War es also gemeint," in G major
15.5 5. "Am Feierabend": "Hätt' ich tausend Arme zu rühren!," in A minor
15.6 6. "Der Neugierige": "Ich frage keine Blume, ich frage keinen Stern," in B major
15.7 7. "Ungeduld": "Ich schnitt' es gern in alle Rinden ein," in A major
15.8 8. "Morgengruss": "Guten Morgen, schöne Müllerin!," in C major
15.9 9. "Des Müllers Blumen": "Am Bach viel kleine Blumen stehn," in A major
15.10 10. "Tränenregen": "Wir sassen so traulich beisammen," in A major
15.11 11. "Mein!": "Bächlein, lass dein Rauschen sein!," in D major
15.12 12. "Pause": "Meine Laute hab ich gehängt an die Wand," in B-flat major
15.13 13. "Mit dem grünen Lautenbande": "Schad um das schöne grüne Band," in B-flat major
15.14 14. "Der Jäger": "Was sucht denn der Jäger am Mühlbach hier?," in C minor
15.15 15. "Eifersucht und Stolz": "Wohin so schnell, so kraus und wild, mein lieber Bach?," in G minor
15.16 16. "Die liebe Farbe": "In Grün will ich mich kleiden," in B minor
15.17 17. "Die böse Farbe": "Ich möchte ziehn in die Welt hinaus," in B major
15.18 18. "Trockne Blumen": "Ihr Blümlein alle, die sie mir gab," in E minor
15.19 19. "Der Müller und der Bach": "Wo ein treues Herze in Liebe vergeht," in G minor
15.20 20. "Des Baches Wiegenlied": "Gute Ruh, gute Ruh! Tu die Augen zu!," in E major

15.21 "Die Winterreise," cycle (c1827, Müller), I: 1. "Gute Nacht": "Fremd bin ich eingezogen,"
   in D minor Op.89, D911
15.22 2. "Die Wetterfahne": "Der Wind spielt mit der Wetterfahne," in A minor
15.23 3. "Gefrorene Tränen": "Gefrorne Tropfen fallen," in F minor
15.24 4. "Erstarrung": "Ich such' im Schnee vergebens," in C minor
15.25 5. "Der Lindenbaum": "Am Brunnen vor dem Tore," in E major
15.26 6. "Wasserflut": "Manche Trän' aus meinen Augen," in F-sharp minor (2nd vers in E minor)
15.27 7. "Auf dem Flusse": "Der du so lustig rauschtest," in E minor
15.28 8. "Rückblick": "Es brennt mir unter beiden Sohlen," in G minor
15.29 9. "Irrlicht": "In die tiefsten Felsengründe," in B minor
15.30 10. "Rast": "Nun merk' ich erst, wie müd' ich bin," in C minor (2nd vers in D minor)
15.31 11. "Frühlingstraum": "Ich träumte von bunten Blumen," in A maj / minor
15.32 12. "Einsamkeit": "Wie eine trübe Wolke durch heit're Lüfte geht," in B minor (2nd vers in D minor)
15.33 II: 13. "Die Post": "Von der Strasse her ein Posthorn klingt," in E-flat major
15.34 14. "Der greise Kopf": "Der Reif hatt' einen weissen Schein," in C minor
15.35 15. "Die Krähe": "Eine Krähe war mit mir," in C minor
15.36 16. "Letzte Hoffnung": "Hie und da ist an den Bäumen," in E-flat major
15.37 17. "Im Dorfe": "Es bellen die Hunde, es rasseln die Ketten," in D major
15.38 18. "Der stürmische Morgen": "Wie hat der Sturm zerrissen," in D minor
15.39 19. "Täuschung": "Ein Licht tanzt freundlich vor mir her," in A major
15.40 20. "Der Wegweiser": "Was vermeid' ich denn die Wege," in G minor
15.41 21. "Das Wirtshaus": "Auf einen Totenacker hat mich mein Weg gebracht," in F major
15.42 22. "Mut": "Fliegt der Schnee mir ins Gesicht," in A minor (2nd vers in G minor)
15.43 23. "Die Nebensonnen": "Drei Sonnen sah ich am Himmel steh'n," in A major (2 vers)
15.44 24. "Der Leiermann": "Drüben hinterm Dorfe steht ein Leiermann," in A minor (2nd vers in B minor)

15.45	"Schwanengesang," cycle (c1828), I: 1. "Liebesbotschaft": "Rauschendes Bächlein, so silbern und hell," in G major (Rellstab)	D957
15.46	2. "Kriegers Ahnung": "In tiefer Ruh liegt um mich her," in C minor (Rellstab)	
15.47	3. "Frühlingssehnsucht": "Säuselnde Lüfte wehend so mild," in B-flat major (Rellstab)	
15.48	4. "Ständchen": "Leise flehen meine Lieder," in D minor (Rellstab)	
15.49	5. "Aufenthalt": "Rauschender Strom, brausender Wald," in E minor (Rellstab)	
15.50	6. "In der Ferne": "Wehe dem Fliehenden, Welt hinaus ziehenden!," in B minor (Rellstab)	
15.51	II: 7. "Abschied": "Ade! du muntre, du fröhliche Stadt, ade!," in E-flat major (Rellstab)	
15.52	8. "Der Atlas": "Ich unglückselger Atlas!," in G minor (Heine)	
15.53	9. "Ihr Bild": "Ich stand in dunkeln Träumen," in B-flat minor (Heine) (also see Wolf's song of 1878)	
15.54	10. "Das Fischermädchen": "Du schönes Fischermädchen," in A-flat major (Heine)	
15.55	11. "Die Stadt": "Am fernen Horizonte," in C minor (Heine)	
15.56	12. "Am Meer": "Das Meer erglänzte weit hinaus," in C major (Heine)	
15.57	13. "Der Doppelgänger": "Still ist die Nacht, es ruhen die Gassen," in B minor (Heine)	
15.58	14. "Die Taubenpost": "Ich hab eine Brieftaub in meinem Sold," in G major (Seidl)	

16. SONGS (w/ pf)

c1811:

16.1	*Song sketch in C minor (c ?1810, w/ out text)*	*D1a*
16.2	"Hagars Klage": "Hier am Hügel heissen Sandes," in C minor (Schücking)	D5
16.3	"Des Mädchens Klage" I: "Der Eichwald brauset," in D minor (c1811 or 12, from Schiller's Wallenstein)	D6
16.4	"Leichenfantasie": "Mit erstorbnem Scheinen," in D minor (ca1811, Schiller)	D7
16.5	"Der Vatermörder": "Ein Vater starb von des Sohnes Hand," in C minor (Pfeffel)	D10

c1812:

16.6	*"Der Geistertanz" I: "Die bretterne Kammer der Toten erbebt," in F minor (Matthisson, frag)*	*D15*
16.7	*"Der Geistertanz" II: "Die bretterne Kammer der Toten erbebt," in F minor (Matthisson, frag)*	*D15a*
16.8	"Quell' innocente figlio" I, in F major (ca1812, Metastasio)	D17
16.9	"Klaglied": "Meine Ruh' ist dahin," in G minor (Rochlitz)	Op.131/3, D23
16.10	"Der Jüngling am Bache" I: "An der Quelle sass der Knabe," in F major (Schiller)	D30
16.11	"Entra l'uomo allor che nasce" I, in E minor (Metastasio)	D33
16.12	"Serbate, o dei custodi" III, in C major (Metastasio)	D35
16.13	"Lebenstraum": "Ich sass an einer Tempelhalle," in C major (ca1810, Baumberg)	D39

c1813:

16.14	"Misero pargoletto" I & II, in G minor (c ?1813, from Metastasio: Demofoonte; setting I: 2 inc vers)	D42
16.15	"Totengräberlied" II: "Grabe, Spaten, grabe!," in E minor (Hölty)	D44
16.16	"Die Schatten": "Freunde, deren Grüfte," in A major (Matthisson)	D50
16.17	"Sehnsucht" I: "Ach, aus dieses Tales Gründen," in D minor (Schiller; B & pf)	D52
16.18	"Verklärung": "Lebensfunke, vom Himmel entglüht," in A minor (Pope transl Herder)	D59
16.19	"Thekla" I: (eine Geisterstimme) I: "Wo ich sei, und wo mich hingewendet," in G major (Schiller)	D73
16.20	"Pensa, che questo istante," in D major (from Metastasio: Alcide al bivio; B & pf; 2 vers)	D76
16.21	"Der Taucher": "Wer wagt es, Rittersmann," in D min (Schiller; B & pf; 2 vers, 2nd vers: former D111)	D77
16.22	"Son fra l'onde," in C major (from Metastasio: Gli orti esperidi; S & pf)	D78
16.23	"Auf den Sieg der Deutschen": "Verschwunden sind die Schmerzen," in F maj (?Schubert; w/ 2vn, vc)	D81
16.24	"Zur Namensfeier des Herrn Andreas Siller": "Des Phöbus Strahlen," in G major (w/ vn & harp)	D83
16.25	"Don Gayseros" (ca1815, from Motte Fouqué's Der Zauberring): 1. "Don Gayseros, Don Gayseros"	D93
16.26	2. "Nächtens klang die süsse Laute" (pf ending lost)	
16.27	3. "An dem jungen Morgenhimmel" (pf ending lost)	

c1814:

16.28	"Adelaide": "Einsam wandelt dein Freund," in A-flat major (Matthisson)	D95
16.29	"Trost. An Elisa": "Lehnst du deine bleichgehärmte Wange," in A minor (Matthisson)	D97
16.30	"Erinnerungen" I: "Am Seegestad, in lauen Vollmondnächten," in B-flat major (Matthisson; 2 vers)	D98
16.31	"Andenken" I: "Ich denke dein," in F major (Matthisson)	D99
16.32	"Geisternähe": "Der Dämmrung Schein durchblinkt den Hain," in E-flat major (Matthisson)	D100
16.33	"Erinnerung": "Kein Rosenschimmer leuchtet dem Tag zur Ruh," in E minor (Matthisson)	D101
16.34	"Die Betende": "Laura betet! Engelharfen hallen," in B major (Matthisson)	D102
16.35	"Die Befreier Europas in Paris": "Sie sind in Paris!," in G major (Mikan; 3 vers)	D104
16.36	"Lied aus der Ferne": "Wenn in des Abends letztem Scheine," in E maj (Matthisson; 2 vers in D maj)	D107
16.37	"Der Abend": "Purpur malt die Tannenhügel," in D minor (Matthisson)	D108
16.38	"Lied der Liebe": "Durch Fichten am Hügel, durch Erlen am Bach," in B-flat major (Matthisson)	D109
16.39	"An Emma": "Weit in nebelgrauer Ferne," in F major (Schiller; 3 vers)	Op.58/2, D113
16.40	"Romanze": "Ein Fräulein klagt' im finstern Turm," in G major (Matthisson; 2 vers)	D114
16.41	"An Laura": "Herzen, die gen Himmel sich erheben," in E major (Matthisson)	D115
16.42	"Der Geistertanz" III: "Die bretterne Kammer der Toten erbebt," in C minor (Matthisson)	D116
16.43	"Das Mädchen aus der Fremde" I: "In einem Tal bei armen Hirten," in A major (Schiller)	D117
16.44	"Gretchen am Spinnrade": "Meine Ruh ist hin, mein Herz ist schwer," in D minor (from Goethe's Faust Part I) (also see Spohr Op.25/3)	Op.2, D118
16.45	"Nachtgesang": "O! gib vom weichem Pfühle," in A-flat major (Goethe)	D119
16.46	"Trost in Tränen": "Wie kommt's, dass du so traurig bist," in F maj (Goethe) (also see Brahms Op.48/5)	D120

16.47 "Schäfers Klagelied": "Da droben auf jenem Berge," in E minor (Goethe; 2nd vers in C min) ..Op.3/1, D121
16.48 "Ammenlied": "Am hohen, hohen Turm," in G minor (Lubi) D122
16.49 "Sehnsucht": "Was zieht mir das Herz so?," in G major (Goethe) (also see Beethoven Op.83/2) D123
16.50 "Am See": "Sitz' ich im Gras am glatten See," in G minor (Mayrhofer; 2 vers) D124
16.51 "Szene aus Faust": "Wie anders, Gretchen, war dir's" (Goethe; w/ ch; 2 vers) D126

c1815:

16.52 "Ballade": "Ein Fräulein schaut vom hohen Turm," in G minor (Kenner) Op.posth126, D134
16.53 "Rastlose Liebe": "Dem Schnee, dem Regen," in E major (Goethe; 2nd vers in D maj 1821) ..Op.5/1, D138
16.54 "Der Mondabend": "Rein und freundlich lacht der Himmel," in A major (Kumpf) Op.posth131/1, D141
16.55 "Geistes-Gruss": "Hoch auf dem alten Turme" (Goethe; 6 vers): Op.92/3, D142
       . Version 1 in E-flat maj / G-flat major
       . Version 2, in E-flat maj / G-flat major
       . Version 3, in D maj / F major
       . Version 4, in E-flat maj / G-flat major
       . Version 5, in E-flat maj / G-flat major
       . Version 6, in E maj / G major (r ?1828)
16.56 "Genügsamkeit": "Dort raget ein Berg aus den Wolken her," in C-sharp minor
       (Schober) Op.posth109/2, D143
16.57 "Romanze": "In der Väter Hallen ruhte," in E major (c1816, Stolberg, sketch) D144
16.58 "Der Sänger": "Was hör' ich draussen vor dem Tor," in D major (from Goethe's Wilhelm Meister;
       2 vers) (also see Schumann Op.98a/2 & Wolf's 10. of: Goethe Lieder) Op.posth117, D149
16.59 "Lodas Gespenst": "Der bleiche, kalte Mond," in G min / B-flat major (c1816, Ossian transl Harold) ... D150
16.60 "Auf einen Kirchhof": "Sei gegrüsst, geweihte Stille," in A major (Schlechta) D151
16.61 "Minona oder die Kunde der Dogge": "Wie treiben die Wolken," in A minor (Bertrand) D152
16.62 "Als ich sie erröten sah": "All' mein Wirken, all' mein Leben," in G major (Ehrlich) D153
16.63 "Das Bild": "Ein Mädchen ist's, das früh und spät mir vor der Seele schwebet," F maj Op.posth165/3, D155
16.64 "Die Erwartung": "Hör' ich das Pförtchen," in B-flat major (c1816, Schiller; 2 vers) Op.posth116, D159
16.65 "Am Flusse" I: "Verfliesset, vielgeliebte Lieder," in D minor (Goethe) D160
16.66 "An Mignon": "Über Tal und Fluss getragen," in G-sharp minor (Goethe; 2nd vers in G min) .Op.19/2, D161
16.67 "Nähe des Geliebten": "Ich denke dein, wenn mir der Sonne Schimmer vom Meere strahlt," in G-flat
       major (Goethe; 2 vers) Op.5/2, D162
16.68 "Sängers Morgenlied" I: "Süsses Licht! aus goldenen Pforten," in G major (Körner) D163
16.69 "Liebesrauch" I: "Glanz des Guten und des Schönen," in D major (Körner, frag) D164
16.70 "Sängers Morgenlied" II: "Süsses Licht! aus goldnen Pforten," in C major (Körner) D165
16.71 "Amphiaraos": "Vor Thebens siebenfach gähnenden Toren," in G minor (Körner) D166
16.72 "Gebet während der Schlacht": "Vater, ich rufe dich!," in B-flat major (Körner) D171
16.73 "Der Morgenstern" I: "Stern der Liebe, Glanzgebilde!," in G-flat major (Körner, sketch) D172
16.74 "Das war ich": "Jüngst träumte mir," in G major (Körner; also frag of 2nd vers in D major 1816) D174
16.75 "Die Sterne": "Was funkelt ihr so mild mich an?," in A-flat major (Fellinger) D176
16.76 "Vergebliche Liebe": "Ja, ich weiss es," in C minor (Bernard) Op.posth173/3, D177
16.77 "Liebesrausch" II: "Dir, Mädchen, schlägt mit leisem Beben," in G major (Körner) D179
16.78 "Sehnsucht der Liebe": "Wie die Nacht mit heil'gem Beben," in G major (Körner; 2nd vers lost) D180
16.79 "Die erste Liebe": "Die erste Liebe füllt das Herz," in G major (Fellinger) D182
16.80 "Die Sterbende": "Heil! dies ist die letzte Zähre," in A-flat major (Matthisson) D186
16.81 "Stimme der Liebe" I: "Abendgewölke schweben hell," in F major (Matthisson) D187
16.82 "Naturgenuss" I: "Im Abendschimmer wallt der Quell," in B-flat major (Matthisson) D188
16.83 "Des Mädchens Klage" II: "Der Eichwald braust," in C minor (Schiller's Wallenstein; 2 vers) .Op.58/3, D191
16.84 "Der Jüngling am Bache" II: "An der Quelle sass der Knabe," in F minor (Schiller) D192
16.85 "An den Mond": "Geuss, lieber Mond," in F minor (Hölty) Op.57/3, D193
16.86 "Die Mainacht": "Wann der silberne Mond," in D minor (Hölty) D194
16.87 "Amalia": "Schön wie Engel voll Walhallas Wonne," in A maj (Schiller's Die Räuber) .Op.posth173/1, D195
16.88 "An die Nachtigall": "Geuss nicht so laut der liebentflammten Lieder," in F-sharp minor (Hölty) (also
       see Brahms Op.46/4) Op.posth172/3, D196
16.89 "An die Apfelbäume, wo ich Julien erblickte": "Ein heilig Säuseln," in A major (Hölty) D197
16.90 "Seufzer": "Die Nachtigall singt überall auf grünen Reisen," in G minor (Hölty) D198
16.91 "Auf den Tod einer Nachtigall" I: "Sie ist dahin," in F-sharp minor (Hölty, sketch) D201
16.92 "Das Traumbild" (Hölty, lost) D204a
16.93 "Liebeständelei": "Süsses Liebchen, komm zu mir!," in E-flat major (Körner) D206
16.94 "Der Liebende": "Beglückt, beglückt, wer dich erblickt," in B-flat major (Hölty) D207
16.95 "Die Nonne": "Es liebt' in Welschland," in A-flat major (Hölty; 2 vers, frag of 1st vers) D208 (D212)
16.96 "Der Liedler": "Gib, Schwester, mir die Harf herab," in A minor (Kenner) Op.38, D209
16.97 "Die Liebe" (Klärchens Lied): "Freudvoll und leidvoll," in B-flat major (from Goethe's Egmont) (also
       see Beethoven Op.84/4 & Liszt S280) D210
16.98 "Adelwold und Emma": "Hoch, und ehern schier von Dauer," in F major (Bertrand) D211
16.99 "Der Traum": "Mir träumt' ich war ein Vögelein," in A major (Hölty) Op.posth172/1, D213
16.100 "Die Laube": "Nimmer werd' ich, nimmer dein vergessen," in A-flat major (Hölty) Op.posth172/2, D214
16.101 "Jägers Abendlied" I: "Im Felde schleich' ich still und wild," in F major (Goethe) D215
16.102 "Meerestille" I: "Tiefe Stille herrscht im Wasser," in C major (Goethe) D215a
16.103 "Meerestille" II: "Tiefe Stille herrscht im Wasser," in C major (Goethe) Op.3/2, D216
16.104 "Kolmas Klage": "Rund um mich Nacht," in C minor (Ossian transl Kenner) D217
16.105 "Grablied": "Er fiel den Tod fürs Vaterland," in F minor (Ossian transl Kenner) D218
16.106 "Das Finden": "Ich hab' ein Mädchen funden," in B-flat major (Kosegarten) D219
16.107 "Der Abend": "Der Abend blüht," in B major (Kosegarten) Op.posth118/2, D221
16.108 "Lieb Minna": "Schwüler Hauch weht mir herüber," in F minor (Stadler) D222

16.109	"Wanderers Nachtlied": "Der du von dem Himmel bist," in G-flat major (Goethe) (also see Liszt S279 & Wolf's 5. of: 6 Poems p1888)	Op.4/3, D224
16.110	"Der Fischer": "Das Wasser rauscht', das Wasser schwoll," in B-flat major (Goethe; 2 vers) (also see R. Strauss AV33)	Op.5/3, D225
16.111	"Erster Verlust": "Ach, wer bringt die schönen Tage," in F minor (Goethe) (also see Mendelssohn Op.99/1)	Op.5/4, D226
16.112	"Idens Nachtgesang": "Vernimm es, Nacht," in B-flat major (Kosegarten)	D227
16.113	"Von Ida": "Der Morgen blüht, der Osten glüht," in F minor (Kosegarten)	D228
16.114	"Die Erscheinung": "Ich lag auf grünen Matten," in E major (Kosegarten)	Op.108/3, D229
16.115	"Die Täuschung": "Im Erlenbusch, im Tannenhain," in E major (Kosegarten)	Op.posth165/4, D230
16.116	"Das Sehnen": "Wehmut, die mich hüllt," in A minor (Kosegarten)	Op.posth172/4, D231
16.117	"Geist der Liebe": "Wer bist du, Geist der Liebe," in E major (Kosegarten)	Op.posth118/1, D233
16.118	"Tischlied": "Mich ergreift, ich weiss nicht wie," in C major (Goethe)	Op.posth118/3, D234
16.119	"Abends unter der Linde" I: "Woher, o namenloses Sehnen," in F major (Kosegarten)	D235
16.120	"Abends unter der Linde" II: "Woher, o namenloses Sehnen," in F major (Kosegarten)	D237
16.121	"Die Mondnacht": "Siehe, wie die Mondesstrahlen," in F-sharp major (Kosegarten)	D238
16.122	"Huldigung": "Ganz verloren, ganz versunken," in E major (Kosegarten)	D240
16.123	"Alles um Liebe": "Was ist es, das die Seele füllt?," in E major (Kosegarten)	D241
16.124	"Die Bürgschaft": "Zu Dionys, dem Tyrannen," in G minor (Schiller)	D246
16.125	"Die Spinnerin": "Als ich still und ruhig spann," in B minor (Goethe)	Op.posth118/6, D247
16.126	"Lob des Tokayers": "O köstlicher Tokayer," in B-flat major (Baumberg)	Op.posth118/4, D248
16.127	*"Die Schlacht" I, in B minor (Schiller, sketch)*	*D249*
16.128	"Das Geheimnis" I: "Sie konnte mir kein Wörtchen sagen," in A-flat major (Schiller)	D250
16.129	"Hoffnung" I: "Es reden und träumen die Menschen viel," in G-flat major (Schiller)	D251
16.130	"Das Mädchen aus der Fremde" II: "In einem Tal bei armen Hirten," in F major (Schiller)	D252
16.131	"Punschlied. Im Norden zu singen": "Auf der Berge," in B-flat major (Schiller; also see D253/2)	D253/1
16.132	"Der Gott und die Bajadere": "Mahadöh, der Herr der Erde," in E-flat major (Goethe)	D254
16.133	"Der Rattenfänger": "Ich bin der wohlbekannte Sänger," in G major (Goethe) (also see Wolf's 11. of: Goethe Lieder)	D255
16.134	"Der Schatzgräber": "Arm am Beutel, krank am Herzen," in D minor (Goethe)	D256
16.135	"Heidenröslein": "Sah ein Knab ein Röslein stehn," in G major (Goethe)	Op.3/3, D257
16.136	"Bundeslied": "In allen guten Stunden," in B-flat major (Goethe)	D258
16.137	"An den Mond" I: "Füllest wieder Busch und Tal," in E-flat major (Goethe)	D259
16.138	"Wonne der Wehmut": "Trocknet nicht, trocknet nicht, Tränen der ewigen Liebe!," in C minor (Goethe) (also see Beethoven Op.83/1)	Op.posth115/2, D260
16.139	"Wer kauft Liebesgötter?": "Von allen schönen Waren," in C major (Goethe)	D261
16.140	"Die Fröhlichkeit": "Wes' Adern leichtes Blut durchspringt," in E major (Prandstetter)	D262
16.141	"Cora an die Sonne": "Nach so vielen trüben Tagen," in E-flat major (Baumberg)	D263
16.142	"Der Morgenkuss": "Durch eine ganze Nacht," in E-flat major (Baumberg; 2nd vers in C major)	D264
16.143	"Abendständchen. An Lina": "Sei sanft wie ihre Seele," in B-flat major (Baumberg)	D265
16.144	"Morgenlied": "Willkommen, rotes Morgenlicht," in F major (Stolberg)	D266
16.145	"An die Sonne": "Sinke, liebe Sonne, sinke," in E-flat major (Baumberg)	Op.posth118/5, D270
16.146	"Der Weiberfreund": "Noch fand von Evens Töchterscharen," in A major (Cowley transl Ratschky)	D271
16.147	"An die Sonne": "Königliche Morgensonne," in E-flat major (Tiedge)	D272
16.148	"Lilla an die Morgenröte": "Wie schön bist du, du güldne Morgenröte," in D major (unknown)	D273
16.149	"Tischlied": "Mein Handwerk geht durch alle Welt," in C major (unknown)	D274
16.150	"Totenkrantz für ein Kind": "Sanft wehn, im Hauch der Abendluft," in G minor (Matthisson)	D275
16.151	"Abendlied": "Gross und rotentflammet," in A major (Stolberg)	D276
16.152	"Ossians Lied nach dem Falle Nathos": "Beugt euch aus euren Wolken nieder," in E major (transl Harold; 2 vers, frag of 1st vers)	D278
16.153	"Das Rosenband": "Im Frühlingsschatten fand ich sie," in A-flat major (Klopstock) (also see R. Strauss Op.36/1)	D280
16.154	"Das Mädchen von Inistore": "Mädchen Inistores," in C minor (from Ossian's Fingal, transl Harold)	D281
16.155	"Cronnan": "Ich sitz' bei der moosigten Quelle," in C min (from Ossian's Carric-Thura, transl Harold)	D282
16.156	"An den Frühling" I: "Willkommen, schöner Jüngling!," in F major (Schiller)	Op.posth172/5, D283
16.157	"Lied": "Es ist so angenehm," in G major (?Schiller)	D284
16.158	"Furcht der Geliebten" (An Cidli): "Cidli, du weinest," in A-flat major (Klopstock; 2 vers)	D285
16.159	"Selma und Selmar": "Weine du nicht, o, die ich innig liebe," in F major (Klopstock; 2 vers)	D286
16.160	"Vaterlandslied": "Ich bin ein deutsches Mädchen," in C major (Klopstock; 2 vers)	D287
16.161	"An Sie": "Zeit, Verkündigerin der besten Freuden," in A-flat major (Klopstock)	D288
16.162	"Die Sommernacht": "Wenn der Schimmer von dem Monde," in C major (Klopstock; 2 vers)	D289
16.163	"Die frühen Gräber": "Willkommen, o silberner Mond," in A minor (Klopstock) (also see Gluck's 6. of: Oden und Lieder, Wq(pp153–154))	D290
16.164	"Dem Unendlichen": "Wie erhebt sich das Herz," in F major (Klopstock; 3 vers, 3rd in G major)	D291
16.165	*"Klage": "Trauer umfliesst mein Leben," in B minor (sketch for D371)*	*D292*
16.166	"Shilric und Vinvela": "Mein Geliebter ist ein Sohn," in B-flat major (from Ossian's Carric-Thura, transl Harold)	D293
16.167	"Hoffnung": "Schaff, das Tagwerk meiner Hände," in F major (ca1816, Goethe; 2nd vers in E major)	D295
16.168	"An den Mond" II: "Füllest wieder Busch und Tal," in A-flat major (ca1816, Goethe)	D296
16.169	"Augenlied": "Süsse Augen, klare Bronnen!," in F major (c ?1817, Mayrhofer; 2 vers)	D297
16.170	"Liane": "Hast du Lianen nicht gesehen?," in C major (Mayrhofer)	D298
16.171	"Der Jüngling an der Quelle": "Leise, rieselnder Quell!," in A major (ca1817, Salis-Seewis)	D300
16.172	"Lambertine": "O Liebe, die mein Herz erfüllet," in E-flat major (Stoll)	D301
16.173	"Labetrank der Liebe": "Wenn im Spiele leiser Töne," in F major (Stoll)	D302
16.174	"An die Geliebte": "O, dass ich dir vom stillen Auge," in G maj (Stoll) (also see Beethoven WoO 140)	D303

16.175 "Wiegenlied": "Schlumm're sanft! Noch an dem Mutterherzen," in F major (Körner) D304
16.176 "Mein Gruss an den Mai": "Sei mir gegrüst, o Mai," in B-flat major (Kumpf) D305
16.177 "Skolie": "Lasst im Morgenstrahl des Mai'n," in B-flat major (Deinhardstein) D306
16.178 "Die Sternenwelten": "Oben drehen sich die grossen," in F major (Jarnik transl Fellinger) D307
16.179 "Die Macht der Liebe": "Überall, wohin mein Auge blicket," in B-flat major (Kalchberg) D308
16.180 "Das gestörte Glück": "Ich hab' ein heisses junges Blut," in F major (Körner) D309
16.181 "Sehnsucht" I: "Nur wer die Sehnsucht kennt," in A-flat major (Goethe; 2nd vers in F major) D310
16.182   "An den Mond," in A major (sketch w/ out text) D311
16.183 "Hektors Abschied": "Will sich Hektor ewig von mir wenden," in F minor (Schiller; 2 vers) Op.58/1, D312
16.184 "Die Sterne": "Wie wohl ist mir im Dunkeln!," in B-flat major (Kosegarten) D313
16.185 "Nachtgesang": "Tiefe Feier schauert um die Welt," in B-flat major (Kosegarten) D314
16.186 "An Rosa" I: "Warum bist du nicht hier," in A-flat major (Kosegarten) D315
16.187 "An Rosa" II: "Rosa, denkst du an mich?," in A-flat major (Kosegarten; 2 vers) D316
16.188 "Idens Schwanenlied": "Wie schaust du aus dem Nebelflor," in F minor (Kosegarten; 2 vers) D317
16.189 "Schwangesang": "Endlich stehn die Pforten offen," in F minor (Kosegarten) D318
16.190 "Luisens Antwort": "Wohl weinen Gottes Engel," in B-flat minor (Kosegarten) D319
16.191 "Der Zufriedene": "Zwar schuf das Glück hienieden," in A major (Reissig) D320
16.192 "Mignon": "Kennst du das Land, wo die Zitronen blühn," in A major (from Goethe's Wilhelm Meister)
           (also see Beethoven Op.75/1, Liszt S275, Schumann Op.79/28 & Wolf's 9. of: Goethe Lieder) D321
16.193 "Hermann und Thusnelda": "Ha, dort kömmt er, mit Schweiss," in E-flat major (Klopstock) D322
16.194 "Klage der Ceres": "Ist der holde Lenz erschienen?," in G maj (Schiller; incl: O so lasst euch, D991) . D323
16.195 "Harfenspieler" I: "Wer sich der Einsamkeit ergibt," in A minor (from Goethe's Wilhelm Meister) D325
16.196   "Lorma" I: "Lorma sass in der Halle von Aldo," in A minor (Ossian transl Harold, frag) D327
16.197 "Erlkönig": "Wer reitet so spät durch Nacht und Wind?," in G minor (Goethe; 4 vers) Op.1, D328
16.198   "Die drei Sänger": "Der König sass beim frohen Mahle," in A major (Bobrik, frag) D329
16.199 "Das Grab" II: "Das Grab ist tief und stille," in C minor (Salis-Seewis; also for ch & pf, D330) D330

c1816:

16.200 "An mein Klavier": "Sanftes Klavier," in A major (Schubart) D342
16.201 "Litanei auf das Fest aller Seelen": "Ruhn in Frieden alle Seelen," in E-flat major (Jacobi; 2 vers) D343
16.202 "Am ersten Maimorgen": "Heute will ich fröhlich, fröhlich sein," in G major (Claudius) D344
16.203 "Der Entfernten" II: "Wohl denk ich allenthalben," in E-flat major (Salis-Seewis) D350
16.204 "Fischerlied" I: "Das Fischergewerbe gibt rüstigen Mut!," in D major (Salis-Seewis) D351
16.205 "Die Nacht": "Du verstörst uns nicht, o Nacht!," in A-flat major (Uz) D358
16.206 "Sehnsucht" II: "Nur wer die Sehnsucht kennt," in D minor (from Goethe's Wilhelm Meister) D359
16.207 "Lied eines Schiffers an die Dioskuren": "Dioskuren, Zwillingssterne, die ihr leuchtet meinem
           Nachen," in A-flat major (Mayrhofer) Op.65/1, D360
16.208 "Am Bach im Frühling": "Du brachst sie nun, die kalte Rinde," in D-flat maj (Schober) Op.posth109/1, D361
16.209 "Zufriedenheit" I: "Ich bin vergnügt," in A major (c1815 or 6, Claudius) D362
16.210 "An Chloen": "Die Munterkeit ist meinen Wangen," in G major (Uz) D363
16.211 "Der König in Thule": "Es war ein König in Thule," in D minor (from Goethe's Faust) (also see
           Liszt S278) Op.5/5, D367
16.212 "Jägers Abendlied" II: "Im Felde schleich ich still und wild," in D-flat major (Goethe) Op.3/4, D368
16.213 "An Schwager Kronos": "Spude dich, Kronos!" in D minor (Goethe) Op.19/1, D369
16.214 "Klage": "Trauer umfliesst mein Leben," in B minor D371
16.215 "An die Natur": "Süsse, heilige Natur," in F major (Stolberg) D372
16.216 "Lied": "Mutter geht durch ihre Kammern," in G minor (from Motte Fouqué's Undine) D373
16.217 "Der Tod Oskars": "Warum öffnest du wieder," in C minor (Ossian transl Harold) D375
16.218   "Lorma" II: "Lorma sass in der Halle," in A minor (Ossian's Die Schlacht von Lora, transl Harold, frag) D376
16.219 "Morgenlied": "Die frohe neubelebte Flur," in C major (unknown) D381
16.220 "Abendlied": "Sanft glänzt die Abendsonne," in F major (unknown) D382
16.221 "Laura am Klavier": "Wenn dein Finger durch die Saiten meistert," in E maj (Schiller; 2nd vers in A) .. D388
16.222 "Des Mädchens Klage" III: "Der Eichwald braust," in C minor (from Schiller's Wallenstein) D389
16.223 "Entzückung an Laura" I: "Laura, über diese Welt," in A major (Schiller) D390
16.224 "Die vier Weltalter": "Wohl perlet im Glase der purpurne Wein," in G major (Schiller) . Op.posth111/3, D391
16.225 "Pflügerlied": "Arbeitsam und wacker, pflügen wir den Acker," in C major (Salis-Seewis) D392
16.226 "Die Einsiedelei" I: "Es rieselt, klar und wehend," in A major (Salis-Seewis) D393
16.227 "An die Harmonie": "Schöpferin beseelter Töne!," in A major (Salis-Seewis) D394
16.228 "Lebensmelodien": "Auf den Wassern wohnt mein stilles Leben," in G major (Schlegel) Op.111/2, D395
16.229   "Gruppe aus dem Tartarus" I: "Horch, wie Murmeln des empörten Meeres," in C minor (Schiller, frag) D396
16.230 "Ritter Toggenburg": "Ritter, treue Schwesterliebe widmet euch dies Herz," in F major (Schiller) D397
16.231 "Frühlingslied" II: "Die Luft ist blau, das Tal ist grün," in G major (Hölty) D398
16.232 "Auf den Tod einer Nachtigall" II: "Sie ist dahin, die Maienlieder tönte," in A minor (Hölty) D399
16.233 "Die Knabenzeit": "Wie glücklich, wem das Knabenkleid," in A major (Hölty) D400
16.234 "Winterlied": "Keine Blumen blühn," in A minor (Hölty) D401
16.235 "Der Flüchtling": "Frisch atmet des Morgens lebendiger Hauch," in B-flat major (Schiller) D402
16.236 "Lied": "Ins stille Land! Wer leitet uns hinüber?" (Salis-Seewis; 4 vers: 1st in G minor, 2nd–4th
           in A minor, 4th version c1823) D403
16.237 "Die Herbstnacht": "Mit leisen Harfentönen sei, Wehmut, mir gegrüsst!," in F major (Salis-Seewis) D404
16.238 "Der Herbstabend": "Abendglockenhalle zittern," in F minor (Salis-Seewis; 2 vers) D405
16.239 "Abschied von der Harfe": "Noch einmal tön, o Harfe," in E minor (Salis-Seewis) D406
16.240 "Beitrag zur fünfjährigen Jubelfeier des Herrn von Salieri," aria (c1816, Schubert; T & pf) D407/2
16.241 "Die verfehlte Stunde": "Quälend ungestilltes Sehnen," in F minor (Schlegel) D409
16.242 "Sprache der Liebe": "Lass dich mit gelinden Schlägen rühren," in E maj (Schlegel) ..Op.posth115/3, D410
16.243 "Daphne am Bach": "Ich hab ein Bächlein funden," in D major (Stolberg) D411

c1818:

16.375	"Auf der Riesenkoppe": "Hoch auf dem Gipfel deiner Gebirge," in D minor (Körner)	D611
16.376	"An den Mond in einer Herbstnacht": "Freundlich ist dein Antlitz," in A major (Schreiber)	D614
16.377	"Grablied für die Mutter": "Hauche milder, Abendluft," in B minor (unknown)	D616
16.378	"Vocal exercise," in C major (w/ out text; 2vv & figured bass)	D619
16.379	"Einsamkeit": "Gib mir die Fülle der Einsamkeit!," in B-flat major (Mayrhofer)	D620
16.380	"Der Blumenbrief": "Euch Blümlein will ich senden," in D major (Schreiber)	D622
16.381	"Das Marienbild": "Sei gegrüsst, du Frau der Huld," in C major (Schreiber)	D623
16.382	"Blondel zu Marien": "In düstrer Nacht," in E-flat minor (unknown)	D626
16.383	"Das Abendrot": "Du heilig, glühend Abendrot!," in E major (Schreiber) Op.posth173/6, D627
16.384	"Sonett" I: "Apollo, lebet noch dein hold Verlangen," in B-flat major (Petrarch transl Schlegel)	D628
16.385	"Sonett" II: "Allein, nachdenklich, wie gelähmt vom Krampfe," in G minor (Petrarch transl Schlegel)	D629
16.386	"Sonett" III: "Nunmehr, da Himmel, Erde schweigt," in C major (Petrarch transl Gries)	D630
16.387	"Blanka": "Wenn mich einsam Lüfte fächeln," in A minor (from Schlegel's Stimmen der Liebe)	D631
16.388	"Vom Mitleiden Mariä": "Als bei dem Kreuz Maria stand," in G minor (Schlegel)	D632

c1819:

16.389	"Der Schmetterling": "Wie soll ich nicht tanzen," in F major (from Schlegel's Abendröte) Op.57/1, D633
16.390	"Die Berge": "Sieht uns der Blick gehoben," in G major (from Schlegel's Abendröte) Op.57/2, D634
16.391	"Sehnsucht" II: "Ach, aus dieses Tales gründen" (ca1821, Schiller; 3 vers) Op.39, D636
16.392	"Hoffnung" II: "Es reden und träumen die Menschen," in B-flat major (Schiller) Op.87/2, D637
16.393	"Der Jüngling am Bache" III: "An der Quelle sass der Knabe," in D minor (Schiller; 2nd vers in C minor) Op.87/3, D638
16.394	"Widerschein" (Schlechta; 2 vers): D639 (D949)
	. Version 1: "Fischer harrt am Brückenbogen," in D major	
	. Version 2: "Tom lehnt harrend auf der Brücke," in B-flat major	
16.395	*"Abend": "Wie ist es denn," in G minor (Tieck, frag)* *D645*
16.396	"Die Gebüsche": "Es wehet kühl und leise," in G major (from Schlegel's Abendröte)	D646
16.397	"Der Wanderer": "Wie deutlich des Mondes Licht zu mir spricht," in D major (Schlegel) Op.65/2, D649
16.398	"Abendbilder": "Still beginnt's im Hain zu tauen," in A minor (Silbert)	D650
16.399	"Himmelsfunken": "Der Odem Gottes weht," in G major (Silbert)	D651
16.400	"Das Mädchen": "Wie so innig, möcht ich sagen," in A major (Schlegel; 2 vers)	D652
16.401	"Bertas Lied in der Nacht": "Nacht umhüllt mit wehendem Flügel," in E-flat minor (Grillparzer)	D653
16.402	"An die Freunde": "Im Wald, im Wald da grabt mich ein," in A minor (Mayrhofer)	D654
16.403	"Marie": "Ich sehe dich in tausend Bildern," in D major (Novalis)	D658
16.404	"Hymne" I: "Wenige wissen das Geheimnis der Liebe," in A minor (Novalis)	D659
16.405	"Hymne" II: "Wenn ich ihn nur habe," in B-flat minor (Novalis)	D660
16.406	"Hymne" III: "Wenn alle untreu werden," in B-flat minor (Novalis)	D661
16.407	"Hymne" IV: "Ich sag es jedem, dass er lebt," in A major (Novalis)	D662
16.408	*"Psalm 13": "Ach, Herr, wie lange," in D-flat major (transl M. Mendelssohn, frag)* *D663*
16.409	"Beim Winde": "Es träumen die Wolken, die Sterne, der Mond," in G minor (Mayrhofer)	D669
16.410	"Die Sternennächte": "In monderhellten Nächten," in D-flat major (Mayrhofer) Op.posth165/2, D670
16.411	"Trost": "Hörnerklage rufen klagend," in E-flat major (Mayrhofer)	D671
16.412	"Nachtstück": "Wenn über Bergen der Nebel breitet," in C-sharp minor (Mayrhofer; 2nd vers in C minor) Op.36/2, D672
16.413	"Die Liebende schreibt": "Ein Blick von deinen Augen in die meinen," in B-flat major (Goethe) (also see Brahms Op.47/5 & Mendelssohn Op.86/3) Op.posth165/1, D673
16.414	"Prometheus": "Bedecke deinen Himmel," in G min (Goethe) (also see Wolf's 49. of: Goethe Lieder) D674
16.415	"Strophe aus Die Götter Griechenlands": "Schöne Welt, wo bist du?," in A min / maj (Schiller; 2 vers) D677

c1820:

16.416	*"Über allen Zauber Liebe": "Sie hüpfte mit mir auf grünem Plan," in G major (Mayrhofer, frag)* *D682*
16.417	"Die Sterne": "Du staunest, o Mensch," in E-flat major (from Schlegel's Abendröte)	D684
16.418	"Morgenlied": "Eh die Sonne früh aufersteht," in A min (from Werner's Die Söhne des Tals) ... Op.4/2, D685
16.419	"Frühlingsglaube": "Die linden Lüfte sind erwacht," in B-flat major (Uhland; 3 vers, 3rd vers in A-flat major) (also see Mendelssohn Op.9/8) Op.20/2, D686
16.420	"Nachthymne": "Hinüber wall ich, und jede Pein," in D major (Novalis)	D687
16.421	"4 Canzonen": 1. "Non t'accostar all'urna," in C major (Vittorelli)	D688
16.422	2. "Guarda, che bianca luna," in G major (Vittorelli)	
16.423	3. "Da quel sembiante appresi," in B-flat major (from Metastasio: L'eroe cinese)	
16.424	4. "Mio ben ricordati," in B-flat minor (from Metastasio: Alessandro nell'Indie)	
16.425	"Abendröte": "Tiefer sinket schon die Sonne," in A major (c1823, Schlegel)	D690
16.426	"Die Vögel": "Wie lieblich und fröhlich," in A major (from Schlegel's Abendröte) Op.posth172/6, D691
16.427	"Der Knabe": "Wenn ich nur ein Vöglein wäre," in A major (from Schlegel's Abendröte)	D692
16.428	"Der Fluss": "Wie rein Gesang sich windet," in B major (from Schlegel's Abendröte)	D693
16.429	"Der Schiffer": "Friedlich lieg ich hingegossen," in D major (Schlegel)	D694
16.430	"Namenstagslied": "Vater, schenk mir diese Stunde," in A major (Stadler)	D695
16.431	"Des Fräuleins Liebeslauchen": "Da unten steht ein Ritter," in A major (Schlechta)	D698
16.432	"Der entsühnte Orest": "Zu meinen Füssen bricht du dich," in C major (Mayrhofer)	D699
16.433	"Freiwilliges Versinken": "Wohin? O Helios!," in D minor (Mayrhofer)	D700
16.434	"Der Jüngling auf dem Hügel": "Ein Jüngling auf dem Hügel," in G major (Hüttenbrenner) Op.8/1, D702
16.435	"Der zürnenden Diana": "Ja, spanne nur den Bogen," in A major (Mayrhofer; 2nd vers in B-flat major) Op.36/1, D707
16.436	"Im Walde" (Waldesnacht): "Windes Rauschen, Gottes Flügel," in C-sharp minor (Schlegel)	D708

16.437 "Lob der Tränen": "Laue Lüfte, Blumendüfte," in D major (c1818, Schlegel; 2 vers) Op.13/2, D711

c1821:

16.438 "Die gefangenen Sänger": "Hörst du von den Nachtigallen," in G major (Schlegel) D712
16.439 "Der Unglückliche": "Die Nacht bricht an," in B minor (from Pichler's Olivier; 2 vers) Op.87/1, D713
16.440 "Versunken": "Voll Locken kraus ein Haupt so rund," in A-flat major (from Goethe's West-östlicher
　　　　 Divan) D715
16.441 "Grenzen der Menschheit": "Wenn der uralte heilige Vater," in E major (Goethe) (also see
　　　　 Wolf's 51. of: Goethe Lieder) D716
16.442 "Suleika" II: "Ach um deine feuchten Schwingen," in B-flat major (from Goethe's West-östlicher
　　　　 Divan) (also see Mendelssohn Op.34/4) Op.31, D717
16.443 "Geheimes": "Über meines Liebchens Äugeln," in A-flat major (from Goethe's West-östlicher
　　　　 Divan) Op.14/2, D719
16.444 "Suleika" I: "Was bedeutet die Bewegung?," in B minor (?Willemer; 2 vers) Op.14/1, D720
16.445 "Mahomets Gesang" II: "Seht den Felsenquell," in C-sharp minor (Goethe, frag) D721
16.446 "Linde Lüfte wehen," in B minor (mS, T, frag) D725
16.447 "Mignon" I: "Heiss mich nicht reden," in B minor (from Goethe's Wilhelm Meister) D726
16.448 "Mignon" II: "So lasst mich scheinen, bis ich werde," in B minor (from Goethe's Wilhelm Meister) (also
　　　　 see Schumann Op.98a/9 & Wolf's 7. of: Goethe Lieder) D727
16.449 "Johanna Sebus"'s "Der Damm zerreisst," in D minor (Goethe, frag) D728
16.450 "Der Blumen Schmerz": "Wie tönt es mir so schaurig," in E minor (Mayláth) Op.posth173/4, D731

c1822:

16.451 "Ihr Grab": "Dort ist ihr Grab," in E-flat major (Engelhardt) D736
16.452 "An die Leier": "Ich will von Atreus' Söhnen," in E-flat major (Bruchmann after Anacreon) Op.56/2, D737
16.453 "Im Haine": "Sonnenstrahlen durch die Tannen," in A major (Bruchmann) Op.56/3, D738
16.454 "Sei mir gegrüsst": "O du Entrissne mir und meinem Kusse," in B-flat major (Rückert) Op.20/1, D741
16.455 "Der Wachtelschlag": "Ach! mir schallt's dorten," in D major (Sauter) Op.68, D742
16.456 "Selige Welt": "Ich treibe auf des Lebens Meer," in A-flat major (Senn) Op.23/2, D743
16.457 "Schwanengesang": "Wie klag ich's aus," in A-flat major (Senn) Op.23/3, D744
16.458 "Die Rose": "Es lockte schöne Wärme," in G maj (from Schlegel's Abendröte; 2nd vers in F) ..Op.73, D745
16.459 "Am See": "In des Sees Wogenspiele," in E-flat major (Bruchmann) D746
16.460 "An Herrn Josef Spaun, Assessor in Linz": "Und nimmer schreibst du?," in C minor (Collin) D749
16.461 "Die Liebe hat gelogen," in C minor (Platen-Hallermünde) Op.23/1, D751
16.462 "Nachtviolen": "Nachtviolen, dunkle Augen, seelenvolle, selig ist es" in C major (Mayrhofer) D752
16.463 "Aus 'Heliopolis' " I: "Im kalten, rauhen Norden," in E minor (from Mayrhofer's Heliopolis) Op.65/3, D753
16.464 "Aus 'Heliopolis' " II: "Fels auf Felsen hingewälzet," in C minor (from Mayrhofer's Heliopolis) D754
16.465 "Du liebst mich nicht": "Mein Herz ist zerrissen, du liebst mich nicht!," in G-sharp minor
　　　　 (Platen-Hallermünde; 2nd vers in A minor) Op.59/1, D756
16.466 "Todesmusik": "In des Todes Feierstunde," in G-flat major (Schober) Op.108/2, D758
16.467 "Schatzgräbers Begehr": "In tiefster Erde ruht ein alt Gesetz," in D minor (Schober; 2 vers) .Op.23/4, D761
16.468 "Schwestergruss": "Im Mondenschein wall ich auf und ab," in F-sharp minor (Bruchmann) D762
16.469 "Der Musensohn": "Durch Feld und Wald zu schweifen," in A-flat major (Goethe; 2nd vers in
　　　　 G major) Op.92/1, D764
16.470 "An die Entfernte": "So hab ich wirklich dich verloren?," in G major (Goethe) D765
16.471 "Am Flusse" II: "Verfliesset, vielgeliebte Lieder," in D major (Goethe) D766
16.472 "Willkommen und Abschied": "Es schlug mein Herz, geschwind, zu Pferde!" in D major (Goethe;
　　　　 2nd vers in C major) Op.56/1, D767

c1823:

16.473 "Wandrers Nachtlied": "Über allen Gipfeln ist Ruh," in B-flat major (c by 1824, Goethe) (also see
　　　　 Liszt S306 & Schumann Op.96/1)..Op.96/3, D768
16.474 "Drang in die Ferne": "Vater, du glaubst es nicht," in A min / major (Leitner) Op.71, D770
16.475 "Der Zwerg": "Im trüben Licht verschwinden schon die Berge," in A minor (Collin) Op.22/1, D771
16.476 "Wehmut": "Wenn ich durch Wald und Fluren geh,' " in D minor (Collin) Op.22/2, D772
16.477 "Auf dem Wasser zu singen": "Mitten im Schimmer der spiegelnden Wellen gleitet," in A-flat major
　　　　 (Stolberg) Op.72, D774
16.478 "Dass sie hier gewesen": "Dass der Ostwind Düfte," in C major (Rückert) Op.59/2, D775
16.479 "Du bist die Ruh": "Du bist die Ruh, der Friede mild," in E-flat major (Rückert) Op.59/3, D776
16.480 "Lachen und Weinen": "Lachen und Weinen zu jeglicher Stunde," in A-flat major (Rückert) ..Op.59/4, D777
16.481 "Greisengesang": "Der Frost hat mir bereifet des Hauses Dach," in B min (Rückert; 2 vers) .Op.60/1, D778
16.482 "Die Wallfahrt": "Meine Tränen im Bussgewand," in F minor (Rückert) D778a
16.483 "Der zürnende Barde": "Wer wagt's, wer wagt's," in G minor (Bruchmann) D785
16.484 "Viola": "Schneeglöcklein, o Schneeglöcklein," in A-flat major (Schober) Op.posth123, D786
16.485 "Die Mutter Erde": "Des Lebens Tag ist schwer und schwül," in A min / major (Stolberg) D788
16.486 "Pilgerweise": "Ich bin ein Waller auf der Erde," in F-sharp minor (Schober) D789
16.487 "Vergissmeinnicht": "Als der Frühling sich vom Herzen," in A-flat major (Schober) D792
16.488 "Das Geheimnis" II: "Sie konnte mir kein Wörtchen sagen," in G major (Schiller) Op.posth173/2, D793
16.489 "Der Pilgrim": "Noch in meines Lebens Lenze," in E major (Schiller; 2nd vers in D major) Op.37/1, D794
16.490 "Romanze zum Drama Rosamunde IIIb": "Der Vollmond strahlt," in F min (Chézy, = 3b. of Op.26, D797) ..
　　　　 .... D799
16.491 "Im Abendrot": "O, wie schön ist diese Welt" (c1824 or 5, Lappe) D799
16.492 "Der Einsame": "Wann meine Grillen schwirren," in G major (c1825, Lappe; 2 vers) Op.41, D800
16.493 "Dithyrambe": "Nimmer, das glaubt mir," in A major (c by 1826, Schiller) Op.60/2, D801

c1824:

16.494   "Der Sieg": "O unbewölktes Leben!," in F major (Mayrhofer) D805
16.495   "Abendstern": "Was weilst du einsam an dem Himmel," in A minor (Mayrhofer) D806
16.496   "Auflösung": "Verbirg dich, Sonne," in G major (Mayrhofer) D807
16.497   "Gondelfahrer" I: "Es tanzen Mond und Sterne," in C major (Mayrhofer) D808
16.498   "Nacht und Träume": "Heil'ge Nacht, du sinkest nieder!," in B maj (c by 1823, Collin; 2 vers) Op.43/2, D827

c1825:

16.499   "Die junge Nonne": "Wie braust durch die Wipfel," in F minor (Craigher de Jachelutta) Op.43/1, D828
16.500   "Abschied": "Leb' wohl, du schöne Erde," melodrama in F major (c1826, from Pratobevera's
         Der Falke) D829
16.501   "Lied der Anne Lyle": "Wärst du bei mir im Lebenstal," in C minor (Scott transl May) Op.85/1, D830
16.502   "Gesang der Norna": "Mich führt mein Weg," in F minor (from Scott's The Pirate, transl
         Spiker) Op.85/2, D831
16.503   "Des Sängers Habe": "Schlagt mein ganzes Glück in Spiltter," in B-flat major (Schlechta) D832
16.504   "Der blinde Knabe": "O sagt, ihr Lieben," in B-flat maj (Cibber transl Craigher; 2 vers) Op.posth101/2, D833
16.505   "Im Walde": "Ich wandre über Berg und Tal," in G minor (Schulze; 2nd vers in B-flat min) Op.93/1, D834
16.506   "Ellens Gesang" I: "Raste, Krieger! Krieg ist aus," in D-flat major (Scott transl Storck) Op.52/1, D837
16.507   "Ellens Gesang" II: "Jäger, ruhe von der Jagd!," in E-flat major (Scott transl Storck) Op.52/2, D838
16.508   "Ellens Gesang" III (An die Jungfrau): "Ave Maria! Jungfrau mild, erhöre einer Jungfrau
         Flehen," in B-flat major (Scott transl Storck) (also see Holst's choral work: Ave Maria maiden
         mild, App.I/35 & Rossini's opera: La donna del lago) Op.52/6, D839
16.509   "Totengräbers Heimweh": "O Menschheit, o Leben, was soll's?," in F min (Craigher de Jachelutta) ... D842
16.510   "Lied des gefangenen Jägers": "Mein Ross so müd," in D minor (Scott transl Storck) Op.52/7, D843
16.511   "Normans Gesang": "Die Nacht bricht bald herein," in C minor (Scott transl Storck) Op.52/5, D846
16.512   "Das Heimweh": "Ach, der Gebirgssohn," in A minor (from Pyrker von Felsö-Eör's Tunisias; 2 vers) .. D851
16.513   "Die Allmacht" I: "Gross ist Jehovah, der Herr," in A major (Felsö-Eör; 2nd vers in C maj) Op.79/2, D852
16.514   "Auf der Bruck": "Frisch trabe sonder Ruh und Rast," in G maj (Schulze; 2nd vers in A-flat) .Op.93/2, D853
16.515   "Fülle der Liebe": "Ein sehnend Streben teilt mir das Herz," in A-flat major (Schlegel) D854
16.516   "Wiedersehn": "Der Frühlingssonne holdes Lächeln," in G major (Schlegel) D855
16.517   "Abendlied für die Entfernte": "Hinaus, mein Blick!," in F major (Schlegel) Op.88/1, D856
16.518   "2 Szenen aus dem Schauspiel Lacrimas" (Schütz): 1. "Ach, was soll," in A major Op.posth124, D857
16.519   2. "Nun, da Schatten niedergleiten," in E major
16.520   "An mein Herz": "O Herz, sei endlich stille," in A minor (Schulze) D860
16.521   "Der liebliche Stern": "Ihr Sternlein, still in der Höhe," in G major (Schulze) D861
16.522   "Um Mitternacht": "Keine Stimme hör ich schallen," in B-flat major (Schulze; 2 vers) Op.88/3, D862
16.523   "An Gott" (c by 1827, Hohlfeld, lost) D863
16.524   "Das Totenhemdchen" (c after 1824, Bauernfeld, lost) D864

c1826:

16.525   "Widerspruch": "Wenn ich durch Busch," in D maj (Seidl, 2nd vers; see 1st for m ch & pf) ..Op.105/1, D865
16.526   "4 Refrainlieder" (c ?1828, Seidl): 1. "Die Unterscheidung": "Die Mutter hat," in G major Op.95, D866
16.527   2. "Bei dir allein": "Bei dir allein empfind ich," in A-flat major
16.528   3. "Die Männer sind méchant": "Du sagtest mir es, Mutter," in A minor
16.529   4. "Irdisches Glück": "So mancher sieht mit finstrer Miene," in D minor
16.530   "Wiegenlied": "Wie sich der Äuglein kindlicher Himmel," in A-flat major (Seidl) Op.105/2, D867
16.531   "Totengräber-Weise": "Nicht so düster und so bleich," in F-sharp minor (Schlechta) D869
16.532   "Der Wanderer an den Mond": "Ich auf der Erd', am Himmel du," in G min / major (Seidl) Op.80/1, D870
16.533   "Das Zügenglöcklein": "Kling die Nacht durch, klinge," in A-flat major (Seidl; 2 vers) Op.80/2, D871
16.534   "O Quell, was strömst du rasch und wild," in G major (Schulze, sketch) D874
16.535   "Im Jänner 1817" (Tiefes Leid): "Ich bin von aller Ruh geschieden," in E minor (Schulze) D876
16.536   "Gesänge aus Wilhelm Meister" (Goethe): 1. "Mignon und der Harfner": "Nur wer," duet
         in B minor (S, T) Op.62, D877
16.537   2. "Lied der Mignon" II: "Heiss' mich nicht reden," in E minor (also see Schumann Op.98a/5
             & Wolf's 5. of: Goethe Lieder)
16.538   3. "Lied der Mignon" III: "So lasst mich scheinen," in B major
16.539   4. "Lied der Mignon" VI: "Nur wer die Sehnsucht kennt," in A minor (also see Beethoven
             WoO 134, Schumann Op.98a/3, Tchaikovsky Op.6/6 & Wolf's 6. of: Goethe Lieder
16.540   "Am Fenster": "Ihr lieben Mauern hold und traut," in F major (Seidl) Op.105/3, D878
16.541   "Sehnsucht": "Die Scheibe friert, der Wind ist rauh," in D minor (Seidl) Op.105/4, D879
16.542   "Im Freien": "Draussen im weiten Nacht steh ich wieder nun," in E-flat major (Seidl) Op.80/3, D880
16.543   "Fischerweise": "Den Fischer fechten Sorgen," in D major (Schlechta; 2 vers) Op.96/4, D881
16.544   "Im Frühling": "Still sitz ich an des Hügels Hang," in G major (Schulze) Op.posth101/1, D882
16.545   "Lebensmut": "O wie dringt das junge Leben," in B-flat major (Schulze) D883
16.546   "Über Wildemann": "Die Winde sausen am Tannenhang," in D minor (Schulze) Op.108/1, D884
16.547   "Trinklied": "Bacchus, feister Fürst des Weins," in C maj (from Shakespeare's Anthony & Cleopatra) . D888
16.548   "Ständchen": "Horch, horch! die Lerch im Ätherblau," in C major (stanza 1 from Shakespeare's
         Cymbeline, transl Schlegel, stanzas 2 & 3 from Reil) (also see Castelnuovo-Tedesco Op.24/VI/2) . D889
16.549   "Hippolits Lied": "Lasst mich, ob ich auch still verglüh," in A minor (Gerstenberg) D890
16.550   "An Silvia": "Was ist Silvia, saget an" in A major (from Shakespeare's The Two Gentlemen of Verone,
         transl Bauernfeld) (also see Castelnuovo-Tedesco Op.24/III/2) Op.106/4, D891

c1827:

16.551   "Fröhliches Scheiden": "Gar fröhlich kann ich scheiden," in F major (Leitner, sketch) D896

17. ARRANGEMENTS OF WORKS BY OTHERS

* * * * *

D = Otto Erich Deutsch: "Franz Schubert. Thematisches Verzeichnis seiner Werke in chronologischer
   Folge." Neuausgabe in deutscher Sprache bearbeitet und herausgegeben von der Editionsleitung
   der Neuen Schubert-Ausgabe und Werner Aderhold. Bärenreiter, 1978.

  Anh. = Anhang (Appendix) in Deutsch's catalog.

1. STAGE WORKS

Operas:

1.1   "Der Corsar" (c1844, Marbach after Byron, unfin) (also see Berlioz: Ouverture du Corsaire,
Op.21, H101, ballet Il Corsaro in Donizetti's opera: Belisario, Verdi's opera: Il Corsaro
& Wolf: Ouvertüre zu Byrons 'Der Korsar') ....

1.2   "Genoveva," 4 acts (c1847–9, Reinick after Tieck & Hebbel; red for pf) Op.81

Incid music:

1.3   "Manfred" (c1848–9, Byron transl Suckow; red for pf) (also see Ives's song Kz123 & Tchaikovsky:
'Manfred Symphony,' in B minor, Op.58) Op.115

1a. SELECTIONS FROM STAGE WORKS

1a.2   "Genoveva," opera: Op.81
      . "Ouvertüre"
      I: 1. "Erhebet Herz," chorus & recit
           2. "Könnt ich mit ... Frieden zieh' in meine," recit & aria (Golo)
           3. "So wenig," duet (Siegfried, Genoveva)
           4. "Dies gilt uns!," recit (Siegfried, Drago, Genoveva, Golo)
           5. "Auf! Auf," d chorus w/ solos (Krieger, Siegfried, Genoveva, Golo)
           6. "Der rauhe," recit & scene (Golo, Genoveva)
           7. "Sieh da welch'," finale (Margaretha, Golo)
      II: 8. "O weh des Scheidens das er that," scene, chorus & recit (Genoveva, Knechte, Golo)
           9. "Wenn ich ein Vöglein wär'," duet (Genoveva, Golo) (= Op.43/1)
          10. "Dem Himmel Dank," duet (Golo, Drago, later Margaretha)
          11. "O du, der über," aria (Genoveva)
          12. "Sacht, sacht, sacht," finale (Knechte, Mägde, Balthasar, Genoveva, Golo, Drago, Margaretha)
      III: 13. "Nichts hält mich mehr," duet (Siegfried, Margaretha)
          14. "Ja wart du bis zum," recit, Lied, duet (Siegfried, Golo)
          15. "Ich sah," finale (Margaretha, Siegfried, Golo, vv & ch behind the scene, Drago's Geist)
        . "Abendlüfte" (Erstes Bild) (2 fem vv)
        . "Wann die Lichter der Erde" (Zweites Bild) (2S, 2T)
        . "Leiser, Leiser Tritt durchs" (Drittes Bild), chorus
      IV: 16. "Steil und steiler," scene (Genoveva, Balthasar, Caspar)
        . "Sie hatten Beid sich herzlich lieb" (Gaunerlied) (2B)
        . "Die letzte" (Genoveva)
          17. "Kennt ihr den Ring?," scene (Golo, Genoveva, Balthasar, Caspar)
          18. "Weib, heuchelt nicht im letzten," scene
          19. "O lass es ruhn dein Aug'auf," duet w/ chorus (Siegfried, Genoveva, Frauen, Männer, Balthasar)
          20. "Bestreut den Weg mit grünen Mai'n," d chorus
          21. "Seit mir gegrüsst nach schwerer Prüfung," finale (Hidulfus, ch, Siegfried, Genoveva)

1a.3   "Manfred," incid music: Op.115
      . "Ouvertüre"
      I: 1. "Gesang der Geister"
           2. "Erscheinung eines Zauberbildes"
           3. "Geisterbannfluch"
           4. "Alpenkuhreigen"
      II: 5. "Zwischenaktmusik"
           6. "Rufung der Alpenfee"
           7. "Hymnus der Geister Ariman's"
           8. "Chor: Wirf in den Staub dich"
           9. "Chor: Zermalmt den Wurm"
          10. "Beschwörung der Astarte"
          11. "Manfreds Ansprache an Astarte"
      III: 12. "Ein Friede kam auf mich"
          13. "Abschied von der Sonne"
          14. "Blick nur hierher" (Manfred)
          15. "Schlussszene. Klostergesang: Requiem aeternam dona eis"

2. SYMPHONIES

2.1   Symphony in G minor, "Zwickau" (c1832–3, unfin: 4th movt in sketches) .... WoO 29
2.2   *Symphony in C min (c1840–1, sketches; Scherzo used in: Bunte Blätter, Op.99 & Adagio of: Sym No.2, Op.61)* ....
2.3   Symphony No.1 in B-flat major, "Spring" (c1841—his 'symphony year') Op.38
2.4   Symphony No.2 in C major (c1845–6) Op.61
2.5   Symphony No.3 in E-flat major, "Rhenish" (c1850) Op.97
2.6   Symphony No.4 in D minor (c1841, r1851) Op.120

3. OTHER ORCHESTRAL WORKS

3.1	"Overture, Scherzo & Finale" (Suite / Symphonette), in E min / major (c1841, r1845)	Op.52
3.2	"Genoveva" Overture, in C minor (c1847; see opera Op.81)	(Op.81)
3.3	"Overture to Schiller's Braut von Messina," in C minor (c1850–1)	Op.100
3.4	"Manfred" Overture, in E-flat minor (c1848–9; see incid music Op.115)	(Op.115)
3.5	"Overture to Shakespeare's Julius Cäsar," in F minor (c1851) (also see overture c by Castelnuovo-Tedesco Op.78 & incid music c by Milhaud Op.158)	Op.128
3.6	"Overture to Goethe's Hermann und Dorothea," in B minor	Op.136

4. CONCERTOS, SOLO INSTR & ORCH

Pf & orch:

4.1	*Piano Concerto in E-flat major (c1828, unfin)*	
4.2	*Piano Concerto in F major (c1829–31, unfin)*	
4.3	*"Introduction and Variations on a theme of Paganini" (c1831, sketches; used in Op.4 & Op.8)*	
4.4	*Piano Concerto in D minor (c1839, 1 movt only)*	
4.5	Piano Concerto in A minor (c1841: 1st movt, c1845: 2nd & 3rd movt, orig 1st movt titled: Fantasie)	Op.54
4.6	"Introduction & Allegro appassionato," in G major (c1849)	Op.92
4.7	"Concert Allegro with Introduction," in D min / major (c1853)	Op.134

Vn & orch:

4.8	"Phantasie," in C major (c1853; vn & orch/pf)	Op.131
4.9	Violin Concerto in D minor (c1853)	WoO 23

Vc & orch:

4.10	Cello Concerto in A minor (c1850; arr Schumann as: Vn Conc, found 1987)	Op.129

Other:

4.11	"Koncertstück," in F major (c1849; 4 hns & orch)	Op.86

5. STRING QUARTETS

5.1	*String Quartet in D major (c1839, sketches)*	
5.2	*String Quartet in E-flat major (c1839, sketches)*	
5.3	"3 String Quartets" (c1842—his 'chamber music year') No.1 in A minor	Op.41
5.4	No.2 in F major	
5.5	No.3 in A major	

6. OTHER CHAMBER MUSIC

5 insts:

6.1	Piano Quintet in E-flat major (c1842—his 'chamber music year'; pf & str qt)	Op.44
6.2	"Andante & Variations" (c1843; 2vc, hn & 2pf, orig vers of Op.46 for 2pf)	WoO 10/1

4 insts:

6.3	Piano Quartet in C major (c1828–30, orig Op.5)	WoO 32
6.4	Piano Quartet in C minor (c1829, p1979)	
6.5	Piano Quartet in B major (c1831–2, unfin)	
6.6	*Quartet (c1838, lost)*	
6.7	Piano Quartet in E-flat major (c1842—his 'chamber music year')	Op.47

3 insts:

6.8	Piano Trio No.1 in D minor (c1847)	Op.63
6.9	Piano Trio No.2 in F major (c1847)	Op.80
6.10	"Phantasiestücke" (c1842; vn, vc & pf): No.1 "Romanze"	Op.88
6.11	No.2 "Humoreske"	
6.12	No.3 "Duett"	
6.13	No.4 "Finale"	
6.14	Piano Trio No.3 in G minor (c1851)	Op.110

Vn & pf:

6.15	Violin Sonata No.1 in A minor (c1851)	Op.105
6.16	Violin Sonata No.2 in D minor (c1851)	Op.121

7. PIANO SONATAS

8. OTHER PIANO WORKS

8.312	No.3 "Menuett"
8.313	No.4 "Ecossaise"
8.314	No.5 "Française"
8.315	No.6 "Ringelreihe"

2 Pf:

8.316   "Andante & Variations," in B-flat major (c1843; orig w/ 2vc & hn) Op.46

Pedal piano:

8.317   "Studien für den Pedal-Flügel," 6 pieces in canon form (c1845): No.1 in C major Op.56
8.318   No.2 in A minor
8.319   No.3 in E major
8.320   No.4 in A-flat major
8.321   No.5 in B minor
8.322   No.6 in B major
8.323   "4 Skizzen für den Pedal-Flügel" (c1845): No.1 in C minor Op.58
8.324   No.2 in C major
8.325   No.3 in F minor
8.326   No.4 in D-flat major

Org / pedal pf or harmonium:

8.327   "6 Fugues on the name of BACH" (c1845; org/pedal pf): No.1 in B-flat major Op.60
8.328   No.2 in B-flat major
8.329   No.3 in G minor
8.330   No.4 in B lfat major
8.331   No.5 in F major
8.332   No.6 in B-flat major
8.333   Piece in F major (c1849; harm, 2 movts only) ....

9. CHORAL WORKS

W/ orch:

9.1   "Psalm 150" (c1822, Biblical; S, A, pf & orch) ....
9.2   "Overture and chorus" (Chor von Landleuten) (c1822) ....
9.3   "Tragödie" (c1841, Heine, orch vers of Op.64/3) ....
9.4   "Das Paradies und die Peri" (c1843, from Moore's Lalla Rookh, transl Flechsig; vv, ch & orch) Op.50
9.5   "Adventlied": "Dein König kommt in Empfang' ihn" (c1848, Rückert; S, ch & orch; red for pf) Op.71
9.6   "Beim Abschied zu singen" (c1847, Feuchtersleben; ch & winds) Op.84
9.7   "Verzweifle nicht im Schmerzenstal" (c1852, Rückert; d ch & orch; see orig motet Op.93) .... (Op.93)
9.8   "Requiem für Mignon" (c1849, from Goethe's Wilhelm Meister; vv, ch & orch) Op.98b
9.9   "Nachtlied" (c1849, Hebbel) Op.108
9.10   "Der Rose Pilgerfahrt," (Mährchen) (c1851, Horn; vv, ch & orch; red for pf): Op.112
        I: 1. "Die Frühlings lüfte" (S)
                2. (Ziemlich lebhaft)
                3. "Wir tanzen, wir tanzen" (Chor der Elfen)
                4. "Und wie sie" (T)
                5. "So sangen sie" (T)
                6. "Bin ein armes Waisenkind" (Rosa)
                7. "Es war der Rose" (T)
                8. "Wie Blätter am" (S)
                9. "Die letzte Scholl hinunter rollt" (T)
                10. "Dank, Herr dir dort im ... Schwesterlein! Hörst du" (Chor der Elfen)
        II: 11. "Ins Haus des Todten" (T)
                12. "Zwischen grünen Bäumen" (S)
                13. "Von dem Greis" (T)
                14. "Bald hat das neue"
                15. "Bist du im Wald gewandelt" (2T, 2B)
                16. "Im Wald gelehnt am" (A)
                17. "Der Abendschlummer" (S)
                18. "O sel'ge Zeit" (S)
                19. "Wer kommt am Sonntags" (B)
                20. "Ei Mühle" (S, A)
                21. "Was klingen denn die" (2T)
                22. "Im Hause des Müllers," chorus
                23. "Und wie ein" (T)
                24. "Röslein" (S, Engelstimmen)
9.11   "Der Königssohn," ballad (c1851, Uhland; vv, ch & orch) Op.116
9.12   "Fest-Overture" (c1852–3, Müller, Claudius; T, ch & orch, on Andre: Rheinweinlied) Op.123
9.13   "Des Sängers Fluch," ballad (c1852, Pohl after Uhland; vv, ch & orch) Op.139

9.14 "Vom Pagen und der Königstochter," 4 ballads (c1852, Geibel; vv, ch & orch): 1. "Der alte König" .. Op.140
9.15   2. "Zwei Reiter"
9.16   3. "Den Runenstein"
9.17   4. "Die Säle funkeln"
9.18 "Das Glück von Edenhall," ballad (c1853, Hasenclever after Uhland; vv, ch & orch) Op.143
9.19 "Neujahrslied" (c1849–50, Rückert) Op.144
9.20 Mass in C minor (c1852–3, Liturgy; S, T, B, ch & orch; red for pf): Op.147
    1. "Kyrie"
    2. "Gloria"
    3. "Credo"
    4. "Offertorium"
    5. "Sanctus"
    6. "Agnus Dei"
9.21 "Requiem" (c1852, Liturgy; ch & orch): Op.148
    1. "Requiem"
    2. "Te decet hymnus"
    3. "Dies irae"
    4. "Liber scriptus"
    5. "Qui Mariam absolvisti"
    6. "Domine Jesu Christe"
    7. "Hostias"
    8. "Sanctus"
    9. "Benedictus"
9.22 "Szenen aus Goethes Faust," 3 parts & 7 scenes (c1844–53, Goethe; vv, ch & orch; red for pf): ..... WoO 3
    . "Ouvertüre"
    I: 1. "Szene im Garten": "Du kanntest mich, o kleiner Engel"
          2. "Gretchen vor dem Bilde der Mater dolorosa": "Ach neige, du Schmerzenreiche"
          3. "Szene im Dom": "Wie anders, Gretchen, war dir's"
    II: 4. "Ariel, Sonnenaufgang": a. "Die ihr dies Haupt umschwebt im luft'gen" (Faust, ch)
          b. "Des Lebens Pulse schlagen"
          5. "Faust's Erblindung. Mitternacht": a. "Ich heisse der Mangel" (4 grauen Weiber)
          b. "Vier sah ich kommen"
          c. "Die Nacht scheint tiefer tief hereinzudringen"
          6. "Faust's Tod": a. "Herbei! herbei! Herein, herein!"
          b. "Ein Sumpf zieht am Gebirge hin"
          c. "Ihn sättigt keine Lust"
    III: 7. "Faust's Verklärung": a. "Waldung, sie schwankt heran"
          b. "Ewiger Wonnebrand"
          c. "Wie Felsen Abgrund mir zu Füssen" (B)
          d. "Gerettet ist das edle Glied" (ch)
          e. "Hier ist die Aussicht frei" (Dr. Marianus)
          f. "Dir, der Unberührbaren" (Dr. Marianus, ch)
          g. "Alles Vergängliche ist nur ein Gleichnis" (Chorus mysticus)

Partsongs (mix ch):

9.23 "5 Lieder" (c1846, Burns transl Gerhard): 1. "Das Hochlandmädchen": "Nicht Damen tönt" Op.55
9.24   2. "Zahnweh": "Wie du mit gift'gem Stachel fast"
9.25   3. "Mich zieht es nach dem Dörfchen hin"
9.26   4. "Die alte, gute Zeit": "Wer lenkt nicht gern den heitern Blick" (also see Beethoven WoO 156/11)
9.27   5. "Hochlandbursch": "Schönster Bursch, den je ich traf"
9.28 "4 Gesänge" (c1846): 1. "Nord oder Süd!" (Lappe) Op.59
9.29   2. "Am Bodensee": "Schwelle die Segel, günstiger Wind!" (Platen)
9.30   3. "Jägerlied": "Zierlich ist des Vogels Tritt im Schnee" (Mörike)
9.31   4. "Gute Nacht": "Die gute Nacht, die ich dir sage" (Rückert)
9.32   (5.) "Hirtenknaben-Gesang": "Heloe! Heloe! Komm du auf unsre Heide" (Hülshoff,
        added later) .... WoO 18
9.33 "Romanzen & Balladen," I (c1849): 1. "Der König von Thule": "Es war ein König" (Goethe) Op.67
9.34   2. "Schön-Rohtraut": "Wie heisst König Ringangs Töchterlein?" (Mörike)
9.35   3. "Heidenröslein": "Sah ein Knab' ein Röslein steh'n" (Goethe)
9.36   4. "Ungewitter": "Auf hohen Burgeszinnen" (Chamisso)
9.37   5. "John Anderson": "John Anderson, mein Lieb!" (Burns transl Gerhard, also see Op.145/4,
        music not related) (also see Shostakovich's 2. of: 8 British and American Folksongs
        arr1943, R. Strauss AV73 & Weber J301)
9.38 "Romanzen & Balladen," II (c1849): 1. "Schnitter Tod": "Es ist ein Schnitter" (Brentano) Op.75
9.39   2. "Im Walde" II: "Es zog eine Hochzeit den Berg entlang" (Eichendorff)
9.40   3. "Der traurige Jäger": "Zur ew'gen Ruh' sie sangen die schöne Müllerin" (Eichendorff)
9.41   4. "Der Rekrut": "Sonst kam mein John mir zu" (Burns transl Gerhard)
9.42   5. "Vom verwundeten Knaben": "Es wollt' ein Mädchen früh aufsteh'n" (from Herder's Volkslieder)
9.43 "4 doppelchörige Gesänge" (c1849): 1. "An die Sterne": "Sterne, in des Himmels" (Rückert) Op.141
9.44   2. "Ungewisses Licht": "Bahnlos und pfadlos" (Zedlitz)
9.45   3. "Zuversicht": "Nach oben musst du blicken" (Zedlitz)
9.46   4. "Talismane": "Gottes ist der Orient!" (Goethe)
9.47 "Romanzen & Balladen," III (c1849–51): 1. "Der Schmidt": "Ich hör' meinen Schatz" (Uhland) Op.145
9.48   2. "Die Nonne": "Sie steht am Zellenfenster" (anon)

9.49   3. "Der Sänger": "Noch singt den Widerhallen" (Uhland)
9.50   4. "John Anderson": "John Anderson, mein Lieb!" (Burns transl Gerhard) (also see Op.67/5, music
            not related)
9.51   5. "Romanze vom Gänsebuben": "Helf' mir Gott" (Malsburg)
9.52   "Romanzen & Balladen," IV (c1849–51): 1. "Brautgesang": "Das Haus benedei ich" (Uhland) Op.146
9.53   2. "Der Bänkelsänger Willie": "O Bänkelsänger Willie" (Burns transl Gerhard)
9.54   3. "Der Traum": "Im schönstem Garten wallten zwei Buhlen" (Uhland)
9.55   4. "Sommerlied": "Seinen Traum, lind wob" (Rückert)
9.56   5. "Das Schifflein": "Ein Schifflein ziehet leise" (Uhland; w/ fl & hn)
9.57   "Des Glockentürmers Töchterlein": "Mein hochgebornes Schätzlein" (c1851, Rückert) ....

Partsongs (m ch):

9.58   "6 Lieder" (c1840): 1. "Der träumende See": "Der See ruht tief im blauen Traum" (Mosen) Op.33
9.59   2. "Die Minnesänger": "Zu dem Wettgesange schreiten" (Heine)
9.60   3. "Die Lotosblume" II: "Die Lotosblume ängstigt" (Heine)
9.61   4. "Der Zecher als Doktrinär": "Was quälte dir dein banges Herz?" (Mosen)
9.62   5. "Rastlose Liebe": "Dem Schnee, dem Regen" (Goethe)
9.63   6. "Frühlingsglocken": "Schneeglöckchen tut läuten" (Reinick)
9.64   "3 Gesänge" (c1847): 1. "Die Rose stand im Tau": "In stiller Bucht" (Eichendorff) Op.62
9.65   2. "Freiheitslied": "Zittr', o Erde dunkle Macht" (Rückert)
9.66   3. "Schlachtgesang": "Mit unserm Arm ist nichts getan" (Klopstock)
9.67   "Ritornelle in canonischen Weisen" (c1847, Rückert): 1. "Die Rose stand im Tau" Op.65
9.68   2. "Lasst Lautenspiel und Becherklang"
9.69   3. "Blüth' oder Schnee!"
9.70   4. "Gebt mir zu trinken!"
9.71   5. "Zürne nicht des Herbstes Wind"
9.72   6. "In Sommertagen rüste den Schlitten"
9.73   7. "In Meeres Mitten ist ein offener Laden"
9.74   8. "Hätte zu einem Traubenkerne" .... WoO 12
9.75   "Zum Anfang": "Mache deinem Meister Ehre" (c1847, Rückert) .... WoO 17
9.76   "3 Freiheitsgesänge" (c1848; winds ad lib): 1. "Zu den Waffen": "Vom Angesicht" (Ullrich) .... WoO 14
9.77   2. "Schwarz-Rot-Gold": "In Kümmernis und Dunkelheit" (Freiligrath) .... WoO 13
9.78   3. "Deutscher Freiheitsgesang": "Der Sieg ist dein, mein Heldenvolk!" (Fürst) .... WoO 15
9.79   "Verzweifle nicht im Schmerzenstal," motet (c1849, Rückert; d ch & org ad lib; see orchd1852) Op.93
9.80   "Jagdlieder" (c1849, from Laube's Jagdbrevier; w/ 4hn): 1. "Zur hohen Jagd": "Frisch auf" Op.137
9.81   2. "Habet acht!": "Habet Acht auf der Jagd"
9.82   3. "Jagdmorgen": "O frischer Morgen, frischer Mut"
9.83   4. "Frühe": "Früh steht der Jäger auf"
9.84   5. "Bei der Flasche": "Wo gibt es wohl noch Jägerei"

Partsongs (fem ch):

9.85   "Romanzen," I (c1849; pf ad lib): 1. "Tamburinschlägerin": "Schwirrend Tamburin" (Ameida) Op.69
9.86   2. "Waldmädchen": "Bin ein Feuer hell" (Eichendorff)
9.87   3. "Klosterfräulein": "Ich armes Klosterfräulein" (Kerner)
9.88   4. "Soldatenbraut" II: "Ach, wenn's nur der König auch wüsst" (Mörike)
9.89   5. "Meerfey": "Still bei Nacht fährt manches Schiff" (Eichendorff)
9.90   6. "Die Kapelle": "Droben stehet die Kapelle" (Uhland)
9.91   "Romanzen," II (c1849, pf ad lib): 1. "Rosmarin": "Es wollt die Jungfrau" (from Des Knaben
            Wunderhorn) Op.91
9.92   2. "Jäger Wohlgemut": "Es jagt' ein Jäger wohlgemut" (from Des Knaben Wunderhorn)
9.93   3. "Der Wassermann": "Es war in des Maien mildem Glanz" (Kerner)
9.94   4. "Das verlassene Mägdelein" II: "Früh wann die Hähne kräh'n" (Mörike)
9.95   5. "Der Bleicherin Nachtlied": "Bleiche, bleiche weisses Lein" (Reinick)
9.96   6. "In Meeres Mitten" (Rückert)

10. SONGS (1–4vv & pf)

c before 1840:

10.1   "Verwandlung": "Wenn der Winter sonst entschand" (c1827, Schulze) ....
10.2   "Lied für XXX": "Leicht wie gaukelnde Sylphiden" (c1827, Schumann) ....
10.3   "11 Songs": 1. "Sehnsucht": "Sterne der blauen" (c1827, Ekert—pseud of Schumann) .... WoO 21/1
10.4   2. "Die Weinende": "Ich sah dich weinen!" (c1827, Byron) .... WoO 21/2
10.5   3. "Erinnerung": "Glück der Engel!" (c1828, Jacobi) .... WoO 21/3
10.6   4. "Kurzes Erwachen": "Ich bin im Mai gegangen" (c1828, Kerner) .... WoO 21/4
10.7   5. "Gesanges Erwachen": "Könnt' ich einmal wieder singen" (c1828, Kerner) .... WoO 21/5
10.8   6. "An Anna" I: "Lange harrt' ich" (c1828, Kerner) .... WoO 21/6
10.9   7. "An Anna" II: "Nicht im Tale" (c1828, Kerner; used in: Pf Son No.1, Op.11) .... WoO 10/2
10.10   8. "Im Herbste": "Zieh' nur, du Sonne" (c1828, Kerner; used in: Pf Son No.2, Op.22) ...... WoO 10/3
10.11   9. "Hirtenknabe": "Bin nur ein armer Hirtenknab" (c1828, Ekert; used in: Intermezzo
            for pf, Op.4/4) .... WoO 10/4
10.12   10. "Der Fischer": "Das Wasser rauscht, das Wasser schwoll" (c1828, Goethe) .... WoO 19
10.13   11. "Klage" (c1828, Jacobi, lost)

10.14	"Vom Reitermann" (Old German) ....
10.15	*"Maultreiberlied" (c1838, lost)* ....

c1840 (his 'song year'—first year of marriage to Clara):

10.16	"Ein Gedanke": "Sie schlingt um meinen Nacken" (c1840, Ferrand) .... WoO 26/1
10.17	"Patriotisches Lied": "Sie sollen ihn nicht haben" (c1840, Becker; 1v, ch & pf) ....
10.18	*"Der Reiter und der Bodensee": "Der Reiter retet durchs helle Tal," ballad (c1840, Schwab, frag)* .... WoO 11/1
10.19	*"Die nächtliche Heerschau": "Nachts um die zwölfte Stunde," ballad (c1840, Zedlitz, frag)* .... WoO 11/2
10.20	"Liederkreis" (c1840, Heine): 1. "Morgens steh' ich auf und frage" (also see Liszt S290) Op.24
10.21	2. "Es treibt mich hin, es treibt mich her!"
10.22	3. "Ich wandelte unter den Bäumen"
10.23	4. "Lieb' Liebchen, leg's Händchen aufs Herze mein"
10.24	5. "Schöne Wiege meiner Leiden"
10.25	6. "Warte, warte, wilder Schiffmann"
10.26	7. "Berg' und Burgen schaun herunter"
10.27	8. "Anfangs wollt' ich fast verzagen" (also see Liszt S311)
10.28	9. "Mit Myrthen und Rosen, lieblich und hold"
10.29	"Myrthen," cycle (c1840): 1. "Widmung": "Du meine Seele, du mein Herz" (Rückert) Op.25
10.30	2. "Freisinn": "Lasst mich nur auf meinem Sattel gelten!" (from Goethe's West-östlicher Divan)
10.31	3. "Der Nussbaum": "Es grünet ein Nussbaum vor dem Haus" (Mosen)
10.32	4. "Jemand": "Mein Herz ist betrübt" (Burns transl Gerhard)
10.33	5. "Lieder aus dem Schenkenbuch im Divan I": "Sitz' ich allein" (Goethe)
10.34	6. "Lieder aus dem Schenkenbuch im Divan II": "Setze mir nicht" (Goethe)
10.35	7. "Die Lotosblume": "Die Lotosblume ängstigt sich vor der Sonne Pracht" (Heine)
10.36	8. "Talismane": "Gottes ist der Orient" (Goethe)
10.37	9. "Lied der Suleika": "Wie mit innigstem Behagen" (Goethe)
10.38	10. "Die Hochländer-Wittwe": "Ich bin gekommen ins Niederland" (Burns transl Gerhard)
10.39	11. "Lieder der Braut aus dem Liebesfrühling I": "Mutter! Mutter! Glaube nicht" (Rückert)
10.40	12. "Lieder der Braut aus dem Liebesfrühling II": "Lass mich ihn am Busen hangen" (Rückert)
10.41	13. "Hochländers Abschied": "Mein Herz ist im Hochland" (Burns transl Gerhard)
10.42	14. "Hochländisches Wiegenlied": "Schlafe, süsser kleiner Donald" (Burns transl Gerhard) (also see Britten Op.41/2)
10.43	15. "Aus den 'Hebräischen Gesängen' ": "Mein Herz ist schwer! Auf von der Wand die Laute" (Byron transl Körner) (also see Balakirev's 13 of: 20 Songs)
10.44	16. "Rätsel": "Es flüstert's der Himmel" (Fanshawe transl Kannegiesser)
10.45	17. "Venetianische Lied I": "Leis' rudern hin" (Moore transl Freiligrath)
10.46	18. "Venetianische Lied II": "Wenn durch die Piazzetta die Abendluft weht" (Moore transl Freiligrath) (also see Mendelssohn Op.57/5)
10.47	19. "Hauptmanns Weib": "Hoch zu Pferd!" (Burns transl Gerhard)
10.48	20. "Weit, weit": "Wie kann ich froh" (Burns transl Gerhard) (also see Beethoven Op.108/14)
10.49	21. "Was will die einsame Träne?" (Heine)
10.50	22. "Niemand": "Ich hab mein Weib allein" (Burns transl Gerhard)
10.51	23. "Im Westen": "Ich schau über Forth hinüber" (Burns transl Gerhard)
10.52	24. "Du bist wie eine Blume" (Heine) (also see Liszt S287 & Wolf's song of 1876)
10.53	25. "Aus den östlichen Rosen": "Ich sende einen Gruss" (Rückert)
10.54	26. "Zum Schluss": "Hier in diesen erdbeklommnen Lüften, wo die Wehmut taut" (Rückert)
10.55	"Lieder und Gesänge," I (c1840): 1. "Sag' an, o lieber Vogel mein" (Hebbel) Op.27
10.56	2. "Dem roten Röslein gleicht mein Lieb" (Burns transl Gerhard) (also see Beach Op.12/3, B5/3, Berg's 33. of: 70 Jugendlieder & Weber J302)
10.57	3. "Was soll ich sagen?": "Mein Aug ist trüb" (Chamisso)
10.58	4. "Jasminenstrauch": "Grün ist der Jasminenstrauch" (Rückert)
10.59	5. "Nur ein lächelnder Blick" (Zimmermann)
10.60	"3 Gedichte" (c1840, Geibel): 1. "Ländliches Lied": "Und wenn die Primel schneeweiss" (2S) Op.29
10.61	2. "Lied": "In meinem Garten die Nelken" (3S)
10.62	3. "Zigeunerleben": "Im Schatten des Waldes" (S, A, T, B, triangle & tambourine ad lib)
10.63	"3 Gedichte" (c1840, Geibel): 1. "Der Knabe mit dem Wunderhorn": "Ich bin ein lust'ger Geselle" Op.30
10.64	2. "Der Page": "Da ich nun entsagen müssen"
10.65	3. "Der Hidalgo": "Es ist so süss zu scherzen"
10.66	"3 Gesänge" (c1840, Chamisso): 1. "Die Löwenbraut": "Mit der Myrtle geschmückt" Op.31
10.67	2. "Die Kartenlegerin": "Schlief die Mutter endlich ein" (after Béranger)
10.68	3. "Die rote Hanne": "Den Säugling an der Brust" (after Béranger; ch ad lib)
10.69	"4 Duette" (c1840; S, T): 1. "Liebesgarten": "Die Liebe ist ein Rosenstrauch" (Reinick) Op.34
10.70	2. "Liebhabers Ständchen": "Wachst du noch, Liebchen" (Burns transl Gerhard)
10.71	3. "Unter'm Fenster": "Wer ist vor meiner Kammertür?" (Burns transl Gerhard)
10.72	4. "Familien-Gemälde": "Grossvater und Grossmutter" (Grün)
10.73	"12 Gedichte" (c1840, Kerner): 1. "Lust der Sturmnacht": "Wenn durch Berg und Tale draussen" Op.35
10.74	2. "Stirb, Lieb' und Freud'!": "Zu Augsburg steht ein hohes Haus"
10.75	3. "Wanderlied": "Wohlauf! noch getrunken den funkelnden Wein!"
10.76	4. "Erstes Grün": "Du junges Grün, du frisches Gras!"
10.77	5. "Sehnsucht nach der Waldgegend": "Wär' ich nie aus euch gegangen"
10.78	6. "Auf das Trinkglas eines verstorbenen Freundes": "Du herrlich Glas, nun stehst du leer"
10.79	7. "Wanderung": "Wohlauf und frisch gewandert ins unbekannte Land!"
10.80	8. "Stille Liebe": "Könnt' ich dich in Liedern preisen"
10.81	9. "Frage": "Wärst du nicht, heil'ger Abendschein!"
10.82	10. "Stille Tränen": "Du bist vom Schlaf erstanden"

10.83	11. "Wer machte dich so krank?": "Dass du so krank geworden, wer hat es denn gemacht?"
10.84	12. "Alte Laute": "Hörst du den Vogel singen?"
10.85	"6 Gedichte" (c1840, Reinick): 1. "Sonntags am Rhein": "Des Sonntags in der Morgenstund" Op.36
10.86	2. "Ständchen": "Komm' in die stille Nacht, Liebchen, was zögerst du?" (also see Wolf's song
	of 1883)
10.87	3. "Nichts schöneres": "Als ich zuerst dich hab gesehn"
10.88	4. "An den Sonnenschein": "O Sonnenschein, o Sonnenschein! Wie scheinst du mir ins Herz hinein"
10.89	5. "Dichters Genesung": "Und wieder hatt ich der Schönsten gedacht"
10.90	6. "Liebesbotschaft": "Wolken, die ihr nach Osten eilt"
10.91	12 "Gedichte aus Liebesfrühling" (c1840, Rückert): 1. "Der Himmel hat eine Träne geweint" Op.37
10.92	*2. "Er ist gekommen" (c by Clara Schumann)*
10.93	3. "O ihr Herren"
10.94	*4. "Liebst du um Schönheit" (c by Clara Schumann) (also see Mahler's 2. of: 5 Rückert-Lieder)*
10.95	5. "Ich hab' in mich gesogen"
10.96	6. "Liebste, was kann dies uns scheiden?"
10.97	7. "Schön ist das Fest des Lenzes" (S, T)
10.98	8. "Flügel! Flügel! um zu fliegen"
10.99	9. "Rose, Meer und Sonne"
10.100	10. "O Sonn', o Meer, o Rose!"
10.101	*11. "Warum willst du andre fragen" (c by Clara Schumann)*
10.102	12. "So wahr die Sonne scheinet" (S, T)
10.103	"Liederkreis" (c1840, Eichendorff; orig Op.77/1): 1. "In der Fremde": "Aus der Heimat hinter den
	Blitzen roth" (also see Brahms Op.3/5) Op.39
10.104	2. "Intermezzo": "Dein Bildnis wunderselig"
10.105	3. "Waldesgespräch": "Es ist schon spät, es ist schon kalt"
10.106	4. "Die Stille": "Es weiss und räth es doch keiner" (also see Mendelssohn Op.99/6)
10.107	5. "Mondnacht": "Es war, als hätt' der Himmel die Erde still geküsst" (also see Brahms WoO 21)
10.108	6. "Schöne Fremde": "Es rauschen die Wipfel und schauern"
10.109	7. "Auf einer Burg": "Eingeschlafen auf der Lauer"
10.110	8. "In der Fremde": "Ich hör' die Bächlein rauschen"
10.111	9. "Wehmut": "Ich kann wohl manchmal singen"
10.112	10. "Zwielicht": "Dämm'rung will die Flügel spreiten"
10.113	11. "Im Walde": "Es zog eine Hochzeit den Berg entlang"
10.114	12. "Frühlingsnacht": "Überm Garten durch die Lüfte"
10.115	"5 Lieder" (c1840): 1. "Märzveilchen": "Der Himmel wölbt sich rein" (Andersen transl Chamisso) Op.40
10.116	2. "Muttertraum": "Die Mutter betet herzig" (Andersen transl Chamisso)
10.117	3. "Der Soldat": "Es geht bei gedämpfter Trommel Klang" (Andersen transl Chamisso)
10.118	4. "Der Spielmann": "Im Städtchen gibt es des Jubels viel" (Andersen transl Chamisso)
10.119	5. "Verratene Liebe": "Da Nachts wir uns küssten" (Chamisso)
10.120	"Frauenliebe und -leben," cycle (c1840, Chamisso): 1. "Seit ich ihn gesehen" Op.42
10.121	2. "Er, der Herrlichste von allen"
10.122	3. "Ich kann's nicht fassen, nicht glauben"
10.123	4. "Du Ring an meinem Finger"
10.124	5. "Helft mir, ihr Schwestern"
10.125	6. "Süsser Freund, du blickest mich verwundert an"
10.126	7. "An meinem Herzen, an meiner Brust"
10.127	8. "Nun hast du mir den ersten Schmerz getan"
10.128	"3 Zweistimmige Lieder" (c1840, 2vv): 1. "Wenn ich ein Vöglein wär" (from Des Knaben Wunderhorn;
	incl as 9. in opera: Genoveva, Op.81) Op.43
10.129	2. "Herbstlied": "Das Laub fällt von den Bäumen" (Mahlmann)
10.130	3. "Schön Blümelein": "Ich bin hinaus gegangen" (Reinick)
10.131	"Romanzen & Balladen," I (c1840): 1. "Der Schatzgräber": "Wenn alle Wälder schliefen"
	(Eichendorff) Op.45
10.132	2. "Frühlingsfahrt": "Es zogen zwei rüst'ge Gesellen" (Eichendorff)
10.133	3. "Abends am Strand": "Wir sassen am Fischerhause" (Heine)
10.134	"Dichterliebe," cycle (c1840, Heine): 1. "Im wunderschönen Monat Mai" Op.48
10.135	2. "Aus meinen Tränen spriessen"
10.136	3. "Die Rose, die Lilie, die Taube, die Sonne" (also see Meyerbeer's song of 1838)
10.137	4. "Wenn ich in deine Augen seh' " (also see Wolf's song of 1876)
10.138	5. "Ich will meine Seele tauchen"
10.139	6. "Im Rhein, im heiligen Strome" (also see Liszt S272)
10.140	7. "Ich grolle nicht, und wenn das Herz auch bricht"
10.141	8. "Und wüssten's die Blumen, die kleinen" (also see Mendelssohn Op.9/10)
10.142	9. "Das ist ein Flöten und Geigen"
10.143	10. "Hör' ich das Liedchen klingen"
10.144	11. "Ein Jüngling liebt ein Mädchen"
10.145	12. "Am leuchtenden Sommermorgen"
10.146	13. "Ich hab' im Traum geweinet"
10.147	14. "Allnächtlich im Traume seh' ich dich" (also see Mendelssohn Op.86/4)
10.148	15. "Aus alten Märchen winkt es"
10.149	16. "Die alten, bösen Lieder"
10.150	"Romanzen & Balladen," II (c1840): 1. "Die beiden Grenadiere": "Nach Frankreich zogen zwei
	Grenadier' " (Heine) (also see Wagner WWV60) Op.49
10.151	2. "Die feindlichen Brüder": "Oben auf des Berges Spitze" (Heine)
10.152	3. "Die Nonne": "Im Garten steht die Nonne" (Fröhlich)

10.153	"Lieder und Gesänge," II: 1. "Sehnsucht": "Ich blick in mein Herz" (c1840, Geibel) Op.51
10.154	2. "Volksliedchen": "Wenn ich früh in den Garten geh" (c1840, Rückert)
10.155	3. "Ich wand're nicht": "Warum soll ich denn wandern" (c1840, Christern)
10.156	4. "Auf dem Rhein": "Auf deinem Grunde haben sie an verborgnem Ort" (c1846, Immermann)
10.157	5. "Liebeslied": "Dir zu eröffnen mein Herz" (c1850, Goethe)
10.158	"Romanzen & Balladen," III (c1840): 1. "Blondels Lied": "Spähend nach dem Eisengitter" (Seidl) Op.53
10.159	2. "Loreley": "Es flüstern und rauschen die Wogen" (Lorenz)
10.160	3. "Der arme Peter" (Heine): a. "Der Hans und die Grete tanzen herum"
	b. "In meiner Brust, da sitzt ein Weh"
	c. "Der arme Peter wankt vorbei"
10.161	"Belsazar": "Die Mitternacht zog näher schon," ballad (c1840, Heine) Op.57

c after 1840:

10.162	"Romanzen & Balladen," IV: 1. "Die Soldatenbraut": "Ach, wenn's nur" (c1847, Mörike) Op.64
10.163	2. "Das verlassne Mägdelein": "Früh wann die Hähne krähn" (c1847, Mörike) (also see Wolf's 7. of: Mörike Lieder)
10.164	3. "Tragödie" (c1841, Heine): a. "Entflieh mit mir und sei mein Weib"
	b. "Es fiel ein Reif in der Frühlingsnacht"
	c. "Auf ihrem Grab, da steht eine Linde" (S, T, from choral project of 1841)
10.165	"Spanisches Liederspiel" (c1849, Geibel): 1. "Erste Begegnung": "Von dem Rosenbusch" (S, A) Op.74
10.166	2. "Intermezzo": "Und schläfst du, mein Mädchen, auf!" (T, B)
10.167	3. "Liebesgram": "Dereinst, dereinst, o Gedanke mein" (S, A)
10.168	4. "In der Nacht": "Alle gingen, Herz, zur Ruh' " (S, T) (also see Wolf's 21. of: Spanisches Liederbuch, nach Heyse und Geibel, II. Weltliche Lieder)
10.169	5. "Es ist verraten": "Dass ihr steht in Liebesglut" (S, A, T, B)
10.170	6. "Melancholie": "Wann, wann erscheint der Morgen" (S)
10.171	7. "Geständnis": "Also lieb ich euch" (T)
10.172	8. "Botschaft": "Nelken wind ich und Jasmin" (S, A)
10.173	9. "Ich bin geliebt": "Mögen alle bösen Zungen" (S, A, T, B)
10.174	10. "Der Kontrabandiste": "Ich bin der Kontrabandiste" (Bar)
10.175	"Lieder und Gesange," III: 1. "Der frohe Wandersmann": "Wem Gott" (c1840, Eichendorff; orig in Op.39) Op.77
10.176	2. "Mein Garten": "Veilchen, Rosmarin, Mimosen" (c1850, Fallersleben)
10.177	3. "Geisternähe": "Was weht um meine Schläfe" (c1850, Halm)
10.178	4. "Stiller Vorwurf": "In einsamen Stunden drängt Wehmut sich auf" (c1840, ?Wolff)
10.179	5. "Aufträge": "Nicht so schnelle, nicht so schnelle!" (c1850, L'Egru)
10.180	"Soldatenlied": "Ein scheckiges Pferd" (c1844, Fallersleben) .... WoO 7
10.181	"Albumblatt für Niels W. Gade": "Auf Wiedersehen" (c1844) .... WoO 8
10.182	"Das Schwert": "Zur Schmiede ging ein junger Held" (c1848, Uhland) ....
10.183	*"Der weisse Hirsch": "Es gingen drei Jäger" (c1848, Uhland, sketches)* ....
10.184	"Die Ammenuhr": "Der Mond, der scheint" (c1848, from Des Knaben Wunderhorn)
10.185	"4 Duette" (c1849; S, T): 1. "Tanzlied": "Eia, wie-flattert der Kranz" (Rückert)................... Op.78
10.186	2. "Er und Sie": "Seh ich in das stille Tal" (Kerner)
10.187	3. "Ich denke dein" (Goethe)
10.188	4. "Wiegenlied": "Schlaf, Kindlein, schlaf" (Hebbel)
10.189	"Sommerruh": "Sommerruh, wie schön bist du" (c1849, Schad, altered by Schumann; 2vv) .... WoO 9
10.190	"Lieder-Album für die Jugend" (c1849): 1. "Der Abendstern": "Du lieblicher Stern" (Fallersleben) Op.79
10.191	2. "Schmetterling": "O Schmetterling, sprich" (Fallersleben)
10.192	3. "Frühlingsbotschaft": "Kuckuck, Kuckuck ruft aus dem Wald" (Fallersleben)
10.193	4. "Frühlingsgruss": "So sei gegrüsst vieltausendmal" (Fallersleben)
10.194	5. "Vom Schlaraffenland": "Kommt, wir wollen uns begeben" (Fallersleben)
10.195	6. "Sonntag": "Der Sonntag ist gekommen" (Fallersleben)
10.196	7. "Zigeunerliedchen" (Geibel from Spanish): a. "Unter die Soldaten ist ein Zigeunerbub gegangen"
10.197	b. "Jeden Morgen, in der Frühe"
10.198	8. "Des Knaben Berglied": "Ich bin vom Berg der Hirtenknab" (Uhland)
10.199	9. "Mailied": "Komm, lieber Mai" (Overbeck; 2vv ad lib)
10.200	10. "Das Käuzlein": "Ich armes Käuzlein kleine" (from Des Knaben Wunderhorn)
10.201	11. "Hinaus in's Freie!": "Wie blüht es im Tale" (Fallersleben)
10.202	12. "Der Sandmann": "Zwei feine Stieflein hab ich an" (Kletke)
10.203	13. "Marienwürmchen": "Marienwürmchen, setze dich" (from Des Knaben Wunderhorn)
10.204	14. "Die Waise": "Der Frühling kehret wieder" (Fallersleben)
10.205	15. "Das Glück": "Vöglein vom Zweig" (Hebbel; 2vv)
10.206	16. "Weihnachtslied": "Als das Christkind ward zur Welt gebracht" (Andersen)
10.207	17. "Die wandelne Glocke": "Es war ein Kind" (Goethe)
10.208	18. "Frühlingslied": "Schneeglöckchen klingen wieder" (Fallersleben; 2vv ad lib)
10.209	19. "Frühlings Ankunft": "Nach diesen trüben Tagen" (Fallersleben)
10.210	20. "Die Schwalben": "Es fliegen zwei Schwalben" (from Des Knaben Wunderhorn; 2vv)
10.211	21. "Kinderwacht": "Wenn fromme Kindlein schlafen gehn" (anon)
10.212	22. "Des Sennen Abschied": "Ihr Matten lebt wohl! Ihr sonnigen Weiden!" (from Schiller's W. Tell)
10.213	23. "Er ist's": "Frühling lässt sein blaues Band" (Mörike) (also see Wolf's 6. of: Mörike Lieder)
10.214	24. "Spinnelied": "Spinn, spinn" (anon; 3vv ad lib)
10.215	25. "Des Buben Schützenlied": "Mit dem Pfeil, dem Bogen" (from Schiller's Wilhelm Tell)
10.216	26. "Schneeglöckchen": "Der Schnee, der gestern noch in Flöckchen" (Rückert)
10.217	27. "Lied Lynceus des Türmers": "Zum Sehen geboren" (Goethe)

10.218   28. "Mignon": "Kennst du das Land, wo die Zitronen blühn" (from Goethe's Wilhelm Meister) (also
          see Beethoven Op.75/1, Liszt S275, Schubert D321 & Wolf's 9. of: Goethe Lieder)
10.219   "3 Gesänge" (c1850): 1. "Resignation": "Lieben, von ganzer Seele lieben" (Buddeus) Op.83
10.220   2. "Die Blume der Ergebung": "Ich bin die Blum' in Garten" (Rückert)
10.221   3. "Der Einsiedler": "Komm, Trost der Welt, du stille Nacht!" (Eichendorff)
10.222   "Der Handschuh": "Vor seinem Löwengarten," ballad (c1850, Schiller) Op.87
10.223   "6 Gesänge" (c1850, Neun): 1. "Es stürmet am Abendhimmel" Op.89
10.224   2. "Heimliches Verschwinden": "Nachts zu unbekannter Stunde"
10.225   3. "Herbstlied": "Durch die Tannen und die Linden"
10.226   4. "Abschied vom Walde": "Nun scheidet vom sterbenden Walde"
10.227   5. "In's Freie": "Mir ist's so eng allüberall!"
10.228   6. "Röselein, Röselein!"
10.229   "6 Gedichte" (c1850, Lenau): 1. "Lied eines Schmiedes": "Fein Rösslein" Op.90
10.230   2. "Meine Rose": "Dem holden Lenzegeschmeide"
10.231   3. "Kommen und Scheiden": "So oft sie kam"
10.232   4. "Die Sennerin": "Schöne Sennin, noch einmal singe"
10.233   5. "Einsamkeit": "Wild verwachs'ne dunkle Fichten"
10.234   6. "Der schwere Abend": "Die dunklen Wolken hingen"
10.235   App. "Requiem": "Ruh' von schmerzensreichen Mühen" (anon, ?after Héloïse)
10.236   "3 Gesänge" (c1849, Byron transl Körner): 1. "Die Tochter Jephtha's": "Da die Heimat" Op.95
10.237   2. "An den Mond": "Schlaflose Sonne, melanchol'scher Stern!" (also see Mendelssohn's 2. of:
          2 Romances of 1834, Rimsky-Korsakov Op.41/1 & Wolf's 3. of: 4 Poems of Heine,
          Shakespeare & Byron)
10.238   3. "Dem Helden": "Dein Tag ist aus, dein Ruhm fing an"
10.239   "Lieder und Gesänge," IV (c1850): 1. "Nachtlied": "Über allen Gipfeln ist Ruh" (Goethe) (also see
          Liszt S306 & Schubert Op.96/3, D768) Op.96
10.240   2. "Schneeglöckchen": "Die Sonne sah die Erde an" (anon)
10.241   3. "Ihre Stimme": "Lass tief in dir mich lesen" (Platen)
10.242   4. "Gesungen!": "Hört ihr im Laube des Regens" (Schöpff)
10.243   5. "Himmel und Erde": "Wie der Bäume kühne Wipfel" (Schöpff)
10.244   "Lieder und Gesänge aus Wilhelm Meister" (c1849, Goethe): 1. "Kennst du das Land?" Op.98a
10.245   2. "Ballade des Harfners": "Was hör ich draussen vor dem Tor" (also see Schubert
          Op.posth 117, D149 & Wolf's 10. of: Goethe Lieder)
10.246   3. "Nur wer die Sehnsucht kennt" (also see Beethoven WoO 134, Schubert Op.62/4, D877,
          Tchaikovsky Op.6/6 & Wolf's 6. of: Goethe Lieder)
10.247   4. "Wer nie sein Brot mit Tränen ass" (also see Liszt S297, Schubert Op.12/2, D480
          & Wolf's 3. of: Goethe Lieder)
10.248   5. "Heiss' mich nicht reden" (also see Schubert Op.62/2, D877/2 & Wolf's 5. of: Goethe Lieder)
10.249   6. "Wer sich der Einsamkeit ergibt" (also see Schubert Op.12/1, D478 & Wolf's 1. of: Goethe
          Lieder)
10.250   7. "Singet nicht in Trauertönen" (also see Wolf's 8. of: Goethe Lieder)
10.251   8. "An die Türen will ich schleichen" (also see Schubert Op.12/3, D479 & Wolf's 2. of: Goethe
          Lieder)
10.252   9. "So lasst mich scheinen" (also see Schubert Op.62/3, D727 & Wolf's 7. of: Goethe Lieder)
10.253   "Minnespiel" (c1849, Rückert): 1. "Lied: Meine Töne still und heiter" (T) Op.101
10.254   2. "Gesang: Liebster, deine Worte stehlen" (S)
10.255   3. "Duett: Ich bin dein Baum, o Gärtner" (A, B)
10.256   4. "Lied: Mein schöner Stern, ich bitte dich" (T)
10.257   5. "Quartett: Schön ist das Fest des Lenzes" (S, A, T, B)
10.258   6. "Lied: O Freund, mein Schirm, mein Schutz!" (A/S)
10.259   7. "Duett: Die tausend Grüsse" (S, T)
10.260   8. "Quartett: So wahr die Sonne scheinet" (S, A, T, B)
10.261   "Mädchenlieder" (c1851, Kuhlmann; S, A or 2S): 1. "Mailied": "Pflücket Rosen" Op.103
10.262   2. "Frühlingslied": "Der Frühling kehret wieder"
10.263   3. "An die Nachtigall": "Bleibe hier und singe, liebe Nachtigall!"
10.264   4. "An den Abendstern": "Schweb empor am Himmel"
10.265   "7 Lieder" (c1851, Kuhlmann): 1. "Mond, meiner Seele Liebling" Op.104
10.266   2. "Viel Glück zur Reise, Schwalben!"
10.267   3. "Du nennst mich armes Mädchen"
10.268   4. "Der Zeisig": "Wir sind ja, Kind im Maie"
10.269   5. "Reich' mir die Hand, o Wolke"
10.270   6. "Die letzten Blumen starben"
10.271   7. "Gekämpft hat meine Barke"
10.272   "Schön' Hedwig": "Im Kreise der Vasallen," declamation (c1849, Hebbel) Op.106
10.273   "6 Gesänge" (c1851–2): 1. "Herzeleid": "Die Weiden lassen matt die Zweige hangen" (Ullrich) Op.107
10.274   2. "Die Fensterscheibe": "Die Fenster klär ich zum Feiertag" (Ullrich)
10.275   3. "Der Gärtner": "Auf ihrem Leibrösslein" (Mörike) (also see Wolf's 17. of: Mörike Lieder)
10.276   4. "Die Spinnerin": "Auf dem Dorf in den Spinnstuben" (Heyse)
10.277   5. "Im Wald": "Ich zieh so allein in den Wald hinein!" (Müller)
10.278   6. "Abendlied": "Es ist so still geworden" (Kinkel)
10.279   "3 Lieder" (c1853; 3 fem vv): 1. "Nänie": "Unter den roten Blumen schlummere" (Bechstein) Op.114
10.280   2. "Triolett": "Senkt die Nacht den sanften Fittig nieder" (L'Egru)
10.281   3. "Spruch": "O blicke, wenn der Sinn dir will die Welt" (Rückert)
10.282   "4 Husarenlieder" (c1851, Lenau; Bar): 1. "Der Husar, trara!" Op.117
10.283   2. "Der leidige Frieden"

10.284	3. "Den grünen Zeigern"
10.285	4. "Da liegt der Feinde gestreckte Schaar"
10.286	"3 Gedichte" (c1851, Pfarrius): 1. "Die Hütte": "Im Wald, in grüner Runde" Op.119
10.287	2. "Warnung": "Es geht der Tag zur Neige"
10.288	3. "Der Bräutigam und die Birke": "Birke, Birke, des Waldes Zier"
10.289	"2 Balladen," declamation (c1852–3): 1. "Ballade vom Haideknaben": "Der Knabe" (Hebbel) Op.122
10.290	2. "Die Flüchtlinge": "Der Hagel klirrt nieder" (Shelley)
10.291	"5 heitere Gesänge" (c1850–1): 1. "Die Meerfee": "Helle Silberglöckklein klingen" (Buddeus) Op.125
10.292	2. "Husarenabzug": "Aus dem dunkeln Tor wallt" (Candidus)
10.293	3. "Jung Volkers Lied": "Und die mich trug im Mutterarm" (Mörike; orig for Op.107/4)
10.294	4. "Frühlingslied": "Das Körnlein springt" (Braun)
10.295	5. "Frühlingslust": "Nun stehen die Rosen in Blüte" (Heyse)
10.296	"5 Lieder & Gesänge": 1. "Sängers Trost": "Weint auch einst kein Liebchen" (c1840, Kerner) Op.127
10.297	2. "Dein Angesicht": "Dein Angesicht, so lieb und schön" (c1840, Heine; orig for Op.48)
10.298	3. "Es leuchtet meine Liebe" (c1840, Heine)
10.299	4. "Mein altes Ross" (c1850, Strachwitz)
10.300	5. "Schlusslied des Narren": "Und als ich ein winzig Bübchen war" (c1840, from Shakespeare's 12th Night) (also see Castelnuovo-Tedesco Op.24/III/3)
10.301	"Frühlingsgrüsse": "Nach langem Frost" (c1851, Lenau) .... WoO 26/2
10.302	"Gedichte der Königin Maria Stuart" (c1852, transl Vincke): 1. "Abschied von Frankreich": "Ich zieh dahin" Op.135
10.303	2. "Nach der Geburt ihres Sohnes": "Herr Jesu Christ"
10.304	3. "An die Königin Elisabeth": "Nur ein Gedanke"
10.305	4. "Abschied von der Welt": "Was nützt die mir noch zugemess'ne Zeit?"
10.306	5. "Gebet": "O Gott, mein Gebieter"
10.307	"Spanische Liebeslieder" (c1849, Geibel): 1. "Vorspiel" (pf duet) Op.138
10.308	2. "Lied: Tief im Herzen trag' ich Pein" (S) (also see Wolf's 23. of: Spanisches Liederbuch, nach Heyse und Geibel, II. Weltliche Lieder)
10.309	3. "Lied: O wie lieblich ist das Mädchen" (T)
10.310	4. "Duett: Bedeckt mich mit Blumen" (S, A)
10.311	5. "Lied: Flutenreicher Ebro" (Bar)
10.312	6. "Intermezzo" (pf duet)
10.313	7. "Lied: Weh, wie zornig ist das Mädchen" (T)
10.314	8. "Lied: Hoch, hoch sind die Berge" (A)
10.315	9. "Duett: Blaue Augen hat das Mädchen" (T, B)
10.316	10. "Quartett: Dunkler Lichtglanz" (S, A, T, B)
10.317	"From Des Sängers Fluch" (c1852, Pohl after Uhland): 1. "Provenzalisches Lied": "In den Talen" ... Op.139
10.318	2. "Ballade": "In der hohen Hall sass König Sifrid"
10.319	"4 Gesänge" (c1840): 1. "Trost im Gesang": "Der Wandrer, dem verschwunden" (Kerner) Op.142
10.320	2. "Lehn' deine Wang' ": "Lehn' deine Wang' an meine Wang" (Heine; orig for Op.48)
10.321	3. "Mädchen-Schwermut": "Kleine Tropfen, seid ihr Tränen" (Bernhard)
10.322	4. "Mein Wagen rollet langsam" (Heine; orig for Op.48) (also see R. Strauss Op.69/4)
10.323	"Mailied" (c1851; 2vv) ....
10.324	"Liedchen von Marie und Papa": "Gern macht' ich dir" (c1852, Schumann; 2vv) .... WoO 26/3
10.325	"Bei Schenkung eines Flügels": "Orange und Myrthe hier" (c1853, Schumann; S, A, T, B) .... WoO 26/4
10.326	"Glockentürmers Töchterlein": "Mein hochgebor'nes Schätzelein" (Rückert) ....
10.327	"Das Käuzlein" II: "Ich armes Käuzlein kleine" (from Des Knaben Wunderhorn) ....
10.328	"Deutscher Blumengarten" (Rückert; 2vv) ....

* * * * *

WoO = Werk ohne Opuszahl (Work w/ out opus number) in K. Hofmann & Siegmar Keil: "Robert Schumann. Thematisches Verzeichnis sämtlicher im Druck erschienenen musikalischen Werke mit Angabe des Jahres ihres Entstehens und Ercheinens." J. Schuberth & Co. Hamburg, 1982.

1. STAGE WORKS

Operas:

1.1	*"The Gypsies," opera (ca1915–8, after Pushkin's poem, frags):*	

extant: . "Duet of Zemfira and Aleko"
  . "Old Man's arietta"
  . vocal trio

1.2	"The Nose," 3 act satiric opera (c1927–8, Zamyatin, Ionin & Preis after Gogol)	Op.15
1.3	"Lady Macbeth of the Mtsensk District," 3 acts (c1930–2, Preis after Leskov's novel; also see opera: Katerina Izmaylova, Op.114) (attacked by the newspaper Pravda in an article 'Chaos Instead of Music' in 1936)	Op.29
1.4	"The Big Lightning" (c1932, Aseyev, abandoned after 9 Nos; compl Rozhdestvensky)	
1.5	*"The Twelve Chairs," 3 act operetta (c1937, after Ilf & Petrov, abandoned draft)*	
1.6	"The Gamblers" (Scenes after Gogol) (c from 1941, after Gogol; 6 m vv & orch, unfin)	
1.7	"Katerina Izmaylova," 4 acts (c1956–63, r vers of: Lady Macbeth, Op.29; also filmed)	Op.114

Operettas:

1.8	"Moscow, Cheremushky," 3 acts (c1957–8, Mass & Chervinsky)	Op.105

Ballets:

1.9	*"Rusalochka" (ca1915–8, on Andersen's fairy tale: The little Mermaid, lost)*	
1.10	"The Age of Gold" (The Golden Age), 3 acts (c1929–30, Ivanovsky)	Op.22
1.11	"The Bolt," 3 acts (c1930–1, Smirnov)	Op.27
1.12	"The Limpid Stream," 3 acts (c1934–5, Lopukhov & Piotrovsky)	Op.39
1.13	"The Dreamers," 4 scenes (c1975, adaptation of ballets Op.22 & Op.27)	

Incid music:

1.14	"The Bedbug" (The Flea) (c1929, Mayakovsky)	Op.19
1.15	"The Shot" (c1929, Bezïmensky)	Op.24
1.16	*"Virgin Land" (c1929, Gorbenko & Lvov, lost)*	*Op.25*
1.17	"Rule, Britannia!" (c1931, Piotrovsky)	Op.28
1.18	"Allegedly Murdered," circus sketch (c1931, Voyevodin & Ryss, 11 of 35 numbers are missing)	Op.31
1.19	"Hamlet" (c1931–2, Shakespeare transl Lozinsky; also see incid music Op.116) (also see incid music c by Honegger H190, Milhaud Op.200, Moniuszko, Prokofiev Op.77 & Tchaikovsky Op.67a)	Op.32
1.20	"The Human Comedy" (c1933–4, Sukhotin after Balzac, part lost)	Op.37
1.21	"Salute to Spain" (c1936, Afinogenov)	Op.44
1.22	"King Lear" (c1940, Shakespeare; music + new Jig & Finale used in 1954 production of 'Hamlet'; also see film score Op.137) (also see incid music c by Balakirev, Debussy L109, Dupré & Khachaturian)	Op.58a
1.23	"Native Country," spectacle (c1942; see orch suite: Native Leningrad)	Op.63
1.24	"Russian River," spectacle (c1944)	Op.66
1.25	"Victorious Spring" (c1945; S, T, ch & orch)	Op.72

Film:

1.26	"New Babylon" (The Assault on Heaven) (c1928–9, for live performance w/ silent film)	Op.18
1.27	"Alone" (All Alone) (c1932, part lost)	Op.26
1.28	"The Golden Mountains" (Happy Street) (c1931, Yutkevich)	Op.30
1.29	"Counterplan" (The Passer-by) (c1932, Ermler & Yutkevich)	Op.33
1.30	*"Genu in Pilae" (c1932, destroyed by Stalin, restored from frags, ?doubtful)*	
1.31	"The Tale of the Priest and His Servant Balda," animated (c1936, after Pushkin)	Op.36
1.32	"Love and Hate" (c1934, Gendelshtein)	Op.38
1.33	"The Youth of Maxim" (The Bolshevik) (Maxim trilogy I) (c1934–5, Kozintsev & Trauberg)	Op.41i
1.34	"The Girl Friends" (Three Women) (c1934–5, Arnshtam; tpt, str qt & pf)	Op.41ii
1.35	"The Return of Maxim" (Maxim trilogy II) (c1936–7, Kozintsev & Trauberg)	Op.45
1.36	"Volochayevka Days" (Intervention in the Far East) (c1936–7, part lost)	Op.48
1.37	"The Vyborg District" (Maxim trilogy III) (c1938, Kozintsev & Trauberg)	Op.50
1.38	"The Friends" (The Pals) (c1938, Arnshtam)	Op.51
1.39	"The Great Citizen," I (c1938, story of party leader Kirov)	Op.52
1.40	"The Man with a Gun" (November) (c1938, Yutkevich)	Op.53
1.41	"The Great Citizen," II (c1938–9, Ermler, story of party leader Kirov, part lost)	Op.55
1.42	"The Silly Little Mouse," animated (c1939, Tsekhanovsky)	Op.56
1.43	"The Adventures of Korzinkina" (A Ticket to the Fifth Zone) (c1940, part lost)	Op.59
1.44	"Zoya" (Who is she?) (c1944, Chirskov & Arnshtam, 9 of 35 numbers lost)	Op.64
1.45	"Simple People" (c1945, Kozintsev & Trauberg, released 1956)	Op.71
1.46	"The Young Guard" (c1947–8, Gerasimov, after Fadeyev's novel, 2 series)	Op.75
1.47	"Pirogov" (c1947, Kozintsev)	Op.76
1.48	"Michurin" (Life in Bloom) (c1948, Dorzenko)	Op.78
1.49	"Encounter at the Elbe" (c1948, Alexandrov, part lost)	Op.80
1.50	"The Fall of Berlin" (c1949, Chiaurelli, 2 series)	Op.82
1.51	"Belinsky" (c1950, released 1953, Kozintsev)	Op.85

1a. SELECTIONS FROM STAGE WORKS

1a.2   "The Nose," opera: Op.15
          I: 1. "Introduction"
                 2. "The barber Ivan Yakovlevich"
                 3. "The Embankment"
                 4. "Entr'acte" (percussion)
                 5. "The bedroom of Kovalyev"
                 6. "Galop"
                 7. "Kazan Cathedral"
          II: 8. "Introduction"
                 9. "In the newspaper dispatch office"
                 10. "Entr'acte"
                 11. "In Kovalyev's apartment"
          III: 12. "On the outskirts of St. Petersburg"
                 13. "In the apartment of Kovalyev and Podtochina"
                 14. "Intermezzo"
          Epilogue: 15. "In Kovalyev's apartment"
                 16. "Nevsky Prospect"

1a.3   "Lady Macbeth of the Mtsensk District," opera: Op.29
          I: 1. "In the Izmailov's house"
                 2. "The Izmailov's courtyard"
                 3. "Katerina's bedroom"
          II: 4. "The Izmailov's couryard at night"
                 5. "Katerina's bedroom"
          III: 6. "The Izmailov's garden before the wedding"
                 7. "At the police station"
                 8. "The wedding feast in the Izmailov's garden"
          IV: 9. "Convict's camp on the road to Siberia"

1a.4   "The Big Lightning," opera: ....
                 1. "Overture"
                 2. "Scene—Tommy and the Manager"
                 3. "Architect's Song"
                 4. "Scene—An American"
                 5. "Matofel's Song"
                 6. "Telephone call"
                 7. "Selyan's Song"
                 8. "Duet of Yegor and Selyan"
                 9. "Model's Procession"

1a.6   "The Gamblers," opera: ....
                 1. "Overture"
                 2. "Scenes in the hotel"
                 3. "Card gambling scene"

1a.8   "Moscow, Cheremushky," operetta:.. Op.105
                 . "Overture-Prologue"
          I/1. "Do not touch!": 1. "Bubentsov and choir of excursionists"
                 2. "Duet: Masha and Bubwntsov"
                 3. "Pantomime"
                 4. "Aria: Boris"
                 5. "Serenade: Boris"
                 6. "Song: Lidochka"
                 7. "A drive through Moscow"
                 . "Dialogue Interlude: 'Reckless love' "
                 8. "Duet: Vava and Drebednev"
                 9. "End of the drive through Moscow"
          I/2. "Registering for a new flat": 10. "Assembly of tenants"

11. "Song: Glushkov, the chauffeur of Marina Grove"
12. "Song: Baburov, the old Muscovite of Teplo Alley"
13. "Song of Cheryomushki"
14. "Scene: Barabashkin with tenants"
15. "Song: Boris"
16. "Scene: Drebednev, Barabashkin, and tenants"
17. "Finale of Act I"
II: . "Musical Interlude: 'Here they are, the keys!' "
18. "Couplets: Barabashkin"
II/3. "Airborne forces": 19. "Duet: Lidochka and Boris"
20. "Duet: Lyusya and Glushkov"
21. "Couplets: Barabashkin and Drebednev"
22. "Duet: Lidochka and Boris"
23. "Scene"
. "Dialogue Interlude"
24. "Song: Lyusya and the builders"
II/4. "Alarm bell": 25. "Duet: Masha and Bubentsov"
26. "Polka with kisses"
27. "Song of Cheryomushki"
. "Dialogue Interlude"
28. "Ballet"
29. "Apotheosis"
30. "Finale of Act II"
III: 31. "Entr'acte"
32. "Scene"
III/5. "Magic hours": 33. "Song: Lidochka"
34. "Blossom Waltz"
35. "Ditty: Barabashkin"
36. "Duet: Lidochka and Boris"
37. "Ditty: Glushkov"
38. "Scene: Barabashkin"
39. "Finale"

1a.10   "The Age of Gold" (The Golden Age), ballet: Op.22
1. "Introduction"
I. "The Golden Age of Industrial Exposition": 2. "Procession of Guests of Honour"
3. "Review of Window Displays"
4. "Demonstration of Exhibits"
5. "Prestidigitator—Barker: Hindu Dance"
6. "Prize fighting for publicity"
7. "Scandal at the Boxing Match"
Scene "Exposition Hall": 8. "Foxtrot: Dance of Flaming Youth"
9. "Director's appearance with Diva"
10. "Adagio of Diva"
11. "Arrival of Soviet Football Team"
12. "Diva's variations"
13. "Soviet Dance"
14. "Soviet Worker invites Diva to a dance"
15. "Dance of Diva and the Fascist"
16. "Dance of the Negro and two Soviet football players"
17. "Waltz: Alleged Bomb plotters—'The Hand of Moscow' "
18. "Confusion among the Fascists"
19. "A Rare Case of Mass Hysteria"
20. "Foxtrot ... foxtrot ... foxtrot"
II. "Street in the City": 21. "Pantomime: Sleuthing by an Agent Provocateur and an Arrest"
Scene "Workers' Stadium": 22. "Workers' Procession to the Stadium"
23. "Pioneers' Dance—Dances: Boxing, Discus-throwing, Tennis, English Hockey & Fencing"
24. "Reception of the Soviet Football Team"
25. "The Football Match"
26. "Interlude: Everybody amuse oneself in one's own way"
27. "Sportive Dance of Western Komsomol members & 4 Sportsmen" (= reorchd Tahiti Trot, Op.16)
28. "General Sportive Dance"
29. " 'The Red Front' " (pre-war anti-fascist organization)
III. "Music Hall" (Divertissement): 30. "Introduction"
31. "Tap-dance: Shoe Shine of the Best Quality"
32. "Tango"
33. "Polka: Once Upon a Time in Geneva—'Angel of Peace' "
34. "Touching Coalition of Classes, slightly fraudulent"
35. "Can-can"
36. "Scene: Liberation of Prisoners. General Exposure"
37. "Finale: Solidarity Dance of Western Workers and the Soviet Team"

1a.11   "The Bolt," ballet: Op.27
I/1. "In the cloakroom": 1. "Gymnastics"
2. "Drinking bout"

I/2. "In the workshop": 1. "Checking the installation of the machines"
 2. "The Charwoman"
 3. "March: Scene of the filling workshop"
 4. "Workshop concert": a. "The Wrecker"
  b. "The Bureaucrat"
  c. "The Blacksmith"
  d. "Industrial March. Dance of the Komsomol members and Pioneers"
 5. "Starting up the workshop"
I/3. "In the cloakroom": 1. "Drinking bout"
 2. "The indignant workers"
I/4. "In the workshop": 1. "At work"
II. "In the Factory Village": 1. "Scene of the Sexton"
 2. "Dance of the Priest"
 3. "The pilgrims"
 4. "Dance: Komsomol Circle"
 5. "Dance of Kozelkov"
 6. "Dance of the cloaked women"
 7. "Dance of the lad"
 8. "Quadrille of the Komsomol members and dance of the Sexton"
 9. "Scene: Priest with the Sexton; departure of the pilgrims and Komsomol"
 10. "Dance pantomime: from the beer-house"
 11. "Scene: vodka and sabotage"
 12. "Kozelkov's Dance with Friends"
 13. "Kozelkov's Dance (in his absence)"
III. "The Club": 1. "March: Red Army"
 2. "Appearance of the agitator-brigade": a. "Maritime conference"
  b. "The aesthetic young ladies"
  c. "The Conciliator"
  d. "Textile workers"
  e. "The Goblin"
  f. "The female Colonial Slave"
 3. "Komsomol Dance"
 4. "Red Army. Dance performance": a. "Infantry and artillery"
  b. "Society of Assistance to Defence, Aviation, and Chemical Protection"
  c. "Bicyclists"
  d. "Red Army, Red Navy and sailors"
  e. "Aviators"
  f. "The Budyonnovtsy Mounted Army"
 5. "Final Dance and Apotheosis"

1a.12 "The Limpid Stream," ballet: Op.39
 I. "Collective Farm" (named 'The Limpid Stream'), I/1. "The wayside halt in early autumn": 1. "Overture"
 2. "Arrival of brigade of artists"
 3. "Scene of the two girl friends" (Zina and the Ballerina)
 4. "Dance-examination"
 5. "Beginning of the intrigue" (Pyotr becomes infatuated with the Ballerina)
 6. "Musical Entr'acte"
 I/2. "The day draws to a close": 7. "Termination of the fieldwork and distribution of presents"
 8. "Benre Dances": a. "Russian Dance"
  b. "Chaconne"
  c. "Weaver's Round Dance"
  d. "Dance of the Milkmaid and the Tractor-driver"
  e. "Waltz of the Classical Dancers"
  f. "Comic Dance"
  g. "Dance of Gorets and Kubanets"
 9. "The jealousy of Zina"
 10. "Zina reveals she was formerly a ballet student"
 11. "Agreement" (between Zina and the Ballerina to change places)
 II. "In a Woodland Clearing": 12. "Picnic and invitation to an evening meeting"
 13. "Scene of the disguising of Zina" (as the Ballerina)
 14. "Entrance and Dance of the Accordionist and Galya"
 15. "Joke over the old summer residents": a. "Entrance to the meeting"
  b. "Variation of the male classical dancer"
  c. "Variation of the Ballerina"
  d. "Coda"
 16. "Adagio of Pyotr and the disguised Zina": a. "Dance of the conspirators"
  b. "Variation of Zina"
  c. "Coda"
 17. "Dance: staging of the play 'Murder' "
 18. "Variation 'Murder' "
 19. "Finale-Coda"
 III. "Harvest Festival": 20. "Musical interjection and swing"
 21. "March: Harvest Festival"
 22. "Waltz"
 23. "Scene of the disclosure of the ruse"

24. "Great Adagio" (reconciliation of Pyotr and Zina)
25. "Variation of the male classical dancer"
26. "Variation of the Ballerina"
27. "Variation of Zina"
28. "Coda"
29. "Final Dance"

1a.14   "The Bedbug" (The Flea), incid music: Op.19
1.–3. "March"
4.–6. "Galop. Foxtrot"
7. "Foxtrot" (Wedding)
8. "Wedding Scene"
9. "Waltz"
10. "Dance" (Foxtrot)
11. "Symphonic Entr'acte"
12. "Fire and Fire Signals"
13. "Fireman's Chorus"
14.–18. "Scene in the Public Garden"
19. "March of the Pioneers"
20. "March of the City Elders"
21. "Flourish"
22. "Waltz"
23. "Closing March"

1a.15   "The Shot," incid music: Op.24
1. "Dundee's Romance"
2. "Choir"
3. "Third Episode"
4. "Fourth Episode"
5. ("Entry of the Heads of Departments")
6. ("Exeunt the Heads of Departments")
7. ("Entry of the Secretaries")
8. ("Entry of the Secretaries")
9. "Ninth Episode"
10. "Tenth Episode"
11. "Eleventh Episode"

1a.17   "Rule, Britannia!," incid music: Op.28
1. "The Internationale"
2. "Infantry March"
3. ("Along the Soviet Route")
4. ("Protest")
5. ("Raising the Banner")
6. ("The Banners are Making a Noise")

1a.18   "Allegedly Murdered," incid music: Op.31
. "Polka"
. "Dance"
. "2 Intermezzi"
. "The Field" (A landscape)
. ("Galop")
. "River-bed"
. "Petrushka"
. "The Storm"
. "The Jugglers"
. "The Waitressess"
. "Paradise": 1. "The Flight of the Cherubs"
       2. "The Flight of the Angels"
. "Adagio"
. "Dance of the temporary Conquerors" (Finale of Act I)
. "Bacchanalia"
. "Waltz"
. "The Archangel Gabriel"
. "Twelve Apostles" (incl vocal solo of the Devil)
. ("Chorus")
. ("Beiburzhuyev's Monologue")

1a.19   "Hamlet," incid music: Op.32
1. "Introduction"
2. "Night watch"
3. "Shepherd's Pipe"
4. "Funeral March"
5. "Exeunt King and Queen"
6. "Dinner Music"
7. "Flourish"

8. "Dance Music"
9. "Finale of First Act"
10. "Entry of Hamlet with the Urchins"
11. "Galop: Ophelia and Polonius"
12. *"Scene: Hamlet and Rosencrantz" (2 frags)*
13. "Arrival of the Players"
14. "Exeunt Polonius, Rosenkrantz and Guildenstern"
15. "Dialogue of Rosencrantz and Guildenstern"
16. "Hunting" (The Chase)
17. "Finale of Second Act" (repeat of last 11 bars of: Hunting)
18. *("Music for the rehearsal of the Strolling Player's spectacle") (8 frags)*
19. "Entry of the Guests"
20. "Scene with Recorder"
21. "Episode after the Scene with Recorder"
22. "Pantomime"
23. "Hamlet carries the corpse of Polonius"
24. "Hamlet carries the corpse of Polonius" (variant)
25. "The King carries away the Queen"
26. "After the word 'Heroic': the Combat"
27. "Removal of the dead Player King"
28. "Monologue of (the King) Claudius"
29. *"Signals to start the Combat" (3 frags)*
30. "Romance at the Banquet" (song)
31. "The Banquet"
32. "Can-can"
33. "Ophelia's Song"
34. "Lullaby"
35. "Introduction to the Churchyard Scene"
36. "Song of the gravedigger" (unacc)
37. "Requiem" (choral)
38. "Tournament"
39. "Flourish"
40. "Heavy Combat"
41. "Slack Combat"
42. "End of the Tournament"
43. "The March of Fortinbras"
44. "The Beggars pass"
45. "Song of Horatio" (unacc)

1a.20   "The Human Comedy," incid music: Op.37
extant: . "Introduction"
. "Overture"
. "Student's Song"
2. "Elegy" (pf)
3. "Waltz" (pf)
. "March"
. "Merry Paris"
. "The Theatre"
. "The Theme of Paris"
. "Cruel Paris"
18. "Gavotte"
. "Addition to Gavotte" (Trio)
. "Flourish"
. "The Panorama of Paris"
. "Panic on the Exchange"
. "Barrel Organ"
. "Bank of the Seine"
. "Casket with Diamonds"
. "Police March"
. "Fanfare"

1a.21   "Salute to Spain," incid music: Op.44
1.–3. "Fanfares" (3 Flourishes)
4. "The Song of Rosita"
5. *(Fragment: Andante)*
6. "March"

1a.22   "King Lear," incid music: Op.58a
1. "Introduction and Ballad of Cordelia"
2. "Return from the Hunt" (red for pf)
3.–12. "The Fool's Songs" (10 brief songs)
13. "Finale of Act I"
14. "Approach of the Storm" (At Regan's Castle)
15. "Scene in the Steppe" (At the hut)
16. "The Blinding of Gloucester"

Interlude: 8. "The Devil's Procession"
   9. "The Bell-ringer and Devils' Dance"
I/2. "The Village and the priest's Household": 10. "Description of the Village"
   11. "Balda and the Priest's Son at Dinner"
   12. "Balda's Work"
   13. "Balda's Song"
   14. "The Priest's Son Dance"
   15. "Balda and the Priest's Daughter Lullaby"
"Evening party of the Peasants" (16.–18.): 16. "What a song"
   17. "Fir-grove, my fir-grove"
   18. "The splinter"
   19. "The Priest's Daughter's Dream"
   20. "The Priest's Daughter's Romance"
   21. "The Priest's Lament"
   22. "The Metropolitan Priest"
   23. "Balda's Farewell"
II/3. "At the Devils": 24. "Introduction"
   25. "Dialogue of the Old Devil and Balda"
   26. "First Dialogue of the Little Devil and Balda"
   27. "Second Dialogue of the Little Devil and Balda"
   28. "Balda's Galop"
   29. "The Rent"
Interlude: 30. "Balda's Return"
Epilogue: 31. "Balda's Welcome"
   32. "Looking for the Priest"
   33. "Three Flicks"
   34. "Final Chorus"

1a.34 "The Girl Friends" (Three Women), film: Op.41ii
     1. "Allegro," in F major
     2. "The Forester's Hut" (Andante), in A minor
     3. "Prelude," in D major

1a.36 "Volochayevka Days" (Intervention in the Far East), film: Op.48
    extant: 1. "Overture"
      2. (w/ out title)
      14. "The Japanese Attack"
      16. (Allegro—Maestoso) (frag)
      . "Thro' the dales and o'er the hills" (The Song of the Far Eastern Partisans) (c by Aturov)
      . "Finale"
      45. (Variant of No.14)
      46. (w/ out title)
      . "Russian Folksong No.1" (Moderato)
      . "Russian Folksong No.2" (Largo)

1a.40 "The Man with a Gun" (November), film: Op.53
     1. "Overture"
     2. "The October"
     3. "Smolny"
     3a. "Smolny"
     4. "Finale"

1a.41 "The Great Citizen," II, film: Op.55
    extant: . "Overture"
      . "Funeral march"
      . "Finale"

1a.44 "Zoya" (Who is she?), film: Op.64
     1. "Allegretto"
     2. "Moderato"
     3. "Adagio"
     4. "Moderato"
     5. "Moderato"
     6. "Moderato—Allegro—Presto"
     7. "Victory" (Adagio)
     8. "The Belfry" (Allegro)
     12. "Moderato"
     13. "Moderato"
     16. "Allegretto"
     20. "Dneprostoi" (Allegretto)
     21. "Adagio"
     22. "The First of May Parade" (Allegretto)
     23. "Arrival of the heroes" (Allegro)
     24. "Allegro"
     25. "Recollection" (Moderato—Allegro)

30. "Moscow" (Adagio)
31. "Song about Zoya" (Simonov)
35. "(Con moto)—Allegro"

1a.49   "Encounter at the Elbe," film: Op.80
       extant: 2. "Tommy's Song": "Things are very good with the Yankees"
           10. (Jazz piece)
           13. "Longing for the Native Country" (Homesickness)
           22. "Moderato"
           23. "Moderato"
           24. "Allegretto"
           25. "Moderato con moto"
           28. "Tommy's Song" (orch vers)
           34. "Song of Peace" (orch vers)

1a.50   "The Fall of Berlin," film: Op.82
       Nos. not incl in the suite: 5. "Beautiful Day" (Dolmatovsky; arr for child ch & pf)
           8. "Allegro"
           9. "Allegretto"
           15. "Overture to Part I"
           17. "Concentration Camp"

1a.53   "Song of the Great Rivers" (Unity and Seven Rivers), film: Op.95
        . "Cover" (Introduction)
           1. "Song of the great Rivers"
           2. "Prologue"
           3. "The Indictment Episode"
           4. "K.K.K." (Klu-Klux-Klan)
           6. "South Africa"
           8. "Hard Labour"
        . "Children. Salt" (va & vc)

1a.54   "The Gadfly," film: Op.97
           1. "Overture"
           2. "The Cliff"
           3. "Youth"
           5. "Confession" (solo org)
           7. "Box on the ear"
           8. "Laughter"
           9. "Barrel Organ"
           10. "Divine Service at the Cathedral" (solo org)
           12. "Exit from the Cathedral"
           13. "Contredance"
           14. "Galop"
           15. "Guitars"
           16. "At the Market Place" (from: Suite for Jazz Orch No.2, dance 1)
           17. "The Rout"
           18. "The Passage of Montanelli"
           19. "Finale"
           20. "The Austrians"
           22. "The River"
           23. "Gemma's Room"

1a.58   "Hamlet," film: Op.116
           1. "Overture 'Elsinore' "
           2. ("Decree of the King")
           3. "Military Music"
           4. ("Royal fanfare")
           5. "Ball at the Palace"
           6. "Story of Horatio and the Ghost"
           7. ("Dance of Ophelia")
           8. "The Ball"
           9. "The Ghost"
           10. "Hamlet's parting with Ophelia"
           11. ("Hamlet in thought or Palace Music")
           12. "Hamlet's monologue: 'What a piece of work is man' "
           13. "Arrival of the Players"
           14. "Hamlet's soliloquy: 'Fie upon't! foh! About my brain' "
           15. "The Presentation"
           16. "Hamlet's soliloquy: 'To be, or not to be' "
           17. ("Preparation for the spectacle")
           18. ("Royal fanfare")
           19. "In the Garden" (Court procession)
           20. "Booth fanfare"
           21. "Scene of the Poisoning"

22. "Flutes"
23. "Conscience"
24. "Hamlet and Gertrude" (The Ghost in the Queen's presence)
25. "Hamlet's soliloquy and scene on board ship"
26. "Song of Ophelia"
27. "The Madness of Ophelia"
28. "Death of Ophelia"
29. ("Song of the Gravedigger")
30. ("Hamlet's monologue: 'Alas, poor Yorick!' ")
31. "War March"
32. "The Duel between Hamlet and Laertes"
33. "Death of Hamlet" ('The rest is silence')
34. "Funeral of Hamlet"

1a.60   "Sofya Perovskaya," film: Op.132
. "March"
. "The Execution"
1. "Allegro"
3. "Allegretto"
. "Waltz"
4. "Moderato"
5. "The Duel"
7. ("The Village")
8. "Voronezh"
9. "Andante"
10. "Allegro"
11. "Allegro"
12. "Moderato"
13. "The Dream"
14. "Allegro"
15. "Adagio"

2. SYMPHONIES

2.1	*"Revolutionary Symphony" (ca1915–8, lost)*	
2.2	Symphony No.1 in F minor (c1923–5, w/ pf)	Op.10
2.3	Symphony No.2 in B major, "To October" (c1927, Bezïmensky; w/ ch in Finale)	Op.14
2.4	Symphony No.3 in E-flat major, "The First of May" (c1929, Kirsanov; w/ ch in Finale)	Op.20
2.5	Symphony No.4 in C minor (c1935–6, p1961)	Op.43
2.6	Symphony No.5 in D minor (c1937; w/ 2harps & pf)	Op.47
2.7	*"Lenin Symphony" (c1938; vv, ch & orch, abandoned)*	
2.8	Symphony No.6 in B minor (c1939; w/ harp)	Op.54
2.9	Symphony No.7 in C major, "Leningrad" (c1941):	Op.60

1. "War"
2. "Memories"
3. "My Native Field"
4. "Victory"

2.10	Symphony No.8 in C minor, "Stalingrad" (c1943)	Op.65
2.11	Symphony No.9 in E-flat major (c1945)	Op.70
2.12	Symphony No.10 in E minor (c1953)	Op.93
2.13	Symphony No.11 in G minor, "The Year 1905" (c1957):	Op.103

1. "Palace Square"
2. "Ninth of January"
3. "Eternal Memory"
4. "The Toscin"

2.14   Symphony No.12 in D minor, "To the Memory of Lenin" / "The Year 1917" (c1961): Op.112
1. "Revolutionary Petrograd"
2. "Razliv"
3. "Aurora"
4. "The Dawn of Humanity"

2.15   Symphony No.13 in B-flat minor, "Babiy Yar" (c1962, Yevtushenko; B, ch & orch): Op.113
1. "Babiy Yar"
2. "Humour" (tune from song Op.62/3)
3. "In the Store"
4. "Fears"
5. "A Career"

2.16   Symphony No.14 (c1969; S, B, strings & perc, in form of a sym song cycle): Op.135
1. "De Profundis" (Lorca transl Tanyanova; w/ B)
2. "Malagueña" (Lorca transl Geleskul; w/ S)
3. "Lorelei" (Apollinaire transl Kudinov; w/ S, B)
4. "The Suicide" (Apollinaire transl Kudinov; w/ S)
5. "On Watch" (Apollinaire transl Kudinov; w/ S)
6. "Madam, look!" (Apollinaire transl Kudinov; w/ S, B)
7. "In Prison—At the Sante Jail" (Apollinaire transl Kudinov; w/ B)

8. "The Zaporozhian Cossack's Reply to the Sultan" (Apollinaire transl Kudinov; w/ B)
9. "O Delvig, Delvig!" (Küchelbecker, w/ B)
10. "The Death of the Poet" (Rilke transl Silman; w/ S)
11. "Conclusion" (Rilke transl Silman; w/ S, B)

2.17 Symphony No.15 in A major (c1971) Op.141
2.18 *Symphony No.16 (c1974–5, unfin: 2 movts started)* ....

3. ORCHESTRAL SUITES

3.1	"The Nose" (c1927–8; T, B & chamber orch, from opera Op.15): No.1 "Overture" Op.15a
3.2	No.2 "Kovalyev's aria" (from Scene 5)
3.3	No.3 "Percussion Interlude" (to Scene 3)
3.4	No.4 "Interlude" (to Scene 6)
3.5	No.5 "Ivan's aria" (from Scene 6)
3.6	No.6 "Kovalyev's monologue" (from Scene 6)
3.7	No.7 "Galop" (from Scene 3)
3.8	*"New Babylon" (restored Rozhdestvensky, from film Op.18): No.1 "War"* .... *(Op.18)*
3.9	*No.2 "Paris"*
3.10	*No.3 "The Siege of Paris"*
3.11	*No.4 "Operetta"*
3.12	*No.5 "Paris has stood for centuries"*
3.13	*No.6 "Versailles"*
3.14	*No.7 "Finale" (orig: Coda of No.6, 'Versailles')*
3.15	"The Bedbug" (from incid music Op.19): No.1 "March" ....(Op.19)
3.16	No.2 "Galop"
3.17	No.3 "Foxtrot"
3.18	No.4 "Waltz"
3.19	No.5 "Intermezzo"
3.20	No.6 "Scene in the Boulevard"
3.21	No.7 "Closing March"
3.22	"The Age of Gold" (p1930, from ballet Op.22): No.1 "Introduction" (= Overture) Op.22a
3.23	No.2 "Adagio" (= Adagio of Diva, from Act I)
3.24	No.3 "Polka" (= Angel of Peace, from Act III)
3.25	No.4 "Russian Dance" (= Soviet Dance, from Act I)
3.26	"The Bolt" (Ballet Suite No.5) (p1933, from ballet Op.27): No.1 "Overture" (Introduction) Op.27a
3.27	No.2 "The Bureaucrat's Dance" (Polka)
3.28	No.3 "The Drayman's Dance" (Variations)
3.29	No.4 "Tango: Kozelkov's Dance with Friends"
3.30	No.5 "Intermezzo" (Interlude)
3.31	No.6 "The Dance of the Colonial Slave"
3.32	No.7 "The Conciliator"
3.33	No.8 "General Dance of Enthusiasm and Apotheosis" (Finale)
3.34	"The Golden Mountains" (c1931, from film Op.30): No.1 "Introduction" Op.30a
3.35	No.2 "Waltz"
3.36	No.3 "Fugue"
3.37	No.4 "Intermezzo"
3.38	No.5 "Funeral march"
3.39	No.6 "Finale" (closing bars of Sym No.3, Op.20 added as a Coda)
3.40	"Hamlet" (c1932, from incid music Op.32): No.1 "Introduction and Night Watch" Op.32a
3.41	No.2 "Funeral March"
3.42	No.3 "Flourish and Dance Music"
3.43	No.4 "The Hunt"
3.44	No.5 "Actors' Pantomime"
3.45	No.6 "Procession"
3.46	No.7 "Musical Pantomime"
3.47	No.8 "The Banquet"
3.48	No.9 "Ophelia's Song" (insts)
3.49	No.10 "Lullaby"
3.50	No.11 "Requiem" (insts)
3.51	No.12 "Tournament"
3.52	No.13 "The March of Fortinbras"
3.53	"The Tale of the Priest and His Servant Balda" (c1933–4, r1935, from film Op.36): No.1 "Overture" Op.36a
3.54	No.2 "The Procession of the Obscurantists" (The Devils' Procession)
3.55	No.3 "Merry-go-round"
3.56	No.4 "Scene in the Bazaar" (Description of the Bazaar)
3.57	No.5 "The Priest's Daughter's Dream" (incl in: Ballet Suite No.2 as: Sentimental Romance)
3.58	No.6 "Finale" (= Overture)
3.59	"Suite for Jazz Orchestra No.1" (c1934): No.1 "Waltz" ....
3.60	No.2 "Polka"
3.61	No.3 "Foxtrot" (Blues)
3.62	"Suite for Jazz Orchestra No.2" (Suite for Variety Stage Orchestra) (c1938): No.1 "March" ....
3.63	No.2 "Dance I" (used in film: The Gadfly, Op.97)
3.64	No.3 "Dance II"
3.65	No.4 "Little Polka"

3.66	No.5 "Lyric Waltz"
3.67	No.6 "Waltz I"
3.68	No.7 "Waltz II"
3.69	No.8 "Finale"
3.70	"The Limpid Stream" (c1945, from ballet Op.39): No.1 "Waltz" (= No.1 of: Ballet Suite No.1) Op.39a
3.71	No.2 ("Russian Popular Dance") (= No.4 of: Ballet Suite No.1)
3.72	No.3 "Galop" (= No.6 of: Ballet Suite No.3)
3.73	No.4 "Adagio" (= No.2 of: Ballet Suite No.2)
3.74	No.5 "Pizzicato" (= No.2 of: Ballet Suite No.1)
3.75	*"Maxim" (assembl Atovmyan 1961, from films Op.45 & Op.89): No.1 "Prelude—'Be bold, brothers' " Op.50a*
3.76	*No.2 "Attack sequence"*
3.77	*No.3 "Death of the old worker"*
3.78	*No.4 "Waltz"*
3.79	*No.5 "Demonstration"*
3.80	*No.6 "Fight at the baricades"*
3.81	*No.7 "Funeral March"*
3.82	*No.8 "Finale"*
3.83	*"The Adventures of Korzinkina" (assembl Rozhdestvensky, from film Op.59): No.1 "Overture" .... (Op.59)*
3.84	*No.2 "March"*
3.85	*No.3 "The Chase" (pf duet)*
3.86	*No.4 "Music in the Restaurant"*
3.87	*No.5 "Intermezzo"*
3.88	*No.6 "Finale"*
3.89	"Native Leningrad" (c1942, from spectacle: Native Country, Op.63): No.1 "Overture—October 1917" ....
3.90	No.2 "Song of the Victorious October" (Song of the River Neva)
3.91	No.3 "Youth Dance" (Dance of the Sailors)
3.92	. "Boldly, friends, on we march!," declamation (from Dzhabayev: Leningrad, I'm Proud of Thee)
3.93	No.4 "Song of Leningrad"
3.94	*"Zoya" (assembl Atovmyan, from film Op.64): No.1 "Introduction: Song about Zoya" (w/ ch) Op.64a*
3.95	*No.2 "Scene—Military Problem"*
3.96	*No.3 "Prelude—Tragedy of a Loss"*
3.97	*No.4 "March—Hero's Victory"*
3.98	*No.5 "Finale—The Heroine's Immortality"*
3.99	*"The Young Guard" (assembl Atovmyan 1951, from film Op.75): No.1 "Prelude" Op.75a*
3.100	*No.2 "By the River"*
3.101	*No.3 "Scherzo"*
3.102	*No.4 "Uneasy Night"*
3.103	*No.5 "Song of the Young Guards"*
3.104	*No.6 "Death of the Heroes"*
3.105	*No.7 "Apotheosis"*
3.106	*"Pirogov" (assembl Atovmyan 1947, from film Op.76): No.1 "Introduction" Op.76a*
3.107	*No.2 "Scene"*
3.108	*No.3 "Waltz"*
3.109	*No.4 "Scherzo"*
3.110	*No.5 "Finale"*
3.111	*"Michurin" (assembl Atovmyan 1964 w/ ch, from film Op.78): No.1 "Overture" Op.78a*
3.112	*No.2 "Winter Garden"*
3.113	*No.3 "Spring Waltz"*
3.114	*No.4 "Reminiscence"*
3.115	*No.5 "Demonstration in the Town Square"*
3.116	*No.6 "Michurin's Monologue"*
3.117	*No.7 "Finale"*
3.118	"Encounter at the Elbe" (c ?1949; w/ vv, from film Op.80): No.1 "Prelude" Op.80a
3.119	No.2 "Longing for the Native Country" (Homesickness)
3.120	No.3 "Dietrich's departure"
3.121	No.4 "In the American Zone"
3.122	No.5 "In the old town"
3.123	No.6 "Marching Song"
3.124	No.7 "Conclusion"
3.125	No.8 "Song of Peace"
3.126	*"Ballet Suite No.1" (assembl Atovmyan 1949): No.1 "Lyric Waltz" (= No.1 of: Suite for Jazz Orch No.1) ....*
3.127	*No.2 "Dance" (Pizzicato) (from ballet: The Limpid Stream, Op.39)*
3.128	*No.3 "Romance" (from ballet: The Limpid Stream, Op.39)*
3.129	*No.4 "Polka" (from ballet: The Limpid Stream, Op.39)*
3.130	*No.5 "Waltz-joke" (from ballet: The Bolt, Op.27)*
3.131	*No.6 "Galop" (from ballet: The Limpid Stream, Op.39)*
3.132	*"The Fall of Berlin" (assembl Atovmyan 1949 w/ ch, from film Op.82): No.1 "Prelude" Op.82a*
3.133	*No.2 "Scene at the river"*
3.134	*No.3 "Attack"*
3.135	*No.4 "In the garden" (vocalise)*
3.136	*No.5 "Storming Zeyelovsky Heights"*
3.137	*No.6 "In the destroyed village"*
3.138	*No.7 "Scene in the metro"*
3.139	*No.8 "Finale"*
3.140	*"Belinsky" (assembl Atovmyan 1960 w/ ch, from film Op.85): No.1 "Overture" Op.85a*

3.141	*No.2 "Sorrowful Ditty" (Girl's Song) (trad)*
3.142	*No.3 "The Strength of the People" (Nekrasov)*
3.143	*No.4 "Interlude"*
3.144	*No.5 "Song without words" (Vocalise)*
3.145	*No.6 "Scene"*
3.146	*No.7 "Finale"*
3.147	*"The Unforgettable Year 1919" (assembl Atovmyan 1954, from film Op.89): No.1 "Introduction"* *Op.89a*
3.148	*No.2 "Romance: the meeting of Shibayev and Katya"*
3.149	*No.3 "Scene from the Sea Battle"*
3.150	*No.4 "Scherzo"*
3.151	*No.5 "The Assault on Beautiful Gorky" (a miniature 'Piano Concerto')*
3.152	*No.6 "Intermezzo"*
3.153	*No.7 "Finale"*
3.154	*"Ballet Suite No.2" (assembl Atovmyan 1951): No.1 "Waltz" (from ballet: The Limpid Stream, Op.39)* ....
3.155	*No.2 "Adagio" (from ballet: The Limpid Stream, Op.39)*
3.156	*No.3 "Polka" (= No.2 of: Suite for Jazz Orch No.1)*
3.157	*No.4 "Sentimental Romance" (from film: The Tale of the Priest, Op.36)*
3.158	*No.5 "Spring Waltz" (from film: Michurin, Op.78)*
3.159	*No.6 "Finale" (Galop) (from ballet: The Limpid Stream, Op.39)*
3.160	*"Ballet Suite No.3" (assembl Atovmyan 1952): No.1 "Waltz" (from incid music: The Human Comedy, Op.37)* ....
3.161	*No.2 "Gavotte" (from incid music: The Human Comedy, Op.37)*
3.162	*No.3 "Dance" (from ballet: The Limpid Stream, Op.39)*
3.163	*No.4 "Elegy" (from incid music: The Human Comedy, Op.37)*
3.164	*No.5 "Waltz" (from ballet: The Limpid Stream, Op.39)*
3.165	*No.6 "Galop" (from ballet: The Limpid Stream, Op.39)*
3.166	*"Ballet Suite No.4" (assembl Atovmyan 1953): No.1 "Prelude" (variations, source unknown)* ....
3.167	*No.2 "Waltz" (from film: Song of the Great Rivers, Op.95)*
3.168	*No.3 "Scherzo" (from ballet: The Limpid Stream, Op.39)*
3.169	*"The Gadfly" (assembl Atovmyan 1955, from film Op.97): No.1 "Overture" (= 1.)* *Op.97a*
3.170	*No.2 "Contredance" (= 13.)*
3.171	*No.3 "People's Holiday" (= 16.)*
3.172	*No.4 "Interlude" (= 17.)*
3.173	*No.5 "Barrel Organ Waltz" (= 9.)*
3.174	*No.6 "Galop" (= 14.)*
3.175	*No.7 "Prelude" (= 15. & 5.)*
3.176	*No.8 "Romance" (= 3. & 7.)*
3.177	*No.9 "Intermezzo" (= 10., 12. & 18.)*
3.178	*No.10 "Nocturne" (= 23.)*
3.179	*No.11 "Scene" (= 2.)*
3.180	*No.12 "Finale" (= 20.)*
3.181	"The First Echelon" (c1955–6; w/ ch, from film Op.99): No.1 "Overture" Op.99a
3.182	No.2 "The Train"
3.183	No.3 "Children's Song" (Vasiliev)
3.184	No.4 "The Field"
3.185	No.5 "Evening Landscape"
3.186	No.6 "The Quarry"
3.187	No.7 "Intermezzo"
3.188	No.8 "Waltz"
3.189	No.9 "The Tender Maiden" (Vasiliev)
3.190	No.10 "The Fire"
3.191	No.11 "The House-Warming"
3.192	*"Five Days—Five Nights" (assembl Atovmyan 1961, from film Op.111): No.1 "Introduction"* *Op.111a*
3.193	*No.2 "Dresden in Ruins"*
3.194	*No.3 "Liberated Dresden"*
3.195	*No.4 "Interlude"*
3.196	*No.5 "Finale"*
3.197	"Katerina Izmaylova" (c ?1956; w/ S, from opera Op.114): No.1 "Entr'acte" (between 1st & 2nd) .. Op.114a
3.198	No.2 "Entr'acte" (between 2nd & 3rd Scene)
3.199	No.3 "Entr'acte" (Passacaglia) (between 4th & 5th Scene)
3.200	No.4 "Entr'acte" (between 6th & 7th Scene)
3.201	No.5 "Entr'acte" (between 7th & 8th Scene)
3.202	*"Hamlet" (assembl Atovmyan 1964, from film Op.116): No.1 "Introduction"* *Op.116a*
3.203	*No.2 "Ball at the Palace"*
3.204	*No.3 "The Ghost"*
3.205	*No.4 "In the Garden"*
3.206	*No.5 "Scene of the Poisoning"*
3.207	*No.6 "Arrival and Scene of the Players"*
3.208	*No.7 "The Duel and Death of Hamlet"*
3.209	*"A Year is Like a Lifetime" (assembl Atovmyan, from film Op.120): No.1 "Overture"* *Op.120a*
3.210	*No.2 "The Barricades"*
3.211	*No.3 "Intermezzo"*
3.212	*No.4 "Farewell" (Monologue)*
3.213	*No.5 "Scene" (Little Waltz)*
3.214	*No.6 "The Battle"*
3.215	*No.7 "Finale"*

4. OTHER ORCHESTRAL WORKS

4.1	"Scherzo," in F-sharp minor (c1919)	Op.1
4.2	"Theme & Variations," in B-flat major (c1921–2; red for pf, Op.3a)	Op.3
4.3	"Scherzo," in E-flat major (c1923–4; used in film: New Babylon, Op.18; red for pf)	Op.7
4.4	*"2 Fragments for Orchestra" (c1927, lost, reconstructed Nikolsky from memory 1946)*	
4.5	"2 Pieces for Dressel's opera 'Kolumbus' " (c1929): No.1 "Entr'acte," in C minor	Op.23
4.6	No.2 "Finale," in C major	
4.7	"Overture for the Green Guild" (c1932, to Dzerzhinsky's spectacle-play: The Green Guild)........	
4.8	"5 Fragments" (c1935, p1965; small orch w/ harp): No.1 "Moderato"	Op.42
4.9	No.2 "Andante"	
4.10	No.3 "Largo"	
4.11	No.4 "Moderato"	
4.12	No.5 "Allegretto"	
4.13	"Solemn March" (c1941; brass band)	
4.14	"3 Pieces for Orchestra" (c1947–8, given Op.77 but unpubd, now Op.77 = Vn Conc No.1)	
4.15	"Festive Overture," in A major (c1954)	Op.96
4.16	"Novorossiisk chimes" (The Fire of Eternal Glory) (c1960)	
4.17	"Overture on Russian and Khirghiz Folksongs" (c1963)	Op.115
4.18	"Mournful—Triumphal Prelude in Memory of the Heroes of Stalingrad" (c1967)	Op.130
4.19	"October," sym poem (c1967)	Op.131
4.20	"March of the Soviet Militia" (c1970; wind band)	Op.139

5. CONCERTOS, SOLO INSTR & ORCH

Pf & orch:

5.1	Piano Concerto No.1 in C minor (c1933; pf, tpt & strings; red for 2pf)	Op.35
5.2	Piano Concerto No.2 in F major (c1957)	Op.102

Vn & orch:

5.3	Violin Concerto No.1 in A minor (c1947–8)	Op.77
5.4	Revision of Violin Concerto No.1 in A minor (r1955; see orig Op.77)....................	Op.99
5.5	Violin Concerto No.2 in C-sharp minor (c1967)	Op.129

Vc & orch:

5.6	Cello Concerto No.1 in E-flat major (c1959)...	Op.107
5.7	Cello Concerto No.2 in G major (c1966)	Op.126

6. STRING QUARTETS

6.1	"2 Movements" (c1931): No.1 "Elegy: Adagio" (from opera: Lady Macbeth, Op.29)	
6.2	No.2 "Polka: Allegretto" (from ballet: The Age of Gold, Op.22)	
6.3	*"12 Preludes for String Quartet" (c1934, lost in 1941)*	
6.4	String Quartet No.1 in C major, "Springtime" (c1938)	Op.49
6.5	String Quartet No.2 in A major (c1944)	Op.68
6.6	String Quartet No.3 in F major (c1946; arr Barshai as: Chamber Symphony, Op.73a):	Op.73
	unpubd titles of movts: 1. "Calm unawareness of the future cataclysm"	
	2. "Rumblings of unrest and anticipation"	
	3. "The forces of war unleashed"	
	4. "Homage to the dead"	
	5. "The eternal question—Why? And for what?"	
6.7	String Quartet No.4 in D major (c1949, p1953; arr Barshai as: Chamber Symphony, Op.83a)	Op.83
6.8	String Quartet No.5 in B-flat major (c1952)	Op.92
6.9	String Quartet No.6 in G major (c1956)	Op.101
6.10	String Quartet No.7 in F-sharp minor (c1960)	Op.108
6.11	String Quartet No.8 in C minor (c1960; arr Barshai as: Chamber Symphony, Op.110a)	Op.110
6.12	String Quartet No.9 in E-flat major (c1964)	Op.117
6.13	String Quartet No.10 in A-flat major (c1964; arr Barshai as: Sym for Strings, Op.118a)	Op.118
6.14	String Quartet No.11 in F minor (c1966)	Op.122
6.15	String Quartet No.12 in D-flat major (c1968)	Op.133
6.16	String Quartet No.13 in B-flat minor (c1969–70)	Op.138
6.17	String Quartet No.14 in F-sharp major (c1973)	Op.142
6.18	String Quartet No.15 in E-flat minor (c1974; arr Rachlevsky as: Requiem for Strings):	Op.144
	1. "Elegy"	
	2. "Serenade"	
	3. "Intermezzo"	
	4. "Nocturne"	
	5. "Funeral March"	
	6. "Epilogue"	

7. OTHER CHAMBER MUSIC

5 or more insts:

7.1	"2 Pieces" (c1924–5; d str qt): No.1 "Prelude," in D minor	Op.11
7.2	No.2 "Scherzo," in G minor	
7.3	Piano Quintet in G minor (c1940)	Op.57

Piano Trios:

7.4	Piano Trio No.1 in C minor (c1923)	Op.8
7.5	Piano Trio No.2 in E minor (c1944)	Op.67

Vn & pf:

7.6	Violin Sonata (c1968)	Op.134

Va & pf:

7.7	Viola Sonata (c1975)	Op.147

Vc & pf:

7.8	*"3 Pieces" (c1923–4, lost)*	*Op.9*
7.9	Cello Sonata in D minor (c1934)	Op.40

1 instr:

7.10	"3 Pieces" (c1940; vn, ?withdrawn): No.1 "Prelude"	(Op.59)
7.11	No.2 "Gavotte"	
7.12	No.3 "Waltz"	

8. PIANO SONATAS

8.1	*Piano Sonata in B-flat minor (ca1924, destroyed by composer)*	
8.2	Piano Sonata No.1 (c1926, orig title: October Symphony)	Op.12
8.3	Piano Sonata No.2 in B minor (c1943)	Op.61

9. OTHER PIANO WORKS

9.1	*"The Soldier" (Ode to Liberty) (c1916, lost)*	
9.2	*"Hymn to Freedom" (c1915–6, lost)*	
9.3	"Funeral March" (c1917, found in 1984; used in: Suite on verses of Michelangelo, Op.145)	
9.4	*"In the Forest" (a trilogy) (ca1915–8, lost)*	
9.5	"Early Piano Pieces" (c1919–20): No.1 "Minuet"	
9.6	No.2 "Prelude"	
9.7	No.3 "Intermezzo"	
9.8	"8 Preludes" (c1919–20): No.1 in G minor	Op.2
9.9	No.2 in G major	
9.10	No.3 in E-flat minor	
9.11	No.4 in B-flat major	
9.12	No.5 in A minor	
9.13	No.6 in F minor	
9.14	No.7 in D-flat major	
9.15	No.8 in D-flat major	
9.16	"5 Preludes" (c1919–21, for collab work: 24 Preludes, w/ Clements & Feldt): No.2 in A minor (= Op.2/5)	
9.17	No.3 in G major (= Op.2/2)	
9.18	No.4 in E minor	
9.19	No.15 in D-flat major (= Op.2/7 or 8)	
9.20	No.18 in F minor (= Op.2/6)	
9.21	"3 Fantastic Dances" (c1920): No.1 "March," in C major	Op.5
9.22	No.2 "Waltz," in G major	
9.23	No.3 "Polka," in C major	
9.24	"Aphorisms" (c1927): No.1 "Recitative"	Op.13
9.25	No.2 "Serenade"	
9.26	No.3 "Nocturne"	
9.27	No.4 "Elegy"	
9.28	No.5 "Funeral March"	
9.29	No.6 "Etude"	
9.30	No.7 "Dance of Death"	
9.31	No.8 "Canon"	
9.32	No.9 "Legend"	
9.33	No.10 "Lullaby"	

9.34   "Preludes" (c1932–3): No.1 in C major Op.34
9.35   No.2 in A minor
9.36   No.3 in G major
9.37   No.4 in E minor
9.38   No.5 in D major, "Velocity étude"
9.39   No.6 in B minor
9.40   No.7 in A major
9.41   No.8 in F-sharp minor
9.42   No.9 in E major
9.43   No.10 in C-sharp minor
9.44   No.11 in B major
9.45   No.12 in G-sharp minor
9.46   No.13 in F-sharp major
9.47   No.14 in E-flat minor, "Zoya Prelude"
9.48   No.15 in D-flat major
9.49   No.16 in B-flat minor
9.50   No.17 in A-flat major
9.51   No.18 in F minor
9.52   No.19 in E-flat major
9.53   No.20 in C minor
9.54   No.21 in B-flat major
9.55   No.22 in G minor
9.56   No.23 in F major
9.57   No.24 in D minor
9.58   "Polka" (arr1935; pf, from ballet: The Golden Age, Op.22a/3; arr for pf duet 1962) ....
9.59   "A Child's Exercise Book" (Children's Tetrad), suite (c1945): No.1 "March" Op.69
9.60   No.2 "Valse"
9.61   No.3 "Sad Tale"
9.62   No.4 "Merry Tale"
9.63   No.5 "The Bear"
9.64   No.6 "Clockwork Doll"
9.65   No.7 "Birthday"
9.66   "Preludes & Fugues" (c1950–1): No.1 in C major (arr Dubinsky for str qt) Op.87
9.67   No.2 in A minor
9.68   No.3 in G major
9.69   No.4 in E minor
9.70   No.5 in D major
9.71   No.6 in B minor
9.72   No.7 in A major
9.73   No.8 in F-sharp minor
9.74   No.9 in E major
9.75   No.10 in C-sharp minor
9.76   No.11 in B major
9.77   No.12 in G-sharp minor
9.78   No.13 in F-sharp major
9.79   No.14 in E-flat minor
9.80   No.15 in D-flat major (arr Dubinsky for str qt)
9.81   No.16 in B-flat minor
9.82   No.17 in A-flat major
9.83   No.18 in F minor
9.84   No.19 in E-flat major
9.85   No.20 in C minor
9.86   No.21 in B-flat major
9.87   No.22 in G minor
9.88   No.23 in F major
9.89   No.24 in D minor
9.90   "Dances of the Dolls," suite (arr1952, from ballet suites): No.1 "Lyric Waltz" (from: Ballet Suite No.3/5) ......
9.91   No.2 "Gavotte" (from: Ballet Suite No.3/2)
9.92   No.3 "Romance" (from: Ballet Suite No.1/3)
9.93   No.4 "Polka" (from: Ballet Suite No.1/2, The Pizzicato Dance)
9.94   No.5 "Waltz-joke" (The Petite Ballerina) (from: Ballet Suite No.1/5)
9.95   No.6 "Hurdy-gurdy" (from: Ballet Suite No.1/4, The Polka)
9.96   No.7 "Dance"
9.97   3 Pieces for collab work: Variations on a theme by Glinka (c1957, theme: Vanya's song in Glinka's
          opera: A Life for the Tsar): No.8 "Adagio" ....
9.98   No.9 "Allegretto"
9.99   No.11 "Moderato maestoso"

          2 Pf:

9.100   "Fantasy" (ca1915–8, lost) ....
9.101   "Suite," in F-sharp minor (c1922): No.1 "Prelude," in F-sharp minor Op.6
9.102   No.2 "Fantastic Dance," in A minor
9.103   No.3 "Nocturne," in D major
9.104   No.4 "Finale," in F-sharp minor

9.105 "Piano Duets for Children" (c1949–54): No.1 "Merry March" ....
9.106 No.2 "Tarantella," in G major & "Prelude," in D-flat major (arr of Khoven: Prelude, Op.87/15)
9.107 "Concertino" (c1953) Op.94
9.108 "Tarantella" (arr1963, from film suite: The Gadfly, Op.97a/3) ....

Arrs by others:

9.109 *"The Human Comedy," suite (arr Solin for pf, from incid music Op.37): No.1 "March"* .... *(Op.37)*
9.110 *No.2 "Gavotte"*
9.111 *No.3 "The Panorama of Paris"*
9.112 *No.4 "Police March"*
9.113 *No.5 "Sarabande"*
9.114 *No.6 "Waltz"*

10. CHORAL WORKS

10.1 "From Karl Marx to Our Own Days," sym poem (c1932, Aseyev; vv, ch & orch, inc)...................................
10.2 *"New Year Madrigal" (c1933, humorous madrigal for New Year celebrations, ?lost)* ....

3 "National Anthem Contest Entries" (c1943):

10.3 1. "Patriotic Song" (Glory to our Soviet Motherland) (Dolmatovsky; ch & pf; orchd)...............................
10.4 2. "Song of the Red Army" (Golodny's Red Army, invincible, collab Kchachaturian)...............................
10.5 3. "National Anthem" (adaptation of Alexandrov: Hymn of the Bolshevik Party, new words Mikhalkov
     & El-Registan, adopted as the National Anthem from 1944) ....

10.6 *"The Heroic Defenders of Moscow," oratorio (c1943, abandoned)*..
10.7 "A Toast to our Motherland" (c1944, Utkin; T, ch & pf)..
10.8 "The Black Sea" (c1944, Alymov & Verkhovsky; B, m ch & pf/bayan) ....
10.9 "Our Native Russia has Gained Strength from the Storms" (c1945, Shchipachev)...................................
10.10 "Poem of the Motherland," cantata (c1947; mS, T, 2Bar, B, ch & orch) Op.74
10.11 "Little Paradise," cantata (c1948, from speeches of party leaders Zhdanov & Shepilov; 4B, ch & pf) ....
10.12 "Hymn to Moscow": "Stand Fast, our inviolable National Shrine" (c1948, Frenkel, music = Op.80a/8) ....
10.13 "To France," song ....
10.14 "Glory to the Shipbuilders," song ....
10.15 "The Song of the Forests," oratorio (c1949, Dolmatovsky; T, B, child ch, ch & orch): Op.81
      1. "When the War was over"
      2. "Clothe the homeland in forests" (The call rings throughout the land)
      3. "Recollection of the past"
      4. "Pioneers plant the forests"
      5. "Young Communists forge onwards"
      6. "A walk into the future"
      7. "Glory"
10.16 "Beautiful Day" (c1950, Dolmatovsky; child ch & pf, from film: The Fall of Berlin, Op.82)............................
10.17 "Our Song" (c1950, Simonov; ch & orch) ....
10.18 "Supporters of Peace March" (c ?1950, Simonov; T, ch & pf) ....
10.19 "10 Poems" (c1951, Revolutionary Poetry of 1870–1917): 1. "Boldly, on we march!" (Radin) Op.88
10.20 2. "One of many" (Tarasov)
10.21 3. "Onto the streets!" (anon)
10.22 4. "The meeting in transit to exile" (Gmyrev)
10.23 5. "To those condemned to death" (Gmyrev)
10.24 6. "The Ninth of January" (Kots)
10.25 7. "The volleys have become silent" (Tarasov)
10.26 8. "They are the victors" (Gmyrev)
10.27 9. "May Day Song" (Kots; boys' ch)
10.28 10. "Song" (Tan-Bogaraz after Whitman: Democratic Vistas; boys' ch)

"10 Russian Folksongs" (Soldiers' Songs) (c1951; 1v/vv, ch & pf):

10.29 1. "All of a sudden there was a clap of thunder over Moscow" (w/ B)...
10.30 2. "Beyond the mountains, beyond the valleys" (w/ T) ....
10.31 3. "Out of the forest of spears and swords" (w/ B) ....
10.32 4. "Nights are dark, the clouds are menacing" (w/ B)..
10.33 5. "A little cuckoo cuckoos" (w/ A)...
10.34 6. "The splinter" (w/ A) ....
10.35 7. "Fir-grove, my fir-grove" (w/ S) ....
10.36 8. "In my dear father's green garden" ....
10.37 9. "I told my sweetheart" (w/ S) ....
10.38 10. "What a song" (w/ B) ....

10.39 "The Sun Shines on Our Motherland," cantata (c1952, Dolmatovsky; child ch, ch & orch)................. Op.90
10.40 "Bird of Peace," song (c1953) ....
10.41 "October Dawn" (c1957, Kharitonov; vv & ch) ....
10.42 "2 Songs" (c1957, Sidorov; ch & pf): 1. "We Cherish the October Dawns in Our Hearts" ....
10.43 2. "We Sing Glory to Our Country"

10.44	"Cultivation," 2 Russian folksongs (arr1957; ch): 1. "Returning Winds" Op.104
10.45	2. "How my husband cruelly beat my child" (As I was a Young Girl)
10.46	"In the Fields Stand the Collective Farms" (c ?1960; child ch & ch)...
10.47	"The Execution of Stepan Razin" (c1964, Yevtushenko; B, ch & orch) Op.119
10.48	"Loyalty," 8 ballads (c1970, Dolmatovsky; m ch): 1. "In some immemorial year" Op.136
10.49	2. "People believing in a flame"
10.50	3. "A great name"
10.51	4. "Revolution banner"
10.52	5. "A difficult season for beauty"
10.53	6. "I want to learn all about him"
10.54	7. "So this is where the people were!"
10.55	8. "On meetings of the young generation"
10.56	*"My Native Country," patriotic oratorio (assembl Silantiev, p1972; narrator, S, 2T, B, ch & orch): ....*
	1. "Overture—'October 1917' " (from spectacle: Native Country, Op.63)
	2. "On Palace Square" (from spectacle: Native Country, Op.63)
	3. "Folk Dance" (from spectacle: Native Country, Op.63)
	4. "Ode to Leningrad" (from spectacle: Native Country, Op.63)
	5. "Song of the Lantern" (from incid music: Victorious Spring, Op.72)
	6. "Lullaby" (from incid music: Victorious Spring, Op.72)
	7. "Battle by the Volga" (from spectacle: Russian River, Op.66)
	8. "Song of Victory" (from incid music: Victorious Spring, Op.72)

11. VOICE & ORCHESTRA

11.1	"2 Fables" (c1922, Krylov; mS & orch): 1. "The Cricket and the Ant" Op.4
11.2	2. "The Ass and the Nightingale"
11.3	"6 Songs" (c1928–32, Japanese poets; T & orch): 1. "Love" (An Epitaph) (c1928) Op.21
11.4	2. "Before suicide" (c1928)
11.5	3. "An indiscreet glance" (c1928)
11.6	4. "For the first and last time" (c1931)
11.7	5. "Love without hope" (c1932)
11.8	6. "Death" (c1932)
	"8 British and American Folksongs" (arr1943, transl Bolotin & Sikorsky; 1v & orch w/ harp):
11.9	1. "The Sailor's Bride": "Blow the wind southerly" (Mickle) ....
11.10	2. "John Anderson, my Jo": "When we were first acquent" (Burns) (also see Schumann Op.67/5, R. Strauss AV73 & Weber J301) ....
11.11	3. "Billy Boy" (Northumbrian capstan shanty) ....
11.12	4. "Oh! the Oak and the Ash" (English air) ....
11.13	5. "Servants of King Arthur" (variant of the English folksong: Three Sons of Rogues) ....
11.14	6. "Coming thro' the Rye" (Burns) ....
11.15	7. "Spring Round Dance": "Come Lasses and Lads" ....
11.16	8. "When Johny Comes Marching Home" (Gilmore)...
11.17	"6 Songs" (c1971; B & small orch, from: 6 Romances, Op.62): 1. "The Wood, the Weed, the Wag" Op.140
11.18	2. "O, Wert thou in the Cauld Blast"
11.19	3. "Macpherson before his Execution"
11.20	4. "Jenny"
11.21	5. "Sonnet No.66"
11.22	6. "The King's Campaign"

12. SONGS (w/ pf)

12.1	"4 Romances" (c1936, Pushkin; arr for harp & strings as Op.46a): 1. "Renaissance" Op.46
12.2	2. "To a young man, sobbing bitterly"
12.3	3. "Premonition"
12.4	4. "Stanzas"
12.5	*"Romance" (c1938 or 41, Heine, not found) ....*
12.6	"6 Romances" (c1942; B & pf; orchd as Op.62a; orchd1971 as Op.140): 1. "The Wood, the Weed, the Wag" (To a Son) (Raleigh transl Pasternak)... Op.62
12.7	2. "O, Wert thou in the Cauld Blast" (In the Fields) (Burns transl Marshak) (also see Mendelssohn's duet Op.63/5)
12.8	3. "Macpherson before his Execution" (Macpherson Farewell) (Burns transl Marshak; tune reused in 2nd movt of Symphony No.13, 'Babiy Yar,' Op.113) (also see Haydn HobXXXIa/182)
12.9	4. "Jenny": "Coming thro' the Rye" (Burns transl Marshak)
12.10	5. "Sonnet No.66": "Tired with all these" (Shakespeare transl Pasternak)
12.11	6. "The King's Campaign" (The Grand Old Duke of York) (trad nursery rhyme transl Marshak)
12.12	"From Jewish Folk Poetry," cycle (c1948; orchd as Op.79a): 1. "Lament for a dead infant" (S, A) Op.79
12.13	2. "The solicitous mother and aunt" (S, A)
12.14	3. "Lullaby: Little son, my fairest" (A)
12.15	4. "Before a long separation" (Farewell) (S, T)
12.16	5. "Warning" (S)
12.17	6. "The abandoned father" (A, T)

12.18	7. "Song of want" (T)
12.19	8. "Winter" (S, A, T)
12.20	9. "The good life" (T)
12.21	10. "Song of the young girl" (S)
12.22	11. "Good fortune" (S, A, T)
12.23	"2 Romances" (c1950, Lermontov): 1. "Ballad: A beautiful maiden sits by the sea" Op.84
12.24	2. "Morning in the Caucasus"
12.25	"4 Songs" (c1950–1, Dolmatovsky): 1. "The Homeland hears" (w/ wordless ch/pf) Op.86
12.26	2. "Rescue me"
12.27	3. "He loves me, he loves me not" (We have many girls in the city)
12.28	4. "Lullaby: Sleep, my darling boy"
12.29	"4 Monologues" (c1952, Pushkin; B & pf): 1. "Estrangements" Op.91
12.30	2. "What does my name mean to you?"
12.31	3. "In the depths of the Siberian mines"
12.32	4. "Farewell"
12.33	"Homesickness" (c1952, Dolmatovsky, from film: Encounter at the Elbe, Op.80/13)...................................
12.34	"We meet this morning" (c1952, from film: Encounter at the Elbe, Op.80)..
12.35	"Greek Songs" (arr1952–3): 1. "Forward" (Song of the Greek Resistance transl Bolotin & Sikorskaya) ......
12.36	2. "Pentozalis" (Cretan folksong transl Bolotin)
12.37	3. (Mount) "Zolongo" (Greek folksong transl Sikorskaya)
12.38	4. "Hymn of the ELAS" (ELAS—Ellenikos Laïkos Apeletherotikos Stratos)
12.39	"5 Romances" (c1954, Dolmatovsky; B & pf): 1. "The Day of our First Meeting" Op.98
12.40	2. "The Day of Declaration of Love"
12.41	3. "The Day of Tiffs"
12.42	4. "The Day of Happiness"
12.43	5. "The Day of Reminiscences"
12.44	"There were kisses," romance (c1954, Dolmatovsky) ....
12.45	"Spanish Songs" (c1956, anon transl Bolotin & Sikorsky; S & pf): 1. "Farewell, Granada" Op.100
12.46	2. "Little Stars"
12.47	3. "First Meeting"
12.48	4. "Round Dance" (A Birth)
12.49	5. "Black Eyes"
12.50	6. "Dream" (Barcarolle)
12.51	"Satires" (Pictures of the Past), 5 songs (c1960, Chorny; S & pf): 1. "To a critic" Op.109
12.52	2. "Spring awakening" (Taste of Spring)
12.53	3. "Descendants" (Progeny)
12.54	4. "Misunderstanding"
12.55	5. "Kreuzer Sonata"
12.56	"A Walk into the Future" (c ?1962, from oratorio: The Song of the Forests, Op.81) ....
12.57	"5 Songs" (c1965, from journal 'Krokodil'; B & pf): 1. "The evidence of one's own manuscript" Op.121
12.58	2. "A desire too difficult to gratify"
12.59	3. "Discretion"
12.60	4. "Irinka and the Shepherd"
12.61	5. "Too much delight"
12.62	"Preface to the Complete Collection of my Works and Thoughts ..." (c1966; B & pf) Op.123
12.63	"Suite of Romances" (c1967, Blok; S & pf trio): 1. "Song of Ophelia" (also see Brahms WoO posth 22,
	Castelnuovo-Tedesco Op.24/VII/1–2, Elgar Op.21/1 & R. Strauss Op.67) Op.127
12.64	2. "Gamayun, the bird of prophecy"
12.65	3. "We were together" (That troubled night)
12.66	4. "The city sleeps" (Deep in sleep)
12.67	5. "The storm"
12.68	6. "Secret signs"
12.69	7. "Music"
12.70	"Spring, spring" (c1967, Pushkin; B & pf) Op.128
12.71	"6 Poems of Marina Tsvetayeva" (c1973; A & pf; orchd as Op.143a): 1. "My poems"...................... Op.143
12.72	2. "Whence such tenderness"
12.73	3. "Hamlet's dialogue with his conscience"
12.74	4. "The Poet and the Tsar"
12.75	5. "No, sounded the drum"
12.76	6. "To Anna Akhmatova"
12.77	"Suite on Verses of Michelangelo" (c1974, transl Efros; B & pf; orchd as Op.145a): 1. "Truth"......... Op.145
12.78	2. "Morning"
12.79	3. "Love"
12.80	4. "Separation"
12.81	5. "Anger"
12.82	6. "Dante"
12.83	7. "To the Exile"
12.84	8. "Creativity" (Art)
12.85	9. "Night—a dialogue"
12.86	10. "Death"
12.87	11. "Immortality"
12.88	"4 Verses of Captain Lebyadkin" (c1974, from Dostoyevsky's The Devils; B & pf): 1. "The Love of
	Captain Lebyadkin" (Miss Lisa Tushin)... Op.146
12.89	2. "The Cockroach"
12.90	3. "The Ball for the Benefit of Governess"

12.91   4. "A shining personality" (A pure soul)
12.92   "La Serenata" (c1970s, Marcello transl Gorchakova; 2 fem vv, vn & pf, from song c by Braga) ....

13. WARTIME CONCERT PARTY PIECES

13.1   "Oath to the People's Commissar" (c1941, Sayanov; B, ch & pf; 2nd vers w/ new words: The Great Day Has Come) ....

"27 Romances and Songs" (c1941; 1v & pf, arrs of works of others for Leningrad frontline concerts):

13.2   1. Beethoven: "Come fill, fill , my good fellow," Op.108/13 (transl Globa; w/ vc & pf) ....
13.3   2. Bizet: "Habanera" (from Act I of opera: Carmen) ....
13.4   3. Zhan Vekerlen: "Pastorale"
13.5   4. Leoncavallo: "Harlequin Serenade" (from Act II of opera: Pagliacci) ....
13.6   5. Rossini: "Alpine shepherds' song" (from opera: Guillaume Tell) ....
13.7   6. Verstovsky: "Gypsy Song"
13.8   7. Gulak-Artemovsky: "From where did you appear?," duet (from: The Zaporozhian Cossack) ....
13.9   8. Gurilyov: "Really, I will tell mama" (Berg) ....
13.10   9. Gurilyov: "The Little Sarafan" (Polezhayev) ....
13.11   10. Dargomyzhky: "What it is like in our street" ....
13.12   11. Dargomyzhky: "Comic Song" ....
13.13   12. Dargomyzhky: "Grenada is clothed in mists" (anon) ....
13.14   13. Dargomyzhky: "Feverishness" (trad) ....
13.15   14. Musorgsky: "Hopak" (Ukrainian poem of Shevchenko: Kaydamaki, transl Mey) ....
13.16   15. Musorgsky: "Parasya's Dumka" (from Act III of opera: Sorochintsy Fair) ....
13.17   16. Musorgsky: "Khivrya's Aria" (from opera: Sorochintsy Fair) ....
13.18   17. Rimsky-Korsakov: "Song of the Varangian (Viking) Merchant" (from Scene 4 of opera: Sadko) ....
13.19   18. Ippolitov-Ivanov: "I am sitting on a little rock" ....
13.20   19. Blanter: "Song about Shchors" (Golodny) ....
13.21   20. Dunayevsky: "Song of the Sea" ....
13.22   21. Dunayevsky: "Anyuta's Song" ....
13.23   22. Dunayevsky: "Sing to us, wind" (Lebedev-Kumach) ....
13.24   23. Dunayevsky: "Oh, good" ....
13.25   24. Milyutin: "Do not touch us" ....
13.26   25. D. & D. Pokrass: "Those are not storm clouds" (Surkov) ....
13.27   26. Danill Pokrass: "Farewell—He was given an order to go to the West" (Isakovsky) ....
13.28   27. Pritsker: "Song of the Young Girl" ....

Other:

13.29   "The Fearless Regiments Are on the Move" (c1941, Rakhmilevich; B, ch & pf) ....
13.30   "Polka," in F-sharp minor (arr1941; 2 harps, from Balakirev's work: Allegretto-Scherzando) ....

14. ARRANGEMENTS OF WORKS OF OTHERS

14.1   Rimsky-Korsakov: "I Waited for Thee in the Grotto," Op.40/4 (orchd1921)...................................
14.2   Youmans: "Tea for Two," song from operetta: No, No, Nanette (orchd1928 as: Tahiti Trot) Op.16
14.3   "2 Pieces by D. Scarlatti" (arr1928; wind band): No.1 "Pastorale" Op.17
14.4   No.2 "Capriccio"
14.5   Stravinsky: "Symphony of Psalms," for ch & orch (transcr1930s; pf duet) ....
14.6   Degeyter: "Internationale," song (orchd1937, adopted as Soviet National Anthem 1917–1944) ....
14.7   Strauss, J. Jr.: "Wiener Blut" (reorchd & ed1940) ....
14.8   Strauss, J. Jr.: "The Excursion Train Polka," Op.281 (reorchd1940)...................................
14.9   Musorgsky: "Boris Godunov," opera (reorchd1940, p1959) Op.58
14.10   Fleishman: "Rothschild's Violin" (Fiddle), chamber opera (compl by 1944, after Chekhov)...........................
14.11   Prokofiev: "War and Peace," opera Op.91 (prepared for publication, vocal score Atovmyan p1958) ....
14.12   Musorgsky: "Khovanshchina," opera (arr for film 1959) Op.106
14.13   Musorgsky: "Songs and Dances of Death" (orchd1962): 1. "Lullaby" ....
14.14   2. "Serenade"
14.15   3. "Trepak"
14.16   4. "The Warrior Captain" (The Field Marshal)
14.17   Davidenko: "2 Choruses" (orchd1962): 1. "To the Tenth Verst" (Ediet) Op.124
14.18   2. "Turmoil in the Street" (Shorin)
14.19   Schumann: Cello Concerto in A minor, Op.129 (reorchd1966) Op.125
14.20   Tishchenko: Cello Concerto No.1 (reorchd1969) ....
14.21   Beethoven: "Song of Mephistopheles in Auerbach's cellar," Op.75/3 (orchd1975) ....

*   *   *   *   *

1. STAGE WORKS

Operas:

1.1	*"The Creation of the Boat" (c1893, sketches)*	
1.2	"Jungfrun i tornet" (The Maiden in the Tower), 1 act (c1896, Herzberg, unpubd; arr for vv, ch & pf 1896)	

Incid music:

1.3	"Näcken" (The Watersprite), 2 songs for a fairy play (c1888, Wennerberg; w/ pf trio, unpubd)	
1.4	"Karelia" (Scenic music for a festival & lottery in aid of education in Viipuri) (c1893, unpubd)	
1.5	"Ödlan" (The Lizard) (c1909, Lybeck; vn & str qnt)	Op.8
1.6	"Press Celebrations," music for pageant (c1899, Bergbom, Leino & Finne)	
1.7	"Kuningas Kristian II" (King Christian II) (c1898, Paul)	Op.27
1.8	"Kuolema" (Death) (c1903, Järnefelt)	(Op.44)
1.9	"Pelléas et Mélisande" (c1905, Maeterlinck)	(Op.46)
1.10	"Belsazars gästabud" (Belshazzar's Feast) (c1906, Procopé)	(Op.51)
1.11	"Svanevit" (Swanwhite) (c1908, Strindberg; suite p1909)	(Op.54)
1.12	"Trettondagsafton" (Twelfth Night), 2 songs (c1909, Shakespeare transl Hagberg; 1v & gui/pf) (also see opera c by Smetana: Viola, T133 & overture c by Castelnuovo-Tedesco Op.73):	Op.60
	1. "Kom nu hit, död!" (Come away, death!) (arr for 1v, harp & strings 1957)	
	2. "Hållilå, uti storm och i regn" (When that I was and a little tiny boy)	
1.13	"Kuolema," 2 add pieces (c1911, for a new production; also see Op.44):	Op.62
	1. "Canzonetta" (strings)	
	2. "Valse romantique" (small orch)	
1.14	"The Language of the Birds," Wedding March for Act III (c1911, Paul, unpubd)	
1.15	"Scaramouche," tragic pantomime (c1913, Knudsen & Bloch)	Op.71
1.16	"Jokamies" (Everyman) (c1916, Hofmannsthal)	Op.83
1.17	"The Tempest" (c1925, Shakespeare transl Lembcke) (also see semi-opera c by Purcell Z631, incid music c by Honegger H48 & Sullivan Op.1)	Op.109

1a. SELECTIONS FROM STAGE WORKS

1a.4	"Karelia," incid music:	
	. "Ouverture" (= Op.10)	
	1. "Alla vivo—Più lento"	
	2. "Moderato assai" (w/ 2vv)	
	3. "Allegro—Moderato" (Moderato = Op.11/1)	
	4. "Tempo di menuetto non troppo lento" (Dansen i rosenlund; r vers as Op.11/2)	
	. "Intermezzo: Alla marcia, moderato" (= Op.11/3)	
	5. "Moderato ma non tanto" (w/ 1v)	
	6. "Vivace"	
	7.–8. "Moderato—Vivace molto—Più presto—Maestoso e largo" (The Finnish National Anthem Maamme / Vårt land c by F. Pacius)	
1a.6	"Press Celebrations," incid music:	
	. "Preludium: Andante" (ma non troppo)	
	1. "Allegro con moto" (r vers as: All'Overture, Op.25/1)	
	2. "Andante, ma non troppo lento"	
	3. "Quasi tempo di menuetto" (r vers as: Festivo, Op.25/3)	
	4. "Tempo di menuetto—Allegro moderato—Allegro molto" (r vers as No.2 of: Scènes, Op.25)	
	5. "Grave"	
	6. "Allegro moderato—Poco allegro" (r vers as ton poem: Finlandia, Op.26)	
1a.7	"King Christian II," incid music:	Op.27
	1a. "Élégie"	
	1b. "Musette"	
	1c. "Menuetto"	
	1d. "Fool's Song of the Spider"	
	2a. "Nocturne"	
	2b. "Serenade"	
	3. "Ballade"	
1a.8	"Kuolema," incid music:	(Op.44)
	1. "Tempo di valse lente—Dans" (r vers as: Valse triste, Op.44)	
	2. "Moderato"	
	3. "Moderato assai—Moderato—Poco adagio" (see note for 4.)	
	4. "Andante" (Scenes 3 & 4 r as: Scene with Cranes, Op.44/2)	
	5. "Moderato"	
	6. "Andante, ma non tanto"	
1a.9	"Pelléas et Mélisande," incid music:	(Op.46)
	1. "Förspiel. Grave e largamente" (= Op.46/1)	
	2. "Act I/2. Andantino con moto" (= Op.46/2)	

3. "Act I/4. Adagio" (= Op.46/2a)
4. "Act II. Förspiel. Commodo" (= Op.46/3)
5. "Act III/1. Förspiel. Con moto" (ma non tanto) (= Op.46/6)
6. "Act III/2. Tranquillo" (r vers as: The three blind Sisters, Op.46/4)
7. "Act III/4. Andantino pastorale" (= Op.46/5)
8. "Act IV/1. Förspiel. Allegretto" (= Op.46/7)
9. "Act IV/2." (w/ out tempo markings)
10. "Act V/2. Förspiel. Andante" (= Op.46/8)

1a.10 "Belshazzar's Feast," incid music: ....(Op.51)
　　　　I:　　1. "Alla marcia" (moderato)
　　　　II:　 2a. "Nocturno"
　　　　　　　2b. "The Jewish Girl's Song"
　　　　III:　3. "Allegretto"
　　　　　　　4. "Dance of Life" (Comodo)
　　　　　　　5. "Dance of Death" (Comodo)
　　　　　　　6. (part of 4. 'aber langsam')
　　　　IV:　 7. "Tempo sostenuto"
　　　　　　　8. "Allegro"
　　　　　　　9. (repeat of 4.) (shortened)
　　　　　　　10. (repeat of 5.)

1a.11 "Swanwhite," incid music: .... (Op.54)
　　　　I:　　1. "Largo" (Hornsignal)
　　　　　　　2. "Commodo"
　　　　　　　3. "Adagio"
　　　　II:　 4. "Lento assai
　　　　　　　5. "Adagio"
　　　　　　　6. "Lento—Allegro"
　　　　　　　7. "Andantino"
　　　　　　　8. "Andante"
　　　　　　　9. "Lento"
　　　　　　　10. "Moderato"
　　　　III:　11. "Allegretto"
　　　　　　　12. "Largamente"
　　　　　　　13. "Adagio"
　　　　　　　14. "Largamente molto"

1a.17 "The Tempest," incid music (Nos. of sections in The Gramophone): Op.109
　　　　excerpts: 1. "Overture"
　　　　I/1:　 2 "Miranda lulled to slumber"
　　　　　　　3. "Ariel approaches"
　　　　　　　4. "Chorus of the Winds"
　　　　　　　5. "Ariel hastens away"
　　　　　　　6. "Come unto these yellow sands" (Ariel's First Song)
　　　　　　　7. "Full fathom five" (Ariel's Second Song)
　　　　II/1:　8. "Entr'acte"
　　　　　　　9. "The oak tree (Ariel) plays the flute"
　　　　　　　10. "While you here do" (Ariel's Third Song)
　　　　II/2: 11. "Interlude" (Caliban)
　　　　　　　12. "The master, the swabber, the boatswain, and I" (Stephano's Song)
　　　　　　　13. "Farewell, master" (Caliban's Song)
　　　　III/1: 14. "Interlude" (Miranda)
　　　　III/2: 15. "Allegro commodo"
　　　　　　　16. "Flout 'em and scout 'em" (Canon)
　　　　III/3: 17. "Antonio—Dance of the Shapes"
　　　　　　　18. "Ariel, like a Harpy"
　　　　　　　19. "Dance 2" (The Shapes dance out)
　　　　IV/1: 20. "Intermezzo"
　　　　　　　21. "Ariel approaches"
　　　　　　　22. "Before you can say 'Come' and 'Go' " (Ariel's Fourth Song)
　　　　　　　23. "The Rainbow"
　　　　　　　24. "Iris's melodrama"
　　　　　　　25. "Honour, riches, marriage blessing" (Juno's Song)
　　　　　　　26. "Dance of the Naiads"
　　　　　　　27. "The harvesters"
　　　　　　　28. "Ariel approaches"
　　　　　　　29. "Ariel hastens away"
　　　　　　　30. "Ariel approaches"
　　　　　　　31. "The dogs"
　　　　V/1: 32. "Overture"
　　　　　　　33. "Where the bee sucks" (Ariel's Fifth Song)
　　　　　　　34. "Cortège"
　　　　　　　35. "Epilogue"

2. SYMPHONIES

3. OTHER ORCHESTRAL WORKS

6. OTHER CHAMBER MUSIC

7 or more insts:

5 insts:

Piano Quartets:

3 insts:

Vn & pf

8. OTHER PIANO WORKS

8.1	Piece in A major (c ?1885) ....
8.2	Piece in A minor (c ?1885) ....
8.3	Piece in E-flat major (c ?1885) ....
8.4	"Con moto, sempre una corda," in D-flat major (c1885) ....
8.5	Piece (?Arrangement) in E major (c ?1886) ....
8.6	Piece (?Arrangement) in E minor (c ?1886) ....
8.7	Short pieces for exercise: No.1 "Variations," in D major (ca1886) ....
8.8	No.2 Piece in E-flat minor (ca1887)
8.9	No.3 Piece in G-flat major (ca1887)
8.10	No.4 Piece in G major (ca1887)
8.11	No.5 Piece in C minor (ca1888)
8.12	No.6 "Menuetto" (ca1888)
8.13	No.7 Piece in D minor (ca1891–4)
8.14	No.8 Piece in B-flat minor (ca1895–8)
8.15	No.9 Piece in C minor (ca1902–5)
8.16	No.10 Piece in D-flat major (ca1918–21)
8.17	"Andante," in E-flat major (c ?1887) ....
8.18	"Molto andante" (c ?1887) ....
8.19	"Au crépuscule" (c1887) ....
8.20	Piece in A-flat major (c1887–8) ....
8.21	"Adagio," in D major (c ?1888) ....
8.22	"Allegretto," in B-flat minor (c ?1888) ....
8.23	"Allegretto," in G minor (c ?1888) ....
8.24	"Andantino," in B major (c ?1888) ....
8.25	"Largo," in A major (c ?1888) ....
8.26	"Più lento—Tempo di valse" (c ?1888) ....
8.27	"Moderato—Presto" (c ?1888) ....
8.28	"Vivace," in D minor (c ?1888) ....
8.29	Piece in E-flat major (c1888–9) ....
8.30	"Allegretto," in E major (c1889) ....
8.31	"Florestan," suite (c1889) ....
8.32	"A Betzy Lerche," waltz in A-flat major (c1889) ....
8.33	"6 Impromptus" (c1893): No.1 "Impromptu" Op.5
8.34	No.2 "Impromptu"
8.35	No.3 "Impromptu"
8.36	No.4 "Impromptu," in E minor (c1892–3)
8.37	No.5 "Impromptu," in B minor (c1890–3; arr for strings ?1893)
8.38	No.6 "Impromptu," in E major (c1890–3; arr for strings ?1893)
8.39	"Allegretto," in F major (c1894–6) ....
8.40	"Lento," in E major (c1895–7) ....
8.41	"18 19 / XII 97" (Allegretto), in G minor (c1897) ....
8.42	"10 Pieces" (c1894–1903): No.1 "Impromptu" (c1894) Op.24
8.43	No.2 "Romance," in A-flat major (c1895)
8.44	No.3 "Caprice" (c1898–9)
8.45	No.4 "Romance" (c1895)
8.46	No.5 "Waltz" (c1895)
8.47	No.6 "Idyll" (c ?1898)
8.48	No.7 "Andantino" (c1895)
8.49	No.8 "Nocturne" (c1900)
8.50	No.9 "Romance," in D-flat major (c1901)
8.51	No.10 "Barcarolle" (c1903)
8.52	"Marche triste" (c1899–1900) ....
8.53	"The Cavalier" (c1900) ....
8.54	Piece in C minor (ca1902–5) ....
8.55	"Finnish Folksongs" (c1903, arrs): No.1 "My beloved" ....
8.56	No.2 "From my heart I love you"
8.57	No.3 "The evening is coming"
8.58	No.4 "The maiden is playing the Kantele"
8.59	No.5 "The brother's murderer"
8.60	No.6 "The wedding memory"
8.61	"Bagatelles" (c1914–6): No.1 "Waltz" Op.34
8.62	No.2 "Dance Air"
8.63	No.3 "Mazurka"
8.64	No.4 "Couplet"
8.65	No.5 "Drollery"
8.66	No.6 "Rêverie"
8.67	No.7 "Pastoral Dance"
8.68	No.8 "The Harper"
8.69	Added later: No.9 "Reconnaissance"
8.70	No.10 "Souvenir"
8.71	"Pensées lyriques" (c1912–4): No.1 "Valsette" Op.40
8.72	No.2 "Chant sans paroles"
8.73	No.3 "Humoresque"

8.149	No.5 "Couplet"
8.150	No.6 "Animoso"
8.151	No.7 "Moment de valse"
8.152	No.8 "Petite marche"
8.153	"5 Romantic Pieces" (c1923): No.1 "Romance" Op.101
8.154	No.2 "Chant du soir"
8.155	No.3 "Scène lyrique"
8.156	No.4 "Humoresque"
8.157	No.5 "Scène romantique"
8.158	"5 Characteristic Impressions" (c1924): No.1 "The Village Church" Op.103
8.159	No.2 "The Fiddler"
8.160	No.3 "The Oarsman"
8.161	No.4 "The Storm"
8.162	No.5 "In Mournful Mood"
8.163	"Episodio, Scena and Canzone" (c1924–7, arr from incid music: Everyman, Op.83) ....
8.164	"Morceau romantique par Jacob de Julin" (c ?1925; see orig for orch) ....
8.165	"5 Esquisses" (c1929): No.1 "Landscape" Op.114
8.166	No.2 "Winter Scene"
8.167	No.3 "Forest Lake"
8.168	No.4 "Song in the Forest"
8.169	No.5 "Spring Vision"

9. ORGAN

9.1	"Postludium," in D minor (c ?1925) ....
9.2	"Preludium," in F major (c ?1925) ....
9.3	"2 Pieces": No.1 "Intrada" (c1925) Op.111
9.4	No.2 "Funeral music" (c1931, memory of Akseli Gallen-Kallela)

10. CHORAL WORKS

10.1	"Up through the air" (c ?1888, Atterbom; ch & pf) ....
10.2	"Alone in the depths of the forest" (c ?1888; ch) ....
10.3	"How pale is all" (c ?1888; ch) ....
10.4	"When spring once more comes to life" (c ?1888; ch) ....
10.5	"Imagine, see how the bird swoops" (c ?1888, Runeberg; ch) ....
10.6	"Ballade": "Ack, hör du fröken gyllenborg" (c1888–9; ch) ....
10.7	"Why kiss you, father, my sweetheart here?" (c1890–1; ch & pf) ....
10.8	"Kullervo," sym poem (c1892, from Kalevala; S, Bar, m ch & orch): Op.7
	1. "Introduction"
	2. "The Youth of Kullervo"
	3. "Kullervo and His Sister" (arr for vv, ch & pf)
	4. "Kullervo Leaves for the War"
	5. "Kullervo's Death" (arr for vv, ch & pf)
10.9	"Rakastava" (The Lover) (c1892, from Kanteletar; m ch; r1894 w/ strings; also see Op.14): ....
	1. "Where is my beloved?"
	2. "Eilaa, Eilaa ..." (My beloved's path)
	3. "Good evening, my little bird"
	4. "Put your hand on my shoulder"
10.10	"Pieces for exercise": 1. Piece in A minor (ca1893–5; ch) ....
10.11	2. "Canon" (ca1895–8; ch) ....
10.12	"Workers' March" (c1893–6, Erkko; ch) ....
10.13	"9 Partsongs" (c1893–1904): 1. "To the Fatherland" (c1899, r1900, r ca1938, Cajander) Op.18
10.14	2. "My brothers abroad" (Aho)
10.15	3. "Fire on the island" (from Kanteletar, Canto 186)
10.16	4. "Busy as a thrush" (from Kanteletar, Canto 219; m ch)
10.17	5. "The woodman's song" (Kivi)
10.18	6. "The song of my heart" (Kivi)
10.19	7. "The broken voice" (from Kanteletar, Canto 57)
10.20	8. "Hail! moon" (from Kalevala)
10.21	9. "The boat journey" (from Kalevala)
10.22	"Impromptu": "Thou who guidest the Stars" (c1902, r1910, Rydberg; fem ch & orch) Op.19
10.23	"Cantata for the Helsinki University Ceremonies of 1894" (c1894, Leino; ch & orch) ....
10.24	"Hymn: Natus in curas" (c1896, Gustafson; ch) Op.21
10.25	"Cantata for the Coronation of Nicholas II" (c1896, Cajander; vv, ch & orch) ....
10.26	"Morning Mist" (c1896, Erkko; child ch) ....
10.27	"Ohi, 'Caroli'!" (c1896–9; ch, arr of Italian folksong)
10.28	"Cantata for the Helsinki University Ceremonies of 1897" (c1897, Koskimies; vv, ch & orch): Op.23
	choral excerpts: 1. "We, the youth of Finland"
	2. "The wind rocks"
	3. "Oh hope, hope you dreamer"
	4. "Many on the sea of life"
	5. "The fading thoughts of the earth"

      6a. "Let thanks ring to the Lord"
      6b. "Blow, blow gentler"
      7. "Love, your realm is vast"
      8. "As the swift current"
      9. "Oh, precious Finland, mother beyond compare"

10.29   "The wind rocks" (c ?1899; S, Bar & ch, arr from No.2 of cantata Op.23) Op.23/2
10.30   "Sandels," improvisation (c1898, r1915, Runeberg; m ch & orch).. Op.28
10.31   "Carminalia" (c1898, Latin student songs; ch, pf/harm): 1. "Ecce novum gaudium" ....
10.32   2. "Angelus emittitur"
10.33   3. "In stadio laboris"
10.34   "Snöfrid," improvisation (c1900, Rydberg; recit, m ch & orch; arr for ch & pf ?1927) Op.29
10.35   "Islossningen i Uleå älv" (The breaking of the ice on the river Uleå), improvisation (c1898, Topelius;
        reciter, m ch & orch) Op.30
10.36   "Laulu Lemminkäiselle" (A song for Lemminkäinen) (c1896, Veijola; ch & orch) Op.31/1
10.37   "Har du mod?" (Have you courage?) (c1904, r1912, Wecksell; m ch & orch) Op.31/2
10.38   "Atenarnes sång" (Song of the Athenians) (c1899, Rydberg; boys' ch, m ch, brass & perc;
        arr w/ orch) Op.31/3
10.39   "Kotikaipaus" (Nostalgia) (c1902, Konow; fem ch) ....
10.40   "Den 25 Oktober 1902. Til Thérèse Hahl" (c1902, Wasatjerna; ch) ....
10.41   "Tulen synty" (The Origin of Fire / Ukko the Firemaker) (c1902, r1910, from Kalevala; Bar, m ch
        & orch) Op.32
10.42   "Ej med klagan" (Not with lamentations) (c1905, Runeberg; ch) ....
10.43   "Vapautettu kuningatar" (The Liberated Queen), cantata (c1906, Cajander; ch & orch) Op.48
10.44   "Listen to the water mill ..." (c1906–7; unison ch)...
10.45   "Kansakoululaisten" (Primary school children's march) (c1910, Pekka; child ch) ....
10.46   "Cantata" (c1911, Konow; fem ch)..
10.47   "2 Partsongs" (c1911–2, Knape & Engström; ch): 1. "People of land and sea" Op.65
10.48   2. "Melody for the bells of Kallio church"
10.49   "Drömmarna" (Dreams) (c1912, Reuter; ch) ....
10.50   "Uusmaalaisten" (Song for the People of Uusimaa) (c1912, Terhi; ch) ....
10.51   "3 Songs for American Schools" (c1913): 1. "Autumn Song" (Dixon; 2vv & pf).................................
10.52   2. "The sun upon the lake is low" (Scott; ch)
10.53   3. "A cavalry catch" (Mcleod; unison m vv & pf)
10.54   "5 Partsongs" (c1914–5; m ch): 1. "Mr. Lager and the fair one" (Fröding) Op.84
10.55   2. "On the mountain" (Gripenberg)
10.56   3. "A dream chord" (Fröding)
10.57   4. "Eternal Eros" (Gripenberg)
10.58   5. "To sea" (Reuter)
10.59   "Kuutamolla" (In the moonlight) (c1916, Suonio; m ch) ....
10.60   "March of the Finnish Jaeger Battalion" (c1917, Nurmio; m ch; orchd ?1917) Op.91/1
10.61   "Fridolins dårskap" (Fridolin's folly) (c1917, Karlfeldt; m ch) ....
10.62   "Brusande rusar en våg" (The roaring of a wave) (c1918, Schybergson; m ch) ....
10.63   "Jone havsfärd" (Jonah's voyage) (c1918, Karlfeldt; m ch) ....
10.64   "Ute hörs stormen" (One hears the storm outside) (c1918, Schybergson; m ch).................................
10.65   "Oma maa" (Our native land), cantata (c1918, Kallio; ch & orch) Op.92
10.66   "Jordens sång" (Song of the Earth), cantata (c1919, Hemmer; ch & orch) Op.93
10.67   "Maan virsi" (Hymn to the Earth), cantata (c1920, Leino; ch & orch) Op.95
10.68   "Viipurin lauluveikkojen kuuniamarssi" (Honour march of the singing brothers of Viipuri) (c1920, Eerola;
        m ch; 2nd vers 1929) ....
10.69   "Scout March" (c1921, Procopé; ch; arr w/ pf 1922, arr for 2vv & pf as: The World Song—of the World
        Association of Girl Guides & Girl Scouts ?1951) Op.91/2
10.70   "Likhet" (Resemblance) (c1922, Runeberg; m ch) ....
10.71   "God's blessing," hymn (c1925; ch & org) Op.107/1
10.72   "3 Introductory Antiphons" (c1925; ch) Op.107/2
10.73   "2 Partsongs" (c1925, Kyösti; m ch): 1. "Humoresque" Op.108
10.74   2. "Wanderers on the long way"
10.75   "Skolsång" (School Song) (c1925–9, Runeberg; ch) ....
10.76   "Song of the 'Skyddskär' " (c1925–9, Runeberg; ch & pf ad lib)..
10.77   "Väinö's song" (c1926, from Kalevala; ch & orch) Op.110
10.78   "You are mighty, O Lord," hymn (c1927, Korpela; ch) ....
10.79   "Masonic Ritual Music" (c1927, r1948; m ch, pf & org): 1. "Introduction" Op.113
10.80   2. "Thoughts be our comfort" (Schiller)
10.81   3. "Introduction and Hymn" (Confucius)
10.82   4. "Marcia" (Goethe)
10.83   5. "Light": "How fair are earth and living!" (Simelius)
10.84   6. "Salem": "Onward, ye brethren" (Rydberg)
10.85   7. "Whosoever hath a love" (Rydberg)
10.86   8. "Ode to Fraternity" (c1946, Sario)
10.87   9. "Hymn of Praise" (c1946, Sario)
10.88   10. "Marche funèbre"
10.89   11. "Ode" (Korpela)
10.90   12. "Finlandia Hymn" (c1938, Sola; ch, arr from ton poem: Finlandia, Op.26)
10.91   "Sittavahti" (The bridge guard) (c1928, Sola; m ch; arr for 1v & pf)...
10.92   "Christmas Song" (c1928–9, Jaakkola; ch; alternative words Forsman) ....
10.93   "Karjalan osa" (Karelia's fate), patriotic march (c1930, Nurminen; m ch & pf) ....

11. VOICE & ORCHESTRA

11.1	"Arioso" (The Maiden's Seasons) (c1893, r1913, Runeberg; S & orch; arr w/ pf ?1911)	Op.3
11.2	"Serenade" (c1895, Stagnelius; Bar & orch)	
11.3	"The Ferrymen's Brides" (c1897, Oksanen; arr w/ pf 1897–9; arr for m ch & orch 1943)	Op.33
11.4	"Luonnotar" (The Spirit of Nature), tone poem (c1913, from Kalevala; S & orch)	Op.70

12. MUSIC FOR RECITATIONS

12.1	"Longing" (c1887, Stagnelius; recit & pf) ....
12.2	"Nights of Jealousy" (c1888, Runeberg; recit & pf trio) ....
12.3	"The Wood Nymph" (The Dryad) (c1895, Rydberg; reciter, pf, 2hn & strings; orig for orch) ....(Op.15)
12.4	"The Countess's Portrait" (c1906, Topelius; strings & orch)..
12.5	"The Lonely Ski Trail" (c1925, Gripenberg; recit & pf; arr w/ harp & strings 1948)............................

13. SONGS (w/ pf)

13.1	"Serenade" (c1888, Runeberg)	
13.2	"A song" (c1888, Baeckman)	
13.3	"When worlds still uncreated were" (c1888–9; w/ ?vc & pf, inc)	
13.4	"Orgies" (c1888–9, Stenbäck)	
13.5	*"The Wood Nymph" (c1888–9, Rydberg, frags)*	
13.6	"Alikeness" (c1890, Runeberg)	
13.7	"Tule, tule kultani," folksong (arr ?1892, inc)	
13.8	"5 Christmas Songs" (c1895–1913): 1. "Now stands Yule at the snowy gate" (Topelius)	Op.1
13.9	2. "Now is Christmas coming" (Topelius)	
13.10	3. "Outside it grows dark" (Topelius)	
13.11	4. "Give me no splendour" (Topelius; arr for 1v & boys' ch/fem ch)	
13.12	5. "High are the snowdrifts" (Joukahainen)	
13.13	"Kullervo's Lament" (p1917–8; Bar & pf, arr from sym poem: Kullervo, Op.7/3)	(Op.7/3)
13.14	"7 Songs of Runeberg": 1. " 'Neath the Fir trees" (c1892)	Op.13
13.15	2. "A hope for a kiss" (c1892)	
13.16	3. "The heart's morning" (c1891)	
13.17	4. "Spring is flying" (c1891; orchd1914)	
13.18	5. "The dream" (c1891)	
13.19	6. "To Fricka" (c1892)	
13.20	7. "The young hunter" (c1891)	
13.21	"7 Songs": 1. "And I questioned then no further" (c1894, Runeberg; orchd1903)	Op.17
13.22	2. "Slumber" (c1894, Tavaststjerna; orchd)	
13.23	3. "Enticement" (c1891, Tavaststjerna; orchd)	
13.24	4. "Astray" (c1894, Tavaststjerna)	
13.25	5. "Dragon-fly" (c ?1894, Levertin)	
13.26	6. "To evening" (c1898, Forsman-Koskimies)	
13.27	7. "Driftwood" (c1898, Calamnius)	
13.28	"Sailing" (c1899, Öhqvist)	
13.29	"Row, row duck" (The blue duck) (c1899, Koskimies)	
13.30	*"Andantino," in E-flat minor (c1899–1903, inc: without words)*	
13.31	*Piece in G major (c1899–1903, inc: without words)*	
13.32	"2 Songs" (c1907–8): 1. "Jubal" (Josephson; orchd)	Op.35
13.33	2. "Theodora" (Gripenberg)	
13.34	"6 Songs" (c1899): 1. "Black roses" (Josephson)...	Op.36
13.35	2. "But my bird is long in homing" (Runeberg)	
13.36	3. "Tennis at Trianon" (Fröding; orchd)	
13.37	4. "Sigh, sedges, sigh" (Fröding)	
13.38	5. "March snow" (Wecksell)	
13.39	6. "The diamond on the March snow" (Wecksell; orchd)	
13.40	"5 Songs": 1. "The first kiss" (c1898, Runeberg)	Op.37
13.41	2. "Little Lasse" (Berceuse) (c1902, Topelius)	
13.42	3. "Sunrise" (c1902, Hedberg)	
13.43	4. "Was it a dream?" (c1902, Wecksell)	
13.44	5. "The maiden's tryst" (c1901, Runeberg)	
13.45	"5 Songs": 1. "Autumn evening" (c1903, Rydberg; orchd1907)...	Op.38
13.46	2. "On a balcony by the sea" (c1902, Rydberg; orchd)	
13.47	3. "In the night" (c1903, Rydberg; orchd)	
13.48	4. "The harper and his son" (c1904, Rydberg)	
13.49	5. "I wish I dwelt in India land" (c1904, Fröding)	
13.50	"The fire has died out" (c1906, Busse-Palmo)	
13.51	"6 Songs" (c1906): 1. "A song of spring" (Fitger)	Op.50
13.52	2. "Longing" (Weiss)	
13.53	3. "A maiden yonder sings" (Susman)	
13.54	4. "O, wert thou here" (Dehmel; orchd)	
13.55	5. "The silent town" (Dehmel)	
13.56	6. "The song of the roses" (Ritter)	

13.57	"8 Songs" (c1909, Josephson): 1. "Älvan and the snail" Op.57
13.58	2. "A little flower in the path"
13.59	3. "The millwheel"
13.60	4. "May"
13.61	5. "The bare tree"
13.62	6. "Duke Magnus"
13.63	7. "The flower of friendship"
13.64	8. "The elf king"
13.65	"Hymn to Thaïs, the Unforgettable" (c1909, Borgström) ....
13.66	"Friendship" (c ?1909, Josephson, words = Op.57/7) ....
13.67	"8 Songs" (c1910): 1. "Slowly as the evening sun" (Tavaststjerna)..................... Op.61
13.68	2. "Lapping waters" (Rydberg)
13.69	3. "When I dream" (Tavaststjerna)
13.70	4. "Romeo" (Tavaststjerna)
13.71	5. "Romance" (Tavaststjerna)
13.72	6. "Dolce far niente" (Tavaststjerna)
13.73	7. "Idle wishes" (Runeberg)
13.74	8. "Spell of springtime" (Gripenberg)
13.75	"6 Songs": 1. "Farewell" (c1914, Rydberg) Op.72
13.76	2. "Orion's belt" (c1914, Topelius)
13.77	3. "The kiss" (c1915, Rydberg)
13.78	4. "The echo nymph" (c1915, Kyösti)
13.79	5. "The wanderer and the brook" (c1915, Greif)
13.80	6. "A hundred ways" (c1907, Runeberg)
13.81	"The Thought" (c1915, Runeberg; 2S & pf) ....
13.82	"6 Songs" (c1916): 1. "The coming of spring" (Tavaststjerna)...................... Op.86
13.83	2. "Longing is my heritage" (Karlfeldt)
13.84	3. "Hidden union" (Snoilsky)
13.85	4. "And is there a thought?" (Tavaststjerna)
13.86	5. "The singer's reward" (Snoilsky)
13.87	6. "Ye sisters, ye brothers" (Lybeck)
13.88	"6 Songs" (c1917): 1. "The anemone" (Franzén) Op.88
13.89	2. "The two roses" (Franzén)
13.90	3. "The star-flower" (The wood anemone) (Franzén)
13.91	4. "The primrose" (Runeberg)
13.92	5. "The thornbush" (Runeberg)
13.93	6. "The flower's destiny" (Runeberg)
13.94	"6 Songs" (c1917, Runeberg): 1. "The North" Op.90
13.95	2. "Her message"
13.96	3. "The morning"
13.97	4. "The bird-catcher"
13.98	5. "Summer night"
13.99	6. "Who has brought you here?"
13.100	"Birthday Song to Grand Mother" (c ?1919, inc) ....
13.101	"Little girls" (c1920, Procopé) ....
13.102	"Narcissus" (c1925, Gripenberg) ....

* * * * *

1. STAGE WORKS

1.1   *"Mysterium" (project) (In his last years Skryabin was preoccupied with the idea of the "Mysterium"—a visionary work combining theatre, painting, dance, and music. Many compositions of those years listed here separately were to be incorporated in this huge mystical work. However, only scarce sketches of the work itself survive.)....*

2. SYMPHONIES

2.1	Symphony No.1 in E major (c1899–1900; w/ mS, T & ch in Finale)	Op.26
2.2	Symphony No.2 in C min / major (c1901)	Op.29
2.3	Symphony No.3 in C minor, "Divine Poem" (c1902–4)	Op.43
2.4	Symphony No.4 in C major, "Poem of Ecstasy" (c1905–8)	Op.54
2.5	Symphony No.5 in F-sharp major, "Prometheus, the Poem of Fire" (c1908–10; w/ pf & ch; based on his 'mystic chord' / 'Prometheus chord'—an underlying dissonant harmony becoming an artificial tonic. This new system of tonal organization will permeate most of his subsequent works. It is compared to Schoenberg's 12-tone method.)	Op.60

3. OTHER ORCHESTRAL WORKS

3.1	"Symphonic Poem," in D minor (c1896–7)	
3.2	"Rêverie," in E major (c1898)	Op.24
3.3	"Andante" (c1899; strings)	

4. PIANO CONCERTOS, PIANO & ORCH

4.1	Piano Concerto in F-sharp minor (c1896)	Op.20

5. STRING QUARTETS

5.1	"Variation No.2," for collab work: Variations on a Russian Theme (c1899)	

6. OTHER CHAMBER MUSIC

6.1	"Romance" (c1890; hn & pf)	

7. PIANO SONATAS

7.1	"Sonate-fantaisie" (c1886)	
7.2	Piano Sonata in E-flat minor (c1887–9)	
7.3	Piano Sonata No.1 in F minor (c1892)	Op.6
7.4	Piano Sonata No.2 in G-sharp minor, "Sonata-Fantasy" (c1892–7)	Op.19
7.5	Piano Sonata No.3 in F-sharp minor, "Etats d'âme" (c1897–8)	Op.23
7.6	Piano Sonata No.4 in F-sharp major (c1903)	Op.30
7.7	Piano Sonata No.5 in F-sharp major, "The Poem of Ecstasy" (c1907)	Op.53
7.8	Piano Sonata No.6 in G major (c1911)	Op.62
7.9	Piano Sonata No.7 in F-sharp major, "White Mass" (c1911)	Op.64
7.10	Piano Sonata No.8 in A major (c1912–3)	Op.66
7.11	Piano Sonata No.9 in F major, "Black Mass" (c1912–3)	Op.68
7.12	Piano Sonata No.10 in C major, "Trill" (c1913)	Op.70

8. OTHER PIANO WORKS

8.1	"Canon" (c1883)	
8.2	"Nocturne," in A-flat major (c1884)	Op.1
8.3	"Valse," in F minor (c1885)	
8.4	"Valse," in G-sharp minor (c1886)	
8.5	"Valse," in D-flat major (c1886)	
8.6	"Variations on a Theme by Mlle Egorova" (c1887)	Op.2
8.7	"3 Pieces" (c1887–9): No.1 "Etude," in C-sharp minor	
8.8	No.2 "Prelude," in B major	
8.9	No.3 "Impromptu-Mazurka," in C major	
8.10	"Feuillet d'album," in A-flat major (c1889)	Op.3
8.11	"10 Mazurkas" (c1889): No.1 in B minor	
8.12	No.2 in F-sharp minor	
8.13	No.3 in G minor	
8.14	No.4 in E major	
8.15	No.5 in D-sharp minor	
8.16	No.6 in C-sharp minor	

*   *   *   *   *

1. STAGE WORKS (operas)

1.1   "Braniboři v Čechách" (The Brandenburgers in Bohemia), 3 acts (c1863, Sabina) .... B124 ..... T90
1.2   "Prodaná Nevěsta" (The Bartered Bride), 2 act comic opera (c1864–70, Sabina; 4 vers): T93
     . Original Version (p1866) .... B131 ....
     . Revised Version 1, 2 acts (r1869) .... B137 ....
     . Revised Version 2, 3 acts (r1869) .... B140 ....
     . Definitive Version, 3 acts (r1869–70) T96
1.3   "Dalibor," 3 act tragic opera (c1867, Wenzig in German): ....
     . Original Version (c1867, Wenzig in German) .... B133 ....
     . Revised Version (r1870, Czech transl Špindler) .... B144 ....
1.4   "Libuše," 3 act festival opera (c1869–72, Wenzig in German; Czech transl Špindler) T107
1.5   "Dvě Vdovy" (The Two Widows), 2 act comic opera (c1873–4, r1877, Züngel after Mallefille) T109
1.6   "Hubička" (The Kiss), 2 act popular opera (c1875–6, Krásnohorská after Světlá) T115
1.7   "Tajemství" (The Secret), 3 act comic opera (c1877–8, Krásnohorská) T118
1.8   "Čertova stěna" (The Devil's Wall), 3 act comic-romantic opera (c1879–82, Krásnohorská) T129
1.9   *"Viola," romantic opera (c1874, 1883–4, Krásnohorská after Shakespeare's 12th Night, inc: frag of Act I) (also*
      see incid music c by Sibelius Op.60 & overture c by Castelnuovo-Tedesco Op.73) T133

1a. SELECTIONS FROM STAGE WORKS

1a.1   "The Brandenburgers in Bohemia," opera: .... B124 ..... T90
     I: 1. "Or is it possible that in this world there could be something nobler than love?," aria (Ludiše)
          2. "O God, arise to our help," trio (Ludiše, Vlčenka, Děčana)
          3. (Ballet)
          4. "Now at last came our time! And the gates were thrown open!," chorus
          5. "You seem to be a burgher's daughter, where then are all your admirers," aria (Jíra)
          6. (Theme)
     II: 7. "O Lord, into the dust we're falling," aria (Old villager)
          8. "O sun, brighten for joy and shine," chorus
          9. "O, how lovely are the scenes of Nature!," aria (Děčana)
         10. "O where is he ... There is no beauty for us," duet (Vlčenka, Ludiše)
         11. "What a lovely dream. That splendid day of my first love!," aria (Ludiše)
         12. "O how blissful, lovely is this moment," duet (Ludiše, Junoš)
         13. "Now then my maidens, my lovely girls! Money is not coming, so we'll be going," aria (Setník)
         14. "Firmly do I believe in freedom," quartet (Ludiše, Vlčenka, Děčana, Setník)
     III: 15. "Introduction" (Tempo di marcia)
         16. "Your image, maiden, like an angel, is caressing me constantly," aria (Tausendmark)
         17. "All of a sudden I am afraid," duet (Ludiše, Děčana)
         18. "The night is quiet, quiet and calm! Everything's sleeping," chorus
         19. "What a sorrow, what a sorrow for her sorely tried father," aria (Old villager)
         20. "You'll be with us, we shall be united without sorrow," duet (Vlčenka, Děčana)

1a.2   "The Bartered Bride," opera (Nos. of sections in The Gramophone): .... B131 ..... T93
         1. "Overture" (also for pf duet 1863)
     I: 2. "Let rejoice, let's be merry while the Lord grants us," opening chorus
          3. "Should I ever happen to learn something like that about you," aria (Mařenka)
          4. "While a mother's love means blessing," duet (Mařenka, Jeník)
          5. "Faithful love cannot be marred by any former pledge or promise," duet (Mařenka, Jeník)
          6. "As I'm saying my dear fellow, you have pledged your word," aria (Kecal)
          7. "Things like these can't be fixed," trio (Ludmilla, Krušina, Kecal)
          8. "He's timid and not used to female society," aria (Kecal)
         9a. "You don't even suspect the hitch there's in it" (Mařenka)
         9b. "And where everybody fails it is his luck to succeed," quartet
         9c. "Polka"
     II: 10. "Beer's no doubt a gift from Heaven," chorus
         11. "Furiant"
         12. "My...my...mother dear sa...sa...sa...said to me," aria (Vašek)
         13. "I know of a maiden fair whose love for you is boundless," duet (Mařenka, Vašek)
          . "Would you like a girl like me?," duet (Mařenka, Vašek)
          . "Now then, my dear man, will you listen to a word or two," duet (Jeník, Kecal)
         14. "Every man maintains his wife is best," aria (Kecal)
         15. "I know a girl, she's got the money," duet (Jeník, Kecal)
        16a. "How could they believe I would ever sell my Mařenka?," aria (Jeník)
        16b. "Come inside, people! Listen to me!" (Kecal)
        16c. "Is it really true that he renouced his sweetheart?," chorus
        16d. "Quite a bargain 'tis! He has for three golden gulden sold his sweetheart," finale
     III: 17. "I can't get it off my mind, my life is at stake!," aria (Vašek)
         18. "March of the Comedians"
         19. "Dance of the Comedians" (Skočná)
        20a. "We will make a graceful little bear of you," duet (Esmeralda, Principal)
        20b. "What? He does not want her?," quartet (Háta, Vašek, Mícha, Kecal)
        20c. "Well then, she's Mařenka, she's your future wife" (Ludmila, Háta, Vašek & others)
         21. "Think it over, Mařenka," sextet (Mařenka, Ludmilla, Háta, Krušina, Mícha, Kecal)

22a. "Oh, what a grief! what burning pain when a loving heart's deceived!," aria (Mařenka)
22b. "That dream of love, how fair it was," aria (Mařenka)
23. "Are you really so stubborn, dear, that you won't learn the truth?," duet (Mařenka, Jeník)
24. "Calm down, calm down, dear," aria (Jeník)
25a. "Now I shall call in your parents," trio (Mařenka, Jeník, Kecal)
25b. "What have you decided, Mařenka? Speak!," chorus
25c. "Oh, he's a cunning man all right! I'm totally defeated!," finale (Kecal)
25d. "Ha ha ha ha," chorus

1a.3   "Dalibor," opera (Nos. of sections in The Gramophone): .... B133 ..... T96
       1. "Overture"
I: 2. "An orphan, abandoned amid some ancient ruins," aria (Jítka)
     . "Entrance of the King" (orch)
     3. "You know by now how our kingdom fair," aria (Vladislav)
     4a. "Oh hear of what I must complain"
     4b. "The sun has set and in the castle we all fell sound asleep," recit (Milada)
     5a. "I won't deny it," recit (Dalibor)
     . "Me female charm has never yet bewitched! A friend to have was my heart's one desire" (Dalibor)
     5b. "When Zdenek mine," aria (Dalibor)
     . "No meaning has my life since Zdenek is away!," duet (Dalibor, Milada)
     6. "Oh, didst thou hear it, friend?," aria (Dalibor)
     . "Here do you see me bending low," aria (Milada)
     7. "What storm in bosom mine is raging?," duet (Milada, Jítka)
II: 8. "Oh yes, yet the gayest in this our world," chorus
     9. "My dearest, my yearning, my heart's delight," duet (Jítka, Vítek)
     10. "Oh, how saddening is a jailer's life," aria (Beneš)
     11. "Oh, goodness! Now so quickly came to me," aria (Milada)
     . "Dalibor's dream" (orch)
     12a. "It was he again" (Dalibor)
     12b. "Oh, Zdenek, just one fleeting touch of hand," aria (Dalibor)
     13. "You're asking who I were! Oh, you haven't even paid attention then to me?," aria (Milada)
     14. "Dalibor, I beg your pardon ... Oh, unspeakable charm of love," duet (Milada, Dalibor)
III: 15. "It will be near to forty years that faithfully I do my task," aria (Beneš)
     16a. "At this late hour"
     16b. "Beautiful aim that any king can follow," aria (Vladislav)
     17a. "It's the third night"
     17b. "Oh, by what marvel thou, o freedom, cometh," aria (Dalibor)
     18. "Let so it be! I'm now prepared to die," aria (Dalibor)
     . (orch)

1a.4   "Libuše," opera: T107
       1. "Prelude"
I: . "Opening" (orch)
     2. "Eternal gods, ye that dwell above the clouds," aria (Libuše)
     3. "You elders, nobles! I come before you here, I, Krok's daughter," aria (Libuše)
II: 4. "My father, before you proclaim your severe judgment," aria (Krasava)
     5. "And so when he in love's sweet yearning," aria (Krasava)
     6. "Without rest onwards & out in the fields," quartet
     7. "The sun is blazing, a peaceful dream is embracing whole nature," aria (Přemysl)
     8. "O, ye lime trees, forefathers' hands have planted you here," aria (Přemysl)
     9. "Ah, look into his face, it shines with happiness," duet (Radovan, Přemysl)
     10. "Peace be with you, my father's quiet gardens," aria (Přemysl)
III: 11. "Introduction" (orch)
     12. "Welcome!," choral scene
     13. "Hail, stronghold of Vyšehrad!," aria (Přemysl)
     14. "O gods almighty," aria (Libuše)
     . "Tableau I" (orch)
     . "Tableau II" (orch)
     . "Tableau III" (orch)
     . "Tableau IV" (orch) (music also in sym poem: Tabor, B120, T120)
     . "Tableau V" (orch)

1a.5   "The Two Widows," opera: T109
       1. "Overture"
I: . "Lovely morning, brilliant sky is greeting us," opening chorus
     . "Tra la la tra la la" (ch)
     . "These are the good, the golden times of harvest-home!" (ch)
     2. "Independently do I rule over my vast estates!," aria (Karolína)
     . "Good morning our gracious lady!," aria (Mumlal)
     . "Ha, ha, ha, ha, ha, ha. What a bit of thrilling news!," trio (Karolína, Anežka, Mumlal)
     3. "O what anxiety my heart is feeling!," quartet (Anežka, Karolína, Ladislav, Mumlal)
     4. "Oh, behold a lonely hunter! A lovely nymph has charmed, bewitched his heart," aria (Ladislav)
     . "You vain little woman," trio (Karolína, Anežka, Ladislav)
II: 5. "Introduction"
     6. "When the Maytime comes, time of love," aria (Ladislav)

    7. "It's decided, it's completed! He's refused and to her ceded!," duet (Karolína, Anežka)
    8. "Your cold resistance hurts my heart. I'm craving for your love," duet (Ladislav, Anežka)
    9. "Oh, what a lovely day! A day made for joy!," aria (Anežka)
    10. "No matter what rouses my anger, I rightaway give vent to it," aria (Mumlal)
    11. "What's the matter, girl? Why this sudden pride?," trio (Toník, Lidka, Mumlal)
    . "Ah, what a painful surprise!," quartet (Karolína, Anežka, Ladislav, Mumlal)
    . "Our Lord must surely love us" (ch)
    12. "Polka" (orch)

1a.6   "The Kiss," opera: T115
    1. "Overture"
    I: . "Today with his friends he has drowned his sorrow," aria (Martinka)
    2. "United? United? Oh, united?," duet (Vendulka, Lukáš)
    . "Let us drink now to their health," aria (Tomeš)
    3. "Never, never in my despair," duet (Vandulka, Lukáš)
    . "Here you are my guiltless child. I shall love you from now on," aria (Vendulka)
    . "Till the wedding shall I wait?," aria (Lukáš)
    . "I only want to kiss your cheek," aria (Lukáš)
    4. "What I've foreseen has now arrived," aria (Paloucký)
    5. "How could he ever forget our love," aria (Vendulka)
    . "I'm, my dear girl, old by now," aria (Martinka)
    6. "Sleep now, my baby dear" (Lullaby) (Vendulka)
    7. "Play musicians, play a jump dance," aria (Lukáš)
    II: 8. "Let's go! Let's go!," aria (Matouš, ch)
    9. "If I knew how to redeem my guilt," aria (Lukáš)
    10. "Just go and pray, you foolish man," aria (Tomeš)
    . "You'll invite two or three women fair and two or three men as witnesses," aria (Tomeš)
    11. "O, why ever did I believe foolishly," trio (Vendulka, Martinka, Matouš)
    12. "Well did he show to me what's hidden in man," duet (Vendulka, Martinka)
    13. "Herald, skylark, herald, a new day" (Lark Song) (Barče)
    14. "O yes, O yes, I forgive you, young man, because I want to have peace!," aria (Paloucký)

1a.7   "The Secret," opera: T118
    1. "Overture"
    I: . "Beautiful corn—there will be enough bread," opening chorus
    2. "O, Rose ... O that he deceives my love," duet (Róza, Bonifác)
    3. "O listen, distant world," aria (Skřivánek)
    . "O sweetheart, still foolishly I did not call you," ensemble
    4. "From your sweet mouth thus I love to hear," duet (Blaženka, Vít)
    5. "Why conceal our happiness," duet (Blaženka, Vít)
    II: 6. "I am a beggar, over the ears in debt," aria (Kalina)
    7. "Why does he enquire further?," aria (Kalina)
    . "With pleasure a deep draught I wish to drink," aria (Kalina)
    8. "Out, out, out; from under the ground," aria (Ghost of Friar Barnabáš)
    9. "When I hear thy horn," aria (Blaženka)
    10. "Why became your heart so sad?," duet (Blaženka, Vít)
    11. "What am I thinking ... You cast down your sweet eyes," recit & aria (Vít)
    . "What man is he who insults me?," aria (Vít)
    12. "O false conjecture! that the yearning of love cares about this vain estate," ensemble
    . "O, if he loved me so," aria (Róza)
    13. "I am a soldier, in battles against the Prussians," aria (Bonifác)
    III: . "Gladly and happy we lend a hand with the hops" (ch)
    14. "How the water from the high slopes," aria (Blaženka)
    . "It is indeed a mere trifle," trio (Róza, Malina, The Mason)
    . "You would not wish to scold me, father," aria (Vít)
    . "Barnabáš was happy, he was truly our good friend" (Skřivánek, Bonifác, ch)

1a.8   "The Devil's Wall," opera: T129
    I: . "Prelude"
    1. "Happy I, he'll come today. Yet there is something which torments me," aria (Katuška)
    2. "Welcome to me, my maiden!," recit (Jarek)
    2a. "Have you, perchance, lost faith in me?," aria (Jarek)
    3. "Thus to rest in your arms forever, lips on lips," duet (Katuška, Jarek)
    4. "That unique woman's beauty touched me so," aria (Vok)
    II: 5. "Where can I flee before so sweet an image?," aria (Jarek)
    6. "It is hard to get accustomed to," aria (Míchálek)
    . "She's like an orphaned bird," aria (Záviš)
    . (orch)
    7. "Cat-like and softly, avoiding noise" (Chorus of Maidens)
    . "Don't worry, we'll get you!" (Chorus of Boys)
    8. "Infernal Dance"
    9. "O God of love, in this horrible moment," aria (Hedvíka)

2. SYMPHONIES

2.1	Symphony in E major, "Triumphal" (c1853–4, r1881) .... Op.6, B92 ..... T59	
2.2	*"Grosse Symphonie" (Grand Symphony) (c1883–4, frag of 1st movt)*	

3. OTHER ORCHESTRAL WORKS

3.1	"Minuet," in B-flat major (c1842) .... B31 ..... T12	
3.2	"Bajader's Galop," in C major (c1842) .... B32 ..... T14	
3.3	Orchestral exercises (c1846)	
3.4	*Overture in D major (c1848, sketch, frag)*	
3.5	"Festival Overture," in D major, "Revolutionary" (c1849, r1883) .... B63 ..... T46	
3.6	*Untitled work in C minor (c1856–7, ?Frithjof; intended for vv, ch & orch, frag)*	
3.7	*"The Viking's Voyage," overture (ca1857, sketch, frag)*	
3.8	*"Cid Campeador (in A minor) e Zimene (in D minor)," tone poem (c1857–8, frags)* BD49	
3.9	"Richard III," sym poem (c1858, after Shakespeare) .... Op.11, B106 ..... T74	
3.10	"Wallenstein's Camp," sym poem (c1859, after Schiller) .... Op.14, B111 ..... T79	
3.11	"Haakon Jarl," sym poem (c1861–2, after Oehlenschläger) .... Op.16, B118 ..... T82	
3.12	"Doktor Faust," prelude (c1862; small orch, to a puppet play by Kopecký) .... B123 ..... T91	
3.13	"To Our Lassies," polka in D major (c1862–3, begun ca1849; arr for pf & orch) .... B125/i T49	
3.14	*"Trasák: Freedom" (ca1862–3, lost/?=B125/i)* B125/ii	
3.15	"Oldřich and Božena," prelude (c1863; small orch, to a puppet play by Kopecký) .... B127 ..... T94	
3.16	"Shakespeare Festival March," in E major (c1864) .... Op.20, B129 ..... T95	
3.17	"Fanfares for the Shakespeare's Richard III" (c1867; brass & timp; during Act II) .... B132 ..... T97	
3.18	"Festive Overture," in C major (c1868, laying of National Theatre foundation stone) .... B136 ... T102	
3.19	"The Bartered Bride," tableau vivant (c1869; chamber orch, from opera T93)	
3.20	"Rybář" (The Fisherman), tableau vivant (c1869, after Goethe; harm, harp & strings) .... B138 ... T103	
3.21	"Libuše's Judgement," tableau vivant (c1869, after poem from Zelenohorský manuscript) .... B139 ... T104	

"Má Vlast" (My Fatherland), cycle of 6 sym poems (red for pf duet 1874–9):

3.22	No.1 "Vyšehrad" (ca1872–4) T110	
3.23	No.2 "Vltava" (Moldau) (c1874) T111	
3.24	No.3 "Šárka" (c1875) T113	
3.25	No.4 "Z českých luhů a hájů" (From Bohemian Woods and Fields) (c1875) T114	
3.26	No.5 "Tábor" (c1878) T120	
3.27	No.6 "Blaník" (c1879) T121	

3.28	*Untitled work in D minor (c1874–8, frag)*	
3.29	"Venkovanka" (The Country Woman), polka in G major (c1879; orig for pf, T123) .... (T123)	
3.30	"Pražský karneval" (Prague Carnival) (c1883, Introduction and Polonaise intended for a sym suite).... T135	

4. CONCERTOS, SOLO INSTR & ORCH

4.1	*?Violin Concerto (c1865, sketch frag)*	
4.2	*"Divertimento on Slavonic songs" (c1869; flugel hn & milit band, lost)* T105	

5. STRING QUARTETS

5.1	*"Polka" (c1839, lost)* B4	
5.2	*"Osmanen Polka" (c1839, lost)* B5	
5.3	*String Quartet in D-flat minor (c1839, lost)* .... B6 .... T3	
5.4	*"Waltz," in F major (c1839–40, lost except for 1st vn part)* B8	
5.5	*"Overture" (c1839–40, written 'according to Mozart's method,' lost)* B10	
5.6	"Fantasia on motives from Bellini's Il pirata" (c1839–40)	
5.7	String Quartet No.1 in E minor, "Z mého života" (From my Life) (c1876) T116	
5.8	String Quartet No.2 in D minor (c1882–3) T131	

6. OTHER CHAMBER MUSIC

3 insts:

6.1	Piano Trio in G minor (c1855–6, r1857) .... Op.15, B96, B104 ..... T64	

Vn & pf:

6.2	"Fantasia on the Bohemian song 'I sowed millet,' " in G minor (c1842–3) .... B35 ..... T16	
6.3	"Z domoviny" (From the Home Country), 2 pieces (c1880): No.1 "Moderato," in A major T128	
6.4	No.2 "Andantino," in G minor	

7. PIANO SONATAS

7.1   Piano Sonata in G minor (c1846; ed Repkova 1949) .... BA76 ..... T35

8. OTHER PIANO WORKS

8.1	*"Waltz" (ca1829–31, lost)*	*B1*	*T1*
8.2	*"Galop" (ca1829–31, lost)*	*B2*	*T2*
8.3	*"Little Galop" (Kvapik), in D major (c1832, inc, lost)*	*B3*	
8.4	"Introduction and Adagio" (c1840, inc)		
8.5	"Galopp di Bravoura," in B-flat major (c1840)	B7	T5
8.6	"Variations on motives from Bellini's opera I Montecchi ed i Capuletti" (c1839–40, inc)	B9	
8.7	"Variations on a theme from Bellini's opera I Montecchi ed i Capuletti" (c1839–40, inc)		
8.8	"Louisina Polka," in E-flat major (c1840)	B12	T4
8.9	"Jiřinková (Dahlia) Polka," in D major (c1840)	B13	T8
8.10	*"Marina Polka," in F major (c1841, frag)*	*B14*	*T9*
8.11	*"Grand Polka," in B-flat minor (c1841, inc sketch)*	*B15*	*T10*
8.12	*"Waltz," in A-flat major (c1841, lost)*	*B16*	
8.13	*"Galop," in B major (c1841, lost)*	*B17*	
8.14	*"Waltz," in A-flat major (c1841, lost)*	*B18*	
8.15	"Nocturne," in F-sharp major	B20	
8.16	*"Katerina Polka" (c1841, lost)*	*B21*	
8.17	*"Elisabeth Polka," in F major (c1841, lost)*	*B22*	*T6*
8.18	"Impromptus" (c1841–2): No.1 in E-flat minor	B23	T7
8.19	No.2 in B minor	B24	T11
8.20	No.3 in A-flat major	*B25*	
8.21	*"Bravoura Waltz," in C-sharp minor (c1842, lost)*	*B26*	
8.22	*"Klara Quadrille" (c1842, lost)*	B27	T17
8.23	"Duo without Words," in E major (c1843)		
8.24	"From a Student's Life," polka in C major (c1842, r1858; ed Löwenbach 1912)	B30, B110	
8.25	"Motivy" (Pensées) (c1842, inc)	B33	T18
8.26	"Quadrille," in B-flat major (c1842)		
8.27	"Etude for the left hand" (c1843)	*B34*	*T19*
8.28	*Untitled (?Rhapsody) in A-flat major (c1843, inc sketch)*	B36	T20
8.29	"Quadrille," in F major (c1843)	B37	T38
8.30	"Souvenir of Plzeň," polka in E-flat major (c1843)	B38	T21
8.31	"Untitled Piece," mazurka-capriccio in C-sharp minor (c1843–4; ed Löwenbach 1912)	B39	T22
8.32	"Waltzes" (c1844; ed Löwenbach 1912): No.1 in C min / E-flat major		
8.33	No.2 in A-flat major		
8.34	No.3 in E-flat maj / G major		
8.35	No.4 in C minor		
8.36	No.5 in A-flat major		
8.37	"Bagatelles and Impromptus" (c1844): No.1 "Innocence," in C major	B40	
8.38	No.2 "Dejection," in A minor		
8.39	No.3 "Idyll," in G major		
8.40	No.4 "Desire," in E minor		
8.41	No.5 "Joy," in D major		
8.42	No.6 "Fairy tale," in B minor		
8.43	No.7 "Love," in A major		
8.44	No.8 "Discord," in F-sharp minor		
8.45	"Composition," in C major ('in Song form') (c1845)		
8.46	"Tragic March," in F minor (c1845)		
8.47	*"Album Leaf," in B-flat major (c1844, frag)*		
8.48	*"Album Leaf," in C major (c1844, frag)*		
8.49	"Album Leaves": No.1 "Moderato," in B major (c1844, for Kolářová)	B41	T31/1
8.50	No.2 "Agitato," in E major (c1845, for Finkeová)	B42	T31/2
8.51	No.3 in C minor (c1845, for Kunz)	B43	T31/3
8.52	No.4 "Lento," in E-flat minor (c1845, for Ulwer)	B44	T31/4
8.53	No.5 "Allegro," in A-flat major (c1845, for Thunová)	B45	T31/5
8.54	*"Lesson," in E-flat major (c1845, frag)*		
8.55	"Nocturne," in E-flat major (c1845)		
8.56	"Composition," in C major (c1845)		
8.57	"Composition," in C minor (c1845)		
8.58	"Figuration on the Chorale 'Bože milostivy bud a vlidny' " (c1845)		
8.59	"Exercises on the building of musical periods" (c1845)		
8.60	9 Fugal Expositions (c1845)		
8.61	"Vivace," in F major (c1845)		
8.62	"Andante," in F major (c1845)		
8.63	"March," in F major (c1845)		
8.64	"March," in C minor (c1845)		
8.65	*"8 Album Leaves" (c1845, frags): No.1 in F major*		
8.66	*No.2 in F minor*		
8.67	*No.3 in D major*		
8.68	*No.4 in D minor*		

8.69	*No.5 in G minor*		
8.70	*No.6 in G-flat minor*		
8.71	*No.7 in F-sharp major*		
8.72	*No.8 in D major*		
8.73	"Pensée fugitive" (Album Leaf), in D minor (c1845)	B46	
8.74	*"8 Praeludien" (c1845, lost/=?B40)*	*B48*	*T27*
8.75	"March of the Warriors," in D major (c1846)	BA43	
8.76	"Country March," in B-flat major (c1846)	BA50	
8.77	"Four-voiced Fugue," in C major (c1845)		
8.78	"Four-voiced Fugue," in A minor (c1845)		
8.79	"Double Fugue," in B major (c1845)		
8.80	"Four-voiced Fugue," in D major (c1845)		
8.81	"Four-voiced Fugue," in A major (c1845)		
8.82	"18 Canons" (c1845)		
8.83	"Double Fugue," in F-sharp minor (c1845)		
8.84	"Four-voiced Fugue," in E major (c1845)		
8.85	"Double Fugue," in C-sharp minor (c1845)		
8.86	"Triumphal March," in E major (c1846)	BA55	
8.87	"4 Canons" (c1846)		
8.88	"Études" (c1846): No.1 "Étude" ('in the form of a Prelude'), in C major	BA57	T28/1
8.89	No.2 "Étude" ('in Song form'), in A minor	BA58	T28/2
8.90	"48 Variations on a theme in F major" (c1846)		
8.91	"Characteristic Variations on the Czech folksong 'I sowed millet," in G major (c1846)	BA60	T29
8.92	"Rondo Movement," in C major		
8.93	"Rondo Movement," in A minor		
8.94	"Rondo Movement," in F major		
8.95	"Rondo Movement," in D minor		
8.96	"Sonata Movement," in C major (c1846)		
8.97	"Sonata Movement," in B-flat major (c1846)		
8.98	"Sonata Movement," in A major (c1846)		
8.99	"Sonata Movement," in D major (c1846, unfin)		
8.100	*"Sonata Movement," in B-flat major (c1846, frag)*		
8.101	"Polka," in E-flat major (c1846)	B50	T37
8.102	*"Fantasia on 4 Bohemian Folk Songs" (c1846, lost)*		
8.103	"Woodland Sensations and Impressions" (Nocturne), in F minor (c1849, r1883)	B53	T52
8.104	"Romance," in B-flat major (c1848, r1883)	B54	
8.105	"Rondo capriccio" (Allegro capriccioso), in B minor (c1849, for Dreyschock)	B55	T48
8.106	"Characteristic Piece," in C major (c1848; ed Hostinský 1912)	B56	
8.107	"6 Characteristic Pieces" (c1848): No.1 "In the Forest," in C major	Op.1, B57	T44
8.108	No.2 "Rising Passion," in C minor		
8.109	No.3 "Shepherdess," in G major		
8.110	No.4 "Desire," in G minor		
8.111	No.5 "Soldier," in D major		
8.112	No.6 "Despair," in D minor		
8.113	"March of the Prague Students' Legion," in F major (c1848)	B58	T45a
8.114	"March of the National Guard," in D major (c1848; arr Pavlis for milit band)	B59	T45b
8.115	"Polka," in F minor (c1848)	B61	
8.116	*"Caprice," in G minor (c1848, orig title: Rapsodie, frag)*	*B62*	*T42*
8.117	"Wedding Scenes" (c1849): No.1 "Wedding Procession," in C major	B64	T41
8.118	No.2 "Bride and Groom," in A-flat major		
8.119	No.3 "Wedding Merriment," in A major		
8.120	"Übungen in den ersten rhythmischen Bildungen," in C major (ca1844–9)	B65	
8.121	"8 Rhythmische Übungen," in C major (c1845)	B66	
8.122	"Thema mit Veränderungen," in G major (ca1844–9)	B67	
8.123	"Fingerübungen auf der Grundlage der Tonleiter," in C major (ca1844–9)	B68	
8.124	16 "Höhere Bildungen" (ca1845–9, Nos.1–12 lost)	B69	
8.125	"A Treasure of Melodies," II (c1850; ed1967): No.1 "Moderato," in C major	B71	
8.126	No.2 in G major		
8.127	No.3 "Toccata," in D major		
8.128	No.4 "Moderato," in A major		
8.129	No.5 "Tempo di marcia," in E major		
8.130	"A Treasure of Melodies," I (c1850; ed1924): No.1 "Preludium," in C major	B72	T50
8.131	No.2 "Capriccio," in A minor		
8.132	No.3 "Vivace," in G major		
8.133	"Album Leaves": No.1 in G major (ca1848–9; ed1903)	B74	
8.134	No.2 in G minor (ca1848–9; ed1903)	B75	
8.135	No.3 in B minor (ca1848–9; ed1903)	B76	
8.136	No.4 in A major (c1849, orig vers of Op.5/1; ed Werner 1958)	B77	
8.137	No.5 "Allegro ma non troppo," in B-flat major (c1849; ed Werner 1958)	B78	
8.138	No.6 in E-flat major (ca1848–50, orig vers of B97)	B79	
8.139	No.7 in B-flat minor (ca1848–50)	B80	
8.140	No.8 in F-sharp minor (ca1848–52, orig vers of Op.4/1)	B81	
8.141	No.9 in E major (ca1848–52, orig vers of Op.3/1)	B82	
8.142	No.10 in G-sharp minor (ca1848–52, orig vers of Op.4/4)	B83	
8.143	No.11 in B-flat major (Toccatina) (c1846, r1883)	B84	

8.144	No.12 in E-flat minor (ca1849–54)	B85
8.145	"6 Album Leaves" (c1849): No.1 "Prelude," in C major	Op.2, B86 ..... T53
8.146	No.2 "Chanson," in A minor	
8.147	No.3 "Vivace," in G major	
8.148	No.4 "Allegro comodo," in E minor	
8.149	No.5 "Moderato con anima," in D major	
8.150	No.6 "Andante ma non troppo," in B minor	
8.151	"Polka," in F-sharp major (c before 1853, orig vers of Op.7/1)	B87
8.152	"Polkas" (ca1852–3, r1883): No.1 in E major	B88 ..... T54
8.153	No.2 in G minor	B89 ..... T55
8.154	No.3 in A major	B90 ..... T56
8.155	"Polka," in F minor (ca1854)	B93
8.156	"Salon Polkas" (c1854): No.1 in F-sharp major (also see B87)	Op.7, B94 ..... T62
8.157	No.2 in F minor	
8.158	No.3 in E major	
8.159	"Poetic Polkas" (c1854): No.1 in E-flat major	Op.8, B95 ..... T63
8.160	No.2 in G minor	
8.161	No.3 in A-flat major	
8.162	"Andante," in E-flat major (c1856, for Emperor Ferdinand)	B97 ..... T65
8.163	Cadenzas for Mozart's Pf Concs (c1856): No.1 in C min (for 1st movt of: Pf Conc No.24, K491) B98
8.164	No.2 in D minor (for 1st & 3rd movts of: Pf Conc No.20 in D minor, K466)	B99
8.165	"Album Leaves" (c1851): No.1 "To Robert Schumann," in E major	Op.3, B100 ..... T67
8.166	No.2 "Wayfarer's Song," in A major	
8.167	No.3 "A roaring, whirling hissing can be heard," in C-sharp minor (from Schiller's Der Taucher)	
8.168	"Sketches," I (c1849): No.1 "Prelude," in F-sharp minor	Op.4, B101 ... T68/i
8.169	No.2 "Idyll," in B major	
8.170	No.3 "Remembrance," in A-flat major	
8.171	No.4 "Relentless Struggle," in G-sharp minor	
8.172	"Sketches, II (c1849): No.1 "Scherzo-Polka," in F-sharp major	Op.5, B102 .. T68/ii
8.173	No.2 "Melancholy," in G-sharp minor	
8.174	No.3 "Happy Countryside," in D-flat major	
8.175	No.4 "Rhapsody," in F minor	
8.176	Cadenza for Beethoven's Piano Concerto No.3, Op.37, 1st movt (c1857, 1st vers)	B103 ..... T85
8.177	*"Ballade," in E minor (c1858, lost, extant inc sketch)*	*B107 ...... T70*
8.178	"Scherzo Etude," in C major (c1858, = 1st vers of: Etude, B113)	B108 ..... T71
8.179	"Vision at the Ball," polka-rhapsody in A min / C major (c1858; ed Hostinský 1912)	B109/i T69
8.180	"Polka," in C major (c1858, vers of: Vision at the Ball, B109/i, T69)	B109/ii
8.181	"Capriccio," in A minor (c1858)	
8.182	"Macbeth and the Witches" (c1859, ?draft for pf & orch or sym poem; ed Hostinský 1912)	B112 ..... T80
8.183	"Concert Etude," in C major (c1858, final vers of B108)	Op.12, B113 ..... T75
8.184	"Bettina Polka," in C major (c1859, r1883)	B114 ..... T81
8.185	"Memories of Bohemia I," polkas (c1859–60): No.1 in A minor	(App to Op.12), B115 ..... T83
8.186	No.2 in E minor	
8.187	"Memories of Bohemia II," polkas (c1861): No.1 in E minor	Op.13, B116 ..... T84
8.188	No.2 in E-flat major	
8.189	*"Maria Stuart" (c1860, sketch, frag; ed Ocadlik 1942)*	
8.190	"On the Sea Shore," concert-étude in G-sharp minor (c1861)	Op.17, B119 ..... T86
8.191	"Album leaf for Marie Proksch," in C major (c1862)	B120
8.192	"Fantasia on Czech National Songs," in B major (c1862)	B121 ..... T88
8.193	Cadenzas for Mozart's Pf Conc No.27 in B-flat major, K595, 1st & 3rd movts (ca1856–64,	
8.194	partly lost)	B130
8.195	"Fantasia on Themes from 'Dalibor' " (c1868, from opera T96)	T100
8.196	"Potpourri from opera Dalibor" (c1873, = r vers of: Fantasia, T100)	T108
8.197	"Fantasia on Themes from 'Libuše' " (c1873, from opera T107)	
8.198	"Dreams" (Rêves), characteristic pieces (c1875): No.1 "Bygone happiness"	T112
8.199	No.2 "Consolation"	
8.200	No.3 "In Bohemia"	
8.201	No.4 "In the drawing-room"	
8.202	No.5 "Near the castle"	
8.203	No.6 "Bohemian festival" (Harvest home)	
8.204	"Czech Dances," I (c1877): No.1 "Polka," in F-sharp minor	T112/i
8.205	No.2 "Polka," in A minor	
8.206	No.3 "Polka," in F major	
8.207	No.4 "Polka," in B-flat major	
8.208	"Czech Dances," II (c1879): No.1 "Furiant"	T112/ii
8.209	No.2 "Slepička" (The hen)	
8.210	No.3 "Oves" (The oats)	
8.211	No.4 "Medvěd" (The bear)	
8.212	No.5 "Cibulička" (The little onion)	
8.213	No.6 "Dupák" (Stamping dance)	
8.214	No.7 "Hulán" (The lancer)	
8.215	No.8 "Obkročák" (The astride dance)	
8.216	No.9 "Sousedská" (The neighbours dance)	
8.217	No.10 "Skočná" (Hop dance)	
8.218	"The Country Woman," polka in G major (c1879; orchd, T123)	T123

8.219   "Andante," in F minor (c1880) T125
8.220   "Romance," in G minor (c1881) T130

Pf duet:

8.221   *"Memories of Nové Mě'sto" (c1840, lost)* .... *B11* ....
8.222   "Overture," in C minor (c1842) .... B28 ..... T13
8.223   "Overture," in A major (c1842) .... B29 ..... T15

2 Pf:

8.224   Untitled work in G minor (c1845; 8 hands) .... B47 ..... T26
8.225   *Piano Sonata in E-flat major (ca1850, sketch, frag)* ....
8.226   "Sonata," in E minor (c1851; 8 hands, in 1 movt) .... B70 ..... T47
8.227   "Youth," rondo in C major (c1851) .... B73 ..... T57

9. ORGAN

9.1   "Preludes" (c1846): No.1 in C major... B52 ..... T36
9.2   No.2 in C minor
9.3   No.3 in G major
9.4   No.4 in G minor
9.5   No.5 in D major
9.6   No.6 in F major

10. CHORAL WORKS

10.1   "Jesu meine Freude," chorale (c1846; ch)..
10.2   "Ich hoffe auf den Herrn," choral fugue (c1846; ch)..
10.3   "Lobet den Herrn," introduction & fugue (c1846; ch) ....
10.4   "Heilig, Heilig ist der Herr Zebaoth" (c1846, Psalm 117; 2ch) ....
10.5   "Scapulis suis obumbrabit tibi Dominus," offertory (c1846; ch, hns, strings & org) .... BA77 ....
10.6   "Meditabitur in mandatis tuis," offertory (à la Händel) (c1846; ch, hns, strings & org)............... BA78 ....
10.7   *"Song in Honour of the Bohemian King" (c1848; ch, lost)* ....
10.8   *"Patriotic Chorus" (c1848; lost)*
10.9   *"The Death of Jan of Husinec" (c1848; ch, lost)* ....
10.10   "Pis eň svobody" (Song of Freedom) (c1848, Kolářová; unison vv & pf; ed Löwenbach 1909) ... B60 ....
10.11   "Pis eň česká" (Song of the Czechs) (c1860, Jan z Hvězdy; m ch; also see cantata T101)..... B117 ....
10.12   "T ři jezdci" (The Three Horsemen) (c1862, Jahn; ch) .... B122 ..... T89
10.13   "Odrodilec" (The Renegade) (c1863, Metli ńskij transl Čelakovský; 2 vers): T92
      . Original Version (d ch) ....
      . Revised Version (r1864; 2T, 2B & m ch)... B126 ....
10.14   "Rolnická" (Farming), hymn (c1868, Trnobranský; m ch) .... B135 ..... T99
10.15   "Česká piseň" (Song of the Czechs), cantata (c1868, Jan z Hvězdy; ch & pf; also d ch
      & orch 1878; also see B117) T101
10.16   "Slavností sbor" (Ceremonial Chorus) (c1870, Züngl; m ch, memory of K. Havlíček) T106
10.17   "Pis eň na m oři" (Song of the Sea) (c1877, Hálek; m ch) T117
10.18   "4 Songs" (c1878; fem ch & pf, pf part lost): 1. "The sun sets behind the mountains" (Sládek)............ T119
10.19   2. "The swallows have come" (Sládek)
10.20   3. "Lullaby" (Sládek)
10.21   4. "My star" (Peška)
10.22   "Věno" (Dowry) (c1880, Šrb-Debrnov; m ch) T126
10.23   "Motlitba" (Prayer) (c1880, Šrb-Debrnov; m ch) T127
10.24   "Heslo" (Motto): "All that we desire" (c1882, Šrb-Debrnov; m ch; 2 settings) T132
10.25   "Naše piseň" (Our Song) (c1883, Šrb-Debrnov; m ch)...T134

11. SONGS (w/ pf)

11.1   "3 Lieder" (c?, juvenilia, p1962): 1. "Nehled boln ě, dívko" ....
11.2   2. "Smutně včela v po ušti"
11.3   3. "Když se slunko zas usmívá"
11.4   *"Hymne zum Johannes von Nepomuk" (c1841, lost)* .... *B19* ....
11.5   "The Wanderer" (c1846, Schiller's Der Pilgrim) ....
11.6   "Pohled mé dívky" (Liebchen's Blick) (My dear eyes) (c1846, Breiger; ed Löwenbach 1909) ..BA70 ..... T32
11.7   "Sbohem!" (Lebewohl!) (Farewell) (c1846, Mehlhop; ed Löwenbach 1909) ....BA71 ..... T33
11.8   "Schmerz der Trennung" (c1846, Wieland) .... B49 ..... T34
11.9   "Vyzvání" (Invitation) (c1846, Jacobi) .... B51 ..... T40
11.10   "Jaro lásky" (Liebesfrühling) (Spring love) (c1853, Rückert) .... B91 ..... T58
11.11   "O Gustave, můj králi" (O Gustav, my king) (c1867, Bozděch, for the Bozděch's tragedy:
      Baron Goertz) .... B134 ..... T98
11.12   "Večerní pisně" (Evening Songs) (c1879, Hálek): 1. "Who can play the golden harp?" T124
11.13   2. "Stone not the Prophet!"

11.14	3. "I dreamt"
11.15	4. "Oh, what joy when dancing!"
11.16	5. "From my songs I will build thee a throne"

12. ARRANGEMENTS OF WORKS OF OTHERS

12.1	Weber: "Jubel-Overtüre," Op.59, J245 (arr1850; 2pf 8 hands) ....
12.2	Schumann: "Canonic Studies" (arr1855; 2pf 8 hands) ....
12.3	Wagner: "Tannhäuser Prelude" (arr1855; 4pf 16 hands) ....
12.4	Beethoven: "March," from incid music: The Ruins of Athens, Op.113 (arr1855; 4pf 16 hands) ....
12.5	Schubert: "Die schöne Müllerin" (arr1857; pf): *No.1 "Trockne Blumen" (Op.25/18,*
	D795/18) (lost) .... Op.10, B105 ..... T72
12.6	No.2 "Der Neugierige" (Op.25/6, D795/18)
12.7	*Schubert: "Thränenragen," Op.25/10, D795/10 (arr1857; pf, lost)* ....
12.8	Mendelssohn: "Fingal's Cave" Overture in B minor, Op.26 (arr1857; 4pf, 16 hands) ....
12.9	Spontini: "Ferdinand Cortez" Overture (arr ?1858; 4pf, 16 hands) ....
12.10	Beethoven: "Fidelio" Overture, Op.72c (arr ca1850–8; 4pf 16 hands) ....
12.11	Beethoven: "Coriolan" Overture, Op.62 (arr ca1850–8; 4pf 16 hands) ....
12.12	Beethoven: "Egmont" Overture, Op.84 (arr ca1850–8; 4pf 16 hands) ....

*   *   *   *   *

B = Bartoš, F.: "Thematic Catalogue" (inc)
T = Teige, K.: "Contributions to the Artistic Work of B. Smetana." Prague, 1896.

SPOHR, Louis (Ludwig)
1784–1859

1. STAGE WORKS

Operas:

1.1	"Alruna, die Eulenkönigin," 3 act romantic grand opera (c1808, Reinhard) .... WoO 49
1.2	"Der Zweikampf mit der Geliebten," 3 act Singspiel (c1810, Schink) .... WoO 50
1.3	"Faust," 2 act romantic opera (c1813, Bernard; r1852 in 3 acts w/ recitatives) .... WoO 51
1.4	"Zemire und Azor," 2 act romantic opera (c1818–9, Ihlée after Marmontel) .... WoO 52
1.5	"Jessonda," 3 act grand opera (c1823, Gehe after Lemierre: La veuve de Malabar) .... WoO 53
1.6	"Der Berggeist," 3 act romantic opera (c1824, Döring & Gehe) .... WoO 54
1.7	"Pietro von Abano," 2 act romantic opera (c1827, Pfeiffer after Tieck) .... WoO 56
1.8	"Der Alchymist," 3 act romantic opera (c1829–30, Pfeiffer after Irving) .... WoO 57
1.9	"Die Kreuzfahrer," 3 act grand opera (c1843–4, L. & M. Spohr after Kotzebue) .... WoO 59

Operettas:

1.10	"Die Prüfung," 1 act operetta (c1806, Henke) .... WoO 48

Incid music:

1.11	"Macbeth" (c1825, Spiker after Shakespeare) (also see operas c by Bloch & Verdi, incid music c by Bacewicz, Khachaturian, Milhaud Op.175 & Sullivan) .... WoO 55
1.12	"Der Sturm von Missolunghi" (Eröffnungsmusik zum 3. Akt) (c1830, Ehlers) .... WoO 4
1.13	"Der Matrose" (c1838, Birnbaum, collab Hauptmann) .... WoO 58

1a. SELECTIONS FROM STAGE WORKS

1a.1   "Alruna, die Eulenkönigin," opera: .... WoO 49
    . "Ouverture" (= Op.21)
- I: 1. "Schön prangt im Jugendglanze," duet (Bertha, Herrmann)
-     2. "Ein Ritter zog aus in den Wald," romanze (Herrmann)
-     3. "Warum laufen und entfliehen wie ein scheues Wild," duet (Franz, Clara)
-     4. "Es sei gewagt! jetzt oder nie!," finale (Herrmann, Bruno, Bertha, Clara, Robert, Franz, Reisige)
- II: 5. "Welch eine Nacht! voll und Graus," introduction (Herrmann, Franz)
-     6. "Dann wirst du hangen am Munde mein," cavatina (Tio)
-     7. "Euer Liebreiz, eure Schönheit," duet (Tio, Franz)
-     8. "Noch kannt ich nicht die Liebe," finale (Alruna, Herrmann, Tio, Franz)
- III: 9. "Hallo, tra-ra, das Hüfthorn schallt!," introduction (Alruna, Jägerinnen)
-     10. "Doch horch! ich höre Hörnerton," melodrama (Tio, Franz)
-     11. "Sie war so gut, so zärtlich und so liebevoll," melodrama (Herrmann, Udos Geist)
-     12. "Hier muss er sein," recit (Alruna, Tio)
-     13. "Ich war vereint, ich hatte ihn gefunden," aria (Bertha)
-     14. "Mein Kind! sei stark!... Lass Gram und Sehnsucht schwinden," scene (Bruno, Bertha)
-     15. "Endlich schlägt die Stund der Rache," finale (Alruna & others)

1a.2   "Der Zweikampf mit der Geliebten," opera: .... WoO 50
    . "Ouverture"
- I: 1. "Lieblich ist des Waldes Kühle," introduction (Enrigue, 4 Wilddiebe, Isabella)
-     2. "Gnäd'ge Fürstin! Ahnen meines Stammes schwör ich," trio (Enrigue, Isabella, Mathilde)
-     3. "Das lasst ein Leben, wie's soll, mir sein!," duet (Decio, Laurette)
-     4. "Ich bin allein. Des Abends Nähe regt die Tätigkeit ... Wie dich nennen?," recit & aria (Mathilde)
-     5. "Lüfte den Schleier, hohe Diana!," finale
- II: 6. "Wie? sie wollen nicht entdekken?," duet (Lauretto, Decio)
-     7. "Von sich selber abgeschieden," aria (Mathilde)
-     8. "Verzeihung! Gnäd'ge Verzeihung mir!," trio (Isabella, Enrigue, Mathilde)
-     9. "Soll ich knieend sie beschwören," finale
- III: 10. (Introduction)
-     11. "Was hör ich? Ich staune und traue mir kaum!," duet (Mathilde, Enrigue)
-     12. "Die Ehre! Ha! wo ist ein Mann ... Durch des Schicksals strenge Bande," recit & aria (Enrigue)
-     13. "Die Stunde der Entscheidung ... Sie naht, der Rache süsse Stunde," recit & aria (Isabella)
-     14. "Marcia"
-     15. "Das Zeichen zum Kampfe, es werd'nun gegeben!," chorus
-     16. "Wieder mein nun, nicht mehr mir verloren!," finale (Isabella & others)

1a.3   "Faust," opera: .... WoO 51
    . "Ouverture" (= Op.60)
- I: 1. "In Sinnenlust so sinnlos leben!," introduction & duet (Faust, Mephistofeles)
-     1a. "Der Hölle selbst will ich ... Liebe ist die zarte Blüte," recit & aria (Faust) (added later)
-     2. "Der Wein erfreut des Menschen Herz," aria & chorus (Wohlhaldt, Chor der Freunde Fausts)
-     3. "Folg dem Freunde mit Vertrauen," duet (Faust, Röschen)
-     4. "Nur der ist frei, der nichts zu lieben hat," duet & chorus (Faust, Franz)
-     5. "Die stille Nacht entweicht ... Ja, ich fühl' es, treue Liebe," scene & aria (Kunigunde)
-     6. "Beflügle den Lauf ... Ja, hoffe Kunigunde!," scene & aria w/ chorus (Hugo, Hugos Gefolge)
-     7. "Ich kann nicht ruhn, ich kann nicht rasten," trio (Röschen, Franz, Mephistofeles)

8. "Nun wohlan! Ich halte Wort," finale
II: 9. "Brenne, Laterne! Nahe und ferne dämmere auf!," introduction (Chor der Hexen, others)
10. "Sende, Himmel, Segensfülle" (Chor der Hochzeitsgäste)
11. "Dürft ich mich nennen, sein eigen," cavatina (Röschen)
12. (Orgel-Zwischenspiel zum Dialog)
13. "Wie ist mir! Welch ein Zwist erhebt ... Blöder Tor! Ich kann hier fragen," scene & aria (Faust)
14. "Lang mögen die Teueren leben," sextet & chorus
. "Pantomimischer Tanz"
15. "Stille noch dies Wutverlangen," aria & chorus (Mephistofeles, Chor der Hexen, Sycorax)
16. "Welch ein Wahn hat mich verblendet," finale (Kunigunde & others)

1a.4   "Zemire und Azor," opera: .... WoO 52
I: 1. "Wo schwarz die Wolken ziehn," overture & introd (Unsichtbarer Geister-Chor, Sander, Ali)
2. "Ich fürchte nichts!," aria (Sander)
3. "Mit neuem Mute, neuer Kraft," romanze (Ali)
4. "Wehe! Wehe!," trio & chorus (Unsichtbarer Geister-Chor, Sander, Ali, Azor)
5. "So nimm aus meinen Händen die Rose nun zurück," trio (Azor, Sander, Ali)
6. "Sanft tragen ihn die leichten Lüfte ... Nein, ich will nicht klagen," recit & rondo (Azor)
7. "Die schwarzen Schatten fliehen," trio (Fatme, Zemire, Lisbe)
8. "Rose wie bist du reizend und mild!," romanze (Zemire)
9. "Sprich, guter Ali, sprich," finale (Zemire, Ali, Sander, Lisbe, Fatme)
II: 10. "Ha, welche Pracht," entr'acte & chorus (Zemire, Ali, Chor von Genien)
11. "Weh' mir! Wo flieh' ich hin!," duet (Zemire, Azor)
12. "O, Himmel, meine Schwestern ... Zemire, teures Kind!," recit & quintet
13. "Unter Palmen schlief ich ein," romanze (Ali)
14. "Lasst die Schwester ziehen," duet (Fatme, Lisbe)
15. "Vergebens sucht in weiter Ferne ... Mein Leiden zu erhöh'n," recit & aria (Azor)
16. "Darf ich meinen Augen trauen! ... Süsses unbekanntes Sehnen," recit & aria (Zemire)
17. "Vernimm aus meinem Munde, du holdes Mädchen," finale (Die Fee & others)

1a.5   "Jessonda," opera: .... WoO 53
. "Ouverture" (= Op.63)
I: 1. "Kalt und starr, doch majestätisch," introduction (Bajaderen, Braminen, Dandau)
2. "Du hast dem Opfer dich entzogen!," recit (Dandau, Nadori)
3. "Aus dieses Tempels heilgen Mauern," duet (Dandau, Nadori)
4. "Was bringst du? Herr, eine wicht'ge Kunde," recit (Dandau, Offizier)
5. "Der auf Morgen-, Abend-Gluten herrlich seinen Thron," aria w/ chorus (Dandau, Braminen)
6. "O Schwester, stille deine Tränen," recit (Jessonda, Amazili)
7. "Als in mitternächt'ger Stunde ... Die ihr Fühlende betrübet," recit & aria (Jessonda)
8. "Erhaben ist's, so still zu leiden," recit (Amazili, Jessonda, Dienerinnen)
9. "So, wie das Rohr zerbrach," finale (Nadori, Amazili, Jessonda)
II: 10. "Kein Sang und Klang auf dieser Welt," introduction (& Waffentanz) (Portugiesen, Tristan, Lopes)
11. "Mit Fülle kriegerischer Ehren ward deine Jugend schon beglükket," recit (Lopes, Tristan)
12. "Der Kriegeslust ergeben," aria (Tristan)
13. "Mein teurer Freund, ich teile dein Gefühl," recit (Lopes, Tristan)
14. "Lasst mich auf Augenblikke allein mit meiner Schwester," recit (Jessonda, Amazili)
15. "Lasst für ihn, den ich geliebet," duet (Jessonda, Amazili)
16. "Still lag auf meiner Seele ... Dass mich Glück mit Rosen kröne," recit & rondo (Nadori)
17. "Was seh ich, unter Blumen wandelt," recit (Nadori, Amazili)
18. "Schönes Mädchen, wirst mich hassen," duet (Nadori, Amazili)
19. "O, neu Gefühl, was mich beseelet," recit (Amazili)
19a. "O, neu Gefühl, was mich beseelet ... O, Welt, so schön und blühend," recit & aria (Amazili)
20. "Aus der Welen heil'gem Schloss," finale (Bajaderen, Jessonda & others)
III: 21. "Introduction"
22. "Mit schwarzem Fittich deckt die Nacht," recit (Lopes)
23. "Durch Fluten, Flammen zu ihr zu streben," recit (Tristan, Lopes)
24. "Entflohen aus des Tempels Hallen," recit (Nadori, Tristan)
25. "Auf! und lasst die Fahnen fliegen!," trio (Nadori, Lopes, Tristan)
26. "Wollet, Götter," chorus (Bajaderen, Braminen, Dandau)
27. "Lasst ab von mir! ... Hohe Götter! Schauet nieder," recit & aria (Jessonda)
28. "Mein Schritt, beflügelt von Entzükken," finale (Amazili & others)

1a.6   "Der Berggeist," opera: .... WoO 54
. "Ouverture" (= Op.73)
I: Scene 1. "Schafft, schafft, schafft," introduction (Chor der Erdgeister, Troll, Berggeist)
2. "Hochzeitsreigen" (Ludmilla, Chor der Dienerinnen)
3. "Er naht! O Freundin, der Geliebte naht" (Alma, Ludmilla)
4. "Oskar, mein Geliebter! Holder Preis des Siegs" (Alma, Oskar, Chor der Dienerinnen)
. "Dich hab ich wieder! Wonnestunde!," duet (Alma, Oskar)
5. "Teuer Sohn, willkommen sei!" (Domoslav, Oskar, Alma)
. "Priestersegen wartet am Altare," trio (Domoslav, Oskar, Alma)
6. "Hier zum ersten Male sah ich den Geliebten" (Alma)
. "Holde Stätte, meiner Liebe Wiege," aria w/ chorus (Alma, Chor der Erdgeister, Berggeist)
7. "Wo weilst du? Alma!" (Oskar, Berggeist, Erdgeister, Diener, Ludmilla, Domoslav)
II: Scene 1. "Jeden Kummer lass entweichen," duet (Berggeist, Alma)

. "O schone mein! Getrennt von meinem Vater," recit (Alma, Berggeist)
. "Nur Wolken!," trio (Alma, Troll, Berggeist)
2. "Ruhig meines Herzens Pochen" (Alma, Ludmillas Gestalt, Chor der Dienerinnen)
3. "Ird'sche Bilder rings um dich hast du versammelt" (Berggeist, Alma, Troll & others)
4. "Solch holdes Kind darf mir nicht allzu schnell entlaufen" (Troll, Ludmillas Gestalt)
. "Solche schlanke Hulldgestalt," duet (Troll, Ludmillas Gestalt)
5. "Beschlossen ist's! Frisch, Troll, zum Tag hinauf!" (Troll)
6. "Hier such ich Ruhe! im öden Felsentale," recit (Oskar)
. "Tief im Grunde rauscht die Flut," aria (Oskar)
7. "Wer ruft den Namen der geliebten Tochter?" (Domoslav, Oskar)
. "Feiger Räuber, höre mich!," duet (Oskar, Domoslav)
8. "Wohin entfliehn?" (Alma, Berggeist)
. "Huldigt der Schönheit, huldigt der Liebe," finale (Berggeist & others)
III: Scene 1. "Von Zweifeln stürmisch wird mein Herz bewegt!" (Alma)
. "Hoffnung! du von Himmelshöhn schwachen Menschen beigesellt," aria (Alma)
2. "Immer trübe noch dein Auge!" (Berggeist, Alma, Troll)
. "Ihr Geister, die mir untertan," trio & chorus (Berggeist, Alma, Troll, Chor der Geister)
3. "Nun zögre nicht! Sprich, welche heitre Kunde bringst du" (Alma, Troll)
. "Felsenpforte! tu dich auf!," trio (Troll, Alma, Ludmilla; Berggeist)
4. "Der Geist! Wir sind verloren!" (Alma, Troll, Berggeist, Ludmilla)
. "Zähle mir genau die Blumen," quartettino (Alma, Berggeist, Ludmilla, Troll)
5. "Gleich zum Werke!" (Berggeist)
. "Ruhig! Zähle! Eins, zwei," aria & chorus (Berggeist, Chor der Erdgeister)
6. "Unsel'ge Stätte!" (Oskar)
7. "Mein Oskar!" (Alma, Oskar, Ludmilla, Troll, Domoslav, Berggeist & others)

1a.7   "Pietro von Abano," opera: .... WoO 56
. "Ouverture"
I: 1. "Seid mir gegrüsst, ihr teuren Hallen ... Ach! umsonst durch ferne Räume," recit & aria (Antonio)
2. "Bricht das Aug' im Todesschmerz" (Chor der Priester und des Volkes)
3. "Auf ewig birgt die teure Hülle," trio & chorus (Eudoxia, Antonio, Podesta, Chor des Volkes)
4. "Hoch! lebe Padua's grosser Meister" (Chor der Studenten)
5. "Vergebt, dass in die ernste Leichenfeier," trio & chorus (Pietro, Podesta, Eudoxia & others)
6. "Hoch! Hoch lebe Padua's grosser Meister" (Chor der Studenten)
7. "Aus dunkeln Wolken ... Es lebt in meinem Herzen," recit & aria (Cäcilia)
8. "Ha, Zauberin! Wo bin ich?... Flieh, Jüngling," duet (Antonio, Cäcilia)
9. "Du bist Todes, frecher Knabe," trio (Ildefonso, Antonio, Cäcilia, Räuber)
10. "Tief unten in kühler Erde," finale (Chor unsichtbarer Geister, Pietro, Beresinth, Cäcilia)
II: 11. "Das Glück entwich aus diesen öden Hallen," aria (Eudoxia)
12. "Ha! teure Gattin ... Ja, mich begleitet Gottes Segen," duet (Podesta, Eudoxia)
13. "Sie schläft! die Wange strahlt in Rosenglut ... Um die Geliebte zu gewinnen," recit & aria (Pietro)
14. "Wo bin ich?... Nur jenseits blüht mir wahres Leben," scene & duet (Antonio, Cäcilia)
15. "Ha! dieses Frevels Kunde," aria (Antonio)
16. "Ich soll sie sehn!... Der Mutter banges Sehnen erhört en güt'ger Gott," aria (Eudoxia)
17. "Willkommen!," quartet & chorus (Chor des Volkes, Cäcilia, Eudoxia, Antonio, Podesta)
18. "So bin ich nun nicht mehr verlassen," quartet & chorus)
19. "Ja, dir Geliebte winkt ... Dein Anblick hat in meine Nacht," duet (Antonio, Cäcilia)
20. "Heil unserm Meister, unserm Herrn!" (Chor der Studenten und des Volkes)
21. "Die Seele flieht in Gottes Hand!," finale (Cäcilia & others)

1a.8   "Der Alchymist," 3 act romantic opera (c1829–30, Pfeiffer after Irving) .... WoO 57
. "Ouverture"
I: 1. "Berg auf, Berg ab, von Fels zu Schlucht," chorus (Chor der Zigeuner, Lopez)
2. "So bin ich verraten, verstossen, verlacht," aria (Paola)
3. "Sie ist's, sie spielt, sie ahnt nicht, wer sie hört!," duettino (Paola, Inez)
4. "Doch atill, wer nahet?," melodrama (Paola, Vasquez, Alonzo, Inez)
5. "O welcher Reiz ist holde Bild ... Trauert nicht, ihr stolzen Hallen," recit & aria (Alonzo)
6. "Ich folg umsonst der Freude Spuren," scene w/ chorus (Ramiro, Chor der Zigeuner, Alonzo)
7. "Fort ist er! Ew'ger Gott! was musst' ich hören!," finale (Alonzo, Vasquez, Inez)
II: 8. "Es ist schon spät ... Ha! mit dem gift'gen Pfeil des Spottes," duet (Ramiro, Paola)
9. "Ha, welch ein Plan!... Ach zu fernen schönen Tagen," recit & aria (Paola)
10. "Der Abend neigt sich zu der Erde nieder," arietta (Inez)
11. "Hinweg du Truggebild ... Der Liebe Blick verklärt mein Wesen," recit & duet (Inez, Alonzo)
12. "Sieh jene Schar sich jubelnd hieher wenden," scene w/ chorus (Inez, Alonzo & others)
13. "Flieht nicht, Senora, höret unsre Bitte," recit (Lopez, Alonzo, Paola)
14. "Abenhamet!," romanza w/ chorus (Paola, Chor der Zigeuner, Inez)
15. "Du bebst, Geliebte? Fort, o fort von hier!," finale (Alonzo, Inez & others)
III: 16. "Glauben—und beten" (Vision) (Vasquez, Inquisitor)
17. "Vor meine Richter ... Du hast, o Gott! mir nicht gegeben," recit & aria (Vasquez)
18. "Von Angst und Sehnsucht ist mein Herz durchdrungen," aria (Inez)
19. "Fliehe nicht vor Männerschritten," ballo (Chor, Ramiro, Inez, Paola)
20. "Weh mir! Was ist euch?... Ha! er spottet meiner Tränen," recit & duet (Inez, Ramiro, Chor)
21. "Auf goldnen Wolken naht der Morgen," finale (Chor des Volkes, Alonzo & others)

1a.9   "Die Kreuzfahrer," opera: .... WoO 59
       I: 1. "Ich sag' ohn' Spott, kein sel'ger Tod," introd & chorus (Chor der Ritter und Knappen & others)
           2. "O Freund, noch herrscht im Lager ... Dir vertrau ich's," recit & duettino (Balduin, Adhemar)
           3. "Hier, hier ist der Wallfahrt Ziel!," scene (Emma, Walther)
           4. "Was begehrt ihr, junger Pilger?," recit (Pförtnerin, Emma, Walther, Cölestine)
           5. "Gesegnet sei! Was führt dich her?," recit (Cölestine, Emma)
           6. "Geleitet dich dein guter Engel heim," duet (Emma, Walther)
           7. "Da geht hin ... Einsam, losgerissen von der Heimat," recit & aria (Emma)
           8. "Bedürft ihr mein, hochwürdge Frau?," scene (Pförtnerin, Cölestine)
           9. "Habe Dank für deine Warnung," duet (Cölestine, Pförtnerin)
         10. "Komm, meine Tochter! Die geweih'ten Mauern," recit (Cölestine, Emma)
         11. "Empfange, Maria, als Christi Verlobte," duet (Cölestine, Emma)
         12. "Seht zu, ob ihr den Schleier ihr entreisst!," finale (Bohemund & others)
      II: 13. "Introduction"
         14. "Du bist ermüdet, Kind," recit (Emir, Fatime)
         15. "Er ist's! o Vater! unser Engel ist's!," trio (Fatime, Emir, Balduin)
         16. "Dein heisser Wunsch, Maria, ist erfüllt," scene (Cölestine, Emma)
         17. "Ein Knappe meldet seinen Ritter an," recit (Pförtnerin, Cölestine, Conrad)
         18. "und diese heil'ge Stätte. Ihr seid im Irrtum," recit (Conrad, Balduin, Cölestine)
         19. "Es schmerzt mich. Conrad löse mir den Helm," scene (Balduin, Emma)
         20. "barmherz'ger Gott! Wer ruft?," ensemble (Pförtnerin, Balduin & others)
         21. "Hört ihr, wie er in blinder Wut uns droht!," recit (Cölestine)
         22. "Ich hoffe, sie der Langmut ... Ich kann hinfort nicht tragen," recit & duet (Cölestine, Emma)
         23. "Es lässt mir keine Ruh. Hört Fräulein!," recit (Pförtnerin, Emma)
         24. "Gott! ich darf ihn wieder lieben," trio (Emma, Pförtnerin, Balduin)
         25. "Ihr seid versammelt?," finale (Cölestine, Chor der Reisigen & others)
     III: 26. "Allein kehr ich zurück ... Verlassen, verzweifelnd," introduction, recit & aria (Balduin)
         27. "Eilt! Man öffnet euch die Pforte," march & recit (Bruno, Balduin)
         28. "Was darf ich tun? Hier fesseln Pflicht und Glaube meinen Arm," duet (Bruno, Balduin)
         29. "So gibt es keine Rettung keine Rache!," scene (Balduin)
         30. "Weine büssende Tränen," chorus w/ solo (Chor der Nonnen, Cölestine)
         31. "Allah segne unsern Herrn," march w/ chorus (Chor der Türken, Emir)
         32. "Lagert euch! Liegt da ein Toter?," recit (Emir, Balduin)
         33. "So fänd ich unter Saracenen," duet & ch (Balduin, Emir, Chor der Türken und Christensklaven)
         34. "Du bist verurteilt durch der Schwestern Spruch!," procession & recit (Cölestine, Emma)
         35. "Gott, der du schauest in der Herzen Tiefen," prayer (Emma)
         36. "Gott, stärke du die Leidende," chorus & recit (Chor der Nonnen, Cölestine, Emma)
         37. "Vollendet! Requiesce in pace," chorus & solo (Cölestine, Chor der Nonnen)
         38. "Was gibt es draussen? welch Getümmel?," finale (Cölestine & others)

1a.10   "Die Prüfung," operetta: .... WoO 48
         . "Ouverture" (= Op.15a)
         1. "Wenn sich zwei Herzen finden," duet (Charis, Edmund)
         2. "Es erblühet neu dem Greise," trio (Natalie, Edmund, Graf)
         3. "Kennst du ein Mädchen Romantik genannt?," duet (Natalie, Graf)
         4. "Noch weilt sie fern ... Nein, ich kann ihr nicht entsagen," recit & aria (Edmund)
         5. "Wohl sind im hesperischen Tale," romanza (Charis)
         6. "Er hat gesiegt!... Alles hat er hingegeben," recit & aria (Natalie)
         7. "Wärs möglich, oder ist's ein Wahn," recit & duet (Natalie, Edmund)
         8. "So reichst du ihm mit Liebe deine Hand," finale (Graf & others)

1a.11   "Macbeth," incid music: .... WoO 55
         . "Ouverture" (= Op.75)
       I: 1. "Scene 1": "Wann kommen wir drei uns wieder entgegen?" (3 Hexen)
         2. "Scene 2" (Der König, Malcolm. Donalbain, Gefolge) (insts)
         3. "Scene 4" (3 Hexen) (insts)
         . "Scene 5" (Macbeth, die Hexen) (insts)
         . "Scene 10" (Der König, Malcolm, Donalbain, Lenox, Gefolge) (= 2.)
         4. "Change of decorations music & Scene 12" (Macbeth) (insts)
      II: 5. "Verschwunden ist die finstre Nacht" (Lied des Pförtners)
     III: . "Scene 2" (= 2.)
     IV: . "Scene 2" (Hekate, 3 Hexen) & "Scene 3" (Vorige, Macbeth, Erscheinungen) (insts)
     V: . "Scene 8" (Marcia)

1a.13   "Der Matrose," incid music: .... WoO 58
         . "Ouverture" (= WoO 7)
        10. "Matrosenlied": "Der Sturmwind braust" (= WoO 80)
        11. "Überleitungsmusik"
        12. "Überleitungsmusik"

2. SYMPHONIES

2.1   Symphony No.1 in E-flat major (c1811) Op.20
2.2   Symphony No.2 in D minor (c1820) Op.49

3. OTHER ORCHESTRAL WORKS

4. CONCERTOS, SOLO INSTR & ORCH

Vn & orch:

5. STRING QUARTETS

6. OTHER CHAMBER MUSIC

6 or more insts:

6.1	Nonet in F major (c1813; fl, ob, cl, hn, bn, vn, va, vc & d bass)	Op.31
6.2	Octet in E major (c1814; cl, 2hn, vn, 2va, vc & d bass)	Op.32
6.3	Double String Quartet No.1 in D minor (c1823)	Op.65
6.4	Double String Quartet No.2 in E-flat major (c1827)	Op.77
6.5	Double String Quartet No.3 in E minor (c1832–3)	Op.87
6.6	Double String Quartet No.4 in G minor (c1847)	Op.136
6.7	String Sextet in C major (c1848; 2vn, 2va & 2vc)	Op.140
6.8	Septet in A minor (c1853; fl, cl, hn, bn, vn, vc & pf)	Op.147

String Quintets:

6.9	"Potpourri on themes by Mozart," in B-flat major (c1807; vn & str qt, d bass ad lib)	Op.22
6.10	String Quintet No.1 in E-flat major (c1814)	Op.33/1
6.11	String Quintet No.2 in G major (c1813)	Op.33/2
6.12	String Quintet No.3 in B minor (c1826)	Op.69
6.13	String Quintet No.4 in A minor (c1833–4)	Op.91
6.14	String Quintet No.5 in G minor (c1838)	Op.106
6.15	String Quintet No.6 in E minor (c1845)	Op.129
6.16	String Quintet No.7 in G minor (c1850)	Op.144

Piano Quintets:

6.17	Piano Quintet No.1 in C minor (c1820, arr from: Quintet, Op.52)	Op.53
6.18	Piano Quintet No.2 in D major (c1845)	Op.130

Other 5 insts:

6.19	Quintet in C minor (c1820; fl, cl, hn, bn & pf; arr for pf qnt, Op.53)	Op.52
6.20	"Fantasia & Variations on a theme of Danzi," in B-flat major (c1814; cl & str qt/pf, arr from Op.118)	Op.81

Piano Trios:

6.21	Piano Trio No.1 in E minor (c1841)	Op.119
6.22	Piano Trio No.2 in F major (c1842)	Op.123
6.23	Piano Trio No.3 in A minor (c1842)	Op.124
6.24	Piano Trio No.4 in B major (c1846)	Op.133
6.25	Piano Trio No.5 in G minor (c1849)	Op.142

Other 3 insts:

6.26	Harp Trio in F minor (c1806; vn, vc & harp)	WoO 28
6.27	Trio in F major (c?; vn, va & gui, attributed to Spohr)	WoO 138

Vn & pf:

6.28	"Romanze," in B-flat major (c1805)	WoO 26
6.29	"Adagio," in E major (c1809)	WoO 32
6.30	"Potpourri," in G major (c1816; orig w/ orch, Op.23)	WoO 34
6.31	"Potpourri," in E-flat major (c1816; orig w/ str trio, Op.24)	Op.42
6.32	"Introduction & Rondo," in E major (c1816)	Op.46
6.33	"Potpourri," in F-sharp minor (c1820, arr of 2 movts from: Vn & Harp Sonata No.4, Op.114)	Op.50
6.34	"Rondo," in G major (c1820, arr of 3 movts from: Vn & Harp Sonata No.5, Op.115)	Op.51
6.35	"Adagio," in G major (c1820)	WoO37
6.36	"Potpourri on Winter's Das unterbrochene Opferfest," in E major (c1821, after Op.80)	Op.56
6.37	"Duo concertant" No.1 in G minor (c1836)	Op.95
6.38	"Duo concertant" No.2 in F major, "Nachklänge einer Reise nach Dresden" (c1836):	Op.96
	1. "Reiselust"	
	2. "Reise"	
	3. "Katholische Kirche"	
	4. "Sächsische Schweiz"	
6.39	"Rondo alla spagnuola," in C major (c1839)	Op.111
6.40	"Duo concertant" No.3 in E major (c1837)	Op.112
6.41	"Fantasia on themes from 'Der Alchymist,' " in D major (c1841)	Op.117
6.42	"6 Duettinen" (Elegisch und humoristisch) (Lieder ohne Worte) (c1843): No.1 "Allegro"	Op.127
6.43	No.2 "Larghetto"	
6.44	No.3 "Andante"	
6.45	No.4 "Adagio"	
6.46	No.5 "Allegro moderato"	
6.47	No.6 "Finale. Vivace"	
6.48	"Barkarole," in G major (c1845)	WoO 38

6.49	"6 Salon Pieces" (c1846–7): No.1 "Barcarolle" (after WoO 38)	Op.135
6.50	No.2 "Scherzo"	
6.51	No.3 "Sarabande"	
6.52	No.4 "Siciliano"	
6.53	No.5 "Air varié"	
6.54	No.6 "Mazurka"	
6.55	"6 Salon Pieces" (c1851): No.1 "Andante"	Op.145
6.56	No.2 "Andante"	
6.57	No.3 "Allegretto"	
6.58	No.4 "Allegro moderato"	
6.59	No.5 "Adagio"	
6.60	No.6 "Rondo. Allegretto"	
6.61	"Rondo," in A minor (c early 1850s, unfin)	WoO 39
6.62	"Salon Piece," in E minor (ca1851, unfin)	WoO 40
6.63	"Scherzino," in D major (ca1856)	WoO 43
6.64	"Salonstück," in D major (ca1857)	WoO 44

Vn & harp:

6.65	Violin & Harp Sonata No.1 in C minor (c1805)	WoO 23
6.66	"Sonatensatz," in G major (c1805, unfin)	WoO 24
6.67	"Introduzione," in G major (c1805)	WoO 25
6.68	"Sonate," in E minor (ca1806)	WoO 27
6.69	Violin & Harp Sonata No.2 in B-flat major (c1806)	Op.16
6.70	Violin & Harp Sonata No.3 in E-flat major (c1806)	Op.113
6.71	Violin & Harp Sonata No.4 in E-flat major (c1811)	Op.114
6.72	Violin & Harp Sonata No.5 in A-flat major (c1809)	Op.115
6.73	"Rondo," in D major (c1813)	WoO 33
6.74	"Fantasia on themes by Handel & Vogler," in B min / A major (c1814; vn & harp/pf)	Op.118
6.75	Violin & Harp Sonata No.6 in A-flat major (c1819)	WoO 36

2 Vn:

6.76	"3 Violin Duets" (ca1796): No.1 in F major	WoO 21
6.77	No.2 in C major	
6.78	No.3 in E-flat major	
6.79	Violin Duet in E-flat major (ca1797)	WoO 22
6.80	Violin Duet No.1 in E-flat major (c1802–3)	Op.3/1
6.81	Violin Duet No.2 in F major (c1802–3)	Op.3/2
6.82	Violin Duet No.3 in G major (c1802–5)	Op.3/3
6.83	Violin Duet No.4 in C major (c1806–7)	Op.9/1
6.84	Violin Duet No.5 in A major (c1806–7)	Op.9/2
6.85	"Kleines Stück," in C major (ca1808)	WoO 30
6.86	Violin Duet No.6 in D minor (c1816)	Op.39/1
6.87	Violin Duet No.7 in E-flat major (c1816)	Op.39/2
6.88	Violin Duet No.8 in E major (c1816)	Op.39/3
6.89	Violin Duet No.9 in A minor (c1824)	Op.67/1
6.90	Violin Duet No.10 in D major (c1824)	Op.67/2
6.91	Violin Duet No.11 in G minor (c1824)	Op.67/3
6.92	"Violinschule" (66 Übungsstücke für 2 Violinen) (c1830–1)	WoO 45
6.93	Violin Duet No.12 in F major (c1854)	Op.148
6.94	Violin Duet No.13 in D major (c1854)	Op.150
6.95	Violin Duet No.14 in C major (c1855)	Op.153

Vn & va:

6.96	Violin & Viola Duo in E minor (c1807)	Op.13

Bn & pf:

6.97	"Adagio," in F major (c1817; bn & pf, arr of 2 movts from: Vn & Harp Sonata No.5, Op.115)	WoO 35

Harp solo:

6.98	"Fantasie," in C minor (c1807)	Op.35
6.99	"Variations on Mehul's Je suis encore dans mon printemps," in F major (c1807)	Op.36
6.100	"Variations," in E-flat major (c1808)	WoO 29

Vn solo:

6.101	Cadenzas for Beethoven: Violin Concerto in D major, Op.61 (p1897)	

7. PIANO SONATAS

8. OTHER PIANO WORKS

9. ORGAN

10. ORATORIOS

10. SELECTIONS FROM ORATORIOS

10a.3   "Des Heilands letzte Stunden," oratorio: .... WoO 62
. "Ouverture"
Part I: . "Senke dich, stille Nacht" (Chor der Freunde und Freundinnen Jesu)
. "So find ich endlich Freunde meines Herrn!," recit (Johannes, Judas)
. "Weh! Judas, Weh! über dich!," aria (Judas)
. "Wer bleibet sein, wenn ihm die Treue brechen," recit (Maria)
. "Und wenn sie alle weichen," aria w/ chorus (Maria, Freundinnen Jesu)
. "Wer naht sich dort?," (arioso) recit (Johannes)
. "Ewig fliesset, meine Zähren!," aria (Petrus)
. "Auch Petrus, du? du Fels, auf den er baute?," recit (Maria)
. "Der du mit Allgewalt über dem Erdkreis thronst" (Freunde und Freundinnen, Jesu, Maria)
. "Die Pforten des Palastes tun sich auf," recit (Johannes)
. "Lasst mit heiligem Erbeben," arioso w/ chorus (Philo, Priester 1., 2. Zeuge)
. "Maria! ach, sie sinkt erblassend ... Bosheit sehn wir siegen," recit & qt (Johannes & others)
. "Treu bin ich dem Gesetz, ihr wisst's," recit (Nicodemus, Joseph von Arimathia)
. "Schmach! Schmach! Schach! Sie folgen dem Lästerer nach" (Priester und Volk)
. "Ihr wollt's! ich rede!," recit & ch (Kaiphas, Priester und Volk, Jesus, Nicodemus)
. "Über uns komme sein Blut" (Chor der priester und des Volks)
Part II: . "Blikke, du strahlende Sonne," chorus & soli (Freunde und Freundinnen Jesu)
. "Wir stehn am Altar, wo das Lamm soll bluten!," recit (Johannes)
. "Arzt, der allen half, hilf dir nun selber!" (Chor der Priester und des Volks)
. "Maria, hör auf ihn, nicht auf die Frevler!," recit (Johannes, Jesus, Maria)
. "Rufe aus der Welt der Mängel," aria (Maria)
. "Jesus, himmlische Liebe!," trio (Freundinnen Jesu)
. "Blick hin, die letzte Stunde naht!," recit & ch (Johanes, Jesus, Freunde und Freundinnen Jesu)
. "In seiner Todesnot dich zu ihm wende," chorus (Freunde und Freundinnen Jesu)
. "Seht! Gott verlässt dich nicht, der ihm vertraut," recit (Johannes, Jesus)
. "Wir sinken in den Staub und feiern," chorus & soli (Freunde und Freundinnen Jesu)
. "Welch drohend Ungewitter" (Chor der Priester und des Volks)
. "Entflöht ihr auch dem Rächer in den Wolken," recit & chorus (Joseph von Arimathia & others)
. "Wir drükken dir die Augen" (Chor der Freunde und Freundinnen Jesu)

10a.4   "Der Fall Babylons," oratorio: .... WoO 63
. "Ouverture"
Part I: 1. "Gott unsrer Väter, hör die Bitten" (Chor der Juden)
2. "O, wie vertraut sind meinem Ohr diese Schmerzenslaute!," recit (Daniel)
3. "Gedenke, Herr," aria (Daniel)
4. "Der Löwe ist vom Lager gesprungen" (Chor der Juden)
5. "Juda's Gott hat geredet," recit (Cyrus)
6. "Grosser Geist vor deinen Willen beug ich mich," aria (Cyrus)
7. "Über Babylon soll flammen gleich des Blitzes Strahl mein Schwert," aria w/ chorus (Cyrus)
8. "Mein süsses Kind, genährt in Kummer," aria (Jüdin)
9. "Freude, Freude bring ich dir," recit (Der Mann)
10. "Juda, Juda, deines Vaters Liebe," duet (Die Frau, der Mann)
11. "Hoch empor die Siegesfahne!" (Chor der Krieger)
12. "Grosse Königin der Städte," recit (Cyrus)
13. "Herr, wir flehn in tiefen Leiden" (Chor und Soli der Juden)
14. "Der Tag ist gekommen, der Tag des Zorns," recit (Daniel)
15. "Kündet laut die grosse Rettung," trio (2. Jüdin, der Mann, 2. Jude)
16. "Nicht länger wird die Herde Judas irren," aria (Jüdin)
17. "Siehe, ich will dich heim suchen" (Chor der Juden)
Part II: 18. "Die festliche Tafel ist freudegekrönt" (Chor der Hofleute)
19. "O ew'ger Bel" (Chor der Priester)
20. "Auf! Auf, lasst uns die festlichen Bräuche beginnen" (Chor der Babylonierinnen)
21. "Ha! die verhassten Sklaven," recit (Belsazar)
22. "Du trotzest mit verruchter Wut, mein Sohn," duet & d ch (Priester und Jungfrauen)
23. "Jetzt füllt mir den weiten Becher bis zum Rande!," recit (Belsazar)
24. "O, mächt'ger König, die Perser stürmen heran," chorus (Soldat, Balylonier)
25. "Erhab'ner Gott von Israel!," recit (Cyrus)
26. "Was ist der Mensch in seinem stolzen Wahne?," aria (Cyrus)
27. "Lasst tönen die Harfen zu festlichen Klängen," quartet (Juden)
28. "Herr! dich fürchten deine Völker" (Chor der Juden)
29. "Welche Bilder schaut mein Blick!" (Vision) (Daniel)
30. "Die Erlösten des Herrn werden ... Ja, Freude wird bald die Stille beleben," recit & aria (Jüdin)
31. "Frohlokket mit Händen, alle Völker," final chorus

11. OTHER SACRED CHORAL

11.1   "Jubilate Deo," offertory in C major (c1815; S, ch, vn & orch) .... WoO 65
11.2   Mass in C minor (c1821; 5vv & d ch) Op.54
11.3   "Hymn to St Cecilia": "Preis dir, Preis! Du Meisterin der Melodien" (c1823, Calenberg; S, ch & pf) ... WoO 67
11.4   "Vater unser" (c1829, Mahlmann; 4vv, ch & orch) .... WoO 67
11.5   "3 Psalms" (c1832, M. Mendelssohn; vv & d ch): 1. "Psalm 8": "Unendlicher! Gott" Op.85
11.6   2. "Psalm 23": "Gott ist mein Hirt, mir wird nicht mangeln"

11.7   3. "Psalm 130": "Aus der Tiefen ruf' ich Gott!"
11.8   "Psalm 24": "Jehova's ist die Erd und was sie erfüllt" (c1836; 4vv, ch & pf) Op.97a
11.9   "Gott, du bist gross," hymn (c1836, Rohdmann; 4vv, ch & pf/orch) Op.98
11.10   "Vater unser": "Um Erden wandeln Monde" (c1838, Klopstock; 2 m ch & orch) .... WoO 70
11.11   "Psalm 128": "Mit ew'gem Segen krönt der Herr" (c1841–2; vv, ch & orch/pf/org) Op.122
11.12   "Psalm 84": "Wie lieblich ist dein heilig Haus" (c1846; 4vv, ch & orch) .... WoO 72
11.13   "Festgesang": "O sel'ge Zeit, wenn junge Herzen" (c1850; A, ch & pf duet) .... WoO 73
11.14   "Requiem" (c1857–8; vv, ch & orch, inc) .... WoO 74

12. SECULAR CHORAL

12.1   "Der Kompass": "Frisch, die Segel aufgezogen" (ca1807; m ch & pf) .... WoO 89
12.2   "Das befreite Deutschland," cantata (c1814, Pichler) .... WoO 64
12.3   "6 Songs" (c1817; m ch): 1. "Hinauf": "Wenn die Dorne dich umsticht" (Grumbach) Op.44
12.4   2. "Rastlose Liebe": "Dem Schnee, dem Regen, dem Wind entgegen" (Goethe)
12.5   3. "Kennt ihr das Land": "Kennt ihr das Land, wo jede Klage schweigt" (Brun)
12.6   4. "Frühlingsorakel": "Du prophet'scher Vogel, du, Blüten sänger, o! Coucou!" (Goethe)
12.7   5. "Trinklied": "Hört! Hört! Brüder hört!"
12.8   6. "Zur Nacht": "Gute Nacht, gute Nacht, allen Müden sei's gebracht!" (Körner)
12.9   "2 Songs" (c1820; m ch): 1. "Flüchtig ist die Zeit": "Rosen pflückte, Rosen blühn" (Gleim) .... WoO 82
12.10   2. "Punschlied": "Auf, ihr Freunde, lasst uns singen! auf! erfüllt ist unser Wunsch!"
12.11   "Chorus for Hell's Die beiden Galeerensklaven" (c1824; S & ch) .... WoO 66
12.12   "Gebet vor der Schlacht": "Barmherziger und gnäd'ger Gott!" (ca1826; m ch, from incid music:
        Der Sturm von Misolunghi, WoO 4) .... WoO 83
12.13   "Hessens Feiergesang" (c1830, Wolff; 1v, unison ch & brass) .... WoO 68
12.14   "Festgesang": "Es schwebt in lichtem Strahlenkranze" (c1832, Wolff; 3S, ch, vn & pf; also vers
        w/ new text) .... WoO 69
12.15   "6 Songs" (c1833; m ch): 1. "Rat": "Will der Trübsinn deine Stirn umziehen" Op.90
12.16   2. "Ständchen": "Komm heraus, tritt aus dem Haus"
12.17   3. "Sängerleben": "Mit der Laute, mit frohen Sinn"
12.18   4. "Sängerfahrt": "Die Sonne hinter den Bergen ruht" (Pfeiffer)
12.19   5. "Alte Liebe": "Blickt im schönsten Frauenkreise lächelnd oft mein Angesicht"
12.20   6. "Trinklied": "Wir sind nicht mehr beim ersten Glas"
12.21   "Lasst uns den Dankgesang erheben," fugue in C major (c1838) .... WoO 85
12.22   "Schill": "Wir trauern um den braven Held, um Schill, er ist nicht mehr!" (c1840; m ch & pf duet) .... WoO 71
12.23   "Grabgesang": "Selig alle, die im Herrn entschliefen" (c1844; m ch) .... WoO 86
12.24   "Festgesang": "O sel'ge Zeit, wenn junge Herzen" (c1850; A, ch & pf duet) .... WoO 73
12.25   "6 Songs" (c1855; ch): 1. "Winterlied": "Der Wind, der saust, der Wald erbraust" (Werra) .... WoO 87
12.26   2. "Die Frühlingszeit": "Wie schön ist doch die Frühlingszeit" (Werra)
12.27   3. "Des Menschen Trost": "Ach, wem ein recht Gedenken blüht, den schmerzet" (Werra)
12.28   4. "Der Sommerabend": "Dieses Schwärmen, dieses Leben" (Holtaus)
12.29   5. "Das deutsche Lied": "Was wirkt das freie Lied?" (Felim)
12.30   6. "Ode": "Himmelanstrebende, geisterbelebende göttliche Kraft" (G. Berlin)
12.31   "Ständchen": "Sei uns gegrüsst im frohen Tönen" (c1856, Kahlert; m ch) .... WoO 88

13. CANONS

13.1   "Lebe wohl, du Vater Brocken" (c1808; 3vv) .... WoO 128
13.2   "Willst du immer weiter schweifen" (c1817; 4vv) .... WoO 129
13.3   "Kanon für 4 Stimmen" (c1817; 4vv) .... WoO 130
13.4   "Kanon für 6 Stimmen" (c1820s; 6vv) .... WoO 132
13.5   "Wer das Scheiden hat erfunden" (c after 1830; 2vv) .... WoO 133
13.6   "Kurz ist der Schmerz" (c1848; 3S) .... WoO 134
13.7   "Auflösung eines Rätselkanons von C. M. von Weber" (c by 1825) .... WoO 135
13.8   "Betracht, o Mensch, die Traurigkeit," geistliches Lied (c1853; 4vv) .... WoO 136

14. VOICE & ORCHESTRA

14.1   "Oscar Umsonst!," scene (c1805; S & orch) .... WoO 75
14.2   "Torni serena l'alma," aria alla polacca (c1811; T, vn solo & orch) .... WoO 76
14.3   "Recitative & aria for opera 'Faust' " (c1818, Döring) .... WoO 77
           1. "Der Hölle selbst will ich segen entringen," recit
           2. "Liebe ist die zarte Blüte," aria
14.4   "Welche seltenen Gefühle," recit (ca1822, for Weigl: Adrian von Ostade) .... WoO 78
14.5   "Scene & aria for opera 'Jessonda' " (c1820s): .... WoO 79
           1. "O neu gefühl, was mich beseelet"
           2. "O Welt, so schön und blühend," aria
14.6   "Matrosenlied": "Der Sturmwind braust" (c1838; T & orch, for incid music) .... WoO 80
14.7   "Tu m'abbandoni, ingrato," scene & aria (c1823; S & orch): Op.71
           1. "E mi lasci così?," recit
           2. "Tu m'abbandoni, ingrato," aria

15. DUETS, TRIOS & QUARTETS (w/ pf)

15.1   "Terzett": "Freunde, Jubel" (ca1808; 3vv & pf) .... WoO 81
15.2   "3 Lieder" (c1838; S, T & pf): 1. "Liebesfragen": "Sag, wie kann man Lieb' erkennen?" (Schulz) Op.107
15.3   2. "Wechselgesang": "Wer lässt hier so lieblich, wer lässt so allein" (Tiedge)
15.4   3. "Liebe": "Wenn im Lenze ringsum alles lacht"
15.5   "3 Lieder" (c1838; 2S & pf): 1. "Abendlied": "Die stille Nacht heisst niedre Sorgen" (Rochlitz) Op.108
15.6   2. "Das Herz": "Es sehnt sich das Herz nach Lust und nach Schmerz"
15.7   3. "Ruhe": "Wenn im letzten Dämmerungsstrahle" (Deuern)
15.8   "Jenseits": "Wo blüht das Tal, wo liebe sich ew'ge Kränze flicht?" (c1838, Bobrich; S, T & pf) .... WoO 98
15.9   "6 Lieder" (c1841–2; S, A, T, B & pf): 1. "Sonnenschein": "Am Wandspalier" (Dräxler-Manfred) Op.120
15.10 2. "Vesper": "Die Abendglokken tönen" (Schweizer)
15.11 3. "Wanderlust": "Lasst mich wandern! ich muss wandern!" (Lyser)
15.12 4. "An die Sterne": "Aus weiter Ferne, liebliche Sterne" (Fr. Spohr)
15.13 5. "Ergebung": "Wen du, mein Gott, mich führst auf Blumenpfade" (Spener)
15.14 6. "Frühlingsgedanken": "Die Knospe sprengt das Haus, und freudig strebt hinaus" (Hagen)
15.15 "Mein Heimatland": "Wo reiner Liebe goldne Strahlen" (c1847, anon from Mecklenburg; 2S & pf) WoO 116
15.16 "3 Lieder" (c1849; 2S & pf): 1. "Der Vogel steigt" (Ebert) .... WoO 117
15.17 2. "Sonntagsfrühe": "Feierlicher Glokkenklang" (Lange)
15.18 3. "Frühlingslied": "Die Fenster sonnen, der Winter ist aus" (Scheurlin)
15.19 "Wenn sich zwei Herzen finden" (c1851, Schad; S, A & pf) .... WoO 120

16. SONGS (w/ pf)

16.1   "6 Lieder" (c1809): 1. "Wiegenlied": "Eia popeia, so leise so lind" (Goechhausen) Op.25
16.2   2. "Schottisch Lied": "Mir ist, als müsst ich dir was sagen"
16.3   3. "Gretchen": "Meine Ruh ist hin, mein Herz ist schwer" (from Goethe's Faust Part I) (also see
       Schubert Op.2, D118)
16.4   4. "Lied der Freude": "Rauschet ihr Meere und wehet ihr Winde!" (Gross)
16.5   5. "Zigeunerlied": "Im Nebelgeriesel, im tiefen Schnee" (Goethe) (also see Busoni Op.55, K295)
16.6   6. "Das Schiffermädchen": "Schwebe, mein tanzender Kahn" (Gyr)
16.7   "Lied des verlassenen Mädchens": "Wie weil' ich so gern" (c1814 or 5, Deinhardstein) .... WoO 90
16.8   "6 Lieder" (c1815): 1. "Mignons Lied": "Kennst du das Land? Wo die Zitronen blühn" (Goethe) Op.37
16.9   2. "Lebenslied": "Schnell geniesst die schnellen Stunden" (Schmidt)
16.10 3. "Die Stimme der Nacht": "Dort im Tal hör ich verhallen" (Cäcilie von W.)
16.11 4. "Getrennte Liebe": "Der Liebe bangen Sorgen erbleicht der Freude Strahl!" (Schmidt)
16.12 5. "Liebesschwärmerei": "Wär ich ein Vögelein, flög ich zu ihm!" (Cäcilie von W.)
16.13 6. "Lied beim Rundetanz": "Auf! es dunkelt; silbern funkelt" (Salis)
16.14 "6 Lieder" (c1815): 1. "Des Mädchens Sehnsucht": "Das Herz ist gewachsen" (Kind) Op.41
16.15 2. "Lied aus Aslauga's Ritter": "Ach, wär' ich nur ein Vögelein!" (Motte-Fouqué)
16.16 3. "An Mignon": "Über Tal und Fluss getragen zieht rein der Sonne Wagen!" (Goethe)
16.17 4. "Klagelied von den drei Rosen": "Drei Rosen hielt ich in Händen" (Buri)
16.18 5. "Der erste Kuss": "Die Lippe brennt, die Wange glüht" (Kartscher)
16.19 6. "Vanitas! vanitatum vanitas": "Ich hab' meine Sach' auf nichts gestellt" (Goethe)
16.20 "Nachgefühl": "Wenn die Reben wieder blühn" (c1819, Goethe) .... WoO 91
16.21 "Was treibt den Waidmann in den Wald" (c1825, Vogel; 1v, hn & harp/pf) .... WoO 92
16.22 "6 Lieder" (c1826): 1. "Frühlingsglaube": "Die Linden Lüfte sind erwacht" (Uhland) Op.72
16.23 2. "Schifferlied der Wasserfee": "Auf Wogen gezogen, von Klängen, Gesängen" (Tieck)
16.24 3. "Ghasel": "Wer hätte wie sie gesehn und nicht auch sie geliebt?" (Adil)
16.25 4. "Beruhigung": "Du armes Herz, was wünschest du?"
16.26 5. "An Rosa Maria": "Du gabst mir längst dein schönes Herz, was geb' ich Dir dafür"
16.27 6. "Schlaflied": "Ruhe, süss Liebchen, im Schatten der grauen dämmernden Nacht" (Tieck)
16.28 "6 Lieder" (c1835–6; A/Bar): 1. "Lied der Harfnerin": "Schweig, o Herz!" Op.94
16.29 2. "Bitte, bitte!": "Bitte, bitte! einen Blick aus den holden blauen Augen" (Schmidt)
16.30 3. "Der Bleicherin Nachtlied": "Wellen blinkten durch die Nacht" (Reinick)
16.31 4. "Ungeduld": "Ich schnitt es gern in alle Rinde ein" (Müller)
16.32 5. "Schwermut": "Als mein Leben voll Blumen hing" (Mahlmann)
16.33 6. "Sonntag und Montag": "Heute ist Sonntag"
16.34 "Das Wirtshaus zu ..." (c1836, Marees; A/Bar) .... WoO 93
16.35 "6 Lieder" (c1836–7; w/ pf/pf duet): 1. "Frühlingsglocken": Schneeglöckchen läuten" (Reinick) Op.101
16.36 2. "Sangeslust": "Das Vöglein singt den ganzen Tag" (Eberwein, = WoO 95)
16.37 3. "Nichts Schöneres": "Als ich zuerst dich hab gesehn" (Reinick)
16.38 4. "Trostlos": "Der Regen rasselt, es saust der Sturm" (Hochwald)
16.39 5. "Schweigen ist ein Ding": "Schweigen ist ein schönes Ding!" (Reinick)
16.40 6. "Gondelfahrt": "In den Wassern der Laguna" (Geibel)
16.41 "6 Lieder" (c1837; w/ cl & pf): 1. "Sei still mein Herz": "Ich wahrte die Hoffnung" (Schweizer) Op.103
16.42 2. "Zweigesang": "Im Fliederbusch ein Vöglein sass" (Reinick)
16.43 3. "Sehnsucht": "Ich blick in mein Herz und ich blick in die Welt" (Geibel)
16.44 4. "Wiegenlied": "Alles still in süsser Ruh" (Fallersleben)
16.45 5. "Das heimliche Lied": "Es gibt geheime Schmerzen" (Koch)
16.46 6. "Wach auf": "Was stehst du lange und sinnest nach?"
16.47 "6 Lieder" (c1838; S/T): 1. "Die Himmelsbraut": "Zu Augsburg steht ein hohes Haus" (Kerner) Op.105
16.48 2. "Der Rosenstrauch": "Das Kind schläft unter dem Rosenstrauch" (Ferrand)
16.49 3. "Ständchen": "Was wekken aus dem Schlummer mich für süsse Klänge doch?" (Uhland)

16.50	4. "An * * * ": "Was treibt mich hin zu dir mit Macht?" (Koch)
16.51	5. "Des Mädchens Klage": "Ich bin so bleich, du bist so rot" (Schweizer)
16.52	6. "Warum nicht?": "Lieben, warum sollt' ich's nicht?"
16.53	"Mitternacht": "Die Wolken ziehen schwarz und hoch" (c1838, Dingelstedt; w/ pf duet) .... WoO 97
16.54	"Verlust": "Am Bach, am Bach, im flüsternden Grass" (c1839, Zimmermann) .... WoO 99
16.55	"An die Geliebte": "Immer mag verklingen" (c1839, from Hugo: Ruy Blas) .... WoO 100
16.56	"Unterwegs": "In die blaue Luft hinaus einen stillen Gruss nach Haus" (c1839, Dingelstedt) .... WoO 101
16.57	"Die 7 Schwestern": "Die Wogen ergriffen vom Loreley-Sang" (c1839, Wihl; w/ pf duet) .... WoO 102
16.58	"Rätselhaft": "Der Frühling ist herangekommen" (c1841; T & pf duet) .... WoO 103
16.59	"Abendlied": "Sternennacht, heil'ge Nacht!" (c1841, Becker) .... WoO 104
16.60	"Lied": "Singet die Nachtigall im dunkeln Wald" (c1841, from Zedlitz: Kerker und Krone) .... WoO 105
16.61	"Wolle keiner mich fragen" (c1842, Geibel) .... WoO 106
16.62	"Tränen": "Was ist's, o Vater, was ich verbrach?" (c1842, Chamisso) .... WoO 108
16.63	"Liebt er mich?" (c1843) .... WoO 109
16.64	"Gruss": "Immortelle! bring' mein 'gute Nacht' ihr hin" (c1843, Braunthal) .... WoO 110
16.65	"Mein Vaterland": "Treue Liebe bis zum Grabe schwör ich dir" (c1844, Fallersleben) .... WoO 111
16.66	"Ermutigung": "Freudig zum Himmel auf blikke mein Herz!" (c1845, Schweizer) .... WoO 112
16.67	"Immerdar liebe": "Kömmt mit dem Lenz auch die Lieb gegangen" (c1845, Göchhausen)............. WoO 113
16.68	"Sehnsucht": "Überall in dem All, mag ich liegen oder stehen" (c1846, ?Meier) .... WoO 114
16.69	"Der Herbst": "Sommer entschwand, Herbstluft durchwehet das Land" (c1847, Lua) .... WoO 115
16.70	"An Sie am Klavier," sonatine w/ song in B-flat major (c1848, Braunthal) Op.138
16.71	"5 Lieder" (c1836–48): 1. "Ständchen": "Atme nur leise" (Simrock, = WoO 94) Op.139
16.72	2. "Maria": "Der Sänger zog durch Wald und Flur" (= WoO 107)
16.73	3. "Jägerlied": "Wenn Eos am Morgen mit rosigem Finger das Dunkel erhellt"
16.74	4. "Lied aus dem 'Märlein von der Wasserfee' ": "Über die Wellen zieht zagend" (Bekmann)
16.75	5. "Was mir wohl übrig bliebe, wenn alles von mir flieht?" (Fallersleben, = WoO 96)
16.76	"Glockenklänge": "Sanft ertönen Morgenglokken" (c1850) .... WoO 118
16.77	"3 Lieder" (c1850, Bodenstedt): 1. "Zuleikha": "Nicht mit Engeln im blauen Himmelszelt" .... WoO 119
16.78	2. "Trinklied": "Füllt mir das Trinkhorn! reicht es herum!"
16.79	3. "Fatima beim Saitenspiel": "Deine Finger rühren die Saiten, und die Saiten mein Herz"
16.80	"Jüngst hört ich, Welchen süssen Lohn" (c1850s, attributed to Spohr) .... WoO 139
16.81	"Erwartung": "Komm in den Garten, ich harre dein" (ca1853, Bassewitz) .... WoO 121
16.82	"Mein Verlangen": "Es ist ein süsses Wähnen im Trauern und in Tränen" (c1854, Werra)............ WoO 122
16.83	"Grüsse": "Fliege auf Windes Schwingen, Blättlein, zu ihr!" (c1855, Linden) .... WoO 123
16.84	"Immer Dasselbe": "Es wogt wie steigende Wellen" (c1856, from Linden: Bühne & Haus) .... WoO 124
16.85	"Wohin": "Wohin du rauschender Strom?" (c1856, Sturm) .... WoO 125
16.86	"6 Lieder" (c1856; Bar, vn & pf): 1. "Abendfeier": "Leise schleich ich mich" (Mahn) Op.154
16.87	2. "Jagdlied": "Seht ihr's dort funkeln in rosiger Pracht?" (Fr. Spohr)
16.88	3. "Töne": "Worte hab ich nicht, um dir zu sagen" (Otto)
16.89	4. "Erlkönig": "Wer reitet so spät durch Nacht und Wind?" (Goethe)
16.90	5. "Der Spielmann und seine Geige": "Vor Gottes Aug', dem Abendrot" (Hozze)
16.91	6. "Abendstille: "Der Tag hat sich zur Ruh gelegt" (Koch)
16.92	"Die verschwiegene Nachtigall": "Unter der Linden an der Heide" (c1857, Vogelweide) .... WoO 126
16.93	"Neue Liebe, neues Leben": "Herz, mein Herz, was soll das geben" (c1858, Goethe) .... WoO 127

17. ARRANGEMENTS OF WORKS OF OTHERS

17.1	Fiorillo: Violin Caprices (add of 2nd vn acc for the teacher 1854) .... WoO 47

* * * * *

WoO = Works without opus numbers in Folker Göthel: "Thematisch-bibliographisches Verzeichnis der Werke von Louis Spohr." Tutzing, 1981.

1. STAGE WORKS

Operas:

1.1   "Atmen gibt das Leben ..." (5–7 min) (c1974–7; orig as chorus; r1977 as opera for ch & orch/tape) ... No.39

"LICHT: Die sieben Tage der Woche," 7-night cycle (one opera for each day of the week, 3 operas completed to date):

1.2   "Donnerstag aus LICHT," 3 act opera, a greeting, and a farewell (c1978–80; 3vv, 8 insts & 3 dancers): ......
     I. "Michaels Jugend" (Kindheit—Mondeva—Examen) No.49
     II. "Michaels Reise um die Erde" No.48
     III. "Michaels Heimkehr" (Festival—Vision); "Donnerstags-Abschied" No.50

1.3   "Samstag aus LICHT," opera in a greeting & 4 scenes (c1981–4; 13 musical performers: 1v, 10 insts, 2 dancers, winds, ballet/mimes, m ch & org): ....
     . "Samstags Gruss" (Luzifer-Gruss)
     Scene 1. "Luzifers Traum"
     2. "Kathinkas Gesang als Luzifers Requiem"
     3. "Luzifers Tanz"
     4. "Luzifers Abschied"

1.4   "Montag aus LICHT," 3 act opera, a greeting, and a farewell (c1984–8; 21 musical performers: 14vv, 6 insts, 1 actor & modern orch: electronic kbd insts, perc, various instr ens, choir groups, vv recorded on tape, 8-track tapes of concrete & electronic sounds, 40-channel sound system, 16-channel sound projection):
     . "Montags-Gruss"
     I. "Evas Erstgeburt"
     II. "Evas Zweitgeburt"
     III. "Evas Zauber"
     . "Montags-Abschied"

Ballet:

1.5   *"Burlesca," pantomime (c1950, Stockhausen; speaker, 4vv, ch, str qt, pf & perc, collab Seuthe, Weiler, ?lost)* ....
1.6   "Der Jahreslauf" (scene from Dienstag aus LICHT) (c1977; ballet, actor, orch & tape; vers for orch) .. No.47

Incid music:

1.7   "Originale" (1 hr 34 min) (c1961, = text + electronic music of: Kontakte, No.12) ....

Film (selection):

1.8   "Musical Forming" (165 min, English) ....
1.9   "Mikrophonie I" (90 min, English) ....
1.10   "Moment-Forming and Integration" (120 min, English) ....
1.11   "Intuitive Music" (60 min, English) ....
1.12   "Questions and Answers on Intuitive Music" (35 min, English) ....
1.13   "4 Criteria of Electronic Music" (105 min, English) ....
1.14   "Questions and Answers on 4 Criteria of Electronic Music" (105 min, English) ....
1.15   "Telemusic" (60 min, English) ....
1.16   "Mantra" (120 min, English) ....
1.17   "Questions and Answers on Mantra" (60 min, English) ....
1.18   "Momente" (45 min 51 sec, English, French, German) ....
1.19   "Microphonie I" (21 min 06 sec, French) ....
1.20   "Stockhausen und die Höhlen von Jeita" (Stockhausen and the Caves of Jeita) (30 min, English)..............
1.21   "Ich werde die Töne—die Weltschau des Karlheinz Stockhausen" (30 min 44 sec, German) ....
1.22   "Internationale Ferienkurse für Neue Musik, Darmstadt 1970. Dokumentation einer Misslungenen Revolution" (Eng, Ger, Fr; from Stockhausen's seminars 'Feedback' and 'Expansion of Dynamics') ....
1.23   "Mantra" (56 min 28 sec, German, English, French, Spanish, Arabic) ....
1.24   "Trans ... und so Weiter" (58 min 43 sec) ....
1.25   "Alphabet für Liège" (60 min, French) ....
1.26   "Inori" (70 min, German; also German vers of 28 min 35 sec; Italian vers of ca 75 min) ....
1.27   "Michaels Reise um die Erde" (ca 50 min, Italian) ....
1.28   " 'Tuning In' with Stockhausen and Singcircle" (ca 49 min, English) ....
1.29   "TG L'UNA" (ca 20 min, Italian) ....
1.30   "Donnerstag aus LICHT im Teatro alla Scala" (Italian) ....
1.31   "Notenschlüssel: Stockhausen und seine Kinder" (43 min 58 sec, German) ....
1.32   "Stockhausen und seine Werke" (44 min 27 sec, German) ....
1.33   "Musique et Electronique avec Karlheinz Stockhausen et George Lewis" (26 min, French video) ....
1.34   "Samstag aus LICHT im Teatro alla Scala" (Italian) ....
1.35   "Blitz" (ca 30 min, Italian) ....
1.36   "Samstag aus LICHT—Karlheinz Stockhausen Zweiter Schöpfungstag" (29 min 45 sec, German) ....
1.37   "Das Welttheater des Karlheinz Stockhausen" (60 min 23 sec, German) ....
1.38   "Hymnen mit Solisten und Orchester" (ca125 min, Hungarian video) ....
1.39   "Kathinkas Gesang de Karlheinz Stockhausen" (33 min 21 sec, French) ....
1.40   "Donnerstag aus LICHT in Covent Garden" (ca 45 min, English) ....
1.41   "Evas Lied" (ca 42 min, German) ....
1.42   "Evas Zauber" (ca 60 min, French video) ....

1a. SELECTIONS FROM STAGE WORKS (for concert performance)

1a.2   "Donnerstag aus LICHT," opera, a greeting, and a farewell: ....
        1978: . "Michaels Reise um die Erde" (Act II), No.48 (tpt & orch)
           . "Eingang und Formel" (tpt, from: Michels Reise, No.48)
           . "Halt" (tpt & d.bass, from: Michaels Reise, No.48)
           . "Kreuzigung" (9 brass insts & electronic org, from: Michaels Reise, No.48)
           . "Mission und Himmelfahrt" (tpt & basset-hn, from: Michaels Reise, No.48)
           . "Donnerstags-Gruss" (8 brass insts, pf & 3 percussionists)
           . "Michaels-Ruf" (8 orchestra players: variable ensemble)
        1978–9: . "Michaels Jugend" (Act I), No.49 (T, S, B, tpt, basset-hn, trbn, pf, electronic org,
             3 dancer-mimes; tapes w/ ch & insts)
           . "Unsichtbare Chöre" (7-track a-capella tape & 8- or 2-track play-back)
           . "Kindheit" (T, S, B, tpt, basset-hn, trbn, dancer & tapes, from: Michaels Jugend, No.49)
           . "Tanze Luceva!" (basset-hn/b cl, from: Michaels Jugend, No.49)
           . "Bijou" (alto fl & b cl, from: Michaels Jugend, No.49)
           . "Mondeva" (Scene 2 of: Michaels Jugend, No.49) (T, tpt, dancer, basset-hn, pf
             & ad lib: 'jury' of S, B, and 2 dancer-mimes, 2 tapes)
           . "Examen" (Scene 3 of: Michaels Jugend, No.49) (T, tpt, dancer, basset-hn, pf
             & ad lib 'jury': S, B & 2 dancer-mimes, 2 tapes)
           . "Klavierstück XII" (Examen) (pf, from: Michaels Jugend, No.49)
        1978–84: . Version for soloists of: Michaels Reise, No.48 (tpt, 9 other players & sound projectionist)
        1980: . "Michaels Heimkehr" (Act III), No.50 (T, S, B, tpt, basset-hn, trbn, 2sax, electronic org,
             3 dancer-mimes, old woman, ch, orch & tapes)
           . "Festival" (T, S, B, tpt, basset-hn, trbn, 2 soprano sax, 3 dancer-mimes, old woman, ch,
             orch & tapes, from: Michaels Heimkehr, No.50)
           . "Drachenkampf" (tpt, trbn, electronic org/synthesizer & 2 dancers ad lib, from: Michaels
             Heimkehr, No.50)
           . "Knabenduett" (2 soprano sax/other insts, from: Michaels Heimkehr, No.50)
           . "Argument" (T, B, electric org/synthesizer & ad lib: tpt, trbn, perc, from: Michaels
             Heimkehr, No.50)
           . "Vision" (T, tpt, dancer, Hammond org, tape & shadow plays ad lib, from: Michaels
             Heimkehr, No.50)

1a.3   "Samstag aus LICHT," opera in a greeting & 4 scenes: ....
        1981: . "Luzifers Traum" (Scene 1) (Piano Piece XIII) (B & pf)
           . "Traum-Formel" (basset-hn, from: Luzifers Traum)
        1982: . "Luzifers Abschied" (Scene 4) (m ch, org, 7trbn live/on tape)
        1982–3: . "Kathinkas Gesang als Luzifers Requiem" (Scene 2) (fl & 6 percussionists or fl solo; vers for fl
             & electronic music; vers for fl & pf)
        1983: . "Luzifers Tanz" (Scene 3) (bass/trbn/euphonium, piccolo tpt, piccolo fl & winds/orch plus
             a stilt-dancer, dancer, ballet/mimes for scenic performance)
           . "Linker Augenbrauentanz" (percussionist, cls & b cls, from: Luzifers Tanz)
           . "Rechter Augentanz" (percussionist, obs, cors anglais, bns, from: Luzifers Tanz)
           . "Nasenflügeltanz" (percussionist & electronic kbd insts ad lib, from: Luzifers Tanz)
           . "Oberlippentanz" (piccolo tpt or piccolo tpt, trbn/euphonium, 2 percussionists & 4–8hns,
             from: Luzifers Tanz)
           . "Zungenspitzentanz" (piccolo or piccolo & ad lib: dancers, percussionist & euphonium/electronic
             kbd insts, from: Luzifers Tanz)
           . "Kinntanz" (trbn/euphonium, 2 percussionists, euphonium, 1 or more alto trbn, 1 or more
             bar/tenor saxhorn, 1 or more b tuba, from: Luzifers Tanz)
        1984: . "Samstags-Gruss" (26 brass players & 2 percussionists)

1a.4   "Montag aus LICHT," 3 act opera, a greeting, and a farewell: ....
        1984: . "Klavierstück XIV" (Geburtstags-Formel) (pf, from: Evas Zweitgeburt)
           . "Evas Spiegel" (basset-hn, from: Evas Zauber)
           . "Susani" (basset-hn, from: Evas Zauber)
        1984–5: . "Botschaft" (basset-hn, alto fl, ch & modern orch, from: Evas Zauber, vers for basset-hn, alto fl
             & ch, vers for basset-hn, alto fl & modern orch)
           . "AVE" (basset-hn & alto fl, from: Evas Zauber)
        1984–6: . "Evas Zauber" (Act III) (basset-hn, alto fl and piccolo, ch, child ch & modern orch)
        1984–7: . "Befruchtung mit Klavierstück" (pf, girls' ch & modern orch, from: Evas Zweitgeburt)
           . "Evas Zweitgeburt" (Act II) (7 boys' vv, basset-hn, 3 'bassettinists': 2 basset-hns + 1v, pf, ch,
             girls' ch & modern orch)
        1984–8: . "Montags-Gruss" (Eva-Gruss) (multiple basset-hns & electronic kbd insts)
        1985: . "Susani's Echo" (alto fl, from: Evas Zauber)
        1986: . "Evas Lied" (7 boy's vv, basset-hn, 3 'bassettinists': 2 basset-hns + 1v, modern orch & fem ch
             ad lib, from: Evas Zweitgeburt)
           . "Wochenkreis" (Die sieben Lieder der Tage), duet (basset-hn & electronic kbd insts,
             from: Evas Zweitgeburt)
           . "Der Kinderfänger" (alto fl and piccolo, basset-hn ad lib, child ch ad lib & modern orch,
             from: Evas Zauber)
           . "Entführung" (piccolo & modern orch ad lib, from: Evas Zauber)
           . "Xi" (basset-hn, from: Montags-Gruss; vers for alto fl/fl)
        1987: . "Evas Erstgeburt" (Act I) (3S, 3T, B, actor, ch, child ch & modern orch)

. "Mädchenprozession" (girls' ch, ch ad lib & modern orch, from: Evas Zweitgeburt)
1988: . "Montags-Abschied" (Eva-Abschied) (child ch, multiple vv and piccolos & electronic kbd insts)

2. ORCHESTRAL WORKS

3. CONCERTOS, SOLO INSTR & ORCH

4. OTHER CHAMBER MUSIC

5. ELECTRONIC MUSIC

8. OTHER PIANO WORKS

8.1	*"Scherzo" (c ?1950, in Hindemith style, unpubd/lost)*	
8.2	*"6 Studien" (c ?1950, destroyed)*	
8.3	"Präludium" (c1951, = pf part of the 1st movt of: Sonatine for vn & pf, No. 1/8)	
8.4	"Piano Pieces I–IV" (ca 8 min) (c1952–3)	No.2
8.5	"Piano Pieces V–X" (c1954–5): . Piano Piece V" (6 min)	No.4
8.6	. "Piano Piece VI" (26 min) (r1961)	
8.7	. "Piano Piece VII" (7 min)	
8.8	. "Piano Piece VIII" (2 min)	
8.9	. "Piano Piece IX" (ca10 min) (not written out until 1961)	
8.10	. "Piano Piece X" (ca 23 min) (not written out until 1961)	
8.11	*"Piano Piece" (c1954, perf1974, unpubd/lost)*	*No.51/2*
8.12	*"Piano Piece" (c1954, perf1974, unpubd/lost)*	*No.61/2*
8.13	"Piano Piece XI" (ca14 min) (c1956, 19 frags on a large sheet of paper, playing order free, tempo indicated at the end of each frag applies to the next one, all repeated 2nd time w/ add instructions, 1 frag played 3rd time)	No.7

Pf duet:

8.14	*"Vision," duo (c1969– , uncompleted)*	

2 Pf:

8.15	"Mantra" (65 min) (c1970)	No.32

9. CHORAL WORKS

9.1	*"3 Chöre" (c ?1950, Stockhausen; 2- & 3-part ch, unpubd/lost): 1. "Gottes Krippen" (God's Cradle)*	
9.2	*2. "Maria"*	
9.3	*3. "Bei dem Kinde" (With the Child)*	
9.4	"Chöre für Doris" (ca15 min) (c1950, Verlaine; ch):	No.1/11
	1. "Die Nachtigall"	
	2. "Armer junger Hirt"	
	3. "Agnus Dei"	
9.5	"Choral": "Wer uns trug mit Schmerzen in dies' Leben" (2 min) (c1950; 4-part ch)	No.1/9
9.6	"Carré" (c1959–60; 4ch & 4orch)	No.10
9.7	"Momente" (80 min) (c1962; S, 4ch & 13 instrumentalists, uses words from Blake's Eternity: '... he who kisses the joy as it flies Lives in Eternity's sun rise') (also see Vaughan Williams' 10. of: 10 Blake Songs)	No.13
9.8	Version of: Momente, No.13 (c1964; enlarged)	No.131/2
9.9	Version of: Momente, No.13 (c1969; enlarged)	No.132/3

10. MISC VOCAL

10.1	"3 Lieder" (17 min) (c1950; A & chamber orch): 1. "Der Rebell" (Baudelaire)	No. 1/10
10.2	2. "Frei" (anon)	
10.3	3. "Der Saitenmann" (anon)	
10.4	"Mikrophonie II" (15 min) (c1965; 12 singers, Hammond org, 4 ring modulators & tape)	No.17
10.5	"Stimmung" (unspecified) (c1968; 2S, mS, T, Bar, B; also 'Paris version' in 1968)	No.24
10.6	"Paris Version" (73 min) (c1968)	No.241/2
10.7	"Am Himmel wandre ich" (12 American Indian Songs) (50 min) (c1971; 2vv)	No.361/2
10.8	"Vortrag über HU" (Musical analysis of INORI) (c1973–4; singer)	No.381/2

11. CADENZAS

11.1	Cadenza for Mozart: Clarinet Conc in A major, K622 (c1978)	
11.2	Cadenza for Mozart: Flute Conc No.1 in G major, K285c (K313) (c1984–5)	
11.3	Cadenza for Mozart: Flute Conc No.2 in D major, K285d (K314) (c1984–5)	
11.4	Cadenza for Leopold Mozart: Trumpet Concerto (c1984)	
11.5	Cadenza for Haydn: Trumpet Conc in E-flat major, HobVIIe/1 (c1983–5)	

* * * * *

Numbers of compositions starting with No. 1/11 by the composer.

1. WALTZES & COTILLONS (pubd for pf, simultaneous arrs for pf duet, also for vn & pf)

1.1	"Walzer mit Coda," in F major (p1818)	
1.2	"Walzer für den Carneval 1820" (p1819–20)	
1.3	"7 Walzer," in F major (p1825)	
1.4	"Täuberl-Walzer" (Walzer in E) (c1826, p1829)	Op.1
1.5	"Döblinger Réunion-Walzer" (p1827)	Op.2
1.6	"Wiener Carneval-Walzer" (p1828)	Op.3
1.7	"Kettenbrücke-Walzer" I (p1828)	Op.4
1.8	"Gesellschafts-Walzer" (p1827)	Op.5
1.9	"Wiener Launen-Walzer" (p1828)	Op.6
1.10	"Walzer à la Paganini" (p1828)	Op.11
1.11	"Krapfen-Waldel-Walzer" (p1828)	Op.12
1.12	(Die beliebten) "Trompeten-Walzer" (p1829)	Op.13
1.13	"Champagner-Walzer" (p1828)	Op.14
1.14	"Erinnerungs-Walzer" (Die so sehr beliebten Erinnerungs-Ländler) (p1829)	Op.15
1.15	"Fort nacheinander!" (p1828)	Op.16
1.16	"Lustlager-Walzer" (p1829)	Op.18
1.17	"Kettenbrücke-Walzer" II (p1829)	Op.19
1.18	"Es ist nur ein Wien!" (p1829)	Op.22
1.19	"Josephstädter Tänze" (p1829)	Op.23
1.20	"Hietzinger Réunion-Walzer" (Weissgärber-Kirchweih-Tänze) (p1829)	Op.24
1.21	"Frohsinn im Gebirge" (p1829)	Op.26
1.22	"Sperls Fest-Walzer" (p1829)	Op.30
1.23	"Des Verfassers beste Laune: Charmant-Walzer" (p1829)	Op.31
1.24	"Schwarz'sche Ball-Tänze" (p1830, from Auber's opera: La muette de Portici)	Op.32
1.25	"Benefice-Walzer" (p1830)	Op.33
1.26	"Gute Meinung—für die Tanzlust" (p1830)	Op.34
1.27	"Souvenir de Baden" (Helenen-Walzer) (p1830)	Op.38
1.28	"Wiener Tivoli-Musik," Book I (p1830)	Op.39a
1.29	"Wiener Tivoli-Musik," Book II (Tivoli-Rutsch-Walzer)	Op.39b
1.30	"Wiener Damen-Toilette-Walzer" (p1830)	Op.40
1.31	"Fra Diavolo-Cotillons" (p1830)	Op.41
1.32	"Tivoli Freudenfest-Tänze" (Tivoli-Fest-Walzer) (p1831)	Op.45
1.33	"Vive la danse!" (p1831)	Op.47
1.34	"Heiter auch in ernster Zeit!" (p1831)	Op.48
1.35	"Das Leben ein Tanz, der Tanz ein Leben!" (p1831)	Op.49
1.36	"Cotillons aus: Die Unbekannte" (p1832, on themes from Bellini's opera: La straniera)	Op.50
1.37	"Hofball-Tänze" (p1832)	Op.51
1.38	"Bajaderen-Walzer" (p1832)	Op.53
1.39	"Alexandra-Walzer" (p1832)	Op.56
1.40	"Zampa-Walzer" (p1832)	Op.57
1.41	"Mein schönster Tag in Baden" (p1832)	Op.58
1.42	"Die vier Temperamente" (p1832)	Op.59
1.43	"Carnevals-Spende" (p1833)	Op.60
1.44	"Tausendsapperment-Walzer" (p1833)	Op.61
1.45	"Der Frohsinn, mein Ziel" (p1833)	Op.63
1.46	"Robert-Tänze" (p1833)	Op.64
1.47	"Mittel gegen den Schlaf" (p1833)	Op.65
1.48	"Erinnerungen an Pesth" (Emlék Pestre) (p1834)	Op.66
1.49	"Gabrielen-Walzer" (p1834)	Op.68
1.50	"Pfennig-Walzer" (p1834)	Op.70
1.51	"Elisabethen-Walzer" (p1834)	Op.71
1.52	"Cotillons aus: Der Zweykampf" (p1834, on themes from Hérold's opera: Le pré aux clercs)	Op.72
1.53	"Iris-Walzer" (p1834)	Op.75
1.54	"Rosa-Walzer" (p1835)	Op.76
1.55	"Erinnerung an Berlin" (p1835)	Op.78
1.56	"Gedankenstriche" (p1835)	Op.79
1.57	"Huldigungs-Walzer" (p1835)	Op.80
1.58	"Grazien-Tänze" (p1835)	Op.81
1.59	"Philomelen-Walzer" (p1835)	Op.82
1.60	"Merkurs-Flügel" (p1836)	Op.83
1.61	"Heimath-Klänge" (p1836)	Op.84
1.62	"Erinnerung an Deutschland" (p1836)	Op.87
1.63	"Die Nachtwandler" (p1836)	Op.88
1.64	"Eisenbahn-Lust-Walzer" (p1836)	Op.89
1.65	"Krönungs-Walzer" (p1837)	Op.91
1.66	"Cotillons aus: Die Hugenotten" (p1837, on themes from Meyerbeer's opera: Les Huguenots)	Op.92
1.67	"Künstler-Ball-Tänze" (p1837)	Op.94
1.68	"Brüssler Spitzen" (p1837)	Op.95
1.69	"Ball-Racketen" (p1837)	Op.96
1.70	"Pilger am Rhein" (p1837)	Op.98
1.71	"Bankett-Tänze" (p1837)	Op.99
1.72	"Paris" (p1838)	Op.101
1.73	"Huldigung der Königin Victoria von Grossbritannien" (p1838; orig pubd as Op.102)	Op.103

1.149   "Soldaten-Lieder" (p1850) Op.242
1.150   "Deutsche Jubellaute" (p1850) Op.247

2. GALOPS (pubd for pf, simultaneous arrs for pf duet, also for vn & pf)

2.1	"Alpenkönig-Galopp" (p1828)	Op.7
2.2	"Champagner-Galopp" (p1828)	Op.8
2.3	"Seufzer-Galopp" (p1828)	Op.9
2.4	"Gesellschafts-Galopp" (Aufgeführt im Saale zum schwarzen Bock) (p1827)	Op.17
2.5	"Chineser-Galopp" (p1828)	Op.20
2.6	"Karolinen-Galopp" (p1827)	Op.21a
2.7	"Kettenbrücke-Galopp" (p1828)	Op.21b
2.8	"Erinnerungs-Galopp" (p1829)	Op.27
2.9	"Hirten-Galopp" (p1829)	Op.28
2.10	"Wettrennen-Galopp" (p1829)	Op.29a
2.11	"Wilhelm Tell-Galopp" (p1829)	Op.29b
2.12	"Einzugs-Galopp" (p1830)	Op.35
2.13	"Ungarische Galoppe" (No.1) (p1831)	Op.36
2.14	"Zweyte ungarische Galoppe" (p1831)	
2.15	"Dritte ungarische Galoppe" (p1831)	
2.16	"Sperl-Galopp" (p1831)	Op.42
2.17	"Bajaderen-Galopp" (p1832)	Op.52
2.18	"Zampa-Galopp" (p1832)	Op.62a
2.19	"Montecchi-Galopp" (p1833)	Op.62b
2.20	"Fortuna-Galopp" (p1834)	Op.69
2.21	"Venetianer-Galopp" (p1834)	Op.74
2.22	"Reise-Galopp" (p1836)	Op.85
2.23	"Ballnacht-Galopp" (p1836)	Op.86
2.24	"Jugendfeuer-Galopp" (p1836)	Op.90
2.25	"Galopp nach 'Hugenotten' " (p1837, on themes from Meyerbeer's opera: Les Huguenots)	Op.93
2.26	"Cachucha-Galopp" (p1837)	Op.97
2.27	"Der Carneval in Paris" (p1838)	Op.100
2.28	"Boulogner-Galopp" (p1839, after Auber's opera: L'ambassadrice)	Op.104
2.29	"Versailler-Galopp" (p1839)	Op.107
2.30	"Gitana-Galopp" (p1839)	Op.108
2.31	"Indianer-Galopp" (p1839)	Op.111
2.32	"Furioso-Galopp" (p1840, on themes by Liszt)	Op.114
2.33	"Gibellinen-Galopp" (p1840)	Op.117

3. QUADRILLES (pubd for pf, simultaneous arrs for pf duet, also for vn & pf)

3.1	"Contre-Tänze" (p1831)	Op.44
3.2	"Contratänze" (p1832)	Op.54
3.3	"Wiener Carnevals-Quadrille" (p1841)	Op.124
3.4	"Jubel-Quadrille" (p1841)	Op.130
3.5	"Mode-Quadrille" (p1842)	Op.138
3.6	"Haute-volée-Quadrille" (p1843)	Op.142
3.7	"Saison-Quadrille" (p1843)	Op.148
3.8	(Kaiser) "Ferdinand-Quadrille" (p1843)	Op.151
3.9	(Kaiserin) "Anna-Quadrille" (p1844)	Op.153
3.10	"Volksgarten-Quadrille" (p1844)	Op.157
3.11	"Redoute-Quadrille" (p1844)	Op.158
3.12	"Orpheus-Quadrille" (p1844)	Op.162
3.13	"Fest-Quadrille" (p1845)	Op.165
3.14	"Haimonskinder-Quadrille" (p1845, on themes from Balfe's opera: Les quatre fils d'Aymon)	Op.169
3.15	"Musen-Quadrille" (p1845)	Op.174
3.16	"Flora-Quadrille" (p1845)	Op.177
3.17	"Stradella-Quadrille" (p1845)	Op.178
3.18	"Amoretten-Quadrille" (p1846)	Op.183
3.19	"Concert-Souvenir-Quadrille" (p1846)	Op.187
3.20	"Zigeunerin-Quadrille" (p1846)	Op.191
3.21	"Eldorado-Quadrille" (p1846)	Op.194
3.22	"Charivari-Quadrille" (p1846)	Op.196
3.23	"Souvenir de Carneval 1847" (p1847)	Op.200
3.24	"Triumph-Quadrille" (p1847)	Op.205
3.25	"Najaden-Quadrille" (p1847)	Op.206
3.26	"Des Teufels Antheil. Beliebte Quadrille" (p1847, after Auber's opera: La part du diable)	Op.211
3.27	"Nádor Kör. Palatinal-Tanz" (p1848)	Op.214
3.28	"Martha-Quadrille" (p1847)	Op.215
3.29	"Schäfer-Quadrille" (p1848)	Op.217
3.30	"Quadrille im militärischen Style" (p1848)	Op.229
3.31	"Huldigungs-Quadrille" (p1849)	Op.233
3.32	"Louisen-Quadrille" (p1849)	Op.234

3.33   "Almacks-Quadrille" (p1849) Op.243
3.34   "Quadrille ohne Titel" (p1850) Op.248

4. MARCHES (pubd for pf, simultaneous arrs for pf duet, also for vn & pf)

4.1   6 "Wiener Bürger-Märsche": No.1 "Original-Parade-Marsch" (p1832) ....
4.2   No.2 "Marsch nach 'Zampa' " (p1832)
4.3   No.3 "Marsch" (after: Robert der Teufel)
4.4   No.4 "Original-Parade-Marsch" (p1834) Op.73
4.5   No.5 "Original-Parade-Marsch" (p1838) Op.102
4.6   No.6 "Esmeralda-Marsch" (p1846) Op.192
4.7   "Parade-Marsch" (p1843) Op.144
4.8   "Österreichischer Fest-Marsch" (p1846) Op.188
4.9   "Österreichischer Defilier-Marsch" (p1847) Op.209
4.10   "Österreichischer National-Garde-Marsch" (p1848) Op.221
4.11   "Marsch der Studenten-Legion" (p1848) Op.223
4.12   "Freiheits-Marsch" (p1848) Op.226
4.13   "Marsch des einigen Deutschlands" (p1848) Op.227
4.14   "Radetzky-Marsch" (p1848) Op.228
4.15   "Brünner National-Garde-Marsch" (p1848) Op.231
4.16   "2 Märsche der königlichen spanischen Nobel-Garde" (p1849): No.1 "Triumph Marsch" Op.240
4.17   No.2 "Manövrir-Marsch"
4.18   "March of the Royal Horse Guards" (p1849; also see altered vers Op.246) ....
4.19   *"Letzter Gedanke von Johann Strauss" (p1849, unfin sketch for: Radetzky-Bankett-Marsch)* ....
4.20   "Jellacic-Marsch" (p1850) Op.244
4.21   "Wiener Jubel-Marsch" (p1850) Op.245
4.22   "Wiener Stadt-Garde-Marsch" (p1850, = altered vers of: March of the Royal Horse Guards) Op.246
4.23   "Trauermarsch, aufgeführt bei Joh. Strauss's Beerdigung" ....

5. POLKAS (pubd for pf, simultaneous arrs for pf duet, also for vn & pf)

5.1   "Beliebte Sperl-Polka" (p1842) Op.133
5.2   "Beliebte Annen-Polka" (p1842) Op.137
5.3   "Salon-Polka" (p1844) Op.161
5.4   "Marianka-Polka" (p1845) Op.173
5.5   "Neujahrs-Polka" (p1846) Op.199
5.6   "Eisele- und Beisele-Sprünge" (p1848) Op.202
5.7   "Beliebte Kathinka-Polka" (p1847) Op.210
5.8   "Fortuna-Polka" (p1848) Op.219
5.9   "Wiener Kreutzer-Polka" (p1848) Op.220
5.10   "Piefke- und Pufke-Polka" (p1849) Op.235
5.11   "Damen-Souvenir-Polka" (p1849) Op.236
5.12   "Alice-Polka" (p1849) Op.238
5.13   "Frederica-Polka" (p1849) Op.239
5.14   "Exeter-Polka" (p1851) Op.249

6. POTPOURRIS (pubd for pf, simultaneous arrs for pf duet, also for vn & pf)

6.1   "Der unzusammenhängende Zusammenhang" (Potpourri No.1) (p1829) Op.25
6.2   "Wiener Tagsbelustigung" (Potpourri No.2) (p1830) Op.37
6.3   "Musikalisches Ragout" (Potpourri No.3) (p1831) Op.46
6.4   "Ein Strauss von Strauss, Aus Tonblumen" (Potpourri No.4) (p1832) Op.55
6.5   "Erste Walzer-Guirlande" (p1834) Op.67
6.6   "Zweyte Walzer-Guirlande" (p1835) Op.77
6.7   "Huldigung der Königin Victoria und Grossbritannien" (p1839, = Op.106) Op.103
6.8   "Musikalischer Telegraph" (Potpourri No.5) (p1839, = Op.103) Op.106
6.9   "Dritte Walzer-Guirlande" (p1840) Op.121
6.10   "Fliegende Blätter" (Grosses Potpourri) (p1851) Op.250

7. FANTASIES (pubd for pf, simultaneous arrs for pf duet, also for vn & pf)

7.1   "Der Carneval in Venedig" (Erinnerung an Ernst), fantasy (p1841) Op.126
7.2   "Melodische Tändeleien" (Fantasie Potpourri), fantasy (p1851) Op.251

8. OTHER WORKS (pubd for pf, simultaneous arrs for pf duet, also for vn & pf)

8.1   "Tempête, Polstertanz und Galoppade" (p1828) Op.10
8.2   "Der Raub der Sabinerinnen. Charakteristisches Tongemälde" (p1831) Op.43

9. MISC WORKS

* * * * *

1. STAGE WORKS

Operas:

1.1   "Ritter Pázmán," 3 act comic opera (c1892, Dóczi after Arany) ....

Operettas (3 acts):

1.2   "Indigo und die vierzig Räuber" (Indigo and the 40 Thieves) (c1871, Steiner): ....
     pubd separately: 1a. "Hier, wo der Palmen schattiger Hain"
           1b. "Der Bajaderen Wahlspruch sei"
           2. "Kennt ihr Männer und ihr Frauen"
           3. "Ahnt mancher wohl"
           4. "Ein lustiger Rath zu sein"
           5a. "Ja so singt man nur in Wien"
           7a. "O ihr Thoren, geistige Zwerge"
           8a. "In des Harems Heiligtume"
           9a. "Willkommen sei, du Sternennacht"
           9b. "Folget eures Hauptmanns Geboth" (Räuberlied)
           10. "Wo die Brandung"
           11. "Nichts kann mich rühren" (Cavatine)
           12. "O Fantaska"
           12a. "Von deinem Arm umfangen"
           12b. "Was sich auch dem Blick mag zeigen"
           14. "Nun wohlan"
           16a. "Lasst frei nun erschallen"
           16b. "Du Schlummersaft mit Zauberkraft"
           20. "Ein Bettler zog zum Wald hinaus" (Romanze)
           21a. "Immer länger, immer weiter"
1.3   "Carneval in Rom" (Roman Carnival) (c1873, Braun & Lindau after Sardou) ....
1.4   "Die Fledermaus" (The Bat) (c1874, Haffner & Genée after Mailhac & Halévy): ....
     pubd separately: 4. "O je, o je, wie rührt mich dies"
           5a. "Glücklich ist, wer vergisst" (Trinklied)
           5b. "Mit mir so spät bei mir so tête à tête"
           7. " 's ist mal bei mir so Sitte"
           8. "Mein Herr Marquis"
           10. "Csárdás für Sopran"
           11a. "Die Majestät wird anerkannt" (Champagnerlied)
           11b. "Brüderlein und Schwesterlein"
           14. "Spiel' ich die Unschuld vom Lande"
1.5   "Cagliostro in Wien" (c1875, Zell & Genée): ....
     pubd separately: 13. "Ha, welch reizendes Gesicht"
1.6   "Prinz Methusalem" (Prince Methusaleh) (c1877, Treumann after Delacour & Wildér): ....
     pubd separately: 1. "Das Tipferl auf dem I"
           2. "Blond muss es sein"
           3. "Du schöner Mai"
           4. "O du, o du mein Ideal!"
1.7   "Blindekuh" (The Blind Cow) (c1878, Kneisel): ....
     pubd separately: 11. "So ein Weiberl"
1.8   "Das Spitzentuch der Königin" (The Queen's Lace Handkerchief) (c1880, Riegen & Genée after Cervantes)
     pubd separately: 1. "Welch' holdes Bild" (Bolero)
           2. "Stets kommt mir wieder in den Sinn" (Trüffel-Couplet)
           3. "Siebzehn Jahre, war ich"
           4. "Wo die wilde Rose erblüht"
           5. "Das ist gegen mein Prinzip"
           6. "In der Nacht mit seiner Zither" (Mondcouplet)
           7. "Höherer Schliff, diplomatischer Kniff"
           8. "Guten Appetit"
1.9   "Der lustige Krieg" (The Merry War) (c1881, Zell & Genée): ....
     pubd separately: 1. "Der Klügere gibt nach" (Couplet)
           2. "Noch kann man ohne Blutvergiessen"
           3b. "Wir machten zusammen aus Holland"
           4. "Für dieses Kriegszuges"
           5. "Von einem Mann liess ich mich küssen"
           6. "Kommen und gehen"
           . "Me Frown, ich wensch"
           7. "Ja, eilen wir geschwind"
           8. "Kommandiert, instruiert"
           9. "Durch Wald und Feld"
           10. "Es war ein lustig Abenteuer"
           11. "Nur für Natur"
           12. "Me Frown, ich wensch" (Holländisches Lied)
           13. "Was ist an einem Kuss gelegen"
           14. "Steh'n wir hier auch kampfbereit"
           16. "Zwei Schlüssel bringen wir" (Schlüssel-Couplet)

17. "Zwei Monat sind es"
18. "Süsse Friedensglocken"
19. "Es harrte kürzlich ziemlich lang" (Discretions-Couplet)

1.10   "Eine Nacht in Venedig" (A Night in Venice) (c1883, Zell & Genée; also vers by Korngold 1923): ....
pubd separately: 2. "Pellegrina rondinella"
3. "Komm in die Gondel" (Gondellied)
4. "Mond hat schwere Klag' erhob'n"
5. "Ninana, Ninana, hier will ich singen"
6. "Alle maskiert"
7. "Venedigs Frauen herzuführen, so ängstlich sind wir nicht"
8. "Mit der Würde, die dir eigen"
9. "Tarantelle"
10. "Was mir der Zufall gab"
11. "Man steckt ein"

1.11   "Der Zigeunerbaron" (The Gypsy Baron) (c1885, Schnitzer after Jókai): ....
pubd separately: 1. "Von des Tajo Strand" (Marsch-Couplet)
2. "Nur keusch und rein" (Sittenkommission-Couplet)
3. "Wer uns getraut"
4. "Als flotter Geist"
5. "Verloren hast du einen Schatz"
6. "Ja, das Schreiben und das Lesen"
7. "Ein Freier meldet sich"
8. "O habet acht" (Zigeunerlied)
9. "Sieh da, ein herrlich Frauenbild"
10. "Wer hat euch denn getraut?"
11. "So voll Fröhlichkeit"
12. "Das wär' kein rechter Schiffersknecht" (Schifferlied)
13. "Ha seht, es winkt" (Schatz-Walzer)
14. "Hier die Hand" (Werberlied und Csárdás)

1.12   "Simplicius" (c1887, Léon): ....
pubd separately: 1. "Aufs Pferd! Aufs Pferd!" (Reiterlied)
2. "Ich denke gern zurück," waltz-romance
3. "Der Frühling lacht"
4. "Also, du bist ein Freiersmann"

1.13   "Fürstin Ninetta" (c1893, Wittmann & Bauer): ....
pubd separately: 1a. "Ade, nun fahre dahin"
2. "Und sage, was von allen diesen Farben"
3. "Fremdenführer bin ich"
4. "Dort, wo Blut und Wutki fliessen"
9. "Schlaf ein, schlaf ein!" (Hypnotisier-Duett)
10. "Als ich ein Backfisch war"
11. "Er soll mich verschmäh'n"
14. "Einst träumte mir"

1.14   "Jabuka" (Das Apfelfest) (c1894, Kalbeck & Davis): ....
pubd separately: . "Im ganzen Land bin ich bekannt" (Entrée-Lied)
. "Vergebens, dass ich spähe," duet
. "Es war einmal, in Märchen," Lied
. "Mit den schlechten Zeiten ist jetzt vorbei" (Bilder-Couplet)
. "Wie die Chroniken vermelden" (Bilder-Couplet)
. "Das Comitat geht in die Höh' " (Couplet)

1.15   "Waldmeister" (c1895, Davis): ....
pubd separately: 1. "Auf feurigem Pferde dahin zu jagen"
2. "Im Walde, wo die Buchen rauschen"
3. "Das Wetter war so scheene"
4. "Das ist ja nicht mehr zu ertragen"
5. "Wir sind brave Müllersknechte"
6. "Allein, allein"
7. "Ja, was ich da mache"
9. "Ist denn soviel dabei?"
10. "Wir gratulieren"
11. "Waldmeister hat es gesagt"
12. "Ja, ä Kleinigkeit ist dazwischen"
15. "Die ganze Nacht durchschwärmt"
16. "Die Liebe kommt, die Liebe geht"
added: . "Sie tun, als wär' das eine Wissenschaft" (Koketterie)

1.16   "Die Göttin der Vernunft" (The Goddess of Reason) (c1897, Willner & Buchbinder): ....
pubd separately: 2. "Soeben hab' ich inspiziert"
3. "Den Säbel an der Seite"
4. "Wir sind die Jakobiner"
5. "In meinem Schlosse behaglich"
6. "In der Schule sang"
7. "Robespierre, der lose Schäker"
8a. "Als Directrice war ich"
9. "O Nachtigall"
10. "Sie sind in meinem Garten"

11. "Wo uns're Fahne weht"
12. "Couplet"
13. "Als ich noch war Grisette"
15. "Heut' ist heut'," waltz (= Op.471)
16. "Beschwerdebuch"
17. "Über Felder"
18. "Frisch gewagt"

Compilations by others:

1.17   *"Wiener Blut" (Viennese Blood / The Viennese Spirit), operetta (arr & ed A. Müller Jr. p1899)* ....
1.18   *"Aschenbrödel" (Cinderella), 3 act ballet (p1901, Regel after Kollmann, adapt & arr Bayer)* ....
1.19   *"Gräfin Pepi," operetta (arr Reitterer p1902, from operettas: Simplicius & Blindekuh)* ....
1.20   *"Tausend und eine Nacht," 2 act operetta (arr Reitterer p1906)* ....
1.21   *"Der Blaue Held" (Carneval in Rom), operetta (arr Stollberg p1912)* ....
1.22   *"Faschingshochzeit," operetta (arr Klein p1921)* ....
1.23   *"Le beau Danube," 2 act ballet (arr & orchd Desormière p1924)* ....
1.24   *"Casanova," musical comedy (arr Benatzky p1928)* ....
1.25   *"Walzer aus Wien," 3 act Singspiel (arr Bittner p1930)* ....
1.26   *"Die Tänzerin Fanny Elssner," operetta (arr Stalle p1935)* ....
1.27   *"Nacht am Bosporus," operetta (arr Schliepe, from operette: Indigo)* ....
1.28   *"Apfelfest" (arr Schulz p1943, from operetta: Jabuka)* ....
1.29   *"Die Straussbuben," 3 act Singspiel (arr Stalla p1946, music also from Josef Strauss)* ....

1a. SELECTIONS FROM STAGE WORKS (Nos. of sections in The Gramophone)

1a.4   "Die Fledermaus," operetta: ....
        excerpts: 1. "Overture"
        I: 2. "Täubchen, das entflattert ist"
              3. "Du darfst heut' nicht"
              4. "Nein, mit solchen Advokaten"
              5. "Komm' mit mir zum Souper"
              6. "So muss allein ich bleiben"
              7. "Trinke, Liebchen, trinke schnell"
              8. "Mein Herr, was dächten Sie"
              9. "Nein, nein, ich zweifle gar nicht mehr"
        II: 10a. "Ein Souper heut uns winkt"
             10b. "Chacun à son goût!"
             11a. "Ach, meine Herr'n und Damen"
             11b. "Mein Herr Marquis"
             12. "Dieser Anstand, so manierlich"
             13. "Klänge der Heimat" (Csárdás)
             14a. "In Feuerstrom der Reben"
             14b. "Brüderlein und Schwesterlein"
             15. "Ballet"
             16. "Genug damit, genug!"
        III: 17. "Spiel' ich die Unschuld"
             18. "Ich stehe voll Zagen"
             19. "O Fledermaus"

1a.10 "Eine Nacht in Venedig," operetta (Korngold's version of 1923): ....
        excerpts: 1. "Overture"
        I: 2. "Wenn vom Lido sacht"
              3. "Ihr Venetianer hört ... Drum sei fröhlich, sei selig, Venetia"
              4. " 'S ist wahr, ich bin nicht ... Wenn du dich kränkst!"
              5. "Seht, oh seht!... Frutti di mare!"
              6. "Evviva, Caramello!... Willkommen, liebe Freunde!"
              7. "Annina! Caramello!... Pellegrina rondinella"
              8. "Alle maskiert, alle maskiert"
              9. "Sei mir gegrüsst, du holdes Venetia!"
             10. "Hier ward es still ... der Mond hat schwere Klag' erhoben"
             11. "Hast du mir ein Kostüm gebracht"
             12. "Komm' in die Gondel, mein Liebchen"
             13. "Messerer Delacqua!"
             14. "Schnell zur Serenade!"
             15. "Kaum dass mein Liebchen die schaukelnde entführt"
        II: 16. "Wo bleibt nur Caramello?... Venedigs Frauen herzuführen"
             17a. "Was mir der Zufall gab"
             17b. "Treu sein, das liegt mir nicht"
             18. "Hör' mich, Annina, komm in die Gondel"
             19. "Sie sagten meinem Liebesfleh'n"
             20. "Solch' ein Wirtshaus lob' ich mir ... Marietta, come va?"
             21. "Ninana, Ninana, hier will ich singen"
             22. "Lasset die Andern tanzen da, tra la la!"

23. "Jetzt ist Zeit ... Horch! von San Marco der Glocken Geläut"
III: 24. "Karneval ruft Euch zum Ball"
25. "Die Tauben von San Marco"
26. "Ach, wie herrlich zu schau'n"
27. "Tacke, tacke, tacke ... Aber wenn man erst gekostet hat"
28. "Wie sichs gebührt, hat es gespürt"

1a.11   "Der Zigeunerbaron," operetta: ....
1a. "Overture"
I: 1b. "Das wär' kein rechter Schifferknecht"
2. "Als flotter Geist"
3a. "So träuschte mich die Ahnung nicht!"
3b. "Ja, das Schreiben und das Lesen"
4. "Just sind es vierundzwanzig Jahre"
5a. "Dem Freier naht die Braut"
5b. "Ein Falter schwirrt ums Licht"
6. "So elend und so treu"
7a. "Arsena! Arsena"
7b. "Ha, was hör' ich da für Klänge"
7c. "Nun zu des bösen Nachbarn Haus," finale
II: 8a. "Entr'acte"
8b. "Mein Aug' bewachte"
9a. "Ein Greis ist mir im Traum erschienen"
9b. "Ha, seht, es winkt"
10. "Auf, auf, vorbei ist die Nacht"
11. "Wer uns getraut"
12. "Her die Hand, es muss ja sein"
13. "Nach Wien!"
III: 14a. "Entr'acte"
15. "Ein Mädchen hat es gar nicht gut"
16. "Von des Tajos Strand"
17. "Hurrah, die Schlacht mitgebracht" (Entrance March)
18. "Heiraten, Vivat!"

2. DANCES FROM STAGE WORKS (pubd for pf, also versions pubd for pf duet / vn & pf and for orch)

"Ritter Pázmán," comic opera:

2.1	"Pázmán Waltz"	
2.2	"Pázmán Polka"	
2.3	"Csárdás"	
2.4	"Eva Waltz"	
2.5	"Pázmán Quadrille"	

"Indigo und die vierzig Räuber," operetta:

2.6	"Shawl-Polka"	Op.343
2.7	"Indigo-Quadrille"	Op.344
2.8	"Auf freiem Fusse," polka française	Op.345
2.9	"Tausend und eine Nacht," waltz	Op.346
2.10	"Aus der Heimath" (From Home), polka-mazurka	Op.347
2.11	"Im Sturmschritt," polka schnell	Op.348
2.12	"Indigo-Marsch"	Op.349
2.13	"Lust'ger Rath," polka française	Op.350
2.14	"Die Bajadere," polka schnell	Op.351

"Roman Carnival," operetta:

2.15	"Vom Donaustrande" (From Danube Shores), polka schnell	Op.356
2.16	"Carnevalsbilder" (Carnival Scenes), waltz	Op.357
2.17	"Nimm sie hin!," polka française	Op.358
2.18	"Gruss aus Österreich" (Greeting from Austria), polka-mazurka	Op.359
2.19	"Rotunde-Quadrille"	Op.360

"Die Fledermaus," operetta:

2.20	"Fledermaus-Polka"	Op.362
2.21	"Fledermaus-Quadrille"	Op.363
2.22	"Tik-Tak," polka schnell	Op.365
2.23	"An der Moldau," polka française	Op.366
2.24	"Du und Du," waltz	Op.367
2.25	"Glücklich ist, wer vergisst," polka-mazurka	Op.368

"Cagliostro in Wien," operetta:

2.26	"Cagliostro-Quadrille"	Op.369
2.27	"Cagliostro-Walzer"	Op.370

"Jabuka" (Das Apfelfest), operetta:

"Waldmeister," operetta:

"Die Göttin der Vernunft," operetta:

"Aschenbrödel," ballet:

3. WALTZES (pubd for pf, also versions pubd for pf duet / vn & pf and for orch)

4. POLKAS (pubd for pf, also versions pubd for pf duet / vn & pf and for orch)

4.89   "Juristen Ball-Polka," polka schnell (p1864) Op.280
4.90   "Vergnügungszug" (Excursion Train), polka schnell (p1864) Op.281
4.91   "Gut bürgerlich," polka française (p1864) Op.282
4.92   "Patronessen-Polka," polka française (p1864) Op.286
4.93   "Newa-Polka," polka française (p1864) Op.288
4.94   " 's gibt nur a Kaiserstadt, 's gibt nur ein Wien," polka schnell (p1865) Op.291
4.95   "Process-Polka," polka schnell (p1865) Op.294
4.96   "Episode," polka française (p1865) Op.296
4.97   "Electrofor-Polka," polka schnell (p1865) Op.297
4.98   "Kreuzfidel," polka française (p1865) Op.301
4.99   "Die Zeitlose," polka française (p1865) Op.302
4.100   "Kinderspiele" (Children's games), polka française (p1865) Op.304
4.101   "Damenspende," polka française (p1866) Op.305
4.102   "Par force!," polka schnell (p1866) Op.308
4.103   "Sylphen-Polka," polka française (p1866) Op.309
4.104   "Tändelei," polka-mazurka (p1866) Op.310
4.105   "Express-Polka," polka schnell (p1866) Op.311
4.106   "Wildfeuer" (Wildfire), polka française (p1866) Op.313
4.107   "Lob der Frauen," polka-mazurka (p1867) Op.315
4.108   "Postillon d'amour," polka française (p1867) Op.317
4.109   "Leichtes Blut" (Light as a Feather), polka schnell (p1867) Op.319
4.110   "Figaro-Polka," polka française (p1867) Op.320
4.111   "Stadt und Land" (Town and Country), polka-mazurka (p1868) Op.322
4.112   "Ein Herz und ein Sinn," polka-mazurka (p1868) Op.323
4.113   "Unter Donner und Blitz" (Thunder and Lighting), polka schnell (p1868) Op.324
4.114   "Freikugeln" (Free-shooting bullets), polka schnell (p1868) Op.326
4.115   "Sängerlust," polka française (p1869, Weyl) Op.328
4.116   "Fata Morgana," polka-mazurka (p1869) Op.330
4.117   "Eljen a Magyar" (Hail to Hungary!), polka schnell (p1869) Op.332
4.118   "Im Krapfenwaldl," polka française (p1870) Op.336
4.119   "Von der Börse" (From the Bourse), polka française (p1870) Op.337
4.120   "Louischen," polka française (p1871) Op.339
4.121   "Frisch heran" (Come on in!), polka schnell (p1880) Op.386
4.122   "Burschenwanderung," polka française (p1881, Seuffert; m ch & orch/pf) Op.389
4.123   "Rasch in der Tat," polka schnell (p1883) Op.409
4.124   "An der Wolga" (On the Volga), polka-mazurka (p1886) Op.425
4.125   "Auf zum Tanze!," polka schnell (p1889) Op.436
4.126   "Durchs Telephon" (p1890) Op.439
4.127   "Unparteiische Kritiken" (Impartial Critics), polka-mazurka (p1892) Op.442

W/ out opus number:

4.128   "Mückenzug-Polka" ....
4.129   "Wo klingen die Lieder," polka-mazurka champêtre ....

5. QUADRILLES (pubd for pf, also versions pubd for pf duet / vn & pf and for orch)

5.1   "Debut-Quadrille" (p1844) Op.2
5.2   "Cytheren-Quadrille" (p1844) Op.6
5.3   " 'Liebesbrunnen' Quadrille" (p1845, on themes from Balfe's opera: Les puits d'amour) Op.10
5.4   "Serben-Quadrille" (p1845) Op.14
5.5   "Elfen-Quadrille" (p1845) Op.16
5.6   "Dämonen-Quadrille" (p1845) Op.19
5.7   "Zigeunerin-Quadrille" (p1845, on themes from Balfe's opera: The Bohemian Girl) Op.24
5.8   "Odeon-Quadrille" (p1846) Op.29
5.9   " 'Die Belagerung von Rochelle' Quadrille" (p1846, on themes from Balfe's opera: The Siege
          of Rochelle) Op.31
5.10   "Alexander-Quadrille" (p1847) Op.33
5.11   "Industrie-Quadrille" (p1847) Op.35
5.12   "Wilhelminen-Quadrille" (p1847) Op.37
5.13   " 'Die Königin von Leon' Quadrille" (p1847, on themes from Baisselot's opera: The Queen of Leon) . Op.40
5.14   "Fest-Quadrille" (p1847) Op.44
5.15   "Martha-Quadrille" (p1848, on themes from Flotow's opera: Martha) Op.46
5.16   "Seladon-Quadrille" (p1848) Op.48
5.17   "Marien-Quadrille" (p1848) Op.51
5.18   "Annika-Quadrille" (p1848) Op.53
5.19   " 'Der Blitz' Quadrille" (p1848, on themes from Halévy's opera: The Attack) Op.59
5.20   "Sanssouci-Quadrille" (p1849) Op.63
5.21   "Nikolai-Quadrille" (p1849, on Russian themes) Op.65
5.22   "Künstler-Quadrille" (Artists' Quadrille) (p1850) Op.71
5.23   "Sofien-Quadrille" (p1850) Op.75
5.24   "Attaque-Quadrille" (p1850) Op.76
5.25   "Bonvivant-Quadrille" (p1850) Op.86
5.26   "Slaven-Ball-Quadrille" (p1850) Op.88
5.27   "Maskenfest-Quadrille" (Masquerade Quadrille) (p1850) Op.92

5.28   "Promenade-Quadrille" (p1850) Op.98
5.29   "Vivat! Quadrille" (p1851) Op.103
5.30   "Tête-à-tête-Quadrille" (p1852) Op.109
5.31   "Melodien-Quadrille" (p1852, on Verdi's melodies) Op.112
5.32   "Hofball-Quadrille" (Court Ball Quadrille) (p1852) Op.116
5.33   "Nocturne-Quadrille" (p1852) Op.120
5.34   "Indra-Quadrille" (p1852, on themes from Flotow's opera: Indra) Op.122
5.35   "Satanella-Quadrille" (p1852) Op.123
5.36   "Motor-Quadrille" (p1853) Op.129
5.37   "Bouquet-Quadrille" (p1853) Op.135
5.38   "Karnevals-Specktakel-Quadrille" (Carnival Sights Quadrille) (p1854) Op.152
5.39   "Nordstern-Quadrille" (Polar Star Quadrille) (p1854, from Meyerbeer's opera: L'étoile du Nord) Op.153
5.40   "Handels-Elite-Quadrille" (Merchantile Élite Quadrille) (p1855) Op.166
5.41   "Bijouterie-Quadrille" (p1855) Op.169
5.42   "Strelna-Terrassen-Quadrille" (p1857) Op.185
5.43   "La berceuse" (p1857) Op.194
5.44   "Le beau-monde" (p1857) Op.199
5.45   "Künstler-Quadrille" (Artists' Quadrille) (p1858) Op.201
5.46   "Dinorah-Quadrille" (p1860, on themes from Meyerbeer's opera: Dinorah) Op.224
5.47   "Orpheus-Quadrille" (p1860) Op.236
5.48   "Neue Melodien-Quadrille" (p1861, on themes from Italian operas) Op.254
5.49   "St. Petersburg" (p1861, on Russian themes, = Romanze No.2 in G minor, Op.255) Op.255
5.50   "Chansonette-Quadrille" (Comic Songs) (p1862, on themes from French ballads) Op.259
5.51   " 'Un ballo in maschera' Quadrille" (p1862, on themes from Verdi's opera: Un ballo in maschera) ... Op.272
5.52   "Lieder-Quadrille" (on favorite themes) (p1863) Op.275
5.53   "Saison-Quadrille" (p1864) Op.283
5.54   "Quadrille on French airs" (p1864) Op.290
5.55   "Afrikanerin-Quadrille" (p1865, on themes from Meyerbeer's opera: L'africaine) Op.299
5.56   "Bal champêtre" (p1865, on French airs) Op.303
5.57   "Ein Tag des Glücks" (Day of Happiness) (p1868, on themes from Auber's opera: Le premier jour
         de bonheur) Op.327
5.58   "Slovanka-Quadrille" (p1871, on Russian airs) Op.338
5.59   "Festival-Quadrille" (Promenade Quadrille) (p1871, on English airs) Op.341
5.60   "Der Lustige Krieg Quadrille" (p1882, on themes from operetta: Der lustige Krieg) Op.402

         W/ out opus number:

5.61   " 'Des Teufels Antheil' Quadrille" (p1847, on themes from Auber's opera: La part du diable) ....

6. MARCHES (pubd for pf, also versions pubd for pf duet / vn & pf and for orch)

6.1   "Patrioten-Marsch" (p1845) Op.8
6.2   "Austria-Marsch" (p1845) Op.20
6.3   "Fest-Marsch" (Kaiser Franz Joseph Festival March) (p1848) Op.49
6.4   "Revolutions-Marsch" (p1848) Op.54
6.5   "Studenten-Marsch" (p1849) Op.56
6.6   "Brünner-Nationalgarde-Marsch" (p1848) Op.58
6.7   "Kaiser Franz Josef Marsch" (p1850) Op.67
6.8   "Triumph-Marsch" (p1850) Op.69
6.9   "Wiener Garnison Marsch" (p1850) Op.77
6.10   "Ottinger Reitermarsch" (p1850) Op.83
6.11   "Kaiser-Jäger-Marsch" (p1850) Op.93
6.12   "Viribus unitis" (p1851) Op.96
6.13   "Grossfürsten-Marsch" (p1852) Op.107
6.14   "Sachsen-Kürassier-Marsch" (p1852) Op.113
6.15   "Wiener Jubel-Gruss-Marsch" (Vienna Jubilee Greeting March) (p1852) Op.115
6.16   "Kaiser Franz Joseph I. Rettungs-Jubel-Marsch" (p1853) Op.126
6.17   "Caroussel-Marsch" (p1853) Op.133
6.18   "Kron-Marsch" (Crown March) (p1853) Op.139
6.19   "Erzherzog Wilhelm Genesungs-Marsch" (p1854) Op.149
6.20   "Napoleon-Marsch" (p1854) Op.156
6.21   "Alliance-Marsch" (p1854) Op.158
6.22   "Krönungs-Marsch" (Coronation March) (p1856) Op.183
6.23   "Fürst Bariatinsky-Marsch" (p1858) Op.212
6.24   "Deutscher Kriegermarsch" (German War March) (p1864) Op.284
6.25   "Verbrüderungs-Marsch" (Broderhood March) (p1864) Op.287
6.26   "Persischer Marsch" (p1864) Op.289
6.27   "Egyptischer Marsch" (p1869) Op.335
6.28   "Jubelfest-Marsch" (Jubilee Festival March) (p1881, Genée; m ch & orch) Op.396
6.29   "Matador-Marsch" (p1883, on themes from operetta: Das Spitzentuch der Königin) Op.406
6.30   "Habsburg Hoch!" (p1883) Op.408
6.31   "Russischer Marsch" (p1886) Op.426
6.32   "Spanischer Marsch" (p1888) Op.433
6.33   "Fest-Marsch" (p1894) Op.452
6.34   "Deutschmeister-Jubiläumsmarsch" (p1896) Op.470

6.35   "Aufs Korn!," march (p1898, Chiavacci) Op.478

W/ out opus number:

6.36   "Serbischer Marsch" (p1847) ....
6.37   "Kaiser Alexander Huldigungs Marsch" (p1864) ....
6.38   "Aufzugs Marsch" (p1883, from operetta: A Night in Venice) ....
6.39   "Freiwillige vor!" (p1887)...
6.40   "Einzugs Marsch" (p1895, from operetta: The Gypsy Baron)..
6.41   "Fanny Marsch oder Polka schnell" (ca1870)..

7. OTHER WORKS (pubd for pf, also versions pubd for pf duet / vn & pf and for orch)

7.1   "Pesther Csárdás" (p1846) Op.23
7.2   "Slaven-Potpourri" (p1847) Op.39
7.3   "Neue Steierische Tänze" (New Styrian Dances) (p1849) Op.61
7.4   "Romanze No.1," in D minor (p1860; vc & orch) Op.243
7.5   "Romanze No.2," in G minor (p1862, = St. Petersburg Quadrille, Op.255) .... (Op.255)
7.6   "Veilchen-Mazurka" (Violet Mazurka) (p1862, on Russian themes) Op.256
7.7   "Perpetuum mobile, Ein musikalischer Scherz" (p1862) Op.257
7.8   "Fest-Polonaise" (p1872; large orch) Op.352
7.9   "Russische Marsch-Fantasie" (p1872) Op.353
7.10   "Im russischen Dorfe" (In a Russian Village), fantasy (p1873; large orch) Op.355
7.11   "Ritter Pázmán" (extracts from comic opera 1892) Op.441
7.12   "Auf dem Tanzboden" (On the Dance Floor) (p1894, music illustration to Defregger's painting)....... Op.454
7.13   "Hochzeits-Präludium" (Wedding Prelude) (p1896; vn, org/harm & harp) Op.469
7.14   "Klänge aus der Raimundzeit" (p1898) Op.479

W/ out opus number:

7.15   "Hommage au public Russe" (Hommage to the Russian Public), potpourri (p1856).............
7.16   "Sängergruss" (p1882; m ch)...
7.17   "D'Hauptsach" (p1887, Anzengruber) ....
7.18   "Bauersleut' im Künstlerhaus" (p1889, Anzengruber) ....
7.19   "Ein Gstanzl vom Tanzl" (Auf der Alm) (p1894, Dóczi) ....
7.20   "Traumbilder," 2 vols (p1889) ....

Unpubd:

7.21   "Tu qui regis totum orbem," gradual (c1844; ch, 2ob, 2cl, 2bn, 2cl, 2bn, 2hn, 3trbn & timp)........................
7.22   "Josefinen-Tänze" ....
7.23   "Dolci pianti," romance (vc & orch) ....
7.24   "Albumblatt für Nikolaus Dumba" ....
7.25   "Wir hab'n uns schon gern g'habt," Lied ....

8. COLLABORATIONS (pubd for pf, also versions pubd for pf duet / vn & pf and for orch)

8.1   "Hinter den Coulissen Quadrille" (p1859, collab Josef Strauss)..
8.2   "Vaterländischer Marsch" (p1859, collab Josef Strauss) ....
8.3   "Monstre-Quadrille" (p1860, collab Josef Strauss) ....
8.4   "Trifolien," waltz (p1865, collab Josef & Eduard Strauss) ....
8.5   "Schützen-Quadrille" (p1868, collab Josef & Eduard Strauss) ....
8.6   "Pizzicato-Polka" (p1870, collab Josef Strauss) ....

* * * * *

Opus number 445 used twice. Opus number 451 not used.

1. STAGE WORKS

Operas:

1.1	"4 Scenes for a Singspiel" (c1876; ch & pf):	AV28

    1. "Im Felsengrund verborgen," chorus (Gnomen)
    2. "Armes Röslein tief im Wald," Lied (Mariechen)
    3. "Was gibt's zu schlafen," ensemble
    . "Das heisst sich schinden spät und früh," aria & recit (Wurzel)
    4. "Das hätten meine jungen Pflanzen," aria (Wurzel)
    . "Szenenmusik" (nach dem Mariechen eingeschlafen ist)

1.2	*"4 Scenes for a Singspiel" (c1876; ch & pf, sketches)*	AV205
1.3	*"Der Kampf mit dem Drachen," 1 act Singspiel (c1876, Körner, sketches):*	AV206

    1. "Adagio"
    2. "Sei willkommen schöner Morgen"
    3. "Ich kannte nur des Lebens Schmerzen," (Herrman)
    4. "Der hat nie das Glück empfunden" (Herrmann, Arnold)
    5. "Ich schwinde, verschwinde, empfinde mich kaum"

1.4	*"Lila," Singspiel (c1878, after Goethe, sketches):*	AV44–45
	. "Arie der Almaide": "Sei nicht beklommen" (S & orch)	AV44
	. "Auf aus der Ruh" (T, ch & orch)	AV45
1.5	"Guntram," 3 acts (c1887–93, r1934–9, Strauss)	Op.25
1.6	*"Fest auf Solhaug," opera (c1888, after Ibsen's play, project)*	AV214
1.7	*"Kaiser und Galiläer," opera (c1888, after Ibsen's play, project)*	AV215
1.8	*"Hans und Gertraud," opera (c1892, project)*	AV216
1.9	*"Till Eulenspiegel bei den Schildbürgern" (c1893–5, project)*	AV219
1.10	*"Lobetanz" (c1894, Bierbaum, project)*	AV220
1.11	*"Lila," Singspiel (c1895–6, after Goethe, project)*	AV221
1.12	*"Schilda" (c1896–7, Sporck, project)*	AV223
1.13	*"Gugeline" (c1898, Bierbaum, project)*	AV224
1.14	*"Ekke und Schnittlein" (c1899, after Cervantes, project)*	AV227
1.15	"Feuersnot," 1 act (c1900–1, Wolzogen)	Op.50
1.16	*"König Ragnar Rauhbeins Tochter" (c1903, Ernst von Wolzogen after Andersen, project)*	AV234
1.17	*"Die heilige Einfalt" (c1903, Elsa L. von Wolzogen, project)*	AV235
1.18	*"Coabbradibosimpur oder Die Bösen Buben von Sevilla" (c1903, Ernst von Wolzogen, project)*	AV236
1.19	"Salome," 1 act staged tone poem (visual + vocal treated as acc to orch music) (c1904–5, after O. Wilde's play transl Lachmann; Salomes Tanz c1905) (also see incid music c by Glazunov)	Op.54
1.20	*"Cesare Borgia" (c1906, project)*	AV237
1.21	*"Savonarola" (c1906, project)*	AV238
1.22	*"Semiramis" (c1906–48, Hofmannsthal after Calderón: Die Tochter der Luft, project)*	AV239
1.23	*"Saul und David" (c1906, Rückert, project)*	AV240
1.24	*"Dantons Tod" (c1906, after Büchner's drama, project)*	AV241
1.25	*"9. Thermidor" (Revolotionsstück von Victorien Sardou) (c1906, project)*	AV242
1.26	"Elektra," 1 act staged tone poem (visual + vocal treated as acc to orch music) (c1906–8, Hofmannsthal)	Op.58
1.27	*"Christinas Heimreise. Casanova-Komödie" (c1908, Hofmannsthal, project)*	AV243
1.28	"Der Rosenkavalier" (The Knight of the Rose), 3 acts (c1909–10, Hofmannsthal)	Op.59
1.29	*"Das steinerne Herz" (c1910–1, Hofmansthal, project)*	AV245
1.30	*"Lucidor" (Figuren zu einer ungeschriebenen Komödie) (c1910–27, Hofmannsthal)*	AV246
1.31	*"Plan zu einer Oper mit Gabriele d'Annunzio" (c1911, project)*	AV248
1.32	*"Plan zu einer Oper mit Karl von Levetzov" (c1911–4, project)*	AV249
1.33	"Ariadne auf Naxos," 1 act (to be played after Molière's play: Der Bürger als Edelmann), 1 act (c1911–2, Hofmannsthal; 2nd vers p1916; also see 3rd vers p1917 as incid music: Der Bürger als Edelmann, Op.60)	Op.60
1.34	"Die Frau ohne Schatten" (The Woman without a Shadow), 3 acts (c1914–7, Hofmannsthal)	Op.65
1.35	*"Die Frau," cycle of 5 comic operas (c1917, collab Bahr, project)*	AV251
1.36	*"Lieber Augustin," pantomime (project)*	AV251a
1.37	*"Groteske 'Circe—Frau Holle' " (project)*	AV251b
1.38	*"Szenarium" (Birinsky, project)*	AV251c
1.39	*"Der Goldene Pfad" (Levetzow, project)*	AV251d
1.40	*"Der Meister von Prag" (Levetzow, project)*	AV251E
1.41	*"Die heilige Eiche" (Levetzow, project)*	AV251f
1.42	*"Das heilige Lachen" (Levetzow, project)*	AV251f
1.43	*"Szenarium 'Nach einer alten Novelle' " (Bahr, project)*	AV252
1.44	*"Iphigenie in Delphi" (c1918, after fragment from Goethe, project)*	AV253
1.45	*"Miles Gloriosus" (c1918, Lenz after Plautus, project)*	AV254
1.46	*"Das Blumenfest" (Ländliche Spieloper) (c1918, after sketch by Hofmannsthal, project)*	Op.72
1.47	"Intermezzo," 2 acts (c1918–23, Strauss, w/ sym inserts)	AV256
1.48	*"Danae oder Die Vernunftheirat" (c1920, Hofmannsthal, project)*	AV257
1.49	*"Peregrinus Proteus" (Peregrin) (c1920–6, Kerr, project)*	Op.75
1.50	"Die Ägyptische Helena," 2 acts (c1924–7, Hofmannsthal; r vers of Act II 1932–3, text Wallerstein)	AV259
1.51	*"Ulrich von Liechtenstein" (c1925, after Hauptmann's comedy, project)*	AV261
1.52	*"Minnesänger—Meistersinger" (c1927–33, project)*	AV262
1.53	*"Dunst" (c1927, after Turgenyev's novel)*	AV263
1.54	*"Achilles auf Skyros," 1 act w/ ballet (c1927–34, Hofmannsthal, project)*	

1.55	*"Der Zwischengatte" (c1927, Hofmannsthal, project)*	*AV264*
1.56	*"Der Fiaker als Graf" (c1927, Hofmannsthal, project)*	*AV265*
1.57	"Arabella," 3 act lyric comedy (c1929–32, Hofmannsthal; 2nd vers 1939)	Op.79
1.58	"Die schweigsame Frau" (The Silent Woman), 3 acts (c1932–5, Zweig after Jonson)	Op.80
1.59	*"Der Rattenfänger von Hameln," Volksoper (c1933, Zweig, project)*	Op.80
1.60	*"Calandria" (c1934, after comedy by Dovizi da Bibbiena, project)*	*AV268*
1.61	*"Amphitryon" (c1934–5, Zweig after Kleist's Lustspiel based on Molière, project)*	*AV269*
1.62	*"Heinrich III (II) oder Der Constanzer Frieden" (c1934, project)*	*AV270*
1.63	*"Mirandolina" (c1934, after Goldoni's Lustspiel)*	*AV271*
1.64	*"Opferspiel" (c1934, Zweig after Faesi's Festspiel)*	*AV272*
1.65	*"Celestina" (c1935–6, Cota & de Roja after Calisto y Melibea, project)*	*AV273*
1.66	*"Catilina" (c1935, after Casti, project)*	*AV274*
1.67	*"Das Weib des Potiphar" (c1935, after Lernet-Holenia's drama, project)*	*AV275*
1.68	*"Alkestis" (c1935–8, after Lernet-Holenia's drama, project of opera/ballet)*	*AV276*
1.69	*"Sardanapal" (c1935, after Byron's poem, project)*	*AV277*
1.70	*"Azteken—Prunkoper" (c1935, after Hauptmann & Stucken, project)*	*AV278*
1.71	"Friedenstag" (Peace Day), 1 act (c1935–6, Gregor)	*AV279*
1.72	"Daphne," 1 act (bukolische Tragödie) (c1936–7, Gregor)	Op.81
1.73	"Die Liebe der Danae" (The Love of Danae), 3 acts (c1938–40, Gregor after Hofmannsthal)	Op.82
1.74	*"Viola" (Was Ihr Wollt) (c1939, after Shakespeare, project)*	Op.83
1.75	*"Gespenstergeschichte" (c1939, Gregor)*	*AV287*
1.76	*"Altenglische Oper" (c1940, after Beaumont & Fletcher, project)*	*AV288*
1.77	*"Jessonda" (c1940, project of new production of Spohr's opera, collab Gregor)*	*AV289*
1.78	"Capriccio" (Conversation Piece for Music), 1 act (c1940–1, collab Krauss)	Op.85
1.79	*"Des Esels Schatten" (c1947–9, Adler after Wieland, sketches; compl Schaller & Haussner)*	*AV300*

Ballets:

1.80	*"Die Flöhe oder Der Schmerzenstanz," ballet-pantomime (c1896, project)*	*AV222*
1.81	*"Lucifer" (c1898, Dehmel, project)*	*AV226*
1.82	*"Kometentanz. Eine astrale Pantomime" (c1900, Scheerbart, project)*	*AV228*
1.83	*"Pan im Busch" (c1900, Bierbaum, project)*	*AV229*
1.84	*"Kythere," 3 acts (c1900, after paintings of Watteau, Boucher & Fragonard, sketches)*	*AV230*
1.85	*"Der Triumph der Zeit" (c1900, Hofmannsthal, project)*	*AV232*
1.86	*"Orest und die Furien" (c1912, Hofmannsthal, project)*	*AV250*
1.87	"Josephs Legende," 1 scene (c1912–4, Kessler & Hofmannsthal)	Op.63
1.88	*"Divertissement" (c1920, Hofmannsthal, project)*	*AV255*
1.89	"Schlagobers," 2 acts (c1921–2, Strauss)	Op.70
1.90	*"Tanzpantomime" (um das Problem der Musik und der Kunst) (c1931, Zweig, project)*	*AV267*
1.91	*"Ballet vor 'Friedenstag' " (c1937–8, project)*	*AV280*
1.92	*"Nefretete und Echnaton" (c1938, project)*	*AV281*
1.93	*"Zenobia" (c1938, project)*	*AV282*
1.94	*"Nausikaa" (c1938–44, project of ballet/opera)*	*AV283*
1.95	*"Lais" (c1938, project)*	*AV284*
1.96	*"Eleusinisches Fest" (c1938, project)*	*AV285*
1.97	*"Camargo" (c1938, project)*	*AV286*
1.98	"Verklungene Feste" (c1940–1, Mlakar, music from Op.86 & AV107, after Fr. Couperin)	AV128
1.99	*"Die Feindinnen" (Die Feindlichen Tänzerinnen) (c1943, Gregor, project)*	*AV292*
1.100	*"Pandora" (c1943, Gregor, project)*	*AV293*
1.101	*"Phaeton" (c1943, Gregor, project)*	*AV294*
1.102	*"Philomela" (c1945, Haas-Heye, project)*	*AV295*
1.103	*"Aphroditens Rache" (Venus & Diana / Venus & Adonis / Diana & Endymion) (c1945–6, Gregor, frag)*	*AV296*

Incid music:

1.104	"Romeo und Julia," 4 acts (c1887, Förster after Shakespeare) (also see opera c by Gounod, ballet c by Prokofiev Op.64, incid music c by Kabalevsky & Milhaud Op.161, film score c by Khachaturian, symphony c by Berlioz Op.17, H79): AV86

    I: . "Tanzlied zu Moresca": "Lasst sie tanzen, sie tanzt so bewegt"
    II: . "Träller-Lied": "Wenn wie der Himmel klar die Sterne"
    III: . "Vor dem Hochzeitsbette": "In diesem Bett mit Tüchern reich erlesen"
    IV: . "Trauermusik"

1.105	"Jägern" (c1891, Iffland, recovered 1972): ....

    1. "Fanfare"
    2. (Slow middle part)
    3. "Allegro vivace" (w/ quote from Beethoven: Symphony No.9 in D minor, Op.125)

1.106	*"Das erhabene Leid der Könige" (c1892, Strauss, project)*	*Av217*
1.107	"Der Bürger als Edelmann" (Le bourgeois gentilhomme) (p1917, Hofmannsthal after Molière, frags from Lully; 3rd vers, also see first 2 vers perf as opera: Ariadne auf Naxos, Op.60)	Op.60

Film:

1.108	*"Der Rosenkavalier" (adapt Alwin & Singer 1925, script Hofmannsthal):*	*AV112*

    incl: . "Military March," in F major (c1925, new composition)
        . "Kampf und Sieg" (see No.1 of: Festmusic zu lebenden Bildern, AV89)

. *"Königsmarsch" (see AVI00)*
. *"Wirbeltanz" (see No.6 of: Dance Suite after Fr. Couperin, AVI07)*

1a. SELECTIONS FROM STAGE WORKS

Op.25

1a.5   "Guntram," opera: ....

       . "Vorspiel"
       I: Scene 1. "Hier, ihr Guten rastet" (Guntram)
               2. "Ein ..." (Guntram)
               3. "Freihild, mein ..." (Herzog)
          . "Vorspiel"
       II: 1. "Einsam sass ich in meiner Kammer" (Narr)
          . "Heil dem Herrscher dessen Seele" (4 Minnesänger)
          . "Ich schaue ein glanzvoll prunkendes Fest" (Guntram)
          . "Ich sehe den Frieden" (Guntram)
               2. "Krieg, Krieg, mein Herzog, Krieg ohn' Ende" (Bote, Herzog)
               3. "Fass ich sie bang" (Freihild)
          . "Vorspiel"
       III: 1. "Et lux perpetua luce," chorus (Mönche)
               2. "Ach! Nein, ach nein! Das ist unmöglich" (Guntram)
               3. "Guntram, Unsel'ger" (Freihild)
               4. "Gegrüst Guntram, grosser Sünder" (Friedhold)
          . "Heil dir, Geliebter" (Freihild)
          . "Wenn du einst die Gauen durchschreitest" (Guntram)
          . "Gönn' mir die Wonne" (Guntram)

Op.50

1a.15   "Feuersnot," opera: ....

       . "Einleitung"
       . "Gebts uns a Holz zum Subendfeuer" (Kinderchor)
       . "Maja, maja, mia mö" (Kinderchor)
       . "Eia, Kind'ln grüss' Euch Gott!" (Ortolf Sentlinger)
       . "Süsse Amarellen" (Diemut)
       . "Ei, ei, ihr bösen Mädigen" (Margret, Elsbeth, Wigelis)
       . "Zu Minka steht a neu' baut's Haus" (Kinderchor)
       . "Lassts den seltsamen Nachbarn aus" (Jörg Pöschel)
       . "Geh' zu, Jörg Pöschel, du bist net recht g'scheit!" (Kunz Gilgensrock, der Bäck und Bräuer)
       . "Ein saub'rer Herr, noch jung an Jahren" (Hämerlein, der Fragner)
       . "Rührts die Trummen, Kindlein singts!" (Tulbeck, der Schäffler)
       . "Hab ihn gesehn unterm Galgen stehn" (Die alte Ursula)
       . "Bockszagel, das sind Altweibergeschichten!" (Kofel der Schmid)
       . "Heh dort! Gebt Ruh!" (Kunrad)
       . "Sonnwend! Sonnwend!" (Kunrad)
       . "Weil jetzt die Sonn' net höher kann" (Mädelnchor)
       . "Wallt's dir im Hirne" (Margret)
       . "Dass ich den Zauber lerne" (Kunrad)
       . "Pfuch! Schamts Euch, Junker Übermut!" (Erstes Zeitmass) (Bürgermeister)
       . "Lebhaftes Walzertempo"
       . "Weil jetzt die Sonn' net höher kann" (Mädelnchor)
       . "Pockszigel! Was wüst' Gelärm und Geschrei" (Burgvogt)
       . "Feuers not!" (Kunrad)
       . "Mittsommernacht! Wehvolle Wacht!" (Diemut)
       . "Leise, leise lasst uns schauen" (Margret, Elsbeth, Wigelis)
       . "Höllenspuk! Satanstrug!" (S, A, T, B)
       . "Oh weh, Herr Schweiker von Gundelfing" (Kunrad)
       . "Mittsommernacht! Wonnige Wacht!" (Diemut)

Op.54

1a.19   "Salome," opera: ....

      Scene 1. "Wie schön, ist die Prinzessin Salome" (Narraboth)
         . "Nach mir wird Einer kommen" (Jochanaan aus der Cisterne)
         2. "Taube" (Narraboth)
         . "Ich will nicht bleiben" (Salome)
         . "Ah!" (Salome)
         3. "Wo ist er, dessen Sündenbecher jetzt voll ist?" (Jochanaan)
         . "Jochanaan!" (Salome)
         . "Zurück Tochter" (Jochanaan)
         . "Sei verflucht, Tochter der blutschänderischen Mutter" (Jochanaan)
         . (Jochanaan geht wieder in die Cisterne hinab)
         4. "Wo ist Salome? Wo ist die Prinzessin?" (Herodes)
         . "Salomes Tanz"
         . "Ah! Herrlich! Wundervoll" (Herodes)
         . "Salome, ich beschwöre dich" (Herodes)
   "Schluss-Scene der Salome": "Ah! Du wolltest mich nicht deinen Mund küssen lassen" (Salome)

1a.26   "Elektra," opera (Nos. of sections in The Gramophone): Op.58
      excerpts: 1. "Wo bleibt Elektra? Ist doch ihre Stunde" (Erste Magd, Zweite Magd)
            2. "Allein! Weh, ganz allein" (Elektra)
            3. "Elektra!" (Chrysothemis)
            4. "Ich kann nicht sitzen und ins Dunkel starren" (Chrysothemis)
            5. "Es geht ein Lärm los"
            6. "Was willst du? Seht doch, dort!" (Klytâmnestra)
            7. "Die Götter! bist doch selber eine Göttin"
            8. "Ich will nichts hören!"
            9. "Ich habe keine guten Nächte"
          10. "Wenn das rechte Blutopfer"
          11. "Was bluten muss?"
          12. "Was sagen sie ihr denn?"
          13. "Orest! Orest ist tot!" (Chrysothemis)
          14. "Platz da! Wer lungert so vor einer Tür?" (Junger Diener)
          15. "Nun muss es hier von uns geschehn"
          16. "Du! Du! denn du bist stark!"
          17. "Nun denn, allein!"
          18. "Was willst du, fremder Mensch?" (Elektra)
          19. "Elektra! Elektra"
          20. "Orest!" (Recognition Scene)
          21. "Du wirst es tun? Allein?"
          22. "Seid ihr von Sinnen" (Der Pfleger)
          23. "Ich habe ihm das Beil nicht geben können!"
          24. "Es muss etwas geschehen sein" (Chrysothemis)
          25. "He! Lichter! Lichter! Ist niemand da" (Aegisth)
          26. "Elektra, Schwester!" (Chrysothemis)
          27. "Ob ich nich höre?"
          28. "Hörst du denn nicht, sie tragen ihn"
          29. "Schweig, und tanze"

1a.28   "Der Rosenkavalier," opera (Nos. of sections in The Gramophone): Op.59
      excerpts: 1. "Prelude"
     I: 2. "Wie du warst! Wie du bist" (Octavian)
           3. "Der Feldmarschall sitzt im krowatischen Wald"
           4. "Selbstverständlich empfängt mich Ihro Gnaden" (Baron)
           5. "Macht das einen lahmen Esel aus mir?" (Baron)
           6a. "I komm' glei"
           6b. "Drei arme adelige Waisen" (Die 3 Waisen)
           7. "Di rigori armato il seno" (Der Sänger)
           8. "Mein lieber Hippolyte"
           9. "Da geht er hin" (Marschallin)
         10. "Ach, du bist wieder da!" (Marschallin, Octavian)
         11. "Die Zeit, die ist ein sonderbar Ding"
     II: 12. "Ein ernster Tag, ein grosser Tag!" (Faninal)
         13. "In dieser feierlichen Stunde der Prüfung" (Sophie)
         14. "Mir ist die Ehre widerfahren" (Presentation of the Rose) (Octavian)
         15. "Ich kenn' Ihn schon recht wohl"
         16. "Jetzt aber kommt mein Herr Zuküftiger" (Sophie)
         17. "Hab' nichts dawider"
         18. "Mit Ihren Augen voll Tränen" (Octavian)
         19. "Herr Baron von Lerchenau!" (Annina)
         20a. "Da lieg' ich!" (Baron)
         20b. "Herr Kavalier!" (Letter Scene)
         20c. "Baron Ochs' Waltz"
    III: 21. "Prelude"
         22. "Hab'n Euer Gnaden" (Der Wirt)
         23. "Nein, nein! I trink' kein Wein" (Octavian)
         24. "Wie die Stund' hingeht"
         25. "Halt! Keiner rührt sich!" (Kommissarius)
         26. "Ihre hochfürstliche Gnaden"
         27. "Ist halt vorbei"
         28. "Mein Gott, es war nicht mehr" (Sophie)
         29. "Heut oder morgen oder den übernächsten Tag"
         30. "Marie Theres' ... Hab' mir's gelobt" (Marschallin)
         31. "Ist ein Traum," finale (Sophie, Octavian)

1a.33   "Ariadne auf Naxos," opera (Nos. of sections in The Gramophone): Op.60
    Prologue: 1. "Introduction"
           2. "Mein Herr Haushofmeister!"
           3. "Du allmächtiger Gott"
           4. "Die ungetreue Zerbinetta"
           5. "Ein Augenblick ist wenig"
           6. "Sein wir wieder gut"
     I: 7. "Ouvertüre"

8. "Schläft sie?"
9. "Wo war ich? Tot?"
10. "Lieben, Hassen, Hoffen, Zagen" (Lied des Harlekin)
11. "Es gibt ein Reich" (Ariadne)
12. "Die Dame gibt mit trübem Sinn sich" (Brighella, Scaramuccio, Harlekin, Truffaldin)
13. "Grossmächtige Prinzessin," recit & aria (Zerbinetta)
14. "Hübsch gepredigt!," recit (Harlekin, Zerbinetta)
15. "Ein schönes Wunder!" (Dryade, Najade)
16. "Circe, Circe, kannst du mich hören?" (Bacchus)
17. "Das waren Zauberworte!"

1a.34   "Die Frau ohne Schatten," opera (Nos. of sections in The Gramophone): Op.65
    excerpts: I: 1. "Licht über'm See, ein fliessender Glanz" (Die Amme)
        2. "Amme! Wachst du?" (Der Kaiser)
        3. "Ist mein Liebster dahin" (Die Kaiserin)
        4. "Wie soll ich denn nicht weinen?" (Des Falken Stimme)
        5. "Amme, um alles, wo find' ich den Schatten?"
        6. "Flight down to Earth"
        7. "Dieb! Da nimm!"
        8. "Sie aus dem Hause"
        9. "Dritthalb Jahr bin ich dein Weib"
        10. "Was wollt ihr hier?"
        11. "Ach, Herrin, süsse Herrin!"
        12. "Hat es dich blutige Tränen gekostet"
        13. "Mutter, Mutter, lass uns nach Hause!" (5 Kinderstimmen)
        14. "Trag' ich die Ware selber zu Markt" (Barak)
        15. "Sie haben es mir gesagt"
    II: 16. "Komm bald wieder nach Haus, mein Gebieter" (Die Amme)
        17. "Was ist nun deine Rede, du Prinzessin"
        18. "Orchestral Interlude"
        19. "Falke, Falke, du wiedergefundener" (Der Kaiser)
        20. "Stille ... O weh, Falke, o weh!"
        21. "Es gibt derer, die haben immer Zeit" (Die Frau)
        22. "Schlange, was hab' ich mit dir zu schaffen"
        23. "Ein Handwerk verstehst du sicher nicht"
        24. "Wer da?"
        25. "Sieh—Amme—sieh" (Die Kaiserin)
        26. "Zum Lebenswasser!," m ch (Stimmen aus dem Innern des Berges)
        27. "Wehe, mein Mann!"
        28. "Es dunkelt, dass ich nicht sehe zur Arbeit" (Barak)
        29. "Es gibt derer"
        30. "Das Weib ist irre"
        31. "Barak, ich hab' es nicht getan!"
    III: 32. "Schweigt doch, ihr Stimmen!" (Die Frau)
        33. "Mir anvertraut"
        34. "Auf, geh nach oben, Mann"
        35. "Sie kommen!"
        36. "Fort mit uns"
        37. "Aus unsern Taten steigt ein Gericht!"
        38. "Was Menschen bedfürfen?"
        39. "Keikobad! Deine Dienerin"
        40. "Weh uns Armen!"
        41. "Vater, bist du's?"
        42. "Goldenen Trank"
        43. "Ach! Weh mir! Mein Liebster starr!"
        44. "Wenn das Herz aus Kristall zerbricht" (Der Kaiser)
        45. "Sind das die Cherubim"
        46. "Engel sind's die von sich sagen!"
        47. "Trifft mich sein Lieben nicht" (Die Frau)
        48. "Nun will ich jubeln" (Barak)
        49. "Vater, dir drohet nichts"
                                                                            .... Op.72
1a.47   "Intermezzo," opera: ....
    I: Scene 1. "Anna, Anna! Wo bleibt denn nur die dumme Gans? (Die Frau)
        2. "Sie Esel! Sehn Sie denn nicht" (Die Frau)
        . "Waltz"
        3. "Ich kann nicht mehr!" (Die Frau)
        4. "Wissen sie, mein Mann" (Die Frau)
        5. "Das ist gut, das soll er nur"
        6. "Frau Notar! Können Sie mir meinen Koffer heraufschicken?" (Der Baron, Die Notarin)
        7. "Tausend Mark will er haben! ... Mein lieber, lieber Bubi!" (Die Frau)
    II: 1. "Ach! Sie kennen sie nicht" (Der Commerzienrat)
        2. "Guten Tag, Herr Notar" (Die Frau, Herr Notar)
        3. "Es ist einfach zum Rasenwerden!" (Robert)
        4. "Anna! Ich hätte den Baron doch nicht dahin schicken sollen" (Die Frau)

     5. "Er kommt! Herrgott, wie ich mich" (Die Frau)
     6. "Da bin ich, gnäd'ge Frau!" (Der Baron, Die Frau)

1a.50   "Die Ägyptische Helena," opera (Nos. of sections in The Gramophone): Op.75
    excerpts: I: 1. "Das Mahl ist gerichtet" (Aithra)
          2. "Ist es wirklich Helena?"
          3. "Wo bin ich?" (Menelas)
          4. "Bei jener Nacht, der keuschen einzig einen"
          5. "Ihr grünen Augen im weissen Gesicht" (Ihr grünen Augen)
          6. "Du bist durchnässt" (Aithra)
          7. "Ai!... Im weissen Gewand" (Aithra)
          8. "Zerspalten das Herz!"
          9a. "Helen's awakening"
          9b. "O Engel!" (Helena, Elfen)
         10. "Das Nötigste nur in eine Truhe"
    II: 11. "Zweite Brautnacht!" (Helena)
         12. "Wo ist das Haus?"
         13. "Aus flirrender Stille was naht heran?" (Menelas)
         14. "Ich werde neben dir reiten!"
         15. "So schön bedient"
         16. "Aithra! Liebe Herrliche!" (Helena)
         17. "O dreifache Törin!"
         18. "Mein Geliebter! Menelas!" (Helena)
         18a. "Funeral march"
         18b. "Mein Geliebter! Menelas!"
         19. "Unter geschlossenem Lid"
         20. "Helena, oder wie ich sonst dich nenne"
         21. "Bei jener Nacht, der keuschen einzig einen"
         22. "Ewig erwählt von diesem Blick!"
         23. "Wie du aufs neue die Nacht durchglänzest"

1a.57   "Arabella," opera (Nos. of sections in The Gramophone): Op.79
    I: 1a. "Ich danke, Fräulein" (Arabella)
        1b. "Aber der Richtige" (Arabella)
        1c. "Mandryka! Der reiche Kerl!"
        2a. "Mein Elemer!" (Arabella)
        2b. "Nach dem Matteo"
    II: 3a. "Sie wollen mich heiraten" (Arabella)
        3b. "So wie Sie sind" (Arabella)
        4. "Und jetzt sag' ich adieu" (Arabella)
    III: 5. "Das war sehr gut" (Arabella)

1a.58   "Die schweigsame Frau," opera: Op.80
      . "Potpourri"
    I: Scene 1. (Die Haushälterin fegt den Staub vom Tisch, macht Ordnung)
         2. "Da eine in deine Takelage" (Morosus)
         3. Ah! Mein Stock!" (Morosus, Barbier)
         4. "Oh Gott, war das ein saurer Empfang!" (Henry, Aminta)
         . "Finale"
    II: 1. "Tempo di Minuetto"
         2. "Euer Gnaden" (Der Barbier)
         3. "Zeit" (Morosus)
         4. "So stumm, mein Kind" (Morosus)
         5. "Ei, ei, wie rasch das Arcanum wirkt!" (Barbier)
         6. "Allegro" (Vanuzzi, Morbio, Haushälterin, Der Barbier)
         7. "Ehre, dem Ehre gebührt!" (Farfallo, Morosus)
         8. "Ist es möglich, Sir Morosus?," chorus (Nachbarn)
         9. "Du bist so still" (Morosus)
        10. "Was geht hier vor?" (Henry, Morosus)
        11. "Ohm, das ist die richtige Art" (Henry)
        12. (Aminta kommt leise heraus, beide umarmen sich)
    III: 1. "Vorhang"
         2. "Oh, gnädigste Frau, der Herr lässt Euch" (Aminta, Haushälterin, Papagei)
         3. "Salute, Maêstro!" (Aminta, Henry, Farfallo)
         . "Sento un certo non so che," aria (Aminta)
         . "Dolce Amor!," duet (Aminta, Henry) (from Legrenzi's opera: Eteocle e Polinice)
         4. "Seine illustre Lordschaft, der chief-Justice" (Barbier)
         5. "Gnädigster Herr ... zwei Karossen sind angefahren" (Haushälterin, Morosus)
         6. "Im Namen Seiner Majestät" (Vanuzzi)
         7. "Meinen submissesten Respect" (Aminta, Barbier, Morbio, Vanuzzi, Farfallo, Morosus)
         8. "Hier diese beiden ehrsamen Damen" (Barbier)
         9. "Sehr wohl, Euer Lordschaft!" (Henry, Vanuzzi)
         . "Willst du wirklich mich nicht kennen?," aria (Henry)
         . "Finale"
        10. (Morosus strahlend beglückt sich in den Sessel zurücklehnend)

1a.71   "Friedenstag," opera: Op.81
. "Hast was gesehn?... Morgen dämmert" (Wachtmeister, Schütze)
. "La rosa, la rosa che un bel fiore" (Piemonteser)
. "Wegtreten von den Scharten! An die Stufen!" (Trauermarsch) (Wachtmeister)
. "In aller pflichtgen Demut" (Bürgmeister)
. "Sieg! Welch ein Fanal" (Prälat, Kommandant)
. "Wie? Niemand hier?" (Maria)
. "Dank dir, Sonne" (Maria)
. "Erwünschtes Zeichen!" (Kommandant)
. "Wo ist der Mann, des Krieges bester Held?" (Holsteiner)
. "Sei uns gegrüsst," chorus (Frauen)
. "Wagt es zu denken" (Maria, 2S, 2T, 4B)

1a.72   "Daphne," opera: Op.82
. "Kleontes! Adrast! Wo bleibst du?" (1. Schäfer, 2. Schäfer)
. "O bleib ... Leb wohl" (Daphne, Schäfer)
. "O wie gerne blieb ich bei" (Daphne)
. "Leukippos du? Ja, ich selbst, ich war der Baum!" (Daphne, Leukippos)
. "Daphne! Wir warten dein" (Daphne, Gaea)
. "Seid ihr um mich, ihr Hirten alle?" (Peneios)
. "Ich grüsse dich, Weiser" (Apollo)
. "Allüberall blühet Dionysos" (Peneios)
. "Allegretto"
. "Zu dir nun, Knabe!" (Apollo)
. "Was erblikke ich?" (Apollo)
. "Daphnes Verwandlung"

1a.73   "Die Liebe der Danae," opera: Op.83
I: . "Wo birgt sich Pollux?" (T, Chor der Gläubiger)
. "O Gold! O süsses Gold!" (Danae, Xanthe)
. "Was bringen die Fürsten? Endet die Not?," chorus
. "Leuchtet mein Traum?" (Danae)
. "Niemals entschwinde, was du gebracht!" (Pollux, 4 Könige, ch)
II: . "Kränze winden wir" (4 Königinnen)
. "Herrliches Spiel!" (Danae)
III: . "Vorspiel"
. "Geliebter! Freund! Bei dir bin ich" (Danae, Midas)
. "Zwischenvorhang"
. "Du schon hier?" (Merkur, Jupiter)
. "Wie sehr er scherzt" (Semele)
. "Schwere Tropfen," chorus
. "Zwischenvorhang"
. "Wie umgibst du mich mit Frieden" (Danae)
. "Maja liebte er" (Jupiter)

1a.78   "Capriccio," opera: Op.85
. "Prelude" (str sextet)
Scene 1. (String sextet behind the scene)
2. (Graf und Gräfin kommen aus dem Salon)
3. "Die Bühne ist fertig" (Direktor)
4. "Sie ist doch gekommen!" (Olivier, Gräfin)
5. "Lassen Sie ihn gewähren" (Gräfin)
6. "Kein Andres, das mir so im Herzen loht" (Flamand)
7. (Flamand allein mit der Gräfin)
8. "Welch köstliche Begegnung! Sie ist reizend, bezaubernd!" (Graf, Gräfin)
9. "Wir kehren zurück in die Welt" (Direktor)
. "Passepied" (Erster Tanz)
. "Ich bin fest entschlossen" (Gigue)
. "Gavotte" (Dritter Tanz)
. "Tanz und Musik stehn im Bann des Rhythmus" (Fuge) (Olivier, Flamand)
. "Addio mia vita, addio non piangere il mio," duet (der italienischen Sänger)
. "Sie lachen ihn aus" (Octet. Part I: Lachensemble)
. "Aber so hört doch! Es kommt ja ganz anders!" (Octet. Part II: Streit-Ensemble)
. "Was hebt sich göttergleich aus hohem Äther?" (Flamand, Olivier)
10. "Wiedersehn!" (Flamand)
11. "Das war ein" (T, 8 Diener)
12. "Herr Direktor!" (Monsieur Taupe)
13. "Andante con moto"
. "Wo ist mein Bruder?" (Gräfin, Haushofmeister)

1a.79   "Des Esels Schatten," opera: AV300
. "Vorspiel"
1. "Hart ist der Weg, die Last ist schwer" (Antrax)
2. "Ihr seid ein Narr," duet (Struthion, Antrax)
3. "Ich möchte am Wiesenrain sitzen" (Lied des Philippides)

4. "Zwei neue Klienten einen für jeden!," duet (Physignatus, Polyphonus)
5. "Da bilden sich die guten Leute immer ein" (Lied des Kenteterion)
6. "Es dreht sich hier nicht um Debatten," trio (Physignatus, Kenteterion, Struthion)
7. "Protektion ist alles hier im Leben," trio (Krobyle)
8a. "La-la-la-la," arietta (Gorgo)
8b. "Wie mächtig wirkt Musik auf manchen Mann," trio (Gorgo, Krobyle, Antrax)
9. "Pantomime der Frösche und Störche"
10. "Dieser Frevel schreit nach Rache," chorus (unison Ts & Bs)
11. "Jahr und Tag sind wir nur brave," chorus (unison)
12. "Die grosse Stunde hat geschlagen" (Ansprache des Philippides)
13. "So geht in Eintracht nun zu Ende" (Finale) (Antrax)

1a.89   "Schlagobers," ballet: Op.70
      I: 1. "Schnell"
            2. "Ländler"
            3. "Konditorküche"
            4. "Tanz der Teeblüte"
            5. "Tanz des Kaffee's"
            6. "Träumerei"
            7. "Tanz des Kakao"
            8. "Auftritt und Tanz des Zuckers"
            9. "Reigen von Tee, Zucker, Kaffee und Kakao"
          10. "Schlagoberwalzer"
     II: 11. "Molto agitato"
          12. "Einzug der Prinzessin Pralinee mit ihrem Hofstaat"
          13. "Langsamer Walzer"
          14. "Tanz der kleinen Pralinees"
          15. "Springtanz der Knallbonbons"
          16. "Galopp"
          17. "Zwischenspiel"
          18. "Menuett"
          19. "Pas de deux"
          20. "Das Chaos"
          21. "Aufruhrpolka"
          22. "Vollbierreigen der Besänftigten"
          23. "Finale. Allgemeiner Tanz"

1a.98   "Verklungene Feste," ballet: AV128
          1.–3. "Vorspiel": 1. (= Divertimento, Op.86/1, La visionnaire)
          1a. (= Divertimento, Op.86/1, Sarabande)
          2. (= Divertimento, Op.86/2, La fine Madelon)
          2a. (= Divertimento, Op.86/2, La douce Janneton)
          2b. (= Divertimento, Op.86/2, La Sézile)
          3. (= Dance Suite, AV107/1, Einzug und feierlicher Reigen)
          4. Dance No.1 "Courante" (= Dance Suite, AV107/2, Courante)
          5. Dance No.2 "Carillon" (= Dance Suite, AV107/3, Carillon)
          6. Dance No.3 "Sarabande" (= Dance Suite, AV107/4, Sarabande)
          7. Dance No.4 "Gavotte" (= Dance Suite, AV107/5, Gavotte)
          8. "Zwischenspiel" (= Divertimento, Op.86/7, Les ombres errantes)
          9. "Aufzug des Triumphwagens der Flora" (= Divertimento, Op.86/5, La trophée)
         10. Dance No.5 "Harlekine" (= Divertimento, Op.89/5, La Linotte effarouchée)
         11. Dance No.6 "Floras Klage" (= Divertimento, Op.86/4, Les fauvettes plaintives)
         12. "Flora und Zephyr" (= Divertimento, Op.86/2, Musette de Taverny)
         13. Dance No.7 "Die befreite Flora" (= Divertimento, Op.86/6, Les tours de passe-passe)
         14. Dance No.8 "Floras Gespielinnen" (= Divertimento, Op.86/2, Musette de Choisy)
         15. Dance No.9 "Wirbeltanz" (= Dance Suite, AV107/6, Wirbeltanz)
         16. "Zwischenspiel" (= Dance Suite, AV107/7, Allemande)
         16a. Dance No.10 "Menuet" (= Dance Suite, AV107/7, Menuett)
         17. "Ausklang" (= Dance Suite, AV107/8, Marsch)

1a.107   "Der Bürger als Edelmann," incid music: Op.60
          1. "Overture to Act I"
          2. "Auftritt des Jourdain"
          3. "Musikalisches Gespräch"
          4. "Minuet"
          5. "The Fencing Master"
          6. "Entrance and Dance of the Tailors"
          7. "Finale of Act I"
          8. "Minuet of Lully"
          9. "Entrance of Cléonte" (after Lully)
         10. "Prelude to Act II" (Intermezzo)
         11. "The Dinner"
         12. "Courante" (in Canonform)
         13. "Finale of Act II"
         14. "Prelude" (alla Sicilienne)

15. "Darf ich heute zu den Geistern sprechen?" (Melodrama) (Jourdain)
16. "Wie mein Gott, so klingeln Sie doch" (Die türkische Zeremonie) (Jourdain)
17. "Finale of Act III"
. "Vertraue hohem Stern" (Madrigal after Lully) (3 Sylphen)

2. SYMPHONIES

		AV69
2.1	Symphony No.1 in D minor (c1880)	Op.12
2.2	Symphony No.2 in F minor (c1883–4)	AV233
2.3	*"Bildersinfonie" (c1901–2, inspired by paintings of Veronese & Hogarth, project)*	Op.53
2.4	"Sinfonia Domestica" (c1902–3)	Op.53
2.5	"Eine Alpensinfonie" (An Alpine Symphony) (c1911–5; large orch w/ org, wind machine, etc; simplified w/out org 1934):	Op.64

1. "Nacht"
2. "Sonnenaufgang"
3. "Der Anstieg"
4. "Eintritt in den Wald"
5. "Wanderung neben dem Bache"
6. "Am Wasserfall"
7. "Auf blumige Wiesen"
8. "Auf der Alm"
9. "Durch Dickicht und Gestrüpp auf Irrwegen"
10. "Auf dem Gletscher"
11. "Gefahrvolle Augenblicke"
12. "Auf dem Gipfel"
13. "Vision"
14. "Nebel steigen auf"
15. "Die Sonne verdüstert"
16. "Elegie"
17. "Stille vor dem Sturm"
18. "Gewitter und Sturm, Abstieg"
19. "Sonnenuntergang"
20. "Ausklang"

2.6	*"Der Antichrist" (c1911–5, project)*	AV247
2.7	*"Sinfonie zu drei Themen," in E-flat major (ca1925, sketches)*	AV260
2.8	*" 'Unvollendete' " (?symphony) (c1948, frag, sketches)*	AV302

3. OTHER ORCHESTRAL WORKS

		AV15
3.1	"Overture" (c1872–3, for Singspiel: Hochlands Treue, short score only)	AV30
3.2	"Concert Overture," in B minor (c1876)	Op.1
3.3	"Festmarsch" (No.1), in E-flat major (c1876; also extract for pf duet)	AV207
3.4	*"Overture," in E minor (c1876, for opera: Ein Studentenstreich, inc sketches)*	AV208
3.5	*"Overture," in E-flat minor (c1876, for opera: Dom Sebastian, inc sketches)*	AV32
3.6	"Serenade," in G major (c1877)	AV209
3.7	*"Andante cantabile," in D major (c1877, inc sketches)*	AV210
3.8	*"Andante," in B-flat major (c1877, inc sketches)*	AV51
3.9	"Overture," in E major (c1878)	AV62
3.10	"Overture," in A minor (c1879)	Op.4
3.11	"Suite," in B-flat major (c1884; 13 winds): No.1 "Präludium"	
3.12	No.2 "Romanze"	
3.13	No.3 "Gavotte"	
3.14	No.4 "Introduktion und Fuge"	Op.7
3.15	"Serenade," in E-flat major (c1881; 13 winds)	AV79
3.16	"Lied ohne Worte," in E-flat major (c1883)	AV80
3.17	"Concert Overture," in C minor (c1883)	AV84
3.18	"Festmarsch" (No.3), in D major (c1884; 2nd vers 1887)	AV212
3.19	*"Suite" (c1886, sketch, mentioned in the letter fo his father)*	Op.16
3.20	"Aus Italien," sym fantasy in G major (c1886; also extract for pf):	

1. "Auf der Campagna"
2. "In Rom's Ruinen"
3. "Am Strande von Sorrent"
4. "Neapolitanisches Volksleben"

		AV87
3.21	"Festmarsch" (No.4), in C major (c1888)	
3.22	"Don Juan," tone poem (Strauss's term, preferred over the older 'symphonic poem') (c1888, after Lenau; choreographed Ashton 1948)	Op.20
3.23	"Macbeth," tone poem (c1886–8, r1889–91, after Shakespeare; also extract for pf duet)	Op.23
3.24	"Tod und Verklärung" (Death and Transfiguration), tone poem (c1889)	Op.24
3.25	"Fanfare" (c1891, for incid music: Jägern of 1891)	AV88a
3.26	"Festmusic zu 'Lebende Bilder' " (c1892):	AV89

1. "Drittes Bild" (after Jacquand; arr for orch 1931 as: Kampf und Zieg)
2. "Viertes Bild" (after Rochussen)
3. "Sechstes Bild" (after Fritjof Smith & Schmidt)

4. CONCERTOS, SOLO INSTR & ORCH

Pf & orch:

Vn & orch:

Vc & orch:

Other instr(s) & orch:

5. STRING QUARTETS

6. OTHER CHAMBER MUSIC

6 insts:

4 insts:

3 insts:

6.8	Piano Trio No.1 in A major (c1877)	AV37
6.9	Piano Trio No.2 in D major (c1878)	AV53
6.10	"Variationen über 's Dirndl is haub auf mi' " (c1882; vn, va & vc)	
6.11	"Fantasie über ein Thema von Paisiello" (c1883; bn, Mundflöte & gui)	
6.12	"Tänze aus 'Capriccio' " (p1943; vn, vc & hpd, from opera: Capriccio, Op.85): No.1 "Passepied"	
6.13	No.2 "Gigue"	
6.14	No.3 "Gavotte"	

Vn & pf:

6.15	*"2 Little Pieces" (c1873, inc sketches): No.1 "Moderato," in G major*	*AV194*
6.16	*No.2 "Largo," in G major*	
6.17	Violin Sonata in E-flat major (c1887)	Op.18
6.18	"Allegretto," in E major (c1948)	AV149

Vc & pf:

6.19	Cello Sonata in F major (c1881–3)	Op.6

Other 2 insts:

6.20	"Introduction, Theme and Variations," in E-flat major (c1878; hn & pf)	AV52
6.21	"Introduction, Theme and Variations," in G major (c1879; fl & pf)	AV56
6.22	"Andante," in C major (c1888; hn & pf, for unfin sonata, recovered 1971)	AV86a
6.23	"Hochzeitspräludium" (c1924, 2 harm)	AV108

1 instr:

6.24	"2 Etüden für Horn" (c ?1873; hn): No.1 "Allegretto," in E-flat major	AV12
6.25	No.2 "Lento—Presto," in E major	
6.26	"Daphne—Etüde," in G major (c1945; vn, on a theme from opera: Daphne, Op.82)	AV141

7. PIANO SONATAS

7.1	Piano Sonata No.1 in E major (c1877)	AV38
7.2	Piano Sonata No.2 in C minor, "Grosse Sonate" (c1879)	AV60
7.3	Piano Sonata in B minor (c1880–1)	Op.5

8. OTHER PIANO WORKS

8.1	"Schneider-Polka" (c1870)	AV1
8.2	"Moderato," in C major (c ?1871)	AV9
8.3	"Panzenburg-Polka" (c1872)	AV10
8.4	Slow movement in G minor (c ?1872)	AV11
8.5	*"Polka, Walzer und andere kleinere Kompositionen" (c ?1872, lost: title page extant)*	*AV152*
8.6	"5 Little Pieces" (c ?1873): No.1 "Allegretto," in C major	AV16
8.7	No.2 "Moderato," in G major	
8.8	No.3 "Allegretto," in C major	
8.9	No.4 "Larghetto," in F major	
8.10	No.5 "Allegro," in D major	
8.11	*Sonatina (No.1), in C major (c ?1873, lost)*	*AV153*
8.12	*Sonatina (No.2), in E major (c ?1873, ?used in: Sonatina No.4, AV195, lost)*	*AV154*
8.13	Sonatina No.1 in C major (c1874)	AV17
8.14	Sonatina No.2 in F major (c1874)	AV18
8.15	Sonatina No.3 in B-flat major (c1874)	AV19
8.16	*Sonatina No.4 in E major (c1874, sketches)*	*AV195*
8.17	*Sonatina No.5 in E-flat major (c1874, lost)*	*AV155*
8.18	*Sonatina No.6 in D major (c1874, lost)*	*AV156*
8.19	*Sonatina No.7 in G minor (c1873, sketches)*	*AV197*
8.20	*Sonatina No.8 in G major (c1873, sketches)*	*AV198*
8.21	*Sonatina No.9 in C minor (c1873, sketches)*	*AV199*
8.22	*Sonatina in E-flat major (c1873, sketches)*	*AV200*
8.23	*"Sonatensatz," in D major (c1873, sketches)*	*AV201*
8.24	*Sonatina in E minor (c1874, sketch)*	*AV202*
8.25	Untitled piece (w/ Maggiore) in C minor (c ?1874)	AV20
8.26	"Fantasie," in C major (c ?1874)	AV21
8.27	"2 Little Pieces" (c ?1875): No.1 "Moderato"	AV22
8.28	No.2 "Andante"	
8.29	*"Allegro assai," in B-flat major (c1875, inc sketches)*	*AV203*
8.30	"12 Variations," in D major (c1878)	AV50
8.31	"Aus alter Zeit. Eine kleine Gavotte" (c1879)	AV57

8.32   "Andante," in C minor (c1879) AV58
8.33   "Skizzen," 5 little pieces (c1879): No.1 "Allegro," in E major AV59
8.34   No.2 "Andante," in G major
8.35   No.3 "Gavotte II," in D major
8.36   No.4 "Gavotte III," in G major
8.37   No.5 "Gavotte IV," in D major (orchd) *AV163*
8.38   *"Hochzeitsmusik" (c1879; pf & child instr, lost)* AV63
8.39   "Scherzo," in B minor (c1879) AV68
8.40   "2 Little Pieces" (c1879–80): No.1 "Andantino," in G major ....
8.41   No.2 "Gavotte," in D major AV70
8.42   "Scherzando," in G major (c1880) AV71
8.43   "Fugue on 4 Themes," in C major (c1880) Op.3
8.44   "5 Klavierstücke" (c1880–1): No.1 "Andante," in B-flat major ....
8.45   No.2 "Allegro vivace scherzando," in E-flat minor
8.46   No.3 "Largo," in C minor
8.47   No.4 "Allegro molto," in A-flat major
8.48   No.5 "Allegro marcatissimo," in D-flat major *AV171*
8.49   *"Albumblatt" (c1882, lost)* AV77
8.50   "Largo," in A minor (c1883) AV78
8.51   "Stiller Waldespfad" (c1883) ....
8.52   "Melodie" (c ?1883) ....
8.53   "Stimmungsbilder" (c1882–4): No.1 "Auf stillem Waldespfad" (Albumleaf No.1 for B. Schlüssel) Op.9
8.54   No.2 "An einsamer Quelle"
8.55   No.3 "Intermezzo" (for Dora Wihan)
8.56   No.4 "Träumerei"
8.57   No.5 "Heidebild"
8.58   14 "Improvisationen und Fuge über ein Originalthema," in A minor (c1884) AV81, AV177
8.59   *Cadenza for Mozart: Piano Concerto No.24 in C minor, K491 (c1885, lost)* *AV179*
8.60   *"2 Stücke für Klavierquartett" (c1893, small frags extant): No.1 "Arabischer Tanz," in D minor* ....
8.61   *No.2 "Liebesliedchen," in G major*
8.62   "Parade-Marsch (No.1) des Regiments Königs-Jäger zu Pferde," in E-flat major (c1905) AV97
8.63   "Parade-Marsch (No.2) für Cavallerie," in D-flat major (c1907) AV98
8.64   "De Brandenburgsche Mars—Präsentiermarsch" (c1905; orchd) AV99
8.65   "Königsmarsch" (Militärischer Festmarsch), in E-flat major (c1905; pf; also for milit orch 1906) AV100
8.66   "Der Einsame" (c1906, pf vers of song Op.51/2) Op.51/2
8.67   "Suite aus 'Capriccio' " (p1944; hpd, from opera Op.85): No.1 "Tanz Passepied. Allegretto" AV138
8.68   No.2 "Tanz Gigue. Allegro molto"
8.69   No.3 "Tanz Tempo di Gavotta. Allegro"

Pf duet:

8.70   "Intermezzo," in F major (c1885) ....

9. CHORAL WORKS

W/ orch:

9.1   *"Festchor" (c ?1880; ch & pf, destroyed 1943)* *AV169*
9.2   "Chorus from Elektra" (c1881, Sophocles in Greek; m ch & small orch) AV74
9.3   "Wandrers Sturmlied": "Wen du nicht verlässest, Genius" (c1884, Goethe; ch & orch) Op.14
9.4   *"Bardengesang" I (c1886, from Kleist: Die Hermannsschlacht, lost; see Op.55)* *AV181*
9.5   "Hymne": "Licht, Du ewiglich Eines" (c1897, Schiller's Votivtafeln; fem ch, brass band & orch) AV91
9.6   "Taillefer": "Wer singt in meinem Hof," ballad (c1902–3, Uhland; S, T, Bar, ch & orch) Op.52
9.7   "Bardengesang" II (c1905, from Klopstock's Hermannsschlacht; m ch & orch) Op.55
9.8   "Die Tageszeiten," cycle (c1927–8, Eichendorff; m ch & orch): 1. "Der Morgen": "Wenn der Hahn" ... Op.76
9.9   2. "Mittagsruh": "Über Bergen, Fluss und Talen"
9.10   3. "Der Abend": "Schweigt der Menschen laute Lust"
9.11   4. "Die Nacht": "Wie schön, hier zu verträumen"
9.12   "Austria": "Wo sich der ewige Schnee" (c1929, Wildgans; m ch & orch) Op.78
9.13   "Olympic Hymn": "Völker! Seid des Volkes Gäste" (c1934, Lubahn, for 1936 Olympic Games) AV119
9.14   *"Besinnung": "Göttlich ist und ewig der Geist" (c1949, Hesse, frag, sketches)* *AV306*

Unacc ch:

9.15   *"Vierstimmiger Satz," in B-flat major (c ?1875, frag)* *AV23*
9.16   *"Vierstimmiger Choralsatz," in B-flat major (c ?1875, frag)* *AV24*
9.17   "2 Lieder" (c1876, Eichendorff): 1. "Morgengesang": "Im Osten geht die Sonne auf" AV25
9.18   2. "Frühlingsnacht": "Über'm Garten durch die Lüfte"
9.19   *"Vierstimmiger Satz," in D minor (c1876, sketches)* *AV26*
9.20   *"Vierstimmiger Satz," in A-flat major (c1876, sketches & notes)* *AV27*
9.21   "4 Sätze zu einer Messe," in D major (c1877): 1. "Kyrie" AV31
9.22   2. "Sanctus"
9.23   3. "Benedictus"
9.24   4. "Agnus Dei"

9.25	"7 Lieder" (c1880; ch / S, A, T, B): 1. "Winterlied": "Mir träumte ich ruhte wieder vor" (Eichendorff) AV67
9.26	2. "Spielmannsweise": "Es stand auf duftiger Aue" (Gensichen)
9.27	3. "Pfingsten": "Frohen Tones laden Glocken" (Böttger)
9.28	4. "Käferlied": "Es war'n einmal drei Käferknaben" (Reinick)
9.29	5. "Waldessang": "Ich hör ein Vöglein locken" (Böttger)
9.30	6. "Schneeglöcklein": "Schneeglöcklein lacht und jubelt" (Böttger)
9.31	7. "Trüb blinken nur die Sterne" (Böttger)
9.32	"Schwäbische Erbschaft": "Der gnäd'ge Herr von Zavelstein" (c1884, Löwe).................... AV83
9.33	"2 Gesänge" (c1897; ch): 1. "Der Abend": "Senke strahlender Gott!" (Schiller) Op.34
9.34	2. "Hymne": "Jakob! Dein verlorner Sohn" (Rückert)
9.35	"Richard Till Khnopff": "Richard Till Khnopff: er lebe hoch!" (c1898; 4vv) ....
9.36	"Soldatenlied": "Wenn man beim Wein sitzt" (c1899, Kopisch; m ch) AV93
9.37	"2 Männerchöre" (c1899, from Herder's Stimmen der Völker; m ch): 1. "Liebe": "Nichts Bessers ist" . Op.42
9.38	2. "Altdeutsches Schlachtlied": "Frisch auf, ihr tapfere Soldaten!"
9.39	"3 Männerchöre" (c1899): 1. "Schlachtgesang": "Kein sel'ger Tod ist in der Welt" (Herder) Op.45
9.40	2. "Lied der Freundschaft": "Der Mensch hat nichts so eigen" (Dach)
9.41	3. "Der Brauttanz": "Tanz, der du Gesetze unsern Füssen gibst" (Dach)
9.42	"Tummel dich guts Weinlein" (arr1905; ch, from folksong of ca1565) ....
9.43	"6 Volksliedbearbeitungen" (c1905–6; m ch): 1. "Geistliche Maien": "Wer sich des Maiens wölle" AV101
9.44	2. "Misslungene Liebesjagd": "Ich schell mein Horn"
9.45	3. "Tummler": "Frisch auf, gut Gesell"
9.46	4. "Hüt' du dich!": "Ich weiss mir ein Maidlein"
9.47	5. "Wächterlied": "Wach auf, wach auf"
9.48	6. "Kuckuck": "Der Gutzgauch auf dem Zaune sass"
9.49	"Deutsche Motette": "Die Schöpfung ist zur Ruh gegangen" (c1913, Rückert; S, A, T, B & ch) Op.62
9.50	"Tüchtigen stellt das schnelle Glück hoch empor," cantata (c1914, Hofmannsthal; m ch)................. AV104
9.51	"Die Göttin im Putzzimmer": "Welche chaotische Haushälterei" (c1935, Rückert)....................... AV120
9.52	"3 Männerchöre" (c1935, Rückert): 1. "Vor den Türen": "Ich habe geklopft" AV123
9.53	2. "Traumlicht": "Ein Licht im Traum hat mich besucht"
9.54	3. "Fröhlich im Maien": "Blühende Frauen, lasset euch schauen"
9.55	"Durch Einsamkeiten": "Durch Einsamkeiten, durch waldwild Geheg" (c1938, Wildgans)............ AV124
9.56	"An den Baum Daphne": "Geliebter Baum!" (c1943, Gregor, epilogue to opera: Daphne, Op.82) AV137
9.57	*"Die Arche Noah," ?oratorio / ?sym poem / ? (c1949, after Krauss, project)...........................AV305*
9.58	*"Besinnung 'Göttlich ist und ewig der Geist" (c1948–9, Hesse; ch & orch, frag, sketches)..........AV306*

10. MISC VOCAL

10.1	"Der weisse Hirsch": "Es gingen drei Jäger wohl auf die Birsch" (c ?1871, Uhland; A, T, B & pf) AV6
10.2	"Das Alphorn": "Ein Alphorn hör' ich schallen" (c ?1878, Kerner; 1v, hn & pf) AV29
10.3	"Utan Svafvel och fosfor" (c1889; 2T, 2B, at a Swedish Matchbox Co. Exhibition Stand) AV88
10.4	"Enoch Arden," melodrama (c1897, Tennyson transl Strodtmann; narrator & pf): Op.38
	. "Vorspiel"
I:	. "Annie Lee, das schmuckste kleine Mädchen"
	. "Annie's Traum"
II:	. "Vorspiel"
	. "Wohl Tag für Tag"
10.5	"Das Schloss am Meere": "Hast du das Schloss gesehen," melodrama (c1899, Uhland; narrator & pf) AV92
10.6	"Hans Huber in Vitznau sei schönstens bedankt," canon in C major (c1903, Strauss) AV95
10.7	"Scatcanon": "S-c-a-t spielen wir fröhlich bei Willy Levin" (c1904, Strauss; m ch) AV95a
10.8	"2 Lieder aus Der Richter von Zalamea" (c1904, Calderón): 1. "Liebesliedchen": "Hör mein
	Liebesliedchen ziehn" (T, gui & harp) AV96
10.9	2. "Lied der Chispa": "Es war ein Bruder Liederlich" (mS, unison m vv, gui & 2 harps)
10.10	"Hymne auf das Haus Kohorn": "Unerschöpflich quillet der Born" (c1925, Strauss; 2T, 2B) AV113
10.11	"Hab Dank, du güt'ger Weisheitsspender" (c1939, Strauss; B) AV126
10.12	"Notschrei aus den Gefilden Lapplands": "Im ganzen Ort gibst keine Kohlen" (c1940) AV127
10.13	"Wer tritt herein": "Wer tritt herein so fesch und schlank?" (c1943, Strauss; S/T) AV136

11. VOICE & ORCHESTRA

11.1	"Arie der Almaide": "Sei nicht beklommen" (c1878, from Goethe's Lila; S & orch, unfin) AV44
11.2	"Der Spielmann und sein Kind": "Es blitzt und kracht es" (c1878, Fallersleben; also w/ pf)................ AV46
11.3	"4 Gesänge": 1. "Verführung": "Der Tag, der schwüle" (c1896–7, Mackay; S/T & orch) Op.33
11.4	2. "Gesang der Apollopriesterin": "Es ist der Tag" (c1896, Bodman; S & orch)
11.5	3. "Hymnus": "Dass du mein Auge wecktest" (c1896, unknown; mS/Bar & orch)
11.6	4. "Pilgers Morgenlied—An Lila": "Morgennebel, Lila" (c1897, Goethe; Bar/B & orch)
11.7	"2 grössere Gesänge" (c1899; A/B & orch): 1. "Notturno": "Hoch hing der Mond" (Dehmel) Op.44
11.8	2. "Nächtlicher Gang": "Die Fahnen flattern im Mitternachtssturm" (Rückert)
11.9	"2 Gesänge" (B & orch): 1. "Das Thal": "Wie willst du dich mir offenbaren" (c1902, Uhland) Op.51
11.10	2. "Der Einsame": "Wo ich bin, mich rings umdunkelt" (c1906, Heine; also see pf vers)
11.11	"3 Hymnen" (c1921, Hölderlin): 1. "Hymne an die Liebe": "Froh der süssen Augenweide" Op.71
11.12	2. "Rückkehr in die Heimat": "Ihr linden Lüfte"
11.13	3. "Liebe": "Wenn ihr Freunde vergesst"
11.14	*"Walzerlied": "Was fiel dem lieben Herrgott ein" (c1921, for Niederberger's operetta, sketch) AV258*

11.15	"Vier letzte Lieder" (4 Last Songs) (c1948): 1. "Frühling": "In dämmrigen Grüften träumte ich lang" (Hesse) AV150
11.16	2. "September": "Der Garten trauert, kühl sinkt in die Blumen der Regen" (Hesse)
11.17	3. "Beim Schlafengehen": "Nun der Tag mich müd' gemacht" (Hesse)
11.18	4. "Im Abendrot": "Wir sind durch Not und Freude gegangen Hand in Hand" (Eichendorff)
11.19	*"Nacht" (c1948, Hesse; S & orch, project)* *AV303*

12. SONGS (w/ pf)

12.1	"Weihnachtslied": "Schlaf wohl, du Himmelsknabe du" (c1870, Schubart) AV2
12.2	"Einkehr": "Bei einem Wirte wundermild" (c1871, Uhland) AV3
12.3	"Winterreise": "Bei diesem kalten Wehen" (c1871, Uhland) AV4
12.4	"Waldkonzert": "Herr Frühling gibt jetzt ein Konzert" (c?1871, Vogel) AV5
12.5	"Der böhmische Musikant": "Es kommt aus fernem Böhmerland" (c?1871, Pletzsch) AV7
12.6	"Herz, mein Herz": "Herz, mein Herz, sei nicht beklommen" (c?1871, Geibel) AV8
12.7	*"Gute Nacht": "Schon fängt es an zu dämmern" (c1871, Geibel, inc sketches)* *AV193*
12.8	*"Des Alpenhirten Abschied": "Ihr Matten lebt wohl!" (c?1872, Schiller, lost)* *AV151*
12.9	"Der müde Wanderer": "Schon sank die Sonne nieder" (c?1873, Fallersleben) AV13
12.10	"Husarenlied": "Husaren müssen reiten" (c1876, Fallersleben) AV14
12.11	"Der Fischer": "Das Wasser rauscht', das Wasser schwoll" (c1877, Goethe) (also see Schubert Op.5/3, D225) AV33
12.12	"Die Drossel": "Ich will ja nicht in Garten geh'n" (c1877, Uhland) AV34
12.13	"Lass ruhn die Toten": "Es steht ein altes Gemäuer" (c1877, Chamisso) AV35
12.14	"Lust und Qual": "Knabe sass ich Fischerknabe" (c1877, Goethe) AV36
12.15	"Spielmann und Zither": "Der Spielmann sass am Felsen" (c1878, Körner) AV40
12.16	"Wiegenlied": "Die Ähren nur noch nicken" (c1878, Fallersleben) AV41
12.17	"Abend- und Morgenrot": "Die Mücke sitzt am Fenster" (c?1878, Fallersleben) AV42
12.18	"Im Walde": "Im Walde im hellen Sonnenschein" (c1878, Geibel) AV43
12.19	"Nebel": "Du trüber Nebel hüllst mir das Tal" (c1878, Lenau) AV47
12.20	"Soldatenlied": "Die Trommeln und Pfeifen, die schallen in's Haus" (c1878, Fallersleben) AV48
12.21	"Das Röslein": "Ein Röslein zog ich mir im Garten" (c1878, Fallersleben) AV49
12.22	*"Für Musik": "Nun die Schatten dunkeln" (c1879, Geibel, lost)* *AV158*
12.23	"3 Lieder" (c1879, Geibel): 1. "Waldesgesang": "Die Liebe sass als Nachtigall" AV55
12.24	*2. "O schneller mein Ross" (lost)* *AV159*
12.25	*3. "Die Lilien glühn in Düften" (lost)* *AV160*
12.26	*"Das rote Laub": "Es rauscht das Laub zu meinen Füssen" (c1879, Geibel, lost)* *AV161*
12.27	*"Frühlingsanfang": "Die Sonne hebt an vom Wolkenzelt" (c1879, Geibel, lost)* *AV162*
12.28	*"Die drei Lieder": "In hoher Hall' sass König Sifrid" (c1879, Uhland, lost)* *AV164*
12.29	"In Vaters Garten heimlich steht ein Blümlein" (c1879, Heine) *AV165*
12.30	*"Der Morgen": "Der ernste Strahl vom Osten her" (c1880, Sallet, lost)* AV66
12.31	"Die erwachte Rose": "Die Knospe träumte von Sonnenschein" (c1880, Sallet) *AV166*
12.32	*"Immer leiser wird mein Schlummer" (c1880, Lingg, lost)* AV72
12.33	"Begegnung": "Die Treppe hinunter gesprungen" (c1880, Gruppe) *AV167*
12.34	*"Mutter, o sing mich zur Ruh" (c1880, Hemans, lost)* AV73
12.35	"John Anderson": "John Anderson, mein Lieb" (c1880, Burns transl Freiligrath) (also see Schumann Op.67/5, Shostakovich's 2. of: 8 British and American Folksongs arr1943 & Weber J301) AV73
12.36	*"Geheiligte Stätte": "Wo zwei sich küssten zum erstenmal" (c1881, Fischer, lost)* *AV170*
12.37	*"Waldesgesang": "Im Waldesweben ist es Ruh' " (c1882, Stieler, lost)* *AV172*
12.38	*"Ballade": "Jung Friedel wallte am Rheinesstrand" (c1882, Becker, lost)* *AV173*
12.39	"Rote Rosen": "Weisst Du die Rose, die Du mir gegeben?" (c1883, Stieler) AV76
12.40	*"Mein Geist ist trüb (c1884, from Byron's Hebräische Melodien, transl Böttger, lost)* *AV175*
12.41	*"Der Dorn ist Zeichen der Verneinung" (c1884, from Bodenstedt's Mirza Schaffy, lost)* *AV176*
12.42	*"Rosenzeichen" (c1885, lost)*
12.43	"8 Lieder aus 'Letzte Blätter' " (c1885, Gilm): 1. "Zueignung": "Ja, du weisst es, teur Seele" (orchd1940) Op.10
12.44	2. "Nichts": "Nennen soll ich, sagt ihr"
12.45	3. "Die Nacht": "Aus dem Walde tritt die Nacht"
12.46	4. "Die Georgine": "Warum so spät erst, Georgine?"
12.47	5. "Geduld": "Geduld, sagst du"
12.48	6. "Die Verschwiegenen": "Ich habe wohl, es sei hier laut"
12.49	7. "Die Zeitlose": "Auf frischgemähten Weideplatz"
12.50	8. "Allerseelen": "Stell' auf den Tisch die duftenden Reseden" AV84a
12.51	"Wer hat's getan?": "Es steht mein Lied in Nacht und Frost" (c1885, Gilm) Op.15
12.52	"5 Lieder" (c1884–6): 1. "Madrigal": "In's Joch beug' ich den Nacken" (Michelangelo) Op.15
12.53	2. "Winternacht": "Mit Regen und Sturmgebrause" (Schack)
12.54	3. "Lob des Leidens": "O schmäht des Lebens Leiden nicht!" (Schack)
12.55	4. "Aus den Liedern der Trauer": "Dem Herzen ähnlich" (Schack)
12.56	5. "Heimkehr": "Leiser schwanken die Äste" (Schack)
12.57	"6 Lieder" (c1885–7, Schack): 1. "Seitdem dein Aug' in meines schaute" Op.17
12.58	2. "Ständchen": "Mach' auf, mach' auf, doch leise, mein Kind"
12.59	3. "Das Geheimnis": "Du fragst mich, Mädchen"
12.60	4. "Aus den Liedern der Trauer": "Von dunklem Schleier umsponnen"
12.61	5. "Nur Muth!": "Lass' das Zagen"
12.62	6. "Barkarole": "Um der fallenden Ruder Spitzen"

12.63	"6 Lieder aus Lotosblättern" (c1887, Schack): 1. "Wozu noch, Mädchen, soll es frommen" Op.19
12.64	2. "Breit' über mein Haupt dein schwarzes Haar"
12.65	3. "Schön sind, doch kalt die Himmelssterne"
12.66	4. "Wie sollten wir geheim sie halten"
12.67	5. "Hoffen und wieder verzagen"
12.68	6. "Mein Herz ist stumm, mein Herz ist kalt"
12.69	"Schlichte Weisen" (c1889, Dahn): 1. "All' mein Gedanken, mein Herz und mein Sinn" Op.21
12.70	2. "Du meines Herzens Krönelein"
12.71	3. "Ach Lieb, ich muss nun scheiden!"
12.72	4. "Ach, weh mir unglückhaftem Mann"
12.73	5. "Die Frauen sind oft fromm und still"
12.74	"Mädchenblumen" (Dahn): 1. "Kornblumen": "Kornblumen nenn' ich die Gestalten" (c1888) Op.22
12.75	2. "Mohnblumen": "Mohnblumen sind die runden" (c1888)
12.76	3. "Epheu": "Aber Epheu nenn' ich jene Mädchen" (c1886–8)
12.77	4. "Wasserrose": "Kennst du die Blume, die Märchenhafte" (c1886–8)
12.78	"2 Lieder" (c1891–3, Lenau): 1. "Frühlingsgedränge": "Frühlingskinder im bunten Gedränge" Op.26
12.79	2. "O wärst du mein": "O wärst du mein, es wär ein schönres Leben"
12.80	"4 Lieder" (c1894): 1. "Ruhe, meine Seele": "Nicht ein Lüftchen regt sich leise" (Henckell; orchd1948) Op.27
12.81	2. "Cäcilie": "Wenn du es wüsstest" (Hart; orchd1897)
12.82	3. "Heimliche Aufforderung": "Auf, hebe die funkelnde Schale empor zum Mund" (Mackay)
12.83	4. "Morgen": "Und morgen wird die Sonne wieder scheinen" (Mackay; orchd1897)
12.84	"3 Lieder" (c1895, Bierbaum): 1. "Traum durch die Dämmerung": "Weite Wiesen im Dämmergrau" .. Op.29
12.85	2. "Schlagende Herzen": "Über Wiesen und Felder ein Knabe ging"
12.86	3. "Nachtgang": "Wir gingen durch die dunkle (stille), milde Nacht"
12.87	"4 Lieder": 1. "Blauer Sommer": "Ein blauer Sommer glanz- und glutenschwer" (c1896, Busse) Op.31
12.88	2. "Wenn ...": "Und wärst du mein Weib" (c1895, Busse)
12.89	3. "Weisser Jasmin": "Bleiche Blüte, Blüte der Liebe" (c1895, Busse)
12.90	4. "Stiller Gang": "Der Abend graut, Herbstfeuer brennen" (c1895, Dehmel; w/ va ad lib)
12.91	"5 Lieder" (c1896): 1. "Ich trage meine Minne" (Henckell) Op.32
12.92	2. "Sehnsucht": "Ich ging den Weg entlang, der einsam lag" (Liliencron)
12.93	3. "Liebeshymnus": "Heil jenem Tag" (Henckell; orchd1897)
12.94	4. "O süsser Mai": "O süsser Mai, o habe du Erbarmen" (Henckell)
12.95	5. "Himmelsboten zu Liebchens Himmelbett": "Der Mondschein" (from Des Knaben Wunderhorn)
12.96	"Wir beide wollen springen": "Es ging ein Wind durchs weite Land" (c1896, Bierbaum) AV90
12.97	*"Vorüber ist der Graus der Nacht" (c ?1896, sketches)* *AV221a*
12.98	"4 Lieder": 1. "Das Rosenband": "Im Frühlingsschatten fand ich sie" (c1897, Klopstock; orchd1897) (also see Schubert D280) Op.36
12.99	2. "Für fünfzehn Pfennige": "Das Mägdlein will ein' Freier hab'n" (c1897, from Des Knaben Wunderhorn)
12.100	3. "Hat gesagt—bleibt' nicht dabei": "Mein Vater hat gesagt" (c1898, from Des Knaben Wunderhorn)
12.101	4. "Anbetung": "Die Liebste steht mir vor den Gedanken" (c1898, Rückert)
12.102	"6 Lieder": 1. "Glückes genug": "Wenn sanft du mir im Arme schliefst" (c1898, Liliencron) Op.37
12.103	2. "Ich liebe dich": "Vier adlige Rosse voran unserm Wagen" (c1898, Liliencron; orchd1943)
12.104	3. "Meinem Kinde": "Du schläfst und sachte neig' ich mich" (c1897, Falke; orchd1897)
12.105	4. "Mein Auge": "Du bist mein Auge!" (c1898, Dehmel; orchd1933)
12.106	5. "Herr Lenz": "Herr Lenz springt heute durch die Stadt" (c1896, Bodman)
12.107	6. "Hochzeitlich Lied": "Lass Akaziendüfte schaukeln" (c1898, Lindner)
12.108	"5 Lieder" (c1898): 1. "Leises Lied": "In einem stillen Garten" (Dehmel) Op.39
12.109	2. "Jung Hexenlied": "Als nachts ich überm Gebirge ritt" (Bierbaum)
12.110	3. "Der Arbeitsmann": "Wir haben ein Bett, wir haben ein Kind" (Dehmel; orchd1918)
12.111	4. "Befreit": "Du wirst nicht weinen" (Dehmel; orchd1933)
12.112	5. "Lied an meinen Sohn": "Der Sturm behorcht mein Vaterhaus" (Dehmel)
12.113	"5 Lieder" (c1899): 1. "Wiegenlied": "Träume, träume, du mein süsses Leben" (Dehmel; orchd ?1900) Op.41
12.114	2. "In der Campagna": "Ich grüsse die Sonne" (Mackay)
12.115	3. "Am Ufer": "Die Welt verstummt" (Dehmel)
12.116	4. "Bruder Liederlich": "Die Feder am Sturmhut in Spiel und Gefahren" (Liliencron)
12.117	5. "Leise Lieder": "Leise Lieder sing ich dir bei Nacht" (Morgenstern)
12.118	"3 Lieder" (c1899, Uhland): 1. "An Sie": "Zeit, Verkündigerin der besten Freuden" (Klopstock) Op.43
12.119	2. "Muttertändelei": "Seht mir doch mein schönes Kind" (Bürger; orchd1900)
12.120	3. "Die Ulme zu Hirsau": "Zu Hirsau in den Trümmern" (Uhland)
12.121	"Weihnachtsgefühl": "Naht die jubelvolle Zeit" (c1899, Greif; Bar & pf) AV94
12.122	"5 Lieder" (Rückert): 1. "Ein Obdach gegen Sturm und Regen" (c1900) Op.46
12.123	2. "Gestern war ich Atlas" (c1899)
12.124	3. "Die sieben Siegel": "Weil ich dich nicht legen kann" (c1899)
12.125	4. "Morgenrot": "Dort, wo der Morgenstern hergeht" (c1900)
12.126	5. "Ich sehe wie in einem Spiegel" (c1900)
12.127	"5 Lieder" (c1900, Uhland): 1. "Auf ein Kind": "Aus der Bedrängnis" Op.47
12.128	2. "Des Dichters Abendgang": "Ergehst du doch im Abendlicht" (orchd1918)
12.129	3. "Rückleben": "An ihrem Grabe kniet' ich festgebunden"
12.130	4. "Einkehr": "Bei einem Wirte wundermild"
12.131	5. "Von den sieben Zechbrüdern": "Ich kenne sieben lust'ge Brüder"

12.132	"5 Lieder" (c1900): 1. "Freundliche Vision": "Nicht im Schlafe hab' ich das geträumt" (Bierbaum; orchd1918) Op.48
12.133	2. "Ich schwebe": "Ich schwebe wie auf Engelsschwingen" (Henckell)
12.134	3. "Kling!": "Kling!... Meine Seele gibt reinen Ton" (Henckell)
12.135	4. "Winterweihe": "In diesen Wintergarten" (Henckell; orchd1918) (also see Schoenberg Op.14/2)
12.136	5. "Winterliebe": "Der Sonne entgegen in Liebesgluten" (Henckell; orchd1918)
12.137	"8 Lieder": 1. "Waldseligkeit": "Der Wald beginnt zu rauchen" (c1901, Dehmel; orchd1918) Op.49
12.138	2. "In goldener Fülle": "Wir schreiten in goldener Fülle" (c1901, Remer)
12.139	3. "Wiegenliedchen": "Bienchen, Bienchen wiegt sich im Sonnenschein" (c1901, Dehmel)
12.140	4. "Das Lied des Steinklopfers": "Ich bin kein Minister" (c1901, Henckell)
12.141	5. "Sie wissen's nicht": "Es wohnt ein kleines Vögelein" (c1901, Panizza)
12.142	6. "Junggesellenschwur": "Weine, weine, weine nur nicht" (c1900, from Des Knaben Wunderhorn)
12.143	7. "Wer lieben will, muss leiden" (c1901, from Mündel's Elsässische Volkslieder)
12.144	8. "Ach, was Kummer, Qual und Schmerzen" (c1901, from Mündel's Elsässische Volkslieder)
12.145	"6 Lieder": 1. "Gefunden": "Ich ging im Walde so für mich hin" (c1903, Goethe) Op.56
12.146	2. "Blindenklage": "Wenn ich dich frage, dem das Leben blüht" (c1903–6, Henckell)
12.147	3. "Im Spätboot": "Aus der Schiffsbank mach' ich meinen Pfühl" (c1903–6, Meyer)
12.148	4. "Mit deinen blauen Augen" (c1903–6, Heine)
12.149	5. "Frühlingsfeier": "Das ist des Frühlings traurige Lust!" (c1903–6, Heine; orchd1933)
12.150	6. "Die heil'gen drei Kön'ge aus Morgenland" (c1903–6, Heine; orchd1906)
12.151	"Der Graf von Rom" (c1906, w/ out text; 2 vers) AV102
12.152	*"Herbstabend" (c before 1910, sketch; compl Henrici)* *AV244*
12.153	"Krämerspiegel" (c1918, from Kerr's Die Händler und die Kunst): 1. "Es war einmal ein Bock" Op.66
12.154	2. "Einst kam der Bock als Bote"
12.155	3. "Es liebte einst ein Hase die salbungsvolle"
12.156	4. "Drei Masken sah ich am Himmel stehn"
12.157	5. "Hast du ein Tongedicht vollbracht"
12.158	6. "O lieber Künstler sei ermahnt"
12.159	7. "Unser Feind ist, grosser Gott"
12.160	8. "Von Händlern wird die Kunst bedroht"
12.161	9. "Es war mal eine Wanze"
12.162	10. "Die Künstler sind die Schöpfer"
12.163	11. "Die Händler und die Macher"
12.164	12. "O Schöpferschwarm, o Händlerkreis"
12.165	"6 Lieder" (c1918, from Shakespeare's Hamlet) (also see Brahms WoO posth 22, Castelnuovo-Tedesco Op.24/VII/1–2, Elgar Op.21/1 & Shostakovich Op.127/1), I. "Lieder der Ophelia": 1. "Wie erkenn ich mein Treulieb" Op.67
12.166	2. "Guten Morgen, 's ist Sankt Valentinstag"
12.167	3. "Sie trugen ihn auf der Bahre bloss"
12.168	II. "Aus den Büchern des Unmuts des Rendsch Nameh" (Goethe): 4. "Wer wird von der Welt"
12.169	5. "Hab ich euch denn je geraten"
12.170	6. "Wanderers Gemütsruhe": "Übers Niederträchtige niemand sich beklage"
12.171	"6 Lieder" (c1918, Brentano): 1. "An die Nacht": "Heilige Nacht!" (orchd1940) Op.68
12.172	2. "Ich wollt ein Sträusslein binden" (orchd1940)
12.173	3. "Säusle, liebe Myrthe!" (orchd1940)
12.174	4. "Als mir dein Lied erklang": "Dein Lied erklang! Ich habe" (orchd1940)
12.175	5. "Amor": "An dem Feuer sass das Kind Amor" (orchd1940)
12.176	6. "Lied der Frauen": "Wenn es stürmt auf den Wogen" (orchd1933)
12.177	"5 kleine Lieder" (c1918): 1. "Der Stern": "Ich sehe ihn wieder den lieblichen Stern" (Arnim) Op.69
12.178	2. "Der Pokal": "Freunde, weihet den Pokal" (Arnim)
12.179	3. "Einerlei": "Ihr Mund ist stets derselbe" (Arnim)
12.180	4. "Waldesfahrt": "Mein Wagen rollet langsam" (Heine) (also see Schumann Op.142/4)
12.181	5. "Schlechtes Wetter": "Das ist ein schlechtes Wetter" (Heine)
12.182	"Sinnspruch": "Alle Menschen gross und klein" (c1919, from Goethe's West-östlicher Divan) AV105
12.183	"Erschaffen und Beleben": "Hans Adam war ein Erdenkloss" (c1922, from Goethe's West-östlicher Divan) (also see Wolf's 33. of: Goethe Lieder) .... (Op.87/2), AV106
12.184	"Durch allen Schall und Klang" (c1925, from Goethe's West-östlicher Divan) AV111
12.185	"Gesänge des Orients" (c1928, transl Bethge): 1. "Ihre Augen": "Deine gewölbten Brauen" (Hafiz) ... Op.77
12.186	2. "Schwung": "Gebt mir meinen Becher!" (Hafiz)
12.187	3. "Liebesgeschenke": "Ich pflückte eine kleine Pfirsichblüte" (from Die chinesische Flöte)
12.188	4. "Die Allmächtige": "Die höchste Macht der Erde" (Hafiz)
12.189	5. "Huldigung": "Die Perlen meiner Seele" (Hafiz)
12.190	"Und dann nicht mehr": "Ich sah sie nur ein einzig mal" (c1929, Rückert; B & pf) .... (Op.87/3), AV114
12.191	"Vom künftigen Alter": "Der Frost hat mir bereifet" (c1929, Rückert; B & pf) .... (Op.87/1), AV115
12.192	"Spruch": "Wie etwas sei leicht" (c1930, from Goethe's West-östlicher Divan) AV116
12.193	*"Lieder" (c1931, Wildgans, project)* *AV266*
12.194	"Das Bächlein": "Du Bächlein silberhell und klar" (c1933, ?Goethe; orchd1935) .... (Op.88/1), AV118
12.195	"Im Sonnenschein": "Noch eine Stunde lasst mich hier verweilen" (c1935, Rückert) .... (Op.87/4), AV121
12.196	"Zugemessne Rhythmen reizen freilich" (c1935, from Goethe's West-östlicher Divan) AV122
12.197	"Sankt Michael": "Ein Mahl für uns und ein Licht für dich" (c1942, Weinheber) .... (Op.88/3), AV129
12.198	"Blick vom oberen Belvedere": "Fülle du! Gezier und schöner" (c1942, Weinheber) .... (Op.88/2), AV130
12.199	"Xenion": "Nichts vom Vergänglichen wie's auch geschah!" (c1942, Goethe) AV131
12.200	*"Malven": "Aus Rosen, Phlox (und) Zin(n)ienflor" (c1948, Knobel, frag)* *AV304*

13. MISC WORKS

13.1 *"Vorstudien zu Harmonielehre und Kontrapunkt" (c1873–6, sketches)* *AV196*
13.2 "Kontrapunktische Studien I. Imitatorische Übungen und Kanons" (c1877–8) AV39
13.3 "Kontrapunktische Studien II. 9 Fugen" (c1878–9) AV54
13.4 "Kontrapunktische Studien III. 3 Fugen" (c1879–80) AV65

14. ARRANGEMENTS OF WORKS OF OTHERS

14.1 Lachner: Nonet in F major (arr1881; pf duet) AV183
14.2 Ritter: Overture to: Der faule Hans (arr1885; pf) AV184a
14.3 Raff: "2 Marches," for: Bernhard von Weimar (arr1885; pf duet): No.1 "Allegro vivace &
   energetico. Trio" AV184
14.4 No.2 "Andante maestoso. Trio"
14.5 Wagner: "Recit of Ada," from opera: Die Feen, WWV32 (add to Act II 1888) AV185
14.6 Gluck: "Iphigenie auf Tauris" (rewritten for the German stage 1889–1890, perf1900) AV186
14.7 Schubert: "Ganymed": "Wie im Morgenglanze," song, Op.19/3, D544 (orchd1897) AV187
14.8 Ritter: "Nun hält Frau Minne Liebeswacht," Op.4/8, from: Liebesnächte (orchd1898) AV188
14.9 Beethoven: 2 Songs (orchd1898): 1. "Zärtliche Liebe": "Ich liebe dich" (Herrosee), WoO123........... AV189
14.10 2. "Wonne der Wehmut": "Trocknet nicht, Tränen der ewigen Liebe" (Goethe), WoO83/1
14.11 Wagner: "Rienzi," opera, WWV49 (orch changes to Introduction, Tercett of Act I & Finale of Act II) ....
14.12 Berlioz: "Instrumentationslehre," Vol.I & II (compl & r1903–4) ....
14.13 Strauss, Franz: "Posthumous Works for Horn" (ed1909–13, collab Rüdel) AV316–7
14.14 Boieldieu: "Princess's aria": "Welche Lust gewährt das Reisen," in: Johann von Paris (reworked 1922) ......
14.15 Beethoven: "Die Ruinen von Athen," incid music, Op.113 (arr1924, text r by Hofmannsthal): AV190
   . "Ouvertüre zu 'Die Geschöpfe des Prometheus' "
   1. "Chor hinter der Szene"
   2. "Duett: Die Grössere—Der Alte"
   3. "Marcia alla turca"
   4. "Duett: Die Grössere—Der Alte"
   5. "Chor der Derwische"
   6. "Melodram: Der Fremde" (c by Strauss)
   7. "Arie: Der Fremde"
   8.–15. "Ballet aus 'Die Geschöpfe des Prometheus"
   16. "Marsch und Chor"
14.16 Mozart: "Idomeneo," 3 act opera, K366 (arr1930, text r by Wallerstein) AV117, AV191
14.17 Schubert: "Walzer," in G-flat major, "Kupelwieser-Walzer," Anh.I/14 (arr1943; pf) AV192

*   *   *   *   *

AV = E. H. Mueller von Asov: "Richard Strauss. Thematisches Verzeichnis." Band I–III. Wien, 1959–74.

1. STAGE WORKS

Operas:

1.1	"Le rossignol" (The Nightingale), 3 act fairy tale (c1908 & 1914, Stravinsky & Mitusov after Andersen) ....
1.2	"Mavra," 1 act buffa (c1921–2, Kochno after Pushkin's tale: The Little House in Kolomna) ....
1.3	"Oedipus rex," 2 act opera-oratorio (c1926–7, r1948, Cocteau after Sophocles, Latin text Daniélou) ....
1.4	"Perséphone," 3 scene melodrama (c1933–4, r1949, Gide): ....

        1. "The Abduction of Persephone"
        2. "Persephone in the Underworld"
        3. "The Rebirth of Persephone"

1.5	"The Rake's Progress," 3 acts (c1948–51, Auden & Kallman after Hogarth) ....

Ballets:

1.6	"L'oiseau de feu" (The Firebird), 2 scene fairy story ballet (c1909–10, Fokin) ....
1.7	"Petrushka," burlesque scenes in 4 tableaux (c1910–1, r1946, Benois) ....
1.8	"Le sacre du printemps" (The Rite of Spring: pictures from pagan Russia) (c1911–3, r1947, Roerich) ....
1.9	"Renard" (Reynard the Fox), burlesque in song & dance (c1915–6, after trad Russian)
1.10	"The Song of the Nightingale" (c1917, based on sym poem: The Song of the Nightingale; also see opera)
1.11	"L'histoire du soldat" (The Soldier's Tale), 2 parts (to be read, played & danced) (c1918, Ramuz) ....
1.12	"Pulcinella," 1 scene (c1919–20, after music of Pergolesi & others, perf1920 w/ sets by Picasso) ....
1.13	"Les noces" (The Wedding), 4 Russian scenes (c1914–7, r1923, after trad Russian) ....
1.14	"Apollon musagète," 2 scenes (c1927–8; strings; r1947 as: Apollo) ....
1.15	"Le baiser de la fée" (The Fairy's Kiss), 4 scenes (c1928, r1950 after Andersen, music after Tchaikovsky).
1.16	"Jeu de cartes" (A Card Game), ballet 'in three deals' (c1936, Stravinsky, Melaïeff) ....
1.17	"Circus Polka" (for the elephant ballet in circus) (c1942, unpubd; arr Reksin for band) ....
1.18	"Ballet Scenes" (c1944, for Rose's revue: The Seven Lively Arts): ....

        1. "Introduction" (Andante)
        2. "Danses" (Moderato)
        3. "Variations" (Con moto)
        4. "Pantomime" (Lento)
        5. "Pas de deux" (Adagio)
        6. "Pantomime" (Agitato ma tempo giusto)
        7. "Variation" (Risoluto)
        8. "Variation" (Andantino)
        9. "Danses" (Con moto)
       10. "Apothèse" (Poco meno mosso)

1.19	"Orpheus," 3 scenes (c1947) ....
1.20	"Agon," ballet for 12 dancers (organized according to the numerical basis of 12-tone method) (c1953–4) ...
1.21	"The Flood" (Noah and the Ark), musical play (for TV performance) (c1961–2, Craft after medieval York & Chester mystery plays) ....

1a. SELECTIONS FROM STAGE WORKS

1a.2	"Mavra," opera: ....

        1. "Overture"
        2. "Parasha's song"
        3. "Hussar's gypsy song"
        4. "Dialogue"
        5. "The mother's song"
        6. "Dialogue"
        7. "Duet"
        8. "Dialogue"
        9. "Quartet"
      10. "Dialogue"
      11. "Duet"
      12. "Dialogue"
      13. "Mavra's song"
      14. "Coda"

1a.6	"The Firebird," ballet (Nos. of sections in The Gramophone): ....

        excerpts: 1. "Introduction"
      I: 2. "Kaschchei's Enchanted Garden"
        3. "Appearance of the Firebird pursued by Ivan Tsarevich"
        4. "Dance of the Firebird"
        5. "Ivan Tsarevich captures the Firebird"
        6. "Supplication of the Firebird"
        7. "Appearance of 13 Enchanted Princesses"
        8. "The Princesses' Game with the Golden Apples" (Scherzo)
        9. "Sudden Appearance of the Ivan Tsarevich"
      10. "The Princesses' Khorovod" (Round Dance)
      11. "Daybreak" (Ivan Tsarevich enters Kashchei's Palace)
      12a. "Magic Carillon"

12b. "Appearance of Kashchei's Guardian Monsters"
12c. "Capture of Ivan Tsarevich"
13a. "Arrival of Kashchei the Immortal"
13b. "His Dialogue with Ivan Tsarevich"
13c. "The Intercession of the Princesses"
14. "Appearance of the Firebird"
15. "Dance of Kashchei's Retinue under the Firebird's Spell"
16. "Infernal Dance of all Kashchei's Subjects"
17. "Lullaby" (The Firebird)
18a. "Kashchei awakens"
18b. "Death of Kashchei"
II: 19a. "Disappearance of the Palace and Dissolution of Kashchei's Enchantments"
19b. "Animation of the Petrified Warriors"
19c. "General Thanksgiving"

1a.7   "Petrushka," ballet (Nos. of sections in The Gramophone): ....
I: 1a. "The Shrove-tide Fair"
        1b. "The Crowds"
        1c. "The Charlatan's Booth"
        1d. "Russian Dance"
II: 2. "Petrushka's Room"
III: 3a. "The Moor's Room"
        3b. "Dance of the Ballerina"
        3c. "Waltz" (Ballerina and Moor)
IV: 4a. "The Shrove-tide Fair" (near evening)
        4b. "Dance of the Wet-Nurses"
        4c. "Dance of the Peasant and the Bear"
        4d. "Dance of the Gypsy Girls"
        4e. "Dance of the Coachmen and Grooms"
        4f. "The Masqueraders"
        4g. "Conclusion" (Petrushka's Death)

1a.8   "The Rite of Spring," ballet (Nos. of sections in The Gramophone): ....
        I. "Adoration of the Earth": 1a. "Introduction"
        1b. "The Augurs of Spring"
        1c. "Ritual Abduction"
        1c. "Spring Round Dances"
        1e. "Games of the Rival Tribes"
        1f. "Procession of the Wise Elder"
        1g. "Adoration of the Earth"
        1h. "Dance of the Earth"
        II. "The Sacrifice": 2a. "Introduction"
        2b. "Mystic Circles of the Young Girls"
        2c. "Glorification of the Chosen Victim"
        2d. "Evocation of the Ancestors"
        2e. "Ritual of the Ancestors"
        2f. "Sacrificial Dance"

1a.11   "The Soldier's Tale," ballet (Nos. of sections in The Gramophone): ....
        1. "The soldier's march"
        2. "Airs by a stream"
        3. "Pastorale"
        4. "Royal march"
        5. "The little concert"
        6. "Three dances": a. "Tango"
           b. "Waltz"
           c. "Ragtime"
        7. "The devil's dance"
        8. "The little chorale"
        9. "The devil's song"
        10. "The great chorale"
        11. "The devil's triumphant march"

1a.13   "The Wedding," ballet (Nos. of sections in The Gramophone): ....
I: 1. "At the Bride's House" (The Tresses)
        2. "At the Bridegroom's House"
        3. "The Bride's Departure"
II: 4. "The Wedding Scene" (The Red Table)

2. SYMPHONIES

2.1   Symphony No.1 in E-flat major (c1905–7, r1913) Op.1
2.2   Symphony in C major (c1939–40) ....
2.3   "Symphony in Three Movements" (c1942–5) ....

3. OTHER ORCHESTRAL WORKS

3.67   "Ode," elegiac chant in 3 parts (c1943, to the memory of Natalia Kussevitsky): ....
        1. "Eulogy"
        2. "Eclogue"
        3. "Epitaph"
3.68   "Scherzo à la russe" (c1944; jazz band, unpubd; orch vers 1943–4) ....
3.69   "Firebird" Ballet Suite No.3 (c1945, reduced orch, from ballet): No.1 "Introduction" ....
3.70   No.2 "Prelude and Dance of the Firebird"
3.71   No.3 "Variations" (Firebird)
3.72   No.4 "Pantomime I"
3.73   No.5 "Pas de deux"
3.74   No.6 "Pantomime II"
3.75   No.7 "Scherzo: Dance of the princesses"
3.76   No.8 "Pantomime III"
3.77   No.9 "Rondo"
3.78   No.10 "Infernal dance"
3.79   No.11 "Lullaby"
3.80   No.12 "Final hymn"
3.81   "Basler Concerto," in D major (c1946; strings, for 20th anniv of Basler Kammerorchester) ....
3.82   "Concertino" (c1952; 12 insts, arr of: Concertino for str qt) ....
3.83   "Tango" (c1953; 19 insts, arr of pf work) ....
3.84   "Greetings Prelude" (c1955, after Summy: Happy Birthday to You) ....
3.85   "8 Instrumental Miniatures" (c1962; 15 insts, arr of: The Five Fingers for pf): No.1 "Andantino" ....
3.86   No.2 "Vivace"
3.87   No.3 "Lento"
3.88   No.4 "Allegretto"
3.89   No.5 "Moderato"
3.90   No.6 "Tempo di marcia"
3.91   No.7 "Larghetto"
3.92   No.8 "Tempo di tango"
3.93   "Variations, Aldous Huxley In Memoriam" (c1963–4) ....
3.94   "Canon on Russian popular tune" (c1965, from Finale of ballet: The Firebird) ....

4. CONCERTOS, SOLO INSTR & ORCH

Pf & orch:

4.1   Piano Concerto (c1923–4, r1950; pf, winds, timp & d basses) ....
4.2   "Capriccio" (c1928–9, r1949) ....
4.3   "Movements" (c1958–9) ....

Vn & orch:

4.4   Violin Concerto in D major (c1931): ....
        1. "Toccata"
        2. "Aria I"
        3. "Aria II"
        4. "Capriccio"

Other:

4.5   "Ebony Concerto" (c1945; cl & jazz band, written for Woody Herman's Band) ....

5. STRING QUARTETS

5.1   "3 Pieces" (c1914, used in: 4 Etudes for orch) ....
5.2   "Concertino," in 1 movt (c1920) ....
5.3   "Double Canon" (Raoul Dufy in memoriam) (c1959) ....

6. OTHER CHAMBER MUSIC

7 or more insts:

6.1   "The Soldier's Tale," suite (c1918; 7 insts, from stage work; also see suite for 3 insts).....................
6.2   "Octet" (c1922–3, r1952; fl, cl, 2bn, C-tpt, A-tpt, trbn & B-minor trbn): ....
        1. "Sinfonia"
        2. "Tema con variationi"
        3. "Finale"
6.3   "Septet" (c1952–3; cl, bn, hn, pf, vn, va & vc) ....

3 insts:

6.4   "The Soldier's Tale," suite (5 sections from suite for 7 insts arr for vn, cl & pf): No.1 "The Soldier's March" .

6.5	No.2 "The Soldier's Fiddle"
6.6	No.3 "Little Concert"
6.7	No.4 "Three Dances: Tango, Waltz and Ragtime"
6.8	No.5 "The Devil's Dance"
6.9	"Epitaphium" (c1959; fl, cl & harp) ....

Vn & pf:

6.10	"Russian Dance" (c1924, from ballet: Petrushka, collab Dushkin) ....
6.11	"Suite after themes & pieces by Pergolesi" (c1925, from ballet: Pulcinella): No.1 "Introductione" ....
6.12	2. "Serenata"
6.13	3. "Tarantella"
6.14	4. "Gavotta con due variationi"
6.15	5. "Minuetto e finale"
6.16	"Firebird Transcriptions" (c1929, collab Dushkin): No.1 "Prélude et Ronde des princesses" ....
6.17	No.2 "Berceuse"
6.18	No.3 "Scherzo" (transcr1933, from: Rondo)
6.19	"Duo concertant" (c1931–2): ....
	1. "Cantilène"
	2. "Eclogue I"
	3. "Eclogue II"
	4. "Gigue"
	5. "Dithyrambe"
6.20	"Songs of the Nightingale & Chinese march" (c1932, from stage work, collab Dushkin) ....
6.21	"Divertimento" (arr1932 from ballet: The Fairy's Kiss, collab Dushkin; also see arr for orch): ....
	1. "Sinfonia"
	2. "Danses suisses"
	3. "Scherzo"
	4. "Pas de deux: Adagio, Variation, Coda"
6.22	"Pastoral" (c1933, arr of: Vocalise, collab Dushkin; arr for vn, ob, hn, cl & bn 1933) ....
6.23	"Chanson russe" (c1937, arr w/ Dushkin from No.2 of opera: Mavra; arr w/ Markevitch for vc & pf) ....
6.24	"Ballad" (arr1947 from ballet: The Fairy's Kiss, collab Gauthier) ....

Vc & pf:

6.25	"Suite italienne" (c1932, arr from ballet: Pulcinella, collab Piatigorsky): No.1 "Introduzione" ....
6.26	No.2 "Serenata"
6.27	No.3 "Aria"
6.28	No.4 "Tarantella, Minuetto e Finale"
6.29	"Suite italienne" (c1932, arr from ballet: Pulcinella, collab Dushkin): No.1 "Introduzione" ....
6.30	No.2 "Serenata"
6.31	No.3 "Tarantella"
6.32	No.4 "Gavotta con due variazioni"
6.33	No.5 "Scherzino"
6.34	No.6 "Minuetto e Finale"

Other 2 insts:

6.35	"Canons" (c1917; 2hn) ....
6.36	"Duet" (c1918; 2bn) ....
6.37	"Lullaby" (p1960; 2 recorders, arr from opera: The Rake's Progress) ....
6.38	"Fanfare for a New Theatre" (c1964; 2tpt) ....

1 instr:

6.39	"Polka" (c1915; cimbalom, arr of No.3 of: 3 Easy Pieces for pf duet) ....
6.40	"Study" (c1917; pianola; arr as No.4 of: 4 Studies for orch) ....
6.41	"3 Pieces for Clarinet Solo" (c1919; cl / A-cl)..
6.42	"Elegy" (c1944; va/vn, in memory of A. Onnou) ....

7. PIANO SONATAS

| 7.1 | Piano Sonata in F-sharp minor (c1903–4)... |
| 7.2 | Piano Sonata (c1924).. |

8. OTHER PIANO WORKS

8.1	"Tarantella" (c1898, unpubd) ....
8.2	"Scherzo" (c1902)...
8.3	"4 Studies" (c1908): No.1 "Con moto" (in C minor) Op.7
8.4	No.2 "Allegro brillante" (in D major)
8.5	No.3 "Andantino" (in E minor)
8.6	No.4 "Vivo" (in F-sharp major)

8.7	"Souvenir d'une marche boche" (c1915) ....
8.8	"Valse pour les enfants" (ca1917) ....
8.9	"Piano Rag-Music" (c1919) ....
8.10	"The Five Fingers," 8 easy pieces (c1921): No.1 "Andantino" ....
8.11	No.2 "Allegro"
8.12	No.3 "Allegretto"
8.13	No.4 "Larghetto"
8.14	No.5 "Moderato"
8.15	No.6 "Lento"
8.16	No.7 "Vivo"
8.17	No.8 "Pesante"
8.18	"3 Movements from Petrushka" (c1921): No.1 "Russian dance" ....
8.19	No.2 "In Petrushka's cell"
8.20	No.3 "The shrove-tide fair"
8.21	"Serenade," in A major (c1925): ....
	1. "Hymn"
	2. "Romance"
	3. "Rondoletto"
	4. "Final Cadence"
8.22	"Tango" (c1940) ....

Pf duet:

8.23	"The Rite of Spring" (c1913, arr from ballet) ....
8.24	"3 Easy Pieces" (c1914–5; orchd as Nos.1–3 of: Suite No.2 for small orch): No.1 "March" ....
8.25	No.2 "Waltz"
8.26	No.3 "Polka"
8.27	"5 Easy Pieces" (c1916–7; Nos.1–4 orchd as: Suite No.1 for small orch): No.1 "Andante" ....
8.28	No.2 "Española"
8.29	No.3 "Balalaika"
8.30	No.4 "Napolitana"
8.31	No.5 "Galop" (orchd1921 as No.4 of: Suite No.2 for small orch)

2 Pf:

8.32	*"Valse des fleurs" (c1914, lost)* ....
8.33	*"Petrushka—3 Movements" (transcr Babin 1924, from ballet): No.1 "Russian dance"* ....
8.34	*No.2 "Petrushka's cell"*
8.35	*No.3 "The shrove-tide fair"*
8.36	"Concerto" (c1931–5): ....
	1. "Con moto"
	2. "Nocturne"
	3. "4 Variations"
	4. "Prelude and Fugue"
8.37	"Sonata" (c1943–4): ....
	1. "Moderato"
	2. "Theme with four variations"
	3. "Allegretto"

9. CHORAL WORKS

9.1	*Cantata (c1904; ch & pf, lost)* ....
9.2	"The King of the Stars," cantata (c1911–2, Balmont transl Calvocoressi; ch & orch) ....
9.3	"Saucers" (Russian Peasant Songs) (c1914–7; fem ch, r1954; ch & 4hn): 1. "On saints' days in Chigaskh"
9.4	2. "Ovsen"
9.5	3. "The pike" (w/ 3vv)
9.6	4. "Master Portly" (w/ 1v)
9.7	"Our Father" (c1926, Slavonic text; r1949 w/ Latin text as: Pater noster) ....
9.8	"Symphony of Psalms" (c1930, r1948, from Psalm 38, 39 & 150; ch & orch) ....
9.9	"Symbol of Faith" (c1932, Slavonic text; ch; r1949 w/ Latin text as: Credo; r1964 w/ Slavonic text) ....
9.10	"Blessed Virgin" (c1934, Slavonic text; ch; r1949 w/ Latin text as: Ave Maria) ....
9.11	"Babel," for collab cantata: Genesis (c1944, p1953, Anders after Genesis; reciter, m ch & orch): ....
	"Genesis": *1. "Prelude" (c by Schoenberg)*
	2. "Creation" (c by Schilkret)
	3. "Fall of man" (c by Tansman)
	4. "Cain and Abel" (c by Milhaud)
	5. "Flood" (c by Castelnuovo-Tedesco)
	6. "Covenant" (c by Toch)
	7. "Babel" (c by Stravinsky)
9.12	"Mass" (c1944–8, Latin text; ch & 2ob, hn, 2bn, 2tpt & 3trbn) ....
9.13	"Cantata" (c1951–2, late medieval English text; S, T, fem ch, 2fl, 2ob, hn & vc) ....
9.14	"Canticum Sacrum Ad Honorem Sancti Marci Nominis," cantata (c1955, Bible; T, Bar, ch & orch): ....
	1. "Dedicato; Euntes in mundum"
	2. "Surge, aquilo"

3. "Ad Ares virtutes horationes"
4. "Brevis motus cantilenae"
5. "Illi autem profecti"

9.15 "Threni: Id Est Lamentationes Jeremiae Prophetae" (serial composition) (c1957–8; S, A, 2T, 2B, ch & orch)
9.16 "A Sermon, a Narrative & a Prayer," cantata (c1960–1, St Paul, Acts, Dekker; A, T, speaker, ch & orch) ....
9.17 "Anthem": "The dove descending breaks the air" (c1962, from Eliot's Little Gidding, part IV in The Four Quartets; ch) ....
9.18 "Introitus. T. S. Eliot in memoriam" (Requiem aeternam) (c1965; m vv & insts) ....
9.19 "Requiem Canticles" (c1965–6; A, B, ch & orch) ....

10. VOICE & ORCHESTRA

10.1 "Faun and Shepherdess," cycle (c1905–6, Pushkin; mS & orch): 1. "Shepherdess" Op.2
10.2 2. "Faun"
10.3 3. "River"
10.4 "Pribaoutki," song games (c1914, trad Russian; 1 m v, fl, ob & 7 insts): 1. "Kornillo" (Onkel Peter) ....
10.5 2. "Natashka"
10.6 3. "The colonel"
10.7 4. "The old man and the hare"
10.8 "Cat's Cradle Songs" (c1915–6, trad Russian; A & 3cl): 1. "The tom-cat" ....
10.9 2. "The tom-cat on the stove"
10.10 3. "Bye-bye"
10.11 4. "O tom-cat, tom-cat"
10.12 "Chanson de Paracha" (c1922–3; S & orch, from opera: Mavra) ....
10.13 "3 Songs from Shakespeare" (serial composition) (c1953; mS, fl, cl & va): 1. "Musick to Heare" ....
10.14 2. "Full Fathom Five" (also see Castelnuovo-Tedesco Op.24/XI/3 & Vaughan Williams' 1. of: 3 Shakespeare Songs)
10.15 3. "When Da(i)sies Pied" (also see Castelnuovo-Tedesco Op.24/VII/3)
10.16 "4 Songs" (c1953–4, Stravinsky; 1v, fl, harp & gui): 1."The Drake" (arr of 1. of: 4 Russian Songs) ....
10.17 2. "A Russian Spiritual" (arr of 4. of: 4 Russian Songs)
10.18 3. "Geese and Swans" (arr of 2. of: 3 Stories for Children)
10.19 4. "Tilimbom" (arr of 1. of: 3 Stories for Children)
10.20 "In Memoriam Dylan Thomas," canons & song (serial composition) (c1954, Dylan Thomas: Do not go gentle into that goodnight; T, str qt & 4trbn) ....
10.21 "Abraham and Isaac," sacred ballad (c1962–3, Genesis 22 in Hebrew; Bar & chamber orch) ....
10.22 "Elegy for J.F.K.": "When a man just dies" (c1964, Auden; Bar & 3cl; r1964 for mS & 3cl) ....

11. SONGS (w/ pf)

11.1 "Storm Cloud," romance (c1902, Pushkin) ....
11.2 "The Mushrooms Going to War" (c1904; B & pf) ....
11.3 "Pastoral" (c1907, wordless; S & pf; arr for: S, ob, hn, cl & bn 1923) ....
11.4 "Deux mélodies" (c1908, Gorodetsky; mS & pf): 1. "Spring" (The Cloister) Op.6
11.5 2. "A Song of the Dew" (Mystic song of the ancient Russian flagellants)
11.6 "Deux poèmes of Paul Verlaine" (c1910; Bar & pf; orchd1951): 1. "Sagesse: Un grand sommeil noir" Op.9
11.7 2. "La bonne chanson: La lune blanche"
11.8 "2 Poems of Balmont" (c1911; S/T & pf; arr w/ 2fl, 2cl, pf & str qt 1954): 1. "Blue Forget-me-not" ....
11.9 2. "The dove"
11.10 "3 Japanese Lyrics" (c1912–3, transl Brandt; S & pf/2fl, 2cl, pf & str qt): 1. "Akahito" ....
11.11 2. "Mazatsumi"
11.12 3. "Tsaraiuki"
11.13 "3 Little songs: recollections of my childhood" (ca1906, r1913; orchd1929–30): 1. "The magpie" ....
11.14 2. "The rook"
11.15 3. "Caw, caw, jackdaw!"
11.16 "3 Tales for Children" (c1915–7, trad Russian): 1. "Tilimbom" (r & orchd1923) ....
11.17 2. "Geese, swans"
11.18 3. "The bear's little song"
11.19 "Berceuse" (c1917, Stravinsky) ....
11.20 "4 Russian Songs" (c1918–9, trad Russian): 1. "The Drake" (Round) ....
11.21 2. "Counting-song"
11.22 3. "Table-mat song"
11.23 4. "Dissident song"
11.24 "Petit Ramusianum harmonique" (c1937, Stravinsky; 1v/unison ch) ....
11.25 "Petit canon pour la fête de Nadia Boulanger" (c1947, Meung; 2T) ....
11.26 "The Owl and the Pussy-cat": "The Owl and the Pussy-cat went to sea" (c1966, Lear) ....

12. REDUCTIONS (for rehearsal or amateur use)

Vocal scores:

12.1 "Faun and Shepherdess" ....
12.2 "The King of the Stars" ....
12.3 "The Nightingale" ....

13. ARRANGEMENTS OF WORKS OF OTHERS

* * * * *

1. STAGE WORKS

Operas & operettas:

1.1	"The Sapphire Necklace" (The False Heiress) (p1867, Chorley, part lost) ....
1.2	"Cox and Box, or The Long-lost Brothers," 1 act (p1866, 1867, Burnard after Morton's Box and Cox) ....
1.3	"The Contrabandista, or The Law of the Ladrones," 2 acts (p1867, Burnard; r as: The Chieftain) ....
1.4	"Thespis, or The Gods Grown Old," 2 acts (p1871, Gilbert) ....
1.5	"Trial by Jury," 1 act (p1875, Gilbert) ....
1.6	"The Zoo," 1 act (p1875, Rowe—pseud of Stevenson) ....
1.7	"The Sorcerer," 2 acts (p1877, r1884, Gilbert) ....
1.8	"HMS Pinafore, or The Lass that Loved a Sailor," 2 acts (p1878, Gilbert) ....
1.9	"The Pirates of Penzance, or The Slave of Duty," 2 acts (p1879, Gilbert) ....
1.10	"Patience, or Bunthorne's Bride," 2 acts (p1881, Gilbert) ....
1.11	"Iolanthe, or The Peer and the Peri," 2 acts (p1882, Gilbert) ....
1.12	"Princess Ida, or Castle Adamant," 3 acts (p1884, Gilbert after Tennyson's The Princess (also see works c by Britten Op.31/2, Holst Op.20a, H80, Delius RTiv/6 & Vaughan Williams' song: The splendour falls) .
1.13	"The Mikado, or The Town of Titipu," 2 acts (p1885, Gilbert) ....
1.14	"Ruddigore, or The Witch's Curse," 2 acts (p1887, Gilbert) ....
1.15	"The Yeomen of the Guard, or The Merryman and his Maid," 2 acts (p1888, Gilbert) ....
1.16	"The Gondoliers, or The King of Barataria," 2 acts (p1889, Gilbert) ....
1.17	"Ivanhoe," 3 act romantic opera (p1891, r1895, Sturgis after Scott; also Ger transl Wittmann) ....
1.18	"Haddon Hall," 2 acts (p1892, Grundy) ....
1.19	"Utopia Ltd, or The Flowers of Progress," 2 acts (p1893, Gilbert) ....
1.20	"The Chieftain," 2 acts (p1894, Burnard, r vers of: The Contrabandista) ....
1.21	"The Grand Duke, or The Statutory Duel," 2 acts (p1896, Gilbert) ....
1.22	"The Beauty Stone," 2 act musical drama (p1898, Pinero & Carr) ....
1.23	"The Rose of Persia, or The Story-teller and the Slave," 2 acts (p1899, Hood) ....
1.24	"The Emerald Isle, or The Caves of Carig-Cleena," 2 acts (p1901, Hood; compl German) ....
1.25	Add accompaniments for Handel's Jephta (p1869) ....

Ballets:

1.26	"L'île enchantée" (p1864, Desplaces) ....
1.27	"Victoria and Merrie England" (p1897, Coppi) ....
1.28	*"Pineapple Poll," ballet (p1951, compiled & arr Mackerras)* ....

Incid music:

1.29	"The Tempest" (p1861, r1862, Shakespeare) (also see semi-opera c by Purcell Z631, incid music c by Honegger H48 & Sibelius Op.10) Op.1
1.30	"The Merchant of Venice" (p1871, Shakespeare) (also see opera c by Castelnuovo-Tedesco Op.181, incid music c by Moniuszko & overture c by Castelnuovo-Tedesco Op.76) ....
1.31	"The Merry Wives of Windsor" (p1874, Shakespeare) (also see opera: Sir John in Love c by Vaughan Williams, incid music c by Khachaturian & Vaughan Williams) ....
1.32	"Henry VIII" (p1877, Shakespeare) ....
1.33	"Macbeth" (p1888, Shakespeare) (also see operas c by Bloch & Verdi, incid music c by Bacewicz, Khachaturian, Milhaud Op.175 & Spohr WoO 55) ....
1.34	"The Foresters, or Robin Hood and his Maid Marian" (p1892, Tennyson) ....
1.35	"King Arthur" (p1895, Carr) ....

1a. SELECTIONS FROM STAGE WORKS (Nos. of sections in The Gramophone)

1a.4	"Thespis, or The Gods Grown Old," comic opera: ....
	excerpts: Act II: 1. "Ballet Music": 1a. "Introduction"
	1b. "Pas de Châles"
	1c. "Valse"
	1d. "St George and the Dragon"
	2. "Galop"
1a.5	"Trial by Jury," operetta: ....
	excerpts: 1. "Hark the hour"
	2a. "Is this the Court"
	2b. "When first my old, old love I knew"
	3. "All hail, great Judge"
	4. "When I, good friends was called to the Bar"
	5. "Swear thou the Jury"
	6. "Comes the broken flower"
	7. "Oh, never since I joined the human race"
	8. "May it please you my lud"
	9. "That she is reeling"
	10. "Oh gentlemen listen"
	11. "That seems a reasonable proposition"
	12. "A nice dilemma we have here"

13. "I love him, I love him, with fervour unceasing"
14. "Oh joy unbounded"

1a.7   "The Sorcerer," operetta: ....
        excerpts: 1. "Overture"
    I: 2. "Ring forth ye bells"
          3a. "Constance, my daughter"
          3b. "When he is here"
          4a. "The air is charged"
          4b. "Time was when Love and I"
          5. "Sir Marmaduke"
          6. "With heart and voice"
          7a. "My kindly friends"
          7b. "Oh happy young heart"
          8. "My child"
          9. "With heart and with voice"
          10. "Welcome joy"
          11. "All is prepared"
          12. "Love feeds on many kinds of food"
          13. "My name is John Wellington Wells"
          14. "Sprites of earth and air ... Let us fly"
          15. "Now to the banquet ... Eat, drink and be gay"
    II: 16. " 'Tis twelve"
          17. "Dear friends, take pity"
          18. "Thou hast the power"
          19. "I rejoice that it's decided"
          20. "Alexis doubt me not"
          21. "Hate me!"
          22. "Oh, my voice is sad and low"
          23. "Oh, joyous boon!"
          24. "Prepare for sad surprises"
          25. "Or he or I must die"

1a.8   "HMS Pinafore, or The Lass that Loved a Sailor," comic operetta: ....
        excerpts: 1. "Overture"
    I: 2. "We sail the ocean blue"
          3a. "Hail, men-o'-war's men"
          3b. "I'm called little Buttercup"
          4a. "But, tell me"
          4b. "The Nightingale"
          4c. "A maiden fair to see"
          5a. "My gallant crew"
          5b. "I am the Captain of the Pinafore"
          6a. "Sir you are sad"
          6b. "Sorry her lot who loves too well"
          7. "Over the bright blue sea"
          8a. "Sir Joseph's barge is seen"
          8b. "Gaily tripping, lightly skipping"
          9. "I am the monarch of the sea"
          10. "When I was a lad I served a term"
          11. "A British tar is a soaring soul"
          12. "Refrain, audacious tar"
          13a. "Can I survive this overbearing"
          13b. "Oh joy, oh rapture unforseen"
          13c. "Let's give three cheers for a sailor's bride"
          14a. "Entr'acte"
    II: 14b. "Fair moon, to thee I sing"
          15. "Things are seldom what they seem"
          16. "The hours creep on apace"
          17. "Never mind the why and wherefore"
          18. "Kind Captain, I've important information"
          19a. "Carefully on tiptoe stealing"
          19b. "He is an Englishman"
          19c. "Did you hear him?"
          20. "Farewell my own"
          21. "A many years ago"
          22. "Oh joy, oh rapture unforseen"

1a.9   "The Pirates of Penzance, or The Slave of Duty," operetta: ....
        excerpts: 1. "Overture"
    I: 2. "Pour, o pour the pirate sherry"
          3. "When Frederic was a little lad"
          4. "Oh better far to live and die"
          5a. "O false one"
          5b. "You told me you were fair"

5c. "What shall I do"
6. "Climbing over rocky mountains"
7a. "Stop ladies pray"
7b. "Oh is there not one maiden breast?"
8. "Poor wandering one"
9. "What ought we to do?"
10. "How beautifully blue the sky"
11. "Stay, we must not lose our senses"
12a. "Hold, monsters"
12b. "Here's a first-class opportunity"
13. "I am the very model of a modern Major-General"
14. "Oh, men of dark and dismal fate"
II: 15. "Oh dry the glistening tear"
16a. "Now Frederic, let your escort"
16b. "When the foeman bares his steel"
17. "Now the Pirates' lair"
18. "When you had left our pirate fold"
19. "Away, away"
20. "All is prepared"
21a. "Stay, Frederick"
21b. "Ah, leave me not"
22a. "Now I'll be brave"
22b. "When a felon's not engaged"
23. "A rollicking band"
24. "With cat-like tread"
25a. "Hush hush not a word"
25b. "Sighing softly"
25c. "Now what is this"
25d. "We triumph now"
25e. "Poor wandering ones"

1a.10 "Patience, or Bunthorne's Bride," operetta: ....
excerpts: 1. "Overture"
I: 2. "Twenty lovesick maidens"
3a. "Still brooding on their mad infatuation"
3b. "I cannot tell what this love may be"
4a. "The Soldiers of the Queen"
4b. "If you are after a receipt"
5. "In a doleful train"
6. "When I first put this uniform on"
7a. "Am I alone and unobserved?"
7b. "If you're anxious for to shine"
8. "Long years ago, fourteen maybe"
9. "Prithee pretty maiden"
10a. "Let the merry cymbals sound"
10b. "True love must single-hearted be"
II: 11. "On such eyes as maidens cherish"
12a. "Sad is that woman's lot"
12b. "Silvered is the raven hair"
13. "Turn, oh turn in this direction"
14. "A magnet hung in a hardware shop"
15. "Love is a plaintive song"
16. "So go to him and say to him"
17. "It's clear that medieval art alone retains its zest"
18. "If Saphir I choose to marry"
19. "When I go out of door"
20. "I'm a Waterloo House young man"
21. "After much debate internal"

1a.11 "Iolanthe, or The Peer and the Peri," comic operetta: ....
excerpts: 1. "Overture"
II: 2. "Tripping hither tripping thither"
3. "Iolanthe"
4. "Good morrow, good mother"
5. "Fare thee well attractive stranger"
6a. "Good morrow, good lover"
6b. "None shall part us"
7. "Loudly let the trumpet bray" (March of the Peers)
8a. "Entrance of Lord Chancellor"
8b. "The law is the true embodiment"
9a. "My well-loved Lord and guardian"
9b. "Of all the young ladies"
10. "Nay tempt me not"
11. "Spurn not the nobly born"
12. "My Lords it may not be"

15. "The sun, whose rays are all ablaze"
16. "Brightly dawns our wedding day"
17. "Here's a how-de-do!"
18. "Miya sama, miya sama"
19. "From every kind of man"
20. "A more humane Mikado"
21. "The criminal cried"
22. "See how the Fates"
23. "The flowers that bloom in the spring"
24a. "Alone, and yet alive"
24b. "Hearts do not break!"
25. "On a tree by a river a little tom-tit" (Tit Willow)
26. "There is beauty in the bellow of the blast"
27. "For he's gone and married Yum-Yum"

1a.14   "Ruddigore, or The Witch's Curse," operetta: ....
excerpts: 1. "Overture" (Geoffrey Toye vers of 1921)
I: 2. "Fair is Rose"
       3. "Sir Rupert Murgatroyd"
       4. "If somebody there chanced to be"
       5. "I know a youth"
       6a. "From the briny sea"
       6b. "I shipped, d'ye see"
       7a. "Hornpipe"
       7b. "My boy, you may take it from me"
       8. "The battle's roar is over"
       9. "If well his suit has sped"
       10. "I sailing o'er life's ocean wide"
       11a. "Cheerily carols the lark"
       11b. "To a garden full of posies"
       12. "Welcome gentry for your entry"
       13. "O why am I moody and sad?"
       14. "You understand?"
       15a. "Hail the bride of seventeen summers"
       15b. "When the buds are blossoming"
       15c. "Hold, bride and bridegroom"
       15d. "As pure and blameless peasant"
       15e. "Within this breast"
       15f. "Farewell"
       15g. "Dance"
II: 16. "I once was as meek"
       17. "Happily coupled"
       18. "In bygone days"
       19. "Painted emblems of a race"
       20. "When the night wind howls" (The Ghosts' High-Noon)
       21. "He yields! He answers to your call!"
       22a. "Away, Remorse!"
       22b. "Ye well-to-do squires"
       23. "I once was a very abandon'd person"
       24. "My eyes are fully open"
       25. "There grew a little flower"
       26. "Oh, happy the lily"
Add item: 27. "Overture" (orig Hamilton Clarke vers of 1887)

1a.15   "The Yeomen of the Guard, or The Merryman and his Maid," operetta: ....
excerpts: 1. "Overture"
I: 2. "When maiden loves, she sits and sighs"
       3. "Tower Warders, Under orders"
       4. "When our gallant Norman foes"
       5. "Alas! I waver to and fro"
       6. "Is life a boon?"
       7. "Here's a man of jollity"
       8. "I have a song to sing, O!"
       9. "Here's a man, maiden"
       10a. "I've jibe and joke and quip and crank"
       10b. "I've wisdom from the East"
       11a. " 'Tis done! I am a bride!"
       11b. "Though tear and long-drawn sigh"
       12. "Were I thy bride"
       13a. "Oh, Sergeant Meryll, it is true"
       13b. "Dids't thou not, oh Leonard Meryll"
       13c. "To thy fraternal care"
       13d. "The prisoner comes to meet his doom"
II: 14a. "Night has spread her pall once more"
       14b. "Warders are ye?"

15. "Oh! a private buffoon"
16. "Hereupon we're both agreed"
17. "Free from his fetters grim"
18. "Strange adventure"
19. "Hark! what was that, sir?"
20. "A man who would woo a fair maid"
21. "When a wooer goes a-wooing"
22. "Rapture, rapture"
23. "Comes the pretty young bride"
Add items: 24. "When jealous torments rack my soul" (Act I)
25. "A laughing boy" (Act I)
26. "Is life a boon?" (orig vers)

1a.16   "The Gondoliers, or The King of Barataria," comic operetta: ....
excerpts: 1. "Overture"
I: 2a. "List and learn"
2b. "Good morrow, pretty maids"
2c. "For the merriest fellow"
2d. "Buon giorno, signorine"
2e. "We're called gondolieri"
2f. "And now to choose our brides"
2g. "Thank you gallant gondolieri"
3. "From the sunny Spanish shore"
4. "In enterprise of martial kind"
5. "O rapture"
6. "There was a time"
7. "I stole the prince"
8. "But, bless my heart consider my position"
9. "Try we lifelong"
10a. "Bridegroom and bride"
10b. "When a merry maiden marries"
11a. "Kind sir you cannot have the heart"
11b. "Then one of us"
II: 12. "Of hapiness the very pith"
13. "Rising early in the morning"
14. "Take a pair of sparkling eyes"
15. "Here we are"
16a. "Dance a cachucha"
16b. "Dance"
17. "There lived a King"
18. "In a contemplative fashion"
19. "With ducal pomp"
20. "On the day"
21a. "To help unhappy commoners"
21b. "Small titles and orders"
22. "I am a courtier grave and serious"
23. "Here is a case unprecedented"
24a. "Now let the loyal lieges"
24b. "The Royal prince"
24c. "This statement we receive"
24d. "Once more gondolieri"

1a.19   "Utopia Ltd, or The Flowers of Progress," operetta: ....
excerpts: I: 1. "In lazy languor"
2a. "O make way for the Wise Men"
2b. "In every mental lore"
3. "Let all your doubts take wing"
4a. "Quaff the nectar"
4b. "A King of autocratic power"
4c. "Although of native maids the cream"
4d. "Bold faced ranger"
5. "First you're born"
6. "Subjected to your heavenly gaze"
7. "Oh maiden rich"
8. "Ah gallant soldier"
9. "It's understood I think"
10. "Oh admirable art"
11a. "Although your royal summons"
11b. "What these may be"
11c. "I'm Captain Corcoran KCB"
11d. "Some seven men form an Association"
II: 12a. "Oh, Zara"
12b. "A tenor all singers above"
13. "Words of love too lordly spoken"
14. "Society has quite forsaken"

15. "Entrance of Court"
16. "Drawing Room Music"
17a. "This ceremonial our wish displays"
17b. "Eagle high"
18. "With fury deep"
19. "If you think that when banded in unity"
20. "With wily brain"
21. "A wonderful joy"
22. "Then I may sing and play?"
23a. "Oh would some demon power"
23b. "When a maid is fifteen years"
24a. "Ah, Lady Sophy"
24b. "Oh rapture unrestrained"
24c. "Tarantella"
25. "Upon our sea-girt land"
26. "There's a little group of isles"

1a.21   "The Grand Duke, or The Statutory Duel," operetta: ....
        excerpts: 1. "Overture"
    I: 2a. "Won't it be a pretty wedding"
          2b. "Pretty Lisa, fair and tasty"
           3. "By the mystic regulation"
           4. "Were I a king in very truth"
           5. "How would I play this part"
           6. "My goodness me ... Ten minutes since, I met a chap"
           7. "About a century since"
           8. "Strange the views some people hold"
           9. "Now take a card"
          10a. "The good Grand Duke"
          10b. "A pattern to professors"
          11. "As o'er our penny roll we sing"
          12. "When you find your a broken down critter"
          13. "Come hither all you people"
    II: 14. "As before you we defile"
          15a. "Your loyalty our Ducal heartstrings touches"
          15b. "At the outset I may mention"
          16. "Yes Ludwig and his Julia are mated ... Take care of him"
          17. "Now Julia come consider it"
          18a. "Your Highness there's a party"
          18b. "With fury indescribable I burn"
          19. "Now away to the wedding we go"
          20. "So ends my dream ... Broken ev'ry promise"
          21. "If the light of love's lingering ember"
          22. "Come, bumpers"
          23. "Why, who is this approaching"
          24. "The Prince of Monte Carlo"
          25. "His Highness we know not"
          26. "We're rigged out in magnificent way"
          27. "Dance"
          28. "Take my advice"
          29a. "Away to the wedding"
          29b. "Well you're a pretty kind of fellow"
          30. "Happy couples lightly treading"

1a.26   "L'île enchantée," ballet: ....
        excerpts: 1. "Prelude"
                  2. "Dance of the Nymphs and Satyrs—pas de Châles"
                  3. "Galop"
                  4. "Storm—Entrance of the Gnomes—Entrance of Fairy Queen"
                  5. "Pas de deux"
                  6. "Mazurka—Variation"
                  7. "Scène des disparitions"
                  8. "Tempo di valse—Variations for Mlle Carmine"
                  9. "Pas de trois" (after Mlle Carmine's Variation)
                 10. "Scène de jalousie"
                 11. "Finale"

1a.28   "Pineapple Poll," ballet: ....
        excerpts: Scene 1: 1. "Opening Dance"
                  2. "Poll's Dance and Pas de deux"
                  3. "Belaye's Solo"
                  4. "Pas de trois"
                  5. "Finale"
        Scene 2: 6. "Poll's Solo"
                  7. "Jasper's Solo"

Scene 3: 8. "Balaye's Solo and Sailors' Dance"
9. "Poll's Solo"
10. "Entry of Belaye with Blanche as His Bride"
11. "Reconciliation"
12. "Grand Finale"

1a.29 "The Tempest," incid music Op.1
excerpts: 1. "Introduction"
3. "Where the bee sucks" (Ariel's Song)
4. "Act III: Prelude"
6. "Banquet Scene"
7. "Act IV: Overture"
10. "Dance of the Nymphs and Reapers"
11. "Act V: Prelude"
12c. "Epilogue"

1a.30 "The Merchant of Venice," incid music: ....
excerpts: 1. "Introduction"
2. "Barcarole" (Sérénade)
3. "Introduction and Bourée"
4. "Danse grotesque"
5. "À la valse"
6. "Melodrama"
7. "Finale"

1a.32 "Henry VIII," incid music: ....
excerpts: 1. "March"
2. "King Henry's song"
3. "Graceful Dance"
4. "Water Music"

2. SYMPHONIES

2.1 Symphony in E major, "Irish" (c1866) ....

3. OTHER ORCHESTRAL WORKS

3.1 "Timon of Athens," overture in C minor (c ?1857, after Shakespeare) (also see masque c by Purcell Z632
& incid music c by Britten) ....
3.2 *"Overture," in D minor (c1858, lost)* ....
3.3 "The Feast of Roses" (Rosenfest), overture (c1860, inspired by Moore's Lalla Rookh) ....
3.4 "Procession March" (The Royal Wedding: Grand March) (c1863; arr for pf 1863) ....
3.5 "Princess of Wales's March" (Marche danoise) (c1863; arr for pf; also for milit band 1863) ....
3.6 "Overture," in C major, "In Memoriam" (c1866) ....
3.7 "Marmion" (A Tale of Flodden Field), overture (c1867, after Scott's narrative poem) ....
3.8 "Overture di Ballo," in E major (c1870, r1889) ....
3.9 "Imperial March" (c1893; arr for pf) ....
3.10 "Victoria and Merrie England" Suite No.1 (from ballet of 1897): No.1 "March of the Druids" ....
3.11 No.2 "Mistletoe—Dance around the Oak Tree"
3.12 No.3 "May Day Festivities"

4. CELLO CONCERTOS, CELLO & ORCH

4.1 *Cello Concerto in D major (c1866, lost except for solo part, reconstr Mackie & Mackerras)* ....

5. STRING QUARTETS

5.1 *String Quartet in D minor (c1859, lost)* ....
5.2 "Romance," in G minor (c1859) ....

6. OTHER CHAMBER MUSIC

Vn & pf:

6.1 "Melody," in D major (orig: Allegro grazioso for pf, Op.2/2) ....

Vc & pf:

6.2 "An Idyll" (c1865) ....
6.3 "Duo concertante" (c1868) ....

7. PIANO SONATAS

7.1   Piano Sonata (c ?1857) ....

8. OTHER PIANO WORKS

8.1   "Scherzo" (c1857) ....
8.2   "Capriccio No.2" (c1857, unfin) ....
8.3   Cadenza for Mozart: Piano Concerto No.23 in A major, K488 (c1859, ?lost) ....
8.4   "Thoughts" (c1862): No.1 "Allegretto con grazia" (later pubd as: Reverie in A major) Op.2
8.5   No.2 "Allegro grazioso" (later pubd for vn & pf as: Melody in D major)
8.6   "Allegro risoluto," in B-flat minor (c1866; ed Parry 1976) ....
8.7   "Day Dreams" (c1867): No.1 "Andante religioso" Op.14
8.8   No.2 "Allegretto grazioso"
8.9   No.3 "Andante"
8.10   No.4 "Tempo di valse"
8.11   No.5 "Andante con molto tenerezza"
8.12   No.6 "A l'hongroise, Allegretto"
8.13   "Twilight" (c1868) Op.12

9. SERVICES & ANTHEMS

Services:

9.1   "Te Deum," in D major (p1866) ....
9.2   "Jubilate & Kyrie," in D major (p1872) ....

Anthems:

9.3   "By the Waters of Babylon" (ca1850) ....
9.4   "Sing unto the Lord" (c1855) ....
9.5   "Psalm 103" (c1856) ....
9.6   "We have heard with our ears" (c1860) ....
9.7   "O love the Lord" (c1864) ....
9.8   "O God, Thou art worthy" (c1867) ....
9.9   "O taste and see" (c1867) ....
9.10   "Rejoice in the Lord" (c1868) ....
9.11   "Sing, O heavens" (c1869) ....
9.12   "I will worship towards thy holy temple" (c1871)...
9.13   "I will mention thy loving-kindness" (c1875)...
9.14   "I will sing of thy power" (c1877)..
9.15   "Hearken unto me" (c1877) ....
9.16   "Turn thy face" (c1878) ....
9.17   "There is none like unto the God of Jeshurun" (p1882, c by Goss, compl Sullivan) ....
9.18   "Who is like unto Thee?" (p1883) ....
9.19   "I will lay me down in peace" (ca1900) ....

10. CHORAL WORKS

W/ orch:

10.1   "Cum sancto spiritu," fugue (c ?1857) ....
10.2   "Psalm" (c ?1858, in German) ....
10.3   "Kenilworth, a Masque of the Days of Queen Elisabeth" (c1864, Chorley; S, A, T, Bar, d ch & orch) ... Op.4
10.4   "The Prodigal Son," oratorio (c1869, Sullivan from Bible) ....
10.5   "On Shore and Sea," dramatic cantata (c1871, Taylor)..
10.6   "Te Deum Laudamus" and "Domine salvam fac reginam" (c1872, Liturgy; ch & milit band/orch) ....
10.7   "The Light of the World," oratorio (c1873, r1890, Sullivan from Bible) ....
10.8   "The Martyr of Antioch," sacred music drama (c1880, Sullivan & Gilbert after Milman; r1898 as opera) ......
10.9   "Ode for the opening of the Colonial and Indian Exhibition": "Welcome, welcome with one voice!" (c1886,
          Tennyson) ....
10.10 "The Golden Legend," cantata (c1886, Bennett after Longfellow)...
10.11 "Ode for the occasion of laying the foundation stone of the Imperial Institute" (c1887, Morris) ....
10.12 "Te Deum Laudamus" (A Thanksgiving for Victory) (c1900; ch & strings, brass, perc & org, last finished
          work) ....

Partsongs:

10.13   Madrigal: "O lady dear" (c1857, ?lost) ....
10.14 "It was a lover and his lass" (c1857, from Shakespeare's As You Like It; 2S & ch) (also see Castelnuovo-
          Tedesco Op.24/II/3, Delius RTv/30/1, Holst H59 & Vaughan Williams' partsong of 1922) ....
10.15 "Sea-side Thoughts": "Beautiful, sublime, and glorious" (c1857, Barton; m ch)..

10.16 "The last night of the year" (p1863, Chorley) ....
10.17 "When love and beauty" (p1898, Chorley, from: The Sapphire Necklace) ....
10.18 "O hush thee, my babie, thy sire was a knight" (p1867, Scott) ....
10.19 "The rainy day" (p1867, Longfellow) ....
10.20 "7 Partsongs" (p1868): 1. "Evening" (Houghton after Goethe) ....
10.21 2. "Joy to the victors" (Scott) ....
10.22 3. "Parting gleams" (Vere) ....
10.23 4. "Echoes" (Moore) (also see Hindemith's 24. of: 25 Songs) ....
10.24 5. "I sing the birth" (Jonson) ....
10.25 6. "The long day closes" (Chorley; m ch) ....
10.26 7. "The beleaguered" (Chorley; m ch) ....
10.27 "All this night bright angels sing" (p1870, Austin after old carol) ....
10.28 "5 Sacred Partsongs" (p1871): 1. "It came upon the midnight clear" ....
10.29 2. "Lead, kindly light" (Newman) ....
10.30 3. "Though sorrow's path" (Kirke White) ....
10.31 4. "Watchman, what of the night?" ....
10.32 5. "The way is long and drear" (Procter) ....
10.33 "2 Choruses" (p1874, adapted from Russian church music): 1. "Turn Thee again" ....
10.34 2. "Mercy and truth" ....
10.35 "Upon the snow-clad earth," carol (p1876) ....
10.36 "Hark! what mean those holy voices?," carol (p1883) ....
10.37 "Wreaths for our graves" (c1897, Massey) ....
10.38 "Fair daffodils" (p1903, Herrick) ....

11. HYMN TUNES

11.1 "Angel voices": "Stars of evening, softly gleaming" (p1872, Whiting) ....
11.2 "Audite audientes me": "I heard the voice of Jesus say" (p1874, Bonar) ....
11.3 "Bethlehem": "While shepherds watched their flocks by night" (p1902, Tate, arr of an old carol) .....
11.4 "Bishopsgarth": "O God, the Ruler of our race" (Whiting) ....
11.5 "Bishopsgarth": "O King of Kings" (p1897, How) ....
11.6 "Bolwell": "Thou, to Whom the sick and dying" (p1902, Thring) ....
11.7 "Carrow": "My God, I thank Thee Who hast made" (p1875, Procter) ....
11.8 "Chapel Royal": "O love that wilt not let me go" (p1902, Matheson) ....
11.9 "Christus": "Show me not only Jesus dying" (p1874, Condor) ....
11.10 "Clarence": "Winter reigneth o'er the land" (p1902, How, arrangement) ....
11.11 "Coena Domini": "Draw nigh, and take the body of the Lord" (p1874, transl Neale) ....
11.12 "Constance": "Who trusts in God, a strong abode" (p1874, transl Kennedy) ....
11.13 "Coronae": "Crown Him with many crowns" (p1874, Bridges) ....
11.14 "Courage, brother": "Courage, brother! do not stumble" (p1872, Macleod) ....
11.15 "Dominion Hymn": "God bless our wide Dominion" (p1880, Lorne) ....
11.16 "Dulce sonans": "At Thine altar, Lord, we gather" (p1874, Whiting) ....
11.17 "Ecclesia": "O where shall rest be found" (p1874, Montgomery) ....
11.18 "Evelyn": "In the hour of my distress" (p1874, Herrick) ....
11.19 "Ever faithful, ever sure": "Let us with a gladsome mind" (p1874, Milton) ....
11.20 "Falfield" (Formosa): "Love divine, all love excelling" (p1867, Wesley) ....
11.21 "Fatherland" (St Edmund): "We are but strangers here" (p1872, Taylor) ....
11.22 "Fortunatus": "Welcome, happy morning! age to age shall say" (p1872, transl Ellerton) ....
11.23 "Gennesareth": "When through the torn sail the wild tempest is streaming" (p1869, Heber) ......
11.24 "Gentle Shepherd" (p1872, anon transl Winkworth) ....
11.25 "Golden sheaves": "To Thee, O Lord, our hearts we raise" (p1874, Dix) ....
11.26 "Hanford": "Jesu, my Saviour, look on me" (p1874, Elliot) ....
11.27 "Holy City": "Sing Alleluia forth in duteous praise" (p1874, Ellerton) ....
11.28 "Hushed was the evening hymn" (p1874, Burns) ....
11.29 "Hymn of the Homeland": "The homeland, the homeland" (p1867, Haweis) ....
11.30 "Lacrymae": "Lord, in this, Thy mercy's day" (p1872, Williams) ....
11.31 "Leominster": "A few more years shall roll" (p1902, Bonar from Martin) ....
11.32 "Light": "Holy Spirit, come in might" (p1902, transl Caswall, arr from Webb's collection) ....
11.33 "Litany No.1": "Jesu, we are far away" (p1875, Pollock) ....
11.34 "Litany No.2": "Jesu, life of those who die" (p1875, Pollock) ....
11.35 "Litany No.3": "Be Thou with us every day" (Pollock) ....
11.36 "Lux eoi": "Hark! a thrilling voice is sounding" (p1874, Caswall) ....
11.37 "Lux in tenebris": "Lead, kindly light" (p1874, Newman) ....
11.38 "Lux mundi": "O Jesu, Thou are standing" (p1872, How) ....
11.39 "Marlborough": "O Strength and Stay upholding all creation" (p1902, trad transl Ellerton) ....
11.40 "Mount Zion": "Rock of Ages, cleft for me" (p1867, Toplady) ....
11.41 "Nearer Home": "For ever with the Lord" (p1902, Montgomery, arr from Woodbury) ....
11.42 "Of Thy love" (St Lucian): "Of Thy love some gracious token" (p1868, Kelly) ....
11.43 "Old 137th": "Great King of nations, hear our prayer" (p1902, Gurney, arr from Genevan Psalter) .....
11.44 "Paradise": "O Paradise!" (p1874, Faber) ....
11.45 "Parting": "With the sweet word of peace" (p1902, Watson, arr of an old melody) ....
11.46 "Pilgrimage": "From Egypt's bondage come" (p1874, Kelly) ....
11.47 "Promissio Patris": "Our Blest Redeemer, ere He breathed" (p1874, Auber) ....
11.48 "Propior Deo": "Nearer, my God, to Thee" (p1872, Adams) ....

11.49	"Rest" (Venite): "Art thou weary, art thou languid" (p1872, transl Neale) ....
11.50	"Resurrexit": "Christ is risen" (p1874, Gurney) ....
11.51	"Safe home": "Safe home, safe home in port" (p1872, transl Neale) ....
11.52	"Springtime": "For all Thy love and goodness" (p1902, Douglas & How, arr from Aldrich) ....
11.53	"St Ann": "The Son of God goes forth to war" (p1869, Heber, arr from Croft) ....
11.54	"St Francis": "Father of heaven, Who hast created all" (p1874, Winkworth) ....
11.55	"St Gertrude": "Onward, Christian soldiers" (p1871, Baring-Gould) ....
11.56	"St Kevin": "Come, ye faithful, raise the strain" (p1872, Neale) ....
11.57	"St Nathaniel": "God moves in a mysterious way" (p1867, Cowper) ....
11.58	"St Mary Magdalene": "Saviour, when in dust to Thee" (p1872, Grant) ....
11.59	"St Millicent": "Let no tears today be shed" (p1874, transl Littledale) ....
11.60	"St Patrick": "He is gone—a cloud of light" (p1874, Stanley) ....
11.61	"Saints of God": "The Saints of God, their conflict past" (p1874, Maclagan) ....
11.62	"St Theresa": "Brightly gleams our banner" (p1874, Potter) ....
11.63	"The long home": "Tender Shepherd, Thou hast still'd" (p1872, Winkworth) ....
11.64	"The roseate hues": "The roseate hues of early dawn" (p1902, Alexander) ....
11.65	"The strain upraise": "The strain upraise in joy and praise" (p1868, transl Neale) ....
11.66	"Thou God of Love": "Thou God of Love, beneath Thy sheltering wings" (p1868, Browne) ....
11.67	"Ultor Omnipotens": "God the all-terrible! King who ordainest" (p1874, Chorley & Ellerton) ....
11.68	"Valete": "Sweet Saviour! bless us ere we go" (p1874, Faber) ....
11.69	"Veni Creator": "Come, Holy Ghost, our souls inspire" (p1874, transl Cosin) ....
11.70	"Victoria": "To mourn our dead we gather here" (p1902, Whiting) ....

Accompaniments to 4 hymns in Helmore's The Hymnal Noted:

11.71	"When in silence and in shadow" (50.) ....
11.72	"Almighty God, who from the flood" (61.) ....
11.73	"Now Christ, ascending whence he came" (83.) ....
11.74	"The world and all its boasted good" (91.) ....

12. SONGS (w/ pf)

12.1	"O Israel," sacred song (p1855) ....
12.2	"Ich möchte hinaus es jauchzen" (c1859, Corrodi) ....
12.3	"Lied mit thränen halbgeschrieben" (c1861, Eichendorff) ....
12.4	"Bride from the North" (p1863, Chorley) ....
12.5	"I heard the nightingale" (p1863, Townsend) ....
12.6	"Sweet day, so cool" (p1864, Herbert) ....
12.7	"The roads should blossom" (c1864) ....
12.8	"Thou art lost to me" (p1865, anon) ....
12.9	"Will he come?" (p1865, Procter) ....
12.10	"Arabian Love Song": "My faint spirit was sitting in the light" (p1866, Shelley) ....
12.11	"5 Shakespeare Songs" (c1863–4): 1. "Orpheus with his lute" ....
12.12	2. "O mistress mine" (Twelfth Night) (also see Castelnuovo-Tedesco Op.24/IV/3 & Vaughan Williams' 3. of: 3 Elisabethan Songs)
12.13	3. "Sigh no more, ladies" (Much Ado About Nothing) (also see Castelnuovo-Tedesco Op.24/IV/1)
12.14	4. "The Willow Song"
12.15	5. "Rosalind" (From East to Western Ind)
12.16	"If doughty deeds" (p1866, Graham) ....
12.17	"She is not fair to outward view" (p1866, Coleridge) (also see Ives Kz18) ....
12.18	"A weary lot is thine, fair maid" (c1866, Scott) ....
12.19	"Over the roof" (p1866, Chorley, from: The Sapphire Necklace) ....
12.20	"County Guy": "Ah! County Guy, the hour is nigh" (p1867, Scott) (also see Castelnuovo-Tedesco's choral work: A Serenade) ....
12.21	"Give" (p1867, Procter) ....
12.22	"In the summers long ago" (p1867, Douglas, music used in: My love beyond the sea) ....
12.23	"The maiden's story" (p1867, Embury) ....
12.24	"What does little birdie say?" (p1867, Tennyson) (also see Delius RTv/29) ....
12.25	"We gathered the roses" (c ?1867, ?lost)
12.26	"I wish to tune my quiv'ring lyre" (p1868, Byron after Anacreon) ....
12.27	"The moon in silent brightness" (p1868, Heber) ....
12.28	"The mother's dream" (p1868, Barnes) ....
12.29	"O fair dove, o fond dove" (p1868, Ingelow) ....
12.30	"O sweet and fair" (p1868, A.F.C.K.) ....
12.31	"The snow lies white" (p1868, Ingelow) ....
12.32	"Dove song" (p1869, Brough; 1v & orch//pf) ....
12.33	"Sad memories" (p1869, Rowe) ....
12.34	"The Troubadour": "Glowing with love, on fire for fame" (p1869, Scott) (also see Weber J296) ....
12.35	"Birds in the night" (p1869, music = Hush'd is the bacon, from: Cox and Box) ....
12.36	"A life that lives for you" (p1870, Lewin) ....
12.37	"Looking back" (p1870, Gray) ....
12.38	"The village chimes" (p1870, Rowe) ....
12.39	"The Window, or the Songs of the Wrens," cycle (p1871, Tennyson): 1. "On the Hill": "The lights and shadows fly!" ....
12.40	2. "At the Window": "Vine, vine and eglantine" (also see Vaughan Williams' song of 1896)

12.41	3. "Gone!": "Gone, till the end of the year"
12.42	4. "Winter": "The frost is here" (also see Vaughan Williams' song of 1896)
12.43	5. "Spring": "Birds' love and birds' song" (also see Vaughan Williams' song of 1896)
12.44	6. "The letter": "Where is another sweet as my sweet?"
12.45	7. "No Answer": "The mist and the rain, the mist and the rain!"
12.46	8. "No Answer": "Winds are loud and you are dumb"
12.47	9. "The Answer": "Two little hands that meet"
12.48	10. "When?": "Sun comes, moon comes"
12.49	11. "Marriage Morning": "Light, so low upon earth"
12.50	"Golden days" (p1872, Lewin) ....
12.51	"Guinevere" (p1872, Lewin) ....
12.52	"None but I can say" (p1872, Lewin) ....
12.53	"Oh! ma charmante" (p1872, Hugo; also see: Oh! bella mia & Sweet dreamer) ....
12.54	"Oh! bella mia" (p1873, Rizelli, Italian vers of: Oh! ma charmante) ....
12.55	"Once again" (p1872, Lewin) ....
12.56	"The sailor's grave" (p1872, Lyte) ....
12.57	"The white plume" (p1872, Douglas) ....
12.58	"Little maid of Arcadee" (p1872, after Gilber from Thespis) ....
12.59	"Coming home" (p1873, Reece; S, mS, music = The Bittercup Stands from: Cox and Box) ....
12.60	"Looking forward" (p1873, Gray) ....
12.61	"There sits a bird in yonder tree" (p1873, from Barham's Ingoldsby Legends) ....
12.62	"2 Songs" (p1873, Burnand, for: The Miller and his Man): 1. "Marquis de Mincepie" ....
12.63	2. "Care is all fiddle-de-dee"
12.64	"The Young Mother" (p1873): 1. "The days are cold" (anon, pubd as: Little darling, sleep again) ....
12.65	2. "Ay de mi, my bird": "O bird that used to press" (Eliot)
12.66	3. "The first departure" (Monro, also see: The Chorister)
12.67	"The Chorister" (p1873, Weatherley, music = The first departure, 3. of: The Young Mother) ....
12.68	"Venetian Serenade" (Nel ciel seren) (p1873, Rizelli transl Rainsom) ....
12.69	"The distant shore" (p1874, Gilbert) ....
12.70	"Living poems" (p1874, Longfellow) ....
12.71	"Mary Morison": "O Mary, at thy window be" (p1874, Burns) (also see Beethoven Op.108/17) ....
12.72	"My dear and only love" (p1874, Marquis of Montrose) ....
12.73	"Sleep, my love" (p1874, Whyte Melville) ....
12.74	"Tender and true" (p1874) ....
12.75	"Thou art weary" (p1874, Procter) ....
12.76	"Love laid his sleepless head" (p1874, Swinburne, used in: The Merry Wives of Windsor) ....
12.77	"Sweet dreamer" (p1872, Farnie, English vers of: Oh! ma charmante) ....
12.78	"Christmas bells at sea" (p1875, Kenney) ....
12.79	"Let me dream again" (p1875, Stevenson) ....
12.80	"The love that loves me not" (p1875, Gilbert) ....
12.81	"The river" (p1875, anon) ....
12.82	"Sweethearts" (p1875, Gilbert; also pubd as duet) ....
12.83	"Thou'rt passing hence, my brother" (p1875, from Hemans's The Highland Message) ....
12.84	"We've ploughed our land" (p1875, anon) ....
12.85	"My dearest heart" (p1876, anon) ....
12.86	"The lost chord" (p1877, Procter) ....
12.87	"Sometimes" (p1877, Lady Lindsay of Balcarres) ....
12.88	"When thou art near" (p1877, Stewart) ....
12.89	"My love beyond the sea" (p1877, Douglas, music = In the summers long ago) ....
12.90	"I would I were a king" (p1878, Cockburn after Hugo) ....
12.91	"Morn, happy morn" (c1878, Wills; 3vv, for play: Olivia) ....
12.92	"Old love letters" (p1879, Cowan) ....
12.93	"St Agnes' Eve": "Deep on the convent-roof" (p1879, Tennyson) ....
12.94	"Edward Gray" (p1880, Tennyson) ....
12.95	"The Sisters": "They have left the doors ajar," duet (p1881, Tennyson) ....
12.96	"In the twilight of our love" (p1881, music = Silver'd is the Raven hair, from: Patience) ....
12.97	"A shadow" (p1886, Procter) ....
12.98	"Ever" (p1887, Mrs. Moore) ....
12.99	"You sleep" (c1889, Mazzucato: E tu nol sai, transl Stephenson, used in: The Profligate) ....
12.100	"Bid me at least good-bye" (c1894, Grundy, for play: An Old Jew) ....
12.101	"The Absent-minded Beggar": "When you've shouted 'Rule Britannia' " (p1899, Kipling) ....
12.102	"O swallow, swallow": "O swallow, swallow, flying, flying South" (p1900, from Tennyson's The Princess; also see operetta: Princess Ida) ....
12.103	"Tears, idle tears": "Tears, idle tears, I know not what they mean" (p1900, from Tennyson's The Princess; also see operetta: Princess Ida) (also see Vaughan Williams' song of 1903) ....
12.104	"My child and I" (p1901, Weatherley) ....
12.105	"To one in paradise" (p1904, Poe) ....
12.106	"Longing for home" (p1904, Ingelow) ....
12.107	"My heart is like a silent lute" (p1904, from Disraeli's Henrietta Temple) ....

* * * * *

1. STAGE WORKS

Juvenilia:

Operas:

Operettas:

Ballets:

      I. "Hala" (On the mountain pasture): 1. "Redyk" (Driving the sheep)
               2. "Scena mimiczna" (Mime scene)
               3. "Marsz zbójnicki" (The Robbers' march)
               4. "Scena mimiczna" (Mime scene)
               5. "Taniec zbójnicki" (The Robbers' dance)
      II. "Wnętrze chałupy" (Inside the hut): 6a. "Wesele" (Wedding)
                          6b. "Cepiny" (Wedding rites)
                          6c. "Pieśń Siuhajów" (The song of young Highlanders)
                         7. "Taniec góralski" (The Highlanders' dance)
                         8. "Wejście Harnasiów" (Arrival of the Highland Robbers—Dance)
     III. "Hala" (On the mountain pasture): 9. "Hala" (On the mountain pasture)

Incid music:

2. SYMPHONIES

3. OTHER ORCHESTRAL WORKS

4. CONCERTOS, SOLO INSTR & ORCH

Pf & orch:

Vn & orch:

5. STRING QUARTETS

6. OTHER CHAMBER MUSIC

3 insts:

6.1	*Piano Trio" (c1907, lost)*	*Op.16, M16*

Vn & pf:

6.2	Violin Sonata in D minor (c1904)	Op.9, M9
6.3	"Romance," in D major (c1910)	Op.23, M23
6.4	"Nocturne & Tarantella" (c1915)	Op.28, M30
6.5	"Mity" (Myths), 3 poems (c1915): No.1 "La fontaine d'Aréthusa"	Op.30, M29
6.6	No.2 "Narcisse"	
6.7	No.3 "Dryades et Pan"	
6.8	"3 Paganini Caprices" (c1918): No.1 in D major (after Caprice No.20, Op.1, MS25)	Op.40, M42
6.9	No.2 in A major (after Caprice No.21, Op.1, MS25)	
6.10	No.3 in A minor (Thema & variations) (after Caprice No.24, Op.1, MS25)	
6.11	"Dance sauvage" (c1923, vn part c by Kochański)	
6.12	"L'aube" (c1923, vn part c by Kochański)	
6.13	"Roxana's Song" (c1924, from opera: King Roger, Op.46; see arr for S & orch)	
6.14	"Lullaby" (La berceuse d'Aïtacho Enia) (c1925)	Op.52, M58

7. PIANO SONATAS

7.1	Piano Sonata No.1 in C minor (c1903–4)	Op.8, M8
7.2	Piano Sonata No.2 in A major (c1910–1)	Op.21, M25
7.3	Piano Sonata No.3 (c1917)	Op.36, M38

8. OTHER PIANO WORKS

8.1	"9 Preludes" (c1899–1900): No.1 in B minor	Op.1, M1
8.2	No.2 in D minor	
8.3	No.3 in D-flat major	
8.4	No.4 in B-flat minor	
8.5	No.5 in D minor	
8.6	No.6 in A minor	
8.7	No.7 in C minor	
8.8	No.8 in E-flat minor	
8.9	No.9 in B-flat minor	
8.10	"4 Etudes" (c1900–2): No.1 in E-flat minor	Op.4, M3
8.11	No.2 in G-flat major	
8.12	No.3 in B-flat minor	
8.13	No.4 in C major	
8.14	"Variations," in B-flat minor (c1901–3)	Op.3, M5
8.15	10 "Variations on a Polish folk theme," in B minor (c1900–4)	Op.10, M10
8.16	"Fantasy," in C major (c1905)	Op.14, M13
8.17	"Prelude and Fugue," in C-sharp minor (c1905–9)	M19
8.18	"Metopy" (Metopes), 3 poems (c1915): No.1 "L'île des sirènes"	Op.29, M31
8.19	No.2 "Calypso"	
8.20	No.3 "Nausicaa"	
8.21	"12 Etudes" (c1916): No.1 "Presto"	Op.33, M34
8.22	No.2 "Andantino soave"	
8.23	No.3 "Vivace assai, agitato"	
8.24	No.4 "Presto"	
8.25	No.5 "Andante espressivo" (c1908)	
8.26	No.6 "Vivace. Agitato e mercato. Vigoroso"	
8.27	No.7 "Allegro molto con brio, burlesco"	
8.28	No.8 "Lento assai, mesto"	
8.29	No.9 "Animato"	
8.30	No.10 "Presto molto agitato, tempestoso"	
8.31	No.11 "Andante soave, rubato"	
8.32	No.12 "Presto energico"	
8.33	"Maski" (Masques) (c1915–6): No.1 "Szecherezade"	Op.34, M35
8.34	No.2 "Clown Tantris"	
8.35	No.3 "Don Juan's Serenade"	
8.36	"20 Mazurkas" (c1924–5)	Op.50, M56
8.37	"Walc romantyczny" (Romantic waltz) (c1925)	M59a
8.38	"4 Polish Dances" (c1926): No.1 "Mazurka"	M60
8.39	No.2 "Krakowiak"	
8.40	No.3 "Oberek"	
8.41	No.4 "Polonaise"	
8.42	"2 Mazurkas" (c1933–4)	Op.62, M73

9. CHORAL WORKS

9.1   "Demeter," cantata (c1917, r1924, Z. Szymanowska after Euripides; A, fem ch & orch) Op.37bis, M39
9.2   "Agave" (c1917, Z. Szymanowska after Euripides; A, fem ch & orch) Op.38, M40
9.3   "Stabat Mater" (c1925–6, medieval Latin sequence transl Jankowski; S, A, Bar, ch & orch): Op.53, M60
        1. "Stała Matka bolejąca"
        2. "I kogóż widząc tak cierpiącą"
        3. "O Matko, źródło wszechmiłości"
        4. "Spraw, niech płaczę z Tobą razem"
        5. "Panno Słodka, racz mozołem"
        6. "Chrystus niech mi będzie grodem"
9.4   "6 Kurpie Songs" (c1928–9, trad; ch): 1. "Hej, wołki moje" M66
9.5   2. "A, chtóz tam puka"
9.6   3. "Niech Jezus Chrystus"
9.7   4. "Bzicem kunia"
9.8   5. "Wyrzundzaj się, dziwce moje"
9.9   6. "Panie muzykancie, prosim zagrać walca"
9.10   "Veni Creator" (c1930, Wyspiański; S, ch, orch & org) Op.57, M67
9.11   "Litany to the Virgin Mary," 2 frags (c1930–3, Liebert; S, fem ch & orch): Op.59, M72
        1. "Dwunastodźwięczna cytra"
        2. "Jak krzak skarlały"

10. VOICE & ORCHESTRA

10.1   "Salome" (ca1904, r1912, Kasprowicz; S & orch) Op.6, M6
10.2   "Penthesilea" (c1908, r1912, from Wyspiański's Achilles; S & orch) Op.18, M18
10.3   "Love-songs of Hafiz" (c1914, Bethe's transl/paraphrase of Arabic, transl Barącz;
     T & orch): 1. "Hafiz' tomb" (also w/ pf, Op.posth) Op.26, M28
10.4   2. "Pearls of my soul"
10.5   3. "Your voice"
10.6   4. "Eternal Youth"
10.7   5. "Drinking song"
10.8   6. "Desires" (orchd song Op.24/1)
10.9   7. "Dance" (orchd song Op.24/4)
10.10   8. "Infatuated East Wind" (orchd song Op.24/5)
10.11 "Roxana's Song" (arr1924; S & orch, from opera: King Roger, Op.46, M55; see arr for vn & pf) ....

11. SONGS (w/ pf)

11.1   "6 Songs" (c1900–2, Tetmajer; 3.–6. also pubd in Ger): 1. "Daleko został cały świat" Op.2, M2
11.2   2. "Tyś nie umarła"
11.3   3. "We mglach" (Vom Felsen)
11.4   4. "Czasem, gdy długo na pół sennie marzę" (Öfters wie betrunken, sitz ich im Traum versunken)
11.5   5. "Słyszałem Ciebię" (Deiner Stimme klang)
11.6   6. "Pielgrzym" (Wohin ich lenk' mein Schritt)
11.7   "3 Fragments from Poems by Jan Kasprowicz" (c1902; pubd in Pol & Fr): 1. "Holy Lord" (O Sainte
        Puissance) (from Holy Lord) Op.5, M4
11.8   2. "I am here and I am crying" (Je souffre, je pleure) (from Holy Lord)
11.9   3. "Błogosławiona niech będzie ta chwila" (Bénie soit l'heure mystérieuse) (from My Evening Song)
11.10 "Łabędź" (The Swan) (c1904, Berent) Op.7, M7
11.11 "4 Songs" (c1904–5, Miciński; pubd in Pol & Ger): 1. "Tak jestem smętny" (Ich bin so trube) Op.11, M11
11.12   2. "W zaczarowanym lesie" (Tief im verzauberten Walde)
11.13   3. "Nade mną leci w szafir morza" (Über mir fliegt im Blaue des Meeres)
11.14   4. "Rycz, burzo" (Brause, o Sturm!)
11.15 "5 Songs" (c1905–7; pubd in Ger & Pol): 1. "Stimme in Dunkeln" (Głos w mroku) (Dehmel transl
        Jachimecki) Op.13, M14
11.16   2. "Christkindlein Wiegenlied" (Kołysanka Dzieciątka Jezus) (from Des Knaben Wunderhorn
        transl Barącz)
11.17   3. "Auf See" (Na morzu) (Dehmel transl Jachimecki)
11.18   4. "Zuleika" (Bodenstedt transl Barącz)
11.19   5. "Die schwarze Laute" (Czarna lutnia) (Bierbaum transl Jachimecki)
11.20 "12 Songs" (c1907; pubd in Ger & Pol): 1. "Hoch in der Frühe" (Wczesnym rankiem) (Dehmel transl
        Fitelberg) Op.17, M17
11.21   2. "Geheimnis" (Tajemnica) (Dehmel transl Fitelberg)
11.22   3. "Werbung" (Zaloty) (Dehmel transl Fitelberg)
11.23   4. "Manche Nacht" (Nocą) (Dehmel transl Fitelberg)
11.24   5. "Aufblick" (Refleksja) (Dehmel transl Fitelberg)
11.25   6. "Verkündigung" (Zwiastowanie) (Dehmel transl Spiess)
11.26   7. "Nach einem Regen" (Po burzy) (Dehmel transl Spiess)
11.27   8. "Entführung" (Zawód) (Dehmel transl Spiess)
11.28   9. "Schlummerlied" (Kołysanka) (Mombert transl F. Szymanowski)
11.29   10. "Seele" (Dusza) (Falke transl F. Szymanowski)
11.30   11. "Fragment" (Der Glübende) (Płomienny) (Mombert transl F. Szymanowski)

11.31	12. "Liebesnacht" (Noc miłosna) (Greif transl F. Szymanowski)
11.32	"6 Songs" (c1909, from Miciński's W Mroku Gwiazd; pubd in Pol, Fr & Ger): 1. "Na księżycu czarnym" (Dans la lune sombre) Op.20, M20
11.33	2. "Święty Franciszek mówi"
11.34	3. "Pachną mi dziwnie twoje złote włosy" (Le doux parfum de tes cheveux me grise)
11.35	4. "W mym sercu" (Mon âme)
11.36	5. "Z mauretańskich śpiewnych sal" (Des pénombres du palais)
11.37	6. "Na pustej trzcinie" (Ses cheveux s'emmêlent)
11.38	"Bunte Lieder" (Barwne Pieśni) (c1910; pubd in Ger & Pol): 1. "Einsiedel" (Pustelnik) (Bulcke) Op.22, M22
11.39	2. "Lied des Mädchens am Fenster" (Pieśń dziewczęcia u okna) (Paquet)
11.40	3. "An kleine Mädchen" (Dla małych dziewczynek) (Faktor)
11.41	4. "Das hat die Sommernacht getan" (Nocy letniej srebrny cud) (Ritter)
11.42	5. "Bestimmung" (Przeznaczenie) (Huch)
11.43	"Love-songs of Hafiz" (c1911, Bethe's transl/paraphrase of Arabic transl Barącz; pubd in Ger & Pol): 1. "Wünsche" (Desires) (orchd1914 & added to Op.26) Op.24, M26
11.44	2. "Die einzige Arzenei" (The only remedy)
11.45	3. "Die brennenden Tulpen" (The glowing tulips)
11.46	4. "Tanz" (Dance) (orchd1914 & added to Op.26)
11.47	5. "Der verliebte Ostwind" (Infatuated East Wind) (orchd1914 & added to Op.26)
11.48	6. "Trauriger Frühling" (A sad spring)
11.49	"Songs of a fairy-tale princess" (c1915, Z. Szymanowska): 1."The lonely moon" (orchd1933)... Op.31, M32
11.50	2. "Nightingale" (orchd1933)
11.51	3. "Golden shoes"
11.52	4. "Dance" (orchd1933)
11.53	5. "Song about wave"
11.54	6. "Feast"
11.55	"3 Songs" (c1915, Davidov; pubd in Pol & Russ): 1. "Wschód słońca" Op.32, M33
11.56	2. "Bezgwiezdne niebo"
11.57	3. "Jesienne słońce"
11.58	"4 Songs" (c1918, Tagore; pubd in Ger transl Effenberger, Pol transl Iwaszkiewicz): 1. "Mein Herz" (Moje serce) Op.41
11.59	2. "Der junge Prinz I" (Młody królewicz I)
11.60	3. "Der junge Prinz I" (Młody królewicz II)
11.61	4. "Das letzte Lied" (Ostatnia pieśń)
11.62	"Pieśni muezina szalonego" (Songs of the Infatuated Muezzin) (c1918, Iwaszkiewicz; pubd in Pol, Ger & Fr; orchd1934): 1. "Allah, Allah, Akbar" Op.42, M44
11.63	2. "O ukochana ma" (O Vielgeliebte)
11.64	3. "Ledwie blask słońca złoci dachy wież" (Früher Morgenstrahl erhellt)
11.65	4. "W południe miasto białe od gorąca" (In Mittagsglut erglänzen)
11.66	5. "O tej godzinie, w której miasto śpi" (Friedvolle Stunde hält die Stadt in Schlaf)
11.67	6. "Odeszłaś w pustynię zachodnią" (O vorbei, o vorüber für ewig)
11.68	"Do dziewczyny", mazurka (c1920) M48
11.69	"O zawiedzionym żołnierzu" (c1920) M49
11.70	"Wyszywała raz Hanka" (c1920, Czyżewski) M50
11.71	"Słopiewnie" (c1921, Tuwim; pubd in Pol, Fr & Ger; orchd1928): 1. "Słowisień" Op.46bis, M51
11.72	2. "Zielone słowa"
11.73	3. "Święty Franciszek"
11.74	4. "Kalinowe dwory"
11.75	5. "Wanda"
11.76	"Trzy Kołysanki" (3 Lullabies) (c1922, Iwaszkiewicz; pubd in Pol, Ger & Fr): 1. "Pochyl się cicho nad kołyską" (Neige dich zu dem schwarzen Wiege) Op.48, M52
11.77	2. "Śpiewam morzu, gwiazdom i tobie" (Meinem Meer, meinem Sternen und dir)
11.78	3. "Biały krąg księżyca olbrzymi" (Des Mondes weisse Scheibe ist riesen Gross)
11.79	"Rymy dziecięce" (Children's rhymes) (c1922–3, Iłłakowiczówna): 1. "Przed zaśnięciem" Op.49, M53
11.80	2. "Jak się najlepiej opędzać od szerzenia"
11.81	3. "Mieszkanie"
11.82	4. "Prosię"
11.83	5. "Gwiazdka"
11.84	6. "Ślub królewny"
11.85	7. "Trzmiel i żuk"
11.86	8. "Święta Krystyna"
11.87	9. "Wiosna"
11.88	10. "Kołysanka lalek"
11.89	11. "Gil i sroka"
11.90	12. "Smutek"
11.91	13. "Wizyta u krowy"
11.92	14. "Kołysanka Krzysi"
11.93	15. "Kot"
11.94	16. "Kołysanka lalki"
11.95	17. "Myszy"
11.96	18. "Zły Lejba"
11.97	19. "Kołysanka gniadego konia"
11.98	20. "Nikczemny szpak"
11.99	"Uplander's song": "Idom se siuhaje dolu, śpiewający" (c1924) M54

11.100	"2 Basque Songs" (c ?1925): 1. "Piękny księżyc" (Argizagi ederra) Op.44, M59
11.101	2. "Ukochane złote włosy" (Maitiak bilhoa holli)
11.102	"Polish Songs" (c1925–6, arrs, other Nos. arr F. Szymanowski): 9. "Idzie żołnierz borem, lasem" M61
11.103	10. "Tam na błoniu błyszczy kwiecie"
11.104	12. "Jak to na wojence ładnie"
11.105	14. "Leci liście z drzewa"
11.106	15. "Hej, strzelcy, wraz"
11.107	16. "Ułani, ułani, malowane dzieci"
11.108	17. "O mój rozmarynie"
11.109	18. "I zabujały siwe łabędzie"
11.110	19. "Gdzież to idziesz, Jasiu"
11.111	"7 Songs" (c1926, Joyce transl Iwaszkiewicz; pubd in Pol & Eng): 1. "Gentle Lady, do not sing" Op.54, M63
11.112	2. "Sleep now, O sleep now"
11.113	3. "Lean out of the window"
11.114	4. "My dove, my beautiful one"
11.115	5. "Strings in the Earth"
11.116	6. "Winds of May"
11.117	7. "Rain has fallen"
11.118	"Vocalise-étude" (c1928) M65
11.119	"12 Kurpie Songs" (c1930–2, trad; pubd in Pol, Ger & Fr): 1. "Lecioły zurazie" (Reiber flogen) . Op.58, M69
11.120	2. "Wysła burzycka" (Wetter und Wind)
11.121	3. "Uwoz, mamo" (Mutter)
11.122	4. "U jeziorecka" (Drüben beim See dort)
11.123	5. "A pod borem siwe kunie" (Dort im Wald)
11.124	6. "Bzicem kunia" (Kriegst die Peitsche)
11.125	7. "Ściani dumbek" (Eiche, zu Fall gekommen)
11.126	8. "Leć, głosie, po rosie" (Über den Wiesentau)
11.127	9. "Zarzyjze, kuniu" (Wiehert, ihr Pferdchen)
11.128	10. "Ciamna nocka, ciamna" (Durch die Nacht)
11.129	11. "Wysły rybki, wysły" (Aus dem See)
11.130	12. "Wsyscy przyjechali" (Alle sind gekommen)

* * * * *

M = Kornel Michałowski: "Karol Szymanowski. Katalog tematyczny dzieł i bibliografia." Kraków, 1967.

Opus numbers 39, 45 & 47 not used.

1. STAGE WORKS

Operas:

1.1	*"The Voyevoda," 3 acts (c1867–8, after Ostrovsky, destroyed Tchaikovsky; reconstr Lamm):* *Op.3*
	extant: . "Ouverture"
	. "Entr'acte & Air de ballet"
1.2	*Introduction, 2 choruses & recit for Auber's opera: Le domino noir (c1868, lost)* ....
1.3	*"Undine" (c1869, Sollogub after Motte Fouqué, part destr):* ....
	extant: 1. "Undine's aria" (reused in incid music: The Snow Maiden, Op.12)
	2. "Act I Finale"
1.4	"Chorus of Flowers & Insects," for projected opera: Mandragora (c1870, Rachinsky; child ch, ch & orch) ...
1.5	"The Oprichnik," 4 acts (c1870–2, after Lazhechnikov) ....
1.6	"Vakula the Smith," 3 acts (c1874, Polonsky after Gogol's Xmas Eve; see r vers: The Slippers) Op.14
1.7	Recitatives for Mozart's opera: The Marriage of Figaro, K492 (Russian adaptation 1875) ....
1.8	"Eugene Onegin," 3 acts (c1877–8, Shilovsky & composer after Pushkin) Op.24
1.9	"The Maid of Orléans" (Jeanne d'Arc), 4 acts (c1878–9, r1882, after Schiller's Die Jungfrau von Orléans) ..
1.10	"Mazeppa," 3 acts (c1881–3, Burenin after Pushkin's Poltava) ....
1.11	"The Slippers" (Oxana's Caprices), 4 act comic-fantastic opera (r1885 of opera: Yakula the Smith, Op.14)
1.12	"The Sorceress" (The Enchantress), 4 acts (c1885–7, Shpazhinsky) ....
1.13	"The Queen of Spades" (Pique Dame), 3 acts (c1890, composer & M. Tchaikovsky after Pushkin) ... Op.68
1.14	"Yolanta," 1 act lyric opera (c1891, M. Tchaikovsky after Hertz: King Rene's Daughter) Op.69

Ballets:

1.15	"The Swan Lake," 4 acts (c1875–6, Begichev & Geltzer) Op.20
1.16	"The Sleeping Beauty," 3 acts (c1888–9, Petipa after Perrault's La belle au bois dormant) Op.66
1.17	"The Nutcracker," 2 acts (c1891–2, Petipa after Hoffmann's Nussknacker und Mausekönig) Op.71

Incid music:

1.18	*"The Romans in the Coliseum" (c1863–4, lost)* ....
1.19	*"Boris Godunov" (c ?1863–4, Pushkin, lost, extant: Fountain Scene)* ....
1.20	2 Numbers for Ostrovsky: Dmitry the Pretender & Vasily Shuysky (c by 1867): ....
	1. "Introduction"
	2. "Mazurka"
1.21	*"The Tangle," recit & couplets for the vaudeville (c1867, Fyodorov, lost)* ....
1.22	"Vous l'ordonnez," couplets for Almaviva in Beaumarchais: Barber of Séville (c1872) ....
1.23	"The Snow Maiden," Russian fairy tale w/ pf music for children (c1873, Ostrovsky) Op.12
1.24	*"La fée," cradle song & waltz (c1879, Feuillet, lost)* ....
1.25	*"Montenegrins Receiving News of Declaration of War on Turkey," tableau (c1880, lost)* ....
1.26	"Do you not hear the nightingale," for Shakespeare: Romeo & Juliet (c1881, transl Sokolovsky; S, T & orch)
1.27	"Domovoy's monologue," melodrama for Ostrovsky: Voyevoda (c1886) ....
1.28	"Hamlet" (c1891, Shakespeare; S, Bar & orch) (also see incid music c by Honegger H190,
	Milhaud Op.200, Moniuszko, Prokofiev Op.77 & Shostakovich Op.32) Op.67a

1a. SELECTIONS FROM STAGE WORKS

1a.8	"Eugene Onegin," opera (Nos. of sections in The Gramophone): Op.24
	excerpts: I: 1. "Introduction"
	6. "I love you, Olga"
	9. "Tatiana's letter scene"
	11. "Maidens, beautiful maidens"
	12. "You have written to me" (Onegin's aria)
	II: 14. "Waltz"
	16. "Triquet'a aria"
	17. "Mazurka"
	19. "In your house"
	21. "Faint echo of my youth" (Lensky's aria)
	III: 23. "Polonaise"
	24. "Here too I'm bored"
	25. "Ecossaise"
	26. "Everyone knows love on earth" (Prince Gremin's aria)
	27. "Can it really be that same Tatiana?" (Onegin's arioso)
	28. "O, what shall I do now"
	29. "Stand up now"
	30. "Onegin, I was younger then"
1a.9	"Jeanne d'Arc," opera: ....
	excerpts: 1a. "Oui, Dieu le veut!"
	1b. "Adieu, fôrets" (Joan's aria)

1a.10   "Mazeppa," opera: ....
. "Introduction"
I: 1. "Choeur des jeunes filles"
2. "Scène, Arioso et Duo"
3. "Scène & Recit"
4. "Choeur et danse" (Hopak)
5. "Scène et arioso"
6. "Scène de la querelle"
7. "Choeur et lamentations de la mère"
8. "Finale"
II: 9. "Scène dans la prison"
10. "Monologue du Mazeppa et Scène avec Orlique"
10a. "Arioso de Mazeppa"
11. "Scène de Mazeppa avec Marie"
12. "Scène de l'apparition de la mère"
13. "Scènes"
14. "Finale"
III: 15. "Entr'acte. La bataille de Poltava" (Tableau symphonique)
16. "Scène et air"
17. "Scène et duo"
18. "Scène de l'apparition de Marie folle"
19. "Finale"
. "Berceuse" (Marie)

1a.13   "The Queen of Spades," opera (Nos. of sections in The Gramophone): Op.68
excerpts: 1. "Introduction"
I: 2. "Shine, sun, bright!"
3a. "How did the play end yesterday"
3b. "I do not know her name"
3c. "If this is the case, we must get to work!"
4a. "At last heaven has sent us a sunny day!"
4b. "But are you sure that she's not noticed you?"
4c. "Happy day, I bless you"
4d. "Tell us, whom are you marrying?"
5. "I feel afraid! There again he is"
6a. "What an old witch, that Countess"
6b. "Once at Versailles"
7. "Se non è vero"
8. " 'Tis evening ... the cloudy spaces darken"
9a. "Fascinating! and delightful!"
9b. "Yes, that's it ... 'My darling friends' "
9c. "Come on, bright-eyed Mashenka"
10. "What a noise you are making"
11a. "It is time now to break up your party"
11b. "You need not shut the door, leave it open"
11c. "What am I crying for, what is it?"
11d. "Stay, I beg of you!"
11e. "Forgive me, loveliest of creatures"
11f. "Liza! Open the door"
11g. "... he who, impelled by burning passion"
II: 12a. "Entr'acte"
12b. "In joy and merriment"
13a. "The host asks his worthy guests"
13b. "I love you beyond all measure"
14. "After the performance wait for me in the hall"
15a. "In the deep shadows"
15b. "Dance of the Shepherds and Shepherdesses"
15c. "My tender friend, my darling shepherd"
15d. "How sweet you are my beauty!"
16a. " 'He who is impelled by burning passion ...' "
16b. "The Empress! Her Majesty!"
17a. "Yes, everything is just as she said"
17b. "And how our noble benefactress enjoys herself"
17c. "Enough of your flatteries!"
17d. "Je crains de lui parles la nuit"
18a. "Don't be frightened!"
18b. "What is all that noise?"
III: 19a. "Entr'acte"
19b. "I do not believe you intended the Countess's death"
20a. "It is terrifying!"
20b. "I have come to you against my will"
21a. "It is close on midnight already"
21b. "Ah! I am weary with sorrow"
22a. "Ah, what if midnight chimes answer"
22b. "Yes, I have come, my darling"

23a. "Drink and make merry!"
23b. "Make your bids!"
24a. "If darling girls could fly like birds"
24b. "When the weather was wet"
25a. "And now, gentlemen, to business"
25b. "What is our life? A game!"
25c. "No more play!"
25d. "Prince! Prince! forgive me!"
25e. "Lord, pardon him!"

1a.15   "The Swan Lake," ballet (Nos. of sections in The Gramophone): Op.20
        excerpts: 1. "Introduction"
      I: 2. "Opening Scene" (Allegro giusto)
           3. "Waltz in A-flat major" (Corps de Ballet)
           4. "Scene—Entrance of Pages" (Allegro moderato)
           5. "Pas de trois": a. "Intrada" (Allegro moderato)
                   b. "Pas de trois I" (Andante Sostenuto)
                   c. "Pas de trois II" (Allegro semplice—Presto)
                   d. "Pas de trois III—Prince" (Moderato)
                   e. "Pas de trois IV" (Allegro)
                   f. "Coda" (Allegro vivace)
           6. "Pas de deux": a. "Waltz in D major"
                   b. "Pas de deux I" (Andante/Adagio)
                   c. "Pas de deux II" (Waltz in B-flat major)
                   d. "Coda" (Allegro molto vivace)
           7. "Pas d'action" (andantino quasi moderato—Allegro)
           8. "Scene—Dusk falls"
           9. "Dance with cups—Polonaise" (Tempo di polacca)
           10. "Finale—Swan theme" (Andante)
     II: 11. "Scene—Swan theme" (Moderato)
           12. "Scene—Benno's entry" (Allegro moderato—Allegro vivo)
           13. "Scene" (Allegro)
           14. "Dances of the swans": a. "Dance 1—Waltz in A major"
                   b. "Dance 2—First Dance of the Queen" (Moderato assai—Molto più mosso)
                   c. "Dance 3—Danse générale" (Waltz in A-flat major)
                   d. "Dance 4—Danses des petites cygnes" (Allegro moderato)
                   e. "Dance 5—Pas d'action: Second Dance of the Queen" (Andante)
                   f. "Coda" (Allegro vivace)
           15. "Scene—Swan theme" (Moderato)
    III: 16. "Scene—Danse de fançailles" (Allegro giusto)
           17. "Dances of the corps de ballet and dwarfs"
           18. "Scene—Entry of guests (Fanfares) and waltz" (in A-flat major)
           19. "Scene" (Allegro—Allegro giusto)
           20. "Pas de six": a. "Intrada" (Moderato assai)
                   b. "Variation 1" (Allegro)
                   c. "Variation 2" (Andante con moto)
                   d. "Variation 3" (Moderato)
                   e. "Variation 4" (Allegro)
                   f. "Variation 5" (Moderato—Allegro semplice)
                   g. "Coda" (Allegro molto vivace)
           21a. "Pas de deux" (add number)
           21b. "Hungarian dance" (Csárdás)
           21c. "Russian dance" (add number)
           22. "Spanish dance"
           23. "Neapolitan dance"
           24. "Mazurka"
           25. "Scène" (Allegro—Valse—Allegro vivo)
    IV: 26. "Entr'acte" (Moderato)
           27. "Scene" (Allegro ma non troppo)
           28. "Dances of the cygnets" (Moderato)
           29. "Scene" (Allegro agitato)
           30a. "Final scene" (Andante)
           30b. "Allegro agitato"
           30c. "Alla breve" (Moderato e maestoso)

1a.16   "The Sleeping Beauty," ballet (Nos. of sections in The Gramophone): Op.66
        excerpts: 1. "Introduction"
    Prologue: 2. "Entrance of King and Court" (March)
           3. "Dance Scene—Entrance of Fairies"
           4. "Pas de six—Fairies present gifts": a. "Intrada"
                   b. "Adagio" (Allegro vivo)
                   c. "Variation 1: Candide"
                   d. "Variation 2: Coulante"
                   e. "Variation 3: Falling crumbs"
                   f. "Variation 4: Song-bird Fairy"

g. "Variation 5: Violente"
h. "Variation 6: Lilac Fairy" (Waltz) (orchd Stravinsky)
i. "Coda"
5. "Finale—La Fée des lilas sort"
I: 6. "Scene—The Palace Garden"
7. "Valse"
8. "Scene—The Four Princes"
9. "Pas d'action": a. "Introduction (Andante) and Adagio" (Rose Adagio)
b. "Dance of Maids of Honour and Pages"
c. "Aurora's Variation" (w/ vn solo)
d. "Coda"
10. "Finale—La Fée des lilas paraît"
II: 11. "Entr'acte and Scene"
12. "Colin-Maillard" (Allegro vivo)
13a. "Scene" (Moderato)
13b. "Danse des duchesses" (Minuet)
13c. "Danse des baronnes" (Gavotte)
13d. "Danse des comtesses"
13e. "Danse de marquises"
14a. "Farandole"
14b. "Danse" (Tempo di Mazurka)
15. "Scene—Arrival of Huntsmen"
16. "Coda": a. "Pas d'action" (Vision) (w/ vc solo)
b. "Variation d'Aurore" (Allegro comodo)
c. "Coda"
17. "Scene" (Allegro agitato)
18. "Panorama" (Andantino)
19. "Entr'acte" (Andante sostenuto) (orchd Stravinsky)
20a. "Entr'acte and Scene—Aurora's sleep"
20b. "Finale" (Breaking of spell) (Allegro agitato)
III: 21. "Marche"
22. "Polacca" (Allegro moderato)
23. "Pas de quarte": a. "Intrada" (Allegro non tanto)
b. "Variation 1—Valse"
c. "Variation 2—Polka" (Silver Fairy)
d. "Variation 3—Saphir"
e. "Variation 4—Diamant"
f. "Coda"
24. "Pas de caractère: Puss in Boots"
25. "Pas de quatre": a. "Adagio" (w/ fl solo)
b. "Variation 1—Cinderella and Prince" (Waltz)
c. "Variation 2—Bluebird and Florisse"
d. "Coda"
26. "Pas de caractère" (Red Riding Hood)
27a. "Pas berrichon" (Hop 'o my Thumb)
27b. "Cinderella and Prince Fortune" (Allegro and Waltz)
28. "Pas de deux": a. "Intrada"
b. "Adagio"
c. "Variation 1—Prince"
d. "Variation 2—Aurora"
e. "Coda" (The Three Ivans) (Allegro vivace)
29. "Sarabande"
30. "Finale": a. "Allegro brillante" (Mazurka)
b. "Apotheosis" (Andante molto maestoso)

1a.17   "The Nutcracker," ballet (Nos. of sections in The Gramophone): Op.71
excerpts: 1a. "Miniature Overture"
I: 1b. "Decoration of the Christmas Tree"
2. "March"
3. "Children's Galop and Entry of the Parents"
4. "Arrival of Drosselmayer"
5. "The Nutcracker and Grandfather Dance"
6. "Departure of the guests—Night"
7. "The Battle and Transformation Scene"
8. "The forest of fir trees in Winter" (Journey Through the Snow)
9. "Waltz of Snowflakes"
II: 10. "The Enchanted Palace of the Kingdom of Sweets" (The Magic Castle)
11. "Arrival of Clara and the Nutcracker"
12. "Divertissement": a. "Chocolate" (Spanish Dance)
b. "Coffee" (Arab Dance)
c. "Tea" (Chinese Dance)
d. "Trépak" (Russian Dance)
e. "Dance of the Mirlitons" (Flutes)
f. "Mother Gigogne and the Clowns"
13. "Waltz of the Flowers"

14a. "Pas de deux" (The Prince and the Sugar-Plum Fairy)
14b. "Variation I" (Tarantella)
14c. "Variation II" (Dance of the Sugar-Plum Fairy)
14d. "Coda"
15. "Final Waltz and Apotheosis"
Add item for 12. "Divertissement": 16. "Gigue" (English Dance) (orchd Lanchbery)

1a.23   "The Snow Maiden," incid music (Nos. of sections in The Gramophone): Op.12
excerpts: 1. "Introduction"
2. "Dance and choirs of the birds"
3. "Winter's monologue"
4. "Carnival procession"
5. "Melodrama"
6. "Interlude"
7. "Lehl's first song"
8. "Lehl's second song"
9. "Interlude"
10. "Chant of the blind bards"
11. "Melodrama"
12. "Chorus of the people and the courtiers"
13. "Round of the young maidens"
14. "Dance of the tumblers"
15. "Lehl's third song"
16. "Brussil's song"
17. "Appearance of the Spirit of the wood"
18. "Interlude. The spring Fairy"
19. "Tsar Berendey's march and chorus"
20. "Final chorus"

1a.28   "Hamlet," incid music (Nos. of sections in The Gramophone): Op.67a
excerpts: 1. "Overture" (from Op.67, shortened & simplified)
2. "Mélodrame" (Act I, Scene 1)
3a. "Fanfare" (Act I, Scene 4)
3b. "Mélodrame" (Act I, Scene 4)
4. "Mélodrame" (Act I, Scene 5)
5. "Entr'acte" (Act II)
6. "Fanfare" (Act II, Scene 2)
7. "Entr'acte" (Act III)
8a. "Fanfare" (Act III, Scene 2)
8b. "Fanfare" (Act III, Scene 2)
8c. "Mélodrame" (Act III, Scene 2)
9. "Entr'acte: Elegy" (Act IV)
10. "Scène d'Ophélie: Mad Scene" (Act IV, Scene 5)
11. "Second Scène d'Ophélie" (Act IV, Scene 5)
12. "Entr'acte" (Act V)
13. "Chant du Fossoyeur" (Act V, Scene 1)
14. "Marche funèbre" (Act V, Scene 1)
15. "Fanfare" (Act V, Scene 2)
16. "Marche finale" (Act V, Scene 2)

2. SYMPHONIES

2.1   Symphony No.1 in G minor, "Winter Daydreams" (c1866; 2nd vers 1866; 3rd vers 1874) Op.13
2.2   Symphony No.2 in C minor, "Little Russian" (c1872, 1879–80; 2 vers; both arr for pf duet) Op.17
2.3   Symphony No.3 in D major, "Polish" (c1875) Op.29
2.4   Symphony No.4 in F minor (c1877–8, ded to his patroness Nadezhda Filaretovna von Meck).......... Op.36
2.5   "Manfred Symphony," in B minor (c1885, after Byron; arr for pf duet 1886) (also see Ives's song Kz123
    & Schumann's incid music: Manfred, Op.115) Op.58
2.6   Symphony No.5 in E minor (c1888).. Op.64
2.7   Symphony No.6 in B minor, "Pathétique" (c1893; arr for pf duet 1893) Op.74
2.8   Symphony No.7 in E-flat maj (c1891–2, sketches: used in: Pf Conc No.3, Op.posth 75 & Andante, Op.posth 79/1).

3. OTHER ORCHESTRAL WORKS

3.1   "Andante ma non troppo," in A major (c1863–4; small orch) ....
3.2   "Agitato and allegro," in E minor (c1863–4; small orch) ....
3.3   "Allegro ma non tanto," in G major (c1863–4; strings)..
3.4   "Allegro vivo," in E major (c1863–4; small orch)..
3.5   "The Storm—Overture," in E min / major (c1864, to Ostrowsky's play: The Storm)....................Op.posth 76
3.6   "Overture," in F major (c1865, small orch; r vers for full orch 1866)..
3.7   "Characteristic Dances" (c1865; r vers: Dances of the Hay Maidens in opera: Voyevoda, Op.3) ....
3.8   "Concert Overture," in C minor (c1865–6) ....
3.9   "Ceremonial Overture," in D major (c1866, on the Danish National Anthem; arr for pf duet 1878) Op.15

4. CONCERTOS, SOLO INSTR & ORCH

Pf & orch:

Vn & orch:

Vc & orch:

Other:

5. STRING QUARTETS

5.1	*"Andante molto," in G major (c1863–4, frag)* ....
5.2	"Allegro vivace," in B-flat major (c1863–4) ....
5.3	"Allegretto," in E major (c1863–4) ....
5.4	String Quartet in B-flat major (c1865, in 1 movt) ....
5.5	String Quartet No.1 in D major (c1871; 2nd movt: Andante cantabile orchd & arr for vc & strings)..... Op.11
5.6	String Quartet No.2 in F major (c1874) Op.22
5.7	String Quartet No.3 in E-flat minor (c1876; Andante funèbre arr for strings, also for vn & pf) Op.30

6. OTHER CHAMBER MUSIC

5 or more insts:

6.1	"Adagio," in F major (c1863–4; wind octet) ....
6.2	"Allegro," in C minor (c1863–4; pf & str qnt) ....
6.3	"Adagio molto," in E-flat major (c1863–4; harp & str qt) ....
6.4	"Prelude" (Andante ma non troppo), in E minor (c1863–4; str qnt) ....
6.5	"Souvenir de Florence," sextet in D major (c1887–90, r1891–2; str sextet / strings) Op.70

4 insts:

6.6	"Adagio," in C major (c1863–4; 4hn) ....

3 insts:

6.7	"Allegretto moderato," in D major (c1863–4; str trio) ....
6.8	Piano Trio in A minor, "In Memory of a Great Artist" (c1881–2) Op.50

Vn & pf:

6.9	"Souvenir d'un lieu cher" (c1878): No.1 "Méditation," in D minor (orchd Glazunov) Op.42
6.10	No.2 "Scherzo," in C minor
6.11	No.3 "Mélodie," in E-flat major (orchd)

7. PIANO SONATAS

7.1	Piano Sonata in C-sharp minor (c1865) ....Op.posth 80
7.2	Piano Sonata in G major (c1878) Op.37

8. OTHER PIANO WORKS

8.1	*"Anastasie-Valse" (c1854, lost)* ....
8.2	*Piece on the theme: By the river, by the bridge, musical joke (c1862, after K. Lyadov, lost)*...............
8.3	*"Allegro," in F minor (c1863–4, frag)* ....
8.4	"Theme & (9) Variations," in A minor (c1863–4)..
8.5	"2 Pieces": No.1 "Scherzo à la russe," in B-flat major (c1867, on Ukrainian tune).................... Op.1
8.6	No.2 "Impromptu," in E-flat minor (c1863–4)
8.7	"Souvenir de Hapsal" (c1867): No.1 "The Castle Ruins," in E minor................................ Op.2
8.8	No.2 "Scherzo," in F major
8.9	No.3 "Song without words," in F major
8.10	"Potpourri on themes from the opera Voyevoda" (c1868) ....
8.11	"Valse-caprice," in D major (c1868) ....
8.12	"Romance," in F minor (c1868) Op.4
8.13	"Valse-scherzo" (No.1), in A major (c1870) Op.5
8.14	"Capriccio," in G-flat major (c1870) Op.7
8.15	"Trois morceaux" (c1870): No.1 "Rêverie," in D major Op.8
8.16	No.2 "Polka de salon," in B-flat major
8.17	No.3 "Mazurka de salon," in D major
8.18	"Deux morceaux" (c1871; arr for vn & pf 1877): No.1 "Nocturne," in F major Op.10
8.19	No.2 "Humoresque," in E minor
8.20	"Six morceaux" (c1873): No.1 "Rêverie du soir," in G minor Op.19
8.21	No.2 "Scherzo humoristique," in D major
8.22	No.3 "Feuillet d'album," in D major
8.23	No.4 "Nocturne," in C-sharp minor (transcr for vc & pf/small orch ca1888)
8.24	No.5 "Capriccioso," in B-flat major
8.25	No.6 "Thème original et (13) variations," in F major
8.26	"Six morceaux composés sur un seul thème" (c1873): No.1 "Prélude," in B major Op.21
8.27	No.2 "Fugue à 4 voix," in G-sharp minor
8.28	No.3 "Impromptu," in C-sharp minor
8.29	No.4 "Marche funèbre," in A-flat minor
8.30	No.5 "Mazurque," in A-flat minor

8.31   No.6 "Scherzo," in A-flat major
8.32   "The Seasons" (c1875–6): No.1 "By the Hearth (January)," in A major Op.37bis
8.33   No.2 "Carnival (February)," in D major
8.34   No.3 "Song of the Lark (March)," in G minor
8.35   No.4 "Snowdrop (April)," in B-flat major
8.36   No.5 "White Nights (May)," in G major
8.37   No.6 "Barcarolle (June)," in G minor
8.38   No.7 "Song of the Reaper (July)," in E-flat major
8.39   No.8 "Harvest (August)," in B minor
8.40   No.9 "The Hunt (September)," in G major
8.41   No.10 "Autumnal Song (October)," in D minor
8.42   No.11 "In the Troika (November)," in E major
8.43   No.12 "Christmas-tide (December)," in A-flat major
8.44   "March for the Volunteer Fleet," in C major (c1878) ....
8.45   "Children's Album: 24 Easy Pieces" (à la Schumann) (c1878): No.1 "Morning Prayer," in G major Op.39
8.46   No.2 "Winter Morning," in B major
8.47   No.3 "Mama," in G major
8.48   No.4 "The Hobby-Horse," in D major
8.49   No.5 "March of the Wooden Soldiers," in D major
8.50   No.6 "The New Doll," in B-flat major
8.51   No.7 "The Sick Doll," in G minor
8.52   No.8 "The Doll's Funeral," in C minor
8.53   No.9 "Waltz," in E-flat major
8.54   No.10 "Polka," in B-flat major
8.55   No.11 "Mazurka," in D minor
8.56   No.12 "Russian Song," in F major
8.57   No.13 "The Peasant plays his harmonika," in B-flat major
8.58   No.14 "Folksong" (Kamarinskaya), in D major
8.59   No.15 "Italian Air," in D major
8.60   No.16 "Old French Air," in G minor
8.61   No.17 "German Air" (Ländler), in E-flat major
8.62   No.18 "Neapolitan Air," in E-flat major
8.63   No.19 "Nanny's Tale," in C major
8.64   No.20 "Baba Yaga," in E minor
8.65   No.21 "Sweet Dreams," in C major
8.66   No.22 "Song of the Lark," in G major
8.67   No.23 "In Church," in E minor
8.68   No.24 "The Organ-grinder sings," in G major Op.40
8.69   "12 Pieces of Moderate Difficulty" (c1878): No.1 "Étude," in G major Op.40
8.70   No.2 "Chanson triste," in G minor
8.71   No.3 "Marche funèbre," in C minor
8.72   No.4 "Mazurka," in C major
8.73   No.5 "Mazurka," in D major
8.74   No.6 "Song without words," in A minor
8.75   No.7 "In the village," in A minor
8.76   No.8 "Valse," in A-flat major
8.77   No.9 "Valse," in F-sharp minor (c1876, r1878)
8.78   No.10 "Russian dance," in A minor
8.79   No.11 "Scherzo," in D minor
8.80   No.12 "Rêverie interrompue," in A-flat major
8.81   "Six morceaux" (c1882): No.1 "Valse de salon," in A-flat major Op.51
8.82   No.2 "Polka peu dansante," in B minor
8.83   No.3 "Menuetto scherzoso," in E-flat major
8.84   No.4 "Natha-valse," in A major (c1878, r1882)
8.85   No.5 "Romance," in F major
8.86   No.6 "Valse sentimentale," in F minor (arr Grunes for vn & pf)
8.87   "Impromptu-caprice," in G major (c1884) ....
8.88   "Dumka" (Russian rustic scene), in C minor (c1886) Op.59
8.89   "Valse-scherzo" (No.2), in A major (c1889) ....
8.90   "Impromptu," in A-flat major (c1889) ....
8.91   "Aveu passionné," in E minor (c ?1892, transcr of episode in sym ballad: The Voyevoda, Op.78) ....
8.92   "Military March," in B-flat major (c1893, for the 98th Yurevsky Infantry Regiment) ....
8.93   "Dix-huit morceaux" (c1893): No.1 "Impromptu," in F minor Op.72
8.94   No.2 "Berceuse," in A-flat major
8.95   No.3 "Tendres reproches," in C-sharp minor
8.96   No.4 "Danse caractéristique," in D major
8.97   No.5 "Méditation," in D major
8.98   No.6 "Mazurque pour danser," in B-flat major
8.99   No.7 "Polacca de concert," in E-flat major
8.100   No.8 "Dialogue," in B major
8.101   No.9 "Un poco di Schumann," in D-flat major
8.102   No.10 "Scherzo-Fantaisie," in E-flat minor
8.103   No.11 "Valse Bleutte," in E-flat major
8.104   No.12 "L'espiègle," in E major
8.105   No.13 "Écho rustique," in E-flat major

8.106   No.14 "Chant élégiaque," in D-flat major
8.107   No.15 "Un poco di Chopin," in C-sharp minor
8.108   No.16 "Valse à cinq temps," in D major
8.109   No.17 "Passé lontain," in E-flat major
8.110   No.18 "Scène dansante" (Invitation au trépak), in C major
8.111   "Impromptu" (Momento lirico), in A-flat major (c ?1893; compl Taneyev) ....

Pf duet:

8.112   "50 Russian Folksongs" (arr for pf duet 1868–9):..
        . Nos.1–25 (from collection of Villebois)
        . Nos.26–46, 48–50 (from collection of Balakirev)
        . No.47 (collected Tchaikovsky)
8.113   *"Funeral March" (c1877, on themes from: The Oprichnik, lost)* ....

9. CHORAL WORKS

9.1   *Oratorio (c ?1863–4, student's work, lost)* ....
9.2   "At Bedtime" (p1863–4, Ogarev; ch; arr for ch & orch p1960) ....
9.3   "Ode to Joy," cantata (c1865–6, Schiller's An die Freude, transl Axakov; S, A, T, B, ch & orch) (also see
        Beethoven: Symphony No.9 in D minor, Op.125 & Schubert Op.posth 111/1, D189) ....
9.4   "Cantata for the opening of the Polytechnic Exhibition in Moscow" (c1872, Polonsky; T, ch & orch) ....
9.5   "Cantata in celebration of the Golden Jubilee of Osip Petrov" (c1875, Nekrasov; T, ch & orch)...................
9.6   "Liturgy of St John Chrysostom" (Messe russe à 4 voix) (c1878; ch; arr for pf 1879): Op.41
        1. "Kyrie eleison"
        2. "Gloria patri"
        3. "Venite adoremus"
        4. "Alleluja"
        5. "Gloria tibi"
        6. "Cherubic Hymn"
        7. "Kyrie eleison"
        8. "Credo"
        9. "Misericordia"
        10. "Te deum"
        11. "Perfectio"
        12. "Amen"
        13. "Pater noster"
        14. "Laudate"
        15. "Benedictus"
9.7   *Cantata (c1881, Pupils of the Patriotic Institute; fem ch, lost)* ....
9.8   "Evening" (c1881, ?Tchaikovsky; m ch) ....
9.9   "Vesper Service," 17 harmonizations of liturgical songs (c1881–2; ch; also w/ pf 1882): Op.52
        1. "Introitus" (from Psalm 104)
        2. "Kyrie eleison"
        3. "Kathesma" (from Psalm 1)
        4. (from Psalm 130)
        5. "Evening Hymn"
        6. "Ave Maria"
        7. (from Psalm 94)
        8. "Polyeleon" (from Psalm 135)
        9. "Troparion"
        10. "Graduale"
        11. "Hymn"
        12. "Katabasis"
        13. "Magnificat"
        14. "Sanctus"
        15. "Theotokion"
        16. "Gloria in excelsis"
        17. "Hymn"
9.10   "Moscow," coronation cantata (c1883, Maykov; mS, Bar, ch & orch) ....
9.11   "3 Cherubic Hymns" (c1884; ch; also w/ pf 1885): 1. "Cherubic Hymn," in F major ....
9.12   2. "Cherubic Hymn," in D major
9.13   3. "Cherubic Hymn," in C major
9.14   "6 Church Songs" (c1885, Liturgy; ch; also w/ pf 1885): 1. "We sing to Thee" ....
9.15   2. "It is very noble"
9.16   3. "Our Father"
9.17   4. "I, a blessed one, choose"
9.18   5. "Let my prayer ascend"
9.19   6. "Today the heavenly powers"
9.20   "Hymn in honour of SS Cyril and Methodius" (c1885, based on Czech hymn; arr for pf) ....
9.21   "School of Jurisprudence Song": "The pure bright flame of truth" (c1885, Tchaikovsky; ch) ....
9.22   "Blessed is he who smiles" (c1887, Grand Duke Konstantin Romanov; m ch) ....
9.23   "An angel crying" (c1887; ch) ....
9.24   "The golden cloud had slept" (c1887, Lermontov; ch) ....

9.25   "Greeting to Anton Rubinstein for his golden jubilee as an artist" (c1889, Polonsky; ch)............................
9.26   "The nightingale" (c1889, Tchaikovsky; ch) ....
9.27   " 'Tis not the Cuckoo in the Dank Pinewood" (c1891, Tsïganov; ch)..
9.28   "Without time, without season" (c1891, Tsïganov; fem ch) ....
9.29   "The merry voice fell silent" (c1891, Pushkin; m ch) ....
9.30   "Spring" (fem ch, lost) ....

10. MISC VOCAL

10.1   "Nature and Love" (c1870, Tchaikovsky; 2S, A, fem ch & pf) ....
10.2   "6 Duets" (c1880; w/ pf): 1. "Evening" (Surikov; S, mS) Op.46
10.3   2. "Scottish ballad: 'Edward' " (trad Scottish transl Tolstoy; S, Bar) (also see Schubert D923)
10.4   3. "Tears" (Tyutchev; S, mS)
10.5   4. "In the garden, near the ford" (Surikov after Shevchenko; S, mS)
10.6   5. "Passion spent" (Tolstoy; S, T)
10.7   6. "Dawn" (Surikov; S, mS; orchd)
10.8   "Night" (c1893, Tchaikovsky; S, A, T, B & pf, on Andantino from Mozart: Fantasia in C minor, K475) ....

11. SONGS (w/ pf)

11.1   "My genius, my angel, my friend" (ca1855–60, from Fet's To Ophelia)..
11.2   "Zemfira's Song" (ca1855–60, from Pushkin's Tsïganï) ....
11.3   "Mezza notte" (ca1855–60) ....
11.4   "Who Goes?" (c?, Apukhtin, lost) ....
11.5   "6 Songs" (c1869): 1. "Do not believe, my friend" (Tolstoy) Op.6
11.6   2. "Not a word, O my friend" (Pleshcheyev after Hartmann's Silence)
11.7   3. "Both painfully and sweetly" (Rostopchina's Words for music)
11.8   4. "A tear trembles" (Tolstoy)
11.9   5. "Why?" (Mey after Heine's Warum sind dann die Rosen so blas?)
11.10   6. "None but the lonely heart" (Mey after Goethe's Nur wer die Sehnsucht kennt) (also see
               Beethoven WoO 134, Schubert Op.62/4, D877, Schumann Op.98a/3 & Wolf's 6. of: Goethe
               Lieder)
11.11 "To forget so soon" (c by 1870, Apukhtin) ....
11.12 "6 Songs" (c1872): 1. "Cradle song" (from Maykov's Modern Greek Songs; arr for pf 1873) Op.16
11.13   2. "Wait!" (Grekov)
11.14   3. "Accept just once" (Fet)
11.15   4. "O sing that song" (Pleshcheyev after Hemans; arr for pf; also for vn & pf 1873)
11.16   5. "Thy radiant image" (Tchaikovsky; arr for pf 1872)
11.17   6. "In dark hell" (from Maykov's Modern Greek Songs)
11.18 "Take my heart away" (c1873, Fet's The Singer) ....
11.19 "Blue eyes of spring" (c1873, Mikhaylov after Heine's Die blauen Frühlingsaugen) ....
11.20 "6 Songs" (c1874–5): 1. "Reconciliation" (Shcherbina) Op.25
11.21   2. "As over the burning ashes" (Tyutchev)
11.22   3. "Mignon's song" (Tyutchev after Goethe's Kennst du das Land, from Wilhelm Meister)
11.23   4. "The Canary" (from Mey's Octaves)
11.24   5. "I never spoke to her" (from Mey's Octaves)
11.25   6. "As they kept on saying: 'Fool' " (from Mey's Song)
11.26 "6 Songs" (c1875): 1. "At bedtime" (Ogarev) Op.27
11.27   2. "Look, yonder cloud" (from Grekov's Stanzas)
11.28   3. "Do not leave me" (from Fet's Melodies)
11.29   4. "Evening" (Mey after Shevchenko)
11.30   5. "Was it the mother who bore me?" (Mey after Mickiewicz's Song)
11.31   6. "My spoiled darling" (Mey after Mickiewicz)
11.32 "6 Songs" (c1875): 1. "No, I shall never tell" (Grekov after Musset's Chanson de fortunio)................ Op.28
11.33   2. "The Corals" (Mey after Kondratowicz)
11.34   3. "Why did I dream of you?" (Mey)
11.35   4. "He loved me so much" (?Apukhtin)
11.36   5. "No answer, or word, or greeting" (Apukhtin)
11.37   6. "The fearful moment" (Tchaikovsky)
11.38 "I should like in a single word" (c1875, Mey after Heine's Die Heimkehr) ....
11.39 "We have not far to walk" (c1875, Grekov)..
11.40 "The Underdog," musical joke (c1876, Tchaikovsky) ....
11.41 "6 Songs" (c1878): 1. "Don Juan's Serenade" (from Tolstoy's Don Juan).. Op.38
11.42   2. "It was in the early spring" (Tolstoy)
11.43   3. "Amid the noise of the ball" (Tolstoy)
11.44   4. "O, if only you could for a moment" (Tolstoy)
11.45   5. "The love of a dead man" (Lermontov)
11.46   6. "Pimpinella" (Tchaikovsky from a Florentine popular song)
11.47 "7 Songs" (c1880): 1. "If only I had known" (Tolstoy) Op.47
11.48   2. "Softly the spirit flew up to heaven" (Tolstoy)
11.49   3. "Dusk fell on the earth" (Berg after Mickiewicz's Morning and Evening)
11.50   4. "Sleep, poor friend" (Tolstoy)
11.51   5. "I bless you, forests" (from Tolstoy's John Damascene)

11.52   6. "Does the day reign?" (Apukhtin; orchd1888)
11.53   7. "Was I not a little blade of grass" (from Surikov's Little Russian Song; arr for vc & strings 1884)
11.54   "16 Children's Songs" (c1883: songs 1.–15.): 1. "Granny and grandson" (Pleshcheyev) Op.54
11.55   2. "The little bird" (Pleshcheyev from Polish: The Snowdrop)
11.56   3. "Spring" (Pleshcheyev from Polish: Country Song)
11.57   4. "My little garden" (Pleshcheyev)
11.58   5. "Legend": "When Jesus Christ was but a child" (Pleshcheyev from English; orchd1884)
11.59   6. "On the bank" (Pleshcheyev from English)
11.60   7. "Winter Evening" (Pleshcheyev)
11.61   8. "The Cuckoo" (Pleshcheyev after Gellert)
11.62   9. "Spring": "The snow is already melting" (Pleshcheyev)
11.63   10. "Lullaby in a storm" (Pleshcheyev)
11.64   11. "The Flower" (Pleshcheyev after Ratisbonne)
11.65   12. "Winter" (Pleshcheyev)
11.66   13. "Spring Song" (Pleshcheyev)
11.67   14. "Autumn" (Pleshcheyev)
11.68   15. "The Swallow" (Surikov after Lenartowicz)
11.69   16. "Child's Song" (c1881, Axakov)
11.70   "6 Songs" (c1884): 1. "Tell me, what in the shade of the branches" (Sollogub) Op.57
11.71   2. "On the golden cornfields" (Tolstoy)
11.72   3. "Do not ask" (Strugovshchikov after 'Heiss mich nicht reden,' from Goethe's Wilhelm Meister)
11.73   4. "Sleep!" (Merezhkovsky)
11.74   5. "Death" (Merezhkovsky)
11.75   6. "Only thou alone" (Pleshcheyev after Kristen)
11.76   "12 Songs" (c1886): 1. "Last night" (Khomyakov's Nachtstück) Op.60
11.77   2. "I'll tell you nothing" (from Fet's cycle: Melodies)
11.78   3. "O, if you knew" (Pleshcheyev)
11.79   4. "The Nightingale" (Pushkin after Karadzic: Songs of the western Slavs)
11.80   5. "Simple words" (Tchaikovsky)
11.81   6. "Frenzied nights" (Apukhtin)
11.82   7. "Gypsy's Song" (Polonsky)
11.83   8. "Forgive" (Nekrasov)
11.84   9. "Night" (Polonsky)
11.85   10. "Behind the window in the shadow" (from Polonsky's Challenge)
11.86   11. "Exploit" (Heroism) (Khomyakov)
11.87   12. "The mild stars shone for us" (from Pleshcheyev's Words for music)
11.88   "6 Songs" (c1887, Grand Duke Konstantin Romanov): 1. "I did not love you at first" Op.63
11.89   2. "I opened the window"
11.90   3. "I do not please you"
11.91   4. "The first meeting"
11.92   5. "The fires in the rooms were already out"
11.93   6. "Serenade": "O child, beneath thy window"
11.94   "6 Songs" (c1888, transl Gorchakova): 1. "Sérénade": "Où vas-tu, souffle d'aurore" (from
                Turquéty's Aurore) Op.65
11.95   2. "Déception" (Collin)
11.96   3. "Sérénade": "J'aime dans le rayon de la limpide aurore" (Collin)
11.97   4. "Qu'importe que l'hiver" (Collin)
11.98   5. "Les larmes" (Blanchecotte)
11.99   6. "Rondel": "Il se cache dans ta grâce" (Collin)
11.100 "Musical joke": plea to composer's nephew V. Davidov" (c1892, Tchaikovsky) ....
11.101 "6 Songs" (c1893, Rathaus): 1. "We sat together" (from cycle: Songs) Op.73
11.102   2. "Night"
11.103   3. "In this moonlight"
11.104   4. "The sun has set"
11.105   5. " 'Mid sombre days" (from cycle: Songs)
11.106   6. "Again, as before, alone"

12. ARRANGEMENTS OF WORKS OF OTHERS

12.1   Weber: Scherzo of Piano Sonata, Op.39, J199 (orchd1863) ....
12.2   Beethoven: 1st movt of Pf Sonata No.17 in D minor, "Tempest," Op.31/2 (orchd ?1863–4; 4 vers)............
12.3   Beethoven: 1st movt of Vn Sonata No.9 in A Major, "Kreutzer," Op.47 (orchd1863–4) ....
12.4   Schumann: "Adagio and Allegro brillante," from: Symphonic Etudes, Op.13 (orchd1864) ....
12.5   Gungl: "Le retour," waltz for pf (orchd1863–4) ....
12.6   Krahl: "Ceremonial March," for pf (orchd1867) ....
12.7   Dargomïzhsky: "Little Russian Kazachok," fantasia for orch (arr1868; pf) ....
12.8   Tarnovskaya: "I remember all," song transcr for pf by Dubuque (arr1868; pf duet) ....
12.9   Dubuque: "Maria-Dagmar," polka for pf (orchd1869) ....
12.10   Rubinstein: "Ivan the Terrible," musical picture for orch (arr1869; pf duet) ....
12.11   Rubinstein: "Don Quixote," musical picture for orch (arr1870; pf duet) ....
12.12   Stradella: "O del mio dolce," aria for 1v & pf (orchd1870) ....
12.13   Cimarosa: "Le faccio un inchino," trio from opera: Il matrimonio segreto (orchd1870) ....
12.14   Dargomïzhsky: "The golden cloud has slept," for 3vv & pf (orchd1870) ....
12.15   Weber: Finale (Perpetuum mobile) from Piano Sonata, Op.24, J138 (transcr1871; pf left hand) ....

12.16   Prokunin: "66 Russian folksongs" (ed1872–3) ....

12.17   Mamontova: "Children's Songs on Russian & Ukrainian Melodies": ....
                    1.–24. (harmonized by 1872)
                25.–43. (harmonized by 1877)

12.18   Haydn: "Gott erhalte den Kaiser," Austrian National Anthem (arr1874; orch) ....

12.19   Schumann: "Ballade vom Haideknaben," Op.121/1, declamation & pf (orchd1874) ....

12.20   Liszt: "Es war ein König in Thule," for): "Gaudeamus igitur" (arr1874; m ch & pf) ....

12.22   Bortnyansky: Complete church music, for ch (ed1881) ....

12.23   Glinka: "Slavsya," from: A Life for the Tsar & Lvov: National Anthem, for ch & pf (orchd1883) ....

12.24   Laroche: "Karmozina," fantasy overture for pf (orchd1888)..

12.25   Menter: "Ungarische Zigeunerweisen," for pf (arr1893; pf & orch) ....

* * * * *

1. STAGE WORKS

Juvenilia (1878–95):

1.1	"A musical exercise book" (c1882, overtures for his toy theatre) ....
1.2	"Tunes 'for a ballet' " (c1891) ....

Operas:

1.3   "Hugh the Drover, or Love in the Stocks," 2 act ballad (c1910–4, p1924, r until 1956, Child): ....
         songs (ch & orch/pf): 1. "Here, Queen uncrown'd" (Mary's song from Act II/2)
                     2. "Hugh's Song of the Road" (Act I)
                     3. "Sweet little linnet" (Hugh's Song, Act I)

1.4   "The Shepherds of the Delectable Mountains," pastoral episode (c1922, Bunyan's The Pilgrim's Progress)
1.5   "Sir John in Love," 4 act opera (c1924–8, after Shakespeare's The Merry Wives of Windsor; also see
         incid music: The Merry Wives of Windsor) ....
1.6   "The Poisoned Kiss," 3 act romantic extravaganza (c1927–9, r until p1957, Sharpe after Garnett): ....
         I. "The magician's haunt in the forest"
         II. "Tormentilla's apartment in Golden Town"
         III. "Room in the Empress's Palace"
1.7   "Raiders to the Sea," 1 act opera (c1925–32, p1936, after Synge) ....
1.8   "Prologue, Episode and Interlude," add scenes to opera: Sir John in Love (perf1933, pubd1936): ....
         1. "Prologue," in B-flat major (before Act I, now withdrawn)
         2. "Episode," in F major (in Act I)
         3. "Interlude," in F minor (between scene 1 & 2 of Act II)
1.9   "The Pilgrim's Progress," 4 act morality (c1949, r1951–2, Bunyan, incorporated: The Shepherds) ....
1.10   "The First Nowell," a Nativity play (c1958, Pakenham; vv, ch & small orch; compl Douglas) ....
1.11   "Thomas the Rhymer," 3 act opera (c1958, inc: pf & vocal score only) ....

Ballets:

1.12   "Pan's Anniversary," masque (c1905, Jonson, collab Holst) ....
1.13   "Old King Cole," ballet (c1923; ch & orch) ....
1.14   "On Christmas Night," folk ballet (c1925–6, Bolm & R.V.W. after Dickens: A Christmas Carol) ....
1.15   "Job, A Masque for Dancing" (c1927–30, Keynes & Raverat after Blake) ....
1.16   "English Folk Dance Society Masque" (c1937): ....
         1. "Overture"
         2. "An E.F.D.S. Medley" (c before ?1937)
1.17   "The Bridal Day," masque (c1938–9, r1952-3, Ursula V.W. after Spenser; also see cantata: Epithalamion)

Pageants:

1.18   "London Pageant" (May Day Scene) (c1911, arr of folk tunes & dances) ....
1.19   "Abinger Pageant" (c1934, Forster) ....
1.20   "England's Pleasant Land" (c1938; ch & milit band, collab w/ others; music used in: Sym No.5 in D major)
1.21   "Solemn Music for Final Scene," for collab masque: Charterhouse (c1950) ....

Incid music:

1.22   "The Pilgrim's Progress," 12 pieces (c1906, Hadley & Onless after Bunyan; S, A, ch & strings) ....
1.23   "The Wasps" (c1909, Aristophanes transl Edwards; T, Bar, ch & orch) ....
1.24   "Bacchae" (c1911, Euripides, inc) ....
1.25   "Iphigenia in Tauris" (c1911, Euripides, inc) ....
1.26   "Electra" (c1911, Euripides, inc) ....
1.27   "The Death of Tintagiles" (c1913, Maeterlinck) ....
1.28   "The Blue Bird" (c1913, unfin: short score only) ....
1.29   "The Merry Wives of Windsor" (c1913, Shakespeare, frag; also see opera: Sir John in Love) (also see incid
         music c by Khachaturian & Sullivan)
1.30   "King Richard II" (c1913, Shakespeare; also see unrelated musically work for radio) (also see incid music
         c by Copland: The Five Kings) ....
1.31   "King Richard III" (c1913, Shakespeare) ....
1.32   "King Henry IV, Part 2" (c1913, Shakespeare) (also see incid music c by Copland: The Five Kings) ....
1.33   "King Henry V" (c1913, Shakespeare, mostly lost) ....
1.34   "The Devil's Disciple" (c1913, Shaw)..

Radio:

1.35   "The Pilgrim's Progress," 38 sections (c1942, Bunyan) ....
1.36   "King Richard II" (c1944, Shakespeare; also see unrelated musically incid music) ....
1.37   "The Mayor of Casterbridge" (c1950, Hardy)..

Film:

1.38   "49th Parallel" (The Invaders) (c1940–1, Powell) ....
1.39   "Coastal Command" (c1942, Dalrymple) ....
1.40   "The People's Land" (c1943, Taylor, music based on trad melodies) ....

1.41   "Flemish Farm" (c1943, Dell) ....
1.42   "Stricken Peninsula" (c1944, Nieter) ....
1.43   "The Loves of Joanna Godden" (c1946, Frend) ....
1.44   "Scott of the Antarctic" (c1948, Frend) ....
1.45   "Dim Little Island" (c1949, Jennings) ....
1.46   *"Bitter Springs" (c1950, Smart, arr & orchd Irving from material supplied by R.V.W.)* ....
1.47   "The England of Elizabeth" (c1955, Taylor): ....
1.48   "The Vision of William Blake" (c1957, dir Benton; also see: 10 Blake Songs) ....

1a. SELECTIONS FROM STAGE WORKS

1a.1   "A musical exercise book," overtures: ....
         1. "Overture to The Major"
         2. "Sonata in F"
         3. "Chant du Matin"
         4. "Overture to The Ram Opera"
         5. "How Doth the Little Busy Bee"
         6. "Sonata in Three Movements" ('op.4')
         7. "Overture to The Galoshes of Happiens"
         8. "Chorale" ('op.9')
         9. "Grand March des Bramas" ('op.10')
       10. "Here I come, creeping," song
       11. "Sketches for a Nativity Scene"

1a.15   "Job, A Masque for Dancing," ballet: ....
     synopsis: Scene 1. "Has thou considered my servant Job?" (I/8)
         2. "So Satan went forth from the presence of the Lord" (I/8)
         3. "Then came a great wind and smote the four corners of the house" (I/19)
         4. "In thoughts from the visions of the night ... fear came upon me" (IV/13–14)
         5. "There came a messenger" (I/14)
         6. "Behold, happy is the man whom God correcteth" (V/17)
         7. "Ye are old and I am very young" (XXXII/6)
         8. "All the Sons of God shouted for joy" (XXXVIII/7)
         9. "So the Lord blessed the latter end of Job more than his beginning" (XLII/12)

1a.18   "London Pageant" (May Day Scene), pageant: ....
         1. "Summer is a-coming in—Henry Martin"
         2. "May Day Songs"
         3. "Nuts in May—Oats and beans"
         4. "Processional Morris—Old Heddon of Founsley—Twanky-dillo"
         5. "Hobby Horse Dance"
         6. "Morris on"
         7. "Processional Morris—Robin Hood and the Pedlar"
         8. "Fanfare of trumpets"
         9. "Staines Morris—Greensleeves"
       10. "Country Gardens—Princess Royal—Shepherds Hey"
       11. "Old woman tossed up in a blanket"
       12. "Follow your lovers"
       13. "Earl of Oxford's March" (Entry of King Henry VIII)

1a.19   "Abinger Pageant," pageant: ....
     arrs: . "Triumphant Music"
         . "Latin hymn: Angelus ad Virginem"
         . "Latin chant: Coelestis Urbs Hierusalem"
         . "Sussex folksong: Twankydillo"
         . "Country Dance: The Triumph"
         . "Country Dance: Haste to the wedding"
         . "Folksong: Seventeen come Sunday"
         . "Folksong: The Sweet Nightingale"
         . "Psalm 84": "How Amiable are Thy Dwellings"
         . "Hymn": "O God our help in ages past"

1a.20   "England's Pleasant Land," pageant: ....
         . "Exit of the Ghosts of the Past"
         . "The Funeral March for the Old Order"
         . "Chorus": "Swiftly they pass, the flying years"

1a.22   "The Pilgrim's Progress," incid music: ....
     extant: 1. "Prelude" (strings, based on hymn-tune: York)
         2. "The Arming of Christian"
         3. "Christian and Apollyon"
         4. "The fight between Christian and Apollyon"
         5. "Vanity Fair" (Down among the dead men) (vocal qt)
         6. "Death of Faithful" (from anthem: Lord, for thy tender mercies' sake)

7. "Final Scene": . "Holy is the Lord" (ch)
   . "Blessed are they that are called to the marriage supper of the Lamb" (S solo)
   . "Alleluias" (from hymn: Sine Nomine)
8. "Epilogue" (strings, based on hymn-tune: York)

1.23   "The Wasps," incid music: ....
       1. "Overture"
   I: 2. "Introduction" (Nocturne)
        3. "Melodrama and Chorus"
        4. "The Wasps' Serenade"
        5. "Chorus"
        6. "Chorus"
        7. "Melodrama and Chorus"
        8. "Melodrama and Chorus"
   II: 9. "Entr'acte and Introduction"
        10. "Melodrama and Chorus"
        11. "March—Past of the Witnesses"
        12. "Parabasis"
   III: 13. "Entr'acte"
        14. "Introduction"
        14a. "Repeat of 13. from letter E"
        15. "Melodrama"
        16. "Chorus"
        17. "Melodrama"
        18. "Chorus and Dance"

1a.24 "Bacchae," incid music: ....
        . "Where is the home for me?," song (Murray after Euripides)

1a.25 "Iphigenia in Tauris," incid music: ....
        . "Prelude"
        . "Chorus I": "Dark of the sea, dark of the sea, gates of the warring water"
        . "Chorus II": "Bird of the sea rocks, of the bursting spray"
        . "Chorus III": "Oh fair the fruits of Leto blow"
        . "Chorus IV": "Go forth in bliss, ye whose lot God shieldeth"

1a.26 "Electra," incid music: ....
        . "Chorus I": "Child of the mighty dead, Electra"
        . "Chorus II": "O for the ships of troy, the beat of oars"
        . "Chorus III": "Onward, O labouring tread"

1a.33   *"King Henry V," incid music:* ....
        extant: 20. "Agincourt Song"
        21. "J'aimons les filles" (for Act III/7)

1a.34 "The Devil's Disciple," incid music: ....
        1. "The British Grenadiers" (arr)
        2. "March from 'Judas Maccabaeus' " (arr from Handel's oratorio, HWV63)
        3. "Yankee Doodle" (verse)

1a.37 "The Mayor of Casterbridge," radio: ....
        1. "Castelbridge"
        2. "Intermezzo"
        3. "Weyhill Fair"

1a.43 "The Loves of Joanna Godden," film: ....
        1. "Main Title"
        2. "Funeral"
        3. "Arthur goes away"
        4. "Waking Ellen"
        5. "Arthur in trap"
        6. "Sheep"
        7. "Farm montage"
        8. "Lamb's foster-mother"
        9. "Marriage banns"
        10. "Driving to Dungeness"
        11. "Martin drowning"
        12. "Ram montage"
        13. "Ellen arriving home"
        14. "Ellen sketching"
        15. "Fairground sequence"
        16. "Fair music"
        17. "Arthur on horseback"
        18. "Night scene"
        19. "Seasons montage"

      20. "Sunrise"
      21. "Ellen riding"
      22. "Foot and mouth"
      23. "Sheep burning"
      24. "End music"
      25. "End titles"

1a.44   "Scott of the Antarctic," film: ....
      1. "Titles. Heroism"
      2. "Titles. Prologue" (the terror and fascination of the Pole)
      3. "Oriana" (Wilson's wife) (not used)
      4. "Dsorn" (Oriana's first meeting with Scott)
      5. & 6. "Scott leaves Oriana" (not used)
      7. "Sculpture scene" (Kathleen Scott and her husband)
      8. "Departure from Ross Island"
      9. "Ice floes"
      10. "Iceberg" (2 vers)
      11. "Penguins"
      12. "Ross Island"
      13. "Aurora"
      14. "Pony march"
      15. "Parhelion"
      16. "Pony march" (not used)
      17. "Pony march and blizzard"
      18. "Distant glacier"
      19. "Climbing glacier"
      20. "Scott on the glacier"
      21. "Scott's decision on how many men to take to the Pole"
      22. "Polar party leaves"
      23. "Amundsen's flag at the Pole"
      24. "The return"
      25. "Death of Evans"
      26. "Death of Oates"
      27. "Only 11 miles" (not used)
      28. "Final shots"

1a.46   *"Bitter Springs," film:* ....
      1. "Main Titles and Opening Music"
      2. "Incidents on the trek"
      3a. "Extrication of wagons from rocky defile"
      3b. "Extrication of wagons from mudhole"
      4. "Dry desert: no water for sheep"
      5. "Night trek: thirsty sheep in dust"
      6. "Arrival at Bitter Springs: smoke signal"

1a.47   "The England of Elizabeth," film: ....
      1. "Titles"
      2. "Street Scenes"
      3. "Countryside"
      4. "Tudor Houses"
      5. "Portraits"
      6. "Elisabeth"
      7. "Hatfield"
      8. "Henry VIII"
      9. "Tintern"
      10. "Books"
      11. "Seamen"
      12. "Dance"
      13. "Wedding Procession"
      14. "Country Dance"
      15. "London"
      16. "Theatres"
      17. "Cradle"
      18. "Map"
      19. "School"
      20. "Charlcote"
      21. "Deer Park"
      22. "Road to London"
      23. "Armada"
      24. "Battle"
      25. "Waves"
      26. "Aftermath"
      27. "More maps"
      28. "Treasures"
      29. "New houses"

30. "Yeoman's Cottage"
31. "Shakespeare Song"
32. "Shakespeare's Tomb"
33. "King's College Introduction"
34. "Conclusion"

2. SYMPHONIES

2.1 Symphony No.1, "A Sea Symphony" (c1903–9, r until 1923, Whitman; S, Bar, ch & orch): ....
    1. "A Song for All Seas, All Ships" (arr Ley for org)
    2. "On the beach at night, alone"
    3. "Scherzo" (The Waves)
    4. "The Explorers"
    . *"The Steersman" (projected 4th movt, discarded)*
2.2 Symphony No.2 in G major, "A London Symphony" (c1912–3, r1920, r until 1953) ....
2.3 Symphony No.3, "Pastoral" (c1921, r1950–1; w/ S/T) ....
2.4 Symphony No.4 in F minor (c1931–4) ....
2.5 Symphony No.5 in D major (c1938–43, r1951) ....
2.6 Symphony No.6 in E minor (c1944–7, r1950) ....
2.7 Symphony No.7, "Sinfonia Antartica" (c1949–52; S, small fem ch & orch, begins w/ recitation of the last
    stanza of Blake's Prometheus Unbound, some music derived from film: Scott of the Antarctic): ....
    1. "Prelude. Andante maestoso"
    2. "Scherzo. Moderato—poco animando"
    3. "Landscape. Lento"
    4. "Epilogue. Alla marcia moderato (ma non troppo)"
2.8 Symphony No.8 in D minor (c1953–5, r1956) ....
2.9 Symphony No.9 in E minor (c1956–7, r1958) ....

3. OTHER ORCHESTRAL WORKS

Juvenilia (1878–95):

3.1 "Happy Day at Gunby" (c1892; vns, vcs, pf & org) ....
3.2 "5 Waltzes" (c1892) ....
3.3 "Fantasia à la valse" (c1892; arr for pf duet) ....

Mature:

3.4 "Serenade," in A minor (c1898): ....
    1. "Prelude"
    2. "Scherzo"
    3. "Intermezzo and Trio"
    4. "Finale"
    . "Romance" (alternative 3rd movt)
3.5 "Bucolic Suite" (c1900): 1. "Allegro," in A minor ....
3.6   2. "Andante," in C major
3.7   3. "Intermezzo: allegretto," in E minor
3.8   4. "Finale: allegro," in A major
3.9 "Heroic Elegy and Triumphal Epilogue" (c1900–1, r1902) ....
3.10 "Burley Heath" (c1903, inc, for planned 4 orch impressions: In the New Forest) ....
3.11 "The Solent" (c1902–3, for planned 4 orch impressions: In the New Forest) ....
3.12   "Symphonic Rhapsody" (c1904, inspired by Rossetti's poem: Echo, destroyed)
3.13 "In the Fen Country," sym impression (c1904, r until 1935; arr for pf) ....
3.14 "2 Impressions" (c1904): No.1 "Harnham Down" ....
3.15   No.2 "Boldre Wood" (lost)
3.16 "Norfolk Rhapsody No.1," in E minor (c1905–6, r1914) ....
3.17 "Norfolk Rhapsody No.2," in D minor (c1906) ....
3.18   "Norfolk Rhapsody No.3," in G min / major (c1906, lost) ....
3.19 "The Wasps—Aristophanic Suite" (c1909, from incid music): No.1 "Overture," in F major ....
3.20   No.2 "Entr'acte," in E modal minor
3.21   No.3 "March—Past of the Kitchen Utensils," in E modal minor
3.22   No.4 "Entr'acte," in G major
3.23   No.5 "Ballet and Final Tableau"
3.24   "Fantasia on English Folk Song" (c1910, studies for an English ballad opera, lost) ....
3.25 "Fantasia on a Theme by Thomas Tallis" (c1910, r until 1919; str qt & d string orch; arr Jacobson for pf) ....
3.26 "English Folk Song Suite" (c1923; milit band; arr Jacob for orch/brass; arr Mullinar for pf): No.1 "March,"
    in F minor (Seventeen come Sunday) ....
3.27   No.2 "Intermezzo," in F minor (My Bonny Boy)
3.28   No.3 "March," in B-flat major (Folk Songs from Somerset)
3.29 "Sea Songs," march (c1923; milit/brass band; transcr for orch 1942) ....
3.30 "Toccata marziale," in B-flat major (c1924; milit band) ....
3.31 "Job" (p1930, concert version of ballet) ....
3.32 "Prelude and Fugue," in C minor (c1930; orig for org 1921) ....
3.33 The Running Set," a fantasia on jig-rhythms (c1933; arr Lasker & Bidder for 2pf) ....

3.34	"Henry V," concert overture (c1933; brass band) ....
3.35	"The Golden Vanity," march (c1933, milit band)..
3.36	"Flourish of Trumpets" (c1935; brass band, for a folk dance festival, based on: Morris Call) ......
3.37	"The Poisoned Kiss" Overture (c1936, from opera)..
3.38	"2 Hymn-Tune Preludes" (c1936; small orch; arr Sumsion for org): No.1 "Eventide," in G major ....
3.39	No.2 "Dominus Regit Me," in B-flat major
3.40	"5 Variants of 'Dives and Lazarus' " (c1939; strings & harp/2harps): ....

. "Introduction and theme," in B modal minor
. "Variant I," in B modal minor
. "Variant II" (Allegro moderato), in B modal minor
. "Variant III," in D modal minor
. "Variant IV" (L'istesso tempo)
. "Variant V" (Adagio), in B modal minor

3.41	"Flourish for Wind Band," overture to a pageant (c1939; milit band) ....
3.42	"Story of a Flemish Farm," suite (p1945, from film): No.1 "The Flag flutters in the wind" ....
3.43	No.2 "Night by the sea. Farewell to the Flag"
3.44	No.3 "Dawn in the barn. The Parting of the Lovers"
3.45	No.4 "In a Belgian café"
3.46	No.5 "The Major goes to face his fate"
3.47	No.6 "The dead man's kit"
3.48	No.7 "The wanderings of the Flag"
3.49	"49th Parallel," suite (p1946, from film): No.1 "Prelude" ....
3.50	No.2 "Warning in a dance hall"
3.51	No.3 "Hudson's Bay": a. "Un canadien errant"
3.52	b. "L'alouette"
3.53	No.4 "Nazis on the prowl"
3.54	No.5 "The Hutterite settlement": a. "Anna's volkslied" (Lasst uns das Kindlein wiegen)
3.55	b. "The wheatfield"
3.56	No.6 "Indian festival"
3.57	No.7 "The lake in the mountains"
3.58	No.8 "Nazi on the run"
3.59	No.9 "Epilogue"
3.60	"Partita" (c1946–8; d string orch, from: Double Trio of 1938) ....
3.61	"Concerto grosso" (c1950; strings in 3 groups): ....

1. "Intrada"
2. "Burlesca Ostinata"
3. "Sarabande"
4. "Scherzo"
5. "March and Reprise"

3.62	"Prelude on an Old Carol Tune" (On Christmas Night) (c1953, for incid music: The Mayor of Casterbridge)
3.63	"Prelude on 3 Welsh Hymn Tunes" (c1955, brass band) ....
3.64	"Variations" (c1957, brass band) ....
3.65	"Flourish for Glorious John (Barbirolli)" (c1957) ....

Misc:

3.66	"Suite for Pipes" (c1939; treble, alto, tenor & bass pipes): No.1 "Intrada," in D major ....
3.67	No.2 "Minuet," in A major & "Trio," in B minor
3.68	No.3 "Valse," in B major
3.69	No.4 "Finale. Jig," in G major
3.70	"Flourish for 3 Trumpets" (c1951; 3tpt)...
3.71	"Diabelleries" (Variations on a theme 'Oh! Where's my little basket gone?') (c1955, collab w/ others).........

Arrs by others:

3.72	*"Coastal Command," suite (arr Mathieson from film score): No.1 "Title"* ....
3.73	*No.2 "Island Station in the Hebrides"*
3.74	*No.3 "Taking off at night"*
3.75	*No.4 "Hudsons take-off from Iceland"*
3.76	*No.5 "Battle of Beauforts"*
3.77	*No.6 "Sunderland goes in close" (quiet determination)*
3.78	*No.7 "JU88 attacks"*
3.79	*No.8 "Finale"*
3.80	*"Suite" (arr Douglas from cantata: Folk Songs of the Four Seasons of 1949):* ....
3.81	*No.1 "To the Ploughboy and May Song"*
3.82	*No.2 "The Green Meadow and An Acre of Land"*
3.83	*No.3 "The Spring of Thyme and The Lark in the Morning"*
3.84	*No.4 "The Cuckoo"*
3.85	*No.5 "Wassail Song and Children's Christmas Song"*
3.86	*"2 Shakespeare Sketches" (arr Mathieson for orch 1955, from: The England of Elisabeth): No.1 "Allegro*
	moderato" (The wind and the rain) ....
3.87	*No.2 "Allegretto—largamente" (It was a lover and his lass)*
3.88	*"3 Portraits from 'The England of Elizabeth,' " suite (arr Mathieson p1964): No.1 "Explorer"* ....
3.89	*No.2 "Poet"*
3.90	*No.3 "Queen"*

4. CONCERTOS, SOLO INSTR & ORCH

Pf & orch:

4.1   "Fantasia" (c1902) ....
4.2   Piano Concerto in C major (c1926–31; rearr w/ Cooper for 2pf & orch 1946)............................

Vn & orch:

4.3   "The Lark Ascending," romance (c1914, r1920, after Meredith's poem; arr w/ pf 1926) ....
4.4   Violin Concerto in D minor, "Concerto accademico" (c1924–5; vn & strings) ....

Va & orch:

4.5   "Flos campi," suite (c1925; va, small wordless ch & small orch): ....
          quotes at each movt from: The Song of Solomon (in Latin & Eng): 1. "As the lily among thorns," in A min
                             2. "For, lo, the winter is past," in G major
                             3. "I sought him whom my soul loveth," in B minor
                             4. "Behold his bed, which is Solomon's," in C minor
                             5. "Return, return, O Shulamite!," in E modal minor
                             6. "Set me as a seal upon thine heart," in B minor
4.6   "Suite for Viola" (c1934; va & small orch): ....
                   1. "Prelude"
                    . "Carol" (arr Sumsion for org as No.4 of: A V. Williams Organ Album p1964)
                    . "Christmas Dance"
                   2. "Ballad"
                    . "Moto perpetuo"
                   3. "Musette" (arr Sumsion for org as No.7 of: A V. Williams Organ Album p1964)
                    . "Polka mélancolique"
                    . "Galop"

Vc & orch:

4.7   "Fantasia on Sussex Folk Tunes" (Sussex Rhapsody) (c1929): ....
                   1. "Salisbury Plain"
                   2. "The Long Whip": 'There was an old man who lived in the city' "
                   3. "Low down in the broom"
                   4. "Bristol Town"
                   5. "I've been to France"
4.8   Cello Concerto (c1953 onwards, sketches from 1942–3, inc: sketches of Scherzo abandoned) ....

Other:

4.9   Oboe Concerto in A minor (c1944; ob & strings) ....
4.10   "Romance," in D-flat major (c1951; harmonica, strings & pf) ....
4.11   Tuba Concerto in F minor (c1954)...
4.12   *"Fantasia on Greensleeves" (arr Greaves for 1/2fl, harp & strings 1934, from opera: Sir John in Love)*...............

5. STRING QUARTETS

5.1   "Finale of a String Quartet" (c1891, juvenilia)...
5.2   String Quartet in C minor (c1897) ....
5.3   String Quartet No.1 in G minor (c1908–9, r1921) ....
5.4   "Household Music. 3 Preludes on Welsh Hymn Tunes" (c1940–1; str qt/4 insts): No.1 "Crug-y-bar," fantasia
5.5   No.2 "St. Denio," scherzo
5.6   No.3 "Aberystwyth," 8 variations (arr Byard for org 1949)
5.7   String Quartet No.2 in A minor, "For Jean on Her Birthday" (c1942–4)...

6. OTHER CHAMBER MUSIC

6 insts:

6.1   "Double Trio" (c1938; string sextet): ....
                   1. "Fantasia"
                   2. "Scherzo Ostinato"
                   3. "Intermezzo" (Homage to Henry Hall)
                   4. "Rondo"

5 insts:

6.2   Quintet in D major (c1898; cl, hn, vn, vc & pf) ....
6.3   Piano Quintet in C minor (c1903, r1904–5; pf, vn, va, vc & d bass)...
6.4   "Ballade and Scherzo" (c1904, r1906; str qnt)...

6.5   "Phantasy Quintet" (c1912; str qnt; Alla Sarabanda arr Ley for org) ....

3 insts:

6.6   Piano Trio in G major (c1888, juvenilia) ....
6.7   Piano Trio in C major (c1895, juvenilia) ....
6.8   "Fantasia on 'Linden Lea' " (c1942-3; ob, cl & bn, arr from song: Linden Lea of 1901) ....

Vn & pf:

6.9   "2 Pieces" (c ?1912, p1923): No.1 "Romance," in F-sharp min / A major ....
6.10   No.2 "Pastorale," in E modal minor
6.11   "The Lark Ascending," romance (c1926, after Meredith's poem; see orig w/ orch 1914) ....
6.12   Violin Sonata in A minor (c1954) ....

Va & pf:

6.13   "Romance" (c?, pubd posth1962) ....

Vc & pf:

6.14   "6 Studies in English Folk Song" (c1926; vc/vn/va/cl & pf): No.1 "Adagio," in E modal minor ....
6.15   No.2 "Andante sostenuto," in E-flat major
6.16   No.3 "Larghetto," in D modal minor
6.17   No.4 "Lento"
6.18   No.5 "Andante tranquillo," in C major
6.19   No.6 "Allegro vivace"

Other 2 insts:

6.20   "Suite de ballet" (c1920; fl & pf): No.1 "Improvisation" ....
6.21   No.2 "Humoresque"
6.22   No.3 "Gavotte"
6.23   No.4 "Passepied"

Arrs by others:

6.24   *"Fantasia on Greensleeves" (arr Mullinar for vn & pf; arr Forbes for vc/va & pf, from opera: Sir John in Love)* ...
6.25   *"Greensleeves" (arr Frank for recorder & pf; arr Quine for gui, from opera: Sir John in Love)* ....
6.26   *"Linden Lea," song (arr Taylor for recorder & pf)* ....

7. PIANO

Juvenilia (1878–95):

7.1   "The Robin's Nest" (c1878) ....
7.2   "Sonatina," in E-flat major (c1890) ....
7.3   "Theme with Variation" (c1891) ....
7.4   "Variation on a Ground Bass by Lully" (c1892) ....
7.5   "Reminiscences of a Walk at Frankham" (c1894): No.1 "A steamy afternoon" ....
7.6   No.2 "Little River Hall"
7.7   No.3 "Anxiety on the Way Home"
7.8   No.4 "Grinham's cottage appears in sight"
7.9   No.5 "Evening comes on"

Mature:

7.10   "Andante sostenuto" (c1904) ....
7.11   "Pezzo ostinato" (c1905) ....
7.12   "6 Short Pieces," suite (c ?1920; arr w/ Brown as: Charterhouse Suite for strings): No.1 "Prelude," in G maj
7.13   No.2 "Slow dance," in E modal minor
7.14   No.3 "Quick dance," in E modal minor
7.15   No.4 "Slow Air," in G modal minor
7.16   No.5 "Rondo," in D modal minor
7.17   No.6 "Pezzo ostinato," in G major
7.18   "Hymn-Tune Prelude on 'Song 13' by Orlando Gibbons," in G major (c1928; arr Roper for org) ....
7.19   "12 Traditional Country Dances," arrs (p1931, collab Karpeles): No.1 "Corn Rigs" ....
7.20   No.2 "Morpeth rant," in D major
7.21   No.3 "Soldier's joy," in E major
7.22   No.4 "Roxburgh Castle," in A major
7.23   No.5 "The Sylph" (tune: Off she goes), in D major
7.24   No.6 "Long eight" (tune: Haste to the wedding), in C major
7.25   No.7 "Three around three" (Pleasures of the town), in A major
7.26   No.8 "Steamboat," in C major
7.27   No.9 "Piper's fancy" (tune: The New Rigged Ship), in A major

7.28   No.10 "The tempest," in F major
7.29   No.11 "The self," in C major
7.30   No.12 "Kitty's rambles," in D major
7.31   "6 Teaching Pieces" (c1934), Book I: No.1 "2-part Invention," in G major ....
7.32   No.2 "2-part Invention," in E-flat major
7.33   II: No.1 "Valse lente," in G modal minor
7.34   No.2 "Nocturne," in A modal minor
7.35   III: No.1 "Canon," in C modal minor
7.36   No.2 "2-part Invention," in F major
7.37   "A Winter Piece" (For Genia) (c1943) ....
7.38   "The Lake in the Mountains" (c1947, from film: 49th Parallel) ....

        Pf duet:

7.39   "Suite" (c1893, juvenilia) ....

        2 Pf:

7.40   "Introduction and Fugue," in G minor (c1945–6) ....

8. ORGAN

8.1   "Organ Overture" (c1890, juvenilia) ....
8.2   "The Old Hundredth" (org acc for the hymn-tune in: Hymns Ancient & Modern p1912) ....
8.3   "3 Preludes on Welsh Hymn-Tunes" (c1920; arr Russell for 2pf): No.1 "Bryn Calfaria," in G modal minor ...
8.4   No.2 "Rhosymedre," in G major (arr Foster for orch)
8.5   No.3 "Hyfrydol," in C major (arr Foster for orch)
8.6   "Prelude and Fugue," in C minor (c1921; arr for orch 1930) ....
8.7   "Passacaglia on B.G.C." (c1933) ....
8.8   "A Wedding Tune for Ann, 27 October 1943" (c1943) ....
8.9   "A Wedding Canon" (c1947) ....
8.10   "2 Preludes on Welsh Folksongs" (c1956): No.1 "Romanza" (The White Rock) ....
8.11   No.2 "Toccata" (St. David's Day)
8.12   "A Vaughan Williams Organ Album" (pubd posth 1964): ....
            No.1 "A Wedding Tune for Ann, 27 October 1943" (c1943, ed Morris)
            No.2 "Greensleeves" (arr Roper 1947, from opera: Sir John in Love)
            No.3 "Toccata" (St. David's Day) (orig No.2 of: 2 Preludes on Welsh Folksongs)
            No.4 "Carol" (arr Sumsion 1938, from: Suite for Viola)
            No.5 "Romanza" (The White Rock) (orig No.1 of: 2 Preludes on Welsh Folksongs)
            No.6 "Prelude: The New Commonwealth" (arr Morris 1960, from: 49th Parallel)
            No.7 "Musette" (arr Sumsion 1938, from: Suite for Viola)
            No.8 "Land of Our Birth" (arr Taylor 1961, from: A Song of Thanksgiving)

9. CHURCH MUSIC

        Juvenilia (1878–95):

9.1   "3 Kyries" (c1889) ....
9.2   "Gloria in excelsis" (c1891; vers w/ Dr. Parry) ....
9.3   "Gloria" (c1891, for R.C.M. exam) ....
9.4   "Super Flumina Babylonis" (c1892, setting for Dr. Parry) ....
9.5   "Vexilla Regis," hymn (c1894; S, ch, strings & org): ....
            1. "Vexilla Regis"
            2. "Impleta sunt"
            3. "O Crux"
            4. "Fons salutis"

        Mature:

9.6   "Mass" (c1897–9; d ch & orch, for degree of Doctor of Music): ....
            1. "Credo"
            2. "Offertorium"
            3. "Sanctus"
            4. "Hosanna"
            5. "Benedictus"
9.7   "O Praise the Lord of Heaven," anthem (c1913, Psalm 148; ch & semi-ch) ....
9.8   "O Clap your Hands," motet (c1920, Psalm 47; ch, brass & org) ....
9.9   "Mass," in G minor (c1920–1; S, A, T, B & ch): ....
        A. Orig version: 1. "Kyrie"
                        2. "Gloria in excelsis"
                        3. "Credo"
                        4. "Sanctus"
                        . "Osanna I"
                        . "Benedictus"

    . "Osanna II"
    5. "Agnus Dei"
  B. Anglican version (adopted Jacobson & r by R.V.W. 1923): 1. "Responses to Commandments"
     2. "Kyrie"
     3. "Creed"
     4. "Sanctus"
     5. "Benedictus"
     6. "Agnus Dei"
     7. "Gloria in excelsis"
    App. "Hosanna"

9.10	"Lord, Thou hast been our Refuge," motet (c1921, Psalm 90; ch, semi-ch & orch/org) ....
9.11	"O Vos Omnes" (Is it Nothing to You?), motet (c1922; A & ch) ....
9.12	"Let us now Praise Famous Men" (c1923, Ecclesiasticus; unison ch & pf/org/small orch) ....
9.13	"The Village Service" (c1925; unison ch & org): 1. "Magnificat," in C major ....
9.14	2. "Nunc Dimittis," in E-flat major
9.15	"Te Deum," in G major (c1928; boys' ch, ch & org/orch) ....
9.16	"Magnificat" (c1932; A, fl, fem ch & orch) ....
9.17	"O How Amiable," anthem (c1934, Psalms 84 & 90; ch & org) ....
9.18	"Festival Te Deum," in F major (c1937; ch & org/orch) ....
9.19	"Liturgical Settings of the Holy Communion" (p1938, trad w/ Benedictus & Agnus Dei) ....
9.20	"Morning, Communion and Evening Services," in D minor (c1939; unison ch, ch & org): ....

    "Morning Service": 1. "Te Deum"
      2. "Benedictus"
      3. "Jubilate"
    "Communion Service": 1. "Kyrie"
      2. "Responses"
      3a. "Before the Gospel"
      3b. "After the Gospel"
      4. "Creed"
      5. "Sursum Corda"
      6. "Sanctus"
      7. "Benedictus qui venit"
      8. "Agnus Dei"
      9. "Gloria"
    "Evening Service": 1. "Magnificat"
      2. "Nunc dimitiis"

9.21	"Deus Misereatur" (Chant for Psalm 67) (c1945) ....
9.22	"The Souls of the Righteous," motet (c1947, Solomon III/1–5; S, T, Bar & ch) ....
9.23	"The Voice out of the Whirlwind," motet (c1947, Book of Job; ch & org/orch, arr from scene 8 of: Job) ....
9.24	"Prayer to the Father of Heaven," motet (c1948, Skelton)...
9.25	"O Taste and See," motet (c1952, Psalm 34; ch w/ org introduction) ....
9.26	"Te Deum and Benedictus" (c1954; unison ch/ch & org/harm/pf) ....
9.27	"The Blessed Son of God" (c1954; ch, arr from Christmas cantata: Hodie) ....
9.28	"A Choral Flourish" (c1956, Psalms; ch, w/ introduction for org/2tpt) ....
9.29	"A Vision of Aeroplanes," motet (c1956, Ezekiel; ch & org)......................................

Arrs by others:

9.30	*"The Twenty-third Psalm" (arr Churchill from stage work: The Pilgrim's Progress)* ....

10. CHORAL WORKS

Juvenilia (1878–95):

10.1	"Music when soft voices die," partsong (c1891, Shelley; m ch) (also see Castelnuovo-Tedesco's choral work of 1951) ....
10.2	"I Heard a Voice from Heaven," anthem (c1891; T & ch) ....
10.3	"Peace, Come Away" (c1895, from Tennyson's In Memoriam; ch & orch) ....

W/ orch:

10.4	"Garden of Proserpine": "Here, where the world is quiet" (c1899, Swinburne; S, ch & orch).......................
10.5	"Willow-wood": "I sat with love upon a woodside well," cantata (c1900–3, Rosseti; Bar/mS & orch/pf; r1908–9 w/ fem ch ad lib) (also see Debussy: La saulaie, L89) ....
10.6	"Toward the Unknown Region" (c1907, r1918, from Whitman's Whispers of Heavenly Death)....................
10.7	"3 Nocturnes" (c1908, from Whitman's Drum Taps; Bar, semi-ch & orch): 1. "Come, O voluptuous sweet-breathed earth"..
10.8	2. "By the bivouac's fitful flame" (ch & pf ad lib; also vers for str qnt)
10.9	3. "Out of the rolling ocean"
10.10	*"Aethiopia. Saluting the Colours" (c1908, Whitman, sketches)*...
10.11	"The Future": "A Wanderer is man from his birth" (c1908, Arnold; S, ch & orch, inc) ....
10.12	"5 Mystical Songs" (c1911, Herbert; Bar, ch ad lib & orch/org): 1. "Easter" ....
10.13	2. "I got me flowers"
10.14	3. "Love bade me welcome"
10.15	4. "The Call" (arr Byard for org)

10.16   5. "Antiphon" (arr Ley for org)
10.17 "Fantasia on Christmas Carols" (c1912; Bar, ch & orch) ....
10.18 "Fanfare": "So he passed over" (c1921; d fem ch, tpts, vc, d bass & bells; used in opera: The Shepherd) ...
10.19 "Sancta Civitas" (The Holy City), oratorio (c1923–5, Revelations; T, Bar, ch, semi-ch, distant ch & orch) ....
10.20 "Benedicite" (c1929, Apocrypha, Austin; S, ch & orch) ....
10.21 "The Hundredth Psalm" (c1929) ....
10.22 "Choral Hymns" (c1929, Coverdale; Bar/T, ch & orch): 1. "Easter Hymn": "Alleluya: Christe is now," in D min
10.23   2. "Christmas Hymn": "Now Blessed be Thou, Christ Jesu," in F major (text after Luther)
10.24   3. "Whitsunday Hymn": "Come, Holy Spirite, most blessed Lorde," in C major (text Luther)
10.25 "Children's Songs for a Spring Festival" (c1929, Farrer; unison ch & strings): 1. "Spring," in F major ....
10.26   2. "The Singers," in D min / major
10.27   3. "An Invitation," in G minor
10.28 "In Windsor Forest," cantata (p1931, Shakespeare, adapted from opera: Sir John in Love): ....
      1. "The Conspiracy" (Sigh no more, ladies), in E minor
      2. "Drinking Song" (Back and side go bare), in A minor
      3. "Falstaff and the Fairies" (Round about in a fair ring-a), in E-flat major
      4. "Wedding Chorus" (See the chariot at hand), in E-flat major
      5. "Epilogue" (Whether men do laugh or weep), in B-flat major
10.29 "The Pilgrim Pavement," hymn (c1934, Partridge; S, ch & orch/org) ....
10.30 "5 Tudor Portraits" (c1935, Skelton; 2vv, ch & orch): 1. "The Tunning of Eleanor Rumming": "Tell you
      I will," ballad ....
10.31   2. "Pretty Bess": "My proper Bess, turn once again to me!," intermezzo (from Speak Parrot)
10.32   3. "Epitaph on John Jayberd of Diss": "Sequitur trigintale, Tale, quale rationale," burlesca
10.33   4. "Jane Scroop" (Her Lament for Philip Sparrow): "Who is there, who?," romanza
10.34   5. "Jolly Rutterkin": "Hoyda, Jolly Rutterkin, hoyda," scherzo (from Jolly Rutterkin & Magnificence)
10.35   *. "Margery Wentworth" (6th Tudor Portrait) (sketches)*
10.36 "Nothing is Here for Tears," choral song (c1936, Milton; unison ch/ch & pf/org/orch) ....
10.37 "Introduction & Scene from 'The Poisoned Kiss' " (c1936; T, ch & orch, from opera) ....
10.38 "Dona Nobis Pacem," cantata (c1936, Whitman & others; S, Bar, ch & orch): ....
      1. "Agnus Dei"
      2. "Beat! beat! Drums!"
      3. "Reconciliation"
      4. "Dirge for two veterans"
      5a. "The Angel of Death"
      5b. "We looked for peace"
      5c. "O man, greatly belowed"
      5d. "The glory of this latter house"
      5e. "Nation shall not lift up a sword against nation"
10.39 "Flourish for a Coronation" (c1937, various; ch & orch): ....
      1. "Let the priest and the prophet anoint him King"
      2. "O prince, desire to be honourable"
      3. "Now gracious God he save our King"
10.40 "Serenade to Music": "How sweet the moonlight sleeps upon this bank!" (c1938, from Shakespeare's
      The Merchant of Venice; 16vv & orch or S, A, T, B, ch & orch) ....
10.41 "The New Commonwealth" (c1940, Child; unison ch & orch/pf, arr of Prelude from film: 49th Parallel) ....
10.42 "6 Choral Songs" (in Time of War) (c1940, from Shelley; unison ch & pf/orch): 1. "A Song of Courage,"
      in E-flat major (There is no work) ....
10.43   2. "A Song of Liberty": "Life may change, but it may fly not," in D modal minor (Hellas)
10.44   3. "A Song of Healing": "Love, from its awful throne of patient power," in A major (Prometheus
      Unbound)
10.45   4. "A Song of Victory," in C modal minor (Prometheus Unbound)
10.46   5. "A Song of Pity, Peace, and Love": "O Spirit vast and deep," in E-flat major (Revolt of Islam)
10.47   6. "A Song of the New Age," in A modal minor (Hellas)
10.48 "England, my England": "What have I done for you," choral song (c1941, Henley; Bar, ch, unison ch
      & orch/pf) ....
10.49 "A Song of Thanksgiving" (c1944, Kipling, Bible & Shakespeare; S, speaker, ch & orch; arr Taylor for org)
10.50 "Folksongs of the Four Seasons," cantata (c1949; fem ch & orch)
10.51 "An Oxford Elegy" (c1947–9, from Arnold's The Scholar-Gypsy & Thyrsis; speaker, small ch & small orch)
10.52 "Fantasia (Quasi Variazione) on the 'Old 104th' Psalm Tune" (c1949, Psalms; pf, ch & orch) ....
10.53 "The Sons of Light," cantata (c1950, Ursula V.W.): ....
      1. "Darkness and Light"
      2. "The Song of the Zodiac"
      3. "The Messengers of Speech"
10.54 "Sun, Moon, Stars & Man," cycle (c1950; unison ch & strings/pf, from cantata: The Sons
      of Light): 1. "Horses of the Sun" ....
10.55   2. "The Rising of the Moon"
10.56   3. "The Procession of the Stars"
10.57   4. "The Song of the Sons of Light"
10.58 "The Old Hundredth Psalm Tune" (c1953; ch, unison ch, orch & org) ....
10.59 "Hodie" (This Day), Christmas cantata (c1953–4; S, T, Bar, ch, boys' ch & orch): ....
      1. "Nowell! Nowell!," prologue (Vespers for Christmas)
      2. "Now the Birth of Jesus Christ," narration (St. Matthew I & St. Luke I)
      3. "It was the winter wild," song (Milton's Hymn on the Morning of Christ's Nativity)
      4. "And it came to pass in those days," narration (St. Luke II)
      5. "The Blessed Son of God," choral (Coverdale after Luther)

6. "And there were in the same country," narration (St. Luke & the Prayer Book)
7. "The Oxen": "Christmas Eve, and twelve of the clock" (Hardy) (also see Britten's choral carol of 1967)
8. "And the shepherds returned," narration
9. "The Shepherds Sing," pastoral (Herbert)
10. "But Mary kept all these things," narration (St. Luke II)
11. "Sweet was the song," lullaby (W. Ballet)
12. "Bright portals of the sky," hymn (Drummond)
13. "Now when Jesus was born," narration (St. Matthew II)
14. "The March of the Three Kings" (Ursula V.W.)
15. "No sad thought his soul affright," choral (anon & Ursula V.W.)
16. "In the beginning," epilogue (John I & Milton's Hymn on the Morning of Christ's Nativity)

10.60   "Epithalamion," cantata (c1957, Vaughan Williams from Spenser; Bar, ch & orch, after masque: The Bridal Day): ....
1. "Prologue": "Early, before the world's light-giving lamp"
2. "Wake Now": "Wake now, my love, awake! for it is time"
3. "The Calling of the Bride": "Now is my love all ready forth to come"
4. "The Minstrels": "Hark how the minstrels 'gin to shrill aloud"
5. "Procession of the Bride": "Lo! where she comes along with portly pace"
6. "The Temple Gates": "Open the temple gates unto my love"
7. "The Bell Ringers": "Ring ye the bells, ye young men of the Town"
8. "The Lover's Song": "Ah! When will this long weary day have end"
9. "The Minstrel's Song": "Now welcome night! thou night so long expected"
10. "Song of the Winged Loves": "The whiles an hundred little winged loves"
11. "Prayer to Juno": "And thou, great Juno! which with awful might"

Hymns (not in Hymnals & Hymn-Tunes):

10.61   "York" (in incid music: The Pilgrim's Progress 1906) ....
10.62   "My Soul, Praise the Lord" (c1934; ch, unison ch & org/string & org) ....
10.63   "All Hail the Power," hymn (c1938; unison ch, ch & org/orch) ....
10.64   "A Hymn of Freedom" (c1939, Briggs; unison ch & pf/org; = 1. of: Wartime Hymns of 1942) ....
10.65   "A Call to the Free Nations" (c1941, Briggs; ch/unison ch; = 2. of: Wartime Hymns of 1942) ....
10.66   "The Airmen's Hymn" (c1942, Lytton; unison ch & pf/org) ....
10.67   "Hymn to St. Margaret" (c1948, Ursula V.W.; unison ch, = 748. in: Hymn for Scotland) ....

Unacc ch or w/ light acc:

10.68   "Sonnet 71": "No longer mourn for me when I am dead" (c1896, Shakespeare) (also see Castelnuovo-Tedesco Op.125 & Kabalevsky Op.52/5) ....
10.69   "Slow, slow, fresh fount" (Echo's Lament of Narcissus), madrigal (c1896, Jonson; d ch) ....
10.70   "Rise early sun," madrigal (c1899, ?Gatty) ....
10.71   "3 Elizabethan Songs," partsongs: 1. "Sweet Day" (ca1896, Herbert) ....
10.72   2. "The Willow Song" (ca1891, from Shakespeare's Othello) (also see Castelnuovo-Tedesco Op.24/V/2)
10.73   3. "O Mistress Mine" (ca1891, from Shakespeare's Twelfth Night) (also see Castelnuovo-Tedesco Op.24/IV/3 & Sullivan's 2. of: 5 Shakespeare Songs)
10.74   "Come Away, Death," partsong (ca1899, from Shakespeare's Twelfth Night) (also see Brahms Op.17/2, Castelnuovo-Tedesco Op.24/I/1 & Holst Op.9a/4, H48/4) ....
10.75   "Ring out ye bells," madrigal (c1902, Sidney) ....
10.76   "Rest": "O earth, lie heavily upon her eyes," partsong (c1902, Rossetti) ....
10.77   "Sound Sleep": "Some are laughing, some are weeping" (c1903, Rossetti; fem ch & pf) ....
10.78   "Fain would I change that note," canzonetta (c1907, anon; 4vv; 2nd vers 1927) ....
10.79   "Love is a sickness" (c1913, Daniel) ....
10.80   "It was a lover and his lass," partsong (c1922, from Shakespeare's As You Like It; fem ch) (also see Castelnuovo-Tedesco Op.24/II/3, Delius RTv/30/1, Holst H59 & Sullivan's partsong of 1857) ....
10.81   "Darest thou now, o Soul" (c1925, Whitman; unison ch & pf/strings) ....
10.82   "Valiant for Truth," motet (c1940, Bunyan; ch & org/pf ad lib, from: The Pilgrim's Progress) ....
10.83   "3 Shakespeare Songs" (c1951): 1. "Full Fathom Five" (also see Castelnuovo-Tedesco Op.24/XI/3 & Stravinsky's 2. of: 3 Shakespeare Songs) ....
10.84   2. "The Cloud-Capp'd Towers"
10.85   3. "Over Hill, Over Dale"
10.86   "Silence and Music" (c1953, Ursula V.W., collab w/ others; = 4. of: A Garland for the Queen) ....
10.87   "Heart's Music" (c1954, Campion) ....
10.88   "Song for a Spring Festival": "All people That On Earth Do Dwell" (c1955, Ursula V.W.) ....

Arrs by others:

10.89   *"A Cotswold Romance," cantata (arr Jacobson 1951, from 1924 synopsis of opera: Hugh the Drover):* ....
1. "The Men of Cotsall"
2. "Sweet Little Linnet"
3. "Song of the Road"
4. "Love at first sight"
5. "The Best Man in England"
6. "Alone and friendless"

       7. "The Fight and its Sequel"
       8. "Hugh in the Stocks" (Gaily I go to die)
       9. "Mary escapes" (alternative vers: "Here, Queen Uncrown'd")
       10. "Freedom at last"
10.90   "Pilgrim's Journey," cantata (arr Morris & Douglas 1962, from stage work: The Pilgrim's Progress): ....
       1. "Cast Thy Burden Upon The Lord"
       2. "Into Thy Hands, O Lord"
       3. "Who Would True Valour See"
       4. "Unto Him That Overcometh"
       5. "Vanity Fair"
       6. "He That is Down"
       7. "The Lord is My Shepherd"
       8. "Alleluia"

11. SONGS (w/ pf)

Juvenilia (1878–95):

11.1	"Crossing the Bar": "Sunset and evening star" (c1892, Tennyson) (also see Ives Ky6) ....
11.2	"Wishes": "Would that the love," ballad love-song (c1893) ....
11.3	"The Virgin's Cradle Song" (c1894, Coleridge) ....
11.4	"To Daffodils" (c1895, Herrick) ....
11.5	"2 Songs from Rumpelstiltskin" (c1895): 1. "Lollipops Song" ....
11.6	2. "Spinning Song"

Mature:

11.7	"Spring": "Birds' love and birds' song," vocal valse (c1896, from Tennyson's The Window) (also see Sullivan's 5. of the song cycle: The Window, or the Songs of the Wrens) ....
11.8	"Vine, vine and eglantine," vocal valse (c1896, from Tennyson's The Window; S, A, T, B & pf) (also see Sullivan's 2. of the song cycle: The Window, or the Songs of the Wrens) ....
11.9	"Winter": "The frost is here," vocal valse (c1896, from Tennyson's The Window; 1v & pf) (also see Sullivan's 4. of the song cycle: The Window, or the Songs of the Wrens) ....
11.10	"Rondel": "Kissing her hair I sat against her feet" (c1895 or 6, Swinburne; A/Bar & pf) ....
11.11	"The Willow Song" (c1897, trad English tune) ....
11.12	"2 Vocal Duets" (c1904, Whitman; S, Bar, pf & str qt w/ vn obbl): 1. "The Last Invocation": "At the last" ......
11.13	2. "The Love-song of the Birds": "Shine! Shine! Shine!"
11.14	"How can the tree but wither?" (c ?1896, Vaux) ....
11.15	"Claribel": "Where Claribel low-lieth" (c ?1896, Tennyson) ....
11.16	"Linden Lea" (In Linden Lea) (c1901, Barnes; w/ orch; also see arr for 3 insts as: Fantasia) ....
11.17	"Boy Johnny": "If you'll busk you as a bride" (c ?1902, Rossetti) ....
11.18	"If I were a Queen" (c ?1902, from Rossetti's Sing-song: a nursery rhyme book) ....
11.19	"Tears, idle tears" (c1903, from Tennyson's The Princess) (also see Sullivan's song of 1900) ....
11.20	"Orpheus with his Lute" I (c1903, from Shakespeare's play: Henry VIII) (also see Castelnuovo-Tedesco Op.24/III/1) ....
11.21	"When I am dead, my dearest" (c1903, Rossetti) ....
11.22	"The Winter's Willow": "There Liddy zot bezide her cow" (c1903, Barnes, in Dorset dialect) ....
11.23	"The House of Life," cycle of 6 sonnets (c1903, Rossetti): 1. "Love-sight": "When do I see thee most" (IV) .
11.24	2. "Silent Noon": "Your hands lie open in the long fresh grass" (XIX)
11.25	3. "Love's Minstrels": "One flame-winged brought a white-winged harp-player" (IX)
11.26	4. "Heart's Heaven": "Sometimes she is a child within mine arms" (XXII)
11.27	5. "Death-in-Love": "There came an image in Life's retinue" (XLVIII)
11.28	6. "Love's Last Gift": "Love to his singer held a glistening leaf" (LIX)
11.29	"Songs of Travel" (c1904, from Stevenson's Songs of Travel; orchd w/ Douglas): 1. "The Vagabond": "Give to me the life I love" (I) ....
11.30	2. "Let Beauty Awake": "Let Beauty awake in the morn from beautiful dreams" (IX)
11.31	3. "The Roadside Fire": "I will make you brooches and toys" (XI)
11.32	4. "Youth and Love": "To the heart of youth the world is a highwayside" (II)
11.33	5. "In Dreams": "In dreams, unhappy, I behold you stand" (IV)
11.34	6. "The infinite shining heavens" (VI)
11.35	7. "Whither must I wander?" (XVI)
11.36	8. "Bright is the Ring of Words" (XIV) (c1901)
11.37	9. "I have trod the upward and the downward slope" (XXII)
11.38	"Blackmwore by the Stour" (c1901, Barnes) ....
11.39	"Ye little birds" (c1905, Heywood) ....
11.40	"A Cradle Song" (c1905, Coleridge) ....
11.41	"The splendour falls" (c1905, from Tennyson's The Princess, IV/1) (also see Britten Op.31/2, Holst Op.20a, H80, Delius RTiv/6 & Sullivan's opera: Princess Ida) ....
11.42	"Dreamland": "Where sunless rivers weep" (c1905, Rossetti) ....
11.43	"Buonaparty": "We be the King's men, hale and hearty" (c1908, Hardy) ....
11.44	"The Sky above the Roof" (c1908, Verlaine transl Dearmer) ....
11.45	"On Wenlock Edge" (c1908–9, Housman; T, pf & str qt ad lib): 1. "On Wenlock Edge the wood's in trouble" (orchd1923) ....
11.46	2. "From far, from eve and morning"
11.47	3. "Is my team ploughing?"

11.48	4. "Oh, when I was in love with you"
11.49	5. "Bredon Hill": "In summertime on Bredon"
11.50	6. "Clun": "In valleys of springs of rivers"
11.51	"4 Hymns" (c1914; T & va obbl/va obbl & strings): 1. "Lord! Come Away" (Taylor) ....
11.52	2. "Who is that fair one?" (Watts)
11.53	3. "Come love, come Lord" (Crashaw)
11.54	4. "Evening hymn" (Bridges from the Greek; orchd)
11.55	"Merciless Beauty," 3 rondels (c1921, Chaucer; S/T, 2vn & vc; also w/ pf): 1. "Your eyën two" ....
11.56	2. "So hath your beauty"
11.57	3. "Since I from love"
11.58	"Dirge for Fidele" (c1922, Shakespeare; 2mS & pf; arr Rowley for org)...
11.59	"4 Poems by Fredegond Shove" (c1922, p1925, Shove): 1. "Motion and Stillness" ....
11.60	2. "Four Nights"
11.61	3. "The New Ghost"
11.62	4. "The Water Mill"
11.63	"Songs from 'Hugh the Drover' " (arr1924): 1. "Alone and Friendless" (Hugh's Song, Act I) ....
11.64	2. "Gaily I go to die" (Hugh's Song, Act II)
11.65	3. "Here on my throne" (Mary's Song, Act II/2)
11.66	4. "Life must be full of care" (Aunt Jane's song, Act I)
11.67	5a. "Cold blows the wind on Cotsall" (The Showman's Song No.1) (Act I) (w/ ch)
11.68	5b. "The Devil and Bonyparty" (The Showman's Song No.2) (Act I) (w/ ch)
11.69	6. "Song of the Road" (Act I)
11.70	7. "Sweet Little Linnet" (Act I)
11.71	8a. "Ah, Love, I've found you" (Act I) (T, S & pf)
11.72	8b. "Hugh my Lover" (Act II/2) (T, S & pf)
11.73	"2 Poems by Seumas O'Sullivan" (c1925, Starkey): 1. "The Twilight People": "It is a whisper"....................
11.74	2. "A Piper": "A Piper in the streets today"
11.75	"3 Songs from Shakespeare" (c1925): 1. "Take, O take, those lips away" (Measure for Measure) (also see
	Beach Op.37/2, B14/2 & Castelnuovo-Tedesco Op.24/IV/2) ....
11.76	2. "When icicles hang by the wall" (Love's Labour's Lost) (T & pf; also unison ch)
11.77	3. "Orpheus with his Lute," II (Henry VIII) (also see Castelnuovo-Tedesco Op.24/III/1)
11.78	"3 Poems by Walt Whitman" (c ?1925): 1. "Nocturne" (from Wispers of Heavenly Death) ....
11.79	2. "A Clear Midnight" (from From Noon to Starry Night)
11.80	3. "Joy, Shipmate, Joy!" (from Songs of Parting)
11.81	"Along the Field," cycle (c1927, r1954, Housman; 1v & vn): 1. "We'll to the woods no more" ....
11.82	2. "Along the field as we came by"
11.83	3. "The half-moon westers low"
11.84	*4. "The Soldier" (destroyed before publication in 1954)*
11.85	5. "Goodbye": "Oh see how thick the goldcup flowers"
11.86	6. "In the morning, in the morning"
11.87	7. "The sigh that heaves the grasses"
11.88	8. "Fancy's Knell": "When lads were home from labour"
11.89	9. "With rue my heart is laden" (also see Barber Op.2/2)
11.90	"The Willow Whistle" (c ?1939, Fuller; 1v & pipe) ....
11.91	"7 Songs from The Pilgrim's Progress" (c before 1951, Bunyan, from stage work): 1. "Watchful's Song" .....
11.92	2. "The Song of the Pilgrim"
11.93	3. "The Pilgrim's Psalm"
11.94	4. "The Song of the Leaves of Life and the Waters of Life"
11.95	5. "The Song of Vanity Fair"
11.96	6. "The Woodcutter's Song" (1v & cl; arr Judge for org)
11.97	7. "The Bird's Song"
11.98	"In the Spring": "My love is the maid" (c1952, Barnes) ....
11.99	"10 Blake Songs" (c1957, Blake; 1v & ob, for film: The Visions): 1. "Infant Joy": "I have no name" ....
11.100	2. "A Poison Tree": "I was angry with my friend"
11.101	3. "The Piper": "Piping down the valleys wild"
11.102	4. "London": "I wander thro' each charter'd street" (also see Britten Op.74/1)
11.103	5. "The Lamb": "Little Lamb who made thee"
11.104	6. "The Shepherd": "How sweet is the Shepherds sweet lot!"
11.105	7. "Ah! Sunflower! weary of time"
11.106	8. "Cruelty has a human heart"
11.107	9. "The Divine Image": "To Mercy, Pity, Peace and Love" (also see 83. of: Songs of Praise
	for Boys and Girls p1929, music not related)
11.108	10. "Eternity": "He who bends to himself a joy" (also see Stockhausen: Momente, No.13)
11.109	"3 Vocalises" (c1958; S & cl): 1. "Prelude" ....
11.110	2. "Scherzo"
11.111	3. "Quasi menuetto"
11.112	"4 Last Songs" (c1954–8, Ursula V.W.): 1. "Procris" ....
11.113	2. "Tired"
11.114	3. "Hands, Eyes and Heart"
11.115	4. "Menelaus on the beach at Pharos"

12. FOLKSONG & CAROL ARRANGEMENTS (arr for 1v/ch & pf/ch)

12.1   "Acre of Land, An" (c ?1934) ....
12.2   "Adieu" (c1903, German transl Ferguson) ....
12.3   "Agincourt Song" (incl in incid music: King Henry V) ....
12.4   "Alister McAlpine's Lament" (c1912, Scottish) ....
12.5   "All in the morning" (On Christmas Day) (c1912) ....
12.6   "Amour de Moy, L' " (c1903, 15th cent French song transl England) ....
12.7   "Angel Gabriel, The" (5. of: 12 Traditional Carols from Herefordshire of 1920) ....
12.8   "As I Walked Out" (5. of: Folksongs from the Eastern Counties of 1908, from Essex) ....

12.9   "Ballade de Jésus Christ, La" (c1904, French) ....
12.10   "Basket of Eggs, A" (used in: Norfolk Rhapsody No.1) ....
12.11   "Birth of the Saviour, The" (7. of: 8 Traditional English Carols of 1919) ....
12.12   "Blake's Cradle Song": "Sweet dreams form a shade" (196. of: The Oxford Book of Carols of 1928, collab
          Shaw) (also see Holst Op.16/5, H69/5) ....
12.13   "Bloody Gardener, The" (7. of: Folksongs from Newfoundland, Vol.I of 1934) ....
12.14   "Bold General Wolfe" (1. of: Folk Songs of England, Vol.V of 1912, w/ Robbins) ....
12.15   "Bold Princess Royal, The" (11. of: Folksongs from the Eastern Counties of 1908, from Norfolk;
          also 7. of: 35 Folksongs, Vol.II of 1935) ....
12.16   "Bold Young Farmer, A" (3. of: Folksongs from the Eastern Counties of 1908, from Essex) ....
12.17   "Bold Young Sailor, A" (used in: Norfolk Rhapsody No.1) ....
12.18   "Bonny Banks of Virgie-O, The" (1. of: Folksongs from Newfoundland, Vol.II of 1934) ....
12.19   "Brewer, The" (4. of: 6 English Folksongs of 1935) ....
12.20   "Bushes and Briars" (1. of: Folksongs from the Eastern Counties of 1908, from Essex) ....

12.21   "Captain Grant" (7. of: Folk Songs of England, Vol.V of 1912, w/ Robbins).................................
12.22   "Captain's Apprentice, The" (8. of: Folksongs from the Eastern Counties of 1908, from Norfolk)....
12.23   "Carter, The" (5. of: Folksongs for Schools of 1912) ....
12.24   "Ca' the Yowes" (Burns: Hark! the Mavis) (also see Britten's 5. of: Vol.V 'British Isles'—Folksong Arrs
          & Haydn HobXXXIa/221) ....
12.25   "Chanson de Quête" (May-day song) (French) ....
12.26   "Cherry-Tree Carol" (As Joseph was a-walking) (2. of: 9 Carols of 1942).................................
12.27   "Children's Christmas Song" (incl in cantata: Folk Songs of the Four Seasons of 1949) ....
12.28   "Christmas Now is Drawing Near" (3. of: 12 Traditional Carols from Herefordshire of 1920) ....
12.29   "Come all you Worthy Christians" (9. of: Folk Songs of England, Vol.V of 1912, collab Robins) ...
12.30   "Come all you Worthy Gentlemen" (used in: Fantasia on Christmas Carols).............................
12.31   "Come Love we God" (1. of: 2 Carols of 1945) ....
12.32   "Cousin Michael" (c1903, German transl Ferguson) ....
12.33   "Coventry Carol" (6. of: 9 Carols of 1942) ....
12.34   "Cruel Mother, The" (2. of: Folksongs from Newfoundland, Vol.I of 1934)..................................
12.35   "Cuckoo, The" (11. of: Folksongs from Newfoundland, Vol.II of 1934) ....
12.36   "Cuckoo and the Nightingale, The" (2. of: Folksongs for Schools of 1912) ....

12.37   "Dark-Eyed Sailor, The" (1. of: 5 English Folksongs of 1913) ....
12.38   "Dives & Lazarus" (9. of: 12 Trad Carols from Herefordshire of 1920; also 9. in: 9 Carols of 1942) ....
12.39   "Down Among the Dead Men" (c1912, Old English air) ....
12.40   "Down in yon Forest" (4. in: 8 Traditional English Carols of 1919) ....
12.41   "Down by the Riverside" (8. of: Folksongs for Schools of 1912) ....

12.42   "Earl Brand" (2. of: Folksongs from Newfoundland, Vol.II of 1934) ....
12.43   "Early in the Spring" (used in cantata: Folksongs of the Four Seasons of 1949) ....
12.44   "Entlaubet ist der Walde" (c1902, 1. in: Two Old German Songs, Eng text Ford) ....

12.45   "Farewell, Lads" (8. of: Folk Songs of England," Vol.V, collab Robins).....................................
12.46   "Farmer's Boy, The" (c1921) ....
12.47   "Farmer's Son so Sweet, A" (c1921) ....
12.48   "Farmyard Song" (10. of: Folksongs for Schools of 1912)...
12.49   "Female Highwayman, The" (4. of: Folksongs for Schools of 1912) ....
12.50   "First Nowell, The" (4. of: 9 Carols of 1942) ....
12.51   "Fox, The" (9. of: Folksongs for Schools of 1912) ....

12.52   "Geordie" (14. of: Folksongs from the Eastern Counties of 1908, from Cambridgeshire) ....
12.53   "God Bless the Master of This House" (c1956)...
12.54   "God Rest You Merry, Gentlemen" (6. of: 12 Traditional Carols from Herefordshire of 1920; also 1. in:
          9 Carols of 1942) ....
12.55   "Golden Carol, The" (Now is Christèmas y-come) (173. of: The Oxford Book of Carols of 1928)............
12.56   "Golden Vanity, The" (1. of: Motherland Songbook, Vol.IV of 1919) ....
12.57   "Green Meadow, The" (incl in cantata: Folk Songs of the Four Seasons of 1949) ....
12.58   "Greensleeves" (incl in: London Pageant of 1911) ....
12.59   "Gypsy Laddie, The" (3. of: Folksongs from Newfoundland of 1934) ....

12.60   "Harry the Tailor" (14. of: Folksongs from the Eastern Counties of 1908, from Cambridgeshire) ....
12.61   "Here's Adieu to all Judges and Juries" (13. of: Folk Songs of England," Vol.V of 1912, collab Robins).......
12.62   "High Germany" (c1923, in Sharp's: Folk Songs of England, Vol.I of 1923) ....
12.63   "Holy Well, The" (2 vers) (1. & 2. of: 12 Traditional Carols from Herefordshire of 1920)............
12.64   "How Cold the Wind Doth Blow" (The Unquiet Grave) (6. of: Folk Songs of England, Vol.V) ....

12.65   "I'll Never Love Thee More" (c1934)..
12.66   "In Bethlehem City" (used in Winter of: Folk Songs of the Four Seasons of 1949) ....

12.67	"I Saw Three Ships" (7. of: 9 Carols of 1942) ....
12.68	"Isle of France, The" (15. of: Folk Songs of England," Vol.V of 1912, collab Robins) ....
12.69	"I will give my love an apple" (6. of: Folksongs for Schools of 1912) ....
12.70	"Jack the Sailor" (6. of: Motherland Songbook, Vol.III of 1919) ....
12.71	"Jean Renaud" (c1903, 15th cent French transl England) ....
12.72	"John Barleycorn" (used in: Norfolk Rhapsody No.3)
12.73	"John Dory" (c ?1934) ....
12.74	"John Raeburn" (used in: Norfolk Rhapsody No.3)
12.75	"Jolly Ploughboy, The" (c1908, from Sussex, 1. of: Folksongs for Schools of 1912; also 18. of 35 Folksongs, Vol.II of 1935) ....
12.76	"Joseph and Mary" (4. of: 12 Traditional Carols from Herefordshire of 1920) ....
12.77	"Just as the tide was flowing" (3. of: 5 English Folksongs of 1913) ....
12.78	"King William" (6. of: 6 English Folksongs of 1935) ....
12.79	"Lark in the Morning, The" (6. of: Folksongs from the Eastern Counties of 1908, from Essex) ....
12.80	"Lawyer, The" (2. of: 2 English Folksongs of 1935; w/ vn) ....
12.81	"Lincolnshire Farmer, The" (12. of: Folksongs from the Eastern Counties of 1908, from Norfolk) ....
12.82	"Loch Lomond" (c1921, Scottish) ....
12.83	"Lord Akeman" (Lord Bateman) (3. of: Folksongs from Newfoundland, Vol.II of 1934) ....
12.84	"Lord at First, The" (5. of: 9 Carols of 1942) ....
12.85	"Lost Lady Found, The" (4. of: Folksongs from the Eastern Counties of 1908, from Essex) ....
12.86	"Lovely Joan" (14. of: Folk Songs of England," Vol.V of 1912, collab Robins) ....
12.87	"Lover's Ghost, The" (4. of: 5 English Folksongs of 1913; 7. of: Folksongs from Newfoundland, Vol.II of 1934) ....
12.88	"Low down in the Broom" (2. of: Folk Songs of England, Vol.V of 1912, collab Robins) ....
12.89	"Maiden's Lament, The" (8. of: Folksongs from Newfoundland, Vol.I of 1934) ....
12.90	"Maid of Islington, The" (12. of: Folk Songs of England, Vol.V of 1912, collab Robins) ....
12.91	"Mannin Veen" (Dear Mona) (c1913, Manx trad) ....
12.92	"Maria Marten" (The Red Barn) (used in: Norfolk Rhapsody No.3) ....
12.93	"May-Day Carol" (5. of: 8 Traditional English Carol of 1919) ....
12.94	"May Song" (incl in cantata: Folk Songs of the Four Seasons of 1949) ....
12.95	"Mermaid, The" (c1921) ....
12.96	"Miraculous Harvest, The" (10. of: 12 Traditional Carols from Herefordshire of 1920) ....
12.97	"Morgenstern, Der" (incl in: Two Old German Songs: see: Entlaubet ist der Walde & Wanderlied) ....
12.98	"Morning Dew, The" (10. of: Folksongs from Newfoundland, Vol.I of 1934) ....
12.99	"Mummers' Carol" (3. of: 9 Carols of 1942) ....
12.100	"My Boy Biilly" (7. of: Folksongs for Schools of 1912) ....
12.101	"New Year's Carol" (7. of: 12 Traditional Carols from Herefordshire of 1920) ....
12.102	"On Board a Ninety-Eight" (7. of: Folksongs from the Eastern Counties of 1908, from Norfolk) ....
12.103	"On Christmas Day" (All in the morning) (1. of: 8 Traditional English Carols of 1919; 8. of: 12 Traditional Carols from Herefordshire of 1920) ....
12.104	"On Christmas Night" (2. of: 8 Traditional English Carols of 1919; 24. of: The Oxford Book of Carols of 1929, w/ Shaw) ....
12.105	"One Man, Two Men" (3. of: 6 English Folksongs of 1935) ....
12.106	"Our Captain Calls" (used in The Arming of Christian in stage work: The Pilgrim's Progress) ....
12.107	"O Who is that raps at my Window?" (5. of: Folk Songs of England, Vol.V of 1912, collab Robins) ....
12.108	"Painful Plough, The" (11. of: Folksongs for Schools of 1912) ....
12.109	"Paradis, Le" (c1952, French) ....
12.110	"Ploughman, The" (2. of: 6 English Folksongs of 1935) ....
12.111	"Pretty Ploughboy, The" (4. of: Folk Songs of England, Vol.V of 1912, collab Robins) ....
12.112	"Proud Nancy" (9. of: Folksongs from Newfoundland, Vol.I of 1934) ....
12.113	"Quand le rossignol" (c1904, French) ....
12.114	"Que Dieu se montre seulement" (c1904, Huguenot battle-hymn) ....
12.115	"Réveillez-vous, Piccars" (c1903, 15th cent French battle-song transl England) ....
12.116	"Robin Hood and the Pedlar" (1. of: 6 English Folksongs of 1935) ....
12.117	"Rolling in the Dew" (5. of: 6 English Folksongs of 1935) ....
12.118	"Saucy bold Robber, The" (10. of: Folksongs from the Eastern Counties of 1908, from Norfolk) ....
12.119	"Saviour's Love, The" (11. of: 12 Traditional Carols from Herefordshire of 1920) ....
12.120	"Searching for Lambs" (1. of: 2 English Folksongs of 1935; w/ vn) ....
12.121	"Seeds of Love, The" (11. of: Folk Songs of England, Vol.V of 1912, collab Robins) ....
12.122	"Servantman and husbandman" (3. of Folksongs for Schools of 1912) ....
12.123	"Seven Virgins, The" (Under the leaves) (12. of: 12 Traditional Carols from Herefordshire of 1920) ....
12.124	"Sheep-shearing, The" ....
12.125	"Sheffield Apprentice, The" (13. of: Folksongs from the Eastern Counties of 1908, from Norfolk) ....
12.126	"She's like the Swallow" (8. of: Folksongs from Newfoundland, Vol.II of 1934) ....
12.127	"Snow in the Street": "From far away we come" (186. of: The Oxford Book of Carols of 1928, collab Shaw)
12.128	"Spanish Ladies, The" (p1912) ....
12.129	"Spring of Thyme, The" (incl in cantata: Folk Songs of the Four Seasons of 1949) ....
12.130	"Springtime of the Year, The" (2. of: 5 English Folksongs of 1913) ....
12.131	"Spurn Point" (used in: Norfolk Rhapsody No.2) ....
12.132	"Summer is a-coming in" (incl in: London Pageant of 1911) ....
12.133	"Sweet William's Ghost" (1. of: Folksongs from Newfoundland, Vol.I of 1934) ....

12.134   "Tarry Trowsers" (2. of: Folksongs from the Eastern Counties, of 1908, from Essex) ....
12.135   "There is a Fountain" (used in: Fantasia on Christmas Carols) ....
12.136   "There is a Flower" (2. of: 2 Carols of 1945) ....
12.137   "Think of Me" (c1903, German transl Ferguson) ....
12.138   "Three Gaelic Songs" (c1954): 1. "Dawn on the hills" ....
12.139   2. "Come let us gather cockles"
12.140   3. "Wake and rise"
12.141   "Thresherman and the Squire, The" (3. of: Folk Songs of England, Vol.V of 1912) ....
12.142   "Tobacco's but an Indian weed" (c ?1934) ....
12.143   "To the Ploughboy" (incl in cantata: Folk Songs of the Four Seasons of 1949) ....
12.144   "Truth sent from Above, The" (6. of: 8 Traditional English Carols of 1919) ....
12.145   "Turkish Lady, The" (10. of: Folk Songs of England, Vol.V of 1912, collab Robins) ....
12.146   "Turtle Dove, The" (c1919) ....
12.147   "Twelve Apostles, The" (3. of: 8 Traditional English Carols of 1919) ....

12.148   "Virgin Most Pure, A" (8. of: 9 Carols of 1942) ....

12.149   "Wanderlied" (c1902, 2. in: Two Old German Songs, Eng text Ford) ....
12.150   "Ward the Pirate" (9. of: Folksongs from the Eastern Counties; 32. of: Folksongs, Vol.II of 1935) ....
12.151   "Wassail Song" (5. of: 5 English Folksongs of 1913; 8. in: 8 Traditional English Carols of 1919) ....
12.152   "We be three Poor Marines" (8. of: Motherland Songbook, Vol.II of 1919) ....
12.153   "World it went Well, The" (c ?1934) ....
12.154   "Winter is Gone, The" (10. of: Folksongs from Newfoundland, Vol.II of 1934) ....

12.155   "Young Floro" (9. of: Folksongs from Newfoundland, Vol.II of 1934) ....
12.156   "Young Henry the Poacher" (used in: Norfolk Rhapsody No.2) ....

         Contributions to "The Oxford Book of Carols" (p1928, text ed Dearmer, music R.V.W. & Shaw):

12.157   orig tunes: 173. "The Golden Carol": "Now is Christèmas y-come" (trad) ....
12.158   185. "Wither's Rocking Hymn": "Sweet baby, sleep! What ails my dear?" (Wither).............................
12.159   186. "Snow in the Street": "From far away we come to you" (Morris) ....
12.160   196. "Blake's Cradle Song": "Sweet dreams, form a shade o'er my lovely infant's head" (Blake) ....
12.161   arrs: 7. "Hereford Carol": "Come all you faithful Christians" ....
12.162   17. "All in the morning": "It was on Christmas Day" ....
12.163   24. "Sussex Carol": "On Christmas night" ....
12.164   31. "Gloucestershire": "Wassail, wassail, all over the town!" ....
12.165   36. "The Salutation Carol": "Nowell, This is the salutation" ....
12.166   39. "This endris night": "This endris night I saw a sight" ....
12.167   43. "The Seven Virgins": "All under the leaves, the leaves of life" ....
12.168   45. "Sussex Mummers' Carol": "O mortal man, remember well" ....
12.169   47. "May Carol": "Awake, awake, good people all" ....
12.170   51. "The Sinners' Redemption": "All you that are to mirth inclined" ....
12.171   53. "The Carnal and the Crane": "As I passed by a riverside" ....
12.172   55. "The Miraculous Harvest": "Rise up, rise up, you merry men all" ....
12.173   57. "Dives and Lazarus": "As it fell out upon one day" ....
12.174   61. "Down in yon forest": "Down in yon forest there stands a hall" ....
12.175   68. "The truth from above": "This is the truth sent from above" ....
12.176   77. "Song of the Crib": "Joseph dearest, Joseph mine" ....
12.177   79. "Quem pastores laudavere": "Quem pastores laudavere" ....
12.178   115. "Joseph and Mary": "O Joseph being an old man truly" ....
12.179   131. "Coverdale's Carol": "Now blessed be thou, Christ Jesu" ....
12.180   132. "Psalm of Sion": "O mother dear, Jerusalem" ....
12.181   134. "If ye would hear": "If ye would hear the angels sing" (w/ Shaw) ....
12.182   138. "O little town": "O little town of Bethlehem" ....
12.183   142. "Children's Song of the nativity": "How far is it to Bethlehem" ....
12.184   Appendix: folk tunes proper to carols in Part I (arr Vaughan Williams): 1. "A Virgin most pure" (4.) ....
12.185   2. "On Christmas Night" (24.) ....
12.186   3. "The Moon shines bright" (46.) ....
12.187   4. "The Holy Well" (56.) ....
12.188   5. "Dives and Lazarus" (57.) ....
12.189   6. "Come all ye worthy Christian men" (60.) ....

         "A Yacre of Land" (ed I. Holst & Ursula V.W. 1961, from manuscript collection of Vaughan Williams):

12.190   1. "A Yacre of Land" ....
12.191   2. "John Reilly" ....
12.192   3. "The Week Before Easter" ....
12.193   4. "Willie Foster" ....
12.194   5. "The Jolly Harin' " ....
12.195   6. "Nine Joys of Mary" ....
12.196   7. "Joseph and his Wedded Wife" ....
12.197   8. "The Lord of Life" ....
12.198   9. "Over the hills and mountains" ....
12.199   10. "The Foxhunt" ....
12.200   11. "Come all you young ploughboys" ....
12.201   12. "A Bold Young Sailor" ....
12.202   13. "The Pretty Ploughboy" ....

12.203	14. "Seventeen Come Sunday" ....
12.204	15. "It was one Morning" ....
12.205	16. "My coffin shall be black" ....

"English Folk Songs from the Southern Appalachian Mountains" (p1967, ed Karpeles):

12.206	incl 9 arrs by Vaughan Williams (ca1938; 1v & pf): 1A. "The Elfin Knight" (The Lovers' Tasks) ....
12.207	7H. "Lord Randal" ....
12.208	19M. "Lord Thomas and Fair Ellinor" ....
12.209	20L. "Fair Margaret and Sweet William" ....
12.210	24M. "Barbara Allen" ....
12.211	35M. "The Daemon Lover" (The House Carpenter) ....
12.212	55A. "The Rich Old Lady" ....
12.213	206B. "The Tree in the Wood" ....
12.214	207D. "The Ten Commandments" (The Twelve Apostles) ....

Misc folk-dance arrs:

12.215	"Minehead Hobby-Horse" (orch) ....
12.216	"Mr. Isaacs Maggot" (c1924; cl, pf, triangle & strings) ....
12.217	"Phil the Flutter's Dancing" (fl & strings) ....

13. CONTRIBUTIONS TO HYMNALS & HYMN-TUNES (arrs & editions)

Purcell Society. The Works of H. Purcell, Vol.XV, "Welcome Songs," Part I (p1906, ed Vaughan Williams):

13.1	1. "Welcome, Viceregent of the mighty King" ....
13.2	2. "Swifter, Isis, swifter flow" ....
13.3	3. "What shall be done on behalf of the man" ....
13.4	4. "The summer's absence unconcerned we bear" ....
13.5	5. "Fly, bold Rebellion" ....

"The English Hymnal" (p1906):

13.6	orig tunes: 152. "Come down, O love Divine" ....
13.7	524. "God be with you till we meet again" ....
13.8	624. "Hail thee, Festival day" ....
13.9	641. "For all the Saints" ....
13.10	arrs of tunes derived from folksongs (w/ copyright): 15. "O Little Town of Bethlehem" ....
13.11	23. "Hark! How all the welkin rings" ....
13.12	186. "Come, let us join the church above" ....
13.13	239. "Saints of God! Lo Jesu's people" ....
13.14	295. " 'Tis winter now, the fallen snow" ....
13.15	299. "When spring unlocks the flowers to paint the laughing soil" ....
13.16	385. "Father hear the prayer we offer" ....
13.17	402. "He who would valiant be" ....
13.18	525. "From Thee all skill and science flow" ....
13.19	562. "O God of earth and altar" ....
13.20	572. "I could not do without Thee" ....
13.21	594. "I love to hear the story" ....
13.22	595. "I think when I read that sweet story of old" ....
13.23	597. "It is a thing most wonderful" ....
13.24	607. "There's a friend for little children" ....
13.25	611. "When Christ was born in Bethlehem" ....
13.26	arrs of tunes (w/ out copyright): 7. "Lo! He comes with clouds descending" ....
13.27	16. "The maker of the sun and moon" ....
13.28	20. "Behold the great Creator" ....
13.29	29. "The great God of heaven" ....
13.30	42. "O worship the Lord in the beauty of holiness" ....
13.31	89. "Soul of Jesus, make me whole" ....
13.32	90. "To my humble supplication" ....
13.33	145. "See the Conqueror mounts in triumph" ....
13.34	212. "I bind unto myself today" ....
13.35	213. "Hail, O star that pointest" ....
13.36	221. "The winter's sleep was long and deep" ....
13.37	249. "O Saviour Jesu, not alone" ....
13.38	268. "God, that madest earth and heaven" ....
13.39	275. "Sweet Saviour, bless us ere we go" ....
13.40	294. "The year is swiftly waning" ....
13.41	308. "Father, see Thy children" ....
13.42	317. "Laud, O Sion, thy salvation" ....
13.43	326. "Of the glorious Body telling" ....
13.44	344. "Thine for ever! God of love" ....
13.45	355. "In Paradise reposing" ....
13.46	379. "Come unto me, ye weary" ....
13.47	388. "Fierce was the wild billow" ....
13.48	389. "Fight the good fight" ....

13.49	390. "Firmly I believe and truly" ....
13.50	417. "Jesu, my Lord, my God, my All" ....
13.51	437. "Love Divine, all loves excelling" ....
13.52	448. "O God of mercy, God of might" ....
13.53	485. "Teach me my God and King" ....
13.54	488. "The church of God a Kingdom is" ....
13.55	490. "The King of Love my shepherd is" ....
13.56	498. "There is a land of pure delight" ....
13.57	514. "Who is this so weak and helpless" ....
13.58	574. "I heard the voice of Jesus say" ....
13.59	579. "Rest of the weary" ....
13.60	591. "Gentle Jesus, meek and mild" ....
13.61	599. "Jesu, tender Shepherd, hear me" ....
13.62	601. "Lord, I would own Thy tender care" ....
13.63	606. "Sing to the Lord the children's hymn" ....
13.64	609. "Through the night Thy angels kept" ....
13.65	638. "Jerusalem, my happy home" ....
13.66	654. "God the Father, God the Son" ....
13.67	656. "See Him in raiment rent" ....
13.68	harmonizations not attrib until the 1933 edition: 18. "From east to west, from shore to shore" ....
13.69	38. "Why, impious Herod" ....
13.70	65. "The fast, as taught by holy lore" ....
13.71	123. "The day draws on with golden light" ....
13.72	125. "The Lamb's high banquet we await" ....
13.73	129. "Christ the Lord is risen again!" ....
13.74	159. "Be present, Holy Trinity" ....
13.75	165. "Father, we praise Thee" ....
13.76	181. "O God, Thy soldiers' crown and guard" ....
13.77	208. "All prophets hail Thee" ....
13.78	242. "Christ, the fair glory" ....
13.79	480. "Soldiers who are Christ's below" ....
13.80	653. "God the Father, God the Word" ....

"The English Hymnal" (p1907, hymns 189., 195., 208., 213. & 250. moved to Part III of the Appendix):

13.81	. "Church Songs" (p1911, collected Baring-Gould, music arr Sheppard & Vaughan Williams: 1.–9., 11.–13., 15.–17., 19.–21., 23.–25.) ....

"Songtime" (rhymes, songs, games, hymns for all occasions in a child's life) (p1915, ed Dearmer):

13.82	incl: 1. "An Acre of Land" ....
13.83	2. "Quem pastores" ....
13.84	3. "Hymns" (from:The English Hymnal): 595. (East Horrdon) ....
13.85	599. (Shipston) ....
13.86	606. (St. Hugh) ....

"Motherland Songbook," I (p1919; unison ch & m ch):

13.87	harmonizations: 13. "O God of earth and altar" ....

"Motherland Songbook," II (p1919, ed Vaughan Williams)

"Motherland Songbook," III (p1919):

13.88	arrs: 1. "The Arethusa" ....
13.89	5. "Full fathom five" ....
13.90	6. "Jack the sailor" ....
13.91	8. "We be three poor marines" ....

"Motherland Songbook," IV (p1919):

13.92	arrs: 1. "The Golden Vanity" ....
13.93	3. "Just as the tide was flowing" ....
13.94	9. "The Spanish Lads" ....

"League of Nations Song Book" (p1921):

13.95	arrs of hymns: 5. "Pilgrim Song" (Monk's Gate) ....
13.96	8. "Chesterton's Hymn" (King's Lynn) ....

24 "Hymns" (p1921, selected from The English Hymnal):

13.97	arrs: 402. "Monk's Gate" ....
13.98	641. "Sine Nomine" ....

"Songs of Praise" (p1925, words ed Dearmer, music ed Vaughan Williams):

13.99	orig tunes: 37. "Magda": "Saviour, again to Thy dear name" ....
13.100	41. "Oakley": "The night is come like to the day" ....
13.101	110. "Sine Nomine": "For all the saints" (first pubd in The English Hymnal) ....

13.102	123. "Cumnor": "Servants of God, or sons" (first pubd in The English Hymnal) ....
13.103	185. "Guildford": "England, arise! The long, long night is over" ....
13.104	217. "Down Ampney": "Come down, O love divine" (first pubd in The English Hymnal of 1906) ....
13.105	406. "Randolph": "God be with you till we meet again" (first pubd in The English Hymnal)..................
13.106	443. "King's Weston": "At the name of Jesus" ....
13.107	445. "Salve Festa Dies": "Hail, Thee, Festival Day" (first pubd in The English Hymnal) ....
13.108	arrs of tunes (not in Hymnal): 12. "Danby": " 'Tis winter now; the fallen snow" ....
13.109	51. "Macht Hoch die Thür": "It was the calm and silent night!" ....
13.110	163. "Valor": "O valiant hearts" ....
13.111	182. "Ach! Wan Doch Jesu, Liebster mein": "Through all the long dark night of years" ....
13.112	200. "Eventide": "Abide with me" ....
13.113	226. "Regina": "Dear Lord and Father of mankind" ....
13.114	246. "Crüger": "Hail to the Lord's Anointed" ....
13.115	249. "Freuen wir uns": "Hark my soul! it is the Lord" ....
13.116	293. "Wächterlied": "Lord Christ, when first Thou can'st to men" ....
13.117	296. "Il Buon Pastor": "Lord of health, Thou life within us"..
13.118	327. "Engadine": "O most mighty, O most holy" ....
13.119	330. "Londonderry": "O son of man, our hero strong and tender" ....
13.120	352. "Essex": "Say not the struggle nought availeth" ....
13.121	353. "Milites": "Soldiers of Christ, arise"...
13.122	372. "St. Gabriel": "Then welcome each rebuff" ....
13.123	408. "Mariners": "Lord, in the hollow of Thy hand"..
13.124	415. "O mentes perfidas": "Thy Kingdom come, O God" ....
13.125	438. "Hardwick": "So here hath been dawning" ....
13.126	440. "Bamberg": The year's at the spring" (also see Beach Op.44/1, B17/1 & Ives Ky2) ....
13.127	442. "Resonet in laudibus": "Who within that stable cries" ....

"Songs of Praise for Boys and Girls" (p1929, ed Dearmer, Vaughan Williams & Shaw):

13.128	orig tunes: 95. "Marathon": "Servants of the great adventure" (in incid music: The Wasps) ....
13.129	arrs: 1. "Hardwick": "So here hath been dawning" ....
13.130	5. "Horsham": "Through the night thy angels kept" ....
13.131	8. "Shipston": "Jesus, tender Shepherd, hear me" ....
13.132	9. "Tavistock": "Matthew, Mark and Luke and John" ....
13.133	13. "Banbury": "The year's at the spring" ....
13.134	23. "Rodmell": "When Christ was born in Bethlehem" ....
13.135	27. "Come, Faithful People": "Come, faithful people, come away" ....
13.136	29. "Bridgwater" (Langport): "See Him in raiment rent" ....
13.137	33. "Solothurn": "Around the Throne of God" ....
13.138	56. "Monk's Gate": "He who would valiant be" ....
13.139	57. "Pleading Saviour": "Heavenly Father, send Thy blessing" ....
13.140	58. "Stowey": "How far is it to Bethlehem? Not very far" ....
13.141	60. "East Horndon": "I think, when I read that sweet story of old" ....
13.142	64. "Herongate": "It is a thing most wonderful" ....
13.143	65. "Quem pastores laudavere": "Jesu, good above all other" ....
13.144	69. "Eardisley": "Lord, I would own Thy tender care" ....
13.145	72. "Hambridge": "O dear and lovely brother" ....
13.146	76. "St. Hugh": "Sing to the Lord the children's hymn"...
13.147	80. "Gosterwood": "The wise may bring their learning" ....
13.148	83. "Epsom": "To Mercy, Pity, Peace and Love" (also see 9. of: 10 Blake Songs) ....
13.149	93. "Resonet in laudibus": "Who within that stable cries" ....
13.150	94. "Magdalena": "Remember all the people" ....
13.151	105. "Magdalena": "We thank Thee, Loving Father" ....
13.152	109. "St. Austin" (Farnham): "O mother dear, Jerusalem" ....

"Hymns for Today," Missionary and Devotional (p1930):

13.153	arrs: 36. "Monk's Gate": "He who would valiant be"..
13.154	79. "Sine Nomine": "For all the saints" ....

14 "Hymns for Sunday School Anniversaries" (p1930, ed Vaughan Williams, Shaw, Dearmer & Briggs):

13.155	c by Vaughan Williams: 12. "Down Ampney": "Come down, O love divine" ....

"Songs of Praise" (p1931, enlarged edition):

13.156	add hymn arrs: 226. "Regina": "Dear Lord and Father of Mankind"...
13.157	330. "Londonderry": "O son of man" ....
13.158	427. "East Horndon": "I think when I read that sweet story of old" ....
13.159	orig tunes: 126. "Mantegna": "Into the woods my master went" ....
13.160	302. "Marathon": "Servants of the great adventure" (in incid music: The Wasps) ....
13.161	319. "Abinger": "I vow to thee my Country" ....
13.162	432. "Famous Men": "Let us now praise famous men" ....
13.163	489. White Gates: "Fierce raged the tempest" ....
13.164	new arrs: 59. "Ah! think not, 'The Lord delayeth' " ....
13.165	65. "Lo He comes" ....
13.166	164. "Sing, brothers, sing and praise your King!" ....
13.167	205. "Hail, glorious spirits"..

13.168	232. "Look up, by failure daunted" ....
13.169	353. "Away in a manger" ....
13.170	393. "City of Peace, our mother dear" ....

"Songs of Praise for Little Children" (p1932):

13.171	arrs: 14. "Hardwick": "So here hath been dawning" ....

"The English Hymnal" (p1933, revised edition):

13.172	added tunes & settings: 18. "Rouen": "From East to West" ....
13.173	58. "O Invidenda Martyrum": "O Boundless Wisdom" ....
13.174	59. "O Invidenda Martyrum": "O Boundless Wisdom" ....
13.175	60. "O Invidenda Martyrum": "O Boundless Wisdom" ....
13.176	91. "Valor": "Weary of earth" ....
13.177	157. "Wicklow": "Our blest redeemer" ....
13.178	273. "Magda": "Saviour, again to Thy dear name" ....
13.179	368. "King's Weston": "At the name of Jesus" ....
13.180	541. "White Gates": "Fierce raged the tempest" ....
13.181	638. "Stalham" (Dunstan): "Jerusalem, my happy home" ....

"Songs of Praise for Little Children" (p1933):

13.182	arrs: 37. "Resonet in Laudibus": "Who within that stable cries" ....
13.183	44. "Forest Green": "O little town of Bethlehem" ....
13.184	45. "Rodmell": "When Christ was born in Bethlehem" ....
13.185	68. "Monk's Gate": "He who would valiant be" ....
13.186	87. "Sine Nomine": "For all the Saints" ....
13.187	113. "White Gates": "Fierce raged the tempest" ....
13.188	135. "Hardwick": "So here hath been dawning" ....
13.189	147. "Randolph": "God be with you till we meet again" ....
13.190	settings to prayers: . "Tuesday": "Almighty God, whose service is perfect freedom" ....
13.191	. "Wednesday": "O God, grant me this day" ....
13.192	. "Thursday": "Eternal Father, who hast called us" ....

"The Daily Service," prayers & hymns for schools (p1936, collab w/ others):

13.193	arrs: 50. "Forest Green": "O little town of Bethlehem" ....
13.194	51. "Rodmell": "When Christ was born in Bethlehem" ....
13.195	90. "Wicklow": "Our blest Redeemer" ....
13.196	91. "Down Ampney": "Come down, O Love Divine" ....
13.197	97. "Sine Domine": "For all the saints" ....
13.198	124. "White Gates": "Fierce raged the tempest" ....
13.199	148. "Hardwick": "So here hath been dawning" ....
13.200	155. "Magda": "Saviour, again to Thy dear name" ....
13.201	164. "Randolph": "God be with you till we meet again" ....
13.202	. "Amen VI" ....
13.203	prayers: 1. "Almighty God, whose service is perfect freedom" ....
13.204	2. "O God, grant me this day" ....
13.205	3. "Eternal Father, who hast called us" ....
13.206	4. "Unto Him that loved us" ....

"Songs of Praise: The Children's Church" (p1936, an order of morning & evening prayer):

13.207	hymns: 87. "Sine Nomine": "For all the saints" ....
13.208	113. "White Gates": "Fierce raged the tempest" ....
13.209	114. "Randolph": "God be with you till we meet again" ....

"The Penguin Book of English Folk Songs," 70 folksongs (ed Vaughan Williams & Lloyd 1959):

13.210	from Vaughan Williams collection: . "All Things are quite silent" ....
13.211	. "Basket of Eggs, The" ....
13.212	. "Blacksmith, The" ....
13.213	. "Broomfield Hill" ....
13.214	. "Devil and the Ploughman, The" ....
13.215	. "Fare thee well, my dearest dear" ....
13.216	. "Green Bed, The" ....
13.217	. "Lovely Joan" ....
13.218	. "Man of Burningham Town, The" ....
13.219	. "On Monday Morning" ....
13.220	. "The Outlandish Knight, The" ....
13.221	. "Oxford City" ....
13.222	. "Ploughman, The" ....
13.223	. "Ratcliffe Highway" ....
13.224	. "Robin Hood and the Pedlar" ....
13.225	. "Sailor in the North Country, A" ....
13.226	. "Salisbury Plain" ....
13.227	. "Young and Single Sailor, The" ....
13.228	. "Young Edwin in the Lowlands Low" ....

14. MISC WORKS (frags in sketch-books)

14.1   *Fragments in a sketch-book (c1897–1902):* ....
         1. Setting of M. Arnold: Dover Beach (compl1899) (also see Barber Op.3)
         2. Horn Sonata (Slow movt, Scherzo & Finale)
         3. "Dirge" (orch, ?incorp in: Heroic Elegy & Triumphal Epilogue)
         4. "Rhapsody" (?sketch for: Symphonic Rhapsody)
         5. "Dramatic March" (?incorp in: Heroic Elegy & Triumphal Epilogue)
         6. Cor anglais tune for 'Ozymandias'
         7. Words for Swinburne: Before the frost
         8. Viola piece
         9. Sketches for: Let us now praise famous men
         10. Ballet tune
         11. "Linden Lea" (tune complete as song)
14.2   *Sketch-books and frags of manuscripts (to1914, not incl sketch-books for: A Sea Symphony)* ....
      A: 1. "Charles Wesley": "Come O thou traveller inknown"
          2. "The Call" (Herbert)
          3. Analysis of Fugue at end of Glazunov's Symphony No.6 in C minor, Op.58
          4. "Clun," song (last verse)
          5. "Rise heart," chorus parts
      B: . Sketch of "Saraband—Helen" (Marlowe's Was this the face; T, ch & orch)
14.3   *Late sketch-books (w/ incomplete works):* ....
      . Settings of Graves's Star Talk: "Are you awake, Gemelli ...?"
      . Settings of Chesterton's In Praise of Wine: "The wine they drink in Paradise"
      . Themes for a string quartet
      . Notes for opera: Belshazzar
      . Sketches for a 'Vibraphone piece'
      . "Exsultate Jubilate" (d ch)
      . "London Calling"
      . "Romance" (org)
      . Sketches of pf continuo for 4 numbers in J. S. Bach: St. Matthew Passion, BWV244
      . Introduction to a masque
      . Folk songs
      . "Prelude" (org)
      . Military march
      . Symphony
      . Sketches for a symphony

15. ARRANGEMENTS OF WORKS OF OTHERS

Juvenilia (1878–95):

15.1   Beethoven: Piano Sonata No.4 in E-flat major, Op.7 (arr1892; orch) ....
15.2   Beethoven: "Largo Appassionato," from: Piano Sonata No.2 in A major, Op.2/2 (arr1892; orch) ....

Mature:

15.3   Purcell: "Welcome Songs" (Purcell Society. The Works of H. Purcel, Vol.XVIII, Part II) (ed1910): 6. "The
        Welcome Song of 1684": "From those serene and rapturous joys" ....
15.4   7. "The Welcome Song of 1685": "Why, why, are all the muses mute?"
15.5   8. "The Welcome Song of 1686": "Ye tuneful muses"
15.6   9. "The Welcome Song of 1687": "Sound the trumpet"
15.7   Purcell: "Evening Hymn," Z193 (arr1912; 1v & strings) ....
15.8   Purcell: "Full Fathom Five," Z631/6b (p1919; see 5. in: Motherland Songbook III) ....
15.9   Purcell: "Our love goes out to English skies," from: The Indian Queen, Z630 (arr1920; ch & strings) ....
15.10   Boyce: "Heart of Oak" (arr1921; unison ch & pf, also for m ch) ....
15.11   Dibolin: "The Lass that Loves a Sailor" (ed & arr1921; S, unison ch/ch & pf) ....
15.12   Foster: "Old Folks at Home" (arr1921; Bar & ch) ....
15.13   Bach, J. S.: Mass in B minor, BWV232 (25 Vocal Exercises 1924, collab Sichel) ....
15.14   Bach, J. S.: "The 'Giant' Fugue," in D minor (arr1925; strings, collab Foster) ....
15.15   Bach, J. S.: "Ach, Bleib bei uns" (free arr1932; pf): No.1 "Choral" (Lento)...
15.16   No.2 "Choral Prelude" (Andante tranquillo, quasi notturno)
15.17   Dvořák: "Te Deum," Op103 (English adaptation 1937) ....
15.18   Meyerbeer: "The Blessing of the Swords," from opera: Hugenots (arr1942; ch & orch) ....
15.19   Bach, J. S.: "Schmücke dich, o liebe Seele" (arr1956; vc & strings) ....
15.20   Hadley: "Fen and Flood," cantata (arr1956; S, Bar & ch, text: Cudworth) ....

* * * * *

VERDI, Giuseppe (Fortunino Francesco)
1813–1901

1. STAGE WORKS (operas)

1.1   "Oberto, conte di San Bonifacio," 2 act dramma (p1839, Solera after Piazza's libretto: Rocester) ....
1.2   "Un giorno di regno, ossia Il finto Stanislao" (King for a Day), 2 act melodramma giocoso (p1840, Romani)
1.3   "Nabucodonosor" (Nabucco), 4 part dramma lirico (p1842, Solera from Cortesi's ballet) ....
1.4   "I Lombardi alla prima Crociata," 4 act dramma lirico (p1843, Solera after Grossi's romance of 1826) ....
1.5   "Ernani," 4 part dramma lirico (p1844, Piave after Hugo's play: Hernani of 1830; the name of the opera
         changed for a time by Austrian censors to: The Pirates of Venice) ('Viva Verdi' used by the Risorgimento
         movement as the acronym for the nationalist cry: Viva Vittorio Emanuele Re d'Italia) ....
1.6   "I due Foscari," 3 act tragedia lirica (p1844, Piave after Byron's play: The Two Foscari of 1821) ....
1.7   "Giovanna d'Arco" (Joan of Arc), 4 act dramma lirico (p1845, Solera after Schiller's Die Jungfrau von
         Orleans of 1801; for a time title changed to: Oriette of Lesbos, see note in opera: Ernani) ....
1.8   "Alzira," 2 act tragedia lirica (p1845, Cammarano after Voltaire's play: Alzire of 1736) ....
1.9   "Attila," 3 act dramma lirico (p1846, Solera & Piave after Werner's play of 1808) ....
1.10   "Macbeth," 4 acts (p1847, Piave & Maffei after Shakespeare; r1865 in French transl Nuitter) (also see
         opera c by Bloch; incid music c by Bacewicz, Khachaturian, Milhaud Op.175, Spohr WoO 55 & Sullivan)
1.11   "I Masnadieri," 4 part tragic opera (p1847, Maffei after Schiller's play: Die Räuber of 1781).......................
1.12   "Jérusalem," 4 acts (p1847, Royer & Vaëz based on Solera's libretto for: I Lombardi of 1843) ....
1.13   "Il Corsaro," 3 act (p1848, Piave after Byron's poem: The Corsair of 1814) (also see Berlioz: Ouverture
         du Corsaire, Op.21, H101, ballet Il Corsaro in Donizetti's opera: Belisario, Schumann's opera:
         Der Corsar & Wolf: Ouvertüre zu Byrons 'Der Korsar')
1.14   "La battaglia di Legnano," 4 act tragedia lirica (p1849, Cammarano after Méry's La Bataille of 1828) ....
1.15   "Luisa Miller," 3 act melodramma tragico (p1849, Cammarano after Schiller's Kabale und Liebe of 1784) ..
1.16   "Stiffelio," 3 acts (p1850, Piave after Souvestre & Bourgeois's play: Le Pasteur) ....
1.17   "Rigoletto" (La Maledizione), 3 act melodramma (p1851, Piave after Hugo's play: Le Roi s'amuse of 1832)
1.18   "Il Trovatore" (The Troubadour), 4 part dramma (p1853, Cammarano after Gutiérrez's play: El Trovador) ..
1.19   "La Traviata" (The Fallen Woman), 3 acts (p1853, Piave after Dumas fils play: La Dame aux camélias) .....
1.20   "Les Vêpres siciliennes" (I vespri siciliani), 5 acts (p1855, Scribe & Duveyrier from libretto for
         Donizetti: Le duc d'Albe) ....
1.21   "Simon Boccanegra," 3 acts (p1857, r1881, Piave after Gutiérrez's play: Simon Bocanegra of 1843) ....
1.22   "Aroldo," 4 acts (p1857, Piave from libretto for: Stiffelio of 1850)...
1.23   "Un ballo in maschera," 3 acts (p1859, Somma from Scribe's libretto for Auber's play: Gustave III of 1833)
1.24   "La forza del destino," 4 acts (p1862, r1869, Piave after Saavedra's play: Don Alvaro of 1835) ....
1.25   "Don Carlo" (Don Carlos), 5 acts (p1867, r1884, Méry & Du Locle after Schiller's play: Don Carlos of 1787)
1.26   "Aida," 4 acts (p1871, Ghislanzoni from Mariette's scenario reworked by Du Locle) ....
1.27   "Otello," 4 act dramma lirico (p1887, Boito after Shakespeare) (also see opera c by Rossini & film score
         c by Khachaturian) ....
1.28   "Falstaff," 3 acts (p1893, Boito after Shakespeare's plays: The Merry Wives of Windsor & Henry IV
         Part I & II) ....

1a. SELECTIONS FROM STAGE WORKS (Nos. of sections in The Gramophone)

1a.1   "Oberto, conte di San Bonifacio," opera: ....
         excerpts: 1. "Overture"
         I: 2a. "Di vermiglia, amabil luce" (ch)
               2b. "Son fra voi! Già parmi udire il fremito" (Riccardo)
               3a. "Ah, sgombro è il loco alfin" (Eleonora)
               3b. "Sotto il paterno tetto" (Eleonora)
               3c. "Oh, potesi nel mio core"
               4. "Oh patria terra, alfina io lti rivedo" (Oberto)
               5a. "Al cader della notte"
               5b. "Guardami! sul mio ciglio"
               5c. "Non ti basto il periglio"
               5d. "Del tuo favour soccorrimi" (Eleonora)
               5e. "Un amplesso riceri, o pentita"
               6. "Findanzata avventurosa" (ch)
               7a. "Basta, basta, o fedeli!" (Cuniza)
               7b. "Cuniza, ah parmi"
               7c. "Il pensier d'amore felice" (Cuniza)
               7d. "Fra il timpre è la speme"
               8. "Alta cagione adunque" (Imelda)
               9. "A, perchè tanto in petto"
               10a. "Son io stresso! A te davanti"
               10b. "Su quella fronte impressa" (Oberto)
               11a. "A me gli amici! Mira!"
               11b. "A quell' aspetto un fremito"
         II: 12. "Infelice! Nel core tradito" (ch)
               13a. "Riccardo! E che gli resta?"
               13b. "Oh, chi torna l'ardente pensiero" (Cuniza)
               13c. "Più che i vezzi e lo splendore"
               14. "Dov'è l'astro che nel cielo" (ch)
               15a. "Ei tarda ancor!" (Oberto)
               15b. "L'orror del tradimento" (Oberto)
               15c. "Ma tu, superbo giovane"

8. "Attila!... Oh, il nobil messo!"
9. "Trado per gli anni, e tremulo" (Ezio)
10. "Vanitosi!"
11. "Qual notte!" (ch)
12. "L'alito del mattin ... Preghiam!"
13. "Quai voci!"
14. "Ella in poter del barbaro!" (Foresto)
15. "Cara patria"
I: 16a. "Liberamente or piangi" (Odabella)
16b. "Oh! nel fuggente nuvolo" (Odabella)
17. "Qual suon di passi!" (Odabella)
18a. "Sì, quell'io son ravvisami" (Foresto)
18b. "Va! Racconta al sacrilego"
18c. "Oh! t'inebria nell'amplesso"
19a. "Uldino! Uldin!" (Attila)
19b. "Mentre gonfiarsi l'anima" (Attila)
19c. "Oltre a quel limite t'attendo"
20. "Parla, imponi" (ch)
21. "No!... non é sogno" (Attila)
II: 22a. "Tregua è cogl'Unni" (Ezio)
22b. "Dagl'immortali vertici" (Ezio)
22c. "Che vien?... Salute ad Ezio"
22d. "È gettata la mie sorte"
23a. "Del ciel l'immensa volta" (ch)
23b. "Ezio, ben vieni!"
23c. "Chi dona luce al cor?" (ch)
23d. "Oh, miei prodi!"
III: 24. "Qui del convegno è il loco" (Foresto)
25. "Che non avrebbe il misero" (Foresto)
26. "Che più s'indugia"
27. "Cessa, seh, cessa"
28. "Te sol, te sol quest'anima"
29. "Non involarti, seguimi"
30a. "Tu, rea donna"
30b. "Nella tenda"

1a.10 "Macbeth," opera: ....
excerpts: 1. "Prelude"
I: 2. "Che faceste? dite su!" (ch)
3a. "Giorno non vidi mai"
3b. "Due vaticini compiuto or sono"
4. "S'allontanarono!"
5a. "Nel dì della vittoria" (Lady Macbeth)
5b. "Vieni! t'affretta!" (Lady Macbeth)
5c. "Ambizioso spirto"
5d. "Or tutti sorgete"
6. "Oh donna mia!" (Macbeth)
7a. "Sappia la sposa mia" (Macbeth)
7b. "Regna il sonno"
7c. "Fatal mia donna!" (Macbeth)
8a. "Di destarlo per tempo" (Macduff)
8b. "Schiudi, inferno, la bocca"
II: 9a. "Perchè mi sfuggi" (Lady Macbeth)
9b. "La luce langue"
10. "Chi osò mandarvi a noi?"
11a. "Studia il passo" (Banco)
11b. "Come dal ciel precipita" (Banco)
12a. "Salve, o Re!" (ch)
12b. "Si colmi il calice" (Lady Macbeth)
12c. "Va' spirto d'abisso!"
III: 13. "Tre volte miagola la gatta" (ch)
14. "Ballet Music"
15a. "Finchè appelli"
15b. "Fuggi, regal fantasima" (Macbeth)
16. "Ondine e Silfidi"
17a. "Ove son io?"
17b. "Ora di morte"
IV: 18. "Patria oppressa!" (ch)
19a. "O figli, o figli miei!" (Macduff)
19b. "Ah, la paterna mano" (Macduff)
20. "Dove siam? che bosco è quello?"
21a. "Vegliammo in van due notti" (Medico)
21b. "Una macchia è qui tutt'ora" (Lady Macbeth)
22a. "Perfidi! All'Anglo contro me v'unite!" (Macbeth)
22b. "Pietà, rispetto, amore"

23. "Ella è morta!" (ch)
24. "Vittoria!" (Finale)

1a.11   "I Masnadieri," opera: ....
excerpts: 1. "Prelude"
I: 2a. "Quando io leggo in Plutarco" (Carlo)
     2b. "O mio castel paterno" (Carlo)
     3a. "Ecco un foglio"
     3b. "Nell'argilla maledetta"
     4a. "Vecchio! spiccai da te" (Francesco)
     4b. "La sua lampada vitale" (Francesco)
     5a. "Trionfo, trionfo!"
     5b. "Tremate o miseri"
     6a. "Venerabile o padre" (Amalia)
     6b. "Lo sguardo avea degl'angeli" (Amalia)
     7a. "Mio Carlo" (Massimiliano)
     7b. "Carlo! io muoio" (Massimiliano)
     8a. "Un messaggero di trista novella" (Francesco)
     8b. "Sul capo mio colpevole"
II: 9a. "Dall'infame banchetto io m'involai" (Amalia)
     9b. "Tu del mio Carlo in seno" (Amalia)
     9c. "Ah, signora!"
     9d. "Carlo vive?"
     10a. "Perchè fuggisti al canto" (Francesco)
     10b. "Io t'amo, Amalia" (Francesco)
     10c. "Tracotante!"
     10d. "Ti scosta, o malnato"
     11a. "Tutto quest'oggi le mani in mano" (ch)
     11b. "I cittadini correano alla festa"
     12a. "Come splendido"
     12b. "Di ladroni attorniato"
     13. "Capitano!"
III: 14. "Dio, ti ringrazio" (Amalia)
     15a. "Qual mare, qual terra da me" (Amalia)
     15b. "Qui nel bosco?"
     15c. "Lassù risplendere"
     16. "Le rube, gli stupri, gl'incendi, le morti" (ch)
     17a. "Ben giunto, o Capitano!" (ch)
     17b. "Tutto è buio e silenzio"
     17c. "Un ignoto"
     17d. "Destatevi, o pietre!"
IV: 18. "Tradimento! Risorgono i defunti!" (Francesco)
     19. "Parea che sorto" (Francesco)
     20a. "M'hai chiamato in quest'ora" (Moser)
     20b. "Precipita dal momte un foribondo"
     21. "Francesco! mio figlio!" (Massimiliano)
     22. "Come il bacio d'un padre amoroso" (Massimiliano)
     23. "Qui son essi!"
     24. "Caduto è il reprobo!"

1a.12   "Jérusalem," opera (Nos. of sections in Chusid's catalogue): ....
     1. "Preludio"
I: 2. "Rec. et Ave Maria": "Non! ce bruit ce n'est rien!," recit (Gaston)
     . "Ave Maria ma voix te prie" (Hélène)
     3. "Choeur": "Enfin voici le jour proprice" (ch)
     4. "Sestetto": "Avant que nous partions" (Le Comte)
     . "Je tremble je tremble encore" (Hélène)
     5. "Choeur et Air": "Viens ô pecheur rebelle" (ch)
     . "Oh! dans l'ombre dans le mystere" (Roger)
     6. "Finale I": "Mais quel tumulte!," finale (Roger)
II: 1. "Rec. et Air": "Grace! mon Dieu!," recit (Roger)
     . "Ô jour fatal ô crime!," aria (Roger)
     2. "Rec. et Air": "Loin des croisés madame" (Isaure)
     . "Quelle ivresse," aria (Hélène)
     3. "Choeur des Pélerins": "O mon Dieu!" (ch)
     . "Marcia": "Ecoutéz ce sont eux!" (ch)
     4. "Rec. Le Comte, Roger le Legat et les Croises": "Dieu soit loué" (Le Comte)
     5. "Rec. et Air Gaston": "L'Emir auprés de lui m'apelle" (Gaston)
     . "Je veux encor entendre," aria (Gaston)
     6. "Rec. et Duo Hélène, Gaston": "Prisonnier dans Ramla" (L'Émir)
     . (Une pensée amère) (Hélène)
III: 1. "Choeur": "Ô belle captive" (ch)
     2. "Ballet": . "Pas de 4"
      . "Galop"
      . "Pas des deux" (Verdi's spelling)

. "Pas Seul"
. "Pas (illegible)"
. "Pas d'ensemble"
3. "Scene et Air Hélène": "Les chrétiens. Ils sont là!" (L'Officier)
. "Mes palintes mes plaintes sont vaines" (Hélène)
4. "Finale III / Marche (illegible)": "Barons et chevaliers," finale (Gaston)
IV: 1. "Choeur / de la procession": "Voici de Josaphat la lugubre vallée" (Roger)
. "Jerusalem! Jerusalem! la sainte la divine citè" (ch)
2. "Trio": "C'est lui" (Hélène)
. "Dieu nous separe Hélène" (Gaston)
3. "Finale Ultima / la bataille"
4. "Finale (cont'd)": "La bataille est gagnée" (Isaure)

1a.13   "Il Corsaro," opera: ....
excerpts: 1. "Prelude"
I: 2. "Come liberi volano i venti" (ch)
3a. "Ah! sì, ben dite"
3b. "Tutto parea sorridere" (Corrado)
3c. "Della brezza col favore"
4. "Sì: de' corsari il fulmine"
5a. "Egli non riede ancora!" (Medora)
5b. "Non so le tetre immagini" (Medora)
6a. "È pur tristo, o Medora" (Corrado)
6b. "No, tu non sai comprendere"
6c. "Tornerai, ma forse spenta"
II: 7. "Oh qual perenne gaudio t'aspetta" (ch)
8a. "Nè sulla terra creatura alcuna" (Gulnara)
8b. "Vola talor dal carcere" (Gulnara)
8c. "Seide celebra con gioia e festa"
8d. "Ah conforto è sol la speme"
9a. "Sol grida di festa" (ch)
9b. "O prodi miei, sorgete"
9c. "Salve, Allah tutta quanta la terra" (Seid)
10a. "Giunge un Dervis" (Uno Schiavo)
10b. "Di, que' ribaldi tremano" (Seid)
11a. "Resta ancora"
11b. "Audace cotanto mostrarti pur sai?"
11c. "Signor, trafiti giacciono"
III: 12. "Alfin questo corsaro è mio prigione!" (Seid)
13a. "Cento leggiadre vergini" (Seid)
13b. "Ma pria togliam dall'anima"
13c. "S'avvicina il tuo momento"
14a. "Eccola!... fingasi" (Seid)
14b. "Sia l'istante maledetto"
15. "Eccomi progioniero!" (Corrado)
16. "Ei dorme?"
17a. "Seid la vuole" (Seid)
17b. "Non sai ti che sulla testa"
18. "Sul capo mio discenda"
19. "La terra, il ciel m'abborrino"
20a. "Voi tacete" (Medora)
20b. "Per me felice" (Corrado)
20c. "O mio Corrado, appressati"

1a.14   "La battaglia di Legnano," opera: ....
excerpts: 1. "Overture"
I: 2. "Viva Italia! Sacro un patto" (ch)
3a. "O magnanima e prima"
3b. "La pia materna mano"
4a. "Viva Italia forte ed una"
4b. "Spento tra la fiamme du Susa"
4c. "Ah! m'abbraccia"
5. "Giulive trombe!"
6. "Plaude all'arrivo Milan dei forti" (ch)
7a. "Voi lo diceste"
7b. "Quante volte come un dono" (Lida)
8. "Che ... signor!"
9. "A frenarti, o cor"
10. "Sposa ... il tuo bel cor" (Rolando)
11a. "È ver? Sei d'altri" (Arrigo)
11b. "T'amai, t'amai qual angelo"
II: 12a. "Udiste?... la grande la forte Milano" (ch)
12b. "Sì, tradi e invano"
13. "Invia la baldanzosa Lombarda Lega"
14a. "Ah! ben vi scorgo"

   14b. "Favellaste acerbi detti"
   15. "A che smarriti e pallidi?" (Federico)
   16. "Le mie possenti squadre"
  III: 17a. "Fra queste dense tenebre" (ch)
   17b. "Campioni della Morte"
   18. "Giuriam d'Italia por fine" (ch, Arrigo)
   19. "Lida, Lida? Ove corri?" (Imelda)
   20. "Di gli ch'è sangue italico" (Rolando)
   21. "Tu m'appellavi" (Arrigo)
   22. "Se al nuovo dì pugnando" (Rolando)
   23. "Rolando? M'ascolta"
   24a. "Regna la notte ancor" (Arrigo)
   24b. "Ah! d'un consorte, o perfidi"
   25. "Vendetta d'un momento" (Rolando)
  IV: 26. "Deus meus, pone illos ut rotam" (ch)
   27. "Vittoria! Vittoria!" (ch)
   28. "Per la salvata Italia"

1a.15 "Luisa Miller," opera: ....
  excerpts: 1. "Overture"
  I: 2a. "Ti desta, o Luisa" (ch)
   2b. "Lo vidi, e'l primo palpito"
   3a. "Mia diletta!"
   3b. "Ferma ed ascolta!" (Wurm)
   3c. "Sacra è la scelta" (Miller)
   4. "Ah! fu giusto"
   5a. "Che mai narrasti!" (Walter)
   5b. "Il mio sangue" (Walter)
   6a. "Quale un sorriso d'amica sorte" (ch)
   6b. "Dall'aule raggianti" (Federica)
   6c. "Deh! La parola amara"
   7a. "Sciogliete i levrieri" (ch)
   7b. "Luisa, non tremer"
   7c. "Fra' mortali ancora oppressa"
  II: 8a. "Ah! Luisa Luisa ove sei?" (ch)
   8b. "Tu puniscimi, o Signore" (Luisa)
   8c. "A brani"
   9a. "Egli delira" (Walter)
   9b. "L'alto retaggio non ho bramato" (Walter)
   9c. "Vien la Duchessa" (Wurm)
   10a. "Il foglio dunque?" (Rodolfo)
   10b. "Oh! fede negar potessi"
   10c. "Quando le sere al placido" (Rodolfo)
   11a. "Di me chiedeste?"
   11b. "L'ara o l'avello apprestami"
  III: 12a. "Come in un giorno solo" (ch)
   12b. "La tomba è un letto" (Luisa)
   13a. "Ah! l'ultima preghiera" (Luisa)
   13b. "Ah, piangi! Il tuo dolore"
   13c. "Avean mio padre i barbari"
   13d. "Padre, ricevi l'estremo addio"

1a.16 "Stiffelio," opera: ....
  excerpts: 1. "Overture"
  I: 2. "Oh santo libro" (Jorg)
   3. "Di qua varcando sul primo albore" (Stiffelio)
   4a. "Son quanti giorno?"
   4b. "Colla cenere disperso"
   4c. "Viva Stiffelio!"
   5a. "Non ha per me un'accento!" (Stiffelio)
   5b. "Vidi dovunque gemere" (Stiffelio)
   5c. "Ah! v'appare in fronte scritto"
   6. "Tosto ei disse!" (Lina)
   7a. "Verrà dovrò risponder!" (Lina)
   7b. "Dite che il fallo a tergere" (Stankar)
   7c. "Ed io pure in faccia agli uomini"
   7d. "Or meco venite"
   8. "M'evitan" (Raffaele)
   9. "Plaudiam!" (ch)
   10. "Cugino, pensaste al sermone?" (Dorotea)
   11. "Oh qual m'invade ed agita"
   12. "Nol volete?"
  II: 13a. "Oh cielo! dove son io!" (Lina)
   13b. "Ah, dagli scanni eterei" (Lina)
   13c. "Perder dunque voi volete"

      14. "Io resto" (Raffaele)
      15a. "Qual rumore!"
      15b. "Santo è il loco"
      15c. "Ah no, è impossibile!"
      16. "Dessa non è"
III: 17a. "Ei fugge e con tal foglio" (Stankar)
      17b. "Lina, pensai che un angelo"
      17c. "Ah, si finisca"
      17d. "In questo teto uno di noi morrà"
      18. "Dite ai fratei che al tempio" (Lina, Stiffelio)
      19a. "Inevitabil fu questo colloquio"
      19b. "Opposto è il calle" (Stiffelio)
      19c. "Non allo sposo volgomi"
      19d. "Egli un patto proponeva"
      19e. "Ah sì, voliamo al tempio"
      20. "Non punirmi, Signor"
      21. "Stiffelio! Eccomi"

1a.17   "Rigoletto," opera: ....
      excerpts: 1. "Prelude"
     I: 2a. "Della mia bella incognita borghese" (Duca)
          2b. "Questa o quella" (Duca)
          3. "Partite? Crudele!"
          4. "Gran nuova! gran nuova!"
          5. "Ch'io gli parli"
          6. "Quel vecchio maledivami" (Rigoletto)
          7. "Pari siamo!" (Rigoletto)
          8. "Figlia!... Mio padre!"
          9. "Ah! veglia, o donna"
          10a. "Signor nè principe"
          10b. "T'amo! T'amo"
          10c. "È il sol dell'anima" (Duca)
          10d. "Addio, addio"
          11a. "Gualtier Maldè" (Gilda)
          11b. "Caro nome" (Gilda)
          12a. "Silenzio"
          12b. "Zitti, zitti"
    II: 13a. "Ella mi fù rapita!" (Duca)
          13b. "Parmi veder le lagrime" (Duca)
          13c. "Scorrendo uniti remota"
          13d. "Possente amor mi chiama"
          14a. "Povero Rigoletto!" (Marullo)
          14b. "Cortigiani, vil razza dannata," aria (Rigoletto)
          15a. "Mio padre!... Tutte le feste al tempio" (Gilda)
          15b. "Ah! Solo per me"
          15c. "Piangi, fanciulla"
          15d. "Sì, vendetta"
    III: 16. "E l'ami?" (Rigoletto)
          17. "La donna è mobile" (Duca)
          18a. "Un dì, se ben rammentomi" (Duca)
          18b. "Bella figlia dell'amore" (Duca)
          19a. "M'odi! ritorna a casa"
          19b. "Ah, più non ragioni!"
          19c. "Storm Music"
          20. "Della vendetta! alfin giunge l'istante" (Rigoletto)
          21a. "Chi è la?"
          21b. "V'ho ingannato! colpevole fui" (Gilda)
          21c. "Lassù in cielo"
      Appendix: 22. "Prends pité de sa jeunesse" (Aria for Maddalena—Paris production)

1a.18   "Il Trovatore," opera: ....
      excerpts: I: 1a. "Introduction"
           1b. "All'erta!" (Ferrando)
           1c. "Di due figli"
           1d. "Abbietta zingara"
           2a. "Che più t'arresti?" (Ines)
           2b. "Come d'aurato"
           2c. "Tacea la notte placida" (Leonora)
           2d. "Di tale amor" (Cabaletta)
           3a. "Tace la notte!"
           3b. "Deserto sulla terra" (Manrico)
           3c. "Non m'inganno"
           3d. "Ah! dalle tenebre"
           3e. "Di geloso amor"
    II: 4a. "Vedi! le fosche notturne spoglie" (Anvil Chorus)

      4b. "Stride la vampa!" (Azucena)
      5a. "Soli or siam!" (Manrico)
      5b. "Condotta all'era in ceppi" (Azucena)
      6a. "Non son tuo figlio?" (Manrico)
      6b. "Mal reggendo all'aspro assalto" (Manrico)
      6c. "Perigliarti ancor languente"
      7a. "Tutto è deserto" (di Luna)
      7b. "Il balen del suo sorriso" (di Luna)
      7c. "Per me ora fatale"
      8a. "Ah! se l'error t'ingombra" (ch)
      8b. "Perchè piangete?"
      8c. "Degg'io volgermi"
      8d. "E deggio e posso creduto" (Leonora)
III: 9a. "Orco dadi ma fra poco" (Soldiers' Chorus)
      9b. "Squilli, echeggi"
      9c. "Ballabile"
      10a. "In bracciò al mio rival!" (di Luna)
      10b. "Giorni poveri vivea" (Azucena)
      10c. "Deh! rallentate"
      11a. "Quale d'armi fragor" (Leonora)
      11b. "Ah! sì, ben mio" (Manrico)
      11c. "Di quella pira"
IV: 12a. "Timor di me?"
      12b. "D'amor sull'ali rosee" (Leonora)
      12c. "Miserere ... Ah, che la morte ognora"
      12d. "Tu vedrai che amore"
      13a. "Udiste? Come albeggi?" (di Luna)
      13b. "Qual voce!"
      13c. "Mira, d'acerbe lagrime" (Leonora)
      13d. "Vivrà! Contende il giubilo"
      14a. "Madre, non dormi?" (Manrico)
      14b. "Se m'ami ancor"
      14c. "Ai nostri monti"
      14d. "Che! Non m'inganno!"
      14e. "Parlar non vuoi?"
      14f. "Ti scosta!"

1a.19 "La Traviata," opera: ....
      excerpts: 1. "Prelude"
I: 2. "Dell'invito trascorsa è già l'ora" (ch)
      3. "Libiamo, ne'lieti calici" (Alfredo) (Brindisi—a drinking / toasting song)
      4a. "Che è ciò?"
      4b. "Un dì, felice"
      5. "Si ridesta in ciel"
      6a. "È strano! È strano!" (Violetta)
      6b. "Ah fors'è lui quest'anima" (Violetta)
      6c. "Follie! Sempre libera"
II: 7a. "Lunge da Lei" (Alfredo)
      7b. "Dei miei bollenti spiriti" (Alfredo)
      7c. "O mio rimorso!"
      8a. "Madamigella Valery?" (Germont)
      8b. "Pura siccome un angelo" (Germont)
      8c. "Bella voi siete"
      8d. "Dite alla giovine"
      9a. "Morrò! La mia memoria"
      9b. "Dammi tu forza o Cielo" (Violetta)
      10a. "Al vivre sol quel core" (Alfredo)
      10b. "Di Provenza il mar" (Germont)
      10c. "Ne rispondi"
      11. "Avrem lieta di maschera la festa" (Flora)
      12a. "Noi siamo zingarelle"
      12b. "Di Madride noi siam Mattadori"
      13. "Alfredo! Voi!"
      14a. "Ogni suo aver tal femmina"
      14b. "Di sprezzo degno!"
III: 15. "Prelude"
      16a. "Annina? Commandate?" (Violetta)
      16b. "Teneste la promessa"
      16c. "Addio del passato" (Violetta)
      17. "Largo al quadrupede" (ch)
      18a. "Signora, Che t'accade" (Annina)
      18b. "Parigi, o cara noi lasceremo" (Alfredo)
      18c. "Gran Dio! morir sì giovine"
      19. "Ah! Violetta" (Germont)

1a.20 "I vespri siciliani," opera: ....
       excerpts: 1. "Overture"
       I: 2a. "In alto mare e battuto dai venti"
             2b. "Deh! tu calma, O Dio possente"
             3. "Arrigo ... Non altro?"
       II: 4a. "O patria"
             4b. "O tu, Palermo" (Procida)
       III: 5. "In braccio alle dovizie"
             6a. "Sogno, o son desto?"
             6b. "Quando al mio sen"
             7. "Ballet—The Four Seasons": a. "Winter"
                          b. "Spring"
                          c. "Summer"
                          d. "Autumn"
       IV: 8a. "È di Monforte il cenno!" (Henri)
             8b. "Giorno di pianto"
             9a. "O sdegni miei, tacete"
             9b. "Arrigo! Ah, parli"
       V: 10. "Si celebri alfine" (ch)
             11. "Mercè, dilette amiche" (Bolero)
             12. "A toi que j'ai chérie" (alternative aria for Act IV)

1a.21 "Simon Boccanegra," opera: ....
       excerpts: Prologue: 1a. "A te l'estremo addio"
                        1b. "Il lacerato spirito"
                        2. "Suona ogni labbro il mio nome"
                        3. "Oh de' Fieschi implacata"
       I: 4. "Come in quest'ora bruna" (Amelia)
              5a. "Orfanella il tetto umile"
              5b. "Figlia! a tal nome io palpito"
             6. "Plebe! Patrizi!"
       II: 7. "Quei due vedesti" (Paolo)
             8a. "O inferno! Amelia qui!"
             8b. "Sento avvampar nell'anima" (Gabriele)
             9a. "Oh! Amelia, ami un nemico"
             9b. "Perdon, perdon Amelia" (Gabriele)
       III: 10a. "M'ardon le tempia"
             10b. "Come un fantasima"
             11. "Piango, perchè mi parla in te"

1a.22 "Aroldo," opera: ....
       excerpts: 1. "Overture"
       I: 2. "Tocchiamo! a gaudio insolito" (ch)
             3. "Ciel, ch'io respiri!"
              4. "Salvami to, gran Dio"
              5. "Egli vieni"
              6. "Sotto il sol di Siria ardente" (Aroldo)
             7. "Ma lagrima ti grondano!"
             8. "Ebben, parlatemi"
             9. "Tosto ei disse!" (Mina)
            10. "Dite che il fallo a tergere" (Egberto)
             11. "Ed io pure in faccia"
             12. "Or meco venite"
             13. "O Mina, tu mi sfuggi" (Godvino)
             14. "E'bello di guerra"
             15. "Eterna vivra in Kenth"
             16. "Vi fi in Palestina"
             17. "Oh, qual m'invade ed agita" (Aroldo)
             18. "Chi ti salve"
       II: 19. "Oh cielo! Ove son io?" (Mina)
             20. "Ah, dagli scanni eterei" (Mina)
             21. "Mina!... Voi qui!" (Godvino)
             22. "Ah, dal sen di quella tomba" (Godvino)
             23. "Io resto" (Godvino)
             24. "Ah! Era vero?" (Aroldo)
             25. "Dessa non è"
             26. "Non punirmi, o Signor"
       III: 27. "Ei fugge! e con tal foglio" (Egberto)
             28. "Mina, pensa che un angelo" (Egberto)
             29. "Oh, gioia inesprimibile"
             30. "L'istante s'avvicina!" (Aroldo)
             31. "Opposto è il calle" (Aroldo)
             32. "Non allo sposo"
             33. "Ah si, voliamo al tempo"
       IV: 34. "Cade il giorno" (ch)

35. "Cantan felici!" (Aroldo)
36. "Angiol di Dio" (Aroldo, Briano)
37. "Al lago" (Burrasca) (ch)
38. "Ah! più non reggo"
39. "Ah, da me fuggi"
40. "Allora che gli anni"

1a.23   "Un ballo in maschera," opera: ....
     excerpts: 1. "Prelude"
     I: 2a. "Posa in pace" (ch)
           2b. "Amici miei ... soldati"
           2c. "La rivedrà nell'estasi" (Riccardo)
           3a. "Conte ... Oh ciel!"
           3b. "Alla vita che t'arride"
           4a. "Il primo giudice"
           4b. "Volta la terrea" (Oscar)
           4c. "Sia condonnata"
           5a. "Zitti ... l'incanto non dèssi turbare" (ch)
           5b. "Re dell'abisso" (Ulrica)
           5c. "Arrivo il primo!"
           5d. "È lui, è lui!"
           6. "Su, fatemi largo"
           7a. "Sentite, la mia Signora"
           7b. "Che v'agita cosi?"
           7c. "Della città all'occaso"
           8a. "Su, profetessa"
           8b. "Di' tu se fedele"
           9. "Chi voi siate"
           10. "È scherzo od è follia"
           11a. "Finisci il vaticinio"
           11b. "O figlio d'Inghiterra"
     II: 12a. "Prelude"
           12b. "Ecco l'orrido campo" (Amelia)
           12c. "Ma dell'arido stelo divulsa" (Amelia)
           13a. "Teco io stò" (Riccardo)
           13b. "M'ami, m'ami"
           13c. "Oh, qual soave brivido"
           14a. "Ahimè! S'appressa alcun" (Amelia)
           14b. "Amico, gelosa"
           14c. "Odi tu come fremono cupi" (Amelia)
           15a. "Seguitemi" (Renato)
           15b. "Ve', se di notte" (Samuel)
     III: 16a. "A tal colpa è nulla il pianto" (Renato)
           16b. "Morrò, ma prima in grazia" (Amelia)
           17a. "Alzati! là tuo figlio" (Renato)
           17b. "Eri tu che macchiavi quell'anima" (Renato)
           18a. "Siam soli Udite" (Renato)
           18b. "Dunque l'onta di tutti sol una!" (Renato)
           19a. "Il messaggio entri"
           19b. "Di che fulgor"
           20a. "Forse la soglia attinse" (Riccardo)
           20b. "Ma se m'è forza perderti" (Riccardo)
           21a. "Fervono amori"
           21b. "Saper vorreste" (Oscar)
           22a. "Ah! perchè qui!"
           22b. "T'amo, si, t'amo"
           23a. "E tu ricevi il mio!"
           23b. "Ah! Morte, infamia"
           23c. "Ella è pura" (Finale)

1a.24   "La forza del destino," opera: ....
     excerpts: 1. "Overture"
     I: 2. "Buona notte, mia figlia" (Marchese)
           3a. "Temea restasse"
           3b. "Me pellegrina ed orfana" (Leonora)
           4a. "Ah! per sempre"
           4b. "Seguirti fino agl'ultimi"
           5a. "È tardi"
           5b. "Vil seduttor!"
     II: 6a. "Holà" (Ballabile)
           6b. "La cena è pronto"
           7a. "Viva la guerra!"
           7b. "Al suon del tamburo" (Preziosilla)
           8a. "Padre Eterno Signor"
           8b. "Viva la buona compagna"

9a. "Poich'imberbe è l'incognito"
9b. "Son Pereda, son ricco d'onore"
10. "Sta bene" (Finale)
11a. "Son giunta! grazie o Dio" (Leonora)
11b. "Madre, madre, pietosa Vergine" (Leonora)
12a. "Chi siete?" (Melitone)
12b. "Chi mi cerca?"
12c. "Or siam soli ..."
12d. "Infelice, delusa, reietta"
12e. "Sull'alba il piede"
13a. "Il santo nome di Dio Signore" (Guardiano)
13b. "La Vergine degli angeli"
III: 14a. "Attenti al gioco" (ch)
14b. "La vita è inferno"
14c. "Oh, tu che in seno agl'angeli" (Alvaro)
15a. "Al tradimento" (Carlo)
15b. "Amici in vita e in morte" (Alvaro, Carlo)
15c. "All'armi!" (ch)
16a. "Arde la mischia!" (Battle Scene)
16b. "Piano, qui posi"
16c. "Solenne in quest'ora"
17a. "Morir! Tremenda cosa!" (Carlo)
17b. "Aura fatale del mio destino" (Carlo)
17c. "Ah! Egli è salvo"
18. "Compagni, sostiamo"
19a. "Nè gustare m'è dato"
19b. "Sleale! Il segreto"
20a. "Lorchè pifferi e Tamburri" (Preziosilla, ch)
20b. "Qua, vivandiere, un sorso"
20c. "A buon mercato"
20d. "Pane, pan per carità"
20e. "Che vergogna!"
21a. "Nella guerra, è la follia"
21b. "Toh, toh! Poffare il mondo"
22a. "Lasciatelo ch'ei vada"
22b. "Rataplan"
IV: 23a. "Fate la carità" (ch)
23b. "Che? Siete all'osteria quieti?" (Melitone)
24a. "Auf! Pazienza non v'ha che basti" (Melitone)
24b. "Del mondo i disinganni" (Guardiano)
25a. "Giunge qualcun"
25b. "Siete il portiere?" (Carlo)
25c. "Invano Alvaro"
25d. "Le minaccie i fieri accenti" (Alvaro)
26. "Pace, pace, mio Dio" (Leonora)
27a. "Io muoio! Confessione!"
27b. "Non imprecare, umiliata"

1a.25 "Don Carlo" (Don Carlos), opera: ....
excerpts: I: 1. "Su, cacciator" (Le cerf s'enfuit sous la ramure) (ch)
2a. "Fontainebleau! Foresta immensa" (Fontainebleau! Forêt immense et solitaire!) (Carlos)
2b. "Io la vidi" (Je l'ai vue et dans son sourire) (Carlos)
3a. "Io suon del corno" (Le bruit du cor) (Carlos)
3b. "Io sono uno stranier" (Je suis un étranger)
3c. "Che mai fate voi?" (Que faites-vous donc?)
3d. "Di qual amor" (De quands transports) (Élisabeth)
4a. "Al fedel ch'ora viene" (A celui qui vous vient) (Carlos)
4b. "L'ora fatale" (L'heure fatale est sonnée!)
5. "Inni di festa" (O chants de fête)
6. "Il glorioso Re di Francia" (Le trè-glorieux Roi de France)
II: 7. "Carlo il sommo Imperatore" (Charles-Quint, l'auguste Empereur) (ch)
8. "Al chiostro di San Giusto" (Au couvent de Saint-Just)
9a. "È lui! desso! l'Infante!" (Le voilà! C'est l'Infant!) (Rodrigue)
9b. "Qual pallor" (Tu pâlis)
9c. "Dio, che nell'alma infondere" (Dieu, tu semas dans nos âmes)
10. "Sotto ai folti" (Sous ces bois) (ch)
11. "Nei giardin del bello" (Au palais des fées) (Eboli)
12. "La Regina!" (La Reine!)
13. "Che mai si fa nel suol francese" (Que fait-on à la cour de France)
14. "Carlo ch'é sol il nostro amor" (L'Infant Carlos)
15a. "Io vengo a domandar" (Je viens solliciter de la Reine) (Carlos)
15b. "Perduta ben, mio sol tesor" (O bien perdu)
15c. "Qual voce" (Par quelle douce voix)
16a. "Il Re!" (Le Roi!) (Thibault)
16b. "Non pianger, mia compagna" (Ô ma chère compagne) (Élisabeth)

17a. "Restate! Presso alla mia persona" (Restez! Auprès de ma personne) (Philippe)
17b. "O Signor, di Fiandre arrivo" (O Roi! J'arrive de Flandre)
III: 18a. "A mezza-notte, ai giardin della Regina" (A minuit, aux jardins de la Reine) (Carlos)
18b. "Sei tu, sei tu" (C'est vous!)
19. "Che disse mai?!" (Que dit-il? Il est en délire)
20. "Spuntato ecco il dì d'esultanza" (Ce jour heureux)
21. "Nel posar sul mio capo la corona" (En plaçant sur mon front)
22. "Sire, no, l'ora estrema" (Sire, la dernière heure)
IV: 23a. "Ella giammai m'amò" (Elle ne m'aime pas!) (Philippe)
23b. "Dormirò sol nel manto mio regal" (Je dormirai dans mon manteau royal)
24a. "Il Grande Inquisitor!... Son io dinanzi al Re?" (Le Grand Inquisiteur!... Suis-je devant le Roi?)
24b. "Nell'ispano suol mai" (Dans ce beau pays)
25a. "Giustizia! o Sire" (Justice! Sire! J'ai foi) (Élisabeth)
25b. "Ah! si maledetto" (Maudit soit le soupçon infâme) (Philippe)
26. "Pietà!" (Pitié pardon pour la femme coupable) (Eboli)
27a. "Ah! più non vedrò" (Ah! Je ne verrai plus la Reine!)
27b. "O don fatale" (O don fatal) (Eboli)
28a. "Son io, mio Carlo" (C'est moi, Carlos!) (Rodrigue)
28b. "Convien qui dirci addio!" (Il faut nous dire adieu!)
28c. "Per me giunto" (Oui, Carlos! C'est mon jour suprême)
28d. "O Carlo, ascolta" (Carlos, écoute)
28e. "Io morrò" (Ah! Je meurs l'âme joyeuse)
29a. "Mio Carlo, a te la spada" (Mon fils, reprenez votre épée) (Philippe)
29b. "Ciel! suona a stormo!" (Ciel! Le tocsin)
V: 30. "Tu che le vanità" (Toi qui sus le néant des grandeurs) (Élisabeth)
31a. "È dessa!... Un detto, un sol" (C'est elle!... Un mot)
31b. "Vago sogno m'arrise" (J'avais fait un beau rêve!)
31c. "Ma lassù ci vedremo" (Au revoir dans un monde)
31d. "Sì, per sempre!" (Oui, pour toujours!)
Add arias: 32. "Io l'ho perduta" (for Italian 4 act version, Scene 1 of Act I)
Omitted prior to 1867: 32. "L'hiver est long!" (Prelude & Introduction, Act I)
33. "Que de fleurs ... Viens Eboli" (Introduction & chorus, Scene 1 of Act III)
34. "Le Ballet de la Reine" (Scene 2 of Act III)
35. "J'ai tout compris" (Élisabeth, Scene 1 of Act IV)
36. "Mons fils, reprenez votre épée" (Finale w/ part 1 reconstructed, Scene 2 of Act IV)
37. "Oui, pour toujours!" (Finale, Act V)

1a.26   "Aida," opera: ....
excerpts: 1. "Prelude"
I: 2. "Si, corre voce che l'Etiope ardisca" (Ramfis)
3a. "Se quel guerrier"
3b. "Celeste Aida" (Radames)
4a. "Quale insolita gioia"
4b. "Vieni o diletta"
5a. "Alta cagion v'aduna"
5b. "Or di vulcano al tempio"
5c. "Sul del Nilo"
6a. "Ritorna vincitor!" (Aida)
6b. "L'insana parola"
6c. "I sacri nomi"
7a. "Possente Possenta—Immenso Ftha" (Gran Sacerdotessa)
7b. "Dance of the Priestesses"
7c. "Mortal diletto"
II: 8a. "Chi mai" (ch)
8b. "Dance of the Moorish slaves"
9a. "Fu la sortè dell' armi" (Amneris)
9b. "Amore, amore"
10a. "Gloria all' Egitto" (ch)
10b. "March" (Grand March)
10c. "Ballabile"
10d. "Vieni, o guerriero"
10e. "Quest' assisa"
11. "O Re, pei sacri Numi"
III: 12a. "O tu che sei d'Osiride" (ch)
12b. "Vieni d'Iside"
12c. "Qui Radames verrà"
12d. "O patria mia"
13. "Ciel mio padre"
14a. "Pur' ti riveggo"
14b. "Fuggiam gli ardor ... Là, tra foreste vergini"
14c. "Tu Amonasro, io son disonorato"
IV: 15a. "Introduction"
15b. "L'abborita rivale" (Amneris)
15c. "Già i sacerdoti"
15d. "Misero appien mi festi"

16a. "Ohimè morir mi sento"
16b. "Spirto del nume"
17a. "La fatal pietra sovra me si chiuse" (Radames)
17b. "Morir si pura e bella"
18a. "Immenso immenso"
18b. "O terra addio"

1a.27 "Otello," opera: ....
  excerpts: I: 1a. "Una vela!" (ch)
   1b. "Esultate!"
   2. "Roderigo, ebben che pensi?"
   3. "Fuoco di gioia!"
   4a. "Roderigo, beviam!"
   4b. "Inaffia l'ugola!" (Brindisi—a drinking or toasting song)
   5a. "Capitano, v'attende"
   5b. "Abbasso le spade!"
   6a. "Già nella notte densa" (Love Duet)
   6b. "Venga la morte!"
  II: 7a. "Non ti crucciar" (Jago)
   7b. "Vanne! la tua meta"
   7c. "Credo in un Dio crudel"
   8a. "Ciò m'accora ..."
   8b. "Dove guardi"
   9. "D'un uom che geme"
   10a. "Desdemona real..."
   10b. "Tu?! Indietro! fuggi!"
   10c. "Ora e per sempre"
   11. "Era la notte" (Dream)
   12a. "Oh! mostruosa colpa!"
   12b. "Ah! mille vite"
   12c. "Si, pel ciel" (Oath Duet)
  III: 13. "La vedetta del porto ha segnalato" (Araldo)
   14a. "Dio ti giocondi"
   14b. "Esterrefatta fisso"
   15. "Dio! mi potevi" (Monologue)
   16a. "Vieni; l'aula è deserta"
   16b. "Questa è una ragna"
   17a. "Quest'è il segnale"
   17b. "Come la ucciderò"
   18a. "Viva! Evviva!"
   18b. "Eccolo! È lui!"
   18c. "A terra!"
   19. "Ballabile": . "Canzone Araba"
    . "Invocazione ad Allah"
    . "Canzone greco"
    . "La Muranese"
  IV: 20a. "Era più calmo?" (Emilia)
   20b. "Mia madre aveva"
   20c. "Piangea cantando" (Willow Song)
   21. "Ave Maria"
   22. "Chi è là?" (Death of Desdemona)
   23. "Niun mi tema"

1a.28 "Falstaff," opera: ....
  excerpts: I: 1. "Falstaff! Olà!"
   2. "So che se andiam la notte"
   3. "Ma è tempo d'assottigliar l'ingegno"
   4a. "Ehi! paggio!"
   4b. "L'Onore! Ladri!"
   5. "Alice ... Meg ... Nannetta"
   6a. "Fulgida Alice! amor t'offro"
   6b. "Quell'otre! quel tino!"
   6c. "È un ribaldo, un furbo, un labro"
   7. "In due parole"
   8a. "Pst, pst, Nannetta"
   8b. "Torno all'assalto"
   9. "Del tuo barbaro diagnostico"
  II: 10a. "Siam pentiti e contriti"
   10b. "Reverenza!"
   11a. "Alice, è mia!"
   11b. "Va vecchio John"
   12. "Signore, v'assista il cielo!"
   13a. "C'è Windsor una dama"
   13b. "V'ascolto"
   14a. "È sogno? o realtà"

14b. "Eccomi qua. Son pronto"
15a. "Presenteremo un bill"
15b. "Giunta all'Albergo della Giarrettiera"
16a. "Fra poco s'incomincia la commedia"
16b. "A noi! Tu la parte farai che ti spetta"
17. "Alfin t'ho colto"
18a. "Quand'ero paggio"
18b. "Voi mi celiate"
19a. "Mia signora!"
19b. "Vien qua"
19c. "Al ladro"
20a. "C'è. C'è"
20b. "Facciamo le viste"
III: 21a. "Ehi! Taverniere!"
21b. "Mondo ladro"
22a. "Reverenza. La bella Alice"
22b. "Quando il rintocco"
23. "Sarai la Fata Regina delle Fate"
24a. "Dal labbro il canto"
24b. "Nossignore! Tu indossa"
25a. "Una, due, tre, quattro"
25b. "Odo un soave passo!"
26a. "Ninfe! Elfi! Silfi!"
26b. "Sul fil d'un soffio etesio"
27a. "Alto là"
27b. "Pizzica, pizzica"
28. "Ogni sorta di gente dozzinale"
29a. "Facciamo il paremtado"
29b. "Tutto nel mondo è burla"

2. ORCHESTRAL WORKS

2.1   *"Barber of Seville" Overture (c early, for performance of Rossini's opera, lost)* ....
2.2   *"La capricciosa" Overture (c ?1825, played before performance of Rigoletto in 1860, lost)* ....

3. STRING QUARTETS

3.1   String Quartet in E minor (c1873) ....

4. PIANO

4.1   "Romanza senza parole" (p1865) ....
4.2   "Waltz" (p1963) ....

5. CHURCH MUSIC

5.1   *"Stabat Mater" (c early, lost)* ....
5.2   *"Domine ad adiuvandum" (c early; T & fl obbl, lost)* ....
5.3   *"Le lamentazioni di Geremia" (c early; Bar, lost)* ....
5.4   *"I deliri di Saul," cantata (c1828; Bar & orch, unpubd, lost)* ....
5.5   "Tantum ergo" (ca1836; T & orch) ....
5.6   "Libera me" (c1868–9; S, ch & orch, for collab work: Requiem for Rossini; incl in: Messa da Requiem) ......
5.7   "Messa da Requiem" (c1874, S, A, T, B, ch & orch, in memory of Manzoni): ....
          1. "Requiem"
          2. "Dies Irae"
          3. "Tuba mirum"
          4. "Liber scriptus"
          5. "Quid sum miser"
          6. "Rex tremendae"
          7. "Recordare"
          8. "Ingemisco"
          9. "Confutatis"
          10. "Lacrymosa"
          11. "Offertorio"
          12. "Sanctus"
          13. "Agnus Dei"
          14. "Lux aeterna"
          15. "Libera me" (c1868–9; see orig for collab work: Requiem for Rossini)
5.8   "Pater noster" (c1880, attrib to Dante, transl from Latin; ch) ....
5.9   "Ave Maria" (c1880, Dante; S & strings; arr for 1v & pf, companion piece to: Pater Noster).......................

* * * * *

1. STAGE WORKS

Operas:

Ballet:

Incid music:

Film:

2. SYMPHONIES

3. OTHER ORCHESTRAL WORKS

4. CONCERTOS, SOLO INSTR & ORCH

Pf & orch:

4.1	"Suíte" (c1913; red for 2pf): No.1 "À Espanha e Portugal"	A068
4.2	No.2 "Ao Brasil"	
4.3	No.3 "À Itália" (Tarantela) (arr for pf, A041)	
4.4	"Folia de um bloco infantil" (c1919, based on: Carnaval das crianças, A157)	A146
4.5	"Choros No.11" (c1928)	A228
4.6	"Momoprecoce," fantasy (c1929, based on A157; transcr for pf & band, A259)	A240
4.7	"Momoprecoce," fantasy (c1931; pf & band; orig for pf & orch, A240)	A259
4.8	"Bachianas brasileiras No.3" (c1938):	A388

            1. "Prelúdio" (Ponteio)
            2. "Fantasia" (Devaneio)
            3. "Ária" (Modinha)
            4. "Tocata" (Picapau)

4.9	"Bachianas brasileiras No.4" (c1941; orig for pf, A264)	A424
4.10	Piano Concerto No.1 (c1945; red for 2 pf)	A453
4.11	Piano Concerto No.2 (c1948; red for 2pf)	A487
4.12	Piano Concerto No.3 (c1952–7; red for 2pf)	A512
4.13	Piano Concerto No.4 (c1952; red for 2pf)	A505
4.14	Piano Concerto No.5 (c1954; red for 2pf)	A521

Vn & orch:

4.15	"Fantasia de movimentos mistos" (c1921; also see w/ pf, A175):	A174

            1. "Alma convulsa"
            2. "Serenidade"
            3. "Contentamento"

4.16	"Martírio dos insectos" (c1925; arr see w/ pf, A214):	A213

            1. "Acigarra no inverno"
            2. "O vagalume na claridade"
            3. "Mariposa na luz" (c1916, used in: Evolução dos aeroplanos, A271)

Vc & orch:

4.17	Cello Concerto No.1 (c1915)	A095
4.18	"Fantasia" (c1945; red for vc & pf)	A454
4.19	Cello Concerto No.2 (c1953; red for vc & pf)	A516

Gui & orch:

4.20	"Introdução aos choros" (c1929)	A239
4.21	Guitar Concerto (c1951; red for gui & pf, A502)	A501

Other:

4.22	"Choros No.8" (c1925; 2pf & orch)	A208
4.23	"Ciranda das sete notas," fantasy (c1933; bn & strings; transcr for bn & pf, A548)	A325
4.24	"Fantasia para saxophone" (c1948; sax/S, 2hn & strings; red for sax & pf)	A490
4.25	Harp Concerto (c1953)	A515
4.26	Harmonica Concerto (c1955; red for harmonica & pf)	A524

5. STRING QUARTETS

5.1	String Quartet No.1 (c1915):	A099

            1. "Cantilena"
            2. "Brincadeira"
            3. "Canto lírico"
            4. "Cançoneta"
            5. "Melancolia"
            6. "Saltando como um Saci"

5.2	String Quartet No.2 (c1915)	A100
5.3	String Quartet No.3, "Quarteto das pipocas" (Pop-corn Quartet) (c1916)	A112
5.4	String Quartet No.4 (c1917)	A129
5.5	String Quartet No.5, "Quarteto Popular No.1" (c1931)	A263
5.6	String Quartet No.6, "II Quarteto brasileiro" (c1938)	A399
5.7	String Quartet No.7 (c1942)	A435
5.8	String Quartet No.8 (c1944)	A446
5.9	String Quartet No.9 (c1945)	A457
5.10	String Quartet No.10 (c1946)	A468
5.11	String Quartet No.11 (c1947)	A481
5.12	String Quartet No.12 (c1950)	A496
5.13	String Quartet No.13 (c1951)	A503

7. GUITAR

8. PIANO

9. SACRED WORKS

10. CHORAL WORKS

W/ acc:

10.37	"Magdalena" Suite No.2 (c1947; vv, ch & orch, from comedy A476): 1. "The Singing Tree" A478
10.38	2. "The Emerald Song"
10.39	3. "Valse d'Espagne"
10.40	"Floresta do Amazonas" (c1958, Vasconcellos; S, m ch & orch, used in film: Green Mansions): 1. "Cair
	da tarde" (arr for 1v & pf, A544; 1v & orch, A545) A551
10.41	2. "Canção de amor" (arr for 1v & orch, A546)
10.42	3. "Melodia Sentimental" (arr for 1v & pf, A556; 1v & orch, A555)
10.43	4. "Veleiros" (arr for 1v & pf, A560; 1v & orch, A561; 1v & 2gui, A562)

Unacc ch:

10.44	"As crianças" (c1908, L. Sales) A018
10.45	"Canção do parachoque" (Bumper Song) (c1925) A203
10.46	"Consolação" (c1932, Mello, theme Mendelssohn) A267
10.47	"Élégie" (c1932; S, T & ch, theme Massenet) A269
10.48	"Fuga No.1" (c1932, transcr from J. S. Bach: The Well-Tempered Clavier) A272
10.49	"Fuga No.5" (c1932, transcr from J. S. Bach: The Well-Tempered Clavier) A273
10.50	"Fuga No.8" (c1932, transcr from J. S. Bach: The Well-Tempered Clavier) A274
10.51	"Fuga No.21" (c1932, transcr from J. S. Bach: The Well-Tempered Clavier) A275
10.52	"Hino às árvores" (c1932; orig melody & text C. Júnior & Arlindo Leal) A285
10.53	"Hino da independência do Brasil" (c1932; orig melody & text Pedro I & Veiga) A286
10.54	"Hino nacional brasileiro" (c1932, Estrada; orig music Silva) A287
10.55	"Iphigénie en Aulide" (c1932, Rollet; orig melody Gluck) A289
10.56	"Lamento" (c1932; orig melody Barreto) A291
10.57	"A Marselhesa" (c1932; from French song c by Rouget de Lisle) A292
10.58	"Meu benzinho," vocal sextet (c1932; 6vv, on popular theme) A293
10.59	"Minha mãe" (Andante) (c1932, Haroldo, theme Beethoven) A294
10.60	"Os moinhos" (Minueto) (c1932, theme Beethoven) A295
10.61	"Moteto" (c1932, adapted from Palestrina's motet) A296
10.62	"Na risonha madrugada" (c1932, Haroldo; fem ch; also for ch; orig melody Haydn) A298
10.63	"Na roça" (c1932, Seixas; orig melody J. Gomes Júnior) A299
10.64	"Pátria" (c1932; w/ milit drums; also for ch/fem ch) A303
10.65	"Prelúdio No.8" (c1932, transcr from J. S. Bach: The Well-Tempered Clavier) A304
10.66	"Prelúdio No.14" (c1932, transcr from J. S. Bach: The Well-Tempered Clavier) A305
10.67	"Prelúdio No.22" (c1932, transcr from J. S. Bach: The Well-Tempered Clavier) A306
10.68	"Rêverie" (c1932; orig melody Schumann) A307
10.69	"O Rio" (c19332; orig melody Dogliani) A308
10.70	"A sementinha" (c1932) A311
10.71	"O tamborzinho" (c1932; fem ch; also for ch; orig melody Leça) A312
10.72	"Terra natal" (c1932, Faustino; fem ch; also for ch, Mozart's theme) A313
10.73	"Valsa" (c1932, adapt from Chopin's waltz) A315
10.74	"Acalentando" (c1933; orig melody & text Salema) A318
10.75	"Canção a José de Alencar" (c1933, Barros) A321
10.76	"Canção da saudade" (c1933, Viana) A322
10.77	"O contra- baixo" (c1933, child ch; orig melody & text Salema) A327
10.78	"As costureiras" (Embolada) (c1933, Villa-Lobos; fem ch) A329
10.79	"Ena-Môkôcê" (Canção de rede) (c1933; 1v, ch & perc, theme from Pareci Indians) A330
10.80	"Invocação à cruz" (c1933, Estrada; orig melody Nepomuceno) A332
10.81	"O felix anima" (c1933, theme Carissimi) A335
10.82	"Papai curumiassú" (Canção de rede) (c1933; 1v & ch, theme from the caboclos of Pará) A336
10.83	"Prólogo do Mefistofle" (c1933, adapt from Boito) A337
10.84	"Serenata" (c1933, transcr from Schubert's Serenade) A339
10.85	"Trenzinho" (c1933, Santoro; also for fem ch) A340
10.86	"A vrgem dos santos" (c1933; fem ch, adapt from Verdi's opera: La forza del destino) A341
10.87	"A Abelhinha" (c1934, Peixoto; orig melody Julião) A342
10.88	"Brincadeira de pegar" (c1934, Braga) A343
10.89	"Gavião de penacho" (c1934, Arinos, arr from orig choral adaptation Braga) A345
10.90	"A infância" (Hino escolar) (c1934, Azevedo Júnior; orig music Braga) A346
10.91	"Prelúdio" (c1934, arr from Rachmaninov's prelude) A349
10.92	"Prelúdio No.4" (c1935, transcr from J. S. Bach: The Well-Tempered Clavier) A350
10.93	"Tico-tico" (c1934, Celso; orig music Lehmann) A351
10.94	"À praia" (c1935, on a popular theme) A352
10.95	"Argentina" (c1935, melody from an Indian dance) A353
10.96	"Ay-ay-ay" (c1935, on a popular Chilean theme) A354
10.97	"Canarinho" (c1935, Salema) A355
10.98	"A canção do barqueiro do Volga" (c1935, Viana; also see for 1v & orch, A319) A356
10.99	"Cânones perpétuos" (c1935, Capistrano, on popular French theme): 1. "Alegria de viver"..............A357
10.100	2. "Companheiros, companheiros"
10.101	"Hino escolar" (c1935, Raymundo; orig melody Goes) A360
10.102	"Tão doce luz" (c1935, ch; orig melody & poetry Salema) A363
10.103	"Vocalismo No.11" (c1935) A364
10.104	"Hino escolar" (Cultura e afeto as nações) (c1936, Teixeira; orig music Nazareth)........A369
10.105	"Quadrilha brasileira" (c1936, Baptista; child ch) A370
10.106	"Redemoinho" (c1936, Salema) A371
10.107	"Rumo à escola" (c1936; orig melody Jardi) A372

11. VOICE & ORCHESTRA

12. SONGS (w/ pf)

12.51	5. "Perversidade"	
12.52	6. "Pudor"	
12.53	7. "Imagem"	
12.54	8. "Verdade" (como ópera lírica)	
12.55	"Poème de l'enfant et de sa mère" (c1923, Villa-Lobos; also see w/ insts, A192) A193
12.56	"Suíte para canto e violino" (c1923, Andrade; 1v & vn): 1. "A menina e a canção" A195
12.57	2. "Quero ser alegre"	
12.58	3. "Sertaneja" (arr w/ vns & vas, A196)	
12.59	"Canção da terra" (c1925, Carvalho; also see for fem ch & orch, A200; fem ch & pf, A201) A202
12.60	"Coleção brasileira" (c1925, G. da Silva Telles; orig w/ orch, A190): 1. "Tempos atrás" A211
12.61	2. "Tristeza"	
12.62	"Serestas" (c1925; also see 10 songs w/ orch, A215): 1. "Pobre cega" (Moreyra) A216
12.63	2. "Anjo da guarda" (Bandeira)	
12.64	3. "Canção da folha morta" (Mariano; also for ch & orch)	
12.65	4. "Saudades da minha vida" (Milano)	
12.66	5. "Modinha" (Bandeira)	
12.67	6. "Na paz do outono" (Carvalho)	
12.68	7. "Cantiga do viúvo" (Andrade)	
12.69	8. "Canção do carreiro" (Couto)	
12.70	9. "Abril" (Couto)	
12.71	10. "Desejo" (Almeida)	
12.72	11. "Redondilha" (Milano)	
12.73	12. "Realejo" (Moreyra)	
12.74	13. "Vôo" (Renault)	
12.75	14. "Serenata" (Nasser)	
12.76	"Filhas de Maria" (c1926, Milano, of the interior of the Candelária church in Rio) A221
12.77	"3 poemas indígenas" (c1926; also see for 1v, ch & orch, A224): 1. "Canidé-Ioune-Sabath" A223
12.78	2. "Teiru" (Canto fúnebre pela morte de um cacique)	
12.79	3. "Iara" (Andrade)	
12.80	"Vira" (c1926, Portuguese melody) A225
12.81	"Fado" (c1929, popular Portuguese melody) A236
12.82	"Suíte sugestiva" (c1929, Andrade, Chalupt & Bandeira; also see for S, Bar & orch, A242): 1. "Ouverture de l'homme tel" (arr for orch, A508) A243
12.83	2. "Prelude, choral et funèbre" (ciné journal)	
12.84	3. "Cloche pied au flic" (comédie)	
12.85	4. "Le recit du peureux" (drame)	
12.86	5. "Charlot aviateur" (comique)	
12.87	6. "L'Enfant et le iouroupari" (tragédie)	
12.88	7. "La marche finale"	
12.89	"Vocalises-Estudos" (c1929) A245
12.90	"Canções indígenas" (c1930): 1. "Pai do Mato" (Poema Ameríndio) (from Pareci Indians) A249
12.91	2. "Ualalocê" (Lenda dos índios Parecis para comemorar a caça) (also see w/ orch, A248)
12.92	3. "Kamalalô" (from Pareci Indians)	
12.93	"Pai do mato" (c1930, Andrade) A253
12.94	"O brasileiro" (Gritos da rua) (c1931; 1v) A255
12.95	"Modinhas e canções," Álbum I (c1935–43; orchd A406): 1. "Canção do marinheiro" (c1936, Vicente) A365
12.96	2. "Lundu da Maquesa de Santos" (c1938, after the play of Correa)
12.97	3. "Cantilena" (Um canto que saiu das senzalas) (c1936, on song from Bahia)
12.98	4. "A gatinha parda" (popular infantil) (c1941)	
12.99	5. "Remeiro de São Francisco"	
12.100	6. "Nhapopê" (c1935, Deodato)	
12.101	7. "Evocação" (c1943, Salema)	
12.102	"Bachianas brasileiras No.5" (orig for 1v & vcs, A389): 1. "Ária" (Cantilena) (c1938, Correa) A390
12.103	2. "Dança" (Martelo) (c1945, Bandeira)	
12.104	"Ária" (c1938; 1v & gui, transcr from 1. of: Bachianas brasileiras No.5, A389; also see A390) A391
12.105	"Tiradentes" (c1939, Correa; arr for 1v & ch; ch & orch, A403; 1v, ch & hpd, A410) A409
12.106	"Hino à vitória" (c1941, Capanema; 1v & pf; orig for ch & band, A428) A430
12.107	"Voz do povo" (Grito de Guerra) (c1942, Villa-Lobos) A436
12.108	"Modinhas e canções," Álbum II (c1943, on children's songs): 1. "Pobre peregrino" A441
12.109	2. "Vida formosa"	
12.110	3. "Nésta rua"	
12.111	4. "Manda tiro, tiro lá"	
12.112	5. "João Cambuête"	
12.113	6. "Na corda da viola"	
12.114	"Poema de Itabira" (Viagem na família) (c1943, Andrade; orig w/ orch, A422) A423
12.115	"Canções de cordialidade" (c1945, Bandeira & Villa-Lobos; orig for orch, A450) A452
12.116	"Duas paisagens" (Deux paysages) (c1946, Sá): 1. "Manhã na praia" A462
12.117	2. "Tarde na Glória"	
12.118	"The Emerald Song" (c1947, Forrest & Wright, from comedy: Magdalena, A476) A471
12.119	"Food for Thought" (c1947, Forrest & Wright; 1v & gui, from comedy: Magdalena, A476) A472
12.120	"Magdalena" (c1947, Forrest & Wright, from comedy: Magdalena, A476) A479
12.121	"My Bus and I" (c1947, Forrest & Wright, popular children's song, from comedy: Magdalena, A476) ... A480
12.122	"Scène de Paris" (c1947, from comedy: Magdalena, A476) A482
12.123	"Big Ben" (London poem) (c1948; also see w/ orch, A485) A484
12.124	"Canção do poeta do século XVIII" (c1948, Ferreira) A486

12.125 "Conselhos" (c1948, Villa-Lobos) A488
12.126 "Coração inquieto" (c1948, Moreaux) A489
12.127 "Dinga-donga" (Poema realista) (c1949; Villa-Lobos) A492
12.128 "Canção de cristal" (c1950, Araújo) A494
12.129 "Samba clássico" (Ode) (c1950, Villa-Lobos; also see w/ orch, A497) A498
12.130 "Canção do poeta do século XVIII" (c1953, Ferreira; 1v & gui) A514
12.131 "Jardim fanado" (Jardim Fané) (c1955, Albuquerque) A525
12.132 "Canção das águas claras" (c1956, Amado; also see w/ orch, A529) A530
12.133 "Eu te amo" (c1956, Vasconcellos; also see w/ orch, A532) A533
12.134 "Modinha" (Seresta No.5) (c1956, Bandeira) A534
12.135 "Poema de palavras" (c1957, Vasconcellos; also see w/ orch, A542) A541
12.136 "Cair da tarde" (c1958, from: Floresta do Amazonas, A551; also see w/ orch, A545) A544
12.137 "Cântico do Colégio Santo André" (c1958, Bandeira) A547
12.138 "Melodia sentimental" (c1958, from: Floresta do Amazonas, A551; also see w/ orch, A555) ... A556
12.139 "Sete vezes" (c1958, Vasconcellos; also see w/ orch, A557) A558
12.140 "Veleiros" (c1958, from: Floresta do Amazonas, A551; also see w/ orch, A561; 1v & 2gui, A562) ... A560
12.141 "Veleiros" (c1958; 1v & 2gui, from: Floresta do Amazonas, A551; also see w/ pf, A560; orch, A561) .. A562

13. EDUCATIONAL WORKS

13.1 "Guia Prático—Estudo Folclórico," 2 vols (a practical guide to musical and artistic education) (c1932–49, melodies collected during his travels; also see accompanying 11 albums for pf listed separately) A276
13.2 "Guia Prático" Album I (c1932; pf): No.1 "Acordei de madrugada" A277
13.3 No.2 "A maré encheu"
13.4 No.3 "A roseira" (2nd vers)
13.5 No.4 "Manquinha"
13.6 No.5 "Na corda da viola"
13.7 "Guia Prático" Album II (c1932; pf): No.1 "Brinquedo" A278
13.8 No.2 "Machadinha"
13.9 No.3 "Espanha"
13.10 No.4 "Samba-le-le"
13.11 No.5 "Senhora Dona Viúva" (1st vers)
13.12 "Guia Prático" Album III (c1932; pf): No.1 "O pastorzinho" A279
13.13 No.2 "João Cambuête"
13.14 No.3 "A freira"
13.15 No.4 "Garibaldi foi à missa"
13.16 No.5 "O pião"
13.17 "Guia Prático" Album IV (c1932; pf): No.1 "O pobre e o rico" A280
13.18 No.2 "Rosa amarela" (2nd vers)
13.19 No.3 "Olha o passarinho, domine"
13.20 No.4 "O gato"
13.21 No.5 "O sim"
13.22 "Guia Prático" Album V (c1932; pf): No.1 "Os pombinhos" A281
13.23 No.2 "Você diz que sabe tudo"
13.24 No.3 "Có-có-có"
13.25 No.4 "O bastião" (Mia gato)
13.26 No.5 "A condessa"
13.27 "Guia Prático" Album VI (c1932; pf): No.1 "Sonho de uma criança" A282
13.28 No.2 "O corcunda"
13.29 No.3 "O carangueijo" (1st vers)
13.30 No.4 "A pombinha voou"
13.31 No.5 "Vamos atrás da serra, Oh! Calunga!"
13.32 "Guia Prático" Album VII (c1932; pf): No.1 "No fundo do meu quintal" A283
13.33 No.2 "Vai, abóbora"
13.34 No.3 "Vamos Maruca"
13.35 No.4 "Os pombinhos"
13.36 No.5 "Anda a roda"
13.37 "Guia Prático" Album VIII (c1935; pf, on popular children's themes): No.1 "O limão" A358
13.38 No.2 "Carambola"
13.39 No.3 "Pobre cega"
13.40 No.4 "Pai Francisco"
13.41 No.5 "Xô! Passarinho!"
13.42 No.6 "Sinh 'Aninha"
13.43 No.7 "Vestidinho branco"
13.44 "Guia Prático" Album IX (c1935; pf, on children's themes): No.1 "Laranjeira pequenina" A359
13.45 No.2 "Pombinha rolinha"
13.46 No.3 "O ciranha, O cirandinha"
13.47 No.4 "A velha que tinha nove filhos"
13.48 No.5 "Constante"
13.49 No.6 "O castelo"
13.50 "Guia Prático" Album X (c1932; pf): No.1 "De flor em flor" A284
13.51 No.2 "Atché"
13.52 No.3 "Nésta rua"
13.53 No.4 "Fui no itororó" (1st vers)

14. INCOMPLETE & FRAGMENTARY WORKS

*   *   *   *   *

A = David P. Appleby: "Heitor Villa-Lobos. A Bio-Bibliography." Greenwood Press. New York, 1988.

1. STAGE WORKS

Operas:

1.1	*"L'Adelaide" (c1735, ?Salvi, lost/=?L'Atenaide)*	*RV695*
1.2	*"Alvilda, regina de' Goti" (c1731, Zeno, lost)*	*RV696*
1.3	*"Agrippo" (c1730, Lalli, lost)*	*RV697*
1.4	*"Aristide" (c1735, Goldoni)*	*RV698*
1.5	"Armida al campo d'Egitto" (c1718, Palazzi, Act II lost, sinfonia in RV710)	RV699
1.6	"Arsilda, regina di Ponto" (c1716, Lalli)	RV700
1.7	*"Artabano, re de' Parti" (c1718, Marchi, modification of RV706, lost)*	*RV701*
1.8	"L'Atenaide o sia Gli affetti generosi" (c1728, Zeno)	RV702
1.9	"Bajazet" (Tamerlano), pasticcio (c1735, Piovene, music compiled Vivaldi from works of others)	RV703
1.10	*"La Candace o siano Li veri amici" (c1720, Silvani & Lalli, lost)*	*RV704*
1.11	"Catone in Utica" (c1737, Metastasio, Act I lost)	RV705
1.12	*"La costanza trionfante degl'amori e de gl'odii" (c1716, Marchi, lost)*	*RV706*
1.13	*"Cunegonda" (c1726, Piovene, lost)*	*RV707*
1.14	*"Doriclea" (c1732, Marchi, modification of RV706, lost)*	*RV708*
1.15	"Dorilla in Tempe" (c1726, Lucchini, sinfonia in RV711)	RV709
1.16	"Ercole su 'I Termodonte" (c1723, Bussani, sinfonia in RV699)	RV710
1.17	"Farnace" (c1727, Lucchini, sinfonia in RV709)	RV711
1.18	*"La fede tradita e vendicata" (c1726, Silvani, lost)*	*RV712*
1.19	*"Feraspe" (c1739, Silvani, lost)*	*RV713*
1.20	"La fida ninfa" (c1732, Maffei; r as: Il giorno felice, KV777)	RV714
1.21	*"Filippo, re di Macedonia" (c1721, Lalli, Acts I & II c by Boniventi, Act III c by Vivaldi, lost)*	*RV715*
1.22	*"Ginevra, principessa di Scozia" (c1736, Salvi, lost)*	*RV716*
1.23	"Giustino" (c1724, Berengani & Pariati, sinfonia in RV111 & R111a)	RV717
1.24	"Griselda" (c1735, Zeno adapted by Goldoni)	RV718
1.25	"L'incoronazione di Dario" (c1717, Morselli)	RV719
1.26	*"Gli inganni per vendetta" (c1720, Palazzi, modification of RV699, lost)*	*RV720*
1.27	*"L'inganno trionfante in amore" (c1725, Noris & Ruggieri, lost)*	*RV721*
1.28	*"Ipermestra" (c1727, Salvi, lost)*	*RV722*
1.29	*"Montezuma" (c1733, Giusti, lost)*	*RV723*
1.30	*"Nerone fatto Cesare," pasticcio (c1715, Norris, some music c by Vivaldi, lost)*	*RV724*
1.31	"L'Olimpiade" (c1734, Metastasio)	RV725
1.32	*"L'oracolo in Messenia" (c1738, Zeno, lost)*	*RV726*
1.33	"Orlando finto pazzo" (c1714, Braccioli)	RV727
1.34	"Orlando" (furioso) (c1727, Braccioli)	RV728
1.35	"Ottone in villa" (c1713, Lalli)	RV729
1.36	*"Rosilena ed Oronta" (c1728, Palazzi, lost)*	*RV730*
1.37	"Rosmira," pasticcio (c1738, Stampiglia, music compiled Vivaldi from works of others)	RV731
1.38	*"Scanderbeg" (c1718, Salvi, lost)*	*RV732*
1.39	*"Semiramide" (c1732, Zeno, lost)*	*RV733*
1.40	*"La Silvia," dramma pastorale (c1721, ?Bissari, lost)*	*RV734*
1.41	*"Siroe, re di Persia" (c1727, Metastasio, lost)*	*RV735*
1.42	"Teuzzone" (c1719, Zeno, sinfonia in RV700)	RV736
1.43	*"Tieteberga" (c1717, Lucchini, lost)*	*RV737*
1.44	"Tito Manlio" (c1720, Noris)	RV738
1.45	"La verità in cimento" (c1720, Palazzi & Lalli)	RV739
1.46	"La virtù trionfante dell'amore e dell'odio ovvero Il Tigrane" (c1724, Silvani, collab Micheli)	RV740
1.47	Misc arias (not in known operas)	RV749
1.48	*"Il giorno felice" (c1737, r vers of: La fida ninfa, RV714, lost)*	*RV777*
1.49	"Tito Manlio," pasticcio (c1720, collab Boni & Giorgio)	RV778

Serenatas:

1.50	"Dall'eccelsa mia reggia" (Gloria e Himeneo) (c ?1725; 2vv)	RV687
1.51	*"Le gare del dovere" (c1719, music lost)*	*RV688*
1.52	*"Le gare della giustitia e della pace" (Catena, lost)*	*RV689*
1.53	"Mio cor, povero cor" (Serenata a tre) (ch)	RV690
1.54	*"Il Mopso," egloga pescatoria (ca1737, Nonnannuci, lost)*	*RV691*
1.55	*"Questa Eurilla gentil" (c1726; ch, music lost)*	*RV692*
1.56	"La Sena festeggiante" (c1729, Lalli; ch, 1st sinfonia = RV117 w/ different 2nd movt)	RV693
1.57	*"L'unione della Pace e di Marte" (c1727; ch, Grossatesta, music lost)*	*RV694*

2. PUBLISHED ORCH / INSTRUMENTAL COLLECTIONS (also see individual works listed separately)

2.1	"Suonate da camera a 3" (p1705 in Venice; 2vn & vle/hpd)	Op.1/1–12
2.2	"Sonate" (p1709 in Venice, p1712–3 in Amsterdam; vn & hpd)	Op.2/1–12
2.3	"L'Estro Armonico," 12 concertos (p1712 in Amsterdam; 1–4 solo insts, strings & cont)	Op.3/1–12
2.4	"La Stravaganza," 12 concertos (p ca1712–3 in Amsterdam; vn, strings & cont)	Op.4/1–12
2.5	"VI Sonate" (p ca1716 in Amsterdam; vn/2vn & cont) (numbers consecutive with Op.2)	Op.5/13–18
2.6	"VI Concerti à 5 stromenti" (p1716–7 in Amsterdam; 3vn, va & cont)	Op.6/1–6
2.7	"Concerti à 5 stromenti," in 2 books (p ca1716–7 in Amsterdam; 3vn, va & cont)	Op.7i/1–6 & Op.7ii/1–6

3. CHAMBER CONCERTOS (p ca1716; insts & cont)

4. CONCERTOS & SINFONIAS (p ca1729–30; strings & cont)

5. VIOLIN CONCERTOS (w/ strings & cont)

6. OTHER CONCERTOS (w/ strings & cont)

6.87	Bassoon Concerto in C major	RV478
6.88	Bassoon Concerto in C major	RV479
6.89	Bassoon Concerto in C minor	RV480
6.90	Bassoon Concerto in D minor	RV481
6.91	Bassoon Concerto in D minor (inc)	RV482
6.92	Bassoon Concerto in E-flat major	RV483
6.93	Bassoon Concerto in E minor	RV484
6.94	Bassoon Concerto in F major (also see RV457)	RV485
6.95	Bassoon Concerto in F major	RV486
6.96	Bassoon Concerto in F major	RV487
6.97	Bassoon Concerto in F major	RV488
6.98	Bassoon Concerto in F major	RV489
6.99	Bassoon Concerto in F major	RV490
6.100	Bassoon Concerto in F major	RV491
6.101	Bassoon Concerto in G major	RV492
6.102	Bassoon Concerto in G major	RV493
6.103	Bassoon Concerto in G major	RV494
6.104	Bassoon Concerto in G minor	RV495
6.105	Bassoon Concerto in G minor	RV496
6.106	Bassoon Concerto in A minor	RV497
6.107	Bassoon Concerto in A minor	RV498
6.108	Bassoon Concerto in A minor	RV499
6.109	Bassoon Concerto in A minor (also see RV463)	RV500
6.110	Bassoon Concerto in B-flat major, "La notte (II)"	RV501
6.111	Bassoon Concerto in B-flat major	RV502
6.112	Bassoon Concerto in B-flat major	RV503
6.113	Bassoon Concerto in B-flat major	RV504

7. DOUBLE CONCERTOS (w/ strings & cont)

7.1	Double Violin Concerto in C major	RV505
7.2	Double Violin Concerto in C major	RV506
7.3	Double Violin Concerto in C major	RV507
7.4	Double Violin Concerto in C major	RV508
7.5	Double Violin Concerto in C minor	RV509
7.6	Double Violin Concerto in C minor	RV510
7.7	Double Violin Concerto in D major	RV511
7.8	Double Violin Concerto in D major	RV512
7.9	Double Violin Concerto in D major	RV513
7.10	Double Violin Concerto in D minor	RV514
7.11	Double Violin Concerto in E-flat major	RV515
7.12	Double Violin Concerto in G major	RV516
7.13	Double Violin Concerto in G minor	RV517
7.14	Double Violin Concerto in A major	RV518
7.15	Double Violin Concerto in A major .... "L'Estro Armonico" Op.3/5,	RV519
7.16	Double Violin Concerto in A major (inc) .... "La Cetra" I/12,	RV520
7.17	Double Violin Concerto in A major	RV521
7.18	Double Violin Concerto in A minor (arr J. S. Bach, BWV593) .... "L'Estro Armonico" Op.3/8,	RV522
7.19	Double Violin Concerto in A minor	RV523
7.20	Double Violin Concerto in B-flat major	RV524
7.21	Double Violin Concerto in B-flat major	RV525
7.22	Double Violin Concerto in B-flat major (inc) .... "La Cetra" I/6,	RV526
7.23	Double Violin Concerto in B-flat major	RV527
7.24	Double Violin Concerto in B-flat major (also see RV381)	RV528
7.25	Double Violin Concerto in B-flat major	RV529
7.26	Double Violin Concerto in B-flat major .... "La Cetra" II Op.9/9,	RV530
7.27	Double Violin Concerto in F major (also see RV767)	RV765
7.28	Double Cello Concerto in G minor	RV531
7.29	Double Mandolin Concerto in G major	RV532
7.30	Double Flute Concerto in C major	RV533
7.31	Double Oboe Concerto in C major	RV534
7.32	Double Oboe Concerto in D minor	RV535
7.33	Double Oboe Concerto in A minor	RV536
7.34	Double Trumpet Concerto in C major	RV537
7.35	Double Horn Concerto in F major (solo vc in 2nd movt)	RV538
7.36	Double Horn Concerto in F major	RV539
7.37	Double Concerto in D minor (va d'amore & lute)	RV540
7.38	Double Concerto in D minor (vn & org)	RV541
7.39	Double Concerto in F major (vn & org)	RV542
7.40	Double Concerto in F major (vn & ob: unison; also see RV139)	RV543
7.41	Double Concerto in F major, "Il Proteo ossia Il mondo al rovescio" (vn & vc; also see RV572)	RV544

7.42 Double Concerto in G major (ob & bn) RV545
7.43 Double Concerto in A major, "All'inglese" (vn & vc; later vers for vn & vc all'inglese) RV546
7.44 Double Concerto in B-flat major (vn & vc) RV547
7.45 Double Concerto in B-flat major (vn & ob) RV548
7.46 Double Concerto in C minor (vn & org; also see RV510) RV766
7.47 Double Concerto in F major (vn & org; also see RV765) RV767
7.48 Double Concerto in C major (vn & org, inc) RV774
7.49 Double Concerto in F major (vn & org, inc) RV775

8. MULTIPLE CONCERTOS (w/ strings & cont)

8.1 Concerto in D major (4vn, vc in 1st movt) .... "L'Estro Armonico" Op.3/1, RV549
8.2 Concerto in E minor (4vn) .... "L'Estro Armonico" Op.3/4, RV550
8.3 Concerto in F major (3vn) RV551
8.4 Concerto in A major, "per eco in lontana" (vn & 3 solo vns) RV552
8.5 Concerto in B-flat major (4vn) RV553
8.6 Concerto in C major (vn, org/vn ad lib & ob) RV554
8.7   Concerto in C major (vn, org/vn ad lib & vc) RV554a
8.8 Concerto in C maj (3vn, ob, 2rec, 2va all'inglese, salmoè, 2vc & 2hpd; also 2tpt & 2vle in 3rd movt) RV555
8.9 Concerto in C major, "per la solennità di S. Lorenzo" (2ob, 2 'claren,' 2rec, 2vn & bn) RV556
8.10 Concerto in C major (4vn) RV557
8.11 Concerto in C major (2vn 'in tromba,' 2rec, 2mand, 2 salmoès, 2 theorbos & vc) RV558
8.12 Concerto in C major (2cl & 2ob) RV559
8.13 Concerto in C major (2cl & 2ob) RV560
8.14 Concerto in C major (vn & 2vc) RV561
8.15 Concerto in D major (vn, 2ob & 2hn) RV562
8.16 Concerto in D major (vn, 2ob, 2hn & timp, different 2nd movt) RV562a
8.17 Concerto in D major (vn & 2ob) RV563
8.18 Concerto in D major (2vn & 2vc) RV564
8.19 Concerto in D major (2vn, 2ob & bn, ?spur) RV564a
8.20 Concerto in D minor (2vn & vc; arr J. S. Bach, BWV596) .... "L'Estro Armonico" Op.3/11, RV565
8.21 Concerto in D minor (2vn, 2rec, 2ob & bn) RV566
8.22 Concerto in F major (4vn & vc) .... "L'Estro Armonico" Op.3/7, RV567
8.23 Concerto in F major (vn, 2ob, 2hn & bn) RV568
8.24 Concerto in F major (vn, 2ob, 2hn & bn, also vc in 3rd movt) RV569
8.25 Concerto in F major, "La tempesta di mare (I)" (fl, ob & bn, also vn in 1st movt; = RV98 reworked,
      also see RV433) RV570
8.26 Concerto in F major (vn, 2ob, 2hn, vc & bn; also see RV99) RV571
8.27 Concerto in F major, "Il Proteo o sia Il mondo al rovescio" (fl, ob, vn, vc & hpd; = RV544 reworked) . RV572
8.28 Concerto in F major (2ob, 2hn & 2bn, lost) RV573
8.29 Concerto in F major (vn, 2trbn da caccia, 2ob, bn, 2vn & 2vc) RV574
8.30 Concerto in G major (2vn & 2vc) RV575
8.31 Concerto in G minor (vn, ob, 2rec, 2ob & bn) RV576
8.32 Concerto in G minor, "per l'orchestra di Dresda" (vn, 2ob, 2rec & bn) RV577
8.33 Concerto in G minor (2vn & vc) .... "L'Estro Armonico" Op.3/2, RV578
8.34 Concerto in B-flat major, "Funebre" (vn, ob, salmoè & 3va all'inglese) RV579
8.35 Concerto in B minor (4vn & vc; arr J. S. Bach, BWV1065) .... "L'Estro Armonico" Op.3/10, RV580
8.36   Concerto in D major (2fl, 2vn & 2bn, lost) RV751

9. CONCERTOS WITH DOUBLE ORCHESTRA (w/ 2 string orch & cont)

9.1 Violin Concerto in C major, "Assontione di Maria Vergine (I)" (also see RV179) RV581
9.2 Violin Concerto in D major, "Assontione di Maria Vergine (II)" (also see RV12) RV582
9.3 Violin Concerto in B-flat major RV583
9.4 Double Concerto in F major (vn & org, solo parts inc) RV584
9.5 Concerto in A major (2vn, 2rec/vc in 3rd movt, 2vn, 2rec & org/vc in 3rd movt) RV585

10. TRIO SONATAS

2vn & cont:

10.1 Trio Sonata in C major (?spur) RV60
10.2 Trio Sonata in C major Op.1/3, RV61
10.3 Trio Sonata in D major Op.1/6, RV62
10.4 Trio Sonata in D minor, "La follia" (theme & 19 variations on old melody / dance: La follia) (also see
      Corelli Op.5/12) Op.1/12, RV63
10.5 Trio Sonata in D minor Op.1/8, RV64
10.6 Trio Sonata in E-flat major Op.1/7, RV65
10.7 Trio Sonata in E major Op.1/4, RV66
10.8 Trio Sonata in E minor Op.1/2, RV67
10.9 Trio Sonata in F major RV68
10.10 Trio Sonata in F major Op.1/5, RV69

11. SOLO SONATAS

Vn & cont:

12. MISC INSTRUMENTAL

13. MASSES & MASS SECTIONS

14. PSALMS

15. HYMNS & SEQUENCES

15.4	"Regina coeli," antiphon in C major (inc)	RV615
15.5	"Salve Regina," antiphon in C minor (d ch)	RV616
15.6	"Salve Regina," antiphon in F major	RV617
15.7	"Salve Regina," antiphon in G minor	RV618
15.8	*"Salve Regina," antiphon (lost)*	*RV619*
15.9	"Sanctorum meritis," hymn in C major	RV620
15.10	"Stabat mater," sequence in F minor	RV621
15.11	*"Te Deum," anthem (lost)*	*RV622*

16. MOTETS

16.1	"Canta in prato," in A major	RV623
16.2	"Carae rosae respirate," in G major	RV624
16.3	"Clarae stellae," in F major	RV625
16.4	"In furore giustissimae irae," in C minor	RV626
16.5	"In turbato mare," in G major	RV627
16.6	"Invicti bellate," in G major	RV628
16.7	"Longe mala umbrae terrores," in G minor	RV629
16.8	"Nulla in mundo pax," in E major	RV630
16.9	"O qui coeli terraeque," in E-flat major	RV631
16.10	"Sum in medio tempestatum," in F major	RV632
16.11	"Vestro Principi divino," in F major	RV633
16.12	"Vos aurae per montes," in A major (Mottetto per la Solennità di S. Antonio)	RV634
16.13	"Ascende laeta," in A major (Dixit)	RV635
16.14	"Canta in prato," in G major (Introduzione al Dixit)	RV636
16.15	"Cur sagittas," in B-flat major (Gloria)	RV637
16.16	"Filiae mestae," in C minor (Miserere)	RV638
16.17	"Jubilate, o amaeni," in D major (Introduzione al Gloria, RV588; 2 vers: S / A)	RV639
16.18	"Longe mala umbrae terrores," in G minor (Gloria)	RV640
16.19	"Non in pratis," in F major (Miserere)	RV641
16.20	"Ostro picta," in D major (Introduzione al Gloria, RV589)	RV642
16.21	*"Aria per la communione," in G major (lost)*	*RV748*

17. ORATORIOS & OTHER SACRED VOCAL

| *17.1* | *"Moyses Deus Pharaonis," oratorio (c1714, lost)* | *RV643* |
| 17.2 | "Juditha triumphans devicta Holofernes barbarie," 2 part oratorio (c1716, Cassetti; arr for 1v & pf): . | RV644 |

    I: 1. "Arma, caedes, vindictae"
          2a. "Felix en fausta dies"
          2b. "Nil arma, nil bella"
          3a. "Mi dux, Domine mi"
          3b. "Matrona immica"
          4a. "Huc accedat Matrona"
          4b. "Quo cum Patriae me"
          5a. "Ne timeas non"
          5b. "Vultus tui vago splendori"
          6a. "Vide, humilis prostata"
          6b. "O quam vaga"
          7a. "Quem vides prope"
          7b. "Quamvis ferro"
          8a. "Quid cerno!"
          8b. "Quanto magis generosa"
          9a. "Magna, o foemina"
          9b. "Sede, o cara"
          10a. "Tu Judex es"
          10b. "Agitata infido flatu"
          11a. "In tentorio supernae"
          11b. "O servi volate"
          12a. "Tu quoque hebraica"
          12b. "Veni, me sequere"
          13a. "Venio, Juditha"
          13b. "Fulgeat sol frontis decorae"
          14a. "In Urbe interim pia"
          14b. "Mundi Tector in Caelo"
    II: 15a. "Summi Regis in mente"
          15b. "O Sydera, o stellae"
          16a. "Jam saeventis in hostem"
          16b. "Nox in umbra dum surgit"
          16c. "Nox obscura tenebrosa"
          17a. "Belligerae meae sorti"
          17b. "Transit aetas"
          18a. "Haec in crastinum serva"
          18b. "Noli o cara te adorantis"

19a. "Tibi dona salutis"
19b. "Plena necate non mero"
20a. "Tormenta mentis tuae"
20b. "Vivat in pace"
21a. "Sic in pace"
21b. "Umbrae carae"
22a. "Quae fortunata es"
22b. "Non ita reducem"
23a. "Jam pergo, postes claudo"
23b. "Summae Astorum Creator"
23c. "In sommo profundo"
24a. "Impii, indigni Tiranni"
24b. "Abra, accipe munus"
24c. "Si fulgida per te"
25a. "Jam non procul"
25b. "Armatae face"
26a. "Quam insolita luce"
26b. "Gaude felix"
27a. "Ita decreto aeterno"
27b. "Salve invicta Juditha"

18. SOLO CANTATAS

1v & cont:

1v, instr(s) & cont:

* * * * *

RV = P. Ryom: "Verzeichnis der Werke A. Vivaldis: kleine Ausgabe." Leipzig, 1974; suppl., Poitiers, 1979.

1. STAGE WORKS

Operas (& music dramas):

1.1	*"Leubald," 5 act Trauerspiel (c1826–8, sketches)*	*WWV1*
1.2	*"Schäferoper" (c ?1830, on Goethe's Die Laune der Verliebten, frag, lost)*	*WWV6*
1.3	*"Die Hochzeit," 3 acts (c1832–3, after Büsching: Ritterzeit und Ritterwesen, frags)*	*WWV31*
1.4	"Die Feen," 3 act romantic (c1833–4, after Gozzi's La donna serpente)	WWV32
1.5	"Das Liebesverbot oder die Novize von Palermo," 2 act comic (c1834–5, after Shakespeare's play Measure for Measure)	WWV38
1.6	*"Die hohe Braut," 5 acts (c1836, after Koenig's novel, project)*	*WWV40*
1.7	*"Männerlist grösser als Frauenlist," 2 act comic (c1838, after '1001 Nights,' lost)*	*WWV48*
1.8	"Rienzi, der Letzte der Tribunen," 5 act grand tragic (c1838–40, r1843, after Bulwer-Lytton's novel transl Bärmann & Mitford's play)	WWV49
1.9	"Der fliegende Holländer" (The Flying Dutchman), 3 act romantic (c1841, r1846, 1852, 1860, on episode from Heine's Memoirs of Herr von Schnabelewopski)	WWV63
1.10	*"Die Sarazenin," 5 acts (c1841, project)*	*WWV66*
1.11	*"Die Bergwerke zu Falun," 3 acts (c1842, Hoffmann, project)*	*WWV67*
1.12	"Tannhäuser und der Sängerkrieg auf dem Wartburg" (Tannhaüser and the Song Contest at the Wartburg), 3 act grand romantic (Wagner; 3 vers):	WWV70
	. Dresden Version (c1843–5, perf1845, titled: Der Venusberg)	
	. Paris Version (c1860–1, perf1861, r of Dresden version w/ additions in French)	
	. Final Version (c1865, perf1865, w/ German transl of Paris additions; new addition 1875)	
1.13	"Lohengrin," 3 act romantic (c1845–47, perf1850, Wagner)	WWV75
1.14	*"Friedrich I," 5 acts (c1846–9, project)*	*WWV76*
1.15	*"Jesus von Nazareth," 5 acts (c1849, project)*	*WWV80*
1.16	*"Achilleus," 3 acts (c1849, project)*	*WWV81*
1.17	*"Wieland der Schmied," 3 acts Heldenoper (c1849–50, project)*	*WWV82*

"Der Ring des Nibelungen" (The Ring of the Nibelung), Bühnenfestspiel für 3 Tage und einen Vorabend (Stage-festival play for 3 days and an introductory evening) (Wagner, 1st draft pubd1848) (new melodic style: 'unendlische Melodie'—rhapsodic semi-recitatives over the continuous symphonic music):

1.18	I. "Vorabend: Das Rheingold" (The Rhine Gold), 4 scenes (c1853–4, perf1869)	WWV86A
1.19	II. "Erster Tag: Die Walküre" (The Valkyrie), 3 acts (c1854–6, perf1870)	WWV86B
1.20	III. "Zweiter Tag: Siegfried," 3 acts (c1856–71, perf1876; orig intended title: Der junge Siegfried)	WWV86C
1.21	IV. "Dritter Tag: Die Götterdämmerung" (Twilight of the Gods) (orig intended title: Siegfrieds Tod), 3 acts (c1869–74, perf1876)	WWV86D

1.22	*"Die Sieger" (c1856, project)*	*WWV89*
1.23	"Tristan und Isolde" (Tristan and Isolde), 3 acts (c1857–1859, perf1865, Wagner)	WWV90
1.24	"Die Meistersinger von Nürnberg" (The Mastersingers of Nuremburg), 3 acts (c1862–7, perf1868, Wagner)	WWV96
1.25	*"Romeo und Julie" (sketches)*	*WWV98*
1.26	*"Luthers Hochzeit" (c1868, project)*	*WWV99*
1.27	*"Ein Lustspiel," 1 act (c1868, project)*	*WWV100*
1.28	*"Eine Kapitulation," 1 act Lustspiel (in antiker Manier) (c1870, project)*	*WWV102*
1.29	"Parsifal," 3 acts (c1878–1882, perf1882, Wagner; orig intended title: Parzival)	WWV111

Incid music:

1.30	*"König Enzio" (c1831–2, Raupach, lost)*	*WWV24B*
1.31	*"Columbus" (c1834–5, Apel, lost; also see: Overture, WWV37A)*	*WWV37B*
1.32	*"Die letzte Heidenverschwörung in Preussen" (c1837, Singer, frag)*	*WWV41*

1a. SELECTIONS FROM STAGE WORKS

1a.4	"Die Feen," opera:	WWV32

  . "Ouvertüre"
- I:
  1. "Introduktion": "Schwinget euch auf" (Feen, Farzana, Zemina, Geister)
  2. "Szene und Rezitativ": "Was seh' ich? Morald, ihr? und Gunther, du?" (Gernot, Morald, Gunther)
  3. "Arie": "Wo find' ich dich, wo wird mir Trost?" (Arindal)
  4. "Rezitativ und Romanze": "Da steht ihr nun" (Gernot, Arindal)
  . "Hexe wohl, Frau Dinovaz genannt," romance
  . "War einst 'ne böse" (Gernot)
  5. "Quartett": "Arindal!... O welch ehrwürdige Gstalt" (Gunther, Arindal, Gernot, Morald)
  6. "Finale" (Arindal, Ada, Morald, Gunther, Gernot, Gefährten, Farzana, Zemina, Feen)
  . "So soll für immer ich nun von dir scheiden," recit (Arindal)
- II:
  1. "Introduktion": "Weh uns, Weh! Wir sind geschlagen!" (Krieger, Volk Lora)
  . "Aria": "O, musst du Hoffnung schwinden" (Lora, Bote, Krieger, Volk)
  2. "Chor und Terzett": "O König, sei gegrüsst" (Chor, Arindal, Morald, Lora)
  3. "Rezitativ": "Wie ist dir's, Gunther" (Gernot, Gunther)
  4. "Duett": "Wie? Seh' ich recht?" (Drolla, Gernot)

. "Rezitativ": "O! Grausame! So habt ihr kein Erbarmen" (Ada, Zemina, Farzana)
. "Szene und Arie" (1st vers): "Ich sollte ihm entsagen," recit (Ada)
. "Ja, dieser Liebe Macht zog hin zu ihm mich ganz" (Ada)
. "Begeistern wird auch ihn die Liebe" (Ada)
5. "Szene und Arie" (2nd vers): "Weh mir, so nah die fürchterliche Stunde," recit (Ada)
. "Begeistern wird auch ihn die Liebe" (Ada)
6. "Finale": "Hört ihr des Sturmes Brausen"
III: 1. "Introduktion" (Chor, Morald, Lora, Drolla, Gunther, Gernot): "Heil sei dem holden Frieden" (ch)
2. (1834 eingefügter Dialog)
3. "Szene und Arie": "Hallo! Hallo! Lasst alle Hunde los!" (Arindal)
. "Szene": "Mein Gatte Arindal" (Ada)
4. "Rezitativ": "So wäre unsre Ada denn gerettet" (Farzana, Zemina)
. "Terzett": "Auf! Auf! Auf! Erwache, Arindal!" (Zemina, Farzana, Arindal)
5. (1834 eingefügter Dialog)
6. "Finale": "Ihr Geister auf" (Chor der Erdgeister)

1a.5 "Das Liebesverbot oder die Novize von Palermo," opera: WWV38
1. "Ouvertüre"
I: 2. "Introduktion": "Ihr Galgenvögel haltet ein" (ch)
3. "Duet": "Salve Regina coeli!" (Chor der Nonnen, Mariana, Isabella)
4. "Duett": "Es ist ein Mann" (Isabella, Luzio)
5. "Arie, Duett, Terzett und Ensemble": "Wie lang er bleibt?" (Brighella)
6. "Finale": "Nun, wird es bald" (Soli, Chor)
II: 7. "Duett": "Wo Isabella bleibt?," recit (Claudio)
8. "Szene und Rezitativ": "So sei's! Für seinen feigen Wankelmut," recit (Isabella)
9. "Terzett": "Wie glücklich" (Luzio, Isabella, Dorella)
. "Rezitativ": "Vernimm, mein Freund, um was ich dich jetzt bitte" (Isabella, Pontio Pilato)
10. "Szene und Arie": "So spät und noch kein Brief von Isabella!," recit (Friedrich)
. "Ja glühend wie des Südens Hauch" (Friedrich)
11. "Finale": "So recht, ihr wackern jungen Leute!" (Antonio)

1a.8 "Rienzi, der Letzte der Tribunen," opera: WWV49
. "Ouvertüre"
I: 1. "Introduktion": "Hier ist's, hier ist's! Frisch auf, ihr Freunde" (Orsini)
2. "Terzett": "O Schwester sprich, was dir geschah" (Rienzi, Irene, Adriano)
3. "Duett": "Er geht und lässt dich meinem Schutz" (Irene, Adriano)
4. "Finale": "Gegrüsst, gegrüsst" (Chor des Volkes, Doppelchor im Lateran, soli)
II: 5. "Introduktion": "Jauchzet ihr Täler! Frohlockt ihr Berge!" (Chor der Friedensboten, soli)
. "Rienzi, nimm des Friedens Gruss!" (Colonna)
6. "Szene, Terzett und Chor": "Colonna, hörtest du das freche Wort?"
7. "Finale": "Erschallet, Feierklänge!" (Chor des Volkes, soli)
. "Ihr Römer, es beginnt das Fest!" (Herold)
"Pantomime" (Musik II)
. "Pantomime und Ballett" (Musik XII)
"Ballett" (Musik II)
A. "Tanz der Frauen" (Musik XII)
"Festlicher Tanz mit Festhaltung der Allegorie" (Musik II)
B. "Waffentanz" (Musik XII)
. "Kampf"
"Festliche Tänze" (Musik II)
C. "Festlicher Tanz" (Musik XII)
"Spätere Fassung des Balletts" (Musik XI):
A. "Introduktion"
B. "Waffenspiel"
C. "Gladiatoren-Kampf"
D. "Auftritt der Jungfrauen"
E. "Festlicher Tanz"
III: 8. "Introd. und Ensemble": "Vernahmt ihr all' die Kunde schon?" (Chor, Baroncelli, Cecco, Rienzi)
9. "Szene und Arie": "Gerechter Gott!," recit (Adriano)
10. "Finale": "Der Tag ist da, die Stunde naht," recit (Rienzi)
. "Schlachthymne": "Santo spirito cavaliere!" (Rienzi)
"Spätere Fassung des Schlusses von No.10" (Musik VIIa):
. "Hört nicht den Rasenden! Den er so wild beklagt," recit (Rienzi)
. "Auf! Auf! Auf, im Triumph" (Chor)
IV: 11. "Introduktion, Terzett und Chor": "Wer war's" (Baroncelli, Chor, Cecco, Adriano)
12. "Finale": "Ihr, nicht beim Feste?," recit (Rienzi)
V: 13. "Introduktion und Gebet": "Allmächtiger Vater" (Rienzi)
14. "Verlässt die Kirche mich," recit (Rienzi, Irene)
15. "Szene und Duo": "Du hier, Irene? Treff' ich dich noch," recit (Adriano, Irene)
16. "Finale": "Herbei! Auf, eilt zu uns!" (Chor des Volkes, Rienzi, Baroncelli, Cecco, Adriano)
"Nachkomponiertes Vorspiel zum 3. Akt" (Musik VI)

1a.9 "Der fliegende Holländer," opera (Nos. of sections in The Gramophone): WWV63
1. "Ouvertüre"
I: 2. "Hojohe! Hallojo!" (Die Matrosen)

    3. "Mit Gewitter und Sturm aus fernem Meer" (Der Steuermann)
    4. "Die Frist ist um," recit (Der Holländer)
    5. "He! Holla! Steuermann!" (Daland)
    6. "Mein Schiff ist fest"
    7. "Blick hin, und überzeuge"
    8. "Wenn aus der Quallen"
    9. "Hei! Wie die Segel schon sich bläh'n!" (Daland)
    10. "Interlude"
II: 11. "Summ' und brumm', du gutes Rädchen" (Spinning Chorus) (Chor der Mädchen)
    12. "Du böses Kind" (Mary)
    13. "Joho hoe! Traft ihr das Schiff" (Senta's Ballad) (Senta)
    14. "Bleib', Senta!," duet (Erik, Senta)
    15. "Ach möchtest du ... Mein Kind, du siehst mich?" (Senta, Daland)
    16. "Mögst du, mein Kind" (Daland)
    17. "Wie aus der Ferne längst vergang'ner Zeiten," duet (Der Holländer, Senta)
    18. "Verzeiht! Mein Volk hält" (Daland)
    19. "Interlude"
III: 20. "Steuermann, lass die Wacht!" (Die Matrosen)
    21. "Jo ho ho hoe!"
    22. "Was musst' ich hören!" (Erik)
    23. "Willst jenes Tags du nicht dich mehr entsinnen" (Erik)
    24. "Verloren! Ach! Verloren!," finale

1a.12   "Tannhäuser und der Sängerkrieg auf dem Wartburg," opera (Nos. of sections in
    The Gramophone): WWV70
I: 1. "Ouvertüre"
    2. "Venusberg Music"
    3. "Geliebter, sag! Wo weilt dein Sinn?" (Venus)
    4. "Dir töne Lob" (Tannhäuser)
    5. "Geliebter, komm! Sieh dort die Grotte" (Venus)
    6. "Stets soll nur dir, nur dir mein Lied ertönen!" (Tannhäuser)
    7. "Frau Holda kam aus dem Berg hervor" (Ein junger Hirt)
    8. "Zu dir wall ich, mein Jesus Christ" (Pilgergesang)
    9. "Als du in kühnen Sange" (Wolfram)
II: 10. "Dich teure Halle grüss' ich wieder" (Elisabeth's Greeting)
    11. "O Fürstin! Gott! Stehet auf!" (Tannhäuser, Elisabeth)
    12. (Entry of the Guests) (Grand March)
    13. "Freudig begrüssen wir die edle Halle" (ch)
    14. "Gar viel und schön" (Landgrave's Address)
    15. "Blick ich umher in diesem edlen Kreise" (Wolfram)
    16. "Heraus zum Kampfe mit uns allen!" (Biterolf)
    17. "O Himmel, lass dich jetzt erflehen" (Wolfram)
    18. "Zurück" (Elisabeth)
    19. "Ein Engel stieg aus lichtem Äther" (Landgraf, Sänger und Ritter)
    20. "Ein furchbares Verbrechen ward begangen" (Landgraf)
III: 21. "Prelude"
    22. "Wohl wüsst' ich hier sie im Gebet zu finden" (Wolfram)
    23. "Beglückt darf nun dich, o Heimat" (Pilgrims' Chorus)
    24. "Allmächt'ge Jungfrau" (Elisabeth's Prayer)
    25a. "Wie Todesahnung Dämm'rung deckt die Lande" (Wolfram)
    25b. "O du mein holder Abendstern" (Wolfram)
    26. "Ich hörte Harfenschlag" (Tannhäuser)
    27. "Inbrunst im Herzen" (Tannhäuser)
    28. "Willkommen, ungetreuer Mann!" (Venus)

1a.13   "Lohengrin," opera (Nos. of sections in The Gramophone): WWV75
    excerpts: 1. "Prelude"
I: 2. "Gott grüss' euch, liebe Männer" (König Heinrich)
    3. "Dank, König, dir" (Friedrich)
    4. "Einsam in trüben Tagen" (Elsa's Dream)
    5a. "Wer hier in Gotteskampf" (Der Heerrufer)
    5b. "In düst'rem Schweigen richtet Gott!... Du trugest zu ihm" (Alle Männer, Elsa)
    6. "Nun sei bedankt" (Lohengrin)
    7. "Nie sollst du mich" (Lohengrin)
    8. "Mein Herr und Gott, nun ruf' ich dich" (Fer König)
II: 9. "Erhebe dich, Genossin meiner Schmach!" (Friedrich)
    10. "Euch Lüften, die mein Klagen so traurig oft erfüllt" (Elsa)
    11. "Elsa!... Wer ruft?" (Ortrud, Elsa)
    12a. "Entweihte Götter!" (Ortrud)
    12b. "Ortrud! Wo bist du?" (Elsa)
    12c. "Du Ärmste kannst wohl nie ermessen" (Elsa)
    13. "Gesegnet soll sie schreiten" (Procession: Die Edlen und Mannen)
    14. "O König! Trugbetörte Fürsten! Haltet ein!" (Friedrich)
    15. "Welch ein Geheimnis muss der Held bewahren" (Der König, die Männer, Frauen und Knaben)
    16. "Mein Held, entgegne kühn dem Ungetreuen!" (Der König)

III: 17. "Prelude"
    18. "Treulich geführt ziehet dahin" (Wedding March)
    19a. "Das süsse Lied verhallt" (Lohengrin)
    19b. "Atmest du nicht mit mir die süssen Düfte?" (Lohengrin)
    19c. "Höchstes Vertraun hast du mir schon zu danken" (Lohengrin)
    20a. "Heil, König Heinrich!" (ch)
    20b. "Habt Dank, ihr Lieben von Brabant" (König Heinrich)
    21. "In fernem Land, unnahbar euren Schritten" (Lohengrin)
    22. "Mein lieber Schwan!" (Lohengrin)

1a.18   "Das Rheingold," opera (Nos. of sections in The Gramophone): WWV86A
    excerpts: I: 1. "Prelude"
        2. "Weia! Waga! Woge, du Welle" (Woglinde, Wellgunde, Flosshilde)
        3. "He he! Ihr Nicker!" (Alberich)
        4. "Garstig glatter glitschriger Glimmer!" (Alberich)
        5. "Lugt, Schwestern" (Woglinde)
        6a. "Der Welt Erbe gewänn' ich zu eigen" (Alberich)
        6b. "Spottet nur zu!" (Alberich)
        7. (Orch interlude)
    II: 8. "Wotan! Gemahl! Erwache!" (Fricka)
        9. "So schirme sie jetzt" (Fricka)
        10. "Sanft schloss Schlaf dein Aug' " (Fasolt)
        11. "Du da, folge uns!" (Fafner)
        12. "Endlich Loge!" (Wotan)
        13. "Immer ist Undank Loges Lohn" (Loge)
        14. "Hör' Wotan, der Harrenden Wort!" (Fafner)
        15a. "Schwester! Brüder! Rettet! Helft!" (Freia)
        15b. "Über Stock und Stein zu Tal" (Loge)
        16. "Jetzt fand ich's! Hört, was euch fehlt" (Loge)
        17. "Wotan, Gemacht, unsel'ger Mann!"
        18a. "Auf, Loge! hinab mit mir!" (Wotan)
        18b. "Nach! Nibelheim fahren wir nieder" (Wotan)
        19. (Descent into Nibelheim) (Orch interlude)
    III: 20. "Hehe! hehe!" (Alberich)
        21. "Nibelheim hier" (Alberich)
        22. "Mit eurem Gefrage" (Mime)
        23. "Was wollt ihr hier?" (Alberich)
        24. "Die in linder Lüfte Wehn da oben ihr lebt" (Alberich)
        25. "Riesenwurm winde sich ringelnd!" (Alberich)
    IV: 26. "Da, Vetter, sitze du fest!" (Loge)
        27. "Wohlan, die Nibelheim rief ich mir nah" (Alberich)
        28. "Bin ich nun frei?" (Alberich's curse)
        29. "Lauschtest du seinem Liebesgruss?" (Loge)
        30. "Halt! Nicht sie berührt" (Fasolt)
        31. "Nicht so leicht und locker gefügt!" (Fafner)
        32. "Freia, die Schöne, schau' ich nicht mehr" (Fasolt)
        33. "Weiche, Wotan, weiche!" (Erda's Warning)
        34. "Hört, ihr Riesen! Zurück, und harret" (Donner)
        35. "Halt, du Gieriger! Gönne mir auch was!" (Fasolt)
        36. "Was gleicht, Wotan, wohl deinem Glücke?" (Loge)
        37. "Schwüles Gedünst schwebt in der Luft" (Donner)
        38. "Zur Burg führt die Brücke" (Froh)
        39. "Abendlich strahlt" (Wotan)
        40. "Ihrem Ende eilen sie zu" (Loge)
        41. "Rheingold! Rheingold! Reines Gold!" (Woglinde, Wellgunde, Wellgunde, Flosshilde)
        42. (Entrance of the Gods into Valhalla) (orch vers)

1a.19   "Die Walküre," opera (Nos. of sections in The Gramophone): WWV86B
    excerpts: I: 1. "Prelude"
        2. "Wess' Herd dies auch sei" (Siegmund)
        3. "Müd am Herd fand ich den Mann" (Sieglinde)
        4. "Friedmund darf ich nicht heissen" (Siegmund)
        5. "Ich weiss ein wildes Geschlecht" (Hunding)
        6. "Ein Schwert verhiess mir der Vater" (Siegmund)
        7. "Schläfst du, Gast?" (Sieglinde)
        8. "Der Männer Sippe sass hier im Saal" (Sieglinde)
        9. "Winterstürme wichen dem Wonnemond" (Siegmund)
        10. "Du bist der Lenz" (Sieglinde)
        11. "War Wälse dein Vater" (Sieglinde)
        12. "Siegmund heiss ich und Siegmund bin ich!" (Siegmund)
    II: 13. "Prelude"
        14. "Nun zäume dein Ross, reisige Maid!" (Wotan)
        15a. "Hojotoho!"
        15b. "Dir rat ich, Vater, rüste dich selbst" (Brünnhilde)
        16. "Der alte Sturm, die alte Müh'!" (Wotan)

17. "So ist es denn aus mit den ewigen Göttern" (Fricka)
18. "Was verlangst du?" (Wotan)
19. "Deiner ew'gen Gattin heilige Ehre" (Fricka)
20. "Schlimm, fürcht ich, schloss der Streit" (Brünnhilde)
21. "Als junger Liebe Lust mir verblich" (Wotan)
22. "Ein andres ist's" (Wotan)
23a. "Ihrem Willen muss ich gewähren" (Wotan)
23b. "So nimmst du von Siegmund den Sieg?" (Brünnhilde)
24. "So sah ich Siegvater nie" (Brünnhilde)
25. "Raste nun hier; gönne dir Ruh'!" (Siegmund)
26. "Siegmund! Sieh auf mich!" (Todesverkündigung) (Brünnhilde)
27. "Du sahest der Walküre sehrenden Blick" (Brünnhilde)
28. "Zauberfest bezähmt ein Schlaf der Holden Schmerz und Harm" (Siegmund)
29a. "Der dort mich ruft" (Siegmund)
29b. "Kehrte der Vater nur heim!" (Sieglinde)
30a. "Zu Ross, dass ich dich rette!" (Brünnhilde)
30b. "Geh hin, Knecht! Knie vor Fricka" (Wotan)
III: 31. "Hojotoho" (Ride of the Valkyries) (Gerhilde)
32. "Schützt mich und helft in höchster Not!" (Brünnhilde)
33. "Nicht sehre dich Sorgen um mich" (Sieglinde)
34. "Wo ist Brünnhild', wo die Verbrecherin?" (Wotan)
35. "Hier bin ich, Vater" (Brünnhilde)
36. "War es schmählich, was ich verbrach" (Brünnhilde)
37. "Weil für dich im Auge das eine ich hielt" (Brünnhilde)
38. "So tatest du, was so gern zu tun ich begehrt" (Wotan)
39a. "Und das ich ihm in Stücken schlug" (Wotan)
39b. "Nicht streb, o Maid, den Mut mir zu stören" (Wotan)
40. "Leb wohl, du kühnes, herrliches Kind!" (Wotan's Farewell)
41. "Der Augen leuchtendes Paar" (Wotan)
42. "Loge, hör! Lausche hieher!" (Wotan)
43. (Magic Fire Music)
44. (Ride of the Valkyries) (concert vers)

excerpts: I: 1. "Prelude"
2. "Zwangvolle Plage! Müh' ohne Zweck!" (Mime)
3. "Hoiho! Hoiho! Hau ein!" (Siegfried)
4. "Als zullendes Kind zog ich dich auf" (Mime)
5. "Vieles lehrtest du, Mime" (Siegfried)
6. "Einst lag wimmernd ein Weib" (Mime)
7. "Soll ich der Kunde glauben" (Siegfried)
8. "Heil dir, weiser Schmied!" (Wanderer)
9. "Hier sitz' ich am Herd und setze mein Haupt" (Wanderer)
10. "Auf wolkigen Höh'n wohnen die Götter" (Wanderer)
11. "Was zu wissen dir frommt, solltest du fragen" (Wanderer)
12. "Verfluchtes Licht! Was flammt dort die Luft?" (Mime)
13. "Bist du es, Kind?" (Mime)
14. "Fühltest du nie im finstren Wald" (Mime)
15. "Her mit den Stücken, fort mit dem Stümper" (Siegfried)
16. "Nothung! Nothung! Neidliches Schwert!" (Forging Song) (Siegfried)
17a. "Hoho! Hoho! Haheil" (Siegfried)
17b. "Schmiede, mein Hammer, ein hartes Schwert!" (Siegfried)
18. "Den der Bruder schuf" (Mime)
II: 19. "Prelude"
20. "In Wald und Nacht" (Alberich)
21a. "Wer naht dort schimmernd im Schatten?" (Alberich)
21b. "Zur Neidhöhle fuhr ich bei Nacht" (Wanderer)
22. "Fafner, Fafner! Erwache, Wurm!" (Wanderer)
23a. "Ich lieg' und besitz,' lasst mich schlafen" (Fafner)
23b. "Nun, Alberich, das schlug fehl" (Wanderer)
24. "Wir sind zur Stelle; bleib hier stehn!" (Mime)
25a. "Dass der mein Vater nicht ist" (Forest Murmurs) (Siegfried)
25b "Forest Murmurs" (concert version)
26a. "Meine Mutter, ein Menschenweib!" (Siegfried)
26b. "Du holdes Vöglein!" (Siegfried)
27. "Siegfried's horn-call"
28. "Haha! Da hätte mein Lied" (Siegfried)
29a. "Da lieg, neidischer Kerl" (Siegfried)
29b. "Wer bist du, kühner Knabe" (Fafner)
30. "Zur Kunde taugt kein Toter" (Siegfried)
31. "Wohin schleichst du eilig und schlau, schlimmer Gesell?" (Alberich)
32. "Willkommen, Siegfried!" (Mime)
33. "Neides Zoll zahlt Nothung" (Siegfried)
34. "Da lieg auch du, dunkler Wurm!" (Siegfried)
35. "Freundliches Vöglein, dich frage ich nun" (Siegfried)

36a. "Nun sing! Ich lausche dem Gesang" (Siegfried)
36b. "Hei! Siegfried erschlug nun den schlimmen Zwerg!" (Stimme des Waldvogels)
III: 37. "Prelude"
38. "Wache, Wala! Wala! Erwach!" (Wanderer)
39. "Stark ruft das Lied" (Erda)
40a. "Weisst du, was Wotan will?" (Wanderer)
40b. "Dir Unweisen ruf' ich ins Ohr" (Wanderer)
41. "Dort seh' ich Siegfried nahn" (Wanderer)
42. "Mein Vöglein schwebte mir fort!" (Siegfried)
43. "Kenntest du mich, kühner Spross" (Wanderer)
44. (Orch interlude)
45a. "Selige Öde auf sonniger Höh'!" (Siegfried)
45b. "Was ruht dort schlummernd im schattigen Tann?" (Siegfried)
46a. "Dass ist kein Mann!" (Siegfried)
46b. "Brennender Zauber zückt mir ins Herz" (Siegfried)
47. "Heil dir, Sonne! Heil dir, Licht!" (Brünnhilde)
48. "O Siegfried! Siegfried! Seliger Held!" (Brünnhilde)
49. "Dort seh' ich Grane" (Brünnhilde)
50. "Ewig war ich, ewig bin ich" (Brünnhilde)

1a.21   "Die Götterdämmerung," opera (Nos. of sections in The Gramophone): WWV86D
excerpts: Prologue: 1a. "Introduction"
       1b. "Welch Licht leuchtet dort?" (Norn 1)
       2. (Dawn) (Orch interlude)
       3. "Zu neuen Taten, teurer Helde" (Brünnhilde)
       4. "O heilige Götter!" (Brünnhilde)
       5. "Siegfried's Rhine Journey" (Orch interlude)
I: 6. "Nun hör, Hagen, sage mir, Held" (Gunther)
       7a. "Was weckst du Zweifel und Zwist!" (Gunther)
       7b. "Brächte Siegfried die Braut dir heim" (Hagen)
       8a. "Heil! Siegfried, teurer Held!" (Hagen)
       8b. "Wer ist Gibichs Sohn?" (Siegfried)
       9. "Begrüsse froh, o Held" (Gunther)
       10. "Willkommen, Gast, in Gibichs Haus!" (Gutrune)
       11. "Hast du, Gunther, ein Weib?" (Siegfried)
       12a. "Blut-Brüderschaft schwöre ein Eid!" (Siegfried)
       12b. "Blühenden Lebens labendes Blut" (Siegfried)
       13. "Hier sitz' ich zur Wacht, wahre den Hof" (Hagen's Watch) (Hagen)
       14. (Orch interlude)
       15. "Altgewohntes Geräusch raunt meinem Ohr die Ferne" (Brünnhilde)
       16a. "Höre mit Sinn, was ich dir sage!" (Walltraute's Narration)
       16b. "Seit er von dir geschieden" (Walltraute's Narration cont'd)
       17. "Da sann ich nach" (Walltraute's Narration cont'd)
       18. "Welch banger Träume Mären" (Brünnhilde)
       19. "Brünnhild'! Ein Freier kam" (Siegfried)
II: 20. "Prelude"
       21. "Schläfst du, Hagen, mein Sohn?" (Alberich)
       22. (Orch interlude)
       23. "Hoiho, Hagen! Müder Mann!" (Siegfried)
       24. "Hoiho! Ihr Gibichsmannen, machet euch auf!" (Hagen)
       25. "Heil dir, Gunther!" (Mannen)
       26. "Brünnhild', die hehrste Frau" (Gunther)
       27a. "Was ist ihr? Ist sie entrückt?" (Mannen)
       27b. "Was müht Brünnhildes Blick?" (Siegfried)
       28. "Helle Wehr! Heilige Waffe!" (Siegfried)
       29. "Welches Unholds List liegt hier verhohlen?" (Brünnhilde)
       30. "Dir hilft kein Hirn" (Hagen)
III: 31. "Prelude"
       32. "Frau Sonne sendet lichte Strahlen" (Die drei Rheintöchter: Woglinde, Wellgunde, Flosshilde)
       33. "Hoiho? Hoiho!" (Stimmen der Mannen, Siegfried)
       34. "Trink, Gunther, trink" (Siegfried)
       35. "Mime heiss ein mürrischer Zwerg" (Siegfried's Narration)
       36. "Brünnhilde, heilige Braut!" (Siegfried)
       37. "Siegfried's Funeral March"
       38. "War das sein Horn?" (Gutrune)
       39. "Schweigt eures Jammers" (Brünnhilde)
       40. "Starke Scheite schichtet mir dort" (Brünnhilde's Immolation)
       41. "Mein Erbe nun nehm' ich zu eigen" (Brünnhilde)
       42. "Fliegt heim, ihr Raben!" (Brünnhilde)
       43. "Zurück vom Ring" (Hagen) (Orch finale)
       44. (Dawn and Siegfried's Rhine Journey) (concert vers)

1a.23   "Tristan und Isolde," opera (Nos. of sections in The Gramophone): WWV90
I: 1. "Prelude"
       2. "Hab acht, Tristan!" (Kurvenal)

3. "Doch nun von Tristan!" (Isolde)
4. "Wie lachend sie mir Lieder singen" (Isolde's Narrative and Curse)
5. "So reihte sie die Mutter" (Brangäne)
6. "Begehrt, Herrin, was ihr wünscht" (Tristan)
II: 7. "Prelude"
8a. "Isolde! Geliebte! Tristan! geliebter" (Tristan, Isolde)
8b. "O eitler Tagesknecht!" (Isolde)
8c. "O sink hernieder" (Beide)
9a. "Einsam wachend" (Brangäne's Warning)
9b. "Lausch Geliebter!"
9c. "So stürben wir" (Tristan)
9d. "Lass' mich sterben!" (Isolde)
10. "Tatest du's wirklich?" (King Marke's Monologue)
11. "O König ... Wohin nun Tristan scheidet" (Tristan)
III: 12. "Prelude"
13. "Die alte Weise—was weckt sie mich?" (Tristan)
14. "Dünkt dich das?" (Tristan)
15. "Wie sie selig"
16. "O diese Sonne!" (Tristan)
17. "Ha! Ich bin's, ich bin's" (Isolde)
18. "Mild und leise" (Liebestod) (Isolde)
19. *"Prelude und Liebestod" (concert vers arr Humperdinck)*

1a.24   "Die Meistersinger von Nürnberg," opera (Nos. of sections in The Gramophone): WWV96
excerpts: 1. "Prelude"
I: 2. "Da zu dir der Heiland kam" (Gemeinde)
3. "Verweilt! Ein Wort! ein einzig Wort!"
4. "Da bin ich! Wer ruft?"
5. "David! Was stehst?"
6. "Mein Herr! Der Singer Meisterschlag"
7. "Der Meister Tön' und Weisen"
8. "Damit, Herr Ritter, ist's so bewandt!"
9. "So bleibt mir einzig der Meister-Lohn!"
10. 'Seid meiner Treue wohl versehen" (Pogner)
11a. "Gott grüsst Euch, Meister"
11b. "Zu einer Freiung und Zunftberatung"
12. "Das schöne Fest, Johannistag" (Pogner's Address)
13. "Vielleicht schon ginget ihr zu weit"
14a. "Wohl, Meister, zur Tagesordnung kehrt"
14b. "Dacht' ich mir's doch!"
15. "Am stillen Herd"
16. "Nun, Meister! Wenn's gefällt"
17. "Was euch zum Liede Richt' und Schnur"
18. " 'Fanget an'—So rief der Lenz" (Trial Song)
19. "Seid Ihr nun fertig?"
20. "Halt! Meister! Nicht so geeilt!"
II: 21. "Johannistag!" (Lehrbuben)
22. "Lass seh'n, ob Meister Sachs zuhaus?" (Pogner)
23a. "Zeig' her!—'s ist gut, Dort an die Tür' " (Sachs)
23b. "Was duftet doch der Flieder" (Fliedermonologue)
24. "Gut'n Abend, Meister!" (Eva)
25. "Das dacht' ich wohl"
26. "Da ist er!... Ja, ihr seid es" (Eva)
27a. "Geliebter, spare den Zorn"
27b. "Hört, ihr Leut, und lasst euch sagen"
27c. "Üble Dinge, die ich da merk"
28a. "Tu's nicht!—Doch horch!"
28b. "Jerum! Jerum!"
29a. "Das Fenster geht auf"
29b. "Freund Sachs! So hört doch nur ein Wort!"
30. "Den Tag seh' ich erscheinen" (Beckmesser's Serenade)
31. "Mit den Schuhen ward ich fertig schier"
32. "Zum Teufel mit dir, verdammter Kerl!" (David)
III: 33. "Prelude"
34. "Gleich, Meister! Hier!" (David)
35. "Am Jordan Sankt Johannes stand"
36. "Wahn! Wahn! Überall Wahn!" (Wahnmonolog)
37. "Grüss Gott, mein Junker!" (Sachs)
38. "Mein Freund! In holder Jugendzeit"
39. "Morgenlich leuchtend" (Prize Song Rehearsal)
40. "Abendlich glühend"
41. "Ein Werbelied! Von Sachs!" (Beckmesser)
42. "Das Gedicht! hier liess ich's"
43a. "So ganz boshaft doch keinen ich fand"
43b. "Sie Evchen!... Grüss Gott, mein Evchen" (Sachs)

44. "Hat man mit dem Schuhwerk"
45. "O Sachs! Mein Freund"
46a. "Mein Kind, von Tristan und Isolde"
46b. "Aha! Da streicht die Lene"
46c. "Ein Kind ward hier geboren"
47. "Selig wie die Sonne" (Quintet)
48. "Sankt Krispin, lobet ihn!" (Die Schuster)
49. "Ihr tanzt?" (Dance of the Apprentices)
50. (Entry of the Masters)
51. "Wach auf! es nahet gen den Tag"
52. "Euch macht ihr's leicht"
53. "Nun denn, wenn's Meistern und Volk beliebt"
54. "Morgen ich leuchte" (Beckmesser)
55. "Das Lied, für wahr, ist nicht von mir"
56. "Morgenlich leuchtend" (Prize Song)
57. "Verachtet mir die Meister nicht" (Sachs' Panegyric)
58. "Ehrt eure deutschen"

1a.29   "Parsifal," opera (Nos. of sections in The Gramophone): WWV111
1. "Prelude"
I: 2. "He! ho! Waldhüter ihr" (Gurnemanz)
3. "Hei! Wie fliegen der Teufelsmähre die Mähnen" (Erster Knappe)
4. "Recht so!—Habt Dank!—Ein wenig Rast" (Amfortas)
5. "Wann alles ratlos steht" (Gurnemanz)
6. "Das ist ein andres" (Gurnemanz)
7. "Titurel, der fromme Held" (Gurnemanz)
8. "Weh! Weh! Hoho! Auf!" (Knappen und Ritter)
9. "Unerhörtes Werk!" (Gurnemanz)
10. "Den Vaterlosen gebar die Mutter" (Kundry)
11. "So recht! So nach des Grales Gnade" (Gurnemanz)
12a. "Vom Bade kehrt der König heim" (Gurnemanz)
12b. (Transformation Scene)
13. "Nun achte wohl ... Zum letzten Liebesmahle" (Gurnemanz)
14a. "Mein Sohn Amfortas, bist du am Amt?" (Titurel)
14b. "Nein! Lasst ihn unenthüllt" (Amfortas)
14c. "Wehvolles Erbe, dem ich verfallen" (Amfortas)
15. " 'Durch Mitleid wissend, der reine Tor" (Knaben und Jünglinge)
II: 16. "Prelude"
17. "Die Zeit ist da" (Klingsor)
18. "Ach! Tiefe Nacht ... Furchtbare Not!" (Kundry)
19. "Hier war das Tosen!" (Blumenmädchen)
20. "Komm, holder Knabe!" (ch)
21. "Dies alles—hab' ich nun geträumt?" (Parsifal)
22. "Ich sah das Kind" (Herzeleide) (Kundry)
23. "Wehe! Wehe! Was tat ich?" (Parsifal)
24. "Amfortas! Die wunde!" (Parsifal)
25. "Grausamer! Fühlst du im Herzen" (Kundry)
26. "Auf Ewigkeit wärst du verdammt mir für eine Stunde" (Parsifal)
III: 27. "Prelude"
28. "Von dorther kam das Stöhnen" (Gurnemanz)
29. "Heil dir, mein Gast!" (Gurnemanz)
30. "Zu ihm, des tiefe Klagen" (Parsifal)
31. "O Gnade! Höchstes Heil!"
32. "Du wuschest mir die Füsse" (Good Friday Music)
33a. (Transformation Scene)
33b. "Geleiten wir im bergenden Schrein" (Ritter des Grales)
34. "Ja, Wehe! Wehe! Weh' über mich!" (Amfortas)
35. "Nur eine Waffe taugt" (Parsifal)
36. (Good Friday music) (concert version)

1a.32   *"Die letzte Heidenverschwörung in Preussen," incid music:* *WWV41*
1. "Marcia, moderato"
. "Hört der Götter Spruch!" (Chor der Priester)
2. "Picullos nimm auf blutigem Altar" (Jünglinge)
3. "Die Flamme sprüht" (Chor der Priester)

2. SYMPHONIES

2.1   Symphony in C major (c1832) WWV29
2.2   Symphony in E major (c1834, inc: 1st movt & 29 bars of Adagio only) WWV35
2.3   *"Sinfonien" (c1846–7, 3 sketches, ?to Lohengrin)* *WWV78*

3. OTHER ORCHESTRAL WORKS

4. CONCERTOS, SOLO INSTR & ORCH

5. STRING QUARTETS

6. OTHER CHAMBER MUSIC

7. PIANO SONATAS

8. OTHER PIANO WORKS

Pf duet:

9. CHORAL WORKS

Doubtful or spurious:

12.12	*Harp Sonata (c1854, ?never composed)*	
12.13	*"Der Berggeist oder Die drei Wünsche," incid music (Gleich, doubtful)*	
12.14	*"Helena," incid music (c ?1844, Euripides, doubtful)*	
12.15	*"Fischerlied" (doubtful)*	
12.16	*"Fanfaren für Signaltrompeten" (doubtful)*	
12.17	*3 sketches (doubtful)*	
12.18	*"Adagio" (cl & str qnt, spur)*	
12.19	*"Wann? Wo? Wie?," duet (spur)*	

13. ARRANGEMENTS OF WORKS OF OTHERS

13.1	*Beethoven: Symphony No.9 in D minor, Op.125 (arr1830; pf, lost)* *WWV9*
13.2	*Haydn: Symphony No.103 in E-flat major, HobI/103 (arr1831–2; pf, lost)* *WWV18*
13.3	*Bellini: aria from opera: Il pirata (orchd1833, from pf score, for use in: La straniera, lost)* *WWV34*

Opera arrs in Riga (c1837–9):

13.4	Bellini: "Norma" (r of orchestration) WWV46A
13.5	Meyerbeer: "Robert toi que j'aime," from opera: Robert le diable (harp part arr for strings) WWWV46B
13.6	Weber: "Jägerchor," section 18. from opera: Euryanthe, J291 (reorchd) WWV46C

Other operatic arrs:

13.7	*Rossini: "Li marinari," duet from: Soirées musicales (pf acc orchd1837–8, lost)* *WWV47*
13.8	Donizetti: "L'elisir d'amore" (arr1840; pf, from vocal score) ....
13.9	*"Suiten für Cornet à pistons" (Opernpotpourris) (c1840, lost)* *WWV62A*
13.10	Donizetti: "La favorite" (arr1840–1; pf, from vocal score) WWV62B
13.11	Herz: "Grande fantaisie sur La romanesca," Op.111 (arr1841; pf duet) WWV62C
13.12	Halévy: "Le guitarrero" (arr1841; pf, from vocal score) WWV62D
13.13	Halévy: "La reine de Chypre" (arr1841–2; pf, from vocal score) WWV62E
13.14	*Auber: "Zanetta" (arr1842, lost)* *WWV62F*
13.15	*Donizetti: "Les martyrs" (arr1839–42, lost)* ....
13.16	Spontini: "La Vestale" (add instrumentation 1844) WWV74
13.17	Gluck: "Iphigénie en Aulide," Wq46 (perf vers 1846–7, vocal score p1858) WWV77
13.18	Palestrina: "Stabat Mater" (perf vers 1848) WWV79
13.19	*Mozart: "Don Giovanni" (perf vers 1850, lost)* *WWV83*
13.20	Gluck: Concert ending of Overture to opera: Iphigénie en Aulide, Wq46 (arr1854) WWV87
13.21	Strauss, J. Jr.: "Wein, Weib und Gesang," waltz, Op.333 (reorchd1875) WWV109

* * * * *

WWV = J. Deathridge, M. Geck, E. Voss: "Wagner Werk-Verzeichnis." Schott. Mainz—London—New York
—Tokyo, 1985.

1. STAGE WORKS

Operas & Singspiels:

1.1	*"Die Macht der Liebe und des Weines," Singspiel (c1798, lost)*	*Anh6*
1.2	*"Eine musicalische Posse," ?a masque (ca1798–1800, lost)*	*Anh7*
1.3	*"Das Waldmädchen," 2 act Romantic-comic opera (c1800, Steinsberg, frags)*	*Anh1*
1.4	"Peter Schmoll und seine Nachbarn," 2 acts (c1801–2, Türk after Crämer; Overture r1807, J54)	J8
1.5	*"Rübezahl," 2 acts (c1804–5, Rhode after popular legend, frags):*	*Anh2*
	extant: . *"Ouvertüre" (frag)*	*Anh27*
	3. "Süss lacht die Liebe den Jüngling an" (Geisterchor)	J44
	7. "Vernahm ich hier nicht ... Wie Bienchen im Frühling," recit & arietta (Kurt, Gnomen)	J45
	10. "Prinzessin! Prinzessin!," quintet (Prinzessin, Klärchen, Kunigunde, Elsbeth, Rübezahl)	J46
1.6	*"Antonius" (und Cleopatra), eine Burleske (c1808, lost)*	*Anh30*
1.7	"Silvana," 3 act Romantic opera (c1808–10, Hiemer after text of Das Waldmädchen)	J87
1.8	"Abu Hassan," 1 act Singspiel (c1810–1, Hiemer after: The 1001 Nights)	J106
1.9	"Der Freischütz," 3 act Romantic opera (c1817–21, Kind after Apel & Laun: Gespensterbuch)	J277
1.10	*"Die drei Pintos," 3 act comic opera (c1820–1, Hell after Seidel, sketches; reconstr & compl Mahler p1888).*	*Anh5*
1.11	"Euryanthe," 3 act grand heroic-Romantic opera (c1822–3, Chézy)	J291
1.12	"Oberon, König der Elfen," 3 act Romantic opera (c1825–6, Planché after Wieland, transl Winkler)	J306

Incid music:

1.13	"Turandot," 5 act Schauspiel (c1809, Gozzi transl Schiller, Overture & 6 instr Nos.)	Op.37, J75
1.14	*"Das österreichische Feldlager," Schauspiel (c1813, lost):*	*Anh43–Anh45*
	. *"Ungarese" (lost)*	*Anh43*
	. *"Ouvertüre" (lost)*	*Anh44*
	. *"Quodlibet" (lost)*	*Anh45*
1.15	"König Yngurd," 5 act Trauerspiel (c1817, Müllner; mS, 11 Nos.):	J214
	incl: . "Lasst den Knaben nicht den Raben" (Lied der Brunhilde, Act V/7)	
1.16	"Donna Diana," Lustspiel (c1817, Moreto, 6 Nos.):	J220
	incl: . "Lasst Fenisens Lob ertönen" (Gastons Rundgesang, Act III/3)	
	. "Darf sich meine Liebe zeigen" (Lied w/ gui, Act III/3)	
1.17	"Heinrich IV, König von Frankreich," 5 act Trauerspiel (c1818, Gehe, 8 instr Nos.)	J237
1.18	"Lieb' um Liebe," 1 act Schauspiel (c1818, Rublack)	J246
1.19	"Der Leuchtthurm," Trauerspiel (c1820, Houwald; harp, 2 melodramas & 2 interludes)	J276
1.20	"Preciosa," 4 act Schauspiel (c1820, Wolff; 1v, ch & orch)	J279
1.21	"Den Sachsen-Sohn vermählet heute," Festspiel (c1822, Robert)	J289

Misc:

1.22	2 Nos. for Haydn: Der Freybrief, HobXXXII/2 (c1809): 1. "Was ich da thu'," rondo alla polacca (T)	J77
1.23	2. "Dich an dies Herz zu drücken" (S, T)	J78
1.24	4 Songs for Kotzebue: Der arme Minnesinger (c1811; w/ gui acc): 1. "Über die Berge mit Ungestüm"	J110
1.25	2. "Rase, Sturmwind, blase"	J111
1.26	3. "Lass mich schlummern, Herzlein, schweige"	J112
1.27	4. "Umringt vom mutherfüllten Heere" (w/ m ch)	J113
1.28	*Chorus for Shakespeare's Romeo & Juliette (c1813, lost)*	*Anh48*
1.29	*"Arrangement of ballet music" (c1814, lost)*	*Anh49*
1.30	"Ah, se Edmondo fosse l'uccisor!," scena & aria for Méhul's opera: Héléna (c1815; S & orch)	Op.52, J178
1.31	2 Songs for Fischer's Singspiel: Der travestirte Aeneas (c1815): 1. "Mein Weib ist capores" (Bar)	J183
1.32	2. "Frau Lieserl, juhe!" (S, B; also arr for orch, J185)	J184
1.33	*"Balletmusik" (c1815, lost)*	*Anh59*
1.34	*Overture to Schauspiel: Lieb' und Versöhnen oder Die Schlacht bei Leipzig (Gubitz, lost)*	*Anh60*
1.35	2 Songs for Gubitz's Festspiel: Lieb' und Versöhnen (c1815): 1. "Wer stets hinter'n Ofen kroch"	J186
1.36	2. "Wie wir voll Glut uns hier zusammenfinden"	J187
1.37	"Was stürmet die Haide herauf," ballad in Reinbeck: Gordon & Montrose (c1815; Bar & harp) Op.47/3, J189	
1.38	*Aria (reworked for Fischer 1816, lost)*	*Anh61*
1.39	*Romanze No.2: "Sei unbekümmert, o Frankenland," for Castelli: Diana von Poitiers (c1816, lost)*	*Anh62*
1.40	"Arietta der Lucinde," for Huber: Das Sternenmädchen im Maidlinger Wald (c1816)	J194
1.41	"Ein König einst gefangen sass," romance for Castelli: Diana von Poitiers (c1816; w/ gui)	J195
1.42	*Fanfare for March, in Isouard's opera: Aschenbrödel (Cendrillon) (c1817, lost)*	*Anh63*
1.43	*"Chor etc.," for Grillparzer's Trauerspiel: Die Ahnfrau (c1817, lost)*	*Anh65*
1.44	"Hold ist der Cyanenkranz," song for Kind: Der Weinberg an der Elbe (c1817; vv & ch)	J222
1.45	*Chorus for Weigl's Singspiel: Das Dorf im Gebirge (c1818, lost)*	*Anh66*
1.46	"Leise weht es" (Alkanzor und Zaide), romance for Kind: Das Nachtlager von Granada (c1818)	J223
1.47	"Sei gegrüsst, Frau Sonne, mir," song for Holbein: Die Drei Wahrzeichen (c1818; T, B & ?acc)	J225
1.48	"In Provence blüht die Liebe," dance & song w/ Andantino for Hell: Das Haus Anglade (c1818; T & ch) J227	
1.49	"Was sag ich?," scena & aria for Cherubini's opera: Lodoïska (c1818; S & orch)	Op.56, J239
1.50	"Heil dir, Sappho!," chorus for Grillparzer: Sappho (c1818; ch, winds & perc)	J240
1.51	"Ein Mädchen ging" (Bach, Echo, Kuss), Kind: Der Abend am Waldrunnen (c1818; w/ pf/gui) Op.71/2, J243	
1.52	*Trombones added to Cherubini's opera: Der Wasserträger (c1820, lost)*	*Anh77*
1.53	"Agnus Dei," for Blankensee's Trauerspiel: Carlo (c1820; ch & winds)	J273
1.54	"Sagt, woher stammt Liebeslust?," song for Shakespeare's The Merchant ... (c1821; 2S, A, ch & gui)	J280
1.55	"Doch welche Töne steigen jetzt hernieder," arioso & recit for Spontini: Olimpia (c1825; B, S)	J305

1a. SELECTIONS FROM STAGE WORKS

1a.4   "Peter Schmoll und seine Nachbarn," opera: J8
         . "Ouvertüre"
      I: 1. "Das sind die schönen Früchte" (Introduction), trio (Minette, Schmoll, Bast)
            2. "Spiele, alter Esel, du," trio (Minette, Schmoll, Bast)
            3. "Im Rheinland eine Dirne war," romance (Minette)
            4. "Der Wüstling verschwendet," aria (Oberbereiter)
            5. "Die Menschen sind schon so!," arietta (Bast)
            6. "Wenn er nur Ruh' und Ordnung hält," trio (Minette, Niclas, Bast)
            7. "Hans Bast! Gieb Acht, Hans Bast!," aria (Bast)
            8. "O Hoffnung, gütigste der Feen," aria (Oberbereiter)
            9. "Dich an dies Herz zu drücken," duet (Minette, Oberbereiter)
           10. "Der edle schöne junge Mann," duet (Minette, Bast)
           11. "Es ist das seligste Vergnügen," trio (Minette, Oberbereiter, Bast)
      II: 12. "Du fröhlicher Jüngling," aria (Minette)
           13. "Ja Gottes Erde ist doch schön," aria (Schmoll)
           14. "Empfanget hier," trio (Minette, Oberbereiter, Greis)
           15. "Wie der bange Pilger zittert," aria (Greis)
           16. "Ein Lügner ist ein grosser Mann," ariette (Bast)
           17. "Fort von hier!," quartet (Minette, Oberbereiter, Schmoll, Bast)
           18. "Fürwahr! Führwahr!," aria (Bast)
           19. "O grosser Gott, ich danke dir!," duet (Minette, Oberbereiter)
           20. "So hab' ich, nach schmerzlich," finale (Minette, Oberbereiter, Schmoll, Greis, Bast)

1a.7   "Silvana," opera: J87
         . "Ouvertüre"
      I: 1. "Das Hifthorn schalt," introduction (Jägerchor mit Fust, Silvana)
            2. "Liegt so ein Unthier ausgestreckt," aria (Krips)
            3. "Halloh! Halloh! Im Wald nur lebt sich's froh!" (Jägerchor)
           4a. "Arme Mathilde!," aria (Rudolf)
           4b. "So soll denn dieses Herz nie Liebe finden?," aria (Rudolf)
            5. "So geh' und führ' aus jener Höhle das Mädchen her!," duet (Rudolf, Krips)
            6. "Ein Mädchen ohne Mängel," arietta (Krips)
            7. "Willst du nicht diesen Aufenthalt," scene (Rudolf, Silvana)
            8. "Geniesst, jedoch bescheiden" (Finale) (Silvana, Chor, Rudolf)
      II: 9. "Wag' es, mir zu widerstreben!," duet (Mechtilde, Adelhart)
          10a. "Weh mir, es ist geschehn!," aria (Mechtilde)
          10b. "Er geht! Er hört mich nicht!," aria (Mechtilde)
           11. "Mechtilde! Mechtilde! / Geliebter!," quartet (Mechtilde, Klärchen, Albert, Kurt)
           12. "Ballo"
           13. "Ich liebe dich!," aria (Rudolf)
           14. "Sah sonst ich ein Mädchen," arietta (Krips)
           15. "Triumph! Triumph" (Finale) (Chor, Mechtilde, Rudolf, Albert, Herold, Adelhart)
      III: 16. "Wie furchtbar die Wolken sich schwärzen!" (Albert, Chor)
           17. "Welch schrecklich Loos fiel mir vom Himmel zu!," aria (Adelhart)
           18. "Nieder mit ihr!," trio (Mechtilde, Rudolph, Adelhart, also Silvana)
           19. "Mit dem Liebesgott im Bunde" (Finale) (Chor)

1a.8   "Abu Hassan," opera: J106
         . "Ouvertüre"
            1. "Liebes Weibchen, reiche Wein!" (Introduction), duet (Fatime, Hassan)
            2. "Was nun zu machen?," aria (Hassan)
            3. "Geld! Geld! Geld! Ich will nicht länger warten!" (Chor der Gläubiger, Hassan, Omar)
            4. "Thränen, Thränen sollst du nicht vergiessen," duet (Fatime, Hassan)
            5. "Wird Philomele trauern," aria (Fatime)
            6. "Siehst du diese grosse Menge," duet (Fatime, Omar)
            7. "Ich such', ich such' in allen Ecken," trio (Fatime, Hassan, Omar)
            8. "Hier liegt, welch martervolles Loos," aria (Fatime) (added 1823)
            9. "Aengstlich klopft es mir im Herzen," trio (Fatime, Hassan, Omar & Chor)
           10. "Heil ist dem Haus beschieden" (Schlusschor)

1a.9   "Der Freischütz," opera: J277
         . "Ouvertüre"
      I: 1. "Victoria! Victoria!... Schau der Herr mich an als König," introduction (Chor, Kilian)
            2. "O diese Sonne!... Lasst lustig die Hörner," trio & chorus (Max, Caspar, Cuno, Chor)
            3. "Nein! länger trag' ich nicht die Qualen," scene & aria (Max)
             . "Durch die Wälder, durch die Auen" (Max)
            4. "Hier im ird'schen Jammerthal," Lied (Caspar)
            5. "Schweig! Schweig! Der Hölle Netz hat dich," aria (Caspar)
      II: 6. "Schelm! Halt fest!," duet (Agathe, Aennchen)
            7. "Kommt ein schlanker Bursch gegangen," arietta (Aennchen)
            8. "Wie nahte mir der Schlummer ... Leise, leise, fromme Weise," scene & aria (Agathe)
            9. "Wie? Was? Entsetzen!," trio (Agathe, Aennchen, Max)
           10. "Milch des Mondes fiel auf's Kraut" (Wolf's Glen Scene), finale (Caspar, Max, Chor)

III: 11. "Entr'acte"
 12. "Und ob die Wolke sie verhülle," cavatina (Agathe)
 13. "Einst träumte meiner sel'gen Base," romance & aria (Aennchen)
 14. "Wir winden dir den Jungfernkranz," folksong (Chor der Brautjungfern mit Solo)
 15. "Was gleicht wohl auf Erden dem Jägervergnügen" (Huntsmen's Chorus)
 16. "Schaut, o schaut!," finale (Agathe, Aennchen, Max, Ottokar, Caspar, Cuno, Eremit, Chor)
 . "Leicht kann des Frommen Herz" (Hermit's Aria)

1a.10   *"Die drei Pintos," opera:* *Anh5*
 I: 1. "Wisst ihr nicht, was wir hier sollen?," introduction (Chor, Clarissa, Laura, Pantaleon)
 2. "Ach! wenn dies du doch vermöchtest," recit & aria (Clarissa)
 3. "Ja, sie wird die Fesseln brechen," duet & trio (Clarissa, Gomez, Laura)
 4. "Wir, die den Musen dienen," duet (Inez, Gaston)
 5. "Also frisch, das Werk begonnen!," trio (Gaston, Pinto, Ambrosio)
 6. "Auf das Wohlsein uns'rer Gäste!," finale (Inez, Gaston, Pinto, Chor)
 II: 7. "Nun da sind wir," duet (Gaston, Ambrosio)

1a.11   "Euryanthe," opera: J291
 . "Ouvertüre"
 I: 1. "Dem Frieden Heil!," introduction (Chor), dance & recit (König, Lysiart, Adolar)
 2. "Unter blüh'nden Mandelbäumen," romance (Adolar)
 3. "Heil Euryanth!," chorus
 . "Ich trag' es nicht!," recit (Adolar, Lysiart, König)
 4. "Wohlan! du kennst mein herrlich Eigenthum," scene & chorus (Adolar, Lysiart, König)
 5. "Glöcklein im Thale," cavatina (Euryanthe)
 . "So einsam bangend," recit (Euryanthe, Eglantine)
 6. "O mein Leid ist unermessen," aria (Eglantine)
 . "Freundin! Geliebte!," recit (Euryanthe, Eglantine)
 7. "Unter ist mein Stern gegangen ... Ja, es wallt mein Herz auf's," duet (Euryanthe, Eglantine)
 8. "Bethörte, die an meine Liebe glaubt," scene (Eglantine)
 . "Er konnte mich um sie verschmäh'n," aria (Eglantine)
 9. "Jubeltöne, Heldensöhne," finale (Chor)
 . "Fröhliche Klänge" (Euryanthe, Eglantine, Bertha, Rudolf, Lysiart)
 II: 10. "Wo berg' ich mich," scene & aria (Lysiart)
 . "Schweigt, glüh'nden Sehens wilde," recit (Eglantine, Lysiart)
 11. "Komm denn, unser Leid zu rächen!," duet (Eglantine, Lysiart)
 12. "Wehen mir Lüfte Ruh'?," aria (Adolar)
 13. "Hin nimm die Seele mein," duet (Euryanthe, Adolar)
 14. "Leuchtend füllt die Königshallen," finale (Chor, Euryanthe, Adolar, Lysiart, König)
 III: 15. "Hier weilest du, hier darf ich ruhn!," introduction & recit (Euryanthe)
 . "Du klagst mich an! Der Tod macht," duet (Euryanthe, Adolar)
 16. "Schirmende Engelschaar," scene (Euryanthe, Adolar)
 17. "So bin ich nun verlassen," scene (Euryanthe)
 . "Hier dicht am Quell, wo Weiden stehn," cavatina (Euryanthe)
 18. "Die Thale dampfen, die Höhen glüh'n!" (Jägerchor)
 . "O seht! Die Schlang' erlegt," recit (König)
 19. "Lasst mich hier in Ruh' erblassen," duet & chorus (Euryanthe, König)
 20. "Zu ihm! Zu ihm! O weilet nicht!," aria w/ chorus (Euryanthe)
 21. "Der Mai, der Mai," scene & chorus (Bertha, Adolar)
 22. "Vernichte kühn das Werk der Tücke," chorus w/ solo (Adolar)
 23. "Hochzeitsmarsch"
 . "Das Frevlerpaar!," scene w/ chorus (Eglantine, Adolar, Lysiart)
 24. "Trotze nicht, Vermessener!," duet w/ chorus (Adolar, Lysiart)
 25. "Lasst ruhn das Schwert," finale (Euryanthe, Eglantine, Adolar, Lysiart, König, Chor)
 Added in 1825: . "Pas de cinq" (to 21.)

1a.12   "Oberon, König der Elfen," opera: J306
 . "Ouvertüre"
 I: 1. "Light, as fairy foot can fall" (Leicht, wie Feentritt nur geht) (Elfenchor)
 2. "Fatal oath!" (Schreckensschwur!), aria (Oberon)
 3. "O, why art thou sleeping, Sir Huon the brave?" (Warum musst du schlafen) (Vision) (Rezia)
 4. "Honour and joy" (Ehre und Heil), ensemble (Oberon, Hüon, Scherasmin, Chor)
 5. "From boyhood trained in battlefield" (Von Jugend auf in dem Kampfgefild) aria (Hüon)
 6. "Haste, gallant knight" (Eil', edler Held), finale (Rezia, Fatime, Chor)
 II: 7. "Glory to the Caliph" (Ehre sei dem mächt'gen Kalifen) (Türkenchor)
 8. "Kleiner Marsch"
 9a. "Melodrama" (after words by Sarazenen: Here's that shall bring assistance)
 9b. "Melodrama" (after words by Oberon: Enough!)
 9c. "Melodrama" (after words by Oberon: Be true, and triumph!"
 10. "A lonely Arab maid" (Arabiens einsam Kind), arietta (Fatime)
 11. "Over the dark blue waters" (Über die blauen Wogen), qt (Rezia, Fatime, Hüon, Scherasmin)
 12. "Spirits of air" (Geister der Luft), scene: solo & chorus (Sturm, Puck, Oberon, Chor)
 12a. "Ruler of this awful hour!" (Vater, hör' mich fleh'n zu dir!), preghiera (Hüon)
 13. "Ocean, thou migthy monster" (Ozean du Ungeheuer!)," scene & aria (Rezia)
 14. "Melodrama" (after words by Abdallah: To the boat, I say!)

15. "O, 't is pleasant" (O, wie wogt es sich), finale (Meermädchen, Oberon, Elfen, Wassernymphen)
III: 16. "O Araby, dear Araby" (Arabien, mein Heimathland), romance (Fatime)
17. "On the banks of sweet Garonne" (An dem Strande der Garonne), duet (Fatime, Scherasmin)
18. "And must I then dissemble" (So muss ich mich verstellen), terzettino (Fatime, Hüon, Scherasmin)
19. "Mourn thou, poor heart, for the joys that are dead" (Traure, mein Herz), cavatina (Rezia)
20. "I revel in hope and joy again!" (Ich jub'le in Glück und Hoffnung neu!), rondo (Hüon)
21. "For thee that beauty" (Für dich hat Schönheit), chorus & ballet (w/ Hüon)
22. "Hark! What notes are swelling?" (Welch Wunderklingen?), finale
. "March"
Added later: . "Yes, even Love to fame must yield!" (Ja, selbst die Liebe weicht), scene & aria (Hüon)

1a.18   "Lieb' um Liebe," incid music: J246
1. "O Vaterland, willkommen unsern" (Schiffer-Chor)
2. "Der Saaten Keim" (Chor der Landleute)
3. "Ländlicher Marsch"
4. "Melodram"
5. "Mein Arm ist schwach," recit (Knabe)
6. "Dem König Heil!," solo & chorus

1a.20   "Preciosa," incid music: J279
1. "Ouvertüre"
I: 2. "Zigeuner-Marsch"
. "Heil Preciosa!," chorus
3. "Lächend sinkt der Abend nieder," melodrama (Preciosa)
4. "Ballo"
5. "Die Stunde ruft, vorbei sind unsre Spiele!," melodrama (Preciosa, Volk)
II: 6. "Im Wald, im Wald, im frischen grünen Wald" (Zigeuner-Chor)
7. "Einsam bin ich nicht alleine" (Lied der Preciosa)
8. "Fröhliche Musik"
9. "Die Sonn' erwacht!" (Zigeuner-Chor)
III: 10. "Ballo"
11. "Zigeuner-Marsch"
IV: 12a. "Es blinken so lustig die Sterne," chorus
12b. "Zigeuner-Marsch" (repeat of 2.)
12c. "Gott, wo bin ich!," melodrama (Preciosa, Donna Clara, Wiarda, Hauptmann, Zigeuner)

1a.21   "Den Sachsen-Sohn vermählet heute," incid music: J289
. "Ouvertüre"
2. "Den Sachsen-Sohn" (Allgemeiner Chor)
3. "Die reine Glut dort" (Chor. Lehrstand)
4. "O Kinder des Thrones" (Mädchen-Chor)
5. "Es ruhen die Waffen der Treue" (Alle)
6. "Lasst die deutschen Königseichen" (Alle)

2. SYMPHONIES

2.1   Symphony No.1 in C major (c1807) Op.19, J50
2.2   Symphony No.2 in C major (c1807) J51

3. OTHER ORCHESTRAL WORKS

3.1   *"Overtura Chinesa" (c1804–5, lost; reworked into Overture to incid music: Turandot, Op.37, J75)* *Anh28*
3.2   "Tusch" (c1806; 20tpt) J47a
3.3   "Grande Ouverture à plusieurs instruments," in E-flat major (c1807, r vers of Overture to: Peter
        Schmoll, J8) Op.8, J54
3.4   "Der Beherrscher der Geister," overture in D minor (r1811 of lost Overture to opera: Rübezahl) Op.27, J122
3.5   "Waltz" (w/ Trio), in E-flat major (c1812; winds, on song: Maienblumlein so schon!, Op.23/3, J117) J149
3.6   *"Marsch für die Prager Schützengarde" (c1814, lost)* *Anh54*
3.7   "Deutscher," in D major (c1815, arr of: Frau Lieserl juhe!, J184, from Fischer: Der travestirte Aeneas) J185
3.8   "Tedesco," in D major (c1816; used in incid music: Preciosa, J279)...J191
3.9   "Jubel-Ouvertüre," in E major (c1818) Op.59, J245
3.10   "Marcia vivace," in D major (c1822; 10tpt & timp; used in opera: Euryanthe, J291) J288
3.11   "March," in C maj (c1826, w/ new Trio; orig for pf duet, J13; arr as: Zu den Fluren for ch & orch, J307) J307

4. CONCERTOS, SOLO INSTR & ORCH

Pf & orch:

4.1   Piano Concerto No.1 in C major (c1810)..Op.11, J98
4.2   Piano Concerto No.2 in E-flat major (c1812) Op.32, J155
4.3   "Concert-Stück," in F minor (c1821) Op.79, J282

Va & orch:

4.4	"6 Variations on 'A Schüsserl und a Reind'rl,' " in C major (c1806)	J49
4.5	"Andante und Rondo Ungarese," in C minor (c1809; also see J158)	Op.35, J79

Vc & orch:

4.6	"Grand Pot-Pourri" (c1808)	Op.20, J64
4.7	"Variations," in F major (c1810)	J94
4.8	*"Concertino" (c?; vc & orch/str qt/pf, lost)*	*Anh82*

Cl & orch:

4.9	Clarinet Concertino in E-flat major (c1811)	Op.26, J109
4.10	Clarinet Concerto No.1 in F minor (c1811)	Op.73, J114
4.11	Clarinet Concerto No.2 in E-flat major (c1811)	Op.74, J118

Other:

4.12	"Romanza Siciliana," in G minor (c1805; fl & orch)	J47
4.13	*"Concertino für Horn" (c1806, lost; reworked into: Horn Concertino, Op.45, J188)*	*Anh29*
4.14	"Adagio und Rondo," in F major (c1811, harmonichord/harmonium)	J115
4.15	Bassoon Concerto in F major (c1811, r1822)	Op.75, J127
4.16	"Andante e Rondo ungarese," in C minor (c1813; bn & orch, r vers of J79)	Op.35, J158
4.17	*"Arbeit" (c1813, for Clement's Concert on Nov. 15, 1813, ?arr of Clement's works, lost)*	*Anh47*
4.18	*"Waltzes" (instrumentation for Brunetti 1814, lost)*	*Anh50*
4.19	*"Waltz," in C major (c1814, for Brunetti, lost)*	*Anh51*
4.20	*"Alt-Vater" (instrumentation for Brunetti 1814, lost)*	*Anh52*
4.21	*"Composition an einem Clarinett-Concert" (c1815, for Hermstedt, lost)*	*Anh57*
4.22	Horn Concertino in E minor (c1815, from lost 1st vers, Anh29)	Op.45, J188

5. STRING QUARTETS

5.1	*Arr of Piano Concerto No.1 in C major, Op.11, J98 (arr1811, lost)*	*Anh37*

6. OTHER CHAMBER MUSIC

3 or more insts:

6.1	*"Drei leichte Trio" (c by 1800; str trio, lost)*	*Anh11–Anh13*
6.2	*"3 Trios" (c by 1801; str trio, lost)*	*Anh24–Anh26*
6.3	"Grand Quatuor," in B-flat major (c1809; pf qt)	J76
6.4	Clarinet Quintet in B-flat major (c1815; cl & str qt)	Op.34, J182
6.5	*"Adagio" (Umarbeitung eines Adagios) (reworked 1815; fl, va/vc & pf, lost)*	*Anh58*
6.6	"Trio," in G minor (c1819; fl, vc & pf)	Op.63, J259

Vn & pf:

6.7	"9 Variations on a Norwegian air," in D minor (c1808)	Op.22, J61
6.8	"6 Sonates progressives" (c1810; vn/fl & pf): No.1 in F major	Op.10, J99
6.9	No.2 in G major	J100
6.10	No.3 in D minor	J101
6.11	No.4 in E-flat major	J102
6.12	No.5 in F major	J103
6.13	No.6 in C major	J104

Vc & pf:

6.14	*"Adagio und Variationen" (c1813; pf & ?vc, lost)*	*Anh42*

Cl & pf:

6.15	"7 Variations on a theme from Silvana," in B-flat major (c1811, from opera J87)	Op.33, J128
6.16	"Grand Duo concertant," in B-flat major (c1815–6)	Op.48, J204

Gui & pf:

6.17	*"Andante" (c1814, lost)*	*Anh53*
6.18	"Divertimento assai facile" (c1816)	Op.38, J207

1 instr:

6.19	*"Adagio für Oboe" (instrumentation 1811, lost)*	*Anh39*

6.20   "Melody," in F major (c1811; cl; pf acc c by Jähns) J119
6.21   "Stück für Guitarre" (c1818; gui, on Klinger's Trauerspiel: Die Zwillinge, lost) *Anh71*

7. PIANO SONATAS

7.1   "3 Piano Sonatas" (c by 1800, lost) *Anh16–Anh18*
7.2   "3 Piano Sonatas" (c by 1801, lost) *Anh20–Anh22*
7.3   Piano Sonata No.1 in C major (c1812, w/ Rondo 'L'infatigable') Op.24, J138
7.4   Piano Sonata No.2 in A-flat major (c1816) Op.39, J199
7.5   Piano Sonata No.3 in D minor (c1816) Op.49, J206
7.6   Piano Sonata No.4 in E minor (c1819–22) Op.70, J287

8. OTHER PIANO WORKS

8.1   "6 Fughetten" (c1798) Op.1, J1–J6
8.2   "6 Variations on an original theme," in C major (c1800) Op.2, J7
8.3   "6 Variationen" (c by 1800, lost) *Anh14*
8.4   "6 Variationen" (c by 1800, lost) *Anh15*
8.5   "6 Variationen" (c by 1800, on song: Lieber Augustin, lost) *Anh19*
8.6   "Einige Variationen" (c by 1801, lost) *Anh23*
8.7   "12 Allemandes" (c1801, Nos.11–12 for pf duet) Op.4, J15–J26
8.8   "6 Ecossaisen" (c1802; arr Kresz for strings): No.1 "Con fuoco," in D major J29
8.9   No.2 "Con tenerezza," in E minor J30
8.10   No.3 in E-flat major J31
8.11   No.4 in E-flat major J32
8.12   No.5 in G minor J33
8.13   No.6 "Affettuoso," in F major J34
8.14   "8 Variations on a theme from Vogler's ballet: Castor and Pollux," in F major (c1804) Op.5, J40
8.15   "6 Variations on Naga's aria from Vogler's opera: Samori," in B-flat maj (c1804, w/ vn & vc ad lib) Op.6, J43
8.16   "7 Variations on Bianchi's Vien quà, Dorina bella," in C major (c1807) Op.7, J53
8.17   "7 Variations on an original theme," in F major (c1808) Op.9, J55
8.18   "Momento Capriccioso" (Capriccio), in B-flat major (c1808) Op.12, J56
8.19   "Grande Polonaise," in E-flat major (c1808) Op.21, J59
8.20   "Klavier-Auszug vom Admiral" (c1811, lost) *Anh33*
8.21   "3 Variationen" (c1811, lost) *Anh34*
8.22   "Walzer und Ecossaisen" (c1812, for Auguste Sebald, lost) *Anh41*
8.23   "7 Variations on 'A peine au sortir de l'enfance' " (c1812, from Méhul's opera: Joseph) Op.28, J141
8.24   "6 Favorit-Walzer der Kaiserin von Frankreich, Marie Louise" (c1812) J143–J148
8.25   "Ecossaise" (c1813, arr from song: Reigen, Op.30/5, J159, lost) *Anh46*
8.26   "9 Variations on a Russian air Schöne Minka," in C minor (c1815) Op.40, J179
8.27   "7 Variations on a Gypsy air," in C major (c1817, on Gipsy song: Woy den czovate) Op.55, J219
8.28   "Rondo brillante" (La gaité), in E-flat major (c1819) Op.62, J252
8.29   "Aufforderung zum Tanze" (Invitation to the Dance), rondo brillant in D-flat major (c1819;
               orchd Berlioz as: Invitation à la valse) Op.65, J260
8.30   "Polacca brillante" (L'hilarité), in E major (c1819) Op.72, J268
8.31   "Etudes" (c1820, lost) *Anh80*
8.32   "Walzer 'für die Kronprinzessin' " (c1825, lost) *Anh81*

Pf duets:

8.33   "6 Easy Little Pieces" (c1801): No.1 "Sonatina" Op.3, J9
8.34   No.2 "Romance" J10
8.35   No.3 "Menuetto" J11
8.36   No.4 "Andante con Variazioni" J12
8.37   No.5 "Marcia maestoso" J13
8.38   No.6 "Rondo" J14
8.39   "6 Pieces" (c1809): No.1 "Moderato" Op.10, J81
8.40   No.2 "Andantino con moto" J82
8.41   No.3 "Andante con Variazioni" J83
8.42   No.4 "Masurik" J84
8.43   No.5 "Adagio" J85
8.44   No.6 "Rondo. Allegro" J86
8.45   "8 Pieces" (c1818–9): No.1 "Moderato" (Arioso) Op.60/1, J248
8.46   No.2 "Allegro" (Alla militare) Op.60/2, J264
8.47   No.3 "Adagio" (Andantino grazioso & Andante) Op.60/3, J253
8.48   No.4 "Allegro" (All'ongarese) Op.60/4, J242
8.49   No.5 "Alla siciliana" Op.60/5, J236
8.50   No.6 "Tema variato" (Air national varié) (on song: Ich hab' mir eins erwählet).............. Op.60/6, J265
8.51   No.7 "Marcia" (Marcia funebre) Op.60/7, J266
8.52   No.8 "Rondo" (scherzando) Op.60/8, J254

9. CHURCH MUSIC

10. CANTATAS

11. OTHER CHORAL WORKS

W/ acc:

. Version: "Schmückt das Haus mit grünen Zweigen" (Illaire)
. Version: "Singet dem Gesang zu Ehren" (anon)
11.15   "Natur und Liebe": "Beglückt, beglückt" (c1818, Kind; 2S, 2T, 2B & pf, also w/ different words): Op.61, J241
. Version: "Freundschaft und Liebe" (Herklots)
11.16   *"Deo rosa" (c1821, Hell; ch & pf, inc)* *Anh3*
11.17   "Wo nehm' ich Blumen her," small cantata (c1823, Hell; ch & pf) J290
11.18   "Reiterlied" II: "Hinaus! Hinaus zum blut'gen Strauss!" (c1825, Reiniger; m ch & pf ad lib) J293
11.19   "Schützenweihe": "Hörnerschall! Überfall!" (c1825, Oertel; m ch & pf ad lib).................... J294
11.20   "Zu den Fluren des heimischen Herdes" (c1826; ch & orch, arr of: March in C major for winds, J307) (J307)

     W/ out acc:

11.21   *"Vierstimmige Gesänge" (ca1798–1800, lost)* *Anh9*
11.22   *"Canons" (ca1798–1800, lost)* *Anh10*
11.23   "Mädchen, ach meide Männerschmeichelei'n," canon (c1802, Breiting) Op.13/6, J35
11.24   "Wenn du in Armen der Liebe," canon (c1802, anon) ....
11.25   "Ein Gärtchen und ein Häuschen drin" (c1803, anon) J36
11.26   "Chorlied" (c1809, text lost) J69
11.27   "Die Sonate soll ich spielen," canon (c1810, Weber) J89
11.28   "Canons zu zwei sind nicht drey," canon (c1810, anon) J90
11.29   "Leck' mich im Angesicht," canon (c1810, anon).. J95
11.30   *"Chor" (c1810, for Singspiel: Abu Hassan, J106, lost)* *Anh32*
11.31   "Das Turnierbankett": "Füllet die Humpen" (c1812, Bornemann; 2T, B & 2ch) Op.68/1, J132
11.32   "Zu dem Reich der Töne schweben," canon (c1814, Gubitz)............................... J164
11.33   "Scheiden und leiden ist einerlei," canon (c1814, anon).................................... J167
11.34   "Leise kömmt der Mond gezogen," canon (c1814) ....
11.35   *"Canon" (c1814, sent to H. Lichtenstein in Berlin, lost)* *Anh55*
11.36   "Leyer und Schwert," Vol.II (c1814, Körner): 1. "Reiterlied" I: "Frisch auf mit raschem Flug!" J172
11.37   2. "Lützow's wilde Jagd": "Was glänzt dort im Walde im Sonnenschein?" J168
11.38   3. "Gebet vor der Schlacht": "Hör' uns, Allmächtiger!" J173
11.39   4. "Männer und Buben": "Das Volk steht auf, der Sturm bricht los!" (w/ pf) J170
11.40   5. "Trinklied vor der Schlacht": "Schlacht, du brichst an!" J171
11.41   6. "Schwertlied": "Du Schwert an meiner Linken" J169
11.42   "Drei Knäbchen lieblich ausstaffiret," burlesque on Mozart: Die Zauberflöte, K620 (c1815, Weber) J180
11.43   "Weil Maria Töne hext," canon (c1816, Gubitz) J193
11.44   "Ei, ei, ei, wie scheint der Mond so hell" (c1818, trad)..................................... Op.64/7, J249
11.45   "Gute Nacht": "Bald heisst es wieder 'Gute Nacht!' " (c1819, Kannegiesser; m ch)................ Op.68/5, J261
11.46   "Freiheitslied": "Ein Kind ist uns geboren!" (c1819, Kannegiesser; m ch) Op.68/3, J262
11.47   "Ermunterung": "Ja, freue dich, so wie du bist" (c1819, Kannegiesser; m ch) Op.68/2, J263
11.48   Double canon (c1819, w/ out text) J272
11.49   "Husarenlied": "Husaren sind gar wack're Truppen" (c1821, Thale; m ch) Op.68/6, J284
11.50   "Schlummerlied": "Sohn der Ruhe, sinke nieder" (c1822, Castelli; m ch) Op.68/4, J285

12. VOICE & ORCHESTRA (concert arias)

12.1   "Il momento s'avvicina," recit & rondo (c1810; S & orch) Op.16, J93
12.2   "Misera me!," scena & aria from: Atalia (c1811; S & orch) Op.50, J121
12.3   "Qual altro attendi disganno maggiore," scena & aria (c1812; T, m ch & orch)..................... J126
12.4   "Signor, se padre sei," scena & aria for opera: Iñes de Castro (c1812; T, 2ch & orch) Op.53, J142
12.5   "Non paventar mia vita," scena & aria for opera: Iñes de Castro (c1815; S & orch) Op.51, J181

13. DUETS

13.1   "Se il mio ben" (c1811, anon; 2A, cl, 2hn & strings; also w/ pf p1815) Op.31/3, J107
13.2   "Mille volte, mio tesoro, se ti" (c1811, anon; 2S & pf).. Op.31/1, J123
13.3   "Va, ti consola, addio!" (c1811, anon; 2S & pf)... Op.31/2, J125
13.4   "Abschied": "O Berlin, ich muss dich lassen" (c1817, trad from: Fliegendes Blatt; 2vv & pf) .. Op.54/4, J208
13.5   "Quodlibet": "So geht es in Schnützelputz-Häusel" (c1817, trad; 2vv & pf) Op.54/2, J209
13.6   "Mailied": "Tra, ri, ro! Der Sommer, der ist do!" (c1817, trad; 2vv & pf) Op.64/2, J210

14. SONGS (w/ pf)

14.1   "Strafpredigt über die französische Musik und Übersetzungswut" (c1801, ?Weber) ....
14.2   "Die Kerze": "Ungern flieht das süsse Leben" (c1802, Matthisson).. J27
14.3   "Umsonst entsagt' ich der lockenden Liebe" (c1802, anon) Op.71/4, J28
14.4   "Entfliehet schnell von mir" (c1803, Seida) J38
14.5   "Ich sah sie hingesunken" (c1804, Swoboda) J41
14.6   "Wiedersehen": "Jüngst sass ich am Grabe der Trauten allein" (c1804, Wallner) Op.30/1, J42
14.7   "Ich denke dein" (c1806, Matthisson).. Op.66/3, J48
14.8   "Liebeszauber": "Mädel, schau' mir in's Gesicht" (c1807, Bürger; w/ gui) Op.13/3, J52
14.9   "Er an Sie": "Ein Echo kenn' ich" (c1808, Lehr) Op.15/6, J57
14.10   "Komisches musikalisches Sendschreiben": "Theuerster Herr Kapellmeister" (c1808, Weber; w/ cont) . J60

15. ARRANGEMENTS OF WORKS OF OTHERS

16. DUBIOUS WORKS

* * * * *

J = F. W. Jähn: "Carl Maria von Weber in seinen Werken. Chronologisch-thematisches Verzeichnis seiner sämmtlichen Compositionen." Verlag der Schlesinger'schen Buch- und Musikhandlung. Berlin, 1871. Unveränderte Neuauflage, Robert Lienau, Berlin Lichterfelde, 1967.

1. STAGE WORKS (operas)

1.1   *"Alladine und Palomides" (c1908, Maeterlinck's No.2 of: Drei mystische Spiele, project)* ....

1.2   *"Die sieben Prinzessinnen" (c1910, Maeterlinck's No.1 of: Drei mystische Spiele, project, lost)* ....

2. SYMPHONIES

2.1   Symphony (c1927–8; small orch) Op.21

2.2   *Movement (c1928, intended for Symphony, Op.21, sketches)* ....

3. OTHER ORCHESTRAL WORKS

3.1   Movement in C sharp minor (c1903; strings) ....

3.2   Movement in C major (c1903; strings) ....

3.3   Movement in F major (c1904) ....

3.4   Movement in D major (Sehr bewegt) (c1904) ....

3.5   Movement in F major (Kräftig bewegt) (c1904) ....

3.6   Movement in D minor (c1904; strings) ....

3.7   "Im Sommerwind" (Idyl for large orchestra) (c1904, after Wille's poem) ....

3.8   "Variations," in D maj / minor (c1905)...

3.9   Movement in B minor (Sehr lebhaft) (c1906)..

3.10   Movement in E major (c1906) ....

3.11   "3 Studies on a Ground" (c1907, related to Op.11): No.1 "Ruhig bewegt" ....

3.12   No.2 (2fl, Eng hn, 2 A-cl, b cl, bn, 4hn, harp, timp & strings)

3.13   No.3 (A-cl, 4hn, harp, timp & strings) Op.1

3.14   *"Passacaglia" (c1908; arr for 2pf-6hands 1918, lost)* ....

3.15   "6 Pieces" (c1909, r1928; arr for chamber ens 1920): No.1 "Etwas bewegte" (r vers: Langsam) Op.6

3.16   No.2 "Bewegt"

3.17   No.3 "Zart bewegt" (r vers: Mässig)

3.18   No.4 "Langsam marcia funebre" (r vers: Sehr mässig)

3.19   No.5 "Sehr langsam"

3.20   No.6 "Zart bewegt" (r vers: Langsam)

3.21   "5 Pieces" (c1911 & 1913; small orch; arr for harm & pf qt 1919): No.1 "Sehr ruhig und zart" Op.10

3.22   No.2 "Lebhaft und zart bewegt"

3.23   No.3 "Sehr langsam und äusserst zart"

3.24   No.4 "Fliessend, äusserst zart"

3.25   No.5 "Sehr fliessend"

3.26   "5 Pieces" (c1913, related to Op.6 & Op.10): No.1 "Bewegt" ....

3.27   No.2 "Langsam" (sostenuto)

3.28   No.3 "Sehr bewegte Viertel"

3.29   No.4 "Langsame Viertel"

3.30   No.5 (Alla breve)

3.31   "8 Fragments" (c1911–3, related to Op.10): No.1 "Andante" ....

3.32   No.2 "Fragment: Langsam"

3.33   No.3 "Fragment"

3.34   No.4 "Fragment"

3.35   No.5 "Fragment"

3.36   No.6 "Fragment"

3.37   No.7 "Fragment"

3.38   No.8 "Fragment: Rasch"

3.39   *"Orchesterstück" (Overture) (c1931, sketches evolved into Op.24)* ....

3.40   *Movement (Sehr rasch) (c1934, ?for Op.24, sketches)* Op.30

3.41   "Variations" (c1940) ....

4. STRING QUARTETS

4.1   "Variations," in F maj / minor (c1903) ....

4.2   Movement in E minor (c1903) ....

4.3   Movement in G major (c1903) ....

4.4   Movement in C minor (c1903) ....

4.5   Movement in C major (c1904) ....

4.6   "Scherzo and Trio," in A minor (c1904) ....

4.7   Movement in B flat major (Schwer) (c1904) ....

4.8   Movement in D maj / minor (c1905) ....

4.9   "Slow Movement" (Langsam, mit bewegtem Ausdruck) (c1905) ....

4.10   String Quartet (Düster und schwer) (c1905) ....

4.11   "Rondo" (Bewegt) (c1906) ....

4.12   Movement in D maj / A major (c1906) ....

4.13   Movement in D major (Sehr lebhaft) (c1906) ....

4.14   Movement in C major (c1906) ....

4.15   Movement in E minor (c1906) ....

4.16   Movement in D minor (c1906) ....

7. CHORAL WORKS

7. CHORAL WORKS

8. VOICE & ORCHESTRA

8.1	"Siegfrieds Schwert": "Jung Siegfried war ein stolzer Knab' " (c1903, Uhland).........................
8.2	"Zum Schluss": "Wen'ge sinds, die mich verstehen" (c1904)..
8.3	"2 Songs" (c1910, Rilke; mS & insts; arr w/ pf 1925): 1. "Du, der ichs nicht sage" Op.8
8.4	2. "Du machst mich allein"
8.5	"Schmerz, immer blick' nach oben" (c1913, Webern; 1v & str qt, associated w/ Op.9)................
8.6	"3 Orchestral Songs" (S & small orch): 1. "Leise Düfte, Blüten so zart" (c1914, Webern) ....
8.7	2. "Kunfttag III": "Nun wird es wieder Lenz" (c1914, George; reconstr Westergaard)
8.8	3. "O sanftes Glühn der Berge" (c1913, Webern)
8.9	"In einer lichten Rose" (c1914, Canto XXXI of Paradise from Dante's Divine Comedy) ....
8.10	"In tiefster Schuld vor einem Augenpaar" (c1914 or later, unknown; 1v & cl, vn, harm) ....
8.11	"8 Songs" (Trakl): 1. "In der Heimat": "Resedenduft durchs kranke Fenster irrt" (c1915; 1v & pf) ....
8.12	2. "In den Nachmittag geflüstert": "Sonne, herbstlich dünn und zag" (c1915; 1v & insts)
8.13	3. "Mit silbernen Sohlen" (c1917; 1v & orch)
8.14	4. "Verklärung": "Wenn es Abend wird" (c1917; 1v & insts/pf)
8.15	5. "Siebengesang des Todes": "Bläulich dämmert der Frühling" (c1917; 1v & orch)
8.16	6. "Nachtergebung": "Mönchin! schliess mich in dein Dunkel" (c1920; 1v & pf)
8.17	7. "Die Heimkehr": "Die Kühle dunkler Jahre" (c1920; 1v & orch)
8.18	8. "Jahr": "Dunkle Stille der Kindheit" (c1921; 1v & cl, va, vc)
8.19	*"Song" (c1917, voice line left blank)*..
8.20	"4 Songs" (also arr w/ pf 1924): 1. "Wiese im Park": "Wie wird mir zeitlos" (c1917, Kraus) Op.13
8.21	2. "Die Einsame": "An dunkelblauem Himmel" (c1914, Wang Seng Yu transl Bethge)
8.22	3. "In der Fremde": "In fremdem Lande" (c1917, Li Tai Po transl Bethge)
8.23	4. "Ein Winterabend": "Wenn der Schnee" (c1918, Trakl)
8.24	"3 Songs" (c1918–20, Kraus): 1. "Vallorbe": "Du himmlisches Geflecht" ....
8.25	2. "Vision des Erblindeten": "So, Mutter, Dank!"
8.26	3. "Flieder": "Nun weiss ich doch"
8.27	"2 Songs" (c1918–20, from Bethge's Die chinesische Flöte): 1. "Nächtliches Bild": "Vom Wind getroffen" ...
8.28	2. "Der Frühlingsregen": "Der holde liebe Frühlingsregen" (also w/ pf)
8.29	"6 Songs" (Trakl; arr w/ pf 1923): 1. "Die Sonne": "Täglich kommt die gelbe Sonne" (c1921) Op.14
8.30	2. "Abendland I": "Mond, als träte ein totes" (c1919)
8.31	3. "Abendland II": "So leise sind die grünen" (c1919)
8.32	4. "Abendland III": "Ihr grossen Städte" (c1917)
8.33	5. "Nacht": "Die Bläue meiner Augen" (c1919)
8.34	6. "Gesang einer gefangenen Amsel": "Dunkler Odem im grünen Gezweig" (c1919)
8.35	"5 Sacred Songs" (also arr w/ pf 1923): 1. "Das Kreuz, das musst' er tragen" (c1921, trad) Op.15
8.36	2. "Morgenlied": "Steht auf, ihr lieben Kinderlein" (c1922, from Des Knaben Wunderhorn)
8.37	3. "In Gottes Namen aufsteh'n" (c1921, trad)
8.38	4. "Mein Weg geht jetzt vorüber" (c1922, trad)
8.39	5. "Fahr hin, o Seel', zu deinem Gott" (c1917, trad)
8.40	"5 Canons" (c1923–4, Latin): 1. "Christus factus est" (for Maundy Thursday; 1v & cl, b cl)............... Op.16
8.41	2. "Dormi Jesu" (from Des Knaben Wunderhorn; 1v & cl)
8.42	3. "Crux fidelis" (for Good Friday; 1v & cl, b cl)
8.43	4. "Asperges me" (for Maundy Thursday; 1v & b cl)
8.44	5. "Crucem tuam adoramus" (for Good Friday; 1v & cl, b cl)
8.45	"Morgenglanz der Ewigkeit" (c1924, from Rosenroth's Freylingshausen Gesangbuch of 1704) ....
8.46	"3 Traditional Rhymes" (c1924–5; S & cl, b cl, vn/va): 1. "Armer Sünder, du" Op.17
8.47	2. "Liebste Jungfrau, wir sind dein"
8.48	3. "Heiland, unsre Missetaten"
8.49	"3 Songs" (c1925; S, E-flat cl & gui): 1. "Schatzerl klein, musst nit traurig sein" (trad) Op.18
8.50	2. "Erlösung": "Mein Kind, sieh an" (from Des Knaben Wunderhorn)
8.51	3. "Ave, Regina coelorum" (Marian Antiphon)
8.52	"Dein Leib geht jetzt der Erde zu" (c1925; 1v & cl, b cl, va) ....
8.53	"Verderben, sterben—ich leb' ohne Trost" (c1925; 1v & insts) ....

9. SONGS (w/ pf)

9.1	"Wolkennacht": "Nacht, dem Zauber" (c1900, Avenarius) ....
9.2	"Vorfrühling" II: "Doch schwer hinschnaubend" (c1900, Avenarius)...............
9.3	"Wehmut": "Darf ich einer Blume still" (c1901, Avenarius)
9.4	"Minnelied": "Du bist mein, ich bin dein" (c1901, anon ca12th cent) ....
9.5	"Du träumst so heiss im Sommerwind" (c1901, unknown)
9.6	"Dämmerstunde": "Im Sessel du, und ich zu deinen Füssen" (c1901, Storm)
9.7	"3 Poems": 1. "Vorfrühling: "Leise tritt auf" (c1899, Avenarius; arr w/ ob, 2hn & harp 1900) ....
9.8	2. "Nachtgebet der Braut": "O Welt, wann darf ich" (c1903, Dehmel)
9.9	3. "Fromm": "Der Mond scheint" (c1902, from Falke's Mit dem Leben)
9.10	"8 Early Songs": 1. "Tief von fern": "Aus des Abends" (c1901, from Dehmel's Erlösungen) ....
9.11	2. "Aufblick": "Über unsere Liebe" (c1903, Dehmel)
9.12	3. "Blumengruss": "Der Strauss, den ich gepflücket" (c1903, Goethe) (also see
	Wolf's 24. of: Goethe Lieder)
9.13	4. "Bild der Liebe": "Vom Wald umgeben" (c1904, from Greif's Neue Lieder und Mären)
9.14	5. "Sommerabend": "Du Sommerabend" (c1903, Weigand)
9.15	6. "Heiter": "Mein Herz ist wie ein See" (c1904, Nietzsche)

9.16	7. "Der Tod": "Ach, es ist so dunkel" (c1903, Claudius)
9.17	8. "Heimgang in der Frühe": "In der Dämmerung" (c1903, from Liliencron's Bunte Beute)
9.18	"Liebeslied": "Ob ich lach" (c1904, Böhm) ....
9.19	"Hochsommernacht": "Stille ruht die weite Welt" (c ?1904, Greif; S, T & pf) ....
9.20	"3 Songs" (c1903–4, Avenarius): 1. "Gefunden": "Nun wir uns lieben" (from Ehe cycle) ....
9.21	2. "Gebet": "Ertrage du's" (from Stimmungen cycle)
9.22	3. "Freunde": "Schmerzen und Freuden" (from Ehe cycle)
9.23	"5 Songs" (c1906–8, Dehmel): 1. "Ideale Landschaft" (c1906, from Weib und Welt) ....
9.24	2. "Am Ufer": "Die Welt verstummt" (c1908, from Weib und Welt)
9.25	3. "Himmelfahrt": "Schwebst du nieder" (c1908, from Weib und Welt)
9.26	4. "Nächtliche Scheu": "Zaghaft vom Gewölk" (c1907, from Aber die Liebe)
9.27	5. "Helle Nacht": "Weich küsst die Zweige" (c1908, from Weib und Welt)
9.28	"5 Songs from 'Der siebente Ring' " (c1908–9, George) (With this work Webern abandons traditional tonality): 1. "Dies ist ein Lied" Op.3
9.29	2. "Im Windesweben"
9.30	3. "An Bachesranft"
9.31	4. "Im Morgentaun"
9.32	5. "Karl reckt der Baum"
9.33	"5 Songs" (c1908–9, George): 1. "Eingang": "Welt der Gestalten" Op.4
9.34	2. "Noch zwingt mich Treue"
9.35	3. "Ja Heil und Dank dir"
9.36	4. "So ich traurig bin"
9.37	5. "Ihr tratet zu dem Herde"
9.38	"4 Songs" (c1908–9, George): 1. "Erwachen aus dem tiefsten Traumesschosse" ....
9.39	2. "Kunfttag" I: "Dem bist du Kind"
9.40	3. "Trauer" I: "So wart, bis ich dies"
9.41	4. "Das lockere Saatgefilde lechzet krank"
9.42	"Meiner Mutter": "Wie oft sah ich die blassen Hände nähen" (c1914 or later, Liliencron) ....
9.43	"Mutig trägst du die Last" (c1914 or later, unknown; also w/ vn, ob & harm) ....
9.44	"4 Songs": 1. "Der Tag ist vergangen" (c1915, trad) Op.12
9.45	2. "Die geheimnisvolle Flöte": "An einem Abend" (c1917, Li Tai Po transl Bethge)
9.46	3. "Schien mir's, als ich sah die Sonne" (c1915, Strindberg transl into German)
9.47	4. "Gleich und Gleich": "Ein Blumenglöckchen" (c1917, Goethe)
9.48	"2 Songs" (c1917–8, Goethe): 1. "Gegenwart": "Alles kündigt dich an!" ....
9.49	2. "Cirrus": "Doch immer höher steigt der edle Drang!"
9.50	"Christkindlein trägt die Sünden der Welt" (c1920, unknown) ....
9.51	*"Nun weiss man erst, was Rosenknospe sei" (c1929, Goethe, sketches)* ....
9.52	*"Cirrus": "Doch immer höher steigt der edle Drang" (c1930, Goethe, sketches)* ....
9.53	"3 Songs from 'Viae inviae' " (c1933–4, Jone): 1. "Das dunkle Herz" Op.23
9.54	2. "Es stürzt aus Höhen Frische"
9.55	3. "Herr Jesus mein"
9.56	"3 Songs" (c1934, from Jone's Die Freunde): 1. "Wie bin ich froh!" Op.25
9.57	2. "Des Herzens Purpurvogel fliegt durch Nacht"
9.58	3. "Sterne, Ihr silbernen Bienen der Nacht"

10. ARRANGEMENTS OF WORKS OF OTHERS

10.1	Wolf, H.: "3 Songs" (from: Mörike Lieder) (orchd1903): 1. "Denk' es, o Seele!" (39.) ....
10.2	2. "Lebe wohl!" (36.)
10.3	3. "Der Knabe und das Immlein" (2.)
10.4	Schubert: "5 Songs" (orchd1903): 1. "Thränenregen" (10. of song cycle: Die schöne Müllerin, Op.25, D795)
10.5	2. "Ihr Bild" (9. of song cycle: Schwanengesang, D957)
10.6	3. "Romance" (3a. of incid music: Rosamunde, Op.26, D797)
10.7	4. "Der Wegweiser" (20. of song cycle: Winterreise, Op.89, D911)
10.8	5. "Du bist die Ruh'," D776
10.9	Schubert: Piano Sonatas (arr1903; orch): 1. 2nd movt of: Pf Sonata No.16 in A minor, Op.42, D845 ....
10.10	2. 3rd movt of: Pf Sonata No.7 in E-flat major, Op.122, D568
10.11	3. 2nd & 3rd movt of: Pf Sonata No.9 in B major, Op.147, D575
10.12	Schoenberg: Prelude and Interludes from: Gurrelieder (arr1909–10; 2pf 8 hands) ....
10.13	Schoenberg: "6 Orchestral Songs," Op.8 (arr1910; w/ pf) ....
10.14	Schoenberg: "Verklärte Nacht," Op.4 (arr1911–2; pf) ....
10.15	Schoenberg: "Pelleas und Melisande," sym poem, Op.5 (arr1911–2; pf) ....
10.16	Schoenberg: "5 Orchestral Pieces," Op.16 (arr1912; pf duet) ....
10.17	Strauss, J. Jr.: "Schatz-Waltzer," Op.418, from operetta: Zigeunerbaron (arr1921; pf qnt & harm) ....
10.18	Schoenberg: "Die glückliche Hand" (The Hand of Fate), drama, Op.18 (arr1921; chamber orch) ....
10.19	Schoenberg: "4 Songs," Op.22 (arr ?1921; w/ insts) ....
10.20	Schoenberg: "Chamber Symphony," Op.9 (arr1922–3; fl/2vn, cl/va, pf, vn, vc & pf) ....
10.21	Liszt: "Arbeiterchor," S82 (arr1924; B, ch & orch; also arr w/ pf) ....
10.22	Schubert: "6 German Dances," D820 (orchd1931) ....
10.23	Bach, J. S.: "Fuga (Ricercata) a 6 voci," from: The Musical Offering, BWV1079 (orchd1934–5) ....
10.24	Wagner-Régeny: "Johanna Balk," opera (arr1939; w/ pf) ....
10.25	Schoeck: "Das Schloss Dürande," opera (arr1941–2; w/ pf) ....
10.26	Casella: "Paganiniana," orch suite, Op.65 (arr1942; pf) ....

* * * * *

WIENIAWSKI, Henryk
1835–1880

1. VIOLIN CONCERTOS, VIOLIN & ORCH

1.1   "Polonaise de concert" (No.1), in D major (ca1852; vn & orch/pf) Op.4
1.2   "Souvenir de Moscou" (ca1852, on Warlamov's songs: Krasnyj sarafan & Osedlaju konia) Op.6
1.3   Violin Concerto No.1 in F-sharp minor (c1852) ....
1.4   "Légende," in G minor (ca1860) Op.14
1.5   "Fantaisie brillante," in A major (ca1865, on themes from Gounod's Faust) Op.17
1.6   "Polonaise brillante" (No.2), in A major (ca1870; vn & orch/pf) Op.21
1.7   Violin Concerto No.2 in D minor (c1862, w/ Finale 'alla Zingara') Op.22

2. VIOLIN & PIANO

2.1   "Variations on an Original Mazurka" (ca1847) ....
2.2   "Grand caprice fantastique sur un thème original" (c1847) Op.1
2.3   *"Aria and Variations," in E major (c before 1848, lost)* ....
2.4   "Allegro de sonate" (c1848, collab brother Józef) Op.2
2.5   "Fantasia and Variations," in E major (c1848) ....
2.6   "Romance" (ca1848) ....
2.7   "Rondo alla polacca," in E minor (c1848) ....
2.8   "Duo concertant" (ca1850, on a theme from Donizetti's Lucia di Lammermoor, collab brother Józef) ....
2.9   "Duo concertant" (ca1850, on Lvov's Russian hymn, collab brother Józef) ....
2.10   "Duo concertant" (ca1850, on a Russian folksong, collab brother Józef) ....
2.11   "Fantasia" (ca1850, on a theme from Meyerbeer's opera: Le prophète) ....
2.12   "Mazur wiejski" (Country Mazur) (ca1850) ....
2.13   "Duet on Finnish themes," 3 duos concertants (ca1851, collab brother Józef) ....
2.14   "Fantasia on a theme from Grétry's Richard Coeur de Lion" (ca1851) ....
2.15   "2 Mazurkas" (ca1851) ....
2.16   "Polonaise triomphale" ....
2.17   "Variations on 'Jechał Kozak zza Dunaju' " (ca1851, on folksong) ....
2.18   "Variations on the Russian National Anthem" (ca1851) ....
2.19   "Variations on Russian hymn" (ca1851; incl in: L'école moderne, Op.10) ....
2.20   "Souvenir de Posen," mazurka in D minor (c1854) Op.3
2.21   "Adagio élégiaque," in A major (ca1852) Op.5
2.22   "Capriccio-valse," in E major (c1852; orchd) Op.7
2.23   "Grand duo polonais" (ca1852, collab brother Józef; 2 vers of Finale): Op.8
       based on: . Moniuszko: "Kozak," dumka in E minor (48. in Vol.II of Dzieła Stanisława Moniuszki)
       . Moniuszko: "Maciek," song in G major (49. in Vol.II of Dzieła Stanisława Moniuszki)
       . Komorowski's song (1st vers of Finale)
       . Wierstowski: "Polonaise," in G major, from opera: Askold's Grave (2nd vers of Finale)
2.24   "Romance sans paroles et Rondo élégant" (ca1852): No.1 "Romance sans paroles" Op.9
2.25   No.2 "Rondo élégant"
2.26   "Kujawiak," in A minor (p ca1853) ....
2.27   "Kujawiak," in C major (p1853) ....
2.28   "Le carnaval russe" (Var et improvisations humoristiques) (ca1853, on song: Po ulice Mostovoy) Op.11
2.29   "2 Mazurkas de salon": No.1 "La champêtre" (Sielanka), in D major (c1850) Op.12
2.30   No.2 "Chanson polonaise," in G minor (c1853)
2.31   *"Fantaisie pastorale" (ca1853, lost)* *Op.13*
2.32   "Variations on an Original Theme" (c1854) Op.15
2.33   "Scherzo-tarantelle," in G minor (c1855) Op.16
2.34   "2 mazurkas caractéristiques" (ca1860): No.1 "Obertas," in G major Op.19
2.35   No.2 "Dudziarz" (The bagpiper)
2.36   "Gigue," in E minor (pubd posth) ....
2.37   "Fantaisie orientale," in A minor (pubd posth) Op.23
2.38   "Reminiscences of San Francisco" (ca1874) Op.24
2.39   *"Rêverie," in F-sharp minor (va & pf, frag; compl Wieckmann 1885)* ....

3. VIOLIN (solo)

3.1   "Nocturne" (c1848) ....
3.2   *Cadenzas to Beethoven: Violin Concerto in D major, Op.61 (c1854, lost)* ....
3.3   "L'école moderne," études-caprices (c1854, collab brother Józef) Op.10
3.4   "Variations on Austrian Natonal Anthem," in G major (c1953, Appendix to: L'école moderne, Op.10) ....
3.5   8 "Études-caprices" (c1862, w/ 2nd vn acc) Op.18
3.6   Cadenzas to Viotti: Violin Concertos Nos.17 & 22 (p1904) ....
3.7   "Romance" (c?, paraphrase of Rubinstein's song: Night, Op.44/1) ....

4. SONGS (w/ pf)

4.1   "Rozumiem" (I have understood): "Pod wierzbami nad strumieniem" (c1854, Minasowicz) ....

* * * * *

1. STAGE WORKS

Operas:

1.1   *"König Alboin," 4 acts (c1876–7, Peitl, unfin, lost, extant frag of 21 bars)* ....
1.2   *Sketch for an unnamed comic opera (c1882–3, Wolf)* ....
1.3   "Der Corregidor," 4 acts (c1895, Mayreder after Alarcón: El sombrero de tres picos): ....
        pubd separately in orch vers: . "Frasquita's Song": "In dem Schatten meiner Locken" (Act I/4)
        . "Corregidor's Song": "Herz, versage nicht geschwind" (Act II/6)
1.4   "Manuel Venegas," 3 acts (c1897, Hoernes after Alarcón: El niño, unfin: Act I/1–5 in vocal score only) ....

Incid music:

1.5   "Prinz Friedrich von Homburg" (c1884, Kleist, inc): ....
        1. "Trauermusic," in B-flat minor (Act II)
        2. "Melodram": "Das Leben nennt der Derwisch der Reise," in F major (Act IV, Scene 3)
        3. Theme in D minor (sketch: 16 bars)
1.6   *"Enleitung zu Hamlet" (Theme for Introduction), in D minor (c1889, 6 bars)* ....
1.7   "Das Fest auf Solhaug" (c1890–1, Ibsen transl Klingenfeld): ....
        1. "Einleitung," in G minor
        2. "Margits Ballade": "Bergkönig ritt durch die Lande," in G minor (arr as song: Gesang Margits)
        3. "Gudmunds erster Gesang": "Ich wandelte sinnend allein," in G major (arr as song)
        4. "Marsch und Chor": "Bei Sang und Spiel," in A major
        5. "Einleitung und Chor": "Nun streichet die Fiedel," in G major
        6. "Chor": "Es locket ins Freie," in A major
        7. "Gudmunds zweiter Gesang": "Ich fuhr wohl übers Wasser," in A min / major (arr as song)
        8. "Einleitung zum dritten Akt," in F major
        9. "Chor": "Wir wünschen Frieden," in F major
        10. "Chor": "Gottes Auge wacht," in G major
1.8   *"Ein Sommernachtstraum" (c1889, Shakespeare transl Schlegel, project)* ....

2. SYMPHONIES

2.1   Symphony in B-flat major (c1876–7, inc; compl Schultz: Finale = orchd vers of: Rondo capriccioso for pf) ..
2.2   *Symphony in G minor (c1877, inc: sketch of 1st movt & frags of 4th movt)* ....
2.3   *Symphony in F minor (c1879, lost)* ....

3. OTHER ORCHESTRAL WORKS

3.1   *"Ouvertüre zu Byrons 'Der Korsar' " (c1877–8, after Byron, lost) (also see Berlioz: Ouverture du Corsaire,*
        Op.21, H101, ballet Il Corsaro in Donizetti's opera: Belisario, Schumann's opera: Der Corsar & Verdi's
        opera: Il Corsaro) ....
3.2   "Penthesilea," sym poem in F minor (c1883–5, after Kleist; r by Hellmesberger 1897; orig vers ed Haas): ..
        1. "Aufbruch der Amazonen nach Troja"
        2. "Der Traum Penthesileas vom Rosenfest"
        3. "Kämpfe, Leidenschaften, Wahnsinn, Vernichtung"
3.3   "Italian Serenade," in G major (arr for small orch 1892, inc) ....
3.4   "Prelude & Intermezzo" (c1895, from opera: Der Corregidor) ....
3.5   *"Dritte Italienische Serenade," in C maj / E major (c1897, sketch)* ....
3.6   *"Tarantella," in C maj / E major (c1897, on: Funiculi, funicula, frag, ?for: Dritte Italienische Serenade)* ....

4. VIOLIN CONCERTOS, VIOLIN & ORCH

4.1   Violin Concerto in D minor (c1875, inc): ....
        . "Maestoso," in D minor
        . "Scherzo and Trio," in A major
        . *"Adagio," in D minor (frag: 25 bars)*

5. STRING QUARTETS

5.1   *String Quartet in D major (c1876, frag: 32 bars)* ....
5.2   String Quartet in D min (c1878–84, inscribed 'Entbehren sollst du, sollst entbehren' from Goethe's Faust) .
5.3   "Intermezzo," in E-flat major (c1882–6) ....
5.4   "Serenade" (Italian Serenade), in G major (c1887; see arr for small orch 1892) ....
5.5   "Langsam" (Serenade movt), in E-flat major (c1889, ?for Italian Serenade) ....

6. OTHER CHAMBER MUSIC

6.1   *Piano Quintet (c1876, frag, lost)* ....
6.2   *Violin Sonata in G minor (c1877, frag)* ....

7. PIANO SONATAS

7.1 Piano Sonata in E-flat maj / D major (c1875, inc) Op.1
7.2 Piano Sonata in D major (c1875, inc) Op.7
7.3 Piano Sonata in G major (c1876, inc) Op.8
7.4 Piano Sonata in G minor (c1876, inc) Op.14
7.5   Piano Sonata in F-sharp minor (c ?1879, lost) ....

8. OTHER PIANO WORKS

8.1 "Variations," in G major (c1875) Op.2
8.2   "Variations," in E maj / A major (ca1875, frag: Var No.4 & beginning of Var No.5) ....
8.3 "Fantasia," in B-flat major (c1876, inc) Op.11
8.4 "Rondo capriccioso," in B-flat major (c1876, intended as Finale of: Sym in B-flat major) Op.15
8.5   "Wellenspiel," in D major (c1877, frag of No.1 of projected set of: 6 Charakterstücke, lost) ....
8.6   "Verlegenheit," in A minor (c1877, intended for: 6 Charakterstücke, frag) ....
8.7 "Humoreske," in G minor (c1877) ....
8.8 "Schlummerlied" (pubd as No.1 of: Aus der Kinderzeit), in G major (c1878; ed Humperdinck w/ added words as: Wiegenlied 1910) ....
8.9 "Scherz und Spiel" (pubd as No.2 of: Aus der Kinderzeit), in G major (c1878) ....
8.10   "Fantasie über Lortzings Zar und Zimmermann" (ca1878, lost) ....
8.11   "Reiseblätter nach Gedichten von N. Lenau" (ca1878–9, lost) ....
8.12   "Fantasia," in C minor (c1878, lost) ....
8.13   "Walzerfinale aus Hans Heiling aus dem Gedächtnis zusammengezogen" (ca1880, frag) ....
8.14 "Albumblatt für Frl. Mizzi Werner" (c1880, r vers of: Schlummerlied of 1878) ....
8.15 "Paraphrase über Die Meistersinger von Nürnberg von Richard Wagner," in G major (ca1880–2) ....
8.16 "Paraphrase über Die Walküre von Richard Wagner," in E minor (ca1880–2) ....
8.17 "Canon," in C major (c1882) ....

Pf duet:

8.18 "March," in E-flat major (c1876, Trio not composed) Op.12

9. CHORAL WORKS

W/ orch:

9.1 "Die Stunden verrauschen": "Ei unter der Linde," in A major (c1878, Kinkel; vv, ch & orch, inc) ....
9.2 "Christnacht," in A major (c1886–9, Platen-Hallermünde; vv, ch & orch; r by Reger & Foll 1903)
9.3 "Elfenlied": "Bunte Schlangen zweigezüngt," in B minor (c1889–1891; S, fem ch & orch, Shakespeare transl Schlegel, for incid music project: Ein Sommernachtstraum) ....
9.4 "Frühlingschor": "Frühling, Herrscher, im sonniger Blau," in A major (arr1898, from opera: Manuel Venegas, ActI/1) ....

W/ pf:

9.5 "Die Stimme des Kindes": "Ein schlafend Kind! o still, o still!," in B minor (c1876, Lenau; ch & pf) Op.10
9.6 "Im stillen Friedhof": "Wenn ich im stillen Friedhof geh'," in F minor (c1876, Pfau; ch & pf) ....

W/ out acc:

9.7   "Wanderlied": "Von dem Berge zu den Hügeln" (c1875, Goethe, lost) Op.4/1*
9.8   "Auf dem See": "Und frische Nahrung," in A major (c1875, Goethe, arr from Op.3/5, frag) Op.4/2*
9.9 "Im Sommer": "Wie Feld und Au," in D major (c1876, Jacobi; m ch) Op.13/1
9.10 "Geistesgruss": "Hoch auf dem alte Turme steht," in C-sharp minor (c1876, Goethe; m ch) Op.13/2
9.11 "Mailied": "Zwischen Weizen und Korn," in D major (c1876, Goethe; m ch) Op.13/3
9.12   "Wanderers Nachtlied" (c1876, Goethe; m ch, lost) ....
9.13   "Die schöne Nacht" (c1876, Goethe; m ch, lost) ....
9.14 "Fröhliche Fahrt": "Glücklich, wer zum Liebchen zieht," in B-flat major (c1876, Hoefer; ed Racek) . Op.17/1
9.15   "Mailied": "Willkommen, lieber schöner Mai," in B-flat major (c1876, Hölty; m ch, frag; ed Racek) ....
9.16 "Grablied": "Wach auf, erwache wieder," in F major (c1876, Lorenzi) ....
9.17 "Gottvertrauen": "An Himmelshöhn die Sterne gehn," in A major (ca1876–81, Mahlmann; ed Racek) ....
9.18   "Wahlspruch": "Das Menschenherz wird nie erkalten" (ca1880–3, m ch, lost) ....
9.19 "6 geistliche Lieder" (c1881, Eichendorff): 1. "Aufblick": "Vergeht mir der Himmel," in E major..................
9.20   2. "Einkehr": "Weil jetzo alles stille ist," in D-flat major (r by Thomas as: Einklang 1903)
9.21   3. "Resignation": "Komm, Trost der Welt, du stille Nacht," in F major
9.22   4. "Letzte Bitte": "Wie ein todeswunder Streiter," in B minor
9.23   5. "Ergebung": "Deine Wille, Herr, geschehe!," in B major (frag of 2nd setting ca1899)
9.24   6. "Erhebung": "So lass' herein nun brechen," in C major

10. SONGS—PUBLISHED BY THE COMPOSER

"6 Songs for a Woman's Voice" (p1888):

10.1	1. "Morgentau": "Der Frühhauch hat gefächelt," in D major (c1877, ?Reinhold) ....
10.2	2. "Das Vöglein": "Vöglein vom Zweig," in E major (c1878, Hebbel) ....
10.3	3. "Die Spinnerin": "O süsse Mutter," in A minor (c1878, Rückert) ....
10.4	4. "Wiegenlied im Sommer": "Vom Berg hinabgestiegen," in F major (c1882, Reinick) ....
10.5	5. "Wiegenlied im Winter": "Schlaf' ein, schlaf' ein," in A-flat major (c1882, Reinick) ....
10.6	6. "Mausfallen-Sprüchlein": "Kleine Gäste, kleines Haus," in F major (c1882, Mörike) ....

"6 Poems of Scheffel, Mörike, Goethe & Kerner" (p1888):

10.7	1. "Wächterlied auf der Wartburg": "Schwingt euch auf," in E-flat maj (c1887, Scheffel; arr for m ch & orch)
10.8	2. "Der König bei der Krönung": "Dir angetrauet am Altare," in E major (c1886, Mörike) ....
10.9	3. "Biterolf" (im Lager von Akkon): "Kampfmüd' und sonnverbrannt," in F major (c1886, Scheffel) ....
10.10	4. "Beherzigung": "Feiger Gedanken," in G min / major (c1887, Goethe) ....
10.11	5. "Wanderers Nachtlied": "Der du von dem Himmel bist," in G-flat maj / B major (c1887, Goethe) (also see Liszt S279 & Schubert Op.4/3, D224)
10.12	6. "Zur Ruh', zur Ruh' ihr müden Glieder," in A-flat major (c1883, Mörike) ....

"Mörike Lieder" (c1888, p1889):

10.13	1. "Der Genesene an die Hoffnung": "Tödlich graute mir der Morgen," in F-sharp min / G-flat major ....
10.14	2. "Der Knabe und das Immlein": "Im Weinberg auf der Höhe," in G min / major ....
10.15	3. "Ein Stündlein wohl vor Tag": "Derweil ich schlafend lag," in G minor ....
10.16	4. "Jägerlied": "Zierlich ist des Vogels Tritt im Schnee," in A major ....
10.17	5. "Der Tambour": "Wenn meine Mutter hexen könnt," in E major ....
10.18	6. "Er ist's": "Frühling lässt sein blaues Band," in G major (orchd1890) (also see Schumann Op.79/23) ....
10.19	7. "Das verlassene Mägdlein": "Früh, wann die Hähne krähn," in A minor (also see Schumann Op.64/2) ..
10.20	8. "Begegnung": "Was doch heut Nacht ein Sturm gewesen," in E-flat major ....
10.21	9. "Nimmersatte Liebe": "So ist die Lieb'! So ist die Lieb'," in A-flat major ....
10.22	10. "Fussreise": "Am frischgeschnittnen Wanderstab," in D major ....
10.23	11. "An eine Äolsharfe": "Angelehnt an die Epheuwand," in E major (also see Brahms Op.19/5) ....
10.24	12. "Verborgenheit": "Lass, o Welt, o lass mich sein!," in E-flat major ....
10.25	13. "Im Frühling": "Hier lieg' ich auf dem Frühlingshügel," in F-sharp minor ....
10.26	14. "Agnes": "Rosenzeit, wie schnell vorbei," in F minor (also see Brahms Op.59/5) ....
10.27	15. "Auf einer Wanderung": "In ein freundliches Städtchen tret ich ein," in E-flat major ....
10.28	16. "Elfenlied": "Bei Nacht im Dorf der Wächter rief: 'Elfe!,' " in F major ....
10.29	17. "Der Gärtner": "Auf ihrem Leibrösslein," in D major (also see Schumann Op.107/3) ....
10.30	18. "Zitronenfalter im April": "Grausame Frühlingssonne," in A min / major ....
10.31	19. "Um Mitternacht": "Gelassen stieg die Nacht ans Land," in C-sharp minor ....
10.32	20. "Auf eine Christblume," I: "Tochter des Wald's," in D major (inc orchd1890) ....
10.33	21. "Auf eine Christblume," II: "Im Winterboden schläft," in F-sharp major ....
10.34	22. "Seufzer": "Dein Liebesfeuer," in E minor (orchd1889) ....
10.35	23. "Auf ein altes Bild": "In grüner Landschaft Sommerflor," in F-sharp minor (orchd1889) ....
10.36	24. "In der Frühe": "Kein Schlaf noch kühlt das Auge mir," in D min / major (orchd1890) ....
10.37	25. "Schlafendes Jesuskind": "Sohn der Jungfrau, Himmelskind!," in F major (orchd1889) ....
10.38	26. "Karwoche": "O Woche! Zeugin heiliger Beschwerde!," in A-flat major (orchd1889) ....
10.39	27. "Zum neuen Jahre—Kirchengesang": "Wie heimlicher Weise," in A major ....
10.40	28. "Gebet": "Herr! schicke was du willt," in E major (orchd1890) ....
10.41	29. "An den Schlaf": "Schlaf! Süsser Schlaf!," in A-flat major (orchd1890) ....
10.42	30. "Neue Liebe": "Kann auch ein Mensch des andern auf der Erde ganz," in B-flat major (orchd1890)......
10.43	31. "Wo find' ich Trost?": "Eine Liebe kenn' ich, die ist treu," in C minor (orchd1890) ....
10.44	32. "An die Geliebte": "Wenn ich, von deinem Anschauin tief gestillt," in E-flat major ....
10.45	33. "Peregrina" I: "Der Spiegel dieser treuen, braunen Augen," in E-flat major (from Maler Nolten) ....
10.46	34. "Peregrina" II: "Warum, Geliebte, denk' ich dein," in G-flat major (from Maler Nolten) ....
10.47	35. "Frage und Antwort": "Fragst du mich," in A-flat major ....
10.48	36. "Lebe wohl": "Lebe wohl!—Du fühlest nicht," in G-flat major ....
10.49	37. "Heimweh": "Anders wird die Welt," in F major ....
10.50	38. "Lied vom Winde": "Sausewind, Brausewind," in F-sharp minor ....
10.51	39. "Denk' es, o Seele!": "Ein Tännlein grünet wo," in D minor (orchd1891) ....
10.52	40. "Der Jäger": "Drei Tage Regen fort und fort," in G minor ....
10.53	41. "Rat einer Alten": "Bin jung gewesen, kann auch mitreden," in E minor ....
10.54	42. "Erstes Liebeslied eines Mädchens": "Was im Netze? Schau einmal!," in A major ....
10.55	43. "Lied eines Verliebten": "In aller Früh," in B minor ....
10.56	44. "Der Feuerreiter": "Sehet ihr am Fensterlein," in B minor (arr for ch & orch 1892) ....
10.57	45. "Nixe Binsefuss": "Des Wassermanns sein Töchterlein," in A minor ....
10.58	46. "Gesang Weylas": "Du bist Orplid, mein Land!," in D-flat major (orchd1890) ....
10.59	47. "Die Geister am Mummelsee": "Vom Berge was kommt dort," in C-sharp minor ....
10.60	48. "Storchenbotschaft": "Des Schäfers sein Haus und das steht auf zwei Rad'," in G min / B-flat major ..
10.61	49. "Zur Warnung": "Einmal, nach einer lustigen Nacht," in A minor ....
10.62	50. "Auftrag—Couplet": "In poetischer Epistel," in F major ....
10.63	51. "Bei einer Trauung": "Vor lauter hochadligen Zeugen," in F minor ....
10.64	52. "Selbstgeständnis": "Ich bin meiner Mutter einzig Kind," in F major ....
10.65	53. "Abschied": "Unangeklopft ein Herr tritt abends bei mir ein," in C min / B-flat major ....

"Eichendorff Lieder" (c1888, p1889):

10.66   1. "Der Freund": "Wer auf den Wogen schliefe," in E major ....
10.67   2. "Der Musikant": "Wandern lieb' ich für mein Leben," in A major ....
10.68   3. "Verschwiegene Liebe": "Über Wipfel und Saaten in den Glanz hinein," in G minor ....
10.69   4. "Das Ständchen": "Auf die Dächer," in D major ....
10.70   5. "Der Soldat," I: "Ist auch schmuck nicht mein Rösslein," in C major (c1887) ....
10.71   6. "Der Soldat," II: "Wagen musst du," in C minor (c1886) ....
10.72   7. "Die Zigeunerin": "Am Kreuzweg, da lausche ich," in A minor (c1887) ....
10.73   8. "Nachtzauber": "Hörst du nicht die Quellen rauschen," in F-sharp major (c1887) ....
10.74   9. "Der Schreckenberger": "Aufs Wohlsein meiner Dame," in G major ....
10.75   10. "Der Glücksritter": "Wenn Fortuna spröde tut," in C major ....
10.76   11. "Lieber alles": "Soldat sein ist gefährlich," in G major ....
10.77   12. "Heimweh": "Wer in die Fremde will wandern," in E-flat major ....
10.78   13. "Der Scholar": "Bei dem angenehmsten Wetter," in A minor ....
10.79   14. "Der verzweifelte Liebhaber": "Studieren will nichts bringen," in G minor ....
10.80   15. "Unfall": "Ich ging bei Nacht," in D minor ....
10.81   16. "Liebesglück": "Ich hab ein Liebchen," in E major ....
10.82   17. "Seemanns Abschied": "Ade, mein Schatz," in F major ....
10.83   18. "Erwartung": "Grüss euch aus Herzensgrund," in E major (c1880) ....
10.84   19. "Die Nacht": "Nacht ist wie ein stilles Meer," in F-sharp minor (c1880) ....
10.85   20. "Waldmädchen": "Bin ein Feuer hell," in G major (c1887) ....

"Goethe Lieder" (c1888–9, p1890):

10.86   1. "Harfenspieler," I: "Wer sich der Einsamkeit ergibt," in G minor (c1888; orchd1890, from Wilhelm Meister) (also see Schubert Op.12/1, D478 & Schumann Op.98a/6) ....
10.87   2. "Harfenspieler," II: "An die Türen will ich schleichen," in C minor (c1888; orchd1890, from Wilhelm Meister) (also see Schubert Op.12/3, D479 & Schumann Op.98a/8) ....
10.88   3. "Harfenspieler," III: "Wer nie sein Brot mit Tränen ass," in F minor (c1888; orchd1890, from Wilhelm Meister) (also see Liszt S297, Schubert Op.12/2, D480 & Schumann Op.98a/4) ....
10.89   4. "Spottlied aus Wilhelm Meister": "Ich armer Teufel, Herr Baron," in F major (c1888) ....
10.90   5. "Mignon," I: "Heiss' mich nicht reden," in F minor (c1888; orchd1890, from Wilhelm Meister) (also see Schubert Op.62/2 D877/2 & Schumann Op.98a/5) ....
10.91   6. "Mignon," II: "Nur wer die Sehnsucht kennt," in G minor (c1888; orchd1893, from Wilhelm Meister) (also see Beethoven WoO134, Schubert Op.62/4, D877, Schumann Op.98a/3 & Tchaikovsky Op.6/6) ....
10.92   7. "Mignon," III: "So lasst mich scheinen, bis ich werde," in A minor (c1888, from Wilhelm Meister) (also see Schubert Op.62/3, D727 & Schumann Op.98a/9) ....
10.93   8. "Philine": "Singet nicht in Trauertönen," in A major (c1888, from Wilhelm Meister) (also see Schumann 98a/7) ....
10.94   9. "Mignon": "Kennst du das Land, wo die Zitronen blühn," in G-flat major (c1888; 2 orchd vers: 1890 & 1893) (also see Beethoven Op.75/1, Liszt S275, Schubert D321 & Schumann Op.79/28) ....
10.95   10. "Der Sänger": "Was hör' ich draussen vor dem Tor," in E major (c1888) (also see Schubert Op.posth 117, D149 & Schumann Op.98a/2) ....
10.96   11. "Der Rattenfänger": "Ich bin der wohlbekannte Sänger," in A minor (c1888; orchd1890) (also see Schubert D255) ....
10.97   12. "Ritter Kurts Brautfahrt": "Mit des Bräutigams Behagen," in F major (c1888) ....
10.98   13. "Gutmann und Gutweib": "Und morgen fällt Sankt Martins Fest," in D major (c1888) ....
10.99   14. "Kophtisches Lied," I: "Lasset Gelehrte sich zanken und streiten," in A-flat major (c1888) ....
10.100 15. "Kophtisches Lied," II: "Geh! Seh gehorche meinen Winken," in D min / G major (c1888) ......
10.101 16. "Frech und froh," I: "Mit Mädchen sich vertragen," in F major (c1888) ....
10.102 17. "Frech und froh," II: "Liebesqual verschmäct mein Herz," in F min / major (c1889) ....
10.103 18. "Beherzigung": "Ach, was soll der Mensch verlangen?," in A min / major (c1888) ....
10.104 19. "Epiphanias": "Die Heiligen drei König' mit ihrem Stern," in G major (c1888; orchd unfin,1894) ....
10.105 20. "St Nepomuks Vorabend": "Lichtlein schwimmen auf dem Strome," in G major (c1888) ....
10.106 21. "Genialisch Treiben": "So wälz ich ohne Unterlass," in A major (c1889) ....
10.107 22. "Der Schäfer": "Es war ein fauler Schäfer," in C minor (c1888) ....
10.108 23. "Der neue Amadis": "Als ich noch ein Knabe war," in G minor (c1889) ....
10.109 24. "Blumengruss": "Der Strauss, den ich gepflücket," in F major (c1888) (also see Webern's 3. of: 8 Early Songs) ....
10.110 25. "Gleich und Gleich": "Ein Blumenglöckchen vom Boden," in E major (c1888) ....
10.111 26. "Die Spröde": "An dem reinsten Frühlingsmorgen," in E major (c1889) ....
10.112 27. "Die Bekehrte": "Bei dem Glanz der Abendröte," in A minor (c1889) ....
10.113 28. "Frühling übers Jahr": "Das Beet, schon lockert sichs in die Höh," in A major (c1888) ....
10.114 29. "Anakreons Grab": "Wo die Rose hier blüht," in D major (c1888; orchd1890 lost; orchd1893) ....
10.115 30. "Dank des Paria": "Grosser Brahma!," in A-flat major (c1888) ....
10.116 31. "Königlich Gebet": "Ha, ich bin der Herr der Welt!," in C major (c1889) ....
10.117 32. "Phänomen": "Wenn zu der Regenwand," in A major (c1889) ....
10.118 33. "Erschaffen und Beleben": "Hans Adam war ein Erdenkloss," in E min / major (c1889) (also see R. Strauss Op.87/2, AV106) ....
10.119 34. "Ob der Koran von Ewigkeit sei?," in A min / major (c1889 from West-östlicher Divan) ....
10.120 35. "Trunken müssen wir alle sein!," in F-sharp minor (c1889) ....
10.121 36. "So lang man nüchtern ist," in A minor (c1889) ....
10.122 37. "Sie haben wegen der Trunkenheit," in G minor (c1889) ....
10.123 38. "Was in der Schenke waren heute," in D minor (c1889) ....
10.124 39. "Nicht Gelegenheit macht Diebe," in F major (c1889) ....

10.125   40. "Hochbeglückt in deiner Liebe," in B-flat major (c1889, Marianne von Willemer r by Goethe) ....
10.126   41. "Als ich auf dem Euphrat schiffte," in A major (c1889, Marianne von Willemer r by Goethe) ....
10.127   42. "Dies zu deuten, bin erbötig," in A major (c1889) ....
10.128   43. "Hätt' ich irgend wohl Bedenken," in A major (c1889) ....
10.129   44. "Komm, Liebchen, komm!," in A-flat major (c1889) ....
10.130   45. "Wie sollt' ich heiter bleiben," in F minor (c1889) ....
10.131   46. "Wenn ich dein gedenke," in F minor (c1889)..
10.132   47. "Locken, haltet mich gefangen," in A major (c1889) ....
10.133   48. "Nimmer will ich dich verlieren," in A major (c1889)...
10.134   49. "Prometheus": "Bedecke deinen Himmel, Zeus," in D minor (c1889; orchd1890) (also see
               Schubert D674)...
10.135   50. "Ganymed": "Wie im Morgenglanze du rings mich anglühst," in D major (c1889; orchd1890 lost) (also
               see Schubert Op.19/3, D544) ....
10.136   51. "Grenzen der Menschheit": "Wenn der uralte heilige Vater," in A minor (c1889) (also see
               Schubert D716)...

        "Spanisches Liederbuch, nach Heyse und Geibel," I. "Geistliche Lieder" (p1891):

10.137   1. "Nun bin ich dein, du aller Blumen Blume," in F major (c1890, Ruiz transl Heyse) ....
10.138   2. "Die du Gott gebarst, du Reine," in A minor (c1889, Nuñes transl Heyse) ....
10.139   3. "Der heilige Joseph singt": "Nun wandre, Maria," in E minor (c1889, Ocaña transl Heyse) ....
10.140   4. "Die ihr schwebet um diese Palmen," in E major (c1889, Vega transl Geibel) ....
10.141   5. "Führ mich, Kind, nach Bethlehem!," in A major (c1889, anon transl Heyse) ....
10.142   6. "Ach, des Knaben Augen sind mir so schön und klar," in F major (c1889, Ubeda transl Heyse) ....
10.143   7. "Mühvoll komm' ich und beladen," in G minor (c1890, Rio transl ?Geibel) ....
10.144   8. "Ach, wie lang' die Seele schlummert!," in E-flat major (c1889, anon transl Geibel) ....
10.145   9. "Herr, was trägt der Boden hier," in E minor (c1889, anon transl Heyse) ....
10.146   10. "Wunden trägst du, mein Geliebter," in B minor (c1889, Valdivielso transl Geibel) ....

        "Spanisches Liederbuch, nach Heyse und Geibel," II. "Weltliche Lieder" (p1891):

10.147   1. "Klinge, klinge, mein Pandero," in G minor (c1889, Almeida transl Geibel) ....
10.148   2. "In dem Schatten meiner Locken," in B-flat major (c1889, anon transl Heyse; orchd ca1895) ....
10.149   3. "Seltsam ist Juanas Weise," in G minor (c1889, anon transl Geibel) ....
10.150   4. "Treibe nur mit Lieben Spott," in G minor (c1889, anon transl Heyse) ....
10.151   5. "Auf dem grünen Balkon mein Mädchen schaut," in A major (c1889, anon transl Heyse) ....
10.152   6. "Wenn du zu den Blumen gehst," in A major (c1889, anon transl Heyse, from opera: Manuel
            Venegas; orchd)
10.153   7. "Wer sein holdes Lieb verloren" (c1889, anon transl Geibel, from opera: Manuel Venegas; orchd) ....
10.154   8. "Ich fuhr über Meer, ich zog über Land," in B minor (c1889, anon transl Heyse) ....
10.155   9. "Blindes Schauen, dunkle Leuchte," in B minor (c1889, Cota transl Heyse) ....
10.156   10. "Eide, so die Liebe schwur," in B minor (c1890, anon transl Heyse) ....
10.157   11. "Herz, verzage nicht geschwind," in E minor (c1889, anon transl Heyse; orchd ca1895) ....
10.158   12. "Sagt, seid Ihr es, feiner Herr," in G major (c1889, anon transl Heyse) ....
10.159   13. "Mögen alle bösen Zungen immer sprechen, was beliebt," in D major (c1890, anon transl Geibel) ....
10.160   14. "Preciosas Sprüchlein gegen Kopfweh": "Köpfchen, Köpfchen, nicht gewimmert," in B-flat major
            (c1889, Cervantes transl Heyse)
10.161   15. "Sagt ihm, dass er zu mir komme," in B minor (c1890, anon transl Heyse) ....
10.162   16. "Bitt' ihn, o Mutter, bitte den Knaben," in G minor (c1889, anon transl Heyse) ....
10.163   17. "Liebe mir im Busen zündet einen Brand," in A minor (c1890, anon transl Heyse) ....
10.164   18. "Schmerzliche Wonnen und wonnige Schmerzen," in A major (c1890, anon transl Geibel) ....
10.165   19. "Trau' nicht der Liebe, mein Liebster, gib acht!," in A minor (c1890, anon transl Heyse) ....
10.166   20. "Ach, im Maien war's, im Maien," in A major (c1890, anon transl Heyse) ....
10.167   21. "Alle gingen, Herz, zur Ruh," in F major (c1889, anon transl Geibel) (also see Schumann Op.74/4) ......
10.168   22. "Dereinst, dereinst, Gedanke mein," in F minor (c1890, Castillejo transl Geibel) ....
10.169   23. "Tief im Herzen trag' ich Pein," in C minor (c1890, Camoens transl Geibel) (also see
            Schumann Op.138/2) ....
10.170   24. "Komm', o Tod, von Nacht umgeben," in D-flat major (c1890, Escriva transl Geibel) ....
10.171   25. "Ob auch finstre Blicke glitten," in B minor (c1890, anon transl Heyse) ....
10.172   26. "Bedeckt mich mit Blumen," in A-flat major (c1889, ?Doceo transl Geibel) ....
10.173   27. "Und schläfst du, mein Mädchen," in E-flat major (c1889, Vicente transl Geibel) ....
10.174   28. "Sie blasen zum Abmarsch," in B-flat major (c1889, anon transl Heyse) ....
10.175   29. "Weint nicht, ihr Äuglein!," im Maien," in B minor (c1890, Vega transl Heyse) ....
10.176   30. "Limusinisch": "Wer tat deinem Füsslein weh?," in A major (c1889, anon transl Heyse) ....
10.177   31. "Deine Mutter, süsses Kind," in F-sharp minor (c1890, Chico transl ?Heyse) ....
10.178   32. "Da nur Leid und Leidenschaft," in B minor (c1890, anon transl Heyse) ....
10.179   33. "Wehe der, die mir verstrickte meinen Geliebten!," in A minor (c1890, Vicente transl Heyse) ....
10.180   34. "Geh', Geliebter, geh' jetzt!," in F-sharp major (c1890, anon transl Geibel; orchd1892 lost) ....

        "Alte Weisen: 6 Poems by Gottfried Keller" (c1890, p1891, Keller):

10.181   1. "Tretet ein, hoher Krieger," in D major ....
10.182   2. "Singt mein Schatz wie ein Fink," in A major ....
10.183   3. "Du milchjunger Knabe, was siehst du mich an?," in A minor (also see Brahms Op.86/1) ....
10.184   4. "Wandl' ich in dem Morgentau," in A major...
10.185   5. "Das Köhlerweib ist trunken," in D minor ....
10.186   6. "Wie glänzt der helle Mond so kalt und fern," in G minor ....

"Italienisches Liederbuch, nach Paul Heyse," Part I (p1892, anon Italian poems transl Heyse):

10.187	1. "Auch kleine Dinge können uns entzücken," in A major (c1891) ....
10.188	2. "Mir ward gesagt, du reisest in die Ferne," in E minor (c1890) ....
10.189	3. "Ihr seid die Allerschönste weit und breit," in A-flat major (c1890) ....
10.190	4. "Gesegnet sei, durch den die Welt entstund," in E-flat major (c1890) ....
10.191	5. "Selig ihr Blinden," in E-flat major (c1890) ....
10.192	6. "Wer rief dich denn? Wer hat dich herbestellt?," in F major (c1890) ....
10.193	7. "Der Mond hat eine schwere Klag' erhoben," in E-flat minor (c1890) ....
10.194	8. "Nun lass uns Frieden schliessen, liebstes Leben," in E-flat major (c1890) ....
10.195	9. "Dass doch gemalt all' deine Reize wären," in F major (c1891) ....
10.196	10. "Du denkst mit einem Fädchen mich zu fangen," in B-flat major (c1891) ....
10.197	11. "Wie lange schon war immer mein Verlangen," in F minor (c1891) ....
10.198	12. "Nein, junger Herr, so treibt man's nicht, fürwahr," in G major (c1891) ....
10.199	13. "Hoffärtig seid Ihr, schönes Kind," in F-sharp minor (c1891) ....
10.200	14. "Geselle, woll'n wir uns in Kutten hüllen?," in D major (c1891) ....
10.201	15. "Mein Liebster ist so klein," in F major (c1891) ....
10.202	16. "Ihr jungen Leute, die ihr zieht ins Feld," in C major (c1891) ....
10.203	17. "Und willst du deinen Liebsten sterben sehen," in A-flat major (c1891) ....
10.204	18. "Heb' auf dein blondes Haupt und schlafe nicht," in A-flat major (c1891) ....
10.205	19. "Wir haben beide lange Zeit geschwiegen," in E-flat major (c1891) ....
10.206	20. "Mein Liebster singt am Haus im Mondenscheine," in G minor (c1891) ....
10.207	21. "Man sagt mir, deine Mutter woll' es nicht," in A minor (c1891) ....
10.208	22. "Ein Ständchen euch zu bringen kam ich her," in C major (c1891) ....

"Italienisches Liederbuch, nach Paul Heyse," Part II (c1896, p1896, anon Italian transl Heyse):

10.209	23. "Was für ein Lied soll dir gesungen werden," in B-flat major ....
10.210	24. "Ich esse nun mein Brot nicht trocken mehr," in E-flat min / major ....
10.211	25. "Mein Liebster hat zu Tische mich geladen," in F major ....
10.212	26. "Ich liess mir sagen und mir ward erzählt," in C minor ....
10.213	27. "Schon streckt' ich aus im Bett die müden Glieder," in A-flat major ....
10.214	28. "Du sagst mir, dass ich keine Fürstin sei," in E-flat major ....
10.215	29. "Wohl kenn' ich Euren Stand, der nicht gering," in C major ....
10.216	30. "Lass sie nur geh'n, die so die Stolze spielt," in G minor ....
10.217	31. "Wie soll ich fröhlich sein und lachen gar," in G minor ....
10.218	32. "Was soll der Zorn, mein Schatz, der dich erhitzt," in C minor ....
10.219	33. "Sterb' ich, so hüllt in Blumen meine Glieder," in A-flat major ....
10.220	34. "Und steht Ihr früh am Morgen auf vom Bette," in E major ....
10.221	35. "Benedeit die sel'ge Mutter," in E-flat major ....
10.222	36. "Wenn du, mein Liebster, steigst zum Himmel auf," in G-flat major ....
10.223	37. "Wie viele Zeit verlor ich, dich zu lieben!," in G minor ....
10.224	38. "Wenn du mich mit den Augen streifst und lachst," in G major ....
10.225	39. "Gesegnet sei das Grün und wer es trägt!," in A major ....
10.226	40. "O wär' dein Haus durchsichtig wie ein Glas," in A minor ....
10.227	41. "Heut' Nacht erhob ich mich um Mitternacht," in D minor ....
10.228	42. "Nicht länger kann ich singen," in A minor ....
10.229	43. "Schweig' einmal still, du garst'ger Schwätzer dort," in A minor ....
10.230	44. "O wüsstest du, wie viel ich deinetwegen," in E minor ....
10.231	45. "Verschling' der Abgrund meines Liebsten Hütte," in D minor ....
10.232	46. "Ich hab' in Penna einen Liebsten wohnen," in F major ....

"3 Poems by Robert Reinick" (p1897, Reinick):

10.233	1. "Gesellenlied": "Kein Meister fällt von Himmel," in C major (c1888) ....
10.234	2. "Morgenstimmung": "Bald ist der Nacht ein End' gemacht," in E major (c1896; arr for ch & orch as: Morgenhymnus 1897) ....
10.235	3. "Skolie": "Reich den Pokal mir," in B major (c1889) ....

"3 Songs from Ibsen's Das Fest auf Solhaug" (c1891, p1897, Ibsen transl Klingenfeld):

10.236	1. "Gesang Margits": "Bergkönig ritt durch die Lande," in G minor ....
10.237	2. "Gudmunds erster Gesang": "Ich wandelte sinnend allein," in G major (r1896) ....
10.238	3. "Gundmunds zweiter Gesang": "Ich fuhr wohl übers Wasser," in A min / major ....

"4 Poems of Heine, Shakespeare & Byron" (p1897):

10.239	1. "Wo wird einst des Wandermüden," in F major (c1888, Heine) ....
10.240	2. "Lied des transferierten Zettel": "Die Schwalbe," in A minor (c1889, Shakespeare transl Schlegel) ....
10.241	3. "Sonne der Schlummerlosen," in C-sharp minor (c1896, Byron transl Gildemeister) (also see Mendelssohn's 2. of: 2 Romances of 1834, Rimsky-Korsakov Op.41/1 & Schumann Op.95/2) ....
10.242	4. "Keine gleicht von allen Schönen" (c1896, Byron transl Gildemeister) (also see Mendelssohn's 1. of: 2 Romances of 1833) ....

"3 Poems by Michelangelo" (c1897, p1898, transl Robert-Tornow):

10.243	1. "Wohl denk' ich oft an mein vergangnes Leben," in G min / major ....
10.244	2. "Alles endet, was entstehet," in C-sharp minor ....
10.245	3. "Fühlt meine Seele das ersehnte Licht von Gott," in E min / major ....

11. OTHER SONGS (unpubd or pubd posthumously)

11.1	*"Das taube Mütterlein" (c1875 or earlier, frag)*	
11.2	*"Soldatenlied" (c1875 or earlier, frag)*	
11.3	*"Der Morgen" (c1875 or earlier, frag)*	
11.4	*"Frühlingslied" (c1875 or earlier, ?lost)*	
11.5	*"Die Sterne" (c1875 or earlier, voice part only, lost)*	
11.6	*"Gebet": "Leise, leise, fromme Weise" (c1875 or earlier, lost)*	
11.7	"Du wirst ja blass," duet in B-flat major (ca1875; S, Bar, inc)	
11.8	"Nacht und Grab": "Sei mir gegrüsst," in C minor (c1875, Zschokke)	Op.3/1
11.9	"Sehnsucht": "Was zieht mir das Herz so," in E major (c1875, Goethe)	Op.3/2
11.10	"Der Fischer": "Das Wasser rauscht', das Wasser schwoll," in C minor (c1875, Goethe)	Op.3/3
11.11	"Wanderlied": "Von dem Berge zu den Hügeln," in G major (c1875, Goethe, inc; arr for ch, Op.4/1) .	Op.3/4
11.12	"Auf dem See": "Und frische Nahrung," in A major (c1875, Goethe; arr for ch, Op.4/2)	Op.3/5
11.13	"Der Raubschütz": "Der alte Müller Jakob," in C minor (c1876, Lenau, inc)	Op.5
11.14	"Frühlingsgrüsse": "Nach langem Frost," in G maj / E major (c1876, Lenau; 2 vers, 1st inc)	Op.6
11.15	"Meeresstille": "Sturm mit seinen Donnerschlägen, in E minor (c1876, Lenau)	Op.9/1
11.16	"Liebesfrühling": "Ich sah den Lenz einmal," in G major (c1876, Lenau)	Op.9/2
11.17	"Erster Verlust": "Ach, wer bringt die schönen Tage," in E-flat major (c1876, Goethe)	Op.9/3
11.18	"Abendglöcklein": "Des Glöckleins Schall," in C-sharp minor (c1876, Zusner)	Op.9/4
11.19	"Mai": "Leichte Silberwolken schweben," in F major (c1876, Goethe; 2 inc vers)	Op.9/5
11.20	"Der goldene Morgen": "Golden lacht und glüht," in B major (c1876)	Op.9/6
11.21	"Perlenfischer": "Du liebes Auge," in A-flat major (c1876, Roquette)	
11.22	"Mailied": "Willkommen, lieber schöner Mai," in F major (c1876, Hölty, inc)	
11.23	*"Ghasél": "Im Wasser wogt die Lillie," in B-flat major (c1876, Platen-Hallermünde, ?spur)*	
11.24	"Stille Sicherheit": "Horch, wie still es wird," in D min / F major (c1876, Lenau)	
11.25	"Scheideblick": "Als ein unergründlich Wonnemeer," in G minor (c1876, Lenau; frag orchd1877)	
11.26	"Ein Grab": "Wenn des Mondes bleiches Licht," in G minor (c1876, Peitl)	
11.27	"Mädchen mit dem roten Mündchen," in F major (c1876, Heine)	
11.28	"Du bist wie eine Blume," in E-flat major (c1876, Heine) (also see Liszt S287 & Schumann Op.25/24)	
11.29	"Wenn ich in deine Augen seh'," in B-flat major (c1876, Heine) (also see Schuman Op.48/4)	
11.30	"Bescheidene Liebe": "Ich bin wie and're Mädchen nicht," in G major (c ?1876–7)	
11.31	"Abendbilder": "Friedlicher Abend," in D-flat major (c1877, Lenau)	
11.32	"Ständchen": "Alles wiegt die stille Nacht," in F major (c1877, Körner)	
11.33	"Andenken": "Ich denke dein," in E major (c1877, Matthison) (also see Beethoven WoO 136)	
11.34	"An * ": "O wag' es nicht," in D minor (c1877, Lenau)	
11.35	"Wanderlied": "Es segeln die Wolken," in A major (c1877, anon)	
11.36	"Die Verlassene": "Hört Ihr dort drüben," in E-flat minor (c1877, inc)	
11.37	"Der Schwalben Heimkehr": "Wenn die Schwalben heimwärts ziehn," in A-flat major (c1877, Herlossohn) .	
11.38	"Das Lied der Waise": "Einsam steh ich und alleine," in A minor (c1877, Steinbach, inc)	
11.39	"Wunsch": "Fort möcht ich reisen weit," in A minor (c1877, Lenau, inc)	
11.40	"Traurige Wege": "Bin mit dir im Wald gegangen," in E-flat minor (c1878, Lenau)	
11.41	"So wahr die Sonne scheinet," in A-flat major (c1878, Rückert)	
11.42	*"Ich sah die blaue unendliche See," in F major (c1878, Fallersleben, frag)*	
11.43	"Nächtliche Wanderung": "Die Nacht ist finster," in C minor (c1878, Lenau)	
11.44	"Auf der Wanderschaft": "Wohl wandert' ich aus," in E major (c1878, Chamisso; 2 vers)	
11.45	"Was soll ich sagen?": "Mein Aug' ist trüb," in G minor (c1878, Chamisso, inc)	
11.46	*"Geschiedensein" (c1878, lost)*	
11.47	"Das Kind am Brunnen": "Frau Amme, Frau Amme," in G major (c1878, Hebbel)	
11.48	"Knabentod": "Vom Berg der Knab," in F-sharp major (c1878, Hebbel)	
11.49	"Sie haben heut' Abend Gesellschaft," in G major (c1878, Heine)	
11.50	"Über Nacht," in E-flat major (c1878, Sturm)	
11.51	"Ich stand in dunkeln Träumen," in A-flat major (c1878, Heine) (also see Schubert D957/9)	
11.52	"Das ist ein Brausen und Heulen," in F minor (c1878, Heine)	
11.53	"Wo ich bin, mich rings umdunkelt," in E minor (c1878, Heine)	
11.54	"Aus meinen grossen Schmerzen," in G minor (c1878, Heine)	
11.55	"Mir träumte von einem Königskind," in C major (c1878, Heine)	
11.56	"Mein Liebchen, wir sassen beisammen," in F-sharp minor (c1878, Heine)	
11.57	"Es blasen die blauen Husaren," in A major (c1878, Heine)	
11.58	"Manch Bild vergessener Zeiten," in C-sharp minor (c1878, Heine, inc)	
11.59	"Frühling, Liebster": "Ich sass an einem Rädchen," in E minor (c1878, Rückert, inc)	
11.60	"Liebesfrühling": "Wie oft schon," in F major (c1878, Fallersleben)	
11.61	"Auf der Wanderung": "Über die Hügel und über die Berge," in C major (c1878, Fallersleben)	
11.62	"Ja, die Schönst! ich sagt es offen," in A major (c1878, Fallersleben)	
11.63	"Gretchen vor dem Andachtsbild": "Ach neige, du Schmerzensreiche," in F minor (c1878, Goethe)	
11.64	"Nach dem Abschiede": "Dunkel sind nun alle Gassen," in E min / G major (c1878, Fallersleben)	
11.65	*"Die Nachtigallen schweigen," in E-flat minor (c1878, Fallersleben, frag)*	
11.66	"Es war ein alter König," in G minor (c1878, Heine)	
11.67	"Mit schwarzen Segeln," in D minor (c1878, Heine)	
11.68	"Spätherbstnebel," in A min / major (c1878, Heine)	
11.69	"Ernst ist der Frühling," in A-flat major (c1878, Heine)	
11.70	*"Schön Hedwig" (c ?1878, Hebbel, lost)*	
11.71	*"Der Kehraus" (c ?1878, Eichendorff, lost)*	
11.72	*"Das zerbrochene Ringlein" (c ?1878, Eichendorff, lost)*	
11.73	*"Der traurige Jäger" (c ?1878, Eichendorff, lost)*	

11.74	*"8 Songs from Des Knaben Wunderhorn" (c ?1878, lost)* ....
11.75	*"Der schwere Abend" (c ?1879, Lenau, lost)* ....
11.76	*"Verschwiegene Liebe," I: "Über Wipfel und Saaten," in G major (c ?1879, Eichendorff, sketch)* ....
11.77	"Herbstentschluss": "Trübe Wolken, Herbstesluft," in G minor (c1879, Lenau) ....
11.78	"Frage nicht": "Wie seht ich Dein," in D-flat major (c1879, Lenau) ....
11.79	"Herbst": "Nun ist es Herbst," in F-sharp minor (c1879, Lenau) ....
11.80	"Herbstklage": "Holder Lenz, du bist dahin," in F minor (c1879, Lenau, inc) ....
11.81	"Wie des Mondes Abbild zittert," in E-flat major (c1880, Lenau) ....
11.82	*"Der kriegslustige Waffenschmied": "Spritze Funken, Säbel klinge," in D major (c1880, Lenau, frag)* ....
11.83	"Nachruf": "Du liebe, treue Leute," in A-flat major (c1880, Eichendorff) ....
11.84	"Nachgruss": "Wie kühl schweift sich's," in E-flat major (c1880, Eichendorff, inc) ....
11.85	"Sterne mit den goldnen Füsschen," in E major (c1880, Heine) ....
11.86	*"Das gelbe Laub erzittert," in E-flat minor (c1880, Heine, frag)* ....
11.87	"Suschens Vogel": "Ich hatt ein Vöglein," in C major (c1880, Mörike) ....
11.88	*"An die Wolke," in F minor (c1881, Lenau, frag)* ....
11.89	"In der Fremde," I: "Da fahr' ich still im Wagen," in F major (c1881, Eichendorff) ....
11.90	*"In der Fremde," II: "Ich geh durch die dunklen Gassen," in G minor (c1882–3, Eichendorff, frag)* ....
11.91	"Wohin mit der Freud?": "Ach, du klarblauer Himmel," in G major (c1882, Reinick) ....
11.92	"Rückkehr": "Mit meinem Saitenspiele," in F-sharp major (c1883, Eichendorff) ....
11.93	"Ständchen": "Komm' in die stille Nacht, Liebchen, was zögerst du?," in D-flat major (c1883, Reinick) (also see Schumann Op.36/2) ....
11.94	"Nachtgruss": "In dem Himmel ruht die Erde," in A-flat major (c1883, Reinick) ....
11.95	"In der Fremde," VI: "Wolken, wälderwärts gegangen," in G minor (c1883, Eichendorff) ....
11.96	"Frühlingsglocken": "Schneeglöcken tut läuten!," in D major (c1883, Reinick) ....
11.97	"Liebesbotschaft": "Wolken, die ihr nach Osten eilt," in A-flat major (c1883, Reinick) ....
11.98	"Liebchen, wo bist du?": "Zaubrer bin ich," in F major (c1883, Reinick) ....
11.99	"In der Fremde," III: "Ich geh durch die dunklen Gassen," in G-sharp minor (c1883, Eichendorff) ....
11.100	"Die Tochter der Heide": "Wasch dich, mein Schwesterchen," in E major (c1884, Mörike) ....
11.101	"Die Kleine": "Zwischen Bergen, liebe Mutter," in E major (c1887, Eichendorff) ....
11.102	*"Die Spröde," in A major (c1889, Goethe, frag, 1st setting)* ....
11.103	"Dem Vaterland": "Das ist ein hohes helles Wort," in C major (c1890, Reinick; arr for m ch & orch) ....
11.104	"Frohe Botschaft": "Hielt die allerschönste Herrin," in E major (c1890, Reinick) ....
11.105	"Pena d'amor": "Ein Himmelssegen ist deine Schönheit" (ca1890, ?Wolf, ?intended as a joke) ....
11.106	*"Irdische & himmlische Liebe": "Zur Schönheit" (c1897, Michelangelo transl Tornow, destroyed Wolf)* ....

12. ARRANGEMENTS OF WORKS OF OTHERS

12.1	Beethoven: Pf Sonata No.14 in C-sharp minor, "Moonlight," Op.27/2 (orchd1876, 3rd movt inc) ....

* * * * *

General: ....
"Dizionario Enciclopedico Universale della Musica e dei Musicisti," diretto da Alberto Basso. Unione
Tipografico—Editrice Torinese, 1985–8.
"The Gramophone Classical Catalogue." Master Edition. No.1. Retail Entertainment Data, London, 1995.
"The International Cyclopedia of Music and Musicians." 11th edition. Thompson, O., ed. Dodd, Mead, 1985.
"The New Grove Dictionary of Music and Musicians." Sadie, S., ed. Macmillan, 1980.
"The Norton/Grove Dictionary of Women Composers." Sadie, J. A. & Samuel, R., ed. Macmillan, 1995.
"Orchestral Catalogue." Compton, S., ed. British Broadcasting Corporation, 1982.
"Piano and Organ Catalogue." British Broadcasting Corporation, 1965.
"Song Catalogue." British Broadcasting Corporation, 1966.
Berkowitz, F. P.: "Popular Titles & Subtitles of Musical Compositions." 2nd edition. Scarecrow, Metuchen, N.J.,
1975.
Fischer-Dieskau, D.: "Texte deutscher Lieder. Ein Handbuch." 4th edition. Deutscher Taschenbuch Verlag,
München, 1977.
Gooch, B. & Thatcher, D.: "A Shakespeare Music Catalogue." Vols.I–V. Clarendon, 1991.
Gooch, B. & Thatcher, D.: "Musical Settings of British Romantic Literature." Vols.I–II. Garland, 1982.
Gooch, B. & Thatcher, D.: "Musical Settings of Early & Mid-Victorian Literature." Garland, 1979.
Gooch, B. & Thatcher, D.: "Musical Settings of Late Victorian & Modern British Literature." Vols.I–II.
Garland, 1976.
Morgan, R. P.: "Twentieth-Century Music." Norton, 1991.

Albéniz, Isaac (Manuel Francisco) (1860–1909, Spanish): ....
Baytelman, P.: "Isaac Albéniz. Chronological List & Thematic Catalog of His Piano Works." Harmonie Park
Press, Michigan,1993.
Fuszek, R. M.: "Piano Music in Collections. An Index." Information Coordinators, Detroit, 1982.
Laplane, G.: "Albéniz: sa vie, son oeuvre." Éditions du Milieu du Monde, Paris, 1956.
Albinoni, Tommaso Giovanni (1671–1750, Italian): ....
Talbot, M.: "Tomaso Albinoni. The Venetian Composer and His World." Clarendon, 1990.
Talbot, M.: "Tomaso Albinoni. Werk und Leben." Adliswil, Zurich, 1980.
Bacewicz, Grażyna (1909–1969, Polish): ....
Rosen, J.: "Grażyna Bacewicz. Her Life and Works." Polish Music History Series. Friends of Polish Music
and University of Southern California School of Music, Los Angeles, 1984.
Bach, Carl Philipp Emanuel (1714–1788, German): ....
Busch, G.: "C. Ph. E. Bach und seine Lieder." Gustav Bosse, Regensburg, 1957.
Clark, S. L.: "C. P. E. Bach Studies." Clarendon, 1988.
Ottenberg, H-G.: "C. P. E. Bach." Transl Ph. J. Whitmore. Oxford University Press, 1987.
Schulenberg, D.: "The Instrumental Music of C. P. E. Bach." UMI Research Press, Ann Arbor., 1984.
Wotquenne, A.: "Thematisches Verzeichnis der Werke von Carl Philipp Emanuel Bach." Breitkopf & Härtel,
1905, r1972.
Bach, Johann (John) Christian (1735–1782, German): ....
Roe, S.: "The Keyboard Music of J. C. Bach." Garland, 1989.
Terry, C. S.: "John Christian Bach." 2nd edition. London University Press, 1967.
Bach, Johann Sebastian (1685–1750, German): ....
Schmiede, W.: "Thematisch-systematisches Verzeichnis der musikalischen Werke von Johann Sebastian
Bach." 2nd edition. Breitkopf & Härtel, Wiesbaden, 1990.
Bach, Wilhelm Friedemann (1710–1784, German): ....
Falck, M.: "Wilhelm Friedemann Bach. Sein Leben und seine Werke mit thematischem Verzeichnis seiner
Kompositionen und zwei Bildern." 2nd edition. Kahnt, Leipzig, 1919.
Balakirev, Mily Alexeyevich (1837–1910, Russian): ....
Garden, E.: "Balakirev. A Critical Study of His Life and Music." Faber & Faber, 1967.
Barber, Samuel (1910–1981, American): ....
Hennessee, D. A.: "Samuel Barber. A Bio-bibliography." Greenwood, 1985.
Heyman, B.: "Samuel Barber: The Composer and His Music." Oxford University Press, 1992.
Bartók, Béla (1881–1945, Hungarian): ....
Antokoletz, E.: "Béla Bartók. A Guide to Research." Garland, 1988.
Dille, D.: "Thematisches Verzeichnis der Jugendwerke Béla Bartóks 1890–1904." Budapest, 1974.
Szöllösy, A.: "Bibliographie des oeuvres musicales et écrits musicologiques de Béla Bartók." In: Szabolcsi, B.,
ed.: "Bartók—Sa vie et son oeuvre." 2nd edition. Budapest, 1968.
Uifalussy, J.: "Bartók Béla." Transl E. West. Budapest—Crescendo, Boston, 1971.
Beach, (née Cheney) Amy Marcy (Mrs. H. H. A. / Mrs. Henry Harris Aubrey) (1867–1944, American): ....
Tuthill, B. C.: "Mrs H. H. A. Beach," in "The Musical Quarterly," Engel, C., ed. Vol. 26, p297. Schirmer, 1940.
Wise Brown, J.: "Amy Beach and Her Chamber Music. Biography, Documents, Style." (Composers of North
America, No.16.) Scarecrow, 1994.
Beethoven, Ludwig van (1770–1827, German): ....
Hess, W.: "Verzeichnis der nicht in der Gesamtausgabe veröffentlichten Werke Ludwig van Beethovens."
Breitkopf & Härtel, Wiesbaden, 1957.
Kinsky, G. & Halm, H.: "Das Werk Beethovens." Henle, Munich, 1955.
Matthews, D.: "Beethoven." Dent, 1985.
Bellini, Vincenzo (1801–1835, Italian): ....
Weinstock, H.: "V. Bellini: His Life and His Operas." Knopf, 1971.
Berg, Alban (Maria Johannes) (1885–1935, Austrian): ....
Carner, M.: "Alban Berg." Transl D. Collins. Jean-Claude Lattes, London, 1979.
Gable, D. & Morgan, R. P., ed.: "A. Berg. Historical & Analytical Perspectives." Clarendon, 1991.
Jarman, D., ed.: "The Berg Companion." Northeastern University Press, Boston, 1989.
Redlich, H. F.: "Alban Berg." Universal Edition, Wien—Zürich—London, 1957.

Berlioz, (Louis-)Hector (1803–1869, French): ....
    Holoman, D. K.: "Catalogue of the Works of Hector Berlioz." Bärenreiter, 1987.
    Macdonald, H. J.: "Berlioz." Dent, 1982.
Bernstein, Leonard (1918–1990, American): ....
    "Leonard Bernstein. A Complete Catalog of His Works. Celebrating His 70th Birthday August 25, 1988." Jalni
        Publications—Boosey & Hawkes, 1988.
    Bernstein, L.: "Findings." Simon & Schuster, 1982.
    Gradenwitz, P.: "Leonard Bernstein." Leamington Spa, Warwickshire, 1987.
Bizet, Georges (Alexandre-César-Léopold) (1838–1875, French): ....
    Dean, W.: "Bizet: His Life and Work." Dent, 1975.
Bloch, Ernest (1880–1959, Swiss-American): ....
    Bloch, S. & Heskes, I.: "Ernest Bloch: Creative Spirit." Jewish Music Council, New York, 1976.
Boccherini, (Ridolfo) Luigi (1743–1805, Italian): ....
    Rothschild, G. de: "Luigi Boccherini: sa vie, son oeuvre." Oxford University Press, 1965.
    Croce, L. della: "Il divino Boccherini." Zanobon, Padova, 1988.
    Gérard, Y.: "Thematic, Bibliographical and Critical Catalogue of the Works of Luigi Boccherini." Transl A. Mayor.
        Oxford University Press, 1969.
Borodin, Alexander Porfiryevich (1833–1887, Russian): ....
    Dianin, S.: "Borodin." Oxford University Press, 1963.
Boulez, Pierre (born 1925, French):..
    Jameux, D.: "Pierre Boulez." Transl S. Bradshaw. Harvard University Press, 1991.
Brahms, Johannes (1833–1897, German): ....
    "Johannes Brahms—Verzeichnis seiner Werke mit einführung von Adolf Aber." Peters, Leipzig, 19—.
    Evans, E.: "Historical, Descriptive and Analytical Account of the Entire Work of Johannes Brahms." London,
        1912–38, 1970.
    MacDonald, M.: "Brahms." Schirmer, 1990.
    McCorkle, M. I.: "J. Brahms. Thematisch-bibliographisches Werkverzeichnis." Henle, Munich, 1984.
Britten, (Edward) Benjamin (1913–1976, English): ....
    "B. Britten: A Complete Catalogue of His Published Works." Boosey & Hawkes—Faber Music, London, 1973.
    Evans, J. & others: "A Britten Source Book." Britten-Pears Library, Aldenburgh, Suffolk, 1987.
    Evans, P. : "The Music of Benjamin Britten." Dent, 1979.
Bruch, Max (Karl August) (1838–1920, German): ....
    Fifield, C.: "Max Bruch. His Life and Works." Braziller, New York, 1988.
    Kämper, D.: "Max Bruch—Studien." Arno Volk, Köln, 1970.
Bruckner, (Josef) Anton (1824–1896, Austrian): ....
    Grasberger, R.: "Werkverzeichnis Anton Bruckner." Schneider, Tutzing, 1977.
    Watson, D.: "Bruckner." Dent, 1975.
Busoni, Ferruccio (Dante Michelangiolo Benvenuto) (1866–1924, Italian): ....
    Kindermann, J.: "Thematisch-chronologisches Verzeichnis der musikalischen Werke von Ferruccio B. Busoni."
        Gustav Bosse, Regensburg, 1980.
    Sablich, S.: "Busoni." Edizioni di Torino, 1982.
Buxtehude, Dietrich (Boxdehude / Buchstehude, Diderich) (ca1637–1707, German / Danish): ....
    Karstädt, G., ed.: "Thematisch-systematisches Verzeichnis der musikalischen Werke von Dietrich Buxtehude:
        Buxtehude-Werke-Verzeichnis (BuxWV)." Breitkopf & Härtel, Wiesbaden, 1974.
    Snyder, K. J.: "Dietrich Buxtehude, Organist in Lübeck." Schirmer, 1987.
Cage, John (Milton) (1912–1992, American): ....
    Dunn, R., ed.: "John Cage." Henmar Press, New York, 1962.
    Griffiths, P.: "Cage." Oxford Studies of Composers (18). Oxford University Press, 1981.
    Kostelanetz, R., ed.: "John Cage." Praeger, 1970.
Castelnuovo-Tedesco, Mario (1895–1968, Italian):...
    (List compiled mostly from sources listed in this bibliography under General)
Cavalli, Francesco (Caletti-Bruni, Pier Francesco) (1602–1676, Italian): ....
    Glover, J.: "Cavalli." St. Martin's Press, 1978.
Chabrier, (Alexis-)Emmanuel (1841–1894, French): ....
    Myers, R.: "Emmanuel Chabrier and His Circle." Dent, 1969.
Charpentier, Marc-Antoine (1634–1704, French): ....
    Cessac, C.: "Marc-Antoine Charpentier." Fayard, 1988.
    Hitchcoock, H. W.: "The Works of Marc-Antoine Charpentier. Catalogue Raisonné." Picard, 1982.
Cherubini, Luigi (Carlo Zanobi Salvatore Maria) (1760–1842, Italian):..
    Bellasis, E.: "Cherubini. Memorials Illustrative of His Life and Work." Da Capo, 1971.
    Della Croce, V.: "Cherubini e i Musicisti Italiani del suo Tempo." Edizioni EDA, Torino, 1986.
Chopin, Fryderyk (Franciszek) (1810–1849, Polish):..
    Brown, M.: "Chopin. An Index of His Works in Chronological Order." 2nd edition. Da Capo, 1972.
    Rehberg, W. & P.: "Frédéric Chopin. Sein Leben und Sein Werk." Artemis, Zürich—Stuttgart, 1949.
    Samson, J., ed.: "The Cambridge Companion to Chopin." Cambridge University Press, 1992.
    Walker, A., ed.: "Frédéric Chopin. Profiles of the Man and the Musician." Taplinger, New York, 1967.
Copland, Aaron (1900–1990, American): ....
    Berger, A.: "Aaron Copland." Greenwood, 1971.
    Butterworth, N.: "The Music of Aaron Copland." Toccata, 1985.
    Skowronski, J.: "Aaron Copland. A Bio-bibliography." Greenwood, 1985.
Corelli, Arcangelo (1653–1713, Italian):...
    Marx, H. J.: "Historisch-kritische Gesamtausgabe der musikalischen Werke. Die Überlieferung der Werke
        Arcangelo Corellis. Catalogue raisonné." Arno Volk Verlag—Hans Gerig, Köln, 1980.
    Pincherle, M.: "Corelli. His Life, His Work." Transl H. Russell. Norton, 1956.

Couperin, François 'Le Grand' (1668–1733, French): ....
    Beaussant, Ph.: "François Couperin." Fayard, 1980.
    Cauchie, M.: "Thematic Index of the Works of François Couperin." Lyrebird—Louise B. M. Dyer—The Ramparts,
        Monaco, 1949.
Debussy, (Achille-)Claude (1862–1918, French): ....
    Lesure, Fr.: "Catalogue de l'oeuvre de Claude Debussy." Minkoff, Genève, 1977.
    Lockspeiser, E.: "Debusy. His Life and Mind." Cassell, London, 1965.
Delius, Frederick (Fritz) (Theodore Albert) (1862–1934, English): ....
    Hutchings, A.: "Delius." Macmillan, London, 1948.
    Jefferson, A.: "Delius." Dent—Octagon, New York, 1972.
    Threlfall, R.: "A Catalogue of the Compositions of F. Delius." Delius Trust, London, 1977.
    Threlfall, R.: "A Supplementary Catalogue." Delius Trust, London, 1986.
    Warlock, P. (Heseltine, Ph.): "Frederick Delius." Bodley Head, London, 1952.
Dohnányi, Ernő (Ernst von) (1877–1960, Hungarian): ....
    (List compiled mostly from sources listed in this bibliography under General)
Donizetti, (Domenico) Gaetano (Maria) (1797–1848, Italian): ....
    Ashbrook, W.: "Donizetti and His Operas." Cambridge University Press, 1982.
    Weinstock, H.: "Donizetti." Pantheon, New York, 1963.
Dupré, Marcel (1886–1971, French): ....
    "Marcel Dupré raconte ..." Bornemann, Paris, 1972.
    Murray, M.: "Marcel Dupré. The Work of a Master Organist." Northeastern University Press, Boston, 1985.
Dvořák, Antonín (Leopold) (1841–1904, Czech): ....
    Burghauser, J.: "Antonín Dvořák. Thematic Catalogue. Bibliography. Survey of Life and Work." Export Artia,
        Prague, 1960.
    Clapham, J.: "Dvořák." David & Charles, New York, 1979.
Elgar, Sir Edward (William) (1857–1934, English): ....
    Kennedy, M.: "Portrait of Elgar." Oxford University Press, 1968.
    Kent, C.: "Edward Elgar. A Guide to Research." Garland, 1993.
    Moore, J. N.: "Edward Elgar. A Creative Life." Oxford University Press, 1984.
    Young, P. Y.: "Elgar. O. M. A Study of a Musician." Collins, London, 1955.
Falla (y Matheu), Manuel de (1876–1946, Spanish): ....
    Burnett, J.: "Manuel de Falla and the Spanish Musical Renaissance." Gollancz, 1979.
    Chase, G., Budwig, A.: "A Bibliography and Research Guide." Garland, 1986.
    Crichton, R.: "Manuel de Falla. Descriptive Catalogue of His Works." Chester Music, 1976.
    Demarquez, S.: "Manuel de Falla." Transl S. Attanasio. Chilton Book Company, 1968.
    Gallego, A.: "Catalogo de Obras de Manuel de Falla." Ministerio de Cultura, Madrid, 1987.
    Hoffelé, J-C.: "Manuel de Falla." Fayard, 1992.
Fauré, Gabriel(-Urbain) (1845–1924, French): ....
    Meister, B.: "19th-Century French Song. Fauré, Chausson, Duparc, & Debussy." Indiana University Press, 1980.
    Nectoux, J-M.: "Gabriel Fauré. A Musical Life." Transl R. Nichols. Cambridge University Press, 1991.
    Suckling, N.: "Fauré." Greenwood, 1979.
Franck, César(-Auguste-Jean-Guillaume-Hubert) (1822–1890, French): ....
    Demuth, N.: "César Franck." Dennis Dobson, London, 1949.
    D'Indy, V.: "César Franck." Dover Publications, New York, 1965.
    Mohr, W.: "Thematisches Werkverzeichnis," in: "César Franck." Schneider, Tutzing, 1969.
Frescobaldi, Girolamo (1583–1643, Italian): ....
    Gallico, C.: "Girolamo Frescobaldi. L'affetto, l'ordito, le metamorfosi." Sansoni, Florence, 1986.
    Hammond, F.: "Girolamo Frescobaldi." Harvard University Press, 1983.
Gershwin, George (Jacob) (1898–1937, American): ....
    Jablonski, E.: "Gershwin. A Biography." Doubleday, 1987.
    Kendall, A.: "Gershwin. A Biography." Harrap, London, 1987.
Glazunov, Alexander Konstantinovich (1865–1936, Russian): ....
    Venturini, D. J.: "Alexander Glazunov. His Life and Works." Aero, Delphos, Ohio, 1992.
Glinka, Mikhail Ivanovich (1804–1857, Russian): ....
    Brown, D.: "Mikhail Glinka. A Biographical and Critical Study." Oxford University Press, 1974.
    Orlova, A.: "Glinka's Life in Music: a Chronicle." Transl R. Hoops. UMI Research Press, 1988.
Gluck, Christoph Willibald (1714–1787, German): ....
    Hopkinson, C.: "A Bibliography of The Printed Works of C. W. von Gluck." Broude, New York, 1967.
    Howard, P.: "Christoph Willibald Gluck. A Guide to Research." Garland, 1987.
    Prod'Homme, J-G.: "Christopf-Willibard Gluck." Fayard, 1985.
    Wotquenne, A.: "Catalogue Thématique des oevres de Chr. W. v. Gluck." Georg Olms Hildesheim, Wiesbaden,
        1967.
Gounod, Charles(-François) (1818–1893, French): ....
    Harding, J.: "Gounod." George Allen & Unwin, London, 1973.
    Prod'Homme, J-G. and Dandelot, A.: "Gounod. Sa vie et ses oeuvres." Minkoff Reprint, Genève, 1973.
Granados (y Campiña), Enrique (1867–1916, Spanish): ....
    Hess, C. A.: "Enrique Granados. A Bio-bibliography." Greenwood, 1991.
    Iglesias, A.: "Enrique Granados. Su obra para piano." Editorial Alpuerto, Madrid, 1985–6.
Grieg, Edvard (Hagerup) (1843–1907, Norwegian): ....
    "Edvard Grieg: Verzeichnis seiner Werke mit Einleitung. Mein Erster Erfolg." Peters, Leipzig, 19—.
Handel, George Frideric (Händel, Georg Friedrich) (1685–1759, German): ....
    Baselt, B.: "Thematisch-systematisches Verzeichnis. Händel-Handbuch." VEB Deutscher Verlag für Musik,
        Leipzig, 1986.
    Labie, J-F.: "Haendel." Robert Laffont, Paris, 1980.
    Parker-Hale, M. A.: "G. F. Handel. A Guide to research." Garland, 1988.

Siegmund-Schultze, W.: "Georg Friedrich Händel. Sein Leben. Sein Work." List Verlag, Munich, 1984.
Haydn, (Franz) Joseph (1732–1809, Austrian): ....
    Geiringer, K.: "Haydn." Gallimard, 1984.
    Hoboken, A. van: "Joseph Haydn. Thematisch-bibliographisches Werkverzeichnis." B. Schott's Söhne, Mainz,
        1957 (Band I), 1971 (Band II), 1978 (Band III).
Hindemith, Paul (1895–1963, German): ....
    "Hindemith-Jahrbuch." 1986/XV. Paul-Hindemith-Institut, Frankfurt / Main. Schott, 1990.
    "Paul Hindemith. Werkverzeichnis. List of Works." Schott, 1985.
    Neumeyer, D.: "The Music of Paul Hindemith." Yale University Press, 1986.
    Skelton, G.: "Paul Hindemith, The Man Behind the Music." Gollancz, 1975.
Holst, Gustav(us Theodore von) (1874–1934, English): ....
    Holst, I.: "A Thematic Catalogue of Gustav Holst's Music." Faber Music, 1974.
    Short, M.: "Gustav Holst. The Man and His Music." Oxford University Press, 1990.
Honegger, Arthur (1892–1955, Swiss): ....
    Delannoy, M.: "Honegger." Slatkine, Genève—Paris, 1985.
    Halbreich, H.: "Arthur Honegger. Un musicien dans la cité des hommes." Fayard / Sacem, 1992.
    Spratt, G. K.: "Catalogue des Oeuvres de Arthur Honegger." Slatkine, Genève—Paris, 1986.
Hummel, Johann Nepomuk (1778–1837, German / Bohemian): ....
    Sachs, J.: "Kapellmeister Hummel in England and France." Detroit Monographs in Musicology Number Six
        Information Coordinators, Detroit, 1977.
    Zimmerschied, D.: "Thematisches Verzeichnis der Werke von Johann Nepomuk Hummel." Musikverlag
        Friedrich Hofmeister, Hofheim am Taunus, 1971.
Ives, Charles Edward (1874–1954, American): ....
    Henderson, C. W.: "The Charles Ives Tunebook." Harmonie Park Press, Michigan, 1990.
    Kirkpatrick, J., ed.: "Charles E. Ives. Memos." Norton, 1972.
Janáček, Leoš (Leo Eugen) (1854–1928, Czech): ....
    Erisman, G.: "Janáček." Éditions du Seuil, 1980.
    Horsbrugh, I.: "Leoš Janáček. The field that prospered." Scribner's, 1982.
    Vogel, J.: "Leoš Janáček. His Life and Works." Transl G. Thomsen-Muchová. Paul Hamlyn, London, 1962.
Kabalevsky, Dmitri Borisovich (1904–1987, Soviet): ....
    Victorov: "Kabalevsky." Izdatelstvo Sovetskiy Kompozitor, Moscow, 1974.
Kalinnikov, Vasily Sergeyevich (1866–1901, Russian): ....
    (List compiled mostly from sources listed in this bibliography under General)
Khachaturian, Aram Ilyich (1903–1978, Soviet / Armenian): ....
    Hudov, G.: "Aram Khachaturian." Moscow, 1962.
    Shneerson, G.: "Aram Khachaturyan." Transl X. Danko. Moscow, 1959.
Kodály, Zoltán (1882–1967, Hungarian): ....
    Amann, J-P.: "Zoltán Kodály." Éditions de l'Aire, Lausanne, 1983.
    Eösze, L.: "Zoltán Kodály. His Life and Work." Transl Farkas & Gulyás. Collet's, London, 1962.
    Young, P. M.: "Zoltán Kodály. A Hungarian Musician." Ernest Benn, London, 1964.
Lalo, Édouard(-Victoire-Antoine) (1823–1892, French): ....
    Servières, G.: "Édouard Lalo. Biographie critique." Renouard, Paris, 1925.
Lehár, Franz (Ferenc) (1870–1948, Austrian): ....
    "Franz Lehár. Thematic Index." Glocken, London, 1985.
    Czech, S.: "Franz Lehár. Sein Weg und sein Werk." Verlagsbuchhandlung Franz Perneder, Vienna, 1968.
Leoncavallo, Ruggiero (1858–1919, Italian): ....
    (List compiled mostly from sources listed in this bibliography under General)
Liszt, Franz (Ferenc) (1811–1886, Hungarian): ....
    "Thematisches Verzeichniss der Werke, Bearbeitungen und Transcriptionen von F. Liszt." Neue vervollständigte
        Ausgabe. Reprinted for H. Baron, London, 1965.
    Walker, A., ed.: "Franz Liszt. The Man and His Music." Barrie & Jenkins, London, 1970.
Lully, Jean-Baptiste (Lulli, Giovanni Battista) (1632–1687, French): ....
    Beaussant, Ph.: "Lully ou Le musicien du Soleil." Gallimard / Théâtre des Champs-Élysées, 1992.
Lutosławski, Witold (1913–1994, Polish): ....
    Stucky, St.: "Lutoslawsky and His Music." Cambridge University Press, 1981.
Mahler, Gustav (1860–1911, Austrian): ....
    Dargie, E. M.: "Music and Poetry in the Songs of Gustav Mahler." Peter Lang, Berne (Switzerland), 1981.
    Filler, S. M.: "Gustav and Alma Mahler. A Guide to Research." Garland, 1989.
    Kennedy, M.: "Mahler." Dent, 1974.
Martinů, Bohuslav (Jan) (1890–1959, Czech): ....
    Červinková, Barancicová, Gebauerová, Pozoutová & Valtrová: "Bohuslav Martinů. Bibliographical Catalogue."
        Praha, 1990.
    Erismann, G.: "Martinů—un musicien à l'éveil des source." Actes Sud, 1990.
Massenet, Jules(-Émile-Frédéric) (1842–1912, French): ....
    Bessand-Massenet, P.: "Massenet." Julliard, Paris.
    Irvine D.: "Massenet. A Chronicle of His Life and Times." Demar Irvine, Seattle, Washington, 1974.
Mendelssohn(-Bartholdy), (Jacob Ludwig) Felix (1809–1847, German): ....
    Kunold, W.: "Felix Mendelssohn Bartholdy und seine Zeit." Laaber, Regensburg, 1984.
    Radcliffe, Ph.: "Mendelssohn." Collier, 1963.
    Tiénot, Y.: "Mendelssohn. Musicien Complet." Lemoine, Paris, 1972.
Messiaen, Olivier(-Eugène-Prosper-Charles) (1908–1992, French): ....
    Griffiths, P.: "Olivier Messiaen and the Music of Time." Cornell University Press, 1985.
    Johnson, R. S.: "Messiaen." Dent, 1975.
    Pauly, R. G., ed.: "Olivier Messiaen. Music and Color. Conversations with Claude Samuel." Amadeus Press,
        Portland, Oregon, 1994.

Meyerbeer, Giacomo (Meyer Beer, Jakob Liebmann) (1791–1864, German): ....
   Becker, H. & G.: "Giacomo Meyerbeer. A Life in Letters." Christopher Helm, London, 1989.
Milhaud, Darius (1892–1974, French): ....
   Beck, G.: "Darius Milhaud. Catalogue chronoligue complet de son oeuvre. Supplément. Oeuvres composées
   de Novembre 1949 à Avril 1956." Heugel, 1956.
   Milhaud, D.: "Notes without Music. An Autobiography." Da Capo, 1970.
   Milhaud, M.: "Catalogue des Oeuvres de Darius Milhaud." Slatkine, Genève—Paris, 1982.
Moniuszko, Stanisław (1819–1872, Polish): ....
   Rudziński, W., ed.: "Dzieła Stanisława Moniuszki," Vols.I–VI. Polskie Wydawnictwo Muzyczne, Kraków,
   1965–74.
Monteverdi, Claudio (Giovanni Antonio) (1567–1643, Italian): ....
   Adams, K. & Kiel, D.: "Claudio Monteverdi. A Guide to Research." Garland, 1989.
   Stattkus, M. H.: "Claudio Monteverdi. Verzeichnis der erhaltenen Werke." (SV) Kleine Ausgabe. Musicverlag
   Stattkus, Bergkamen, 1985.
Mozart, (Johannes Chrisostomus) Wolfgang(us) Amadeus (Theophilus Sigismundus) (1756–1791, Austrian): ....
   Köchel, L. R. von: "Chronologisch-thematisches Verzeichnis sämtlicher Tonwerke Wolfgang Amadé Mozarts."
   Sechste Auflage bearbeitet von Franz Giegling, Zürich, Alexander Weinmann, Wien, Gerd Sievers,
   Wiesbaden. Breitkopf & Härtel, Wiesbaden, 1964.
Musorgsky, Modest Petrovich (1839–1881, Russian): ....
   Calvocoressi, M. D.: "Modest Mussorgsky. His Life and Works." Rockliff Publishing, 1956.
   Reilly, E. R.: "The Music of Mussorgsky. A Guide to the Editions." Musical Newsletter, New York, 1980.
   Riesemann, O. von: "Moussorgsky." Transl P. England. Knopf, 1929.
Nielsen, Carl (August) (1865–1931, Danish): ....
   "Carl Nielsen. The Catalogue." Wilhelm Hansen. Snekkersten, Denmark, 1964.
   Fog, D. & Schousboe, T.: "Carl Nielsen kompositioner: en bibliografi." Nyt Nordisk Forlag—Arnold Busck,
   Copenhagen, 1965.
   Simpson, R.: "Carl Nielsen. Symphonist." Taplinger, New York, 1979.
Offenbach, Jacques (Jacob) (1819–1880, French): ....
   Faris, A.: "Jacques Offenbach." Faber & Faber, 1980.
   Gammond, P.: "Offenbach. His Life and Times." Midas Books, 1980.
Orff, Carl (1895–1982, German): ....
   Liess, A.: "Carl Orff. Idee und Werk." Atlantis, Zürich, 1977.
Paderewski, Ignacy Jan (1860–1941, Polish): ....
   Zamoyski, A.: "Paderewski." Collins, 1982.
Paganini, Niccolò (1782–1840, Italian): ....
   Moretti, M. R., Sorrento, A.: "Catalogo Tematico delle musiche di Niccolò Paganini." Comune di Genova, 1982.
   Neill, E.: "Nicolo Paganini." Fayard, 1991.
Penderecki, Krzysztof (born 1933, Polish): ....
   Robinson, R.: "K. Penderecki. A Guide to His Works." Prestige, Princeton, 1983.
   Schwinger, W.: "K. Penderecki, his life and work." Schott, 1989.
Poulenc, Francis (Jean Marcel) (1899–1963, French): ....
   Bernac, P.: "Francis Poulenc. The Man and His Songs." Gollancz, 1977.
   Bloch, F.: "Phonographies II. Francis Poulenc. 1928–1982." Bibliothèque Nationale, Paris, 1984.
   Hell, H.: "Francis Poulenc. Musicien français." Fayard, 1978.
   Keck, G. R.: "Francis Poulenc. A Bio-bibliography." Greenwood, 1990.
Prokofiev, Sergey Sergeyevich (1891–1953, Soviet): ....
   Moisson-Franckhauser, S.: "Serge Prokofiev et les courants esthétiques de son temps." Publications
   Orientalistes de France, 1974.
   Nestyev, I. V.: "Prokofiev." Transl F. Jonas. Stanford University Press, 1960.
Puccini, Giacomo (Antonio Domenico Michele Secondo Maria) (1858–1924, Italian): ....
   Carner, M.: "Puccini." Jean-Claude Lattes, Paris, 1983.
   Hopkinson, C.: "A Bibliography of the Works of Giacomo Puccini." Broude, New York, 1968.
Purcell, Henry (1659–1695, English): ....
   Zimmerman, F. B.: "Henry Purcell. An Analytical Catalogue of His Music." Macmillan, St Martin's Press, 1963.
   Zimmerman, F. B.: "Henry Purcell. A Guide to Research." Garland, 1989.
Rachmaninov, Sergey Vasilyevich (1873–1943, Russian): ....
   Norris, G.: "Rakhmaninov." Dent, 1976.
   Palmieri, R.: "S. V. Rachmaninov. A Guide to Research." Garland, 1985.
   Threlfall, R. & Norris, G.: "A Catalogue of the Compositions of S. Rachmaninoff." Scolar, London, 1982.
Rameau, Jean-Philippe (1683–1764, French): ....
   Girdlestone, C.: "Jean-Philippe Rameau. His Life and Work." Dover Publications, New York, 1969.
Ravel, (Joseph) Maurice (1875–1937, French): ....
   "Catalogue de l'oeuvre de Maurice Ravel." Fondation Maurice Ravel—Durand, Paris, 1954.
   Nichols, R.: "Ravel." Dent, 1977.
Respighi, Ottorino (1879–1936, Italian): ....
   Battaglia, Bellingardi & others: "Ottorino Respighi." Edizioni Rai Radiotelevisione Italiana, Torino, 1985.
   Pedarra, P.: "Catalogo delle composizioni di Ottorino Respighi." 1985.
Rimsky-Korsakov, Nicolay Andreyevich (1844–1908, Russian): ....
   Seaman, G. R.: "N. A. Rimsky-Korsakov. A Guide to Research." Garland, 1988.
   Yastrebtsev, V.: "Reminiscences of Rimsky-Korsakov." Ed & transl F. Jonas. Columbia University Press, 1985.
Rodrigo, Joaquín (born 1901, Spanish): ....
   Sopeña, F.: "Joaquín Rodrigo." Ediciones y Publicaciones Españolas, Madrid, 1946.
Rossini, Gioachino (Antonio) (1792–1868, Italian): ....
   "Quaderni Rossiniani, a cura della Fondazione Rossini." Pesaro, 1954–.
   Kendall, A.: "Gioacchino Rossini. The Reluctant Hero." Gollancz, 1992.

Osborne, R.: "Rossini." Dent, 1986.
Roussel, Albert (Charles Paul Marie) (1869–1937, French): ....
    "Catalogue de l'oeuvre d'Albert Roussel." Paris, 1947.
    Basil, D.: "Albert Roussel." Barrie and Rockliff, London, 1961.
    Labelle, N.: "Catalogue Raisonné de l'Oeuvre de Albert Roussel." Musicologica Neolovaniensia, Studia 6,
        Louvain-La-Neuve, 1992.
Saint-Saëns, (Charles-)Camille (1835–1921, French): ....
    (List compiled mostly from sources listed in this bibliography under General)
Sarasate (y Navascuéz), Pablo (Martín Melitón) de (1844–1908, Spanish): ....
    (List compiled mostly from sources listed in this bibliography under General)
Satie, Érik(-Alfred-Leslie) (1866–1925, French): ....
    Gillmor, A. M.: "Satie." Twayne, Boston, 1988.
Scarlatti, (Pietro) Alessandro (Gaspare) (1660–1725, Italian): ....
    Dent, E. J.: "Alessandro Scarlatti: His Life and Works." Edward Arnold, London, 1960.
    Rostirolla, G.: "Catalogo generale delle opere di Alessandro Scarlatti," in R. Pagano & Lino Bianchi:
        "Alessandro Scarlatti." Edizioni Rai Radiotelevisione Italiana, Torino, 1972.
Scarlatti, (Giuseppe) Domenico (1685–1757, Italian): ....
    Boyd, M.: "Domenico Scarlatti—Master of Music." Weidenfeld & Nicolson, London, 1986.
    Kirkpatrick, R.: "Domenico Scarlatti." Princeton University Press, 1953.
Schoenberg (Schönberg), Arnold (Franz Walter) (1874–1951, Austrian): ....
    MacDonald, M.: "Schoenberg." Dent, 1976.
Schubert, Franz (Peter) (1797–1828, Austrian): ....
    Brown, M. J. E.: "Schubert: a Critical Biography." Da Capo, 1977.
    Deutsch, O. E.: "Franz Schubert. Thematisches Verzeichnis seiner Werke in chronologischer Folge."
        Neuausgabe in deutscher Sprache bearbeitet und herausgegeben von der Editionsleitung der Neuen
        Schubert-Ausgabe und Werner Aderhold. Bärenreiter, 1978.
Schumann, Robert (Alexander) (1810–1856, German): ....
    Chissell, J.: "Schumann." Collier, London, 1948, r1967.
    Hofmann, K. & Keil, S.: "Robert Schumann. Thematisches Verzeichnis sämtlicher im Druck erschienen
        musikalischen Werke mit Angabe des Jahnres ihres Entstehens und Erscheines." 5th edition. Schuberth,
        Hamburg, 1982.
    Sams, E.: "The Songs of Robert Schumann." 2nd edition. Eulenburg, London, 1975.
Shostakovich, Dmitry Dmitryevich (1906–1975, Soviet): ....
    Hulme, D. C.: "D. Shostakovich. A Catalogue, Bibliography and Discography." Clarendon, 1991.
    MacDonald, M.: "Dmitri Shostakovich. A Complete Catalogue." Boosey & Hawkes, 1977.
Sibelius, Jean (Jan) (Julius Christian) (1865–1957, Finnish): ....
    Kilpeläinen, K.: "The Jean Sibelius Musical Manuscripts at Helsinki University Library. A Complete Catalogue."
        Breitkopf & Härtel, 1991.
    Ringbom, N-E.: "Jean Sibelius. A Master and His Work." University of Oklahoma Press, 1954.
Skryabin, Alexander Nicolayevich (1872–1915, Russian): ....
    Hull, A. E.: "A Great Russian Tone-Poet. Scriabin." Kegan Paul—Trench—Trubner, London, 1916.
    Schloezer, B. de: "Scriabin. Artist and Mystic." Transl N. Slonimsky. University of California Press, 1987.
Smetana, Bedřich (1824–1884, Czech): ....
    Bennett, J. R.: "Smetana on 3000 Records." Oakwood, 1974.
    Large, B.: "Smetana." Duckworth, London, 1970.
Spohr, Louis (Ludwig) (1784–1859, German): ....
    Katow, P.: "Louis Spohr. Persönlichkeit und Werk." RTL Edition, 1983.
    Göthel, F.: "Thematisch-Bibliographisches Verzeichnis der Werke von Louis Spohr." Schneider, Tutzing, 1981.
Stockhausen, Karlheinz (born 1928, German): ....
    Harvey, J.: "The Music of Stockhausen." University of California Press, 1975.
    Maconie, R.: "The Works of Karlheinz Stockhausen." 2nd edition. Clarendon, 1990.
    Wörner, K. H.: "Stockhausen. Life and Work." Transl & ed B. Hopkins. University of California Press, 1973.
Strauss (I), Johann (Baptist) Sr. (1804–1849, Austrian): ....
    Weinmann, A.: "Verzeichnis Sämtlicher Werke von Johann Strauss, Vater und Sohn." Krenn, Vienna, 1956.
Strauss (II), Johann (Baptist) Jr. (1825–1899, Austrian): ....
    Ewen, D.: "Tales from the Vienna Woods. The Story of Johann Strauss." Holt, Rinehart and Winston,
        1944, 1966.
    Weinmann, A.: "Verzeichnis Sämtlicher Werke von Johann Strauss, Vater und Sohn." Krenn, Vienna, 1956.
Strauss, Richard (Georg) (1864–1949, German): ....
    Asov, E. H. Mueller von: "Richard Strauss. Thematisches Verzeichnis," Band I–III. Doblinger (B. Herzmansky),
        Vienna, 1959–74.
    Del Mar, N.: "Richard Strauss. A Critical Commentary on His Life and Works." Barrie & Rockliff, London, 1962.
    Krause, E.: "Richard Strauss." Breitkopf und Härtel, Leipzig, 1955.
    Trenner, F.: "Richard Strauss. Werkverzeichnis." Doblinger, Vienna—Munich, 1985.
Stravinsky, Igor Fyodorovich (1882–1971, Russian): ....
    "Igor Strawinsky. A Complete Catalogue of His Published Works." Boosey & Hawkes, London, 1957.
    Lerma, D-R. de, as assisted by Ahrens, T. J.: "Igor Fedorovitch Stravinsky, 1882–1971; A Practical Guide to
        Publications of His Music." Kent State University Press, 1974.
    White, E. W.: "Stravinsky. A Critical Survey." Philosophical Library, New York, 1948.
Sullivan, Sir Arthur (Seymour) (1842–1900, English): ....
    Jacobs, A.: "Arthur Sullivan. A Victorian Musician." Oxford University Press, 1984.
Szymanowski, Karol (Maciej) (1882–1937, Polish): ....
    Chylińska, T.: "Szymanowski." Polskie Wydawnictwo Muzyczne, Kraków, 1982.
    Samson, J.: "The Music of Szymanowski." Kahn & Averkill, London, 1990.

Tchaikovsky, Pyotr Ilyich (1840–1893, Russian): ....
  "Systematisches Verzeichnis der Werke von P. I. Tschaikovsky. Ein Handbuch für die Musikpraxis."
  Herausgegeben vom Tschaikowsky-Studio Institut International. Sikorski, Hamburg, 1973.
  Abraham, G.: "The Music of Tchaikovsky." Norton, 1974.
  Jurgenson, B., ed.: "Catalogue Thèmatique des oeuvres de P. Tschaïkowsky." 1897. Reprinted Stephen
    Austin and Sons for H. Baron, London, 1965.
  Warrack, J.: "Tchaikovsky." Hamish Hamilton, London, 1973.
Vaughan Williams, Ralph (1872–1958, English):..
  Butterworth, N.: "Ralph Vaughan Williams. A Guide to Research." Garland, 1990.
  Day, J.: "Vaughan Williams." Dent—Octagon, 1961.
  Kennedy, M.: "A Catalogue of the Works of Ralph Vaugan Williams." Oxford University Press, 1982.
Verdi, Giuseppe (Fortunino Francesco) (1813–1901, Italian): ....
  Chusid, M.: "Music Indexes and Bibliographies. No.5. A Catalog of Verdi's Operas." Joseph Boonin,
    Hackensack, N.J., 1974.
  Hopkinson, C.: "A Bibliography of the Works of Giuseppe Verdi." Broude, New York, 1973.
  Osborne, C.: "The Complete Operas of Verdi." Gollancz, 1969.
Villa-Lobos, Heitor (1887–1959, Brasilian):...
  Appleby, D. P.: "Heitor Villa-Lobos. A Bio-bibliography." Greenwood, 1988.
  Schic, A. S.: "Villa Lobos. Souvenirs de l'indien blanc." Actes Sud, 1987.
Vivaldi, Antonio (Lucio) (1678–1741, Italian): ....
  Talbot, M.: "Vivaldi." Dent, 1978.
  Ryom, P.: "Verzeichnis der Werke Antonio Vivaldis: kleine Ausgabe." Leipzig, 1974; suppl., Poitiers, 1979.
Wagner, (Wilhelm) Richard (1813–1883, German): ....
  Deathridge, J., Geck, M., Voss, E.: "Wagner Werk-Verzeichnis." Schott, 1985.
Weber, Carl Maria (Friedrich Ernst) von (1786–1826, German):..
  Jähn, F. W.: "Carl Maria von Weber in seinen Werken. Chronologisch-thematisches Verzeichnis seiner
    sämmtlichen Compositionen." Verlag der Schlesinger'schen Buch- und Musikhandlung, Berlin, 1871.
    Unveränderte Neuauflage Robert Lienau, Berlin—Lichterfelde, 1967.
  Warrack, J.: "Carl Maria von Weber." Cambridge University Press, 1976.
Webern, Anton (Friedrich Wilhelm von) (1883–1945, Austrian): ....
  Kolneder, W.: "Anton Webern. An Introduction to His Works." Transl H. Searle. Faber & Faber, London, 1968.
  Moldenhauer, H. & R.: "Anton von Webern. A Chronicle of His Life and Work." Knopf, 1979.
Wieniawski, Henryk (1835–1880, Polish): ....
  Reiss, J. W.: "Wieniawski." Polskie Wydawnictwo Muzyczne, Kraków, 1985.
Wolf, Hugo (Filipp Jakob) (1860–1903, Austrian): ....
  "Hugo Wolf. Verzeichnis seiner Werke mit einer Einführung von Paul Müller." Peters, Leipzig, 1908.
  Ossenkop, D.: "Hugo Wolf. A Guide to Research." Garland, 1988.

* * * * *

KEYS:

English:	French:	German:
C major	ut majeur	C-dur
C minor	ut mineur	c-moll
C-sharp major	ut dièse majeur	Cis-dur
C-sharp minor	ut dièse mineur	cis-moll
D major	ré majeur	D-dur
D minor	ré mineur	d-moll
E-flat major	mi bémol majeur	Es-dur
E-flat minor	mi bémol mineur	es-moll
E major	mi majeur	E-dur
E minor	mi mineur	e-moll
F major	fa majeur	F-dur
F minor	fa mineur	f-moll
F-sharp major	fa dièse majeur	Fis-dur
F-sharp minor	fa dièse mineur	fis-moll
G major	sol majeur	G-dur
G minor	sol mineur	g-moll
A-flat major	la bémol majeur	As-dur
G-sharp minor	sol dièse mineur	gis-moll
A major	la majeur	A-dur
A minor	la mineur	a-moll
B-flat major	si bémol majeur	B-dur
B-flat minor	si bémol mineur	b-moll
B major	si majeur	H-dur
B minor	si mineur	h-moll